Webster's

New Spanish

Dictionary

Wiley Publishing, Inc.

Contents/Índice

Preface   iv
Prefacio   v

Structure of Entries   vi
Estructura de las entradas   vii

Abbreviations/Abreviaturas   viii

Spanish Pronunciation Guide   xi
Pronunciación del inglés   xiv

SPANISH-ENGLISH DICTIONARY   1–350
DICCIONARIO ESPAÑOL-INGLÉS

Spanish Verbs   (i)
Verbos irregulares ingleses   (xiii)

ENGLISH-SPANISH DICTIONARY   1-414
DICCIONARIO INGLÉS-ESPAÑOL

Preface

This new pocket-sized dictionary is aimed at students at beginner and intermediate level. It covers all the essential words and phrases needed and packs a wealth of vocabulary into its pages.

Content is fully up to date with the latest changes in language and in the world. In particular, there is excellent coverage of computing terms (including e-mail and the Internet), as well as Latin American Spanish.

A number of extra features add to the effectiveness of the dictionary as a learning tool. We have included false friend boxes to help the user avoid common translation pitfalls, and grammar notes to indicate correct usage. In the pronunciation guides, special attention has been given to the problems Spanish speakers encounter in pronouncing English.

As regards presentation, adverbs and phrasal verbs have separate entries, and each part of speech within an entry starts on a new line. This makes for a clear layout of the text, so the book is easy to consult.

Prefacio

Este nuevo diccionario de bolsillo, dirigido a estudiantes de nivel elemental e intermedio, recoge todas las palabras y expresiones básicas, incluyéndose en sus páginas una gran cantidad de vocabulario.

El contenido refleja los cambios en el lenguaje y en el mundo. En particular, contiene una excelente selección de términos de informática (además del correo electrónico e Internet) y del español de América.

La utilidad del diccionario como herramienta de aprendizaje ha sido potenciada con varios elementos adicionales. Hemos incluido cuadros sobre falsos amigos para evitar trampas en las traducciones y notas gramaticales que indican el uso correcto de las palabras. Las guías sobre la pronunciación prestan especial atención a los problemas que tienen los hablantes nativos de español al pronunciar el inglés.

En lo que respecta a la presentación, los adverbios y los "phrasal verbs" tienen entradas individuales, y cada categoría gramatical comienza en una nueva línea. Esto hace que la presentación del texto sea más clara y que el libro sea fácil de consultar.

Structure of Entries

> **ceviche** *nm* = raw fish marinated in lemon and garlic

● The equals sign = introduces an explanation when there is no direct translation.

> **inocentada** *nf Fam* ≃ April Fool's joke; **hacer una i. a algn** to play an April Fool's joke on sb

● The sign ≃ introduces a word that has a roughly equivalent status but is not identical.

> **aflojar 1** *vt* to loosen
> **2** *vi (viento etc)* to weaken, to grow weak
> **3 aflojarse** *vpr* to come *o* work loose; *(rueda)* to go down

● The different grammatical categories are cleary indicated, introduced by a bold Arabic numeral.

> **abrir²** (*pp* **abierto**) **1** *vi* to open
> **2** *vt* (**a**) to open; *(cremallera)* to undo (**b**) *(gas, grifo)* to turn on (**c**) *Jur* **a. (un) expediente** to start proceedings
> **3 abrirse** *vpr* (**a**) to open; *Fig* **a. paso** to make one's way (**b**) *Fam* **¡me abro!** I'm off!

● Usage and field labels are clearly shown.

> **reconocer** [34] *vt* (**a**) to recognize (**b**) *(admitir)* to recognize, to admit (**c**) *Med (paciente)* to examine

● A number before an irregular Spanish verb refers the user to the verb tables in the middle of the book for information on how to conjugate it.

> **bland** [blænd] *adj (food)* soso(a)
>
> Note that the Spanish word **blando** is a false friend and is never a translation for the English word **bland**. In Spanish, **blando** means "soft".

● Usage notes warn the user when a word is a false friend.

> **acodarse** *vpr* to lean (**en** on)

● The most common prepositions used are given after the translation.

> **acústica** *nf* acoustics *sing*

● The number of a translation is indicated where this is ambiguous.

Estructura de las entradas

> **ceviche** *nm* = raw fish marinated in lemon and garlic

- Cuando no es posible dar una traducción se ofrece una explicación precedida por el signo igual (=).

> **inocentada** *nf Fam* ≃ April Fool's joke; **hacer una i. a algn** to play an April Fool's joke on sb

- El signo ≃ precede a una traducción que tiene un significado aproximado pero no idéntico.

> **aflojar** **1** *vt* to loosen
> **2** *vi (viento etc)* to weaken, to grow weak
> **3** **aflojarse** *vpr* to come *o* work loose; *(rueda)* to go down

- Las diferentes categorías gramaticales están separadas por un número en negrita.

> **abrir²** (*pp* **abierto**) **1** *vi* to open
> **2** *vt* (**a**) to open; *(cremallera)* to undo (**b**) *(gas, grifo)* to turn on (**c**) *Jur* **a. (un) expediente** to start proceedings
> **3** **abrirse** *vpr* (**a**) to open; *Fig* **a. paso** to make one's way (**b**) *Fam* **¡me abro!** I'm off!

- Las marcas de uso y de campo semántico están claramente indicadas.

> **reconocer** [34] *vt o*(**a**) to recognize (**b**) *(admitir)* to recognize, to admit (**c**) *Med (paciente)* to examine

- Los números que aparecen detrás de los verbos irregulares remiten a las tablas verbales que se encuentran en el medio del diccionario.

> **blando,-a** *adj* soft
>
> *ℓ* Observa que la palabra inglesa **bland** es un falso amigo y no es la traducción de la palabra española **blando**. En inglés, **bland** significa "soso".

- Las notas de uso informan sobre los falsos amigos.

> **acodarse** *vpr* to lean (**en** on)

- Las preposiciones más comunes aparecen después de las traducciones.

> **acústica** *nf* acoustics *sing*

- El número de la traducción aparece en los casos en los que éste es ambiguo.

Abbreviations used in this dictionary
Abreviaturas usadas en este diccionario

abbreviation	*abbr, abr*	abreviatura
adjective	*adj*	adjetivo
adverb	*adv*	adverbio
agriculture	*Agr*	agricultura
somebody, someone	*algn*	alguien
Latin American Spanish	*Am*	español de América
anatomy	*Anat*	anatomía
Andean Spanish (Bolivia, Chile, Colombia, Ecuador, Peru)	*Andes*	español andino (Bolivia, Chile, Colombia, Ecuador, Perú)
approximately	*aprox*	aproximadamente
architecture	*Archit*	arquitectura
Argentinian Spanish	*Arg*	español de Argentina
architecture	*Arquit*	arquitectura
article	*art*	artículo
astronomy	*Astron*	astronomía
Australian	*Austral*	australiano
motoring	*Aut*	automóviles
auxiliary	*aux*	auxiliar
aviation	*Av*	aviación
biology	*Biol*	biología
Bolivian Spanish	*Bol*	español de Bolivia
botany	*Bot*	botánica
British English	*Br*	inglés británico
Central American Spanish	*CAm*	español centroamericano
Canary Islands Spanish	*Can*	español de Canarias
Caribbean Spanish (Cuba, Puerto Rico, Dominican Republic, Venezuela)	*Carib*	español caribeño (Cuba, Puerto Rico, República Dominicana, Venezuela)
chemistry	*Chem*	química
Chilean Spanish	*Chile*	español de Chile
cinema	*Cin*	cine
Colombian Spanish	*Col*	español de Colombia
commerce	*Com*	comercio
comparative	*comp*	comparativo
computers	*Comput*	informática
conditional	*cond*	condicional
conjunction	*conj*	conjunción
building industry	*Constr*	construcción
sewing	*Cost*	costura
Costa Rican Spanish	*CRica*	español de Costa Rica
Spanish from the Southern Cone region (Argentina, Uruguay, Paraguay, Chile)	*CSur*	español del Cono Sur (Argentina, Uruguay, Paraguay, Chile)
Cuban Spanish	*Cuba*	español de Cuba
cookery	*Culin*	cocina
definite	*def*	definido
defective	*defect*	defectivo
demonstrative	*dem*	demostrativo
sport	*Dep*	deporte
economics	*Econ*	economía
Ecuadorian Spanish	*Ecuad*	español de Ecuador
education	*Educ*	educación
electricity	*Elec*	electricidad
especially	*esp*	especialmente
Peninsular Spanish	*Esp*	español de España
etcetera	*etc*	etcétera
euphemism	*Euph, Euf*	eufemismo
feminine	*f*	femenino

familiar	*Fam*	familiar
pharmacy	*Farm*	farmacia
railways	*Ferroc*	ferrocarriles
figurative use	*Fig*	uso figurado
finance	*Fin*	finanzas
physics	*Fís*	física
formal use	*Fml*	uso formal
photography	*Fot*	fotografía
feminine plural	*fpl*	plural femenino
football	*Ftb*	fútbol
future	*fut*	futuro
geography	*Geog*	geografía
geology	*Geol*	geología
geometry	*Geom*	geometría
present participle	*ger*	gerundio
Guatemalan Spanish	*Guat*	español de Guatemala
history	*Hist*	historia
humorous	*Hum*	humorístico
imperative	*imperat*	imperativo
imperfect	*imperf*	imperfecto
impersonal	*impers*	impersonal
printing	*Impr*	imprenta
industry	*Ind*	industria
indefinite	*indef*	indefinido
indeterminate	*indet*	indeterminado
indicative	*indic*	indicativo
infinitive	*infin*	infinitivo
computers	*Informát*	informática
insurance	*Ins*	seguros
interjection	*interj*	interjección
interrogative	*interr*	interrogativo
invariable	*inv*	invariable
ironic	*Irón*	irónico
law	*Jur*	derecho
linguistics	*Ling*	lingüística
literature	*Lit*	literatura
phrase	*loc*	locución
masculine	*m*	masculino
mathematics	*Math, Mat*	matemáticas
medicine	*Med*	medicina
meteorology	*Met*	meteorología
Mexican Spanish	*Méx*	español de México
military	*Mil*	militar
mining	*Min*	minas
masculine plural	*mpl*	plural masculino
music	*Mus, Mús*	música
noun	*n*	nombre
nautical	*Naut, Náut*	náutica
neuter	*neut*	neutro
feminine noun	*nf*	nombre femenino
plural feminine noun	*nfpl*	nombre femenino plural
masculine noun	*nm*	nombre masculino
masculine and feminine noun	*nmf/nm,f*	nombre masculino y femenino
plural masculine noun	*nmpl*	nombre masculino plural
plural noun	*npl*	nombre plural
optics	*Opt*	óptica
ornithology	*Orn*	ornitología
Panamanian Spanish	*Pan*	español de Panamá
Paraguayan Spanish	*Par*	español de Paraguay
pejorative	*Pej*	peyorativo
personal	*pers*	personal
Peruvian Spanish	*Perú*	español de Perú
pejorative	*Pey*	peyorativo
pharmacy	*Pharm*	farmacia

photography	*Phot*	fotografía
physics	*Phys*	física
plural	*pl*	plural
politics	*Pol*	política
possessive	*pos, poss*	posesivo
past participle	*pp*	participio pasado
prefix	*pref*	prefijo
preposition	*prep*	preposición
present	*pres*	presente
present participle	*pres p*	gerundio
Puerto Rican Spanish	*PRico*	español de Puerto Rico
pronoun	*pron*	pronombre
psychology	*Psi, Psy*	psicología
past tense	*pt*	pretérito
chemistry	*Quím*	química
radio	*Rad*	radio
railways	*Rail*	ferrocarriles
relative	*rel*	relativo
religion	*Rel*	religión
Spanish from the River Plate region (Argentina, Uruguay, Paraguay)	*RP*	español de los países ribereños del Río de la Plata
somebody, someone	*sb*	alguien
Scottish	*Scot*	escocés
insurance	*Seg*	seguros
singular	*sing*	singular
something	*sth*	algo
subjunctive	*subj*	subjuntivo
superlative	*superl*	superlativo
bullfighting	*Taurom*	tauromaquia
technical	*Tech, Téc*	técnica
telephones	*Tel*	teléfonos
textiles	*Tex*	textiles
theatre	*Th*	teatro
television	*TV*	televisión
typography	*Typ*	tipografía
university	*Univ*	universidad
Uruguayan Spanish	*Urug*	español de Uruguay
American English	*US*	inglés norteamericano
usually	*usu*	usualmente
verb	*v*	verbo
auxiliary verb	*v aux*	verbo auxiliar
Venezuelan Spanish	*Ven*	español de Venezuela
intransitive verb	*vi*	verbo intransitivo
impersonal verb	*v impers*	verbo impersonal
reflexive verb	*vpr*	verbo pronominal
transitive verb	*vt*	verbo transitivo
vulgar	*Vulg*	vulgar
zoology	*Zool*	zoología
cultural equivalent	≃	equivalente cultural
registered trademark	®	marca registrada

Spanish Pronunciation Guide

The pronunciation of most Spanish words is predictable as there is a close match between spelling and pronunciation. The table below gives an explanation of that pronunciation. In the dictionary text therefore, pronunciation is only given when the word does not follow these rules, usually because it is a word of foreign origin. In these cases, the IPA (International Phonetic Alphabet) is used (see column 2 of the table below).

Letter in Spanish	IPA Symbol	Example in Spanish	Pronunciation (example in English)
Vowels			
Note that all vowel sounds in Spanish are shorter than in English			
a	a	ala	Similar to the sound in "father" but more central
e	e	ecó	Similar to the sound in "met"
i	i	iris	Like the vowel sound in "meat" but much shorter
o	o	oso	off, on
u	u	uva	Like the vowel sound in "soon" but much shorter
Semiconsonants			
"i" in the diphthongs: ia, ie, io, iu	j	hiato, hielo, avión, viuda	yes
"u" in the diphthongs: ua, ue, ui, uo	w	suave, fuego, huida	win
Consonants			
b	b	bomba (at beginning of word or after m)	boom
	β	abajo (all other contexts)	A "b" pronounced without quite closing the lips completely

Spanish Pronunciation Guide

Letter in Spanish	IPA Symbol	Example in Spanish	Pronunciation (example in English)
c	θ (in Spain)	ceño (before e) cinco (before i)	thanks (in Spain)
	s (in Latin America and southern Spain)		sun (in Latin America and southern Spain)
	k	casa (all other contexts)	cat
ch	tʃ	caucho	arch
d	d	donde (at beginning of word or after n) aldea (after l)	day
	ð	adorno (all other contexts)	Similar to the sound in "mother" but less strong
f	f	furia	fire
g	χ	gema (before e) girasol (before i)	Like an "h" but pronounced at the back of the throat (similar to Scottish "loch")
	g	gato (at beginning of word) lengua (after n)	goose
	ɣ	agua (all other contexts)	Like a "w" pronounced while trying to say "g"
j	χ	jabalí	Like an "h" but pronounced at the back of the throat (similar to Scottish "loch")
l	l	lado	lake
ll	j	lluvia	million
	ʒ		In some regions (eg the Rio de la Plata area of South America) it is pronounced like the "s" in "pleasure"
m	m	mano	man
n	n	nulo	no
	ŋ	manco, fango (before c and g)	parking
ñ	ɲ	año	onion
p	p	papa	pool

Letter in Spanish	IPA Symbol	Example in Spanish	Pronunciation (example in English)
r	r	dorado (in between vowels) hablar (at end of syllable or word)	A rolled "r" sound (similar to Scottish "r")
	rr	rosa (at beginning of word) alrededor (after l) enredo (after n)	A much longer rolled "r" sound (similar to Scottish "r")
rr	rr	arroyo	A much longer rolled "r" sound (similar to Scottish "r")
s	s	saco	sound
sh	ʃ	show	show
t	t	tela	tea
v	b	invierno (after "n")	boom
	β	ave (all other contexts)	A "b" pronounced without quite closing the lips completely
x	ks	examen	extra
y	j	ayer	yellow
	ʒ		In some regions (eg the Rio de la Plata area of South America) it is pronounced like the "s" in "pleasure"
z	θ (in Spain)	zapato	thanks (in Spain)
	s (in Latin America and southern Spain)		sun (in Latin America and southern Spain)

Pronunciación del inglés

Para ilustrar la pronunciación inglesa, en este diccionario utilizamos los símbolos del AFI (Alfabeto Fonético Internacional). En el siguiente cuadro, para cada sonido del inglés hay ejemplos de palabras en inglés y palabras en español donde aparece un sonido similar. En los casos en los que no hay sonido similar en español, ofrecemos una explicación de cómo pronunciarlos.

Carácter AFI	Ejemplo en inglés	Ejemplo en español
Consonantes		
[b]	ba**bb**le	**b**e**b**é
[d]	**d**ig	**d**e**d**o
[dʒ]	**g**iant, ji**g**	se pronuncia como [ʒ] en "plea**s**ure" pero con una "**d**" adelante, o como "**gi**" en italiano: **Gi**ovanna
[f]	**f**it, **ph**ysics	**f**aro
[g]	**g**rey, bi**g**	**g**ris
[h]	**h**appy	"**h**" aspirada
[j]	**y**ellow	se pronuncia como "**y**" o "**ll**" en España: **y**o, **ll**uvia
[k]	**c**lay, ki**ck**	**c**asa
[l]	**l**ip	**l**abio
	pi**ll**	pape**l**
[m]	**mu**m**m**y	**m**a**m**á
[n]	**n**ip, pi**n**	**n**ada
[ŋ]	si**ng**	se pronuncia como "**n**" antes de "**c**": ba**n**co
[p]	**p**i**p**	**p**a**p**á
[r]	**r**ig, w**r**ite	sonido entre "**r**" y "**rr**"
[s]	**s**ick, **sc**ience	**s**apo
[ʃ]	**sh**ip, na**ti**on	**sh**ow
[t]	**t**ip, bu**tt**	**t**ela
[tʃ]	**ch**ip, ba**tch**	cau**ch**o
[θ]	**th**ick	**z**apato (como se pronuncia en España)

Carácter AFI	Ejemplo en inglés	Ejemplo en español
[ð]	**th**is	se pronuncia como la "**d**" de "ha**d**a" pero más fuerte
[v]	**v**ague, gi**v**e	se pronuncia como "**v**" de **v**ida, con los dientes apoyados sobre el labio inferior
[w]	**w**it, **w**hy	**wh**isky
[z]	**z**ip, phy**s**ics	"**s**" con sonido zumbante
[ʒ]	plea**s**ure	se pronuncia como "**y**" o "**ll**" en el Río de la Plata: **y**o, **ll**uvia
[χ]	lo**ch**	**j**ota

Vocales

En inglés, las vocales marcadas con dos puntos son mucho más alargadas

[æ]	rag	se pronuncia "**a**" con posición bucal para "**e**"
[ɑː]	l**ar**ge, b**a**th	"**a**" muy alargada
[ʌ]	c**u**p	"**a**" breve y cerrada
[e]	s**e**t	se pronuncia como "**e**" de **e**lefant**e** pero más corta
[ɜː]	c**ur**tain, w**ere**	se pronuncia como una "**e**" larga con posición bucal entre "**o**" y "**e**"
[ə]	utt**er**	se pronuncia como "**e**" con posición bucal para "**o**"
[ɪ]	b**i**g, w**o**men	"**i**" breve, a medio camino entre "**e**" e "**i**"
[iː]	l**ea**k, w**ee**	"**i**" muy alargada
[ɒ]	l**o**ck	"**o**" abierta
[ɔː]	w**a**ll, c**o**rk	"**o**" cerrada y alargada
[ʊ]	p**u**t, l**oo**k	"**u**" breve
[uː]	m**oo**n	"**u**" muy alargada

Pronunciación del inglés

Carácter AFI	Ejemplo en inglés	Ejemplo en español
Diptongos		
[aɪ]	why, high, lie	aire
[aʊ]	how	aura
[eə]	bear	"ea" pronunciado muy brevemente y con sonido de "e" más marcado que el de "a"
[eɪ]	day, make, main	reina
[əʊ]	show, go	"ou" como en COU
[ɪə]	here, gear	hielo pronunciado con el sonido de "i" más marcado y alargado que el de "e"
[ɔɪ]	boy, soil	voy
[ʊə]	poor	cuerno pronunciado con el sonido de "u" más marcado y alargado que el de "e"

Spanish – English
Español – Inglés

A, a [a] *nf (la letra)* A, a
a (*abr* **área**) area
a *prep*

> **a** combines with the article **el** to form the contraction **al** (e.g. **al centro** to the centre).

(**a**) *(dirección)* to; **ir a Colombia** to go to Colombia; **llegar a Valencia** to arrive in Valencia; **subir al tren** to get on the train; **ir al cine** to go to the cinema; **vete a casa** go home

(**b**) *(lugar)* at, on; **a la derecha** on the right; **a la entrada** at the entrance; **a lo lejos** in the distance; **a mi lado** at *o* by my side, next to me; **al sol** in the sun; **a la mesa** at (the) table

(**c**) *(tiempo)* at; **a las doce** at twelve o'clock; **a los sesenta años** at the age of sixty; **a los tres meses/la media hora** three months/half an hour later; **al final** in the end; **al principio** at first

(**d**) *(distancia)* away; **a 100 km de aquí** 100 km from here

(**e**) *(manera)* **a la inglesa** (in the) English fashion *o* manner *o* style; **escrito a máquina** typed, typewritten; **a mano** by hand

(**f**) *(proporción)* **a 90 km por hora** at 90 km an hour; **a 300 pesetas el kilo** 300 pesetas a kilo; **tres veces a la semana** three times a week

(**g**) *Dep* **ganar cuatro a dos** to win four (to) two

(**h**) *(complemento indirecto)* to; *(procedencia)* from; **díselo a Javier** tell Javier; **te lo di a ti** I gave it to you; **comprarle algo a algn** to buy sth from sb; *(para algn)* to buy sth for sb; *(complemento directo de persona)* **saludé a tu tía** I said hello to your aunt

(**i**) *Fam* **ir a por algn/algo** to go and fetch sb/sth

(**j**) *(verbo + a + infin)* to; **aprender a nadar** to learn (how) to swim; **fueron a ayudarle** they went to help him

(**k**) *(nombre + a + infin)* **distancia a recorrer** distance to be covered

(**l**) **a decir verdad** to tell (you) the truth; **a no ser por ...** if it were not for ...; **a no ser**

que unless; **a ver** let's see; **¡a comer!** lunch/dinner/*etc* is ready!; **¡a dormir!** bedtime!; **¿a que no lo haces?** *(desafío)* I bet you don't do it!
abad *nm* abbot
abadía *nf* abbey
abajeño,-a *nm,f Am* lowlander
abajo 1 *adv* (**a**) *(en una casa)* downstairs; **el piso de a.** the downstairs flat (**b**) *(dirección)* down, downwards; **ahí/aquí a.** down there/here; **la parte de a.** the bottom (part); **más a.** further down; **hacia a.** down, downwards; **calle a.** down the street; **echar algo a.** to knock sth down; **venirse a.** *(edificio)* to fall down; *Fig (proyecto)* to fall through
2 *interj* **¡a. la censura!** down with censorship!
abalanzarse [40] *vpr* **a. sobre/contra** to rush towards
abalear *vt Andes, CAm, Ven* to shoot at
abalorio *nm* (**a**) *(cuenta)* glass bead (**b**) *(baratija)* trinket
abanderado,-a *nm,f* standard bearer
abandonado,-a *adj* (**a**) abandoned; **tiene a su familia muy abandonada** he takes absolutely no interest in his family (**b**) *(desaseado)* untidy, unkempt
abandonar 1 *vt* (**a**) *(lugar)* to leave, to quit; *(persona, cosa)* to abandon; *(proyecto, plan)* to give up (**b**) *Dep (carrera)* to drop out of
2 abandonarse *vpr* to let oneself go
abandono *nm* (**a**) *(acción)* abandoning, desertion (**b**) *(de proyecto, idea)* giving up (**c**) *(descuido)* neglect
abanicarse *vpr* to fan oneself
abanico *nm* (**a**) fan (**b**) *(gama)* range; **un amplio a. de posibilidades** a wide range of possibilities
abaratar 1 *vt* to cut *o* reduce the price of
2 abaratarse *vpr (artículos)* to become cheaper, to come down in price; *(precios)* to come down
abarcar [44] *vt (incluir)* to cover
abarrotado,-a *adj* packed, crammed (**de** with)
abarrotar *vt* to pack, to cram (**de** with); **el público abarrotaba la sala** the room

was packed (with people)

abarrote *nm Andes, CAm, Méx* grocer's (shop), grocery store; **abarrotes** groceries; **tienda de abarrotes** grocer's (shop), grocery store

abarrotería *nf Andes, CAm, Méx* grocer's (shop), grocery store

abarrotero,-a *nm,f Andes, CAm, Méx* grocer

abastecedor,-a *nm,f* supplier

abastecer [33] **1** *vt* to supply
 2 abastecerse *vpr* **a. de** to be supplied with

abastecimiento *nm* supplying; **a. de agua** water supply

abasto *nm* (**a**) *Fam* **no doy a.** I can't cope, I can't keep up (**b**) **mercado de abastos** wholesale food market

abatible *adj* folding, collapsible; **asiento a.** reclining seat

abatido,-a *adj* downcast

abatir 1 *vt* (**a**) *(derribar)* to knock down, to pull down (**b**) *(matar)* to kill; **a. a tiros** to shoot down (**c**) *(desanimar)* to depress, to dishearten
 2 abatirse *vpr* *(desanimarse)* to lose heart, to become depressed

abdicación *nf* abdication

abdicar [44] *vt & vi* to abdicate

abdomen *nm* abdomen

abdominales *nmpl* sit-ups

abecedario *nm* alphabet

abedul *nm* birch

abeja *nf* bee; **a. reina** queen bee

abejorro *nm* bumblebee

aberración *nf* aberration

aberrante *adj* deviant

abertura *nf* *(hueco)* opening, gap; *(grieta)* crack, slit

abertzale *adj & nmf* Basque nationalist

abeto *nm Bot* fir (tree); **a. rojo** spruce

abierto,-a *adj* (**a**) open; *(grifo)* (turned) on; **a. de par en par** wide open (**b**) *(persona)* open-minded

abigarrado,-a *adj (mezclado)* jumbled, mixed up

abismal *adj* abysmal; *Fig* **una diferencia a.** a world of a difference

abismo *nm* abyss; *Fig* **al borde del a.** on the brink of ruin; *Fig* **entre ellos media un a.** they are worlds apart

ablandar 1 *vt* to soften
 2 ablandarse *vpr* (**a**) to soften, to go soft (**b**) *Fig (persona)* to mellow

abnegación *nf* abnegation, self-denial

abnegado,-a *adj* selfless, self-sacrificing

abocado,-a *adj* (**a**) **está a. al fracaso** it is doomed to failure (**b**) *(vino)* medium dry

abochornar *vt* to shame, to embarrass

abofetear *vt* to slap

abogacía *nf* legal profession

abogado,-a *nm,f* lawyer, solicitor; *(en tribunal supremo)* lawyer, *Br* barrister; **a. de oficio** legal aid lawyer; **a. defensor** counsel for the defense; **a. del diablo** devil's advocate; **a. laboralista** union lawyer

abogar [42] *vt* to plead; **a. a favor de** to plead for, to defend; **a. por algo** to advocate *o* champion sth

abolengo *nm* ancestry, lineage

abolición *nf* abolition

abolir *vt defect* to abolish

abolladura *nf* dent

abollar *vt* to dent

abominable *adj* abominable

abominar *vt & vi* **a. (de)** to abominate, to loathe

abonado,-a 1 *nm,f* subscriber
 2 *adj Fin (pagado)* paid; **a. en cuenta** credited

abonar 1 *vt* (**a**) *Agr* to fertilize (**b**) *(pagar)* to pay (for) (**c**) *(subscribir)* to subscribe
 2 abonarse *vpr* to subscribe (**a** to)

abonero,-a *nm,f Méx* hawker, street trader

abono *nm* (**a**) *Agr (producto)* fertilizer; *(estiércol)* manure (**b**) *(pago)* payment (**c**) *(a revista etc)* subscription; *(billete)* season ticket (**d**) *Méx (plazo)* instalment; **pagar en abonos** to pay by instalments

abordar *vt (persona)* to approach; *(barco)* to board; **a. un asunto** to tackle a subject

aborigen *(pl* **aborígenes**) **1** *adj* native, indigenous; *esp Austral* aboriginal
 2 *nmf* native; *esp Austral* aborigine

aborrecer [33] *vt* to detest, to loathe

abortar 1 *vi (involuntariamente)* to miscarry, to have a miscarriage; *(intencionadamente)* to abort, to have an abortion
 2 *vt* to abort

abortista *nmf* abortionist

aborto *nm* miscarriage; *(provocado)* abortion

abotargado,-a *adj* swollen

abotonar *vt (ropa)* to button (up)

abovedado,-a *adj* vaulted, arched

abracadabra *nm* abracadabra

abrasador,-a *adj* scorching

abrasar 1 *vt & vi* to scorch
 2 abrasarse *vpr* to burn

abrazadera *nf* clamp

abrazar [40] **1** *vt* to embrace, to hug; *Fig (doctrina)* to embrace

2 abrazarse *vpr* **a. a algn** to embrace sb; **se abrazaron** they embraced each other

abrazo *nm* embrace, hug; **un a., abrazos** *(en carta)* best wishes

abrecartas *nm inv* letter-opener, paperknife

abrefácil *nm Com* **caja con a.** easy-open carton

abrelatas *nm inv* tin-opener, *US* can opener

abreviar [43] 1 (**a**) *vt* to shorten; *(texto)* to abridge; *(palabra)* to abbreviate

2 *vi* to be quick o brief; **para a.** to cut a long story short

abreviatura *nf* abbreviation

abridor *nm (de latas, botellas)* opener

abrigado,-a *adj* wrapped-up; **ir muy a.** to be well wrapped-up

abrigar [42] *vt* (**a**) to keep warm; **esta chaqueta abriga mucho** this cardigan is very warm (**b**) *(proteger)* to protect, to shelter (**c**) *(esperanza)* to cherish; *(duda)* to have, to harbour

abrigo *nm* (**a**) *(prenda)* coat, overcoat; **ropa de a.** warm clothes (**b**) **al a. de** protected o sheltered from

abril *nm* April

abrillantador *nm* polish

abrillantar *vt* to polish

abrir [1] *nm* **en un a. y cerrar de ojos** in the twinkling of an eye

abrir [2] (*pp* **abierto**) **1** *vi* to open

2 *vt* (**a**) to open; *(cremallera)* to undo (**b**) *(gas, grifo)* to turn on (**c**) *Jur* **a. (un) expediente** to start proceedings

3 abrirse *vpr* (**a**) to open; *Fig* **a. paso** to make one's way (**b**) *Fam* **¡me abro!** I'm off!

abrochar *vt,* **abrocharse** *vpr (botones)* to do up; *(camisa)* to button (up); *(cinturón)* to fasten; *(zapatos)* to tie up; *(cremallera)* to do up

abrumado,-a *adj* overwhelmed

abrumador,-a *adj* overwhelming

abrumar *vt* to overwhelm, to crush; **tantos problemas me abruman** all these problems are getting on top of me

abrupto,-a *adj* (**a**) *(terreno)* steep, abrupt (**b**) *Fig* abrupt, sudden

absceso *nm* abscess

absentismo *nm* absenteeism; **a. laboral** absenteeism from work

absolución *nf* (**a**) *Rel* absolution (**b**) *Jur* acquittal

absolutamente *adv* absolutely, completely; **a. nada** nothing at all

absoluto,-a *adj* absolute; **en a.** not at all, by no means

absolutorio,-a *adj Jur* **sentencia absolutoria** verdict of not guilty

absolver [4] (*pp* **absuelto**) *vt* (**a**) *Rel* to absolve (**b**) *Jur* to acquit

absorbente *adj* (**a**) *(papel)* absorbent (**b**) *Fig* absorbing, engrossing

absorber *vt* to absorb

absorción *nf* absorption

absorto,-a *adj* absorbed, engrossed (**en** in)

abstemio,-a 1 *adj* teetotal, abstemious

2 *nm,f* teetotaller

abstención *nf* abstention

abstenerse [24] *vpr* to abstain (**de** from); *(privarse)* to refrain (**de** from)

abstinencia *nf* abstinence; **síndrome de a.** withdrawal symptoms

abstracción *nf* abstraction

abstracto,-a *adj* abstract

abstraer [25] 1 *vt* to abstract

2 abstraerse *vpr* to become lost in thought

abstraído,-a *adj (ensimismado)* absorbed, engrossed (**en** in); *(distraído)* absent-minded

absuelto,-a *pp de* **absolver**

absurdo,-a 1 *adj* absurd

2 *nm* absurdity, absurd thing

abuchear *vt* to boo, to jeer at

abucheo *nm* booing, jeering

abuela *nf* grandmother; *Fam* grandma, granny; *Fig* old woman

abuelo *nm* (**a**) grandfather; *Fam* grandad, grandpa; *Fig* old man (**b**) **abuelos** grandparents

abulense 1 *adj* of/from Avila

2 *nmf* person from Avila

abulia *nf* apathy, lack of willpower

abultado,-a *adj* bulky, big

abultar 1 *vi* to be bulky; **abulta mucho** it takes up a lot of space

2 *vt* to exaggerate

abundancia *nf* abundance, plenty; *Fig* **nadar en la a.** to be rolling in money

abundante *adj* abundant, plentiful

abundar *vi* to abound, to be plentiful

abur *interj Fam* cheerio!, see you!

aburrido,-a *adj* (**a**) **ser a.** to be boring (**b**) **estar a.** to be bored; **estar a. de** *(harto)* to be tired of

aburrimiento *nm* boredom; **¡qué a.!** how boring!, what a bore!

aburrir 1 *vt* to bore

2 aburrirse *vpr* to get bored; **a. como una ostra** to be bored stiff

abusado,-a *adj Méx* astute, shrewd

abusar *vi* (**a**) *(propasarse)* to go too far (**b**) **a. de** *(situación, persona)* to take (unfair) advantage of; *(poder, amabilidad)* to abuse; **a. de la bebida/del tabaco** to drink/smoke too much *o* to excess; *Jur* **a. de un niño/una mujer** to abuse a child/woman

abusivo,-a *adj (precio)* exorbitant

abuso *nm* abuse

abyecto,-a *adj* abject

a. C. (*abr* antes de Cristo) BC

a/c *Com* (*abr* **a cuenta**) on account

acá *adv* (**a**) *(lugar)* here, over here; **más a.** nearer; **¡ven a.!** come here! (**b**) **de entonces a.** since then

acabado,-a 1 *adj* (**a**) *(terminado)* finished (**b**) *Fig (persona)* worn-out, spent
2 *nm* finish

acabar 1 *vt* to finish (off); *(completar)* to complete
2 *vi* (**a**) to finish, to end; **a. bien** to have a happy ending; **a. con algo** *(terminarlo)* to finish sth; *(romperlo)* to break sth (**b**) **a. de ...** to have just ...; **acaba de entrar** he has just come in; **no acaba de convencerme** I'm not quite convinced (**c**) **acabaron casándose** *o* **por casarse** they ended up getting married; **acabó en la cárcel** he ended up in jail
3 acabarse *vpr* to finish, to come to an end; **se nos acabó la gasolina** we ran out of *Br* petrol *o US* gas; *Fam* **¡se acabó!** that's that!

acabóse *nm Fam* **esto es el a.** this is the end

acacia *nf* acacia

academia *nf* academy; **a. de idiomas** language school

académico,-a *adj & nm,f* academic

acaecer [33] *v impers* to happen, to occur

acallar *vt* to silence

acalorado,-a *adj* (**a**) hot (**b**) *Fig (excitado)* worked up, excited; *(debate etc)* heated, angry

acalorarse *vpr* (**a**) to get warm *o* hot (**b**) *Fig* to get excited *o* worked up

acampada *nf* camping; **ir de a.** to go camping; **zona de a.** camp site, *US* campground

acampanado,-a *adj* bell-shaped; *(prendas)* flared

acampar *vi* to camp

acantilado *nm* cliff

acantonar *vt (tropas)* to billet, to quarter (**en** in)

acaparar *vt* (**a**) *(productos)* to hoard; *(el mercado)* to corner (**b**) *Fig* to monopolize

acápite *nm Am (párrafo)* paragraph

acaramelado,-a *adj* (**a**) *(color)* caramel-coloured (**b**) *(pareja)* lovey-dovey, starry-eyed

acariciar [43] *vt* to caress; *(pelo, animal)* to stroke; *(esperanza)* to cherish

acarrear *vt* (**a**) *(transportar)* to carry, to transport (**b**) *Fig (conllevar)* to entail

acaso *adv* perhaps, maybe; **¿a. no te lo dije?** did I not tell you, by any chance?; **por si a.** just in case; **si a. viene ...** if he should come ...

acatamiento *nm* respect; *(de la ley)* observance

acatar *vt* to observe, to comply with

acatarrado,-a *adj* **estar a.** to have a cold

acatarrarse *vpr* to catch a cold

acaudalado,-a *adj* rich, wealthy

acaudalar *vt* to accumulate, to amass

acaudillar *vt* to lead

acceder *vi* **a. a** *(consentir)* to accede to, to consent to; *(tener acceso)* to gain admittance to; *Informát* to access

accesible *adj* accessible; *(persona)* approachable

acceso *nm* (**a**) *(entrada)* access, entry; *Informát* **a. al azar, a. directo** random access; *Univ* **prueba de a.** entrance examination; **a. a Internet** Internet access (**b**) *(carretera)* approach, access (**c**) *Med & Fig* fit

accesorio,-a *adj & nm* accessory

accidentado,-a 1 *adj (terreno)* uneven, hilly; *(viaje, vida)* eventful
2 *nm,f* casualty, accident victim

accidental *adj* accidental; **un encuentro a.** a chance meeting

accidente *nm* (**a**) accident; **por a.** by chance; **a. laboral** industrial accident (**b**) *Geog* **accidentes geográficos** geographical features

acción *nf* (**a**) action; *(acto)* act; **poner en a.** to put into action; **ponerse en a.** to go into action; **campo de a.** field of action; **película de a.** adventure film (**b**) *Fin* share

accionar *vt* to drive

accionista *nmf* shareholder

acebo *nm (hoja)* holly; *(árbol)* holly tree

acechar *vt* to lie in wait for; **un grave peligro nos acecha** great danger awaits us

acecho *nm* **estar al a. de** *(esperar)* to lie in wait for

acedía *nf (pez)* dab

aceite *nm* oil; **a. de girasol/maíz/oliva** sunflower/corn/olive oil

aceitera *nf* (**a**) *Culin* oil bottle; **aceiteras** oil and vinegar set (**b**) *Aut* oil can

aceitero,-a 1 *adj* oil
  2 *nm,f* oil merchant
aceitoso,-a *adj* oily
aceituna *nf* olive; **a. rellena** stuffed olive
aceitunado,-a *adj* olive, olive-coloured
aceitunero,-a *nm,f* (**a**) *(recolector)* olive picker *o* harvester (**b**) *(vendedor)* olive seller
acelerado,-a *adj* accelerated, fast
acelerador *nm Aut* accelerator
acelerar *vt* to accelerate
acento *nm* (**a**) accent; *(de palabra)* stress (**b**) *(énfasis)* stress, emphasis
acentuar [30] 1 *vt* (**a**) to stress (**b**) *Fig* to emphasize, to stress
  2 acentuarse *vpr Fig* to become more pronounced *o* noticeable
aceña *nf* watermill
acepción *nf* meaning, sense
aceptable *adj* acceptable
aceptación *nf* (**a**) acceptance (**b**) **tener poca a.** to have little success, not to be popular
aceptar *vt* to accept
acequia *nf* irrigation ditch *o* channel
acera *nf Br* pavement, *US* sidewalk; *Fam Pey* **ser de la a. de enfrente** to be gay *o* queer
acerado *nm* pavement
acerbo,-a *adj* harsh, bitter
acerca *adv* **a. de** about
acercamiento *nm* bringing together, coming together; *Pol* rapprochement
acercar [44] 1 *vt* to bring near *o* nearer, to bring (over); *Fig* to bring together; **¿te acerco a casa?** can I give you a lift home?
  2 acercarse *vpr* (**a**) **acercarse (a)** to approach (**b**) *(ir)* to go; *(venir)* to come
acerico *nm* pincushion
acero *nm* steel; **a. inoxidable** stainless steel
acérrimo,-a *adj (partidario)* staunch; *(enemigo)* bitter
acertado,-a *adj* (**a**) *(solución)* right, correct; *(decisión)* wise (**b**) **no estuviste muy a. al decir eso** it wasn't very wise of you to say that
acertante 1 *nmf* winner
  2 *adj* winning
acertar [1] 1 *vt (pregunta)* to get right; *(adivinar)* to guess correctly; **a. las quinielas** to win the pools
  2 *vi* to be right; **acertó con la calle que buscaba** she found the street she was looking for
acertijo *nm* riddle
acervo *nm* **a. cultural** cultural tradition *o* heritage

achacar [44] *vt (atribuir)* to attribute
achacoso,-a *adj* ailing, unwell
achaque *nm* ailment, complaint
achicar [44] 1 *vt* (**a**) *(amilanar)* to intimidate (**b**) *(encoger)* to reduce, to make smaller (**c**) *(barco)* to bale out
  2 achicarse *vpr* (**a**) *(amilanarse)* to lose heart (**b**) *(encogerse)* to get smaller
achicharrar *vt* to burn to a crisp
achicoria *nf* chicory
achinado,-a *adj* (**a**) *(ojos)* slanting (**b**) *Am* Indian-looking
acholado,-a *adj Andes Pey* half-caste
achuchar *vt (empujar)* to shove
achuchón *nm (empujón)* push, shove
aciago,-a *adj* ill-fated, fateful
acicalado,-a *adj* well-dressed, smart
acicalarse *vpr* to dress up, to smarten up
acicate *nm Fig (aliciente)* spur, incentive
acidez *nf (de sabor)* sharpness, sourness; *Quím* acidity; *Med* **a. de estómago** heartburn
ácido,-a 1 *adj (sabor)* sharp, tart; *Quím* acidic; *Fig (tono)* harsh
  2 *nm Quím* acid
acierto *nm (buena decisión)* good choice *o* idea; **con gran a.** very wisely
aclamación *nf* acclamation, acclaim
aclamar *vt* to acclaim
aclaración *nf* explanation
aclarado *nm* rinsing, rinse
aclarar 1 *vt* (**a**) *(explicar)* to clarify, to explain; *(color)* to lighten, to make lighter (**b**) *(enjuagar)* to rinse
  2 *v impers Met* to clear (up)
  3 aclararse *vpr* (**a**) *(decidirse)* to make up one's mind; *(entender)* to understand (**b**) *Met* to clear (up)
aclaratorio,-a *adj* explanatory
aclimatación *nf Br* acclimatization, *US* acclimation
aclimatar 1 *vt Br* to acclimatize, *US* to acclimate (**a** to)
  2 aclimatarse *vpr Fig* **a. a algo** to get used to sth
acné *nf* acne
acobardar 1 *vt* to frighten
  2 acobardarse *vpr* to get frightened, to lose one's nerve
acodarse *vpr* to lean (**en** on)
acogedor,-a *adj* cosy, warm
acoger [53] 1 *vt* (**a**) *(recibir)* to receive; *(a invitado)* to welcome (**b**) *(persona desvalida)* to take in
  2 acogerse *vpr Fig* **a. a** to take refuge in; *(amnistía)* to avail oneself of; **a. a la ley** to have recourse to the law
acogida *nf* reception, welcome

acojonado,-a *adj muy Fam* shit-scared

acojonante *adj muy Fam* damn *o Br* bloody great *o* terrific

acojonarse *vpr muy Fam (acobardarse)* to shit oneself, to be shit-scared

acolchar *vt (rellenar)* to pad; *(prenda)* to quilt

acometer *vt* (**a**) *(emprender)* to undertake (**b**) *(atacar)* to attack

acometida *nf (ataque)* attack; *(de gas etc)* connection

acomodado,-a *adj* well-off, well-to-do

acomodador,-a *nm,f (hombre)* usher; *(mujer)* usherette

acomodar 1 *vt* (**a**) *(alojar)* to lodge, to accommodate (**b**) *(en cine etc)* to find a place for
　2 acomodarse *vpr* (**a**) to make oneself comfortable (**b**) *(adaptarse)* to adapt

acomodaticio,-a *adj* (**a**) accommodating, easy-going (**b**) *Pey* pliable

acompañante 1 *nmf* companion
　2 *adj* accompanying

acompañar *vt* (**a**) to accompany; **le acompañó hasta la puerta** she saw him to the door; **me acompañó al médico** he came with me to see the doctor; **¿te acompaño a casa?** can I walk you home?; *Fml* **le acompaño en el sentimiento** my condolences (**b**) *(adjuntar)* to enclose

acompasado,-a *adj (rítmico)* rhythmic

acomplejado,-a *adj* **estar a.** to have a complex (**por** about)

acomplejar 1 *vt* **a. alguien** to give sb a complex
　2 acomplejarse *vpr* **a. por** to develop a complex about

acondicionado,-a *adj* **aire a.** air conditioning

acondicionador *nm* conditioner

acondicionar *vt* to prepare, to set up; *(mejorar)* to improve; *(cabello)* to condition

acongojar *vt* to distress

aconsejable *adj* advisable

aconsejar *vt* to advise

acontecer [33] *v impers* to happen, to take place

acontecimiento *nm* event

acopio *nm* store, stock; **hacer a. de** to store

acoplar 1 *vt* (**a**) to fit (together), to join (**b**) *Téc* to couple, to connect
　2 acoplarse *vpr (nave espacial)* to dock

acorazado,-a 1 *adj* armoured, armour-plated
　2 *nm* battleship

acordado,-a *adj* agreed; **según lo a.** as agreed

acordar [2] 1 *vt* to agree; *(decidir)* to decide
　2 acordarse *vpr* to remember; **no me acuerdo (de Silvia)** I can't remember (Silvia)

acorde 1 *adj* in agreement
　2 *nm Mús* chord

acordeón *nm* (**a**) *(instrument)* accordion (**b**) *Col, Méx Fam (en examen)* crib

acordonado,-a *adj* cordoned off, sealed off

acordonar *vt* (**a**) *(zona)* to cordon off, to seal off (**b**) *(atar)* to lace up

acorralar *vt* to corner

acortar *vt* to shorten; **a. distancias** to cut down the distance

acosar *vt* to harass; *Fig* **a. a algn a preguntas** to bombard sb with questions

acoso *nm* harassment; **a. sexual** sexual harassment

acostar [2] 1 *vt* to put to bed
　2 acostarse *vpr* (**a**) to go to bed (**b**) *Fam* **a. con algn** to sleep with sb, to go to bed with sb

acostumbrado,-a *adj* (**a**) usual, customary; **es lo a.** it is the custom (**b**) **a. al frío/calor** used to the cold/heat

acostumbrar 1 *vi* **a. a** *(soler)* to be in the habit of
　2 *vt* **a. a algn a algo** *(habituar)* to get sb used to sth
　3 acostumbrarse *vpr (habituarse)* **a. a algo** to get used to sth

acotación *nf* (**a**) *(en escrito)* (marginal) note; *Teatro* stage direction (**b**) *(en mapa)* elevation mark

acotamiento *nm Méx (arcén)* verge; *(de autopista) Br* hard shoulder, *US* shoulder

acotar *vt* (**a**) *(área)* to enclose; *Fig (tema)* to delimit (**b**) *(texto)* to annotate (**c**) *(mapa)* to mark with elevations

ácrata *adj & nmf* anarchist

acre¹ *adj* (**a**) *(sabor)* sour, bitter; *(olor)* acrid (**b**) *Fig (palabras)* bitter, harsh; *(crítica)* biting

acre² *nm (medida)* acre

acrecentar [1] *vt* to increase

acreditación *nf* badge

acreditar *vt* (**a**) to be a credit to (**b**) *(probar)* to prove (**c**) *(embajador)* to accredit (**d**) *Fin* to credit

acreditativo,-a *adj* which proves, which gives proof

acreedor,-a *nm,f Com* creditor

acribillar *vt* to riddle, to pepper; **a. a algn a balazos** to riddle sb with bullets

acrílico,-a *adj* acrylic

acriollarse *vpr Am* to adopt native ways

acritud *nf (mordacidad)* acrimony
acrobacia *nf* acrobatics *sing*
acróbata *nmf* acrobat
acta *nf* (**a**) *(de reunión)* minutes, record (**b**) *(certificado)* certificate, official document; **a. notarial** affidavit; **A. Única (Europea)** Single European Act

> Takes the masculine articles **el** and **un**.

actitud *nf* attitude
activar *vt* (**a**) to activate (**b**) *(avivar)* to liven up
actividad *nf* activity
activista *nmf* activist
activo,-a **1** *adj* active; **en a.** on active service
   2 *nm Fin* assets
acto *nm* (**a**) act, action; **a. sexual** sexual intercourse; **en el a.** at once; **a. seguido** immediately afterwards; *Mil* **en a. de servicio** in action; **hacer a. de presencia** to put in an appearance (**b**) *(ceremonia)* ceremony (**c**) *Teatro* act
actor *nm* actor
actriz *nf* actress
actuación *nf* (**a**) performance (**b**) *(intervención)* intervention, action
actual *adj* current, present; *(al día)* up-to-date; **un tema muy a.** a very topical subject
actualidad *nf* (**a**) present time; **en la a.** at present; **estar de a.** to be fashionable; **temas de a.** topical subjects (**b**) *(hechos)* current affairs
actualizar [**40**] *vt* to update, to bring up to date; *Informát (software, hardware)* to upgrade
actualmente *adv (hoy en día)* nowadays, these days; *(ahora)* at the moment, at present

> Observa que las palabras inglesas **actual** y **actually** son falsos amigos y no son la traducción de las palabras españolas **actual** y **actualmente**. En inglés, **actual** significa "real, verdadero", y **actually** significa "en realidad".

actuar [**30**] *vi* (**a**) to act; **a. como** *o* **de** to act as (**b**) *Cin & Teatro* to perform, to act
acuarela *nf* watercolour
Acuario *nm* Aquarius
acuario *nm* aquarium
acuartelar *vt* to confine to barracks
acuático,-a *adj* aquatic; **esquí a.** water-skiing
acuchillar *vt* to knife, to stab
acuciante *adj* urgent, pressing
acuciar [**43**] *vt* to urge on

acudir *vi (ir)* to go; *(venir)* to come, to arrive; **nadie acudió en su ayuda** nobody came to help him; **no sé dónde a.** I don't know where to turn
acueducto *nm* aqueduct
acuerdo *nm* agreement; **¡de a.!** all right!, O.K.!; **de a. con** in accordance with; **de común a.** by common consent; **estar de a. en algo** to agree on sth; **ponerse de a.** to agree; **a. marco** framework agreement
acumular **1** *vt* to accumulate
   2 acumularse *vpr* (**a**) to accumulate, to build up (**b**) *(gente)* to crowd
acunar *vt* to rock
acuñar *vt (moneda)* to mint; *(frase)* to coin
acuoso,-a *adj* watery; *(jugoso)* juicy
acupuntura *nf* acupuncture
acurrucarse [**44**] *vpr* to curl up, to snuggle up
acusación *nf* (**a**) accusation (**b**) *Jur* charge
acusado,-a **1** *nm,f* accused, defendant
   2 *adj (marcado)* marked, noticeable
acusar **1** *vt* (**a**) to accuse (**de** of); *Jur* to charge (**de** with) (**b**) *(golpe etc)* to feel; *Fig* **su cara acusaba el cansancio** his face showed his exhaustion (**c**) *Com* **a. recibo** to acknowledge receipt
   2 acusarse *vpr* (**a**) *(acentuarse)* to become more pronounced (**b**) *Fig (notarse)* to show
acuse *nm* **a. de recibo** acknowledgment of receipt
acusica *adj & nmf Fam* telltale
acústica *nf* acoustics *sing*
acústico,-a *adj* acoustic
adán *nm Fam* untidy *o* slovenly person
adaptable *adj* adaptable
adaptación *nf* adaptation
adaptador *nm* adapter
adaptar **1** *vt* (**a**) to adapt (**b**) *(ajustar)* to adjust
   2 adaptarse *vpr* to adapt oneself (**a** to)
adecentar *vt* to tidy (up), to clean (up)
adecuado,-a *adj* appropriate, suitable
adecuar [**47**] *vt* to adapt
adefesio *nm (persona)* freak; *(cosa)* monstrosity
a. de J.C. (*abr* **antes de Jesucristo**) BC
adelantado,-a *adj* (**a**) advanced; *(desarrollado)* developed; *(precoz)* precocious (**b**) *(reloj)* fast (**c**) **pagar por a.** to pay in advance
adelantamiento *nm* overtaking; **hacer un a.** to overtake
adelantar **1** *vt* (**a**) to move *o* bring forward; *(reloj)* to put forward; *Fig* to

advance (**b**) *Aut* to overtake (**c**) *(fecha)* to bring forward; *Fig* **a. (los) acontecimientos** to get ahead of oneself

2 *vi* (**a**) to advance (**b**) *(progresar)* to make progress (**c**) *(reloj)* to be fast

3 adelantarse *vpr* (**a**) *(ir delante)* to go ahead (**b**) *(reloj)* to gain, to be fast (**c**) **el verano se ha adelantado** we are having an early summer

adelante 1 *adv* forward; **más a.** *(lugar)* further on; *(tiempo)* later; **seguir a.** to keep going, to carry on; **llevar a. un plan** to carry out a plan

2 *interj* **¡a!** come in!

adelanto *nm* (**a**) advance; *(progreso)* progress (**b**) **el reloj lleva diez minutos de a.** the watch is ten minutes fast (**c**) *(de dinero)* advance payment

adelfa *nf* oleander, rosebay

adelgazamiento *nm* slimming

adelgazar [40] *vi* to slim, to lose weight

ademán *nm* (**a**) gesture (**b**) **ademanes** manners

además *adv* moreover, furthermore; **a., no lo he visto nunca** what's more, I've never seen him; **a. de él** besides him

adentrarse *vpr* **a. en** *(bosque)* to go deep into; *(asunto)* to study thoroughly

adentro 1 *adv* *(dentro)* inside; **mar a.** out to sea; **tierra a.** inland

2 *nmpl* **decir algo para sus adentros** to say sth to oneself

adepto,-a *nm,f* follower, supporter

Observa que la palabra inglesa **adept** es un falso amigo y no es la traducción de la palabra española **adepto**. En inglés, **adept** significa "experto".

---

aderezar [40] *vt* *(comida)* to season; *(ensalada)* to dress

aderezo *nm* *(de comida)* seasoning; *(de ensalada)* dressing

adeudar 1 *vt* to owe

2 adeudarse *vpr* to get into debt

adherencia *nf* adherence; *Aut* roadholding

adherir [5] 1 *vt* to stick on

2 adherirse *vpr* **a. a** to adhere to; *(partido)* to join

adhesión *nf* adhesion; *(a partido)* joining; *(a teoría)* adherence

adhesivo,-a *adj & nm* adhesive

adicción *nf* addiction; **crear a.** to be addictive

adición *nf* addition

adicional *adj* additional

adicto,-a 1 *nm,f* addict

2 *adj* addicted (**a** to)

adiestrar *vt* to train

adinerado,-a 1 *adj* wealthy, rich

2 *nm,f* rich person

adiós *(pl* **adioses***)* **1** *interj* goodbye; *Fam* bye-bye; *(al cruzarse)* hello

2 *nm* goodbye

aditivo,-a *adj & nm* additive

adivinanza *nf* riddle, puzzle

adivinar *vt* to guess; **a. el pensamiento de algn** to read sb's mind

adivino,-a *nm,f* fortune-teller

adjetivo,-a 1 *nm* adjective

2 *adj* adjectival

adjudicación *nf* award; *(en subasta)* sale

adjudicar [44] 1 *vt* (**a**) *(premio, contrato)* to award (**b**) *(en subasta)* to sell

2 adjudicarse *vpr* to appropriate, to take over

adjuntar *vt* to enclose

adjunto,-a 1 *adj* (**a**) enclosed, attached (**b**) *Educ* assistant

2 *nm,f* *Educ* assistant teacher

adm., admón. *(abr* **administración***)* admin.

administración *nf* (**a**) *(gobierno)* administration, authorities; *Pol* **a. central** central government; **a. pública** civil service (**b**) *(de empresa)* administration, management (**c**) *(oficina)* (branch) office

administrador,-a 1 *nm,f* administrator

2 *adj* administrating

administrar 1 *vt* (**a**) to administer (**b**) *(dirigir)* to run, to manage

2 administrarse *vpr* to manage one's own money

administrativo,-a 1 *adj* administrative

2 *nm,f* *(funcionario)* official

admirable *adj* admirable

admiración *nf* (**a**) admiration; **causar a.** to impress (**b**) *Ling* exclamation mark

admirador,-a *nm,f* admirer

admirar 1 *vt* (**a**) to admire (**b**) *(sorprender)* to amaze, to astonish

2 admirarse *vpr* to be amazed, to be astonished

admisible *adj* admissible, acceptable

admisión *nf* admission; **reservado el derecho de a.** *(en letrero)* the management reserves the right to refuse admission

admitir *vt* (**a**) to admit, to let in (**b**) *(aceptar)* to accept; **no se admiten cheques** *(en letrero)* no cheques accepted (**c**) *(tolerar)* to allow (**d**) *(reconocer)* to admit, to acknowledge; **admito que mentí** I admit that I lied

admonición *nf* warning

ADN *nm* *(abr* **ácido desoxirribonucleico***)* DNA

adobar vt Culin to marinate
adobe nm adobe
adobo nm marinade
adoctrinar vt to indoctrinate
adolecer [33] vi a. de (carecer de) to lack; Fig Fml to suffer from
adolescencia nf adolescence
adolescente adj & nmf adolescent
adonde adv where
adónde adv interr where (to)?
adondequiera adv wherever
adopción nf adoption
adoptar vt to adopt
adoptivo,-a adj (hijo) adopted; (padres) adoptive; Fig país a. country of adoption
adoquín nm cobble, paving stone
adorable adj adorable
adorar vt (a) Rel to worship (b) Fig to adore
adormecer [33] 1 vt to send to sleep, to make sleepy
　2 adormecerse vpr (a) (dormirse) to doze off (b) (brazo etc) to go to sleep, to go numb
adormecido,-a adj sleepy, drowsy
adormilarse vpr to doze, to drowse
adornar vt to adorn, to decorate
adorno nm decoration, adornment; de a. decorative
adosado,-a adj adjacent; (casa) semidetached
adquirir [31] vt to acquire; (comprar) to purchase
adquisición nf acquisition; (compra) buy, purchase
adquisitivo,-a adj poder a. purchasing power
adrede adv deliberately, on purpose
adrenalina nf adrenalin
adriático,-a nm el (Mar) A. the Adriatic (Sea)
adscribir (pp adscrito) **1** vt (a) (atribuir) to ascribe to (b) (a un trabajo) to appoint to
　2 adscribirse vpr to affiliate (a to)
adscrito,-a pp de adscribir
aduana nf customs
aduanero,-a 1 adj customs
　2 nm,f customs officer
aducir [10] vt (motivo, pretexto) to give
adueñarse vpr a. de to take over; (pánico etc) to take hold of
aduje pt indef de aducir
adulación nf adulation
adular vt to adulate
adulterar vt to adulterate
adulterio nm adultery
adúltero,-a 1 adj adulterous

　2 nm,f (hombre) adulterer; (mujer) adulteress
adulto,-a adj & nm,f adult
adusto,-a adj harsh, severe
aduzco indic pres de aducir
advenedizo,-a adj & nm,f upstart
advenimiento nm advent, coming
adverbio nm adverb
adversario,-a 1 nm,f adversary, opponent
　2 adj opposing
adversidad nf adversity; (revés) setback
adverso,-a adj adverse
advertencia nf warning
advertido,-a adj warned; (informado) informed; estás o quedas a. you've been warned
advertir [5] vt (a) to warn; (informar) to inform, to advise; Fam te advierto que yo tampoco lo vi mind you, I didn't see it either (b) (notar) to realize, to notice
adviento nm Advent
adyacente adj adjacent
aéreo,-a adj (a) aerial (b) Av air; tráfico a. air traffic; Com por vía aerea by air
aero- pref aero-
aeróbic nm aerobics sing
aerodinámico,-a adj aerodynamic; de línea aerodinámica streamlined
aeródromo nm aerodrome
aeromodelismo nm aeroplane modelling
aeromoza nf Am air hostess
aeronáutica nf aeronautics sing
aeronáutico,-a adj la industria aeronáutica the aeronautics industry
aeronave nf airship
aeroplano nm light aeroplane
aeropuerto nm airport
aerosol nm aerosol
aerostático,-a adj globo a. hot-air balloon
a/f (abr a favor) in favour
afable adj affable
afamado,-a adj famous, well-known
afán nm (pl afanes) (a) (esfuerzo) effort (b) (celo) zeal
afanador,-a nm,f Méx cleaner
afanar 1 vt Fam (robar) to pinch
　2 afanarse vpr a. por conseguir algo to do one's best to achieve sth
afanoso,-a adj (a) (persona) keen, eager (b) (tarea) hard, tough
afección nf disease
afectación nf affectation
afectado,-a adj affected
afectar vt a. to affect; le afectó mucho she was deeply affected; nos afecta a

todos it concerns all of us
afecto *nm* affection; **tomarle a. a algn** to become fond of sb
afectuoso,-a *adj* affectionate
afeitado *nm* shave
afeitar *vt*, **afeitarse** *vpr* to shave
afeminado,-a *adj* effeminate
aferrado,-a *adj* **a. a** clinging to
aferrar 1 *vt Náut* to anchor, to moor
  2 **aferrarse** *vpr* to clutch, to cling; *Fig* **a. a una creencia** to cling to a belief
Afganistán *n* Afghanistan
afgano,-a *adj & nm,f* Afghan
afianzamiento *nm* strengthening, reinforcement
afianzar [40] 1 *vt* to strengthen, to reinforce
  2 **afianzarse** *vpr (persona)* to become established
afiche *nm Am* poster
afición *nf* (**a**) liking; **tiene a. por la música** he is fond of music (**b**) *Dep* **la a.** the fans
aficionado,-a 1 *nm,f* (**a**) enthusiast; **un a. a la música** a music lover (**b**) *(no profesional)* amateur
  2 *adj* (**a**) keen, fond; **ser a. a algo** to be fond of sth (**b**) *(no profesional)* amateur
aficionarse *vpr* to become fond (**a** of), to take a liking (**a** to)
afilado,-a *adj* sharp
afilar *vt* to sharpen
afiliación *nf* affiliation
afiliado,-a *nm,f* member
afiliarse [43] *vpr* to become a member
afín *adj (semejante)* kindred, similar; *(relacionado)* related
afinar *vt* (**a**) *(puntería)* to sharpen (**b**) *(instrumento)* to tune
afincarse [44] *vpr* to settle down
afinidad *nf* affinity
afirmación *nf* affirmation; **afirmaciones** *(declaración)* statement
afirmar (**a**) *vt (aseverar)* to state, to declare (**b**) *(afianzar)* to strengthen, to reinforce
afirmativo,-a *adj* affirmative; **en caso a.** ... if the answer is yes ...
aflicción *nf* affliction
afligir [57] 1 *vt* to afflict
  2 **afligirse** *vpr* to grieve, to be distressed
aflojar 1 *vt* to loosen
  2 *vi (viento etc)* to weaken, to grow weak
  3 **aflojarse** *vpr* to come *o* work loose; *(rueda)* to go down
aflorar *vi (río)* to come to the surface; *(sentimiento)* to surface, to show
afluencia *nf* inflow, influx; **gran a. de**

público great numbers of people
afluente *nm* tributary
afluir [37] *vi* to flow (**a** into)
afónico,-a *adj* **estar a.** to have lost one's voice
aforismo *nm* aphorism
aforo *nm (capacidad)* seating capacity
afortunado,-a *adj* fortunate; **las Islas Afortunadas** the Canaries
afrenta *nf Fml* affront
Africa *n* Africa
africano,-a *adj & nm,f* African
afrodisíaco,-a *adj & nm* aphrodisiac
afrontar *vt* to confront, to face; **a. las consecuencias** to face the consequences
afuera 1 *adv* outside; **la parte de a.** the outside; **más a.** further out; **salir a.** to come *o* go out
  2 *nfpl* **afueras** outskirts
agachar 1 *vt* to lower
  2 **agacharse** *vpr* to duck
agalla *nf* (**a**) *(de pez)* gill (**b**) **tiene agallas** she's got guts
agarraderas *nfpl Fam* **tener buenas a.** to be well-connected
agarrado,-a *adj* (**a**) *Fam* stingy, tight (**b**) **baile a.** cheek-to-cheek dancing
agarrar 1 *vt* (**a**) to grasp, to seize; **agárralo fuerte** hold it tight (**b**) *Am (tomar)* to take; **a. un taxi** to take a taxi (**c**) *Fam (pillar)* to catch; **a. una borrachera** to get drunk *o* pissed
  2 **agarrarse** *vpr* to hold on; **agarraos bien** hold tight
agarrotarse *vpr* (**a**) *(músculo)* to stiffen (**b**) *(máquina)* to seize up
agasajar *vt* to smother with attentions
ágata *nf* agate

Takes the masculine articles **el** and **un**.

agazaparse *vpr* to crouch (down)
agencia *nf* agency; *(sucursal)* branch; **a. de viajes** travel agency; **a. de seguros** insurance agency; **a. inmobiliaria** estate agency
agenciarse [43] *vpr* (**a**) to get oneself; **se agenció una moto** he got himself a motorbike (**b**) **agenciárselas** to manage
agenda *nf* diary
agente *nmf* agent; **a. de policía** *(hombre)* policeman; *(mujer)* policewoman; **a. de bolsa** stockbroker; **a. de seguros** insurance broker
agigantado,-a *adj* **a pasos agigantados** by leaps and bounds
ágil *adj* agile
agilidad *nf* agility
agilización *nf* speeding up

agilizar [40] *vt (trámites)* to speed up
agitación *nf (intranquilidad)* restlessness; *(social, político)* unrest
agitado,-a *adj* agitated; *(persona)* anxious; *(mar)* rough; **una vida muy agitada** a very hectic life
agitar 1 *vt (botella)* to shake; *(multitud)* to agitate
    2 agitarse *vpr (persona)* to become agitated; *(mar)* to become rough
aglomeración *nf* agglomeration; *(de gente)* crowd
aglomerar 1 *vt* to bring together
    2 aglomerarse *vpr* to mass *o* gather together
agnóstico,-a *adj & nm,f* agnostic
agobiado,-a *adj Fig* **a. de problemas** snowed under with problems; *Fig* **a. de trabajo** up to one's eyes in work
agobiante *adj (trabajo)* overwhelming; *(lugar)* claustrophobic; *(calor)* oppressive; *(persona)* tiresome, tiring
agobiar [43] 1 *vt* to overwhelm
    2 agobiarse *vpr (con problemas)* to be over-anxious; *(por el calor)* to suffocate
agobio *nm* (**a**) *(angustia)* anxiety (**b**) *(sofoco)* suffocation
agolpamiento *nm* crowd, crush
agolparse *vpr* to crowd, to throng
agonía *nf* dying breath, last gasp
agonizante *adj* dying
agonizar [40] *vi* to be dying
agosto *nm* August; *Fam* **hacer su a.** to make a packet
agotado,-a *adj* (**a**) *(cansado)* exhausted, worn out (**b**) *Com* sold out; *(existencias)* exhausted; *(libro)* out of print
agotador,-a *adj* exhausting
agotamiento *nm* exhaustion
agotar 1 *vt* (**a**) *(cansar)* to exhaust, to wear out (**b**) *(acabar)* to exhaust, to use up (completely)
    2 agotarse *vpr* (**a**) *(acabarse)* to run out, to be used up; *Com* to be sold out (**b**) *(persona)* to become exhausted *o* tired out
agraciado,-a *adj* (**a**) *(hermoso)* pretty (**b**) *(ganador)* winning; **ser a. con** to win
agradable *adj* pleasant
agradar *vi* to please; **no me agrada** I don't like it
agradecer [33] *vt* (**a**) *(dar las gracias)* to thank for; **les agradezco su atención** (I) thank you for your attention; **te lo agradezco mucho** thank you very much (**b**) *(estar agradecido)* to be grateful to; **te agradecería que vinieras** I'd be grateful if you'd come (**c**) *(uso impers)* **siempre se**

agradece un descanso a rest is always welcome
agradecido,-a *adj* grateful; **le estoy muy a.** I am very grateful to you
agradecimiento *nm* gratitude
agrado *nm* pleasure; **no es de su a.** it isn't to his liking
agrandar 1 *vt* to enlarge, to make larger
    2 agrandarse *vpr* to enlarge, to become larger
agrario,-a *adj* agrarian; **política agraria** agricultural policy
agravamiento *nm* aggravation
agravante 1 *adj Jur* aggravating
    2 *nm Jur* aggravating circumstance
agravar 1 *vt* to aggravate
    2 agravarse *vpr* to worsen, to get worse
agraviar [43] *vt* to offend, to insult
agravio *nm* offense, insult
agredir *vt defect* to assault
agregación *nf* aggregation
agregado,-a 1 *adj Educ* **profesor a.** *(escuela)* secondary school teacher; *Univ* assistant teacher
    2 *nm,f Pol* attaché
agregar [42] 1 *vt* (**a**) *(añadir)* to add (**b**) *(destinar)* to appoint
    2 agregarse *vpr* **a. a** to join
agresión *nf* aggression
agresividad *nf* aggressiveness
agresivo,-a *adj* aggressive
agresor,-a 1 *nm,f* aggressor, attacker
    2 *adj* attacking
agriarse *vpr* to turn sour
agrícola *adj* agricultural
agricultor,-a *nm,f* farmer
agricultura *nf* agriculture; **a. biológica** *o* **ecológica** organic farming
agridulce *adj* bittersweet
agrietar 1 *vt* to crack; *(piel, labios)* to chap
    2 agrietarse *vpr* to crack; *(piel)* to get chapped
agringarse [42] *vpr Am Pey* to behave like a gringo
agrio,-a 1 *adj* sour
    2 *nmpl* **agrios** citrus fruits
agrónomo,-a *nm,f* **(ingeniero) a.** agronomist
agropecuario,-a *adj* farming, agricultural
agrupación *nf* association
agrupar 1 *vt* to group
    2 agruparse *vpr* (**a**) *(congregarse)* to group together, to form a group (**b**) *(asociarse)* to associate
agua *nf* water; **a. potable** drinking water; **a. corriente/del grifo** running/tap water;

a. dulce/salada fresh/salt water; **a. mineral sin/con gas** still/fizzy o sparkling mineral water; **a. de colonia** (eau de) cologne; *Fig* **estar con el a. al cuello** to be up to one's neck in it; **aguas jurisdiccionales** territorial waters; **aguas residuales** sewage

Takes the masculine articles **el** and **un**.

aguacate *nm* (*árbol*) avocado; (*fruto*) avocado (pear)

aguacero *nm* shower, downpour

aguado,-a *adj* watered down

aguafiestas *nmf inv* spoilsport, wet blanket

aguafuerte *nm* (**a**) *Arte* etching (**b**) *Quím* nitric acid

aguamala *nf Carib, Col, Ecuad, Méx* jellyfish

aguamarina *nf* aquamarine

aguamiel *nm o nf* (**a**) *Am* (*bebida*) = water mixed with honey or cane syrup (**b**) *Carib, Méx* (*jugo*) maguey juice

aguanieve *nf* sleet

aguantar 1 *vt* (**a**) (*soportar*) to tolerate; **no lo aguanto más** I can't stand it any longer (**b**) (*sostener*) to support, to hold; **aguanta esto** hold this (**c**) **aguanta la respiración** hold your breath

2 **aguantarse** *vpr* (**a**) (*contenerse*) to keep back; (*lágrimas*) to hold back; **no pude aguantarme la risa** I couldn't help laughing (**b**) (*resignarse*) to resign oneself

aguante *nm* endurance; **tener mucho a.** (*ser paciente*) to be very patient; (*tener resistencia*) to be strong, to have a lot of stamina

aguar [45] *vt* to water down; *Fig* **a. la fiesta a algn** to spoil sb's fun

aguardar 1 *vt* to await

2 *vi* to wait

aguardiente *nm* liquor, brandy

aguarrás *nm* turpentine

aguatero,-a *nm,f Am* water seller

aguaviva *nf RP* jellyfish

agudeza *nf* (**a**) sharpness; (*del dolor*) acuteness (**b**) *Fig* (*ingenio*) witticism, witty saying

agudización *nf* (**a**) sharpening (**b**) (*empeoramiento*) worsening

agudizar [40] 1 *vt* to intensify, to make more acute

2 **agudizarse** *vpr* to intensify, to become more acute

agudo,-a *adj* (*dolor*) acute; (*voz*) high-pitched; (*sonido*) treble, high; *Fig* (*ingenioso*) witty; *Fig* (*sentido*) sharp, keen

agüero *nm* omen

aguijón *nm* sting; *Fig* (*estímulo*) spur

águila *nf* eagle; **á. real** golden eagle; *Méx* **¿á. o sol?** heads or tails?

Takes the masculine articles **el** and **un**.

aguileño,-a *adj* aquiline; **nariz aguileña** aquiline nose

aguinaldo *nm* Christmas box; **pedir el a.** to go carol singing

agüita *nf Chile* (herbal) tea

aguja *nf* (**a**) needle; (*de reloj*) hand; (*de tocadiscos*) stylus (**b**) *Arquit* spire (**c**) *Ferroc* point, *US* switch

agujerear *vt* to make holes in

agujero *nm* (**a**) hole; **a. negro** black hole (**b**) *Econ* deficit, shortfall

agujetas *nfpl* stiffness; **tener a.** to be stiff

agur *interj Fam* bye!, see you!

aguzar [40] *vt* (**a**) (*afilar*) to sharpen (**b**) *Fig* **a. el oído** to prick up one's ears; **a. la vista** to look attentively; **aguzar el ingenio** to sharpen one's wits

ahí *adv* there; **a. está** there he/she/it is; **ve por a.** go that way; **está por a.** it's over there; **setenta o por a.** seventy or thereabouts; **de a.** hence

ahijado,-a *nm,f* godchild; (*niño*) godson; (*niña*) goddaughter; **ahijados** godchildren

ahínco *nm* eagerness; **con a.** eagerly

ahíto,-a *adj* (*de comida*) full, stuffed; (*harto*) fed up

ahogado,-a 1 *adj* (**a**) (*en líquido*) drowned; **morir a.** to drown (**b**) (*asfixiado*) suffocated

2 *nm,f* drowned person

ahogar [42] 1 *vt* (**a**) (*en líquido*) to drown (**b**) (*asfixiar*) to suffocate

2 **ahogarse** *vpr* (**a**) (*en líquido*) to drown, to be drowned; *Fig* **a. en un vaso de agua** to make a mountain out of a molehill (**b**) (*asfixiarse*) to suffocate (**c**) (*motor*) to be flooded

ahondar 1 *vt* to deepen

2 *vi* to go deep; *Fig* **a. en un problema** to go into a problem in depth

ahora 1 *adv* (**a**) (*en este momento*) now; **a. mismo** right now; **de a. en adelante** from now on; **por a.** for the time being (**b**) **a. voy** I'm coming; **a. vuelvo** I'll be back in a minute (**c**) **hasta a.** (*hasta el momento*) until now, so far; (*hasta luego*) see you later

2 *conj* **a. bien** (*sin embargo*) however; (*y bueno*) well then

ahorcado,-a 1 *nm,f* hanged person

2 *adj* hanged

ahorcar [44] 1 *vt* to hang
 2 ahorcarse *vpr* to hang oneself
ahorita, ahoritica *adv Andes, CAm, Carib, Méx Fam* (**a**) *(en el presente)* (right) now; **a. voy** I'm just coming (**b**) *(pronto)* in a second (**c**) *(hace poco)* just now, a few minutes ago
ahorrador,-a *adj* thrifty
ahorrar 1 *vt* to save
 2 ahorrarse *vpr* **ahórrate los comentarios** keep your comments to yourself
ahorrativo,-a *adj* thrifty
ahorro *nm* (**a**) saving; **a. energético** energy saving (**b**) **ahorros** savings; *Fin* **caja de ahorros** savings bank
ahuecar [44] *vt* (**a**) to hollow out; *Fam* **a. el ala** to clear off, to beat it (**b**) *(voz)* to deepen
ahuevado,-a *adj Andes, CAm Fam (tonto)* **estar a. con algo** to be bowled over by sth
ahumado,-a *adj (cristal, jamón)* smoked; *(bacon)* smoky; **salmón a.** smoked salmon
ahumar 1 *vt* to smoke
 2 *vi (echar humo)* to smoke, to give off smoke
ahuyentar *vt* to scare away
aindiado,-a *adj Am* Indian-like
airado,-a *adj* angry
airar 1 *vt* to anger
 2 airarse *vpr* to get angry
airbag ['era, air'a] *nm (pl* **airbags**) airbag
aire *nm* (**a**) air; **a. acondicionado** air conditioning; **al a.** *(hacia arriba)* into the air; *(al descubierto)* uncovered; **al a. libre** in the open air; **en el a.** *(pendiente)* in the air; *Rad* on the air; **hacerse a.** to fan oneself; **saltar por los aires** to blow up; **tomar el a.** to get some fresh air; **necesito un cambio de aires** I need a change of scene (**b**) *Aut* choke (**c**) *(viento)* wind; **hace a.** it's windy (**d**) *(aspecto)* air, appearance (**e**) **él va a su a.** he goes his own sweet way (**f**) **darse aires** to put on airs
airear *vt (ropa, lugar)* to air; *Fig (asunto)* to publicize
airoso,-a *adj* graceful, elegant; *Fig* **salir a. de una situación** to come out of a situation with flying colours
aislacionismo *nm* isolationism
aislado,-a *adj* (**a**) isolated (**b**) *Téc* insulated
aislamiento *nm* (**a**) isolation (**b**) *Téc* insulation
aislante 1 *adj* **cinta a.** insulating tape
 2 *nm* insulator
aislar *vt* (**a**) to isolate (**b**) *Téc* to insulate
ajar *vt* to wear out

ajedrez *nm* (**a**) *(juego)* chess (**b**) *(piezas y tablero)* chess set
ajeno,-a *adj* belonging to other people; **los bienes ajenos** other peoples' goods; **por causas ajenas a nuestra voluntad** for reasons beyond our control
ajetreado,-a *adj* (very) busy, hectic
ajetreo *nm* activity, hard work, bustle
ají *nm* (**a**) *Andes, RP (pimiento)* chilli (pepper) (**b**) *Andes, RP (salsa)* = sauce made from oil, vinegar, garlic and chilli
ajiaco *nm* (**a**) *Andes, Carib (estofado)* = chilli-based stew (**b**) *Méx (estofado con ajo)* = tripe stew flavoured with garlic
ajillo *nm Culin* **al a.** fried with garlic
ajo *nm* garlic; **cabeza/diente de a.** head/clove of garlic; *Fam* **estar en el a.** to be in on it
ajonjolí *nm* sesame
ajorca *nf* bracelet; *(en el tobillo)* anklet
ajuar *nm (de novia)* trousseau
ajustado,-a *adj* tight
ajustador,-a *nm,f* fitter
ajustar *vt* (**a**) to adjust (**b**) *(apretar)* to tighten (**c**) *Fin (cuenta)* to settle; *Fig* **ajustarle las cuentas a algn** to settle a score with sb
ajuste *nm* (**a**) adjustment; *Téc* assembly; *TV* **carta de a.** test card (**b**) *(de precio)* fixing; *(de cuenta)* settlement; *Fig* **a. de cuentas** settling of scores
ajusticiar [43] *vt* to execute
al *(contracción de* **a** + **el**) (**a**) *ver* **a** (**b**) (**al** + *infin*) **al salir** on leaving; **está al caer** it's about to happen; **al parecer** apparently
ala 1 *nf* (**a**) wing; *Fig* **cortarle las alas a algn** to clip sb's wings (**b**) *(de sombrero)* brim
 2 *nmf Dep* winger

> Takes the masculine articles **el** and **un**.

alabanza *nf* praise
alabar *vt* to praise
alabastro *nm* alabaster
alacena *nf* (food) cupboard
alacrán *nm* scorpion
alambicado,-a *adj* intricate
alambique *nm* still
alambrada *nf*, **alambrado** *nm* wire fence
alambrar *vt* to fence with wire
alambre *nm* wire; **a. de púas** barbed wire
alambrista *nmf* tightrope walker
alameda *nf* (**a**) poplar grove (**b**) *(paseo)* avenue, boulevard
álamo *nm* poplar
alano,-a *nm,f* **(perro) a.** mastiff
alarde *nm* *(ostentación)* bragging,

boasting; **hacer a. de** to show off

alardear *vi* to brag, to boast; **a. de rico** *o* **de riqueza** to flaunt one's wealth

alargadera *nf Elec* extension

alargado,-a *adj* elongated

alargar [42] 1 *vt* (**a**) to lengthen; *(estirar)* to stretch; **ella alargó la mano para cogerlo** she stretched out her hand to get it (**b**) *(prolongar)* to prolong, to extend (**c**) *(dar)* to pass, to hand over; **alárgame ese jersey** can you pass me that sweater?

2 **alargarse** *vpr* (**a**) to get longer (**b**) *(prolongarse)* to go on (**c**) **¿puedes a. a casa?** can you give me a lift home?

alarido *nm* screech, shriek; **dar un a.** to howl

alarma *nf* alarm; **la a. saltó** the alarm went off; **falsa a.** false alarm; **señal de a.** alarm (signal)

alarmado,-a *adj* alarmed

alarmante *adj* alarming

alarmar 1 *vt* to alarm

2 **alarmarse** *vpr* to be alarmed

alazán,-ana *adj & nm,f* **(caballo) a.** chestnut

alba *nf* dawn, daybreak

> Takes the masculine articles **el** and **un**.

albacea *nmf (hombre)* executor; *(mujer)* executrix

albahaca *nf* basil

albanés,-esa *adj & nm,f* Albanian

Albania *n* Albania

albañal *nm* sewer, drain

albañil *nm* bricklayer

albañilería *nf* bricklaying; **pared de a.** *(obra)* brick wall

albarán *nm Com* delivery note, despatch note

albaricoque *nm* apricot

albaricoquero *nm* apricot tree

albatros *nm inv* albatross

albedrío *nm* will; **libre a.** free will

alberca *nf* (**a**) *(depósito)* water tank (**b**) *Méx (piscina)* swimming pool

albergar [42] 1 *vt (alojar)* to house, to accommodate; *Fig (sentimientos)* to cherish, to harbour

2 **albergarse** *vpr* to stay

albergue *nm* hostel; **a. juvenil** youth hostel

albino,-a *adj & nm,f* albino

albóndiga *nf* meatball

albores *nmpl* beginning; **en los a. de ...** at the beginning of ...

albornoz *nm* bathrobe

alborotado,-a *adj* (**a**) worked up, agitated (**b**) *(desordenado)* untidy, messy (**c**)

(mar) rough; *(tiempo)* stormy

alborotar 1 *vt* (**a**) *(agitar)* to agitate, to work up (**b**) *(desordenar)* to make untidy, to turn upside down

2 *vi* to kick up a racket

3 **alborotarse** *vpr* (**a**) to get excited *o* worked up (**b**) *(mar)* to get rough; *(tiempo)* to get stormy

alboroto *nm* (**a**) *(jaleo)* din, racket (**b**) *(desorden)* disturbance, uproar

alborozo *nm* merriment, gaiety

albufera *nf* lagoon

álbum *nm* album

alcachofa *nf* (**a**) *Bot* artichoke (**b**) *(de tubo, regadera)* rose, sprinkler

alcalde *nm* mayor

alcaldesa *nf* mayoress

alcaldía *nf* (**a**) *(cargo)* mayorship (**b**) *(oficina)* mayor's office

alcalino,-a *adj* alkaline

alcance *nm* (**a**) reach; **al a. de cualquiera** within everybody's reach; **dar a. a** to catch up with; **fuera del a. de los niños** out of the reach of children (**b**) *Fig* scope; *(de noticia)* importance

alcancía *nf* money box; *(cerdito)* piggy bank

alcanfor *nm* camphor

alcantarilla *nf* sewer; *(boca)* drain

alcantarillado *nm* sewer system

alcanzar [40] 1 *vt* (**a**) to reach; *(persona)* to catch up with; **la producción alcanza dos mil unidades** production is up to two thousand units (**b**) **alcánzame la sal** *(pasar)* pass me the salt (**c**) *(conseguir)* to attain, to achieve

2 *vi (ser suficiente)* to be sufficient; **con un kilo no alcanza para todos** one kilo won't be enough for all of us

alcaparra *nf (fruto)* caper; *(planta)* caper bush

alcatraz *nm Orn* gannet

alcaucil *nm RP* artichoke

alcayata *nf* hook

alcazaba *nf* fortress, citadel

alcázar *nm* (**a**) *(fortaleza)* fortress, citadel (**b**) *(castillo)* castle, palace

alcista 1 *adj (bolsa)* rising, bullish; **tendencia a.** upward tendency

2 *nmf (bolsa)* bull

alcoba *nf* bedroom

> 🖉 Observa que la palabra inglesa **alcove** es un falso amigo y no es la traducción de la palabra española **alcoba**. En inglés, **alcove** significa "hueco".

alcohol *nm* alcohol

alcoholemia *nf* blood alcohol level;

prueba de a. Breathalyser® test
alcohólico,-a adj & nm,f alcoholic
alcoholímetro nm Breathalyser®
alcoholismo nm alcoholism
alcoholizado,-a adj & nm,f alcoholic
alcornoque nm cork oak
alcurnia nf lineage, ancestry; **de alta a.** of noble lineage
alcuzcuz nm couscous
aldaba nf (llamador) door knocker
aldabonazo nm (**a**) loud knock (**b**) (advertencia) warning
aldea nf village
aldeano,-a 1 adj village
 2 nm,f villager
aleación nf alloy
aleatorio,-a adj random
alebrestarse vpr Col (ponerse nervioso) to get nervous o excited
aleccionador,-a adj (instructivo) instructive; (ejemplar) exemplary
aleccionar vt (instruir) to teach, to instruct; (adiestrar) to train
aledaño,-a 1 adj adjoining, adjacent
 2 nmpl aledaños outskirts
alegar [42] vt (**a**) (aducir) to claim; Jur to allege (**b**) (presentar) to put forward
alegato nm argument
alegoría nf allegory
alegrar 1 vt (**a**) (complacer) to make happy o glad; **me alegra que se lo hayas dicho** I am glad you told her (**b**) Fig (avivar) to enliven, to brighten up
 2 alegrarse vpr to be glad, to be happy; **me alegro de verte** I am pleased to see you; **me alegro por ti** I am happy for you
alegre adj (**a**) (contento) happy, glad (**b**) (color) bright; (música) lively; (lugar) pleasant, cheerful (**c**) Fig (borracho) tipsy, merry
alegría nf joy, happiness
alejado,-a adj far away, remote
alejar 1 vt to move further away
 2 alejarse vpr to go away, to move away; **no te alejes de mí** keep close to me
aleluya nm o nf hallelujah, alleluia
alemán,-ana 1 adj & nm,f German
 2 nm (idioma) German
Alemania n Germany; **A. del Este/Oeste** East/West Germany; **A. Occidental/Oriental** West/East Germany
alentador,-a adj encouraging; **un panorama poco a.** a rather bleak outlook
alentar [1] vt Fig to encourage
alergia nf allergy
alérgico,-a adj allergic
alero nm eaves
alerón nm Av aileron

alerta nf & adj alert; **estar en estado de a.** to be (on the) alert
alertar vt to alert (**de** to); **nos alertó del peligro** he alerted us to the danger
aleta nf (de pez) fin; (de foca, de nadador) flipper
aletargado,-a adj lethargic
aletargar [42] 1 vt to make lethargic
 2 aletargarse vpr to become lethargic
aletear vi to flutter o flap its wings
alevín nm (pescado) young fish; Fig (principiante) beginner
alevosía nf (traición) treachery; (premeditación) premeditation
alevoso,-a adj (persona) treacherous; (acto) premeditated
alfabético,-a adj alphabetic
alfabetización nf teaching to read and write; **campaña de a.** literacy campaign
alfabeto nm alphabet
alfajor nm CSur = large biscuit filled with toffee and coated with coconut
alfalfa nf lucerne, alfalfa
alfarería nf (**a**) (arte) pottery (**b**) (taller) potter's workshop; (tienda) pottery shop
alfarero,-a nm,f potter
alféizar nm sill, windowsill
alférez nm second lieutenant
alfil nm bishop
alfiler nm pin; (broche) pin, brooch; (de corbata) tiepin; (para tender) peg; Andes, RP, Ven **a. de gancho** (imperdible) safety pin
alfiletero nm pin box, pin case
alfombra nf rug; (moqueta) carpet
alfombrar vt to carpet
alfombrilla nf rug, mat
alforja nf (para caballos) saddlebag; (para hombro) knapsack
alga nf alga; (marina) seaweed

Takes the masculine articles **el** and **un**.

algarabía nf hubbub, hullabaloo
algarrobo nm carob tree
algazara nf din, row
álgebra nf algebra

Takes the masculine articles **el** and **un**.

álgido,-a adj culminating, critical; **el punto a.** the climax
algo 1 pron indef (**a**) (afirmativo) something; (interrogativo) anything; **a. así** something like that; **¿a. más?** anything else?; **por a. será** there must be a reason for it; Fam **a. es a.** it's better than nothing (**b**) (cantidad indeterminada) some; **¿queda a. de pastel?** is there any cake left?

2 *adv (un poco)* quite, somewhat; **se siente a. mejor** she's feeling a bit better

algodón *nm* cotton; **a. (hidrófilo)** *Br* cotton wool, *US* absorbent cotton; **a. de azúcar** *Br* candy floss, *US* cotton candy

algodonero,-a 1 *nm,f* cotton grower
2 *adj* cotton

alguacil *nm* bailiff

alguien *pron indef (afirmativo)* somebody, someone; *(interrogativo)* anybody, anyone

alguno,-a 1 *adj* (**a**) *(delante de nombre)* *(afirmativo)* some; *(interrogativo)* any; **algunos días** some days; **algunas veces** some times; **alguna que otra vez** now and then; **¿has tomado alguna medicina?** have you taken any medicine?; **¿le has visto alguna vez?** have you ever seen him? (**b**) *(después de nombre)* not at all; **no vino persona alguna** nobody came

> **algún** is used instead of **alguno** before masculine singular nouns (e.g. **algún día** some day).

2 *pron indef* (**a**) someone, somebody; **a. dirá que ...** someone might say that ...; **a. que otro** some (**b**) **algunos,-as** some (people)

alhaja *nf* jewel

alhelí *nm (pl* **alhelíes)** wallflower, stock

aliado,-a 1 *adj* allied
2 *nm,f* **los Aliados** the Allies

alianza *nf* (**a**) *(pacto)* alliance (**b**) *(anillo)* wedding ring

aliarse [29] *vpr* to become allies, to form an alliance

alias *adv & nm inv* alias

alicaído,-a *adj* (**a**) *Fig (débil)* weak, feeble (**b**) *Fig (deprimido)* down, depressed

alicatar *vt* to tile

alicates *nmpl* pliers

aliciente *nm* (**a**) *(atractivo)* lure, charm (**b**) *(incentivo)* incentive

alienación *nf* alienation

alienado,-a *adj* insane, deranged

alienar *vt* to alienate

alienígena *adj & nmf* alien

aliento *nm* (**a**) *(respiración)* breath; **sin a.** breathless (**b**) *(ánimo)* encouragement

aligerar 1 *vt (acelerar)* to speed up; **a. el paso** to quicken one's pace
2 *vi Fam* **¡aligera!** hurry up!

alijo *nm* haul; **un a. de drogas** a consignment of drugs

alimaña *nf* vermin

alimentación *nf (comida)* food; *(acción)* feeding; *Téc* supply

alimentar 1 *vt* (**a**) *(dar alimento)* to feed; *(ser nutritivo)* to be nutritious (**b**) *Fig (sentimientos)* to nourish (**c**) *Informát* to feed; *Téc* to supply
2 alimentarse *vpr* **a. con** *o* **de** to live on

alimentario,-a *adj* food

alimenticio,-a *adj* nutritious; **productos alimenticios** food products, foodstuffs; **valor a.** nutritional value

alimento *nm* (**a**) *(comida)* food (**b**) *Fig* **tiene poco a.** it is not very nourishing

alimón *adv* **al a.** together

alineación *nf* (**a**) alignment (**b**) *Dep (equipo)* line-up

alineado,-a *adj* aligned, lined-up; **países no alineados** non-aligned countries

alineamiento *nm* alignment

alinear 1 *vt* to align, to line up
2 alinearse *vpr* to line up

aliñar *vt* to season, to flavour; *(ensalada)* to dress

aliño *nm* seasoning, dressing

alioli *nm* garlic mayonnaise

alisar *vt,* **alisarse** *vpr* to smooth

aliscafo, alíscafo *nm RP* hydrofoil

alistar 1 *vt Mil* to recruit, to enlist
2 alistarse *vpr* (**a**) *Mil* to enlist, to enrol (**b**) *Am (prepararse)* to get ready

aliviar [43] 1 *vt (dolor)* to soothe, to relieve; *(carga)* to lighten, to make lighter
2 aliviarse *vpr (dolor)* to diminish, to get better

alivio *nm* relief

aljibe *nm* cistern, tank

allá *adv* (**a**) *(lugar alejado)* there, over there; **a. abajo/arriba** down/up there; **¡a. voy!** here I go!; **más a.** further on; **más a. de** beyond; **el más a.** the beyond (**b**) *(tiempo)* **a. por los años veinte** back in the twenties (**c**) **a. tú** that's your problem

allanamiento *nm Jur* **a. de morada** breaking and entering

allanar *vt* (**a**) *(terreno)* to level, to flatten; *Fig (camino)* to smooth (**b**) *Jur* to break into

allegado,-a 1 *adj* close
2 *nm,f* close friend

allende *adv Fml* beyond; **a. los mares** overseas

allí *adv* there, over there; **a. abajo/arriba** down/up there; **de a. para acá** back and forth; **por a.** *(movimiento)* that way; *(posición)* over there

alma *nf* soul; **no había ni un a.** there was not a soul

> Takes the masculine articles **el** and **un**.

almacén *nm* (**a**) *(local)* warehouse; *(habitación)* storeroom (**b**) *Com* **(grandes) almacenes** department store (**c**) *Andes,*

RP (de alimentos) grocer's (shop), grocery store

almacenaje *nm* storage, warehousing

almacenamiento *nm* storage, warehousing; *Informát* storage

almacenar *vt* to store

almacenista *nmf (vendedor)* wholesaler; *(propietario)* warehouse owner

almanaque *nm* calendar

almeja *nf* clam; *muy Fam* pussy

almena *nf* merlon

almendra *nf* almond; **a. garapiñada** sugared almond

almendro *nm* almond tree

almiar *nm* haystack

almíbar *nm* syrup

almidón *nm* starch

almidonar *vt* to starch

alminar *nm* minaret

almirante *nm* admiral

almizcle *nm* musk

almohada *nf* pillow; *Fam* **consultarlo con la a.** to sleep on it

almohadilla *nf* (small) cushion

almohadón *nm* large pillow, cushion

almorrana *nf Fam* pile

almorzar [2] 1 *vi* to have lunch

   2 *vt* to have for lunch

almuerzo *nm* lunch

aló *interj Andes, Carib (al teléfono)* hello!

alocado,-a *adj* thoughtless, rash

alocución *nf* speech, address

alojamiento *nm* accommodation; **dar a.** to accommodate

alojar 1 *vt* to accommodate

   2 alojarse *vpr* to stay

alondra *nf* lark; **a. común** skylark

alpaca *nf* alpaca

alpargata *nf* canvas sandal, espadrille

Alpes *npl* **los A.** the Alps

alpinismo *nm* mountaineering, climbing

alpinista *nmf* mountaineer, climber

alpino,-a *adj* Alpine; **esquí a.** downhill skiing

alquilar *vt* to hire; *(pisos, casas)* to rent; **se alquila** *(en letrero)* to let

alquiler *nm* (a) *(de pisos, casas)* renting, letting; **a. de coches** car hire; **de a.** *(pisos, casas)* to let, rented; *(coche)* for hire; *(televisión)* for rent (b) *(precio)* hire, rental; *(de pisos, casas)* rent

alquimia *nf* alchemy

alquitrán *nm* tar

alrededor 1 *adv (lugar)* round, around; **mira a.** look around; **a. de la mesa** round the table; **a. de las dos** around two o'clock; **a. de quince** about fifteen;

   2 *nmpl* **alrededores** surrounding area;

en los alrededores de Murcia in the area round Murcia

alta *nf* **dar de** *o* **el a.** *(a un enfermo)* to discharge from hospital

> Takes the masculine articles **el** and **un**.

altamente *adv* highly, extremely

altanería *nf* arrogance

altanero,-a *adj* arrogant

altar *nm* altar

altavoz *nm* loudspeaker

alterable *adj* changeable

alteración *nf* (a) *(cambio)* alteration (b) *(alboroto)* quarrel, row; **a. del orden público** disturbance of the peace (c) *(excitación)* agitation

alterar 1 *vt* to alter, to change; **a. el orden público** to disturb the peace

   2 alterarse *vpr* (a) *(cambiar)* to change (b) *(inquietarse)* to be upset (c) *(alimentos)* to go off

altercado *nm* quarrel, argument

alternar 1 *vt* to alternate

   2 *vi (relacionarse)* to meet people, to socialize

   3 alternarse *vpr* to alternate

alternativa *nf* alternative

alternativo,-a *adj* alternative

alterno,-a *adj* alternate; **días alternos** alternate days

alteza *nf* Highness; **Su A. Real** His/Her Royal Highness

altibajos *nmpl Fig* ups and downs

altiplano *nm* high plateau

altísimo *nm* **el A.** the Almighty

altisonante *adj* grandiloquent

altitud *nf* altitude

altivez *nf* arrogance, haughtiness

altivo,-a *adj* arrogant, haughty

alto¹ *nm* (a) *(interrupción)* stop, break (b) *Mil* halt; **dar el a.** to order to halt; **un a. el fuego** a cease-fire

alto²,-a 1 *adj (persona, árbol, edificio)* tall; *(montaña, techo, presión)* high; *(sonido)* loud; *Fig (precio, tecnología)* high; *(tono)* high-pitched; **los pisos altos** the top floors; **en lo a.** at the top; **alta sociedad** high society; **clase alta** upper class; **en voz alta** aloud, in a loud voice; **a altas horas de la noche** late at night

   2 *adv* (a) high, high up (b) *(sonar, hablar etc)* loud, loudly; **pon la radio más alta** turn the radio up; **¡habla más a.!** speak up!

   3 *nm* (a) *(altura)* height; **¿cuánto tiene de a.?** how tall/high is it?; *Fig* **por todo lo a.** in a grand way (b) *(elevación)* hill

altoparlante *nm Am* loudspeaker

altozano *nm* hillock, hill
altramuz *nm* lupin
altruista **1** *adj* altruistic
  2 *nmf* altruist
altura *nf* (**a**) height; **de 10 m de a.** 10 m high (**b**) *(nivel)* level; **a la misma a.** on the same level; *Geog* on the same latitude; **a la a. del cine** by the cinema; *Fig* **estar a la a. de las circunstancias** to meet the challenge; *Fig* **no está a su a.** he does not measure up to him; *Fig* **a estas alturas** at this stage (**c**) *Rel* **alturas** heaven
alubia *nf* bean
alucinación *nf* hallucination
alucinado,-a *adj Fam* amazed
alucinante *adj Fam* brilliant, mind-blowing
alucinar **1** *vt* to hallucinate; *Fig (encantar)* to fascinate
  2 *vi Fam* to be amazed, to be spaced out
alucinógeno,-a **1** *adj* hallucinogenic
  2 *nm* hallucinogen
alud *nm* avalanche
aludido,-a *adj Fig* **darse por a.** to take it personally
aludir *vi* to allude to, to mention
alumbrado,-a **1** *adj* lit
  2 *nm Elec* lighting; **a. público** street lighting
alumbrar **1** *vt (iluminar)* to light, to illuminate
  2 *vi (parir)* to give birth
aluminio *nm* aluminium
alumnado *nm (de colegio)* pupils; *Univ* student body
alumno,-a *nm,f* (**a**) *(de colegio)* pupil; **a. externo** day pupil; **a. interno** boarder (**b**) *Univ* student
alusión *nf* allusion, mention
aluvión *nm* downpour; *Fig* **un a. de preguntas** a barrage of questions
alverja, alverjana *nf Am* pea
alza *nf* (**a**) rise; **en a.** rising; **jugar al a.** *(bolsa)* to bull the market (**b**) *Mil* sight

Takes the masculine articles **el** and **un**.

alzado,-a **1** *adj* raised, lifted; **votación a mano alzada** vote by a show of hands
  2 *nm Arquit* elevation
alzamiento *nm (rebelión)* uprising
alzar **[40]** **1** *vt* to raise, to lift; **a. el vuelo** to take off; **a. los ojos/la vista** to look up; **álzate el cuello** turn your collar up
  2 alzarse *vpr* (**a**) *(levantarse)* to get up, to rise (**b**) *(rebelarse)* to rise, to rebel (**c**) **a. con la victoria** to win, to be victorious
AM *nf (abr* **amplitude modulation**) AM
a.m. *adv* a.m.

ama *nf (señora)* lady of the house; *(dueña)* owner; **a. de casa** housewife; **a. de llaves** housekeeper

Takes the masculine articles **el** and **un**.

amabilidad *nf* kindness; *Fml* **tenga la a. de esperar** would you be so kind as to wait?
amable *adj* kind, nice; *Fml* **¿sería usted tan a. de ayudarme?** would you be so kind as to help me?
amado,-a **1** *adj* loved, beloved
  2 *nm,f* sweetheart
amaestrar *vt* to train; *(domar)* to tame
amagar **[42]** *vt (amenazar)* to threaten; **amaga tormenta** a storm is threatening
amago *nm* (**a**) *(indicio)* first sign; **a. de infarto** onset of a heart attack (**b**) *(intento)* attempt (**c**) *Fig (amenaza)* threat
amainar *vi (viento etc)* to drop, to die down
amalgama *nf* amalgam
amalgamar *vt* to amalgamate
amamantar *vt* to breast-feed; *Zool* to suckle
amancay *nm Andes* amaryllis
amancebarse *vpr* to cohabit
amanecer **[33]** **1** *v impers* to dawn; **¿a qué hora amanece?** when does it get light?; **amaneció lluvioso** it was rainy at daybreak
  2 *vi* **amanecimos en Finlandia** we were in Finland at daybreak; **amaneció muy enfermo** he woke up feeling very ill
  3 *nm* dawn, daybreak; **al a.** at dawn
amanerado,-a *adj* mannered, affected
amansar *vt* (**a**) to tame (**b**) *Fig (apaciguar)* to tame, to calm
amante *nmf* lover; **a. del arte** art lover
amañar *vt* to fix, to fiddle; *(elecciones)* to rig
amapola *nf* poppy
amar **1** *vt* to love
  2 amarse *vpr* to love each other
amaraje *nm Av* landing at sea
amargado,-a **1** *adj (rencoroso)* embittered, bitter; *Fam (agobiado)* pissed off; **estoy a. con los exámenes** I'm pissed off with the exams
  2 *nm,f* bitter person
amargar **[42]** **1** *vt* to make bitter; *Fig* to embitter, to sour
  2 amargarse *vpr Fig* to become embittered o bitter; **no te amargues por eso** don't let that make you bitter
amargo,-a *adj* bitter
amargor *nm,* **amargura** *nf* bitterness
amarillento,-a *adj* yellowish

amarillo,-a *adj & nm* yellow; **prensa amarilla** gutter press

amarilloso,-a *adj Ven* yellowish

amarra *nf* mooring rope; **soltar amarras** to cast off, to let go

amarradero *nm* mooring

amarrar *vt Náut* to moor, to tie up; *(atar)* to tie (up), to bind

amarrete,-a *adj Andes, RP Fam* mean, tight

amasar *vt* (**a**) *Culin* to knead (**b**) *Fig (fortuna)* to amass

amasiato *nm CAm, Méx* cohabitation, common-law marriage

amasijo *nm Fam* hotchpotch, jumble

amasio,-a *nm,f CAm, Méx* live-in lover, common-law partner

amateur *adj & nmf* amateur

amatista *nf* amethyst

amazona *nf* (**a**) *(jinete)* horsewoman (**b**) *(en mitología)* Amazon

Amazonas *n* **el A.** the Amazon

amazónico,-a *adj* Amazonian

ambages *nmpl* **hablar sin a.** to go straight to the point

ámbar *nm* amber

Amberes *n* Antwerp

ambición *nf* ambition

ambicionar *vt* to have as an ambition; **ambiciona ser presidente** his ambition is to become president

ambicioso,-a 1 *adj* ambitious
  2 *nm,f* ambitious person

ambidextro,-a *nm,f* ambidextrous person

ambientación *nf Cin & Teatro* setting

ambientado,-a *adj (bar etc)* lively

ambientador *nm* air freshener

ambiental *adj* environmental

ambientar 1 *vt* (**a**) *(bar etc)* to liven up (**b**) *Cin & Teatro* to set
  2 ambientarse *vpr (adaptarse)* to get used to

ambiente 1 *nm* (**a**) *(gen)* environment; *Fig (medio)* environment, milieu (**b**) *Andes, RP (habitación)* room
  2 *adj* environmental; **temperatura a.** room temperature

ambigüedad *nf* ambiguity

ambiguo,-a *adj* ambiguous

ámbito *nm* field, sphere; **empresa de a. nacional** nationwide company

ambos,-as *adj pl Fml* both; **por a. lados** on both sides

ambulancia *nf* ambulance

ambulante *adj* travelling, mobile; **biblioteca a.** mobile library

ambulatorio *nm* surgery, clinic

amedrentar *vt* to frighten, to scare

amén[1] *nm* amen

amén[2] *adv* **a. de** in addition to

amenaza *nf* threat

amenazador,-a, amenazante *adj* threatening, menacing

amenazar [40] *vt* to threaten; **a. de muerte a algn** to threaten to kill sb

amenizar [40] *vt* to liven up

ameno,-a *adj* entertaining

América *n* America; **A. Central/del Norte/ del Sur** Central/North/South America

americana *nf (prenda)* jacket

americano,-a *adj & nm,f* American

amerindio,-a *adj & nm,f* Amerindian, American Indian

ameritar *vt Am* to deserve

amerizar [40] *vi* to land at sea

ametralladora *nf* machine gun

ametrallar *vt* to machine-gun

amianto *nm* asbestos

amigable *adj* friendly

amígdala *nf* tonsil

amigdalitis *nf* tonsillitis

amigo,-a 1 *nm,f* friend; **hacerse a. de** to make friends with; **hacerse amigos** to become friends; **son muy amigos** they are very good friends
  2 *adj (aficionado)* fond (**de** of)

amilanar 1 *vt* to frighten, to scare
  2 amilanarse *vpr* to be frightened *o* daunted

aminorar *vt* to reduce; **a. el paso** to slow down

amistad *nf* (**a**) friendship (**b**) **amistades** friends

amistoso,-a *adj* friendly

amnesia *nf* amnesia

amnistía *nf* amnesty

amo *nm* (**a**) *(dueño)* owner (**b**) *(señor)* master

amodorrarse *vpr* to become sleepy *o* drowsy

amoldar 1 *vt* to adapt, to adjust
  2 amoldarse *vpr* to adapt oneself

amonestación *nf* (**a**) rebuke, reprimand; *Dep* warning (**b**) *Rel* **amonestaciones** banns

amonestar *vt* (**a**) *(advertir)* to rebuke, to reprimand; *Dep* to warn (**b**) *Rel* to publish the banns of

amoniaco, amoníaco *nm* ammonia

amontonar 1 *vt* to pile up, to heap up
  2 amontonarse *vpr* to pile up, to heap up; *(gente)* to crowd together

amor *nm* love; **hacer el a.** to make love; **a. propio** self-esteem; **¡por el a. de Dios!** for God's sake!

amoral *adj* amoral

amoratado,-a *adj (de frío)* blue with cold; *(de un golpe)* black and blue

amordazar [40] *vt (perro)* to muzzle; *(persona)* to gag

amorfo,-a *adj* amorphous

amorío *nm* love affair, flirtation

amoroso,-a *adj* loving, affectionate

amortajar *vt* to shroud, to wrap in a shroud

amortiguador *nm Aut* shock absorber

amortiguar [45] *vt (golpe)* to cushion; *(ruido)* to muffle; *(luz)* to subdue

amortización *nf* repayment

amortizar [40] *vt* to pay off

amotinado,-a *nm,f* rioter; *Mil* mutineer

amotinamiento *nm* riot, rioting; *Mil* mutiny

amotinar 1 *vt* to incite to riot; *Mil* to incite to mutiny

 2 amotinarse *upr* to rise up; *Mil* to mutiny

amparar 1 *vt* to protect

 2 ampararse *upr* to seek refuge

amparo *nm* protection, shelter; **al a. de la ley** under the protection of the law

amperio *nm* ampère, amp

ampliación *nf* enlargement; *(de plazo, casa)* extension

ampliar [29] *vt* to enlarge; *(casa, plazo)* to extend

amplificador *nm* amplifier

amplificar [44] *vt* to amplify

amplio,-a *adj* large, roomy; *(ancho)* wide, broad; **en el sentido más a. de la palabra** in the broadest sense of the word

amplitud *nf* (a) spaciousness; **a. de miras** broad-mindedness (b) *(de espacio)* room, space (c) *Fís* amplitude

ampolla *nf* (a) *Med* blister; *Fig* **levantar ampollas** to raise people's hackles (b) *(de medicina)* ampoule

ampuloso,-a *adj* pompous, bombastic

amputar *vt Med* to amputate; *Fig* to cut out

amueblar *vt* to furnish

amuermar *vt Fam* (a) *(atontar)* to make feel dopey *o* groggy (b) *(aburrir)* to bore

amuleto *nm* amulet; **a. de la suerte** lucky charm

amurallar *vt* to wall, to fortify

anacronismo *nm* anachronism

ánade *nm* duck; **á. real** mallard

anales *nmpl* annals

analfabetismo *nm* illiteracy

analfabeto,-a *nm,f* illiterate

analgésico,-a *adj & nm* analgesic

análisis *nm inv* analysis; **a. de sangre** blood test

analista *nmf* analyst

analizar [40] *vt* to analyse

analogía *nf* analogy

analógico,-a *adj* analogue

análogo,-a *adj* analogous, similar

ananá *nm (pl* **ananaes)**, **ananás** *nm (pl* **ananases)** pineapple

anaquel *nm* shelf

anaranjado,-a *adj & nm* orange

anarquía *nf* anarchy

anarquismo *nm* anarchism

anarquista *adj & nmf* anarchist

anatomía *nf* anatomy

anatómico,-a *adj* anatomical

anca *nf* haunch; **ancas de rana** frogs' legs

> Takes the masculine articles **el** and **un**.

ancestral *adj* ancestral

ancho,-a 1 *adj* wide, broad; **a lo a.** breadthwise; **te está muy a.** it's too big for you

 2 *nm* (a) *(anchura)* width, breadth; **2 m de a.** 2 m wide; **¿qué a. tiene?** how wide is it? (b) *Cost* width

 3 *nfpl Fam* **a mis** *o* **tus anchas** at ease, comfortable

anchoa *nf* anchovy

anchura *nf* width, breadth

anciano,-a 1 *adj* very old

 2 *nm,f* old person; **los ancianos** old people

ancla *nf* anchor

> Takes the masculine articles **el** and **un**.

anclar *vt & vi* to anchor

andadas *nfpl* **volver a las a.** to go back to one's old tricks

andaderas *nfpl* baby-walker

andadura *nf* walking

ándale *interj CAm, Méx Fam* come on!

Andalucía *n* Andalusia

andaluz,-a *adj & nm,f* Andalusian

andamiaje, andamio *nm* scaffolding

andanza *nf* adventure, happening

andar¹ *nm* **a.** *o* **andares** *nmpl* walk, gait

andar² [8] 1 *vi* (a) to walk (b) *(coche etc)* to move; **este coche anda despacio** this car goes very slowly (c) *(funcionar)* to work; **esto no anda** this doesn't work (d) *Fam* **anda por los cuarenta** he's about forty; **anda siempre diciendo que ...** he's always saying that ...; **¿cómo andamos de tiempo?** how are we off for time?; **tu bolso debe a. por ahí** your bag must be over there somewhere

 2 *vt (recorrer)* to walk

andariego,-a *adj* fond of walking

andén *nm* (a) *(en estación)* platform (b)

Andes, CAm (acera) Br pavement, *US* sidewalk (**c**) *Andes (bancal de tierra)* terrace
Andes *nmpl* Andes
andinismo *nm Am* mountaineering
andinista *nmf Am* mountaineer
andino,-a *adj & nm,f* Andean
andrajo *nm* rag, tatter
andrajoso,-a *adj* ragged, tattered
androide *nm* android
andurriales *nmpl Fam* out-of-the-way place
anécdota *nf* anecdote
anecdótico,-a *adj* anecdotal
anegar [42] *vt,* **anegarse** *vpr* to flood
anejo,-a 1 *adj* attached, joined (**a** to)
  2 *nm* appendix
anemia *nf* anaemia
anestesia *nf* anaesthesia
anestésico,-a *adj & nm* anaesthetic
anexar *vt* to annex
anexión *nf* annexation
anexionar *vt* to annex
anexo,-a 1 *adj* attached, joined (**a** to)
  2 *nm* appendix
anfetamina *nf* amphetamine
anfibio,-a 1 *adj* amphibious
  2 *nm* amphibian
anfiteatro *nm* (**a**) amphitheatre (**b**) *Cin & Teatro* gallery
anfitrión,-ona *nm,f* host, *f* hostess
ángel *nm* (**a**) angel; **á. de la guarda** guardian angel (**b**) *Am (micrófono)* hand-held microphone
angelical, angélico,-a *adj* angelic
angina *nf* angina; **tener anginas** to have tonsillitis; *Med* **a. de pecho** angina pectoris
anglófono,-a 1 *adj* English-speaking
  2 *nm,f* English speaker
anglosajón,-ona *adj & nm,f* Anglo-Saxon
Angola *n* Angola
angosto,-a *adj Fml* narrow
anguila *nf* eel; **a. de mar** conger eel
angula *nf* elver
angular *adj* angular; *Fot* **(objetivo) gran a.** wide-angle lens; **piedra a.** cornerstone
ángulo *nm* angle; *(rincón)* corner
angustia *nf* anguish
angustiar [43] *vt* to distress
angustioso,-a *adj* distressing
anhelar *vt* to long for, to yearn for
anhelo *nm* longing, yearning
anhídrido *nm* **a. carbónico** carbon dioxide
anidar *vi* to nest

anilla *nf* ring; **carpeta de anillas** ring-binder
anillo *nm* ring; **a. de boda** wedding ring
ánima *nf* soul

Takes the masculine articles **el** and **un**.

animación *nf (diversión)* entertainment
animado,-a *adj (fiesta etc)* lively
animador,-a *nm,f* (**a**) entertainer; *TV* presenter; **a. cultural** cultural organizer (**b**) *Dep* cheerleader
animadversión *nf* ill feeling, animosity
animal 1 *nm* animal; *Fig (basto)* brute; *(necio)* dunce
  2 *adj* animal
animar 1 *vt* (**a**) *(alentar)* to encourage (**b**) *(alegrar) (persona)* to cheer up; *(fiesta, bar)* to liven up, to brighten up
  2 animarse *vpr* (**a**) *(persona)* to cheer up; *(fiesta, reunión)* to brighten up (**b**) **¿te animas a venir?** do you fancy coming along?
anímico,-a *adj* **estado a.** frame *o* state of mind
ánimo *nm* (**a**) *(espíritu)* spirit; **estado de á.** frame *o* state of mind (**b**) **con á. de** *(intención)* with the intention of (**c**) *(valor, coraje)* courage; **dar ánimos a** to encourage; **¡á.!** cheer up!
animosidad *nf* animosity
animoso,-a *adj* cheerful
aniñado,-a *adj* childlike; *Pey* childish
aniquilación *nf* annihilation
aniquilar *vt* to annihilate
anís *nm* (**a**) *(bebida)* anisette (**b**) *(grano)* aniseed
anisete *nm* anisette
aniversario *nm* anniversary
ano *nm* anus
anoche *adv* last night; *(por la tarde)* yesterday evening; **antes de a.** the night before last
anochecer [33] 1 *v impers* to get dark; **cuando anochece** at nightfall, at dusk
  2 *vi* to be somewhere at dusk; **anochecimos en Cuenca** we were in Cuenca at dusk
  3 *nm* nightfall, dusk
anodino,-a *adj (insustancial)* insubstantial; *(soso)* insipid, dull
anomalía *nf* anomaly
anómalo,-a *adj* anomalous
anonadado,-a *adj* **me quedé/dejó a.** I was astonished
anonimato *nm* anonymity; **permanecer en el a.** to remain anonymous *o* nameless
anónimo,-a 1 *adj* (**a**) *(desconocido)*

anonymous (**b**) *Com* **sociedad anónima** public liability company, *US* incorporated company

2 *nm (carta)* anonymous letter

anorak *nm* (*pl* **anoraks**) anorak

anorexia *nf* anorexia

anormal 1 *adj* (**a**) abnormal (**b**) *(inhabitual)* unusual; **una situación a.** an irregular situation (**c**) *Med* subnormal

2 *nmf Med* subnormal person

anotación *nf* (**a**) annotation (**b**) *(apunte)* note

anotar 1 *vt* (**a**) to annotate (**b**) *(apuntar)* to take down, to make a note of

2 anotarse *vpr RP (en curso)* to enrol

anquilosado,-a *adj Fig* fossilized; **a. en el pasado** locked in the past

anquilosarse *vpr Fig* to stagnate

ansia *nf* (**a**) *(deseo)* longing, yearning (**b**) *(ansiedad)* anxiety (**c**) *Med* sick feeling

> Takes the masculine articles **el** and **un**.

ansiar [29] *vt* to long for, to yearn for

ansiedad *nf* anxiety; **con a.** anxiously

ansioso,-a *adj* (**a**) *(deseoso)* eager (**por** for) (**b**) *(avaricioso)* greedy

antagónico,-a *adj* antagonistic

antagonismo *nm* antagonism

antagonista 1 *adj* antagonistic

2 *nmf* antagonist

antaño *adv* in the past, formerly

antártico,-a 1 *adj* Antarctic

2 *nm* **el A.** the Antarctic

Antártida *nf* Antarctica

ante¹ *nm* (**a**) *Zool* elk, moose (**b**) *(piel)* suede

ante² *prep* (**a**) before, in the presence of; *Jur* **a. notario** in the presence of a notary; **a. todo** most of all (**b**) *(en vista de)* faced with, in view of; **a. la crisis energética** faced with the energy crisis

anteanoche *adv* the night before last

anteayer *adv* the day before yesterday

antecedente 1 *adj* previous

2 *nm* antecedent

3 *nmpl* (**a**) **antecedentes** *(historial)* record; *Jur* **antecedentes penales** criminal record (**b**) *Fig* **poner en antecedentes** to put in the picture

anteceder *vt* to precede, to go before

antecesor,-a *nm,f* (**a**) *(en un cargo)* predecessor (**b**) *(antepasado)* ancestor

antedicho,-a *adj* above-mentioned

antelación *nf* notice; **con poca a.** at short notice; **con un mes de a.** a month beforehand, with a month's notice

antemano *adv* **de a.** beforehand, in advance

antena *nf* (**a**) *Rad & TV* aerial; **a. parabólica** satellite dish; **en a.** on the air (**b**) *Zool* antenna, feeler

anteojo *nm* (**a**) telescope (**b**) **anteojos** *(binoculares)* binoculars; *Am (gafas)* glasses, spectacles

antepasado,-a *nm,f* ancestor

antepecho *nm (de ventana)* sill; *(pretil)* parapet, guardrail

antepenúltimo,-a *adj* antepenultimate; **el capítulo a.** the last chapter but two

anteponer [19] *(pp* **antepuesto)** *vt Fig* to give preference to

anteproyecto *nm* preliminary plan, draft; *Pol* **a. de ley** draft bill

antepuesto,-a *pp de* **anteponer**

antepuse *pt indef de* **anteponer**

anterior *adj* (**a**) previous; **el día a.** the day before (**b**) *(delantero)* front; **parte a.** front part

anterioridad *nf* **con a.** before; **con a. a** prior to, before

anteriormente *adv* previously, before

antes *adv* (**a**) *(tiempo)* before; **a. de las tres** before three o'clock; **mucho a.** long before; **la noche a.** the night before; **cuanto a.** as soon as possible (**b**) *(antaño)* in the past; **a. llovía más** it used to rain more in the past (**c**) *(lugar)* before; **a. del semáforo** before the traffic lights (**d**) **a. prefiero hacerlo yo** I'd rather do it myself; **a. (bien)** on the contrary

antesala *nf* antechamber, anteroom; *Fig* **en la a. de** on the eve of

anti- *pref* anti-

antiadherente *adj* nonstick

antiaéreo,-a *adj* anti-aircraft

antibiótico,-a *adj & nm* antibiotic

anticaspa *adj* anti-dandruff

anticiclón *nm* anticyclone, high pressure area

anticipación *nf* bringing forward; **con a.** in advance

anticipadamente *adv* in advance

anticipado,-a *adj* brought forward; **elecciones anticipadas** early elections; **gracias anticipadas** thanks in advance; *Com* **por a.** in advance

anticipar 1 *vt (acontecimiento)* to bring forward; *(dinero)* to pay in advance; **no anticipemos acontecimientos** we'll cross that bridge when we come to it

2 anticiparse *vpr* (**a**) *(adelantarse)* to beat to it; **iba a decírtelo, pero él se me anticipó** I was going to tell you, but he beat me to it (**b**) *(llegar pronto)* to arrive early; *Fig* **a. a su tiempo** to be ahead of one's time

anticipo *nm (adelanto)* advance; **pedir un a.** to ask for an advance (on one's wages)

anticonceptivo,-a *adj & nm* contraceptive

anticongelante *adj & nm (de radiador)* antifreeze; *(de parabrisas)* de-icer

anticonstitucional *adj* unconstitutional

anticuado,-a *adj* antiquated

anticuario,-a *nm,f* antique dealer

anticucho *nm Andes (brocheta)* kebab

anticuerpo *nm* antibody

antídoto *nm* antidote

antier *adv Am Fam* the day before yesterday

antiestético,-a *adj* ugly, unsightly

antifaz *nm* mask

antigás *adj* **careta/mascarilla a.** gas mask

antigualla *nf Pey* museum piece

antigüedad *nf* (**a**) *(período histórico)* antiquity; **en la a.** in olden days, in former times (**b**) *(en cargo)* seniority (**c**) **tienda de antigüedades** antique shop

antiguo,-a *adj* (**a**) old, ancient (**b**) *(pasado de moda)* old-fashioned (**c**) *(en cargo)* senior (**d**) *(anterior)* former

antihigiénico,-a *adj* unhygienic, unhealthy

antihistamínico,-a *adj & nm* antihistamine

Antillas *nfpl* **las A.** the West Indies, the Antilles

antinatural *adj* unnatural, contrary to nature

antiniebla *adj inv* **luces a.** foglights

antipatía *nf* antipathy, dislike; **tener a. a** to dislike

antipático,-a *adj* unpleasant; **Pedro me es a.** I don't like Pedro

antípodas *nfpl* **las A.** the Antipodes

antiquísimo,-a *(superl de* **antiguo**) *adj* very old, ancient

antirrobo 1 *adj inv* antitheft; **alarma a.** burglar alarm; *(para coche)* car alarm
   2 *nm (para coche)* car alarm; *(para casa)* burglar alarm

antisemita 1 *adj* anti-Semitic
   2 *nmf* anti-Semite

antiséptico,-a *adj & nm* antiseptic

antítesis *nf inv* antithesis

antivirus *nm inv Informát* antivirus system

antojadizo,-a *adj* capricious, unpredictable

antojarse *vpr* (**a**) **cuando se me antoja** when I feel like it; **se le antojó un helado** he fancied an ice-cream (**b**) *(suponer)* **se me antoja que no lo sabe** I have the feeling that he doesn't know

antojitos *nmpl Méx* snacks, appetizers

antojo *nm* (**a**) *(capricho)* whim, caprice; *(de embarazada)* craving; **a su a.** in one's own way, as one pleases (**b**) *(en la piel)* birthmark

antología *nf* anthology

antonomasia *nf* **por a.** par excellence

antorcha *nf* torch

antro *nm* dump, hole; *Fig* **a. de perdición** den of vice

antropología *nf* anthropology

antropólogo,-a *nm,f* anthropologist

anual *adj* annual; **ingresos anuales** yearly income

anualidad *nf* annual payment, annuity

anuario *nm* yearbook

anudar *vt* (**a**) *(atar)* to knot, to tie (**b**) *Fig (unir)* to join, to bring together

anulación *nf* cancellation; *(de matrimonio)* annulment; *(de ley)* repeal

anular¹ *nm* ring finger

anular² *vt* (**a**) *Com (pedido)* to cancel; *Dep (gol)* to disallow; *(matrimonio)* to annul; *Jur (ley)* to repeal (**b**) *Informát* to delete

anunciador,-a *adj* **empresa anunciadora** advertising company

anunciante *nm* advertiser

anunciar [43] 1 *vt* (**a**) *(producto etc)* to advertise (**b**) *(avisar)* to announce
   2 anunciarse *vpr* to advertise oneself; **a. en un periódico** to put an advert in a newspaper

anuncio *nm* (**a**) *(comercial)* advertisement, advert, ad (**b**) *(aviso)* announcement (**c**) *(cartel)* notice, poster

anzuelo *nm* (fish) hook

añadidura *nf* addition; **por a.** besides, on top of everything else

añadir *vt* to add (**a** to)

añejo,-a *adj* (**a**) *(vino, queso)* mature (**b**) *(estropeado)* stale

añicos *nmpl* smithereens; **hacer a.** to smash to smithereens

añil 1 *adj* indigo, blue
   2 *nm* (**a**) *Bot* indigo plant (**b**) *(color)* indigo

año *nm* (**a**) year; **el a. pasado** last year; **el a. que viene** next year; **hace años** a long time ago, years ago; **los años noventa** the nineties; **todo el a.** all the year (round); **a. luz** light year (**b**) **¿cuántos años tienes?** how old are you?; **tiene seis años** he's six years old; **entrado en años** getting on

añoranza *nf* longing, yearning

añorar *vt (pasado)* to long for, to yearn for; *(país)* to feel homesick for, to miss

APA *nf (abr* **Asociación de Padres de Alumnos**) = Spanish association for parents of schoolchildren, ≃ PTA

> Takes the masculine articles **el** and **un.**

apabullar *vt* to bewilder

apacentar [1] *vt* to put out to pasture, to graze

apacible *adj* mild, calm

apaciguar [45] 1 *vt (calmar)* to pacify, to appease

2 apaciguarse *vpr (persona)* to calm down; *(tormenta)* to abate

apadrinar *vt* (**a**) *(en bautizo)* to act as godfather to; *(en boda)* to be best man for (**b**) *(artista)* to sponsor

apagado,-a *adj* (**a**) *(luz, cigarro)* out (**b**) *(color)* dull; *(voz)* sad; *(mirada)* expressionless, lifeless; *(carácter, persona)* spiritless

apagar [42] *vt (fuego)* to put out; *(luz, tele etc)* to turn off, to switch off; *(color)* to soften; *(sed)* to quench

apagón *nm* power cut, blackout

apaisado,-a *adj* (**a**) oblong (**b**) *(papel)* landscape

apalabrar *vt (concertar)* to make a verbal agreement on

apalancar [44] 1 *vt* to lever up

2 apalancarse *vpr Fam* to ensconce oneself, to settle down

apalear¹ *vt* to beat, to thrash

apalear² *vt Agr (grano)* to winnow

apañar 1 *vt* to mend, to fix

2 apañarse *vpr Fam* **apañárselas** to manage

apaño *nm* mend, repair

apapachar *vt Méx Fam (mimar)* to cuddle; *(consentir)* to spoil

apapacho *nm Méx Fam (mimo)* cuddle

aparador *nm (mueble)* sideboard; *(de tienda)* shop window

aparato *nm* (**a**) (piece of) apparatus; *(dispositivo)* device; *(instrumento)* instrument; **a. de radio/televisión** radio/television set; **a. digestivo** digestive system; **a. eléctrico** thunder and lightning (**b**) *Tel* **¿quién está al a.?** who's speaking? (**c**) *(ostentación)* display

aparatoso,-a *adj* (**a**) *(pomposo)* ostentatious, showy (**b**) *(espectacular)* spectacular (**c**) *(grande)* bulky

aparcamiento *nm (en la calle)* parking place; *(parking) Br* car park, *US* parking lot

aparcar [44] *vt* to park

aparcería *nf Agr* sharecropping

apareamiento *nm* (**a**) *(de cosas)* pairing off (**b**) *(de animales)* mating

aparear *vt,* **aparearse** *vpr* to mate

aparecer [33] 1 *vi* (**a**) to appear; **no aparece en mi lista** he is not on my list (**b**) to turn up, to show up; **¿apareció el dinero?** did the money turn up?; **no apareció nadie** nobody turned up

2 aparecerse *vpr* to appear

aparejado,-a *adj* **llevar** *o* **traer a.** to entail

aparejador,-a *nm,f* quantity surveyor

aparejar *vt* (**a**) *(caballo)* to harness (**b**) *(emparejar)* to pair off

aparejo *nm* (**a**) *(equipo)* equipment (**b**) *(de caballo)* harness

aparentar 1 *vt* (**a**) *(fingir)* to affect (**b**) *(tener aspecto)* to look; **no aparenta esa edad** she doesn't look that age

2 *vi* to show off

aparente *adj* (**a**) apparent; **sin motivo a.** for no apparent reason (**b**) *Fam (conveniente)* suitable

aparición *nf* (**a**) appearance (**b**) *(visión)* apparition

apariencia *nf* appearance; **en a.** apparently; *Fig* **guardar las apariencias** to keep up appearances

apartado,-a 1 *adj (lugar)* remote, isolated; **mantente a. de él** keep away from him

2 *nm* (**a**) *(párrafo)* section, paragraph (**b**) **a. de correos** Post Office Box

apartamento *nm* (small) flat, apartment

apartar 1 *vt* (**a**) *(alejar)* to move away, to remove; **a. la mirada** to look away (**b**) *(guardar)* to put aside

2 *vi* **¡aparta!** move out of the way!

3 apartarse *vpr (alejarse)* to move over, to move away; **apártate de en medio** move out of the way

aparte 1 *adv* (**a**) aside; **ponlo a.** put it aside; **modestia/bromas a.** modesty/joking apart (**b**) **eso hay que pagarlo a.** *(separadamente)* you have to pay for that separately (**c**) **a. de eso** *(además)* besides that; *(excepto)* apart from that (**d**) **eso es caso a.** that's completely different

2 *nm* (**a**) *Teatro* aside (**b**) *Ling* **punto y a.** full stop, new paragraph

apasionado,-a 1 *adj* passionate; **a. de la música** very fond of music

2 *nm,f* enthusiast

apasionante *adj* exciting

apasionar *vt* to excite, to thrill; **le apasiona el jazz** he is mad about jazz

apatía *nf* apathy

apático,-a 1 *adj* apathetic
  2 *nm,f* apathetic person
apátrida 1 *adj* stateless
  2 *nmf* stateless person
apdo. (*abr* **apartado**) P.O. Box
apeadero *nm* halt
apearse *vpr* (*de un autobús, tren*) to get off, to alight; (*de un coche*) to get out; **se apeó en Jerez** he got off in Jerez
apechugar [42] *vi* **a. con** to shoulder
apedrear *vt* to throw stones at
apegado,-a *adj* devoted, attached (**a** to)
apegarse [42] *vpr* to become devoted *o* attached (**a** to)
apego *nm* love, affection; **tener a. a** to be attached to
apelación *nf* appeal; **interponer a.** to lodge an appeal
apelar *vi* (**a**)*Jur* to appeal (**b**) (*recurrir*) to resort (**a** to)
apellidarse *vpr* to have as a surname, to be called
apellido *nm* surname; **a. de soltera** maiden name
apelmazado,-a *adj* stodgy
apelotonar 1 *vt* to pile up, to put into a pile
  2 apelotonarse *vpr* (*gente*) to crowd together
apenado,-a *adj* (**a**) (*entristecido*) sad (**b**) *Andes, CAm, Carib, Méx* (*avergonzado*) ashamed, embarrassed
apenar 1 *vt* to sadden
  2 apenarse *vpr* (**a**) (*entristecerse*) to be saddened (**b**) *Andes, CAm, Carib, Méx* (*avergonzarse*) to be ashamed, to be embarrassed
apenas *adv* (**a**) (*casi no*) hardly, scarcely; **a. come** he hardly eats anything; **a. (si) hay nieve** there is hardly any snow (**b**) (*tan pronto como*) scarcely; **a. llegó, sonó el teléfono** no sooner had he arrived than the phone rang
apéndice *nm* appendix
apendicitis *nf* appendicitis
apercibir 1 *vt* to warn
  2 apercibirse *vpr* **apercibirse (de)** to notice
aperitivo *nm* (*bebida*) apéritif; (*comida*) appetizer
apero *nm* (*usu pl*) equipment, tools; **aperos de labranza** farming implements
apertura *nf* (**a**) (*comienzo*) opening (**b**) *Pol* liberalization
apestar 1 *vi* to stink (**a** of)
  2 *vt* to infect with the plague
apetecer [33] *vi* **¿qué te apetece para cenar?** what would you like for supper?;

¿te apetece ir al cine? do you fancy going to the cinema?
apetecible *adj* tempting, inviting
apetito *nm* appetite; **tengo mucho a.** I'm really hungry
apetitoso,-a *adj* appetizing, tempting; (*comida*) delicious, tasty
apiadarse *vpr* to take pity (**de** on)
ápice *nm* (**a**) (*punta*) apex (**b**) *Fig* **ni un á.** not a bit
apicultura *nf* beekeeping, apiculture
apilar *vt*, **apilarse** *vpr* to pile up, to heap up
apiñarse *vpr* to crowd together
apio *nm* celery
apisonadora *nf* roadroller, steamroller
apisonar *vt* to roll
aplacar [44] 1 *vt* to placate, to calm
  2 aplacarse *vpr* to calm down
aplanar *vt* to level
aplastante *adj* crushing; *Pol* **victoria a.** landslide victory
aplastar *vt* (**a**) to flatten, to squash (**b**) *Fig* (*vencer*) to crush
aplatanarse *vpr* *Fam* to become lethargic
aplaudir *vt* (**a**) to clap, to applaud (**b**) *Fig* to applaud
aplauso *nm* applause
aplazamiento *nm* postponement, adjournment; (*de un pago*) deferment
aplazar [40] *vt* to postpone, to adjourn; *Fin* (*pago*) to defer
aplicación *nf* application
aplicado,-a *adj* hard-working
aplicar [44] 1 *vt* to apply
  2 aplicarse *vpr* (**a**) (*esforzarse*) to apply oneself, to work hard (**b**) (*norma, ley*) to apply, to be applicable
aplique *nm* wall light, wall lamp
aplomo *nm* aplomb
apocado,-a *adj* shy, timid
apocamiento *nm* timidity, lack of self-confidence
apocarse [44] *vpr* to become frightened
apodar *vt* to nickname
apoderado,-a *nm,f* (**a**) agent, representative (**b**) (*de torero, deportista*) manager
apoderarse *vpr* to take possession (**de** of), to seize; *Fig* **el miedo se apoderó de ella** she was seized by fear
apodo *nm* nickname
apogeo *nm* height; **estar en pleno a.** (*fama etc*) to be at its height
apolillarse *vpr* to get moth-eaten
apolítico,-a *adj* apolitical
apología *nf* apology, defence
apoltronarse *vpr* *Fam* to vegetate

apoplejía *nf* apoplexy
apoquinar *vt Fam* to cough up, to fork out
aporrear *vt* to beat, to hit, to thrash; *(puerta)* to bang; *Fam* **a. el piano** to bang (away) on the piano
aportación *nf* contribution
aportar 1 *vt* to contribute
   2 *vi Náut* to reach port
aposentarse *vpr* to stay, to lodge
aposento *nm* room
aposta *adv* on purpose, intentionally
apostar[1] **[2] 1** *vt* to bet; **te apuesto una cena a que no viene** I bet you a dinner that he won't come
   2 *vi* to bet (**por** on); **a. a los caballos** to bet on horses; **apuesto a que sí viene** I bet she will come
   3 apostarse *vpr* to bet; **me apuesto lo que quieras** I bet you anything
apostar[2] *vt (situar)* to post, to station
apostilla *nf* note
apóstol *nm* apostle
apóstrofo *nm* apostrophe
apostura *nf* good bearing
apoteósico,-a *adj* enormous, tremendous
apoyacabezas *nm Aut* headrest
apoyar 1 *vt* (**a**) to lean (**b**) *(causa)* to support
   2 apoyarse *vpr* (**a**) **a. en** to lean on; **apóyate en mi brazo** take my arm (**b**) **a. en** *(opinión)* to be based on, to rest on
apoyo *nm* support
apreciable *adj* appreciable, noticeable
apreciación *nf* appreciation
apreciar [43] 1 *vt* (**a**) to appreciate (**b**) *(percibir)* to notice, to see
   2 apreciarse *vpr* to be noticeable
aprecio *nm* regard, esteem; **tener a. a algn** to be fond of sb
aprehender *vt (alijo, botín)* to apprehend, to seize
aprehensión *nf* seizure
apremiante *adj* urgent, pressing
apremiar [43] *vi* to be urgent; **el tiempo apremia** time is at a premium
aprender *vt* to learn; **así aprenderás** that'll teach you
aprendiz,-a *nm,f* apprentice, trainee
aprendizaje *nm* (**a**) learning (**b**) *(instrucción)* apprenticeship, traineeship
aprensión *nf* apprehension
aprensivo,-a *adj* apprehensive
apresar *vt* to seize, to capture
aprestar 1 *vt* to prepare, to get ready
   2 aprestarse *vpr* to get ready
apresurado,-a *adj (persona)* in a hurry; *(cosa)* hurried

apresuramiento *nm* haste, hurry
apresurar 1 *vt (paso etc)* to speed up
   2 apresurarse *vpr* to hurry up
apretado,-a *adj* (**a**) *(ropa, cordón)* tight; **íbamos todos apretados en el coche** we were all squashed together in the car (**b**) *(día, agenda)* busy
apretar [1] 1 *vt (botón)* to press; *(nudo, tornillo)* to tighten; **a. el gatillo** to pull the trigger; **me aprietan las botas** these boots are too tight for me
   2 *vi* **apretaba el calor** it was really hot
   3 apretarse *vpr* to squeeze together, to cram together; *Fig* **a. el cinturón** to tighten one's belt
apretón *nm* squeeze; **a. de manos** handshake
apretujar 1 *vt* to squeeze, to crush
   2 apretujarse *vpr* to squeeze together, to cram together
aprieto *nm* tight spot, fix, jam; **poner a algn en un a.** to put sb in an awkward position
aprisa *adv* quickly
aprisionar *vt (atrapar)* to trap
aprobación *nf* approval
aprobado *nm Educ* pass
aprobar [2] *vt* (**a**) *(autorizar)* to approve (**b**) *(estar de acuerdo con)* to approve of (**c**) *Educ* to pass (**d**) *Pol (ley)* to pass
aprontar 1 *vt (preparar)* to quickly prepare o get ready
   2 aprontarse *vpr RP (prepararse)* to get ready; **aprontate para cuando llegue tu papá!** just wait till your father gets back!
apropiado,-a *adj* suitable, appropriate
apropiarse [43] *vpr* to appropriate
aprovechado,-a *adj* (**a**) **mal a.** *(recurso, tiempo)* wasted; **bien a.** put to good use (**b**) *(espacio)* well-planned (**c**) *(egoísta)* self-seeking
aprovechamiento *nm* use
aprovechar 1 *vt* (**a**) to make good use of, to make the most of; **aprovechamos bien la tarde** we've done lots of things this afternoon (**b**) *(recursos etc)* to take advantage of; **a. la ocasión** to seize the opportunity
   2 *vi* **¡que aproveche!** enjoy your meal!, bon appétit!
   3 aprovecharse *vpr* to use to one's advantage, to take advantage; **a. de algn** to take advantage of sb; **a. de algo** to make the most of sth
aprovisionar *vt* to supply, to provide; **a. las tropas** to give supplies to the troops
aproximación *nf* (**a**) approximation (**b**) *(en lotería)* consolation prize

aproximadamente *adv* approximately, roughly

aproximado,-a *adj* approximate; **un cálculo a.** a rough estimate

aproximar 1 *vt* to bring *o* put nearer

  2 aproximarse *vpr* **aproximarse (a)** to approach

aproximativo,-a *adj* approximate, rough

aptitud *nf* aptitude; **prueba de a.** aptitude test

apto,-a *adj* (**a**) *(apropiado)* suitable, appropriate; *Cin* **a. para todos los públicos** *Br* U, *US* G (**b**) *(capacitado)* capable, able (**c**) *Educ* passed

apuesta *nf* bet, wager

apuesto,-a *adj* good-looking; *(hombre)* handsome

apunado,-a *adj Andes* **estar a.** to have altitude sickness

apunarse *vpr Andes* to get altitude sickness

apuntador,-a *nm,f Teatro* prompter

apuntalar *vt* to prop up, to shore up, to underpin

apuntar 1 *vt* (**a**) *(con arma)* to aim (**b**) *(señalar)* to point out (**c**) *(anotar)* to note down, to make a note of (**d**) *(indicar)* to indicate, to suggest; **todo parece a. a ...** everything seems to point to ...

  2 *vi* **cuando apunta el día** when day breaks

  3 apuntarse *vpr* (**a**) *(en una lista)* to put one's name down (**b**) *Fam* **¿te apuntas?** are you game?; **me apunto** count me in

apunte *nm (usu pl)* note; **tomar apuntes** to take notes

apuñalar *vt* to stab

apurado,-a 1 *adj* (**a**) *(necesitado)* in need; **a. de dinero** hard up for money; **a. de tiempo** in a hurry (**b**) *(preocupado)* worried; *(avergonzado)* embarrassed (**c**) *(situación)* awkward, difficult (**d**) *(afeitado)* close

  2 *nm (afeitado)* close shave

apurar 1 *vt* (**a**) *(terminar)* to finish off, to end (**b**) *(preocupar)* to worry

  2 apurarse *vpr* (**a**) *(preocuparse)* to worry, to get worried; **no te apures** don't worry (**b**) *(darse prisa)* to rush, to hurry, to pester; **apúrate** get a move on

apuro *nm* (**a**) *(situación difícil)* tight spot, fix, jam; **estar en un a.** to be in a tight spot (**b**) *(escasez de dinero)* hardship; **pasar apuros** to be hard up (**c**) *(vergüenza)* embarrassment; **¡qué a.!** how embarrassing!

aquejado,-a *adj* suffering (**de** from)

aquel,-ella *adj dem* (**a**) that; **a. niño** that boy (**b**) **aquellos,-as** those; **aquellas niñas** those girls

aquél,-élla *pron dem m,f* (**a**) that one; *(el anterior)* the former; **aquél/aquélla ... éste/ésta** the former ... the latter (**b**) **todo a. que** anyone who, whoever (**c**) **aquéllos,-as** those; *(los anteriores)* the former

> Note that **aquél** and its various forms can be written without an accent when there is no risk of confusion with the adjective.

aquella *adj dem f ver* **aquel**

aquélla *pron dem f ver* **aquél**

aquello *pron neut f* that, it

aquellos,-as *adj dem pl ver* **aquel,-ella**

aquéllos,-as *pron dem m,fpl ver* **aquél, -élla**

aquí *adv* (**a**) *(lugar)* here; **a. arriba/fuera** up/out here; **a. está** here it is; **a. mismo** right here; **de a. para allá** up and down, to and fro; **hasta a.** this far; **por a., por favor** this way please; **está por a.** it's around here somewhere (**b**) *(tiempo)* **de a. en adelante** from now on; **de aquí a junio** between now and June; **hasta a.** up till now

aquietar *vt* to pacify, to calm down

ara *nf Fml* **en aras de** for the sake of

> Takes the masculine articles **el** and **un**.

árabe 1 *adj (de Arabia)* Arab

  2 *nmf (persona)* Arab

  3 *nm (idioma)* Arabic

Arabia *n* Arabia; **A. Saudita** Saudi Arabia

arado *nm* plough

Aragón *n* Aragon

aragonés,-esa *adj & nm,f* Aragonese

arancel *nm* tariff, customs duty

arancelario,-a *adj* tariff, duty; **derechos arancelarios** duties; **barreras arancelarias** customs barriers

arandela *nf Téc* washer; *(anilla)* ring

araña *nf* (**a**) spider (**b**) *(lámpara)* chandelier

arañar *vt* to scratch

arañazo *nm* scratch

arar *vt* to plough

araucaria *nf* araucaria, monkey puzzle tree

arbitraje *nm* (**a**) arbitration (**b**) *Dep* refereeing; *Ten* umpiring

arbitrar *vt* (**a**) to arbitrate (**b**) *Dep* to referee; *Ten* to umpire

arbitrariedad *nf* (**a**) arbitrariness (**b**) *(acto)* arbitrary action

arbitrario,-a *adj* arbitrary

arbitrio *nm (voluntad)* will; *(juicio)* judgement

árbitro,-a *nm,f* (**a**) *Dep* referee; *(de tenis)* umpire (**b**) *(mediador)* arbitrator
árbol *nm* (**a**) *Bot* tree (**b**) *Téc* shaft (**c**) *Náut* mast (**d**) *(gráfico)* tree (diagram); **á. genealógico** family *o* genealogical tree
arbolado,-a 1 *adj* wooded
2 *nm* woodland
arboleda *nf* grove
arbusto *nm* bush, shrub
arca *nf* (**a**) chest (**b**) *(para caudales)* strongbox, safe; **arcas públicas** Treasury

Takes the masculine articles **el** and **un**.

arcada *nf* (**a**) arcade; *(de puente)* arch (**b**) *(náusea)* retching
arcaico,-a *adj* archaic
arcén *nm* verge; *(de autopista) Br* hard shoulder, *US* shoulder
archi- *pref* super-
archiconocido,-a *adj* extremely well-known
archipiélago *nm* archipelago
archivador *nm* filing cabinet
archivar *vt* (**a**) *(documento etc)* to file (away) (**b**) *(caso, asunto)* to shelve (**c**) *Informát* to save
archivo *nm* (**a**) file (**b**) *(archivador)* filing cabinet (**c**) **archivos** archives (**d**) *Informát* file; **a. adjunto** attachment
arcilla *nf* clay
arco *nm* (**a**) *Arquit* arch (**b**) *Mat & Elec* arc (**c**) *(de violín)* bow (**d**) *(para flechas)* bow; **tiro con a.** archery (**e**) **a. iris** rainbow (**f**) *Am Dep (portería)* goal, goalmouth
arder *vi* to burn; *Fam* **la conversación está que arde** the conversation is really heating up; **Juan está que arde** Juan is really fuming
ardid *nm* scheme, plot
ardiente *adj* (**a**) *(encendido)* burning; **capilla a.** chapel of rest (**b**) *Fig (fervoroso)* eager
ardilla *nf* squirrel
ardor *nm* (**a**) heat; *Med* **a. de estómago** heartburn (**b**) *Fig* ardour, fervour
ardoroso,-a *adj Fig* ardent, passionate
arduo,-a *adj* arduous
área *nf* (**a**) area; *Dep* penalty area (**b**) *(medida)* are *(100 square metres)*

Takes the masculine articles **el** and **un**.

arena *nf* (**a**) sand; **playa de a.** sandy beach (**b**) *Taurom* bullring
arengar [42] *vt* to harangue
arenisca *nf* sandstone
arenoso,-a *adj* sandy
arenque *nm* herring; *Culin* **a. ahumado** kipper

arepa *nf Carib, Col* = pancake made of maize flour
arete *nm Andes, Méx* earring
argamasa *nf* mortar
Argel *n* Algiers
Argelia *n* Algeria
argelino,-a *adj & nm,f* Algerian
Argentina *n* Argentina
argentino,-a *adj & nm,f* Argentinian, Argentine
argolla *nf* (**a**) *(aro)* (large) ring (**b**) *Col, Méx (alianza)* wedding ring
argot *nm (popular)* slang; *(técnico)* jargon
argucia *nf* ruse
argüende *nm Méx Fam* (**a**) *(alboroto)* rumpus, shindy; **armar (un) a.** to kick up a rumpus (**b**) *(enredo, confusión)* mess, trouble; **meterse en un a.** to get into a mess
argüir [62] *vt* (**a**) *(deducir)* to deduce, to conclude (**b**) *(argumentar)* to argue
argumentación *nf* argument
argumentar *vt* = **argüir**
argumento *nm* (**a**) *Lit & Teatro (trama)* plot (**b**) *(razonamiento)* argument
arguyo *indic pres de* **argüir**
aridez *nf* aridity; *Fig* dryness
árido,-a *adj* arid; *Fig* dry
Aries *nm* Aries
ariete *nm Mil* battering ram
ario,-a *adj & nm,f* Aryan
arisco,-a *adj (persona)* unfriendly, stand-offish; *(animal)* unfriendly
arista *nf* edge
aristocracia *nf* aristocracy
aristócrata *nmf* aristocrat
aristocrático,-a *adj* aristocratic
aritmética *nf* arithmetic
arma *nf* weapon; **a. blanca** knife; **a. de fuego** firearm; **a. homicida** murder weapon; **a. nuclear** nuclear weapon; *Fig* **a. de doble filo** double-edged sword

Takes the masculine articles **el** and **un**.

armada *nf* navy
armado,-a *adj* armed; **ir a.** to be armed; **lucha armada** armed struggle
armador,-a *nm,f* shipowner
armadura *nf* (**a**) *(armazón)* frame (**b**) *Hist* suit of armour
armamentista *adj* arms; **la carrera a.** the arms race
armamento *nm* armaments; **a. nuclear** nuclear weapons
armar 1 *vt* (**a**) *(tropa, soldado)* to arm (**b**) *(piezas)* to fit *o* put together, to assemble (**c**) *Fam* **armaron un escándalo** they created a scandal

2 armarse *vpr* to arm oneself; *Fig* **a. de paciencia** to summon up one's patience; *Fig* **a. de valor** to pluck up courage; *Fam* **se armó la gorda** all hell broke loose

armario *nm (para ropa)* wardrobe; *(de cocina)* cupboard; **a. empotrado** built-in wardrobe *o* cupboard

armatoste *nm (cosa)* monstrosity

armazón *nm* frame; *(de madera)* timberwork; *Arquit* shell

Armenia *n* Armenia

armería *nf* gunsmith's (shop)

armiño *nm* ermine

armisticio *nm* armistice

armonía *nf* harmony

armonioso,-a *adj* harmonious

armonizar [40] *vt & vi* to harmonize

aro *nm* (**a**) *(gen)* hoop; *Fam* **pasar por el a.** to knuckle under (**b**) *Am (pendiente)* earring

aroma *nm* aroma; *(de vino)* bouquet

aromático,-a *adj* aromatic

arpa *nf* harp

> Takes the masculine articles **el** and **un**.

arpía *nf (en mitología)* harpy; *Fig* harpy, old witch

arpón *nm* harpoon

arquear *vt,* **arquearse** *vpr* to bend, to curve

arqueología *nf* archaeology

arqueólogo,-a *nm,f* archaeologist

arquero,-a *nm,f* (**a**) *(tirador)* archer (**b**) *Am (portero de fútbol)* goalkeeper

arquetipo *nm* archetype

arquitecto,-a *nm,f* architect

arquitectónico,-a *adj* architectural

arquitectura *nf* architecture

arrabalero,-a *adj Pey* coarse

arrabales *nmpl* slums

arraigado,-a *adj* deeply rooted

arraigar [42] *vi* to take root

arraigo *nm Fig* roots; **una tradición con mucho a.** a deeply-rooted tradition

arrancar [44] 1 *vt* (**a**) *(planta)* to uproot, to pull up; **a. de raíz** to uproot (**b**) *(extraer)* to pull *o* tear off *o* out; *(diente, pelo)* to pull out; *Fig (confesión etc)* to extract; **arranca una hoja del cuaderno** tear a page out of the notebook (**c**) *(coche, motor)* to start; *Informát* to boot

2 *vi* (**a**) *Aut & Téc* to start; *Informát* to boot (up) (**b**) *(empezar)* to begin; **a. a llorar** to burst out crying

arranque *nm* (**a**) *Aut & Téc* starting (**b**) *(comienzo)* start (**c**) *Fam (arrebato)* outburst, fit

arrasar 1 *vt* to devastate, to destroy

2 *vi (en elecciones etc)* to win by a landslide

arrastrado,-a *Fam* **1** *adj* wretched

2 *nm,f* bad egg

arrastrar 1 *vt* to pull (along), to drag (along); **vas arrastrando el vestido** your dress is trailing on the ground; **lo arrastró la corriente** he was swept away by the current

2 arrastrarse *vpr* to drag oneself; *Fig (humillarse)* to crawl

arrastre *nm* (**a**) pulling, dragging; *Fam* **para el a.** *(persona)* on one's last legs; *(cosa)* done for (**b**) **(pesca de) a.** trawling (**c**) *Am Fam* **tener a.** to have a lot of influence

arrayán *nm* myrtle

arre *interj* gee up!, giddy up!

arrear *vt* (**a**) to spur on; *(caballos)* to urge on (**b**) *Fam (bofetada)* to give

arrebatador,-a *adj Fig* captivating, fascinating

arrebatar 1 *vt (coger)* to snatch, to seize; *Fig (cautivar)* to captivate, to fascinate

2 arrebatarse *vpr (enfurecerse)* to become furious; *(exaltarse)* to get carried away

arrebato *nm* outburst, fit

arreciar [43] *vi (viento, tormenta)* to get worse

arrecife *nm* reef

arreglado,-a *adj* (**a**) *(reparado)* repaired, fixed (**b**) *(solucionado)* settled (**c**) *(habitación)* tidy, neat (**d**) *(persona)* well-dressed, smart

arreglar 1 *vt* (**a**) to arrange; *(problema)* to sort out; *(habitación)* to tidy; *(papeles)* to put in order (**b**) *(reparar)* to repair, to fix (**c**) *(vestir)* to get ready

2 arreglarse *vpr* (**a**) *(vestirse)* to get ready (**b**) *Fam* **arreglárselas** to manage (**c**) *(reconciliarse)* to make up

arreglo *nm* (**a**) arrangement; *(acuerdo)* compromise (**b**) *(reparación)* repair; **no tiene a.** it is beyond repair; *Fam* **¡no tienes a.!** you're hopeless! (**c**) *Fml* **con a. a** in accordance with

arrellanarse *vpr* to sit back

arremangarse [42] *vpr* to roll one's sleeves *o* trousers up

arremeter *vi* to attack

arremolinarse *vpr* to whirl about; *Fig (gente)* to crowd together, to cram together

arrendamiento *nm* (**a**) *(alquiler)* renting (**b**) *(precio)* rent

arrendar [1] *vt (piso)* to rent; *(dar en arriendo)* to let on lease; *(tomar en* *arriendo)* to take on lease

arrendatario,-a *nm,f* leaseholder, lessee; *(inquilino)* tenant

arreos *nmpl* (**a**) *(de caballería)* harness, trappings (**b**) *(adornos)* adornments

arrepentido,-a *adj* regretful

arrepentimiento *nm* regret

arrepentirse [5] *vpr* **a. de** to regret; *Rel* to repent

arrestar *vt* to arrest, to detain; *(encarcelar)* to put in prison

arresto *nm* arrest; *Jur* **a. domiciliario** house arrest

arriar [29] *vt (bandera)* to strike; *(velas)* to lower

arriba 1 *adv* up; *(encima)* on the top; **ahí a.** up there; **de a. abajo** from top to bottom; *Fam* **mirar a algn de a. abajo** to look sb up and down; **desde a.** from above; **hacia a.** upwards; **de un millón para a.** from one million upwards; **más a.** higher up, further up; **a. del todo** right on *o* at the top; **la parte de a.** the top (part); **vive a.** he lives upstairs; **véase más a.** see above

2 *interj* get up!, up you get!; **¡a. la República!** long live the Republic!; **¡a. las manos!** hands up!

3 *prep Am* **a. (de)** on top of

arribar *vi* to reach port, to arrive

arribeño,-a *Am* **1** *adj* highland

2 *nm,f* highlander

arribista *nmf* parvenu, social climber

arriendo *nm* lease; *(de un piso)* renting; **dar en a.** to let out on lease; **tomar en a.** to take on lease

arriesgado,-a *adj* (**a**) *(peligroso)* risky (**b**) *(temerario)* fearless, daring

arriesgar [42] 1 *vt* to risk

2 arriesgarse *vpr* to risk; **se arriesga demasiado** he's taking too many risks

arrimar 1 *vt* to move closer, to bring near *o* nearer; *Fam* **a. el hombro** to lend a hand

2 arrimarse *vpr* to move *o* get close, to come near *o* nearer

arrinconar *vt* (**a**) *(poner en un rincón)* to put in a corner (**b**) *(abandonar)* to put away, to lay aside (**c**) *(acorralar)* to corner

arrobo *nm* rapture, enthralment

arrocero,-a *adj* **la industria arrocera** the rice industry

arrodillarse *vpr* to kneel down

arrogancia *nf* arrogance

arrogante *adj* arrogant

arrojadizo,-a *adj* **arma arrojadiza** missile

arrojado,-a *adj (osado)* bold, daring

arrojar 1 *vt* (**a**) *(tirar)* to throw, to fling (**b**) *Com (saldo)* to show

2 arrojarse *vpr* to throw oneself, to fling oneself

arrojo *nm* daring, courage

arrollador,-a *adj Fig* overwhelming; *(éxito)* resounding; *(personalidad)* captivating

arrollar *vt* **1** *(atropellar)* to run over, to knock down

2 *vi Dep & Pol* to win easily

arropar 1 *vt* to wrap up; *(en la cama)* to tuck in

2 arroparse *vpr* to wrap oneself up

arrostrar *vt* to face

arroyo *nm* brook, stream

arroz *nm* rice; **a. con leche** rice pudding

arruga *nf (en la piel)* wrinkle; *(en la ropa)* crease

arrugar [42] 1 *vt (piel)* to wrinkle; *(ropa)* to crease; *(papel)* to crumple (up)

2 arrugarse *vpr (piel)* to wrinkle; *(ropa)* to crease

arruinado,-a *adj* bankrupt, ruined

arruinar 1 *vt* to ruin

2 arruinarse *vpr* to be ruined

arrullar 1 *vt (bebé)* to lull

2 *vi (paloma)* to coo

arrullo *nm* (**a**) *(de paloma)* cooing (**b**) *(nana)* lullaby

arrumaco *nm Fam* kissing and hugging; *(halago)* flattery

arsenal *nm* arsenal

arsénico *nm* arsenic

arte *nm o nf* (**a**) art; **bellas artes** fine arts; *Fam* **por amor al a.** for the love of it (**b**) *(habilidad)* skill

Takes the masculine articles **el** and **un**.

artefacto *nm* device; **a. explosivo** explosive device

arteria *nf* artery; *(carretera)* highway

artesanal *adj* handmade

artesanía *nf* (**a**) *(cualidad)* craftsmanship (**b**) *(objetos)* crafts, handicrafts

artesano,-a 1 *nm,f* craftsman, *f* craftswoman

2 *adj* handmade

ártico,-a 1 *adj* arctic; **el océano Á.** the Arctic Ocean

2 *nm* **el Á.** the Arctic

articulación *nf* (**a**) *Anat* joint, articulation (**b**) *Téc* joint

articulado,-a *adj (tren etc)* articulated

articular *vt* to articulate

artículo *nm* article; **a. de fondo** leader (article)

artífice *nmf* author; *Fig* **el a. del acuerdo** the architect of the agreement

artificial *adj* artificial; *Tex* man-made *o* synthetic

artificio *nm* (**a**) artifice; **fuego de a.** firework (**b**) *(artimaña)* ruse

artillería *nf* artillery; **a. antiaérea** anti-aircraft guns

artillero *nm* artilleryman

artilugio *nm* gadget, device

artimaña *nf* trick, ruse

artista *nmf* artist; **a. de cine** film star

artístico,-a *adj* artistic

artritis *nf* arthritis

arveja *nf Andes, Carib, RP* pea

arzobispo *nm* archbishop

as *nm* ace

asa *nf* handle

> Takes the masculine articles **el** and **un**.

asado,-a 1 *adj Culin* roast; **pollo a.** roast chicken; *Fig* **a. de calor** roasting, boiling hot

2 *nm Culin* roast; *Col, CSur (barbacoa)* barbecue

asaduras *nfpl* offal; *(de ave)* giblets

asalariado,-a 1 *adj* salaried

2 *nm,f* wage earner, salaried worker

asaltador,-a *nm,f,* **asaltante** *nmf* attacker; *(en un robo)* robber

asaltar *vt* to assault, to attack; *(banco)* to rob; *Fig* to assail

asalto *nm* (**a**) assault, attack; **a. a un banco** bank robbery (**b**) *(en boxeo)* round

asamblea *nf* meeting; **a. general** general meeting

asar 1 *vt* to roast

2 asarse *vpr Fig* to be roasting, to be boiling hot

ascendencia *nf* ancestry, ancestors; **de a. escocesa** of Scottish descent

ascender [3] 1 *vt (en un cargo)* to promote

2 *vi* (**a**) to move upward; *(temperatura)* to rise; **la factura asciende a ...** the bill adds up to ... (**b**) *(al trono)* to ascend (**c**) *(de categoría)* to be promoted

ascendiente *nmf* ancestor

ascensión *nf* (**a**) climb (**b**) *(al trono)* accession

ascenso *nm* promotion; *(subida)* rise

ascensor *nm Br* lift, *US* elevator

asco *nm* disgust, repugnance; **me da a.** it makes me (feel) sick; **¡qué a.!** how disgusting *o* revolting!

ascua *nf* ember; *Fig* **en ascuas** on tenterhooks

> Takes the masculine articles **el** and **un**.

aseado,-a *adj* tidy, neat

asear 1 *vt* to clean, to tidy up

2 asearse *vpr* to wash, to get washed

asediar [43] *vt* to besiege

asedio *nm* siege

asegurado,-a *adj* (**a**) insured (**b**) *(indudable)* secure

asegurador,-a 1 *adj* insurance

2 *nm,f* insurer

asegurar 1 *vt* (**a**) to insure (**b**) *(garantizar)* **me aseguró que ...** he assured me that ...; **a. el éxito de un proyecto** to ensure the success of a project (**c**) *(cuerda)* to fasten

2 asegurarse *vpr* (**a**) to make sure; **a. de que ...** to make sure that ... (**b**) *Seg* to insure oneself

asemejarse *vpr* **a. a** to look like

asentado,-a *adj (establecido)* established, settled

asentamiento *nm* settlement

asentar [1] 1 *vt* **a. la cabeza** to settle down

2 asentarse *vpr* (**a**) *(establecerse)* to settle down, to establish oneself (**b**) *(té, polvo)* to settle

asentimiento *nm* assent, consent

asentir [5] *vi* to assent, to agree; **a. con la cabeza** to nod

aseo *nm* (**a**) cleanliness, tidiness (**b**) **aseos** *o* **(cuarto de) a.** bathroom; *(retrete)* toilet

asequible *adj* affordable; *(comprensible)* easy to understand; *(alcanzable)* attainable

aserrín *nm* sawdust

asesinar *vt* to murder; *(rey, ministro)* to assassinate

asesinato *nm* murder; *(de rey, ministro)* assassination

asesino,-a 1 *adj* murderous

2 *nm,f* killer; *(hombre)* murderer; *(mujer)* murderess; *Pol* assassin

asesor,-a 1 *nm,f* adviser; **a. fiscal** tax adviser

2 *adj* advisory

asesoramiento *nm* (**a**) *(acción)* advising (**b**) *(consejo)* advice

asesorar 1 *vt* (**a**) to advise, to give (professional) advice to (**b**) *Com* to act as consultant to

2 asesorarse *vpr* to consult

asesoría *nf* consultant's office

asestar *vt* to deal; **a. un golpe a algn** to deal sb a blow

aseverar *vt* to assert

asfalto *nm* asphalt

asfixia *nf* asphyxiation, suffocation

asfixiante *adj* asphyxiating, suffocating; *Fam* **hace un calor a.** it's stifling

asfixiar [43] *vt*, **asfixiarse** *vpr* to asphyxiate, to suffocate

así *adv* (**a**) *(de esta manera)* like this *o* that, this way, thus; **ponlo a.** put it this way; **a. de grande/alto** this big/tall; **algo a.** something like this *o* that; **¿no es a.?** isn't that so *o* right?; **a. es la vida** such is life; **a. a.** so-so; **a. sin más,** *Am* **a. no más** *o* **nomás** just like that (**b**) **a las seis o a.** around six o'clock; **diez años o a.** ten years more or less (**c**) **a. como** as well as (**d**) **a. tenga que ...** *(aunque)* even if I have to ... (**e**) **aun a.** and despite that (**f**) **a. pues** so; **a. que ...** so ... (**g**) **a. que llegues** as soon as

Asia *n* Asia; **A. Menor** Asia Minor

asiático,-a *adj & nm,f* Asian

asidero *nm* *(asa)* handle; *Fig* pretext, excuse

asiduidad *nf* assiduity; **con a.** frequently, regularly

asiduo,-a 1 *adj* assiduous
   2 *nm,f* regular customer

asiento *nm* (**a**) seat; **a. trasero/delantero** front/back seat; **tome a.** take a seat (**b**) *(poso)* sediment (**c**) *Fin* entry

asignación *nf* (**a**) *(de dinero)* assignment, allocation (**b**) *(de puesto)* appointment (**c**) *(paga)* allowance

asignar *vt* (**a**) to assign, to allocate (**b**) *(nombrar)* to appoint

asignatura *nf* subject; **a. pendiente** failed subject

asilado,-a *nm,f* refugee

asilar *vt* to grant *o* give political asylum to

asilo *nm* asylum; **a. de ancianos** old people's home; *Pol* **a. político** political asylum

asimilación *nf* assimilation

asimilar *vt* to assimilate

asimismo *adv* also, as well

asir [46] *vt* to grasp, to seize

asistencia *nf* (**a**) *(presencia)* attendance; **falta de a.** absence (**b**) **a. médica/técnica** medical/technical assistance (**c**) *(público)* audience, public

asistenta *nf* charlady, cleaning lady

asistente 1 *adj* attending; **el público a.** the audience
   2 *nmf* (**a**) *(ayudante)* assistant; **a. social** social worker (**b**) **los asistentes** the public

asistido,-a *adj* assisted; **a. por ordenador** computer-assisted; *Aut* **dirección asistida** power steering

asistir 1 *vt* to assist, to help
   2 *vi* **a.** (**a**) to attend, to be present (at)

asma *nf* asthma

Takes the masculine articles **el** and **un**.

asno *nm* donkey, ass

asociación *nf* association

asociado,-a 1 *adj* associated
   2 *nm,f* associate, partner

asociar [43] 1 *vt* to associate
   2 asociarse *vpr* (**a**) to be associated (**b**) *Com* to become partners

asolar [2] *vt* to devastate, to destroy

asomar 1 *vt* to put out, to stick out; **asomó la cabeza por la ventana** he put his head out of the window
   2 *vi* to appear
   3 asomarse *vpr* (**a**) to lean out; **a. a la ventana** to lean out of the window (**b**) *(entrar)* to pop in; *(salir)* to pop out

asombrar 1 *vt* to amaze, to astonish
   2 asombrarse *vpr* to be astonished; **a. de algo** to be amazed at sth

asombro *nm* amazement, astonishment

asombroso,-a *adj* amazing, astonishing

asomo *nm* trace, hint

asonada *nf* putsch, uprising

asorocharse *vpr Andes* to get altitude sickness

aspa *nf* (**a**) *(de molino)* arm; *(de ventilador)* blade (**b**) *(cruz)* cross

Takes the masculine articles **el** and **un**.

aspaviento *nm* **hacer aspavientos** to wave one's arms about

aspecto *nm* (**a**) look, appearance (**b**) *(de un asunto)* aspect

aspereza *nf* roughness; *Fig* **limar asperezas** to smooth things over

áspero,-a *adj* rough; *Fig (carácter)* surly

aspersión *nf* sprinkling

aspersor *nm* sprinkler

aspiración *nf* (**a**) inhalation, breathing in (**b**) *(pretensión)* aspiration

aspiradora *nf* vacuum cleaner

aspirante *nmf* candidate, applicant

aspirar 1 *vt* (**a**) *(respirar)* to inhale, to breathe in (**b**) *Téc (absorber)* to suck in, to draw in
   2 *vi Fig* **a. a algo** to aspire after sth

aspirina *nf* aspirin

asquear *vt* to disgust

asquerosidad *nf* filthy *o* revolting thing; **¡qué a.!** how revolting!

asqueroso,-a 1 *adj* *(sucio)* filthy; *(desagradable)* revolting, disgusting
   2 *nm,f* filthy *o* revolting person

asta *nf* (**a**) *(de bandera)* staff, pole; **a media a.** at half-mast (**b**) *Zool (cuerno)* horn

Takes the masculine articles **el** and **un**.

asterisco *nm* asterisk

astilla *nf* splinter
astillero *nm* shipyard
astral *adj* astral; **carta a.** birth chart
astringente *adj & nm* astringent
astro *nm* star
astrología *nf* astrology
astrólogo,-a *nm,f* astrologer
astronauta *nmf* astronaut
astronave *nf* spaceship
astronomía *nf* astronomy
astronómico,-a *adj* astronomical
astrónomo,-a *nm,f* astronomer
astucia *nf* shrewdness; *(artimaña)* ruse
asturiano,-a *adj & nm,f* Asturian
Asturias *n* Asturias
astuto,-a *adj* astute, shrewd
asumir *vt* to assume
asunción *nf* assumption
asunto *nm* (a) subject; **no es a. tuyo** it's none of your business (b) **Asuntos Exteriores** Foreign Affairs
asustar 1 *vt* to frighten, to scare
2 asustarse *vpr* to be frightened, to be scared
atacante *nmf* attacker, assailant
atacar [44] *vt* to attack, to assault; *Fig* **me ataca los nervios** he gets on my nerves
atado,-a *adj* tied; *(ocupado)* tied up
atadura *nf Fig* hindrance
atajar *vi* to take a shortcut (**por** across o through)
atajo *nm* (a) shortcut (b) *(grupo)* bunch
atalaya *nf* watchtower
atañer *v impers* to concern, to have to do with; **eso no te atañe** that has nothing to do with you
ataque *nm* (a) attack, assault; **a. aéreo** air raid (b) *Med* fit; **a. cardíaco** o **al corazón** heart attack; **a. de nervios/tos** fit of hysterics/coughing
atar 1 *vt* (a) to tie; *Fig* **a. cabos** to put two and two together; *Fam* **loco de a.** as mad as a hatter (b) *Fig* to tie down
2 atarse *vpr Fig* to get tied up; **átate los zapatos** do your shoes up
atardecer [33] 1 *v impers* to get o grow dark
2 *nm* evening, dusk
atareado,-a *adj* busy
atascado,-a *adj* stuck
atascar [44] 1 *vt (bloquear)* to block, to obstruct
2 atascarse *vpr* (a) *(bloquearse)* to become obstructed, to become blocked (b) *Fig (estancarse)* to get bogged down
atasco *nm* traffic jam
ataúd *nm* coffin

ataviarse [29] *vpr* to dress oneself up
atavío *nm* dress, attire
ate *nm Méx* quince jelly
atemorizar [40] *vt* to frighten, to scare
atemperar *vt* to moderate, to temper
Atenas *n* Athens
atención 1 *nf* attention; **llamar la a.** to attract attention; **prestar/poner a.** to pay attention (**a** to)
2 *interj* attention!
atender [3] 1 *vt* to attend to; *(petición)* to agree to
2 *vi (alumno)* to pay attention (**a** to)
atenerse [24] *vpr* (**a**) *(a reglas etc)* to abide (**a** by); **a. a las consecuencias** to bear the consequences (**b**) *(remitirse)* to go by; **me atengo a sus palabras** I'm going by what he said; **no saber a qué a.** not to know what to expect
atentado *nm* attack; **a. terrorista** terrorist attack
atentamente *adv* **le saluda a.** *(en carta)* yours sincerely o faithfully
atentar *vi* **a. a** o **contra** to commit a crime against; **a. contra la vida de algn** to make an attempt on sb's life
atento,-a *adj* (**a**) attentive; **estar a. a** to be mindful o aware of (**b**) *(amable)* thoughtful, considerate; **atentos saludos de** *(en carta)* yours faithfully
atenuante 1 *adj* attenuating
2 *nm Jur* extenuating circumstance
atenuar [30] *vt* (**a**) to attenuate; *Jur* to extenuate (**b**) *(importancia)* to lessen, to diminish
ateo,-a 1 *adj* atheistic
2 *nm,f* atheist
aterciopelado,-a *adj* velvety; *(vino)* smooth
aterido,-a *adj* **a. de frío** stiff with cold, numb
aterrador,-a *adj* terrifying
aterrar 1 *vt* to terrify
2 aterrarse *vpr* to be terrified
aterrizaje *nm Av* landing; **a. forzoso** forced landing
aterrizar [40] *vi* to land
aterrorizar [40] 1 *vt* to terrify; *Mil & Pol* to terrorize
2 aterrorizarse *vpr* to be terrified
atesorar *vt* to accumulate; *(dinero)* to hoard
atestado¹ *nm Jur* affidavit, statement; **atestados** testimonials
atestado²,-a *adj* packed, crammed; **estaba a. de gente** it was full of people
atestar¹ *vt Jur* to testify

atestar² *vt (abarrotar)* to pack, to cram (**de** with)

atestiguar [45] *vt* (**a**)*Jur* to testify to (**b**) *Fig* to vouch for

atiborrar 1 *vt* to pack, to stuff (**de** with)
  2 atiborrarse *vpr Fam* to stuff oneself (**de** with)

ático *nm* attic

atinado,-a *adj (juicioso)* sensible; *(pertinente)* pertinent

atinar *vi* to get it right; **a. a hacer algo** to succeed in doing sth; **a. al blanco** to hit the target; **atinó con la solución** he found the solution

atingencia *nf Am* connection; *(observación)* comment

atípico,-a *adj* atypical

atisbar *vt* to make out

atisbo *nm Fig* slight sign, inkling

atizar [40] *vt* (**a**) *(fuego)* to poke, to stoke (**b**) *Fig (rebelión)* to stir up; *(pasión)* to rouse, to excite

atlántico,-a 1 *adj* Atlantic
  2 *nm* **el (océano) A.** the Atlantic (Ocean)

atlas *nm inv* atlas

atleta *nmf* athlete

atlético,-a *adj* athletic

atletismo *nm* athletics *sing*

atmósfera *nf* atmosphere

atmosférico,-a *adj* atmospheric

atole, atol *nm CAm, Méx* = drink made of corn meal

atolladero *nm* fix, jam; **estar en un a.** to be in a jam

atolondrado,-a *adj* stunned, bewildered; *(atontado)* stupid

atolondrar 1 *vt* to confuse, to bewilder
  2 atolondrarse *vpr* to be confused, to bewildered

atómico,-a *adj* atomic

átomo *nm* atom

atónito,-a *adj* amazed, astonished

atontado,-a *adj* (**a**) *(tonto)* silly, foolish (**b**) *(aturdido)* bewildered, amazed

atontar 1 *vt* to confuse, to bewilder
  2 atontarse *vpr* to be *o* get confused, to be bewildered

atorarse *vpr* (**a**) *(atragantarse)* to choke (**con** on) (**b**) *Am (atascarse)* to get stuck

atormentar 1 *vt* to torment
  2 atormentarse *vpr* to torment oneself, to suffer agonies

atornillar *vt* to screw on

atorón *nm Méx* traffic jam

atorrante *adj CSur (holgazán)* lazy

atosigar [42] *vt* to harass

atracador,-a *nm,f (de banco)* (bank) robber; *(en la calle)* attacker, mugger

atracar [44] 1 *vt* to hold up; *(persona)* to rob
  2 *vi Náut* to come alongside, to tie up
  3 atracarse *vpr (de comida)* to stuff oneself (**de** with), to gorge oneself (**de** on)

atracción *nf* attraction; **parque de atracciones** funfair

atraco *nm* hold-up, robbery; **a. a mano armada** armed robbery

atracón *nm Fam* binge, blowout; **darse un a. de comer** to make a pig of oneself

atractivo,-a 1 *adj* attractive, appealing
  2 *nm* attraction, appeal

atraer [25] *vt* to attract

atragantarse *vpr* to choke (**con** on), to swallow the wrong way; *Fig* **esa chica se me ha atragantado** I can't stand that girl

atraigo *indic pres de* **atraer**

atraje *pt indef de* **atraer**

atrancar [44] 1 *vt (puerta)* to bolt
  2 atrancarse *vpr* to get stuck; *(al hablar, leer)* to get bogged down

atrapar *vt* to catch

atrás *adv* (**a**) *(lugar)* at the back, behind; **hacia/para a.** backwards; **puerta de a.** back *o* rear door; *Fig* **echarse a.** to back out (**b**) *(tiempo)* previously, in the past, ago; **un año a.** a year ago; **venir de muy a.** to go *o* date back a long time

atrasado,-a *adj* late, slow; *(pago)* overdue; *(reloj)* slow; *(país)* backward; *Prensa* **número a.** back number

atrasar 1 *vt* to put back
  2 *vi (reloj)* to be slow
  3 atrasarse *vpr* (**a**) to remain *o* stay behind, to lag behind (**b**) *(tren)* to be late

atraso *nm* (**a**) delay (**b**) *(de país)* backwardness (**c**) *Fin* **atrasos** arrears

atravesado,-a *adj (cruzado)* lying crosswise; *(persona)* difficult; **lo tengo a.** I can't stand him

atravesar [1] 1 *vt* (**a**) *(calle)* to cross (**b**) *(muro)* to pierce, to go through (**c**) *(poner a través)* to lay across, to put across, to put crosswise
  2 atravesarse *vpr* to get in the way; *Fig* **se me ha atravesado Luis** I can't stand Luis

atrayente *adj* attractive

atreverse *vpr* to dare; **a. a hacer algo** to dare to do sth

atrevido,-a *adj* (**a**) *(osado)* daring, bold (**b**) *(insolente)* insolent, impudent (**c**) *(ropa etc)* daring, risqué

atrevimiento *nm* (**a**) *(osadía)* daring, audacity (**b**) *(insolencia)* insolence, impudence

atribuir [37] 1 *vt* to attribute, to ascribe
  2 atribuirse *vpr* to assume

atribular *vt* to afflict
atributo *nm* attribute
atril *nm* music stand
atrochar *vi* to take a short cut
atrocidad *nf* atrocity
atrofiar [43] *vt,* **atrofiarse** *vpr* to atrophy
atropellado,-a *adj* hasty, impetuous
atropellar *vt* to knock down, to run over
atropello *nm* (**a**) *Aut* knocking down, running over (**b**) *(abuso)* abuse
atroz *adj* (**a**) *(bárbaro)* atrocious (**b**) *Fam (hambre, frío)* enormous, tremendous
ATS *nmf* (*abr* **ayudante técnico sanitario**) = qualified Spanish nurse
atuendo *nm* dress, attire
atún *nm* tuna, tunny
aturdido,-a *adj* stunned, dazed
aturdimiento *nm* confusion, bewilderment
aturdir *vt* (**a**) *(con un golpe)* to stun, to daze (**b**) *(confundir)* to bewilder, to confuse
aturrullar *vt* to confuse, to bewilder
atuve *pt indef de* **atenerse**
audacia *nf* audacity
audaz *adj* audacious, bold
audible *adj* audible
audición *nf* (**a**) hearing (**b**) *Teatro* audition
audiencia *nf* (**a**) *(público)* audience; *TV & Rad* **horas de máxima a.** prime time; **índice de a.** viewing figures, ratings (**b**) *(entrevista)* audience (**c**) *Jur* court hearing
audiovisual *adj* audio-visual
auditivo,-a 1 *adj* auditory; **comprensión auditiva** listening comprehension
  2 *nm* receiver
auditor *nm Fin* auditor
auditorio *nm* (**a**) *(público)* audience (**b**) *(sala)* auditorium, hall
auge *nm* peak; *Econ* boom; *Fig* **estar en a.** to be thriving *o* booming
augurar *vt* to augur
augurio *nm* omen
aula *nf* *(en colegio)* classroom; *Univ* lecture room; **a. magna** amphitheatre

Takes the masculine articles **el** and **un**.

aulaga *nf* gorse
aullar *vt* to howl, to yell
aullido *nm* howl, yell
aumentar 1 *vt* to increase; *(precios)* to put up; *(producción)* to step up; *Fot* to enlarge; *Opt* to magnify
  2 *vi (precios)* to go up, to rise; *(valor)* to appreciate

3 aumentarse *vpr* to increase, to be on the increase
aumento *nm* increase; *Opt* magnification; **a. de precios** rise in prices; **ir en a.** to be on the increase
aun *adv* even; **a. así** even so, even then; **a. más** even more
aún *adv* still; *(en negativas)* yet; **a. está aquí** he's still here; **ella no ha venido a.** she hasn't come yet
aunar *vt* to unite, to join
aunque *conj* although, though; *(enfático)* even if, even though; **a. no vengas** even if you don't come
aúpa *interj* up!, get up!
aura *nf* aura

Takes the masculine articles **el** and **un**.

aureola *nf* halo
auricular *nm* (**a**) *Tel* receiver (**b**) **auriculares** earphones, headphones
aurora *nf* daybreak, dawn
auscultar *vt* to sound (with a stethoscope)
ausencia *nf* absence
ausentarse *vpr* to leave
ausente 1 *adj* absent
  2 *nmf* absentee
ausentismo *nm Am* absenteeism
austeridad *nf* austerity
austero,-a *adj* austere
austral 1 *adj* southern
  2 *nm Fin* = former standard monetary unit of Argentina
Australia *n* Australia
australiano,-a *adj & nm,f* Australian
Austria *n* Austria
austríaco,-a *adj & nm,f* Austrian
autenticidad *nf* authenticity
auténtico,-a *adj* authentic
autentificar [44] *vt* to authenticate
autismo *nm* autism
autista *adj* autistic
auto¹ *nm RP (coche)* car
auto² *nm Jur* decree, writ; **autos** *(pleito)* papers, documents
autoadhesivo,-a *adj* self-adhesive
autobiografía *nf* autobiography
autobiográfico,-a *adj* autobiographical
autobombo *nm Fam* self-praise, blowing one's own trumpet
autobús *nm* bus
autocar *nm* coach
autocrítica *nf* self-criticism
autóctono,-a *adj* indigenous
autodefensa *nf* self-defence
autodisciplina *nf* self-discipline
autoedición *nf Informát* desktop publishing

autoescuela *nf* driving school, school of motoring

autogobierno *nm* self-government

autógrafo *nm* autograph

autómata *nm* automaton

automático,-a *adj* automatic

automatización *nf* automation

automatizar [40] *vt* to automate

automotor,-a 1 *adj* self-propelled

2 *nm Ferroc* diesel train

automóvil *nm* car

automovilismo *nm* motoring

automovilista *nmf* motorist

automovilístico,-a *adj* car; **accidente a.** car accident

autonomía *nf* (**a**) autonomy (**b**) *(región)* autonomous region

autonómico,-a *adj* autonomous, self-governing; **elecciones autonómicas** elections for the autonomous parliament; **televisión autónomica** regional television

autónomo,-a *adj* autonomous

autopista *nf* motorway; *Informát* **autopista de la información** information superhighway

autopsia *nf* autopsy, postmortem

autor,-a *nm,f (hombre)* author; *(mujer)* authoress; *(de crimen)* perpetrator

autoridad *nf* authority

autoritario,-a *adj* authoritarian

autorizado,-a *adj* authoritative, official

autorizar [40] *vt* to authorize

autorretrato *nm* self-portrait

autoservicio *nm* self-service; *(supermercado)* supermarket

autostop *nm* hitch-hiking; **hacer a.** to hitch-hike

autostopista *nmf* hitch-hiker

autosuficiencia *nf* self-sufficiency

autosuficiente *adj* self-sufficient

auxiliar [43] 1 *adj & nmf* auxiliary, assistant

2 *vt* to help, to assist

auxilio *nm* help, assistance; **primeros auxilios** first aid

auyama *nf Carib, Col* pumpkin

Av. (*abr* **Avenida**) Ave

aval *nm Com & Fin* endorsement

avalancha *nf* avalanche

avalar *vt* to guarantee, to endorse

avance *nm* (**a**) advance (**b**) *Fin* advance payment (**c**)*TV* **a. informativo** news summary, *US* news in brief

avanzado,-a *adj* advanced; **de avanzada edad** advanced in years

avanzar [40] *vt* to advance

avaricia *nf* avarice

avaricioso,-a *adj* greedy

avaro,-a 1 *adj* avaricious, miserly

2 *nm,f* miser

avasallar *vt* to subdue

avatares *nmpl* quirks

Avda. = **Av.**

AVE *nf* (*abr* **Alta Velocidad Española**) High Speed Train

ave *nf* bird; **aves de corral** poultry; **a. de rapiña** bird of prey

Takes the masculine articles **el** and **un**.

avecinarse *vpr* to approach, to come near

avellana *nf* hazelnut

avellano *nm* hazelnut tree

avena *nf* oats

avendré *indic fut de* **avenir**

avenencia *nf* compromise

avengo *indic pres de* **avenir**

avenida *nf* avenue

avenido,-a *adj* **bien/mal avenidos** on good/bad terms

avenir [27] 1 *vt* to reconcile

2 avenirse *vpr* to be on good terms; *(consentir)* to agree (**en** to)

aventajado,-a *adj (destacado)* outstanding, exceptional; *(en cabeza)* in the lead

aventajar *vt* (**a**) to be ahead *o* in front of (**a** of) (**b**) *(superar)* to surpass, to outdo

aventar [1] 1 *vt* (**a**) *Agr* to winnow (**b**) *(el fuego)* to fan (**c**) *Andes, CAm, Méx (tirar)* to throw (**d**) *CAm, Méx, Perú (empujar)* to push, to shove

2 aventarse *vpr Méx* (**a**) *(tirarse)* to throw oneself (**b**) *(atreverse)* **a. a hacer algo** to dare to do sth

aventón *nm Méx* **dar a. a algn** to give sb a ride; **pedir a.** to hitch a ride

aventura *nf* (**a**) adventure (**b**) *(amorosa)* (love) affair

aventurado,-a *adj* risky

aventurarse *vpr* to venture

aventurero,-a *adj* adventurous

avergonzado,-a *adj* ashamed

avergonzar [63] 1 *vt* to shame

2 avergonzarse *vpr* to be ashamed (**de** of)

avería *nf* breakdown

averiado,-a *adj* out of order; *(coche)* broken down

averiar [29] 1 *vt* to break

2 averiarse *vpr (estropearse)* to malfunction, to go wrong; *(coche)* to break down

averiguación *nf* enquiry

averiguar [45] *vt* to ascertain

aversión *nf* aversion

avestruz *nm* ostrich

aviación *nf* (**a**) aviation; **accidente de a.** plane crash; **a. civil** civil aviation (**b**) *Mil* air force

aviador,-a *nm,f* aviator, flier; *Mil (piloto)* air force pilot

aviar [29] *vt (preparar)* to prepare, to get ready

avícola *adj* poultry

avicultura *nf* aviculture; *(de aves de corral)* poultry keeping

avidez *nf* avidity, eagerness

ávido,-a *adj* avid; **a. de** eager for

avinagrado,-a *adj* vinegary, sour; *Fig* sour

avinagrarse *vpr* to turn sour; *Fig* to become sour *o* bitter

avión¹ *nm* aircraft, *Br* aeroplane, *US* airplane; **viajar en a.** to fly, to go by plane; **por a.** *(en carta)* airmail

avión² *nm Orn* martin

avioneta *nf* light aircraft *o* plane

avíos *nmpl Culin* ingredients

avisar *vt* (**a**) *(informar)* to inform; **avísame cuando hayas acabado** let me know when you finish (**b**) *(advertir)* to warn; **ya te avisé** I warned you (**c**) *(llamar)* to call for; **a. a la policía** to notify the police; **a. al médico** to send for the doctor

aviso *nm* (**a**) notice; *(advertencia)* warning; *(nota)* note; **hasta nuevo a.** until further notice; **sin previo a.** without notice (**b**) **estar sobre a.** to know what's going on, to be in on it (**c**) *Am (anuncio)* advertisement; **a. clasificado** classified advertisement

avispa *nf* wasp

avispado,-a *adj Fam* quick-witted

avispero *nm (nido)* wasps' nest

avistar *vt* to see, to sight

avituallamiento *nm* provisioning

avivar *vt (fuego)* to stoke (up); *(pasión)* to intensify; *(paso)* to quicken

avizor,-a *adj* **estar ojo a.** to be on the alert *o* on the lookout

axila *nf* armpit, axilla

axioma *nm* axiom

ay *interj (dolor)* ouch!

aya *nf (niñera)* nanny

> Takes the masculine articles **el** and **un**.

ayer 1 *adv* yesterday; **a. por la mañana/ por la tarde** yesterday morning/afternoon; **a. por la noche** last night; **antes de a.** the day before yesterday
    2 *nm* **el a.** yesteryear

ayuda *nf* help, assistance; **ir en a. de algn**

to come to sb's assistance; **a. al desarrollo** development aid

ayudante *nmf* assistant; *Med* **a. técnico-sanitario** nurse

ayudar 1 *vt* to help; **¿en qué puedo ayudarte?** (how) can I help you?
    2 ayudarse *vpr* (**a**) *(unos a otros)* to help (**b**) **a. de** to use, to make use of

ayunar *vi* to fast

ayunas *nfpl* **en a.** without having eaten breakfast

ayuno *nm* fasting; **guardar/hacer a.** to fast

ayuntamiento *nm (institución)* town council; *(edificio)* town hall

azabache *nm* jet; **negro a.** jet black

azada *nf* hoe

azafata *nf* (**a**) *Av* air hostess (**b**) *(de congresos)* stewardess; *(de concurso)* hostess

azafate *nm Andes (bandeja)* tray

azafrán *nm* saffron

azahar *nm (del naranjo)* orange blossom; *(del limonero)* lemon blossom

azar *nm* chance; **por a.** by chance; **al a.** at random; **juegos de a.** games of chance; **los azares de la vida** the ups and downs of life

azaroso,-a *adj* hazardous, dangerous

azogue *nm* mercury, quicksilver

azorado,-a *adj* embarrassed

azorar 1 *vt* to embarrass
    2 azorarse *vpr* to be embarrassed

Azores *nfpl* **las (Islas) A.** the Azores

azotar *vt* to beat; *(con látigo)* to whip, to flog; *Fig* to scourge

azote *nm* (**a**) *(golpe)* smacking; *(latigazo)* lash, stroke (of the whip) (**b**) *Fig* scourge

azotea *nf* flat roof

azteca *adj & nmf* Aztec

azúcar *nm o nf* sugar; **a. blanco** refined sugar; **a. moreno** brown sugar

azucarado,-a *adj* sweetened

azucarero,-a 1 *nm o nf* sugar bowl
    2 *adj* sugar

azucena *nf* white lily

azufre *nm* sulphur

azul *adj & nm* blue; **a. celeste** sky blue; **a. marino** navy blue; **a. turquesa** turquoise; **sangre a.** blue blood

azulado,-a *adj* bluish

azulejo *nm (glazed)* tile

azuzar [40] *vt* **a. los perros a algn** to set the dogs on sb

B

B, b [be] *nf (la letra)* B, b

baba *nf* dribble; *Fig* **se le caía la b.** he was delighted

babear *vi (niño)* to dribble; *(adulto, animal)* to slobber

babel *nm o nf* bedlam

babero *nm* bib

Babia *n Fig* **estar en B.** to be daydreaming

babor *nm Náut* port, port side

babosa *nf* slug

babosada *nf CAm, Méx Fam (disparate)* daft thing

baboso,-a 1 *adj* (**a**) *Fam (despreciable)* slimy (**b**) *Am Fam (tonto)* daft, stupid
2 *nm,f Fam* (**a**) *(persona despreciable)* creep (**b**) *Am (tonto)* twit, idiot

babucha *nf* slipper

baca *nf Aut* roof rack

bacalao *nm (pez)* cod

bache *nm* (**a**) *(en carretera)* pot hole (**b**) *Av* air pocket (**c**) *Fig* bad patch; **pasar un b.** to go through a bad patch

bachillerato *nm* = academically orientated Spanish secondary school course for pupils aged 14-17

bacilo *nm* bacillus

bacon *nm* bacon

bacteria *nf* bacterium; **bacterias** bacteria

bacteriológico,-a *adj* bacteriological; **guerra bacteriológica** germ warfare

báculo *nm* walking stick; *(de obispo)* crosier

badén *nm Aut* bump

bádminton *nm* badminton

bafle *nm* loudspeaker

bagaje *nm* baggage

bagatela *nf (baratija)* knick-knack; *Fig* trifle

Bagdad *n* Baghdad

Bahamas *npl* **las (Islas) B.** the Bahamas

bahía *nf* bay

baila(d)or,-a *nm,f* flamenco dancer

bailar *vt & vi* to dance; *Fig* **b. al son que le tocan** to toe the line; *Fam* **¡que me quiten lo baila(d)o!** but at least I had a good time!

bailarín,-ina *nm,f* dancer; *(clásico)* ballet dancer

baile *nm* (**a**) *(danza)* dance (**b**) *(fiesta popular)* dance; *(formal)* ball; **b. de disfraces** fancy dress ball

baja *nf* (**a**) drop, fall; *Fin* **jugar a la b.** to bear (**b**) *Mil* loss, casualty (**c**) **dar de b. a algn** *(despedir)* to lay sb off; **darse de b.** *(por enfermedad)* to take sick leave; *(de un club)* to resign (**de** from), to drop out (**de** of)

bajada *nf* (**a**) *(descenso)* descent (**b**) *(cuesta)* slope (**c**) **b. de bandera** *(de taxi)* minimum fare

bajamar *nf* low tide

bajar 1 *vt* (**a**) to come/go down; **b. la escalera** to come/go downstairs (**b**) *(descender)* to bring/get/take down; *(volumen)* to turn down; *(voz, telón)* to lower; *(precios etc)* to reduce, to cut; *(persiana)* to let down; *(cabeza)* to bow o lower
2 *vi* (**a**) to go/come down (**b**) *(apearse)* to get off; *(de un coche)* to get out (**de** of) (**c**) *(disminuir)* to fall, to drop
3 bajarse *vpr* (**a**) to come/go down (**b**) *(apearse)* to get off; *(de un coche)* to get out (**de** of)

bajativo *nm Andes, RP (licor)* digestive liqueur; *(tisana)* herbal tea

bajeza *nf* despicable action

bajial *nm Perú* lowland

bajinis: • por lo bajinis *loc adv Fam* on the sly

bajío *nm* (**a**) sandbank (**b**) *(terreno bajo)* lowland

bajista 1 *adj Fin* bearish; **tendencia b.** downward trend
2 *nmf* (**a**) *Fin* bear (**b**) *Mús* bass guitarist

bajo,-a 1 *adj* (**a**) low; *(persona)* short; *(sonido)* faint, soft; **en voz baja** in a low voice; **planta baja** ground floor; **de baja calidad** of poor quality; **la clase baja** the lower class (**b**) *Fig (vil)* base, contemptible
2 *nm* (**a**) *Mús* bass (**b**) *(planta baja)* ground floor
3 *adv* low; **hablar b.** to speak quietly; *Fig* **por lo b.** on the sly
4 *prep* (**a**) *(lugar)* under, underneath; **b. tierra** underground; **b. la lluvia** in the rain (**b**) *Pol & Hist* under; **b. la República** under the Republic (**c**) **b. cero** *(temperatura)*

below zero (**d**) *Jur* under; **b. juramento** under oath; **b. pena de muerte** on pain of death; **b. fianza** on bail

bajón *nm* (**a**) *(bajada)* sharp fall, decline (**b**) *Com* slump (**c**) *(de salud)* relapse, deterioration

bajorrelieve *nm* bas-relief

bajura *nf* **pesca de b.** coastal fishing

bala *nf* bullet; *Fig* **como una b.** like a shot

balacear *vt Am (tirotear)* to shoot

balacera *nf Am* shootout

balada *nf* ballad

baladí *adj* (*pl* **baladíes**) trivial

balance *nm* (**a**) *Fin* balance; *(declaración)* balance sheet; *Fig* **hacer b. de una situación** to take stock of a situation (**b**) *(resultado)* outcome

balancear 1 *vt* to rock

2 balancearse *vpr (en mecedora)* to rock; *(en columpio)* to swing

balanceo *nm* rocking, swinging; *(de barco, avión)* rolling; *Am Aut* wheel balance

balanza *nf* scales; *Fig* **estar en la b.** to be in the balance *o* in danger; **b. comercial** balance of trade; **b. de pagos** balance of payments

balar *vi* to bleat

balaustrada *nf* balustrade, railing

balazo *nm* (**a**) *(disparo)* shot; **matar a algn de un b.** to shoot sb dead (**b**) *(herida)* bullet wound

balboa *nm Fin* = standard monetary unit of Panama

balbucear *vi (adulto)* to stutter, stammer; *(niño)* to babble

balbuceo *nm (de adulto)* stuttering, stammering; *(de niño)* babbling

balbucir *vi defect* = **balbucear**

Balcanes *nmpl* **los B.** the Balkans

balcón *nm* balcony

baldado,-a *adj Fam* shattered

baldar *vt* to cripple, to maim

balde¹ *nm* pail, bucket

balde² *loc adv* (**a**) **de b.** *(gratis)* free (**b**) **en b.** *(en vano)* in vain

baldío,-a *adj (terreno)* uncultivated, waste; *(esfuerzo)* vain, useless

baldosa *nf* (ceramic) floor tile; *(para pavimentar)* flagstone, paving stone

balear¹ 1 *adj* Balearic

2 *nmf* person from the Balearic Islands

balear² *vt Am (disparar)* to shoot

Baleares *npl* **las (Islas) B.** the Balearic Islands

baleo *nm Am* shootout

balido *nm* bleating, bleat

balística *nf* ballistics *sing*

balístico,-a *adj* ballistic

baliza *nf* (**a**) *Náut* buoy (**b**) *Av* beacon

ballena *nf* whale

ballet *nm* ballet

balneario *nm* spa, health resort

balompié *nm* football

balón *nm* (**a**) ball, football; *Fig* **b. de oxígeno** boost (**b**) *(bombona)* gas cylinder

baloncesto *nm* basketball

balonmano *nm* handball

balonvolea *nm* volleyball

balsa *nf* (**a**) *Náut* raft (**b**) *Fig* **como una b. de aceite** very quiet

bálsamo *nm* balsam, balm

balsero,-a *nm,f (de Cuba)* = refugee fleeing Cuba on a raft

Báltico *nm* **el (Mar) B.** the Baltic (Sea)

baluarte *nm Fig* stronghold

bambas® *nfpl* trainers

bambolear *vi*, **bambolearse** *vpr* to swing; *(persona, árbol)* to sway; *(mesa, silla)* to wobble

bambú *nm* (*pl* **bambúes**) bamboo

banal *adj* banal, trivial

banalidad *nf* triviality, banality

banana *nf* banana

banano *nm (árbol)* banana tree; *Col (fruto)* banana

banca *nf* (**a**) *(asiento)* bench (**b**) *Com & Fin* (the) banks; *(actividad)* banking; **b. electrónica** electronic banking (**c**) *(en juegos)* bank

bancario,-a *adj* banking

bancarrota *nf Fin* bankruptcy; **estar en b.** to be bankrupt

banco *nm* (**a**) bench (**b**) *Com & Fin* bank (**c**) **b. de arena** sandbank (**d**) *(de peces)* shoal, school (**e**) *Geol* layer

banda *nf* (**a**) *Mús* band (**b**) *Cin* **b. sonora** sound track (**c**) *(de pájaros)* flock (**d**) *(cinta)* sash (**e**) *(lado)* side; *Ftb* **línea de b.** touchline; **saque de b.** throw-in

bandada *nf* flock

bandazo *nm* **dar bandazos** to lurch

bandeja *nf* tray; *Fig* **servir algo a algn en b.** to hand sth to sb on a plate

bandera *nf* flag; **b. azul** *(en playa)* blue flag

banderín *nf* pennant, small flag

bandido *nm* bandit, outlaw

bando¹ *nm* (**a**) *Jur (edicto)* edict, proclamation (**b**) **bandos** banns

bando² *nm* faction, side; **pasarse al otro b.** to go over to the other side, to change allegiances

bandolero *nm* bandit, outlaw

banquero,-a *nm,f* banker

banqueta *nf* (**a**) *(asiento)* stool (**b**) *(para*

los pies) footstool (**c**) *CAm, Méx (acera) Br* pavement, *US* sidewalk

banquete *nm* banquet, feast; **b. de bodas** wedding reception

banquillo *nm* (**a**) *Jur* dock (**b**) *Dep* bench

banquina *nf RP (arcén)* verge; *(de autopista) Br* hard shoulder, *US* shoulder

bañadera *nf* (**a**) *Arg (bañera)* bath (**b**) *RP (vehículo)* minibus

bañado *nm Bol, RP (terreno)* marshy area

bañador *nm (de mujer)* bathing *o* swimming costume; *(de hombre)* swimming trunks

bañar 1 *vt* (**a**) to bath (**b**) *(cubrir)* to coat, to cover; **b. en oro** to goldplate

2 bañarse *vpr (en baño)* to have *o* take a bath; *(en mar, piscina)* to go for a swim; *Am (ducharse)* to have a shower

bañera *nf* bath, bathtub

bañista *nmf* bather, swimmer

baño *nm* (**a**) bath; **tomar un b.** to have *o* take a bath; *Fig* **darse un b. de sol** to sunbathe; **b. de sangre** bloodbath (**b**) *(de oro etc)* coat; *(de chocolate etc)* coating, covering (**c**) *(cuarto de baño)* bathroom; *(lavabo)* toilet

bar *nm* bar, pub

barahúnda *nf* din, uproar

baraja *nf* pack, deck

barajar *vt (cartas)* to shuffle; *Fig (nombres, cifras)* to juggle with

baranda, barandilla *nf (de escalera)* handrail, banister; *(de balcón)* handrail

baratija *nf* trinket, knick-knack

baratillo *nm* flea market

barato,-a 1 *adj* cheap

2 *adv* cheaply

baraúnda *nf* din, uproar

barba *nf* (**a**) *Anat* chin (**b**) *(pelo)* beard; *Fig* **100 pesetas por b.** 100 pesetas a head

barbacoa *nf* barbecue

barbaridad *nf* (**a**) atrocity (**b**) *(disparate)* piece of nonsense; **no digas barbaridades** don't talk nonsense (**c**) **una b.** a lot; **costar una b.** to cost a fortune

barbarie *nf* savagery, cruelty

bárbaro,-a 1 *adj* (**a**) *Hist* barbarian (**b**) *(cruel)* barbaric, barbarous (**c**) *Fam (enorme)* massive (**d**) *RP Fam (estupendo)* tremendous, terrific

2 *nm,f Hist* barbarian

barbecho *nm* fallow land; **dejar en b.** to leave fallow

barbería *nf* barber's (shop)

barbero *nm* barber

barbilla *nf* chin

barbitúrico *nm* barbiturate

barbudo,-a *adj* with a heavy beard

barca *nf* small boat

barcaza *nf* lighter

barcelonés,-esa 1 *adj* of/from Barcelona

2 *nm,f* person from Barcelona

barco *nm* boat, ship; **b. de pasajeros** liner; **b. de vapor** steamer

baremo *nm* scale

barítono *nm* baritone

barlovento *nm* windward

barman *nm* barman

barniz *nm* (**a**) *(en madera)* varnish; *(en cerámica)* glaze (**b**) *Fig* veneer

barnizar [40] *vt (madera)* to varnish; *(cerámica)* to glaze

barómetro *nm* barometer

barón *nm* baron

baronesa *nf* baroness

barquero,-a *nm,f (hombre)* boatman; *(mujer)* boatwoman

barquillo *nm* wafer

barra *nf* (**a**) bar; **b. de pan** French loaf, baguette; **b. de labios** lipstick (**b**) *(mostrador)* bar; **b. americana** = bar where hostesses chat with clients (**c**) *Dep* **b. fija** horizontal bar; **barras paralelas** parallel bars (**d**) *Andes, RP Fam (grupo de amigos)* gang, group of friends; **b. brava** = group of violent soccer supporters

barraca *nf* (**a**) *(caseta)* shack, hut (**b**) *(en Valencia y Murcia)* thatched farmhouse

barracón *nm Mil* prefabricated hut

barranco *nm (despeñadero)* cliff, precipice; *(torrentera)* gully, ravine

barranquismo *nm Dep* canyoning

barrena *nf* twist drill

barrenar *vt Téc* to drill

barrendero,-a *nm,f* sweeper, street sweeper

barreno *nm* (**a**) *(taladro)* large drill (**b**) *Min* charge

barreño *nm* tub

barrer 1 *vt* to sweep

2 *vi (en elecciones)* to win by a landslide

barrera *nf* barrier

barriada *nf* (**a**) *(barrio popular)* neighbourhood, area (**b**) *Am (barrio de chabolas)* shanty town

barricada *nf* barricade

barrida *nf* landslide victory

barriga *nf* belly; *Fam* tummy

barrigón,-ona, barrigudo,-a *adj* potbellied

barril *nm* barrel; **cerveza de b.** draught beer

barrillo *nm* pimple, spot

barrio *nm* area, district; **del b.** local; **el B. Gótico** the Gothic Quarter; **b. chino**

red-light district; **barrios bajos** slums
barrizal *nm* mire, quagmire
barro *nm* (**a**) *(lodo)* mud (**b**) *(arcilla)* clay; **objetos de b.** earthenware
barroco,-a *adj* baroque
barruntar *vt (sospechar)* to suspect; *(presentir)* to have a feeling
barrunto *nm (presentimiento)* feeling, presentiment; *(sospecha)* suspicion
bartola: • **a la bartola** *loc adv Fam* **tenderse** *o* **tumbarse a la b.** to laze around, to idle away one's time
bártulos *nmpl Fam* things, bits and pieces
barullo *nm (alboroto)* row, din; *(confusión)* confusion
basar 1 *vt* to base (**en** on)
2 basarse *vpr (teoría, película)* **b. en** to be based on; **¿en qué te basas para decir eso?** what grounds do you have for saying that?
basca *nf Fam* people, crowd
báscula *nf* scales; *(para camiones)* weighbridge
bascular *vi* to tilt
base *nf* (**a**) base; **sueldo b.** minimum wage; *Informát* **b. de datos** database (**b**) *(de argumento, teoría)* basis; **en b. a** on the basis of; **a b. de estudiar** by studying; **a b. de productos naturales** using natural products (**c**) *(de partido)* grass roots; **miembro de b.** rank and file member (**d**) *(nociones)* grounding
básico,-a *adj* basic
basílica *nf* basilica
básquet *nm* basketball
bastante 1 *adj* (**a**) *(suficiente)* enough; **b. tiempo/comida** enough time/food; **bastantes platos** enough plates (**b**) *(abundante)* quite a lot of; **hace b. calor/frío** it's quite hot/cold; **bastantes amigos** quite a lot of friends
2 *adv* (**a**) *(suficiente)* enough; **con esto hay b.** that is enough; **no soy lo b. rico (como) para ...** I am not rich enough to ... (**b**) *(considerablemente)* fairly, quite; **me gusta b.** I quite like it; **vamos b. al cine** we go to the cinema quite *o* fairly often
bastar 1 *vi* to be sufficient *o* enough, to suffice; **basta con tres** three will be enough; **¡basta de tonterías!** enough of this nonsense!; **basta con tocarlo para que se abra** you only have to touch it and it opens; **¡basta (ya)!** that's enough!, that will do!
2 bastarse *vpr* **b. a sí mismo** to be self-sufficient, to rely only on oneself
bastardilla *nf Impr* italics

bastardo,-a *adj & nm,f* bastard
bastidor *nm* (**a**) frame (**b**) *Teatro* **bastidores** wings; *Fig* **entre bastidores** behind the scenes
bastión *nm* bastion
basto,-a *adj (cosa)* rough, coarse; *(persona)* coarse, uncouth
bastón *nm* stick, walking stick
bastos *nmpl Naipes* ≃ clubs
basura *nf Br* rubbish, *US* garbage, *US* trash
basurero *nm* (**a**) *(persona) Br* dustman, *US* garbage man (**b**) *(lugar) Br* rubbish tip *o* dump, *US* garbage dump
bata *nf (para casa)* dressing gown; *(de médico etc)* white coat; *(de científico)* lab coat
batacazo *nm* (**a**) crash, bang (**b**) *CSur Fam (triunfo inesperado)* surprise victory;
batalla *nf* battle; **librar b.** to do *o* join battle; **b. campal** pitched battle
batallar *vi* to fight, quarrel
batallón *nm* battalion
batata *nf* sweet potato
batatazo *nm Am* = **batacazo**
bate *nm Dep* bat; **b. de béisbol** baseball bat
batear 1 *vi* to bat
2 *vt* to hit
batería 1 *nf* (**a**) battery (**b**) *Mús* drums (**c**) **b. de cocina** pots and pans, set of pans
2 *nmf* drummer
batiburrillo *nm* jumble, mess
batida *nf* (**a**) *(de la policía)* raid (**b**) *(en caza)* beat
batido,-a 1 *adj* (**a**) *Culin* whipped (**b**) *Dep* **tierra batida** clay
2 *nm* milk shake
batidora *nf (eléctrica)* mixer
batiente *adj* **reírse a mandíbula b.** to laugh one's head off
batín *nm* short dressing gown
batir 1 *vt* (**a**) to beat (**b**) *(huevo)* to beat; *(nata)* to whip, to whisk (**c**) *(récord)* to break (**d**) *(en caza)* to beat
2 batirse *vpr* to fight
batuta *nf Mús* baton; *Fig* **llevar la b.** to be in charge
baúl *nm* (**a**) *(cofre)* trunk (**b**) *RP (maletero) Br* boot, *US* trunk
bautismo *nm* baptism, christening
bautizar [40] *vt* to baptize, to christen; *(vino)* to water down
bautizo *nm* baptism, christening
Baviera *n* Bavaria
baya *nf* berry
bayeta *nf* floorcloth
bayo,-a *adj* whitish yellow

bayoneta *nf* bayonet

baza *nf* trick; *Fig* **meter b.** to butt in

bazar *nm* bazaar

bazo *nm* spleen

bazofia *nf* rubbish

be *nf (letra)* b; *Am* **be baja** *o* **corta** v *(to distinguish from "b")*; *Am* **be alta** *o* **grande** *o* **larga** b *(to distinguish from "v")*

beatería *nf* sanctimoniousness

beato,-a *adj (piadoso)* devout; *Pey* prudish, sanctimonious

bebe,-a *nm,f Andes, RP* baby

bebé *nm* baby; **b. probeta** test-tube baby

bebedero *nm* drinking trough, water trough

bebedor,-a *nm,f* (hard *o* heavy) drinker

beber *vt & vi* to drink

bebible *adj* drinkable

bebida *nf* drink; **darse a la b.** to take to drink

bebido,-a *adj* drunk

beca *nf* grant

becar [44] *vt* to award a grant to

becario,-a *nm,f* grant holder

becerro *nm* calf

bechamel *nf* bechamel; **salsa b.** bechamel sauce, white sauce

becuadro *nm Mús* natural sign

bedel *nm* beadle

begonia *nf* begonia

beige *adj & nm inv* beige

béisbol *nm* baseball

bejuco *nm (en América)* liana; *(en Asia)* rattan

Belén *n* Bethlehem

belén *nm* nativity scene, crib

belga *adj & nmf* Belgian

Bélgica *n* Belgium

Belgrado *n* Belgrade

Belice *n* Belize

bélico,-a *adj* warlike, bellicose; *(preparativos etc)* war; **material b.** armaments

belicoso,-a *adj* warlike, bellicose; *(agresivo)* aggressive

beligerancia *nf* belligerence

beligerante *adj* belligerent; **los países beligerantes** the countries at war

bellaco,-a 1 *adj* wicked, roguish

2 *nm,f* scoundrel, rogue

belleza *nf* beauty

bello,-a *adj* beautiful

bellota *nf Bot* acorn; *Fig* **animal de b.** blockhead

bemol 1 *adj Mús* flat

2 *nm* **esto tiene bemoles** this is a tough one

bencina *nf Chile (gasolina) Br* petrol, *US* gas

bencinera *nf Chile Br* petrol station, *US* gas station

bendecir [12] *vt* to bless; **b. la mesa** to say grace; **¡Dios te bendiga!** God bless you!

bendición *nf* blessing

bendito,-a 1 *adj* blessed; *(maldito)* damned

2 *nm,f (bonachón)* good sort, kind soul; *(tontorrón)* simple soul

beneficencia *nf* beneficence, charity

beneficiado,-a *adj* favoured; **salir b. de algo** to do well out of sth

beneficiar [43] 1 *vt* to benefit

2 beneficiarse *vpr* **b. de** *o* **con algo** to profit from *o* by sth

beneficiario,-a *nm,f* beneficiary; **margen b.** profit margin

beneficio *nm* (**a**) *Com & Fin* profit (**b**) *(bien)* benefit; **en b. propio** in one's own interest; **un concierto a b. de …** a concert in aid of …

beneficioso,-a *adj* beneficial

benéfico,-a *adj* charitable

benemérita *nf* **la B.** the Spanish Civil Guard

beneplácito *nm Fml* approval, consent

benevolencia *nf* benevolence

benevolente, benévolo,-a *adj* benevolent

bengala *nf* flare

benigno,-a *adj (persona)* gentle, benign; *(clima)* mild; *(tumor)* benign

benjamín,-ina *nm,f* youngest child

beodo,-a *adj* drunk

berberecho *nm* (common) cockle

berbiquí *nm Téc* drill

berenjena *nf Br* aubergine, *US* eggplant

Berlín *n* Berlin

berlina *nf (coche)* saloon; *(carruaje)* sedan

berlinés,-esa 1 *adj* of/from Berlin

2 *nm,f* Berliner

berma *nf Andes (arcén)* verge; *(de autopista) Br* hard shoulder, *US* shoulder

bermejo,-a *adj* reddish

bermellón *nm* vermilion

Bermudas 1 *nfpl* **las (Islas) B.** Bermuda

2 *nmpl* **bermudas** *(prenda)* Bermuda shorts

Berna *n* Bern

berrear *vi* to bellow, low

berrido *nm* bellowing, lowing

berrinche *nm Fam* rage, tantrum

berro *nm* cress, watercress

berza *nf* cabbage

besar 1 *vt* to kiss

2 besarse *vpr* to kiss

beso *nm* kiss

bestia 1 *nf* beast, animal; **b. de carga** beast of burden
2 *nmf Fam Fig* brute, beast
3 *adj Fig* brutish, boorish; **a lo b.** rudely
bestial *adj* bestial; *Fam (enorme)* huge, tremendous; *(extraordinario)* fantastic, terrific
bestialidad *nf* (**a**) *Fam (estupidez)* stupidity (**b**) *(crueldad)* act of cruelty (**c**) *Fam* **una b. de** tons of, stacks of
best-seller *nm* best-seller
besugo *nm* (**a**) *(pez)* sea bream (**b**) *(persona)* idiot, half-wit
besuquear *Fam* **1** *vt* to kiss, to cover with kisses
2 besuquearse *vpr* to smooch
betabel *nf Méx Br* beetroot, *US* beet
betarraga *nf Andes Br* beetroot, *US* beet
betún *nm (para el calzado)* shoe polish; *Quím* bitumen
biberón *nm* baby's bottle, feeding bottle
Biblia *nf* Bible
bíblico,-a *adj* biblical
bibliografía *nf* bibliography
bibliorato *nm RP* file
biblioteca *nf* (**a**) *(institución)* library; **b. ambulante** mobile library (**b**) *RP (mueble)* bookcase
bibliotecario,-a *nm,f* librarian
bicameral *adj Pol* bicameral, two-chamber
bicarbonato *nm* bicarbonate; **b. sódico** bicarbonate of soda
bicentenario *nm Br* bicentenary, *US* bicentennial
bíceps *nm inv* biceps
bicha *nf* snake
bicho *nm* (**a**) bug, insect; **¿qué b. te ha picado?** what's bugging you? (**b**) *Taurom* bull (**c**) *Fam* **todo b. viviente** every living soul; **un b. raro** a weirdo, an oddball
bici *nf Fam* bike
bicicleta *nf* bicycle; **montar en b.** to ride a bicycle
bicolor *adj* two-coloured; *Pol* **gobierno b.** two-party government
bidé *nm* bidet
bidón *nm* drum
biela *nf Aut* connecting rod
Bielorrusia *n* Belarus
bien¹ 1 *adv* (**a**) *(correctamente)* well; **habla b. (el) inglés** she speaks English well; **responder b.** to answer correctly; **hiciste b. en decírmelo** you were right to tell me; **las cosas le van b.** things are going well for him; **¡b.!** good!, great!; **¡muy b.!** excellent, first class!; **¡qué b.!** great!, fantastic!

(**b**) *(de salud)* well; **sentirse/encontrarse/estar b.** to feel well
(**c**) **vivir b.** to be comfortably off; **¡está b.!** *(¡de acuerdo!)* fine!, all right!; **¡ya está b.!** that's (quite) enough!; **aquí se está muy b.** it's really nice here; **esta falda te sienta b.** this skirt suits you; *Fam* **ese libro está muy b.** that book is very good; *Fam* **su novia está muy b.** his girlfriend is very nice
(**d**) *(intensificador)* very, quite; **b. temprano** very early, nice and early; **b. caliente** pretty hot; **b. es verdad que ...** it's quite clear that ...
(**e**) **más b.** rather, a little
(**f**) **b. podía haberme avisado** she might have let me know
(**g**) *(de buena gana)* willingly, gladly; **b. me tomaría una cerveza** I'd really love a beer
2 *conj* **ahora b.** now, now then; **o b.** or, or else; **b. ... o b. ...** either ... or ...; **no b.** as soon as; **no b. llegó ...** no sooner had she arrived than ...; **si b.** although, even if
3 *adj* **la gente b.** the wealthy, the upper classes
bien² ** *nm* (a**) *(bondad)* good; **el b. y el mal** good and evil; **un hombre/familia de b.** a good man/family (**b**) *(bienestar)* **por el b. de** for the good of; **lo hace por tu b.** he does it for your sake (**c**) **bienes** goods; **bienes de equipo** capital goods; **bienes gananciales** communal property; **bienes inmuebles** real estate; **bienes de consumo** consumer goods
bienal *nf* biennial exhibition
bienestar *nm (personal)* well-being, contentment; *(comodidad)* ease, comfort; **la sociedad del b.** the affluent society
bienhechor,-a *nm,f (hombre)* benefactor; *(mujer)* benefactress
bienintencionado,-a *adj* well-meaning, well-intentioned
bienio *nm* biennium, two-year period
bienvenida *nf* welcome; **dar la b. a algn** to welcome sb
bienvenido,-a *adj* welcome
bife *nm Andes, RP (bistec)* steak
bifocal *adj* bifocal; **gafas bifocales** bifocals
bifurcación *nf* bifurcation; *(de la carretera)* fork
bifurcarse [44] *vpr* to fork, to branch off
bigamia *nf* bigamy
bígamo,-a 1 *adj* bigamous
2 *nm,f* bigamist
bigote *nm (de persona)* moustache; *(de animal) (usu pl)* whiskers

ℓ Observa que la palabra inglesa **bigot** es un falso amigo y no es la traducción de la palabra española **bigote**. En inglés, **bigot** significa "intolerante".

bilateral *adj* bilateral; **acuerdo b.** bilateral agreement
bilbaíno,-a 1 *adj* of/from Bilbao
   2 *nm,f* person from Bilbao
bilingüe *adj* bilingual
bilis *nf* bile
billar *nm* (**a**) *(juego)* billiards *sing;* **b. americano** pool; **b. ruso** snooker (**b**) *(mesa)* billiard table
billete *nm* (**a**) ticket; **b. de ida** *Br* single (ticket), *US* one-way ticket; **b. de ida y vuelta** *Br* return (ticket), *US* round-trip (ticket); (**b**) *(de banco) Br* note, *US* bill; **un b. de mil pesetas** a thousand peseta note
billetera *nf,* **billetero** *nm* wallet, *US* billfold
billón *nm* trillion
bimensual *adj* twice-monthly, bimonthly
bimotor 1 *adj* twin-engined
   2 *nm* twin-engined plane
binario,-a *adj* binary
bingo *nm* (**a**) *(juego)* bingo (**b**) *(sala)* bingo hall
binomio *nm* binomial
biodegradable *adj* biodegradable
biofísica *nf* biophysics *sing*
biografía *nf* biography
biográfico,-a *adj* biographical
biógrafo,-a *nm,f* biographer
biología *nf* biology
biológico,-a *adj* biological; *(agricultura, productos)* organic
biólogo,-a *nm,f* biologist
biomasa *nf* bio-mass
biombo *nm* (folding) screen
biopsia *nf* biopsy
bioquímica *nf* biochemistry
bioquímico,-a 1 *adj* biochemical
   2 *nm,f* biochemist
bióxido *nm* dioxide; **b. de carbono** carbon dioxide
bipartidismo *nm* two-party system
biquini *nm* bikini
birlar *vt Fam* to pinch, to nick
Birmania *n* Burma
birmano,-a *adj & nm,f* Burmese
birome *nf RP* ballpoint pen, *Br* Biro®
birrete *nm* cap, beret; *Rel* biretta; *Univ* mortar-board
birria *nf Fam* rubbish
bis 1 *nm* encore
   2 *adv* twice

bisabuela *nf* great-grandmother
bisabuelo *nm* great-grandfather; **bisabuelos** great-grandparents
bisagra *nf* hinge; **partido b.** party holding the balance of power
bisbisar, bisbisear *vt* to whisper
bisexual *adj & nmf* bisexual
bisiesto *adj* **año b.** leap year
bisnieto,-a *nm,f (niño)* great-grandson; *(niña)* great-granddaughter; **mis bisnietos** my great-grandchildren
bisonte *nm* bison, American buffalo
bisoño,-a *adj* inexperienced
bisté, bistec *nm* steak
bisturí *nm* scalpel
bisutería *nf* imitation jewellery
bit *nm Informát* bit
bíter *nm* bitters
bizantino,-a *adj Fig* **discusiones bizantinas** hair-splitting arguments
bizco,-a 1 *adj* cross-eyed
   2 *nm,f* cross-eyed person
bizcocho *nm* sponge cake
biznieto,-a *nm,f* = **bisnieto,-a**
blanca *nf Fam* **estar sin b.** to be flat broke
blanco¹,-a 1 *adj* white; *(tez)* fair
   2 *nm,f (hombre)* white man; *(mujer)* white woman; **los blancos** whites
blanco² *nm* (**a**) *(color)* white (**b**) *(hueco)* blank; **dejó la hoja en b.** he left the page blank; **votos en b.** blank votes; *Fig* **pasar la noche en b.** to have a sleepless night; **me quedé en b.** my mind went blank (**c**) *(diana)* target; **dar en el b.** to hit the target; *Fig* **ser el b. de todas las miradas** to be the centre of attention
blancura *nf* whiteness
blandengue *adj Pey* weak, soft
blandir *vt* to brandish
blando,-a *adj* soft

ℓ Observa que la palabra inglesa **bland** es un falso amigo y no es la traducción de la palabra española **blando**. En inglés, **bland** significa "soso".

blanquear *vt* (**a**) to whiten (**b**) *(encalar)* to whitewash (**c**) *(dinero)* to launder
blanquecino,-a *adj* whitish
blanqueo *nm* (**a**) whitening (**b**) *(encalado)* whitewashing (**c**) *(de dinero)* laundering
blanquillo *nm CAm, Méx (huevo)* egg
blasfemar *vi* to blaspheme (**contra** against)
blasfemia *nf* blasphemy
blasón *nm* coat of arms
bledo *nm Fam* **me importa un b.** I couldn't give a damn

blindado,-a *adj Mil* armoured, armour-plated; *(antibalas)* bullet-proof; **coche b.** bullet-proof car; **puerta blindada** reinforced door, security door

blindaje *nm* armour; *(vehículo)* armour plating

bloc *nm* pad; **b. de notas** notepad

bloomer ['blumer], **blúmer** *nm CAm, Carib* panties, *Br* knickers

bloque *nm* (**a**) block; **en b.** en bloc; **b. de pisos** *BR* (block of) flats, *US* apartment block (**b**) *Pol* bloc; **el b. comunista** the Communist Bloc

bloquear *vt* (**a**) to block (**b**) *Mil* to blockade

bloqueo *nm* blockade; *Dep* block

blues *nm* blues

blusa *nf* blouse

blusón *nm* loose blouse, smock

bluyín *nm*, **bluyines** *nmpl Andes, Ven* jeans

boato *nm* show, ostentation

bobada *nf* nonsense; **decir bobadas** to talk nonsense

bobalicón,-ona *Fam* **1** *adj* simple, stupid **2** *nm,f* simpleton, idiot

bobería *nf* = bobada

bobina *nf* (**a**) reel (**b**) *Elec* coil

bobo,-a **1** *adj (tonto)* stupid, silly; *(ingenuo)* naïve **2** *nm,f* fool

boca *nf* (**a**) mouth; **b. abajo** face downward; **b. arriba** face upward; *Fig* **a pedir de b.** in accordance with one's wishes; *Fig* **andar de b. en b.** to be the talk of the town; *Fam* **¡cierra la b!** shut up!; *Fam* **con la b. abierta** open-mouthed; *Fam* **se le hizo la b. agua** his mouth watered; **el b. a b.** kiss of life, mouth-to-mouth resuscitation (**b**) **la b. del metro** the entrance to the *Br* underground *o US* subway station; **b. de riego** hydrant

bocacalle *nf* entrance to a street

bocadillo *nm* (**a**) *(con pan)* sandwich; **un b. de jamón/tortilla** a ham/an omelette sandwich (**b**) *(de cómic)* balloon

bocado *nm* (**a**) *(mordedura)* bite (**b**) *(de caballo)* bit

bocajarro: • **a bocajarro** *loc adv* point-blank

bocanada *nf* (**a**) *(de vino)* mouthful (**b**) *(de humo)* puff; **una b. de viento** a gust of wind

bocata *nm* sandwich

bocazas *nmf inv Fam* bigmouth, blabbermouth

boceto *nm Arte* sketch, outline; *(esquema)* outline, plan

bochinche *nm Fam* uproar; **armar un b.** to kick up a row

bochorno *nm* (**a**) *(tiempo)* sultry *o* close weather; *(calor sofocante)* stifling heat (**b**) *Fig (vergüenza)* shame, embarrassment

bochornoso,-a *adj* (**a**) *(tiempo)* sultry, close, muggy; *(calor)* stifling (**b**) *Fig (vergonzoso)* shameful, embarrassing

bocina *nf* horn; **tocar la b.** to blow *o* sound one's horn

bocinazo *nm* hoot, toot

bocón,-ona *nm,f Am Fam* bigmouth

boda *nf* wedding, marriage; **bodas de plata** silver wedding

bodega *nf* (**a**) wine cellar; *(tienda)* wine shop (**b**) *Náut* hold (**c**) *(almacén)* warehouse (**d**) *Am* grocery store, grocer's (shop)

bodegón *nm* still-life

bodrio *nm Fam* rubbish, trash

body *nm* bodystocking, leotard

BOE *nm* (*abr* **Boletín Oficial del Estado**) Official Gazette

bofetada *nf,* **bofetón** *nm* slap on the face; **dar una b./un b. a algn** to slap sb's face

boga *nf Fig* **estar en b.** to be in vogue

bogar [42] *vi* (**a**) *(remar)* to row (**b**) *(navegar)* to sail

bogavante *nm* lobster

bogotano,-a **1** *adj* of/from Bogotá **2** *nm,f* person from Bogotá

bohío *nm Am* hut, cabin

boicot *nm* (*pl* **boicots**) boycott

boicotear *vt* to boycott

boicoteo *nm* boycott

bóiler *nm Méx* boiler

boina *nf* beret

bol *nm* bowl

bola *nf* (**a**) ball; *(canica)* marble; **b. de nieve** snowball; **no dar pie con b.** to be unable to do anything right (**b**) *Fam (mentira)* fib, lie; **meter bolas** to tell fibs (**c**) *(rumor)* rumour; **corre la b. por ahí de que te has echado novio** they say you've got yourself a boyfriend

bolchevique *adj & nmf* Bolshevik

bolear *vt Méx (sacar brillo)* to shine, to polish

bolera *nf* bowling alley

bolería *nf Méx* shoeshine store

boleta *nf* (**a**) *Méx, RP (para votar)* ballot, voting slip (**b**) *CSur (comprobante)* receipt (**c**) *CAm, CSur (multa)* parking ticket (**d**) *Méx (boletín)* (school) report card

boletería *nf Am (de cine, teatro)* box office; *(de estación)* ticket office

boletero,-a *nm,f Am* box office attendant

boletín *nm* bulletin; **B. Oficial del Estado** Official Gazette

boleto *nm* (**a**) *(de rifa)* ticket (**b**) *Am (de tren, metro)* ticket (**c**) *Méx (para espectáculo)* ticket

boli *nm Fam* pen, *Br* Biro®

boliche *nm* (**a**) *(juego)* bowling (**b**) *(bola)* jack (**c**) *(lugar)* bowling alley (**d**) *CSur Fam (bar)* small bar

bólido *nm Aut* racing car

bolígrafo *nm* ballpoint (pen), *Br* Biro®

bolita *nf CSur (bola)* marble; **jugar a las bolitas** to play marbles

bolívar *nm Fin* = standard monetary unit of Venezuela

Bolivia *n* Bolivia

boliviano,-a *adj & nm,f* Bolivian

bollar *vt* to dent

bollo *nm* (**a**) *Culin* bun, bread roll (**b**) *(abolladura)* dent

bolo¹ *nm (pieza)* skittle, pin; **bolos** *(juego)* (ten-pin) bowling

bolo²,-a *nm,f CAm Fam (borracho)* drunk

bolsa¹ *nf* bag; *Méx (de mano) Br* handbag, *US* purse; *Av* **b. de aire** air pocket; **b. de deportes** sports bag; **b. de la compra** shopping bag; **b. de viaje** travel bag

bolsa² *nf Fin* Stock Exchange; **jugar a la b.** to play the market

bolsillo *nm (en prenda)* pocket; **de b.** pocket, pocket-size; **libro de b.** paperback; **lo pagó de su b.** he paid for it out of his own pocket

bolso *nm Br* handbag, *US* purse

boludear *vi RP Fam* (**a**) *(hacer tonterías)* to mess about (**b**) *(decir tonterías)* to talk rubbish (**c**) *(perder el tiempo)* to waste one's time

boludo,-a *nm,f RP Fam (estúpido)* idiot, twit

bomba¹ *nf* pump; *Andes, Ven (gasolinera) Br* petrol station, *US* gas station; **b. de aire** air pump; **b. de incendios** fire engine; *Andes, Ven* **b. (de gasolina)** *(surtidor) Br* petrol pump, *US* gas pump

bomba² *nf* bomb; **b. atómica/de hidrógeno/de neutrones** atomic/hydrogen/neutron bomb; **b. de relojería** time bomb; **b. fétida** stink bomb; *Fam* **noticia b.** shattering piece of news; *Fam* **pasarlo b.** to have a whale of a time

bombacha *nf RP (braga)* panties, *Br* knickers; **bombachas** *(pantalones)* = loose-fitting trousers worn by cowboys

bombardear *vt* to bomb, to shell; **b. a algn a preguntas** to bombard sb with questions

bombardeo *nm* bombing, bombardment

bombardero *nm Av* bomber

bombazo *nm* bomb blast

bombear *vt* (**a**) *(agua etc)* to pump (**b**) *(pelota)* to blow up

bombeo *nm (de líquido)* pumping; **estación de b.** pumping station

bombero,-a *nm,f* (**a**) *(de incendios)* firefighter; *(hombre)* fireman; *(mujer)* firewoman; **cuerpo de bomberos** *Br* fire brigade, *US* fire department; **parque de bomberos** fire station (**b**) *Ven (de gasolinera) Br* petrol-pump *o US* gas-pump attendant

bombilla *nf* (light) bulb

bombillo *nm CAm, Carib, Col, Méx* light bulb

bombín *nm* bowler hat

bombita *nf RP* light bulb

bombo *nm* (**a**) *Mús* bass drum; *Fig* **a b. y platillo(s)** with a great song and dance; *Fam* **darse b.** to blow one's own trumpet (**b**) *(de sorteo)* lottery drum

bombón *nm* chocolate

bombona *nf* cylinder; **b. de butano** butane gas cylinder

bombonera *nf* chocolate box

bonachón,-ona *adj* good-natured, easygoing

bonaerense 1 *adj* of/from Buenos Aires **2** *nmf* person from Buenos Aires

bonanza *nf* (**a**) *Náut (tiempo)* fair weather; *(mar)* calm at sea (**b**) *Fig (prosperidad)* prosperity

bondad *nf* goodness; *Fml* **tenga la b. de esperar** please be so kind as to wait

bondadoso,-a *adj* kind, good-natured

bonete *nm Rel* cap, biretta; *Univ* mortarboard

boniato *nm* sweet potato

bonificación *nf* bonus

bonificar **[44]** *vt Com* to give a bonus to

bonito¹,-a *adj* pretty, nice

bonito² *nm* tuna

bono *nm* (**a**) *(vale)* voucher (**b**) *Fin* bond, debenture; **bonos del tesoro** *o* **del Estado** Treasury bonds

bono-bus *nm* bus pass

boom *nm* boom

boomerang *nm* boomerang

boquerón *nm* anchovy

boquete *nm* hole

boquiabierto,-a *adj* open-mouthed; **se quedó b.** he was flabbergasted

boquilla *nf* (**a**) *(de cigarro)* tip; *(de pipa)* mouthpiece; **decir algo de b.** to pay lip service to sth (**b**) *Mús* mouthpiece (**c**) *(orificio)* opening

borbotar, borbotear *vi* to bubble
borbotón *nm* bubbling; *Fig* **salir a borbotones** to gush forth
borda *nf Náut* gunwale; **arrojar** *o* **echar por la b.** to throw overboard; **fuera b.** *(motor)* outboard motor
bordado,-a 1 *adj* embroidered; **el examen me salió b.** I made a good job of that exam
   2 *nm* embroidery
bordar *vt* (**a**) to embroider (**b**) *Fig* to do excellently
borde¹ *nm (de mesa, camino)* edge; *Cost* hem, edge; *(de vasija)* rim, brim; **al b. de** on the brink of, on the verge of; **al b. del mar** at the seaside
borde² *Fam* **1** *adj* stroppy
   2 *nmf* stroppy person
bordear *vt* to go round the edge of, to skirt
bordillo *nm Br* kerb, *US* curb
bordo *nm* **a b.** on board; **subir a b.** to go on board
bordó *adj inv RP* maroon, burgundy
borla *nf* tassel
borne *nm Elec* terminal
borra *nf* (**a**) *(pelusa)* fluff (**b**) *(poso)* sediment, dregs
borrachera *nf (embriaguez)* drunkenness; **agarrarse** *o* **cogerse una b.** to get drunk;
borracho,-a 1 *adj* (**a**) *(bebido)* drunk; **estar b.** to be drunk (**b**) *(bizcocho)* with rum
   2 *nm,f* drunkard, drunk
borrador *nm* (**a**) *(escrito)* rough copy, first draft (**b**) *(croquis)* rough *o* preliminary sketch (**c**) *(de pizarra)* duster
borraja *nf* **quedar en agua de borrajas** to come to nothing, to fizzle *o* peter out
borrar 1 *vt* (**a**) *(con goma)* to erase, to rub out; *(pizarra)* to clean (**b**) *Informát* to delete
   2 borrarse *vpr (de un club etc)* to drop out, to withdraw
borrasca *nf* area of low pressure
borrascoso,-a *adj* stormy
borrego,-a *nm,f* (**a**) yearling lamb (**b**) *Fam (persona)* sheep
borrico *nm* ass, donkey; *Fam Fig* ass, dimwit
borrón *nm* blot, smudge
borroso,-a *adj* blurred; **veo b.** I can't see clearly, everything's blurred
Bosnia *n* Bosnia; **B. y Herzegóvina** Bosnia-Herzegovina
bosnio,-a *adj & nm,f* Bosnian
bosque *nm* wood

bosquejar *vt (dibujo)* to sketch, outline; *(plan)* to draft, to outline
bosquejo *nm (de dibujo)* sketch, study; *(de plan)* draft, outline
bostezar [40] *vi* to yawn
bostezo *nm* yawn
bota *nf* (**a**) boot; *Fig* **ponerse las botas** to make a killing (**b**) *(de vino)* wineskin
botana *nf Méx* snack, appetizer
botánica *nf* botany
botánico,-a 1 *adj* botanic; **jardín b.** botanic gardens
   2 *nm,f* botanist
botar 1 *vi* (**a**) *(saltar)* to jump (**b**) *(pelota)* to bounce
   2 *vt* (**a**) *(barco)* to launch (**b**) *(pelota)* to bounce (**c**) *Am (arrojar)* to throw out
botarate *nmf* madcap, fool
bote¹ *nm* (**a**) jump, bound; **dar botes** to jump up and down; **de un b.** with one leap (**b**) *(de pelota)* bounce, rebound
bote² *nm (lata)* can, tin; *(para propinas)* jar *o* box for tips; *(en lotería)* jackpot; *Fam* **chupar del b.** to scrounge
bote³ *nm (lancha)* boat; **b. salvavidas** lifeboat
bote⁴ *nm* **de b. en b.** packed, full to bursting
botella *nf* (**a**) bottle (**b**) *Cuba (autostop)* **dar b. a algn** to give sb a lift; **hacer b.** to hitchhike
botellín *nm* small bottle
botepronto *nm Fam* **a b.** all of a sudden
botica *nf* pharmacy, *Br* chemist's (shop), *US* drugstore; *Fam* **hay de todo como en b.** there's everything under the sun
boticario,-a *nm,f* pharmacist, *Br* chemist, *US* druggist
botijo *nm* earthenware pitcher *(with spout and handle)*
botín¹ *nm (de un robo)* loot, booty
botín² *nm (calzado)* ankle boot
botiquín *nm* (**a**) medicine chest *o* cabinet; *(portátil)* first-aid kit (**b**) *(enfermería)* first-aid post
botón *nm* button; **pulsar el b.** to press the button; **b. de muestra** sample
botones *nm inv (en hotel)* bellboy, *US* bellhop; *(recadero)* messenger, errand boy
boutique *nf* boutique
bóveda *nf* vault
bovino,-a *adj* bovine; **ganado b.** cattle
box *nm (pl* **boxes)** (**a**) *(de caballo)* stall (**b**) *(de coches)* pit (**c**) *Am (boxeo)* boxing
boxeador *nm* boxer
boxear *vi* to box
boxeo *nm* boxing

boya *nf* (**a**) *Náut* buoy (**b**) *(corcho)* float
boyante *adj* buoyant
boy-scout *nm* boy scout
bozal *nm* (**a**) *(para perro)* muzzle (**b**) *Am (cabestro)* halter
bracero *nm* (day) labourer
bragas *nfpl* panties, *Br* knickers
bragueta *nf (de pantalón etc)* fly, flies
braguetazo *nm Fam* **dar el b.** to marry for money
braille *nm* braille
bramar *vi* to low, to bellow
bramido *nm* lowing, bellowing
brandy *nm* brandy
branquia *nf* gill
brasa *nf* ember, red-hot coal; **chuletas a la b.** barbecued chops
brasero *nm* brazier
brasier *nm Carib, Col, Méx* bra
Brasil *n* Brazil
brasileño,-a, *RP* **brasilero,-a** *adj & nm,f* Brazilian
bravata *nf* piece o act of bravado
bravo,-a 1 *adj* (**a**) *(valiente)* brave, courageous (**b**) *(feroz)* fierce, ferocious; **un toro b.** a fighting bull (**c**) *(mar)* rough, stormy
  2 *interj* ¡**b.!** well done!, bravo!
bravucón,-ona *nm,f* boaster, braggart
bravura *nf* (**a**) *(de animal)* ferocity, fierceness (**b**) *(de persona)* courage, bravery (**c**) *(de toro)* fighting spirit
braza *nf* (**a**) *Náut* fathom (**b**) *(en natación)* breaststroke; **nadar a b.** to do the breaststroke
brazada *nf (en natación)* stroke
brazalete *nm* (**a**) *(insignia)* armband (**b**) *(pulsera)* bracelet
brazo *nm* arm; *(de animal)* foreleg; *(de sillón, tocadiscos)* arm; **en brazos** in one's arms; **ir del b.** to walk arm in arm; *Fig* **con los brazos abiertos** with open arms; *Fig* **no dar su b. a torcer** not to give in, stand firm; **b. de gitano** = type of Swiss roll containing cream
brea *nf* tar, pitch
brebaje *nm* concoction, brew
brecha *nf (en muro)* opening, gap; *Mil & Fig* breach; *Fig* **estar siempre en la b.** to be always in the thick of things
brécol *nm* broccoli
bregar [42] *vi* to fight
Bretaña *nf* (**a**) Brittany (**b**) **Gran B.** Great Britain
brete *nm Fig* **poner a algn en un b.** to put sb in a tight spot
bretel *nm CSur* strap; **un vestido sin breteles** a strapless dress

breva *nf* early fig; *Fam* **de higos a brevas** once in a blue moon; *Fam* ¡**no caerá esa b.!** no such luck!
breve *adj* brief; **en b., en breves momentos** shortly, soon; **en breves palabras** in short
brevedad *nf* briefness; *(concision)* brevity; **con la mayor b. posible** as soon as possible
brevet *nm Chile (de avión)* pilot's licence; *Ecuad, Perú (de automóvil) Br* driving licence, *US* driver's license; *RP (de velero)* sailor's licence
brezo *nm* heather
bribón,-ona 1 *adj* roguish, dishonest
  2 *nm,f* rogue, rascal
bricolaje *nm* do-it-yourself, DIY
brida *nf* (**a**) *(rienda)* rein, bridle (**b**) *Téc* flange
bridge *nm Naipes* bridge
brigada 1 *nf* (**a**) *Mil* brigade (**b**) *(de policías)* squad; **b. antiterrorista** anti-terrorist squad
  2 *nm Mil* sergeant major
brigadier *nm* brigadier
brillante 1 *adj* brilliant
  2 *nm* diamond
brillantez *nf* brilliance
brillantina *nf* brilliantine
brillar *vi (resplandecer)* to shine; *(ojos, joyas)* to sparkle; *(lentejuelas etc)* to glitter; **b. por su ausencia** to be conspicuous by one's absence
brillo *nm (resplandor)* shine; *(del sol, de la luna)* brightness; *(de lentejuelas etc)* glittering; *(del cabello, tela)* sheen; *(de color)* brilliance; *(de pantalla)* brightness; *(de zapatos)* shine; **sacar b. a** to shine, to polish
brilloso,-a *adj Am* shining
brincar [44] *vi* to skip
brinco *nm* skip
brindar 1 *vi* to drink a toast; **b. por algn/algo** to drink to sb/sth
  2 *vt* (**a**) *(oportunidad)* to offer, to provide (**b**) *Taurom* to dedicate (**a** to)
  3 brindarse *vpr* to offer (**a** to), to volunteer (**a** to)
brindis *nm* (**a**) toast (**b**) *Taurom* dedication (of the bull)
brío *nm* energy
brioso,-a *adj* energetic, vigorous
brisa *nf* breeze; **b. marina** sea breeze
británico,-a 1 *adj* British; **las Islas Británicas** the British Isles
  2 *nm,f* Briton; **los británicos** the British
brizna *nf (de hierba)* blade; *(de carne)* string

broca *nf Téc* bit
brocha *nf (para pintar)* paintbrush; **b. de afeitar** shaving brush
broche *nm* (**a**) *(joya)* brooch; *Fig* **poner el b. de oro** to finish with a flourish (**b**) *(de vestido)* fastener
bróculi *nm* broccoli
broma *nf (chiste)* joke; **bromas aparte** joking apart; **en b.** as a joke; **¡ni en b.!** not on your life!; **b. pesada** practical joke; **gastar una b.** to play a joke
bromear *vi* to joke
bromista 1 *adj* fond of joking *o* playing jokes
   2 *nmf* joker, prankster
bronca *nf* (**a**) *(riña)* quarrel, row (**b**) **echar una b. a algn** to bawl sb out (**c**) *RP Fam (rabia)* **me da b.** it hacks me off; **el jefe le tiene b.** the boss can't stand him
bronce *nm* bronze
bronceado,-a 1 *adj* suntanned, tanned
   2 *nm* suntan, tan
bronceador,-a 1 *adj* **leche bronceadora** suntan cream
   2 *nm* suntan cream *o* lotion
broncearse *vpr* to get a tan *o* a suntan
bronco,-a *adj* rough, coarse
bronquitis *nf inv* bronchitis
brotar *vi (planta)* to sprout; *(agua)* to spring, to gush; *(lágrimas)* to well up; *(epidemia)* to break out
brote *nm* (**a**) *Bot (renuevo)* bud, shoot; *(de agua)* gushing (**b**) *(de epidemia, violencia)* outbreak
bruces: •de bruces *loc adv* face downwards; **se cayó de b.** he fell flat on his face
bruja *nf* witch, sorceress
brujería *nf* witchcraft, sorcery
brujo,-a 1 *nm* wizard, sorcerer
   2 *adj Méx Fam* **estar b.** to be broke
brújula *nf* compass
bruma *nf* mist
brumoso,-a *adj* misty
bruñir *vt* to polish
brusco,-a *adj* (**a**) *(persona)* brusque, abrupt (**b**) *(repentino)* sudden, sharp
Bruselas *n* Brussels; **coles de B.** Brussels sprouts
brusquedad *nf* brusqueness, abruptness
brutal *adj* brutal
brutalidad *nf* brutality
bruto,-a 1 *adj* (**a**) *(necio)* stupid, thick; *(grosero)* coarse, uncouth (**b**) *Fin* gross; **peso b.** gross weight (**c**) **un diamante en b.** an uncut diamond
   2 *nm,f* blockhead, brute

búcaro *nm* earthenware jug
bucear *vi* to swim under water
buche *nm* maw; *(de ave)* craw; *Fam (estómago)* belly, stomach
bucle *nm* curl, ringlet
budín *nm* pudding
budismo *nm* Buddhism
budista *adj & nmf* Buddhist
buen *adj (delante de un nombre masculino singular)* good; **¡b. viaje!** have a good trip!; *ver* **bueno,-a**
buenamente *adv* **haz lo que b. puedas** just do what you can; **si b. puedes** if you possibly can
buenaventura *nf* good fortune, good luck; **echar la b. a algn** to tell sb's fortune
bueno,-a 1 *adj* (**a**) good; **un alumno muy b.** a very good pupil; **una buena película** a good film; **lo b.** the good thing
   (**b**) *(amable) (con* **ser**) good, kind; **el b. de Carlos** good old Carlos; **es muy buena persona** he's a very kind soul
   (**c**) *(sano) (con* **estar**) well, in good health
   (**d**) *(tiempo)* good; **hoy hace buen tiempo** it's fine today; **mañana hará b.** it will be fine *o* a nice day tomorrow
   (**e**) *(conveniente)* good; **no es b. comer tanto** it's not good for you to eat so much; **sería b. que vinieras** it would be a good idea if you came
   (**f**) *(considerable)* considerable; **un buen número de** a good number of; **una buena cantidad** a considerable amount
   (**g**) *(grande)* good, big; **un buen trozo de pastel** a nice *o* good big piece of cake
   (**h**) *Fam (atractivo)* gorgeous, sexy; **¡Rosa está muy buena!** Rosa's a bit of all right!; **una tía buena** a good-looking girl
   (**i**) *Irón* fine, real, proper; **¡en buen lío te has metido!** that's a fine mess you've got yourself into!
   (**j**) **¡buenas!** *(saludos)* hello!; **buenas tardes** *(desde mediodía hasta las cinco)* good afternoon; *(desde las cinco)* good evening; **buenas noches** *(al llegar)* good evening; *(al irse)* good night; **buenos días** good morning
   (**k**) *(locuciones)* **de buenas a primeras** suddenly, all at once; **estar de buenas** to be in a good mood; **los buenos tiempos** the good old days; **por las buenas** willingly; **por las buenas o por las malas** willy-nilly; *Irón* **¡buena la has hecho!** that's done it!; **un susto de los buenos** a real fright; *Irón* **¡estaría b.!** I should jolly well hope not!; *Irón* **librarse de una buena** to get off scot free

buen is used instead of **bueno** before masculine singular nouns (e.g. **buen hombre** good man). The comparative form of **bueno** is **mejor** (better), and the superlative form is **el mejor** (masculine) or **la mejor** (feminine) (the best).

2 *interj* (**a**) *(vale)* all right, OK (**b**) *(expresa sorpresa)* hey! (**c**) *Col, Méx (al teléfono)* hello

buey *nm* ox, bullock

búfalo,-a *nm,f* buffalo

bufanda *nf* scarf

bufar *vi* (**a**) *(toro)* to snort; *(caballo)* to neigh (**b**) *(persona)* to be fuming

bufé *nm* buffet; **b. libre** self-service buffet meal

bufete *nm (despacho de abogado)* lawyer's office

buffet *nm* (*pl* **buffets**) = **bufé**

bufido *nm (de toro)* snort; *(de caballo)* neigh

bufón,-ona *nm,f* clown, buffoon

buhardilla *nf* attic, garret

búho *nm* owl; **b. real** eagle owl

buhonero,-a *nm,f* pedlar, hawker

buitre *nm* vulture

bujía *nf* (**a**) *Aut* spark plug (**b**) *Fís* candlepower

bulbo *nm* bulb

buldog *nm* bulldog

bulevar *nm* boulevard

Bulgaria *n* Bulgaria

búlgaro,-a *adj & nm,f* Bulgarian

bulín *nm RP Fam* bachelor pad

bulla *nf* (**a**) *(muchedumbre)* crowd, mob (**b**) *(ruido)* din; **armar b.** to kick up a din

bullicio *nm* din, hubbub

bullir *vi* (**a**) *(hervir)* to boil, to bubble (up) (**b**) **b. de gente** to be teeming with people

bulto *nm* (**a**) *(cosa indistinta)* shape, form (**b**) *(maleta, caja)* piece of luggage (**c**) *Med* lump (**d**) **hacer mucho b.** to be very bulky; *Fam* **escurrir el b.** to pass the buck

bumerán, bumerang *nm* boomerang

bungalow *nm* bungalow

búnker *nm* bunker

buñuelo *nm* doughnut

BUP *nm (abr* **Bachillerato Unificado Polivalente**) = academically orientated Spanish secondary school course for pupils aged 14-17

buque *nm* ship; **b. de guerra** warship; **b. de pasajeros** liner, passenger ship; **b. insignia** flagship

burbuja *nf* bubble; **hacer burbujas** to bubble, make bubbles

burbujear *vi* to bubble

burdel *nm* brothel

Burdeos *n* Bordeaux

burdo,-a *adj* coarse, rough

burgalés,-esa 1 *adj* of/from Burgos
2 *nm,f* person from Burgos

burgués,-esa *adj & nm,f* bourgeois

burguesía *nf* bourgeoisie

burla *nf* gibe, jeer; **hacer b. de algo/algn** to make fun of sth/sb; **hacer b. a algn** to stick one's tongue out at sb

burladero *nm Taurom* refuge in bullring

burlar 1 *vt* (**a**) *(engañar)* to deceive (**b**) *(eludir)* to dodge, to evade
2 burlarse *vpr* to make fun (**de** of), to laugh (**de** at)

burlón,-ona *adj* mocking

buró *nm* (**a**) *Pol* executive committee (**b**) *(escritorio)* bureau, desk (**c**) *Méx (mesa de noche)* bedside table

burocracia *nf* bureaucracy

burócrata *nmf* bureaucrat

burocrático,-a *adj* bureaucratic

buromática *nf* office automation

burrada *nf (comentario)* stupid *o* foolish remark; *(hecho)* stupid *o* foolish act

burro,-a 1 *nm,f* (**a**) donkey, ass; *Fam Fig* **bajarse del b.** to climb *o* back down (**b**) *Fam (estúpido)* dimwit, blockhead (**c**) **b. de carga** dogsbody, drudge
2 *adj Fam* (**a**) *(necio)* stupid, dumb (**b**) *(obstinado)* stubborn

bursátil *adj* stock-market

bus *nm* bus

busca *nf* search; **ir en b. de** to go in search of

buscapersonas *nm* pager

buscapleitos *nmf inv* troublemaker

buscar [44] 1 *vt* (**a**) to look *o* search for; **b. una palabra en el diccionario** to look up a word in the dictionary (**b**) **ir a b. algo** to go and get sth, to fetch sth; **fue a buscarme a la estación** she picked me up at the station
2 buscarse *vpr Fam* **b. la vida** to try and earn one's living; *Fam* **te la estás buscando** you're asking for it; **se busca** *(en anuncios)* wanted

buseta *nf Col, CRica, Ecuad, Ven* minibus

búsqueda *nf* search, quest; *Informát* search

busto *nm* bust

butaca *nf* (**a**) *(sillón)* armchair, easy chair (**b**) *Cin & Teatro* seat; **b. de platea** *o* **patio** seat in the stalls

butano *nm* butane; **(gas) b.** butane gas

butifarra *nf* sausage

buzo *nm* (**a**) *(persona)* diver (**b**) *Arg, Col (sudadera)* sweatshirt (**c**) *Col, Urug (jersey)* sweater, *Br* jumper

buzón *nm Br* letter box, *US* mailbox; *Informát (de correo electrónico)* (electronic) mailbox; **echar una carta al b.** to *Br* post *o US* mail a letter; **b. de voz** voice mail

byte *nm Informát* byte

C, c [θe] *nf (la letra)* C, c

C (**a**) (*abr* **Celsius**) C (**b**) (*abr* **centígrado**) C

c/ (**a**) (*abr* **calle**) St; Rd (**b**) (*abr* **cargo**) cargo, freight (**c**) (*abr* **cuenta**) a/c

C., Ca (*abr* **compañía**) Co

cabal 1 *adj* (**a**) (*exacto*) exact, precise (**b**) (*honesto*) honest, upright

2 *nmpl Fam* **no está en sus cabales** he's not in his right mind

cábala *nf Fig* **hacer cábalas sobre algo** to speculate about sth

cabalgadura *nf* mount

cabalgar [42] *vt & vi* to ride

cabalgata *nf* cavalcade; **la c. de los Reyes Magos** the procession of the Three Wise Men

caballa *nf* mackerel

caballar *adj* **ganado c.** horses

caballería *nf* (**a**) (*cabalgadura*) mount, steed (**b**) *Mil* cavalry

caballeriza *nf* stable

caballero *nm* (**a**) gentleman; **¿qué desea, c.?** can I help you, sir?; **ropa de c.** menswear (**b**) *Hist* knight (**c**) **caballeros** (*en letrero*) gents

caballeroso,-a *adj* gentlemanly, chivalrous

caballete *nm* (**a**) (*de pintor*) easel (**b**) *Téc* trestle (**c**) (*de nariz*) bridge

caballito *nm* (**a**) **c. de mar** seahorse (**b**) **caballitos** merry-go-round, *US* carousel

caballo *nm* (**a**) horse; **a c.** on horseback; **montar a c.** to ride; *Fig* **a c. entre ...** halfway between ... (**b**) *Téc* **c. de vapor** horse power (**c**) (*pieza de ajedrez*) knight (**d**) *Naipes* queen (**e**) *Fam (heroína)* horse, smack

cabaña *nf* cabin

cabaret *nm* (*pl* **cabarets**) cabaret

cabecear 1 *vi* to nod

2 *vt Dep* to head

cabecera *nf* (**a**) top, head (**b**) *Impr* headline

cabecilla *nmf* leader

cabellera *nf* head of hair

cabello *nm* (**a**) hair (**b**) *Culin* **c. de ángel** = sweet made of gourd and syrup

cabelludo,-a *adj* **cuero c.** scalp

caber [9] *vi* (**a**) to fit, to be (able to be) contained; **cabe en el maletero** it fits in the boot; **¿cabemos todos?** is there room for all of us?; **en este coche/jarro caben ...** this car/jug holds ...; **no cabe por la puerta** it won't go through the door; **no c. en sí de gozo** to be beside oneself with joy; **no me cabe en la cabeza** I can't understand it; **no cabe duda** there is no doubt; **cabe la posibilidad de que ...** there is a possibility *o* chance that ...; **no está mal dentro de lo que cabe** it isn't bad, under the circumstances

(**b**) **cabe señalar que ...** we should point out that ...

(**c**) *Mat* **doce entre cuatro caben a tres** four into twelve goes three (times)

cabestrillo *nm* sling

cabeza 1 *nf* head; **en c.** in the lead; **por c.** a head, per person; *Fig* **a la c. de** at the front *o* top of; *Fig* **estar mal de la c.** to be a mental case; **c. de turco** scapegoat; **el** *o* **la c. de familia** the head of the family

2 *nm* **c. rapada** skinhead

cabezada *nf* (**a**) (*golpe*) butt, blow on the head (**b**) *Fam* **echar una c.** to have a snooze; **dar cabezadas** to nod

cabezal *nm Téc* head; (*de tocadiscos*) pick-up

cabezota *Fam* **1** *adj* pigheaded

2 *nmf* pigheaded person

cabezudo *nm* = carnival figure with a huge head

cabida *nf* capacity; **dar c. a** to leave room for

cabildo *nm Rel* chapter

cabina *nf* cabin; **c. telefónica** telephone box, telephone booth

cabinera *nf Col* air hostess

cabizbajo,-a *adj* crestfallen

cable *nm* cable; *Fam* **echarle un c. a algn** to give sb a hand

cableoperador *nm* cable company, cable operator

cabo *nm* (**a**) (*extremo*) end; **al c. de** after; **de c. a rabo** from start to finish (**b**) *Mil* corporal; (*policía*) sergeant (**c**) *Náut* rope, cable; *Fig* **atar cabos** to put two and two together; *Fig* **no dejar ningún c.**

suelto to leave no loose ends (**d**) *Geog* cape; **Ciudad del C.** Cape Town; **C. Verde** Cape Verde

cabra *nf* goat; *Fam* **estar como una c.** to be off one's head

cabré *indic fut de* **caber**

cabreado,-a *adj muy Fam* pissed off

cabrear *muy Fam* **1** *vt* to make angry, *Br* to piss off

   2 cabrearse *vpr* to get *Br* pissed off *o US* pissed

cabreo *nm muy Fam* anger

cabrío,-a *adj* **macho c.** billy goat; **ganado c.** goats

cabriola *nf* skip

cabrito *nm Zool* kid

cabro,-a *nm,f Chile Fam* kid

cabrón,-ona *nm,f Vulg (hombre) Br* bastard, *US* asshole; *(woman)* bitch

cabronada *nf muy Fam* dirty trick

cabuya *nf* (**a**) *(planta)* agave (**b**) *(fibra)* fibre hemp (**c**) *CAm, Col, Ven (cuerda)* rope

caca *nf Fam* poopoo

cacahuete, *CAm, Méx* **cacahuate** *nm* peanut

cacao *nm* (**a**) *Bot* cacao (**b**) *(polvo, bebida)* cocoa (**c**) *Fam (lío)* mess

cacarear 1 *vi (gallina)* to cluck

   2 *vt Fig* to boast about

cacareo *nm* (**a**) *(de gallina)* clucking (**b**) *Fig* boasting, bragging

cacatúa *nf* cockatoo

cacereño,-a 1 *adj* of/from Cáceres

   2 *nm,f* person from Cáceres

cacería *nf* (**a**) *(actividad)* hunting, shooting (**b**) *(partida)* hunt, shoot

cacerola *nf* saucepan

cacha *nf Fam (muslo)* thigh; **estar cachas** to be really muscular

cachalote *nm* sperm whale

cacharro *nm* (**a**) earthenware pot *o* jar (**b**) *Fam (cosa)* thing, piece of junk (**c**) **cacharros** *(de cocina)* pots and pans

caché *nm Informát* (**memoria**) **c.** cache memory

cachear *vt* to frisk, to search

cachemir *nm,* **cachemira** *nf* cashmere

cacheo *nm* frisk, frisking

cachetada *nf Am* slap

cachete *nm* (**a**) *(bofetada)* slap (**b**) *Am (mejilla)* cheek

cachila *nf RP (automóvil)* vintage car

cachimba *nf* (**a**) *(pipa)* pipe (**b**) *RP (pozo)* well

cachiporra *nf* club, truncheon

cachivache *nm Fam* thing, knick-knack

cacho¹ *nm Fam (pedazo)* bit, piece; *Fig* **¡qué c. de animal!** what a nasty piece of work!

cacho² *nm Andes, Ven (cuerno)* horn

cachondearse *vpr Fam* **c. de** to take the mickey out of

cachondeo *nm Fam* laugh; **tomar algo a c.** to take sth as a joke

cachondo,-a *adj Fam* (**a**) *(sexualmente)* randy (**b**) *(divertido)* funny

cachorro,-a *nm,f (de perro)* pup, puppy; *(de gato)* kitten; *(de otros animales)* cub, baby

cacique *nm (jefe)* local boss

caco *nm Fam* thief

cacofonía *nf* cacophony

cacto *nm,* **cactus** *nm inv Bot* cactus

cada *adj (de dos)* each; *(de varios)* each, every; **c. día** every day; **c. dos días** every second day; **c. vez más** more and more; **¿c. cuánto?** how often?; **c. dos por tres** every other minute; **cuatro de c. diez** four out of (every) ten; **¡tienes c. cosa!** you come up with some fine ideas!

cadalso *nm* scaffold

cadáver *nm (de persona)* corpse, (dead) body; *(de animal)* body, carcass; **ingresar c.** to be dead on arrival

cadena *nf* (**a**) chain; *(correa de perro)* lead, leash (**b**) *TV* channel (**c**) *Ind* line; **c. de montaje** assembly line; **trabajo en c.** assembly line work (**d**) *Geog* **c. montañosa** mountain range (**e**) *Jur* **c. perpetua** life imprisonment (**f**) *Aut* **cadenas** tyre chains

cadencia *nf* rhythm; *Mús* cadenza

cadera *nf* hip

cadete *nm* cadet; *RP (chico de los recados)* errand boy, office junior

caducar [**44**] *vi* to expire

caducidad *nf* expiry; **fecha de c.** *(en alimentos)* ≃ sell-by date; *(en medicinas)* to be used before

caduco,-a *adj* (**a**) *Bot* deciduous (**b**) *(anticuado)* out-of-date

caer [**39**] **1** *vi* (**a**) to fall; **dejar c.** to drop; *Fig* **está al c.** *(llegar)* he'll arrive any minute now; *(ocurrir)* it's on the way

   (**b**) *(fecha)* to be; **su cumpleaños cae en sábado** his birthday falls on a Saturday

   (**c**) *(entender)* to understand, to see; **ya caigo** I get it; **no caí** I didn't twig

   (**d**) *(hallarse)* to be; **cae por Granada** it is somewhere near Granada

   (**e**) **me cae bien/mal** I like/don't like her

   (**f**) **al c. el día** in the evening; **al c. la noche** at nightfall

   2 caerse *vpr* to fall (down); **me caí de la moto** I fell off the motorbike; **se le ha cayó**

el pañuelo she dropped her handkerchief
café *nm* (**a**) coffee; **c. solo/con leche** black/white coffee (**b**) *(cafetería)* café
cafeína *nf* caffeine
cafetal *nm* coffee plantation
cafetera *nf* coffee-maker
cafetería *nf* snack bar, coffee bar; *Ferroc* buffet car
cafetero,-a *adj* (**a**) coffee (**b**) *Fam* **es muy c.** *(persona)* he loves coffee
cafiche *nm Andes Fam (proxeneta)* pimp
cafre *nmf* savage, beast
cagado,-a *adj muy Fam (cobarde)* coward; **estar c. de miedo** to be shit-scared
cagar [42] *muy Fam* **1** *vi* (**a**) to (have a) shit (**b**) *(estropear)* to ruin, to spoil; **cagarla** to cock it up
　2 cagarse *vpr* to shit oneself; **c. de miedo** to be shit-scared; **¡me cago en diez!** *Br* bloody hell!, *US* goddamn it!
caída *nf* (**a**) fall; *(de pelo, diente)* loss (**b**) *(de precios)* drop (**c**) *Pol* downfall, collapse
caído,-a **1** *adj* fallen
　2 *nmpl* **los caídos** the fallen
caigo *indic pres de* **caer**
caimán *nm* alligator
Cairo *n* **El C.** Cairo
caja *nf* (**a**) box; **c. fuerte** safe; *Fam TV* **la c. tonta** the idiot box (**b**) *(de leche etc)* carton (**c**) *(de embalaje)* crate, case; **una c. de cerveza** a crate of beer (**d**) *Fin (en tienda)* cash desk; *(en banco)* cashier's desk (**e**) *Aut* **c. de cambios** gearbox (**f**) *Com* **c. de ahorros** *o* **de pensiones** savings bank (**g**) *(féretro)* coffin
cajero,-a *nm,f* cashier; **c. automático** cash point, cash dispenser
cajetilla *nf* packet, pack
cajón *nm* (**a**) *(en un mueble)* drawer; *Fig* **c. de sastre** jumble; *Fam* **de c.** obvious, self-evident (**b**) *(caja grande)* crate, chest
cajuela *nf CAm, Méx (maletero) Br* boot, *US* trunk
cal¹ *nf* lime; *Fig* **a c. y canto** hermetically; *Fam* **una de c. y otra de arena** six of one and half a dozen of the other
cal² *(abr* **caloría(s))** cal
cala *nf* (**a**) *Geog* creek, cove (**b**) *Náut* hold
calabacín *nm Bot* (**a**) *(pequeño) Br* courgette, *US* zucchini (**b**) *(grande) Br* marrow, *US* squash
calabaza *nf* pumpkin, gourd
calabobos *nm inv Fam* drizzle
calabozo *nm* (**a**) *(prisión)* jail, prison (**b**) *(celda)* cell
calada *nf Fam (de cigarrillo)* drag, puff

calado,-a 1 *adj* soaked
　2 *nm Náut* draught
calamar *nm* squid *inv*; *Culin* **calamares a la romana** squid fried in batter
calambre *nm* (**a**) *Elec (descarga)* electric shock; **ese cable da c.** that wire is live (**b**) *(en músculo)* cramp
calamidad *nf* calamity
calaña *nf* kind, sort; **una persona de mala c.** a bad sort
calar 1 *vt* (**a**) *(mojar)* to soak, to drench (**b**) *(agujerear)* to pierce, to penetrate (**c**) *Fam (a alguien)* to rumble; **¡te hemos calado!** we've got your number!
　2 *vi* (**a**) *(prenda)* to let in water (**b**) *Náut* to draw
　3 calarse *vpr* (**a**) *(prenda, techo)* to let in water; *(mojarse)* to get soaked (**b**) *(el sombrero)* to pull down (**c**) *Aut* to stall
calavera 1 *nf* (**a**) *(cráneo)* skull (**b**) *Méx Aut* **calaveras** tail lights
　2 *nm* tearaway
calcar [44] *vt* (**a**) *(un dibujo)* to trace (**b**) *Fig (imitar)* to copy, to imitate
calceta *nf* (**a**) *(prenda)* stocking (**b**) **hacer c.** to knit
calcetín *nm* sock
calcinar *vt* to burn
calcio *nm* calcium
calco *nm* tracing; **papel de c.** carbon paper
calcomanía *nf* transfer
calculadora *nf* calculator
calcular *vt* (**a**) *Mat* to calculate (**b**) *(evaluar)* to (make an) estimate (**c**) *(suponer)* to figure, to guess
cálculo *nm* (**a**) calculation; **según mis cálculos** by my reckoning (**b**) *Med* gallstone (**c**) *Mat* calculus
caldear *vt* to heat up
caldera *nf* (**a**) *(industrial)* boiler; *(olla)* cauldron (**b**) *Urug (hervidor)* kettle
caldereta *nf* stew
calderilla *nf* small change
caldo *nm* stock, broth; **c. de cultivo** culture medium; *Fig* breeding ground
calé *adj & nm* gypsy
calefacción *nf* heating; **c. central** central heating
calefaccionar *vt CSur (calentar)* to heat (up), to warm (up)
calefactor *nm* heater
calefón *nm CSur (calentador)* water heater
caleidoscopio *nm* kaleidoscope
calendario *nm* calendar
calentador *nm* heater
calentamiento *nm Dep* warm-up

calentar [1] 1 *vt* (**a**) *(agua, horno)* to heat; *(comida, habitación)* to warm up; *Fig* **no me calientes la cabeza** don't bug me (**b**) *Fam (pegar)* to smack (**c**) *Fam (excitar)* to arouse (sexually), to turn on
   2 calentarse *upr* (**a**) to get hot *o* warm, to heat up (**b**) *Fig* **se calentaron los ánimos** people became very excited
calentón,-ona, calentorro,-a *adj Fam* randy
calentura *nf* fever, temperature
calesita *nf RP* merry-go-round, carousel
calibrar *vt* to gauge, to bore
calibre *nm* (**a**) *(de arma)* calibre (**b**) *Fig (importancia)* importance
calidad *nf* (**a**) quality; **de primera c.** first-class; **un vino de c.** good-quality wine (**b**) **en c. de** as
cálido,-a *adj* warm; **una cálida acogida** a warm welcome
calidoscopio *nm* = caleidoscopio
caliente *adj* (**a**) hot (**b**) *Fig (debate)* heated; **en c.** in the heat of the moment (**c**) *Fam (cachondo)* hot, randy
calificación *nf* (**a**) qualification (**b**) *Educ* mark
calificar [44] *vt* (**a**) to describe (**de** as); **le calificó de inmoral** he called him immoral (**b**) *(examen)* to mark, to grade
calificativo *nm* epithet
caligrafía *nf* calligraphy; *(modo de escribir)* handwriting
calima *nf* haze, mist
calimocho *nm* = drink made with wine and Coca-Cola®
calina *nf* = calima
cáliz *nm* chalice
caliza *nf* limestone
calizo,-a *adj* lime
callado,-a *adj* quiet; **te lo tenías muy c.** you were keeping that quiet
callar 1 *vi* (**a**) *(dejar de hablar)* to stop talking; **¡calla!** be quiet!, *Fam* shut up! (**b**) *(no hablar)* to keep quiet, to say nothing
   2 *vt (noticia)* not to mention, to keep to oneself
   3 •callarse *upr* to stop talking, to be quiet; **¡cállate!** shut up!
calle *nf* (**a**) street, road; **c. de dirección única** one-way street; **c. mayor** *Br* high street, *US* main street; **el hombre de la c.** the man in the street (**b**) *Dep* lane
calleja *nf* narrow street
callejero,-a 1 *nm (mapa)* street directory
   2 *adj* street; **gato c.** alley cat
callejón *nm* back alley *o* street; **c. sin salida** cul-de-sac, dead end
callejuela *nf* narrow street, lane

callista *nmf* chiropodist
callo *nm* (**a**) *Med* callus, corn; *Fam* **dar el c.** to slog (**b**) *Culin* **callos** tripe
calma *nf* (**a**) calm; **¡c.!** calm down!; **en c.** calm; **tómatelo con c.** take it easy (**b**) *Met* calm weather; **c. chicha** dead calm
calmante *nm* painkiller
calmar 1 *vt (persona)* to calm (down); *(dolor)* to soothe, to relieve
   2 calmarse *upr* (**a**) *(persona)* to calm down (**b**) *(dolor, viento)* to ease off
caló *nm* gypsy dialect
calor *nm* (**a**) heat; **hace c.** it's hot; **tengo c.** I'm hot; **entrar en c.** to warm up (**b**) *Fig (afecto)* warmth
caloría *nf* calorie
calote *nm RP Fam* swindle
calumnia *nf* (**a**) calumny (**b**) *Jur* slander
calumniar [43] *vt* (**a**) to calumniate (**b**) *Jur* to slander
caluroso,-a *adj* hot; *(acogida etc)* warm
calva *nf* bald patch
calvicie *nf* baldness
calvinismo *nm* Calvinism
calvo,-a 1 *adj* bald; **ni tanto ni tan c.** neither one extreme nor the other
   2 *nm* bald man
calza *nf* wedge
calzada *nf* road, carriageway
calzado *nm* shoes, footwear
calzador *nm* shoehorn
calzar [40] 1 *vt* (**a**) *(poner calzado)* to put shoes on; **¿qué número calzas?** what size do you take? (**b**) *(mueble)* to wedge
   2 calzarse c. los zapatos *upr* to put on one's shoes
calzón *nm* (**a**) *Dep* shorts (**b**) *Andes, RP* **calzones** *(bragas)* panties, *Br* knickers (**c**) *Méx* **calzones** *(calzoncillos)* underpants
calzonazos *nm inv Fam* henpecked husband
calzoncillos *nmpl* underpants, pants
calzoneta *nm CAm* swimming trunks
cama *nf* bed; **estar en** *o* **guardar c.** to be confined to bed; **hacer la c.** to make the bed; **irse a la c.** to go to bed; **c. doble/sencilla** double/single bed; **c. turca** couch
camada *nf* litter; *(de pájaros)* brood
camafeo *nm* cameo
camaleón *nm* chameleon
cámara 1 *nf* (**a**) *(aparato)* camera; **a c. lenta** in slow motion (**b**) *Pol* Chamber, House; **C. Alta/Baja** Upper/Lower House (**c**) *Aut* inner tube (**d**) *(habitación)* room, chamber; **c. de gas** gas chamber; **c. frigorífica** cold-storage room; **música de c.** chamber music

2 *nmf (hombre)* cameraman; *(mujer)* camerawoman

camarada *nmf* comrade

camaradería *nf* camaraderie

camarera *nf (de hotel)* chambermaid

camarero,-a *nm,f* (**a**) *(de restaurante)* *(hombre)* waiter; *(mujer)* waitress; *(trás la barra) (hombre)* barman; *(mujer)* barmaid (**b**) *(de avión) (hombre)* steward; *(mujer)* stewardess

camarilla *nf* clique

camarón *nm* (common) prawn

camarote *nm* cabin

camba *Bol Fam* **1** *adj* of/from the forested lowland region of Bolivia

2 *nmf* person from the forested lowland region of Bolivia

cambalache *nm RP (tienda)* junk shop

cambiante *adj* changing; *(carácter)* changeable

cambiar [43] 1 *vt* (**a**) to change; **c. algo de sitio** to move sth (**b**) *(intercambiar)* to swap, to exchange (**c**) *(dinero)* to change

2 *vi* to change; **c. de casa** to move (house); **c. de idea** to change one's mind; **c. de trabajo** to get another job; **c. de velocidad** to change gear

3 cambiarse *vpr* (**a**) *(de ropa)* to change (clothes) (**b**) *(de casa)* to move (house)

cambiazo *nm Fam* switch

cambio *nm* (**a**) change; *(de impresiones)* exchange; **c. de planes** change of plans; **un c. en la opinión pública** a shift in public opinion; *Fig* **a c. de** in exchange for; **en c.** on the other hand (**b**) *(dinero)* change; **¿tienes c. de mil pesetas?** have you got change for a thousand pesetas? (**c**) *Fin (de divisas)* exchange; *(de acciones)* price (**d**) *Aut* gear change; **c. automático** automatic transmission

cambista *nmf* moneychanger

Camboya *n* Cambodia

cambur *nm Ven (plátano)* banana

camelar *vt*, **camelarse** *vpr Fam* (**a**) to cajole (**b**) *(galantear)* to win over

camelia *nf* camellia

camello,-a 1 *nm,f* camel

2 *nm Fam (traficante de drogas)* (drug) pusher

camellón *nm Col, Méx (en avenida) Br* central reservation, *US* median (strip)

camelo *nm Fam* (**a**) *(engaño)* hoax (**b**) *(trola)* cock-and-bull story

camerino *nm* dressing room

Camerún *n* Cameroon

camilla *nf* (**a**) stretcher (**b**) **mesa c.** = small round table under which a heater is placed

caminante *nmf* walker

caminar 1 *vi* to walk

2 *vt* to cover, to travel; **caminaron 10 km** they walked for 10 km

caminata *nf* long walk

camino *nm* (**a**) *(ruta)* route, way; **ir c. de** to be going to; **ponerse en c.** to set off; *Fig* **ir por buen/mal c.** to be on the right/wrong track; **abrirse c.** to break through; **a medio c.** half-way; **en el c. a o de c. a** on the way to; **estar en c.** to be on the way; **nos coge o pilla de c.** it is on the way (**b**) *(vía)* path, track (**c**) *(modo)* way

camión *nm* (**a**) truck, *Br* lorry; **c. cisterna** tanker; **c. de la basura** *Br* dustcart, *US* garbage truck; **c. frigorífico** refrigerated truck (**b**) *CAm, Méx (autobús)* bus

camionero,-a *nm,f* truck o *Br* lorry driver

camioneta *nf* van

camisa *nf* shirt; **en mangas de c.** in one's shirtsleeves; *Fig* **cambiar de c.** to change sides; **c. de fuerza** straightjacket

camiseta *nf* (**a**) *(de uso interior) Br* vest, *US* undershirt (**b**) *(de uso exterior)* T-shirt (**c**) *Dep* shirt; **sudar la c.** to run oneself into the ground

camisón *nm* nightdress, *Fam* nightie

camomila *nf* camomile

camorra *nf Fam* trouble

camorrista 1 *adj* quarrelsome, rowdy

2 *nmf* troublemaker

camote *nm Andes, CAm, Méx (batata)* sweet potato

campal *adj* **batalla c.** pitched battle

campamento *nm* camp

campana *nf* bell; **pantalones de campana** bell-bottom trousers

campanada *nf* peal o ring of a bell

campanario *nm* belfry, bell tower

campanilla *nf* (**a**) small bell (**b**) *Anat* uvula (**c**) *Bot* bell flower

campante *adj Fam* **se quedó tan c.** he didn't bat an eyelid

campaña *nf* (**a**) campaign; **c. electoral** election campaign; **c. publicitaria** advertising campaign (**b**) *Mil* campaign; **hospital/ambulancia de c.** field hospital/ambulance (**c**) *RP (campo)* countryside

campar *vi Fam* **c. por sus respetos** to do as one pleases

campechano,-a *adj* unpretentious

campeón,-ona *nm,f* champion; **c. mundial** world champion

campeonato *nm* championship; **un tonto de c.** an utter idiot

campera *nf* (**a**) **camperas** *(botas)* cowboy boots (**b**) *RP (chaqueta)* jacket

campero,-a *adj* country, rural; **(botas) camperas** leather boots
campesino,-a *nm,f (hombre)* countryman; *(mujer)* countrywoman
campestre *adj* rural
camping *nm* campsite; **hacer o ir de c.** to go camping
campiña *nf* open country
campista *nmf* camper
campo *nm* (**a**) country, countryside; **a c. traviesa o través** cross-country; **trabaja (en) el c.** he works (on) the land; **trabajo de c.** fieldwork (**b**) *(parcela)* field (**c**) *Fís & Fot* field (**d**) *(ámbito)* field; **c. de acción** field of action; *Mil* **c. de batalla** battlefield; **c. de concentración** concentration camp; **c. de trabajo** work camp (**e**) *Dep* field; *(de fútbol)* pitch; *(de golf)* course (**f**) *RP (hacienda)* farm (**g**) *Andes (sitio)* room, space
camposanto *nm* cemetery
camuflaje *nm* camouflage
camuflar *vt* to camouflage
cana *nf (gris)* grey hair; *(blanco)* white hair; **tener canas** to have grey hair; *Fam* **echar una c. al aire** to let one's hair down
Canadá *n* Canada
canadiense *adj & nmf* Canadian
canal *nf* (**a**) *(artificial)* canal; *(natural)* channel; **C. de la Mancha** English Channel (**b**) *TV, Elec & Informát* channel
canalizar [40] *vt* to channel
canalla 1 *nm* swine, rotter
2 *nf* riffraff, mob
canallesco,-a *adj* rotten, despicable
canalón *nm* gutter
canapé *nm* (**a**) *Culin* canapé (**b**) *(sofá)* couch, sofa
canario,-a 1 *adj & nm,f* Canarian; **Islas Canarias** Canary Islands, Canaries
2 *nm Orn* canary
canasta *nf* basket
canastilla *nf* small basket; *(de un bebé)* layette
canasto *nm* big basket, hamper
cancán *nm* frilly petticoat; *RP* **cancanes** *(leotardos) Br* tights, *US* pantyhose
cancela *nf* wrought-iron gate
cancelación *nf* cancellation
cancelar *vt* (**a**) *(acto etc)* to cancel (**b**) *(deuda)* to pay off (**c**) *Chile, Ven (compra)* to pay for
cáncer *nm* cancer; **c. de pulmón/mama** lung/breast cancer
cancerbero,-a *nm,f Ftb* goalkeeper
cancerígeno,-a *adj* carcinogenic
canceroso,-a *adj* cancerous
cancha *nf* ground; *Ten* court

canchero,-a *adj RP Fam (desenvuelto)* streetwise, savvy
canciller *nm* chancellor
cancillería *nf Am* foreign ministry
canción *nf* song
candado *nm* padlock
candela *nf* fire
candelabro *nm* candelabrum
candelero *nm* candlestick; *Fig* **en el c.** at the top
candente *adj* red-hot; *Fig* **tema c.** topical issue
candidato,-a *nm,f* candidate; *(a un puesto)* applicant
candidatura *nf* (**a**) *(lista)* list of candidates (**b**) **presentar su c.** to submit one's application
candidez *nf* candour
cándido,-a *adj* ingenuous, naive

> ⚠ Observa que la palabra inglesa **candid** es un falso amigo y no es la traducción de la palabra española **cándido**. En inglés, **candid** significa "franco, sincero".

candil *nm* oil lamp; *Méx (candelabro)* chandelier
candilejas *nfpl Teatro* footlights
candor *nm* innocence, naivety

> ⚠ Observa que la palabra inglesa **candour** es un falso amigo y no es la traducción de la palabra española **candor**. En inglés, **candour** significa "sinceridad, franqueza".

candoroso,-a *adj* innocent, pure
canela *nf* cinnamon
canelones *nmpl* cannelloni
cangrejo *nm (de mar)* crab; *(de río)* freshwater crayfish
canguro 1 *nm* kangaroo
2 *nmf Fam* baby-sitter
caníbal *adj & nmf* cannibal
canica *nf* marble
caniche *nm* poodle
canícula *nf* dog days, midsummer heat
canijo,-a *adj Fam* puny, weak
canilla *nf* (**a**) *Fam (espinilla)* shinbone (**b**) *RP (grifo) Br* tap, *US* faucet
canillera *nf Am (cobardía)* cowardice; *(miedo)* fear
canillita *nm Andes, RP* newspaper vendor
canino,-a 1 *adj* canine; *Fam* **tener un hambre canina** to be starving
2 *nm (colmillo)* canine
canjear *vt* to exchange
cano,-a *adj (blanco)* white; *(gris)* grey
canoa *nf* canoe
canódromo *nm* dog *o* greyhound track

canon *nm* (**a**) canon, norm (**b**) *Mús & Rel* canon (**c**) *Com* royalty
canónigo *nm* canon
canonizar [40] *vt* to canonize
canoso,-a *adj* (*de pelo blanco*) white-haired; (*de pelo gris*) grey-haired; (*pelo*) white, grey
cansado,-a *adj* (**a**) (*agotado*) tired, weary; **estar c.** to be tired (**b**) **ser c.** (*pesado*) to be boring o tiresome
cansador,-a *adj Andes, RP* (*que cansa*) tiring; (*que aburre*) boring
cansancio *nm* tiredness, weariness; *Fam* **estoy muerto de c.** I'm on my last legs
cansar 1 *vt* to tire
   2 *vi* to be tiring
   3 cansarse *vpr* to get tired; **se cansó de esperar** he got fed up (with) waiting
Cantabria *n* Cantabria
cantábrico,-a *adj* Cantabrian; **Mar C.** Bay of Biscay
cántabro,-a *adj & nm,f* Cantabrian
cantaleta *nf Am* **la misma c.** the same old story
cantante 1 *nmf* singer
   2 *adj* singing; **llevar la voz c.** to rule the roost
cantaor,-a *nm,f* flamenco singer
cantar¹ *vt & vi* (**a**) *Mús* to sing; *Fig* **en menos que canta un gallo** in a flash (**b**) *Fam* (*confesar*) to sing, to spill the beans (**c**) *Fam* (*oler mal*) to hum
cantar² *nm Literario* song; *Fam* **¡eso es otro c.!** that's a totally different thing!
cantarín,-ina *adj* (*voz*) singsong
cántaro *nm* pitcher; *Fig* **llover a cántaros** to rain cats and dogs
cante *nm* (**a**) (*canto*) singing; **c. hondo, c. jondo** flamenco (**b**) *Fam* **dar el c.** to attract attention
cantegril *nm Urug* shanty town
cantera *nf* (**a**) (*de piedra*) quarry (**b**) *Fig Ftb* young players
cantero *nm* (**a**) (*masón*) stonemason (**b**) *Cuba, RP* (*parterre*) flowerbed
cantidad 1 *nf* quantity; (*de dinero*) amount, sum; **en c.** a lot; *Fam* **c. de gente** thousands of people
   2 *adv Fam* a lot; **me gusta c.** I love it
cantimplora *nf* water bottle
cantina *nf* canteen
cantinero,-a *nm,f* bar attendant
canto¹ *nm* (**a**) (*arte*) singing (**b**) (*canción*) song
canto² *nm* (*borde*) edge; **de c.** on its side
canto³ *nm* (*guijarro*) pebble, stone; **c. rodado** (*grande*) boulder; (*pequeño*) pebble

cantor,-a 1 *adj* singing; **pájaro c.** songbird
   2 *nm,f* singer
canturrear *vi* to hum, to croon
canutas *nfpl Fam* **pasarlas c.** to have a hard time
canuto *nm* (**a**) (*tubo*) tube (**b**) *Fam* (*porro*) joint
caña *nf* (**a**) (*vaso*) glass; (*de cerveza*) glass of beer (**b**) *Bot* reed; (*tallo*) cane, stem; **c. de azúcar** sugar cane (**c**) (*de pescar*) rod (**d**) *Fam* **darle c. al coche** to go at full speed (**e**) *Andes, Cuba, RP* (*aguardiente*) cane spirit, cheap rum
cañada *nf* gully, ravine
cáñamo *nm* hemp
cañería *nf* (piece of) piping; **cañerías** plumbing
cañero,-a *nm,f Am* (*trabajador*) = worker on sugar plantation
cañí *adj & nmf* (*pl* **cañís**) *Fam* gypsy
caño *nm* (*tubo*) tube; (*tubería*) pipe
cañón *nm* (**a**) cannon; *Fig* **estar siempre al pie del c.** to be always ready for a fight (**b**) (*de fusil*) barrel (**c**) *Geog* canyon
cañonazo *nm* gunshot
caoba *nf* mahogany
caos *nm* chaos
caótico,-a *adj* chaotic
cap. (*abr* **capítulo**) ch
capa *nf* (**a**) (*prenda*) cloak, cape; **de c. caída** low-spirited (**b**) (*de pintura*) layer, coat; *Culin* coating (**c**) *Geol* stratum, layer
capacidad *nf* (**a**) (*cabida*) capacity (**b**) (*aptitud*) capacity, ability
capacitación *nf* qualification
capacitar *vt* (*autorizar*) to authorize
capar *vt* to castrate
caparazón *nm* shell
capataz,-a *nm,f* (*hombre*) foreman; (*mujer*) forewoman
capaz *adj* (**a**) capable, able; **ser c. de hacer algo** (*tener la habilidad de*) to be able to do sth; (*atreverse a*) to dare to do sth; **si se entera es c. de despedirle** if he finds out, he could quite easily sack him (**b**) *Am* **es c. que** it is likely that
capcioso,-a *adj* captious; **pregunta capciosa** catch question
capea *nf* amateur bullfight
capear *vt* (*dificultad etc*) to dodge, to shirk; *Fig* **c. el temporal** to weather the storm
capellán *nm* chaplain
caperuza *nf* hood
capicúa *adj* **número c.** reversible number; **palabra c.** palindrome

capilar *adj* hair; **loción c.** hair lotion
capilla *nf* chapel; **c. ardiente** chapel of rest
capirote *nm Fam* **tonto de c.** silly idiot
capital 1 *nf* capital
   2 *nm Fin* capital; **c. activo** *o* **social** working *o* share capital
   3 *adj* capital, main; **de importancia c.** of capital importance; **pena c.** capital punishment
capitalismo *nm* capitalism
capitalista *adj & nmf* capitalist
capitalizar [40] *vt* to capitalize
capitán,-ana *nm,f* captain; **c. general** *Br* field marshal, *US* general of the army
capitanear *vt* (**a**) *Mil & Náut* to captain, to command (**b**) *(dirigir)* to lead; *Dep* to captain
capitulación *nf* agreement; *Mil* capitulation; **capitulaciones matrimoniales** marriage settlement
capitular *vi* (**a**) *Mil* to capitulate, to surrender (**b**) *(convenir)* to reach an agreement
capítulo *nm* (**a**) *(de libro)* chapter (**b**) *Fig* **dentro del c. de ...** *(tema)* under the heading of ...
capó *nm Aut Br* bonnet, *US* hood
capón *nm* rap on the head with the knuckles
capota *nf Aut* folding hood *o* top
capote *nm* (**a**)*Taurom* cape (**b**) *Mil* greatcoat
capricho *nm* (**a**) *(antojo)* whim, caprice (**b**) *Mús* caprice, capriccio
caprichoso,-a *adj* whimsical
Capricornio *nm* Capricorn
cápsula *nf* capsule
captar *vt* (**a**) *(ondas)* to receive, to pick up (**b**) *(comprender)* to understand, to grasp (**c**) *(interés etc)* to attract
captura *nf* capture
capturar *vt* *(criminal)* to capture; *(cazar, pescar)* to catch; *Mil* to seize
capucha *nf* hood
capuchino *nm (café)* cappuccino
capullo *nm* (**a**) *(de insecto)* cocoon (**b**) *Bot* bud (**c**) *Vulg (prepucio)* foreskin (**d**) *muy Fam (persona despreciable) Br* dickhead, *US* jerk
caqui 1 *adj (color)* khaki
   2 *nm (fruto)* persimmon
cara 1 *nf* (**a**) face; **c. a c.** face to face; **c. a la pared** facing the wall; **poner mala c.** to pull a long face; **tener buena/mala c.** to look good/bad; *Fig* **c. de circunstancias** serious look; *Fig* **dar la c.** to face the consequences (of one's acts); *Fig* **dar la**

c. por algn to stand up for sb; *Fig* **(de) c. a** with a view to; *Fig* **echarle a algn algo en c.** to reproach sb for sth; *Fig* **plantar c. a algn** to face up to sb
   (**b**) *(lado)* side; *(de moneda)* right side; **¿c. o cruz?** heads or tails?; **echar algo a c. o cruz** to toss (a coin) for sth
   (**c**) *Fam (desfachatez)* cheek, nerve; **¡qué c. (más dura) tienes!** what a cheek you've got!
   2 *nm Fam (desvergonzado)* cheeky person
carabela *nf* caravel
carabina *nf* (**a**) *(arma)* carbine, rifle (**b**) *(persona)* chaperon
carabinero *nm* (**a**) *(marisco)* scarlet shrimp, = type of large red prawn (**b**) *Chile (policía)* military policeman
caracense 1 *adj* of/from Guadalajara
   2 *nmf* person from Guadalajara
caracol 1 *nm* (**a**) *(de tierra)* snail; *Am* shell (**b**) *(rizo)* kiss-curl
   2 *interj* **¡caracoles!** good heavens!
caracola *nf* conch
carácter *nm* (*pl* **caracteres**) (**a**) *(temperamento)* character; **de mucho c.** with a strong character; **tener buen/mal c.** to be good-natured/bad-tempered (**b**) *Fig (índole)* nature; **con c. de invitado** as a guest (**c**) *Impr* character
característica *nf* characteristic
característico,-a *adj* characteristic
caracterizar [40] *vt* to characterize
caradura *nmf Fam* cheeky devil; **¡qué c. eres!** you're so cheeky!
carajillo *nm Fam* = coffee with a dash of brandy
carajo *interj Vulg* shit!; **¡vete al c.!** go to hell!
caramba *interj Fam (sorpresa)* good grief!; *(enfado)* damn it!
carámbano *nm* icicle
carambola *nf Br* cannon, *US* carom
caramelo *nm* (**a**) *(dulce) Br* (boiled) sweet, *US* candy (**b**) *(azúcar quemado)* caramel; *Culin* **a punto de c.** syrupy
carantoña *nf* caress
caraota *nf Ven* bean
caraqueño,-a 1 *adj* of/from Caracas
   2 *nm,f* person from Caracas
carátula *nf* (**a**) *(cubierta)* cover (**b**) *(máscara)* mask
caravana *nf* (**a**) *(vehículo)* caravan (**b**) *(de tráfico) Br* tailback, *US* backup (**c**) *Urug (aro, pendiente)* earring
caray *interj* God!, good heavens!
carbón *nm* coal; **c. vegetal** charcoal; **c. mineral** coal

carboncillo *nm* charcoal

carbonero *nm* coal merchant

carbónico,-a *adj* carbonic; **agua carbónica** mineral water

carbonilla *nf* coal dust

carbonizar [40] 1 *vt* to carbonize, to char; **morir carbonizado** to be burnt to death

2 carbonizarse *upr* to carbonize, to char

carbono *nm* carbon

carburador *nm* carburettor

carburante *nm* fuel

carburar *vi Fam (funcionar)* to work properly

carca *adj & nmf Fam* old fogey; *Pol* reactionary

carcaj *nm* quiver

carcajada *nf* guffaw

carcamal *nm Fam* old fogey

cárcel *nf* prison, jail

carcelario,-a *adj* prison, jail

carcelero,-a *nm,f* jailer, warder

carcoma *nf* woodworm

carcomer 1 *vt* to eat away

2 carcomerse *upr* to be consumed (**de** with)

cardar *vt* (**a**) *(lana, algodón)* to card (**b**) *(pelo)* to backcomb

cardenal *nm* (**a**) *Rel* cardinal (**b**) *Med* bruise

cárdeno,-a *adj* purple

cardiaco,-a, cardíaco,-a 1 *adj* cardiac, heart; **ataque c.** heart attack

2 *nm,f* person with a heart condition

cardinal *adj* cardinal; **punto/número c.** cardinal point/number

cardiólogo,-a *nm,f* cardiologist

cardo *nm (con espinas)* thistle

carear *vt* (**a**)*Jur* to bring two people face to face (**b**) *(cotejar)* to compare

carecer [33] *vi* **c. de** to lack

carencia *nf* lack (**de** of)

carente *adj* lacking; **c. de interés** lacking interest

careo *nm Jur* confrontation

carestía *nf* (**a**) *(falta)* lack, shortage (**b**) *Fin* high price o cost

careta *nf* mask; **c. antigás** gas mask

carey *nm* tortoiseshell

carezco *indic pres de* **carecer**

carga *nf* (**a**) *(acción)* loading (**b**) *(cosa cargada)* load; *(de avión, barco)* cargo, freight; *Fig* **c. afectiva** emotional content (**c**) *Fin (gasto)* debit; **c. fiscal** tax charge (**d**) *Fig (obligación)* burden (**e**) *Mil & Elec* charge

cargado,-a *adj* (**a**) loaded (**b**) *(bebida)* strong; **un café c.** a strong coffee (**c**)

(ambiente) heavy; **atmósfera cargada** stuffy atmosphere (**d**) *Fig* burdened; **c. de deudas** up to one's eyes in debt (**e**) *Elec* charged

cargamento *nm* (**a**) *(carga)* load (**b**) *(mercancías)* cargo, freight

cargante *adj Fam* annoying

cargar [42] 1 *vt* (**a**) to load; *(mechero, pluma)* to fill; *(batería)* to charge; *Fig* **c. las culpas a algn** to put the blame on sb (**b**) *Com* to charge; **cárguelo a mi cuenta** charge it to my account; *Fam Educ* **me han cargado las matemáticas** I failed maths

2 *vi* (**a**) **c. con** *(llevar)* to carry; *Fig* **c. con la responsabilidad** to take the responsibility; *Fig* **c. con las consecuencias** to suffer the consequences (**b**) *Mil* **c. contra** to charge

3 cargarse *upr* (**a**) *Fam* **te la vas a c.** you're asking for trouble and you're going to get it (**b**) *Fam (estropear)* to smash, to ruin (**c**) *Fam (matar)* to kill, to bump off

cargo *nm* (**a**) *(puesto)* post, position; **alto c.** *(puesto)* top job, high ranking position; *(persona)* top person (**b**) **estar al c. de** to be in charge of; **correr a c. de** *(gastos)* to be met by; **hacerse c. de** to take charge of; **hazte c. de mi situación** please try to understand my situation; **c. de conciencia** weight on one's conscience (**c**) *Fin* charge, debit; **con c. a mi cuenta** charged to my account (**d**) *Jur* charge, accusation

cargosear *vt CSur* to annoy, to pester

cargoso,-a *adj CSur* annoying

carguero *nm* (**a**) *(avión)* transport plane (**b**) *(barco)* freighter

cariarse *upr* to decay

caribe *nm (idioma)* Carib; **el (mar) C.** the Caribbean Sea

caricatura *nf* caricature

caricaturizar [40] *vt* to caricature

caricia *nf* caress, stroke

caridad *nf* charity

caries *nf inv* decay, caries

carilla *nf* page, side of a piece of paper

cariño *nm* (**a**) *(amor)* affection; **coger/ tener c. a algo/algn** to grow/to be fond of sth/sb; **con c.** *(en carta)* love (**b**) *(querido)* darling (**c**) *(abrazo)* cuddle

cariñoso,-a *adj* loving, affectionate

carisma *nm* charisma

carismático,-a *adj* charismatic

caritativo,-a *adj* charitable

cariz *nm* look

carmesí *adj & nm* crimson

carmín *nm* (**de color**) **c.** carmine; **c. (de labios)** lipstick

carnal *adj* (**a**) *(de carne)* carnal (**b**) *(pariente)* first; **primo c.** first cousin
carnaval *nm* carnival
carne *nf* (**a**) flesh; *Fam* **ser de c. y hueso** to be only human; *Fig* **c. de cañón** cannon fodder; **c. de gallina** goosepimples; **c. viva** raw flesh (**b**) *(alimento)* meat; **c. de cerdo/cordero/ternera/vaca** pork/lamb/veal/beef (**c**) *(de fruta)* pulp
carné *nm* card; **c. de conducir** *Br* driving licence, *US* driver's license; **c. de identidad** identity card
carnear *vt Andes, RP (sacrificar)* to slaughter, to butcher
carnero *nm* ram; *Culin* mutton
carnet *nm* = **carné**
carnicería *nf* (**a**) butcher's (shop) (**b**) *Fig (masacre)* slaughter
carnicero,-a *nm,f* butcher
cárnico,-a *adj* **productos cárnicos** meat products
carnitas *nfpl Méx* = small pieces of fried or grilled pork
carnívoro,-a 1 *adj* carnivorous
   2 *nm,f* carnivore
carnoso,-a *adj* fleshy
caro,-a 1 *adj* expensive, dear
   2 *adv* **salir c.** to cost a lot; **te costará c.** *(amenaza)* you'll pay dearly for this
carozo *nm RP (de fruta, aceituna)* stone, *US* pit
carpa *nf* (**a**) *(pez)* carp (**b**) *(de circo)* big top; *(en parque, la calle)* marquee (**c**) *Am (de camping)* tent
Cárpatos *nmpl* Carpathians
carpeta *nf* file, folder

> 📖 Observa que la palabra inglesa **carpet** es un falso amigo y no es la traducción de la palabra española **carpeta**. En inglés, **carpet** significa "alfombra".

carpetazo *nm* **dar c. a un asunto** to shelve a matter
carpintería *nf* (**a**) *(oficio)* carpentry; **c. metálica** metalwork (**b**) *(taller)* carpenter's (shop)
carpintero,-a *nm,f* carpenter
carraca *nf* rattle
carraspear *vi* to clear one's throat
carraspeo *nm* clearing of the throat
carraspera *nf* hoarseness
carrera *nf* (**a**) run; *(de media)* run, ladder; **a la c.** in a hurry (**b**) *(competición)* race; **c. contra reloj** race against the clock; **c. de coches** rally, meeting; **echar una c. a algn** to race sb; **c. de armamentos** arms race (**c**) *(estudios)* university course; **hacer la c. de derecho/físicas** to study law/

physics (at university) (**d**) *(profesión)* career, profession
carrerilla *nf* run; **tomar c.** to take a run; **de c.** parrot fashion
carreta *nf* cart
carrete *nm (de hilo)* reel; *(de película)* spool; *(de cable)* coil
carretera *nf* road; **c. de acceso** access road; *(en autopista)* slip road; **c. de circunvalación** *Br* ring road, *US* beltway; **c. comarcal** minor road; *Méx* **c. de cuota** toll road; **c. nacional** *Br* ≃ A road, *US* ≃ state highway
carretero,-a *adj Am* road; **un accidente c.** a road accident
carretilla *nf* wheelbarrow
carricoche *nm* caravan
carril *nm* (**a**) *Ferroc* rail (**b**) *Aut* lane
carrillo *nm* cheek; *Fam* **comer a dos carrillos** to devour, to gobble up
carriola *nf* (**a**) *(cama)* truckle bed (**b**) *Méx (coche de bebé)* *Br* pram, *US* baby carriage
carro *nm* (**a**) *(carreta)* cart; *RP Fam* **¡pará el c.!** hold your horses! (**b**) *Mil* **c. de combate** tank (**c**) *(de máquina de escribir)* carriage (**d**) *Andes, CAm, Carib, Méx* car (**e**) *Méx (vagón)* car; **c. comedor** dining car
carrocería *nf Aut* bodywork
carroña *nf* carrion
carroza 1 *nf* (**a**) *(coche de caballos)* coach, carriage (**b**) *(de carnaval)* float
   2 *nmf Fam* old fogey
carruaje *nm* carriage, coach
carrusel *nm Andes* roundabout, merry-go-round
carta *nf* (**a**) letter; **c. certificada/urgente** registered/express letter (**b**) *(menú)* menu; **a la c.** à la carte; **c. de vinos** wine list (**c**) *Naipes* card; **echar las cartas a algn** to tell sb's fortune; *Fig* **poner las cartas sobre la mesa** to put *o* lay one's cards on the table, to come clean (**d**) *Geog (mapa)* chart (**e**) *Fig* **adquirir c. de naturaleza** to become widely accepted; **tomar cartas en un asunto** to take part in an affair
cartabón *nm* set square
cartearse *vpr* to correspond (**con** with), to exchange letters (**con** with)
cartel *nm* poster; **pegar/fijar carteles** to put *o* stick up bills
cartél *nm Com* cartel
cartelera *nf* billboard, *Br* hoarding; *Prensa* **c. de espectáculos** entertainments section *o* page
cartera *nf* (**a**) *(de bolsillo)* wallet, *US*

billfold (**b**) *(de mano)* handbag; *(para documentos etc)* briefcase; *(de colegial)* satchel, schoolbag (**c**) *Pol (ministerio)* portfolio (**d**) *Com* portfolio; **c. de pedidos** order book

carterista *nm* pickpocket

cartero,-a *nm,f (hombre) Br* postman, *US* mailman; *(mujer) Br* postwoman, *US* mailwoman

cartilla *nf* (**a**) *(libreta)* book; **c. de ahorros** savings book (**b**) *(libro)* first reader; *Fam* **leerle la c. a algn** to tell sb off

cartografía *nf* cartography

cartón *nm* (**a**) *(material)* card, cardboard; **c. piedra** papier mâché (**b**) *(de cigarrillos)* carton

cartucho *nm* (**a**) *(de balas)* cartridge (**b**) *(de papel)* cone

cartulina *nf* card

casa *nf* (**a**) *(edificio)* house; **c. de huéspedes** boarding house; **c. de socorro** first-aid post (**b**) *(hogar)* home; **vete a c.** go home; **en c. de Daniel** at Daniel's; **de andar por c.** everyday (**c**) *(empresa)* company, firm; **c. matriz/principal** head/central office

casación *nf Jur* annulment

casadero,-a *adj* of marrying age

casado,-a **1** *adj* married
  2 *nm,f* married person; **los recién casados** the newlyweds

casamiento *nm* marriage; *(boda)* wedding

casar¹ **1** *vt* to marry
  2 *vi* to match, to go o fit together
  3 **casarse** *vpr* to marry, to get married; **c. por la iglesia/por lo civil** to get married in church/in a registry office

casar² *vt Jur* to annul, to quash

cascabel *nm* bell

cascada *nf* waterfall, cascade

cascanueces *nm inv* nutcracker

cascar [**44**] **1** *vt* (**a**) to crack (**b**) *Fam* **cascarla** to kick the bucket, to snuff it
  2 *vi Fam (charlar)* to chat away
  3 **cascarse** *vpr* to crack

cáscara *nf* shell; *(de fruta)* skin, peel; *(de grano)* husk

cascarón *nm* eggshell

cascarrabias *nmf inv Fam* short-tempered person

casco *nm* (**a**) *(para la cabeza)* helmet (**b**) *(de caballo)* hoof (**c**) *(envase)* empty bottle (**d**) **c. urbano** city centre (**e**) *(de barco)* hull (**f**) **cascos** *(auriculares)* headphones

cascote *nm* piece of rubble o debris

caserío *nm* country house

casero,-a **1** *adj* (**a**) *(hecho en casa)* homemade (**b**) *(persona)* home-loving
  2 *nm,f (dueño) (hombre)* landlord; *(mujer)* landlady

caseta *nf* hut, booth; *(de feria, exposición)* stand, stall; *Méx* **c. de cobro** tollbooth; *Méx* **c. telefónica** phone box, phone booth

casete **1** *nm (magnetófono)* cassette player o recorder
  2 *nf (cinta)* cassette (tape)

casi *adv* almost, nearly; **c. mil personas** almost one thousand people; **c. ni me acuerdo** I can hardly remember it; **c. nunca** hardly ever; **c. nadie** hardly anyone; **c. me caigo** I almost fell

casilla *nf* (**a**) *(de casillero)* pigeonhole; *Andes, RP* **c. de correos** PO Box; *CAm, Carib, Méx* **c. postal** PO Box (**b**) *(recuadro)* box (**c**) *Fig* **sacar a algn de sus casillas** to drive sb mad

casillero *nm* pigeonholes

casino *nm* casino

caso *nm* case; **el c. es que ...** the fact o thing is that ...; **el c. Mattei** the Mattei affair; **(en) c. contrario** otherwise; **en c. de necesidad** if need be; **en cualquier c.** in any case; **en el mejor/peor de los casos** at best/worst; **en ese c.** in such a case; **en todo c.** in any case; **en un c. extremo, en último c.** as a last resort; **hacer c. a o de algn** to pay attention to sb; **hacer c. omiso de** to take no notice of; **no venir al c.** to be beside the point; **pongamos por c.** let's say

caspa *nf* dandruff

casquete *nm* (**a**) *(de bala)* case, shell (**b**) *Geog* **c. polar** polar cap

> ⚠ Observa que la palabra inglesa **casket** es un falso amigo y no es la traducción de la palabra española **casquete**. En inglés, **casket** significa "cofre, ataúd".

casquillo *nm (de bala)* case

cassette *nm & nf* = **casete**

casta *nf* (**a**) *(linaje)* lineage, descent (**b**) *(animales)* breed; **de c.** thoroughbred, purebred (**c**) *(división social)* caste

castaña *nf* chestnut; *Fig* **sacarle a algn las castañas del fuego** to save sb's bacon

castañetear *vi (dientes)* to chatter

castaño,-a **1** *adj* chestnut-brown; *(pelo, ojos)* brown, dark
  2 *nm Bot* chestnut

castañuela *nf* castanet

castellano,-a **1** *adj* Castilian
  2 *nm,f (persona)* Castilian
  3 *nm (idioma)* Spanish, Castilian

castidad *nf* chastity
castigar [42] *vt* (**a**) to punish (**b**) *(dañar)* to harm, to ruin (**c**) *Jur & Dep* to penalize
castigo *nm* punishment; *Jur* penalty; *Dep* **área de c.** penalty area
Castilla *n* Castile
castillo *nm* castle
castizo,-a *adj* pure, authentic
casto,-a *adj* chaste
castor *nm* beaver
castrar *vt* to castrate
castrense *adj* military
casual 1 *adj* accidental, chance
  2 *nm Fam* chance
casualidad *nf* chance, coincidence; **de** *o* **por c.** by chance; **dio la c. que ...** it so happened that ...; **¿tienes un lápiz, por c.?** do you happen to have a pencil?; **¡que c.!** what a coincidence!

📖 Observa que la palabra inglesa **casualty** es un falso amigo y no es la traducción de la palabra española **casualidad**. En inglés, **casualty** significa "víctima".

---

casualmente *adv* by chance
cata *nf* tasting
cataclismo *nm* cataclysm
catador,-a *nm,f* taster
catalán,-ana 1 *adj & nm,f* Catalan
  2 *nm (idioma)* Catalan
catalejo *nm* telescope
catalepsia *nf* catalepsy
catalizador *nm* catalyst; *Aut* catalytic converter
catalizar [40] *vt Fig* to act as a catalyst for
catalogar [42] *vt* (**a**) to catalogue (**b**) *(clasificar)* to classify
catálogo *nm* catalogue
Cataluña *n* Catalonia
cataplasma *nf* (**a**) *Farm* cataplasm, poultice (**b**) *Fam (pelmazo)* bore
catapulta *nf* catapult; *Fig* springboard
catapultar *vt* to catapult
catar *vt* to taste
catarata *nf* (**a**) waterfall (**b**) *Med* cataract
catarro *nm* (common) cold
catastral *adj* **valor c.** rateable value
catastro *nm* land registry
catástrofe *nf* catastrophe
catastrófico,-a *adj* catastrophic
catear *vt* (**a**) *Fam (suspender)* to fail, *US* to flunk (**b**) *Am (casa)* to search
catecismo *nm* catechism
cátedra *nf* (professorial) chair; **le han dado la c.** they have appointed him professor
catedral *nf* cathedral

catedrático,-a *nm,f Educ* (**a**) *Univ* professor (**b**) *(de instituto)* head of department
categoría *nf* category; *Fig* class; **de c.** *(persona)* important; *(vino etc)* quality
categórico,-a *adj* categoric; **un no c.** a flat refusal
cateto,-a *nm,f Pey* yokel, bumpkin
catire,-a *adj Carib (rubio)* blond, blonde
catolicismo *nm* Catholicism
católico,-a *adj & nm,f* Catholic
catorce *adj & nm inv* fourteen
catre *nm Fam* bed
Cáucaso *n* Caucasus
cauce *nm* (**a**) *(de un río)* bed (**b**) *Fig (canal)* channel; **cauces oficiales** official channels
caucho *nm* (**a**) rubber (**b**) *Am (cubierta)* tyre
caudal *nm* (**a**) *(de un río)* flow (**b**) *(riqueza)* wealth, riches
caudaloso,-a *adj (río)* plentiful
caudillo *nm* leader, head
causa *nf* (**a**) cause; **a** *o* **por c. de** because of (**b**) *(ideal)* cause (**c**) *Jur (caso)* case; *(juicio)* trial
causante 1 *adj* causal, causing
  2 *nmf* **el c. del incendio** the person who caused the fire
causar *vt* to cause, to bring about; **me causa un gran placer** it gives me great pleasure; **c. buena/mala impresión** to make a good/bad impression
cáustico,-a *adj* caustic
cautela *nf* caution
cautivar *vt* (**a**) to capture, to take prisoner (**b**) *Fig (fascinar)* to captivate
cautiverio *nm,* **cautividad** *nf* captivity
cautivo,-a *adj & nm,f* captive
cauto,-a *adj* cautious, wary
cava 1 *nf (bodega)* wine cellar
  2 *nm (vino espumoso)* cava, champagne
cavar *vt* to dig
caverna *nf* cave; **hombre de las cavernas** caveman
cavernícola *nmf* cave dweller
caviar *nm* caviar
cavidad *nf* cavity
cavilar *vt* to ponder
cayado *nm* (**a**) *(de pastor)* crook (**b**) *(de obispo)* crosier, crozier
cayuco *nm Am* small flat-bottomed canoe
caza 1 *nf* (**a**) hunting; **ir de c.** to go hunting; **c. furtiva** poaching (**b**) *(animales)* game; **c. mayor/menor** big/small game (**c**) *Fig (persecución)* hunt; **c. de brujas** witch hunt

2 *nm Av* fighter, fighter plane

cazabe *nm Am* cassava bread

cazabombardero *nm Av* fighter bomber

cazador,-a *nm,f* hunter; **c. furtivo** poacher

cazadora *nf* (waist-length) jacket

cazar [40] *vt* to hunt; *Fam* **cazarlas al vuelo** to be quick on the uptake

cazatalentos *nmf inv* head-hunter

cazo *nm* (**a**) *(cacerola)* saucepan (**b**) *(cucharón)* ladle

cazuela *nf* saucepan; *(guiso)* casserole, stew; **a la c.** stewed

c/c *(abr* **cuenta corriente**) c/a

CC. OO. *nfpl (abr* **Comisiones Obreras**) = Spanish left-wing trade union

CD-ROM *nm* CD-ROM

cebada *nf* barley

cebar 1 *vt* (**a**) *(animal)* to fatten; *(persona)* to feed up (**b**) *(anzuelo)* to bait (**c**) *(fuego, caldera)* to stoke, to fuel; *(máquina, arma)* to prime (**d**) *RP (mate)* to prepare, to brew

2 cebarse *upr* **c. con** *(ensañarse)* to delight in tormenting

cebo *nm* bait

cebolla *nf* onion

cebolleta *nf* (**a**) *(especie)* chives (**b**) *(cebolla tierna)* spring onion

cebra *nf* zebra; **paso de c.** *Br* zebra crossing, *US* crosswalk

cecear *vi* to lisp

ceceo *nm* lisp

cedazo *nm* sieve

ceder 1 *vt* to give, to hand over; *Aut* **c. el paso** to give way

2 *vi* (**a**) *(cuerda, cable)* to give way (**b**) *(lluvia, calor)* to diminish, to slacken (**c**) *(consentir)* to give in

cederrón *nm* CD-ROM

cedro *nm* cedar

cédula *nf* (**a**) document, certificate; *Am* **c. de identidad** identity card (**b**) *Com & Fin* bond, certificate, warrant

C(E)E *nf (abr* **Comunidad (Económica) Europea**) E(E)C

cegador,-a *adj* blinding

cegar [1] *vt* (**a**) to blind (**b**) *(puerta, ventana)* to wall up

ceguera *nf* blindness

CEI *(abr* **Comunidad de Estados Independientes**) CIS

Ceilán *n* Ceylon

ceja *nf* eyebrow

cejar *vi* **c. en el empeño** to give up

celada *nf* trap, ambush

celador,-a *nm,f* attendant; *(de una cárcel)* warder

celda *nf* cell; **c. de castigo** punishment cell

celebración *nf* (**a**) *(festejo)* celebration (**b**) *(de juicio etc)* holding

celebrar 1 *vt* (**a**) to celebrate; **celebro que todo saliera bien** I'm glad everything went well (**b**) *(reunión, juicio, elecciones)* to hold (**c**) *(triunfo)* to laud

2 celebrarse *vpr* to take place, to be held

célebre *adj* famous, well-known

celebridad *nf* (**a**) celebrity, fame (**b**) *(persona)* celebrity

celeste 1 *adj* (**a**) *(de cielo)* celestial (**b**) *(color)* sky-blue

2 *nm* sky blue

celestial *adj* celestial, heavenly

celibato *nm* celibacy

célibe *adj & nmf* celibate

celo *nm* (**a**) zeal (**b**) **en c.** *(macho)* in rut; *(hembra)* on o in heat (**c**) **celos** jealousy; **tener celos (de algn)** to be jealous (of sb)

celo® *nm Fam Br* Sellotape®, *US* Scotch tape®

celofán *nm* cellophane®

celosía *nf* lattice

celoso,-a *adj* (**a**) jealous (**b**) *(cumplidor)* conscientious

celta 1 *adj* Celtic

2 *nmf* Celt

3 *nm (idioma)* Celtic

célula *nf* cell

celular 1 *adj* (**a**) cellular (**b**) **coche c.** police van (**c**) *Am* **teléfono c.** mobile phone, cellphone

2 *nm Am* mobile, cellphone

celulitis *nf inv* cellulitis

celuloide *nm* celluloid

celulosa *nf* cellulose

cementerio *nm* cemetery, graveyard; **c. de coches** scrapyard

cemento *nm* cement; **c. armado** reinforced cement

cena *nf* evening meal; *(antes de acostarse)* supper; **la Ultima C.** the Last Supper

cenagal *nm* marsh, swamp

cenar 1 *vi* to have supper o dinner

2 *vt* to have for supper o dinner

cencerro *nm* cowbell

cenefa *nf (de ropa)* edging, trimming; *(de suelo, techo)* ornamental border, frieze

cenetista 1 *adj* = of or related to the CNT (Confederación Nacional del Trabajo)

2 *nmf* member of the CNT

cenicero *nm* ashtray

cenit *nm* zenith

ceniza *nf* ash

cenizo *nm Fam (gafe)* jinx

censo *nm* census; **c. electoral** electoral roll

censor *nm* censor

censura *nf* (**a**) censorship (**b**) *Pol* **moción de c.** vote of no confidence

censurar *vt* (**a**) *(libro, película)* to censor (**b**) *(criticar)* to censure, to criticize

centavo *nm Am Fin* cent, centavo

centella *nf* spark

centellear *vi* to flash, to sparkle

centelleo *nm* flashing, sparkling

centena *nf,* **centenar** *nm* hundred; **a centenares** in hundreds

centenario *nm* centenary, hundredth anniversary

centeno *nm* rye

centésimo,-a *adj & nm,f* hundredth

centígrado,-a *adj* centigrade

centilitro *nm* centilitre

centímetro *nm* centimetre

céntimo *nm* cent

centinela *nm* sentry

centollo *nm* spider crab

centrado,-a *adj* (**a**) centred (**b**) *(equilibrado)* balanced

central 1 *adj* central
   2 *nf* (**a**) *Elec* **c. nuclear/térmica** nuclear/coal-fired power station (**b**) *(oficina principal)* head office

centralismo *nm* centralism

centralita *nf Tel* switchboard

centralizar [40] *vt* to centralize

centrar 1 *vt* (**a**) to centre (**b**) *(esfuerzos, atención)* to concentrate, to centre (**en** on)
   2 centrarse *vpr* (**a**) to be centred *o* based (**b**) **c. en** *(concentrarse)* to concentrate on

céntrico,-a *adj* centrally situated; **zona céntrica** centrally situated area

centrifugar [42] *vt* to centrifuge; *(ropa)* to spin-dry

centrista *Pol* **1** *adj* centre; **partido c.** centre party
   2 *nmf* centrist

centro *nm* (**a**) middle, centre; **c. de la ciudad** town *o* city centre (**b**) *(establecimiento)* institution, centre; **c. comercial** shopping centre

Centroamérica *n* Central America

centroamericano,-a *adj & nm,f* Central American

centrocampista *nmf Ftb* midfielder

centuria *nf* century

ceñido,-a *adj* tight-fitting, clinging

ceñirse [6] *vpr* (**a**) *(atenerse, limitarse)* to limit oneself, to stick (**a** to); **c. al tema** to keep to the subject; **ciñéndonos a este caso en concreto** coming down to this particular case (**b**) **c. a** *(prenda)* to cling to

ceño *nm* scowl, frown; **con el c. fruncido** frowning

CEOE *nf (abr* **Confederación Española de Organizaciones Empresariales)** = Spanish employers' organization, ≃ CBI

cepa *nf* (**a**) *(de vid)* vine (**b**) *Fig* **vasco de pura c.** *(origen)* Basque through and through

cepillar 1 *vt* (**a**) to brush (**b**) *(en carpintería)* to plane (down) (**c**) *Fam (robar)* to pinch
   2 cepillarse *vpr* (**a**) *(con cepillo)* to brush (**b**) *Fam (matar)* to do in (**c**) *muy Fam* to lay

cepillo *nm* brush; *(en carpintería)* plane; **c. de dientes** toothbrush; **c. del pelo** hairbrush

cepo *nm* (**a**) *(para cazar)* trap (**b**) *Aut* clamp

CEPYME *nf (abr* **Confederación Española de la Pequeña y Mediana Empresa)** = Spanish confederation of small and medium-sized businesses

cera *nf* wax; *(de abeja)* beeswax

cerámica *nf* ceramics *sing*

cerca¹ *adv* (**a**) near, close; **ven más c.** come closer; **ya estamos c.** we are almost there (**b**) **c. de** *(al lado de)* near, close to; **el colegio está c. de mi casa** the school is near my house (**c**) **c. de** *(casi)* nearly, around; **c. de cien personas** about one hundred people (**d**) **de c.** closely; **lo vi muy de c.** I saw it close up

cerca² *nf* fence, wall

cercado *nm* (**a**) *(lugar cerrado)* enclosure (**b**) *(valla)* fence, wall

cercanía *nf* (**a**) proximity, nearness (**b**) **cercanías** outskirts, suburbs; **(tren de) cercanías** suburban train

cercano,-a *adj* nearby; **el C. Oriente** the Near East

cercar [44] *vt* (**a**) *(tapiar)* to fence, to enclose (**b**) *(rodear)* to surround

cercenar *vt* to cut off, to amputate

cerciorar 1 *vt* to assure
   2 cerciorarse *vpr* to make sure

cerco *nm* (**a**) circle, ring (**b**) *Mil (sitio)* siege; **poner c. (a una ciudad)** to besiege (a town)

cerda *nf* (**a**) *Zool* sow (**b**) *(pelo)* bristle; **cepillo de c.** bristle brush

Cerdeña *n* Sardinia

cerdo *nm* (**a**) pig (**b**) *(carne)* pork (**c**) *Fam* pig, arsehole

cereal *nm* cereal

cerebral *adj* (**a**) cerebral (**b**) *(frío)* calculating

cerebro *nm* brain; *Fig (inteligencia)* brains

ceremonia nf ceremony

ceremonioso,-a adj ceremonious, formal; Pey pompous, stiff

cereza nf cherry

cerezo nm cherry tree

cerilla nf match

cerillo nm CAm, Méx match

cernerse [3] vpr Fig to loom (**sobre** above)

cernícalo nm kestrel

cernirse [54] vpr = cernerse

cero nm zero; Dep nil; Fig **partir de c.** to start from scratch; Fig **ser un c. a la izquierda** to be useless o a good-for-nothing

cerquillo nm Am Br fringe, US bangs

cerrado,-a adj (**a**) closed, shut; **a puerta cerrada** behind closed doors (**b**) (reservado) reserved; (intransigente) uncompromising, unyielding; Fam (torpe) thick; (acento) broad; (curva) tight, sharp (**c**) (barba) bushy

cerradura nf lock

cerrajero,-a nm,f locksmith

cerrar [1] 1 vt to shut, to close; (grifo, gas) to turn off; (luz) to turn off, to switch off; (cremallera) to do up; (negocio) to close down; (cuenta) to close; (carta) to seal; (puños) to clench; **c. con llave** to lock; **c. el paso a algn** to block sb's way; Fam **c. el pico** to shut one's trap

2 vi to close, to shut

3 **cerrarse** vpr to close, to shut; Fam **c. en banda** to stick to one's guns

cerro nm hill; Fig **irse por los cerros de Ubeda** to beat around the bush

cerrojo nm bolt; **echar el c. (de una puerta)** to bolt (a door)

certamen nm competition, contest

certero,-a adj accurate

certeza, certidumbre nf certainty; **saber (algo) con c.** to be certain (of sth); **tener la c. de que ...** to be sure o certain that ...

certificado,-a 1 adj (**a**) certified (**b**) (correo) registered

2 nm certificate

certificar [44] vt (**a**) to certify (**b**) (carta) to register

cervatillo nm fawn

cervecería nf (**a**) (bar) pub, bar (**b**) (fábrica) brewery

cerveza nf beer; **c. de barril** draught beer; **c. dorada** o **ligera** lager; **c. negra** stout

cervical adj cervical

cesante adj (destituido) dismissed, Br sacked; CSur, Méx (parado) unemployed

cesantear vt CSur to make redundant

cesar 1 vi **c. (de)** to stop, to cease; **sin c.** incessantly

2 vt (empleado) to dismiss, Br to sack

cesárea nf Caesarean (section)

cese nm (**a**) cessation, suspension (**b**) (despido) dismissal

Cesid nm (abr **Centro Superior de Investigación de la Defensa**) = Spanish military intelligence and espionage service

césped nm lawn, grass

cesta nf basket; **c. de Navidad** Christmas hamper

cesto nm basket

cetáceo nm cetacean, whale

cetrino,-a adj sallow

cetro nm sceptre

Ceuta n Ceuta

ceutí 1 adj of/from Ceuta

2 nmf person from Ceuta

ceviche nm = raw fish marinated in lemon and garlic

chabacano,-a 1 adj cheap

2 nm Méx (fruto) apricot; (árbol) apricot tree

chabola nf shack; **barrio de chabolas** shanty town

chacal nm jackal

chacarero,-a nm,f Andes, RP farmer

chacha nf maid

cháchara nf Fam small talk, chinwag; **estar de c.** to have a yap

chachi adj smashing

chacinados nmpl RP pork products

chacinería nf pork butcher's (shop)

chacra nf Andes, RP farm

chafar vt (**a**) Fam (plan etc) to ruin, to spoil (**b**) (aplastar) to squash, to flatten

chal nm shawl

chalado,-a adj Fam crazy, nuts (**por** about)

chalé nm (pl **chalés**) = chalet

chaleco nm Br waistcoat, US vest; (de punto) sleeveless pullover; **c. antibalas** bullet-proof vest; **c. salvavidas** life jacket

chalet nm villa

chalupa nf (**a**) (embarcación) boat, launch (**b**) Méx (torta) = small tortilla with a raised rim to contain a filling

chamaco,-a nm,f Méx Fam kid

chamarra nf sheepskin jacket

chamba nf CAm, Méx, Perú, Ven Fam (trabajo) job

chambelán nm chamberlain

chambergo nm heavy coat

chambón,-ona nm,f Am Fam sloppy o shoddy worker

chamizo nm thatched hut

champa nf CAm (tienda de campaña) tent

champán, champaña *nm o nf* champagne

champiñón *nm* mushroom

champú *nm* shampoo

chamuscar [44] *vt* to singe, to scorch

chamusquina *nf* singeing, scorching; *Fam* **esto me huele a c.** there's something fishy going on here

chancaca *nf CAm (torta)* syrup cake

chance 1 *nm Am* opportunity
  2 *adv Méx* maybe

chancear *vi Am* to joke, to horse around

chanchada *nf Am* (**a**) *(porquería)* **no hagas chanchadas** stop that, don't be disgusting! (**b**) *Fam (jugarreta)* dirty trick

chancho,-a *nm,f Am* pig, hog, *f* sow

chanchullo *nm Fam* fiddle, wangle

chancla *nf Br* flip-flop, *US* thong

chanclo *nm (zueco)* clog; *(de goma)* overshoe, galosh

chándal *nm* track *o* jogging suit

changa *nf Bol, RP (trabajo temporal)* odd job

changador *nm RP (cargador)* porter

changarro *nm Méx* small shop

chantaje *nm* blackmail; **hacer c. a algn** to blackmail sb

chantajear *vt* to blackmail

chantajista *nmf* blackmailer

chanza *nf* joke

chapa *nf* (**a**) *(de metal)* sheet (**b**) *(de madera)* panel-board (**c**) *(tapón)* bottle top, cap (**d**) *(de adorno)* badge (**e**) *RP Br* number plate, *US* license plate (**f**) *Col (cerradura)* lock

chapado,-a *adj (metal)* plated; **c. en oro** gold-plated; *Fig* **c. a la antigua** old-fashioned

chaparro *nm Bot* holm oak

chaparrón *nm* downpour, heavy shower

chapopote *nm Carib, Méx* bitumen, pitch

chapotear *vi* to splash about, to paddle

chapucero,-a *adj (trabajo)* slapdash, shoddy; *(persona)* bungling

chapulín *nm CAm, Méx (saltamontes)* grasshopper

chapurrear *vt* to speak badly *o* with difficulty; **sólo chapurreaba el francés** he spoke only a few words of French

chapuza *nf* (**a**) *(trabajo mal hecho)* shoddy piece of work (**b**) *(trabajo ocasional)* odd job

chapuzón *nm (baño corto)* dip; **darse un c.** to have a dip

chaqué *nm* morning coat

chaqueta *nf* jacket; *Pol* **cambiar de c.** to change sides

chaquetero,-a *nm,f Fam Pol* turncoat

chaquetilla *nf* short jacket

charanga *nf Mús* brass band

charca *nf* pond, pool

charco *nm* puddle

charcutería *nf* delicatessen

charla *nf (conversación)* talk, chat; *(conferencia)* informal lecture *o* address; *Informát* chat

charlar *vi* to talk, to chat; *Informát* to chat

charlatán,-ana 1 *adj (parlanchín)* talkative; *(chismoso)* gossipy
  2 *nm,f* (**a**) *(parlanchín)* chatterbox; *(chismoso)* gossip; *(bocazas)* bigmouth (**b**) *(embaucador)* trickster, charmer

charol *nm* (**a**) *(piel)* patent leather; **zapatos de c.** patent leather shoes (**b**) *Andes (bandeja)* tray

charola *nf CAm, Méx* tray

charqui *nm Andes, RP (carne)* jerked *o* salted beef

chárter *adj inv* **(vuelo) c.** charter (flight)

chasca *nf Andes (greña)* mop of hair

chascar [44] *vt (lengua)* to click; *(dedos)* to snap; *(látigo)* to crack

chascarrillo *nm* shaggy dog story

chasco *nm Fam* disappointment; **llevarse un c.** to be disappointed

chasis *nm inv* chassis

chasquear *vt (lengua)* to click; *(dedos)* to snap; *(látigo)* to crack

chasqui *nm* = Inca messenger or courier

chasquido *nm (de la lengua)* click; *(de los dedos)* snap; *(de látigo, madera)* crack

chatarra *nf* scrap (metal), scrap iron; *Fam* junk

chato,-a 1 *adj* (**a**) *(nariz)* snub; *(persona)* snub-nosed (**b**) *(objeto)* flat, flattened (**c**) *PRico, RP Fam (sin ambiciones)* commonplace; **una vida chata** a humdrum existence
  2 *nm* (small) glass of wine

chau *interj Andes, RP Fam* bye!, see you!

chaucha 1 *adj RP Fam* dull, boring
  2 *nf Bol, RP* green bean

chauvinista *adj & nmf* chauvinist

chaval,-a *nm,f Fam (chico)* boy, lad; *(chica)* girl

chaveta *nf* (**a**) *(clavija)* cotter pin (**b**) *Fam (cabeza)* nut, head; **perder la c.** *(volverse loco)* to go off one's rocker (**c**) *Andes (navaja)* penknife

chavo,-a *Fam* **1** *nm,f Méx (chico)* guy; *(chica)* girl
  2 *nm (dinero)* **no tener un c.** to be broke

che *interj RP Fam* **¿qué hacés, c.?, ¿cómo andás, c.?** how are things *o* how's it going, then?; **c., ¡vení para acá!** over here, you!

checo,-a *adj* Czech
checoslovaco,-a 1 *adj* Czechoslovakian, Czech
  2 *nm,f (persona)* Czechoslovakian, Czechoslovak, Czech
Checoslovaquia *n* Czechoslovakia
chele,-a *CAm* **1** *adj (rubio)* blond, blonde; *(de piel blanca)* fair-skinned
  2 *nm,f (rubio)* blond(e) person; *(de piel blanca)* fair-skinned person
chelín *nm* shilling
chepa *nf Fam* hump
cheque *nm* cheque; **c. al portador** cheque payable to bearer; **c. de viaje** *o* **(de) viajero** traveller's cheque
chequeo *nm Med* checkup; *Aut* service
chévere *adj Andes, CAm, Carib, Méx Fam* great, fantastic
chic *adj inv* chic, elegant
chicano,-a *adj & nm,f* chicano
chicha¹ *nf Andes* = alcoholic drink made from fermented maize
chicha² *adj inv Náut* **calma c.** dead calm
chícharo *nm CAm, Méx* pea
chicharra *nf* (**a**) *(insecto)* cicada (**b**) *Méx, RP (timbre)* electric buzzer
chiche *nm* (**a**) *Andes, RP Fam (juguete)* toy (**b**) *Andes, RP (adorno)* delicate ornament (**c**) *CAm, Méx muy Fam (pecho)* tit
chichón *nm* bump, lump
chichonera *nf* helmet
chicle *nm* chewing gum
chico,-a 1 *nm,f (muchacho)* boy, lad; *(muchacha)* girl
  2 *adj* small, little
chicoria *nf* chicory
chicote *nm Am (látigo)* whip
chiflado,-a *adj Fam* mad, crazy (**por** about)
chiflar *vt* (**a**) *(silbar)* to hiss (at), to boo (at) (**b**) *Fam* **le chiflan las motos** he's really into motorbikes
chiflido *nm Am* whistle, whistling
chigüín,-ina *nm,f CAm Fam* kid
chiita *adj & nmf* Shiite
chilango,-a *Méx Fam* **1** *adj* of/from Mexico City
  2 *nm,f* person from Mexico City
Chile *n* Chile
chile *nm* chilli (pepper)
chileno,-a *adj & nm,f* Chilean
chillar *vi (persona)* to scream, to shriek; *(ratón)* to squeak; *(frenos)* to screech, to squeal; *(puerta)* to creak, to squeak
chillido *nm (de persona)* scream, shriek; *(de ratón)* squeak; *(de frenos)* screech, squeal; *(de puerta)* creaking, squeaking
chillón,-ona *adj* (**a**) *(voz)* shrill, high-

pitched; *(sonido)* harsh, strident (**b**) *(color)* loud, gaudy
chilpotle *nm Méx* = smoked or pickled jalapeño chilli
chimbo,-a *adj Col, Ven Fam* (**a**) *(de mala calidad)* crap, useless (**b**) *(complicado)* screwed-up
chimenea *nf* (**a**) *(hogar abierto)* fireplace, hearth (**b**) *(conducto)* chimney; *(de barco)* funnel, stack
chimichurri *nm RP* = barbecue sauce made from garlic, parsley, herbs and vinegar
China *n* China
china *nf* (**a**) pebble, small stone; *Fam* **tocarle a uno la c.** to get the short straw (**b**) *Fam (droga)* deal

> 🖉 Observa que la palabra inglesa **china** es un falso amigo y no es la traducción de la palabra española **china**. En inglés, **china** significa "loza, porcelana".

chinampa *nf Méx* = man-made island for growing flowers, fruit and vegetables, found in Xochimilco near Mexico City
chinche 1 *nf* bug, bedbug; *Fam* **caer como chinches** to fall like flies
  2 *nmf Fam* nuisance, pest
chincheta *nf Br* drawing pin, *US* thumbtack
chinchín *interj* **¡c.!** cheers!, (to) your (good) health!
chinchulín *nm*, **chinchulines** *nmpl Andes, RP (plato)* = piece of sheep or cow intestine, plaited and then roasted
chinesco,-a *adj* **sombras chinescas** shadow theatre
chingado,-a *adj muy Fam (estropeado)* bust, *Br* knackered
chingana *nf Perú Fam* bar
chingar [42] *vt* (**a**) *(fastidiar)* to annoy (**b**) *muy Fam (estropear)* to bust, *Br* to knacker (**c**) *Vulg (joder)* to fuck, to screw
chino¹ *nm (piedrecita)* pebble, stone
chino²,-a *adj* (**a**) *(de la China)* Chinese; *Fam* **eso me suena a c.** it's all Greek to me (**b**) *Am (mestizo)* of mixed ancestry
chip *nm (pl* chips) *Informát* chip
chipirón *nm* baby squid
Chipre *n* Cyprus
chipriota *adj & nmf* Cypriot
chiqueo *nm Méx* cuddle
chiquilín,-ina *nm,f RP* small boy, *f* small girl
chiquillo,-a *nm,f* kid
chiquito,-a *adj* tiny
chirimiri *nm* drizzle, fine misty rain
chirimoya *nf* custard apple

chiringuito *nm (en playa etc)* refreshment stall; *(en carretera)* roadside snack bar

chiripa *nf* fluke, lucky stroke; *Fam Fig* **de o por c.** by a fluke, by chance; **cogió el tren por c.** it was sheer luck that he caught the train

chiripá *nm (pl* **chiripaes)** *Bol, CSur* = garment worn by gauchos as trousers

chirla *nf* small clam

chirona *nf Fam* clink, nick

chirriar [29] *vi (puerta etc)* to creak; *(frenos)* to screech, to squeal

chirrido *nm (de puerta etc)* crack, cracking; *(de frenos)* screech, squeal

chisme *nm* (**a**) *(habladuría)* piece of gossip (**b**) *Fam (trasto)* knick-knack; *(cosa)* thing

chismorrear *vi Fam* to gossip

chismorreo *nm Fam* gossip, gossiping

chismoso,-a 1 *adj* gossipy
    2 *nm,f* gossip

chispa *nf* (**a**) spark; **echar chispas** to fume (**b**) *Fam (un poco)* bit, tiny amount (**c**) *Fam (agudeza)* wit, sparkle; *(viveza)* liveliness

chispear *vi* (**a**) to spark, to throw out sparks (**b**) *(lloviznar)* to spit

chiste *nm* joke; **contar un c.** to tell a joke; **c. verde** blue joke, dirty joke

chistera *nf* top hat

chistoso,-a *adj (persona)* funny, witty; *(anécdota)* funny, amusing

chivarse *vpr Fam* to tell tales

chivatazo *nm Fam* tip-off; **dar el c.** to squeal

chivato,-a 1 *nm,f Fam (delator) Br* grass, *US* rat; *(acusica)* telltale
    2 *nm* (**a**) *(luz)* warning light (**b**) *(alarma)* alarm bell (**c**) *Ven Fam (pez gordo)* big cheese

chivito *nm Urug* = steak sandwich *(containing cheese and salad)*

chivo,-a *nm,f Zool* kid, young goat; *Fig* **c. expiatorio** scapegoat

chocante *adj* (**a**) *(persona)* off-putting (**b**) *(sorprendente)* surprising, startling; *(raro)* strange

chocar [44] 1 *vi* (**a**) *(topar)* to crash, to collide; **c. con o contra** to run into, to collide with (**b**) *(en discusión)* to clash
    2 *vt* (**a**) to knock; *(la mano)* to shake; *Fam* **¡chócala!, ¡choca esos cinco!** shake (on it)!, put it there! (**b**) *(sorprender)* to surprise

chochear *vi* (**a**) to be senile *o* in one's dotage (**b**) **c. con algn** to dote on sb

chocho,-a 1 *adj (senil)* senile; **viejo c.** old dodderer
    2 *nm* (**a**) *(altramuz)* lupin (**b**) *muy Fam Br* fanny, *US* beaver

choclo *nm Andes, RP (mazorca)* corncob, ear of maize *o US* corn; *(granos)* sweetcorn; *(cultivo)* maize, *US* corn

chocolate *nm* (**a**) chocolate; **c. con leche** milk chocolate (**b**) *Fam (droga)* dope

chocolatina *nf* bar of chocolate, chocolate bar

chófer *nm (pl* **chóferes**), *Am* **chofer** *nm (pl* **choferes**) driver; *(particular)* chauffeur

chollo *nm Fam (ganga)* bargain, snip

chomba *nf Arg* polo shirt

chompa *nf Andes* sweater, *Br* jumper

chompipe *nm CAm, Méx* turkey

chongo *nm Méx* (**a**) *(moño)* bun (**b**) **chongos zamoranos** *(dulce)* = Mexican dessert made from milk curds, served in syrup

chonta *nf Am* palm tree

chop *nm CSur* (**a**) *(jarra)* beer mug/glass (**b**) *(cerveza)* (glass of) beer

chopo *nm* poplar

chopp *nm CSur* = **chop**

choque *nm* (**a**) impact; *(de coches etc)* crash, collision; **c. frontal** head-on collision; **c. múltiple** pile-up (**b**) *Fig (contienda)* clash

choricear, chorizar *vt Fam* to pinch

chorizo *nm* (**a**) chorizo, highly-seasoned pork sausage (**b**) *Fam (ratero)* thief, pickpocket

chorlito *nm Orn* plover; *Fam Fig* **cabeza de c.** scatterbrain

choro *nm Andes* mussel

chorra *Fam* **1** *nmf (tonto)* idiot, fool
    2 *nf (suerte)* luck

chorrada *nf Fam* piece of nonsense

chorrear *vi* to drip, to trickle; *Fam* **c. de sudor** to pour with sweat; *Fam* **tengo el abrigo chorreando** my coat is dripping wet

chorro *nm* (**a**) *(de agua etc)* spurt; *(muy fino)* trickle; **salir a chorros** to gush forth (**b**) *Téc* jet (**c**) *Fig* stream, flood

chovinismo *nm* chauvinism

chovinista 1 *adj* chauvinistic
    2 *nmf* chauvinist

choza *nf* hut, shack

christmas *nm* Christmas card

chubasco *nm* heavy shower, downpour

chubasquero *nm* raincoat

chúcaro,-a *adj Andes, CAm, RP* (**a**) *(animal)* wild (**b**) *(persona)* unsociable

chuchería *nf Fam Br* sweet, *US* candy

chueco,-a 1 *adj Am (torcido)* twisted;

(patizambo) bowlegged; *Méx, Ven Fam (cojo)* lame

  2 *nm,f Am (patizambo)* bowlegged person; *Méx, Ven Fam (cojo)* lame person

chufa *nf* groundnut

chulear *vi Fam* to strut around; **c. de** to go on about

chuleta *nf* (**a**) chop, cutlet; **c. de cerdo** pork chop (**b**) *Educ Fam* crib

chullo *nm Andes* woollen cap

chulo,-a *Fam* **1** *nm,f* show-off

  2 *nm (proxeneta)* pimp

  3 *adj (bonito)* smashing

chungo,-a *adj Fam* dodgy

chuño *nm Andes, RP* potato starch

chupa *nf Arg* short jacket

chupachups® *nm* lollipop

chupacirios *nmf inv Fam Pey* holy Joe

chupado,-a *adj* (**a**) *(flaco)* skinny, thin (**b**) *Fam* **está c.** it's dead easy

chupamedias *nmf Andes, RP, Ven Fam* toady, sycophant

chupar **1** *vt* (**a**) to suck (**b**) *(lamer)* to lick (**c**) *(absorber)* to soak up, to absorb

  2 *vi* to suck

  3 chuparse *vpr* (**a**) **está para c. los dedos** it's really mouthwatering (**b**) *Fam* to put up with; **nos chupamos toda la película** we sat through the whole film

chupatintas *nm inv Pey* penpusher

chupe *nm Andes, Arg* stew

chupete *nm Br* dummy, *US* pacifier

chupi *adj Fam* great, terrific, fantastic

chupón *nm* (**a**) lollipop (**b**) *(desatrancador)* plunger

churrasco *nm* barbecued meat

churrería *nf* fritter shop

churrete *nm* dirty mark, grease spot

churro *nm* (**a**) = dough formed into sticks or rings, fried in oil and covered in sugar (**b**) *Fam (chapuza)* mess

chusco *nm* chunk of stale bread; *Mil Fam* ration bread

chusma *nf* rabble, mob

chutar **1** *vi* (**a**) *Dep (a gol)* to shoot (**b**) *Fam* **¡y vas que chutas!** and then you're well away!

  2 chutarse *vpr Fam (drogas)* to shoot up

chute *nm* (**a**) *Dep* shot (**b**) *Fam (drogas)* fix

CI *nm (abr* **coeficiente intelectual**) IQ

Cía., cía *(abr* **compañía**) Co

cianuro *nm* cyanide

cibercafé *nm Informát* Internet cafe, cybercafe

ciberespacio *nm Informát* cyberspace

cibernética *nf* cybernetics *sing*

cicatero,-a **1** *adj* stingy, mean

  2 *nm,f* miser

cicatriz *nf* scar

cicatrizar [40] *vt & vi Med* to heal

cíclico,-a *adj* cyclical

ciclismo *nm* cycling

ciclista **1** *adj* cycling

  2 *nmf* cyclist

ciclo *nm* cycle; *(de conferencias etc)* course, series

ciclocróss *nm* cyclo-cross

ciclomotor *nm* moped

ciclón *nm* cyclone

ciego,-a **1** *adj (persona)* blind; *Fam (borracho)* blind drunk; *(de droga)* stoned; **a ciegas** blindly

  2 *nm,f* blind person; **los ciegos** the blind

cielo *nm* (**a**) sky (**b**) *Rel* heaven; *Fig* **caído del c.** *(oportuno)* heaven-sent; *(inesperado)* out of the blue; **¡c. santo!** good heavens! (**c**) *Arquit* **c. raso** ceiling (**d**) **c. de la boca** roof of the mouth

ciempiés *nm inv* centipede

cien *adj & nm inv* hundred; **c. libras** a o one hundred pounds; **c. por c.** one hundred percent

ciénaga *nf* marsh, bog

ciencia *nf* (**a**) science; *Fig* **saber algo a c. cierta** to know sth for certain; **c. ficción** science fiction; **c. infusa** intuition; **ciencias ocultas** the occult (**b**) *(conocimiento)* knowledge

cieno *nm* mud, mire

científico,-a **1** *adj* scientific

  2 *nm,f* scientist

cientista *nmf CSur* **c. social** social scientist

ciento *adj* hundred; **c. tres** one hundred and three; **por c.** percent

cierne *nm Fig* **en ciernes** budding

cierre *nm* (**a**) *(acción)* closing, shutting; *(de fábrica)* shutdown; *TV* close-down; **c. patronal** lockout (**b**) *(de bolso)* clasp; *(de puerta)* catch; *(prenda)* fastener; **c. de seguridad** safety lock; **c. centralizado** central locking; *Am* **c. relámpago** *Br* zip, *US* zipper

cierto,-a **1** *adj* (**a**) *(verdadero)* true; *(seguro)* certain; **estar en lo c.** to be right; **lo c. es que ...** the fact is that ...; **por c.** by the way (**b**) *(algún)* certain; **ciertas personas** certain o some people

  2 *adv* certainly

ciervo,-a *nm,f* deer; *(macho)* stag; *(hembra)* doe, hind

cifra *nf* (**a**) *(número)* figure, number (**b**) *(código)* cipher, code

cifrar *vt* to express in figures

cigala *nf* Norway lobster, scampi
cigarra *nf* cicada
cigarrillo *nm* cigarette
cigarro *nm* (**a**) *(puro)* cigar (**b**) *(cigarrillo)* cigarette
cigüeña *nf* (**a**) *Orn* stork (**b**) *Téc* crank
cigüeñal *nm* crankshaft
cilindrada *nf Aut* cylinder capacity
cilíndrico,-a *adj* cylindrical
cilindro *nm* cylinder
cima *nf* summit
cimbrearse *vpr* to sway
cimentar *vt* to lay the foundations of; *Fig (amistad)* to strengthen
cimientos *nmpl* foundations; **echar** *o* **poner los c.** to lay the foundations
cinc *nm* zinc
cincel *nm* chisel
cincelar *vt* to chisel
cinco *adj & nm inv* five
cincuenta *adj & nm inv* fifty
cine *nm* (**a**) *(local)* cinema, *US* movie theater (**b**) *(arte)* cinema; **c. mudo/sonoro** silent/talking films
cineasta *nmf* movie director, movie maker
cinéfilo,-a *nm,f (que va al cine)* (keen) moviegoer *o Br* filmgoer; *(que entiende de cine)* movie *o Br* film buff
cinematográfico,-a *adj* cinematographic; **la industria cinematográfica** the movie *o Br* film industry
cíngaro,-a *adj & nm,f* gypsy
cínico,-a 1 *adj* shameless
   2 *nm,f* shameless person; **es un c.** he's shameless, he has no shame

> [!NOTE]
> ⚠ Observa que la palabra inglesa **cynic** es un falso amigo y no es la traducción de la palabra española **cínico**. En inglés, **cynic** significa tanto "descreído, suspicaz" como "desaprensivo".

cinismo *nm* shamelessness

> [!NOTE]
> ⚠ Observa que la palabra inglesa **cynicism** es un falso amigo y no es la traducción de la palabra española **cinismo**. En inglés, **cynicism** significa "descreimiento, suspicacia".

cinta *nf* (**a**) *(tira)* band, strip; *(para adornar)* ribbon; *Cost* braid, edging (**b**) *Téc & Mús* tape; **c. adhesiva/aislante** adhesive/insulating tape; **c. de vídeo** video tape; **c. transportadora** conveyor belt (**c**) *Cin* film
cinto *nm* belt
cintura *nf* waist
cinturón *nm* belt; *Fig* **apretarse el c.** to tighten one's belt; **c. de seguridad** safety belt; *Am* **c. de miseria** = slum or shanty

town area round a large city
ciprés *nm* cypress
circense *adj* circus
circo *nm* circus
circuito *nm* circuit
circulación *nf* (**a**) circulation (**b**) *Aut (tráfico)* traffic
circular 1 *adj & nf* circular
   2 *vi (moverse)* to circulate; *(líquido)* to flow; *(tren, autobús)* to run; *Fig (rumor)* to go round; **circule por la izquierda** *(en letrero)* keep to the left
circulatorio,-a *adj* circulatory; *Aut* **un caos c.** traffic chaos
círculo *nm* circle; *Fig* **c. vicioso** vicious circle
circuncisión *nf* circumcision
circundante *adj* surrounding
circundar *vt* to surround, to encircle
circunferencia *nf* circumference
circunloquio *nm* circumlocution
circunscribirse (*pp* **circunscrito**) *vpr* **c. a** to confine *o* limit oneself to
circunscripción *nf* district; **c. electoral** constituency
circunscrito,-a *adj* circumscribed
circunspecto,-a *adj* circumspect
circunstancia *nf* circumstance; **en estas circunstancias ...** under the circumstances ...
circunstancial *adj* circumstantial
cirio *nm* wax candle
cirrosis *nf* cirrhosis
ciruela *nf* plum; **c. claudia** greengage; **c. pasa** prune
ciruelo *nm* plum tree
cirugía *nf* surgery; **c. estética** *o* **plástica** plastic surgery
cirujano,-a *nm,f* surgeon
cisma *nm* (**a**) *Rel* schism (**b**) *Pol* split
cisne *nm* swan
cisterna *nf* cistern, tank
cistitis *nf inv* cystitis
cita *nf* (**a**) appointment; **darse c.** to come together (**b**) *(amorosa)* date (**c**) *(mención)* quotation
citación *nf Jur* citation, summons *sing*
citado,-a *adj* aforementioned
citar 1 *vt* (**a**) *(dar cita)* to arrange to meet, to make an appointment with (**b**) *(mencionar)* to quote (**c**) *Jur* to summons
   2 citarse *vpr* to arrange to meet, to make a date (**con** with)
cítrico,-a 1 *adj* citric, citrus
   2 *nmpl* **cítricos** citrus fruits
ciudad *nf* town; *(capital)* city; *Méx* **c. perdida** shanty town
ciudadanía *nf* citizenship

ciudadano,-a 1 *nm,f* citizen; **el c. de a pie** the man in the street
   2 *adj* civic
cívico,-a *adj* civic
civil 1 *adj* (**a**) civil; **matrimonio c.** civil marriage (**b**) *Mil* civilian
   2 *nm* member of the Guardia Civil
civilización *nf* civilization
civilizado,-a *adj* civilized
civilizar [40] *vt* to civilize
civismo *nm* (**a**) *(urbanidad)* public-spiritedness (**b**) *(cortesía)* civility
cizaña *nf Bot* bearded darnel; *Fig* **sembrar c.** to sow discord
cl (*abr* **centilitro(s)**) cl
clamar *vt* to cry out for, to clamour for
clamor *nm* clamour
clamoroso,-a *adj* resounding
clan *nm* clan
clandestinidad *nf* **en la c.** underground
clandestino,-a *adj* clandestine, underground; **aborto c.** backstreet abortion
clara *nf (de huevo)* white
claraboya *nf* skylight
clarear *vi* (**a**) *(amanecer)* to dawn (**b**) *(despejar)* to clear up (**c**) *(transparentar)* to wear thin, to become transparent
clarete *adj & nm* claret
claridad *nf* (**a**) *(luz)* light, brightness (**b**) *(inteligibilidad)* clarity; **con c.** clearly
clarificador,-a *adj* clarifying
clarificar [44] *vt* to clarify
clarín *nm* bugle
clarinete *nm* clarinet
clarividente 1 *adj* (**a**) far-sighted (**b**) *(lúcido)* lucid
   2 *nmf (persona)* clairvoyant
claro,-a 1 *adj* (**a**) clear; **dejar algo c.** to make sth clear (**b**) *(líquido, salsa)* thin (**c**) *(color)* light
   2 *interj* of course!; **¡c. que no!** of course not!; **¡c. que sí!** certainly!
   3 *nm* (**a**) *(espacio)* gap, space; *(en un bosque)* clearing (**b**) *Met* bright spell
   4 *adv* clearly
clase *nf* (**a**) *(grupo)* class; **c. alta/media** upper/middle class; **clases pasivas** pensioners; **primera/segunda c.** first/second class (**b**) *(tipo)* kind, sort; **toda c. de ...** all kinds of ... (**c**) *Educ (curso)* class; *(aula)* classroom; **c. particular** private class *o* lesson (**d**) *(estilo)* class; **tener c.** to have class
clásico,-a 1 *adj* classical; *(típico)* classic; *(en el vestir)* classic
   2 *nm* classic
clasificación *nf* (**a**) classification; *Dep* league table (**b**) *(para campeonato,*

concurso) qualification
clasificar [44] 1 *vt* to classify, to class
   2 clasificarse *vpr Dep* to qualify
claudicar [44] *vi* to give in
claustro *nm* (**a**) *Arquit* cloister (**b**) *(reunión)* staff meeting
claustrofobia *nf* claustrophobia
cláusula *nf* clause
clausura *nf* (**a**) *(cierre)* closure; **ceremonia de c.** closing ceremony (**b**) *Rel* enclosure
clausurar *vt* to close
clavadista *nmf CAm, Méx* diver
clavar 1 *vt* (**a**) to nail; *(clavo)* to bang *o* hammer in; *(estaca)* to drive in (**b**) *Fam (timar)* to sting *o* fleece
   2 clavarse *vpr* **c. una astilla** to get a splinter
clave 1 *nf* key; **la palabra c.** the key word
   2 *nm* harpsichord
clavel *nm* carnation
clavícula *nf* collarbone
clavija *nf Téc* jack
clavo *nm* (**a**) nail; *Fig* **dar en el c.** to hit the nail on the head (**b**) *Bot* clove
claxon *nm* (*pl* **cláxones**) horn; **tocar el c.** to sound the horn
clemencia *nf* mercy, clemency
clementina *nf* clementine
cleptómano,-a *adj & nm,f* kleptomaniac
clerical *adj* clerical
clericó *nm RP* = drink made of white wine and fruit
clérigo *nm* priest
clero *nm* clergy
cliché *nm* (**a**) *Fig (tópico)* cliché (**b**) *Fot* negative (**c**) *Impr* plate
cliente *nmf* customer, client
clientela *nf* clientele
clima *nm* climate
climatizado,-a *adj* air-conditioned
climatizar [40] *vt* to air-condition
clímax *nm inv* climax
clínica *nf* clinic
clínico,-a *adj* clinical
clip *nm* clip
clítoris *nm inv* clitoris
cloaca *nf* sewer, drain
clorhídrico,-a *adj* hydrochloric
cloro *nm* chlorine
cloroformo *nm* chloroform
cloruro *nm* chloride; **c. sódico** sodium chloride
clóset *nm* (*pl* **clósets**) *Am* fitted cupboard
club *nm* (*pl* **clubs** *o* **clubes**) club; **c. náutico** yacht club
cm (*abr* **centímetro(s)**) cm
CNT *nf* (*abr* **Confederación Nacional del**

Trabajo) = Spanish anarchist trade union federation

coacción *nf* coercion

coaccionar *vt* to coerce

coactivo,-a *adj* coercive

coadyuvar *vt* to assist

coagular *vt & vi*, **coagularse** *vpr* to coagulate; *(sangre)* to clot; *(leche)* to curdle

coágulo *nm* coagulum, clot

coalición *nf* coalition

coartada *nf* alibi

coartar *vt* to restrict

coba *nf Fam* **dar c. a algn** to soft-soap sb

cobalto *nm* cobalt

cobarde 1 *adj* cowardly
  2 *nmf* coward

cobardía *nf* cowardice

cobaya *nf* guinea pig

cobertizo *nm* shed, shack

cobertor *nm* bedspread

cobertura *nf* cover; *(de noticia)* coverage

cobija *nf Am* blanket

cobijar 1 *vt* to shelter
  2 cobijarse *vpr* to take shelter

cobijo *nm* shelter; *Fig (protección)* protection

cobra *nf* cobra

cobrador,-a *nm,f* (**a**) *(de autobús)* *(hombre)* conductor; *(mujer)* conductress (**b**) *(de luz, agua etc)* collector

cobrar 1 *vt* (**a**) *(dinero)* to charge; *(cheque)* to cash; *(salario)* to earn (**b**) *Fig (fuerza)* to gain, to get; **c. ánimos** to take courage *o* heart; **c. importancia** to become important
  2 *vi Fam* to catch it
  3 cobrarse *vpr* **¿se cobra?** *(al pagar)* take it out of this, please

cobre *nm* (**a**) copper (**b**) *Am (moneda)* copper cent

cobrizo,-a *adj* copper, copper-coloured

cobro *nm (pago)* collecting; *(de cheque)* cashing; *Tel* **llamada a c. revertido** *Br* reverse-charge call, *US* collect call

coca *nf* (**a**) *Bot* coca (**b**) *Fam (droga)* cocaine, coke

cocaína *nf* cocaine

cocainómano,-a *nm,f* cocaine addict

cocalero,-a *Bol, Perú* **1** *adj* **región cocalera** coca-producing area; **productor c.** coca farmer *o* producer
  2 *nm,f* coca farmer *o* producer

cocción *nf* cooking; *(en agua)* boiling; *(en horno)* baking

cocer [41] 1 *vt* to cook; *(hervir)* to boil; *(hornear)* to bake
  2 *vi (hervir)* to boil

3 cocerse *vpr* (**a**) *(comida)* to cook; *(hervir)* to boil; *(hornear)* to bake (**b**) *(tramarse)* to be going on

cochambroso,-a *adj* squalid

coche *nm* (**a**) car; **en c.** by car; **c. de carreras** racing car; **c. de bomberos** fire engine; **c. fúnebre** hearse (**b**) *Ferroc* carriage, coach; **c. cama** sleeping car, sleeper (**c**) *(de caballos)* carriage, coach

cochecito *nm (de niño) Br* pram, *US* baby carriage

cochera *nf* (**a**) garage (**b**) *(de autobuses)* depot

cochinillo *nm* suckling pig

cochino,-a 1 *nm,f* (**a**) *(macho)* pig; *(hembra)* sow (**b**) *Fam (persona)* filthy person, pig
  2 *adj (sucio)* filthy, disgusting

cocido *nm* stew

cociente *nm* quotient

cocina *nf* (**a**) kitchen (**b**) *(aparato)* cooker, stove; **c. eléctrica/de gas** electric/gas cooker (**c**) *(arte)* cooking; **c. casera** home cooking; **c. española** Spanish cooking *o* cuisine

cocinar *vt & vi* to cook

cocinero,-a *nm,f* cook

cocktail *nm* = **cóctel**

coco¹ *nm* coconut; *Fam (cabeza)* nut; **comerle el c. a algn** to brainwash sb; **comerse el c.** to get obsessed

coco² *nm Fam (fantasma)* bogeyman

cocodrilo *nm* crocodile

cocoliche *nm RP Fam* = pidgin Spanish spoken by Italian immigrants

cocotero *nm* coconut palm

cóctel *nm* cocktail; **c. Molotov** Molotov cocktail

coctelera *nf* cocktail shaker

codazo *nm* (**a**) *(señal)* nudge with one's elbow (**b**) *(golpe)* blow with one's elbow

codearse *vpr* to rub shoulders (**con** with), to hobnob (**con** with)

codeína *nf* codeine

codicia *nf* greed

codiciar [43] *vt* to covet

codicioso,-a *adj* covetous, greedy

codificar [44] *vt (ley)* to codify; *(mensajes)* to encode

código *nm* code; **c. de circulación** highway code; **c. postal** *Br* postcode, postal code, *US* zip code

codo *nm* elbow; *Fig* **c. con c.** side by side; *Fam* **hablar por los codos** to talk nonstop

codorniz *nf* quail

coeficiente *nm* (**a**) coefficient (**b**) *(grado)* rate; **c. intelectual** intelligence quotient

coercitivo,-a *adj* coercive
coetáneo,-a *adj & nm,f* contemporary
coexistencia *nf* coexistence
coexistir *vi* to coexist
cofia *nf* bonnet
cofradía *nf (hermandad)* brotherhood; *(asociación)* association
cofre *nm (arca)* trunk, chest; *(para joyas)* box, casket
coger [53] 1 *vt* (**a**) to take; *(del suelo)* to pick (up); *(fruta, flores)* to pick; *(asir)* to seize, to take hold of; *(bus, tren)* to take, to catch; *(pelota, ladrón, resfriado)* to catch; *(entender)* to grasp; *(costumbre)* to pick up; *(velocidad, fuerza)* to gather; *(atropellar)* to run over, to knock down
(**b**) *Am Vulg* to fuck
2 *vi Fam* **cogió y se fue** he upped and left
3 cogerse *vpr (agarrarse)* to hold on
cogida *nf* goring
cogollo *nm (de lechuga)* heart
cogotazo *nm Fam* blow on the back of the neck
cogote *nm* nape *o* back of the neck
cohabitación *nf* cohabitation
cohabitar *vi* to live together, to cohabit
cohecho *nm Jur* bribery
coherencia *nf* coherence
coherente *adj* coherent
cohesión *nf* cohesion
cohete *nm* rocket; **c. espacial** space rocket
cohibido,-a *adj* inhibited
cohibir 1 *vt* to inhibit
2 cohibirse *vpr* to feel inhibited
COI *nm Dep* (*abr* **Comité Olímpico Internacional**) IOC
coima *nf Andes, RP Fam* bribe, *Br* backhander
coincidencia *nf* coincidence
coincidir *vi* (**a**) to coincide (**b**) *(concordar)* to agree; **todos coincidieron en señalar que** everyone agreed that (**c**) *(encontrarse)* to meet by chance
coito *nm* coitus, intercourse
cojear *vi (persona)* to limp, to hobble; *(mueble)* to wobble
cojera *nf* limp
cojín *nm* cushion
cojinete *nm Téc* bearing; **c. de agujas/bolas** needle/ball bearing
cojo,-a 1 *adj (persona)* lame; *(mueble)* rickety
2 *nm,f* lame person
cojón *nm Vulg* ball; **de cojones** *(estupendo)* fucking brilliant *o* good; *(pésimo)* fucking awful *o* bad
cojonudo,-a *adj muy Fam Br* bloody

o US goddamn brilliant
cojudez *nf Andes muy Fam* **¡qué c.!** *(acto)* what a *Br* bloody *o US* goddamn stupid thing to do!; *(dicho)* what a *Br* bloody *o US* goddamn stupid thing to say!
cojudo,-a *adj Andes muy Fam Br* bloody *o US* goddamn stupid
col *nf* cabbage; **c. de Bruselas** Brussels sprout
cola¹ *nf* (**a**) *(de animal)* tail; *(de vestido)* train; *(de pelo)* ponytail; *Am (de persona) Br* bum, *US* fanny; **a la c.** at the back *o* rear; *Fam* **traer c.** to have consequences (**b**) *(fila) Br* queue, *US* line; **hacer c.** *Br* to queue (up), *US* to stand in line
cola² *nf (pegamento)* glue
colaboración *nf* (**a**) collaboration (**b**) *Prensa* contribution
colaboracionismo *nm Pol* collaboration
colaborador,-a 1 *nm,f* (**a**) collaborator (**b**) *Prensa* contributor
2 *adj* collaborating
colaborar *vi* to collaborate, to cooperate
colación *nf* **sacar** *o* **traer (algo) a c.** to bring (sth) up
colada *nf* wash, laundry; **hacer la c.** to do the washing *o* laundry
colador *nm* colander, sieve; *(de té, café)* strainer
colapsar 1 *vt* to bring to a standstill
2 colapsarse *vpr* to come to a standstill
colapso *nm* (**a**) *Med* collapse (**b**) *Aut* **c. circulatorio** traffic jam, hold-up
colar [2] 1 *vt* (**a**) *(líquido)* to strain, to filter (**b**) *(por agujero)* to slip
2 *vi Fam* **esa mentira no cuela** that lie won't wash
3 colarse *vpr* (**a**) to slip in; *(a fiesta)* to gatecrash; *(en una cola)* to jump the queue (**b**) *Fam (pasarse)* to go too far
colateral *adj* collateral
colcha *nf* bedspread
colchón *nm* mattress
colchoneta *nf* air bed
colear *vi* (**a**) to wag its tail; *Fam* **vivito y coleando** alive and kicking (**b**) *Fam* **el asunto aún colea** we haven't heard the last of it yet
colección *nf* collection
coleccionable *adj & nm* collectable
coleccionar *vt* to collect
coleccionista *nmf* collector
colecta *nf* collection
colectividad *nf* community
colectivo,-a 1 *adj* collective
2 *nm* (**a**) *(asociación)* association (**b**) *Andes (taxi)* (collective) taxi (**c**) *Arg (autobús)* bus

colega *nmf* (**a**) colleague (**b**) *Fam (amigo)* pal, *Br* mate, *US* buddy

colegiado,-a *nm,f Dep* referee

colegial,-ala 1 *adj (escolar)* school

2 *nm,f (alumno)* schoolboy; *(alumna)* schoolgirl; **los colegiales** the schoolchildren

colegio *nm* (**a**) *(escuela)* school; **c. privado** private school, *Br* public *o* independent school (**b**) *(profesional)* association, college; **c. de abogados** the Bar; *Pol* **c. electoral** electoral college (**c**) *Univ* **c. mayor** *o* **universitario** hall of residence

colegir [**58**] *vt* to infer, to deduce

cólera¹ *nf* anger, rage

cólera² *nm Med* cholera

colérico,-a *adj* furious

colesterol *nm* cholesterol

coleta *nf* pigtail, ponytail; *Fig* **cortarse la c.** to retire

coletazo *nm* **dar los últimos coletazos** to be on one's last legs

coletilla *nf* postcript

colgado,-a *adj* (**a**) *Fam* **dejar (a algn) c.** to leave (sb) in the lurch (**b**) *Fam* weird; *(drogado)* high

colgante 1 *nm (joya)* pendant

2 *adj* hanging

colgar [**2**] **1** *vt* (**a**) to hang (up); *(colada)* to hang (out) (**b**) *(ahorcar)* to hang

2 *vi* (**a**) to hang (**de** from); *Fig* **c. de un hilo** to hang by a thread (**b**) *Tel* to hang up

3 colgarse *vpr (ahorcarse)* to hang oneself

colibrí *nm* hummingbird

cólico *nm* colic

coliflor *nf* cauliflower

colijo *indic pres de* **colegir**

colilla *nf* (cigarette) end *o* butt

colimba *nf Arg Fam* military service

colina *nf* hill

colindante *adj* adjoining, adjacent

colindar *vi* to be adjacent (**con** to)

colirio *nm* eye-drops

colisión *nf* collision, crash; *(de ideas)* clash

colisionar *vi* to collide, to crash

colitis *nf* colitis

colla *Bol* **1** *adj* of/from the altiplano

2 *nmf* = indigenous person from the altiplano

collage *nm* collage

collar *nm* (**a**) *(adorno)* necklace (**b**) *(de perro)* collar

colmado,-a *adj* full, filled; *(cucharada)* heaped

colmar *vt* (**a**) to fill (right up); *(vaso, copa)* to fill to the brim; *Fig* to shower (**de** with) (**b**) *(ambiciones)* to fulfil, to satisfy

colmena *nf* beehive

colmillo *nm* eye *o* canine tooth; *Zool (de carnívoro)* fang; *(de jabalí, elefante)* tusk

colmo *nm* height; **el c. de** the height of; **¡eso es el c.!** that's the last straw!; **para c.** to top it all

colocación *nf* (**a**) *(acto)* positioning (**b**) *(disposición)* lay-out (**c**) *(empleo)* job, employment

colocado,-a *adj* (**a**) *(empleado)* employed (**b**) *Fam (drogado)* high

colocar [**44**] **1** *vt* (**a**) to place, to put (**b**) *Fin (invertir)* to invest (**c**) *(emplear)* to give work to (**d**) *Fam (drogar)* to stone

2 colocarse *vpr* (**a**) *(situarse)* to put oneself (**b**) *(emplearse)* to take a job (**de** as) (**c**) *Fam (drogarse)* to get high

colofón *nm* (**a**) *(apéndice)* colophon (**b**) *Fig* climax

Colombia *n* Colombia

colombiano,-a *adj & nm,f* Colombian

Colón *n* Columbus

colón *nm Fin* = standard monetary unit of Costa Rica and El Salvador

colonia¹ *nf* colony; *(campamento)* summer camp; *Méx (barrio)* district

colonia² *nf (perfume)* cologne

colonial *adj* colonial

colonialismo *nm* colonialism

colonización *nf* colonization

colonizar [**40**] *vt* to colonize

coloquial *adj* colloquial

coloquio *nm* discussion, colloquium

color *nm* colour; *Cin & Fot* **en c.** in colour; **de colores** multicoloured; **persona de c.** coloured person

colorado,-a 1 *adj* red; **ponerse c.** to blush

2 *nm* red

> *ℓ* Observa que la palabra inglesa **coloured** es un falso amigo y no es la traducción de la palabra española **colorado**. En inglés, **coloured** significa "coloreado".

colorante *nm* colouring

colorear *vt* to colour

colorete *nm* rouge

colorido *nm* colour

colorín *nm* goldfinch

colosal *adj* colossal

columna *nf* column; *Anat* **c. vertebral** vertebral column, spinal column

columpiar [**43**] **1** *vt* to swing

2 columpiarse *vpr* to swing

columpio *nm* swing

coma¹ *nf* (**a**) *Ling & Mús* comma (**b**) *Mat*

point; **tres c. cinco** three point five
coma² *nm Med* coma
comadre *nf* (**a**) *(madrina)* = godmother of one's child, or mother of one's godchild (**b**) *Am Fam (amiga)* friend
comadreja *nf* weasel
comadreo *nm* gossip, gossiping
comadrona *nf* midwife
comal *nm CAm, Méx* = flat clay or metal dish used for baking "tortillas"
comandancia *nf* command
comandante *nm* (**a**) *Mil* commander, commanding officer (**b**) *Av* captain
comandar *vt* to command
comando *nm* (**a**) *Mil* commando (**b**) *Informát* command
comarca *nf* region
comarcal *adj* regional
comba *nf* (**a**) *(curvatura)* curve, bend (**b**) *(cuerda)* skipping rope; **saltar a la c.** to skip, *US* to jump rope
combar *vt* to bend
combate *nm* combat; *(en boxeo)* fight; *Mil* battle; **fuera de c.** out for the count; *(eliminado)* out of action
combatiente 1 *adj* fighting
2 *nmf* combatant
combatir 1 *vt* to combat
2 *vi* **c. contra** to fight against
combativo,-a *adj* spirited, aggressive
combinación *nf* (**a**) combination (**b**) *(prenda)* slip
combinado,-a 1 *adj* combined
2 *nm* (**a**) *(cóctel)* cocktail (**b**) *Dep* line-up
combinar *vt*, **combinarse** *vpr* to combine
combustible 1 *nm* fuel
2 *adj* combustible
combustión *nf* combustion
comedia *nf* comedy
comediante,-a *nm,f (hombre)* actor; *(mujer)* actress
comedido,-a *adj* self-restrained, reserved
comedor *nm* dining room
comensal *nmf* companion at table
comentar *vt* **c. algo con algn** to talk sth over with sb; **me han comentado que** I've been told that
comentario *nm* (**a**) comment, remark; *(crítica)* commentary; **sin c.** no comment (**b**) **comentarios** *(cotilleos)* gossip
comentarista *nmf* commentator
comenzar [51] *vt & vi* to begin, to start; **comenzó a llover** it started raining *o* to rain; **comenzó diciendo que ...** he started by saying that ...

comer 1 *vt* (**a**) to eat (**b**) *(en juegos)* to take, to capture
2 *vi* to eat; **dar de c. a algn** to feed sb
3 comerse *vpr* (**a**) to eat (**b**) *Fig (saltarse)* to skip
comercial *adj* commercial
comercialización *nf* marketing
comercializar [40] *vt* to market
comerciante *nmf* merchant
comerciar [43] *vi* to trade; **comercia con oro** he trades in gold
comercio *nm* (**a**) commerce, trade; **c. exterior** foreign trade; *Informát* **c. electrónico** e-commerce; **c. justo** fair trade (**b**) *(tienda)* shop
comestible 1 *adj* edible
2 *nmpl* **comestibles** food, foodstuff(s); **tienda de comestibles** grocer's shop, *US* grocery store
cometa 1 *nm Astron* comet
2 *nf (juguete)* kite
cometer *vt (error, falta)* to make; *(delito, crimen)* to commit
cometido *nm* (**a**) *(tarea)* task, assignment (**b**) *(deber)* duty; **cumplir su c.** to do one's duty
comezón *nm* itch
cómic *nm* comic
comicios *nmpl* elections
cómico,-a 1 *adj* (**a**) comical, funny (**b**) *Teatro* **actor c.** comedian
2 *nm,f* comic; *(hombre)* comedian; *(mujer)* comedienne
comida *nf* (**a**) *(alimento)* food (**b**) *(almuerzo, cena)* meal
comidilla *nf Fam* **la c. del pueblo** the talk of the town
comienzo *nm* beginning, start; **a comienzos de** at the beginning of; **dar c. (a algo)** to begin *o* start (sth)
comillas *nfpl* inverted commas; **entre c.** in inverted commas
comilón,-ona 1 *adj* greedy, gluttonous
2 *nm,f* big eater, glutton
comilona *nf Fam* big meal, feast
comino *nm* cumin, cummin; *Fam* **me importa un c.** I don't give a damn (about it)
comisaría *nf* police station
comisario *nm* (**a**) *(de policía)* police inspector (**b**) *(delegado)* commissioner; **c. europeo** European Commissioner
comisión *nf* (**a**) *Com (retribución)* commission; **a** *o* **con c.** on a commission basis (**b**) *(comité)* committee; **la C. Europea** the European Commission
comité *nm* committee
comitiva *nf* suite, retinue

como 1 *adv* (**a**) *(manera)* how; **me gusta c. cantas** I like the way you sing; **dilo c. quieras** say it however you like
(**b**) *(comparación)* as; **blanco c. la nieve** as white as snow; **habla c. su padre** he talks like his father
(**c**) *(según)* as; **c. decíamos ayer** as we were saying yesterday
(**d**) *(en calidad de)* as; **c. presidente** as president; **lo compré c. recuerdo** I bought it as a souvenir
(**e**) *(aproximadamente)* about; **c. a la mitad de camino** halfway; **c. unos diez** about ten
2 *conj* (**a**) *(+ subjunctive) (si)* if; **c. no estudies vas a suspender** if you don't study hard, you'll fail
(**b**) *(porque)* as, since; **c. no venías me marché** as you didn't come, I left
(**c**) **c. si** as if; **c. si nada** *o* **tal cosa** as if nothing had happened; *Fam* **c. si lo viera** I can imagine perfectly well

cómo 1 *adv* (**a**) **¿c.?** *(¿perdón?)* what?
(**b**) *(interrogativo)* how; **¿c. estás?** how are you?; **¿c. lo sabes?** how do you know?; **¿c. es de grande/ancho?** how big/wide is it?; **¿a c. están los tomates?** how much are the tomatoes?; **¿c. es que no viniste a la fiesta?** *(por qué)* how come you didn't come to the party?; *Fam* **¿c. es eso?** how come?
(**c**) *(exclamativo)* how; **¡c. has crecido!** you've really grown a lot!; **¡c. no!** but of course!
2 *nm* **el c. y el porqué** the whys and wherefores

cómoda *nf* chest of drawers

comodidad *nf* (**a**) comfort (**b**) *(conveniencia)* convenience

> 🖉 Observa que la palabra inglesa **commodity** es un falso amigo y no es la traducción de la palabra española **comodidad**. En inglés, **commodity** significa "producto básico".

comodín *nm Naipes* joker

cómodo,-a *adj* (**a**) comfortable; **ponerse c.** to make oneself comfortable (**b**) *(útil)* handy, convenient

comoquiera *adv* (**a**) however, whatever way; **c. que sea** one way or another (**b**) **c. que no estaba enterado** *(puesto que)* as he didn't know

compa *nmf Fam* pal, *Br* mate, *US* buddy

compacto,-a *adj* compact; **disco c.** compact disc

compadecer [33] 1 *vt* to feel sorry for, to pity

2 compadecerse *vpr* to have *o* take pity (**de** on)

compadre *nm* (**a**) *(padrino)* = godfather of one's child, or father of one's godchild (**b**) *Am Fam (amigo)* friend, mate

compadrear *vi RP* to brag, to boast

compaginar *vt* to combine

compañerismo *nm* companionship, comradeship

compañero,-a *nm,f* companion; **c. de colegio** school friend; **c. de piso** flat-mate

compañía *nf* company; **hacer c. (a algn)** to keep (sb) company; **c. de seguros/de teatro** insurance/theatre company

comparable *adj* comparable

comparación *nf* comparison; **en c.** comparatively; **en c. con** compared to; **sin c.** beyond compare

comparar *vt* to compare (**con** with)

comparativo,-a *adj & nm* comparative

comparecencia *nf* appearance

comparecer [33] *vi Jur* to appear (**ante** before)

comparsa *nf* band of revellers

compartimento, compartimiento *nm* compartment; **c. de primera/segunda clase** first-/second-class compartment

compartir *vt* to share

compás *nm* (**a**) *Téc* (pair of) compasses (**b**) *Náut* compass (**c**) *Mús (división)* time; *(intervalo)* beat; *(ritmo)* rhythm; **c. de espera** *Mús* bar rest; *Fig (pausa)* delay; **al c. de** in time to

compasión *nf* compassion, pity; **tener c. (de algn)** to feel sorry (for sb)

compasivo,-a *adj* compassionate

compatible *adj* compatible

compatriota *nmf* compatriot; *(hombre)* fellow countryman; *(mujer)* fellow countrywoman

compendiar [43] *vt* to abridge, to summarize

compendio *nm* compendium

compenetrarse *vpr* to understand each other *o* one another

compensación *nf* compensation

compensar 1 *vt* *(pérdida, error)* to make up for; *(indemnizar)* to compensate (for)
2 *vi* to be worthwhile; **este trabajo no compensa** this job's not worth my time

competencia *nf* (**a**) *(rivalidad, empresas rivales)* competition (**b**) *(capacidad)* competence (**c**) *(incumbencia)* field, province; **no es de mi c.** it's not up to me

competente *adj* competent

competición *nf* competition, contest

competido,-a *adj* hard-fought

competidor,-a 1 *nm,f* (**a**) *Com & Dep*

competitor (**b**) *(participante)* contestant **2** *adj* competing
competir [6] *vi* to compete (**con** with *o* against; **en** in; **por** for)
competitividad *nf* competitivity
competitivo,-a *adj* competitive
compilar *vt* to compile
compinche *nmf* (**a**) *(compañero)* chum, pal (**b**) *(cómplice)* accomplice
complacencia *nf* (**a**) *(satisfacción)* satisfaction (**b**) *(indulgencia)* indulgence

> *ℓ* Observa que la palabra inglesa **complacency** es un falso amigo y no es la traducción de la palabra española **complacencia**. En inglés, **complacency** significa "autocomplacencia".

complacer [60] 1 *vt* to please; *Fml* **me complace presentarles a ...** it gives me great pleasure to introduce to you ...
2 complacerse *vpr* to delight (**en** in), to take pleasure (**en** in)
complaciente *adj* obliging
complejidad *nf* complexity
complejo,-a *adj & nm* complex
complementar 1 *vt* to complement
2 complementarse *vpr* to complement (each other), to be complementary to (each other)
complementario,-a *adj* complementary
complemento *nm* complement; *Ling* object
completamente *adv* completely
completar *vt* to complete
completo,-a *adj* (**a**) *(terminado)* complete; **por c.** completely (**b**) *(lleno)* full; **al c.** full up to capacity
complexión *nf* build; **de c. fuerte** well-built

> *ℓ* Observa que la palabra inglesa **complexion** es un falso amigo y no es la traducción de la palabra española **complexión**. En inglés, **complexion** significa "tez".

complicación *nf* complication
complicado,-a *adj* (**a**) *(complejo)* complicated (**b**) *(implicado)* involved
complicar [44] 1 *vt* (**a**) to complicate (**b**) **c. en** *(involucrar)* to involve in
2 complicarse *vpr* to get complicated; **c. la vida** to make life difficult for oneself
cómplice *nmf* accomplice
complot *nm* (*pl* **complots**) conspiracy, plot
componente 1 *adj* component
2 *nm* (**a**) *(pieza)* component; *(ingrediente)* ingredient (**b**) *(persona)* member

componer [19] (*pp* **compuesto**) **1** *vt* (**a**) *(formar)* to compose, to make up (**b**) *Mús & Lit* to compose (**c**) *(reparar)* to mend, to repair
2 componerse *vpr* (**a**) **c. de** *(consistir)* to be made up of, to consist of (**b**) *(arreglarse)* to dress up (**c**) *Fam* **componérselas** to manage
comportamiento *nm* behaviour
comportar 1 *vt* to entail, to involve
2 comportarse *vpr* to behave; **c. mal** to misbehave
composición *nf* composition
compositor,-a *nm,f* composer
compostelano,-a *adj* from Santiago de Compostela
compostura *nf* composure
compota *nf* compote
compra *nf* *(acción)* buying; *(cosa comprada)* purchase, buy; **ir de c.** to go shopping
comprador,-a *nm,f* purchaser, buyer
comprar *vt* (**a**) to buy (**b**) *Fig (sobornar)* to bribe, to buy off
compraventa *nf* buying and selling; **contrato de c.** contract of sale
comprender *vt* (**a**) *(entender)* to understand; **se comprende** it's understandable (**b**) *(contener)* to comprise, to include
comprensible *adj* understandable
comprensión *nf* understanding
comprensivo,-a *adj* understanding

> *ℓ* Observa que la palabra inglesa **comprehensive** es un falso amigo y no es la traducción de la palabra española **comprensivo**. En inglés, **comprehensive** significa "amplio, detallado".

compresa *nf* (**a**) *(para mujer)* sanitary towel (**b**) *Med* compress
comprimido,-a 1 *nm Farm* tablet
2 *adj* compressed; **escopeta de aire c.** air rifle
comprimir *vt* to compress
comprobante *nm* *(de compra etc)* voucher, receipt
comprobar [2] *vt* to check
comprometer 1 *vt* (**a**) *(arriesgar)* to compromise, to jeopardize (**b**) *(obligar)* to compel, to force
2 comprometerse *vpr* (**a**) **c. a hacer algo** to undertake to do sth (**b**) *(novios)* to become engaged
comprometido,-a *adj* (**a**) *(situación)* difficult (**b**) *(para casarse)* engaged
compromiso *nm* (**a**) *(obligación)* obligation, commitment; **sin c.** without obligation; **por c.** out of a sense of duty (**b**) **poner (a algn) en un c.** to put (sb) in a

difficult o embarrassing situation (**c**) *(acuerdo)* agreement; *Fml* **c. matrimonial** engagement; **soltero y sin c.** single and unattached

> ⚠ Observa que la palabra inglesa **compromise** es un falso amigo y no es la traducción de la palabra española **compromiso**. En inglés, **compromise** significa "solución negociada".

compuesto,-a 1 *adj* (**a**) compound (**b**) **c. de** composed of
   2 *nm* compound
compulsar *vt* to make a certified true copy of
compungido,-a *adj (arrepentido)* remorseful; *(triste)* sorrowful, sad
compuse *pt indef de* **componer**
computadora *nf* computer
cómputo *nm* calculation
comulgar [42] *vi* (**a**) to receive Holy Communion (**b**) *Fig* **no comulgo con sus ideas** I don't share his ideas
común 1 *adj* (**a**) common; **de c. acuerdo** by common consent; **hacer algo en c.** to do sth jointly; **poco c.** unusual; **por lo c.** generally (**b**) *(compartido)* shared, communal; **amigos comunes** mutual friends
   2 *nm Br Pol* **los Comunes** the Commons
comuna *nf Am (municipalidad)* municipality
comunal *adj* communal
comunero,-a *nm,f Perú, Méx (indígena)* = member of an indigenous village community
comunicación *nf* (**a**) communication; **ponerse en c. (con algn)** to get in touch (with sb) (**b**) *(comunicado)* communication; **c. oficial** communiqué (**c**) *Tel* connection; **se nos cortó la c.** we were cut off (**d**) *(unión)* link, connection
comunicado,-a 1 *adj* **una zona bien comunicada** a well-served zone; **dos ciudades bien comunicadas** two towns with good connections (between them)
   2 *nm* communiqué; **c. de prensa** press release
comunicar [44] 1 *vt* to communicate; **comuníquenoslo lo antes posible** let us know as soon as possible
   2 *vi* (**a**) to communicate (**b**) *Tel* to be engaged; **está comunicando** it's engaged
   3 comunicarse *upr* to communicate
comunicativo,-a *adj* communicative
comunidad *nf* community; **C. Europea** European Community; **C. de Estados Independientes** Commonwealth of Independent States
comunión *nf* communion
comunismo *nm* communism
comunista *adj & nmf* communist
comunitario,-a *adj* (**a**) of o relating to the community (**b**) *(de UE)* of o relating to the EU; **la política agraria comunitaria** the common agricultural policy
con *prep* (**a**) with; **córtalo c. las tijeras** cut it with the scissors; **voy cómodo c. este jersey** I'm comfortable in this sweater
   (**b**) *(compañía)* with; **vine c. mi hermana** I came with my sister
   (**c**) **c. ese frío/niebla** in that cold/fog; **estar c. (la) gripe** to have the flu
   (**d**) *(contenido)* with; **una bolsa c. dinero** a bag (full) of money
   (**e**) *(a)* to; **habló c. todos** he spoke to everybody; **sé amable c. ella** be nice to her
   (**f**) *(con infinitivo)* **c. llamar será suficiente** it will be enough just to phone
   (**g**) *(+ que + subjuntivo)* **bastará c. que lo esboces** a general idea will do
   (**h**) **c. tal (de) que ...** provided that ...; **c. todo (y eso)** even so
conato *nm* attempt; **c. de asesinato** attempted murder
concebible *adj* conceivable, imaginable
concebir [6] 1 *vt* (**a**) *(plan, hijo)* to conceive (**b**) *(entender)* to understand
   2 *vi (mujer)* to become pregnant, to conceive
conceder *vt* to grant; *(premio)* to award
concejal,-a *nm,f* town councillor
concejo *nm* council
concentración *nf* concentration; *(de manifestantes)* gathering; *(de coches, motos)* rally; *(de equipo)* base
concentrado *nm* concentrate
concentrar 1 *vt* to concentrate
   2 concentrarse *upr* (**a**) to concentrate (**en** on) (**b**) *(reunirse)* to gather
concepción *nf* conception
concepto *nm* (**a**) *(idea)* concept; **tener buen/mal c. de** to have a good/a bad opinion of; **bajo/por ningún c.** under no circumstances (**b**) **en c. de** under the heading of (**c**) *(en factura)* item
concerniente *adj* **c.** (**a**) concerning, regarding; *Fml* **en lo c. a** with regard to
concernir [54] *v impers* (**a**) *(afectar)* to concern; **en lo que a mí concierne** as far as I am concerned; **en lo que concierne a** with regard/respect to (**b**) *(corresponder)* to be up to
concertación *nf* compromise, agreement

concertar [1] 1 *vt* (**a**) *(cita)* to arrange; *(precio)* to agree on; *(acuerdo)* to reach (**b**) *(una acción etc)* to plan, to co-ordinate
2 *vi* to agree, to tally

concesión *nf* (**a**) concession (**b**) *(de un premio, contrato)* awarding

concesionario,-a *nm,f* dealer

concha *nf* (**a**) *Zool (caparazón)* shell; *(carey)* tortoiseshell (**b**) *Andes, RP Vulg Br* fanny, *US* beaver (**c**) *Ven (de árbol)* bark; *(de fruta)* peel, rind; *(del pan)* crust; *(de huevo)* shell

conchabarse *vpr* to gang up

concheto,-a *RP Fam* **1** *adj* posh
2 *nm,f* rich kid

conchudo,-a *nm,f Perú, RP Vulg* prick, *Br* dickhead

conciencia *nf* (**a**) conscience; **tener la c. tranquila** with a clear conscience (**b**) *(conocimiento)* consciousness, awareness; **a c.** conscientiously; **tener/tomar c. (de algo)** to be/to become aware (of sth)

concienciar [43], *Am* **concientizar [40] 1** *vt* **c. de** to make aware of
2 concienciarse *vpr* to become aware (de of)

concienzudo,-a *adj* conscientious

concierto *nm* (**a**) *Mús* concert; *(composición)* concerto (**b**) *(acuerdo)* agreement

conciliar [43] *vt* to reconcile; **c. el sueño** to get to sleep

concilio *nm* council

conciso,-a *adj* concise

conciudadano,-a *nm,f* fellow citizen

concluir [37] *vt* to conclude

conclusión *nf* conclusion; **sacar una c.** to draw a conclusion

concluyente *adj* conclusive

concomerse *vpr* to be consumed; **c. de envidia** to be green with envy

concordar [2] 1 *vi* to agree; **esto no concuerda con lo que dijo ayer** this doesn't fit in with what he said yesterday
2 *vt* to bring into agreement

concordia *nf* concord

concretamente *adv* specifically

concretar *vt (precisar)* to specify, to state explicitly; *(fecha, hora)* to fix

concreto,-a 1 *adj* (**a**) *(preciso, real)* concrete (**b**) *(particular)* specific; **en c.** specifically; **en el caso c. de ...** in the specific case of ...
2 *nm Am* concrete

concurrencia *nf* (**a**) *(de dos cosas)* concurrence (**b**) *(público)* audience

concurrido,-a *adj* crowded, busy

concurrir *vi* (**a**) *(gente)* to converge (**en** on), to meet (**en** in) (**b**) *(coincidir)* to concur, to coincide (**c**) *(participar)* to compete; *(en elecciones)* to be a candidate

concursante *nmf* (**a**) contestant, competitor (**b**) *(para un empleo)* candidate

concursar *vi* to compete, to take part

concurso *nm* (**a**) *(competición)* competition; *(de belleza etc)* contest; *TV* quiz show; **presentar (una obra) a c.** to invite tenders (for a piece of work) (**b**) *Fml (ayuda)* help

---

> Observa que la palabra inglesa **concourse** es un falso amigo y no es la traducción de la palabra española **concurso**. En inglés, **concourse** significa "vestíbulo".

---

condal *adj* of o relating to a count; **la Ciudad C.** Barcelona

conde *nm* count

condecoración *nf* decoration

condecorar *vt* to decorate

condena *nf* (**a**) *Jur* sentence (**b**) *(desaprobación)* condemnation, disapproval

condenado,-a 1 *adj* (**a**) *Jur* convicted; **c. a muerte** condemned to death (**b**) *Rel & Fam* damned; **c. al fracaso** doomed to failure
2 *nm,f* (**a**) *Jur* convicted person; *(a muerte)* condemned person (**b**) *Rel* damned person

condenar 1 *vt* (**a**) *Jur* to convict, to find guilty; **c. a algn a muerte** to condemn sb to death (**b**) *(desaprobar)* to condemn
2 condenarse *vpr Rel* to be damned

condensado,-a *adj* condensed; **leche condensada** condensed milk

condensador *nm* condenser

condensar *vt,* **condensarse** *vpr* to condense

condesa *nf* countess

condescender [3] *vi* (**a**) to condescend (**b**) *(ceder)* to comply (with), to consent (to)

condescendiente *adj* (**a**) *(displicente)* condescending (**b**) *(complaciente)* complacent

condición *nf* (**a**) condition; **en buenas/ malas condiciones** in good/bad condition; **condiciones de trabajo** working conditions; **con la c. de que ...** on the condition that ... (**b**) *(manera de ser)* nature, character (**c**) **en su c. de director** *(calidad)* in his capacity as director

condicional *adj* conditional

condicionar *vt* (**a**) to condition (**b**) **una**

cosa condiciona la otra one thing determines the other

condimentar *vt* to season, to flavour

condimento *nm* seasoning, flavouring

condolerse [4] *vpr* **c. de** to sympathize with

condominio *nm Am (edificio) Br* block of flats, *US* condominium

condón *nm* condom

condonar *vt (ofensa)* to condone; *(deuda)* to cancel

cóndor *nm* condor

conducir [10] 1 *vt (coche)* to drive; *(electricidad)* to conduct
  2 *vi* (**a**) *Aut* to drive; **permiso de c.** *Br* driving licence, *US* driver's license (**b**) *(camino, actitud)* to lead; **eso no conduce a nada** this leads nowhere

conducta *nf* behaviour, conduct; **mala c.** misbehaviour, misconduct

conducto *nm* (**a**) *(tubería)* pipe; *Fig* **por conductos oficiales** through official channels (**b**) *Anat* duct, canal

conductor,-a 1 *nm,f Aut* driver
  2 *nm Elec* conductor

conectar *vt* (**a**) to connect up (**b**) *Elec* to plug in, to switch on

coneja *nf* doe rabbit

conejillo *nm* **c. de Indias** guinea pig

conejo *nm* rabbit

conexión *nf* connection

confabularse *vpr* to conspire, to plot

confección *nf* (**a**) *Cost* dressmaking, tailoring; **la industria de la c.** the rag trade (**b**) *(de un plan etc)* making, making up

confeccionar *vt* to make (up)

confederación *nf* confederation

conferencia *nf* (**a**) lecture; **dar una c. (sobre algo)** to give a lecture (on sth) (**b**) **c. de prensa** press conference (**c**) *Tel* long-distance call

conferenciante *nmf* lecturer

conferir [5] *vt Fml (honor, privilegio)* to confer

confesar [1] 1 *vt* to confess, to admit; *(crimen)* to own up to; *Rel (pecados)* to confess
  2 *vi Jur* to own up
  3 • confesarse *vpr* to confess; **c. culpable** to admit one's guilt; *Rel* to go to confession

confesión *nf* confession, admission; *Rel* confession

confesionario *nm Rel* confessional

confeti *nm (pl* **confetis***)* confetti

confiado,-a *adj* (**a**) *(seguro)* self-confident (**b**) *(crédulo)* gullible, unsuspecting

confianza *nf* (**a**) *(seguridad)* confidence;

tener c. en uno mismo to be self-confident (**b**) **de c.** reliable (**c**) **tener c. con algn** to be on intimate terms with sb; **con toda c.** in all confidence; **tomarse (demasiadas) confianzas** to take liberties

confiar [29] 1 *vt (entregar)* to entrust; *(información, secreto)* to confide
  2 *vi* **c. en** to trust; **confío en ella** I trust her; **no confíes en su ayuda** don't count on his help
  3 confiarse *vpr* to confide (**en** *o* **a** in); **c. demasiado** to be over-confident

confidencia *nf* confidence

confidencial *adj* confidential

confidente,-a *nm,f* (**a**) *(hombre)* confidant; *(mujer)* confidante (**b**) *(de la policía)* informer

configuración *nf* configuration; *Informát* configuration

configurar *vt* to shape, to form

confín *nm* limit, boundary

confinar *vt Jur* to confine

confirmación *nf* confirmation

confirmar *vt* to confirm; *Prov* **la excepción confirma la regla** the exception proves the rule

confiscar [44] *vt* to confiscate

confite *nm Br* sweet, *US* candy

confitería *nf* (**a**) confectioner's (shop), *US* candy store (**b**) *CSur* café

confitura *nf* preserve, jam

conflagración *nf Fig* **c. mundial** world war

conflictividad *nf* **c. laboral** industrial unrest

conflictivo,-a *adj (asunto)* controversial; *(época)* unsettled; **niño c.** problem child

conflicto *nm* conflict; **c. laboral** industrial dispute

confluencia *nf* confluence

confluir [37] *vi* to converge; *(caminos, ríos)* to meet, to come together

conformar 1 *vt* to shape
  2 conformarse *vpr* to resign oneself, to be content

conforme 1 *adj* (**a**) *(satisfecho)* satisfied; **c.** agreed, all right; **no estoy c.** I don't agree (**b**) **c. a** in accordance *o* keeping with
  2 *conj* (**a**) *(según, como)* as; **c. lo vi/lo oí** as I saw/heard it (**b**) *(a medida que)* as; **la policía los detenía c. iban saliendo** the police were arresting them as they came out

conformidad *nf* (**a**) approval, consent (**b**) **en c. con** in conformity with

conformismo *nm* conformity

conformista *adj & nmf* conformist

confort nm (pl **conforts**) comfort; **todo c.** (en anuncio) all mod cons

confortable adj comfortable

confortar vt to comfort

confraternizar [40] vi to fraternize

confrontación nf (**a**) (enfrentamiento) confrontation (**b**) (comparación) contrast

confrontar vt (**a**) to confront (**b**) (cotejar) to compare, to collate

confundir 1 vt (**a**) to confuse (**con** with); **c. a una persona con otra** to mistake somebody for somebody else (**b**) (persona) to mislead (**c**) (turbar) to confound

2 confundirse vpr (**a**) (equivocarse) to be mistaken; Tel **se ha confundido** you've got the wrong number (**b**) (mezclarse) to mingle; **se confundió entre el gentío** he disappeared into the crowd

confusión nf confusion

confuso,-a adj (**a**) confused; (formas, recuerdo) blurred, vague (**b**) (mezclado) mixed up

congelación nf (**a**) freezing (**b**) Fin freeze; **c. salarial** wage freeze (**c**) Med frostbite

congelado,-a 1 adj frozen; Med frostbitten

2 nmpl **congelados** frozen food

congelador nm freezer

congelar 1 vt to freeze

2 congelarse vpr (**a**) to freeze; Fam **me estoy congelando** I'm freezing (**b**) Med to get o become frostbitten

congeniar [43] vi to get on (**con** with)

congénito,-a adj congenital

congestión nf congestion; Med **c. cerebral** stroke

congestionar vt to congest

conglomerado nm conglomerate

conglomerar vt, **conglomerarse** vpr to conglomerate

congoja nf sorrow, grief

congraciarse [43] vpr to ingratiate oneself (**con** with)

congratular vt Fml to congratulate (**por** on)

congregación nf congregation

congregar [42] vt, **congregarse** vpr to congregate, to assemble

congresista nmf member of a congress

congreso nm congress, conference; Pol **c. de los Diputados** Br ≃ Parliament, US ≃ Congress

congrio nm conger (eel)

congruente adj coherent, suitable

conjetura nf conjecture; **por c.** by guesswork

conjeturar vt to conjecture

conjugación nf conjugation

conjugar [42] vt to conjugate; Fig (planes, opiniones) to combine

conjunción nf conjunction

conjuntar vt to co-ordinate

conjuntivitis nf conjunctivitis

conjunto,-a 1 nm (**a**) (grupo) collection, group (**b**) (todo) whole; **de c.** overall; **en c.** on the whole (**c**) Mús (pop) group, band (**d**) (prenda) outfit, ensemble (**e**) Mat set (**f**) Dep team

2 adj joint

conjurar 1 vt to exorcise; (peligro) to ward off

2 conjurarse vpr to conspire, to plot

conjuro nm (**a**) (exorcismo) exorcism (**b**) (encantamiento) spell, incantation

conllevar vt to entail

conmemoración nf commemoration

conmemorar vt to commemorate

conmigo pron pers with me; **vino c.** he came with me; **él habló c.** he talked to me

conminar vt to threaten, to menace

conmoción nf commotion, shock; **c. cerebral** concussion

conmocionar vt to shock; Med to concuss

conmovedor,-a adj touching; **una película conmovedora** a moving film

conmover [4] vt to touch, to move

conmutador nm (**a**) Elec switch (**b**) Am Tel switchboard

conmutar vt to exchange; Jur to commute; Elec to commutate

connivencia nf connivance, collusion

connotación nf connotation

cono nm cone; **C. Sur** South America

conocedor,-a adj & nm,f expert; (de vino, arte etc) connoisseur

conocer [34] 1 vt (**a**) to know; **dar (algo/algn) a c.** to make (sth/sb) known (**b**) (a una persona) to meet (**c**) (reconocer) to recognize; **te conocí por la voz** I recognized you by your voice

2 conocerse vpr (dos personas) to know each other; (por primera vez) to meet

conocido,-a 1 adj known; (famoso) well-known

2 nm,f acquaintance

conocimiento nm (**a**) knowledge; **con c. de causa** with full knowledge of the facts (**b**) (conciencia) consciousness; **perder/recobrar el c.** to lose/regain consciousness (**c**) **conocimientos** knowledge

conque conj so

conquense 1 adj of/from Cuenca

2 nmf person from Cuenca

conquista *nf* conquest

conquistador,-a *nm,f* conqueror

conquistar *vt (país, ciudad)* to conquer; *Fig (puesto, título)* to win; *(a una persona)* to win over

consabido,-a *adj* (**a**) *(bien conocido)* well-known (**b**) *(usual)* familiar, usual

consagración *nf* (**a**) *Rel* consecration (**b**) *(de un artista)* recognition

consagrar 1 *vt* (**a**) *Rel* to consecrate (**b**) *(artista)* to confirm (**c**) *(tiempo, vida)* to devote

  2 consagrarse *vpr* **c. a** *(dedicarse)* to devote oneself to, to dedicate oneself to (**b**) *(lograr fama)* to establish oneself

consciente *adj* (**a**) conscious, aware; **ser c. de algo** to be aware of sth (**b**) *Med* conscious

conscripto *nm Andes, Arg* conscript

consecución *nf* (**a**) *(de un objetivo)* achievement (**b**) *(obtención)* obtaining

consecuencia *nf* (**a**) consequence; **a** *o* **como c. de** as a consequence *o* result of; **en c.** therefore; **tener** *o* **traer (malas) consecuencias** to have (ill) effects; **sacar como** *o* **en c.** to come to a conclusion (**b**) *(coherencia)* consistency; **actuar en c.** to be consistent

consecuente *adj* consistent

consecutivo,-a *adj* consecutive; **tres días consecutivos** three days in a row

conseguir [6] *vt* (**a**) to get, to obtain; *(objetivo)* to achieve (**b**) **conseguí terminar** I managed to finish

consejero,-a *nm,f* (**a**) *(asesor)* adviser (**b**) *Pol* councillor (**c**) *Com* **c. delegado** managing director

consejo *nm* (**a**) *(recomendación)* advice; **un c.** a piece of advice (**b**) *(junta)* council; **c. de ministros** cabinet; *(reunión)* cabinet meeting; **c. de administración** board of directors; **c. de guerra** court martial

consenso *nm* consensus

consensuar *vt* to approve by consensus

consentido,-a *adj* spoiled

consentimiento *nm* consent

consentir [5] 1 *vt* (**a**) *(tolerar)* to allow, to permit; **no consientas que haga eso** don't allow him to do that (**b**) *(mimar)* to spoil

  2 *vi* to consent; **c. en** to agree to

conserje *nm* commissionaire; *(en escuela etc)* janitor

conserva *nf* tinned *o* canned food

conservación *nf* (**a**) preservation (**b**) *(mantenimiento)* maintenance, upkeep

conservador,-a 1 *adj & nm,f* conservative; *Pol* Conservative

  2 *nm (de museo)* curator

conservadurismo *nm* conservatism

conservante *nm* preservative

conservar 1 *vt* to conserve, to preserve; *(mantener)* to keep up, to maintain; *(alimentos)* to preserve

  2 conservarse *vpr* (**a**) *(tradición etc)* to survive (**b**) **c. bien** *(persona)* to age well

conservatorio *nm* conservatory

considerable *adj* considerable

consideración *nf* (**a**) consideration; **tomar algo en c.** to take sth into account (**b**) *(respeto)* regard (**c**) **de c.** important, considerable; **herido de c.** seriously injured

considerado,-a *adj* (**a**) *(atento)* considerate, thoughtful (**b**) **estar bien/mal c.** to be well/badly thought of

considerar *vt* to consider; **lo considero imposible** I think it's impossible

consigna *nf* (**a**) *(para maletas) Br* left-luggage office, *US* checkroom (**b**) *Mil* orders, instructions

consignar *vt* (**a**) *(puesto)* to allocate; *(cantidad)* to assign (**b**) *(mercancía)* to ship, to dispatch

consigo¹ *pron pers* (**a**) *(tercera persona) (hombre)* with him; *(mujer)* with her; *(cosa, animal)* with it; *(plural)* with them; *(usted)* with you (**b**) **hablar c. mismo** to speak to oneself

consigo² *indic pres de* **conseguir**

consiguiente *adj* resulting, consequent; **por c.** therefore, consequently

consistencia *nf* (**a**) consistency (**b**) *(de argumento)* soundness

consistente *adj* (**a**) *(firme)* firm, solid (**b**) *(teoría)* sound (**c**) **c. en** consisting of

> *Observa que la palabra inglesa **consistent** es un falso amigo y no es la traducción de la palabra española **consistente**. En inglés, **consistent** significa "consecuente".*

consistir *vi* to consist (**en** of); **el secreto consiste en tener paciencia** the secret lies in being patient

consistorial *adj* **casa c.** town hall

consola *nf* console table; *Informát* console

consolación *nf* consolation; **premio de c.** consolation prize

consolador,-a 1 *adj* consoling, comforting

  2 *nm* dildo

consolar [2] 1 *vt* to console, to comfort

  2 consolarse *vpr* to console oneself, to take comfort (**con** from)

consolidar *vt*, **consolidarse** *vpr* to consolidate

consomé nm clear soup, consommé
consonancia nf **en c. con** in keeping with
consonante adj & nf consonant
consorcio nm consortium
consorte 1 adj **príncipe c.** prince consort
 2 nmf (cónyuge) partner, spouse
conspicuo,-a adj prominent, outstanding
conspiración nf conspiracy, plot
conspirar vi to conspire, to plot
constancia nf (**a**) constancy, perseverance (**b**) (testimonio) proof, evidence; **dejar c. de algo** to put sth on record
constante 1 adj constant; (persona) steadfast
 2 nf constant feature; Mat constant
constantemente adv constantly
constar vi (**a**) (figurar) to figure, to be included (**en** in); **c. en acta** to be on record (**b**) **me consta que ...** I am absolutely certain that ... (**c**) **c. de** to be made up of, to consist of
constatar vt to state; (comprobar) to check
constelación nf constellation
consternación nf consternation
consternar vt to dismay
constipado,-a 1 adj **estar c.** to have a cold o a chill
 2 nm cold, chill

> ℓ Observa que la palabra inglesa **constipated** es un falso amigo y no es la traducción de la palabra española **constipado**. En inglés, **constipated** significa "estreñido".

constiparse vpr to catch a cold o a chill
constitución nf constitution
constitucional adj constitutional
constituir [37] 1 vt (**a**) (formar) to constitute; **estar constituido por** to consist of (**b**) (suponer) to represent (**c**) (fundar) to constitute, to set up
 2 constituirse vpr **c. en** to set oneself up as
constituyente adj & nmf constituent
constreñir [6] vt (**a**) (forzar) to compel, to force (**b**) (oprimir) to restrict (**c**) Med to constrict
construcción nf (**a**) construction; (sector) the building industry; **en c.** under construction (**b**) (edificio) building
constructivo,-a adj constructive
constructor,-a 1 nm,f builder
 2 adj **empresa constructora** builders, construction company
construir [37] vt to build, to manufacture

> ℓ Observa que el verbo inglés **to construe** es un falso amigo y no es la traducción del verbo español **construir**. En inglés, **to construe** significa "interpretar".

consuelo nm consolation
cónsul nmf consul
consulado nm consulate
consulta nf (**a**) consultation; **obra de c.** reference book (**b**) Med surgery; (despacho) consulting room; **horas de c.** surgery hours
consultar vt to consult, to seek advice (**con** from); (libro) to look up
consultivo,-a adj consultative, advisory
consultorio nm (**a**) Med medical centre (**b**) Prensa problem page, advice column
consumado,-a adj (**a**) consummated; **hecho c.** fait accompli, accomplished fact (**b**) Fig (artista) consummate
consumar vt to complete, to carry out; (crimen) to commit
consumición nf (**a**) consumption (**b**) (bebida) drink
consumidor,-a 1 nm,f consumer
 2 adj consuming
consumir 1 vt to consume
 2 consumirse vpr (al hervir) to boil away; Fig (persona) to waste away
consumismo nm consumerism
consumo nm consumption; **bienes de c.** consumer goods; **sociedad de c.** consumer society
contabilidad nf Com (**a**) (profesión) accountancy (**b**) (de empresa, sociedad) accounting, book-keeping
contabilizar [40] vt Com to enter in the books; Dep to score
contable nmf accountant
contactar vi **c. con** to contact, to get in touch with
contacto nm contact; Aut ignition; **perder el c.** to lose touch; **ponerse en c.** to get in touch
contado,-a 1 adj few and far between; **contadas veces** very seldom; **tiene los días contados** his days are numbered
 2 nm **pagar al c.** to pay cash
contador,-ora 1 nm,f Am (persona) accountant; **c. público** Br chartered accountant, US certified public accountant
 2 nm (aparato) meter; **c. de agua** water meter
contagiar [43] 1 vt Med to pass on
 2 contagiarse vpr (**a**) (persona) to get infected (**b**) (enfermedad) to be contagious
contagio nm contagion

contagioso,-a *adj* contagious; *Fam (risa)* infectious

contaminación *nf* contamination; *(del aire)* pollution

contaminar *vt* to contaminate; *(aire, agua)* to pollute

contante *adj* **dinero c. (y sonante)** hard *o* ready cash

contar [2] 1 *vt* (**a**) *(sumar)* to count (**b**) *(narrar)* to tell
   2 *vi* (**a**) to count (**b**) **c. con** *(confiar en)* to count on; *(tener)* to have
   3 contarse *vpr Fam* **¿qué te cuentas?** how's it going?

contemplación *nf* contemplation; *Fam* **no andarse con contemplaciones** to make no bones about it

contemplar *vt* to contemplate; *(considerar)* to consider; *(estipular)* to stipulate

contemporáneo,-a *adj & nm,f* contemporary

contención *nf* **muro de c.** retaining wall; **c. salarial** wage restraint

contencioso,-a 1 *adj* contentious; *Jur* litigious
   2 *nm Jur* legal dispute

contendiente *nmf* contender, contestant

contenedor *nm* container

contener [24] 1 *vt* (**a**) to contain (**b**) *(pasiones etc)* to restrain, to hold back
   2 contenerse *vpr* to control oneself, to hold (oneself) back

contenido *nm* content, contents

contentar 1 *vt* (**a**) *(satisfacer)* to please (**b**) *(alegrar)* to cheer up
   2 contentarse *vpr* (**a**) *(conformarse)* to make do (**con** with), to be satisfied (**con** with) (**b**) *(alegrarse)* to cheer up

contento,-a *adj* happy, pleased (**con** with)

contestación *nf* answer; **dar c.** to answer

contestador *nm* **c. automático** answering machine

contestar *vt* (**a**) to answer (**b**) *Fam (replicar)* to answer back

contestatario,-a *adj* anti-establishment

contexto *nm* context

contienda *nf* struggle

contigo *pron pers* with you

contiguo,-a *adj* contiguous (**a** to), adjoining

continente *nm* (**a**) *Geog* continent (**b**) *(compostura)* countenance

contingencia *nf* contingency

contingente *nm* contingent

continuación *nf* continuation; **a c.** next

continuamente *adv* continuously

continuar [30] *vt & vi* to continue, to carry on (with); **continúa en Francia** he's still in France; **continuará** to be continued

continuidad *nf* continuity

continuo,-a 1 *adj* (**a**) continuous; *Aut* **línea continua** solid white line (**b**) *(reiterado)* continual, constant
   2 *nm* continuum

contonearse *vpr* to swing one's hips

contorno *nm* (**a**) outline (**b**) **contornos** surroundings, environment

contorsión *nf* contortion

contorsionarse *vpr* to contort *o* twist oneself

contra 1 *prep* against; **en c. de** against
   2 *nm* **los pros y los contras** the pros and cons

contraataque *nm* counterattack

contrabajo *nm* double bass

contrabandista *nmf* smuggler; **c. de armas** gunrunner

contrabando *nm* smuggling; **c. de armas** gunrunning; **pasar algo de c.** to smuggle sth in

contracción *nf* contraction

contracepción *nf* contraception

contrachapado *nm* plywood

contracorriente 1 *nf* crosscurrent
   2 *adv* **ir (a) c.** to go against the tide

contradecir [12] *(pp* **contradicho***)* *vt* to contradict

contradicción *nf* contradiction

contradictorio,-a *adj* contradictory

contraer [25] 1 *vt* to contract; **c. matrimonio con algn** to marry sb
   2 contraerse *vpr* to contract

contraigo *indic pres de* **contraer**

contraindicación *nf* contraindication

contraje *pt indef de* **contraer**

contralor *nm Am* = inspector of public spending

contraloría *nf Am* = office controlling public spending

contraluz *nm* view against the light; **a c.** against the light

contramaestre *nm* (**a**) *(en buque)* boatswain (**b**) *(capataz)* foreman

contramano: • a contramano *loc adv* the wrong way *o* direction

contrapartida *nf* **en c.** in return

contrapelo: • a contrapelo *loc adv* the wrong way; *Fig* against the grain

contrapesar *vt* (**a**) to counterbalance, to counterpoise (**b**) *Fig (compensar)* to offset, to balance

contrapeso *nm* counterweight

contraportada *nf* back page

contraposición *nf* contrast

contraproducente *adj* counterproductive

contraprogramación *nf TV* competitive scheduling

contrapunto *nm* counterpoint

contrariamente *adv* **c. a ...** contrary to ...

contrariar [29] *vt* (a) *(oponerse a)* to oppose, to go against (b) *(disgustar)* to upset

contrariedad *nf* (a) *(contratiempo)* obstacle, setback (b) *(disgusto)* annoyance

contrario,-a 1 *adj* (a) opposite; **lo c. de** the opposite of; **en el lado/sentido c.** on the other side/in the other direction; **al c., por el c.** on the contrary; **de lo c.** otherwise; **todo lo c.** quite the opposite (b) *(perjudicial)* contrary (**a** to)
2 *nm,f* opponent, rival
3 *nf* **llevar la contraria** to be contrary

contrarrestar *vt* to offset, to counteract

contrasentido *nm* contradiction

contraseña *nf* password

contrastar *vt* to contrast (**con** with)

contraste *nm* (a) contrast (b) *(en oro, plata)* hallmark

contrata *nf* contract

contratar *vt* to hire, to engage

contratiempo *nm* setback, hitch

contratista *nmf* contractor

contrato *nm* contract; **c. de trabajo** work contract; **c. de alquiler** lease, leasing agreement; **c. basura** short-term contract with poor conditions

contravenir [27] *vt* to contravene, to infringe

contraventana *nf* shutter

contribución *nf* (a) contribution (b) *(impuesto)* tax

contribuir [37] **1** *vt* to contribute (**a** to)
2 *vi* (a) to contribute (b) *(pagar impuestos)* to pay taxes

contribuyente *nmf* taxpayer

contrincante *nmf* rival, opponent

control *nm* (a) control; **c. a distancia** remote control (b) *(inspección)* check; *(de policía etc)* checkpoint

controlador,-a *nm,f* **c. (aéreo)** air traffic controller

controlar 1 *vt* (a) to control (b) *(comprobar)* to check
2 controlarse *upr* to control oneself

controversia *nf* controversy

controvertido,-a *adj* controversial

contumaz *adj* obstinate

contundente *adj* (a) *(arma)* blunt (b) *(argumento)* forceful, convincing

contusión *nf* contusion, bruise

conuco *nm Carib, Col* small farm, *Br* smallholding

convalecencia *nf* convalescence

convaleciente *adj & nmf* convalescent

convalidar *vt* to validate; *(documento)* to ratify

convencer [49] *vt* to convince; **c. a algn de algo** to convince sb about sth

convencimiento *nm* conviction; **tener el c. de que ...** to be convinced that ...

convención *nf* convention

convencional *adj* conventional

convenido,-a *adj* agreed; **según lo c.** as agreed

conveniencia *nf* (a) *(provecho)* convenience (b) **conveniencias sociales** social proprieties

conveniente *adj* (a) *(oportuno)* convenient; *(aconsejable)* advisable (b) *(precio)* good, fair

convenio *nm* agreement; **c. laboral** agreement on salary and conditions

convenir [27] *vt & vi* (a) *(acordar)* to agree; **c. una fecha** to agree on a date; **sueldo a c.** salary negotiable; **c. en** to agree on (b) *(ser oportuno)* to suit, to be good for; **conviene recordar que ...** it's as well to remember that ...

convento *nm (de monjas)* convent; *(de monjes)* monastery

convergente *adj* convergent

converger [53] *vi* to converge

conversación *nf* conversation

conversada *nf Am Fam* chat

conversar *vi* to converse, to talk

conversión *nf* conversion

converso,-a *nm,f* convert

convertible *adj* convertible

convertir [54] **1** *vt* to change, to convert
2 convertirse *upr* (a) **c. en** to turn into, to become (b) *Rel* to be converted (**a** to)

convexo,-a *adj* convex

convicción *nf* conviction; **tengo la c. de que ...** I am convinced that ..

convicto,-a *adj* convicted

convidado,-a *adj & nm,f* guest

convidar *vt* to invite

convincente *adj* convincing

convite *nm* reception

convivencia *nf* life together; *Fig* coexistence

convivir *vi* to live together; *Fig* to coexist (**con** with)

convocar [44] *vt* to summon; *(reunión, elecciones)* to call

convocatoria *nf* (a) *(a huelga etc)* call (b) *Educ* diet

convulsión *nf Med* convulsion; *(agitación social)* upheaval
convulsivo,-a *adj* convulsive
conyugal *adj* conjugal; **vida c.** married life
cónyuge *nmf* spouse; **cónyuges** married couple, husband and wife
coña *nf muy Fam* **estar de c.** to be joking
coñac *nm* brandy, cognac
coñazo *nm muy Fam* pain, drag; **dar el c.** to be a real pain
coño 1 *nm Vulg* cunt
2 *interj Vulg* for fuck's sake!
cooperación *nf* co-operation
cooperador,-a *nm,f* collaborator, co-operator
cooperante *nmf* aid worker
cooperar *vi* to co-operate (**con** with)
cooperativa *nf* co-operative
coordenada *nf* co-ordinate
coordinación *nf* co-ordination
coordinador,-a *nm,f* co-ordinator
coordinadora *nf* co-ordinating committee; **c. general** joint committee
coordinar *vt* to co-ordinate
copa *nf* (**a**) glass; **tomar una c.** to have a drink (**b**) *(de árbol)* top (**c**) *Dep* cup (**d**) *Naipes* **copas** hearts
copar *vt* to take up
copartícipe *adj & nmf (socio)* partner; *(colaborador)* collaborator; *(copropietario)* joint owner, co-owner
Copenhague *n* Copenhagen
copetín *nm RP* pre-lunch/pre-dinner drinks
copia *nf* copy; *Informát* **c. de seguridad** backup; *Informát* **hacer una c. de seguridad de algo** to back up sth
copiar [43] *vt* to copy
copiloto *nm Av* copilot; *Aut* co-driver
copioso,-a *adj* abundant, copious
copistería *nf* photocopying service
copla *nf* verse, couplet
copo *nm* flake; *(de nieve)* snowflake; **copos de maíz** cornflakes
coproducción *nf* co-production, joint production
cópula *nf* (**a**) *(coito)* copulation, intercourse (**b**) *Ling* conjunction
copular *vt* to copulate (**con** with)
coqueta *nf* dressing table
coquetear *vi* to flirt (**con** with)
coqueto,-a 1 *adj* coquettish
2 *nm,f* flirt
coraje *nm* (**a**) *(valor)* courage (**b**) *(ira)* anger, annoyance; *Fig* **dar c. a algn** to infuriate sb; **¡qué c.!** how maddening!
coral¹ *nm Zool* coral

coral² *nf Mús* choral, chorale
Corán *nm* Koran
coraza *nf* armour; *Fig* protection
corazón *nm* (**a**) heart; *Fig* **de (todo) c.** in all sincerity; *Fig* **tener buen c.** to be kindhearted (**b**) *(parte central)* heart; *(de fruta)* core (**c**) *Naipes* **corazones** hearts
corazonada *nf* hunch, feeling
corbata *nf* tie, *US* necktie; **con c.** wearing a tie
Córcega *n* Corsica
corchete *nm* (**a**) *Impr* square bracket (**b**) *Cost* hook and eye, snap fastener
corcho *nm* cork; *(de pesca)* float
cordel *nm* rope, cord
cordero,-a *nm,f* lamb
cordial *adj* cordial, warm
cordialidad *nf* cordiality, warmth
cordillera *nf* mountain chain *o* range
córdoba *nm Fin* = monetary unit of Nicaragua
cordón *nm* string; *(de zapatos)* shoelace; *Anat* **c. umbilical** umbilical cord; **c. policial** police cordon; *CSur, Cuba (de la vereda) Br* kerb, *US* curb
cordura *nf* common sense
Corea *n* Korea; **C. del Norte/Sur** North/South Korea
coreano,-a *adj & nm,f* Korean
corear *vt* (**a**) *(cantar a coro)* to sing in chorus (**b**) *(aclamar)* to applaud
coreografía *nf* choreography
cornada *nf Taurom* goring
corneja *nf* crow
córner *nm Ftb* corner (kick); **sacar un c.** to take a corner
corneta *nf* bugle; **c. de llaves** cornet
cornisa *nf* cornice
cornudo *nm Fam (marido)* cuckold
coro *nm Mús* choir; *Teatro* chorus; *Fig* **a c.** all together
corona *nf* (**a**) crown (**b**) *(de flores etc)* wreath, garland; **c. funeraria** funeral wreath
coronación *nf* (**a**) coronation (**b**) *Fig (culminación)* crowning point
coronar *vt* to crown
coronel *nm* colonel
coronilla *nf* crown of the head; *Fam* **estar hasta la c. (de)** to be fed up (with)
corpiño *nm (vestido)* bodice; *Arg (sostén)* bra
corporación *nf* corporation
corporal *adj* corporal; **castigo c.** corporal punishment; **olor c.** body odour, BO
corporativo,-a *adj* corporative
corpulento,-a *adj* corpulent, stout
corpus *nm* corpus

corral *nm* farmyard, *US* corral; *(de casa)* courtyard

correa *nf* (**a**) *(tira)* strap; *(de reloj)* watchstrap; *(de pantalón)* belt; *(de perro)* lead, leash (**b**)*Téc* belt

corrección *nf* (**a**) *(rectificación)* correction (**b**) *(urbanidad)* courtesy, politeness

correcto,-a *adj* (**a**) *(sin errores)* correct (**b**) *(educado)* polite, courteous (**con** to); *(conducta)* proper

corredera *nf* **puerta/ventana de c.** sliding door/window

corredizo,-a *adj* sliding; **nudo c.** slip-knot; **techo c.** sunroof

corredor,-a *nm,f* (**a**) *Dep* runner (**b**) *Fin* **c. de bolsa** stockbroker

corregir [58] 1 *vt* to correct

2 corregirse *vpr* to mend one's ways

correo *nm* (**a**) post, mail; **echar al c.** to post; **por c.** by post; **c. aéreo** airmail; **c. certificado** registered post; *Informát* **c. electrónico** electronic mail, e-mail; *Informát* **me envió un c. (electrónico)** *(un mensaje)* she e-mailed me, she sent me an e-mail; **(tren) c.** mail train (**b**) **correos** *(edificio)* post office

correr 1 *vi* (**a**) to run; *(coche)* to go fast; *(conductor)* to drive fast; *(viento)* to blow; *Fig* **no corras, habla más despacio** don't rush, speak slower; **c. prisa** to be urgent (**b**) **c. con los gastos** to foot the bill; **corre a mi cargo** I'll take care of it

2 *vt* (**a**) *(cortina)* to draw; *(cerrojo)* to close; *(aventura etc)* to have; **c. el riesgo** *o* **peligro** to run the risk (**b**) *(mover)* to pull up, to draw up

3 correrse *vpr* (**a**) *(moverse)* to move over (**b**) *Fam* **c. una juerga** to go on a spree (**c**) *muy Fam (tener orgasmo)* to come

correspondencia *nf* (**a**) correspondence (**b**) *Ferroc* connection

corresponder 1 *vi* (**a**) to correspond (**a** to; **con** with) (**b**) *(incumbir)* to concern, to be incumbent upon; **esta tarea te corresponde a ti** it's your job to do this (**c**) *(pertenecer)* to belong; **me dieron lo que me correspondía** they gave me my share

2 corresponderse *vpr* (**a**) *(ajustarse)* to correspond (**b**) *(dos cosas)* to tally; **no se corresponde con la descripción** it does not match the description (**c**) *(dos personas)* to love each other

correspondiente *adj* corresponding (**a** to)

corresponsal *nmf* correspondent

corrida *nf* **c. (de toros)** bullfight

corrido,-a *adj* (**a**) *(avergonzado)*

abashed (**b**) **de c.** without stopping; **se lo sabe de c.** she knows it by heart

corriente 1 *adj* (**a**) *(común)* common (**b**) *(agua)* running (**c**) *(mes, año)* current, present; **el diez del c.** the tenth of this month (**d**) *Fin (cuenta)* current (**e**) **estar al c.** to be up to date

2 *nf* (**a**) current, stream; *Fig* **ir** *o* **navegar contra c.** to go against the tide; *Fam* **seguirle** *o* **llevarle la c. a algn** to humour sb; *Elec* **c. eléctrica** (electric) current (**b**) *(de aire)* draught (**c**) *(tendencia)* trend, current

corrijo *indic pres de* **corregir**

corrillo *nm* small group of people talking; *Fig* clique

corro *nm* (**a**) circle, ring (**b**) *(juego)* ring-a-ring-a-roses

corroborar *vt* to corroborate

corroer [38] *vt* to corrode; *Fig* **la envidia le corroe** envy eats away at him

corromper 1*vt* (**a**) *(pudrir)* to turn bad, to rot (**b**) *(pervertir)* to corrupt, to pervert

2 corromperse *vpr* (**a**) *(pudrirse)* to go bad, to rot (**b**) *(pervertirse)* to become corrupted

corrosivo,-a *adj* corrosive; *Fig (mordaz)* caustic

corrupción *nf* (**a**) *(putrefacción)* rot, decay (**b**) *Fig* corruption; *Jur* **c. de menores** corruption of minors

corrupto,-a *adj* corrupt

corsé *nm* corset

cortacésped *nm o nf* lawnmower

cortado,-a 1 *adj* (**a**) cut (up) (**b**) *(leche)* sour (**c**) *(labios)* chapped (**d**) *Fam (tímido)* shy

2 *nm* small coffee with a dash of milk

cortafuego *nm* firebreak

cortapisa *nf Fig* restriction, limitation

cortar 1 *vt* (**a**) to cut; *(carne)* to carve; *(árbol)* to cut down; *Fam* **c. por lo sano** to take drastic measures; *Fam* **cortó con su novio** she split up with her boyfriend (**b**) *(piel)* to chap, to crack (**c**) *(luz, teléfono)* to cut off (**d**) *(paso, carretera)* to block

2 cortarse *vpr* (**a**) *(herirse)* to cut oneself (**b**) **c. el pelo** to have one's hair cut (**c**) *(leche etc)* to curdle (**d**) *Tel* **se cortó la comunicación** we were cut off (**e**) *Fam (aturdirse)* to become all shy

cortaúñas *nm inv* nail clippers

corte¹ *nm* (**a**) cut; **c. de pelo** haircut; *TV* **c. publicitario** commercial break; **c. de mangas** ≃ V-sign (**b**) *(sección)* section; **c. transversal** cross section (**c**) *Fam* rebuff; **dar un c. a algn** to cut sb dead

corte² *nf* (**a**) *(real)* court (**b**) **Las Cortes** (Spanish) Parliament

cortejar *vt* to court

cortejo *nm* (**a**) *(galanteo)* courting (**b**) *(comitiva)* entourage, retinue; **c. fúnebre** funeral cortège

cortés *adj* courteous, polite

cortesía *nf* courtesy, politeness

corteza *nf* *(de árbol)* bark; *(de queso)* rind; *(de pan)* crust

cortijo *nm* Andalusian farm *o* farmhouse

cortina *nf* curtain; **c. de humo** smoke screen

corto,-a 1 *adj* (**a**) *(distancia, tiempo)* short; *Fam* **c. de luces** dim-witted; **c. de vista** short-sighted; *Aut* **luz corta** dipped headlights (**b**) *Fam* **quedarse c.** *(calcular mal)* to underestimate (**c**) *(apocado)* timid, shy
 2 *nm Cin* short (film)

cortocircuito *nm* short circuit

cortometraje *nm* short (film)

corvo,-a *adj* curved, bent

cosa *nf* (**a**) thing; **no he visto c. igual** I've never seen anything like it; **no ser gran c.** not to be up to much (**b**) *(asunto)* matter, business; **eso es c. tuya** that's your business *o* affair; **eso es otra c.** that's different (**c**) **hace c. de una hora** about an hour ago

coscorrón *nm* knock *o* blow on the head

cosecha *nf* (**a**) *Agr* harvest, crop (**b**) *(año del vino)* vintage

cosechadora *nf* combine harvester

cosechar *vt* to harvest, to gather (in)

coser *vt* (**a**) to sew; *Fam* **es c. y cantar** it's a piece of cake (**b**) *Med* to stitch up

cosmético,-a *adj & nm* cosmetic

cósmico,-a *adj* cosmic

cosmonauta *nmf* cosmonaut

cosmopolita *adj & nmf* cosmopolitan

cosmos *nm inv* cosmos

coso *nm* (**a**) *Taurom* bullring (**b**) *CSur Fam (objeto)* whatnot, thing

cosquillas *nfpl* tickling; **hacer c. a algn** to tickle sb; **tener c.** to be ticklish

cosquilleo *nm* tickling

costa¹ *nf* coast; *(litoral)* coastline; *(playa)* beach, seaside

costa² *nf* **a c. de** at the expense of; **a toda c.** at all costs, at any price; **vive a c. mía** he lives off me

costado *nm* side; **de c.** sideways; **es catalana por los cuatro costados** she's Catalan through and through

costal *nm* sack

costanera *nf CSur* seaside promenade

costar [2] *vi* (**a**) to cost; **¿cuánto cuesta?** how much is it?; **c. barato/caro** to be

cheap/expensive (**b**) *Fig* **te va a c. caro** you'll pay dearly for this; **c. trabajo** *o* **mucho** to be hard; **me cuesta hablar francés** I find it difficult to speak French; **cueste lo que cueste** at any cost

costarricense *adj & nmf*, **costarriqueño,-a** *adj & nm,f* Costa Rican

coste *nm* cost; **a precio de c.** (at) cost price; **c. de la vida** cost of living

costear 1 *vt* to afford, to pay for; **c. los gastos** to foot the bill
 2 costearse *vpr* to pay for

costero,-a 1 *adj* coastal; **ciudad costera** seaside town
 2 *nf Méx* **costera** seaside promenade

costilla *nf* (**a**) *Anat* rib (**b**) *Culin* cutlet

costo¹ *nm* cost

costo² *nm Fam (hachís)* dope, shit, stuff

costoso,-a *adj* costly, expensive

costra *nf* crust; *Med* scab

costumbre *nf* (**a**) *(hábito)* habit; **como de c.** as usual; **tengo la c. de levantarme temprano** I usually get up early; **tenía la c. de ...** he used to ... (**b**) *(tradición)* custom

costura *nf* (**a**) sewing (**b**) *(confección)* dressmaking; **alta c.** haute couture (**c**) *(línea de puntadas)* seam

costurera *nf* seamstress

costurero *nm* sewing basket

cota *nf Geog* height above sea level; *Fig* rating

cotejar *vt* to compare

cotidiano,-a *adj* daily; **vida cotidiana** everyday life

cotilla *nmf Fam* busybody, gossip

cotillear *vi Fam* to gossip (**de** about)

cotilleo *nm Fam* gossip

cotización *nf* (**a**) *Fin* (market) price, quotation (**b**) *(cuota)* membership fees, subscription

cotizar [40] 1 *vt Fin* to quote
 2 *vi* to pay national insurance
 3 cotizarse *vpr Fin* **c. a** to sell at

coto *nm* (**a**) enclosure, reserve; **c. de caza** game reserve (**b**) **poner c. a** to put a stop to

cotorra *nf* parrot; *Fig (persona)* chatterbox

COU *nm Educ (abr* **Curso de Orientación Universitaria**) = one-year course which prepares students aged 17-18 for Spanish university entrance examinations

country ['kauntri] *nm Arg* = luxury suburban housing development

coyote *nm* coyote, prairie wolf

coyuntura *nf* (**a**) *Anat* articulation, joint (**b**) *Fig (circunstancia)* juncture; **la c.**

económica the economic situation
coz *nf* kick; **dar una c.** to kick
C.P. (*abr* **código postal**) *Br* postcode, *US* zip code
crac(k) *nm* (**a**) *Fin* crash (**b**) *(droga)* crack
cráneo *nm* cranium, skull
cráter *nm* crater
creación *nf* creation
creador,-a *nm,f* creator
crear *vt* to create
creatividad *nf* creativity
creativo,-a *adj* creative
crecer [33] *vi* (**a**) to grow; **c. en importancia** to become more important (**b**) *(al tricotar)* to increase
creces *nfpl* **con c.** fully, in full; **devolver con c.** to return with interest
crecido,-a *adj (persona)* grown-up
creciente *adj* growing, increasing; **cuarto c.** crescent
crecimiento *nm* growth
credencial *adj* credential; **(cartas) credenciales** credentials
credibilidad *nf* credibility
crédito *nm* (**a**) *Com & Fin* credit (**b**) *(confianza)* belief; **dar c. a** to believe
credo *nm* creed
crédulo,-a *adj* credulous, gullible
creencia *nf* belief
creer [36] **1** *vt* (**a**) to believe (**b**) *(pensar)* to think; **creo que no** I don't think so; **creo que sí** I think so; **ya lo creo** I should think so
2 *vi* to believe; **c. en** to believe in
3 creerse *vpr* (**a**) to consider oneself to be; **¿qué te has creído?** what *o* who do you think you are? (**b**) **no me lo creo** I can't believe it
creíble *adj* credible, believable
creído,-a **1** *adj* arrogant, vain
2 *nm,f* big head
crema *nf* cream
cremallera *nf Br* zip (fastener), *US* zipper
crematorio *nm* **(horno) c.** crematorium
cremoso,-a *adj* creamy
crepe *nm* crêpe, pancake
crepería *nf* creperie
crepitar *vi* to crackle
crepúsculo *nm* twilight
crespo,-a *adj* frizzy
crespón *nm* crepe
cresta *nf* (**a**) crest; *(de gallo)* comb (**b**) *(de punk)* mohican
Creta *n* Crete
cretino,-a **1** *adj* stupid, cretinous
2 *nm,f* cretin
creyente *nmf* believer
crezco *indic pres de* **crecer**

cría *nf* (**a**) *(cachorro)* young (**b**) *(crianza)* breeding, raising
criada *nf* maid
criadero *nm* nursery
criadilla *nf Culin* bull's testicle
criado,-a **1** *adj* **mal c.** spoilt
2 *nm,f* servant
crianza *nf (de animales)* breeding; *Fig* **vinos de c.** vintage wines
criar [29] *vt* (**a**) *(animales)* to breed, to raise; *(niños)* to bring up, to rear (**b**) *(producir)* to have, to grow
criatura *nf* (**a**) (living) creature (**b**) *(crío)* baby, child
criba *nf* sieve
cribar *vt* to sieve, to sift
crimen *nm* (*pl* **crímenes**) murder; **c. de guerra** war crime
criminal *nmf & adj* criminal
crin *nf*, **crines** *nfpl* mane
crío,-a **1** *nm Fam* kid
2 *adj* babyish
criollo,-a *adj & nm,f* Creole
críquet *nm* cricket
crisantemo *nm* chrysanthemum
crisis *nf inv* (**a**) crisis (**b**) *(ataque)* fit, attack; **c. nerviosa** nervous breakdown
crispación *nf* tension
crispar *vt* to make tense; *Fig* **eso me crispa los nervios** that sets my nerves on edge
cristal *nm* (**a**) crystal; **c. de roca** rock crystal (**b**) *(vidrio)* glass; *(de gafas)* lense; *(de ventana)* (window) pane
cristalera *nf* window
cristalería *nf (conjunto)* glassware; *(vasos)* glasses
cristalino,-a *adj* crystal clear
cristalizar [40] *vi* to crystallize
cristiandad *nf* Christendom
cristianismo *nm* Christianity
cristiano,-a *adj & nm,f* Christian
Cristo *nm* Christ
criterio *nm* (**a**) *(pauta)* criterion (**b**) *(opinión)* opinion (**c**) *(discernimiento)* discretion; **lo dejo a tu c.** I'll leave it up to you
crítica *nf* (**a**) criticism (**b**) *Prensa* review; **tener buena c.** to get good reviews (**c**) *(conjunto de críticos)* critics
criticar [44] **1** *vt* to criticize
2 *vi (murmurar)* to gossip
crítico,-a **1** *adj* critical
2 *nm,f* critic
criticón,-ona *nm,f Fam* fault-finder
Croacia *n* Croatia
croar *vi* to croak
croata **1** *adj* Croatian
2 *nmf* Croat, Croatian

croché *nm* crochet
croissant *nm* croissant
crol *nm* crawl
cromo *nm* (**a**) *(metal)* chromium, chrome (**b**) *(estampa)* picture card
cromosoma *nm* chromosome
crónica *nf* (**a**) account, chronicle (**b**) *Prensa* feature, article
crónico,-a *adj* chronic
cronista *nmf Prensa* feature writer
cronología *nf* chronology
cronológico,-a *adj* chronological
cronometrar *vt* to time
cronómetro *nm* stopwatch
croqueta *nf* croquette
croquis *nm inv* sketch
cruce *nm* (**a**) crossing; *(de carreteras)* crossroads; *(de razas)* crossbreeding (**b**) *Tel* crossed line
crucero *nm Náut* cruise; *(barco)* cruiser
crucial *adj* crucial
crucificar [44] *vt* to crucify
crucifijo *nm* crucifix
crucigrama *nm* crossword (puzzle)
crudeza *nf* crudeness, coarseness
crudo,-a 1 *adj* (**a**) raw; *(comida)* underdone; *Fam Fig* **lo veo muy c.** it doesn't look too good (**b**) *(clima)* harsh (**c**) *(color)* cream
  2 *nm (petróleo)* crude
cruel *adj* cruel
crueldad *nf* cruelty; *Fig (del clima)* severity
cruento,-a *adj* bloody
crujido *nm (de puerta)* creak, creaking; *(de dientes)* grinding
crujiente *adj* crunchy
crujir *vi (madera)* to creak; *(comida)* to crunch; *(dientes)* to grind
cruz *nf* (**a**) cross; **C. Roja** Red Cross; **c. gamada** swastika (**b**) **¿cara o c.?** ≃ heads or tails?
cruza *nf Am* cross, crossbreed
cruzada *nf* crusade
cruzado,-a 1 *adj* (**a**) crossed; **con los brazos cruzados** arms folded (**b**) *Cost* double-breasted (**c**) *(atravesado)* lying across (**d**) *(animal)* crossbred
  2 *nm Hist* crusader
cruzar [40] 1 *vt* (**a**) to cross (**b**) *(palabras, miradas)* to exchange (**c**) *(animal, planta)* to cross, to crossbreed
  2 *vi (atravesar)* to cross
  3 cruzarse *vpr* to cross; **c. con algn** to pass sb
cta. *Com (abr* **cuenta**) a/c
cta. cte. *Com (abr* **cuenta corriente**) c/a
c/u (*abr* **cada uno**) ea

cuaderno *nm* notebook
cuadra *nf* (**a**) *(establo)* stable (**b**) *Am* block (of houses)
cuadrado,-a 1 *adj* (**a**) *Geom* square (**b**) *(complexión física)* broad, stocky (**c**) *Fig (mente)* rigid
  2 *nm* (**a**) *Geom* square (**b**) *Mat* square; **elevar (un número) al c.** to square (a number)
cuadrar 1 *vt* (**a**) *Mat* to square (**b**) *Andes (aparcar)* to park
  2 *vi (coincidir)* to square, to agree (**con** with); *(sumas, cifras)* to tally
  3 cuadrarse *vpr (soldado)* to stand to attention
cuadriculado,-a *adj* **papel c.** square paper
cuadrilátero,-a 1 *adj* quadrilateral
  2 *nm (en boxeo)* ring
cuadrilla *nf (equipo)* gang, team; *Mil* squad; *Taurom* bullfighter's team
cuadro *nm* (**a**) *Geom* square; **tela a cuadros** checked cloth (**b**) *Arte* painting, picture (**c**) *Teatro* scene (**d**) *Elec & Téc* panel; **c. de mandos** control panel (**e**) *(gráfico)* chart, graph
cuádruple *adj* quadruple, fourfold
cuajada *nf* curd
cuajar 1 *vt (leche)* to curdle; *(sangre)* to clot
  2 *vi* (**a**) *(nieve)* to lie (**b**) *(moda)* to catch on; *(plan, esfuerzo)* to get off the ground
cual 1 *pron rel (precedido de artículo)* (**a**) *(persona) (sujeto)* who; *(objeto)* whom (**b**) *(cosa)* which
  2 *pron* (**a**) **tal c.** exactly as (**b**) *Literario (comparativo)* such as, like
cuál 1 *pron interr* which (one)?, what?; **¿c. quieres?** which one do you want?
  2 *adj interr* which
  3 *loc adv* **a c. más tonto** each more stupid than the other
cualidad *nf* quality
cualificado,-a *adj* qualified
cualquier *adj indef* any; **c. cosa** anything; **en c. momento** at any moment o time
cualquiera (*pl* **cualesquiera**) **1** *adj indef* (**a**) *(indefinido)* any; **un profesor c.** any teacher (**b**) *(corriente)* ordinary

> Note that **cualquier** is used before singular nouns (e.g. **cualquier hombre** any man).

  2 *pron indef* (**a**) *(persona)* anybody; **c. te lo puede decir** anybody can tell you (**b**) *(cosa, animal)* anyone (**c**) **c. que sea** whatever it is
  3 *nmf Fig* **ser un c.** to be a nobody; **es una c.** she's a tart

cuando 1 *adv* *(de tiempo)* when; **c. más** at the most; **c. menos** at least; **de c. en c., de vez en c.** from time to time

2 *conj* **(a)** *(temporal)* when; **c. quieras** whenever you want; **c. vengas** when you come **(b)** *(condicional) (si)* if **(c)** *(concesiva) (aunque)* **(aun) c.** even if

3 *prep* during, at the time of; **c. la guerra** during the war; **c. niño** as a child

cuándo *adv interr* when?; **¿desde c.?** since when?; **¿para c. lo quieres?** when do you want it for?

cuantía *nf* quantity, amount

cuantioso,-a *adj* substantial, considerable

cuanto,-a 1 *adj* all; **gasta c. dinero gana** he spends all the money *o* as much as he earns; **unas cuantas niñas** a few girls

2 *pron rel* as much as; **coma c. quiera** eat as much as you want; **regala todo c. tiene** he gives away everything he's got

3 *pron indef pl* **unos cuantos** a few

4 *adv* **(a)** *(tiempo)* **c. antes** as soon as possible; **en c.** as soon as

(b) *(cantidad)* **c. más ... más** the more ... the more; **c. más lo miro, más me gusta** the more I look at it, the more I like it; **cuantas más personas (haya) mejor** the more the merrier

(c) en c. a with respect to, regarding; **en c. a Juan** as for Juan, as far as Juan is concerned

cuánto,-a 1 *adj & pron interr (sing)* how much?; *(pl)* how many?; **¿cuántas veces?** how many times?; **¿c. es?** how much is it?

2 *adv* how, how much; **¡cuánta gente hay!** what a lot of people there are!

cuarenta *adj & nm inv* forty; *Fam* **cantarle a algn las c.** to give sb a piece of one's mind

cuarentena *nf Med* quarantine

cuarentón,-ona *nm,f* forty-year-old

cuaresma *nf* Lent

cuartear *vt* to quarter

cuartel *nm Mil* barracks; *Fig* **no dar c.** to give no quarter

cuartelada *nf,* **cuartelazo** *nm* putsch, military uprising

cuartelillo *nm Mil* post, station

cuarteto *nm* quartet

cuartilla *nf* sheet of paper

cuarto,-a 1 *nm* **(a)** *(habitación)* room; **c. de baño** bathroom; **c. de estar** living room **(b)** *(cuarta parte)* quarter; **c. de hora** quarter of an hour; *Dep* **cuartos de final** quarter finals **(c)** *Fam* **cuartos** *(dinero)* dough, money

2 *adj & nm,f* fourth

cuarzo *nm* quartz

cuate *nmf Méx Fam* pal, *Br* mate, *US* buddy

cuatro 1 *adj & nm inv* four

2 *nm Fam* a few; **cayeron c. gotas** it rained a little bit

cuatrocientos,-as *adj & nm* four hundred

Cuba *n* Cuba

cuba *nf* cask, barrel; *Fam* **como una c.** (as) drunk as a lord

cubalibre *nm* rum/gin and coke

cubano,-a *adj & nm,f* Cuban

cubata *nm Fam* = cubalibre

cubertería *nf* cutlery

cúbico,-a *adj* cubic; *Mat* **raíz cúbica** cube root

cubierta *nf* **(a)** cover **(b)** *(de rueda)* tyre **(c)** *Náut* deck **(d)** *(techo)* roof

cubierto,-a 1 *adj* **(a)** covered; *(piscina)* indoors; *(cielo)* overcast **(b)** *(trabajo, plaza)* filled

2 *nm* **(a)** *(en la mesa)* place setting **(b)** **cubiertos** cutlery

cubil *nm* lair

cubismo *nm* cubism

cubito *nm* little cube; **c. de hielo** ice cube

cubo *nm* **(a)** bucket; **c. de la basura** rubbish bin **(b)** *Mat* cube **(c)** *(de rueda)* hub

cubrecama *nm* bedspread

cubrir *(pp* **cubierto)** **1** *vt* to cover

2 **cubrirse** *vpr (cielo)* to become overcast

cucaracha *nf* cockroach

cuchara *nf* spoon

cucharada *nf* spoonful; **c. rasa/colmada** level/heaped spoonful

cucharilla *nf* teaspoon; **c. de café** coffee spoon

cucharón *nm* ladle

cuchichear *vi* to whisper

cuchicheo *nm* whispering

cuchilla *nf* blade; **c. de afeitar** razor blade

cuchillada *nf,* **cuchillazo** *nm* stab

cuchillo *nm* knife

cuchitril *nm Fam* hovel, hole

cuclillas • **en cuclillas** *loc adv* **en c.** crouching; **ponerse en c.** to crouch down

cuco,-a 1 *nm* cuckoo

2 *adj Fam (astuto)* shrewd, crafty

cucurucho *nm* **(a)** *(para helado)* cornet **(b)** *(de papel)* paper cone

cuello *nm* **(a)** neck **(b)** *(de camisa etc)* collar

cuenca *nf* **(a)** *Geog* basin **(b)** *(de los ojos)* socket

cuenco *nm* earthenware bowl

cuenta *nf* **(a)** *(factura)* bill **(b)** *Fin (de*

banco) account; **c. corriente** current account (**c**) *(cálculo)* count; **hacer cuentas** to do sums; **c. atrás** countdown (**d**) *(de collar)* bead (**e**) *(locuciones)* **caer en la c., darse c.** to realize; **dar c.** to report; **tener en c.** to take into account; **traer c.** to be worthwhile; **más sillas de la c.** too many chairs; **en resumidas cuentas** in short; **pedir cuentas** to ask for an explanation; **trabajar por c. propia** to be self-employed

cuentagotas *nm inv* dropper

cuentakilómetros *nm inv (distancia)* mileometer; *(velocidad)* speedometer

cuento *nm* story; *Lit* short story; **contar un c.** to tell a story; *Fig* **eso no viene a c.** that's beside the point; **c. chino** tall story; **c. de hadas** fairy story

cuerda *nf* (**a**) *(cordel)* rope; *Fig* **bajo c.** dishonestly; **c. floja** tightrope; **cuerdas vocales** vocal chords (**b**) *(de instrumento)* string (**c**) *(del reloj)* spring; **dar c. al reloj** to wind up a watch

cuerdo,-a *adj* sane

cueriza *nf Andes Fam* beating, leathering

cuerno *nm* horn; *(de ciervo)* antler; *Fam* **¡vete al c.!** get lost!; *Fam* **ponerle cuernos a algn** to be unfaithful to sb

cuero *nm* (**a**) *leather;* **chaqueta de c.** leather jacket (**b**) **c. cabelludo** scalp; *Fam* **en cueros (vivos)** (stark) naked

cuerpo *nm* (**a**) *body;* **de c. entero** full-length; *Fig* **tomar c.** to take shape (**b**) *(cadáver)* corpse; **de c. presente** lying in state (**c**) *(parte)* section, part (**d**) *(grupo)* corps, force; **c. de bomberos** fire brigade; **c. diplomático** diplomatic corps

cuervo *nm* raven

cuesta **1** *nf* slope; **c. abajo** downhill; **c. arriba** uphill
2 *loc adv* **a cuestas** on one's back *o* shoulders

cuestión *nf* (**a**) *(asunto)* matter, question; **es c. de vida o muerte** it's a matter of life or death; **en c. de unas horas** in just a few hours (**b**) *(pregunta)* question

cuestionario *nm* questionnaire

cueva *nf* cave

cuezo *indic pres de* **cocer**

cuico,-a *nm,f Méx Fam* cop

cuidado **1** *nm* (**a**) *care;* **con c.** carefully; **tener c.** to be careful; **estar al c. de** *(cosa)* to be in charge of; *(persona)* to look after; **me trae sin c.** I couldn't care less (**b**) *Med* **cuidados intensivos** intensive care
2 *interj* **¡c.!** look out!, watch out!; **¡c. con lo que dices!** watch what you say!; **¡c. con el escalón!** mind the step!

cuidadoso,-a *adj* careful

cuidar **1** *vt* to care for, to look after; **c. de que todo salga bien** to make sure that everything goes all right; **c. los detalles** to pay attention to details
2 cuidarse *vpr* **cuídate** look after yourself

cuitlacoche *nm CAm, Méx* corn smut, = edible fungus which grows on maize

culata *nf* (**a**) *(de arma)* butt (**b**) *Aut* cylinder head

culebra *nf* snake

culebrilla *nf Med* ringworm

culebrón *nm* soap opera

culinario,-a *adj* culinary

culminación *nf* culmination

culminante *adj (punto)* highest; *(momento)* culminating

culminar *vi* to culminate

culo *nm* (**a**) *Fam (trasero)* backside; *Vulg* **¡vete a tomar por c.!** fuck off! (**b**) *(de recipiente)* bottom

culpa *nf* (**a**) *blame;* **echar la c. a algn** to put the blame on sb; **fue c. mía** it was my fault; **por tu c.** because of you (**b**) *(culpabilidad)* guilt

culpabilidad *nf* guilt, culpability

culpable **1** *nmf* offender, culprit
2 *adj* guilty; *Jur* **declararse c.** to plead guilty

culpar *vt* to blame; **c. a algn de un delito** to accuse sb of an offence

cultivado,-a *adj* (**a**) *Agr* cultivated (**b**) *(con cultura)* cultured, refined

cultivar *vt* (**a**) to cultivate (**b**) *Biol* to culture

cultivo *nm* (**a**) cultivation; *(planta)* crop (**b**) *Biol* culture

culto,-a **1** *adj* educated; *(palabra)* learned
2 *nm* cult; *Rel* worship

cultura *nf* culture

cultural *adj* cultural

culturismo *nm* body building

culturista *nmf* body builder

cumbre *nf* (**a**) *(de montaña)* summit, top; **(conferencia) c.** summit conference (**b**) *Fig (culminación)* pinnacle

cumple *nm Fam* birthday

cumpleaños *nm inv* birthday; **¡feliz c.!** happy birthday!

cumplido,-a **1** *adj* (**a**) completed; *(plazo)* expired; **misión cumplida** mission accomplished (**b**) *(cortés)* polite
2 *nm* compliment

cumplidor,-a *adj* reliable, dependable

cumplimiento *nm* fulfilment; **c. de la ley** observance of the law

cumplir **1** *vt* (**a**) to carry out, to fulfil; *(deseo)* to fulfil; *(promesa)* to keep;

(sentencia) to serve (**b**) **ayer cumplí veinte años** I was twenty (years old) yesterday

2 *vi* (**a**) *(plazo)* to expire, to end (**b**) **c. con el deber** to do one's duty

3 cumplirse *vpr* (**a**) *(deseo, sueño)* to be fulfilled, to come true (**b**) *(plazo)* to expire

cúmulo *nm* pile, load

cuna *nf* (**a**) cot (**b**) *Fig (origen)* cradle

cundir *vi* (**a**) **me cunde mucho el trabajo** *o* **el tiempo** I seem to get a lot done (**b**) *(extenderse)* to spread; **cundió el pánico** panic spread; **cundió la voz de que ...** rumour had it that ...

cuneta *nf (de la carretera)* gutter; **quedarse en la c.** to be left behind

cuña *nf* (**a**) *(pieza)* wedge; **c. publicitaria** commercial break (**b**) *Andes, RP Fam (enchufe)* **tener c.** to have friends in high places

cuñado,-a *nm,f (hombre)* brother-in-law; *(mujer)* sister-in-law

cuño *nm* **de nuevo c.** newly-coined

cuota *nf* (**a**) *(de club etc)* membership fees, dues (**b**) *(porción)* quota, share (**c**) *Méx* **carretera de c.** toll road

cupe *pt indef de* **caber**

cupiera *subj imperf de* **caber**

cupo *nm* ceiling; *Mil* **excedente de c.** exempt from military service

cupón *nm* coupon, voucher

cúpula *nf* dome, cupola; *(líderes)* leadership

cura 1 *nm Rel* priest

2 *nf Med* cure; *Fig* **no tiene c.** there's no remedy

curación *nf* cure, treatment

curandero,-a *nm,f* quack

curar 1 *vt* (**a**) *(sanar)* to cure; *(herida)* to dress; *(enfermedad)* to treat (**b**) *(carne, pescado)* to cure

2 *vi (sanar)* to recover, to get well; *(herida)* to heal up

3 •**curarse** *vpr* to recover, to get well; *(herida)* to heal up; **c. en salud** to make sure

curcuncho,-a *adj Andes Fam* hunchbacked

curiosear *vi* to pry

curiosidad *nf* curiosity; **tener c. de** to be curious about

curioso,-a 1 *adj* (**a**) *(indiscreto)* curious, inquisitive (**b**) *(extraño)* strange, odd; **lo c. es que ...** the strange thing is that ... (**c**) *(limpio)* neat, tidy

2 *nm,f* (**a**) *(mirón)* onlooker (**b**) *(chismoso)* nosey-parker, busybody

curita *nf Am Br* sticking-plaster, *US* Band-aid®

currante *nmf Fam* worker

currar, currelar *vi Fam* to graft, to grind

currículum *nm (pl* **curricula**) **c. vitae** curriculum vitae

curro *nm Fam* job

cursar *vt (estudiar)* to study; *(enviar)* to send

cursi *adj* vulgar

cursillo *nm* short course; **c. de reciclaje** refresher course

cursivo,-a *adj* **letra cursiva** italics

curso *nm* (**a**) *(año académico)* year; *(clase)* class (**b**) *Fig* **año/mes en c.** current year/month; **en el c. de** during (**c**) *(de acontecimientos, río)* course (**d**) *Fin* **moneda de c. legal** legal tender

cursor *nm* cursor

curtido,-a *adj* (**a**) *(piel)* weatherbeaten; *(cuero)* tanned (**b**) *Fig (persona)* hardened

curtiembre *nf Andes, RP* tannery

curtir *vt* (**a**) *(cuero)* to tan (**b**) *Fig (avezar)* to harden, to toughen

curva *nf* (**a**) curve (**b**) *(en carretera)* bend; **c. cerrada** sharp bend

curvilíneo,-a *adj* curvaceous

curvo,-a *adj* curved

cuscús *nm* couscous

cúspide *nf* summit, peak; *Fig* peak

custodia *nf* custody

custodiar [43] *vt* to watch over

cutáneo,-a *adj* cutaneous, skin; *Med* **erupción cutánea** rash

cutícula *nf* cuticle

cutis *nm* complexion

cuyo,-a *pron rel & pos (de persona)* whose; *(de cosa)* of which; **en c. caso** in which case

cv *(abr* **caballos de vapor**) hp

D

D, d [de] *nf (la letra)* D, d
D. (*abr* **don**) Mr
Da. (*abr* **doña**) Mrs/Miss
dactilar *adj* **huellas dactilares** fingerprints
dádiva *nf (regalo)* gift, present; *(donativo)* donation
dadivoso,-a *adj* generous
dado¹,-a *adj* (**a**) given; **en un momento d.** at a certain point (**b**) **ser d. a** to be given to (**c**) **d. que** since, given that
dado² *nm* die, dice
daga *nf* dagger
dalia *nf* dahlia
dálmata *nm* Dalmatian (dog)
daltónico,-a *adj* colour-blind
dama *nf* (**a**) *(señora)* lady (**b**) *(en damas)* king (**c**) **damas** *(juego)* Br draughts, US checkers
damasco *nm* (**a**) *(tela)* damask (**b**) *Andes, CAm, Carib, RP (albaricoque)* apricot
damnificado,-a *nm,f* victim, injured person
danés,-esa 1 *adj* Danish
2 *nm,f (persona)* Dane
3 *nm* (**a**) *(idioma)* Danish (**b**) **gran d.** *(perro)* Great Dane
Danubio *nm* **el D.** the Danube
danza *nf* dancing; *(baile)* dance
danzar [40] *vt & vi* to dance
dañar *vt (cosa)* to damage; *(persona)* to hurt, to harm
dañino,-a *adj* harmful, damaging (**para** to)
daño *nm (a cosa)* damage; *(a persona) (físico)* hurt; *(perjuicio)* harm; **se hizo d. en la pierna** he hurt his leg; *Jur* **daños y perjuicios** (legal) damages
dar [11] 1 *vt* (**a**) to give; *(recado, recuerdos)* to pass on, to give; *(noticia)* to tell
(**b**) *(mano de pintura, cera)* to apply, to put on
(**c**) *(película)* to show, to screen; *(fiesta)* to throw, to give
(**d**) *(cosecha)* to produce, to yield; *(fruto, flores)* to bear; *(beneficio, interés)* to give, to yield
(**e**) *(bofetada etc)* to deal; **d. a algn en la cabeza** to hit sb on the head

(**f**) **dale a la luz** switch the light on; **d. la mano a algn** to shake hands with sb; **d. los buenos días/las buenas noches a algn** to say good morning/good evening to sb; **me da lo mismo, me da igual** it's all the same to me; **¿qué más da?** what difference does it make?
(**g**) *(hora)* to strike; **ya han dado las nueve** it's gone nine (o'clock)
(**h**) **d. de comer a** to feed
(**i**) **d. a conocer** *(noticia)* to release; **d. a entender a algn que ...** to give sb to understand that ...
(**j**) **d. por** *(considerar)* to assume, to consider; **lo dieron por muerto** he was assumed dead, he was given up for dead; **d. por descontado/sabido** to take for granted, to assume
2 *vi* (**a**) **me dio un ataque de tos/risa** I had a coughing fit/an attack of the giggles
(**b**) **d. a** *(ventana, habitación)* to look out onto, to overlook; *(puerta)* to open onto, to lead to
(**c**) **d. con** *(persona)* to come across; **d. con la solución** to hit upon the solution
(**d**) **d. de sí** *(ropa)* to stretch, to give
(**e**) **d. en** to hit; **el sol me daba en los ojos** the sun was (shining) in my eyes
(**f**) **d. para** to be enough *o* sufficient for; **el presupuesto no da para más** the budget will not stretch any further
(**g**) **le dio por nadar** he took it into his head to go swimming
(**h**) **d. que hablar** to set people talking; **el suceso dio que pensar** the incident gave people food for thought
3 darse *upr* (**a**) **se dio un caso extraño** something strange happened
(**b**) *(hallarse)* to be found, to exist
(**c**) **d. a** to take to; **se dio a la bebida** he took to drink
(**d**) **d. con** *o* **contra** to bump *o* crash into
(**e**) **dárselas de** to consider oneself
(**f**) **d. por satisfecho** to feel satisfied; **d. por vencido** to give in
(**g**) **se le da bien/mal el francés** she's good/bad at French
dardo *nm* dart

dársena *nf* dock
datar 1 *vt* to date
  2 *vi* **d. de** to date back to o from
dátil *nm* date
dato *nm* (**a**) piece of information; **datos personales** personal details (**b**) *Informát* **datos** data
d.C. (*abr* **después de Cristo**) AD
dcha. (*abr* **derecha**) rt.
de *prep*

> **de** combines with the article **el** to form the contraction **del** (e.g. **del hombre** of the man).

  (**a**) *(pertenencia)* of; **el título de la novela** the title of the novel; **el coche/hermano de Sofía** Sofía's car/brother; **las bicicletas de los niños** the boys' bicycles
  (**b**) *(procedencia)* from; **de Madrid a Valencia** from Madrid to Valencia; **soy de Palencia** I'm from o I come from Palencia
  (**c**) *(descripción)* **el niño de ojos azules** the boy with blue eyes; **el señor de la chaqueta** the man in the jacket; **el bobo del niño** the silly boy; **un reloj de oro** a gold watch; **un joven de veinte años** a young man of twenty
  (**d**) *(contenido)* of; **un saco de patatas** a sack of potatoes
  (**e**) **gafas de sol** sunglasses; **goma de borrar** eraser, *Br* rubber
  (**f**) *(oficio)* by, as; **es arquitecto de profesión** he's an architect by profession; **trabaja de secretaria** she's working as a secretary
  (**g**) *(acerca de)* about; **curso de informática** computer course
  (**h**) *(tiempo)* **a las tres de la tarde** at three in the afternoon; **de día** by day; **de noche** at night; **de lunes a jueves** from Monday to Thursday; **de pequeño** as a child; **de año en año** year in year out
  (**i**) *(precio)* at; **patatas de 30 pesetas el kilo** potatoes at 30 pesetas a kilo
  (**j**) **una avenida de 15 km** an avenue 15 km long; **una botella de litro** a litre bottle
  (**k**) *(con superlativo)* in; **el más largo de España** the longest in Spain
  (**l**) *(causa)* with, because of; **llorar de alegría** to cry with joy; **morir de hambre** to die of hunger
  (**m**) *(condicional)* **de haber llegado antes** if he had arrived before; **de no ser así** if that wasn't o weren't the case; **de ser cierto** if it was o were true
  (**n**) **lo mismo de siempre** the usual thing
  (**o**) **de cuatro en cuatro** in fours, four at a time

deambular *vi* to saunter, to stroll
debajo *adv* underneath, below; **el mío es el de d.** mine is the one below; **está d. de la mesa** it's under the table; **por d. de lo normal** below normal; **salió por d. del coche** he came out from under the car
debate *nm* debate
debatir 1 *vt* to debate
  2 debatirse *vpr* to struggle; **d. entre la vida y la muerte** to fight for one's life
debe *nm Com* debit, debit side
deber¹ *nm* (**a**) duty; **cumplir con su d.** to do one's duty (**b**) *Educ* **deberes** homework
deber² **1** *vt (dinero, explicación)* to owe
  2 *vi* (**a**) must, to have to; **debe (de) comer** he must eat; **debe (de) irse ahora** she has to leave now; **la factura debe pagarse mañana** the bill must be paid tomorrow; **el tren debe llegar a las dos** the train is expected to arrive at two
  (**b**) *(consejo)* **deberías visitar a tus padres** you ought to visit your parents; **debería haber ido ayer** I should have gone yesterday; **no debiste hacerlo** you shouldn't have done it
  (**c**) *(suposición)* **deben de estar fuera** they must be out
  3 deberse *vpr* **d. a** to be due to; **esto se debe a la falta de agua** this is due to lack of water
debidamente *adv* duly, properly
debido,-a *adj* (**a**) due; **a su d. tiempo** in due course; **con el d. respeto** with due respect (**b**) *(adecuado)* proper; **más de lo d.** too much; **tomaron las debidas precauciones** they took the proper precautions; **como es d.** properly (**c**) **d. a** because of, due to; **d. a que** because of the fact that
débil *adj* weak; *(luz)* dim; **punto d.** weak spot
debilidad *nf* weakness; *Fig* **tener d. por** *(persona)* to have a soft spot for; *(cosa)* to have a weakness for
debilitamiento *nm* weakening
debilitar 1 *vt* to weaken, to debilitate
  2 debilitarse *vpr* to weaken, to grow weak
débito *nm* (**a**) *(deuda)* debt (**b**) *(debe)* debit
debut *nm* début, debut
debutar *vi* to make one's début o debut
década *nf* decade; **en la d. de los noventa** during the nineties
decadencia *nf* decadence
decadente *adj & nmf* decadent
decaer [39] *vi* to deteriorate

decaído,-a *adj* down
decaimiento *nm* (**a**) *(debilidad)* weakness (**b**) *(desaliento)* low spirits
decano,-a *nm,f Univ* dean
decantarse *vpr* to lean towards; **d. por** to come down on the side of
decapitar *vt* to behead, to decapitate
decena *nf* (about) ten; **una d. de veces** (about) ten times; **por decenas** in tens
decencia *nf* (**a**) *(decoro)* decency (**b**) *(honradez)* honesty
decenio *nm* decade
decente *adj* decent; *(decoroso)* modest
decepción *nf* disappointment

> ⚠ Observa que la palabra inglesa **deception** es un falso amigo y no es la traducción de la palabra española **decepción**. En inglés, **deception** significa "engaño".

decepcionante *adj* disappointing
decepcionar *vt* to disappoint
decididamente *adv* (**a**) *(resueltamente)* resolutely (**b**) *(definitivamente)* definitely
decidido,-a *adj* determined, resolute
decidir 1 *vt & vi* to decide
  2 decidirse *vpr* to make up one's mind; **d. a hacer algo** to make up one's mind to do sth; **d. por algo** to decide on sth
décima *nf* tenth
decimal *adj & nm* decimal; **el sistema métrico d.** the decimal system
décimo,-a 1 *adj & nm,f* tenth
  2 *nm* (**a**) *(parte)* tenth (**b**) *(billete de lotería)* tenth part of a lottery ticket
decir[1] *nm* saying
decir[2] **[12]** *(pp* **dicho**) **1** *vt* (**a**) to say; **dice que no quiere venir** he says he doesn't want to come
  (**b**) **d. una mentira/la verdad** to tell a lie/the truth
  (**c**) *Tel* **dígame** hello
  (**d**) **¿qué me dices del nuevo jefe?** what do you think of the new boss?
  (**e**) *(mostrar)* to tell, to show; **su cara dice que está mintiendo** you can tell from his face that he's lying
  (**f**) *(sugerir)* to mean; **esta película no me dice nada** this film doesn't appeal to me; **¿qué te dice el cuadro?** what does the picture mean to you?
  (**g**) **querer d.** to mean
  (**h**) *(locuciones)* **es d.** that is (to say); **por así decirlo** as it were, so to speak; **digamos** let's say; **digo yo** in my opinion; **el qué dirán** what people say; **ni que d. tiene** needless to say; **¡no me digas!** really!; **¡y que lo digas!** you bet!
  2 decirse *vpr* **¿cómo se dice "mesa" en**

inglés? how do you say "mesa" in English?; **se dice que ...** they say that ...; **sé lo que me digo** I know what I am saying
decisión *nf* (**a**) decision; **tomar una d.** to take o make a decision (**b**) *(resolución)* determination; **con d.** decisively
decisivo,-a *adj* decisive
decisorio,-a *adj* decision-making
declamar *vt & vi* to declaim, to recite
declaración *nf* (**a**) declaration; **d. de (la) renta** tax declaration o return (**b**) *(afirmación)* statement; **hacer declaraciones** to comment (**c**) *Jur* **prestar d.** to give evidence
declarante *nmf Jur* witness
declarar 1 *vt* (**a**) to declare; **d. la guerra a** to declare war on (**b**) *(afirmar)* to state (**c**) *Jur* **d. culpable/inocente a algn** to find sb guilty/not guilty
  2 *vi* (**a**) to declare (**b**) *Jur* to testify
  3 declararse *vpr* (**a**) **d. a favor/en contra de** to declare oneself in favour of/against; **d. en huelga** to go on strike; **d. a algn** to declare one's love for sb (**b**) *(guerra, incendio)* to start, to break out (**c**) *Jur* **d. culpable** to plead guilty
declinar *vt & vi* to decline
declive *nm* (**a**) *(del terreno)* incline, slope (**b**) *(de imperio etc)* decline
decolaje *nm Am* take-off
decolar *vi Am* to take off
decolorante *nm* bleaching agent
decolorar 1 *vt* to fade; *(pelo)* to bleach
  2 decolorarse *vpr* to fade
decomisar *vt* to confiscate, to seize
decoración *nf* decoration
decorado *nm* scenery, set
decorador,-a *nm,f* (**a**) decorator (**b**) *Teatro* set designer
decorar *vt* to decorate
decorativo,-a *adj* decorative
decoro *nm* (**a**) *(respeto)* dignity, decorum (**b**) *(pudor)* modesty, decency
decoroso,-a *adj* (**a**) *(correcto)* seemly, decorous (**b**) *(decente)* decent, modest
decrecer **[33]** *vi* to decrease, to diminish
decrépito,-a *adj* decrepit
decretar *vt* to decree
decreto *nm* decree; **d.-ley** decree
dedal *nm* thimble
dedicación *nf* dedication
dedicar **[44]** **1** *vt* to dedicate; *(tiempo, esfuerzos)* to devote (**a** to)
  2 dedicarse *vpr* **¿a qué se dedica Vd.?** what do you do for a living?; **los fines de semana ella se dedica a pescar** at weekends she spends her time fishing
dedicatoria *nf* dedication

dedillo *nm* **saber algo al d.** to have sth at one's fingertips, to know sth very well

dedo *nm* *(de la mano)* finger; *(del pie)* toe; **d. anular/corazón/índice/meñique** ring/middle/index/little finger; **d. pulgar, d. gordo** thumb; *RP* **hacer d.** to hitchhike; *Fig* **elegir a algn a d.** to hand-pick sb

deducción *nf* deduction

deducible *adj Com* deductible

deducir [10] 1 *vt* (**a**) to deduce, to infer (**b**) *Com* to deduct
2 deducirse *vpr* **de aquí se deduce que ...** from this it follows that ...

deductivo,-a *adj* deductive

defecar [44] *vi* to defecate

defecto *nm* defect, fault; **d. físico** physical defect

defectuoso,-a *adj* defective, faulty

defender [3] 1 *vt* to defend (**de** from); **d. del frío/viento** to shelter from the cold/wind
2 defenderse *vpr* (**a**) to defend oneself (**b**) *Fam* **se defiende en francés** he can get by in French

defendido,-a *adj Jur* defendant

defensa 1 *nf* defence; **en d. propia, en legítima d.** in self-defence; **salir en d. de algn** to come out in defence of sb
2 *nm Dep* defender, back

defensiva *nf* defensive; **estar/ponerse a la d.** to be/go on the defensive

defensivo,-a *adj* defensive

defensor,-a *nm,f* defender; **abogado d.** counsel for the defence; **el defensor del pueblo** the ombudsman

deferencia *nf* deference; **en** *o* **por d. a** out of deference for

deficiencia *nf* deficiency, shortcoming; **d. mental** mental deficiency; **d. renal** kidney failure

deficiente 1 *adj* deficient
2 *nmf* **d. mental** mentally retarded person
3 *nm Educ* fail

déficit *nm* (*pl* **déficits**) deficit; *(carencia)* shortage

deficitario,-a *adj* showing a deficit

definición *nf* definition; **por d.** by definition

definido,-a *adj* clear; *Ling* definite

definir *vt* to define

definitivamente *adv* (**a**) *(para siempre)* for good, once and for all (**b**) *(con toda seguridad)* definitely

definitivo,-a *adj* definitive; **en definitiva** in short

deflación *nf Econ* deflation

deflacionista *adj Econ* deflationary

deformación *nf* deformation

deformar 1 *vt* to deform, to put out of shape; *(cara)* to disfigure; *Fig (la verdad, una imagen)* to distort
2 deformarse *vpr* to go out of shape, to become distorted

deforme *adj* deformed; *(objeto)* misshapen

defraudación *nf* fraud; **d. fiscal** tax evasion

defraudar *vt* (**a**) *(decepcionar)* to disappoint (**b**) *(al fisco)* to defraud, to cheat; **d. a Hacienda** to evade taxes

defunción *nf Fml* decease, demise

degeneración *nf* degeneration

degenerado,-a *adj & nm,f* degenerate

degenerar *vi* to degenerate

degollar [2] *vt* to behead

degradación *nf* degradation

degradante *adj* degrading

degradar *vt* to degrade

degustación *nf* tasting

degustar *vt* to taste, to sample

dehesa *nf* pasture, meadow

deificar [44] *vt* to deify

dejadez *nf* slovenliness

dejado,-a *adj* (**a**) *(descuidado)* untidy, slovenly (**b**) *(negligente)* negligent, careless (**c**) *Fam* **d. de la mano de Dios** godforsaken

dejar 1 *vt* (**a**) to leave; **déjame en paz** leave me alone; **d. dicho** to leave word *o* a message
(**b**) *(prestar)* to lend
(**c**) *(abandonar)* to give up; **d. algo por imposible** to give sth up; **dejé el tabaco y la bebida** I gave up smoking and drinking
(**d**) *(permitir)* to let, to allow; **d. caer** to drop; **d. entrar/salir** to let in/out
(**e**) *(omitir)* to leave out, to omit
(**f**) *(ganancias)* to produce
(**g**) *(+ adj)* to make; **d. triste** to make sad; **d. preocupado/sorprendido** to worry/surprise
(**h**) *(posponer)* **dejaron el viaje para el verano** they put the trip off until the summer
2 *v aux* **d. de** + *inf* to stop, to give up; **dejó de fumar el año pasado** he gave up smoking last year; **no deja de llamarme** she's always phoning me up
3 dejarse *vpr* (**a**) **me he dejado las llaves dentro** I've left the keys inside (**b**) *(locuciones)* **d. barba** to grow a beard; **d. caer** to flop down; **d. llevar por** to be influenced by

del *(contracción de* **de** + **el**) *ver* **de**

delantal *nm* apron

delante *adv* (**a**) in front; **la entrada de d.** the front entrance (**b**) **d. de** in front of; *(en serie)* ahead of (**c**) **por d.** in front; **se lo lleva todo por d.** he destroys everything in his path; **tiene toda la vida por d.** he has his whole life ahead of him

delantera *nf* (**a**) *(ventaja)* lead; **tomar la d.** take the lead (**b**) *Ftb* forward line, forwards

delantero,-a 1 *adj* front
  2 *nm Ftb* forward; **d. centro** centre forward

delatar *vt* (**a**) to inform against (**b**) *Fig* to give away

delator,-a *nm,f* informer

delegación *nf* (**a**) *(acto, delegados)* delegation (**b**) *(oficina)* local office, branch; **D. de Hacienda** Tax Office (**c**) *Méx (distrito municipal)* district; *(comisaría)* police station

delegado,-a *nm,f* (**a**) delegate; **d. de Hacienda** chief tax inspector (**b**) *Com* representative

delegar [42] *vt* to delegate (**en** to)

deleitar 1 *vt* to delight
  2 deleitarse *vpr* to delight in, to take delight in

deleite *nm* delight

deletrear *vt* to spell (out)

deleznable *adj* brittle

delfín *nm* dolphin

delgadez *nf* slimness

delgado,-a *adj* slim; *(capa)* fine

deliberación *nf* deliberation

deliberado,-a *adj* deliberate

deliberar *vi* to deliberate (on), to consider

delicadeza *nf* (**a**) *(finura)* delicacy, daintiness (**b**) *(tacto)* tactfulness; **falta de d.** tactlessness

delicado,-a *adj* (**a**) delicate (**b**) *(exigente)* fussy, hard to please (**c**) *(sensible)* hypersensitive

delicia *nf* delight; **hacer las delicias de algn** to delight sb

delicioso,-a *adj (comida)* delicious; *(agradable)* delightful

delictivo,-a *adj* criminal, punishable

delimitar *vt* to delimit

delincuencia *nf* delinquency

delincuente *adj & nmf* delinquent; **d. juvenil** juvenile delinquent

delineante *nmf (hombre)* draughtsman; *(mujer)* draughtswoman

delinear *vt* to delineate, to outline

delinquir [48] *vi* to break the law, to commit an offence

delirante *adj* delirious

delirar *vi* to be delirious

delirio *nm* delirium; **delirios de grandeza** delusions of grandeur

delito *nm* crime, offence

delta *nm* delta; **ala d.** hang-glider

demacrado,-a *adj* emaciated

demagogia *nf* demagogy

demagogo,-a *nm,f* demagogue

demanda *nf* (**a**) *Jur* lawsuit (**b**) *Com* demand

demandado,-a 1 *nm,f* defendant
  2 *adj* in demand

demandante *nmf* claimant

demandar *vt* to sue

demarcar [44] *vt* to demarcate

demás 1 *adj* **los/las d.** the rest of; **la d. gente** the rest of the people
  2 *pron* **lo/los/las d.** the rest; **por lo d.** otherwise, apart from that; **y d.** etcetera

demasía *nf* **en d.** excessively

demasiado,-a 1 *adj (singular)* too much; *(plural)* too many; **hay demasiada comida** there is too much food; **quieres demasiadas cosas** you want too many things
  2 *adv* too (much); **es d. grande/caro** it is too big/dear; **fumas/trabajas d.** you smoke/work too much

demencia *nf* dementia, insanity

demente 1 *adj* insane, mad
  2 *nmf* mental patient

democracia *nf* democracy

demócrata 1 *adj* democratic
  2 *nmf* democrat

democrático,-a *adj* democratic

democratizar [40] *vt* to democratize

demografía *nf* demography

demográfico,-a *adj* demographic; **crecimiento d.** population growth

demoledor,-a *adj Fig* devastating

demoler [4] *vt* to demolish

demonio *nm* devil, demon; *Fam* **¿cómo/dónde demonios ...?** how/where the hell ...?; *Fam* **¡demonio(s)!** hell!, damn!; *Fam* **¡d. de niño!** you little devil!

demora *nf* delay

demorar 1 *vt* (**a**) *(retrasar)* to delay, to hold up (**b**) *(tardar)* **demoraron tres días en pintar la casa** it took them three days to paint the house
  2 *vi Am (tardar)* **¡no demores!** don't be late!; **demorar en hacer algo** *(llevar tiempo)* to take one's time doing sth; *(retrasarse)* to take too long doing sth; **no demoraron en venir** they came immediately
  3 demorarse *vpr* (**a**) *(retrasarse)* to be delayed, to be held up (**b**) *(detenerse)* to dally

demostrable *adj* demonstrable
demostración *nf* demonstration; **una d. de fuerza/afecto** a show of strength
demostrar [2] *vt* (**a**) *(mostrar)* to show, to demonstrate (**b**) *(evidenciar)* to prove
demudado,-a *adj* pale
denegar [1] *vt* to refuse; *Jur* **d. una demanda** to dismiss a claim
denigrante *adj* humiliating
denigrar *vt* to humiliate
denominación *nf* denomination; **d. de origen** *(vinos)* = guarantee of region of origin
denominado,-a *adj* so-called
denominador *nm* denominator
denominar *vt* to name, to designate
denotar *vt* to denote
densidad *nf* density; **d. de población** population density
denso,-a *adj* dense
dentadura *nf* teeth, set of teeth; **d. postiza** false teeth, dentures
dental *adj* dental
dentera *nf* **me da d.** it sets my teeth on edge
dentífrico,-a 1 *adj* **pasta/crema dentífrica** toothpaste
2 *nm* toothpaste
dentista *nmf* dentist
dentro *adv* (**a**) *(en el interior)* inside; **aquí d.** in here; **por d.** (on the) inside; **por d. está triste** deep down (inside) he feels sad (**b**) **d. de** *(lugar)* inside (**c**) **d. de poco** shortly, soon; **d. de un mes** in a month's time; **d. de lo que cabe** all things considered
denuncia *nf* (**a**) *Jur* report (**b**) *(crítica)* denunciation
denunciar [43] *vt* (**a**) *(delito)* to report (**a** to) (**b**) *(criticar)* to denounce
deparar *vt* to give; **no sabemos qué nos depara el destino** we don't know what fate has in store for us
departamento *nm* (**a**) department (**b**) *Ferroc* compartment (**c**) *(territorial)* province, district (**d**) *Arg (piso) Br* flat, *US* apartment
dependencia *nf* (**a**) dependence (**de** on) (**b**) **dependencias** premises
depender *vi* to depend (**de** on); *(económicamente)* to be dependent (**de** on)
dependienta *nf* shop assistant
dependiente 1 *adj* dependent (**de** on)
2 *nm* shop assistant
depilación *nf* depilation; **d. a la cera** waxing
depilar *vt* to remove the hair from; *(cejas)* to pluck

depilatorio,-a *adj & nm* depilatory; **crema depilatoria** hair-remover, hair-removing cream
deplorable *adj* deplorable
deplorar *vt* to deplore
deponer [19] *(pp* **depuesto**) *vt* (**a**) *(destituir)* to remove from office; *(líder)* to depose (**b**) *(actitud)* to abandon
deportado,-a *nm,f* deportee, deported person
deportar *vt* to deport
deporte *nm* sport; **hacer d.** to practise sports; **d. de aventura** adventure sport
deportista 1 *nmf (hombre)* sportsman; *(mujer)* sportswoman
2 *adj* sporty
deportividad *nf* sportsmanship
deportivo,-a 1 *adj* sports; **club/chaqueta d.** sports club/jacket
2 *nm Aut* sports car
deposición *nf* removal from office; *(de un líder)* deposition
depositar 1 *vt* (**a**) *Fin* to deposit (**b**) *(colocar)* to place, to put
2 depositarse *vpr* to settle
depósito *nm* (**a**) *Fin* deposit; **en d.** on deposit (**b**) *(de agua, gasolina)* tank (**c**) **d. de basuras** rubbish tip *o* dump; **d. de cadáveres** mortuary, morgue
depravación *nf* depravity
depravar *vt* to deprave
depre *nf Fam* downer, depression
depreciación *nf* depreciation
depreciar [43] 1 *vt* to reduce the value of
2 depreciarse *vpr* to depreciate, to lose value
depredador,-a 1 *adj* predatory
2 *nm,f* predator
depresión *nf* depression; **d. nerviosa** nervous breakdown
depresivo,-a *adj* depressive
deprimente *adj* depressing
deprimido,-a *adj* depressed
deprimir 1 *vt* to depress
2 deprimirse *vpr* to get depressed
deprisa *adv* quickly
depuesto,-a *pp de* **deponer**
depuración *nf* (**a**) *(del agua)* purification (**b**) *(purga)* purge
depurador,-a *adj* **planta depuradora** purification plant
depuradora *nf* purifier
depurar *vt* (**a**) *(agua)* to purify (**b**) *(partido)* to purge (**c**) *(estilo)* to refine
derecha *nf* (**a**) *(mano)* right hand (**b**) *(lugar)* right, right-hand side; **a la d.** to o on the right, on the right hand side (**c**) *Pol* **la d.** the right; **de derechas** right-wing

derechista *nmf* right-winger
derecho,-a 1 *adj* (**a**) *(de la derecha)* right (**b**) *(recto)* upright, straight
2 *nm* (**a**) *(privilegio)* right; **derechos civiles/humanos** civil/human rights; **tener d. a** to be entitled to, to have the right to; **estar en su d.** to be within one's rights; **no hay d.** it's not fair; **d. de admisión** right to refuse admission (**b**)*Jur* law; **d. penal/político** criminal/constitutional law (**c**) *Com* **derechos** duties; **derechos de autor** royalties; **derechos de matrícula** enrolment fees
3 *adv* **siga todo d.** go straight ahead
deriva *nf* drift; **ir a la d.** to drift
derivado *nm* *(producto)* derivative, byproduct
derivar 1 *vt* to divert; *(conversación)* to steer
2 *vi* (**a**) to drift (**b**) **d. de** to derive from
3 derivarse *vpr* (**a**) **d. de** *(proceder)* to result o stem from (**b**) **d. de** *Ling* to be derived from
dermatitis *nf inv* dermatitis
dermatólogo,-a *nm,f* dermatologist
derogar [42] *vt* to repeal
derramamiento *nm* spilling; **d. de sangre** bloodshed
derramar 1 *vt* to spill; *(lágrimas)* to shed
2 derramarse *vpr* to spill
derrame *nm* *Med* discharge; **d. cerebral** brain haemorrhage
derrapar *vi* to skid
derredor *nm* **en d. de** round, around
derretir [6] *vt,* **derretirse** *vpr* to melt; *(hielo, nieve)* to thaw
derribar *vt* (**a**) *(edificio)* to pull down, to knock down (**b**) *(avión)* to shoot down (**c**) *(gobierno)* to bring down
derrocar [44] *vt* to bring down; *(violentamente)* to overthrow
derrochador,-a 1 *adj* wasteful
2 *nm,f* wasteful person, squanderer
derrochar *vt* to waste, to squander
derroche *nm* (**a**) *(de dinero, energía)* waste, squandering (**b**) *(abundancia)* profusion, abundance
derrota *nf* (**a**) defeat (**b**) *Náut* (ship's) course
derrotar *vt* to defeat, to beat
derrotero *nm* (**a**) *Fig* path, course o plan of action (**b**) *Náut* sailing directions
derrotista *adj & nmf* defeatist
derruido,-a *adj* in ruins
derruir [37] *vt* to demolish
derrumbar 1 *vt (edificio)* to knock down, to pull down
2 derrumbarse *vpr* to collapse, to fall

down; *(techo)* to fall in, to cave in
desabastecido,-a *adj* **d. de** out of
desaborido,-a 1 *adj* (**a**) *(comida)* tasteless (**b**) *Fig (persona)* dull
2 *nm,f Fig* dull person
desabrido,-a *adj* (**a**) *(comida)* tasteless (**b**) *(tiempo)* unpleasant (**c**) *Fig (tono)* harsh; *(persona)* moody, irritable
desabrigado,-a *adj* **ir/estar d.** to be lightly dressed
desabrochar 1 *vt* to undo
2 desabrocharse *vpr* (**a**) **desabróchate la camisa** undo your shirt (**b**) *(prenda)* to come undone
desacatar *vt* to disobey
desacato *nm* lack of respect, disrespect (**a** for); *Jur* **d. al tribunal** contempt of court
desacertado,-a *adj* unwise
desacierto *nm* mistake, error
desaconsejar *vt* to advise against
desacorde *adj* **estar d. con** to be in disagreement with
desacreditar *vt* (**a**) *(desprestigiar)* to discredit, to bring into discredit (**b**) *(criticar)* to disparage
desactivador,-a *nm,f* bomb disposal expert
desactivar *vt (bomba)* to defuse
desacuerdo *nm* disagreement
desafiante *adj* defiant
desafiar [29] *vt* to challenge
desafinado,-a *adj* out of tune
desafinar 1 *vi* to sing out of tune; *(instrumento)* to play out of tune
2 *vt* to put out of tune
3 desafinarse *vpr* to go out of tune
desafío *nm* challenge
desaforado,-a *adj* wild
desafortunado,-a *adj* unlucky, unfortunate
desagradable *adj* unpleasant, disagreeable
desagradar *vi* to displease
desagradecido,-a 1 *adj* ungrateful
2 *nm,f* ungrateful person
desagrado *nm* displeasure
desagraviar [43] *vt* to make amends for
desaguar [45] *vt* to drain
desagüe *nm* *(vaciado)* drain; *(cañería)* waste pipe, drainpipe
desaguisado *nm* mess
desahogado,-a *adj* (**a**) *(acomodado)* well-off, well-to-do (**b**) *(espacioso)* spacious, roomy
desahogarse [42] *vpr* to let off steam; **se desahogó de su depresión** he got his depression out of his system

desahogo *nm* (**a**) *(alivio)* relief (**b**) **vivir con d.** to live comfortably

desahuciado,-a *adj* (**a**) *(enfermo)* hopeless (**b**) *(inquilino)* evicted

desahuciar [43] *vt* (**a**) *(desalojar)* to evict (**b**) *(enfermo)* to deprive of all hope

desahucio *nm* eviction

desairado,-a *adj* (**a**) *(humillado)* spurned (**b**) *(sin gracia)* awkward

desairar *vt* to slight, to snub

desaire *nm* slight, rebuff

desajustar 1 *vt* to upset

2 desajustarse *vpr (piezas)* to come apart

desajuste *nm* upset; **d. económico** economic imbalance; **un d. de horarios** clashing timetables

desalentador,-a *adj* discouraging, disheartening

desalentar [1] 1 *vt* to discourage, to dishearten

2 desalentarse *vpr* to get discouraged, to lose heart

desaliento *nm* discouragement

desaliñado,-a *adj* scruffy, untidy

desaliño *nm* scruffiness, untidiness

desalmado,-a *adj* cruel, heartless

desalojamiento *nm (de inquilino)* eviction; *(de público)* removal; *(de lugar)* evacuation

desalojar *vt* (**a**) *(inquilino)* to evict; *(público)* to move on; *(lugar)* to evacuate (**b**) *(abandonar)* to move out of, to abandon

desalojo *nm* = desalojamiento

desamor *nm* lack of affection

desamortizar [40] *vt* to alienate, to disentail

desamparado,-a 1 *adj (persona)* helpless, unprotected; *(lugar)* abandoned, forsaken

2 *nm,f* helpless o abandoned person

desamparar *vt* (**a**) to abandon, to desert (**b**) *Jur* to renounce, to relinquish

desamparo *nm* helplessness

desamueblado,-a *adj* unfurnished

desandar [8] *vt* **d. lo andado** to retrace one's steps

desangrarse *vpr* to lose (a lot of) blood

desanimado,-a *adj* (**a**) *(persona)* downhearted, dejected (**b**) *(fiesta etc)* dull, lifeless

desanimar 1 *vt* to discourage, to dishearten

2 desanimarse *vpr* to lose heart, to get discouraged

desánimo *nm* discouragement, dejection

desapacible *adj* unpleasant

desaparecer [33] *vi* to disappear

desaparecido,-a 1 *adj* missing

2 *nm,f* missing person

desaparición *nf* disappearance

desapego *nm* indifference, lack of affection

desapercibido,-a *adj* (**a**) *(inadvertido)* unnoticed; **pasar d.** to go unnoticed (**b**) *(desprevenido)* unprepared

desaprensivo,-a 1 *adj* unscrupulous

2 *nm,f* unscrupulous person

desaprobar [2] *vt* (**a**) *(no aprobar)* to disapprove of (**b**) *(rechazar)* to reject

desaprovechar *vt (dinero, tiempo)* to waste; **d. una ocasión** to fail to make the most of an opportunity

desarmable *adj* that can be taken to pieces

desarmador *nm Méx* screwdriver

desarmar *vt* (**a**) *(desmontar)* to dismantle, to take to pieces (**b**) *Mil* to disarm

desarme *nm* disarmament; **d. nuclear** nuclear disarmament

desarraigado,-a *adj* rootless, without roots

desarraigar [42] *vt* to uproot

desarraigo *nm* rootlessness

desarreglado,-a *adj* (**a**) *(lugar)* untidy (**b**) *(persona)* untidy, slovenly

desarreglar *vt* (**a**) *(desordenar)* to make untidy, to mess up (**b**) *(planes etc)* to spoil, to upset

desarreglo *nm* difference of opinion

desarrollado,-a *adj* developed; **país d.** developed country

desarrollar 1 *vt* to develop

2 desarrollarse *vpr* (**a**) *(persona, enfermedad)* to develop (**b**) *(tener lugar)* to take place

desarrollo *nm* development; **países en vías de d.** developing countries

desarticular *vt* to dismantle; **d. un complot** to foil a plot

desaseado,-a *adj* unkempt

desasir [46] 1 *vt* to release

2 desasirse *vpr* to get loose; **d. de** to free o rid oneself of

desasosegar [1] *vt* to make restless o uneasy

desasosiego *nm* restlessness, uneasiness

desastrado,-a 1 *adj* untidy, scruffy

2 *nm,f* scruffy person

desastre *nm* disaster; **eres un d.** you're just hopeless

desastroso,-a *adj* disastrous

desatar 1 *vt* to untie, to undo; *(provocar)* to unleash

2 desatarse *vpr* (**a**) *(zapato, cordón)* to come undone (**b**) *(tormenta)* to break; *(pasión)* to run wild

desatascar [44] *vt* to unblock, to clear

desatender [3] *vt* to neglect, not to pay attention to

desatento,-a *adj* inattentive; *(descortés)* impolite, discourteous

desatinado,-a *adj* unwise

desatino *nm* blunder

desatornillar *vt* to unscrew

desatrancar [44] *vt* to unblock; *(puerta)* to unbolt

desautorizar [40] *vt* (**a**) to disallow (**b**) *(huelga etc)* to ban, to forbid (**c**) *(desmentir)* to deny

desavenencia *nf* disagreement

desaventajado,-a *adj* at a disadvantage

desayunar 1 *vi* to have breakfast; *Fml* to breakfast

2 *vt* to have for breakfast

desayuno *nm* breakfast

desazón *nf* unease

desazonar *vt* to cause unease to, to worry

desbancar [44] *vt* to oust

desbandada *nf* scattering; **hubo una d. general** everyone scattered

desbandarse *vpr* to scatter, to disperse

desbarajuste *nm* confusion, disorder

desbaratar *vt* to ruin, to wreck; *(jersey)* to unravel

desbloquear *vt* (**a**) *(negociaciones)* to get going again (**b**) *(créditos, precios)* to unfreeze

desbocado,-a *adj (caballo)* runaway

desbocarse *vpr (caballo)* to bolt, to run away

desbolado,-a *RP Fam* **1** *adj* messy, untidy

2 *nm,f* untidy person

desbolarse *vpr RP Fam* to undress, to strip

desbole *nm RP Fam* mess, chaos

desbordante *adj* overflowing, bursting

desbordar 1 *vt* to overflow; *Fig* to overwhelm

2 *vi* to overflow (**de** with)

2 desbordarse *vpr* to overflow, to flood

descabalgar [42] *vi* to dismount

descabellado,-a *adj* crazy, wild

descafeinado,-a *adj* (**a**) *(café)* decaffeinated (**b**) *Fig* watered-down, diluted

descalabrar *vt* (**a**) to wound in the head (**b**) *Fig* to damage, to harm

descalabro *nm* setback, misfortune

descalificar [44] *vt* to disqualify

descalzarse [40] *vpr* to take one's shoes off

descalzo,-a *adj* barefoot

descambiar [43] *vt* to exchange

descaminado,-a *adj Fig* **ir d.** to be on the wrong track

descampado *nm* waste ground

descansado,-a *adj* (**a**) *(persona)* rested (**b**) *(vida, trabajo)* restful

descansar *vi* (**a**) to rest, to have a rest; *(corto tiempo)* to take a break (**b**) *Euf* **que en paz descanse** may he/she rest in peace

descansillo *nm* landing

descanso *nm* (**a**) rest, break; **un día de d.** a day off (**b**) *Cin & Teatro* interval; *Dep* half-time, interval (**c**) *(alivio)* relief (**d**) *(rellano)* landing

descapotable *adj & nm* convertible

descarado,-a 1 *adj* (**a**) *(insolente)* cheeky, insolent; *(desvergonzado)* shameless (**b**) *Fam* **d. que sí/no** *(por supuesto)* of course/course not

2 *nm,f* cheeky person

descarga *nf* (**a**) unloading (**b**) *Elec & Mil* discharge

descargar [42] 1 *vt* (**a**) to unload (**b**) *Elec* to discharge (**c**) *(disparar)* to fire; *(golpe)* to deal

2 *vi (tormenta)* to burst

3 descargarse *vpr (batería)* to go flat

descargo *nm Jur* discharge; **testigo de d.** witness for the defence

descarnado,-a *adj* crude

descaro *nm* cheek, nerve; **¡qué d.!** what a cheek!

descarriar [29] 1 *vt* to lead astray, to put on the wrong road

2 descarriarse *vpr* to go astray, to lose one's way

descarrilar *vi* to go off the rails, to be derailed

descartar 1 *vt* to rule out

2 descartarse *vpr Naipes* to discard cards; **me descarté de un cinco** I got rid of a five

descascarillarse *vpr* to chip, to peel

descendencia *nf* descendants; **morir sin d.** to die without issue

descendente *adj* descending, downward

descender [3] 1 *vi* (**a**) *(temperatura, nivel)* to fall, to drop (**b**) **d. de** to descend from

2 *vt* to lower

descendiente *nmf* descendant

descenso *nm* (**a**) descent; *(de temperatura)* fall, drop (**b**) *Dep* relegation

descentrado,-a *adj* off-centre

descentralizar [40] *vt* to decentralize

descifrar *vt* to decipher; *(mensaje)* to decode; *(misterio)* to solve; *(motivos, causas)* to figure out

descojonarse *vpr muy Fam (reírse)* to piss oneself laughing

descolgar [2] 1 *vt (el teléfono)* to pick up; *(cuadro, cortinas)* to take down
  2 descolgarse *vpr* to let oneself down, to slide down

descolorido,-a *adj* faded

descombros *nmpl* rubble, debris

descompasado,-a *adj* inconsistent

descomponer [19] *(pp* **descompuesto***)* **1** *vt* (**a**) to break down (**b**) *(corromper)* to rot, to decompose
  2 descomponerse *vpr* (**a**) *(corromperse)* to rot, to decompose (**b**) *(ponerse nervioso)* to lose one's cool (**c**) *Am (el tiempo)* to turn nasty

descomposición *nf* (**a**) *(de carne)* decomposition, rotting; *(de país)* disintegration (**b**) *Quím* breakdown

descompostura *nf* (**a**) *Am (malestar)* unpleasant turn (**b**) *Méx, RP (avería)* breakdown

descompuesto,-a *adj* (**a**) *(podrido)* rotten, decomposed (**b**) *(furioso)* furious

descompuse *pt indef de* **descomponer**

descomunal *adj* huge, massive

desconcertante *adj* disconcerting

desconcertar [1] 1 *vt* to disconcert
  2 desconcertarse *vpr* to be bewildered, to be puzzled

desconchón *nm* bare patch

desconcierto *nm* chaos, confusion

desconectar *vt* to disconnect

desconexión *nf* disconnection

desconfiado,-a *adj* distrustful, wary

desconfianza *nf* distrust, mistrust

desconfiar [29] *vi* **d. (de)** to distrust, to mistrust

descongelar *vt (nevera)* to defrost; *(créditos)* to unfreeze

descongestionar *vt* to clear

desconocer [34] *vt* not to know, to be unaware of

desconocido,-a 1 *adj* unknown; *(irreconocible)* unrecognizable
  2 *nm* **lo d.** the unknown
  3 *nm,f* stranger

desconsiderado,-a 1 *adj* inconsiderate, thoughtless
  2 *nm,f* inconsiderate o thoughtless person

desconsolado,-a *adj* disconsolate, grief-stricken

desconsuelo *nm* grief, sorrow

descontado,-a *adj Fam* **dar por d.** to take for granted; **por d.** needless to say, of course

descontar [2] *vt* (**a**) to deduct (**b**) *Dep (tiempo)* to add on

descontento,-a 1 *adj* unhappy
  2 *nm* dissatisfaction

descontrol *nm Fam* lack of control; **había un d. total** it was absolute chaos

descontrolarse *vpr* to lose control

desconvocar *vt* to call off

descorchar *vt* to uncork

descornarse [2] *vpr Fam (trabajar)* to slave (away)

descorrer *vt* to draw back

descortés *adj* impolite, discourteous

descortesía *nf* discourtesy, impoliteness

descoser *vt* to unstitch, to unpick

descosido *nm (en camisa etc)* open seam; *Fam* **como un d.** like mad, wildly

descoyuntar *vt* to dislocate

descrédito *nm* disrepute, discredit

descremado,-a *adj* skimmed

describir *(pp* **descrito***) vt* to describe

descripción *nf* description

descriptivo,-a *adj* descriptive

descrito,-a *pp de* **describir**

descuajaringar [42] *vt Fam* to pull o take to pieces

descuartizar [40] *vt* to cut up, to cut into pieces

descubierto,-a 1 *adj* open, uncovered; **a cielo d.** in the open
  2 *nm* (**a**) *Fin* overdraft (**b**) **al d.** in the open; **poner al d.** to uncover, to bring out into the open

descubridor,-a *nm,f* discoverer

descubrimiento *nm* discovery

descubrir *(pp* **descubierto***) vt* to discover; *(conspiración)* to uncover; *(placa)* to unveil

descuento *nm* discount

descuidado,-a *adj* (**a**) *(desaseado)* untidy, neglected (**b**) *(negligente)* careless, negligent (**c**) *(desprevenido)* off one's guard

descuidar 1 *vt* to neglect, to overlook
  2 *vi* **descuida, voy yo** don't worry, I'll go
  3 descuidarse *vpr (despistarse)* to be careless; **como te descuides, llegarás tarde** if you don't watch out, you'll be late

descuido *nm* (**a**) oversight, mistake; **por d.** inadvertently, by mistake (**b**) *(negligencia)* negligence, carelessness

desde *adv* (**a**) *(tiempo)* since; **d. ahora** from now on; **d. el lunes/entonces** since Monday/then; **espero d. hace media hora** I've been waiting for half an hour; **no lo he visto d. hace un año** I haven't seen him for a year; **¿d. cuándo?** since when?; **d. siempre** always

(**b**) *(lugar)* from; **d. aquí** from here; **d. arriba/abajo** from above/below

(**c**) **d. luego** of course

(**d**) **d. que** ever since; **d. que lo conozco** ever since I've known him

desdecir [12] (*pp* **desdicho**) **1** *vi* **d. de** not to live up to

2 desdecirse *vpr* to go back on one's word

desdén *nm* disdain

desdentado,-a *adj* toothless

desdeñar *vt* to disdain

desdeñoso,-a *adj* disdainful

desdibujarse *vpr* to become blurred *o* faint

desdicha *nf* misfortune; **por d.** unfortunately

desdichado,-a 1 *adj* unfortunate

2 *nm,f* poor devil, wretch

desdigo *indic pres de* **desdecir**

desdiré *indic fut de* **desdecir**

desdoblar *vt* to unfold

deseable *adj* desirable

desear *vt* (**a**) to desire; **deja mucho que d.** it leaves a lot to be desired (**b**) *(querer)* to want; **¿qué desea?** can I help you?; **estoy deseando que vengas** I'm looking forward to your coming (**c**) **te deseo buena suerte/feliz Navidad** I wish you good luck/a merry Christmas

desecar [44] *vt* to dry up

desechable *adj* disposable, throw-away

desechar *vt* (**a**) *(tirar)* to discard, to throw out *o* away (**b**) *(oferta)* to turn down, to refuse; *(idea, proyecto)* to drop, to discard

desechos *nmpl* waste

desembalar *vt* to unpack

desembarcar [44] 1 *vt* *(mercancías)* to unload; *(personas)* to disembark

2 *vi* to disembark

desembarco, desembarque *nm* *(de mercancías)* unloading; *(de personas)* disembarkation

desembocadura *nf* mouth

desembocar [44] *vi* **d. en** *(río)* to flow into; *(calle, situación)* to lead to

desembolsar *vt* to pay out

desembolso *nm* expenditure

desembragar [42] *vt* *Aut* to declutch

desembrollar *vt* *Fam* (**a**) *(aclarar)* to clarify, to clear up (**b**) *(desenredar)* to disentangle

desembuchar *vt* *Fig* to blurt out; *Fam* **¡desembucha!** out with it!

desempañar *vt* to wipe the condensation from; *Aut* to demist

desempaquetar *vt* to unpack, to unwrap

desempatar *vi* *Dep* to break the deadlock

desempate *nm* play-off; **partido de d.** play-off, deciding match

desempeñar *vt* (**a**) *(cargo)* to hold, to occupy; *(función)* to fulfil; *(papel)* to play (**b**) *(recuperar)* to redeem

desempleado,-a 1 *adj* unemployed, out of work

2 *nm,f* unemployed person; **los desempleados** the unemployed

desempleo *nm* unemployment; **cobrar el d.** to be on the dole

desempolvar *vt* (**a**) to dust (**b**) *Fig (pasado)* to revive

desencadenar 1 *vt* (**a**) to unchain (**b**) *(provocar)* to unleash

2 desencadenarse *vpr* (**a**) *(prisionero)* to break loose; *(viento, pasión)* to rage (**b**) *(conflicto)* to start, to break out

desencajar 1 *vt* *(pieza)* to knock out; *(hueso)* to dislocate

2 desencajarse *vpr* (**a**) *(pieza)* to come out; *(hueso)* to become dislocated (**b**) *(cara)* to become distorted

desencaminado,-a *adj* = **descaminado,-a**

desencanto *nm* disenchantment

desenchufar *vt* to unplug

desenfadado,-a *adj* carefree, free and easy

desenfado *nm* ease

desenfocado,-a *adj* out of focus

desenfoque *nm* incorrect focusing; *Fig (de asunto)* wrong approach

desenfrenado,-a *adj* frantic, uncontrolled; *(vicio, pasión)* unbridled

desenfreno *nm* debauchery

desenganchar *vt* to unhook; *(vagón)* to uncouple

desengañar 1 *vt* **d. a algn** to open sb's eyes

2 desengañarse *vpr* (**a**) to be disappointed (**b**) *Fam* **¡desengáñate!** get real!

desengaño *nm* disappointment; **llevarse** *o* **sufrir un d. con algo** to be disappointed in sth

desengrasar *vt* to degrease, to remove the grease from

desenlace *nm* (**a**) result, outcome; **un feliz d.** a happy end (**b**) *Cin & Teatro* ending, dénouement

desenmarañar *vt* *(pelo)* to untangle; *(problema)* to unravel; *(asunto)* to sort out

desenmascarar *vt* to unmask

desenredar *vt* to untangle, to disentangle

desenrollar *vt* to unroll; *(cable)* to unwind

desenroscar [44] *vt* to unscrew

desentenderse [3] *vpr* **se desentendió de mi problema** he didn't want to have anything to do with my problem

desenterrar [1] *vt* (**a**) *(cadáver)* to exhume, to disinter; *(tesoro etc)* to dig up (**b**) *(recuerdo)* to revive

desentonar *vi* (**a**) *Mús* to sing out of tune, to be out of tune (**b**) *(colores etc)* not to match (**c**) *(persona, comentario)* to be out of place

desentrañar *vt* *(misterio)* to unravel, to get to the bottom of

desentrenado,-a *adj* out of training *o* shape

desentumecer [33] *vt* to put the feeling back into

desenvoltura *nf* ease

desenvolver [4] (*pp* **desenvuelto**) **1** *vt* to unwrap
2 desenvolverse *vpr* (**a**) *(persona)* to manage, to cope (**b**) *(hecho)* to develop

desenvuelto,-a *adj* relaxed

deseo *nm* wish; *(sexual)* desire; **formular un d.** to make a wish

deseoso,-a *adj* eager; **estar d. de** be eager to

desequilibrado,-a 1 *adj* unbalanced
2 *nm,f* unbalanced person

desequilibrar 1 *vt* to unbalance, to throw off balance
2 desequilibrarse *vpr* to become mentally disturbed

desequilibrio *nm* imbalance; **d. mental** mental disorder

deserción *nf* desertion

desertar *vi* to desert

desértico,-a *adj* desert

desertización *nf* desertification

desertor,-a *nm,f* deserter

desesperación *nf* *(desesperanza)* despair; *(exasperación)* desperation

desesperado,-a *adj* (**a**) *(sin esperanza)* desperate, hopeless (**b**) *(exasperado)* exasperated, infuriated

desesperante *adj* exasperating

desesperar 1 *vt* to drive to despair; *(exasperar)* to exasperate
2 desesperarse *vpr* to despair

desestabilizar [40] *vt* to destabilize

desestatización *nf Am* privatization

desestatizar *vt Am* to privatize

desestimar *vt* to reject

desfachatez *nf* cheek, nerve

desfalco *nm* embezzlement, misappropriation

desfallecer [33] *vi* (**a**) *(debilitarse)* to feel faint; *(desmayarse)* to faint (**b**) *(desanimarse)* to lose heart

desfasado,-a *adj* (**a**) outdated (**b**) *(persona)* old-fashioned, behind the times (**c**)*Téc* out of phase

desfase *nm* gap; **d. horario** time lag

desfavorable *adj* unfavourable

desfigurar *vt (cara)* to disfigure; *(verdad)* to distort

desfiladero *nm* narrow pass

desfilar *vi* (**a**) to march in single file (**b**) *Mil* to march past, to parade

desfile *nm Mil* parade, march past; **d. de modas** fashion show

desfogar [42] 1 *vt* to give vent to
2 desfogarse *vpr* to let off steam

desgajar 1 *vt (arrancar)* to rip *o* tear out; *(rama)* to tear off
2 desgajarse *vpr* to come off

desgana *nf* (**a**) *(inapetencia)* lack of appetite (**b**) *(apatía)* apathy, indifference; **con d.** reluctantly, unwillingly

desganado,-a *adj* (**a**) **estar d.** *(inapetente)* to have no appetite (**b**) *(apático)* apathetic

desgañitarse *vpr Fam* to shout oneself hoarse

desgarbado,-a *adj* ungraceful, ungainly

desgarrador,-a *adj* harrowing

desgarrar *vt* to tear

desgarrón *nm* big tear, rip

desgastar 1 *vt* to wear out
2 desgastarse *vpr (consumirse)* to wear out; *(persona)* to wear oneself out

desgaste *nm* wear; **d. del poder** wear and tear of power

desgracia *nf* (**a**) misfortune; **por d.** unfortunately (**b**) *(deshonor)* disgrace (**c**) **desgracias personales** loss of life

desgraciadamente *adv* unfortunately

desgraciado,-a 1 *adj* unfortunate; *(infeliz)* unhappy
2 *nm,f* unfortunate person; **un pobre d.** a poor devil

desgravable *adj* tax-deductible

desgravación *nf* deduction; **d. fiscal** tax deduction

desgravar *vt* to deduct

desguazar [40] *vt (un barco)* to break up; *Aut* to scrap

deshabitado,-a *adj* uninhabited, unoccupied

deshabitar *vt* to abandon, to vacate

deshacer [15] (*pp* **deshecho**) **1** *vt* (**a**) *(paquete)* to undo; *(maleta)* to unpack (**b**) *(plan)* to destroy, to ruin (**c**) *(acuerdo)* to break off (**d**) *(disolver)* to dissolve; *(derretir)* to melt

2 deshacerse *vpr* (**a**) to come undone *o* untied (**b**) **d. de algn/algo** to get rid of sb/sth (**c**) *(afligirse)* to go to pieces; **d. en lágrimas** to cry one's eyes out (**d**) *(disolverse)* to dissolve; *(derretirse)* to melt (**e**) *(niebla)* to fade away, to disappear

deshecho,-a *adj* (**a**) *(cama)* unmade; *(maleta)* unpacked; *(paquete)* unwrapped (**b**) *(roto)* broken, smashed (**c**) *(disuelto)* dissolved; *(derretido)* melted (**d**) *(abatido)* devastated, shattered (**e**) *(cansado)* exhausted, tired out

desheredar *vt* to disinherit

deshidratar *vt* to dehydrate

deshielo *nm* thaw

deshilachar *vt* to fray

deshilvanado,-a *adj Fig (inconexo)* disjointed

deshonesto,-a *adj* (**a**) dishonest (**b**) *(indecente)* indecent, improper

deshonor *nm,* **deshonra** *nf* dishonour

deshonrar *vt* (**a**) to dishonour (**b**) *(a la familia etc)* to bring disgrace on

deshora: • **a deshora** *loc adv* at an inconvenient time; **comer a d.** to eat at odd times

deshuesar *vt (carne)* to bone; *(fruta)* to stone

deshumanizar [40] *vt* to dehumanize

desidia *nf* apathy

desierto,-a 1 *nm* desert

2 *adj* (**a**) *(deshabitado)* uninhabited (**b**) *(vacío)* empty, deserted (**c**) *(premio)* void

designación *nf* designation

designar *vt* (**a**) to designate (**b**) *(fecha, lugar)* to fix

designio *nm* intention, plan

desigual *adj* (**a**) uneven (**b**) *(lucha)* unequal (**c**) *(carácter)* changeable

desigualdad *nf* (**a**) inequality (**b**) *(del terreno)* unevenness

desilusión *nf* disappointment, disillusionment

desilusionar *vt* to disappoint, to disillusion

desinfectante *adj & nm* disinfectant

desinfectar *vt* to disinfect

desinflar 1 *vt* to deflate; *(rueda)* to let down

2 desinflarse *vpr* to go flat

desintegración *nf* disintegration

desintegrar *vt,* **desintegrarse** *vpr* to disintegrate

desinterés *nm* (**a**) *(indiferencia)* lack of interest, apathy (**b**) *(generosidad)* unselfishness

desinteresado,-a *adj* selfless, unselfish

desintoxicar [44] 1 *vt* to detoxicate; *(de alcohol)* to dry out

2 desintoxicarse *vpr Med* to detoxicate oneself; *(de alcohol)* to dry out

desistir *vi* to desist

deslavazado,-a *adj* disjointed

deslave *nm Am* landslide *(caused by flooding or rain)*

desleal *adj* disloyal; *(competencia)* unfair

deslealtad *nf* disloyalty

deslenguado,-a *adj (insolente)* insolent, cheeky; *(grosero)* coarse, foul-mouthed

desliar [29] *vt* to unwrap

desligar [42] 1 *vt* (**a**) *(separar)* to separate (**b**) *(desatar)* to untie, to unfasten

2 desligarse *vpr* **d. de** to disassociate oneself from

desliz *nm* mistake, slip; **cometer** *o* **tener un d.** to slip up

deslizar [40] 1 *vi* to slide

2 deslizarse *vpr* (**a**) *(patinar)* to slide (**b**) *(fluir)* to flow

deslucir [35] *vt* (**a**) *(espectáculo)* to spoil (**b**) *(metal)* to make dull

deslumbrador,-a, deslumbrante *adj* dazzling; *Fig* stunning

deslumbrar *vt* to dazzle

desmadrarse *vpr Fam* to go wild

desmadre *nm Fam* hullabaloo

desmandarse *vpr* to get out of hand, to run wild; *(caballo)* to bolt

desmano: • **a desmano** *loc adv* out of the way; **me coge a d.** it is out of my way

desmantelar *vt* (**a**) to dismantle (**b**) *Náut* to dismast, to unrig

desmaquillador,-a 1 *nm* make-up remover

2 *adj* **leche desmaquilladora** cleansing cream

desmaquillarse *vpr* to remove one's make-up

desmarcarse [44] *vpr Dep* to lose one's marker

desmayado,-a *adj* unconscious; **caer d.** to faint

desmayarse *vpr* to faint

desmayo *nm* faint, fainting fit; **tener un d.** to faint

desmedido,-a *adj* disproportionate, out of all proportion; *(ambición)* unbounded

desmejorar *vi,* **desmejorarse** *vpr* to deteriorate, to go downhill

desmelenarse *vpr Fam* to let one's hair down

desmembración *nf,* **desmembramiento** *nm* dismemberment

desmemoriado,-a *adj* forgetful, absent-minded

desmentir [5] *vt* to deny

desmenuzar [40] *vt* (**a**) *(deshacer)* to break into little pieces, to crumble; *(carne)* to cut into little pieces (**b**) *(asunto)* to examine in detail

desmerecer [33] *vi* to lose value

desmesura *nf* excess

desmesurado,-a *adj* excessive

desmilitarizar [40] *vt* to demilitarize

desmontable *adj* that can be taken to pieces

desmontar 1 *vt* (**a**) *(desarmar)* to take to pieces, to dismantle (**b**) *(allanar)* to level **2** *vi* **d. (de)** to dismount, to get off

desmoralizar [40] *vt* to demoralize

desmoronarse *vpr* to crumble, to fall to pieces

desnatado,-a *adj (leche)* skimmed

desnivel *nm (en el terreno)* drop, difference in height

desnivelar *vt* to throw out of balance

desnucarse [44] *vpr* to break one's neck

desnuclearizar *vt* to denuclearize

desnudar 1 *vt* to undress **2 desnudarse** *vpr* to get undressed

desnudismo *nm* nudism

desnudista *adj & nmf* nudist

desnudo,-a 1 *adj* naked, nude **2** *nm Arte* nude

desnutrición *nf* malnutrition

desnutrido,-a *adj* undernourished

desobedecer [33] *vt* to disobey

desobediencia *nf* disobedience

desobediente 1 *adj* disobedient **2** *nmf* disobedient person

desocupado,-a *adj* (**a**) *(vacío)* empty, vacant (**b**) *(ocioso)* free, not busy (**c**) *(sin empleo)* unemployed

desocupar *vt* to empty, to vacate

desodorante *adj & nm* deodorant

desolación *nf* desolation

desolar *vt* to devastate

desollar [2] 1 *vt* to skin **2 •desollarse** *vpr* to scrape; **me desollé el brazo** I scraped my arm

desorbitado,-a *adj (precio)* exorbitant

desorden *nm* untidiness, mess; **¡qué d.!** what a mess!; **d. público** civil disorder

desordenado,-a *adj* messy, untidy

desordenar *vt* to make untidy, to mess up

desorganizar [40] *vt* to disorganize, to disrupt

desorientación *nf* disorientation

desorientar 1 *vt* to disorientate **2 desorientarse** *vpr* to lose one's sense of direction, to lose one's bearings; *Fig* to become disorientated

despabilado,-a *adj* (**a**) *(sin sueño)* wide awake (**b**) *(listo)* quick, smart

despachar *vt* (**a**) *(asunto)* to get through (**b**) *(correo)* to send, to dispatch (**c**) *(en tienda)* to serve (**d**) *Fam (despedir)* to send packing, to sack (**e**) *Am (facturar)* to check in

despacho *nm* (**a**) *(oficina)* office; *(en casa)* study (**b**) *(venta)* sale (**c**) *(comunicación)* dispatch

despachurrar *vt Fam* to squash, to flatten

despacio *adv* (**a**) *(lentamente)* slowly (**b**) *(en voz baja)* quietly

despampanante *adj Fam* stunning

desparpajo *nm* self-assurance; **con d.** in a carefree manner

desparramar *vt,* **desparramarse** *vpr* to spread, to scatter; *(líquido)* to spill

despavorido,-a *adj* terrified

despecho *nm* spite; **por d.** out of spite

despectivo,-a *adj* derogatory, disparaging

despedazar [40] *vt* to cut o tear to pieces

despedida *nf* farewell, goodbye; **d. de soltera/soltero** hen/stag party

despedido,-a *adj* **salir d.** to be off like a shot

despedir [6] 1 *vt* (**a**) *(empleado)* to fire, *Br* to sack (**b**) *(decir adiós)* to see off, to say goodbye to (**c**) *(olor, humo etc)* to give off **2 despedirse** *vpr* (**a**) *(decir adiós)* to say goodbye (**de** to) (**b**) *Fig* to forget, to give up; **ya puedes despedirte del coche** you can say goodbye to the car

despegado,-a *adj* (**a**) unstuck (**b**) *(persona)* couldn't-care-less

despegar [42] 1 *vt* to take off, to detach **2** *vi Av* to take off **3 despegarse** *vpr* to come unstuck

despego *nm* detachment

despegue *nm* take-off

despeinado,-a *adj* dishevelled, with untidy hair

despejado,-a *adj* clear; *(cielo)* cloudless

despejar 1 *vt* to clear; *(misterio, dudas)* to clear up **2 despejarse** *vpr* (**a**) *(cielo)* to clear (**b**) *(persona)* to clear one's head

despeje *nm Dep* clearance

despellejar *vt* to skin

despelotarse *vpr Fam* (**a**) *(desnudarse)* to strip (**b**) **d. de risa** to laugh one's head off

despensa *nf* pantry, larder
despeñadero *nm* cliff, precipice
despeñarse *vpr* to go over a cliff
desperdiciar [43] *vt* to waste; *(oportunidad)* to throw away
desperdicio *nm* (**a**) *(acto)* waste (**b**) **desperdicios** *(basura)* rubbish; *(desechos)* scraps, leftovers
desperdigar [42] *vt,* **desperdigarse** *vpr* to scatter, to separate
desperezarse [40] *vpr* to stretch (oneself)
desperfecto *nm* (**a**) *(defecto)* flaw, imperfection (**b**) *(daño)* damage
despertador *nm* alarm clock
despertar [1] **1** *vt* to wake (up), to awaken; *Fig (sentimiento etc)* to arouse
2 despertarse *vpr* to wake (up)
despiadado,-a *adj* merciless
despido *nm* dismissal, sacking
despierto,-a *adj* (**a**) *(desvelado)* awake (**b**) *(vivo)* quick, sharp
despilfarrar *vt* to waste, to squander
despilfarro *nm* wasting, squandering
despintar *vi,* **despintarse** *vpr (ropa)* to fade
despiole *nm RP Fam* rumpus, shindy
despistado,-a 1 *adj* (**a**) *(olvidadizo)* scatterbrained (**b**) *(confuso)* confused
2 *nm,f* scatterbrain
despistar 1 *vt* (**a**) *(hacer perder la pista a)* to lose, to throw off one's scent (**b**) *Fig* to mislead
2 despistarse *vpr* (**a**) *(perderse)* to get lost (**b**) *(distraerse)* to switch off
despiste *nm* (**a**) *(cualidad)* absentmindedness (**b**) *(error)* slip-up
desplazamiento *nm (viaje)* trip, journey; **dietas de d.** travelling expenses
desplazar [40] 1 *vt* to displace
2 desplazarse *vpr* to travel
desplegar [1] 1 *vt* (**a**) to open (out), to spread (out) (**b**) *(energías etc)* to use, to deploy
2 desplegarse *vpr* (**a**) *(abrirse)* to open (out), to spread (out) (**b**) *Mil* to deploy
despliegue *nm* (**a**) *Mil* deployment (**b**) *(de medios etc)* display
desplomarse *vpr* to collapse; *(precios)* to slump, to fall sharply
desplumar *vt* to pluck
despoblar [2] *vt* to depopulate
despojar *vt* (**a**) to strip (**de** of) (**b**) *Fig* to divest, to deprive (**de** of)
despojo *nm* (**a**) stripping (**b**) **despojos** leftovers, scraps
desposado,-a *adj Fml* newly-wed
desposar *vt Fml* to marry

desposeer [36] *vt* **d. de** to dispossess of; *(autoridad)* to strip of
desposeído *nm* **los desposeídos** the have-nots
déspota *nmf* despot
despótico,-a *adj* despotic
despotismo *nm* despotism
despotricar [44] *vi* to rant and rave (**contra** about)
despreciable *adj* despicable, contemptible; *(cantidad)* negligible
despreciar [43] *vt* (**a**) *(desdeñar)* to scorn, to despise (**b**) *(rechazar)* to reject, to spurn
desprecio *nm* (**a**) *(desdén)* scorn, disdain (**b**) *(desaire)* slight, snub
desprender 1 *vt* (**a**) *(separar)* to remove, to detach (**b**) *(olor, humo etc)* to give off
2 desprenderse *vpr* (**a**) *(soltarse)* to come off *o* away (**b**) **d. de** to rid oneself of, to free oneself from (**c**) **de aquí se desprende que ...** it can be deduced from this that ...
desprendido,-a *adj Fig* generous, unselfish
desprendimiento *nm* (**a**) loosening, detachment; **d. de tierras** landslide (**b**) *Fig (generosidad)* generosity, unselfishness
despreocupado,-a *adj* (**a**) *(tranquilo)* unconcerned (**b**) *(descuidado)* careless; *(estilo)* casual
despreocuparse *vpr* (**a**) *(tranquilizarse)* to stop worrying (**b**) *(desentenderse)* to be unconcerned, to be indifferent (**de** to)
desprestigiar [43] *vt* to discredit, to run down
desprestigio *nm* discredit, loss of reputation; **campaña de d.** smear campaign
desprevenido,-a *adj* unprepared; **coger** *o* **pillar a algn d.** to catch sb unawares
desprolijo,-a *adj Am (casa)* messy, untidy; *(cuaderno)* untidy; *(persona)* unkempt, dishevelled
desproporción *nf* disproportion, lack of proportion
desproporcionado,-a *adj* disproportionate
desprovisto,-a *adj* **d. (de)** lacking, without, devoid (of)
después *adv* (**a**) afterwards, later; *(entonces)* then; *(seguidamente)* next; **una semana d.** a week later; **poco d.** soon after (**b**) *(lugar)* next (**c**) **d. de** after; **d. de la guerra** after the war; **mi calle está d. de la tuya** my street is the one after yours; **d. de cenar** after eating; **d. de todo** after

all (**d**) **d. de que** after; **d. de que vi-niera** after he came

despuntar 1 *vt* to blunt, to make blunt
  2 *vi* (**a**) *(día)* to dawn (**b**) *(destacar)* to excel, to stand out

desquiciar [43] 1 *vt (persona)* to unhinge
  2 desquiciarse *vpr (persona)* to go crazy

desquitarse *vpr* to take revenge (**de** for)

desquite *nm* revenge

destacado,-a *adj* outstanding

destacamento *nm* detachment

destacar [44] 1 *vt Fig* to emphasize, to stress
  2 *vi* to stand out
  3 destacarse *vpr* to stand out

destajo *nm* piecework; **trabajar a d.** to do piecework

destapador *nm Am* bottle opener

destapar 1 *vt* to take the lid off; *(botella)* to open; *Fig (asunto)* to uncover; *RP (caño)* to unblock
  2 destaparse *vpr* to get uncovered

destartalado,-a *adj* rambling; *(desvencijado)* ramshackle

destello *nm* flash, sparkle

destemplado,-a *adj* (**a**) *(voz, gesto)* sharp, snappy; **con cajas destempladas** rudely, brusquely (**b**) *(tiempo)* unpleasant (**c**) *(enfermo)* indisposed, out of sorts (**d**) *Mús* out of tune, discordant

desteñir [6] 1 *vt & vi* to discolour
  2 desteñirse *vpr* to lose colour, to fade

desternillarse *vpr* **d. (de risa)** to split one's sides laughing

desterrar [1] *vt* to exile

destiempo: • **a destiempo** *loc adv* at the wrong time o moment

destierro *nm* exile

destilado,-a *adj* distilled; **agua destilada** distilled water

destilar *vt* to distil

destilería *nf* distillery

destinado,-a *adj* destined, bound; *Fig* **d. al fracaso** doomed to failure

destinar *vt* (**a**) *(dinero etc)* to set aside, to assign (**b**) *(empleado)* to appoint

destinatario,-a *nm,f* (**a**) *(de carta)* addressee (**b**) *(de mercancías)* consignee

destino *nm* (**a**) *(rumbo)* destination; **el avión con d. a Bilbao** the plane to Bilbao (**b**) *(sino)* fate, fortune (**c**) *(de empleo)* post

destitución *nf* dismissal from office

destituir [37] *vt* to dismiss o remove from office

destornillador *nm* screwdriver

destornillar *vt* to unscrew

destreza *nf* skill

destrozado,-a *adj* (**a**) *(roto)* torn-up, smashed (**b**) *(cansado)* worn-out, exhausted (**c**) *(abatido)* shattered

destrozar [40] *vt* (**a**) *(destruir)* to destroy; *(rasgar)* to tear to shreds o pieces (**b**) *(afligir)* to shatter; *(vida, reputación)* to ruin

destrozo *nm* (**a**) destruction (**b**) **destrozos** damage

destrucción *nf* destruction

destructivo,-a *adj* destructive

destructor,-a 1 *adj* destructive
  2 *nm Náut* destroyer

destruir [37] *vt* to destroy

desubicado,-a *nm,f Andes, RP* **ser un d.** to have no idea how to behave, to be clueless

desusado,-a *adj* old-fashioned, outdated

desuso *nm* disuse; **caer en d.** to fall into disuse; **en d.** obsolete, outdated

desvalido,-a *adj* defenceless

desvalijar *vt (robar)* to clean out, to rob; *(casa, tienda)* to burgle

desvalorizar [40] *vt* to devalue

desván *nm* attic, loft

desvanecerse [33] *vpr* (**a**) *(disiparse)* to vanish, to fade away (**b**) *(desmayarse)* to faint

desvariar [29] *vi* to talk nonsense

desvarío *nm* (**a**) *(delirio)* raving, delirium (**b**) *(disparate)* nonsense

desvelado,-a *adj* awake, wide awake

desvelar 1 *vt* to keep awake
  2 desvelarse *vpr* (**a**) *(despabilarse)* to stay awake (**b**) *(desvivirse)* to devote oneself (**por** to) (**c**) *CAm, Méx (quedarse despierto)* to stay up o awake

desvencijar 1 *vt* to take apart
  2 desvencijarse *vpr* to fall apart

desventaja *nf* (**a**) disadvantage; **estar en d.** to be at a disadvantage (**b**) *(inconveniente)* drawback

desventura *nf* misfortune, bad luck

desvergonzado,-a 1 *adj* (**a**) *(indecente)* shameless (**b**) *(descarado)* insolent
  2 *nm,f* (**a**) *(sinvergüenza)* shameless person (**b**) *(fresco)* insolent o cheeky person

desvergüenza *nf* (**a**) *(indecencia)* shamelessness (**b**) *(atrevimiento)* insolence; **tuvo la d. de negarlo** he had the cheek to deny it (**c**) *(impertinencia)* insolent o rude remark

desvestir [6] 1 *vt* to undress
  2 desvestirse *vpr* to undress, to get undressed

desviación *nf* deviation; *(de carretera)*

diversion, detour; *Med* **d. de columna** slipped disc

desviar [29] 1 *vt (río, carretera)* to divert; *(golpe, conversación)* to deflect; **d. la mirada** to look away

2 desviarse *vpr* to go off course; *(coche)* to turn off; *Fig* **d. del tema** to digress

desvincular 1 *vt* to separate

2 desvincularse *vpr* to separate, to cut oneself off

desvío *nm* diversion, detour

desvirgar [42] *vt* to deflower

desvirtuar [30] *vt* to distort

desvivirse *vpr* to bend over backwards

detalladamente *adv* in (great) detail

detallado,-a *adj* detailed, thorough

detallar *vt* to give the details of

detalle *nm* (a) detail; **entrar en detalles** to go into details (b) *(delicadeza)* nice thought, nicety; **¡qué d.!** how nice!, how sweet! (c) *(toque decorativo)* touch, ornament

detallista 1 *adj* perfectionist

2 *nmf Com* retailer

detectar *vt* to detect

detective *nmf* detective; **d. privado** private detective *o* eye

detector,-a *nm,f* detector; **d. de incendios** fire detector

detención *nf* (a)*Jur* detention, arrest (b) **con d.** carefully, thoroughly

detener [24] 1 *vt* (a) to stop, to halt (b) *Jur (arrestar)* to arrest, to detain

2 detenerse *vpr* to stop

detenidamente *adv* carefully, thoroughly

detenido,-a 1 *adj* (a) *(parado)* standing still, stopped (b) *(arrestado)* detained (c) *(minucioso)* detailed, thorough

2 *nm,f* detainee, person under arrest

detenimiento *nm* **con d.** carefully, thoroughly

detentar *vt* to hold

detergente *adj & nm* detergent

deteriorar 1 *vt* to spoil, to damage

2 deteriorarse *vpr* (a) *(estropearse)* to get damaged (b) *(empeorar)* to get worse

deterioro *nm* (a) *(empeoramiento)* deterioration, worsening (b) *(daño)* damage; **ir en d. de** to be to the detriment of

determinación *nf* (a) determination; **con d.** determinedly (b) *(decisión)* decision

determinado,-a *adj* (a) *(preciso)* definite, precise (b) *(resuelto)* decisive, resolute (c) *Ling* definite

determinante *adj* decisive

determinar 1 *vt* (a) *(fecha etc)* to fix, to

set (b) *(decidir)* to decide on (c) *(condicionar)* to determine (d) *(ocasionar)* to bring about

2 determinarse *vpr* to make up one's mind to

detestable *adj* detestable, repulsive

detestar *vt* to detest, to hate

detonante *nm* detonator; *Fig* trigger

detonar *vt* to detonate

detractor,-a *nm,f* detractor

detrás *adv* (a) behind, on *o* at the back (**de** of) (b) **d. de** behind

detrimento *nm* detriment; **en d. de** to the detriment of

detuve *pt indef de* **detener**

deuda *nf* debt; **estoy en d. contigo** *(monetaria)* I am in debt to you; *(moral)* I am indebted to you; **d. del Estado** public debt; **d. pública** national debt

deudor,-a 1 *adj* indebted

2 *nm,f* debtor

devaluación *nf* devaluation

devaluar [30] *vt* to devalue

devanar 1 *vt (hilo)* to wind; *(alambre)* to coil

2 devanarse *vpr Fam* **d. los sesos** to rack one's brains

devaneo *nm* dabbling

devastador,-a *adj* devastating

devastar *vt* to devastate, to ravage

devengar [42] *vt Com* to earn, to accrue

devenir [27] *vi* to become

devoción *nf* (a) *Rel* devoutness (b) *(al trabajo etc)* devotion; *Fam* **Juan no es santo de mi d.** Juan isn't really my cup of tea

devolución *nf* (a) giving back, return; *Com* refund, repayment (b) *Jur* devolution

devolver [4] *(pp* **devuelto)** **1** *vt* to give back, to return; *(dinero)* to refund

2 *vi (vomitar)* to vomit, to throw *o* bring up

3 devolverse *vpr Am* to go *o* come back, to return

devorar *vt* to devour

devoto,-a 1 *adj* pious, devout

2 *nm,f* (a) *Rel* pious person (b) *(seguidor)* devotee

devuelto,-a *pp de* **devolver**

DF *nm (abr* **Distrito Federal***) (en México)* Mexico City

DGI *nf RP (abr* **Dirección General Impositiva***) Br* ≃ Inland Revenue, *US* ≃ IRS

DGT *nf (abr* **Dirección General de Tráfico***)* = government department responsible for road transport

di (a) *pt indef de* **dar** (b) *imperat de* **decir**

día *nm* day; **¿qué d. es hoy?** what's the date today?; **d. a d.** day by day; **de d.** by day; **durante el d.** during the daytime; **de un d. para otro** overnight; **un d. sí y otro no** every other day; **pan del d.** fresh bread; **hoy (en) d.** nowadays; **el d. de mañana** in the future; *Fig* **estar al d.** to be up to date; *Fig* **poner al d.** to bring up to date; **d. festivo** holiday; **d. laborable** working day; **d. libre** free day, day off; **es de d.** it is daylight; **hace buen/mal d.** it's a nice/bad day, the weather is nice/bad today

diabetes *nf* diabetes

diabético,-a *adj & nm,f* diabetic

diablo *nm* devil; *Fam* **¡al d. con ...!** to hell with ...!; *Fam* **vete al d.** get lost; *Fam* **¿qué/ cómo diablos ...?** what/how the hell ...?

diablura *nf* mischief

diácono *nm* deacon

diadema *nf* tiara

diáfano,-a *adj* clear

diafragma *nm* diaphragm; *Fot* aperture; *Med* cap

diagnosis *nf inv* diagnosis

diagnosticar [44] *vt* to diagnose

diagnóstico *nm* diagnosis

diagonal *adj & nf* diagonal; **en d.** diagonally

diagrama *nm* diagram; *Informát* **d. de flujo** flowchart

dial *nm* dial

dialecto *nm* dialect

dialogar [42] *vi* to have a conversation; *(para negociar)* to talk

diálogo *nm* dialogue

diamante *nm* diamond

diámetro *nm* diameter

diana *nf* (**a**) *Mil* reveille (**b**) *(blanco)* bull's eye

diapositiva *nf* slide

diariamente *adv* daily, every day

diariero,-a *nm,f Andes, RP* newspaper seller

diario,-a 1 *nm* (**a**) *Prensa* (daily) newspaper (**b**) *(memorias)* diary; *Náut* **d. de a bordo, d. de navegación** logbook
2 *adj* daily; **a d.** daily, every day

diarrea *nf* diarrhoea

diatriba *nf* diatribe

dibujante *nmf* (**a**) drawer (**b**) *(de cómic)* cartoonist (**c**) *Téc (hombre)* draughtsman; *(mujer)* draughtswoman

dibujar *vt* to draw

dibujo *nm* (**a**) drawing; **dibujos animados** cartoons (**b**) *(arte)* drawing; **d. artístico** artistic drawing; **d. lineal** draughtsmanship

diccionario *nm* dictionary; **buscar/mirar una palabra en el d.** to look up a word in the dictionary

dicha *nf* happiness

dicharachero,-a *adj* talkative and witty

dicho,-a *adj* (**a**) said; **mejor d.** or rather; **d. de otro modo** to put it another way; **d. sea de paso** let it be said in passing; **d. y hecho** no sooner said than done (**b**) **dicha persona** *(mencionado)* the abovementioned person

dichoso,-a *adj* (**a**) *(feliz)* happy (**b**) *Fam* damned; **¡este d. trabajo!** this damned job!

diciembre *nm* December

dictado *nm* dictation; *Fig* **dictados** dictates

dictador,-a *nm,f* dictator

dictadura *nf* dictatorship

dictáfono® *nm* Dictaphone®

dictamen *nm* *(juicio)* ruling; *(informe)* report

dictaminar *vi* to rule (**sobre** on)

dictar *vt* (**a**) to dictate (**b**) *(ley)* to enact; *(sentencia)* to pass

dictatorial *adj* dictatorial

didáctico,-a *adj* didactic

diecinueve *adj & nm inv* nineteen

dieciocho *adj & nm inv* eighteen

dieciséis *adj & nm inv* sixteen

diecisiete *adj & nm inv* seventeen

diente *nm* tooth; *Téc* cog; *(de ajo)* clove; **d. de leche** milk tooth; **dientes postizos** false teeth; *Fig* **hablar entre dientes** to mumble; *Fig* **poner los dientes largos a algn** to make sb green with envy

diera *subj imperf de* **dar**

diéresis *nf inv* diaeresis

diesel *adj & nm* diesel

diestra *nf* right hand

diestro,-a 1 *adj* (**a**) *(hábil)* skilful, clever (**b**) **a d. y siniestro** right, left and centre
2 *nm Taurom* bullfighter, matador

dieta *nf* (**a**) diet; **estar a d.** to be on a diet (**b**) **dietas** expenses *o* subsistence allowance

dietética *nf* dietetics *sing*

dietista *nmf* dietician

diez *adj & nm inv* ten

difamación *nf* defamation, slander; *(escrita)* libel

difamar *vt* to defame, to slander; *(por escrito)* to libel

diferencia *nf* difference; **a d. de** unlike

diferencial 1 *adj* distinguishing
2 *nm* differential

diferenciar [43] 1 *vt* to differentiate, to distinguish (**entre** between)

2 diferenciarse *vpr* to differ (**de** from), to be different (**de** from)
diferente 1 *adj* different (**de** from *o US* than)
   2 *adv* differently
diferido,-a *adj TV* **en d.** recorded
difícil *adj* difficult, hard; **d. de creer/hacer** difficult to believe/do; **es d. que venga** it is unlikely that she'll come
dificultad *nf* difficulty; *(aprieto)* trouble, problem
dificultar *vt* to make difficult
dificultoso,-a *adj* difficult, hard
difuminar *vt* to blur
difundir *vt,* **difundirse** *vpr* to spread
difunto,-a 1 *adj* late, deceased
   2 *nm,f* deceased
difusión *nf* (**a**) *(de noticia)* spreading; **tener gran d.** to be widely broadcast (**b**) *Rad & TV* broadcasting
difuso,-a *adj* diffuse
digerir [**5**] *vt* to digest; *Fig* to assimilate
digestión *nf* digestion; **corte de d.** sudden indigestion
digestivo,-a *adj* easy to digest
digitador,-a *nm,f Am* keyboarder
digital *adj* digital; **huellas digitales** fingerprints; **tocadiscos d.** CD player
digitalizar *vt* digitize
digitar *vt Am* to key
dígito *nm* digit
dignarse *vpr* **d. (a)** to deign to, to condescend to
dignidad *nf* dignity
digno,-a *adj* (**a**) *(merecedor)* worthy; **d. de admiración** worthy of admiration; **d. de mención/verse** worth mentioning/ seeing (**b**) *(decoroso)* decent, good
digo *indic pres de* **decir**
dije *pt indef de* **decir**
dilación *nf* delay, hold-up; **sin d.** without delay
dilatado,-a *adj* (**a**) *(agrandado)* dilated (**b**) *(vasto)* vast, extensive
dilatar 1 *vt* (**a**) *(agrandar)* to expand (**b**) *(pupila)* to dilate
   2 dilatarse *vpr* (**a**) *(agrandarse)* to expand (**b**) *(pupila)* to dilate
dilema *nm* dilemma
diligencia *nf* (**a**) diligence; **con d.** diligently (**b**) **diligencias** formalities
diligente *adj* diligent
dilucidar *vt* to elucidate, to clarify
diluir [**37**] **1** *vt* to dilute
   2 diluirse *vpr* to dilute
diluviar [**43**] *v impers* to pour with rain
diluvio *nm* flood; **el D. (Universal)** the Flood

diluyo *indic pres de* **diluir**
dimensión *nf* (**a**) dimension, size; **de gran d.** very large (**b**) *Fig (importancia)* importance
diminutivo,-a *adj & nm* diminutive
diminuto,-a *adj* minute, tiny
dimisión *nf* resignation; **presentar la d.** to hand in one's resignation
dimitir *vi* to resign (**de** from); **d. de un cargo** to give in *o* tender one's resignation
Dinamarca *n* Denmark
dinámica *nf* dynamics *sing*
dinámico,-a *adj* dynamic
dinamita *nf* dynamite
dinamitar *vt* to dynamite
dinamo, dínamo *nf* dynamo
dinar *nm Fin* dinar
dinastía *nf* dynasty
dineral *nm Fam* fortune
dinero *nm* money; **d. contante (y sonante)** cash; **d. efectivo** *o* **en metálico** cash; **gente de d.** wealthy people
dinosaurio *nm* dinosaur
diócesis *nf inv* diocese
dios *nm* god; **¡D. mío!** my God!; **¡por D.!** for goodness sake!; **a la buena de D.** any old how; **hacer algo como D. manda** to do sth properly; *Fam* **ni d.** nobody; *Fam* **todo d.** everybody
diosa *nf* goddess
diploma *nm* diploma
diplomacia *nf* diplomacy
diplomarse *vpr* to graduate
diplomático,-a 1 *adj* diplomatic; **cuerpo d.** diplomatic corps
   2 *nm,f* diplomat
diptongo *nm* diphthong
diputación *nf* **d. provincial** ≃ county council
diputado,-a *nm,f Br* ≃ Member of Parliament, MP; *US (hombre)* Congressman; *(mujer)* Congresswoman; **Congreso de Diputados** *Br* ≃ House of Commons, *US* ≃ Congress; **d. provincial** ≃ county councillor
dique *nm* dike
diré *fut de* **decir**
dirección *nf* (**a**) direction; *Aut (en letrero)* **d. prohibida** no entry; **calle de d. única** one-way street (**b**) *(señas)* address; *Informát* **d. de correo electrónico** e-mail address (**c**) *Cin & Teatro* direction (**d**) *(destino)* destination (**e**) *Aut & Téc* steering (**f**) *(dirigentes)* management; *(cargo)* directorship; *(de un partido)* leadership; *(de un colegio)* headship
direccional *nm Col, Méx Aut Br* indicator, *US* turn signal

directa *nf Aut* top gear
directamente *adv* directly, straight away
directiva *nf* board of directors, management
directivo,-a *adj* directive; **junta directiva** board of directors
directo,-a *adj* direct; *TV & Rad* **en d.** live
director,-a *nm,f* director; *(de colegio)* *(hombre)* headmaster; *(mujer)* headmistress; *(de periódico)* editor; **d. de cine** (film) director; **d. de orquesta** conductor; **d. gerente** managing director
directorio *nm Informát* directory; *Andes, Méx* **d. telefónico** telephone directory
directriz *nf* directive; *Mat* directrix
dirigente **1** *adj* leading; **clase d.** ruling class
    2 *nmf* leader
dirigir **[57]** **1** *vt* to direct; *(empresa)* to manage; *(negocio, colegio)* to run; *(orquesta)* to conduct; *(partido)* to lead; *(periódico)* to edit; *(coche, barco)* to steer; **d. la palabra a algn** to speak to sb
    2 dirigirse *vpr* (**a**) **d. a** *o* **hacia** to go to, to make one's way towards (**b**) *(escribir)* to write; **diríjase al apartado de correos 42** write to PO Box 42 (**c**) *(hablar)* to speak
discapacidad *nf* disability
discar *vt Andes, RP* to dial
discernir **[54]** *vt* to discern
disciplina *nf* discipline
disciplinado,-a *adj* disciplined
discípulo,-a *nm,f* disciple
disco *nm* (**a**) disc; **d. de freno** brake disc (**b**) *Mús* record; **d. compacto** compact disc (**c**) *Informát* disk; **d. duro** *o* **fijo/ flexible** hard/floppy disk (**d**) *Dep* discus (**e**) *Tel* dial
discográfico,-a *adj* **casa/compañía discográfica** record company
disconforme *adj* **estar d. con** to disagree with
discontinuo,-a *adj* discontinuous; *Aut* **línea discontinua** broken line
discordante *adj* discordant; **ser la nota d.** to be the odd man out
discordia *nf* discord; **la manzana de la d.** the bone of contention; **sembrar d.** to sow discord
discoteca *nf* (**a**) *(lugar)* discotheque (**b**) *(colección)* record collection
discreción *nf* (**a**) discretion (**b**) **a d.** at will
discrecional *adj* optional; **servicio d.** special service
discrepancia *nf (desacuerdo)* disagreement; *(diferencia)* discrepancy
discrepar *vi (disentir)* to disagree (**de** with; **en** on); *(diferenciarse)* to be different (**de** from)
discreto,-a *adj* (**a**) discreet (**b**) *(mediocre)* average
discriminación *nf* discrimination
discriminar *vt* (**a**) to discriminate against (**b**) *Fml (diferenciar)* to discriminate between, to distinguish
disculpa *nf* excuse; **dar disculpas** to make excuses; **pedir disculpas a algn** to apologize to sb
disculpar **1** *vt* to excuse
    2 disculparse *vpr* to apologize (**por** for)
discurrir *vi* (**a**) *(reflexionar)* to think (**b**) *Fig (transcurrir)* to pass, to go by (**c**) *Fml (río)* to wander
discurso *nm* speech; **dar** *o* **pronunciar un d.** to make a speech
discusión *nf* argument
discutir **1** *vi* to argue (**de** about)
    2 *vt* to discuss, to talk about
disecar **[44]** *vt* (**a**) *(animal)* to stuff (**b**) *(planta)* to dry
diseminar *vt* to disseminate, to spread
disentir **[54]** *vi* to dissent, to disagree (**de** with)
diseñar *vt* to design
diseño *nm* design; **d. de interiores** interior design
disertar *vi* to expound (**sobre** on *o* upon)
disfraz *nm* disguise; *(para fiesta)* fancy dress; **fiesta de disfraces** fancy dress party
disfrazar **[40]** **1** *vt* to disguise
    2 disfrazarse *vpr* to disguise oneself; **d. de pirata** to dress up as a pirate
disfrutar **1** *vi* (**a**) *(gozar)* to enjoy oneself (**b**) *(poseer)* **d. (de)** to enjoy
    2 *vt* to enjoy
disgregar **[42]** *vt* (**a**) to disintegrate, to break up (**b**) *(dispersar)* to disperse
disgustado,-a *adj* upset, displeased
disgustar **1** *vt* to upset
    2 disgustarse *vpr* (**a**) *(molestarse)* to get upset, to be annoyed (**b**) *(dos amigos)* to quarrel

> *Observa que el verbo inglés* **to disgust** *es un falso amigo y no es la traducción del verbo español* **disgustar**. *En inglés,* **to disgust** *significa "repugnar, indignar".*

disgusto *nm* (**a**) *(preocupación)* annoyance; **llevarse un d.** to get upset; **dar un d. a algn** to upset sb (**b**) *(desgracia)* trouble; **a d.** unwillingly; **sentirse** *o* **estar a d.** to feel ill at ease (**c**) *(desavenencia)* fall-out, disagreement

📝 Observa que la palabra inglesa **disgust** es un falso amigo y no es la traducción de la palabra española **disgusto**. En inglés, **disgust** significa "repugnancia, asco".

disidente *adj & nmf* dissident
disimuladamente *adv* surreptitiously
disimulado,-a *adj* (**a**) *(persona)* sly, crafty (**b**) *(oculto)* hidden, concealed
disimular *vt* to conceal, to hide
disimulo *nm* pretence
disipar 1 *vt (niebla)* to drive away; *(temor, duda)* to dispel
  2 **disiparse** *vpr (gaseosa)* to go flat; *(niebla, temor etc)* to disappear
disketera *nf Informát* disk drive
dislexia *nf* dyslexia
dislocar [44] *vt* to dislocate
disminución *nf* decrease
disminuir [37] 1 *vt* to reduce
  2 *vi* to diminish
disolución *nf* dissolution
disolvente *adj & nm* solvent
disolver [4] *(pp disuelto) vt* to dissolve
disparar 1 *vt (pistola etc)* to fire; *(flecha, balón)* to shoot; **d. a algn** to shoot at sb
  2 **dispararse** *vpr* (**a**) *(arma)* to go off, to fire (**b**) *(precios)* to rocket
disparatado,-a *adj* absurd
disparate *nm* (**a**) *(dicho)* nonsense; **decir disparates** to talk nonsense (**b**) *(acto)* foolish act
disparidad *nf* disparity
disparo *nm* shot; *Dep* **d. a puerta** shot
dispensar *vt* (**a**) *(disculpar)* to pardon, to forgive (**b**) *(eximir)* to exempt
dispersar 1 *vt* to disperse; *(esparcir)* to scatter
  2 **dispersarse** *vpr* to disperse
disperso,-a *adj (separado)* dispersed; *(esparcido)* scattered
displicencia *nf* condescension, disdain
displicente *adj* condescending, disdainful
disponer [19] *(pp dispuesto)* 1 *vt* (**a**) *(arreglar)* to arrange, to set out (**b**) *(ordenar)* to order
  2 *vi* **d. de** to have at one's disposal
  3 **disponerse** *vpr* to prepare, to get ready
disponible *adj* available
disposición *nf* (**a**) *(uso)* disposal; **a su d.** at your disposal *o* service (**b**) *(colocación)* arrangement, layout (**c**) **no estar en d. de** not to be prepared to (**d**) *(orden)* order, law
dispositivo *nm* device
dispuesto,-a *adj* (**a**) *(ordenado)* arranged (**b**) *(a punto)* ready (**c**) *(decidido)*

determined; **no estar d. a** not to be prepared to (**d**) **según lo d. por la ley** in accordance with what the law stipulates
disputa *nf (discusión)* argument; *(contienda)* contest
disputar 1 *vt* (**a**) *(premio)* to compete for (**b**) *Dep (partido)* to play
  2 **disputarse** *vpr (premio)* to compete for
disquete *nm Informát* diskette, floppy disk
disquetera *nf Informát* disk drive
distancia *nf* distance; **a d.** from a distance
distanciamiento *nm* distancing
distanciar [43] 1 *vt* to separate
  2 **distanciarse** *vpr* to become separated; *(de otra persona)* to distance oneself
distante *adj* distant, far-off
distar *vi* to be distant *o* away; *Fig* to be far from; **dista mucho de ser perfecto** it's far from (being) perfect
distender [3] *vt Fig* to ease, to relax
distensión *nf Pol* détente
distinción *nf* distinction; **a d. de** unlike; **sin d. de** irrespective of
distinguido,-a *adj* distinguished
distinguir [59] 1 *vt* (**a**) *(diferenciar)* to distinguish (**b**) *(reconocer)* to recognize (**c**) *(honrar)* to honour
  2 *vi (diferenciar)* to discriminate
  3 **distinguirse** *vpr* to distinguish oneself
distintivo,-a 1 *adj* distinctive, distinguishing
  2 *nm* distinctive sign *o* mark
distinto,-a *adj* different
distorsión *nf* (**a**) distortion (**b**) *Med* sprain
distracción *nf* (**a**) entertainment; *(pasatiempo)* pastime, hobby (**b**) *(descuido)* distraction, absent-mindedness
distraer [25] 1 *vt* (**a**) *(atención)* to distract (**b**) *(divertir)* to entertain, to amuse
  2 **distraerse** *vpr* (**a**) *(divertirse)* to amuse oneself (**b**) *(abstraerse)* to let one's mind wander
distraído,-a *adj* (**a**) *(divertido)* entertaining (**b**) *(abstraído)* absent-minded
distribución *nf* (**a**) distribution (**b**) *(disposición)* layout
distribuidor,-a 1 *adj* distributing
  2 *nm,f* (**a**) distributor (**b**) *Com* wholesaler
distribuir [37] *vt* to distribute; *(trabajo)* to share out
distrito *nm* district; **d. postal** postal district
disturbio *nm* riot, disturbance
disuadir *vt* to dissuade

disuasión *nf* dissuasion
disuelto,-a *pp de* disolver
DIU *nm* (*abr* **dispositivo intrauterino**) IUD
diurético,-a *adj & nm* diuretic
diurno,-a *adj* daytime
divagar [42] *vi* to digress, to wander
diván *nm* divan, couch
divergencia *nf* divergence
divergente *adj* diverging
diversidad *nf* diversity
diversificar [44] **1** *vt* to diversify
  2 diversificarse *upr* to be diversified *o* varied; *(empresa)* to diversify
diversión *nf* fun
diverso,-a *adj* different; **diversos** several, various
divertido,-a *adj* amusing, funny
divertir [5] **1** *vt* to amuse, to entertain
  2 divertirse *upr* to enjoy oneself, to have a good time; **¡que te diviertas!** enjoy yourself!, have fun!
dividendo *nm* dividend
dividir **1** *vt* to divide (**en** into); *Mat* **15 dividido entre 3** 15 divided by 3
  2 dividirse *upr* to divide, to split up
divinidad *nf* divinity
divino,-a *adj* divine
divisa *nf* (**a**) *(emblema)* symbol, emblem (**b**) *Com* **divisas** foreign currency
divisar *vt* to make out, to discern
división *nf* division
divisorio,-a *adj* dividing
divorciado,-a **1** *adj* divorced
  2 *nm,f (hombre)* divorcé; *(mujer)* divorcée
divorciar [43] **1** *vt* to divorce
  2 divorciarse *upr* to get divorced; **se divorció de él** she divorced him, she got a divorce from him
divorcio *nm* divorce
divulgación *nf* disclosure
divulgar [42] *vt* to disclose; *Rad & TV* to broadcast
dizque *advAndes, Carib, Méx* apparently
DNI *nm* (*abr* **Documento Nacional de Identidad**) Identity Card, ID card
do *nm Mús (de solfa)* doh, do; *(de escala diatónica)* C; **do de pecho** high C
doberman *nm* Doberman (pinscher)
dobladillo *nm* hem
doblaje *nm Cin* dubbing
doblar **1** *vt* (**a**) to double; **me dobla la edad** he is twice as old as I am (**b**) *(plegar)* to fold *o* turn up (**c**) *(torcer)* to bend (**d**) *(la esquina)* to go round (**e**) *(película)* to dub
  2 *vi* (**a**) *(girar)* to turn; **d. a la derecha/**

izquierda to turn right/left (**b**) *(campanas)* to toll
  3 doblarse *upr* (**a**) *(plegarse)* to fold (**b**) *(torcerse)* to bend
doble **1** *adj* double; **arma de d. filo** double-edged weapon
  2 *nm* (**a**) double; **gana el d. que tú** she earns twice as much as you do (**b**) *Dep* **dobles** doubles
doblegar [42] **1** *vt* to bend
  2 doblegarse *upr* to give in
doblez **1** *nm (pliegue)* fold
  2 *nm o nf Fig* two-facedness, hypocrisy
doce *adj & nm inv* twelve
docena *nf* dozen
docencia *nf* teaching
docente *adj* teaching; **centro d.** educational centre
dócil *adj* docile
doctor,-a *nm,f* doctor
doctorado *nm Univ* doctorate, PhD
doctrina *nf* doctrine
documentación *nf* documentation; *(DNI, de conducir etc)* papers
documental *adj & nm* documentary
documentar **1** *vt* to document
  2 documentarse *upr* **d. (sobre)** to research, to get information (about *o* on)
documento *nm* document; **d. nacional de identidad** identity card
dogma *nm* dogma
dogmático,-a *adj & nm,f* dogmatic
dogo *nm* bulldog
dólar *nm* dollar
dolarización *nf* dollarization
dolencia *nf* ailment
doler [4] **1** *vi* to hurt, to ache; **me duele la cabeza** I've got a headache; **me duele la mano** my hand is sore
  2 dolerse *upr* to be sorry *o* sad
dolido,-a *adj* **estar d.** to be hurt
dolor *nm* (**a**) *Med* pain; **d. de cabeza** headache; **d. de muelas** toothache (**b**) *(pena)* grief, sorrow
dolorido,-a *adj* (**a**) *(dañado)* sore, aching (**b**) *(apenado)* hurt
doloroso,-a *adj* painful
domar *vt* to tame; *(caballo)* to break in
domesticar [44] *vt* to domesticate; *(animal)* to tame
doméstico,-a *adj* domestic; **animal d.** pet
domiciliación *nf* payment by standing order
domiciliar [43] *vt* (**a**) to house (**b**) *Fin* to pay by standing order
domiciliario,-a *adj* **arresto d.** house arrest

domicilio *nm* home, residence; *(señas)* address; **sin d. fijo** of no fixed abode; **d. fiscal** registered office

dominación *nf* domination

dominante *adj* (**a**) dominant (**b**) *(déspota)* domineering

dominar 1 *vt* (**a**) to dominate, to rule (**b**) *(situación)* to control; *(idioma)* to speak very well; *(asunto)* to master; *(paisaje etc)* to overlook

　2 *vi* (**a**) to dominate (**b**) *(resaltar)* to stand out

　3 dominarse *vpr* to control oneself

domingo *nm inv* Sunday; **D. de Resurrección** *o* **Pascua** Easter Sunday

dominguero,-a *nm,f Fam (excursionista)* weekend tripper; *(conductor)* weekend driver

dominical 1 *adj* Sunday

　2 *nm (suplemento)* Sunday supplement

dominicano,-a *adj & nm,f* Dominican; **República Dominicana** Dominican Republic

dominio *nm* (**a**) *(poder)* control; *(de un idioma)* command; **d. de sí mismo** self-control (**b**) *(ámbito)* scope, sphere; **ser del d. público** to be public knowledge (**c**) *(territorio)* dominion (**d**) *Informát* domain

dominó, dómino *nm* dominoes

don[1] *nm* (**a**) *(habilidad)* gift, talent; **tener el d. de** to have a knack for; **tener d. de gentes** to get on well with people (**b**) *(regalo)* present, gift

don[2] *nm* **Señor D. José García** Mr José Garcia; **D. Fulano de Tal** Mr So-and-So; **un d. nadie** a nobody

donaire *nm* grace, elegance

donante *nmf* donor; *Med* **d. de sangre** blood donor

donar *vt Fml* to donate; *(sangre)* to give

donativo *nm* donation

doncella *nf Literario* (**a**) *(joven)* maid, maiden (**b**) *(criada)* maid, housemaid

donde *adv rel* where; **a** *o* **en d.** where; **de** *o* **desde d.** from where; **está d. lo dejaste** it is where you left it; *Fam* **está d. su tía** he's at his aunt's

---

donde combines with the preposition **a** to form **adonde** when following a noun, a pronoun or an adverb expressing location (e.g. **el sitio adonde vamos** the place where we're going; **es allí adonde iban** that's where they were going).

---

dónde *adv interr* where?; **¿de d. eres?** where are you from?; **¿por d. se va a la playa?** which way is it to the beach?

---

dónde can combine with the preposition **a** to form **adónde** (e.g. **¿adónde vamos?** where are we going?).

---

dondequiera *adv* everywhere; **d. que vaya** wherever I go

donostiarra 1 *adj* of/from San Sebastián

　2 *nmf* person from San Sebastián

doña *nf* **(Señora) D. Leonor Benítez** Mrs Leonor Benítez

dopaje *nm Dep* drug-taking

dopar 1 *vt (caballo etc)* to dope

　2 doparse *vpr* to take drugs

doping *nm Dep* drug-taking

doquier, doquiera *adv Literario* **por d.** everywhere

dorada *nf (pez)* gilthead bream

dorado,-a 1 *adj* golden

　2 *nm Téc* gilding

dorar *vt* (**a**) to gild (**b**) *Culin* to brown

dormido,-a *adj* (**a**) asleep; **quedarse d.** to fall asleep; *(no despertarse)* to oversleep, to sleep in (**b**) *(pierna, brazo)* numb

dormilón,-ona 1 *adj Fam* sleepyheaded

　2 *nm,f* sleepyhead

　3 *nf Ven* **dormilona** nightdress

dormir [7] 1 *vi* to sleep; **tener ganas de d.** to feel sleepy;

　2 *vt* **d. la siesta** to have an afternoon nap

　3 dormirse *vpr* to fall asleep; **se me ha dormido el brazo** my arm has gone to sleep

dormitar *vi* to doze, to snooze

dormitorio *nm* (**a**) *(de una casa)* bedroom (**b**) *(de colegio, residencia)* dormitory; **ciudad d.** dormitory town

dorsal 1 *adj* **espina d.** spine

　2 *nm Dep* number

dorso *nm* back; **instrucciones al d.** instructions over; **véase al d.** see overleaf

dos *adj & nm inv* two; **los d.** both; **nosotros/vosotros d.** both of us/you; *Fam* **cada d. por tres** every other minute; *Fam* **en un d. por tres** in a flash

doscientos,-as *adj & nm* two hundred

dosel *nm* canopy

dosificación *nf* dosage

dosificar [44] *vt* (**a**) to dose (**b**) *(esfuerzos, energías)* to measure

dosis *nf inv* dose

dossier *nm* dossier

dotación *nf (dinero)* grant; *(personal)* personnel, staff; *(de barco)* crew

dotado,-a *adj* (**a**) *(persona)* gifted (**b**) *(equipado)* equipped; **d. de** provided with

dotar *vt* **d. de** to provide with

dote *nf* (**a**) *(de novia)* dowry (**b**) **dotes** *(talento)* gift, talent

doy *indic pres de* **dar**
dpto. (*abr* **departamento**) Dept
Dr. (*abr* **doctor**) Dr
Dra. (*abr* **doctora**) Dr
dragar [42] *vt* to dredge
dragón *nm* dragon
drama *nm* drama
dramático,-a *adj* dramatic
dramatismo *nm* drama, dramatic quality
dramaturgo,-a *nm,f* playwright, dramatist
drástico,-a *adj* drastic
drenar *vt* to drain
driblar *vi* to dribble
droga *nf* drug; **d. blanda/dura** soft/hard drug
drogadicto,-a *nm,f* drug addict
drogar [42] 1 *vt* to drug
  2 drogarse *vpr* to drug oneself, to take drugs
droguería *nf* hardware and household goods shop
dto. (*abr* **descuento**) discount
dual *adj* dual
dualidad *nf* duality
dubitativo,-a *adj* doubtful
Dublín *n* Dublin
dublinés,-esa 1 *adj* of/from Dublin
  2 *nm,f* Dubliner
ducha *nf* shower; **darse/tomar una d.** to take/have a shower
ducharse *vpr* to shower, to have *o* take a shower
ducho,-a *adj* expert; **ser d. en** to be well versed in
duda *nf* doubt; **sin d.** without a doubt; **no cabe d.** (there is) no doubt; **poner algo en d.** to question sth; **sacar a algn de dudas** to dispel sb's doubts
dudar 1 *vi* (**a**) to doubt (**b**) (*vacilar*) to hesitate (**en** to); **dudaba entre ir o quedarme** I hesitated whether to go *o* to stay (**c**) **d. de algn** (*desconfiar*) to suspect sb
  2 *vt* to doubt
dudoso,-a *adj* (**a**) **ser d.** (*incierto*) to be uncertain *o* doubtful (**b**) **estar d.** (*indeciso*) to be undecided (**c**) (*poco honrado*) dubious
duelo¹ *nm* (*combate*) duel
duelo² *nm* (*luto*) mourning
duende *nm* (**a**) (*espíritu*) goblin, elf (**b**) (*encanto*) magic, charm

dueña *nf* owner; (*de pensión*) landlady
dueño *nm* owner; (*de casa etc*) landlord; *Fig* **ser d. de sí mismo** to be self-possessed
Duero *n* **el D.** the Douro
dulce 1 *adj* (**a**) (*sabor*) sweet (**b**) (*carácter, voz*) gentle (**c**) (*metal*) soft (**d**) **agua d.** fresh water
  2 *nm* (**a**) *Culin* (*pastel*) cake (**b**) (*caramelo*) *Br* sweet, *US* candy
dulzura *nf* (**a**) sweetness (**b**) *Fig* gentleness, softness
duna *nf* dune
dúo *nm* duet
duodécimo,-a *adj & nm,f* twelfth
dúplex *nm* (**a**) (*piso*) duplex, duplex apartment (**b**) *Tel* link-up
duplicado,-a 1 *adj* **por d.** in duplicate
  2 *nm* duplicate, copy
duplicar [44] 1 *vt* to duplicate; (*cifras*) to double
  2 duplicarse *vpr* to double
duplo,-a *adj & nm,f* double
duque *nm* duke
duquesa *nf* duchess
duración *nf* duration, length; **disco de larga d.** long-playing record
duradero,-a *adj* durable, lasting
durante *prep* during; **d. el día** during the day; **d. todo el día** all day long; **viví en La Coruña d. un año** I lived in La Coruña for a year
durar *vi* (**a**) to last (**b**) (*ropa, calzado*) to wear well, to last
durazno *nm* (*fruto*) peach; (*árbol*) peach tree
dúrex *nm Méx Br* Sellotape®, *US* Scotch tape®
dureza *nf* (**a**) hardness; (*severidad*) harshness, severity (**b**) (*callosidad*) corn

🖉 Observa que la palabra inglesa **duress** es un falso amigo y no es la traducción de la palabra española **dureza**. En inglés, **duress** significa "coacción".

duro,-a 1 *adj* (**a**) hard; *Dep* **juego d.** rough play (**b**) (*resistente*) tough; (*severo*) hard (**c**) (*clima*) harsh
  2 *nm* (*moneda*) 5-peseta coin
  3 *adv* hard; **trabajar d.** to work hard
DVD *nm Informát* (*abr* **Disco Versátil Digital**) DVD

E, e [e] *nf (la letra)* E, e
E (*abr* **Este**) E
e *conj* and

> **e** is used instead of **y** in front of words beginning with "i" or "hi" (e.g. **apoyo e interés** support and interest; **corazón e hígado** heart and liver).

ebanista *nm* cabinet-maker
ébano *nm* ebony
ebrio,-a *adj* inebriated; **e. de dicha** drunk with joy
ebullición *nf* boiling; **punto de e.** boiling point
eccema *nm* eczema
echar 1 *vt* (**a**) *(lanzar)* to throw; *Fig* **e. una mano** to give a hand; *Fig* **e. una mirada/una ojeada** to have a look/a quick look *o* glance
  (**b**) *(carta)* to post; *(vino, agua)* to pour; **e. sal al estofado** to put salt in the stew; **e. gasolina al coche** to put *Br* petrol *o US* gas in the car
  (**c**) *(expulsar)* to throw out; *(despedir)* to fire, *Br* to sack
  (**d**) *(humo, olor etc)* to give off
  (**e**) *Fam (película)* to show
  (**f**) **le echó 37 años** he reckoned she was about 37
  (**g**) **e. de menos** *o* **en falta** to miss
  (**h**) **e. abajo** *(edificio)* to demolish
  2 *vi* (+ **a** + *infin*) *(empezar)* to begin to; **echó a correr** he ran off
  3 echarse *vpr* (**a**) *(tumbarse)* to lie down; *(lanzarse)* to throw oneself; *Fig* **la noche se nos echó encima** it was night before we knew it
  (**b**) **échate a un lado** stand aside; *Fig* **e. atrás** to get cold feet
  (**c**) *Fam* **e. novio/novia** to get a boyfriend/girlfriend
  (**d**) (+ **a** + *infin*) *(empezar)* to begin to; **e. a llorar** to burst into tears; **e. a reír** to burst out laughing; **e. a perder** *(comida)* to go bad
ecléctico,-a *adj & nm,f* eclectic
eclesiástico,-a 1 *adj* ecclesiastical
  2 *nm* clergyman
eclipsar *vt* to eclipse

eclipse *nm* eclipse
eco *nm* echo; *Fig* **hacerse e. de una noticia** to publish an item of news; **tener e.** to arouse interest
ecografía *nf* scan
ecología *nf* ecology
ecológico,-a *adj* ecological; *(alimentos)* organic; *(detergente)* environmentally-friendly
ecologista 1 *adj* ecological; *Pol* **partido e.** ecology party
  2 *nmf* ecologist
economía *nf* (**a**) economy; **con e.** economically (**b**) *(ciencia)* economics *sing*
económico,-a *adj* (**a**) economic (**b**) *(barato)* economical, inexpensive (**c**) *(persona)* thrifty
economista *nmf* economist
economizar [40] *vt & vi* to economize
ecosistema *nm* ecosystem
ecotasa *nf* ecotax
ecoturismo *nm* ecotourism
ecuación *nf* equation
Ecuador *n* Ecuador
ecuador *nm Geog* equator
ecualizador *nm* **e. (gráfico)** graphic equalizer
ecuánime *adj* (**a**) *(temperamento)* equable, even-tempered (**b**) *(juicio)* impartial
ecuatorial *adj* equatorial; **Guinea E.** Equatorial Guinea
ecuatoriano,-a *adj & nm,f* Ecuadorian
ecuestre *adj* equestrian
ecuménico,-a *adj* ecumenical
eczema *nm* eczema
edad *nf* age; **¿qué e. tienes?** how old are you?; **la tercera e.** senior citizens; **E. Media** Middle Ages
edición *nf* (**a**) *(publicación)* publication; *(de sellos)* issue (**b**) *(conjunto de ejemplares)* edition
edicto *nm* edict, proclamation
edificante *adj* edifying
edificar [44] *vt* to build
edificio *nm* building
edil,-a *nm,f* town councillor
Edimburgo *n* Edinburgh
editar *vt* (**a**) *(libro, periódico)* to publish;

(disco) to release (**b**) *Informát* to edit
editor,-a 1 *adj* publishing
  2 *nm,f* publisher
editorial 1 *adj* publishing
  2 *nf* publishers, publishing house
  3 *nm Prensa* editorial, leader article
edredón *nm Br* duvet, *US* comforter
educación *nf* (**a**) education; **e. física** physical education (**b**) *(formación)* upbringing (**c**) **buena/mala e.** *(modales)* good/bad manners; **falta de e.** bad manners
educado,-a *adj* polite
educador,-a 1 *adj* educating
  2 *nm,f* educationalist
educar [44] *vt (hijos)* to raise; *(alumnos)* to educate; *(la voz)* to train
educativo,-a *adj* educational; **sistema e.** education system
edulcorante *nm* sweetener
EE.UU. *(abr* **Estados Unidos**) USA
efectista *adj* spectacular
efectivamente *adv* quite!, yes indeed!
efectividad *nf* effectiveness
efectivo,-a 1 *adj* effective; **hacer algo e.** to carry sth out; *Fin* **hacer e. un cheque** to cash a cheque
  2 *nm* (**a**) *Fin* **en e.** in cash (**b**) *Mil* **efectivos** forces
efecto *nm* (**a**) *(resultado)* effect; **efectos especiales/sonoros** special/sound effects; **efectos personales** personal belongings *o* effects; **a efectos de ...** for the purposes of ...; **en e.** quite!, yes indeed! (**b**) *(impresión)* impression; **causar** *o* **hacer e.** to make an impression (**c**) *Dep* spin
efectuar [30] *vt* to carry out; *(viaje)* to make; *Com (pedido)* to place
efeméride *nf* event
efervescente *adj* effervescent; **aspirina e.** soluble aspirin
eficacia *nf (de persona)* efficiency; *(de remedio etc)* effectiveness
eficaz *adj (persona)* efficient; *(remedio, medida etc)* effective
eficiencia *nf* efficiency
eficiente *adj* efficient
efigie *nf* effigy
efímero,-a *adj* ephemeral
efusivo,-a *adj* effusive
EGB *nf Educ (abr* **Enseñanza General Básica**) = formerly, stage of Spanish education system for pupils aged 6-14
Egeo *n* **el (Mar) E.** the Aegean Sea
egipcio,-a *adj & nm,f* Egyptian
Egipto *n* Egypt
egocéntrico,-a *adj* egocentric, self-centred

egoísmo *nm* egoism, selfishness
egoísta 1 *adj* ego(t)istic, selfish
  2 *nmf* ego(t)ist, selfish person
egregio,-a *adj* eminent, illustrious
egresar *vi Am* to leave school, *US* to graduate
Eire *n* Eire, Republic of Ireland
ej. *(abr* **ejemplo**) example
eje *nm* (**a**) *Téc (de rueda)* axle; *(de máquina)* shaft (**b**) *Mat* axis (**c**) *Hist* **El E.** the Axis
ejecución *nf* (**a**) *(de orden)* carrying out (**b**) *(ajusticiamiento)* execution (**c**) *Mús* performance
ejecutar *vt* (**a**) *(orden)* to carry out (**b**) *(ajusticiar)* to execute (**c**) *Mús* to perform, to play (**d**) *Informát* to run
ejecutiva *nf Pol* executive
ejecutivo,-a 1 *adj* executive; *Pol* **el poder e.** the government
  2 *nm* executive
ejecutor,-a *nm,f* (**a**) *Jur* executor (**b**) *(verdugo)* executioner
ejemplar 1 *nm* (**a**) *(de libro)* copy; *(de revista, periódico)* number, issue (**b**) *(espécimen)* specimen
  2 *adj* exemplary, model
ejemplificar [44] *vt* to exemplify
ejemplo *nm* example; **por e.** for example; **dar e.** to set an example
ejercer [49] 1 *vt* (**a**) *(profesión etc)* to practise (**b**) *(influencia)* to exert (**c**) **e. el derecho de/a ...** to exercise one's right to ...
  2 *vi* to practise (**de** as)
ejercicio *nm* (**a**) exercise; *(de profesión)* practice; **hacer e.** to take *o* do exercise (**b**) *Fin* tax year; **e. económico** financial *o* fiscal year
ejercitar *vt* to practise
ejército *nm* army
ejote *nm CAm, Méx* green bean
el 1 *art def m* (**a**) the (**b**) *(no se traduce)* **el Sr. García** Mr. García; **el hambre/destino** hunger/fate (**c**) *(con partes del cuerpo, prendas de vestir)* **me he cortado el dedo** I've cut my finger; **métetelo en el bolsillo** put it in your pocket (**d**) *(con días de la semana)* **el lunes** on Monday

---

el is used instead of **la** before feminine nouns which are stressed on the first syllable and begin with "a" or "ha" (e.g. **el agua, el hacha**). Note that **el** combines with the prepositions **a** and **de** to produce the contracted forms **al** and **del**.

---

2 *pron* (**a**) the one; **el de las once** the eleven o'clock one; **el que tienes en la mano** the one you've got in your hand; **el**

que quieras whichever one you want (**b**) *(no se traduce)* **el de tu amigo** your friend's
él *pron pers* (**a**) *(sujeto) (persona)* he; *(animal, cosa)* it (**b**) *(complemento) (persona)* him; *(animal, cosa)* it

> Usually omitted in Spanish as a subject except for emphasis or contrast.

elaboración *nf* (**a**) *(de un producto)* manufacture, production (**b**) *(de una idea)* working out, development
elaborar *vt* (**a**) *(producto)* to manufacture, to produce (**b**) *(teoría)* to develop
elasticidad *nf* elasticity; *Fig* flexibility
elástico,-a *adj & nm* elastic
elección *nf* choice; *Pol* election
elector,-a *nm,f* elector
electorado *nm* electorate
electoral *adj* electoral; **campaña e.** election campaign; **colegio e.** polling station
electoralismo *nm* electioneering
electricidad *nf* electricity
electricista *nmf* electrician
eléctrico,-a *adj* electric
electrificar [44] *vt* to electrify
electrizar [40] *vt* to electrify
electrochoque *nm* electric shock therapy
electrocutar *vt* to electrocute
electrodo *nm* electrode
electrodoméstico *nm* (domestic) electrical appliance
electroimán *nm* electromagnet
electromagnético,-a *adj* electromagnetic
electrón *nm* electron
electrónica *nf* electronics *sing*
electrónico,-a *adj* electronic
elefante *nm* elephant
elegancia *nf* elegance
elegante *adj* elegant
elegía *nf* elegy
elegir [58] *vt* (**a**) to choose (**b**) *Pol* to elect
elemental *adj* (**a**) *(fundamental)* basic, fundamental (**b**) *(simple)* elementary
elemento *nm* (**a**) element (**b**) *(componente)* component, part (**c**) *(individuo)* type, individual (**d**) **elementos** elements; *(fundamentos)* rudiments
elepé *nm* LP (record)
elevación *nf* elevation; **e. de precios** rise in prices; **e. del terreno** rise in the ground
elevado,-a *adj* (**a**) high; *(edificio)* tall (**b**) *(pensamiento etc)* lofty, noble
elevalunas *nm inv Aut* **e. eléctrico** electric windows

elevar 1 *vt* to raise
  2 elevarse *vpr* (**a**) *(subir)* to rise; *(edificio)* to stand (**b**) **e. a** *(cantidad)* to amount o come to
elijo *indic pres de* **elegir**
eliminación *nf* elimination
eliminar *vt* to eliminate
eliminatoria *nf Dep* heat, qualifying round
eliminatorio,-a *adj* qualifying, eliminatory
élite *nf* elite, élite
elitista *adj* elitist
elixir *nm (enjuage bucal)* mouthwash; *Literario* elixir
ella *pron pers f* (**a**) *(sujeto)* she; *(animal, cosa)* it, she (**b**) *(complemento)* her; *(animal, cosa)* it, her

> Usually omitted in Spanish as a subject except for emphasis or contrast.

ellas *pron pers fpl ver* **ellos**
ello *pron pers neut* it; **por e.** for that reason
ellos *pron pers mpl*
  (**a**) *(sujeto)* they (**b**) *(complemento)* them

> Usually omitted in Spanish as a subject except for emphasis or contrast.

elocuencia *nf* eloquence
elocuente *adj* eloquent; **los hechos son elocuentes** the facts speak for themselves
elogiar [43] *vt* to praise
elogio *nm* praise
elote *nm CAm, Méx* corncob, ear of maize
El Salvador *n* El Salvador
elucidar *vt* to elucidate
eludir *vt* to avoid
emanar *vi* to emanate; *Fig* **e. de** *(derivar)* to derive o come from
emancipar 1 *vt* to emancipate
  2 emanciparse *vpr* to become emancipated
embadurnar *vt* to daub, to smear (**de** with)
embajada *nf* embassy
embajador,-a *nm,f* ambassador
embalaje *nm* packing, packaging
embalar *vt* to pack
embalarse *vpr* to speed up; *Fig* **no te embales** hold your horses
embalsamar *vt* to embalm
embalsar 1 *vt* to dam; *(problema)* to contain
  2 embalsarse *vpr* to form a pool
embalse *nm* dam, reservoir
embarazada 1 *adj* pregnant; **dejar e.** to get pregnant

2 *nf* pregnant woman, expectant mother

> 🖉 Observa que la palabra inglesa **embarrassed** es un falso amigo y no es la traducción de la palabra española **embarazada**. En inglés **embarrassed** significa "avergonzado".

embarazar [40] *vt Fig* to hinder
embarazo *nm* (**a**) *(preñez)* pregnancy (**b**) *(obstáculo)* obstacle (**c**) *(turbación)* embarrassment
embarazoso,-a *adj* awkward, embarrassing
embarcación *nf* (**a**) *(nave)* boat, craft (**b**) *(embarco)* embarkation
embarcadero *nm* quay
embarcar [44] 1 *vt* to ship
2 *vi* to embark, to go on board
3 embarcarse *vpr* (**a**) *Náut* **e. (en)** to go on board; *Av* to board (**b**) **e. en un proyecto** to embark on a project
embarco *nm* embarkation
embargar [42] *vt* (**a**) *Jur* to seize, to impound (**b**) *Fig* **le embarga la emoción** he's overwhelmed with joy
embargo *nm* (**a**) *Jur* seizure of property (**b**) *Com & Pol* embargo (**c**) **sin e.** however, nevertheless
embarque *nm (de persona)* boarding; *(de mercancías)* loading; **tarjeta de e.** boarding card
embarrancar [44] *vi*, **embarrancarse** *vpr Náut* to run aground
embaucador,-a 1 *adj* deceitful
2 *nm,f* swindler, cheat
embaucar [44] *vt* to swindle, to cheat
embeber 1 *vt* to soak up
2 embeberse *vpr* to become absorbed *o* engrossed
embelesar *vt* to fascinate
embellecer [33] *vt* to embellish
embestida *nf* (**a**) onslaught (**b**) *Taurom* charge
embestir [6] *vt* (**a**) *Taurom* to charge (**b**) *(atacar)* to attack
emblandecer [33] 1 *vt* to soften
2 emblandecerse *vpr Fig* to relent
emblema *nm* emblem
embobado,-a *adj* fascinated
embobarse *vpr* to be fascinated *o* besotted (**con** by)
embolia *nf* embolism
émbolo *nm* piston
embolsar *vt*, **embolsarse** *vpr* to pocket
emborrachar *vt*, **emborracharse** *vpr* to get drunk
emboscada *nf* ambush; **tender una e.** to lay an ambush

embotar *vt* to blunt; *Fig (sentidos)* to dull; *(mente)* to befuddle
embotellado *nm* bottling
embotellamiento *nm Aut* traffic jam
embotellar *vt* (**a**) to bottle (**b**) *(tráfico)* to block
embragar [42] *vi Aut* to engage the clutch
embrague *nm* clutch
embravecerse [33] *vpr* (**a**) *(enfadarse)* to become enraged (**b**) *(mar)* to become rough
embriagador,-a *adj* intoxicating
embriagar [42] 1 *vt* to intoxicate; *Fig* to enrapture
2 embriagarse *vpr* to get drunk; *Fig* to be enraptured
embriaguez *nf* intoxication
embridar *vt* to bridle
embrión *nm* embryo
embrollar 1 *vt* to confuse, to muddle
2 embrollarse *vpr* to get muddled *o* confused
embrollo *nm* (**a**) *(lío)* muddle, confusion (**b**) *(aprieto)* fix, jam
embrujado,-a *adj (persona)* bewitched; *(sitio)* haunted
embrujo *nm* spell, charm; *Fig* attraction, fascination
embrutecer [33] *vt* to stultify
embuchar *vt* to stuff
embudo *nm* funnel
embuste *nm* lie, trick
embustero,-a *nm,f* cheater, liar
embutido *nm* sausage
embutir *vt* (**a**) *(carne)* to stuff (**b**) *(meter)* to stuff *o* cram *o* squeeze (**en** into) (**c**) *(incrustar)* to inlay
emergencia *nf* emergency; **salida de e.** emergency exit; **en caso de e.** in an emergency
emerger [53] *vi* to emerge
emigración *nf* emigration; *(de pájaros)* migration
emigrado,-a *nm,f* emigrant; *Pol* émigré
emigrante *adj & nmf* emigrant
emigrar *vi* to emigrate; *(pájaros)* to migrate
emilio *nm Fam Informát* e-mail (message)
eminencia *nf* eminence; *(genio)* genius
eminente *adj* eminent
emirato *nm* emirate
emisario,-a *nm,f* emissary
emisión *nf* (**a**) emission (**b**) *(de bonos, sellos)* issue (**c**) *Rad & TV* broadcasting
emisora *nf* radio *o* television station
emitir *vt* (**a**) to emit; *(luz, calor)* to give off

(**b**) *(opinión, juicio)* to express (**c**) *Rad & TV* to transmit (**d**) *(bonos, sellos)* to issue

emoción *nf* (**a**) emotion (**b**) *(excitación)* excitement; **¡qué e.!** how exciting!

emocionado,-a *adj* deeply moved *o* touched

emocionante *adj* (**a**) *(conmovedor)* moving, touching (**b**) *(excitante)* exciting, thrilling

emocionar 1 *vt* (**a**) *(conmover)* to move, to touch (**b**) *(excitar)* to thrill

　2 emocionarse *vpr* (**a**) *(conmoverse)* to be moved (**b**) *(excitarse)* to get excited

emotivo,-a *adj* emotional

empacar [44] *vt* (**a**) *(mercancías)* to pack (**b**) *Am* to annoy

empachar *vt* to give indigestion to

empacho *nm (de comida)* indigestion, upset stomach; *Fig* surfeit

empadronar *vt,* **empadronarse** *vpr* to register

empalagar [42] *vi* to pall

empalagoso,-a *adj* (**a**) *(dulce)* sickly sweet (**b**) *Fig (persona)* smarmy

empalizada *nf* fence

empalmar 1 *vt* (**a**) *(unir)* to join; *(cuerdas, cables)* to splice (**b**) *Ftb* to volley

　2 *vi* to converge; *Ferroc* to connect

　3 empalmarse *vpr Vulg* to get a hard-on

empalme *nm* (**a**) connection (**b**) *Ferroc* junction; *(en carretera)* intersection, T-junction

empanada *nf* pie

empanadilla *nf* pasty

empanado,-a *adj (filete etc)* breaded, in breadcrumbs

empantanarse *vpr* (**a**) *(inundarse)* to become flooded (**b**) *Fig* to be bogged down

empañar *vt,* **empañarse** *vpr (cristales)* to steam up

empapado,-a *adj* soaked

empapar 1 *vt* (**a**) *(mojar)* to soak (**b**) *(absorber)* to soak up

　2 empaparse *vpr* (**a**) *(persona)* to get soaked (**b**) *Fam Fig* **empaparse (de)** to take in

empapelar *vt* to wallpaper

empaque *nm* bearing, presence

empaquetar *vt* to pack

emparedado *nm* sandwich

emparejar *vt (cosas)* to match; *(personas)* to pair off

empastar *vt (diente)* to fill

empaste *nm (de diente)* filling

empatado,-a *adj* drawn; **estar/ir empatados** to be drawing

empatar 1 *vi Dep* to tie, to draw

　2 *vt* (**a**) *Dep* **e. el partido** to equalize (**b**) *Am (unir)* to join

empate *nm Dep* draw, tie

empecinarse *vpr* to dig one's heels in

empedernido,-a *adj (fumador, bebedor)* hardened

empedrado,-a 1 *adj* cobbled

　2 *nm* (**a**) *(adoquines)* cobblestones (**b**) *(acción)* paving

empeine *nm* instep

empellón *nm* push, shove

empeñar 1 *vt* to pawn

　2 empeñarse *vpr* (**a**) *(insistir)* to insist (**en** on), to be determined (**en** to) (**b**) *(endeudarse)* to get into debt

empeño *nm* (**a**) *(insistencia)* insistence; **poner e. en algo** to put a lot of effort into sth (**b**) *(deuda)* pledge; **casa de empeños** pawnshop

empeoramiento *nm* deterioration, worsening

empeorar 1 *vi* to deteriorate, to worsen

　2 *vt* to make worse

　3 empeorarse *vpr* to deteriorate, to worsen

empequeñecer [33] *vt Fig* to belittle

emperador *nm* emperor

emperatriz *nf* empress

emperifollarse *vpr Fam* to get dolled up

emperrarse *vpr* to dig one's heels in, to become stubborn

empezar [51] *vt & vi (a hacer algo)* to begin; *(algo)* to start, to commence

empinado,-a *adj (cuesta)* steep

empinar 1 *vt* to raise; *Fam* **e. el codo** to drink

　2 empinarse *vpr (persona)* to stand on tiptoe

empírico,-a *adj* empirical

emplasto *nm* poultice

emplazamiento *nm* (**a**) *(colocación)* site, location (**b**) *Jur* summons *sing*

emplazar ¹ [40] *vt* to locate, to situate

emplazar ² [40] *vt* (**a**) *Jur* to summons (**b**) *(a una reunión etc)* to call

empleado,-a *nm,f* employee; *(de oficina, banco)* clerk; **empleada del hogar** servant, maid

emplear *vt* (**a**) *(usar)* to use; *(contratar)* to employ (**b**) *(dinero, tiempo)* to spend

empleo *nm* (**a**) *(oficio)* job; *Pol* employment (**b**) *(uso)* use; **modo de e.** instructions for use

emplomar *vt Am (diente)* to fill

empobrecer [33] 1 *vt* to impoverish

　2 empobrecerse *vpr* to become impoverished *o* poor

empobrecimiento *nm* impoverishment

empollar *vt* (**a**) *(huevos)* to sit on (**b**) *Fam (estudiar)* to bone up on, *Br* to swot up

empollón,-ona *nm,f Br Fam* swot, *US* grind

empolvar 1 *vt* to cover in dust

2 empolvarse *vpr (la cara)* to powder

emponzoñar *vt* to poison

emporcar [44] *vt* to foul, to dirty

emporio *nm* (**a**) *Com* emporium, trading *o* commercial centre (**b**) *Am* department store

emporrarse *vpr Fam* to get high

empotrado,-a *adj* fitted

emprendedor,-a *adj* enterprising

emprender *vt* to undertake; *Fam* **emprenderla con algn** to pick on sb

empresa *nf* (**a**) *Com & Ind* firm, company; **e. punto com** dot com (company); **e. de trabajo temporal** temping agency (**b**) *Pol* **la libre e.** free enterprise (**c**) *(tarea)* undertaking

empresariado *nm* employers

empresarial *adj* (**a**) *(de empresa)* business; **(ciencias) empresariales** business studies (**b**) *(espíritu)* entrepreneurial; **organización e.** employers' organization

empresario,-a *nm,f* (**a**) *(hombre)* businessman; *(mujer)* businesswoman (**b**) *(patrón)* employer

empréstito *nm Fin* debenture loan

empujar *vt* to push, to shove

empuje *nm* push; *Fig (brío)* verve, get-up-and-go

empujón *nm* push, shove; **dar empujones** to push and shove

empuñadura *nf (de espada)* hilt

empuñar *vt* to grasp, to seize

emular *vt* to emulate

emulsión *nf* emulsion

en *prep* (**a**) *(posición)* in, on, at; **en Madrid/Bolivia** in Madrid/Bolivia; **en la mesa** on the table; **en el bolso** in the bag; **en casa/el trabajo** at home/work

(**b**) *(movimiento)* into; **entró en el cuarto** he went into the room

(**c**) *(tiempo)* in, on, at; **en 1940** in 1940; **en verano** in summer; *Am* **en la mañana** in the morning; **cae en martes** it falls on a Tuesday; **en ese momento** at that moment

(**d**) *(transporte)* by, in; **en coche/tren** by car/train; **en avión** by air

(**e**) *(modo)* **en español** in Spanish; **en broma** jokingly; **en serio** seriously

(**f**) *(reducción, aumento)* by; **los precios aumentaron en un diez por ciento** the prices went up by ten percent

(**g**) *(tema, materia)* at, in; **bueno en**

deportes good at sports; **experto en política** expert in politics

(**h**) *(división, separación)* in; **lo dividió en tres partes** he divided it in three

(**i**) *(con infinitivo)* **fue rápido en responder** he was quick to answer; **la conocí en el andar** I recognized her by her walk; **ser sobrio en el vestir** to dress simply

enaguas *nfpl* underskirt, petticoat

enajenación *nf,* **enajenamiento** *nm* alienation; **e. mental** mental derangement, insanity

enajenar 1 *vt* (**a**) *Jur* to alienate (**b**) *(turbar)* to drive insane

2 enajenarse *vpr (enloquecer)* to go insane

enaltecer [33] *vt* (**a**) *(alabar)* to praise, to extol (**b**) *(ennoblecer)* to do credit to

enamorado,-a 1 *adj* in love

2 *nm,f* person in love

enamorar 1 *vt* to win the heart of

2 enamorarse *vpr* to fall in love (**de** with)

enano,-a *adj & nm,f* dwarf

enardecer [33] 1 *vt* *(sentimientos)* to rouse, to stir up; *(persona)* to fill with enthusiasm

2 enardecerse *vpr Fig* to become excited

encabezamiento *nm (de carta)* heading; *(de periódico)* headline; *(préambulo)* foreword, preamble

encabezar [40] *vt* (**a**) *(carta, lista)* to head; *(periódico)* to lead (**b**) *(rebelión, carrera, movimiento)* to lead

encabritarse *vpr* (**a**) *(caballo)* to rear (up) (**b**) *Fig (persona)* to get cross

encadenar *vt* to chain

encajar 1 *vt* (**a**) *(ajustar)* to insert; **e. la puerta** to push the door to (**b**) *Fam (asimilar)* to take (**c**) *(comentario)* to get in; **e. un golpe a algn** to land sb a blow

2 *vi* (**a**) *(ajustarse)* to fit (**b**) *Fig* **e. con** to fit (in) with, to square with

encaje *nm* lace

encalar *vt* to whitewash

encallar *vi* (**a**) *Náut* to run aground (**b**) *Fig* to flounder, to fail

encaminado,-a *adj* **estar bien/mal e.** to be on the right/wrong track

encaminar 1 *vt* to direct

2 encaminarse *vpr* to head (**a** for; **hacia** towards)

encandilar *vt* to dazzle

encantado,-a *adj* (**a**) *(contento)* delighted; **e. de conocerle** pleased to meet you (**b**) *(embrujado)* enchanted

encantador,-a 1 *adj* charming, delightful

2 *nm,f* magician

encantamiento *nm* spell

encantar *vt (hechizar)* to bewitch, to cast a spell on; *Fig* **me encanta nadar** I love swimming

encanto *nm* (**a**) *(atractivo)* charm; **ser un e.** to be charming (**b**) *(hechizo)* spell

encapricharse *vpr* **e. con** to set one's mind on; *(encariñarse)* to take a fancy to; *(enamorarse)* to get a crush on

encapuchado,-a *adj* hooded

encaramarse *vpr* to climb up

encarar 1 *vt* to face, to confront

　　2 encararse *vpr* **e. con** to face up to

encarcelar *vt* to imprison, to jail

encarecer [33] 1 *vt* to put up the price of

　　2 encarecerse *vpr* to go up (in price)

encarecidamente *adv* earnestly, insistently; **le rogamos e. que …** we would earnestly request you to …

encarecimiento *nm* increase *o* rise in price

encargado,-a 1 *nm,f Com (hombre)* manager; *(mujer)* manager, manageress; *(responsable)* person in charge

　　2 *adj* in charge

encargar [42] 1 *vt* (**a**) to put in charge of, to entrust with (**b**) *Com (mercancías)* to order, to place an order for; *(encuesta)* to commission

　　2 encargarse *vpr* **e. de** to see to, to deal with

encargo *nm* (**a**) *Com* order; **hecho de e.** *(a petición)* made to order (**b**) *(recado)* errand (**c**) *(tarea)* job, assignment

encariñarse *vpr* **e. con** to become fond of, to get attached to

encarnación *nf* incarnation, embodiment

encarnado,-a *adj (rojo)* red

encarnar *vt* to personify, to embody

encarnizado,-a *adj* fierce

encarrilar *vt (coche, tren)* to put on the road *o* rails; *Fig* to put on the right track

encasillar *vt* to pigeonhole

encausar *vt* to prosecute

encauzar [40] *vt* to channel

encenagarse [42] *vpr* to get covered in mud

encendedor *nm* lighter

encender [3] 1 *vt* (**a**) *(luz, radio, tele)* to switch on, to put on; *(cigarro, vela, fuego)* to light; *(cerilla)* to strike, to light (**b**) *Fig* to inflame, to stir up

　　2 encenderse *vpr* (**a**) *(fuego)* to catch; *(luz)* to go *o* come on (**b**) *(cara)* to blush, to go red

encendido *nm* ignition

encerado *nm (pizarra)* blackboard

encerar *vt* to wax, polish

encerrar [1] 1 *vt* (**a**) to shut in; *(con llave)* to lock in (**b**) *Fig (contener)* to contain, to include

　　2 encerrarse *vpr* to shut oneself up *o* in; *(con llave)* to lock oneself in

encestar *vi Dep* to score (a basket)

enchaquetado,-a *adj* smartly dressed

encharcar [44] 1 *vt* to flood, to swamp

　　2 encharcarse *vpr* to get flooded

enchilada *nf Culin* = stuffed corn tortilla seasoned with chilli

enchironar *vt Fam* to put away

enchufado,-a 1 *adj Fam* **estar e.** to have good connections *o* contacts

　　2 *nm,f Fam (favorito)* pet

enchufar *vt* (**a**) *Elec* to plug in (**b**) *(unir)* to join, to connect (**c**) *Fam (para un trabajo)* to pull strings for

enchufe *nm* (**a**) *Elec (hembra)* socket; *(macho)* plug (**b**) *Fam* contact

enchufismo *nm Fam* string-pulling

encía *nf* gum

enciclopedia *nf* encyclopedia

encierro *nm Pol (protesta)* sit-in

encima *adv* (**a**) on top; *(arriba)* above; *(en el aire)* overhead; **déjalo e.** put it on top; **¿llevas cambio e.?** do you have any change on you?; *Fig* **quitarse algo de e.** to get rid of sth; **ahí e.** up there (**b**) *(además)* besides (**c**) **e. de** *(sobre)* on; *(en el aire)* above; *Fig (además)* besides; **e. de la mesa** on the table (**d**) **por e.** above; *Fig* **por e. de sus posibilidades** beyond his abilities; **leer un libro por e.** to skip through a book

encimera *nf (de cocina)* worktop

encina *nf* holm oak

encinta *adj* pregnant

enclaustrarse *vpr* to shut oneself up

enclave *nm* enclave

enclenque *adj (débil)* puny; *(enfermizo)* sickly

encoger [53] 1 *vi (contraerse)* to contract; *(prenda)* to shrink

　　2 *vt* to contract; *(prenda)* to shrink

　　3 encogerse *vpr (contraerse)* to contract; *(prenda)* to shrink; **e. de hombros** to shrug (one's shoulders)

encolar *vt (papel)* to paste; *(madera)* to glue

encolerizar [40] 1 *vt* to infuriate, to anger

　　2 encolerizarse *vpr* to become furious

encomendar [1] 1 *vt* to entrust with, to put in charge of

　　2 encomendarse *vpr* **e. a** to entrust oneself to

encomienda *nf* (**a**) assignment, mission (**b**) *(paquete postal)* parcel

encomio *nm* praise

enconado,-a *adj* (**a**) *(discusión)* bitter, fierce (**b**) *Med* inflamed, sore

enconarse *vpr* (**a**) *(exasperarse)* to get angry *o* irritated (**b**) *Med (herida)* to become inflamed *o* sore

encono *nm* spitefulness, ill feeling

encontrado,-a *adj (contrario)* conflicting

encontrar [2] 1 *vt* (**a**) *(hallar)* to find; **no lo encuentro** I can't find it; **lo encuentro muy agradable** I find it very pleasant (**b**) *(dar con)* to meet; *(problema)* to run into, to come up against

2 **encontrarse** *vpr* (**a**) *(persona)* to meet (**b**) *(sentirse)* to feel, to be; **e. a gusto** feel comfortable (**c**) *(estar)* to be

encontronazo *nm* (**a**) *(choque)* collision, crash (**b**) *Fig (de ideas etc)* clash

encorvar 1 *vt* to bend

2 **encorvarse** *vpr* to stoop *o* bend (over)

encrespar 1 *vt* (**a**) *(pelo)* to curl (**b**) *(mar)* to make choppy *o* rough (**c**) *Fig (enfurecer)* to infuriate

2 **encresparse** *vpr* (**a**) *(mar)* to get rough (**b**) *Fig (enfurecerse)* to get cross *o* irritated

encrucijada *nf* crossroads

encrudecer [33] *vi*, **encrudecerse** *vpr* to get worse

encuadernación *nf* (**a**) *(oficio)* bookbinding (**b**) *(cubierta)* binding

encuadernador,-a *nm,f* bookbinder

encuadernar *vt* to bind

encuadrar *vt* (**a**) *(imagen etc)* to frame (**b**) *Fig (encajar)* to fit, to insert

encuadre *nm Cin & TV* framing

encubierto,-a *adj (secreto)* hidden; *(operación)* covert

encubridor,-a *nm,f Jur* accessory (after the fact), abettor

encubrir *vt* to conceal

encuentro *nm* (**a**) encounter, meeting (**b**) *Dep* meeting, match; **e. amistoso** friendly (match)

encuesta *nf* (**a**) *(sondeo)* (opinion) poll, survey (**b**) *(investigación)* investigation, inquiry

encuestador,-a *nm,f* pollster

encuestar *vt* to poll

encumbrar 1 *vt* to exalt

2 **encumbrarse** *vpr* to rise to a high (social) position

ende: • **por ende** *loc adv* therefore

endeble *adj* weak, feeble

endeblez *nf* weakness, feebleness

endémico,-a *adj Med* endemic; *Fig* chronic

endemoniado,-a *adj* (**a**) *(poseso)* possessed (**b**) *Fig (travieso)* mischievous

enderezar [40] 1 *vt (poner derecho)* to straighten out; *(poner vertical)* to set upright

2 **enderezarse** *vpr* to straighten up

endeudarse *vpr* to get *o* fall into debt

endiablado,-a *adj* (**a**) *(poseso)* possessed (**b**) *(travieso)* mischievous, devilish

endibia *nf* endive

endiosar *vt* to deify

endomingarse [42] *vpr Fam* to put on one's Sunday best

endosar *vt* (**a**) *(cheque)* to endorse (**b**) *Fam* **e. algo a algn** *(tarea)* to lumber sb with sthg

endrina *nf Bot* sloe

endrogarse [42] *vpr Am* to take drugs, to use drugs

endulzar [40] *vt* to sweeten

endurecer [33] 1 *vt* to harden

2 **endurecerse** *vpr* to harden, to become hard

enebro *nm* juniper

enema *nm* enema

enemigo,-a 1 *adj* enemy; **soy e. de la bebida** I'm against drink

2 *nm,f* enemy

enemistad *nf* hostility, enmity

enemistar 1 *vt* to set at odds, to cause a rift between

2 **enemistarse** *vpr* to become enemies; **e. con algn** to fall out with sb

energético,-a *adj* energy

energía *nf* energy; **e. hidráulica/nuclear** hydro-electric/nuclear power; *Fig* **e. vital** vitality

enérgico,-a *adj* energetic; *(decisión)* firm; *(tono)* emphatic

energúmeno,-a *nm,f Fam (hombre)* madman; *(mujer)* mad woman; **ponerse como un e.** to go up the wall

enero *nm* January

enervante *adj* enervating

enervar *vt* to enervate

enésimo,-a *adj* (**a**) *Mat* nth (**b**) *Fam* umpteenth; **por enésima vez** for the umpteenth time

enfadado,-a *adj (enojado)* angry; *(molesto)* annoyed; **estamos enfadados** we've fallen out with each other

enfadar 1 *vt* to make angry *o* annoyed

2 **enfadarse** *vpr* (**a**) to get angry (**con** with) (**b**) *(dos personas)* to fall out

enfado *nm* anger; *(desavenencia)* fall-out

enfangarse [42] *vpr* to get muddy; *Fig* to

get involved (in dirty business)

énfasis *nm inv* emphasis, stress; **poner e. en algo** to lay stress on sth

enfático,-a *adj* emphatic

enfatizar [40] *vt* to emphasize, to stress

enfermar *vi,* **enfermarse** *upr* to become *o* fall ill, to be taken ill

enfermedad *nf* illness; *(contagiosa)* disease

enfermería *nf* infirmary

enfermero,-a *nm,f (mujer)* nurse; *(hombre)* male nurse

enfermizo,-a *adj* unhealthy, sickly

enfermo,-a 1 *adj* ill; **caer e.** to be taken ill; *Fam* **esa gente me pone e.** those people make me sick
2 *nm,f* ill person; *(paciente)* patient

enfervorizar [40] *vt* to enthuse

enfilar *vi* **e. hacia** to make for

enflaquecer [33] *vt (adelgazar)* to make thin; *(debilitar)* to weaken

enfocado,-a *adj Fot* **bien/mal enfocado** in/out of focus

enfocar [44] *vt* (**a**) *(imagen)* to focus; *(persona)* to focus on (**b**) *(tema)* to approach (**c**) *(con linterna)* to shine a light on

enfoque *nm* (**a**) focus; *(acción)* focusing (**b**) *(de un tema)* approach

enfrentamiento *nm* clash

enfrentar 1 *vt* (**a**) *(situación, peligro)* to confront (**b**) *(enemistar)* to set at odds
2 enfrentarse *upr* (**a**) **e. con** *o* **a** to face up to, to confront (**b**) *Dep* **enfrentarse (a)** *(rival)* to meet

enfrente *adv* (**a**) opposite, facing; **la casa de e.** the house opposite *o* across the road (**b**) **e. de.** opposite (to), facing; **e. del colegio** opposite the school

enfriamiento *nm* (**a**) *(proceso)* cooling (**b**) *Med (catarro)* cold, chill

enfriar [29] 1 *vt* to cool (down), to chill
2 *vi* to cool down
3 enfriarse *upr* (**a**) to get *o* go cold (**b**) *(resfriarse)* to get *o* catch a cold (**c**) *Fig (pasión)* to cool down

enfurecer [33] 1 *vt* to enrage, to infuriate
2 enfurecerse *upr* to get furious, to lose one's temper

enfurruñarse *upr Fam* to sulk

engalanar 1 *vt* to deck out, to adorn
2 engalanarse *upr* to dress up, to get dressed up

enganchado,-a *adj Fam* **estar e. (a la droga)** to be hooked (on drugs)

enganchar 1 *vt* (**a**) to hook; *Ferroc* to couple (**b**) *Fam (pillar)* to nab
2 engancharse *upr* to get caught *o*

hooked; *Fam (a la droga)* to get hooked

enganche *nm (gancho)* hook; *Ferroc* coupling

engañabobos *nm inv (persona)* con man, confidence trickster; *(truco)* con trick

engañar 1 *vt* to deceive, to mislead; *(estafar)* to cheat, to trick; *(mentir a)* to lie to; *(al marido, mujer)* to be unfaithful to
2 engañarse *upr* to deceive oneself

engañifa *nf Fam* swindle

engaño *nm* (**a**) deceit; *(estafa)* fraud, swindle; *(mentira)* lie (**b**) *(error)* mistake, misunderstanding

engañoso,-a *adj (palabras)* deceitful; *(apariencias)* deceptive; *(consejo)* misleading

engarzar [40] *vt* (**a**) *(unir)* to link (**b**) *(engastar)* to mount, to set

engastar *vt* to set, to mount

engatusar *vt Fam* to coax; **e. a algn para que haga algo** to coax sb into doing sth

engendrar *vt* (**a**) *Biol* to engender (**b**) *Fig* to give rise to, to cause

engendro *nm* freak

englobar *vt* to include

engomar *vt* to gum, to glue

engordar 1 *vt* to fatten (up), to make fat
2 *vi* (**a**) to put on weight, to get fat; **he engordado 3 kilos** I've put on 3 kilos (**b**) *(comida, bebida)* to be fattening

engorro *nm Fam* bother, nuisance

engorroso,-a *adj Fam* bothersome, tiresome

engranaje *nm* (**a**) *Téc* gearing (**b**) *Fig* machinery

engranar *vt Téc* to engage

engrandecer [33] *vt* to exalt

engrasar *vt* (**a**) *(lubricar)* to lubricate, to oil (**b**) *(manchar)* to make greasy, to stain with grease

engrase *nm* lubrication

engreído,-a *adj* vain, conceited

engreírse [56] *upr* to become vain *o* conceited

engrosar [2] *vt (incrementar)* to enlarge; *(cantidad)* to increase, to swell

engrudo *nm* paste

enguatar *vt* to pad

engullir *vt* to gobble up

enharinar *vt* to cover with flour

enhebrar *vt* to thread

enhorabuena *nf* congratulations; **dar la e. a algn** to congratulate sb

enigma *nm* enigma

enigmático,-a *adj* enigmatic

enjabonar *vt* to soap

enjalbegar [42] *vt* to whitewash

enjambre *nm* swarm

enjaular *vt* (**a**) *(animal)* to cage (**b**) *Fam* to put inside, to put in jail

enjuagar [42] *vt* to rinse

enjuague *nm* rinse; **e. bucal** mouthwash

enjugar [42] *vt*, **enjugarse** *vpr* (**a**) *(secar)* to mop up; *(lágrimas)* to wipe away (**b**) *(deuda, déficit)* to clear, to wipe out

enjuiciamiento *nm* (**a**) *(opinión)* judgement (**b**) *Jur (civil)* lawsuit; *(criminal)* trial, prosecution

enjuiciar [43] *vt* (**a**) *(juzgar)* to judge, to examine (**b**) *Jur (criminal)* to indict, to prosecute

enjundia *nf Fig (sustancia)* substance; *(importancia)* importance

enjuto,-a *adj* lean, skinny

enlace *nm* (**a**) *(unión)* link, connection; **e. químico** chemical bond (**b**) *Ferroc* connection (**c**) *(casamiento)* marriage (**d**) *(persona)* liaison officer; **e. sindical** shop steward

enlatado,-a *adj* canned, tinned

enlatar *vt* to can, to tin

enlazar [40] *vt & vi* to link, to connect (**con** with)

enlodar *vt* (**a**) *(enfangar)* to muddy, to cover with mud (**b**) *Fig (reputación)* to stain, to besmirch

enloquecedor,-a *adj* maddening

enloquecer [33] 1 *vi* to go mad

2 *vt* (**a**) *(volver loco)* to drive mad (**b**) *Fam* **me enloquecen las motos** I'm mad about motorbikes

3 enloquecerse *vpr* e. to go mad, to go out of one's mind

enlosar *vt* to tile

enlucir [35] *vt (pared)* to plaster; *(plata, oro)* to polish

enlutado,-a *adj* in mourning

enmadrado,-a *adj* **estar e.** to be tied to one's mother's apron strings

enmarañar 1 *vt* (**a**) *(pelo)* to tangle (**b**) *Fig (complicar)* to complicate, confuse

2 enmarañarse *vpr* (**a**) *(pelo)* to get tangled (**b**) *Fig (situación)* to get confused, to get into a mess o a muddle

enmarcar [44] *vt* to frame

enmascarar 1 *vt* (**a**) to mask (**b**) *(problema, la verdad)* to mask, to disguise

2 enmascararse *vpr* to put on a mask

enmendar [1] 1 *vt (corregir)* to correct, to put right; *Jur* to amend

2 enmendarse *vpr (persona)* to reform, to mend one's ways

enmienda *nf* correction; *Jur & Pol* amendment

enmohecerse [33] *vpr (metal)* to rust, to get rusty; *Bot* to go mouldy

enmoquetar *vt* to carpet

enmudecer [33] *vi (callar)* to fall silent; *Fig* to be dumbstruck

ennegrecer [33] *vt*, **ennegrecerse** *vpr* to blacken, to turn black

ennoblecer *vt* to ennoble

enojadizo,-a *adj* irritable, touchy

enojado,-a *adj (enojado)* angry; *(molesto)* annoyed;

enojar 1 *vt* to anger, to annoy

2 enojarse *vpr* to get angry, to lose one's temper

enojo *nm* anger, annoyance

enorgullecer [33] 1 *vt* to fill with pride

2 enorgullecerse *vpr* to be o feel proud (**de** of)

enorme *adj* enormous

enormidad *nf* enormity; *Fam* **una e. loads**

enraizado,-a *adj* rooted

enraizar [40] *vi*, **enraizarse** *vpr (persona)* to put down roots; *(planta, costumbre)* to take root

enrarecerse [33] *vpr (aire)* to become rarefied

enredadera *nf* climbing plant, creeper

enredar 1 *vt* (**a**) *(pelo)* to entangle, to tangle up (**b**) *Fig (asunto)* to confuse, to complicate (**c**) *Fig (implicar)* to involve (**en** in) (**d**) *(confundir)* to mix up

2 enredarse *vpr* (**a**) *(pelo)* to get entangled, to get tangled (up) o in a tangle (**b**) *Fig (asunto)* to get complicated o confused (**c**) *Fig* **e. con** *(involucrarse)* to get involved with (**d**) *(confundirse)* to get mixed up

enredo *nm* (**a**) *(maraña)* tangle (**b**) *Fig (lío)* muddle, mess

enrejado *nm (de ventana)* lattice

enrevesado,-a *adj* complicated, difficult

enriquecer [33] 1 *vt* to make rich; *Fig* to enrich

2 enriquecerse *vpr* to get o become rich, to prosper; *Fig* to become enriched

enrocar [44] *vi (en ajedrez)* to castle

enrojecer [33] 1 *vt* to redden, to turn red

2 *vi (ruborizarse)* to blush

3 enrojecerse *vpr* to blush

enrolarse *vpr* to enrol, to sign on; *Mil* to enlist, to join up

enrollado,-a *adj* (**a**) rolled up (**b**) *(persona)* great (**c**) *Fam* **estar e. con algn** *(estar saliendo con)* to go out with sb

enrollar 1 *vt* to roll up; *(cable)* to coil; *(hilo)* to wind up

2 enrollarse *vpr* (**a**) *Fam (hablar)* to chatter, to go on and on (**b**) *Fam* **e. con**

algn *(tener relaciones)* to have an affair with sb

🔏 Observa que el verbo inglés **to enrol** es un falso amigo y no es la traducción del verbo español **enrollar**. En inglés, **to enrol** significa "matricular, inscribir".

---

enroque *nm (en ajedrez)* castling
enroscar [44] 1 *vt* (**a**) to coil (round), to wind (**b**) *(tornillo, tapón)* to screw in *o* on
  2 enroscarse *vpr* to coil, to wind
ensaimada *nf* = kind of spiral pastry from Majorca
ensalada *nf* salad
ensaladera *nf* salad bowl
ensaladilla *nf* **e. rusa** Russian salad
ensalzar [40] *vt (enaltecer)* to exalt; *(elogiar)* to praise, to extol
ensamblador *nm Informát* assembler
ensamblaje *nm Téc* assembly
ensamblar *vt* to assemble
ensanchar 1 *vt* to enlarge, to widen; *Cost* to let out
  2 ensancharse *vpr* to get wider
ensanche *nm* enlargement, widening; *(de ciudad)* urban development
ensangrentado,-a *adj* bloodstained, covered in blood
ensangrentar [1] *vt* to stain with blood, to cover in blood
ensañarse *vpr* **e. con** to be brutal with; *(cebarse)* to delight in tormenting
ensartar *vt* (**a**) *(perlas etc)* to string together (**b**) *(mentiras etc)* to reel off, to rattle off
ensayar *vt* to test, to try out; *Teatro* to rehearse; *Mús* to practise
ensayista *nmf* essayist
ensayo *nm* (**a**) *(prueba)* test, trial (**b**) *Teatro* rehearsal; **e. general** dress rehearsal (**c**) *(escrito)* essay
enseguida, en seguida *adv (inmediatamente)* at once, straight away; *(poco después)* in a minute, soon; **e. voy** I'll be right there
ensenada *nf* inlet, cove
enseña *nf* ensign, standard
enseñanza *nf* (**a**) *(educación)* education (**b**) *(de idioma etc)* teaching (**c**) **enseñanzas** teachings
enseñar *vt* (**a**) to teach; **e. a algn a hacer algo** to teach sb how to do sth (**b**) *(mostrar)* to show; *(señalar)* to point out
enseres *nmpl (bártulos)* belongings, goods; *(de trabajo)* tools
ensillar *vt* to saddle (up)
ensimismado,-a *adj (en la lectura etc)* engrossed; *(abstraído)* lost in thought

ensimismarse *vpr (en la lectura etc)* to become engrossed; *(abstraerse)* to be lost in thought
ensombrecer [33] 1 *vt* to cast a shadow over
  2 ensombrecerse *vpr* to darken
ensopar *vt Am* to soak
ensordecedor,-a *adj* deafening
ensordecer [33] 1 *vt* to deafen
  2 *vi* to go deaf
ensortijado,-a *adj* curly
ensuciar [43] 1 *vt* (**a**) to get dirty (**b**) *Fig (reputación)* to harm, to damage
  2 ensuciarse *vpr* to get dirty
ensueño *nm* dream; **una casa de e.** a dream house
entablado *nm* (**a**) *(entarimado)* planking, planks (**b**) *(suelo)* wooden floor
entablar *vt* (**a**) *(conversación)* to open, to begin; *(amistad)* to strike up; *(negocios)* to start (**b**) *(en juegos de tablero)* to set up (**c**) *(pleito)* to initiate
entablillar *vt Med* to splint
entallado,-a *adj (vestido)* close-fitting; *(camisa)* fitted
entallar 1 *vt* to take in at the waist
  2 *vi* to fit at the waist
entarimado *nm* parquet floor
entarimar *vt* to cover with parquet
ente *nm* (**a**) *(institución)* organization, body; **e. público** public service organization (**b**) *(ser)* being
entendederas *nfpl Fam* brains; **ser duro de e.** to be slow on the uptake
entender [3] 1 *vt (comprender)* to understand; **a mi e.** to my way of thinking; **dar a algn a e. que ...** to give sb to understand that ...
  2 *vi* (**a**) *(comprender)* to understand (**b**) **e. de** *(saber)* to know about
  3 entenderse *vpr* (**a**) *(comprenderse)* to be understood, to be meant (**b**) *Fam* **e. (bien) con** to get on (well) with
entendido,-a 1 *nm,f* expert
  2 *adj* **tengo e. que ...** I understand that ...
entendimiento *nm* understanding
enterado,-a 1 *adj* knowledgeable, well-informed; **estar e.** to be in the know; **estar e. de ...** to be aware of ...
  2 *nm,f (listillo)* know-all
enteramente *adv* entirely, completely
enterar 1 *vt* to inform (**de** about *o* of)
  2 enterarse *vpr* to find out; **me he enterado de que ...** I understand ...; **ni me enteré** I didn't even realize it
entereza *nf* strength of character
enternecedor,-a *adj* moving, touching
enternecer [33] 1 *vt* to move, to touch

2 enternecerse *vpr* to be moved *o* touched

entero,-a 1 *adj* (**a**) *(completo)* entire, whole; **por e.** completely (**b**) *Fig (íntegro)* honest, upright (**c**) *Fig (firme)* strong

2 *nm* (**a**) *Mat* whole number (**b**) *Fin* point

enterrador *nm* gravedigger

enterramiento *nm* burial

enterrar [1] *vt* to bury

entidad *nf* organization; **e. comercial** company, firm

entierro *nm* (**a**) burial (**b**) *(ceremonia)* funeral

entomología *nf* entomology

entonación *nf* intonation

entonar 1 *vt* (**a**) *(canto)* to sing (**b**) *Med* to tone up

2 *vi* to be in harmony, to be in tune (**con** with)

entonces *adv* then; **por aquel e.** at that time; **el e. ministro** the then minister

entornar *vt (ojos etc)* to half-close; *(puerta)* to leave ajar

entorno *nm* environment

entorpecer [33] *vt (obstaculizar)* to hinder, to impede

entrada *nf* (**a**) entrance (**b**) *(billete)* ticket; *(recaudación)* takings (**c**) **de e.** for a start (**d**) *Culin* entrée (**e**) *Com* entry; *(pago inicial)* down payment, deposit; **e. de capital** capital inflow (**f**) *Com* **entradas** *(ingresos)* receipts, takings (**g**) *(en la frente)* receding hairline

entrado,-a *adj* **e. en años** advanced in years; **hasta bien entrada la noche** well into the night

entramado *nm* framework; *(de sistema etc)* network

entramparse *vpr Fam* to get into debt

entrante 1 *adj* coming; **el mes e.** next month; **el ministro e.** the incoming minister

2 *Culin* starter

entrañable *adj* (**a**) *(lugar)* intimate, close (**b**) *(persona)* affectionate, warmhearted

entrañar *vt* to entail

entrañas *nfpl* bowels

entrar 1 *vi* (**a**) to come in, to go in, to enter; *Fig* **no me entran las matemáticas** I can't get the hang of maths (**b**) *(encajar)* to fit (**c**) **el año que entra** next year, the coming year (**d**) *(venir)* to come over; **me entró dolor de cabeza** I got a headache; **me entraron ganas de reír** I felt like laughing

2 *vt* (**a**) to introduce (**b**) *Informát* to enter

entre *prep* (**a**) *(dos)* between (**b**) *(más de dos)* among(st)

entreabierto,-a *adj (ojos etc)* half-open; *(puerta)* ajar

entreacto *nm* interval, intermission

entrecejo *nm* space between the eyebrows; **fruncir el e.** to frown, to knit one's brow

entrecortado,-a *adj (voz)* faltering, hesitant

entrecot *nm* fillet steak

entrecruzar [40] *vt,* **entrecruzarse** *vpr* to entwine

entredicho *nm* (**a**) *Jur* injunction (**b**) **estar en e.** to be suspect; **poner algo en e.** to bring sth into question

entrega *nf* (**a**) *(de productos)* delivery; *(de premios)* presentation (**b**) *(fascículo)* part, instalment (**c**) *(devoción)* selflessness

entregar [42] 1 *vt* to hand over; *(deberes etc)* to give in, to hand in; *Com* to deliver

2 entregarse *vpr* (**a**) *(rendirse)* to give in, to surrender (**b**) **e. a** to devote oneself to; *Pey* to indulge in

entreguismo *nm Pol* appeasement

entrelazar [40] *vt,* **entrelazarse** *vpr* to entwine

entremedias *adv* in between; *(mientras tanto)* meanwhile, in the meantime

entremés *nm Culin* hors d'oeuvres

entremeterse *vpr* = entrometerse

entremezclarse *vpr* to mix, to mingle

entrenador,-a *nm,f* trainer, coach

entrenamiento *nm* training

entrenar *vi,* **entrenarse** *vpr* to train

entrepierna *nf* crotch, crutch

entresacar [44] *vt* to pick out, to select

entresijos *nmpl* nooks and crannies

entresuelo *nm* mezzanine

entretanto 1 *adv* meanwhile

2 *nm* **en el e.** in the meantime

entretejer *vt* to interweave

entretención *nf Am* amusement, entertainment

entretener [24] 1 *vt* (**a**) *(divertir)* to entertain, to amuse (**b**) *(retrasar)* to delay; *(detener)* to hold up, to detain

2 entretenerse *vpr* (**a**) *(distraerse)* to amuse oneself, to while away the time (**b**) *(retrasarse)* to be delayed, to be held up

entretenido,-a *adj* enjoyable, entertaining

entretenimiento *nm* entertainment, amusement

entretiempo: •de entretiempo *loc adj* **ropa de e.** lightweight clothing

entrever [28] *vt* to glimpse, to catch sight of; *Fig* **dejó e. que ...** she hinted that ...

entrevista *nf* interview

entrevistador,-a *nm,f* interviewer

entrevistar 1 *vt* to interview

2 entrevistarse *upr* **e. con algn** to have an interview with sb

entristecer [33] 1 *vt* to sadden, to make sad

2 entristecerse *upr* to be sad (**por** about)

entrometerse *upr* to meddle, to interfere (**en** in)

entrometido,-a 1 *nm,f* meddler, busybody

2 *adj* interfering

entroncar *vi* to connect

entumecer [33] 1 *vt* to numb

2 entumecerse *upr* to go numb

entumecido,-a *adj* numb

enturbiar [43] 1 *vt* (**a**) *(agua)* to make cloudy (**b**) *Fig (asunto)* to cloud, to obscure

2 enturbiarse *upr* to become cloudy

entusiasmar 1 *vt* to fill with enthusiasm

2 entusiasmarse *upr* to get excited *o* enthusiastic (**con** about)

entusiasmo *nm* enthusiasm; **con e.** enthusiastically

entusiasta 1 *adj* enthusiastic, keen (**de** on)

2 *nmf* enthusiast

enumerar *vt* to enumerate

enunciado *nm (de teoría, problema)* wording

envainar *vt* to sheathe

envanecer [33] 1 *vt* to make proud *o* vain

2 envanecerse *upr* to become conceited *o* proud, to give oneself airs

envasado,-a 1 *nm (en botella)* bottling; *(en paquete)* packing; *(en lata)* canning

2 *adj* **e. al vacío** vacuum-packed

envasar *vt (embotellar)* to bottle; *(empaquetar)* to pack; *(enlatar)* to can, to tin

envase *nm* (**a**) *(acto)* packing; *(de botella)* bottling; *(de lata)* canning (**b**) *(recipiente)* container (**c**) *(botella vacía)* empty

envejecer [33] 1 *vi* to grow old

2 *vt* to age

envejecimiento *nm* ageing

envenenar *vt* to poison

envergadura *nf* (**a**) *(importancia)* importance, scope; **de gran e.** large-scale (**b**) *(de pájaro, avión)* span, wingspan; *Náut* breadth (of sail)

envés *nm* other side

envestidura *nf* investiture

enviado,-a *nm,f* envoy; *Prensa* **e.**

especial special correspondent

enviar [29] *vt* to send

enviciarse [43] *upr* to become addicted (**con** to)

envidia *nf* envy; **tener e. de algn** to envy sb

envidiable *adj* enviable

envidiar [43] *vt* to envy; **no tener nada que e.** to be in no way inferior (**a** to)

envidioso,-a *adj* envious

> Observa que la palabra inglesa **invidious** es un falso amigo y no es la traducción de la palabra española **envidioso**. En inglés, **invidious** significa "ingrato" o "injusto".

envilecer [33] *vt* to degrade, to debase

envío *nm* sending; *(remesa)* consignment; *(paquete)* parcel; **gastos de e.** postage and packing; **e. contra reembolso** cash on delivery

enviudar *vi (hombre)* to become a widower, to lose one's wife; *(mujer)* to become a widow, to lose one's husband

envoltorio *nm*, **envoltura** *nf* wrapper, wrapping

envolver [4] *(pp envuelto)* **1** *vt* (**a**) *(con papel)* to wrap (**b**) *(cubrir)* to envelop (**c**) *(en complot etc)* to involve (**en** in)

2 envolverse *upr* (**a**) to wrap oneself up (**en** in) (**b**) *(implicarse)* to become involved (**en** in)

enyesar *vt* to plaster; *Med* to put in plaster

enzima *nf* enzyme

épica *nf* epic poetry

epicentro *nm* epicentre

épico,-a *adj* epic

epidemia *nf* epidemic

epilepsia *nf* epilepsy

epílogo *nm* epilogue

episcopal *adj* episcopal

episodio *nm* episode

epístola *nf* epistle

epitafio *nm* epitaph

epíteto *nm* epithet

época *nf* time; *Hist* period, epoch; *Agr* season; **en esta é. del año** at this time of the year; **hacer é.** to be a landmark; **mueble de é.** period furniture

equidad *nf* equity

equilátero *nm* equilateral

equilibrar *vt* to balance

equilibrio *nm* balance

equilibrismo *nm* balancing act

equilibrista *nmf* (**a**) tightrope walker (**b**) *Am Pol* opportunist

equipaje *nm* luggage; **hacer el e.** to pack, do the packing

equipar *vt* to equip, to furnish (**con** *o* **de** with)

equiparable *adj* comparable (**a** to; **con** with)

equiparar *vt* to compare (**con** with), to liken (**con** to)

equipo *nm* (**a**) *(de expertos, jugadores)* team (**b**) *(aparatos)* equipment; **e. de alta fidelidad** hi-fi stereo system (**c**) *(ropas)* outfit

equis *nf* = name of the letter X in Spanish

equitación *nf* horse *o US* horseback riding

equitativo,-a *adj* equitable, fair

equivalente *adj* equivalent

equivaler [26] *vi* to be equivalent (**a** to)

equivocación *nf* error, mistake

equivocado,-a *adj* mistaken, wrong

equivocar [44] **1** *vt* to mix up

2 equivocarse *vpr* to make a mistake; *Tel* **se equivocó de número** he dialled the wrong number; **se equivocó de fecha** he got the wrong date

equívoco,-a 1 *adj* equivocal, misleading

2 *nm* misunderstanding

era¹ *nf (época)* era, age

era² *nf Agr* threshing floor

era³ *pt indef de* **ser**

erario *nm* exchequer, treasury

eras *pt indef de* **ser**

erección *nf* erection

erecto,-a *adj* upright; *(pene)* erect

eres *indic pres de* **ser**

erguir [55] **1** *vt* to erect

2 erguirse *vpr* to straighten up, to stand/ sit up straight

erial *nm* uncultivated land

erigir [57] **1** *vt* to erect

2 erigirse *vpr* **e. en algo** to set oneself up in sth

erizado,-a *adj* bristly, prickly

erizarse [40] *vpr* to bristle, to stand on end

erizo *nm* hedgehog; **e. de mar** *o* **marino** sea urchin

ermita *nf* hermitage

> *ℓ* Observa que la palabra inglesa **hermit** es un falso amigo y no es la traducción de la palabra española **ermita**. En inglés, **hermit** significa "ermitaño".

ermitaño,-a *nm,f* hermit

erosión *nf* erosion

erosionar *vt* to erode

erótico,-a *adj* erotic

erotismo *nm* eroticism

erradicar [44] *vt* to eradicate

errante *adj* wandering

errar [50] **1** *vt* to miss, to get wrong

2 *vi* (**a**) *(vagar)* to wander, to roam (**b**) *(fallar)* to err

errata *nf* erratum, misprint

erre *nf* **e. que e.** stubbornly, pigheadedly

erróneo,-a *adj* erroneous, wrong

error *nm* error, mistake; *Informát* bug; **por e.** by mistake, in error; *Impr* **e. de imprenta** misprint; **caer en un e.** to make a mistake

Ertzaintza *nf* = Basque police force

eructar *vi* to belch, to burp

eructo *nm* belch, burp

erudición *nf* erudition

erudito,-a 1 *adj* erudite, learned

2 *nm,f* scholar

erupción *nf* (**a**) *(de volcán)* eruption (**b**) *(en la piel)* rash

es *indic pres de* **ser**

esa *adj dem ver* **ese**

ésa *pron dem ver* **ése**

esbelto,-a *adj* slender

esbirro *nm* henchman

esbozar [40] *vt* to sketch, to outline

esbozo *nm* sketch, outline, rough draft

escabeche *nm* brine

escabechina *nf* massacre

escabroso,-a *adj* (**a**) *(espinoso)* tricky (**b**) *(indecente)* crude

escabullirse *vpr* to slip away, to scuttle *o* scurry off

escacharrar *vt Fam* to break

escafandra *nf* diving suit; **e. espacial** spacesuit

escala *nf* (**a**) scale; *(de colores)* range; **e. musical** scale; **en gran e.** on a large scale (**b**) *(parada)* *Náut* port of call; *Av* stopover; **hacer e. en** to call in at, to stop over in (**c**) *(escalera)* ladder, stepladder

escalada *nf* (**a**) climb (**b**) *Fig (de violencia)* escalation; *(de precios)* rise

escalador,-a *nm,f* climber, mountaineer

> *ℓ* Observa que la palabra inglesa **escalator** es un falso amigo y no es la traducción de la palabra española **escalador**. En inglés, **escalator** significa "escalera mecánica".

escalafón *nm (graduación)* rank; *(de salarios)* salary *o* wage scale

escalar *vt* to climb, to scale

escaldar *vt* to scald

escalera *nf* (**a**) stair; **e. de incendios** fire escape; **e. mecánica** escalator; **e. de caracol** spiral staircase (**b**) *(escala)* ladder (**c**) *Naipes* run

escalerilla *nf (de piscina)* steps; *Náut* gangway; *Av* (boarding) ramp

escalfar *vt* to poach

escalinata *nf* stoop

escalofriante *adj* hair-raising, blood-curdling

escalofrío *nm* shiver; **me dio un e.** it gave me the shivers

escalón *nm* step; **e. lateral** *(en letrero)* ramp

escalonar *vt* to place at intervals, to space out

escalope *nm* escalope

escalpelo *nm* scalpel

escama *nf Zool* scale; *(de jabón)* flake

escamarse *vpr* to smell a rat, to become suspicious

escamotear *vt Fam* to diddle out of, to do out of

escampar *vi* to stop raining, to clear up

escanciar [43] *vt (vino)* to pour out, to serve

escandalizar [40] **1** *vt* to scandalize, to shock

     2 escandalizarse *vpr* to be shocked (**de** at o by)

escándalo *nm* (**a**) *(alboroto)* racket, din; **armar un e.** to kick up a fuss (**b**) *(desvergüenza)* scandal

escandaloso,-a *adj* (**a**) *(ruidoso)* noisy, rowdy (**b**) *(ofensivo)* scandalous

Escandinavia *n* Scandinavia

escandinavo,-a *adj & nm,f* Scandinavian

escáner *nm Med & Informát* scanner

escaño *nm Parl* seat

escapada *nf* (**a**) *(de prisión)* escape; *(en ciclismo)* breakaway (**b**) *(viaje rápido)* flying visit, quick trip

> ℓ Observa que la palabra inglesa **escapade** es un falso amigo y no es la traducción de la palabra española **escapada**. En inglés, **escapade** significa "aventura".

escapar 1 *vi* to escape, to run away

     2 escaparse *vpr* (**a**) to escape, to run away; **se me escapó de las manos** it slipped out of my hands; **se me escapó el tren** I missed the train (**b**) *(gas etc)* to leak, to escape

escaparate *nm* shop window

escapatoria *nf* escape; **no tener e.** to have no way out

escape *nm* (**a**) *(de gas etc)* leak, escape (**b**) *Téc* exhaust; **tubo de e.** exhaust (pipe) (**c**) *(huida)* escape; *(escapatoria)* way out

escaquearse *vpr Fam* to duck out; **e. de hacer algo** to worm one's way out of doing sth

escarabajo *nm* beetle

escaramuza *nf Mil* skirmish; *Fig (riña)* squabble, brush

escarbar *vt* (**a**) *(suelo)* to scratch; *(fuego)* to poke (**b**) *Fig* to inquire into, to investigate

escarceo *nm* attempt

escarcha *nf* hoarfrost, frost

escarchado,-a *adj (fruta)* crystallized, candied

escardar *vt* to hoe

escardillo *nm* weeding hoe

escarlata *adj* scarlet

escarlatina *nf* scarlet fever

escarmentar [1] *vi* to learn one's lesson

escarmiento *nm* punishment, lesson

escarnio *nm* derision, mockery

escarola *nf* curly endive

escarpado,-a *adj (paisaje)* craggy; *(pendiente)* steep

escasear *vi* to be scarce

escasez *nf* scarcity

escaso,-a *adj* scarce; *(dinero)* tight; *(conocimientos)* scant; **e. de dinero** short of money

escatimar *vt* to skimp on; **no escatimó esfuerzos para ...** he spared no efforts to ...

escayola *nf* (**a**) plaster of Paris, stucco (**b**) *Med* plaster

escayolar *vt Med* to put in plaster

escena *nf* (**a**) scene (**b**) *(escenario)* stage; **poner en e.** to stage

escenario *nm* (**a**) *Teatro* stage (**b**) *(entorno)* scenario; *(de crimen)* scene; *(de película)* setting

escénico,-a *adj* scenic

escenografía *nf Cin* set design; *Teatro* stage design

escepticismo *nm* scepticism

escéptico,-a *adj & nm,f* sceptic

escindirse *vpr* to split (off) (**en** into)

escisión *nf* split

esclarecer [33] *vt* to shed light on

esclava *nf* bangle

esclavitud *nf* slavery

esclavizar [40] *vt* to enslave

esclavo,-a *adj & nm,f* slave

esclusa *nf* lock, sluicegate

escoba *nf* brush, broom

escocer [41] **1** *vi* to sting, to smart

     2 escocerse *vpr (piel)* to chafe

escocés,-esa 1 *adj* Scottish, Scots; **falda escocesa** kilt

     2 *nm,f (hombre)* Scotsman; *(mujer)* Scotswoman

Escocia *n* Scotland

escoger [53] *vt* to choose

escogido,-a *adj* chosen, selected;

(producto) choice, select; *Lit* **obras escogidas** selected works
escolar 1 *adj (curso, año)* school
  2 *nmf (niño)* schoolboy; *(niña)* schoolgirl
escolaridad *nf* schooling
escollo *nm* reef; *Fig* pitfall
escolta *nf* escort
escoltar *vt* to escort
escombros *nmpl* rubbish, debris
esconder 1 *vt* to hide (**de** from), to conceal (**de** from)
  2 esconderse *vpr* to hide (**de** from)
escondidas *adv* **a e.** secretly
escondite *nm* (**a**) *(lugar)* hiding place, hide-out (**b**) *(juego)* hide-and-seek
escondrijo *nm* hiding place, hide-out
escopeta *nf* shotgun; **e. de aire comprimido** air gun; **e. de cañones recortados** sawn-off shotgun
escopetazo *nm* gunshot
escorbuto *nm* scurvy
escoria *nf* (**a**) *(de metal)* slag (**b**) *Fig* scum, dregs
Escorpio *nm* Scorpio
escorpión *nm* scorpion
escotado,-a *adj* low-cut
escote *nm* low neckline
escotilla *nf* hatch, hatchway
escozor *nm* stinging, smarting
escribiente *nmf* clerk
escribir *(pp escrito)* **1** *vt* to write; **e. a mano** to write in longhand; **e. a máquina** to type
  2 escribirse *vpr* (**a**) *(dos personas)* to write to each other, to correspond (**b**) **se escribe con h** it is spelt with an h
escrito,-a 1 *adj* written; **e. a mano** handwritten, in longhand; **por e.** in writing
  2 *nm* writing
escritor,-a *nm,f* writer
escritorio *nm* (**a**) *(mueble)* writing desk, bureau; *(oficina)* office (**b**) *Informát* desktop
escritura *nf* (**a**) *Jur* deed, document; **e. de propiedad** title deed (**b**) *Rel* **Sagradas Escrituras** Holy Scriptures
escrúpulo *nm* (**a**) scruple; **una persona sin escrúpulos** an unscrupulous person (**b**) *(esmero)* care (**c**) **me da e.** *(asco)* it makes me feel squeamish
escrupuloso,-a *adj* (**a**) *(honesto)* scrupulous (**b**) *(meticuloso)* painstaking (**c**) *(delicado)* squeamish
escrutar *vt* (**a**) to scrutinize (**b**) *(votos)* to count
escrutinio *nm* (**a**) scrutiny (**b**) *(de votos)* count

escuadra *nf* (**a**) *(instrumento)* square (**b**) *Mil* squad; *Náut* squadron; *Dep* team; *(de coches)* fleet
escuadrilla *nf Náut* squadron
escuadrón *nm Av* squadron
escuálido,-a *adj* emaciated
escucha *nf* listening; **escuchas telefónicas** phone tapping; **estar a la e. de** to be listening out for
escuchar 1 *vt* to listen to; *(oír)* to hear
  2 *vi* to listen; *(oír)* to hear
escudarse *vpr Fig* **e. en algo** to hide behind sth
escudería *nf* motor racing team
escudilla *nf* bowl
escudo *nm* (**a**) *(arma defensiva)* shield (**b**) *(blasón)* coat of arms
escudriñar *vt* to scrutinize
escuela *nf* school; **e. de Bellas Artes** Art School; **e. de conducir/de idiomas** driving/language school
escueto,-a *adj* plain, unadorned
escuezo *indic pres de* **escocer**
esculcar [44] *vt Am* to search
esculpir *vt* to sculpt; *(madera)* to carve; *(metal)* to engrave
escultor,-a *nm,f (hombre)* sculptor; *(mujer)* sculptress; *(de madera)* woodcarver; *(de metales)* engraver
escultura *nf* sculpture
escultural *adj* sculptural; *(persona)* statuesque
escupidera *nf* (**a**) *(recipiente)* spittoon (**b**) *(orinal)* chamberpot
escupir 1 *vi* to spit
  2 *vt* to spit out
escupitajo *nm Fam* spit
escurreplatos *nm inv* dish rack
escurridizo,-a *adj* (**a**) *(resbaladizo)* slippery (**b**) *Fig (huidizo)* elusive, slippery
escurridor *nm* colander; *(escurreplatos)* dish rack
escurrir 1 *vt (plato, vaso)* to drain; *(ropa)* to wring out; **e. el bulto** to wriggle out
  2 escurrirse *vpr* (**a**) *(platos etc)* to drip (**b**) *(escaparse)* to run o slip away (**c**) *(resbalarse)* to slip
escúter *nm (motor)* scooter
ese,-a *adj dem* (**a**) that (**b**) **esos,-as** those
ése,-a *pron dem m,f* (**a**) that one (**b**) **ésos,-as** those (ones); *Fam* **¡ni por ésas!** no way!; *Fam* **¡no me vengas con ésas!** come off it!

Note that **ése** and its various forms can be written without an accent when there is no risk of confusion with the adjective.

esencia *nf* essence

esencial *adj* essential; **lo e.** the main thing

esencialmente *adv* essentially

esfera *nf* (**a**) sphere; *Fig* sphere, field (**b**) *(de reloj de pulsera)* dial; *(de reloj de pared)* face

esférico,-a 1 *adj* spherical

2 *nm (balón)* ball

esfinge *nf* sphinx

esforzarse [2] *vpr* to make an effort (**por** to)

esfuerzo *nm* effort

esfumarse *vpr Fam* to beat it

esgrima *nf Dep* fencing

esgrimir *vt* to wield

esguince *nm* sprain

eslabón *nm* link

eslavo,-a 1 *adj* Slav, Slavonic

2 *nm,f (persona)* Slav

3 *nm (idioma)* Slavonic

eslip *nm* (*pl* **eslips**) men's briefs, underpants

eslogan *nm* (*pl* **eslóganes**) slogan; **e. publicitario** advertising slogan

eslora *nf Náut* length

eslovaco,-a 1 *adj & nm,f* Slovak, Slovakian

2 *nm (idioma)* Slovak

Eslovaquia *n* Slovakia

Eslovenia *n* Slovenia

esloveno,-a 1 *adj & nm,f* Slovene

2 *nm (idioma)* Slovene

esmaltar *vt* to enamel

esmalte *nm* enamel; *(de uñas)* nail polish *o* varnish

esmerado,-a *adj* painstaking, careful

esmeralda *nf* emerald

esmerarse *vpr* to be careful; *(esforzarse)* to go to great lengths

esmero *nm* great care

esmoquin *nm* (*pl* **esmóquines**) dinner jacket, *US* tuxedo

esnifar *vt Fam (drogas)* to sniff

esnob (*pl* **esnobs**) **1** *adj (persona)* snobbish; *(restaurante etc)* posh

2 *nmf* snob

esnobismo *nm* snobbery, snobbishness

ESO *nf* (*abr* **Enseñanza Secundaria Obligatoria**) = mainstream secondary education in Spain for pupils aged 12-16

eso *pron neut* that; **¡e. es!** that's it!; **por e.** that's why; *Fam* **a e. de las diez** around ten; *Fam* **e. de las Navidades sale muy caro** this whole Christmas thing costs a fortune

esófago *nm* oesophagus

esos,-as *adj dem pl ver* **ese,-a**

ésos,-as *pron dem m,fpl ver* **ése,-a**

esotérico,-a *adj* esoteric

espabilado,-a *adj* (**a**) *(despierto)* wide awake (**b**) *(niño)* bright

espabilar 1 *vt* to wake up

2 espabilarse *vpr* to wake up, to waken up

espachurrar *vt* to squash

espacial *adj* spatial, spacial; **nave e.** space ship

espaciar [43] *vt* to space out

espacio *nm* (**a**) space; *(de tiempo)* length; **a doble e.** double-spaced (**b**) *Rad & TV* programme

espacioso,-a *adj* spacious, roomy

espada 1 *nf* (**a**) sword; **estar entre la e. y la pared** to be between the devil and the deep blue sea; **pez e.** swordfish (**b**) *Naipes* spade

2 *nm Taurom* matador

> *Observa que la palabra inglesa* **spade** *es un falso amigo y no es la traducción de la palabra española* **espada**. *En inglés,* **spade** *significa "pala".*

espadaña *nf* belfry

espaguetis *nmpl* spaghetti

espalda *nf* (**a**) *Anat* back; **espaldas** back; **a espaldas de algn** behind sb's back; **por la e.** from behind; **volver la e. a algn** to turn one's back on sb; *Fam* **e. mojada** wetback (**b**) *(en natación)* backstroke

espaldar *nm (de silla)* back

espaldilla *nf* shoulder blade

espantapájaros *nm inv* scarecrow

espantar 1 *vt* (**a**) *(asustar)* to frighten, to scare (**b**) *(ahuyentar)* to frighten away

2 espantarse *vpr* to get *o* feel frightened (**de** of), to get *o* feel scared (**de** of)

espanto *nm* fright; *Fam* **de e.** dreadful, shocking

espantoso,-a *adj* dreadful

España *n* Spain

español,-a 1 *adj* Spanish

2 *nm,f* Spaniard; **los españoles** the Spanish

3 *nm (idioma)* Spanish

esparadrapo *nm* sticking plaster

esparcimiento *nm (relajación)* relaxation

esparcir [52] **1** *vt (papeles, semillas)* to scatter; *Fig (rumor)* to spread

2 esparcirse *vpr* (**a**) to be scattered (**b**) *(relajarse)* to relax

espárrago *nm* asparagus

espartano,-a *adj Fig* spartan

espasmo *nm* spasm

espástico,-a *adj* spastic

espátula *nf Culin* spatula; *Arte* palette

knife; *Téc* stripping knife; *(de albañil)* trowel

especia *nf* spice

especial *adj* special; **en e.** especially; **e. para ...** suitable for ...

especialidad *nf* speciality, *US* specialty; *Educ* main subject

especialista *nmf* specialist

especializarse **[40]** *vpr* to specialize (**en** in)

especialmente *adv (exclusivamente)* specially; *(muy)* especially

especie *nf* (**a**) *Biol* species *inv* (**b**) *(clase)* kind; **una e. de salsa** a kind of sauce (**c**) *Com* **en e.** in kind

específicamente *adv* specifically

especificar **[44]** *vt* to specify

específico,-a *adj* specific; **peso e.** specific gravity

espécimen *nm* (*pl* **especímenes**) specimen

espectacular *adj* spectacular

espectacularidad *nf* **de gran e.** really spectacular

espectáculo *nm* (**a**) *(escena)* spectacle, sight; *Fam* **dar un e.** to make a spectacle of oneself (**b**) *Teatro, Cin & TV* show; **montar un e.** to put on a show

espectador,-a *nm,f Dep* spectator; *(de accidente)* onlooker; *Teatro & Cin* member of the audience; **los espectadores** the audience; *TV* the viewers

espectro *nm* (**a**) *Fís* spectrum (**b**) *(fantasma)* spectre (**c**) *(gama)* range

especulación *nf* speculation; **e. del suelo** land speculation

especulador,-a *nm,f Fin* speculator

especular *vi* to speculate

especulativo,-a *adj* speculative

espejismo *nm* mirage

espejo *nm* mirror; *Aut* **e. retrovisor** rearview mirror

espeleología *nf* potholing, speleology

espeluznante *adj* hair-raising, horrifying

espera *nf* wait; **en e. de ...** waiting for ...; **a la e. de** expecting; **sala de e.** waiting room

esperanza *nf* hope; **tener la e. puesta en algo** to have one's hopes pinned on sth; **e. de vida** life expectancy; **en estado de buena e.** expecting, pregnant

esperanzador,-a *adj* encouraging

esperanzar *vt* to give hope to

esperar **1** *vi* (**a**) *(aguardar)* to wait (**b**) *(tener esperanza de)* to hope

2 *vt* (**a**) *(aguardar)* to wait for; **espero a mi hermano** I'm waiting for my brother

(**b**) *(tener esperanza de)* to hope for; **espero que sí** I hope so; **espero que vengas** I hope you'll come (**c**) *(estar a la espera de)* to expect; **te esperábamos ayer** we were expecting you yesterday (**d**) *Fig (bebé)* to expect

esperma (**a**) *nm Biol* sperm (**b**) *Am (vela)* candle

espermaticida *nm* spermicide

espermatozoide *nm* spermatozoid

esperpéntico,-a *adj Fam* grotesque

espesar **1** *vt* to thicken

2 espesarse *vpr* to thicken, to get thicker

espeso,-a *adj (bosque, niebla)* dense; *(líquido)* thick; *(masa)* stiff

espesor *nm* thickness; **3 m de e.** 3 m thick

espesura *nf* denseness

espetar *vt Fig* to spit out

espía *nmf* spy

espiar **[29]** **1** *vi* to spy

2 *vt* to spy on

espichar *vi Fam* **espichar(la)** *(morir)* to kick the bucket

espiga *nf* (**a**) *(de trigo)* ear (**b**) *Téc* pin

espigado,-a *adj* slender

espina *nf* (**a**) *Bot* thorn (**b**) *(de pescado)* bone (**c**) *Anat* **e. dorsal** spinal column, spine (**d**) *Fig* **ése me da mala e.** there's something fishy about that one

espinaca *nf* spinach

espinal *adj* spinal; **médula e.** spinal marrow

espinazo *nm* spine, backbone

espinilla *nf* (**a**) *Anat* shin (**b**) *(en la piel)* spot

espinillera *nf Dep* shin pad

espino *nm* hawthorn; **alambre de e.** barbed wire

espionaje *nm* spying, espionage; **novela de e.** spy story

espiral *adj & nf* spiral

espirar *vi* to breathe out, to exhale

espiritismo *nm* spiritualism

espíritu *nm* (**a**) spirit; **e. deportivo** sportsmanship (**b**) *Rel (alma)* soul; **el E. Santo** the Holy Ghost

espiritual *adj* spiritual

espléndido,-a *adj* (**a**) *(magnífico)* splendid (**b**) *(generoso)* lavish, generous

esplendor *nm* splendour

esplendoroso,-a *adj* magnificent

espliego *nm* lavender

espolear *vt* to spur on

espolio *nm* = expolio

espolvorear *vt* to sprinkle (**de** with)

esponja *nf* sponge

esponjoso,-a *adj* spongy; *(bizcocho)* light

esponsales *nmpl* betrothal, engagement
espontaneidad *nf* spontaneity; **con e.** naturally
espontáneo,-a 1 *adj* spontaneous
2 *nm Taurom* = spectator who spontaneously joins in the bullfight
esporádico,-a *adj* sporadic
esposado,-a *adj* (**a**) *(recién casado)* newly married (**b**) *(con esposas)* handcuffed
esposar *vt* to handcuff
esposas *nfpl* handcuffs
esposo,-a *nm,f* spouse; *(hombre)* husband; *(mujer)* wife
esprint *nm* sprint
esprintar *vi* to sprint
espuela *nf* spur
espuerta *nf* hod
espuma *nf* foam; *(de olas)* surf; *(de cerveza)* froth, head; *(de jabón)* lather; **e. de afeitar** shaving foam
espumoso,-a *adj* frothy; *(vino)* sparkling
esputo *nm* spit
esquela *nf* notice, announcement; **e. mortuoria** announcement of a death
esquelético,-a *adj* (**a**) *Anat* skeletal (**b**) *(flaco)* skinny
esqueleto *nm* (**a**) skeleton (**b**) *Constr* framework
esquema *nm* diagram
esquemático,-a *adj* *(escueto)* schematic; *(con diagramas)* diagrammatic
esquí *nm* (**a**) *(objeto)* ski (**b**) *(deporte)* skiing; **e. acuático** waterskiing
esquiador,-a *nm,f* skier
esquiar [29] *vi* to ski
esquilar *vt* to shear
esquimal *adj & nmf* Eskimo
esquina *nf* corner; *Dep* **saque de e.** corner (kick)
esquinazo *nm* **dar e. a algn** to give sb the slip
esquirla *nf* splinter
esquirol *nm Ind* blackleg, scab
esquivar *vt* *(a una persona)* to avoid; *(un golpe)* to dodge
esquivo,-a *adj* cold, aloof
esquizofrenia *nf* schizophrenia
esquizofrénico,-a *adj & nm,f* schizophrenic
esta *adj dem ver* **este,-a**
ésta *pron dem f ver* **éste,-a**
está *indic pres de* **estar**
estabilidad *nf* stability
estabilizar [40] *vt* to stabilize
estable *adj* stable
establecer [33] 1 *vt* to establish; *(fundar)* to set up, to found; *(récord)* to set
2 establecerse *vpr* to settle

establecimiento *nm* establishment
establo *nm* cow shed
estaca *nf* stake, post; *(de tienda de campaña)* peg
estacada *nf* fence; *Fig* **dejar a algn en la e.** to leave sb in the lurch
estacazo *nm* blow with a stick
estación *nf* (**a**) station; **e. de servicio** service station; **e. de esquí** ski resort (**b**) *(del año)* season
estacional *adj* seasonal
estacionamiento *nm Aut (acción)* parking; *(lugar) Br* car park, *US* parking lot
estacionar *vt*, **estacionarse** *vpr Aut* to park
estacionario,-a *adj* stationary
estada *nf*, **estadía** *nf Am* stay
estadio *nm* (**a**) *Dep* stadium (**b**) *(fase)* stage, phase
estadista *nmf Pol (hombre)* statesman; *(mujer)* stateswoman
estadística *nf* statistics *sing*; **una e.** a statistic
estado *nm* (**a**) *Pol* state (**b**) *(situación)* state, condition; **en buen e.** in good condition; **e. de salud** condition, state of health; **e. de excepción** state of emergency; **estar en e.** to be pregnant; **e. civil** marital status; *Com* **e. de cuentas** statement of accounts (**c**) *Mil* **e. mayor** general staff
Estados Unidos *npl* the United States
estadounidense 1 *adj* United States, American
2 *nmf* American
estafa *nf* swindle
estafador,-a *nm,f* swindler
estafar *vt* to swindle
estafeta *nf* **e. de Correos** sub-post office
estalactita *nf* stalactite
estalagmita *nf* stalagmite
estallar *vi* (**a**) to burst; *(bomba)* to explode, to go off; *(guerra)* to break out (**b**) *Fig (de cólera etc)* to explode; **e. en sollozos** to burst into tears
estallido *nm* explosion; *(de guerra)* outbreak
estambre *nm Bot* stamen
Estambul *n* Istanbul
estamento *nm Hist* estate; *Fig (grupo)* group
estampa *nf* print, image

> ⚘ Observa que la palabra inglesa **stamp** es un falso amigo y no es la traducción de la palabra española **estampa**. En inglés, **stamp** significa "sello, tampón".

estampado,-a 1 *adj (tela)* printed

2 *nm* (**a**) *(tela)* print (**b**) *(proceso)* printing

estampar *vt* (**a**) *(tela)* to print (**b**) *(dejar impreso)* to imprint (**c**) *Fig (bofetada, beso)* to plant, to place

estampida *nf* (**a**) *(estampido)* bang (**b**) *(carrera rápida)* stampede; **de e.** suddenly

estampido *nm* bang

estampilla *nf Am* (postage) stamp

estancado,-a *adj (agua)* stagnant; *Fig* static, at a standstill; **quedarse e.** to get stuck *o* bogged down

estancar [44] 1 *vt* (**a**) *(agua)* to hold back (**b**) *Fig (asunto)* to block; *(negociaciones)* to bring to a standstill
2 estancarse *vpr* to stagnate; *Fig* to get bogged down

estancia *nf* (**a**) *(permanencia)* stay (**b**) *(habitación)* room (**c**) *Am (hacienda)* ranch, farm

estanco,-a 1 *nm* tobacconist's
2 *adj* watertight

estándar *(pl* **estándares***) adj & nm* standard

estandarizar [40] *vt* to standardize

estandarte *nm* standard, banner

estanque *nm* pool, pond

estanquero,-a *nm,f* tobacconist

estante *nm* shelf; *(para libros)* bookcase

estantería *nf* shelves, shelving

estaño *nm* tin

estar [13] 1 *vi* (**a**) to be; **está en la playa** he is at the beach; **e. en casa** to be in, to be at home; **estamos en Caracas** we are in Caracas; **¿está tu madre?** is your mother in?; **¿cómo estás?** how are you?; **los precios están bajos** prices are low; **el problema está en el dinero** the problem is money; **e. en lo cierto** to be right; **e. en todo** not to miss a trick
(**b**) *(+ adj)* to be; **está cansado/enfermo** he's tired/ill; **está vacío** it's empty
(**c**) *(+ adv)* to be; **está bien/mal** it's all right/wrong; **e. mal de dinero** he's short of money; **estará enseguida** it'll be ready in a minute
(**d**) *(+ ger)* to be; **está escribiendo** she is writing; **estaba comiendo** he was eating
(**e**) *(+ a + fecha)* to be; **¿a cuántos estamos?** what's the date (today)?; **estamos a 2 de Noviembre** it is the 2nd of November
(**f**) *(+ precio)* to be at; **están a 100 pesetas el kilo** they're at 100 pesetas a kilo
(**g**) *(locuciones)* **e. al caer** to be just round the corner; **¿estamos?** OK?

(**h**) *(+ de)* **e. de más** not to be needed; **e. de paseo** to be out for a walk; **e. de vacaciones/viaje** to be (away) on holiday/a trip; **estoy de jefe hoy** I'm the boss today
(**i**) *(+ para)* **estará para las seis** it will be finished by six; **hoy no estoy para bromas** I'm in no mood for jokes today; **el tren está para salir** the train is just about to leave
(**j**) *(+ por)* **está por hacer** it has still to be done; **eso está por ver** it remains to be seen; **estoy por esperar** *(a favor de)* I'm for waiting
(**k**) *(+ con)* to have; **e. con la gripe** to have the flu, to be down with flu; **estoy con Jaime** *(de acuerdo con)* I agree with Jaime
(**l**) *(+ sin)* to have no; **e. sin luz/agua** to have no light/water
(**m**) *(+ que)* **está que se duerme** he is nearly asleep; *Fam* **está que rabia** he's hopping mad
2 estarse *vpr* **¡estáte quieto!** keep still!, stop fidgeting!

estatal *adj* state; **enseñanza e.** state education

estático,-a *adj* static

estatua *nf* statue

estatura *nf* (**a**) height; **¿cuál es tu e.?** how tall are you? (**b**) *(renombre)* stature

estatus *nm* status; **e. quo** status quo

estatutario,-a *adj* statutory

estatuto *nm Jur* statute; *(de ciudad)* by-law; *(de empresa etc)* rules

este¹ 1 *adj* eastern; *(dirección)* easterly
2 *nm* east; **al e. de** to the east of

este²,-a *adj dem* (**a**) this (**b**) **estos,-as** these

éste,-a *pron dem m,f* (**a**) this one; **aquél ... é.** the former ... the latter (**b**) **éstos,-as** these (ones); **aquéllos ... é.** the former ... the latter

> Note that **éste** and its various forms can be written without an accent when there is no risk of confusion with the adjective.

esté *subj pres de* **estar**

estela *nf (de barco)* wake; *(de avión)* vapour trail; *(de cometa)* tail

estelar *adj* (**a**) *Astron* stellar (**b**) *Fig Cin & Teatro* star

estentóreo,-a *adj* stentorian, thundering

estepa *nf* steppe

estera *nf* rush mat

estercolero *nm* dunghill; *Fig* pigsty

estéreo *nm & adj* stereo

estereofónico,-a *adj* stereophonic, stereo

estereotipar *vt* to stereotype

estereotipo *nm* stereotype

estéril *adj* (**a**) sterile (**b**) *Fig (esfuerzo)* futile

esterilidad *nf* (**a**) sterility (**b**) *Fig* futility, uselessness

esterilizar [40] *vt* to sterilize

esterilla *nf* small mat

esterlina *adj & nf* sterling; **libra e.** pound (sterling)

esternón *nm* sternum, breastbone

estero *nm Am* marsh, swamp

estertor *nm* death rattle

estética *nf* aesthetics *sing*

esteticienne, esteticista *nf* beautician

estético,-a *adj* aesthetic; **cirugía estética** plastic surgery

estibador *nm* docker, stevedore

estiércol *nm* manure, dung

estigma *nm* stigma; *Rel* stigmata

estilarse *vpr* to be in vogue, to be fashionable

estilete *nm (punzón)* stylus; *(puñal)* stiletto

estilístico,-a *adj* stylistic

estilizar [40] *vt* to stylize

estilo *nm* (**a**) style; *(modo)* manner, fashion; **algo por el e.** something like that; **e. de vida** way of life (**b**) *(en natación)* stroke (**c**) *Ling* **e. directo/indirecto** direct/indirect speech

estilográfica *nf* (**pluma**) **e.** fountain pen

estima *nf* esteem, respect

estimación *nf* (**a**) *(estima)* esteem, respect (**b**) *(valoración)* evaluation; *(cálculo aproximado)* estimate

estimado,-a *adj* esteemed, respected; **E. Señor** *(en carta)* Dear Sir

estimar *vt* (**a**) *(apreciar)* to esteem (**b**) *(considerar)* to consider, to think; **lo estimo conveniente** I think it appropriate (**c**) *(valorar)* to value

estimativo,-a *adj* approximate, estimated

estimulante 1 *adj* stimulating
2 *nm* stimulant

estimular *vt* (**a**) to stimulate (**b**) *Fig* to encourage

estímulo *nm Biol & Fís* stimulus; *Fig* encouragement

estío *nm* summer

estipendio *nm* stipend, fee

estipular *vt* to stipulate

estirado,-a *adj Fig* stiff

estirar 1 *vt* to stretch; *Fig (dinero)* to spin out; *Fig* **e. la pata** to kick the bucket

2 estirarse *vpr* to stretch

estirón *nm* pull, jerk, tug; *Fam* **dar** *o* **pegar un e.** to shoot up *o* grow quickly

estirpe *nf* stock, pedigree

estival *adj* summer; **época e.** summertime

esto *pron neut* this, this thing, this matter; *Fam* **e. de la fiesta** this business about the party

estocada *nf Taurom* stab

Estocolmo *n* Stockholm

estofado *nm* stew

estoico,-a 1 *adj* stoical
2 *nm,f* stoic

estómago *nm* stomach; **dolor de e.** stomach ache

Estonia *n* Estonia

estonio,-a 1 *adj & nm,f* Estonian
2 *nm (lengua)* Estonian

estoque *nm Taurom* sword

estorbar 1 *vt* (**a**) *(dificultar)* to hinder, to get in the way of (**b**) *(molestar)* to disturb
2 *vi* to be in the way

estorbo *nm* (**a**) *(obstáculo)* obstruction, obstacle (**b**) *(molestia)* nuisance

estornino *nm* starling

estornudar *vi* to sneeze

estornudo *nm* sneeze

estos,-as *adj dem pl ver* **este,-a**

éstos,-as *pron dem m,fpl ver* **éste,-a**

estoy *indic pres de* **estar**

estrabismo *nm* squint

estrado *nm* platform; *Mús* bandstand; *Jur* stand

estrafalario,-a *adj Fam* outlandish

estragos *nmpl* **hacer e. en** to wreak havoc with *o* on

estrambótico,-a *adj Fam* outlandish, eccentric

estrangulador,-a *nm,f* strangler

estrangular *vt* to strangle; *Med* to strangulate

estraperlo *nm* black market; **tabaco de e.** black market cigarettes

Estrasburgo *n* Strasbourg

estratagema *nf Mil* stratagem; *Fam* trick, ruse

estratega *nmf* strategist

estrategia *nf* strategy

estratégico,-a *adj* strategic

estratificar [44] *vt* to stratify

estrato *nm* stratum

estraza *nf* **papel de e.** brown paper

estrechamente *adv (íntimamente)* closely, intimately; **e. relacionados** closely related

estrechamiento *nm* (**a**) narrowing; **e. de calzada** *(en letrero)* road narrows (**b**)

(de amistad etc) tightening
estrechar 1 *vt* (**a**) to make narrow (**b**) *(mano)* to shake; *(lazos de amistad)* to tighten; **me estrechó entre sus brazos** he hugged me
  2 estrecharse *vpr* to narrow, to become narrower

> 🖉 Observa que el verbo inglés **to stretch** es un falso amigo y no es la traducción del verbo español **estrechar**. En inglés, **to stretch** significa "estirar, desplegar".

estrechez *nf* (**a**) narrowness; *Fig* **e. de miras** narrow-mindedness (**b**) *Fig (dificultad económica)* want, need; **pasar estrecheces** to be hard up
estrecho,-a 1 *adj* (**a**) narrow; *(ropa, zapato)* tight; *(amistad, relación)* close, intimate (**b**) *Fig* **e. de miras** narrow-minded
  2 *nm Geog* strait, straits
estregar *vt* to scrub
estrella *nf* star; **e. de cine** film star; *Zool* **e. de mar** starfish; **e. fugaz** shooting star
estrellado,-a *adj* (**a**) *(en forma de estrella)* star-shaped (**b**) *(cielo)* starry (**c**) *(huevos)* scrambled
estrellar 1 *vt Fam* to smash
  2 estrellarse *vpr (morir)* to die in a car crash; *Aut & Av* **e. contra** *(chocar)* to crash into
estrellato *nm* stardom
estremecedor,-a *adj* bloodcurdling
estremecer [33] *vt*, **estremecerse** *vpr* to shake
estrenar *vt* (**a**) to use for the first time; *(ropa)* to wear for the first time (**b**) *Teatro & Cin* to premiere
estreno *nm Teatro* first performance; *Cin* premiere
estreñido,-a *adj* constipated
estreñimiento *nm* constipation
estrépito *nm* din, racket
estrepitoso,-a *adj* deafening; *Fig (fracaso)* spectacular
estrés *nm* stress
estresante *adj* stressful
estría *nf* (**a**) *(en la piel)* stretch mark (**b**) *Arquit* flute, fluting
estribar *vi* **e. en** to lie in, to be based on
estribillo *nm (en canción)* chorus; *(en poema)* refrain
estribo *nm* (**a**) stirrup; *Fig* **perder los estribos** to lose one's temper, to lose one's head (**b**) *Arquit* buttress; *(de puente)* pier, support
estribor *nm* starboard
estricto,-a *adj* strict

estridente *adj* strident
estrofa *nf* verse
estropajo *nm* scourer
estropear 1 *vt (máquina, cosecha)* to damage; *(fiesta, plan)* to spoil, to ruin; *(pelo, manos)* to ruin
  2 estropearse *vpr* to be ruined; *(máquina)* to break down
estropicio *nm Fam (destrozo)* damage; *(ruido)* crash, clatter
estructura *nf* structure; *(armazón)* frame, framework
estructurar *vt* to structure
estruendo *nm* roar
estrujar 1 *vt (limón etc)* to squeeze; *(ropa)* to wring; *(apretar)* to crush
  2 estrujarse *vpr Fam* **e. los sesos** *o* **el cerebro** to rack one's brains
estrujón *nm* tight squeeze, big hug
estuche *nm* case; *(para lápices)* pencil case
estuco *nm* stucco
estudiante *nmf* student
estudiantil *adj* student
estudiar [43] *vt & vi* to study
estudio *nm* (**a**) study; *(encuesta)* survey; *Com* **e. de mercado** market research (**b**) *(sala)* studio; **e. cinematográfico/de grabación** film/recording studio (**c**) *(apartamento)* studio (flat) (**d**) **estudios** studies
estudioso,-a 1 *adj* studious
  2 *nm,f* specialist
estufa *nf (calentador)* heater; *(de leña)* stove
estupefaciente *nm* drug, narcotic
estupefacto,-a *adj* astounded, flabbergasted
estupendamente *adv* marvellously, wonderfully
estupendo,-a *adj* super, marvellous; **¡e.!** great!
estupidez *nf* stupidity
estúpido,-a 1 *adj* stupid
  2 *nm,f* idiot
estupor *nm* amazement, astonishment
estuve *pt indef de* **estar**
esvástica *nf* swastika
ETA *nf (abr* **Euzkadi Ta Askatasuna** *(Patria Vasca y Libertad))* ETA
etapa *nf* stage; **por etapas** in stages
etarra *nmf* = member of ETA
etc. *(abr* **etcétera***)* etc
etcétera *adv* etcetera
éter *nm* ether
etéreo,-a *adj* ethereal
eternidad *nf* eternity; *Fam* **una e.** ages
eterno,-a *adj* eternal
ética *nf* ethic; *(ciencia)* ethics *sing*

ético,-a *adj* ethical
etílico,-a *adj* ethylic; **alcohol e.** ethyl alcohol; **en estado e.** intoxicated; **intoxicación etílica** alcohol poisoning
etimología *nf* etymology
etimológico,-a *adj* etymological
etiope, etíope *adj & nmf* Ethiopian
Etiopía *nf* Ethiopia
etiqueta *nf* (a) *(de producto)* label (b) *(ceremonia)* etiquette; **de e.** formal
etiquetar *vt* to label
etnia *nf* ethnic group
étnico,-a *adj* ethnic
ETT *nf* (*abr* **Empresa de Trabajo Temporal**) temping agency
eucalipto *nm* eucalyptus
eucaristía *nf* eucharist
eufemismo *nm* euphemism
euforia *nf* euphoria
eufórico,-a *adj* euphoric
eureka *interj* eureka!
euro *nm (moneda)* euro
eurocomunismo *nm* Eurocommunism
eurodiputado,-a *nm,f* Euro MP
euromisil *nm* Euromissile
Europa *n* Europe
europeísmo *nm* Europeanism
europeizar [40] *vt* to europeanize
europeo,-a *adj & nm,f* European
euscalduna 1 *adj* Basque; *(que habla vasco)* Basque-speaking
   2 *nmf* Basque speaker
euskera *adj & nm* Basque
eutanasia *nf* euthanasia
evacuación *nf* evacuation
evacuar [47] *vt* to evacuate
evadir 1 *vt (respuesta, peligro, impuestos)* to avoid; *(responsabilidad)* to shirk
   2 **evadirse** *vpr* to escape
evaluación *nf* evaluation; *Educ* assessment; **e. continua** continuous assessment
evaluar [30] *vt* to evaluate, to assess
evangélico,-a *adj* evangelical
evangelio *nm* gospel
evangelista *nm* evangelist
evaporación *nf* evaporation
evaporar 1 *vt* to evaporate
   2 **evaporarse** *vpr* to evaporate; *Fig* to vanish
evasión *nf (fuga)* escape; *Fig* evasion; **e. fiscal** *o* **de impuestos** tax evasion
evasiva *nf* evasive answer
evasivo,-a *adj* evasive
evento *nm* (a) *(acontecimiento)* event (b) *(incidente)* contingency, unforeseen event
eventual *adj* (a) *(posible)* possible;

(gastos) incidental (b) *(trabajo, obrero)* casual, temporary
eventualidad *nf* contingency
eventualmente *adv* by chance; **los problemas que e. surjan** such problems as may arise

> ℓ Observa que las palabras inglesas **eventual** y **eventually** son falsos amigos y no son la traducción de las palabras españolas **eventual** y **eventualmente**. En inglés, **eventual** significa "final" o "consiguiente" y **eventually** "finalmente".

evidencia *nf* obviousness; **poner a algn en e.** to show sb up
evidenciar [43] *vt* to show, to demonstrate
evidente *adj* obvious
evidentemente *adv* obviously
evitar *vt* to avoid; *(prevenir)* to prevent; *(desastre)* to avert
evocador,-a *adj* evocative
evocar [44] *vt (traer a la memoria)* to evoke; *(acordarse de)* to recall
evolución *nf* evolution; *(desarrollo)* development
evolucionar *vi* to develop; *Biol* to evolve; **el enfermo evoluciona favorablemente** the patient is improving
ex 1 *pref* former, ex-; **ex alumno** former pupil, ex-student; **ex combatiente** *Br* ex-serviceman, *f* ex-servicewoman, *US* (war) veteran; **ex marido** ex-husband
   2 *nmf Fam* **mi ex** my ex
exabrupto *nm* sharp comment
exacerbar 1 *vt* (a) *(agravar)* to exacerbate, to aggravate (b) *(irritar)* to exasperate, to irritate
   2 **exacerbarse** *vpr* (a) *(agravarse)* to get worse (b) *(irritarse)* to feel exasperated
exactamente *adv* exactly, precisely
exactitud *nf* accuracy; **con e.** precisely
exacto,-a *adj* exact; **¡e.!** precisely!; **para ser e.** to be precise
exageración *nf* exaggeration
exagerado,-a *adj* exaggerated; *(excesivo)* excessive
exagerar 1 *vt* to exaggerate
   2 *vi* to overdo it
exaltado,-a 1 *adj (persona)* excitable, hot-headed
   2 *nm,f Fam* fanatic
exaltar 1 *vt (ensalzar)* to praise, to extol
   2 **exaltarse** *vpr (acalorarse)* to get overexcited, to get carried away
examen *nm* examination, exam; **e. de conducir** driving test; *Med* **e. médico** checkup

examinador,-a *nm,f* examiner
examinar 1 *vt* to examine
 2 examinarse *vpr* to take *o* sit an examination
exasperante *adj* exasperating
exasperar 1 *vt* to exasperate
 2 exasperarse *vpr* to become exasperated
Exc., Exca., Exc.a (*abr* **Excelencia**) Excellency
excavación *nf* excavation; (*en arqueología*) dig
excavadora *nf* digger
excavar *vt* to excavate, to dig
excedencia *nf* leave (of absence)
excedente *adj & nm* excess, surplus
exceder 1 *vt* to exceed, to surpass
 2 excederse *vpr* to go too far
excelencia *nf* (**a**) excellence; **por e.** par excellence (**b**) (*título*) **Su E.** His/Her Excellency
excelente *adj* excellent
excelso,-a *adj* sublime, lofty
excentricidad *nf* eccentricity
excéntrico,-a *adj* eccentric
excepción *nf* exception; **a e. de** with the exception of, except for; **de e.** exceptional; *Pol* **estado de e.** state of emergency
excepcional *adj* exceptional
excepto *adv* except (for), apart from
exceptuar [30] *vt* to except, to exclude
excesivo,-a *adj* excessive
exceso *nm* excess; **en e.** in excess, excessively; **e. de equipaje** excess baggage; **e. de velocidad** speeding
excitable *adj* excitable
excitación *nf* (*sentimiento*) excitement
excitante 1 *adj* exciting; *Med* stimulating
 2 *nm* stimulant
excitar 1 *vt* to excite
 2 excitarse *vpr* to get excited
exclamación *nf* exclamation
exclamar *vt & vi* to exclaim, to cry out
excluir [37] *vt* to exclude; (*rechazar*) to reject
exclusión *nf* exclusion
exclusiva *nf* *Prensa* exclusive; *Com* sole right
exclusive *adv* (*en fechas*) exclusive
exclusivo,-a *adj* exclusive
Excma. (*abr* **Excelentísima**) Most Excellent
Excmo. (*abr* **Excelentísimo**) Most Excellent
excomulgar [42] *vt Rel* to excommunicate
excomunión *nf* excommunication
excremento *nm* excrement

exculpar *vt* to exonerate
excursión *nf* excursion
excursionista *nmf* tripper; (*a pie*) hiker
excusa *nf* (*pretexto*) excuse; (*disculpa*) apology
excusado *nm* (*retrete*) toilet
excusar 1 *vt* (**a**) (*justificar*) to excuse (**b**) (*eximir*) to exempt (**de** from)
 2 excusarse *vpr* (*disculparse*) to apologize
execrar *vt* to execrate, to abhor
exención *nf* exemption; **e. de impuestos** tax exemption
exento,-a *adj* exempt, free (**de** from)
exequias *nfpl* funeral rites
exhalar *vt* to exhale, to breathe out; (*gas*) to give off, to emit; (*suspiro*) to heave
exhaustivo,-a *adj* exhaustive
exhausto,-a *adj* exhausted
exhibición *nf* exhibition
exhibicionista *nmf* exhibitionist
exhibir 1 *vt* (**a**) (*mostrar*) to exhibit, to display (**b**) (*lucir*) to show off
 2 exhibirse *vpr* to show off, to make an exhibition of oneself
exhortar *vt* to exhort
exhumar *vt* to exhume
exigencia *nf* (**a**) demand (**b**) (*requisito*) requirement
exigente *adj* demanding, exacting
exigir [57] *vt* to demand
exiguo,-a *adj* minute
exilado,-a 1 *adj* exiled, in exile
 2 *nm,f* exile
exilar 1 *vt* to exile, to send into exile
 2 exilarse *vpr* to go into exile
exiliado,-a *adj & nm,f =* **exilado,-a**
exiliar [43] *vt,* **exiliarse** *vpr =* **exilar**
exilio *nm* exile
eximio,-a *adj* distinguished, eminent
eximir *vt* to exempt (**de** from)
existencia *nf* (**a**) (*vida*) existence (**b**) *Com* **existencias** stock, stocks
existente *adj* existing; *Com* in stock
existir *vi* to exist, to be (in existence)
éxito *nm* success; **con é.** successfully; **tener é.** to be successful

---

🖉 Observa que la palabra inglesa **exit** es un falso amigo y no es la traducción de la palabra española **éxito**. En inglés, **exit** significa "salida".

---

exitoso,-a *adj* successful
éxodo *nm* exodus
exonerar *vt* to exonerate
exorbitante *adj* exorbitant, excessive
exorcista *nmf* exorcist
exorcizar [40] *vt* to exorcize

exótico,-a *adj* exotic
expandir 1 *vt* to expand
   2 expandirse *vpr (gas etc)* to expand; *(noticia)* to spread
expansión *nf* (**a**) expansion; *(de noticia)* spreading (**b**) *(diversión)* relaxation, recreation
expansionarse *vpr Fig (divertirse)* to relax, to let one's hair down
expatriado,-a *adj & nm,f* expatriate
expatriar [29] *vt* to exile, to banish
   2 expatriarse *vpr* to leave one's country
expectación *nf* excitement
expectativa *nf* expectancy; **estar a la e. de** to be on the lookout for
expectorante *nm* expectorant
expedición *nf* expedition
expedientar *vt* to place under enquiry
expediente *nm* (**a**) *(informe)* dossier, record; *(ficha)* file; *Educ* **e. académico** student's record; **abrirle e. a algn** to place sb under enquiry (**b**) *Jur* proceedings, action
expedir [6] *vt* (**a**) *(carta)* to send, to dispatch (**b**) *(pasaporte etc)* to issue
expedito,-a *adj* free, clear
expendedor,-a 1 *nm,f* seller
   2 *nm* **e. automático** vending machine
expendeduría *nf* tobacconist's
expensas *nfpl* **a e. de** at the expense of
experiencia *nf* (**a**) experience; **por e.** from experience (**b**) *(experimento)* experiment
experimentado,-a *adj* experienced
experimental *adj* experimental
experimentar 1 *vi* to experiment
   2 *vt* to undergo; *(aumento)* to show; *(pérdida)* to suffer; *(sensación)* to experience, to feel; *Med* **e. una mejoría** to improve, to make progress
experimento *nm* experiment
experto,-a *nm,f* expert
expiar [29] *vt* to expiate, to atone for
expirar *vi* to expire
explanada *nf* esplanade
explayarse *vpr* to talk at length (about)
explicación *nf* explanation
explicar [44] 1 *vt* to explain
   2 explicarse *vpr (persona)* to explain (oneself); **no me lo explico** I can't understand it
explicativo,-a *adj* explanatory
explícito,-a *adj* explicit
exploración *nf* exploration; *Téc* scanning; *Med (interna)* exploration; *(externa)* examination; *Mil* reconnaissance
explorador,-a *nm,f* (**a**) *(persona)* explorer (**b**) *Med* probe; *Téc* scanner

explorar *vt* to explore; *Med (internamente)* to explore; *(externamente)* to examine; *Téc* to scan; *Mil* to reconnoitre
explosión *nf* explosion, blast; **hacer e.** to explode; **motor de e.** internal combustion engine; **e. demográfica** population explosion
explosionar *vt & vi* to explode, to blow up
explosivo,-a *adj & nm* explosive
explotación *nf* (**a**) *(abuso)* exploitation (**b**) *(uso)* exploitation, working; *Agr* cultivation (of land); *(granja)* farm
explotador,-a *nm,f* exploiter
explotar 1 *vi (bomba)* to explode, to go off
   2 *vt* (**a**) *(aprovechar)* to exploit; *(recursos)* to tap; *(tierra)* to cultivate (**b**) *(abusar de)* to exploit
expoliar [43] *vt* to plunder, to pillage
exponente *nmf* exponent
exponer [19] *(pp* **expuesto**) **1** *vt* (**a**) *(mostrar)* to exhibit, to display (**b**) *(explicar)* to expound, to put forward (**c**) *(arriesgar)* to expose
   2 exponerse *vpr* to expose oneself (**a** to); **te expones a perder el trabajo** you run the risk of losing your job
exportación *nf* export
exportador,-a 1 *adj* exporting
   2 *nm,f* exporter
exportar *vt* to export
exposición *nf* (**a**) *Arte* exhibition; **e. universal** world fair; **sala de exposiciones** gallery (**b**) *(de hechos, ideas)* exposé (**c**) *Fot* exposure
exprés *adj* express; **(olla) e.** pressure cooker; **(café) e.** espresso (coffee)
expresamente *adv* specifically, expressly
expresar 1 *vt* to express; *(manifestar)* to state
   2 expresarse *vpr* to express oneself
expresión *nf* expression; **la mínima e.** the bare minimum
expresivo,-a *adj* expressive
expreso,-a 1 *adj* express; **con el fin e. de** with the express purpose of
   2 *nm Ferroc* express (train)
   3 *adv* on purpose, deliberately
exprimidor *nm* squeezer, juicer
exprimir *vt (limón)* to squeeze; *(zumo)* to squeeze out; *Fig (persona)* to exploit, to bleed dry
expropiar [43] *vt* to expropriate
expuesto,-a *adj* (**a**) *(sin protección)* exposed; **estar e. a** to be exposed to (**b**) *(peligroso)* risky, dangerous (**c**) *(exhibido)* on display, on show

expulsar *vt* (**a**) to expel, to throw out; *Dep (jugador)* to send off (**b**) *(gas etc)* to belch out

expulsión *nf* expulsion; *Dep* sending off

expurgar [42] *vt* to expurgate; *Fig* to purge

expuse *pt indef de* **exponer**

exquisito,-a *adj* exquisite; *(comida)* delicious; *(gusto)* refined

extasiado,-a *adj* ecstatic; **quedarse e.** to go into ecstasies o raptures

extasiarse [29] *vpr* to go into ecstasies o raptures

éxtasis *nm inv* ecstasy

extender [3] 1 *vt* (**a**) to extend; *(agrandar)* to enlarge (**b**) *(mantel, mapa)* to spread (out), to open (out); *(mano, brazo)* to stretch (out) (**c**) *(crema, mantequilla)* to spread (**d**) *(cheque)* to make out; *(documento)* to draw up; *(certificado)* to issue
2 extenderse *vpr* (**a**) *(en el tiempo)* to extend, to last (**b**) *(en el espacio)* to spread out, to stretch (**c**) *(rumor, noticia)* to spread, to extend (**d**) *Fig (hablar demasiado)* to go on

extendido,-a *adj* (**a**) extended; *(mapa, plano)* spread out, open; *(mano, brazo)* outstretched (**b**) *(costumbre, rumor)* widespread

extensible *adj* extending

extensión *nf (de libro etc)* length; *(de cuerpo)* size; *(de terreno)* area, expanse; *(edificio anexo)* extension; **en toda la e. de la palabra** in every sense of the word; **por e.** by extension

extensivo,-a *adj* **hacer e.** to extend; **ser e. a** to cover

extenso,-a *adj (terreno)* extensive; *(libro, película)* long

extenuar [30] 1 *vt* to exhaust
2 extenuarse *vpr* to exhaust oneself

exterior 1 *adj* (**a**) *(de fuera)* outer; *(puerta)* outside (**b**) *(política, deuda)* foreign; *Pol* **Ministerio de Asuntos Exteriores** Ministry of Foreign Affairs, *Br* ≃ Foreign Office, *US* ≃ State Department
2 *nm* (**a**) *(parte de fuera)* exterior, outside (**b**) *(extranjero)* abroad (**c**) **exteriores** *Cin* location

exteriorizar [40] *vt* to show

exteriormente *adv* outwardly

exterminar *vt* to exterminate

exterminio *nm* extermination

externalización *nf Com* outsourcing

externo,-a 1 *adj* external; *Farm* **de uso e.** for external use only
2 *nm,f Educ* day pupil

extinción *nf* extinction

extinguir [59] 1 *vt (fuego)* to extinguish, to put out; *(raza)* to wipe out
2 extinguirse *vpr (fuego)* to go out; *(especie)* to become extinct, to die out

extinto,-a *adj* extinct

extintor *nm* fire extinguisher

extirpar *vt* (**a**) *Med* to remove (**b**) *Fig* to eradicate, to stamp out

extorsión *nf* extortion

extorsionar *vt* to extort

extra 1 *adj* (**a**) *(suplementario)* extra; **horas e.** overtime; **paga e.** bonus (**b**) *(superior)* top-quality
2 *nm* extra
3 *nmf Cin & Teatro* extra

extra- *pref* extra-; **extramatrimonial** extramarital

extracción *nf* (**a**) extraction (**b**) *(en lotería)* draw

extracto *nm* (**a**) extract; **e. de fresa** strawberry extract; **e. de regaliz** liquorice; *Fin* **e. de cuenta** statement of account (**b**) *(resumen)* summary

extractor *nm* extractor

extradición *nf* extradition

extraer [25] *vt* to extract, to take out

extraescolar *adj (actividad etc)* extracurricular

extrafino,-a *adj* superfine

extralimitarse *vpr* to overstep the mark

extranjería *nf* **ley de e.** law on aliens

extranjero,-a 1 *adj* foreign
2 *nm,f* foreigner
3 *nm* abroad; **en el e.** abroad

extrañar 1 *vt* (**a**) *(sorprender)* to surprise; **no es de e.** it's hardly surprising (**b**) *Am (echar de menos)* to miss
2 extrañarse *vpr* **e. de** to be surprised at

extrañeza *nf* (**a**) *(sorpresa)* surprise, astonishment (**b**) *(singularidad)* strangeness

extraño,-a 1 *adj* strange; *Med* **cuerpo e.** foreign body
2 *nm,f* stranger

extraoficial *adj* unofficial

extraordinaria *nf (paga)* bonus

extraordinario,-a *adj* extraordinary; *Prensa* **edición extraordinaria** special edition

extrarradio *nm* outskirts, suburbs

extraterrestre *nmf* alien

extravagancia *nf* extravagance

extravagante *adj* odd, outlandish

extravertido,-a *adj* = **extrovertido,-a**

extraviado,-a *adj* lost, missing

extraviar [29] 1 *vt* to mislay, to lose
2 extraviarse *vpr* to be missing, to get mislaid

extremadamente *adv* extremely

extremado,-a *adj* extreme

Extremadura *n* Estremadura

extremar 1 *vt* **e. la prudencia** to be extremely careful

2 extremarse *vpr* to take great pains, to do one's utmost

extremaunción *nf* extreme unction

extremeño,-a 1 *adj* of/from Estremadura

2 *nm,f* person from Estremadura

extremidad *nf* (**a**) *(extremo)* end, tip (**b**) *Anat (miembro)* limb, extremity

extremista *adj & nmf* extremist

extremo,-a 1 *nm (de calle, cable)* end; *(máximo)* extreme; **en e.** very much; **en último e.** as a last resort

2 *nm,f (en fútbol)* winger; **e. derecha/ izquierda** outside right/left

3 *adj* extreme; **E. Oriente** Far East

extrovertido,-a *adj & nm,f* extrovert

exuberante *adj* exuberant; *(vegetación)* lush, abundant

eyaculación *nf* ejaculation; **e. precoz** premature ejaculation

eyacular *vi* to ejaculate

eyectable *adj* **asiento e.** ejector seat

F

F, f ['efe] *nf (la letra)* F, f
fa *nm Mús* F
fabada *nf* stew of beans, pork sausage and bacon
fábrica *nf* factory; **marca de f.** trademark; **precio de f.** factory *o* ex-works price

> 🖉 Observa que la palabra inglesa **fabric** es un falso amigo y no es la traducción de la palabra española **fábrica**. En inglés, **fabric** significa "tejido".

fabricación *nf* manufacture; **de f. casera** home-made; **de f. propia** our own make; **f. en cadena** mass production
fabricante *nmf* manufacturer
fabricar [44] *vt* (**a**) *Ind* to manufacture (**b**) *Fig (mentiras etc)* to fabricate
fabril *adj* manufacturing
fábula *nf* fable
fabuloso,-a *adj* fabulous
faca *nf* large curved knife
facción *nf* (**a**) *Pol* faction (**b**) **facciones** *(rasgos)* features
faccioso,-a 1 *adj* seditious
　2 *nm,f* rebel
faceta *nf* facet
facha¹ *nf Fam* appearance, look
facha² *nmf Pey* fascist
fachada *nf* façade
facial *adj* facial
fácil *adj* (**a**) easy; **f. de comprender** easy to understand (**b**) *(probable)* likely, probable; **es f. que ...** it's (quite) likely that ...
facilidad *nf* (**a**) *(sencillez)* easiness (**b**) *(soltura)* ease (**c**) *(servicio)* facility; **dar facilidades** to make things easy; *Com* **facilidades de pago** easy terms (**d**) **f. para los idiomas** gift for languages
facilitar *vt (proporcionar)* to provide, to supply (**a** with)
fácilmente *adv* easily
facineroso,-a *adj* criminal
facsímil, facsímile *nm* facsimile
factible *adj* feasible
fáctico,-a *adj* **poderes fácticos** vested interests
factor *nm* (**a**) factor (**b**) *Ferroc* luggage clerk

factoría *nf (fábrica)* factory
factura *nf* (**a**) *Com* invoice (**b**) *Arg (bollo)* = rolls and pastries
facturación *nf* (**a**) *Com* invoicing (**b**) *(de equipajes) (en aeropuerto)* check-in; *(en estación)* registration
facturar *vt* (**a**) *Com* to invoice (**b**) *(en aeropuerto)* to check in; *(en estación)* to register
facultad *nf* faculty; **facultades mentales** faculties
facultativo,-a 1 *adj* optional
　2 *nm,f* doctor
faena *nf* (**a**) *(tarea)* task (**b**) *Fam (mala pasada)* dirty trick (**c**)*Taurom* performance
faenar *vi* to fish
fagot *nm Mús* bassoon
fainá *nf Urug (plato)* = baked dough made with chickpea flour and olive oil, served with pizza
faisán *nm* pheasant
faja *nf* (**a**) *(corsé)* girdle, corset (**b**) *(banda)* sash (**c**) *(de terreno)* strip
fajo *nm (de ropa etc)* bundle; *(de billetes)* wad
falacia *nf* fallacy
falaz *adj* (**a**) *(erróneo)* fallacious (**b**) *(engañoso)* deceitful
falda *nf* (**a**) *(prenda)* skirt; **f. pantalón** culottes (**b**) *(de montaña)* slope, hillside (**c**) *(de mesa)* cover (**d**) *(regazo)* lap
faldero,-a *adj* **perro f.** lapdog
falencia *nf* (**a**) *Am Com (bancarrota)* bankruptcy (**b**) *CSur (error)* fault
falla¹ *nf Am (defecto)* defect, fault
falla² *nf Geol* fault
fallar¹ **1** *vi Jur* to rule
　2 *vt (premio)* to award
fallar² **1** *vi* to fail; **le falló la puntería** he missed his aim; *Fig* **no me falles** don't let me down
　2 *vt* to miss
fallecer [33] *vi Fml* to pass away, to die
fallecido,-a *adj* deceased
fallecimiento *nm* demise
fallido,-a *adj* unsuccessful, vain
fallo¹ *nm* (**a**) *(error)* mistake; **f. humano** human error (**b**) *(del corazón, de los frenos)* failure

fallo² *nm* (**a**)*Jur* judgement, sentence (**b**) *(en concurso)* awarding

falluto,-a *RP Fam* **1** *adj* phoney, hypocritical

2 *nm,f* hypocrite

falo *nm* phallus

falsear *vt* (**a**) *(informe etc)* to falsify; *(hechos, la verdad)* to distort (**b**) *(moneda)* to forge

falsedad *nf* (**a**) falseness, *(doblez)* hypocrisy (**b**) *(mentira)* falsehood

falsificar [44] *vt* to falsify; *(cuadro, firma, moneda)* to forge

falso,-a *adj* (**a**) false; **dar un paso en f.** *(tropezar)* to trip, to stumble; *Fig* to make a blunder; **jurar en f.** to commit perjury (**b**) *(persona)* insincere

falta *nf* (**a**) *(carencia)* lack; **por f. de** for want o lack of; **sin f.** without fail; **f. de educación** bad manners

(**b**) *(escasez)* shortage

(**c**) *(ausencia)* absence; **echar algo/a algn en f.** to miss sth/sb

(**d**) *(error)* mistake; *(defecto)* fault, defect; **f. de ortografía** spelling mistake; **sacar faltas a algo/a algn** to find fault with sth/sb

(**e**)*Jur* misdemeanour

(**f**) *(en fútbol)* foul; *(en tenis)* fault

(**g**) **hacer f.** to be necessary; **(nos) hace f. una escalera** we need a ladder; **harán f. dos personas para mover el piano** it'll take two people to move the piano; **no hace f. que ...** there is no need for ...

faltante *nm Am* deficit

faltar *vi* (**a**) *(no estar)* to be missing; **¿quién falta?** who is missing?

(**b**) *(escasear)* to be lacking o needed; **le falta confianza en sí mismo** he lacks confidence in himself; **¡lo que me faltaba!** that's all I needed!; **¡no faltaría o faltaba más!** *(por supuesto)* (but) of course!

(**c**) *(quedar)* to be left; **¿cuántos kilómetros faltan para Managua?** how many kilometres is it to Managua?; **ya falta poco para las vacaciones** it won't be long now till the holidays; **faltó poco para que me cayera** I very nearly fell

(**d**) **f. a la verdad** not to tell the truth; **f. al deber** to fail in one's duty; **f. a su palabra/promesa** to break one's word/promise; **f. al respeto a algn** to treat sb with disrespect

falto,-a *adj* **f. de** lacking in

fama *nf* (**a**) fame, renown; **de f. mundial** world-famous (**b**) *(reputación)* reputation

famélico,-a *adj* starving, famished

familia *nf* family; **estar en f.** to be among friends; **f. numerosa** large family

familiar 1 *adj* (**a**) *(de la familia)* family; **empresa f.** family business (**b**) *(conocido)* familiar

2 *nmf* relation, relative

familiaridad *nf* familiarity

familiarizarse [40] *vpr* **f. con** to familiarize oneself with

famoso,-a 1 *adj* famous

2 *nm* famous person

fan *nmf* fan

fanático,-a 1 *adj* fanatical

2 *nm,f* fanatic

fanatismo *nm* fanaticism

fanfarrón,-ona *Fam* **1** *adj* boastful

2 *nm,f* show-off

fanfarronear *vi Fam* *(chulear)* to show off; *(bravear)* to brag, to boast

fango *nm* (**a**) *(barro)* mud (**b**) *Fig* degradation

fantasear *vi* to daydream, to dream

fantasía *nf* fantasy; **joya de f.** imitation jewellery

fantasioso,-a *adj* imaginative

fantasma *nm* (**a**) *(espectro)* ghost (**b**) *Fam (fanfarrón)* braggart, show-off

fantasmal *adj* ghostly

fantástico,-a *adj* fantastic

fantoche *nm Pey* nincompoop, ninny

faraón *nm* Pharaoh

fardar *vi Fam* to show off

fardo *nm* bundle

farfullar *vt* to jabber

faringe *nf* pharynx

faringitis *nf* pharyngitis

fariseo,-a *nm,f (falso)* hypocrite

farmacéutico,-a 1 *adj* pharmaceutical

2 *nm,f* pharmacist, *Br* chemist, *US* druggist

farmacia *nf* (**a**) *(tienda) Br* chemist's (shop), *US* drugstore (**b**) *(ciencia)* pharmacology

fármaco *nm* medicine, medication

faro *nm* (**a**) *(torre)* lighthouse (**b**) *(de coche)* headlight, headlamp

farol *nm* (**a**) lantern; *(en la calle)* streetlight, streetlamp (**b**) *Fam (fanfarronada)* bragging; **tirarse un f.** to brag (**c**) *(en naipes)* bluff

farola *nf* streetlight, streetlamp

farolear *vi Fam* to brag

farolillo *nm Fig* **ser el f. rojo** to bring up the rear

farragoso,-a *adj* confused, rambling

farruco,-a *adj Fam* cocky

farsa *nf* farce

farsante *nmf* fake, impostor

fascículo *nm Impr* instalment

fascinador,-a, fascinante *adj* fascinating

fascinar *vt* to fascinate

fascismo *nm* fascism

fascista *adj & nmf* fascist

fase *nf* (a) *(etapa)* phase, stage (b) *Elec & Fís* phase

fastidiado,-a *adj Fam* (a) *(roto)* broken (b) *(enfermo)* sick; **tiene el estómago f.** he's got a bad stomach

fastidiar [43] 1 *vt* (a) *(molestar)* to annoy, to bother; *(dañar)* to hurt; *Fam* **¡no fastidies!** you're kidding! (b) *Fam (estropear)* to damage, to ruin; *(planes)* to spoil
  2 fastidiarse *vpr* (a) *(aguantarse)* to put up with it, to resign oneself; **que se fastidie** that's his tough luck (b) *Fam (estropearse)* to get damaged, to break down (c) **me he fastidiado el tobillo** I've hurt my ankle

fastidio *nm* nuisance

fastuoso,-a *adj* (a) *(acto)* splendid, lavish (b) *(persona)* lavish, ostentatious

fatal 1 *adj* (a) *Fam (muy malo)* awful, dreadful (b) *(mortal)* deadly, fatal (c) *(inexorable)* fateful, inevitable
  2 *adv Fam* awfully, terribly; **lo pasó f.** he had a rotten time

fatalidad *nf* (a) *(destino)* fate (b) *(desgracia)* misfortune

> 🖉 Observa que la palabra inglesa **fatality** es un falso amigo y no es la traducción de la palabra española **fatalidad**. En inglés, **fatality** significa "víctima mortal".

fatalista 1 *adj* fatalistic
  2 *nmf* fatalist

fatiga *nf* (a) *(cansancio)* fatigue (b) **fatigas** *(dificultades)* troubles, difficulties

fatigar [42] 1 *vt* to tire, to weary
  2 fatigarse *vpr* to tire, to become tired

fatigoso,-a *adj* tiring, exhausting

fatuo,-a *adj* (a) *(envanecido)* vain, conceited (b) *(necio)* fatuous, foolish

fauces *nfpl Fig* jaws

fauna *nf* fauna

favor *nm* favour; **por f.** please; **¿puedes hacerme un f.?** can you do me a favour?; **estar a f. de** to be in favour of; **haga el f. de** sentarse please sit down

favorable *adj* favourable; **f. a** in favour of

favorecedor,-a *adj* flattering

favorecer [33] *vt* (a) to favour (b) *(sentar bien)* to flatter

favoritismo *nm* favouritism

favorito,-a *adj & nm,f* favourite

faz *nf* (*pl* **faces**) *Literario (cara)* face

fe *nf* (a) faith; **de buena/mala fe** with good/dishonest intentions (b) *(certificado)* certificate; **fe de bautismo/matrimonio** baptism/marriage certificate (c) *Impr* **fe de erratas** errata

fealdad *nf* ugliness

febrero *nm* February

febril *adj* (a) *Med* feverish (b) *(actividad)* hectic

fecha *nf* (a) date; **f. límite** *o* **tope** deadline; **f. de caducidad** sell-by date; **hasta la f.** so far; **en f. próxima** at an early date (b) **fechas** *(época)* time; **el año pasado por estas fechas** this time last year

fechar *vt* to date

fechoría *nf* *(de niños)* mischief; *Literario* misdeed

fécula *nf* starch

fecundación *nf* fertilization; **f. in vitro** in vitro fertilization

fecundar *vt* to fertilize

fecundo,-a *adj* fertile

federación *nf* federation

federal *adj & nmf* federal

fehaciente *adj* (a) *Fml* authentic, reliable (b) *Jur* irrefutable; **documento** *o* **prueba f.** irrefutable proof

felicidad *nf* happiness; **(muchas) felicidades** *(en cumpleaños)* many happy returns

felicitación *nf* **tarjeta de f.** greetings card

felicitar *vt* to congratulate (**por** on); **¡te felicito!** congratulations!

feligrés,-esa *nm,f* parishioner

felino,-a *adj & nm* feline

feliz *adj* (a) *(contento)* happy; **¡felices Navidades!** Happy *o* Merry Christmas! (b) *(decisión etc)* fortunate

felonía *nf* treachery

felpa *nf* (a) *Tex* plush; **oso** *o* **osito de f.** teddy bear (b) *(para el pelo)* hairband

felpudo *nm* mat, doormat

femenino,-a *adj* feminine; *(equipo, ropa)* women's; **el sexo f.** the female sex, women

feminismo *nm* feminism

feminista *adj & nmf* feminist

fémur *nm* femur

fenecer [33] *vi Euf* to pass away, to die

fenomenal 1 *adj* (a) phenomenal (b) *Fam (fantástico)* great, terrific
  2 *adv Fam* wonderfully, marvellously; **lo pasamos f.** we had a fantastic time

fenómeno,-a 1 *nm* (a) phenomenon (b) *(prodigio)* genius (c) *(monstruo)* freak

2 *adj Fam* fantastic, terrific
3 *interj* fantastic!, terrific!
feo,-a 1 *adj* ugly; *(asunto etc)* nasty
  2 *nm Fam* **hacerle un f. a algn** to offend
  sb
féretro *nm* coffin
feria *nf* fair; **f. de muestras/del libro**
  trade/book fair
feriado,-a *Am* **1** *adj* **día f.** (public) holiday
  2 *nm* (public) holiday
ferial *adj* **recinto f.** *(de exposiciones)* exhibition centre; *(de fiestas)* fairground
ferina *adj* **tos f.** whooping cough
fermentar *vi* to ferment
fermento *nm* ferment
ferocidad *nf* ferocity, fierceness
feroz *adj* fierce, ferocious; **el lobo f.** the
  big bad wolf
férreo,-a *adj* ferreous; *Fig* iron
ferretería *nf* ironmonger's (shop), hardware store
ferrocarril *nm Br* railway, *US* railroad
ferroviario,-a *adj* rail, *Br* railway
ferry *nm* ferry
fértil *adj* fertile
fertilidad *nf* fertility
fertilizante 1 *adj* fertilizing
  2 *nm* fertilizer
fertilizar [40] *vt* to fertilize
ferviente *adj* fervent
fervor *nm* fervour
fervoroso,-a *adj* fervent
festejar *vt* to celebrate
festejos *nmpl* festivities
festín *nm* feast, banquet
festival *nm* festival
festividad *nf* festivity
festivo,-a 1 *adj* (**a**) *(ambiente etc)* festive
  (**b**) **día f.** holiday
  2 *nm* holiday
feta *nf RP* slice
fetal *adj* foetal
fetiche *nm* fetish
fétido,-a *adj* stinking, fetid
feto *nm* foetus
feudalismo *nm* feudalism
feudo *nm* fief; *Pol* stronghold
FEVE *nm* (*abr* **Ferrocarriles de Vía Estre-
  cha**) = Spanish narrow-gauge railways
FF.AA. *nfpl* (*abr* **Fuerzas Armadas**) Armed
  Forces
FF.CC. *nmpl* (*abr* **ferrocarriles**) railways
fiabilidad *nf* reliability, trustworthiness
fiable *adj* reliable, trustworthy
fiaca *nf Méx, CSur Fam (pereza)* laziness
fiador,-a *nm,f* guarantor; **salir** *o* **ser f. de
  algn** *(pagar fianza)* to stand bail for sb;
  (avalar) to vouch for sb

fiambre *nm* (**a**) *Culin* cold meat (**b**) *Fam
  (cadáver)* stiff, corpse
fiambrera *nf* lunch box
fianza *nf (depósito)* deposit; *Jur* bail; **en
  libertad bajo f.** on bail
fiar [29] 1 *vt* (**a**) *(avalar)* to guarantee (**b**)
  (vender sin cobrar) to sell on credit
  2 fiarse *vpr* **fiarse (de)** to trust
fiasco *nm* fiasco
fibra *nf* fibre; *(de madera)* grain; **f. de
  vidrio** fibreglass
ficción *nf* fiction
ficha *nf* (**a**) *(tarjeta)* filing card; **f. técnica**
  specifications,   technical   data;   *Cin*
  credits (**b**) *(en juegos)* counter; *(de ajedrez)* piece, man; *(de dominó)* domino
fichado,-a *adj* **está f. por la policía** he has
  a police record
fichaje *nm Dep* signing
fichar 1 *vt* (**a**) to put on file (**b**) *Dep* to sign
  up
  2 *vi* (**a**) *(en el trabajo) (al entrar)* to clock
  in; *(al salir)* to clock out (**b**) *Dep* to sign
fichero *nm* card index
ficticio,-a *adj* fictitious
fidedigno,-a *adj* reliable, trustworthy;
  fuentes fidedignas reliable sources
fidelidad *nf* faithfulness; **alta f.** high
  fidelity, hi-fi
fideo *nm* noodle
fiebre *nf* fever; **tener f.** to have a temperature
fiel 1 *adj* (**a**) *(leal)* faithful, loyal (**b**)
  (exacto) accurate, exact
  2 *nm* (**a**) *(de balanza)* needle, pointer
  (**b**) *Rel* **los fieles** the congregation
fieltro *nm* felt
fiera *nf* (**a**) wild animal; *Fam* **estaba hecho una f.** he was hopping mad (**b**)
  Taurom bull
fiero,-a *adj (salvaje)* wild; *(feroz)* fierce,
  ferocious
fierro *nm Am (hierro)* iron
fiesta *nf* (**a**) *(entre amigos)* party (**b**) **día
  de f.** holiday (**c**) *Rel* feast; **f. de guardar**
  holy day of obligation (**d**) *(festividad)*
  celebration, festivity
figura *nf* figure
figurado,-a *adj* figurative; **en sentido f.**
  figuratively
figurar 1 *vi (en lista)* to figure
  2 figurarse *vpr* (**a**) to imagine, to suppose; **ya me lo figuraba** I thought as
  much (**b**) **¡figúrate!, ¡figúrese!** just imagine!
figurinista *nmf Teatro & Cin* costume
  designer
fijador *nm* (**a**) *(gomina)* gel (**b**) *Fot* fixative

fijamente *adv* mirar f. to stare
fijar 1 *vt* to fix; **prohibido f. carteles** *(en letrero)* post no bills
 2 fijarse *vpr* (**a**) *(darse cuenta)* to notice (**b**) *(poner atención)* to pay attention, to watch
fijo,-a *adj* (**a**) fixed; **sin domicilio f.** of no fixed abode (**b**) *(trabajo)* steady
fila *nf* (**a**) file; **en f. india** in single file; **poner en f.** to line up (**b**) *(de cine, teatro)* row (**c**) *Mil* **filas** ranks; **llamar a algn a filas** to call sb up; **¡rompan filas!** fall out!, dismiss!
filamento *nm* filament
filantropía *nf* philanthropy
filántropo,-a *nm,f* philanthropist
filarmónico,-a *adj* philharmonic
filatelia *nf* philately, stamp collecting
filete *nm (de carne, pescado)* fillet
filiación *nf Pol* affiliation
filial 1 *adj* (**a**) *(de hijos)* filial (**b**) *Com* subsidiary
 2 *nf Com* subsidiary
filigrana *nf* (**a**) filigree (**b**) *Fig* **filigranas** intricacy, intricate work
Filipinas *npl* **(las) F.** (the) Philippines
filipino,-a *adj & nm,f* Philippine, Filipino
film *nm* film
filmar *vt* to film, to shoot
filme *nm* film
fílmico,-a *adj* film
filmoteca *nf (archivo)* film library
filo *nm* (cutting) edge; **al f. de la medianoche** on the stroke of midnight; *Fig* **de doble f.** double-edged
filón *nm* (**a**) *Min* seam, vein (**b**) *Fig (buen negocio)* gold mine
filoso,-a *adj Am* sharp
filosofal *adj* **piedra f.** philosopher's stone
filosofía *nf* philosophy; *Fig* **con f.** philosophically
filosófico,-a *adj* philosophical
filósofo,-a *nm,f* philosopher
filtración *nf* filtration; *(de información)* leak
filtrar 1 *vt* (**a**) to filter (**b**) *(información)* to leak
 2 • filtrarse *vpr* (**a**) *(líquido)* to seep (**b**) *(información)* to leak out
filtro *nm* filter
fin *nm* (**a**) *(final)* end; **dar** *o* **poner f. a** to put an end to; **llegar** *o* **tocar a su f.** to come to an end; **en f.** anyway; **¡por** *o* **al f.!** at last!; **f. de semana** weekend; **al f. y al cabo** when all's said and done; **noche de F. de Año** New Year's Eve (**b**) *(objetivo)* purpose, aim; **a f. de** in order to, so as to;

a f. de que in order that, so that; **con el f. de** with the intention of
final 1 *adj* final
 2 *nm* end; **al f.** in the end; **f. de línea** terminal; **f. feliz** happy ending; **a finales de octubre** at the end of October
 3 *nf Dep* final
finalidad *nf* purpose, aim
finalista 1 *nmf* finalist
 2 *adj* in the final
finalizar [40] *vt & vi* to end, to finish
finalmente *adv* finally
financiación *nf* financing
financiar [43] *vt* to finance
financiero,-a 1 *adj* financial
 2 *nm,f* financier
financista *nmf Am* financier, financial expert
finanzas *nfpl* finances
finca *nf (inmueble)* property; *(de campo)* country house
finés,-esa *adj & nm,f* = finlandés,-esa
fingido,-a *adj* feigned, false; **nombre f.** assumed name
fingir [57] 1 *vt* to feign
 2 fingirse *vpr* to pretend to be
finlandés,-esa 1 *adj* Finnish
 2 *nm,f (persona)* Finn
 3 *nm (idioma)* Finnish
Finlandia *n* Finland
fino,-a 1 *adj* (**a**) *(hilo, capa)* fine (**b**) *(flaco)* thin (**c**) *(educado)* refined, polite (**d**) *(oído)* sharp, acute; *(olfato)* keen (**e**) *(humor, ironía)* subtle
 2 *nm (vino)* = type of dry sherry
finta *nf (en boxeo)* feint; *(en fútbol)* dummy
finura *nf* (**a**) *(refinamiento)* refinement, politeness (**b**) *(sutileza)* subtlety
firma *nf* (**a**) signature (**b**) *(empresa)* firm, company
firmamento *nm* firmament
firmante *adj & nmf* signatory; **el** *o* **la abajo f.** the undersigned
firmar *vt* to sign
firme 1 *adj* (**a**) firm; *Fig* **mantenerse f.** to hold one's ground; **tierra f.** terra firma (**b**) *Mil* **¡firmes!** attention!
 2 *nm (de carretera)* road surface
 3 *adv* hard
firmemente *adv* firmly
firmeza *nf* firmness
fiscal 1 *adj* fiscal, tax
 2 *nmf Jur* public prosecutor, *US* district attorney
fisco *nm* treasury, exchequer
fisgar [42] *vi Fam* to snoop, to pry
fisgón,-ona *nm,f* snooper

fisgonear *vi* to snoop, to pry
física *nf* physics *sing*
físico,-a 1 *adj* physical
  2 *nm,f (profesión)* physicist
  3 *nm* physique
fisión *nf* fission
fisioterapeuta *nmf* physiotherapist
fisioterapia *nf Med* physiotherapy
fisonomía *nf* physiognomy
fisonomista *nmf Fam* **ser buen/mal f.** to be good/no good at remembering faces
fisura *nf* fissure
flácido,-a *adj* flaccid, flabby
flaco,-a 1 *adj* (**a**) *(delgado)* skinny (**b**) *Fig* **punto f.** weak spot
  2 *nm,f Am Fam (como apelativo)* **¿cómo estás, flaca?** hey, how are you doing?
flagelar *vt* to flagellate
flagelo *nm (látigo)* whip; *Fig* scourge
flagrante *adj* flagrant; **en f. delito** red-handed
flamante *adj* (**a**) **nuevecito f.** *(nuevo)* brand-new (**b**) *(vistoso)* splendid, brilliant
flamenco,-a 1 *adj* (**a**) *Mús* flamenco (**b**) *(de Flandes)* Flemish
  2 *nm* (**a**) *Mús* flamenco (**b**) *Orn* flamingo (**c**) *(idioma)* Flemish
flan *nm* crème caramel

> ℓ Observa que la palabra inglesa **flan** es un falso amigo y no es la traducción de la palabra española **flan**. En inglés, **flan** significa "tarta".

flanco *nm* flank, side
flanquear *vt* to flank
flaquear *vi (fuerzas, piernas)* to weaken, to give way
flaqueza *nf* weakness
flash *nm Fot* flash
flato *nm* wind, flatulence
flatulencia *nf* flatulence
flauta *nf* flute; **f. dulce** recorder
flautín *nm (instrumento)* piccolo
flautista *nmf Mús* flute player, flautist, *US* flutist
flecha *nf* arrow
flechazo *nm Fig (enamoramiento)* love at first sight
fleco *nm* fringe
flema *nf* phlegm
flemático,-a *adj* phlegmatic
flemón *nm* gumboil, abscess
flequillo *nm Br* fringe, *US* bangs
fletar *vt* to charter
flete *nm* (**a**) *(alquiler)* charter (**b**) *(carga)* freight
flexibilidad *nf* flexibility
flexible *adj* flexible

flexión *nf* (**a**) *Gram* inflection (**b**) **flexiones** push-ups, *Br* press-ups
flexionar *vt* to bend; *(músculo)* to flex
flexo *nm* reading lamp
flipante *adj Fam* great, cool
flipar *vt Fam* **le flipan las motos** he's crazy about motorbikes
flirtear *vi* to flirt
flirteo *nm* flirting
flojear *vi (ventas etc)* to fall off, to go down; *(piernas)* to weaken, to grow weak; *(memoria)* to fail; *Andes Fam (holgazanear)* to laze around o about
flojedad *nf* weakness
flojera *nf Fam* weakness, faintness
flojo,-a *adj* (**a**) *(tornillo, cuerda etc)* loose, slack (**b**) *(perezoso)* lazy, idle; *(exámen, trabajo, resultado)* poor
flor *nf* (**a**) flower; **en f.** in blossom; *Fig* **en la f. de la vida** in the prime of life; *Fig* **la f. y nata** the cream (of society) (**b**) **a f. de piel** skin-deep
flora *nf* flora
floreado,-a *adj* flowery
florecer [33] *vi* (**a**) *(plantas)* to flower (**b**) *Fig (negocio)* to flourish, to thrive
floreciente *adj Fig* flourishing, prosperous
Florencia *n* Florence
florero *nm* vase
floricultura *nf* flower growing, floriculture
florido,-a *adj* (**a**) *(con flores)* flowery (**b**) *(estilo)* florid
floripondio *nm Pey (adorno)* heavy ornamentation
florista *nmf* florist
floristería *nf* florist's (shop)
flota *nf* fleet
flotador *nm* (**a**) *(de pesca)* float (**b**) *(para nadar)* rubber ring
flotar *vi* to float
flote *nm* floating; **a f.** afloat; **sacar a f. un negocio** to put a business on a sound footing
flotilla *nf* flotilla
fluctuación *nf* fluctuation
fluctuar [30] *vi* to fluctuate
fluidez *nf* fluency
fluido,-a 1 *adj* fluid; *(estilo etc)* fluent
  2 *nm* fluid; **f. eléctrico** current
fluir [37] *vi* to flow
flujo *nm* (**a**) flow (**b**) rising tide; **f. y reflujo** ebb and flow (**c**) *Fís* flux (**d**) *Med* discharge (**e**) *Informát* stream
flúor *nm* fluorine
fluorescente *adj* fluorescent
fluvial *adj* river

FM *nf* (*abr* **Frecuencia Modulada**) FM

FMI *nm* (*abr* **Fondo Monetario Internacional**) IMF

fobia *nf* phobia (**a** about)

foca *nf* seal

foco *nm* (**a**) *Elec* spotlight, floodlight (**b**) *(de ideas, revolución etc)* centre, focal point (**c**) *Am (de coche)* (car) headlight; *(farola)* street light (**d**) *Col, Méx (bombilla)* light bulb

fofo,-a *adj* soft; *(persona)* flabby

fogata *nf* bonfire

fogón *nm (de cocina)* ring

fogonazo *nm* flash

fogosidad *nf* ardour, fire

fogoso,-a *adj* fiery, spirited

fogueo *nm* **cartucho de f.** blank cartridge

fólder *nm Andes, CAm, Méx (carpeta)* folder

folio *nm* sheet of paper

folklore *nm* folklore

folklórico,-a *adj* **música folklórica** folk music

follaje *nm* foliage

follar *muy Fam* (**a**) *vi* to screw, to shag

2 *vt (suspender)* to fail

3 **follarse** *upr* **f. a algn** to screw sb, to shag sb

folletín *nm* (**a**) *(relato)* newspaper serial (**b**) *Fig* melodrama

folleto *nm* leaflet; *(turístico)* brochure

follón *nm Fam* (**a**) *(alboroto)* rumpus, shindy; **armar (un) f.** to kick up a rumpus (**b**) *(enredo, confusión)* mess, trouble; **meterse en un f.** to get into a mess (**c**) **un f. de** *(montón)* a load of

follonero,-a *nm,f* troublemaker

fomentar *vt* to promote

fomento *nm* promotion

fonda *nf* inn

fondear *vi* to anchor

fondista *nmf Dep* long-distance runner

fondo¹ *nm* (**a**) *(parte más baja)* bottom; **a f.** thoroughly; **al f. de la calle** at the bottom of the street; **tocar f.** *Náut* to touch bottom; *Fig* to reach rock bottom; *Fig* **en el f. es bueno** deep down he's kind; **bajos fondos** dregs of society; **doble f.** false bottom

(**b**) *(de habitación)* back; *(de pasillo)* end

(**c**) *(segundo término)* background; **música de f.** background music

(**d**) *Prensa* **artículo de f.** leading article

(**e**) *Dep* **corredor de f.** long-distance runner; **esquí de f.** cross-country skiing

(**f**) *RP (patio)* back patio

(**g**) *Carib, Méx (prenda)* petticoat

fondo² *nm Fin* fund; **cheque sin fondos** bad cheque; *Fam* **f. común** kitty

fonendoscopio *nm* stethoscope

fonética *nf* phonetics *sing*

fonético,-a *adj* phonetic

fono *nm Am Fam* phone

fontanería *nf* plumbing

fontanero,-a *nm,f* plumber

footing *nm* jogging; **hacer f.** to go jogging

forajido,-a *nm,f* outlaw

foráneo,-a *adj* foreign

forastero,-a *nm,f* outsider, stranger

forcejear *vi* to wrestle, to struggle

forcejeo *nm* struggle

fórceps *nm inv* forceps

forense 1 *adj* forensic

2 *nmf* **(médico) f.** forensic surgeon

forestal *adj* forest; **repoblación f.** reafforestation

forjado,-a *adj* wrought

forjar *vt (metal)* to forge; *Fig* to create, to make

forma *nf* (**a**) form, shape; **en f. de L** L-shaped; **¿qué f. tiene?** what shape is it? (**b**) *(manera)* way; **de esta f.** in this way; **de f. que** so that; **de todas formas** anyway, in any case; **no hubo f. de convencerla** there was no way we could convince her; **f. de pago** method of payment (**c**) *Dep* form; **estar en f.** to be on form; **estar en baja f.** to be off form (**d**) *Rel* **Sagrada F.** Host (**e**) **formas** *(modales)* manners

formación *nf* (**a**) formation (**b**) *(educación)* upbringing (**c**) *(enseñanza)* training; **f. profesional** vocational training

formal *adj* (**a**) formal (**b**) *(serio)* serious, serious-minded (**c**) *(fiable)* reliable, dependable

formalidad *nf* (**a**) formality (**b**) *(seriedad)* seriousness (**c**) *(fiabilidad)* reliability (**d**) **formalidades** *(trámites)* formalities

formalizar [40] 1 *vt* to formalize

2 **formalizarse** *upr* to settle down

formar 1 *vt* (**a**) to form; **f. parte de algo** to be a part of sth (**b**) *(educar)* to bring up; *(enseñar)* to educate, to train

2 **formarse** *upr* (**a**) to be formed, to form; **se formó un charco** a puddle formed; **f. una impresión de algo** to get an impression of sth (**b**) *(educarse)* to be educated o trained

formatear *vt Informát* to format

formato *nm* format; *(del papel)* size

formica® *nf* Formica®

formidable *adj* (**a**) *(estupendo)* wonderful, terrific (**b**) *(espantoso)* formidable

fórmula *nf* formula; *Aut* **f. uno** formula one

formular *vt (quejas, peticiones)* to make; *(deseo)* to express; *(pregunta)* to ask; *(una teoría)* to formulate

formulario *nm* form

fornicación *nf* fornication

fornicar [44] *vi* to fornicate

fornido,-a *adj* strapping, hefty

foro *nm* (**a**) forum (**b**) *(mesa redonda)* round table (**c**) *Teatro* back (of the stage) (**d**) *Jur* law court, court of justice

forofo,-a *nm,f Fam* fan, supporter

forrado,-a *adj* lined; *Fam* **estar f.** to be well-heeled, to be well-off

forraje *nm* fodder

forrar 1 *vt (por dentro)* to line; *(por fuera)* to cover
   2 forrarse *vpr Fam (de dinero)* to make a packet

forro *nm* (**a**) *(por dentro)* lining; *(por fuera)* cover, case (**b**) *RP Fam (preservativo)* rubber, condom

fortalecer [33] *vt* to fortify, to strengthen

fortaleza *nf* (**a**) strength; *(de espíritu)* fortitude (**b**) *Mil* fortress, stronghold

fortificante 1 *adj* fortifying
   2 *nm* tonic

fortificar [44] *vt* to fortify

fortísimo,-a *adj* very strong

fortuito,-a *adj* fortuitous

fortuna *nf* (**a**) *(destino)* fortune, fate (**b**) *(suerte)* luck; **por f.** fortunately (**c**) *(capital)* fortune

forzado,-a *adj* forced; **a marchas forzadas** at a brisk pace; **trabajos forzados** hard labour

forzar [2] *vt* (**a**) *(obligar)* to force; **f. a algn a hacer algo** to force sb to do sth (**b**) *(puerta, candado)* to force, to break open

forzosamente *adv* necessarily

forzoso,-a *adj* obligatory, compulsory; *Av* **aterrizaje f.** forced landing

fosa *nf* (**a**) *(sepultura)* grave (**b**) *(hoyo)* pit (**c**) *Anat* **fosas nasales** nostrils

fosforescente *adj* phosphorescent

fósforo *nm (cerilla)* match

fósil *adj & nm* fossil

fosilizarse [40] *vpr* to fossilize, to become fossilized

foso *nm* (**a**) *(hoyo)* pit (**b**) *(de fortificación)* moat (**c**) *(en garage)* inspection pit

foto *nf Fam* photo; **sacar/echar una f.** to take a photo

fotocopia *nf* photocopy

fotocopiadora *nf* photocopier

fotocopiar [43] *vt* to photocopy

fotogénico,-a *adj* photogenic

fotografía *nf* (**a**) photograph; **echar** *o* **hacer** *o* **sacar fotografías** to take photographs (**b**) *(arte)* photography

fotografiar [29] *vt* to photograph, to take a photograph of

fotográfico,-a *adj* photographic

fotógrafo,-a *nm,f* photographer

fotograma *nm* still, shot

fotomatón *nm* passport photo machine

fotómetro *nm* light meter, exposure meter

FP *nf Educ (abr* **Formación Profesional***)* vocational training

frac *nm (pl* **fracs** *o* **fraques***)* dress coat, tails

fracasado,-a 1 *adj* unsuccessful
   2 *nm,f (persona)* failure

fracasar *vi* to fail

fracaso *nm* failure

> 📝 Observa que la palabra inglesa **fracas** es un falso amigo y no es la traducción de la palabra española **fracaso**. En inglés, **fracas** significa "gresca, refriega".

---

fracción *nf* (**a**) fraction (**b**) *Pol* faction

fraccionamiento *nm Méx (urbanización)* housing estate

fraccionar *vt,* **fraccionarse** *vpr* to break up, to split up

fraccionario,-a *adj* fractional; **moneda fraccionaria** small change

fractura *nf* fracture

fracturar *vt,* **fracturarse** *vpr* to fracture, to break

fragancia *nf* fragrance

fragata *nf* frigate

frágil *adj* (**a**) *(quebradizo)* fragile (**b**) *(débil)* frail

fragmentar 1 *vt* to fragment
   2 fragmentarse *vpr* to break up

fragmento *nm* fragment; *(de novela etc)* passage

fragor *nm* din

fragua *nf* forge

fraguar [45] *vt* (**a**) *(metal)* to forge (**b**) *(plan)* to think up, to fabricate; *(conspiración)* to hatch

fraile *nm* friar, monk

frailecillo *nm* puffin

frambuesa *nf* raspberry

francamente *adv* frankly

francés,-esa 1 *adj* French; *Culin* **tortilla francesa** plain omelette
   2 *nm,f (hombre)* Frenchman; *(mujer)* Frenchwoman
   3 *nm (idioma)* French

Francfort, Francfurt *n* Frankfurt; *Culin* **salchicha estilo f.** frankfurter

Francia *n* France

francmasón,-ona *nm,f* freemason
franco¹,-a *adj* (**a**) *(persona)* frank (**b**) *Com* **f. a bordo** free on board; **f. fábrica** ex-works; **puerto f.** free port (**c**) *CSur (día)* **me dieron el día f.** they gave me the day off
franco² *nm Fin (moneda)* franc
francotirador,-a *nm,f* sniper
franela *nf* (**a**) *(paño)* flannel (**b**) *Bol, Col, Ven (camiseta)* T-shirt
franja *nf (de terreno)* strip; *(de bandera)* stripe; *Cost* fringe, border
franquear *vt* (**a**) *(atravesar)* to cross; *Fig (dificultad, obstáculo)* to overcome (**b**) *(carta)* to frank (**c**) *(camino, paso)* to free, to clear
franqueo *nm* postage
franqueza *nf* frankness
franquicia *nf* exemption; *Com* franchise
franquismo *nm Hist* (**a**) *(ideología)* Francoism (**b**) **el f.** *(régimen)* the Franco regime
franquista *adj & nmf* Francoist
frasco *nm* small bottle, flask
frase *nf (oración)* sentence; *(expresión)* phrase; **f. hecha** set phrase *o* expression
fraternidad *nf* brotherhood, fraternity
fraternizar [40] *vi* to fraternize
fraterno,-a *adj* fraternal, brotherly
fraude *nm* fraud; **f. fiscal** tax evasion
fraudulento,-a *adj* fraudulent
fray *nm Rel* brother
frazada *nf Am* blanket
frecuencia *nf* frequency; **con f.** frequently, often
frecuentar *vt* to frequent
frecuente *adj* frequent
frecuentemente *adv* frequently, often
fregadero *nm* (kitchen) sink
fregado¹ *nm* (**a**) *(lavado)* washing (**b**) *Fam (follón)* racket
fregado²,-a *adj Am Fam* (**a**) *(persona) (difícil)* tiresome, annoying (**b**) *(objeto) (roto)* broken
fregar [1] *vt* (**a**) *(lavar)* to wash; *(suelo)* to mop (**b**) *Am Fam (molestar)* to annoy, to irritate (**c**) *Am Fam (romper)* to bust, to break
fregón,-ona *adj Am* annoying
fregona *nf* mop
freidora *nf* (deep fat) fryer
freír [56] *(pp frito)* **1** *vt* to fry
  2 freírse *upr* to fry; *Fig* **f. de calor** to be roasting
frenar *vt* to brake; *Fig (inflación etc)* to slow down; *(impulsos)* to restrain
frenazo *nm* sudden braking; **dar un f.** to jam on the brakes

frenesí *nm* frenzy
frenético,-a *adj* frantic
freno *nm* (**a**) brake; **pisar/soltar el f.** to press/release the brake; **f. de disco/tambor** disc/drum brake; **f. de mano** handbrake (**b**) *(de caballería)* bit (**c**) *Fig* curb, check; **poner f. a algo** to curb sth
frente 1 *nm* front; **al f. de** at the head of; **chocar de f.** to crash head on; **hacer f. a algo** to face sth, to stand up to sth
  2 *nf Anat* forehead; **f. a f.** face to face
  3 *adv* **f. a** in front of, opposite
fresa *nf* (**a**) strawberry (**b**) *Téc* milling cutter
fresca *nf Fam* cheeky remark
fresco,-a 1 *adj* (**a**) *(frío)* cool (**b**) *(comida, fruta)* fresh (**c**) *(reciente)* fresh, new (**d**) *(descarado)* cheeky, shameless; **se quedó tan f.** he didn't bat an eyelid; **¡qué f.!** what a nerve!
  2 *nm* (**a**) *(frescor)* fresh air, cool air; **al f.** in the cool; **hace f.** it's chilly (**b**) *Arte* fresco
frescor *nm* freshness
frescura *nf* (**a**) freshness (**b**) *(desvergüenza)* cheek, nerve
fresno *nm* ash tree
fresón *nm* (large) strawberry
frialdad *nf* coldness
fríamente *adv* coolly
fricción *nf* (**a**) friction (**b**) *(masaje)* massage
friega *nf* rub
friegaplatos *nmf inv (persona)* dishwasher
frigider *nm Andes* refrigerator, fridge
frígido,-a *adj* frigid
frigorífico,-a 1 *nm* refrigerator, fridge
  2 *adj* **cámara frigorífica** cold store
frijol, fríjol *nm Andes, CAm, Carib, Méx* bean
frío,-a 1 *adj* (**a**) cold (**b**) *(indiferente)* cold, cool, indifferent; **su comentario me dejó f.** her remark left me cold
  2 *nm* cold; **hace f.** it's cold
friolento,-a *adj Am* sensitive to the cold
friolera *nf Fam* **la f. de diez mil pesetas/ dos horas** a mere ten thousand pesetas/ two hours
friolero,-a *adj* sensitive to the cold
fritanga *nf* fried food; *Am* greasy food
frito,-a 1 *adj* (**a**) *Culin* fried (**b**) *Fam* exasperated, fed up; **me tienes f.** I'm sick to death of you
  2 *nm* **fritos** fried food
frívolo,-a *adj* frivolous
frondoso,-a *adj* leafy, luxuriant
frontera *nf* frontier

fronterizo,-a *adj* frontier, border; **países fronterizos** neighbouring countries
frontón *nm Dep* pelota
frotar 1 *vt* to rub
  2 frotarse *vpr* to rub; **f. las manos** to rub one's hands together
fructífero,-a *adj (árbol)* fruit-bearing; *(esfuerzo)* fruitful
frugal *adj* frugal
fruncir [52] *vt* (**a**) *Cost* to gather (**b**) *(labios)* to purse, to pucker; **f. el ceño** to frown, to knit one's brow
frustración *nf* frustration
frustrado,-a *adj* frustrated; **intento f.** unsuccessful attempt
frustrante *adj* frustrating
frustrar 1 *vt* to frustrate; *(defraudar)* to disappoint
  2 frustrarse *vpr* (**a**) *(esperanza)* to fail, to go awry (**b**) *(persona)* to be frustrated *o* disappointed
fruta *nf* fruit; **f. del tiempo** fresh fruit
frutería *nf* fruit shop
frutero,-a 1 *nm,f* fruiterer
  2 *nm* fruit dish *o* bowl
frutilla *nf Bol, CSur, Ecuad* strawberry
fruto *nm* fruit; **frutos secos** nuts; **dar f.** to bear fruit; *Fig (dar buen resultado)* to be fruitful; **sacar f. de algo** to profit from sth
fu *interj* **ni fu ni fa** so-so
fucsia *nf* fuchsia
fuego *nm* (**a**) fire; **fuegos artificiales** fireworks (**b**) *(lumbre)* light; **¿me da f., por favor?** have you got a light, please? (**c**) *Culin* **a f. lento** on a low flame; *(al horno)* in a slow oven
fuel, fuel-oil *nm* diesel
fuente *nf* (**a**) fountain; *Chile, Col, Méx, Ven* **f. de soda** *(cafetería)* cafe *(serving soft drinks and alcohol)* (**b**) *(recipiente)* dish, serving dish (**c**) *(de información)* source
fuera¹ *adv* (**a**) outside, out; **quédate f.** stay outside; **sal f.** go out; **desde f.** from (the) outside; **por f.** on the outside; **la puerta de f.** the outer door (**b**) **f. de** out of; **f. de serie** extraordinary; *Fig* **estar f. de sí** to be beside oneself (**c**) *Dep* **el equipo de f.** the away team; **jugar f.** to play away; **f. de juego** offside
fuera² **1** *subj imperf de* **ir**
  2 *subj imperf de* **ser**
fuero *nm* (**a**) *Hist* code of laws (**b**) *Fig* **en tu f. interno** deep down, in your heart of hearts
fuerte 1 *adj* strong; *(dolor)* severe; *(sonido)* loud; *(comida)* heavy; **el plato f.** the main course; *Fig* the most important event

  2 *nm* (**a**) *(fortaleza)* fort (**b**) *(punto fuerte)* forte, strong point
  3 *adv* **¡abrázame f.!** hold me tight!; **comer f.** to eat a lot; **¡habla más f.!** speak up!; **¡pégale f.!** hit him hard!
fuerza *nf* (**a**) *(fortaleza)* strength; *Fig* **a f. de** by dint of (**b**) *(violencia)* force; **a la f.** *(por obligación)* of necessity; *(con violencia)* by force; **por f.** of necessity; **f. mayor** force majeure (**c**) *Fís* force (**d**) *(cuerpo)* force; **las fuerzas del orden** the forces of law and order; **f. aérea** air force; **fuerzas armadas** armed forces
fuese 1 *subj imperf de* **ir**
  2 *subj imperf de* **ser**
fuete *nm Am* whip
fuga *nf* (**a**) *(huida)* escape; **darse a la f.** to take flight (**b**) *(de gas etc)* leak
fugarse [42] *vpr* to escape; **f. de casa** to run away from home
fugaz *adj* fleeting, brief
fugitivo,-a *nm,f* fugitive
fui 1 *pt indef de* **ir**
  2 *pt indef de* **ser**
fulana *nf* whore, tart
fulano,-a *nm,f* so-and-so; *(hombre)* what's-his-name; *(mujer)* what's-her-name; **Doña Fulana de tal** Mrs So-and-so
fular *nm* headscarf
fulgor *nm Literario* brilliance, glow
fullería *nf* cheating; **hacer fullerías** to cheat
fullero,-a 1 *adj* cheating
  2 *nm,f* cheat
fulminante *adj (cese)* summary; *(muerte, enfermedad)* sudden; *(mirada)* withering
fulminar *vt Fig* to strike dead; **f. a algn con la mirada** to look daggers at sb
fumada *nf Am (calada)* pull, drag
fumado,-a *adj Fam (colocado)* stoned
fumador,-a *nm,f* smoker; **los no fumadores** nonsmokers
fumar 1 *vt & vi* to smoke; **no f.** *(en letrero)* no smoking
  2 fumarse *vpr* to smoke; **f. un cigarro** to smoke a cigarette

> *𝒫* Observa que el verbo inglés **to fume** es un falso amigo y no es la traducción del verbo español **fumar**. En inglés, **to fume** significa "despedir humo".

fumigar [42] *vt* to fumigate
funambulista *nmf*, **funámbulo,-a** *nm,f* tightrope walker
función *nf* (**a**) function; **en f. de** according to (**b**) *(cargo)* duties; **entrar en funciones** to take up one's duties; **presidente**

en funciones acting president (**c**) *Cin &
Teatro* performance
funcionamiento *nm* operation; **poner/
entrar en f.** to put/come into operation
funcionar *vi* to work; **no funciona** *(en
letrero)* out of order
funcionario,-a *nm,f* civil servant; **f. público** public official
funda *nf* cover; *(de gafas etc)* case; *(de
espada)* sheath; **f. de almohada** pillowcase
fundación *nf* foundation
fundador,-a *nm,f* founder
fundamental *adj* fundamental
fundamentar *vt* to base (**en** on)
fundamento *nm* basis, grounds; **sin f.**
unfounded
fundar 1 *vt* (**a**) *(empresa)* to found (**b**)
(teoría) to base, to found
  2 fundarse *vpr* (**a**) *(empresa)* to be founded (**b**) *(teoría)* to be based (**en** on)

⎿ Observa que el verbo inglés **to fund** es
un falso amigo y no es la traducción del verbo español **fundar**. En inglés, **to fund** significa "financiar".

fundición *nf* (**a**) *(de metales)* smelting
(**b**) *(fábrica)* foundry
fundir 1 *vt* (**a**) to melt; *(bombilla, plomos)*
to blow (**b**) *(unir)* to unite, to join
  2 fundirse *vpr* (**a**) *(derretirse)* to melt (**b**)
(bombilla, plomos) to blow (**c**) *(unirse)* to
merge (**d**) *RP Fam (arruinarse)* to go bust,
to be ruined
fúnebre *adj* (**a**) *(mortuorio)* funeral; **coche f.** hearse (**b**) *(lúgubre)* mournful,
lugubrious
funeral *nm* funeral
funeraria *nf* undertaker's, *US* funeral
home

funesto,-a *adj* ill-fated, fatal; *(consecuencias)* disastrous
fungir [57] *vi Méx* to act (**de** o **como** as)
funicular *nm* funicular (railway)
furcia *nf Pey* whore, tart
furgón *nm Aut* van
furgoneta *nf* van
furia *nf* fury; **ponerse hecho una f.** to
become furious, to fly into a rage
furibundo,-a *adj* furious, enraged
furioso,-a *adj* furious; **ponerse f.** to get
furious
furor *nm* fury, rage; *Fig* **hacer f.** to be all
the rage
furtivo,-a *adj* furtive, stealthy; **caza/pes-
ca furtiva** poaching; **cazador/pescador f.**
poacher
furúnculo *nm Med* boil
fuselaje *nm* fuselage
fusible *nm* fuse
fusil *nm* gun, rifle
fusilamiento *nm* shooting, execution
fusilar *vt* to shoot, to execute
fusión *nf* (**a**) *(de metales)* fusion; *(del
hielo)* thawing, melting; **punto de f.** melting point (**b**) *Com* merger
fusionar *vt,* **fusionarse** *vpr* (**a**) *Fís* to
fuse (**b**) *Com* to merge
fustán *nm Am* petticoat
fútbol *nm* soccer, *Br* football
futbolín *nm Br* table football, *US* foosball
futbolista *nmf* soccer player, *Br* footballer
fútil *adj* futile, trivial
futilidad *nf* futility, triviality
futurista *adj* futuristic
futuro,-a 1 *adj* future
  2 *nm* future; **en un f. próximo** in the near
future; *CSur, Méx* **a f.** in the future

G, g [xe] *nf (la letra)* G, g
gabán *nm* overcoat
gabardina *nf (prenda)* raincoat
gabinete *nm* (**a**) *(despacho)* study; **g. de abogados** lawyers' office (**b**) *Pol* cabinet
gaceta *nf* gazette
gachas *nfpl* porridge
gacho,-a *adj* **con la cabeza gacha** hanging one's head
gaditano,-a 1 *adj* of/from Cadiz
  2 *nm,f* person from Cadiz
gafar *vt Fam* to put a jinx on, to bring bad luck to
gafas *nfpl* glasses, spectacles; **g. de sol** sunglasses
gafe *adj & nm Fam* **ser g.** to be a jinx

✍ Observa que la palabra inglesa **gaffe** es un falso amigo y no es la traducción de la palabra española **gafe**. En inglés, **gaffe** significa "metedura de pata, desliz".

---

gafete *nm Méx* badge
gaita *nf* bagpipes
gajes *nmpl Fam Irón* **g. del oficio** occupational hazards
gajo *nm* (**a**) *(de naranja, pomelo etc)* segment (**b**) *(rama desprendida)* torn-off branch
gala *nf* (**a**) *(vestido)* full dress; **de g.** dressed up; *(ciudad)* decked out (**b**) *(espectáculo)* gala; **hacer g. de** to glory in (**c**) **galas** finery
galán *nm* (**a**) handsome young man; *Hum* ladies' man (**b**) *Teatro* leading man
galante *adj* gallant
galantear *vt* to court
galanteo *nm* courtship
galantería *nf* gallantry
galápago *nm* turtle
galardón *nm* prize
galardonado,-a *nm,f* prizewinner
galardonar *vt* to award a prize to
galaxia *nf* galaxy
galeón *nm* galleon
galeote *nm* galley slave
galera *nf* (**a**) *Náut* galley (**b**) *(carro)* covered wagon (**c**) *Impr* galley proof
galería *nf* (**a**) *Arquit* covered balcony (**b**)

(museo) art gallery (**c**) *Teatro* gallery, gods
Gales *n* (**el país de**) **G.** Wales
galés,-esa 1 *adj* Welsh
  2 *nm,f (hombre)* Welshman; *(mujer)* Welshwoman; **los galeses** the Welsh
  3 *nm (idioma)* Welsh
galgo *nm* greyhound
Galicia *n* Galicia
galimatías *nm inv Fam* gibberish
gallardo *adj* (**a**) *(apuesto)* smart (**b**) *(valeroso)* brave
gallego,-a 1 *adj* (**a**) Galician (**b**) *CSur, Cuba Pey* Spanish
  2 *nm,f* (**a**) Galician, person from Galicia (**b**) *CSur, Cuba Pey* Spaniard
  3 *nm (idioma)* Galician
galleta *nf* (**a**) *Culin Br* biscuit, *US* cookie (**b**) *Fam (cachete)* slap
gallina 1 *nf* hen
  2 *nmf Fam* coward, chicken
gallinero *nm* (**a**) hen run (**b**) *Teatro* **el g.** the gods
gallito *nm Fam (peleón)* bully
gallo *nm* (**a**) cock, rooster; *Fam Fig* **en menos que un canto de g.** before you could say Jack Robinson (**b**) *Fam Mús* off-key note
galón¹ *nm Mil* stripe
galón² *nm (medida)* gallon, *Br* = 4.55 l, *US* = 3.79 l
galopante *adj Fig (inflación etc)* galloping
galopar *vi* to gallop
galope *nm* gallop; **a g. tendido** flat out
galpón *nm Am* shed
gama *nf* range; *Mús* scale
gamba *nf* prawn
gamberrismo *nm* hooliganism
gamberro,-a 1 *nm,f* hooligan
  2 *adj* uncouth
gamo *nm* fallow deer
gamonal *nm Andes, CAm, Ven* local boss
gamuza *nf* (**a**) *Zool* chamois (**b**) *(trapo)* chamois o shammy leather
gana *nf* (**a**) *(deseo)* wish (**de** for); **de buena g.** willingly; **de mala g.** reluctantly; *Fam* **no me da la g.** I don't feel like it (**b**) **tener ganas de (hacer) algo** to feel like

(doing) sth; **quedarse con las ganas** not to manage (**c**) *(apetito)* appetite; **comer con ganas** to eat heartily

ganadería *nf* (**a**) *(crianza)* livestock farming (**b**) *(conjunto de ganado)* livestock

ganadero,-a *nm,f* livestock farmer

ganado *nm* (**a**) livestock (**b**) *Fam Fig (gente)* crowd

ganador,-a 1 *adj* winning
  2 *nm,f* winner

ganancia *nf* profit

ganar 1 *vt* (**a**) *(sueldo)* to earn (**b**) *(victoria)* to win (**c**) *(aventajar)* to beat (**d**) *(alcanzar)* to reach
  2 ganarse *vpr* (**a**) to earn; **g. el pan** to earn one's daily bread (**b**) *(merecer)* to deserve; **se lo ha ganado** he deserves it

ganchillo *nm* crochet work

gancho *nm* (**a**) hook (**b**) *Fam Fig (gracia, atractivo)* charm (**c**) *Andes, CAm, Méx (horquilla)* hairpin (**d**) *Andes, CAm, Méx, Ven (percha)* hanger

gandul,-a *nm,f* loafer

ganga *nf* bargain

gangoso,-a *adj* nasal

gangrena *nf* gangrene

gansada *nf Fam* silly thing to say/do

ganso,-a 1 *nm,f* (**a**) goose; *(macho)* gander (**b**) *Fam* dolt
  2 *adj Fam* ginormous; **pasta gansa** bread, dough

ganzúa *nf* picklock

gañán *nm (obrero)* farmhand; *Fam (bribón)* cheat

garabatear *vt & vi* to scribble

garabato *nm* scrawl

garaje *nm* garage

garante *nmf Fin* guarantor

garantía *nf* (**a**) guarantee (**b**) *Jur (fianza)* bond, security

garantizar [40] *vt* to guarantee

garbanzo *nm* chickpea

garbeo *nm Fam (paseo)* stroll; **darse un g.** to go for a stroll

garbo *nm* grace

garfio *nm* hook, grappling iron

gargajo *nm* spit

garganta *nf* (**a**) throat (**b**) *(desfiladero)* narrow pass

gargantilla *nf* short necklace

gárgaras *nfpl* (**a**) gargling; *Fam* **¡vete a hacer g.!** get lost! (**b**) *Am (licor)* gargling solution

gárgola *nf* gargoyle

garita *nf (caseta)* hut; *Mil* sentry box

garito *nm Fam* joint

garra *nf* (**a**) *Zool* claw; *(de ave)* talon (**b**) *Fig (fuerza)* force; **tener g.** to be compelling

garrafa *nf* carafe

garrafal *adj* monumental

garrapata *nf* tick

garrote *nm* (**a**) *(porra)* club (**b**) *Jur* garrotte

garrucha *nf* pulley

gárrulo,-a *adj Fig* garrulous

garúa *nf Andes, RP, Ven* drizzle

garza *nf* heron

gas *nm* (**a**) gas; **g. ciudad** town gas; **gases (nocivos)** fumes; **g. de escape** exhaust fumes (**b**) *(en bebida)* fizz; **agua con g.** fizzy water (**c**) *Med* **gases** flatulence

gasa *nf* gauze

gaseosa *nf* lemonade

gasfitería *nf Chile, Ecuad, Perú* plumber's (shop)

gasfitero,-a *nm,f Chile, Ecuad, Perú* plumber

gasoducto *nm* gas pipeline

gasoil, gasóleo *nm* diesel oil

gasolina *nf Br* petrol, *US* gasoline

gasolinera, *Méx* **gasolinería** *nf Br* petrol *o US* gas station

gastado,-a *adj (zapatos etc)* worn-out; *Fig (frase)* hackneyed

gastar 1 *vt* (**a**) *(consumir) (dinero, tiempo)* to spend; *(gasolina, electricidad)* to consume (**b**) *Fig (malgastar)* to waste (**c**) *(ropa)* to wear; **¿qué número gastas?** what size do you take? (**d**) **g. una broma a algn** to play a practical joke on sb
  2 gastarse *vpr* (**a**) *(zapatos etc)* to wear out (**b**) *(gasolina etc)* to run out

gasto *nm* expenditure; **gastos** expenses; **gastos de viaje** travelling expenses

gatas: • a gatas *loc adv* on all fours

gatear *vi* (**a**) to crawl (**b**) *(trepar)* to climb

gatillo *nm (de armas)* trigger; **apretar el g.** to pull the trigger

gato *nm* (**a**) cat (**b**) *Aut & Téc* jack

gauchada *nf CSur* favour

gaucho,-a 1 *adj RP Fam (servicial)* helpful, obliging
  2 *nm,f* gaucho

gaveta *nf* (**a**) *(cajón)* drawer (**b**) *Am Aut (guantera)* glove compartment

gavilán *nm Orn* sparrowhawk

gavilla *nf (de ramillas etc)* sheaf

gaviota *nf* seagull

gay *adj inv & nm (pl* **gays***)* homosexual, gay

gazapo *nm* (**a**) *(error)* misprint (**b**) *Zool* young rabbit

gaznate *nm* gullet

gazpacho *nm Culin* gazpacho

gel *nm* gel; **g. (de ducha)** shower gel
gelatina *nf (ingrediente)* gelatin; *Culin* jelly
gema *nf* gem
gemelo,-a 1 *adj & nm,f* (identical) twin
  2 *nmpl* **gemelos** (**a**) *(de camisa)* cufflinks (**b**) *(anteojos)* binoculars
gemido *nm* groan
Géminis *nm* Gemini
gemir [6] *vi* to groan
generación *nf* generation
general 1 *adj* general; **por lo** *o* **en g.** in general, generally;
  2 *nm Mil & Rel* general
Generalitat *nf* Catalan/Valencian/Balearic parliament
generalización *nf* (**a**) generalization (**b**) *(extensión)* spread
generalizar [40] 1 *vt* (**a**) to generalize (**b**) *(extender)* to spread
  2 generalizarse *vpr* to become widespread *o* common
generalmente *adv* generally
generar *vt* to generate
género *nm* (**a**) *(clase)* kind, sort (**b**) *Arte & Lit* genre (**c**) *(mercancía)* article (**d**) *Ling* gender (**e**) *Biol* genus; **el g. humano** mankind
generosidad *nf* generosity
generoso,-a *adj* (**a**) generous (**con** to) (**b**) *(vino)* full-bodied
Génesis *nm Rel* Genesis
genética *nf* genetics *sing*
genético,-a *adj* genetic
genial *adj* brilliant; *Fam* terrific

ℓ Observa que la palabra inglesa **genial** es un falso amigo y no es la traducción de la palabra española **genial**. En inglés, **genial** significa "cordial, amable".

genio *nm* (**a**) *(carácter)* temperament; *(mal carácter)* temper; **estar de mal g.** to be in a bad mood (**b**) *(facultad)* genius
genocidio *nm* genocide
Génova *n* Genoa
gente *nf* (**a**) people (**b**) *(familia)* folks (**c**) *Am* respectable people
gentil *adj* (**a**) *(amable)* kind (**b**) *(pagano)* pagan

ℓ Observa que la palabra inglesa **genteel** es un falso amigo y no es la traducción de la palabra española **gentil**. En inglés, **genteel** significa "fino, distinguido".

gentileza *nf* kindness; *Fml* **por g. de** by courtesy of
gentío *nm* crowd
gentuza *nf Pey* riffraff

genuino,-a *adj (puro)* genuine; *(verdadero)* authentic
geografía *nf* geography
geología *nf* geology
geometría *nf* geometry
geranio *nm* geranium
gerencia *nf* management
gerente *nmf* manager
germano,-a 1 *adj* German, Germanic
  2 *nm,f* German
gérmen *nm* (**a**) *Biol* germ (**b**) *Fig (inicio)* germ; *(fuente)* origin
germinar *vi* to germinate
gerundio *nm* gerund
gesta *nf* heroic exploit
gestación *nf* gestation
gestar *vt* to gestate
gesticular *vi* to gesticulate
gestión *nf* (**a**) *(administración)* management (**b**) **gestiones** *(negociaciones)* negotiations; *(trámites)* formalities
gestionar *vt* to take steps to acquire *o* obtain; *(negociar)* to negotiate
gesto *nm* (**a**) *(mueca)* face (**b**) *(con las manos)* gesture
gestor,-a *nm,f* ≃ solicitor
giba *nf* hump
gibar *vt Fam* to annoy
Gibraltar *n* Gibraltar; **el peñón de G.** the Rock of Gibraltar
gibraltareño,-a 1 *adj* of/from Gibraltar
  2 *nm,f* Gibraltarian
gigante,-a 1 *nm,f* giant
  2 *adj* giant, enormous
gigantesco,-a *adj* gigantic
gigoló *nm* gigolo
gil, gila *nm,f CSur Fam* twit, idiot
gili, gilí *nm muy Fam* = **gilipollas**
gilipollas *nmf muy Fam Br* prat, *US* dork
gimnasia *nf* gymnastics
gimnasio *nm* gymnasium
gimotear *vi* to whine
Ginebra *n* Geneva
ginebra *nf (bebida)* gin
ginecología *nf* gynaecology
ginecólogo,-a *nm,f* gynaecologist
gira *nf Teatro & Mús* tour
girar 1 *vi* (**a**) *(dar vueltas)* to spin (**b**) **g. a la derecha/izquierda** to turn right/left
  2 *vt Fin* (**a**) *(expedir)* to draw (**b**) *(dinero)* to transfer
girasol *nm* sunflower
giratorio,-a *adj* revolving
giro *nm* (**a**) *(vuelta)* turn (**b**) *(de acontecimientos)* direction (**c**) *(frase)* turn of phrase (**d**) *Fin* draft; **g. telegráfico** money order; **g. postal** postal *o* money order

gis *nm Andes, Méx* chalk
gitano,-a *adj & nm,f* gypsy, gipsy
glacial *adj* icy
glaciar *nm* glacier
glándula *nf* gland
glasear *vt Culin* to glaze
global *adj* comprehensive; **precio g.** all-inclusive price
globalmente *adv* as a whole
globo *nm* (**a**) balloon (**b**) *(esfera)* globe (**c**) *(lámpara)* globe, glass lampshade
glóbulo *nm* globule
gloria *nf* (**a**) *(fama)* glory (**b**) *Rel* heaven; *Fam Fig* **estar en la g.** to be in seventh heaven (**c**) *Fam (delicia)* delight
glorieta *nf* (**a**) *(plazoleta)* small square (**b**) *(encrucijada de calles) Br* roundabout, *US* traffic circle (**c**) *(en un jardín)* arbour
glorificar [44] *vt* to glorify
glorioso,-a *adj* glorious
glosa *nf* (**a**) gloss (**b**) *Lit (comentario)* notes, commentary
glosar *vt* (**a**) *(explicar)* to gloss; *(texto)* to interpret (**b**) *(comentar)* to comment on
glosario *nm* glossary
glotón,-ona **1** *adj* greedy
   2 *nm,f* glutton
glotonería *nf* gluttony
glucosa *nf Quím* glucose
gobernación *nf* government; *Pol & Hist* **Ministerio de la G.** *Br* ≃ Home Office, *US* ≃ Department of the Interior
gobernador,-a *nm,f* governor
gobernante *adj* ruling
gobernar [1] **1** *vt* to govern; *(un país)* to rule
   2 *vi Náut* to steer
gobiernista *Am* **1** *adj* government
   2 *nmf* government supporter
gobierno *nm* (**a**) *Pol* government (**b**) *(mando)* running (**c**) *Náut* steering (**d**) *Náut (timón)* rudder
goce *nm* enjoyment
gofio *nm Am Can* roasted maize meal
gol *nm* goal
goleada *nf* lots of goals; **ganar por g.** to win by a barrowload
golear *vt* to hammer
golf *nm* golf; **palo de g.** golf club
golfista *nmf* golfer
golfo¹,-a **1** *nm,f* good-for-nothing
   2 *nf* **golfa** *Fam Pey* tart
golfo² *nm Geog* gulf; **el g. Pérsico** the Persian Gulf
golondrina *nf* swallow
golosina *nf Br* sweet, *US* candy
goloso,-a *adj* sweet-toothed

golpe *nm* (**a**) blow; *(llamada)* knock; *(puñetazo)* punch; **de g.** all of a sudden; **g. de estado** coup d'état; **g. de suerte** stroke of luck; **no dar ni g.** not to lift a finger (**b**) *Aut* bump (**c**) *(desgracia)* blow; **un duro g.** a great blow (**d**) *(de humor)* witticism
golpear *vt* to hit; *(con el puño)* to punch; *(puerta, cabeza)* to bang
golpiza *nf Am* beating
goma *nf* (**a**) rubber; **g. de pegar** glue; **g. de borrar** eraser, *Br* rubber (**b**) *(elástica)* rubber band (**c**) *Cuba, CSur (neumático)* tyre (**d**) *Fam (preservativo)* rubber
gomaespuma *nf* foam rubber
gomal *nm Am Agr* rubber plantation
gomería *nf CSur* tyre centre
gomero *nm Am* (**a**) *Bot* gum tree (**b**) *(recolector)* rubber collector
gomina *nf* hair cream
góndola *nf* (**a**) *(embarcación)* gondola (**b**) *Bol, Chile (autobús)* (long distance) bus
gordo,-a **1** *adj* (**a**) *(carnoso)* fat (**b**) *(grueso)* thick (**c**) *(importante)* big; **me cae g.** I can't stand him; **de g.** in a big way
   2 *nm,f* (**a**) fat person; *Fam* fatty (**b**) *Am Fam (como apelativo)* **¿cómo estás, gorda?** hey, how are you doing?
   3 *nm* **el g.** *(de lotería)* the jackpot
gordura *nf* fatness
gorgorito *nm* trill
gorila *nm* (**a**) gorilla (**b**) *Fig (en discoteca etc)* bouncer
gorjear **1** *vi* to chirp
   2 • **gorjearse** *vpr Am* **g. de algn** to laugh at sb's expense
gorjeo *nm* chirping
gorra *nf* cap; *(con visera)* peaked cap; *Fam* **de g.** free
gorrión *nm* sparrow
gorro *nm* (**a**) cap (**b**) *Fam* **estar hasta el g. (de)** to be up to here (with)
gorrón,-ona *nm,f* sponger
gota *nf* (**a**) drop; *(de sudor)* bead; **g. a g.** drop by drop; **ni g.** not a bit (**b**) *Med* gout
gotear *v impers* to drip; **el techo gotea** there's a leak in the ceiling
gotera *nf* leak
gótico,-a *adj* Gothic
gozar [40] **1** *vt* to enjoy
   2 *vi (disfrutar)* **g. (de)** to enjoy
gozne *nm* hinge
gozo *nm* pleasure
grabación *nf* recording
grabado *nm* (**a**) *(arte)* engraving (**b**) *(dibujo)* drawing
grabadora *nf* tape recorder

grabar vt (**a**) (sonidos, imágenes) to record (**b**) Informát to save (**c**) Arte to engrave

gracia nf (**a**) (atractivo) grace (**b**) (chiste) joke; **hacer** o **tener g.** to be funny (**c**) (indulto) pardon

gracias nfpl (agradecimiento) thanks; **g. a Dios** thank God, thank goodness; **g. a** thanks to; **muchas** o **muchísimas g.** thank you very much

gracioso,-a 1 adj (**a**) (divertido) funny (**b**) (garboso) graceful

  2 nm,f Teatro comic character

grada nf (**a**) (peldaño) step (**b**) **gradas** (en estadio) terraces

gradación nf (**a**) gradation (**b**) Mús scale

graderío nm tiers of seats; Dep terraces, US bleachers

gradiente 1 nm gradient

  2 nf Am slope

grado nm (**a**) degree (**b**) Mil rank (**c**) **de buen g.** willingly, gladly

graduable adj adjustable

graduación nf (**a**) gradation (**b**) Mil rank

graduado,-a nm,f graduate

gradual adj gradual

gradualmente adv gradually

graduar [30] **1** vt (**a**) Educ & Mil to confer degree o a rank on (**b**) (regular) to regulate

  2 graduarse vpr (**a**) Educ & Mil to graduate (**b**) **g. la vista** to have one's eyes tested

gráfico,-a 1 adj graphic; **diseño g.** graphic design

  2 nm graph

grafista nmf graphic designer

gragea nf Med pill

grajo,-a 1 nm,f Orn rook

  2 nm Am body odour

gral. (abr **General**) gen

gramática nf grammar

gramo nm gram, gramme

gran adj = **grande**

grana adj scarlet

granada nf (**a**) (fruto) pomegranate (**b**) Mil grenade

granate 1 adj inv (color) maroon

  2 nm (color) maroon

Gran Bretaña n Great Britain

grande adj (**a**) (tamaño) big, large; Fig (persona) great (**b**) (cantidad) large; **vivir a lo g.** to live in style; Fig **pasarlo en g.** to have a great time

> **gran** is used instead of **grande** before masculine singular nouns (e.g. **gran hombre** great man).

grandeza nf (**a**) (importancia) greatness (**b**) (grandiosidad) grandeur; **delirios de g.** delusions of grandeur

grandioso,-a adj grandiose

granel: • a granel loc adv (sin medir exactamente) loose

granero nm Agr granary

granito nm granite

granizada nf, **granizado** nm iced drink

granizar [40] v impers to hail

granizo nm hail

granja nf farm

granjear vt, **granjearse** vpr to gain

granjero,-a nm,f farmer

grano nm (**a**) grain; (de café) bean; **ir al g.** to get to the point (**b**) (espinilla) spot

granuja nm (**a**) (pilluelo) ragamuffin (**b**) (estafador) con-man

grapa nf (**a**) staple (**b**) Constr cramp (**c**) CSur (bebida) grappa

grapadora nf stapler

grapar vt to staple

grasa nf grease

grasiento,-a adj greasy

graso,-a adj (pelo) greasy; (materia) fatty

gratificar [44] vt (**a**) (satisfacer) to gratify (**b**) (recompensar) to reward

gratinar vt Culin to cook in a sauce until golden brown

gratis adj inv & adv free

gratitud nf gratitude

grato,-a adj pleasant

gratuito,-a adj (**a**) (de balde) free (of charge) (**b**) (arbitrario) gratuitous

grava nf (guijas) gravel; (en carretera) chippings

gravamen nm Jur (**a**) (carga) burden (**b**) (impuesto) tax

gravar vt Jur (**a**) (cargar) to burden (**b**) (impuestos) to tax

grave adj (**a**) (importante) serious (**b**) (muy enfermo) seriously ill (**c**) (voz, nota) low

gravedad nf (**a**) (seriedad, importancia) seriousness (**b**) Fís gravity

gravilla nf chippings

gravitar vi (**a**) Fís to gravitate (**b**) **g. sobre** to rest on

gravoso,-a adj (**a**) (costoso) costly (**b**) (molesto) burdensome

graznar vi to squawk; (de pato) to quack; (de cuervo) to caw

graznido nm (un sonido) squawk; (varios) squawking; (de pato) quack; (de cuervo) caw

Grecia n Greece

gregario,-a adj gregarious; **instinto g.** herd instinct

gremio *nm* (**a**) *Hist* guild (**b**) *(profesión)* profession

greña *nf* lock of entangled hair; *Fam* **andar a la g.** to squabble

gres *nm* **artículos de g.** stoneware

gresca *nf* (**a**) *(bulla)* racket (**b**) *(riña)* row

griego,-a *adj & nm,f* Greek

grieta *nf* crack; *(en la piel)* chap

grifo *nm* (**a**) *(llave) Br* tap, *US* faucet (**b**) *Perú (gasolinera) Br* petrol station, *US* gas station

grillete *nm* shackle

grillo *nm* cricket

gringo,-a *Fam* **1** *adj* (**a**) *(estadounidense)* gringo, American (**b**) *Am (extranjero)* foreign

2 *nm,f* (**a**) *(estadounidense)* gringo, American (**b**) *Am (extranjero)* = non-Spanish-speaking foreigner

gripa *nf Col, Méx* flu

gripe *nf* flu

gris *adj & nm* grey

grisáceo,-a *adj* greyish

gritar *vt & vi* to shout

grito *nm* shout; **a voz en g.** at the top of one's voice

Groenlandia *n* Greenland

grosella *nf (fruto)* redcurrant; **g. negra** blackcurrant; **g. silvestre** gooseberry

grosería *nf* (**a**) *(ordinariez)* rude word *o* expression (**b**) *(rusticidad)* rudeness

grosero,-a *adj (tosco)* coarse; *(maleducado)* rude

grosor *nm* thickness

grotesco,-a *adj* grotesque

grúa *nf* (**a**) *Constr* crane (**b**) *Aut Br* breakdown van *o* truck, *US* tow truck

grueso,-a **1** *adj* thick; *(persona)* stout

2 *nm (parte principal)* bulk

grulla *nf Orn* crane

grumo *nm* lump; *(de leche)* curd

gruñido *nm* grunt

gruñir *vi* to grunt

gruñón,-ona *adj* grumpy

grupa *nf* hindquarters

grupo *nm* (**a**) group; *Informát* **g. de noticias** newsgroup (**b**) *Téc* unit, set

gruta *nf* cave

guaca *nf Am (sepultura)* = pre-Columbian Indian tomb

guacal *nm* (**a**) *CAm, Méx (calabaza)* calabash (**b**) *Carib, Col, Méx (jaula)* cage

guacamayo,-a *nm,f Orn* macaw

guacamol, guacamole *nm Culin* guacamole

guachafita *nf Am* uproar

guachimán *nm Am* night watchman

guacho,-a *adj & nm,f Andes, RP* (**a**) *muy Fam (persona huérfana)* orphan (**b**) *Fam (sinvergüenza)* bastard, swine

guaco *nm Am (cerámica)* = pottery object found in pre-Columbian Indian tomb

guadaña *nf* scythe

guagua¹ *nf Can, Cuba* bus

guagua² *nf Andes* baby

guajiro,-a *nm,f Cuba Fam (campesino)* peasant

guajolote *nm CAm, Méx* (**a**) *(pavo)* turkey (**b**) *(tonto)* fool, idiot

guampa *nf Bol, CSur* horn

guanajo *nm Carib* turkey

guantazo *nm* slap

guante *nm* glove

guantera *nf Aut* glove compartment

guapo,-a *adj* (**a**) *(hombre)* handsome, good-looking; *(mujer)* pretty, good-looking (**b**) *Am (matón)* bully

guaraca *nf Am* sling

guarache *nm Méx (sandalia)* sandal

guarangada *nf Bol, CSur* rude remark

guarango,-a *adj Bol, CSur* rude

guarda *nmf* guard; **g. jurado** security guard

guardabarros *nm inv Aut Br* mudguard, *US* fender

guardabosque *nmf* gamekeeper

guardacoches *nmf inv* parking attendant

guardacostas *nm inv (persona)* coastguard; *(embarcación)* coastguard vessel

guardaespaldas *nmf inv* bodyguard

guardafangos *nm inv Andes, CAm, Carib Aut Br* mudguard, *US* fender

guardameta *nmf Dep* goalkeeper

guardapolvo *nm* overalls

guardar **1** *vt* (**a**) *(conservar)* to keep (**b**) *(un secreto)* to keep; **g. silencio** to remain silent; **g. cama** to stay in bed (**c**) *(poner en un sitio)* to put away (**d**) *(reservar)* to keep (**e**) *Informát* to save

2 guardarse *vpr* **g. de hacer algo** *(abstenerse)* to be careful not to do sth; **guardársela a algn** to have it in for sb

guardarropa *nm* (**a**) *(cuarto)* cloakroom (**b**) *(armario)* wardrobe

guardería *nf* **g. infantil** nursery (school)

guardia **1** *nf* (**a**) *(vigilancia)* watch (**b**) **la G. Civil** the civil guard (**c**) *(turno de servicio)* duty; *Mil* guard duty; **de g.** on duty; **farmacia de g.** duty chemist

2 *nmf* policeman; *(mujer)* policewoman

guardián,-ana *nm,f* watchman

guarecer [**33**] **1** *vt* to shelter

2 guarecerse *vpr* to take shelter *o* refuge (**de** from)

guarida *nf (de animal)* lair; *(refugio)* hideout

guarismo *nm* digit
guarnecer [33] *vt* (**a**) *Culin* to garnish (**b**) *(dotar)* to provide (**de** with) (**c**) *Mil* to garrison
guarnición *nf* (**a**) *Culin* garnish (**b**) *Mil* garrison
guarro,-a 1 *adj* filthy
  2 *nm,f* pig
guarura *nm Méx Fam* bodyguard
guasa *nf* mockery
guasearse *vpr Fam* **g. de** to make fun of
guaso,-a *adj Am* peasant
guasón,-ona 1 *adj* humorous
  2 *nm,f* joker
guata *nf* (**a**) *(relleno)* padding (**b**) *Am (barriga)* paunch
Guatemala *n* (**a**) *(país)* Guatemala (**b**) *(ciudad)* Guatemala City
guatemalteco,-a *adj & nm,f* Guatemalan
guay *adj inv Fam* brilliant, terrific
guayabera *nf* short jacket
guayabo,-a *nm,f Am Fig (chica bonita)* pretty young girl; *(chico guapo)* good-looking boy
guepardo *nm* cheetah
güero,-a *adj Méx Fam* blond, blonde
guerra *nf* war; **en g.** at war; **g. bacteriológica** germ warfare; **g. civil/fría/mundial/nuclear** civil/cold/world/nuclear war; *Fam* **dar g.** to be a real nuisance
guerrero,-a 1 *nm,f* warrior
  2 *adj* warlike
guerrilla *nf* (**a**) *(partida armada)* guerrilla force o band (**b**) *(lucha)* guerrilla warfare
güevón,-ona *nm,f Andes, Arg, Ven muy Fam (estúpido) Br* prat, *US* dork
guía 1 *nmf (persona)* guide
  2 *nf* (**a**) *(norma)* guideline (**b**) *(libro)* guide; *(lista)* directory; **g. de teléfonos** telephone directory
guiar [29] 1 *vt* (**a**) *(indicar el camino)* to guide (**b**) *Aut* to drive; *Náut* to steer; *(caballo, bici)* to ride
  2 guiarse *vpr* **g. por** to be guided by, to go by
guija *nf* pebble
guijarro *nm* pebble
guinda *nf (fruto)* morello (cherry)

guindilla *nf* chilli
guineo *nm Andes, CAm* banana
guiñapo *nm* (**a**) *(andrajo)* rag (**b**) *Fig (persona)* wreck; **poner a algn como un g.** to tear sb to pieces
guiñar *vt* to wink
guiño *nm* wink
guión *nm* (**a**) *Cin & TV* script (**b**) *Ling* hyphen, dash (**c**) *(esquema)* sketch
guionista *nmf* scriptwriter
guiri *nmf Fam* foreigner
guirigay *nm* hubbub
guirnalda *nf* garland
guisa *nf* way, manner; **a g. de** as, by way of
guisado *nm Culin* stew
guisante *nm* pea
guisar *vt* to cook
guiso *nm* dish; *(guisado)* stew
guita *nf* (**a**) *(cuerda)* rope (**b**) *Fam* dough
guitarra 1 *nf* guitar
  2 *nmf* guitarist
guitarreada *nf CSur* singalong *(to guitars)*
guitarrista *nmf* guitarist
gula *nf* gluttony
gurí,-isa *nm,f RP Fam (niño)* kid, child; *(joven) (hombre)* lad; *(mujer)* lass
gusano *nm* worm; *(oruga)* caterpillar; *Fam Pey (exiliado cubano)* = anti-Castro Cuban living in exile; **g. de seda** silkworm
gustar 1 *vt* (**a**) **me gusta el vino** I like wine; **me gustaban los caramelos** I used to like sweets; **me gusta nadar** I like swimming; **me gustaría ir** I would like to go (**b**) *Fml* **¿gustas?** would you like some?; **cuando gustes** whenever you like
  2 *vi* **g. de** to enjoy
gusto *nm* (**a**) *(sentido)* taste (**b**) *(en fórmulas de cortesía)* pleasure; **con (mucho) g.** with (great) pleasure; **tanto g.** pleased to meet you (**c**) **estar a g.** to feel comfortable o at ease; **por g.** for the sake of it; **ser de buen/mal g.** to be in good/bad taste; **tener buen/mal g.** to have good/bad taste; **tenemos el gusto de comunicarle que ...** we are pleased to inform you that ...
gutural *adj* guttural

H, h [atʃe] *nf (la letra)* H,h; **bomba H** H-bomb

ha *indic pres de* **haber**

haba *nf* broad bean

Takes the masculine articles **el** and **un**.

Habana *nf* **La H.** Havana

habano *nm* Havana cigar

haber **[14]** **1** *v aux* (**a**) *(en tiempos compuestos)* to have; **lo he visto** I have seen it; **ya lo había hecho** he had already done it
(**b**) **h. de** + *infin (obligación)* to have to; **has de ser bueno** you must be good
2 *v impers (special form of present tense:* **hay**) (**a**) *(existir, estar) (singular used also with plural nouns)* **hay** there is/are; **había** there was/were; **había un gato en el tejado** there was a cat on the roof; **había muchos libros** there were a lot of books; **hay 500 km entre Madrid y Granada** it's 500 km from Madrid to Granada
(**b**) **h. que** + *infin* it is necessary to; **hay que trabajar** you've got to *o* you must work; **habrá que comprobarlo** I/you/we/ *etc* will have to check it
(**c**) *(tener lugar)* **habrá una fiesta** there will be a party; **hoy hay partido** there's a match today; **los accidentes habidos en esta carretera** the accidents which have happened on this road
(**d**) **había una vez ...** once upon a time ...; **no hay de qué** you're welcome, don't mention it; **¿qué hay?** how are things?
3 *nm* (**a**) *Fin* credit; **haberes** assets
(**b**) **en su h.** in his possession

habichuela *nf (judía)* kidney bean; *Carib, Col (judía verde)* green bean

hábil *adj* (**a**) *(diestro)* skilful (**b**) *(astuto)* smart (**c**) **días hábiles** working days

habilidad *nf* (**a**) *(destreza)* skill (**b**) *(astucia)* cleverness

habilitar *vt* (**a**) *(espacio)* to fit out (**b**) *(persona)* to entitle (**c**) *Fin (financiar)* to finance

habiloso,-a *adj Chile* shrewd, astute

habitación *nf (cuarto)* room; *(dormitorio)* bedroom; **h. individual/doble** single/ double room

habitante *nmf* inhabitant

habitar **1** *vt* to live in, to inhabit
2 *vi* to live

hábitat *nm* (*pl* **hábitats**) habitat

hábito *nm* (**a**) *(costumbre)* habit (**b**) *Rel* habit

habitual *adj* usual, habitual; *(cliente, lector)* regular

habituar **[30]** **1** *vt* to accustom (**a** to)
2 habituarse *vpr* **habituarse a** to get used to, to become accustomed to

habla *nf* (**a**) *(idioma)* language; **países de h. española** Spanish-speaking countries (**b**) *(facultad de hablar)* speech; **quedarse sin h.** to be left speechless (**c**) *Tel* **¡al h.!** speaking!

Takes the masculine articles **el** and **un**.

hablado,-a *adj* spoken; **el inglés h.** spoken English; **mal h.** coarse, foul-mouthed

hablador,-a *adj (parlanchín)* talkative; *(chismoso)* gossipy

habladuría *nf (rumor)* rumour; *(chisme)* piece of gossip

hablante *nmf* speaker

hablar **1** *vi* (**a**) to speak, to talk; **h. con algn** to speak to sb (**b**) **¡ni h.!** certainly not!; *Fam* **¡quién fue a h.!** look who's talking!
2 *vt* (**a**) *(idioma)* to speak; **habla alemán** he speaks German (**b**) *(tratar un asunto)* to talk over, to discuss
3 hablarse *vpr* (**a**) to speak *o* talk to one another (**b**) **se habla español** *(en letrero)* Spanish spoken

habré *indic fut de* **haber**

hacendado,-a *nm,f Am* farmer

hacendoso,-a *adj* hardworking

hacer **[15]** **1** *vt* (**a**) *(crear, producir, fabricar)* to make; **h. una casa** to build a house
(**b**) *(obrar, ejecutar)* to do; **eso no se hace** it isn't done; **hazme un favor** do me a favour; **¿qué haces?** *(en este momento)* what are you doing?; *(para vivir)* what do you do (for a living)?; **tengo mucho que h.** I have a lot to do; **h. deporte** to do sports; **h. una carrera/medicina** to do a degree/medicine
(**c**) *(conseguir) (amigos, dinero)* to make
(**d**) *(obligar)* to make; **hazle callar/**

trabajar make him shut up/work
(**e**) *(arreglar)* to make; **h. la cama** to
make the bed
(**f**) *Mat (sumar)* to make; **y con éste
hacen cien** and that makes a hundred
(**g**) *(dar aspecto)* to make look; **el negro
le hace más delgado** black makes him
look slimmer
(**h**) *(sustituyendo a otro verbo)* to do; **ya
no puedo leer como solía hacerlo** I can't
read as well as I used to
(**i**) *(representar)* to play; **h. el bueno** to
play the (part of the) goody
(**j**) **¡bien hecho!** well done!
2 *vi* (**a**) *(actuar)* to play; **hizo de Desdé-
mona** she played Desdemona
(**b**) **h. por** *o* **para** + *infin* to try to; **hice por
venir** I tried to come
(**c**) *(fingir)* to pretend; **h. como si** to act
as if
(**d**) *(convenir)* to be suitable; **a las ocho
si te hace** will eight o'clock be all right for
you?
3 *v impers* (**a**) **hace calor/frío** it's hot/
cold
(**b**) *(tiempo transcurrido)* ago; **hace mucho (tiempo)** a long time ago; **hace dos
días que no le veo** I haven't seen him for
two days; **hace dos años que vivo en
Glasgow** I've been living in Glasgow for
two years
4 hacerse *upr* (**a**) *(volverse)* to become,
to grow; **h. viejo** to grow old
(**b**) *(simular)* to pretend; **h. el dormido** to
pretend to be sleeping
(**c**) **h. con** *(apropiarse)* to get hold of
(**d**) **h. a** *(habituarse)* to get used to;
enseguida me hago a todo I soon get
used to anything
hacha *nf* (**a**) *(herramienta)* axe (**b**) *Fam*
ser un h. en algo to be an ace *o* a wizard at
sth

Takes the masculine articles **el** and **un**.

hachís *nm* hashish
hacia *prep* (**a**) *(dirección)* towards, to; **h.
abajo** down, downwards; **h. adelante** forwards; **h. arriba** up, upwards; **h. atrás**
back, backwards (**b**) *(tiempo)* at about,
at around; **h. las tres** at about three
o'clock
hacienda *nf* (**a**) *Am (finca agrícola)* estate, *US* ranch (**b**) *Fin* Treasury; **h. pública**
public funds *o* finances; **Ministerio de H.**
= Exchequer, Treasury
hacinamiento *nm* (**a**) *Agr* stacking; *Fig
(montón)* piling (**b**) *(de gente)* overcrowding

hacinar 1 *vt Agr* to stack; *Fig (amontonar)*
to pile up, to heap up
2 hacinarse *upr* **h. en** *(gente)* to be
packed into
hada *nf* fairy; **cuento de hadas** fairy tale;
h. madrina fairy godmother

Takes the masculine articles **el** and **un**.

hado *nm* destiny
hago *indic pres de* **hacer**
halagar [42] *vt* to flatter
halago *nm* flattery
halagüeño,-a *adj (noticia, impresión)*
promising
halcón *nm* falcon; **h. peregrino** peregrine
(falcon)
hálito *nm* (**a**) *(aliento)* breath (**b**) *(vapor)*
vapour
hallar 1 *vt (encontrar)* to find; *(averiguar)*
to find out; *(descubrir)* to discover
2 hallarse *upr (estar)* to be, to find oneself; *(estar situado)* to be situated
hallazgo *nm* (**a**) *(descubrimiento)* discovery (**b**) *(cosa encontrada)* find
hamaca *nf* hammock; *(mecedora)* rocking chair
hambre *nf (apetito)* hunger; *(inanición)*
starvation; *(catástrofe)* famine; **tener h.**
to be hungry

Takes the masculine articles **el** and **un**.

hambriento,-a *adj* starving
hamburguesa *nf* hamburger
hampa *nf* underworld

Takes the masculine articles **el** and **un**.

han *indic pres de* **haber**
harapo *nm* rag; **hecho un h.** in tatters
haré *indic fut de* **hacer**
harén *nm (pl harenes)* harem
harina *nf* flour
hartar 1 *vt* (**a**) *(cansar, fastidiar)* to annoy
(**b**) *(atiborrar)* to satiate; **el dulce harta
enseguida** sweet things soon fill you up
2 hartarse *upr* (**a**) *(saciar el apetito)* to
eat one's fill (**b**) *(cansarse)* to get fed up
(**de** with), to grow tired (**de** of)
harto,-a 1 *adj* (**a**) *(de comida)* full (**b**)
(cansado) fed up; **¡me tienes h.!** I'm fed
up with you!; **estoy h. de trabajar** I'm fed
up working (**c**) *Andes, CAm, Carib, Méx
(mucho)* lots of; **tiene h. dinero** he's got
lots of money
2 *adv* (**a**) *Fml (muy)* very (**b**) *Andes,
CAm, Carib, Méx (muy, mucho)* really
hartura *nf* bellyful; **¡qué h.!** what a drag!
has *indic pres de* **haber**
hasta 1 *prep* (**a**) *(lugar)* up to, as far as,

down to (**b**) *(tiempo)* until, till, up to; **h. el domingo** until Sunday; **h. el final** right to the end; **h. la fecha** up to now; **h. luego** see you later (**c**) *(con cantidad)* up to, as many as (**d**) *(incluso)* even (**e**) *CAm, Col, Méx (no antes de)* **pintaremos la casa h. fin de mes** we won't paint the house till the end of the month
  2 *conj* **h. que** until
hastiado,-a *adj* sick, tired (**de** of)
hastiar [29] *vt* to sicken
hastío *nm* weariness
hato *nm* bundle
hay *indic pres de* **haber**
Haya *nf* **La H.** The Hague
haya¹ *nf* (**a**) *Bot (árbol)* beech (**b**) *(madera)* beech (wood)

> Takes the masculine articles **el** and **un**.

haya² *subj pres de* **haber**
haz¹ *nm* (**a**) *Agr* sheaf (**b**) *(de luz)* shaft
haz² *nf (de hoja)* top side
haz³ *imperat de* **hacer**
hazaña *nf* deed, exploit
hazmerreír *nm* laughing stock
he¹ *adv* **he ahí/aquí ...** there/here you have ...
he² *indic pres de* **haber**
hebilla *nf* buckle
hebra *nf* thread; *(de carne)* sinew; *(de madera)* grain; **pegar la h.** to chat
hebreo,-a 1 *adj* Hebrew
  2 *nm,f* Hebrew
hecatombe *nf* disaster
hechicería *nf* witchcraft
hechicero,-a 1 *adj* bewitching
  2 *nm,f (hombre)* wizard, sorcerer; *(mujer)* witch, sorceress
hechizar [40] *vt* (**a**) *(embrujar)* to cast a spell on (**b**) *Fig (fascinar)* to bewitch, to charm
hechizo *nm* (**a**) *(embrujo)* spell (**b**) *Fig (fascinación)* fascination, charm
hecho,-a 1 *adj* (**a**) made, done; **¡bien h.!** well done! (**b**) *(carne)* done (**c**) *(persona)* mature (**d**) *(frase)* set; *(ropa)* ready-made
  2 *nm* (**a**) *(realidad)* fact; **de h.** in fact; **el h. es que ...** the fact is that ... (**b**) *(acto)* act, deed (**c**) *(suceso)* event, incident
hechura *nf (forma)* shape; *Cost* cut
hectárea *nf* hectare
hectolitro *nm* hectolitre
heder [3] *vi* to stink, to smell foul
hediondo,-a *adj* foul-smelling
hedor *nm* stink, stench
hegemonía *nf* hegemony
helada *nf* frost

heladera *nf* *RP (nevera)* refrigerator, fridge
heladería *nf* ice-cream parlour
helado,-a 1 *nm* ice cream
  2 *adj* (**a**) *(muy frío)* frozen, freezing cold; **estoy h. (de frío)** I'm frozen (**b**) *Fig* **quedarse h.** *(atónito)* to be flabbergasted
helar [1] 1 *vt (congelar)* to freeze
  2 *v impers* to freeze; **anoche heló** there was a frost last night
  3 helarse *vpr (congelarse)* to freeze
helecho *nm Bot* fern
hélice *nf* (**a**) *Av & Náut* propeller (**b**) *Anat, Arquit & Mat* helix
helicóptero *nm Av* helicopter
helipuerto *nm Av* heliport
hematoma *nm Med* haematoma
hembra *nf* (**a**) *Bot & Zool* female (**b**) *(mujer)* woman (**c**) *Téc* female; *(de tornillo)* nut; *(de enchufe)* socket
hemiciclo *nm Fam* (Spanish) parliament
hemisferio *nm* hemisphere
hemorragia *nf Med* haemorrhage
hemos *indic pres de* **haber**
henchir [6] *vt* to stuff
hender [3] *vt (resquebrajar)* to crack, to split; *Fig (olas)* to cut
hendidura *nf* crack
hendir [5] *vt =* **hender**
heno *nm* hay
heráldica *nf* heraldry
herbicida *nm* weedkiller, herbicide
herbívoro,-a 1 *adj* herbivorous, grass-eating
  2 *nm,f Zool* herbivore
herbolario *nm* herbalist's (shop)
herboso,-a *adj* grassy
hercio *nm* Herz
heredad *nf* (**a**) *(finca)* country estate (**b**) *(conjunto de bienes)* private estate
heredar *vt* (**a**) *Jur* to inherit (**b**) **ha heredado la sonrisa de su madre** she's got her mother's smile
heredero,-a *nm,f (hombre)* heir; *(mujer)* heiress; **príncipe h.** crown prince
hereditario,-a *adj* hereditary
hereje *nmf Rel* heretic
herejía *nf Rel* heresy
herencia *nf* (**a**) *Jur* inheritance, legacy (**b**) *Biol* heredity
herida *nf (lesión)* injury; *(corte)* wound
herido,-a *nm,f* injured person; **no hubo heridos** there were no casualties
herir [5] 1 *vt* (**a**) *(físicamente) (lesionar)* to injure; *(cortar)* to wound (**b**) *(emocionalmente)* to hurt, to wound (**c**) *(vista)* to offend
  2 herirse *vpr* to injure o hurt oneself

hermana *nf* (**a**) sister (**b**) *Rel (monja)* sister

hermanado,-a *adj* twinned; **ciudad hermanada** twin town

hermanar 1 *vt* (**a**) *(personas)* to unite spiritually (**b**) *(ciudades)* to twin (**c**) *(unir)* to unite, to combine

2 hermanarse *vpr* (**a**) *(ciudades)* to twin (**b**) *(combinar)* to combine

hermanastro,-a *nm,f (hombre)* stepbrother; *(mujer)* stepsister

hermandad *nf* (**a**) *(grupo)* fraternity, brotherhood, sisterhood (**b**) *(relación)* brotherhood, sisterhood

hermano *nm* (**a**) brother; **h. político** brother-in-law; **primo h.** first cousin (**b**) *Rel (fraile)* brother (**c**) **hermanos** brothers and sisters

herméticamente *adv* **h. cerrado** hermetically sealed

hermético,-a *adj* (**a**) *(cierre)* hermetic, airtight (**b**) *Fig (abstruso)* secretive

hermetismo *nm* airtightness; *Fig* impenetrability

hermoso,-a *adj* beautiful, lovely; *(grande)* fine

hermosura *nf* beauty

héroe *nm* hero

heroico,-a *adj* heroic

heroína *nf* (**a**) *(mujer)* heroine (**b**) *(droga)* heroin

heroinómano,-a *nm,f* heroin addict

heroísmo *nm* heroism

herrador *nm* blacksmith

herradura *nf* horseshoe

herramienta *nf Téc* tool; **caja de herramientas** toolbox

herrar [1] *vt* (**a**) *(caballo)* to shoe (**b**) *(ganado)* to brand

herrería *nf* forge, smithy

herrero *nm* blacksmith, smith

herrumbre *nf* rust

hervidero *nm Fig (lugar)* hotbed

hervir [5] 1 *vt (hacer bullir)* to boil
2 *vi (**a**) Culin* to boil; **romper a h.** to come to the boil (**b**) *(abundar)* to swarm, to seethe (**de** with)

heterodoxo,-a *adj* unorthodox

heterogéneo,-a *adj* heterogeneous

hez *nf* (**a**) *(usu pl) (poso)* sediment, dregs (**b**) **heces** faeces

hiato *nm Ling* hiatus

híbrido,-a *adj & nm,f* hybrid

hice *pt indef de* hacer

hiciste *pt indef de* hacer

hidalgo *nm Hist* nobleman, gentleman

hidalguía *nf* nobility; *Fig* chivalry, gentlemanliness

hidratación *nf* (**a**) *Quím* hydration (**b**) *(de la piel)* moisturizing

hidratante *adj* moisturizing; **crema/leche h.** moisturizing cream/lotion

hidráulico,-a *adj* hydraulic; **energía hidráulica** hydro-electric energy

hidroavión *nm* seaplane, *US* hydroplane

hidrocarburo *nm* hydrocarbon

hidrófilo,-a *adj* absorbent; **algodón h.** *Br* cotton wool, *Am* absorbent cotton

hidrógeno *nm Quím* hydrogen

hidroterapia *nf Med* hydrotherapy

hiedra *nf* ivy

hiel *nf* (**a**) *Anat* bile (**b**) *Fig* bitterness, gall

hielo *nm* ice; *Fig* **romper el h.** to break the ice

hiena *nf* hyena

hierba *nf* (**a**) grass; **mala h.** *Bot* weed; *Fig (persona)* bad lot; *Fam Hum* **y otras hierbas** among others (**b**) *Culin* herb; **h. luisa** lemon verbena (**c**) *Fam (marihuana)* grass

hierbabuena *nf* mint

hierro *nm* (**a**) *(metal)* iron; **h. forjado** wrought iron (**b**) *(punta de arma)* head, point (**c**) *(marca en el ganado)* brand

hígado *nm* (**a**) *Anat* liver (**b**) *Euf* guts

higiene *nf* hygiene

higiénico,-a *adj* hygienic; **papel h.** toilet paper

higo *nm Fam Fig* **hecho un h.** wizened, crumpled

higuera *nf Bot* fig tree

hija *nf* daughter

hijastro,-a *nm,f (hombre)* stepson; *(mujer)* stepdaughter

hijo *nm* (**a**) son, child; *Pey* **h. de papá** rich kid; *Vulg* **h. de puta** o *Méx* **de la chingada** bastard, *US* asshole (**b**) **hijos** children

hijoputa *nm Vulg* bastard, *US* asshole

hilacha *nf,* **hilacho** *nm* loose o hanging thread

hilandería *nf* mill; *(de algodón)* cotton mill

hilandero,-a *nm,f* spinner

hilar *vt & vi* (**a**) to spin (**b**) *Fig (idea, plan)* to work out; **h. muy fino** to split hairs

hilaridad *nf* hilarity, mirth

hilera *nf* line, row

hilo *nm* (**a**) *Cost* thread; *(grueso)* yarn (**b**) *Fig (de historia, discurso)* thread; *(de pensamiento)* train; **perder el h.** to lose the thread; **h. musical** background music (**c**) *Tex* linen

hilvanar *vt* (**a**) *Cost* to tack, to baste (**b**) *Fig (ideas etc)* to outline

himno *nm* hymn; **h. nacional** national anthem

hincapié *nm* **hacer h. en** *(insistir)* to insist on; *(subrayar)* to emphasize, to stress

hincar [44] 1 *vt (clavar)* to drive (in); **h. el diente a** to sink one's teeth into
2 hincarse *vpr* **h. de rodillas** to kneel (down)

hincha *Fam* **1** *nmf Ftb* fan, supporter
2 *nf (antipatía)* grudge, dislike; **me tiene h.** he's got it in for me

hinchada *nf Ftb Fam* fans, supporters

hinchado,-a *adj* (**a**) inflated, blown up (**b**) *Med (cara etc)* swollen, puffed up; *(estómago)* bloated (**c**) *Fig (estilo)* bombastic, pompous

hinchar 1 *vt* (**a**) *(inflar)* to inflate, to blow up (**b**) *Fig (exagerar)* to inflate, to exaggerate
2 hincharse *vpr* (**a**) *Med* to swell (up) (**b**) *Fam* **me hinché de comida** I stuffed myself; **me hinché de llorar** I cried for all I was worth

hinchazón *nf Med* swelling

hindú *adj & nmf* Hindu

hipermercado *nm* hypermarket

hipertensión *nf* high blood pressure

hípica *nf* (horse) riding

hípico,-a *adj* horse; **club h.** riding club

hipnotizar [40] *vt* to hypnotize

hipo *nm* hiccups, hiccough; **me ha dado h.** it's given me the hiccups

hipocondríaco,-a *adj & nm,f* hypochondriac

hipocresía *nf* hypocrisy

hipócrita 1 *adj* hypocritical
2 *nmf* hypocrite

hipódromo *nm* racetrack, racecourse

hipopótamo *nm* hippopotamus

hipoteca *nf Fin* mortgage

hipotecar [44] *vt* (**a**) *Fin* to mortgage (**b**) *Fig* to jeopardize

hipótesis *nf inv* hypothesis

hipotético,-a *adj* hypothetical

hiriente *adj* offensive, wounding; *(palabras)* cutting

hirsuto,-a *adj* hirsute, hairy; *(cerdoso)* bristly

hispánico,-a *adj* Hispanic, Spanish

hispanidad *nf* **el Día de la H.** Columbus Day *(12 October)*

hispano,-a 1 *adj (español)* Spanish; *(español y sudamericano)* Hispanic; *(sudamericano)* Spanish American
2 *nm,f (hispanoamericano)* Spanish American; *(estadounidense)* Hispanic

Hispanoamérica *nf* Latin America

hispanoamericano,-a *adj & nm,f* Latin American

hispanohablante 1 *adj* Spanish-speaking
2 *nmf* Spanish speaker

histeria *nf* hysteria; **un ataque de h.** hysterics

histérico,-a *adj* hysterical; *Fam Fig* **me pones h.** you're driving me mad

historia *nf* (**a**) history; **esto pasará a la h.** this will go down in history (**b**) *(narración)* story, tale; *Fam* **¡déjate de historias!** don't give me that!

historiador,-a *nm,f* historian

historial *nm* (**a**) *Med* medical record, case history (**b**) *(antecedentes)* background

historiar [29] *vt* to recount

histórico,-a *adj* (**a**) historical (**b**) *(auténtico)* factual, true; **hechos históricos** true facts (**c**) *(de gran importancia)* historic, memorable

historieta *nf* (**a**) *(cuento)* short story, tale (**b**) *(tira cómica)* comic strip

hito *nm* milestone; **mirar de h. en h.** to stare at

hizo *pt indef de* **hacer**

hnos. (*abr* **Hermanos**) Bros

hocico *nm* (**a**) *(de animal)* snout (**b**) *(de persona)* mug, snout; *Fam* **meter los hocicos en algo** to stick *o* poke one's nose into sth

hogar *nm* (**a**) *(casa)* home (**b**) *(de la chimenea)* hearth, fireplace (**c**) *Fig* **formar** *o* **crear un h.** *(familia)* to start a family

hogareño,-a *adj (vida)* home, family; *(persona)* home-loving, stay-at-home

hoguera *nf* bonfire

hoja *nf* (**a**) *Bot* leaf (**b**) *(pétalo)* petal (**c**) *(de papel)* sheet, leaf; **h. de cálculo** spreadsheet (**d**) *(de libro)* leaf, page (**e**) *(de metal)* sheet (**f**) *(de cuchillo, espada)* blade (**g**) *(impreso)* hand-out, printed sheet (**h**) *(de puerta o ventana)* leaf

hojalata *nf* tin, tin plate

hojaldre *nm Culin* puff pastry

hojarasca *nf* fallen *o* dead leaves

hojear *vt* to leaf through, to flick through

hola *interj* hello!, hullo!, hi!

Holanda *n* Holland

holandés,-esa 1 *adj* Dutch
2 *nm,f (hombre)* Dutchman; *(mujer)* Dutchwoman
3 *nm (idioma)* Dutch

holding *nm Fin* holding company

holgado,-a *adj* (**a**) *(ropa)* loose, baggy (**b**) *(económicamente)* comfortable (**c**) *(espacio)* roomy; **andar h. de tiempo** to have plenty of time

holgar [2] *vi* (**a**) *(no trabajar)* to be idle

(**b**) *(sobrar)* **huelga decir que ...** it goes without saying that ...

holgazán,-ana 1 *adj* lazy, idle

2 *nm,f* lazybones, layabout

holgura *nf* (**a**) *(ropa)* looseness (**b**) *(espacio)* space, roominess; *Téc* play, give (**c**) *(bienestar económico)* affluence, comfort; **vivir con h.** to be comfortably off, to be well-off

hollar [2] *vt Fig* to walk on; **terrenos jamás hollados** uncharted territory

hollín *nm* soot

hombre 1 *nm* (**a**) man; **de h. a h.** man-to-man; **¡pobre h.!** poor chap!; **ser muy h.** to be every inch a man; **h. de estado** statesman; **h. de negocios** businessman (**b**) *(especie)* mankind, man

2 *interj* (**a**) *(saludo)* hey!, hey there!; **¡h., Juan!** hey, Juan! (**b**) **¡sí h.!, ¡h. claro!** *(enfático)* sure!, you bet!; **¡anda, h.!** *(incredulidad)* oh come on!

hombrera *nf* shoulder pad

hombría *nf* manliness, virility

hombrillo *nm Ven (arcén)* verge; *(de autopista)* Br hard shoulder, US shoulder

hombro *nm* shoulder; **a hombros** on one's shoulders; **encogerse de hombros** to shrug one's shoulders; **mirar a algn por encima del h.** to look down one's nose at sb

hombruno,-a *adj* mannish, butch

homenaje *nm* homage, tribute; **rendir h. a algn** to pay homage *o* tribute to sb

homenajear *vt* to pay tribute to

homicida 1 *nmf (hombre)* murderer; *(mujer)* murderess

2 *adj* homicidal; **el arma h.** the murder weapon

homicidio *nm* homicide

homogéneo,-a *adj* homogeneous, uniform

homologable *adj* comparable (**con** with)

homologar [42] *vt* to give official approval *o* recognition to

homólogo,-a 1 *adj (equiparable)* comparable

2 *nm,f (persona con mismas condiciones)* counterpart

homosexual *adj & nmf* homosexual

homosexualidad *nf* homosexuality

honda *nf (arma)* sling

hondo,-a *adj* (**a**) *(profundo)* deep; **plato h.** soup dish (**b**) *Fig (pesar)* profound, deep

hondonada *nf Geog* hollow, depression

hondura *nf* depth; *Fig* **meterse en honduras** *(profundizar)* to go into too much detail

Honduras *n* Honduras

hondureño,-a *adj & nm,f* Honduran

honestidad *nf* (**a**) *(honradez)* honesty, uprightness (**b**) *(decencia)* modesty

honesto,-a *adj* (**a**) *(honrado)* honest, upright (**b**) *(decente)* modest

hongo *nm* (**a**) *Bot* fungus; **h. venenoso** toadstool (**b**) *(sombrero) Br* bowler (hat), *US* derby

honor *nm* (**a**) *(virtud)* honour; **palabra de h.** word of honour (**b**) **en h. a la verdad ...** to be fair ...; **es un h. para mí** it's an honour for me (**c**) **hacer h. a** to live up to

honorable *adj* honourable; *Pol* **el h.** = head of the Catalan government

honorario,-a 1 *adj* honorary

2 *nmpl* **honorarios** fees, fee

honorífico,-a *adj* honorary

honra *nf* (**a**) *(dignidad)* dignity, self-esteem (**b**) *(fama)* reputation, good name (**c**) *(honor)* honour; **me cabe la h. de ...** I have the honour of ...; **¡a mucha h.!** and proud of it!

honradez *nf* honesty, integrity

honrado,-a *adj* (**a**) *(de fiar)* honest (**b**) *(decente)* upright, respectable

honrar *vt* (**a**) *(respetar)* to honour (**b**) *(enaltecer)* to be a credit to

honrilla *nf* self-respect, pride

honroso,-a *adj (loable)* honourable

hora *nf* (**a**) hour; **media h.** half an hour; **a altas horas de la madrugada** in the small hours; **dar la h.** to strike the hour; **(trabajo) por horas** (work) paid by the hour; **h. punta,** *Am* **h. pico** *(de mucho tráfico)* rush hour; *(de agua, electricidad)* peak times; **horas extra** overtime (hours) (**b**) *Fig* time; **¿qué h. es?** what time is it?; **a su h.** at the proper time; **a última h.** at the last moment; **la h. de la verdad** the moment of truth (**c**) *(cita)* appointment; **pedir h.** *(al médico etc)* to ask for an appointment

horadar *vt (perforar)* to drill *o* bore a hole in

horario,-a 1 *nm* timetable, *US* schedule

2 *adj* time; *Rad* **señal horaria** pips

horca *nf* gallows *sing*

horcajada: • **a horcajadas** *loc adv* astride

horchata *nf Culin* = sweet, milky drink made from chufa nuts or almonds

horda *nf* horde, mob

horizonte *nm* horizon

horma *nf (de zapato)* last

hormiga *nf* ant

hormigón *nm Constr* concrete; **h. armado** reinforced concrete

hormiguear *vi* to itch, to tingle; **me hormigueaba la pierna** I had pins and needles in my leg

hormigueo *nm* (**a**) pins and needles, tingling *o* itching sensation (**b**) *Fig* anxiety

hormiguero *nm* (**a**) anthill (**b**) *Fig* **ser un h.** *(lugar)* to be swarming (with people)

hormona *nf* hormone

hornada *nf* (**a**) *(pan)* batch (**b**) *Fig* set, batch

hornillo *nm* *(de cocinar)* stove; *(placa)* hotplate

horno *nm* *(cocina)* oven; *Téc* furnace; *(para cerámica, ladrillos)* kiln; *Culin* **pescado al h.** baked fish; *Fam Fig* **esta habitación es un h.** this room is boiling hot

Hornos *n* **Cabo de H.** Cape Horn

horóscopo *nm* horoscope

horquilla *nf* (**a**) *(del pelo)* hairpin, *Br* hair-grip, *US* bobby-pin (**b**) *(estadística)* chart (**c**) **h. de precios** price range

horrendo,-a *adj* horrifying, horrible

hórreo *nm* *Agr* granary

horrible *adj* horrible, dreadful, awful

horripilante *adj* hair-raising, scary

horror *nm* (**a**) horror, terror; **¡qué h.!** how awful!; *Fam* **tengo h. a las motos** I hate motorbikes (**b**) *Fam Fig* **me gusta horrores** *(muchísimo)* I like it an awful lot

horrorizar [40] *vt* to horrify, to terrify

horroroso,-a *adj* (**a**) *(que da miedo)* horrifying, terrifying (**b**) *Fam (muy feo)* hideous, ghastly (**c**) *Fam (malísimo)* awful, dreadful

hortaliza *nf* vegetable

hortelano,-a *nm,f Br* market gardener, *US* truck farmer

hortensia *nf Bot* hydrangea

hortera *adj Fam (persona)* flashy; *(cosa)* tacky, kitsch

horterada *nf Fam* tacky thing *o* act

hosco,-a *adj* (**a**) *(poco sociable)* surly, sullen (**b**) *(tenebroso)* dark, gloomy (**c**) *(difícil)* tough

hospedaje *nm* lodgings, *Br* accommodation, *US* accommodations

hospedar 1 *vt* to put up, to lodge
2 hospedarse *vpr* to stay (**en** at)

hospicio *nm* orphanage

hospital *nm* hospital

hospitalario,-a *adj* (**a**) *(acogedor)* hospitable (**b**) *Med* hospital; **instalaciones hospitalarias** hospital facilities

hospitalidad *nf* hospitality

hospitalizar [40] *vt* to take *o* send into hospital, to hospitalize

hostal *nm* guest house

hostelería *nf (negocio)* catering business; *(estudios)* hotel management

hostelero,-a *nm,f (hombre)* landlord; *(mujer)* landlady

hostería *nf CSur* inn, lodging house

hostia 1 *nf* (**a**) *Rel* host (**b**) *Vulg (tortazo)* bash (**c**) *Vulg* **estar de mala h.** to be in a foul mood; **ser la h.** *(fantástico)* to be *Br* bloody *o US* goddamn amazing; *(penoso)* to be *Br* bloody *o US* goddamn awful
2 *interj Vulg* damn! *Br* bloody hell!

hostiar [29] *vt Vulg* to bash, to sock

hostigar [42] *vt* (**a**) to harass (**b**) *(caballerías)* to whip

hostil *adj* hostile

hostilidad *nf* hostility

hotel *nm* hotel

hotelero,-a 1 *adj* hotel; **el sector h.** the hotel sector
2 *nm,f* hotel-keeper, hotelier

hoy *adv* (**a**) *(día)* today (**b**) *Fig (presente)* now; **h. (en) día** nowadays; **h. por h.** at the present time

hoya *nf Geog* dale, valley

hoyo *nm* (**a**) *(agujero)* hole, pit (**b**) *(sepultura)* grave (**c**) *(de golf)* hole

hoyuelo *nm* dimple

hoz *nf Agr* sickle; **la h. y el martillo** the hammer and sickle

HR *nm* (*abr* **Hostal Residencia**) boarding house

huachafo,-a *adj Perú Fam* tacky

huasipungo *nm Andes* = plot of land given to Indian for his own use in exchange for work on the landowner's farm

huaso,-a *nm,f Chile Fam* farmer, peasant

hube *pt indef de* haber

hubiera *subj imperf de* haber

hucha *nf* piggy bank

hueco,-a 1 *adj* (**a**) *(vacío)* empty, hollow (**b**) *(sonido)* resonant
2 *nm* (**a**) *(cavidad)* hollow, hole (**b**) *(sitio no ocupado)* empty space (**c**) *(rato libre)* free time

huele *indic pres de* oler

huelga *nf* strike; **estar en** *o* **de h.** to be on strike; **h. de brazos caídos** go-slow; **h. de celo** work-to-rule

huelguista *nmf* striker

huella *nf* (**a**) *(del pie)* footprint; *(coche)* track; **h. dactilar** fingerprint (**b**) *Fig (vestigio)* trace, sign; **dejar h.** to leave one's mark

huérfano,-a *nm,f* orphan

huero,-a *adj Fig* empty

huerta *nf Agr* (**a**) *(parcela) Br* market garden, *US* truck farm (**b**) *(región)* = irrigated area used for cultivation

huerto *nm (de verduras)* vegetable garden, kitchen garden; *(de frutales)* orchard

hueso *nm* (**a**) *Anat* bone; **estar en los**

huesos to be all skin and bone (**b**) *(de fruto)* stone, *US* pit (**c**) *Fig (difícil)* hard work; *(profesor)* hard nut (**d**) *Méx (enchufe)* contact

huésped,-a *nm,f (invitado)* guest; *(en hotel etc)* lodger, boarder; **casa de huéspedes** guesthouse

hueste *nf Mil* army, host

huesudo,-a *adj* bony

huevada *nf Andes, RP muy Fam (dicho)* garbage, bullshit, *Br* bollocks

huevera *nf (caja)* egg box

huevo *nm* (**a**) egg; **h. duro** hard-boiled egg; **h. escalfado** poached egg; **h. frito** fried egg; **h. pasado por agua,** *Am* **h. tibio** *o* **a la copa** soft-boiled egg; **huevos revueltos** scrambled eggs (**b**) *muy Fam (usu pl)* balls; **hacer algo por huevos** to do sth even if it kills you; **tener huevos** to have guts

huida *nf* flight, escape

huidizo,-a *adj* elusive

huipil *nm CAm, Méx* = traditional Indian woman's dress or blouse

huir [37] *vi* to run away (**de** from), to flee; **h. de la cárcel** to escape from prison; **h. de algn** to avoid sb

hule *nm* (**a**) *(tela impermeable)* oilcloth, oilskin (**b**) *(de mesa)* tablecloth (**c**) *Am* rubber

hulla *nf* soft coal

humanidad *nf* (**a**) *(género humano)* humanity, mankind (**b**) *(cualidad)* humanity, humaneness (**c**) *(bondad)* compassion, kindness

humanitario,-a *adj* humanitarian

humano,-a 1 *adj* (**a**) *(relativo al hombre)* human (**b**) *(compasivo)* humane
2 *nm* human (being); **ser h.** human being

humear *vi (echar humo)* to smoke; *(arrojar vapor)* to steam, to be steaming hot

humedad *nf (atmosférica)* humidity; *(de lugar)* dampness; **a prueba de h.** damp-proof

humedecer [33] **1** *vt* to moisten, to dampen
2 humedecerse *vpr* to become damp *o* wet *o* moist

húmedo,-a *adj (casa, ropa)* damp; *(clima)* humid, damp, moist

humildad *nf* humility; *(pobreza)* humbleness

humilde *adj* humble, modest; *(pobre)* poor

humillación *nf* humiliation

humillante *adj* humiliating, humbling

humillar 1 *vt (rebajar)* to humiliate, to humble
2 humillarse *vpr* **humillarse ante algn** to humble oneself before sb

humita *nf Andes, Arg (pasta de maíz)* = paste made of mashed maize *o US* corn, used to make steamed dumplings

humo *nm* (**a**) smoke; *(gas)* fumes; *(vapor)* vapour, steam (**b**) ¡**qué humos tiene!** she thinks a lot of herself!

humor *nm* (**a**) *(genio)* mood; **estar de buen/mal h.** to be in a good/bad mood (**b**) *(carácter)* temper; **es persona de mal h.** he's bad-tempered (**c**) *(gracia)* humour; **sentido del h.** sense of humour

humorismo *nm* humour

humorista *nmf* humorist; **h. gráfico** cartoonist

humorístico,-a *adj* humorous, funny

hundido,-a *adj* (**a**) *(barco)* sunken; *(ojos)* deep-set (**b**) *Fig (abatido)* down, demoralized

hundimiento *nm* (**a**) *(de edificio)* collapse (**b**) *(de barco)* sinking (**c**) *(de tierra)* subsidence (**d**) *Fig Fin* crash, slump; *(ruina)* downfall

hundir 1 *vt* (**a**) *(barco)* to sink (**b**) *(edificio)* to bring *o* knock down (**c**) *Fig (desmoralizar)* to demoralize
2 hundirse *vpr* (**a**) *(barco)* to sink (**b**) *(edificio)* to collapse (**c**) *Fig (empresa)* to collapse, to crash

húngaro,-a 1 *adj* Hungarian
2 *nm,f (persona)* Hungarian
3 *nm (idioma)* Hungarian

Hungría *n* Hungary

huracán *nm* hurricane

huraño,-a *adj Pey* unsociable

hurgar [42] **1** *vi (fisgar)* to poke one's nose in
2 *vt (fuego etc)* to poke, to rake
3 hurgarse *vpr* **h. las narices** to pick one's nose

hurón,-ona 1 *nm Zool* ferret
2 *nm,f Fam Fig (fisgón)* busybody, nosey-parker

hurraca *nf Orn* = **urraca**

hurtadillas *adv* **a h.** stealthily, on the sly

hurtar *vt* to steal, to pilfer

hurto *nm* petty theft, pilfering

husmear 1 *vt (olfatear)* to sniff out, to scent
2 *vi Fig (curiosear)* to snoop, to pry

huyo *indic pres de* **huir**

I, i [i] *nf (la letra)* I, i; **i griega** Y, y

IB *nm Educ (abr* **Instituto de Bachillerato**) ≃ state secondary school

ib. (*abr* **ibídem**) ibid.

ibérico,-a *adj* Iberian

Iberoamérica *n* Latin America

iberoamericano,-a *adj & nm,f* Latin American

iceberg *nm (pl* **icebergs**) iceberg

ICONA *nm Antes (abr* **Instituto Nacional para la Conservación de la Naturaleza**) = Spanish national institute for conservation

icono *nm* icon; *Informát* icon

iconoclasta 1 *adj* iconoclastic
   2 *nmf* iconoclast

iconografía *nf* iconography

ictericia *nf Med* jaundice

íd. (*abr* **ídem**) id

I+D (*abr* **Investigación más Desarrollo**) R&D

ida *nf* **billete de i. y vuelta** *Br* return ticket, *US* round-trip ticket; **idas y venidas** comings and goings

idea *nf* (**a**) idea; **i. fija** fixed idea (**b**) *(noción)* idea; **hacerse a la i. de** to get used to the idea of; *Fam* **ni i.** no idea, not a clue (**c**) *(opinión)* opinion; **cambiar de i.** to change one's mind (**d**) *(intención)* intention; **a mala i.** on purpose

ideal *adj & nm* ideal

idealismo *nm* idealism

idealista 1 *adj* idealistic
   2 *nmf* idealist

idealizar [40] *vt* to idealize, to glorify

idear *vt* (**a**) *(inventar)* to devise, to invent (**b**) *(concebir)* to think up, to conceive

ídem *adv* idem, ditto; *Fam* **í. de í.** exactly the same

idéntico,-a *adj* identical

identidad *nf* (**a**) identity; **carnet de i.** identity card (**b**) *(semejanza)* identity, sameness

identificación *nf* identification

identificar [44] **1** *vt* to identify
   2 identificarse *vpr* to identify oneself; *Fig* **i. con** to identify with

ideología *nf* ideology

ideológico,-a *adj* ideological

idílico,-a *adj* idyllic

idilio *nm* (**a**) *Lit* idyll (**b**) *Fig (romance)* romance, love affair

idioma *nm* language

idiomático,-a *adj* idiomatic

idiosincrasia *nf* idiosyncrasy

idiota 1 *adj* idiotic, stupid
   2 *nmf* idiot, fool

idiotez *nf* idiocy, stupidity

ido,-a *adj* (**a**) *(distraído)* absent-minded (**b**) *Fam (chiflado)* crazy, nuts

idólatra 1 *adj* idolatrous
   2 *nmf (hombre)* idolater; *(mujer)* idolatress

idolatrar *vt* to worship; *Fig* to idolize

idolatría *nf* idolatry

ídolo *nm* idol

idóneo,-a *adj* suitable, fit

iglesia *nf* (**a**) *(edificio)* church (**b**) **la I.** *(institución)* the Church

ignominia *nf* ignominy

ignominioso,-a *adj* ignominious, shameful

ignorancia *nf* ignorance

ignorante 1 *adj* (**a**) *(sin instrucción)* ignorant (**b**) *(no informado)* ignorant, unaware (**de** of)
   2 *nmf* ignoramus

ignorar 1 *vt* (**a**) *(algo)* not to know (**b**) *(a algn)* to ignore
   2 ignorarse *vpr* to be unknown

ignoto,-a *adj* unknown

igual 1 *adj* (**a**) *(idéntico)* the same, alike; **son todos iguales** they're all the same; **es i.** it doesn't matter; **i. que** the same as (**b**) *(equivalente)* equal; **a partes iguales** fifty-fifty (**c**) *Dep (empatados)* even; **treinta iguales** thirty all (**d**) *Mat* equal; **tres más tres i. a seis** three plus three equals six (**e**) **al i. que** just like (**f**) **por i.** equally
   2 *nm* equal; **de i. a i.** on an equal footing; **sin i.** unique, unrivalled
   3 *adv* (**a**) **lo haces i. que yo** you do it the same way I do (**b**) *(probablemente)* probably; **i. vengo** I'll probably come (**c**) *Andes, RP (aún así)* anyway, still; **estaba nublado pero i. fuimos a la playa** it was cloudy but we still went to the beach *o* we went to the beach anyway

igualar 1 *vt* (**a**) to make equal (**b**) *(nivelar)* to level (**c**) *Dep* **i. el partido** to equalize, to square the match
2 igualarse *vpr* (**a**) to be equal (**b**) **igualarse con algn** to place oneself on an equal footing with sb
igualdad *nf* (**a**) equality; **i. ante la ley** equality before the law (**b**) *(identidad)* sameness; **en i. de condiciones** on equal terms
igualitario,-a *adj* egalitarian
igualmente *adv* equally; *(también)* also, likewise; *Fam* **encantado de conocerlo –** **¡i.!** pleased to meet you – likewise!
ijada *nf,* **ijar** *nm Anat* flank
ikastola *nf* = primary school in the Basque Country where classes are given entirely in Basque
ikurriña *nf* = Basque national flag
ilegal *adj* illegal
ilegalidad *nf* illegality
ilegalmente *adv* illegally
ilegible *adj* illegible, unreadable
ilegítimo,-a *adj* illegitimate
ileso,-a *adj* unhurt, unharmed
ilícito,-a *adj* illicit, unlawful
ilimitado,-a *adj* unlimited, limitless
Ilmo. (*abr* **Ilustrísimo**) His Excellence *o* Excellency
ilógico,-a *adj* illogical
iluminación *nf (alumbrado)* illumination, lighting
iluminar *vt* (**a**) to illuminate, to light (up) (**b**) *Fig (a persona)* to enlighten; *(tema)* to throw light upon
ilusión *nf* (**a**) *(esperanza)* hope; *(esperanza vana)* illusion, delusion; **hacerse ilusiones** to build up one's hopes (**b**) *(sueño)* dream (**c**) *(emoción)* excitement, thrill; **me hace i. verla** I'm looking forward to seeing her; **¡qué i.!** how exciting!
ilusionar 1 *vt* (**a**) *(esperanzar)* to build up sb's hopes (**b**) *(entusiasmar)* to excite, to thrill
2 ilusionarse *vpr* (**a**) *(esperanzarse)* to build up one's hopes (**b**) *(entusiasmarse)* to be excited *o* thrilled (**con** about)
iluso,-a *adj* easily deceived, gullible
ilusorio,-a *adj* illusory, unreal
ilustración *nf* (**a**) *(grabado)* illustration, picture; *(ejemplo)* illustration (**b**) *(erudición)* learning, erudition; *Hist* **la I.** the Enlightenment
ilustrado,-a *adj* (**a**) *(con dibujos, ejemplos)* illustrated (**b**) *(erudito)* learned, erudite
ilustrar 1 *vt* (**a**) to illustrate (**b**) *(aclarar)* to explain, to make clear

2 ilustrarse *vpr* to acquire knowledge (**sobre** of), to learn (**sobre** about)
ilustrativo,-a *adj* illustrative
ilustre *adj* illustrious, distinguished
imagen *nf* (**a**) image; **ser la viva i. de algn** to be the spitting image of sb; **tener buena i.** to have a good image (**b**) *Rel* image, statue (**c**) *TV* picture
imaginación *nf* imagination; **eso son imaginaciones tuyas** you're imagining things
imaginar 1 *vt* to imagine
2 imaginarse *vpr* to imagine; **me imagino que sí** I suppose so
imaginario,-a *adj* imaginary
imaginativo,-a *adj* imaginative
imán *nm* magnet
imbatible *adj* unbeatable
imbatido,-a *adj* unbeaten, undefeated
imbécil 1 *adj* stupid, silly
2 *nmf* idiot, imbecile
imbecilidad *nf* stupidity, imbecility
imborrable *adj* indelible
imbuir [37] *vt Fml* to imbue
imitación *nf* imitation
imitar *vt* to imitate; *(gestos)* to mimic; **este collar imita al oro** this necklace is imitation gold
impaciencia *nf* impatience
impacientar 1 *vt* **i. a algn** to make sb lose patience, to exasperate sb
2 impacientarse *vpr* to get *o* grow impatient (**por** at)
impaciente *adj (deseoso)* impatient; *(intranquilo)* anxious
impactante *adj* **una noticia i.** a sensational piece of news
impactar *vt* to shock, to stun
impacto *nm* impact; *Mil* hit
impar *adj Mat* odd; **número i.** odd number
imparable *adj Dep* unstoppable
imparcial *adj* impartial, unbiased
imparcialidad *nf* impartiality
impartir *vt (clases)* to give
impasible *adj* impassive
impávido,-a *adj* fearless
impecable *adj* impeccable
impedido,-a 1 *adj* disabled, handicapped
2 *nm,f* disabled *o* handicapped person
impedimento *nm* impediment; *(obstáculo)* hindrance, obstacle
impedir [6] *vt (obstaculizar)* to impede, to hinder; *(imposibilitar)* to prevent, to stop; **i. el paso** to block the way
impeler *vt Téc* to drive, to propel; *Fig* to drive, to impel

impenetrable *adj* impenetrable

impenitente *adj Rel* impenitent, unrepentant

impensable *adj* unthinkable

impepinable *adj Fam* dead sure, certain

imperante *adj (gobernante)* ruling; *(predominante)* prevailing

imperar *vi (gobernar)* to rule; *(predominar)* to prevail

imperativo,-a 1 *adj* imperative
2 *nm Ling* imperative

imperceptible *adj* imperceptible

imperdible *nm* safety pin

imperdonable *adj* unforgivable, inexcusable

imperecedero,-a *adj* imperishable; *Fig* enduring

imperfección *nf* (a) imperfection (b) *(defecto)* defect, fault

imperfecto,-a *adj* (a) imperfect, fallible (b) *(defectuoso)* defective, faulty (c) *Ling* imperfect

imperial *adj* imperial

imperialismo *nm* imperialism

impericia *nf* incompetence

imperio *nm* empire; **el i. de la ley** the rule of law

imperioso,-a *adj* (a) *(autoritario)* imperious (b) *(ineludible)* urgent, imperative; **una necesidad imperiosa** a pressing need

impermeable 1 *adj* impermeable, impervious; *(ropa)* waterproof
2 *nm* raincoat, mac

impersonal *adj* impersonal

impertérrito,-a *adj* undaunted, fearless

impertinencia *nf* impertinence

impertinente 1 *adj (insolente)* impertinent; *(inoportuno)* irrelevant
2 *nmpl* **impertinentes** lorgnette

imperturbable *adj* imperturbable, unruffled

ímpetu *nm* (a) *(impulso)* impetus, momentum (b) *(violencia)* violence (c) *(energía)* energy

impetuosidad *nf* (a) *(violencia)* violence (b) *(fogosidad)* impetuosity, impulsiveness

impetuoso,-a *adj* (a) *(violento)* violent (b) *(fogoso)* impetuous, impulsive

impío,-a *adj* ungodly, irreligious

implacable *adj* relentless, implacable

implantar *vt (costumbres)* to implant, to instil; *(reformas)* to introduce; *Med* to implant

implicación *nf (participación)* involvement; *(significado)* implication

implicancia *nf CSur* implication

implicar **[44]** *vt* (a) *(involucrar)* to involve, to implicate (**en** in) (b) *(conllevar)* to imply

implícito,-a *adj* implicit, implied

implorar *vt* to implore, to beg

impoluto,-a *adj* pure, spotless

imponente *adj* (a) *(impresionante)* imposing, impressive (b) *(sobrecogedor)* stunning (c) *Fam (atractivo)* terrific, tremendous, smashing

imponer [19] *(pp* **impuesto)** **1** *vt* (a) to impose (b) *(respeto)* to inspire (c) *Fin* to deposit
2 *vi (impresionar)* to be impressive;
3 imponerse *vpr* (a) *(infundir respeto)* to command respect (b) *(prevalecer)* to prevail (c) *(ser necesario)* to be necessary

imponible *adj Fin* taxable

impopular *adj* unpopular, disliked

importación *nf (mercancía)* import; *(acción)* importing; **artículos de i.** imported goods

importancia *nf* importance, significance; **dar i. a** to attach importance to; **sin i.** unimportant

importante *adj* important, significant; **una suma i.** a considerable sum

importar¹ 1 *vi* (a) *(atañer)* **eso no te importa a tí** that doesn't concern you, that's none of your business (b) *(tener importancia)* to be important; **no importa** it doesn't matter; *Fam* **me importa un bledo** *o* **un pito** I couldn't care less (c) *(molestar)* **¿te importaría repetirlo?** would you mind repeating it?; **¿te importa si fumo?** do you mind if I smoke?
2 *vt (valer)* to amount to; **los libros importan 2.000 pesetas** the books come to 2,000 pesetas

importar² *vt* to import

importe *nm Com & Fin* amount, total

importunar *vt* to bother, to pester

imposibilidad *nf* impossibility

imposibilitar *vt* (a) *(impedir)* to make impossible, to prevent (b) *(incapacitar)* to disable, to cripple

imposible *adj* impossible; **me es i. hacerlo** I can't (possibly) do it

imposición *nf* (a) *(disciplina, condiciones)* imposing (b) *Fin* deposit; *(impuesto)* taxation

impostor,-a *nm,f (farsante)* impostor

impotencia *nf* powerlessness, helplessness; *Med* impotence

impotente *adj* powerless, helpless; *Med* impotent

impracticable *adj* (a) *(inviable)* impracticable, unviable (b) *(camino)* impassable

imprecar [44] *vt* to imprecate, to curse
imprecisión *nf* imprecision, vagueness
impreciso,-a *adj* imprecise, vague
impregnar 1 *vt* to impregnate (**de** with)
  2 impregnarse *upr* to become impregnated
imprenta *nf* (**a**) *(taller)* printer's, print works (**b**) *(aparato)* printing press (**c**) **libertad de i.** freedom of the press
imprescindible *adj* essential, indispensable
impresentable *adj* unpresentable
impresión *nf* (**a**) *Fig (efecto)* impression; **causar i.** to make an impression (**b**) *Fig (opinión)* impression; **cambiar impresiones** to exchange impressions (**c**) *Impr (acto)* printing; *(edición)* edition (**d**) *(huella)* impression, imprint
impresionable *adj* impressionable
impresionante *adj* impressive, striking; *Fam* **un error i.** *(tremendo)* a terrible mistake
impresionar *vt* (**a**) *(causar admiración)* to impress; *(sorprender)* to stun, to shock (**b**) *Fot* to expose
impresionismo *nm Arte* impressionism
impresionista *adj & nmf* impressionist
impreso,-a 1 *adj* printed
  2 *nm* (**a**) *(papel, folleto)* printed matter (**b**) *(formulario)* form; **i. de solicitud** application form (**c**) **impresos** *(de correos)* printed matter
impresora *nf Informát* printer; **i. láser** laser printer; **i. de chorro de tinta** inkjet printer
imprevisible *adj* unforeseeable, unpredictable
imprevisión *nf* lack of foresight
imprevisto,-a 1 *adj* unforeseen, unexpected
  2 *nm (incidente)* unforeseen event
imprimir *(pp* **impreso)** *vt* (**a**) *Impr & Informát* to print (**b**) *(marcar)* to stamp
improbable *adj* improbable, unlikely
ímprobo,-a *adj (inmoral)* dishonest, corrupt
improcedente *adj* (**a**) inappropriate, unsuitable (**b**) *Jur* inadmissible
improductivo,-a *adj* unproductive
improperio *nm* insult, offensive remark
impropio,-a *adj (inadecuado)* inappropriate, unsuitable; **i. de** uncharacteristic of
improvisación *nf* improvisation; *Mús* extemporization
improvisado,-a *adj (espontáneo)* improvised, impromptu, ad lib; *(provisional)* makeshift; **discurso i.** impromptu speech

improvisar *vt* to improvise; *Mús* to extemporize
improviso *adj* **de i.** unexpectedly, suddenly; *Fam* **coger** *o* **pillar a algn de i.** to catch sb unawares
imprudencia *nf* imprudence, rashness; *(indiscreción)* indiscretion
imprudente *adj* imprudent, unwise; *(indiscreto)* indiscreet
impudicia *nf (falta de pudor)* immodesty; *(desvergüenza)* shamelessness
impudor *nm* immodesty; *(desvergüenza)* shamelessness
impuesto,-a 1 *nm Fin* tax; **i. sobre la renta** income tax; **libre de impuestos** tax-free; **i. sobre el valor añadido** value-added tax
  2 *adj* imposed
impugnar *vt (teoría)* to refute, to disprove; *(decisión)* to challenge, to contest
impulsar *vt* to impel, to drive
impulsivo,-a *adj* impulsive
impulso *nm* impulse, thrust; *Dep* **tomar i.** to take a run-up
impune *adj* unpunished
impunemente *adv* with impunity
impunidad *nf* impunity
impureza *nf* impurity
impuro,-a *adj* impure
impuse *pt indef de* **imponer**
imputar *vt* to impute, to attribute
inabarcable *adj* unfathomable
inabordable *adj* unapproachable, inaccessible
inacabable *adj* interminable, endless
inaccesible *adj* inaccessible
inaceptable *adj* unacceptable
inactividad *nf* inactivity; *Fin* lull, stagnation
inactivo,-a *adj* inactive
inadaptación *nf* maladjustment
inadaptado,-a 1 *adj* maladjusted
  2 *nm,f* misfit
inadecuado,-a *adj* unsuitable, inappropriate
inadmisible *adj* inadmissible
inadvertido,-a *adj (desapercibido)* unnoticed, unseen; **pasar i.** to escape notice, to pass unnoticed
inagotable *adj* (**a**) *(recursos etc)* inexhaustible (**b**) *(persona)* tireless, indefatigable
inaguantable *adj* unbearable, intolerable
inalámbrico,-a 1 *adj* cordless
  2 *nm* cordless telephone
inalcanzable *adj* unattainable, unachievable

inalterable *adj* (**a**) unalterable (**b**) *(persona)* impassive, imperturbable
inamovible *adj* immovable, fixed
inanición *nf* starvation; *Med* inanition
inanimado,-a *adj* inanimate
inapreciable *adj* (**a**) *(valioso)* invaluable, inestimable (**b**) *(insignificante)* insignificant, trivial
inasequible *adj* (**a**) *(producto)* unaffordable (**b**) *(meta)* unattainable, unachievable (**c**) *(persona)* unapproachable, inaccessible (**d**) *(cuestión)* incomprehensible
inaudito,-a *adj* (**a**) *(sin precedente)* unprecedented (**b**) *Fig (escandaloso)* outrageous
inauguración *nf* inauguration, opening
inaugural *adj* inaugural, opening; **ceremonia i.** inaugural ceremony
inaugurar *vt* to inaugurate, to open
inca *adj & nmf* Inca
incalculable *adj* incalculable, indeterminate
incandescente *adj* white-hot, incandescent
incansable *adj* tireless, indefatigable
incapacidad *nf* (**a**) incapacity, inability; **i. física** physical disability (**b**) *(incompetencia)* incompetence, inefficiency
incapacitado,-a *adj (imposibilitado)* incapacitated, disabled; *(desautorizado)* incapacitated
incapacitar *vt* (**a**) to incapacitate, to disable (**b**) *(inhabilitar)* to disqualify, to make unfit (**para** for)
incapaz *adj* (**a**) unable (**de** to), incapable (**de** of); **soy i. de continuar** I can't go on (**b**) *Jur* unfit
incario *nm* = period of the Inca empire
incautación *nf Jur* seizure, confiscation
incautarse *vpr Jur* **i. de** to seize, to confiscate
incauto,-a *adj* (**a**) *(imprudente)* incautious, unwary (**b**) *(crédulo)* gullible
incendiar [43] **1** *vt* to set fire to, to set alight
  2 incendiarse *vpr* to catch fire
incendiario,-a 1 *adj* incendiary; *Fig (discurso etc)* inflammatory
  2 *nm,f (persona)* arsonist, fire-raiser
incendio *nm* fire; **i. forestal** forest fire
incentivar *vt* to give an incentive to
incentivo *nm* incentive
incertidumbre *nf* uncertainty, doubt
incesante *adj* incessant, never-ending
incesto *nm* incest
incestuoso,-a *adj* incestuous
incidencia *nf* (**a**) *(repercusión)* impact,

effect; **la huelga tuvo escasa i.** the strike had little effect (**b**) *(hecho)* incident (**c**) *Fís* incidence
incidente *nm* incident
incidir *vi* (**a**) *(incurrir)* to fall (**en** into) (**b**) **i. en** *(afectar)* to affect, to influence
incienso *nm* incense
incierto,-a *adj (inseguro)* uncertain
incineración *nf (de basuras)* incineration; *(de cadáveres)* cremation
incinerar *vt (basura)* to incinerate; *(cadáveres)* to cremate
incipiente *adj* incipient, budding
incisión *nf* incision, cut
incisivo,-a 1 *adj (mordaz)* incisive, cutting; *(cortante)* sharp
  2 *nm Anat* incisor
inciso *nm (paréntesis)* digression; **a modo de i.** in passing, incidentally
incitación *nf* incitement
incitante *adj* (**a**) *(instigador)* inciting (**b**) *(provocativo)* provocative
incitar *vt* to incite, to urge
incivil *adj* uncivil, rude
inclemencia *nf* inclemency, harshness
inclemente *adj* inclement, harsh
inclinación *nf* (**a**) *(de terreno)* slope, incline; *(del cuerpo)* stoop (**b**) *(reverencia)* bow (**c**) *Fig (tendencia)* tendency, inclination, penchant
inclinado,-a *adj* inclined, slanting; *Fig* **me siento i. a creerle** I feel inclined to believe him
inclinar 1 *vt* (**a**) to incline, to bend; *(cabeza)* to nod (**b**) *Fig (persuadir)* to persuade, to induce
  2 inclinarse *vpr* (**a**) to lean, to slope, to incline (**b**) *(al saludar)* to bow; **i. ante** to bow down to (**c**) *Fig (optar)* **i. a** to feel inclined to; **me inclino por éste** I'd rather have this one, I prefer this one
incluido,-a *adj* (**a**) *(después del sustantivo)* included; *(antes del sustantivo)* including; **servicio no i.** service not included; **i. I.V.A.** including VAT; **todos pagan, incluidos los niños** everyone has to pay, including children (**b**) *(adjunto)* enclosed
incluir [37] *vt* (**a**) to include (**b**) *(contener)* to contain, to comprise (**c**) *(adjuntar)* to enclose
inclusión *nf* inclusion
inclusive *adv* (**a**) *(incluido)* inclusive; **de martes a viernes i.** from Tuesday to Friday inclusive; **hasta la lección ocho i.** up to and including lesson eight (**b**) *(incluso)* even
incluso *adv* even; **i. mi madre** even my mother

incoar *vt defectJur* to initiate
incógnita *nf* (**a**) *Mat* unknown quantity, unknown (**b**) *(misterio)* mystery
incógnito *nm* **de i.** incognito
incoherencia *nf* incoherence
incoherente *adj* incoherent
incoloro,-a *adj* colourless
incólume *adj Fml* unharmed; **salir i.** to escape unharmed
incombustible *adj* incombustible, fireproof
incomodar 1 *vt* (**a**) *(causar molestia)* to inconvenience, to put out (**b**) *(fastidiar)* to bother, to annoy
  2 incomodarse *vpr* (**a**) *(tomarse molestias)* to put oneself out, to go out of one's way (**b**) *(disgustarse)* to get annoyed *o* angry
incomodidad *nf (falta de comodidad)* discomfort; *(molestia)* inconvenience
incómodo,-a *adj* uncomfortable; **sentirse i.** to feel uncomfortable *o* awkward
incompatibilidad *nf* incompatibility; *Jur* **i. de caracteres** mutual incompatibility
incompatible *adj* incompatible
incompetencia *nf* incompetence
incompetente *adj & nmf* incompetent
incompleto,-a *adj* incomplete; *(inacabado)* unfinished
incomprensible *adj* incomprehensible
incomprensión *nf* lack of understanding, failure to understand; *(indiferencia)* lack of sympathy
incomunicado,-a *adj* (**a**) *(aislado)* isolated; **el pueblo se quedó i.** the town was cut off (**b**) *(en la cárcel)* in solitary confinement
incomunicar [44] *vt* (**a**) *(ciudad)* to isolate, to cut off (**b**) *(recluso)* to place in solitary confinement
inconcebible *adj* inconceivable, unthinkable
inconcluso,-a *adj* unfinished
incondicional 1 *adj* unconditional; *(apoyo)* wholehearted; *(amigo)* faithful; *(partidario)* staunch
  2 *nm* die-hard
inconexo,-a *adj (incoherente)* incoherent, confused
inconformismo *nm* nonconformity
inconformista *adj & nmf* nonconformist
inconfundible *adj* unmistakable, obvious
incongruencia *nf* incongruity
incongruente *adj* incongruous
inconmensurable *adj* immeasurable, vast

inconsciencia *nf Med* unconsciousness; *Fig (irreflexión)* thoughtlessness; *(irresponsabilidad)* irresponsibility
inconsciente *adj* (**a**) *(con* **estar)** *(desmayado)* unconscious (**b**) *(con* ser*) (despreocupado)* unaware (**de** of); *Fig (irreflexivo)* thoughtless, irresponsible
inconsecuente *adj* inconsistent
inconsistente *adj* flimsy; *(argumento)* weak
inconstancia *nf* inconstancy, fickleness
inconstante *adj* inconstant, fickle
incontable *adj* countless, innumerable
incontenible *adj* uncontrollable, irrepressible
incontestable *adj* indisputable, unquestionable
incontinencia *nf* incontinence
incontrolable *adj* uncontrollable
incontrolado,-a 1 *adj* uncontrolled
  2 *nm,f* troublemaker
inconveniencia *nf* (**a**) inconvenience (**b**) *(impropiedad)* unsuitability
inconveniente 1 *adj* (**a**) inconvenient (**b**) *(inapropiado)* unsuitable
  2 *nm* (**a**) *(objeción)* objection; **poner inconvenientes** to raise objections (**b**) *(desventaja)* disadvantage, drawback; *(problema)* difficulty; **¿tienes i. en acompañarme?** would you mind coming with me?
incordiar [43] *vt Fam* to bother, to pester
incordio *nm Fam* nuisance, pain
incorporación *nf* incorporation
incorporar 1 *vt* (**a**) to incorporate (**en** into) (**b**) *(levantar)* to help to sit up
  2 incorporarse *vpr* (**a**) **i. a** *(sociedad)* to join; *(trabajo)* to start; *Mil* **i. a filas** to join up (**b**) *(en la cama)* to sit up
incorrección *nf* (**a**) *(falta)* incorrectness, inaccuracy; *(gramatical)* mistake (**b**) *(descortesía)* discourtesy, impropriety
incorrecto,-a *adj* (**a**) *(equivocado)* incorrect, inaccurate (**b**) *(grosero)* impolite, discourteous
incorregible *adj* incorrigible
incrédulo,-a 1 *adj* (**a**) incredulous, disbelieving (**b**) *Rel* unbelieving
  2 *nm,f* (**a**) disbeliever (**b**) *Rel* unbeliever
increíble *adj* incredible, unbelievable
incrementar 1 *vt* to increase
  2 incrementarse *vpr* to increase
incremento *nm (aumento)* increase; *(crecimiento)* growth; **i. de la temperatura** rise in temperature
increpar *vt Fml* to rebuke, to reprimand
incruento,-a *adj* bloodless
incrustar *vt* (**a**) *(insertar)* to encrust *o*

incrust (**b**) *(embutir)* to inlay; **incrustado con perlas** inlaid with pearls

incubadora *nf* incubator

incubar *vt* to incubate

incuestionable *adj* unquestionable, indisputable

inculcar [44] *vt (principios, ideas)* to instil (**en** into)

inculpado,-a *nm,f* **el i.** the accused

inculpar *vt* to accuse (**de** of), to blame (**de** for); *Jur* to charge (**de** with)

inculto,-a 1 *adj (ignorante)* uneducated, uncouth
2 *nm,f* ignoramus

incultura *nf (ignorancia)* ignorance, lack of culture

incumbencia *nf* **no es de mi i.** it doesn't come within my province, it isn't my concern

incumbir *vi* to be incumbent (**a** upon); **esto no te incumbe** this is none of your business

incumplimiento *nm (de un deber)* non-fulfilment; *(de una orden)* failure to execute; **i. de contrato** breach of contract

incumplir *vt* not to fulfil; *(deber)* to fail to fulfil; *(promesa, contrato)* to break; *(orden)* to fail to carry out

incurrir *vi (cometer)* to fall (**en** into); **i. en delito** to commit a crime; **i. en (un) error** to fall into error

incursión *nf* raid, incursion

incursionar *vi Am* (**a**) *(en ciudad, territorio)* to make an incursion (**b**) **i. en algo** *(tema, asunto)* to dabble in sth

indagar [42] *vt* to investigate, to inquire into

indebido,-a *adj* (**a**) *(desconsiderado)* improper, undue (**b**) *(ilegal)* unlawful, illegal

indecencia *nf* indecency, obscenity

indecente *adj* (**a**) *(impúdico)* indecent (**b**) *(impresentable)* dreadful

indecible *adj* unspeakable; *(inefable)* indescribable; **sufrir lo i.** to suffer agonies

indecisión *nf* indecision, hesitation

indeciso,-a *adj* (**a**) *(vacilante)* hesitant, irresolute (**b**) *(resultados etc)* inconclusive

indefenso,-a *adj* defenceless, helpless

indefinidamente *adv* indefinitely

indefinido,-a *adj* (**a**) *(indeterminado)* indefinite; *(impreciso)* undefined, vague (**b**) *Ling* indefinite

indeleble *adj* indelible

indemne *adj (persona)* unharmed, unhurt; *(cosa)* undamaged

indemnización *nf* (**a**) *(acto)* indemnification (**b**) *Fin (compensación)* indemnity,

compensation; **i. por despido** redundancy payment

indemnizar [40] *vt* to indemnify, to compensate (**por** for)

independencia *nf* independence

independiente *adj (libre)* independent; *(individualista)* self-reliant

independientemente *adv* (**a**) independently (**de** of) (**b**) *(aparte de)* regardless, irrespective (**de** of)

independizar [40] 1 *vt* to make independent, to grant independence to
2 independizarse *vpr* to become independent

indescifrable *adj* indecipherable

indescriptible *adj* indescribable

indeseable *adj & nmf* undesirable

indeterminación *nf* indecision, irresolution

indeterminado,-a *adj* (**a**) indefinite; *(impreciso)* vague (**b**) *(persona)* irresolute (**c**) *Ling* indefinite

India *nf* **(la) I.** India

Indias *nfpl* **(las) I.** the Indies; **las I. Orientales/Occidentales** the East/West Indies

indicación *nf* (**a**) *(señal)* indication, sign (**b**) *(instrucción)* instruction, direction; **por i. de algn** at sb's suggestion

indicado,-a *adj* right, suitable; **a la hora indicada** at the specified time; **en el momento menos i.** at the worst possible moment

indicador *nm* (**a**) indicator (**b**) *Téc* gauge, dial, meter; *Aut* **i. del nivel de aceite** (oil) dipstick; *Aut* **i. de velocidad** speedometer

indicar [44] *vt (señalar)* to indicate, to show, to point out; **¿me podría i. el camino?** could you show me the way?

indicativo,-a *adj* (**a**) indicative (**de** of) (**b**) *Ling* **(modo) i.** indicative (mood)

índice *nm* (**a**) *(de libro)* index, table of contents (**b**) *(relación)* rate; **í. de natalidad/mortalidad** birth/death rate; *Fin* **í. de precios** price index (**c**) *Anat (dedo)* **í.** index finger, forefinger

indicio *nm* (**a**) *(señal)* indication, sign, token (**de** of) (**b**) *Jur* **indicios** *(prueba)* evidence

índico,-a *adj* Indian; **Océano Í.** Indian Ocean

indiferencia *nf* indifference, apathy

indiferente *adj* (**a**) *(no importante)* unimportant; **me es i.** it makes no difference to me (**b**) *(apático)* indifferent

indígena 1 *adj* indigenous, native (**de** to)
2 *nmf* native (**de** of)

indigencia *nf Fml* poverty, indigence

indigente *adj Fml* needy, poverty-stricken

indigestarse *vpr* (**a**) **se le indigestó la comida** the meal gave her indigestion (**b**) *(sufrir indigestión)* to get indigestion

indigestión *nf* indigestion

indigesto,-a *adj (comida)* indigestible, difficult to digest; **me siento i.** I've got indigestion

indignación *nf* indignation

indignado,-a *adj* indignant (**por** at *o* about)

indignante *adj* outrageous, infuriating

indignar 1 *vt* to infuriate, to make angry
  2 indignarse *vpr* to be *o* feel indignant (**por** at *o* about)

indigno,-a *adj* (**a**) unworthy (**de** of) (**b**) *(despreciable)* wretched, dreadful

indio,-a *adj & nm,f* Indian; **en fila india** in single file; *Fam* **hacer el i.** to act the fool

indirecta *nf Fam (insinuación)* hint, insinuation; **tirar** *o* **lanzar una i.** to drop a hint; **coger la i.** to get the message

indirecto,-a *adj* indirect; *Ling* **estilo i.** indirect *o* reported speech

indisciplinado,-a *adj* undisciplined, unruly

indiscreción *nf* indiscretion; *(comentario)* tactless remark

indiscreto,-a *adj* indiscreet, tactless

indiscutible *adj* indisputable, unquestionable

indispensable *adj* indispensable, essential

indisponer [19] *(pp indispuesto)* **1** *vt* to upset, to make unwell
  2 indisponerse *vpr* (**a**) to fall ill, to become unwell (**b**) *Fig* **i. con algn** to fall out with sb

indispuesto,-a *adj* indisposed, unwell

indispuse *pt indef de* **indisponer**

indistintamente *adv* **pueden escribir en inglés o en español i.** you can write in English or Spanish, it doesn't matter which

indistinto,-a *adj (indiferente)* immaterial, inconsequential

individual 1 *adj* individual; **habitación i.** single room
  2 *nmpl Dep* **individuales** singles

individualismo *nm* individualism

individualista 1 *adj* individualistic
  2 *nmf* individualist

individuo *nm* (**a**) individual (**b**) *(tío)* bloke, guy

índole *nf* (**a**) *(carácter)* character, nature (**b**) *(clase, tipo)* kind, sort

indolencia *nf* indolence, laziness

indolente 1 *adj* indolent, lazy
  2 *nmf* idler

indomable *adj* (**a**) *(animal)* untamable (**b**) *(pueblo)* ungovernable, unruly; *(niño)* uncontrollable; *(pasión)* indomitable

indómito,-a *adj* (**a**) *(no domado)* untamed; *(indomable)* untamable (**b**) *(pueblo)* unruly; *(persona)* uncontrollable

Indonesia *n* Indonesia

inducir [10] *vt* (**a**) *(incitar, mover)* to lead, to induce; **i. a error** to lead into error, to mislead (**b**) *Elec (corriente)* to induce

inductivo,-a *adj* inductive

indudable *adj* indubitable, unquestionable; **es i. que** there is no doubt that

induje *pt indef de* **inducir**

indulgencia *nf* indulgence, leniency

indulgente *adj* indulgent (**con** towards), lenient (**con** with)

indultar *vt Jur* to pardon

indulto *nm Jur* pardon, amnesty

indumentaria *nf* clothing, clothes

industria *nf* industry

industrial 1 *adj* industrial
  2 *nmf* industrialist

industrialización *nf* industrialization

industrializar [40] *vt* to industrialize

induzco *indic pres de* **inducir**

INE *nm (abr* **Instituto Nacional de Estadística***)* = organization that publishes official statistics about Spain

inédito,-a *adj* (**a**) *(libro, texto)* unpublished (**b**) *(nuevo)* completely new; *(desconocido)* unknown

inefable *adj* ineffable, indescribable

ineficacia *nf (ineptitud)* inefficiency; *(inutilidad)* ineffectiveness

ineficaz *adj (inepto)* inefficient; *(inefectivo)* ineffective

ineludible *adj* inescapable, unavoidable

INEM *nm (abr* **Instituto Nacional de Empleo***)* = Spanish department of employment

ineptitud *nf* ineptitude, incompetence

inepto,-a 1 *adj* inept, incompetent
  2 *nm,f* incompetent person

inequívoco,-a *adj* unmistakable, unequivocal

inercia *nf* (**a**) *Fís* inertia (**b**) *Fig (pasividad)* inertia, passivity; **hacer algo por i.** to do sth out of habit

inerte *adj (inanimado)* inert; *(inmóvil)* motionless

inesperado,-a *adj (fortuito)* unexpected, unforeseen; *(imprevisto)* sudden

inestabilidad *nf* instability

inestable *adj* unstable, unsteady

inestimable *adj* inestimable, invaluable
inevitable *adj* inevitable, unavoidable
inexistente *adj* non-existent
inexorable *adj* inexorable
inexperiencia *nf* lack of experience
inexperto,-a *adj (inexperto)* inexpert; *(sin experiencia)* inexperienced
inexplicable *adj* inexplicable
inexpugnable *adj Mil* impregnable
infalible *adj* infallible
infamar *vt* to defame, to slander
infame *adj (vil)* infamous, vile; *(despreciable)* dreadful, awful
infamia *nf* disgrace, infamy
infancia *nf* childhood, infancy
infanta *nf* infanta, princess
infante *nm* (a) infante, prince (b) *Mil* infantryman
infantería *nf Mil* infantry; **la i. de marina** the marines
infantil *adj* (a) **literatura i.** *(para niños)* children's literature (b) *(aniñado)* childlike; *Pey* childish, infantile
infarto *nm Med* infarction, infarct; **i. (de miocardio)** heart attack, coronary thrombosis; *Fam* **de i.** thrilling, stunning
infatigable *adj* indefatigable, tireless
infección *nf* infection
infeccioso,-a *adj* infectious
infectar 1 *vt* to infect
　2 infectarse *vpr* to become infected (**de** with)
infeliz 1 *adj* unhappy; *(desdichado)* unfortunate
　2 *nmf Fam* simpleton; **es un pobre i.** he is a poor devil
inferior 1 *adj* (a) *(más bajo)* lower (b) *(calidad)* inferior; **de calidad i.** of inferior quality (c) *(cantidad)* lower, less; **i. a la media** below average
　2 *nmf (persona)* subordinate, inferior
inferioridad *nf* inferiority; **estar en i. de condiciones** to be at a disadvantage; **complejo de i.** inferiority complex
inferir [5] *vt Literario (deducir)* to infer, to deduce (**de** from)
infernal *adj* infernal, hellish; *Fig* **había un ruido i.** there was a hell of a noise
infestar *vt* (a) **infestado de** *(parásitos)* infested with; *(plantas)* overgrown with (b) *Fig (llenar)* to overrun, to invade; **infestado de turistas** swarming with tourists (c) *(infectar)* to infect
inficción *nf Méx* pollution
infidelidad *nf* infidelity, unfaithfulness
infiel 1 *adj (desleal)* unfaithful
　2 *nmf Rel* infidel
infierno *nm* (a) *Rel* hell (b) *Fig (tormento)*

hell; **su vida es un i.** his life is sheer hell (c) *(horno)* inferno; **en verano esto es un i.** in summer it's like an inferno here; *Fam* **¡vete al i.!** go to hell!, get lost!
infiltración *nf (de agua)* infiltration; *(de noticia)* leak
infiltrado,-a *nm,f* infiltrator
infiltrar 1 *vt* to infiltrate; *(noticia)* to leak
　2 infiltrarse *vpr* to infiltrate (**en** into)
ínfimo,-a *adj Fml (mínimo)* extremely low; **detalle í.** smallest detail; **ínfima calidad** very poor quality
infinidad *nf* (a) infinity (b) *(sinfín)* great number; **en i. de ocasiones** on countless occasions
infinitivo,-a *adj & nm Ling* infinitive
infinito,-a 1 *adj* infinite, endless
　2 *nm* infinity
　3 *adv Fam (muchísimo)* infinitely, immensely
inflación *nf Econ* inflation
inflacionario,-a, inflacionista *adj Econ* inflationary
inflamable *adj* flammable
inflamación *nf Med* inflammation
inflamar 1 *vt* (a) *Med* to inflame (b) *(encender)* to set on fire, to ignite
　2 inflamarse *vpr* (a) *Med* to become inflamed (b) *(incendiarse)* to catch fire
inflar 1 *vt* (a) *(hinchar)* to inflate, to blow up; *Náut (vela)* to swell (b) *Fig (exagerar)* to exaggerate
　2 inflarse *vpr* (a) to inflate; *Náut (vela)* to swell (b) *Fam* **i. de** to overdo; **se inflaron de macarrones** they stuffed themselves with macaroni
inflexible *adj* inflexible
infligir [57] *vt* to inflict
influencia *nf* influence; **ejercer** *o* **tener i. sobre algn** to have an influence on *o* upon sb; **tener influencias** to be influential; **tráfico de influencias** Old-Boy network
influenciar [43] *vt* to influence
influir [37] 1 *vt* to influence
　2 *vi* (a) to have influence (b) **i. en** *o* **sobre** to influence, to have an influence on
influjo *nm* influence
influyente *adj* influential
información *nf* (a) information; **oficina de i.** information bureau (b) **una i.** *(noticia)* a piece of news, news *sing* (c) *Tel Br* directory enquiries, *US* information (d) *(referencias)* references
informado,-a *adj* informed; **de fuentes bien informadas** from well-informed sources

informal *adj* (**a**) *(reunión, cena)* informal (**b**) *(comportamiento)* casual (**c**) *(persona)* unreliable, untrustworthy

informalidad *nf (incumplimiento)* unreliability; *(desenfado)* informality

informar 1 *vt* to inform (**de** of); *(dar informes)* to report

2 informarse *vpr (procurarse noticias)* to find out (**de** about); *(enterarse)* to inquire (**de** about)

informática *nf* computing, information technology

informático,-a 1 *adj* computer, computing

2 *nm,f* (computer) technician

informativo,-a 1 *adj* (**a**) *Rad & TV* news; **boletín i.** news (broadcast) (**b**) *(explicativo)* informative, explanatory

2 *nm Rad & TV* news bulletin

informe *nm* (**a**) report (**b**) **informes** references; **pedir informes sobre algn** to make inquiries about sb

infracción *nf (de ley)* infringement, breach (**de** of)

infractor,-a *nm,f* offender

infraestructura *nf* infrastructure

in fraganti *loc adv* in the act; **coger** *o* **pillar a algn i.** to catch sb redhanded

infrahumano,-a *adj* subhuman

infranqueable *adj* impassable; *Fig* insurmountable

infrarrojo,-a *adj* infrared

infrautilizar *vt* to underutilize

infringir [**57**] *vt* to infringe, to contravene; **i. una ley** to break a law

infructuoso,-a *adj* fruitless, unsuccessful

infundado,-a *adj* unfounded, groundless

infundir *vt* to infuse; *Fig* to instil; **i. dudas** to give rise to doubt; **i. respeto** to command respect

infusión *nf* infusion

infuso,-a *adj Fam Irón* **ciencia infusa** sheer genius

ingeniar [**43**] **1** *vt* to invent, to devise

2 ingeniarse *vpr* **ingeniárselas para hacer algo** to manage to do sth

ingeniería *nf* engineering

ingeniero,-a *nm,f* engineer; **i. agrónomo** agricultural engineer; **i. de caminos** civil engineer; **i. de minas/montes** mining/forestry engineer; **i. de telecomunicaciones** telecommunications engineer; **i. técnico** technician

ingenio *nm* (**a**) *(talento)* talent; *(inventiva)* inventiveness, creativeness; *(agudeza)* wit (**b**) *(aparato)* device

ingenioso,-a *adj* ingenious, clever; *(vivaz)* witty

ingente *adj* huge, enormous

ingenuidad *nf* ingenuousness, naïveté

ingenuo,-a 1 *adj* ingenuous, naïve

2 *nm,f* naïve person

ingerir [**5**] *vt (comida)* to ingest, to consume; *(líquidos, alcohol)* to drink, to consume

Inglaterra *n* England

ingle *nf Anat* groin

inglés,-esa 1 *adj* English

2 *nm,f (hombre)* Englishman; *(mujer)* Englishwoman; **los ingleses** the English

3 *nm (idioma)* English

ingratitud *nf* ingratitude, ungratefulness

ingrato,-a 1 *adj* (**a**) *(persona)* ungrateful (**b**) *(noticia)* unpleasant (**c**) *(trabajo)* thankless, unrewarding (**d**) *(tierra)* unproductive

2 *nm,f* ungrateful person

ingrediente *nm* ingredient

ingresar 1 *vt* (**a**) *Fin* to deposit, to pay in (**b**) *Med* to admit; **la ingresaron en el hospital** she was admitted to hospital

2 *vi* (**a**) to enter; **i. en el ejército** to enlist in the army, to join the army; **i. en un club** to join a club (**b**) **i. cadáver** to be dead on arrival

ingreso *nm* (**a**) *Fin* deposit; **hacer un i. en una cuenta** to pay money into an account (**b**) *(entrada)* entry (**en** into); *(admisión)* admission (**en** to) (**c**) **ingresos** *(sueldo, renta)* income; *(beneficios)* revenue

inhábil *adj* (**a**) *(incapaz)* unfit; **i. para el trabajo** unfit for work (**b**) **día i.** non-working day

inhabilitación *nf* (**a**) *Fml (incapacidad)* disablement (**b**) *Jur* disqualification

inhabilitar *vt* (**a**) *Fml (incapacitar)* to disable; **inhabilitado para el trabajo** unfit for work (**b**) *Jur* to disqualify

inhabitable *adj* uninhabitable

> Observa que la palabra inglesa **inhabitable** es un falso amigo y no es la traducción de la palabra española **inhabitable**. En inglés, **inhabitable** significa "habitable".

inhalación *nf* inhalation

inhalador *nm Med* inhaler

inhalar *vt* to inhale

inherente *adj* inherent (**a** in)

inhibición *nf* inhibition

inhibir 1 *vt* to inhibit

2 inhibirse *vpr* (**a**) *(cohibirse)* to be *o* feel inhibited (**b**) *(abstenerse)* to refrain (**de** from)

inhóspito,-a *adj* inhospitable
inhumación *nf* burial
inhumano,-a *adj* inhumane; *(cruel)* inhuman
inhumar *vt* to bury
INI *nm Antes* (*abr* **Instituto Nacional de Industria**) = Spanish governmental organization that promotes industry
inicial *adj & nf* initial; **punto i.** starting point
iniciar [43] 1 *vt* (**a**) *(empezar)* to begin, to start; *(discusión)* to initiate; *(una cosa nueva)* to pioneer (**b**) *(introducir)* to initiate
    2 iniciarse *vpr* (**a**) **i. en algo** *(aprender)* to start to study sth (**b**) *(empezar)* to begin, to start
iniciativa *nf* initiative; **i. privada** private enterprise; **por i. propia** on one's own initiative
inicio *nm* beginning, start; **a inicios de** at the beginning of
inimitable *adj* inimitable
ininterrumpido,-a *adj* uninterrupted, continuous
iniquidad *nf* iniquity
injerencia *nf* interference, meddling (**en** in)
injerirse *vpr* to interfere, to meddle (**en** in)
injertar *vt Agr & Med* to graft
injerto *nm* graft
injuria *nf (insulto)* insult, affront; *(agravio)* outrage
injuriar [43] *vt (insultar)* to insult; *(ultrajar)* to outrage
injusticia *nf* injustice, unfairness
injustificado,-a *adj* unjustified
injusto,-a *adj* unjust, unfair
inmaculado,-a *adj* immaculate
inmadurez *nf* immaturity
inmaduro,-a *adj* immature
inmediaciones *nfpl* neighbourhood
inmediatamente *adv* immediately, at once
inmediato,-a *adj* (**a**) *(en el tiempo)* immediate; **de i.** at once (**b**) *(en el espacio)* next (**a** to), adjoining
inmejorable *adj (trabajo)* excellent; *(precio)* unbeatable
inmemorial *adj* immemorial; **desde tiempos inmemoriales** since time immemorial
inmensidad *nf* immensity, enormity
inmenso,-a *adj* immense, vast
inmerecido,-a *adj* undeserved, unmerited
inmersión *nf* immersion; *(de submarino)* dive

inmerso,-a *adj* immersed (**en** in)
inmigración *nf* immigration
inmigrante *adj & nmf* immigrant
inmigrar *vi* to immigrate
inminente *adj* imminent, impending
inmiscuirse [37] *vpr* to interfere, to meddle (**en** in)
inmobiliaria *nf Br* estate agent's, *US* real estate company
inmobiliario,-a *adj* property, *US* realestate; **agente i.** *Br* estate agent, *US* realtor
inmolar *vt Fml* to immolate, to sacrifice
inmoral *adj* immoral
inmoralidad *nf* immorality
inmortal *adj & nmf* immortal
inmortalidad *nf* immortality
inmortalizar [40] *vt* to immortalize
inmóvil *adj* motionless, immobile
inmovilista *adj* ultra-conservative
inmovilizar [40] *vt* (**a**) *(persona, cosa)* to immobilize (**b**) *Fin (capital)* to immobilize, to tie up
inmueble 1 *adj* **bienes inmuebles** real estate
    2 *nm* building
inmundicia *nf* (**a**) *(suciedad)* dirt, filth; *Fig* dirtiness (**b**) *(basura)* rubbish, refuse
inmundo,-a *adj* dirty, filthy; *Fig* nasty
inmune *adj* immune (**a** to), exempt (**de** from)
inmunidad *nf* immunity (**contra** against); **i. diplomática/parlamentaria** diplomatic/parliamentary immunity
inmunizar [40] *vt* to immunize (**contra** against)
inmutarse *vpr* to change countenance; **ni se inmutó** he didn't turn a hair
innato,-a *adj* innate, inborn
innecesario,-a *adj* unnecessary
innegable *adj* undeniable
innovación *nf* innovation
innovar *vt & vi* to innovate
innumerable *adj* innumerable, countless
inocencia *nf* (**a**) innocence (**b**) *(ingenuidad)* naïveté
inocentada *nf Fam* ≃ April Fool's joke; **hacer una i. a algn** to play an April Fool's joke on sb
inocente 1 *adj* innocent
    2 *nmf* innocent; **día de los Inocentes** Holy Innocents' Day, 28 December, ≃ April Fools' Day
inocuo,-a *adj* innocuous
inodoro,-a 1 *adj* odourless
    2 *nm* toilet, lavatory
inofensivo,-a *adj* harmless

inolvidable *adj* unforgettable

inoperante *adj* ineffective

inopia *nf Fig* **estar en la i.** to be in the clouds, to be miles away

inopinado,-a *adj* unexpected

inoportuno,-a *adj* inappropriate; **llegó en un momento muy i.** he turned up at a very awkward moment

inorgánico,-a *adj* inorganic

inoxidable *adj* **acero i.** stainless steel

inquebrantable *adj Fig* unshakable; *(persona)* unyielding

inquietante *adj* worrying

inquietar 1 *vt* to worry

   2 inquietarse *vpr* to worry (**por** about)

inquieto,-a *adj* (**a**) *(preocupado)* worried (**por** about) (**b**) *(intranquilo)* restless (**c**) *(emprendedor)* eager

inquietud *nf* (**a**) *(preocupación)* worry (**b**) *(agitación)* restlessness (**c**) *(anhelo)* eagerness

inquilino,-a *nm,f* tenant

inquirir [31] *vt* to investigate

inquisitivo,-a *adj* inquisitive

inri *nm Fam* insult; **para más** *o* **mayor i.** to make matters worse

insaciable *adj* insatiable

insalubre *adj* unhealthy

INSALUD *nm* (*abr* **Instituto Nacional de la Salud**) = Spanish national health service, *Br* ≃ NHS, *US* ≃ Medicaid

insano,-a *adj* (**a**) *(loco)* insane, mad (**b**) *(insalubre)* unhealthy

insatisfecho,-a *adj* dissatisfied

inscribir (*pp* **inscrito**) **1** *vt* (**a**) *(registrar)* to register; **i. a un niño en el registro civil** to register a child's birth (**b**) *(matricular)* to enrol (**c**) *(grabar)* to inscribe

   2 inscribirse *vpr* (**a**) *(registrarse)* to register; *(hacerse miembro)* to join (**b**) *(matricularse)* to enrol

inscripción *nf* (**a**) *(matriculación)* enrolment, registration (**b**) *(escrito etc)* inscription

insecticida *nm* insecticide

insecto *nm* insect

inseguridad *nf* (**a**) *(falta de confianza)* insecurity (**b**) *(duda)* uncertainty (**c**) *(peligro)* lack of safety; **la i. ciudadana** the breakdown of law and order

inseguro,-a *adj* (**a**) *(poco confiado)* insecure (**b**) *(dubitativo)* uncertain (**c**) *(peligroso)* unsafe

inseminar *vt* to inseminate

insensatez *nf* foolishness

insensato,-a 1 *adj* foolish

   2 *nm,f* fool

insensibilidad *nf* insensitivity

insensible *adj* (**a**) *(indiferente)* insensitive (**a** to), unfeeling (**b**) *(imperceptible)* imperceptible (**c**) *Med* numb

inseparable *adj* inseparable

insertar *vt* to insert

inservible *adj* useless

insidia *nf* (**a**) *(trampa)* malicious ploy (**b**) *(malicia)* maliciousness

insidioso,-a *adj* insidious

insigne *adj* distinguished

insignia *nf* (**a**) *(emblema)* badge (**b**) *(bandera)* flag

insignificancia *nf* (**a**) *(intrascendencia)* insignificance (**b**) *(nadería)* trifle

insignificante *adj* insignificant

insinuación *nf* insinuation

insinuante *adj* insinuating; *(atrevido)* forward

insinuar [30] 1 *vt* to insinuate

   2 insinuarse *vpr* **i. a algn** to make advances to sb

insípido,-a *adj* insipid; *Fig* dull, flat

insistencia *nf* insistence; **con i.** insistently

insistente *adj* insistent

insistir *vi* to insist (**en** on); **insistió en ese punto** he stressed that point

insociable *adj* unsociable

insolación *nf Med* sunstroke; **coger una i.** to get sunstroke

insolencia *nf* insolence

insolente *adj* insolent

insolidaridad *nf* unsupportive stance

insólito,-a *adj* *(poco usual)* unusual; *(extraño)* strange, odd

insoluble *adj* insoluble

insolvencia *nf Fin* insolvency

insolvente *adj Fin* insolvent

insomnio *nm* insomnia; **noche de i.** sleepless night

insondable *adj* unfathomable

insonorizado,-a *adj* soundproof

insonorizar [40] *vt* to soundproof

insoportable *adj* unbearable

insospechado,-a *adj* unsuspected

insostenible *adj* untenable

inspección *nf* inspection

inspeccionar *vt* to inspect

inspector,-a *nm,f* inspector; **i. de Hacienda** tax inspector

inspiración *nf* (**a**) inspiration (**b**) *(inhalación)* inhalation

inspirado,-a *adj* inspired

inspirar 1 *vt* (**a**) to inspire (**b**) *(inhalar)* to inhale, to breathe in

   2 inspirarse *vpr* **i. en** to be inspired by

instalación *nf* installation; **instalaciones deportivas** sports facilities

instalar 1 *vt* (**a**) to install (**b**) *(puesto, tienda)* to set up
 2 instalarse *vpr (persona)* to settle (down)
instancia *nf* (**a**) *(solicitud)* request; **a instancia(s) de** at the request of (**b**) *(escrito)* application form (**c**) *Jur* **tribunal de primera i.** court of first instance (**d**) **en primera i.** first of all; **en última i.** as a last resort

> ♟ Observa que la palabra inglesa **instance** es un falso amigo y no es la traducción de la palabra española **instancia**. En inglés, **instance** significa "caso, ejemplo".

instantánea *nf* snapshot
instantáneamente *adv* instantly
instantáneo,-a *adj* instantaneous; **café i.** instant coffee
instante *nm* instant, moment; **a cada i.** constantly; **al i.** immediately, right away; **por instantes** with every second; **¡un i.!** just a moment!
instar *vt* to urge
instauración *nf* founding
instaurar *vt* to found
instigador,-a *nm,f* instigator
instigar [42] *vt* to instigate; **i. a la rebelión** to incite a rebellion
instintivo,-a *adj* instinctive
instinto *nm* instinct; **por i.** instinctively; **i. de conservación** survival instinct
institución *nf* institution
instituir [37] *vt* to institute
instituto *nm* (**a**) institute (**b**) *Educ Br* state secondary school, *US* high school
institutriz *nf* governess
instituyo *indic pres de* **instituir**
instrucción *nf* (**a**) *(educación)* education (**b**) *(usu pl) (indicación)* instruction; **instrucciones para el** *o* **de uso** directions for use (**c**) *Jur* preliminary investigation; **la i. del sumario** proceedings; **juez de i.** examining magistrate (**d**) *Mil* drill
instructivo,-a *adj* instructive
instruido,-a *adj* educated, well-educated
instruir [37] *vt* (**a**) to instruct (**b**) *(enseñar)* to educate (**c**) *Mil* to drill (**d**) *Jur* to investigate
instrumental *adj* instrumental
instrumento *nm* instrument
insubordinación *nf* insubordination
insubordinado,-a *adj* insubordinate
insubordinarse *vpr (sublevarse)* to rebel (**contra** against)
insuficiencia *nf* insufficiency
insuficiente 1 *adj* insufficient

2 *nm Educ (nota)* fail
insufrible *adj* insufferable
insular 1 *adj* insular, island
 2 *nmf* islander
insulso,-a *adj* insipid
insultante *adj* insulting
insultar *vt* to insult
insulto *nm* insult
insumisión *nf* = refusal to do military service
insumiso,-a 1 *adj* unsubmissive
 2 *nm* = person who refuses to do military service
insuperable *adj* (**a**) *(inmejorable)* unsurpassable (**b**) *(problema)* insurmountable
insurgente *adj & nmf* insurgent
insurrección *nf* insurrection
intachable *adj* irreproachable; **conducta i.** impeccable behaviour
intacto,-a *adj* intact
integral 1 *adj* integral; *Culin* **pan i.** wholemeal bread; **arroz i.** brown rice
 2 *nf Mat* integral
integrante 1 *adj* integral; **ser parte i. de** to be an integral part of
 2 *nmf* member
integrar 1 *vt (formar)* to compose, to make up; **el equipo lo integran once jugadores** there are eleven players in the team
 2 integrarse *vpr* to integrate (**en** with)
integridad *nf* integrity
íntegro,-a *adj* (**a**) *(entero)* whole, entire; *Cin & Lit* **versión íntegra** unabridged version (**b**) *(honrado)* upright
intelecto *nm* intellect
intelectual *adj & nmf* intellectual
inteligencia *nf (intelecto)* intelligence; **cociente de i.** intelligence quotient, IQ
inteligente *adj* intelligent
inteligible *adj* intelligible
intemperie *nf* bad weather; **a la i.** in the open (air)
intempestivo,-a *adj* untimely
intención *nf* intention; **con i.** deliberately, on purpose; **con segunda** *o* **doble i.** with an ulterior motive; **tener la i. de hacer algo** to intend to do sth.
intencionadamente *adv* on purpose
intencionado,-a *adj* deliberate
intencional *adj* intentional
intendencia *nf* (**a**) *RP (corporación municipal)* town council, *US* city council (**b**) *RP (edificio)* town hall, *US* city hall (**c**) *Chile (gobernación)* administrative region
intendente *nm* (**a**) *RP (alcalde)* mayor (**b**) *Chile (gobernador)* governor

intensidad *nf* intensity; *(del viento)* force
intensificar [44] *vt*, **intensificarse** *vpr* to intensify; *(amistad)* to strengthen
intensivo,-a *adj* intensive; *Agr* **cultivo i.** intensive farming; *Educ* **curso i.** crash course
intenso,-a *adj* intense
intentar *vt* to try, to attempt; *Fam* **¡inténtalo!** give it a go!
intento *nm* attempt; **i. de suicidio** attempted suicide
intentona *nf* putsch
inter- *pref* inter-
intercalar *vt* to insert
intercambiar [43] *vt* to exchange
intercambio *nm* exchange; **i. comercial** trade
interceder *vi* to intercede
interceptar *vt* (**a**) *(detener)* to intercept (**b**) *(carretera)* to block; *(tráfico)* to hold up
intercesión *nf* intercession
intercontinental *adj* intercontinental
interdicto *nm* prohibition
interés *nm* (**a**) interest; **poner i. en** to take an interest in; **tener i. en** *o* **por** to be interested in (**b**) *(provecho personal)* self-interest; **hacer algo (sólo) por i.** to do sth out of self-interest; **intereses creados** vested interests (**c**) *Fin* interest; **con un i. del 11 por ciento** at an interest of 11 percent; **tipos de i.** interest rates
interesado,-a 1 *adj* (**a**) interested (**en** in); **las partes interesadas** the interested parties (**b**) *(egoísta)* selfish
2 *nm,f* interested person; **los interesados** those interested *o* concerned
interesante *adj* interesting
interesar 1 *vt* (**a**) *(tener interés)* to interest; **la poesía no me interesa nada** poetry doesn't interest me at all (**b**) *(concernir)* to concern
2 *vi* *(ser importante)* to be of interest, to be important; **interesaría llegar pronto** it is important to get there early
3 interesarse *vpr* **i. por** *o* **en** to be interested in; **se interesó por ti** he asked about *o* after you
interferencia *nf* interference; *Rad & TV* jamming
interferir [5] *vt* (**a**) to interfere with; *(plan)* to upset (**b**) *Rad & TV* to jam
interfono *nm Tel* intercom
interinidad *nf* (**a**) *(temporalidad)* temporariness (**b**) *(empleo)* temporary employment
interino,-a 1 *adj* *(persona)* acting
2 *nm,f* *(trabajador temporal)* temporary worker

interior 1 *adj* (**a**) inner, inside, interior; **habitación i.** inner room; **ropa i.** underwear (**b**) *Pol* domestic, internal (**c**) *Geog* inland
2 *nm* (**a**) inside, interior; *Fig* **en su i. no estaba de acuerdo** deep down she disagreed (**b**) *Geog* interior; *Pol* **Ministerio del I.** *Br* ≃ Home Office, *US* ≃ Department of the Interior
interiorizar [40] *vt* to internalize
interjección *nf Ling* interjection
interlocutor,-a *nm,f* speaker; *(negociador)* negotiator
intermediario *nm Com* middleman
intermedio,-a 1 *adj* intermediate
2 *nm TV (intervalo)* break
interminable *adj* endless
intermitente 1 *adj* intermittent
2 *nm Aut Br* indicator, *US* turn signal
internacional *adj* international
internado,-a 1 *nm,f* inmate
2 *nm (colegio)* boarding-school
internar 1 *vt (en hospital)* to confine
2 internarse *vpr* (**a**) *(penetrar)* to advance (**en** into) (**b**) *Dep* to break through
internauta *nmf Informát* Net user
Internet *nf Informát* Internet; **está en I.** it's on the Internet
interno,-a 1 *adj* (**a**) internal; **por vía interna** internally (**b**) *Pol* domestic
2 *nm,f (alumno)* boarder; *Med (enfermo)* patient; *(preso)* inmate
3 *nm RP (extensión)* (telephone) extension; **i. 28, por favor** extension 28, please
interponer [19] *(pp* **interpuesto)** **1** *vt* to insert; *Jur* **i. un recurso** to give notice of appeal
2 interponerse *vpr* to intervene
interpretación *nf* (**a**) interpretation (**b**) *Mús & Teatro* performance
interpretar *vt* (**a**) to interpret (**b**) *Teatro (papel)* to play; *(obra)* to perform; *Mús (concierto)* to play, to perform; *(canción)* to sing
intérprete *nmf* (**a**) *(traductor)* interpreter (**b**) *Teatro* performer; *Mús (cantante)* singer; *(músico)* performer
interpuse *pt indef de* **interponer**
interrogación *nf* interrogation; *Ling* **(signo de) i.** question *o* interrogation mark
interrogante *nf Fig* question mark
interrogar [42] *vt* to question; *(testigo etc)* to interrogate
interrogatorio *nm* interrogation
interrumpir *vt* to interrupt; *(tráfico)* to block
interrupción *nf* interruption; **i. del embarazo** termination of pregnancy

interruptor *nm Elec* switch
intersección *nf* intersection
interurbano,-a *adj* intercity; *Tel* **conferencia interurbana** long-distance call
intervalo *nm* interval; **habrá intervalos de lluvia** there will be periods of rain
intervención *nf* (a) *(participación)* intervention, participation (**en** in); *(aportación)* contribution (**en** to) (b) *Med* intervention
intervenir [27] 1 *vi (mediar)* to intervene (**en** in); *(participar)* to take part (**en** in); *(contribuir)* to contribute (**en** to)
   2 *vt* (a) *(confiscar)* to confiscate, to seize (b) *Tel (teléfono)* to tap (c) *Med* to operate on
interventor,-a *nm,f (supervisor)* inspector; *Fin* **i. (de cuentas)** auditor
interviú *nf* (*pl* **interviús**) interview
intestino,-a 1 *adj (luchas)* internal
   2 *nm Anat* intestine
intimar *vi* to become close (**con** to)
intimidad *nf (amistad)* intimacy; *(vida privada)* private life; *(privacidad)* privacy; **en la i.** privately, in private
intimidar *vt* to intimidate
íntimo,-a 1 *adj* (a) *(intimate)* (b) *(vida)* private; **una boda íntima** a quiet wedding (c) *(amistad)* close
   2 *nm,f* close friend, intimate
intolerable *adj* intolerable
intolerancia *nf* intolerance
intolerante 1 *adj* intolerant
   2 *nmf* intolerant person
intoxicación *nf* poisoning; **i. alimentaria** food poisoning

> ⚠ Observa que la palabra inglesa **intoxication** es un falso amigo y no es la traducción de la palabra española **intoxicación**. En inglés, **intoxication** significa "embriaguez".

intoxicar [44] *vt* to poison

> ⚠ Observa que el verbo inglés **to intoxicate** es un falso amigo y no es la traducción del verbo español **intoxicar**. En inglés, **to intoxicate** significa "embriagar, emborrachar".

intra- *pref* intra-
intranet *nf Informát* intranet
intranquilidad *nf* worry
intranquilizarse *vpr* to get worried
intranquilo,-a *adj (preocupado)* worried; *(agitado)* restless
intransigente *adj* intransigent
intransitable *adj* impassable
intransitivo,-a *adj Ling* intransitive
intratable *adj* (a) *(problema)* intractable

(b) *(persona)* unsociable
intrépido,-a *adj* intrepid
intriga *nf* intrigue; *Cin & Teatro* plot
intrigante 1 *adj* (a) *(interesante)* intriguing, interesting (b) *(maquinador)* scheming
   2 *nmf (persona)* schemer
intrigar [42] 1 *vt (interesar)* to intrigue, to interest
   2 *vi (maquinar)* to plot
intrincado,-a *adj* (a) *(cuestión, problema)* intricate (b) *(bosque)* dense
intrínseco,-a *adj* intrinsic
introducción *nf* introduction
introducir [10] *vt* (a) to introduce (b) *(meter)* to insert, to put in
intromisión *nf (injerencia)* meddling; **perdón por la i.** forgive the intrusion
introspectivo,-a *adj* introspective
introvertido,-a 1 *adj* introverted
   2 *nm,f* introvert
intruso,-a 1 *adj* intrusive
   2 *nm,f* intruder; *Jur* trespasser
intuición *nf* intuition
intuir [37] *vt* to know by intuition
intuitivo,-a *adj* intuitive
inundación *nf* flood
inundar *vt* to flood; *Fig (de trabajo etc)* to swamp
inusitado,-a *adj* unusual
inútil 1 *adj* (a) useless; *(esfuerzo, intento)* vain, pointless (b) *Mil* unfit (for service)
   2 *nmf Fam* good-for-nothing
inutilidad *nf* uselessness
inutilizar [40] *vt* to make o render useless; *(máquina etc)* to put out of action
invadir *vt* to invade; *Fig* **los estudiantes invadieron la calle** students poured out onto the street
invalidar *vt* to invalidate
invalidez *nf* (a) *Jur (nulidad)* invalidity (b) *Med (minusvalía)* disability
inválido,-a 1 *adj* (a) *Jur (nulo)* invalid (b) *Med (minusválido)* disabled, handicapped
   2 *nm,f Med* disabled o handicapped person
invariable *adj* invariable
invasión *nf* invasion
invasor,-a 1 *adj* invading
   2 *nm,f* invader
invencible *adj* (a) *(enemigo)* invincible (b) *(obstáculo)* insurmountable
invención *nf (invento)* invention; *(mentira)* fabrication
inventar *vt* to invent; *(excusa, mentira)* to make up, to concoct
inventario *nm* inventory

inventiva *nf* inventiveness; *(imaginación)* imagination
invento *nm* invention
inventor,-a *nm,f* inventor
invernadero *nm* greenhouse; **efecto i.** greenhouse effect
invernal *adj* winter, wintry
invernar [1] *vi* to hibernate
inverosímil *adj* unlikely, improbable
inversión *nf* (**a**) inversion (**b**) *Fin* investment
inverso,-a *adj* opposite; **en sentido i.** in the opposite direction; **en orden i.** in reverse order
inversor,-a *nm,f Fin* investor
invertebrado,-a *adj & nm Zool* invertebrate
invertido,-a 1 *adj* inverted, reversed **2** *nm,f* homosexual
invertir [5] *vt* (**a**) *(orden)* to invert, to reverse (**b**) *(dinero)* to invest (**en** in); *(tiempo)* to spend (**en** on)
investidura *nf* investiture; *Pol* vote of confidence
investigación *nf* (**a**) *(policial etc)* investigation (**b**) *(científica)* research
investigador,-a *nm,f* (**a**) *(detective)* investigator (**b**) *(científico)* researcher, research worker
investigar [42] *vt* to research; *(indagar)* to investigate
investir [6] *vt* to invest
invidente 1 *adj* unsighted **2** *nmf* unsighted person
invierno *nm* winter
invisible *adj* invisible
invitación *nf* invitation
invitado,-a 1 *adj* invited; **artista i.** guest artist **2** *nm,f* guest
invitar *vt* to invite; **hoy invito yo** it's on me today; **me invitó a una copa** he treated me to a drink
invocar [44] *vt* to invoke
involucrar 1 *vt* to involve (**en** in) **2 involucrarse** *upr* to get involved (**en** in)
involuntario,-a *adj* involuntary; *(impremeditado)* unintentional
invulnerable *adj* invulnerable
inyección *nf* injection; **poner una i.** to give an injection
inyectar *vt* to inject (**en** into); **i. algo a algn** to inject sb with sth
IPC *nm (abr* **Índice de Precios al Consumo)** RPI
ir [16] 1 *vi* (**a**) to go; **¡vamos!** let's go!; **voy a Lima** I'm going to Lima; **¡ya voy!** (I'm) coming!

(**b**) *(río, camino)* to lead; **esta carretera va a la frontera** this road leads to the border
(**c**) *(funcionar)* to work (properly); **el ascensor no va** the lift is out of order
(**d**) *(desenvolverse)* **¿cómo le va el nuevo trabajo?** how is he getting on in his new job?; **¿cómo te va?** how are things?, how are you doing?
(**e**) *(sentar bien)* to suit; **el verde te va mucho** green really suits you
(**f**) *(combinar)* to match; **el rojo no va con el verde** red doesn't go with green
(**g**) *(vestir)* to wear; **ir con falda** to wear a skirt; **ir de blanco/de uniforme** to be dressed in white/in uniform
(**h**) *Fam (importar, concernir)* to concern; **eso va por ti también** and the same goes for you; **ni me va ni me viene** I don't care one way or the other
(**i**) *Fam (comportarse)* to act; **ir de guapo por la vida** to be a flash Harry
(**j**) **va para abogado** he's studying to be a lawyer
(**k**) (**ir + por**) **ir por la derecha** to keep (to the) right; *(ir a buscar)* **ve (a) por agua** go and fetch some water; *(haber llegado)* **voy por la página 90** I've got as far as page 90
(**l**) *(locuciones)* **a eso iba** I was coming to that; **¡ahí va!** catch!; **en lo que va de año** so far this year; **ir a parar** to end up; **¡qué va!** of course not!, nothing of the sort!; **va a lo suyo** he looks after his own interests; **¡vamos a ver!** let's see!; **¡vaya!** fancy that!; **¡vaya moto!** what a bike!
2 *v aux* (**a**) (**ir** + *gerundio*) **ir andando** to go on foot; **va mejorando** she's improving
(**b**) (**ir** + *pp*) **ya van rotos tres** three (of them) have already been broken
(**c**) (**ir a** + *inf*) **iba a decir que** I was going to say that; **va a llover** it's going to rain; **vas a caerte** you'll fall
3 irse *upr* (**a**) *(marcharse)* to go away, to leave; **me voy** I'm off; **¡vámonos!** let's go!; **¡vete!** go away!; **vete a casa** go home
(**b**) *(líquido, gas) (escaparse)* to leak
(**c**) *(direcciones)* **¿por dónde se va a ...?** which is the way to ...? **por aquí se va al río** this is the way to the river
ira *nf* wrath, rage, anger
iracundo,-a *adj* (**a**) *(irascible)* irascible (**b**) *(enfadado)* irate, angry
Irak *n* Iraq
Irán *n* Iran
iraní *adj & nmf (pl* **iraníes)** Iranian
Iraq *n =* **Irak**
iraquí *adj & nmf (pl* **iraquíes)** Iraqi

irascible *adj* irascible, irritable
iris *nm inv Anat* iris; **arco i.** rainbow
Irlanda *n* Ireland; **I. del Norte** Northern Ireland
irlandés,-esa 1 *adj* Irish
  2 *nm,f (hombre)* Irishman; *(mujer)* Irishwoman; **los irlandeses** the Irish
  3 *nm (idioma)* Irish
ironía *nf* irony
irónico,-a *adj* ironic
IRPF *nm Econ (abr* **impuesto sobre la renta de las personas físicas**) income tax
irracional *adj* irrational
irradiar [43] *vt* (**a**) *(emitir)* to radiate (**b**) *Am Fig (expulsar)* to expel
irreal *adj* unreal
irrealizable *adj* unattainable, unfeasible; *Fig* unreachable
irreconocible *adj* unrecognizable
irregular *adj* irregular
irregularidad *nf* irregularity
irremediable *adj* irremediable, incurable
irremplazable *adj* irreplaceable
irreparable *adj* irreparable
irreprochable *adj* irreproachable, blameless
irresistible *adj* (**a**) *(impulso, persona)* irresistible (**b**) *(insoportable)* unbearable
irresoluto,-a *adj* irresolute
irresponsable *adj* irresponsible
irrestricto,-a *adj Am* unconditional, complete
irreverente *adj* irreverent
irrigación *nf* irrigation
irrigar [42] *vt* to irrigate, to water
irrisorio,-a *adj* derisory, ridiculous
irritación *nf* irritation
irritante *adj* irritating
irritar 1 *vt* (**a**) *(enfadar)* to irritate, to exasperate (**b**) *Med* to irritate

  2 irritarse *vpr* (**a**) *(enfadarse)* to lose one's temper, to get angry (**b**) *Med* to become irritated
irrompible *adj* unbreakable
irrumpir *vi* to burst (**en** into)
isla *nf* island, isle
islam *nm Rel* Islam
islámico,-a *adj* Islamic
islandés,-esa 1 *adj* Icelandic
  2 *nm,f (persona)* Icelander
  3 *nm (idioma)* Icelandic
Islandia *n* Iceland
isleño,-a 1 *adj* island
  2 *nm,f* islander
islote *nm* small island
ismo *nm Fam* ism
Israel *n* Israel
israelí *adj & nmf (pl* **israelíes**) Israeli
istmo *nm Geog* isthmus
itacate *nm Méx* packed lunch
Italia *n* Italy
italiano,-a 1 *adj* Italian
  2 *nm,f (persona)* Italian
  3 *nm (idioma)* Italian
itinerante *adj* itinerant, itinerating
itinerario *nm* itinerary, route
IVA *nm Econ (abr* **impuesto sobre el valor añadido**)VAT
izar [40] *vt* to hoist, to raise
izqda., izqda *(abr* **izquierda**) left
izqdo., izqdo *(abr* **izquierdo**) left
izquierda *nf* (**a**) left; **a la i.** on the left; **girar a la i.** to turn left (**b**) *(mano)* left hand (**c**) *Pol* **la i.** the left; **de izquierdas** left-wing
izquierdista *Pol* **1** *adj* leftist, left-wing
  2 *nmf* leftist, left-winger
izquierdo,-a *adj* (**a**) left; **brazo i.** left arm (**b**) *(zurdo)* left-handed
izquierdoso,-a *adj Fam* leftish

J, j ['xota] *nf (la letra)* J, j
jabalí *nm (pl* **jabalíes**) wild boar
jabalina *nf Dep* javelin
jabón *nm* soap; **j. de afeitar/tocador** shaving/toilet soap
jabonera *nf* soap dish
jaca *nf* gelding
jacal *nm Méx* hut
jacinto *nm Bot* hyacinth
jactancia *nf* boastfulness
jactancioso,-a 1 *adj* boastful
2 *nm,f* braggart
jactarse *upr* to boast, to brag (**de** about)
jadeante *adj* panting, breathless
jadear *vi* to pant, to gasp
jadeo *nm* panting, gasping
jaez *nm Pey (ralea)* kind, sort
jaiba *nf Andes, CAm, Carib, Méx (cangrejo)* crayfish
jalar 1 *vt* (**a**) *Fam (comer)* to wolf down (**b**) *Andes, CAm, Carib, Méx (tirar)* to pull
2 jalarse *upr Fam (comerse)* to wolf down, to scoff
jalbegar [42] *vt* to whitewash
jalea *nf* jelly; **j. real** royal jelly
jalear *vt (animar)* to cheer (on)
jaleo *nm (alboroto)* din, racket; *(riña)* row; *(confusión)* muddle; **armar j.** to make a racket
jalón¹ *nm (estaca)* stake; *Fig (hito)* milestone
jalón² *nm* (**a**) *(tirón)* pull, tug (**b**) *Am Aut* lift
jamaicano,-a *adj & nm,f* Jamaican
jamar *vt Fam* to scoff, to eat
jamás *adv* (**a**) never; **j. he estado allí** I have never been there (**b**) ever; **el mejor libro que j. se ha escrito** the best book ever written (**c**) **nunca j.** never again; **por siempre j.** for ever (and ever)
jamba *nf Arquit* jamb
jamón *nm* ham; **j. de York/serrano** boiled/cured ham
jamona *adj Fam* buxom
Japón *n* (**el**) **J.** Japan
japonés,-esa 1 *adj* Japanese
2 *nm,f (persona)* Japanese; **los japoneses** the Japanese
3 *nm (idioma)* Japanese

japuta *nf (pez)* Ray's bream
jaque *nm (en ajedrez)* check; **dar j. a** to check; **j. mate** checkmate; **j. al rey** check; *Fig* **estar en j.** to be stymied
jaqueca *nf* migraine
jara *nf Bot* rock rose
jarabe *nm* syrup; **j. para la tos** cough mixture
jarana *nf Fam* (**a**) *(juerga)* wild party, spree; **ir de j.** to go on a spree *o* a binge (**b**) *(jaleo)* racket, din
jaranero,-a 1 *adj* fun-loving, party-loving
2 *nm,f* pleasure seeker, party-lover
jardín *nm* garden; **j. botánico** botanical garden; **j. de infancia** nursery school, kindergarten
jardinería *nf* gardening
jardinero *nm* gardener
jarra *nf* pitcher; **j. de cerveza** beer mug; *Fig* **de** *o* **en jarras** (with) arms akimbo, hands on hips
jarro *nm (recipiente)* jug; *(contenido)* jugful; *Fig* **echar un j. de agua fría a** to pour cold water on
jarrón *nm* vase; *(en arqueología)* urn
jaspe *nm* jasper; **como el j.** spotless, like a new pin
Jauja *nf Fig* promised land; **¡esto es J.!** this is the life!
jaula *nf (para animales)* cage
jauría *nf* pack of hounds
jazmín *nm Bot* jasmine
J.C. *(abr* **Jesucristo)** J.C.
jeba = **jeva**
jebo,-a = **jevo,-a**
jeep [jip] *nm Aut* jeep
jefa *nf* female boss, manageress
jefatura *nf* (**a**) *(cargo, dirección)* leadership (**b**) *(sede)* central office; **j. de policía** police headquarters
jefe *nm* (**a**) head, chief, boss; *Com* manager; **j. de estación** stationmaster; **j. de redacción** editor-in-chief; **j. de ventas** sales manager (**b**) *Pol* leader; **J. de Estado** Head of State (**c**) *Mil* officer in command; **comandante en j.** commander-in-chief
Jehová *nm* Jehovah; **testigos de J.** Jehovah's Witnesses

jején *nm Am* gnat
jengibre *nm Bot* ginger
jeque *nm* sheik, sheikh
jerarquía *nf* (**a**) hierarchy (**b**) *(categoría)* rank
jerárquico,-a *adj* hierarchical
jeremías *nmf inv* whiner, whinger
jerez *nm* sherry
jerga *nf (argot) (técnica)* jargon; *(vulgar)* slang; **la j. legal** legal jargon
jerigonza *nf* (**a**) *(extravagancia)* oddness (**b**) *(galimatías)* gibberish
jeringa *nf Med* syringe; *Aut* **j. de engrase** grease gun
jeringar [42] *vt Fam* (**a**) *(molestar)* to pester, to annoy (**b**) *(romper)* to break
jeringuilla *nf* (hypodermic) syringe
jeroglífico,-a 1 *adj* hieroglyphic
 2 *nm* (**a**) *Ling* hieroglyph, hieroglyphic (**b**) *(juego)* rebus
jersey *nm (pl* **jerseis**) sweater, *Br* jumper
Jerusalén *n* Jerusalem
Jesucristo *nm* Jesus Christ
jesuita *adj & nmf* Jesuit
Jesús 1 *nm* Jesus
 2 *interj* (**a**) *(expresa sorpresa)* good heavens! (**b**) *(al estornudar)* bless you!
jet *nf* jet set
jeta *nf Fam* (**a**) *(descaro)* cheek; **tener j.** to be cheeky, to have a nerve (**b**) *(cara)* mug, face (**c**) *(hocico)* snout
jet-set *nf* jet set
jeva *nf Carib Fam (mujer)* chick, *Br* bird
jevo,-a *nm,f Ven Fam (novio)* guy, boyfriend; *(novia)* girl, girlfriend
jíbaro,-a *nm,f Am* peasant
jícama *nf* yam bean, jicama
jícara *nf CAm, Méx, Ven (bol)* small cup; *(calabaza)* gourd
jilguero *nm Orn* goldfinch
jilipollas *nmf inv muy Fam* = **gilipollas**
jinete *nm* rider, horseman
jinetera *nf Cuba Fam* prostitute
jiñar *vi muy Fam* to shit
jirafa *nf* (**a**) giraffe (**b**) *(de micrófono)* boom
jirón *nm* (**a**) *(trozo desgarrado)* shred, strip; *(pedazo suelto)* bit, scrap; **hecho jirones** in shreds o tatters (**b**) *Perú (calle)* street
jitomate *nm Méx* tomato
JJOO *nmpl (abr* **Juegos Olímpicos)** Olympic Games
jocoso,-a *adj* funny, humorous
joda *nf RP muy Fam* (**a**) *(fastidio)* pain, drag (**b**) *(broma)* joke; **decir/hacer algo en j.** to say/do sth as a joke (**c**) *(juerga)* wild party

joder *Vulg* **1** *interj* shit!, *Br* bloody hell!
 2 *vt* (**a**) *(fastidiar)* to piss off; **¡no me jodas!** come on, don't give me that! (**b**) *(copular)* to fuck (**c**) *(echar a perder)* to screw up; **¡la jodiste!** you screwed it up! (**d**) *(romper)* to bugger
 3 joderse *vpr* (**a**) *(aguantarse)* to put up with it; **¡hay que j.!** you'll just have to grin and bear it! (**b**) *(echarse a perder)* to get screwed up; **¡se jodió el invento!** that's really screwed things up!; **¡que se joda!** to hell with him! (**c**) *(romperse)* to go bust
jodido,-a *adj Vulg* (**a**) *(maldito)* damned, *Br* bloody (**b**) *(molesto)* annoying (**c**) *(enfermo)* in a bad way; *(cansado)* knackered, exhausted (**d**) *(estropeado, roto)* bust, kaput, buggered (**e**) *(difícil)* shitty
jodienda *nf Vulg* (**a**) *(coito)* fuck (**b**) *(molestia)* pain in the arse
jofaina *nf* washbasin
jogging ['jogin]￼ *nm Urug (ropa)* track o jogging suit
jolgorio *nm Fam (juerga)* binge; *(algazara)* fun
jolín, jolines *interj Fam (sorpresa)* gosh!, good grief!; *(enfado)* blast!, damn!
Jordania *n* Jordan
jornada *nf* (**a**) **j. (laboral)** *(día de trabajo)* working day; **j. intensiva** continuous working day; **j. partida** working day with a lunch break; **trabajo de media j./j. completa** part-time/full-time work (**b**) **jornadas** conference
jornal *nm (paga)* day's wage; **trabajar a j.** to be paid by the day

> Observa que la palabra inglesa **journal** es un falso amigo y no es la traducción de la palabra española **jornal**. En inglés, **journal** significa "revista, diario".

jornalero,-a *nm,f* day labourer
joroba 1 *nf (jiba)* hump
 2 *interj* drat!
jorobado,-a 1 *adj* hunchbacked
 2 *nm,f* hunchback
jorobar *Fam* **1** *vt* (**a**) *(fastidiar)* to annoy, to bother; **me joroba** it really gets up my nose; **¡no jorobes!** *(incredulidad)* pull the other one! (**b**) *(estropear)* to ruin, to wreck
 2 jorobarse *vpr* (**a**) *(fastidiarse)* to grin and bear it (**b**) *(estropearse)* to break
jorongo *nm Méx (manta)* blanket (**b**) *(poncho)* poncho
jota¹ *nf* (**a**) = name of the letter J in Spanish (**b**) *(cantidad mínima)* jot, scrap; **ni j.** not an iota; **no entiendo ni j.** I don't understand a thing

jota² *nf Mús* = Spanish dance and music
joven 1 *adj* young; **de aspecto j.** young-looking
    2 *nmf (hombre)* youth, young man; *(mujer)* girl, young woman; **de j.** as a young man/woman; **los jóvenes** young people, youth
jovial *adj* jovial, good-humoured
joya *nf* (**a**) jewel, piece of jewellery; **joyas de imitación** imitation jewellery (**b**) *Fig* **ser una j.** *(persona)* to be a real treasure *o* gem
joyería *nf (tienda)* jewellery shop, jeweller's (shop)
joyero,-a 1 *nm,f* jeweller
    2 *nm* jewel case *o* box
juanete *nm (en el pie)* bunion
jubilación *nf* (**a**) *(acción)* retirement; **j. anticipada** early retirement (**b**) *(pensión)* pension
jubilado,-a 1 *adj* retired
    2 *nm,f* retired person, pensioner; **los jubilados** retired people
jubilar 1 *vt (retirar)* to retire, to pension off; *Fam Fig* to get rid of, to ditch
    2 jubilarse *vpr (retirarse)* to retire, to go into retirement
júbilo *nm* jubilation, joy
jubón *nm* doublet, jerkin
judería *nf (barrio)* Jewish quarter
judía *nf* bean; **j. verde** French bean, green bean
judicial *adj* judicial; **vía j.** legal channels
judío,-a 1 *adj* Jewish
    2 *nm,f* Jew
judo *nm Dep* judo
juego *nm* (**a**) game; **j. de azar** game of chance; **j. de cartas** card game; *Fig* **j. de manos** sleight of hand; *Fig* **j. de palabras** play on words, pun; **j. de rol** fantasy role-playing game; *Fig* **j. limpio/sucio** fair/foul play (**b**) *Dep* game; **Juegos Olímpicos** Olympic Games; **terreno de j.** *Ten* court; *Ftb* field; **fuera de j.** offside (**c**) *(apuestas)* gambling; *Fig* **poner algo en j.** to put sth at stake (**d**) *(conjunto de piezas)* set; **j. de café/té** coffee/tea service; *Fig* **ir a j. con** to match
juerga *nf Fam* binge, rave-up; **ir de j.** to go on a binge
juerguista 1 *adj* fun-loving
    2 *nmf* fun-loving person, raver
jueves *nm inv* Thursday; **J. Santo** Maundy Thursday
juez *nmf* judge; **j. de instrucción** examining magistrate; **j. de paz** justice of the peace; *Dep* **j. de salida** starter; **j. de línea** linesman

jugada *nf* (**a**) move; *(en billar)* shot (**b**) *Fam* dirty trick
jugador,-a *nm,f* player; *(apostador)* gambler
jugar [32] 1 *vi* (**a**) to play; **j. a(l) fútbol/tenis** to play football/tennis; *Fig* **j. sucio** to play dirty (**b**) **j. con** *(no tomar en serio)* to toy with
    2 *vt* (**a**) to play (**b**) *(apostar)* to bet, to stake
    3 jugarse *vpr* (**a**) *(arriesgar)* to risk; *Fam* **j. el pellejo** to risk one's neck (**b**) *(apostar)* to bet, to stake
jugarreta *nf Fam* dirty trick
jugo *nm* juice; *Fig* **sacar el j. a** *(aprovechar)* to make the most of; *(explotar)* to squeeze dry
jugoso,-a *adj* (**a**) juicy; **un filete j.** a juicy steak (**b**) *Fig (sustancioso)* substantial, meaty; **un tema j.** a meaty topic
juguete *nm* toy; **pistola de j.** toy gun; *Fig* **ser el j. de algn** to be sb's plaything
juguetear *vi* to play
juguetón,-ona *adj* playful
juicio *nm* (**a**) *(facultad mental)* judgement, discernment; *(opinión)* opinion, judgement; **a j. de** in the opinion of; **a mi j.** in my opinion (**b**) *(sensatez)* reason, common sense; **en su sano j.** in one's right mind; **perder el j.** to go mad *o* insane (**c**) *Jur* trial, lawsuit; **llevar a algn a j.** to take legal action against sb, to sue sb
juicioso,-a *adj* judicious, wise
julepe *nm PRico, RP Fam (susto)* scare, fright; **dar un j. a algn** to give sb a scare
julio *nm* July
junco *nm Bot* rush
jungla *nf* jungle
junio *nm* June
júnior *adj Dep* junior; **campeonato j. de golf** junior golf championship
junta *nf* (**a**) *(reunión)* meeting, assembly; *Pol* **j. de gobierno** cabinet meeting (**b**) *(dirección)* board, committee; **j. directiva** board of directors (**c**) *Mil* junta; **j. militar** military junta (**d**) *(parlamento regional)* regional parliament (**e**) *Téc* joint
juntar 1 *vt* (**a**) *(unir)* to join, to put together; *(piezas)* to assemble (**b**) *(reunir) (sellos)* to collect; *(dinero)* to raise
    2 juntarse *vpr* (**a**) *(unirse)* to join; *(ríos, caminos)* to meet; *(personas)* to gather (**b**) *(amancebarse)* to live together
junto,-a 1 *adj* together; **dos mesas juntas** two tables side by side; **todos juntos** all together
    2 *adv* **j. con** together with; **j. a** next to

juntura *nf* (**a**) *Téc* joint, seam (**b**) *Anat* joint

jura *nf (acción)* oath; *(ceremonia)* swearing in; **j. de bandera** oath of allegiance to the flag

jurado *nm* (**a**) *(tribunal)* jury; *(en un concurso)* panel of judges, jury (**b**) *(miembro del tribunal)* juror, member of the jury

juramento *nm* (**a**)*Jur* oath; **bajo j.** under oath (**b**) *(blasfemia)* swearword, curse

jurar 1 *vi Jur & Rel* to swear, to take an oath

2 *vt* to swear; **j. el cargo** to take the oath of office; **j. por Dios** to swear to God

3 **jurarse** *vpr Fam* **jurársela(s) a algn** to have it in for sb

jurel *nm (pez)* scad, horse mackerel

jurídico,-a *adj* legal

jurisdicción *nf* jurisdiction

jurisdiccional *adj* jurisdictional; **aguas jurisdiccionales** territorial waters

jurista *nmf* jurist, lawyer

justamente *adv* ¡**j.!** precisely!; **j. detrás de** right behind

justicia *nf* justice; **tomarse la j. por su mano** to take the law into one's own hands

justicialismo *nm Pol* = Argentinian nationalistic political movement founded by Juan Domingo Perón

justicialista *adj Pol* = belonging or related to "justicialismo"

justiciero,-a *adj* severe

justificable *adj* justifiable

justificación *nf* justification

justificado,-a *adj* justified, well-grounded

justificante *nm* written proof; **j. de pago** proof of payment

justificar [44] 1 *vt* to justify

2 **justificarse** *vpr* to clear oneself, to justify oneself

justo,-a 1 *adj* (**a**) just, fair, right; **un trato j.** a fair deal (**b**) *(apretado) (ropa)* tight; **estamos justos de tiempo** we're pressed for time (**c**) *(exacto)* right, accurate; **la palabra justa** the right word (**d**) *(preciso)* **llegamos en el momento j. en que salían** we arrived just as they were leaving (**e**) **lo j.** just enough

2 *nm,f* just *o* righteous person; **los justos** the just, the righteous

3 *adv (exactamente)* exactly, precisely; **j. al lado** right beside

juvenil 1 *adj (aspecto)* youthful, young; **ropa j.** young people's clothes; **delincuencia j.** juvenile delinquency

2 *nmf* **los juveniles** the juveniles

juventud *nf* (**a**) *(edad)* youth (**b**) *(jóvenes)* young people

juzgado *nm* court, tribunal; **j. de guardia** police court

juzgar [42] *vt* to judge; **a j. por ...** judging by...

K, k [ka] *nf (la letra)* K, k
ka *nf* = name of the letter K in Spanish
kárate *nm Dep* karate
karateka *nmf Dep* person who does karate
Kenia *n* Kenya
kermés [ker'mes] (*pl* **kermeses**), **kermesse** [ker'mes] (*pl* **kermesses**) *nf* fair, kermesse
Kg, kg (*abr* **kilogramo(s)**) kg
kilo *nm* (**a**) *(medida)* kilo; *Fam* **pesa un k.** it weighs a ton (**b**) *Fam (millón)* a million pesetas
kilogramo *nm* kilogram, kilogramme
kilolitro *nm* kilolitre

kilometraje *nm* ≃ mileage
kilométrico,-a *adj* kilometric, kilometrical; **billete k.** multiple-journey ticket
kilómetro *nm* kilometre
kilovatio *nm* kilowatt; **k. hora** kilowatt-hour
kínder *nm Andes, Méx* kindergarten, nursery school
kiosco *nm* = **quiosco**
kiwi *nm* (**a**) *Orn* kiwi (**b**) *(fruto)* kiwi (fruit), Chinese gooseberry
Kleenex® *nm* Kleenex®, tissue
Km, km (*abr* **kilómetro(s)**) km
Kw, kw (*abr* **kilovatio(s)**) kW

L, l ['ele] *nf (la letra)* L, l
l (*abr* **litro(s)**) l
la¹ 1 *art def f* the; **la mesa** the table
 2 *pron dem* the one; **la del vestido azul** the one in the blue dress; **la que vino ayer** the one who came yesterday; *ver* **el**
la² *pron pers f (persona)* her; *(usted)* you; *(cosa)* it; **la invitaré** I'll invite her along; **no la dejes abierta** don't leave it open; **ya la avisaremos, señora** we'll let you know, madam; *ver* **le**
la³ *nm Mús* la, A
laberinto *nm* labyrinth
labia *nf Fam* loquacity; *Pey* glibness; **tener mucha l.** to have the gift of the gab
labio *nm* lip
labor *nf* (**a**) job, task; **l. de equipo** teamwork; **(de profesión) sus labores** housewife (**b**) *Agr* farmwork (**c**) *(de costura)* needlework, sewing
laborable *adj* (**a**) **día l.** *(no festivo)* working day (**b**) *Agr* arable
laboral *adj* industrial; **accidente l.** industrial accident; **conflictividad l.** industrial unrest; **jornada l.** working day; **Universidad L.** technical training college
laboratorio *nm* laboratory
laborioso,-a *adj* (**a**) *(persona)* hardworking (**b**) *(tarea)* laborious
laborista *Pol* **1** *adj* Labour; **partido l.** Labour Party
 2 *nmf* Labour (Party) member/supporter
labrado,-a *adj Arte* carved
labrador,-a *nm,f (granjero)* farmer; *(trabajador)* farm worker
labranza *nf* farming
labrar 1 *vt* (**a**) *Agr* to till (**b**) *(madera)* to carve; *(piedra)* to cut; *(metal)* to work
 2 labrarse *vpr Fig* **l. un porvenir** to build a future for oneself
laburar *vi RP Fam* to work
laburo *nm RP Fam* job
laca *nf* (**a**) hair lacquer, hairspray; **l. de uñas** nail polish *o* varnish (**b**) *Arte* lacquer
lacio,-a *adj* (**a**) *(pelo)* lank, limp (**b**) **qué l.!** *(soso)* what a weed!
lacónico,-a *adj* laconic; *(conciso)* terse

lacra *nf* evil, curse; **una l. social** a scourge of society
lacrar *vt* to seal with wax
lacre *nm* sealing wax
lacrimógeno,-a *adj* (**a**) **gas l.** tear gas (**b**) *Fig* **una película lacrimógena** a tearjerker
lactar *vi* to breast-feed
lácteo,-a *adj* **productos lácteos** milk *o* dairy products; *Astron* **Vía Láctea** Milky Way
ladear 1 *vt (inclinar)* to tilt; *(cabeza)* to lean
 2 ladearse *vpr* (**a**) *(inclinarse)* to lean, to tilt (**b**) *(desviarse)* to go off to one side
ladera *nf* slope
ladino,-a 1 *adj (astuto)* cunning, crafty
 2 *nm,f CAm, Méx, Ven (no blanco)* = Spanish-speaking person of mixed race
lado *nm* (**a**) side; **a un l.** aside; **al l.** close by, nearby; **al l. de** next to, beside; **ponte de l.** stand sideways (**b**) *(en direcciones)* direction; **por todos lados** on/from all sides (**c**) *Fig* **dar de l. a algn** to coldshoulder sb; **por otro l.** *(además)* moreover; **por un l. ..., por otro l. ...** on the one hand ..., on the other hand ...
ladrar *vi* to bark
ladrillo *nm* (**a**) *Constr* brick (**b**) *Fam (pesado)* bore, drag
ladrón,-ona 1 *nm,f* thief, robber; **¡al l.!** stop thief!
 2 *nm Elec* multiple socket
lagartija *nf* small lizard
lagarto *nm* lizard
lago *nm* lake
lágrima *nf* (**a**) tear; **llorar a l. viva** to cry one's eyes out (**b**) *(en lámpara)* teardrop
lagrimoso,-a *adj* tearful
laguna *nf* (**a**) small lake (**b**) *Fig (hueco)* gap
La Haya *n* The Hague
laico,-a 1 *adj* lay
 2 *nm,f* lay person; *(hombre)* layman; *(mujer)* laywoman
lameculos *nmf inv muy Fam* bootlicker, arselicker
lamentable *adj* regrettable; *(infame)* lamentable

lamentar 1 *vt* to regret; **lo lamento** I'm sorry
  2 lamentarse *vpr* to complain
lamento *nm* moan, wail
lamer *vt* to lick
lámina *nf* (**a**) sheet, plate; **l. de acero** steel sheet (**b**) *Impr* plate
laminado,-a 1 *adj* (**a**) laminated (**b**) *(metales)* rolled; **acero l.** rolled steel
  2 *nm* lamination
laminar *vt (metal)* to roll
lámpara *nf* (**a**) lamp; **l. de pie** standard lamp (**b**) *Elec (bombilla)* bulb (**c**) *Rad* valve
lamparón *nm Fam* oil *o* grease stain
lana *nf* (**a**) *(de oveja)* wool; **pura l. virgen** pure new wool (**b**) *Andes, Méx Fam (dinero)* dough, cash
lanar *adj* **ganado l.** sheep
lance *nm Literario (episodio)* event, incident

> Observa que la palabra inglesa **lance** es un falso amigo y no es la traducción de la palabra española **lance**. En inglés, **lance** significa "lanza".

lanceta *nf Andes, Méx* sting
lancha *nf* motorboat, launch; **l. motora** speedboat; **l. neumática** rubber dinghy; **l. salvavidas** lifeboat
langosta *nf* (**a**) lobster (**b**) *(insecto)* locust
langostino *nm* king prawn
languidecer [33] *vi* to languish
lánguido,-a *adj* languid; *(sin vigor)* listless
lanudo,-a *adj* woolly, fleecy; *(peludo)* furry
lanza *nf* spear, lance; **punta de l.** spearhead; *Fig* **romper una l. en favor de algn/de algo** to defend sb/sth
lanzadera *nf* shuttle; **l. espacial** space shuttle
lanzado,-a *adj Fam* reckless; **ir l.** to tear along
lanzagranadas *nm inv Mil* grenade launcher
lanzamiento *nm* (**a**) throwing, hurling (**b**) *Dep (de disco, jabalina)* throw; *(de peso)* put (**c**) *Mil (de cohete etc)* launching (**d**) *Com* launch; **precio de l.** launch price (**e**) *Náut* launch
lanzar [40] 1 *vt* (**a**) *(arrojar)* to throw, to fling (**b**) *Fig (grito)* to let out (**c**) *Náut, Com & Mil* to launch
  2 lanzarse *vpr* (**a**) *(arrojarse)* to throw *o* hurl oneself; **l. al suelo** to throw oneself to the ground (**b**) *(emprender)* **l. a** to embark

on; **l. a los negocios** to go into business (**c**) *Fam (irse, largarse)* to scram
lapa *nf* (**a**) *Zool* limpet (**b**) **es una verdadera l.** he/she sticks to you like glue
lapicera *nf CSur* ballpoint (pen), *Br* Biro®; **l. fuente** fountain pen
lapicero *nm* (**a**) *(lápiz)* pencil (**b**) *CAm, Perú (bolígrafo)* ballpoint (pen), *Br* Biro®
lápida *nf* headstone
lapidario,-a *adj* lapidary
lápiz *nm* pencil; **l. labial** *o* **de labios** lipstick; **l. de ojos** eyeliner
lapso *nm* (**a**) *(periodo de tiempo)* period (**b**) *(error)* lapse, slip
lapsus *nm* slip; **l. linguae** slip of the tongue
largar [42] 1 *vt* (**a**) *Fam (golpe, discurso, dinero)* to give (**b**) *Náut* **l. amarras** to cast off
  2 largarse *vpr Fam* to clear off, to split; **¡lárgate!** beat it!
largas *nfpl* **dar l. a algo** to put sth off
largavistas *nm inv Bol, CSur* binoculars
largo,-a 1 *adj* (**a**) *(espacio)* long; *(tiempo)* long, lengthy; **pasamos un mes l. allí** we spent a good month there; **a lo l. de** *(espacio)* along; *(tiempo)* through; **a la larga** in the long run (**b**) *(excesivo)* too long; **se hizo l. el día** the day dragged on (**c**) **largos años** many years
  2 *nm* (**a**) *(longitud)* length; **¿cuánto tiene de l.?** how long is it? (**b**) *Mús* largo
  3 *adv* **l. y tendido** at length; *Fam* **¡l. (de aquí)!** clear off!; **esto va para l.** this is going to last a long time

> Observa que la palabra inglesa **large** es un falso amigo y no es la traducción de la palabra española **largo**. En inglés, **large** significa "grande".

largometraje *nm* feature film, full-length film
laringe *nf* larynx
laringitis *nf* laryngitis
las¹ 1 *art def fpl* the; **l. sillas** the chairs; **lávate l. manos** wash your hands; *(no se traduce)* **me gustan l. flores** I like flowers
  2 *pron* **l. que** *(personas)* the ones who, those who; *(objetos)* the ones that, those that; **toma l. que quieras** take whichever ones you want; *ver* **la** *y* **los**
las² *pron pers fpl (ellas)* them; *(ustedes)* you; **l. llamaré mañana (a ustedes)** I'll call you tomorrow; **no l. rompas** don't break them; **Pepa es de l. mías** Pepa thinks the way I do; *ver* **los**
lasaña *nf* lasagna, lasagne
lascivo,-a *adj* lewd, lecherous

láser *nm inv* laser; **impresora l.** laser printer

lástima *nf* pity; **¡qué l.!** what a pity!, what a shame!; **es una l. que ...** it's a pity (that) ...; **estar hecho una l.** to be a sorry sight; **tener l. a algn** to feel sorry for sb

lastimar *vt* to hurt, to injure

lastre *nm* (**a**) *(peso)* ballast (**b**) *Fig* dead weight

lata¹ *nf* (**a**) *(envase)* tin, can; **en l.** tinned, canned (**b**) *(hojalata)* tin(plate); **hecho de l.** made of tin

lata² *nf Fam* nuisance, drag; **dar la l.** to be a nuisance *o* a pest

latente *adj* latent

lateral 1 *adj* side, lateral; **salió por la puerta l.** he went out by the side door; **escalón l.** *(en letrero)* ramp
   2 *nm* side passage; *Aut* **(carril) l.** side lane

latido *nm (del corazón)* beat

latifundio *nm* large landed estate

latigazo *nm* (**a**) *(lash)* lash (**b**) *Fam (trago)* drink, swig

látigo *nm* whip

latín *nm* Latin

latino,-a 1 *adj* Latin; **América Latina** Latin America
   2 *nm,f* Latin American

Latinoamérica *nf* Latin America

latinomericano,-a *adj & nm,f* Latin American

latir *vi* to beat

latitud *nf* (**a**) *Geog* latitude (**b**) **latitudes** region, area

latón *nm* brass

latoso,-a *adj Fam* annoying

laucha *nf Am* mouse

laúd *nm* lute

laurel *nm Bot* laurel, (sweet) bay; *Culin* bay leaf; *Fig* **dormirse en los laureles** to rest on one's laurels

lava *nf* lava

lavable *adj* washable

lavabo *nm* (**a**) *(pila)* washbasin (**b**) *(cuarto de aseo)* washroom (**c**) *(retrete)* lavatory, toilet

lavadero *nm (de coches)* carwash

lavado *nm* wash, washing; *Fig* **l. de cerebro** brainwashing; **l. en seco** dry-cleaning

lavadora *nf* washing machine

lavanda *nf* lavender

lavandería *nf* (**a**) *(automática) Br* launderette, *US* Laundromat® (**b**) *(atendida por personal)* laundry

lavaplatos *nm inv* dishwasher

lavar *vt* to wash; **l. en seco** to dry-clean

lavativa *nf* enema

lavatorio *nm Andes, RP (lavabo) Br* washbasin, *US* washbowl

lavavajillas *nm inv* dishwasher

laxante *adj & nm* laxative

laxar *vt (vientre)* to loosen

laxitud *nf* laxity, laxness

lazada *nf (nudo)* bow

lazarillo *nm* **perro l.** guide dog, *US* seeing-eye dog

lazo *nm* (**a**) *(adorno)* bow (**b**) *(nudo)* knot; **l. corredizo** slipknot (**c**) *(para reses)* lasso (**d**) *Fig (usu pl) (vínculo)* tie, bond

le 1 *pron pers mf (objeto indirecto)* (*a él*) (to) him; (*a ella*) (to) her; (*a cosa*) (to) it; (*a usted*) (to) you; **lávale la cara** wash his face; **le compraré uno** I'll buy one for her; **¿qué le pasa (a usted)?** what's the matter with you?
   2 *pron pers m (objeto directo)* (*él*) him; (*usted*) you; **no le oigo** I can't hear him; **no quiero molestarle** I don't wish to disturb you

leal 1 *adj* loyal, faithful
   2 *nmf* loyalist

lealtad *nf* loyalty, faithfulness

lebrel *nm* greyhound

lección *nf* lesson; *Fig* **dar una l. a algn** to teach sb a lesson; *Fig* **te servirá de l.** let that be a lesson to you

leche *nf* (**a**) milk; *Anat* **dientes de l.** milk teeth; **l. descremada** *o* **desnatada** skim *o* skimmed milk (**b**) *Fam* **mala l.** badness (**c**) **l.!** damn! (**d**) *muy Fam (golpe)* knock; **dar** *o* **pegar una l. a algn** to clobber sb (**e**) *Vulg* semen

lechera *nf* (**a**) *(vasija)* churn (**b**) *muy Fam* police car

lechería *nf* dairy, creamery

lechero,-a 1 *adj* milk, dairy; **central lechera** dairy co-operative; **vaca lechera** milk cow
   2 *nm* milkman

lecho *nm Lit* bed; **l. del río** river-bed; **l. mortuorio** death-bed

lechón *nm* sucking-pig

lechosa *nf Carib* papaya

lechoso,-a *adj* milky

lechuga *nf* lettuce

lechuza *nf* owl

lectivo,-a *adj* school; **horas lectivas** teaching hours

lector,-a 1 *nm,f* (**a**) *(persona)* reader (**b**) *Univ* lector, (language) assistant
   2 *nm* **l. de microfichas** *(aparato)* microfiche reader

lectura *nf* reading

leer [36] *vt* to read; **léenos el menú** read

out the menu for us; *Fig* **l. entre líneas** to read between the lines

legado *nm (herencia)* legacy

legajo *nm* bundle (of papers)

legal *adj* (**a**) *Jur* legal, lawful; **requisitos legales** legal formalities (**b**) *Fam (persona)* honest, trustworthy

legalidad *nf* legality, lawfulness

legalizar [40] *vt* to legalize; *(documento)* to authenticate

legaña *nf* sleep

legar [42] *vt (propiedad etc)* to bequeath; *Fig (tradiciones etc)* to hand down, to pass on

legendario,-a *adj* legendary

legión *nf* legion

legionella *nf* Legionnaire's Disease

legislación *nf* legislation

legislar *vi* to legislate

legislativo,-a *adj* legislative; **el poder l.** parliament

legislatura *nf* legislature

legitimar *vt* to legitimize; *(legalizar)* to legalize

legitimidad *nf Jur* legitimacy; *(licitud)* justice

legítimo,-a *adj* (**a**) *Jur* legitimate; **en legítima defensa** in self-defence (**b**) *(auténtico)* authentic, real; **oro l.** pure gold

lego,-a 1 *adj Rel* lay

2 *nm* (**a**) layman; **ser l. en la materia** to be a layman in the subject (**b**) *Rel* lay brother

legua *nf (medida)* league; *Fig* **se nota a la l.** it stands out a mile

legumbres *nfpl* pulses

lejanía *nf* distance

lejano,-a *adj* distant, far-off; **parientes lejanos** distant relatives; **el L. Oriente** the Far East

lejía *nf* bleach

lejos *adv* far (away); **a lo l.** in the distance; **de l.** from a distance; *Fig* **ir demasiado l.** to go too far; *Fig* **llegar l.** to go a long way; *Fig* **sin ir más l.** to take an obvious example

lelo,-a *Fam* **1** *adj* stupid, silly

2 *nm,f* ninny

lema *nm* (**a**) *(divisa)* motto, slogan (**b**) *(contraseña)* code name

lencería *nf* (**a**) *(prendas)* lingerie (**b**) *(ropa blanca)* linen (goods)

lendakari *nm* = head of the Basque government

lengua *nf* (**a**) tongue; *Fig* **malas lenguas** gossips; *Fam Fig* **irse de la l.** to spill the beans; *Fam Fig* **tirarle a algn de la l.** to draw sb out (**b**) *Ling* language; **l. materna**

native *o* mother tongue

lenguado *nm (pez)* sole

lenguaje *nm* language; *Informát* language; **l. corporal** body language

lengüeta *nf* (**a**) *(de zapato)* tongue (**b**) *Mús* reed

lente 1 *nf* lens; **l. de contacto** contact lens

2 *nm Am* **lentes** *(gafas)* glasses, spectacles; **l. de contacto** contact lens

lenteja *nf* lentil

lentejuela *nf* sequin, spangle

lentilla *nf* contact lens

lentitud *nf* slowness; **con l.** slowly

lento,-a *adj* slow; **a fuego l.** on a low heat

leña *nf* (**a**) firewood; *Fig* **echar l. al fuego** to add fuel to the fire (**b**) *Fam (golpes)* knocks

leñazo *nm Fam (golpe)* blow, smash

leñe *interj Fam* damn it!

leño *nm* (**a**) log (**b**) *Fam (persona)* blockhead, halfwit

león *nm* lion

leona *nf* lioness

leonera *nf* lion's den; *Fig (habitación)* den

leopardo *nm* leopard

leotardos *nmpl* thick tights

lépero,-a *adj Fam* (**a**) *CAm, Méx (vulgar)* coarse, vulgar (**b**) *Cuba (ladino)* smart, crafty

lepra *nf* leprosy

leproso,-a 1 *adj* leprous

2 *nm,f* leper

les 1 *pron pers mfpl (objeto indirecto) (a ellos,-as)* them; *(a ustedes)* you; **dales el dinero** give them the money; **l. he comprado un regalo** I've bought you a present

2 *pron pers mpl (objeto directo) (ellos)* them; *(ustedes)* you; **l. esperaré** I shall wait for you; **no quiero molestarles** I don't wish to disturb you

lesbiana *nf* lesbian

leseras *nfpl Chile Fam (tonterías)* nonsense, *Br* rubbish

lesión *nf* (**a**) *(corporal)* injury (**b**) *Jur (perjuicio)* damage

lesionar *vt* to injure

leso,-a *adj Jur* **crimen de lesa humanidad** crime against humanity

letal *adj* lethal, deadly

letanía *nf* litany

letargo *nm* lethargy

letón,-ona 1 *adj* Latvian

2 *nm,f* Latvian

3 *nm (idioma)* Latvian, Lettish

Letonia *n* Latvia

letra *nf* (**a**) letter; **l. de imprenta** block capitals; **l. mayúscula** capital letter; **l.**

minúscula small letter; **l. pequeña** small print (**b**) *(escritura)* (hand)writing (**c**) *Mús (texto)* lyrics, words (**d**) *Fin* **l. (de cambio)** bill of exchange, draft (**e**) *Univ* **letras** arts

letrado,-a *nm,f* lawyer

letrero *nm (aviso)* notice, sign; *(cartel)* poster; **l. luminoso** neon sign

leucemia *nf* leukaemia

levadizo,-a *adj* **puente l.** drawbridge

levadura *nf* yeast; **l. en polvo** baking powder

levantamiento *nm* (**a**) raising, lifting; *Dep* **l. de pesos** weightlifting (**b**) *(insurrección)* uprising, insurrection

levantar 1 *vt* (**a**) to raise, to lift; *(mano, voz)* to raise; *(edificio)* to erect; *Fig (ánimos)* to raise; **l. los ojos** to look up (**b**) *(castigo)* to suspend
2 levantarse *vpr* (**a**) *(ponerse de pie)* to stand up, to rise (**b**) *(salir de la cama)* to get up (**c**) *(concluir)* to finish; **se levanta la sesión** the meeting is closed (**d**) *Pol* to rise, to revolt; **l. en armas** to rise up in arms (**e**) *(viento)* to come up; *(tormenta)* to gather

levante *nm* (**a**) (**el**) **L.** Levante, = the regions of Valencia and Murcia (**b**) *(viento)* east wind, Levanter

levar *vt* **l. ancla** to weigh anchor

leve *adj (ligero)* light; *Fig (de poca importancia)* slight

levedad *nf (ligereza)* lightness; *Fig* slightness; *Fig (de ánimo)* levity; **heridas de l.** minor injuries

levemente *adv* slightly

levitar *vi* to levitate

léxico,-a *Ling* **1** *nm (diccionario)* lexicon; *(vocabulario)* vocabulary, word list
2 *adj* lexical

ley *nf* (**a**) law; *Parl* bill, act; **aprobar una l.** to pass a bill (**b**) **oro de l.** pure gold; **plata de l.** sterling silver

leyenda *nf* (**a**) *(relato)* legend (**b**) *(en un mapa)* legend; *(en una moneda)* inscription; *(bajo ilustración)* caption

liar [29] 1 *vt* (**a**) *(envolver)* to wrap up; *(un cigarrillo)* to roll (**b**) *(enredar)* to muddle up; *(confundir)* to confuse
2 liarse *vpr* (**a**) *(embarullarse)* to get muddled up (**b**) *Fam (salir con)* to get involved; *(besarse)* to neck (**c**) **l. a bofetadas** to come to blows

libanés,-esa *adj & nm,f* Lebanese

Líbano *n* **el L.** the Lebanon

libelo *nm (difamación)* lampoon, satire

libélula *nf* dragonfly

liberación *nf (de país)* liberation; *(de*

rehén) release, freeing

liberal 1 *adj* (**a**) liberal; *(carácter)* open-minded; *Pol* **Partido L.** Liberal Party; **profesión l.** profession (**b**) *(generoso)* generous, liberal
2 *nmf* liberal

liberalizar [40] *vt* to liberalize

liberar *vt (país)* to liberate; *(prisionero)* to free, to release

líbero *nm Ftb* sweeper

libertad *nf* freedom, liberty; **en l.** free; *Jur* (**en**) **l. bajo palabra/fianza** (on) parole/bail; *Jur* (**en**) **l. condicional** (on) parole; **l. de comercio** free trade; **l. de expresión** freedom of speech

libertador,-a *nm,f* liberator

libertar *vt* to set free, to release

libertinaje *nm* licentiousness

libertino,-a *adj & nm,f* libertine

Libia *n* Libya

libio,-a *adj & nm,f* Libyan

libra *nf (moneda, peso)* pound; **l. esterlina** pound sterling

librador,-a *nm,f Fin* drawer

librar 1 *vt* (**a**) to free; *Jur* to free, to release (**b**) *Com (una letra)* to draw (**c**) **l. batalla** to do o join battle
2 *vi* **libro los martes** *(no ir a trabajar)* I have Tuesdays off
3 librarse *vpr* to escape; **l. de algn** to get rid of sb

libre *adj* free; **entrada l.** *(gratis)* admission free; *(sin restricción)* open to the public; **l. cambio** free trade; **l. de impuestos** tax-free

librecambio, librecambismo *nm* free trade

librería *nf* (**a**) *(tienda)* bookshop, *US* bookstore (**b**) *(estante)* bookcase

> Observa que la palabra inglesa **library** es un falso amigo y no es la traducción de la palabra española **librería**. En inglés, **library** significa "biblioteca".

librero,-a 1 *nm,f* bookseller
2 *nm CAm, Col, Méx (mueble)* bookcase

> Observa que la palabra inglesa **librarian** es un falso amigo y no es la traducción de la palabra española **librero**. En inglés, **librarian** significa "bibliotecario".

libreta *nf* notebook; **l. (de ahorro)** savings book

libretista *nmf Am Cin* screenwriter, scriptwriter

libreto *nm Am Cin* script

libro *nm* book; **l. de texto** textbook; *Com* **l. de caja** cashbook; *Fin* **l. mayor** ledger

liceal *nmf Urug Br* secondary school *o US* high school pupil

liceano,-a *nm,f Chile Br* secondary school *o US* high school pupil

liceísta *nmf Ven Br* secondary school *o US* high school pupil

licencia *nf* (**a**) *(permiso)* permission; *(documentos)* permit, licence; **l. de armas/ caza** gun/hunting licence (**b**) *(libertad abusiva)* licence, licentiousness (**c**) *Am Aut Br* driving licence, *US* driver's license

licenciado,-a *nm,f* (**a**) *Univ* graduate; **l. en Ciencias** Bachelor of Science (**b**) *Am* lawyer

licenciar [43] 1 *vt* (**a**) *Mil* to discharge (**b**) *Univ* to confer a degree on
  2 **licenciarse** *vpr Univ* to graduate

licenciatura *nf Univ (título)* (bachelor's) degree (course); *(carrera)* degree (course)

liceo *nm* (**a**) *(sociedad literaria)* literary society (**b**) *(escuela) Br* secondary school, *US* high school

licitar *vt Com (pujar)* to bid for

lícito,-a *adj (permisible)* allowed; *Jur* lawful

licor *nm* liquor, spirits

licuadora *nf* liquidizer

licuar [30] *vt* to liquidize

lid *nf (combate)* contest

líder *nmf* leader

liderar *vt* to lead, to head

liderato, liderazgo *nm* leadership; *Dep* top *o* first position

lidia *nf* bullfight, bullfighting

lidiador *nm* bullfighter

lidiar [43] 1 *vt Taurom* to fight
  2 *vi* to fight; **l. con** to contend with, to fight against

liebre *nf* (**a**) hare (**b**) *Dep* pacemaker

liendre *nf* nit

lienzo *nm* (**a**) *Tex* linen (**b**) *Arte* canvas

lifting *nm* face-lift

liga *nf* (**a**) *Dep & Pol* league; **hacer buena l.** to get on well together (**b**) *(prenda)* garter

ligamento *nm* ligament

ligar [42] 1 *vt* (**a**) to join; *Fig (dos personas)* to unite (**b**) *Fam (coger)* to get
  2 *vi Fam* **l. con algn** *(seducir)* to *Br* get off *o US* make out with sb
  3 **ligarse** *vpr (vincularse)* to become attached (**a** to)

ligazón *nf* bond, tie

ligeramente *adv* (**a**) *(levemente)* lightly (**b**) *(un poco)* slightly

ligereza *nf* (**a**) lightness; *(de tela, argumento)* flimsiness (**b**) *(frivolidad)* flippancy; *(acto)* indiscretion; *(dicho)* indiscreet remark (**c**) *(rapidez)* speed

ligero,-a 1 *adj* (**a**) *(peso)* light, lightweight; **l. de ropa** lightly clad (**b**) *(ágil)* light on one's feet; *(veloz)* swift, quick (**c**) *(leve)* slight; **brisa/comida ligera** light breeze/meal (**d**) **a la ligera** lightly
  2 *adv (rápido)* fast, swiftly

light *adj inv (tabaco)* mild; *Fig (persona)* lightweight

ligón,-ona *adj & nm,f Fam (hombre)* ladies' man; **es muy ligona** she's hot stuff

ligue *nm* pick-up

liguero,-a 1 *adj Dep* league; **partido l.** league match
  2 *nm Br* suspender belt, *US* garter belt

lija *nf* sandpaper; **papel de l.** sandpaper

lijar *vt* to sand *o* sandpaper (down)

lila¹ 1 *nm (color)* lilac
  2 *nf (flor)* lilac
  3 *adj inv* lilac

lila² *Fam* 1 *adj (tonto)* dumb, stupid
  2 *nmf (tonto)* twit

lima¹ *nf (fruto)* lime

lima² *nf (herramienta)* file; **l. de uñas** nail-file

limar *vt* to file; *Fig* **l. asperezas** to smooth things over

limbo *nm* limbo

limitación *nf* limitation; **l. de velocidad** speed limit

limitar 1 *vt* to limit, to restrict
  2 *vi* to border; **l. con** to border on

límite *nm* limit; *Geog & Pol* boundary, border; **caso l.** borderline case; **fecha l.** deadline; **velocidad l.** maximum speed

limítrofe *adj* neighbouring

limo *nm* slime

limón *nm* lemon

limonada *nf* lemon squash

limonero *nm* lemon tree

limosna *nf* alms; **pedir l.** to beg

limpiabotas *nm inv* bootblack, shoeshine

limpiacristales *nm inv* window cleaner

limpiador,-a 1 *adj* cleansing
  2 *nm,f (persona)* cleaner
  3 *nm (producto)* cleaner

limpiaparabrisas *nm inv Br* windscreen *o US* windshield wiper

limpiar [43] *vt* (**a**) to clean; *(con un trapo)* to wipe; *(zapatos)* to polish; *Fig* to cleanse (**b**) *Fam (hurtar)* to pinch, to nick

limpieza *nf (calidad)* cleanliness; *(acción)* cleaning; *Fig (integridad)* integrity; **con l.** cleanly

limpio,-a 1 *adj* (**a**) *(aseado)* clean (**b**) *Dep*

juego l. fair play (**c**) *Fin (neto)* net; **beneficios en l.** net profit (**d**) *Fam* **pasar algo a l.** to produce a fair copy of sth
   2 *adv* fairly; **jugar l.** to play fair
linaje *nm* lineage
linaza *nf* **aceite de l.** linseed oil
lince *nm* lynx; **tiene ojos de l.** he's eagle-eyed
linchar *vt* to lynch; *Fam (pegar)* to beat up
lindante *adj* bordering
lindar *vi* **l. con** to border on
linde *nm o nf* boundary, limit
lindero,-a 1 *adj* bordering, adjoining
   2 *nm* boundary, limit
lindo,-a 1 *adj (bonito)* pretty, lovely; **de lo l.** a great deal
   2 *adv Am (bien)* nicely
línea *nf* (**a**) line; **l. aérea** airline; **en líneas generales** roughly speaking; *Informát* **fuera de l.** off-line; **en l.** on-line (**b**) **guardar la l.** to watch one's figure
lineal *adj* linear; **dibujo l.** line drawing
lingote *nm* ingot; *(de oro, plata)* bar
lingüista *nmf* linguist
lino *nm* (**a**) *Bot* flax (**b**) *Tex* linen
linterna *nf* torch
linyera *nmf CSur (vagabundo)* tramp, *US* bum
lío *nm* (**a**) *(paquete)* bundle (**b**) *Fam (embrollo)* mess, muddle; **hacerse un l.** to get mixed up; **meterse en líos** to get into trouble; **armar un l.** to kick up a fuss (**c**) *Fam (relación amorosa)* affair
lioso,-a *adj Fam (asunto)* confusing
lipotimia *nf* fainting fit
liquidación *nf* (**a**) *Com (saldo)* clearance sale (**b**) *Fin* liquidation
liquidar 1 *vt Com (deuda, cuenta)* to settle; *(mercancías)* to sell off
   2 liquidarse *vpr Fam* (**a**) *(gastar)* to spend (**b**) **l. a algn** *(matar)* to bump sb off
liquidez *nf Fin* liquidity
líquido,-a 1 *adj* (**a**) liquid (**b**) *Fin* net
   2 *nm* (**a**) *(fluido)* liquid (**b**) *Fin* liquid assets; **l. imponible** taxable income
lira *nf (moneda)* lira
lírico,-a *adj* lyrical
lirio *nm* iris
lirismo *nm* lyricism
lirón *nm* dormouse; *Fig* **dormir como un l.** to sleep like a log
Lisboa *n* Lisbon
lisiado,-a 1 *adj* crippled
   2 *nm,f* cripple
lisiar [43] *vt* to maim, to cripple
liso,-a 1 *adj* (**a**) *(superficie)* smooth, even; *Dep* **los cien metros lisos** the one hundred metres sprint (**b**) *(pelo, falda)* straight (**c**)

(tela) self-coloured (**d**) *Am (desvergonzado)* rude (**e**) **lisa y llanamente** purely and simply
lisonjero,-a 1 *adj* flattering
   2 *nm,f* flatterer
lista *nf* (**a**) *(relación)* list; **l. de espera** waiting list; *(en avión)* standby; **pasar l.** to call the register o the roll; *Informát* **l. de correo** mailing list (**b**) *(franja)* stripe; **a listas** striped
listado,-a 1 *adj* striped
   2 *nm* list; *Informát* listing
listar *vt Am* to list
listín *nm* **l. telefónico** telephone directory
listo,-a *adj* (**a**) **ser l.** *(inteligente)* to be clever o smart (**b**) **estar l.** *(a punto)* to be ready
listón *nm Dep* bar; *Fig* **subir el l.** to raise the requirements level
litera *nf (cama)* bunk bed; *(en tren)* couchette
literal *adj* literal
literario,-a *adj* literary
literato,-a *nm,f* writer, author

> 🖉 Observa que la palabra inglesa **literate** es un falso amigo y no es la traducción de la palabra española **literato**. En inglés, **literate** significa "alfabetizado".

literatura *nf* literature
litigar [42] *vi Jur* to litigate
litigio *nm Jur* lawsuit; *Fig* dispute; **en l.** in dispute
litografía *nf* (**a**) *(técnica)* lithography (**b**) *(imagen)* lithograph
litoral 1 *nm* coast, seaboard
   2 *adj* coastal
litro *nm* litre
Lituania *n* Lithuania
lituano,-a 1 *adj & nm,f* Lithuanian
   2 *nm (idioma)* Lithuanian
liturgia *nf* liturgy
liviano,-a *adj (de poco peso)* lightweight
lívido,-a *adj* livid
living ['liin] *(pl livings)* *nm* living room
liza *nf* contest
llaga *nf* sore; *(herida)* wound
llama *nf* flame; **en llamas** in flames, ablaze
llamada *nf* call; *Tel* **l. interurbana** long-distance call; **señal de l.** ringing tone
llamado,-a 1 *adj* so-called
   2 *nm Am* (**a**) *(en general)* call; *(a la puerta)* knock; *(con timbre)* ring (**b**) *(telefónico)* call; **hacer un l.** to make a phone call (**c**) *(apelación)* appeal, call; **hacer un l. a algn para que haga algo** to call upon sb to do sth; **hacer un l. a la huelga** to call a strike

llamamiento *nm* appeal
llamar 1 *vt* (**a**) to call; **l. (por teléfono)** to ring up, to call (**b**) *(atraer)* to draw, to attract; **l. la atención** to attract attention
  2 *vi (a la puerta)* to knock
  3 llamarse *vpr* to be called; **¿cómo te llamas?** what's your name?
llamarada *nf* blaze
llamativo,-a *adj* (**a**) *(color, ropa)* loud, flashy (**b**) *(persona)* striking
llanero,-a *nm,f (del llano)* plainsman, *f* plainswoman
llaneza *nf (sencillez)* simplicity
llano,-a 1 *adj* (**a**) *(superficie)* flat, level (**b**) *(claro)* clear (**c**) *(sencillo)* simple; **el pueblo l.** the common people
  2 *nm* plain
llanta *nf* (**a**) *(de rueda)* wheel rim (**b**) *Am (neumático)* tyre
llanto *nm* crying, weeping
llanura *nf* plain
llave *nf* (**a**) key; **cerrar con l.** to lock; **llaves en mano** *(en anuncio)* available for immediate occupation; *Aut* **l. de contacto** ignition key (**b**) *Téc* spanner; **l. inglesa** adjustable spanner (**c**) *(interruptor)* switch; **l. de paso** stopcock (**d**) *(en lucha)* lock (**e**) *Impr* brace (**f**) *Chile, Méx (grifo) Br* tap, *US* faucet
llavero *nm* key-ring
llegada *nf* arrival; *Dep* finish
llegar [42] 1 *vi* (**a**) to arrive; **l. a Madrid** to arrive in Madrid (**b**) *(ser bastante)* to be enough (**c**) *(alcanzar)* **l. a** to reach; **¿llegas al techo?** can you reach the ceiling? (**d**) *Fig* **l. a las manos** to come to blows; **l. a presidente** to become president (**e**) **l. a + *inf*** to go so far as to (**f**) **l. a ser** to become
  2 llegarse *vpr* to stop by
llenar 1 *vt* (**a**) to fill; *(cubrir)* to cover (**b**) *(satisfacer)* to satisfy
  2 *vi (comida)* to be filling
  3 llenarse *vpr* to fill (up), to become full
lleno,-a 1 *adj* full (up); *Fig* **de l.** fully
  2 *nm Teatro* full house
llevadero,-a *adj* bearable, tolerable
llevar 1 *vt* (**a**) to take; *(hacia el oyente)* to bring; **¿adónde llevas eso?** where are you taking that?; **te llevaré un regalo** I'll bring you a present
  (**b**) *(transportar)* to carry; **dejarse l.** to get carried away
  (**c**) *(prenda)* to wear; **llevaba falda** she was wearing a skirt
  (**d**) *(soportar)* to bear; **¿cómo lleva lo de su enfermedad?** how's he bearing up?
  (**e**) *(tiempo)* **llevo dos años aquí** I've been here for two years; **esto lleva mucho tiempo** this takes a long time
  (**f**) *(negocio)* to be in charge of
  2 *v aux* (**a**) **l. + *gerundio*** to have been + *present participle*; **llevo dos años estudiando español** I've been studying Spanish for two years
  (**b**) **l. + *participio pasado*** to have + *past participle*; **llevaba escritas seis cartas** I had written six letters
  3 llevarse *vpr* (**a**) to take away; *(premio)* to win; *(recibir)* to get
  (**b**) *(arrastrar)* to carry away
  (**c**) *(estar de moda)* to be fashionable
  (**d**) **l. bien con algn** to get on well with sb
llorar *vi* to cry; *Lit* to weep
llorica *nmf Fam* crybaby
lloriquear *vi* to whimper, to snivel
llorón,-ona *adj* **un bebé l.** a baby which cries a lot
lloroso,-a *adj* tearful
llover [4] *v impers* to rain
llovizna *nf* drizzle
lloviznar *v impers* to drizzle
lluvia *nf* rain; **una l. de** lots of; **l. radiactiva** fallout; **l. ácida** acid rain
lluvioso,-a *adj* rainy
lo¹ *art neut* the; **lo mejor** the best (part); **lo mismo** the same thing; **lo mío** mine; **lo tuyo** yours
lo² *pron pers m & neut* (**a**) *(cosa)* it; **debes hacerlo** you must do it; **no lo creo** I don't think so; *(no se traduce)* **no se lo dije** I didn't tell her; *ver* **le** (**b**) **lo que ...** what ...; **no sé lo que pasa** I don't know what's going on (**c**) **lo cual ...** which ... (**d**) **lo de ...** the business of ...; **cuéntame lo del juicio** tell me about the trial
loable *adj* praiseworthy, laudable
loar *vt* to praise
lobo *nm* wolf; **como boca de l.** pitch-dark; *Fam* **¡menos lobos!** pull the other one!
lóbrego,-a *adj* gloomy
lóbulo *nm* lobe
local 1 *adj* local
  2 *nm (recinto)* premises, site
localidad *nf* (**a**) *(pueblo)* locality; *(en impreso)* place of residence (**b**) *Cin & Teatro (asiento)* seat; *(entrada)* ticket
localizar [40] *vt* (**a**) *(encontrar)* to find (**b**) *(fuego, dolor)* to localize
loción *nf* lotion
loco,-a 1 *adj* mad, crazy; **a lo l.** crazily; **l. por** crazy about; **volverse l.** to go mad; *Fam* **¡ni l.!** I'd sooner die!
  2 *nm,f* madman, *f* madwoman; **hacerse el l.** to act the fool
  3 *nm Chile (molusco)* = type of abalone

locomotora *nf* locomotive
locomotriz *adj* locomotive
locuaz *adj* loquacious, talkative
locución *nf* phrase
locura *nf* (*enfermedad*) madness, insanity; **con l.** madly; *Fam* **esto es una l.** this is crazy
locutor,-a *nm,f TV & Rad* presenter
locutorio *nm* telephone booth
lodo *nm* mud
logaritmo *nm* logarithm
lógica *nf* logic; **no tiene l.** there's no logic to it
lógico,-a *adj* logical; **era l. que ocurriera** it was bound to happen
logística *nf* logistics *sing o pl*
logotipo *nm* logo
lograr *vt* (**a**) to get, to obtain; (*premio*) to win; (*ambición*) to achieve (**b**) **l. hacer algo** to manage to do sth
logro *nm* achievement
loma *nf* hillock, rise
lombriz *nf* worm, earthworm
lomo *nm* (**a**) back; **a lomo(s)** on the back (**b**) *Culin* loin (**c**) (*de libro*) spine
lona *nf* canvas
loncha *nf* slice; **l. de bacon** rasher of bacon
lonche *nm* (**a**) *Méx, Perú, Ven (merienda)* (*en escuela*) mid-morning snack; (*en casa*) (afternoon) tea (**b**) *Méx, Ven (comida rápida)* (mid-morning) snack, *Br* elevenses
lonchería *nf Méx* snack-bar
londinense 1 *adj* of/from London
2 *nmf* Londoner
Londres *n* London
longaniza *nf* spicy (pork) sausage
longevo,-a *adj* long-lived
longitud *nf* (**a**) length; **2 m de l.** 2 m long; **l. de onda** wavelength; *Dep* **salto de l.** long jump (**b**) *Geog* longitude
lonja¹ *nf (loncha)* slice; **l. de bacon** rasher of bacon
lonja² *nf* **l. de pescado** fish market
loquería *nf Am* mental asylum, mental hospital
lord *nm* (*pl* **lores**) lord; *Br Parl* **Cámara de los Lores** House of Lords
loro *nm* parrot
los¹ 1 *art def mpl* the; **l. libros** the books; **cierra l. ojos** close your eyes; **l. García** the Garcías; *ver* **el, las** *y* **lo**
2 *pron* **l. que** (*personas*) those who; (*cosas*) the ones (that); **toma l. que quieras** take whichever ones you want; **esos son l. míos/tuyos** these are mine/yours; *ver* **les**

los² *pron pers mpl* them; **¿l. has visto?** have you seen them?
losa *nf* (stone) slab, flagstone
lote *nm* (**a**) set (**b**) *Com* lot (**c**) *Informát* batch (**d**) *Fam* **darse el l.** to pet (**e**) *Am (solar)* plot (of land)
loteamiento *nm Bol, Urug* parcelling out, division into plots
loteo *nm Chile, Col* = **loteamiento**
lotería *nf* lottery; **me tocó la l.** I won a prize in the lottery
lotización *nf Ecuad, Perú* = **loteamiento**
loto 1 *nm Bot* lotus
2 *nf (lotería)* lottery
loza *nf* (**a**) (*material*) earthenware (**b**) (*de cocina*) crockery
lozano,-a *adj* (**a**) (*persona*) healthy-looking (**b**) (*plantas*) lush, luxuriant
Ltda. (*abr* **Limitada**) Ltd
lubricante *nm* lubricant
lubricar [44] *vt* to lubricate
lucero *nm* (bright) star
lucha *nf* (**a**) fight, struggle; **l. de clases** class struggle (**b**) *Dep* wrestling; **l. libre** freestyle wrestling
luchador,-a *nm,f* (**a**) fighter (**b**) *Dep* wrestler
luchar *vi* (**a**) to fight, to struggle (**b**) *Dep* to wrestle
lucidez *nf* lucidity
lúcido,-a *adj* lucid, clear
luciérnaga *nf* glow-worm
lucir [35] 1 *vi* (**a**) (*brillar*) to shine (**b**) *Am (parecer)* to seem (**c**) *Fam (compensar)* **no le luce lo que estudia** his studies don't get him anywhere
2 *vt (ropas)* to sport; (*talento*) to display
3 lucirse *vpr* (**a**) (*hacer buen papel*) to do very well (**b**) (*pavonearse*) to show off
lucrativo,-a *adj* lucrative, profitable
lucro *nm* profit, gain; **afán de l.** greed for money
lúcuma *nf Andes* lucuma, = sweet, pear-shaped fruit
lúdico,-a *adj* relating to games, recreational
luego 1 *adv* (**a**) (*después*) then, next, afterwards (**b**) (*más tarde*) later (on); **¡hasta l.!** so long!; **l. de** after (**c**) **desde l.** of course (**d**) *Chile, Ven (pronto)* soon; *Méx Fam* **l. l.** *o* **l. lueguito** right *o* straight away
2 *conj* therefore
lugar *nm* (**a**) place; **en primer l.** in the first place; **en l. de** instead of; **sin l. a dudas** without a doubt; **tener l.** to take place (**b**) **dar l. a** to cause, to give rise to
lugareño,-a *adj & nm,f* local

lugarteniente *nmf* lieutenant
lúgubre *adj* gloomy, lugubrious
lujo *nm* luxury; **productos de l.** luxury products; **no puedo permitirme ese l.** I can't afford that
lujoso,-a *adj* luxurious
lujuria *nf* lust

ℓ Observa que la palabra inglesa **luxury** es un falso amigo y no es la traducción de la palabra española **lujuria**. En inglés, **luxury** significa "lujo".

---

lujurioso,-a *adj* lecherous, lustful
lumbre *nf* fire
lumbrera *nf* luminary
luminoso,-a *adj* luminous; *Fig* bright
luna *nf* (a) moon; *Fig* **estar en la l.** to have one's head in the clouds; **l. creciente/llena** crescent/full moon; *Fig* **l. de miel** honeymoon (b) *(de escaparate)* pane; *(espejo)* mirror
lunar 1 *adj* lunar
   2 *nm (redondel)* dot; *(en la piel)* mole, beauty spot; **vestido de lunares** spotted dress
lunático,-a *nm,f* lunatic

lunes *nm inv* Monday; **vendré el l.** I'll come on Monday
lupa *nf* magnifying glass
luso,-a *adj & nm,f* Portuguese
lustrabotas *nm inv*, **lustrador,-a** *nm,f Andes, RP* bootblack
lustradora *nf Andes, RP* floor polisher
lustrar *vt* to polish; *(zapatos)* to shine
lustre *nm (brillo)* shine, lustre; *Fig (esplendor)* splendour, glory; **dar** *o* **sacar l. a algo** to polish sth
lustro *nm* five-year period
lustroso,-a *adj* shiny, glossy
luto *nm* mourning
Luxemburgo *n* Luxembourg
luz *nf* (a) light; **apagar la l.** to put out the light; **a la l. de** in the light of; **a todas luces** obviously; *Fig* **dar a l.** *(parir)* to give birth to; *Fig* **dar l. verde a** to give the green light to (b) *Aut* light; **luces de cruce** dipped headlights; **luces de posición** sidelights; **l. larga** headlights (c) **luces** *(inteligencia)* intelligence; **corto de luces** dim-witted (d) **traje de luces** bullfighter's costume
luzco *indic pres de* **lucir**

M, m ['eme] *nf (la letra)* M, m
m (**a**) (*abr* **metro(s)**) m (**b**) (*abr* **minuto(s)**) min
macabro,-a *adj* macabre
macana *nf* (**a**) *Andes, Carib, Méx (palo)* club (**b**) *CSur, Perú, Ven Fam (fastidio)* pain, drag
macanear *vt CSur, Ven (hacer mal)* to botch, to do badly
macanudo,-a *adj Fam* great, terrific
macarra *nm Fam* yob
macarrón *nm* (**a**) macaroon (**b**) *Elec* sheath
macarrones *nmpl* macaroni
macedonia *nf* fruit salad
macerar *vt* to macerate
maceta *nf (tiesto)* plant-pot, flowerpot
machacar [44] 1 *vt* (**a**) to crush; *Dep* to smash (**b**) *Fam (estudiar con ahínco) Br* to swot up on, *US* to bone up on (**c**) *Fam (insistir en)* to harp on about, to go on about
  2 *vi* (**a**) *Fam (insistir mucho)* to harp on, to go on (**b**) *Fam (estudiar con ahínco) Br* to swot, *US* to grind (**c**) *(en baloncesto)* to smash
machacón,-ona *Fam* 1 *adj (repetitivo)* repetitious; *(pesado)* boring, tiresome
  2 *nm,f (muy estudioso) Br* swot, *US* grind
machamartillo: •**a machamartillo** *loc adv (con firmeza)* firmly; *(con obstinación)* obstinately
machete *nm* (**a**) *(arma)* machete (**b**) *Arg Fam (chuleta)* crib
machismo *nm* machismo, male chauvinism
machista *adj & nm* male chauvinist
macho 1 *adj* (**a**) *(animal, planta)* male (**b**) *Fam (viril)* manly, virile, macho
  2 *nm* (**a**) *(animal, planta)* male (**b**) *Téc (pieza)* male piece *o* part; *(de enchufe)* plug (**c**) *Fam (hombre viril)* macho, he-man, tough guy
machote *nm Am (borrador)* rough draft
macilento,-a *adj* gaunt
macizo,-a 1 *adj* (**a**) *(sólido)* solid; **de oro m.** of solid gold (**b**) *(robusto)* solid, robust; *Fam (atractivo)* well-built
  2 *nm (masa sólida)* mass

macramé *nm* macramé
macro *nf Informát* macro
macro- *pref* macro-
macroeconomía *nf* macroeconomics *sing*
macuto *nm (morral)* knapsack, haversack
madeja *nf (de lana etc)* hank, skein
madera *nf* (**a**) wood; *(de construcción)* timber, *US* lumber; **de m.** wood, wooden (**b**) *Fig* **tiene m. de líder** he has all the makings of a leader
madero *nm* (**a**) *(de construcción)* timber; *(leño)* log (**b**) *muy Fam (policía)* cop; **los maderos** the fuzz *pl*
madrastra *nf* stepmother
madre 1 *nf* (**a**) mother; **es m. de tres hijos** she is a mother of three (children); **m. adoptiva** adoptive mother; **m. alquilada** surrogate mother; **m. de familia** mother, housewife; **m. política** mother-in-law; **m. soltera** unmarried mother; *Fig* **la m. patria** one's motherland; *Méx muy Fam* **me vale m.** I couldn't give a damn *o Br* a toss (**b**) *(de río)* bed
  2 *interj* **¡m. de Dios!, ¡m. mía!** good heavens!
madreperla *nf (nácar)* mother-of-pearl
madreselva *nf* honeysuckle
Madrid *n* Madrid
madriguera *nf* burrow, hole
madrileño,-a 1 *adj* of/from Madrid
  2 *nm,f* person from Madrid
madrina *nf* (**a**) *(de bautizo)* godmother (**b**) *(de boda)* ≃ bridesmaid (**c**) *Fig (protectora)* protectress
madrugada *nf* (**a**) dawn; **de m.** in the wee small hours (**b**) early morning; **las tres de la m.** three o'clock in the morning
madrugador,-a 1 *adj* early-rising
  2 *nm,f* early riser
madrugar [42] *vi* to get up early
madurar 1 *vt Fig (un plan)* to think out
  2 *vi* (**a**) *(persona)* to mature (**b**) *(fruta)* to ripen
madurez *nf* (**a**) maturity (**b**) *(de la fruta)* ripeness
maduro,-a *adj* (**a**) mature; **de edad madura** middle-aged (**b**) *(fruta)* ripe

maestría *nf* mastery; **con m.** masterfully

maestro,-a 1 *nm,f* (**a**) *Educ* teacher; **m. de escuela** schoolteacher (**b**) *Méx (en universidad) Br* lecturer, *US* professor (**c**) *(especialista)* master; **m. de obras** foreman (**d**) *Mús* maestro

2 *adj* **obra maestra** masterpiece; **llave maestra** master key

mafia *nf* mafia

mafioso,-a 1 *adj* of/relating to the mafia

2 *nm,f* member of the mafia, mafioso

magdalena *nf* bun, cake

magia *nf* magic; **por arte de m.** as if by magic

mágico,-a *adj* (**a**) magic (**b**) *Fig (maravilloso)* magical, wonderful

magisterio *nm* teaching

magistrado,-a *nm,f* judge; *Am* **primer m.** prime minister

magistral *adj (excelente)* masterly; **una jugada m.** a master stroke

magistratura *nf* magistracy

magnánimo,-a *adj* magnanimous

magnate *nm* magnate, tycoon

magnesio *nm* magnesium

magnético,-a *adj* magnetic

magnetizar [40] *vt* (**a**) *(imantar)* to magnetize (**b**) *Fig (hipnotizar)* to hypnotize

magnetofón, magnetófono *nm* tape recorder

magnetofónico,-a *adj* magnetic

magnífico,-a *adj* magnificent, splendid

magnitud *nf* magnitude, dimension; **de primera m.** of the first order

magno,-a *adj Literario* great; **aula magna** main amphitheatre

mago,-a *nm,f* wizard, magician; **los tres Reyes Magos** the Three Wise Men, the Three Kings

magrear *vt muy Fam* to grope

magro,-a 1 *nm (de cerdo)* lean meat

2 *adj (sin grasa)* lean

magullar 1 *vt* to bruise, to damage

2 magullarse *vpr* to get bruised, to get damaged

mahometano,-a *adj & nm,f Rel* Mohammedan, Muslim

mahonesa *nf* mayonnaise

maillot *nm (malla)* leotard; *Dep* shirt

maíz *nm* maize, *US* corn

maizal *nm* field of maize *o US* corn

majadería *nf* silly thing, absurdity

majadero,-a *nm,f* fool, idiot

majara, majareta *adj Fam* loony, nutty

majestad *nf* majesty

majestuosidad *nf* majesty

majestuoso,-a *adj* majestic, stately

majo,-a *adj (bonito)* pretty, nice; *Fam* *(simpático)* nice; **tiene un hijo muy m.** she's got a lovely little boy; *Fam* **ven aquí, m.** come here, dear

mal 1 *nm* (**a**) evil, wrong (**b**) *(daño)* harm; **no le deseo ningún m.** I don't wish him any harm (**c**) *(enfermedad)* illness, disease; *Fam* **el m. de las vacas locas** mad cow disease

2 *adj* bad; **un m. año** a bad year; *ver* **malo,-a**

3 *adv* badly, wrong; **lo hizo muy m.** he did it very badly; **menos m. que ...** it's a good job (that) ...; **no está (nada) m.** it is not bad (at all); **te oigo/veo (muy) m.** I can hardly hear/see you; **tomar a m.** *(enfadarse)* to take badly

malabar *adj* **(juegos) malabares** juggling

malabarista *nmf* juggler

malapata *nf Fam (mala suerte)* bad luck

malaria *nf* malaria

malcriado,-a 1 *adj* ill-mannered, ill-bred

2 *nm,f* ill-mannered *o* uncivil person

malcriar [29] *vt* to spoil

maldad *nf* (**a**) badness, evil (**b**) *(acción perversa)* evil *o* wicked thing

maldecir [12] 1 *vt* to curse

2 *vi* (**a**) *(blasfemar)* to curse (**b**) *(criticar)* to speak ill (**de** of)

maldición 1 *nf* curse

2 *interj* damnation!

maldito,-a *adj* (**a**) *Fam (molesto)* damned, *Br* bloody (**b**) *(endemoniado)* damned, cursed; **¡maldita sea!** damn it!

maleante *adj & nmf* criminal

malear 1 *vt Fig* to corrupt, to pervert

2 malearse *vpr* to go bad

maleducado,-a 1 *adj* bad-mannered

2 *nm,f* bad-mannered person

maleficio *nm (hechizo)* curse, spell

maléfico,-a *adj* evil, harmful

malentendido *nm* misunderstanding

malestar *nm* (**a**) *(molestia)* discomfort (**b**) *Fig (inquietud)* uneasiness; **tengo m.** I feel uneasy

maleta 1 *nf* suitcase, case; **hacer la m.** to pack one's things *o* case

2 *nm Fam (persona)* bungler

maletero *nm Aut Br* boot, *US* trunk

maletín *nm* briefcase

malévolo,-a *adj* malevolent

maleza *nf* (**a**) *(arbustos)* thicket, undergrowth (**b**) *(malas hierbas)* weeds

malgastar *vt & vi* to waste, to squander

malhablado,-a 1 *adj* foul-mouthed

2 *nm,f* foul-mouthed person

malhechor,-a *nm,f* wrongdoer, criminal

malhumor *nm* bad temper *o* mood; **de m.** in a bad temper *o* mood

malicia *nf* (**a**) *(mala intención)* malice, maliciousness (**b**) *(astucia)* cunning, slyness (**c**) *(maldad)* badness, evil

malicioso,-a 1 *adj* malicious, spiteful

2 *nm,f* malicious o spiteful person

maligno,-a *adj* malignant

malintencionado,-a 1 *adj* ill-intentioned

2 *nm,f* ill-intentioned person

malla *nf* (**a**) *(prenda)* leotard (**b**) *(red)* mesh (**c**) *Perú, RP (bañador)* swimsuit, swimming costume

Mallorca *n* Majorca

mallorquín,-ina *adj & nm,f* Majorcan

malo,-a 1 *adj* (**a**) bad; **un año m.** a bad year; **estar a malas** to be on bad terms; **por las malas** by force (**b**) *(persona) (malvado)* wicked, bad; *(travieso)* naughty (**c**) *(de poca calidad)* bad, poor; **una mala canción/comida** a poor song/meal (**d**) *(perjudicial)* harmful; **el tabaco es m.** tobacco is harmful (**e**) **lo m. es que ...** the problem is that ... (**f**) *(enfermo)* ill, sick

> **Mal** is used instead of **malo** before masculine singular nouns (e.g. **un mal ejemplo** a bad example). The comparative form of **malo** (= worse) is **peor**, the superlative forms (= the worst) are **el peor** (masculine) and **la peor** (feminine).

2 *nm,f Fam* **el m.** the baddy o villain

malograr 1 *vt Andes (estropear)* to make a mess of, to ruin

2 malograrse *vpr* (**a**) *(fracasar)* to fail, to fall through (**b**) *Andes (estropearse) (el tiempo)* to turn nasty; *(máquina)* to break down; *(alimento)* to go off, to spoil

maloliente *adj* foul-smelling

malparado,-a *adj* **salir m.** to end up in a sorry state

malpensado,-a 1 *adj* nasty-minded

2 *nm,f* nasty-minded person

malsonante *adj (grosero)* rude, offensive; **palabras malsonantes** foul language

malta *nf (cebada)* malt

maltratado,-a *adj* battered

maltratar *vt* to ill-treat, to mistreat

maltrecho,-a *adj* in a sorry state, wrecked

malva 1 *adj inv* mauve

2 *nm (color)* mauve

3 *nf Bot* mallow

malvado,-a 1 *adj* evil, wicked

2 *nm,f* villain, evil person

malvender *vt* to sell at a loss

malversar *vt* to misappropriate, to embezzle

Malvinas *npl* **las (Islas) M.** the Falkland Islands

malviviente *nmf CSur* criminal

malvivir *vi* to live very badly

mama *nf* (**a**) *(de mujer)* breast; *(de animal)* teat (**b**) *Fam (mamá)* mum, mummy

mamá *nf Fam* mum, mummy; *Col, Méx Fam* **m. grande** grandma

mamada *nf* (**a**) *(bebé)* feed (**b**) *Vulg (felatio)* blowjob

mamadera *nf Am* feeding bottle

mamar *vt (leche)* to suck; *Fig (adquirir)* to absorb

mamarracho,-a *nm,f Fam (persona)* ridiculous-looking person, mess, sight; *(cosa)* mess

mameluco *nm Fig* (**a**) fool, idiot, dimwit (**b**) *Am* boiler suit

mamey *nm* (**a**) *(árbol)* mamey, mammee (**b**) *(fruto)* mamey, mammee (apple)

mamífero,-a *nm,f* mammal

mamón *nm muy Fam Br* prat, *US* jerk

mampara *nf* screen

mamporro *nm Fam* wallop

mampostería *nf* masonry

mamut *nm* mammoth

manada *nf* (**a**) *Zool (de vacas, elefantes)* herd; *(de ovejas)* flock; *(de lobos, perros)* pack; *(de leones)* pride (**b**) *Fam (multitud)* crowd, mob; **en manada(s)** in crowds

manager *nmf Dep & Mús* manager

manantial *nm* spring

manar 1 *vi* to flow, to run (**de** from)

2 *vt* to run with, to flow with; **la herida manaba sangre** blood flowed from his wound

manazas *nmf inv Fam* ham-fisted person

mancebo *nm* (**a**) *(de farmacia)* assistant (**b**) *Literario (muchacho)* young man

Mancha *n* **el Canal de la M.** the English Channel

mancha *nf* stain, spot; **m. solar** sunspot; **m. de tinta/vino** ink/wine stain

manchado,-a *adj* dirty, stained; **leche manchada** milky coffee

manchar 1 *vt* to stain, to dirty; *Fig* to stain, to blemish

2 mancharse *vpr* to get dirty

manchego,-a 1 *adj* of/from La Mancha

2 *nm,f* person from La Mancha

manco,-a 1 *adj* (**a**) *(de un brazo)* one-armed *(sin brazos)* armless (**b**) *(de una mano)* one-handed; *(sin manos)* handless

2 *nm,f* (**a**) *(de brazos)* one-armed/armless person (**b**) *(de manos)* one-handed/handless person

mancomunidad *nf* community, association

mancornas, mancuernas *nfpl CAm, Chile, Col, Méx, Ven* cufflinks

mandado *nm (recado)* order, errand; **hacer un m.** to run an errand

mandamás *nmf (pl* **mandamases**) *Fam* bigwig, boss

mandamiento *nm* (**a**) *(orden)* order, command (**b**) **los Diez Mandamientos** the Ten Commandments

mandar *vt* (**a**) to order; *Fam* **¿mande?** pardon? (**b**) *(grupo)* to lead, to be in charge *o* command of; *Mil* to command (**c**) *(enviar)* to send; **m. (a) por** to send for; **m. algo por correo** to post sth, to send sth by post; **m. recuerdos** to send regards

mandarina *nf* mandarin (orange), tangerine

mandatario,-a *nm,f Pol* president

mandato *nm* (**a**) *(orden)* order, command (**b**) *Jur* writ, warrant (**c**) *Pol (legislatura)* mandate, term of office

mandíbula *nf* jaw; *Fam* **reír a m. batiente** to laugh one's head off

mandil *nm* apron

Mandinga *nm Am* the Devil

mando *nm* (**a**) *(autoridad)* command, control (**b**) **los altos mandos del ejército** high-ranking army officers (**c**) *Téc (control)* controls; *Aut* **cuadro** *o* **tablero de mandos** dashboard; **m. a distancia** remote control; **palanca de m.** *Téc* control lever; *(de avión, videojuego)* joystick

mandón,-ona 1 *adj Fam* bossy, domineering
2 *nm,f Fam* bossy *o* domineering person
3 *nm Am* (mine) foreman

manecilla *nf (de reloj)* hand

manejable *adj* manageable; *(herramienta)* easy-to-use; *(coche)* manoeuvrable

manejar 1 *vt* (**a**) *(máquina)* to handle, to operate; *Fig (situación)* to handle (**b**) *(negocio)* to run, to manage (**c**) *Fig (a otra persona)* to domineer, to boss about (**d**) *Am (coche)* to drive
2 *vi Am (conducir)* to drive
3 manejarse *vpr* to manage

manejo *nm* (**a**) *(uso)* handling, use; **de fácil m.** easy-to-use (**b**) *Fig (de un negocio)* management; *(de un coche)* driving (**c**) *Fig* tricks

manera *nf* (**a**) way, manner; **a mi/tu m.** (in) my/your way; **de cualquier m.** *(mal)* carelessly, any old how; *(en cualquier caso)* in any case; **de esta m.** in this way; **de ninguna m.** in no way, certainly not; **de todas maneras** anyway, at any rate, in any case; **es mi m. de ser** that's the way I

am; **no hay m.** it's impossible (**b**) **de m. que** so; **de tal m. que** in such a way that (**c**) **maneras** manners; **de buenas maneras** politely

manga *nf* (**a**) sleeve; **de m. corta/larga** short-/long-sleeved; **sin mangas** sleeveless; *Fig* **hacer un corte de mangas a algn** ≃ to give sb the fingers; *Fig* **m. por hombro** messy and untidy; *Fig* **sacarse algo de la m.** to pull sth out of one's hat (**b**) *(de riego)* hose (**c**) *(del mar)* arm (**d**) *Dep* leg, round; *Ten* set

mangante *nmf Fam* thief

mangar [42] *vt Fam* to pinch, to nick, to swipe

mango *nm* (**a**) *(asa)* handle (**b**) *RP Fam (dinero)* **no tengo un m.** I haven't got a bean, I'm broke

mangonear *vi Fam* (**a**) *(entrometerse)* to meddle (**b**) *(dar órdenes)* to throw one's weight around

manguera *nf* hose

mangui *nmf Fam* thief

manguito *nm* (**a**) *(para las mangas)* oversleeve; *(para flotar)* armband (**b**) *Téc* sleeve

maní *nm (pl* **maníes**) peanut

manía *nf* (**a**) dislike, ill will; **me tiene m.** he has it in for me (**b**) *(costumbre)* habit; **tiene la m. de llegar tarde** he's always arriving late (**c**) *(afición exagerada)* craze; **la m. de las motos** the motorbike craze (**d**) *Med* mania

maniaco,-a, maníaco,-a *adj & nm,f Psi* manic; *Fam (obseso)* maniac

maniatar *vt* to tie the hands of

maniático,-a 1 *adj* fussy
2 *nm,f* fusspot

manicomio *nm* mental hospital

manicura *nf* manicure

manido,-a *adj* (**a**) *(comida)* off (**b**) *(asunto)* trite, hackneyed

manifestación *nf* (**a**) demonstration (**b**) *(expresión)* manifestation, expression

manifestante *nmf* demonstrator

manifestar [1] 1 *vt* (**a**) *(declarar)* to state, to declare (**b**) *(mostrar)* to show, to display
2 manifestarse *vpr* (**a**) *(por la calle)* to demonstrate (**b**) *(declararse)* to declare oneself; **se manifestó contrario a …** he spoke out against …

manifiesto,-a 1 *adj* clear, obvious; **poner de m.** *(revelar)* to reveal, to show; *(hacer patente)* to make clear
2 *nm* manifesto

manigua *nf Am Geog* scrubland

manilla *nf* (**a**) *(de reloj)* hand (**b**) *Am (palanca)* lever

manillar *nm* handlebar

maniobra *nf* manoeuvre

maniobrar *vi* to manoeuvre

manipulación *nf* manipulation

manipular *vt* to manipulate; *(máquina)* to handle

maniquí *nm (muñeco)* dummy

manitas *nmf inv Fam* (**a**) **ser un m.** to be handy, to be very good with one's hands (**b**) **hacer m.** to hold hands

manito *nm Méx Fam* pal, *Br* mate, *US* buddy

manivela *nf Téc* crank

manjar *nm* dish, food

mano 1 *nf* (**a**) hand; **a m.** *(sin máquina)* by hand; *(asequible)* at hand; **escrito a m.** hand-written; **hecho a m.** hand-made; **a m. armada** armed; **estrechar la m. a algn** to shake hands with sb; **de segunda m.** second-hand; **echar una m. a algn** to give sb a hand; **¡manos a la obra!** shoulders to the wheel!; **meter m. a** *(un problema)* to tackle; *Fam* to touch up; **traerse algo entre manos** to be up to sth; **equipaje de m.** hand luggage (**b**) *(lado)* side; **a m. derecha/izquierda** on the right/left(-hand side) (**c**) **m. de pintura** coat of paint (**d**) **m. de obra** labour (force) (**e**) *RP (dirección)* direction *(of traffic)*; **calle de una/doble m.** one-/two-way street

2 *nm Andes, CAm, Carib, Méx Fam* pal, *Br* mate, *US* buddy

manojo *nm* bunch; **ser un m. de nervios** to be a bundle of nerves

manopla *nf* mitten

manoseado,-a *adj (objeto)* worn(-out); *(tema)* hackneyed

manosear *vt* to touch repeatedly, to finger; *Fam* to paw

manotazo *nm* cuff, slap

mansalva: • **a mansalva** *loc adv (en gran cantidad)* galore

mansedumbre *nf* (**a**) *(de persona)* meekness, gentleness (**b**) *(de animal)* tameness, docility

manso,-a *adj* (**a**) *(persona)* gentle, meek (**b**) *(animal)* tame, docile (**c**) *Chile (extraordinario)* great

manta 1 *nf* (**a**) blanket; **m. eléctrica** electric blanket (**b**) *(zurra)* beating, hiding (**c**) *Ven (vestido)* = traditional costume worn by women from Guajira

2 *nmf Fam* lazy person, idler

manteca *nf* (**a**) *(de animal)* fat; **m. de cacao/cacahuete** cocoa/peanut butter; **m. de cerdo** lard (**b**) *Am (mantequilla)* butter

mantecado *nm* shortcake

mantel *nm* tablecloth

> 🖉 Observa que la palabra inglesa **mantle** es un falso amigo y no es la traducción de la palabra española **mantel**. En inglés, **mantle** significa "manto, capa".

mantener [24] 1 *vt* (**a**) *(conservar)* to keep; **mantén el fuego encendido** keep the fire burning; **m. la línea** to keep in trim (**b**) *(entrevista, reunión)* to have; **m. correspondencia con algn** to correspond with sb (**c**) *(ideas, opiniones)* to defend, to maintain (**d**) *(familia)* to support, to feed (**e**) *(peso)* to support, to hold up

2 mantenerse *vpr* (**a**) *(sostenerse)* to stand (**b**) **m. firme** *(perseverar)* to hold one's ground (**c**) *(sustentarse)* to live (**de on**)

mantenimiento *nm* (**a**) *Téc* maintenance, upkeep; **servicio de m.** maintenance service (**b**) *(alimento)* sustenance, support (**c**) **gimnasia y m.** keep fit

mantequilla *nf* butter

manto *nm* cloak

mantón *nm* shawl

mantuve *pt indef de* **mantener**

manual 1 *adj* manual; **trabajo m.** manual labour; *Educ* **trabajos manuales** handicrafts

2 *nm* manual, handbook

manubrio *nm Am (manillar)* handlebars

manufactura *nf* (**a**) *(fabricación)* manufacture (**b**) *(fábrica)* factory

manufacturar *vt* to manufacture

manuscrito *nm* manuscript

manutención *nf* maintenance

manzana *nf* (**a**) apple (**b**) *(de edificios)* block

manzanilla *nf* (**a**) *Bot* camomile (**b**) *(infusión)* camomile tea (**c**) *(vino)* manzanilla

maña *nf* (**a**) *(astucia)* cunning (**b**) *(habilidad)* skill

mañana 1 *nf* morning; **a las dos de la m.** at two in the morning; **de m.** early in the morning; **por la m.** in the morning

2 *nm* tomorrow, the future

3 *adv* tomorrow; **¡hasta m.!** see you tomorrow! **m. por la m.** tomorrow morning; **pasado m.** the day after tomorrow

mañanitas *nfpl Méx* birthday song

mañoco *nm Ven* tapioca

mañoso,-a *adj* skilful

mapa *nm* map; **m. mudo** blank map; *Fam* **borrar del m.** to wipe out

maqueta *nf* (**a**) *(miniatura)* scale model, maquette (**b**) *Mús* demo (tape)

maquiavélico,-a *adj* Machiavellian

maquila *nf Méx (of machines)* assembly
maquiladora *nf Méx* assembly plant
maquillaje *nm* make-up
maquillar 1 *vt* to make up
  2 **maquillarse** *vpr* (**a**) *(ponerse maquillaje)* to put one's make-up on, to make (oneself) up (**b**) *(usar maquillaje)* to wear make-up
máquina *nf* (**a**) machine; **escrito a m.** typewritten; **hecho a m.** machine-made; *Fam* **a toda m.** at full speed **m. de afeitar (eléctrica)** (electric) razor *o* shaver; **m. de coser** sewing machine; **m. de escribir** typewriter; **m. fotográfica** *o* **de fotos** camera; **m. tragaperras** *o Am* **tragamonedas** slot machine, one-armed bandit (**b**) *CAm, Cuba (coche)* car
maquinar *vt* to machinate, to plot
maquinaria *nf* (**a**) machinery, machines (**b**) *(de reloj etc) (mecanismo)* mechanism, works
maquinilla *nf* **m. de afeitar** safety razor
maquinista *nmf (de tren)* engine driver
mar 1 *nm o nf* (**a**) sea; **en alta m.** on the high seas; **m. adentro** out to sea; **por m.** by sea; **m. gruesa** heavy sea; **m. picada** rough sea (**b**) *Fam* **está la m. de guapa** she's looking really beautiful; **llover a mares** to rain cats and dogs

Note that the feminine is used in literary language, by people such as fishermen with a close connection with the sea, and in some idiomatic expressions.

  2 *nm* sea; **M. del Norte** North Sea; **M. Muerto/Negro** Dead/Black Sea
maracuyá *nf* passion fruit
maraña *nf* tangle
maratón *nm* marathon
maratoniano,-a *adj* marathon
maravilla *nf* marvel, wonder; **de m.** wonderfully; **¡qué m. de película!** what a wonderful film!; *Fam* **a las mil maravillas** marvellously
maravillar 1 *vt* to amaze, to astonish
  2 **maravillarse** *vpr* to marvel (**con** at), to wonder (**con** at)
maravilloso,-a *adj* wonderful, marvellous
marca *nf* (**a**) mark, sign (**b**) *Com* brand, make; **ropa de m.** brand-name clothes; **m. de fábrica** trademark; **m. registrada** registered trademark (**c**) *Dep (récord)* record; **batir la m. mundial** to break the world record
marcador *nm* (**a**) marker (**b**) *Dep (tablero)* scoreboard; *(persona)* scorer (**c**) *Am (rotulador)* felt-tip pen; *Méx (fluorescente)* highlighter pen

marcaje *nm Dep* marking
marcapasos *nm inv Med* pacemaker
marcar [44] 1 *vt* (**a**) to mark (**b**) *Tel* to dial (**c**) *(indicar)* to indicate, to show; **el contador marca 1.327** the meter reads 1,327 (**d**) *Dep (gol, puntos)* to score; *(a jugador)* to mark (**e**) *(cabello)* to set
  2 **marcarse** *vpr Fam* **m. un farol** to show off, to boast
marcha *nf* (**a**) march; **hacer algo sobre la m.** to do sth as one goes along; **a marchas forzadas** against the clock (**b**) **estar en m.** *(vehículo)* to be in motion; *(máquina)* to be working; *(proyecto etc)* to be under way; **poner en m.** to start (**c**) *Aut* gear; **m. atrás** reverse (gear) (**d**) *Mús* march (**e**) *Fam (juerga)* **hay mucha m.** there's lots going on; **ella tiene mucha m.** she likes a good time
marchante,-a *nm,f* (**a**) *(de arte)* dealer (**b**) *CAm, Méx, Ven Fam (cliente)* customer, patron
marchar 1 *vi* (**a**) *(ir)* to go, to walk; *Fam* **¡marchando!** on your way!; **¡una cerveza! – ¡marchando!** a beer, please! – coming right up! (**b**) *(aparato)* to be on; **m. bien** *(negocio)* to be going well (**c**) *Mil* to march
  2 **marcharse** *vpr (irse)* to leave, to go away
marchitar *vt*, **marchitarse** *vpr* to shrivel, to wither
marchito,-a *adj* shrivelled, withered
marchoso,-a *Fam* 1 *adj (persona)* fun-loving, wild
  2 *nm,f* raver, fun-lover
marcial *adj* martial; **artes marciales** martial arts
marcianitos *nmpl (juego)* space invaders
marciano,-a *adj & nm,f* Martian
marco *nm* (**a**) *(de cuadro etc)* frame (**b**) *Fig (ámbito)* framework; **acuerdo m.** framework agreement (**c**) *Fin (moneda)* mark
marea *nf* (**a**) tide; **m. alta/baja** high/low tide; **m. negra** oil slick (**b**) *Fig (multitud)* crowd, mob
mareado,-a *adj* (**a**) sick; *(en un avión)* airsick; *(en un coche)* car-sick, travel-sick; *(en el mar)* seasick (**b**) *Euf (bebido)* tipsy (**c**) *(aturdido)* dizzy
marear 1 *vt* (**a**) to make sick; *(en el mar)* to make seasick; *(en un avión)* to make airsick; *(en un coche)* to make car-sick *o* travel-sick (**b**) *(aturdir)* to make dizzy (**c**) *Fam (fastidiar)* to annoy, to pester (**d**) *Culin* to stir

2 marearse *vpr* (**a**) to get sick/seasick/airsick/car-sick *o* travel-sick (**b**) *(quedar aturdido)* to get dizzy (**c**) *Euf (emborracharse)* to get tipsy

mareo *nm* (**a**) *(náusea)* sickness; *(en el mar)* seasickness; *(en un avión)* airsickness; *(en un coche)* car-sickness, travel-sickness (**b**) *(aturdimiento)* dizziness, light-headedness

marfil *nm* ivory

margarina *nf* margarine

margarita *nf* daisy

margen 1 *nm* (**a**) border, edge; *Fig* **dejar algn/algo al m.** to leave sb/sth out; *Fig* **mantenerse al m.** not to get involved; **al m. de** leaving aside (**b**) *(del papel)* margin (**c**) *Com* **m. beneficiario** profit margin

2 *nf (de río)* bank

marginación *nf (exclusión)* exclusion

marginado,-a 1 *adj* excluded

2 *nm,f* dropout

marginal *adj* (**a**) marginal (**b**) *Pol* fringe

marginar *vt (de un grupo, sociedad)* to leave out, to exclude

maría *nf Fam* (**a**) *(droga)* marijuana, pot (**b**) *Educ (asignatura fácil)* easy subject (**c**) *(ama de casa)* housewife

marica *nm Fam* queer, *Br* poof, *US* fag

maricón *nm muy Fam* queer, *Br* poof, *US* fag

marido *nm* husband

mariguana, marihuana, marijuana *nf* marijuana

marimacho *nm Fam* mannish woman, butch woman

marimandón,-ona *nm,f Fam* domineering person

marimorena *nf Fam* row, fuss; *Fam* **armar(se) la m.** to kick up a racket

marina *nf* (**a**) *Náut* seamanship (**b**) *Mil* navy; **m. de guerra** navy; **m. mercante** merchant navy (**c**) *Geog (zona costera)* seacoast

marinero,-a 1 *nm* sailor, seaman

2 *adj* seafaring

marino,-a 1 *adj* marine; **brisa marina** sea breeze

2 *nm* sailor

marioneta *nf* marionette, puppet

mariposa *nf* (**a**) *(insecto)* butterfly (**b**) *(lamparilla)* oil lamp (**c**) *(en natación)* butterfly

mariposear *vi Fig* (**a**) *(flirtear)* to flirt (**b**) *(ser inconstante)* to be fickle

mariposón *nm* (**a**) *(galanteador)* flirt (**b**) *Fam (marica)* fairy, pansy

mariquita 1 *nf (insecto) Br* ladybird, *US* ladybug

2 *nm Fam (marica)* queer, *Br* poof, *US* fag

mariscal *nm Mil* marshal; **m. de campo** *Br* field marshal, *US* general of the army

marisco *nm* shellfish; **mariscos** seafood

marisma *nf* marsh

marisquería *nf* seafood restaurant, shellfish bar

marítimo,-a *adj* maritime, sea; **ciudad marítima** coastal town; **paseo m.** promenade

mármol *nm* marble

marmóreo,-a *adj* marble

maroma *nf* (**a**) *Náut* cable (**b**) *(cuerda)* thick rope

marqués *nm* marquis

marquesa *nf* marchioness

marquesina *nf* canopy; **m. (del autobús)** bus shelter

marquetería *nf* marquetry, inlaid work

marrano,-a 1 *adj (sucio)* filthy, dirty

2 *nm,f* (**a**) *Fam (persona)* dirty pig, slob (**b**) *(animal)* pig

marras: • **de marras** *loc adv* **el individuo de m.** the man in question

marrón 1 *adj (color)* brown

2 *nm* (**a**) *(color)* brown (**b**) *Fam (condena)* sentence

marroquí *adj & nmf* Moroccan

marroquinería *nf* leather goods

Marruecos *n* Morocco

marrullero,-a 1 *adj* cajoling, wheedling

2 *nm,f* cajoler, wheedler

Marte *n* Mars

martes *nm inv* Tuesday; **m. y trece** ≃ Friday the thirteenth

martillero *nm CSur* auctioneer

martillo *nm* hammer

mártir *nmf* martyr

martirio *nm* (**a**) martyrdom (**b**) *Fig (fastidio)* torment

martirizar [40] *vt* (**a**) to martyr (**b**) *Fig (fastidiar)* to torture, to torment

marxista *adj & nmf* Marxist

marzo *nm* March

mas *conj Literario* but

más 1 *adv* (**a**) *(adicional)* more; **no tengo m.** I haven't got any more

(**b**) *(comparativo)* more; **es m. alta/inteligente que yo** she's taller/more intelligent than me; **tengo m. dinero que tú** I've more money than you; **m. gente de la que esperas** more people than you're expecting; **m. de** *(con numerales, cantidad)* more than, over

(**c**) *(superlativo)* most; **es el m. bonito/caro** it's the prettiest/most expensive

(**d**) *interj* so ..., what a ...; **¡qué casa m. bonita!** what a lovely house! **¡está m.**

guapa! she looks so beautiful!
(**e**) *(después de pron interr e indef)* else; **¿algo m.?** anything else?; **no, nada m.** no, nothing else; **¿quién m.?** who else?; **nadie/alguien m.** nobody/somebody else
(**f**) **cada día** *o* **vez m.** more and more; **estar de m.** to be unnecessary; **traje uno de m.** I brought a spare one; **es m.** what's more, furthermore; **lo m. posible** as much as possible; **m. bien** rather; **m. o menos** more or less; **m. aún** even more; **¿qué m. da?** what's the difference?; **todo lo m.** at the most
(**g**) **por m.** *(+ adj/adv) + que (+ subjunctive)* however (much), no matter how (much); **por m. fuerte que sea** however strong he may be; **por m. que grites no te oirá nadie** no matter how much you shout nobody will hear you
2 *nm inv* **los m.** the majority, most people; **sus m. y sus menos** its pros and cons
3 *prep Mat* plus; **dos m. dos** two plus *o* and two

masa *nf* (**a**) mass (**b**) *(de cosas)* bulk, volume; **m. salarial** total wage bill (**c**) *(gente)* mass; **en m.** en masse; **medios de comunicación de masas** mass media (**d**) *Culin* dough (**e**) *Constr* mortar (**f**) *RP (pastelito)* shortcake cookie
masacrar *vt* to massacre
masacre *nf* massacre
masaje *nm* massage; **dar masaje(s)** (**a**) to massage
masajista *nmf (hombre)* masseur; *(mujer)* masseuse
mascar [44] *vt & vi* to chew, to masticate
máscara *nf* mask; **m. de gas** gas mask; **traje de m.** fancy dress

> ⚠ Observa que la palabra inglesa **mascara** es un falso amigo y no es la traducción de la palabra española **máscara**. En inglés, **mascara** significa "rímel".

mascarilla *nf* (**a**) mask; **m. de oxígeno** oxygen mask (**b**) *Med* face mask (**c**) *(cosmética)* face pack
mascota *nf* mascot
masculino,-a *adj* (**a**) *Zool & Bot* male (**b**) *(de hombre)* male, manly; **una voz masculina** a manly voice (**c**) *(para hombre)* men's; **ropa masculina** men's clothes, menswear (**d**) *Ling* masculine
mascullar *vt* to mumble
masificación *nf* overcrowding
masificado,-a *adj* overcrowded
masilla *nf* putty
masivo,-a *adj* massive
masón *nm* freemason, mason

masonería *nf* freemasonry, masonry
masoquista 1 *adj* masochistic
2 *nmf* masochist
máster *nm* master's degree
masticar [44] *vt* to chew
mástil *nm* (**a**) *(asta)* mast, pole (**b**) *Náut* mast (**c**) *(de guitarra)* neck
mastín *nm* mastiff
masturbación *nf* masturbation
masturbar *vt*, **masturbarse** *vpr* to masturbate
mata *nf* (**a**) *(matorral)* bush, shrub; **m. de pelo** head of hair (**b**) *(ramita)* sprig
matadero *nm* slaughterhouse, abattoir
matador *nm* matador, bullfighter
matadura *nf* sore
matambre *nm Andes, RP* = flank steak rolled with boiled egg, olives and red pepper, which is cooked, then sliced and served cold
matamoscas *nm inv (pala)* fly swat
matanza *nf* slaughter
matar *vt* (**a**) to kill; *Fam* **m. el hambre/el tiempo** to kill one's hunger/the time; *Fam* **que me maten si ...** I'll be damned if ... (**b**) *(cigarro, bebida)* to finish off (**c**) *(sello)* to frank
matasellos *nm inv* postmark
matasuegras *nm inv* party blower
mate¹ *adj (sin brillo)* matt
mate² *nm (en ajedrez)* mate; **jaque m.** checkmate
mate³ *nm (infusión)* maté
matemática *nf*, **matemáticas** *nfpl* mathematics *sing*
matemático,-a 1 *adj* mathematical
2 *nm,f* mathematician
materia *nf* (**a**) matter; **m. prima** raw material (**b**) *(tema)* matter, question; **índice de materias** table of contents (**c**) *Educ (asignatura)* subject
material 1 *adj* material, physical; **daños materiales** damage to property
2 *nm* (**a**) material; **m. escolar/de construcción** teaching/building material *o* materials (**b**) *(equipo)* equipment; **m. de oficina** office equipment
materialista *adj & nmf* materialist
materialmente *adv* physically
maternal *adj* maternal, motherly
maternidad *nf* maternity, motherhood
materno,-a *adj* maternal; **abuelo m.** maternal grandfather; **lengua materna** native *o* mother tongue
mates *nfpl Fam Br* maths *sing*, *US* math
matinal *adj* morning; **televisión m.** breakfast television
matiz *nm* (**a**) *(de color)* shade (**b**) *(de*

palabra) shade of meaning, nuance; **un m. irónico** a touch of irony

matización *nf* **hacer una m.** to add a rider

matizar [40] *vt* (**a**) *Fig (precisar)* to be more precise o explicit about (**b**) *Arte* to blend, to harmonize (**c**) *Fig (palabras, discurso)* to tinge; *(voz)* to vary, to modulate

matón,-ona *nm,f Fam* thug, bully

matorral *nm* brushwood, thicket

matraca *nf (ruido)* rattle; *Fam* **dar la m. a algn** to pester o bother sb

matrero,-a *nm,f Am (bandolero)* bandit, brigand

matriarcado *nm* matriarchy

matrícula *nf* (**a**) registration; **derechos de m.** registration fee; **m. de honor** distinction; **plazo de m.** registration period (**b**) *Aut (número) Br* registration number, *US* license number; *(placa) Br* number plate, *US* license plate

matriculación *nf* registration

matricular *vt*, **matricularse** *upr* to register

matrimonial *adj* matrimonial; **agencia m.** marriage bureau; **enlace m.** wedding; **vida m.** married life

matrimonio *nm* (**a**) marriage; **m. civil/religioso** registry office/church wedding; **contraer m.** to marry; **cama de m.** double bed (**b**) *(pareja casada)* married couple; **el m. y los niños** the couple and their children; **el m. Romero** Mr and Mrs Romero, the Romeros

matriz *nf* (**a**) *Anat* womb, uterus (**b**) *Mat* matrix (**c**) *(de documento) (original)* original, master copy (**d**) *Téc* mould (**e**) **casa m.** parent company

matrona *nf* midwife

matutino,-a *adj* morning; **prensa matutina** morning papers

maullar *vi* to miaow

maullido *nm* miaowing, miaow

maxilar *nm* jaw, jawbone

máxima *nf* (**a**) *Met* maximum temperature (**b**) *(aforismo)* maxim

máxime *adv* especially, all the more so

máximo,-a 1 *adj* maximum, highest; **la máxima puntuación** the highest score

2 *nm* maximum; **al m.** to the utmost; **como m.** *(como mucho)* at the most; *(lo más tarde)* at the latest

mayo *nm* May

mayonesa *nf* mayonnaise

mayor 1 *adj* (**a**) *(comparativo) (tamaño)* larger, bigger (**que** than); *(edad)* older, elder; **m. que yo** older than me (**b**) *(superlativo) (tamaño)* largest, biggest;

(edad) oldest, eldest; **la m. parte** the majority; **la m. parte de las veces** most often (**c**) *(adulto)* grown-up; **ser m. de edad** to be of age (**d**) *(maduro)* elderly, mature (**e**) *(principal)* major, main; *Educ* **colegio m.** hall of residence (**f**) *Mús* major (**g**) *Com* **al por m.** wholesale; *Fig (en abundancia)* by the score, galore

2 *nm* (**a**) *Mil* major (**b**) **mayores** *(adultos)* grown-ups, adults

mayordomo *nm* butler

mayoreo *nm Andes, Méx Com* wholesale

mayoría *nf* majority; **en su m.** in the main; **la m. de los niños** most children; **m. absoluta/relativa** absolute/relative majority; **m. de edad** majority

mayorista 1 *adj* wholesale

2 *nmf* wholesaler; **precios de m.** wholesale prices

mayoritario,-a *adj* majority; **un gobierno m.** a majority government

mayúscula *nf* capital letter

mayúsculo,-a *adj* (**a**) *Ling (letra)* capital (**b**) *(error)* very big, enormous

mazacote *nm* (**a**) *Culin* solid mass, stodge (**b**) *(mezcla confusa)* hotchpotch

mazapán *nm* marzipan

mazmorra *nf* dungeon

mazo *nm* mallet

mazorca *nf Agr* cob

me *pron pers* (**a**) *(objeto directo)* me; **no me mires** don't look at me (**b**) *(objeto indirecto)* me, to me, for me; **¿me das un caramelo?** will you give me a sweet?; **me lo dio** he gave it to me; **me es difícil hacerlo** it is difficult for me to do it (**c**) *(pron reflexivo)* myself; **me he cortado** I've cut myself; **me voy/muero** *(no se traduce)* I'm off/dying

meada *nf Fam* piss; **echar una m.** to have a piss

meadero *nm Fam Br* bog, *US* john

meandro *nm* meander

mear *Fam* **1** *vi* to (have a) piss

2 mearse *upr* to wet oneself; *Fig* **m. de risa** to piss oneself (laughing)

MEC *nm* *(abr* **Ministerio de Educación y Ciencia)** = Spanish ministry of education and science

mecachis *interj Fam* darn it!, damn it!

mecánica *nf* (**a**) *(ciencia)* mechanics *sing* (**b**) *(mecanismo)* mechanism, works

mecánico,-a 1 *adj* mechanical

2 *nm,f* mechanic

mecanismo *nm* mechanism

mecanizar [40] *vt* to mechanize

mecanografía *nf* typewriting, typing

mecanografiar [29] *vt* to type

mecanógrafo,-a *nm,f* typist
mecapal *nm CAm, Méx* = porter's leather harness
mecedora *nf* rocking-chair
mecenas *nmf inv* patron
mecer [49] 1 *vt* to rock
  2 mecerse *vpr* to swing, to rock
mecha *nf* (**a**) *(de vela)* wick (**b**) *Mil & Min* fuse; *Fam* **aguantar m.** to grin and bear it (**c**) *(de pelo)* streak; **hacerse mechas** to have one's hair streaked
mechar *vt (carne)* to lard
mechero *nm* (cigarette) lighter
mechón *nm* (**a**) *(de pelo)* lock (**b**) *(de lana)* tuft
medalla 1 *nf* medal
  2 *nmf Dep (campeón)* medallist
medallón *nm* medallion
media *nf* (**a**) stocking; *Am (calcetín)* sock (**b**) *(promedio)* average; *Mat* mean; **m. aritmética/geométrica** arithmetic/geometric mean (**c**) **a medias** *(incompleto)* unfinished; *(entre dos)* half and half; **ir a medias** to go halves

> *Observa que la palabra inglesa* **media** *es un falso amigo y no es la traducción de la palabra española* **media**. *En inglés,* **media** *significa "medios de comunicación".*

mediación *nf* mediation, intervention; **por m. de un amigo** through a friend
mediado,-a *adj* half-full, half-empty; **a mediados de mes/semana** about the middle of the month/week
mediador,-a *nm,f* mediator
medialuna *nf* (**a**) *(símbolo musulmán)* crescent (**b**) *Am Culin (pasta)* croissant
mediano,-a *adj* (**a**) middling, average (**b**) *(tamaño)* medium-sized
medianoche *nf* midnight
mediante *prep* by means of, with the help of, using; **Dios m.** God willing
mediar [43] *vi* (**a**) *(intervenir)* to mediate, to intervene; **m. en favor de** *o* **por algn** to intercede on behalf of sb (**b**) *(tiempo)* to pass; **mediaron tres semanas** three weeks passed
mediático,-a *adj* media
medicación *nf* medication, medical treatment
medicamento *nm* medicine, medicament
medicina *nf* medicine; **estudiante de m.** medical student, medic
médico,-a 1 *nm,f* doctor; **m. de cabecera** family doctor, general practitioner, GP
  2 *adj* medical
medida *nf* (**a**) measure; **a (la) m.** *(ropa)* made-to-measure; **a m. que avanzaba** as he advanced; **en gran m.** to a great extent (**b**) *(dimensión)* measurement (**c**) *(disposición)* measure; **adoptar** *o* **tomar medidas** to take steps; **m. represiva** deterrent
medidor *nm Am (contador)* meter
medieval *adj* medieval
medievo *nm* Middle Ages
medio,-a 1 *adj* (**a**) half; **a m. camino** halfway; **m. kilo** half a kilo; **una hora y media** one and a half hours, an hour and a half (**b**) *(intermedio)* middle; **a media mañana/tarde** in the middle of the morning/afternoon; **clase media** middle class; **punto m.** middle ground (**c**) *(normal)* average; **salario m.** average wage
  2 *adv* half; **está m. muerta** she is half dead
  3 *nm* (**a**) *(mitad)* half (**b**) *(centro)* middle; **en m. (de)** *(en el centro)* in the middle (of); *(entre dos)* in between (**c**) **medios de transporte** means of transport; **por m. de ...** by means of ...; **medios económicos** means; **medios de comunicación** (mass) media (**d**) **m. ambiente** environment (**e**) *Dep (jugador)* half back
medioambiental *adj* environmental
medioambientalista *nmf* environmentalist
mediocre *adj* mediocre
mediocridad *nf* mediocrity
mediodía *nm* (**a**) *(hora exacta)* midday, noon (**b**) *(período aproximado)* early afternoon, lunch-time (**c**) *(sur)* south
medir [6] 1 *vt* (**a**) *(distancia, superficie, temperatura)* to measure (**b**) *(moderar)* to weigh; **mide tus palabras** weigh your words
  2 *vi* to measure, to be; **¿cuánto mides?** how tall are you?; **mide 2 m** he is 2 m tall; **mide 2 m de alto/ancho/largo** it is 2 m high/wide/long
meditar *vt & vi* to meditate, to ponder; **m. sobre algo** to ponder over sth
mediterráneo,-a 1 *adj* Mediterranean
  2 *nm* **el M.** the Mediterranean
medrar *vi* to climb the social ladder
medroso,-a *adj* (**a**) *(temeroso)* fearful, faint-hearted (**b**) *(que causa miedo)* frightening
médula *nf* (**a**) marrow; **m. ósea** bone marrow (**b**) *Fig (lo más profundo)* marrow, pith; **hasta la m.** to the marrow
medusa *nf* jellyfish
megafonía *nf* public-address system, PA system
megáfono *nm* megaphone
megalito *nm* megalith

megalómano,-a *adj* megalomaniac
mejicano,-a *adj & nm,f* Mexican
Méjico *n* Mexico; **ciudad de M.** Mexico City; **Nuevo M.** New Mexico
mejilla *nf* cheek
mejillón *nm* mussel
mejor 1 *adj* (a) *(comparativo)* better (**que** than); **el m. de los dos** the better of the two; **es m. no decírselo** it's better not to tell her; **es m. que vayas** you'd better go (b) *(superlativo)* best; **el m. de los tres** the best of the three; **tu m. amiga** your best friend; **lo m.** the best thing
   2 *adv* (a) *(comparativo)* better (**que** than); **cada vez m.** better and better; **ella conduce m.** she drives better; **m. dicho** or rather; **¡mucho** o **tanto m.!** so much the better! (b) *(superlativo)* best; **es el que m. canta** he is the one who sings the best; **a lo m.** *(quizás)* perhaps; *(ojalá)* hopefully
mejora *nf* improvement
mejorar 1 *vt* to improve; **m. la red vial** to improve the road system; **m. una marca** o **un récord** to break a record
   2 *vi* to improve, to get better
   3 mejorarse *upr* to get better; **¡que te mejores!** get well soon!
mejoría *nf* improvement
melancolía *nf* melancholy
melancólico,-a *adj* melancholic, melancholy
melé *nf Dep* scrum
melena *nf* (head of) hair; *(de león)* mane
Melilla *n* Melilla
melindroso,-a 1 *adj* affected, fussy, finicky
   2 *nm,f* affected o finicky person
mella *nf* (a) *(hendedura)* nick, notch; *(en plato, taza etc)* chip (b) *(en dentadura)* gap (c) *Fig* impression; **hacer m. en algn** to make an impression on sb
mellado,-a *adj (sin dientes)* gap-toothed
mellizo,-a *adj & nm,f* twin
melocotón *nm* peach
melodía *nf* melody, tune
melodrama *nm* melodrama
melón *nm* (a) *(fruto)* melon (b) *Fam (tonto)* ninny (c) *muy Fam* **melones** *(tetas)* boobs
melopea *nf Fam* **coger** o **agarrar/llevar una m.** to get/be drunk o pissed
meloso,-a *adj* sweet, honeyed
membrana *nf* membrane
membresía *nf Am* membership
membrete *nm* letterhead
membrillo *nm* (a) *Bot* quince; *(árbol)* quince tree; *(dulce)* quince preserve o jelly (b) *Fam (tonto)* dimwit

memela *nf Méx* = thick corn tortilla
memo,-a *Fam* **1** *adj* silly, stupid
   2 *nm,f* nincompoop, ninny
memorable *adj* memorable
memorándum *nm* (*pl* **memorándums**) memorandum
memoria *nf* (a) memory; **aprender/saber algo de m.** to learn/know sth by heart; **irse de la m.** to slip one's mind (b) *(informe)* report, statement; **m. anual** annual report (c) *(recuerdo)* memory, recollection (d) **memorias** *(biografía)* memoirs
memorístico,-a *adj* acquired by memory
memorizar [40] *vt* to memorize
menaje *nm* furniture and furnishing; **m. de cocina** kitchen equipment o utensils
mención *nf* mention; **m. honorífica** honourable mention
mencionar *vt* to mention
mendicidad *nf* begging
mendigar [42] *vt & vi* to beg
mendigo,-a *nm,f* beggar
mendrugo *nm* (a) crust o chunk (of stale bread) (b) *(tonto)* dimwit
mene *nm Ven* = deposit of oil at surface level
menear 1 *vt* to shake, to move; *(cola)* to wag, to waggle; *Fam (culo)* to wiggle
   2 menearse *upr* to move, to shake; *Fam* **una tormenta de no te menees** a hell of a storm; *Vulg* **meneársela** to wank
meneo *nm* shake; *(de cola)* wag, waggle; *(de culo)* wiggle
menester *nm* (a) **es m.** it is necessary (b) **menesteres** *(deberes)* jobs
menestra *nf* vegetable stew
mengano,-a *nm,f Fam* so-and-so, what's-his- o her-name
menguante *adj* waning, on the wane; **cuarto m.** last quarter
menguar [45] 1 *vt* (a) to diminish, to reduce (b) *(en labor de punto)* to decrease
   2 *vi* (a) to diminish, to decrease (b) *(la luna)* to wane
menopausia *nf Med* menopause
menor 1 *adj* (a) *(comparativo) (de tamaño)* smaller (**que** than); *(de edad)* younger (**que** than); **mal m.** the lesser of two evils; **el m. de los dos** the smaller of the two; **ser m. de edad** to be a minor o under age (b) *(superlativo) (de tamaño)* smallest; *(de intensidad)* least, slightest; *(de edad)* youngest; **al m. ruido** at the slightest noise; **el m. de los tres** the youngest of the three; **es la m.** she's the

youngest child (**c**) *Mús* minor (**d**) *Com* **al por m.** retail

2 *nmf* minor; *Jur* **tribunal de menores** juvenile court

menos 1 *adj* (**a**) *(comparativo) (con singular)* less; *(con plural)* fewer; **m. dinero/ leche/ tiempo que** less money/milk/time than; **m. libros/pisos que** fewer books/ flats than; *(con cláusula)* **tiene m. años de lo que parece** he's younger than he looks (**b**) *(superlativo)* **fui el que perdí m. dinero** I lost the least money

2 *adv* (**a**) **m. de** *(con singular)* less than; *(con plural)* fewer than, less than; **m. de media hora** less than half an hour

(**b**) *(superlativo) (con singular)* least; *(con plural)* the fewest; *(con cantidad)* the least; **el m. inteligente de la clase** the least intelligent boy in the class; **ayer fue cuando vinieron m. personas** yesterday was when the fewest people came

3 *(locuciones)* **a m. que** (+ *subjunctive*) unless; **al** *o* **por lo m.** at least; **echar a algn de m.** to miss sb; **eso es lo de m.** that's the least of it; **¡m. mal!** just as well!; **nada m. que** no less *o* no fewer than; **ni mucho m.** far from it

4 *prep* (**a**) but, except; **todo m. eso** anything but that

(**b**) *Mat* minus; **tres m. uno** three minus one

menoscabar *vt* (**a**) *(perjudicar)* to damage (**b**) *Fig (desacreditar)* to discredit

menoscabo *nm* harm, damage; **ir en m. de algo** to be to the detriment of sth

menospreciar [43] *vt* to scorn, to disdain

menosprecio *nm* contempt, scorn, disdain

mensáfono *nm* pager

mensaje *nm* message

mensajero,-a *nm,f* messenger, courier

menso,-a *adj Méx Fam* foolish, stupid

menstruación *nf* menstruation

mensual *adj* monthly; **dos visitas mensuales** two visits a month

mensualidad *nf (pago)* monthly payment; *(sueldo)* monthly salary *o* wage

menta *nf* (**a**) *Bot* mint (**b**) *(licor)* crème de menthe

mental *adj* mental

mentalidad *nf* mentality; **de m. abierta/ cerrada** open-/narrow-minded

mentalizar [40] 1 *vt (concienciar)* to make aware

2 mentalizarse *vpr* (**a**) *(concienciarse)* to become aware (**b**) *(hacerse a la idea)* to come to terms (**a** with)

mentar [1] *vt* to mention, to name

mente *nf* mind; **se me quedó la m. en blanco** my mind went blank; **m. abierta/ tolerante/cerrada** open/broad/closed mind

mentecato,-a *nm,f* fool, idiot

mentir [5] *vi* to lie, to tell lies

mentira *nf* lie; **aunque parezca m.** strange as it may seem; **parece m.** it is unbelievable

mentiroso,-a 1 *adj* lying

2 *nm,f* liar

mentís *nm* denial

mentón *nm Anat* chin

menú *nm* menu

menudeo *nm Andes, Méx Com* retailing

menudillos *nmpl* giblets

menudo,-a 1 *adj* minute, tiny; *(irónico)* tremendous; **la gente menuda** the little ones; **¡m. lío/susto!** what a mess/fright!

2 *adv* **a m.** often

meñique *adj & nm* **(dedo) m.** little finger

meollo *nm* (**a**) *Fig (quid)* essence (**b**) *(miga)* crumb

mercado *nm* market; **M. Común** Common Market; **m. negro** black market; **m. único** single market; **sacar algo al m.** to put sth on the market

mercadotecnia *nf* marketing

mercancía *nf* commodity, goods

mercante *adj* merchant; **barco/marina m.** merchant ship/navy

mercantil *adj* mercantile, commercial

merced *nf Fml* favour, grace; **a m. de** at the mercy of

mercenario,-a *adj & nm,f* mercenary

mercería *nf Br* haberdasher's (shop), *US* notions store

MERCOSUR *nm* (*abr* **Mercado Común del Sur**) = South American economic community consisting of Argentina, Brazil, Paraguay and Uruguay

mercurio *nm* (**a**) *Quím* mercury, quicksilver (**b**) **M.** Mercury

merecer [33] 1 *vt* (**a**) to deserve (**b**) *(uso impers)* **no merece la pena hacerlo** it's not worth while doing it

2 merecerse *vpr* to deserve

merecido,-a 1 *adj* deserved; **ella lo tiene m.** *(recompensa)* she deserves it; *(castigo)* it serves her right

2 *nm* just deserts

merendar [1] *vt* to have as an afternoon snack, to have for tea

2 *vi* to have an afternoon snack, to have tea

merendero *nm (establecimiento)* tea

room, snack-bar; *(en el campo)* picnic spot

merengue *nm Culin* meringue

merezco *indic pres de* **merecer**

meridiano *nm* meridian

meridional 1 *adj* southern

2 *nmf* southerner

merienda *nf* afternoon snack, tea

mérito *nm* merit, worth; **hacer méritos para algo** to strive to deserve sth

merluza *nf (pez)* hake

merma *nf* decrease, reduction

mermar 1 *vt* to cause to decrease *o* diminish

2 *vi* to decrease, to diminish

3 **mermarse** *vpr* to decrease, to diminish

mermelada *nf* (**a**) jam; **m. de fresa** strawberry jam (**b**) *(de agrios)* marmalade; **m. de naranja** orange marmalade

mero,-a *adj* mere, pure; **por el m. hecho de** through the mere fact of

merodear *vi* to prowl

mes *nm* (**a**) month; **el m. pasado/que viene** last/next month (**b**) *(cobro)* monthly salary *o* wages; *(pago)* monthly payment (**c**) *Fam (menstruación)* period

mesa *nf* (**a**) table; **poner/recoger la m.** to set/clear the table; *(de despacho etc)* desk; **m. redonda** round table (**b**) *(junta directiva)* board, executive; **el presidente de la m.** the chairman; **m. electoral** electoral college

mesada *nf* (**a**) *Am (dinero)* monthly payment (**b**) *RP (para adolescentes)* (monthly) pocket money, *US* (monthly) allowance (**c**) *RP (encimera)* worktop

mesero,-a *nm,f CAm, Col, Méx* waiter, *f* waitress

meseta *nf* plateau, tableland, meseta; **la M.** the plateau of Castile

mesilla *nf* **m. de noche** bedside table

mesón *nm* = old-style tavern

mesonero,-a *nm,f* (**a**) *(en mesón)* innkeeper (**b**) *Chile, Ven (camarero)* waiter, *f* waitress

mestizo,-a *adj & nm,f* half-breed, half-caste, mestizo

mesura *nf Fml* moderation, restraint

♪ Observa que la palabra inglesa **measure** es un falso amigo y no es la traducción de la palabra española **mesura**. En inglés, **measure** significa "medida".

---

meta *nf* (**a**) *(objetivo)* goal, aim, objective (**b**) *(de carrera)* finish, finishing line (**c**) *Ftb (portería)* goal

metafísica *nf* metaphysics *sing*

metáfora *nf* metaphor

metal *nm* (**a**) metal; **metales preciosos** precious metals (**b**) *(timbre de la voz)* timbre (**c**) *Mús* brass

metálico,-a 1 *adj* metallic

2 *nm* cash; **pagar en m.** to pay (in) cash

metalizado,-a *adj* metallic

metalúrgico,-a 1 *adj* metallurgical

2 *nm,f* metallurgist

metate *nm Guat, Méx* grinding stone

metedura *nf Fam* **m. de pata** blunder

meteorito *nm* meteorite

meteorología *nf* meteorology

meteorológico,-a *adj* meteorological; **parte m.** weather report *o* forecast

meter 1 *vt* (**a**) *(poner)* to put (**en** in); *Fig* **m. las narices en algo** to poke one's nose into sth (**b**) *(comprometer)* to involve (**en** in), to get mixed up (**en** in) (**c**) *Fam Fig (dar)* to give; **m. un rollo** to go on and on; **m. prisa a algn** to hurry sb up (**d**) *(hacer)* to make; **m. ruido** to make a noise

2 **meterse** *vpr* (**a**) *(entrar)* to go *o* come in, to get into (**en**) *(estar)* to be; **¿dónde te habías metido?** where have you been (all this time)? (**c**) *(entrometerse)* to meddle (**d**) **m. con algn** *(en broma)* to get at sb

meterete *nmf RP Fam* meddler

metete *nmf Andes, CAm Fam* meddler, busybody

metiche *nmf Méx, Ven Fam* meddler

meticuloso,-a *adj* meticulous

metido,-a *adj Fam* **estar muy m. en algo** to be deeply involved in sth; **m. en años** getting on (in years)

metódico,-a *adj* methodical

método *nm* (**a**) method (**b**) *Educ* course

metodología *nf* methodology

metomentodo *nmf inv Fam* busybody

metralleta *nf* submachine-gun

métrico,-a *adj* metric; **sistema m.** metric system

metro *nm* (**a**) *(medida)* metre (**b**) *(tren) Br* underground, *Br* tube, *US* subway

metrópoli *nf* metropolis

metropolitano,-a 1 *adj* metropolitan

2 *nm Fml Br* underground, *Br* tube, *US* subway

mexicano,-a *adj & nm,f* Mexican

México *n* Mexico

mezcla *nf* (**a**) *(acción)* mixing, blending; *Rad & Cin* mixing (**b**) *(producto)* mixture, blend

mezclar 1 *vt* (**a**) *(dos o más cosas)* to mix, to blend (**b**) *(desordenar)* to mix up (**c**) *(involucrar)* to involve, to mix up

2 **mezclarse** *vpr* (**a**) *(cosas)* to get mixed up; *(gente)* to mingle (**b**) *(relacionarse)* to get involved (**con** with)

mezcolanza *nf Fml* strange mixture, hotch-potch

mezquino,-a *adj* (**a**) *(persona)* mean, stingy (**b**) *(sueldo)* miserable

mezquita *nf* mosque

m/g *(abr* **miligramo**) mg

mi¹ *adj* my; **mi casa/trabajo** my house/ job; **mis cosas/libros** my things/books

mi² *nm Mús* E; **mi menor** E minor

mí *pron pers* me; **a mí me dio tres** he gave me three; **compra otro para mí** buy one for me too; **por mí mismo** just by myself

mía *adj & pron pos f ver* **mío**

miaja *nf* crumb; *Fig* bit

miche *nm Ven (aguardiente)* = cane spirit flavoured with herbs and spices

michelín *nm Fam* spare tyre

mico *nm* (**a**) *Zool* long-tailed monkey (**b**) *Fam (pequeñajo)* little kid

micra *nf (medida)* micron

micro 1 *nm Fam* mike, microphone

  2 *nm o nf Arg, Chile (microbús)* minibus

microbio *nm* microbe

microbús *nm* (**a**) *(autobús)* minibus (**b**) *Méx (taxi)* (collective) taxi

microchip *nm* (*pl* **microchips**) *Informát* microchip

microficha *nf* microfiche

micrófono *nm* microphone

microonda *nf* **un (horno) microondas** a microwave (oven)

microscopio *nm* microscope

miedica *nmf Fam* scaredy-cat

miedo *nm (pavor)* fear; *(temor)* apprehension; **una película de m.** a horror film; **tener m. de algn/algo** to be afraid of sb/ sth; *Fam* **lo pasamos de m.** we had a fantastic time; **un calor de m.** sizzling heat

miedoso,-a *adj* fearful

miel *nf* honey; **luna de m.** honeymoon

miembro *nm* (**a**) *(socio)* member; **estado m.** member state (**b**) *Anat* limb; **m. viril** penis

mientras 1 *conj* (**a**) *(al mismo tiempo que)* while (**b**) *(durante el tiempo que)* when, while; **m. viví en Barcelona** when I lived in Barcelona (**c**) **m. que** *(por el contrario)* whereas (**d**) *Fam (cuanto más)* **m. más/ menos ...** the more/less ...

  2 *adv* **m. (tanto)** meanwhile, in the meantime

miércoles *nm inv* Wednesday; **M. de Ceniza** Ash Wednesday

mierda *nf Vulg* (**a**) shit; **ese libro es una m.** that book is crap; **¡vete a la m.!** piss off! (**b**) *Fig (porquería)* dirt, filth (**c**) *(borrachera)* bender

miga *nf (de pan etc)* crumb; *Fig* **hacer buenas migas con algn** to get on well with sb

migaja *nf* (**a**) *(de pan)* crumb (**b**) *Fig* bit, scrap (**c**) **migajas** *(del pan)* crumbs; *Fig* leftovers

migra *nf Méx Fam Pey* = US police border patrol

migraña *nf Med* migraine

mil *adj & nm* thousand; **m. pesetas** a *o* one thousand pesetas

milagro *nm* miracle

milagroso,-a *adj* miraculous

milanesa *nf (de ternera)* Wiener schnitzel, breaded veal escalope

milano *nm Orn* kite; **m. real** red kite

milenario,-a 1 *adj* millenarian, millennial

  2 *nm* millennium

milenio *nm* millennium

milésimo,-a *adj & nm,f* thousandth

mili *nf Fam* military *o* national service; **hacer la m.** to do one's military service

milicia *nf (ejército)* militia; *(servicio militar)* military service

milico *nm Andes, RP Fam Pey (militar)* soldier; **los milicos tomaron el poder** the military took power

milímetro *nm* millimetre

militar 1 *adj* military

  2 *nm* military man, soldier

  3 *vi Pol (en un partido)* to be a member

milla *nf* mile

millar *nm* thousand

millón *nm* million

millonario,-a *adj & nm,f* millionaire

milpa *nf CAm, Méx* cornfield

mimar *vt* to spoil, to pamper

⚠ Observa que el verbo inglés **to mime** es un falso amigo y no es la traducción del verbo español **mimar**. En inglés, **to mime** significa "representar con gestos".

---

mimbre *nm* wicker

mimetismo *nm* mimicry

mímica *nf* mimicry

mimo *nm* (**a**) *(delicadeza)* care (**b**) *Fig (zalamería)* pampering (**c**) *Teatro (actor)* mime

mina *nf* (**a**) mine; **ingeniero de minas** mining engineer (**b**) *(explosivo)* mine; **campo de minas** minefield (**c**) *(de lápiz)* lead; **lápiz de m.** propelling pencil (**d**) *Fig (ganga)* gold mine

minar *vt* (**a**) *Mil & Min* to mine (**b**) *Fig (desgastar)* to undermine

mineral 1 *adj* mineral

  2 *nm* ore

minería *nf* (**a**) *Min* mining (**b**) *Ind* mining industry

minero,-a 1 *nm,f* miner

2 *adj* mining

miniatura *nf* miniature

minifalda *nf* miniskirt

minifundio *nm* smallholding

mínima *nf* minimum temperature

minimizar *vt* to minimize

mínimo,-a 1 *adj* (**a**) *(muy pequeño)* minute, tiny (**b**) *Mat & Téc* minimum, lowest; **m. común múltiplo** lowest common denominator

2 *nm* minimum; **como m.** at least; **ni lo más m.** not in the least

minipimer® *nm o nf* liquidizer, blender

ministerio *nm* (**a**) *Pol Br* ministry, *US* department (**b**) *Rel* ministry

ministro,-a *nm,f* (**a**) *Pol* minister; **primer m.** Prime Minister (**b**) *Rel* minister

minoría *nf* minority; *Jur* **m. de edad** minority

minoritario,-a *adj* minority

minucioso,-a *adj* (**a**) *(persona)* meticulous (**b**) *(informe, trabajo etc)* minute, detailed

minúsculo,-a *adj* minuscule, minute; **letra minúscula** lower-case o small letter

minusválido,-a 1 *adj* handicapped, disabled

2 *nm,f* handicapped person, disabled person

minuta *nf* (**a**) *(cuenta)* lawyer's bill (**b**) *(menú)* menu (**c**) *RP (comida)* one-plate meal

minutero *nm* minute hand

minuto *nm* minute

mío,-a 1 *adj pos* of mine; **un amigo m.** a friend of mine; **no es asunto m.** it is none of my business

2 *pron pos* mine; **ese libro es m.** that book is mine; **lo m. es el tenis** tennis is my strong point; *Fam* **los míos** my people o folks

miope *nmf* myopic o short-sighted person

miopía *nf* myopia, short-sightedness

mira *nf* (**a**) *Téc* sight (**b**) *Fig (objetivo)* aim, target; **con miras a** with a view to; **amplitud de miras** broad-mindedness

mirada *nf* look; **lanzar** o **echar una m. a** to glance at; **levantar la m.** to raise one's eyes; **m. fija** stare

mirador *nm* (**a**) *(lugar con vista)* viewpoint (**b**) *(balcón)* bay window, windowed balcony

mirar 1 *vt* (**a**) to look at (**b**) *(observar)* to watch (**c**) **m. por algn/algo** *(cuidar)* to look after sb/sth (**d**) *(procurar)* to see;

mira que no le pase nada see that nothing happens to him

2 *vi (dar a)* to look, to face; **la casa mira al sur** the house faces south

mirilla *nf* spyhole, peephole

mirlo *nm* blackbird

misa *nf* mass

misántropo,-a 1 *adj* misanthropic

2 *nm,f* misanthrope, misanthropist

miscelánea *nf Méx (tienda)* = small general store

miserable 1 *adj* (**a**) *(mezquino) (persona)* despicable; *(sueldo etc)* miserable (**b**) *(pobre)* wretched, poor; **una vida m.** a wretched life

2 *nmf* (**a**) *(mezquino)* miser (**b**) *(canalla)* wretch

miseria *nf* (**a**) *(pobreza extrema)* extreme poverty (**b**) *(insignificancia)* pittance; **ganar una m.** to earn next to nothing (**c**) *(tacañería)* miserliness, meanness

misericordia *nf* mercy, compassion

mísero,-a *adj* miserable, wretched

misil *nm* missile; **m. tierra-aire** surface-to-air missile

misión *nf* mission; **m. cumplida** mission accomplished

misionero,-a *nm,f* missionary

mismísimo,-a *adj superl Fam* (**a**) *(preciso)* very; **en el m. centro** right in the centre (**b**) *(en persona)* in person

mismo,-a 1 *adj* (**a**) same (**b**) *(uso enfático)* **yo m.** I myself; **aquí m.** right here

2 *pron* same; **es el m. de ayer** it's the same one as yesterday; **estamos en las mismas** we're back to square one; **lo m.** the same (thing); **dar** o **ser lo m.** to make no difference; **por eso m.** that is why; **por uno** o **sí m.** by oneself

3 *adv* (**a**) *(por ejemplo)* for instance; **que venga algn, Juan m.** ask one of them to come, Juan, for instance (**b**) **así m.** likewise

misógino,-a 1 *adj* misogynous

2 *nm,f* misogynist

miss *nf* beauty queen

míster *nm Ftb* coach, trainer

misterio *nm* mystery

misterioso,-a *adj* mysterious

mitad *nf* (**a**) half; **a m. de camino** halfway there; **a m. de precio** half-price (**b**) *(centro)* middle; **en la m. del primer acto** halfway through the first act; *Fam* **eso me parte por la m.** that really screws things up for me

mítico,-a *adj* mythical

mitigar [42] *vt Fml* to mitigate, to palliate; *(luz)* to reduce

mitin *nm Pol* meeting, rally
mito *nm* myth
mitología *nf* mythology
mitote *nm Méx Fam (alboroto)* racket
mixto,-a *adj* mixed
moai *nm* = statue of giant head found on Easter Island
mobiliario *nm* furniture
moca *nm* mocha
mochila *nf* rucksack, backpack
mochuelo *nm Zool* little owl
moción *nf* motion; **m. de censura** vote of censure
moco *nm* snot; **sonarse los mocos** to blow one's nose
mocoso,-a *nm,f Fam* brat
moda *nf* (**a**) fashion; **a la m., de m.** in fashion; **pasado de m.** old-fashioned (**b**) *(furor pasajero)* craze
modales *nmpl* manners
modalidad *nf* form, category; *Com* **m. de pago** method of payment; *Dep* **m. deportiva** sport
modelar *vt* to model, to shape
modélico,-a *adj* model
modelo **1** *adj inv & nm* model
   2 *nmf* (fashion) model; **desfile de modelos** fashion show
módem *nm Informát* modem; **m. fax** fax modem
moderación *nf* moderation
moderado,-a *adj* moderate; **un m. aumento de temperatura** a mild increase in temperature
moderador,-a *nm,f* chairperson; *(hombre)* chairman; *(mujer)* chairwoman
moderar **1** *vt* (**a**) to moderate; *(velocidad)* to reduce (**b**) *(debate)* to chair
   2 moderarse *vpr* to be moderate
modernizar [40] *vt*, **modernizarse** *vpr* to modernize
moderno,-a *adj* modern
modestia *nf* modesty; **m. aparte** without wishing to be immodest
modesto,-a *adj* modest
módico,-a *adj* moderate; **una módica suma** a modest o small sum
modificar [44] *vt* to modify
modismo *nm* idiom
modisto,-a *nm,f* (**a**) *(diseñador)* fashion designer (**b**) *(sastre) (hombre)* couturier; *(mujer)* couturière
modo *nm* (**a**) *(manera)* way, manner; **m. de empleo** instructions for use; = **manera** (**b**) **modos** manners (**c**) *Ling* mood
modorra *nf (somnolencia)* drowsiness
modoso,-a *adj* (**a**) *(educado)* well-behaved (**b**) *(recatado)* modest

modulación *nf* modulation
modular *vt* to modulate
módulo *nm* module
mofa *nf* mockery; **en tono de m.** in a gibing tone
mofarse *vpr* to laugh (**de** at), to make fun (**de** of)
moflete *nm* chubby cheek
mogollón *nm Fam* (**a**) **m. de** loads of; **me gusta un m.** I like it loads (**b**) *(confusión)* commotion; *(ruido)* racket
moho *nm* (**a**) *Bot* mould (**b**) *(de metales)* rust
mohoso,-a *adj* (**a**) mouldy (**b**) *(oxidado)* rusty
mojado,-a *adj (empapado)* wet; *(húmedo)* damp
mojar **1** *vt* (**a**) to wet; *(humedecer)* to damp; **m. pan en la leche** to dip o dunk bread in one's milk (**b**) *muy Fam* **mojarla** to have it off
   2 mojarse *vpr* to get wet
mojón *nm* (**a**) **m. kilométrico** ≃ milestone (**b**) *muy Fam (mierda)* shit
moka *nm* mocha
molar **1** *vi Fam* **me mola cantidad** I really love it, it's brilliant
   2 *adj & nm Anat* molar
molcajete *nm Méx* mortar
molde *nm* mould; **letras de m.** printed letters; **pan de m.** ≃ sliced bread
moldeador *nm (del pelo)* wave
moldear *vt* to mould
mole **1** *nf* mass, bulk
   2 *nm Méx* (**a**) *(salsa)* = thick, cooked chilli sauce (**b**) *(guiso)* = dish served in "mole" sauce
molécula *nf* molecule
moler [4] *vt* (**a**) *(triturar)* to grind (**b**) **m. a algn a golpes** to beat sb up
molestar **1** *vt* (**a**) *(incomodar)* to disturb, to bother (**b**) *Fml* to bother; **¿le molestaría esperar fuera?** would you mind waiting outside? (**c**) *(causar malestar a)* to hurt
   2 molestarse *vpr* (**a**) *(tomarse la molestia)* to bother (**b**) *(ofenderse)* to take offence, to get upset
molestia *nf* (**a**) bother; **no es ninguna m.** it is no trouble at all; **perdone las molestias** forgive the inconvenience (**b**) *Med (dolor)* trouble, slight pain
molesto,-a *adj* (**a**) *(irritante)* annoying, upsetting (**b**) **estar m. con algn** *(enfadado)* to be annoyed o upset with sb
molinillo *nm* grinder
molino *nm* mill; **m. de agua** watermill; **m. de viento** windmill

mollera *nf Fam* brains; **duro de m.** *(tonto)* dense, thick; *(testarudo)* pigheaded
molón,-ona *adj Fam* flashy, showy
momentáneo,-a *adj* momentary
momento *nm* (**a**) *(instante)* moment; **al m.** at once; **por momentos** by the minute (**b**) *(periodo)* time; **de m.** for the time being; **en cualquier m.** at any time
momia *nf* mummy
mona *nf Fam* **coger una m.** to get drunk; **dormir la m.** to sleep it off
Mónaco *n* Monaco
monada *nf Fam* **¡qué m.!** how cute!
monaguillo *nm Rel* altar boy
monarca *nmf* monarch
monarquía *nf* monarchy
monasterio *nm Rel* monastery
monda *nf* (**a**) *(piel)* peel, skin (**b**) *Fam* **ser la m.** *(divertido)* to be a scream
mondadientes *nm inv* toothpick
mondar 1 *vt* to peel
   2 mondarse *vpr Fam* **m. (de risa)** to laugh one's head off
moneda *nf* (**a**) *(pieza)* coin; **m. suelta** small change; **acuñar m.** to mint money (**b**) *Fin* currency; **m. única** single currency
monedero *nm* purse
monería *nf Fam* = monada
monetario,-a *adj* monetary
mongol 1 *adj* Mongolian
   2 *nmf (persona)* Mongolian
   3 *nm (idioma)* Mongolian
mongólico,-a *Med* **1** *adj* Down's syndrome
   2 *nm,f* **ser m.** to have Down's syndrome
monigote *nm* (**a**) *Pey (persona)* wimp (**b**) *(dibujo)* rough drawing o sketch (of a person)
monitor,-a *nm,f* monitor; *(profesor)* instructor
monja *nf* nun
monje *nm* monk
mono,-a 1 *nm* (**a**) monkey (**b**) *(prenda) (de trabajo)* boiler suit, overalls; *(de vestir)* catsuit; *Ven (de deporte)* track o jogging suit (**c**) *Fam (droga)* cold turkey
   2 *adj Fam (bonito)* pretty, cute
monobloque *nm Arg* tower block
monográfico,-a 1 *adj* monographic
   2 *nm* monograph
monólogo *nm* monologue
monopolio *nm* monopoly
monopolizar [40] *vt* to monopolize
monótono,-a *adj* monotonous
monserga *nf Fam* drag
monstruo *nm* (**a**) monster (**b**) *(genio)* genius

monstruoso,-a *adj* (**a**) *(repugnante)* monstrous (**b**) *(enorme)* massive, huge
monta *nf Fig* **de poca m.** of little importance
montacargas *nm inv Br* service lift, *US* freight elevator
montado,-a 1 *adj (nata)* whipped
   2 *nm* sandwich
montador,-a *nm,f* (**a**) *(operario)* fitter (**b**) *Cin & TV* film editor (**c**) *Teatro* producer
montaje *nm* (**a**) *Téc (instalación)* fitting; *(ensamblaje)* assembling; **cadena de m.** assembly line (**b**) *Cin* editing and mounting (**c**)*Teatro* staging (**d**) *Fot* montage (**e**) *Fam (farsa)* farce
montante *nm* (**a**) *Fin* amount (**b**) *(de puerta)* post
montaña *nf* mountain; **m. rusa** big dipper
montañismo *nm* mountaineering
montañoso,-a *adj* mountainous
montar 1 *vi* (**a**) *(subirse)* to get in; *(en bici, a caballo)* to ride (**b**) *Fin (ascender)* **m. a** to amount to, to come to
   2 *vt* (**a**) *(colocar)* to put on (**b**) *(máquina etc)* to assemble, *(negocio)* to set up, to start (**c**) *Culin* to whip (**d**) *Cin & Fot (película)* to edit, to mount; *(fotografía)* to mount (**e**) *Teatro (obra)* to stage, to mount (**f**) *Zool (cubrir)* to mount
   3 montarse *vpr* (**a**) *(subirse)* to get on; *(en coche)* to get in (**en** to) (**b**) *Fam (armarse)* to break out; *Fam* **montárselo bien** to have things (nicely) worked out o set up
monte *nm* (**a**) *(montaña)* mountain; *(con nombre propio)* mount; **de m.** wild (**b**) **el m.** *(zona)* the hills
montés *adj (animal)* wild
monto *nm* total
montón *nm* heap, pile; **un m. de** a load of; *Fam* **me gusta un m.** I really love it; *Fam* **del m.** run-of-the-mill, nothing special
montura *nf* (**a**) *(cabalgadura)* mount (**b**) *(de gafas)* frame
monumento *nm* monument
monzón *nm* monsoon
moño *nm* (**a**) *(de pelo)* bun (**b**) *Am (lazo)* bow
MOPU *nm* (*abr* **Ministerio de Obras Públicas y Urbanismo**) = Spanish ministry of public works and town planning
moquear *vi* to have a runny nose
moqueta *nf* fitted carpet
mora *nf (zarzamora)* blackberry
morado,-a 1 *adj* purple; *Fam* **pasarlas**

moradas to have a tough time; **ponerse m.** to stuff oneself
  2 *nm* purple
moral 1 *adj* moral
  2 *nf* (**a**) *(ética)* morals (**b**) *(ánimo)* morale, spirits; **levantar la m. a algn** to raise sb's spirits
moraleja *nf* moral
moralista 1 *adj* moralistic
  2 *nmf* moralist
moratoria *nf* moratorium
morbo *nm Fam (interés malsano)* morbid curiosity
morboso,-a *adj (malsano)* morbid
morcilla *nf Br* black pudding, *US* blood sausage; *Fam* **que le den m.** he can drop dead for all I care
mordaz *adj* biting
mordaza *nf* gag
mordedura *nf* bite
morder [4] *vt* to bite; **me ha mordido** it has bitten me; *Fig* **m. el anzuelo** to take the bait
mordida *nf CAm, Méx (soborno)* bribe
mordisco *nm* bite
mordisquear *vt* to nibble (at)
moreno,-a 1 *adj* (**a**) *(pelo)* dark-haired; *(piel)* dark-skinned (**b**) *(bronceado)* tanned; **ponerse m.** to get a suntan; **pan/azúcar m.** brown bread/sugar
  2 *nm,f (persona) (de pelo)* dark-haired person; *(de piel)* dark-skinned person
morera *nf Bot* white mulberry
moretón *nm Fam* bruise
morfina *nf* morphine
morfinómano,-a 1 *nm,f* morphine addict
  2 *adj* addicted to morphine
morgue *nf Am* morgue
moribundo,-a *adj & nm,f* moribund
morir [7] **1** *vi* to die; **m. de frío/hambre/cáncer** to die of cold/hunger/cancer; **m. de amor o pena** to die from a broken heart
  2 morirse *vpr* to die; **m. de hambre** to starve to death; *Fig* to be starving; **m. de aburrimiento** to be bored to death; **m. de ganas (de hacer algo)** to be dying (to do sth); **m. de risa** to die laughing
mormón,-ona *adj & nm,f* Mormon
moro,-a *nm,f* (**a**) *Hist* Moor; *Fam* **no hay moros en la costa** the coast is clear (**b**) *Pey (musulmán)* Muslim; *(árabe)* Arab
morocho,-a 1 *adj* (**a**) *Andes, RP (moreno)* dark-haired (**b**) *Ven (gemelo)* twin
  2 *nm,f* (**a**) *Andes, RP (moreno)* dark-haired person (**b**) *Ven (gemelo)* twin
moronga *nf CAm, Méx Br* black pudding, *US* blood sausage

moroso,-a *nm,f* bad debtor

🖉 Observa que la palabra inglesa **morose** es un falso amigo y no es la traducción de la palabra española **moroso**. En inglés, **morose** significa "hosco, huraño".

morral *nm* (**a**) *(para pienso)* nosebag (**b**) *Mil* haversack; *(de cazador)* game bag
morralla *nf* (**a**) *(cosas sin valor)* rubbish, junk (**b**) *(chusma)* scum
morrear *vt,* **morrearse** *vpr Fam* to snog
morreo *nm Fam* snog
morro *nm* (**a**) *(de animal) (hocico)* snout (**b**) *Fam (de persona)* mouth, (thick) lips; **caerse de m.** to fall flat on one's face; **por los morros** without so much as a by-your-leave; *Fam* **¡vaya m.!** what a cheek! (**c**) *(de coche)* nose
morrón *adj* **pimiento m.** (fleshy) red pepper
morsa *nf* walrus
morse *nm* Morse
mortadela *nf* mortadella
mortaja *nf* shroud
mortal 1 *adj* (**a**) mortal (**b**) *(mortífero)* fatal; **un accidente m.** a fatal accident
  2 *nmf* mortal
mortalidad *nf* mortality; **índice de m.** death rate
mortandad *nf* death toll
mortecino,-a *adj* colourless
mortero *nm Culin & Mil* mortar
mortífero,-a *adj* deadly, lethal
mortificar [44] *vt* to mortify
mortuorio,-a *adj* death; **lecho m.** deathbed
moruno,-a *adj* Moorish; *Culin* **pincho m.** ≃ kebab
mosaico *nm* mosaic
mosca *nf* fly; **peso m.** flyweight; *Fam* **estar m.** *(suspicaz)* to be suspicious; *(borracho)* to be pissed; *Fam* **por si las moscas** just in case; *Fam* **¿qué m. te ha picado?** what's biting you?
moscada *adj* **nuez m.** nutmeg
moscardón *nm* (**a**) *(insecto)* blowfly (**b**) *Fam (pesado)* pest
moscovita *adj & nmf* Muscovite
Moscú *n* Moscow
mosquearse *vpr Fam* (**a**) *(enfadarse)* to get cross (**b**) *(sospechar)* to smell a rat
mosquetero *nm Hist* musketeer
mosquitero *nm (red)* mosquito net
mosquito *nm* mosquito
mostaza *nf Bot & Culin* mustard
mosto *nm (bebida)* grape juice; *(del vino)* must

mostrador *nm* (**a**) *(de tienda)* counter (**b**) *(de bar)* bar

mostrar 1 *vt* to show; **muéstramelo** show it to me

2 mostrarse *vpr* to be; **se mostró muy comprensiva** she was very understanding

mostrenco,-a 1 *nm,f* (**a**) *(ignorante)* blockhead (**b**) *(gordo)* very fat person

2 *adj* (*de dueño*) ownerless; **bienes mostrencos** ownerless property

mota *nf* speck

mote¹ *nm* *(apodo)* nickname; **poner m. a algn** to give sb a nickname

mote² *nm Andes* stewed maize *o US* corn

moteado,-a *adj* dotted

motín *nm* *(amotinamiento)* mutiny; *(disturbio)* riot

motivación *nf* motivation

motivar *vt* (**a**) *(causar)* to cause, to give rise to (**b**) *(inducir)* to motivate

motivo *nm* (**a**) *(causa)* reason; *(usu pl)* grounds; **con este** *o* **tal m.** for this reason; **con m. de** on the occasion of; **sin m.** for no reason at all; **bajo ningún m.** under no circumstances (**b**) *Arte & Mús* motif, leit-motiv

moto *nf Aut* motorbike; **m. náutica** *o* **acuática** jet ski

motocicleta *nf* motorbike

motociclismo *nm* motorcycling

motociclista *nmf* motorcyclist

motocross *nm* motocross

motoneta *nf Am* (motor) scooter

motonetista *nmf Am* scooter rider

motor,-a 1 *nm* *(grande)* engine; *(pequeño)* motor; **m. de reacción** jet engine; **m. de explosión** internal combustion engine; **m. eléctrico** electric motor; *Informát* **m. de busca** search engine

2 *adj Téc* motive

motora *nf* motorboat

motorista *nmf* motorcyclist

motorizar [40] 1 *vt* to motorize

2 motorizarse *vpr Fam* to get oneself a car *o* motorbike

motosierra *nf* power saw

motriz *adj* **fuerza m.** motive power

movedizo,-a *adj* **arenas movedizas** quicksand

mover [4] 1 *vt* (**a**) to move; **m. algo de su sitio** to move sth out of its place (**b**) *(hacer funcionar)* to drive; **el motor mueve el coche** the engine drives the car

2 moverse *vpr* (**a**) to move (**b**) *Fam (gestionar)* to do everything possible (**c**) *(darse prisa)* to hurry up; **¡muévete!** get a move on!

movida *nf Fam* **hay mucha m.** there's a lot going on

movido,-a *adj* (**a**) *Fot* blurred (**b**) *(ocupado)* busy

móvil 1 *adj* mobile; **teléfono m.** mobile phone; *TV & Rad* **unidad m.** outside broadcast unit

2 *nm* (**a**) *(de delito)* motive (**b**) *(teléfono)* mobile

movilización *nf* mobilization

movilizar [40] *vt* to mobilize

movimiento *nm* (**a**) *(gen)* movement; *Fís & Téc* motion; **(poner algo) en m.** (to set sth) in motion; **m. sísmico** earth tremor (**b**) *(actividad)* activity (**c**) *Com & Fin (entradas y salidas)* operations (**d**) *Hist* **el M.** the Falangist Movement

moviola *nf Cin & TV* (**a**) *(cámara)* editing projector (**b**) *(repetición)* action replay

moza *nf* lass, young girl

mozo,-a *nm,f* (**a**) *(niño)* young boy, young lad; *(niña)* young girl (**b**) *(de estación)* porter (**c**) *Mil* conscript (**d**) *Perú, RP (camarero)* waiter, *f* waitress

mucamo,-a *nm,f Andes, RP (en hotel)* chamberperson, *f* chambermaid

muchacha *nf* girl

muchachada *nf Am* group of youngsters

muchacho *nm* boy

muchedumbre *nf (de gente)* crowd

mucho,-a 1 *adj* (**a**) *sing (usu en frases afirmativas)* a lot of, lots of; *(usu en frases negativas)* much; **m. tiempo** a long time; **tengo m. sueño/mucha sed** I am very sleepy/thirsty; **hay m. tonto suelto** there are lots of idiots around; **¿bebes m. café?** – **no, no m.** do you drink a lot of coffee? – no, not much

(**b**) *(demasiado)* **es m. coche para mí** this car is a bit too much for me

(**c**) **muchos,-as** *(usu en frases afirmativas)* a lot of, lots of; *(usu en frases neg)* many; **tiene muchos años** he is very old

2 *pron* (**a**) a lot, a great deal; **¿cuánta leche queda? – mucha** how much milk is there left? – a lot

(**b**) **muchos,-as** a lot, lots, many; **¿cuántos libros tienes? – muchos** how many books have you got? – lots *o* a lot; **muchos creemos que ...** many of us believe that ...

3 *adv* (**a**) a lot, very much; **lo siento m.** I'm very sorry; **como m.** at the most; **con m.** by far; **m. antes/después** long before/after; **¡ni m. menos!** no way!; **por m. (que)** (*+ subjunctive*) however much

(**b**) *(tiempo)* **hace m. que no viene por aquí** he has not been to see us for a long time (**c**) *(a menudo)* often; **vamos m. al cine** we go to the cinema quite often

muda *nf (de ropa)* change of clothes

mudanza *nf* move; **estar de m.** to be moving; **camión de m.** removal van

mudar 1 *vt* (**a**) *(ropa)* to change (**b**) *(plumas, pelo)* to moult; *(piel)* to shed, to slough

2 mudarse *vpr* **m. de casa/ropa** to move house/to change one's clothes

mudo,-a 1 *adj* (**a**) *(que no habla)* dumb; **cine m.** silent films (**b**) *Fig (callado)* speechless

2 *nm,f* mute

mueble 1 *nm* piece of furniture; **muebles** furniture; **con/sin muebles** furnished/unfurnished; **m. bar** cocktail cabinet

2 *adj* movable

mueca *nf* (**a**) *(de burla)* mocking face; **hacer muecas** to pull faces (**b**) *(de dolor, asco)* grimace

muela *nf* (**a**) *Anat* molar; **dolor de muelas** toothache; **m. del juicio** wisdom tooth (**b**) *Téc (de molino)* millstone

muelle¹ *nm* spring

muelle² *nm Náut* dock

muermo *nm Fam (tedio)* boredom; *(rollo)* drag

muerte *nf* death; **m. natural** natural death; **dar m. a algn** to kill sb; **odiar a algn a m.** to loathe sb; *Fam* **de mala m.** lousy, rotten; *Fam* **un susto de m.** the fright of one's life

muerto,-a 1 *adj* dead; **caer m.** to drop dead; **m. de hambre** starving; **m. de frío** frozen to death; **m. de miedo** scared stiff; **m. de risa** laughing one's head off; **horas muertas** spare time; *Aut* **(en) punto m.** (in) neutral

2 *nm,f* (**a**) *(difunto)* dead person; **hacerse el m.** to pretend to be dead; *Fam* **cargar con el m.** to do the dirty work (**b**) *(víctima)* fatality; **hubo dos muertos** two (people) died

muesca *nf* notch

muestra *nf* (**a**) *(espécimen)* sample, specimen (**b**) *(modelo a copiar)* model (**c**) *(prueba, señal)* sign; **dar muestras de** to show signs of; **m. de cariño/respeto** token of affection/respect; **una m. más de ...** yet another example of ...

muestral *adj* error m. margin of error

muestreo *nm* sampling

mugido *nm (de vaca)* moo; *(de toro)* bellow

mugir [57] *vi (vaca)* to moo, to low; *(toro)* to bellow

mugre *nf* filth

mugriento,-a *adj* filthy

mujer *nf* (**a**) woman; **dos mujeres** two women; **m. de la limpieza** cleaner; **m. de su casa** houseproud woman (**b**) *(esposa)* wife; **su futura m.** his bride-to-be

mujeriego 1 *adj* woman-chasing

2 *nm* womanizer, woman chaser

muleta *nf* (**a**) *(prótesis)* crutch (**b**) *Taurom* muleta

muletilla *nf* pet word o phrase

mullido,-a *adj* soft

mulo *nm* mule

multa *nf* fine; *Aut* ticket

multar *vt* to fine

multi- *pref* multi-

multicolor *adj* multicoloured

multicopista *nf* duplicator

multilateral *adj* multilateral

multinacional *adj & nf* multinational

múltiple *adj* (**a**) multiple; **accidente m.** pile-up (**b**) **múltiples** *(muchos)* many

multiplicación *nf Mat* multiplication

multiplicar [44] 1 *vt & vi* to multiply (**por** by)

2 multiplicarse *vpr (reproducirse, aumentar)* to multiply

múltiplo,-a *adj & nm* multiple

multirriesgo *adj inv* **póliza m.** multiple risk policy

multitud *nf* (**a**) *(de personas)* crowd (**b**) *(de cosas)* multitude

mundano,-a *adj* worldly

> 🖊 Observa que la palabra inglesa **mundane** es un falso amigo y no es la traducción de la palabra española **mundano**. En inglés, **mundane** significa "prosaico".

mundial 1 *adj* worldwide; **campeón m.** world champion; **de fama m.** world-famous

2 *nm* world championship

mundialmente *adv* **m. famoso** world-famous, famous worldwide

mundo *nm* world; **todo el m.** everyone; **correr** o **ver m.** to travel widely; **nada del otro m.** nothing special; **el otro m.** the hereafter

munición *nf* ammunition

municipal 1 *adj* municipal

2 *nm (municipal)* policeman

municipio *nm* (**a**) *(territorio)* municipality (**b**) *(ayuntamiento)* town council

muñeca *nf* (**a**) *(espécimen)* wrist (**b**) *(juguete, muchacha)* doll (**c**) *Andes, RP Fam* **tener m.** *(enchufe)* to have friends in high places; *(habilidad)* to have the knack

muñeco *nm (juguete)* (little) boy doll; **m. de trapo** rag doll; **m. de nieve** snowman

muñequera *nf* wristband

muñón *nm Anat* stump
muralla *nf* wall
Murcia *n* Murcia
murciélago *nm Zool* bat
murmullo *nm* murmur
murmuración *nf* gossip
murmurar *vi* (**a**) *(criticar)* to gossip (**b**) *(susurrar)* to whisper; *(refunfuñar)* to grumble (**c**) *Fig (río)* to murmur
muro *nm* wall
murrio,-a *adj Fam* sad, blue
musa *nf* muse
musaraña *nf Fam* **estar mirando a** *o* **pensando en las musarañas** to be daydreaming *o* in the clouds
musculatura *nf* musculature; **desarrollar la m.** to develop one's muscles
músculo *nm* muscle
musculoso,-a *adj* muscular
museo *nm* museum; **m. de arte** *o* **pintura** art gallery
musgo *nm* moss
música *nf* music; **m. clásica** classical music; **m. de fondo** background music
musical 1 *adj* musical
  2 *nm* musical

músico,-a 1 *adj* musical
  2 *nm,f* musician
muslo *nm* thigh
mustio,-a *adj* (**a**) *(plantas)* wilted, withered (**b**) *(persona)* sad, gloomy
musulmán,-ana *adj & nm,f* Muslim, Moslem
mutación *nf Biol* mutation
mutilación *nf* mutilation
mutilado,-a *nm,f* disabled person; **m. de guerra** disabled serviceman
mutilar *vt* to mutilate
mutis *nm Teatro* exit
mutua *nf* mutual benefit society
mutual *nf Arg, Chile, Perú* mutual benefit society
mutualidad *nf* (**a**) *(reciprocidad)* mutuality (**b**) *(asociación)* mutual benefit society
mutuo,-a *adj* mutual
muy *adv* very; **m. bueno/malo** very good/bad; **¡m. bien!** very good!; *Fam* **m. mucho** very much; **M. señor mío** Dear Sir; **m. de los andaluces** typically Andalusian; **m. de mañana/noche** very early/late

N, n ['ene] *nf (la letra)* N, n
N *(abr* **Norte)** N
n/ *(abr* **nuestro,-a)** our
nabo *nm* (**a**) *Bot* turnip (**b**) *Vulg (pene)*
prick
nácar *nm* mother-of-pearl
nacer [60] *vi* (**a**) to be born; **al n.** at birth;
nací en Montoro I was born in Montoro;
Fam Fig **n. de pie** to be born under a lucky
star (**b**) *(pájaro)* to hatch (out) (**c**) *(pelo)*
to begin to grow (**d**) *(río)* to rise
nacido,-a *adj* born; **n. de padre español**
born of a Spanish father; **recién n.** newborn; *Fig* **mal n.** despicable, mean
naciente *adj (nuevo)* new, recent; *(sol)*
rising
nacimiento *nm* (**a**) birth; **sordo de n.**
deaf from birth; **lugar de n.** birthplace,
place of birth (**b**) *Fig (principio)* origin,
beginning; *(de río)* source (**c**) *(belén)*
Nativity scene, crib
nación *nf* nation; **las Naciones Unidas** the
United Nations
nacional 1 *adj* (**a**) national (**b**) *(producto,
mercado)* domestic; **vuelos nacionales**
domestic flights
  2 *nmf* national; *Hist* **los nacionales** the
Francoist forces
nacionalidad *nf* nationality
nacionalismo *nm* nationalism
nacionalista *adj & nmf* nationalist
nacionalizar [40] 1 *vt* (**a**) *Econ (banca,
industria)* to nationalize (**b**) *(naturalizar)*
to naturalize
  2 nacionalizarse *upr* to become naturalized; **n. español** to take up Spanish citizenship
nada 1 *pron* (**a**) *(como respuesta)* nothing;
¿qué quieres? – n. what do you want? –
nothing
  (**b**) *(con verbo)* not ... anything; *(enfático)* nothing; **no sé n.** I don't know
anything; **yo no digo n.** I'm saying nothing
  (**c**) *(con otro negativo)* anything; **no
hace nunca n.** he never does anything;
nadie sabía n. nobody knew anything
  (**d**) *(en ciertas construcciones)* anything;
más que n. more than anything; **sin decir**

n. without saying anything; **casi n.** hardly
anything
  (**e**) **gracias – de n.** thanks – don't mention it; *Fam* **para n.** not at all; **casi n.**
almost nothing; **como si n.** just like that;
un rasguño de n. an insignificant little
scratch; **n. de eso** nothing of the kind; **n.
de n.** nothing at all; **n. más verla** as soon
as he saw her
  2 *adv* not at all; **no me gusta n.** I don't
like it at all; **no lo encuentro n. interesante** I don't find it remotely interesting
  3 *nf* nothingness; **salir de la n.** to come
out of nowhere
nadador,-a *nm,f* swimmer
nadar *vi* (**a**) *Dep* to swim; **n. a braza** to do
the breaststroke (**b**) *(flotar)* to float
nadie 1 *pron* (**a**) *(como respuesta)* no one,
nobody; **¿quién vino? – n.** who came? –
no one (**b**) *(con verbo)* not ... anyone, not
... anybody; *(enfático)* no one, nobody;
no conozco a n. I don't know anyone *o*
anybody; **no vi a n.** I saw no one (**c**) *(con
otro negativo)* anyone, anybody; **nunca
habla con n.** he never speaks to anybody
(**d**) *(en ciertas construcciones)* anybody,
anyone; **más que n.** more than anyone;
sin decírselo a n. without telling anyone;
casi n. hardly anyone
  2 *nm* nobody; **ser un don n.** to be a
nobody
nado: • **a nado** *loc adv* swimming; **cruzar**
o **pasar a n.** to swim across
NAFTA *nm* (*abr* **North American Free
Trade Agreement)** NAFTA
nafta *nf RP (gasolina) Br* petrol, *US*
gas(oline)
nahua, náhuatl 1 *adj* Nahuatl
  2 *nmf (individuo)* Nahuatl (Indian)
nailon *nm* nylon
naipe *nm* playing card
nalga *nf* buttock; **nalgas** bottom, buttocks
nana *nf* (**a**) *(canción)* lullaby (**b**) *Col, Méx
(niñera)* nanny
napalm *nm* napalm
napias *nfpl Fam* snout
Nápoles *n* Naples
napolitano,-a *adj & nm,f* Neapolitan

naranja 1 *nf* orange; *Fig* **mi media n.** my better half
  2 *adj & nm (color)* orange
naranjada *nf* orangeade
naranjo *nm* orange tree
narciso *nm* (**a**) *(blanco)* narcissus; *(amarillo)* daffodil (**b**) *Fig (hombre)* narcissist
narcótico *nm* narcotic; *(droga)* drug
narcotizar [40] *vt (drogar)* to drug
narcotraficante *nmf* drug trafficker
narcotráfico *nm* drug trafficking
nariz *nf* (**a**) nose; *Fam* **me da en la n. que ...** I've got this feeling that ... (**b**) *Fam* **narices** nose; *Fam* **en mis (propias) narices** right under my very nose; *Fam* **estar hasta las narices de** to be totally fed up with; *Fam* **meter las narices en algo** to poke one's nose into sth; *Fam* **por narices** because I say so; *Fam* **tocarle a algn las narices** to get on sb's wick
narración *nf* narration
narrar *vt* to narrate, to tell
narrativo,-a *adj & nf* narrative
nata *nf* (**a**) cream; **n. batida** *o* **montada** whipped cream (**b**) *(de leche hervida)* skin (**c**) *Fig* cream, best
natación *nf Dep* swimming
natal *adj* **mi país n.** my native country; **su pueblo n.** his home town
natalicio *nm Fml* birthday
natalidad *nf* birth rate; **control de n.** birth control
natillas *nfpl Culin* custard
natividad *nf* Nativity
nativo,-a *adj & nm,f* native
nato,-a *adj* born
natura *nf Literario* nature; **contra n.** against nature
natural 1 *adj* natural; *(fruta, flor)* fresh; **de tamaño n.** life-size; **en estado n.** in its natural state; *Jur* **hijo n.** illegitimate child
  2 *nmf* native
naturaleza *nf* (**a**) nature; **en plena n.** in the wild, in unspoilt countryside; *Arte* **n. muerta** still life (**b**) *(complexión)* physical constitution
naturalidad *nf (sencillez)* naturalness; **con n.** naturally, straightforwardly
naturalismo *nm* naturalism
naturalista 1 *adj* naturalistic
  2 *nmf* naturalist
naturalización *nf* naturalization
naturalizar [40] 1 *vt* to naturalize
  2 naturalizarse *vpr* to become naturalized
naturalmente *adv* naturally; **¡n.!** of course!
naturismo *nm* naturism

naturista *nmf* naturist
naufragar [42] *vi (barco)* to sink, to be wrecked; *(persona)* to be shipwrecked
naufragio *nm Náut* shipwreck
náufrago,-a *nm,f* shipwrecked person, castaway
náusea *nf (usu pl)* nausea, sickness; **me da n.** it makes me sick; **sentir náuseas** to feel sick
nauseabundo,-a *adj* nauseating, sickening
náutico,-a *adj* nautical
navaja *nf* (**a**) *(cuchillo)* penknife, pocketknife; **n. de afeitar** razor (**b**) *(molusco)* razor-shell
navajada *nf*, **navajazo** *nm* stab, gash
navajero *nm Fam* thug
naval *adj* naval
Navarra *n* Navarre
navarro,-a 1 *adj* Navarrese, of/from Navarre
  2 *nm,f* person from Navarre
nave *nf* (**a**) ship; **n. (espacial)** spaceship, spacecraft (**b**) *Ind* plant, building (**c**) *(de iglesia)* nave; **n. lateral** aisle
navegable *adj* navigable
navegación *nf* navigation; **n. costera** coastal shipping
navegador *nm Informát* browser
navegar [42] *vi* (**a**) to navigate, to sail (**b**) *Av* to navigate, to fly (**c**) **n. por Internet** to surf the Net
Navidad(es) *nf(pl)* Christmas; **árbol de Navidad** Christmas tree; **Feliz Navidad, Felices Navidades** Merry Christmas
navideño,-a *adj* Christmas
navío *nm* ship
nazi *adj & nmf* Nazi
nazismo *nm* Nazism
n/c., n/cta. *(abr* **nuestra cuenta**) our account, our acct
neblina *nf* mist, thin fog
nebulosa *nf Astron* nebula
nebuloso,-a *adj* (**a**) *Met* cloudy, hazy (**b**) *Fig* nebulous, vague
necedad *nf* (**a**) *(estupidez)* stupidity, foolishness (**b**) *(tontería)* stupid thing to say *o* to do
necesario,-a *adj* necessary; **es n. hacerlo** it has to be done; **es n. que vayas** you must go; **no es n. que vayas** there is no need for you to go; **si fuera n.** if need be
neceser *nm (de aseo)* toilet bag; *(de maquillaje)* make-up bag
necesidad *nf* (**a**) necessity, need; **artículos de primera n.** essentials; **por n.** of necessity; **tener n. de** to need (**b**) *(pobreza)* poverty, hardship (**c**) **hacer**

sus **necesidades** to relieve oneself
necesitado,-a 1 *adj (pobre)* needy, poor;
n. de in need of
  2 *nmpl* **los necesitados** the needy
necesitar *vt* to need; **se necesita chico** *(en
anuncios)* boy wanted
necio,-a 1 *adj* (**a**) *(tonto)* silly, stupid (**b**)
Méx (pesado) boring
  2 *nm,f* (**a**) *(tonto)* fool, idiot (**b**) *Méx
(pesado)* bore
necrología *nf* obituary
néctar *nm* nectar
nectarina *nf* nectarine
neerlandés,-esa 1 *adj* Dutch, of/from
the Netherlands
  2 *nm,f (persona) (hombre)* Dutchman;
(mujer) Dutchwoman; **los neerlandeses**
the Dutch
  3 *nm (idioma)* Dutch
nefasto,-a *adj* (**a**) *(perjudicial)* harmful
(**b**) *(funesto)* unlucky, ill-fated (**c**) *(inútil)*
hopeless
negación *nf* (**a**) negation (**b**) *(negativa)*
denial; *(rechazo)* refusal (**c**) *Ling* negative
negado,-a 1 *adj* **ser n. para algo** to be
hopeless *o* useless at sth
  2 *nm,f* no-hoper
negar [1] 1 *vt* (**a**) to deny; **negó haberlo
robado** he denied stealing it (**b**) *(rechazar)* to refuse, to deny; **le negaron la beca**
they refused him the grant
  2 negarse *vpr* to refuse (**a** to)
negativa *nf* denial
negativo,-a *adj & nm* negative
negligencia *nf* negligence
negociación *nf* negotiation
negociado *nm Andes, RP (chanchullo)*
shady deal
negociador,-a *adj* negotiating; **comité n.**
negotiating committee
negociante *nmf* dealer; *(hombre)* businessman; *(mujer)* businesswoman
negociar [43] 1 *vt Fin & Pol* to negotiate
  2 *vi (comerciar)* to do business, to
deal
negocio *nm Com & Fin* business; *(transacción)* deal, transaction; *(asunto)* affair;
hombre de negocios businessman; **mujer de negocios** businesswoman
negra *nf* (**a**) *Fig (mala suerte)* bad luck;
tener la n. to be very unlucky (**b**) *Mús Br*
crotchet, *US* quarter note
negrilla, negrita *adj & nf Impr* bold
(face)
negro,-a 1 *adj* (**a**) black; **estar n.** *(bronceado)* to be suntanned (**b**) *Fig (suerte)*
awful; *(desesperado)* desperate; *(furioso)*

furious; **verlo todo n.** to be very pessimistic; **vérselas negras para hacer algo** to
have a tough time doing sth
  2 *nm,f (hombre)* black; *(mujer)* black
(woman)
  3 *nm (color)* black
nene,-a *nm,f (niño)* baby boy; *(niña)* baby
girl
nenúfar *nm Bot* waterlily
**neocelandés,-esa, neozelandés,-esa
1** *adj* of/from New Zealand
  2 *nm,f* New Zealander
neoclásico,-a *adj Arte & Lit* neoclassic,
neoclassical
neologismo *nm* neologism
neón *nm* neon
neoyorquino,-a 1 *adj* of/from NewYork
  2 *nm,f* NewYorker
neozelandés,-esa *adj & nm,f* = **neocelandés,-esa**
nepotismo *nm* nepotism
Neptuno *n* Neptune
nervio *nm* (**a**) *Anat & Bot* nerve; *(de la
carne)* sinew (**b**) *Fig (fuerza, vigor)* nerve,
courage (**c**) **nervios** nerves; **ataque de
nervios** fit of hysterics; **ser un manojo de
nervios** to be a bundle of nerves; **tener
los nervios de acero** to have nerves of
steel
nerviosismo *nm* nerves
nervioso,-a *adj* (**a**) nervous; **poner n. a
algn** to get on sb's nerves (**b**) *(inquieto)*
fidgety
neto,-a *adj* (**a**) *(peso, cantidad)* net (**b**)
(nítido) neat, clear
neumático,-a 1 *adj* pneumatic
  2 *nm* tyre; **n. de recambio** spare tyre
neumonía *nf* pneumonia
neurálgico,-a *adj* neuralgic; *Fig* **punto n.**
nerve centre
neurólogo,-a *nm,f* neurologist
neurosis *nf* neurosis
neurótico,-a *adj & nm,f* neurotic
neutral *adj* neutral
neutralidad *nf* neutrality
neutralizar [40] *vt* to neutralize
neutro,-a *adj* (**a**) *(imparcial)* neutral (**b**)
Ling neuter
neutrón *nm Fís* neutron; **bomba de neutrones** neutron bomb
nevada *nf* snowfall
nevar [1] *v impers* to snow
nevera *nf* (**a**) *(frigorífico)* refrigerator,
fridge (**b**) *(portátil)* cool box
nexo *nm* connection, link
ni *conj* (**a**) **no ... ni, ni ... ni** neither ... nor,
not ... or; **no tengo tiempo ni dinero** I
have got neither time nor money; **ni ha**

venido ni ha llamado he hasn't come or phoned; **no vengas ni hoy ni mañana** don't come today or tomorrow (**b**) *(ni siquiera)* not even; **ni por dinero** not even for money; **ni se te ocurra** don't even think about it; **¡ni hablar!** no way!

Nicaragua *n* Nicaragua

nicaragüense *adj & nmf* Nicaraguan

nicho *nm* niche

nicotina *nf* nicotine

nido *nm* nest

niebla *nf* fog; **hay mucha n.** it is very foggy

nieto,-a *nm,f (niño)* grandson; *(niña)* granddaughter; **mis nietos** my grandchildren

nieve *nf* (**a**) *Met* snow; *Culin* **a punto de n.** (beaten) stiff (**b**) *Fam (cocaína)* snow (**c**) *Carib, Méx (granizado)* = drink of flavoured crushed ice

nigeriano,-a *adj & nm,f* Nigerian

Nilo *n* **el N.** the Nile

nilón *nm Tex* nylon

nimio,-a *adj (insignificante)* insignificant, petty

ninfómana *nf* nymphomaniac

ninguno,-a 1 *adj* (**a**) *(con verbo)* not ... any; **no leí ninguna revista** I didn't read any magazines; **no tiene ninguna gracia** it is not funny at all (**b**) **en ninguna parte** nowhere; **de ningún modo** no way

> **Ningún** is used instead of **ninguno** before masculine singular nouns (e.g. **ningún hombre** no man).

2 *pron* (**a**) *(persona)* nobody, no one; **n. lo vio** no one saw it; **n. de los dos** neither of the two; **n. de ellos** none of them (**b**) *(cosa)* not ... any of them; *(enfático)* none of them; **me gusta n.** I don't like any of them; **no vi n.** I saw none of them

niña *nf* (**a**) girl; *ver* **niño,-a** (**b**) *Anat* pupil; *Fig* **es la n. de sus ojos** she's the apple of his eye

niñera *nf* nursemaid, nanny

niñez *nf* infancy; *(a partir de los cuatro años)* childhood

niño,-a *nm,f* (**a**) child; *(muchacho)* (small) boy; *(muchacha)* (little) girl; **de n.** as a child; **n. prodigio** child prodigy; *Pey* **n. bien** *o* **de papá** rich boy, rich kid; *Pey* **n. bonito** *o* **mimado** mummy's/daddy's boy (**b**) *(bebé)* baby (**c**) **niños** children; *Fig* **juego de niños** child's play (**d**) *Met* **el N.** el Niño

nipón,-ona *adj & nm,f* Japanese; **los nipones** the Japanese

níquel *nm* nickel

niqui *nm* T-shirt

níspero *nm (fruto)* medlar; *(árbol)* medlar tree

nítido,-a *adj (claro)* clear; *(imagen)* sharp

nitrógeno *nm* nitrogen

nitroglicerina *nf* nitroglycerine

nivel *nm* (**a**) *(altura)* level; **a n. del mar** at sea level (**b**) *(categoría)* standard; **n. de vida** standard of living (**c**) *(instrumento)* level; **n. de aire** spirit level (**d**) *Ferroc* **paso a n.** *Br* level crossing, *US* grade crossing

nivelar *vt* (**a**) to level out *o* off (**b**) *(equilibrar)* to balance out

n *(abr número)* no

no 1 *adv* (**a**) *(como respuesta)* no; **¿te gusta? – no** do you like it? – no (**b**) *(en otros contextos)* not; **no vi a nadie** I didn't see anyone; **aún no** not yet; **ya no** no longer, not any more; **no sin antes ...** not without first ...; **¿por qué no?** why not? (**c**) **no fumar/aparcar** *(en letrero)* no smoking/parking (**d**) **no sea que** (+ *subjunctive*) in case (**e**) **es rubia, ¿no?** she's blonde, isn't she?; **llegaron anoche, ¿no?** they arrived yesterday, didn't they? (**f**) *(como prefijo negativo)* non; **la no violencia** non-violence

2 *nm* no; **un no rotundo** a definite no

noble 1 *adj* noble

2 *nmf (hombre)* nobleman; *(mujer)* noblewoman; **los nobles** the nobility

nobleza *nf* nobility

noche *nf* evening; *(después de las diez)* night, night-time; **de n., por la n.** at night; **esta n.** tonight; **mañana por la n.** tomorrow night *o* evening; **buenas noches** *(saludo)* good evening; *(despedida)* good night; **son las nueve de la n.** it's nine p.m.

nochebuena *nf* Christmas Eve

nochero *nm CSur (vigilante)* nightwatchman

nochevieja *nf* New Year's Eve

noción *nf* (**a**) notion, idea (**b**) **nociones** smattering, basic knowledge; **nociones de español** a smattering of Spanish

nocivo,-a *adj* noxious, harmful

noctámbulo,-a *nm,f* sleepwalker; *Fam* nightbird

nocturno,-a *adj* (**a**) night; **vida nocturna** night life; **clases nocturnas** evening classes (**b**) *Bot & Zool* nocturnal

nodriza *nf* (**a**) *(ama)* wet nurse (**b**) **buque n.** supply ship

nogal *nm Bot* walnut (tree)

nómada 1 *adj* nomadic

2 *nmf* nomad

nombrado,-a *adj (célebre)* famous, well-known

nombramiento *nm* appointment
nombrar *vt* (**a**) *(designar)* to name, to appoint; **n. a algn director** to appoint sb director (**b**) *(mencionar)* to name, to mention
nombre *nm* (**a**) name; **n. de pila** Christian name; **n. y apellidos** full name; *Informát* **n. de dominio** domain name; **a n. de** addressed to; **en n. de** on behalf of (**b**) *Ling* noun; **n. propio** proper noun
nómina *nf* (**a**) *(de sueldo)* pay slip (**b**) *(plantilla)* payroll
nominar *vt* to nominate
nominativo,-a *adj* **cheque n.** a cheque made out to
non *nm* (**a**) *Mat* odd number; **pares y nones** odds and evens (**b**) *Fam* **nones** *(negación)* no; **decir (que) nones** to refuse
nono,-a *adj* = **noveno,-a**
norcoreano,-a *adj & nm,f* North Korean
nordeste *nm* = **noreste**
nórdico,-a 1 *adj* (**a**) *(del norte)* northern (**b**) *(escandinavo)* Nordic
  2 *nm,f* Nordic person
noreste *nm* northeast
noria *nf* (**a**) *(de feria)* big wheel (**b**) *(para agua)* water wheel
norirlandés,-esa 1 *adj* Northern Irish
  2 *nm,f (persona) (hombre)* Northern Irishman; *(mujer)* Northern Irishwoman; **los norirlandeses** the Northern Irish
norma *nf* norm; **n. de seguridad** safety standard
normal *adj* normal, usual; **lo n.** the normal thing, what usually happens
normalidad *nf* normality; **volver a la n.** to return to normal
normalizar [40] 1 *vt* to normalize, to restore to normal
  2 **normalizarse** *vpr* to return to normal
normativa *nf* rules
noroeste *nm* northwest
norte *nm* (**a**) north; **al n. de** to the north of (**b**) *Fig* aim, goal
norteafricano,-a *adj & nm,f* North African
Norteamérica *n* North America
norteamericano,-a *adj & nm,f* (North) American
norteño,-a 1 *adj* northern
  2 *nm,f* Northerner
Noruega *n* Norway
noruego,-a 1 *adj* Norwegian
  2 *nm,f* Norwegian
  3 *nm (idioma)* Norwegian
nos 1 *pron pers (directo)* us; *(indirecto)* (to) us; **n. ha visto** he has seen us; **n. trajo un** regalo he brought us a present; **n. lo dio** he gave it to us
  2 *pron (reflexivo)* ourselves; *(recíproco)* each other; **n. hemos divertido mucho** we enjoyed ourselves a lot; **n. queremos mucho** we love each other very much
nosotros,-as *pron pers pl* (**a**) *(sujeto)* we; **n. lo vimos** we saw it; **somos n.** it is us (**b**) *(complemento)* us; **con n.** with us

> Usually omitted in Spanish except for emphasis or contrast.

nostalgia *nf* nostalgia; *(morriña)* homesickness
nostálgico,-a *adj* nostalgic; *(con morriña)* homesick
nota *nf* (**a**) *(anotación)* note (**b**) *Educ* mark, grade; **sacar buenas notas** to get good marks (**c**) *Fig (detalle)* element, quality; **la n. dominante** the prevailing quality (**d**) *Mús* note; *Fam* **dar la n.** to make oneself noticed
notable 1 *adj (apreciable)* noticeable; *(destacado)* outstanding, remarkable
  2 *nm (nota)* very good
notar 1 *vt (percibir)* to notice, to note
  2 **notarse** *vpr* to be noticeable o evident, to show; **no se nota** it doesn't show; **se nota que ...** one can see that ...
notaría *nf (despacho)* notary's office
notarial *adj* notarial; **acta n.** affidavit
notario,-a *nm,f* notary (public), solicitor
noticia *nf* news *sing*; **una n.** a piece of news; **una buena n.** good news; **no tengo n. de esto** I don't know anything about it

> ℓ Observa que la palabra inglesa **notice** es un falso amigo y no es la traducción de la palabra española **noticia**. En inglés, **notice** significa "aviso, anuncio".

noticiario, *Am* **noticiero** *nm* (**a**) *Cin* newsreel (**b**) *Rad & TV* television news *sing*
notificación *nf* notification; **sin n. previa** without (previous) notice; *Jur* **n. judicial** summons *sing*
notificar [44] *vt* to notify
notorio,-a *adj* (**a**) *(evidente)* obvious, evident (**b**) *(famoso)* famous, well-known

> ℓ Observa que la palabra inglesa **notorious** es un falso amigo y no es la traducción de la palabra española **notorio**. En inglés, **notorious** significa "tristemente célebre".

novatada *nf* (**a**) *(broma)* rough joke, rag (**b**) **pagar la n.** to learn the hard way
novato,-a 1 *adj (persona)* inexperienced; *Fam* green

2 *nm,f* (**a**) *(principiante)* novice, beginner (**b**) *Univ* fresher

novecientos,-as *adj & nm* nine hundred

novedad *nf* (**a**) *(cosa nueva)* novelty; **últimas novedades** latest arrivals (**b**) *(cambio)* change, development (**c**) *(cualidad)* newness

novedoso,-a *adj* (**a**) *(nuevo)* new, full of novelties (**b**) *(innovador)* innovative

novel 1 *adj* new, inexperienced
2 *nmf* beginner, novice

novela *nf Lit* novel; **n. corta** short story; **n. policíaca** detective story

novelero,-a *adj* (**a**) fond of new things (**b**) *(fantasioso)* highly imaginative

novelesco,-a *adj* (**a**) *(de novela)* novelistic, fictional (**b**) *(extraordinario)* bizarre, fantastic

novelista *nmf* novelist

noveno,-a *adj & nm* ninth; **novena parte** ninth

noventa *adj & nm inv* ninety

novia *nf* (**a**) *(amiga)* girlfriend (**b**) *(prometida)* fiancée (**c**) *(en boda)* bride

noviar *vi CSur, Méx* **n. con algn** to go out with sb; **novian hace tiempo** they've been going out together for a while

noviazgo *nm* engagement

noviembre *nm* November

novillada *nf Taurom* = bullfight with young bulls

novillero,-a *nm,f Taurom* apprentice matador

novillo,-a *nm,f* (**a**) *(toro)* young bull; *(vaca)* young cow (**b**) *Fam Educ* **hacer novillos** to play *Br* truant *o US* hooky

novio *nm* (**a**) *(amigo)* boyfriend (**b**) *(prometido)* fiancé (**c**) *(en boda)* bridegroom; **los novios** the bride and groom

nubarrón *nm Fam* storm cloud

nube *nf* cloud; *Fig* **vivir en las nubes** to have one's head in the clouds; *Fig* **poner a algn por las nubes** to praise sb to the skies

nublado,-a *adj* cloudy, overcast

nublarse *vpr* to become cloudy, to cloud over; *Fig* **se le nubló la vista** his eyes clouded over

nuboso,-a *adj* cloudy

nuca *nf* nape, back of the neck

nuclear *adj* nuclear; **central n.** nuclear power station

núcleo *nm* nucleus; *(parte central)* core; **n. urbano** city centre

nudillo *nm (usu pl)* knuckle

nudista *adj & nmf* nudist

nudo *nm* (**a**) knot; **hacer un n.** to tie a knot; *Fig* **se me hizo un n. en la garganta** I

got a lump in my throat (**b**) *(punto principal)* crux, core (**c**) *(de comunicaciones)* centre

nuera *nf* daughter-in-law

nuestro,-a 1 *adj pos* (**a**) our; **nuestra familia** our family (**b**) *(después del sustantivo)* of ours; **un amigo n.** a friend of ours
2 *pron pos* ours; **este libro es n.** this book is ours

nuevamente *adv* again

Nueva Zelanda *n* New Zealand

nueve *adj & nm inv* nine

nuevo,-a 1 *adj* (**a**) new; *Fam* **¿qué hay de n.?** what's new?; **de n.** again; **Nueva York** New York; **Nueva Zelanda** New Zealand (**b**) *(adicional)* further
2 *nm,f* newcomer; *(principiante)* beginner

nuez *nf* (**a**) walnut; **n. moscada** nutmeg (**b**) *Anat* **n. (de Adán)** Adam's apple

nulidad *nf* (**a**) *(ineptitud)* incompetence (**b**) *Jur* nullity

nulo,-a *adj* (**a**) *(inepto)* useless, totally incapable (**b**) *(sin valor)* null and void, invalid; **voto n.** invalid vote (**c**) **crecimiento n.** zero growth

núm. *(abr* **número**) no

numeral *adj & nm* numeral

numerar *vt* to number

numerario,-a 1 *adj* **profesor no n.** teacher on a temporary contract
2 *nm* (**a**) *(miembro)* full member (**b**) *(dinero)* cash

numérico,-a *adj* numerical

número *nm* (**a**) number; **n. de matrícula** *Br* registration number, *US* license number; **n. de serie** serial number; *Fig* **sin n.** countless (**b**) *Prensa* number, issue; **n. atrasado** back number (**c**) *(de zapatos)* size (**d**) *(en espectáculo)* sketch, act; *Fam* **montar un n.** to make a scene

numeroso,-a *adj* numerous

nunca *adv* (**a**) *(como respuesta)* never; **¿cuándo volverás? – n.** when will you come back? – never (**b**) *(con verbo)* never; *(enfático)* not … ever; **no he estado n. en España** I've never been to Spain; **yo no haría n. eso** I wouldn't ever do that (**c**) *(en ciertas construcciones)* ever; **casi n.** hardly ever; **más que n.** more than ever (**d**) **n. jamás** never ever; *(futuro)* never again

nupcial *adj* wedding, nuptial; **marcha n.** wedding march

nupcias *nfpl Fml* wedding, nuptials; **casarse en segundas n.** to marry again

nutrición *nf* nutrition

nutricionista *nmf* nutritionist

nutrir 1 *vt* to nourish, to feed
  2 nutrirse *vpr* to feed (**de** *o* **con** on)

nutritivo,-a *adj* nutritious, nourishing;
  valor n. nutritional value

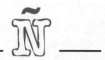

ñandutí *nm Par* fine lace
ñapa *nf Ven Fam* bonus, extra

ñato,-a *adj Andes, RP* snub-nosed

O, o [o] *nf (la letra)* O, o

o *conj* or; **jueves o viernes** Thursday or Friday; **o ... o** either ... or; **o sea** that is (to say), in other words

> **u** is used instead of **o** in front of words beginning with "o" or "ho" (e.g. **mujer u hombre** woman or man). Note that **ó** (with acute accent) is used between figures.

O. (*abr* **Oeste**) W

oasis *nm inv* oasis

obcecado,-a *adj Fig* stubborn

obcecar [44] **1** *vt Fig* to blind; **la ira lo obceca** he is blinded by anger

  2 obcecarse *vpr Fig* to refuse to budge; *(obsesionarse)* to become obsessed

obedecer [33] **1** *vt* to obey

  2 *vi* **o. a** *(provenir)* to be due to; **¿a qué obedece esa actitud?** what's the reason behind this attitude?

obediencia *nf* obedience

obediente *adj* obedient

obertura *nf* overture

obesidad *nf* obesity

obeso,-a *adj* obese

óbice *nm* obstacle; **eso no es ó. para que yo no lo haga** it won't prevent me from doing it

obispo *nm* bishop

objeción *nf* objection; **poner una o.** to raise an objection, to object

objetar 1 *vt* **no tengo nada que o.** I've got no objections

  2 *vi Mil* to be a conscientious objector

objetividad *nf* objectivity

objetivo,-a 1 *nm* (**a**) *(fin, meta)* objective, aim (**b**) *Mil* target (**c**) *Cin & Fot* lens; **o. zoom** zoom lens

  2 *adj* objective

objeto *nm* (**a**) object; **objetos perdidos** lost property; **mujer o.** sex object (**b**) *(fin)* aim, purpose; **con o. de ...** in order to ...; **tiene por o. ...** it is designed to ... (**c**) *Ling* object

objetor,-a 1 *nm,f* objector; **o. de conciencia** conscientious objector

  2 *adj* objecting, dissenting

obligación *nf* (**a**) *(deber)* obligation; **por o.** out of a sense of duty; **tengo o. de ...** I

have to ... (**b**) *Fin* bond, debenture

obligado,-a *adj* obliged; **verse o estar o. a** to be obliged to

obligar [42] *vt* to compel, to force

obligatorio,-a *adj* compulsory, obligatory

obra *nf* (**a**) *(trabajo)* (piece of) work; **por o. de** thanks to (**b**) *Arte* work; **o. maestra** masterpiece (**c**) *(acto)* deed (**d**) *Constr* building site (**e**) **obras** *(arreglos)* repairs; **carretera en obras** *(en letrero)* roadworks; **cerrado por obras** *(en letrero)* closed for repairs

obrar 1 *vi* (**a**) *(proceder)* to act, to behave; **o. bien/mal** to do the right/wrong thing (**b**) *Fml* **obra en nuestro poder ...** we are in receipt of ...

  2 *vt (milagro)* to work

obrero,-a 1 *nm,f* worker, labourer

  2 *adj* working; **clase obrera** working class; **movimiento o.** labour movement

obscenidad *nf* obscenity

obsceno,-a *adj* obscene

obscurecer [33] **1** *v impers* to get dark

  2 *vt* to darken

  3 obscurecerse *vpr (nublarse)* to become cloudy

obscuridad *nf* darkness; *Fig* obscurity

obscuro,-a *adj* (**a**) dark (**b**) *Fig (origen, idea)* obscure; *(futuro)* uncertain, gloomy; *(asunto)* shady; *(nublado)* overcast

obsequiar [43] *vt* to give away

obsequio *nm* gift, present

observación *nf* observation

observador,-a 1 *nm,f* observer

  2 *adj* observant

observancia *nf* observance

observar *vt* (**a**) *(mirar)* to observe, to watch (**b**) *(notar)* to notice (**c**) *(cumplir)* to observe

observatorio *nm* observatory

obsesión *nf* obsession

obsesionar 1 *vt* to obsess; **estoy obsesionado con eso** I can't get it out of my mind

  2 obsesionarse *vpr* to get obsessed

obsesivo,-a *adj* obsessive

obseso,-a *nm,f* obsessed person; **un o. sexual** a sex maniac

obsoleto,-a *adj* obsolete
obstaculizar [40] *vt* to obstruct, to get in the way of
obstáculo *nm* obstacle
obstante: • **no obstante 1** *loc adv* nevertheless
  2 *prep* notwithstanding
obstetricia *nf* obstetrics *sing*
obstinación *nf* obstinacy
obstinado,-a *adj* obstinate
obstinarse *vpr* to persist (**en** in)
obstrucción *nf* obstruction; *Med* blockage
obstruir [37] 1 *vt* (**a**) *(salida, paso)* to block, to obstruct (**b**) *(progreso)* to impede, to block
  2 obstruirse *vpr* to get blocked up
obtención *nf* obtaining
obtener [24] 1 *vt* *(alcanzar)* to obtain, to get
  2 obtenerse *vpr* **o. de** *(provenir)* to come from
obturador *nm Fot* shutter
obtuso,-a *adj* obtuse
obús *nm* shell
obviar [43] *vt* *(problema)* to get round
obvio,-a *adj* obvious
oca *nf* goose
ocasión *nf* (**a**) *(momento)* occasion; **con o. de ...** on the occasion of ...; **en cierta o.** once (**b**) *(oportunidad)* opportunity, chance; **aprovechar una o.** to make the most of an opportunity (**c**) *Com* bargain; **de o.** cheap; **precios de o.** bargain prices
ocasional *adj* (**a**) *(eventual)* occasional; **trabajo o.** casual work; **de forma o.** occasionally (**b**) *(fortuito)* accidental, chance
ocasionar *vt* to cause, to bring about
ocaso *nm* *(anochecer)* sunset; *Fig (declive)* fall, decline
occidental *adj* western, occidental
occidente *nm* west; **el O.** the West
OCDE *nf* (*abr* **Organización para la Cooperación y el Desarrollo Económico**) OECD
Oceanía *n* Oceania
oceánico,-a *adj* oceanic
océano *nm* ocean
ochenta *adj & nm inv* eighty
ocho *adj & nm inv* eight
ochocientos,-as *adj & nm* eight hundred
ocio *nm* leisure; **en mis ratos de o.** in my spare *o* leisure time
ocioso,-a *adj* (**a**) *(inactivo)* idle (**b**) *(inútil)* pointless
ocre *nm* ochre
octavilla *nf* *(panfleto)* handout, leaflet
octavo,-a *adj & nm,f* eighth

octogenario,-a *adj & nm,f* octogenarian
octogésimo,-a *adj & nm,f* eightieth
octubre *nm* October
ocular *adj* **testigo o.** eye witness
oculista *nmf* ophthalmologist
ocultar 1 *vt* to conceal, to hide; **o. algo a algn** to hide sth from sb
  2 ocultarse *vpr* to hide
oculto,-a *adj* concealed, hidden
ocupación *nf* occupation
ocupado,-a *adj* *(persona)* busy; *(asiento)* taken; *(aseos, teléfono)* engaged; *(puesto de trabajo)* filled
ocupante *nmf* *(de casa)* occupant, occupier; *(ilegal)* squatter; *(de vehículo)* occupant
ocupar 1 *vt* (**a**) to occupy (**b**) *(espacio, tiempo)* to take up; *(cargo)* to hold, to fill (**c**) *CAm, Méx (usar, emplear)* to use
  2 ocuparse *vpr* **o. de** *(cuidar)* to look after; *(encargarse)* to see to
ocurrencia *nf* *(agudeza)* witty remark, wisecrack; *(idea)* bright idea

---

  Observa que la palabra inglesa **occurrence** es un falso amigo y no es la traducción de la palabra española **ocurrencia**. En inglés, **occurrence** significa "suceso, incidencia".

---

ocurrente *adj* witty
ocurrir 1 *v impers* to happen, to occur; **¿qué ocurre?** what's going on?; **¿qué te ocurre?** what's the matter with you?
  2 ocurrirse *vpr* **no se me ocurre nada** I can't think of anything; **se me ocurre que ...** it occurs to me that ...
odiar [43] *vt* to detest, to hate; **odio tener que ...** I hate having to ...
odio *nm* hatred, loathing; **mirada de o.** hateful look
odioso,-a *adj* hateful
odontología *nf* dentistry, odontology
odontólogo,-a *nm,f* dental surgeon, odontologist
odre *nm* wineskin
OEA *nf* (*abr* **Organización de Estados Americanos**) OAS
oeste *nm* west
ofender 1 *vt* to offend
  2 ofenderse *vpr* to get offended (**por** by), to take offence (**por** at)
ofensa *nf* offence
ofensiva *nf* offensive
ofensivo,-a *adj* offensive
oferta *nf* offer; *Fin & Ind* bid, tender, proposal; *Com* **de** *o* **en o.** on (special) offer; **o. y demanda** supply and demand
ofertar *vt* to offer

off *adj* **voz en o.** *Cin & TV* voice-over; *Teatro* voice offstage

offset *nm Impr* offset

oficial 1 *adj* official

  2 *nmf* (**a**) *Mil & Náut* officer (**b**) *(empleado)* clerk (**c**) *(obrero)* skilled worker

oficialismo *nm Am* (**a**) **el o.** *(gobierno)* the Government (**b**) **el o.** *(partidarios del gobierno)* government supporters

oficialista *Am* **1** *adj* pro-government

  2 *nmf* government supporter

oficina *nf* office; **o. de empleo** *Br* job centre, *US* job office; **o. de turismo** tourist office; **o. de correos** post office; **horas/ horario de o.** business hours

oficinista *nmf* office worker, clerk

oficio *nm* (**a**) *(ocupación)* job, occupation; *(profesión)* trade; **ser del o.** to be in the trade (**b**) *(comunicación oficial)* official letter *o* note; **de o.** ex-officio; **abogado de o.** state-appointed lawyer (**c**) *Rel* service

oficioso,-a *adj (noticia, fuente)* unofficial

> 🖉 Observa que la palabra inglesa **officious** es un falso amigo y no es la traducción de la palabra española **oficioso**. En inglés, **officious** significa "excesivamente celoso o diligente".

ofimática *nf* office automation

ofimático,-a *adj Informát* **paquete o.** business package

ofrecer [33] 1 *vt* (**a**) to offer (**b**) *(aspecto)* to present

  2 ofrecerse *vpr* (**a**) *(prestarse)* to offer, to volunteer (**b**) *(situación)* to present itself (**c**) *Fml* **¿qué se le ofrece?** what can I do for you?

ofrecimiento *nm* offering

ofrendar *vt Rel* to offer up

ofrezco *indic pres de* **ofrecer**

oftalmología *nf* ophthalmology

oftalmólogo,-a *nm,f* ophthalmologist

ofuscación *nf,* **ofuscamiento** *nm* blinding, dazzling

ofuscar [44] *vt* (**a**) *Fig (confundir)* to blind (**b**) *(deslumbrar)* to dazzle

oídas: • de oídas *loc adv* by hearsay

oído *nm* (**a**) *(sentido)* hearing (**b**) *(órgano)* ear; **aprender de o.** to learn by ear; *Fig* **hacer oídos sordos** to turn a deaf ear

oír [17] *vt* to hear; **¡oye!** hey!; **¡oiga!** excuse me!; *Fam* **como lo oyes** believe it or not

OIT *nf (abr* **Organización Internacional del Trabajo**) ILO

ojal *nm* buttonhole

ojalá 1 *interj* let's hope so!, I hope so!

  2 *conj (+ subjunctive)* **¡o. sea cierto!** I hope it's true!

ojeada *nf* **echar una o.** to have a quick look

ojeras *nfpl* rings *o* bags under the eyes

ojeriza *nf* dislike

ojo 1 *nm* (**a**) eye; **o. morado** black eye; **ojos saltones** bulging eyes; *Fig* **a ojos vista** clearly, openly; *Fig* **calcular a o.** to guess; *Fam* **no pegué o.** I didn't sleep a wink (**b**) *(de aguja)* eye; *(de cerradura)* keyhole (**c**) *(de un puente)* span

  2 *interj* careful!, look out!

ojota *nf* (**a**) *Méx (sandalia)* sandal (**b**) *RP (chancletas) Br* flip-flop, *US* thong

okupa *nmf* squatter

ola *nf* wave; **o. de calor** heat wave

ole, olé *interj* bravo!

oleada *nf* wave; *Fig* **o. de turistas** influx of tourists

oleaje *nm* swell

óleo *nm Arte* oil; **pintura** *o* **cuadro al ó.** oil painting

oleoducto *nm* pipeline

oler [65] 1 *vt* (**a**) *(percibir olor)* to smell (**b**) *Fig (adivinar)* to smell, to feel

  2 *vi* (**a**) *(exhalar)* to smell; **o. a** to smell of; **o. bien/mal** to smell good/bad (**b**) *Fig (parecer)* to smack (**a** of)

  3 olerse *vpr Fig (adivinar)* to feel, to sense; **me lo olía** I thought as much

olfatear *vt* (**a**) *(oler)* to sniff (**b**) *Fig (indagar)* to pry into

olfato *nm* sense of smell; *Fig* good nose, instinct

oligarquía *nf* oligarchy

olimpiada *nf Dep* Olympiad, Olympic Games; **las olimpiadas** the Olympic Games

olímpicamente *adv* **paso o. de estudiar** I couldn't give a damn about studying

olímpico,-a *adj* Olympic; **Juegos Olímpicos** Olympic Games

oliva *nf* olive; **aceite de o.** olive oil

olivar *nm* olive grove

olivo *nm* olive (tree)

olla *nf* saucepan, pot; **o. exprés** *o* **a presión** pressure cooker

olmo *nm* smooth-leaved elm

olor *nm* smell; **o. corporal** body odour

oloroso,-a *adj* fragrant, sweet-smelling

OLP *nf (abr* **Organización para la Liberación de Palestina**) PLO

olvidadizo,-a *adj* forgetful

olvidar 1 *vt* (**a**) to forget; *Fam* **¡olvídame!** leave me alone! (**b**) **olvidé el paraguas allí** I left my umbrella there

  2 olvidarse *vpr* to forget; **se me ha olvidado hacerlo** I forgot to do it

olvido *nm* (**a**) *(desmemoria)* oblivion (**b**) *(lapsus)* oversight
ombligo *nm* navel
ominoso,-a *adj* shameful
omisión *nf* omission
omiso,-a *adj* **hacer caso o. de** to take no notice of
omitir *vt* to omit, to leave out
ómnibus *nm* (*pl* **ómnibus** *o* **omnibuses**) *Cuba, Urug* bus
omnipotente *adj* omnipotent, almighty
omnipresente *adj* omnipresent
omnisciente *adj* omniscient, all-knowing
omnívoro,-a 1 *adj* omnivorous
2 *nm,f* omnivore
omóplato, omoplato *nm* shoulder blade
OMS *nf* (*abr* **Organización Mundial de la Salud**) WHO
ONCE *nf* (*abr* **Organización Nacional de Ciegos Españoles**) ≃ RNIB
once 1 *adj inv* eleven
2 *nm inv* eleven; *Ftb* eleven, team
onda *nf* (**a**) *Fís* wave; *Fam Fig* **estar en la o.** to be with it; **o. expansiva** shock wave; *Rad* **o. larga/media/corta** long/medium/short wave (**b**) *(en el agua)* ripple (**c**) *(de pelo)* wave (**d**) *Méx, RP* **¿qué o.?** *(¿qué tal?)* how's it going?, how are things?
ondear *vi* (**a**) *(bandera)* to flutter (**b**) *(de agua)* to ripple
ondulación *nf* undulation; *(de agua)* ripple
ondulado,-a *adj* *(pelo)* wavy; *(paisaje)* rolling
ondulante *adj* undulating
ondular 1 *vt* *(el pelo)* to wave
2 *vi* *(moverse)* to undulate
oneroso,-a *adj* *(impuesto)* heavy
ONG *nf inv* (*abr* **Organización no Gubernamental**) NGO
onomástica *nf* saint's day
onomatopeya *nf* onomatopoeia
ONU *nf* (*abr* **Organización de las Naciones Unidas**) UN(O)
onubense 1 *adj* of/from Huelva
2 *nmf* person from Huelva
onza *nf* *(medida)* ounce
OPA *nf* (*abr* **Oferta Pública de Adquisición**) takeover bid
opaco,-a *adj* opaque
ópalo *nm* opal
opción *nf* (**a**) *(elección)* option, choice; *(alternativa)* alternative (**b**) *(posibilidad)* opportunity, chance
opcional *adj* optional
open *nm* *Dep* open

OPEP *nf* (*abr* **Organización de los Países Exportadores de Petróleo**) OPEC
ópera *nf* *Mús* opera
operación *nf* (**a**) *Med* operation; **o. quirúrgica** surgical operation (**b**) *Fin* transaction, deal; **operaciones bursátiles** stock exchange transactions (**c**) *Mat* operation
operador,-a *nm,f* (**a**) *(técnico)* operator (**b**) *Cin (de cámara) (hombre)* cameraman; *(mujer)* camerawoman; *(del proyector)* projectionist (**c**) *Tel* operator
operante *adj* operative
operar 1 *vt* (**a**) *Med* **o. a algn (de algo)** to operate on sb (for sth) (**b**) *(cambio etc)* to bring about
2 *vi Fin* to deal, to do business (**con** with)
3 operarse *vpr* (**a**) *Med* to have an operation (**de** for) (**b**) *(producirse)* to occur, to come about
operario,-a *nm,f* operator; *(obrero)* worker
operativo,-a 1 *adj* operative
2 *nm Am* operation
opereta *nf* operetta
opinar *vi* (**a**) *(pensar)* to think (**b**) *(declarar)* to give one's opinion, to be of the opinion
opinión *nf* *(juicio)* opinion; **cambiar de o.** to change one's mind
opio *nm* opium
oponente *nmf* opponent
oponer [19] (*pp* **opuesto**) **1** *vt* *(resistencia)* to offer
2 oponerse *vpr* *(estar en contra)* to be opposed; **se opone a aceptarlo** he refuses to accept it
oporto *nm* *(vino)* port
oportunidad *nf* opportunity, chance
oportunista *adj & nmf* opportunist
oportuno,-a *adj* (**a**) *(adecuado)* timely; **¡qué o.!** what good timing! (**b**) *(conveniente)* appropriate; **si te parece o.** if you think it appropriate
oposición *nf* (**a**) opposition (**b**) *(examen)* competitive examination
opositar *vi* = to sit a competitive examination
opositor,-a *nm,f* (**a**) *(candidato)* = candidate for a competitive examination (**b**) *Am Pol* opponent
opresión *nf* oppression; **o. en el pecho** tightness of the chest
opresivo,-a *adj* oppressive
opresor,-a 1 *nm,f* oppressor
2 *adj* oppressive, oppressing
oprimir *vt* (**a**) *(pulsar)* to press (**b**) *(subyugar)* to oppress

oprobio *nm* ignominy, opprobrium
optar *vi* (**a**) *(elegir)* to choose (**entre** between); **opté por ir yo mismo** I decided to go myself (**b**) *(aspirar)* to apply (**a** for); **puede o. a medalla** he's in with a chance of winning a medal
optativo,-a *adj* optional
óptica *nf* (**a**) *(tienda)* optician's (shop) (**b**) *(punto de vista)* angle
óptico,-a 1 *adj* optical
　2 *nm,f* optician
optimismo *nm* optimism
optimista 1 *adj* optimistic
　2 *nmf* optimist
óptimo,-a *adj* optimum, excellent
opuesto,-a *adj* (**a**) *(contrario)* contrary; **en direcciones opuestas** in opposite directions; **gustos opuestos** conflicting tastes (**b**) *(de enfrente)* opposite; **el extremo o.** the other end
opulencia *nf* opulence
opulento,-a *adj* opulent
opuse *pt indef de* **oponer**
oración *nf* (**a**) *Rel* prayer (**b**) *Ling* clause, sentence
oráculo *nm* oracle
orador,-a *nm,f* speaker, orator
oral *adj* oral; *Med* **por vía o.** to be taken orally
órale *interj Méx Fam* (**a**) *(venga)* come on! (**b**) *(de acuerdo)* right!, sure!
orangután *nm* orang-outang, orang-utan
orar *vi Rel* to pray
oratoria *nf* oratory
órbita *nf* (**a**) orbit (**b**) *Anat* eye socket
orden 1 *nm* order; **o. público** law and order; **por o. alfabético** in alphabetical order; **de primer o.** first-rate; **o. del día** agenda; **del o. de** approximately
　2 *nf* (**a**) *(mandato)* order; *Mil* **¡a la o.!** sir! (**b**) *Jur* warrant, order; **o. de registro** search warrant; **o. judicial** court order
ordenado,-a *adj* tidy
ordenador *nm* computer; **o. personal** personal computer
ordenamiento *nm* ordering
ordenanza 1 *nm* *(empleado)* office boy
　2 *nf* regulations; **o. municipal** bylaw
ordenar 1 *vt* (**a**) *(organizar)* to put in order; *(habitación)* to tidy up (**b**) *(mandar)* to order (**c**) *Am (pedir)* to order
　2 ordenarse *vpr Rel* to be ordained (**de** as), to take holy orders
ordeñar *vt* to milk
ordinario,-a *adj* (**a**) *(corriente)* ordinary, common (**b**) *(grosero)* vulgar, common
orégano *nm* oregano, marjoram

oreja *nf* ear; *(de sillón)* wing
orejero,-a *nm,f Am (soplón)* grass
orfanato *nm* orphanage
orfebre *nm (del oro)* goldsmith; *(de la plata)* silversmith
orfebrería *nf* gold/silver work
orfelinato *nm* orphanage
orgánico,-a *adj* organic
organigrama *nm* organization chart; *Informát* flow chart
organismo *nm* (**a**) *(ser vivo)* organism (**b**) *(institución)* organization, body
organista *nmf* organist
organización *nf* organization
organizado,-a *adj* organized; **viaje o.** package tour
organizador,-a 1 *adj* organizing
　2 *nm,f* organizer
organizar [40] 1 *vt* to organize
　2 organizarse *vpr Fig (armarse)* to happen
órgano *nm* organ
orgasmo *nm* orgasm
orgía *nf* orgy
orgullo *nm* (**a**) *(propia estima)* pride (**b**) *(arrogancia)* arrogance
orgulloso,-a *adj* (**a**) **estar o.** *(satisfecho)* to be proud (**b**) **ser o.** *(arrogante)* to be arrogant *o* haughty
orientación *nf* (**a**) *(dirección)* orientation, direction (**b**) *(guía)* guidance; **curso de o.** induction course
oriental 1 *adj* (**a**) *(del este)* eastern, oriental; *(del Lejano Oriente)* oriental (**b**) *Am (uruguayo)* Uruguayan
　2 *nmf* (**a**) *(del Lejano Oriente)* oriental (**b**) *Am (uruguayo)* Uruguayan
orientar 1 *vt* (**a**) *(enfocar)* to aim (**a** at), to intend (**a** for); **orientado al consumo** intended for consumption (**b**) *(indicar camino)* to give directions to; *Fig (aconsejar)* to advise (**c**) **una casa orientada al sur** a house facing south (**d**) *(esfuerzo)* to direct
　2 orientarse *vpr (encontar el camino)* to get one's bearings, to find one's way about
oriente *nm* East, Orient; **el Extremo** *o* **Lejano/Medio/Próximo O.** the Far/Middle/Near East
orificio *nm* hole, opening; *Anat & Téc* orifice; **o. de entrada** inlet; **o. de salida** outlet
origen *nm* origin; **país de o.** country of origin; **dar o. a** to give rise to
original *adj & nm* original
originalidad *nf* originality
originar 1 *vt* to cause, to give rise to

2 originarse *vpr* to originate
originariamente *adv* originally
originario,-a *adj* native
orilla *nf (borde)* edge; *(del río)* bank; *(del mar)* shore
orillero,-a *adj Am (persona)* suburban
orín[1] *nm (herrumbre)* rust
orín[2] *nm (usu pl) (orina)* urine
orina *nf* urine
orinal *nm* chamberpot; *Fam* potty
orinar 1 *vi* to urinate
2 orinarse *vpr* to wet oneself
oriundo,-a *adj* **ser o. de** to come from
orla *nf Univ* graduation photograph
ornamentar *vt* to adorn, to embellish
ornamento *nm* ornament
ornar *vt* to adorn, to embellish
ornato *nm (atavío)* finery; *(adorno)* decoration
ornitología *nf* ornithology
ornitólogo,-a *nm,f* ornithologist
oro *nm* (**a**) gold; **de o.** gold, golden; **o. de ley** fine gold (**b**) *Naipes* **oros** *(baraja española)* ≃ diamonds
orquesta *nf* orchestra; *(de verbena)* dance band
orquestar *vt* to orchestrate
orquídea *nf* orchid
ortiga *nf* (stinging) nettle
ortodoxia *nf* orthodoxy
ortodoxo,-a *adj* orthodox
ortografía *nf* orthography, spelling; **faltas de o.** spelling mistakes
ortográfico,-a *adj* orthographic, orthographical; **signos ortográficos** punctuation
ortopédico,-a *adj* orthopaedic; **pierna ortopédica** artificial leg
oruga *nf* caterpillar
orzuelo *nm Med* sty, stye
os *pron pers pl* (**a**) *(complemento directo)* you; **os veo mañana** I'll see you tomorrow (**b**) *(complemento indirecto)* you, to you; **os daré el dinero** I'll give you the money; **os escribiré** I'll write to you (**c**) *(con verbo reflexivo)* yourselves (**d**) *(con verbo recíproco)* each other; **os queréis mucho** you love each other very much
osa *nf* **O. Mayor** *Br* Great Bear, *US* Big Dipper; **O. Menor** *Br* Little Bear, *US* Little Dipper
osadía *nf* (**a**) *(audacia)* daring (**b**) *(desvergüenza)* impudence
osado,-a *adj* (**a**) *(audaz)* daring (**b**) *(desvergonzado)* shameless
osar *vi* to dare
osario *nm* ossuary
Óscar *nm Cin* Oscar

oscilación *nf* (**a**) oscillation (**b**) *(de precios)* fluctuation
oscilante *adj* (**a**) oscillating (**b**) *(precios)* fluctuating
oscilar *vi* (**a**) *Fís* to oscillate (**b**) *(variar)* to vary, to fluctuate
oscuras: • a oscuras *loc adv* in the dark; **nos quedamos a o.** we were left in darkness
oscurecer [33] *v impers, vt & vpr* = **obscurecer**
oscuridad *nf* = **obscuridad**
oscuro,-a *adj* = **obscuro,-a**
óseo,-a *adj* osseous, bony; **tejido ó.** bone tissue
osito *nm Fam* **o. (de peluche)** teddy bear
ósmosis, osmosis *nf inv* osmosis
oso *nm* bear; **o. polar** polar bear; **o. hormiguero** anteater; **o. marino** fur seal; *Fam Fig* **hacer el o.** to play the fool
ostensible *adj* ostensible
ostentación *nf* ostentation; **hacer o. de algo** to show sth off
ostentar *vt* (**a**) *(lucir)* to flaunt (**b**) *(cargo)* to hold
ostentoso,-a *adj* ostentatious
osteópata *nmf* osteopath
osteopatía *nf* osteopathy
ostión *nm* (**a**) *Méx (ostra)* large oyster (**b**) *Chile (vieira)* scallop
ostra *nf* oyster; *Fig* **aburrirse como una o.** to be bored stiff; *Fam* **¡ostras!** *Br* crikey!, *US* gee!
ostracismo *nm* ostracism
OTAN *nf* (*abr* **Organización del Tratado del Atlántico Norte**) NATO
otear *vt (horizonte)* to scan, to search
OTI *nf* (*abr* **Organización de Televisiones Iberoamericanas**) = association of all Spanish-speaking television networks
otitis *nf inv* infection and inflammation of the ear, otitis
otoñal *adj* autumn, *US* fall
otoño *nm* autumn, *US* fall
otorgamiento *nm (concesión)* granting; *(de un premio)* award
otorgar [42] *vt* (**a**) *(premio)* to award (**a** to); **o. un indulto** to grant pardon (**b**) *(permiso)* to grant (**a** to)
otorrinolaringólogo,-a *nm,f* ear, nose and throat specialist
otro,-a 1 *adj indef* (**a**) *(sin artículo) (sing)* another; *(pl)* other; **o. coche** another car; **otras personas** other people (**b**) *(con artículo definido)* other; **el o. coche** the other car (**c**) **otra cosa** something else; **otra vez** again
2 *pron indef* (**a**) *(sin artículo) (sing)*

another (one); *(pl) (personas)* others; *(cosas)* other ones; **dame o.** give me another (one); **no es mío, es de o.** it's not mine, it's somebody else's (**b**) *(con artículo definido) (sing)* **el o./la otra** the other (one); *(pl) (personas)* **los otros/las otras** the others; *(cosas)* the other ones (**c**) **hacer o. tanto** to do likewise

ovación *nf* ovation

ovacionar *vt* to give an ovation to, to applaud

oval, ovalado,-a *adj* oval

óvalo *nm* oval

ovario *nm* ovary

oveja *nf* sheep; *(hembra)* ewe; *Fig* **la o. negra** the black sheep

overol *nm Am* overalls

ovillo *nm* ball (of wool); *Fig* **hacerse un o.** to curl up into a ball

ovino,-a *adj* ovine; **ganado o.** sheep *pl*

OVNI *nm (abr* **objeto volador no identificado)** UFO

ovular 1 *adj* ovular
　2 *vi* to ovulate

óvulo *nm* ovule

oxidación *nf (metal)* rusting

oxidado,-a *adj (metal)* rusty; *Fig* **su inglés está un poco o.** her English is a bit rusty

oxidar 1 *vt Quím* to oxidize; *(metales)* to rust
　2 oxidarse *vpr Quím* to oxidize; *(metales)* to rust, to go rusty

óxido *nm* (**a**) oxide; **ó. de carbono** carbon monoxide (**b**) *(orín)* rust

oxigenado,-a *adj* oxygenated; **agua oxigenada** (hydrogen) peroxide

oxígeno *nm* oxygen; **bomba de o.** oxygen cylinder *o* tank

oye *indic pres & imperat de* **oír**

oyente *nmf* (**a**) *Rad* listener (**b**) *Univ* occasional student

ozono *nm* ozone; **capa de o.** ozone layer

P

P, p [pe] *nf (la letra)* P, p
pabellón *nm* (**a**) **p. de deportes** sports centre (**b**) *(en feria)* stand (**c**) *(bloque)* wing (**d**) *(bandera)* flag
pábulo *nm Fml Fig* fuel; **dar p. a** to encourage
pacer [60] *vt & vi* to graze, to pasture
pachá *nm Fam Fig* **vivir como un p.** to live like a king
Pachamama *n* Mother Earth
pachanguero,-a *adj Fam Pey (música)* catchy
pachón,-ona *nm,f (perro)* pointer
pachorra *nf Fam* sluggishness; **tener p.** to be phlegmatic
paciencia *nf* patience; **armarse de p.** to grin and bear it
paciente *adj & nmf* patient
pacificación *nf* pacification
pacificador,-a 1 *adj* pacifying
  2 *nm,f* peacemaker
pacificar [44] 1 *vt* to pacify; *Fig (apaciguar)* to appease, to calm
  2 pacificarse *vpr* to calm down
Pacífico *nm* **el (océano) P.** the Pacific (Ocean)
pacífico,-a *adj* peaceful
pacifismo *nm* pacifism
pacifista *adj & nmf* pacifist
paco *nm Andes, Pan Fam (policía)* cop
pacotilla *nf Fam* **de p.** second-rate
pactar *vt* to agree to
pacto *nm* pact; **el P. de Varsovia** the Warsaw Pact; **p. de caballeros** gentlemen's agreement
padecer [33] *vt & vi* to suffer; **padece del corazón** he suffers from heart trouble
padecimiento *nm* suffering
padrastro *nm* (**a**) stepfather (**b**) *(pellejo)* hangnail
padrazo *nm* easy-going *o* indulgent father
padre 1 *nm* (**a**) father; **p. de familia** family man (**b**) **padres** parents
  2 *adj inv Fam* (**a**) *(tremendo)* huge; **pegarse la vida p.** to live like a king (**b**) *Méx (genial)* great
padrenuestro *nm* Lord's Prayer
padrino *nm* (**a**) *(de bautizo)* godfather;

(de boda) best man; **padrinos** godparents (**b**) *(espónsor)* sponsor
padrísimo,-a *adj Méx Fam* fantastic, great
padrón *nm* census
padrote *nm Méx Fam (proxeneta)* pimp
paella *nf* paella, = rice dish made with vegetables, meat and/or seafood
paellera *nf* paella pan
pág *(abr* **página***)* p
paga *nf (salario)* wage; *(de niños)* pocket money; **p. extra** bonus
pagadero,-a *adj* payable; *Fin* **cheque p. al portador** cheque payable to bearer
pagador,-a *nm,f* payer
pagano,-a *adj & nm,f* pagan, heathen
pagar [42] *vt* (**a**) to pay; **p. en metálico** *o* **al contado** to pay cash; **p. por** *(producto, mala acción)* to pay for; *Fig* **(ella) lo ha pagado caro** she's paid dearly for it (**b**) *(recompensar)* to repay
pagaré *nm Fin* promissory note, IOU; **p. del tesoro** treasury note
página *nf* page; **en la p. 3** on page 3; *Fig* **una p. importante de la historia** an important chapter in history; *Informát* **p. personal** home page; *Informát* **p. web** web page
pago *nm* payment; **p. adelantado** *o* **anticipado** advance payment; **p. contra reembolso** cash on delivery; **p. inicial** down payment; **p. por visión** pay-per-view
paila *nf Andes, CAm, Carib* (frying) pan
paipái, paipay *nm (pl* **paipáis***)* = large palm fan
país *nm* country, land; **vino del p.** local wine; **P. Vasco** Basque Country; **P. Valenciano** Valencia
paisaje *nm* landscape, scenery
paisano,-a 1 *adj* of the same country
  2 *nm,f (compatriota)* fellow countryman/countrywoman, compatriot; **en traje de p.** in plain clothes
Países Bajos *npl* **(los) P.** the Netherlands, the Low Countries
paja *nf* (**a**) straw (**b**) *Fam Fig (bazofia)* padding, waffle (**c**) *Vulg* **hacerse una p.** to wank

pajar *nm (almacén)* straw loft; *(en el exterior)* straw rick

pajarita *nf* (**a**) bow tie (**b**) *(de papel)* paper bird

pájaro *nm* (**a**) bird; **Madrid a vista de p.** a bird's-eye view of Madrid; **p. carpintero** woodpecker (**b**) *Fam* **tener pájaros** to have daft ideas

pajita, pajilla *nf* (drinking) straw

Pakistán *n* Pakistan

pakistaní *adj & nmf* Pakistani

pala *nf* (**a**) shovel; *(de jardinero)* spade; *(de cocina)* slice (**b**) *Dep (de ping-pong, frontón)* bat, *US* paddle; *(de remo)* blade

palabra *nf* (**a**) word; **de p.** by word of mouth; **dirigir la p. a algn** to address sb; **juego de palabras** pun (**b**) *(promesa)* word; **p. de honor** word of honour (**c**) *(turno para hablar)* right to speak; **tener la p.** to have the floor

palabrería *nf* palaver

palabrota *nf* swearword

palacio *nm (grande)* palace; *(pequeño)* mansion; **P. de Justicia** Law Courts

paladar *nm* (**a**) palate (**b**) *(sabor)* taste

paladear *vt* to savour, to relish

palanca *nf* (**a**) lever (**b**) *(manecilla)* handle, stick; *Aut* **p. de cambio** *Br* gearstick, *US* gearshift; **p. de mando** control lever (**c**) *Dep (trampolín)* diving board

palangana *nf* washbasin

palco *nm* box

paleolítico,-a *adj* palaeolithic, paleolithic

paleontología *nf* palaeontology, paleontology

Palestina *n* Palestine

palestino,-a *adj & nm,f* Palestinian

palestra *nf* arena; *Fig* **salir** *o* **saltar a la p.** to enter the fray, to take the field

paleta *nf* (**a**) *(espátula)* slice (**b**) *(de pintor)* palette; *(de albañil)* trowel (**c**) *Dep (de pingpong)* bat (**d**) *CAm, Méx (pirulí)* lollipop; *(polo) Br* ice lolly, *US* Popsicle®

paletilla *nf* (**a**) shoulder blade (**b**) *Culin* shoulder

paleto,-a *Fam Pey* **1** *adj* unsophisticated, boorish

2 *nm,f* country bumpkin, yokel

paliar [43] *vt* to alleviate, to palliate

paliativo,-a *adj & nm* palliative

palidecer [33] *vi* (**a**) *(persona)* to turn pale (**b**) *Fig (disminuir)* to diminish, to be on the wane

palidez *nf* paleness, pallor

pálido,-a *adj* pale

palillero *nm* toothpick case

palillo *nm* (**a**) *(mondadientes)* toothpick;

palillos chinos chopsticks (**b**) *Mús* drumstick

palio *nm* (**a**) canopy (**b**) *Rel* pallium

palique *nm Fam* chat, small talk

paliza *nf* (**a**) *(zurra)* thrashing, beating; **darle a algn una p.** to beat sb up (**b**) *(derrota)* beating (**c**) *Fam (pesadez)* bore, pain (in the neck)

palma *nf* (**a**) *Anat* palm (**b**) *Bot* palm tree (**c**) **hacer palmas** to applaud

palmada *nf* (**a**) *(golpe)* slap (**b**) **palmadas** applause, clapping

palmar *vt Fam* **palmarla** to snuff it, to kick the bucket

palmarés *nm* (**a**) *(historial)* service record (**b**) *(vencedores)* list of winners

palmatoria *nf* candlestick

palmera *nf* palm tree

palmo *nm (medida)* span; *Fig* **p. a p.** inch by inch

palo *nm* (**a**) stick; *(vara)* rod; *(de escoba)* broomstick; *Fig* **a p. seco** on its own (**b**) *(golpe)* blow; *Fig* **dar un p. a algn** to let sb down (**c**) **de p.** wooden (**d**) *Dep (de portería)* woodwork (**e**) *(de golf)* club (**f**) *Naipes* suit

paloma *nf* pigeon; *Lit* dove; **p. mensajera** homing *o* carrier pigeon

palomar *nm* pigeon house, dovecot

palomilla *nf* (**a**) grain moth (**b**) *(tuerca)* wing *o* butterfly nut

palomitas (de maíz) *nfpl* popcorn

palpable *adj* palpable

palpar *vt* to touch, to feel; *Med* to palpate

palpitación *nf* palpitation, throbbing

palpitante *adj* palpitating, throbbing; *(asunto)* burning

palpitar *vi* to palpitate, to throb

palta *nf Andes, RP (fruto)* avocado

palúdico,-a *adj* malarial

paludismo *nm* malaria

palurdo,-a *adj* uncouth, boorish

pamela *nf* broad-brimmed hat

pampa *nf* pampa, pampas

pamplina *nf Fam* nonsense

pan *nm* bread; **p. de molde** loaf of bread; **p. integral** wholemeal *o* wholewheat bread; **p. rallado** breadcrumbs; **p. dulce** *Méx* cake; *RP* = type of fruitcake eaten at Christmas; *Arg* **p. lactal** sliced bread; *Fam Fig* **más bueno que el p.** as good as gold; *Fam Fig* **es p. comido** it's a piece of cake

pana *nf* corduroy

panacea *nf* panacea

panadería *nf* baker's (shop), bakery

panadero,-a *nm,f* baker

panal *nm* honeycomb

Panamá *n* Panama

panamá *nm (sombrero)* Panama hat
panameño,-a *adj & nm,f* Panamanian
pancarta *nf* placard; *(en manifestación)* banner
pancho *nm RP (perrito caliente)* hot dog
páncreas *nm inv* pancreas
panda[1] *nm* panda
panda[2] *nf* gang
pandereta *nf* tambourine
pandilla *nf Fam* gang
panecillo *nm* bread roll
panel *nm* panel
panera *nf* bread-basket
pánfilo,-a *adj Fam (bobo)* silly, stupid; *(crédulo)* gullible
panfleto *nm* lampoon, political pamphlet
pánico *nm* panic; **sembrar el p.** to cause panic
panocha *nf Bot* corn cob; *(de trigo etc)* ear
panoli *nmf Fam* idiot
panorama *nm (vista)* panorama, view; *Fig* panorama
panorámico,-a *adj* panoramic
panqueque *nm Am* pancake
pantaleta *nf*, **pantaletas** *nfpl Carib, Méx (bragas)* panties, *Br* knickers
pantalla *nf* (**a**) *Cin, TV & Informát* screen (**b**) *(de lámpara)* shade (**c**) *Fig* **servir de p.** to act as a decoy
pantalón *nm (usu pl)* trousers, *US* pants; **p. vaquero** jeans
pantano *nm Geog* (**a**) *(natural)* marsh, bog (**b**) *(artificial)* reservoir
panteón *nm* pantheon, mausoleum; **p. familiar** family vault
pantera *nf* panther
pantimedias *nfpl Méx Br* tights, *US* pantyhose
pantomima *nf Teatro* pantomime, mime; *Pey (farsa)* farce
pantorrilla *nf Anat* calf
pantry *nm Ven (comedor diario)* = family dining area off kitchen
pants *nmpl Méx* track *o* jogging suit
pantufla *nf* slipper
panty *nm* (pair of) *Br* tights, *US* pantyhose

⚠ Observa que la palabra inglesa **panties** es un falso amigo y no es la traducción de la palabra española **panty**. En inglés, **panties** significa "bragas".

panza *nf Fam* belly, paunch
panzada *nf Fam* bellyful
panzudo,-a, panzón,-ona *adj* pot-bellied, paunchy
pañal *nm Br* nappy, *US* diaper; *Fig* **estar en pañales** to be in one's infancy
paño *nm* (**a**) cloth material; *(de lana)* woollen cloth; *(para polvo)* duster, rag; *(de cocina)* dishcloth; *Fig* **paños calientes** half-measures (**b**) *paños (ropa)* clothes; **en paños menores** in one's underclothes
pañoleta *nf* (**a**) shawl (**b**) *Taurom* bullfighter's tie
pañuelo *nm* handkerchief; *(pañoleta)* shawl
Papa *nm* **el P.** the Pope
papa *nf* potato; *Fam* **no saber ni p. (de algo)** not to have the faintest idea (about sth); *Am* **papas fritas** *Br* chips, *US* (French) fries; *(de bolsa) Br* crisps, *US* (potato) chips
papá *nm Fam* dad, daddy
papada *nf* double chin
papagayo *nm* (**a**) *(animal)* parrot (**b**) *Carib, Méx (cometa)* kite
papalote *nm CAm, Méx* kite
papamoscas *nm inv* flycatcher
papanatas *nmf inv* sucker, twit
paparrucha(da) *nf* (piece of) nonsense
papaya *nf* papaya *o* pawpaw fruit
papear *vi Fam* to eat
papel *nm* (**a**) paper; *(hoja)* piece *o* sheet of paper; **papeles** *(documentos)* documents, identification papers; **p. higiénico** toilet paper; **p. carbón** carbon paper; **p. de carta** writing paper, stationery; *Chile* **p. confort** toilet paper; **p. de aluminio/de estraza** aluminium foil/brown paper; **p. de fumar** cigarette paper; **p. de lija** sandpaper; *Fin* **p. moneda** paper money, banknotes; **p. pintado** wallpaper; *Cuba* **p. sanitario** toilet paper; **p. secante** blotting paper; *Guat, Ven* **p. toilette** *o* **tualé** toilet paper (**b**) *Cin & Teatro* role, part
papeleo *nm Fam* paperwork
papelera *nf (en despacho)* wastepaper basket; *(en calle)* litter bin
papelería *nf (tienda)* stationer's (shop)
papeleta *nf* (**a**) *(de rifa)* ticket; *(de votación)* ballot paper; *(de resultados)* report (**b**) *Fam (dificultad)* tricky problem, difficult job
papeo *nm Fam* grub
paperas *nfpl Med* mumps *sing*
papilla *nf* pap, mush; *(de niños)* baby food
papista *nmf* papist
Papúa Nueva Guinea *n* Papua New Guinea
paquete *nm* (**a**) *(de cigarrillos etc)* packet; *(postal)* parcel, package (**b**) *(conjunto)* set, package; *Fin* **p. de acciones** share package (**c**) *Informát* software

package (**d**) *Fam (castigo)* punishment (**e**) *muy Fam (genitales)* packet, bulge

Paquistán *n* Pakistan

paquistaní *adj & nmf* Pakistani

par 1 *adj Mat* even

2 *nm* (**a**) *(pareja)* pair; *(dos)* couple (**b**) *Mat* even number; **pares y nones** odds and evens (**c**) *(noble)* peer (**d**) *(locuciones)* **a la p.** *(a la vez)* at the same time; **de p. en p.** wide open; *Fig* **sin p.** matchless

para *prep* (**a**) for; **bueno p. la salud** good for your health; **¿p. qué?** what for?; **p. ser inglés habla muy bien español** for an Englishman he speaks very good Spanish (**b**) *(finalidad)* to, in order to; **p. terminar antes** *to o* in order to finish earlier; **p. que lo disfrutes** for you to enjoy (**c**) *(tiempo)* by; **p. entonces** by then (**d**) *(a punto de)* **está p. salir** it's about to leave (**e**) *(locuciones)* **decir p. sí** to say to oneself; **ir p. viejo** to be getting old; **no es p. tanto** it's not as bad as all that; **p. mí** in my opinion

parábola *nf* (**a**) *Geom* parabola (**b**) *Rel* parable

parabólico,-a *adj* parabolic; *TV* **antena parabólica** satellite dish

parabrisas *nm inv Aut Br* windscreen, *US* windshield

paraca *nm Fam* para(chutist)

paracaídas *nm inv* parachute

paracaidista *nmf Dep* parachutist; *Mil* paratrooper

parachoques *nm inv Br* bumper, *US* fender

parada *nf* (**a**) stop; **p. de autobús** bus stop; **p. de taxis** taxi stand *o* rank (**b**) *Ftb* save, stop

paradero *nm* (**a**) *(lugar)* whereabouts *sing* (**b**) *Méx, Perú (apeadero)* stop

parado,-a 1 *adj* (**a**) stopped, stationary; *(quieto)* still; *(fábrica)* at a standstill; *Fig* **salir bien/mal p.** to come off well/badly (**b**) *(desempleado)* unemployed, out of work (**c**) *Fig (lento)* slow (**d**) *Am (de pie)* standing

2 *nm,f* unemployed person

paradoja *nf* paradox

paradójico,-a *adj* paradoxical

parador *nm* roadside inn; **p. nacional** *o* **de turismo** state-run hotel

parafernalia *nf* paraphernalia *pl*

parafrasear *vt* to paraphrase

paráfrasis *nf inv* paraphrase

paragolpes *nm inv RP (de automóvil) Br* bumper, *US* fender

paraguas *nm inv* umbrella

Paraguay *n* Paraguay

paragüero *nm* umbrella stand

paraíso *nm* (**a**) paradise; **p. terrenal** heaven on earth; *Fin* **p. fiscal** tax haven (**b**) *Teatro* gods, gallery

paraje *nm* spot, place

paralelo,-a *adj & nm* parallel

parálisis *nf inv* paralysis; **p. infantil** poliomyelitis

paralítico,-a *adj & nm,f* paralytic

paralización *nf* (**a**) *Med* paralysis (**b**) *(detención)* halting, stopping

paralizar [40] 1 *vt* to paralyse; *(circulación)* to stop

2 paralizarse *vpr Fig* to come to a standstill

parámetro *nm* parameter

paramilitar *adj* paramilitary

páramo *nm* bleak plain *o* plateau, moor

parangón *nm Fml* comparison; **sin p.** incomparable

paranoia *nf* paranoia

paranoico,-a *adj & nm,f* paranoiac, paranoid

parapente *nm (desde montaña)* paragliding, parapenting

parapeto *nm* (**a**) parapet (**b**) *(de defensa)* barricade

parapléjico,-a *adj & nm,f* paraplegic

parar 1 *vt* (**a**) to stop (**b**) *Dep* to save (**c**) *Am (levantar)* to raise

2 *vi* (**a**) to stop; **p. de hacer algo** to stop doing sth; **sin p.** non-stop, without stopping; *Fam* **no p.** to be always on the go (**b**) *(alojarse)* to stay (**c**) *(acabar)* **fue a p. a la cárcel** he ended up in jail

3 pararse *vpr* (**a**) to stop; **p. a pensar** to stop to think (**b**) *Am (ponerse en pie)* to stand up

pararrayos *nm inv* lightning rod *o* conductor

parásito,-a 1 *adj* parasitic

2 *nm* parasite

parasol *nm* sunshade, parasol

parcela *nf* plot

parche *nm* (**a**) patch (**b**) *(emplasto)* plaster (**c**) *Pey (chapuza)* botched-up *o* slapdash job

parchís *nm Br* ludo, *US* Parcheesi®

parcial 1 *adj* (**a**) *(partidario)* biased (**b**) *(no completo)* partial; **a tiempo p.** part-time

2 *nm* **(examen) p.** class examination

parcialmente *adv* partially, partly

parco,-a *adj (moderado)* sparing; *(frugal)* scant

pardillo,-a 1 *nm,f Pey* yokel, bumpkin

2 *nm Orn* linnet

pardo,-a *adj (marrón)* brown; *(gris)* dark grey

parecer[1] *nm* (**a**) *(opinión)* opinion (**b**) *(aspecto)* appearance

parecer[2] **[33] 1** *vi* to seem, to look (like); **parece difícil** it seems *o* looks difficult; **parecía (de) cera** it looked like wax; *(uso impers)* **parece que no arranca** it looks as if it won't start; **como te parezca** whatever you like; **¿te parece?** is that okay with you?; **parece que sí/no** I think/don't think so; **¿qué te parece?** what do you think of it?

2 parecerse (**a**) *vpr* to be alike; **no se parecen** they're not alike (**b**) **p. a** to look like, to resemble; **se parecen a su madre** they look like their mother

parecido,-a 1 *adj* (**a**) alike, similar (**b**) **bien p.** good-looking

2 *nm* likeness, resemblance; **tener p. con algn** to bear a resemblance to sb

pared *nf* wall

paredón *nm* (**a**) thick wall (**b**) *Fam* **le llevaron al p.** he was shot by firing squad

pareja *nf* (**a**) pair; **por parejas** in pairs (**b**) *(hombre y mujer)* couple; *(hijo e hija)* boy and girl; **hacen buena p.** they make a nice couple, they're well matched; **p. de hecho** = common-law heterosexual *o* homosexual relationship (**c**) *(en naipes)* pair; **doble p.** two pairs (**d**) *(de baile, juego)* partner

parejo,-a *adj* (**a**) *(parecido)* similar, alike (**b**) **ir parejos** to be neck and neck

parentela *nf Fam* relations, relatives

parentesco *nm* relationship, kinship

paréntesis *nm inv* (**a**) parenthesis, bracket; **entre p.** in parentheses *o* brackets (**b**) *(descanso)* break, interruption; *(digresión)* digression

parezco *indic pres de* **parecer**

paria *nmf* pariah

parida *nf Fam* silly thing

pariente *nmf* relative, relation

> 🖉 Observa que la palabra inglesa **parent** es un falso amigo y no es la traducción de la palabra española **pariente**. En inglés, **parent** significa tanto "padre" como "madre".

parir *vt & vi* to give birth (to)

París *n* Paris

parking *nm Br* car park, *US* parking lot

parlamentario,-a 1 *adj* parliamentary

2 *nm,f Br* Member of Parliament, MP, *US* Congressman, *f* Congresswoman

parlamento *nm* parliament

parlanchín,-ina *adj Fam* talkative, chatty

parné *nm Fam* dough, cash

paro *nm* (**a**) *(huelga)* strike, stoppage (**b**) *(desempleo)* unemployment; **estar en p.** to be unemployed; **cobrar el p.** *Br* to be on the dole

parodia *nf* parody

parodiar [43] *vt* to parody

parpadear *vi (ojos)* to blink; *Fig (luz)* to flicker

parpadeo *nm (de ojos)* blinking; *Fig (de luz)* flickering

párpado *nm* eyelid

parque *nm* (**a**) park; **p. de atracciones** funfair; **p. zoológico** zoo; **p. nacional/ natural** national park/nature reserve; **p. eólico** wind farm (**b**) *(de niños)* playpen (**c**) **p. móvil** total number of cars

parqué *nm* parquet

parqueadero *nm Carib, Col, Pan Br* car park, *US* parking lot

parquear *vt Carib, Col, Pan* to park

parquet *nm* = **parqué**

parquímetro *nm Aut* parking meter

parra *nf* grapevine

párrafo *nm* paragraph

parranda *nf Fam* spree

parricidio *nm* parricide

parrilla *nf* (**a**) *Culin* grill; **pescado a la p.** grilled fish (**b**) *Téc* grate (**c**) *Aut & Dep* starting grid

párroco *nm* parish priest

parronal *nm Chile* vineyard

parroquia *nf* parish; *(iglesia)* parish church

parroquiano,-a *nm,f* (regular) customer

parsimonia *nf* phlegm, calmness

parte 1 *nf* (**a**) *(sección)* part (**b**) *(en una repartición)* share (**c**) *(lugar)* place, spot; **en** *o* **por todas partes** everywhere; **se fue por otra p.** he went another way (**d**) *Jur* party (**e**) *(bando)* side; **estoy de tu p.** I'm on your side (**f**) *Euf* **partes** *(genitales)* private parts (**g**) *(locuciones)* **por mi p.** as far as I am concerned; **de p. de ...** on behalf of ...; *Tel* **¿de p. de quién?** who's calling?; **en gran p.** to a large extent; **en p.** partly; **la mayor p.** the majority; **por otra p.** on the other hand; **tomar p. en** to take part in

2 *nm (informe)* report

partición *nf (reparto)* division, sharing out; *(de herencia)* partition; *(de territorio)* partition

participación *nf* (**a**) participation (**b**) *Fin (acción)* share; **p. en los beneficios** profit-sharing (**c**) *(en lotería)* part of a lottery ticket (**d**) *(notificación)* notice, notification

participante 1 *adj* participating

2 *nmf* participant

participar 1 *vi* (**a**) to take part, to participate (**en** in) (**b**) *Fin* to have a share (**en** in) (**c**) *Fig* **p. de** to share

2 *vt* (*notificar*) to notify

partícipe *nmf* (**a**) participant; **hacer p. de algo** (*notificar*) to inform about sth (**b**) *Com & Fin* partner

participio *nm Ling* participle

partícula *nf* particle

particular 1 *adj* (**a**) (*concreto*) particular (**b**) (*privado*) private, personal (**c**) (*raro*) peculiar

2 *nmf* (*individuo*) private individual

3 *nm* (*asunto*) subject, matter

particularidad *nf* special feature

partida *nf* (**a**) (*salida*) departure (**b**) *Com* (*remesa*) batch, consignment (**c**) (*juego*) game (**d**) *Fin* (*entrada*) item (**e**) *Jur* (*certificado*) certificate; **p. de nacimiento** birth certificate

partidario,-a 1 *adj* **ser/no ser p. de algo** to be for/against sth

2 *nm,f* supporter, follower; **es p. del aborto** he is in favour of abortion

partidista *adj* biased, partisan

partido *nm* (**a**) *Pol* party (**b**) *Dep* match, game; **p. amistoso** friendly game; **p. de vuelta** return match (**c**) (*provecho*) advantage; **sacar p. de** to profit from (**d**) *Jur* (*distrito*) district (**e**) **tomar p. por** to side with (**f**) **ser un buen p.** to be a good catch

partir 1 *vt* to break; (*dividir*) to split, to divide; (*cortar*) to cut; **p. a algn por la mitad** to mess things up for sb

2 *vi* (**a**) (*marcharse*) to leave, to set out *o* off (**b**) **a p. de** from

3 partirse *vpr* to split (up), to break (up); *Fam* **p. de risa** to split one's sides laughing

partisano,-a *nm,f* partisan

partitura *nf Mús* score

parto *nm* childbirth, labour; **estar de p.** to be in labour

parvulario *nm* nursery school, kindergarten

párvulo,-a *nm,f* infant

pasa *nf* raisin; **p. de Corinto** currant

pasable *adj* passable, tolerable

pasaboca *nm Col* snack, appetizer

pasacalle *nm Col, Urug* banner (*hung across street*)

pasada *nf* (**a**) **de p.** in passing (**b**) (*jugarreta*) dirty trick (**c**) *Fam* **¡eso es una p.!** it's too much!

pasadizo *nm* corridor, passage

pasado,-a 1 *adj* (**a**) (*último*) last; **el año/lunes p.** last year/Monday (**b**) (*anticuado*) dated, old-fashioned; **p. (de moda)** out of date *o* fashion (**c**) (*alimento*) bad

(**d**) *Culin* cooked; **lo quiero muy p.** I want it well done (**e**) **p. mañana** the day after tomorrow

2 *nm* past

pasador *nm* (**a**) (*prenda*) pin, clasp; (*para el pelo*) (hair) slide (**b**) (*pestillo*) bolt, fastener

pasaje *nm* (**a**) passage (**b**) (*calle*) alley (**c**) (*pasajeros*) passengers (**d**) (*billete*) ticket

pasajero,-a 1 *adj* passing, temporary; **aventura pasajera** fling

2 *nm,f* passenger

pasamanos *nm inv* (*barra*) handrail; (*de escalera*) banister, bannister

pasamontañas *nm inv* balaclava

pasapalo *nm Ven* snack, appetizer

pasaporte *nm* passport

pasapurés *nm inv Culin* potato masher

pasar 1 *vt* (**a**) to pass; (*objeto*) to pass, to give; (*mensaje*) to give; (*página*) to turn; (*trasladar*) to move; **p. algo a limpio** to make a clean copy of sth

(**b**) (*tiempo*) to spend, to pass; **p. el rato** to kill time

(**c**) (*padecer*) to suffer, to endure; **p. hambre** to go hungry

(**d**) (*río, calle*) to cross; (*barrera*) to pass through *o* over; (*límite*) to go beyond

(**e**) (*perdonar*) to forgive, to tolerate; **p. algo (por alto)** to overlook sth

(**f**) (*introducir*) to insert, to put through

(**g**) (*examen*) to pass

(**h**) *Cin* to run, to show

2 *vi* (**a**) to pass; **¿ha pasado el autobús?** has the bus gone by?; **ha pasado un hombre** a man has gone past; **p. de largo** to go by (without stopping); **el tren pasa por Burgos** the train goes via Burgos; **pasa por casa mañana** come round to my house tomorrow

(**b**) **p. a** (*continuar*) to go on to; **p. a ser** to become

(**c**) (*entrar*) to come in

(**d**) (*tiempo*) to pass, to go by

(**e**) **p. sin** to do without; *Fam* **paso de tí** I couldn't care less about you; *Fam* **yo paso** count me out

3 *v impers* (*suceder*) to happen; **¿qué pasa aquí?** what's going on here?; **¿qué te pasa?** what's the matter?; *Fam* **¿qué pasa?** (*saludo*) how are you?; **pase lo que pase** whatever happens, come what may

4 pasarse *vpr* (**a**) **se me pasó la ocasión** I missed my chance; **se le pasó llamarme** he forgot to phone me

(**b**) (*gastar tiempo*) to spend *o* pass time;

pasárselo bien/mal to have a good/bad time

(**c**) *(comida)* to go off

(**d**) *Fam (excederse)* to go too far; **no te pases** don't overdo it

(**e**) **pásate por mi casa** call round at my place

pasarela *nf (puente)* footbridge; *(de barco)* gangway; *(de moda)* catwalk

pasatiempo *nm* pastime, hobby

pascua *nf* (**a**) Easter (**b**) **pascuas** *(Navidad)* Christmas; **¡felices Pascuas!** Merry Christmas!

pascualina *nf RP, Ven* = pie made with spinach and hard-boiled egg

pase *nm* (**a**) pass, permit (**b**) *Cin* showing

pasear 1 *vi* to go for a walk, to take a walk

2 *vt* (**a**) *(persona)* to take for a walk; *(perro)* to walk (**b**) *Fig (exhibir)* to show off

3 pasearse *vpr* to go for a walk

paseíllo *nm Taurom* opening parade

paseo *nm* (**a**) walk; *(en bicicleta, caballo)* ride; *(en coche)* drive; **dar un p.** to go for a walk/a ride (**b**) *(avenida)* avenue

pasillo *nm* corridor; *Av* **p. aéreo** air corridor

pasión *nf* passion

pasional *adj* passionate; **crimen p.** crime of passion

pasividad *nf* passivity, passiveness

pasivo,-a 1 *adj* passive; *(inactivo)* inactive

2 *nm Com* liabilities

pasmado,-a *adj (asombrado)* astounded, amazed; *(atontado)* flabbergasted; **dejar p.** to astonish; **quedarse p.** to be amazed

pasmo *nm* astonishment, amazement

paso¹,-a *adj* **ciruela pasa** prune; **uva pasa** raisin

paso² *nm* (**a**) step; *(modo de andar)* gait, walk; *(ruido al andar)* footstep; *Mil* **llevar el p.** to keep in step; *Fig* **a dos pasos** a short distance away; *Fig* **seguir los pasos de algn** to follow in sb's footsteps

(**b**) *(camino)* passage, way; **abrirse p.** to force one's way through; *Aut* **ceda el p.** *(en letrero)* give way; **prohibido el p.** *(en letrero)* no entry; **p. a nivel** *Br* level crossing, *US* grade crossing; **p. de cebra** zebra crossing; **p. de peatones** *Br* pedestrian crossing, *US* crosswalk; **p. elevado** *Br* flyover, *US* overpass; **p. subterráneo** *(para peatones)* subway; *(para coches)* underpass

(**c**) *(acción)* passage, passing; **a su p. por la ciudad** when he was in town; **el p. del tiempo** the passage of time; **estar de p.** to be just passing through

(**d**) **p. de montaña** mountain pass

pasodoble *nm* paso doble

pasota *nmf Fam* waster

pasta *nf* (**a**) paste; **p. de dientes** *o* **dentífrica** toothpaste (**b**) *(de pan, pasteles)* dough; *(italiana)* pasta (**c**) *(galleta) Br* biscuit, *US* cookie (**d**) *Fam (dinero)* dough, bread

pastar *vt & vi* to graze, to pasture

pastel *nm* (**a**) cake; *(de carne, fruta)* pie (**b**) *Arte* pastel (**c**) *Fam* **descubrir el p.** to spill the beans

pastelería *nf* (**a**) *(tienda)* confectioner's (shop) (**b**) *(dulces)* confectionery

pastelero,-a *nm,f* pastry cook, confectioner

pastiche *nm* (**a**) pastiche (**b**) *Fam (chapuza)* botch(-up)

pastilla *nf* (**a**) tablet, pill; **pastillas para la tos** cough drops (**b**) *(de jabón)* bar (**c**) *Fam* **a toda p.** at full speed

pastizal *nm* grazing land, pasture

pasto *nm* (**a**) *(hierba)* grass (**b**) *(alimento)* fodder; **ser p. de** to fall prey to (**c**) *Am (césped)* lawn, grass

pastor,-a 1 *nm,f* shepherd; *(mujer)* shepherdess; **perro p.** sheepdog

2 *nm* (**a**) *Rel* pastor, minister (**b**) *(perro)* **p. alemán** Alsatian

pastoreo *nm* shepherding

pastoso,-a *adj* pasty; *(lengua)* furry

pata 1 *nf* leg; *Fig* **patas arriba** upside down; **estirar la p.** to kick the bucket; **mala p.** bad luck; **meter la p.** to put one's foot in it; **p. de gallo** crow's foot

2 *nm Perú Fam (amigo)* pal, *Br* mate, *US* buddy

patada *nf (puntapié)* kick, stamp

patalear *vi* to stamp one's feet (with rage)

pataleo *nm* kicking; *(de rabia)* stamping

patán *nm* bumpkin, yokel

patata *nf* potato; **patatas fritas** *Br* chips, *US* (French) fries; *(de bolsa) Br* crisps, *US* (potato) chips

patatús *nm inv Fam* dizzy spell, queer turn

paté *nm* pâté

patear 1 *vt (pelota)* to kick; *(pisotear)* to stamp on

2 *vi (patalear)* to stamp (one's foot with rage)

patentar *vt* to patent

patente 1 *nf* (**a**) *(autorización)* licence; *(de invención)* patent (**b**) *CSur (matrícula) Br* number plate, *US* license plate

2 *adj (evidente)* patent, obvious

pateo *nm* stamping; *(abucheo)* boo(ing), jeer(ing)

paternal *adj* paternal, fatherly

paternalista *adj* paternalistic

paternidad *nf* paternity, fatherhood

paterno,-a *adj* paternal

patético,-a *adj* moving

patíbulo *nm* scaffold, gallows *sing*

patidifuso,-a *adj Fam* dumbfounded, flabbergasted

patilla *nf* (**a**) *(de gafas)* leg (**b**) **patillas** *(pelo)* sideburns

patín *nm* (**a**) skate; *(patinete)* scooter; **p. de ruedas/de hielo** roller-/ice-skate; **p. en línea** rollerblade (**b**) *Náut* pedal boat

patinaje *nm* skating; **p. artístico** figure skating; **p. sobre hielo/ruedas** ice-/roller-skating

patinar *vi* (**a**) to skate; *(sobre ruedas)* to roller-skate; *(sobre hielo)* to ice-skate (**b**) *(deslizarse)* to slide; *(resbalar)* to slip; *(vehículo)* to skid (**c**) *Fam (equivocarse)* to put one's foot in it, to slip up

patinazo *nm* (**a**) skid (**b**) *Fam (equivocación)* blunder, boob

patinete *nm* scooter

patio *nm* (**a**) *(de una casa)* yard, patio; *(de recreo)* playground (**b**) *Teatro & Cin* **p. de butacas** stalls

pato *nm* duck; *Fam* **pagar el p.** to carry the can

patochada *nf* blunder, boob

patógeno,-a *adj* pathogenic

patología *nf* pathology

patológico,-a *adj* pathological

patoso,-a *adj* clumsy, awkward

patota *nf Perú, RP (de gamberros)* street gang

patraña *nf* nonsense

patria *nf* fatherland, native country; **madre p.** motherland; **p. chica** one's home town/region

patriarca *nm* patriarch

patrimonio *nm (bienes)* wealth; *(herencia)* inheritance

patriota *nmf* patriot

patriótico,-a *adj* patriotic

patriotismo *nm* patriotism

patrocinador,-a 1 *adj* sponsoring
  2 *nm,f* sponsor

patrocinar *vt* to sponsor

patrocinio *nm* sponsorship, patronage

patrón,-ona 1 *nm,f* (**a**) *(jefe)* boss (**b**) *(de pensión) (hombre)* landlord; *(mujer)* landlady (**c**) *Rel* patron saint
  2 *nm* (**a**) pattern (**b**) *(medida)* standard

patronal 1 *adj* employers'; **cierre p.** lockout; **clase p.** managerial class

  2 *nf (dirección)* management

patronato, patronazgo *nm* (**a**) *(institución benéfica)* foundation (**b**) *(protección)* patronage

patrono,-a *nm,f* (**a**) boss; *(empresario)* employer (**b**) *Rel* patron saint

patrulla *nf* (**a**) patrol; **estar de p.** to be on patrol; **coche p.** patrol car (**b**) *(grupo)* group, band; **p. de rescate** rescue party; **p. ciudadana** vigilante group

patrullar 1 *vt* to patrol
  2 *vi* to be on patrol

patrullero *nm CSur (auto)* police (patrol) car

paulatino,-a *adj* gradual

paupérrimo,-a *adj* extremely poor, poverty-stricken

pausa *nf* pause, break; *Mús* rest

pausado,-a *adj* unhurried, calm

pauta *nf* guidelines

pava *nf* (**a**) *Fam* **pelar la p.** to chat (**b**) *Arg (tetera)* kettle

pavada *nf RP (tontería)* stupid thing

pavesa *nf* ash

pavimentar *vt* to pave

pavimento *nm (de carretera)* road (surface), *US* pavement; *(de acera)* paving; *(de habitación)* flooring

pavo *nm* (**a**) turkey; *Fam* **no ser moco de p.** to be nothing to scoff at (**b**) *Fam (tonto)* twit; *Fam* **estar en la edad del p.** to be growing up

pavonearse *upr Fam* to show off, to strut

pavoneo *nm Fam* showing off, strutting

pavor *nm* terror, dread

pay *nm Chile, Méx, Ven* pie

payaso *nm* clown; **hacer el p.** to act the clown

payés,-esa *nm,f* = Catalan or Balearic peasant

payo,-a *nm,f* non-gipsy person

paz *nf* peace; *(sosiego)* peacefulness; *Fam* **¡déjame en p.!** leave me alone!, **hacer las paces** to make (it) up

pazguato,-a *adj* (**a**) *(estúpido)* silly, stupid (**b**) *(mojigato)* prudish

PC *nm (abr* **personal computer**) PC

PCE *nm Pol (abr* **Partido Comunista de España**) = Spanish Communist party

pe *nf Fam* **de pe a pa** from A to Z

peaje *nm* toll; **autopista de p.** *Br* toll motorway, *US* turnpike

peatón *nm* pedestrian

peca *nf* freckle

pecado *nm Rel* sin; **p. capital** *o* **mortal** deadly sin

pecador,-a *nm,f* sinner

pecaminoso,-a *adj* sinful

pecar [44] *vi* to sin; *Fig* **p. por defecto** to fall short of the mark

pecera *nf* fish bowl, fish tank

pecho *nm* (**a**) chest; *(de mujer)* breast, bust; *(de animal)* breast; **dar el p. (a un bebé)** to breast-feed (a baby); *Fig* **to-mar(se) (algo) a p.** to take (sth) to heart (**b**) *Am (en natación)* breaststroke; **nadar p.** to do the breaststroke

pechuga *nf* (**a**) *(de ave)* breast (**b**) *Fam (de mujer)* boob

pectoral *adj* pectoral, chest

peculiar *adj (raro)* peculiar; *(característico)* characteristic

peculiaridad *nf* peculiarity

pedagogía *nf* pedagogy

pedagógico,-a *adj* pedagogical

pedal *nm* pedal

pedalear *vi* to pedal

pedante 1 *adj* pedantic
　　2 *nmf* pedant

pedantería *nf* pedantry

pedazo *nm* piece, bit; **a pedazos** in pieces; **caerse a pedazos** to fall apart *o* to pieces; **hacer pedazos** to break *o* tear to pieces, to smash (up); *Fam* **¡qué p. de coche!** what a terrific car!

pederasta *nm* pederast

pedernal *nm* flint

pedestal *nm* pedestal

pediatra *nmf* paediatrician

pediatría *nf* paediatrics *sing*

pedicuro,-a *nm,f* chiropodist, *US* podiatrist

pedido *nm* (**a**) *Com* order; **hacer un p. a** to place an order with (**b**) *(petición)* request

pedigrí *nm* pedigree

pedir [6] *vt* (**a**) to ask (for); **p. algo a algn** to ask sb for sth; **te pido que te quedes** I'm asking you to stay; **p. prestado** to borrow; *Fig* **p. cuentas** to ask for an explanation (**b**) *Com & (en bar etc)* to order (**c**) *(mendigar)* to beg

pedo *nm Fam* (**a**) fart; **tirarse un p.** to fart (**b**) *(borrachera)* bender

pedrada *nf (golpe)* blow from a stone; *(lanzamiento)* throw of a stone

pedrea *nf (en lotería)* small prizes

pedregoso,-a *adj* stony, rocky

pedrería *nf* precious stones, gems

pedrisco *nm* hailstorm

pega *nf* (**a**) *Fam (objeción)* objection; **poner pegas** to find fault (**b**) **de p.** *(falso)* sham

pegadizo,-a *adj* catchy

pegado,-a *adj* (**a**) *(adherido)* stuck (**b**) *(quemado)* burnt

pegajoso,-a *adj (pegadizo)* sticky; *Fig (persona)* tiresome, hard to get rid of

pegamento *nm* glue

pegar [42] 1 *vt* (**a**) *(adherir)* to stick; *(con pegamento)* to glue; *(coser)* to sew on; *Fam* **no pegó ojo** he didn't sleep a wink; **p. fuego a** to set fire to
　　(**b**) *(golpear)* to hit
　　(**c**) **p. un grito** to shout; **p. un salto** to jump
　　(**d**) *Fam (contagiar)* to give; **me ha pegado sus manías** I've caught his bad habits
　　(**e**) *(arrimar)* **p. algo a** *o* **contra algo** to put *o* place sth against sth
　　2 *vi* (**a**) *(adherirse)* to stick
　　(**b**) *(armonizar)* to match, to go; **el azul no pega con el verde** blue and green don't go together *o* don't match; *Fig* **ella no pegaría aquí** she wouldn't fit in here
　　(**c**) *(sol)* to beat down
　　3 pegarse *vpr* (**a**) *(adherirse)* to stick; *(pelearse)* to fight
　　(**b**) *Fam (darse)* to have, to get; **p. un tiro** to shoot oneself
　　(**c**) *(comida)* to get burnt; **se me ha pegado el sol** I've got a touch of the sun
　　(**d**) *Fam* **pegársela a algn** to trick *o* deceive sb
　　(**e**) *(arrimarse)* to get close
　　(**f**) *Fam Fig* to stick
　　(**g**) *Med (enfermedad)* to be catching *o* contagious; *Fig (melodía)* to be catchy

pegatina *nf* sticker

peinado *nm* hairstyle, *Fam* hairdo

peinar 1 *vt* (**a**) *(pelo)* to comb (**b**) *(registrar)* to comb
　　2 peinarse *vpr* to comb one's hair

peine *nm* comb

peineta *nf* = ornamental comb worn in hair

pela *nf Fam* peseta

pelado,-a 1 *adj* (**a**) *(cabeza)* shorn; *(piel, fruta)* peeled; *(terreno)* bare (**b**) *Fam* **saqué un cinco p.** *(en escuela)* I just scraped a pass; **a grito p.** shouting and bawling (**c**) *Fam (arruinado)* broke, penniless (**d**) *(desvergonzado)* impudent, insolent
　　2 *nm Fam* haircut
　　3 *nm,f* (**a**) *Andes Fam (niño, adolescente)* kid (**b**) *CAm, Méx Fam (pobre)* poor person

peladura *nf* peeling

pelagatos *nmf inv Fam* poor devil, nobody

pelaje *nm* (**a**) fur, hair (**b**) *Pey (apariencia)* looks, appearance

pelambrera *nf Fam* mop (of hair), long/thick hair

pelapatatas *nm inv* potato peeler

pelar 1 *vt (cortar el pelo a)* to cut the hair of; *(fruta, patata)* to peel; *Fam* **hace un frío que pela** it's brass monkey weather
　2 *vi (despellejar)* to peel
　3 pelarse *vpr* (**a**) *(cortarse el pelo)* to get one's hair cut (**b**) *Fam* **corre que se las pela** she runs like the wind

peldaño *nm* step; *(de escalera de mano)* rung

pelea *nf* fight; *(riña)* row, quarrel; **buscar p.** to look for trouble

peleado,-a *adj* **estar p. (con algn)** not to be on speaking terms (with sb)

pelear 1 *vi* to fight; *(reñir)* to quarrel
　2 pelearse *vpr* (**a**) to fight; *(reñir)* to quarrel (**b**) *(enemistarse)* to fall out

pelele *nm (muñeco)* straw puppet; *Fig* puppet

peleón,-ona *adj* (**a**) quarrelsome, aggressive (**b**) *(vino)* cheap

peletería *nf* furrier's; *(tienda)* fur shop

peletero,-a *nm,f* furrier

peliagudo,-a *adj* difficult, tricky

pelícano *nm* pelican

película *nf* (**a**) *Cin* movie, *Br* film; **p. de miedo** *o* **terror** horror film; **p. del Oeste** Western; *Fam* **de p.** fabulous (**b**) *Fot* film

peligrar *vi* to be in danger, to be threatened; **hacer p.** to endanger, to jeopardize

peligro *nm* danger; *(riesgo)* risk; **con p. de ...** at the risk of ...; **correr (el) p. de ...** to run the risk of ...; **poner en p.** to endanger

peligroso,-a *adj* dangerous, risky

pelirrojo,-a 1 *adj* red-haired; *(anaranjado)* ginger-haired
　2 *nm,f* redhead

pellejo *nm* (**a**) *(piel)* skin (**b**) *(odre)* wineskin (**c**) *Fam* **arriesgar** *o* **jugarse el p.** to risk one's neck

pelliza *nf* fur jacket

pellizcar [44] *vt* to pinch, to nip

pellizco *nm* pinch, nip

pelma *nmf,* **pelmazo,-a** *nm,f (persona)* bore, drag

pelo *nm* (**a**) hair; **cortarse el p.** *(uno mismo)* to cut one's hair; *(en la peluquería)* to have one's hair cut; *Fig* **no tiene ni un p. de tonto** he's no fool; *Fig* **no tener pelos en la lengua** to be very outspoken; *Fig* **tomar el p. a algn** to pull sb's leg, to take the mickey out of sb; *Fam* **con pelos y señales** in full detail; *Fam* **por los pelos** by the skin of one's teeth; *Fam* **me puso el p. de punta** it gave me the creeps (**b**) *(de animal)* fur, coat, hair (**c**) *Tex (de una tela)* nap, pile (**d**) *(cerda)* bristle

pelón,-ona *adj (sin pelo)* bald

pelota 1 *nf* (**a**) ball; *Fam* **devolver la p.** to give tit for tat (**b**) *Dep* pelota (**c**) *Fam (cabeza)* nut (**d**) **hacer la p. a algn** to toady to sb, to butter sb up (**e**) *muy Fam* **pelotas** *(testículos)* balls; **en pelotas** *Br* starkers, *US* butt-naked
　2 *nmf Fam (pelotillero)* crawler

pelotari *nm* pelota player

pelotear *vi Dep* to kick a ball around; *Ten* to knock up

peloteo *nm Ten* knock-up

pelotilla *nf Fam* **hacer la p. (a algn)** to fawn (on sb)

pelotillero,-a *nm,f Fam* crawler

pelotón *nm* (**a**) *Mil* squad (**b**) *Fam (grupo)* small crowd, bunch; *(en ciclismo)* pack (**c**) *(amasijo)* bundle

pelotudo,-a *adj RP Fam* (**a**) *(estúpido)* stupid (**b**) *(grande)* great big, massive

peluca *nf* wig

peluche *nm* **osito de p.** teddy bear

peludo,-a *adj* hairy, furry

peluquería *nf* hairdresser's (shop)

peluquero,-a *nm,f* hairdresser

peluquín *nm* toupee

pelusa, pelusilla *nf* (**a**) fluff; *(de planta)* down (**b**) *Fam* jealousy

pelvis *nf inv* pelvis

pena *nf* (**a**) *(tristeza)* grief, sorrow; *Fig* **me da p. de ella** I feel sorry for her; **¡qué p.!** what a pity! (**b**) *(dificultad)* hardships, trouble; **no merece** *o* **vale la p. (ir)** it's not worth while (going); **a duras penas** with great difficulty (**c**) *(castigo)* punishment, penalty; **p. de muerte** *o* **capital** death penalty (**d**) *CAm, Carib, Col, Méx (vergüenza)* shame, embarrassment; **me da p.** I'm ashamed of it

penacho *nm* (**a**) *(de ave)* crest, tuft (**b**) *Mil (de plumas)* plume

penal 1 *adj* penal; *Jur* **código p.** penal code
　2 *nm* prison, jail

penalidad *nf (usu pl)* hardships, troubles

penalización *nf* penalization; *Dep* penalty

penalizar [40] *vt* to penalize

penalti *nm Dep (pl* **penaltis***)* penalty; *Fam* **casarse de p.** to have a shotgun wedding

penar 1 *vt* to punish
　2 *vi* to be in torment, to suffer

pendejo,-a *nm,f muy Fam* (**a**) *Am (tonto)* jerk, idiot (**b**) *RP Pey (adolescente)* kid

pendenciero,-a *adj* quarrelsome, argumentative

pendiente 1 *adj* (**a**) *(por resolver)* pending; *Educ* **asignatura p.** failed subject;

Com **p. de pago** unpaid (**b**) **estar p. de** *(esperar)* to be waiting for; *(vigilar)* to be on the lookout for (**c**) *(colgante)* hanging (**de** from)
  2 *nm (joya)* earring
  3 *nf* slope; *(de tejado)* pitch
pendón *nm* (**a**) *(bandera)* banner (**b**) *Pey (mujer)* slut, whore; *(hombre)* playboy
péndulo *nm* pendulum
pene *nm* penis
penetración *nf* penetration; *(perspicacia)* insight, perception
penetrante *adj* penetrating; *(frío, voz, mirada)* piercing; *Fig (inteligencia)* sharp, acute
penetrar **1** *vt* to penetrate; **p. un misterio** to get to the bottom of a mystery
  2 *vi (entrar)* to go o get (**en** in)
penicilina *nf* penicillin
península *nf* peninsula
penique *nm* penny, *pl* pence
penitencia *nf* penance
penitenciaría *nf* prison
penitenciario,-a *adj* penitentiary, prison
penoso,-a *adj* (**a**) *(lamentable)* sorry, distressing (**b**) *(laborioso)* laborious, difficult (**c**) *CAm, Carib, Col, Méx (vergonzoso)* shy
pensado,-a *adj* (**a**) thought out; **bien p., ...** on reflection, ...; **en el momento menos p.** when least expected; **mal p.** twisted; **tener algo p.** to have sth planned, to have sth in mind; **tengo p. ir** I intend to go (**b**) *(concebido)* designed
pensamiento *nm* (**a**) thought (**b**) *(máxima)* saying, motto (**c**) *Bot* pansy
pensar [1] **1** *vi* to think (**en** of o about; **sobre** about o over); *Fig* **sin p.** *(con precipitación)* without thinking; *(involuntariamente)* involuntarily
  2 *vt* (**a**) to think (**de** of); *(considerar)* to think over o about; **piénsalo bien** think it over; *Fam* **¡ni pensarlo!** not on your life! (**b**) *(proponerse)* to intend; **pienso quedarme** I plan to stay (**c**) *(concebir)* to make; **p. un plan** to make a plan; **p. una solución** to find a solution
pensativo,-a *adj* pensive, thoughtful
pensión *nf* (**a**) *(residencia)* boarding house; *(hotel)* guesthouse; **media p.** half board; **p. completa** full board (**b**) *(paga)* pension, allowance; **p. vitalicia** life annuity
pensionista *nmf* pensioner
pentágono *nm* pentagon
pentagrama *nm* staff, stave
penthouse [pent'χaus] *nm CSur, Ven* penthouse

penúltimo,-a *adj & nm,f* next to the last, penultimate
penumbra *nf* penumbra, half-light
penuria *nf* scarcity, shortage
peña *nf* (**a**) rock, crag (**b**) *(de amigos)* club (**c**) *Fam (gente)* people
peñasco *nm* rock, crag
peñón *nm* rock; **el P. de Gibraltar** the Rock of Gibraltar
peón *nm* (**a**) unskilled labourer; **p. agrícola** farmhand (**b**) *(en ajedrez)* pawn
peonada *nf* day's work
peonza *nf* (spinning) top
peor **1** *adj* (**a**) *(comparativo)* worse (**b**) *(superlativo)* worst; **en el p. de los casos** if the worst comes to the worst; **lo p. es que** the worst of it is that
  2 *adv* (**a**) *(comparativo)* worse; **¡p. para mí/ti/etc.!** too bad! (**b**) *(superlativo)* worst
pepa *nf Col, Ven (carozo)* stone, *US* pit *(of fruit)*
pepenador,-a *nm,f CAm, Méx* scavenger *(on rubbish tip)*
pepián *nm CAm, Méx* = sauce thickened with ground nuts or seeds
pepinillo *nm* gherkin
pepino *nm* cucumber; *Fam* **me importa un p.** I don't give a hoot
pepita *nf (de fruta)* pip, seed; *(de metal)* nugget
pepitoria *nf* fricassee; **pollo en p.** fricassee of chicken
peque *nm Fam (niño)* kid
pequeño,-a **1** *adj* small, little; *(bajo)* short
  2 *nm,f* child; **de p.** as a child
Pequín *n* Peking
pera *nf* (**a**) *Bot* pear; **p. de agua** juicy pear (**b**) *CSur Fam (mentón)* chin
peral *nm* pear tree
percance *nm* mishap, setback
percatarse *vpr* **p. de** to realize
percepción *nf* perception
perceptible *adj* (**a**) perceptible (**b**) *Fin* receivable, payable
percha *nf (colgador)* (coat) hanger; *(de gallina)* perch
perchero *nm* clothes rack
percibir *vt* (**a**) *(notar)* to perceive, to notice (**b**) *(cobrar)* to receive
percusión *nf* percussion
perdedor,-a **1** *adj* losing
  2 *nm,f* loser
perder [3] **1** *vt* (**a**) to lose (**b**) *(tren, autobús)* to miss; *(tiempo)* to waste; *(oportunidad)* to miss (**c**) *(pervertir)* to be the ruin o downfall of

2 *vi* to lose; **echar (algo) a p.** to spoil (sth); **echarse a p.** to be spoilt; **salir perdiendo** to come off worst

3 perderse *vpr* (**a**) *(extraviarse) (persona)* to get lost; **se me ha perdido la llave** I've lost my key; **no te lo pierdas** don't miss it (**b**) *(pervertirse)* to go to rack and ruin

perdición *nf* undoing, downfall

pérdida *nf* (**a**) loss; **no tiene p.** you can't miss it (**b**) *(de tiempo, esfuerzos)* waste (**c**) *Mil* **pérdidas** losses

perdido,-a *adj* (**a**) *(extraviado)* lost (**b**) *Fam (sucio)* filthy (**c**) *Fam* **loco p.** mad as a hatter (**d**) **estar p. por algn** *(enamorado)* to be crazy about sb (**e**) *(acabado)* finished; **¡estoy p.!** I'm a goner!

perdigón *nm* pellet

perdiguero,-a *adj* partridge-hunting; **perro p.** setter

perdiz *nf* partridge

perdón *nm* pardon, forgiveness; **¡p.!** sorry!; **pedir p.** to apologize

perdonar *vt* (**a**) *(remitir)* to forgive (**b**) **¡perdone!** sorry!; **perdone que le moleste** sorry for bothering you (**c**) *(eximir)* to pardon; **perdonarle la vida a algn** to spare sb's life; **p. una deuda** to write off a debt

perdurable *adj* (**a**) *(eterno)* everlasting (**b**) *(duradero)* durable, long-lasting

perdurar *vi* (**a**) *(durar)* to endure, to last (**b**) *(persistir)* to persist, to continue to exist

perecedero,-a *adj* perishable; **artículos perecederos** perishables

perecer [33] *vi* to perish, to die

peregrinación *nf*, **peregrinaje** *nm* pilgrimage

peregrino,-a 1 *nm,f* pilgrim

2 *adj* **ideas peregrinas** crazy ideas

perejil *nm* parsley

perenne *adj* perennial, everlasting

perentorio,-a *adj* peremptory, urgent

pereza *nf* laziness, idleness

perezoso,-a *adj (vago)* lazy, idle

perfección *nf* perfection; **a la p.** to perfection

perfeccionamiento *nm* (**a**) *(acción)* perfecting (**b**) *(mejora)* improvement

perfeccionar *vt* to perfect; *(mejorar)* to improve, to make better

perfeccionista *adj & nmf* perfectionist

perfectamente *adv* perfectly; **¡p.!** *(de acuerdo)* agreed!, all right!

perfecto,-a *adj* perfect

perfidia *nf* perfidy, treachery

perfil *nm* (**a**) profile; *(contorno)* outline, contour; **de p.** in profile (**b**) *Geom* cross-section

perfilar 1 *vt (dar forma a)* to shape, to outline

2 perfilarse *vpr (tomar forma)* to take shape

perforación *nf*, **perforado** *nm* perforation; *Min* drilling, boring; *Informát (de tarjetas)* punching

perforadora *nf* punch; *Min* drill; *Informát* **p. de teclado** keypunch

perforar *vt* to perforate; *Min* to drill, to bore; *Informát* to punch

perfumar 1 *vt* to perfume

2 perfumarse *vpr* to put on perfume

perfume *nm* perfume, scent

pergamino *nm* parchment

pericia *nf* expertise, skill

periferia *nf* periphery; *(alrededores)* outskirts

periférico,-a 1 *adj* peripheral

2 *nm* (**a**) *Informát* peripheral (**b**) *CAm, Méx (carretera) Br* ring road, *US* beltway

perífrasis *nf inv* periphrasis, long-winded explanation

perilla *nf (barba)* goatee; *Fam* **de perilla(s)** *(oportuno)* at the right moment; *(útil)* very handy

perímetro *nm* perimeter

periódico,-a 1 *nm* newspaper

2 *adj* periodic(al); *Quím* **tabla periódica** periodic table

periodismo *nm* journalism

periodista *nmf* journalist, reporter

periodo, período *nm* period

peripecia *nf* sudden change, vicissitude

periplo *nm* voyage, tour

periquete *nm Fam* **en un p.** in a jiffy

periquito *nm* budgerigar, *Fam* budgie

periscopio *nm* periscope

peritaje *nm (estudios)* technical studies

perito,-a *nm,f* technician, expert; **p. industrial/agrónomo** ≃ industrial/agricultural expert

peritonitis *nf* peritonitis

perjudicar [44] *vt* to harm, to injure; *(intereses)* to prejudice

perjudicial *adj* prejudicial, harmful

perjuicio *nm* harm, damage; **en p. de** to the detriment of; **sin p. de** without prejudice to

perjurar *vi* to commit perjury

perjurio *nm* perjury

perla *nf* pearl; *Fig (persona)* gem, jewel; *Fam* **me viene de perlas** it's just the ticket

permanecer [33] *vi* to remain, to stay

permanencia *nf* (**a**) *(inmutabilidad)* permanence (**b**) *(estancia)* stay

permanente 1 *adj* permanent
    2 *nf (de pelo)* permanent wave, perm; **hacerse la p.** to have one's hair permed
permisivo,-a *adj* permissive
permiso *nm* (**a**) *(autorización)* permission (**b**) *(licencia)* licence, permit; **p. de conducir** *Br* driving licence, *US* driver's license; **p. de residencia/trabajo** residence/work permit (**c**) *Mil* leave; **estar de p.** to be on leave
permitir 1 *vt* to permit, to allow; **¿me permite?** may I?
    2 permitirse *vpr* (**a**) to permit o allow oneself; **me permito recordarle que** let me remind you that (**b**) **no se permite fumar** *(en letrero)* no smoking
permutar *vt* to exchange
pernicioso,-a *adj* pernicious
pernil *nm (de pantalón)* leg; *(jamón)* leg of pork
pernocta *nf Mil* **(pase de) p.** overnight pass
pero 1 *conj* but; **p., ¿qué pasa aquí?** now, what's going on here?
    2 *nm* objection
perogrullada *nf* truism, platitude
perol *nm* large saucepan, pot
perorata *nf* boring speech
perpendicular *adj & nf* perpendicular
perpetrar *vt* to perpetrate, to commit
perpetuar [30] *vt* to perpetuate
perpetuo,-a *adj* perpetual, everlasting; *Jur* **cadena perpetua** life imprisonment
perplejidad *nf* perplexity, bewilderment
perplejo,-a *adj* perplexed, bewildered
perra *nf* (**a**) bitch (**b**) *Fam (moneda)* penny; **estar sin una p.** to be broke
perrera *nf* kennel, kennels
perrería *nf Fam* dirty trick
perro,-a 1 *nm* dog; *Fam* **un día de perros** a lousy day; *Fam* **vida de perros** dog's life; *Culin* **p. caliente** hot dog
    2 *adj Fam (vago)* lazy
persecución *nf* (**a**) pursuit (**b**) *Pol (represión)* persecution
perseguir [6] *vt* (**a**) to pursue, to chase; *(correr trás)* to run after, to follow (**b**) *(reprimir)* to persecute
perseverante *adj* persevering
perseverar *vi* (**a**) to persevere, to persist (**b**) *(durar)* to last
persiana *nf* blinds
pérsico,-a *adj* Persian; **golfo P.** Persian Gulf
persignarse *vpr* to cross oneself
persistencia *nf* persistence
persistente *adj* persistent
persistir *vi* to persist

persona *nf* person; **algunas personas** some people; *Fam* **p. mayor** grown-up
personaje *nm* (**a**) *Cin, Lit & Teatro* character (**b**) *(celebridad)* celebrity, important person
personal 1 *adj* personal, private
    2 *nm* (**a**) *(plantilla)* staff, personnel (**b**) *Fam (gente)* people
personalidad *nf* personality
personarse *vpr* to present oneself, to appear in person
personero,-a *nm,f Am* representative
personificar [44] *vt* to personify
perspectiva *nf* (**a**) perspective (**b**) *(futuro)* prospect
perspicacia *nf* insight, perspicacity
perspicaz *adj* sharp, perspicacious
persuadir *vt* to persuade; **estar persuadido de que** to be convinced that
persuasión *nf* persuasion
persuasivo,-a *adj* persuasive, convincing
pertenecer [33] *vi* to belong (**a** to)
perteneciente *adj* belonging
pertenencia *nf* (**a**) possessions, property (**b**) *(a un partido etc)* affiliation, membership
pértiga *nf* pole; *Dep* **salto con p.** pole vault
pertinaz *adj* (**a**) persistent (**b**) *(obstinado)* obstinate, stubborn
pertinente *adj* (**a**) pertinent, relevant (**b**) *(apropiado)* appropriate
perturbación *nf* disturbance; **p. del orden público** breach of the peace; *Med* **p. mental** mental disorder
perturbado,-a *adj* (mentally) deranged o unbalanced
perturbador,-a 1 *adj* disturbing
    2 *nm,f* unruly person
perturbar *vt (el orden)* to disturb
Perú *n* Peru
peruano,-a *adj & nm,f* Peruvian
perversión *nf* perversion
perverso,-a *adj* perverse, evil
pervertir [5] *vt* to pervert, to corrupt
pervivir *vi* to survive
pesa *nf* weight; **levantamiento de pesas** weightlifting
pesadez *nf* (**a**) heaviness; *(de estómago)* fullness (**b**) *Fam (fastidio)* drag, nuisance
pesadilla *nf* nightmare; **de p.** nightmarish
pesado,-a 1 *adj* (**a**) heavy (**b**) *(aburrido)* tedious, dull; **¡qué p.!** what a drag!
    2 *nm,f* bore
pesadumbre *nf* grief, affliction
pésame *nm* condolences, sympathy; **dar**

el **p.** to offer one's condolences; **mi más sentido p.** my deepest sympathy
pesar 1 *vt* to weigh; *Fig (entristecer)* to grieve
  2 *vi* (**a**) to weigh; **¿cuánto pesas?** how much do you weigh? (**b**) *(ser pesado)* to be heavy (**c**) *Fig (tener importancia)* **este factor pesa mucho** this is a very important factor
  3 *nm* (**a**) *(pena)* sorrow, grief (**b**) *(arrepentimiento)* regret; **a su p.** to his regret (**c**) **a p. de** in spite of
pesaroso,-a *adj* (**a**) *(triste)* sorrowful, sad (**b**) *(arrepentido)* regretful, sorry
pesca *nf* fishing; *Fam* **y toda la p.** and all that
pescadería *nf* fish shop, fishmonger's (shop)
pescadero,-a *nm,f* fishmonger
pescadilla *nf* young hake
pescado *nm* fish
pescador,-a 1 *adj* fishing
  2 *nm,f (hombre)* fisherman; *(mujer)* fisherwoman
pescante *nm* (**a**) *(de carruaje)* coachman's seat (**b**) *Constr* jib, boom (**c**) *Náut* davit
pescar [44] 1 *vi* to fish
  2 *vt* (**a**) to fish (**b**) *Fam (coger)* to catch
pescozada *nf*, **pescozón** *nm* slap on the neck/head
pescuezo *nm Fam* neck
pese a (que) *loc adv* in spite of (the fact that)
pesebre *nm* manger, stall
pesero *nm CAm, Méx* fixed-rate taxi service
peseta *nf* peseta
pesetero,-a *nm,f* skinflint
pesimismo *nm* pessimism
pesimista 1 *adj* pessimistic
  2 *nmf* pessimist
pésimo,-a *adj* very bad, awful, terrible
peso *nm* (**a**) weight; **al p.** by weight; **p. bruto/neto** gross/net weight; *Fig* **me quité un p. de encima** it took a load off my mind; **p. mosca/pesado** *(en boxeo)* flyweight/heavyweight (**b**) *(importancia)* importance; **de p.** *(persona)* influential; *(razón)* convincing
pespunte *nm* backstitch
pesquero,-a 1 *adj* fishing
  2 *nm* fishing boat
pesquisa *nf* inquiry
pestaña *nf* (**a**) eyelash, lash (**b**) *Téc* flange; *(de neumático)* rim
pestañear *vi* to blink; **sin p.** without batting an eyelid

peste *nf* (**a**) *(hedor)* stench, stink (**b**) *Med* plague; *Hist* **la p. negra** the Black Death (**c**) **decir** *o* **echar pestes** to curse
pesticida *nm* pesticide
pestilencia *nf* stench, stink
pestilente *adj* stinking, foul
pestillo *nm* bolt, latch
petaca *nf* (**a**) *(para cigarrillos)* cigarette case; *(para bebidas)* flask (**b**) *Méx (maleta)* suitcase (**c**) *Méx* **petacas** *(nalgas)* buttocks
petaco *nm (de juego)* flipper; **máquina de petacos** pinball machine
pétalo *nm* petal
petardo *nm* (**a**) firecracker, firework; *Mil* petard (**b**) *Fam (persona aburrida)* bore (**c**) *(droga)* joint
petate *nm Mil* luggage
petición *nf* request; *Jur* petition, plea
petiso,-a *adj Andes, RP Fam* short
peto *nm* **pantalón de p.** dungarees
petrificar [44] *vt*, **petrificarse** *vpr* to petrify
petróleo *nm* petroleum, oil

> 🖊 Observa que en el inglés británico **petrol** es un falso amigo y no es la traducción de la palabra española **petróleo**. En inglés británico, **petrol** significa "gasolina".

petrolero *nm* oil tanker
petulante *adj* arrogant, vain

> 🖊 Observa que la palabra inglesa **petulant** es un falso amigo y no es la traducción de la palabra española **petulante**. En inglés, **petulant** significa "caprichoso".

petunia *nf* petunia
peyorativo,-a *adj* pejorative, derogatory
pez¹ *nm* fish; **ella está como p. en el agua** she's in her element; **p. gordo** big shot
pez² *nf* pitch, tar
pezón *nm* nipple
pezuña *nf* hoof
piadoso,-a *adj* (**a**) *(devoto)* pious (**b**) *(compasivo)* compassionate; **mentira piadosa** white lie
pianista *nmf* pianist, piano player
piano *nm* piano
piar [29] *vi* to chirp, to tweet
piara *nf* herd of pigs
PIB *nm Fin* (*abr* **producto interior bruto**) GDP
pibe,-a *nm,f Fam* (**a**) *(hombre)* guy; *(mujer)* girl (**b**) *RP (niño)* kid, boy; *(niña)* kid, girl
picada *nf RP (tapas)* appetizers, snacks
picadero *nm* riding school
picadillo *nm* (**a**) *(de carne)* *Br* minced *o*

US ground meat; *(de verduras)* vegetable salad (**b**) *Chile (tapas)* appetizers, snacks
picado,-a 1 *adj* (**a**) *(carne) Br* minced, *US* ground (**b**) *(fruta)* bad; *(diente)* decayed (**c**) *(mar)* choppy (**d**) *Fam (enfadado)* narked (**e**) **estar p. con** *(en competición)* to be at loggerheads with
2 *nm Av* dive; **caer en p.** to plummet
picador *nm Taurom* mounted bullfighter, picador
picadora *nf Br* mincer, *US* grinder
picadura *nf* (**a**) *(mordedura)* bite; *(de avispa, abeja)* sting (**b**) *(en fruta)* spot; *Med (de viruela)* pockmark; *(en diente)* decay, caries *sing; (en metalurgia)* pitting
picajoso,-a 1 *adj* touchy
2 *nm,f* touchy person
picante *adj* (**a**) *Culin* hot, spicy (**b**) *Fig (chiste etc)* risqué, spicy
picantería *nf Andes* cheap restaurant
picapica *nm* **(polvos de) p.** itching powder
picaporte *nm (aldaba)* door knocker; *(pomo)* door handle
picar [44] 1 *vt* (**a**) *(de insecto, serpiente)* to bite; *(de avispas, abejas)* to sting; *(barba)* to prick (**b**) *(comer) (aves)* to peck (at); *(persona)* to nibble, to pick at (**c**) *(de pez)* to bite (**d**) *(perforar)* to prick, to puncture (**e**) *Culin (carne) Br* to mince, *US* to grind (**f**) *(incitar)* to incite, to goad; **p. la curiosidad (de algn)** to arouse (sb's) curiosity
2 *vi* (**a**) *(escocer)* to itch; *(herida)* to smart; *(el sol)* to burn (**b**) *Culin* to be hot (**c**) *(pez)* to bite (**d**) *Fig (dejarse engañar)* to swallow it
3 picarse *vpr* (**a**) *(hacerse rivales)* to be at loggerheads (**b**) *(fruta)* to spot, to rot; *(ropa)* to become moth-eaten; *(dientes)* to decay (**c**) *(enfadarse)* to get cross (**d**) *(drogadicto)* to shoot up
picardía *nf* (**a**) *(astucia)* craftiness (**b**) *(palabrota)* swearword (**c**) *(prenda)* baby-doll pyjamas
pícaro,-a 1 *adj* (**a**) *(travieso)* naughty, mischievous; *(astuto)* sly, crafty (**b**) *(procaz)* risqué
2 *nm,f* rascal, rogue
picatoste *nm* crouton
pichi *nm Br* pinafore dress, *US* jumper
pichincha *nf RP Fam* snip, bargain
pichón *nm* young pigeon; **tiro al** *o* **de p.** pigeon shooting
pickles ['pikles] *nmpl RP* pickles
pico *nm* (**a**) *(de ave)* beak, bill; *Fam (boca)* mouth; **tener un p. de oro** to have the gift of the gab (**b**) *(punta)* corner (**c**) *Geog* peak (**d**) *(herramienta)* pick, pickaxe (**e**)

(cantidad) odd amount; **cincuenta y p.** fifty odd; **las dos y p.** just after two (**f**) *(drogas)* fix
picoleto *nm Fam* civil guard
picor *nm* itch, tingling
picoso,-a *adj Méx* spicy, hot
picotazo *nm* peck
picotear *vt & vi* (**a**) *(pájaro)* to peck (**b**) *(comer)* to nibble
pictórico,-a *adj* pictorial
pídola *nf* leapfrog
pie *nm* (**a**) *(de persona)* foot; **pies** feet; **a p.** on foot; **de p.** standing up; **de pies a cabeza** from head to foot; **en p.** standing; **el acuerdo sigue en p.** the agreement still stands; **hacer p.** to touch the bottom; **perder p.** to get out of one's depth; *Fig* **a pies juntillas** blindly; *Fig* **al p. de la letra** to the letter, word for word; *Fig* **con buen/mal p.** on the right/wrong footing; *Fig* **con pies de plomo** gingerly, cautiously; *Fig* **dar p. a** to give cause for (**b**) *(de instrumento)* stand; *(de copa)* stem (**c**) *(de página)* foot; *(de una ilustración)* caption; **p. de página** foot of the page (**d**) *(medida)* foot (**e**) *Teatro* cue (**f**) *Lit* foot
piedad *nf* (**a**) devoutness, piety (**b**) *(compasión)* compassion, pity
piedra *nf* stone; *(de mechero)* flint; **poner la primera p.** to lay the foundation stone; *Fam Fig* **me dejó** *o* **me quedé de p.** I was flabbergasted
piel *nf* (**a**) skin; **p. de gallina** goose pimples (**b**) *(de fruta, de patata)* skin, peel (**c**) *(cuero)* leather; *(con pelo)* fur
pienso *nm* fodder, feed; **piensos compuestos** mixed feed
pierna *nf* leg
pieza *nf* (**a**) piece, part; **p. de recambio** spare part; *Fig* **me dejó** *o* **me quedé de una p.** I was speechless *o* dumbfounded *o* flabbergasted (**b**) *(habitación)* room (**c**) *Teatro* play
pigmento *nm* pigment
pigmeo,-a 1 *adj* pigmy; *Fig* pygmean
2 *nm,f* Pygmy, Pigmy; *Fig* pygmy, pigmy
pijama *nm* pyjamas
pijo,-a *Fam* **1** *adj* posh; **un barrio p.** a posh area
2 *nm,f (chico)* poor little rich boy; *(chica)* poor little rich girl
3 *nm (pene)* willy
pila *nf* (**a**) *Elec* battery (**b**) *(montón)* pile, heap; *Fig* **una p. de** *(muchos)* piles *o* heaps *o* loads of (**c**) *(lavadero)* basin (**d**) *Fig* **nombre de p.** Christian name
pilar *nm* (**a**) *Arquit* pillar (**b**) *(fuente)* waterhole

píldora *nf* pill; **p. abortiva** morning-after pill; *Fig* **dorar la p. a algn** to butter sb up

pileta *nf* (**a**) *(pila)* sink (**b**) *Am (piscina)* swimming pool

pilila *nf Fam Br* willy, *US* peter

pillaje *nm* looting, pillage

pillar 1 *vt* (**a**) *(robar)* to plunder, to loot (**b**) *(coger)* to catch; *(alcanzar)* to catch up with; **lo pilló un coche** he was run over by a car (**c**) *Fam* to be; **me pilla un poco lejos** it's a bit far for *o* from me

2 pillarse *vpr* to catch; **p. un dedo/una mano** to catch one's finger/hand

pillo,-a 1 *adj* (**a**) *(travieso)* naughty (**b**) *(astuto)* sly, cunning

2 *nm,f* rogue

pilotar *vt Av* to pilot, to fly; *Aut* to drive; *Náut* to pilot, to steer

piloto *nm* (**a**) *Av & Náut* pilot; *Aut* driver; **piso p.** show flat; **programa p.** pilot programme (**b**) *(luz)* pilot lamp *o* light

piltrafa *nf* (**a**) *Fam* weakling; **estar hecho una p.** to be on one's last legs (**b**) *(desecho)* scraps

pimentón *nm* paprika, red pepper

pimienta *nf* pepper

pimiento *nm* *(fruto)* pepper; *(planta)* pimiento; **p. morrón** sweet pepper; *Fam* **me importa un p.** I don't give a damn, I couldn't care less

pimpollo *nm* (**a**) *Bot* shoot (**b**) *Fam (hombre)* handsome young man; *(mujer)* elegant young woman

pinacoteca *nf* art gallery

pináculo *nm* pinnacle

pinar *nm* pine grove, pine wood

pincel *nm* brush, paintbrush

pincelada *nf* brushstroke, stroke of a brush

pinchadiscos *nmf inv Fam* disc jockey, DJ

pinchar 1 *vt* (**a**) *(punzar)* to prick; *(balón, globo)* to burst; *(rueda)* to puncture (**b**) *Fam (incitar)* to prod; *(molestar)* to get at, to nag (**c**) *Med* to inject, to give an injection to (**d**) *Tel* to bug

2 *vi* (**a**) *Aut* to get a puncture (**b**) *Fam* **ni pincha ni corta** he cuts no ice

> ♪ Observa que el verbo inglés **to pinch** es un falso amigo y no es la traducción del verbo español **pinchar**. En inglés, **to pinch** significa "pellizcar".

pinchazo *nm* (**a**) *(punzadura)* prick; *Aut* puncture, blowout (**b**) *(de dolor)* sudden *o* sharp pain

pinche *nm* (**a**) **p. de cocina** kitchen assistant (**b**) *Am (bribón)* rogue

pinchito *nm (de carne)* = type of kebab

pincho *nm* (**a**) *(púa)* barb (**b**) **p. moruno** ≃ shish kebab; **p. de tortilla** = small portion of omelette

ping-pong® *nm* table tennis, ping-pong

pingüe *adj* abundant, plentiful; **pingües beneficios** fat profits

pingüino *nm* penguin

pino *nm* pine; *Fig* **hacer el p.** to do a handstand; *Fam* **en el quinto p.** in the back of beyond

pinole *nm Am* maize *o US* corn drink

pinta 1 *nf* (**a**) *Fam (aspecto)* look; **tiene p. de ser interesante** it looks interesting (**b**) *(mota)* dot; *(lunar)* spot (**c**) *(medida)* pint

2 *nmf Fam* shameless person

pintada *nf* graffiti

pintado,-a *adj* **recién p.** *(en letrero)* wet paint; *Fam Fig* **nos viene que ni p.** it is just the ticket; *Fam Fig* **te está que ni p.** it suits you to a tee

pintar 1 *vt* (**a**) *(dar color)* to paint (**b**) *(dibujar)* to draw, to sketch

2 *vi (importar)* to count; *Fig* **yo aquí no pinto nada** I am out of place here

3 pintarse *vpr* (**a**) *(maquillarse)* to put make-up on (**b**) *Fam* **pintárselas** to manage

pintarraj(e)ar *vt* to daub

pintor,-a *nm,f* painter

pintoresco,-a *adj* (**a**) *(lugar)* picturesque (**b**) *(raro)* eccentric, bizarre

pintura *nf* (**a**) painting; **p. rupestre** cave painting; *Fam Fig* **no la puedo ver ni en p.** I can't stand the sight of her (**b**) *(materia)* paint

pinza *nf (para depilar)* tweezers; *(para tender)* *Br* clothes peg, *US* clothespin; *(de animal)* pincer, nipper; *Téc* tongs

piña *nf* (**a**) *(de pino)* pine cone; *(ananás)* pineapple (**b**) *Fig (grupo)* clan, clique (**c**) *Fam (golpe)* thump

piñón *nm* (**a**) pine seed *o* nut (**b**) *Téc* pinion

pío¹ *nm Fam* **no dijo ni p.** there wasn't a cheep out of him

pío²,-a *adj* pious

piojo *nm* louse

piola *adj RP Fam* (**a**) *(simpático)* fun (**b**) *Irón (listo)* smart, clever (**c**) *(lugar)* cosy

piolín *nm Am* cord

pionero,-a *nm,f* pioneer

pipa *nf* (**a**) *(de fumar)* pipe; **fumar en p.** to smoke a pipe (**b**) *(de fruta)* pip; *(de girasol)* sunflower seed

pipí *nm Fam* pee, *Br* wee-wee; **hacer p.** to pee, *Br* to wee-wee

pique *nm* (**a**) resentment (**b**) *(rivalidad)* needle (**c**) **a p. de** on the point of (**d**) **irse**

a p. *Náut* to sink; *(un plan)* to fall through; *(un negocio)* to go bust

piqueta *nf* pickaxe

piquete *nm* (**a**) *(de huelga)* picket (**b**) *Mil* **p. de ejecución** firing squad

pira *nf* pyre

pirado,-a *adj Fam* crazy

piragua *nf* canoe

piragüismo *nm* canoeing

piragüista *nmf* canoeist

pirámide *nf* pyramid

piraña *nf* piranha

pirarse, pirárselas *vpr Fam* to clear off, to hop it

pirata *adj & nmf* pirate

piratear *vt Fig* to pirate

Pirineo(s) *nm(pl)* Pyrenees

pirita *nf* pyrite

pirómano,-a *nm,f Med* pyromaniac; *Jur* arsonist

piropo *nm* **echar un p.** to pay a compliment

pirueta *nf* pirouette; *Fig Pol* **hacer una p.** to do a U-turn

pirulí *nm* lollipop; *TV* television tower

pis *nm Fam* pee, *Br* wee-wee; **hacer p.** to have a pee, *Br* to wee-wee

pisada *nf* step, footstep; *(huella)* footprint

pisapapeles *nm inv* paperweight

pisar *vt* to tread on, to step on

piscifactoría *nf* fish farm

piscina *nf* swimming pool

pisco *nm* pisco, = Andean grape brandy

piscolabis *nm inv Fam* snack

piso *nm* (**a**) apartment, *Br* flat; *Pol* **p. franco** safe house (**b**) *(planta)* floor; *(de carretera)* surface

pisotear *vt (aplastar)* to stamp on; *(pisar)* to trample on

pisotón *nm* **me dio un p.** he stood on my foot

pista *nf* (**a**) track; **p. de baile** dance floor; *Dep* **p. de esquí** ski run *o* slope; *Dep* **p. de patinaje** ice rink; *Dep* **p. de tenis** tennis court; **p. de aterrizaje** landing strip; **p. de despegue** runway (**b**) *(rastro)* trail, track (**c**) **dame una p.** give me a clue

pistacho *nm* pistachio nut

pisto *nm Culin* ≃ ratatouille

pistola *nf* (**a**) gun, pistol (**b**) *(para pintar)* spray gun

pistolero *nm* gunman, gangster

pistón *nm* (**a**) *Téc (émbolo)* piston (**b**) *(de arma)* cartridge cap (**c**) *Mús* key

pita *nf* agave

pitada *nf* (**a**) *(silbidos de protesta)* booing, whistling (**b**) *Am Fam (calada)* drag, puff

pitar 1 *vt* (**a**) *(silbato)* to blow (**b**) *Dep* **el árbitro pitó un penalti** the referee awarded a penalty

2 *vi* (**a**) to whistle (**b**) *Aut* to toot one's horn (**c**) *Dep* to referee (**d**) *Fam* **salir pitando** to fly off

pitido *nm* whistle

pitillera *nf* cigarette case

pitillo *nm* (**a**) *(cigarrillo)* cigarette (**b**) *Col (paja)* drinking straw

pito *nm* (**a**) whistle; *Aut* horn; *Fam* **me importa un p.** I don't give a hoot (**b**) *Fam (cigarrillo)* fag (**c**) *Fam (pene)* prick, willie

pitón *nm* (**a**) *(serpiente)* python (**b**) *(de toro)* horn

pitorreo *nm Fam* scoffing, teasing; **hacer algo de p.** to do sth for a laugh

pivot, pivote *nmf* pivot

pizarra *nf* (**a**) *(encerado)* blackboard (**b**) *(roca, material)* slate

pizarrón *nm Am (encerado)* blackboard

pizca *nf* little bit, tiny piece; **ni p.** not a bit; **una p. de sal** a pinch of salt

placa *nf* (**a**) plate (**b**) *(conmemorativa)* plaque

placaje *nm Dep* tackle

placentero,-a *adj* pleasant, agreeable

placer [33] 1 *vt* to please

2 *nm* pleasure; **ha sido un p. (conocerle)** it's been a pleasure (meeting you); *Fml* **tengo el p. de** it gives me great pleasure to; **un viaje de p.** a holiday trip

placidez *nf* placidity

plácido,-a *adj* placid, easy-going

plaga *nf* (**a**) plague (**b**) *Agr* pest, blight

plagar [42] *vt* to cover, to fill

plagiar [43] *vt* (**a**) *(copiar)* to plagiarize (**b**) *Andes, CAm, Méx (secuestrar)* to kidnap

plagiario,-a *nm,f Andes, CAm, Méx (secuestrador)* kidnapper

plagio *nm* plagiarism

plan *nm* (**a**) *(proyecto)* plan (**b**) *(programa)* scheme, programme; *Educ* **p. de estudios** syllabus; **estar a p.** to be on a diet (**c**) *Fam* **en p. de broma** for a laugh; **si te pones en ese p.** if you're going to be like that (about it); **en p. barato** cheaply (**d**) *Fam (cita)* date

plana *nf* (**a**) page; **a toda p.** full page; **primera p.** front page (**b**) *Mil* **p. mayor** staff

plancha *nf* (**a**) iron; *(de metal)* plate (**b**) *Culin* hotplate; **sardinas a la p.** grilled sardines (**c**) *Impr* plate

planchado *nm* ironing

planchar *vt* to iron

planchazo *nm Fam* blunder, boob
planeador *nm* glider
planear 1 *vt* to plan
  2 *vi* to glide
planeta *nm* planet
planetario,-a 1 *adj* planetary
  2 *nm* planetarium
planicie *nf* plain
planificación *nf* planning; **p. familiar** family planning
planificar [44] *vt* to plan
planilla *nf Am* application form
plano,-a 1 *nm* (**a**) *(de ciudad)* map; *Arquit* plan, draft (**b**) *Cin* shot; **un primer p.** a close-up; *Fig* **estar en primer/segundo p.** to be in the limelight/in the background (**c**) *Mat* plane
  2 *adj* flat, even
planta *nf* (**a**) plant (**b**) *(del pie)* sole (**c**) *(piso)* floor, storey; **p. baja** *Br* ground floor, *US* first floor
plantación *nf* (**a**) plantation (**b**) *(acción)* planting
plantado,-a *adj Fam* **dejar a algn p.** to stand sb up
plantar 1 *vt* (**a**) *(árboles, campo)* to plant (**b**) *(poner)* to put, to place; **p. cara a algn** to stand up to sb (**c**) *Fam* **p. a algn en la calle** to throw sb out; **le ha plantado su novia** his girlfriend has ditched him
  2 plantarse *upr* (**a**) to stand (**b**) *(llegar)* to arrive; **en cinco minutos se plantó aquí** he got here in five minutes flat
planteamiento *nm (enfoque)* approach
plantear 1 *vt* (**a**) *(problema)* to pose, to raise (**b**) *(planear)* to plan (**c**) *(proponer)* to put forward (**d**) *(exponer)* to present
  2 plantearse *upr* (**a**) *(considerar)* to consider (**b**) *(problema)* to arise
plantel *nm Fig* cadre, clique
plantilla *nf* (**a**) *(personal)* staff, personnel (**b**) *(de zapato)* insole (**c**) *(patrón)* model, pattern
plantón *nm Fam* **dar un p. a algn** to stand sb up
plañir *vi* to mourn
plasmar 1 *vt* (**a**) *(reproducir)* to capture (**b**) *(expresar)* to express
  2 plasmarse *upr* **p. en** to take the shape of
plasta *nmf Fam* bore
plástico,-a 1 *adj* plastic
  2 *nm* (**a**) plastic (**b**) *(disco)* record
plastificar [44] *vt* to coat *o* cover with plastic
plastilina® *nf* Plasticine®
plata *nf* (**a**) silver; *(objetos de plata)* silverware; *Fam* **hablar en p.** to lay (it) on

the line; **p. de ley** sterling silver (**b**) *Am* money
plataforma *nf* platform
plátano *nm* (**a**) *(fruta)* banana (**b**) *(árbol)* plane tree; **falso p.** sycamore
platea *nf Cin & Teatro Br* stalls, *US* orchestra
platear *vt* to silver-plate
platense 1 *adj* of/from the River Plate
  2 *nmf* person from the River Plate
plática *nf CAm, Méx* chat, talk
platicar [44] *vi CAm, Méx* to chat, to talk
platillo *nm* (**a**) saucer; **p. volante** flying saucer (**b**) *Mús* cymbal
platina *nf (de tocadiscos)* deck; **doble p.** double deck
platino *nm* (**a**) platinum (**b**) *Aut* **platinos** contact breaker, points
plato *nm* (**a**) plate, dish (**b**) *(parte de una comida)* course; **de primer p.** for starters; **p. fuerte** main course; **p. combinado** one-course meal (**c**) *(guiso)* dish (**d**) *(de balanza)* pan, tray (**e**) *(de tocadiscos)* turntable
plató *nm Cin & TV* (film) set
platudo,-a *adj Am Fam* loaded, rolling in it
plausible *adj* (**a**) *(admisible)* plausible, acceptable (**b**) *(loable)* commendable
playa *nf* (**a**) beach; *(costa)* seaside (**b**) *Am* **p. de estacionamiento** *Br* car park, *US* parking lot
playera *nf* (**a**) *(zapatilla) Br* sandshoe, *US* sneaker (**b**) *Méx (camiseta)* teeshirt
plaza *nf* (**a**) square (**b**) *(mercado)* market, marketplace (**c**) *Aut* seat (**d**) *(laboral)* post, position (**e**) **p. de toros** bullring
plazo *nm* (**a**) *(periodo)* time, period; *(término)* deadline; **a corto/largo p.** in the short term/in the long run; **el p. termina el viernes** Friday is the deadline (**b**) *Fin* **comprar a plazos** to buy on *Br* hire purchase *o US* an installment plan; **en seis plazos** in six instalments
pleamar *nf* high tide
plebe *nf* masses, plebs
plebeyo,-a 1 *adj* plebeian
  2 *nm,f* plebeian, pleb
plebiscito *nm* plebiscite
plegable *adj* folding, collapsible
plegar [1] **1** *vt* to fold
  2 plegarse *upr* to give way, to bow
plegaria *nf* prayer
pleitear *vi* to conduct a lawsuit, to plead
pleito *nm* (**a**) *Jur* lawsuit, litigation; **poner un p. (a algn)** to sue (sb) (**b**) *Am (discusión)* argument
plenilunio *nm* full moon

plenitud *nf* plenitude, fullness; **en la p. de la vida** in the prime of life

pleno,-a 1 *adj* full; **en plena noche** in the middle of the night; **los empleados en p.** the entire staff

2 *nm* plenary meeting

pletórico,-a *adj* abundant

plexiglás® *nm* (*plástico*) Perspex®, *US* Plexiglass®

pliego *nm* (**a**) (*hoja*) sheet *o* piece of paper; **p. de condiciones** bidding specifications (**b**) (*carta*) sealed letter

pliegue *nm* (**a**) fold (**b**) (*de vestido*) pleat

plinto *nm Dep* horse

plisar *vt* to pleat

plomería *nf Méx, RP, Ven* plumber's

plomero *nm Méx, RP, Ven* plumber

plomizo,-a *adj* lead, leaden; (*color*) lead-coloured

plomo *nm* (**a**) (*en metalurgia*) lead (**b**) *Elec* (*fusible*) fuse (**c**) (*bala*) slug, pellet

pluma *nf* (**a**) feather (**b**) (*estilográfica*) fountain pen (**c**) *Carib, Méx* (*bolígrafo*) (ballpoint) pen

plumaje *nm* plumage

plumazo *nm* **de un p.** at a stroke

plumero *nm* (**a**) (*para el polvo*) feather duster (**b**) *Fam* **se te ve el p.** I can see through you

plumier *nm* pencil box

plural *adj & nm* plural

pluralismo *nm* pluralism

pluriempleo *nm* moonlighting

plus *nm* bonus, bonus payment

plusmarca *nf* record

plusmarquista *nmf* record breaker

plusvalía *nf* capital gain

Plza. (*abr* **Plaza**) Sq

población *nf* (**a**) (*ciudad*) town; (*pueblo*) village (**b**) (*habitantes*) population (**c**) *Chile* (*barrio*) **p. (callampa)** shanty town

poblado,-a *adj* (**a**) populated; *Fig* **p. de** full of (**b**) (*barba*) bushy, thick

poblador,-a *nm,f* settler

poblar [2] *vt* (**a**) (*con gente*) to settle, to people; (*con plantas*) to plant (**b**) (*vivir*) to inhabit

pobre 1 *adj* poor; ¡**p.!** poor thing!; **un hombre p.** a poor man; **un p. hombre** a poor devil

2 *nmf* poor person; **los pobres** the poor

pobreza *nf* poverty; *Fig* (*de medios, recursos*) lack

pocho,-a *adj* (**a**) (*fruta*) bad, overripe (**b**) *Fig* (*persona*) (*débil*) off-colour; (*triste*) depressed, down (**c**) *Méx Fam* (*americanizado*) Americanized

pochoclo *nm Arg* popcorn

pocilga *nf* pigsty

pocillo *nm RP* (**a**) (*pequeño*) small cup (**b**) *Méx, Ven* (*grande*) enamel mug

pócima, poción *nf* potion; *Pey* concoction, brew

poco,-a 1 *nm* (**a**) **un p.** (*con adj o adv*) a little; **un p. tarde/frío** a little late/cold

(**b**) **un p.** (*con sustantivo*) a little; **un p. de azúcar** a little sugar

2 *adj* (**a**) not much, little; **p. sitio/tiempo** not much *o* little space/time; **poca cosa** not much

(**b**) **pocos,-as** not many, few; **pocas personas** not many *o* few people

(**c**) **unos,-as pocos,-as** a few

3 *pron* (**a**) (*escasa cantidad*) not much; **queda p.** there isn't much left

(**b**) (*breve tiempo*) **p. antes/después** shortly *o* a little before/afterwards; **a p. de** shortly *o* a little after; **dentro de p.** soon

(**c**) **pocos,-as** (*cosas*) few, not many; **tengo muy pocos** I have very few, I don't have very many

(**d**) **pocos,-as** (*personas*) few people, not many people; **vinieron pocos** few people came, not many people came

4 *adv* (**a**) (*con verbo*) not (very) much, little; **ella come p.** she doesn't eat much, she eats little

(**b**) (*con adj*) not very; **es p. probable** it's not very likely

(**c**) (*en frases*) **p. a p.** little by little, gradually; **por p.** almost

podadera, *Am* **podadora** *nf* garden shears

podar *vt* to prune

poder[1] *nm* power; *Econ* **p. adquisitivo** purchasing power

poder[2] **[18] 1** *vi* (**a**) (*capacidad*) to be able to; **no puede hablar** she can't speak; **no podré llamarte** I won't be able to phone; **no puedo más** I can't take any more; **guapa a más no p.** unbelievably pretty

(**b**) (*permiso*) may, might; ¿**puedo pasar?** can *o* may I come in?; ¿**se puede (entrar)?** may I (come in)?; **aquí no se puede fumar** you can't smoke here

(**c**) (*uso impers*) (*posibilidad*) may, might; **puede que no lo sepan** they may *o* might not know; **no puede ser** that's impossible; **puede (ser) (que sí)** maybe, perhaps

(**d**) (*deber*) **podrías haberme advertido** you might have warned me

(**e**) to cope (**con** with); **no puede con**

tanto trabajo he can't cope with so much work

  2 *vt (batir)* to be stronger than; **les puede a todos** he can take on anybody

poderoso,-a *adj* powerful

podio, pódium *nm Dep* podium

podré *indic fut de* **poder**

podrido,-a *adj* (**a**) *(putrefacto)* rotten, putrid (**b**) *(corrupto)* corrupt; *Fam* **p. de dinero** *o Am* **en plata** stinking rich (**c**) *RP Fam (harto)* fed up, sick

podrir *vt defect* = **pudrir**

poema *nm* poem

poesía *nf* (**a**) *(género)* poetry (**b**) *(poema)* poem

poeta *nmf* poet

poético,-a *adj* poetic

póker *nm* poker

polaco,-a 1 *adj* Polish

  2 *nm,f* Pole

  3 *nm (idioma)* Polish

polaridad *nf* polarity

polarizar [40] *vt* (**a**) *Fís* to polarize (**b**) *Fig (ánimo, atención)* to concentrate

polea *nf* pulley

polémica *nf* controversy

polémico,-a *adj* controversial

polemizar [40] *vi* to argue, to debate

polen *nm* pollen

polera *nf RP* polo shirt

poli *Fam* **1** *nmf* cop

  2 *nf* **la p.** the fuzz *pl*

poli- *pref* poly-

policía 1 *nf* police (force)

  2 *nmf (hombre)* policeman; *(mujer)* policewoman

policíaco,-a, policiaco,-a, policial *adj* police; **novela/película policíaca** detective story/film

polideportivo *nm* sports centre

poliéster *nm* polyester

polietileno *nm Br* polythene, *US* polyethylene

polifacético,-a *adj* versatile, many-sided; **es un hombre muy p.** he's a man of many talents

poligamia *nf* polygamy

políglota *adj & nmf* polyglot

polígono *nm* polygon; **p. industrial** industrial estate

polilla *nf* moth

poliomielitis *nf* polio, poliomyelitis

politécnico,-a *adj & nm* polytechnic

política *nf* (**a**) politics *sing* (**b**) *(estrategia)* policy

políticamente *adv* **p. correcto** politically correct

político,-a 1 *adj* (**a**) political (**b**)

(pariente) in-law; **hermano p.** brother-in-law; **su familia política** her in-laws

  2 *nm,f* politician

póliza *nf* (**a**) *(sello)* stamp (**b**) **p. de seguros** insurance policy

polizón *nm* stowaway

polla *nf* (**a**) *Vulg (pene)* prick (**b**) *Orn* **p. de agua** moorhen

pollera *nf* (**a**) *RP (occidental)* skirt (**b**) *Andes (indígena)* = long skirt worn by Indian women

pollo *nm* (**a**) chicken (**b**) *Fam (joven)* lad

polo *nm* (**a**) *Elec & Geog* pole; **P. Norte/ Sur** North/South Pole (**b**) *(helado) Br* ice lolly, *US* Popsicle® (**c**) *(prenda)* sports shirt, polo neck (sweater) (**d**) *Dep* polo

pololear *vi Chile Fam* to go out (together)

pololo,-a *nm,f Chile Fam* boyfriend, *f* girlfriend

Polonia *n* Poland

poltrona *nf* easy chair

polución *nf* pollution

polvareda *nf* cloud of dust

polvera *nf* powder compact

polvo *nm* (**a**) dust; **limpiar** *o* **quitar el p.** to dust; **en p.** powdered; **polvo(s) de talco** talcum powder (**b**) *Fam* **estar hecho p.** *(cansado)* to be *Br* knackered *o US* bushed; *(deprimido)* to be depressed (**c**) *muy Fam* **echar un p.** to have a screw

pólvora *nf* gunpowder

polvoriento,-a *adj* dusty

polvorín *nm* gunpowder arsenal; *Fig* powder keg

polvorón *nm* sweet pastry

pomada *nf* ointment

pomelo *nm (fruto)* grapefruit; *(árbol)* grapefruit tree

pómez *adj inv* **piedra p.** pumice (stone)

pomo *nm (de puerta)* knob

pompa *nf* (**a**) bubble (**b**) *(ostentación)* pomp (**c**) *Méx Fam* **pompas** botty

pompis *nm inv Fam* botty

pomposo,-a *adj* pompous

pómulo *nm* cheekbone

ponchar 1 *vt* (**a**) *CAm, Carib, Méx (rueda)* to puncture (**b**) *Am (en béisbol)* to strike out

  2 poncharse *vpr* (**a**) *CAm, Carib, Méx (rueda)* to get a puncture (**b**) *Am (en béisbol)* to strike out

ponche *nm* punch

poncho *nm* poncho

ponderar *vt* (**a**) *(asunto)* to weigh up *o* consider (**b**) *(alabar)* to praise

pondré *indic fut de* **poner**

ponencia *nf* paper

poner [19] (*pp* **puesto**) **1** *vt* (**a**) to put;
(*mesa, huevo*) to lay; (*gesto*) to make;
(*multa*) to impose; (*telegrama*) to send;
(*negocio*) to set up
  (**b**) (*tele, radio etc*) to turn *o* switch on
  (**c**) (*+ adj*) to make; **p. triste a algn** to
make sb sad; **p. colorado a algn** to make
sb blush
  (**d**) **¿qué llevaba puesto?** what was he
wearing?
  (**e**) (*decir*) **¿qué pone aquí?** what does it
say here?
  (**f**) (*suponer*) to suppose; **pongamos que
Ana no viene** supposing Ana doesn't turn
up
  (**g**) *TV & Cin* to put on, to show; **¿qué
ponen en la tele?** what's on the telly?
  (**h**) *Tel* **ponme con Manuel** put me
through to Manuel
  (**i**) (*nombrar*) **le pondremos (de nombre)
Pilar** we are going to call her Pilar
2 *v impers Am Fam* (*parecer*) **se me pone
que ...** it seems to me that ...
3 ponerse *vpr* (**a**) to put oneself; **ponte
en mi lugar** put yourself in my place;
ponte más cerca come closer
  (**b**) (*vestirse*) to put on; **ella se puso el
jersey** she put her sweater on
  (**c**) (*+ adj*) to become; **p. furioso/malo**
to become furious/ill
  (**d**) (*sol*) to set
  (**e**) *Tel* **p. al teléfono** to answer the
phone
  (**f**) **p. a** to start to; **p. a trabajar** to get
down to work
poney *nm* pony
pongo *indic pres de* **poner**
poniente *nm* (**a**) (*occidente*) West (**b**)
(*viento*) westerly (wind)
ponqué *nm Col,Ven* = large sponge cake,
filled with cream and/or fruit, and covered in icing or chocolate
pontífice *nm* Pontiff; **el Sumo P.** His Holiness the Pope
ponzoña *nf* (**a**) venom, poison (**b**) **tener
p.** (*tristeza*) to be down in the dumps
ponzoñoso,-a *adj* (**a**) venomous, poisonous (**b**) (*triste*) down in the dumps
popa *nf* stern; *Fig* **ir viento en p.** to go full
speed ahead
popote *nm Méx* drinking straw
populacho *nm Pey* plebs, masses
popular *adj* (**a**) folk; **arte/música p.** folk
art/music (**b**) (*medida*) popular (**c**) (*actor*) well-known
popularidad *nf* popularity
popularizar [40] *vt* to popularize
populoso,-a *adj* densely populated

popurrí *nm Mús* medley
póquer *nm* poker
por *prep* (**a**) (*agente*) by; **pintado p. Picasso** painted by Picasso
  (**b**) **p. qué** why
  (**c**) (*causa*) because of; **p. sus ideas**
because of her ideas; **p. necesidad/amor**
out of need/love; **suspendió p. no estudiar** he failed because he didn't study
  (**d**) (*tiempo*) **p. la mañana/noche** in the
morning/at night; **p. ahora** for the time
being; **p. entonces** at that time
  (**e**) (*en favor de*) for; **lo hago p. mi
hermano** I'm doing it for my brother('s
sake)
  (**f**) (*lugar*) **pasamos p. Córdoba** we went
through Córdoba; **p. ahí** over there; **¿p.
dónde vamos?** which way are we taking *o*
going?; **p. la calle** in the street; **mirar p. la
ventana** to look out the window; **entrar p.
la ventana** to get in through the window
  (**g**) (*medio*) by; **p. avión/correo** by
plane/post
  (**h**) (*a cambio de*) for; **cambiar algo p.
otra cosa** to exchange sth for something
else
  (**i**) (*distributivo*) **p. cabeza** a head, per
person; **p. hora/mes** per hour/month
  (**j**) *Mat* **dos p. tres, seis** two times three is
six; **un 10 p. ciento** 10 percent
  (**k**) (*con infinitivo*) in order to, so as to;
hablar p. hablar to talk for the sake of it
  (**l**) (*locuciones*) **p. así decirlo** so to
speak; **p. más** *o* **muy ... que sea** no matter
how ... he/she is; **p. mí** as far as I'm
concerned
porcelana *nf* porcelain
porcentaje *nm* percentage
porche *nm* porch
porcino,-a *adj* **ganado p.** pigs
porción *nf* portion, part
pordiosero,-a *nm,f* tramp, *US* bum
porfía *nf* (*obstinación*) obstinacy, stubbornness
porfolio *nm* portfolio
pormenor *nm* detail; **venta al p.** retail
porno *adj inv Fam* porn
pornografía *nf* pornography
pornográfico,-a *adj* pornographic
poro *nm* pore
poroso,-a *adj* porous
poroto *nm RP* (*judía*) kidney bean
porque *conj* (**a**) (*causal*) because; **¡p. no!**
just because! (**b**) (*final*) (*+ subjunctive*)
so that, in order that
porqué *nm* reason
porquería *nf* (**a**) (*suciedad*) dirt, filth (**b**)
(*birria*) *Br* rubbish, *US* garbage (**c**) *Fam*

(chuchería) junk food, *Br* rubbish
porra *nf* (**a**) *(de policía)* truncheon, baton (**b**) *Fam (locuciones)* ¡una **p.**! *Br* rubbish!, *US* garbage!; ¡vete a la **p.**! get lost!
porrazo *nm* thump
porro *nm* (**a**) *Fam (de droga)* joint (**b**) *Am (puerro)* leek
porrón *nm* = glass bottle with a spout coming out of its base, used for drinking wine
portaaviones *nm inv* aircraft carrier
portada *nf* (**a**) *(de libro etc)* cover; *(de periódico)* front page; *(de disco)* sleeve (**b**) *(fachada)* front, facade
portador,-a *nm,f Com* bearer; *Med* carrier
portaequipajes *nm inv* (**a**) *Aut (maletero) Br* boot, *US* trunk; *(baca)* roof rack (**b**) *(carrito)* luggage trolley
portafolios *nm inv* briefcase
portal *nm* (**a**) *(zaguán)* porch, entrance hall (**b**) *(puerta de la calle)* main door (**c**) **p. de Belén** Nativity scene (**d**) *Informát* portal
portamaletas *nm inv* = **portaequipajes**
portaminas *nm inv* propelling pencil
portamonedas *nm inv* purse
portarse *vpr* to behave; **p. mal** to misbehave
portátil *adj* portable
portaviones *nm inv* = **portaaviones**
portavoz *nmf* spokesperson; *(hombre)* spokesman; *(mujer)* spokeswoman
portazo *nm* oímos un **p.** we heard a slam *o* bang; **dar un p.** to slam the door
porte *nm* (**a**) *(aspecto)* bearing (**b**) *(transporte)* carriage
portento *nm* (**a**) *(cosa)* wonder, marvel (**b**) *(persona)* genius
portentoso,-a *adj* extraordinary, prodigious
porteño,-a **1** *adj* of/from Buenos Aires **2** *nm,f* person from Buenos Aires
portería *nf* (**a**) porter's lodge (**b**) *Dep* goal
portero,-a *nm,f* (**a**) *(de vivienda)* porter, caretaker; **p. automático** Entryphone® (**b**) *Dep* goalkeeper
pórtico *nm* (**a**) *(portal)* portico, porch (**b**) *(con arcadas)* arcade
portorriqueño,-a *adj & nm,f* Puerto Rican
portuario,-a *adj* harbour, port
Portugal *n* Portugal
portugués,-esa **1** *adj* Portuguese **2** *nm (idioma)* Portuguese
porvenir *nm* future; **sin p.** with no prospects

pos *adv* en **p. de** after
pos- *pref* post-
posada *nf* inn
posaderas *nfpl Fam* buttocks
posadero,-a *nm,f* innkeeper
posar **1** *vi (para retrato etc)* to pose **2** *vt* to put *o* lay down **3 posarse** *vpr* to settle, to alight
posdata *nf* postscript
pose *nf* (**a**) *(postura)* pose (**b**) *(afectación)* posing
poseedor,-a *nm,f* possessor
poseer [36] *vt* to possess, to own
poseído,-a *adj* possessed
posesión *nf* possession; **estar en p. de** to have; **tomar p. (de un cargo)** to take up (a post)
posesivo,-a *adj* possessive
poseso,-a *adj & nm,f* possessed
posguerra *nf* postwar period
posibilidad *nf* possibility; *(oportunidad)* chance
posibilitar *vt* to make possible
posible **1** *adj* possible; **de ser p.** if possible; **en (la medida de) lo p.** as far as possible; **haré todo lo p.** I'll do everything I can; **lo antes p.** as soon as possible; **es p. que venga** he might come **2** *nmpl* **posibles** means
posición *nf* position
positivo,-a *adj* positive
posmoderno,-a *adj* postmodern
poso *nm* dregs, sediment
posponer [19] *vt* (**a**) *(aplazar)* to postpone, to put off (**b**) *(relegar)* to put in second place *o* behind, to relegate
post- *pref* post-
posta *nf* a **p.** on purpose
postal **1** *adj* postal **2** *nf* postcard
poste *nm* pole; *Dep (de portería)* post
póster *nm* poster
postergar [42] *vt* (**a**) *(relegar)* to relegate (**b**) *(retrasar)* to delay; *(aplazar)* to postpone
posteridad *nf* posterity; **pasar a la p.** to go down in history
posterior *adj* (**a**) *(lugar)* posterior, rear (**b**) *(tiempo)* later (**a** than), subsequent (**a** to)
posterioridad *nf* posteriority; **con p.** later
posteriormente *adv* subsequently, later
postgraduado,-a *adj & nm,f* postgraduate
postigo *nm* *(de puerta)* wicket; *(de ventana)* shutter
postín *nm Fam* boasting, showing off;

darse p. to show off, to swank; **de p.** posh, swanky
postizo,-a 1 *adj* false, artificial; **dentadura postiza** false teeth, dentures
2 *nm* hairpiece
postor *nm* bidder
postrarse *vpr* to prostrate oneself, to kneel down
postre *nm* dessert, sweet
postrero,-a *adj* last

> **Postrer** is used instead of **postrero** before masculine singular nouns (e.g. **el postrer día** the last day).

postrimería *nf (usu pl)* last part o period
postular 1 *vt* (**a**) *(defender)* to call for (**b**) *Am (candidatar)* to propose, to nominate
2 *vi (en colecta)* to collect
3 postularse *vpr Am* (**a**) *Pol (para cargo)* to stand, to run (**b**) *(para trabajo)* to apply (**para** for)
póstumo,-a *adj* posthumous
postura *nf* (**a**) position, posture (**b**) *Fig (actitud)* attitude
pos(t)venta *adj* **servicio p.** after-sales service
potable *adj* drinkable; **agua p./no p.** drinking water/not drinking water
potaje *nm* hotpot, stew
pote *nm* pot; *(jarra)* jug
potencia *nf* power; **en p.** potential
potencial 1 *adj* potential
2 *nm* (**a**) potential; **p. eléctrico** voltage; **p. humano** manpower (**b**) *Ling* conditional (tense)
potenciar [43] *vt* to promote, to strengthen
potente *adj* powerful, strong
potestad *nf* power, authority
potingue *nm* *Fam Pey* (**a**) *(bebida)* concoction (**b**) *(maquillaje)* make-up, face cream/lotion
potra *nf Fam* luck
potrero *nm Am* field, pasture
potro *nm Zool* colt; *(de gimnasia)* horse
poyo *nm* stone bench
pozo *nm* well; *Min* shaft, pit
pozole *nm* *CAm, Carib, Méx (guiso)* = stew made with maize kernels, pork or chicken and vegetables
PP *nm (abr* **Partido Popular**) = Spanish political party to the right of the political spectrum
práctica *nf* (**a**) practice; **en la p.** in practice (**b**) *(formación)* placement; **período de prácticas** practical training period
practicante 1 *adj Rel* practising
2 *nmf Med* medical assistant

practicar [44] 1 *vt* to practise; *(operación)* to carry out
2 *vi* to practise
práctico,-a *adj* practical; *(útil)* handy, useful
pradera *nf* meadow
prado *nm* meadow, field
Praga *n* Prague
pragmático,-a 1 *adj* pragmatic
2 *nm,f* pragmatist
pre- *pref* pre-
preámbulo *nm* (**a**) *(introducción)* preamble (**b**) *(rodeo)* circumlocution
preaviso *nm* previous warning, notice
precalentamiento *nm* warm-up
precalentar [1] *vt* to preheat
precario,-a *adj* precarious
precaución *nf* (**a**) *(cautela)* caution; **con p.** cautiously (**b**) *(medida)* precaution
precaver 1 *vt* to guard against
2 precaverse *vpr* to take precautions (**de** o **contra** against)
precavido,-a *adj* cautious, prudent
precedencia *nf* precedence, priority
precedente 1 *adj* preceding
2 *nmf* predecessor
3 *nm* precedent; **sin p.** unprecedented
preceder *vt* to precede
precepto *nm* precept
preciarse [43] *vpr* to fancy oneself (**de** as)
precintar *vt* to seal
precinto *nm* seal

> Observa que la palabra inglesa **precinct** es un falso amigo y no es la traducción de la palabra española **precinto**. En inglés, **precinct** significa "recinto" o "distrito".

precio *nm* price; **p. de coste** cost price; **a cualquier p.** at any price
preciosidad *nf* (**a**) *(hermosura) (cosa)* lovely thing; *(persona)* darling (**b**) *Fml (cualidad)* preciousness
precioso,-a *adj* (**a**) *(hermoso)* lovely, beautiful (**b**) *(valioso)* precious, valuable
precipicio *nm* precipice
precipitación *nf* (**a**) *(prisa)* haste (**b**) *(lluvia)* rainfall
precipitado,-a *adj* *(apresurado)* hasty, hurried; *(irreflexivo)* rash
precipitar 1 *vt* (**a**) *(acelerar)* to hurry, to rush (**b**) *(arrojar)* to throw, to hurl down
2 precipitarse *vpr* (**a**) *(persona)* to hurl oneself; *(acontecimientos)* to gather speed (**b**) *(actuar irreflexivamente)* to hurry, to rush
precisamente *adv* *(con precisión)* precisely; *(exactamente)* exactly; **p. por**

eso for that very reason

precisar vt (**a**) (determinar) to determine, to give full details of; (especificar) to specify (**b**) (necesitar) to require, to need

precisión nf (**a**) (exactitud) precision, accuracy; **con p.** precisely, accurately (**b**) (aclaración) clarification

preciso,-a adj (**a**) (necesario) necessary, essential (**b**) (exacto) accurate, exact; **en este p. momento** at this very moment (**c**) (claro) concise, clear

preconizar [40] vt to advocate

precoz adj (**a**) (persona) precocious (**b**) (fruta) early

precursor,-a nm,f precursor

predecesor,-a nm,f predecessor

predecir [12] (pp **predicho**) vt to foretell, to predict

predestinado,-a adj predestined

predeterminar vt to predetermine

predicado nm predicate

predicador,-a nm,f preacher

predicar [44] vt to preach

predicción nf prediction, forecast

predice indic pres de **predecir**

predije pt indef de **predecir**

predilección nf predilection

predilecto,-a adj favourite, preferred

predisponer [19] (pp **predispuesto**) vt to predispose

predisposición nf predisposition

predominante adj predominant

predominar vi to predominate

predominio nm predominance

preescolar adj preschool; **en p.** in the nursery school

prefabricado,-a adj prefabricated

prefacio nm preface

preferencia nf preference

preferente adj preferable, preferential

preferible adj preferable; **es p. que no vengas** you'd better not come

preferido,-a nm,f favourite

preferir [5] vt to prefer

prefijo nm (**a**) Tel Br dialling code, US area code (**b**) Ling prefix

pregonar vt (anunciar) to announce publicly; Fig (divulgar) to reveal, to disclose

pregunta nf question; **hacer una p.** to ask a question

preguntar 1 vt to ask; **p. algo a algn** to ask sb sth; **p. por algn** to ask after o about sb

2 preguntarse vpr to wonder; **me pregunto si ...** I wonder whether ...

preguntón,-ona nm,f Fam busybody

prehistoria nf prehistory

prehistórico,-a adj prehistoric

prejuicio nm prejudice; **tener prejuicios** to be prejudiced, to be biased

preliminar adj & nm preliminary

preludio nm prelude

prematrimonial adj premarital

prematuro,-a adj premature

premeditación nf premeditation; **con p.** deliberately

premeditado,-a adj premeditated, deliberate

premiado,-a adj prize-winning

premiar [43] vt (**a**) to award a prize to (**b**) (recompensar) to reward

premio nm prize, award; (recompensa) reward

premisa nf premise

premonición nf premonition

premura nf (urgencia) urgency; **p. de tiempo** haste

prenatal adj antenatal, prenatal

prenda nf (**a**) (prenda) garment (**b**) (garantía) token, pledge

prendar 1 vt to captivate, to delight

2 prendarse vpr (enamorarse) to fall in love (**de** with)

prendedor nm brooch, pin

prender 1 vt (**a**) (sujetar) to fasten, to attach; (con alfileres) to pin (**b**) **p. fuego a** to set fire to (**c**) (arrestar) to arrest

2 vi (fuego) to catch; (madera) to catch fire; (planta) to take root

3 prenderse vpr to catch fire

prensa nf press; Fig **tener buena/mala p.** to have a good/bad press

prensar vt to press

preñado,-a adj (**a**) pregnant (**b**) Fig (lleno) pregnant (**de** with), full (**de** of)

preñar vt (mujer) to make pregnant; (animal) to impregnate

preocupación nf worry, concern

preocupado,-a adj worried, concerned

preocupar 1 vt to worry; **me preocupa que llegue tan tarde** I'm worried about him arriving so late

2 preocuparse vpr to worry, to get worried (**por** about); **no te preocupes** don't worry; **p. de algn** to look after sb; **p. de algo** to see to sth

preparación nf preparation; (formación) training

preparado,-a 1 adj (**a**) (dispuesto) ready, prepared; **comidas preparadas** ready-cooked meals (**b**) (capacitado) trained, qualified

2 nm Farm preparation

preparador,-a nm,f coach, trainer

preparar 1 vt (**a**) to prepare, to get ready;

p. un examen to prepare for an exam (**b**) *Dep (entrenar)* to train, to coach

2 prepararse *upr* (**a**) to prepare oneself, to get ready (**b**) *Dep (entrenarse)* to train
preparativo *nm* preparation
preparatorio,-a *adj* preparatory
preponderante *adj* preponderant
preposición *nf Ling* preposition
prepotente *adj* domineering; *(arrogante)* overbearing
prerrogativa *nf* prerogative
presa *nf* (**a**) prey; *Fig* **ser p. de** to be a victim of; **p. del pánico** panic-stricken (**b**) *(embalse)* dam
presagiar [**43**] *vt* to predict, to foretell
presagio *nm* (**a**) *(señal)* omen; **buen/mal p.** good/bad omen (**b**) *(premonición)* premonition
presbiteriano,-a *adj & nm,f* Presbyterian
presbítero *nm* priest
prescindir *vi* **p. de** to do without
prescribir (*pp* **prescrito**) *vt* to prescribe
prescripción *nf* prescription; **p. facultativa** medical prescription
presencia *nf* presence; **hacer acto de p.** to put in an appearance; **p. de ánimo** presence of mind
presencial *adj* **testigo p.** eyewitness
presenciar [**43**] *vt (ver)* to witness
presentable *adj* presentable; **no estoy p.** I'm not dressed for the occasion
presentación *nf* presentation; *(aspecto)* appearance; *(de personas)* introduction
presentador,-a *nm,f Rad & TV* presenter, host, *f* hostess
presentar 1 *vt* (**a**) to present; *(mostrar)* to show, to display; *(ofrecer)* to offer (**b**) *(una persona a otra)* to introduce; **le presento al doctor Ruiz** may I introduce you to Dr Ruiz

2 presentarse *upr* (**a**) *(comparecer)* to present oneself; *(inesperadamente)* to turn *o* come up (**b**) *(ocasión, oportunidad)* to present itself, to arise (**c**) *(candidato)* to stand; **p. a unas elecciones** to stand for election, *US* to run for office; **p. a un examen** to sit an examination (**d**) *(darse a conocer)* to introduce oneself (**a** to)
presente 1 *adj* present; **la p. (carta)** this letter; **hacer p.** to declare, to state; **tener p.** *(tener en cuenta)* to bear in mind; *(recordar)* to remember

2 *nm* present
presentimiento *nm* presentiment, premonition; **tengo el p. de que ...** I have the feeling that ...

presentir [**5**] *vt* to have a presentiment *o* premonition of; **presiento que lloverá** I've got the feeling that it's going to rain
preservación *nf* preservation, protection
preservar *vt* to preserve, to protect (**de** from; **contra** against)
preservativo *nm* sheath, condom
presidencia *nf* (**a**) *Pol* presidency (**b**) *(de una reunión) (hombre)* chairmanship; *(mujer)* chairwomanship
presidenciable *nmf Am* potential president
presidencial *adj* presidential
presidente,-a *nm,f* (**a**) *Pol* president; **p. del gobierno** Prime Minister, Premier (**b**) *(de una reunión)* chairperson
presidiario,-a *nm,f* prisoner, convict
presidio *nm* prison, penitentiary
presidir *vt* (**a**) *Pol* to rule, to head (**b**) *(reunión)* to chair, to preside over
presión *nf* pressure; **a** *o* **bajo p.** under pressure; **grupo de p.** pressure group, lobby; **p. arterial** *o* **sanguínea** blood pressure; **p. atmosférica** atmospheric pressure
presionar *vt* to press; *Fig* to pressurize, to put pressure on
preso,-a 1 *adj* imprisoned

2 *nm,f* prisoner
prestación *nf* (**a**) service (**b**) **prestaciones** *(de coche etc)* performance
prestado,-a *adj* **dejar p.** to lend; **pedir p.** to borrow; **vivir de p.** to scrounge
prestamista *nmf* moneylender
préstamo *nm* loan
prestar 1 *vt* (**a**) to lend, to loan; **¿me prestas tu pluma?** can I borrow your pen? (**b**) *(atención)* to pay; *(ayuda)* to give; *(servicio)* to do

2 prestarse *upr* (**a**) *(ofrecerse)* to offer oneself (**a** to) (**b**) **p. a** *(dar motivo)* to cause; **se presta a (crear) malentendidos** it makes for misunderstandings
presteza *nf* promptness; **con p.** promptly
prestidigitador,-a *nm,f* conjuror, magician
prestigiar [**43**] *vt* to give prestige to
prestigio *nm* prestige
prestigioso,-a *adj* prestigious
presto,-a *adj Fml* (**a**) *(dispuesto)* ready, prepared (**b**) *(rápido)* swift, prompt
presumible *adj* probable, likely
presumido,-a *adj* **1** vain, conceited

2 *nm,f* vain person
presumir 1 *vt (suponer)* to presume, to suppose

2 *vi* (**a**) *(ser vanidoso)* to show off (**b**)

presume de guapo he thinks he's good-looking

presunción *nf* (**a**) *(suposición)* presumption, supposition (**b**) *(vanidad)* vanity, conceit

presunto,-a *adj* supposed; *Jur* alleged

presuntuoso,-a *adj* (**a**) *(vanidoso)* vain, conceited (**b**) *(pretencioso)* pretentious, showy

> ✍ Observa que la palabra inglesa **presumptuous** es un falso amigo y no es la traducción de la palabra española **presuntuoso**. En inglés, **presumptuous** significa "impertinente".

presuponer [19] *(pp* presupuesto*) vt* to presuppose

presupuestar *vt* to budget for; *(importe)* to estimate for

presupuestario,-a *adj* budgetary

presupuesto *nm* (**a**) *Fin* budget; *(cálculo)* estimate (**b**) *(supuesto)* supposition, assumption

presuroso,-a *adj (rápido)* quick; *(con prisa)* in a hurry

pretencioso,-a *adj* pretentious

pretender *vt* (**a**) *(intentar)* to try; **¿qué pretendes insinuar?** what are you getting at? (**b**) *(afirmar)* to claim (**c**) *(aspirar a)* to try for (**d**) *(cortejar)* to court, to woo

pretendiente,-a *nm,f* (**a**) *(al trono)* pretender (**b**) *(a un cargo)* applicant, candidate (**c**) *(amante)* suitor

pretensión *nf* (**a**) *(aspiración)* aim, aspiration (**b**) *(presunción)* pretentiousness

pretérito,-a 1 *adj* past, former
   2 *nm Ling* preterite, simple past tense

pretextar *vt* to plead, to allege

pretexto *nm* pretext, excuse

pretil *nm* parapet

prevalecer [33] *vi* to prevail

prevaler [26] *vi* = prevalecer

prevención *nf* (**a**) *(precaución)* prevention; **en p. de** as a prevention against (**b**) *(medida)* precaution

prevenir [27] *vt* (**a**) *(preparar)* to prepare, to get ready (**b**) *(prever)* to prevent, to forestall; *(evitar)* to avoid; **para p. la gripe** to prevent flu; *Prov* **más vale p. que curar** prevention is better than cure (**c**) *(advertir)* to warn

preventivo,-a *adj* preventive; *(medidas)* precautionary; *Jur* **detención** *o* **prisión preventiva** remand in custody

prever [28] *(pp* previsto*) vt* (**a**) *(prevenir)* to foresee, to forecast (**b**) *(preparar de antemano)* to cater for

previo,-a *adj* previous, prior; **p. pago de su importe** only on payment; **sin p. aviso** without prior notice

previsible *adj* predictable

previsión *nf* (**a**) *(predicción)* forecast; **p. del tiempo** weather forecast (**b**) *(precaución)* precaution; **en p. de** as a precaution against (**c**) *Andes, RP* **p. social** social security

previsor,-a *adj* careful, far-sighted

previsto,-a *adj* foreseen, forecast; **según lo p.** as expected

prieto,-a *adj* (**a**) *(ceñido)* tight; **íbamos muy prietos en el coche** we were really squashed together in the car (**b**) *Méx Fam (moreno)* dark-skinned

prima *nf* (**a**) *(gratificación)* bonus; **p. de seguro** insurance premium (**b**) *(persona)* ver **primo,-a**

primacía *nf* primacy

primar 1 *vi* to have priority, to prevail
   2 *vt* to give a bonus to

primario,-a *adj* primary

primavera *nf* spring

primer *adj (delante de nm)* ver **primero,-a**

primera *nf* (**a**) *(en tren)* first class (**b**) *Aut (marcha)* first gear (**c**) **a la p.** at the first attempt; *Fam* **de p.** great, first-class

primero,-a 1 *adj* first; **a primera hora de la mañana** first thing in the morning; **primera página** *o* **plana** front page; **de primera necesidad** basic

> **Primer** is used instead of **primero** before masculine singular nouns (e.g. **el primer hombre** the first man).

   2 *nm,f* first; **a primero(s) de mes** at the beginning of the month
   3 *adv* (**a**) first (**b**) *(más bien)* rather, sooner; ver **primera**

primicia *nf* novelty; **p. informativa** scoop; **p. mundial** world premiere

primitivo,-a *adj* (**a**) primitive (**b**) *(tosco)* coarse, rough

primo,-a 1 *nm,f* (**a**) cousin; **p. hermano** first cousin (**b**) *Fam (tonto)* fool, drip, dunce
   2 *adj* (**a**) **materia prima** raw material (**b**) *(número)* prime

primogénito,-a *adj & nm,f* first-born

primor *nm* (**a**) *(delicadeza)* delicacy (**b**) *(belleza)* beauty

primordial *adj* essential, fundamental

primoroso,-a *adj* delicate, exquisite

princesa *nf* princess

principado *nm* principality

principal *adj* main, principal; **lo p. es que ...** the main thing is that ...; **puerta p.** front door

príncipe *nm* prince
principiante 1 *adj* novice
2 *nmf* beginner, novice
principio *nm* (**a**) beginning, start; **a principio(s) de** at the beginning of; **al p., en un p.** at first, in the beginning (**b**) *(fundamento)* principle; **en p.** in principle (**c**) **principios** rudiments, basics
pringar [42] 1 *vt (ensuciar)* to make greasy/dirty
2 *vi Fam (trabajar)* to work hard
3 **pringarse** *vpr* (**a**) *(ensuciarse)* to get greasy/dirty (**b**) *Fam (meterse de lleno)* to get involved
pringoso,-a *adj (grasiento)* greasy; *(sucio)* dirty
pringue *nm (grasa)* grease
prior,-a *nm,f (hombre)* prior; *(mujer)* prioress
priori: • a priori *loc adv* a priori
prioridad *nf* priority
prioritario,-a *adj* priority
prisa *nf* (**a**) *(rapidez)* hurry; **date p.** hurry up; **tener p.** to be in a hurry; **de/a p.** in a hurry (**b**) **correr p.** to be urgent; **me corre mucha p.** I need it right away
prisión *nf* prison, jail
prisionero,-a *nm,f* prisoner
prisma *nm* prism
prismáticos *nmpl* binoculars, field glasses
priva *nf Fam* booze
privación *nf* deprivation
privado,-a *adj* private
privar 1 *vt (despojar)* to deprive (**de** of)
2 *vi* (**a**) *Fam (gustar)* to like; *(estar de moda)* to be fashionable o popular (**b**) *Fam (beber)* to booze
3 **privarse** *vpr (abstenerse)* to deprive oneself (**de** of), to go without
privativo,-a *adj* exclusive (**de** of)
privilegiado,-a 1 *adj* privileged
2 *nm,f* privileged person
privilegio *nm* privilege
pro 1 *nm* advantage; **los pros y los contras** the pros and cons; **en p. de** in favour of
2 *prep* in favour of; **campaña p. desarme** campaign for disarmament, disarmament campaign
pro- *pref* pro-
proa *nf* prow, bows
probabilidad *nf* probability, likelihood; **tiene pocas probabilidades** he stands little chance
probable *adj* probable, likely; **es p. que llueva** it'll probably rain
probador *nm* fitting room
probar [2] 1 *vt* (**a**) *(comida, bebida)* to try

(**b**) *(comprobar)* to test, to check (**c**) *(intentar)* to try (**d**) *(demostrar)* to prove, to show
2 *vi* to try; **p. a** to attempt o try to
3 **probarse** *vpr (ropa)* to try on
probeta *nf* test tube; **niño p.** test-tube baby
problema *nm* problem
problemático,-a *adj* problematic
procedencia *nf* origin, source
procedente *adj* (**a**) *(originario)* coming (**de** from) (**b**) *(adecuado)* appropriate; *Jur* proper
proceder 1 *vi* (**a**) **p. de** *(provenir)* to come from (**b**) *(actuar)* to act (**c**) *(ser oportuno)* to be advisable o appropriate; *Jur* **la protesta no procede** objection overruled (**d**) **p. a** *(continuar)* to go on to
2 *nm (comportamiento)* behaviour
procedimiento *nm* (**a**) *(método)* procedure (**b**) *Jur (trámites)* proceedings
procesado,-a 1 *nm,f* accused
2 *nm Informát* processing
procesador *nm* processor; **p. de textos** word processor
procesamiento *nm* (**a**) *Jur* prosecution (**b**) *Informát* **p. de datos/textos** data/word processing
procesar *vt* (**a**) *Jur* to prosecute (**b**) *(elaborar, transformar)* to process; *Informát* to process
procesión *nf* procession
proceso *nm* (**a**) process; *Informát* **p. de datos** data processing (**b**) *Jur* trial
proclamación *nf* proclamation
proclamar *vt* to proclaim
proclive *adj* prone, inclined
procreación *nf* procreation
procrear *vt* to procreate
procurador,-a *nm,f Jur* attorney
procuraduría *nf Méx* **p. general** Ministry of Justice
procurar *vt* (**a**) *(intentar)* to try, to attempt; **procura que no te vean** make sure they don't see you (**b**) *(proporcionar)* (to manage) to get
prodigar [42] *Fml* **1** *vt (dar generosamente)* to lavish
2 **prodigarse** *vpr* **p. en** to be lavish in
prodigio *nm* prodigy, miracle; **hacer prodigios** to work wonders; **niño p.** child prodigy
prodigioso,-a *adj (sobrenatural)* prodigious; *(maravilloso)* wonderful, marvellous
pródigo,-a *adj* generous, lavish; **ella es pródiga en regalos** she's very generous with presents

producción *nf (acción)* production; *(producto)* product; *Cin* production; **p. en cadena/serie** assembly-line/mass production

producir [10] 1 *vt* (**a**) to produce; *(fruto, cosecha)* to yield, to bear; *(ganancias)* to yield (**b**) *Fig (originar)* to cause, to bring about

2 producirse *upr* to take place, to happen

productividad *nf* productivity

productivo,-a *adj* productive; *(beneficioso)* profitable

producto *nm* product; *Agr (producción)* produce

productor,-a 1 *adj* producing

2 *nm,f* producer

proeza *nf* heroic deed, exploit

profanación *nf* desecration, profanation

profanar *vt* to desecrate, to profane

profano,-a 1 *adj* profane, secular

2 *nm,f (hombre)* layman; *(mujer)* laywoman

profecía *nf* prophecy

proferir [31] *vt* to utter; **p. insultos** to hurl insults

profesar *vt* to profess

profesión *nf* profession; **de p.** by profession

profesional *adj & nmf* professional

profesionista *adj & nmf Méx* professional

profeso *adv* **ex p.** intentionally

profesor,-a *nm,f* teacher; *Univ* lecturer

profesorado *nm (profesión)* teaching; *(grupo de profesores)* staff

profeta *nm* prophet

profetizar [40] *vt* to prophesy, to foretell

profiláctico,-a 1 *adj* prophylactic

2 *nm* condom

prófugo,-a 1 *adj & nm,f* fugitive

2 *nm Mil* deserter

profundidad *nf* depth; **un metro de p.** one metre deep *o* in depth; *Fig (de ideas etc)* profundity, depth

profundizar [40] *vt & vi (cavar)* to deepen; *Fig (examinar)* to study in depth

profundo,-a *adj* deep; *Fig (idea, sentimiento)* profound

profusión *nf* profusion

progenitor,-a *nm,f (antepasado)* ancestor, progenitor; **progenitores** *(padres)* parents

programa *nm* programme; *Informát* program; *Educ* syllabus

programación *nf Rad & TV* programme planning

programador,-a *nm,f Informát* programmer

programar *vt* to programme; *Informát* to program

progre *adj & nmf Fam* trendy, lefty

progresar *vi* to progress, to make progress

progresista *adj & nmf* progressive

progresivo,-a *adj* progressive

progreso *nm* progress; **hace grandes progresos** he's making great progress

prohibición *nf* prohibition, ban

prohibido,-a *adj* forbidden, prohibited; **prohibida la entrada** *(en letrero)* no admittance; **p. aparcar/fumar** *(en letrero)* no parking/smoking

prohibir *vt* to forbid, to prohibit; **se prohíbe pasar** *(en letrero)* no admittance *o* entry

prohibitivo,-a, prohibitorio,-a *adj* prohibitive

prójimo,-a *nm,f* one's fellow man, one's neighbour

proletariado *nm* proletariat

proletario,-a *adj & nm,f* proletarian

proliferar *vi* to proliferate

prolífico,-a *adj* prolific

prolijo,-a *adj* verbose, long-winded

prólogo *nm* prologue

prolongación *nf* prolonging, extension, prolongation

prolongado,-a *adj* long

prolongar [42] 1 *vt (alargar)* to prolong, to extend

2 prolongarse *upr (continuar)* to carry on

promedio *nm* average; **como p.** on average

promesa *nf* promise; *Fig* **la joven p. de la música** the promising young musician

prometedor,-a *adj* promising

prometer 1 *vt* to promise; **te lo prometo** I promise

2 *vi* to be promising

3 prometerse *upr (pareja)* to get engaged

prometido,-a 1 *adj* promised

2 *nm,f (hombre)* fiancé; *(mujer)* fiancée

prominente *adj (elevado)* protruding, projecting; *(importante)* prominent

promiscuo,-a *adj* promiscuous

promoción *nf* promotion; *Educ* **p. universitaria** class, year

promocionar *vt (cosas)* to promote; *(personas)* to give promotion to

promotor,-a 1 *adj* promoting

2 *nm,f* promoter

promover [4] *vt* (**a**) *(cosas, personas)* to promote; *(juicio, querella)* to initiate (**b**) *(causar)* to cause, to give rise to

promulgar [42] *vt* to promulgate

pronombre *nm* pronoun

pronosticar [44] *vt* to predict, to forecast; *Med* to make a prognosis of

pronóstico *nm (del tiempo)* forecast; *Med* prognosis

pronto,-a 1 *adj* quick, prompt; *Fml (dispuesto)* prepared

2 *nm (impulso)* sudden impulse

3 *adv* (**a**) *(deprisa)* quickly, rapidly; **al p.** at first; **de p.** suddenly; **por de** *o* **lo p.** *(para empezar)* to start with (**b**) *(temprano)* soon, early; **¡hasta p.!** see you soon!

pronunciación *nf* pronunciation

pronunciamiento *nm* (**a**) *Mil* uprising, insurrection (**b**) *Jur* pronouncement

pronunciar [43] 1 *vt* to pronounce; *(discurso)* to deliver

2 pronunciarse *vpr* (**a**) *(opinar)* to declare oneself (**b**) *(sublevarse)* to rise up

propagación *nf* propagation, spreading

propagador,-a *nm,f* propagator

propaganda *nf (política)* propaganda; *(comercial)* advertising, publicity

propagar [42] 1 *vt* to propagate, to spread

2 propagarse *vpr* to spread

propano *nm* propane

propasarse *vpr* to go too far

propensión *nf* tendency, inclination

propenso,-a *adj* (**a**) *(inclinado)* prone, inclined (**b**) *Med* susceptible

propiamente *adv* **p. dicho** strictly speaking

propiciar [43] *vt* (**a**) *(causar)* to cause (**b**) *Am (patrocinar)* to sponsor

propicio,-a *adj* propitious, suitable; **ser p. a** to be inclined to

propiedad *nf* (**a**) *(posesión)* ownership; *(cosa poseída)* property (**b**) *(cualidad)* property, quality; *Fig* **con p.** properly, appropriately

propietario,-a *nm,f* owner

propina *nf* tip; **dar p. (a algn)** to tip (sb)

propinar *vt* to give

propio,-a *adj* (**a**) *(de uno)* own; **en su propia casa** in his own house (**b**) *(correcto)* suitable, appropriate; **juegos propios para su edad** games suitable for their age (**c**) *(característico)* typical, peculiar (**d**) *(mismo) (hombre)* himself; *(mujer)* herself; *(animal, cosa)* itself; **el p. autor** the author himself (**e**) **propios,-as** themselves; **los propios inquilinos** the tenants themselves (**f**) *Ling* proper

proponer [19] *(pp* **propuesto)** **1** *vt* to propose, to suggest

2 proponerse *vpr* to intend

proporción *nf* (**a**) proportion; **en p. con** in proportion to (**b**) **proporciones** *(tamaño)* size

proporcionado,-a *adj (mesurado)* proportionate, in proportion

proporcional *adj* proportional

proporcionar *vt (dar)* to give, to supply, to provide

proposición *nf* (**a**) *(propuesta)* proposal (**b**) *(oración)* clause

propósito *nm* (**a**) *(intención)* intention (**b**) **a p.** *(por cierto)* by the way; *(adrede)* on purpose, intentionally; **a p. de viajes ...** speaking of travelling ...

propuesta *nf* suggestion, proposal

propuesto,-a *pp de* **proponer**

propugnar *vt* to advocate

propulsar *vt (vehículo)* to drive; *Fig (idea)* to promote

propulsión *nf* propulsion

propulsor,-a *nm,f Fig (persona)* promoter

propuse *pt indef de* **proponer**

prórroga *nf* (**a**) *(prolongación)* extension; *Dep Br* extra time, *US* overtime (**b**) *(aplazamiento)* postponement; *Mil* deferment

prorrogar [42] *vt* (**a**) *(prolongar)* to extend (**b**) *(aplazar)* to postpone; *Mil* to defer

prorrumpir *vi* to burst (**en** into)

prosa *nf* prose

proscrito,-a 1 *adj (persona)* exiled, banished; *(cosa)* banned

2 *nm,f* exile, outlaw

proseguir [6] *vt & vi* to carry on, to continue

prospección *nf* (**a**) *Min* prospect (**b**) *Com* survey

prospecto *nm* leaflet, prospectus

prosperar *vi (negocio, país)* to prosper, to thrive; *(propuesta)* to be accepted

prosperidad *nf* prosperity

próspero,-a *adj* prosperous, thriving; **¡p. año nuevo!** Happy New Year!

prostíbulo *nm* brothel

prostitución *nf* prostitution

prostituir [37] 1 *vt* to prostitute

2 prostituirse *vpr* to prostitute oneself

prostituta *nf* prostitute

protagonista *nmf* (**a**) main character, leading role; **¿quién es el p.?** who plays the lead? (**b**) *Fig (centro)* centre of attraction

protagonizar [40] *vt* to play the lead in, to star in

protección *nf* protection

proteccionismo *nm* protectionism

protector,-a 1 *adj* protecting, protective

2 *nm,f* protector

proteger [53] *vt* to protect, to defend
protegido,-a *nm,f (hombre)* protégé; *(mujer)* protégée
proteína *nf* protein
prótesis *nf inv* prosthesis
protesta *nf* protest; *Jur* objection
protestante *adj & nmf Rel* Protestant
protestar *vi* (**a**) to protest; *Jur* to object (**b**) *Fam (quejarse)* to complain
protestón,-ona *nm,f* moaner, grumbler
protocolo *nm* protocol
protón *nm* proton
prototipo *nm* prototype
protuberancia *nf* protuberance
protuberante *adj* protuberant, bulging
prov. (*abr* **provincia**) prov
provecho *nm* profit, benefit; **¡buen p.!** enjoy your meal!; **sacar p. de algo** to benefit from sth
provechoso,-a *adj* beneficial
proveedor,-a *nm,f* supplier, purveyor; *Informât* **p. de acceso (a Internet)** Internet access provider
proveer [36] (*pp* **provisto**) *vt* to supply, to provide
proveniente *adj (procedente)* coming; *(resultante)* arising, resulting
provenir [27] *vi* **p. de** to come from
proverbio *nm* proverb
providencia *nf* providence
provincia *nf* province
provincial *adj* provincial
provinciano,-a *adj & nm,f Pey* provincial
provisión *nf* provision
provisional, *Am* **provisorio,-a** *adj* provisional
provisto,-a *adj* **p. de** equipped with
provocación *nf* provocation
provocado,-a *adj* provoked, caused; **incendio p.** arson
provocador,-a 1 *nm,f* instigator, agent provocateur
  2 *adj* provocative
provocar [44] *vt* (**a**) *(causar)* to cause; **p. un incendio** to start a fire (**b**) *(instigar)* to provoke (**c**) *Carib, Col, Méx Fam (apetecer)* **¿te provoca ir al cine?** would you like to go to the movies?, *Br* do you fancy going to the cinema?; **¿qué te provoca?** what would you like to do?, *Br* what do you fancy doing?
provocativo,-a *adj* provocative
proxeneta *nmf* procurer, pimp
próximamente *adv (pronto)* soon; *Cin & Teatro (en letrero)* coming soon
proximidad *nf* proximity, closeness; **en las proximidades de** close to, in the vicinity of

próximo,-a *adj* (**a**) *(cercano)* near, close (**b**) *(siguiente)* next
proyección *nf* (**a**) projection (**b**) *Cin* showing
proyectar *vt* (**a**) *(luz)* to project (**b**) *(planear)* to plan (**c**) *Cin* to show
proyectil *nm* projectile
proyecto *nm (plan)* project, plan; **tener algo en p.** to be planning sth; **p. de ley** bill
proyector *nm Cin* projector
prudencia *nf* prudence, discretion; *(moderación)* care
prudente *adj* prudent, sensible; *(conductor)* careful; **a una hora p.** at a reasonable time
prueba *nf* (**a**) proof; **en p. de** as a sign of (**b**) *(examen etc)* test; **a p.** on trial; **a p. de agua/balas** waterproof/bullet-proof; **haz la p.** try it (**c**) *Dep* event
pseudo *adj* pseud, pseudo
psicoanálisis *nm inv* psychoanalysis
psicodélico,-a *adj* psychedelic
psicología *nf* psychology
psicológico,-a *adj* psychological
psicólogo,-a *nm,f* psychologist
psicópata *nmf* psychopath
psicosis *nf inv* psychosis
psicotécnico,-a *adj* psychometric
psicoterapeuta 1 *nmf* psychotherapist
  2 *adj* psychotherapeutic
psicoterapia *nf* psychotherapy
psicótico,-a *adj & nm,f* psychotic
psique *nf* psyche
psiquiatra *nmf* psychiatrist
psiquiatría *nf* psychiatry
psiquiátrico,-a 1 *adj* psychiatric; **hospital p.** psychiatric hospital
  2 *nm* psychiatric hospital
psíquico,-a *adj* psychic
PSOE *nm Pol* (*abr* **Partido Socialista Obrero Español**) = Spanish political party to the centre-left of the political spectrum
pta(s). (*abr* **peseta(s)**) peseta(s)
púa *nf* (**a**) *(de planta)* thorn; *(de animal)* quill, spine; *(de peine)* tooth; **alambre de púas** barbed wire (**b**) *Mús* plectrum
pub *nm* (*pl* **pubs, pubes**) pub
pubertad *nf* puberty
publicación *nf* publication
publicar [44] *vt* (**a**) *(libro etc)* to publish (**b**) *(secreto)* to publicize
publicidad *nf* (**a**) *Com* advertising (**b**) *(conocimiento público)* publicity
publicitario,-a *adj* advertising
público,-a 1 *adj* public
  2 *nm* public; *Teatro* audience; *Dep* spectators

pucha *interj Andes, RP Fam Euf* (**a**) *(lamento) Br* sugar!, *US* shoot!; **¡p. digo, ya son las doce!** oh, *Br* sugar o *US* shoot! it's twelve o'clock already! (**b**) *(sorpresa)* wow!; **¿cincuenta años? ¡la p.!** fifty years old? get away! o never! (**c**) *(enojo) Br* sugar!, *US* shoot!; **¡la p.!, perdí las llaves** *Br* sugar o *US* shoot! I've lost my keys!

pucherazo *nm* rigging of an election

puchero *nm* (**a**) *(olla)* cooking pot; *(cocido)* stew (**b**) **hacer pucheros** to pout

pucho *nm CSur* dog-end

pude *pt indef de* **poder**

pudendo,-a *adj* **partes pudendas** private parts

púdico,-a *adj* modest

pudiente *adj* rich, wealthy

pudor *nm* modesty

pudoroso,-a *adj* modest

pudrir *vt* defect, **pudrirse** *vpr* to rot, to decay

pueblerino,-a *adj Pey (provinciano)* countrified, provincial

pueblo *nm* (**a**) *(población) (pequeña)* village; *(grande)* town (**b**) *(gente)* people; **el p. español** the Spanish people

puente *nm* (**a**) bridge; *Av* **p. aéreo** *(civil)* air shuttle service; *Mil* airlift; **p. colgante** suspension bridge; **p. levadizo** drawbridge (**b**) *(entre dos fiestas)* ≃ long weekend

puerco,-a 1 *adj* filthy

2 *nm,f* pig

3 *nm* **p. espín** porcupine

puericultura *nf* paediatrics *sing*

pueril *adj* childish, puerile

puerro *nm* leek

puerta *nf* door; *(verja, en aeropuerto)* gate; *Dep* goal; **p. corredera/giratoria** sliding/revolving door; *Fig* **a las puertas, en puertas** imminent; *Fig* **a p. cerrada** behind closed doors

puerto *nm* (**a**) *(de mar)* port, harbour; **p. deportivo** marina (**b**) *(de montaña)* (mountain) pass

Puerto Rico *n* Puerto Rico

puertorriqueño,-a *adj & nm,f* Puerto Rican

pues *conj* (**a**) *(puesto que)* as, since (**b**) *(por lo tanto)* therefore (**c**) *(entonces)* so (**d**) *(para reforzar)* **¡p. claro que sí!** but of course!; **p. como iba diciendo** well, as I was saying; **¡p. mejor!** so much the better!; **¡p. no!** certainly not! (**e**) *(como pregunta)* **¿p.?** why?

puesta *nf* (**a**) **p. de sol** sunset (**b**) *Fig* **p. a punto** tuning, adjusting; *Fig* **p. al día** updating; *Teatro* **p. en escena** staging;

p. en marcha starting-up, start-up; *ver* **puesto,-a**

puestero,-a *nm,f Am* stallholder

puesto,-a 1 *conj* **p. que** since, as

2 *nm* (**a**) *(lugar)* place; *(asiento)* seat (**b**) *(empleo)* position, post, job; **p. de trabajo** job, post (**c**) *(tienda)* stall (**d**) *Mil* post

3 *adj* (**a**) *(colocado)* set, put (**b**) **llevar p.** *(ropa)* to have on; *Fam* **ir muy p.** to be all dressed up (**c**) *Fam (borracho)* drunk (**d**) *Fam* **estar p. en una materia** to be well up in a subject

púgil *nm* boxer

pugilato *nm* boxing

pugna *nf* battle, fight

pugnar *vi* to fight, to struggle (**por** for)

puja *nf (acción)* bidding; *(cantidad)* bid

pujante *adj* thriving, prosperous

pujanza *nf* strength, vigour

pujar *vi* (**a**) *(pugnar)* to struggle (**b**) *(en una subasta)* to bid higher

pulcro,-a *adj* (extremely) neat

pulga *nf* flea; *Fam* **tener malas pulgas** to be nasty, to have a nasty streak

pulgada *nf* inch

pulgar *nm* thumb

pulimentar *vt* to polish

pulir *vt* (**a**) *(metal, madera)* to polish (**b**) *(mejorar)* to polish up

pulla *nf* dig

pulmón *nm* lung

pulmonía *nf* pneumonia

pulóver *nm* pullover

pulpa *nf* pulp

pulpería *nf Am* store

púlpito *nm* pulpit

pulpo *nm* octopus

pulque *nm CAm, Méx* pulque, = fermented maguey juice

pulquería *nf CAm, Méx* "pulque" bar

pulsación *nf* pulsation; *(en mecanografía)* stroke, tap; **pulsaciones por minuto** ≃ keystrokes per minute

pulsar *vt (timbre, botón)* to press; *(tecla)* to hit, to strike

pulsera *nf (aro)* bracelet; *(de reloj)* watchstrap; **reloj de p.** wristwatch

pulso *nm* (**a**) pulse; *Fig* **tomar el p. a la opinión pública** to sound out opinion (**b**) *(mano firme)* steady hand; **a p.** freehand; **ganarse algo a p.** to deserve sth (**c**) *Fig* trial of strength; **echarse un p.** to armwrestle

pulverizador *nm* spray, atomizer

pulverizar [40] *vt (sólidos)* to pulverize; *(líquidos)* to spray; *(un récord)* to smash

puma *nm* puma

puna *nf Andes* (**a**) high moor (**b**) *(mal)*

mountain o altitude sickness
pundonor *nm* self-respect, self-esteem
punta *nf* (**a**) *(extremo)* tip; *(extremo afilado)* point; *(de cabello)* end; **sacar p. a un lápiz** to sharpen a pencil; **tecnología p.** state-of-the-art technology; **me pone los nervios de p.** he makes me very nervous (**b**) *(periodo)* peak; **hora p.** rush hour (**c**) *(pequeña cantidad)* bit; **una p. de sal** a pinch of salt (**d**) *(clavo)* nail
puntada *nf Am (dolor)* stabbing pain
puntaje *nm Am (calificación) Br* mark, *US* grade; *(en concursos, competiciones)* score
puntal *nm* prop; *(travesaño)* beam; *Fig (soporte)* pillar, support
puntapié *nm* kick
puntear *vt* (**a**) *(dibujar)* to dot (**b**) *Mús (guitarra)* to pluck
punteo *nm* plucking
puntería *nf* aim; **tener buena/mala p.** to be a good/bad shot
puntero,-a 1 *adj* leading
    2 *nm,f CSur Dep* back
puntiagudo,-a *adj* pointed, sharp
puntilla *nf* (**a**) *(encaje)* lace (**b**) **dar la p.** *Taurom* to finish (the bull) off; *Fig (liquidar)* to finish off (**c**) **de puntillas** on tiptoe
puntilloso,-a *adj* touchy
punto *nm* (**a**) point; **a p.** ready; *Culin* **en su p.** just right; **a p. de** on the point of; **hasta cierto p.** to a certain o some extent; **p. muerto** *Aut* neutral; *Fig (impase)* deadlock; **p. de vista** point of view (**b**) *(marca)* dot; **línea de puntos** dotted line (**c**) *(lugar)* place, point (**d**) **p. y seguido** full stop; **p. y coma** semicolon; **dos puntos** colon; **p. y aparte** full stop, new paragraph (**e**) *(tiempo)* **en p.** sharp, on the dot (**f**) *Dep (tanto)* point (**g**) *Cost & Med* stitch; **hacer p.** to knit
puntuable *adj Dep* **una prueba p. para** a race counting towards
puntuación *nf* (**a**) *Ling* punctuation (**b**) *Dep* score (**c**) *Educ* mark
puntual 1 *adj* (**a**) punctual (**b**) *(exacto)* accurate, precise (**c**) *(caso)* specific
    2 *adv* punctually
puntualidad *nf* punctuality
puntualizar [40] *vt* to specify, to clarify
puntuar [30] **1** *vt* (**a**) *(al escribir)* to punctuate (**b**) *Educ (calificar)* to mark
    2 *vi Dep* (**a**) *(marcar)* to score (**b**) *(ser puntuable)* to count
punzada *nf (de dolor)* sudden sharp pain
punzante *adj (objeto)* sharp; *(dolor)* acute, piercing

punzar [40] *vt Téc* to punch
puñado *nm* handful; *Fam* **a puñados** by the score, galore
puñal *nm* dagger
puñalada *nf* stab; *Fig* **p. trapera** stab in the back
puñeta *nf Fam* **hacer la p. a algn** to pester sb, to annoy sb; **¡puñetas!** damn!; **¡vete a hacer puñetas!** go to hell!
puñetazo *nm* punch
puño *nm* (**a**) fist (**b**) *(de camisa etc)* cuff (**c**) *(de herramienta)* handle
pupa *nf* (**a**) *(herida)* cold sore (**b**) *Fam (daño)* pain
pupila *nf (de ojo)* pupil
pupilo,-a *nm,f* pupil
pupitre *nm* desk
purasangre *adj & nm* thoroughbred
puré *nm* purée; **p. de patata** mashed potatoes; **p. de verduras** thick vegetable soup
pureta *nmf* old fogey
pureza *nf* (**a**) purity (**b**) *(castidad)* chastity
purga *nf Med* purgative; *Fig* purge
purgante *adj & nm* purgative
purgar [42] *vt Med & Fig* to purge
purgatorio *nm* purgatory
purificación *nf* purification
purificar [44] *vt* to purify
purista *nmf* purist
puritano,-a 1 *adj* puritanical
    2 *nm,f* puritan, Puritan
puro,-a 1 *adj* (**a**) *(sin mezclas)* pure; **aire p.** fresh air; **la pura verdad** the plain truth; *Pol* **p. y duro** hardline (**b**) *(mero)* sheer, mere; **por pura curiosidad** out of sheer curiosity (**c**) *(casto)* chaste, pure
    2 *nm (cigarro)* cigar
púrpura *adj inv* purple
purpúreo,-a *adj* purple
pus *nm* pus
puse *pt indef de* **poner**
pusilánime *adj* faint-hearted
pústula *nf* sore, pustule
puta *nf Vulg* whore; **de p. madre** great, terrific; **de p. pena** *Br* bloody o *US* goddamn awful; **no tengo ni p. idea** I haven't (got) a *Br* bloody o *US* goddamn clue; **pasarlas putas** to go through hell, to have a rotten time
putada *nf Vulg* dirty trick
puteada *nf RP muy Fam (insulto)* swear-word
putear *vt* (**a**) *Vulg (fastidiar)* to fuck o piss around (**b**) *RP muy Fam (insultar)* **p. a algn** to call sb for everything, to call sb every name under the sun

puticlub *nm Fam* brothel
puto,-a 1 *adj Vulg* fucking
  2 *nm* male prostitute, stud
putrefacto,-a, pútrido,-a *adj* putrefied, rotten
puzzle *nm* jigsaw puzzle

PVC *nm* (*abr* **cloruro de polivinilo**) PVC
PVP *nm* (*abr* **precio de venta al público**) RRP
PYME *nf* (*abr* **Pequeña y Mediana Empresa**) SME
Pza. (*abr* **Plaza**) Sq

Q, q [ku] *nf (la letra)* Q, q

que¹ *pron rel* (**a**) *(sujeto) (persona)* who; *(cosa)* that, which; **el hombre q. vino** the man who came; **la bomba q. estalló** the bomb that *o* which went off (**b**) *(complemento) (persona) no se traduce o* that *o* who *o Fml* whom; *(cosa) no se traduce o* that, which; **la chica q. conocí** the girl (that *o* who *o* whom) I met; **el coche q. compré** the car (that *o* which) I bought (**c**) **lo q.** what; **lo q. más me gusta** what I like best (**d**) *(con infinitivo) no se traduce*; **hay mucho q. hacer** there's a lot to do

que² *conj* (**a**) *no se traduce o* that; **dijo q. llamaría** he said (that) he would call; **quiero q. vengas** I want you to come (**b**) *(consecutivo) no se traduce o* that; *(en comparativas)* than; **habla tan bajo q. no se le oye** he speaks so quietly (that) he can't be heard; **más alto q. yo** taller than me (**c**) *(causal) no se traduce* **date deprisa q. no tenemos mucho tiempo** hurry up, we haven't got much time (**d**) *(enfático) no se traduce* **¡q. no!** no!; **¡q. te calles!** I said be quiet! (**e**) *(deseo, mandato) (+ subjunctive) no se traduce*; **¡q. te diviertas!** enjoy yourself! (**f**) *(final)* so that; **ven q. te dé un beso** come and let me give you a kiss (**g**) *(disyuntivo)* whether; **me da igual q. suba o no** it doesn't matter to me whether he comes up or not (**h**) *(locuciones)* **¿a q. no ...?** I bet you can't ...!; **q. yo sepa** as far as I know; **yo q. tú** if I were you

qué 1 *pron interr* (**a**) what; **¿q. quieres?** what do you want?; *Fam* **¿y q.?** so what? (**b**) *(exclamativo) (+ adj)* how; **¡q. bonito!** how pretty! (**c**) *(+ n)* what a; **¡q. lástima!** what a pity! (**d**) *Fam* **¡q. de ...!** what a lot of ...! **2** *adj interr* which; **¿q. libro quieres?** which book do you want?

quebrada *nf Am* stream

quebradero *nm Fig* **q. de cabeza** headache

quebradizo,-a *adj (débil)* fragile; *(cabello, hielo)* brittle

quebrado *nm Mat* fraction

quebradura *nf* (**a**) *(grieta)* crack (**b**) *Med* hernia, rupture

quebrantamiento *nm (de una ley)* violation, infringement

quebrantar 1 *vt (promesa, ley)* to break **2 quebrantarse** *vpr* to break down

quebrar [1] 1 *vt (romper)* to break **2** *vi Fin* to go bankrupt **3 quebrarse** *vpr* to break; *Med* to rupture oneself

queda *nf* **toque de q.** curfew

quedar 1 *vi* (**a**) *(restar)* to be left, to remain; **quedan dos** there are two left (**b**) *(en un lugar)* to arrange to meet; **quedamos en el bar** I'll meet you in the bar (**c**) **me queda corta** *(ropa)* it is too short for me; **quedaría muy bien allí** *(objeto)* it would look very nice there (**d**) *(acordar)* to agree (**en** to); **¿en qué quedamos?** so what's it to be? (**e**) *(estar situado)* to be; **¿dónde queda la estación?** where's the station? (**f**) *(terminar)* to end; **¿en qué quedó la película?** how did the film end? (**g**) *(locuciones)* **q. en ridículo** to make a fool of oneself; **q. bien/mal** to make a good/bad impression **2 quedarse** *vpr* (**a**) *(permanecer)* to stay; **se quedó en casa** she stayed (at) home; **q. sin dinero/pan** to run out of money/bread; **q. con hambre** to still be hungry (**b**) **q. (con)** *(retener)* to keep; **quédese (con) el cambio** keep the change (**c**) *Fam* **q. con algn** to make a fool of sb

quedo *adv* softly, quietly

quehacer *nm* task, chore

queja *nf* complaint; *(de dolor)* groan, moan

quejarse *vpr* to complain (**de** about)

quejica *Fam* **1** *adj* grumpy **2** *nmf* moaner

quejido *nm* groan, cry

quemado,-a *adj* (**a**) burnt, burned; *(del sol)* sunburnt (**b**) *Fig (agotado)* burnt-out

quemador *nm (de cocina etc)* burner

quemadura *nf* burn

quemar 1 *vt* to burn; *Fig (agotar)* to burn out

2 *vi* to be burning hot; **este café quema** this coffee's boiling hot

3 quemarse *upr Fig* to burn oneself out

quemarropa: •a quemarropa *loc adv* point-blank

quemazón *nf* smarting

quena *nf* Andean flute

quepo *indic pres de* **caber**

queque *nm Andes, CAm, Méx* sponge (cake)

querella *nf Jur* lawsuit

querer [20] 1 *vt* (**a**) *(amar)* to love (**b**) *(desear)* to want; **¿cuánto quiere por la casa?** how much does he want for the house?; **sin q.** without meaning to; **queriendo** on purpose; **¡por lo que más quieras!** for heaven's sake!; **¿quiere pasarme el pan?** would you pass me the bread? (**c**) **q. decir** to mean (**d**) **no quiso darme permiso** he refused me permission

2 quererse *upr* to love each other

3 *nm* love, affection

querido,-a 1 *adj* dear, beloved; **q. amigo** *(en carta)* dear friend

2 *nm,f (amante)* lover; *(mujer)* mistress

queroseno *nm* kerosene, kerosine

querré *indic fut de* **querer**

quesadilla *nf CAm, Méx* = filled fried tortilla

queso *nm* cheese; **q. rallado** grated cheese; **q. de cerdo** *Br* brawn, *US* head-cheese

quetzal *nm (moneda)* = standard monetary unit of Guatemala

quiché *adj & nm* Quiché

quicio *nm* (**a**) *(de puerta)* doorpost (**b**) *Fig* **fuera de q.** beside oneself; **sacar de q.** *(a algn)* to infuriate; *(algo)* to take too far

quid *nm* crux; **has dado en el q.** you've hit the nail on the head

quiebra *nf Fin (bancarrota)* bankruptcy; *(crack)* crash

quiebro *nm (con el cuerpo)* dodge; *Ftb* dribbling

quien *pron rel* (**a**) *(con prep)* no se traduce *o Fml* whom; **el hombre con q. vino** the man she came with; *Fml* the man with whom she came (**b**) *(indefinido)* whoever, anyone who; **q. quiera venir que venga** whoever wants to can come; **hay q. dice lo contrario** some people say the opposite; *Fig* **q. más q. menos** everybody

quién *pron interr* (**a**) *(sujeto)* who?; **¿q. es?** who is it? (**b**) *(complemento)* who, *Fml* whom; **¿para q. es?** who is it for?; **¿de q. es esa bici?** whose bike is that?

quienquiera *pron indef* (*pl* **quienesquiera**) whoever

quieto,-a *adj* still; *(mar)* calm; **¡estáte q.!** keep still!, don't move!

quietud *nf* stillness; *(calma)* calm

quijada *nf* jawbone

quilate *nm* carat

quilla *nf* keel

quillango *nm Arg, Chile* hide blanket

quilo *nm* = **kilo**

quilombo *nm RP muy Fam* (**a**) *(burdel)* whorehouse (**b**) *(lío, desorden)* godawful ruckus *o* rumpus

quimera *nf Fig* fantasy, pipe dream

química *nf* chemistry

químico,-a 1 *adj* chemical

2 *nm,f* chemist

quimioterapia *nf* chemotherapy

quimono *nm* kimono

quincalla *nf* metal pots and pans, tinware

quince *adj & nm inv* fifteen

quinceañero,-a *adj & nm,f* fifteen-year-old

quincena *nf* fortnight, two weeks

quincenal *adj* fortnightly

quincho *nm CSur* (**a**) *(techo)* thatched roof (**b**) *(refugio)* thatched shelter

quiniela *nf* football pools

quinientos,-as *adj & nm* five hundred

quinina *nf* quinine

quinqué *nm* oil lamp

quinquenal *adj* quinquennial, five-year

quinqui *nm Fam* delinquent, petty criminal

quinta *nf* (**a**) *(casa)* country house (**b**) *Mil* call-up year

quintaesencia *nf* quintessence

quintal *nm (medida)* = 46 kg; **q. métrico** ≃ 100 kg

quinteto *nm* quintet

quinto,-a 1 *adj & nm,f* fifth

2 *nm Mil* conscript, recruit

quiosco *nm* kiosk; **q. de periódicos** newspaper stand

quirófano *nm* operating theatre

quiromancia *nf* palmistry

quirúrgico,-a *adj* surgical

quise *indic fut de* **querer**

quisque, quisqui *pron Fam* **todo** *o* **cada q.** everyone, everybody

quisquilloso,-a 1 *adj* fussy, finicky

2 *nm,f* fusspot

quiste *nm* cyst

quitaesmalte(s) *nm inv* nail varnish *o* polish remover

quitamanchas *nm inv* stain remover

quitanieves *nm* (máquina) **q.** snow-plough

quitar 1 *vt* (**a**) to remove; *(ropa)* to take off; *(la mesa)* to clear; *(mancha)* to remove; *(dolor)* to relieve; *(hipo)* to stop; *(sed)* to quench; *(hambre)* to take away

(**b**) *(apartar)* to take away, to take off; *Fig* **q. importancia a algo** to play sth down; *Fig* **q. las ganas a algn** to put sb off

(**c**) *(robar)* to steal, to take; *Fig (tiempo)* to take up; *(sitio)* to take

(**d**) *(descontar)* to take off

(**e**) *Fam (apagar)* to turn off

(**f**) **eso no quita para que ...** that's no reason not to be ...

(**g**) **¡quita!** go away!

2 quitarse *vpr* (**a**) *(apartarse)* to move away

(**b**) *(mancha)* to come out; *(dolor)* to go away; **se me han quitado las ganas** I don't feel like it any more

(**c**) *(ropa, gafas)* to take off

(**d**) **q. de beber/fumar** to give up drinking/smoking

(**e**) **q. a algn de encima** to get rid of sb

> Observa que el verbo inglés **to quit** es un falso amigo y no es la traducción del verbo español **quitar**. En inglés, **to quit** significa "dejar, abandonar".

quizá(s) *adv* perhaps, maybe

R

R, r ['erre] *nf (la letra)* R, r

rábano *nm* radish; *Fam* **me importa un r.** I couldn't care less

rabia *nf* (**a**) *Fig (ira)* fury, rage; **¡qué r.!** how annoying!; **me da r.** it gets up my nose; **me tiene r.** he's got it in for me (**b**) *Med* rabies *sing*

rabiar [43] *vi* (**a**) *Fig (sufrir)* to be in great pain (**b**) *Fig (enfadar)* to rage; **hacer r. a algn** to make sb see red (**c**) *Med* to have rabies

rabieta *nf Fam* tantrum; **coger una r.** to throw a tantrum

rabillo *nm (del ojo)* corner

rabino *nm* rabbi

rabioso,-a *adj* (**a**) *Med* rabid; **perro r.** rabid dog (**b**) *Fig (enfadado)* furious (**c**) **de rabiosa actualidad** up-to-the-minute

rabo *nm* tail; *(de fruta etc)* stalk

racanear *vi Fam (ser tacaño)* to be stingy

rácano,-a *adj Fam (tacaño)* stingy, mean

racha *nf (de viento)* gust, squall; *Fam (período)* spell, patch; **a rachas** in fits and starts

racial *adj* **discriminación r.** racial discrimination; **disturbios raciales** race riots

racimo *nm* bunch, cluster

raciocinio *nm* reason

ración *nf* portion

racional *adj* rational

racionalizar [40] *vt* to rationalize

racionamiento *nm* rationing; **cartilla de r.** ration book

racionar *vt (limitar)* to ration; *(repartir)* to ration out

racismo *nm* racism

racista *adj & nmf* racist

radar *nm (pl* **radares***) Téc* radar

radiación *nf* radiation

radiactividad *nf* radioactivity

radiactivo,-a *adj* radioactive

radiador *nm* radiator

radial *adj* (**a**) *(en forma de estrella)* radial (**b**) *Am (de la radio)* radio

radiante *adj* radiant (**de** with)

radiar [43] *vt* to broadcast, to transmit

radical *adj* radical

radicalizar [40] *vt*, **radicalizarse** *vpr (conflicto)* to intensify; *(postura)* to harden

radicar [44] *vi (estar)* to be (situated) (**en** in), to be rooted (**en** in)

radio 1 *nf* radio; *(aparato)* radio (set)

2 *nm* (**a**) radius; **r. de acción** field of action, scope (**b**) *(de rueda)* spoke

radioactividad *nf* radioactivity

radioactivo,-a *adj* radioactive

radioaficionado,-a *nm,f* radio ham

radiocasete *nm (pl* **radiocasetes***)* radio cassette

radioescucha *nmf* listener

radiograbador *nm*, **radiograbadora** *nf CSur* radio cassette

radiografía *nf (imagen)* X-ray

radioyente *nmf* listener

ráfaga *nf (de viento)* gust, squall; *(de disparos)* burst

raído,-a *adj* (**a**) *(gastado)* worn (**b**) *Fam (desvergonzado)* insolent

raigambre *nf* roots

raíl *nm* rail

raíz *nf (pl* **raíces***)* root; **r. cuadrada** square root; *Fig* **a r. de** as a result of

raja *nf (corte)* cut, slit; *(hendidura)* crack, split

rajar 1 *vt (hender)* to crack, to split; *Fam (acuchillar)* to cut up

2 *vi Fam* to backbite

3 rajarse *vpr* (**a**) *(partirse)* to crack, to split (**b**) *Fam (echarse atrás)* to back out (**c**) *Am (acobardarse)* to chicken out

rajatabla: • a rajatabla *loc adv* strictly

ralea *nf Pey* type, sort

ralentí *nm* neutral; **estar al r.** to be ticking over

ralentizar *vt* to slow down

rallado,-a *adj* **queso r.** grated cheese; **pan r.** breadcrumbs

rallador *nm* grater

ralladura *nf* gratings

rallar *vt* to grate

ralo,-a *adj* sparse, thin

rama *nf* branch; *Fam* **andarse** *o* **irse por las ramas** to beat about the bush

ramaje *nm* branches

ramalazo *nm Fam (toque)* touch

rambla *nf (avenida)* boulevard, avenue

ramera *nf* prostitute, whore

ramificación *nf* ramification

ramificarse [44] *vpr* to ramify, to branch (out)

ramillete *nm (de flores)* posy

ramo *nm* (**a**) *(de flores)* bunch, bouquet (**b**) *(sector)* branch

rampa *nf* ramp; **r. de lanzamiento** launch pad

ramplón,-ona *adj* coarse, vulgar

rana *nf* frog; *Fam* **salir r.** to be a disappointment

ranchero,-a *nm,f (granjero)* rancher, farmer

rancho *nm* (**a**) *(granja)* ranch (**b**) *Mil (comida)* mess (**c**) *RP (en la playa)* = thatched beachside building (**d**) *CSur, Ven (en la ciudad)* shack, shanty

rancio,-a *adj* (**a**) *(comida)* stale (**b**) *(antiguo)* ancient

rango *nm* rank; *(jerarquía elevada)* high social standing

ranura *nf* slot

rapar *vt (afeitar)* to shave; *(pelo)* to crop

rapaz¹ *adj* predatory; **ave r.** bird of prey

rapaz²,-aza *nm,f (muchacho)* lad; *(muchacha)* lass

rape *nm* (**a**) *(pez)* angler fish (**b**) *Fam* **cortado al r.** close-cropped

rapidez *nf* speed, rapidity

rápido,-a 1 *adj* quick, fast, rapid
  2 *adv* quickly
  3 *nm* (**a**) *(tren)* fast train (**b**) **rápidos** *(de un río)* rapids

rapiña *nf* robbery, theft; **ave de r.** bird of prey

raptar *vt* to kidnap, to abduct

rapto *nm* (**a**) *(secuestro)* kidnapping, abduction (**b**) *Fig (arrebato)* outburst, fit

raqueta *nf* (**a**) *(de tenis)* racket; *(de ping-pong)* *Br* bat, *US* paddle (**b**) *(de nieve)* snowshoe

raquítico,-a *adj Fam (escaso)* small, meagre; *(delgado)* emaciated

raquitismo *nm* rickets *sing*

rareza *nf* (**a**) rarity, rareness (**b**) *(extravagancia)* eccentricity

raro,-a *adj* (**a**) rare; **rara vez** seldom (**b**) *(extraño)* odd, strange

ras *nm* level; **a r. de** (on a) level with; **a r. de tierra** at ground level

rasante 1 *nf Aut* **cambio de r.** brow of a hill
  2 *adj (vuelo)* low

rasar *vt (nivelar)* to level

rasca *nf Fam (frío)* cold

rascacielos *nm inv* skyscraper

rascar [44] 1 *vt (con las uñas)* to scratch; *(guitarra)* to strum
  2 *vi* to chafe

rasero *nm Fig* **medir con el mismo r.** to treat impartially

rasgado,-a *adj (ojos)* slit, almond-shaped

rasgar [42] *vt* to tear, to rip

rasgo *nm (característica)* characteristic, feature; *(de la cara)* feature; *Fig* **a grandes rasgos** broadly speaking

rasgón *nm* tear, rip

rasguñar *vt* to scratch, to scrape

rasguño *nm* scratch, scrape

rasilla *nf (ladrillo)* tile

raso,-a 1 *adj (llano)* flat, level; *(vuelo)* low; *(cielo)* clear, cloudless; **soldado r.** private
  2 *nm* satin

raspa *nf (de pescado)* bone, backbone

raspador *nm* scraper

raspadura *nf (ralladura)* scraping, scrapings

raspar 1 *vt (limar)* to scrape (off)
  2 *vi (ropa etc)* to chafe

rasposo,-a *adj* rough, sharp

rastra *nf Agr* harrow; **a la r., a rastras** dragging; *Fig (de mal grado)* grudgingly

rastreador *nm* tracker

rastrear *vt (zona)* to comb

rastreo *nm* search

rastrero,-a *adj* creeping; *Fig (despreciable)* vile, base

rastrillo *nm* (**a**) rake (**b**) *Fam (mercadillo)* flea market

rastro *nm* (**a**) trace, sign; *(en el suelo)* track, trail (**b**) **el R.** = the Madrid flea market

rastrojo *nm* stubble

rasurar *vt*, **rasurarse** *vpr* to shave

rata 1 *nf* rat
  2 *nm Fam (tacaño)* mean o stingy person

ratero,-a *nm,f* pickpocket

raticida *nm* rat poison

ratificar [44] *vt* to ratify

rato *nm* (**a**) *(momento)* while, time; **a ratos** at times; **al poco r.** shortly after; **hay para r.** it'll take a while; **pasar un buen/mal r.** to have a good/bad time; **ratos libres** free time (**b**) *Fam* **un r.** *(mucho)* very, a lot

ratón *nm* mouse; *Informát* mouse

ratonera *nf* mousetrap

raudal *nm* torrent, flood; *Fig* **a raudales** in abundance

raya *nf* (**a**) *(línea)* line; *(del pantalón)* crease; *(del pelo)* parting; **camisa a rayas** striped shirt (**b**) *Fig* **tener a r.** to keep at bay; **pasarse de la r.** to go over the score (**c**) *(de droga)* fix, dose

rayano,-a *adj* bordering (**en** on)

rayar 1 *vt (arañar)* to scratch

2 *vi* **r. en** *o* **con** to border on
rayo *nm* (**a**) ray, beam; **rayos X** X-rays (**b**) *(relámpago)* (flash of) lightning; **¡mal r. la parta!** to hell with her!
rayón *nm* rayon
rayuela *nf* hopscotch
raza *nf* (**a**) *(humana)* race (**b**) *(de animal)* breed (**c**) *Perú (descaro)* cheek, nerve
razón *nf* (**a**) *(facultad)* reason; **uso de r.** power of reasoning (**b**) *(motivo)* reason; **r. de más para** all the more reason to (**c**) *(justicia)* rightness, justice; **dar la r. a algn** to say that sb is right; **tienes r.** you're right (**d**) *(proporción)* ratio, rate; **a r. de** at the rate of (**e**) **r. aquí** *(en letrero)* enquire within, apply within
razonable *adj* reasonable
razonado,-a *adj* reasoned, well-reasoned
razonamiento *nm* reasoning
razonar 1 *vt (argumentar)* to reason out
2 *vi (discurrir)* to reason
RDA *nf Hist* (*abr* **República Democrática Alemana** *o* **de Alemania**) GDR
re- *pref* re-
reacción *nf* reaction; **avión de r.** jet (plane); **r. en cadena** chain reaction
reaccionar *vi* to react
reaccionario,-a *adj & nm,f* reactionary
reacio,-a *adj* reluctant, unwilling
reactor *nm* reactor; *(avión)* jet (plane)
readaptación *nf* rehabilitation; **r. profesional** industrial retraining
reafirmar *vt* to reaffirm, to reassert
reagrupar *vt*, **reagruparse** *vpr* to regroup
reajuste *nm* readjustment; *Com* **r. de plantillas** downsizing; **r. ministerial** cabinet reshuffle
real¹ *adj (efectivo, verdadero)* real; **en la vida r.** in real life
real² *adj (regio)* royal
realce *nm (relieve)* relief; *Fig (esplendor)* splendour
realeza *nf* royalty
realidad *nf* reality; **en r.** in fact, actually; **la r. es que ...** the fact of the matter is that ...
realismo *nm* realism
realista 1 *adj* realistic
2 *nmf* realist
realizable *adj* feasible
realización *nf (ejecución)* carrying out; *Cin & TV* production
realizador,-a *nm,f Cin & TV* producer
realizar [40] 1 *vt* (**a**) *(hacer)* to carry out; *(ambición)* to achieve, to fulfil (**b**) *Cin & TV* to produce (**c**) *Fin* to realize

2 realizarse *vpr (persona)* to fulfil oneself; *(sueño)* to come true
realmente *adv* really; *(en realidad)* actually, in fact
realzar [40] *vt (recalcar)* to highlight; *Fig (belleza, importancia)* to enhance, to heighten
reanimación *nf* revival
reanimar *vt*, **reanimarse** *vpr* to revive
reanudación *nf* renewal, resumption, re-establishment; **r. de las clases** return to school
reanudar 1 *vt* to renew, to resume; **r. el paso** *o* **la marcha** to set off again; **r. las clases** to go back to school
2 reanudarse *vpr* to start again, to resume
reaparición *nf* reappearance, recurrence; *(de artista etc)* comeback
reapertura *nf* reopening
rearme *nm* rearmament
reaseguro *nm* reinsurance
reavivar *vt* to revive
rebaja *nf (descuento)* reduction, discount; **rebajas** sales; **precio de r.** sale price
rebajar 1 *vt* (**a**) *(precio)* to cut, to reduce; *(cantidad)* to take off (**b**) *(color)* to tone down, to soften; *(intensidad)* to diminish (**c**) *(trabajador)* to excuse, to exempt (**de** from) (**d**) *(humillar)* to humiliate
2 rebajarse *vpr (humillarse)* to humble oneself
rebanada *nf* slice
rebanar *vt* to slice, to cut into slices
rebañar *vt (plato etc)* to finish off
rebaño *nm (de ovejas)* flock; *(de otros animales)* herd
rebasar *vt* (**a**) *(exceder)* to exceed, to go beyond (**b**) *Aut* to overtake
rebatir *vt* to refute

> 🖋 Observa que la palabra inglesa **rebate** es un falso amigo y no es la traducción del verbo español **rebatir**. En inglés, **rebate** significa "devolución".

rebeca *nf* cardigan
rebelarse *vpr* to rebel, to revolt
rebelde 1 *nmf* rebel
2 *adj* rebellious; *Fig* **una tos r.** a persistent cough
rebeldía *nf* (**a**) rebelliousness (**b**) *Jur* default
rebelión *nf* rebellion, revolt
rebenque *nm RP* whip
reblandecer [33] *vt* to soften
rebobinar *vt* to rewind
rebosante *adj* overflowing (**de** with), brimming (**de** with)

rebosar 1 *vi* to overflow, to brim over; *Fig* **r. de** to be overflowing *o* brimming with **2** *vt (irradiar)* to radiate

rebotar *vi (pelota)* to bounce, to rebound; *(bala)* to ricochet

rebote *nm (de pelota)* bounce, rebound; *(de bala)* ricochet; **de r.** on the rebound

rebozar [40] *vt* to coat in breadcrumbs/ batter

rebozo *nm Am* wrap, shawl

rebullir *vi,* **rebullirse** *vpr* to stir

rebuscado,-a *adj* recherché

rebuznar *vi* to bray

recabar *vt (información)* to obtain, to manage to get

recado *nm (mandado)* errand; *(mensaje)* message; **dejar un r.** to leave a message

recaer [39] *vi* (**a**) *Med* to relapse (**b**) *(culpa, responsabilidad)* to fall (**sobre** on)

recaída *nf* relapse

recalcar [44] *vt* to stress, to emphasize

recalcitrante *adj* recalcitrant

recalentar [1] *vt (comida)* to reheat, to warm up; *(calentar demasiado)* to overheat

recámara *nf* (**a**) *(de rueda)* tube (**b**) *(habitación)* dressing room (**c**) *CAm, Col, Méx (dormitorio)* bedroom

recamarera *nf CAm, Col, Méx* chambermaid

recambiar [43] *vt* to change (over)

recambio *nm* (**a**) *(repuesto)* spare (part); **rueda de r.** spare wheel (**b**) *(de pluma etc)* refill

recapacitar *vi* to reflect, to think

recargable *adj (pluma)* refillable; *(mechero)* rechargeable

recargado,-a *adj* overloaded; *Fig (estilo)* overelaborate, affected

recargar [42] 1 *vt* (**a**) *Elec* to recharge (**b**) *(sobrecargar)* to overload; *(adornar mucho)* to overelaborate (**c**) *Fin* to increase **2 recargarse** *vpr Méx (apoyarse)* to lean (**contra** against)

recargo *nm* extra charge, surcharge

recatado,-a *adj (prudente)* prudent, cautious; *(modesto)* modest, decent

recato *nm (cautela)* caution, prudence; *(pudor)* modesty

recaudación *nf (cobro)* collection; *(cantidad recaudada)* takings; *Dep* gate

recaudador,-a *nm,f* tax collector

recaudar *vt* to collect

recaudo *nm* **estar a buen r.** to be in safekeeping

recelar *vi* **r. de** to distrust

recelo *nm* suspicion, distrust

receloso,-a *adj* suspicious, distrustful

recepción *nf* reception; *(en hotel)* reception (desk)

recepcionista *nmf* receptionist

receptivo,-a *adj* receptive

receptor,-a 1 *nm,f (persona)* recipient **2** *nm Rad & TV* receiver

recesión *nf* recession

receta *nf* recipe; *Med* prescription

recetar *vt Med* to prescribe

rechace *nm Dep* clearance

rechazar [40] *vt* to reject, to turn down; *Mil* to repel, to drive back

rechazo *nm* rejection

rechiflar *vt* (**a**) *(silbar)* to hiss, to boo (**b**) *(mofarse)* to mock, to jeer at

rechinar *vi (madera)* to creak; *(metal)* to squeak, to screech; *(dientes)* to chatter

rechistar *vi* **sin r.** that's final

rechoncho,-a *adj Fam* chubby, tubby

rechupete: • **de rechupete** *loc Fam* **me sé el tema de r.** I know the subject inside out; **la comida estaba de r.** the food was mouthwateringly good

recibidor *nm* entrance hall

recibimiento *nm* reception, welcome

recibir 1 *vt* to receive; *(en casa)* to welcome; *(en la estación etc)* to meet **2 recibirse** *vpr Am (graduarse)* to graduate, to qualify (**de** as)

recibo *nm* (**a**) *(factura)* invoice, bill; *(resguardo)* receipt; **r. de la luz** electricity bill (**b**) **acusar r. de** to acknowledge receipt of

reciclado,-a 1 *adj* recycled **2** *nm (reciclaje)* recycling

reciclaje *nm (de residuos)* recycling; *Fig (renovación)* retraining; **curso de r.** refresher course

reciclar *vt (residuos)* to recycle; *Fig (profesores etc)* to retrain

recién *adv* (**a**) *(recientemente) (antes de pp)* recently, newly; **café r. hecho** freshly made coffee; **r. casados** newlyweds; **r. nacido** newborn baby (**b**) *Am (hace poco)* recently

reciente *adj* recent

recientemente *adv* recently, lately

recinto *nm (cercado)* enclosure; **r. comercial** shopping precinct

recio,-a 1 *adj (robusto)* strong, sturdy; *(grueso)* thick; *(voz)* loud **2** *adv* hard

recipiente *nm* receptacle, container

Observa que la palabra inglesa **recipient** es un falso amigo y no es la traducción de la palabra española **recipiente**. En inglés, **recipient** significa "receptor, destinatario".

recíproco,-a *adj* reciprocal
recital *nm Mús* recital; *Lit* reading
recitar *vt* to recite
reclamación *nf* (**a**) *(demanda)* claim, demand (**b**) *(queja)* complaint
reclamar 1 *vt* to claim, to demand
   2 *vi* (**a**) to protest (**contra** against) (**b**) *Jur* to appeal
reclamo *nm* (**a**) *(publicitario)* appeal (**b**) *(en caza)* decoy bird, lure; *Fig* inducement (**c**) *Am (queja)* complaint (**d**) *Am (reivindicación)* claim
reclinar 1 *vt* to lean (**sobre** on)
   2 reclinarse *vpr* to lean back, to recline
recluir [37] *vt* to shut away, to lock away; *(encarcelar)* to imprison, to intern
reclusión *nf* seclusion; *(encarcelamiento)* imprisonment, internment
recluso,-a *nm,f* prisoner

>   Observa que la palabra inglesa **recluse** es un falso amigo y no es la traducción de la palabra española **recluso**. En inglés, **recluse** significa "solitario".

recluta *nmf* recruit
reclutamiento *nm (voluntario)* recruitment; *(obligatorio)* conscription
recobrar 1 *vt* to recover, to retrieve; *(conocimiento)* to regain; **r. el aliento** to get one's breath back
   2 recobrarse *vpr* to recover, to recuperate
recochineo *nm Fam* mockery
recodo *nm (de río)* twist, turn; *(de camino)* bend
recogedor *nm* dustpan
recoger [53] 1 *vt* (**a**) *(del suelo etc)* to pick up (**b**) *(datos etc)* to gather, to collect (**c**) *(ordenar, limpiar)* to clean; **r. la mesa** to clear the table (**d**) *(ira buscar)* to pick up, to fetch (**e**) *(cosecha)* to gather, to pick
   2 recogerse *vpr* (**a**) *(irse a casa)* to go home (**b**) *(pelo)* to lift up
recogida *nf* collection; *Agr (cosecha)* harvest, harvesting
recolección *nf Agr* harvest, harvesting; *(recogida)* collection, gathering

>   Observa que la palabra inglesa **recollection** es un falso amigo y no es la traducción de la palabra española **recolección**. En inglés, **recollection** significa "recuerdo".

recomendable *adj* recommendable
recomendación *nf* recommendation, reference
recomendado,-a *adj Am (carta, paquete)* registered
recomendar [1] *vt* to recommend

recompensa *nf* reward
recompensar *vt* to reward
recomponer [19] (*pp* **recompuesto**) *vt* to repair, to mend
reconciliación *nf* reconciliation
reconciliar [43] 1 *vt* to reconcile
   2 reconciliarse *vpr* to be reconciled
recóndito,-a *adj* hidden, secret
reconfortante *adj* comforting
reconfortar *vt* to comfort
reconocer [34] *vt* (**a**) to recognize (**b**) *(admitir)* to recognize, to admit (**c**) *Med (paciente)* to examine
reconocimiento *nm* (**a**) recognition (**b**) *Med* examination, checkup
reconquista *nf* reconquest
reconstituyente *nm* tonic
reconstruir [37] *vt* to reconstruct
reconversión *nf* reconversion; **r. industrial** industrial redeployment
reconvertir [5] *vt* to reconvert; *Ind* to modernize
recopilación *nf* (**a**) *(resumen)* summary, résumé (**b**) *(compendio)* compilation, collection
recopilar *vt* to compile, to collect
récord *nm* record
recordar [2] 1 *vt* (**a**) *(rememorar)* to remember (**b**) **r. algo a algn** to remind sb of sth
   2 *vi* to remember
recordatorio *nm (aviso)* reminder; *(de defunción)* notice of death
recordman *nm* record holder
recorrer *vt (distancia)* to cover, to travel; *(país)* to tour, to travel through o round; *(ciudad)* to visit, to walk round
recorrido *nm*, *Am* **recorrida** *nf (distancia)* distance travelled; *(trayecto)* trip, journey; *(itinerario)* itinerary, route
recortable *adj & nm* cutout
recortar *vt* to cut out
recorte *nm (acción, de periódico)* cutting; *(de pelo)* trim, cut; *Fig (de salarios etc)* cut
recostado,-a *adj* reclining, leaning
recostar [2] 1 *vt* to lean
   2 recostarse *vpr (tumbarse)* to lie down
recoveco *nm (curva)* turn, bend; *(rincón)* nook, corner
recreación *nf* recreation
recrear 1 *vt* (**a**) *(divertir)* to amuse, to entertain (**b**) *(crear de nuevo)* to recreate
   2 recrearse *vpr* to amuse oneself, to enjoy oneself; **r. con** to take pleasure o delight in
recreativo,-a *adj* recreational
recreo *nm* (**a**) *(diversión)* recreation (**b**) *(en el colegio)* break, recreation

recriminar *vt* to recriminate; *(reprochar)* to reproach

recrudecer [33] *vt*, **recrudecerse** *vpr* to worsen

recrudecimiento *nm* worsening

recta *nf Geom* straight line; *(de carretera)* straight stretch; *Dep* **la r. final** the home straight

rectangular *adj* rectangular

rectángulo *nm* rectangle

rectificación *nf* rectification; *(corrección)* correction

rectificar [44] *vt* to rectify; *(corregir)* to correct, to remedy

rectilíneo,-a *adj* straight

rectitud *nf* straightness; *Fig* uprightness, rectitude

recto,-a 1 *adj* (**a**) *(derecho)* straight (**b**) *(honesto)* upright, honest (**c**) *Geom* right
  2 *nm Anat* rectum
  3 *adv* straight (on)

rector,-a 1 *adj (principio)* guiding, ruling
  2 *nm,f* rector

recua *nf Fig* string, series

recuadro *nm Prensa* box

recubrir *(pp* **recubierto)** *vt* to cover

recuento *nm* count; **hacer (el) r. de** to count

recuerdo *nm* (**a**) *(memoria)* memory (**b**) *(regalo etc)* souvenir (**c**) **recuerdos** regards

recuperación *nf* recovery; *(examen)* resit

recuperar 1 *vt (salud)* to recover; *(conocimiento)* to regain; *(tiempo, clases)* to make up
  2 recuperarse *vpr* to recover

recurrir *vi* (**a**) *Jur* to appeal (**b**) **r. a** *(a algn)* to turn to; *(a algo)* to make use of, to resort to

> 🖉 Observa que el verbo inglés **to recur** es un falso amigo y no es la traducción del verbo español **recurrir**. En inglés, **to recur** significa "repetirse".

recurso *nm* (**a**) resource; **recursos naturales** natural resources; **como último r.** as a last resort (**b**) *Jur* appeal

recusar *vt* to challenge, to object to

red *nf* net; *(sistema)* network; *Com (cadena)* chain of supermarkets; *Fig (trampa)* trap; **la R.** *(Internet)* the Net

redacción *nf (escrito)* composition, essay; *(acción)* writing; *Prensa* editing; *(redactores)* editorial staff

redactar *vt* to draft; *Prensa* to edit

redactor,-a *nm,f Prensa* editor

redada *nf* **r. policial** *(en un solo sitio)* raid;

(en varios lugares a la vez) round-up

redentor,-a *nm,f* redeemer

redicho,-a *adj Fam* affected, pretentious

redil *nm* fold, sheepfold

redimir *vt* to redeem

rédito *nm* yield, interest

redituable *adj* interest-yielding

redoblar 1 *vt* to redouble
  2 *vi (tambor)* to roll

redoble *nm* roll; *(de campanas)* peal

redomado,-a *adj* utter, out-and-out

redonda *nf* **a la r.** around

redondear *vt (objeto)* to round, to make round; *(cantidad)* to round up

redondel *nm Fam (círculo)* circle, ring; *Taurom* ring, arena

redondo,-a *adj* (**a**) round; *Fig* **caer r.** to collapse (**b**) *(rotundo)* categorical; *(perfecto)* perfect

reducción *nf* reduction

reducido,-a *adj (disminuido)* reduced, decreased; *(pequeño)* limited, small

reducir [10] 1 *vt (disminuir)* to reduce
  2 reducirse *vpr* (**a**) *(disminuirse)* to be reduced, to diminish (**b**) *(limitarse)* to confine oneself

redundancia *nf* redundancy, superfluousness; **valga la r.** if I might say so again

redundante *adj* redundant

redundar *vi* **r. en** *(resultar)* to result in, to lead to

reduplicar [44] *vt* to redouble

reembolsar *vt* to reimburse; *(deuda)* to repay; *(importe)* to refund

reembolso *nm* reimbursement; *(de deuda)* repayment; *(devolución)* refund; **contra r.** cash on delivery

reemplazar [40] *vt* to replace (**con** with)

reemplazo *nm* replacement; *Mil* call-up

reestructuración *nf* restructuring

reestructurar *vt* to restructure

ref. (*abr* **referencia**) ref

refacción *nf* (**a**) *Andes, CAm, RP, Ven (reparación)* repair (**b**) *Méx (recambio)* spare part

refaccionar *vt Am* to repair, to do up

refectorio *nm* refectory, canteen

referencia *nf* reference; **con r. a** with reference to

referéndum *nm* (*pl* **referéndums**) referendum

referente *adj* **r. a** concerning, regarding

referir [5] 1 *vt* to tell, to relate
  2 referirse *vpr (aludir)* to refer (**a** to); **¿a qué te refieres?** what do you mean?

refilón: • de refilón *loc adv (de pasada)* briefly

refinado,-a *adj* refined
refinamiento *nm* refinement
refinar *vt* to refine
refinería *nf* refinery
reflector,-a 1 *adj* reflecting
2 *nm Elec* spotlight, searchlight
reflejar 1 *vt* to reflect
2 reflejarse *vpr* to be reflected (**en** in)
reflejo,-a 1 *nm* (**a**) *(imagen)* reflection
(**b**) *(destello)* gleam, glint (**c**) *Anat* reflex
(**d**) **reflejos** *(en el cabello)* streaks, highlights
2 *adj (movimiento)* reflex
reflexión *nf* reflection
reflexionar *vi* to reflect (**sobre** on), to think (**sobre** about)
reflexivo,-a *adj* (**a**) *(persona)* thoughtful
(**b**) *Ling* reflexive
reflujo *nm* ebb (tide)
reforma *nf* (**a**) reform; **r. fiscal** tax reform
(**b**) *(reparación)* repair
reformador,-a *nm,f* reformer
reformar 1 *vt* to reform; *(edificio)* to renovate
2 reformarse *vpr* to reform
reformatorio *nm* reformatory, reform school
reforzar [2] *vt* to reinforce, to strengthen
refractario,-a *adj* (**a**) *Téc* heat-resistant
(**b**) *(persona)* unwilling, reluctant
refrán *nm* proverb, saying
refregar [1] *vt* to rub vigorously; *Fig* **no me lo refriegues** don't rub it in
refrenar 1 *vt (contener)* to restrain, to curb
2 refrenarse *vpr* to restrain oneself
refrendar *vt (firmar)* to endorse, to countersign; *(aprobar)* to approve
refrescante *adj* refreshing
refrescar [44] 1 *vt* to refresh
2 *vi* (**a**) *(tiempo)* to turn cool (**b**) *(bebida)* to be refreshing
3 refrescarse *vpr* to cool down
refresco *nm* soft drink, refreshments
refriega *nf (lucha)* scuffle, brawl; *(escaramuza)* skirmish
refrigeración *nf (enfriamiento)* refrigeration; *(aire acondicionado)* air conditioning
refrigerado,-a *adj* air-conditioned
refrigerador *nm* refrigerator, fridge
refrigerar *vt* to refrigerate; *(habitación)* to air-condition
refrigerio *nm* snack, refreshments
refuerzo *nm* reinforcement, strengthening
refugiado,-a *adj & nm,f* refugee

refugiarse [43] *vpr* to shelter, to take refuge
refugio *nm* refuge
refulgente *adj* radiant, brilliant
refulgir [57] *vi (brillar)* to shine; *(resplandecer)* to glitter, to sparkle
refunfuñar *vi* to grumble, to moan
refutar *vt* to refute
regadera *nf* (**a**) *(para regar)* watering can; *Fam* **estar como una r.** to be as mad as a hatter (**b**) *Col, Méx, Ven (ducha)* shower
regadío *nm (tierra)* irrigated land
regalado,-a *adj* (**a**) *(gratis)* free; *(muy barato)* dirt-cheap (**b**) **una vida regalada** an easy life
regalar *vt* (**a**) *(dar)* to give (as a present); *(en ofertas etc)* to give away (**b**) **r. el oído a algn** to flatter sb
regaliz *nm* liquorice
regalo *nm* (**a**) gift, present; **de r.** as a present (**b**) *(comodidad)* pleasure, comfort
regalón,-ona *adj CSur Fam (niño)* spoilt
regañadientes: • a regañadientes *loc adv* reluctantly, unwillingly
regañar 1 *vt Fam* to scold, to tell off
2 *vi* to nag
regañina *nf* scolding, telling-off
regañón,-ona *nm,f Fam* nag
regar [1] *vt* to water
regata *nf* boat race
regatear 1 *vi* (**a**) to haggle, to bargain (**b**) *Dep* to dribble
2 *vt* **no r. esfuerzos** to spare no effort
regateo *nm* (**a**) *(de precios)* haggling (**b**) *Dep* dribbling
regazo *nm* lap
regeneración *nf* regeneration
regenerar *vt* to regenerate
regentar *vt* to rule, to govern; *(cargo)* to hold
regente *nmf* (**a**) *Pol* regent (**b**) *(director)* manager (**c**) *Méx (alcalde)* mayor, *f* mayoress
régimen *nm* (*pl* **regímenes**) (**a**) *Pol* regime (**b**) *Med* diet; **estar a r.** to be on a diet
regimiento *nm* regiment
regio,-a *adj* (**a**) *(real)* royal, regal (**b**) *(suntuoso)* sumptuous, luxurious; *Am (magnífico)* splendid, majestic
región *nf* region
regional *adj* regional
regionalista *adj & nmf* regionalist
regir [58] 1 *vt* to govern
2 *vi* to be in force
3 regirse *vpr* to be guided, to go (**por** by)
registrado,-a *adj* (**a**) *(patentado, inscrito)*

registered; **marca registrada** registered trademark (**b**) *Am (certificado)* registered
registrador,-a *adj* **caja registradora** cash register
registradora *nf Am* cash register
registrar 1 *vt* (**a**) *(examinar)* to inspect; *(cachear)* to frisk (**b**) *(inscribir)* to register (**c**) *(grabar)* to record
 2 registrarse *vpr* (**a**) *(inscribirse)* to register, to enrol (**b**) *(detectarse)* to be recorded
registro *nm* (**a**) inspection (**b**) *(inscripción)* registration, recording; *(oficina)* registry office (**c**) *Mús* register
regla *nf* (**a**) *(norma)* rule; **en r.** in order; **por r. general** as a (general) rule; **r. de oro** golden rule (**b**) *(instrumento)* ruler (**c**) *Mat* rule (**d**) *Med (periodo)* period
reglamentación *nf* (**a**) *(acción)* regulation (**b**) *(reglamento)* regulations, rules
reglamentar *vt* to regulate
reglamentario,-a *adj* statutory; *Mil* **arma reglamentaria** regulation gun
reglamento *nm* regulations, rules
reglar *vt* to regulate
regocijar 1 *vt* to delight, to amuse
 2 regocijarse *vpr* to be delighted, to rejoice
regocijo *nm (placer)* delight, joy; *(alborozo)* rejoicing, merriment
regodearse *vpr Fam* to delight (**con** in)
regodeo *nm Fam* delight
regordete,-a *adj Fam* plump, chubby
regresar 1 *vi* to return
 2 *vt Andes, CAm, Carib, Méx (devolver)* to give back
 3 regresarse *vpr Andes, CAm, Carib, Méx (yendo)* to go back, to return; *(viniendo)* to come back, to return
regresión *nf* regression; *(decaimiento)* deterioration, decline
regreso *nm* return
reguero *nm (corriente)* trickle; *(de humo)* trail
regulable *adj* adjustable
regular 1 *vt* (**a**) to regulate, to control (**b**) *(ajustar)* to adjust
 2 *adj* (**a**) regular; **por lo r.** as a rule; **vuelo r.** scheduled flight (**b**) *Fam (mediano)* average, so-so
 3 *adv* so-so
regularidad *nf* regularity; **con r.** regularly
regularizar [40] *vt* to regularize
regusto *nm* aftertaste
rehabilitar *vt* to rehabilitate; *(edificio)* to convert
rehacer [15] (*pp* **rehecho**) **1** *vt* to redo

 2 rehacerse *vpr (recuperarse)* to recover, to recuperate
rehén *nm* hostage
rehogar [42] *vt* to brown
rehuir [37] *vt* to shun, to avoid
rehusar *vt* to refuse
reina *nf* queen
reinado *nm* reign
reinante *adj (que reina)* reigning, ruling; *(prevaleciente)* prevailing
reinar *vi* to reign
reincidente *nmf Jur* recidivist
reincidir *vi* to relapse, to fall back (**en** into)
reincorporarse *vpr* **r. al trabajo** to return to work
reino *nm* kingdom; **el R. Unido** the United Kingdom
reinserción *nf* reintegration
reinsertar *vt*, **reinsertarse** *vpr* to reintegrate
reintegrar *vt* (**a**) *(trabajador)* to reinstate (**b**) *(dinero)* to reimburse, to refund
reintegro *nm (en lotería)* winning of one's stake
reír [56] 1 *vi* to laugh
 2 reírse *vpr* (**a**) to laugh (**b**) *(mofarse)* to laugh (**de** at), to make fun (**de** of)
reiterar *vt* to reiterate, to repeat
reivindicación *nf* claim, demand
reivindicar [44] *vt* to claim, to demand; **el atentado fue reivindicado por los terroristas** the terrorists claimed responsibility for the attack
reivindicativo,-a *adj* protest
reja *nf* (**a**) *(de ventana)* grill, grating; *Fam* **estar entre rejas** to be behind bars (**b**) *Agr* ploughshare
rejilla *nf (de ventana, ventilador, radiador)* grill; *(de horno)* gridiron; *(para equipaje)* luggage rack
rejoneador,-a *nm,f Taurom* = bullfighter on horseback
rejonear *vt Taurom* to fight on horseback
rejuvenecer [33] *vt* to rejuvenate
relación *nf* (**a**) relationship; *(conexión)* connection, link; **con** *o* **en r. a** with regard to; **relaciones públicas** public relations (**b**) *(lista)* list (**c**) *(relato)* account (**d**) *Mat & Téc* ratio
relacionado,-a *adj* related (**con** to), connected (**con** with)
relacionar 1 *vt* to relate (**con** to), to connect (**con** with)
 2 •relacionarse *vpr* (**a**) to be related, to be connected (**b**) *(alternar)* to mix, to get acquainted
relajación *nf* relaxation

relajante *adj* relaxing
relajar 1 *vt* to relax
  2 relajarse *vpr* to relax; *(moral)* to deteriorate
relajo *nm Am Fam (alboroto)* racket, din
relamerse *vpr* to lick one's lips
relamido,-a *adj (afectado)* affected; *(pulcro)* prim and proper
relámpago *nm* flash of lightning; *Fig* **pasó como un r.** he flashed past; *Fig* **visita r.** flying visit
relampaguear *v impers* to flash
relanzar *vt* to relaunch
relatar *vt* to narrate, to relate
relatividad *nf* relativity
relativo,-a *adj* relative (**a** to); **en lo r. a** with regard to, concerning
relato *nm (cuento)* tale, story
relax *nm Fam* relaxation
relegar [42] *vt* to relegate
relente *nm* dew
relevancia *nf* importance

> *ℓ* Observa que la palabra inglesa **relevance** es un falso amigo y no es la traducción de la palabra española **relevancia**. En inglés, **relevance** significa "pertinencia".

relevante *adj* important
relevar 1 *vt* to relieve, to take over from; **fue relevado del cargo** he was relieved of his duties
  2 relevarse *vpr (turnarse)* to relieve one another
relevo *nm* relief; *Dep* relay
relieve *nm Arte* relief; *Fig* **poner de r.** to emphasize
religión *nf* religion
religioso,-a 1 *adj* religious
  2 *nm,f (hombre)* monk; *(mujer)* nun
relinchar *vi* to neigh, to whinny
relincho *nm* neigh, whinny
reliquia *nf* relic
rellamada *nf Tel* redial
rellano *nm* landing
rellenar *vt* (**a**) *(impreso etc)* to fill in (**b**) *(un ave)* to stuff; *(un pastel)* to fill
relleno,-a 1 *nm (de aves)* stuffing; *(de pasteles)* filling
  2 *adj* stuffed
reloj *nm* clock; *(de pulsera)* watch; **r. de arena** hourglass; **r. de sol** sundial; **r. despertador** alarm clock
relojería *nf (tienda)* watchmaker's, clockmaker's; **bomba de r.** time bomb
relojero,-a *nm,f* watchmaker, clockmaker
reluciente *adj* shining, gleaming
relucir [35] *vi (brillar)* to shine, to gleam; **sacar a r. un tema** to bring up a subject

relumbrar *vi* to shine, to gleam
reluzco *indic pres de* **relucir**
remachar *vt* to drive home, to hammer home
remache *nm* rivet
remanente *nm (restos)* remainder; *(extra)* surplus
remangar [42] *vt*, **remangarse** *vpr (mangas, pantalones)* to roll up; *(camisa)* to tuck up
remanso *nm* pool; *(lugar tranquilo)* quiet place
remar *vi* to row
remarcar [44] *vt* to stress, to underline

> *ℓ* Observa que el verbo inglés **to remark** es un falso amigo y no es la traducción del verbo español **remarcar**. En inglés, **to remark** significa "comentar, observar".

rematadamente *adv* **r. loco** as mad as a hatter
rematar *vt* (**a**) to finish off, to put the finishing touches to (**b**) *Com* to sell off cheaply (**c**) *Dep* to shoot
remate *nm* (**a**) *(final)* end, finish; **para r.** to crown it all (**b**) *Dep* shot at goal (**c**) **de r.** utter, utterly
rembolsar *vt* = reembolsar
rembolso *nm* = reembolso
remedar *vt* to imitate, to copy
remediar [43] *vt* (**a**) to remedy; *(enmendar)* to repair, to make good (**b**) *(evitar)* to avoid, to prevent; **no pude remediarlo** I couldn't help it
remedio *nm (cura)* remedy, cure; *(solución)* solution; **¡qué r.!** what else can I do?; **no hay más r.** there's no choice; **sin r.** without fail; *Fam* **¡no tienes r.!** you're hopeless!
remedo *nm (imitación)* imitation, copy; *(parodia)* parody
rememorar *vt* to remember, to recall
remendar [1] *vt (ropa)* to patch
remera *nf RP (prenda)* T-shirt
remero,-a *nm,f* rower
remesa *nf (de mercancías)* consignment, shipment; *(de dinero)* remittance
remiendo *nm (parche)* patch
remilgado,-a *adj (afectado)* affected; *(melindroso)* fussy, finicky; *(gazmoño)* prudish
remilgo *nm* affectation; *(gazmoñería)* prudishness
reminiscencia *nf* reminiscence
remise *nm RP* taxi *(in private car without meter)*
remisero,-a *nm,f RP* taxi driver *(of private car without meter)*

remiso,-a *adj* reluctant
remite *nm (en carta)* = sender's name and address
remitente *nmf* sender
remitir 1 *vt* (a) *(enviar)* to send (b) *(referir)* to refer
2 *vi (fiebre, temporal)* to subside
3 **remitirse** *vpr* **si nos remitimos a los hechos** if we look at the facts; **remítase a la página 10** see page 10
remo *nm* oar; *(deporte)* rowing
remoción *nf Andes, RP (de objetos)* transport, removal; *(de heridos)* transport
remodelación *nf (modificación)* reshaping; *(reorganización)* reorganization; *Pol* **r. ministerial** *o* **del gobierno** cabinet reshuffle
remodelar *vt* to reshape; *(reorganizar)* to reorganize
remojar *vt* to soak (**en** in)
remojo *nm* **dejar** *o* **poner en r.** to soak, to leave to soak
remojón *nm Fam* **darse un r.** to go for a dip
remolacha *nf Br* beetroot, *US* beet
remolcador *nm* (a) *Náut* tug, tugboat (b) *Aut Br* breakdown van *o* truck, *US* tow truck
remolcar [44] *vt* to tow
remolino *nm (de agua)* whirlpool, eddy; *(de aire)* whirlwind
remolón,-ona 1 *adj* lazy
2 *nm,f* **hacerse el r.** to shirk, to slack
remolonear *vi* to shirk, to slack
remolque *nm (acción)* towing; *(vehículo)* trailer; *Fig* **ir a r. de algn** to trundle along behind sb
remontar 1 *vt* (a) *(subir)* to go up (b) *(superar)* to overcome
2 **remontarse** *vpr* (a) *(pájaros, aviones)* to soar (b) *(datar)* to go back, to date back (**a** to)
remorder [4] *vt* to trouble; **me remuerde la conciencia por ...** I've got a bad conscience about ...
remordimiento *nm* remorse
remoto,-a *adj* remote, faraway; **no tengo la más remota idea** I haven't got the faintest idea
remover [4] *vt* (a) *(trasladar)* to move over (b) *(tierra)* to turn over; *(líquido)* to shake up; *(comida etc)* to stir; *(asunto)* to stir up

⚠ Observa que el verbo inglés **to remove** es un falso amigo y no es la traducción del verbo español **remover**. En inglés, **to remove** significa "quitar, despedir".

remozar [40] *vt* to modernize
remplazar [40] *vt* = **reemplazar**
remplazo *nm* = **reemplazo**
remuneración *nf* remuneration
remunerar *vt* to remunerate
renacentista *adj* Renaissance
renacer [60] *vi* to be reborn; *Fig (revivir)* to revive, to come back to life
renacimiento *nm* **el R.** the Renaissance
renacuajo *nm* tadpole; *Fam (niño pequeño)* shrimp
renal *adj* kidney; **insuficiencia r.** kidney failure
rencilla *nf* quarrel
rencor *nm* rancour; *(resentimiento)* resentment; **guardar r. a algn** to have a grudge against sb
rencoroso,-a *adj (hostil)* rancorous; *(resentido)* resentful
rendición *nf* surrender
rendido,-a *adj (muy cansado)* exhausted, worn out
rendija *nf* crack, split
rendimiento *nm (producción)* yield, output; *(de máquina, motor)* efficiency, performance
rendir [6] 1 *vt* (a) *(fruto, beneficios)* to yield, to produce (b) *(cansar)* to exhaust, to wear out (c) **r. culto a** to worship; **r. homenaje a** to pay homage to
2 *vi (dar beneficios)* to pay, to be profitable
3 **rendirse** *vpr* (a) to surrender, to give in; **¡me rindo!** I give up! (b) *(cansarse)* to wear oneself out
renegado,-a *adj & nm,f* renegade
renegar [1] *vt* **r. de** to renounce, to disown
renegrido,-a *adj* blackened
RENFE *nf (abr* **Red Nacional de los Ferrocarriles Españoles)** = Spanish state railway company
renglón *nm* line; **a r. seguido** immediately afterwards
rengo,-a *adj Andes, RP* lame
renguear *vi Andes, RP* to limp, to hobble
reno *nm* reindeer
renombrado,-a *adj* renowned, famous
renombre *nm* renown, fame
renovable *adj* renewable
renovación *nf (de contrato, pasaporte)* renewal; *(de una casa)* renovation
renovar [2] *vt* to renew; *(edificio)* to renovate
renta *nf* (a) *Fin (ingresos)* income; *(beneficio)* interest, return; **r. per cápita** per capita income; **r. fija** fixed-interest security (b) *(alquiler)* rent

rentable *adj* profitable

rentar 1 *vt (rendir)* to produce, to yield; *Méx (alquilar)* to rent
  2 *vi* to be profitable

renuncia *nf* (**a**) renunciation (**b**) *(dimisión)* resignation

renunciar [43] *vi* (**a**) **r. a** to renounce, to give up; *(no aceptar)* to decline (**b**) *(dimitir)* to resign

reñido,-a *adj (disputado)* tough, hard-fought

reñir [6] 1 *vt (regañar)* to scold, to tell off
  2 *vi (discutir)* to quarrel, to argue; *(pelear)* to fight; **r. con algn** to fall out with sb

reo *nmf (acusado)* defendant, accused; *(culpable)* culprit

reojo: • **de reojo** *loc adv* **mirar algo de r.** to look at sth out of the corner of one's eye

reparación *nf* repair; *(compensación)* reparation, amends

reparar 1 *vt* to repair; *(ofensa, injuria)* to make amends for; *(daño)* to make good
  2 *vi* **r. en** *(darse cuenta de)* to notice; *(reflexionar sobre)* to think about

reparo *nm* **no tener reparos en** not to hesitate to; **me da r.** I feel embarrassed

repartidor,-a *nm,f* distributor

repartir *vt* (**a**) *(dividir)* to distribute, to share out (**b**) *(regalo, premio)* to give out, to hand out (**c**) *(correo)* to deliver; *Naipes* to deal

reparto *nm* (**a**) distribution, sharing out (**b**) *(distribución)* handing out; *(de mercancías)* delivery (**c**) *Cin & Teatro* cast

repasador *nm RP (trapo)* tea towel

repasar *vt* (**a**) to revise, to go over (**b**) *(ropa)* to mend

repaso *nm* revision

repatear *vt Fam* to annoy, to turn off

repatriar [29] *vt* to repatriate

repecho *nm* short steep slope

repelente *adj* repulsive, repellent; *Fam* **niño r.** little know-all

repeler *vt (rechazar)* to repel, to repulse; *(repugnar)* to disgust

repente *nm Fam (arrebato)* fit, outburst; **de r.** suddenly, all of a sudden

repentino,-a *adj* sudden

repercusión *nf* repercussion

repercutir *vi* (**a**) *(sonido)* to resound, to reverberate; *(objeto)* to rebound (**b**) *Fig* **r. en** to have repercussions on, to affect

repertorio *nm* repertoire, repertory

repesca *nf Fam* second chance; *(examen)* resit

repetición *nf* repetition; **r. de la jugada** action replay

repetido,-a *adj* **repetidas veces** repeatedly

repetidor,-a 1 *adj* repeating
  2 *nm,f Fam Educ* = student who is repeating a year

repetir [6] 1 *vt* (**a**) to repeat (**b**) *(plato)* to have a second helping
  2 *vi Educ* to repeat a year
  3 repetirse *vpr* (**a**) *(persona)* to repeat oneself (**b**) *(hecho)* to recur (**c**) **el pepino se repite** cucumber repeats (on me/you/him/*etc*)

repicar [44] *vt (las campanas)* to peal, to ring out

repipi *adj Fam* **niño r.** little know-all

repique *nm (de campanas)* peal, ringing

repiquetear *vt & vi (campanas)* to ring; *(tambor)* to beat

repisa *nf* shelf, ledge

replantear *vt*, **replantearse** *vpr* to reconsider, to rethink

replegarse [1] *vpr* to fall back, to retreat

repleto,-a *adj* full (up), jam-packed; **r. de** packed with, crammed with

réplica *nf* (**a**) answer, reply (**b**) *(copia)* replica

replicar [44] 1 *vt* to answer back
  2 *vi* (**a**) to reply, to retort (**b**) *(objetar)* to argue (**c**) *Jur* to answer

repliegue *nm Mil* withdrawal, retreat

repoblación *nf* repopulation; **r. forestal** reafforestation

repoblar [2] *vt* to repopulate; *(bosque)* to reafforest

repollo *nm* cabbage

reponer [19] 1 *vt* (**a**) to put back, to replace (**b**) *Teatro (obra)* to put on again; *Cin (película)* to rerun; *TV (programa)* to repeat
  2 reponerse *vpr* **r. de** to recover from, to get over

reportaje *nm Prensa & Rad* report; *(noticias)* article, news item

reportar 1 *vt (beneficios etc)* to bring; *Am (informar)* to report
  2 reportarse *vpr Am (presentarse)* to report (**a** to)

reporte *nm Méx (informe)* report; *(noticia)* news item *o* report; **recibí reportes de mi hermano** I was sent news by my brother; **el r. del tiempo** the weather report *o* forecast

reportero,-a *nm,f* reporter

reposar 1 *vt* to rest (**en** on)
  2 *vi (descansar)* to rest, to take a rest; *(té)* to infuse; *(comida)* to stand

reposera *nf RP Br* sun-lounger, *US* beach recliner

reposición *nf* TV repeat; *Cin* rerun, re-showing

reposo *nm* rest; **en r.** at rest

repostar *vt* *(provisiones)* to stock up with; *Aut (gasolina)* to fill up with

repostería *nf* confectionery; *(tienda)* confectioner's (shop)

repostero,-a *nm,f* confectioner

reprender *vt* to reprimand, to scold

represalia *nf* *(usu pl)* reprisals, retaliation

representación *nf* (**a**) representation (**b**) *Teatro* performance

representante *nmf* representative

representar *vt* (**a**) to represent (**b**) *(significar)* to mean, to represent (**c**) *Teatro (obra)* to perform

representativo,-a *adj* representative

represión *nf* repression

represivo,-a *adj* repressive

reprimenda *nf* reprimand

reprimir *vt* to repress

reprobar [2] *vt* *(cosa)* to condemn; *(a persona)* to reproach, to reprove; *Am (estudiante, examen)* to fail

réprobo,-a *adj & nm,f* reprobate

reprochable *adj* reproachable

reprochar *vt* to reproach; **r. algo a algn** to reproach sb for sth

reproche *nm* reproach

reproducción *nf* reproduction

reproducir [10] 1 *vt* to reproduce

2 reproducirse *vpr* (**a**) to reproduce, to breed (**b**) *(repetirse)* to recur, to happen again

reproductor,-a *adj* reproductive

reptar *vi* to slither

reptil *nm* reptile

república *nf* republic; **la R. Checa** the Czech Republic

republicano,-a *adj & nm,f* republican

repudiar [43] *vt* to repudiate

repuesto *nm* *(recambio)* spare part, spare; *Aut* **rueda de r.** spare wheel

repugnancia *nf* loathing, disgust

repugnante *adj* disgusting, revolting

repugnar *vt* to disgust, to revolt

repujar *vt* to emboss

repulsa *nf* rebuff

repulsión *nf* repulsion, repugnance

repulsivo,-a *adj* repulsive, revolting

repuntar *vi Am (mejorar)* to improve

repunte *nm Am (recuperación)* recovery; *(aumento)* rise, increase; **un r. en las ventas** an improvement o increase in sales

repuse *pt indef de* **reponer**

reputación *nf* reputation

reputar *vt* to consider, to deem

requemar *vt* to scorch

requerimiento *nm* (**a**) *(súplica)* request (**b**) *Jur (aviso)* summons *sing*

> 🖋 Observa que la palabra inglesa **require-ment** es un falso amigo y no es la traducción de la palabra española **requerimiento**. En inglés, **requirement** significa "requisito".

requerir [5] *vt* (**a**) to require (**b**) *(solicitar)* to request (**c**) *Jur (avisar)* to summon

requesón *nm* cottage cheese

requete- *pref Fam* really, very, incredibly; **requetebueno** brilliant

réquiem *nm (pl* **réquiems**) requiem

requisa *nf* (**a**) *(inspección)* inspection (**b**) *Mil* requisition

requisar *vt* to requisition

requisito *nm* requirement, requisite

res *nf* animal

resabiado,-a *adj Pey* pedantic

resabio *nm* (**a**) *(mal sabor)* unpleasant o bad aftertaste (**b**) *(vicio)* bad habit

resaca *nf* (**a**) hangover (**b**) *Náut* undertow, undercurrent

resaltar *vi* (**a**) *(sobresalir)* to project, to jut out (**b**) *Fig* to stand out

resarcir [52] *vt* to compensate

resbalada *nf Am Fam* slip

resbaladizo,-a *adj* slippery

resbalar *vi,* **resbalarse** *vpr* to slip; *Aut* to skid

resbalón *nm* slip

rescatar *vt (persona)* to rescue; *(objeto)* to recover

rescate *nm* (**a**) *(salvamento)* rescue; *(recuperación)* recovery (**b**) *(suma)* ransom

rescindir *vt* to rescind, to annul; *(contrato)* to cancel

rescisión *nf* rescission, annulment

rescoldo *nm* (**a**) embers (**b**) *Fig (recelo)* lingering doubt

resecarse [44] *vpr* to dry up, to become parched

reseco,-a *adj* very dry, parched

resentido,-a *adj* resentful

resentimiento *nm* resentment

resentirse [5] *vpr* (**a**) **r. de** to suffer from, to feel the effects of (**b**) *(ofenderse)* to feel offended; **r. por algo** to take offence at sth, to feel bitter about sth

reseña *nf* review; *Prensa* write-up

reserva 1 *nf* (**a**) *(de entradas etc)* reservation, booking (**b**) *(provisión)* reserve, stock; **un vino de r.** a vintage wine (**c**) *Mil* reserve, reserves (**d**) *(duda)* reservation

2 *nmf Dep* reserve, substitute

reservado,-a 1 *adj (persona)* reserved, quiet
  2 *nm* private room
reservar 1 *vt* (**a**) *(billetes etc)* to reserve, to book (**b**) *(dinero, tiempo etc)* to keep, to save
  2 reservarse *vpr* (**a**) to save oneself (**para** for) (**b**) *(sentimientos)* to keep to oneself (**c**) **r. el derecho de** to reserve the right to
resfriado,-a 1 *nm (catarro)* cold; **coger un r.** to catch (a) cold
  2 *adj* **estar r.** to have a cold
resfriarse *vpr* to catch (a) cold
resfrío *nm Andes, RP* cold
resguardar *vt (proteger)* to protect, to shelter (**de** from)
resguardo *nm* (**a**) *(recibo)* receipt (**b**) *(protección)* protection, shelter
residencia *nf* residence; **r. de ancianos** old people's home
residencial *adj* residential
residente *adj & nmf* resident
residir *vi* to reside, to live (**en** in); *Fig* to lie (**en** in)
residuo *nm* (**a**) residue (**b**) **residuos** waste
resignación *nf* resignation
resignado,-a *adj* resigned
resignarse *vpr* to resign oneself (**a** to)
resina *nf* resin
resistencia *nf* (**a**) resistance (**b**) *(aguante)* endurance, stamina (**c**) *Elec* element
resistente *adj* (**a**) resistant (**a** to) (**b**) *(fuerte)* tough, hardy
resistir 1 *vi* (**a**) to resist (**b**) *(aguantar)* to hold (out)
  2 *vt (situación, persona)* to put up with; *(tentación)* to resist
  3 resistirse *vpr* to resist; *(oponerse)* to offer resistance; *(negarse)* to refuse
resollar [2] *vi* to breathe heavily; *(con silbido)* to wheeze
resolución *nf* (**a**) *(solución)* solution (**b**) *(decisión)* resolution
resolver [4] *(pp* **resuelto**) **1** *vt (problema)* to solve; *(asunto)* to settle
  2 *vi (decidir)* to resolve, to decide
  3 resolverse *vpr* (**a**) *(solucionarse)* to be solved (**b**) *(decidirse)* to resolve, to make up one's mind (**a** to)
resonancia *nf* (**a**) *(sonora)* resonance (**b**) *(repercusión)* repercussions
resonar [2] *vi* to resound; *(tener eco)* to echo
resoplar *vi (respirar)* to breathe heavily; *(de cansancio)* to puff and pant; *(de enfado)* to huff and puff
resoplido *nm (silbido)* wheezing; *(de cansancio)* panting; *(de enfado)* snort
resorte *nm* (**a**) *(muelle)* spring (**b**) *Fig* means

> *Observa que la palabra inglesa* **resort** *es un falso amigo y no es la traducción de la palabra española* **resorte**. *En inglés,* **resort** *significa "recurso" o "lugar de vacaciones".*

respaldar *vt* to support, to back (up)
respaldo *nm (de silla etc)* back; *Fig (apoyo)* support, backing
respectar *vt* to concern, to regard; **por lo que a mí respecta** as far as I'm concerned
respectivo,-a *adj* respective; **en lo r. a** with regard to, regarding
respecto *nm*
  al r., a este r. in this respect; **con r. a, r. a, r. de** with regard to; **r. a mí** as for me, as far as I am concerned
respetable 1 *adj* respectable
  2 *nm Fam* **el r.** the audience
respetar *vt* to respect; **hacerse r. de todos** to command everyone's respect
respeto *nm* (**a**) respect; **por r.** out of consideration (**b**) *(recelo)* fear
respetuoso,-a *adj* respectful
respingar [42] *vi* to shy
respingo *nm* start, jump
respingón,-ona *adj (nariz)* snub, upturned
respiración *nf (acción)* breathing, respiration; *(aliento)* breath; **r. artificial** artificial resuscitation
respirar *vi* to breathe; **¡por fin respiro!** well, that's a relief!
respiratorio,-a *adj* respiratory
respiro *nm* (**a**) breathing (**b**) *(descanso)* breather, break
resplandecer [33] *vi* to shine
resplandeciente *adj (brillante)* shining; *(esplendoroso)* resplendent, radiant
resplandor *nm (brillo)* brightness; *(muy intenso)* brilliance; *(de fuego)* glow, blaze
responder 1 *vt* to answer
  2 *vi* (**a**) *(una carta)* to reply (**b**) *(reaccionar)* to respond (**c**) *(protestar)* to answer back (**d**) **r. de algn** to be responsible for sb; **r. por algn** to vouch for sb
respondón,-ona *adj Fam* argumentative, cheeky
responsabilidad *nf* responsibility
responsabilizar [40] 1 *vt* to make *o* hold responsible (**de** for)
  2 responsabilizarse *vpr* to assume *o* claim responsibility (**de** for)

responsable 1 *adj* responsible

  2 *nmf* **el/la r.** *(encargado)* the person in charge; *(de robo etc)* the perpetrator

respuesta *nf* answer, reply; *(reacción)* response

resquebrajarse *vpr* to crack

resquemor *nm* resentment, ill feeling

resquicio *nm* crack, chink

resta *nf* subtraction

restablecer [33] 1 *vt* to re-establish; *(el orden)* to restore

  2 restablecerse *vpr Med* to recover

restablecimiento *nm* (a) re-establishment; *(del orden etc)* restoration (b) *Med* recovery

restante *adj* remaining; **lo r.** the rest, the remainder

restar 1 *vt* (a) *Mat* to subtract, to take away (b) **r. importancia a algo** to play sth down

  2 *vi (quedar)* to be left, to remain

restauración *nf* restoration

restaurador,-a 1 *nm,f* restorer

  2 *adj* restoring

restaurante *nm* restaurant

restaurar *vt* to restore

restitución *nf* restitution

restituir [37] *vt (restablecer)* to restore; *(devolver)* to return, to give back

resto *nm* (a) rest, remainder; *Mat* remainder (b) **restos** remains; *(de comida)* leftovers

restregar [1] *vt* to rub hard, to scrub

restricción *nf* restriction

restrictivo,-a *adj* restrictive

restringir [57] *vt* to restrict, to limit

resucitar *vt & vi* to resuscitate

resuello *nm* breath, gasp

resuelto,-a *adj (decidido)* resolute, determined

resultado *nm* result; *(consecuencia)* outcome; **dar buen r.** to work, to give results

resultante *adj* resulting

resultar *vi* (a) *(ser)* to turn o work out; **así resulta más barato** it works out cheaper this way; **me resultó fácil** it turned out to be easy for me (b) *(ocurrir)* **resulta que ...** the thing is ...; **y ahora resulta que no puede venir** and now it turns out that she can't come (c) *(tener éxito)* to be successful; **la fiesta no resultó** the party wasn't a success

resultas *nfpl* **a r. de** as a result of

resumen *nm* summary; **en r.** in short, to sum up

resumir 1 *vt* to sum up; *(recapitular)* to summarize

  2 resumirse *vpr* (a) *(abreviarse)* **se resume en pocas palabras** it can be summed up in a few words (b) **r. en** *(saldarse con)* to result in

> ℓ Observa que la palabra inglesa **resume** es un falso amigo y no es la traducción de la palabra española **resumir**. En inglés, **resume** significa "reanudar".

resurgir [57] *vi* to reappear

resurrección *nf* resurrection

retablo *nm* altarpiece

retaguardia *nf* rearguard

retahíla *nf* series *sing*, string

retal *nm (pedazo)* scrap

retar *vt* to challenge

retardarse *vpr* to be delayed

retardo *nm* delay

retazo *nm (pedazo)* scrap; *(fragmento)* fragment, piece

rete- *pref Méx Fam* very

retén *nm* (a) **r. (de bomberos)** squad (of firefighters) (b) *Am (prisión)* reformatory, reform school

retención *nf* retention; *Fin* withholding; **r. de tráfico** (traffic) hold-up, traffic jam

retener [24] *vt* (a) *(conservar)* to retain (b) *Fin (descontar)* to deduct (c) *(detener)* to detain

reticencia *nf* reticence, reserve

reticente *adj* reticent, reserved

retina *nf* retina

retintín *nm (tono irónico)* innuendo, sarcastic tone

retirada *nf* retreat, withdrawal

retirado,-a 1 *adj* (a) *(alejado)* remote (b) *(jubilado)* retired

  2 *nm,f* retired person, *US* retiree

retirar 1 *vt* to take away, to remove; *(dinero)* to withdraw; *(ofensa)* to take back

  2 retirarse *vpr* (a) *(apartarse)* to withdraw, to draw back; *(irse)* to retire (b) *(jubilarse)* to retire (c) *Mil* to retreat, to withdraw

retiro *nm* (a) *(jubilación)* retirement; *(pensión)* pension (b) *(lugar tranquilo)* retreat (c) *Rel* retreat

reto *nm* challenge

retocar [44] *vt* to touch up

retoño *nm (rebrote)* shoot, sprout; *Fig (niño)* kid

retoque *nm* retouching, touching up; **los últimos retoques** the finishing touches

retorcer [41] 1 *vt (cuerda, hilo)* to twist; *(ropa)* to wring (out)

  2 retorcerse *vpr* to twist, to become twisted; **r. de dolor** to writhe in pain

retorcido,-a *adj Fig* twisted

retórica *nf* rhetoric
retórico,-a *adj* rhetorical
retornable *adj* returnable; **envase no r.** non-deposit bottle
retornar 1 *vt* to return, to give back
2 *vi* to return, to come back, to go back
retorno *nm* return
retortijón *nm (dolor)* stomach cramp
retozar [40] *vi* to frolic, to romp
retracción *nf* retraction
retractar 1 *vt* to retract
2 retractarse *vpr* **r. (de)** to retract, to take back
retraerse *vpr (retirarse)* to withdraw; *(por miedo)* to shy away
retraído,-a *adj* shy, reserved
retraimiento *nm (timidez)* shyness
retransmisión *nf* broadcast, transmission
retransmitir *vt* to broadcast
retrasado,-a 1 *adj* (**a**) *(tren)* late; *(reloj)* slow; **voy r.** I'm behind schedule (**b**) *(país)* backward, underdeveloped (**c**) *(mental)* retarded, backward
2 *nm,f* **r. (mental)** mentally retarded person
retrasar 1 *vt* (**a**) *(retardar)* to slow down (**b**) *(atrasar)* to delay, to postpone (**c**) *(reloj)* to put back
2 retrasarse *vpr* to be late, to be delayed; *(reloj)* to be slow
retraso *nm* delay; **con r.** late; **una hora de r.** an hour behind schedule; **r. mental** mental deficiency
retratar 1 *vt (pintar)* to paint a portrait of; *Fot* to take a photograph of; *Fig (describir)* to describe, to depict
2 retratarse *vpr* *Fot* to have one's photograph taken
retrato *nm (pintura)* portrait; *Fot* photograph; **r. robot** identikit picture, Photofit® picture; **ser el vivo r. de** to be the spitting image of
retreta *nf* retreat
retrete *nm* lavatory, toilet
retribución *nf (pago)* payment; *(recompensa)* reward

> ✍ Observa que la palabra inglesa **retribution** es un falso amigo y no es la traducción de la palabra española **retribución**. En inglés, **retribution** significa "represalias".

retribuir *vt (pagar)* to pay; *(recompensar)* to reward
retro *adj inv Fam (retrógrado)* reactionary; *(antiguo)* old-fashioned
retroactivo,-a *adj* retroactive; **con efecto r.** retrospectively

retroceder *vi* to move back, to back away
retroceso *nm* (**a**) *(movimiento)* backward movement (**b**) *Med* deterioration, worsening (**c**) *Econ* recession
retrógrado,-a *adj & nm,f (reaccionario)* reactionary
retropropulsión *nf Av* jet propulsion
retrospectivo,-a *adj & nf* retrospective
retrovisor *nm Aut* rear-view mirror
retumbar *vi (resonar)* to resound, to echo; *(tronar)* to thunder, to boom
retuve *pt indef de* **retener**
reúma *nm* rheumatism
reumático,-a *adj & nm,f* rheumatic
reumatismo *nm* rheumatism
reunión *nf* meeting; *(reencuentro)* reunion
reunir 1 *vt* to gather together; *(dinero)* to raise; *(cualidades)* to have, to possess; *(requisitos)* to fulfil
2 reunirse *vpr* to meet, to gather; **r. con algn** to meet sb
revalidar *vt* to ratify, to confirm; *Dep (título)* to retain
revalorizar [40] *vt,* **revalorizarse** *vpr (moneda)* to revalue
revancha *nf* revenge; *Dep* return match
revanchista *adj* vengeful, vindictive
revelación *nf* revelation
revelado *nm Fot* developing
revelar *vt* (**a**) to reveal, to disclose (**b**) *Fot (película)* to develop
revender *vt (entradas)* to tout
reventa *nf (de entradas)* touting
reventado,-a *adj Fam (cansado)* knackered
reventar [1] 1 *vt* (**a**) to burst (**b**) *(romper)* to break, to smash (**c**) *(fastidiar)* to annoy, to bother
2 *vi (estallar)* to burst; **r. de ganas de hacer algo** to be dying to do sth; **está que revienta** he's bursting at the seams
3 reventarse *vpr (estallar)* to burst, to explode
reventón *nm (de neumático)* blowout, puncture, flat tyre
reverberación *nf* reverberation
reverberar *vi* to reverberate
reverencia *nf* (**a**) *(respeto)* reverence (**b**) *(inclinación) (de hombre)* bow; *(de mujer)* curtsy
reverenciar [43] *vt* to revere, to venerate
reverendo,-a *adj & nm,f* reverend
reversa *nf Méx* reverse
reversible *adj* reversible
reverso *nm* reverse, back
revertido,-a *adj* **llamada a cobro r.** *Br*

reverse-charge call, *US* collect call
revertir [5] *vi* to result (**en** in)
revés *nm* (**a**) *(reverso)* reverse; **al** *o* **del r.** *(al contrario)* the other way round; *(la parte interior en el exterior)* inside out; *(boca abajo)* upside down; *(la parte de detrás delante)* back to front; **al r. de lo que dicen** contrary to what they say (**b**) *(bofetada)* slap; *Ten* backhand (stroke) (**c**) *Fig (contrariedad)* setback, reverse; **los reveses de la vida** life's misfortunes; **reveses de fortuna** setbacks, blows of fate
revestimiento *nm Téc* covering, coating
revestir [6] *vt* (**a**) *(recubrir)* to cover (**de** with), to coat (**de** with), to line (**de** with) (**b**) *Fig* **la herida no reviste importancia** the wound is not serious
revisar *vt* to check; *(coche)* to service
revisión *nf* checking; *(de coche)* service, overhaul; **r. médica** checkup
revisor,-a *nm,f* ticket inspector
revista *nf* (**a**) magazine (**b**) **pasar r. a** to inspect, to review (**c**) *Teatro* revue
revitalizar [40] *vt* to revitalize
revivido,-a *adj* revived
revivir *vt & vi* to revive
revocar [44] *vt* to revoke, to repeal
revolcar [2] **1** *vt Fam (oponente)* to floor, to crush
2 revolcarse *vpr* to roll about
revolcón *nm* fall, tumble; *Fam (sexual)* romp
revolotear *vi* to fly about, to flutter about
revoltijo, revoltillo *nm* mess, jumble
revoltoso,-a *adj (travieso)* mischievous, naughty
revolución *nf* revolution
revolucionar *vt* to revolutionize
revolucionario,-a *adj & nm,f* revolutionary
revolver [4] (*pp* **revuelto**) **1** *vt (mezclar)* to stir, to mix; *(desordenar)* to mess up; **me revuelve el estómago** it turns my stomach
2 revolverse *vpr* (**a**) *(agitarse)* to roll (**b**) *Fig* **r. contra algn** to turn against sb (**c**) *(el tiempo)* to turn stormy; *(el mar)* to become rough

> *Observa que el verbo inglés* **to revolve** *es un falso amigo y no es la traducción del verbo español* **revolver***. En inglés,* **to revolve** *significa "girar".*

revólver *nm* (*pl* **revólveres**) revolver
revuelo *nm Fig* stir, commotion
revuelta *nf* (**a**) *(insurrección)* revolt (**b**) *(curva)* bend, turn

revuelto,-a *adj* (**a**) *(desordenado)* jumbled, in a mess (**b**) *(tiempo)* stormy, unsettled; *(mar)* rough (**c**) *(agitado)* excited
revulsivo,-a *adj & nm* revulsive
rey *nm* king; *Rel* (**el día de**) **Reyes** (the) Epiphany, 6 January
reyerta *nf* quarrel, dispute
rezagado,-a *nm,f* straggler, latecomer
rezagarse *vpr* to lag *o* fall behind
rezar [40] **1** *vi* (**a**) *(orar)* to pray (**b**) *(decir)* to say, to read
2 *vt (oración)* to say
rezo *nm* prayer
rezumar *vt* to ooze; *Fig* to exude
RFA *nf Hist* (*abr* **República Federal de Alemania**) FRG
ría *nf* estuary
riada *nf* flood
ribera *nf* *(de río)* bank; *(zona)* riverside, waterfront
ribete *nm* edging, border
ribetear *vt* to edge, to border
ricamente *adv Fam* **tan r.** very well
rico,-a **1** *adj* (**a**) **ser r.** *(adinerado)* to be rich *o* wealthy; *(abundante)* to be rich; *(bonito)* to be lovely *o* adorable; *(fértil)* to be rich *o* fertile (**b**) **estar r.** *(delicioso)* to be delicious
2 *nm,f* rich person
rictus *nm inv* grin
ridiculez *nf* ridiculous thing; *(cualidad)* ridiculousness
ridiculizar [40] *vt* to ridicule
ridículo,-a **1** *adj* ridiculous
2 *nm* ridicule; **hacer el r., quedar en r.** to make a fool of oneself; **poner a algn en r.** to make a fool of sb
riego *nm* watering, irrigation; **r. sanguíneo** blood circulation
riel *nm* rail
rienda *nf* rein; *Fig* **dar r. suelta a** to give free rein to; *Fig* **llevar las riendas** to hold the reins, to be in control
riesgo *nm* risk; **correr el r. de** to run the risk of; **seguro a todo r.** fully comprehensive insurance
riesgoso,-a *adj Am* risky
rifa *nf* raffle
rifar *vt* to raffle (off)
rifle *nm* rifle
rigidez *nf* rigidity, stiffness; *Fig (severidad)* strictness, inflexibility
rígido,-a *adj* rigid, stiff; *Fig (severo)* strict, inflexible
rigor *nm* rigour; *(severidad)* severity; **con r.** rigorously; **de r.** indispensable
rigurosamente *adv* rigorously; *(meticulosamente)* meticulously; *(severamente)*

severely; **r. cierto** absolutely true

riguroso,-a *adj* rigorous; *(severo)* severe, strict

rijo *indic pres de* **regir**

rima *nf* rhyme

rimar *vt & vi* to rhyme (**con** with)

rimbombante *adj (lenguaje)* pompous, pretentious

rímel *nm* mascara

Rin *n* el **R.** the Rhine

rincón *nm* corner; *Fam (lugar remoto)* nook

rinoceronte *nm* rhinoceros

riña *nf (pelea)* fight; *(discusión)* row, quarrel

riñón *nm* kidney; *Fam* **costar un r.** to cost an arm and a leg; *Med* **r. artificial** kidney machine

río *nm* river; **r. abajo** downstream; **r. arriba** upstream

rioja *nm* Rioja (wine)

rioplatense *adj* of/from the River Plate region

ripio *nm (palabras de relleno)* waffle; *Fam* **no perder r.** not to miss a trick

riqueza *nf* (a) wealth (b) *(cualidad)* wealthiness

risa *nf* laugh; *(carcajadas)* laughter; **es (cosa) de r.** it's laughable; **me da r.** it makes me laugh; **tomarse algo a r.** to laugh sth off; *Fig* **morirse** *o* **mondarse de r.** to die *o* fall about laughing; *Fam* **mi hermano es una r.** my brother is a laugh; *Fam Fig* **tener algo muerto de r.** to leave sth lying around

risco *nm* crag, cliff

risible *adj* laughable

risilla, risita *nf* giggle, titter; *(risa falsa)* false laugh

risotada *nf* guffaw

ristra *nf* string

ristre *nm* **en r.** at the ready

risueño,-a *adj* smiling

rítmico,-a *adj* rhythmic; **gimnasia rítmica** eurhythmics *sing*

ritmo *nm* (a) rhythm (b) *(paso)* rate; **llevar un buen r. de trabajo** to work at a good pace

rito *nm* (a) rite (b) *(ritual)* ritual

ritual *adj & nm* ritual

rival *adj & nmf* rival

rivalidad *nf* rivalry

rivalizar [40] *vi* to rival (**en** in)

rizado,-a *adj* (a) *(pelo)* curly (b) *(mar)* choppy

rizar [40] 1 *vt (pelo)* to curl; *(tela, papel)* to crease; *Fig* **r. el rizo** to make things even more complicated

2 rizarse *vpr (pelo)* to curl, to go curly

rizo *nm* (a) *(de pelo)* curl (b) *(en el agua)* ripple

RNE *nf (abr* **Radio Nacional de España**) = Spanish state radio station

robalo *nm (pez)* bass

robar *vt* (a) *(objeto)* to steal; *(banco, persona)* to rob; *(casa)* to burgle; *Fig* **en aquel supermercado te roban** they really rip you off in that supermarket (b) *Naipes* to draw

roble *nm* oak (tree)

robledal, robledo *nm* oak grove *o* wood

robo *nm* robbery, theft; *(en casa)* burglary; *Fam (timo)* rip-off

robot *nm (pl* **robots**) robot; **r. de cocina** food processor

robótica *nf* robotics *sing*

robustecer [33] *vt* to strengthen

robusto,-a *adj* robust, sturdy

roca *nf* rock

rocalla *nf* pebbles, stone chippings

rocambolesco,-a *adj* incredible, far-fetched

roce *nm* (a) *(fricción)* rubbing; *(en la piel)* chafing (b) *(marca) (en la pared etc)* scuff mark; *(en la piel)* chafing mark, graze (c) *(contacto ligero)* brush, light touch (d) *Fam (trato entre personas)* contact (e) *Fam (discusión)* brush

rociar [29] *vt (salpicar)* to spray, to sprinkle

rocín *nm* nag, hack

rocío *nm* dew

Rocosas *nfpl* las **R.** the Rockies

rocoso,-a *adj* rocky, stony

rodaballo *nm (pez)* turbot

rodado,-a *adj* (a) *(piedra)* smooth, rounded; **canto r.** boulder (b) **tráfico r.** road traffic, vehicular traffic

rodaja *nf* slice; **en rodajas** sliced

rodaje *nm* (a) *(filmación)* filming, shooting (b) *Aut* running in

Ródano *n* el **R.** the Rhone

rodante *adj* rolling

rodar [2] 1 *vt (película etc)* to film, to shoot

2 *vi* to roll, to turn

rodear 1 *vt* to surround, to encircle

2 rodearse *vpr* to surround oneself (**de** with)

rodeo *nm* (a) *(desvío)* detour (b) *(al hablar)* evasiveness; **andarse con rodeos** to beat about the bush; **no andarse con rodeos** to get straight to the point (c) *Am* rodeo

rodilla *nf* knee; **de rodillas** *(arrodillado)* kneeling; **hincarse** *o* **ponerse de rodillas**

to kneel down, to go down on one's knees
rodillera *nf (de pantalón)* knee patch;
Dep knee pad
rodillo *nm* roller; **r. de cocina** rolling pin
rododendro *nm* rhododendron
roedor *nm* rodent
roer [38] *vt (hueso)* to gnaw; *(galleta)* to
nibble at; *Fig (conciencia)* to gnaw at, to
nag at; *Fig* **un hueso duro de r.** a hard nut
to crack
rogar [2] *vt (pedir)* to request, to ask;
(implorar) to beg; **hacerse de r.** to play
hard to get; **se ruega silencio** *(en letrero)*
silence please; **rogamos disculpen la molestia** please forgive the inconvenience
roído,-a *adj* gnawed, eaten away
rojizo,-a *adj* reddish
rojo,-a 1 *adj* (**a**) red; *Fin* **estar en números
rojos** to be in the red (**b**) *Pol (comunista)*
red
　2 *nm (color)* red; **al r. vivo** *(caliente)* red-
hot; *Fig (tenso)* very tense
　3 *nm,f Pol (comunista)* red
rol *nm* role; **juego de r.** role play
rollizo,-a *adj* chubby, plump
rollo *nm* (**a**) *(de papel etc)* roll (**b**) *Fam
(pesadez)* drag, bore; **es el mismo r. de
siempre** it's the same old story; **un r. de
libro** a boring book (**c**) *Fam (amorío)*
affair
Roma *n* Rome
romana *nf* **calamares a la r.** = squid in
batter
romance *nm* (**a**) *(aventura amorosa)* romance (**b**) *(idioma)* Romance; *Fig* **hablar
en r.** to speak plainly (**c**) *Lit* narrative
poem, ballad
románico,-a *adj & nm* Romanesque
romanticismo *nm* romanticism
romántico,-a *adj & nm,f* romantic
rombo *nm* rhombus
romería *nf Rel* pilgrimage
romero *nm Bot* rosemary
romo,-a *adj* (**a**) blunt (**b**) *(nariz)* snub
rompecabezas *nm inv (juego)* (jigsaw)
puzzle; *Fig (problema)* riddle, puzzle
rompeolas *nm inv* breakwater, jetty
romper *(pp* **roto) 1** *vt* (**a**) to break;
(papel, tela) to tear; *(vajilla, cristal)* to
smash, to shatter (**b**) *(relaciones)* to
break off
　2 *vi* (**a**) *(olas, día)* to break (**b**) *(acabar)*
to break (**con** with); **rompió con su novio**
she broke it off with her boyfriend (**c**) **r. a
llorar** to burst out crying; **r. en llanto** to
burst into tears
　3 romperse *vpr* to break; *(papel, tela)* to
tear; **se rompió por la mitad** it broke o

split in half; *Fig* **r. la cabeza** to rack one's
brains
rompevientos *nm RP (jersey)* polo neck
jersey; *(anorak)* anorak
rompimiento *nm Am* breaking off
ron *nm* rum
roncar [44] *vi* to snore
roncha *nf (en la piel)* swelling, lump
ronco,-a *adj* hoarse; **quedarse r.** to lose
one's voice
ronda *nf* (**a**) round; *(patrulla)* patrol (**b**)
(carretera) ring road; *(paseo)* avenue (**c**)
pagar una r. to pay for a round of drinks
rondar 1 *vt* (**a**) *(vigilar)* to patrol, to do the
rounds of (**b**) *Pey (merodear)* to prowl
around, to hang about (**c**) *(estar cerca
de)* to be about o approximately; **ronda
los cuarenta** she is about forty
　2 *vi* (**a**) *(vigilar)* to patrol (**b**) *(merodear)*
to prowl around, to roam around
ronquera *nf* hoarseness
ronquido *nm* snore
ronronear *vi* to purr
ronroneo *nm* purring
roña *nf* (**a**) *(mugre)* filth, dirt (**b**) *(sarna)*
mange
roñica *Fam* **1** *adj* mean, stingy
　2 *nmf* scrooge, miser
roñoso,-a *adj* (**a**) *(mugriento)* filthy, dirty
(**b**) *(sarnoso)* mangy (**c**) *Fam (tacaño)*
mean, stingy
ropa *nf* clothes, clothing; *Fig* **a quema r.**
point-blank; **r. blanca** (household) linen;
r. interior underwear

> 🖉 Observa que la palabra inglesa **rope** es
> un falso amigo y no es la traducción de la
> palabra española **ropa**. En inglés, **rope** sig-
> nifica "cuerda, soga".

ropaje *nm* clothes
ropero *nm* **(armario)** r. wardrobe
roque *nm* (**a**) *(en ajedrez)* rook (**b**) *Fam*
quedarse r. to fall fast asleep
rosa 1 *adj inv (color)* pink; **novela r.** romantic novel
　2 *nf Bot* rose; *(en la piel)* birthmark; **r. de
los vientos** compass (rose)
　3 *nm (color)* pink
rosáceo,-a *adj* rose-coloured, rosy
rosado,-a 1 *adj (color)* pink, rosy; *(vino)*
rosé
　2 *nm (vino)* rosé
rosal *nm* rosebush
rosaleda *nf* rose garden
rosario *nm Rel* rosary; *(sarta)* string, series *sing*
rosbif *nm* roast beef
rosca *nf* (**a**) *(de tornillo)* thread; **tapón de**

r. screw top; *Fig* **pasarse de r.** to go too far (**b**) *(espiral)* spiral, coil

rosco *nm (pastel)* = ring-shaped roll or pastry; *Fam* **no comerse un r.** not to get one's oats

rosetón *nm* rose window

rosquilla *nf* ring-shaped pastry; *Fam Fig* **venderse como rosquillas** to sell like hot cakes

rosticería *nf Chile, Méx* = shop selling roast chicken

rostro *nm* face; *Fam* **tener mucho r.** to have a lot of nerve; *Fam* **¡vaya r.!** what a cheek!

> ⁄ Observa que la palabra inglesa **rostrum** es un falso amigo y no es la traducción de la palabra española **rostro**. En inglés, **rostrum** significa "estrado".

rotación *nf* rotation

rotativo,-a 1 *adj* rotary, revolving
   2 *nm* newspaper

roto,-a 1 *adj* broken; *(papel)* torn; *(ropa)* in tatters, tattered
   2 *nm (agujero)* hole, tear
   3 *nm,f Chile Fam (trabajador)* worker

rotoso,-a *adj Andes, RP* ragged, in tatters

rótula *nf* (**a**) *Anat* kneecap (**b**) *Téc* ball-and-socket joint

rotulador *nm* felt-tip pen

rotular *vt* to letter, to label

rótulo *nm (letrero)* sign, notice; *(titular)* title, heading

rotundo,-a *adj* categorical; **éxito r.** resounding success; **un no r.** a flat refusal

rotura *nf (ruptura)* breaking; *Med* fracture

roturar *vt* to plough

roulotte *nf Br* caravan, *US* trailer

rozadura *nf* scratch, abrasion

rozamiento *nm* rubbing, friction

rozar [40] 1 *vt* to touch, to rub against, to brush against
   2 *vi* to rub
   3 rozarse *upr* to rub, to brush (**con** against)

Rte. (*abr* **remite, remitente**) sender

RTVE *nf* (*abr* **Radiotelevisión Española**) = Spanish state broadcasting company

ruana *nf Andes* poncho

rubéola *nf* German measles *sing*, rubella

rubí *nm* (*pl* **rubíes**) ruby

rubicundo,-a *adj* rosy, reddish

rubio,-a 1 *adj (pelo, persona)* fair, blond, *f* blonde; **r. de bote** peroxide blonde; **tabaco r.** Virginia tobacco
   2 *nm,f* blond, *f* blonde

rublo *nm* rouble

rubor *nm* blush, flush

ruborizarse [40] *upr* to blush, to go red

ruboroso,-a *adj* blushing, bashful

rúbrica *nf* (**a**) *(de firma)* = flourish added to a signature (**b**) *(título)* title, heading

rubricar [44] *vt* (**a**) *(firmar)* to sign with a flourish (**b**) *(respaldar)* to endorse, to ratify

rudeza *nf* roughness, coarseness

rudimentario,-a *adj* rudimentary

rudimento *nm* rudiment

rudo,-a *adj* rough, coarse

rueda *nf* (**a**) wheel; *Aut* **r. de recambio** spare wheel; *Aut* **r. delantera/trasera** front/rear wheel; **r. de prensa** press conference; *Fam* **ir sobre ruedas** to go very smoothly (**b**) *(rodaja)* round slice

ruedo *nm* (**a**) *Taurom* bullring, arena (**b**) *(de falda)* hem

ruego *nm* request

rufián *nm* villain, scoundrel

rugby *nm* rugby

rugido *nm (de animal)* roar; *(del viento)* howl; *(de tripas)* rumbling

rugir [57] *vi* to roar; *(viento)* to howl

rugoso,-a *adj* rough

ruibarbo *nm* rhubarb

ruido *nm* noise; *(sonido)* sound; *(jaleo)* din, row; *Fig* stir, commotion; **hacer r.** to make a noise

ruidoso,-a *adj* noisy, loud

ruin *adj* (**a**) *(vil)* vile, despicable (**b**) *(tacaño)* mean, stingy

ruina *nf* ruin; *(derrumbamiento)* collapse; *(de persona)* downfall

ruindad *nf* vileness, meanness; *(acto)* mean act, low trick

ruinoso,-a *adj* dilapidated, tumbledown

ruiseñor *nm* nightingale

ruleta *nf* roulette

ruletear *vi CAm, Méx Fam (en taxi)* to drive a taxi

ruletero *nm CAm, Méx Fam (de taxi)* taxi driver

rulo *nm* (**a**) *(para el pelo)* curler, roller (**b**) *Culin* rolling pin

rulot(a) *nf* (*pl* **rulots**) *Br* caravan, *US* trailer

ruma *nf Andes, Ven* heap, pile

Rumanía, Rumania *n* Romania

rumba *nf* rhumba, rumba

rumbo *nm* direction, course; **(con) r. a** bound for, heading for

rumiante *nm* ruminant

rumiar [43] 1 *vt* (**a**) *(mascar)* to chew (**b**) *Fig (pensar)* to ruminate, to reflect on, to chew over
   2 *vi* to ruminate, to chew the cud

rumor *nm* (**a**) rumour (**b**) *(murmullo)* murmur

rumorearse *v impers* to be rumoured

runrún, runruneo *nm* buzz, noise

rupestre *adj* **pintura r.** cave painting

ruptura *nf* breaking; *(de relaciones)* breaking off

rural *adj* rural, country

Rusia *n* Russia

ruso,-a *adj & nm,f* Russian

rústico,-a *adj* rustic, rural

ruta *nf* route, road

rutilar *vi* to sparkle

rutina *nf* routine; **por r.** as a matter of course

rutinario,-a *adj* routine

S, s ['ese] *nf (la letra)* S, s

S (*abr* **Sur**) S

S. (*abr* **San, Santo**) St

s. (*abr* **siglo**) c

S.A. (*abr* **Sociedad Anónima**) *Br* ≃ PLC, *US* ≃ Inc

sábado *nm* Saturday

sabana *nf* savannah

sábana *nf* sheet; *Fam* **se me pegaron las sábanas** I overslept

sabandija *nf (insecto)* creepy-crawly; *(persona)* creep

sabañón *nm* chilblain

sabático,-a *adj* sabbatical

sabelotodo *nmf inv* know-all

saber¹ *nm* knowledge

saber² [21] 1 *vt* (**a**) to know; **hacer s.** to inform; **para que lo sepas** for your information; **que yo sepa** as far as I know; **vete tú a s.** goodness knows; **¡y yo qué sé!** how should I know!; *Fig* **a s.** namely (**b**) *(tener habilidad)* to be able to; **¿sabes cocinar?** can you cook?; **¿sabes hablar inglés?** can you speak English? (**c**) *(enterarse)* to learn, to find out; **lo supe ayer** I found this out yesterday

2 *vi* (**a**) *(tener sabor)* to taste (**a** of); **sabe a fresa** it tastes of strawberries; *Fig* **me sabe mal** I feel guilty *o* bad about that (**b**) *Am (soler)* to be accustomed to

sabido,-a *adj* known; **como es s.** as everyone knows

sabiduría *nf* wisdom

sabiendas: • **a sabiendas** *loc adv* **lo hizo a s.** he did it in the full knowledge of what he was doing; **a s. de que ...** knowing full well that ...

sabihondo,-a *nm,f Fam (sabelotodo)* know-all; *(pedante)* pedant

sabio,-a 1 *adj (prudente)* wise

2 *nm,f* scholar

sabiondo,-a *nm,f Fam* = sabihondo,-a

sable *nm* sabre

sabor *nm (gusto)* taste, flavour; **con s. a limón** lemon-flavoured; **sin s.** tasteless; **me deja mal s. de boca** it leaves a bad taste in my mouth

saborear *vt (degustar)* to taste; *Fig (apreciar)* to savour

sabotaje *nm* sabotage

saboteador,-a *nm,f* saboteur

sabotear *vt* to sabotage

sabré *indic fut de* saber

sabroso,-a *adj* (**a**) tasty; *(delicioso)* delicious (**b**) *(agradable)* delightful

sabueso *nm* bloodhound

sacacorchos *nm inv* corkscrew

sacamuelas *nmf inv Fam* dentist

sacapuntas *nm inv* pencil sharpener

sacar [44] *vt* (**a**) to take out; *(con más fuerza)* to pull out; **s. dinero del banco** to withdraw money from the bank; **s. la lengua** to stick one's tongue out; *Fig* **s. faltas a algo** to find fault with sth; *Fig* **s. adelante** to help to get on; **s. provecho de algo** to benefit from sth; **s. algo en claro** *o* **en limpio** to make sense of sth (**b**) *(obtener)* to get; *(dinero)* to get, to make; *(conclusiones)* to draw, to reach; *(entrada)* to get, to buy (**c**) *(producto, libro, disco)* to bring out; *(nueva moda)* to bring in (**d**) *(fotografía)* to take; *(fotocopia)* to make (**e**) *Ten* to serve; *Ftb* to kick off

sacarina *nf* saccharin

sacerdotal *adj* priestly

sacerdote *nm* priest; **sumo s.** high priest

saciar [43] *vt* to satiate; *(sed)* to quench; *(deseos, hambre)* to satisfy; *(ambiciones)* to fulfil

saciedad *nf* satiety; **repetir algo hasta la s.** to repeat sth ad nauseam

saco *nm* (**a**) sack; **s. de dormir** sleeping bag (**b**) *Mil* **entrar a s. en una ciudad** to pillage a town (**c**) *Am (chaqueta)* jacket

sacralizar [40] *vt* to consecrate

sacramento *nm* sacrament

sacrificar [44] **1** *vt* to sacrifice

2 sacrificarse *vpr* to make a sacrifice *o* sacrifices

sacrificio *nm* sacrifice

sacrilegio *nm* sacrilege

sacrílego,-a *adj* sacrilegious

sacristán *nm* verger, sexton

sacristía *nf* vestry, sacristy

sacro,-a *adj* sacred

sacudida *nf* (**a**) shake; *(espasmo)* jolt, jerk; **s. eléctrica** electric shock (**b**) *(de terremoto)* tremor

sacudir *vt* (**a**) *(agitar)* to shake; *(alfombra, sábana)* to shake out; *(arena, polvo)* to shake off (**b**) *(golpear)* to beat (**c**) *(conmover)* to shock, to stun

sádico,-a 1 *adj* sadistic
  2 *nm,f* sadist

sadismo *nm* sadism

sadomasoquista 1 *adj* sadomasochistic
  2 *nmf* sadomasochist

saeta *nf* (**a**) *(dardo)* dart (**b**) *(canción)* = popular religious song

safari *nm* *(cacería)* safari; *(parque)* safari park

sagacidad *nf* *Fml (listeza)* cleverness; *(astucia)* astuteness, shrewdness

sagaz *adj* *(listo)* clever; *(astuto)* astute, shrewd

Sagitario *nm* Sagittarius

sagrado,-a *adj* sacred

sagrario *nm* tabernacle

Sáhara *n* Sahara

saharaui *adj* & *nmf* Saharan

sahariana *nf* safari jacket

sainete *nm Teatro* comic sketch, one-act farce

sajón,-ona *adj* & *nm,f* Saxon

sal¹ *nf* (**a**) salt; **s. fina** table salt; **s. gema** salt crystals; **s. gorda** cooking salt (**b**) *Fig (gracia)* wit

sal² *imperat de* **salir**

sala *nf* room; *(en un hospital)* ward; *Jur* courtroom; **s. de estar** lounge, living room; **s. de espera** waiting room; **s. de exposiciones** exhibition hall; **s. de fiestas** nightclub, discotheque; **s. de lectura** reading room

saladito *nm RP* savoury snack o appetizer

salado,-a *adj* (**a**) *(con sal)* salted; *(con exceso de sal)* salty; **agua salada** salt water (**b**) *Fig (encantador)* charming (**c**) *Am (infortunado)* unlucky

salamandra *nf* salamander

salamanquesa *nf* gecko

salame, salami *nm* salami

salar *vt* to salt, to add salt to

salarial *adj* salary, wage

salario *nm* salary, wages; **s. mínimo** minimum wage

salazones *nfpl* salted meat o fish

salchicha *nf* sausage

salchichón *nm* = salami-type sausage

salchichonería *nf Méx* delicatessen

saldar *vt* (**a**) *Fin (cuenta)* to settle; *(deuda)* to pay off (**b**) *Com (vender barato)* to sell off (**c**) *Fig (diferencias)* to settle, to resolve

saldo *nm* (**a**) **saldos** sales; **a precio de s.** at bargain prices (**b**) *Fin* balance (**c**) *(de*

una deuda) liquidation, settlement (**d**) *(resto de mercancía)* remainder, leftover

saldré *indic fut de* **salir**

saledizo,-a *adj* projecting

salero *nm* (**a**) *(recipiente)* saltcellar (**b**) *Fig (gracia)* charm

salgo *indic pres de* **salir**

salida *nf* (**a**) *(partida)* departure; *(puerta etc)* exit, way out; **callejón sin s.** dead end; **s. de emergencia** emergency exit (**b**) *Dep* start; **línea de s.** starting line; **s. nula** false start (**c**) **te vi a la s. del cine** I saw you leaving the cinema (**d**) *(de un astro)* rising; **s. del sol** sunrise (**e**) *(profesional)* opening; *Com* outlet (**f**) *(recurso)* solution, way out; **no tengo otra s.** I have no other option (**g**) *Fam (ocurrencia)* witty remark, witticism (**h**) *Informát* output

salido,-a *adj* (**a**) prominent, projecting (**b**) *muy Fam (persona)* horny

saliente *adj* (**a**) projecting, prominent; *Fig* outstanding (**b**) *(cesante)* outgoing

salina *nf* salt mine

salino,-a *adj* saline

salir [22] 1 *vi* (**a**) *(de un sitio)* to go out, to leave; *(venir de dentro)* to come out; **salió de la habitación** she left the room; **s. de la carretera** to turn off the road
  (**b**) *(tren etc)* to depart
  (**c**) *(novios)* to go out (**con** with)
  (**d**) *(aparecer)* to appear; *(revista, disco)* to come out; *(ley)* to come in; *(trabajo, vacante)* to come up
  (**e**) *(resultar)* to turn out, to turn out to be; **el pequeño les ha salido muy listo** their son has turned out to be very clever; **¿cómo te salió el examen?** how did your exam go?; **s. ganando** to come out ahead o on top; **salió presidente** he was elected president
  (**f**) **s. a** *(precio)* to come to, to work out at; **s. barato/caro** to work out cheap/expensive
  (**g**) **ha salido al abuelo** she takes after her grandfather
  (**h**) *(problema)* to work out; **esta cuenta no me sale** I can't work this sum out
  (**i**) **¡con qué cosas sales!** the things you come out with!
  2 **salirse** *vpr* (**a**) *(líquido, gas)* to leak (out); *Fig* **s. de lo normal** to be out of the ordinary; **se salió de la carretera** he went off the road
  (**b**) *Fam* **s. con la suya** to get one's own way

saliva *nf* saliva

salivar *vi* to salivate

salivazo *nm* spit

salmantino,-a 1 *adj* of/from Salamanca **2** *nm,f* person from Salamanca
salmo *nm* psalm
salmón 1 *nm (pescado)* salmon **2** *adj inv (color)* salmon pink, salmon
salmonete *nm (pescado)* red mullet
salmorejo *nm (salsa)* = sauce made from vinegar, water, pepper and salt
salmuera *nf* brine
salobre *adj (agua)* brackish; *(gusto)* salty, briny
salón *nm* (**a**) *(en una casa)* lounge, sitting room (**b**) **s. de actos** assembly hall; **s. de baile** dance hall (**c**) **s. de belleza** beauty salon; **s. de té** tearoom, teashop (**d**) **s. del automóvil** motor show
salpicadera *nf Méx Br* mudguard, *US* fender
salpicadura *nf* splashing
salpicar [44] *vt* (**a**) *(rociar)* to splash; **me salpicó el abrigo de barro** he splashed mud on my coat (**b**) *Fig (esparcir)* to sprinkle
salpicón *nm* (**a**) splash (**b**) *Culin* cocktail
salpimentar [1] *vt* to season
salpullido *nm* rash
salsa *nf* sauce; *(de carne)* gravy; *Fig* **en su (propia) s.** in one's element
saltador,-a *nm,f Dep* jumper
saltamontes *nm inv* grasshopper
saltar 1 *vt (obstáculo, valla)* to jump (over) **2** *vi* (**a**) to jump; *Fig* **s. a la vista** to be obvious (**b**) *(cristal etc)* to break, to shatter; *(plomos)* to go, to blow (**c**) *(desprenderse)* to come off (**d**) *(encolerizarse)* to explode, to blow up; **por menos de nada salta** the smallest thing makes him explode **3 saltarse** *vpr* (**a**) *(omitir)* to skip, to miss out; **s. el semáforo/turno** to jump the lights/the queue (**b**) *(botón)* to come off; **se me saltaron las lágrimas** tears came to my eyes
salteado,-a *adj* (**a**) *(espaciado)* spaced out (**b**) *Culin* sauté, sautéed
saltear *vt Culin* to sauté
saltimbanqui *nmf* acrobat, tumbler
salto *nm* (**a**) *(acción)* jump, leap; *Fig (paso adelante)* leap forward; **a saltos** in leaps and bounds; **dar** *o* **pegar un s.** to jump, to leap; **de un s.** in a flash; *Fig* **a s. de mata** every now and then; **s. de agua** waterfall; **s. de cama** negligée (**b**) *Dep* jump; **s. de altura** high jump; **s. de longitud** long jump; **s. mortal** somersault
saltón,-ona *adj* prominent; **ojos saltones** bulging eyes
salubre *adj* salubrious

salubridad *nf* healthiness; **por razones de s.** for health reasons
salud *nf* health; **beber a la s. de algn** to drink to sb's health; *Fam* **¡s.!** cheers!
saludable *adj* (**a**) *(sano)* healthy, wholesome (**b**) *Fig (beneficioso)* good, beneficial
saludar *vt* (**a**) *(decir hola a)* to say hello to, to greet; **saluda de mi parte a** give my regards to; **le saluda atentamente** *(en una carta)* yours faithfully (**b**) *Mil* to salute
saludo *nm* (**a**) greeting; **un s. de** best wishes from (**b**) *Mil* salute
salva *nf Mil* salvo, volley
salvación *nf* salvation
salvado *nm* bran
salvador,-a 1 *nm,f* saviour; *(rescatador)* rescuer **2** *nm* **El S.** El Salvador
salvadoreño,-a *adj & nm,f* Salvadoran, Salvadorian
salvaguarda *nf (defensa)* protection
salvaguardar *vt* to safeguard (**de** from), to protect (**de** from)
salvaguardia *nf* = salvaguarda
salvajada *nf* brutal act
salvaje *adj* (**a**) *Bot* wild, uncultivated; *Zool* wild; *(pueblo, tribu)* savage, uncivilized (**b**) *Fam (violento)* savage, wild
salvajismo *nm* savagery
salvamento, salvamiento *nm* rescue
salvar 1 *vt* (**a**) to save, to rescue (**de** from) (**b**) *(obstáculo)* to clear; *(dificultad)* to get round, to overcome (**c**) *(exceptuar)* to exclude, to except; **salvando ciertos errores** except for a few mistakes **2 salvarse** *vpr* (**a**) *(sobrevivir)* to survive, to come out alive; *Fam (escaparse)* to escape (**de** from); **¡sálvese quien pueda!** every man for himself!; *Fam* **s. por los pelos** to have a narrow escape (**b**) *Rel* to be saved, to save one's soul
salvavidas *nm inv* life belt
salvedad *nf* (**a**) *(excepción)* exception (**b**) *(reserva)* proviso
salvia *nf Bot* sage
salvo,-a 1 *adj* unharmed, safe; **a s.** safe **2** *adv (exceptuando)* except (for); **s. que** unless
salvoconducto *nm* safe-conduct
san *adj* saint
sanar 1 *vt (curar)* to cure, to heal **2** *vi* (**a**) *(persona)* to recover, to get better (**b**) *(herida)* to heal
sanatorio *nm* sanatorium
sanción *nf* (**a**) sanction (**b**) *(aprobación)* sanction, approval (**c**) *Jur* penalty
sancionar *vt* (**a**) *(castigar)* to penalize

(**b**) *(aprobar)* to sanction
sancochar *vt* to parboil; *Am* = to boil in water and salt
sancocho *nm Andes, Ven (comida)* = stew of beef, chicken or fish, vegetables and green bananas
sandalia *nf* sandal
sándalo *nm* sandalwood
sandez *nf* piece of nonsense
sandía *nf* watermelon
sándwich *nm* sandwich
sandwichera *nf* toasted sandwich maker
saneamiento *nm (de terreno)* drainage, draining; *(de una empresa)* reorganization
sanear *vt (terrenos)* to drain; *(empresa)* to reorganize
sangrar **1** *vt* (**a**) to bleed (**b**) *Fam (sacar dinero)* to bleed dry
2 *vi* to bleed
sangre *nf* blood; **donar s.** to give blood; **s. fría** sangfroid; **a s. fría** in cold blood
sangría *nf* (**a**) *Med* bleeding, bloodletting; *Fig* drain (**b**) *(timo)* rip-off (**c**) *(bebida)* sangria
sangriento,-a *adj (guerra etc)* bloody
sanguijuela *nf* leech, bloodsucker
sanguinario,-a *adj* bloodthirsty
sanguíneo,-a *adj* blood; **grupo s.** blood group
sanidad *nf* health; **Ministerio de S.** Department of Health

> ℓ Observa que la palabra inglesa **sanity** es un falso amigo y no es la traducción de la palabra española **sanidad**. En inglés, **sanity** significa "cordura, sensatez".

sanitario,-a **1** *adj* health
2 *nm* toilet
sano,-a *adj* (**a**) *(bien de salud)* healthy; **s. y salvo** safe and sound (**b**) *(comida)* healthy, wholesome (**c**) **en su s. juicio** in one's right mind

> ℓ Observa que la palabra inglesa **sane** es un falso amigo y no es la traducción de la palabra española **sano**. En inglés, **sane** significa "cuerdo, sensato".

Santa Claus, *Méx, Ven* **Santa Clos** *n* Santa Claus
santería *nf* (**a**) *(religión)* santería, = form of religion common in the Caribbean, in which people allegedly have contact with the spirit world (**b**) *Am (tienda)* = shop selling religious mementos such as statues of saints
santero,-a *nm,f (curandero)* = faith

healer who calls on the saints to assist with the healing process
santiamén *nm Fam* **en un s.** in a flash, in no time at all
santidad *nf* saintliness, holiness
santificar **[44]** *vt* to sanctify
santiguarse **[45]** *upr* to cross oneself
santo,-a **1** *adj* (**a**) holy, sacred (**b**) *(bueno)* saintly; **un s. varón** a saint
2 *nm,f* (**a**) saint; *Fam* **¡por todos los santos!** for heaven's sake!; *Fig* **se me fue el s. al cielo** I clean forgot (**b**) *(día onomástico)* saint's day; *Fig* **¿a s. de qué?** why on earth?
santuario *nm* sanctuary, shrine
saña *nf* fury; **con s.** furiously
sapo *nm* toad; *Fam* **echar sapos y culebras** to rant and rave
saque *nm* (**a**) *Ftb* **s. inicial** kick-off; **s. de banda** throw-in; **s. de esquina** corner kick (**b**) *Ten* service
saquear *vt (ciudad)* to sack, to plunder; *(casas, tiendas)* to loot
saqueo *nm (de ciudades)* sacking, plundering; *(de casa, tienda)* looting
S.A.R. (*abr* **Su Alteza Real**) H.R.H.
sarampión *nm* measles *sing*
sarao *nm* knees-up
sarcasmo *nm* sarcasm
sarcástico,-a *adj* sarcastic
sarcófago *nm* sarcophagus
sardana *nf* sardana, = Catalan dance and music
sardina *nf* sardine
sardónico,-a *adj* sardonic
sargento *nm* sergeant
sarmiento *nm* vine shoot
sarna *nf Med* scabies *sing*; *Zool* mange
sarpullido *nm* rash
sarracina *nf* massacre
sarro *nm (sedimento)* deposit; *(en los dientes)* tartar; *(en la lengua)* fur
sarta *nf* string
sartén *nf* frying pan, *US* fry-pan; *Fig* **tener la s. por el mango** to have the upper hand
sastre *nm* tailor
Satanás *n* Satan
satánico,-a *adj* satanic
satélite *nm* satellite; *Fig* **país s.** satellite state; **televisión vía s.** satellite TV
satén *nm* satin
satinar *vt* to gloss, to make glossy
sátira *nf* satire
satírico,-a *adj* satirical
satirizar **[40]** *vt* to satirize
satisfacción *nf* satisfaction; **s. de un deseo** fulfilment of a desire

satisfacer [15] (*pp* **satisfecho**) *vt* (**a**) (*deseos, necesidades*) to satisfy (**b**) (*requisitos*) to meet, to satisfy (**c**) (*deuda*) to pay
satisfactorio,-a *adj* satisfactory
satisfecho,-a *adj* satisfied; **me doy por s.** that's good enough for me; **s. de sí mismo** self-satisfied, smug
saturar *vt* to saturate
Saturno *n* Saturn
sauce *nm* willow; **s. llorón** weeping willow
saudí, saudita *adj & nmf* Saudi; **Arabia Saudita** Saudi Arabia
sauna *nf* sauna
savia *nf* sap
saxo *nm Fam Mús* sax
saxofón *nm* saxophone
saxofonista *nmf* saxophonist
sayo *nm* cassock, smock
sazonar *vt* to season, to flavour
s/c. (*abr* **su cuenta**) your account
Sdad. (*abr* **sociedad**) Soc.
se¹ *pron* (**a**) (*reflexivo*) (*objeto directo*) (*a él mismo*) himself; (*animal*) itself; (*a ella misma*) herself; (*animal*) itself; (*a usted mismo*) yourself; (*a ellos mismos*) themselves; (*a ustedes mismos*) yourselves (**b**) (*objeto indirecto*) (*a él mismo*) (to/for) himself; (*animal*) (to/for) itself; (*a ella misma*) (to/for) herself; (*animal*) (to/for) itself; (*a usted mismo*) (to/for) yourself; (*a ellos mismos*) (to/for) themselves; (*a ustedes mismos*) (to/for) yourselves; **se compró un nuevo coche** he bought himself a new car; **todos los días se lava el pelo** she washes her hair every day (**c**) (*recíproco*) one another, each other (**d**) (*voz pasiva*) **el vino se guarda en cubas** wine is kept in casks (**e**) (*impersonal*) **nunca se sabe** you never know; **se habla inglés** (*en letrero*) English spoken here; **se dice que ...** it is said that ...
se² *pron pers* (*a él*) (to/for) him; (*a ella*) (to/for) her; (*a usted o ustedes*) (to/for) you; (*a ellos*) (to/for) them; **se lo diré en cuanto les vea** I'll tell them as soon as I see them; **¿se lo explico?** shall I explain it to you?; **¿se lo has dado ya?** have you given it to him yet?
sé¹ *indic pres de* **saber**
sé² *imperat de* **ser**
S.E. (*abr* **Su Excelencia**) HE
sea *subj pres de* **ser**
sebo *nm* (*grasa*) fat
secado *nm* drying
secador *nm* dryer; **s. de pelo** hairdryer

secadora *nf* tumble dryer
secano *nm* dry land
secante *adj* **papel s.** blotting paper
secar [44] **1** *vt* to dry
  2 secarse *vpr* (**a**) to dry; **sécate** dry yourself; **s. las manos** to dry one's hands (**b**) (*marchitarse*) to dry up, to wither
sección *nf* section
seco,-a *adj* (**a**) dry; **frutos secos** dried fruit; **limpieza en s.** dry-cleaning; *Fig* **a palo s.** on its own; *Fig* **a secas** just, only (**b**) (*tono*) curt, sharp; (*golpe, ruido*) sharp; *Fig* **frenar en s.** to pull up sharply; *Fig* **parar en s.** to stop dead (**c**) (*delgado*) skinny
secreción *nf* secretion
secretaría *nf* (*oficina*) secretary's office; **S. de Estado** (*en España*) = government department under the control of a *Br* junior minister *o US* under-secretary; (*en Latinoamérica*) department, *Br* ministry; (*en Estados Unidos*) State Department
secretariado *nm* (**a**) (*oficina*) secretariat (**b**) *Educ* secretarial course
secretario,-a *nm,f* secretary; **s. de dirección** secretary to the director; **s. de Estado** (*en España*) *Br* junior minister, *US* under-secretary; (*en Latinoamérica*) minister; (*en Estados Unidos*) Secretary of State
secreto,-a 1 *adj* secret; **en s.** in secret, secretly
  2 *nm* secret; **guardar un s.** to keep a secret; **con mucho s.** in great secrecy
secta *nf* sect
sectario,-a *adj* sectarian
sector *nm* (**a**) sector (**b**) (*zona*) area; **un s. de la ciudad** an area of the city
sectorial *adj* sectoral
secuela *nf* consequence
secuencia *nf* sequence
secuestrador,-a *nm,f* (**a**) (*de persona*) kidnapper; (*de un avión*) hijacker (**b**) *Jur* sequestrator
secuestrar *vt* (**a**) (*persona*) to kidnap; (*aviones*) to hijack (**b**) *Jur* to confiscate
secuestro *nm* (**a**) (*de persona*) kidnapping; (*de un avión*) hijacking (**b**) *Jur* confiscation
secular *adj* (**a**) *Rel* secular, lay (**b**) (*antiquísimo*) ancient, age-old
secundar *vt* to back
secundario,-a *adj* secondary
secuoya *nf Bot* redwood, sequoia; **s. gigante** giant sequoia
sed *nf* thirst; **tener s.** to be thirsty
seda *nf* silk
sedal *nm* fishing line

sedante *adj & nm* sedative
sede *nf* (**a**) headquarters, head office; *(de gobierno)* seat (**b**) **la Santa S.** the Holy See
sedentario,-a *adj* sedentary
sedición *nf* sedition
sedicioso,-a 1 *adj* rebellious
  2 *nm,f* rebel
sediento,-a *adj* thirsty; *Fig* **s. de poder** hungry for power
sedimentario,-a *adj* sedimentary
sedimentarse *vpr* to settle
sedimento *nm* sediment, deposit
sedoso,-a *adj* silky, silken
seducción *nf* seduction
seducir [10] *vt* to seduce; *(persuadir)* to tempt
seductor,-a 1 *adj* seductive; *(persuasivo)* tempting
  2 *nm,f* seducer
segadora *nf* *(máquina)* reaper, harvester
segar [1] *vt* to reap, to cut
seglar 1 *adj* secular, lay
  2 *nmf* lay person; *(hombre)* layman; *(mujer)* laywoman
segmento *nm* segment
segregación *nf* (**a**) *(separación)* segregation (**b**) *(secreción)* secretion
segregar [42] *vt* (**a**) *(separar)* to segregate (**b**) *(secretar)* to secrete
seguida *nf* **en s.** immediately, straight away
seguido,-a 1 *adj* (**a**) *(continuo)* continuous (**b**) *(consecutivo)* consecutive, successive; **tres veces seguidas** on three consecutive occasions; **tres lunes seguidos** three Mondays in a row
  2 *adv* (**a**) *(en línea recta)* straight on; **todo s.** straight on *o* ahead (**b**) *Am (a menudo)* often
seguidor,-a *nm,f* follower
seguimiento *nm* (**a**) pursuit (**b**) *Prensa* in- depth coverage (**c**) **estación de s. (espacial)** tracking station
seguir [6] **1** *vt* (**a**) to follow (**b**) *(camino)* to continue (**c**) *(perseguir)* to chase
  2 *vi* (**a**) to follow (**b**) **s. +** *ger (continuar)* to continue, to go on, to keep on; **siguió hablando** he continued *o* went on *o* kept on speaking (**c**) **s. +** *adj/pp* to continue to be, to be still; **sigo resfriado** I've still got the cold; **sigue con vida** he's still alive
  3 **seguirse** *vpr* to follow, to ensue
según 1 *prep* (**a**) according to; **s. la Biblia** according to the Bible (**b**) *(en función de)* depending on; **varía s. el tiempo (que haga)** it varies depending on the weather
  2 *adv* (**a**) depending on; **s. estén las cosas** depending on how things stand;

¿vendrás mañana? – s. will you come tomorrow? – it depends (**b**) *(tal como)* just as; **estaba s. lo dejé** it was just as I had left it (**c**) *(a medida que)* as; **s. iba leyendo ...** as I read on ...
segundero *nm* second hand
segundo¹,-a 1 *adj* second; *Fig* **decir algo con segundas (intenciones)** to say sth with a double meaning
  2 *nm,f (de una serie)* second (one)
segundo² *nm (tiempo)* second; **sesenta segundos** sixty seconds
seguramente *adv* (**a**) *(seguro)* surely (**b**) *(probablemente)* most probably; **s. no lloverá** it isn't likely to rain
seguridad *nf* (**a**) security; **cerradura de s.** security lock (**b**) *(física)* safety; **s. en carretera** road safety; **para mayor s.** to be on the safe side (**c**) *(confianza)* confidence; **s. en sí mismo** self-confidence (**d**) *(certeza)* sureness; **con toda s.** most probably; **tener la s. de que ...** to be certain that ... (**e**) **S. Social** ≃ Social Security, *Br* ≃ National Health Service (**f**) *(fiabilidad)* reliability
seguro,-a 1 *adj* (**a**) *(cierto)* sure; **estoy s. de que ...** I am sure that ...; **dar algo por s.** to take sth for granted (**b**) *(libre de peligro)* safe; *Fig* **ir sobre s.** to play safe (**c**) *(protegido)* secure (**d**) *(fiable)* reliable (**e**) **está segura de ella misma** she has self-confidence (**f**) *(firme)* steady, firm
  2 *nm Seg* insurance; **s. a todo riesgo** fully comprehensive insurance; **s. contra terceros** third-party insurance; **s. de vida** life insurance (**b**) *(dispositivo)* safety catch *o* device (**c**) *CAm, Méx (imperdible)* safety pin
  3 *adv* for sure, definitely
seis *adj & nm inv* six
seiscientos,-as *adj & nm* six hundred
seísmo *nm (terremoto)* earthquake; *(temblor de tierra)* earth tremor
selección *nf* (**a**) selection (**b**) *Dep* team
seleccionador,-a *nm,f* (**a**) selector (**b**) *Dep* manager
seleccionar *vt* to select
selectividad *nf* selectivity; *Univ* **(prueba de) s.** entrance examination
selectivo,-a *adj* selective
selecto,-a *adj* select; **ambiente s.** exclusive atmosphere
self-service *nm* self-service cafeteria
sellar *vt (documento)* to seal; *(carta)* to stamp
sello *nm* (**a**) *(de correos)* stamp; *(para documentos)* seal (**b**) *(precinto)* seal
selva *nf* jungle

semáforo *nm* traffic lights
semana *nf* week; **entre s.** during the week; **S. Santa** Holy Week
semanada *nf Am Br* (weekly) pocket money, *US* (weekly) allowance
semanal *adj & nm* weekly
semanario *nm* weekly magazine
semblante *nm Literario (cara)* face; *Fig (aspecto)* look
sembrado *nm* sown field
sembrar [1] *vt* (**a**) *Agr* to sow (**b**) *Fig* **s. el pánico** to spread panic
semejante 1 *adj* (**a**) *(parecido)* similar; **nunca he visto nada s.** I've never seen anything like it (**b**) *Pey (comparativo)* such; **s. desvergüenza** such insolence
   2 *nm (prójimo)* fellow being
semejanza *nf* similarity, likeness
semen *nm* semen
semental *nm* stud
semestral *adj* half-yearly
semestre *nm* six-month period, semester
semicírculo *nm* semicircle
semifinal *nf* semifinal
semifinalista *nmf* semifinalist
semilla *nf* seed
semillero *nm* seedbed
seminario *nm* (**a**) *Educ* seminar (**b**) *Rel* seminary
sémola *nf* semolina
Sena *n* **el S.** the Seine
senado *nm* senate
senador,-a *nm,f* senator
sencillez *nf* simplicity
sencillo,-a 1 *adj* (**a**) *(fácil)* simple, easy (**b**) *(natural)* natural, unaffected (**c**) *(billete)* single (**d**) *(sin adornos)* simple, plain
   2 *nm Andes, CAm, Méx Fam (cambio)* loose change
senda *nf*, **sendero** *nm* path
sendos,-as *adj pl* one each; **con sendas carteras** each carrying a briefcase
senil *adj* senile
seno *nm* (**a**) *(pecho)* breast (**b**) *Fig* bosom, heart; **en el s. de** within (**c**) *Mat* sine
sensación *nf* (**a**) sensation, feeling; **tengo la s. de que ...** I have a feeling that ... (**b**) *(impresión)* sensation; **causar s.** to cause a sensation
sensacional *adj* sensational
sensacionalista *adj* sensationalist; **prensa s.** gutter press
sensato,-a *adj* sensible
sensibilizar [40] *vt* to make aware; **s. a la opinión pública** to increase public awareness

sensible *adj* (**a**) sensitive (**b**) *(perceptible)* perceptible
sensiblemente *adv* noticeably, considerably

> Observa que la palabra inglesa **sensible** es un falso amigo y no es la traducción de la palabra española **sensible**. En inglés, **sensible** significa tanto "sensato" como "práctico".

sensiblero,-a *adj* over-sentimental, mawkish
sensitivo,-a *adj* sense; **órgano s.** sense organ
sensorial, sensorio,-a *adj* sensory
sensual *adj* sensual
sensualidad *nf* sensuality
sentada *nf* (**a**) sitting (**b**) *Fam (protesta)* sit-in (demonstration)
sentado,-a *adj (establecido)* established, settled; **dar algo por s.** to take sth for granted; **dejar s. que ...** to make it clear that ...
sentar [1] 1 *vt* (**a**) to sit (**b**) *(establecer)* to establish; **s. las bases** to lay the foundations
   2 *vi* (**a**) *(color, ropa etc)* to suit; **el pelo corto te sienta mal** short hair doesn't suit you (**b**) **s. bien/mal a** *(comida)* to agree/disagree with; **la sopa te sentará bien** the soup will do you good (**c**) **le sentó mal la broma** she didn't like the joke
   3 sentarse *vpr* to sit, to sit down
sentencia *nf* (**a**) sentence; **visto para s.** ready for judgement (**b**) *(aforismo)* maxim, saying
sentenciar [43] *vt Jur* to sentence (**a** to)
sentido,-a 1 *nm* (**a**) sense; **los cinco sentidos** the five senses; **s. común** common sense; **s. del humor** sense of humour (**b**) *(significado)* meaning; **doble s.** double meaning; **no tiene s.** it doesn't make sense (**c**) *(dirección)* direction; **(de) s. único** one-way (**d**) *(conciencia)* consciousness; **perder el s.** to faint
   2 *adj* deeply felt; *Fml* **mi más s. pésame** my deepest sympathy
sentimental 1 *adj* sentimental; **vida s.** love life
   2 *nmf* sentimental person
sentimiento *nm* (**a**) feeling (**b**) *(pesar)* sorrow, grief; *Fml* **le acompaño en el s.** my deepest sympathy
sentir¹ *nm* (**a**) *(sentimiento)* feeling (**b**) *(opinión)* opinion, view
sentir² [5] 1 *vt* (**a**) to feel; **s. hambre/calor** to feel hungry/hot (**b**) *(lamentar)* to regret, to be sorry about; **lo siento**

(mucho) I'm (very) sorry; **siento molestarle** I'm sorry to bother you
  2 sentirse *vpr* to feel; **me siento mal** I feel ill; **s. con ánimos de hacer algo** to feel like doing sth

senyera *nf* Catalan flag

seña *nf* (**a**) mark (**b**) *(gesto)* sign; **hacer señas a algn** to signal to sb (**c**) *(indicio)* sign (**d**) **señas** *(dirección)* address

señal *nf* (**a**) *(indicio)* sign, indication; **en s. de** as a sign of, as a token of (**b**) *(placa)* sign; **s. de tráfico** road sign (**c**) *(gesto etc)* signal, sign (**d**) *(marca)* mark; *(vestigio)* trace (**e**) *Tel* tone; **s. de llamada** *Br* dialling tone, *US* dial tone (**f**) *Com* deposit

señalado,-a *adj (importante)* important; **un día s.** a red-letter day

señalar *vt* (**a**) *(indicar)* to mark, to indicate; **s. con el dedo** to point at (**b**) *(resaltar)* to point out (**c**) *(precio, fecha)* to fix, to arrange

señalero *nm* *Urug Br* indicator, *US* turn signal

señor *nm* (**a**) *(hombre)* man; *(caballero)* gentleman (**b**) *Rel* **El S.** the Lord (**c**) *(con apellido)* Mr; *(tratamiento de respeto)* sir; **el Sr. Gutiérrez** Mr Gutiérrez; **muy s. mío** *(en carta)* Dear Sir (**d**) *(con título) (no se traduce)* **el s. ministro** the Minister

señora *nf* (**a**) *(mujer)* woman, *Fml* lady; **¡señoras y señores!** ladies and gentlemen! (**b**) *Rel* **Nuestra S.** Our Lady (**c**) *(con apellido)* Mrs; *(tratamiento de respeto)* madam; **la Sra. Salinas** Mrs Salinas; **muy s. mía** *(en carta)* Dear Madam (**d**) *(con título) (no se traduce)* **la s. ministra** the Minister (**e**) *(esposa)* wife

señoría *nf* (**a**) *Jur (hombre)* lordship; *(mujer)* ladyship (**b**) *Pol* **sus señorías** the honourable gentlemen

señorita *nf* (**a**) *(joven)* young woman, *Fml* young lady (**b**) *(tratamiento de respeto)* Miss; **S. Padilla** Miss Padilla (**c**) *Educ* **la s.** the teacher, Miss

señuelo *nm (en caza)* decoy

sepa *subj pres de* **saber**

separación *nf* (**a**) separation; *Jur* **s. conyugal** legal separation (**b**) *(espacio)* space, gap

separado,-a *adj* (**a**) separate; **por s.** separately, individually (**b**) *(divorciado)* separated

separar 1 *vt* (**a**) to separate (**b**) *(desunir)* to detach, to remove (**c**) *(dividir)* to divide, to separate (**d**) *(apartar)* to move away
  2 separarse *vpr* (**a**) to separate, to part

company (**b**) *(matrimonio)* to separate (**c**) *(apartarse)* to move away (**de** from)

separata *nf* offprint

separatismo *nm* separatism

separatista *adj & nmf* separatist

separo *nm Méx* (prison) cell

sepia 1 *nf (pez)* cuttlefish
  2 *adj & nm (color)* sepia

septentrional *adj* northern

septiembre *nm* September; **el 5 de s.** the 5th of September; **en s.** in September

séptimo,-a *adj & nm,f* seventh; **la** *o* **una séptima parte** a seventh

sepulcral *adj (silencio)* deathly

sepulcro *nm* tomb

sepultura *nf* grave

sepulturero,-a *nm,f* gravedigger

sequía *nf* drought

séquito *nm* entourage, retinue

ser¹ *nm* being; **s. humano** human being; **s. vivo** living being

ser² **[23]** *vi* (**a**) *(+ adj)* to be; **es alto y rubio** he is tall and fair; **el edificio es gris** the building is grey
  (**b**) *(+ profesión)* to be a(n); **Rafael es músico** Rafael is a musician
  (**c**) **s. de** *(procedencia)* to be *o* come from; **¿de dónde eres?** where are you from?, where do you come from?
  (**d**) **s. de** *(+ material)* to be made of
  (**e**) **s. de** *(+ poseedor)* to belong to; **el perro es de Miguel** the dog belongs to Miguel; **¿de quién es este abrigo?** whose coat is this?
  (**f**) **s. para** *(finalidad)* to be for; **esta agua es para lavar** this water is for washing
  (**g**) *(+ día, hora)* to be; **hoy es 2 de noviembre** today is the 2nd of November; **son las cinco de la tarde** it's five o'clock
  (**h**) *(+ cantidad)* **¿cuántos estaremos en la fiesta?** how many of us will there be at the party?
  (**i**) *(costar)* to be, to cost; **¿cuánto es?** how much is it?
  (**j**) *(tener lugar)* to be; **el estreno será mañana** tomorrow is the opening night
  (**k**) **¿qué es de Gonzalo?** what has become of Gonzalo?
  (**l**) *(auxiliar en pasiva)* to be; **fue asesinado** he was murdered
  (**m**) *(locuciones)* **¿cómo es eso?, ¿cómo puede s.?** how can that be?; **es más** furthermore; **es que ...** it's just that ...; **como sea** anyhow; **lo que sea** whatever; **o sea** that is (to say); **por si fuera poco** to top it all; **sea como sea** in any case, be that as it may; **a no s. que** unless; **de no s.**

por ... had it not been for ...; **eso era de esperar** it was to be expected

> The auxiliary verb **ser** is used with the past participle of a verb to form the passive (e.g. **la película fue criticada** the film was criticized).

serenarse *vpr* to calm down
serenidad *nf* serenity
sereno¹ *nm (vigilante)* nightwatchman
sereno²,-a *adj* (**a**) *(severo)* calm (**b**) *Fam* **estar s.** *(sobrio)* to be sober
serial *nm Rad & TV* serial
serie *nf* (**a**) series *sing*; **fabricación en s.** mass production; **lleva ABS de s.** it has ABS fitted as standard; **fuera de s.** out of the ordinary (**b**) *Rad & TV* series *sing*
seriedad *nf* (**a**) seriousness (**b**) *(formalidad)* reliability, dependability; **falta de s.** irresponsibility
serio,-a *adj* (**a**) *(severo)* serious; **en s.** seriously (**b**) *(formal)* reliable, responsible
sermón *nm* sermon
sermonear *vt & vi Fam* to lecture
seropositivo,-a *adj* HIV-positive
serpentear *vi (zigzaguear)* to wind one's way, to meander
serpentina *nf (de papel)* streamer
serpiente *nf* snake; **s. de cascabel** rattlesnake; **s. pitón** python
serranía *nf* mountainous area/country
serrar [1] *vt* to saw
serrín *nm* sawdust
serrucho *nm* handsaw
servicial *adj* helpful, obliging
servicio *nm* (**a**) service; **s. a domicilio** delivery service (**b**) *Mil* service; **s. militar** military service; **estar de s.** to be on duty (**c**) **servicios** *(retrete)* toilet, *US* rest room
servidor,-a *nm,f* servant; *Fam* **un s.** yours truly
servil *adj* servile
servilleta *nf* serviette, napkin
servilletero *nm* serviette ring, napkin ring
servio,-a *adj & nm,f* Serbian
servir [6] 1 *vt* to serve; **¿en qué puedo servirle?** what can I do for you?, may I help you?; **¿te sirvo una copa?** will I pour you a drink?
2 *vi* (**a**) to serve (**b**) *(valer)* to be useful, to be suitable; **no sirve de nada llorar** it's no use crying; **ya no sirve** it's no use; **¿para qué sirve esto?** what is this (used) for? (**c**) **s. de** to serve as, to act as
3 servirse *vpr* (**a**) *(comida etc)* to help oneself (**b**) *Fml* **sírvase comunicarnos su**

decisión please inform us of your decision
sésamo *nm* sesame
sesenta *adj & nm inv* sixty
sesgar [42] *vt* (**a**) *(cortar)* to cut diagonally (**b**) *(torcer)* to slant
sesgo *nm Fig* slant, turn; **tomar un s. favorable** to take a turn for the better
sesión *nf* (**a**) *(reunión)* meeting, session; *Jur* session, sitting (**b**) *Cin* showing
seso *nm* brain
set *nm Ten* set
seta *nf (comestible)* mushroom; **s. venenosa** toadstool
setecientos,-as *adj & nm* seven hundred
setenta *adj & nm inv* seventy
setiembre *nm* September
seto *nm* hedge
seudónimo *nm* pseudonym; *(de escritores)* pen name
severidad *nf* severity
severo,-a *adj* severe
Sevilla *n* Seville
sexismo *nm* sexism
sexista *adj* sexist
sexo *nm* (**a**) sex (**b**) *(órgano)* genitals
sexólogo,-a *nm,f* sexologist
sexto,-a *adj & nm,f* sixth
sexual *adj* sexual; **vida s.** sex life
sexualidad *nf* sexuality
sexy *adj* sexy
s/f. (*abr* **su favor**) your favour
shock *nm* shock
short *nm RP* swimming trunks
show *nm* show
si¹ *conj* (**a**) *(condicional)* if; **como si** as if; **si no** if not; **si quieres** if you like, if you wish (**b**) *(pregunta indirecta)* whether, if; **me preguntó si me gustaba** he asked me if I liked it; **no sé si ir o no** *(disyuntivo)* I don't know whether to go or not (**c**) *(sorpresa)* **¡si está llorando!** but she's crying!
si² *nm* (*pl* **sis**) *Mús* B; *(en solfeo)* ti
sí¹ *pron pers* (**a**) *(singular) (él)* himself; *(ella)* herself; *(cosa)* itself; *(plural)* themselves; **de por sí, en sí** in itself; **hablaban entre sí** they were talking among themselves *o* to each other; **por sí mismo** by himself (**b**) *(uno mismo)* oneself; **decir para sí** to say to oneself
sí² *adv* (**a**) yes; **dije que sí** I said yes, I accepted, I agreed; **porque sí** just because; **¡que sí!** yes, I tell you!; **un día sí y otro no** every other day (**b**) *(uso enfático) (no se traduce)* **sí que me gusta** of course I like it; **¡eso sí que no!** certainly not!
2 *nm* (*pl* **síes**) yes; **los síes** *(en parlamento)* the ayes

siamés,-esa *nm,f* Siamese twin
sibarita *nmf* sybarite
sicario *nm* hired gunman; *Fam* hitman
Sicilia *n* Sicily
sico- = **psico-**
sicómoro *nm* sycamore
sida *nm* (*abr* **síndrome de inmunodeficiencia adquirida**) AIDS
sidecar *nm* sidecar
siderurgia *nf* iron and steel industry
siderúrgico,-a *adj* iron and steel; **la industria siderúrgica** the iron and steel industry
sidra *nf Br* cider, *US* hard cider
siempre *adv* (**a**) always; **s. pasa lo mismo** it's always the same; **como s.** as usual; **a la hora de s.** at the usual time; **eso es así desde s.** it has always been like that; **para s.** for ever; **s. que** (*cada vez que*) whenever; (*a condición de que*) provided, as long as; **s. y cuando** provided, as long as (**b**) *Am* (*todavía*) still; **s. viven allí** they still live there (**c**) *Méx Fam* (*enfático*) still; **s. sí quiero ir** I still want to go; **s. no me marcho** I'm still not leaving
sien *nf* temple
sierra *nf* (**a**) saw; **s. mecánica** power saw (**b**) *Geog* mountain range, sierra
siervo,-a *nm,f* slave
siesta *nf* siesta, nap; **dormir la s.** to have a siesta *o* an afternoon nap
siete 1 *adj* seven
2 *nm inv* seven
3 *nf RP Fam Euf* **¡la gran s.!** *Br* sugar!, *US* shoot!
sietemesino,-a *nm,f* seven-month baby, premature baby
sífilis *nf inv* syphilis
sifón *nm* siphon; **whisky con s.** whisky and soda
sig. (*abr* **siguiente**) following
sigilo *nm* secrecy; **entrar con mucho s.** to tiptoe in
sigilosamente *adv* (*secretamente*) secretly; **entró s. en la habitación** she crept *o* slipped into the room
sigiloso,-a *adj* secretive
sigla *nf* acronym
siglo *nm* century; **el s. veintiuno** the twenty-first century; *Fam* **hace siglos que no le veo** I haven't seen him for ages
signatario,-a *adj & nm,f* signatory
significación *nf* (**a**) (*sentido*) meaning (**b**) (*importancia*) significance
significado *nm* meaning
significar [44] *vt* to mean
significativo,-a *adj* significant; (*expresivo*) meaningful

signo *nm* (**a**) sign; **s. del zodiaco** zodiac sign (**b**) *Ling* mark; **s. de interrogación** question mark
sigo *indic pres de* **seguir**
siguiente *adj* following, next; **¡el s.!** next, please!; **al día s.** the following day
sílaba *nf* syllable
silbar *vi* to whistle; (*abuchear*) to hiss, to boo
silbato *nm* whistle
silbido *nm* whistle, whistling; (*agudo*) hiss
silenciador *nm* (*de arma*) silencer; (*de coche, moto*) *Br* silencer, *US* muffler
silenciar [43] *vt* (**a**) (*un sonido*) to muffle (**b**) (*noticia*) to hush up
silencio *nm* silence; **imponer s. a algn** to make sb be quiet
silencioso,-a *adj* (*persona*) quiet; (*motor etc*) silent
silicio *nm* silicon
silicona *nf* silicone
silla *nf* (**a**) chair; **s. de ruedas** wheelchair; **s. giratoria** swivel chair (**b**) (*de montura*) saddle
sillín *nm* saddle
sillón *nm* armchair
silo *nm* silo
silueta *nf* silhouette; (*de cuerpo*) figure
silvestre *adj* wild
simbólico,-a *adj* symbolic; **precio s.** token price
simbolizar [40] *vt* to symbolize
símbolo *nm* symbol
simetría *nf* symmetry
simétrico,-a *adj* symmetrical
simiente *nf* seed
similar *adj* similar
similitud *nf* similarity
simio *nm* monkey
simpatía *nf* liking, affection; **le tengo mucha s.** I am very fond of him

> *♪* Observa que la palabra inglesa **sympathy** es un falso amigo y no es la traducción de la palabra española **simpatía**. En inglés, **sympathy** significa tanto "compasión" como "comprensión".

simpático,-a *adj* (*amable*) nice, likeable; **me cae s.** I like him

> *♪* Observa que la palabra inglesa **sympathetic** es un falso amigo y no es la traducción de la palabra española **simpático**. En inglés, **sympathetic** significa tanto "comprensivo" como "compasivo".

simpatizante *nmf* sympathizer
simpatizar [40] *vi* (**a**) to sympathize

(**con** with) (**b**) *(llevarse bien)* to hit it off (**con** with)

simple 1 *adj* (**a**) simple (**b**) *(fácil)* simple, easy (**c**) *(mero)* mere (**d**) *(persona)* simple, simple-minded
  2 *nm (persona)* simpleton

simpleza *nf* simple-mindedness; *(tontería)* nonsense

simplificar [44] *vt* to simplify

simposio *nm* symposium

simulacro *nm* sham, pretence; **un s. de ataque** a mock attack

simular *vt* to simulate

simultanear *vt* to combine; **simultanea el trabajo y los estudios** he's working and studying at the same time

simultáneo,-a *adj* simultaneous

sin *prep* (**a**) without; **s. dinero/tí** without money/you; **estamos s. pan** we're out of bread; **s. hacer nada** without doing anything; **cerveza s.** alcohol-free beer; **s. más ni más** without further ado (**b**) *(+ inf)* **está s. secar** it hasn't been dried

sinagoga *nf* synagogue

sincerarse *vpr* to open one's heart (**con** to)

sinceridad *nf* sincerity; **con toda s.** in all sincerity

sincero,-a *adj* sincere

sincronizar [40] *vt* to synchronize

sindical *adj* (*Br* trade *o US* labor) union

sindicalista *nmf* union member, *Br* trade unionist

sindicar *vt Andes, RP, Ven* to accuse

sindicato *nm* union, trade union

síndrome *nm* syndrome

sinfín *nm* endless number; **un s. de** lots of

sinfonía *nf* symphony

singani *nm Bol* grape brandy

single *nm* (**a**) *(disco)* single, 7-inch (**b**) *CSur (habitación)* single room

singular 1 *adj* (**a**) singular (**b**) *(excepcional)* exceptional, unique (**c**) *(raro)* peculiar, odd
  2 *nm Ling* singular; **en s.** in the singular

siniestrado,-a *adj* stricken

siniestro,-a 1 *adj* sinister, ominous
  2 *nm* disaster, catastrophe

sino¹ *nm Fml* fate, destiny

sino² *conj* (**a**) but; **no fui a Madrid, s. a Barcelona** I didn't go to Madrid but to Barcelona (**b**) *(excepto)* **nadie s. él** no one but him; **no quiero s. que me oigan** I only want them to listen (to me)

sinónimo,-a 1 *adj* synonymous
  2 *nm* synonym

sinóptico,-a *adj* **cuadro s.** diagram, chart

sinsabor *nm (usu pl)* trouble, worry

sintético,-a *adj* synthetic

sintetizador *nm* synthesizer

sintetizar [40] *vt* to synthesize

síntoma *nm* symptom

sintonía *nf* (**a**) *Elec & Rad* tuning (**b**) *Mús & Rad (de programa)* signature tune (**c**) *Fig* harmony

sintonizador *nm Rad* tuning knob

sintonizar [40] *vt* (**a**) *Rad* to tune in to (**b**) *(simpatizar)* **sintonizaron muy bien** they clicked straight away

sinuoso,-a *adj (camino)* winding

sinvergüenza 1 *adj (desvergonzado)* shameless; *(descarado)* cheeky
  2 *nmf (desvergonzado)* rogue; *(caradura)* cheeky devil

sionismo *nm* Zionism

siquiera 1 *adv (por lo menos)* at least; **ni s.** not even
  2 *conj Fml (aunque)* although, even though

sirena *nf* (**a**) siren, mermaid (**b**) *(señal acústica)* siren

Siria *n* Syria

sirimiri *nm* fine drizzle

sirio,-a *adj & nm,f* Syrian

sirviente,-a *nm,f* servant

sisar *vt (hurtar)* to pilfer, to filch

sisear *vi* to hiss

sísmico,-a *adj* seismic

sismógrafo *nm* seismograph

sistema *nm* system; **por s.** as a rule; **s. nervioso** nervous system; **s. montañoso** mountain chain

sistemático,-a *adj* systematic

sitiar [43] *vt* to besiege

sitio¹ *nm* (**a**) *(lugar)* place; **en cualquier s.** anywhere; **en todos los sitios** everywhere; *Fig* **quedarse en el s.** to die (**b**) *(espacio)* room; **hacer s.** to make room (**c**) *Méx (parada de taxis)* taxi stand *o Br* rank

sitio² *nm* siege; **estado de s.** state of emergency

sito,-a *adj Fml* situated, located

situación *nf* (**a**) situation; **su s. económica es buena** his financial position is good (**b**) *(ubicación)* situation, location

situado,-a *adj* situated; *Fig* **estar bien s.** to have a good position

situar [30] 1 *vt* to locate
  2 situarse *vpr* to be situated *o* located

sketch *nm Cin & Teatro* sketch

S.L. *(abr* **Sociedad Limitada**) *Br* ≃ Ltd, *US* ≃ Inc

slip *nm* underpants

slogan *nm* slogan

S.M. (*abr* **Su Majestad**) *(rey)* His Majesty; *(reina)* Her Majesty

smoking *nm* dinner jacket, *US* tuxedo

s/n. (*abr* **sin número**) = abbreviation used in addresses after the street name, where the building has no number

snob *adj & nmf* = esnob

snobismo *nm* = esnobismo

so¹ *prep* (*bajo*) under; **so pena de** under penalty of

so² *nm Fam* ¡**so imbécil!** you damned idiot!

sobaco *nm* armpit

sobar *Fam* **1** *vt* (*manosear*) to fondle, to paw
  2 *vi* (*dormir*) to sleep

soberanía *nf* sovereignty

soberano,-a 1 *adj* (**a**) sovereign (**b**) *Fam* huge, great
  2 *nm,f* (*monarca*) sovereign

soberbia *nf* pride

soberbio,-a *adj* (**a**) proud (**b**) (*magnífico*) splendid, magnificent

sobón,-ona *nm,f Fam* **ser un s.** to be fresh *o* all hands

sobornar *vt* to bribe

soborno *nm* (*acción*) bribery; (*dinero etc*) bribe

sobra *nf* (**a**) **de s.** (*no necesario*) superfluous; **tener de s.** to have plenty; **estar de s.** not to be needed; **saber algo de s.** to know sth only too well (**b**) **sobras** (*restos*) leftovers

sobradamente *adv* only too well

sobrado,-a *adj* (*que sobra*) abundant, more than enough; **sobradas veces** repeatedly; **andar s. de tiempo/dinero** to have plenty of time/money

sobrante 1 *adj* remaining, spare
  2 *nm* surplus, excess

sobrar *vi* (**a**) to be more than enough, (*sing*) to be too much, (*pl*) to be too many; **sobran tres sillas** there are three chairs too many; **sobran comentarios** I've nothing further to add; *Fam* **tú sobras aquí** you are not wanted here (**b**) (*quedar*) to be left over; **ha sobrado carne** there's still some meat left

sobrasada *nf* sausage spread

sobre¹ *nm* (**a**) (*para carta*) envelope (**b**) (*de sopa etc*) packet

sobre² *prep* (**a**) (*encima de*) on, upon, on top of (**b**) (*por encima de*) over, above (**c**) (*acerca de*) about, on (**d**) (*aproximadamente*) about; **vendré s. las ocho** I'll come at about eight o'clock (**e**) **s. todo** especially, above all

sobre- *pref* super-, over-

sobrealimentado,-a *adj* overfed

sobrecarga *nf* overload

sobrecargar [42] *vt* to overload

sobrecogedor,-a *adj* dramatic, awesome

sobrecoger [53] *vt* (*conmover*) to shock

sobredosis *nf inv* overdose

sobreentenderse *vpr* **se sobreentiende** that goes without saying

sobregiro *nm* overdraft

sobrehumano,-a *adj* superhuman

sobreimpresión *nf Fot & Cin* superimposing

sobrellevar *vt* to endure, to bear

sobremesa¹ *nf* afternoon

sobremesa² *nf* **ordenador de s.** desktop computer

sobrenatural *adj* supernatural

sobrenombre *nm* nickname

sobrepasar 1 *vt* to exceed, to surpass; (*rival*) to beat
  2 sobrepasarse *vpr* to go too far

sobrepeso *nm* (*de carga*) overload, excess weight; (*de persona*) excess weight

sobreponerse *vpr* (**a**) **s. a** (*superar*) to overcome; **s. al dolor** to overcome pain (**b**) (*animarse*) to pull oneself together

sobreproducción *nf* overproduction

sobresaliente 1 *nm* (*nota*) ≃ A
  2 *adj* (*que destaca*) outstanding, excellent

sobresalir [22] *vi* to stick out, to protrude; *Fig* (*destacar*) to stand out, to excel

sobresaltar 1 *vt* to startle
  2 sobresaltarse *vpr* to be startled, to start

sobresalto *nm* (*movimiento*) start; (*susto*) fright

sobreseer [36] *vt Jur* to stay; **s. una causa** to stay proceedings

sobretiempo *nm Andes* (**a**) (*en trabajo*) overtime (**b**) (*en deporte*) *Br* extra time, *US* overtime

sobretodo *nm* (*abrigo*) overcoat; (*guardapolvo*) overalls

sobrevalorar *vt* to overestimate

sobrevenir [27] *vi* to happen unexpectedly

sobreviviente 1 *adj* surviving
  2 *nmf* survivor

sobrevivir *vi* to survive

sobrevolar [2] *vt* to fly over

sobriedad *nf* sobriety; (*en la bebida*) soberness

sobrina *nf* niece

sobrino *nm* nephew

sobrio,-a *adj* sober

socarrón,-ona *adj* (**a**) (*sarcástico*) sarcastic (**b**) (*astuto*) sly, cunning

socavar *vt Fig* to undermine

socavón *nm (bache)* pothole
sociable *adj* sociable, friendly
social *adj* social
socialdemócrata 1 *adj* social democratic
  2 *nmf* social democrat
socialismo *nm* socialism
socialista *adj & nmf* socialist
socializar [40] *vt* to socialize
sociedad *nf* (a) society; **s. de consumo**
consumer society (**b**) *(asociación)* association, society (**c**) *Com* company; **s.
anónima** *Br* public (limited) company,
US incorporated company; **s. limitada**
private limited company
socio,-a *nm,f* (a) *(miembro)* member; **hacerse s. de un club** to become a member
of a club, to join a club (**b**) *Com (asociado)* partner
sociología *nf* sociology
sociológico,-a *adj* sociological
sociólogo,-a *nm,f* sociologist
socorrer *vt* to help, to assist
socorrido,-a *adj* handy, useful
socorrista *nmf* life-saver, lifeguard
socorro *nm* help, assistance; **¡s.!** help!;
  puesto de s. first-aid post
soda *nf* soda water
soez *adj* vulgar, crude
sofá *nm* (*pl* **sofás**) sofa, settee; **s. cama**
sofa bed, studio couch
Sofía *n* Sofia
sofisticado,-a *adj* sophisticated
sofocado,-a *adj* suffocated
sofocante *adj* suffocating, stifling; **hacía
un calor s.** it was unbearably hot
sofocar [44] 1 *vt* (a) *(ahogar)* to suffocate, to smother (**b**) *(incendio)* to extinguish, to put out
  2 sofocarse *vpr* (a) *(ahogarse)* to suffocate, to stifle (**b**) *Fam (irritarse)* to get
upset
sofoco *nm Fig (vergüenza)* embarrassment; **le dio un s.** *(disgusto)* it gave her
quite a turn
sofocón *nm Fam* shock; **llevarse un s.** to
get upset
sofreír [56] *vt* to fry lightly, to brown
sofrito *nm* = fried tomato and onion
sauce
software *nm* software
soga *nf* rope; *Fig* **estar con la s. al cuello** to
be in dire straits
soja *nf* (a) *(planta, fruto) Br* soya bean, *US*
soy bean (**b**) *(proteína)* soya
sojuzgar [42] *vt* to subjugate
sol¹ *nm* (a) sun (**b**) *(luz)* sunlight; *(luz y
calor)* sunshine; **hace s.** it's sunny, the sun

is shining; **tomar el s.** to sunbathe; **al** *o*
bajo el s. in the sun; **de s. a s.** from sunrise
to sunset (**c**) *Fin* = standard monetary
unit of Peru
sol² *nm Mús* G; *(solfeo)* so
solamente *adv* only; **no s.** not only; **s. con
mirarte lo sé** I know just by looking at
you; **s. que ...** except that ...
solapa *nf (de chaqueta)* lapel; *(de sobre,
bolsillo, libro)* flap
solapadamente *adv* stealthily, in an underhand way
solapado,-a *adj (persona)* sly
solapamiento *nm* overlap
solapar 1 *vt Fig* to conceal, to cover up
  2 *vi* to overlap
solar¹ *adj* solar; **luz s.** sunlight
solar² *nm (terreno)* plot; *(en obras)* building site
solario, solárium *nm* sunbed
solaz *nm Fml (descanso)* rest, relaxation;
(esparcimiento) recreation, entertainment
solazarse [40] *vpr (relajar)* to relax; *(divertir)* to entertain oneself, to amuse
oneself
soldado *nm* soldier; **s. raso** private
soldador,-a 1 *nm,f* welder
  2 *nm* soldering iron
soldar [2] *vt (cable)* to solder; *(chapa)* to
weld
soleado,-a *adj* sunny
soledad *nf (estado)* solitude; *(sentimiento)* loneliness
solemne *adj* (a) *(majestuoso)* solemn (**b**)
Pey downright
solemnidad *nf* solemnity
soler [4] *vi defect* (a) *(en presente)* to be in
the habit of; **solemos ir en coche** we
usually go by car; **sueles equivocarte**
you are usually wrong (**b**) *(en pasado)*
solía pasear por aquí he used to walk
round here
solera *nf Fig* tradition; **de s.** old-estab-
lished; **vino de s.** vintage wine
solfa *nf* (a) *Mús* solfa; *Fam* **poner en s.** to
ridicule (**b**) *Fam (paliza)* thrashing, beating
solicitar *vt (información etc)* to request,
to ask for; *(trabajo)* to apply for
solícito,-a *adj* obliging, attentive
solicitud *nf (petición)* request; *(de trabajo)* application
solidaridad *nf* solidarity
solidario,-a *adj* (a) supportive; **una sociedad solidaria** a caring society (**b**) *Jur*
jointly responsible
solidarizarse *vpr* to show one's solidarity
(**con** with)

solidez *nf* solidity, strength
sólido,-a *adj* solid, strong
soliloquio *nm* soliloquy
solista *nmf* soloist
solitario,-a 1 *adj (que está solo)* solitary, lone; *(que se siente solo)* lonely
  2 *nm* (**a**) *(diamante)* solitaire (**b**) *Naipes* solitaire, patience
soliviantar *vt (irritar)* to irritate
sollozar [40] *vi* to sob
sollozo *nm* sob
solo,-a 1 *adj* (**a**) only, single; **ni un s. día** not a single day; **una sola vez** only once, just once (**b**) *(solitario)* lonely (**c**) **hablar s.** to talk to oneself; **se enciende s.** it switches itself on automatically; **a solas** alone, by oneself
  2 *nm Mús* solo
sólo *adv* only; **tan s.** only; **no s. ... sino (también)** not only ... but (also); **con s., (tan) s. con** just by

Note that the adverb **sólo** can be written without an accent when there is no risk of confusion with the adjective.

solomillo *nm* sirloin
soltar [2] 1 *vt* (**a**) *(desasir)* to let go of; **¡suéltame!** let me go! (**b**) *(prisionero)* to release (**c**) *(humo, olor)* to give off (**d**) *(bofetada)* to deal; *(carcajada)* to let out; **me soltó un rollo** he bored me to tears
  2 **soltarse** *vpr* (**a**) *(desatarse)* to come loose (**b**) *(perro etc)* to get loose, to break loose (**c**) *(desprenderse)* to come off
soltero,-a 1 *adj* single, unmarried
  2 *nm (hombre)* bachelor, single man
  3 *nf* **soltera** *(mujer)* single woman, spinster
solterón, -ona *nm,f* old bachelor, *f* old maid
soltura *nf (agilidad)* agility; *(seguridad)* confidence, assurance; **habla italiano con s.** he speaks Italian fluently
soluble *adj* soluble; **café s.** instant coffee
solución *nf* solution
solucionar *vt* to solve; *(arreglar)* to settle
solvencia *nf* (**a**) *Fin* solvency (**b**) *(fiabilidad)* reliability; **fuentes de toda s.** completely reliable sources
solventar *vt (problema)* to solve, to resolve; *(deuda, asunto)* to settle
solvente *adj* (**a**) *Fin* solvent (**b**) *(fiable)* reliable
sombra *nf* (**a**) shade (**b**) *(silueta proyectada)* shadow; **s. de ojos** eyeshadow; **sin s. de duda** beyond a shadow of doubt (**c**)

tener buena s. *(tener suerte)* to be lucky
sombrero *nm* hat; **s. de copa** top hat; **s. hongo** bowler hat
sombrilla *nf* parasol, sunshade
sombrío,-a *adj (oscuro)* dark; *(tenebroso)* sombre, gloomy; *Fig (persona)* gloomy, sullen
somero,-a *adj* superficial, shallow
someter 1 *vt* (**a**) to subject; **s. a prueba** to put to the test; **s. algo a votación** to put sth to the vote (**b**) *(rebeldes)* to subdue, to put down
  2 **someterse** *vpr* (**a**) *(subordinarse)* to submit (**b**) *(rendirse)* to surrender, to yield (**c**) **s. a un tratamiento** to undergo treatment
somier *nm (pl* **somieres**) spring mattress
somnífero *nm* sleeping pill
somnoliento,-a *adj* sleepy, drowsy
son *nm* sound; **al s. del tambor** to the sound of the drum; **venir en s. de paz** to come in peace
sonado,-a *adj* (**a**) much talked of (**b**) *(trastocado)* mad, crazy
sonajero *nm* baby's rattle
sonámbulo,-a *nm,f* somnambulist, sleepwalker
sonar [2] 1 *vi* (**a**) to sound; **s. a** to sound like; **suena bien** it sounds good (**b**) *(timbre, teléfono)* to ring; **sonaron las cinco** the clock struck five (**c**) **tu nombre/cara me suena** your name/face rings a bell
  2 **sonarse** *vpr* **s. (la nariz)** to blow one's nose
sonda *nf* (**a**) *Med* sound, probe (**b**) **s. espacial** space probe
sondear *vt* (**a**) *(opinión)* to test, to sound out (**b**) *Med* to sound, to probe (**c**) *Náut* to sound
sondeo *nm* (**a**) *(encuesta)* poll (**b**) *Med* sounding, probing (**c**) *Náut* sounding
soneto *nm Lit* sonnet
sonido *nm* sound
sonoro,-a *adj* (**a**) *Cin* sound; **banda sonora** soundtrack (**b**) *(resonante)* loud, resounding (**c**) *Ling* voiced
sonreír [56] *vi,* **sonreírse** *vpr* to smile; **me sonrió** he smiled at me
sonriente *adj* smiling
sonrisa *nf* smile
sonrojarse *vpr* to blush
sonrojo *nm* blush
sonsacar [44] *vt* to wheedle; *(secreto)* to worm out
sonso,-a *adj Am* foolish, silly
soñador,-a *nm,f* dreamer
soñar [2] *vt & vi* (**a**) to dream; **s. con** to dream of o about; *Fig* **¡ni soñarlo!** not on

your life! (**b**) *(fantasear)* to daydream, to dream

soñoliento,-a *adj* sleepy, drowsy

sopa *nf* soup; **s. juliana** spring vegetable soup; *Fig* **quedar hecho una s.** to get soaked to the skin

sope *nm Méx* = fried corn tortilla, with beans and cheese or other toppings

sopera *nf* soup tureen

sopero,-a *adj* **cucharada sopera** soup spoon

sopesar *vt* to try the weight of; *Fig* to weigh up

sopetón *nm Fam* slap; **de s.** all of a sudden

soplado *nm* glass-blowing

soplagaitas *nmf inv Fam (estúpido, pesado)* jerk, *Br* prat

soplar 1 *vi (viento)* to blow
   2 *vt* (**a**) *(polvo etc)* to blow away; *(para enfriar)* to blow on (**b**) *(para apagar)* to blow out (**c**) *(para inflar)* to blow up (**d**) *(en examen etc)* **me sopló las respuestas** he whispered the answers to me

soplete *nm* blowlamp, blowtorch

soplido *nm* blow, puff

soplillo *nm* fan; *Fam* **orejas de s.** sticky-out ears

soplo *nm* (**a**) *(acción)* blow, puff; *(de viento)* gust (**b**) *Med* murmur

soplón,-ona *nm,f Fam (niño)* telltale, sneak; *(delator) Br* grass, *US* rat

soporífero,-a *adj* (**a**) *(que adormece)* soporific, sleep-inducing (**b**) *(aburrido)* boring, dull

soportable *adj* bearable

soportal *nm* porch; **soportales** arcade

soportar *vt* (**a**) *(peso)* to support, to bear (**b**) *Fig (calor, ruido)* to bear, to endure; *(situación)* to put up with, to bear; **no te soporto** I can't stand you

soporte *nm* support; **s. publicitario** advertising medium

soprano *nmf* soprano

sorber *vt* (**a**) *(beber)* to sip (**b**) *(absorber)* to soak up, to absorb

sorbete *nm* sorbet, sherbet

sorbo *nm* sip; *(trago)* gulp; **de un s.** in one gulp

sordera *nf* deafness

sórdido,-a *adj* squalid, sordid

sordo,-a 1 *adj* (**a**) *(persona)* deaf; **s. como una tapia** stone-deaf (**b**) *(golpe, ruido, dolor)* dull
   2 *nm,f* deaf person; **los sordos** the deaf *pl*; *Fam Fig* **hacerse el s.** to turn a deaf ear

sordomudez *nf* deaf-muteness

sordomudo,-a 1 *adj* deaf and dumb, deaf-mute

   2 *nm,f* deaf and dumb person, deaf-mute

soroche *nm Andes, Arg (mal de altura)* altitude sickness

sorprendente *adj* surprising

sorprender *vt* (**a**) *(extrañar)* to surprise (**b**) *(coger desprevenido)* to catch unawares, to take by surprise

sorpresa *nf* surprise; **coger de** *o* **por s.** to take by surprise

sorpresivo,-a *adj Am* unexpected, surprising

sortear *vt* (**a**) to draw *o* cast lots for; *(rifar)* to raffle (off) (**b**) *(evitar)* to avoid, to get round

sorteo *nm* draw; *(rifa)* raffle

sortija *nf* ring

sortilegio *nm* spell

S.O.S. *nm* SOS

sosa *nf* soda; **s. cáustica** caustic soda

sosegado,-a *adj (tranquilo)* calm, quiet; *(pacífico)* peaceful

sosegar [1] 1 *vt* to calm, to quieten
   2 sosegarse *vpr* to calm down

sosiego *nm (calma)* calmness; *(paz)* peace, tranquillity

soslayo: • de soslayo *loc adv* **mirar de s.** to look sideways (at)

soso,-a *adj* lacking in salt; *Fig (persona)* insipid, dull

sospecha *nf* suspicion

sospechar 1 *vi (desconfiar)* to suspect; **s. de algn** to suspect sb
   2 *vt (pensar)* to suspect

sospechoso,-a 1 *adj* suspicious; **s. de** suspected of
   2 *nm,f* suspect

sostén *nm* (**a**) *(apoyo)* support (**b**) *(sustento)* sustenance (**c**) *(prenda)* bra, brassière

sostener [24] 1 *vt* (**a**) *(sujetar)* to support, to hold up (**b**) *(con la mano)* to hold (**c**) *Fig (teoría etc)* to defend, to uphold; **s. que ...** to maintain that ... (**d**) *(conversación)* to hold, to sustain (**e**) *(familia)* to support
   2 sostenerse *vpr* (**a**) *(mantenerse)* to support oneself (**b**) *(permanecer)* to stay, to remain

sostenido,-a *adj* (**a**) *(continuado)* sustained (**b**) *Mús* sharp

sostuve *pt indef de* **sostener**

sota *nf Naipes* jack, knave

sotana *nf* cassock, soutane

sótano *nm* basement, cellar

soto *nm* grove

soviético,-a *adj & nm,f* Soviet; *Hist* **la Unión Soviética** the Soviet Union

soy *indic pres de* **ser**

soya *nf* = **soja**

SP (*abr* **servicio público**) = sign indicating public transport vehicle

sport: •de sport *loc adj* casual, sports; **chaqueta de s.** sports jacket

spot *nm* (*pl* **spots**) *TV* commercial, advert, ad

spray *nm* (*pl* **sprays**) spray

sprint *nm* sprint

Sr. (*abr* **Señor**) Mr

Sra. (*abr* **Señora**) Mrs

S.R.C., s.r.c. (*abr* **se ruega contestación**) please reply, R.S.V.P.

Srta. (*abr* **Señorita**) Miss

SS *nf* (*abr* **Seguridad Social**) Social Security

SS.AA. (*abr* **Sus Altezas**) Their Royal Highnesses

Sta., sta. (*abr* **Santa**) St

stand *nm* *Com* stand

standard *adj & nm* standard

status *nm inv* status

Sto., sto. (*abr* **Santo**) St

su *adj pos* (*de él*) his; (*de ella*) her; (*de usted, ustedes*) your; (*de animales o cosas*) its; (*impersonal*) one's; (*de ellos*) their; **su coche** his/her/your/their car; **su pata** its leg; **sus libros** his/her/your/their books; **sus patas** its legs

suave *adj* (**a**) smooth; (*luz, voz etc*) soft (**b**) *Met* (*templado*) mild

> 🖉 Observa que la palabra inglesa **suave** es un falso amigo y no es la traducción de la palabra española **suave**. En inglés, **suave** significa "fino, cortés".

suavidad *nf* (**a**) smoothness; (*dulzura*) softness (**b**) *Met* mildness

suavizante *nm* (*para el pelo*) (hair) conditioner; (*para la ropa*) fabric softener

suavizar [40] **1** *vt* to smooth (out)
2 suavizarse *vpr* (*temperatura*) to get milder; (*persona*) to calm down

subacuático,-a *adj* underwater

subalimentado,-a *adj* undernourished, underfed

subalterno,-a *adj & nm,f* subordinate, subaltern

subarrendar [1] *vt* *Com* to sublet, to sublease

subasta *nf* auction

subastar *vt* to auction (off), to sell at auction

subcampeón *nm* *Dep* runner-up

subconsciente *adj & nm* subconscious

subcontratación *nf* *Com* outsourcing

subdesarrollado,-a *adj* underdeveloped

subdesarrollo *nm* underdevelopment

subdirector,-a *nm,f* assistant director/manager

súbdito,-a *nm,f* subject, citizen; **s. francés** French citizen

subdividir *vt* to subdivide

subestimar *vt* to underestimate

subida *nf* (**a**) (*de temperatura*) rise; (*de precios, salarios*) rise, increase (**b**) (*ascenso*) ascent, climb (**c**) (*pendiente*) slope, hill (**d**) *Fam* (*drogas*) high

subido,-a *adj* **s. de tono** daring, risqué

subir 1 *vt* (**a**) to go up (**b**) (*llevar arriba*) to take up, to bring up (**c**) (*cabeza, mano*) to lift, to raise (**d**) (*precio, salario*) to raise, to put up (**e**) (*volumen*) to turn up; (*voz*) to raise
2 *vi* (**a**) (*ir arriba*) to go up, to come up (**b**) **s. a** (*un coche*) to get into; (*un autobús*) to get on; (*un barco, avión, tren*) to board, to get on (**c**) (*aumentar*) to rise, to go up
3 subirse *vpr* (**a**) to climb up; *Fig* **el vino se le subió a la cabeza** the wine went to his head (**b**) **s. a** (*un coche*) to get into; (*un autobús, avión, tren*) to get on, to board; (*caballo, bici*) to get on (**c**) (*cremallera*) to do up; (*mangas*) to roll up

súbitamente *adv* suddenly

súbito,-a *adj* sudden

subjetivo,-a *adj* subjective

sublevación *nf* rising, rebellion

sublevar 1 *vt* *Fig* (*indignar*) to infuriate, to enrage
2 sublevarse *vpr* to rebel, to revolt

sublime *adj* sublime

submarinismo *nm* skin-diving

submarino,-a 1 *adj* submarine, underwater
2 *nm* submarine

subnormal 1 *adj* mentally handicapped
2 *nmf* mentally handicapped person

suboficial *nm* (**a**) *Mil* noncommissioned officer (**b**) *Náut* petty officer

subordinado,-a *adj & nm,f* subordinate

subordinar *vt* to subordinate

subproducto *nm* by-product

subrayar *vt* to underline; *Fig* (*recalcar*) to emphasize, to stress

subrepticio,-a *adj* surreptitious

subrutina *nf* subroutine

subsanar *vt* (*error*) to rectify, to put right; (*daño*) to make up for

subscribir (*pp* **subscrito**) *vt* = **suscribir**

subscripción *nf* subscription

subsecretario,-a *nm,f* undersecretary

subsidiario,-a *adj* subsidiary

subsidio *nm* allowance, benefit; **s. de desempleo** unemployment benefit

subsistencia *nf* subsistence

subsistir *vi* to subsist, to remain; *(vivir)* to live on, to survive

subsuelo *nm* subsoil

subte *nm RP Br* underground, *Br* tube, *US* subway

subterráneo,-a 1 *adj* underground
   2 *nm (túnel)* tunnel, underground passage

subtítulo *nm* subtitle

suburbano,-a *adj* suburban

suburbio *nm (barrio pobre)* slums; *(barrio periférico)* suburb

subvención *nf* subsidy

subvencionar *vt* to subsidize

subversión *nf* subversion

subversivo,-a *adj* subversive

subyacente *adj* underlying

subyugar [42] *vt* to subjugate

succionar *vt* to suck (in)

sucedáneo,-a *adj & nm* substitute

suceder 1 *vi* (**a**) *(ocurrir)* (uso impers) to happen, to occur; **¿qué sucede?** what's going on?, what's the matter? (**b**) *(seguir)* to follow, to succeed
   2 sucederse *vpr* to follow one another, to come one after the other

sucesión *nf* (**a**) *(serie)* series *sing*, succession (**b**) *(al trono)* succession (**c**) *(descendencia)* issue, heirs

sucesivamente *adv* **y así s.** and so on

sucesivo,-a *adj* following, successive; **en lo s.** from now on

suceso *nm (hecho)* event, occurrence; *(incidente)* incident; *Prensa* **sección de sucesos** accident and crime reports

---
📖 Observa que la palabra inglesa **success** es un falso amigo y no es la traducción de la palabra española **suceso**. En inglés, **success** significa "éxito".
---

sucesor,-a *nm,f* successor

suciedad *nf* (**a**) *(dirt)* (**b**) *(calidad)* dirtiness

sucinto,-a *adj* concise, succinct

sucio,-a 1 *adj* dirty; **en s.** in rough; *Fig* **juego s.** foul play; *Fig* **negocio s.** shady business
   2 *adv* **jugar s.** to play dirty

sucre *nm Fin* = standard monetary unit of Ecuador

suculento,-a *adj* succulent, juicy

sucumbir *vi* to succumb, to yield

sucursal *nf Com & Fin* branch, branch office

sudaca *nmf Pey* South American

sudadera *nf* sweatshirt

Sudáfrica *n* South Africa

sudafricano,-a *adj & nm,f* South African

Sudamérica *n* South America

sudamericano,-a *adj & nm,f* South American

sudar *vt & vi* to sweat; *Fam Fig* **s. la gota gorda** to sweat blood

sudeste *nm* southeast

sudoeste *nm* southwest

sudor *nm* sweat; *Fig* **con el s. de mi frente** by the sweat of my brow

sudoroso,-a *adj* sweaty

Suecia *n* Sweden

sueco,-a 1 *adj* Swedish
   2 *nm,f (persona)* Swede
   3 *nm (idioma)* Swedish

suegra *nf* mother-in-law

suegro *nm* father-in-law; **mis suegros** my in-laws

suela *nf (de zapato)* sole

sueldo *nm* salary, wages

suelo *nm* (**a**) *(superficie)* ground; *(de interior)* floor; *Fig* **estar por los suelos** *(precios)* to be rock-bottom (**b**) *(territorio)* soil, land (**c**) *(campo, terreno)* land; **s. cultivable** arable land (**d**) *(de carretera)* surface

suelto,-a 1 *adj* (**a**) loose; *(desatado)* undone (**b**) *Fig* **dinero s.** loose change; **hojas sueltas** loose sheets (of paper); **se venden sueltos** they are sold singly *o* separately *o* loose (**c**) *(en libertad)* free; *(huido)* at large (**d**) *(vestido, camisa)* loose, loose-fitting
   2 *nm (dinero)* (loose) change

sueño *nm* (**a**) sleep; *(ganas de dormir)* sleepiness; **tener s.** to feel *o* be sleepy (**b**) *(cosa soñada)* dream

suero *nm Med* serum; *(de la leche)* whey

suerte *nf* (**a**) *(fortuna)* luck; **por s.** fortunately; **probar s.** to try one's luck; **tener s.** to be lucky; **¡que tengas s.!** good luck! (**b**) **echar algo a suertes** to draw lots for sth (**c**) *(destino)* fate, destiny (**d**) *Fml (género)* kind, sort, type

suéter *nm* sweater

suficiencia *nf* (**a**) *(engreimiento)* smugness, complacency (**b**) *Educ* **prueba de s.** final exam

suficiente 1 *adj (bastante)* sufficient, enough
   2 *nm Educ* pass

suficientemente *adv* sufficiently; **no es lo s. rico como para …** he isn't rich enough to …

sufijo *nm* suffix

sufragar [42] 1 *vt* (*gastos*) to pay, to defray

2 *vi Am* to vote (**por** for)

sufragio *nm Pol* suffrage; (*voto*) vote

sufrido,-a *adj* (*persona*) long-suffering

sufrimiento *nm* suffering

sufrir 1 *vi* to suffer; **s. del corazón** to have a heart condition

2 *vt* (**a**) (*accidente*) to have; (*operación*) to undergo; (*dificultades, cambios*) to experience; **s. dolores de cabeza** to suffer from headaches (**b**) (*aguantar*) to bear, to put up with

sugerencia *nf* suggestion

sugerente *adj* suggestive

sugerir [5] *vt* to suggest

sugestión *nf* suggestion

sugestionar *vt* to influence, to persuade

sugestivo,-a *adj* suggestive; (*atractivo*) alluring

suiche *nm Andes, Ven* switch

suicida 1 *nmf* (*persona*) suicide

2 *adj* suicidal

suicidarse *vpr* to commit suicide, to kill oneself

suicidio *nm* suicide

suite *nf* suite

Suiza *n* Switzerland

suizo,-a 1 *adj* Swiss

2 *nm,f* (*persona*) Swiss

3 *nm Culin* éclair

sujetador *nm* (*prenda*) bra, brassière

sujetar 1 *vt* (**a**) (*agarrar*) to hold (**b**) (*fijar*) to hold down, to hold in place (**c**) *Fig* (*someter*) to restrain

2 **sujetarse** *vpr* (*agarrarse*) to hold on

sujeto,-a 1 *nm* subject; (*individuo*) fellow, individual

2 *adj* (*atado*) fastened, secure; **s. a** (*sometido*) subject to, liable to

sulfato *nm* sulphate

sulfurar 1 *vt Fam* (*exasperar*) to exasperate, to infuriate

2 **sulfurarse** *vpr Fam* to lose one's temper, to blow one's top

sultán *nm* sultan

suma *nf* (**a**) (*cantidad*) sum, amount (**b**) *Mat* sum, addition; **s. total** sum total (**c**) **en s.** in short

sumamente *adv* extremely, highly

sumar 1 *vt Mat* to add, to add up

2 **sumarse** *vpr* **s. a** (*huelga*) to join; (*propuesta*) to support

sumario,-a 1 *adj* summary, brief; *Jur* **juicio s.** summary proceedings

2 *nm Jur* summary

sumarísimo,-a *adj Jur* swift, expeditious

sumergible *adj & nm* submersible

sumergir [57] 1 *vt* to submerge, to submerse; (*hundir*) to sink, to plunge

2 **sumergirse** *vpr* to submerge, to go underwater; (*hundirse*) to sink

sumidero *nm* drain, sewer

suministrar *vt* to supply, to provide; **s. algo a algn** to supply sb with sth

suministro *nm* supply

sumir *vt* (*hundir*) to sink, to plunge; *Fig* to plunge

sumiso,-a *adj* submissive, obedient

sumo,-a *adj* (*supremo*) supreme; **con s. cuidado** with extreme care; **a lo s.** at (the) most

suntuoso,-a *adj* sumptuous, magnificent

supe *pt indef de* **saber**

supeditar *vt* to subject (**a** to)

super- *pref* super-

súper *Fam* **1** *adj* super, great

2 *nm* (**a**) (*supermercado*) supermarket (**b**) (*gasolina*) 4-star

superado,-a *adj* outdated, obsolete

superar 1 *vt* (**a**) (*obstáculo etc*) to overcome, to surmount; (*prueba*) to pass (**b**) (*aventajar*) to surpass, to excel

2 **superarse** *vpr* to improve o better oneself

superávit *nm* surplus

superdotado,-a 1 *adj* exceptionally gifted

2 *nm,f* genius

superficial *adj* superficial

superficialidad *nf* superficiality

superficie *nf* surface; (*área*) area; *Com* **grandes superficies** hypermarkets

superfluo,-a *adj* superfluous

superhombre *nm* superman

superior 1 *adj* (**a**) (*posición*) top, upper (**b**) (*cantidad*) greater, higher, larger (**a** than) (**c**) (*calidad*) superior; **calidad s.** top quality (**d**) *Educ* higher

2 *nm* (*jefe*) superior

superioridad *nf* superiority

supermán *nm* (*pl* **supermanes**) superman

supermercado *nm* supermarket

superpoblación *nf* overpopulation

superponer [19] *vt* to superimpose

superpotencia *nf* superpower

superproducción *nf* (**a**) *Ind* overproduction (**b**) *Cin* mammoth production

supersónico,-a *adj* supersonic

superstición *nf* superstition

supersticioso,-a *adj* superstitious

supervisar *vt* to supervise

supervisor,-a *nm,f* supervisor

supervivencia *nf* survival

supino,-a *adj* (**a**) *(boca arriba)* supine, face up (**b**) *Fig (absoluto)* total absolute
súpito,-a *adj Am* sudden
suplantar *vt* to supplant, to take the place of
suplementario,-a *adj* supplementary, additional
suplemento *nm* supplement; **sin s.** without extra charge
suplente *adj & nmf (sustituto)* substitute, deputy; *Dep* substitute
supletorio,-a *adj* supplementary, additional; **cama supletoria** extra bed; **teléfono s.** extension
súplica *nf* entreaty, plea
suplicar [44] *vt* to beseech, to beg
suplicio *nm (tortura)* torture; *Fig (tormento)* torment
suplir *vt* (**a**) *(reemplazar)* to replace, to substitute (**b**) *(compensar)* to make up for
suponer [19] *(pp* supuesto*)* *vt* (**a**) *(significar)* to mean (**b**) *(implicar)* to entail (**c**) *(representar)* to account for (**d**) *(pensar)* to suppose; **supongo que sí** I suppose so; **supongamos que ...** let's assume that ... (**e**) *(adivinar)* to guess; **(me) lo suponía** I guessed as much
suposición *nf* supposition
supositorio *nm* suppository
supremacía *nf* supremacy
supremo,-a *adj* supreme
supresión *nf (de una ley etc)* abolition; *(de restricciones)* lifting; *(de una palabra)* deletion; *(de una rebelión)* suppression; *(omisión)* omission
suprimir *vt* (**a**) *(ley, impuesto)* to abolish; *(restricción)* to lift; *(palabra)* to delete, to take/leave out; *(rebelión)* to suppress (**b**) *(omitir)* to omit
supuesto,-a 1 *adj* (**a**) *(asumido)* supposed, assumed; **¡por s.!** of course!; **dar algo por s.** to take sth for granted (**b**) *(presunto)* alleged
  2 *nm* assumption; **en el s. de que** on the assumption that
supurar *vi* to suppurate, to fester
supuse *pt indef de* **suponer**
sur *nm* south
Suramérica *n* South America
suramericano,-a *adj & nm,f* South American
surcar [44] *vt Agr* to plough; *Fig (olas)* to cut through
surco *nm Agr* furrow; *(en un disco)* groove
sureño,-a 1 *adj* southern
  2 *nm,f* southerner
sureste *nm* = **sudeste**
surf(ing) *nm Dep* surfing

surfista *nmf* surfer
surgir [57] *vi (aparecer)* to arise, to emerge, to appear; *(problema, dificultad)* to crop up
suroeste *nm* = **sudoeste**
surrealista *adj & nmf* surrealist
surtido,-a 1 *adj* (**a**) *(variado)* assorted (**b**) **bien s.** well-stocked
  2 *nm* selection, assortment
surtidor *nm* spout; **s. de gasolina** *Br* petrol pump, *US* gas pump
surtir *vt* (**a**) to supply, to provide (**b**) **s. efecto** to have the desired effect
susceptible *adj* susceptible; *(quisquilloso)* oversensitive, touchy
suscitar *vt (provocar)* to cause, to provoke; *(rebelión)* to stir up, to arouse; *(interés etc)* to arouse
suscribir *(pp* suscrito*)* **1** *vt* (**a**) to subscribe to, to endorse (**b**) *Fml (firmar)* to sign
  2 suscribirse *vpr* to subscribe (**a** to)
suscripción *nf* subscription
susodicho,-a *adj* above-mentioned, aforesaid
suspender 1 *vt* (**a**) *(ley)* to suspend; *(reunión)* to adjourn (**b**) *(examen)* to fail; **me han suspendido** I've failed (the exam) (**c**) *(colgar)* to hang, to suspend
  2 *vi Educ* **he suspendido** I've failed
suspense *nm* suspense; **novela/película de s.** thriller
suspensión *nf* (**a**) hanging (up), suspension (**b**) *Aut* suspension (**c**) *Fin & Jur* **s. de pagos** suspension of payments
suspensivo,-a *adj* **puntos suspensivos** suspension points
suspenso *nm* (**a**) *Educ* fail (**b**) **en s.** *(asunto, trabajo)* pending; **estar en s.** to be pending
suspicacia *nf* suspiciousness
suspicaz *adj* suspicious; *(desconfiado)* distrustful
suspirar *vi* to sigh
suspiro *nm* sigh
sustancia *nf* substance
sustancial *adj* (**a**) substantial (**b**) *(fundamental)* essential, fundamental
sustantivo,-a 1 *adj* substantive
  2 *nm Ling* noun
sustentar *vt* (**a**) *(peso)* to support (**b**) *(familia)* to maintain, to support (**c**) *(teoría)* to support, to defend
sustento *nm* (**a**) *(alimento)* sustenance, food (**b**) *(apoyo)* support
sustitución *nf* substitution, replacement
sustituir [37] *vt* to substitute, to replace
sustituto,-a *nm,f* substitute, stand-in

susto *nm* fright, scare; **llevarse** *o* **darse un s.** to get a fright

sustraer [25] *vt* (**a**) *Mat* to subtract (**b**) *(robar)* to steal, to remove

sustrato *nm* substratum

susurrar *vt* to whisper

susurro *nm* whisper

sutil *adj* (**a**) *(diferencia, pregunta)* subtle (**b**) *(delgado)* thin, fine (**c**) *(aroma)* delicate

sutileza *nf* (**a**) *(dicho)* subtlety (**b**) *(finura)* fineness

suyo,-a *adj & pron pos (de él)* his; *(de ella)* hers; *(de usted, ustedes)* yours; *(de animal o cosa)* its; *(de ellos, ellas)* theirs; **los zapatos no son suyos** the shoes aren't hers; **varios amigos suyos** several friends of his/hers/yours/theirs; *Fam* **es muy s.** he's very aloof; *Fam* **hacer de las suyas** to be up to one's tricks; *Fam* **ir (cada uno) a lo s.** to mind one's own business; *Fam* **salirse con la suya** to get one's (own) way

svástica *nf* swastika

T, t [te] *nf (la letra)* T, t
t (*abr* **tonelada(s)**) t
tabacalero,-a 1 *nm,f (vendedor)* tobacco trader
  2 *nf* **LaTabacalera** = Spanish state tobacco monopoly
tabaco *nm* (**a**) *(planta, hoja)* tobacco; **t. rubio** Virginia tobacco (**b**) *(cigarrillos)* cigarettes
tábano *nm* horsefly
tabaquismo *nm* nicotine poisoning
tabarra *nf Fam* nuisance, bore; **dar la t.** to go on and on
tabasco® *nm* Tabasco® sauce
taberna *nf* pub, bar; *(antiguamente)* tavern
tabernero,-a *nm,f* publican; *(hombre)* landlord; *(mujer)* landlady
tabique *nm* (**a**) *(pared)* partition (wall) (**b**) *Anat* **t. nasal** nasal wall
tabla *nf* (**a**) board; *Dep* **t. de surf** surfboard; *Dep* **t. de windsurf** sailboard (**b**) *(de vestido)* pleat (**c**) *Mat* table (**d**) **tablas** *(en ajedrez)* stalemate, draw; **quedar en tablas** *(juego)* to end in a draw (**e**)*Taurom* **tablas** fence (**f**) *Teatro* **las tablas** the stage; *Fig* **tener (muchas) tablas** to be an old hand
tablado *nm* (**a**) *(plataforma)* wooden platform (**b**)*Teatro* stage
tablao *nm Fam* = flamenco bar or show
tablero *nm* (**a**) *(tablón)* panel, board; **t. de mandos** *(de coche)* dash(board) (**b**) *(en juegos)* board; **t. de ajedrez** chessboard
tableta *nf (de chocolate)* bar
tablón *nm* plank; *(en construcción)* beam; **t. de anuncios** *Br* noticeboard, *US* bulletin board
tabú *adj & nm* (*pl* **tabúes**) taboo
tabular *vt* to tabulate
taburete *nm* stool
tacaño,-a 1 *adj* mean, stingy
  2 *nm,f* miser
tacatá, tacataca *nm* baby-walker
tacha *nf (defecto)* flaw, defect; **sin t.** flawless, without blemish
tachar *vt* (**a**) to cross out (**b**) *Fig* **t. de** to accuse of

tachero *nm RP Fam (de taxi)* taxi driver
tacho *nm Am* bucket
tachón *nm (borrón)* crossing out
tachuela *nf* tack, stud
tácito,-a *adj* tacit
taciturno,-a *adj* (**a**) *(callado)* taciturn (**b**) *(triste)* sullen
taco *nm* (**a**) plug; *(de billetes)* wad; *(de bota de fútbol)* stud; *(en billar)* cue (**b**) *(cubo) (de jamón, queso)* cube, piece (**c**) *Culin (tortilla de maíz)* taco, = rolled-up tortilla pancake (**d**) *Fam (palabrota)* swearword (**e**) *Fam (lío)* mess, muddle; **armarse** *o* **hacerse un t.** to get all mixed up (**f**) **me gusta un t.** I like it a lot (**g**)*Fam* **tacos** *(años)* years
tacón *nm* heel; **zapatos de t.** high-heeled shoes
taconeo *nm (pisada)* heel-tapping; *(golpe)* stamping with the heels
táctica *nf* tactics
táctico,-a *adj* tactical
táctil *adj* tactile; **pantalla t.** touch screen
tacto *nm* (**a**) *(sentido)* touch (**b**) *Fig (delicadeza)* tact; **tener t.** to be tactful
taekwondo *nm* tae kwon do
tafetán *nm* taffeta
tahur *nm* cardsharp
tailandés,-esa 1 *adj* Thai
  2 *nm,f (persona)* Thai; **los tailandeses** theThai *o*Thais
  3 *nm (idioma)* Thai
Tailandia *n*Thailand
taimado,-a *adj* sly, crafty
tajada *nf* (**a**) slice; *Fig* **sacar** *o* **llevarse t.** to take one's share (**b**) *Fam (borrachera)* drunkenness
tajante *adj* incisive
Tajo *n* **el T.** theTagus
tal 1 *adj* (**a**) *(semejante)* such; *(más sustantivo singular contable)* such a; **en tales condiciones** in such conditions; **nunca dije t. cosa** I never said such a thing
  (**b**) *(indeterminado)* such and such; **t. día y a t. hora** such and such a day and at such and such a time
  (**c**) *(persona)* person called ...; **te llamó una t. Amelia** someone called Amelia phoned you

(**d**) *(locuciones)* **t. vez** perhaps, maybe; **como si t. cosa** as if nothing had happened

2 *adv* (**a**) *(así)* just; **t. cual** just as it is; **t. (y) como** just as

(**b**) **¿qué t.?** how are things?; **¿qué t. ese vino?** how do you find this wine?

3 *conj* as; **con t. (de) que** (+ *subjunctive*) so long as, provided

4 *pron (cosa)* something; *(persona)* someone, somebody; **t. para cual** two of a kind; **y t. y cual** and so on

tala *nf* tree felling

taladradora *nf* drill

taladrar *vt* to drill; *(pared)* to bore through; *(papeles)* to punch

taladro *nm* (**a**) *(herramienta)* drill (**b**) *(agujero)* hole

talante *nm* (**a**) *(carácter)* disposition (**b**) *(voluntad)* **de buen t.** willingly; **de mal t.** unwillingly, reluctantly

talar *vt (árboles)* to fell, to cut down

talco *nm* talc; **polvos de t.** talcum powder

talega *nf* bag, sack

talego *nm* (**a**) long bag, long sack (**b**) *Fam (cárcel)* clink, hole (**c**) *Fam (mil pesetas)* = 1,000 peseta note

talento *nm* talent

Talgo *nm* = fast passenger train

talismán *nm* talisman, lucky charm

talla *nf* (**a**) *(de prenda)* size; **¿qué t. usas?** what size are you? (**b**) *(estatura)* height; *Fig* stature; *Fig* **dar la t.** to make the grade (**c**) *(escultura)* carving, sculpture (**d**) *(tallado)* cutting, carving

tallado *nm (de madera)* carving; *(de piedras preciosas)* cutting; *(de metales)* engraving

tallar *vt* (**a**) *(madera, piedra)* to carve, to shape; *(piedras preciosas)* to cut; *(metales)* to engrave (**b**) *(medir)* to measure the height of

tallarines *nmpl* tagliatelle

talle *nm* (**a**) *(cintura)* waist (**b**) *(cuerpo)* *(de hombre)* build, physique; *(de mujer)* figure, shape

taller *nm* (**a**) *(obrador)* workshop; *Aut* **t. de reparaciones** garage (**b**) *Ind* factory, mill

tallo *nm* stem, stalk

talón *nm* (**a**) *(del pie)* heel (**b**) *(cheque)* cheque

♪ Observa que la palabra inglesa **talon** es un falso amigo y no es la traducción de la palabra española **talón**. En inglés, **talon** significa "garra".

talonario *nm (de cheques)* cheque book; *(de billetes)* book of tickets

tamal *nm (comida)* tamale, = steamed maize dumpling with savoury or sweet filling, wrapped in maize husks or a banana leaf

tamaño,-a 1 *adj* such a big, so big a

2 *nm* size; **de gran t.** large; **del t. de** as large as, as big as

tamarindo *nm* tamarind

tambalearse *vpr (persona)* to stagger; *(mesa)* to wobble; *Fig* to teeter

tambero *nm Am (mesonero)* innkeeper, landlord

también *adv (igualmente)* too, also, as well; **tú t. puedes venir** you can come too; **¿lo harás? yo t.** are you going to do it? so am I

tambo *nm RP (granja)* dairy farm

tambor *nm* (**a**) *(Mús, de lavadora, de freno)* drum (**b**) *Anat* eardrum

Támesis *n* **el T.** the Thames

tamiz *nm* sieve

tamizar [40] *vt* to sieve

tampoco *adv* (**a**) *(en afirmativas)* nor, neither; **Juan no vendrá y María t.** Juan won't come and neither will Maria; **no lo sé – yo t.** I don't know – neither do I (**b**) *(en negativas)* either, not ... either; **la Bolsa no sube, pero t. baja** the stock market isn't going up, but it's not going down either

tampón *nm* tampon

tan *adv* (**a**) such; *(más sustantivo singular contable)* such a; **es t. listo** he's such a clever fellow; **no me gusta t. dulce** I don't like it so sweet; **¡qué gente t. agradable!** such nice people!; **¡qué vestido t. bonito!** what a beautiful dress! (**b**) *(comparativo)* **t. ... como** as ... as; **t. alto como tú** as tall as you (are) (**c**) *(consecutivo)* so ... (that); **iba t. deprisa que no lo ví** he was going so fast that I couldn't see him (**d**) **t. siquiera** at least; **t. sólo** only

tanda *nf (conjunto)* batch, lot; *(serie)* series *sing*; **por tandas** in groups

tándem *nm* tandem

tanga *nm* tanga

tangente *nf* tangent; *Fig* **salirse** *o* **escaparse por la t.** to go off at a tangent

Tánger *n* Tangier

tangible *adj* tangible

tango *nm* tango

tanguería *nf* = nightclub for tango dancing

tanguero,-a *nm,f (aficionado)* tango enthusiast

tanque *nm* tank

tantear 1 *vt* (**a**) *Fig* **t. a algn** to sound sb

out; **t. el terreno** to see how the land lies (**b**) *(calcular)* to estimate, to guess

2 *vi Dep* to (keep) score

tanteo *nm* (**a**) *(cálculo)* estimate, guess (**b**) *Dep* score

tanto,-a 1 *nm* (**a**) *(punto)* point

(**b**) *(cantidad imprecisa)* so much, a certain amount; **t. por ciento** percentage

(**c**) **un t.** a bit; **la casa es un t. pequeña** the house is rather *o* somewhat small

(**d**) **estar al t.** *(informado)* to be informed; *(pendiente)* to be on the lookout

2 *adj* (**a**) *(+ singular)* so much; *(+ plural)* so many; **no le des t. dinero** don't give him so much money; **¡ha pasado t. tiempo!** it's been so long!; **no comas tantas manzanas** don't eat so many apples

(**b**) **cincuenta y tantas personas** fifty odd people; **en el año sesenta y tantos** in nineteen sixty something

(**c**) **t. como** as much as; **tantos,-as como** as many as

3 *pron* (**a**) *(+ singular)* so much; **otro t.** as much again, the same again; **no es** *o* **hay para t.** it's not that bad

(**b**) *(+ plural)* so many; **otros tantos** as many again; **uno de tantos** run-of-the-mill; *Fam* **a las tantas** very late, at an unearthly hour

4 *adv* (**a**) *(cantidad)* so much; **t. mejor/ peor** so much the better/worse; **t. más cuanto que** all the more so because

(**b**) *(tiempo)* so long

(**c**) *(frecuencia)* so often

(**d**) **t. ... como** both ... and; **t. tú como yo** both you and I; **t. si vienes como si no** whether you come or not

(**e**) *(locuciones)* **por lo t.** therefore; **¡y t.!** oh yes!, and how!

tañer *vt* to play

tapa *nf* (**a**) *(cubierta)* lid; *Andes, RP (de botella)* top; *(de libro)* cover; *(de zapato)* heelplate; *Aut (de cilindro)* head (**b**) *(aperitivo)* appetizer, snack

tapadera *nf (tapa)* cover, lid; *Fig* cover, front

tapadillo *nm* **hacer algo de t.** to do sth secretly

tapado *nm CSur (abrigo)* overcoat

tapar 1 *vt* (**a**) to cover; *(botella etc)* to put the lid/top on; *(con ropas o mantas)* to wrap up (**b**) *(ocultar)* to hide; *(vista)* to block (**c**) *(encubrir)* to cover up

2 taparse *vpr (cubrirse)* to cover oneself; *(abrigarse)* to wrap up

taparrabos *nm inv* loincloth

tapete *nm* (table) cover; *Fig* **poner algo sobre el t.** to table sth

tapia *nf* garden wall

tapiar [43] *vt* (**a**) *(área)* to wall off (**b**) *(puerta, ventana etc)* to wall, to close up

tapicería *nf* (**a**) tapestry; *(de muebles, coche)* upholstery (**b**) *(tienda)* upholsterer's shop/workshop

tapioca *nf* tapioca

tapiz *nm* tapestry

tapizar [40] *vt* to upholster

tapón *nm* (**a**) *(de lavabo etc)* stopper, plug; *(de botella)* cap, cork; **t. de rosca** screw-on cap (**b**) *(de oídos)* earplug (**c**) *(en baloncesto)* block (**d**) *Aut* traffic jam (**e**) *Am (plomo)* fuse

taponar 1 *vt* (**a**) *(tubería, hueco)* to plug (**b**) *Med (herida)* to tampon

2 taponarse *vpr* **se me han taponado los oídos** my ears are blocked up

taquería *nf Méx (quiosco)* taco stall; *(restaurante)* taco restaurant

taquigrafía *nf* shorthand

taquígrafo,-a *nm,f* shorthand writer

taquilla *nf* (**a**) ticket office, booking office; *Cin & Teatro* box-office; **un éxito de t.** a box-office success (**b**) *(recaudación)* takings (**c**) *(armario)* locker

taquillero,-a 1 *adj* popular; **película taquillera** box-office hit

2 *nm,f* booking *o* ticket clerk

tara *nf* (**a**) *(peso)* tare (**b**) *(defecto)* defect, fault

tarántula *nf* tarantula

tararear *vt* to hum

tardanza *nf* delay

tardar 1 *vt (llevar tiempo)* to take; **¿cuánto va a t.?** how long will it take?; **tardé dos horas en venir** it took me two hours to get here

2 *vi (demorar)* to take long; **si tarda mucho, me voy** if it takes much longer, I'm going; **no tardes** don't be long; **a más t.** at the latest

3 tardarse *vpr* **¿cuánto se tarda en llegar?** how long does it take to get there?

tarde 1 *nf* (**a**) *(hasta las cinco)* afternoon (**b**) *(después de las cinco)* evening (**c**) **la t. noche** late evening

2 *adv* (**a**) late; **siento llegar t.** sorry I'm late (**b**) *(locuciones)* **de t. en t.** very rarely, not very often; **(más) t. o (más) temprano** sooner or later

tardío,-a *adj* late, belated

tardo,-a *adj* slow

tarea *nf* job, task; **tareas** *(de ama de casa)* housework; *(de estudiante)* homework

tarifa *nf* (**a**) *(precio)* tariff, rate; *(en transportes)* fare (**b**) *(lista de precios)* price list

tarima *nf* platform, dais

tarjeta *nf* card; **t. postal** postcard; **t. de crédito** credit card; **t. de visita** *Br* visiting card, *US* calling card; *Informát* **t. perforada** punch *o* punched card

tarraconense 1 *adj* of/from Tarragona

2 *nmf* person from Tarragona

tarro *nm* (**a**) *(vasija)* jar, pot, tub (**b**) *Fam (cabeza)* bonce (**c**) *Am (lata)* tin, can

tarta *nf* tart, pie

tartamudear *vi* to stutter, to stammer

tartamudo,-a 1 *adj* stuttering, stammering

2 *nm,f* stutterer, stammerer

tartana *nf Fam (coche viejo)* banger, heap

tártaro,-a *adj* **salsa tártara** tartar sauce

tartera *nf* (**a**) *(fiambrera)* lunch box (**b**) *(cazuela)* baking tin

tarugo *nm* (**a**) *(de madera)* lump of wood (**b**) *Fam (persona)* blockhead

tarumba *adj Fam* crazy, mad; **estar t.** to be bonkers

tasa *nf* (**a**) *(precio)* fee; **tasas académicas** course fees (**b**) *(impuesto)* tax; **tasas de aeropuerto** airport tax (**c**) *(índice)* rate; **t. de natalidad/mortalidad** birth/death rate (**d**) *(valoración)* valuation, appraisal

tasación *nf* valuation

tasador,-a *nm,f* valuer

tasar *vt* (**a**) *(valorar)* to value; **t. una casa en 10 millones de pesetas** to value a house at 10 million pesetas (**b**) *(poner precio)* to set *o* fix the price of

tasca *nf Fam* bar, pub

tata 1 *nf (niñera)* nanny

2 *nm Am Fam (papá)* dad, daddy, *US* pop

tatarabuelo,-a *nm,f* great-great-grandfather, *f* great-great-grandmother; **tatarabuelos** great-great-grandparents

tataranieto,-a *nm,f* great-great-grandson, *f* great-great-granddaughter; **tataranietos** great-great-grandchildren

tatuaje *nm* tattoo

tatuar [30] *vt* to tattoo

taurino,-a *adj* bullfighting

Tauro *nm* Taurus

tauromaquia *nf* tauromachy, (art of) bullfighting

taxativo,-a *adj* categorical

taxi *nm* taxi

taxímetro *nm* taximeter, clock

taxista *nmf* taxi driver

taza *nf* (**a**) cup; **una t. de café** *(recipiente)* coffee cup; *(contenido)* a cup of coffee (**b**) *(de retrete)* bowl

tazón *nm* bowl

te *pron pers* (**a**) *(complemento directo)* you; *(complemento indirecto)* (to/for) you; **no quiero verte** I don't want to see

you; **te compraré uno** I'll buy one for you, I'll buy you one; **te lo dije** I told you so (**b**) *(reflexivo)* yourself; **lávate** wash yourself; *(sin traducción)* **bébetelo todo** drink it up; **no te vayas** don't go

té *nm* (*pl* **tés**) tea; **té con limón** lemon tea

tea *nf* torch

teatral *adj* (**a**) **grupo t.** theatre company; **obra t.** play (**b**) *Fig (teatrero)* theatrical

teatrero,-a *adj* theatrical

teatro *nm* (**a**) theatre; **obra de t.** play; **autor de t.** playwright (**b**) *Lit* drama

tebeo *nm* children's comic

techar *vt* to roof

techo *nm* *(de habitación)* ceiling; *(tejado)* roof; *Aut* **t. corredizo** sun roof

tecla *nf* key; *Fig* **dar en la t.** to get it right

teclado *nm* keyboard; *Informát* **t. expandido** expanded keyboard

teclear 1 *vt* to key in

2 *vi* to drum with one's fingers

técnica *nf* (**a**) *(tecnología)* technology (**b**) *(método)* technique (**c**) *(habilidad)* skill

técnico,-a 1 *adj* technical

2 *nm,f* technician, technical expert

tecnicolor® *nm* Technicolor®

tecno- *pref* techno-

tecnócrata *nmf* technocrat

tecnología *nf* technology

tecnológico,-a *adj* technological

tecolote *nm CAm, Méx (búho)* owl

tedio *nm* tedium, boredom

tedioso,-a *adj* tedious, boring

teja *nf Constr* tile; *Fam Fig* **a toca t.** on the nail

tejado *nm* roof

tejanos *nmpl* jeans

tejemaneje *nm Fam* (**a**) *(actividad)* bustle, fuss (**b**) *(maquinación)* intrigue, scheming

tejer *vt* *(en el telar)* to weave; *(hacer punto)* to knit; *(telaraña)* to spin; *Fig (plan)* to plot, to scheme

tejido *nm* (**a**) fabric; **t. de punto** knitted fabric (**b**) *Anat* tissue

tejo *nm Fam* **tirar los tejos a algn** to make a play for sb

tejón *nm* badger

tel. (*abr* **teléfono**) tel.

tela *nf* (**a**) *Tex* material, fabric, cloth; *(de la leche)* skin; **t. de araña** cobweb; **t. metálica** gauze (**b**) *Fam (dinero)* dough (**c**) *Arte* canvas (**d**) *Fig* **poner en t. de juicio** to question; *Fig* **tiene mucha t.** it's not an easy thing

telar *nm Tex* loom

telaraña *nf* cobweb, spider's web

tele *nf Fam* telly, TV
telearrastre *nm* ski lift
telebanca *nf* telephone banking, home banking
telebasura *nf Fam* junk TV
telecabina *nf* cable car
telecomunicaciones *nfpl* telecommunications
telediario *nm* *TV* television news bulletin
teledirigido,-a *adj* remote-controlled
telefax *nm* telefax, fax
teleférico *nm* cable car/railway
telefilm, telefilme *nm* TV film
telefonazo *nm* **dar un t. (a algn)** to give (sb) a ring
telefonear *vt & vi* to telephone, to phone
telefonía *nf* **t. móvil** mobile phones
telefónica *nf* **Compañía T.** ≃ British Telecom
telefónico,-a *adj* telephone; **llamada telefónica** telephone call
telefonista *nmf* (telephone) operator
teléfono *nm* telephone, phone; **t. portátil** portable telephone; **t. móvil** car phone; **está hablando por t.** she's on the phone; **te llamó por t.** she phoned you
telegrafiar [29] *vt* to telegraph, to wire
telegráfico,-a *adj* telegraphic; **giro t.** giro, money order
telégrafo *nm* (**a**) telegraph (**b**) **telégrafos** post office
telegrama *nm* telegram, cable
teleimpresor *nm,* **teleimpresora** *nf* teleprinter
telele *nm Fam* **darle a uno un t.** to have a fit
telemando *nm* remote control (unit)
telenovela *nf* television serial
teleobjetivo *nm* telephoto lens *sing*
telepático,-a *adj* telepathic
telescopio *nm* telescope
teleserie *nf* television series *sing*
telesilla *nm* chair lift
telespectador,-a *nm,f* TV viewer
telesquí *nm* ski lift
teletexto *nm* teletext
teletienda *nf* home shopping programme
teletipo *nm* teleprinter
teletrabajador,-a *nm,f* teleworker
teletrabajo *nm* teleworking
televidente *nmf* TV viewer
televisar *vt* to televise
televisión *nf* (**a**) (*sistema*) television (**b**) *Fam* (*aparato*) television set; **t. en color/en blanco y negro** colour/black-and-white television; **t. digital** digital television;

t. por cable cable television; **ver la t.** to watch television
televisivo,-a *adj* television; **espacio t.** television programme
televisor *nm* television set
télex *nm inv* telex
telón *nm Teatro* curtain; *Pol & Hist* **t. de acero** Iron Curtain; **t. de fondo** *Teatro* backdrop; *Fig* background
telonero,-a *adj* (**grupo**) **t.** support band
tema *nm* (**a**) (*asunto*) topic, subject; (*de examen*) subject; **temas de actualidad** current affairs (**b**) *Mús* theme
temario *nm* (*de examen*) programme
temática *nf* subject matter
temático,-a *adj* thematic
temblar [1] *vi* (*de frío*) to shiver; (*de miedo*) to tremble (**de** with); (*voz*) to quiver; (*pulso*) to shake
tembleque *nm Fam* shaking fit
temblón,-ona *adj Fam* trembling, shaky
temblor *nm* tremor, shudder; **t. de tierra** earth tremor
tembloroso,-a, tembloso,-a *adj* shaking; (*voz*) quivering; (*de frío*) shivering; (*de miedo*) trembling; **manos temblorosas** shaky hands
temer 1 *vt* to fear, to be afraid of; **temo que esté muerto** I fear he's dead; **temo que no podrá recibirte** I'm afraid (that) he won't be able to see you
2 *vi* to be afraid
3 temerse *vpr* to fear, to be afraid; **¡me lo temía!** I was afraid this would happen!
temerario,-a *adj* reckless, rash
temeridad *nf* (**a**) (*actitud*) temerity, rashness (**b**) (*acto temerario*) reckless act
temeroso,-a *adj* (**a**) fearful, timid (**b**) (*temible*) frightful
temible *adj* fearful, frightful
temor *nm* (**a**) fear (**b**) (*recelo*) worry, apprehension
témpano *nm* ice floe
temperamental *adj* temperamental
temperamento *nm* temperament; **tener t.** to have a strong character
temperatura *nf* temperature
tempestad *nf* storm; *Fig* turmoil, uproar
tempestuoso,-a *adj* stormy, tempestuous
templado,-a *adj* (**a**) (*agua*) lukewarm; (*clima*) mild, temperate (**b**) *Mús* (*afinado*) tuned
templanza *nf* moderation, restraint
templar *vt* (**a**) to moderate (**b**) (*algo frío*) to warm up; (*algo caliente*) to cool down (**c**) *Mús* (*instrumento*) to tune (**d**) *Téc* (*metal*) to temper

temple *nm* (**a**) *(fortaleza)* boldness, courage (**b**) *Arte* tempera

templete *nm* bandstand

templo *nm* temple

temporada *nf* (**a**) season; **t. alta** high *o* peak season; **t. baja** low *o* off season (**b**) *(período)* period, time; **por temporadas** on and off

temporal 1 *adj* temporary, provisional
  2 *nm* storm

temporario,-a *adj Am* temporary

temporero,-a *nm,f* seasonal *o* temporary worker

tempranero,-a *adj* (**a**) *(persona)* early-rising (**b**) *(cosecha)* early

temprano,-a *adj & adv* early

tenacidad *nf* (**a**) *(perseverancia)* tenacity, perseverance (**b**) *(de metal)* tensile strength

tenacillas *nfpl (para pelo)* curling tongs

tenaz *adj* tenacious

tenaza *nf,* **tenazas** *nfpl (herramienta)* pliers, pincers; *(para el fuego)* tongs

tendedero *nm* clothes line, drying place

tendencia *nf* tendency

tendencioso,-a *adj* tendentious, biased

tender [3] 1 *vt* (**a**) *(mantel etc)* to spread out; *(para secar)* to hang out (**b**) *Am (cama)* to make; *(mesa)* to set, to lay (**c**) *(red)* to cast; *(puente)* to build; *(vía, cable)* to lay; *(trampa)* to lay, to set (**d**) *(mano)* to stretch *o* hold out (**e**) *(tumbar)* to lay
  2 *vi* to tend (**a** to), to have a tendency (**a** to)
  3 tenderse *vpr* to lie down, to stretch out

tenderete *nm (puesto)* market stall

tendero,-a *nm,f* shopkeeper

tendido *nm* (**a**) *(de vía, cable)* laying; *(de puente)* construction; **t. eléctrico** electrical installation (**b**) *Taurom (asientos)* = front tiers of seats

tendón *nm* tendon, sinew

tenebroso,-a *adj (sombrío)* dark, gloomy; *(siniestro)* sinister, shady

tenedor *nm* fork

teneduría *nf* **t. de libros** bookkeeping

tenencia *nf Jur* **t. ilícita de armas** illegal possession of arms

tener [24] 1 *vt* (**a**) to have, to have got; **tenemos un examen** we've got *o* we have an exam; **va a t. un niño** she's going to have a baby, she's expecting; **¡ahí (lo) tienes!** here you are!
  (**b**) *(poseer)* to own, to possess
  (**c**) *(sostener)* to hold; **tenme el bolso un momento** hold my bag a minute; **ten, es para ti** take this *o* here you are, it's for you
  (**d**) **t. calor/frío** to be hot/cold; **t. cariño**

a algn to be fond of sb; **t. miedo** to be frightened
  (**e**) *(edad)* to be; **tiene dieciocho (años)** he's eighteen (years old)
  (**f**) *Am (llevar)* **tengo tres años aquí** I've been here for three years
  (**g**) *(medida)* **la casa tiene 100 metros cuadrados** the house is 100 square metres
  (**h**) *(contener)* to hold, to contain
  (**i**) *(mantener)* to keep; **me tuvo despierto toda la noche** he kept me up all night
  (**j**) **t. por** *(considerar)* to consider, to think; **me tienen por estúpido** they think I'm a fool; **ten por seguro que lloverá** you can be sure it'll rain
  (**k**) **t. que** to have (got) to; **tengo que irme** I must leave; **tienes/tendrías que verlo** you must/should see it
  2 tenerse *vpr* (**a**) **t. en pie** to stand (up)
  (**b**) **t. por** *(considerarse)* to think *o* consider oneself; **se tiene por muy inteligente** he thinks he's very intelligent

tenga *subj pres de* **tener**

tengo *indic pres de* **tener**

teniente *nm* (**a**) *Mil* lieutenant (**b**) **t. (de) alcalde** deputy mayor

tenis *nm* tennis

tenista *nmf* tennis player

tenor[1] *nm Mús* tenor

tenor[2] *nm* **a t. de** according to

tensar *vt (cable etc)* to tighten; *(arco)* to draw

tensión *nf* (**a**) tension; **en t.** tense (**b**) *Elec* tension, voltage (**c**) *Med* **t. arterial** blood pressure; **t. nerviosa** nervous strain (**d**) *Téc* stress

tenso,-a *adj* (**a**) *(cuerda, cable)* tense, taut (**b**) *(persona)* tense; *(relaciones)* strained

tentación *nf* temptation

tentáculo *nm* tentacle

tentador,-a *adj* tempting

tentar [1] *vt* (**a**) *(palpar)* to feel, to touch (**b**) *(incitar)* to tempt

tentativa *nf* attempt; *Jur* **t. de asesinato** attempted murder

tentempié *nm Fam (pl* **tentempiés)** (**a**) *(comida)* snack, bite (**b**) *(juguete)* tumbler

tenue *adj* (**a**) *(luz, sonido)* subdued, faint (**b**) *(delgado)* thin, light

teñir [6] 1 *vt* (**a**) *(pelo etc)* to dye (**b**) *Fig* to tinge with
  2 teñirse *vpr* **t. el pelo** to dye one's hair

teocalli *nm Hist* = Mexican pyramid

teología *nf* theology

teorema *nm* theorem

teoría *nf* theory; **en t.** theoretically

teórico,-a *adj* theoretical
teorizar [40] *vi* to theorize (**sobre** on)
tepache *nm* = mildly alcoholic Mexican drink made from fermented pineapple peelings and unrefined sugar
tequila *nm* tequila
terapeuta *nmf* therapist
terapia *nf* therapy
tercer *adj* third; **el t. mundo** the third world
tercerización *nf Am Com* outsourcing
tercermundista *adj* third-world
tercero,-a 1 *adj* third

> Tercer is used instead of tercero before masculine singular nouns (e.g. **el tercer piso** the third floor).

  2 *nm,f (de una serie)* third; **a la tercera va la vencida** third time lucky
  3 *nm (mediador)* mediator; *Jur* third party
terceto *nm Mús* trio
terciar [43] 1 *vi* (**a**) *(mediar)* to mediate, to arbitrate (**b**) *(participar)* to take part, to participate
  2 terciarse *vpr* **si se tercia** should the occasion arise
terciario,-a *adj* tertiary
tercio *nm* (**a**) *(parte)* (one) third (**b**) *(de cerveza)* = medium-sized bottle of beer (**c**) *Taurom* stage, part *(of a bullfight)*
terciopelo *nm* velvet
terco,-a *adj* stubborn, obstinate
tereré *nm Arg, Par (mate)* = refreshing drink made from maté in cold water with lemon juice
tergiversar *vt (verdad)* to distort; *(palabras)* to twist
termal *adj* thermal
termas *nfpl (baños)* spa, hot baths *o* springs
térmico,-a *adj* thermal; **central térmica** coal- fired power station
terminación *nf* completion
terminal 1 *adj* terminal
  2 *nf* (**a**) *(de aeropuerto)* terminal; *(de autobús)* terminus (**b**) *Elec & Informát* terminal
terminante *adj* (**a**) *(categórico)* categorical, final (**b**) *(dato, resultado)* conclusive
terminantemente *adv* categorically; **t. prohibido** strictly forbidden
terminar 1 *vt (acabar)* to finish, to complete; *(completamente)* to finish off
  2 *vi* (**a**) *(acabarse)* to finish, to end; **termina en seis** it ends with a six; **no termina de convencerse** he still isn't quite

convinced (**b**) *(ir a parar)* to end up (**en** in); **terminó por comprarlo** he ended up buying it (**c**) **t. con** *(eliminar)* to put an end to
  3 terminarse *vpr* (**a**) to finish, to end, to be over (**b**) *(vino, dinero etc)* to run out
término *nm* (**a**) *(final)* end, finish (**b**) *(palabra)* term, word; **en otros términos** in other words; **en términos generales** generally speaking (**c**) **t. municipal** district (**d**) **por t. medio** on average (**e**) *Fig* **en último t.** as a last resort
terminología *nf* terminology
termo *nm* Thermos® (flask), flask
termodinámico,-a *adj* thermodynamic
termómetro *nm* thermometer
termonuclear *adj* thermonuclear
termostato *nm* thermostat
ternera *nf* calf; *(carne)* veal
ternero *nm* calf
terno *nm Andes, Méx (traje)* three-piece suit
ternura *nf* tenderness
terquedad *nf* stubbornness, obstinacy
terracota *nf* terracotta
terraja *adj RP Fam (persona)* flashy; *(cosa)* tacky, kitsch
terrajada *nf RP Fam* tacky thing/act
terral *nm Am (polvareda)* dust cloud
Terranova *n* Newfoundland
terraplén *nm* embankment
terráqueo,-a *adj* **globo t.** *(tierra)* (the) earth; *(esfera)* globe
terrateniente *nmf* landowner
terremoto *nm* earthquake
terrenal *adj* **un paraíso t.** a heaven on earth
terreno *nm* (**a**) *(tierra)* (piece of) land, ground; *Geol* terrain; *(campo)* field; **ganar/perder t.** to gain/lose ground (**b**) *Dep* field, ground (**c**) *Fig* field, sphere
terrestre *adj* (**a**) *(de la tierra)* terrestrial, earthly (**b**) *(por tierra)* by land; **por vía t.** by land
terrible *adj* terrible, awful
terrícola *nmf (en ciencia ficción)* earthling
terrier *nm* terrier
territorio *nm* territory
terrón *nm (de azúcar)* lump; *(de tierra)* clod
terror *nm* terror; *Cin* horror
terrorífico,-a *adj* terrifying, frightening
terrorismo *nm* terrorism
terrorista *adj & nmf* terrorist
terroso,-a *adj (color)* earth-coloured
terruño *nm (terreno)* piece of land; *(patria chica)* homeland, native land
terso,-a *adj* smooth

tersura *nf* smoothness

tertulia *nf* get-together; **t. literaria** literary gathering

tesina *nf* first degree dissertation

tesis *nf inv* thesis; *(opinión)* view, theory

tesón *nm* tenacity, firmness

tesorero,-a *nm,f* treasurer

tesoro *nm* (**a**) treasure (**b**) *(erario)* exchequer; **T. Público** Treasury

test *nm* test

testaferro *nm* front man

testamentario,-a *Jur* **1** *adj* testamentary
  2 *nm,f* executor

testamento *nm* (**a**) *Jur* will; **hacer** *o* **otorgar t.** to make *o* draw up one's will (**b**) *Rel* Testament

testar *vi* to make *o* draw up one's will

testarudo,-a *adj* stubborn, obstinate

testear *vt CSur* to test

testículo *nm* testicle

testificar [44] *vt* to testify

testigo 1 *nmf* witness; *Jur* **t. de cargo/descargo** witness for the prosecution/defence; *Jur* **t. ocular/presencial** eyewitness; *Rel* **Testigos de Jehová** Jehovah's Witnesses
  2 *nm Dep* baton

testimoniar [43] *vt* (**a**) *(dar testimonio)* to testify to, to attest to (**b**) *(mostrar)* to show

testimonio *nm Jur* testimony; *(prueba)* evidence, proof

teta *nf Fam* (**a**) tit, boob; **niño de t.** breastfeeding baby (**b**) *(de vaca)* udder

tétanos *nm* tetanus

tetera *nf* teapot

tetero *nm Col, Ven (biberón)* baby's bottle

tetilla *nf* (**a**) *Anat* man's nipple (**b**) *(de biberón)* (rubber) teat

tetina *nf* (rubber) teat

tétrico,-a *adj* gloomy, dull

textil *adj & nm* textile

texto *nm* text; **libro de t.** textbook

textual *adj* textual; *(exacto)* literal; **en palabras textuales** literally

textura *nf Tex* texture; *(en minerales)* structure

tez *nf* complexion

ti *pron pers* you; **es para ti** it's for you; **hazlo por ti** do it for your own sake; **piensas demasiado en ti mismo** you think too much about yourself

tía *nf* (**a**) *(pariente)* aunt (**b**) *Fam (mujer)* girl, woman

tianguis *nm inv CAm, Méx* open-air market

tibieza *nf* tepidity; *Fig* lack of enthusiasm

tibio,-a *adj* tepid, lukewarm; *Fam* **ponerse t. de cerveza** to get pissed

tiburón *nm* shark

tic *nm* (*pl* **tiques**) tic, twitch; **t. nervioso** nervous tic *o* twitch

ticket *nm* (*pl* **tickets**) *(billete)* ticket; *(recibo)* receipt

tictac *nm* tick-tock, ticking

tiempo *nm* (**a**) time; **a t.** in time; **a su (debido) t.** in due course; **a un t., al mismo t.** at the same time; **al poco t.** soon afterwards; **antes de t.** (too) early *o* soon; **con el t.** in the course of time, with time; **con t.** in advance; **¿cuánto t.?** how long?; **¿cuánto t. hace?** how long ago?; **demasiado t.** too long; **estar a t. de** to still have time to; **hacer t.** to kill time; **¿nos da t. de llegar?** have we got (enough) time to get there?; **t. libre** free time; *Fig* **dar t. al t.** to let matters take their course
  (**b**) *(meteorológico)* weather; **¿qué t. hace?** what's the weather like?; **hace buen/mal t.** the weather is good/bad
  (**c**) *(edad)* age; **¿cuánto** *o* **qué t. tiene tu niño?** how old is your baby/child?
  (**d**) *Mús* movement
  (**e**) *Dep* half
  (**f**) *Ling* tense

tienda *nf* (**a**) shop, store; **ir de tiendas** to go shopping (**b**) **t. (de campaña)** tent

tienta *nf* **a tientas** by touch; **andar a tientas** to feel one's way; **buscar (algo) a tientas** to grope (for sth)

tiento *nm* tact; **con t.** tactfully

tierno,-a *adj* (**a**) *(blando)* tender, soft (**b**) *(reciente)* fresh

tierra *nf* (**a**) *(planeta)* earth (**b**) *Agr* land, soil (**c**) *(continente)* land; **tocar t.** to land (**d**) *(país)* country; **t. de nadie** no-man's-land (**e**) *(suelo)* ground; *Fig* **echar** *o* **tirar por t.** to spoil (**f**) *Elec* **(toma de) t.** *Br* earth, *US* ground

tierral *nm Am* cloud of dust

tieso,-a *adj (rígido)* stiff, rigid; *(erguido)* upright, erect

tiesto *nm* flowerpot

tifoidea *nf* **(fiebre) t.** typhoid (fever)

tifón *nm* typhoon

tifus *nm inv* typhus (fever)

tigre *nm* tiger; *Am* jaguar

tijeras *nfpl* (pair of) scissors

tijereta *nf* (**a**) *(insecto)* earwig (**b**) *Dep* scissors

tila *nf (flor)* lime *o* linden blossom; *(infusión)* lime *o* linden blossom tea

tildar *vt* to call, to brand; **me tildó de ladrón** he called me a thief

tilde *nf* written accent

tilín *nm (sonido)* ting-a-ling; *Fig* **José le hace t.** she fancies José
tilma *nf Méx* woollen blanket
tilo *nm* lime tree
timar *vt* to swindle; **me han timado** they did me
timbal *nm* kettledrum
timbrar *vt (carta)* to stamp; *(documento)* to seal
timbre *nm* (**a**) *(de la puerta)* bell (**b**) *(sello)* stamp, seal; *Fin* fiscal *o* revenue stamp (**c**) *Mús (sonido)* timbre
timidez *nf* shyness, timidity
tímido,-a *adj* shy, timid; *Fig (mejoría)* light; *(intento)* cautious
timo *nm* swindle, fiddle; **es un t.** it's a rip-off
timón *nm* (**a**) *Náut & Av* rudder; **golpe de t.** U-turn (**b**) *Andes Aut* steering wheel
timonel *nm* helmsman
tímpano *nm Anat* eardrum
tina *nf* (**a**) *(tinaja)* pitcher (**b**) *(gran cuba)* vat (**c**) *CAm, Col, Méx (bañera)* bathtub
tinaja *nf* large earthenware jar
tinerfeño,-a **1** *adj* of/from Tenerife
  2 *nm,f* person from Tenerife
tinglado *nm* (**a**) *(intriga)* intrigue (**b**) *(cobertizo)* shed
tinieblas *nfpl* darkness
tino *nm* (**a**) *(puntería)* (good) aim; **tener buen t.** to be a good shot (**b**) *(tacto)* (common) sense, good judgement
tinta *nf* (**a**) ink; **t. china** Indian ink; **t. simpática** invisible ink (**b**) *Fig* **medias tintas** ambiguities, half measures
tintar *vt* to dye
tinte *nm* (**a**) dye (**b**) *Fig (matiz)* shade, overtone
tintero *nm* inkpot, inkwell; *Fig* **se quedó en el t.** it wasn't said
tintinear *vi (vidrio)* to clink; *(campana)* to jingle, to tinkle
tintineo *nm (de vidrio)* clinking; *(de campana)* jingling
tinto,-a **1** *adj (vino)* red
  2 *nm* (**a**) *(vino)* red wine (**b**) *Col, Ven (café)* black coffee
tintorería *nf* dry-cleaner's
tintura *nf* (**a**) *(colorante)* dye (**b**) *Quím* tincture; **t. de yodo** iodine
tío *nm* (**a**) *(pariente)* uncle; **mis tíos** my uncle and aunt (**b**) *Fam* guy, *Br* bloke
tiovivo *nm* roundabout, merry-go-round
tipazo *nm Fam* good figure
tipear *vt & vi Am* to type
típico,-a *adj* (**a**) typical; **eso es t. de Antonio** that's just like Antonio (**b**) *(baile, traje)* traditional

tipificar [**44**] *vt* (**a**) *(normalizar)* to standardize (**b**) *(caracterizar)* to typify
tipismo *nm* local colour
tipo *nm* (**a**) *(clase)* type, kind (**b**) *Fam (persona)* guy, *Br* bloke; **t. raro** weirdo (**c**) *Anat (de hombre)* build, physique; *(de mujer)* figure; *Fig* **jugarse el t.** to risk one's neck; **aguantar el t.** to keep one's cool *o* head (**d**) *Fin* rate; **t. bancario** *o* **de descuento** bank rate; **t. de cambio/interés** rate of exchange/interest (**e**) **el político t. de la izquierda** the typical left-wing politician
tipografía *nf* typography
tipográfico,-a *adj* typographic; **error t.** printing error
tipógrafo,-a *nm,f* typographer
tiquismiquis *Fam* **1** *nmf inv* fusspot
  2 *nmpl* (**a**) *(escrúpulos)* silly scruples (**b**) *(rencillas)* bickering
tira *nf* (**a**) *(banda, cinta)* strip (**b**) *(de dibujos)* comic strip (**c**) *Fam* **la t. de gente** a lot *o* loads of people (**d**) *Méx Fam* **la t.** *(la policía)* the cops (**e**) **t. y afloja** tug of war
tirabuzón *nm* ringlet
tirachinas *nm inv Br* catapult, *US* slingshot
tirada *nf* (**a**) *(lanzamiento)* throw (**b**) *(impresión)* print run
tirado,-a *adj Fam* (**a**) *(precio)* dirt-cheap (**b**) *(examen)* dead easy (**c**) *Fam* **dejar t. (a algn)** to let (sb) down
tirador *nm* (**a**) *(persona)* marksman (**b**) *(pomo)* knob, handle; *(cordón)* bell pull (**c**) *(tirachinas) Br* catapult, *US* slingshot
tiraje *nm Am* print run
tiralíneas *nm inv* tracer, drawing *o* ruling pen
tiranía *nf* tyranny
tiránico,-a *adj* tyrannical
tiranizar [**40**] *vt* to tyrannize
tirano,-a *nm,f* tyrant
tirante **1** *adj (cable etc)* tight, taut; *(situación, relación)* tense
  2 *nm* (**a**) *(de vestido etc)* strap; **tirantes** *Br* braces, *US* suspenders (**b**) *Téc* brace, stay
tirar **1** *vt* (**a**) *(echar)* to throw
  (**b**) *(dejar caer)* to drop
  (**c**) *(desechar)* to throw away; *Fig (dinero)* to squander
  (**d**) *(derribar)* to knock down; **t. la puerta (abajo)** to smash the door in
  (**e**) *(foto)* to take
  (**f**) *Impr* to print
  (**g**) *(beso)* to blow
  2 *vi* (**a**) **t. de** *(cuerda, puerta)* to pull

(**b**) *(chimenea, estufa)* to draw
(**c**) *(funcionar)* to work, to run
(**d**) **ir tirando** to get by
(**e**) **t. a** to tend towards; **tira a rojo** it's reddish
(**f**) **tira a la izquierda** turn left; **¡venga, tira ya!** come on, get going!
(**g**) *(disparar)* to shoot, to fire; *Ftb* **t. a puerta** to shoot at goal
3 tirarse *vpr* (**a**) *(lanzarse)* to throw *o* hurl oneself; **t. de cabeza al agua** to dive into the water
(**b**) *(tumbarse)* to lie down
(**c**) *Fam (tiempo)* to spend; **me tiré una hora esperando** I waited (for) a good hour
(**d**) *Vulg* **t. a algn** to lay sb
tirita® *nf* Elastoplast®, Band-aid®, plaster
tiritar *vi* to shiver, to shake
tiro *nm* (**a**) *(lanzamiento)* throw (**b**) *(disparo, ruido)* shot; *Ftb* **t. a gol** shot at goal; **t. al blanco** target shooting; **t. al plato** clay pigeon shooting; **t. con arco** archery (**c**) *(de vestido)* shoulder width (**d**) *(de chimenea)* draught; **animal de t.** draught animal
tirón *nm* pull, tug; *(del bolso)* snatch; *Fam* **de un t.** in one go
tirotear *vt* to shoot at, to snipe at
tiroteo *nm* shooting, firing to and fro
tirria *nf Fam* dislike; **le tengo t.** I dislike him, I can't stand him
tísico,-a *adj* tubercular, consumptive
tisis *nf inv* tuberculosis, consumption
tisú *nm* tissue, paper hankie
títere *nm (marioneta)* puppet; **no dejar t. con cabeza** to spare no one
titilar *vi (luz)* to flicker; *(estrella)* to twinkle
titiritero,-a *nm,f* (**a**) puppeteer (**b**) *(acróbata)* travelling acrobat
titubeante *adj (indeciso)* hesitant; *(al hablar)* stammering
titubear *vi* (**a**) *(dudar)* to hesitate, to waver (**b**) *(al hablar)* to stammer
titubeo *nm* (**a**) *(duda)* hesitation (**b**) *(al hablar)* stammering
titulación *nf* qualifications
titulado,-a *adj (licenciado)* graduate; *(diplomado)* qualified
titular¹ 1 *nmf (persona)* holder
2 *nm Prensa* headline
3 *adj* appointed, official
titular² 1 *vt (poner título)* to call
2 titularse *vpr* (**a**) *(película etc)* to be called; **¿cómo se titula?** what is it called?
(**b**) *Educ* to graduate (**en** in)
titularidad *nf Educ* tenure

titulitis 1 *nf* obsession with qualifications
2 *nm Fam* certificate
título *nm* (**a**) title (**b**) *Educ* degree; *(diploma)* diploma (**c**) *Prensa (titular)* headline (**d**) **a t. de ejemplo** by way of example
tiza *nf* chalk; **una t.** a piece of chalk
tiznada *nf Am* **hijo de la t.** son of a bitch
tiznar *vt* to blacken (with soot)
tizne *nm* soot
tizón *nm* half-burnt stick, brand
tlapalería *nf Méx* ironmonger's (shop)
toalla *nf* towel; **tirar la t.** to throw in the towel
toallero *nm* towel *Br* rail *o US* bar
tobera *nf* nozzle
tobillo *nm* ankle
tobogán *nm* slide, chute
toca *nf (sombrero)* headdress; *(de monja)* wimple
tocadiscos *nm inv* record player; **t. digital** *o* **compacto** CD player
tocado¹ *nm* (**a**) *(peinado)* coiffure, hairdo (**b**) *(prenda)* headdress
tocado²,-a *adj Fam* crazy, touched
tocador *nm* (**a**) *(mueble)* dressing table (**b**) *(habitación)* dressing room; **t. de señoras** powder room
tocante a *loc adv* **en lo t. a ...** with reference to ...
tocar [44] 1 *vt* (**a**) to touch; *Fam Fig* **toca madera** touch wood (**b**) *(instrumento, canción)* to play; *(timbre, campana)* to ring; *(bocina)* to blow (**c**) *(tema, asunto)* to touch on (**d**) *(afectar)* to concern; **por lo que a mí me toca** as far as I am concerned
2 *vi* (**a**) **¿a quién le toca?** *(en juegos)* whose turn is it? (**b**) **me tocó el gordo** *(en rifa)* I won the jackpot (**c**) **t. con** to be next to; *Fig* **t. a su fin** to be coming to an end (**d**) *(llamar)* **t. a la puerta** to knock on the door
3 tocarse *vpr (una cosa con otra)* to touch each other; **¿os tocáis algo?** *(ser parientes)* are you related?
tocarse *vpr (cubrirse)* to cover one's head
tocata 1 *nf Mús* toccata
2 *nm Fam* record player
tocateja: • **a tocateja** *loc adv* **pagar a t.** to pay on the nail
tocayo,-a *nm,f* namesake
tocho *nm Fam (libro grande)* tome
tocino *nm* lard; **t. ahumado** smoked bacon; **t. de cielo** = sweet made with egg yolk
tocólogo,-a *nm,f* obstetrician
tocuyo *nm Am* coarse cotton cloth

todavía *adv* (**a**) *(aún)* still; *(en negativas)* yet; **t. la quiere** he still loves her; **t. no** not yet; **no mires t.** don't look yet (**b**) *(para reforzar)* even, still; **t. más/menos** even more/less

todo,-a 1 *adj* (**a**) all; **t. el pan** all the bread; **t. el mundo** (absolutely) everybody; **t. el día** all day, the whole *o* entire day; *Fam* **t. quisqui** every Tom, Dick and Harry

(**b**) *(cada)* every; **t. ciudadano de más de dieciocho años** every citizen over eighteen years of age

(**c**) *(entero)* complete, thorough; **es toda una mujer** she is every inch a woman

(**d**) **todos,-as** all; *(con expresiones de tiempo)* every; **todos los niños** all the children; **todos los martes** every Tuesday

2 *nm (totalidad)* whole

3 *pron* (**a**) *(sin excluir nada)* all, everything; **ante t.** first of all; **con t.** in spite of everything; **del t.** completely; **después de t.** after all; **eso es t.** that's all, that's it; **estar en t.** to be really with it; **hay de t.** there are all sorts; **lo sé t.** I know all about it; **t. lo contrario** quite the contrary *o* opposite; **t. lo más** at the most

(**b**) *(cualquiera)* anybody; **t. aquél** *o* **el que quiera** anybody who wants (to)

(**c**) *(cada uno)* **todos aprobamos** we all passed; **todos fueron** they all went

4 *adv* completely, totally; **volvió t. sucio** he was all dirty when he got back

todopoderoso,-a *adj* all-powerful, almighty

todoterreno *nm* all-terrain vehicle

toga *nf* (**a**) gown, robe (**b**) *Hist* toga

Tokio *n* Tokyo

toldo *nm* (**a**) *(cubierta)* awning (**b**) *Am (cabaña)* tent, teepee

tolerancia *nf* tolerance

tolerante *adj* tolerant

tolerar *vt* to tolerate; *(situación)* to stand; *(gente)* to put up with

toma *nf* (**a**) *(acción)* taking; *Elec* **t. de corriente** plug, socket (**b**) *Med* dose (**c**) *Mil* capture (**d**) *Cin* take, shot (**e**) **t. de posesión** swearing in (**f**) *Fam Fig* **t. y daca** give and take

tomado,-a *adj* (**a**) *(voz)* hoarse (**b**) *Am (borracho)* drunk (**c**) **tenerla tomada con algn** to have it in for sb

tomadura *nf Fam* **t. de pelo** leg-pull; *(timo)* rip-off

tomar 1 *vt* (**a**) *(coger)* to take; *(autobús, tren)* to catch; *(decisión)* to make, to take; **toma** here (you are); **t. el sol** to sunbathe; *Av* **t. tierra** to land; *Fam* **tomarla con algn**

to have it in for sb (**b**) *(comer, beber)* to have (**c**) **t. algo a mal** to take sth badly; **t. en serio/broma** to take seriously/as a joke (**d**) *(confundir)* to take (**por** for) (**e**) *Mil* to take

2 *vi Am (beber alcohol)* to drink

3 tomarse *vpr* (**a**) *(comer)* to eat; *(beber)* to drink (**b**) *Fam* **no te lo tomes así** don't take it like that

tomate *nm* tomato; **salsa de t.** *(de lata)* tomato sauce; *(de botella)* ketchup

tomavistas *nm inv* cine *o* movie camera

tómbola *nf* tombola

tomillo *nm* thyme

tomo *nm* volume; *Fam* **de t. y lomo** utter, out-and-out

ton *nm* **sin t. ni son** without rhyme or reason

tonada *nf* (**a**) *Mús* tune, song (**b**) *Am (acento)* accent

tonalidad *nf* tonality

tonel *nm* barrel, cask

tonelada *nf* ton; **t. métrica** tonne

tonelaje *nm* tonnage

tonelero,-a *nm,f* cooper

tongo *nm* fix

tónico,-a 1 *nm Med* tonic; *(cosmético)* skin tonic

2 *nf* tónica (**a**) *(tendencia)* tendency, trend; **tónica general** overall trend (**b**) *(bebida)* tonic (water) (**c**) *Mús* tonic

3 *adj* (**a**) *Ling* tonic, stressed (**b**) *Mús & Med* tonic

tonificante *adj* invigorating

tonificar [44] *vt* to tone up, to invigorate

tono *nm* tone; **a t. con** in tune *o* harmony with; **subir de t.** *o* **el t.** to speak louder; **un t. alto/bajo** a high/low pitch; *Fig* **darse t.** to put on airs; *Fig* **fuera de t.** inappropriate, out of place; **dar el t.** to set the tone

tontear *vi* (**a**) to act the clown, to fool about (**b**) *(galantear)* to flirt

tontería *nf* (**a**) stupidity, silliness (**b**) *(dicho, hecho)* silly *o* stupid thing (**c**) *(insignificancia)* trifle

tonto,-a 1 *adj* silly, dumb

2 *nm,f* fool, idiot; **t. de remate** *o* **de capirote** prize idiot

topacio *nm* topaz

topadora *nf RP* bulldozer

toparse *vpr* **t. con** to bump into; *(dificultades)* to run up against, to encounter; **t. con algo** to come across sth

tope 1 *nm* (**a**) *(límite)* limit, end; *Fam* **a t.** *(al máximo)* flat out; *Fig* **estar hasta los topes** to be full up; **fecha t.** deadline (**b**) *Téc* stop, check (**c**) *Ferroc* buffer

2 *adv Fam* incredibly; **t. difícil** really difficult

tópico,-a 1 *nm* cliché

2 *adj Med & Farm* for external use

> ℓ Observa que la palabra inglesa **topic** es un falso amigo y no es la traducción de la palabra española **tópico**. En inglés, **topic** significa "tema".

topo *nm* mole

topografía *nf* topography

topónimo *nm* place name

toque *nm* (**a**) *(touch; Fam* **dar un t. a algn** *(avisar)* to let sb know; *(advertir)* to warn sb (**b**) *(de campanas)* peal; *Fig* warning; **t. de queda** curfew

toquetear *vt* to fiddle with, to finger

toquilla *nf* (knitted) shawl

tórax *nm* thorax

torbellino *nm* (**a**) *(de viento)* whirlwind (**b**) *Fig (confusión)* whirl, turmoil

torcedura *nf (acción)* twist, twisting; *Med* sprain

torcer [41] 1 *vt* (**a**) *(metal)* to bend; *(cuerda, hilo)* to twist; *Med* to sprain; *Fig (esquina)* to turn (**b**) *(inclinar)* to slant

2 *vi* to turn (left o right)

3 torcerse *vpr* (**a**) *(doblarse)* to twist, to bend (**b**) *Med* **se me torció el tobillo** I sprained my ankle (**c**) *(plan)* to fall through (**d**) *(desviarse)* to go off to the side

torcido,-a *adj* twisted; *(ladeado)* slanted, lopsided; *(corbata)* crooked

tordo,-a 1 *adj* dapple-grey

2 *nm Orn* thrush

torear 1 *vt* to fight; *Fam* **t. a algn** to tease o confuse sb; *Fam* **t. un asunto** to tackle a matter skilfully

2 *vi* to fight

toreo *nm* bullfighting

torero,-a *nm,f* bullfighter

tormenta *nf* storm

tormento *nm (tortura)* torture; *(padecimiento)* torment

tormentoso,-a *adj* stormy

tornado *nm* tornado

tornar *Fml* **1** *vt (convertir)* to transform, to turn (**en** into)

2 *vi (regresar)* to return, to go back; **t. en sí** to regain consciousness

3 tornarse *vpr* to become, to turn

tornasolado,-a *adj* iridescent

torneo *nm* (**a**) *Dep* tournament (**b**) *Hist* tourney, joust

tornillo *nm* screw

torniquete *nm* (**a**) turnstile (**b**) *Med* tourniquet

torno *nm* (**a**) *Téc* lathe; *(de alfarero)*

wheel (**b**) **en t. a** *(alrededor de)* around; *(acerca de)* about

toro *nm* bull; **¿te gustan los toros?** do you like bullfighting?

toronja *nf* grapefruit

torpe *adj* (**a**) *(sin habilidad)* clumsy (**b**) *(tonto)* dim, thick (**c**) *(movimiento)* slow, awkward

torpedear *vt* to torpedo

torpedo *nm* torpedo

torpeza *nf* (**a**) *(física)* clumsiness; *(mental)* dimness, stupidity (**b**) *(lentitud)* slowness, heaviness (**c**) *(error)* blunder

torre *nf* (**a**) tower (**b**) *Mil & Náut* turret (**c**) *(en ajedrez)* rook, castle

torrefacto,-a *adj* roasted; **café t.** high roast coffee

torrencial *adj* torrential

torrente *nm* (**a**) *(de agua)* torrent (**b**) *Fig* **t. de voz** strong o powerful voice

torrezno *nm* = rasher of fried bacon

tórrido,-a *adj* torrid

torrija *nf* French toast

torsión *nf* (**a**) *(torcedura)* twist, twisting (**b**) *Téc* torsion

torso *nm* (**a**) *Anat* torso (**b**) *Arte* bust

torta *nf* (**a**) *Culin* cake (**b**) *Fam (golpe)* slap, punch

tortazo *nm Fam* (**a**) *(bofetada)* slap, punch (**b**) *(golpe)* whack, thump

tortícolis *nf inv* crick in the neck

tortilla *nf* (**a**) *(egg)* omelette; **t. francesa/española** (plain)/potato omelette (**b**) *Am* tortilla

tortillera *nf muy Fam* dyke, lesbian

tórtola *nf* dove

tortuga *nf (de tierra)* tortoise, *US* turtle; *(de mar)* turtle

tortuoso,-a *adj* tortuous

tortura *nf* torture

torturar *vt* to torture

tos *nf* cough; **t. ferina** whooping cough

tosco,-a *adj (basto)* rustic, rough; *(persona)* uncouth

toser *vi* to cough

tosquedad *nf* roughness

tostada *nf* (slice of) toast

tostado,-a *adj* (**a**) *(pan)* toasted (**b**) *(moreno)* tanned, brown

tostador *nm* toaster

tostar [2] *vt (pan)* to toast; *(café)* to roast; *(carne, pescado)* to brown; *Fig (la piel)* to tan

tostón *nm* (**a**) *Culin (pan frito)* crouton (**b**) *Fam (tabarra)* bore, drag

total 1 *adj (completo)* total

2 *nm* (**a**) *(todo)* whole; **en t.** in all (**b**) *Mat* total

3 *adv* so, in short; **¿t. para qué?** what's the point anyhow?; *Fam* **t. que ...** so ...; **t., tampoco te hará caso** he won't listen to you anyway

totalidad *nf* whole, totality; **la t. de** all of; **en su t.** as a whole

totalitario,-a *adj* totalitarian

totalizar [40] 1 *vt* to total
2 *vi* to amount to

tóxico,-a 1 *adj* toxic, poisonous
2 *nm* poison

toxicología *nf* toxicology

toxicólogo,-a *nm,f* toxicologist

toxicomanía *nf* drug addiction

toxicómano,-a *Med* **1** *adj* addicted to drugs
2 *nm,f* drug addict

tozudo,-a *adj* obstinate, stubborn

traba *nf* (**a**) *(de rueda)* chock; *(enlace)* bond, tie (**b**) *Fig (obstáculo)* hindrance, obstacle

trabajador,-a 1 *nm,f* worker, labourer
2 *adj* hard-working

trabajar 1 *vi* to work; **trabaja mucho** he works hard; **t. de camarera** to work as a waitress
2 *vt* (**a**) to work (on); *(la tierra)* to till (**b**) *(asignatura etc)* to work on (**c**) *Fam (convencer)* to (try to) persuade

trabajo *nm* (**a**) *(ocupación)* work; **t. a destajo** piecework; **t. eventual** casual labour; **trabajos manuales** arts and crafts (**b**) *(empleo)* employment, job (**c**) *(tarea)* task, job (**d**) *Educ (redacción)* report, paper (**e**) *(esfuerzo)* effort; **cuesta t. creerlo** it's hard to believe

trabajoadicto,-a *nm,f* workaholic

trabajoso,-a *adj (laborioso)* hard, laborious; *(difícil)* difficult

trabalenguas *nm inv* tongue twister

trabar 1 *vt* (**a**) *(sujetar)* to lock, to fasten; *(un plan)* to obstruct (**b**) *(conversación, amistad)* to start, to strike up (**c**) *Culin* to thicken
2 trabarse *vpr* (**a**) *(cuerdas)* to get tangled up (**b**) *Fig* **se le trabó la lengua** he got tongue-tied

trabazón *nf (de ideas)* link

trabilla *nf (de pantalón)* belt loop

trabuco *nm* blunderbuss

tracción *nf* traction; *Aut* **t. delantera/ trasera** front-/rear-wheel drive; *Aut* **t. en las cuatro ruedas** four-wheel drive

tractor *nm* tractor

tradición *nf* tradition

tradicional *adj* traditional

traducción *nf* translation; **t. directa/inversa** translation from/into a foreign language

traducir [10] 1 *vt* to translate (**a** into)
2 traducirse *vpr Fig* to result (**en** in)

traductor,-a *nm,f* translator

traer [25] 1 *vt* (**a**) to bring; **trae** give it to me (**b**) *(llevar puesto)* to wear (**c**) *(llevar consigo)* to carry (**d**) *(problemas)* to cause; **traerá como consecuencia ...** it will result in ...
2 traerse *vpr (llevar consigo)* to bring along; *Fig* **¿qué se trae entre manos?** what is he up to?

traficante *nmf (de drogas etc)* trafficker, pusher

traficar [44] *vi (ilegalmente)* to traffic (**con** in)

tráfico *nm* (**a**) *Aut* traffic; **t. rodado** road traffic (**b**) *Com* traffic, trade; **t. de drogas** drug traffic

tragaluz *nm* skylight

tragaperras *nf inv* **(máquina) t.** slot machine

tragar [42] 1 *vt* (**a**) *(ingerir)* to swallow (**b**) *Fam (engullir)* to gobble up, to tuck away (**c**) *Fig (a una persona)* to stand, to stomach (**d**) *Fig (creer)* to believe, to swallow
2 tragarse *vpr* (**a**) *(ingerir)* to swallow (**b**) *Fig (creer)* to believe, to swallow

tragedia *nf* tragedy

trágico,-a *adj* tragic

trago *nm* (**a**) *(bebida)* swig; **de un t.** in one go (**b**) *Fig* **pasar un mal t.** to have a bad time of it

tragón,-ona *nm,f* glutton, big eater

traición *nf* treason, betrayal; **a t.** treacherously; **alta t.** high treason

traicionar *vt* to betray; *(delatar)* to give away, to betray

traicionero,-a *adj* treacherous

traidor,-a 1 *adj* treacherous
2 *nm,f* traitor

traigo *indic pres de* **traer**

tráiler *nm (pl* **tráilers)** (**a**) *Cin* trailer, *US* preview (**b**) *Aut Br* articulated lorry, *US* semitrailer (**c**) *Méx (casa rodante) Br* caravan, *US* trailer

traje¹ *nm* (**a**) *(de hombre)* suit; **t. de baño** bathing suit *o* costume, swimsuit; **t. de paisano** civilian clothes; **t. de luces** bullfighter's costume (**b**) *(de mujer)* dress; **t. de chaqueta** two-piece suit; **t. de novia** wedding dress

traje² *pt indef de* **traer**

trajeado,-a *adj Fam* sharp, dapper

trajearse *vpr* to dress up

trajín *nm Fam* comings and goings, hustle and bustle

trajinar *vi* to run *o* bustle about

trama nf (**a**)*Tex* weft, woof (**b**) *Lit* plot
tramar vt to plot, to cook up; ¿qué tramas? what are you up to?
tramitar vt (**a**) *(gestionar)* to take the necessary (legal) steps to obtain (**b**) *Fml (despachar)* to convey, to transmit (**c**) *Com, Jur & Fin* to carry out, to process
trámite nm *(paso)* step; *(formalidad)* formality; *Com, Jur & Fin* procedures, proceedings
tramo nm *(de carretera)* section, stretch; *(de escalera)* flight
tramoya nf *(maquinaria)* stage machinery; *(trama)* plot, scheme
trampa nf (**a**) *(de caza)* trap, snare (**b**) *(puerta)* trapdoor (**c**) *(engaño)* fiddle; **hacer trampa(s)** to cheat (**d**) *(truco)* trick

> Observa que la palabra inglesa **tramp** es un falso amigo y no es la traducción de la palabra española **trampa**. En inglés, **tramp** significa "vagabundo".

trampilla nf trapdoor, hatch
trampolín nm (**a**) *(de piscina)* diving board (**b**) *(de esquí)* ski jump

> Observa que la palabra inglesa **trampoline** es un falso amigo y no es la traducción de la palabra española **trampolín**. En inglés, **trampoline** significa "cama elástica".

tramposo,-a adj deceitful
  2 nm,f cheat; *Naipes* cardsharp
tranca nf (**a**) *(garrote)* cudgel; *Fam* **a trancas y barrancas** with great difficulty (**b**) *(en puerta, ventana)* bar
trancar 1 vt *(asegurar) (con cerrojo)* to bolt; *(con tranca)* to bar
  2 **trancarse** vpr *Am (atorarse)* to get stuck; **la llave se trancó en la cerradura** the key got stuck in the lock
trance nm (**a**) *(coyuntura)* (critical) moment; **estar en t. de ...** to be on the point of ... (**b**) *(éxtasis)* trance
tranquilidad nf calmness, tranquillity; **con t.** calmly; **pídemelo con toda t.** don't hesitate to ask me
tranquilizante nm tranquillizer
tranquilizar [40] 1 vt to calm down; **lo dijo para tranquilizarme** he said it to reassure me
  2 **tranquilizarse** vpr *(calmarse)* to calm down
tranquillo nm *Fig* knack; **coger el t. a algo** to get the knack of sth
tranquilo,-a adj (**a**) *(persona, lugar)* calm; *(agua)* still; *(conciencia)* clear; *Fam* **tú t.** don't you worry (**b**) *(despreocupado)* placid, easy-going

transacción nf transaction, deal
transar vi *Am Fam* (**a**) *(transigir)* to compromise, to give in (**b**) *(negociar)* to negotiate
transatlántico,-a 1 adj transatlantic
  2 nm *Náut* (ocean) liner
transbordador nm (car) ferry; **t. espacial** space shuttle
transbordar 1 vt to transfer; *Náut (mercancías)* to tranship
  2 vi *Ferroc* to change trains, *US* to transfer
transbordo nm (**a**) *Ferroc* change, *US* transfer; **hacer t.** to change, *US* to transfer (**b**) *Náut* transhipment
transcurrir vi (**a**) *(tiempo)* to pass, to go by (**b**) *(acontecer)* to take place
transcurso nm course o passing (of time); **en el t. de** in the course of, during
transeúnte nmf (**a**) *(peatón)* passer-by (**b**) *(residente temporal)* temporary resident
transferencia nf transference; *Fin* transfer; **t. bancaria** banker's order
transferible adj transferable
transferir [5] vt to transfer; *Informát* to download
transformación nf transformation
transformador nm *Elec* transformer
transformar 1 vt to transform, to change
  2 **transformarse** vpr to change, to turn (**en** into); *(algo plegable)* to convert
tránsfuga nmf (**a**) *Mil* deserter (**b**) *Pol* turncoat
transfusión nf transfusion
transgénico,-a 1 adj transgenic
  2 nmpl **transgénicos** GM foods
transgredir vt *defect* to transgress, to break
transgresor,-a nm,f transgressor, lawbreaker
transición nf transition
transido,-a adj *Fml* **t. de angustia** overcome by anxiety; **t. de dolor** racked with pain
transigente adj tolerant
transigir [57] vi to compromise
transistor nm transistor
transitable adj passable
transitado,-a adj *(carretera)* busy
transitar vi to pass
transitivo,-a adj transitive
tránsito nm (**a**) *Aut* traffic (**b**) *(movimiento)* movement, passage; **pasajeros en t.** passengers in transit
transitorio,-a adj transitory
translucirse [35] vpr = traslucirse
transmisión nf (**a**) transmission (**b**) *Téc*

drive; **t. delantera/trasera** front-/rear-wheel drive (**c**) *Rad & TV* transmission, broadcast

transmisor *nm* transmitter

transmitir *vt* (**a**) to transmit, to pass on (**b**) *Rad & TV* to transmit, to broadcast (**c**) *Jur* to transfer, to hand down

transparencia *nf* (**a**) transparency; *Pol* openness (**b**) *Fot* slide

transparentarse *vpr* to be transparent; **esta tela se transparenta** this is see-through material; **se le transparentaban las bragas** you could see her panties

transparente 1 *adj* transparent; *Pol* open **2** *nm* (**a**) *(visillo)* net curtain (**b**) *(pantalla)* shade, blind

transpiración *nf* perspiration

transpirar *vi* to perspire

transplante *nm* transplant; *Med* **t. de corazón/córnea** heart/eye transplant

transponer [19] 1 *vt* *(mudar de sitio)* to transpose, to move about **2 transponerse** *vpr* *(desmayarse)* to faint

transportar *vt* to transport; *(pasajeros)* to carry; *(mercancías)* to ship

transporte *nm* (**a**) transport (**b**) *Com* freight; **t. de mercancías** freight transport; **t. marítimo** shipment

transportista *nmf* carrier

transvase *nm* (**a**) *(de líquidos)* decanting (**b**) *(de ríos)* transfer

transversal *adj* transverse, cross

tranvía *nm Br* tram, tramcar, *US* streetcar

trapecio *nm* trapeze

trapecista *nmf* trapeze artist

trapero,-a 1 *nm Br* rag-and-bone man, *US* junkman **2** *adj* **puñalada trapera** stab in the back

trapichear *vi* to be up to something

trapicheo *nm* jiggery-pokery

trapo *nm* (**a**) *(viejo, roto)* rag (**b**) *(bayeta)* cloth; **t. de cocina** dishcloth; **t. del polvo** duster; *Fam* **poner (a algn) como un t. (sucio)** to tear (sb) apart

tráquea *nf* trachea, windpipe

traqueteo *nm* rattle, clatter

tras *prep* (**a**) *(después de)* after; **uno t. otro** one after the other (**b**) *(detrás)* behind; **sentados uno t. otro** sitting one behind the other (**c**) **andar/ir t.** to be after; **la policía iba t. ella** the police were after her

trasatlántico,-a *adj & nm* = transatlántico,-a

trasbordador *nm* = transbordador

trasbordar *vt & vi* = transbordar

trasbordo *nm* = transbordo

trascendencia *nf* (**a**) *(importancia)* importance, significance (**b**) *(en filosofía)* transcendence

trascendental, trascendente *adj* (**a**) significant, far-reaching (**b**) *(en filosofía)* transcendental

trascender [3] *vi* (**a**) *(noticia)* to become known, to leak out (**b**) *(tener consecuencias)* to have far-reaching consequences (**c**) **t. de** to go beyond

trascurrir *vi* = transcurrir

trascurso *nm* = transcurso

trasero,-a 1 *adj* back, rear; **en la parte trasera** at the back **2** *nm Euf* backside

trasferencia *nf* = transferencia

trasferible *adj* = transferible

trasferir [5] *vt* = transferir

trasfondo *nm* background

trasformación *nf* = transformación

trasformador *nm* = transformador

trasformar *vt* = transformar

trásfuga *nmf* = tránsfuga

trasfusión *nf* = transfusión

trasgredir *vt* = transgredir

trasgresor,-a *nm,f* = transgresor,-a

trashumancia *nf* = seasonal movement of livestock

trasiego *nm* comings and goings, hustle and bustle

trasladar 1 *vt* *(cosa)* to move; *(persona)* to move, to transfer **2 trasladarse** *vpr* to go, to move

traslado *nm* *(de casa)* move, removal; *(de personal)* transfer; *Educ* **t. de expediente** transfer of student record

traslucirse [35] *vpr* to show (through)

trasluz *nm* **mirar algo al t.** to hold sth against the light

trasmano *nm* **a t.** out of reach; **(me) coge a t.** it's out of my way

trasmisión *nf* = transmisión

trasmisor *nm* = transmisor

trasmitir *vt* = transmitir

trasnochado,-a *adj* *(desfasado)* old, hackneyed

trasnochador,-a 1 *adj* given to staying up late **2** *nm,f* night bird, nighthawk

trasnochar *vi* to stay up (very) late

traspapelarse *vpr* to get mislaid *o* misplaced

trasparencia *nf* = transparencia

trasparentarse *vpr* = transparentarse

trasparente *adj & nm* = transparente

traspasar *vt* (**a**) *(atravesar)* to go through; *(río)* to cross (**b**) *(negocio, local)* to transfer; **se traspasa** *(en letrero)* for sale (**c**) *Fig (exceder)* to exceed, to go beyond

> ✐ Observa que el verbo inglés **to trespass** es un falso amigo y no es la traducción del verbo español **traspasar**. En inglés, **to trespass** significa "entrar sin autorización".

traspaso *nm* (**a**) *(de propiedad etc)* transfer (**b**) *Com (venta)* sale
traspié *nm* (*pl* **traspiés**) stumble, trip; **dar un t.** to trip; *Fig* to slip up
traspiración *nf* = transpiración
traspirar *vi* = transpirar
trasplante *nm* = transplante
trasponer [19] *vt* = transponer
trasportar *vt* = transportar
trasporte *nm* = transporte
traspuesto,-a *adj* **quedarse t.** to faint
trasquilar *vt (oveja)* to shear; *(pelo)* to crop
trastabillar *vi (tambalearse)* to stagger, to totter
trastada *nf Fam* **hacer trastadas** to be up to mischief
trastazo *nm Fam* wallop, thump
traste¹ *nm Mús* fret
traste² *nm* (**a**) *(trasto)* piece of junk (**b**) *Andes, CAm, Carib, Méx* **trastes** dirty dishes; **fregar los trastes** to wash the dishes, *US* to do the washing-up (**c**) *CSur Fam (trasero)* bottom (**d**) *Fig* **dar al t. con un plan** to spoil a plan; **irse al t.** to fall through
trastear *vi (revolver)* to rummage about
trastero *nm* (**cuarto**) **t.** junk room
trastienda *nf* back shop
trasto *nm (objeto cualquiera)* thing; *(cosa inservible)* piece of junk
trastocar [44] *vt* = trastornar
trastornado,-a *adj (loco)* mad, unhinged
trastornar 1 *vt* (**a**) *(planes)* to disrupt (**b**) *Fig (persona)* to unhinge
  2 trastornarse *vpr (enloquecer)* to go out of one's mind, to go mad
trastorno *nm (molestia)* trouble, inconvenience; **t. mental** mental disorder *o* disturbance
trasvase *nm* = transvase
trasversal *adj* = transversal
trata *nf* slave trade *o* traffic; **t. de blancas** white slave trade
tratable *adj* easy to get along with, congenial
tratado *nm* (**a**) *(pacto)* treaty (**b**) *(estudio)* treatise
tratamiento *nm* (**a**) treatment (**b**) *Téc* processing, treatment (**c**) *Informát*

processing; **t. de textos** word processing
tratar 1 *vt* (**a**) *(atender)* to treat; **t. bien/mal** to treat well/badly (**b**) *Med* to treat (**c**) *(asunto)* to discuss (**d**) *Informát & Téc* to process (**e**) **me trata de tú** he addresses me as "tu"
  2 *vi* (**a**) **t. de** *(intentar)* to try (**b**) **t. de** *o* **sobre** *o* **acerca** to be about; **¿de qué trata?** what is it about? (**c**) **t. con** *(tener tratos)* to deal with; *(negociar)* to negotiate with; *(relacionarse)* to move among (**d**) *Com* **t. en** to deal in
  3 tratarse *vpr* (**a**) *(relacionarse)* to be on speaking terms (**b**) **se trata de** *(es cuestión de)* it's a question of; **se trata de un caso excepcional** it's an exceptional case
tratativas *nfpl CSur* negotiation
trato *nm* (**a**) *(de personas)* manner; *(contacto)* contact; **malos tratos** ill-treatment (**b**) *(acuerdo)* agreement; **¡t. hecho!** it's a deal! (**c**) *Com* deal
trauma *nm* trauma
traumático,-a *adj* traumatic
traumatizar *vt Med* to traumatize; *Fam* to shock
través 1 *prep* (**a**) **a t. de** *(superficie)* across, over; *(agujero etc)* through; **a t. del río** across the river; **a t. del agujero** through the hole (**b**) *Fig* **a t. de** through; **a t. del periódico** through the newspaper
  2 *adv* **de t.** *(transversalmente)* crosswise; *(de lado)* sideways
  3 *nm* (*pl* **traveses**) *Fig (desgracia)* misfortune
travesaño *nm Ftb* crossbar
travesía *nf (viaje)* crossing
travesti, travestí *nmf* transvestite

> ✐ Observa que la palabra inglesa **travesty** es un falso amigo y no es la traducción de la palabra española **travesti**. En inglés, **travesty** significa "parodia burda".

travesura *nf* mischief, childish prank
travieso,-a *adj* mischievous
trayecto *nm* (**a**) *(distancia)* distance; *(recorrido)* route; *(trecho)* stretch (**b**) *(viaje)* journey
trayectoria *nf* (**a**) *(de proyectil, geométrica)* trajectory (**b**) *Fig (orientación)* line, course
traza *nf* (**a**) *(apariencia)* looks, appearance; **no lleva trazas de curarse** it doesn't look as if he's going to get better (**b**) *Arquit* plan, design
trazado *nm* (**a**) *(plano)* layout, plan (**b**) *(de carretera, ferrocarril)* route
trazar [40] *vt (línea)* to draw; *(plano)* to design; *Fig (plan)* to sketch out

trazo *nm* (**a**) *(línea)* line (**b**) *(de letra)* stroke

trébol *nm* (**a**) trefoil (**b**) *Naipes* club

trece 1 *adj inv* thirteen

  2 *nm inv* thirteen; *Fig* **estar** *o* **mantenerse** *o* **seguir en sus t.** to stick to one's guns

trecho *nm* distance, way; *(tramo)* stretch; **de t. en t.** from time to time

tregua *nf Mil* truce; *Fig* respite

treinta *adj & nm inv* thirty

treintavo,-a *adj & nm* thirtieth

treintena *nf* **una t. de** (about) thirty

tremendista *adj* over the top

tremendo,-a *adj* (**a**) *(terrible)* terrible, dreadful (**b**) *(muy grande)* enormous; *Fig* tremendous

trementina *nf* turpentine

trémulo,-a *adj Literario (vacilante)* quivering, tremulous; *(luz)* flickering

tren *nm* (**a**) train (**b**) *Av* **t. de aterrizaje** undercarriage; **t. de lavado** car wash (**c**) **t. de vida** lifestyle

trenca *nf* duffle coat

trenza *nf (de pelo)* plait, *esp US* braid

trepador,-a *adj* climbing

trepar *vt & vi* to climb

trepidante *adj* vibrating, shaking; *Fig* **lleva un ritmo de vida t.** he leads a hectic *o* frantic life

trepidar *vi* to vibrate, to shake

tres 1 *adj inv (cardinal)* three; *(ordinal)* third; *Fam* **de t. al cuarto** cheap, of little value

  2 *nm (pl* **treses***)* three; **t. en raya** *Br* noughts and crosses, *US* tick-tack-toe

trescientos,-as *adj & nm* three hundred

tresillo *nm* (**a**) *(mueble)* (three-piece) suite (**b**) *Mús* triplet

treta *nf* trick, ruse

triángulo *nm* triangle; *Fig* **t. amoroso** eternal triangle

tribal *adj* tribal

tribu *nf* tribe

tribuna *nf* (**a**) *(plataforma)* rostrum, dais; **t. de (la) prensa** press box (**b**) *Dep* stand

tribunal *nm* (**a**) *Jur* court; **t. de apelación** court of appeal; **T. Supremo** *Br* High Court, *US* Supreme Court; **t. (tutelar) de menores** juvenile court (**b**) *(de examen)* board of examiners

tributar *vt* to pay

tributario,-a *adj* **sistema t.** tax system

tributo *nm* (**a**) *Com* tax (**b**) **pagar t. a** *(homenaje)* to pay tribute to

triciclo *nm* tricycle

tricornio *nm* three-cornered hat

tridimensional *adj* three-dimensional

trienio *nm* three-year period

trifásico,-a 1 *adj Elec* three-phase

  2 *nm* adapter

trigésimo,-a *adj & nm,f* thirtieth; **t. primero** thirty-first

trigo *nm* wheat

trigueño,-a *adj Am (pelo)* dark brown; *(persona)* olive-skinned

trilla *nf* threshing

trillado,-a *adj Fig* well-worn

trilladora *nf* threshing machine; **t. segadora** combine harvester

trillar *vt* to thresh

trilogía *nf* trilogy

trimestral *adj* quarterly, three-monthly

trimestre *nm* quarter; *Educ* term

trinar *vi* (**a**) to warble (**b**) *Fam* to rage, to fume; **Santiago está que trina** Santiago is really fuming

trincar¹ **[44]** *vt Fam (capturar)* to catch

trincar² *vt Fam* to drink

trinchar *vt (carne)* to carve, to slice (up)

trinchera *nf* trench

trineo *nm* sledge, sleigh

Trinidad *nf* **la Santísima T.** the Holy Trinity

trino *nm* (**a**) warble, trill (**b**) *Mús* trill

trío *nm* trio

tripa *nf* (**a**) *(intestino)* gut, intestine; *Fam* tummy; **dolor de t.** stomach ache (**b**) **tripas** innards

triple *adj & nm* triple

triplicado,-a *adj* triplicate; **por t.** in triplicate

triplicar [44] *vt* to triple, to treble

trípode *nm* tripod

tríptico *nm* (**a**) *(cuadro)* triptych (**b**) *(folleto)* leaflet

tripulación *nf* crew

tripulante *nmf* crew member

tripular *vt* to man

triquiñuela *nf Fam* trick, dodge

tris *nm* **estar en un t. de** to be on the verge of

triste *adj* (**a**) *(persona, situación)* sad (**b**) *(lugar)* gloomy

tristeza *nf* sadness

triturar *vt (machacar)* to grind (up)

triunfador,-a 1 *adj* winning

  2 *nm,f* winner

triunfal *adj* triumphant

triunfar *vi* to triumph

triunfo *nm* (**a**) *(victoria)* triumph, victory; *Dep* win (**b**) *(éxito)* success

trivial *adj* trivial

trivialidad *nf* triviality

trivializar *vt* to trivialize, to minimize

triza *nf* bit, fragment; **hacer trizas** to tear to shreds

trocar [64] *vt* to barter

trocear *vt* to cut up (into bits o pieces)

trochemoche: •**a trochemoche** *loc adv Fam* haphazardly

trofeo *nm* trophy

trola *nf Fam* fib

trolebús *nm* trolleybus

tromba *nf* **t. de agua** violent downpour

trombón *nm* trombone

trombosis *nf inv* thrombosis

trompa *nf* (**a**) *Mús* horn (**b**) *(de elefante)* trunk (**c**) *Anat* tube (**d**) *Fam* **estar t.** to be sloshed o plastered

trompazo *nm Fam* bump; **darse** o **pegarse un t.** to have a bump

trompeta *nf* trumpet

trompetista *nmf* trumpet player, trumpeter

trompicón *nm* trip, stumble; **hacer algo a trompicones** to do sth in fits and starts

trompo *nm* spinning top

tronar [2] 1 *vi* to thunder

2 *vt Méx Fam* (**a**) *(destruir, acabar con)* to destroy; **este remedio es para t. anginas** this remedy will clear up tonsillitis (**b**) *(reprobar)* to fail

tronchar 1 *vt (rama, tronco)* to cut down, to fell; *Fig (esperanzas etc)* to destroy

2 troncharse *vpr* **t. de risa** to split one's sides with laughter

troncho *nm* stem, stalk

tronco *nm* (**a**) *Anat* trunk, torso (**b**) *Bot (de árbol)* trunk; *(leño)* log; *Fam Fig* **dormir como un t.** to sleep like a log

tronera *nf* (**a**) *(de billar)* pocket (**b**) *(ventana)* small window; *(de fortificación)* loophole; *Náut* porthole

trono *nm* throne

tropa *nf* (**a**) squad (**b**) **tropas** troops

tropel *nm* throng, mob; **en t.** in a mad rush

tropezar [1] *vi* (**a**) to trip, to stumble (**con** on) (**b**) **t. con algo** to come across sth; **t. con algn/dificultades** to run into sb/difficulties

tropezón *nm* (**a**) *(traspié)* trip, stumble; **dar un t.** to trip (**b**) *(error)* slip-up, faux pas (**c**) *(de comida)* chunk of meat

tropical *adj* tropical

trópico *nm* tropic

tropiezo 1 *nm* (**a**) *(obstáculo)* trip (**b**) *Fig (error)* blunder, faux pas

2 *indic pres de* **tropezar**

trotamundos *nmf inv* globetrotter

trotar *vi* to trot

trote *nm* (**a**) trot; **al t.** at a trot (**b**) *Fam* **ya no está para esos trotes** he cannot keep up the pace any more

trovador *nm* troubadour

trozar *vt Am (carne)* to cut up; *(res, tronco)* to butcher, to cut up

trozo *nm* piece

trucar [44] *vt* to doctor, to alter

trucha *nf* trout

truco *nm* (**a**) *(ardid)* trick; **aquí hay t.** there's something fishy going on here (**b**) **coger el t. (a algo)** to get the knack o hang (of sth)

truculento,-a *adj* horrifying, terrifying

⚠️ Observa que la palabra inglesa **truculent** es un falso amigo y no es la traducción de la palabra española **truculento**. En inglés, **truculent** significa "agresivo, airado".

trueno *nm* thunder; **un t.** a thunderclap

trueque *nm* barter

trufa *nf* truffle

truhán,-ana *nm,f* rogue, crook

truncar [44] *vt* to truncate; *Fig (vida etc)* to cut short; *Fig (esperanzas)* to shatter

trusa *nf Méx (calzoncillo)* underpants; *(braga)* panties, *Br* knickers

trust *nm (pl* **trusts***)* trust, cartel

tu *adj pos* your; **tu libro** your book; **tus libros** your books

tú *pron* you; **de tú a tú** on equal terms

Usually omitted in Spanish except for emphasis or contrast.

tuba *nf* tuba

tubérculo *nm* (**a**) *Bot* tuber (**b**) *Med* tubercle

tuberculosis *nf inv* tuberculosis

tubería *nf* (**a**) *(de agua)* piping, pipes (**b**) *(de gas)* pipeline

tubo *nm* (**a**) tube; **t. de ensayo** test tube (**b**) *(tubería)* pipe; *Aut* **t. de escape** exhaust (pipe)

tucán *nm* toucan

tuerca *nf* nut

tuerto,-a 1 *adj* one-eyed, blind in one eye

2 *nm,f* one-eyed person

tuerzo *indic pres de* **torcer**

tuétano *nm* marrow; **hasta el t.** to one's fingertips

tufo *nm* foul odour o smell

tugurio *nm* hovel

tul *nm* tulle

tulipa *nf* small tulip

tulipán *nm* tulip

tullido,-a *adj* crippled, disabled

tullir *vt* to cripple

tumba *nf* grave, tomb

tumbar 1 *vt* to knock down o over

2 tumbarse *vpr (acostarse)* to lie down, to stretch out

tumbo *nm* **dar tumbos** to reel
tumbona *nf Br* sun-lounger, *US* beach recliner
tumor *nm* tumour
tumulto *nm* tumult, commotion
tumultuoso,-a *adj* tumultuous, riotous
tuna *nf* (**a**) *(agrupación musical)* = group of student minstrels (**b**) *Am (higo chumbo)* prickly pear

> 🖉 Observa que la palabra inglesa **tuna** es un falso amigo y no es la traducción de la palabra española **tuna**. En inglés, **tuna** significa "atún, bonito".

tunante,-a *nm,f* rogue, crook
túnel *nm* tunnel; **el t. del Canal de la Mancha** the Channel Tunnel
Túnez *n* (**a**) *(país)* Tunisia (**b**) *(ciudad)* Tunis
túnica *nf* tunic
tuno,-a 1 *nm,f (bribón)* rogue, crook
 2 *nm* = member of a "tuna"
tuntún: • **al tuntún** *loc adv* haphazardly, any old how
tupé *nm* *(pl* **tupés**) *(flequillo)* quiff
tupido,-a *adj* thick, dense
turba¹ *nf (combustible)* peat
turba² *nf (muchedumbre)* mob, crowd
turbado,-a *adj* (**a**) *(alterado)* disturbed (**b**) *(preocupado)* worried, anxious (**c**) *(desconcertado)* confused
turbante *nm* turban
turbar 1 *vt* (**a**) *(alterar)* to unsettle (**b**) *(preocupar)* to upset o worry (**c**) *(desconcertar)* to baffle, to put off
 2 turbarse *vpr* (**a**) *(preocuparse)* to be o become upset (**b**) *(desconcertarse)* to be o become confused o baffled
turbina *nf* turbine
turbio,-a *adj (agua)* cloudy; *(negocio etc)* shady, dubious

turborreactor *nm* turbojet (engine)
turbulencia *nf* turbulence
turbulento,-a *adj* turbulent
turco,-a 1 *adj* Turkish
 2 *nm,f (persona)* Turk; *Fig* **cabeza de t.** scapegoat
 3 *nm (idioma)* Turkish
turismo *nm* (**a**) tourism; **ir de t.** to go touring; **t. rural** rural tourism (**b**) *Aut* car
turista *nmf* tourist
turístico,-a *adj* tourist; **de interés t.** of interest to tourists
turnarse *vpr* to take turns
turno *nm* (**a**) *(en juegos etc)* turn, go (**b**) *(de trabajo)* shift; **estar de t.** to be on duty; **t. de día/noche** day/night shift
turquesa *adj inv & nf* turquoise
Turquía *n* Turkey
turrón *nm* nougat
tute *nm Fam* **darse un t. de algo** to go to town doing sth
tutear 1 *vt* = to address as "tú"
 2 tutearse *vpr* = to address each other as "tú"
tutela *nf* (**a**) *Jur* guardianship, tutelage (**b**) *Fig (protección)* protection, guidance
tuteo *nm* = use of the "tú" form of address
tutor *nm* (**a**) *Jur* guardian (**b**) *Educ* tutor
tuve *pt indef de* **tener**
tuyo,-a 1 *adj pos (con personas)* of yours; *(con objetos)* one of your; **¿es amigo t.?** is he a friend of yours?; **unas amigas tuyas** some friends of yours; **un libro t.** one of your books
 2 *pron pos* yours; **éste es t.** this one is yours; *Fam* **los tuyos** *(familiares)* your family
TV *nf (abr* **televisión**) TV
TVE *nf (abr* **Televisión Española**) = Spanish state television network

U, u [u] *nf (la letra)* U, u

u *conj (delante de palabras que empiecen por* **o** *o* **ho**) or; **siete u ocho** seven or eight; **ayer u hoy** yesterday or today

ubicación *nf* location, position

ubicar [44] 1 *vt Am (situar)* to locate, to situate

2 ubicarse *vpr* to be situated *o* located

ubicuo,-a *adj* ubiquitous

ubre *nf* udder

Ucrania *n* Ukraine

ucraniano,-a *adj & nm,f* Ukrainian

Ud. (*abr* **usted**) you

Uds. (*abr* **ustedes**) you

UE *nf* (*abr* **Unión Europea**) EU

UEM *nf* (*abr* **unión económica y monetaria**) EMU

ufanarse *vpr* to boast (**de** of)

ufano,-a *adj* conceited

ugetista *adj* = relating to the UGT

UGT *nf* (*abr* **Unión General de los Trabajadores**) = major socialist trade union in Spain

ujier *nm* usher

úlcera *nf* ulcer

ulcerar *vt*, **ulcerarse** *vpr* to ulcerate

ulterior *adj (siguiente)* subsequent

últimamente *adv* lately, recently

ultimar *vt* (**a**) *(terminar)* to finalize (**b**) *Am (matar)* to kill, to finish off

ultimátum *nm* (*pl* **ultimátums**) ultimatum

último,-a 1 *adj* (**a**) last; **el ú. día** the last day; **por ú.** finally (**b**) *(más reciente)* latest; **últimas noticias** latest news (**c**) *(más alto)* top; **el ú. piso** the top flat (**d**) *(más bajo)* lowest (**e**) *(más lejano)* back, last; **la última fila** the back row (**f**) *(definitivo)* final

2 *nm,f* **llegar el ú.** to arrive last; **a últimos de mes** at the end of the month; **en las últimas** on one's last legs; *Fam* **a la última** up to the minute; **el ú. de la lista** the lowest in the list

ultra *nmf* extreme right-winger; **los ultras** the extreme right

ultra- *pref* ultra-

ultraderecha *nf Pol* extreme right

ultraderechista *Pol* **1** *adj* extreme right-wing

2 *nmf* extreme right-winger

ultraizquierda *nf* extreme left

ultrajar *vt* to outrage, to offend

ultraje *nm* outrage, offence

ultramar *nm* overseas (countries), abroad; **del** *o* **en u.** overseas

ultramarinos *nmpl* groceries; **tienda de u.** greengrocer's (shop)

ultranza: • **a ultranza** *loc adv* (**a**) *(a todo trance)* at all costs, at any price; **defender algo a u.** to defend sth to the death (**b**) *(acérrimo)* out-and-out, extreme

ultrasónico,-a *adj* ultrasonic

ultratumba *nf* afterlife

ultravioleta *adj inv* ultraviolet

ulular *vi (viento)* to howl; *(búho)* to hoot

umbral *nm* threshold

umbrío,-a, umbroso,-a *adj* shady

un, una 1 *art indet* (**a**) a; *(antes de vocal)* an; **un coche** a car; **un huevo** an egg; **una flor** a flower (**b**) **unos,-as** some; **unas flores** some flowers

2 *adj (delante de nm sing)* one; **un chico y dos chicas** one boy and two girls; *ver también* **uno,-a**

unánime *adj* unanimous

unanimidad *nf* unanimity; **por u.** unanimously

unción *nf* unction

undécimo,-a *adj* eleventh

UNED *nf* (*abr* **Universidad Nacional de Educación a Distancia**) = Spanish open university

ungir [57] *vt Rel* to anoint

ungüento *nm* ointment

únicamente *adv* only, solely

único,-a *adj* (**a**) *(solo)* only; **es el ú. que tengo** it's the only one I've got; **hijo ú.** only child; **lo ú. que quiero** the only thing I want; **el Mercado Ú.** the Single Market; **el Acta Única** the Single European Act (**b**) *(extraordinario)* unique

unidad *nf* (**a**) unit (**b**) *(cohesión)* unity

unido,-a *adj* united; **están muy unidos** they are very attached to one another; **una familia muy unida** a very close family

unifamiliar *adj* **vivienda u.** detached house

unificación *nf* unification

unificar [44] *vt* to unify
uniformar *vt* (**a**) *(igualar)* to make uniform, to standardize (**b**) *(poner un uniforme a)* to put into uniform, to give a uniform to
uniforme 1 *nm (prenda)* uniform
  2 *adj* (**a**) *(igual)* uniform (**b**) *(superficie)* even
uniformidad *nf* (**a**) *(igualdad)* uniformity (**b**) *(de superficie)* evenness
unilateral *adj* unilateral
unión *nf* union
Unión Soviética *n* Soviet Union
unir 1 *vt* (*juntar*) to unite, to join (together); **esta carretera une las dos comarcas** this road links both districts
  2 unirse *vpr* (*juntarse*) to unite, to join
unisex *adj inv* unisex
unísono *nm* unison; **al u.** in unison
unitario,-a *adj* unitary; **precio u.** unit price
universal *adj* universal; **historia u.** world history
universidad *nf* university; **u. a distancia** ≃ Open University; **u. laboral** technical college
universitario,-a 1 *adj* university
  2 *nm,f* university student
universo *nm* universe
uno,-a 1 *nm inv* one; **el u.** (number) one; **el u. de mayo** the first of May
  2 *nf* **es la una** *(hora)* it's one o'clock
  3 *adj* **unos,-as** some; **unas cajas** some boxes; **habrá unos** *o* **unas veinte** there must be around twenty
  4 *pron* (**a**) one; **u. (de ellos), una (de ellas)** one of them; **unos cuantos** a few; **se miraron el u. al otro** they looked at each other; **de u. en u.** one by one; **un trás otro** one after the other; **una de dos** one of the two
  (**b**) *(persona)* someone, somebody; **u. que pasaba por allí** some passer-by; **vive con u.** she's living with some man; **unos ... otros** some people ... others
  (**c**) *(impers)* you, one; **u. tiene que ...** you have to ...
untar *vt* to grease, to smear; *(mantequilla)* to spread
untura *nf* ointment
uña *nf* (**a**) nail; **morderse** *o* **comerse las uñas** to bite one's fingernails; *Fig* **ser u. y carne** to be hand in glove (**b**) *Zool (garra)* claw; *(pezuña)* hoof
uperizado,-a *adj* **leche uperizada** UHT milk
Urales *nmpl* **los U.** the Urals
uranio *nm* uranium

Urano *nm* Uranus
urbanidad *nf* urbanity, politeness
urbanismo *nm* town planning
urbanístico,-a *adj* town-planning
urbanización *nf* (**a**) *(barrio)* housing development *o* estate (**b**) *(proceso)* urbanization
urbanizar *vt* to build up
urbano,-a *adj* urban, city; **guardia u.** (traffic) policeman
urbe *nf* large city
urdimbre *nf* (**a**) *Tex* warp (**b**) *(trama)* intrigue
urdir *vt* (**a**) *Tex* to warp (**b**) *(tramar)* to plot, to scheme
urgencia *nf* (**a**) urgency (**b**) *(emergencia)* emergency
urgente *adj* urgent; **correo u.** express mail
urgir [57] *vi* to be urgent *o* pressing; **me urge (tenerlo)** I need it urgently
urinario *nm* urinal
urna *nf* (**a**) *Pol* ballot box (**b**) *(vasija)* urn
urólogo,-a *nm,f Med* urologist
urraca *nf* magpie
URSS *nf Hist* (*abr* **Unión de Repúblicas Socialistas Soviéticas**) USSR
urticaria *nf Med* hives
Uruguay *n* Uruguay
uruguayo,-a *adj* & *nm,f* Uruguayan
usado,-a *adj (ropa)* second-hand, used
usanza *nf Literario* **a la antigua u.** in the old style
usar 1 *vt* (**a**) to use (**b**) *(prenda)* to wear
  2 usarse *vpr* to be used *o* in fashion
usina *nf Am (central eléctrica)* power station; **u. nuclear** nuclear power station
uso *nm* (**a**) use; *Farm* **u. externo/tópico** external/local application (**b**) *(de poder, privilegio)* exercise (**c**) *(de prenda)* wearing; **haga u. del casco** wear a helmet (**d**) *(costumbre)* usage, custom; **al u.** conventional
usted *(pl* **ustedes**) *pron pers Fml* you; **¿quién es u.?, ¿quiénes son ustedes?** who are you?

> Usually omitted in Spanish except for emphasis or contrast. Although formal in peninsular Spanish, it is not necessarily so in Latin American Spanish.

usual *adj* usual, common
usuario,-a *nm,f* user
usura *nf* usury
usurero,-a *nm,f* usurer
usurpar *vt* to usurp
utensilio *nm* utensil; *(herramienta)* tool
útero *nm* uterus, womb

útil 1 *adj* useful; *(día)* working
  2 *nm (herramienta)* tool, instrument
utilidad *nf* usefulness, utility; *(beneficio)* profit
utilitario,-a 1 *nm (coche)* utility vehicle
  2 *adj* utilitarian
utilización *nf* use, utilization

utilizar [40] *vt* to use, to utilize
utopía *nf* utopia
utópico,-a *adj & nm,f* utopian
uva *nf* grape; **u. blanca** green grape
UVI *nf* (*abr* **unidad de vigilancia intensiva**) ICU
úvula *nf* uvula

V, v [ˈue] *nf (la letra)* V, v

V *Elec (abr* **voltio(s)**) V

vaca *nf* (**a**) cow (**b**) *(carne)* beef

vacaciones *nfpl Br* holidays, *US* vacation; *(viaje)* holiday; **durante las v.** during the holidays; **estar/irse de v.** to be/go on holiday

vacacionista *nmf Am Br* holidaymaker, *US* vacationer

vacante 1 *adj* vacant
   2 *nf* vacancy

vaciar [29] 1 *vt* (**a**) *(recipiente)* to empty; *(contenido)* to empty out (**b**) *(terreno)* to hollow out (**c**) *Arte* to cast, to mould
   2 vaciarse *upr* to empty

vacilación *nf* hesitation

vacilante *adj (persona)* hesitant, irresolute (**b**) *(voz)* hesitant, faltering (**c**) *(luz)* flickering

vacilar *vi* (**a**) *(dudar)* to hesitate; **sin v.** without hesitation (**b**) *(voz)* to falter (**c**) *(luz)* to flicker (**d**) *Fam (jactarse)* to show off

vacilón,-ona *Fam* **1** *adj* (**a**) *(fanfarrón)* swanky (**b**) *(bromista)* jokey, teasing (**c**) *CAm, Méx Fam (juerguista)* fond of partying
   2 *nm,f* (**a**) *(fanfarrón)* show-off (**b**) *(bromista)* tease
   3 *nm Carib (fiesta)* party

vacío,-a 1 *adj* (**a**) empty; *(hueco)* hollow (**b**) *(sin ocupar)* vacant, unoccupied
   2 *nm* (**a**) emptiness, void (**b**) *(hueco)* gap; *(espacio)* (empty) space (**c**) *Fís* vacuum; **envasado al v.** vacuum-packed

vacuna *nf* vaccine

vacunación *nf* vaccination

vacunar **1** *vt* to vaccinate (**contra** against); *Fig* to inure
   2 vacunarse *upr* to get oneself vaccinated

vacuno,-a *adj* bovine; **ganado v.** cattle

vacuo,-a *adj* vacuous, empty

vadear *vt (río)* to ford; *Fig (dificultad)* to overcome

vado *nm* (**a**) *(de un río)* ford (**b**) *Aut* **v. permanente** *(en letrero)* keep clear

vagabundear *vi* to wander, to roam

vagabundo,-a 1 *adj (errante)* wandering; *Pey* vagrant; **perro v.** stray dog
   2 *nm,f* wanderer; *(sin casa)* tramp, *US* hobo; *Pey* vagrant, tramp

vagancia *nf* idleness, laziness

vagar [42] *vi* to wander about, to roam about

vagido *nm* cry *(of a newborn baby)*

vagina *nf* vagina

vago,-a 1 *adj* (**a**) *(perezoso)* lazy (**b**) *(indefinido)* vague
   2 *nm,f* (**a**) *(holgazán)* layabout (**b**) *Jur* vagrant

vagón *nm (para pasajeros)* carriage, coach, *US* car; *(para mercancías)* truck, wagon, *US* freight car, *US* boxcar

vaguedad *nf* vagueness

vaho *nm (de aliento)* breath; *(vapor)* vapour

vaina 1 *nf* (**a**) *(de espada)* sheath, scabbard (**b**) *Bot* pod (**c**) *Col, Perú, Ven muy Fam (molestia)* bother, pain (in the neck); **¡qué v.!** what a pain!
   2 *nmf (persona)* dimwit

vainilla *nf* vanilla

vaivén *nm* (**a**) *(oscilación)* swinging, to-and-fro movement (**b**) *(de gente)* coming and going, bustle; *Fig* **vaivenes** ups and downs

vajilla *nf* crockery, dishes; **una v.** a set of dishes, a dinner service

valdré *indic fut de* **valer**

vale¹ *interj* all right!, O.K.!

vale² *nm* (**a**) *(comprobante)* voucher (**b**) *(pagaré)* promissory note, IOU (**c**) *Méx, Ven Fam (amigo)* pal, *Br* mate, *US* buddy

valedero,-a *adj* valid

valenciano,-a *adj* Valencian

valentía *nf* courage, bravery

valentón,-ona *Pey* **1** *adj* bragging, boastful
   2 *nm,f* braggart

valer [26] 1 *vt* (**a**) to be worth; **no vale nada** it is worthless; **vale una fortuna** it is worth a fortune; **no vale la pena (ir)** it's not worth while (going) (**b**) *(costar)* to cost; **¿cuánto vale?** how much is it? (**c**) *(proporcionar)* to earn
   2 *vi* (**a**) *(servir)* to be useful, to be of use (**b**) *(ser válido)* to be valid, to count; **no**

vale hacer trampa cheating isn't on (**c**) **más vale** it is better; **más vale que te vayas ya** you had better leave now
   3 valerse *vpr* **v. de** to use, to make use of; **v. por sí mismo** to be able to manage on one's own
valeroso,-a *adj* brave, courageous
valgo *indic pres de* **valer**
valía *nf* value, worth
validez *nf* validity
válido,-a *adj* valid
valiente *adj* (**a**) *(valeroso)* brave, courageous (**b**) *Irón* ¡**v. amigo eres tú!** a fine friend you are!
valija *nf* (**a**) *(maleta)* case, suitcase; **v. diplomática** diplomatic bag (**b**) *(de correos)* mailbag
valioso,-a *adj* valuable
valla *nf* (**a**) *(cerca)* fence; *(muro)* wall; **v. publicitaria** billboard, *Br* hoarding (**b**) *Dep* hurdle; **los 100 metros vallas** the 100 metres hurdle race
vallado *nm* fence
vallar *vt* to fence (in)
valle *nm* valley
vallisoletano,-a 1 *adj* of/from Valladolid
   2 *nm,f* person from Valladolid
valor *nm* (**a**) *(valía)* value, worth; *(precio)* price; **objetos de v.** valuables; **sin v.** worthless; **v. alimenticio** food value (**b**) *(valentía)* courage (**c**) *Fin* **valores** securities, bonds
valoración *nf* valuation
valorar *vt* to value, to calculate the value of
valorización *nf* (**a**) *(tasación)* valuation (**b**) *(revalorización)* appreciation
valorizar [40] *vt* (**a**) *(tasar)* to value (**b**) *(revalorizar)* to raise the value of
vals *nm* waltz; **bailar el v.** to waltz
válvula *nf* valve; **v. de seguridad** safety valve
vampiro *nm* vampire
vanagloriarse [43] *vpr* to boast (**de** of)
vandalismo *nm* vandalism
vándalo,-a *nm,f* vandal
vanguardia *nf* (**a**) avant-garde, vanguard; *Fig* **ir a la v. de** to be at the forefront of (**b**) *Mil* vanguard, van
vanguardista 1 *adj* avant-garde
   2 *nmf* avant-gardist
vanidad *nf* vanity
vanidoso,-a *adj* vain, conceited
vano,-a *adj* (**a**) *(vanidoso)* vain, conceited (**b**) *(esfuerzo, esperanza)* vain, futile; **en v.** in vain
vapor *nm* (**a**) *(de agua hirviendo)* steam;

Culin **al v.** steamed (**b**) *(gas)* vapour; **v. de agua** water vapour
vaporizador *nm* vaporizer, spray
vaporizar [40] 1 *vt* to vaporize
   2 vaporizarse *vpr* to vaporize, to evaporate
vaporoso,-a *adj* vaporous
vapulear *vt* *(físicamente)* to shake; *(con palabras)* to slate
vaqueriza *nf* cowshed
vaquero,-a 1 *nm* cowherd, cowboy
   2 *adj* **pantalón v.** jeans, pair of jeans
   3 *nmpl* **vaqueros** *(prenda)* jeans, pair of jeans
vara *nf* pole, rod
varar 1 *vt* to beach, to dock
   2 *vi* to run aground
variable *adj & nf* variable
variación *nf* variation
variado,-a *adj* varied; **galletas variadas** assorted *Br* biscuits *o US* cookies
variante *nf* variant; *Aut* detour
variar [29] 1 *vt* to vary, to change
   2 *vi* to vary, to change; *Irón* **para v.** as usual, just for a change
varice, várice *nf* = **variz**
varicela *nf* chickenpox
variedad *nf* (**a**) variety (**b**) *Teatro* **variedades** variety show
varilla *nf* *(vara)* rod, stick; *(de abanico, paraguas)* rib
variopinto,-a *adj* diverse, assorted; **un público v.** a varied audience
varios,-as *adj* several
varita *nf* **v. mágica** magic wand
variz *nf* varicose vein
varón *nm* *(hombre)* man; *(chico)* boy; **hijo v.** male child; **sexo v.** male sex
varonil *adj* manly, virile
Varsovia *n* Warsaw
vas *indic pres de* **ir**
vasallo,-a *nm,f* *Hist* vassal
vasco,-a *adj* Basque; **el País V.** the Basque Country
vascuence *nm* *(idioma)* Basque
vasectomía *nf* vasectomy
vaselina *nf* Vaseline®
vasija *nf* pot
vaso *nm* (**a**) *(para beber)* glass (**b**) *Anat* vessel

   ✐ Observa que la palabra inglesa **vase** es un falso amigo y no es la traducción de la palabra española **vaso**. En inglés, **vase** significa "jarrón".

vástago *nm* (**a**) *Bot* shoot (**b**) *Fig (hilo)* offspring (**c**) *Téc* rod, stem
vasto,-a *adj* vast

Vaticano *nm* el V. the Vatican
vaticinar *vt* to prophesy, to predict
vaticinio *nm* prophecy, prediction
vatio *nm* watt
vaya¹ *interj* ¡v. lío! what a mess!
vaya² *subj pres de* ir
Vd., Vds. (*abr* **usted, ustedes**) you
ve 1 *imperat de* ir
　2 *indic pres de* **ver**
vecinal *adj* local
vecindad *nf,* **vecindario** *nm* (**a**) (*área*) neighbourhood, vicinity (**b**) (*vecinos*) community, residents (**c**) *Méx (inquilinato)* tenement house
vecino,-a 1 *nm,f* (**a**) (*persona*) neighbour; **el v. de al lado** the next-door neighbour (**b**) (*residente*) resident
　2 *adj* neighbouring, nearby
veda *nf (de caza)* closed season; **levantar la v.** to open the season
vedado,-a *adj* **coto v. de caza** private hunting ground
vedar *vt* to forbid, to prohibit
vega *nf* fertile plain *o* lowland
vegetación *nf* (**a**) *Bot* vegetation (**b**) *Med* **vegetaciones** adenoids
vegetal *nm* vegetable
vegetar *vi Fig* to vegetate
vegetariano,-a *adj & nm,f* vegetarian
vehemencia *nf* vehemence
vehemente *adj* vehement
vehículo *nm* vehicle
veinte *adj & nm inv* twenty
veintena *nf (veinte)* twenty; **una v. de** about twenty
vejación *nf* humiliation
vejar *vt* to humiliate
vejatorio,-a *adj* humiliating
vejez *nf* old age
vejiga *nf* bladder
vela¹ *nf* (**a**) candle (**b**) *Fam* **quedarse a dos velas** to be in the dark (**c**) **pasar la noche en v.** to have a sleepless night
vela² *nf Náut* sail
velada *nf* evening (party)
velado,-a *adj* (**a**) (*oculto*) veiled, hidden (**b**) *Fot* blurred
velador 1 *nm* (**a**) (*mesa*) table (**b**) *Andes, Méx (mesilla de noche)* bedside table (**c**) *Méx, RP (lámpara)* bedside lamp
　2 *nm Méx (sereno)* nightwatchman
velar¹ *vi* (**a**) **v. por** to watch over (**b**) (*hacer guardia*) to keep watch
velar² *Fot* **1** *vt* to blur
　2 velarse *vpr* to become blurred
velatorio *nm* vigil, wake
veleidad *nf* fickleness
veleidoso,-a *adj* fickle

velero *nm* sailing boat *o* ship
veleta 1 *nf* weather vane, weathercock
　2 *nmf Fam* fickle *o* changeable person
veliz *nf Méx* suitcase, case
vello *nm* hair
vellón *nm* fleece
velloso,-a, velludo,-a *adj* downy
velo *nm* veil
velocidad *nf* (**a**) (*rapidez*) speed; (*de proyectil etc*) velocity; *Aut* **v. máxima** speed limit; *Informát* **v. de transmisión** bit rate; *Informát* **v. operativa** operating speed (**b**) *Aut (marcha)* gear
velocímetro *nm* speedometer
velocista *nmf* sprinter
velódromo *nm* cycle track, velodrome
veloz 1 *adj* swift, rapid
　2 *adv* quickly, fast
vena *nf* vein
venado *nm* deer, stag; *Culin* venison
vencedor,-a 1 *nm,f* winner
　2 *adj* winning
vencejo *nm Orn* swift
vencer [49] 1 *vt* (**a**) (*al enemigo*) to defeat; (*al contrincante*) to beat (**b**) (*dificultad*) to overcome, to surmount
　2 *vi* (**a**) (*pago, deuda*) to fall due, to be payable (**b**) (*plazo*) to expire
　3 vencerse *vpr (torcerse)* to warp
vencido,-a *adj* (**a**) *Mil (derrotado)* defeated; *Dep* beaten; *Fig* **darse por v.** to give up, to accept defeat (**b**) (*pago, deuda*) due, payable (**c**) (*plazo*) expired (**d**) *Fam* **a la tercera va la vencida** third time lucky
vencimiento *nm* (**a**) *Com* maturity (**b**) (*de un plazo*) expiry
venda *nf* bandage
vendaje *nm* dressing
vendar *vt* to bandage; *Fig* **v. los ojos a algn** to blindfold sb
vendaval *nm* gale
vendedor,-a *nm,f* seller; (*hombre*) salesman; (*mujer*) saleswoman
vender 1 *vt* to sell; **v. a plazos/al contado** to sell on credit/for cash; **v. al por mayor/menor** to (sell) wholesale/retail
　2 venderse *vpr* (**a**) to sell; **este disco se vende bien** this record is selling well; **se vende** (*en letrero*) for sale (**b**) (*claudicar*) to sell out
vendimia *nf* grape harvest
vendré *indic fut de* venir
Venecia *n* Venice
veneno *nm* poison; (*de serpiente*) venom
venenoso,-a *adj* poisonous
venerable *adj* venerable
veneración *nf* veneration
venerar *vt* to venerate, to revere

venéreo,-a *adj* venereal
venero *nm* spring
venezolano,-a *adj & nm,f* Venezuelan
Venezuela *n* Venezuela
venga *subj pres de* venir
venganza *nf* vengeance, revenge
vengar [42] 1 *vt* to avenge
   2 vengarse *vpr* to avenge oneself; **v. de algn** to take revenge on sb
vengativo,-a *adj* vengeful, vindictive
vengo *indic pres de* venir
venia *nf* (a) *Fml (permiso)* permission (b) *(perdón)* pardon
venial *adj* venial
venida *nf* coming, arrival
venidero,-a *adj* future, coming
venir [27] 1 *vi* (a) to come; *Fig* **v. a menos** to come down in the world; *Fig* **v. al mundo** to be born; **el año que viene** next year; *Fig* **me viene a la memoria** I remember; *Fam* **¡venga ya!** *(vamos)* come on!; *(expresa incredulidad)* come off it! (b) **v. grande/pequeño** *(ropa)* to be too big/small; **v. mal/bien** to be inconvenient/convenient; **el metro me viene muy bien** I find the *Br* underground *o US* subway very handy (c) *(en pasivas)* **esto vino provocado por ...** this was brought about by ... (d) **esto viene ocurriendo desde hace mucho tiempo** this has been going on for a long time now
   2 venirse *vpr* **v. abajo** to collapse
venta *nf* (a) sale; **en v.** for sale; **a la v.** on sale; **v. a plazos/al contado** credit/cash sale; **v. al por mayor/al por menor** wholesale/retail (b) *(posada)* country inn
ventaja *nf* advantage; **llevar v. a** to have the advantage over; **le sacó 2 m de v.** he beat him by 2 m
ventajoso,-a *adj* advantageous
ventana *nf* (a) window (b) *(de la nariz)* nostril
ventanal *nm* large window
ventanilla *nf* (a) window (b) *(de la nariz)* nostril
ventanuco *nm* small window
ventilación *nf* ventilation; **sin v.** unventilated
ventilador *nm* ventilator; *(de coche)* fan
ventilar 1 *vt* (a) *(habitación)* to ventilate, to air (b) *Fig (opinión)* to air
   2 ventilarse *vpr Fam (terminar)* to finish off
ventisca *nf* blizzard; *(de nieve)* snowstorm
ventosa *nf* sucker; *Med* cupping glass
ventosear *vi* to break wind
ventoso,-a *adj* windy

ventrílocuo,-a *nm,f* ventriloquist
ventura *nf* (a) *(felicidad)* happiness (b) *(suerte)* luck; *(casualidad)* chance
venturoso,-a *adj* lucky, fortunate
Venus *nm* Venus
veo-veo *nm Fam* **el (juego del) v.** I-spy
ver¹ *nm* **de buen v.** good-looking
ver² [28] 1 *vt* (a) to see; *(televisión)* to watch; **a v.** let me see, let's see; **a v. si escribes** I hope you'll write; **(ya) veremos** we'll see; *Fam* **había un jaleo que no veas** you should have seen the fuss that was made; **no veo por qué** I can't see why; **a mi modo de v.** as I see it (b) **no tener nada que v. con** to have nothing to do with
   2 verse *vpr* (a) *(imagen etc)* to be seen (b) *(encontrarse con algn)* to meet, to see each other; **¡nos vemos!** see you later! (c) **no se pueden ni v.** *(soportarse)* they can't stand (the sight of) each other (d) *Am* **te ves divina** you look divine
vera *nf* edge, border; **a la v. de** beside, next to
veracidad *nf* veracity, truthfulness
veraneante *nmf Br* holidaymaker, *US* (summer) vacationer
veranear *vi* to spend one's summer *Br* holiday *o US* vacation
veraneo *nm* summer *Br* holiday *o US* vacation
veraniego,-a *adj* summer
veranillo *nm* Indian summer; **el v. de San Juan** *(en el hemisferio sur)* = warm spell around 24 June; **el v. de San Martín** *(en el hemisferio norte)* = warm spell around 11 November
verano *nm* summer
veras *nfpl* **de v.** really, seriously
veraz *adj* veracious, truthful
verbal *adj* verbal
verbena *nf* street party
verbo *nm* verb
verborrea *nf Fam* verbosity, verbal diarrhoea
verdad *nf* (a) truth; **es v.** it is true; **a decir v.** to tell the truth; **¡de v!.** really!, truly!; **un amigo de v.** a real friend (b) *(en frase afirmativa)* **está muy bien, ¿(no es) v.?** it is very good, isn't it?; *(en frase negativa)* **no te gusta, ¿v.?** you don't like it, do you?
verdaderamente *adv* truly, really
verdadero,-a *adj* true, real
verde 1 *adj* (a) green (b) *(fruta)* unripe (c) *Fam (chiste, película)* blue; **viejo v.** dirty old man (d) *Fam Fig* **poner v. a algn** to call sb every name under the sun
   2 *nm* (a) *(color)* green (b) *Pol* **los verdes** the Greens

verdear *vi* to turn green
verdor *nm* (*color*) greenness; (*de plantas*) verdure
verdoso,-a *adj* greenish
verdugo,-a 1 *nm* executioner
 2 *nm,f Fig* tyrant
verdulería *nf* greengrocer's (shop)
verdulero,-a *nm,f* greengrocer
verdura *nf* vegetables, greens
vereda *nf* (**a**) (*camino*) path, lane (**b**) *CSur, Perú* (*acera*) *Br* pavement, *US* sidewalk
veredicto *nm* verdict
verga *nf* penis
vergonzoso,-a *adj* (**a**) (*penoso*) shameful, disgraceful (**b**) (*tímido*) shy, bashful
vergüenza *nf* (**a**) shame; **¿no te da v.?** aren't you ashamed?, have you no shame?; **¡es una v.!** it's a disgrace! (**b**) (*timidez*) shyness, bashfulness; **tener v.** to be shy; **me da v.** I'm too embarrassed
vericueto *nm* winding path; *Fig* **los vericuetos** the ins and outs
verídico,-a *adj* truthful, true
verificar [44] 1 *vt* (*comprobar*) to check
 2 **verificarse** *vpr* to take place, to occur
verja *nf* (*reja*) grating; (*cerca*) railing, railings; (*puerta*) iron gate
vermut, vermú *nm* (*pl* **vermús**) (**a**) (*licor*) vermouth (**b**) (*aperitivo*) aperitif (**c**) *Andes, RP* (*en cine*) early evening showing; (*en teatro*) early evening performance
verosímil *adj* probable, likely; (*creíble*) credible
verruga *nf* wart
versado,-a *adj* well-versed (**en** in)
versar *vi* **v. sobre** to be about, to deal with
versátil *adj* (**a**) versatile (**b**) (*voluble*) changeable, inconstant
versatilidad *nf* (**a**) versatility (**b**) (*volubilidad*) changeableness, inconstancy
versículo *nm* verse
versión *nf* version; **película en v. original** film in the original language
verso *nm* (**a**) (*poesía*) verse (**b**) (*línea*) line
vértebra *nf* vertebra
vertebrado,-a *adj & nm* vertebrate
vertedero *nm* (*de basura*) *Br* rubbish tip *o* dump, *US* garbage dump
verter [3] 1 *vt* (**a**) to pour (out) (**b**) (*basura*) to dump
 2 *vi* (*río*) to flow, to run (**a** into)
vertical *adj* vertical
vértice *nm* vertex
vertiente *nf* (**a**) (*de una montaña, un tejado*) slope; *Fig* aspect (**b**) *Am* (*manantial*) spring

vertiginoso,-a *adj* dizzy, giddy; *Fig* (*velocidad*) breakneck
vértigo *nm* vertigo; **me da v.** it makes me dizzy
vesícula *nf* vesicle; **v. biliar** gall bladder
vespa® *nf* (motor) scooter
vespertino,-a 1 *adj* evening
 2 *nm Prensa* evening newspaper
vespino® *nm* moped
vestíbulo *nm* (*de casa*) hall; (*de edificio público*) foyer
vestido,-a 1 *nm* (*ropa*) clothes; (*de mujer*) dress
 2 *adj* dressed; **policía v. de paisano** plain-clothes policeman
vestidura *nf* clothing, clothes
vestigio *nm* vestige, trace
vestimenta *nf* clothes, garments
vestir [6] 1 *vt* (**a**) (*a algn*) to dress (**b**) (*llevar puesto*) to wear
 2 *vi* (**a**) to dress; **ropa de (mucho) v.** formal dress (**b**) *Fam* **la seda viste mucho** silk always looks very elegant
 3 **vestirse** *vpr* (**a**) to get dressed, to dress (**b**) **v. de** to wear, to dress in; (*disfrazarse*) to disguise oneself as, to dress up as
vestuario *nm* (**a**) (*conjunto de vestidos*) clothes, wardrobe; *Teatro* wardrobe, costumes (**b**) (*camerino*) dressing room (**c**) *Dep* changing room
veta *nf Min* vein, seam; (*de carne*) streak
vetar *vt* to veto
veterano,-a *adj & nm,f* veteran
veterinario,-a 1 *nm,f* vet, *Br* veterinary surgeon, *US* veterinarian
 2 *nf veterinaria* veterinary medicine *o* science
veto *nm* veto; **derecho a v.** power *o* right of veto
vetusto,-a *adj Fml* ancient
vez *nf* (**a**) time; **una v.** once; **dos veces** twice; **cinco veces** five times; **a** *o* **algunas veces** sometimes; **cada v.** each *o* every time; **cada v. más** more and more; **de v. en cuando** now and again, every now and then; **¿le has visto alguna v.?** have you ever seen him?; **otra v.** again; **a la v.** at the same time; **tal v.** perhaps, maybe; **de una v.** in one go; **de una v. para siempre** once and for all; **en v. de** instead of; **érase** *o* **había una v.** (*en cuentos etc*) once upon a time (**b**) (*turno*) turn (**c**) **hacer las veces de** to do duty as
v.g(r). (*abr* **verbigracia**) eg
vía 1 *nf* (**a**) *Ferroc* track, line (**b**) (*camino*) road; **v. pública** public thoroughfare; **V. Láctea** Milky Way (**c**) *Anat* passage, tract; *Farm* **(por) v. oral** to be taken orally (**d**)

Fig **por v. oficial** through official channels; **por v. aérea/marítima** by air/sea (**e**) **en vías de** in the process of; **países en vías de desarrollo** developing countries
   2 *prep (a través de)* via, through; **v. París** via Paris; **transmisión v. satélite** satellite transmission
viable *adj* viable
viaducto *nm* viaduct
viajante *nmf* commercial traveller, travelling salesman, *f* saleswoman
viajar *vi* to travel
viaje *nm (recorrido)* journey, trip; *(largo, en barco)* voyage; **¡buen v.!** bon voyage!, have a good trip!; **estar de v.** to be away (on a trip); **irse** *o* **marcharse de v.** to go on a journey *o* trip; **v. de negocios** business trip; **v. de novios** honeymoon
viajero,-a 1 *nm,f* (**a**) traveller (**b**) *(en transporte público)* passenger
   2 *adj* **cheque v.** traveller's cheque
vianda *nf RP* (**a**) *(tentempié)* packed lunch (**b**) *(fiambrera)* lunchbox
viandante *nmf* passer-by
viario,-a *adj* road, highway; **red viaria** road network
víbora *nf* viper
vibración *nf* vibration
vibrador *nm* vibrator
vibrar *vt & vi* to vibrate
vicario,-a *nm,f* vicar
vicepresidente,-a *nm,f* (**a**) *Pol* vice-president (**b**) *(de compañía, comité)* vice-chairperson; *(hombre)* vice-chairman; *(mujer)* vice-chairwoman
vicesecretario,-a *nm,f* assistant secretary
viceversa *adv* vice versa
viciado,-a *adj* (**a**) *(corrompido)* corrupt (**b**) *(aire)* foul
viciar [43] 1 *vt* (**a**) *(corromper)* to corrupt (**b**) *(estropear)* to waste
   2 viciarse *vpr* (**a**) *(deformarse)* to go out of shape (**b**) *(corromperse)* to become corrupted
vicio *nm* (**a**) vice (**b**) *(mala costumbre)* bad habit (**c**) *Fam (destreza)* skill
vicioso,-a 1 *adj* (**a**) *(persona)* depraved, perverted (**b**) **círculo v.** vicious circle
   2 *nm,f* depraved person; **v. del trabajo** workaholic
vicisitud *nf (usu pl)* vicissitude
víctima *nf* victim
victimar *vt Am* to kill, to murder
victimario,-a *nm,f Am* killer, murderer
victoria *nf* victory
victorioso,-a *adj* victorious
vicuña *nf* vicuña

vid *nf* vine, grapevine
vida *nf* life; *(período)* lifetime; **de toda la v.** lifelong; **en mi v.** never in my life; **de por v.** for life; **ganarse la v.** to earn one's living; **¿qué es de tu v.?** how's life?; **estar con/sin v.** to be alive/dead
vidente *nmf* clairvoyant
vídeo *nm* video; **grabar en v.** to videotape
videocámara *nf* video camera
videoclub *nm* video club
videoconferencia *nf* videoconferencing; *(sesión)* videoconference
videojuego *nm* video game
vidriera *nf* (**a**) stained-glass window (**b**) *Am (escaparate)* shop window
vidrio *nm* glass
viejo,-a 1 *adj* old; **hacerse v.** to grow old; **un v. amigo** an old friend
   2 *nm,f* (**a**) *(hombre, padre)* old man; *(mujer, madre)* old woman; **los viejos** old people; *Fam* **mis viejos** my parents (**b**) *RP Fam* **¡mi v.!** *(apelativo cariñoso)* young man *o* fellow!; **¡mi vieja!** *(apelativo cariñoso)* my dear! (**c**) *Chile* **el V. de Pascua** *o* **Pascuero** Father Christmas
   3 *nf* **vieja** *Col, Méx, Ven Fam (mujer, chica)* chick, *Br* bird, *US* broad
Viena *n* Vienna
vienés,-esa *adj & nm,f* Viennese
viento *nm* wind; **hace** *o* **sopla mucho v.** it is very windy; *Fam Fig* **¡vete a tomar v.!** get lost!
vientre *nm* (**a**) belly; **hacer de v.** to have a bowel movement (**b**) *(útero)* womb
viernes *nm inv* Friday; **V. Santo** Good Friday
Vietnam *n* Vietnam
vietnamita *adj & nmf* Vietnamese
viga *nf (de madera)* beam; *(de hierro)* girder
vigencia *nf* validity; **entrar en v.** to come into force *o* effect
vigente *adj* in force
vigésimo,-a *adj & nm,f* twentieth
vigía 1 *nf* watchtower, lookout post
   2 *nmf* lookout; *(hombre)* watchman; *(mujer)* watchwoman
vigilancia *nf* vigilance, watchfulness; *Med* **unidad de v. intensiva** intensive care unit
vigilante *nm* watchman; *(de banco)* guard
vigilar 1 *vt* to watch; *(un lugar)* to guard; **vigila que no entren** make sure they don't get in
   2 *vi (gen)* to keep watch
vigilia *nf* (**a**) vigil (**b**) *(víspera)* eve (**c**) *Rel (abstinencia)* abstinence

vigor *nm* (**a**) vigour; *(fuerza)* strength (**b**) **en v.** in force
vigoroso,-a *adj* vigorous
VIH *nm* (*abr* **Virus de la Inmunodeficiencia Humana**) HIV
vikingo,-a *adj & nm* Viking
vil *adj Fml* vile, base
vileza *nf* (**a**) vileness, baseness (**b**) *(acto)* vile act, despicable deed
vilipendiar [43] *vt Fml* to vilify, to revile
villa *nf* (**a**) *(población)* town (**b**) *(casa)* villa, country house (**c**) *Arg* **v. miseria** shanty town
villancico *nm* (Christmas) carol
vilo: • en vilo *loc adv (persona)* on tenterhooks; *(cosa)* up in the air
vinagre *nm* vinegar
vinagrera *nf* **vinagreras** oil and vinegar cruets, cruet (stand)
vinagreta *nf* vinaigrette sauce
vinajeras *nfpl* cruets
vincha *nf Am* headband
vinculante *adj* binding
vincular *vt* to link, to bind; *(relacionar)* to relate, to connect
vínculo *nm* link
vine *pt indef de* **venir**
vinícola *adj* wine-producing
vinicultor,-a *nm,f* wine producer
vinicultura *nf* wine production *o* growing
vinilo *nm* vinyl
vino *nm* wine; **tomar un v.** to have a glass of wine; **v. blanco/tinto/dulce/seco** white/red/sweet/dry wine; **v. rosado** rosé
viña *nf* vineyard
viñedo *nm* vineyard
viñeta *nf* illustration
viola *nf* viola
violación *nf* (**a**) *(de una persona)* rape (**b**) *(de ley, derecho)* violation, infringement
violador *nm* rapist
violar *vt* (**a**) *(persona)* to rape (**b**) *(ley, derecho)* to violate, to infringe
violencia *nf* (**a**) violence; **la no v.** non-violence (**b**) *(incomodidad)* embarrassment
violentar *vt* (**a**) *(forzar)* to force, to break open; *(sitio)* to break into, to enter by force (**b**) *(enojar)* to infuriate
violento,-a *adj* (**a**) violent (**b**) *(situación)* embarrassing, awkward (**c**) **sentirse v.** *(incómodo)* to feel embarrassed *o* awkward
violeta 1 *adj & nm (color)* violet
2 *nf (flor)* violet
violín *nm* violin; *Fam* fiddle

violinista *nmf* violinist
violón *nm* double bass
violoncelista, violonchelista *nmf* cellist
violoncelo, violonchelo *nm* violoncello, cello
viraje *nm* (**a**) turn (**b**) *Fig* about-face, U-turn
virar *vi* (**a**) *(girar)* to turn round (**b**) *Fig* to change
virgen 1 *adj* (**a**) *(persona, selva)* virgin (**b**) *(aceite, lana)* pure; *(cinta)* blank
2 *nmf* virgin; *Fam* **ser un viva la v.** to be a devil-may-care person
virginidad *nf* virginity
Virgo *nm* Virgo
virgo *nm* hymen
virguería *nf Fam* gem, marvel; **hacer virguerías** to work wonders, to be a dab hand
virguero,-a *adj Fam* smart, great; **esta camisa es muy virguera** that shirt is the business
vírico,-a *adj* viral
viril *adj* virile, manly; **miembro v.** penis
virilidad *nf* virility
virtual *adj* virtual
virtud *nf* (**a**) virtue; *Fig* **en v. de** by virtue of (**b**) *(propiedad)* property, quality
virtuoso,-a 1 *adj* virtuous
2 *nm,f* (**a**) virtuous person (**b**) *(músico)* virtuoso
viruela *nf* smallpox; **viruelas** pockmarks
virulé: • a la virulé *loc adj Fam* (**a**) *(torcido)* crooked, twisted (**b**) **un ojo a la v.** a black eye
virulencia *nf* virulence
virulento,-a *adj* virulent
virus *nm inv* virus
visado *nm*, *Am* **visa** *nf* visa
víscera *nf* (**a**) internal organ (**b**) **vísceras** viscera, entrails
visceral *adj* (**a**) *Anat* visceral (**b**) *Fig* profound, deep-rooted
viscoso,-a *adj* viscous
visera *nf (de gorra)* peak; *(de casco)* visor
visibilidad *nf* visibility; **curva con mala v.** blind corner
visible *adj* visible; *(evidente)* evident
visillo *nm* small lace *o* net curtain
visión *nf* (**a**) vision (**b**) *(vista)* sight; *Fig* **v. de conjunto** overall view; **con v. de futuro** forward-looking (**c**) *(aparición)* vision
visionario,-a *nm,f* visionary; *(iluso)* person who imagines things
visita *nf* (**a**) *(acción)* visit; **hacer una v.** to pay a visit; **estar de v.** to be visiting (**b**) *(invitado)* visitor, guest

visitador,-a *nm,f Farm* pharmaceutical salesman, *f* saleswoman

visitante 1 *nmf* visitor
  2 *adj (equipo)* away

visitar *vt* to visit

vislumbrar *vt* to glimpse

viso *nm* (**a**) *(reflejo)* sheen (**b**) *Fig* **tener visos de** to seem, to appear

visón *nm* mink

visor *nm Fot* viewfinder

> Observa que la palabra inglesa **visor** es un falso amigo y no es la traducción de la palabra española **visor**. En inglés, **visor** significa "visera".

víspera *nf (día anterior)* day before; *(de festivo)* eve; **en vísperas de** in the period leading up to

vista *nf* (**a**) sight; **a la v.** visible; **a primera** *o* **simple v.** at first sight, on the face of it; **con vistas a** with a view to; **en v. de** in view of, considering; **corto de v.** short-sighted; **conocer a algn de v.** to know sb by sight; **perder de v. a** to lose sight of; **quítalo de mi v.** take it away; *Fig* **tener mucha v. para** to have a good eye for; *Fig* **volver la v. atrás** to look back; *Fam* **¡hasta la v.!** goodbye!, see you!; *Fam* **hacer la v. gorda** to turn a blind eye (**b**) *(panorama)* view; **con vista(s) al mar** overlooking the sea (**c**)*Jur* trial, hearing

vistazo *nm* glance; **echar un v. a algo** *(ojear)* to have a (quick) look at sth; *(tener cuidado de)* to keep an eye on sth

visto,-a 1 *adj* (**a**) **está v. que ...** it is obvious that ...; **por lo v.** evidently, apparently; **v. que** in view of the fact that, seeing *o* given that (**b**) **estar bien v.** to be well looked upon, to be considered acceptable; **estar mal v.** to be frowned upon (**c**) **estar muy v.** to be old hat
  2 *nm* **v. bueno** approval, O.K.

vistoso,-a *adj* eye-catching

visual *adj* visual; **campo v.** field of vision

visualizar [40] *vt* to visualize; *(película)* to view

vital *adj* (**a**) vital (**b**) *(persona)* full of vitality

vitalicio,-a *adj* life, for life; **pensión/cargo v.** life pension/permanent post

vitalidad *nf* vitality

vitamina *nf* vitamin

vitamínico,-a *adj* vitamin; **complejo v.** multivitamins

viticultor,-a *nm,f* wine grower

viticultura *nf* wine growing

vitorear *vt* to cheer

vítreo,-a *adj* vitreous

vitrina *nf (aparador)* glass *o* display cabinet; *(de exposición)* glass case, showcase; *Am (escaparate)* shop window

vituallas *nfpl* provisions

vituperar *vt* to condemn

vituperio *nm* condemnation

viudo,-a *nm,f (hombre)* widower; *(mujer)* widow

viva *interj* **¡v.!** hurrah!

vivacidad *nf* vivacity

vivaracho,-a *adj Fam* lively, sprightly

vivaz *adj* (**a**) lively, vivacious (**b**) *(perspicaz)* sharp, quick-witted

vivencias *nfpl* personal experience

víveres *nmpl* provisions, supplies

vivero *nm (de plantas)* nursery; *(de peces)* fish farm *o* hatchery; *Fig* breeding ground, hotbed

viveza *nf* (**a**) liveliness, vivacity; *(en los ojos)* sparkle (**b**) *(agudeza)* sharpness, quick-wittedness

vividor,-a *nm,f Pey* sponger, scrounger

vivienda *nf* (**a**) housing (**b**) *(casa)* house; *(piso)* flat

vivir 1 *vi* to live; **vive de sus ahorros** she lives off her savings; **viven de la pesca** they make their living by fishing
  2 *vt* to live through
  3 *nm* life

vivito,-a *adj Fam* **v. y coleando** alive and kicking

vivo,-a 1 *adj* (**a**) alive; **de viva voz** verbally, by word of mouth; **en v.** *(programa)* live; *Fam* **es el v. retrato** *o* **la viva imagen de** she is the spitting image of (**b**) **al rojo v.** red-hot (**c**) *(vivaz)* lively, vivacious (**d**) *(listo)* sharp, clever (**e**) *(color)* vivid, bright (**f**) *(descripción)* lively, graphic
  2 *nm,f* **los vivos** the living

Vizcaya *n* **el golfo de V.** the Bay of Biscay

V. B. *(abr* **visto bueno**) *(en documento)* approved

vocablo *nm* word, term

vocabulario *nm* vocabulary

vocación *nf* vocation, calling; **con v. europea** with leanings towards Europe

vocacional *adj* vocational

vocal 1 *nf Ling* vowel
  2 *nmf* member

vocalista *nmf Mús* vocalist, singer

vocalizar [40] *vt & vi* to vocalize

voceador,-a *nm,f Am* vendor

vocerío *nm* shouting

vocero,-a *nm,f Am* spokesperson; *(hombre)* spokesman; *(mujer)* spokeswoman

vociferante *adj* vociferous

vociferar *vt & vi* to vociferate

vodka *nm* vodka

vol. (*abr* **volumen**) vol
volado,-a *adj Fam* estar **v.** to have a screw loose
volador,-a *adj* flying
volandas: • en **volandas** *loc adv (por el aire)* in the air, flying through the air
volante 1 *nm* (**a**) *Aut* steering wheel; **ir al v.** to be driving; **un as del v.** a motor-racing champion (**b**) *Cost* frill, ruffle (**c**) *Med* note
　2 *adj* flying; **platillo v.** flying saucer
volantín *nm (cometa)* small kite
volar [2] 1 *vi* (**a**) to fly; *Fig* **lo hizo volando** he did it in a flash (**b**) *Fam (desaparecer)* to disappear, to vanish
　2 *vt (edificios)* to blow up; *(caja fuerte)* to blow open; *Min* to blast
　3 volarse *vpr (papel etc)* to be blown away
volátil *adj* volatile
volatinero,-a *nm,f* acrobat
volcán *nm* volcano
volcánico,-a *adj* volcanic
volcar [2] 1 *vt* (**a**) *(cubo etc)* to knock over; *(barco, bote)* to capsize (**b**) *(vaciar)* to empty out (**c**) *(tiempo)* to invest
　2 *vi (coche)* to turn over; *(barco)* to capsize
　3 volcarse *vpr* (**a**) *(vaso, jarra)* to fall over, to tip over; *(coche)* to turn over; *(barco)* to capsize (**b**) *Fig* **v. con** to do one's utmost for
voleibol *nm* volleyball
voleo *nm Fig* **a(l) v.** at random, haphazardly
voltaje *nm* voltage
voltear 1 *vt* (**a**) *(dar la vuelta a)* to turn upside down (**b**) *CSur (derribar)* to knock over (**c**) *Andes, CAm, Carib, Méx (cabeza)* to turn; **v. la espalda a algn** to turn one's back on sb
　2 *vi* (**a**) to turn *o* roll over (**b**) *Méx (doblar la esquina)* to go round
　3 voltearse *vpr* (**a**) *Andes, CAm, Carib, Méx (volverse)* to turn around (**b**) *Méx (vehículo)* to turn over
voltereta *nf* somersault
voltio *nm* volt
voluble *adj* fickle, changeable

📖 Observa que la palabra inglesa **voluble** es un falso amigo y no es la traducción de la palabra española **voluble**. En inglés, **voluble** significa "locuaz".

---

volumen *nm* volume
voluminoso,-a *adj* voluminous; *(enorme)* massive, bulky
voluntad *nf* will; **fuerza de v.** willpower;

tiene mucha **v.** he is very strong-willed; **a v.** at will
voluntario,-a 1 *adj* voluntary
　2 *nm,f* volunteer; **ofrecerse v.** to volunteer
voluntarioso,-a *adj* willing
voluptuoso,-a *adj* voluptuous
volver [4] (*pp* **vuelto**) **1** *vi* (**a**) to return; *(venir)* to come back; *(ir)* to go back; **v. en sí** to come round, to recover consciousness (**b**) **v. a hacer algo** to do sth again
　2 *vt* (**a**) *(convertir)* to turn, to make; **me vas a v. loco** you are driving me mad (**b**) *(dar vuelta a)* to turn; *(boca abajo)* to turn upside down; *(de fuera adentro)* to turn inside out; *(de atrás adelante)* to turn back to front; *(dar la vuelta a)* to turn over; **volverle la espalda a algn** to turn one's back on sb; *Fig* **v. la vista atrás** to look back; **al v. la esquina** on turning the corner
　3 volverse *vpr* (**a**) to turn (**b**) *(regresar)* *(venir)* to come back; *(ir)* to go back (**c**) *(convertirse)* to become; **v. loco,-a** to go mad
vomitar 1 *vi* to vomit, to be sick; **tengo ganas de v.** I feel sick, I want to be sick
　2 *vt* to vomit, to bring up
vómito *nm (lo vomitado)* vomit; *(acción)* vomiting
vomitona *nf Fam* vomit
voracidad *nf* voracity, voraciousness
vorágine *nf* whirlpool; *Fig* maelstrom
voraz *adj* voracious; *Fig* raging, fierce
vórtice *nm* vortex
vos *pron pers Am (tú)* you

The **vos** form is used alongside **tú** in many Latin American countries, and in some countries (Argentina, Paraguay and Uruguay) is the preferred form.

---

vosotros,-as *pron pers pl* (**a**) *(sujeto)* you (**b**) *(con prep)* you; **entre v.** among yourselves; **sin vosotras** without you

---

Usually omitted in Spanish except for emphasis or contrast. In Latin America, **vosotros** is not used. Instead, **ustedes** is used as the second person plural in all contexts, without necessarily suggesting formality.

---

votación *nf* (**a**) *(voto)* vote, ballot (**b**) *(acción)* voting
votante *nmf* voter
votar *vi* to vote; **v. a algn** to vote (for) sb
voto *nm* (**a**) vote; **tener v.** to have the right to vote; **v. secreto** secret ballot (**b**) *Rel* vow

vox *nf* **esto es v. populi** this is common knowledge

voy *indic pres de* **ir**

voz *nf* (**a**) voice; **en v. alta** aloud; **en v. baja** in a low voice; **a media v.** in a low voice, softly; **de viva v.** verbally (**b**) *(grito)* shout; **a voces** shouting; **dar voces** to shout; *Fig* **estar pidiendo algo a voces** to be crying out for sth; *Fig* **secreto a voces** open secret; **a v. en grito** at the top of one's voice (**c**) **no tener ni v. ni voto** to have no say in the matter; *Fig* **llevar la v. cantante** to rule the roost (**d**) *Gram* **v. pasiva** passive voice

vudú *nm* voodoo

vuelco *nm* upset, tumble; **dar un v.** *(coche)* to overturn; *Fig* **me dio un v. el corazón** my heart missed a beat

vuelo *nm* (**a**) flight; **v. chárter/regular** charter/scheduled flight; **v. sin motor** gliding; *Fig* **cazarlas** *o* **cogerlas al v.** to be quick on the uptake (**b**) *Cost* **una falda de v.** a full skirt

vuelta *nf* (**a**) *(regreso)* return; *(viaje)* return journey; **a v. de correo** by return of post; **estar de v.** to be back; *Dep* **partido de v.** return match (**b**) *(giro)* turn; *(en carreras)* lap; *Dep (ciclista)* tour; **dar media v.** to turn round; *Fig* **la cabeza me da vueltas** my head is spinning; *Fig* **no le des más vueltas** stop worrying about it; **v. de campana** somersault (**c**) *(dinero)* change (**d**) **dar una v.** *(a pie)* to go for a walk *o* stroll; *(en coche)* to go for a drive *o* a spin (in the car) (**e**) *Fig* **no tiene v. de hoja** there's no doubt about it

vuelto,-a 1 *adj* **jersey de cuello v.** rollneck sweater

2 *nm Am* change

vuestro,-a 1 *adj pos (antes del sustantivo)* your; *(después del sustantivo)* of yours; **v. libro** your book; **un amigo v.** a friend of yours

2 *pron pos* yours; **éstos son los vuestros** these are yours; **lo v.** what is yours, what belongs to you

vulgar *adj* (**a**) vulgar (**b**) **el término v.** the everyday term

vulgaridad *nf* vulgarity

vulgarizar [40] *vt (popularizar)* to popularize

vulgarmente *adv* **v. llamado** commonly known as

vulgo *nm* **el v.** the common people; *Pey* the masses

vulnerable *adj* vulnerable

vulnerar *vt (ley, acuerdo)* to violate

vulva *nf* vulva

W, w [ueˈðole] *nf (la letra)* W, w
W *(abr vatio(s))* W
walkie-talkie *nm* walkie-talkie
walkman® *nm* Walkman®
wáter *nm (pl* **wáteres**) *Fam* toilet
waterpolo *nm* water polo
Web, web [web] *Informát* **1** *nf (World Wide Web)* la **W.** the Web
  2 *nm o nf (página web)* web site
whisky *nm (escocés)* whisky; *(irlandés, US)* whiskey
windsurf, windsurfing *nm* windsurfing
windsurfista *nmf* windsurfer

xenofobia *nf* xenophobia
xenófobo,-a 1 *adj* xenophobic
  2 *nm,f* xenophobe

Y, y [iriˈea] *nf (la letra)* Y, y
y *conj* (**a**) and; **una chica alta y morena** a tall, dark-haired girl; **son las tres y cuarto** it's a quarter past three (**b**) **¿y qué?** so what?; **¿y si no llega a tiempo?** what if he doesn't arrive in time?; **¿y tú?** what about you?; **¿y eso?** how come?; **y eso que** although, even though; **¡y tanto!** you bet!, and how!; *ver* **e**
ya 1 *adv* (**a**) already; **ya lo sabía** I already knew; **ya en la Edad Media** as far back as the Middle Ages (**b**) *(ahora mismo)* now; **es preciso actuar ya** it is vital that we act now; **¡hazlo ya!** do it at once!; **ya mismo** right away (**c**) *(en el futuro)* **ya hablaremos luego** we'll talk about it later; **ya nos veremos** see you!; **ya verás** you'll see (**d**) **ya no** no longer; **ya no viene por aquí** he doesn't come round here any more (**e**) *(refuerza el verbo)* **ya era hora** about time too; **ya lo creo** of course, I should think so; **¡ya voy!** coming!; **¡ya está!** that's it!
  2 *conj* **ya que** since
yacaré *nm* cayman
yacer [61] *vi* to lie, to be lying
yacimiento *nm* bed, deposit; **yacimientos petrolíferos** oilfields
yaguar *nm* jaguar
yanqui *Pey* **1** *adj* Yankee
  2 *nmf* Yankee, Yank
yarará *nf Am* = large poisonous snake

yaraví *nm Am* = Quechuan song
yarda *nf* yard
yate *nm* yacht
yaya *nf Am Bot* lance-wood; *Fam (abuela)* granny
yedra *nf* = hiedra
yegua *nf* mare
yema *nf* (**a**) *(de huevo)* yolk (**b**) *Bot* bud (**c**) **y. del dedo** fingertip (**d**) *Culin* = sweet made from sugar and egg yolk
Yemen *n* Yemen
yen *nm (moneda)* yen
yendo *ger de* **ir**
yerba *nf* (**a**) = **hierba** (**b**) *RP* maté; **y. mate** yerba maté
yerbatero,-a *Am* **1** *nm,f (curandero)* = witch doctor who uses herbs
  2 *adj* maté
yermo,-a *adj* (**a**) *(baldío)* barren, uncultivated (**b**) *(despoblado)* deserted, uninhabited
yerno *nm* son-in-law
yerro *indic pres de* **errar**
yeso *nm* (**a**) *Geol* gypsum (**b**) *Constr* plaster
Yibuti *n* Djibouti
yiu-yitsu *nm* ju-jitsu
yo *pron pers* I; **entre tú y yo** between you and me; **¿quién es? – soy yo** who is it? – it's me; **yo no** not me; **yo que tú** if I were you; **yo mismo** I myself

> Usually omitted as a personal pronoun in Spanish except for emphasis or contrast.

yodo *nm* iodine
yoga *nm* yoga
yogur *nm* yogurt, yoghurt
yogurtera *nf* yoghurt maker
yonqui *nmf Fam* junkie, drug addict
yoyo, yoyó *nm* yo-yo
yuca *nf* yucca
Yucatán *n* Yucatan
yudo *nm* judo
yudoka *nmf* judoka
yugo *nm* yoke
Yugoslavia *n* Yugoslavia
yugoslavo,-a, yugoeslavo,-a *adj & nm,f* Yugoslav, Yugoslavian
yugular *nf* jugular

yunque *nm* anvil
yunta *nf* yoke *o* team of oxen
yuxtaponer [19] (*pp* **yuxtapuesto**) *vt* to juxtapose

yuxtaposición *nf* juxtaposition
yuyo *nm* (**a**) *CSur (mala hierba)* weed; *(hierba medicinal)* medicinal herb (**b**) *Andes (hierba silvestre)* wild herb

Z, z ['θeta] *nf (la letra)* Z, z
zacate *nm CAm, Méx* fodder
zafarse *vpr (librarse)* to get away (**de** from), to escape (**de** from)
zafio,-a *adj* uncouth
zafiro *nm* sapphire
zaga *nf* **a la z.** behind, at the rear
zaguán *nm* hall, hallway
zaherir *vt* to hurt
zahúrda *nf* pigsty
zaino,-a *adj (caballo)* chestnut; *(toro)* black
Zaire *n* Zaire
zalamería *nf* flattery
zalamero,-a 1 *nm,f* flatterer, fawner
2 *adj* flattering, fawning
zamarra *nf (prenda)* sheepskin jacket
Zambia *n* Zambia
zambo,-a 1 *adj* (**a**) *(patizambo)* knock-kneed (**b**) *Am (persona)* half Indian and half Negro
2 *nm,f Am (persona)* = person who is half Indian and half Negro
zambomba *nf* = kind of primitive drum
zambullida *nf* plunge
zambullirse *vpr* to plunge
zamparse *vpr Fam* to gobble down
zanahoria *nf* carrot
zancada *nf* stride
zancadilla *nf* **ponerle la z. a algn** to trip sb up
zanco *nm* stilt
zancudo,-a 1 *adj* (**a**) long-legged (**b**) *Orn* wading; **ave zancuda** wading bird, wader
2 *nm Am* mosquito
zángano,-a 1 *nm (insecto)* drone
2 *nm,f Fam (persona)* idler, lazybones *inv*
zanja *nf* ditch, trench
zanjar *vt (asunto)* to settle
zapallito *nm CSur Br* courgette, *US* zucchini
zapallo *nm Andes, RP* sweet pumpkin
zapata *nf* (**a**) *(cuña)* wedge (**b**) *Téc* shoe
zapatear *vi* to tap one's feet
zapatería *nf* shoe shop
zapatero,-a *nm,f (vendedor)* shoe dealer; *(fabricante)* shoemaker, cobbler

zapatilla *nf* slipper; **zapatillas de deporte** trainers
zapato *nm* shoe; **zapatos de tacón** high-heeled shoes
zar *nm* czar, tsar
Zaragoza *n* Saragossa
zaragozano,-a 1 *adj* of/from Saragossa
2 *nm,f* person from Saragossa
zarandear *vt* to shake
zarandeo *nm* shaking
zarcillo *nm* (**a**) *(pendiente)* earring (**b**) *Bot* tendril
zarina *nf* czarina, tsarina
zarpa *nf* claw
zarpar *vi* to weigh anchor, to set sail
zarpazo *nm* clawing; **dar** *o* **pegar un z. a** to claw
zarza *nf* bramble, blackberry bush
zarzal *nm* bramble patch
zarzamora *nf (zarza)* blackberry bush; *(fruto)* blackberry
zarzuela *nf* (**a**) = Spanish operetta (**b**) **la Z.** = royal residence in Madrid (**c**) *Culin* = fish stew
zenit *nm* zenith
zigzag *nm* (*pl* **zigzags** *o* **zigzagues**) zigzag
zigzaguear *vi* to zigzag
Zimbabwe *n* Zimbabwe
zinc *nm* zinc
zíper *nm CAm, Méx Br* zip, *US* zipper
zócalo *nm* (**a**) *(de pared)* skirting board (**b**) *(pedestal)* plinth
zodiaco, zodíaco *nm* zodiac; **signo del z.** sign of the zodiac
zona *nf* zone; *(región)* region; **z. euro** euro zone; **z. verde** park
zoo *nm* zoo
zoología *nf* zoology
zoológico,-a 1 *adj* zoological; **parque z.** zoo
2 *nm* zoo
zoom *nm Cin & Fot* zoom
zopenco,-a *nm,f Fam* dope, halfwit
zopilote *nm Am* buzzard
zoquete 1 *nmf Fam* blockhead
2 *nm CSur (calcetín)* ankle sock
zorra *nf* (**a**) vixen (**b**) *Fam* slut
zorro,-a 1 *nm* fox

2 *adj* (**a**) *(astuto)* cunning, sly (**b**) *muy Fam* **no tengo ni zorra (idea)** I haven't got a *Br* bloody *o US* goddamn clue

zorzal *nm Orn* thrush

zozobrar *vi* to be in danger of going under

zueco *nm* clog

zumbado,-a *adj Fam* crazy, mad

zumbar 1 *vi* to buzz, to hum; **me zumban los oídos** my ears are buzzing; *Fam* **salir zumbando** to zoom off

    2 *vt Fam* to thrash

zumbido *nm* buzzing, humming

zumo *nm* juice

zurcir [**52**] *vt Cost* to darn; *Fam* **¡que te zurzan!** go to hell!

zurda *nf (mano)* left hand

zurdo,-a 1 *nm,f (persona)* left-handed person

    2 *adj* left-handed

zurrar *vt (pegar)* to beat, to flog

zutano,-a *nm,f Fam* so-and-so; *(hombre)* what's-his-name; *(mujer)* what's-her-name

Spanish Verbs

◆

Regular Spelling Changes

The rules of spelling in Spanish cause a number of verbs to have regular spelling changes. These are listed below.

Spanish verbs fall into three groups depending on whether their infinitive ends in **-ar, -er** or **-ir.** The stem of the verb is the part which is left when the **-ar, -er** or **-ir** is removed from the infinitive. For example, the stem of **tomar** is **tom**, the stem of **beber** is **beb**, and the stem of **salir** is **sal**.

In the examples given below, the following indicators are used:

> (**1**) = first person singular present indicative
> (**2**) = present subjunctive, all persons
> (**3**) = first person singular preterite

Verbs ending in -ar

Verbs with a stem ending in **c**, for example **buscar**

The **c** changes to **qu** in:

> (**2**) busque, busques, busque, busquemos, busquéis, busquen
> (**3**) busqué

Verbs with a stem ending in **g**, for example **cargar**

The **g** changes to **gu** in:

> (**2**) cargue, cargues, cargue, carguemos, carguéis, carguen
> (**3**) cargué

Verbs with a stem ending in **gu**, for example **averiguar**

The **gu** changes to **gü** in:

> (**2**) averigüe, averigües, averigüe, averigüemos, averigüéis, averigüen
> (**3**) averigüé

Verbs with a stem ending in **z**, for example **realizar**

The **z** changes to **c** in:

> (**2**) realice, realices, realice, realicemos, realicéis, realicen
> (**3**) realicé

Verbs ending in -er *or* -ir

Verbs with a stem ending in **c**, for example **esparcir**

The **c** changes to **z** in:

      (**1**) esparzo
      (**2**) esparza, esparzas, esparza, esparzamos, esparzáis, esparzan

Verbs with a stem ending in **g**, for example **coger**

The **g** changes to **j** in:

      (**1**) cojo
      (**2**) coja, cojas, coja, cojamos, cojáis, cojan

Verbs with a stem ending in **qu**, for example **delinquir**

The **qu** changes to **c** in:

      (**1**) delinco
      (**2**) delinca, delincas, delinca, delincamos, delincáis, delincan

Verbs with a stem ending in **gu**, for example **distinguir**

The **gu** changes to **g** in:

      (**1**) distingo
      (**2**) distinga, distingas, distinga, distingamos, distingáis, distingan

Models for Regular Conjugation

TOMAR to take

INDICATIVE

PRESENT	FUTURE	CONDITIONAL
1. tomo	tomaré	tomaría
2. tomas	tomarás	tomarías
3. toma	tomará	tomaría
1. tomamos	tomaremos	tomaríamos
2. tomáis	tomaréis	tomarías
3. toman	tomarán	tomarían

IMPERFECT	PRETERITE	PERFECT
1. tomaba	tomé	he tomado
2. tomabas	tomaste	has tomado
3. tomaba	tomó	ha tomado
1. tomábamos	tomamos	hemos tomado
2. tomabais	tomasteis	habéis tomado
3. tomaban	tomaron	han tomado

FUTURE PERFECT	CONDITIONAL PERFECT	PLUPERFECT
1. habré tomado	habría tomado	había tomado
2. habrás tomado	habrías tomado	habías tomado
3. habrá tomado	habría tomado	había tomado
1. habremos tomado	habríamos tomado	habíamos tomado
2. habréis tomado	habríais tomado	habíais tomado
3. habrán tomado	habrían tomado	habían tomado

SUBJUNCTIVE

PRESENT	IMPERFECT	PERFECT/PLUPERFECT
1. tome	tom-ara/ase	haya/hubiera* tomado
2. tomes	tom-aras/ases	hayas/hubieras tomado
3. tome	tom-ara/ase	haya/hubiera tomado
1. tomemos	tom-áramos/ásemos	hayamos/hubiéramos tomado
2. toméis	tom-arais/aseis	hayáis/hubierais tomado
3. tomen	tom-aran/asen	hayan/hubieran tomado

IMPERATIVE   INFINITIVE   PARTICIPLE

(tú) toma	PRESENT	PRESENT
(Vd) tome	tomar	tomando
(nosotros) tomemos		
(vosotros) tomad	PERFECT	PAST
(Vds) tomen	haber tomado	tomado

* the alternative form 'hubiese' etc is also possible

COMER to eat

INDICATIVE

PRESENT	FUTURE	CONDITIONAL
1. como	comeré	comería
2. comes	comerás	comerías
3. come	comerá	comería
1. comemos	comeremos	comeríamos
2. coméis	comeréis	comeríais
3. comen	comerán	comerían

IMPERFECT	PRETERITE	PERFECT
1. comía	comí	he comido
2. comías	comiste	has comido
3. comía	comió	ha comido
1. comíamos	comimos	hemos comido
2. comíais	comisteis	habéis comido
3. comían	comieron	han comido

FUTURE PERFECT	CONDITIONAL PERFECT	PLUPERFECT
1. habré comido	habría comido	había comido
2. habrás comido	habrías comido	habías comido
3. habrá comido	habría comido	había comido
1. habremos comido	habríamos comido	habíamos comido
2. habréis comido	habríais comido	habías comido
3. habrán comido	habrían comido	habían comido

SUBJUNCTIVE

PRESENT	IMPERFECT	PERFECT/PLUPERFECT
1. coma	com-iera/iese	haya/hubiera* comido
2. comas	com-ieras/ieses	hayas/hubieras comido
3. coma	com-iera/iese	haya/hubiera comido
1. comamos	com-iéramos/iésemos	hayamos/hubiéramos comido
2. comáis	com-ierais/ieseis	hayáis/hubierais comido
3. coman	com-ieran/iesen	hayan/hubieran comido

IMPERATIVE	INFINITIVE	PARTICIPLE
(tú) come	**PRESENT**	**PRESENT**
(Vd) coma	comer	comiendo
(nosotros) comamos		
(vosotros) comed	**PERFECT**	**PAST**
(Vds) coman	haber comido	comido

* the alternative form 'hubiese' etc is also possible

PARTIR to leave

| INDICATIVE |

PRESENT	FUTURE	CONDITIONAL
1. parto	partiré	partiría
2. partes	partirás	partirías
3. parte	partirá	partiría
1. partimos	partiremos	partiríamos
2. partís	partiréis	partiríais
3. parten	partirán	partirían

IMPERFECT	PRETERITE	PERFECT
1. partía	partí	he partido
2. partías	partiste	has partido
3. partía	partió	ha partido
1. partíamos	partimos	hemos partido
2. partíais	partisteis	habéis partido
3. partían	partieron	han partido

FUTURE PERFECT	CONDITIONAL PERFECT	PLUPERFECT
1. habré partido	habría partido	había partido
2. habrás partido	habrías partido	habías partido
3. habrá partido	habría partido	había partido
1. habremos partido	habríamos partido	habíamos partido
2. habréis partido	habríais partido	habíais partido
3. habrán partido	habrían partido	habían partido

| SUBJUNCTIVE |

PRESENT	IMPERFECT	PERFECT/PLUPERFECT
parta	parti-era/ese	haya/hubiera* partido
partas	parti-eras/eses	hayas/hubieras partido
parta	parti-era/ese	haya/hubiera partido
partamos	parti-éramos/ésemos	hayamos/hubiéramos partido
partáis	parti-erais/eseis	hayáis/hubierais partido
partan	parti-eran/esen	hayan/hubieran partido

| IMPERATIVE | | INFINITIVE | | PARTICIPLE |

IMPERATIVE	INFINITIVE	PARTICIPLE
(tú) parte	**PRESENT**	**PRESENT**
(Vd) parta	partir	partiendo
(nosotros) partamos		
(vosotros) partid	**PERFECT**	**PAST**
(Vds) partan	haber partido	partido

* the alternative form 'hubiese' etc is also possible

Models for Irregular Conjugation

[1] **pensar PRES** pienso, piensas, piensa, pensamos, pensáis, piensan; **PRES SUBJ** piense, pienses, piense, pensemos, penséis, piensen; **IMPERAT** piensa, piense, pensemos, pensad, piensen

[2] **contar PRES** cuento, cuentas, cuenta, contamos, contáis, cuentan; **PRES SUBJ** cuente, cuentes, cuente, contemos, contéis, cuenten; **IMPERAT** cuenta, cuente, contemos, contad, cuenten

[3] **perder PRES** pierdo, pierdes, pierde, perdemos, perdéis, pierden; **PRES SUBJ** pierda, pierdas, pierda, perdamos, perdáis, pierdan; **IMPERAT** pierde, pierda, perdamos, perded, pierdan

[4] **morder PRES** muerdo, muerdes, muerde, mordemos, mordéis, muerden; **PRES SUBJ** muerda, muerdas, muerda, mordamos, mordáis, muerdan; **IMPERAT** muerde, muerda, mordamos, morded, muerdan

[5] **sentir PRES** siento, sientes, siente, sentimos, sentís, sienten; **PRES SUBJ** sienta, sientas, sienta, sintamos, sintáis, sientan; **PRES P** sintiendo; **IMPERAT** siente, sienta, sintamos, sentid, sientan

[6] **vestir PRES** visto, vistes, viste, vestimos, vestís, visten; **PRES SUBJ** vista, vistas, vista, vistamos, vistáis, vistan; **PRES P** vistiendo; **IMPERAT** viste, vista, vistamos, vestid, vistan

[7] **dormir PRES** duermo, duermes, duerme, dormimos, dormís, duermen; **PRES SUBJ** duerma, duermas, duerma, durmamos, durmáis, duerman; **PRES P** durmiendo; **IMPERAT** duerme, duerma, durmamos, dormid, duerman

[8] **andar PRET** anduve, anduviste, anduvo, anduvimos, anduvisteis, anduvieron; **IMPERF SUBJ** anduviera/anduviese

[9] **caber PRES** quepo, cabes, cabe, cabemos, cabéis, caben; **PRES SUBJ** quepa, quepas, quepa, quepamos, quepáis, quepan; **FUT** cabré; **COND** cabría; **PRET** cupe, cupiste, cupo, cupimos, cupisteis, cupieron; **IMPERF SUBJ** cupiera/cupiese; **IMPERAT** cabe, quepa, quepamos, cabed, quepan

[10] **conducir PRES** conduzco, conduces, conduce, conducimos, conducís, conducen; **PRES SUBJ** conduzca, conduzcas, conduzca, conduzcamos, conduzcáis, conduzcan; **PRET** conduje, condujiste, condujo, condujimos, condujisteis, condujeron; **IMPERF SUBJ** condujera/condujese; **IMPERAT** conduce, conduzca, conduzcamos, conducid, conduzcan

[11] **dar PRES** doy, das, da, damos, dais, dan; **PRES SUBJ** dé, des, dé, demos, deis, den; **PRET** di, diste, dio, dimos, disteis, dieron; **IMPERF SUBJ** diera/diese; **IMPERAT** da, dé, demos, dad, den

[12] **decir PRES** digo, dices, dice, decimos, decís, dicen; **PRES SUBJ** diga, digas, diga, digamos, digáis, digan; **FUT** diré; **COND** diría; **PRET** dije, dijiste, dijo, dijimos, dijisteis, dijeron; **IMPERF SUBJ** dijera/dijese; **PRES P** diciendo; **PP** dicho; **IMPERAT** di, diga, digamos, decid, digan

[13] **ESTAR** to be

INDICATIVE

PRESENT	FUTURE	CONDITIONAL
1. estoy	estaré	estaría
2. estás	estarás	estarías
3. está	estará	estaría
1. estamos	estaremos	estaríamos
2. estáis	estaréis	estaríais
3. están	estarán	estarían

IMPERFECT	PRETERITE	PERFECT
1. estaba	estuve	he estado
2. estabas	estuviste	has estado
3. estaba	estuvo	ha estado
1. estábamos	estuvimos	hemos estado
2. estabais	estuvisteis	habéis estado
3. estaban	estuvieron	han estado

FUTURE PERFECT	CONDITIONAL PERFECT	PLUPERFECT
1. habré estado	habría estado	había estado
2. habrás estado	habrías estado	habías estado
3. habrá estado	habría estado	había estado
1. habremos estado	habríamos estado	habíamos estado
2. habréis estado	habríais estado	habíais estado
3. habrán estado	habrían estado	habían estado

SUBJUNCTIVE

PRESENT	IMPERFECT	PERFECT/PLUPERFECT
1. esté	estuv-iera/iese	haya/hubiera* estado
2. estés	estuv-ieras/ieses	hayas/hubieras estado
3. esté	estuv-iera/iese	haya/hubiera estado
1. estemos	esuv-iéramos/iésemos	hayamos/hubiéramos estado
2. estéis	estuv-ierais/ieseis	hayáis/hubierais estado
3. estén	estuv-ieran/iesen	hayan/hubieran estado

IMPERATIVE	INFINITIVE	PARTICIPLE
(tú) está	**PRESENT**	**PRESENT**
(Vd) esté	estar	estando
(nosotros) estemos		
(vosotros) estad	**PERFECT**	**PAST**
(Vds) estén	haber estado	estado

* the alternative form 'hubiese' etc is also possible

[14] **HABER** to have (*auxiliary*)

INDICATIVE

PRESENT	FUTURE	CONDITIONAL
1. he	habré	habría
2. has	habrás	habrías
3. ha/hay*	habrá	habría
1. hemos	habremos	habríamos
2. habéis	habréis	habríais
3. han	habrán	habrían

IMPERFECT	PRETERITE	PERFECT
1. había	hube	
2. habías	hubiste	
3. había	hubo	ha habido*
1. habíamos	hubimos	
2. habíais	hubisteis	
3. habían	hubieron	

FUTURE PERFECT	CONDITIONAL PERFECT	PLUPERFECT
1.		
2.		
3. habrá habido*	habría habido*	había habido*
1.		
2.		
3.		

SUBJUNCTIVE

PRESENT	IMPERFECT	PERFECT/PLUPERFECT
1. haya	hub-iera/iese	
2. hayas	hub-ieras/ieses	
3. haya	hub-iera/iese	haya/hubiera** habido*
1. hayamos	hub-iéramos/iésemos	
2. hayáis	hub-ierais/ieseis	
3. hayan	hub-ieran/iesen	

INFINITIVE   PARTICIPLE

INFINITIVE	PARTICIPLE
PRESENT	**PRESENT**
haber	habiendo
PERFECT	**PAST**
haber habido*	habido

* 'haber' is an auxiliary verb used with the participle of another verb to form compound tenses (eg he bebido - I have drunk). 'hay' means 'there is/are' and all third person singular forms in their respective tenses have this meaning. The forms highlighted with an asterisk are used only for this latter construction.

** the alternative form 'hubiese' is also possible.

[15] **hacer PRES** hago, haces, hace, hacemos, hacéis, hacen; **PRES SUBJ** haga, hagas, haga hagamos, hagáis, hagan; **FUT** haré; **COND** haría; **PRET** hice, hiciste, hizo, hicimos, hicisteis, hicieron; **IMPERF SUBJ** hiciera/hiciese; **PP** hecho; **IMPERAT** haz, haga, hagamos, haced, hagan

[16] **ir PRES** voy, vas, va, vamos, vais, van; **PRES SUBJ** vaya, vayas, vaya, vayamos, vayáis, vayan; **IMPERF** iba, ibas, iba, íbamos, ibais, iban; **PRET** fui, fuiste, fue, fuimos, fuisteis, fueron; **IMPERF SUBJ** fuera/fuese; **PRES P** yendo; **IMPERAT** ve, vaya, vamos, id, vayan

[17] **oir PRES** oigo, oyes, oye, oímos, oís, oyen; **PRES SUBJ** oiga, oigas, oiga, oigamos, oigáis, oigan; **PRET** oí, oíste, oyó, oímos, oísteis, oyeron; **IMPERF SUBJ** oyera/oyese; **PRES P** oyendo; **PP** oído; **IMPERAT** oye, oiga, oigamos, oíd, oigan

[18] **poder PRES** puedo, puedes, puede, podemos, podéis, pueden; **PRES SUBJ** pueda, puedas, pueda, podamos, podáis, puedan; **FUT** podré; **COND** podría; **PRET** pude, pudiste, pudo, pudimos, pudisteis, pudieron; **IMPERF SUBJ** pudiera/pudiese; **PRES P** pudiendo; **IMPERAT** puede, pueda, podamos, poded, puedan

[19] **poner PRES** pongo, pones, pone, ponemos, ponéis, ponen; **PRES SUBJ** ponga, pongas, ponga, pongamos, pongáis, pongan; **FUT** pondré; **PRET** puse, pusiste, puso, pusimos, pusisteis, pusieron; **IMPERF SUBJ** pusiera/pusiese; **PP** puesto; **IMPERAT** pon, ponga, pongamos, poned, pongan

[20] **querer PRES** quiero, quieres, quiere, queremos, queréis, quieren; **PRES SUBJ** quiera, quieras, quiera, queramos, queráis, quieran; **FUT** querré; **COND** querría; **PRET** quise, quisiste, quiso, quisimos, quisisteis, quisieron; **IMPERF SUBJ** quisiera/quisiese; **IMPERAT** quiere, quiera, queramos, quered, quieran

[21] **saber PRES** sé, sabes, sabe, sabemos, sabéis, saben; **PRES SUBJ** sepa, sepas, sepa, sepamos, sepáis, sepan; **FUT** sabré; **COND** sabría; **PRET** supe, supiste, supo, supimos, supisteis, supieron; **IMPERF SUBJ** supiera/supiese; **IMPERAT** sabe, sepa, sepamos, sabed, sepan

[22] **salir PRES** salgo, sales, sale, salimos, salís, salen; **PRES SUBJ** salga, salgas, salga, salgamos, salgáis, salgan; **FUT** saldré; **COND** saldría; **IMPERAT** sal, salga salgamos, salid, salgan

[23] **ser PRES** soy, eres, es, somos, sois, son; **PRES SUBJ** sea, seas, sea, seamos, seáis, sean; **IMPERF** era, eras, era, éramos, erais, eran; **PRET** fui, fuiste, fue, fuimos, fuisteis, fueron; **IMPERF SUBJ** fuera/fuese; **IMPERAT** sé, sea, seamos, sed, sean

[24] **tener PRES** tengo, tienes, tiene, tenemos, tenéis, tienen; **PRES SUBJ** tenga, tengas, tenga, tengamos, tengáis, tengan; **FUT** tendré; **COND** tendría; **PRET** tuve, tuviste, tuvo, tuvimos, tuvisteis, tuvieron; **IMPERF SUBJ** tuviera/tuviese; **IMPERAT** ten, tenga, tengamos, tened tengan

[25] **traer PRES** traigo, traes, trae, traemos, traéis, traen; **PRES SUBJ** traiga, traigas, traiga, traigamos, traigáis, traigan; **PRET** traje, trajiste, trajo, trajimos, trajisteis, trajeron; **IMPERF SUBJ** trajera/trajese; **IMPERAT** trae, traiga, traigamos, traed, traigan

[26] **valer PRES** valgo, vales, vale, valemos, valéis, valen; **PRES SUBJ** valga, valgas, valga, valgamos, valgáis, valgan; **FUT** valdré; **COND** valdría; **IMPERAT** vale, valga, valemos, valed, valgan

[27] **venir PRES** vengo, vienes, viene, venimos, venís, vienen; **PRES SUBJ** venga, vengas, venga, vengamos, vengáis, vengan; **FUT** vendré; **COND** vendría; **PRET** vine, viniste, vino, vinimos, vinisteis, vinieron; **IMPERF SUBJ** viniera/viniese; **PRES P** viniendo; **IMPERAT** ven, venga, vengamos, venid, vengan

[28] **ver PRES** veo, ves, ve, vemos, veis, ven; **PRES SUBJ** vea, veas, vea, veamos, veáis, vean; **IMPERF** veía, veías, veía, veíamos, veíais, veían; **PRET** vi, viste, vio, vimos, visteis, vieron; **IMPERF SUBJ** viera/viese; **IMPERAT** ve, vea, veamos, ved, vean

[29] **desviar PRES** desvío, desvías, desvía, desviamos, desviáis, desvían; **PRES SUBJ** desvíe, desvíes, desvíe, desviemos, desviéis, desvíen; **IMPERAT** desvía, desvíe, desviemos, desviéis, desvíen

[30] **continuar PRES** continúo, continúas, continúa, continuamos, continuáis, continúan; **PRES SUBJ** continúe, continúes, continúe, continuemos, continuéis, continúen; **IMPERAT** continúa, continúe, continuemos, continuad, continúen

[31] **adquirir PRES** adquiero, adquieres, adquiere, adquirimos, adquirís, adquieren; **PRES SUBJ** adquiera, adquiras, adquiera, adquiramos, adquiráis, adquieran; **IMPERAT** adquiere, adquiera, adquiramos, adquirid, adquieran

[32] **jugar PRES** juego, juegas, juega, jugamos, jugáis, juegan; **PRES SUBJ** juegue, juegues, juegue, juguemos, juguéis, jueguen; **IMPERAT** juega, juegue, juguemos, jugad, jueguen

[33] **agradecer PRES** agradezco, agradeces, agradece, agradecemos, agradecéis, agradecen; **PRES SUBJ** agradezca, agradezcas, agradezca, agradezcamos, agradezcáis, agradezcan; **IMPERAT** agradece, agradezca, agradezcamos, agradeced, agradezcan

[34] **conocer PRES** conozco, conoces, conoce, conocemos, conocéis, conocen; **PRES SUBJ** conozca, conozcas, conozca, conozcamos, conozcáis, conozcan; **IMPERAT** conoce, conozca, conozcamos, conoced, conozcan

[35] **lucir PRES** luzco, luces, luce, lucimos, lucís, lucen; **PRES SUBJ** luzca, luzcas, luzca, luzcamos, luzcáis, luzcan; **IMPERAT** luce, luzca, luzcamos, lucid, luzcan

[36] **leer PRET** leí, leíste, leyó, leímos, leísteis, leyeron; **IMPERF SUBJ** leyera/leyese; **PRES P** leyendo; **PP** leído; **IMPERAT** lee, lea, leamos, leed, lean

[37] **huir PRES** huyo, huyes, huye, huimos, huís, huyen; **PRES SUBJ** huya, huyas, huya, huyamos, huyáis, huyan; **PRET** huí, huiste, huyó, huimos, huisteis, huyeron; **IMPERF SUBJ** huyera/huyese; **PRES P** huyendo; **PP** huido; **IMPERAT** huye, huya, huyamos, huid, huyan

[38] **roer PRES** roo/roigo/royo, roes, roe, roemos, roéis, roen; **PRES SUBJ** roa/roiga/roya, roas, roa, roamos, roáis, roan; **PRET** roí, roíste, royó, roímos, roísteis, royeron; **IMPERF SUBJ** royera/royese; **PRES P** royendo; **PP** roído; **IMPERAT** roe, roa, roamos, roed, roan

[39] **caer PRES** caigo, caes, cae, caemos, caéis, caen; **PRES SUBJ** caiga, caigas, caiga, caigamos, caigáis, caigan; **PRES P** cayendo; **PP** caído; **IMPERAT** cae, caiga caigamos, caed, caigan

[40] **cazar PRET** cacé, cazaste, cazó, cazamos, cazasteis, cazaron; **PRES SUBJ** cace, caces, cacen, cacemos, cacéis, cacen

[41] **cocer PRES** cuezo, cueces, cuece, cocemos, cocéis, cuecen; **PRES SUBJ** cueza, cuezas, cueza, cozamos, cozáis, cuezan; **IMPERAT** cuece, cueza, cozamos, cozed, cuezan

[42] **llegar PRET** llegué, llegaste, llegó, llegamos, llegasteis, llegaron; **PRES SUBJ** llegue, llegues, llegue, lleguemos, lleguéis, lleguen

[43] **cambiar PRES** cambio, cambias, cambia, cambiamos, cambiáis, cambian; **PRES SUBJ** cambie, cambies, cambie, cambiemos, cambiéis, cambien; **IMPERAT** cambia, cambie, cambiemos, cambiad, cambien

[44] **sacar PRET** saqué, sacaste, sacó, sacamos, sacasteis, sacaron; **PRES SUBJ** saque, saques, saque, saquemos, saquéis, saquen; **IMPERAT** saca, saque, saquemos, sacad, saquen

[45] **averiguar PRET** averigüé, averiguaste, averiguó, averiguamos, averiguasteis, averiguaron; **PRES SUBJ** averigüe, averigües, averigüe, averigüemos, averigüéis, averigüen; **IMPERAT** averigua, averigüe, averigüemos, averiguad, averigüen

[46] **asir PRES** asgo, ases, ase, asimos, asís, asen; **PRES SUBJ** asga, asgas, asga, asgamos, asgáis, asgan; **IMPERAT** asc, asga, asgamos, asid, asgan

[47] **adecuar PRES** adecuo, adecuas, adecua, adecuamos, adecuáis, adecuan; **PRES SUBJ** adecue, adecues, adecue, adecuemos, adecuéis, adecuen; **IMPERAT** adecua, adecuen, adecuemos, adecuad, adecuen

[48] **delinquir PRES** delinco, delinques, delinque, delinquimos, delinquís, delinquen; **PRES SUBJ** delinca, delincas, delinca, delincamos, delincáis, delincan; **IMPERAT** delinque, delinca, delincamos, delinquid, delincan

[49] **mecer PRES** mezo, meces, mece, mecemos, mecéis, mecen; **PRES SUBJ** meza, mezas, meza, mezamos, mezáis, mezan; **IMPERAT** mece, meza, mezamos, meced, mezan

[50] **errar PRES** yerro, yerras, yerra, erramos, erráis, yerran; **PRES SUBJ** yerre, yerres, yerre, erremos, erréis, yerren; **IMPERAT** yerra, yerre, erremos, errad, yerren

[51] **comenzar PRES** comienzo, comienzas, comienza, comenzamos, comenzáis, comienzan; **PRES SUBJ** comience, comiences, comience, comencemos, comencéis, comiencen; **IMPERAT** comienza, comience, comencemos, comenzad, comiencen

[52] **zurcir PRES** zurzo, zurces, zurce, zurcimos, zurcís, zurcen; **PRES SUBJ** zurza, zurzas, zurza, zurzamos, zurzáis, zurzan; **IMPERAT** zurce, zurza, zurzamos, zurcid, zurzan

[53] **proteger PRES** protejo, proteges, protege, protegemos, protegéis, protegen; **PRES SUBJ** proteja, protejas, proteja, protejamos, protejáis, protejan; **IMPERAT** protege, proteja, protejamos, proteged, protejan

[54] **discernir PRES** discierno, disciernes, discierne, discernimos, discernís, disciernen; **PRES SUBJ** discierna, disciernas, discierna, discernamos, discernáis, disciernan; **IMPERAT** discierne, discierna, discernamos, discernid, disciernan

[55] **erguir PRES** irgo/yergo, irgues/yergues, irgue/yergue, erguimos, erguís, irguen/yerguen; **PRET** erguí, erguiste, irguió, erguimos, erguisteis, irguieron; **PRES SUBJ** irga/yerga, irgas/yergas, irga/yerga, irgamos/yergamos, irgáis/ yergáis, irgan/yergan; **IMPERF SUBJ** irguiera/irguiese; **IMPERAT** irgue/yergue, irga/yerga, irgamos/yergamos, erguid, irgan/yergan

[56] **reír PRES** río, ríes, ríe, reímos, reís, ríen; **PRET** reí, reíste, rió, reímos, reísteis, rieron; **PRES SUBJ** ría, rías, ría, riamos, riáis, rían; **IMPERF SUBJ** riera/ riese; **IMPERAT** ríe, ría, riamos, reíd, rían

[57] **dirigir PRES** dirijo, diriges, dirige, dirigimos, dirigís, dirigen; **PRES SUBJ** dirija, dirijas, dirija, dirijamos, dirijáis, dirijan; **IMPERAT** dirige, dirija, dirijamos, dirigid, dirijan

[58] **regir PRES** rijo, riges, rige, regimos, regís, rigen; **PRES SUBJ** rija, rijas, rija, rijamos, rijáis, rijan; **IMPERAT** rige, rija, rijamos, regid, rijan

[59] **distinguir PRES** distingo, distingues, distingue, distinguimos, distinguís, distinguen; **PRES SUBJ** distinga, distingas, distinga, distingamos, distingáis, distingan; **IMPERAT** distingue, distinga, distingamos, distinguid, distingan

[60] **nacer PRES** nazco, naces, nace, nacemos, nacéis, nacen; **PRES SUBJ** nazca, nazcas, nazca, nazcamos, nazcáis, nazcan; **IMPERAT** nace, nazca, nazcamos, naced, nazcan

[61] **yacer PRES** yazco/yazgo/yago, yaces, yace, yacemos, yacéis, yacen; **PRES SUBJ** yazca/yazga/yaga; **IMPERAT** yace/yaz, yazca/yazga/yaga, yazcamos/ yazgamos/yagamos, yaced, yazcan/yazgan/yagan

[62] **argüir PRES** arguyo, arguyes, arguye, argüimos, argüís, arguyen; **PRET** argüí, argüiste, arguyó, argüimos, argüisteis, arguyeron; **PRES SUBJ** arguya, arguyas, arguya, arguyamos, arguyáis, arguyan; **IMPERF SUBJ** arguyera/ arguyese; **IMPERAT** arguye, arguya, arguyamos, argüid, arguyan

[63] **avergonzar PRES** avergüenzo, avergüenzas, avergüenza, avergonzamos, avergonzáis, avergüenzan; **PRET** avergoncé, avergonzaste, avergonzó, avergonzamos, avergonzasteis, avergonzaron; **PRES SUBJ** avergüence, avergüences, avergüence, avergoncemos, avergoncéis, avergüencen; **IMPERAT** avergüenza, avergüence, avergoncemos, avergonzad, avergüencen

[64] **trocar PRES** trueco, truecas, trueca, trocamos, trocáis, truecan; **PRET** troqué, trocaste, trocó, trocamos, trocasteis, trocaron; **PRES SUBJ** trueque, trueques, trueque, troquemos, troquéis, truequen; **IMPERAT** trueca, trueque, troquemos, trocad, truequen

[65] **oler PRES** huelo, hueles, huele, olemos, oléis, huelen; **PRES SUBJ** huela, huelas, huela, olamos, oláis, huelan; **IMPERAT** huele, huela, olamos, oled, huelan

Verbos irregulares ingleses

INFINITIVO	PRETÉRITO	PARTICIPIO
arise	arose	arisen
awake	awoke	awoken
awaken	awoke, awakened	awakened, awoken
be	were/was	been
bear	bore	borne
beat	beat	beaten
become	became	become
begin	began	begun
bend	bent	bent
beseech	besought, beseeched	besought, beseeched
bet	bet, betted	bet, betted
bid	bade, bid	bidden, bid
bind	bound	bound
bite	bit	bitten
bleed	bled	bled
blow	blew	blown
break	broke	broken
breed	bred	bred
bring	brought	brought
build	built	built
burn	burnt, burned	burnt, burned
burst	burst	burst
buy	bought	bought
cast	cast	cast
catch	caught	caught
choose	chose	chosen
cling	clung	clung
clothe	clad, clothed	clad, clothed
come	came	come
cost	cost	cost
creep	crept	crept
cut	cut	cut
deal	dealt	dealt
dig	dug	dug
do	did	done
draw	drew	drawn
dream	dreamt, dreamed	dreamt, dreamed
drink	drank	drunk
drive	drove	driven
dwell	dwelt	dwelt
eat	ate	eaten
fall	fell	fallen
feed	fed	fed
feel	felt	felt

INFINITIVO	PRETÉRITO	PARTICIPIO
fight	fought	fought
find	found	found
flee	fled	fled
fling	flung	flung
fly	flew	flown
forget	forgot	forgotten
forgive	forgave	forgiven
forsake	forsook	forsaken
freeze	froze	frozen
get	got	got, *US* gotten
give	gave	given
go	went	gone
grind	ground	ground
grow	grew	grown
hang	hung/hanged	hung/hanged
have	had	had
hear	heard	heard
hide	hid	hidden
hit	hit	hit
hold	held	held
hurt	hurt	hurt
keep	kept	kept
kneel	knelt	knelt
knit	knitted, knit	knitted, knit
know	knew	known
lay	laid	laid
lead	led	led
lean	leant, leaned	leant, leaned
leap	leapt, leaped	leapt, leaped
learn	learnt, learned	learnt, learned
leave	left	left
lend	lent	lent
let	let	let
lie	lay	lain
light	lit	lit
lose	lost	lost
make	made	made
mean	meant	meant
meet	met	met
mow	mowed	mown, mowed
pay	paid	paid
put	put	put
quit	quit	quit
read	read	read
rend	rent	rent
rid	rid	rid
ride	rode	ridden
ring	rang	rung
rise	rose	risen
run	ran	run
saw	sawed	sawn, sawed

INFINITIVO	PRETÉRITO	PARTICIPIO
say	said	said
see	saw	seen
seek	sought	sought
sell	sold	sold
send	sent	sent
set	set	set
sew	sewed	sewn
shake	shook	shaken
shear	sheared	shorn, sheared
shed	shed	shed
shine	shone	shone
shoe	shod	shod
shoot	shot	shot
show	showed	shown
shrink	shrank	shrunk
shut	shut	shut
sing	sang	sung
sink	sank	sunk
sit	sat	sat
slay	slew	slain
sleep	slept	slept
slide	slid	slid
sling	slung	slung
slink	slunk	slunk
slit	slit	slit
smell	smelled, smelt	smelled, smelt
sow	sowed	sown, sowed
speak	spoke	spoken
speed	sped, speeded	sped, speeded
spell	spelt, spelled	spelt, spelled
spend	spent	spent
spill	spilt, spilled	spilt, spilled
spin	span	spun
spit	spat	spat
split	split	split
spoil	spoilt, spoiled	spoilt, spoiled
spread	spread	spread
spring	sprang	sprung
stand	stood	stood
steal	stole	stolen
stick	stuck	stuck
sting	stung	stung
stink	stank, stunk	stunk
strew	strewed	strewed, strewn
stride	strode	stridden
strike	struck	struck
string	strung	strung
strive	strove	striven
swear	swore	sworn
sweep	swept	swept
swell	swelled	swollen

INFINITIVO	PRETÉRITO	PARTICIPIO
swing	swung	swung
swim	swam	swum
take	took	taken
teach	taught	taught
tear	tore	torn
tell	told	told
think	thought	thought
thrive	thrived, throve	thrived, thriven
throw	threw	thrown
thrust	thrust	thrust
tread	trod	trodden
wake	woke	woken
wear	wore	worn
weave	wove	woven
weep	wept	wept
wet	wet	wet
win	won	won
wind	wound	wound
wring	wrung	wrung
write	wrote	written

English – Spanish
Inglés – Español

A, a [eɪ] *n* (**a**) *(the letter)* A, a *f* (**b**) *Mus* A la *m* (**c**) *Br* **A road** ≃ carretera *f* nacional

a [eɪ, *unstressed* ə] *indef art (before vowel or silent h* **an**) (**a**) un, una; **a man/a woman** un hombre/una mujer; **he has a big nose** tiene la nariz grande (**b**) *(omitted in Spanish)* **half a litre/an hour** medio litro/media hora; **a hundred/thousand people** cien/mil personas; **let's have a drink** vamos a beber algo; **he's a teacher** es profesor; **what a pity** qué pena (**c**) *(each)* **60 pence a kilo** 60 peniques el kilo; **to eat grapes two at a time** comer las uvas de dos en dos; **three times a week** tres veces a la semana (**d**) *(a certain)* un/una tal; **a Mr Rees phoned** llamó un tal Sr. Rees

AA [eɪˈeɪ] *n* (**a**) *(abbr* **Alcoholics Anonymous***)* AA, alcohólicos *mpl* anónimos (**b**) *(abbr* **Automobile Association***)* ≃ AC

AAA [eɪeɪˈeɪ] *n* (**a**) *Br (abbr* **Amateur Athletic Association***)* = federación británica de atletismo aficionado (**b**) *US (abbr* **American Automobile Association***)* ≃ AC

aback [əˈbæk] *adv* **to be taken a.** quedarse de una pieza (**by** por)

abandon [əˈbændən] **1** *n* desenfreno *m*; **with reckless a.** desenfrenadamente

2 *vt (child)* abandonar; *(job)* dejar; *(project)* renunciar a

abase [əˈbeɪs] *vt* **to a. oneself** humillarse

abashed [əˈbæʃt] *adj* desconcertado(a)

abate [əˈbeɪt] *vi (anger)* apaciguarse; *(storm)* amainar

abattoir [ˈæbətwɑː(r)] *n* matadero *m*

abbey [ˈæbɪ] *n* abadía *f*

abbot [ˈæbət] *n* abad *m*

abbreviate [əˈbriːvɪeɪt] *vt* abreviar

abbreviation [əbriːvɪˈeɪʃən] *n* abreviatura *f*

abdicate [ˈæbdɪkeɪt] *vt & vi* abdicar

abdication [æbdɪˈkeɪʃən] *n* abdicación *f*

abdomen [ˈæbdəmən] *n* abdomen *m*

abduct [æbˈdʌkt] *vt* raptar, secuestrar

aberration [æbəˈreɪʃən] *n* aberración *f*

abet [əˈbet] *vt* **to aid and a. sb** ser cómplice de algn

abeyance [əˈbeɪəns] *n* **to be in a.** estar en desuso

abhor [əbˈhɔː(r)] *vt* aborrecer

abhorrent [əbˈhɒrənt] *adj* aborrecible

abide [əˈbaɪd] *vt* aguantar; **I can't a. it** no lo aguanto

  ▸ **abide by** *vt insep (promise)* cumplir con; *(rules)* atenerse a

ability [əˈbɪlɪtɪ] *n (capability)* capacidad *f*, aptitud *f*; *(talent)* talento *m*

abject [ˈæbdʒekt] *adj (state)* miserable; *(apology)* rastrero(a)

ablaze [əˈbleɪz] *adj & adv* en llamas, ardiendo

able [ˈeɪbəl] *adj (capable)* capaz; **will you be a. to come on Tuesday?** ¿podrás venir el martes?

able-bodied [eɪbəlˈbɒdɪd] *adj* sano(a); **a. seaman** marinero *m* de primera

abnormal [æbˈnɔːməl] *adj* anormal

abnormally [æbˈnɔːməlɪ] *adv* anormalmente; *(large)* extraordinariamente

aboard [əˈbɔːd] **1** *adv* a bordo; **to go a.** *(ship)* embarcarse; *(train)* subir

  2 *prep* a bordo de

abode [əˈbəʊd] *n Jur* **of no fixed a.** sin domicilio fijo

abolish [əˈbɒlɪʃ] *vt* abolir

abolition [æbəˈlɪʃən] *n* abolición *f*

abominable [əˈbɒmɪnəbəl] *adj* abominable; *(dreadful)* terrible

aborigine [æbəˈrɪdʒɪnɪ] *n* aborigen *mf* australiano(a)

abort [əˈbɔːt] **1** *vt Med* hacer abortar; *Fig (plan etc)* archivar

  2 *vi Med* abortar

abortion [əˈbɔːʃən] *n Med* aborto *m*; **a. law** ley *f* del aborto; **to have an a.** abortar

abortive [əˈbɔːtɪv] *adj (plan)* fracasado(a); *(attempt)* frustrado(a)

abound [əˈbaʊnd] *vi* **to a. in** *or* **with** abundar en

about [əˈbaʊt] *adv & prep* (**a**) *(concerning)* acerca de, sobre; **a programme a. Paris** un programa sobre París; **to be worried a. sth** estar preocupado(a) por algo; **to speak a. sth** hablar de algo; **what's it all a.?** *(what's happening?)* ¿qué pasa?; *(story etc)* ¿de qué se trata?; *Fam* **how a. a game of tennis?** ¿qué te parece un partido de tenis?

(**b**) *(around)* por todas partes; **don't leave things lying a.** no dejes las cosas por medio; **there's nobody a.** no hay nadie; **to look a.** mirar alrededor; **to rush a.** correr de un lado para otro; **we went for a walk a.** the town dimos una vuelta por el pueblo

(**c**) *(approximately)* más o menos; **it's a. three o'clock** son más o menos las tres; **it's a. time you got up** ya es hora de que te levantes; **it's just a. finished** está casi terminado; **she's a. forty** tiene unos cuarenta años

(**d**) **it's a. to start** está a punto de empezar; **not to be a. to do sth** no estar dispuesto(a) a hacer algo

about-turn [əbaʊt'tɜːn], *US* **about-face** [əbaʊt'feɪs] *n* media vuelta *f*; **to do an a.** dar media vuelta; *Fig* cambiar de idea por completo

above [ə'bʌv] *adv & prep* (**a**) *(higher than)* encima de, sobre, arriba; **100 m a. sea level** 100 m sobre el nivel del mar; **it's a. the door** está encima de la puerta; **the flat a.** el piso de arriba (**b**) *(greater than)* superior (a); **amounts a. £10** cantidades superiores a las 10 libras; *Fig* **a policy imposed from a.** una política impuesta desde arriba (**c**) **a. all** sobre todo; **he's not a. stealing** es capaz incluso de robar (**d**) *(in book etc)* más arriba

above-board [ə'bʌv'bɔːd] *adj (scheme)* legítimo(a)

above-mentioned [ə'bʌvmenʃənd] *adj* susodicho(a)

abrasive [ə'breɪsɪv] **1** *adj (substance)* abrasivo(a); *Fig (voice, wit etc)* cáustico(a)

2 *n* abrasivo *m*

abreast [ə'brest] *adv* **to walk three a.** ir de tres en fondo; *Fig* **to keep a. of things** mantenerse al día

abridged [ə'brɪdʒd] *adj (book)* abreviado(a)

abroad [ə'brɔːd] *adv* **to be a.** estar en el extranjero; **to go a.** irse al extranjero

abrupt [ə'brʌpt] *adj (manner)* brusco(a); *(tone)* áspero(a); *(change)* súbito(a)

abruptly [ə'brʌptlɪ] *adv (act)* bruscamente; *(speak)* con aspereza; *(change)* repentinamente

abscess ['æbses] *n* absceso *m*; *(on gum)* flemón *m*

abscond [əb'skɒnd] *vi* huir

absence ['æbsəns] *n (of person)* ausencia *f*; *(of thing)* falta *f*

absent ['æbsənt] *adj* ausente; *Fig* **an a. look** una mirada distraída

absentee [æbsən'tiː] *n* ausente *mf*

absenteeism [æbsən'tiːɪzəm] *n* absentismo *m*

absently ['æbsəntlɪ] *adv* distraídamente

absent-minded [æbsənt'maɪndɪd] *adj* distraído(a)

absolute ['æbsəluːt] *adj* absoluto(a); *(failure)* total; *(truth)* puro(a); **it's an a. disgrace** es una auténtica vergüenza

absolutely [æbsə'luːtlɪ] **1** *adv (completely)* completamente; **a. not** en absoluto; **you're a. right** tienes toda la razón

2 *interj* **a.!** ¡desde luego!

absolve [əb'zɒlv] *vt* absolver (**from** de)

absorb [əb'zɔːb] *vt (liquid)* absorber; *(sound, blow)* amortiguar; *Fig* **to be absorbed in sth** estar absorto(a) en algo

absorbing [əb'zɔːbɪŋ] *adj (book, work)* absorbente

abstain [əb'steɪn] *vi* abstenerse (**from** de)

abstemious [əb'stiːmɪəs] *adj* abstemio(a)

abstention [əb'stenʃən] *n* abstención *f*

abstinence ['æbstɪnəns] *n* abstinencia *f*

abstract ['æbstrækt] **1** *adj* abstracto(a)

2 *n (of thesis etc)* resumen *m*

abstruse [əb'struːs] *adj* abstruso(a)

absurd [əb'sɜːd] *adj* absurdo(a)

abundance [ə'bʌndəns] *n* abundancia *f*

abundant [ə'bʌndənt] *adj* abundante, rico(a) (**in** en)

abuse **1** *n* [ə'bjuːs] (**a**) *(ill-treatment)* malos tratos; *(misuse)* abuso *m* (**b**) *(insults)* injurias *fpl*

2 *vt* [ə'bjuːz] (**a**) *(ill-treat)* maltratar; *(misuse)* abusar de (**b**) *(insult)* injuriar

abusive [əb'juːsɪv] *adj (insulting)* insultante

abysmal [ə'bɪzməl] *adj (conditions)* extremo(a); *Fam (very bad)* fatal, pésimo(a)

abyss [ə'bɪs] *n* abismo *m*; *Fig* extremo *m*

AC [eɪ'siː] *(abbr* **alternating current***)* CA

academic [ækə'demɪk] **1** *adj* académico(a); *(career)* universitario(a); *(discussion)* teórico(a); **a. year** año *m* escolar

2 *n* académico(a) *m,f*

academy [ə'kædəmɪ] *n (society)* academia *f*; *Educ* instituto *m* de enseñanza media; **a. of music** conservatorio *m*

accede [æk'siːd] *vi* acceder (**to** a)

accelerate [æk'seləreɪt] **1** *vt (engine)* acelerar; *(step)* aligerar

2 *vi (car, engine)* acelerar

acceleration [ækselə'reɪʃən] *n* aceleración *f*

accelerator [æk'seləreɪtə(r)] *n* acelerador *m*

accent ['æksənt] *n* acento *m*

accentuate [æk'sentʃʋeɪt] *vt* subrayar

accept [ək'sept] *vt & vi* aceptar; *(theory)* admitir; **do you a. that ...?** ¿estás de acuerdo en que ...?

acceptable [ək'septəbəl] *adj (satisfactory)* aceptable; *(tolerable)* admisible

acceptance [ək'septəns] *n (act of accepting)* aceptación *f*; *(good reception)* aprobación *f*

access ['ækses] *n* acceso *m*; *Comput* **a. provider** proveedor *m* de acceso (a Internet); **a. road** carretera *f* de acceso; **to have a. to sth** tener libre acceso a algo

accessible [ək'sesəbəl] *adj (place, position)* accesible; *(person)* asequible

accession [ək'seʃən] *n* subida *f* (al trono)

accessory [ək'sesərɪ] *n* (**a**) *Jur* cómplice *mf* (**b**) **accessories** accesorios *mpl*; *(for outfit)* complementos *mpl*

accident ['æksɪdənt] *n* accidente *m*; *(coincidence)* casualidad *f*; **it was an a. on my part** lo hice sin querer; **car a.** accidente *m* de carretera; **by a.** por casualidad

accidental [æksɪ'dentəl] *adj* fortuito(a); *(unintended)* imprevisto(a)

accidentally [æksɪ'dentəlɪ] *adv (by chance)* por casualidad; **he did it a.** lo hizo sin querer

accident-prone ['æksɪdəntprəʊn] *adj* propenso(a) a los accidentes

acclaim [ə'kleɪm] **1** *n* aclamación *f* **2** *vt* aclamar

acclimatization [əklaɪmətaɪ'zeɪʃən], *US* **acclimation** [æklɪ'meɪʃən] *n* aclimatación *f*

acclimatize [ə'klaɪmətaɪz], *US* **acclimate** ['æklɪmeɪt] *vt* aclimatar

acclimatized [ə'klaɪmətaɪzd] *adj* aclimatado(a); **to become a.** aclimatarse

accolade ['ækəleɪd] *n* elogio *m*

accommodate [ə'kɒmədeɪt] *vt* (**a**) *(guests)* alojar (**b**) **to a. sb's wishes** complacer a algn

accommodating [ə'kɒmədeɪtɪŋ] *adj (obliging)* complaciente; *(understanding)* comprensivo(a)

accommodation [əkɒmə'deɪʃən] *n* (*US* also *accommodations*) *(lodgings)* alojamiento *m*

accompany [ə'kʌmpənɪ] *vt* acompañar

accomplice [ə'kʌmplɪs] *n* cómplice *mf*

accomplish [ə'kʌmplɪʃ] *vt (aim)* conseguir; *(task, mission)* llevar a cabo

accomplished [ə'kʌmplɪʃt] *adj* dotado(a), experto(a)

accomplishment [ə'kʌmplɪʃmənt] *n* (**a**) *(of task)* realización *f*; *(of duty)* cumplimiento *m* (**b**) **accomplishments** *(talents)* dotes *fpl*

accord [ə'kɔːd] **1** *n (agreement)* acuerdo *m*; **of her/his own a.** espontáneamente **2** *vt (honour etc)* conceder

accordance [ə'kɔːdəns] *n* **in a. with** de acuerdo con

according [ə'kɔːdɪŋ] *prep* **a. to** según; **everything went a. to plan** todo salió conforme a los planes

accordingly [ə'kɔːdɪŋlɪ] *adv* (**a**) **to act a.** *(appropriately)* obrar según y conforme (**b**) *(therefore)* así pues

accordion [ə'kɔːdɪən] *n* acordeón *m*

account [ə'kaʊnt] *n* (**a**) *(report)* informe *m*; **by all accounts** al decir de todos (**b**) **I was fearful on her a.** sufría por ella; **it's of no a.** no tiene importancia; **on a. of** a causa de; **on no a.** bajo ningún concepto; **to take a. of, to take into a.** tener en cuenta (**c**) *Com* cuenta *f*; **to keep the accounts** llevar las cuentas; **accounts department** servicio *m* de contabilidad; **to open/close an a.** abrir/cancelar una cuenta; **current a.** cuenta corriente; **a. number** número *m* de cuenta

▸ **account for** *vt insep (explain)* explicar

accountable [ə'kaʊntəbəl] *adj* **to be a. to sb for sth** ser responsable ante algn de algo

accountancy [ə'kaʊntənsɪ] *n* contabilidad *f*

accountant [ə'kaʊntənt] *n* contable *mf*

accredited [ə'kredɪtɪd] *adj* acreditado(a)

accrue [ə'kruː] *vi (interest)* acumularse

accumulate [ə'kjuːmjʊleɪt] **1** *vt* acumular; *(fortune)* amasar **2** *vi* acumularse

accuracy ['ækjʊrəsɪ] *n (of number etc)* exactitud *f*; *(of shot, criticism)* certeza *f*

accurate ['ækjʊrət] *adj (number)* exacto(a); *(shot, criticism)* certero(a); *(answer)* correcto(a); *(observation)* acertado(a); *(instrument)* de precisión; *(translation)* fiel

accusation [ækjʊ'zeɪʃən] *n* acusación *f*

accuse [ə'kjuːz] *vt* acusar

accused [ə'kjuːzd] *n* **the a.** el/la acusado(a)

accustom [ə'kʌstəm] *vt* acostumbrar; **to be accustomed to doing sth** estar acostumbrado(a) a hacer algo

ace [eɪs] *n* (**a**) *Cards & Fig* as *m* (**b**) *(in tennis)* ace *m*

acetate ['æsɪteɪt] *n* acetato *m*
acetone ['æsɪtəʊn] *n* acetona *f*
ache [eɪk] **1** *n* dolor *m*; **aches and pains** achaques *mpl*
2 *vi* doler; **my back aches** me duele la espalda
achieve [ə'tʃiːv] *vt (attain)* conseguir, alcanzar; *(accomplish)* llevar a cabo, realizar
achievement [ə'tʃiːvmənt] *n (attainment)* logro *m*; *(completion)* realización *f*; *(feat)* hazaña *f*
acid ['æsɪd] **1** *adj* ácido(a); *(taste)* agrio(a); *(remark)* mordaz; **a. rain** lluvia ácida; *Fig* **a. test** prueba decisiva
2 *n* ácido *m*
acknowledge [ək'nɒlɪdʒ] *vt* (**a**) *(recognize)* reconocer; *(claim, defeat)* admitir; *(present)* agradecer; *(letter)* acusar recibo de (**b**) *(greet)* saludar
acknowledgement [ək'nɒlɪdʒmənt] *n* (**a**) *(recognition)* reconocimiento *m*; *(of letter)* acuse *m* de recibo (**b**) **acknowledgements** *(in preface)* menciones *fpl*
acne ['æknɪ] *n* acné *m*
acorn ['eɪkɔːn] *n* bellota *f*
acoustic [ə'kuːstɪk] **1** *adj* acústico(a)
2 *npl* **acoustics** acústica *f*
acquaint [ə'kweɪnt] *vt* **to a. sb with the facts** informar a algn de los detalles; **to be acquainted with the procedure** estar al corriente de como se procede; **to be acquainted with sb** conocer a algn
acquaintance [ə'kweɪntəns] *n* (**a**) conocimiento *m*; **to make sb's a.** conocer a algn (**b**) *(person)* conocido(a) *m,f*
acquiesce [ækwɪ'es] *vi* consentir (**in** en)
acquiescent [ækwɪ'esənt] *adj* conforme
acquire [ə'kwaɪə(r)] *vt* adquirir
acquisition [ækwɪ'zɪʃən] *n* adquisición *f*
acquisitive [ə'kwɪzɪtɪv] *adj* codicioso(a)
acquit [ə'kwɪt] *vt* (**a**) *Jur* **to a. sb of sth** absolver a algn de algo (**b**) **to a. oneself well** defenderse bien
acquittal [ə'kwɪtəl] *n* absolución *f*
acre ['eɪkə(r)] *n* acre *m* (= *aprox 40,47 áreas*)
acrid ['ækrɪd] *adj (smell, taste)* acre
acrimonious [ækrɪ'məʊnɪəs] *adj (remark)* cáustico(a); *(dispute)* enconado(a)
acrobat ['ækrəbæt] *n* acróbata *mf*
across [ə'krɒs] **1** *adv* a través; **the river is 30 m a.** el río mide 30 m de ancho; **to go a.** atravesar; **to run a.** atravesar corriendo
2 *prep* (**a**) a través de; **they live a. the road** viven enfrente; **to go a. the street** cruzar la calle (**b**) *(at the other side of)* al otro lado de

acrylic [ə'krɪlɪk] *adj* acrílico(a)
act [ækt] **1** *n* (**a**) *(action)* acto *m*, acción *f*; **a. of God** caso *m* de fuerza mayor (**b**) *(in parliament)* ley *f*, decreto *m* (**c**)*Th* acto *m*; *(turn in show)* número *m*
2 *vt Th (part)* interpretar; *(character)* representar; *Fig* **to a. the fool** hacer el tonto
3 *vi* (**a**)*Th* hacer teatro; *Cin* hacer cine; *Fig (pretend)* fingir (**b**) *(behave)* comportarse (**c**) *(take action)* actuar, obrar; **to a. on sb's advice** seguir el consejo de algn (**d**)*(work)* funcionar; *(drug etc)* actuar; **to a. as a deterrent** servir de disuasivo (**e**) **to a. as director** hacer de director
▸ **act out** *vt sep* exteriorizar
▸ **act up** *vi Fam (machine)* funcionar mal; *(child)* dar guerra
acting ['æktɪŋ] **1** *adj* interino(a)
2 *n (profession)* teatro *m*; **he's done some a.** ha hecho algo de teatro
action ['ækʃən] *n* (**a**) *(deed)* acción *f*; *Mil* acción de combate; **to be out of a.** *(person)* estar fuera de servicio; *(machine)* estar estropeado(a); **to take a.** tomar medidas (**b**) *Jur* demanda *f* (**c**) *TV* **a. replay** repetición *f*
activate ['æktɪveɪt] *vt* activar
active ['æktɪv] *adj* activo(a); *(energetic)* vigoroso(a); *(interest)* vivo(a); *Ling* **a. voice** voz activa
activist ['æktɪvɪst] *n* activista *mf*
activity [æk'tɪvɪtɪ] *n (of person)* actividad *f*; *(on street etc)* bullicio *m*
actor ['æktə(r)] *n* actor *m*
actress ['æktrɪs] *n* actriz *f*
actual ['æktʃʊəl] *adj* real, verdadero(a)

📝 Note that the Spanish word **actual** is a false friend and is never a translation for the English word **actual**. In Spanish, **actual** means "current, up-to-date, topical".

---

actually ['æktʃʊəlɪ] *adv (really)* en efecto, realmente; *(even)* incluso, hasta; *(in fact)* de hecho

---

📝 Note that the Spanish word **actualmente** is a false friend and is never a translation for the English word **actually**. In Spanish, **actualmente** means "nowadays, at the moment".

---

acumen ['ækjʊmən] *n* perspicacia *f*
acupuncture ['ækjʊpʌŋktʃə(r)] *n* acupuntura *f*
acute [ə'kjuːt] *adj* agudo(a); *(pain)* intenso(a); *(hearing)* muy fino(a); *(shortage)* grave; *(mind)* perspicaz
AD [eɪ'diː] (*abbr* **Anno Domini**) d.J.C., d.C.

ad [æd] *n Fam* anuncio *m*

adamant ['ædəmənt] *adj* firme, inflexible

adapt [ə'dæpt] **1** *vt* adaptar (**to** a); **to a. oneself to sth** adaptarse a algo
   2 *vi* adaptarse

adaptable [ə'dæptəbəl] *adj (instrument)* ajustable; **he's very a.** se amolda fácilmente a las circunstancias

adaptation [ædəp'teɪʃən] *n* adaptación *f*

adapter, adaptor [ə'dæptə(r)] *n Elec* ladrón *m*

add [æd] **1** *vt (numbers)* sumar; *(one thing to another)* añadir
   2 *vi (count)* sumar
   ▸ **add to** *vt insep* aumentar
   ▸ **add up 1** *vt sep* sumar
   2 *vi (numbers)* sumar; *Fig* **it doesn't a. up** no tiene sentido; **it doesn't a. up to much** no es gran cosa

added ['ædɪd] *adj* adicional

adder ['ædə(r)] *n* víbora *f*

addict ['ædɪkt] *n* adicto(a) *m,f*; *Fam* **television a.** teleadicto(a) *m,f*

addicted [ə'dɪktɪd] *adj* adicto(a); **to become a. to sth** enviciarse con algo

addiction [ə'dɪkʃən] *n (to gambling etc)* vicio *m*; *(to drugs)* adicción *f*

addictive [ə'dɪktɪv] *adj* que crea adicción

addition [ə'dɪʃən] *n Math* adición *f*; *(increase)* aumento *m*; **an a. to the family** un nuevo miembro de la familia; **in a. to** además de

additional [ə'dɪʃənəl] *adj* adicional

additive ['ædɪtɪv] *n* aditivo *m*

address [ə'dres] **1** *n* (**a**) *(on letter)* dirección *f*, señas *fpl* (**b**) *(speech)* discurso *m*
   2 *vt* (**a**) *(letter)* dirigir (**b**) *(speak to)* dirigirse (**to** a); **to a. the floor** tomar la palabra (**c**) *(use form of address to)* tratar de

adenoids ['ædɪnɔɪdz] *npl* vegetaciones *fpl* (adenoideas)

adept [ə'dept] **1** *adj* experto(a) (**at** en)
   2 *n* experto(a) *m,f*

> ✍ Note that the Spanish word **adepto** is a false friend and is never a translation for the English word **adept**. In Spanish, **adepto** means "follower, supporter".

adequate ['ædɪkwɪt] *adj (enough)* suficiente; *(satisfactory)* adecuado(a)

adhere [əd'hɪə(r)] *vi (stick)* pegarse (**to** a)
   ▸ **adhere to** *vt insep (policy)* adherirse a; *(contract)* cumplir con

adherent [əd'hɪərənt] *n* partidario(a) *m,f*

adhesive [əd'hiːsɪv] **1** *adj* adhesivo(a); *(sticky)* pegajoso(a); **a. tape** cinta adhesiva
   2 *n* adhesivo *m*

ad hoc [æd'hɒk] *adj (remark)* improvisado(a); **an a. committee** un comité especial

ad infinitum [ædɪnfɪ'naɪtəm] *adv* hasta el infinito

adjacent [ə'dʒeɪsənt] *adj (building)* contiguo(a); *(land)* colindante; **a. to** contiguo(a) a

adjective ['ædʒɪktɪv] *n* adjetivo *m*

adjoining [ə'dʒɔɪnɪŋ] *adj* contiguo(a); *(land)* colindante; **the a. room** la habitación de al lado

adjourn [ə'dʒɜːn] **1** *vt (postpone)* aplazar; *(court)* levantar
   2 *vi* aplazarse (**until** hasta)

adjudicate [ə'dʒuːdɪkeɪt] *vt* juzgar

adjudicator [ə'dʒuːdɪkeɪtə(r)] *n* juez(a) *m,f*

adjust [ə'dʒʌst] **1** *vt (machine etc)* ajustar; *Fig (methods)* variar
   2 *vi (person)* adaptarse (**to** a)

adjustable [ə'dʒʌstəbəl] *adj* ajustable

adjustment [ə'dʒʌstmənt] *n* (**a**) *(to machine etc)* ajuste *m*; *(by person)* adaptación *f* (**b**) *(change)* modificación *f*

ad lib [æd'lɪb] **1** *adv (speak)* sin preparación; *(continue)* a voluntad
   2 *adj (speech)* improvisado(a)
   3 **ad-lib** *vi* improvisar

administer [əd'mɪnɪstə(r)] *vt (country)* gobernar; *(justice)* administrar

administration [ədmɪnɪ'streɪʃən] *n (of country)* gobierno *m*; *(of justice)* administración *f*; *(governing body)* dirección *f*

administrative [əd'mɪnɪstrətɪv] *adj* administrativo(a)

admirable [æd'mərəbəl] *adj* admirable

admiral ['ædmərəl] *n* almirante *m*

admiration [ædmə'reɪʃən] *n* admiración *f*

admire [əd'maɪə(r)] *vt* admirar

admirer [əd'maɪərə(r)] *n* admirador(a) *m,f*

admissible [əd'mɪsəbəl] *adj* admisible

admission [əd'mɪʃən] *n* (**a**) *(to school etc)* ingreso *m*; *(price)* entrada *f* (**b**) *(of fact)* reconocimiento *m*; *(confession)* confesión *f*

admit [əd'mɪt] *vt* (**a**) *(person)* dejar entrar; **to be admitted to hospital** ser ingresado(a) en el hospital (**b**) *(acknowledge)* reconocer; *(crime, guilt)* confesar

admittance [əd'mɪtəns] *n (entry)* entrada *f*

admittedly [əd'mɪtɪdlɪ] *adv* la verdad es que ...

admonish [əd'mɒnɪʃ] *vt* amonestar

ad nauseam [æd'nɔːzɪæm] *adv* hasta la saciedad

ado [ə'duː] *n* **without further a.** sin más

adolescence [ædə'lesəns] *n* adolescencia *f*

adolescent [ædə'lesənt] *n* adolescente *mf*

adopt [ə'dɒpt] *vt* adoptar; *(suggestion)* aceptar

adopted [ə'dɒptɪd] *adj* **a. child** hijo(a) *m,f* adoptivo(a)

adoption [ə'dɒpʃən] *n* adopción *f*; **country of a.** país adoptivo

adore [ə'dɔː(r)] *vt* adorar

adorn [ə'dɔːn] *vt* adornar

adornment [ə'dɔːnmənt] *n* adorno *m*

adrenalin [ə'drenəlɪn] *n* adrenalina *f*

Adriatic [eɪdrɪ'ætɪk] *adj* **the A. (Sea)** el (mar) Adriático

adrift [ə'drɪft] *adv* **to come a.** *(boat)* irse a la deriva; *(rope)* soltarse; *Fig* **to go a.** *(plans)* ir a la deriva

adult ['ædʌlt] **1** *adj (person)* adulto(a), mayor; *(film, education)* para adultos
2 *n* adulto(a) *m,f*

adulterate [ə'dʌltəreɪt] *vt* adulterar

adulterer [ə'dʌltərə(r)] *n* adúltero *m*

adulteress [ə'dʌltrɪs] *n* adúltera *f*

adultery [ə'dʌltərɪ] *n* adulterio *m*

advance [əd'vɑːns] **1** *n* (**a**) *(movement)* avance *m*; *Fig (progress)* progreso *m*; **to have sth ready in a.** tener algo preparado de antemano; **to make advances (to)** *(person)* insinuarse (a) (**b**) *(loan)* anticipo *m*
2 *adj (before time)* adelantado(a); *Cin & Th* **a. bookings** reservas *fpl* por adelantado
3 *vt* (**a**) *(troops)* avanzar; *(time, date)* adelantar (**b**) *(idea)* proponer; *(opinion)* dar (**c**) *Fin (sum of money)* anticipar
4 *vi (move forward)* avanzar, adelantarse; *(make progress)* hacer progresos; *(gain promotion)* ascender

advanced [əd'vɑːnst] *adj (developed)* avanzado(a); *(student)* adelantado(a); *(course)* superior; *Educ* **A. level** examen *m* superior de segunda enseñanza, ≃ COU *m*

advancement [əd'vɑːnsmənt] *n (progress)* adelanto *m*; *(promotion)* ascenso *m*

advantage [əd'vɑːntɪdʒ] *n* ventaja *f*; *(in tennis)* **a. Velasco** ventaja para Velasco; **to**

take a. of sb/sth abusar de algn/aprovechar algo

advantageous [ædvən'teɪdʒəs] *adj* ventajoso(a)

advent ['ædvent] *n (arrival)* llegada *f*; *(of Christ)* advenimiento *m*; **A.** Adviento *m*

adventure [əd'ventʃə(r)] *n* aventura *f*; **a. sport** deporte *m* de aventura

adventurous [əd'ventʃərəs] *adj* aventurero(a)

adverb ['ædvɜːb] *n* adverbio *m*

adversary ['ædvəsərɪ] *n* adversario(a) *m,f*

adverse ['ædvɜːs] *adj (effect)* desfavorable; *(conditions)* adverso(a); *(winds)* contrario(a)

adversity [əd'vɜːsɪtɪ] *n* adversidad *f*

advert ['ædvɜːt] *n Fam* anuncio *m*

advertise ['ædvətaɪz] **1** *vt* anunciar
2 *vi* hacer publicidad; *(in newspaper)* poner un anuncio; **to a. for sth/sb** buscar algo/a algn mediante un anuncio

advertisement [əd'vɜːtɪsmənt] *n* anuncio *m*; **advertisements** publicidad *f*

advertiser ['ædvətaɪzə(r)] *n* anunciante *mf*

advertising ['ædvətaɪzɪŋ] **1** *n* publicidad *f*, propaganda *f*; *(in newspaper)* anuncios *mpl*
2 *adj* publicitario(a); **a. agency** agencia *f* de publicidad

advice [əd'vaɪs] *n* consejos *mpl*; **a piece of a.** un consejo; **to take legal a. on a matter** consultar el caso con un abogado; **to take sb's a.** seguir los consejos de algn

advisable [əd'vaɪzəbəl] *adj* aconsejable

advise [əd'vaɪz] *vt* aconsejar; *(on business etc)* asesorar; **I a. you to do it** te aconsejo que lo hagas

adviser [əd'vaɪzə(r)] *n* consejero(a) *m,f*; *(in business etc)* asesor(a) *m,f*

advisory [əd'vaɪzərɪ] *adj* asesor(a)

advocate **1** *n* ['ædvəkɪt] *Scot Jur* abogado(a) *m,f*; *(supporter)* defensor(a) *m,f*
2 *vt* ['ædvəkeɪt] *(reform)* abogar por; *(plan)* apoyar

aerial ['eərɪəl] **1** *adj* aéreo(a)
2 *n* antena *f*

aerobics [eə'rəʊbɪks] *n sing* aerobic *m*

aerodrome ['eərədrəʊm] *n Br* aeródromo *m*

aerodynamics [eərəʊdaɪ'næmɪks] *n sing* aerodinámica *f*

aeroplane ['eərəpleɪn] *n Br* avión *m*

aerosol ['eərəsɒl] *n* aerosol *m*

aerospace ['eərəʊspeɪs] *adj* aeroespacial

aesthetic [iːsˈθetɪk] *adj* estético(a)
afar [əˈfɑː(r)] *adv* lejos; **from a.** desde lejos
affair [əˈfeə(r)] *n (matter)* asunto *m*; *(event)* acontecimiento *m*; **that's my a.** eso es asunto mío; **business affairs** negocios *mpl*; **foreign affairs** asuntos exteriores; **love a.** aventura amorosa
affect [əˈfekt] *vt (person, health)* afectar; *(prices, future)* influir en; *(touch emotionally)* conmover
affected [əˈfektɪd] *adj* (**a**) *(unnatural)* afectado(a) (**b**) *(influenced)* influido(a) (**c**) *(touched emotionally)* conmovido(a) (**d**) *(pretended)* fingido(a)
affection [əˈfekʃən] *n* afecto *m*, cariño *m*
affectionate [əˈfekʃənɪt] *adj* cariñoso(a)
affidavit [æfɪˈdeɪvɪt] *n* declaración escrita y jurada
affiliated [əˈfɪlɪeɪtɪd] *adj* afiliado(a); **to be/become a. (to** *or* **with)** afiliarse (a)
affinity [əˈfɪnɪtɪ] *n* afinidad *f*; *(liking)* simpatía *f*
affirm [əˈfɜːm] *vt* afirmar, sostener
affirmation [æfəˈmeɪʃən] *n* afirmación *f*
affirmative [əˈfɜːmətɪv] **1** *adj* afirmativo(a)
   2 *n* **he answered in the a.** contestó que sí
affix [əˈfɪks] *vt (stamp)* pegar
afflict [əˈflɪkt] *vt* afligir
affluence [ˈæflʊəns] *n* opulencia *f*
affluent [ˈæflʊənt] *adj (society)* opulento(a); *(person)* rico(a)
afford [əˈfɔːd] *vt* (**a**) *(be able to buy)* permitirse el lujo de; **I can't a. a new car** no puedo pagar un coche nuevo (**b**) *(be able to do)* permitirse; **you can't a. to miss the opportunity** no puedes perderte la ocasión
affront [əˈfrʌnt] **1** *n* afrenta *f*
   2 *vt* afrentar
afield [əˈfiːld] *adv* **far a.** muy lejos
afloat [əˈfləʊt] *adv* **to keep a.** mantenerse a flote
afoot [əˈfʊt] *adv* **there's a plan a.** hay un proyecto en marcha; **there's something strange a.** se está tramando algo
aforementioned [əˈfɔːmenʃənd], **aforesaid** [əˈfɔːsed] *adj* susodicho(a)
afraid [əˈfreɪd] *adj* (**a**) **to be a.** tener miedo (**of sb** a algn; **of sth** de algo); **I'm a. of it** me da miedo (**b**) **I'm a. not** me temo que no; **I'm a. so** me temo que sí; **I'm a. you're wrong** me temo que estás equivocado(a)
afresh [əˈfreʃ] *adv* de nuevo

Africa [ˈæfrɪkə] *n* Africa
African [ˈæfrɪkən] *adj & n* africano(a) *(m,f)*
Afro [ˈæfrəʊ] *adj & n Fam (hairstyle)* afro *(m)*
aft [ɑːft] *adv* en popa; **to go a.** ir en popa
after [ˈɑːftə(r)] **1** *adv* después; **soon a.** poco después; **the day a.** el día siguiente
   2 *prep* (**a**) *(later)* después de; *US* **it's ten a. five** son las cinco y diez; **soon a. arriving** al poco rato de llegar; **the day a. tomorrow** pasado mañana
   (**b**) *(behind)* detrás de, tras; **a. you!** ¡pase usted!; **they went in one a. the other** entraron uno tras otro; **the police are a. them** la policía anda tras ellos
   (**c**) *(about)* por; **they asked a. you** preguntaron por ti; **what's he a.?** ¿qué pretende?
   (**d**) **he takes a. his uncle** se parece a su tío; **she was named a. her grandmother** le llamaron como a su abuela
   3 *conj* después (de) que; **a. it happened** después de que ocurriera
after-effect [ˈɑːftərɪfekt] *n* efecto secundario
afterlife [ˈɑːftəlaɪf] *n* vida *f* después de la muerte
aftermath [ˈɑːftəmæθ] *n* secuelas *fpl*
afternoon [ɑːftəˈnuːn] *n* tarde *f*; **good a.!** ¡buenas tardes!; **in the a.** por la tarde
afternoons [ɑːftəˈnuːnz] *adv US* por las tardes
afters [ˈɑːftəz] *npl Fam* postre *m*
after-sales service [ɑːftəseɪlzˈsɜːvɪs] *n Com* servicio *m* posventa
aftershave (lotion) [ˈɑːftəʃeɪv(ˈləʊʃən)] *n* loción *f* para después del afeitado
afterthought [ˈɑːftəθɔːt] *n* ocurrencia *f* tardía
afterwards [ˈɑːftəwədz] *adv* después, más tarde
again [əˈgen] *adv* (**a**) otra vez, de nuevo; **I tried a. and a.** lo intenté una y otra vez; **to do sth a.** volver a hacer algo; **never a.!** ¡nunca más!; **now and a.** de vez en cuando; **once a.** otra vez (**b**) *(besides)* además; **then a.** por otra parte
against [əˈgenst] *prep* (**a**) *(touching)* contra (**b**) *(opposing)* contra, en contra (de); **a. the grain** a contrapelo; **it's a. the law** es ilegal (**c**) **as a.** en contraste con, comparado con
age [eɪdʒ] **1** *n* (**a**) edad *f*; **she's eighteen years of a.** tiene dieciocho años; **to be under a.** ser menor de edad; **to come of a.** llegar a la mayoría de edad; **a. limit** límite *m* de edad; **old a.** vejez *f* (**b**) *(period)*

época *f*; **the Iron A.** la Edad de Hierro (**c**) *Fam (long time)* eternidad *f*; **it's ages since I last saw her** hace siglos que no la veo

2 *vt & vi* envejecer

aged¹ [eɪdʒd] *adj* de *or* a la edad de

aged² ['eɪdʒɪd] *npl* **the a.** los ancianos

agency ['eɪdʒənsɪ] *n* (**a**) *Com* agencia *f* (**b**) **by the a. of** por medio de

agenda [ə'dʒendə] *n* orden *m* del día

agent ['eɪdʒənt] *n* agente *mf*; *(representative)* representante *mf*

aggravate ['ægrəveɪt] *vt (worsen)* agravar; *(annoy)* molestar

aggregate ['ægrɪgɪt] *n* conjunto *m*; **on a.** en conjunto

aggression [ə'greʃən] *n* agresión *f*

aggressive [ə'gresɪv] *adj (violent)* agresivo(a), violento(a); *(dynamic)* dinámico(a)

aggrieved [ə'griːvd] *adj* apenado(a)

aghast [ə'gɑːst] *adj* espantado(a)

agile ['ædʒaɪl] *adj* ágil

agitate ['ædʒɪteɪt] **1** *vt (shake)* agitar; *Fig (worry)* perturbar

2 *vi Pol* **to a. against sth** hacer campaña en contra de algo

agitator ['ædʒɪteɪtə(r)] *n Pol* agitador(a) *m,f*

AGM [eɪdʒiː'em] *n (abbr* **annual general meeting**) junta *f* general anual

agnostic [æg'nɒstɪk] *n* agnóstico(a) *m,f*

ago [ə'gəʊ] *adv* **a long time a.** hace mucho tiempo; **as long a. as 1910** ya en 1910; **a week a.** hace una semana; **how long a.?** ¿hace cuánto tiempo?

agog [ə'gɒg] *adj* ansioso(a)

agonizing ['ægənaɪzɪŋ] *adj (pain)* atroz; *(decision)* desesperante

agony ['ægənɪ] *n* dolor *m* muy fuerte; *(anguish)* angustia *f*; **he was in a. with his back** tenía un dolor insoportable de espalda

agree [ə'griː] **1** *vi* (**a**) *(be in agreement)* estar de acuerdo; *(reach agreement)* ponerse de acuerdo; *(consent)* consentir; **to a. to do sth** consentir en hacer algo; **to a. with sb** estar de acuerdo con algn (**b**) *(harmonize) (things)* concordar; *(people)* congeniar; **onions don't a. with me** la cebolla no me sienta bien

2 *vt* acordar

agreeable [ə'griːəbəl] *adj (pleasant)* agradable; *(person)* simpático(a); *(in agreement)* de acuerdo

agreement [ə'griːmənt] *n (arrangement)* acuerdo *m*; *Com* contrato *m*; **to reach an a.** llegar a un acuerdo

agricultural [ægrɪ'kʌltʃərəl] *adj* agrícola; *(college)* de agricultura

agriculture ['ægrɪkʌltʃə(r)] *n* agricultura *f*

aground [ə'graʊnd] *adv* **to run a.** encallar, varar

ahead [ə'hed] *adv* delante; *(early)* antes; **go a.!** ¡adelante!; **to be a.** llevar la ventaja; **to go a.** ir adelante; *Fig* **to go a. with sth** llevar algo adelante; *(start)* comenzar algo; **to get a.** triunfar; **to look a.** pensar en el futuro

aid [eɪd] **1** *n* ayuda *f*; *(rescue)* auxilio *m*; **in a. of** a beneficio de; **to come to the a. of sb** acudir en ayuda de algn; **a. worker** cooperante *mf*

2 *vt* ayudar; **to a. and abet sb** ser cómplice de algn

aide [eɪd] *n* ayudante *mf*

AIDS [eɪdz] *n* (*abbr* **Acquired Immune Deficiency Syndrome**) sida *m*

ailing ['eɪlɪŋ] *adj* achacoso(a)

ailment ['eɪlmənt] *n* enfermedad *f* (leve), achaque *m*

aim [eɪm] **1** *n (with weapon)* puntería *f*; *(target)* propósito *m*

2 *vt (gun)* apuntar (**at** a *or* hacia); *(attack, action)* dirigir (**at** a *or* hacia)

► **aim at** *vt insep (target)* tirar para; **to a. at doing sth** tener pensado hacer algo

► **aim to** *vt insep* **to a. to do sth** tener la intención de hacer algo

aimless ['eɪmlɪs] *adj* sin objeto, sin propósito

aimlessly ['eɪmlɪslɪ] *adv (wander)* sin rumbo fijo

air [eə(r)] **1** *n* (**a**) aire *m*; **to travel by a.** viajar en avión; **to throw sth up in the a.** lanzar algo al aire; *Fig* **it's still in the a.** todavía queda por resolver; *Aut* **a. bag** airbag *m*; **a. base** base aérea; **a. bed** colchón *m* hinchable; **a. conditioning** aire acondicionado; **A. Force** Fuerzas Aéreas; **a. freshener** ambientador *m*; **a. gun** pistola *f* de aire comprimido; **a. hostess** azafata *f*; **a. letter** carta aérea; **a. pocket** bache *m*; **a. pressure** presión atmosférica; **a. raid** ataque aéreo; **a. terminal** terminal aérea; **a. traffic control** control *m* de tráfico aéreo; **a. traffic controller** controlador(a) *m,f* aéreo(a)

(**b**) *Rad & TV* **to be on the a.** *(programme)* estar emitiendo; *(person)* estar transmitiendo

(**c**) *(appearance)* aspecto *m*

2 *vt (bed, clothes)* airear; *(room)* ventilar; *Fig (grievance)* airear; *(knowledge)* hacer alarde de

airborne ['eəbɔːn] *adj (aircraft)* en vuelo; *(troops)* aerotransportado(a)
air-conditioned ['eəkɒndɪʃənd] *adj* climatizado(a)
aircraft ['eəkrɑːft] *n (pl aircraft)* avión *m*; **a. carrier** portaviones *m inv*
airfield ['eəfiːld] *n* campo *m* de aviación
airlift ['eəlɪft] *n* puente aéreo
airline ['eəlaɪn] *n* línea aérea
airlock ['eəlɒk] *n (in pipe)* bolsa *f* de aire; *(in spacecraft)* esclusa *f* de aire
airmail ['eəmeɪl] *n* correo aéreo; **by a.** por avión
airplane ['eəpleɪn] *n US* avión *m*
airport ['eəpɔːt] *n* aeropuerto *m*; **a. tax** tasas *fpl* de aeropuerto
airsick ['eəsɪk] *adj* **to be a.** marearse en avión
airstrip ['eəstrɪp] *n* pista *f* de aterrizaje
airtight ['eətaɪt] *adj* hermético(a)
airy ['eərɪ] *adj* (**airier, airiest**) *(well-ventilated)* bien ventilado(a); *(vague, carefree)* ligero(a)
aisle [aɪl] *n (in church)* nave *f*; *(in theatre)* pasillo *m*
ajar [ə'dʒɑː(r)] *adj & adv* entreabierto(a)
akin [ə'kɪn] *adj* semejante
alacrity [ə'lækrɪtɪ] *n* **with a.** con presteza
à la mode [ælə'məʊd] *adj US (dessert)* con helado
alarm [ə'lɑːm] **1** *n* (**a**) alarma *f*; **a. clock** despertador *m* (**b**) *(fear)* inquietud *f*; **to cause a.** provocar temor
   2 *vt* alarmar
alas [ə'læs] *interj* ¡ay!, ¡ay de mí!
albatross ['ælbətrɒs] *n* albatros *m*
albeit [ɔːl'biːɪt] *conj* aunque, no obstante
album ['ælbəm] *n* álbum *m*
alcohol ['ælkəhɒl] *n* alcohol *m*
alcoholic [ælkə'hɒlɪk] *adj & n* alcohólico(a) *(m,f)*
alcopop ['ælkəʊpɒp] *n Br* refresco *m* con alcohol
alcove ['ælkəʊv] *n* hueco *m*

> 🖉 Note that the Spanish word **alcoba** is a false friend and is never a translation for the English word **alcove**. In Spanish, **alcoba** means "bedroom".

ale [eɪl] *n* cerveza *f*; **brown/pale a.** cerveza negra/rubia
alert [ə'lɜːt] **1** *adj* alerta; *(lively)* despabilado(a)
   2 *n* alerta *m*; **to be on the a.** estar alerta
   3 *vt* **to a. sb to sth** avisar a algn de algo
A-level ['eɪlevəl] *n Br Educ (abbr* **Advanced level**) = examen final o diploma

en una asignatura de los estudios pre-universitarios
algae ['ældʒiː] *npl* algas *fpl*
algebra ['ældʒɪbrə] *n* álgebra *f*
Algeria [æl'dʒɪərɪə] *n* Argelia
Algerian [æl'dʒɪərɪən] *adj & n* argelino(a) *(m,f)*
Algiers [æl'dʒɪəz] *n* Argel
alias ['eɪlɪəs] **1** *n* alias *m*
   2 *adv* alias
alibi ['ælɪbaɪ] *n* coartada *f*
alien ['eɪlɪən] **1** *adj (foreign)* extranjero(a); *(from space)* extraterrestre; **a. to** ajeno(a) a
   2 *n (foreigner)* extranjero(a) *m,f*; *(from space)* extraterrestre *mf*
alienate ['eɪlɪəneɪt] *vt* (**a**) **to a. sb** ofender a algn; **to a. oneself from sb** alejarse de algn (**b**) *Jur* enajenar
alight¹ [ə'laɪt] *adj (on fire)* ardiendo(a)
alight² [ə'laɪt] *vi (get off)* apearse (**from** de)
align [ə'laɪn] *vt* alinear
alike [ə'laɪk] **1** *adj (similar)* parecidos(as); *(the same)* iguales
   2 *adv (in the same way)* de la misma manera, igualmente; **dressed a.** vestidos(as) iguales
alimony ['ælɪmənɪ] *n Jur* pensión alimenticia
alive [ə'laɪv] *adj* vivo(a); *Fig (teeming)* lleno(a) (**with** de); **to be a.** estar vivo(a)
alkaline ['ælkəlaɪn] *adj* alcalino(a)
all [ɔːl] **1** *adj* todo(a), todos(as); **a. year** *(durante)* todo el año; **a. kinds of things** todo tipo de cosas; **at a. hours** a todas horas; **at a. times** siempre; **she works a. the time** siempre está trabajando; **a. six of us were there** los seis estábamos allí
   2 *pron* todo(a), todos(as); **after a.** al fin y al cabo; **a. of his work** toda su obra; **a. of us** todos(as) nosotros(as); **a. who saw it** todos los que lo vieron; **a. you can do is wait** lo único que puedes hacer es esperar; **I don't like it at a.** no me gusta en absoluto; **is that a.?** ¿eso es todo?; **most of** *or* **above a.** sobre todo; **once and for a.** de una vez por todas; **thanks – not at a.** gracias – de nada; **a. in a.** en conjunto; **that's a.** ya está; **the score was one a.** empataron a uno
   3 *adv* **a. by myself** completamente solo(a); **a. at once** *(suddenly)* de repente; *(altogether)* de una vez; **a. the better** tanto mejor; **a. the same** de todos modos; **he knew a. along** lo sabía desde el principio; **if it's a. the same to you** si no te importa; **it's a. but impossible** es casi

imposible; **I'm not a. that tired** no estoy tan cansado(a) como eso

4 *n* **to give one's a.** darse por completo

Allah ['ælə] *n* Alá *m*

allay [ə'leɪ] *vt (fears, doubts)* apaciguar

allegation [ælɪ'geɪʃən] *n* alegato *m*

allege [ə'ledʒ] *vt* sostener, pretender (**that** que)

allegedly [ə'ledʒɪdlɪ] *adv* supuestamente

allegiance [ə'liːdʒəns] *n* lealtad *f*

allergic [ə'lɜːdʒɪk] *adj* alérgico(a) (**to** a)

allergy ['ælədʒɪ] *n* alergia *f*

alleviate [ə'liːvɪeɪt] *vt (pain)* aliviar

alley ['ælɪ] *n* callejón *m*

alliance [ə'laɪəns] *n* alianza *f*

allied ['ælaɪd] *adj* aliado(a)

alligator ['ælɪgeɪtə(r)] *n* caimán *m*

all-in ['ɔːlɪn] *adj (price)* todo incluido; *Sport* **a. wrestling** lucha *f* libre

alliteration [əlɪtə'reɪʃən] *n* aliteración *f*

all-night ['ɔːlnaɪt] *adj (café etc)* abierto(a) toda la noche; *(vigil)* que dura toda la noche

allocate ['æləkeɪt] *vt* destinar (**to** para)

allocation [ælə'keɪʃən] *n* (**a**) *(distribution)* asignación *f* (**b**) *(amount allocated)* cuota *f*

allot [ə'lɒt] *vt* asignar

allotment [ə'lɒtmənt] *n* (**a**) *(distribution)* asignación *f* (**b**) *(land)* parcela *f*

all-out ['ɔːlaʊt] **1** *adj (effort)* supremo(a); *(attack)* concentrado(a)

2 all out *adv* **to go all out to do sth** emplearse a fondo para hacer algo

allow [ə'laʊ] *vt* (**a**) *(permit)* permitir; *(a request)* acceder a; **to a. sb to do sth** permitir que algn haga algo (**b**) *(allot) (time)* dejar; *(money)* destinar

▸ **allow for** *vt insep* tener en cuenta

allowance [ə'laʊəns] *n (payment)* pensión *f*, subvención *f*; *(discount)* descuento *m*; **to make allowances for sb/sth** disculpar a algn/tener algo en cuenta; **tax a.** desgravación *f* fiscal; **travel a.** dietas *fpl* de viaje

alloy ['ælɔɪ] *n* aleación *f*

all right [ɔːl'raɪt] **1** *adj (okay)* bien; **thank you very much – that's a.** muchas gracias – de nada

2 *adv* (**a**) *(well)* bien (**b**) *(definitely)* sin duda (**c**) *(okay)* de acuerdo, vale

all-round ['ɔːlraʊnd] *adj (athlete etc)* completo(a)

all-terrain [ɔːltə'reɪn] *adj* **a. vehicle** todoterreno *m*

all-time ['ɔːltaɪm] *adj* **an a. low** una baja sin antecedente; **the a. greats** los grandes de siempre

allude [ə'luːd] *vi* **to a. to** aludir a

alluring [ə'ljʊərɪŋ] *adj* atractivo(a)

allusion [ə'luːʒən] *n* alusión *f*

ally ['ælaɪ] **1** *n* aliado(a) *m,f*

2 *vt* **to a. oneself to/with sb** aliarse a/con algn

almighty [ɔːl'maɪtɪ] **1** *adj (all-powerful)* todopoderoso(a)

2 *n* **the A.** El Todopoderoso

almond ['ɑːmənd] *n* almendra *f*

almost ['ɔːlməʊst] *adv* casi

alms [ɑːmz] *npl* limosna *f*

aloft [ə'lɒft] *adv* arriba

alone [ə'ləʊn] **1** *adj* solo(a); **can I speak to you a.?** ¿puedo hablar contigo a solas?; **let a.** ni mucho menos; **leave it a.!** ¡no lo toques!; **leave me a.** déjame en paz; **to be a.** estar solo(a)

2 *adv* solamente, sólo

along [ə'lɒŋ] **1** *adv* **come a.!** ¡anda, ven!; **he'll be a. in ten minutes** llegará dentro de diez minutos; **a. with** junto con

2 *prep (the length of)* a lo largo de; **to walk a. the street** andar por la calle; **it's just a. the street** está un poco más abajo

alongside [ə'lɒŋsaɪd] **1** *adv Naut* de costado

2 *prep* al lado de

aloof [ə'luːf] **1** *adj (person)* distante

2 *adv* **to keep oneself a. (from)** mantenerse a distancia (de)

aloud [ə'laʊd] *adv* en voz alta

alphabet ['ælfəbet] *n* alfabeto *m*

alphabetical [ælfə'betɪkəl] *adj* alfabético(a)

alphabetically [ælfə'betɪkəlɪ] *adv* por orden alfabético

alpine ['ælpaɪn] *adj* alpino(a)

Alps [ælps] *npl* **the A.** los Alpes

already [ɔːl'redɪ] *adv* ya

alright [ɔːl'raɪt] *adj & adv* = **all right**

Alsatian [æl'seɪʃən] *n* pastor *m* alemán

also ['ɔːlsəʊ] *adv* también, además

also-ran ['ɔːlsəʊræn] *n Fam (person)* segundón(ona) *m,f*

altar ['ɔːltə(r)] *n* altar *m*

alter ['ɔːltə(r)] **1** *vt (plan)* cambiar, retocar; *(project)* modificar; *(clothing)* arreglar; *(timetable)* revisar

2 *vi* cambiar, cambiarse

alteration [ɔːltə'reɪʃən] *n (to plan)* cambio *m*; *(to project)* modificación *f*; *(to clothing)* arreglo *m*; *(to timetable)* revisión *f*; **alterations** *(to building)* reformas *fpl*

alternate 1 *adj* [ɔːl'tɜːnɪt] alterno(a); **on a. days** cada dos días

2 *vt* ['ɔːltəneɪt] alternar

alternately [ɔːlˈtɜːnɪtlɪ] adv **a. hot and cold** ahora caliente, ahora frío

alternative [ɔːlˈtɜːnətɪv] **1** adj alternativo(a)
2 n alternativa f; **I have no a. but to accept** no tengo más remedio que aceptar

alternatively [ɔːlˈtɜːnətɪvlɪ] adv o bien; **a., you could walk** o bien podrías ir andando

alternator [ˈɔːltəneɪtə(r)] n Aut alternador m

although [ɔːlˈðəʊ] conj aunque

altitude [ˈæltɪtjuːd] n altitud f

alto [ˈæltəʊ] adj & n (male singer, instrument) alto (m); (female singer) contralto (f)

altogether [ɔːltəˈɡeðə(r)] adv (in total) en conjunto, en total; (completely) completamente, del todo

altruism [ˈæltruːɪzəm] n altruismo m

aluminium [æljʊˈmɪnɪəm], US **aluminum** [əˈluːmɪnəm] n aluminio m

alumnus [əˈlʌmnəs] n (pl alumni [əˈlʌmnaɪ]) US antiguo alumno

always [ˈɔːlweɪz] adv siempre

AM [eɪˈem] Rad (abbr **amplitude modulation**) AM

am [æm] 1st person sing pres of **be**

a.m. [eɪˈem] (abbr **ante meridiem**) a.m., de la mañana

amalgamate [əˈmælɡəmeɪt] **1** vt (metals) amalgamar
2 vi (metals) amalgamarse; (companies) fusionarse

amalgamation [əmælɡəˈmeɪʃən] n fusión f

amass [əˈmæs] vt (money) amontonar; (information) acumular

amateur [ˈæmətə(r)] **1** n amateur mf, aficionado(a) m,f
2 adj aficionado(a); Pej (work etc) chapucero(a)

amateurish [ˈæmətərɪʃ] adj chapucero(a)

amaze [əˈmeɪz] vt asombrar, pasmar; **to be amazed at sth** quedarse pasmado(a) de algo

amazement [əˈmeɪzmənt] n asombro m, sorpresa f

amazing [əˈmeɪzɪŋ] adj asombroso(a), increíble

ambassador [æmˈbæsədə(r)] n embajador(a) m,f

amber [ˈæmbə(r)] **1** n ámbar m
2 adj ambarino(a); (traffic light) amarillo(a)

ambiguity [æmbɪˈɡjuːɪtɪ] n ambigüedad f

ambiguous [æmˈbɪɡjʊəs] adj ambiguo(a)

ambition [æmˈbɪʃən] n ambición f

ambitious [æmˈbɪʃəs] adj ambicioso(a)

ambivalent [æmˈbɪvələnt] adj ambivalente

amble [ˈæmbəl] vi deambular

ambulance [ˈæmbjʊləns] n ambulancia f; **a. man** ambulanciero m

ambush [ˈæmbʊʃ] **1** n emboscada f
2 vt tender una emboscada a; Fig atacar por sorpresa

amen [ɑːˈmen] interj amén

amenable [əˈmiːnəbəl] adj **I'd be quite a. to doing that** no me importaría nada hacer eso; **a. to reason** razonable

amend [əˈmend] vt (law) enmendar; (error) subsanar

amendment [əˈmendmənt] n enmienda f

amends [əˈmendz] npl **to make a. to sb for sth** compensar a algn por algo

amenities [əˈmiːnɪtɪz] npl comodidades fpl

America [əˈmerɪkə] n (continent) América f; (USA) (los) Estados Unidos; **South A.** América del Sur, Sudamérica f

American [əˈmerɪkən] adj & n americano(a) (m,f); (of USA) norteamericano(a) (m,f), estadounidense (mf)

amiable [ˈeɪmɪəbəl] adj amable, afable

amicable [ˈæmɪkəbəl] adj amistoso(a)

amid(st) [ˈæmɪd(st)] prep entre, en medio de

amiss [əˈmɪs] adj & adv mal; **there's sth a.** algo anda mal; **to take sth a.** tomar algo a mal

ammonia [əˈməʊnɪə] n amoníaco m

ammunition [æmjʊˈnɪʃən] n municiones fpl

amnesia [æmˈniːʒə] n amnesia f

amnesty [ˈæmnɪstɪ] n amnistía f

amok [əˈmɒk] adv Fig **to run a.** (child) desmadrarse; (inflation etc) dispararse

among(st) [əˈmʌŋ(st)] prep entre

amoral [eɪˈmɒrəl] adj amoral

amorous [ˈæmərəs] adj cariñoso(a)

amorphous [əˈmɔːfəs] adj amorfo(a)

amount [əˈmaʊnt] n cantidad f; (of money) suma f; (of bill) importe m
▶**amount to** vt insep ascender a; Fig equivaler a

amp [æmp], **ampère** [ˈæmpeə(r)] n amperio m

amphetamine [æmˈfetəmiːn] n anfetamina f

amphibian [æmˈfɪbɪən] adj & n anfibio(a) (m)

amphibious [æmˈfɪbɪəs] *adj* anfibio(a)
amphitheatre [ˈæmfɪθɪətə(r)] *n* anfiteatro *m*
ample [ˈæmpəl] *adj (enough)* bastante; *(more than enough)* abundante; *(large)* amplio(a)
amplifier [ˈæmplɪfaɪə(r)] *n* amplificador *m*
amputate [ˈæmpjʊteɪt] *vt* amputar
amuck [əˈmʌk] *adv* = amok
amuse [əˈmjuːz] *vt* divertir, entretener
amusement [əˈmjuːzmənt] *n (enjoyment)* diversión *f*; *(laughter)* risa *f*; *(pastime)* pasatiempo *m*; **a. arcade** salón *m* de juegos; **a. park** parque *m* de atracciones
amusing [əˈmjuːzɪŋ] *adj* divertido(a)
an [æn, *unstressed* ən] *see* **a**
anabolic steroid [ænəbɒlɪkˈstɪərɔɪd] *n* esteroide *m* anabolizante
anaemia [əˈniːmɪə] *n* anemia *f*
anaemic [əˈniːmɪk] *adj* anémico(a); *Fig (weak)* débil
anaesthetic [ænɪsˈθetɪk] *n* anestesia *f*
anaesthetist [əˈniːsθətɪst] *n* anestesista *mf*
analog(ue) [ˈænəlɒg] *n* análogo *m*; **a. computer** ordenador analógico, *Am* computadora analógica; **a. watch** reloj *m* de agujas
analogy [əˈnælədʒɪ] *n* analogía *f*
analyse [ˈænəlaɪz] *vt* analizar
analysis [əˈnælɪsɪs] *n* (*pl* **analyses** [əˈnælɪsiːz]) análisis *m inv*
analyst [ˈænəlɪst] *n* analista *mf*; *(psychoanalyst)* psicoanalista *mf*
analytic(al) [ænəˈlɪtɪk(əl)] *adj* analítico(a)
analyze [ˈænəlaɪz] *vt US* = **analyse**
anarchist [ˈænəkɪst] *n* anarquista *mf*
anarchy [ˈænəkɪ] *n* anarquía *f*
anathema [əˈnæθəmə] *n* **the very idea was a. to him** le repugnaba sólo de pensarlo
anatomy [əˈnætəmɪ] *n* anatomía *f*
ancestor [ˈænsestə(r)] *n* antepasado *m*
anchor [ˈæŋkə(r)] **1** *n Naut* ancla *f*; *Fig* áncora *f*; **to drop a.** echar el ancla; **to weigh a.** zarpar
2 *vt Naut* anclar; *Fig (fix securely)* sujetar
3 *vi* anclar
anchovy [ˈæntʃəvɪ] *n* anchoa *f*
ancient [ˈeɪnʃənt] *adj* antiguo(a)
ancillary [ænˈsɪlərɪ] *adj & n* auxiliar *(mf)*
and [ænd, *unstressed* ənd, ən] *conj* y; *(before i-, hi-)* e; **a hundred a. one** ciento uno; **a. so on** etcétera; **Bill a. Pat** Bill y Pat; **Chinese a. Indian** chino e indio; **come a. see us** ven a vernos; **four a. a half** cuatro y

medio; **she cried a. cried** no paró de llorar; **try a. help me** trata de ayudarme; **wait a. see** espera a ver; **worse a. worse** cada vez peor
Andalusia [ændəˈluːzɪə] *n* Andalucía
Andalusian [ændəˈluːzɪən] *adj* andaluz(a)
Andes [ˈændiːz] *npl* **the A.** los Andes
Andorra [ænˈdɔːrə] *n* Andorra
anecdote [ˈænɪkdəʊt] *n* anécdota *f*
anemia [əˈniːmɪə] *n US* = **anaemia**
anesthetic [ænɪsˈθetɪk] *n US* = **anaesthetic**
angel [ˈeɪndʒəl] *n* ángel *m*
anger [ˈæŋgə(r)] **1** *n* cólera *f*
2 *vt* enojar
angina [ænˈdʒaɪnə] *n* angina *f* (de pecho)
angle [ˈæŋgəl] *n* ángulo *m*; *Fig* punto *m* de vista
angler [ˈæŋglə(r)] *n* pescador(a) *m,f* de caña
Anglican [ˈæŋglɪkən] *adj & n* anglicano(a) *(m,f)*
Anglo-Saxon [æŋgləʊˈsæksən] *adj & n* anglosajón(ona) *(m,f)*
Angola [æŋˈgəʊlə] *n* Angola
angrily [ˈæŋgrɪlɪ] *adv* furiosamente
angry [ˈæŋgrɪ] *adj* (**angrier, angriest**) *(person etc)* enfadado(a); *(voice)* airado(a); **to get a. with sb about sth** enfadarse con algn por algo
anguish [ˈæŋgwɪʃ] *n* angustia *f*
angular [ˈæŋgjʊlə(r)] *adj (shape)* angular; *(face)* anguloso(a)
animal [ˈænɪməl] **1** *adj* animal
2 *n* animal *m*; *Fig* bestia *f*
animate 1 *adj* [ˈænɪmɪt] vivo(a)
2 *vt* [ˈænɪmeɪt] animar; *Fig* estimular
animated [ˈænɪmeɪtɪd] *adj (lively)* animado(a)
animosity [ænɪˈmɒsɪtɪ] *n* animosidad *f*
aniseed [ˈænɪsiːd] *n* anís *m*
ankle [ˈæŋkəl] *n* tobillo *m*; **a. boots** botines *mpl*; **a. socks** calcetines cortos
annex [əˈneks] *vt (territory)* anexionar
annexe, *US* **annex** [ˈæneks] *n (building)* (edificio *m*) anexo *m*
annihilate [əˈnaɪəleɪt] *vt* aniquilar
anniversary [ænɪˈvɜːsərɪ] *n* aniversario *m*; **wedding a.** aniversario de bodas
announce [əˈnaʊns] *vt* anunciar; *(news)* comunicar; *(fact)* hacer saber
announcement [əˈnaʊnsmənt] *n* anuncio *m*; *(news)* comunicación *f*; *(statement)* declaración *f*
announcer [əˈnaʊnsə(r)] *n TV & Rad* locutor(a) *m,f*
annoy [əˈnɔɪ] *vt* molestar, fastidiar; **to**

get annoyed enfadarse, molestarse
annoyance [ə'nɔɪəns] n *(feeling)* enojo m; *(thing)* molestia f, fastidio m
annoying [ə'nɔɪɪŋ] adj molesto(a), fastidioso(a)
annual ['ænjʊəl] **1** adj anual
2 n *(book)* anuario m; *(plant)* anual m
annually ['ænjʊəlɪ] adv anualmente
annul [ə'nʌl] vt anular
annulment [ə'nʌlmənt] n anulación f
anomaly [ə'nɒməlɪ] n anomalía f
anonymity [ænə'nɪmɪtɪ] n anonimato m
anonymous [ə'nɒnɪməs] adj anónimo(a)
anorak ['ænəræk] n anorak m
anorexia [ænə'reksɪə] n anorexia f
another [ə'nʌðə(r)] **1** adj otro(a); **a. one** otro(a); **without a. word** sin más
2 pron otro(a); **have a.** toma otro(a); **to love one a.** quererse el uno al otro
Ansaphone® ['ɑːnsəfəʊn] n mensáfono m
answer ['ɑːnsə(r)] **1** n *(to letter etc)* contestación f; *(to question)* respuesta f; *(to problem)* solución f; **in a. to your letter** contestando a su carta; **there's no a.** *(on telephone)* no contestan; *(at door)* no abren
2 vt contestar a; *(problem)* resolver; *(door)* abrir; *(phone)* contestar
3 vi contestar, responder
▶ **answer back** vi replicar; **don't a. back!** ¡no seas respondón!
▶ **answer for** vt insep responder de; **he's got a lot to a. for** es responsable de muchas cosas
▶ **answer to** vt insep *(name)* responder a; *(description)* corresponder a
answerable ['ɑːnsərəbəl] adj **to be a. to sb for sth** ser responsable ante algn de algo
answering machine ['ɑːnsərɪŋməʃiːn] n contestador automático
ant [ænt] n hormiga f; **a. hill** hormiguero m
antagonism [æn'tægənɪzəm] n antagonismo m (**between** entre), hostilidad f (**towards** hacia)
antagonize [æn'tægənaɪz] vt enemistar, malquistar
Antarctic [æn'tɑːktɪk] **1** adj antártico(a); **A. Ocean** océano Antártico
2 n **the A.** la Antártida
Antarctica [æn'tɑːktɪkə] n Antártida
antecedent [æntɪ'siːdənt] n antecedente m
antelope ['æntɪləʊp] n antílope m
antenatal [æntɪ'neɪtəl] adj antenatal; *(clinic)* prenatal

antenna [æn'tenə] n (**a**) *(pl* **antennae** [æn'teniː]) *(of animal, insect)* antena f (**b**) *(pl* **antennas**) *TV & Rad* antena f
anthem ['ænθəm] n motete m; **national a.** himno m nacional
anthology [æn'θɒlədʒɪ] n antología f
anthracite ['ænθrəsaɪt] n antracita f
anthropology [ænθrə'pɒlədʒɪ] n antropología f
anti-aircraft [æntɪ'eəkrɑːft] adj antiaéreo(a)
antibiotic [æntɪbaɪ'ɒtɪk] n antibiótico m
antibody ['æntɪbɒdɪ] n anticuerpo m
anticipate [æn'tɪsɪpeɪt] vt (**a**) *(expect)* esperar (**b**) *(predict)* prever; *(get ahead of)* anticiparse a, adelantarse a
anticipation [æntɪsɪ'peɪʃən] n *(expectation)* esperanza f; *(expectancy)* ilusión f
anticlimax [æntɪ'klaɪmæks] n *(disappointment)* decepción f
anticlockwise [æntɪ'klɒkwaɪz] adv Br en sentido opuesto al de las agujas del reloj
antics ['æntɪks] npl payasadas fpl; *(naughtiness)* travesuras fpl
anticyclone [æntɪ'saɪkləʊn] n anticiclón m
antidote ['æntɪdəʊt] n antídoto m
antifreeze ['æntɪfriːz] n anticongelante m
antihistamine [æntɪ'hɪstəmɪn] n antihistamínico m
antinuclear [æntɪ'njuːklɪə(r)] adj antinuclear
antipathy [æn'tɪpəθɪ] n antipatía f (**to** a)
antiquated ['æntɪkweɪtɪd] adj anticuado(a)
antique [æn'tiːk] **1** adj antiguo(a)
2 n antigüedad f; **a. dealer** anticuario(a) m,f; **a. shop** tienda f de antigüedades
antiquity [æn'tɪkwɪtɪ] n antigüedad f
anti-Semitism [æntɪ'semɪtɪzəm] n antisemitismo m
antiseptic [æntɪ'septɪk] adj & n antiséptico(a) *(m)*
antisocial [æntɪ'səʊʃəl] adj *(delinquent)* antisocial; *(unsociable)* insociable
antithesis [æn'tɪθɪsɪs] n antítesis f
antivirus ['æntɪˌvaɪrəs] adj Comput *(program, software)* antivirus
antler ['æntlə(r)] n cuerna f; **antlers** cornamenta f
Antwerp ['æntwɜːp] n Amberes
anus ['eɪnəs] n ano m
anvil ['ænvɪl] n yunque m
anxiety [æŋ'zaɪtɪ] n *(concern)* inquietud f; *(worry)* preocupación f; *(fear)* angustia f; *(eagerness)* ansia f
anxious ['æŋkʃəs] adj *(concerned)*

inquieto(a); *(worried)* preocupado(a); *(fearful)* angustiado(a); *(eager)* ansioso(a); **to be a. about sth** estar preocupado(a) por algo

any ['enɪ] **1** *adj (in questions, conditionals)* algún(una); *(in negative clauses)* ningún(una); *(no matter which)* cualquier(a); *(every)* todo(a); **a. doctor will say the same** cualquier médico te dirá lo mismo; **are there a. seats left?** ¿quedan plazas?; **at a. moment** en cualquier momento; **have you a. apples?** ¿tienes manzanas?; **have you a. money?** ¿tienes (algo de) dinero?; **I don't have a. time** no tengo tiempo; **in a. case** de todas formas **2** *pron (in questions)* alguno(a); *(in negative clauses)* ninguno(a); *(no matter which)* cualquiera; **do they have a.?** ¿tienen alguno?; **I don't want a.** no quiero ninguno(a); **I need some paper, have you a.?** necesito papel, ¿tienes?; **you can have a. (one)** coge el/la que quieras **3** *adv* **is there a. more?** ¿hay más?; **I used to like it, but not a. more/longer** antes me gustaba pero ya no; **is he a. better?** ¿está mejor?

anybody ['enɪbɒdɪ] *pron (in questions, conditionals)* alguien, alguno(a); *(in negative clauses)* nadie, ninguno(a); *(no matter who)* cualquiera; **a. but me** cualquiera menos yo; **bring a. you like** trae a quien quieras; **do you see a. over there?** ¿ves a alguien allí?; **I can't find a.** no encuentro a nadie

anyhow ['enɪhaʊ] *adv* **(a)** *(in spite of that)* en todo caso, de todas formas; *(changing the subject)* bueno, pues **(b)** *(carelessly)* desordenadamente, de cualquier modo *or* forma

anyone ['enɪwʌn] *pron* = **anybody**

anyplace ['enɪpleɪs] *adv US* = **anywhere**

anything ['enɪθɪŋ] **1** *pron (in questions, conditionals)* algo, alguna cosa; *(in negative clauses)* nada; *(no matter what)* cualquier cosa; **a. but that** cualquier cosa menos eso; **a. else?** ¿algo más?; **can I do a. for you?** ¿puedo ayudarte en algo?; **hardly a.** casi nada; **if a., I'd buy the big one** de comprar uno compraría el grande; **to run/work like a.** correr/trabajar a más no poder **2** *adv* **is this a. like what you wanted?** ¿viene a ser éste lo que querías?

anyway ['enɪweɪ] *adv* = **anyhow** (a)

anywhere ['enɪweə(r)] *adv* **(a)** *(in questions, conditionals) (situation)* en alguna parte; *(movement)* a alguna parte; **could it be a. else?** ¿podría estar en otro sitio?

(b) *(in negative clauses) (situation)* en ninguna parte; *(movement)* a ninguna parte; *(no matter where)* dondequiera, en cualquier parte; **go a. you like** ve a donde quieras; **we aren't a. near finished** no hemos terminado ni mucho menos

apart [ə'pɑːt] *adv* **(a)** aparte; **to fall a.** deshacerse; **to take sth a.** desmontar algo **(b)** *(distant)* alejado(a); *(separate)* separado(a); **to be poles a.** ser polos opuestos; **you can't tell the twins a.** no se puede distinguir los mellizos el uno del otro **(c)** **a. from** aparte de

apartheid [ə'pɑːtheɪt] *n* apartheid *m*

apartment [ə'pɑːtmənt] *n (large room)* salón *m*; *US (flat)* piso *m*, apartamento *m*; **a. block** bloque *m* de pisos

apathetic [æpə'θetɪk] *adj* apático(a)

apathy ['æpəθɪ] *n* apatía *f*

ape [eɪp] **1** *n* mono *m*
2 *vt* imitar, copiar

apéritif [ə'perɪtiːf] *n* aperitivo *m*

aperture ['æpətʃə(r)] *n (hole, crack)* resquicio *m*, rendija *f*; *Phot* abertura *f*

apex ['eɪpeks] *n (of triangle)* vértice *m*; *Fig* cumbre *f*

aphrodisiac [æfrə'dɪzɪæk] *n* afrodisíaco *m*

apiece [ə'piːs] *adv* cada uno(a)

aplomb [ə'plɒm] *n* aplomo *m*

apocalypse [ə'pɒkəlɪps] *n* apocalipsis *m inv*

apolitical [eɪpə'lɪtɪkəl] *adj* apolítico(a)

apologetic [əpɒlə'dʒetɪk] *adj (remorseful)* de disculpa; **he was very a.** pidió mil perdones

apologetically [əpɒlə'dʒetɪklɪ] *adv* disculpándose, pidiendo perdón

apologize [ə'pɒlədʒaɪz] *vi (say sorry)* disculparse; **they apologized to us for the delay** se disculparon con nosotros por el retraso

apology [ə'pɒlədʒɪ] *n* disculpa *f*, excusa *f*; *Fam* **what an a. for a meal!** ¡vaya birria de comida!

apoplectic [æpə'plektɪk] *adj Med* apopléctico(a); *Fam* **to be a. with rage** estar furioso(a)

apostle [ə'pɒsəl] *n* apóstol *m*

apostrophe [ə'pɒstrəfɪ] *n* apóstrofo *m*

appal, *US* **appall** [ə'pɔːl] *vt* horrorizar; **to be appalled by sth** quedar horrorizado(a) por algo

appalling [ə'pɔːlɪŋ] *adj (horrifying)* horroroso(a); *Fam (very bad)* pésimo(a), fatal

apparatus [æpə'reɪtəs] *n* aparato *m*; *(equipment)* equipo *m*

apparent [ə'pærənt] *adj (obvious)* evidente; *(seeming)* aparente; **to become a.** ponerse de manifiesto

apparently [ə'pærəntlı] *adv (seemingly)* por lo visto

apparition [æpə'rıʃən] *n* aparición *f*

appeal [ə'pi:l] **1** *n* (**a**) *(request)* solicitud *f*; *(plea)* súplica *f* (**b**) *(attraction)* atractivo *m*; *(interest)* interés *m* (**c**) *Jur* apelación *f* **2** *vi* (**a**) *(plead)* rogar, suplicar (**to** a); **to a. for help** solicitar ayuda (**b**) *(attract)* atraer; *(interest)* interesar; **it doesn't a. to me** no me dice nada (**c**) *Jur* apelar

appealing [ə'pi:lıŋ] *adj (moving)* conmovedor(a); *(attractive)* atractivo(a); *(tempting)* atrayente

appear [ə'pıə(r)] *vi* (**a**) *(become visible)* aparecer; *(publicly)* presentarse; *(on stage)* actuar; **to a. before a court** comparecer ante un tribunal; **to a. on television** salir en la televisión (**b**) *(seem)* parecer; **he appears relaxed** parece relajado; **so it appears** según parece

appearance [ə'pıərəns] *n* (**a**) *(becoming visible)* aparición *f*; *(publicly)* presentación *f*; *(on stage)* actuación *f*; *(before court)* comparecencia *f*; *(of book etc)* publicación *f*; **to put in an a.** hacer acto de presencia (**b**) *(look)* apariencia *f*, aspecto *m*; **to all appearances** al parecer

appease [ə'pi:z] *vt* apaciguar; *(curiosity)* satisfacer

appeasement [ə'pi:zmənt] *n Pol* entreguismo *m*

appendices [ə'pendısi:z] *pl of* **appendix**

appendicitis [əpendı'saıtıs] *n* apendicitis *f*

appendix [ə'pendıks] *n* (*pl* **appendices**) apéndice *m*

appetite ['æpıtaıt] *n* apetito *m*; *Fig* deseo *m*

appetizer ['æpıtaızə(r)] *n (drink)* aperitivo *m*; *(snack)* tapa *f*, pincho *m*

applaud [ə'plɔːd] *vt & vi* aplaudir

applause [ə'plɔːz] *n* aplausos *mpl*

apple ['æpəl] *n* manzana *f*; **a. tree** manzano *m*

appliance [ə'plaıəns] *n* dispositivo *m*

applicable [ə'plıkəbəl] *adj* aplicable

applicant ['æplıkənt] *n (for post)* candidato(a) *m,f*; *(to court, for tickets)* solicitante *mf*

application [æplı'keıʃən] *n* (**a**) *(of cream)* aplicación *f* (**b**) *(for post etc)* solicitud *f*; **a. form** solicitud; **job a.** solicitud de empleo (**c**) *(effort)* aplicación *f*; **she lacks a.** no se aplica

applied [ə'plaıd] *adj* aplicado(a)

apply [ə'plaı] **1** *vt* aplicar; *(brake)* echar; *(law)* recurrir a; *(force)* usar; **to a. oneself to** dedicarse a

2 *vi* (**a**) *(refer)* aplicarse (**to** a) (**b**) *(for job)* presentar una solicitud; *(for information, to court)* presentar una petición

▸ **apply for** *vt insep (post, information)* solicitar; *(tickets)* pedir

appoint [ə'pɔınt] *vt (person)* nombrar; *(time, place etc)* fijar, señalar

appointment [ə'pɔıntmənt] *n* (**a**) *(to post)* nombramiento *m*; *(post)* cargo *m* (**b**) *(meeting)* cita *f*; **to make an a. with** citarse con; *(at doctor's)* pedir hora a

apportion [ə'pɔːʃən] *vt Fig (blame)* echar

appraisal [ə'preızəl] *n* evaluación *f*

appreciable [ə'priːʃəbəl] *adj (difference)* apreciable; *(sum)* importante

appreciate [ə'priːʃıeıt] **1** *vt* (**a**) *(be thankful for)* agradecer (**b**) *(understand)* entender (**c**) *(value)* apreciar, valorar

2 *vi (increase in value)* apreciarse

appreciation [əpriːʃı'eıʃən] *n* (**a**) *(of help, advice)* agradecimiento *m*; *(of difficulty)* comprensión *f*; *(of wine etc)* aprecio *m*; *(appraisal)* evaluación *f* (**b**) *(increase in value)* apreciación *f*

appreciative [ə'priːʃıətıv] *adj (thankful)* agradecido(a); *(responsive)* apreciativo(a)

apprehend [æprı'hend] *vt (arrest)* detener

apprehension [æprı'henʃən] *n* (**a**) *(arrest)* detención *f* (**b**) *(fear)* aprensión *f*

apprehensive [æprı'hensıv] *adj (fearful)* aprensivo(a)

apprentice [ə'prentıs] *n* aprendiz(a) *m,f*

apprenticeship [ə'prentısʃıp] *n* aprendizaje *m*

approach [ə'prəʊtʃ] **1** *n* (**a**) *(coming near)* acercamiento *m*; *(to town)* acceso *m*; **a. road** vía *f* de acceso (**b**) *(to problem)* enfoque *m*

2 *vt (come near to)* acercarse a; *(be similar to)* aproximarse a; *Fig (problem)* abordar; *(person)* dirigirse a; **to a. sb about sth** dirigirse a algn a propósito de algo

3 *vi* acercarse

approachable [ə'prəʊtʃəbəl] *adj (person)* accesible

appropriate¹ [ə'prəʊprıət] *adj (suitable)* apropiado(a), adecuado(a); *(convenient)* oportuno(a)

appropriate² [ə'prəʊprıeıt] *vt (allocate)* asignar; *(steal)* apropiarse de

approval [ə'pruːvəl] *n* aprobación *f*, visto

bueno; *Com* **to get sth on a.** adquirir algo sin compromiso de compra
approve [ə'pru:v] *vt* aprobar; **approved school** reformatorio *m*
▸ **approve of** *vt insep* aprobar
approving [ə'pru:vɪŋ] *adj (look etc)* aprobatorio(a)
approx [ə'prɒks] (*abbr* **approximately**) aprox.
approximate 1 *adj* [ə'prɒksɪmɪt] aproximado(a)
   2 *vt* [ə'prɒksɪmeɪt] aproximarse a
approximately [ə'prɒksɪmɪtlɪ] *adv* aproximadamente
apricot ['eɪprɪkɒt] *n* albaricoque *m*, *Am* damasco *m*, *Méx* chabacano *m*
April ['eɪprəl] *n* abril *m*; **A. Fools' Day** día *m* uno de abril, ≃ día de los Inocentes (28 de diciembre)
apron ['eɪprən] *n* delantal *m*; *(for workman)* mandil *m*
apt [æpt] *adj* (**a**) *(suitable)* apropiado(a); *(remark)* acertado(a), oportuno(a); *(name)* justo(a); *(description)* exacto(a) (**b**) **to be a. to do sth** ser propenso(a) a hacer algo
aptitude ['æptɪtju:d] *n* capacidad *f*; **a. test** prueba *f* de aptitud
aptly ['æptlɪ] *adv* acertadamente
aqualung ['ækwəlʌŋ] *n* botella *f* de oxígeno
aquamarine [ækwəmə'ri:n] **1** *n (gem)* aguamarina *f*
   2 *adj* de color de aguamarina
aquarium [ə'kweərɪəm] *n* acuario *m*
Aquarius [ə'kweərɪəs] *n* Acuario *m*
aquatic [ə'kwætɪk] *adj* acuático(a)
aqueduct ['ækwɪdʌkt] *n* acueducto *m*
Arab ['ærəb] *adj & n* árabe *(mf)*
Arabian [ə'reɪbɪən] *adj* árabe
Arabic ['ærəbɪk] **1** *adj* árabe, arábigo(a); **A. numerals** numeración arábiga
   2 *n (language)* árabe *m*
arable ['ærəbəl] *adj* cultivable
Aragon ['ærəgən] *n* Aragón
arbitrary ['ɑ:bɪtrərɪ] *adj* arbitrario(a)
arbitrate ['ɑ:bɪtreɪt] *vt & vi* arbitrar
arbitration [ɑ:bɪ'treɪʃən] *n* arbitraje *m*
arc [ɑ:k] *n* arco *m*; **a. lamp** arco voltaico
arcade [ɑ:'keɪd] *n* arcada *f*; *(passageway)* pasaje *m*; **shopping a.** galerías *fpl* (comerciales)
arch [ɑ:tʃ] **1** *n* (**a**) *Archit* arco *m*; *(vault)* bóveda *f* (**b**) *Anat* empeine *m*
   2 *vt (back)* arquear
archaeologist [ɑ:kɪ'ɒlədʒɪst] *n* arqueólogo(a) *m,f*
archaeology [ɑ:kɪ'ɒlədʒɪ] *n* arqueología *f*

archaic [ɑ:'keɪɪk] *adj* arcaico(a)
archbishop [ɑ:tʃ'bɪʃəp] *n* arzobispo *m*
arched [ɑ:tʃt] *adj* arqueado(a)
archeologist [ɑ:kɪ'ɒlədʒɪst] *n US* = **archaeologist**
archeology [ɑ:kɪ'ɒlədʒɪ] *n US* = **archaeology**
archer ['ɑ:tʃə(r)] *n* arquero(a) *m,f*
archery ['ɑ:tʃərɪ] *n* tiro *m* con arco
archetypal ['ɑ:kɪtaɪpəl] *adj* arquetípico(a)
archipelago [ɑ:kɪ'pelɪgəʊ] *n* archipiélago *m*
architect ['ɑ:kɪtekt] *n* arquitecto(a) *m,f*
architectural [ɑ:kɪ'tektʃərəl] *adj* arquitectónico(a)
architecture ['ɑ:kɪtektʃə(r)] *n* arquitectura *f*
archives ['ɑ:kaɪvz] *npl* archivos *mpl*
archway ['ɑ:tʃweɪ] *n (arch)* arco *m*; *(vault)* bóveda *f*; *(in church)* atrio *m*; *(passage)* pasaje *m*
arctic ['ɑ:ktɪk] **1** *adj* ártico(a); **A. Circle** círculo *m* polar Ártico
   2 *n* **the A.** el Ártico
ardent ['ɑ:dənt] *adj (supporter etc)* apasionado(a); *(desire)* ardiente
ardour, *US* **ardor** ['ɑ:də(r)] *n* pasión *f*, ardor *m*
arduous ['ɑ:djʊəs] *adj* arduo(a), penoso(a)
are [ɑ:(r)] *2nd person sing pres, 1st, 2nd, 3rd person pl pres of* **be**
area ['eərɪə] *n (surface)* área *f*, superficie *f*; *(space)* extensión *f*; *(region)* región *f*; *(of town)* zona *f*; *Fig (field)* campo *m*; *US Tel* **a. code** prefijo *m* local
arena [ə'ri:nə] *n (stadium)* estadio *m*; *(bullring)* plaza *f*; *(circus)* pista *f*; *Fig (stage)* campo *m* de batalla
Argentina [ɑ:dʒən'ti:nə] *n* Argentina
Argentinian [ɑ:dʒən'tɪnɪən] *adj & n* argentino(a) *(m,f)*
arguable ['ɑ:gjʊəbəl] *adj* discutible
arguably ['ɑ:gjʊəblɪ] *adv* **it's a. the best** hay quienes dicen que es el mejor
argue ['ɑ:gju:] **1** *vt (reason)* discutir; *(point of view)* mantener
   2 *vi (quarrel)* discutir; *(reason)* argumentar, razonar; **to a. for** abogar por; **to a. against sth** ponerse en contra de algo
argument ['ɑ:gjʊmənt] *n (reason)* argumento *m* (**for** a favor de; **against** en contra de); *(quarrel)* discusión *f*, disputa *f*; **for the sake of a.** por decir algo
argumentative [ɑ:gjʊ'mentətɪv] *adj* **she's very a.** le gusta discutir por todo
aria ['ɑ:rɪə] *n* aria *f*

arid ['ærɪd] *adj* árido(a)

Aries ['eəriːz] *n* Aries *m*

arise [ə'raɪz] *vi* (*pt* **arose**; *pp* **arisen** [ə'rɪzən]) (*get up*) levantarse; (*happen*) surgir; **should the occasion a.** si se presenta la ocasión

aristocracy [ærɪ'stɒkrəsɪ] *n* aristocracia *f*

aristocrat ['ærɪstəkræt] *n* aristócrata *mf*

arithmetic [ə'rɪθmətɪk] *n* aritmética *f*

ark [ɑːk] *n* arca *f*; **Noah's A.** el arca de Noé

arm [ɑːm] **1** *n* (**a**) brazo *m*; (*of garment*) manga *f*; **to walk a. in a.** ir cogidos(as) del brazo (**b**) *Mil* **arms** armas *fpl*; **arms race** carrera armamentística; **coat of arms** escudo *m*
    2 *vt* armar; **to a.** **oneself against sth** armarse contra algo

armaments ['ɑːməmənts] *npl* armamentos *mpl*

armchair ['ɑːmtʃeə(r)] *n* sillón *m*

armed ['ɑːmd] *adj* armado(a); **a. forces** fuerzas armadas; **a. robbery** robo *m* a mano armada

Armenia [ɑː'miːnɪə] *n* Armenia

armistice ['ɑːmɪstɪs] *n* armisticio *m*

armour, *US* **armor** ['ɑːmə(r)] *n* (*on vehicle*) blindaje *m*; (**suit of**) **a.** armadura *f*

armoured car, *US* **armored car** [ɑːməd'kɑː(r)] *n* coche *m* blindado

armour-plated ['ɑːmə'pleɪtɪd] *adj* acorazado(a)

armoury, *US* **armory** ['ɑːmərɪ] *n* arsenal *m*

armpit ['ɑːmpɪt] *n* axila *f*, sobaco *m*

army ['ɑːmɪ] *n* ejército *m*

aroma [ə'rəʊmə] *n* aroma *m*

arose [ə'rəʊz] *pt of* **arise**

around [ə'raʊnd] **1** *adv* alrededor; **all a.** por todos los lados; **are the children a.?** ¿están los niños por aquí?; **he looked a.** miró (a su) alrededor
    2 *prep* (**a**) alrededor de; **a. the corner** a la vuelta de la esquina; **a. here** por aquí (**b**) (*approximately*) aproximadamente

arouse [ə'raʊz] *vt* despertar; (*sexually*) excitar

arrange [ə'reɪndʒ] **1** *vt* (**a**) (*order*) ordenar; (*hair, flowers*) arreglar; *Mus* adaptar (**b**) (*plan*) organizar; (*agree on*) quedar en; **to a. a time** fijar una hora; **arranged marriage** boda arreglada
    2 *vi* **I shall a. for him to be there** lo arreglaré para que pueda asistir

arrangement [ə'reɪndʒmənt] *n* (**a**) (*display*) colocación *f*; *Mus* adaptación *f* (**b**) (*agreement*) acuerdo *m* (**c**) **arrangements** (*plans*) planes *mpl*; (*preparations*) preparativos *mpl*

array [ə'reɪ] *n* colección *f*; **a great a. of goods** un gran surtido de productos

arrears [ə'rɪəz] *npl* atrasos *mpl*; **to be in a. with the rent** estar atrasado(a) con el alquiler; **to be paid in a.** cobrar con retraso

arrest [ə'rest] **1** *n* detención *f*; **to be under a.** estar detenido(a)
    2 *vt* (*criminal*) detener; *Fig* (*progress*) frenar

arresting [ə'restɪŋ] *adj* llamativo(a)

arrival [ə'raɪvəl] *n* llegada *f*; **a new a.** un(a) recién llegado(a)

arrive [ə'raɪv] *vi* llegar (**at/in** a)

arrogance ['ærəgəns] *n* arrogancia *f*

arrogant ['ærəgənt] *adj* arrogante

arrow ['ærəʊ] *n* flecha *f*

arse ['ɑːs] *n Vulg* culo *m*

arsenal ['ɑːsənəl] *n* arsenal *m*

arsenic ['ɑːsənɪk] *n* arsénico *m*

arson ['ɑːsən] *n* incendio *m* provocado

art [ɑːt] *n* (**a**) arte *m*; (*drawing*) dibujo *m*; **the arts** las bellas artes; **arts and crafts** artes *fpl* y oficios *mpl*; **a. gallery** galería *f* de arte (**b**) **arts** (*branch of knowledge*) letras *fpl*

artefact ['ɑːtɪfækt] *n* artefacto *m*; (*in archaeology*) objeto *m* de arte

artery ['ɑːtərɪ] *n* arteria *f*

artful ['ɑːtfʊl] *adj* (*cunning*) ladino(a)

arthritis [ɑː'θraɪtɪs] *n* artritis *f*

artichoke ['ɑːtɪtʃəʊk] *n* alcachofa *f*, *RP* alcaucil *m*

article ['ɑːtɪkəl] *n* (**a**) artículo *m*; *Press* artículo; **a. of clothing** prenda *f* de vestir (**b**) *Jur* **articles** contrato *m* de aprendizaje

articulate¹ [ɑː'tɪkjʊlɪt] *adj* (*speech*) claro(a); (*person*) que se expresa bien

articulate² [ɑː'tɪkjʊleɪt] *vt & vi* articular; (*words*) pronunciar; *Br* **articulated lorry** camión articulado

artificial [ɑːtɪ'fɪʃəl] *adj* artificial; (*limb*) postizo(a); **a. intelligence** inteligencia *f* artificial

artillery [ɑː'tɪlərɪ] *n* artillería *f*

artisan ['ɑːtɪzæn] *n* artesano(a) *m,f*

artist ['ɑːtɪst] *n* artista *mf*; (*painter*) pintor(a) *m,f*

artistic [ɑː'tɪstɪk] *adj* artístico(a)

artistry ['ɑːtɪstrɪ] *n* arte *m*, talento artístico

as [æz, *unstressed* əz] **1** *adv & conj* (**a**) (*comparison*) **as ... as ...** tan ... como ...; **as far as** hasta; *Fig* **as far as I'm concerned** por lo que a mi respecta; **as many as** tantos(as) como; **as much as** tanto(a) como; **as tall as me** tan alto(a) como yo; **as opposed to** a diferencia de; **as little as**

£5 tan sólos 5 libras ; **as soon as they arrive** en cuanto lleguen; **I'll stay as long as I can** quedaré todo el tiempo que pueda; **just as big** igual de grande; **three times as fast** tres veces más rápido; **the same as** igual que

(**b**) *(manner)* como; **as a rule** por regla general; **as you know** como ya sabéis; **as you like** como quieras; **do as I say** haz lo que yo te digo; **he's working as a doctor** está trabajando de médico; **I thought as much** ya me lo suponía; **it serves as a table** sirve de mesa; **leave it as it is** déjalo tal como está; **he was dressed as a pirate** iba vestido de pirata

(**c**) *(while, when)* mientras (que); **as a child** de niño(a); **as I was eating** mientras comía; **as we were leaving, we saw Pat** al salir vimos a Pat

(**d**) *(though)* aunque; **be that as it may** por mucho que así sea; **young as he is** aunque es joven

(**e**) *(because)* como, ya que

(**f**) *(and so)* igual que; **as do I** igual que yo; **as well** también

(**g**) *(purpose)* para; **so as to do sth** para hacer algo

(**h**) **as for my brother** en cuanto a mi hermano

(**i**) **as from, as of** a partir de

(**j**) **to act as if** actuar como si *(+ subj)*; **it looks as if the concert is off** parece ser que no habrá concierto

(**k**) **it's late enough as it is** ya es muy tarde; **as it were** por así decirlo

(**l**) **as long as** *(only if)* siempre que, con tal de que

(**m**) **as regards** en cuanto a, por lo que se refiere a; **as usual** como siempre; **as yet** aún, todavía

2 *rel pron* **such as** tal(es) como

asbestos [æz'bestəs] *n* amianto *m*, asbesto *m*

ascend [ə'send] *vi* subir, ascender

ascendancy [ə'sendənsı] *n* dominio *m*, influencia *f*

ascendant [ə'sendənt] *n* **to be in the a.** estar en auge

ascent [ə'sent] *n* subida *f*

ascertain [æsə'teın] *vt* averiguar, enterarse de

ascribe [ə'skraıb] *vt* **to a. sth to sb/sth** imputar algo a alguien/algo

aseptic [ə'septık] *adj* aséptico(a)

ash¹ [æʃ] *n Bot* fresno *m*

ash² [æʃ] *n* ceniza *f*; **a. bin,** *US* **a. can** cubo *m* de la basura; *Rel* **A. Wednesday** miércoles *m inv* de ceniza

ashamed [ə'ʃeımd] *adj* avergonzado(a); **you ought to be a. of yourself!** ¡te debería dar vergüenza!

ashen ['æʃən] *adj (face)* pálido(a)

ashore [ə'ʃɔ:(r)] *adv (position)* en tierra; **to go a.** desembarcar; **to swim a.** nadar hacia tierra

ashtray ['æʃtreı] *n* cenicero *m*

Asia ['eıʒə] *n* Asia; **A. Minor** Asia Menor

Asian ['eıʒən] *adj & n* asiático(a) *(m,f)*

aside [ə'saıd] **1** *adv* al lado, aparte; **to cast a.** echar a un lado; **to stand a.** apartarse

2 *prep* **a. from** *(apart from)* aparte de; *(as well as)* además de

3 *n Th* aparte *m*

ask [ɑ:sk] **1** *vt* (**a**) preguntar; **to a. sb a question** hacer una pregunta a algn (**b**) *(request)* pedir, solicitar; **she asked me to post it** me pidió que lo echara al buzón (**c**) *(invite)* invitar

2 *vi (inquire)* preguntar; *(request)* pedir

▸ **ask after** *vt insep* **to a. after sb** preguntar por algn

▸ **ask for** *vt insep (help)* pedir, solicitar; *(person)* preguntar por

▸ **ask out** *vt sep* **to a. sb out** invitar a algn a salir

askance [ə'skæns] *adv* **to look a. at sb** mirar a algn con recelo

askew [ə'skju:] **1** *adj* ladeado(a)

2 *adv* de lado

asleep [ə'sli:p] *adj (person)* dormido(a); *(limb)* adormecido(a); **to fall a.** quedarse dormido(a)

asparagus [ə'spærəgəs] *n inv* espárragos *mpl*

aspect ['æspekt] *n* (**a**) *(of question)* aspecto *m* (**b**) *(of building)* orientación *f*

aspersions [ə'spɜ:ʃənz] *npl* **to cast a. on sb** difamar a algn

asphalt ['æsfælt] *n* asfalto *m*

asphyxiation [æsfıksı'eıʃən] *n* asfixia *f*

aspiration [æspə'reıʃən] *n* aspiración *f*

aspire [ə'spaıə(r)] *vi* **to a. to** aspirar a

aspirin ['æsprın] *n* aspirina *f*

ass¹ [æs] *n Zool* asno(a) *m,f*, burro(a) *m,f*; *Fam Fig* burro(a)

ass² [æs] *n US Vulg* culo *m*

assailant [ə'seılənt] *n* agresor(a) *m,f*, atacante *mf*

assassin [ə'sæsın] *n* asesino(a) *m,f*

assassinate [ə'sæsıneıt] *vt* asesinar

assassination [əsæsı'neıʃən] *n* asesinato *m*

assault [ə'sɔ:lt] **1** *n Mil* ataque *m* (**on** a); *Jur* agresión *f*

2 *vt Mil* asaltar, atacar; *Jur* agredir; *(sexually)* violar

assemble [əˈsembəl] **1** vt (people) reunir, juntar; (furniture) montar **2** vi (people) reunirse, juntarse

assembly [əˈsemblɪ] n reunión f, asamblea f; Tech montaje m; Ind **a. line** cadena f de montaje; Educ **morning a.** servicio m matinal

assent [əˈsent] **1** n (agreement) asentimiento m; (consent) consentimiento m; (approval) aprobación f **2** vi asentir, consentir (**to** en)

assert [əˈsɜːt] vt afirmar; **to a. oneself** imponerse; **to a. one's rights** hacer valer sus derechos

assertive [əˈsɜːtɪv] adj enérgico(a)

assess [əˈses] vt (estimate value) valorar; (damages, price) calcular; (tax) gravar; Fig (effect) evaluar

assessment [əˈsesmənt] n (of value) valoración f; (of damages etc) cálculo m; (of taxes) gravamen m; Fig juicio m

assessor [əˈsesə(r)] n asesor(a) m,f

asset [ˈæset] n (**a**) ventaja f; **to be an a.** (person) ser de gran valor (**b**) Fin **assets** bienes mpl; **fixed assets** bienes raíces

asshole [ˈæshəʊl] n US Vulg (unpleasant person) hijo(a) m,f de puta, cabrón(ona) m,f

assiduous [əˈsɪdjʊəs] adj asiduo(a)

assign [əˈsaɪn] vt (task) asignar; (property etc) ceder; **to a. sb to a job** designar a algn para un trabajo

assignment [əˈsaɪnmənt] n (allocation) asignación f; (task) tarea f; (mission) misión f; (appointment) cita f

assimilate [əˈsɪmɪleɪt] vt asimilar

assist [əˈsɪst] vt & vi ayudar

assistance [əˈsɪstəns] n ayuda f, auxilio m

assistant [əˈsɪstənt] n ayudante mf; **a. manager** subdirector(a) m,f; **shop a.** dependiente(a) m,f; (**language**) **a.** lector(a) m,f

associate¹ [əˈsəʊʃɪeɪt] **1** vt (ideas) relacionar; (companies) asociar; **to be associated with sth** estar relacionado(a) con algo **2** vi **to a. with** tratar con

associate² [əˈsəʊʃɪt] **1** adj asociado(a) **2** n (colleague) colega mf; (partner) socio(a) m,f; (accomplice) cómplice mf

association [əsəʊsɪˈeɪʃən] n asociación f; (company) sociedad f

assorted [əˈsɔːtɪd] adj surtido(a), variado(a)

assortment [əˈsɔːtmənt] n surtido m, variedad f

assume [əˈsjuːm] **1** vt (power) asumir;

(attitude, name) adoptar; **an assumed name** un nombre falso **2** vi (suppose) suponer

assumption [əˈsʌmpʃən] n (**a**) (of power) toma f; **a. of office** toma de posesión (**b**) (supposition) suposición f

assurance [əˈʃʊərəns] n (**a**) (guarantee) garantía f (**b**) (confidence) confianza f (**c**) (insurance) seguro m

assure [əˈʃʊə(r)] vt asegurar

asterisk [ˈæstərɪsk] n asterisco m

astern [əˈstɜːn] adv a popa

asthma [ˈæsmə] n asma f

astonish [əˈstɒnɪʃ] vt asombrar, pasmar; **I was astonished** me quedé pasmado(a)

astonishing [əˈstɒnɪʃɪŋ] adj asombroso(a), pasmoso(a)

astonishment [əˈstɒnɪʃmənt] n asombro m; **to my a.** para gran sorpresa mía

astound [əˈstaʊnd] vt asombrar, pasmar

astray [əˈstreɪ] adv **to go a.** extraviarse; Fig equivocarse; **to lead sb a.** llevar a algn por mal camino

astride [əˈstraɪd] prep a horcajadas sobre

astrology [əˈstrɒlədʒɪ] n astrología f

astronaut [ˈæstrənɔːt] n astronauta mf

astronomer [əˈstrɒnəmə(r)] n astrónomo(a) m,f

astronomical [æstrəˈnɒmɪkəl] adj astronómico(a)

astronomy [əˈstrɒnəmɪ] n astronomía f

Asturias [æˈstʊərɪæs] n Asturias

astute [əˈstjuːt] adj astuto(a)

asylum [əˈsaɪləm] n (**a**) (protection) asilo m; **to seek political a.** pedir asilo político (**b**) **mental a.** manicomio m

at [æt, unstressed ət] prep (**a**) (position) a, en; **at school/work** en el colegio/trabajo; **at the window** a la ventana; **at the top** en lo alto

(**b**) (direction) a; **to be angry at sb/sth** enfadarse con algn/por algo; **to laugh at sb** reírse de algn; **to look at sth/sb** mirar algo/a algn; **to shout at sb** gritarle a algn

(**c**) (time) a; **at Easter/Christmas** en Semana Santa/Navidad; **at six o'clock** a las seis; **at first** al principio; **at last** por fin; **at once** enseguida; **at that time** entonces; **at the moment** ahora

(**d**) (manner) a, en; **at best/worst** en el mejor/peor de los casos; **at hand** a mano; **at least** por lo menos; **not at all** en absoluto; (don't mention it) de nada

(**e**) (rate) a; **they retail at 100 pesetas each** se venden a 100 pesetas la unidad; **two at a time** de dos en dos

ate [et, eɪt] pt of **eat**

atheist [ˈeɪθɪɪst] n ateo(a) m,f

Athens [ˈæθɪnz] *n* Atenas
athlete [ˈæθliːt] *n* atleta *mf*
athletic [æθˈletɪk] **1** *adj* atlético(a); *(sporty)* deportista
2 *npl* **athletics** atletismo *m*
Atlantic [ətˈlæntɪk] *adj* **the A. (Ocean)** el (océano) Atlántico
atlas [ˈætləs] *n* atlas *m*
atmosphere [ˈætməsfɪə(r)] *n* atmósfera *f*; *Fig (ambience)* ambiente *m*
atmospheric [ætməsˈferɪk] *adj* atmosférico(a)
atom [ˈætəm] *n* átomo *m*; **a. bomb** bomba atómica
atomic [əˈtɒmɪk] *adj* atómico(a)
atone [əˈtəʊn] *vi* **to a. for** expiar
atrocious [əˈtrəʊʃəs] *adj* atroz
attach [əˈtætʃ] *vt (stick)* pegar; *(fasten)* sujetar; *(document)* adjuntar; **to a. importance to sth** dar importancia a algo; *Fig* **to be attached to** *(be fond of)* tener cariño a
attaché [əˈtæʃeɪ] *n* agregado(a) *m,f*; **a. case** maletín *m*
attachment [əˈtætʃmənt] *n* **(a)** *Tech* accesorio *m*; *(action)* acoplamiento *m* **(b)** *(fondness)* apego *m* (**to** por) **(c)** *Comput (to e-mail)* archivo adjunto, anexo *m*
attack [əˈtæk] **1** *n* **(a)** *(assault)* ataque *m*, asalto *m*; **an a. on sb's life** un atentado contra la vida de algn **(b)** *Med* ataque *m*
2 *vt (assault)* atacar, asaltar; *Fig (problem)* abordar; *(job)* emprender; *Fig (criticize)* atacar
attacker [əˈtækə(r)] *n* asaltante *mf*, agresor(a) *m,f*
attain [əˈteɪn] *vt (aim)* lograr; *(rank, age)* llegar a
attainment [əˈteɪnmənt] *n (achievement)* logro *m*; *(skill)* talento *m*
attempt [əˈtempt] **1** *n* intento *m*, tentativa *f*; **at the second a.** a la segunda; **an a. on sb's life** un atentado contra la vida de algn
2 *vt* intentar; **to a. to do sth** tratar de *or* intentar hacer algo; *Jur* **attempted murder/rape** intento *m* de asesinato/violación
attend [əˈtend] **1** *vt (be present at)* asistir a; *(care for, wait on)* atender
2 *vi (be present)* asistir; *(pay attention)* prestar atención
▸ **attend to** *vt insep (business)* ocuparse de; *(in shop)* atender a
attendance [əˈtendəns] *n* asistencia *f*
attendant [əˈtendənt] *n (in cinema etc)* acomodador(a) *m,f*; *(in museum)* guía *mf*; *(in car park)* vigilante(a) *m,f*

attention [əˈtenʃən] *n* **(a)** atención *f*; **for the a. of Miss Jones** a la atención de la Srta. Jones; **pay a.!** ¡atiende!; **to pay a. to sb/sth** prestar atención a algn/algo **(b)** *Mil* **a.!** ¡firmes!; **to stand to a.** estar firmes
attentive [əˈtentɪv] *adj (listener)* atento(a); *(helpful)* solícito(a)
attest [əˈtest] *vi* **to a. to** dar testimonio a
attic [ˈætɪk] *n* ático *m*
attire [əˈtaɪə(r)] *n* *Fml* traje *m*
attitude [ˈætɪtjuːd] *n* actitud *f*; *(position of body)* postura *f*; **an a. of mind** un estado de ánimo
attorney [əˈtɜːnɪ] *n* **(a)** *US (lawyer)* abogado(a) *m,f*; **A. General** ≃ Ministro(a) *m,f* de Justicia; **district a.** fiscal *mf* **(b)** *Jur* **power of a.** poderes *mpl*
attract [əˈtrækt] *vt* atraer; **to a. attention** llamar la atención; **to a. a waiter's attention** llamar a un camarero
attraction [əˈtrækʃən] *n* **(a)** *(power)* atracción *f* **(b)** *(attractive thing)* atractivo *m*; *(charm)* encanto *m*; *(incentive)* aliciente *m*; **the main a.** el número fuerte
attractive [əˈtræktɪv] *adj* atractivo(a); *(good-looking)* guapo(a); *(idea, proposition)* atrayente
attribute¹ [ˈætrɪbjuːt] *n (quality)* atributo *m*
attribute² [əˈtrɪbjuːt] *vt* atribuir
attrition [əˈtrɪʃən] *n* **war of a.** guerra *f* de desgaste
aubergine [ˈəʊbəʒiːn] *n* *Br* berenjena *f*
auburn [ˈɔːbən] *adj* castaño rojizo *inv*
auction [ˈɔːkʃən] **1** *n* subasta *f*
2 *vt* subastar
auctioneer [ɔːkʃəˈnɪə(r)] *n* subastador(a) *m,f*
audacious [ɔːˈdeɪʃəs] *adj (daring)* audaz; *(bold)* atrevido(a); *(impudent)* descarado(a)
audible [ˈɔːdɪbəl] *adj* audible
audience [ˈɔːdɪəns] *n* **(a)** *(spectators)* público *m*; *(at concert, conference)* auditorio *m*; *(television)* telespectadores *mpl* **(b)** *(meeting)* audiencia *f*
audio-visual [ɔːdɪəʊˈvɪzjʊəl] *adj* audiovisual; **a. aids** apoyo *m* audiovisual
audit [ˈɔːdɪt] **1** *n* revisión *f* de cuentas
2 *vt* revisar, intervenir
audition [ɔːˈdɪʃən] **1** *n* prueba *f*
2 *vt* **to a. sb for a part** probar a algn para un papel
auditor [ˈɔːdɪtə(r)] *n* revisor(a) *m,f* de cuentas
auditorium [ɔːdɪˈtɔːrɪəm] *n* auditorio *m*
augment [ɔːgˈment] *vt* aumentar

augur [ˈɔːgə(r)] *vi* **to a. well** ser de buen agüero

August [ˈɔːgəst] *n* agosto *m*

aunt [ɑːnt] *n* (*also Fam* **auntie, aunty** [ˈɑːntɪ]) tía *f*

au pair [əʊˈpeə(r)] *n* **a. (girl)** au pair *f*

aura [ˈɔːrə] *n* aura *f*; *Rel* aureola *f*

aural [ˈɔːrəl] *adj* auditivo(a), del oído

auspices [ˈɔːspɪsɪz] *npl* **under the a. of** bajo los auspicios de

auspicious [ɔːˈspɪʃəs] *adj* de buen augurio

austere [ɒˈstɪə(r)] *adj* austero(a)

austerity [ɒˈsterɪtɪ] *n* austeridad *f*

Australia [ɒˈstreɪlɪə] *n* Australia

Australian [ɒˈstreɪlɪən] *adj & n* australiano(a) *(m,f)*

Austria [ˈɒstrɪə] *n* Austria

Austrian [ˈɒstrɪən] *adj & n* austríaco(a) *(m,f)*

authentic [ɔːˈθentɪk] *adj* auténtico(a)

author [ˈɔːθə(r)] *n* autor(a) *m,f*

authoritarian [ɔːθɒrɪˈteərɪən] *adj* autoritario(a)

authoritative [ɔːˈθɒrɪtətɪv] *adj* (*reliable*) autorizado(a); (*authoritarian*) autoritario(a)

authority [ɔːˈθɒrɪtɪ] *n* autoridad *f*; **local a.** ayuntamiento *m*

authorize [ˈɔːθəraɪz] *vt* autorizar; (*payment etc*) aprobar; **to a. sb to do sth** autorizar a algn a hacer algo

auto [ˈɔːtəʊ] *n US* coche *m*, *Andes, CAm, Carib, Méx* carro *m*

autobiography [ɔːtəʊbaɪˈɒgrəfɪ] *n* autobiografía *f*

autograph [ˈɔːtəgrɑːf] **1** *n* autógrafo *m*
2 *vt* (*sign*) firmar; (*book, photo*) dedicar

automata [ɔːˈtɒmətə] *pl of* **automaton**

automatic [ɔːtəˈmætɪk] **1** *adj* automático(a)
2 *n* (*car*) coche automático; (*gun*) pistola automática

automatically [ɔːtəˈmætɪklɪ] *adv* automáticamente

automation [ɔːtəˈmeɪʃən] *n* automatización *f*; **office a.** ofimática *f*

automaton [ɔːˈtɒmətɒn] *n* (*pl* **automata**) autómata *m*

automobile [ˈɔːtəməbiːl] *n US* coche *m*, automóvil *m*, *Andes, CAm, Carib, Méx* carro *m*

autonomous [ɔːˈtɒnəməs] *adj* autónomo(a)

autonomy [ɔːˈtɒnəmɪ] *n* autonomía *f*

autopsy [ˈɔːtɒpsɪ] *n* autopsia *f*

autumn [ˈɔːtəm] *n* otoño *m*

auxiliary [ɔːgˈzɪljərɪ] *adj* auxiliar

Av., av. (*abbr* **Avenue**) Av., Avda.

avail [əˈveɪl] **1** *n* **to no a.** en vano
2 *vt* **to a. oneself of sth** aprovecharse de algo

available [əˈveɪləbəl] *adj* (*thing*) disponible; (*person*) libre

avalanche [ˈævəlɑːnʃ] *n* avalancha *f*

avarice [ˈævərɪs] *n* avaricia *f*

Ave (*abbr* **Avenue**) Av., Avda.

avenge [əˈvendʒ] *vt* vengar

avenue [ˈævɪnjuː] *n* avenida *f*; *Fig* vía *f*

average [ˈævərɪdʒ] **1** *n* promedio *m*, media *f*; **on a.** por término medio
2 *adj* medio(a); (*condition*) regular
3 *vt* sacar la media de; **he averages eight hours' work a day** trabaja una media de ocho horas al día
▸ **average out at** *vt insep* salir a una media de

averse [əˈvɜːs] *adj* **to be a. to sth** ser reacio(a) a algo

aversion [əˈvɜːʃən] *n* (*feeling*) aversión *f*; (*thing*) bestia negra

avert [əˈvɜːt] *vt* (*eyes, thoughts*) apartar (**from** de); (*accident*) impedir; (*danger*) evitar

avid [ˈævɪd] *adj* (*reader*) voraz

avidly [ˈævɪdlɪ] *adv* vorazmente

avocado [ævəˈkɑːdəʊ] *n* **a. (pear)** aguacate *m*, *Andes, RP* palta *f*

avoid [əˈvɔɪd] *vt* evitar; (*question*) eludir

avoidable [əˈvɔɪdəbəl] *adj* evitable

await [əˈweɪt] *vt* esperar, aguardar

awake [əˈweɪk] **1** *adj* despierto(a); **to be a.** estar despierto(a)
2 *vt* (*pt* **awoke, awaked**; *pp* **awoken, awaked**) despertar

awaken [əˈweɪkən] *vt & vi* (*pt* **awakened**; *pp* **awoken**) = **awake 2**

awakening [əˈweɪkənɪŋ] *n* despertar *m*

award [əˈwɔːd] **1** *n* (*prize*) premio *m*; (*medal*) condecoración *f*; *Jur* indemnización *f*; (*grant*) beca *f*
2 *vt* (*prize*) conceder, otorgar; (*medal*) dar; (*damages*) adjudicar

aware [əˈweə(r)] *adj* (*informed*) enterado(a); **not that I'm a. of** que yo sepa no; **to be a. of sth** ser consciente de algo; **to become a. of sth** darse cuenta de algo

awareness [əˈweənɪs] *n* conciencia *f* (**of** de)

awash [əˈwɒʃ] *adj* inundado(a) (**with** de)

away [əˈweɪ] *adv* **far a.** lejos; **go a.!** ¡lárgate!; **it's 3 miles a.** está a 3 millas (de distancia); **keep a. from the fire!** ¡no te acerques al fuego!; **right a.** en seguida; **to be a.** (*absent*) estar ausente; (*out*) estar fuera; **to die a.** desvanecerse; **to give sth**

a. regalar algo; *(secret)* revelar algo; **to go a.** irse; *Sport* **to play a.** jugar fuera; **to turn a.** volver la cara; **to work a.** trabajar

awe [ɔː] *n (fear)* temor *m*; *(amazement)* asombro *m*; **he was in a. of his father** le intimidaba su padre

awe-inspiring ['ɔːɪnspaɪərɪŋ] *adj* impresionante, imponente

awesome ['ɔːsəm] *adj* impresionante

awful ['ɔːfʊl] *adj Fam* espantoso(a); **an a. lot of work** muchísimo trabajo

awfully ['ɔːfʊlɪ] *adv Fam* terriblemente

awkward ['ɔːkwəd] *adj (clumsy)* torpe; *(difficult)* pesado(a); *(object)* incómodo(a); *(moment)* inoportuno(a); *(situation)* embarazoso(a); *(problem)* difícil

awning ['ɔːnɪŋ] *n (on ship)* toldo *m*; *(on shop)* marquesina *f*

awoke [ə'wəʊk] *pt of* **awake**

awoken [ə'wəʊkən] *pp of* **awake, awaken**

axe, *US* **ax** [æks] **1** *n* hacha *f*
2 *vt Fig (jobs)* eliminar; *(costs)* reducir; *(plan)* cancelar; *(person)* despedir

axis ['æksɪs] *n (pl* **axes** ['æksiːz]) eje *m*

axle ['æksəl] *n* eje *m*; *Tech* árbol *m*

ayatollah [aɪə'tɒlə] *n* ayatolá *m*

Aztec ['æztek] *adj & n* azteca *(mf)*

B, b [biː] *n* (**a**) *(the letter)* B, b *f*; *Br Aut* **B road** carretera secundaria (**b**) *Mus* **B** si *m*; **B flat** si bemol

BA [biːˈeɪ] *n* (*abbr* **Bachelor of Arts**) *(person)* licenciado(a) *m,f* en Filosofía y Letras

babble [ˈbæbəl] *vi* *(baby)* balbucear; *(brook)* murmurar

babe [beɪb] *n* (**a**) *(baby)* bebé *m* (**b**) *US Fam* **hi, b.!** ¡hola, guapa!

baboon [bəˈbuːn] *n* zambo *m*

baby [ˈbeɪbɪ] *n* (**a**) bebé *m*; *(young child)* niño(a) *m,f*; *Br* **B. Buggy**® sillita *f* de paseo *or* de niño; *US* **b. buggy** *or* **carriage** cochecito *m* de niño; **b. face** cara *f* de niño (**b**) *(animal)* cría *f* (**c**) *Fam (darling)* querido(a) *m,f*

baby-sit [ˈbeɪbɪsɪt] *vi* hacer de canguro

baby-sitter [ˈbeɪbɪsɪtə(r)] *n* canguro *mf*

baby-walker [ˈbeɪbɪwɔːkə(r)] *n* tacataca *m*

bachelor [ˈbætʃələ(r)] *n* (**a**) soltero *m* (**b**) *Univ* licenciado(a) *m,f*; **B. of Arts/Science** licenciado(a) *m,f* en Filosofía y Letras/ Ciencias

back [bæk] **1** *n* (**a**) *(of person)* espalda *f*; *(of animal)* lomo *m*; **b. to front** al revés; *Fig* **to get sb's b. up** poner negro a algn; *Fig* **to have one's b. to the wall** estar en un aprieto

(**b**) *(of book)* lomo *m*; *(of chair)* respaldo *m*; *(of coin)* reverso *m*; *(of hand)* dorso *m*; *(of house, car)* parte *f* de atrás; *Fig* **he knows Leeds like the b. of his hand** se conoce Leeds como la palma de la mano

(**c**) *(of stage, cupboard)* fondo *m*; *Fam* **at the b. of beyond** en el quinto pino

(**d**) *Ftb* defensa *mf*

(**e**) *US* **in b. (of)** *(behind)* en la parte de atrás (de), detrás (de); *(to the rear of)* al fondo (de)

2 *adj* (**a**) trasero(a), de atrás; **b. door** puerta *f* de atrás; **b. seat** asiento *m* de detrás; *Fig* **to take a b. seat** pasar al segundo plano; *Aut* **b. wheel** rueda trasera

(**b**) **b. rent** alquiler atrasado; **b. pay** atrasos *mpl*; *Press* **b. number** número *m* atrasado

3 *adv* (**a**) *(to the rear)* atrás; *(towards the rear)* hacia atrás; **b. and forth** de acá para allá

(**b**) **some years b.** hace unos años

4 *vt* (**a**) *(support)* apoyar, respaldar

(**b**) *Fin* financiar

(**c**) *(bet on)* apostar por

(**d**) *(car etc)* dar marcha atrás a

5 *vi* (**a**) *(move backwards)* retroceder

(**b**) *(car etc)* dar marcha atrás

▸ **back away** *vi* retirarse

▸ **back down** *vi* echarse atrás

▸ **back off** *vi* desistir

▸ **back out** *vi* *(withdraw)* retractarse, volverse atrás

▸ **back up 1** *vt sep* (**a**) *(support)* apoyar (**b**) *Comput (file)* hacer una copia de seguridad de

2 *vi* *Aut* ir marcha atrás

backache [ˈbækeɪk] *n* dolor *m* de espalda

backbencher [bækˈbentʃə(r)] *n* diputado(a) *m,f* que no es ministro

backbiting [ˈbækbaɪtɪŋ] *n* murmuración *f*

backbone [ˈbækbəʊn] *n* *Anat* columna *f*

backcloth [ˈbækklɒθ] *n* telón *m* de fondo

backdate [bækˈdeɪt] *vt* antedatar

backdated [bækˈdeɪtɪd] *adj* con efecto retroactivo

backdrop [ˈbækdrɒp] *n* telón *m* de fondo

backer [ˈbækə(r)] *n* (**a**) *Fin* promotor(a) *m,f* (**b**) *Pol* partidario(a) *m,f* (**c**) *(person who bets)* apostante *mf*

backfire [bækˈfaɪə(r)] *vi* (**a**) *Aut* petardear (**b**) *Fig* **our plan backfired** nos salió el tiro por la culata

background [ˈbækgraʊnd] *n* (**a**) fondo *m*; **to stay in the b.** quedarse en segundo plano; **b. music** música *f* de fondo (**b**) *(origin)* origen *m*; *(past)* pasado *m*; *(education)* formación *f* (**c**) *(circumstances)* antecedentes *mpl* (**d**) *(atmosphere)* ambiente *m*

backhand [ˈbækhænd] *n* *Sport* revés *m*

backhanded [ˈbækhændɪd] *adj* equívoco(a), ambiguo(a)

backhander [ˈbækhændə(r)] *n* *Fam (bribe)* soborno *m*

backing [ˈbækɪŋ] *n* (**a**) *(support)* apoyo

m; *Com & Fin* respaldo financiero (**b**) *Mus* acompañamiento *m*

backlash [ˈbæklæʃ] *n* reacción violenta y repentina

backlog [ˈbæklɒg] *n* **to have a b.** of work tener un montón de trabajo atrasado

backpack [ˈbækpæk] *n* mochila *f*

backpedal [bækˈpedəl] *vi Fam* dar marcha atrás

backside [bækˈsaɪd] *n Fam* trasero *m*, culo *m*

backstage [bækˈsteɪdʒ] *adv* entre bastidores

backstroke [ˈbækstrəʊk] *n* espalda *f*

backtrack [ˈbæktræk] *vi Fig* volverse atrás

backup [ˈbækʌp] *n* (**a**) *(support)* apoyo *m*, respaldo *m*; *Comput* **b. (file)** fichero *m* de apoyo (**b**) *US (of traffic)* caravana *f*

backward [ˈbækwəd] **1** *adj* (**a**) *(movement)* hacia atrás (**b**) *(country)* subdesarrollado(a); *(child)* retrasado(a)
2 *adv esp US* hacia atrás

backwards [ˈbækwədz] *adv* hacia atrás; **to walk b.** andar de espaldas

backyard [bækˈjɑːd] *n* patio trasero; *US* jardín trasero

bacon [ˈbeɪkən] *n* tocino *m*, beicon *m*

bacteria [bækˈtɪərɪə] *npl* bacterias *fpl*

bad [bæd] **1** *adj* (**worse, worst**) (**a**) *(poor)* malo(a); **to go from b. to worse** ir de mal en peor (**b**) *(decayed)* podrido(a); **to go b.** echarse a perder (**c**) **that's too b.!** ¡qué pena! (**d**) *(wicked)* malo(a); **to use b. language** ser mal hablado(a) (**e**) *(accident)* grave; *(headache)* fuerte (**f**) *(ill)* enfermo(a) (**g**) **b. debt** deuda *f* incobrable
2 *n* lo malo

bade [beɪd] *pt of* **bid**

badge [bædʒ] *n* insignia *f*; *(metal disc)* chapa *f*

badger [ˈbædʒə(r)] **1** *n* tejón *m*
2 *vt* acosar

badly [ˈbædlɪ] *adv* (**a**) mal; **he did b. in the exam** le salió mal el examen; **to be b. off** andar mal de dinero (**b**) *(seriously)* gravemente (**c**) *(very much)* mucho; **to miss sb b.** echar mucho de menos a algn; **we need it b.** nos hace mucha falta

badminton [ˈbædmɪntən] *n* bádminton *m*

bad-tempered [bædˈtempəd] *adj* **to be b.** *(temperament)* tener mal genio; *(temporarily)* estar de mal humor

baffle [ˈbæfəl] **1** *vt* desconcertar
2 *n Tech* pantalla acústica

baffling [ˈbæflɪŋ] *adj* incomprensible, enigmático(a)

bag [bæg] **1** *n* (**a**) *(large)* bolsa *f*; *(handbag)* bolso *m*, cartera *f*, *Méx* bolsa; *Fam* **bags of** montones de; **travel b.** bolsa de viaje (**b**) *(hunting)* caza *f*; *Fam* **it's in the b.** es cosa hecha (**c**) *Pej* **old b.** *(woman)* bruja *f* (**d**) **bags** *(under eyes)* ojeras *fpl*
2 *vt* (**a**) *(put into sacks)* meter en sacos (**b**) *Fam* coger

baggage [ˈbægɪdʒ] *n* (**a**) equipaje *m* (**b**) *Mil* bagaje *m*

baggy [ˈbægɪ] *adj* (**baggier, baggiest**) holgado(a); **b. trousers** pantalones anchos

bagpipes [ˈbægpaɪps] *npl* gaita *f*

Bahamas [bəˈhɑːməz] *npl* **the B.** las Bahamas

bail¹ [beɪl] *n Jur* fianza *f*; **on b.** bajo fianza; **to stand b. for sb** salir fiador por algn
▸ **bail out** *vt sep Fig (person)* sacar de un apuro

bail² [beɪl] *vi Naut* **to b. (out)** achicar

bailiff [ˈbeɪlɪf] *n* (**a**) *Jur* alguacil *m* (**b**) *(steward)* administrador *m*

bait [beɪt] **1** *n* cebo *m*; **to rise to the b.** tragar el anzuelo, picar
2 *vt* (**a**) *(for fishing)* cebar (**b**) *(torment)* hostigar

baize [beɪz] *n* bayeta *f*; **green b.** tapete *m* verde

bake [beɪk] **1** *vt* (**a**) cocer al horno (**b**) *(harden)* endurecer
2 *vi Fam* hacer mucho calor

baked [beɪkt] *adj* al horno; **b. potato** patata *f or Am* papa *f* al horno

baker [ˈbeɪkə(r)] *n* panadero(a) *m,f*

bakery [ˈbeɪkərɪ] *n* panadería *f*

baking [ˈbeɪkɪŋ] *n* cocción *f*; **b. dish** fuente *f* para horno; **b. powder** levadura *f* en polvo; **b. tin** molde *m*

balaclava [bæləˈklɑːvə] *n* pasamontañas *m inv*

balance [ˈbæləns] **1** *n* (**a**) *(scales)* balanza *f*; *Fig* **to hang in the b.** estar en juego (**b**) *(equilibrium)* equilibrio *m*; *Pol* **b. of power** equilibrio de fuerzas (**c**) *Fin* saldo *m*; **b. of payments** balanza *f* de pagos; **b. sheet** balance *m*; **credit b.** saldo acreedor (**d**) *(remainder)* resto *m*
2 *vt* (**a**) poner en equilibrio (**on** en) (**b**) *(budget)* equilibrar; **to b. the books** hacer el balance (**c**) *(weigh up)* sopesar
3 *vi* guardar el equilibrio
▸ **balance out** *vi (figures)* corresponderse

balanced [ˈbælənst] *adj* equilibrado(a)

balcony [ˈbælkənɪ] *n* balcón *m*; *Th* anfiteatro *m*

bald [bɔːld] *adj* (**a**) *(person)* calvo(a) (**b**)

(tyre) desgastado(a) (**c**) *(style)* escueto(a)

baldness [ˈbɔːldnɪs] *n* (**a**) *(of person)* calvicie *f* (**b**) *(of tyre)* desgaste *m* (**c**) *(of style)* sencillez *f*

bale¹ [beɪl] **1** *n (of cloth)* fardo *m*
  2 *vt* embalar

bale² [beɪl] *vt* = **bail²**
  ▸ **bale out 1** *vi Av* saltar en paracaídas de un avión
  2 *vt sep Fig (person)* sacar de apuros a

Balearic [bælɪˈærɪk] *adj* **the B. Islands** las Islas Baleares

baleful [ˈbeɪlfʊl] *adj* funesto(a), siniestro(a)

Balkan [ˈbɔːlkən] *adj* **the Balkans** los Balcanes

ball¹ [bɔːl] *n* (**a**) *(in cricket, tennis etc)* pelota *f*; *Ftb* balón *m*; *(in billiards, golf etc)* bola *f*; *Fig* **the b. is in your court** ahora te toca a tí; *Fig* **to play b. with sb** cooperar con algn; *Fam* **to be on the b.** ser un espabilado; *Tech* **b. bearing** rodamiento *m* de bolas (**b**) *(of paper)* bola *f*; *(of wool)* ovillo *m* (**c**) *US* béisbol *m*; *Fig* **it's a whole new b. game** es otra historia (**d**) *very Fam* **balls** cojones *mpl*

ball² [bɔːl] *n (dance)* baile *m*

ballad [ˈbæləd] *n* balada *f*

ballast [ˈbæləst] *n Naut* lastre *m*

ballerina [bæləˈriːnə] *n* bailarina *f*

ballet [ˈbæleɪ] *n* ballet *m*; **b. dancer** bailarín(ina) *m,f*

ballistic [bəˈlɪstɪk] *adj* balístico(a)

ballistics [bəˈlɪstɪks] *n sing* balística *f*

balloon [bəˈluːn] **1** *n* (**a**) globo *m* (**b**) *(in cartoon)* bocadillo *m*
  2 *vi* hincharse; *Fig* aumentar rápidamente

ballot [ˈbælət] **1** *n* votación *f*; **b. box** urna *f*; **b. paper** papeleta *f*
  2 *vt* someter a votación

ballpoint (pen) [ˈbɔːlpɔɪnt(ˈpen)] *n* bolígrafo *m*, *CSur* lapicera *f*

ballroom [ˈbɔːlruːm] *n* salón *m* de baile

ballyhoo [bælɪˈhuː] *n Fam (fuss)* jaleo *m*

balm [bɑːm] *n* bálsamo *m*

balmy [ˈbɑːmɪ] *adj* (**balmier, balmiest**) *(weather)* suave

Baltic [ˈbɔːltɪk] *adj* báltico(a); **the B. (Sea)** el (mar) Báltico

balustrade [ˈbæləstreɪd] *n* barandilla *f*

bamboo [bæmˈbuː] *n* bambú *m*

bamboozle [bæmˈbuːzəl] *vt Fam* (**a**) *(puzzle)* dejar perplejo (**b**) *(trick)* engañar, embaucar

ban [bæn] **1** *n* prohibición *f*
  2 *vt* (**a**) *(prohibit)* prohibir (**b**) *(exclude)* excluir

banal [bəˈnɑːl] *adj* banal, trivial

banana [bəˈnɑːnə] *n* plátano *m*, banana *f*, *Col* banano *m*, *Ven* cambur *m*; *Fam* **to go bananas** volverse loco(a)

band [bænd] **1** *n* (**a**) *(strip)* tira *f*; *(ribbon)* cinta *f* (**b**) *(stripe)* raya *f* (**c**) *Rad* banda *f* (**d**) *(group)* grupo *m*; *(of youths)* pandilla *f*; *(of thieves)* banda *f* (**e**) *Mus* banda *f*
  2 *vi* **to b. together** unirse, juntarse

bandage [ˈbændɪdʒ] **1** *n* venda *f*
  2 *vt* vendar

Band-Aid® [ˈbændeɪd] *n US* tirita® *f*, *Am* curita *f*

B & B [biːənˈbiː] *n (abbr* **bed and breakfast***) (hotel)* = hostal familiar en el que el desayuno está incluido en el precio de la habitación

bandit [ˈbændɪt] *n* bandido *m*

bandstand [ˈbændstænd] *n* quiosco *m* de música

bandwagon [ˈbændwægən] *n Fig* **to jump on the b.** subirse al tren

bandy [ˈbændɪ] **1** *vt (words, ideas)* intercambiar
  2 *adj* (**bandier, bandiest**) torcido(a) hacia fuera
  ▸ **bandy about** *vt sep (ideas)* propagar, difundir

bandy-legged [ˈbændɪˈleg(ɪ)d] *adj* patizambo(a)

bang [bæŋ] **1** *n* (**a**) *(blow)* golpe *m* (**b**) *(noise)* ruido *m*; *(explosion)* estallido *m*; *(of gun)* estampido *m*; **to shut the door with a b.** dar un portazo
  2 *npl US* **bangs** flequillo *m*, *Am* cerquillo *m (corto)*
  3 *vt* golpear; **to b. sth shut** cerrar algo de golpe
  4 *vi* golpear; **to b. shut** cerrarse de golpe
  5 *interj (blow)* ¡zas!; **b., b.!** *(of gun)* ¡pum, pum!
  6 *adv Fam* justo

banger [ˈbæŋə(r)] *n* (**a**) *(firework)* petardo *m* (**b**) *Fam (sausage)* salchicha *f* (**c**) *Fam* **old b.** *(car)* tartana *f*

bangle [ˈbæŋgəl] *n* brazalete *m*

banish [ˈbænɪʃ] *vt* desterrar

banister [ˈbænɪstə(r)] *n* pasamanos *m inv*

bank¹ [bæŋk] **1** *n* (**a**) *Com & Fin* banco *m*; **b. account** cuenta bancaria; **b. card** tarjeta bancaria; **b. clerk** empleado(a) *m,f* de banca; **b. draft** letra bancaria; **b. holiday** fiesta *f* nacional; **b. statement** extracto *m* de cuenta (**b**) *(in gambling)* banca *f* (**c**) *(store)* banco *m*

2 *vt Com & Fin* depositar, ingresar
3 *vi Com & Fin* **to b. with** tener una cuenta en
► **bank on** *vt insep* contar con
bank² [bæŋk] **1** *n* (**a**) *(mound)* loma *f*; *(embankment)* terraplén *m* (**b**) *(of river)* ribera *f*; *(edge)* orilla *f*
2 *vt Av* ladear
3 *vi Av* ladearse
bankbook ['bæŋkbʊk] *n* libreta *f* de ahorros
banker ['bæŋkə(r)] *n* banquero(a) *m,f*
banking ['bæŋkɪŋ] *n* banca *f*
banknote ['bæŋknəʊt] *n* billete *m* de banco
bankrupt ['bæŋkrʌpt] **1** *adj* en quiebra; **to go b.** quebrar
2 *vt* llevar a la bancarrota
bankruptcy ['bæŋkrʌptsɪ] *n* quiebra *f*, bancarrota *f*
banner ['bænə(r)] *n* *(in demonstration)* pancarta *f*; *(flag)* bandera *f*
banns [bænz] *npl* amonestaciones *fpl*
banquet ['bæŋkwɪt] *n* banquete *m*
banter ['bæntə(r)] **1** *n* bromas *fpl*
2 *vi* bromear
bap [bæp] *n* bollo *m*, panecillo *m*
baptism ['bæptɪzəm] *n* bautismo *m*
baptize [bæp'taɪz] *vt* bautizar
bar [bɑː(r)] **1** *n* (**a**) *(of gold)* barra *f*; *(of chocolate)* tableta *f*; *(of soap)* pastilla *f*; *Com* **b. code** código *m* de barras (**b**) *(of cage)* barrote *m*; *Fam* **to be behind bars** estar en la cárcel (**c**) *(obstacle)* obstáculo *m* (**d**) *Jur (dock)* banquillo *m*; *(court)* tribunal *m* (**e**) *Jur* **the B.** *(profession)* abogacía *f*, *(body of lawyers)* colegio *m* de abogados (**f**) *(pub)* bar *m*; *(counter)* barra *f* (**g**) *Mus* compás *m*
2 *vt* (**a**) *(door)* atrancar; *(road)* cortar (**b**) *(exclude)* excluir (**from** de) (**c**) *(prohibit)* prohibir
3 *prep* salvo; **b. none** sin excepción
barbarian [bɑː'beərɪən] *adj & n* bárbaro(a) *(m,f)*
barbaric [bɑː'bærɪk] *adj* bárbaro(a)
barbecue ['bɑːbɪkjuː] **1** *n* barbacoa *f*
2 *vt* asar a la parrilla
barbed [bɑːbd] *adj* (**a**) **b. wire** alambre *m* de púas (**b**) *Fig (remark)* mordaz
barber ['bɑːbə(r)] *n* barbero(a) *m,f*; **b.'s (shop)** barbería *f*
barbiturate [bɑː'bɪtjʊrɪt] *n* barbitúrico *m*
bare [beə(r)] **1** *adj* (**a**) desnudo(a); *(head)* descubierto(a); *(foot)* descalzo(a); *(room)* sin muebles; **to lay b.** poner al descubierto; **with his b. hands** sólo con las manos (**b**) *(basic)* mero(a); **the**

b. minimum lo mínimo
2 *vt* desnudar; *(uncover)* descubrir
bareback(ed) ['beə'bæk(t)] *adv* **to ride b.** montar un caballo a pelo
barefaced ['beəfeɪst] *adj* desvergonzado(a)
barefoot ['beə'fʊt] *adj & adv* descalzo(a)
barely ['beəlɪ] *adv* apenas
bargain ['bɑːgɪn] **1** *n* (**a**) *(agreement)* pacto *m*; *(deal)* negocio *m*; **into the b.** por añadidura, además; **to drive a hard b.** imponer condiciones duras; **to strike a b.** cerrar un trato (**b**) *(cheap purchase)* ganga *f*; **b. price** precio *m* de oferta
2 *vi* (**a**) negociar (**b**) *(haggle)* regatear
► **bargain for** *vt insep* esperar, contar con
barge [bɑːdʒ] **1** *n* gabarra *f*
2 *vt Fam* **to b. into** *(room)* irrumpir en; *(person)* tropezar con
► **barge in** *vi Fam* (**a**) *(go in)* entrar sin permiso (**b**) *(interfere)* entrometerse
baritone ['bærɪtəʊn] *adj & n* barítono *(m)*
bark¹ [bɑːk] **1** *n* ladrido *m*
2 *vi (dog)* ladrar
bark² [bɑːk] *n Bot* corteza *f*
barley ['bɑːlɪ] *n* cebada *f*; **b. sugar** azúcar *m* cande
barmaid ['bɑːmeɪd] *n* camarera *f*
barman ['bɑːmən] *n* camarero *m*, barman *m*
barn [bɑːn] *n* granero *m*; **b. dance** baile *m* popular
barnacle ['bɑːnəkəl] *n* percebe *m*
barometer [bə'rɒmɪtə(r)] *n* barómetro *m*
baron ['bærən] *n* barón *m*
baroness ['bærənɪs] *n* baronesa *f*
baroque [bə'rɒk] *adj* barroco(a)
barrack ['bærək] *vt* abuchear
barracks ['bærəks] *n Mil* cuartel *m*
barrage ['bærɑːʒ] *n* (**a**) *(dam)* presa *f* (**b**) *Mil* barrera *f* de fuego (**c**) *Fig (of questions)* lluvia *f*
barrel ['bærəl] *n* (**a**) *(of wine)* tonel *m*; *(of beer, oil)* barril *m* (**b**) *(of firearm)* cañón *m*
barren ['bærən] *adj* estéril; *(land)* yermo(a)
barricade [bærɪ'keɪd] **1** *n* barricada *f*
2 *vt* levantar barricadas; **to b. oneself in** parapetarse
barrier ['bærɪə(r)] *n* barrera *f*
barrister ['bærɪstə(r)] *n Br* abogado(a) *m,f (capacitado(a) para ejercer ante tribunales superiores)*
barrow ['bærəʊ] *n* carretilla *f*
bartender ['bɑːtendə(r)] *n US* camarero *m*, barman *m*
barter ['bɑːtə(r)] *vt* trocar (**for** por)
base [beɪs] **1** *n* base *f*; *(foot)* pie *m*; *(of*

column) basa *f; Sport (of team)* concentración *f;* **air/naval b.** base *f* aérea/naval
2 *vt* (**a**) basar, fundar (**on** en) (**b**) *(troops)* estacionar
3 *adj* (**a**) *(despicable)* bajo(a), despreciable (**b**) *(metals)* común
baseball ['beɪsbɔːl] *n* béisbol *m*
baseline ['beɪslaɪn] *n (in tennis)* línea *f* de saque
basement ['beɪsmənt] *n* sótano *m*
bases ['beɪsiːz] *pl of* **basis**
bash [bæʃ] **1** *n (heavy blow)* golpetazo *m; (dent)* bollo *m; Fam (attempt)* intento *m*
2 *vt* golpear
bashful ['bæʃfʊl] *adj* tímido(a)
basic ['beɪsɪk] **1** *adj* básico(a); **b. pay** sueldo *m* base
2 *npl* **basics** lo fundamental
basically ['beɪsɪklɪ] *adv* fundamentalmente
basil ['bæzəl] *n* albahaca *f*
basin ['beɪsən] *n* (**a**) *(washbowl)* palangana *f; (for washing up)* barreño *m; (in bathroom)* lavabo *m; (dish)* cuenco *m* (**b**) *(of river)* cuenca *f*
basis ['beɪsɪs] *n (pl* **bases**) base *f;* **on the b. of** en base a
bask [bɑːsk] *vi* tostarse; **to b. in the sun** tomar el sol
basket ['bɑːskɪt] *n* cesta *f,* cesto *m*
basketball ['bɑːskɪtbɔːl] *n* baloncesto *m*
Basque [bæsk, bɑːsk] **1** *adj* vasco(a); **B. Country** País Vasco, Euskadi; **B. flag** ikurriña *f;* **B. nationalist** abertzale *mf*
2 *n* (**a**) *(person)* vasco(a) *m,f* (**b**) *(language)* vasco *m,* euskera *m*
bass¹ [bæs] *n inv (seawater)* lubina *f; (freshwater)* perca *f*
bass² [beɪs] **1** *n* (**a**) *(singer)* bajo *m* (**b**) *(notes)* graves *mpl;* **b. drum** bombo *m;* **b. guitar** bajo *m*
2 *adj* bajo(a)
bassoon [bə'suːn] *n* fagot *m*
bastard ['bɑːstəd, 'bæstəd] **1** *n* (**a**) bastardo(a) *m,f* (**b**) *Pej* cabrón *m,* hijo *m* de puta; **poor b.!** ¡el pobre!
2 *adj* bastardo(a)
baste [beɪst] *vt Culin* untar
bastion ['bæstɪən] *n* baluarte *m,* bastión *m*
bat¹ [bæt] **1** *n (in cricket, baseball)* bate *m; (in table tennis)* pala *f; Fig* **to do sth off one's own b.** hacer algo por cuenta propia
2 *vi (in cricket, baseball)* batear
bat² [bæt] *n Zool* murciélago *m*
bat³ [bæt] *vt Fam* **without batting an eyelid** sin pestañear

batch [bætʃ] *n (of bread)* hornada *f; (of goods)* lote *m; Comput* **b. processing** procesamiento *m* por lotes
bated ['beɪtɪd] *adj* **with b. breath** sin respirar
bath [bɑːθ] **1** *n* (**a**) baño *m;* **to have a b.** bañarse; **b. towel** toalla *f* de baño (**b**) *(tub)* bañera *f* (**c**) **baths** piscina *f* municipal
2 *vt* bañar
bathe [beɪð] **1** *vi* bañarse
2 *vt* (**a**) *(wound)* lavar (**b**) **he was bathed in sweat** *(covered)* estaba empapado de sudor
bather ['beɪðə(r)] *n* bañista *mf*
bathing ['beɪðɪŋ] *n* baño *m;* **b. cap** gorro *m* de baño; **b. costume** traje *m* de baño; **b. trunks** bañador *m* de hombre
bathrobe ['bɑːθrəʊb] *n* albornoz *m*
bathroom ['bɑːθruːm] *n* cuarto *m* de baño
bathtub ['bɑːθtʌb] *n* bañera *f*
baton ['bætən, 'bætɒn] *n* (**a**) *Mus* batuta *f* (**b**) *(truncheon)* porra *f* (**c**) *Sport* testigo *m*
battalion [bə'tæljən] *n* batallón *m*
batter¹ ['bætə(r)] *vt* aporrear, apalear
batter² ['bætə(r)] *n (in cricket, baseball)* bateador(a) *m,f*
batter³ ['bætə(r)] *Culin* **1** *n* pasta *f* (para rebozar); **fish in b.** pescado rebozado
2 *vt* rebozar
battered ['bætəd] *adj (car)* abollado(a); *(person)* maltratado(a)
battering ['bætərɪŋ] *n* paliza *f;* **to take a b.** recibir una paliza; *Mil* **b. ram** ariete *m*
battery ['bætərɪ] *n* (**a**) *(for torch, radio)* pila *f; Aut* batería *f* (**b**) *Jur* **assault and b.** lesiones *fpl*
battle ['bætəl] **1** *n* batalla *f; Fig* lucha *f;* **to do b.** librar batalla; *Fig* **b. cry** lema *m*
2 *vi* luchar
battlefield ['bætəlfiːld] *n* campo *m* de batalla
battleship ['bætəlʃɪp] *n* acorazado *m*
bauble ['bɔːbəl] *n* chuchería *f*
bawdy ['bɔːdɪ] *adj (joke etc)* verde
bawl [bɔːl] *vi* gritar, chillar
bay¹ [beɪ] *n Geog* bahía *f; (large)* golfo *m;* **B. of Biscay** golfo de Vizcaya; **B. of Bengal** golfo de Bengala
bay² [beɪ] *n* (**a**) *(recess)* hueco *m;* **b. window** ventana salediza (**b**) *(in factory)* nave *f;* **cargo b.** bodega *f* de carga
bay³ [beɪ] *n* laurel *m*
bay⁴ [beɪ] **1** *vi (dog)* aullar
2 *n* ladrido *m; Fig* **at b.** acorralado(a); *Fig* **to keep sb at b.** mantener a algn a raya

bayonet [ˈbeɪənɪt] *n* bayoneta *f*

bazaar [bəˈzɑː(r)] *n* (**a**) *(market)* bazar *m* (**b**) **(church) b.** *(charity sale)* rastrillo benéfico

BBC [biːbiːˈsiː] *n* (*abbr* **British Broadcasting Corporation**) BBC *f*

BC [biːˈsiː] (*abbr* **before Christ**) a.d.C.

be [biː, *unstressed* bɪ]

> En el inglés hablado, y en el escrito en estilo coloquial, el verbo **be** se contrae de forma que **I am** se transforma en **I'm, he/she/it is** se transforman en **he's/she's/it's** y **you/we/they are** se transforman en **you're/we're/they're**. Las formas negativas **is not, are not, was not** y **were not** se transforman en **isn't, aren't, wasn't** y **weren't**.

1 *vi* (*pres 1st person sing* **am**; *3rd person sing* **is**; *2nd person sing & all persons pl* **are**; *pt 1st & 3rd persons sing* **was**; *2nd person sing & all persons pl* **were**; *pp* **been**) (**a**) ser; **he is very tall** es muy alto; **Madrid is the capital** Madrid es la capital; **sugar is sweet** el azúcar es dulce

(**b**) *(nationality, occupation)* ser; **he's Italian** es italiano

(**c**) *(origin, ownership)* ser; **the car is Domingo's** el coche es de Domingo; **this painting is by Goya** este cuadro es de Goya

(**d**) *(price)* costar; *(total)* ser; **a return ticket is £24** un billete de ida y vuelta cuesta £24; **how much is a kilo of cod?** ¿a cuánto está el kilo de bacalao?; **how much is it?** ¿cuánto es?

(**e**) *(temporary state)* estar; **how are you? – I'm very well** ¿cómo estás? – estoy muy bien; **this soup is cold** esta sopa está fría; **to be cold/afraid/hungry** tener frío/miedo/hambre; **to be lucky** tener suerte

(**f**) *(location)* estar; **Aberdeen is in Scotland** Aberdeen está en Escocia; **Birmingham is 200 miles from London** Birmingham está a 200 millas de Londres

(**g**) *(age)* tener; **she is thirty (years old)** tiene treinta años

2 *v aux* (**a**) *(with pres p)* estar; **he is writing a letter** está escribiendo una carta; **she was singing** estaba cantando; **they are leaving next week** se van la semana que viene; **we have been waiting for a long time** hace mucho que estamos esperando; **he is coming** *(emphatic)* es seguro que viene

(**b**) *(passive)* ser; **he was murdered** fue asesinado; **she is allowed to smoke** se le permite fumar

(**c**) *(obligation)* **I am to see him this afternoon** debo verle esta tarde; **you are not to smoke here** no se puede fumar aquí

3 *v impers* (**a**) *(with* **there***)* haber; **there is, there are** hay; **there was, there were** había; **there will be** habrá; **there would be** habría; **there have been a lot of complaints** ha habido muchas quejas; **there were ten of us** éramos diez

(**b**) *(with it)* **it's late** es tarde; **it is said that** se dice que; **who is it? – it's me** ¿quién es? – soy yo; **what is it?** ¿qué pasa?

(**c**) *(weather)* **it's foggy** hay niebla; **it's cold/hot** hace frío/calor

(**d**) *(time)* ser; **it's one o'clock** es la una; **it's four o'clock** son las cuatro

(**e**) *(date)* **it's the 11th/Tuesday today** hoy es 11/martes

(**f**) *(in tag questions)* **it's lovely, isn't it?** es bonito, ¿no?; **you're happy, aren't you?** estás contento, ¿verdad? **he's not very clever, is he?** no es muy listo, ¿verdad?

(**g**) *(unreal conditions)* **if I was/were you ...** yo en tu lugar...; **if you were a millionaire ...** si fueras millonario...

(**h**) *pres & past perfect (visit, go)* estar, ir; **I've been to Paris** he estado en París

beach [biːtʃ] **1** *n* playa *f*
2 *vt* varar

beacon [ˈbiːkən] *n* (**a**) *Av & Naut* baliza *f* (**b**) *(lighthouse)* faro *m*

bead [biːd] *n* (**a**) *(of necklace etc)* cuenta *f*; **glass b.** abalorio *m* (**b**) *(of liquid)* gota *f*

beady [ˈbiːdɪ] *adj* (**beadier, beadiest**) *(eyes)* pequeños y brillantes

beagle [ˈbiːgəl] *n* beagle *m*

beak [biːk] *n* (**a**) *(of bird)* pico *m* (**b**) *Fam (nose)* nariz ganchuda

beaker [ˈbiːkə(r)] *n* (tumbler) taza alta, jarra *f*

beam [biːm] **1** *n* (**a**) *Archit* viga *f* (**b**) *(of light)* rayo *m*; *Phys* haz *m* (**c**) *(in gymnastics)* barra fija (**d**) *(smile)* sonrisa *f* radiante

2 *vi* (**a**) *(sun)* brillar (**b**) *(smile)* sonreír
3 *vt* (**a**) *(broadcast)* difundir, emitir (**b**) *(transmit)* transmitir

beaming [ˈbiːmɪŋ] *adj (smiling)* radiante

bean [biːn] *n* alubia *f*, judía *f*, *Andes, CAm, Carib, Méx* frijol *m*, *RP* poroto *m*; *Fam* **to spill the beans** descubrir el pastel; **baked beans** = alubias cocidas en salsa de tomate; **broad b.** haba *f*; **butter b.** judía blanca, *Andes, CAm, Carib, Méx* frijol blanco, *RP* poroto de manteca; **coffee b.**

grano *m* de café; **green/runner b.** judía verde, *Bol, RP* chaucha *f*, *CAm* ejote *m*, *Col, Cuba* habichuela *f*, *Chile* poroto verde, *Ven* vainita *f*; **haricot b.** alubia; **kidney b.** frijol

beansprout ['biːnspraʊt] *n* brote *m* de soja

bear¹ [beə(r)] (*pt* **bore**; *pp* **borne**) **1** *vt* (**a**) *(carry)* llevar

(**b**) *(support)* sostener

(**c**) *(endure)* soportar, aguantar; **I can't b. him** no lo soporto

(**d**) *(fruit)* dar; *Fin (interest)* devengar

(**e**) **to b. a resemblance to** parecerse a

(**f**) **to b. a grudge against sb** guardar rencor a algn; **to b. in mind** tener presente

(**g**) **to b. witness** atestiguar

(**h**) (*pt* **born** *passive only, not followed by* **by**) *(give birth to)* dar a luz; **he was born in Wakefield** nació en Wakefield

2 *vi (turn)* girar, torcer; **to b. left** girar a la izquierda

▶ **bear down** *vi (approach)* correr (**on** sobre)

▶ **bear out** *vt sep (confirm)* confirmar

▶ **bear up** *vi (endure)* resistir

▶ **bear with** *vt insep* tener paciencia con

bear² [beə(r)] *n* (**a**) oso *m*; **b. cub** osezno *m*; *Astron* **Great B.** Osa *f* Mayor; **Little B.** Osa Menor (**b**) *Fin* bajista *mf*

beard [bɪəd] *n* barba *f*

bearer ['beərə(r)] *n* portador(a) *m,f*; *(of passport, office)* titular *mf*

bearing ['beərɪŋ] *n* (**a**) *(posture)* porte *m* (**b**) *(relevance)* relación *f*; **to have a b. on** estar relacionado(a) con (**c**)*Tech* cojinete *m* (**d**) *Naut* **bearings** posición *f*, orientación *f*; **to get one's bearings** orientarse; **to lose one's bearings** desorientarse

beast [biːst] *n* (**a**) bestia *f*; **b. of burden** bestia de carga (**b**) *Fig* bestia *f*, bruto *m* (**c**) **beasts** *(cattle)* reses *fpl*

beastly ['biːstlɪ] *adj* (**beastlier, beastliest**) *Fam* asqueroso(a)

beat [biːt] **1** *vt* (*pt* **beat**; *pp* **beaten** ['biːtən]) (**a**) *(hit)* pegar, golpear; *(clothes)* sacudir; *(drum)* tocar; **off the beaten track** en un lugar muy apartado; *Fam* **b. it!** ¡lárgate!

(**b**) *Culin* batir

(**c**) *(defeat)* batir, vencer; **we b. them 5–2** les ganamos 5 a 2

(**d**) **to b. a retreat** batirse en retirada

(**e**) *Mus (time)* marcar

(**f**) **to b. the traffic** evitar los embotellamientos de tráfico

(**g**) *Fam (puzzle)* extrañar; **it beats me** no lo entiendo

2 *vi* (**a**) *(heart)* latir

(**b**) *(strike)* dar golpes; *Fig* **to b. about the bush** andarse por las ramas

3 *n* (**a**) *(of heart)* latido *m*

(**b**) *Mus* ritmo *m*, compás *m*

(**c**) *(of policeman)* ronda *f*

4 *adj Fam (exhausted)* agotado(a)

▶ **beat down** *vi (sun)* apretar

▶ **beat off** *vt sep* rechazar

▶ **beat up** *vt sep Fam* dar una paliza a

beating ['biːtɪŋ] *n* (**a**) *(thrashing)* paliza *f* (**b**) *(defeat)* derrota *f* (**c**) *(of drum)* toque *m* (**d**) *(of heart)* latido *m*

beautician [bjuːˈtɪʃən] *n* esteticista *mf*

beautiful ['bjuːtɪfʊl] *adj* hermoso(a), bello(a); *(delicious)* delicioso(a); **b. people** gente guapa

beauty ['bjuːtɪ] *n* belleza *f*, hermosura *f*; **b. contest** concurso *m* de belleza; **b. queen** miss *f*; **b. salon** salón *m* de belleza; **b. spot** *(on face)* lunar *m*; *(place)* lugar pintoresco

beaver ['biːvə(r)] **1** *n* castor *m*

2 *vi* **to b. away at sth** meterse de lleno en algo

became [bɪˈkeɪm] *pt of* **become**

because [bɪˈkɒz] **1** *conj* porque

2 *prep* **b. of** a causa de, debido a

beckon ['bekən] *vt & vi* llamar (con la mano); **to b. to sb** llamar a algn con señas

become [bɪˈkʌm] **1** *vi* (*pt* **became**; *pp* **become**) *(a teacher, doctor)* hacerse; *(boring, jealous, suspicious)* volverse; *(old, difficult, stronger)* hacerse; *(happy, sad, thin)* ponerse; **to b. angry/interested** enfadarse/interesarse; **what will b. of him?** ¿qué va a ser de él?

2 *vt Fml (of clothes, colour)* sentar bien a

becoming [bɪˈkʌmɪŋ] *adj* (**a**) *(dress)* favorecedor(a) (**b**) *(behaviour)* conveniente, apropiado(a)

bed [bed] *n* (**a**) cama *f*; **to get out of b.** levantarse de la cama; **to go to b.** acostarse; **to make the b.** hacer la cama; *Br* **b. and breakfast** *(service)* cama y desayuno *m*; *(sign)* pensión *f*; **b. linen** ropa *f* de cama (**b**) *(of river)* lecho *m*; *(of sea)* fondo *m* (**c**) *Geol* capa *f* (**d**) *(flower)* **b.** arriate *m*

bedbug ['bedbʌg] *n* chinche *f*

bedclothes ['bedkləʊðz] *npl*, **bedding** ['bedɪŋ] *n* ropa *f* de cama

bedlam ['bedləm] *n* algarabía *f*, alboroto *m*

bedraggled [bɪˈdrægəld] *adj (wet)* mojado(a); *(dirty)* ensuciado(a)

bedridden ['bedrɪdən] *adj* postrado(a) en cama

bedroom ['bedruːm] *n* dormitorio *m*

bedside ['bedsaɪd] *n* **at sb's b.** junto a la cama de algn; **b. table** mesilla *f* de noche

bedsit ['bedsɪt] *n Fam,* **bedsitter** [bed'sɪtə(r)] *n* estudio *m*

bedspread ['bedspred] *n* colcha *f*

bedtime ['bedtaɪm] *n* hora *f* de acostarse

bee [biː] *n* abeja *f*

beech [biːtʃ] *n* haya *f*

beef [biːf] *n* carne *f* de vaca, *Méx* carne de res; **roast b.** rosbif *m*
▶ **beef up** *vt sep Fam* reforzar

beefburger ['biːfbɜːgə(r)] *n* hamburguesa *f*

beefsteak ['biːfsteɪk] *n* bistec *m*

beehive ['biːhaɪv] *n* colmena *f*

beeline ['biːlaɪn] *n Fam* **to make a b. for sth** ir directo hacia algo

been [biːn, bɪn] *pp of* **be**

beep [biːp] *n (of apparatus)* pitido *m; (of horn)* pito *m*

beer [bɪə(r)] *n* cerveza *f;* **a glass of b.** una caña

beet [biːt] *n US* remolacha *f, Andes* betarraga *f, Méx* betabel *f; US* **red b.** remolacha

beetle ['biːtəl] *n* escarabajo *m*

beetroot ['biːtruːt] *n Br* remolacha *f, Andes* betarraga *f, Méx* betabel *f*

befit [bɪ'fɪt] *vt* convenir a, corresponder a

before [bɪ'fɔː(r)] **1** *conj* (a) *(earlier than)* antes de que (+ *subj*), antes de (+ *infin*); **b. she goes** antes de que se vaya; **b. leaving** antes de salir (b) *(rather than)* antes que (+ *infin*)
2 *prep* (a) *(place)* delante de; *(in the presence of)* ante (b) *(order, time)* antes de; **b. Christ** antes de Cristo; **b. long** dentro de poco; **b. 1950** antes de 1950; **I saw it b. you** lo vi antes que tú
3 *adv* (a) *(time)* antes; **I have met him b.** ya lo conozco; **not long b.** poco antes; **the night b.** la noche anterior (b) *(place)* delante, por delante

beforehand [bɪ'fɔːhænd] *adv* (a) *(earlier)* antes (b) *(in advance)* de antemano, con anticipación

befriend [bɪ'frend] *vt* trabar amistad con

beg [beg] **1** *vt* (a) *(money etc)* pedir (b) *(beseech)* rogar, suplicar; **I b. your pardon!** ¡perdone usted!; **I b. your pardon?** ¿cómo ha dicho usted?
2 *vi* (a) *(solicit)* mendigar; *(dog)* pedir; **to b. for money** pedir limosna (b) **to b.**

for help/mercy *(beseech)* implorar ayuda/compasión

began [bɪ'gæn] *pt of* **begin**

beggar ['begə(r)] *n* (a) mendigo(a) *m,f* (b) *Fam Euph (chap)* tío *m*

begin [bɪ'gɪn] *vt & vi (pt* **began;** *pp* **begun)** empezar, comenzar; **to b. again** volver a empezar; **to b. at the beginning** empezar por el principio; **to b. doing** *or* **to do sth** empezar a hacer algo; **to b. with ...** *(initially)* para empezar ...

beginner [bɪ'gɪnə(r)] *n* principiante *mf*

beginning [bɪ'gɪnɪŋ] *n* (a) principio *m,* comienzo *m;* **at the b. of May** a principios de mayo; **from the b.** desde el principio; **in the b.** al principio (b) *(origin)* origen *m*

begonia [bɪ'gəʊnɪə] *n* begonia *f*

begrudge [bɪ'grʌdʒ] *vt* dar de mala gana; *(envy)* envidiar

beguile [bɪ'gaɪl] *vt (charm)* seducir

begun [bɪ'gʌn] *pp of* **begin**

behalf [bɪ'hɑːf] *n* **on b. of,** *US* **in b. of** en nombre de, de parte de; **don't worry on my b.** no te preocupes por mí

behave [bɪ'heɪv] *vi* (a) *(person)* portarse, comportarse; **b. yourself!** ¡pórtate bien!; **to b. well/badly** portarse bien/mal (b) *(machine)* funcionar

behaviour, *US* **behavior** [bɪ'heɪvjə(r)] *n* (a) *(of person)* comportamiento *m,* conducta *f* (b) *(of machine)* funcionamiento *m*

behead [bɪ'hed] *vt* decapitar

beheld [bɪ'held] *pt & pp of* **behold**

behind [bɪ'haɪnd] **1** *prep* (a) detrás de; **b. sb's back** a espaldas de algn; **b. the scenes** entre bastidores; **to be b. sb** apoyar a algn; **what motive was there b. the crime?** ¿cuál fue el móvil del crimen? (b) **b. the times** *(less advanced than)* anticuado(a)
2 *adv* (a) *(in the rear)* detrás, atrás; **I've left my umbrella b.** se me ha olvidado el paraguas (b) **to be b. with one's payments** *(late)* estar atrasado(a) en los pagos
3 *n Fam* trasero *m*

behold [bɪ'həʊld] *vt (pt & pp* **beheld)** *Literary* contemplar

beige [beɪʒ] *adj & n* beige *(m)*

being ['biːɪŋ] *n* (a) ser *m* (b) *(existence)* existencia *f;* **to come into b.** nacer

Belarus [beləˈruːs] *n* Bielorrusia

belated [bɪ'leɪtɪd] *adj* tardío(a)

belch [beltʃ] **1** *vi (person)* eructar
2 *vt (smoke, flames)* vomitar, arrojar
3 *n* eructo *m*

beleaguered [bɪˈliːgəd] *adj* asediado(a)
belfry [ˈbelfrɪ] *n* campanario *m*
Belgian [ˈbeldʒən] *adj & n* belga *(mf)*
Belgium [ˈbeldʒəm] *n* Bélgica
Belgrade [belˈgreɪd] *n* Belgrado
belie [bɪˈlaɪ] *vt* desmentir
belief [bɪˈliːf] *n* (**a**) creencia *f*; **beyond b.**
increíble (**b**) *(opinion)* opinión *f* (**c**)
(faith) fe *f* (**d**) *(confidence)* confianza *f*
(**in** en)
believe [bɪˈliːv] **1** *vi* (**a**) *(have faith)* creer
(**b**) **to b. in** *(be in favour of)* ser partida-
rio(a) de (**c**) *(think)* creer; **I b. so** creo que
sí
   2 *vt* creer
believer [bɪˈliːvə(r)] *n* (**a**) *Rel* creyente *mf*
(**b**) partidario(a) *m,f* (**in** de)
belittle [bɪˈlɪtəl] *vt* *(person)* menospreciar; *(problem)* minimizar
bell [bel] *n* *(of church)* campana *f*; *(small)*
campanilla *f*; *(of school, door, bicycle etc)*
timbre *m*; *(on cat)* cascabel *m*; *(on cow)*
cencerro *m*; *Fig* **that rings a b.** eso me
suena; **b. jar** campana; **b. tower** campanario *m*
bell-bottoms [ˈbelbɒtəmz] *npl* pantalones *mpl* de campana
bellboy [ˈbelbɔɪ], *US* **bellhop** [ˈbelhɒp]
n botones *m inv*
belligerent [bɪˈlɪdʒərənt] *adj* agresivo(a)
bellow [ˈbeləʊ] *vi* *(bull)* bramar; *(person)*
rugir
bellows [ˈbeləʊz] *npl* **(pair of) b.** fuelle *m*
belly [ˈbelɪ] *n* (**a**) *(of person)* barriga *f*; **b.**
flop panzazo *m* (**b**) *(of animal)* panza *f*
bellyache [ˈbelɪeɪk] *n* *Fam* dolor *m* de
vientre
belong [bɪˈlɒŋ] *vi* (**a**) pertenecer (**to** a)
(**b**) *(be a member)* ser socio(a) (**to** de); *Pol*
to b. to a party ser miembro de un
partido (**c**) *(have a proper place)* corresponder; **this chair belongs here** esta silla
va aquí
belongings [bɪˈlɒŋɪŋz] *npl* efectos *mpl*
personales
beloved [bɪˈlʌvɪd, bɪˈlʌvd] **1** *adj* ama-
do(a), querido(a)
   2 *n* amado(a) *m,f*
below [bɪˈləʊ] **1** *prep* debajo de; **b. av-**
erage por debajo de la media; **10 degrees**
b. zero 10 grados bajo cero
   2 *adv* abajo; **above and b.** arriba y abajo;
see b. véase más abajo
belt [belt] **1** *n* (**a**) cinturón *m*; **blow below**
the b. golpe bajo (**b**) *Tech* correa *f*, cinta *f*
(**c**) *(area)* zona *f*
   2 *vt* *Fam* pegar una paliza a
▸ **belt along** *vi* *Fam* ir a todo gas

▸ **belt out** *vt sep* *Fam* *(song)* cantar a voz
en grito
▸ **belt up** *vi* *Fam* callarse
beltway [ˈbeltweɪ] *n* *US* carretera *f* de
circunvalación
bemused [bɪˈmjuːzd] *adj* perplejo(a)
bench [bentʃ] *n* (**a**) *(seat)* banco *m* (**b**)
(in parliament) escaño *m* (**c**) *Jur* **the b.**
(judges) la magistratura (**d**) *Sport* banquillo *m* (**e**) **b. mark** *Geol* cota *f* de referencia; *Fig* punto *m* de referencia
bend [bend] **1** *vt* (*pt & pp* **bent**) doblar;
(back) encorvar; *(head)* inclinar; *Fam* **to**
b. the rules hacer una excepción
   2 *vi* (**a**) doblarse; *(road)* torcerse (**b**) **to**
b. (over) inclinarse; *Fam* **he bends over**
backwards to please her hace lo imposible por complacerla
   3 *n* *(in river, road)* curva *f*; *(in pipe)*
recodo *m*; *Br Fam* **round the b.** loco(a)
perdido(a)
▸ **bend down** *vi* inclinarse
beneath [bɪˈniːθ] **1** *prep* *(below)* bajo,
debajo de; *Fig* **it's b. him** es indigno de él
   2 *adv* debajo
benefactor [ˈbenɪfæktə(r)] *n* bienhe-
chor(a) *m,f*
beneficial [benɪˈfɪʃəl] *adj* (**a**) *(doing*
good) benéfico(a) (**b**) *(advantageous)*
beneficioso(a)
beneficiary [benɪˈfɪʃərɪ] *n* beneficia-
rio(a) *m,f*
benefit [ˈbenɪfɪt] **1** *vt* beneficiar
   2 *vi* sacar provecho (**from** *or* **by** de)
   3 *n* (**a**) *(advantage)* beneficio *m*, provecho *m*; **for the b. of** en beneficio de; **I did**
it for your b. lo hice por tu bien (**b**)
(allowance) subsidio *m*; **unemployment**
b. subsidio de desempleo (**c**) *(event)* función benéfica
benevolent [bɪˈnevələnt] *adj* benévo-
lo(a)
Bengal [beŋˈgɔːl] *n* Bengala
benign [bɪˈnaɪn] *adj* benigno(a)
bent [bent] **1** *adj* (**a**) *(curved)* curvado(a)
(**b**) **to be b. on doing sth** *(determined)*
estar empeñado(a) en hacer algo (**c**) *Fam*
(corrupt) deshonesto(a) (**d**) *very Fam*
(homosexual) gay (**e**) *pt & pp* of **bend**
   2 *n* *(inclination)* inclinación *f* (**towards**
hacia)
benzine [ˈbenziːn] *n* *Chem* bencina *f*
bequeath [bɪˈkwiːð] *vt* *Jur* legar
bequest [bɪˈkwest] *n* *Jur* legado *m*
bereaved [bɪˈriːvd] *npl* **the b.** los familiares del/de un difunto
bereavement [bɪˈriːvmənt] *n* *(mourning)*
duelo *m*

bereft [bɪˈreft] *adj* **b. of** privado(a) de

beret [ˈbereɪ] *n* boina *f*

Berlin [bɜːˈlɪn] *n* Berlín

Bermuda [bəˈmjuːdə] *n* las (Islas) Bermudas; **B. shorts** bermudas *fpl*

Bern [bɜːn] *n* Berna

berry [ˈberɪ] *n* baya *f*

berserk [bəˈsɜːk, bəˈzɜːk] *adj* **to go b.** volverse loco(a)

berth [bɜːθ] *Naut* **1** *n* (**a**) *(mooring)* amarradero *m*; *Fig* **to give sb a wide b.** evitar a algn (**b**) *(bed)* litera *f*
2 *vi* atracar

beseech [bɪˈsiːtʃ] *vt* (*pt & pp* **besought** *or* **beseeched**) suplicar, implorar

beset [bɪˈset] *vt* (*pt & pp* **beset**) acosar; **it is b. with dangers** está plagado de peligros

beside [bɪˈsaɪd] *prep* (**a**) *(next to)* al lado de, junto a (**b**) *(compared with)* comparado con (**c**) **he was b. himself with joy** estaba loco de alegría; **that's b. the point** eso no viene al caso; **to be b. oneself** estar fuera de sí

besides [bɪˈsaɪdz] **1** *prep* (**a**) *(in addition to)* además de (**b**) *(except)* excepto, menos; **no one b. me** nadie más que yo
2 *adv* además

besiege [bɪˈsiːdʒ] *vt (city)* sitiar; *Fig* asediar

besought [bɪˈsɔːt] *pt & pp of* **beseech**

best [best] **1** *adj (superl of* **good**) mejor; **b. man** ≃ padrino *m* de boda; **her b. friend** su mejor amiga; **the b. thing would be to phone them** lo mejor sería llamarles; **we had to wait the b. part of a year** tuvimos que esperar casi un año; **with b. wishes from Mary** *(in letter)* con mis mejores deseos, Mary
2 *adv (superl of* **well**) mejor; **as b. I can** lo mejor que pueda; **I like this one b.** éste es el que más me gusta; **the world's b. dressed man** el hombre mejor vestido del mundo
3 *n* **the b.** el/la/lo mejor; **all the b.!** ¡que te vaya bien!; **at b.** a lo más; **to be at one's b.** estar en plena forma; **to do one's b.** hacer todo lo posible; **to make the b. of sth** sacar el mejor partido de algo; **to the b. of my knowledge** que yo sepa

bestiality [bestɪˈælɪtɪ] *n* bestialidad *f*

bestow [bɪˈstəʊ] *vt (favour etc)* conceder; *(honours, power)* otorgar (**on** a); *(title etc)* conferir (**on** a)

best-seller [bestˈselə(r)] *n* best-seller *m*

best-selling [ˈbestselɪŋ] *adj* **a b. author** un autor de superventas

bet [bet] **1** *n* apuesta *f*

2 *vt (pt* **bet** *or* **betted**) apostar

3 *vi* apostar (**on** por); *Fam* **you b.!** ¡y tanto!

Bethlehem [ˈbeθlɪhem] *n* Belén

betray [bɪˈtreɪ] *vt* (**a**) traicionar (**b**) *(be unfaithful to)* engañar (**c**) *(reveal)* revelar

betrayal [bɪˈtreɪəl] *n* traición *f*

better [ˈbetə(r)] **1** *adj* (**a**) *(comp of* **good**) mejor; **that's b.!** ¡así está mejor!; **the weather is b. than last week** hace mejor tiempo que la semana pasada; **to be no b. than ...** no ser más que ...; **to get b.** mejorar
(**b**) *(healthier)* mejor (de salud)
(**c**) **b. off** *(better)* mejor; *(richer)* más rico(a); **you'd be b. off going home** lo mejor es que te vayas a casa
(**d**) **the b. part of the day** la mayor parte del día
2 *adv (comp of* **well**) (**a**) mejor; **all the b., so much the b.** tanto mejor; **b. and b.** cada vez mejor; *Prov* **b. late than never** más vale tarde que nunca
(**b**) **we had b. leave** más vale que nos vayamos
(**c**) **to think b. of** *(plan)* cambiar de
3 *n* mejor; **a change for the b.** una mejora; **to get the b. of sb** vencer a algn
4 *vt* (**a**) *(improve)* mejorar
(**b**) *(surpass)* superar

betting [ˈbetɪŋ] *n* apuestas *fpl*; *Br* **b. shop** quiosco *m* de apuestas

between [bɪˈtwiːn] **1** *prep* entre; **b. you and me** entre nosotros; **closed b. one and two** cerrado de una a dos
2 *adv* **in b.** *(position)* en medio; *(time)* entretanto, mientras (tanto)

beverage [ˈbevərɪdʒ] *n* bebida *f*

bevy [ˈbevɪ] *n* bandada *f*

beware [bɪˈweə(r)] *vi* tener cuidado (**of** con); **b.!** ¡cuidado!; **b. of the dog** *(sign)* cuidado con el perro

bewildered [bɪˈwɪldəd] *adj* desconcertado(a)

bewilderment [bɪˈwɪldəmənt] *n* desconcierto *m*

bewitching [bɪˈwɪtʃɪŋ] *adj* fascinador(a)

beyond [bɪˈjɒnd] **1** *prep* más allá de; **b. belief** increíble; **b. doubt** sin lugar a dudas; **it is b. me why ...** no comprendo por qué ...; **it's b. a joke** eso ya no tiene gracia; **she is b. caring** ya no le importa; **this task is b. me** no puedo con esta tarea
2 *adv* más allá, más lejos

bias [ˈbaɪəs] *n (tendency)* tendencia *f* (**towards** hacia); *(prejudice)* prejuicio *m*

bias(s)ed [ˈbaɪəst] *adj* parcial; **to be b.**

against sth/sb tener prejuicio en contra de algo/algn

bib [bɪb] *n (for baby)* babero *m*; *(of apron)* peto *m*

Bible ['baɪbəl] *n* Biblia *f*; *Fam* **B. basher, B. thumper** evangelista *mf*

bibliography [bɪblɪ'ɒgrəfɪ] *n* bibliografía *f*

bicarbonate [baɪ'kɑːbənɪt] *n* bicarbonato *m*; **b. of soda** bicarbonato sódico

bicentenary [baɪsen'tiːnərɪ], *US* **bicentennial** [baɪsen'tenɪəl] *n* bicentenario *m*

biceps ['baɪseps] *n* bíceps *m*

bicker ['bɪkə(r)] *vi* reñir

bicycle ['baɪsɪkəl] *n* bicicleta *f*; **b. pump** bomba *f* (de aire); **to go by b.** ir en bicicleta

bid [bɪd] **1** *vt* (*pt* **bid** *or* **bade**; *pp* **bid** *or* **bidden** ['bɪdən]) (**a**) *(say)* decir; **to b. sb farewell** despedirse de algn (**b**) *(command)* mandar, ordenar; **she bade him be quiet** le mandó que se callase (**c**) *(invite)* invitar; **he bade me sit down** me invitó a sentarme (**d**) *(at auction)* (*pt & pp* **bid**) pujar

2 *vi* (*pt & pp* **bid**) *(at auction)* pujar (**for** por)

3 *n* (**a**) *(offer)* oferta *f* (**b**) *(at auction)* puja *f* (**c**) *(attempt)* intento *m*, tentativa *f*

bidder ['bɪdə(r)] *n* **the highest b.** el mejor postor

bidding ['bɪdɪŋ] *n* (**a**) *(at auction)* puja *f* (**b**) *(order)* orden *f*; **to do sb's b.** cumplir la orden de algn

bide [baɪd] *vt* (*pt* **bided** *or* **bode**; *pp* **bided**) esperar; **to b. one's time** esperar el momento oportuno

bidet ['biːdeɪ] *n* bidé *m*

bifocal [baɪ'fəʊkəl] **1** *adj* bifocal

2 *npl* **bifocals** lentes *fpl* bifocales

big [bɪg] **1** *adj* grande (**gran** *before singular noun*); **a b. clock** un reloj grande; **a b. surprise** una gran sorpresa; **my b. brother** mi hermano mayor; *Fam Ironic* **b. deal!** ¿y qué?; **b. business** los grandes negocios; **b. dipper** montaña rusa; *US Astron* **B. Dipper** Osa *f* Mayor; **b. toe** dedo gordo del pie; *Fam* **b. gun, b. shot** pez gordo; *Fam* **to make the b. time** tener éxito; *Fam* **b. top** carpa *f*

2 *adv* (**a**) *(on a grand scale)* a lo grande (**b**) *(well)* de manera excepcional

bigamy ['bɪgəmɪ] *n* bigamia *f*

bighead ['bɪghed] *n Fam* creído(a) *m,f*, engreído(a) *m,f*

bigheaded [bɪg'hedɪd] *adj* creído(a), engreído(a)

bigot ['bɪgət] *n* intolerante *mf*

bigoted ['bɪgətɪd] *adj* intolerante

bigotry ['bɪgətrɪ] *n* intolerancia *f*

bigwig ['bɪgwɪg] *n Fam* pez gordo

bike [baɪk] *n Fam* (*abbr* **bicycle** *or* **motorbike**) *(bicycle)* bici *f*; *(motorcycle)* moto *f*; **on your b.!** ¡vete de aquí!

bikini [bɪ'kiːnɪ] *n* bikini *m*

bilateral [baɪ'lætərəl] *adj* bilateral

bile [baɪl] *n* bilis *f*

bilingual [baɪ'lɪŋgwəl] *adj* bilingüe

Bill [bɪl] *n Br Fam* **the Old B.** la poli

bill¹ [bɪl] **1** *n* (**a**) *(for gas etc)* factura *f*, recibo *m* (**b**) *esp Br (in restaurant)* cuenta *f* (**c**) *Parl* proyecto *m* de ley (**d**) *US (banknote)* billete *m* de banco (**e**) *(poster)* cartel *m*; **on the b.** en cartel; **post no bills** *(sign)* prohibido fijar carteles; *Th* **to top the b.** encabezar el reparto; **b. of exchange** letra *f* de cambio; *Pol* **B. of Rights** declaración *f* de derechos

2 *vt* (**a**) *(send bill to)* facturar (**b**) *Th* programar

bill² [bɪl] *n (of bird)* pico *m*

billboard ['bɪlbɔːd] *n (hoarding)* cartelera *f*

billet ['bɪlɪt] **1** *n* alojamiento *m*

2 *vt* alojar

billfold ['bɪlfəʊld] *n US* cartera *f*, billetero *m*

billiards ['bɪljədz] *n sing* billar *m*

billion ['bɪljən] *n US* mil millones *mpl*; *Br Old-fashioned* billón *m*

billionaire [bɪljə'neə(r)] *n* multimillonario(a) *m,f*

billow ['bɪləʊ] **1** *n (of water)* ola *f*; *(of smoke)* nube *f*

2 *vi (sea)* ondear; *(sail)* hincharse

billy goat ['bɪlɪgəʊt] *n* macho cabrío

bin [bɪn] *n (for storage)* cajón *m*; **bread b.** panera *f*; **(rubbish) b.** cubo *m* de la basura

binary ['baɪnərɪ] *adj* **b. number** número binario

bind [baɪnd] *vt* (*pt & pp* **bound**) (**a**) *(tie up)* atar (**b**) *Med (bandage)* vendar (**c**) *(book)* encuadernar (**d**) *(require)* obligar (**e**) *(join etc)* unir

▸ **bind over** *vt sep Jur* obligar legalmente

binder ['baɪndə(r)] *n (file)* carpeta *f*

binding ['baɪndɪŋ] *adj (promise)* comprometedor(a); *(contract)* vinculante

binge [bɪndʒ] *n Fam* borrachera *f*; **to go on a b.** irse de juerga

bingo ['bɪŋgəʊ] *n* bingo *m*

binoculars [bɪˈnɒkjʊləz] *npl* prismáticos *mpl*, gemelos *mpl*

biochemistry [baɪəʊˈkemɪstrɪ] *n* bioquímica *f*

biodegradable [baɪəʊdɪˈgreɪdəbəl] *adj* biodegradable

biography [baɪˈɒgrəfɪ] *n* biografía *f*

biological [baɪəˈlɒdʒɪkəl] *adj* biológico(a); **b. warfare** guerra biológica

biologist [baɪˈɒlədʒɪst] *n* biólogo(a) *m,f*

biology [baɪˈɒlədʒɪ] *n* biología *f*

biorhythm [ˈbaɪəʊrɪðəm] *n* biorritmo *m*

biosphere [ˈbaɪəsfɪə(r)] *n* biosfera *f*

birch [bɜːtʃ] **1** *n* (a) *Bot* abedul *m* (b) *(rod)* vara *f* (de abedul)
2 *vt* azotar

bird [bɜːd] *n* (a) pájaro *m*, ave *f*; *Fig* **to kill two birds with one stone** matar dos pájaros de un tiro; **they're birds of a feather** son tal para cual; **b. of prey** ave de rapiña (b) *Br Fam (girl)* tía *f*, chica *f*

birdcage [ˈbɜːdkeɪdʒ] *n* jaula *f*

birdie [ˈbɜːdɪ] *n (in golf)* birdie *m*

bird's-eye view [bɜːdzaɪˈvjuː] *n* vista *f* de pájaro

bird-watcher [ˈbɜːdwɒtʃə(r)] *n* ornitólogo(a) *m,f*

Biro® [ˈbaɪrəʊ] *n Fam* boli *m*

birth [bɜːθ] *n* (a) nacimiento *m*; *(childbirth)* parto *m*; **by b.** de nacimiento; **to give b. to a child** dar a luz a un niño; **b. certificate** partida *f* de nacimiento; **b. control** *(family planning)* control *m* de la natalidad; *(contraception)* métodos anticonceptivos; **b. rate** índice *m* de natalidad (b) **of noble b.** *(parentage)* de noble linaje

birthday [ˈbɜːθdeɪ] *n* cumpleaños *m inv*

birthmark [ˈbɜːθmɑːk] *n* antojo *m*

birthplace [ˈbɜːθpleɪs] *n* lugar *m* de nacimiento

Biscay [ˈbɪskeɪ] *n* Vizcaya; **the Bay of B.** el golfo de Vizcaya

biscuit [ˈbɪskɪt] *n* (a) *Br (sweet, salted)* galleta *f*; *Fam* **that really takes the b.!** ¡eso ya es el colmo! (b) *US (savoury)* bollo *m*, bizcocho *m*

bisect [baɪˈsekt] *vt* bisegmentar; *Geom* bisecar

bisexual [baɪˈseksjʊəl] *adj* bisexual

bishop [ˈbɪʃəp] *n* (a) *Rel* obispo *m* (b) *(in chess)* alfil *m*

bison [ˈbaɪsən] *n inv* bisonte *m*

bit¹ [bɪt] *n* (a) *(small piece)* trozo *m*, pedazo *m*; **to smash sth to bits** hacer añicos algo; *Fig* **thrilled to bits** muy emocionado(a); *Fig* **to do one's b.** poner de su parte (b) *(small quantity)* poco *m*; **a**

b. of sugar un poco de azúcar; **a b. of advice** un consejo; **a b. of news** una noticia; **bits and pieces** trastos *mpl*; *Fig* **b. by b.** poco a poco (c) **a b.** *(slightly)* un poco; **a b. longer** un ratito más; **a b. worried** un poco preocupado (d) *(coin)* moneda *f*

bit² [bɪt] *n (of tool)* broca *f*

bit³ [bɪt] *n Comput* bit *m*

bit⁴ [bɪt] *pt of* **bite**

bitch [bɪtʃ] **1** *n* (a) *Zool (female)* hembra *f*; *(dog)* perra *f* (b) *Fam (spiteful woman)* bruja *f*
2 *vi Fam* **to b. (about)** *(criticize)* criticar

bitchy [ˈbɪtʃɪ] *adj Fam (spiteful)* maldiciente; *(malicious)* malicioso(a); *(malevolent)* malintencionado(a)

bite [baɪt] **1** *n* (a) *(act)* mordisco *m* (b) *(wound)* mordedura *f*; **(insect) b.** picadura *f* (c) *(mouthful)* bocado *m* (d) *Fam (snack)* bocado *m*
2 *vt (pt* **bit;** *pp* **bitten)** morder; *(insect)* picar; **to b. one's nails** morderse las uñas; *Fig* **to b. the dust** *(suffer defeat)* morder el polvo; *(die)* palmarla; *Fam* **to b. sb's head off** echarle una bronca a algn
3 *vi* (a) morder; *(insect)* picar (b) *Fig (take effect)* surtir efecto (c) *(fish)* picar

biting [ˈbaɪtɪŋ] *adj (wind)* cortante; *Fig (criticism)* mordaz

bitten [ˈbɪtən] *pp of* **bite**

bitter [ˈbɪtə(r)] **1** *adj* (a) amargo(a) (b) *(weather)* glacial; *(wind)* cortante (c) *(person)* amargado(a) (d) *(struggle)* enconado(a); *(hatred)* implacable
2 *n* (a) *(beer)* cerveza amarga (b) **bitters** bíter *m*

bitterly [ˈbɪtəlɪ] *adv* **she was b. disappointed** sufrió una terrible decepción

bitterness [ˈbɪtənɪs] *n* (a) amargura *f* (b) *(of weather)* crudeza *f* (c) *(of person)* rencor *m*

bittersweet [bɪtəˈswiːt] *adj* agridulce

bitumen [ˈbɪtjʊmɪn] *n* betún *m*

bizarre [bɪˈzɑː(r)] *adj (odd)* extraño(a); *(eccentric)* estrafalario(a)

blab [blæb] *vi Fam* parlotear; *(let out a secret)* chivarse

black [blæk] **1** *adj* (a) *(colour)* negro(a); **a b. and white television** un televisor en blanco y negro; *Fig* **b. and blue** amoratado(a); **to put sth down in b. and white** poner algo por escrito; *Av* **b. box** caja negra; **b. coffee** café solo; **b. eye** ojo morado; **b. hole** agujero negro; **b. humour** humor negro; **b. magic** magia negra; **b. market** mercado negro; *Br* **b. pudding** morcilla *f*; **the B. Sea** el Mar

Negro; *Aut* **b. spot** punto negro; *Br* **the B. Country** = la región de los Midlands; *Fig* **b. sheep** oveja negra
 (**b**) *(gloomy)* negro(a); *Fig* **a b. day** un día aciago
 2 *n* (**a**) *(colour)* negro *m*
 (**b**) *(person)* negro(a) *m,f*
 3 *vt* (**a**) *(make black)* ennegrecer
 (**b**) *(polish)* lustrar
 (**c**) *(boycott)* boicotear
 ▸ **black out 1** *vt sep* (**a**) *(extinguish lights in)* apagar las luces de (**b**) *(censor)* censurar
 2 *vi (faint)* desmayarse

blackberry ['blækbərɪ] *n* zarzamora *f*
blackbird ['blækbɜːd] *n* mirlo *m*
blackboard ['blækbɔːd] *n* pizarra *f*, encerado *m*
blackcurrant [blæk'kʌrənt] *n* grosella negra
blacken ['blækən] *vt* (**a**) *(make black)* ennegrecer (**b**) *Fig (defame)* manchar
blackhead ['blækhed] *n* espinilla *f*
blackjack ['blækdʒæk] *n Cards* veintiuna *f*
blackleg ['blækleg] *n* esquirol *m*
blacklist ['blæklɪst] *n* lista negra
blackmail ['blækmeɪl] **1** *n* chantaje *m*
 2 *vt* chantajear
blackout ['blækaʊt] *n* (**a**) *(of lights)* apagón *m* (**b**) *Rad & TV* censura *f* (**c**) *(fainting)* pérdida *f* de conocimiento
blacksmith ['blæksmɪθ] *n* herrero *m*
bladder ['blædə(r)] *n* vejiga *f*; **gall b.** vesícula *f* biliar
blade [bleɪd] *n* (**a**) *(of grass)* brizna *f* (**b**) *(of knife etc)* hoja *f* (**c**) *(of propeller, oar)* pala *f*
blame [bleɪm] **1** *n* culpa *f*; **to take the b. for sth** asumir la responsabilidad de algo
 2 *vt* echar la culpa a; **he is to b.** él tiene la culpa
blameless ['bleɪmlɪs] *adj (person)* inocente; *(conduct)* intachable
blancmange [blə'mɒnʒ] *n* = tipo de budín dulce
bland [blænd] *adj (food)* soso(a)

> ✎ Note that the Spanish word **blando** is a false friend and is never a translation for the English word **bland**. In Spanish, **blando** means "soft".

blank [blæŋk] **1** *adj* (**a**) *(without writing)* en blanco; *Fin* **b. cheque** cheque *m* en blanco (**b**) *(empty)* vacío(a); **a. b. look** una mirada inexpresiva (**c**) **a b. refusal** *(absolute)* una negativa rotunda
 2 *n* (**a**) *(space)* espacio *m* en blanco; **to draw a b.** no tener éxito (**b**) *Mil* cartucho

m de fogueo (**c**) *US (form)* impreso *m*
blanket ['blæŋkɪt] **1** *n* manta *f*, *Am* frazada *f*, cobija *f*; *Fig* capa *f*
 2 *adj* general
blare [bleə(r)] *vi* resonar
 ▸ **blare out** *vt sep* pregonar
blasé ['blɑːzeɪ] *adj* de vuelta (de todo)
blasphemous ['blæsfəməs] *adj* blasfemo(a)
blasphemy ['blæsfəmɪ] *n* blasfemia *f*
blast [blɑːst] **1** *n* (**a**) *(of wind)* ráfaga *f* (**b**) *(of horn etc)* toque *m*; **at full b.** a toda marcha (**c**) *(explosion)* explosión *f*; **b. furnace** alto horno (**d**) *(shock wave)* onda *f* de choque
 2 *vt* (**a**) *(blow up)* volar; *Fam* **b. (it)!** ¡maldito sea! (**b**) *Fig (destroy)* arruinar (**c**) *Fig (criticize)* criticar
blasted ['blɑːstɪd] *adj* maldito(a)
blast-off ['blɑːstɒf] *n* despegue *m*
blatant ['bleɪtənt] *adj (very obvious)* evidente; *(shameless)* descarado(a); **a b. lie** una mentira patente
blaze¹ [bleɪz] **1** *n* (**a**) *(burst of flame)* llamarada *f* (**b**) *(fierce fire)* incendio *m* (**c**) *(of sun)* resplandor *m* (**d**) *Fig (of anger)* arranque *m*
 2 *vi* (**a**) *(fire)* arder (**b**) *(sun etc)* brillar
blaze² [bleɪz] *vt* **to b. a trail** abrir un camino
blazer ['bleɪzə(r)] *n* chaqueta *f* sport
bleach [bliːtʃ] **1** *n (household)* lejía *f*
 2 *vt* (**a**) *(whiten)* blanquear; *(fade)* descolorir (**b**) *(hair)* decolorar
bleachers ['bliːtʃəz] *npl US Sport (seats)* gradas *fpl*
bleak [bliːk] *adj* (**a**) *(countryside)* desolado(a) (**b**) *(weather)* desapacible (**c**) *(future)* poco prometedor(a)
bleary ['blɪərɪ] *adj (blearier, bleariest)* *(eyes) (due to tears)* lloroso(a); *(due to tiredness)* cansado(a)
bleary-eyed [blɪərɪ'aɪd] *adj* con los ojos llorosos/cansados
bleat [bliːt] **1** *n* balido *m*
 2 *vi (animal)* balar
bleed [bliːd] **1** *vi (pt & pp* **bled** [bled]) sangrar
 2 *vt Med* sangrar; *Fam* **to b. sb dry** sacarle a algn hasta el último céntimo
bleeding ['bliːdɪŋ] **1** *n (loss of blood)* pérdida *f* de sangre
 2 *adj* (**a**) *Med* sangrante (**b**) *Fam Pej* puñetero(a)
bleep [bliːp] **1** *n* bip *m*, pitido *m*
 2 *vi* pitar
bleeper ['bliːpə(r)] *n Fam* busca *m*, buscapersonas *m inv*

blemish ['blemɪʃ] *n (flaw)* defecto *m*; *(on fruit)* maca *f*; *Fig* mancha *f*; *Fig* **without b.** sin tacha

blend [blend] **1** *n* mezcla *f*
2 *vt (mix)* mezclar; *(colours)* armonizar
3 *vi (mix)* mezclarse; *(colours)* armonizar

blender ['blendə(r)] *n* licuadora *f*

bless [bles] *vt (pt & pp* **blessed** *or* **blest**) (**a**) bendecir; *Fam* **b. you!** *(after a sneeze)* ¡Jesús! (**b**) **blessed with good eyesight** dotado(a) de buena vista

blessing ['blesɪŋ] *n* bendición *f*; *(advantage)* ventaja *f*; **a mixed b.** una ventaja relativa

blest [blest] *pt & pp of* **bless**

blew [blu:] *pt of* **blow**

blight [blaɪt] **1** *n* plaga *f*
2 *vt Fig (spoil)* arruinar; *(frustrate)* frustrar

blimey ['blaɪmɪ] *interj Fam* ¡caramba!, ¡caray!

blind [blaɪnd] **1** *adj* ciego(a); **a b. man** un ciego; **a b. woman** una ciega; *Fig* **b. faith** fe ciega; *Fig* **to turn a b. eye** hacer la vista gorda; **b. alley** callejón *m* sin salida; *Aut* **b. corner** curva *f* sin visibilidad; **b. spot** ángulo muerto; *Fam* **b. date** cita *f* a ciegas
2 *adv* a ciegas; *Fam* **to get b. drunk** agarrar una curda
3 *n* (**a**) *(on window)* persiana *f* (**b**) *pl* **the b.** los ciegos
4 *vt* (**a**) cegar, dejar ciego; *Fig* **blinded by ambition** cegado por la ambición (**b**) *(dazzle)* deslumbrar

blinders ['blaɪndəz] *npl US* anteojeras *fpl*

blindfold ['blaɪndfəʊld] **1** *n* venda *f*
2 *vt* vendar los ojos a

blinding ['blaɪndɪŋ] *adj* cegador(a), deslumbrante

blindly ['blaɪndlɪ] *adv* a ciegas, ciegamente

blindness ['blaɪndnɪs] *n* ceguera *f*

blink [blɪŋk] *vi (eyes)* pestañear; *(lights)* parpadear

blinkered ['blɪŋkəd] *adj Fig* de miras estrechas

blinkers ['blɪŋkəz] *npl (on horse)* anteojeras *fpl*

bliss [blɪs] *n* felicidad *f*; **it was b.!** ¡fue maravilloso!

blissful ['blɪsfʊl] *adj (happy)* feliz; *(marvellous)* maravilloso(a)

blister ['blɪstə(r)] **1** *n (on skin)* ampolla *f*; *(on paint)* burbuja *f*
2 *vi* ampollarse

blithe [blaɪð] *adj* alegre

blithely ['blaɪðlɪ] *adv* alegremente

blitz [blɪts] **1** *n* bombardeo aéreo
2 *vt* bombardear

blizzard ['blɪzəd] *n* ventisca *f*

bloated ['bləʊtɪd] *adj* hinchado(a)

blob [blɒb] *n (drop)* gota *f*; *(spot)* mancha *f*

bloc [blɒk] *n Pol* bloque *m*

block [blɒk] **1** *n* (**a**) bloque *m*; *(of wood)* taco *m*; **in b. capitals** en mayúsculas (**b**) **a b. of flats** un bloque de pisos (**c**) *(group of buildings)* manzana *f* (**d**) *(obstruction)* bloqueo *m* (**e**) *Fin* **a b. of shares** un paquete de acciones (**f**) *Fam (head)* coco *m*
2 *vt* (**a**) *(obstruct)* obstruir; *Aut* **road blocked** *(sign)* carretera cortada; **to b. the way** cerrar el paso (**b**) *Sport (player)* obstaculizar (**c**) *Fin* bloquear
► **block up** *vt sep* bloquear, obstruir; **to get blocked up** *(pipe)* obstruirse

blockade [blɒ'keɪd] *n* bloqueo *m*

blockage ['blɒkɪdʒ] *n* bloqueo *m*, obstrucción *f*; *(traffic jam)* atasco *m*

blockbuster ['blɒkbʌstə(r)] *n Fam* exitazo *m*; *Cin & TV* gran éxito *m* de taquilla; *(book)* éxito de ventas

bloke [bləʊk] *n Fam* tío *m*, tipo *m*

blond [blɒnd] *adj & n* rubio *(m)*

blonde [blɒnd] *adj & n* rubia *(f)*

blood [blʌd] *n* (**a**) sangre *f*; **b. bank** banco *m* de sangre; **b. cell** glóbulo *m*; **b. donor** donante *mf* de sangre; **b. group** grupo sanguíneo; **b. pressure** tensión *f* arterial; *US* **b. sausage** morcilla *f*; **b. test** análisis *m* de sangre; **b. transfusion** transfusión *f* de sangre; **b. vessel** vaso sanguíneo; **blue b.** sangre azul; **high/low b. pressure** hipertensión *f*/hipotensión *f* (**b**) *(race)* sangre *f*, raza *f*

bloodbath ['blʌdbɑ:θ] *n Fig* baño *m* de sangre

bloodhound ['blʌdhaʊnd] *n* sabueso *m*

bloodshed ['blʌdʃed] *n* derramamiento *m* de sangre

bloodshot ['blʌdʃɒt] *adj* inyectado(a) de sangre

bloodstream ['blʌdstri:m] *n* corriente sanguínea

bloodthirsty ['blʌdθɜ:stɪ] *adj* sanguinario(a)

bloody ['blʌdɪ] **1** *adj* (**bloodier, bloodiest**) (**a**) *(battle)* sangriento(a) (**b**) *(bloodstained)* manchado(a) de sangre (**c**) *Br very Fam (damned)* condenado(a), puñetero(a), *Andes* cojudo(a), *Méx* pinche
2 *adv Br very Fam* **it's b. difficult!** ¡joder, qué difícil!; **not b. likely!** ¡ni de coña!

bloody-minded [blʌdɪˈmaɪndɪd] *adj Fam* terco(a)

bloom [bluːm] **1** *n* (**a**) *(flower)* flor *f*; **in full b.** en flor (**b**) *(on fruit)* vello *m*
2 *vi (blossom)* florecer

blooming [ˈbluːmɪŋ] *adj* (**a**) *(blossoming)* floreciente (**b**) *Fam Euph (damned)* maldito(a), condenado(a)

blossom [ˈblɒsəm] **1** *n (flower)* flor *f*
2 *vi* florecer; *Fig* **to b. out** alcanzar la plenitud

blot [blɒt] **1** *n (of ink)* borrón *m*; *Fig* mancha *f*
2 *vt* (**a**) *(with ink)* emborronar (**b**) *(dry)* secar
3 *vi (ink)* correrse
► **blot out** *vt sep (memories)* borrar; *(view)* ocultar

blotchy [ˈblɒtʃɪ] *adj* (**blotchier, blotchiest**) *(skin etc)* enrojecido(a); *(paint etc)* cubierto(a) de manchas

blotting-paper [ˈblɒtɪŋpeɪpə(r)] *n* papel *m* secante

blouse [blaʊz] *n* blusa *f*

blow¹ [bləʊ] *n* golpe *m*; **to come to blows** llegar a las manos; **it came as a terrible b.** fue un duro golpe

blow² [bləʊ] **1** *vi (pt* **blew**; *pp* **blown**) (**a**) *(wind)* soplar; **to b. shut** cerrarse de golpe (**b**) *(fuse)* fundirse (**c**) *(tyre)* reventar
2 *vt* (**a**) *(kiss)* mandar (**b**) *(trumpet etc)* tocar; *Fig* **to b. one's own trumpet** darse bombo (**c**) *(one's nose)* sonarse (**d**) *(fuse)* fundir (**e**) *Fam (waste)* despilfarrar (**f**) *Fam (chances)* dar al traste con (**g**) *(explode)* volar; *Fig* **to b. sb's cover** descubrir la tapadera de algn; *Fam* **to b. one's top** salirse de sus casillas
► **blow away** *vt sep & vi* = **blow off**
► **blow down** *vt sep* derribar
► **blow off 1** *vt sep (by wind)* llevarse
2 *vi (hat)* salir volando
► **blow out 1** *vt sep* apagar
2 *vi* apagarse
► **blow over** *vi (storm)* calmarse; *(scandal)* olvidarse
► **blow up 1** *vt sep* (**a**) *(building)* volar (**b**) *(inflate)* inflar (**c**) *Phot* ampliar
2 *vi (explode)* explotar

blowlamp [ˈbləʊlæmp] *n* soplete *m*

blown [bləʊn] *pp of* **blow**

blowout [ˈbləʊaʊt] *n Aut* reventón *m*; *Fam (meal)* comilona *f*

blowtorch [ˈbləʊtɔːtʃ] *n US* soplete *m*

blow-up [ˈbləʊʌp] *n Phot* ampliación *f*

blubber [ˈblʌbə(r)] **1** *n* grasa *f* de ballena
2 *vi Fam* llorar a moco tendido

bludgeon [ˈblʌdʒən] *vt* aporrear; *Fig* **to b. sb into doing sth** forzar a algn a hacer algo

blue [bluː] **1** *adj* (**a**) *(colour)* azul; *Fig* **once in a b. moon** de higos a brevas; *Fam* **to scream b. murder** gritar como un loco; **b. jeans** vaqueros *mpl*, tejanos *mpl* (**b**) *(sad)* triste; **to feel b.** sentirse deprimido (**c**) *(obscene)* verde; **b. joke** chiste *m* verde
2 *n* (**a**) *(colour)* azul *m*; *Fam* **the boys in b.** los maderos (**b**) **out of the b.** *(suddenly)* de repente; *(unexpectedly)* como llovido del cielo

bluebell [ˈbluːbel] *n* campanilla *f*

blueberry [ˈbluːbərɪ] *n* arándano *m*

bluebottle [ˈbluːbɒtəl] *n* moscarda *f*, mosca *f* azul

blue-collar [ˈbluːkɒlə(r)] *adj* **b. worker** obrero(a) *m,f*

blueprint [ˈbluːprɪnt] *n* anteproyecto *m*

blues [bluːz] *n* (**a**) *Mus* **the b.** el blues (**b**) *Fam (sadness)* tristeza *f*, melancolía *f*; **to have the b.** sentirse deprimido

bluetit [ˈbluːtɪt] *n* herrerillo *m* común

bluff [blʌf] **1** *n (trick)* farol *m*; **to call sb's b.** hacer que algn ponga sus cartas encima de la mesa
2 *adj (abrupt)* brusco(a); *(forthright)* francote(a)
3 *vi* tirarse un farol; **to b. one's way through sth** hacer colar algo

blunder [ˈblʌndə(r)] **1** *n* metedura *f* de pata; *Fam* patinazo *m*
2 *vi* meter la pata, pegar un patinazo

blunt [blʌnt] **1** *adj* (**a**) *(knife)* desafilado(a); *(pencil)* despuntado(a); **b. instrument** instrumento *m* contundente (**b**) *(frank)* directo(a), francote(a); *(statement)* tajante
2 *vt (pencil)* despuntar; *(knife)* desafilar

bluntly [ˈblʌntlɪ] *adv* francamente

blur [blɜː(r)] **1** *n* aspecto borroso
2 *vt (windows)* empañar; *(shape)* desdibujar; *(memory)* enturbiar

blurb [blɜːb] *n (in book)* resumen *m*

blurred [blɜːd] *adj* borroso(a)

blurt [blɜːt] *vt* **to b. out** dejar escapar

blush [blʌʃ] **1** *n* rubor *m*
2 *vi* ruborizarse

blusher [ˈblʌʃə(r)] *n* colorete *m*

blustery [ˈblʌstərɪ] *adj* borrascoso(a)

boar [bɔː(r)] *n* verraco *m*; **wild b.** jabalí *m*

board [bɔːd] **1** *n* (**a**) *(plank)* tabla *f* (**b**) *(work surface)* mesa *f*; *(blackboard)* pizarra *f*; *(for games)* tablero *m* (**c**) *(meals)* pensión *f*; **full b.** pensión completa; **b. and lodging** casa *f* y comida (**d**) *(committee)* junta *f*, consejo *m*; **b. of directors**

consejo de administración; **b. room** sala f del consejo (**e**) *Naut* **on b.** a bordo (**f**) *Fig* **above b.** en regla; **across-the-b.** general; **to let sth go by the b.** abandonar algo
2 *vt (ship, plane etc)* embarcarse en, subir a
3 *vi* (**a**) *(lodge)* alojarse (**b**) *(at school)* estar interno(a)
▸ **board up** *vt sep* tapar

boarder ['bɔːdə(r)] *n* (**a**) *(in boarding house)* huésped *mf* (**b**) *(at school)* interno(a) *m,f*

boarding ['bɔːdɪŋ] *n* (**a**) *(embarkation)* embarque *m*; **b. card, b. pass** tarjeta f de embarque (**b**) *(lodging)* alojamiento *m*, pensión f; **b. house** pensión; **b. school** internado *m*

boardwalk ['bɔːdwɔːk] *n US* paseo marítimo entarimado

boast [bəʊst] 1 *n* jactancia f, alarde *m*
2 *vi* jactarse, alardear (**about** de)
3 *vt* presumir de, alardear de; **the town boasts an Olympic swimming pool** la ciudad disfruta de una piscina olímpica

boat [bəʊt] *n* barco *m*; *(small)* barca f, bote *m*; *(launch)* lancha f; *(large)* buque *m*; *Fig* **we're all in the same b.** todos estamos en el mismo barco; **fishing b.** barco de pesca

boater ['bəʊtə(r)] *n* canotié *m*, canotier *m*

boatswain ['bəʊsən] *n* contramaestre *m*

boatyard ['bəʊtjɑːd] *n* astillero *m*

bob [bɒb] 1 *n* (**a**) *(haircut)* pelo *m* a lo chico (**b**) *Fam (pl* **bob**) *(shilling)* chelín *m*
2 *vi* **to b. up and down** subir y bajar

bobbin ['bɒbɪn] *n (of sewing machine)* canilla f; *(for lace-making)* bolillo *m*

bobby ['bɒbɪ] *n Br Fam (policeman)* poli *m*

bobby-pin ['bɒbɪpɪn] *n US (hairgrip)* horquilla f

bobsleigh ['bɒbsleɪ] *n* bobsleigh *m*

bode¹ [bəʊd] *pt of* **bide**

bode² [bəʊd] *vt & vi* presagiar; **to b. well/ill** ser de buen/mal agüero

bodice ['bɒdɪs] *n* (**a**) *(sleeveless undergarment)* corpiño *m* (**b**) *(of dress)* cuerpo *m*

bodily ['bɒdɪlɪ] 1 *adj* físico(a); **b. harm** daños *mpl* corporales
2 *adv* **to carry sb b.** llevar a algn en brazos

body ['bɒdɪ] *n* (**a**) cuerpo *m*; **b. language** expresión f corporal; **b. odour** olor *m* corporal; **b. piercing** perforaciones *fpl* en el cuerpo, piercing *m* (**b**) *(corpse)* cadáver *m* (**c**) *(main part)* parte f principal (**d**) *Aut* carrocería f; *Naut* casco *m* (**e**)

(organization) organismo *m*; *(profession)* cuerpo *m*; **the b. politic** el estado (**f**) *(group of people)* conjunto *m*, grupo *m*

body-blow ['bɒdɪbləʊ] *n Fig* duro golpe

body-builder ['bɒdɪbɪldə(r)] *n* culturista *mf*

body-building ['bɒdɪbɪldɪŋ] *n* culturismo *m*

bodyguard ['bɒdɪgɑːd] *n* guardaespaldas *mf inv*

bodywork ['bɒdɪwɜːk] *n Aut* carrocería f

Boer ['bəʊə(r)] *adj* **the B. War** la guerra del Transvaal

bog [bɒg] *n* (**a**) ciénaga f (**b**) *Br very Fam (lavatory)* meódromo *m*
▸ **bog down** *vt sep* **to get bogged down** atascarse

bogey ['bəʊgɪ] *n* (**a**) *(spectre)* espectro *m*, fantasma *m* (**b**) *(bugbear)* pesadilla f (**c**) *(in golf)* bogey *m* (**d**) *Fam (mucus)* moco *m*

boggle ['bɒgəl] *vi Fam* **the mind boggles!** ¡es alucinante!

bogus ['bəʊgəs] *adj* falso(a); **b. company** compañía f fantasma

boil¹ [bɔɪl] 1 *n* **to come to the b.** empezar a hervir
2 *vt (water)* hervir; *(food)* cocer; *(egg)* cocer, pasar por agua
3 *vi* hervir; *Fig* **to b. with rage** estar furioso(a)
▸ **boil down** *vi* reducirse (**to** a)
▸ **boil over** *vi (milk)* salirse

boil² [bɔɪl] *n Med* furúnculo *m*

boiled [bɔɪld] *adj* **b. egg** huevo cocido *or* pasado por agua

boiler ['bɔɪlə(r)] *n* caldera f; *Br* **b. suit** mono *m*

boiling ['bɔɪlɪŋ] *adj* **b. water** agua hirviendo; **it's b. hot** *(food)* quema; *(weather)* hace un calor agobiante; **b. point** punto *m* de ebullición

boisterous ['bɔɪstərəs] *adj* (**a**) *(person, party)* bullicioso(a) (**b**) *(weather)* borrascoso(a)

bold [bəʊld] *adj* (**a**) *(brave)* valiente (**b**) *(daring)* audaz (**c**) *(features)* marcado(a); *Typ* **b. type** negrita f (**d**) *(impudent)* descarado(a)

Bolivia [bə'lɪvɪə] *n* Bolivia

Bolivian [bə'lɪvɪən] *adj & n* boliviano(a) *(m,f)*

bollard ['bɒlɑːd] *n Aut* baliza f

bollocks ['bɒləks] *npl Br very Fam* cojones *mpl*; **b.!** *(disagreement)* ¡y un huevo!

Bolshevik ['bɒlʃəvɪk] *adj & n* bolchevique *(mf)*

bolster ['bəʊlstə(r)] **1** *n (pillow)* cabezal *m*, travesaño *m*
2 *vt (strengthen)* reforzar; *(support)* apoyar

bolt [bəʊlt] **1** *n* (**a**) *(on door)* cerrojo *m*; *(small)* pestillo *m* (**b**) *Tech* perno *m*, tornillo *m* (**c**) *(of lightning)* rayo *m* (**d**) *(crossbow)* flecha *f*
2 *vt* (**a**) *(lock)* cerrar con cerrojo (**b**)*Tech* sujetar con pernos (**c**) *Fam (food)* engullir
3 *vi (person)* largarse; *(horse)* desbocarse
4 *adv* **b. upright** derecho

bomb [bɒm] **1** *n* bomba *f*; *Br Fam* **to cost a b.** costar un ojo de la cara; **b. disposal squad** brigada *f* de artificieros; **b. scare** amenaza *f* de bomba; **car b.** cochebomba *m*; **letter b.** carta-bomba *f*
2 *vt (city etc)* bombardear; *(by terrorists)* volar
3 *vi Fam* **to b. (along)** *(car)* ir a toda pastilla

bombard [bɒm'bɑːd] *vt* bombardear

bombardment [bɒm'bɑːdmənt] *n* bombardeo *m*

bombastic [bɒm'bæstɪk] *adj* rimbombante

bomber ['bɒmə(r)] *n* (**a**) *Av* bombardero *m*; **b. jacket** cazadora *f* (**b**) terrorista *mf* que coloca bombas

bombshell ['bɒmʃel] *n* (**a**) *Mil* obús *m* (**b**) *Fig (surprise)* bomba *f* (**c**) *Fam* **a blonde b.** una rubia explosiva

bona fide ['bəʊnə'faɪdɪ] *adj* (**a**) *(genuine)* auténtico(a) (**b**) *(in good faith)* bienintencionado(a)

bond [bɒnd] **1** *n* (**a**) *(link)* lazo *m*, vínculo *m* (**b**) *Fin* bono *m* (**c**)*Jur (bail)* fianza *f* (**d**) *(binding agreement)* acuerdo *m* (**e**) *(warehouse)* depósito *m*; **in b.** en depósito (**f**) *US (guarantee)* garantía *f* (**g**) **bonds** *(shackles)* cadenas *fpl*
2 *vt* (**a**) *(join)* pegar (**b**) *(merchandise)* poner en depósito

bondage ['bɒndɪdʒ] *n* esclavitud *f*

bone [bəʊn] **1** *n* (**a**) hueso *m*; *(in fish)* espina *f*; *Fig* **b. of contention** manzana *f* de la discordia; *Fig* **he made no bones about it** no trató de disimularlo; **b. china** porcelana fina (**b**) **bones** *(remains)* restos *mpl*; **the bare bones** lo esencial
2 *vt (meat)* deshuesar; *(fish)* quitar las espinas a
▸ **bone up on** *vt insep Fam* empollar

bone-dry ['bəʊn'draɪ] *adj* completamente seco(a)

bone-idle ['bəʊn'aɪdəl] *adj* gandul(a)

bonfire ['bɒnfaɪə(r)] *n* hoguera *f*, fogata *f*; *Br* **B. Night** = fiesta del 5 de noviembre en que de noche se hacen hogueras y hay fuegos artificiales

bonkers ['bɒŋkəz] *adj Br Fam* chalado(a)

bonnet ['bɒnɪt] *n* (**a**) *(child's)* gorra *f* (**b**) *BrAut* capó *m*

bonus ['bəʊnəs] *n* (**a**) *(on wages)* prima *f* (**b**) *Fin (on shares)* dividendo *m* extraordinario (**c**) *Br Ins* beneficio *m*

bony ['bəʊnɪ] *adj* (**bonier, boniest**) *(person)* huesudo(a); *(fish)* lleno(a) de espinas

boo [buː] **1** *interj* ¡bu!
2 *n* abucheo *m*
3 *vt* abuchear

boob [buːb] *n Br Fam* (**a**) *(silly mistake)* patinazo *m* (**b**) **boobs** *(breasts)* tetas *fpl*

booby ['buːbɪ] *n* **b. prize** premio *m* de consolación; **b. trap** trampa *f*; *Mil* trampa explosiva

boogie ['buːgɪ] *vi Fam* bailar

book [bʊk] **1** *n* (**a**) libro *m*; *Fig* **in my b.** según mi punto de vista; *Fig* **by the b.** según las reglas; **b. end** sujetalibros *m inv*; *Br* **b. token** vale *m* para comprar libros; **savings b.** libreta *f* de ahorros (**b**) *(of stamps)* carpeta *f*; *(of matches)* cajetilla *f* (**c**) *Com* **books** cuentas *fpl*; **to keep the books** llevar las cuentas
2 *vt* (**a**) *(reserve)* reservar; *(return flight)* cerrar (**b**) *(engage)* contratar (**c**) *(by police)* poner una multa a (**d**) *Ftb* amonestar
▸ **book into** *vt insep (hotel)* reservar una habitación en
▸ **book out** *vi (of hotel)* marcharse
▸ **book up** *vt sep* **booked up** *(sign)* completo

booking ['bʊkɪŋ] *n esp Br (reservation)* reserva *f*; **b. office** taquilla *f*

bookmaker ['bʊkmeɪkə(r)] *n* corredor(a) *m,f* de apuestas

bookseller ['bʊkselə(r)] *n* librero(a) *m,f*

bookshelf ['bʊkʃelf] *n* **bookshelves** estantería *f*

bookshop ['bʊkʃɒp] *n* librería *f*

bookstall ['bʊkstɔːl] *n* quiosco *m*

bookstore ['bʊkstɔː(r)] *n US* librería *f*

bookworm ['bʊkwɜːm] *n Fam* ratón *m* de biblioteca

boom¹ [buːm] **1** *n* (**a**) *(noise)* estampido *m*, trueno *m* (**b**) *(sudden prosperity)* boom *m*, auge *m*
2 *vi* (**a**) *(thunder)* retumbar; *(cannon)* tronar (**b**) *(prosper)* estar en auge

boom² [buːm] *n (of microphone)* jirafa *f*

boomerang [ˈbuːməræŋ] *n* bumerang *m*, bumerán *m*

booming [ˈbuːmɪŋ] *adj* (**a**) (*voice, thunder*) que retumba (**b**) (*prosperous*) en auge

boon [buːn] *n* (*blessing*) bendición *f*

boost [buːst] **1** *n* estímulo *m*, empujón *m*
2 *vt* (**a**) (*increase*) aumentar (**b**) **to b. sb's confidence** subirle la moral a algn (**c**) (*tourism, exports*) fomentar (**d**) (*voltage*) elevar

booster [ˈbuːstə(r)] *n* (**a**) *Elec* elevador *m* de voltaje (**b**) *Rad & TV (amplifier)* amplificador *m* (**c**) *Med* **b. (shot)** revacunación *f*

boot¹ [buːt] **1** *n* (**a**) bota *f*; (*short*) botín *m*; *Fig* **he's too big for his boots** es muy creído; *Fam* **to put the b. in** pisotear; *Fam* **she got the b.** la echaron (del trabajo); **b. polish** betún *m* (**b**) *Br Aut* maletero *m*, *CAm, Méx* cajuela *f*, *RP* baúl *m*
2 *vt Fam* (**a**) *Ftb (ball)* chutar (**b**) **to b. (out)** echar a patadas (**c**) *Comput* arrancar
3 *vi Comput* **to b. (up)** arrancar

boot² [buːt] *n* **to b.** además

bootblack [ˈbuːtblæk] *n esp US* limpiabotas *mf inv*

booth [buːð, buːθ] *n* (**a**) (*in language lab etc*) cabina *f*; **telephone b.** cabina telefónica (**b**) (*at fair*) puesto *m*

bootleg [ˈbuːtleg] *adj* de contrabando

bootlegger [ˈbuːtlegə(r)] *n* contrabandista *m*

booty [ˈbuːtɪ] *n* botín *m*

booze [buːz] *Fam* **1** *n* priva *f*
2 *vi* privar

bop [bɒp] **1** *n* (**a**) *Mus* be-bop *m* (**b**) *Fam (dance)* baile *m*
2 *vi Fam (dance)* bailar

Bordeaux [bɔːˈdəʊ] *n* (**a**) (*city*) Burdeos (**b**) (*wine*) burdeos *m*

border [ˈbɔːdə(r)] **1** *n* (**a**) borde *m*, margen *m* (**b**) *Sewing* ribete *m* (**c**) (*frontier*) frontera *f*; **b. town** pueblo fronterizo (**d**) (*flowerbed*) arriate *m*
2 *vt Sewing* ribetear
▸ **border on** *vt insep* (**a**) *Geog* lindar con (**b**) *Fig* rayar en

borderline [ˈbɔːdəlaɪn] **1** *n* (**a**) (*border*) frontera *f* (**b**) (*dividing line*) línea divisoria
2 *adj* (**a**) (*on the border*) fronterizo(a) (**b**) *Fig (case etc)* dudoso(a)

bore¹ [bɔː(r)] **1** *vt Tech* taladrar, perforar
2 *n* (**a**) *Tech (hole)* taladro *m* (**b**) (*of gun*) calibre *m*

bore² [bɔː(r)] **1** *vt* aburrir

2 *n* (*person*) pesado(a) *m,f*, pelma *mf*; (*thing*) lata *f*, rollo *m*; **what a b.!** ¡qué rollo!

bore³ [bɔː(r)] *pt of* **bear**

bored [bɔːd] *adj* aburrido(a); **to be b. stiff** *or* **to tears** estar aburrido(a) como una ostra

boredom [ˈbɔːdəm] *n* aburrimiento *m*

boring [ˈbɔːrɪŋ] *adj* (*uninteresting*) aburrido(a); (*tedious*) pesado(a), latoso(a)

born [bɔːn] **1** *pp of* **bear**; **to be b.** nacer; **I wasn't b. yesterday** no nací ayer
2 *adj* (*having natural ability*) nato(a); **b. poet** poeta nato

born-again [ˈbɔːnəgen] *adj Rel* converso(a)

borne [bɔːn] *pp of* **bear**

borough [ˈbʌrə] *n* (**a**) (*town*) ciudad *f*; *US* (*municipality*) municipio *m* (**b**) *esp Br* (*constituency*) distrito *m* electoral

borrow [ˈbɒrəʊ] **1** *vt* (**a**) pedir *or* tomar prestado; **can I b. your pen?** ¿me dejas tu bolígrafo? (**b**) (*ideas etc*) apropiarse
2 *vi* pedir *or* tomar prestado

borstal [ˈbɔːstəl] *n Br Fam* reformatorio *m*

Bosnia [ˈbɒznɪə] *n* Bosnia

Bosnia-Herzegovina
[ˈbɒznɪəhɜːtsəgəˈviːnə] *n* Bosnia y Hercegóvina

Bosnian [ˈbɒznɪən] *adj & n* bosnio(a) (*m,f*)

bosom [ˈbʊzəm] *n* (**a**) (*breast*) pecho *m*; (*breasts*) pechos *mpl*; **b. friend** amigo(a) *m,f* del alma (**b**) *Fig* seno *m*

boss [bɒs] *n* (**a**) (*head*) jefe(a) *m,f*; (*factory owner etc*) patrón(ona) *m,f* (**b**) *esp US Pol* jefe *m*; *Pej* cacique *m*
2 *vt* **to b. sb about** *or* **around** mandar sobre algn

bossy [ˈbɒsɪ] *adj* (**bossier, bossiest**) *Fam* mandón(ona)

bosun [ˈbəʊsən] *n* contramaestre *m*

botanic(al) [bəˈtænɪk(əl)] *adj* botánico(a); **b. garden** jardín botánico

botany [ˈbɒtənɪ] *n* botánica *f*

botch [bɒtʃ] **1** *vt* chapucear; **a botched job** una chapuza
2 *n* chapuza *f*

both [bəʊθ] **1** *adj* ambos(as), los dos/las dos; **b. men are teachers** ambos son profesores; **hold it with b. hands** sujétalo con las dos manos
2 *pron* **b. (of them)** ambos(as), los dos/las dos; **b. of you** vosotros dos
3 *conj* a la vez; **b. England and Spain are in Europe** tanto Inglaterra como España están en Europa

bother [ˈbɒðə(r)] **1** *vt* (**a**) (*disturb*) molestar; (*be a nuisance to*) dar la lata a (**b**) *(worry)* preocupar; *Fam* **I can't be bothered** no tengo ganas

2 *vi* molestarse; **don't b. about me** no te preocupes por mí; **he didn't b. shaving** no se molestó en afeitarse

3 *n* (**a**) *(disturbance)* molestia *f*; *(nuisance)* lata *f* (**b**) *(trouble)* problemas *mpl*

4 *interj Br* ¡maldito sea!

bothersome ['bɒðəsəm] *adj* molesto(a)

bottle ['bɒtəl] **1** *n* (**a**) *(of perfume, ink)* frasco *m*; *Fam* **to hit the b.** darle a la bebida; **baby's b.** biberón *m*; **b. opener** abrebotellas *m inv* (**b**) *Br Fam* **to have a lot of b.** *(nerve)* tener muchas agallas

2 *vt (wine)* embotellar; *(fruit)* enfrascar

▸ **bottle out** *vi Br Fam* encogerse

▸ **bottle up** *vt sep* reprimir

bottle-bank ['bɒtəlbæŋk] *n* contenedor *m* de vidrio

bottled ['bɒtəld] *adj (beer, wine)* en botella, embotellado(a); *(fruit)* envasado(a)

bottle-green ['bɒtəlgriːn] *adj* verde botella

bottleneck ['bɒtəlnek] *n Aut* embotellamiento *m*, atasco *m*

bottom ['bɒtəm] **1** *adj* (**a**) *(lowest)* más bajo(a); *(drawer, shelf)* de abayo; *Aut* **b. gear** primera *f* (**b**) *(last)* último(a); **b. line** *Fin* saldo *m* final; *Fig* resultado *m* final

2 *n* (**a**) *(part)* parte *f* inferior; *(of sea, garden, street, box)* fondo *m*; *(of bottle)* culo *m*; *(of page, hill)* pie *m*; *Educ* **to be (at) the b. of the class** ser el último/la última de la clase; **to touch b.** tocar fondo; *Fam* **bottoms up!** ¡salud! (**b**) **to get to the b. of a matter** llegar al meollo de una cuestión; **who is at the b. of all this?** ¿quién está detrás de todo esto? (**c**) *(buttocks)* trasero *m*

▸ **bottom out** *vi Fin* tocar fondo

bottomless ['bɒtəmlɪs] *adj (pit)* sin fondo; *(mystery)* insondable

boudoir ['buːdwɑː(r)] *n* tocador *m*

bough [baʊ] *n* rama *f*

bought [bɔːt] *pt & pp of* **buy**

bouillon ['buːjɒn] *n* caldo *m*

boulder ['bəʊldə(r)] *n* canto rodado *m*

boulevard ['buːlvɑː(r)] *n* bulevar *m*

bounce [baʊns] **1** *vi* (**a**) *(ball)* rebotar (**b**) *(jump)* saltar (**c**) *Fam (cheque)* ser rechazado (por el banco)

2 *vt (ball)* botar

3 *n* (**a**) *(of ball)* bote *m* (**b**) *(jump)* salto *m* (**c**) *(energy)* vitalidad *f*

▸ **bounce back** *vi (recover health)* recuperarse, recobrarse

bouncer ['baʊnsə(r)] *n Fam* gorila *m*

bound[1] [baʊnd] *adj* (**a**) *(tied up)* atado(a) (**b**) *(book)* encuadernado(a) (**c**) *(obliged)* obligado(a) (**d**) **b. (up)** *(linked)* vinculado(a) (**with a**) (**e**) **it's b. to happen** sucederá con toda seguridad; **it was b. to fail** estaba destinado al fracaso

bound[2] [baʊnd] **1** *vi* saltar

2 *n* salto *m*

bound[3] [baʊnd] *pt & pp of* **bind**

bound[4] [baʊnd] *adj* **b. for** con destino a, rumbo a; **to be b. for** dirigirse a

boundary ['baʊndərɪ] *n* límite *m*

boundless ['baʊndlɪs] *adj* ilimitado(a), sin límites

bounds [baʊndz] *npl* **beyond the b. of reality** más allá de la realidad; **her ambition knows no b.** su ambición no conoce límites; **the river is out of b.** está prohibido bajar al río

bounty ['baʊntɪ] *n* prima *f*, gratificación *f*

bouquet *n* (**a**) [buːˈkeɪ, bəʊˈkeɪ] *(of flowers)* ramillete *m* (**b**) [buːˈkeɪ] *(of wine)* aroma *m*, buqué *m*

bourbon ['bɜːbən] *n US (whiskey)* whisky americano, bourbon *m*

bourgeois ['bʊəʒwɑː] *adj & n* burgués(esa) *(m,f)*

bourgeoisie [bʊəʒwɑːˈziː] *n* burguesía *f*

bout [baʊt] *n* (**a**) *(of work)* turno *m*; *(of illness)* ataque *m* (**b**) *(in boxing)* combate *m*

boutique [buːˈtiːk] *n* boutique *f*, tienda *f*

bow[1] [baʊ] **1** *vi* (**a**) hacer una reverencia (**b**) *(give in)* ceder

2 *n (with head, body)* reverencia *f*

▸ **bow out** *vi* retirarse (**of** de)

bow[2] [bəʊ] *n* (**a**) *Sport & Mus* arco *m*; *Fig* **to have more than one string to one's b.** ser una persona de recursos (**b**) *(knot)* lazo *m*; **b. tie** pajarita *f*

bow[3] [baʊ] *n esp Naut* proa *f*

bowel ['baʊəl] *n* (**a**) intestino *m* (**b**) **bowels** entrañas *fpl*

bowl[1] [bəʊl] *n* (**a**) *(dish)* cuenco *m*; *(for soup)* tazón *m*; *(for washing hands)* palangana *f*; *(for washing clothes, dishes)* barreño *m*; *(of toilet)* taza *f* (**b**) *Geol* cuenca *f*

bowl[2] [bəʊl] **1** *n* bola *f*

2 *vt (in cricket)* lanzar

3 *vi* (**a**) *(play bowls)* jugar a los bolos (**b**) *(in cricket)* lanzar la pelota

▸ **bowl along** *vi Fam (car)* ir volando

▸ **bowl out** *vt sep (in cricket)* eliminar

▸ **bowl over** *vt sep* (**a**) *(knock down)* derribar (**b**) *Fig (astonish)* desconcertar

bow-legged ['bəʊleg(ɪ)d] *adj* patizambo(a)

bowler¹ [ˈbəʊlə(r)] *n (in cricket)* lanzador(a) *m,f*

bowler² [ˈbəʊlə(r)] *n (hat)* bombín *m*

bowling [ˈbəʊlɪŋ] *n (game)* bolos *mpl*; **b. alley** bolera *f*; **b. ball** bola *f* (de jugar a los bolos)

bowls [bəʊlz] *npl Sport* bolos *mpl*

box¹ [bɒks] **1** *n* (**a**) caja *f*; *(large)* cajón *m*; *(of matches)* cajetilla *f*; **jewellery b.** joyero *m*; *Th* **b. office** taquilla *f*; **b. office success** éxito taquillero (**b**) *Press* recuadro *m* (**c**) *Th* palco *m* (**d**) *Br Fam (television)* caja tonta
  2 *vt (pack)* embalar

box² [bɒks] *Sport* **1** *vi* boxear
  2 *vt (hit)* pegar; **to b. sb's ears** dar un cachete a algn

boxcar [ˈbɒkskɑː(r)] *n US* vagón *m* de mercancías, furgón *m* (de mercancías)

boxer [ˈbɒksə(r)] *n* (**a**) boxeador *m* (**b**) *(dog)* bóxer *m*

boxing [ˈbɒksɪŋ] *n* boxeo *m*; **b. ring** cuadrilátero *m*

Boxing Day [ˈbɒksɪŋdeɪ] *n Br* = el día de San Esteban *(26 de diciembre)*

boxroom [ˈbɒksruːm] *n* trastero *m*

boy [bɔɪ] *n* (**a**) *(child)* niño *m*, chico *m*; *(youth)* joven *m*; **b. band** = grupo musical juvenil compuesto por adolescentes varones; *Fam* **oh b.!** ¡vaya! (**b**) *(son)* hijo *m*

boycott [ˈbɔɪkɒt] **1** *n* boicot *m*
  2 *vt* boicotear

boyfriend [ˈbɔɪfrend] *n* novio *m*; *(live-in)* compañero *m*

boyhood [ˈbɔɪhʊd] *n* niñez *f*, juventud *f*

boyish [ˈbɔɪɪʃ] *adj* juvenil, de muchacho

bra [brɑː] *n* sostén *m*, *Esp* sujetador *m*, *Carib, Col, Méx* brasier *m*, *RP* corpiño *m*

brace [breɪs] **1** *n* (**a**) *(clamp)* abrazadera *f*; *(of drill)* berbiquí *m*; *(for teeth)* aparato *m* (**b**) *(of wood)* puntal *m* (**c**) *(pair)* par *m* (**d**) *Br* **braces** tirantes *mpl*
  2 *vt* (**a**) *(wall)* apuntalar (**b**) *(strengthen)* reforzar (**c**) **to b. oneself** prepararse (**for** para)
  ▸ **brace up** *vi* cobrar ánimo

bracelet [ˈbreɪslɪt] *n* pulsera *f*

bracing [ˈbreɪsɪŋ] *adj (wind)* fresco(a); *(stimulating)* tonificante

bracken [ˈbrækən] *n* helecho *m*

bracket [ˈbrækɪt] **1** *n* (**a**) *Typ (round)* paréntesis *m*; *(square)* corchete *m*; *(curly)* llave *f*; **in brackets** entre paréntesis (**b**) *(support)* soporte *m*; *(for lamp)* brazo *m*; *(shelf)* repisa *f* (**c**) *(for tax)* sector *m*
  2 *vt* (**a**) *Ling (phrase etc)* poner entre paréntesis (**b**) *(group together)* agrupar, juntar

brag [bræg] *vi* jactarse (**about** de)

braggart [ˈbrægət] *n* fanfarrón(ona) *m,f*

braid [breɪd] **1** *vt* trenzar
  2 *n* (**a**) *Sewing* galón *m* (**b**) *esp US (plait)* trenza *f*

Braille [breɪl] *n* braille *m*

brain [breɪn] *n* (**a**) cerebro *m*; **she's got cars on the b.** está obsesionada por los coches; *Med* **b. death** muerte *f* cerebral; *Fig* **b. drain** fuga *f* de cerebros; **b. wave** idea *f* genial (**b**) *Fam* **brains** inteligencia *f*; **to have brains** ser inteligente; *Br* **brains** *or US* **b. trust** grupo *m* de expertos (**c**) *Culin* **brains** sesos *mpl*

brainchild [ˈbreɪntʃaɪld] *n* invento *m*, idea *f* genial

brainpower [ˈbreɪnpaʊə(r)] *n* capacidad *f* intelectual

brainstorm [ˈbreɪnstɔːm] *n* (**a**) *(outburst)* arranque *m* (**b**) *(brainwave)* genialidad *f*, lluvia *f* de ideas

brainwash [ˈbreɪnwɒʃ] *vt* lavar el cerebro a

brainy [ˈbreɪnɪ] *adj* (**brainier, brainiest**) *Fam* listo(a)

braise [breɪz] *vt* cocer a fuego lento

brake [breɪk] **1** *n Aut (also pl)* freno *m*; **b. drum** tambor *m* del freno; **b. fluid** líquido *m* de frenos; **b. light** luz *f* de freno
  2 *vi* frenar, echar el freno

bramble [ˈbræmbəl] *n* zarza *f*, zarzamora *f*

bran [bræn] *n* salvado *m*

branch [brɑːntʃ] **1** *n* (*of tree)* rama *f*; *(of road)* bifurcación *f*; *(of science etc)* ramo *m*; *Com* **b. (office)** sucursal *f*
  2 *vi (road)* bifurcarse
  ▸ **branch off** *vi* desviarse
  ▸ **branch out** *vi* diversificarse

brand [brænd] **1** *n* (**a**) *Com* marca *f*; **b. name** marca de fábrica (**b**) *(type)* clase *f* (**c**) *(on cattle)* hierro *m*
  2 *vt* (**a**) *(animal)* marcar con hierro candente (**b**) *(label)* tildar

brandish [ˈbrændɪʃ] *vt* blandir

brand-new [ˈbrændˈnjuː] *adj* flamante

brandy [ˈbrændɪ] *n* coñac *m*, brandy *m*

brash [bræʃ] *adj* (**a**) *(impudent)* descarado(a) (**b**) *(reckless)* temerario(a) (**c**) *(loud, showy)* chillón(ona)

brass [brɑːs] *n* latón *m*; *Fam (money)* pasta *f*; *Mus* instrumentos *mpl* de metal; **b. band** banda *f* de metal

brassiere [ˈbræzɪə(r)] *n* sostén *m*, sujetador *m*

brat [bræt] *n Fam* mocoso(a) *m,f*

bravado [brəˈvɑːdəʊ] *n* bravuconería *f*

brave [breɪv] **1** *adj* valiente, valeroso(a)

2 *n US* (**Indian**) **b.** guerrero *m* indio
3 *vt* (**a**) *(face)* hacer frente a (**b**) *(defy)* desafiar
bravely ['breɪvlɪ] *adv* valientemente
bravery ['breɪvərɪ] *n* valentía *f*, valor *m*
bravo [brɑː'vəʊ] *interj* ¡bravo!
brawl [brɔːl] **1** *n* reyerta *f*
2 *vi* pelearse
brawn [brɔːn] *n* (**a**) *(strength)* fuerza física (**b**) *Br Culin* queso *m* de cerdo
bray [breɪ] **1** *n (of donkey)* rebuzno *m*
2 *vi* rebuznar
brazen ['breɪzən] *adj* descarado(a)
Brazil [brə'zɪl] *n* (el) Brasil
brazil [brə'zɪl] *n* **b. nut** nuez *f* del Brasil
Brazilian [brə'zɪlɪən] *adj & n* brasileño(a) *(m,f)*
breach [briːtʃ] **1** *n* (**a**) *(in wall)* brecha *f* (**b**) *(violation)* incumplimiento *m*; **b. of confidence** abuso *m* de confianza; **b. of contract** incumplimiento de contrato; **b. of the law** violación *f* de la ley; **b. of the peace** alteración *f* del orden público (**c**) *(in relations)* ruptura *f*
2 *vt* violar
bread [bred] *n* (**a**) *(food)* pan *m*; **b. and butter** pan con mantequilla, *Am* pan con manteca; *Fig* **our daily b.** el pan nuestro de cada día (**b**) *Fam (money)* pasta *f*, *Am* plata *f*
breadboard ['bredbɔːd] *n* tabla *f* (para cortar el pan)
breadcrumb ['bredkrʌm] *n* miga *f* de pan; **breadcrumbs** pan rallado
breadline ['bredlaɪn] *n Fam* miseria *f*; **to be on the b.** vivir en la miseria
breadth [bredθ] *n* (**a**) *(width)* anchura *f*; **it is 2 m in b.** tiene 2 m de ancho (**b**) *(extent)* amplitud *f*
breadwinner ['bredwɪnə(r)] *n* cabeza *mf* de familia
break [breɪk] **1** *vt* (*pt* **broke**; *pp* **broken**) (**a**) *(romper)*; **to b. a leg** romperse la pierna; **to b. a record** batir un récord; **to b. even** no tener ni ganancias ni pérdidas; *Fig* **to b. one's back** matarse a trabajar; *Fig* **to b. sb's heart** partirle el corazón a algn; *Fig* **to b. the ice** romper el hielo (**b**) *(fail to keep)* faltar a; **to b. a contract** romper un contrato; **to b. the law** violar la ley
(**c**) *(destroy)* destrozar; *Fin* arruinar
(**d**) *(interrupt)* interrumpir
(**e**) *(code)* descifrar
(**f**) *(fall)* amortiguar
(**g**) **she broke the news to him** le comunicó la noticia

2 *vi* (**a**) romperse; *(clouds)* dispersarse; *(waves)* romper
(**b**) *(storm)* estallar
(**c**) *(voice)* cambiar
(**d**) *(health)* resentirse
(**e**) **when day breaks** al rayar el alba
(**f**) *(story)* divulgarse
3 *n* (**a**) *(fracture)* rotura *f*; *(crack)* grieta *f*; *(opening)* abertura *f*
(**b**) *(in relationship)* ruptura *f*
(**c**) *(pause)* pausa *f*, descanso *m*; *(at school)* recreo *m*; **to take a b.** descansar un rato; *(holiday)* tomar unos días libres; **without a b.** sin parar
(**d**) *Fam (chance)* oportunidad *f*; **a lucky b.** un golpe de suerte
▸ **break away** *vi* (**a**) *(become separate)* desprenderse (**from** de) (**b**) *(escape)* escaparse
▸ **break down 1** *vt sep* (**a**) *(door)* derribar (**b**) *(resistance)* acabar con (**c**) *(costs)* desglosar
2 *vi* (**a**) *Aut* tener una avería (**b**) *(resistance)* ceder (**c**) *(health)* debilitarse (**d**) *(weep)* ponerse a llorar
▸ **break in 1** *vt sep* acostumbrar; **to b. in a pair of shoes** cogerle la forma a los zapatos
2 *vi (burglar)* entrar por la fuerza
▸ **break into** *vt insep* (**a**) *(burgle) (house)* allanar; *(safe)* forzar (**b**) **to b. into song** empezar a cantar
▸ **break off 1** *vt sep* partir
2 *vi* (**a**) *(become detached)* desprenderse (**b**) *(talks)* interrumpirse (**c**) *(stop)* pararse
▸ **break out** *vi* (**a**) *(prisoners)* escaparse (**b**) *(war etc)* estallar; **she broke out in a rash** le salió un sarpullido
▸ **break through 1** *vt insep* (**a**) *(crowd)* abrirse paso por; *(cordon)* romper (**b**) *(clouds)* atravesar
2 *vi* (**a**) *(crowd)* abrirse paso (**b**) *(sun)* salir
▸ **break up 1** *vt sep* *(object)* romper; *(car)* desguazar; *(crowd)* disolver
2 *vi* (**a**) *(object)* romperse (**b**) *(crowd)* disolverse; *(meeting)* levantarse (**c**) *(relationship)* fracasar; *(couple)* separarse (**d**) *Educ* terminar
▸ **break with** *vt insep (past)* romper con
breakable ['breɪkəbəl] *adj* frágil
breakage ['breɪkɪdʒ] *n (breaking)* rotura *f*
breakaway ['breɪkəweɪ] *adj* disidente
breakdown ['breɪkdaʊn] *n* (**a**) *Aut* avería *f*; *Br* **b. truck** *or* **van** grúa *f* (**b**) (**nervous**) **b.** crisis nerviosa (**c**) *(in communications)*

ruptura *f* (**d**) *(analysis)* análisis *m*; *Fin* desglose *m*

breaker ['breɪkə(r)] *n* (**a**) *(wave)* ola *f* grande (**b**) *Tech* trituradora *f* (**c**) *(switch)* interruptor automático

breakfast ['brekfəst] **1** *n* desayuno *m*; **to have b.** desayunar

2 *vi* desayunar

break-in ['breɪkɪn] *n* robo *m* *(con allanamiento de morada)*

breaking ['breɪkɪŋ] *n* (**a**) rotura *f*; **b. point** punto *m* de ruptura (**b**) *Jur* **b. and entering** allanamiento *m* de morada

breakthrough ['breɪkθruː] *n* paso *m* adelante, avance *m*

breakwater ['breɪkwɔːtə(r)] *n* rompeolas *m inv*

breast [brest] *n* *(chest)* pecho *m*; *(of woman)* pecho, seno *m*; *(of chicken etc)* pechuga *f*; *Fig* **to make a clean b. of it** dar la cara

breast-feed ['brestfiːd] *vt* dar el pecho a, amamantar a

breaststroke ['breststrəʊk] *n* braza *f*

breath [breθ] *n* (**a**) aliento *m*; *(breathing)* respiración *f*; **in the same b.** al mismo tiempo; **to catch one's b.** sin aliento; **to draw b.** recobrar el aliento; **to draw b.** respirar; **under one's b.** en voz baja; *Fig* **to take sb's b. away** dejar pasmado a algn; *Aut* **b. test** alcoholemia *f* (**b**) **to go out for a b. of fresh air** salir a tomar el aire

Breathalyser®, *US* **Breathalyzer**® ['breθəlaɪzə(r)] *n Br* alcoholímetro *m*

breathe [briːð] **1** *vt* respirar; **to b. a sigh of relief** dar un suspiro de alivio

2 *vi* respirar; **to b. in** aspirar; **to b. out** espirar; **to b. heavily** resoplar

breather ['briːðə(r)] *n Fam (rest)* descanso *m*

breathing ['briːðɪŋ] *n* respiración *f*; **b. space** pausa *f*, respiro *m*

breathless ['breθlɪs] *adj* sin aliento, jadeante

breathtaking ['breθteɪkɪŋ] *adj* impresionante

bred [bred] *pt & pp of* **breed**

breeches ['brɪtʃɪz, 'briːtʃɪz] *npl* bombachos *mpl*; **knee b., riding b.** pantalones *mpl* de montar

breed [briːd] **1** *n* *(of animal)* raza *f*; *Fig (class)* clase *f*

2 *vt* *(pt & pp* **bred***)* *(animals)* criar; *Fig (ideas)* engendrar

3 *vi* *(animals)* reproducirse

breeder ['briːdə(r)] *n* (**a**) *(person)* criador(a) *m,f* (**b**) **(fast) b. reactor** reactor *m* generador

breeding ['briːdɪŋ] *n* (**a**) *(of animals)* cría *f*; *Fig* **b. ground** caldo *m* de cultivo (**b**) *(of person)* educación *f*

breeze [briːz] **1** *n* brisa *f*; *Constr* **b. block** bloque *m* de cemento

2 *vi* **to b. in/out** entrar/salir despreocupadamente

breezy ['briːzɪ] *adj* (**breezier, breeziest**) (**a**) *(weather)* ventoso(a) (**b**) *(person)* despreocupado(a)

brevity ['brevɪtɪ] *n* brevedad *f*

brew [bruː] **1** *vt* *(beer)* elaborar; *(hot drink)* preparar

2 *vi* *(tea)* reposar; *Fig* **a storm is brewing** se prepara una tormenta; *Fam* **something's brewing** algo se está cociendo

3 *n* (**a**) *(of tea)* infusión *f*; *Fam (of beer)* birra *f* (**b**) *(magic potion)* brebaje *m*

brewer ['bruːə(r)] *n* cervecero(a) *m,f*

brewery ['bruːərɪ] *n* cervecería *f*

brewing ['bruːɪŋ] **1** *adj* cervecero(a)

2 *n* *(of beer)* elaboración *f* de la cerveza

briar ['braɪə(r)] *n* brezo *m*

bribe [braɪb] **1** *vt* sobornar

2 *n* soborno *m*

bribery ['braɪbərɪ] *n* soborno *m*

bric-a-brac ['brɪkəbræk] *n* baratijas *fpl*

brick [brɪk] *n* ladrillo *m*; *Fam (reliable person)* persona *f* de confianza

bricklayer ['brɪkleɪə(r)] *n* albañil *m*

brickwork ['brɪkwɜːk] *n* ladrillos *mpl*

bridal ['braɪdəl] *adj* nupcial

bride [braɪd] *n* novia *f*; **the b. and groom** los novios

bridegroom ['braɪdgruːm] *n* novio *m*

bridesmaid ['braɪdzmeɪd] *n* dama *f* de honor

bridge¹ [brɪdʒ] **1** *n* puente *m*; *(of nose)* caballete *m*; *(of ship)* puente de mando

2 *vt* (**a**) *(river)* tender un puente sobre (**b**) *(gap)* llenar; *Fin* **bridging loan** crédito *m* a corto plazo

bridge² [brɪdʒ] *n Cards* bridge *m*

bridle ['braɪdəl] **1** *n* brida *f*; *(bit)* freno *m*; **b. path** camino *m* de herradura

2 *vt (horse)* embridar

brief [briːf] **1** *adj* (**a**) *(short)* breve (**b**) *(concise)* conciso(a)

2 *n* (**a**) *(report)* informe *m*; **in b.** en resumen (**b**) *Jur* expediente *m* (**c**) *Mil* instrucciones *fpl* (**d**) **briefs** *(for men)* calzoncillos *mpl*; *(for women)* bragas *fpl*

3 *vt* (**a**) *(inform)* informar (**b**) *(instruct)* dar instrucciones a

briefcase ['briːfkeɪs] *n* cartera *f*, portafolios *m inv*

briefing ['briːfɪŋ] *n* *(meeting)* reunión informativa

briefly [ˈbriːflɪ] *adv* brevemente; **as b. as possible** con la mayor brevedad (posible)

brigade [brɪˈgeɪd] *n* brigada *f*

brigadier [brɪgəˈdɪə(r)] *n* general *m* de brigada

bright [braɪt] *adj* (**a**) *(light, sun, eyes)* brillante; *(colour)* vivo(a); *(day)* claro(a) (**b**) *(cheerful)* alegre; **to look on the b. side** mirar el lado bueno (**c**) *(clever)* listo(a), espabilado(a) (**d**) *(promising)* prometedor(a)

brighten [ˈbraɪtən] *vi (prospects)* mejorarse; *(face)* iluminarse
▸ **brighten up 1** *vt sep (room etc)* alegrar **2** *vi (weather)* despejarse; *(person)* animarse

brightly [ˈbraɪtlɪ] *adv* brillantemente

brightness [ˈbraɪtnɪs] *n* (**a**) *(of sun)* resplandor *m*; *(of day)* claridad *f*; *(of colour)* viveza *f* (**b**) *(cleverness)* inteligencia *f*

brilliance [ˈbrɪljəns] *n* (**a**) *(of light)* brillo *m*; *(of colour)* viveza *f* (**b**) *(of person)* brillantez *f*

brilliant [ˈbrɪljənt] **1** *adj* brillante; *(idea)* genial; *Fam (very good)* estupendo(a) **2** *n* brillante *m*

brim [brɪm] **1** *n* borde *m*; *(of hat)* ala *f*; **full to the b.** lleno hasta el borde **2** *vi* rebosar (**with** de)
▸ **brim over** *vi* rebosar

brine [braɪn] *n* salmuera *f*

bring [brɪŋ] *vt (pt & pp* **brought**) (**a**) *(carry, take)* traer; **could you b. that book?** ¿podrías traerme el libro? (**b**) *(take to a different position)* llevar; **the war brought hunger to many homes** la guerra llevó el hambre a muchos hogares (**c**) *(cause)* provocar; **he brought it upon himself** se lo buscó (**d**) *(persuade)* convencer; **how did they b. themselves to do it?** ¿cómo llegaron a hacerlo? (**e**) *(lead)* llevar (**f**) **to b. an action against** acusar
▸ **bring about** *vt sep* provocar
▸ **bring along** *vt sep* traer
▸ **bring back** *vt sep* (**a**) *(return)* devolver (**b**) *(reintroduce)* volver a introducir (**c**) *(make one remember)* traerle a la memoria
▸ **bring down** *vt sep* (**a**) *(from upstairs)* bajar (**b**) *(government)* derribar; *Th* **to b. the house down** echar el teatro abajo con los aplausos (**c**) *(reduce)* rebajar
▸ **bring forward** *vt sep* (**a**) *(meeting etc)* adelantar (**b**) *(present)* presentar (**c**) *Fin* **brought forward** suma y sigue

▸ **bring in** *vt sep* (**a**) *(yield)* dar (**b**) *(show in)* hacer entrar (**c**) *(law etc)* introducir; *(fashion)* lanzar
▸ **bring off** *vt sep* lograr, conseguir
▸ **bring on** *vt sep* provocar
▸ **bring out** *vt sep* (**a**) *(publish)* publicar (**b**) *(reveal)* recalcar; **he brings out the worst in me** despierta lo peor que hay en mí
▸ **bring round** *vt sep* (**a**) *(revive)* hacer volver en sí (**b**) *(persuade)* convencer
▸ **bring to** *vt sep* reanimar
▸ **bring up** *vt sep* (**a**) *(educate)* criar, educar (**b**) *(subject)* plantear (**c**) *(vomit)* devolver

brink [brɪŋk] *n (edge)* borde *m*; *Fig* **on the b. of ruin** al borde de la ruina; **on the b. of tears** a punto de llorar

brisk [brɪsk] *adj* enérgico(a); *(pace)* rápido(a); *(trade)* activo(a); *(weather)* fresco(a)

bristle [ˈbrɪsəl] **1** *n* cerda *f* **2** *vi* (**a**) erizarse (**b**) *(show anger)* enfurecer (**at** con)
▸ **bristle with** *vt insep (be full of)* estar lleno(a) de

Brit [brɪt] *n Fam* británico(a) *m,f*

Britain [ˈbrɪtən] *n* (**Great**) **B.** Gran Bretaña

British [ˈbrɪtɪʃ] **1** *adj* británico(a); **the B. Isles** las Islas Británicas **2** *npl* **the B.** los británicos

brittle [ˈbrɪtəl] *adj* quebradizo(a), frágil

broach [brəʊtʃ] *vt (subject)* abordar

broad [brɔːd] **1** *adj* (**a**) *(wide)* ancho(a); *(large)* extenso(a) (**b**) **a b. hint** *(clear)* una indirecta clara (**c**) *(daylight)* pleno(a) (**d**) *(not detailed)* general (**e**) *(accent)* marcado(a), cerrado(a) **2** *n US Fam (woman)* tía *f*, chica *f*

broadcast [ˈbrɔːdkɑːst] *Rad & TV* **1** *n* emisión *f* **2** *vt (pt & pp* **broadcast**) emitir, transmitir

broadcaster [ˈbrɔːdkɑːstə(r)] *n* locutor(a) *m,f*

broadcasting [ˈbrɔːdkɑːstɪŋ] *n Rad* radiodifusión *f*; *TV* transmisión *f*; *Rad* **b. station** emisora *f*

broaden [ˈbrɔːdən] *vt* ensanchar

broadly [ˈbrɔːdlɪ] *adv* en términos generales

broad-minded [brɔːdˈmaɪndɪd] *adj* liberal, tolerante

broadsheet [ˈbrɔːdʃiːt] *n* folleto *m*

broccoli [ˈbrɒkəlɪ] *n* brécol *m*

brochure [ˈbrəʊʃə(r), ˈbrəʊʃʊə(r)] *n* folleto *m*

broil [brɔɪl] *vt US* asar a la parrilla

broiler [ˈbrɔɪlə(r)] *n* (**a**) *(chicken)* pollo *m* (tomatero) (**b**) *US (grill)* parrilla *f*

broke [brəʊk] **1** *adj Fam* **to be (flat) b.** estar sin blanca
2 *pt of* **break**

broken [ˈbrəʊkən] **1** *adj* (**a**) roto(a); *(machinery)* averiado(a); *(leg)* fracturado(a) (**b**) *(home)* deshecho(a); *(person)* destrozado(a); *(ground)* accidentado(a); **to speak b. English** chapurrear el inglés
2 *pp of* **break**

broken-hearted [brəʊkənˈhɑːtɪd] *adj Fig* con el corazón destrozado

broker [ˈbrəʊkə(r)] *n* corredor *m*, agente *mf* de Bolsa

brolly [ˈbrɒlɪ] *n Fam* paraguas *m inv*

bronchitis [brɒŋˈkaɪtɪs] *n* bronquitis *f*

bronze [brɒnz] **1** *n* bronce *m*
2 *adj (material)* de bronce; *(colour)* bronceado(a)

bronzed [brɒnzd] *adj (suntanned)* bronceado(a)

brooch [brəʊtʃ] *n* broche *m*

brood [bruːd] **1** *n (birds)* cría *f*; *Hum (children)* prole *m*
2 *vi (hen)* empollar; *Fig (ponder)* rumiar; *Fig* **to b. over a problem** darle vueltas a un problema

broody [ˈbruːdɪ] *adj* (**a**) *Fam (woman)* con ganas de tener hijos (**b**) *(pensive)* pensativo(a) (**c**) *(moody)* melancólico(a)

brook¹ [brʊk] *n* arroyo *m*

brook² [brʊk] *vt (usu in negative)* soportar, aguantar

broom [bruːm] *n* (**a**) escoba *f* (**b**) *Bot* retama *f*

broomstick [ˈbruːmstɪk] *n* palo *m* de escoba

Bros *Com (abbr* **Brothers**) Hnos

broth [brɒθ] *n* caldo *m*

brothel [ˈbrɒθəl] *n* burdel *m*

brother [ˈbrʌðə(r)] *n* hermano *m*; **brothers and sisters** hermanos

brotherhood [ˈbrʌðəhʊd] *n* hermandad *f*

brother-in-law [ˈbrʌðərɪnlɔː] *n* cuñado *m*

brotherly [ˈbrʌðəlɪ] *adj* fraternal

brought [brɔːt] *pt & pp of* **bring**

brow [braʊ] *n* (**a**) *(forehead)* frente *f* (**b**) *(eyebrow)* ceja *f* (**c**) *(of hill)* cima *f*

brown [braʊn] **1** *adj* (**a**) marrón; *(hair, eyes)* castaño(a); **b. bread** pan *m* integral; **b. paper** papel *m* de estraza; **b. sugar** azúcar moreno (**b**) *(tanned)* moreno(a)
2 *n* marrón *m*
3 *vt Culin* dorar; *(tan)* broncear

Brownie [ˈbraʊnɪ] *n* niña exploradora

brownish [ˈbraʊnɪʃ] *adj* pardusco(a)

browse [braʊz] **1** *vi (in shop)* mirar; *(through book)* hojear
2 *vt Comput* **to b. the Web** navegar por la Web
3 *n* **to have a b. (in)** dar un vistazo (a)

browser [ˈbraʊzə(r)] *n Comput* navegador *m*

bruise [bruːz] **1** *n* morado *m*, cardenal *m*
2 *vt (body)* contusionar; *(fruit)* estropear
3 *vi (body)* magullarse; *(fruit)* estropearse

brunch [brʌntʃ] *n* = combinación de desayuno y almuerzo

brunette [bruːˈnet] *adj & n* morena *(f)*

brunt [brʌnt] *n* **the b.** lo peor; **to bear the b.** llevar el peso

brush¹ [brʌʃ] **1** *n* (**a**) *(for hair, teeth)* cepillo *m*; *Art* pincel *m*; *(for housepainting)* brocha *f* (**b**) *(with the law)* roce *m*
2 *vt* (**a**) cepillar; **to b. one's hair** cepillarse el pelo; **to b. one's teeth** cepillarse los dientes (**b**) *(touch lightly)* rozar
3 *vi* **to b. against** rozar al pasar
▸ **brush aside** *vt sep* dejar de lado
▸ **brush off** *vt sep* ignorar
▸ **brush up** *vt sep* repasar

brush² [brʌʃ] *n (undergrowth)* broza *f*, maleza *f*

brushwood [ˈbrʌʃwʊd] *n* maleza *f*

brusque [bruːsk, brʊsk] *adj* brusco(a); *(words)* áspero(a)

Brussels [ˈbrʌsəlz] *n* Bruselas

brutal [ˈbruːtəl] *adj* brutal, cruel

brute [bruːt] **1** *adj* bruto(a); **b. force** fuerza bruta
2 *n (animal)* bruto *m*; *(person)* bestia *f*

BSc [biːesˈsiː] *n (abbr* **Bachelor of Science**) *(person)* licenciado(a) *m,f* en Ciencias

bubble [ˈbʌbəl] **1** *n* burbuja *f*; **b. bath** espuma *f* de baño; **b. gum** chicle *m*; **soap b.** pompa *f* de jabón
2 *vi* burbujear; *Culin* borbotear

bubbly [ˈbʌblɪ] **1** *adj* (**bubblier, bubbliest**) efervescente
2 *n Fam* champán *m*, cava *m*

buck¹ [bʌk] **1** *n Zool* macho *m*; *(male deer)* ciervo *m*; *(male goat)* macho cabrío; *Fam* **to pass the b. to sb** echarle el muerto a algn
2 *vi (horse)* corcovear
▸ **buck up 1** *vt sep Fam* **b. your ideas up!** ¡espabílate!
2 *vi (cheer up)* animarse

buck² [bʌk] *n US Fam* dólar *m*

bucket [ˈbʌkɪt] **1** *n* cubo *m*; *Fam* **it rained buckets** llovía a cántaros
2 *vi Fam (rain)* llover a cántaros
buckle [ˈbʌkəl] **1** *n* hebilla *f*
2 *vt* abrochar con hebilla
3 *vi* (**a**) *(wall, metal)* combarse (**b**) *(knees)* doblarse
bud [bʌd] **1** *n (shoot)* brote *m*; *(flower)* capullo *m*
2 *vi* brotar; *Fig* florecer
Buddhism [ˈbʊdɪzəm] *n* budismo *m*
budding [ˈbʌdɪŋ] *adj* en ciernes
buddy [ˈbʌdɪ] *n US Fam* amigote *m*, compinche *m*
budge [bʌdʒ] *vi* (**a**) *(move)* moverse (**b**) *(yield)* ceder
budgerigar [ˈbʌdʒərɪgɑː(r)] *n* periquito *m*
budget [ˈbʌdʒɪt] **1** *n* presupuesto *m*; *Br Pol* **the B.** ≃ los Presupuestos Generales del Estado
2 *vi* hacer un presupuesto (**for** para)
budgie [ˈbʌdʒɪ] *n Fam* = budgerigar
buff¹ [bʌf] **1** *adj & n (colour)* color *(m)* de ante
2 *vt* dar brillo a
buff² [bʌf] *n Fam (enthusiast)* aficionado(a) *m,f*
buffalo [ˈbʌfələʊ] *n (pl* **buffaloes** *or* **buffalo***)* búfalo *m*
buffer [ˈbʌfə(r)] **1** *n* (**a**) *(device)* amortiguador *m*; *Rail* tope *m*; **b. zone** zona *f* de seguridad (**b**) *Comput* memoria intermedia
2 *vt* amortiguar
buffet¹ [ˈbʊfeɪ] *n* (**a**) *(snack bar)* bar *m*; *(at railway station)* cantina *f*; *Rail* **b. car** coche *m* restaurante (**b**) *(self-service meal)* bufet *m* libre (**c**) *(item of furniture)* aparador *m*
buffet² [ˈbʌfɪt] *vt* golpear
buffoon [bəˈfuːn] *n* bufón *m*, payaso *m*
bug [bʌg] **1** *n* (**a**) *(insect)* bicho *m* (**b**) *Fam (microbe)* microbio *m*; **the flu b.** el virus de la gripe (**c**) *(hidden microphone)* micrófono oculto (**d**) *Comput* error *m*
2 *vt Fam* (**a**) **to b. a room** ocultar micrófonos en una habitación; **to b. a phone** pinchar un teléfono (**b**) *(annoy)* fastidiar, molestar
bugger [ˈbʌgə(r)] **1** *n* (**a**) sodomita *m* (**b**) *very Fam Pej (person)* gilipollas *mf inv*; *(thing)* coñazo *m*; **poor b.!** ¡el pobre!
2 *interj very Fam Pej* ¡joder!
3 *vt* sodomizar
▶ **bugger about** *very Fam* **1** *vi* hacer chorradas
2 *vt sep* **they really buggered him about**

se las hicieron pasar canutas
▶ **bugger off** *vi very Fam Pej* pirarse; **b. off!** ¡vete a la mierda!
▶ **bugger up** *vt sep very Fam* jorobar
buggy [ˈbʌgɪ] *n* (**a**) *Br (baby's pushchair)* cochecito *m* de niño (**b**) *US (pram)* cochecito *m* (de niño)
bugle [ˈbjuːgəl] *n* bugle *m*
build [bɪld] **1** *vt (pt & pp* **built***)* construir
2 *n (physique)* tipo *m*, físico *m*
▶ **build up** *vt sep (accumulate)* acumular; **to b. up a reputation** labrarse una buena reputación
builder [ˈbɪldə(r)] *n* constructor(a) *m,f*; *(contractor)* contratista *mf*
building [ˈbɪldɪŋ] *n* edificio *m*, construcción *f*; **b. site** obra *f*; **b. society** sociedad hipotecaria
build-up [ˈbɪldʌp] *n* (**a**) *(accumulation)* aumento *m*; *(of gas)* acumulación *f* (**b**) *(publicity)* propaganda *f*
built [bɪlt] *pt & pp of* build
built-in [ˈbɪltˈɪn] *adj* (**a**) *(cupboard)* empotrado(a) (**b**) *(incorporated)* incorporado(a)
built-up [bɪltˈʌp] *adj* urbanizado(a)
bulb [bʌlb] *n* (**a**) *Bot* bulbo *m* (**b**) *(light bulb)* bombilla *f*
Bulgaria [bʌlˈgeərɪə] *n* Bulgaria
Bulgarian [bʌlˈgeərɪən] **1** *adj* búlgaro(a)
2 *n* (**a**) *(person)* búlgaro(a) *m,f* (**b**) *(language)* búlgaro *m*
bulge [bʌldʒ] **1** *n* protuberancia *f*; *(in pocket)* bulto *m*
2 *vi (swell)* hincharse; *(be full)* estar repleto(a)
bulk [bʌlk] *n* (**a**) *(mass)* masa *f*, volumen *m*; *Com* **in b.** a granel; **to buy sth in b.** comprar algo al por mayor (**b**) *(greater part)* mayor parte *f*
bulky [ˈbʌlkɪ] *adj* (**bulkier, bulkiest**) (**a**) *(large)* voluminoso(a) (**b**) **this crate is rather b.** esta caja es un armatoste
bull [bʊl] *n* (**a**) toro *m*; *Fig* **to take the b. by the horns** coger al toro por los cuernos (**b**) *Fin* **b. market** mercado *m* al alza
bulldog [ˈbʊldɒg] *n* buldog *m*
bulldoze [ˈbʊldəʊz] *vt (land)* nivelar; *(building)* derribar
bulldozer [ˈbʊldəʊzə(r)] *n* bulldozer *m*
bullet [ˈbʊlɪt] *n* bala *f*; **b. wound** balazo *m*
bulletin [ˈbʊlɪtɪn] *n* boletín *m*; *Rad & TV* **news b.** boletín de noticias; *US* **b. board** tablón *m* de anuncios
bullet-proof [ˈbʊlɪtpruːf] *adj* a prueba de balas; **b. vest** chaleco *m* antibalas
bullfight [ˈbʊlfaɪt] *n* corrida *f* de toros
bullfighter [ˈbʊlfaɪtə(r)] *n* torero(a) *m,f*

bullfighting ['bʊlfaɪtɪŋ] *n* los toros *mpl*; *(art)* tauromaquia *f*

bullion ['bʊljən] *n (gold, silver)* lingote *m*

bullish ['bʊlɪʃ] *adj Fin (market)* en alza

bullock ['bʊlək] *n* buey *m*

bullring ['bʊlrɪŋ] *n* plaza *f* de toros

bull's-eye ['bʊlzaɪ] *n (of target)* blanco *m*

bully ['bʊlɪ] **1** *n* matón *m*

  2 *vt (terrorize)* intimidar; *(bulldoze)* tiranizar

  3 *interj Ironic* b. for you! ¡bravo!

bulwark ['bʊlwək] *n* baluarte *m*

bum¹ [bʌm] *n Fam (bottom)* culo *m*

bum² [bʌm] *Fam* **1** *n* (**a**) *US (tramp)* vagabundo *m* (**b**) *(idler)* holgazán(ana) *m,f*

  2 *vi* gorronear

  ► **bum around** *vi Fam* vaguear

bumblebee ['bʌmbəlbiː] *n* abejorro *m*

bumbling ['bʌmblɪŋ] *adj* torpe

bump [bʌmp] **1** *n* (**a**) *(swelling)* chichón *m*; *(lump)* abolladura *f*; *(on road)* bache *m* (**b**) *(blow)* choque *m*, golpe *m* (**c**) *(jolt)* sacudida *f*

  2 *vt* golpear; **to b. one's head** darse un golpe en la cabeza

  3 *vi* chocar (**into** contra)

  ► **bump into** *vt insep (meet)* tropezar con

  ► **bump off** *vt sep Fam* liquidar

bumper ['bʌmpə(r)] **1** *adj* abundante; **b. edition** edición *f* especial

  2 *n Aut* parachoques *m inv*

bumptious ['bʌmpʃəs] *adj* presuntuoso(a), engreído(a)

bumpy ['bʌmpɪ] *adj* (**bumpier, bumpiest**) con muchos baches

bun [bʌn] *n* (**a**) *(bread)* panecillo *m*; *(sweet)* bollo *m*; *Fig Euph* **she's got a b. in the oven** está preñada (**b**) *(of hair)* moño *m*

bunch [bʌntʃ] **1** *n (of keys)* manojo *m*; *(of flowers)* ramo *m*; *(of grapes)* racimo *m*; *(of people)* grupo *m*; *(gang)* pandilla *f*

  2 *vi* **to b. together** juntarse, agruparse

bundle ['bʌndəl] **1** *n (of clothes)* bulto *m*, fardo *m*; *(of papers)* fajo *m*; *(of wood)* haz *m*

  2 *vt* (**a**) *(make a bundle of)* liar, atar (**b**) *(push)* empujar

bung [bʌŋ] **1** *n* tapón *m*

  2 *vt Fam* (**a**) *(throw)* arrojar (**b**) *(put)* meter

  ► **bung up** *vt sep Fam* atascar

bungalow ['bʌŋgələʊ] *n* chalé *m*, bungalow *m*

bungle ['bʌŋgəl] *vt* chapucear

bunion ['bʌnjən] *n* juanete *m*

bunk [bʌŋk] *n (bed)* litera *f*

bunker ['bʌŋkə(r)] *n* (**a**) *(coal)* carbonera *f* (**b**) *Mil* búnker *m* (**c**) *(in golf)* búnker *m*

bunny ['bʌnɪ] *n Fam (baby talk)* **b. (rabbit)** conejito *m*

bunting ['bʌntɪŋ] *n (material)* lanilla *f*; *(flags)* banderines *mpl*; *Naut* empavesada *f*

buoy [bɔɪ] *n* boya *f*

  ► **buoy up** *vt sep* (**a**) *(keep afloat)* mantener a flote (**b**) *(person, spirits)* alentar, animar

buoyancy ['bɔɪənsɪ] *n* (**a**) *(of object)* flotabilidad *f* (**b**) *Fin* tendencia *f* alcista (**c**) *(optimism)* optimismo *m*

buoyant ['bɔɪənt] *adj* (**a**) *(object)* flotante (**b**) *Fin* con tendencia alcista (**c**) *(optimistic)* optimista

burble ['bɜːbəl] *vi* (**a**) *(stream)* murmurar; *(baby)* balbucear (**b**) *(talk quickly)* farfullar

burden ['bɜːdən] **1** *n* carga *f*; *Fig* **to be a b. to sb** ser una carga para algn

  2 *vt* cargar (**with** con)

bureau ['bjʊərəʊ] *n* (*pl* **bureaux**) (**a**) *(desk)* escritorio *m* (**b**) *(office)* agencia *f*, oficina *f* (**c**) *US (chest of drawers)* cómoda *f* (**d**) *US Pol* departamento *m* del Estado

bureaucracy [bjʊəˈrɒkrəsɪ] *n* burocracia *f*

bureaucrat ['bjʊərəkræt] *n* burócrata *mf*

bureaucratic [bjʊərəˈkrætɪk] *adj* burocrático(a)

burgeon ['bɜːdʒən] *vi* florecer

burger ['bɜːgə(r)] *n Fam (hamburger)* hamburguesa *f*

burglar ['bɜːglə(r)] *n* ladrón(ona) *m,f*; **b. alarm** alarma *f* antirrobo

burglarize ['bɜːgləraɪz] *vt US* robar, desvalijar

burglary ['bɜːglərɪ] *n* robo *m* con allanamiento de morada

burgle ['bɜːgəl] *vt* robar, desvalijar

burial ['berɪəl] *n* entierro *m*

burly ['bɜːlɪ] *adj* (**burlier, burliest**) fornido(a), fuerte

Burma ['bɜːmə] *n* Birmania

Burmese [bɜːˈmiːz] **1** *adj* birmano(a)

  2 *n* (**a**) *(person)* birmano(a) *m,f* (**b**) *(language)* birmano *m*

burn [bɜːn] **1** *n* quemadura *f*

  2 *vt* (*pt & pp* **burnt** *or* **burned**) quemar

  3 *vi* (**a**) *(fire)* arder; *(building, food)* quemarse (**b**) *(lamp)* estar encendido(a) (**c**) *(sore)* escocer

  ► **burn down 1** *vt sep* incendiar

  2 *vi* incendiarse

  ► **burn out** *vi (people)* quemarse

▸ **burn up** *vt sep (energy, calories)* quemar

burner ['bɜːnə(r)] *n* quemador *m*

burning ['bɜːnɪŋ] *adj* (**a**) *(on fire)* incendiado(a); *(hot)* abrasador(a) (**b**) *(passionate)* ardiente (**c**) **a b. question** una cuestión candente

burnt [bɜːnt] **1** *adj* quemado(a); **b. almonds** almendras tostadas
2 *pt & pp of* **burn**

burp [bɜːp] **1** *n* eructo *m*
2 *vi* eructar

burrow ['bʌrəʊ] **1** *n* madriguera *f*; *(for rabbits)* conejera *f*
2 *vi* (**a**) hacer una madriguera (**b**) *(search)* hurgar

bursar ['bɜːsə(r)] *n* tesorero(a) *m,f*

bursary ['bɜːsərɪ] *n* beca *f*

burst [bɜːst] **1** *n* (**a**) *(explosion)* estallido *m*; *(of tyre)* reventón *m* (**b**) *(of applause)* arranque *m*; *(rage)* arrebato *m*; **b. of gunfire** ráfaga *f* de tiros; **b. of laughter** carcajadas *fpl*
2 *vt* (*pt & pp* **burst**) *(balloon)* reventar; *Fig* **the river b. its banks** el río se salió de madre
3 *vi* (**a**) reventarse; *(shell)* estallar (**b**) *(enter suddenly)* irrumpir (**into** en)
▸ **burst into** *vt insep* **to b. into laughter/tears** echarse a reír/allorar
▸ **burst open** *vi* abrirse violentamente
▸ **burst out** *vi* **to b. out laughing** echarse a reír

bursting ['bɜːstɪŋ] *adj* **the bar was b. with people** el bar estaba atestado de gente; *Fam* **to be b. to do sth** reventar por hacer algo

bury ['berɪ] *vt* (**a**) enterrar; **to be buried in thought** estar absorto en pensamientos (**b**) *(hide)* ocultar

bus [bʌs] *n* (*pl* **buses**, *US* **busses**) autobús *m*, *Andes, CAm, Ven* buseta *f*, *Arg* colectivo *m*, *CAm, Méx* camión *m*, *Chile* micro *m*, *Cuba* guagua *f*, *Urug* ómnibus *m*; **b. conductor** revisor *m*; **b. driver** conductor(a) *m,f*; **b. stop** parada *f* de autobús

bush [bʊʃ] *n* (**a**) *(shrub)* arbusto *m* (**b**) *Austral* **the b.** el monte; *Fam* **b. telegraph** radio *f* macuto

bushy ['bʊʃɪ] *adj* espeso(a), tupido(a)

business ['bɪznɪs] *n* (**a**) *(commerce)* negocios *mpl*; **how's b.?** ¿cómo andan los negocios?; **to be away on b.** estar en viaje de negocios; **b. deal** negocio *m*; **b. hours** horas *fpl* de oficina; **b. trip** viaje *m* de negocios (**b**) *(firm)* empresa *f* (**c**) *(matter)* asunto *m*; **I mean b.** estoy hablando en serio; **it's no b. of mine** no es asunto mío; **to make it one's b. to ...**

encargarse de ...; **to get down to b.** ir al grano; **to go about one's b.** ocuparse de sus asuntos

businesslike ['bɪznɪslaɪk] *adj (practical)* eficiente; *(methodical)* metódico(a); *(serious)* serio(a)

businessman ['bɪznɪsmən] *n* hombre *m* de negocios

businesswoman ['bɪznɪswʊmən] *n* mujer *f* de negocios

busker ['bʌskə(r)] *n Fam* músico(a) *m,f* callejero(a)

bust¹ [bʌst] *n* (**a**) *(of woman)* pecho *m* (**b**) *Art* busto *m*

bust² [bʌst] *Fam* **1** *vt* (**a**) estropear (**b**) *(person)* trincar; *(place)* hacer una redada en
2 *adj* (**a**) *(damaged)* estropeado(a) (**b**) **to go b.** *(bankrupt)* quebrar

bustle ['bʌsəl] **1** *n (activity, noise)* bullicio *m*
2 *vi* **to b. about** ir y venir

bustling ['bʌslɪŋ] *adj* bullicioso(a)

bust-up ['bʌstʌp] *n Fam* riña *f*, pelea *f*

busy ['bɪzɪ] **1** *adj* (**a**) ocupado(a), atareado(a); *(life)* ajetreado(a); *(street)* concurrido(a) (**b**) *esp US Tel* ocupado(a); **b. signal** señal *f* de comunicando
2 *vt* **to b. oneself doing sth** ocuparse haciendo algo

busybody ['bɪzɪbɒdɪ] *n* entrometido(a) *m,f*

but [bʌt] **1** *conj* (**a**) pero; **b. yet** a pesar de todo (**b**) *(after negative)* sino; **not two b. three** no dos sino tres; **she's not Spanish b. Portuguese** no es española sino portuguesa
2 *adv* **had we b. known** de haberlo sabido; **we can b. try** al menos podemos intentarlo; **b. for her we would have drowned** si no hubiera sido por ella, nos habríamos ahogado
3 *prep* salvo, menos; **everyone b. her** todos menos ella; **he's anything b. handsome** es todo menos guapo
4 *npl* **ifs and buts** pegas *fpl*

butane ['bjuːteɪn] *n* butano *m*; **b. gas** gas butano

butcher ['bʊtʃə(r)] **1** *n* carnicero(a) *m,f*; **b.'s (shop)** carnicería *f*
2 *vt (animals)* matar; *(people)* masacrar

butler ['bʌtlə(r)] *n* mayordomo *m*

butt¹ [bʌt] *n* (**a**) *(end)* extremo *m*; *(of rifle)* culata *f*; *(of cigarette)* colilla *f* (**b**) **he was the b. of all the jokes** era el blanco de todas las bromas (**c**) *US Fam (bottom)* culo *m*

butt² [bʌt] **1** *n (with head)* cabezazo *m*

2 *vt (strike with head)* dar un cabezazo a
▸ **butt in** *vi* entrar en la conversación
butt³ [bʌt] *n (barrel)* tonel *m*
butter ['bʌtə(r)] **1** *n* mantequilla *f, Am*
manteca *f*; **b. dish** mantequera *f*
　2 *vt* untar con mantequilla *or Am* manteca
buttercup ['bʌtəkʌp] *n* ranúnculo *m*,
botón *m* de oro
butterfingers ['bʌtəfɪŋgəz] *n sing Fam*
manazas *mf inv*
butterfly ['bʌtəflaɪ] *n* mariposa *f*
buttock ['bʌtək] *n* nalga *f*; **buttocks** nalgas *fpl*
button ['bʌtən] **1** *n* (**a**) *(on clothes, machine)* botón *m* (**b**) *US (badge)* chapa *f*
　2 *vt* **to b. (up)** abrochar(se), abotonar(se)
buttonhole ['bʌtənhəʊl] *n* ojal *m*
buttress ['bʌtrɪs] **1** *n* (**a**) contrafuerte *m*
(**b**) *(support)* apoyo *m*
　2 *vt* apuntalar; *Fig* reforzar, apoyar
buxom ['bʌksəm] *adj (woman)* pechugona
buy [baɪ] **1** *n* compra *f*; **a good b.** una
ganga
　2 *vt (pt & pp* **bought**) (**a**) comprar; **she
bought that car from a neighbour**
compró ese coche a un vecino (**b**) *Fam
(believe)* tragar
▸ **buy off** *vt sep* sobornar
▸ **buy out** *vt sep* adquirir la parte de
▸ **buy up** *vt sep* comprar en grandes cantidades
buyer ['baɪə(r)] *n* comprador(a) *m,f*
buzz [bʌz] **1** *n* (**a**) *(of bee)* zumbido *m*; *(of
conversation)* rumor *m* (**b**) *Fam (telephone call)* telefonazo *m*
　2 *vi* zumbar
buzzer ['bʌzə(r)] *n* timbre *m*
by [baɪ] **1** *prep* (**a**) *(indicating agent)* por;
composed by Bach compuesto(a) por
Bach; **a film by Almodóvar** una película
de Almodóvar
　(**b**) *(via)* por; **he left by the back door**
salió por la puerta trasera
　(**c**) *(manner)* por; **by car/train** en coche/
tren; **by credit card** con tarjeta de crédito;
by chance por casualidad; **by oneself**
solo(a); **made by hand** hecho(a) a mano;
**you can obtain a ticket by filling in the
coupon** puede conseguir una entrada
llenando el cupón
　(**d**) *(amount)* por; **little by little** poco a
poco; **they are sold by the dozen** se

venden por docenas; **to be paid by the
hour** cobrar por horas
　(**e**) **by far** con mucho; **he won by a foot**
ganó por un pie
　(**f**) *(beside)* al lado de, junto a; **side by
side** juntos
　(**g**) **to walk by a building** *(pass)* pasar
por delante de un edificio
　(**h**) *(time)* para; **by now** ya; **by then** para
entonces; **we have to be there by nine**
tenemos que estar allí para las nueve; **by
the time we arrive** (para) cuando lleguemos; **by this time next year** el año que
viene por estas fechas
　(**i**) *(during)* de; **by day/night** de día/
noche
　(**j**) *(in an oath)* por; **by God!** ¡por Dios!
　(**k**) *Math* por
　(**l**) *(according to)* según; **is that O.K. by
you?** ¿te viene bien?
　(**m**) **he had two children by his first
wife** tuvo dos hijos con su primera esposa
　(**n**) *(phrases)* **bit by bit** poco a poco; **day
by day** día a día; **what do you mean by
that?** ¿qué quieres decir con eso?; **by the
way** a propósito
　2 *adv* (**a**) **to go by** *(past)* pasar; **she just
walked by** pasó de largo
　(**b**) **by and by** con el tiempo; **by and
large** en conjunto
bye [baɪ] **1** *n* **by the b.** por cierto
　2 *interj Fam* ¡hasta luego!
bye-bye ['baɪ'baɪ] *interj Fam* ¡adiós!,
¡hasta luego!
by-election ['baɪɪlekʃən] *n* elección *f*
parcial
bygone ['baɪgɒn] **1** *adj* pasado(a)
　2 *npl* **let bygones be bygones** lo pasado
pasado está
by-law ['baɪlɔ:] *n* ley *f* municipal
bypass ['baɪpɑ:s] **1** *n* (**a**) *(road)* carretera
f de circunvalación (**b**) *Med* **b. surgery**
cirugía *f* de by-pass
　2 *vt* evitar
by-product ['baɪprɒdʌkt] *n Chem & Ind*
derivado *m*, subproducto *m*; *Fig* consecuencia *f*
byroad ['baɪrəʊd] *n* carretera secundaria
bystander ['baɪstændə(r)] *n* testigo *mf*
byte [baɪt] *n Comput* byte *m*, octeto *m*
byword ['baɪwɜ:d] *n* **it became a b. for
modernity** se convirtió en sinónimo de
modernidad

C, c [siː] *n* (**a**) *(the letter)* C, c *f* (**b**) *Mus* **C** do *m*

C (**a**) *(abbr* **Celsius**) C (**b**) *(abbr* **centigrade**) C

cab [kæb] *n US* taxi *m*; **c. driver** taxista *mf*

cabaret [ˈkæbəreɪ] *n* cabaret *m*

cabbage [ˈkæbɪdʒ] *n* col *f*, berza *f*; **red c.** (col) lombarda *f*

cabin [ˈkæbɪn] *n* (**a**) *(hut)* choza *f*; **log c.** cabaña *f* (**b**) *Naut* camarote *m* (**c**) *(of lorry, plane)* cabina *f*

cabinet [ˈkæbɪnɪt] *n* (**a**) *(item of furniture)* armario *m*; *(glass-fronted)* vitrina *f*; **c. maker** ebanista *mf* (**b**) *Pol* gabinete *m*, consejo *m* de ministros

cable [ˈkeɪbəl] **1** *n* cable *m*; **c. car** teleférico *m*; **c. company** cableoperador(a) *m,f*; **c. TV** televisión *f* por cable
2 *vt & vi* cablegrafiar, telegrafiar

caboose [kəˈbuːs] *n US (on train)* furgón *m* de cola

cache [kæʃ] *n* (**a**) *(place)* alijo *m* (**b**) *Comput* caché *f*

cackle [ˈkækəl] *vi* cacarear

cactus [ˈkæktəs] *n (pl* **cacti** [ˈkæktaɪ]) cactus *m*

CAD [kæd] *n (abbr* **computer-aided or -assisted design**) CAD *m*

cad [kæd] *n Br Fam* canalla *m*

caddie [ˈkædɪ] *n (in golf)* cadi *m*

cadet [kəˈdet] *n Mil* cadete *m*

cadge [kædʒ] *vt & vi Fam* gorronear

Caesarean [siːˈzeərɪən] *n Med* **she had a C.** le hicieron una cesárea; **C. section** operación *f* cesárea

café [ˈkæfeɪ], **cafeteria** [kæfɪˈtɪərɪə] *n* cafetería *f*

caffeine [ˈkæfiːn] *n* cafeína *f*

cage [keɪdʒ] **1** *n* jaula *f*
2 *vt* enjaular

cagey [ˈkeɪdʒɪ] *adj* (**cagier, cagiest**) *Fam* reservado(a)

cagoule [kəˈguːl] *n (garment)* canguro *m*

Cairo [ˈkaɪrəʊ] *n* (el) Cairo

cajole [kəˈdʒəʊl] *vt* engatusar

cake [keɪk] **1** *n* (**a**) pastel *m*, tarta *f*; *Fam Fig* **it's a piece of c.** está chupado; **birthday c.** pastel de cumpleaños; **c. shop** pastelería *f* (**b**) *(of soap)* pastilla *f*

2 *vi (mud)* endurecerse
3 *vt* **caked with ...** cubierto(a) de ...

calamity [kəˈlæmɪtɪ] *n* calamidad *f*

calcium [ˈkælsɪəm] *n* calcio *m*

calculate [ˈkælkjʊleɪt] *vt* calcular

calculated [ˈkælkjʊleɪtɪd] *adj* intencionado(a)

calculating [ˈkælkjʊleɪtɪŋ] *adj* (**a**) **c. machine** calculadora *f* (**b**) *Pej (person)* calculador(a)

calculation [kælkjʊˈleɪʃən] *n* cálculo *m*

calculator [ˈkælkjʊleɪtə(r)] *n* calculadora *f*

calendar [ˈkælɪndə(r)] *n* calendario *m*; **c. year** año *m* civil

calf[1] [kɑːf] *n (pl* **calves**) *(of cattle)* becerro(a) *m,f*, ternero(a) *m,f*; *(of other animals)* cría *f*

calf[2] [kɑːf] *n (pl* **calves**) *Anat* pantorrilla *f*

calfskin [ˈkɑːfskɪn] *n* piel *f* de becerro

calibre, *US* **caliber** [ˈkælɪbə(r)] *n* calibre *m*

call [kɔːl] **1** *vt* (**a**) llamar; **to c. sb names** poner verde a algn; **what's he called?** ¿cómo se llama?
(**b**) *(meeting etc)* convocar; **to c. sth to mind** traer algo a la memoria
2 *vi* (**a**) llamar; *Tel* **who's calling?** ¿de parte de quién?
(**b**) **to c. at sb's (house)** pasar por casa de algn; **to c. for sth/sb** pasar a recoger algo/a algn
(**c**) *(trains)* parar
(**d**) **to c. for** *(require)* exigir; **that wasn't called for** eso no estaba justificado
3 *n* (**a**) llamada *f*, grito *m*
(**b**) *(visit)* visita *f*; **to pay a c. on sb** visitar a algn
(**c**) *Tel* **(phone) c.** llamada *f*, *Am* llamado *m*; **c. box** cabina telefónica; **c. centre** centro *m* de atención telefónica
(**d**) *Med* **to be on c.** estar de guardia
(**e**) **there's no c. for you to worry** no hay motivo para que te preocupes

▸ **call away** *vt sep* **to be called away on business** tener que ausentarse por motivos de trabajo

▸ **call back** *vi (phone again)* llamar otra vez; *(visit again)* volver

▸ **call in 1** *vt sep (doctor)* llamar
2 *vi* (**a**) **I'll c. in tomorrow** *(visit)* mañana me paso (**b**) *Naut* hacer escala (**at** en)
▸ **call off** *vt sep* suspender
▸ **call on** *vt insep* (**a**) visitar (**b**) **to c. on sb for support** recurrir a algn en busca de apoyo
▸ **call out 1** *vt sep* (**a**) *(shout)* gritar (**b**) *(doctor)* hacer venir; *(workers)* convocar a la huelga
2 *vi* gritar
▸ **call up** *vt sep* (**a**) *Tel* llamar (por teléfono) (**b**) *Mil* llamar a filas, reclutar
caller ['kɔːlə(r)] *n* visita *mf*; *Tel* persona *f* que llama
calling ['kɔːlɪŋ] *n esp Rel* llamada *f*, vocación *f*; *US* **c. card** tarjeta *f* de visita;
callous ['kæləs] *adj* insensible, duro(a)
call-up ['kɔːlʌp] *n* llamamiento *m* a filas
calm [kɑːm] **1** *adj* (**a**) *(weather, sea)* en calma (**b**) *(relaxed)* tranquilo(a); **keep c.!** ¡tranquilo(a)!
2 *n* (**a**) *(of weather, sea)* calma *f* (**b**) *(tranquillity)* tranquilidad *f*
3 *vt* calmar, tranquilizar
4 *vi* **to c. (down)** calmarse, tranquilizarse
Calor Gas® ['kæləgæs] *n* (gas *m*) butano *m*
calorie, calory ['kælərɪ] *n* caloría *f*
calve [kɑːv] *vi (cow)* parir (un becerro)
calves [kɑːvz] *pl of* **calf¹, calf²**
Cambodia [kæm'bəʊdɪə] *n* Camboya
came [keɪm] *pt of* **come**
camel ['kæməl] *n* camello(a) *m,f*
cameo ['kæmɪəʊ] *n* camafeo *m*
camera ['kæmərə] *n* (**a**) cámara *f or* máquina *f* fotográfica; *Cin & TV* cámara (**b**) *Jur* **in c.** a puerta cerrada
cameraman ['kæmərəmən] *n* cámara *m*
Cameroon [kæmə'ruːn] *n* Camerún
camomile ['kæməmaɪl] *n* camomila *f*; **c. tea** (infusión *f* de) manzanilla *f*
camouflage ['kæməflɑːʒ] **1** *n* camuflaje *m*
2 *vt* camuflar
camp¹ [kæmp] **1** *n* campamento *m*; **c. bed** cama *f* plegable; **c. site** camping *m*
2 *vi* **to go camping** ir de camping
camp² [kæmp] *adj Fam* afeminado(a); *(affected)* amanerado(a)
campaign [kæm'peɪn] **1** *n* campaña *f*
2 *vi* **to c. for/against** hacer campaña a favor de/en contra de
campaigner [kæm'peɪnə(r)] *n* defensor(a) *m,f* (**for** de)
camper ['kæmpə(r)] *n* (**a**) *(person)* campista *mf* (**b**) *US (vehicle)* caravana *f*

camping ['kæmpɪŋ] *n* **c. ground, c. site** camping *m*
campus ['kæmpəs] *n* campus *m*, ciudad universitaria
can¹ [kæn, *unstressed* kən] *v aux (pt* **could**)

> El verbo **can** carece de infinitivo, de gerundio y de participio. En infinitivo o en participio, se empleará la forma correspondiente de **be able to**, por ejemplo: **he wanted to be able to speak English**; **she has always been able to swim**. En el inglés hablado, y en el escrito en estilo coloquial, la forma negativa **cannot** se transforma en **can't** y la forma negativa **could not** se transforma en **couldn't**.

(**a**) *(be able to)* poder; **he could have come** podría haber venido; **I'll phone you as soon as I c.** te llamaré en cuanto pueda; **she can't do it** no puede hacerlo; **I can't understand why** no entiendo por qué (**b**) *(know how to)* saber; **c. you ski?** ¿sabes esquiar?; **I can't speak English** no sé hablar inglés (**c**) *(be permitted to)* poder; **he can't go out tonight** no le dejan salir esta noche (**d**) *(be possible)* poder; **she could have forgotten** puede (ser) que lo haya olvidado; **they can't be very poor** no deben ser muy pobres; **what c. it be?** ¿qué será?
can² [kæn] **1** *n* (**a**) *(of oil)* bidón *m* (**b**) *US (tin)* lata *f*, bote *m*; **c. opener** abrelatas *m inv*
2 *vt* (**a**) *(fish, fruit)* envasar, enlatar (**b**) *US Fam* desestimar
Canada ['kænədə] *n* Canadá
Canadian [kə'neɪdɪən] *adj & n* canadiense *(mf)*
canal [kə'næl] *n* canal *m*
canary [kə'neərɪ] *n* canario *m*
Canary Islands [kə'neərɪaɪləndz] *npl* (Islas *fpl*) Canarias *fpl*
cancel ['kænsəl] *vt (train, contract)* cancelar; *Com* anular; *(permission)* retirar; *(decree)* revocar
cancellation [kænsɪ'leɪʃən] *n* cancelación *f*; *Com* anulación *f*
cancer ['kænsə(r)] *n* (**a**) *Med* cáncer *m*; **breast c.** cáncer de mama; **c. research** cancerología *f* (**b**) **C.** *(in astrology)* Cáncer *m*
candelabra [kændɪ'lɑːbrə] *n* candelabro *m*
candid ['kændɪd] *adj* franco(a), sincero(a)

> ⚠ Note that the Spanish word **cándido** is a false friend and is never a translation for the English word **candid**. In Spanish, **cándido** means "ingenuous, naïve".

candidate [ˈkændɪdeɪt, ˈkændɪdɪt] n candidato(a) m,f; (in exam) opositor(a) m,f
candle [ˈkændəl] n vela f; (in church) cirio m
candlelight [ˈkændəllaɪt] n luz f de vela; **by c.** a la luz de las velas
candlestick [ˈkændəlstɪk] n candelero m, palmatoria f; (in church) cirial m
candour, US candor [ˈkændə(r)] n sinceridad f, ranqueza f

> ⚠ Note that the Spanish word **candor** is a false friend and is never a translation for the English word **candour**. In Spanish, **candor** means "innocence, naïvety".

candy [ˈkændɪ] n US caramelo m; **c. store** confitería f
candyfloss [ˈkændɪflɒs] n Br algodón m dulce
cane [keɪn] 1 n (a) Bot caña f; **c. sugar** azúcar m de caña (b) (wicker) mimbre m (c) (walking stick) bastón m; (for punishment) palmeta f
2 vt castigar con la palmeta
canine [ˈkeɪnaɪn] adj Zool canino(a); **c. tooth** colmillo m
canister [ˈkænɪstə(r)] n bote m
canned [kænd] adj enlatado(a); **c. foods** conservas fpl
cannelloni [kænəˈləʊnɪ] n canelones mpl
cannibal [ˈkænɪbəl] adj & n caníbal (mf)
cannon [ˈkænən] 1 n (a) (pl cannons or cannon) cañón m; Fig **c. fodder** carne f de cañón (b) Br (in billiards, snooker) carambola f
2 vi chocar (into contra)
cannonball [ˈkænənbɔːl] n bala f de cañón
cannot [ˈkænɒt, kæˈnɒt] = can not
canoe [kəˈnuː] n canoa f; Sport piragua f
canon [ˈkænən] n Rel canon m
canopy [ˈkænəpɪ] n (a) (on throne) dosel m (b) (awning) toldo m
can't [kɑːnt] = can not
Cantabria [kænˈtæbrɪə] n Cantabria
cantankerous [kænˈtæŋkərəs] adj intratable
canteen [kænˈtiːn] n (a) (restaurant) cantina f (b) (set of cutlery) juego m de cubiertos (c) (flask) cantimplora f
canter [ˈkæntə(r)] 1 n medio galope
2 vi ir a medio galope
canvas [ˈkænvəs] n (a) Tex lona f (b) (painting) lienzo m
canvass [ˈkænvəs] vi (a) Pol hacer propaganda electoral (b) Com hacer promoción, buscar clientes

canvasser [ˈkænvəsə(r)] n Pol = persona que hace propaganda electoral de puerta en puerta
canyon [ˈkænjən] n cañón m; **the Grand C.** el Gran Cañón
canyoning [ˈkænjənɪŋ] n Sport barranquismo m
cap [kæp] 1 n (a) gorro m; (soldier's) gorra f (b) Br Sport **to win a c.** ser seleccionado(a) para el equipo de Inglaterra (c) (of pen) capuchón m; (of bottle) chapa f
2 vt (a) (bottle) poner la chapa a; Fig **to c. it all** para colmo (b) Br Sport seleccionar
capability [keɪpəˈbɪlɪtɪ] n habilidad f
capable [ˈkeɪpəbəl] adj (a) (skilful) hábil (b) (able) capaz (of de)
capacity [kəˈpæsɪtɪ] n (a) capacidad f (b) (position) puesto m; **in her c. as manageress** en calidad de gerente
cape¹ [keɪp] n (garment) capa f
cape² [keɪp] n Geog cabo m, promontorio m; **C. Horn** Cabo de Hornos; **C. Town** Ciudad del Cabo; **C. Verde** Cabo Verde
caper [ˈkeɪpə(r)] n (prank) travesura f
capital [ˈkæpɪtəl] 1 n (a) (town) capital f (b) Fin capital m; **c. expenditure** inversión f de capital (c) (letter) mayúscula f
2 adj (a) (city) capital (b) **c. punishment** pena f capital (c) (primary) primordial (d) **c. letter** mayúscula f
capitalism [ˈkæpɪtəlɪzəm] n capitalismo m
capitalist [ˈkæpɪtəlɪst] adj & n capitalista (mf)
capitalize [ˈkæpɪtəlaɪz] vi Fin capitalizar; Fig **to c. on sth** sacar provecho or beneficio de algo
capitulate [kəˈpɪtjʊleɪt] vi capitular
cappuccino [kæpəˈtʃiːnəʊ] n (café m) capuchino m
Capricorn [ˈkæprɪkɔːn] n Capricornio m
capsicum [ˈkæpsɪkəm] n pimiento m
capsize [kæpˈsaɪz] 1 vt hacer zozobrar
2 vi zozobrar
capsule [ˈkæpsjuːl] n cápsula f
captain [ˈkæptɪn] 1 n capitán m
2 vt capitanear
caption [ˈkæpʃən] n (under picture) leyenda f; Cin subtítulo m
captivating [ˈkæptɪveɪtɪŋ] adj seductor(a)
captive [ˈkæptɪv] 1 n cautivo(a) m,f
2 adj cautivo(a)
captivity [kæpˈtɪvɪtɪ] n cautiverio m
capture [ˈkæptʃə(r)] 1 vt (a) capturar, apresar; Mil (town) tomar (b) (market)

acaparar (**c**) *Fig (mood)* captar
  2 *n (of fugitive)* captura *f*; *(of town)* toma *f*

car [kɑː(r)] *n* (**a**) coche *m, Andes, CAm, Carib, Méx* carro *m, RP* auto *m*; **c. ferry** transbordador *m* para coches; *Br* **c. park** parking *m*, aparcamiento *m*; **c. wash** túnel *m* de lavado (**b**) *US Rail* coche *m*

carafe [kəˈræf, kəˈrɑːf] *n* garrafa *f*

caramel [ˈkærəməl] *n* azúcar *m* quemado; *(sweet)* caramelo *m*

carat [ˈkærət] *n* quilate *m*

caravan [ˈkærəvæn] *n* (**a**) *(vehicle)* remolque *m*, caravana *f* (**b**) *(in desert)* caravana *f*

carbohydrate [kɑːbəʊˈhaɪdreɪt] *n* hidrato *m* de carbono, carbohidrato *m*

carbon [ˈkɑːbən] *n* carbono *m*; **c. copy** copia *f* al papel carbón; *Fig* copia exacta; **c. dioxide** dióxido *m* de carbono; **c. paper** papel *m* carbón

carburettor [kɑːbjʊˈretə(r)], *US* **carburetor** [ˈkɑːrbəreɪtər] *n* carburador *m*

carcass [ˈkɑːkəs] *n* res muerta

card [kɑːd] *n* (**a**) tarjeta *f*; *(of cardboard)* cartulina *f*; **birthday/Christmas c.** tarjeta de cumpleaños/de Navidad (**b**) *(in file)* ficha *f*; *(identity)* carnet *m*; **c. index** fichero *m* (**c**) **pack of cards** baraja *f*, cartas *fpl*; **(playing) c.** naipe *m*, carta; *Fig Br* **on** *or US* **in the cards** previsto

cardboard [ˈkɑːdbɔːd] *n* cartón *m*; **c. box** caja *f* de carton; **c. cutout** recortable *m*

cardiac [ˈkɑːdɪæk] *adj* cardíaco(a); **c. arrest** paro cardíaco

cardigan [ˈkɑːdɪɡən] *n* rebeca *f*

cardinal [ˈkɑːdɪnəl] **1** *n Rel* cardenal *m*
  2 *adj* cardinal; **c. numbers** números *mpl* cardinales

care [keə(r)] **1** *vi (be concerned)* preocuparse (**about** por); **I don't c.** no me importa; *Fam* **for all I c.** me trae sin cuidado; *Fam* **he couldn't c. less** le importa un bledo
  2 *n* (**a**) *(attention, protection)* cuidado *m*, atención *f*; **c. of ...** *(on letter)* al cuidado de ...; **medical c.** asistencia *f* médica; **to take c. of** cuidar; *(business)* ocuparse de (**b**) *(carefulness)* cuidado *m*; **take c.** *(be careful)* ten cuidado; *(as farewell)* ¡cuídate! (**c**) *(worry)* preocupación *f*
  ▸ **care for** *vt insep* (**a**) *(look after)* cuidar (**b**) *(like)* gustar, interesar; **would you c. for a coffee?** ¿te apetece un café?

career [kəˈrɪə(r)] **1** *n* carrera *f*
  2 *vi* correr a toda velocidad

carefree [ˈkeəfriː] *adj* despreocupado(a)

careful [ˈkeəfʊl] *adj* cuidadoso(a); *(cautious)* prudente; **be c.!** ¡ojo!; **to be c.** tener cuidado

carefully [ˈkeəfʊlɪ] *adv (painstakingly)* cuidadosamente; *(cautiously)* con cuidado

careless [ˈkeəlɪs] *adj* descuidado(a); *(about clothes)* desaliñado(a); *(driving)* negligente; **a c. mistake** un descuido

carelessly [ˈkeəlɪslɪ] *adv* descuidadamente, a la ligera

carelessness [ˈkeəlɪsnɪs] *n* descuido *m*

caress [kəˈres] **1** *n* caricia *f*
  2 *vt* acariciar

caretaker [ˈkeəteɪkə(r)] *n (in school etc)* bedel *mf*; *(in block of flats)* portero(a) *m,f*

carfare [ˈkɑːrfeər] *n US* (precio *m* del) billete *m* *or Am* boleto *m*

cargo [ˈkɑːɡəʊ] *n (pl* **cargoes** *or* **cargos**) carga *f*, cargamento *m*; *Naut* **c. boat** buque *m* de carga, carguero *m*

Caribbean [kærɪˈbɪən, *US* kəˈrɪbɪən] *adj* caribe, caribeño(a); **the C. (Sea)** el (mar) Caribe

caricature [ˈkærɪkətjʊə(r)] *n* caricatura *f*

caring [ˈkeərɪŋ] *adj* solidario(a)

carnage [ˈkɑːnɪdʒ] *n Fig* carnicería *f*

carnal [ˈkɑːnəl] *adj* carnal

carnation [kɑːˈneɪʃən] *n* clavel *m*

carnival [ˈkɑːnɪvəl] *n* carnaval *m*

carnivorous [kɑːˈnɪvərəs] *adj* carnívoro(a)

carol [ˈkærəl] *n* villancico *m*

carom [ˈkærəm] *n US (in billiards, pool)* carambola *f*

carousel [kærəˈsel] *n US* tiovivo *m*

carp¹ [kɑːp] *n (fish)* carpa *f*

carp² [kɑːp] *vi* refunfuñar

carpenter [ˈkɑːpɪntə(r)] *n* carpintero(a) *m,f*

carpentry [ˈkɑːpɪntrɪ] *n* carpintería *f*

carpet [ˈkɑːpɪt] **1** *n* alfombra *f*
  2 *vt Fig* **carpeted with** cubierto(a) de

> ✎ Note that the Spanish word **carpeta** is a false friend and is never a translation for the English word **carpet**. In Spanish, **carpeta** means "file, folder".

carriage [ˈkærɪdʒ] *n* (**a**) *(horse-drawn)* carruaje *m*; *Rail* vagón *m*, coche *m*; *(of gun)* cureña *f*; *(of typewriter)* carro *m* (**b**) *(of goods)* porte *m*, transporte *m*

carriageway [ˈkærɪdʒweɪ] *n Br* carril *m*, autovía *f*; **dual c.** autovía

carrier [ˈkærɪə(r)] *n* (**a**) *(company)* transportista *mf*; *Br* **c. bag** bolsa *f* de plástico; **c. pigeon** paloma mensajera (**b**) *Med* portador(a) *m,f*

carrot [ˈkærət] *n* zanahoria *f*
carry [ˈkærɪ] **1** *vt* (**a**) llevar; *(goods)* transportar (**b**) *(stock)* tener; *(responsibility, penalty)* conllevar, implicar (**c**) **the motion was carried** se aprobó la moción (**d**) *(disease)* ser portador(a) de
  2 *vi (sound)* oírse
  ▸ **carry away** *vt sep* llevarse; **to get carried away** entusiasmarse
  ▸ **carry forward** *vt sep Fin* **carried forward** suma y sigue
  ▸ **carry off** *vt sep (prize)* llevarse; *Fam* **to c. it off** salir airoso(a)
  ▸ **carry on** **1** *vt sep* continuar; *(conversation)* mantener
  2 *vi* (**a**) continuar, seguir adelante; **c. on!** ¡adelante! (**b**) *Fam (make a fuss)* hacer una escena; **don't c. on about it!** ¡no te enrolles! (**c**) *Fam* **to c. on with sb** estar liado(a) con algn
  ▸ **carry out** *vt sep (plan)* llevar a cabo, realizar; *(test)* verificar
carryall [ˈkærɪɔːl] *n US* bolsa *f (de viaje o de deporte)*
carrycot [ˈkærɪkɒt] *n Br* cuna *f* portátil
carsick [ˈkɑːsɪk] *adj* mareado(a) (en el coche)
cart [kɑːt] **1** *n (horse-drawn)* carro *m*; *(handcart)* carretilla *f*; *US (in supermarket)* carrito *m*
  2 *vt* carretear
cartel [kɑːˈtel] *n* cártel *m*
carton [ˈkɑːtən] *n (of cream etc)* caja *f*
cartoon [kɑːˈtuːn] *n (strip)* tira cómica, historieta *f*; *Art* cartón *m*; *(animated)* dibujos *mpl* animados
cartoonist [kɑːˈtuːnɪst] *n* caricaturista *mf*
cartridge [ˈkɑːtrɪdʒ] *n* (**a**) cartucho *m* (**b**) *(for pen)* recambio *m*; **c. paper** papel guarro
carve [kɑːv] *vt* (**a**) *(wood)* tallar; *(stone, metal)* cincelar, esculpir (**b**) *(meat)* trinchar
cascade [kæˈskeɪd] *n* cascada *f*
case¹ [keɪs] *n* (**a**) caso *m*; **a c. in point** un buen ejemplo; **in any c.** en cualquier caso, de todas formas; **in c. of doubt** en caso de duda; **just in c.** por si acaso (**b**) *Med* caso *m*; **c. history** historial clínico (**c**) *Jur* causa *f*
case² [keɪs] *n* (**a**) *(suitcase)* maleta *f*, *Méx* petaca *f*, *RP* valija *f*; *(small)* estuche *m*; *(soft)* funda *f* (**b**) **a c. of wine** una caja de botellas de vino (**c**) *Typ* **lower c.** minúscula *f*; **upper c.** mayúscula *f*
cash [kæʃ] **1** *n* dinero efectivo; **to pay c.** pagar al contado *or* en efectivo; **c. desk** caja *f*; **c. on delivery** entrega *f* contra reembolso; **c. dispenser** cajero automático; **c. register** caja registradora
  2 *vt (cheque)* cobrar
  ▸ **cash in 1** *vi Fam Fig* **to c. in on sth** sacar provecho de algo
  2 *vt sep* hacer efectivo(a)
cash-and-carry [kæʃənˈkærɪ] *adj & adv* = de venta al por mayor y pago al contado
cashew [ˈkæʃuː] *n* **c. (nut)** anacardo *m*
cashier [kæˈʃɪə(r)] *n* cajero(a) *m,f*
cashmere [ˈkæʃmɪə(r)] *n* cachemira *f*
casino [kəˈsiːnəʊ] *n* casino *m*
cask [kɑːsk] *n* tonel *m*, barril *m*
casket [ˈkɑːskɪt] *n (box)* cofre *m*; *US (coffin)* ataúd *m*

> 🛈 Note that the Spanish word **casquete** is a false friend and is never a translation for the English word **casket**. In Spanish, **casquete** means "shell case".

casserole [ˈkæsərəʊl] *n* (**a**) *(container)* cacerola *f* (**b**) *Culin* guisado *m*
cassette [kəˈset] *n* cassette *f*; **c. recorder** cassette *m*
cast [kɑːst] **1** *vt (pt & pp* **cast***)* (**a**) *(net, fishing line)* echar, arrojar; *(light)* proyectar; *(glance)* lanzar; *(anchor)* echar; *(vote)* emitir; *(skin)* mudar (**b**) *Fig* **to c. doubts on sth** poner algo en duda; **to c. suspicion on sb** levantar sospechas sobre algn (**c**) *(metal)* moldear; **c. iron** hierro fundido (**d**) *Th (play)* hacer el reparto de
  2 *n* (**a**) *(mould)* molde *m*; *(product)* pieza *f* (**b**) *Med* **(plaster) c.** escayola *f* (**c**) *Th* reparto *m*
  ▸ **cast off** *vi Naut* soltar (las) amarras
castanets [kæstəˈnets] *npl* castañuelas *fpl*
castaway [ˈkɑːstəweɪ] *n* náufrago(a) *m,f*
caste [kɑːst] *n* casta *f*
caster [ˈkɑːstə(r)] *n* **c. sugar** azúcar *m or f* extrafino(a)
Castile [kæˈstiːl] *n* Castilla
Castilian [kæˈstɪlɪən] **1** *adj* castellano(a)
  2 *n* **C. (Spanish)** *(language)* castellano *m*
casting [ˈkɑːstɪŋ] *n* **c. vote** voto *m* de calidad
cast-iron [ˈkɑːstaɪən] *adj* de hierro fundido
castle [ˈkɑːsəl] **1** *n* (**a**) castillo *m* (**b**) *(in chess)* torre *f*
  2 *vi (in chess)* enrocar
castor¹ [ˈkɑːstə(r)] *n* **c. oil** aceite *m* de ricino
castor² [ˈkɑːstə(r)] *n (on furniture)* ruedecilla *f*
castrate [kæˈstreɪt] *vt* castrar

casual [ˈkæʒjʊəl] *adj* (**a**) *(meeting etc)* fortuito(a) (**b**) *(worker)* eventual (**c**) *(clothes)* (de) sport (**d**) *(visit)* de paso (**e**) *(person, attitude)* despreocupado(a), informal

casualty [ˈkæʒjʊəltɪ] *n* (**a**) *Mil* baja *f*; **casualties** pérdidas *fpl* (**b**) *(injured)* herido(a) *m,f*

> 🖉 Note that the Spanish word **casualidad** is a false friend and is never a translation for the English word **casualty**. In Spanish, **casualidad** means "chance, coincidence".

cat [kæt] *n* gato(a) *m,f*; *Fig* **to let the c. out of the bag** descubrir el pastel

Catalan [ˈkætəlæn] **1** *adj* catalán(ana) **2** *n* (**a**) *(person)* catalán(ana) *m,f* (**b**) *(language)* catalán *m*

catalogue, *US* **catalog** [ˈkætəlɒg] **1** *n* catálogo *m* **2** *vt* catalogar

Catalonia [kætəˈləʊnɪə] *n* Cataluña

catalyst [ˈkætəlɪst] *n* catalizador *m*

catapult [ˈkætəpʌlt] *n Br* tirachinas *m inv*

catarrh [kəˈtɑː(r)] *n* catarro *m*

catastrophe [kəˈtæstrəfɪ] *n* catástrofe *f*

catastrophic [kætəˈstrɒfɪk] *adj* catastrófico(a)

catch [kætʃ] **1** *vt* (*pt & pp* **caught**) (**a**) *(ball, thief)* coger; *(fish)* pescar; *(mouse etc)* atrapar; *(train, bus)* coger, *Am* agarrar; **to c. a cold** coger un resfriado; **to c. fire** *(log)* prenderse; *(building)* incendiarse; **to c. hold of** agarrar; **to c. sb's eye** captar la atención de algn; **to c. sight of** entrever (**b**) *(surprise)* pillar, sorprender (**c**) *(hear)* entender (**d**) **to c. one's breath** *(hold)* sostener la respiración; *(recover)* recuperar el aliento

2 *vi* *(sleeve etc)* engancharse (**on** en); *(fire)* encenderse

3 *n* (**a**) *(of ball)* parada *f*; *(of fish)* presa *f* (**b**) *(on door)* pestillo *m* (**c**) *(drawback)* pega *f*; **c. question** pregunta *f* con pega (**d**) **c. phrase** slogan *m*

▸ **catch on** *vi Fam* (**a**) *(become popular)* ganar popularidad (**b**) *(understand)* caer en la cuenta

▸ **catch out** *vt sep Fam* **to c. sb out** pillar a algn cometiendo una falta

▸ **catch up** *vi* (**a**) **to c. up with sb** *(reach)* alcanzar a algn (**b**) *(with news)* ponerse al corriente (**on** de); **to c. up on sleep** recuperar el sueño perdido; **to c. up with work** ponerse al día de trabajo

catching [ˈkætʃɪŋ] *adj (disease)* contagioso(a)

catchment [ˈkætʃmənt] *n* **c. area** zona *f* de captación

catchword [ˈkætʃwɜːd] *n* lema *m*

catchy [ˈkætʃɪ] *adj* (**catchier, catchiest**) *Fam (tune)* pegadizo(a)

categoric(al) [kætɪˈgɒrɪk(əl)] *adj* categórico(a)

categorize [ˈkætɪgəraɪz] *vt* clasificar

category [ˈkætɪgərɪ] *n* categoría *f*

cater [ˈkeɪtə(r)] *vi* (**a**) **to c. for** *(wedding etc)* proveer comida para (**b**) **to c. for** *(taste)* atender a

caterer [ˈkeɪtərə(r)] *n* proveedor(a) *m,f*

catering [ˈkeɪtərɪŋ] *n* abastecimiento *m* (de comidas por encargo)

caterpillar [ˈkætəpɪlə(r)] *n* (**a**) oruga *f* (**b**) **c. (tractor)** tractor *m* de oruga

cathedral [kəˈθiːdrəl] *n* catedral *f*

Catholic [ˈkæθəlɪk] *adj & n* católico(a) *(m,f)*

catholic [ˈkæθəlɪk] *adj* católico(a)

Catholicism [kəˈθɒlɪsɪzəm] *n* catolicismo *m*

cat's-eye® [ˈkætsaɪ] *n Br* captafaro *m*, = baliza reflectante en la calzada

cattle [ˈkætəl] *npl* ganado *m* (vacuno)

catty [ˈkætɪ] *adj* (**cattier, cattiest**) *Fam (remark)* malintencionado(a); *(person)* malicioso(a)

catwalk [ˈkætwɔːk] *n* pasarela *f*

Caucasian [kɔːˈkeɪzɪən] *adj & n* caucásico(a) *(m,f)*, blanco(a) *(m,f)*

caucus [ˈkɔːkəs] *n* comité *m* central, ejecutiva *f*

caught [kɔːt] *pt & pp of* **catch**

cauliflower [ˈkɒlɪflaʊə(r)] *n* coliflor *f*

cause [kɔːz] **1** *n* (**a**) *(origin)* causa *f* (**b**) *(reason)* motivo *m* (**c**) **for a good c.** por una buena causa

2 *vt* causar; **to c. sb to do sth** hacer que algn haga algo

caustic [ˈkɔːstɪk] *adj* cáustico(a); *Fig* mordaz

caution [ˈkɔːʃən] **1** *n* (**a**) *(care)* cautela *f*, prudencia *f* (**b**) *(warning)* aviso *m*, advertencia *f* (**c**) *Br Jur* represión *f* **2** *vt* advertir, amonestar

cautious [ˈkɔːʃəs] *adj* cauteloso(a), prudente

cavalcade [kævəlˈkeɪd] *n* cabalgata *f*

cavalier [kævəˈlɪə(r)] **1** *adj* arrogante **2** *n* caballero *m*

cavalry [ˈkævəlrɪ] *n* caballería *f*

cave [keɪv] *n* cueva *f*

▸ **cave in** *vi (roof etc)* derrumbarse, hundirse

caveman ['keɪvmæn] *n* hombre *m* de las cavernas

cavern ['kævən] *n* caverna *f*

caviar(e) ['kævɪɑː(r)] *n* caviar *m*

cavity ['kævɪtɪ] *n* (a) *(hole)* cavidad *f* (b) *(in tooth)* caries *f inv*

cavort [kə'vɔːt] *vi* retozar, brincar

CB [siː'biː] *(abbr* **C**itizens' **B**and) banda ciudadana

CBI [siːbiː'aɪ] *n Br (abbr* **Confederation of British Industry)** ≃ CEOE *f*

cc [siː'siː] *(abbr* **c**ubic **c**entimetre(**s**)) cc

CD [siː'diː] *n (abbr* **c**ompact **d**isc) CD *m*; **CD player** (lector *m or* reproductor *m* de) CD *m*

CD-ROM [siːdiː'rɒm] *n Comput (abbr* **c**ompact **d**isc **r**ead-**o**nly **m**emory) CD-ROM *m*

cease [siːs] **1** *vt* cesar; **to c. doing** *or* **to do sth** dejar de hacer algo
  2 *vi* terminar

cease-fire [siːs'faɪə(r)] *n* alto *m* el fuego

ceaseless ['siːslɪs] *adj* incesante

cedar ['siːdə(r)] *n* cedro *m*

cede [siːd] *vt* ceder

ceiling ['siːlɪŋ] *n* techo *m*

celebrate ['selɪbreɪt] **1** *vt (occasion)* celebrar
  2 *vi* divertirse

celebrated ['selɪbreɪtɪd] *adj* célebre

celebration [selɪ'breɪʃən] *n* (a) celebración *f* (b) **celebrations** festividades *fpl*

celebrity [sɪ'lebrɪtɪ] *n* celebridad *f*

celery ['selərɪ] *n* apio *m*

celibate ['selɪbɪt] *adj & n* célibe *(mf)*

cell [sel] *n* (a) *(in prison)* celda *f* (b) *Biol & Pol* célula *f* (c) *Elec* pila *f*

cellar ['selə(r)] *n* sótano *m*; *(for wine)* bodega *f*

cello ['tʃeləʊ] *n* violoncelo *m*

cellophane® ['seləfeɪn] *n Br* celofán *m*

celluloid ['seljʊlɔɪd] *n* celuloide *m*

cellulose ['seljʊləʊs] *n* celulosa *f*

Celsius ['selsɪəs] *adj* Celsio

Celt [kelt, selt] *n* celta *mf*

Celtic ['keltɪk, 'seltɪk] **1** *n (language)* celta *m*
  2 *adj* celta

cement [sɪ'ment] **1** *n* cemento *m*; **c. mixer** hormigonera *f*
  2 *vt Constr* unir con cemento; *Fig (friendship)* cimentar

cemetery ['semɪtrɪ] *n* cementerio *m*

censor ['sensə(r)] **1** *n* censor(a) *m,f*
  2 *vt* censurar

censorship ['sensəʃɪp] *n* censura *f*

censure ['senʃə(r)] **1** *n* censura *f*
  2 *vt* censurar

census ['sensəs] *n* censo *m*

cent [sent] *n* (a) centavo *m*, céntimo *m* (b) **per c.** por ciento

centenary [sen'tiːnərɪ] *n* centenario *m*

center ['sentər] *n & vt US* = **centre**

centigrade ['sentɪgreɪd] *adj* centígrado(a)

centilitre, *US* **centiliter** ['sentɪliːtə(r)] *n* centilitro *m*

centimetre, *US* **centimeter** ['sentɪmiːtə(r)] *n* centímetro *m*

centipede ['sentɪpiːd] *n* ciempiés *m inv*

central ['sentrəl] *adj* central; **c. heating** calefacción *f* central; **C. America** Centroamérica; **C. American** centroamericano(a) *m,f*; *Br* **c. reservation** *(on motorway)* mediana *f*, *Col, Méx* camellón *m*

centralize ['sentrəlaɪz] *vt* centralizar

centrally ['sentrəlɪ] *adv* **c. heated** con calefacción central; **c. situated** céntrico(a)

centre ['sentə(r)] **1** *n* centro *m*; **town c.** centro de la ciudad; *Ftb* **c. forward** delantero centro; *Ftb* **c. half** medio centro; *Pol* **c. party** partido *m* centrista; **sports c.** centro deportivo
  2 *vt (attention etc)* centrar *(*on en)

century ['sentʃərɪ] *n* siglo *m*; **the nineteenth c.** el siglo diecinueve

ceramic [sɪ'ræmɪk] **1** *n* cerámica *f*
  2 *adj* de cerámica

ceramics [sɪ'ræmɪks] *n sing* cerámica *f*

cereal ['sɪərɪəl] *n* cereal *m*

cerebral ['serɪbrəl, sɪ'riːbrəl] *adj* cerebral; **c. palsy** parálisis *f* cerebral

ceremony ['serɪmənɪ] *n* ceremonia *f*

certain ['sɜːtən] **1** *adj* (a) *(sure)* seguro(a); **to be c.** estar seguro(a); **to make c. of sth** asegurarse de algo (b) **to a c. extent** hasta cierto punto (c) *(not known)* cierto(a); **a c. Miss Ward** una tal señorita Ward (d) *(true)* cierto(a)
  2 *adv* **for c.** a ciencia cierta

certainly ['sɜːtənlɪ] *adv* desde luego; **c. not** de ninguna manera

certainty ['sɜːtəntɪ] *n* certeza *f*; *(assurance)* seguridad *f*

certificate [sə'tɪfɪkɪt] *n* certificado *m*; *Educ* diploma *m*

certified [sə'tɪfaɪd] *adj* certificado(a); *(copy)* compulsado(a); *US* **c. public accountant** censor(a) *m,f* jurado(a) de cuentas, auditor(a) *m,f*, *Am* contador(a) *m,f* público(a)

certify ['sɜːtɪfaɪ] *vt* certificar

cervical ['sɜːvɪkəl, sə'vaɪkəl] *adj* **c. cancer** cáncer *m* del útero; **c. smear** frotis *m* cervical

cervix ['sɜːvɪks] *n* (**a**) *(uterus)* cuello *m* del útero (**b**) *(neck)* cerviz *f*, cuello *m*
cessation [se'seɪʃən] *n* cese *m*
cesspit ['sespɪt] *n* pozo negro
Ceylon [sɪ'lɒn] *n* Ceilán
cf [siː'ef] (*abbr* **confer, compare**) cf., cfr.
chafe [tʃeɪf] **1** *vt (make sore)* rozar
2 *vi (skin)* irritarse; *(item of clothing)* rozar
chaffinch ['tʃæfɪntʃ] *n* pinzón *m* vulgar
chagrin ['ʃægrɪn] *n* disgusto *m*, desilusión *f*
chain [tʃeɪn] **1** *n* cadena *f*; *Fig (of events)* serie *f*; **c. of mountains** cordillera *f*; **c. reaction** reacción *f* en cadena; **c. saw** sierra mecánica
2 *vt* **to c. (up)** encadenar
chain-smoke ['tʃeɪnsməʊk] *vi* fumar un pitillo tras otro
chair [tʃeə(r)] **1** *n* (**a**) silla *f*; *(with arms)* sillón *m*; **c. lift** telesilla *m* (**b**) *(position)* presidencia *f*; *Univ* cátedra *f*
2 *vt* presidir
chairman ['tʃeəmən] *n* presidente *m*
chairperson ['tʃeəpɜːsən] *n* presidente(a) *m,f*
chalet ['ʃæleɪ] *n* chalet *m*, chalé *m*
chalk [tʃɔːk] *n (for writing)* tiza *f*
▶ **chalk up** *vt sep Fam (victory etc)* apuntarse
challenge ['tʃælɪndʒ] **1** *vt* (**a**) retar, desafiar; **to c. sb to do sth** retar a algn a que haga algo (**b**) *(authority etc)* poner a prueba; *(statement)* poner en duda (**c**) *Mil* dar el alto a
2 *n* (**a**) reto *m*, desafío *m* (**b**) *Mil* quién vive *m*
challenging ['tʃælɪndʒɪŋ] *adj (idea)* desafiante; *(task)* que presenta un desafío
chamber ['tʃeɪmbə(r)] *n* (**a**) *(hall)* cámara *f*; **C. of Commerce** Cámara de Comercio (**b**) *Mus* **c. music** música *f* de cámara (**c**) *BrJur* **chambers** gabinete *m*
chambermaid ['tʃeɪmbəmeɪd] *n* camarera *f*
chameleon [kə'miːlɪən] *n* camaleón *m*
champagne [ʃæm'peɪn] *n* *(French)* champán *m*; *(from Catalonia)* cava *m*
champion ['tʃæmpɪən] *n* campeón(ona) *m,f*; *Fig* **c. of human rights** defensor(a) *m,f* de los derechos humanos
championship ['tʃæmpɪənʃɪp] *n* campeonato *m*
chance [tʃɑːns] **1** *n* (**a**) *(fortune)* casualidad *f*, azar *m*; **by c.** por casualidad; **to take a c.** arriesgarse; **c. meeting** encuentro *m* casual (**b**) *(likelihood)* posibilidad *f*; **(the) chances are that ...** lo más posible

es que ... (**c**) *(opportunity)* oportunidad *f*
2 *vt* arriesgar
▶ **chance upon** *vt insep* encontrar por casualidad
chancellor ['tʃɑːnsələ(r)] *n* (**a**) *(head of state, in embassy)* canciller *m* (**b**) *Br Univ* rector(a) *m,f* (**c**) *Br* **C. of the Exchequer** ≃ ministro(a) *m,f* de Hacienda
chandelier [ʃændɪ'lɪə(r)] *n* araña *f* (de luces)
change [tʃeɪndʒ] **1** *vt* cambiar; **to c. gear** cambiar de marcha; **to c. one's mind/the subject** cambiar de opinión/de tema; **to c. trains** hacer transbordo; **to get changed** cambiarse de ropa; *Fig* **to c. hands** cambiar de dueño(a)
2 *vi* cambiar, cambiarse; **to c. for the better/worse** mejorar/empeorar; **to c. into** convertirse en
3 *n* (**a**) cambio *m*; **for a c.** para variar; **c. of heart** cambio de parecer; **c. of scene** cambio de aires (**b**) *(money)* cambio *m*; *(after purchase)* vuelta *f*; **small c.** suelto *m*
▶ **change over** *vi* cambiarse
changeable ['tʃeɪndʒəbəl] *adj (weather)* variable; *(person)* inconstante
changeover ['tʃeɪndʒəʊvə(r)] *n* conversión *f*
changing ['tʃeɪndʒɪŋ] **1** *n* (**a**) **c. room** vestuario *m* (**b**) *Mil* relevo *m* (de la guardia)
2 *adj* cambiante
channel ['tʃænəl] **1** *n* (**a**) *Geog* canal *m*; *(of river)* cauce *m*; **the C. Islands** las Islas Anglonormandas; **the English C.** el Canal de la Mancha (**b**) *(administrative)* vía *f* (**c**) *TV & Rad* canal *m*, cadena *f*
2 *vt Fig (ideas etc)* canalizar, encauzar
chant [tʃɑːnt] **1** *n* *Rel* cántico *m*; *(of demonstrators)* slogan *m*
2 *vt & vi Rel* cantar; *(demonstrators)* corear
chaos ['keɪɒs] *n* caos *m*
chaotic [keɪ'ɒtɪk] *adj* caótico(a)
chap [tʃæp] *n Fam* chico *m*, tío *m*
chapel ['tʃæpəl] *n* capilla *f*
chaperon(e) ['ʃæpərəʊn] *n* carabina *f*
chaplain ['tʃæplɪn] *n* capellán *m*
chapter ['tʃæptə(r)] *n* (**a**) capítulo *m* (**b**) *Rel* cabildo *m*
char [tʃɑː(r)] *vt* chamuscar, carbonizar
character ['kærɪktə(r)] *n* (**a**) carácter *m* (**b**) *Fam (person)* tipo *m* (**c**) *Th* personaje *m*
characteristic [kærɪktə'rɪstɪk] **1** *n* característica *f*
2 *adj* característico(a)

characterize [ˈkærɪktəraɪz] *vt* caracterizar

charcoal [ˈtʃɑːkəʊl] *n* carbón *m* vegetal; *Art* **c. drawing** carboncillo *m*; **c. grey** gris marengo *or* oscuro

charge [tʃɑːdʒ] **1** *vt* (**a**) cobrar; **c. it to my account** cárguelo en mi cuenta (**b**) **to c. sb with a crime** acusar a algn de un crimen (**c**) *Mil* cargar contra (**d**) *Elec* cargar

  2 *vi Elec & Mil* cargar; **to c. about** andar a lo loco

  3 *n* (**a**) *(cost)* precio *m*; **bank charges** comisión *f*; **free of c.** gratis; **service c.** servicio *m*; **c. account** cuenta *f* corriente (**b**) **to be in c. of** estar a cargo de; **to take c. of** hacerse cargo de (**c**) *Jur* cargo *m*, acusación *f* (**d**) *(explosive)* carga explosiva (**e**) *Elec* carga *f*

charged [tʃɑːdʒd] *adj Fig* emotivo(a)

charismatic [kærɪzˈmætɪk] *adj* carismático(a)

charitable [ˈtʃærɪtəbəl] *adj (person)* caritativo(a); *(organization)* benéfico(a)

charity [ˈtʃærɪtɪ] *n* caridad *f*; *(organization)* institución benéfica

charlady [ˈtʃɑːleɪdɪ] *n Br* mujer *f* de la limpieza

charlatan [ˈʃɑːlətən] *n (doctor)* curandero(a) *m,f*

charm [tʃɑːm] **1** *n* (**a**) *(quality)* encanto *m* (**b**) *(spell)* hechizo *m*; **lucky c.** amuleto *m*

  2 *vt* encantar

charming [ˈtʃɑːmɪŋ] *adj* encantador(a)

chart [tʃɑːt] **1** *n* (**a**) *(giving information)* tabla *f*; *(graph)* gráfico *m* (**b**) *(map)* carta *f* de navegación (**c**) *Mus* **the charts** la lista de éxitos

  2 *vt Av & Naut (on map)* trazar

charter [ˈtʃɑːtə(r)] **1** *n* (**a**) *(of institution)* estatutos *mpl*; *(of rights)* carta *f* (**b**) **c. flight** vuelo *m* chárter

  2 *vt (plane, boat)* fletar

chartered accountant [tʃɑːtədəˈkaʊntənt] *n Br* censor(a) *m,f* jurado(a) de cuentas, *Am* contador(a) *m,f* público(a)

chase [tʃeɪs] **1** *vt* perseguir; *(hunt)* cazar

  2 *n* persecución *f*; *(hunt)* caza *f*

chasm [ˈkæzəm] *n Geog* sima *f*; *Fig* abismo *m*

chassis [ˈʃæsɪ] *n* chasis *m inv*

chastise [tʃæsˈtaɪz] *vt* castigar

chastity [ˈtʃæstɪtɪ] *n* castidad *f*

chat [tʃæt] **1** *n* (**a**) *(informal conversation)* charla *f*; *Br* **c. show** coloquio *m* (**b**) *Comput* charla *f*; **c. room** sala *f* de conversación

  2 *vi* (**a**) *(talk informally)* charlar (**b**) *Comput* charlar (**to** *or* **with** con)

  ▸ **chat up** *vt sep Br Fam* **to chat sb up** (intentar) ligar con algn

chatter [ˈtʃætə(r)] **1** *vi (person)* parlotear; *(bird)* piar; *(teeth)* castañetear

  2 *n (of person)* parloteo *m*; *(of birds)* gorjeo *m*; *(of teeth)* castañeteo *m*

chatterbox [ˈtʃætəbɒks] *n Fam* parlanchín(ina) *m,f*

chatty [ˈtʃætɪ] *adj* (**chattier, chattiest**) hablador(a)

chauffeur [ˈʃəʊfə(r), ʃəʊˈfɜː(r)] *n* chófer *m*

chauvinism [ˈʃəʊvɪnɪzəm] *n* chovinismo *m*; **male c.** machismo *m*

chauvinist [ˈʃəʊvɪnɪst] *adj & n* chovinista *(mf)*; **male c.** machista *m*

cheap [tʃiːp] **1** *adj* barato(a); *(fare)* económico(a); *(joke)* de mal gusto; *(contemptible)* bajo(a); *Fam* **dirt c.** tirado(a)

  2 *n Br Fam* **on the c.** en plan barato

  3 *adv* barato

cheapen [ˈtʃiːpən] *vt Fig* degradar

cheaply [ˈtʃiːplɪ] *adv* barato, en plan económico

cheat [tʃiːt] **1** *vt* engañar; **to c. sb out of sth** estafar algo a algn

  2 *vi* (**a**) *(at games)* hacer trampa; *(in exam etc)* copiar(se) (**b**) *Fam (husband, wife)* poner cuernos (**on** a)

  3 *n (trickster)* tramposo(a) *m,f*

check [tʃek] **1** *vt* (**a**) repasar; *(facts)* comprobar; *(tickets)* controlar; *(tyres, oil)* revisar (**b**) *(impulse)* refrenar; *(growth)* retardar (**c**) *(stop)* detener (**d**) *(in chess)* dar jaque a

  2 *vi* comprobar

  3 *n* (**a**) *(of documents etc)* revisión *f*; *(of facts)* comprobación *f* (**b**) *(in chess)* jaque *m* (**c**) *(pattern)* cuadro *m* (**d**) **to keep in c.** *(feelings)* contener; *(enemy)* mantener a raya (**e**) *US* = **cheque**

  ▸ **check in** *vi (at airport)* facturar; *(at hotel)* registrarse (**at** en)

  ▸ **check out 1** *vi (of hotel)* dejar el hotel

  2 *vt sep (facts)* verificar

  ▸ **check up** *vi* **to c. up on sb** hacer averiguaciones sobre algn; **to c. up on sth** comprobar algo

checked [tʃekt] *adj* a cuadros

checker [ˈtʃekər] *n US (cashier)* cajero(a) *m,f*

checkered [ˈtʃekərd] *adj US =* **chequered**

checkers [ˈtʃekərz] *n sing US (game)* damas *fpl*

check-in [ˈtʃekɪn] *n* **c. desk** *(at airport)* mostrador *m* de facturación

checkmate ['tʃekmeɪt] **1** *n* jaque mate *m*
2 *vt* dar (jaque) mate a; *Fig* poner en un callejón sin salida

checkout ['tʃekaʊt] *n (counter)* caja *f*

checkpoint ['tʃekpɔɪnt] *n* control *m*

checkroom ['tʃekruːm] *n US (for coats, hats)* guardarropa *m*; *(for luggage)* consigna *f*

checkup ['tʃekʌp] *n Med* chequeo *m*, examen médico

cheek [tʃiːk] *n* (**a**) mejilla *f* (**b**) *Fam (nerve)* cara *f*; **what c.!** ¡vaya jeta!

cheekbone ['tʃiːkbəʊn] *n* pómulo *m*

cheeky ['tʃiːkɪ] *adj* (**cheekier, cheekiest**) *Fam* fresco(a), descarado(a)

cheep [tʃiːp] **1** *n (of bird)* pío *m*
2 *vi* piar

cheer [tʃɪə(r)] **1** *vi* aplaudir, aclamar
2 *vt* (**a**) *(applaud)* vitorear, aclamar (**b**) *(make hopeful)* animar
3 *n* viva *m*; **cheers** aplausos *mpl*; *Fam* **cheers!** *(thank you)* ¡gracias!; *(before drinking)* ¡salud!
▸ **cheer up 1** *vi* animarse
2 *vt sep* **to c. sb up** alegrar *or* animar a algn

cheerful ['tʃɪəfʊl] *adj* alegre

cheerio [tʃɪərɪ'əʊ] *interj Br Fam* ¡hasta luego!

cheese [tʃiːz] *n* queso *m*

cheesecake ['tʃiːzkeɪk] *n* tarta *f* de queso

cheetah ['tʃiːtə] *n* guepardo *m*

chef [ʃef] *n* chef *m*

chemical ['kemɪkəl] **1** *n* sustancia química, producto químico
2 *adj* químico(a)

chemist ['kemɪst] *n* (**a**) químico(a) *m,f* (**b**) *Br* **c.'s (shop)** farmacia *f*; **(dispensing) c.** farmacéutico(a) *m,f*

chemistry ['kemɪstrɪ] *n* química *f*

cheque [tʃek] *n* cheque *m*; **to pay by c.** pagar con (un) cheque; **c. book** talonario *m* (de cheques); **c. card** tarjeta *f* de identificación bancaria

chequered ['tʃekəd] *adj* a cuadros; *Fig* **a c. career** una carrera con altibajos

cherish ['tʃerɪʃ] *vt* (**a**) *(person)* tenerle mucho cariño a (**b**) *Fig (hopes etc)* abrigar

cherry ['tʃerɪ] *n* cereza *f*

chess [tʃes] *n* ajedrez *m*

chessboard ['tʃesbɔːd] *n* tablero *m* de ajedrez

chesspiece ['tʃespiːs] *n* pieza *f* de ajedrez

chest [tʃest] *n* (**a**) *Anat* pecho *m* (**b**) *(for linen)* arca *f*; *(for valuables)* cofre *m*; **c. of drawers** cómoda *f*

chestnut ['tʃesnʌt] *n (tree, colour)* castaño *m*; *(nut)* castaña *f*

chew [tʃuː] *vt* masticar, mascar

chewing gum ['tʃuːɪŋgʌm] *n* chicle *m*

chic [ʃiːk] *adj* elegante

chick [tʃɪk] *n* (**a**) *(young chicken)* pollito *m* (**b**) *Fam (woman)* nena *f*, *Arg* piba *f*, *Méx* chava *f*

chicken ['tʃɪkɪn] **1** *n* (**a**) pollo *m* (**b**) *Fam (coward)* gallina *mf*
2 *vi Fam* **to c. out** rajarse (por miedo)

chickenpox ['tʃɪkɪnpɒks] *n* varicela *f*

chickpea ['tʃɪkpiː] *n* garbanzo *m*

chicory ['tʃɪkərɪ] *n* achicoria *f*

chief [tʃiːf] **1** *n* jefe *m*
2 *adj* principal

chiefly ['tʃiːflɪ] *adv (above all)* sobre todo; *(mainly)* principalmente

chiffon ['ʃɪfɒn] *n* gasa *f*

chilblain ['tʃɪlbleɪn] *n* sabañón *m*

child [tʃaɪld] *n (pl* **children***)* niño(a) *m,f*; *(son)* hijo *m*; *(daughter)* hija *f*; **c. minder** = persona que cuida niños en su propia casa

childbirth ['tʃaɪldbɜːθ] *n* parto *m*

childhood ['tʃaɪldhʊd] *n* infancia *f*, niñez *f*

childish ['tʃaɪldɪʃ] *adj* pueril, aniñado(a)

childlike ['tʃaɪldlaɪk] *adj* infantil

children ['tʃɪldrən] *pl of* **child**

Chile ['tʃɪlɪ] *n* Chile

Chilean ['tʃɪlɪən] *adj & n* chileno(a) *(m,f)*

chili ['tʃɪlɪ] *n* = **chilli**

chill [tʃɪl] **1** *n* (**a**) *Med* resfriado *m* (**b**) *(coldness)* fresco *m*
2 *adj* frío(a)
3 *vt (meat)* refrigerar; *(wine)* enfriar

chilli ['tʃɪlɪ] *n* chile *m*

chilly ['tʃɪlɪ] *adj* (**chillier, chilliest**) frío(a)

chime [tʃaɪm] **1** *n (peal)* campanada *f*
2 *vt* **to c. five o'clock** *(of clock)* dar las cinco
3 *vi* sonar
▸ **chime in** *vi Fam* intervenir

chimney ['tʃɪmnɪ] *n* chimenea *f*; **c. sweep** deshollinador *m*

chimpanzee [tʃɪmpæn'ziː] *n* chimpancé *m*

chin [tʃɪn] *n* barbilla *f*, mentón *m*; **double c.** papada *f*

China ['tʃaɪnə] *n* China

china ['tʃaɪnə] *n* loza *f*, porcelana *f*

⌀ Note that the Spanish word **china** is a false friend and is never a translation for the English word **china**. In Spanish, **china** means "pebble, small stone".

Chinese [tʃaɪ'niːz] **1** *adj* chino(a)

2 *n* (**a**) *(person)* chino(a) *m,f* (**b**) *(language)* chino *m*

chink¹ [tʃɪŋk] *n (opening)* resquicio *m*; *(crack)* grieta *f*

chink² [tʃɪŋk] **1** *vi* tintinear
2 *n* tintineo *m*

chip [tʃɪp] **1** *n* (**a**) *(of wood)* astilla f; *(of stone)* lasca *f*; *(in cup)* mella *f* (**b**) *Br Culin* **chips** patatas *or Am* papas fritas; *US* (**potato**) **chips** *(crisps)* patatas *or Am* papas fritas *(de bolsa)* (**c**) *Comput* chip *m* (**d**) *(in gambling)* ficha *f*
2 *vt (wood)* astillar; *(stone)* resquebrajar; *(china, glass)* mellar
3 *vi (wood)* astillarse; *(china, glass)* mellarse; *(paint)* descocharse
▸**chip in** *vi Fam* (**a**) meterse (**b**) *(with money)* poner algo (de dinero)

chiropodist [kɪˈrɒpədɪst] *n* pedicuro(a) *m,f*

chirp [tʃɜːp] *vi (birds)* gorjear

chisel [ˈtʃɪzəl] *n* cincel *m*

chit [tʃɪt] *n* nota *f*; *(small invoice)* vale *m*

chitchat [ˈtʃɪtʃæt] *n Fam* palique *m*

chivalry [ˈʃɪvəlrɪ] *n* caballerosidad *f*

chives [tʃaɪvz] *npl* cebolleta *f*

chlorine [ˈklɔːriːn] *n* cloro *m*

chock-a-block [tʃɒkəˈblɒk], **chock-full** [tʃɒkˈfʊl] *adj Fam* (lleno(a)) hasta los topes

chocolate [ˈtʃɒkəlɪt] **1** *n* chocolate *m*; **chocolates** bombones *mpl*
2 *adj* de chocolate

choice [tʃɔɪs] **1** *n* elección *f*; **a wide c.** un gran surtido; **by c.** por gusto
2 *adj* selecto(a)

choir [ˈkwaɪə(r)] *n* coro *m*, coral *f*

choirboy [ˈkwaɪəbɔɪ] *n* niño *m* de coro

choke [tʃəʊk] **1** *vt* (**a**) *(person)* ahogar (**b**) *(obstruct)* obstruir
2 *vi* ahogarse; **to c. on food** atragantarse con la comida
3 *n Aut* estárter *m*
▸**choke back** *vt sep (emotions)* tragarse

cholera [ˈkɒlərə] *n* cólera *m*

cholesterol [kəˈlestərɒl] *n* colesterol *m*

choose [tʃuːz] **1** *vt (pt* **chose**; *pp* **chosen)** escoger, elegir; *(decide on)* optar por
2 *vi* escoger, elegir

choos(e)y [ˈtʃuːzɪ] *adj* (**choosier, choosiest**) *Fam* exigente

chop [tʃɒp] **1** *vt* (**a**) *(wood)* cortar; *(tree)* talar (**b**) *Culin* cortar a pedacitos
2 *n* (**a**) *(blow)* tajo *m*; *(with axe)* hachazo *m* (**b**) *Culin* chuleta *f*

chopper [ˈtʃɒpə(r)] *n Fam* helicóptero *m*

choppy [ˈtʃɒpɪ] *adj* (**choppier, choppiest**) *(sea)* picado(a)

chopsticks [ˈtʃɒpstɪks] *npl* palillos *mpl*

chord [kɔːd] *n Mus* acorde *m*; *Fig* **it strikes a c.** (me) suena

chore [tʃɔː(r)] *n* quehacer *m*, tarea *f*

chortle [ˈtʃɔːtəl] *vi* reír con ganas

chorus [ˈkɔːrəs] *n Mus & Th* coro *m*; *(in a song)* estribillo *m*; **c. girl** corista *f*

chose [tʃəʊz] *pt of* **choose**

chosen [ˈtʃəʊzən] *pp of* **choose**

Christ [kraɪst] *n* Cristo *m*, Jesucristo *m*

christen [ˈkrɪsən] *vt* bautizar

christening [ˈkrɪsənɪŋ] *n* bautizo *m*

Christian [ˈkrɪstʃən] **1** *adj* cristiano(a); **c. name** nombre *m* de pila
2 *n* cristiano(a) *m,f*

Christianity [krɪstɪˈænɪtɪ] *n* cristianismo *m*

Christmas [ˈkrɪsməs] *n* Navidad *f*; **merry C.!** ¡feliz Navidad!; **C. carol** villancico *m*; **C. Day** día *m* de Navidad; **C. Eve** Nochebuena *f*

chrome [krəʊm] *n* cromo *m*

chromium [ˈkrəʊmɪəm] *n* cromo *m*; **c. plating** cromado *m*

chromosome [ˈkrəʊməsəʊm] *n* cromosoma *m*

chronic [ˈkrɒnɪk] *adj* crónico(a)

chronicle [ˈkrɒnɪkəl] **1** *n* crónica *f*
2 *vt* hacer la crónica de

chronological [krɒnəˈlɒdʒɪkəl] *adj* cronológico(a)

chrysanthemum [krɪˈsænθəməm] *n* crisantemo *m*

chubby [ˈtʃʌbɪ] *adj* (**chubbier, chubbiest**) rellenito(a)

chuck [tʃʌk] *vt Fam* tirar; **to c. one's job in** *or* **up** dejar el trabajo; **to c. sb out** echar a algn; **to c. sth away** *or* **out** tirar algo

chuckle [ˈtʃʌkəl] **1** *vi* reír entre dientes
2 *n* sonrisita *f*

chug [tʃʌg] *vi* traquetear

chum [tʃʌm] *n* compinche *mf*, compañero(a) *m,f*

chunk [tʃʌŋk] *n Fam* cacho *m*, pedazo *m*

church [tʃɜːtʃ] *n* iglesia *f*; **to go to c.** ir a misa; **C. of England** Iglesia Anglicana

churchyard [ˈtʃɜːtʃjɑːd] *n* cementerio *m*, campo santo

churlish [ˈtʃɜːlɪʃ] *adj* grosero(a)

churn [tʃɜːn] **1** *n (for butter)* mantequera *f*; *Br (for milk)* lechera *f*
2 *vt (butter)* hacer
3 *vi* revolverse, agitarse
▸**churn out** *vt sep Fam* producir en serie

chute [ʃuːt] *n (channel)* conducto *m*; *(slide)* tobogán *m*

chutney [ˈtʃʌtnɪ] *n* conserva *f* (de frutas) picante

CIA [siːaɪˈeɪ] *n US* (*abbr* **Central Intelligence Agency**) CIA *f*

CID [siːaɪˈdiː] *n Br* (*abbr* **Criminal Investigation Department**) = policía judicial británica

cider [ˈsaɪdə(r)] *n* sidra *f*

cigar [sɪˈgɑː(r)] *n* puro *m*

cigarette [sɪgəˈret] *n* cigarrillo *m*; **c. case** pitillera *f*; **c. end** colilla *f*; **c. holder** boquilla *f*; **c. lighter** mechero *m*

Cinderella [sɪndəˈrelə] *n* Cenicienta *f*

cine camera [ˈsɪnɪkæmərə] *n Br* cámara cinematográfica

cinema [ˈsɪnɪmə] *n* (**a**) *Br (building)* cine *m* (**b**) *(art)* cine *m*

cinnamon [ˈsɪnəmən] *n* canela *f*

cipher [ˈsaɪfə(r)] *n (numeral)* cifra *f*

circle [ˈsɜːkəl] **1** *n* (**a**) círculo *m*; *(of people)* corro *m*; **in business circles** en el mundo de los negocios (**b**) *Th* anfiteatro *m*
    2 *vt (surround)* rodear; *(move round)* dar la vuelta a
    3 *vi* dar vueltas

circuit [ˈsɜːkɪt] *n* (**a**) *(journey)* recorrido *m* (**b**) *Elec* circuito *m* (**c**) *Sport (events)* liga *f*; *Br (track)* circuito *m* (**d**) *Br Jur* **c. judge** juez *mf* de distrito

circular [ˈsɜːkjʊlə(r)] *adj & n* circular (*f*)

circulate [ˈsɜːkjʊleɪt] **1** *vt (news)* hacer circular
    2 *vi* circular

circulation [sɜːkjʊˈleɪʃən] *n* (**a**) *(of blood)* circulación *f* (**b**) *(of newspaper)* tirada *f*

circumcise [ˈsɜːkəmsaɪz] *vt* circuncidar

circumference [səˈkʌmfərəns] *n* circunferencia *f*

circumspect [ˈsɜːkəmspekt] *adj* prudente

circumstance [ˈsɜːkəmstəns] *n (usu pl)* circunstancia *f*; **under no circumstances** en ningún caso; **economic circumstances** situación económica

circumvent [sɜːkəmˈvent] *vt Fig* burlar

circus [ˈsɜːkəs] *n* circo *m*

cirrhosis [sɪˈrəʊsɪs] *n* cirrosis *f*

CIS [siːaɪˈes] *n* (*abbr* **Commonwealth of Independent States**) CEI *f*

cistern [ˈsɪstən] *n* cisterna *f*

cite [saɪt] *vt (quote)* citar

citizen [ˈsɪtɪzən] *n* ciudadano(a) *m,f*

citizenship [ˈsɪtɪzənʃɪp] *n* ciudadanía *f*

citrus [ˈsɪtrəs] *adj* **c. fruits** agrios *mpl*

city [ˈsɪtɪ] *n* (**a**) ciudad *f*; *US* **c. council** ayuntamiento *m*; *US* **c. hall** ayuntamiento (**b**) *Fin* **the C.** = el centro financiero de Londres

civic [ˈsɪvɪk] *adj* cívico(a); *Br* **c. centre** centro cívico; **c. duties** obligaciones cívicas

civil [ˈsɪvəl] *adj* (**a**) civil; **c. defence** defensa *f* civil; **c. rights** derechos *mpl* civiles; **c. servant** funcionario(a) *m,f*; *Pol* **c. service** administración pública (**b**) *(polite)* cortés, educado(a)

civilian [sɪˈvɪljən] *adj & n* civil *(mf)*; **c. clothing** traje *m* de paisano

civilization [sɪvɪlaɪˈzeɪʃən] *n* civilización *f*

civilized [ˈsɪvɪlaɪzd] *adj* civilizado(a)

clad [klæd] **1** *adj Literary* vestido(a)
    2 *pt & pp of* **clothe**

claim [kleɪm] **1** *vt* (**a**) *(benefits, rights)* reclamar; *Jur (compensation)* exigir (**b**) *(assert)* afirmar
    2 *n* (**a**) *(demand)* reclamación *f*; *Jur* demanda *f*; **to put in a c.** reclamar una indemnización (**b**) *(right)* derecho *m* (**c**) *(assertion)* pretensión *f*

claimant [ˈkleɪmənt] *n Jur* demandante *mf*

clairvoyant [kleəˈvɔɪənt] *n* clarividente *mf*

clam [klæm] *n* almeja *f*
    ▶ **clam up** *vi Fam* callarse

clamber [ˈklæmbə(r)] *vi* trepar (**over** por)

clammy [ˈklæmɪ] *adj* (**clammier, clammiest**) *(weather)* bochornoso(a); *(hand)* pegajoso(a)

clamour, *US* **clamor** [ˈklæmə(r)] **1** *n* clamor *m*
    2 *vi* clamar; **to c. for** pedir a gritos

clamp [klæmp] **1** *n (for carpentry)* tornillo *m* de banco; *Tech* abrazadera *f*; **wheel c.** cepo *m*
    2 *vt* sujetar con abrazaderas
    ▶ **clamp down on** *vt insep* aumentar los esfuerzos contra

clan [klæn] *n* clan *m*

clandestine [klænˈdestɪn] *adj* clandestino(a)

clang [klæŋ] **1** *vi* sonar
    2 *n* sonido metálico

clap [klæp] **1** *vi* aplaudir
    2 *n* (**a**) palmada *f* (**b**) **a c. of thunder** un trueno

clapping [ˈklæpɪŋ] *n* aplausos *mpl*

claret [ˈklærət] *n Br (wine)* clarete *m*; *(colour)* burdeos *m*

clarify [ˈklærɪfaɪ] *vt* aclarar

clarinet [klærɪˈnet] *n* clarinete *m*

clarity [ˈklærɪtɪ] *n* claridad *f*

clash [klæʃ] **1** *vi* (**a**) *(cymbals)* sonar; *(swords)* chocar; *Fig (disagree)* estar en

desacuerdo (**b**) *(colours)* desentonar (**c**) *(dates)* coincidir
2 *n* (**a**) *(sound)* sonido *m* (**b**) *(fight)* choque *m*; *Fig (conflict)* conflicto *m*
clasp [klɑːsp] **1** *n* (**a**) *(on belt)* cierre *m*; *(on necklace)* broche *m* (**b**) *(grasp)* apretón *m*; **c. knife** navaja *f*
2 *vt (object)* agarrar; **to c. hands** juntar las manos
class [klɑːs] **1** *n* clase *f*; **c. struggle** lucha *f* de clases; *US Educ* **c. of '84** promoción *f* de 1984; *Rail* **second c. ticket** billete *m* de segunda (clase)
2 *vt* clasificar
classic [ˈklæsɪk] **1** *adj* clásico(a)
2 *n* (**a**) *(author)* autor clásico; *(work)* obra clásica (**b**) **the classics** *(literature)* las obras clásicas; **classics** *(languages)* clásicas *fpl*
classical [ˈklæsɪkəl] *adj* clásico(a)
classified [ˈklæsɪfaɪd] *adj (information)* secreto(a); **c. advertisements** anuncios *mpl* por palabras
classify [ˈklæsɪfaɪ] *vt* clasificar
classless [ˈklɑːslɪs] *adj* sin clases
classmate [ˈklɑːsmeɪt] *n* compañero(a) *m,f* de clase
classroom [ˈklɑːsruːm] *n* aula *f*, clase *f*
clatter [ˈklætə(r)] **1** *vi* hacer ruido; *(things falling)* hacer estrépito
2 *n* ruido *m*, estrépito *m*
clause [klɔːz] *n* (**a**) *Jur* cláusula *f* (**b**) *Ling* oración *f*
claw [klɔː] **1** *n (of bird, lion)* garra *f*; *(of cat)* uña *f*; *(of crab)* pinza *f*
2 *vt* agarrar, arañar; *(tear)* desgarrar
▸ **claw at** *vt insep* agarrar, arañar
clay [kleɪ] *n* arcilla *f*; **c. pigeon shooting** tiro *m* al plato
clean [kliːn] **1** *adj* (**a**) limpio(a) (**b**) *(unmarked, pure)* sin defecto; **a c. copy** una copia en limpio; **to have a c. record** no tener antecedentes (penales) (**c**) *(not obscene)* decente (**d**) *Fig* **to make a c. sweep of it** arrasar
2 *adv* (**a**) **to play c.** jugar limpio; *Fam* **to come c.** confesarlo todo (**b**) *Fam* por completo; **it went c. through the middle** pasó justo por el medio
3 *vt (room)* limpiar; **to c. one's teeth** lavarse los dientes
▸ **clean out** *vt sep (room)* limpiar a fondo
▸ **clean up** *vt sep & vi* limpiar
clean-cut [ˈkliːnˈkʌt] *adj (person)* limpio(a), pulcro(a)
cleaner [ˈkliːnə(r)] *n* limpiador(a) *m,f*
cleaning [ˈkliːnɪŋ] *n* limpieza *f*
cleanliness [ˈklenlɪnɪs] *n* limpieza *f*

cleanse [klenz] *vt* limpiar
cleansing [ˈklenzɪŋ] *n* **c. lotion** leche limpiadora
clear [klɪə(r)] **1** *adj* (**a**) claro(a); *(road, day)* despejado(a); **c. conscience** conciencia tranquila (**b**) *(obvious)* claro(a); **to make sth c.** aclarar algo (**c**) *(majority)* absoluto(a); *(profit)* neto(a); **three c. days** tres días completos (**d**) *(free)* libre
2 *adv* (**a**) *Fig* **loud and c.** claramente (**b**) **stand c.!** ¡apártese!; **to stay c. of** evitar
3 *vt* (**a**) *(room)* vaciar; *Com* liquidar; **to c. one's throat** aclararse la garganta; **to c. the table** quitar la mesa (**b**) *(authorize)* autorizar (**c**) *(hurdle)* salvar (**d**) **to c. sb of a charge** exculpar a algn de un delito
4 *vi (sky)* despejarse
▸ **clear away** *vt sep* quitar
▸ **clear off** *vi Fam* largarse; **c. off!** ¡largo!
▸ **clear out** *vt sep (room)* limpiar a fondo; *(cupboard)* vaciar
▸ **clear up 1** *vt sep* (**a**) *(tidy)* recoger; *(arrange)* ordenar (**b**) *(mystery)* resolver; *(misunderstanding)* aclarar
2 *vi (weather)* despejarse; *(problem)* desaparecer
clearance [ˈklɪərəns] *n* (**a**) *(of area)* despeje *m*; *Com* **c. sale** liquidación *f* (de existencias) (**b**) *(space)* espacio *m* libre (**c**) *(authorization)* autorización *f*
clear-cut [klɪəˈkʌt] *adj* claro(a)
clearing [ˈklɪərɪŋ] *n* (**a**) *(in wood)* claro *m* (**b**) *(of rubbish)* limpieza *f* (**c**) *(of cheque)* compensación *f*
clearly [ˈklɪəlɪ] *adv* (**a**) claramente (**b**) *(at start of sentence)* evidentemente
clearway [ˈklɪəweɪ] *n Br* = carretera donde está prohibido parar
cleaver [ˈkliːvə(r)] *n* cuchillo *m* de carnicero
clef [klef] *n* clave *f*; **bass/treble c.** clave de fa/de sol
cleft [kleft] *n* hendidura *f*, grieta *f*
clementine [ˈkleməntaɪn] *n* clementina *f*
clench [klentʃ] *vt (teeth, fist)* apretar
clergy [ˈklɜːdʒɪ] *n* clero *m*
clergyman [ˈklɜːdʒɪmən] *n* clérigo *m*
clerical [ˈklerɪkəl] *adj* (**a**) *Rel* clerical (**b**) *(staff, work)* de oficina
clerk [klɑːk, *US* klɜːrk] *n* (**a**) *(office worker)* oficinista *mf*; *(civil servant)* funcionario(a) *m,f* (**b**) *US Com* dependiente(a) *m,f*, vendedor(a) *m,f*
clever [ˈklevə(r)] *adj* (**a**) *(person)* inteligente, listo(a); **to be c. at sth** tener aptitud para algo; *Fam* **c. Dick** sabiondo(a) *m,f* (**b**) *(argument)* ingenioso(a)

cliché [ˈkliːʃeɪ] *n* cliché *m*
click [klɪk] **1** *n (sound)* clic *m*
  2 *vt (tongue)* chasquear
  3 *vi* **it didn't c.** *(I didn't realize)* no me di
cuenta
client [ˈklaɪənt] *n* cliente *mf*
clientele [kliːɒnˈtel] *n* clientela *f*
cliff [klɪf] *n* acantilado *m*
climate [ˈklaɪmɪt] *n* clima *m*
climax [ˈklaɪmæks] *n* (**a**) *(peak)* clímax
m, punto *m* culminante (**b**) *(sexual)* orgasmo *m*
climb [klaɪm] **1** *vt (ladder)* subir a; *(mountain)* escalar; *(tree)* trepar a
  2 *vi (plants)* trepar; *Av* subir; *Fig (socially)* ascender
  3 *n* subida *f*, ascensión *f*
  ▸ **climb down** *vi* bajar; *Fig* volverse atrás
climber [ˈklaɪmə(r)] *n* alpinista *mf*, *Am*
andinista *mf*
climbing [ˈklaɪmɪŋ] *n Sport* montañismo
m, alpinismo *m*, *Am* andinismo *m*
clinch [klɪntʃ] **1** *vt* resolver; *(deal)* cerrar
  2 *n Fam* abrazo apasionado
cling [klɪŋ] *vi (pt & pp* **clung**) *(hang on)*
agarrarse; *(clothes)* ajustarse; *(smell)* pegarse; **to c. together** unirse
clinic [ˈklɪnɪk] *n (in state hospital)* ambulatorio *m*; *(specialized)* clínica *f*
clinical [ˈklɪnɪkəl] *adj* (**a**) *Med* clínico(a)
  (**b**) *(detached)* frío(a)
clink [klɪŋk] **1** *vi* tintinear
  2 *n* tintineo *m*
clip¹ [klɪp] **1** *vt (cut)* cortar; *(ticket)* picar
  2 *n* (**a**) *(of film)* extracto *m* (**b**) *(with
scissors)* tijeretada *f*
clip² [klɪp] **1** *n (for hair)* pasador *m*; *(for
paper)* clip *m*, sujetapapeles *m inv*;
(brooch) clip
  2 *vt* sujetar
clippers [ˈklɪpəz] *npl (for hair)* maquinilla *f* para rapar; *(for nails)* cortauñas
m inv; *(for hedge)* tijeras *fpl* de podar
clipping [ˈklɪpɪŋ] *n* recorte *m*
clique [kliːk] *n Pej* camarilla *f*
cloak [kləʊk] **1** *n (garment)* capa *f*
  2 *vt* encubrir
cloakroom [ˈkləʊkruːm] *n* guardarropa
m; *Euph (toilets)* servicios *mpl*
clock [klɒk] **1** *n* reloj *m*
  2 *vt (race)* cronometrar
  ▸ **clock in, clock on** *vi* fichar
  ▸ **clock off, clock out** *vi* fichar a la salida
  ▸ **clock up** *vt sep (mileage)* hacer
clockwise [ˈklɒkwaɪz] *adj & adv* en el
sentido de las agujas del reloj
clockwork [ˈklɒkwɜːk] *n* mecanismo *m*;
c. toy juguete *m* de cuerda

clog [klɒg] **1** *vt* obstruir; *(pipe)* atascar; **to
get clogged up** atascarse
  2 *n (footwear)* zueco *m*
cloister [ˈklɔɪstə(r)] *n* claustro *m*
close¹ [kləʊs] **1** *adj* (**a**) *(in space, time)*
cercano(a); *(print, weave)* compacto(a);
(encounter) cara a cara; *(contact)* direc-
to(a); **c. to** cerca de; **c. together** jun-
tos(as); *Fig* **we had a c. shave** nos
libramos por los pelos (**b**) *(relationship)*
estrecho(a); *(friend)* íntimo(a) (**c**) *(inspection)* detallado(a); *(watch)* atento(a)
(**d**) *(contest)* reñido(a); **a c. resemblance**
un gran parecido (**e**) *(air)* cargado(a);
(weather) bochornoso(a) (**f**) *(secretive)*
reservado(a) (**g**) **c. season** *(in hunting)*
veda *f*
  2 *adv* cerca; **they live c. by** *or* **c. at hand**
viven cerca; **to stand c. together** estar
apretados(as)
close² [kləʊz] **1** *vt* (**a**) cerrar; **closing time**
hora *f* de cierre (**b**) *(end)* concluir, terminar; *(meeting)* levantar
  2 *vi* (**a**) *(shut)* cerrar, cerrarse (**b**) *(end)*
concluirse, terminarse
  3 *n* fin *m*, final *m*
  ▸ **close down** *vi (business)* cerrar para
siempre; *Rad & TV* cerrar
  ▸ **close in** *vi* **to c. in on sb** rodear a algn
closed [kləʊzd] *adj* cerrado(a); *Ind* **c.
shop** = empresa que emplea solamente
a miembros de un sindicato
close-knit [kləʊsˈnɪt] *adj Fig* unido(a)
closely [ˈkləʊslɪ] *adv* (**a**) *(tightly)* estrechamente, muy; **c. contested** muy reñi-
do(a); **they are c. related** *(people)* son
parientes próximos (**b**) *(attentively)* con
atención; **to follow (events) c.** seguir de
cerca (los acontecimientos)
closet [ˈklɒzɪt] *n US* armario *m*
close-up [ˈkləʊsʌp] *n* primer plano *m*
closure [ˈkləʊʒə(r)] *n* cierre *m*
clot [klɒt] **1** *n* (**a**) *(of blood)* coágulo *m*;
Med **c. on the brain** embolia *f* cerebral (**b**)
Br Fam tonto(a) *m,f*
  2 *vi* coagularse
cloth [klɒθ] *n* tela *f*, paño *m*; *(rag)* trapo
m; *(tablecloth)* mantel *m*
clothe [kləʊð] *vt (pt & pp* **clothed** *or* **clad**)
vestir (**in** *or* **with** de); *Fig* revestir, cubrir
(**in** *or* **with** de)
clothes [kləʊðz] *npl* ropa *f*, vestidos *mpl*;
c. brush cepillo *m* de la ropa; **c. hanger**
percha *f*; **c. horse** tendedero *m* plegable;
c. line tendedero *m*; **c. peg** *or US* **pin** pinza
f
clothing [ˈkləʊðɪŋ] *n* ropa *f*
cloud [klaʊd] **1** *n* nube *f*

2 *vt* nublar; *Fig* **to c. the issue** complicar el asunto

3 *vi* **to c. over** nublarse

cloudy ['klaʊdɪ] *adj* (**cloudier, cloudiest**) (**a**) *(sky)* nublado(a) (**b**) *(liquid)* turbio(a)

clout [klaʊt] *Fam* **1** *n* (**a**) *(blow)* tortazo *m* (**b**) *(influence)* influencia *f*

2 *vt* dar un tortazo a

clove[1] [kləʊv] *n (spice)* clavo *m*

clove[2] [kləʊv] *n (of garlic)* diente *m*

clover ['kləʊvə(r)] *n* trébol *m*

clown [klaʊn] **1** *n* payaso *m*

2 *vi* **to c. (about** or **around)** hacer el payaso

cloying ['klɔɪɪŋ] *adj* empalagoso(a)

club [klʌb] **1** *n* (**a**) *(society)* club *m*; **sports c.** club deportivo (**b**) *(heavy stick)* garrote *m*, porra *f*; *(in golf)* palo *m* (**c**) *Cards* trébol *m* (**d**) *Culin* **c. sandwich** sándwich *m* doble; *US* **c. soda** soda *f*

2 *vt* aporrear

3 *vi* **to c. together** pagar entre varios

clubhouse ['klʌbhaʊs] *n* sede *f* de un club

cluck [klʌk] **1** *n* cloqueo *m*

2 *vi* cloquear

clue [kluː] *n (sign)* indicio *m*; *(to mystery)* pista *f*; *(in crossword)* clave *f*; *Fam* **I haven't a c.** no tengo ni idea

clump [klʌmp] *n (of trees)* grupo *m*; *(of plants)* mata *f*

clumsy ['klʌmzɪ] *adj* (**clumsier, clumsiest**) desmañado(a), torpe; *(awkward)* tosco(a)

clung [klʌŋ] *pt* & *pp of* **cling**

cluster ['klʌstə(r)] **1** *n* grupo *m*; *(of grapes)* racimo *m*

2 *vi* agruparse

clutch [klʌtʃ] **1** *vt* agarrar

2 *vi Fig* **to c. at straws** aferrarse a cualquier cosa

3 *n* (**a**) *Aut* embrague *m* (**b**) *Fig* **to fall into sb's clutches** caer en las garras de algn

clutter ['klʌtə(r)] *vt* **to c. (up)** llenar, atestar

cm *(abbr* **centimetre(s)**) cm

CND [siːen'diː] *n Br (abbr* **Campaign for Nuclear Disarmament**) = organización británica en favor del desarme nuclear

Co (**a**) *Com (abbr* **Company**) Cía. (**b**) *abbr* **County**

c/o [siːˈəʊ] *(abbr* **care of**) en el domicilio de

coach [kəʊtʃ] **1** *n* (**a**) *Aut* autocar *m*; *(carriage)* carruaje *m*; **c. tour** excursión *f* en autocar (**b**) *Rail* coche *m*, vagón *m* (**c**) *Sport* entrenador(a) *m,f*

2 *vt Sport* entrenar; *Educ* dar clases particulares a

coagulate [kəʊˈægjʊleɪt] *vi* coagularse

coal [kəʊl] *n* carbón *m*, hulla *f*; **c. bunker** carbonera *f*; **c. merchant** carbonero *m*; **c. mine** mina *f* de carbón

coalfield ['kəʊlfiːld] *n* yacimiento *m* de carbón

coalition [kəʊəˈlɪʃən] *n* coalición *f*

coarse [kɔːs] *adj (material)* basto(a); *(skin)* áspero(a); *(language)* grosero(a), ordinario(a)

coast [kəʊst] **1** *n* costa *f*, litoral *m*; *Fam Fig* **the c. is clear** no hay moros en la costa

2 *vi Aut* ir en punto muerto

coastal ['kəʊstəl] *adj* costero(a)

coaster ['kəʊstə(r)] *n (mat)* salvamanteles *m inv*

coastguard ['kəʊstgɑːd] *n* guardacostas *m inv*

coastline ['kəʊstlaɪn] *n* litoral *m*, costa *f*

coat [kəʊt] **1** *n* (**a**) *(overcoat)* abrigo *m*; *(short)* chaquetón *m*; **c. hanger** percha *f* (**b**) *(of animal)* pelo *m* (**c**) *(of paint)* mano *f*, capa *f* (**d**) **c. of arms** escudo *m* de armas

2 *vt* cubrir (**with** de); *(with liquid)* bañar (**with** en)

coating ['kəʊtɪŋ] *n* capa *f*, baño *m*

coax [kəʊks] *vt* engatusar

cob [kɒb] *n* mazorca *f*

cobble ['kɒbəl] *n* adoquín *m*

cobbler ['kɒblə(r)] *n* zapatero *m*

cobweb ['kɒbweb] *n* telaraña *f*

cocaine [kəˈkeɪn] *n* cocaína *f*

cock [kɒk] **1** *n* (**a**) *Orn* gallo *m*; *(male bird)* macho *m* (**b**) *(on gun)* percutor *m* (**c**)*Vulg (penis)* polla *f*

2 *vt (gun)* amartillar; *(ears)* erguir

▶ **cock up** *vt sep Br very Fam* chapucear

cocker ['kɒkə(r)] *n* **c. spaniel** cocker *m*

cockerel ['kɒkərəl] *n* gallo *m* joven

cockeyed ['kɒkaɪd] *adj Fam (lopsided)* torcido(a); *(scheme)* disparatado(a)

cockle ['kɒkəl] *n* berberecho *m*

cockney ['kɒknɪ] **1** *adj* = del East End londinense

2 *n* = persona del East End londinense

cockpit ['kɒkpɪt] *n* cabina *f* del piloto

cockroach ['kɒkrəʊtʃ] *n* cucaracha *f*

cocktail ['kɒkteɪl] *n* cóctel *m*; **c. lounge** bar *m*; **c. party** cóctel; **prawn c.** cóctel de gambas; **Molotov c.** cóctel Molotov

cocky ['kɒkɪ] *adj* (**cockier, cockiest**) *Fam* creído(a)

cocoa ['kəʊkəʊ] *n* cacao *m*

coconut ['kəʊkənʌt] *n* coco *m*

cocoon [kəˈkuːn] *n* capullo *m*

COD [siːəʊˈdiː] *Br* (*abbr* **cash on delivery**) CAE

cod [kɒd] *n* bacalao *m*; **c. liver oil** aceite *m* de hígado de bacalao

code [kəʊd] **1** *n* código *m*; (*symbol*) clave *f*; *Tel* prefijo *m*
2 *vt* (*message*) cifrar, poner en clave

co-ed [kəʊˈed] *Fam* **1** *adj* mixto(a)
2 *n* colegio mixto

coerce [kəʊˈɜːs] *vt* coaccionar

coercion [kəʊˈɜːʃən] *n* coacción *f*

coexist [kəʊɪgˈzɪst] *vi* coexistir

coffee [ˈkɒfɪ] *n* café *m*; **c. bar/shop** cafetería *f*; **c. break** descanso *m*; **c. table** mesita *f* de café

coffeepot [ˈkɒfɪpɒt] *n* cafetera *f*

coffer [ˈkɒfə(r)] *n* arca *f*

coffin [ˈkɒfɪn] *n* ataúd *m*

cog [kɒg] *n* diente *m*

cognac [ˈkɒnjæk] *n* coñac *m*

coherent [kəʊˈhɪərənt] *adj* coherente

coil [kɔɪl] **1** *vt* **to c. (up)** enrollar
2 *vi* enroscarse
3 *n* (**a**) (*loop*) vuelta *f*; (*of rope*) rollo *m*; (*of hair*) rizo *m* (**b**) (*contraceptive*) espiral *f* (**c**) *Elec* carrete *m*, bobina *f*

coin [kɔɪn] **1** *n* moneda *f*
2 *vt* (**a**) (*money*) acuñar (**b**) *Fig* **to c. a phrase** por así decirlo

coinage [ˈkɔɪnɪdʒ] *n* moneda *f*, sistema monetario

coincide [kəʊɪnˈsaɪd] *vi* coincidir (**with** con)

coincidence [kəʊˈɪnsɪdəns] *n* coincidencia *f*

coincidental [kəʊɪnsɪˈdentəl] *adj* casual

coincidentally [kəʊɪnsɪˈdentəlɪ] *adv* por casualidad *or* coincidencia

Coke® [kəʊk] *n Fam* Coca-Cola® *f*

coke [kəʊk] *n* (*coal*) coque *m*

colander [ˈkɒləndə(r)] *n* colador *m*

cold [kəʊld] **1** *adj* frío(a); **I'm c.** tengo frío; **it's c.** (*weather*) hace frío; (*thing*) está frío(a); *Fig* **to get c. feet** (about doing sth) entrarle miedo a algn (de hacer algo); **c. cream** crema *f* hidratante; *Fig* **it leaves me c.** no me dice nada; **c. war** guerra fría
2 *n* (**a**) frío *m* (**b**) *Med* resfriado *m*; **to catch a c.** resfriarse, acatarrarse; **to have a c.** estar resfriado(a); **c. sore** herpes *m* (en el labio)

cold-blooded [kəʊldˈblʌdɪd] *adj* (**a**) (*animal*) de sangre fría (**b**) *Fig* (*person*) frío(a); (*crime*) a sangre fría

coleslaw [ˈkəʊlslɔː] *n* ensalada *f* de col

collaborate [kəˈlæbəreɪt] *vi* colaborar (**with** con)

collaborator [kəˈlæbəreɪtə(r)] *n Pol* colaboracionista *mf*

collapse [kəˈlæps] **1** *vi* (*break down*) derrumbarse; (*cave in*) hundirse; *Fig* (*prices*) caer en picado; *Med* sufrir un colapso
2 *vt* (*table*) plegar
3 *n* (*breaking down*) derrumbamiento *m*; (*caving in*) hundimiento *m*; *Med* colapso *m*

collapsible [kəˈlæpsəbəl] *adj* plegable

collar [ˈkɒlə(r)] **1** *n* (*of garment*) cuello *m*; (*for dog*) collar *m*
2 *vt Fam* pescar, agarrar

collarbone [ˈkɒləbəʊn] *n* clavícula *f*

collateral [kɒˈlætərəl] **1** *n Fin* garantía subsidiaria
2 *adj* colateral

colleague [ˈkɒliːg] *n* colega *mf*

collect [kəˈlekt] **1** *vt* (**a**) (*gather*) recoger (**b**) (*stamps etc*) coleccionar (**c**) (*taxes*) recaudar
2 *vi* (**a**) (*people*) reunirse (**b**) (*for charity*) hacer una colecta (**for** para)
3 *adj US* **c. call** llamada *f or Am* llamado *m* a cobro revertido
4 *adv US Tel* **to call c.** llamar a cobro revertido

collection [kəˈlekʃən] *n* (**a**) (*of mail*) recogida *f*; (*of money*) colecta *f* (**b**) (*of stamps*) colección *f* (**c**) (*of taxes*) recaudación *f* (**d**) (*of people*) grupo *m*

collective [kəˈlektɪv] **1** *adj* colectivo(a); **c. bargaining** negociación colectiva
2 *n* colectivo *m*

collector [kəˈlektə(r)] *n* (**a**) (*of stamps*) coleccionista *mf* (**b**) **tax c.** recaudador(a) *m,f* (de impuestos)

college [ˈkɒlɪdʒ] *n* colegio *m*; (*of university*) colegio mayor; *US* (*university*) universidad *f*

collide [kəˈlaɪd] *vi* chocar, colisionar

collie [ˈkɒlɪ] *n* perro *m* pastor escocés

colliery [ˈkɒljərɪ] *n Br* mina *f* de carbón

collision [kəˈlɪʒən] *n* choque *m*

colloquial [kəˈləʊkwɪəl] *adj* coloquial

collusion [kəˈluːʒən] *n* conspiración *f*

cologne [kəˈləʊn] *n* (agua *f* de) colonia *f*

Colombia [kəˈlɒmbɪə] *n* Colombia

Colombian [kəˈlɒmbɪən] *adj & n* colombiano(a) (*m,f*)

colon¹ [ˈkəʊlən] *n Typ* dos puntos *mpl*

colon² [ˈkəʊlən] *n Anat* colon *m*

colonel [ˈkɜːnəl] *n* coronel *m*

colonial [kəˈləʊnɪəl] *adj* colonial

colonize [ˈkɒlənaɪz] *vt* colonizar

colony [ˈkɒlənɪ] *n* colonia *f*

color [ˈkʌlər] *n*, *vt & vi US* = **colour**

colossal [kəˈlɒsəl] *adj* colosal

colour ['kʌlə(r)] **1** n (**a**) color m; **what c. is it?** ¿de qué color es?; **c. film/television** película f/televisión f en color; **c. scheme** combinación f de colores (**b**) *(race)* color m; **c. bar** discriminación f racial (**c**) **colours** Br Sport colores mpl; Mil (flag) bandera f

2 vt colorear

3 vi **to c. (up)** ruborizarse

colour-blind ['kʌləblaɪnd] adj daltónico(a)

Coloured ['kʌləd] adj de color

coloured ['kʌləd] adj (photograph) en color

> Note that the Spanish word **colorado** is a false friend and is never a translation for the English word **coloured**. In Spanish, **colorado** means "red".

colourful ['kʌləfʊl] adj (**a**) con muchos colores (**b**) Fig lleno(a) de color; (person) pintoresco(a)

colouring ['kʌlərɪŋ] n (colour) colorido m

colourless ['kʌlələs] adj incoloro(a); Fig soso(a)

colt [kəʊlt] n potro m

column ['kɒləm] n columna f

columnist ['kɒləmnɪst] n columnista mf

coma ['kəʊmə] n coma m; **to go into a c.** entrar en coma

comb [kəʊm] **1** n peine m

2 vt peinar; **to c. one's hair** peinarse

combat ['kɒmbæt] **1** n combate m

2 vt (enemy, disease) combatir

3 vi combatir (**against** contra)

combination [kɒmbɪ'neɪʃən] n combinación f

combine [kəm'baɪn] **1** vt combinar

2 vi combinarse; (companies) asociarse

3 n ['kɒmbaɪn] (**a**) Com asociación f (**b**) **c. harvester** cosechadora f

combustion [kəm'bʌstʃən] n combustión f

come [kʌm] vi (pt **came**; pp **come**) (**a**) venir; (arrive) llegar; **coming!** ¡voy!; **to c. and go** ir y venir; Fig **in years to c.** en el futuro

(**b**) **to c. apart/undone** desatarse/soltarse

(**c**) (happen) suceder; **that's what comes of being too impatient** es lo que pasa por ser demasiado impaciente; Fam **how c.?** ¿y eso?

(**d**) **I came to believe that ...** llegué a creer que ...

(**e**) Fig **c. what may** pase lo que pase

(**f**) very Fam (have orgasm) correrse

▸ **come about** vi ocurrir, suceder

▸ **come across 1** vt insep (thing) encontrar por casualidad; **to c. across sb** tropezar con algn

2 vi Fig **to c. across well** causar buena impresión

▸ **come along** vi (**a**) (arrive) venir; **c. along!** ¡venga! (**b**) (make progress) progresar

▸ **come away** vi (leave) salir; (part) desprenderse (**from** de)

▸ **come back** vi (return) volver

▸ **come before** vt insep (**a**) preceder (**b**) (court) comparecer ante

▸ **come by** vt insep adquirir

▸ **come down** vi bajar; (rain) caer; (building) ser derribado(a); **to c. down with the flu** coger la gripe

▸ **come forward** vi (advance) avanzar; (volunteer) ofrecerse

▸ **come in** vi (**a**) (enter) entrar; **c. in!** ¡pase! (**b**) (arrive) (train) llegar; (tide) subir; Fam Fig **where do I c. in?** y yo ¿qué pinto? (**c**) **to c. in handy** venir bien (**d**) **to c. in for** ser objeto de

▸ **come into** vt insep (**a**) (enter) entrar en (**b**) (inherit) heredar

▸ **come off 1** vt insep (fall from) caerse de; Fam **c. off it!** ¡venga ya!

2 vi (**a**) (fall) caerse; (stain) quitarse; (button) caerse (**b**) Fam (take place) pasar; (succeed) salir bien; **to c. off badly** salir mal

▸ **come on** vi (**a**) **c. on!** (hurry) ¡venga! (**b**) (make progress) progresar (**c**) (rain, illness) comenzar

▸ **come out** vi (**a**) salir (**of** de); (book) aparecer; (product) estrenarse; (facts) revelarse (**b**) (stain) quitarse; (colour) desteñir (**c**) **to c. out against/in favour of sth** declararse en contra/a favor de algo; Br Ind **to c. out (on strike)** declararse en huelga (**d**) (turn out) salir

▸ **come over 1** vi venir

2 vt insep (**a**) (hill) aparecer en lo alto de (**b**) Fam **what's c. over you?** ¿qué te pasa?

▸ **come round 1** vt insep (corner) dar la vuelta a

2 vi (**a**) (visit) venir (**b**) (regain consciousness) volver en sí (**c**) **to c. round to sb's way of thinking** dejarse convencer por algn

▸ **come through 1** vt insep (**a**) (cross) cruzar (**b**) (illness) recuperarse de; (accident) sobrevivir

2 vi (message) llegar

▸ **come to 1** vi (regain consciousness) volver en sí

2 *vt insep* (**a**) *Fig* **to c. to one's senses** recobrar la razón (**b**) *(amount to)* costar (**c**) *(arrive at)* llegar a; **to c. to an end** terminar; *Fam* **c. to that** a propósito
▸ **come under** *vt insep Fig* **to c. under fire from sb** ser criticado(a) por algn
▸ **come up** *vi* (**a**) *(rise)* subir; *(approach)* acercarse (**to** a) (**b**) *(difficulty, question)* surgir; **to c. up with a solution** encontrar una solución; **to c. up against problems** encontrarse con problemas (**c**) *(sun)* salir (**d**) **to c. up to** igualar; **to c. up to sb's expectations** satisfacer a algn (**e**) *Fam* **three chips, coming up!** ¡van tres de patatas fritas!
▸ **come upon** *vt insep* = **come across**
comeback ['kʌmbæk] *n Fam* (**a**) *(of person)* reaparición *f*; **to make a c.** reaparecer (**b**) *(answer)* réplica *f*
comedian [kə'miːdɪən] *n* cómico *m*
comedienne [kəmiːdɪ'en] *n* cómica *f*
comedown ['kʌmdaʊn] *n Fam* desilusión *f*, revés *m*
comedy ['kɒmɪdɪ] *n* comedia *f*
comet ['kɒmɪt] *n* cometa *m*
comeuppance [kʌm'ʌpəns] *n Fam* **to get one's c.** llevarse su merecido
comfort ['kʌmfət] **1** *n* (**a**) comodidad *f*; *US* **c. station** servicios *mpl* (**b**) *(consolation)* consuelo *m*; **to take c. in** *or* **from sth** consolarse con algo
2 *vt* consolar
comfortable ['kʌmfətəbəl] *adj (chair, person, margin)* cómodo(a); *(temperature)* agradable
comfortably ['kʌmfətəblɪ] *adv (win)* con facilidad; **to be c. off** vivir cómodamente
comforter ['kʌmfətə(r)] *n* (**a**) *Br (scarf)* bufanda *f* (**b**) *(for baby)* chupete *m* (**c**) *US (quilt)* edredón *m*
comforting ['kʌmfətɪŋ] *adj* consolador(a)
comic ['kɒmɪk] **1** *adj* cómico(a); **c. strip** tira cómica, historieta *f*
2 *n* (**a**) *(person)* cómico(a) *m,f* (**b**) *Press* tebeo *m*, comic *m*
coming ['kʌmɪŋ] **1** *adj (year)* próximo(a); *(generation)* futuro(a)
2 *n* venida *f*, llegada *f*; **comings and goings** idas *fpl* y venidas; *Fig* **c. and going** ajetreo *m*
comma ['kɒmə] *n* coma *f*
command [kə'mɑːnd] **1** *vt* (**a**) mandar (**b**) *(respect)* infundir; *(sympathy)* merecer; *(money etc)* disponer de
2 *n* (**a**) *(order)* orden *f*; *(authority)* mando *m*; **to be at sb's c.** estar a las órdenes

de algn (**b**) *(of language)* dominio *m* (**c**) *(disposal)* disposición *f* (**d**) *Comput* comando *m*, instrucción *f*
commandeer [kɒmən'dɪə(r)] *vt* requisar
commander [kə'mɑːndə(r)] *n* comandante *m*
commanding [kə'mɑːndɪŋ] *adj* dominante; *Mil* **c. officer** comandante *m*
commandment [kə'mɑːndmənt] *n* mandamiento *m*
commando [kə'mɑːndəʊ] *n* comando *m*
commemorate [kə'meməreɪt] *vt* conmemorar
commence [kə'mens] *vt & vi Fml* comenzar
commend [kə'mend] *vt* (**a**) *(praise)* alabar, elogiar (**b**) *(entrust)* encomendar (**c**) *(recommend)* recomendar
commensurate [kə'menʃərɪt] *adj* proporcional; **c. to** *or* **with** en proporción con
comment ['kɒment] **1** *n* comentario *m*; **no c.** sin comentario
2 *vi* hacer comentarios
commentary ['kɒməntərɪ] *n* comentario *m*
commentator ['kɒmənteɪtə(r)] *n* comentarista *mf*
commerce ['kɒmɜːs] *n* comercio *m*
commercial [kə'mɜːʃəl] **1** *adj* comercial; *TV* **c. break** corte publicitario
2 *n TV* anuncio *m*
commiserate [kə'mɪzəreɪt] *vi* compadecerse (**with** de)
commission [kə'mɪʃən] **1** *n* (**a**) *Mil* despacho *m* (de oficial); **out of c.** fuera de servicio (**b**) *(of inquiry)* comisión *f*; *(job)* encargo *m* (**c**) *(payment)* comisión *f*
2 *vt* (**a**) *Mil* nombrar (**b**) *(order)* encargar (**c**) *Naut* poner en servicio
commissionaire [kəmɪʃə'neə(r)] *n Br* portero *m*
commissioner [kə'mɪʃənə(r)] *n (official)* comisario *m*; **c. of police** comisario de policía
commit [kə'mɪt] *vt* (**a**) *(crime)* cometer; **to c. suicide** suicidarse (**b**) **to c. oneself (to do sth)** comprometerse (a hacer algo) (**c**) **to c. sth to sb's care** confiar algo a algn
commitment [kə'mɪtmənt] *n* compromiso *m*
committee [kə'mɪtɪ] *n* comisión *f*, comité *m*
commode [kə'məʊd] *n (chair)* silla *f* con orinal; *(chest of drawers)* cómoda *f*
commodity [kə'mɒdɪtɪ] *n* producto *m* básico

📝 Note that the Spanish word **comodidad** is a false friend and is never a translation for the English word **commodity**. In Spanish, **comodidad** means "comfort, convenience".

common [ˈkɒmən] **1** *adj* (**a**) común; **that's c. knowledge** eso lo sabe todo el mundo; **c. law** derecho consuetudinario; **C. Market** Mercado *m* Común; *Br* **c. room** sala *f* de profesores/de estudiantes (**b**) *(ordinary)* corriente (**c**) *(vulgar)* ordinario(a), maleducado(a)
   2 *n (land)* campo *m or* terreno *m* comunal

commonplace [ˈkɒmənpleɪs] *adj* corriente

Commons [ˈkɒmənz] *npl Br* **the (House of) C.** (la Cámara de) los Comunes

Commonwealth [ˈkɒmənwelθ] *n Br* **the C.** la Commonwealth; **C. of Independent States** Comunidad *f* de Estados Independientes

commotion [kəˈməʊʃən] *n* alboroto *m*

commune¹ [kəˈmjuːn] *vi (converse)* conversar íntimamente; *(with nature)* estar en comunión (**with** con)

commune² [ˈkɒmjuːn] *n* comuna *f*

communicate [kəˈmjuːnɪkeɪt] **1** *vi* comunicarse (**with** con)
   2 *vt* comunicar

communication [kəmjuːnɪˈkeɪʃən] *n* (**a**) comunicación *f* (**b**) *Br Rail* **c. cord** timbre *m* de alarma

communion [kəˈmjuːnɪən] *n* comunión *f*; **to take c.** comulgar

communiqué [kəˈmjuːnɪkeɪ] *n* comunicado *m* oficial

communism [ˈkɒmjʊnɪzəm] *n* comunismo *m*

communist [ˈkɒmjʊnɪst] *adj & n* comunista *(mf)*

community [kəˈmjuːnɪtɪ] *n* comunidad *f*; *(people)* colectividad *f*; **c. centre** centro *m* social

commute [kəˈmjuːt] **1** *vi* = viajar diariamente al lugar de trabajo
   2 *vt Jur* conmutar

commuter [kəˈmjuːtə(r)] *n* = persona que viaja diariamente al lugar de trabajo

compact¹ 1 *adj* [kəmˈpækt] compacto(a); *(style)* conciso(a)
   2 *n* [ˈkɒmpækt] *(for powder)* polvera *f*

compact² [ˈkɒmpækt] *n Pol* pacto *m*

compact disc [ˈkɒmpækt'dɪsk] *n* disco compacto

companion [kəmˈpænjən] *n* compañero(a) *m,f*

companionship [kəmˈpænjənʃɪp] *n* compañerismo *m*

company [ˈkʌmpənɪ] *n* (**a**) compañía *f*; **to keep sb c.** hacer compañía a algn (**b**) *Com* empresa *f*, compañía *f*

comparable [ˈkɒmpərəbəl] *adj* comparable (**to** *or* **with** con)

comparative [kəmˈpærətɪv] **1** *adj* comparativo(a); *(relative)* relativo(a)
   2 *n Ling* comparativo *m*

comparatively [kəmˈpærətɪvlɪ] *adv* relativamente

compare [kəmˈpeə(r)] **1** *vt* comparar (**to** *or* **with** con); **(as) compared with** en comparación con
   2 *vi* compararse

comparison [kəmˈpærɪsən] *n* comparación *f*; **by c.** en comparación; **there's no c.** no se puede comparar

compartment [kəmˈpɑːtmənt] *n (section)* compartimiento *m*; *Rail* departamento *m*

compass [ˈkʌmpəs] *n* (**a**) brújula *f* (**b**) **(pair of) compasses** compás *m* (**c**) *Fig (range)* límites *mpl*

compassion [kəmˈpæʃən] *n* compasión *f*

compassionate [kəmˈpæʃənət] *adj* compasivo(a)

compatible [kəmˈpætəbəl] *adj* compatible

compel [kəmˈpel] *vt* (**a**) *(oblige)* obligar; **to c. sb to do sth** obligar a algn a hacer algo (**b**) *(admiration)* despertar

compelling [kəmˈpelɪŋ] *adj* irresistible

compensate [ˈkɒmpənseɪt] **1** *vt* compensar; **to c. sb for sth** indemnizar a algn de algo
   2 *vi* compensar

compensation [kɒmpənˈseɪʃən] *n* compensación *f*; *(for loss)* indemnización *f*

compere [ˈkɒmpeə(r)] *n Br* animador(a) *m,f*

compete [kəmˈpiːt] *vi* competir

competence [ˈkɒmpɪtəns] *n* (**a**) *(ability)* aptitud *f* (**b**) *(of court etc)* competencia *f*

competent [ˈkɒmpɪtənt] *adj* competente

competition [kɒmpɪˈtɪʃən] *n* (**a**) *(contest)* concurso *m* (**b**) *Com* competencia *f*

competitive [kəmˈpetɪtɪv] *adj* competitivo(a)

competitor [kəmˈpetɪtə(r)] *n* competidor(a) *m,f*

compilation [kɒmpɪˈleɪʃən] *n* recopilación *f*

compile [kəmˈpaɪl] *vt* compilar, recopilar

complacency [kəmˈpleɪsənsɪ] *n* autocomplacencia *f*

> 🖉 Note that the Spanish word **complacencia** is a false friend and is never a translation for the English word **complacency**. In Spanish, **complacencia** means "satisfaction, indulgence".

complacent [kəm'pleɪsənt] *adj* autocomplaciente

complain [kəm'pleɪn] *vi* quejarse (**of/about** de)

complaint [kəm'pleɪnt] *n* (**a**) queja *f*; *Com* reclamación *f* (**b**) *Jur* demanda *f* (**c**) *Med* enfermedad *f*

complement ['kɒmplɪmənt] **1** *n* (**a**) complemento *m* (**b**) *Naut* dotación *f*
2 *vt* complementar

complementary [kɒmplɪ'mentərɪ] *adj* complementario(a)

complete [kəm'pliːt] **1** *adj* (**a**) *(entire)* completo(a) (**b**) *(absolute)* total
2 *vt* completar; **to c. a form** rellenar un formulario

completely [kəm'pliːtlɪ] *adv* completamente, por completo

completion [kəm'pliːʃən] *n* terminación *f*; **near c.** casi terminado(a); **on c.** en cuanto se termine

complex ['kɒmpleks] **1** *adj* complejo(a)
2 *n* complejo *m*; **inferiority c.** complejo de inferioridad

complexion [kəm'plekʃən] *n* tez *f*; *Fig* aspecto *m*

> 🖉 Note that the Spanish word **complexión** is a false friend and is never a translation for the English word **complexion**. In Spanish, **complexión** means "build".

compliance [kəm'plaɪəns] *n* conformidad *f*; **in c. with** de acuerdo con

complicate ['kɒmplɪkeɪt] *vt* complicar

complicated ['kɒmplɪkeɪtɪd] *adj* complicado(a)

complication [kɒmplɪ'keɪʃən] *n* complicación *f*

complicity [kəm'plɪsɪtɪ] *n* complicidad *f*

compliment 1 *n* ['kɒmplɪmənt] (**a**) cumplido *m*; **to pay sb a c.** hacerle un cumplido a algn (**b**) **compliments** saludos *mpl*
2 *vt* ['kɒmplɪment] felicitar; **to c. sb on sth** felicitar a algn por algo

complimentary [kɒmplɪ'mentərɪ] *adj* (**a**) *(praising)* elogioso(a) (**b**) *(free)* gratis

comply [kəm'plaɪ] *vi* obedecer; **to c. with** *(order)* cumplir con; *(request)* acceder a

component [kəm'pəʊnənt] **1** *n* componente *m*
2 *adj* componente; **c. part** parte *f*

compose [kəm'pəʊz] *vt* & *vi* (**a**) componer; **to be composed of** componerse de (**b**) **to c. oneself** calmarse

composed [kəm'pəʊzd] *adj (calm)* sereno(a)

composer [kəm'pəʊzə(r)] *n* compositor(a) *m,f*

composite ['kɒmpəzɪt] *adj* compuesto(a)

composition [kɒmpə'zɪʃən] *n* composición *f*; *(essay)* redacción *f*

compost ['kɒmpɒst] *n* abono *m*

composure [kəm'pəʊʒə(r)] *n* calma *f*, serenidad *f*

compound¹ ['kɒmpaʊnd] **1** *n* compuesto *m*
2 *adj* compuesto(a); *(fracture)* complicado(a)
3 *vt* [kəm'paʊnd] *(problem)* agravar

compound² ['kɒmpaʊnd] *n (enclosure)* recinto *m*

comprehend [kɒmprɪ'hend] *vt* comprender

comprehensible [kɒmprɪ'hensəbəl] *adj* comprensible

comprehension [kɒmprɪ'henʃən] *n* comprensión *f*

comprehensive [kɒmprɪ'hensɪv] *adj* (**a**) *(knowledge)* amplio(a); *(study)* detallado(a) (**b**) *Ins* a todo riesgo (**c**) *Br* **c. school** ≃ instituto *m* de segunda enseñanza

> 🖉 Note that the Spanish word **comprensivo** is a false friend and is never a translation for the English word **comprehensive**. In Spanish, **comprensivo** means "understanding".

compress 1 *vt* [kəm'pres] comprimir
2 *n* ['kɒmpres] compresa *f*

comprise [kəm'praɪz] *vt* comprender; *(consist of)* constar de

compromise ['kɒmprəmaɪz] **1** *n* solución *f* negociada; **to reach a c.** llegar a un acuerdo
2 *vi (two people)* llegar a un acuerdo; *(individual)* transigir
3 *vt (person)* comprometer

> 🖉 Note that the Spanish word **compromiso** is a false friend and is never a translation for the English word **compromise**. In Spanish, **compromiso** means "obligation, commitment, agreement".

compulsion [kəm'pʌlʃən] *n* obligación *f*

compulsive [kəm'pʌlsɪv] *adj* compulsivo(a)

compulsory [kəm'pʌlsərɪ] *adj* obligatorio(a)

computer [kəmˈpjuːtə(r)] *n* ordenador *m*, *Am* computadora *f*; **c. programmer** programador(a) *m,f* de ordenadores; **c. science** informática *f*; **personal c.** ordenador personal, *Am* computadora personal

computerize [kəmˈpjuːtəraɪz] *vt* informatizar

computing [kəmˈpjuːtɪŋ] *n* informática *f*

comrade [ˈkɒmreɪd] *n* (**a**) *(companion)* compañero(a) *m,f* (**b**) *Pol* camarada *mf*

comradeship [ˈkɒmreɪdʃɪp] *n* camaradería *f*

con [kɒn] *Fam* **1** *vt* estafar, timar
  2 *n* estafa *f*, camelo *m*; **c. man** estafador *m*

concave [ˈkɒnkeɪv] *adj* cóncavo(a)

conceal [kənˈsiːl] *vt* ocultar; *(emotions)* disimular

concede [kənˈsiːd] *vt* conceder

conceit [kənˈsiːt] *n* presunción *f*, vanidad *f*

conceited [kənˈsiːtɪd] *adj* presuntuoso(a)

conceivable [kənˈsiːvəbəl] *adj* concebible

conceive [kənˈsiːv] *vt & vi* concebir

concentrate [ˈkɒnsəntreɪt] **1** *vt* concentrar
  2 *vi* **to c. on sth** concentrarse en algo

concentration [kɒnsənˈtreɪʃən] *n* concentración *f*; **c. camp** campo *m* de concentración

concept [ˈkɒnsept] *n* concepto *m*

conception [kənˈsepʃən] *n Med* concepción *f*; *(understanding)* concepto *m*, idea *f*

concern [kənˈsɜːn] **1** *vt* (**a**) concernir, afectar; **as far as I'm concerned** por lo que a mí se refiere (**b**) *(worry)* preocupar
  2 *n* (**a**) **it's no c. of mine** no es asunto mío (**b**) *(worry)* preocupación *f* (**c**) *Com* negocio *m*

concerned [kənˈsɜːnd] *adj* (**a**) *(affected)* afectado(a) (**b**) *(worried)* preocupado(a) (**about** por)

concerning [kənˈsɜːnɪŋ] *prep* con respecto a, en cuanto a

concert [ˈkɒnsət, ˈkɒnsɜːt] *n Mus* concierto *m*; **c. hall** sala *f* de conciertos

concerted [kənˈsɜːtɪd] *adj* concertado(a)

concertina [kɒnsəˈtiːnə] *n* concertina *f*

concerto [kənˈtʃɜːtəʊ] *n* concierto *m*

concession [kənˈseʃən] *n* (**a**) concesión *f*; **tax c.** privilegio *m* fiscal (**b**) *Com* reducción *f*

concise [kənˈsaɪs] *adj* conciso(a)

conclude [kənˈkluːd] *vt & vi* concluir

conclusion [kənˈkluːʒən] *n* conclusión *f*; **to reach a c.** llegar a una conclusión

conclusive [kənˈkluːsɪv] *adj* concluyente

concoct [kənˈkɒkt] *vt (dish)* confeccionar; *Fig (plan)* fraguar; *(excuse)* inventar

concoction [kənˈkɒkʃən] *n (mixture)* mezcolanza *f*; *Pej (brew)* brebaje *m*

concourse [ˈkɒŋkɔːs] *n* explanada *f*

> 🖉 Note that the Spanish word **concurso** is a false friend and is never a translation for the English word **concourse**. In Spanish, **concurso** means "competition, contest".

concrete [ˈkɒnkriːt] **1** *n* hormigón *m*; **c. mixer** hormigonera *f*
  2 *adj* (**a**) *(definite)* concreto(a) (**b**) *(made of concrete)* de hormigón

concur [kənˈkɜː(r)] *vi* (**a**) **to c. with** *(agree)* estar de acuerdo con (**b**) *(coincide)* coincidir

concurrent [kənˈkʌrənt] *adj* simultáneo(a)

concussion [kənˈkʌʃən] *n* conmoción *f* cerebral

condemn [kənˈdem] *vt* condenar

condemnation [kɒndemˈneɪʃən] *n* condena *f*

condensation [kɒndenˈseɪʃən] *n* condensación *f*

condense [kənˈdens] **1** *vt* condensar
  2 *vi* condensarse

condensed [kənˈdenst] *adj* **c. milk** leche condensada

condescending [kɒndɪˈsendɪŋ] *adj* condescendiente

condition [kənˈdɪʃən] **1** *n* condición *f*; **to be in good c.** estar en buen estado; **on c. that ...** a condición de que ...; **on one c.** con una condición; **heart c.** enfermedad cardíaca; **conditions** *(circumstances)* circunstancias *fpl*
  2 *vt* condicionar

conditional [kənˈdɪʃənəl] *adj* condicional

conditioner [kənˈdɪʃənə(r)] *n* acondicionador *m*

condolences [kənˈdəʊlənsɪz] *npl* pésame *m*; **please accept my c.** le acompaño en el sentimiento

condom [ˈkɒndəm] *n* preservativo *m*

condominium [kɒndəˈmɪnɪəm] *n US (building)* = bloque de apartamentos poseídos por diferentes propietarios; *(apartment)* apartamento *m*, piso *m* (en propiedad)

condone [kənˈdəʊn] *vt* perdonar, consentir

condor [ˈkɒndɔː(r)] *n* cóndor *m*

conducive [kənˈdjuːsɪv] *adj* conducente

conduct 1 *n* [ˈkɒndʌkt] *(behaviour)*

conducta f, comportamiento m
2 vt [kən'dʌkt] *(lead)* guiar; *(business, orchestra)* dirigir; **conducted tour** visita acompañada; **to c. oneself** comportarse
3 vi *Mus* dirigir
conductor [kən'dʌktə(r)] n (**a**) Br *(on bus)* cobrador m (**b**) US *Rail* revisor(a) m,f (**c**) *Mus* director(a) m,f (**d**) *Phys* conductor m
conductress [kən'dʌktrɪs] n *(on bus)* cobradora f
cone [kəʊn] n (**a**) cono m; **ice-cream c.** cucurucho m (**b**) *Bot* piña f
confectioner [kən'fekʃənə(r)] n confitero(a) m,f; **c.'s (shop)** confitería f
confectionery [kən'fekʃənərɪ] n dulces mpl
confederate [kən'fedərɪt] **1** adj confederado(a)
2 n confederado(a) m,f; *Jur* cómplice mf
confer [kən'fɜː(r)] **1** vt **to c. a title on sb** conferir un título a algn
2 vi consultar
conference ['kɒnfərəns] n conferencia f
confess [kən'fes] **1** vi confesar; *Rel* confesarse
2 vt confesar
confession [kən'feʃən] n confesión f
confessional [kən'feʃənəl] n confesionario m
confetti [kən'fetɪ] n confeti m
confide [kən'faɪd] vi **to c. in sb** confiar en algn
confidence ['kɒnfɪdəns] n (**a**) confianza f; **vote of c./no c.** voto m de confianza/de censura; **c. trick** camelo m (**b**) *(secret)* confidencia f; **in c.** en confianza
confident ['kɒnfɪdənt] adj seguro(a)
confidential [kɒnfɪ'denʃəl] adj *(secret)* confidencial; *(entrusted)* de confianza
confine [kən'faɪn] vt encerrar; *Fig* limitar
confinement [kən'faɪnmənt] n (**a**) *(prison)* prisión f; **to be in solitary c.** estar incomunicado(a) (**b**) *Med* parto m
confirm [kən'fɜːm] vt confirmar
confirmation [kɒnfə'meɪʃən] n confirmación f
confirmed [kən'fɜːmd] adj empedernido(a)
confiscate ['kɒnfɪskeɪt] vt confiscar
conflict 1 n ['kɒnflɪkt] conflicto m
2 vi [kən'flɪkt] chocar (**with** con)
conflicting [kən'flɪktɪŋ] adj contradictorio(a)
conform [kən'fɔːm] vi conformarse; **to c. to** or **with** *(customs)* amoldarse a; *(rules)* someterse a

confound [kən'faʊnd] vt confundir, desconcertar
confront [kən'frʌnt] vt hacer frente a
confrontation [kɒnfrʌn'teɪʃən] n confrontación f
confuse [kən'fjuːz] vt *(person)* despistar; *(thing)* confundir (**with** con); **to get confused** confundirse
confused [kən'fjuːzd] adj *(person)* confundido(a); *(mind, ideas)* confuso(a)
confusing [kən'fjuːzɪŋ] adj confuso(a)
confusion [kən'fjuːʒən] n confusión f
congeal [kən'dʒiːl] vi coagularse
congenial [kən'dʒiːnɪəl] adj agradable
congenital [kən'dʒenɪtəl] adj congénito(a)
congested [kən'dʒestɪd] adj (**a**) *(street)* repleto(a) de gente; *(city)* superpoblado(a) (**b**) *Med* congestionado(a)
congestion [kən'dʒestʃən] n congestión f
conglomeration [kənglɒmə'reɪʃən] n conglomeración f
congratulate [kən'grætjʊleɪt] vt felicitar
congratulations [kəngrætjʊ'leɪʃənz] npl felicitaciones fpl; **c.!** ¡enhorabuena!
congregate ['kɒŋgrɪgeɪt] vi congregarse
congregation [kɒŋgrɪ'geɪʃən] n *(group)* congregación f; *Rel* fieles mpl
congress ['kɒŋgres] n (**a**) *(conference)* congreso m (**b**) US *Pol* **C.** el Congreso *(de los Estados Unidos)*
Congressman ['kɒŋgresmən] n US *Pol* congresista m, Am congresal m
Congresswoman ['kɒŋgreswʊmən] n US *Pol* congresista f, Am congresal f
conifer ['kɒnɪfə(r)] n conífera f
conjecture [kən'dʒektʃə(r)] **1** n conjetura f
2 vt conjeturar
3 vi hacer conjeturas
conjugal ['kɒndʒʊgəl] adj conyugal
conjugate ['kɒndʒʊgeɪt] vt conjugar
conjunction [kən'dʒʌŋkʃən] n conjunción f; *Fig* **in c. with** conjuntamente con
conjunctivitis [kəndʒʌŋktɪ'vaɪtɪs] n conjuntivitis f
conjure ['kʌndʒə(r)] **1** vt **to c. (up)** *(magician)* hacer aparecer; *(memories)* evocar
2 vi hacer juegos de manos
conjurer ['kʌndʒərə(r)] n prestidigitador(a) m,f
conker ['kɒŋkə(r)] n *Fam* castaña f
connect [kə'nekt] **1** vt (**a**) *(join)* juntar, unir; *(wires)* empalmar; *Fig* **to be connected by marriage** estar emparentado(a) por matrimonio (**b**) *(install)* instalar; *Elec*

conectar (**c**) *Tel (person)* poner (**d**) *Fig (associate)* asociar

2 *vi* unirse; *(rooms)* comunicarse; *(train, flight)* enlazar *or* empalmar (**with** con)

connected [kəˈnektɪd] *adj* unido(a); *(events)* relacionado(a); *Fig* **to be well c.** *(person) (socially)* estar bien relacionado(a)

connection [kəˈnekʃən] *n* (**a**) *(joint)* juntura *f*, unión *f*; *Elec* conexión *f*; *Tel* instalación *f* (**b**) *Rail* correspondencia *f* (**c**) *Fig (of ideas)* relación *f*; **in c. with** *(regarding)* con respecto a (**d**) *(person)* contacto *m*

connive [kəˈnaɪv] *vi* **to c. at** hacer la vista gorda con

connoisseur [kɒnɪˈsɜː(r)] *n* conocedor(a) *m,f*

connotation [kɒnəˈteɪʃən] *n* connotación *f*

conquer [ˈkɒŋkə(r)] *vt (enemy, bad habit)* vencer; *(country)* conquistar

conqueror [ˈkɒŋkərə(r)] *n* conquistador *m*

conquest [ˈkɒŋkwest] *n* conquista *f*

conscience [ˈkɒnʃəns] *n* conciencia *f*; **to have a clear c.** tener la conciencia tranquila; **to have a guilty c.** sentirse culpable

conscientious [kɒnʃɪˈenʃəs] *adj* concienzudo(a); **c. objector** objetor(a) *m,f* de conciencia

conscious [ˈkɒnʃəs] *adj (aware)* consciente; *(choice etc)* deliberado(a)

consciousness [ˈkɒnʃəsnɪs] *n Med* conocimiento *m*; *(awareness)* conciencia *f*

conscript [ˈkɒnskrɪpt] *n* recluta *m*

conscription [kənˈskrɪpʃən] *n* servicio *m* militar obligatorio

consecrate [ˈkɒnsɪkreɪt] *vt* consagrar

consecutive [kənˈsekjʊtɪv] *adj* consecutivo(a)

consensus [kənˈsensəs] *n* consenso *m*

consent [kənˈsent] **1** *n* consentimiento *m*; **by common c.** de común acuerdo

2 *vi* consentir (**to** en)

consequence [ˈkɒnsɪkwəns] *n* consecuencia *f*

consequent [ˈkɒnsɪkwənt] *adj* consiguiente

consequently [ˈkɒnsɪkwəntlɪ] *adv* por consiguiente

conservation [kɒnsəˈveɪʃən] *n* conservación *f*

conservative [kənˈsɜːvətɪv] **1** *adj* cauteloso(a)

2 *adj & n Pol* **C.** conservador(a) *(m,f)*

conservatory [kənˈsɜːvətrɪ] *n* (**a**) *(greenhouse)* invernadero *m* (**b**) *Mus* conservatorio *m*

conserve 1 *vt* [kənˈsɜːv] conservar

2 *n* [ˈkɒnsɜːv] conserva *f*

consider [kənˈsɪdə(r)] *vt* (**a**) *(ponder on, regard)* considerar; **to c. doing sth** pensar hacer algo (**b**) *(keep in mind)* tener en cuenta

considerable [kənˈsɪdərəbəl] *adj* considerable

considerably [kənˈsɪdərəblɪ] *adv* bastante

considerate [kənˈsɪdərɪt] *adj* considerado(a)

consideration [kənsɪdəˈreɪʃən] *n* consideración *f*; **without due c.** sin reflexión

considering [kənˈsɪdərɪŋ] *prep* teniendo en cuenta

consign [kənˈsaɪn] *vt Com* consignar; *Fig* entregar

consignment [kənˈsaɪnmənt] *n* envío *m*

consist [kənˈsɪst] *vi* **to c. of** consistir en

consistency [kənˈsɪstənsɪ] *n* (**a**) *(of actions)* consecuencia *f* (**b**) *(of mixture)* consistencia *f*

consistent [kənˈsɪstənt] *adj* consecuente; **c. with** de acuerdo con

> **Note** that the Spanish word **consistente** is a false friend and is never a translation for the English word **consistent**. In Spanish, **consistente** means "firm, solid, sound".

consolation [kɒnsəˈleɪʃən] *n* consuelo *m*; **c. prize** premio *m* de consolación

console¹ [kənˈsəʊl] *vt* consolar

console² [ˈkɒnsəʊl] *n* consola *f*

consolidate [kənˈsɒlɪdeɪt] **1** *vt* consolidar

2 *vi* consolidarse

consonant [ˈkɒnsənənt] *n* consonante *f*

consortium [kənˈsɔːtɪəm] *n* consorcio *m*

conspicuous [kənˈspɪkjʊəs] *adj (striking)* llamativo(a); *(easily seen)* visible; *(mistake)* evidente

conspiracy [kənˈspɪrəsɪ] *n* conjura *f*

conspire [kənˈspaɪə(r)] *vi* conspirar

constable [ˈkʌnstəbəl] *n* policía *m*, guardia *m*; **chief c.** jefe *m* de policía

constabulary [kənˈstæbjʊlərɪ] *n Br* comisaría *f*

constant [ˈkɒnstənt] **1** *adj* constante; *(continuous)* incesante; *(loyal)* fiel, leal

2 *n* constante *f*

constellation [kɒnstɪˈleɪʃən] *n* constelación *f*

consternation [kɒnstəˈneɪʃən] *n* consternación *f*

constipated [ˈkɒnstɪpeɪtɪd] *adj* **to be c.** estar estreñido(a)

> *Note that the Spanish word **constipado** is a false friend and is never a translation for the English word **constipated**. In Spanish, **constipado** means both "cold, chill" and "suffering from a cold".*

constipation [kɒnstɪˈpeɪʃən] *n* estreñimiento *m*
constituency [kənˈstɪtjʊənsɪ] *n* circunscripción *f* electoral
constituent [kənˈstɪtjʊənt] **1** *adj (component)* constituyente
2 *n* (**a**) *(part)* componente *m* (**b**) *Pol* votante *mf*
constitute [ˈkɒnstɪtjuːt] *vt* constituir
constitution [kɒnstɪˈtjuːʃən] *n* constitución *f*
constitutional [kɒnstɪˈtjuːʃənəl] *adj* constitucional
constrained [kənˈstreɪnd] *adj* **to feel c. to do sth** sentirse obligado(a) a hacer algo
constraint [kənˈstreɪnt] *n* coacción *f*; **to feel c. in sb's presence** sentirse cohibido(a) ante algn
construct [kənˈstrʌkt] *vt* construir
construction [kənˈstrʌkʃən] *n* construcción *f*
constructive [kənˈstrʌktɪv] *adj* constructivo(a)
construe [kənˈstruː] *vt* interpretar

> *Note that the Spanish verb **construir** is a false friend and is never a translation for the English verb **to construe**. In Spanish, **construir** means "to build, to manufacture".*

consul [ˈkɒnsəl] *n* cónsul *mf*
consulate [ˈkɒnsjʊlɪt] *n* consulado *m*
consult [kənˈsʌlt] *vt & vi* consultar (**about** sobre)
consultant [kənˈsʌltənt] *n Med* especialista *mf*; *Com & Ind* asesor(a) *m,f*
consultation [kɒnsəlˈteɪʃən] *n* consulta *f*
consulting [kənˈsʌltɪŋ] *adj* **c. room** consulta *f*
consume [kənˈsjuːm] *vt* consumir
consumer [kənˈsjuːmə(r)] *n* consumidor(a) *m,f*; **c. goods** bienes *mpl* de consumo
consummate **1** *vt* [ˈkɒnsəmeɪt] consumar
2 *adj* [ˈkɒnsəmɪt] consumado(a)
consumption [kənˈsʌmpʃən] *n* (**a**) *(of food)* consumo *m*; **fit for c.** apto(a) para el consumo (**b**) *Med* tisis *f*
cont. (*abbr* **continued**) sigue

contact [ˈkɒntækt] **1** *n* contacto *m*; **c. lenses** lentes *fpl* de contacto
2 *vt* ponerse en contacto con
contagious [kənˈteɪdʒəs] *adj* contagioso(a)
contain [kənˈteɪn] *vt* contener; **to c. oneself** contenerse
container [kənˈteɪnə(r)] *n* (**a**) *(box, package)* recipiente *m*; *(bottle)* envase *m* (**b**) *Naut* contenedor *m*
contaminate [kənˈtæmɪneɪt] *vt* contaminar
contamination [kəntæmɪˈneɪʃən] *n* contaminación *f*
contd. (*abbr* **continued**) sigue
contemplate [ˈkɒntempleɪt] *vt* (**a**) *(consider)* considerar, pensar en (**b**) *(look at)* contemplar
contemporary [kənˈtemprərɪ] *adj & n* contemporáneo(a) *(m,f)*
contempt [kənˈtempt] *n* desprecio *m*; **to hold in c.** despreciar; **c. of court** desacato *m* a los tribunales
contemptible [kənˈtemptəbəl] *adj* despreciable
contemptuous [kənˈtemptjʊəs] *adj* despectivo(a)
contend [kənˈtend] **1** *vi* competir; *Fig* **there are many problems to c. with** se han planteado muchos problemas
2 *vt* afirmar
contender [kənˈtendə(r)] *n* contendiente *mf*
content[1] [ˈkɒntent] *n* contenido *m*; **table of contents** índice *m* de materias
content[2] [kənˈtent] **1** *adj* contento(a)
2 *vt* contentar
3 *n* contento *m*; **to one's heart's c.** todo lo que uno quiera
contented [kənˈtentɪd] *adj* contento(a), satisfecho(a)
contention [kənˈtenʃən] *n* (**a**) *(dispute)* controversia *f* (**b**) *(point)* punto *m* de vista
contentment [kənˈtentmənt] *n* contento *m*
contest 1 *n* [ˈkɒntest] concurso *m*; *Sport* prueba *f*
2 *vt* [kənˈtest] (**a**) *(matter)* rebatir; *(verdict)* impugnar; *Fig (will)* disputar (**b**) *Pol (seat)* luchar por
contestant [kənˈtestənt] *n* concursante *mf*
context [ˈkɒntekst] *n* contexto *m*
continent [ˈkɒntɪnənt] *n* continente *m*; **(on) the C.** (en) Europa
continental [kɒntɪˈnentəl] *adj* (**a**) continental; **c. shelf** plataforma *f* continental

(**b**) *Br* **C.** europeo(a); **c. quilt** edredón *m* de pluma

contingency [kən'tɪndʒənsɪ] *n* contingencia *f*; **c. plans** planes *mpl* para casos de emergencia

contingent [kən'tɪndʒənt] *adj & n* contingente *(m)*

continual [kən'tɪnjʊəl] *adj* continuo(a), constante

continuation [kəntɪnjʊ'eɪʃən] *n (sequel etc)* continuación *f*; *(extension)* prolongación *f*

continue [kən'tɪnjuː] *vt & vi* continuar, seguir; **to c. to do sth** seguir *or* continuar haciendo algo

continuous [kən'tɪnjʊəs] *adj* continuo(a)

contort [kən'tɔːt] *vt* retorcer

contortion [kən'tɔːʃən] *n* contorsión *f*

contour ['kɒntʊə(r)] *n* contorno *m*; **c. line** línea *f* de nivel

contraband ['kɒntrəbænd] *n* contrabando *m*

contraception [kɒntrə'sepʃən] *n* anticoncepción *f*

contraceptive [kɒntrə'septɪv] *adj & n* anticonceptivo *(m)*

contract 1 *vi* [kən'trækt] *Phys* contraerse
  2 *vt* (**a**) contraer (**b**) **to c. to do sth** *(make agreement)* comprometerse por contrato a hacer algo
  3 *n* ['kɒntrækt] contrato *m*; **to enter into a c.** hacer un contrato

contraction [kən'trækʃən] *n* contracción *f*

contractor [kən'træktə(r)] *n* contratista *mf*

contradict [kɒntrə'dɪkt] *vt* contradecir

contradiction [kɒntrə'dɪkʃən] *n* contradicción *f*; **it's a c. in terms** no tiene lógica

contradictory [kɒntrə'dɪktərɪ] *adj* contradictorio(a)

contraption [kən'træpʃən] *n Fam* cacharro *m*

contrary ['kɒntrərɪ] **1** *adj* (**a**) *(opposite)* contrario(a) (**b**) [kən'treərɪ] *(awkward)* terco(a)
  2 *n* **on the c.** todo lo contrario; **unless I tell you to the c.** a menos que te diga lo contrario
  3 *adv* **c. to** en contra de

contrast 1 *vi* [kən'trɑːst] contrastar
  2 *n* ['kɒntrɑːst] contraste *m*

contrasting [kən'trɑːstɪŋ] *adj* opuesto(a)

contravene [kɒntrə'viːn] *vt* contravenir

contribute [kən'trɪbjuːt] **1** *vt (money)* contribuir con; *(ideas, information)* aportar

2 *vi* (**a**) contribuir; *(in discussion)* participar (**b**) *Press* colaborar (**to** en)

contribution [kɒntrɪ'bjuːʃən] *n* (**a**) *(of money)* contribución *f*; *(of ideas etc)* aportación *f* (**b**) *Press* colaboración *f*

contributor [kən'trɪbjʊtə(r)] *n (to newspaper)* colaborador(a) *m,f*

contrive [kən'traɪv] *vt* inventar, idear; **to c. to do sth** buscar la forma de hacer algo

contrived [kən'traɪvd] *adj* artificial, forzado(a)

control [kən'trəʊl] **1** *vt* controlar; *(person, animal)* dominar; *(vehicle)* manejar; **to c. one's temper** controlarse
  2 *n* (**a**) *(power)* control *m*, dominio *m*; *(authority)* autoridad *f*; **out of c.** fuera de control; **to be in c.** estar al mando; **to be under c.** *(situation)* estar bajo control; **to go out of c.** descontrolarse; **to lose c.** perder los estribos (**b**) *Aut & Av (device)* mando *m*; *Rad & TV* botón *m* de control; **c. panel** tablero *m* de instrumentos; **c. room** sala *f* de control; *Av* **c. tower** torre *f* de control

controversial [kɒntrə'vɜːʃəl] *adj* controvertido(a), polémico(a)

controversy ['kɒntrəvɜːsɪ, kən'trɒvəsɪ] *n* polémica *f*

conurbation [kɒnɜː'beɪʃən] *n* conurbación *f*

convalesce [kɒnvə'les] *vi* convalecer

convalescence [kɒnvə'lesəns] *n* convalecencia *f*

convalescent [kɒnvə'lesənt] *adj* convaleciente; **c. home** clínica *f* de reposo

convene [kən'viːn] **1** *vt* convocar
  2 *vi* reunirse

convenience [kən'viːnɪəns] *n* conveniencia *f*, comodidad *f*; **all modern conveniences** todas las comodidades; **at your c.** cuando le convenga; **c. food** comida precocinada; *Br Euph* **public conveniences** aseos públicos

convenient [kən'viːnɪənt] *adj (time, arrangement)* conveniente, oportuno(a); *(place)* bien situado(a)

convent ['kɒnvənt] *n* convento *m*

convention [kən'venʃən] *n* convención *f*

conventional [kən'venʃənəl] *adj* clásico(a); *(behaviour)* convencional

converge [kən'vɜːdʒ] *vi* convergir

conversant [kən'vɜːsənt] *adj Fml* **to be c. with a subject** ser versado(a) en una materia

conversation [kɒnvə'seɪʃən] *n* conversación *f*

conversational [kɒnvə'seɪʃənəl] *adj* coloquial

converse¹ [kən'vɜːs] *vi* conversar

converse² ['kɒnvɜːs] *n* the c. lo opuesto

conversely ['kɒnvɜːslɪ] *adv* a la inversa

conversion [kən'vɜːʃən] *n Math & Rel* conversión *f* (**to** a; **into** en)

convert 1 *vt* [kən'vɜːt] convertir
  2 *n* ['kɒnvɜːt] converso(a) *m,f*

convertible [kən'vɜːtəbəl] **1** *adj* convertible
  2 *n Aut* descapotable *m*

convex ['kɒnveks, kɒn'veks] *adj* convexo(a)

convey [kən'veɪ] *vt* (a) *(carry)* transportar (**b**) *(sound)* transmitir; *(idea)* comunicar

conveyor [kən'veɪə(r)] *n* c. **belt** cinta transportadora

convict 1 *vt* [kən'vɪkt] declarar culpable a, condenar
  2 *n* ['kɒnvɪkt] presidiario(a) *m,f*

conviction [kən'vɪkʃən] *n* (a) *(belief)* creencia *f*, convicción *f* (b) *Jur* condena *f*

convince [kən'vɪns] *vt* convencer

convincing [kən'vɪnsɪŋ] *adj* convincente

convoluted ['kɒnvəluːtɪd] *adj* intrincado(a)

convoy ['kɒnvɔɪ] *n* convoy *m*

convulse [kən'vʌls] *vt* convulsionar; *Fam* **to be convulsed with laughter** troncharse de risa

convulsion [kən'vʌlʃən] *n* convulsión *f*

coo [kuː] *vi (pigeon)* arrullar

cook [kʊk] **1** *vt* cocinar, guisar; *(dinner)* preparar; *Fam* **to c. the books** falsificar las cuentas
  2 *vi (person)* cocinar, guisar; *(food)* cocerse
  3 *n* cocinero(a) *m,f*

cookbook ['kʊkbʊk] *n US* libro *m* de cocina

cooker ['kʊkə(r)] *n* cocina *f*

cookery ['kʊkərɪ] *n* cocina *f*; c. **book** libro *m* de cocina

cookie ['kʊkɪ] *n US* galleta *f*

cooking ['kʊkɪŋ] *n* cocina *f*

cool [kuːl] **1** *adj* (a) fresco(a); **it's c.** *(weather)* hace fresquito (b) *Fig (calm)* tranquilo(a); *(reserved)* frío(a)
  2 *n* (a) *(coolness)* fresco *m* (b) *Fam* **to lose one's c.** perder la calma
  3 *vt (air)* refrescar; *(drink)* enfriar
  4 *adv Fam* **to play it c.** hacer como si nada
  ▸**cool down, cool off** *vi Fig* calmarse; *(feelings)* enfriarse

coolness ['kuːlnɪs] *n* (a) *Fig (calmness)* calma *f*, *(composure)* aplomo *m* (b) *Fam (nerve, cheek)* frescura *f*

coop [kuːp] **1** *n* gallinero *m*
  2 *vt* **to c. (up)** encerrar

co-operate [kəʊ'ɒpəreɪt] *vi* cooperar

co-operation [kəʊɒpə'reɪʃən] *n* cooperación *f*

co-operative [kəʊ'ɒpərətɪv] **1** *adj (helpful)* cooperador(a)
  2 *n* cooperativa *f*

co-ordinate 1 *vt* [kəʊ'ɔːdɪneɪt] coordinar
  2 *n* [kəʊ'ɔːdɪnɪt] (a) *Math* coordenada *f* (b) **co-ordinates** *(clothes)* conjunto *m*

co-ordination [kəʊɔːdɪ'neɪʃən] *n* coordinación *f*

cop [kɒp] *Fam* **1** *n (policeman)* poli *m*
  2 *vt* **you'll c. it** te vas a ganar una buena
  ▸**cop out** *vi* rajarse

cope [kəʊp] *vi* arreglárselas; **to c. with** *(person, work)* poder con; *(problem)* hacer frente a

Copenhagen [kəʊpən'heɪgən] *n* Copenhague

copious ['kəʊpɪəs] *adj* copioso(a), abundante

copper¹ ['kɒpə(r)] **1** *n (metal)* cobre *m*
  2 *adj (colour)* cobrizo(a)

copper² ['kɒpə(r)] *n Fam* poli *mf*

coppice ['kɒpɪs], **copse** [kɒps] *n* arboleda *f*, bosquecillo *m*

copulate ['kɒpjʊleɪt] *vi* copular

copy ['kɒpɪ] **1** *n* (a) copia *f* (b) *(of book)* ejemplar *m*
  2 *vt & vi* copiar

copycat ['kɒpɪkæt] *n Fam* copión(ona) *m,f*

copyright ['kɒpɪraɪt] *n* derechos *mpl* de autor

coral ['kɒrəl] *n* coral *m*; c. **reef** arrecife *m* de coral

cord [kɔːd] *n* (a) *(string)* cuerda *f*; *Elec* cordón *m* (b) *Tex (corduroy)* pana *f*; **cords** pantalones *mpl* de pana

cordial ['kɔːdɪəl] **1** *adj* cordial
  2 *n* licor *m*

cordon ['kɔːdən] **1** *n* cordón *m*
  2 *vt* **to c. off a street** acordonar una calle

corduroy ['kɔːdərɔɪ] *n* pana *f*

core [kɔː(r)] **1** *n (of fruit)* corazón *m*; *Elec* núcleo *m*; *Fig* **the hard c.** los incondicionales
  2 *vt* quitarle el corazón a

coriander [kɒrɪ'ændə(r)] *n* culantro *m*

cork [kɔːk] *n* corcho *m*; c. **oak** alcornoque *m*

corkscrew ['kɔːkskruː] *n* sacacorchos *m inv*

corn¹ [kɔːn] *n* cereal *m*; *(grain)* granos *mpl*; *(maize)* maíz *m*; **c. on the cob**

mazorca *f* de maíz *or Andes, RP* choclo, *Méx* elote *m*

corn² [kɔːn] *n Med* callo *m*

corncob ['kɔːnkɒb] *n* mazorca *f*

cornea ['kɔːnɪə] *n* córnea *f*

corner ['kɔːnə(r)] **1** *n* (**a**) *(of street)* esquina *f*; *(bend in road)* curva *f*; **round the c.** a la vuelta de la esquina; *Ftb* **c. kick** córner *m*; **c. shop** tienda pequeña de barrio (**b**) *(of room)* rincón *m*

2 *vt* (**a**) *(enemy)* arrinconar (**b**) *Com* acaparar

3 *vi Aut* tomar una curva

cornerstone ['kɔːnəstəʊn] *n* piedra *f* angular

cornet ['kɔːnɪt] *n* (**a**) *Mus* corneta *f* (**b**) *Br (for ice cream)* cucurucho *m*

cornflakes ['kɔːnfleɪks] *npl* copos *mpl* de maíz, cornflakes *mpl*

cornflour ['kɔːnflaʊə(r)], *US* **cornstarch** ['kɔːnstɑːtʃ] *n* harina *f* de maíz

Cornwall ['kɔːnwəl] *n* Cornualles

corny ['kɔːnɪ] *adj* (**cornier, corniest**) *Fam* gastado(a)

corollary [kə'rɒlərɪ] *n* corolario *m*

coronary ['kɒrənərɪ] *adj* coronario(a); **c. thrombosis** trombosis coronaria

coronation [kɒrə'neɪʃən] *n* coronación *f*

coroner ['kɒrənə(r)] *n* juez *mf* de instrucción

corporal¹ ['kɔːpərəl] *adj* corporal; **c. punishment** castigo *m* corporal

corporal² ['kɔːpərəl] *n Mil* cabo *m*

corporate ['kɔːpərɪt] *adj* corporativo(a)

corporation [kɔːpə'reɪʃən] *n* (**a**) *(business)* sociedad anónima (**b**) *(of city)* ayuntamiento *m*

corps [kɔː(r)] *n* (*pl* **corps** [kɔːz]) cuerpo *m*

corpse [kɔːps] *n* cadáver *m*

corpulent ['kɔːpjʊlənt] *adj* corpulento(a)

corpuscle ['kɔːpʌsəl] *n* corpúsculo *m*

corral [kə'rɑːl] *n US* corral *m*

correct [kə'rekt] **1** *vt* (**a**) *(mistake)* corregir (**b**) *(child)* reprender

2 *adj* correcto(a), exacto(a); *(behaviour)* formal

correction [kə'rekʃən] *n* corrección *f*

correlation [kɒrə'leɪʃən] *n* correlación *f*

correspond [kɒrɪ'spɒnd] *vi* (**a**) corresponder; **to c. to** equivaler a (**b**) *(by letter)* escribirse

correspondence [kɒrɪ'spɒndəns] *n* correspondencia *f*; **c. course** curso *m* por correspondencia

correspondent [kɒrɪ'spɒndənt] *n Press* corresponsal *mf*; **special c.** enviado(a) *m,f* especial

corridor ['kɒrɪdɔː(r)] *n* pasillo *m*

corroborate [kə'rɒbəreɪt] *vt* corroborar

corrode [kə'rəʊd] **1** *vt* corroer

2 *vi* corroerse

corrosion [kə'rəʊʒən] *n* corrosión *f*

corrugated ['kɒrʊgeɪtɪd] *adj* **c. iron** hierro ondulado

corrupt [kə'rʌpt] **1** *adj* *(person)* corrompido(a), corrupto(a); *(actions)* deshonesto(a)

2 *vt & vi* corromper

corruption [kə'rʌpʃən] *n* corrupción *f*

corset ['kɔːsɪt] *n* *(garment)* faja *f*

Corsica ['kɔːsɪkə] *n* Córcega

cortège [kɔː'teɪʒ] *n* cortejo *m*, comitiva *f*

cosh [kɒʃ] *n Br* porra *f*

cosmetic [kɒz'metɪk] **1** *n* cosmético *m*

2 *adj* cosmético(a); **c. surgery** cirugía plástica

cosmic ['kɒzmɪk] *adj* cósmico(a)

cosmonaut ['kɒzmənɔːt] *n* cosmonauta *mf*

cosmopolitan [kɒzmə'pɒlɪtən] *adj* cosmopolita

cosset ['kɒsɪt] *vt* mimar

cost [kɒst] **1** *n* *(price)* precio *m*, coste *m*; **c. of living** coste de la vida; **to count the c.** considerar las desventajas; **at all costs** a toda costa

2 *vt & vi* (*pt & pp* **cost**) costar, valer; **how much does it c.?** ¿cuánto cuesta?; **whatever it costs** cueste lo que cueste

3 *vt* (*pt & pp* **costed**) *Com & Ind* calcular el coste de

co-star ['kəʊstɑː(r)] *n Cin & Th* coprotagonista *mf*

Costa Rica [kɒstə'riːkə] *n* Costa Rica

Costa Rican [kɒstə'riːkən] *adj & n* costarricense (*mf*)

cost-effective [kɒstɪ'fektɪv] *adj* rentable

costly ['kɒstlɪ] *adj* (**costlier, costliest**) costoso(a)

costume ['kɒstjuːm] *n* traje *m*; **swimming c.** bañador *m*; **c. jewellery** bisutería *f*

cosy ['kəʊzɪ] *adj* (**cosier, cosiest**) *(atmosphere)* acogedor(a); *(bed)* calentito(a); **it's c. in here** aquí se está bien

cot [kɒt] *n* (**a**) *Br (for child)* cuna *f* (**b**) *US (folding bed)* catre *m*, cama *f* plegable

cottage ['kɒtɪdʒ] *n* casa *f* de campo; **c. cheese** queso fresco; **c. industry** industria casera; *Br* **c. pie** = pastel de carne picada con puré de patatas *or Am* papas

cotton ['kɒtən] *n* (**a**) *Bot* algodonero *m*; *Tex* algodón *m*; *Br* **c. wool,** *US* **absorbent c.** algodón hidrófilo (**b**) *(thread)* hilo *m*

▸ **cotton on** *vi Fam* **to c. on to sth** caer en la cuenta de algo

couch [kaʊtʃ] *n* sofá *m*; *(in surgery)* camilla *f*

couchette [kuː'ʃet] *n Rail* litera *f*

cough [kɒf] **1** *vi* toser

2 *n* tos *f*; **c. drop** pastilla *f* para la tos; **c. mixture** jarabe *m* para la tos

► **cough up** *vt sep Fam* **to c. up the money** soltar la pasta

could [kʊd] *v aux see* **can¹**

council ['kaʊnsəl] *n (body)* consejo *m*; *Br* **c. house** vivienda *f* de protección oficial; **town c.** consejo municipal, ayuntamiento *m*

councillor, *US* **councilor** ['kaʊnsələ(r)] *n* concejal *mf*

counsel ['kaʊnsəl] **1** *n* (**a**) *(advice)* consejo *m* (**b**) *Jur* abogado(a) *m,f*

2 *vt* aconsejar

counsellor, *US* **counselor** ['kaʊnsələ(r)] *n* (**a**) *(adviser)* asesor(a) *m,f* (**b**) *US Jur* abogado(a) *m,f*

count¹ [kaʊnt] **1** *vt* (**a**) contar (**b**) *Fig* **to c. oneself lucky** considerarse afortunado(a)

2 *vi* contar; **that doesn't c.** eso no vale; **to c. to ten** contar hasta diez

3 *n* (**a**) cuenta *f*; *(total)* recuento *m* (**b**) *Jur* cargo *m*

► **count on** *vt insep* contar con

count² [kaʊnt] *n (nobleman)* conde *m*

countdown ['kaʊntdaʊn] *n* cuenta *f* atrás

countenance ['kaʊntɪnəns] **1** *n* semblante *m*, rostro *m*

2 *vt* aprobar

counter¹ ['kaʊntə(r)] *n* (**a**) *(in shop)* mostrador *m*; *(in bank)* ventanilla *f* (**b**) *(in board games)* ficha *f*

counter² ['kaʊntə(r)] *n* contador *m*

counter³ ['kaʊntə(r)] **1** *adv* **c. to** en contra de

2 *vt (attack)* contestar a; *(trend)* contrarrestar

3 *vi* contestar

counteract [kaʊntər'ækt] *vt* contrarrestar

counterattack ['kaʊntərətæk] *n* contraataque *m*

counter-clockwise ['kaʊntə'klɒkwaɪz] *adv US* en sentido opuesto al de las agujas del reloj

counterfeit ['kaʊntəfɪt] **1** *adj* falsificado(a); **c. coin** moneda falsa

2 *n* falsificación *f*

3 *vt* falsificar

counterfoil ['kaʊntəfɔɪl] *n Br (of cheque)* matriz *f*

countermand [kaʊntə'mɑːnd] *vt (command)* revocar; *Com (order)* anular

counterpart ['kaʊntəpɑːt] *n* homólogo(a) *m,f*

counterproductive [kaʊntəprə'dʌktɪv] *adj* contraproducente

countersign ['kaʊntəsaɪn] *vt* refrendar

countess ['kaʊntɪs] *n* condesa *f*

countless ['kaʊntlɪs] *adj* innumerable, incontable

country ['kʌntrɪ] *n* (**a**) *(state)* país *m*; **native c.** patria *f* (**b**) *(rural area)* campo *m*; **c. dancing** baile *m* popular

countryman ['kʌntrɪmən] *n* (**a**) *(rural)* hombre *m* del campo (**b**) *(compatriot)* compatriota *m*

countryside ['kʌntrɪsaɪd] *n (area)* campo *m*; *(scenery)* paisaje *m*

county ['kaʊntɪ] *n* condado *m*

coup [kuː] *n (pl coups* [kuːz]*)* golpe *m*; **c. d'etat** golpe de estado

couple ['kʌpəl] **1** *n* (**a**) *(of people)* pareja *f*; **a married c.** un matrimonio (**b**) *(of things)* par *m*; *Fam* **a c. of times** un par de veces

2 *vt (wagons)* enganchar

coupling ['kʌplɪŋ] *n Rail* enganche *m*

coupon ['kuːpɒn] *n* (**a**) cupón *m* (**b**) *Br Ftb* quiniela *f*

courage ['kʌrɪdʒ] *n* coraje *m*, valentía *f*

courageous [kə'reɪdʒəs] *adj* valeroso(a), valiente

courgette [kʊə'ʒet] *n Br* calabacín *m*, *CSur* zapallito *m*

courier ['kʊrɪə(r)] *n* (**a**) *(messenger)* mensajero(a) *m,f* (**b**) *(guide)* guía *mf* turístico(a)

course [kɔːs] *n* (**a**) *(of river)* curso *m*; *Naut & Av* rumbo *m* (**b**) *Fig* desarrollo *m*; **in the c. of construction** en vías de construcción; **in the c. of time** con el tiempo (**c**) *(series)* ciclo *m*; **a c. of treatment** un tratamiento (**d**) *Educ* curso *m*; *Univ* asignatura *f* (**e**) *(for golf)* campo *m*; *(for horseracing)* hipódromo *m* (**f**) *Culin* plato *m* (**g**) **of c.** claro, por supuesto; **of c. not!** ¡claro que no!

court [kɔːt] **1** *n* (**a**) *Jur* tribunal *m*; **c. martial** consejo *m* de guerra; **c. order** orden *f* judicial (**b**) *(royal)* corte *f* (**c**) *Sport* pista *f*, cancha *f*

2 *vt (woman)* hacer la corte a; *Fig* **to c. danger** buscar el peligro; *Fig* **to c. disaster** exponerse al desastre

3 *vi (couple)* tener relaciones

courteous ['kɜːtɪəs] *adj* cortés

courtesy ['kɜːtɪsɪ] *n* (**a**) cortesía *f*, educación *f* (**b**) **by c. of** por cortesía de

courthouse ['kɔːthaʊs] *n US* palacio *m* de justicia

courtier ['kɔːtɪə(r)] *n* cortesano(a) *m,f*
court-martial [kɔːt'mɑːʃəl] *vt* someter a consejo de guerra
courtroom ['kɔːtruːm] *n* sala *f* de justicia
courtyard ['kɔːtjɑːd] *n* patio *m*
cousin ['kʌzən] *n* primo(a) *m,f*; **first c.** primo(a) hermano(a)
cove [kəʊv] *n* cala *f*, ensenada *f*
covenant ['kʌvənənt] *n* convenio *m*, pacto *m*
cover ['kʌvə(r)] **1** *vt* (**a**) cubrir (**with** de); *(furniture)* revestir (**with** de); *(with lid)* tapar
 (**b**) *(hide)* disimular
 (**c**) *(protect)* abrigar
 (**d**) *(distance)* recorrer
 (**e**) *Press* investigar
 (**f**) *(deal with)* abarcar
 (**g**) *(include)* incluir
 (**h**) *Sport* marcar
 2 *vi* **to c. for sb** sustituir a algn
 3 *n* (**a**) cubierta *f*; *(lid)* tapa *f*; *(on bed)* manta *f*, *Am* frazada *f*, cobija *f*; *(of chair etc)* funda *f*
 (**b**) *(of book)* tapa *f*; *(of magazine)* portada *f*; **c. girl** modelo *f* de revista
 (**c**) *(in restaurant)* cubierto *m*
 (**d**) **under separate c.** por separado
 (**e**) *Ins* **full c.** cobertura completa; *Br* **c. note** seguro *m* provisional
 (**f**) *(protection)* abrigo *m*; **to take c.** abrigarse; **under c.** al abrigo; *(indoors)* bajo techo
 ▸ **cover up 1** *vt sep* (**a**) cubrir (**b**) *(crime)* encubrir
 2 *vi* (**a**) *(person)* abrigarse (**b**) **to c. up for sb** encubrir a algn
coverage ['kʌvərɪdʒ] *n* cobertura *f*
coveralls ['kʌvərɔːlz] *npl US* mono *m*
covering ['kʌvərɪŋ] **1** *n* cubierta *f*, envoltura *f*
 2 *adj (letter)* explicatorio(a)
covert ['kʌvət] *adj* disimulado(a), secreto(a)
cover-up ['kʌvərʌp] *n* encubrimiento *m*
covet ['kʌvɪt] *vt* codiciar
cow¹ [kaʊ] *n* vaca *f*; *Pej (woman)* arpía *f*, bruja *f*
cow² [kaʊ] *vt* intimidar
coward ['kaʊəd] *n* cobarde *mf*
cowardice ['kaʊədɪs] *n* cobardía *f*
cowardly ['kaʊədlɪ] *adj* cobarde
cowboy ['kaʊbɔɪ] *n* vaquero *m*
cower ['kaʊə(r)] *vi (with fear)* encogerse
cox [kɒks] *n* timonel *m*
coy [kɔɪ] *adj (shy)* tímido(a); *(demure)* coquetón(ona)
cozy ['kəʊzɪ] *adj US* = **cosy**

crab [kræb] *n* (**a**) cangrejo *m* (**b**) **c. apple** manzana *f* silvestre
crack [kræk] **1** *vt* (**a**) *(cup)* partir; *(bone)* fracturar; *(nut)* cascar; *(safe)* forzar (**b**) *(whip)* hacer restallar (**c**) *Fig (problem)* dar con la solución de; *(joke)* contar
 2 *vi* (**a**) *(glass)* partirse; *(wall)* agrietarse (**b**) *(whip)* restallar (**c**) *Fam* **to get cracking on sth** ponerse a hacer algo
 3 *n* (**a**) *(in cup)* raja *f*; *(in wall, ground)* grieta *f* (**b**) *(of whip)* restallido *m*; *(of gun)* detonación *f* (**c**) *Fam (blow)* golpetazo *m* (**d**) *Fam* **to have a c. at sth** *(attempt)* intentar hacer algo (**e**) *Fam (wisecrack)* réplica aguda (**f**) *Fam (drug)* crack *m*
 4 *adj Fam* de primera
 ▸ **crack down on** *vt insep* atajar con mano dura
 ▸ **crack up** *vi Fam Fig (go mad)* desquiciarse; *(with laughter)* partirse de risa
cracker ['krækə(r)] *n* (**a**) *(biscuit)* galleta salada (**b**) *(firework)* petardo *m*
crackle ['krækəl] *vi* crujir; *(fire)* crepitar
cradle ['kreɪdəl] *n (baby's)* cuna *f*
craft [krɑːft] *n* (**a**) *(occupation)* oficio *m*; *(art)* arte *m*; *(skill)* destreza *f* (**b**) *(cunning)* maña *f* (**c**) *Naut* embarcación *f*
craftsman ['krɑːftsmən] *n* artesano *m*
craftsmanship ['krɑːftsmənʃɪp] *n* arte *f*
crafty ['krɑːftɪ] *adj* (**craftier, craftiest**) astuto(a)
crag [kræg] *n* peña *f*, peñasco *m*
cram [kræm] **1** *vt* atiborrar; **crammed with** atestado(a) de
 2 *vi Fam Educ* empollar
cramp¹ [kræmp] *n Med* calambre *m*; **cramps** retortijones *mpl*
cramp² [kræmp] *vt (development etc)* poner trabas a
cramped [kræmpt] *adj* atestado(a); *(writing)* apretado(a)
cranberry ['krænbərɪ] *n* arándano *m*
crane [kreɪn] **1** *n* (**a**) *Zool* grulla *f* común (**b**) *(device)* grúa *f*
 2 *vt* estirar
crank [kræŋk] *n* (**a**) *Tech* manivela *f* (**b**) *Fam (eccentric)* tío raro
crankshaft ['kræŋkʃɑːft] *n* árbol *m* del cigüeñal
cranny ['krænɪ] *n Fig* **in every nook and c.** en todos los rincones
crap [kræp] *n Fam* mierda *f*
crash [kræʃ] **1** *vt* **to c. one's car** tener un accidente con el coche
 2 *vi* (**a**) *(car, plane)* estrellarse; *(collide)* chocar; **to c. into** estrellarse contra (**b**) *Com* quebrar
 3 *n* (**a**) *(noise)* estrépito *m* (**b**) *(collision)*

choque *m*; **car/plane c.** accidente *m* de coche/avión; *Fig* **c. course** curso intensivo; **c. helmet** casco *m* protector (**c**) *Com* quiebra *f*

crash-land [kræʃ'lænd] *vi* hacer un aterrizaje forzoso

crass [kræs] *adj (person)* grosero(a); *(error)* garrafal

crate [kreɪt] *n* caja *f*, cajón *m (para embalaje)*

crater ['kreɪtə(r)] *n* cráter *m*

cravat [krə'væt] *n* pañuelo *m (de hombre)*

crave [kreɪv] *vi* **to c. for sth** ansiar algo

craving ['kreɪvɪŋ] *n* ansia *f*; *(in pregnancy)* antojo *m*

crawfish ['krɔːfɪʃ] *n* langosta *f*

crawl [krɔːl] **1** *vi (baby)* gatear; *(vehicle)* avanzar lentamente; *Fig* **to c. to sb** arrastrarse a los pies de algn

   2 *n (swimming)* crol *m*

crayfish ['kreɪfɪʃ] *n* cangrejo *m* de río

crayon ['kreɪɒn] *n* cera *f*

craze [kreɪz] *n* manía *f*; *(fashion)* moda *f*; **it's the latest c.** es el último grito

crazy ['kreɪzɪ] *adj* (**crazier, craziest**) *Fam* loco(a), chalado(a); *Br* **c. paving** pavimento *m* en mosaico

creak [kriːk] *vi (floor)* crujir; *(hinge)* chirriar

cream [kriːm] **1** *n* (**a**) *(of milk)* nata *f*; **c.-coloured** color crema; *Fig* **the c.** la flor y nata; **c. cheese** queso *m* crema (**b**) *(cosmetic)* crema *f*

   2 *vt* (**a**) *(milk)* desnatar (**b**) *Culin* batir; **creamed potatoes** puré *m* de patatas *or Am* papas

creamy ['kriːmɪ] *adj* (**creamier, creamiest**) cremoso(a)

crease [kriːs] **1** *n (wrinkle)* arruga *f*; *(fold)* pliegue *m*; *(on trousers)* raya *f*

   2 *vt (clothes)* arrugar

   3 *vi* arrugarse

create [kriː'eɪt] *vt* crear

creation [kriː'eɪʃən] *n* creación *f*

creative [kriː'eɪtɪv] *adj (person)* creativo(a)

creativity [kriːeɪ'tɪvɪtɪ] *n* creatividad *f*

creator [kriː'eɪtə(r)] *n* creador(a) *m,f*

creature ['kriːtʃə(r)] *n (animal)* criatura *f*

crèche [kreɪʃ, kreʃ] *n* guardería *f*

credence ['kriːdəns] *n* **to give c. to** dar crédito a

credentials [krɪ'denʃəlz] *npl* credenciales *fpl*

credible ['kredɪbəl] *adj* creíble

credit ['kredɪt] **1** *n* (**a**) *Com* crédito *m*; **on c.** a crédito; **c. card** tarjeta *f* de crédito (**b**) **to give c. to sb for sth** reconocer algo a

algn (**c**) *(benefit)* honor *m*; **to be a c. to** hacer honor a (**d**) *Cin & TV* **credits** créditos *mpl*

   2 *vt* (**a**) *Com* abonar (**b**) *(believe)* creer (**c**) *Fig* atribuir; **he is credited with having** se le atribuye haber

creditor ['kredɪtə(r)] *n* acreedor(a) *m,f*

creed [kriːd] *n* credo *m*

creek [kriːk] *n* (**a**) *Br* cala *f* (**b**) *US & Austral* riachuelo *m*

creep [kriːp] **1** *vi (pt & pp* **crept***)* andar silenciosamente; *(insect)* arrastrarse; *(plant)* trepar; **to c. up on sb** sorprender a algn

   2 *n Fam (person)* pelotillero(a) *m,f*

creeper ['kriːpə(r)] *n Bot* trepadora *f*

creepy ['kriːpɪ] *adj* (**creepier, creepiest**) *Fam* espeluznante

cremate [krɪ'meɪt] *vt* incinerar

crematorium [kremə'tɔːrɪəm] *n* crematorio *m*

crêpe [kreɪp] *n* (**a**) *Tex* crepé *m* (**b**) **c. paper** papel *m* crespón

crept [krept] *pt & pp of* **creep**

crescendo [krɪ'ʃendəʊ] *n* crescendo *m*

crescent ['kresənt] **1** *n (shape)* medialuna *f*; *Br (street)* calle *f* en medialuna

   2 *adj* creciente

cress [kres] *n* berro *m*

crest [krest] *n* (**a**) *(of cock, wave)* cresta *f*; *(on helmet)* penacho *m*; *(of hill)* cima *f* (**b**) *(heraldic)* blasón *m*

crestfallen ['krestfɔːlən] *adj* abatido(a)

Crete [kriːt] *n* Creta

cretin ['kretɪn] *n* cretino(a) *m,f*

crevasse [krɪ'væs] *n* grieta *f*, fisura *f*

crevice ['krevɪs] *n* grieta *f*, hendedura *f*

crew [kruː] *n Av & Naut* tripulación *f*; **c. cut** corte *m* al rape; **c.-neck sweater** jersey *m* con cuello redondo

crib [krɪb] **1** *n* (**a**) *(manger)* pesebre *m* (**b**) *(for baby)* cuna *f* (**c**) *Fam (in exam)* chuleta *f*, *Arg* machete *m*, *Col, Méx* acordeón *m*

   2 *vt Fam* (**a**) *(copy)* copiar (**b**) *(steal)* quitar

crick [krɪk] *n Fam* **a c. in the neck** una tortícolis

cricket¹ ['krɪkɪt] *n (insect)* grillo *m*

cricket² ['krɪkɪt] *n Sport* cricket *m*

crikey ['kraɪkɪ] *interj Fam Old-fashioned* ¡caramba!

crime [kraɪm] *n* delincuencia *f*; *(offence)* delito *m*

criminal ['krɪmɪnəl] *adj & n* criminal *(mf)*; **c. law** derecho *m* penal; **c. record** antecedentes *mpl* penales

crimson ['krɪmzən] *adj & n* carmesí *(m)*

cringe [krɪndʒ] *vi* abatirse, encogerse

crinkle ['krɪŋkəl] *vt* fruncir, arrugar
cripple ['krɪpəl] **1** *n* lisiado(a) *m,f*, mutilado(a) *m,f*
  2 *vt* mutilar, dejar cojo(a); *Fig* paralizar
crisis ['kraɪsɪs] *n* (*pl* **crises** ['kraɪsiːz]) crisis *f inv*
crisp [krɪsp] **1** *adj* crujiente; (*lettuce*) fresco(a); (*banknote*) nuevo(a); (*weather*) frío(a) y seco(a); *Fig* (*style*) directo(a)
  2 *n Br* **(potato) c.** patata *or Am* papa frita
crisscross ['krɪskrɒs] *n* líneas entrecruzadas
criterion [kraɪ'tɪərɪən] *n* (*pl* **criteria** [kraɪ'tɪərɪə]) criterio *m*
critic ['krɪtɪk] *n Art & Th* crítico(a) *m,f*
critical ['krɪtɪkəl] *adj* crítico(a)
critically ['krɪtɪkəlɪ] *adv* críticamente; **c. ill** gravemente enfermo(a)
criticism ['krɪtɪsɪzəm] *n* crítica *f*
criticize ['krɪtɪsaɪz] *vt* criticar
croak [krəʊk] *vi* (*frog*) croar; (*raven*) graznar; (*person*) hablar con voz ronca
Croat ['krəʊæt] **1** *adj* croata
  2 *n* (**a**) (*person*) croata *mf* (**b**) (*language*) croata *m*
Croatia [krəʊ'eɪʃə] *n* Croacia
Croatian [krəʊ'eɪʃən] *adj & n* = **Croat**
crochet ['krəʊʃeɪ] *n* ganchillo *m*
crockery ['krɒkərɪ] *n* loza *f*
crocodile ['krɒkədaɪl] *n* cocodrilo *m*
crocus ['krəʊkəs] *n* azafrán *m*
crony ['krəʊnɪ] *n* compinche *mf*
crook [krʊk] **1** *n* (**a**) (*of shepherd*) cayado *m* (**b**) *Fam* caco *m*
  2 *vt* (*arm*) doblar
crooked ['krʊkɪd] *adj* (**a**) (*stick, picture*) torcido(a); (*path*) tortuoso(a) (**b**) *Fam* (*dishonest*) deshonesto(a)
crop [krɒp] **1** *n* (**a**) cultivo *m*; (*harvest*) cosecha *f*; (*of hair*) mata *f* (**b**) (*whip*) fusta *f*
  2 *vt* (*hair*) rapar; (*grass*) cortar
  ▸ **crop up** *vi Fam* surgir, presentarse
croquet ['krəʊkeɪ] *n* croquet *m*
cross [krɒs] **1** *n* (**a**) cruz *f* (**b**) (*breeds*) cruce *m* (**c**) **c. section** sección *f* transversal
  2 *vt* (**a**) cruzar (**b**) *Rel* **to c. oneself** hacer la señal de la cruz; *Fam* **c. my heart!** ¡te lo juro! (**c**) (*thwart*) contrariar
  3 *vi* cruzar; (*roads*) cruzarse; **to c. over** cruzar
  4 *adj* (**a**) *Fig* **they are at c. purposes** hay un malentendido entre ellos (**b**) (*angry*) enfadado(a)
  ▸ **cross off, cross out** *vt sep* tachar, rayar
crossbar ['krɒsbɑː(r)] *n* travesaño *m*

cross-country 1 *adj* ['krɒskʌntrɪ] **c. race** cros *m*
  2 *adv* [krɒs'kʌntrɪ] campo través
cross-examine [krɒsɪg'zæmɪn] *vt* interrogar
cross-eyed ['krɒsaɪd] *adj* bizco(a)
crossfire ['krɒsfaɪə(r)] *n* fuego cruzado
crossing ['krɒsɪŋ] *n* cruce *m*; **pedestrian c.** paso *m* de peatones; **sea c.** travesía *f*
cross-legged [krɒs'leg(ɪ)d] *adj* con las piernas cruzadas
cross-reference [krɒs'refərəns] *n* remisión *f*
crossroads ['krɒsrəʊdz] *n* cruce *m*; *Fig* encrucijada *f*
crosswalk ['krɒswɔːk] *n US* paso *m* de peatones
crosswind ['krɒswɪnd] *n* viento *m* lateral
crossword ['krɒswɜːd] *n* **c. (puzzle)** crucigrama *m*
crotch [krɒtʃ] *n* entrepierna *f*
crotchet ['krɒtʃɪt] *n Br Mus* negra *f*
crotchety ['krɒtʃɪtɪ] *adj Fam* gruñón(ona)
crouch [kraʊtʃ] *vi* **to c. (down)** agacharse
crow¹ [krəʊ] *n* cuervo *m*; *Fig* **as the c. flies** en línea recta; **c.'s-feet** patas *fpl* de gallo
crow² [krəʊ] **1** *vi* (**a**) (*cock*) cantar; *Fig* **to c. over sth** jactarse de algo (**b**) (*baby*) balbucir
  2 *n* (*of cock*) canto *m*
crowbar ['krəʊbɑː(r)] *n* palanca *f*
crowd [kraʊd] **1** *n* muchedumbre *f*; *Fam* (*gang*) pandilla *f*; **the c.** el populacho
  2 *vt* (*streets*) llenar
  3 *vi* apiñarse; **to c. in/out** entrar/salir en tropel
crowded ['kraʊdɪd] *adj* atestado(a), lleno(a)
crown [kraʊn] **1** *n* (**a**) corona *f*; (*garland*) guirnalda *f*; **the c. jewels** las joyas de la corona; *Br Jur* **c. court** tribunal *m* superior; **C. Prince** príncipe heredero (**b**) *Anat* coronilla *f*; (*of hat, tree*) copa *f*
  2 *vt* coronar; *Fam Fig* **to c. it all** y para más inri
crucial ['kruːʃəl] *adj* decisivo(a)
crucifix ['kruːsɪfɪks] *n* crucifijo *m*
crucifixion [kruːsɪ'fɪkʃən] *n* crucifixión *f*
crucify ['kruːsɪfaɪ] *vt* crucificar
crude [kruːd] *adj* (**a**) (*manners, style*) tosco(a), grosero(a); (*tool*) primitivo(a) (**b**) **c. oil** crudo *m*
cruel [kruːəl] *adj* cruel (**to** con)
cruelty ['kruːəltɪ] *n* crueldad *f* (**to** hacia)
cruet ['kruːɪt] *n* **c. set** vinagreras *fpl*
cruise [kruːz] **1** *vi* (**a**) *Naut* hacer un crucero (**b**) *Aut* viajar a velocidad constante;

Av viajar a velocidad de crucero
2 *n* (**a**) *Naut* crucero *m* (**b**) **c. missile** misil teledirigido
cruiser ['kru:zə(r)] *n* (barco *m*) crucero *m*
crumb [krʌm] *n* miga *f*, migaja *f*
crumble ['krʌmbəl] **1** *vt* desmigar
2 *vi* (*wall*) desmoronarse; *Fig* (*hopes*) desvanecerse
crumbly ['krʌmblɪ] *adj* (**crumblier, crumbliest**) que se desmigaja
crumpet ['krʌmpɪt] *n Br* = clase de crepe grueso que se puede tostar
crumple ['krʌmpəl] *vt* arrugar
crunch [krʌntʃ] **1** *vt* (*food*) ronchar; (*with feet*) hacer crujir
2 *n Fam* **when it comes to the c.** a la hora de la verdad
crunchy ['krʌntʃɪ] *adj* (**crunchier, crunchiest**) crujiente
crusade [kru:'seɪd] *n* cruzada *f*
crush [krʌʃ] **1** *vt* aplastar; (*wrinkle*) arrugar; (*grind*) moler; (*squeeze*) exprimir
2 *n* (**a**) (*of people*) gentío *m* (**b**) **orange c.** naranjada *f*
crushing ['krʌʃɪŋ] *adj Fig* (*defeat, reply*) aplastante
crust [krʌst] *n* corteza *f*
crutch [krʌtʃ] *n Med* muleta *f*; *Fig* apoyo *m*
crux [krʌks] *n* **the c. of the matter** el quid de la cuestión
cry [kraɪ] **1** *vi* (*pt & pp* **cried**) (**a**) gritar (**b**) (*weep*) llorar
2 *vt* gritar; *Fig* **to c. wolf** dar una falsa alarma
3 *n* (**a**) grito *m* (**b**) (*weep*) llanto *m*
▸ **cry off** *vi Fam* rajarse
▸ **cry out** *vi* gritar; **to c. out for sth** pedir algo a gritos
crying ['kraɪɪŋ] *adj* **it's a c. shame** es una vergüenza
cryptic ['krɪptɪk] *adj* enigmático(a)
crystal ['krɪstəl] *n* cristal *m*
crystal-clear [krɪstəl'klɪə(r)] *adj* claro(a) como el agua
crystallize ['krɪstəlaɪz] **1** *vt* cristalizar
2 *vi* cristalizarse
cub [kʌb] *n* (**a**) (*animal*) cachorro *m* (**b**) (*junior scout*) niño *m* explorador
Cuba ['kju:bə] *n* Cuba
Cuban ['kju:bən] *adj & n* cubano(a) (*m,f*)
cubbyhole ['kʌbɪhəʊl] *n* cuchitril *m*
cube [kju:b] **1** *n* cubo *m*; (*of sugar*) terrón *m*; **c. root** raíz cúbica
2 *vt Math* elevar al cubo
cubic ['kju:bɪk] *adj* cúbico(a)
cubicle ['kju:bɪkəl] *n* cubículo *m*; (*at swimming pool*) caseta *f*

cuckoo ['kʊku:] **1** *n* cuco *m*; **c. clock** reloj *m* de cuco
2 *adj Fam* lelo(a)
cucumber ['kju:kʌmbə(r)] *n* pepino *m*
cuddle ['kʌdəl] **1** *vt* abrazar
2 *vi* abrazarse
cuddly ['kʌdlɪ] *adj* **c. toy** muñeco *m* de peluche
cue¹ [kju:] *n Th* pie *m*
cue² [kju:] *n* (*in billiards*) taco *m*; **c. ball** bola blanca
cuff¹ [kʌf] *n* (*of sleeve*) puño *m*; *US* (*of trousers*) dobladillo *m*; *Fig* **to do sth off the c.** improvisar algo
cuff² [kʌf] **1** *vt* abofetear
2 *n* bofetada *f*
cufflinks ['kʌflɪŋks] *npl* gemelos *mpl*
cul-de-sac ['kʌldəsæk] *n* callejón *m* sin salida
cull [kʌl] *vt* (**a**) (*choose*) escoger (**b**) (*animals*) eliminar
culminate ['kʌlmɪneɪt] *vi* **to c. in** terminar en
culmination [kʌlmɪ'neɪʃən] *n* culminación *f*, punto *m* culminante
culottes [kju:'lɒts] *npl* falda-pantalón *f*
culprit ['kʌlprɪt] *n* culpable *mf*
cult [kʌlt] *n* culto *m*; **c. figure** ídolo *m*
cultivate ['kʌltɪveɪt] *vt* cultivar
cultivated ['kʌltɪveɪtɪd] *adj* (*person*) culto(a)
cultivation [kʌltɪ'veɪʃən] *n* cultivo *m* (de la tierra)
cultural ['kʌltʃərəl] *adj* cultural
culture ['kʌltʃə(r)] *n* cultura *f*
cultured ['kʌltʃəd] *adj* = **cultivated**
cumbersome ['kʌmbəsəm] *adj* (*awkward*) incómodo(a); (*bulky*) voluminoso(a)
cum(m)in ['kʌmɪn] *n* comino *m*
cumulative ['kju:mjʊlətɪv] *adj* acumulativo(a)
cunning ['kʌnɪŋ] **1** *adj* astuto(a)
2 *n* astucia *f*
cup [kʌp] **1** *n* taza *f*; *Sport* copa *f*; **C. Final** final *f* de copa; **c. tie** partido *m* de copa
2 *vt* (*hands*) ahuecar
cupboard ['kʌbəd] *n* armario *m*; (*on wall*) alacena *f*
curate ['kjʊərɪt] *n* cura *m* coadjutor
curator [kjʊə'reɪtə(r)] *n* conservador(a) *m,f*
curb [kɜ:b] **1** *n* (**a**) (*limit*) freno *m* (**b**) *US* (*kerb*) bordillo *m*
2 *vt* (*horse*) refrenar; *Fig* (*public spending*) contener
curd [kɜ:d] *n* cuajada *f*
curdle ['kɜ:dəl] *vi* cuajarse

cure [kjʊə(r)] **1** vt curar
2 n (remedy) cura f, remedio m
curfew ['kɜːfjuː] n toque m de queda
curiosity [kjʊərɪ'ɒsɪtɪ] n curiosidad f
curious ['kjʊərɪəs] adj (**a**) (inquisitive) curioso(a) (**b**) (odd) extraño(a)
curl [kɜːl] **1** vt (hair) rizar; (lip) fruncir
2 vi rizarse
3 n (of hair) rizo m; (of smoke) espiral f
▸ **curl up** vi enroscarse
curly ['kɜːlɪ] adj (**curlier, curliest**) rizado(a)
currant ['kʌrənt] n pasa f (de Corinto)
currency ['kʌrənsɪ] n (**a**) moneda f; **foreign c.** divisa f (**b**) **to gain c.** cobrar fuerza
current ['kʌrənt] **1** adj (**a**) (opinion) general; (word) en uso; (year) en curso; **c. account** cuenta f corriente; **c. affairs** actualidad f (política); Fin **c. assets** activo m disponible (**b**) **the c. issue** (of magazine, newspaper) el último número
2 n corriente f
currently ['kʌrəntlɪ] adv actualmente
curriculum [kə'rɪkjʊləm] n (pl **curricula** [kə'rɪkjʊlə]) plan m de estudios; **c. vitae** curriculum m (vitae)
curry¹ ['kʌrɪ] n curry m; **chicken c.** pollo m al curry
curry² ['kʌrɪ] vt **to c. favour with** congraciarse con
curse [kɜːs] **1** n maldición f; (oath) palabrota f; Fig azote m
2 vt maldecir
3 vi blasfemar
cursor ['kɜːsə(r)] n cursor m
cursory ['kɜːsərɪ] adj rápido(a)
curt [kɜːt] adj brusco(a), seco(a)
curtail [kɜː'teɪl] vt (expenses) reducir; (text) acortar
curtain ['kɜːtən] n cortina f; Th telón m; Fig velo m
curts(e)y ['kɜːtsɪ] **1** n reverencia f
2 vi hacer una reverencia (**to** a)
curve [kɜːv] **1** n curva f
2 vt encorvar
3 vi torcerse, describir una curva
cushion ['kʊʃən] **1** n cojín m; (large) almohadón m; (of billiard table) banda f
2 vt Fig amortiguar; (person) proteger
cushy ['kʊʃɪ] adj (**cushier, cushiest**) Fam cómodo(a)
custard ['kʌstəd] n natillas fpl; **c. powder** polvos mpl para natillas
custodian [kʌ'stəʊdɪən] n conserje mf, guarda mf
custody ['kʌstədɪ] n custodia f; **to take into c.** detener

custom ['kʌstəm] n (**a**) (habit) costumbre f (**b**) Com clientela f
customary ['kʌstəmərɪ] adj habitual
customer ['kʌstəmə(r)] n cliente mf
customize ['kʌstəmaɪz] vt hacer por encargo
custom-made [kʌstəm'meɪd] adj hecho(a) a la medida
customs ['kʌstəmz] n sing or pl aduana f; **c. duty** derechos mpl de aduana; **c. officer** agente mf de aduana
cut [kʌt] **1** vt (pt & pp **cut**) (**a**) cortar; (stone) tallar; (record) grabar; **he's cutting a tooth** le está saliendo un diente; **to c. one's finger** cortarse el dedo; Fig **to c. a long story short** en resumidas cuentas; Fig **to c. corners** recortar presupuestos (**b**) (reduce) reducir
(**c**) (divide up) dividir (**into** en)
2 n (**a**) corte m; (in skin) cortadura f; (wound) herida f; (with knife) cuchillada f (**b**) (of meat) clase f de carne
(**c**) (reduction) reducción f
(**d**) Fig **to be a c. above sb** estar por encima de algn
3 adj cortado(a); (price) reducido(a); Fig **c. and dried** convenido(a) de antemano; **c. glass** cristal tallado
4 vi (**a**) cortar; Fam Fig **to c. loose** romper con todo
(**b**) Cin **c.!** ¡corten!
▸ **cut back** vt sep (expenses) reducir; (production) disminuir
▸ **cut down 1** vt sep (tree) talar
2 vt insep **to c. down on** reducir
▸ **cut in** vi (driver) adelantar bruscamente
▸ **cut off** vt sep (water etc) cortar; (place) aislar; (heir) excluir; Tel **I've been c. off** me han cortado (la comunicación)
▸ **cut out 1** vt sep (**a**) (from newspaper) recortar; (person) **to be c. out for sth** estar hecho(a) para algo (**b**) (delete) suprimir
2 vi (engine) calarse
▸ **cut up** vt sep cortar en pedazos
cutback ['kʌtbæk] n reducción f (**in** de)
cute [kjuːt] adj mono(a), lindo(a); US Fam Pej listillo(a)
cuticle ['kjuːtɪkəl] n cutícula f
cutlery ['kʌtlərɪ] n cubiertos mpl
cutlet ['kʌtlɪt] n chuleta f
cut-price [kʌt'praɪs] adj (article) a precio rebajado
cutthroat ['kʌtθrəʊt] **1** n asesino(a) m,f, matón m
2 adj (cruel) cruel; (competition) feroz
cutting ['kʌtɪŋ] **1** n (from newspaper)

recorte *m*; *Rail* tajo *m*
  2 *adj* cortante; *(remark)* mordaz
CV, cv [siː'viː] *n* (*abbr* **curriculum vitae**) CV *m*
cwt. (*abbr* **hundredweight**) *(metric)* 50 kg; *(imperial) Br* = 50,8 kg; *US* = 45,36 kg
cyanide ['saɪənaɪd] *n* cianuro *m*
cybercafe ['saɪbəkæfeɪ] *n Comput* ciber-café *m*
cyberspace ['saɪbəspeɪs] *n Comput* cibe-respacio *m*
cycle ['saɪkəl] **1** *n* (**a**) ciclo *m* (**b**) *(bicycle)* bicicleta *f*; *(motorcycle)* moto *f*
  2 *vi* ir en bicicleta
cycling ['saɪklɪŋ] *n* ciclismo *m*
cyclist ['saɪklɪst] *n* ciclista *mf*
cyclone ['saɪkləʊn] *n* ciclón *m*
cygnet ['sɪgnɪt] *n* pollo *m* de cisne
cylinder ['sɪlɪndə(r)] *n* (**a**) cilindro *m* (**b**) *(for gas)* bombona *f*
cymbal ['sɪmbəl] *n* címbalo *m*, platillo *m*
cynic ['sɪnɪk] *n* descreído(a) *m,f*, suspi-caz *mf*

> ♫ Note that the Spanish word **cínico** is a false friend and is never a translation for the English word **cynic**. In Spanish, **cínico** means "shameless person".

cynical ['sɪnɪkəl] *adj* (**a**) *(sceptical)* des-creído(a), suspicaz (**b**) *(unscrupulous)* desaprensivo(a), sin escrúpulos

> ♫ Note that the Spanish word **cínico** is a false friend and is never a translation for the English word **cynical**. In Spanish, **cínico** means "shameless".

cynicism ['sɪnɪsɪzəm] *n* descreimiento *m*, suspicacia *f*

> ♫ Note that the Spanish word **cinismo** is a false friend and is never a translation for the English word **cynicism**. In Spanish, **cinismo** means "shamelessness".

cypress ['saɪprəs] *n* ciprés *m*
Cypriot ['sɪprɪət] *adj & n* chipriota *(mf)*
Cyprus ['saɪprəs] *n* Chipre
cyst [sɪst] *n* quiste *m*
cystitis [sɪ'staɪtɪs] *n* cistitis *f*
czar [zɑː(r)] *n* zar *m*
Czech [tʃek] **1** *adj* checo(a); **the C. Re-public** la República Checa
  2 *n* (**a**) *(person)* checo(a) *m,f* (**b**) *(language)* checo *m*
Czechoslovakia [tʃekəʊslə'vækɪə] *n* Checoslovaquia

D

D, d [diː] *n* (**a**) *(the letter)* D, d *f* (**b**) *Mus* D re *m*

D.A. [diːˈeɪ] *n US* (*abbr* **district attorney**) fiscal *mf* (del distrito)

dab [dæb] **1** *n (small quantity)* toque *m*
  2 *vt* (**a**) *(apply)* aplicar (**b**) *(touch lightly)* tocar ligeramente

dabble [ˈdæbəl] *vi* **to d. in politics** meterse en política

dachshund [ˈdækshʊnd] *n* perro *m* salchicha

dad [dæd], **daddy** [ˈdædɪ] *n Fam* papá *m*, papi *m*

daddy-longlegs [dædɪˈlɒŋlegz] *n inv Fam* (**a**) *Br (cranefly)* típula *f* (**b**) *US (spider)* segador *m*

daffodil [ˈdæfədɪl] *n* narciso *m*

daft [dɑːft] *adj Br Fam* chalado(a); *(idea)* tonto(a)

dagger [ˈdægə(r)] *n* puñal *m*, daga *f*

dahlia [ˈdeɪlɪə] *n* dalia *f*

daily [ˈdeɪlɪ] **1** *adj* diario(a), cotidiano(a)
  2 *adv* diariamente; **three times d.** tres veces al día
  3 *n* (**a**) *(newspaper)* diario *m* (**b**) *Br Fam (cleaning lady)* asistenta *f*

dainty [ˈdeɪntɪ] *adj* (**daintier, daintiest**) *(flower)* delicado(a); *(child)* precioso(a); *(food)* exquisito(a)

dairy [ˈdeərɪ] *n (on farm)* vaquería *f*; *(shop)* lechería *f*; **d. farming** industria lechera; **d. produce** productos lácteos

dais [ˈdeɪɪs] *n (in hall)* tarima *f*; *(in ceremony)* estrado *m*

daisy [ˈdeɪzɪ] *n* margarita *f*

daisywheel [ˈdeɪzɪwiːl] *n (printer)* margarita *f*

dale [deɪl] *n* valle *m*, hondonada *f*

Dalmatian [dælˈmeɪʃən] *n* (perro *m*) dálmata *m*

dam [dæm] **1** *n (barrier)* dique *m*; *(lake)* presa *f*
  2 *vt (water)* represar
  ▸ **dam up** *vt sep Fig (emotion)* contener

damage [ˈdæmɪdʒ] **1** *n* (**a**) daño *m*; *(to health, reputation)* perjuicio *m*; *(to relationship)* deterioro *m* (**b**) *Jur* **damages** daños *mpl* y perjuicios *mpl*
  2 *vt (harm)* dañar, hacer daño a; *(spoil)* estropear; *(undermine)* perjudicar

damaging [ˈdæmɪdʒɪŋ] *adj* perjudicial

damn [dæm] **1** *vt* condenar
  2 *interj Fam* **d. (it)!** ¡maldito(a) sea!; **well, I'll be damned!** ¡vaya por Dios!
  3 *n Fam* **I don't give a d.** me importa un bledo
  4 *adj Fam* maldito(a)
  5 *adv Fam* muy, sumamente

damned [dæmd] *adj & adv* = **damn**

damnedest [ˈdæmdɪst] *n Fam* **to do one's d. to ...** hacer todo lo posible para ...

damning [ˈdæmɪŋ] *adj (evidence)* irrefutable; *(criticism)* mordaz

damp [dæmp] **1** *adj* húmedo(a); *(wet)* mojado(a)
  2 *n* humedad *f*
  3 *vt* (**a**) *(for ironing)* humedecer (**b**) **to d. (down)** *(fire)* sofocar; *Fig (violence)* frenar

dampen [ˈdæmpən] *vt* humedecer; *Fig* frenar

damper [ˈdæmpə(r)] *n Fig* **to put a d. on sth** poner freno a algo

damsel [ˈdæmzəl] *n Literary* doncella *f*

damson [ˈdæmzən] *n* ciruela damascena

dance [dɑːns] **1** *n* baile *m*; *(classical, tribal)* danza *f*; **d. band** orquesta *f* de baile; **d. floor** pista *f* de baile; **d. hall** salón *m* de baile
  2 *vi & vt* bailar

dancer [ˈdɑːnsə(r)] *n (by profession)* bailarín(ina) *m,f*

dandelion [ˈdændɪlaɪən] *n* diente *m* de león

dandruff [ˈdændrəf] *n* caspa *f*

Dane [deɪn] *n* danés(esa) *m,f*

danger [ˈdeɪndʒə(r)] *n* (**a**) *(risk)* riesgo *m*; *(of war etc)* amenaza *f* (**b**) *(peril)* peligro *m*; **d.** *(sign)* peligro; **out of d.** fuera de peligro

dangerous [ˈdeɪndʒərəs] *adj* peligroso(a); *(risky)* arriesgado(a); *(harmful)* nocivo(a); *(illness)* grave

dangerously [ˈdeɪndʒərəslɪ] *adv* peligrosamente

dangle [ˈdæŋgəl] **1** *vi (hang)* colgar; *(swing)* balancearse
  2 *vt (legs)* colgar; *(bait)* dejar colgado(a);

(swing) balancear en el aire

Danish ['deɪnɪʃ] **1** *adj* danés(esa); **D. pastry** pastel *m* de hojaldre

2 *n (language)* danés *m*

dapper ['dæpə(r)] *adj* pulcro(a)

dappled ['dæpəld] *adj (shade)* moteado(a)

dare [deə(r)] **1** *vi* atreverse, osar; **he doesn't d. be late** no se atreve a llegar tarde; **how d. you!** ¿cómo te atreves?; *esp Br* **I d. say** quizás; *Ironic* ya (lo creo)

2 *vt (challenge)* desafiar

3 *n* desafío *m*

daredevil ['deədevəl] *adj & n* atrevido(a) *(m,f)*, temerario(a) *(m,f)*

daring ['deərɪŋ] **1** *adj* **(a)** *(bold)* audaz, osado(a) **(b)** *(clothes)* atrevido(a)

2 *n* atrevimiento *m*, osadía *f*

dark [dɑːk] **1** *adj* **(a)** *(room, colour)* oscuro(a); *(hair, complexion)* moreno(a); *(eyes, future)* negro(a) **(b)** *Fig (gloomy)* triste **(c)** *Fig* **to be a d. horse** ser una incógnita; *(discreet)* ser una caja de sorpresas **(d)** *Fig (sinister)* siniestro(a)

2 *n* **(a)** *(darkness)* oscuridad *f*, tinieblas *fpl*; **after d.** después del anochecer **(b)** *Fig* **to be in the d. (about)** estar a oscuras (sobre)

darken ['dɑːkən] **1** *vt (sky)* oscurecer; *(colour)* hacer más oscuro(a)

2 *vi* oscurecerse; *(sky)* nublarse; *Fig (face)* ensombrecerse

darkness ['dɑːknɪs] *n* oscuridad *f*, tinieblas *fpl*

darkroom ['dɑːkruːm] *n* cuarto oscuro

darling ['dɑːlɪŋ] *adj & n* querido(a) *(m,f)*

darn [dɑːn] **1** *vt* zurcir

2 *n* zurcido *m*

dart [dɑːt] **1** *n* **(a)** *(missile)* dardo *m* **(b)** **darts** *sing* dardos *mpl*

2 *vi (fly about)* revolotear; **to d. in/out** entrar/salir corriendo

dartboard ['dɑːtbɔːd] *n* diana *f*

dash [dæʃ] **1** *n* **(a)** *(rush)* carrera *f* **(b)** *esp US (race)* sprint *m* **(c)** *(small amount)* poquito *m*; *(of salt)* pizca *f*; *(of liquid)* gota *f* **(d)** *Typ* guión largo; *(hyphen)* guión **(e)** *(vitality)* brío *m*

2 *vt* **(a)** *(throw)* arrojar **(b)** *(smash)* estrellar; *Fig* **to d. sb's hopes** desvanecer las esperanzas de algn

3 *vi (rush)* correr; **to d. around** correr de un lado a otro; **to d. out** salir corriendo; *Fam* **I must d.!** ¡me voy pitando!

► dash off *vi* salir corriendo

dashboard ['dæʃbɔːd] *n Aut* salpicadero *m*

dashing ['dæʃɪŋ] *adj (appearance)* garboso(a)

data ['deɪtə, 'dɑːtə] *npl* datos *mpl*; **d. bank** *or* **base** banco *m* de datos; **d. processing** *(act)* proceso *m* de datos; *(science)* informática *f*; **d. protection act** ley *f* de informática

date¹ [deɪt] **1** *n* **(a)** fecha *f*; **what's the d. today?** ¿qué día es hoy?; **out of d.** *(ideas)* anticuado(a); *(expression)* desusado(a); *(invalid)* caducado(a); **to d.** hasta la fecha; *Fig* **to be up to d.** estar al día; **d. of birth** fecha de nacimiento **(b)** *(social event)* compromiso *m*; *Fam (with girl, boy)* cita *f* **(c)** *US Fam (person dated)* ligue *m*

2 *vt (ruins)* datar

3 *vi (ideas)* quedar anticuado(a)

► date back to, date from *vt insep* remontar a, datar de

date² [deɪt] *n (fruit)* dátil *m*; **d. palm** datilera *f*

dated ['deɪtɪd] *adj (idea)* anticuado(a); *(fashion)* pasado(a) de moda; *(expression)* desusado(a)

daub [dɔːb] *vt* embadurnar; *(with oil, grease)* untar

daughter ['dɔːtə(r)] *n* hija *f*

daughter-in-law ['dɔːtərɪnlɔː] *n* nuera *f*, hija política

daunting ['dɔːntɪŋ] *adj* desalentador(a)

dawdle ['dɔːdəl] *vi Fam (walk slowly)* andar despacio; *(waste time)* perder el tiempo

dawn [dɔːn] **1** *n* alba *f*, amanecer *m*

2 *vi* **(a)** *(day)* amanecer **(b)** *Fig (age, hope)* comenzar **(c)** *Fig* **suddenly it dawned on him that ...** de repente cayó en la cuenta de que ...

day [deɪ] *n* **(a)** día *m*; **d. in, d. out** día tras día; **d. by d.** diariamente; **good d.!** ¡buenos días!; **once a d.** una vez al día; **one of these days** un día de éstos; **(on) the next** *or* **following d.** el *or* al día siguiente; **the d. after tomorrow** pasado mañana; **the d. before yesterday** anteayer; **the other d.** el otro día; *Fig* **to live from d. to d.** vivir al día; *Fig* **to win the d.** llevarse la palma; *Fam* **to call it a d.** *(finish)* dar por acabado un trabajo; *(give up)* darse por vencido(a); *Fam* **to make sb's d.** alegrarle a algn el día; *Br Rail* **d. return (ticket)** billete *m* de ida y vuelta para el mismo día; **d. trip** excursión *f* de un día **(b)** *(daylight)* día *m*; **by d.** de día; **d. and night** de día y de noche; *Br* **d. shift** turno *m* de día **(c)** *(period of work)* jornada *f*; **an eight-hour d.** una jornada de ocho horas; **paid**

by the d. pagado(a) a jornal; **d. off** día de fiesta; **I'll take a d. off tomorrow** mañana me tomaré el día libre

(**d**) *(era)* época *f*; **in those days** en aquellos tiempos; **these days, in this d. and age** hoy (en) día

daybreak ['deɪbreɪk] *n* amanecer *m*

daydream ['deɪdriːm] **1** *n* ensueño *m*; *(vain hope)* fantasía *f*

2 *vi* soñar despierto(a); *(hope vainly)* hacerse ilusiones

daylight ['deɪlaɪt] *n* luz *f* del día; **in broad d.** en pleno día; **to scare the (living) daylights out of sb** pegarle a algn un susto de muerte

daytime ['deɪtaɪm] *n* día *m*; **in the d.** de día

day-to-day ['deɪtədeɪ] *adj* cotidiano(a), diario(a)

daze [deɪz] *n* aturdimiento *m*; **in a d.** aturdido(a)

dazed [deɪzd] *adj* aturdido(a), atontado(a)

dazzle ['dæzəl] *vt* deslumbrar

D-day ['diːdeɪ] *n* día *m* D

deacon ['diːkən] *n* diácono *m*

dead [ded] **1** *adj* (**a**) muerto(a); **he was shot d.** le mataron a tiros; **to be d.** estar muerto(a); *Fam Fig* **over my d. body!** ¡sobre mi cadáver!; **d. man** muerto *m*

(**b**) *(machine)* averiado(a); *(phone)* cortado(a)

(**c**) *(numb)* entumecido(a); *(limb)* adormecido(a); **my leg's gone d.** se me ha dormido la pierna

(**d**) *(silence, secrecy)* total; **d. end** callejón *m* sin salida; *Sport* **d. heat** empate *m*; *Fam* **d. loss** inútil *m*, birria *f*

2 *adv* (**a**) *(exactly)* justo; **d. on time** a la hora en punto

(**b**) **to stop d.** pararse en seco

(**c**) *(very)* muy; *Fam* **d. beat, d. tired** rendido(a); *Fam* **it's d. easy!** ¡está chupado(a)!; *Aut* **d. slow** *(sign)* al paso; *Fam* **you're d. right** tienes toda la razón

3 *n* (**a**) **the d.** *pl* los muertos

(**b**) **at d. of night** a altas horas de la noche

deaden ['dedən] *vt (impact, noise)* amortiguar; *Fig (pain, feeling)* calmar, aliviar

deadline ['dedlaɪn] *n (date)* fecha *f* tope; *(time)* hora *f* tope; **we have to meet the d.** tenemos que hacerlo dentro del plazo

deadlock ['dedlɒk] *n* punto muerto

deadly ['dedlɪ] **1** *adj* (**deadlier, deadliest**) mortal; *(weapon)* mortífero(a); *(aim)* certero(a)

2 *adv (extremely)* terriblemente, sumamente

deadpan ['dedpæn] *adj Fam (face)* sin expresión; *(humour)* guasón(ona)

deaf [def] **1** *adj* sordo(a); *Fig* **to turn a d. ear** hacerse el sordo; **d. mute** sordomudo(a) *m,f*

2 *npl* **the d.** los sordos; **the d. and dumb** los sordomudos

deafen ['defən] *vt* ensordecer

deafening ['defənɪŋ] *adj* ensordecedor(a)

deafness ['defnɪs] *n* sordera *f*

deal [diːl] **1** *n* (**a**) *Com & Pol* trato *m*, pacto *m*; **business d.** negocio *m*, transacción *f*; **to do a d. with sb** *(transaction)* cerrar un trato con algn; *(agreement)* pactar algo con algn; *Fam* **it's a d.!** ¡trato hecho! (**b**) *(amount)* cantidad *f*; **a good d. of criticism** muchas críticas; **a good d. slower** mucho más despacio (**c**) *Cards* reparto *m*

2 *vt (pt & pp* **dealt**) (**a**) *Cards* dar (**to** a) (**b**) **to d. sb a blow** asestarle un golpe a algn

▸ **deal in** *vt insep (goods)* comerciar en, tratar en; *(drugs)* traficar con

▸ **deal out** *vt sep* repartir

▸ **deal with** *vt insep (firm, person)* tratar con; *(subject, problem)* abordar, ocuparse de; *(in book etc)* tratar de

dealer ['diːlə(r)] *n* (**a**) *Com (in goods)* comerciante *mf*; *(in drugs)* traficante *mf* (**b**) *Cards* repartidor(a) *m,f*

dealings ['diːlɪŋz] *npl* (**a**) *(relations)* trato *m* (**b**) *Com* negocios *mpl*

dealt [delt] *pt & pp of* **deal**

dean [diːn] *n* (**a**) *Rel* deán *m* (**b**) *Univ* decano *m*

dear [dɪə(r)] **1** *adj* (**a**) *(loved)* querido(a); **to hold sth/sb d.** apreciar mucho algo/a algn (**b**) *(in letter)* Querido(a); *Fam* **D. Andrew** Querido Andrew; *Fml* **D. Madam** Estimada señora; *Fml* **D. Sir(s)** Muy señor(es) mío(s) (**c**) **it is very d. to me** *(precious)* le tengo un gran cariño (**d**) *Br (expensive)* caro(a)

2 *n* querido(a) *m,f*; **my d.** mi vida

3 *interj* **oh d.!, d. me!** *(surprise)* ¡caramba!; *(disappointment)* ¡qué pena!

dearly ['dɪəlɪ] *adv* muchísimo; *Fig* **he paid d. for his mistake** su error le costó caro

dearth [dɜːθ] *n Fml* escasez *f*

death [deθ] *n* (**a**) muerte *f*; *Fml* fallecimiento *m*; **to put sb to d.** dar muerte a algn; *Fam* **to be bored to d.** aburrirse como una ostra; *Fam* **to be scared to d.** estar muerto(a) de miedo; *Fam Fig* **to be**

sick to d. of estar hasta la coronilla de; **d. certificate** certificado *m* de defunción; **d. penalty, d. sentence** pena *f* de muerte; **d. rate** índice *m* de mortalidad; **d. squad** escuadrón *m* de la muerte (**b**) *Fig (end)* fin *m*

deathbed ['deθbed] *n* **to be on one's d.** estar en el lecho de muerte

deathly ['deθlɪ] *adj* (**deathlier, deathliest**) *(silence)* sepulcral; **d. pale** pálido(a) como un muerto

debacle [deɪ'bɑːkəl] *n* debacle *f*

debar [dɪ'bɑː(r)] *vt Fml* excluir, prohibir

debase [dɪ'beɪs] *vt Fig* envilecer; **to d. oneself** humillarse

debatable [dɪ'beɪtəbəl] *adj* discutible

debate [dɪ'beɪt] **1** *n* debate *m*; **a heated d.** una discusión acalorada
2 *vt* (**a**) *(discuss)* discutir (**b**) *(wonder about)* dar vueltas a
3 *vi* discutir

debateable dɪ'beɪtəbəl] *adj* = debatable

debauchery [dɪ'bɔːtʃərɪ] *n* libertinaje *m*

debilitating [dɪ'bɪlɪteɪtɪŋ] *adj* debilitante; *(heat, climate)* agotador(a)

debit ['debɪt] **1** *n* débito *m*; **d. balance** saldo negativo
2 *vt* **d. Mr Jones with £20** cargar la suma de 20 libras en la cuenta del Sr. Jones

debris ['debriː, 'deɪbriː] *n sing* escombros *mpl*

debt [det] *n* deuda *f*; **to be deeply in d.** estar cargado(a) de deudas; *Fig* **to be in sb's d.** estar en deuda con algn

debtor ['detə(r)] *n* deudor(a) *m,f*

debug [diː'bʌg] *vt Comput* eliminar fallos de

debunk [diː'bʌŋk] *vt Fam* desacreditar, desprestigiar

debut ['debjuː, 'deɪbjuː] *n* debut *m*; **to make one's d.** debutar

debutante ['debjʊtɑːnt] *n* debutante *f*

decade [de'keɪd, 'dekeɪd] *n* decenio *m*, década *f*

decadence ['dekədəns] *n* decadencia *f*

decadent ['dekədənt] *adj* decadente

decaffeinated [dɪ'kæfɪneɪtɪd] *adj* descafeinado(a)

decanter [dɪ'kæntə(r)] *n* jarra *f*, jarro *m*

decapitate [dɪ'kæpɪteɪt] *vt* decapitar

decay [dɪ'keɪ] **1** *n* *(of food, body)* descomposición *f*; *(of teeth)* caries *f inv*; *(of buildings)* desmoronamiento *m*; *Fig* decadencia *f*
2 *vi* descomponerse; *(teeth)* cariarse; *(building)* deteriorarse; *Fig* corromperse

deceased [dɪ'siːst] *adj Fml* difunto(a), fallecido(a)

deceit [dɪ'siːt] *n* (**a**) *(dishonesty)* falta *f* de honradez, falsedad *f* (**b**) *(trick)* engaño *m*, mentira *f*

deceitful [dɪ'siːtfʊl] *adj* falso(a)

deceive [dɪ'siːv] *vt (mislead)* engañar; *(lie to)* mentir

December [dɪ'sembə(r)] *n* diciembre *m*

decency ['diːsənsɪ] *n* decencia *f*; *(modesty)* pudor *m*; *(morality)* moralidad *f*

decent ['diːsənt] *adj* decente; *(person)* honrado(a); *Fam (kind)* simpático(a)

decentralize [diː'sentrəlaɪz] *vt* descentralizar

deception [dɪ'sepʃən] *n* engaño *m*

> Note that the Spanish word **decepción** is a false friend and is never a translation for the English word **deception**. In Spanish, **decepción** means "disappointment".

deceptive [dɪ'septɪv] *adj* engañoso(a)

deceptively [dɪ'septɪvlɪ] *adv* **it looks d. simple** parece engañosamente sencillo(a)

decibel ['desɪbel] *n* decibelio *m*

decide [dɪ'saɪd] **1** *vt* (**a**) decidir; **to d. to do sth** decidir hacer algo (**b**) *(matter, question)* resolver, determinar
2 *vi (reach decision)* decidirse; **to d. against sth** decidirse en contra de algo
▶ **decide on** *vt insep (choose)* optar por

decided [dɪ'saɪdɪd] *adj* (**a**) *(noticeable)* marcado(a) (**b**) *(resolute)* decidido(a); *(views)* categórico(a)

decidedly [dɪ'saɪdɪdlɪ] *adv Fml* (**a**) *(clearly)* indudablemente (**b**) *(resolutely)* decididamente

deciding [dɪ'saɪdɪŋ] *adj* decisivo(a)

deciduous [dɪ'sɪdjʊəs] *adj* de hoja caduca

decimal ['desɪməl] **1** *adj* decimal; **d. point** coma *f* (de fracción decimal)
2 *n* decimal *m*

decimate ['desɪmeɪt] *vt* diezmar

decipher [dɪ'saɪfə(r)] *vt* descifrar

decision [dɪ'sɪʒən] *n* (**a**) decisión *f*; *Jur* fallo *m*; **to come to a d.** llegar a una decisión; **to make a d.** tomar una decisión (**b**) *(resolution)* resolución *f*

decisive [dɪ'saɪsɪv] *adj* (**a**) *(resolute)* decidido(a), resuelto(a) (**b**) *(conclusive)* decisivo(a)

deck [dek] **1** *n* (**a**) *(of ship)* cubierta *f*; **on/ below d.** en/bajo cubierta; **d. chair** tumbona *f* (**b**) *(of bus)* piso *m*; **top d.** piso de arriba (**c**) *esp US (of cards)* baraja *f* (**d**) *(of record player)* plato *m*
2 *vt* **to d. out** adornar

declaration [deklə'reɪʃən] *n* declaración *f*

declare [dɪ'kleə(r)] *vt* declarar; *(winner, innocence)* proclamar; *(decision)* manifestar

declared [dɪ'kleəd] *adj (opponent)* declarado(a); *(intention)* manifiesto(a)

decline [dɪ'klaɪn] **1** *n* (**a**) *(decrease)* disminución *f* (**b**) *(deterioration)* deterioro *m*; *(of health)* empeoramiento *m*; **to fall into d.** empezar a decaer
  2 *vi* (**a**) *(decrease)* disminuir; *(amount)* bajar; *(business)* decaer (**b**) *(deteriorate)* deteriorarse; *(health)* empeorar (**c**) *(refuse)* negarse
  3 *vt* (**a**) *(refuse)* rechazar (**b**) *Ling* declinar

declutch [dɪ'klʌtʃ] *vi* soltar el embrague

decode [diː'kəʊd] *vt* descifrar

decompose [diːkəm'pəʊz] *vi* descomponerse

décor ['deɪkɔː(r)] *n* decoración *f*; *Th* decorado *m*

decorate ['dekəreɪt] *vt* (**a**) *(adorn)* decorar, adornar (**with** con) (**b**) *(paint)* pintar; *(wallpaper)* empapelar (**c**) *(honour)* condecorar

decoration [dekə'reɪʃən] *n* (**a**) *(decor)* decoración *f*; **Christmas decorations** adornos navideños (**b**) *(medal)* condecoración *f*

decorative ['dekərətɪv] *adj* decorativo(a)

decorator ['dekəreɪtə(r)] *n* decorador(a) *m,f*; *(painter)* pintor(a) *m,f*; *(paperhanger)* empapelador(a) *m,f*

decorum [dɪ'kɔːrəm] *n* decoro *m*

decoy ['diːkɔɪ] *n Fig* señuelo *m*

decrease 1 *n* ['diːkriːs] disminución *f*; *(in speed, size, price)* reducción *f*
  2 *vi* [dɪ'kriːs] disminuir; *(strength)* menguar; *(price, temperature)* bajar; *(speed, size)* reducir
  3 *vt* disminuir, reducir; *(price, temperature)* bajar

decree [dɪ'kriː] **1** *n* (**a**) *Pol & Rel* decreto *m* (**b**) *esp US Jur* sentencia *f*; **d. absolute** sentencia definitiva de divorcio; **d. nisi** sentencia provisional de divorcio
  2 *vt Pol & Rel* decretar, pronunciar

decrepit [dɪ'krepɪt] *adj* decrépito(a)

dedicate ['dedɪkeɪt] *vt* consagrar, dedicar

dedicated ['dedɪkeɪtɪd] *adj* ardiente; **d. to** entregado(a) a

dedication [dedɪ'keɪʃən] *n (act)* dedicación *f*; *(commitment)* entrega *f*; *(in book)* dedicatoria *f*

deduce [dɪ'djuːs] *vt* deducir (**from** de)

deduct [dɪ'dʌkt] *vt* descontar (**from** de)

deduction [dɪ'dʌkʃən] *n* (**a**) *(conclusion)* conclusión *f* (**b**) *(subtraction)* descuento *m*

deed [diːd] *n* (**a**) *(act)* acto *m*; *(feat)* hazaña *f* (**b**) *Jur* escritura *f*; **title deeds** título *m* de propiedad

deem [diːm] *vt Fml* estimar

deep [diːp] **1** *adj* (**a**) profundo(a); *(breath, sigh)* hondo(a); **it's 10 m d.** tiene 10 m de profundidad (**b**) *(voice)* grave; *(shame)* grande; *(interest)* vivo(a) (**c**) *(colour)* oscuro(a) (**d**) *(serious)* grave
  2 *adv* **to dig d.** cavar hondo; **to be d. in thought** estar absorto(a); **to look d. into sb's eyes** penetrar a algn con la mirada; *Fig* **nine d.** de nueve en fondo

deepen ['diːpən] **1** *vt (well)* profundizar, ahondar; *Fig (knowledge)* aumentar
  2 *vi (river etc)* hacerse más hondo *or* profundo; *Fig (knowledge)* aumentar; *(colour, emotion)* intensificarse; *(sound, voice)* hacerse más grave

deep-freeze [diːp'friːz] **1** *n* congelador *m*
  2 *vt* congelar

deep-fry [diːp'fraɪ] *vt* freír en mucho aceite

deeply ['diːplɪ] *adv* profundamente; *(breathe)* hondo; **to be d. in debt** estar cargado(a) de deudas

deep-rooted [diːp'ruːtɪd] *adj Fig* arraigado(a)

deep-seated [diːp'siːtɪd] *adj Fig* arraigado(a)

deep-set [diːp'set] *adj (eyes)* hundido(a)

deer [dɪə(r)] *n inv* ciervo *m*

deface [dɪ'feɪs] *vt (book, poster)* garabatear

de facto [deɪ'fæktəʊ] *adj & adv Fml* de hecho

defamation [defə'meɪʃən] *n* difamación *f*

default [dɪ'fɔːlt] **1** *vi* (**a**) *(not act)* faltar a sus compromisos (**b**) *Jur* estar en rebeldía (**c**) *(not pay)* suspender pagos
  2 *n* (**a**) *(failure to act)* omisión *f* (**b**) *(failure to pay)* incumplimiento *m* de pago (**c**) *Jur* rebeldía *f*; **in d. of** a falta de; **to win by d.** ganar por incomparecencia del adversario

defaulter [dɪ'fɔːltə(r)] *n (on loan)* moroso(a) *m,f*; *Jur & Mil* rebelde *mf*

defeat [dɪ'fiːt] **1** *vt* (**a**) derrotar, vencer; *(motion)* rechazar (**b**) *Fig* frustrar
  2 *n* (**a**) *(of army, team)* derrota *f*; *(of motion)* rechazo *m* (**b**) *Fig* fracaso *m*

defeatist [dɪˈfiːtɪst] *adj & n* derrotista *(mf)*

defect 1 *n* [ˈdiːfekt] defecto *m; (flaw)* desperfecto *m*
2 *vi* [dɪˈfekt] desertar (**from** de); *(from country)* huir

defective [dɪˈfektɪv] *adj (faulty)* defectuoso(a); *(flawed)* con desperfectos; *(lacking)* incompleto(a)

defector [dɪˈfektə(r)] *n Pol* tránsfuga *mf,* trásfuga *mf*

defence [dɪˈfens] *n* (**a**) defensa *f;* **the Ministry of D.** el Ministerio de Defensa; **to come to sb's d.** salir en defensa de algn (**b**) *usu sing Jur* defensa *f* (**c**) *Sport* [*Br* dɪˈfens, *US* ˈdiːfens] **the d.** la defensa

defenceless [dɪˈfenslɪs] *adj* indefenso(a)

defend [dɪˈfend] *vt* defender

defendant [dɪˈfendənt] *n Jur* acusado(a) *m,f*

defender [dɪˈfendə(r)] *n* defensor(a) *m,f; Sport* defensa *m*

defending [dɪˈfendɪŋ] *adj Sport* defensor(a); **d. champion** campeón(ona) *m,f* titular

defense [dɪˈfens, ˈdiːfens] *n US* = **defence**

defensive [dɪˈfensɪv] **1** *adj* defensivo(a)
2 *n* **to be on the d.** estar a la defensiva

defer¹ [dɪˈfɜː(r)] *vt* aplazar, retrasar

defer² [dɪˈfɜː(r)] *vi* **to d. to** deferir a

deference [ˈdefərəns] *n Fml* deferencia *f,* respeto *m;* **out of** *or* **in d. to** por respeto *or* por deferencia a

defiance [dɪˈfaɪəns] *n* (**a**) *(challenge)* desafío *m;* **in d. of** a despecho de (**b**) *(resistance)* resistencia *f*

defiant [dɪˈfaɪənt] *adj (challenging)* desafiante; *(bold)* insolente

deficiency [dɪˈfɪʃənsɪ] *n* (**a**) *(lack)* falta *f,* carencia *f* (**b**) *(shortcoming)* defecto *m*

deficient [dɪˈfɪʃənt] *adj* deficiente; **to be d. in sth** carecer de algo

deficit [ˈdefɪsɪt] *n* déficit *m*

defile [dɪˈfaɪl] *vt Fml* (**a**) *(mind)* corromper; *(honour)* manchar; *(woman)* deshonrar (**b**) *(desecrate)* profanar

define [dɪˈfaɪn] *vt* definir; *(duties, powers)* delimitar

definite [ˈdefɪnɪt] *adj* (**a**) *(clear)* claro(a); *(progress)* notable (**b**) *(date, place)* determinado(a); **is it d.?** ¿es seguro?

definitely [ˈdefɪnɪtlɪ] **1** *adv* sin duda; **he was d. drunk** no cabe duda de que estaba borracho
2 *interj* ¡desde luego!

definition [defɪˈnɪʃən] *n* definición *f;* **by d.** por definición

definitive [dɪˈfɪnɪtɪv] *adj* definitivo(a)

deflate [dɪˈfleɪt] *vt* (**a**) *(tyre etc)* desinflar (**b**) *Fig* rebajar; **to d. sb** hacer bajar los humos a algn (**c**) **to d. the economy** tomar medidas deflacionistas

deflationary [dɪˈfleɪʃənərɪ] *adj Econ* deflacionista

deflect [dɪˈflekt] *vt* desviar

deflection [dɪˈflekʃən] *n* desviación *f*

deforestation [diːfɒrɪˈsteɪʃən] *n* deforestación *f*

deformed [dɪˈfɔːmd] *adj* deforme

deformity [dɪˈfɔːmɪtɪ] *n* deformidad *f*

defraud [dɪˈfrɔːd] *vt* estafar

defrost [diːˈfrɒst] *vt* (**a**) *(freezer, food)* descongelar (**b**) *US (windscreen)* desempañar

deft [deft] *adj* hábil, diestro(a)

defunct [dɪˈfʌŋkt] *adj (person)* difunto(a); *(thing)* en desuso

defuse [diːˈfjuːz] *vt (bomb)* desactivar; *Fig* **to d. a situation** reducir la tensión de una situación

defy [dɪˈfaɪ] *vt* (**a**) *(person)* desafiar; *(law, order)* contravenir (**b**) *(challenge)* retar, desafiar

degenerate 1 *vi* [dɪˈdʒenəreɪt] degenerar (**into** en)
2 *adj & n* [dɪˈdʒenərɪt] degenerado(a) *(m,f)*

degrading [dɪˈgreɪdɪŋ] *adj* degradante

degree [dɪˈgriː] *n* (**a**) grado *m;* **to some d.** hasta cierto punto (**b**) *(stage)* etapa *f;* **by degrees** poco a poco (**c**) *(qualification)* título *m; (doctorate)* doctorado *m;* **to have a d. in science** ser licenciado(a) en ciencias

dehydrated [diːhaɪˈdreɪtɪd] *adj (person)* deshidratado(a); *(vegetables)* seco(a)

de-ice [diːˈaɪs] *vt* quitar el hielo a, deshelar

de-icer [diːˈaɪsə(r)] *n* anticongelante *m*

deign [deɪn] *vi* dignarse

deity [ˈdeɪɪtɪ] *n* deidad *f*

dejected [dɪˈdʒektɪd] *adj* desalentado(a), abatido(a)

delay [dɪˈleɪ] **1** *vt* (**a**) *(flight, train)* retrasar; *(person)* entretener; **delayed action** acción retardada (**b**) *(postpone)* aplazar
2 *vi* **don't d.** no lo deje para más tarde
3 *n* retraso *m*

delectable [dɪˈlektəbəl] *adj* delicioso(a)

delegate 1 *n* [ˈdelɪgɪt] delegado(a) *m,f*
2 *vt* [ˈdelɪgeɪt] delegar (**to** en); **to d. sb to do sth** encargar a algn que haga algo

delegation [delɪˈgeɪʃən] *n* delegación *f*

delete [dɪˈliːt] *vt* tachar, suprimir

deliberate 1 *adj* [dɪˈlɪbərɪt] *(intentional)*

deliberado(a), intencionado(a); *(studied)* premeditado(a); *(careful)* prudente; *(unhurried)* pausado(a)
  2 *vt* [dɪˈlɪbəreɪt] deliberar
  3 *vi* deliberar (**on** *or* **about** sobre)
deliberately [dɪˈlɪbərɪtlɪ] *adv (intentionally)* a propósito; *(unhurriedly)* pausadamente
deliberation [dɪlɪbəˈreɪʃən] *n* (**a**) *esp pl (consideration)* deliberación *f* (**b**) *(care)* cuidado *m*; *(unhurriedness)* pausa *f*
delicacy [ˈdelɪkəsɪ] *n* (**a**) delicadeza *f* (**b**) *(food)* manjar *m* (exquisito)
delicate [ˈdelɪkɪt] *adj* delicado(a); *(handiwork)* fino(a); *(instrument)* sensible; *(flavour)* sutil
delicious [dɪˈlɪʃəs] *adj* delicioso(a)
delight [dɪˈlaɪt] **1** *n* (**a**) *(pleasure)* placer *m*; **he took d. in it** le encantó (**b**) *(source of pleasure)* encanto *m*, delicia *f*
  2 *vt* encantar
delighted [dɪˈlaɪtɪd] *adj* encantado(a); *(smile)* de alegría; **I'm d. to see you** me alegro mucho de verte
delightful [dɪˈlaɪtfʊl] *adj* encantador(a); *(view, person)* muy agradable; *(meal, weather)* delicioso(a)
delinquency [dɪˈlɪŋkwənsɪ] *n* delincuencia *f*; **juvenile d.** delincuencia juvenil
delinquent [dɪˈlɪŋkwənt] *adj & n* delincuente *(mf)*
delirious [dɪˈlɪrɪəs] *adj* delirante
deliver [dɪˈlɪvə(r)] *vt* (**a**) *(goods)* repartir, entregar; *(message)* dar; *(order)* despachar; *Fig* **to d. the goods** cumplir con la obligación (**b**) *(blow)* asestar; *(speech, verdict)* pronunciar (**c**) *Med* ayudar en el nacimiento de (**d**) *Fml (rescue)* liberar
delivery [dɪˈlɪvərɪ] *n* (**a**) *(of goods)* reparto *m*, entrega *f*; **to take d. of an order** recibir un pedido; **d. note** albarán *m* de entrega; *Br* **d. van** furgoneta *f* de reparto (**b**) *(of speech)* declamación *f* (**c**) *(of baby)* parto *m*
delta [ˈdeltə] *n Geog* delta *m*
delude [dɪˈluːd] *vt* engañar; **don't d. yourself** no te hagas ilusiones
deluge [ˈdeljuːdʒ] **1** *n (flood)* inundación *f*; *(rain)* diluvio *m*; *Fig (of letters etc)* avalancha *f*
  2 *vt Fml* inundar
delusion [dɪˈluːʒən] *n* (**a**) *(state, act)* engaño *m* (**b**) *(false belief)* ilusión *f* (vana); **delusions of grandeur** delirios *mpl* de grandeza
de luxe [dəˈlʌks, dəˈlʊks] *adj* de lujo *inv*
delve [delv] *vi* **to d. into** *(pocket)* hurgar

en; *(subject)* profundizar en
demand [dɪˈmɑːnd] **1** *n* (**a**) solicitud *f*; *(for pay rise, rights)* reclamación *f*; *(need)* necesidad *f*; **on d.** a petición (**b**) *(claim)* exigencia *f*; **to be in d.** ser solicitado(a) (**c**) *Econ* demanda *f*
  2 *vt* (**a**) exigir; *(rights)* reclamar; **to d. that ...** insistir en que ... (+ *subj*) (**b**) *(need)* requerir
demanding [dɪˈmɑːndɪŋ] *adj* (**a**) *(person)* exigente (**b**) *(job)* agotador(a)
demean [dɪˈmiːn] *vt Fml* **to d. oneself** rebajarse
demeaning [dɪˈmiːnɪŋ] *adj Fml* humillante
demeanour, *US* **demeanor** [dɪˈmiːnə(r)] *n Fml* (**a**) *(behaviour)* comportamiento *m*, conducta *f* (**b**) *(bearing)* porte *m*
demented [dɪˈmentɪd] *adj Med* demente; *Fam* loco(a)
demise [dɪˈmaɪz] *n Fml (death)* fallecimiento *m*; *Fig (of institution)* desaparición *f*; *(of ambition etc)* fracaso *m*
demist [diːˈmɪst] *vt Aut* desempañar
demo [ˈdeməʊ] *n Fam* manifestación *f*; **d. tape** maqueta *f*
demobilize [diːˈməʊbɪlaɪz] *vt* desmovilizar
democracy [dɪˈmɒkrəsɪ] *n* democracia *f*
democrat [ˈdeməkræt] *n* demócrata *mf*; *Pol* **Christian D.** democratacristiano(a) *m,f*; **Social D.** socialdemócrata *mf*
democratic [deməˈkrætɪk] *adj* democrático(a); *US Pol* **D. party** partido *m* demócrata
demographic [deməˈgræfɪk] *adj* demográfico(a)
demolish [dɪˈmɒlɪʃ] *vt (building)* derribar, demoler; *Fig (theory, proposal)* echar por tierra
demolition [deməˈlɪʃən] *n* demolición *f*
demon [ˈdiːmən] *n* demonio *m*
demonstrate [ˈdemənstreɪt] **1** *vt* demostrar
  2 *vi Pol* manifestarse
demonstration [demənˈstreɪʃən] *n* (**a**) *(proof)* demostración *f*, prueba *f* (**b**) *(explanation)* explicación *f* (**c**) *Pol* manifestación *f*
demonstrative [dɪˈmɒnstrətɪv] *adj* expresivo(a)
demonstrator [ˈdemənstreɪtə(r)] *n* manifestante *mf*
demoralize [dɪˈmɒrəlaɪz] *vt* desmoralizar
demoralizing [dɪˈmɒrəlaɪzɪŋ] *adj* desmoralizador(a), desmoralizante

demote [dɪ'məʊt] vt rebajar de graduación a

demure [dɪ'mjʊə(r)] adj (person) recatado(a)

den [den] n (a) (of animal) guarida f (b) Fam (study) estudio m

denial [dɪ'naɪəl] n (a) (of charge) desmentido m (b) (of rights) denegación f; (of request) negativa f

denim ['denɪm] n dril m; **d. skirt** falda tejana; **denims** tejanos mpl, vaqueros mpl

Denmark ['denmɑːk] n Dinamarca

denomination [dɪnɒmɪ'neɪʃən] n (a) Rel confesión f (b) Fin (of coins) valor m

denominator [dɪ'nɒmɪneɪtə(r)] n denominador m

denote [dɪ'nəʊt] vt (show) indicar; (mean) significar

denounce [dɪ'naʊns] vt denunciar; (criticize) censurar

dense [dens] adj (a) denso(a); (crowd) numeroso(a) (b) Fam (stupid) torpe

densely ['densli] adv densamente

density ['densɪtɪ] n densidad f

dent [dent] 1 n abolladura f
2 vt (car) abollar

dental ['dentəl] adj dental; **d. floss** hilo m dental; **d. surgeon** odontólogo(a) m,f; **d. surgery** (place) clínica f dental; (treatment) cirugía f dental

dentist ['dentɪst] n dentista mf

dentistry ['dentɪstrɪ] n odontología f

denture ['dentʃə(r)] n (usu pl) dentadura postiza

denunciation [dɪnʌnsɪ'eɪʃən] n denuncia f, condena f

deny [dɪ'naɪ] vt (a) (repudiate) negar; (rumour, report) desmentir; (charge) rechazar (b) (refuse) negar

deodorant [diː'əʊdərənt] n desodorante m

depart [dɪ'pɑːt] vi marcharse, irse; Fig (from subject) desviarse (**from** de)

department [dɪ'pɑːtmənt] n sección f; (in university) departamento m; (in government) ministerio m; **d. store** grandes almacenes mpl; US **D. of the Interior** Ministerio m del Interior

departure [dɪ'pɑːtʃə(r)] n partida f; Av & Rail salida f; Av **d. lounge** sala f de embarque

depend [dɪ'pend] 1 vi (rely) fiarse (**on** or **upon** de)
2 v impers (be determined by) depender (**on** or **upon** de); **it depends on the weather** según el tiempo que haga; **that depends** según

dependable [dɪ'pendəbəl] adj (person)

responsable, fiable; (income) seguro(a); (machine) fiable

dependant, US **dependent** [dɪ'pendənt] n dependiente mf

dependence [dɪ'pendəns] n dependencia f

dependent [dɪ'pendənt] 1 adj dependiente; **to be d. on sth** depender de algo
2 n US = **dependant**

depict [dɪ'pɪkt] vt Art representar; Fig describir

deplete [dɪ'pliːt] vt reducir

deplorable [dɪ'plɔːrəbəl] adj lamentable

deplore [dɪ'plɔː(r)] vt deplorar

deploy [dɪ'plɔɪ] vt Mil desplegar; Fig utilizar

depopulate [diː'pɒpjʊleɪt] vt despoblar

deport [dɪ'pɔːt] vt expulsar (**from** de; **to** a)

deportation [diːpɔː'teɪʃən] n expulsión f

deportment [dɪ'pɔːtmənt] n Fml porte m

depose [dɪ'pəʊz] vt deponer

deposit [dɪ'pɒzɪt] 1 n (a) sedimento m; Min yacimiento m; (in wine) poso m (b) (in bank) depósito m; **d. account** cuenta f de ahorros (c) Com (on purchase) señal f; (on rented car, flat) depósito m; (on house) entrada f
2 vt depositar; (into account) ingresar

deposition [depə'zɪʃən] n (a) (of leader) destitución f (b) Jur (of witness) declaración f

depositor [dɪ'pɒzɪtə(r)] n depositante mf

depot ['depəʊ] n almacén m; Mil depósito m; (bus garage) garaje m (de autobuses); US (bus station) estación f de autobuses

depraved [dɪ'preɪvd] adj (person) depravado(a)

deprecate ['deprɪkeɪt] vt desaprobar, censurar

depreciate [dɪ'priːʃɪeɪt] vi depreciarse

depreciation [dɪpriːʃɪ'eɪʃən] n depreciación f

depress [dɪ'pres] vt (a) (person) deprimir (b) Econ (profits) reducir; (trade) dificultar (c) Fml (switch, lever etc) presionar; (clutch, piano pedal) pisar

depressed [dɪ'prest] adj (a) (person) deprimido(a); **to get d.** deprimirse (b) (market) en crisis (c) (surface) hundido(a)

depressing [dɪ'presɪŋ] adj deprimente

depression [dɪ'preʃən] n depresión f

deprivation [deprɪ'veɪʃən] n (hardship) privación f; (loss) pérdida f

deprive [dɪ'praɪv] vt privar (**of** de)

deprived [dɪ'praɪvd] adj necesitado(a)

dept (*abbr* **department**) dpt, dpto
depth [depθ] *n* (**a**) profundidad *f* (**b**) *Fig (of emotion)* intensidad *f*; *(of thought)* complejidad *f*; **to be in the depths of despair** estar completamente desesperado(a); **in d.** a fondo
deputation [depjʊ'teɪʃən] *n* delegación *f*
deputy ['depjʊtɪ] *n* (**a**) *(substitute)* suplente *mf*; **d. chairman** vicepresidente *m*; **d. head** subdirector(a) *m,f* (**b**) *Pol* diputado(a) *m,f*
derail [dɪ'reɪl] *vt* hacer descarrilar
deranged [dɪ'reɪndʒd] *adj* trastornado(a)
derby *n* (**a**) ['dɑːbɪ] *Sport* prueba *f* (**b**) ['dɜːrbɪ] *US* sombrero hongo
derelict ['derɪlɪkt] *adj* abandonado(a), en ruinas
deride [dɪ'raɪd] *vt* ridiculizar, burlarse de
derisive [dɪ'raɪsɪv] *adj* burlón(ona)
derisory [dɪ'raɪsərɪ] *adj* irrisorio(a)
derivative [dɪ'rɪvətɪv] **1** *adj (art, writing)* sin originalidad
  2 *n (of word, substance)* derivado *m*
derive [dɪ'raɪv] **1** *vt* sacar
  2 *vi (word)* derivarse (**from** de); *(skill)* provenir (**from** de)
derogatory [dɪ'rɒgətərɪ] *adj (remark, article)* despectivo(a); *(meaning)* peyorativo(a)
derrick ['derɪk] *n* torre *f* de perforación
descend [dɪ'send] **1** *vi* descender; **to d. from** *(be related to)* descender de
  2 *vt (stairs)* bajar
descendant [dɪ'sendənt] *n* descendiente *mf*
descent [dɪ'sent] *n* (**a**) descenso *m* (**b**) *Fig (into madness, poverty)* caída *f* (**c**) *(slope)* declive *m* (**d**) *(ancestry)* ascendencia *f*
describe [dɪ'skraɪb] *vt* (**a**) describir (**b**) *(circle)* trazar
description [dɪ'skrɪpʃən] *n* (**a**) descripción *f*; **to defy d.** superar la descripción (**b**) *(type)* clase *f*
desecrate ['desɪkreɪt] *vt* profanar
desert[1] ['dezət] *n* desierto *m*
desert[2] [dɪ'zɜːt] **1** *vt (place, family)* abandonar
  2 *vi Mil* desertar (**from** de)
deserter [dɪ'zɜːtə(r)] *n* desertor(a) *m,f*
desertion [dɪ'zɜːʃən] *n* abandono *m*; *Pol* defección *f*; *Mil* deserción *f*
deserts [dɪ'zɜːts] *npl* **to get one's just d.** llevarse su merecido
deserve [dɪ'zɜːv] *vt (rest, punishment)* merecer; *(prize, praise)* ser digno(a) de
deservedly [dɪ'zɜːvɪdlɪ] *adv* con (toda) razón

deserving [dɪ'zɜːvɪŋ] *adj (person)* de valía; *(cause)* meritorio(a)
design [dɪ'zaɪn] **1** *n* (**a**) diseño *m* (**b**) *(drawing, blueprint)* plano *m* (**c**) *(layout)* disposición *f* (**d**) *(pattern)* dibujo *m* (**e**) *Fig (scheme)* intención *f*; **by d.** a propósito; *Fam* **to have designs on** tener puestas las miras en
  2 *vt* diseñar
designate **1** *vt* ['dezɪgneɪt] (**a**) *(appoint)* designar, nombrar (**b**) *Fml (boundary)* señalar
  2 *adj* ['dezɪgnɪt] designado(a)
designer [dɪ'zaɪnə(r)] *n Art* diseñador(a) *m,f*; **d. jeans** pantalones *mpl* de marca
desirable [dɪ'zaɪərəbəl] *adj* deseable; *(asset, offer)* atractivo(a)
desire [dɪ'zaɪə(r)] **1** *n* deseo *m*; **I haven't the slightest d. to go** no me apetece nada ir
  2 *vt* desear
desist [dɪ'zɪst] *vi Fml* desistir (**from** de)
desk [desk] *n (in school)* pupitre *m*; *(in office)* escritorio *m*; *US* **d. clerk** recepcionista *mf*; **d. job** trabajo *m* de oficina; **news d.** redacción *f*; **reception d.** recepción *f*
desktop ['desktɒp] *n Comput* escritorio *m*; **d. computer** ordenador *m* de sobremesa, *Am* computadora *f* de mesa; **d. publishing** autoedición *f*
desolate ['desəlɪt] *adj* (**a**) *(uninhabited)* desierto(a); *(barren)* yermo(a) (**b**) *(person)* desconsolado(a)
desolation [desə'leɪʃən] *n* (**a**) *(of place)* desolación *f*; *(by destruction)* asolamiento *m* (**b**) *(of person)* desconsuelo *m*
despair [dɪ'speə(r)] **1** *n* desesperación *f*; **to drive sb to d.** desesperar a algn
  2 *vi* desesperar(se) (**of** de)
despairing [dɪ'speərɪŋ] *adj* desesperado(a)
despatch [dɪ'spætʃ] *n & vt* = **dispatch**
desperate ['despərɪt] *adj* (**a**) desesperado(a); *(struggle)* encarnizado(a) (**b**) *(need)* apremiante
desperately ['despərɪtlɪ] *adv (recklessly)* desesperadamente; *(struggle)* encarnizadamente; *(ill)* gravemente; *(in love)* locamente; *(difficult)* sumamente
desperation [despə'reɪʃən] *n* desesperación *f*; **in d.** a la desesperada
despicable [dɪ'spɪkəbəl] *adj* despreciable; *(behaviour)* indigno(a)
despise [dɪ'spaɪz] *vt* despreciar, menospreciar
despite [dɪ'spaɪt] *prep Fml* a pesar de
despondent [dɪ'spɒndənt] *adj* abatido(a)

despot ['despɒt] *n* déspota *mf*
dessert [dɪ'zɜːt] *n* postre *m*; **d. wine** vino *m* dulce
dessertspoon [dɪ'zɜːtspuːn] *n* (**a**) cuchara *f* de postre (**b**) **dessertspoon(ful)** *(measure)* cucharada *f* de postre
destination [destɪ'neɪʃən] *n* destino *m*
destined ['destɪnd] *adj* (**a**) **d. to fail** condenado(a) al fracaso (**b**) *(bound)* con destino (**for** a)
destiny ['destɪnɪ] *n* destino *m*
destitute ['destɪtjuːt] *adj* indigente
destroy [dɪ'strɔɪ] *vt* destruir; *(vehicle, old furniture)* destrozar
destroyer [dɪ'strɔɪə(r)] *n Naut* destructor *m*
destruction [dɪ'strʌkʃən] *n* destrucción *f*; *Fig* ruina *f*
destructive [dɪ'strʌktɪv] *adj (gale etc)* destructor(a); *(tendency, criticism)* destructivo(a)
detach [dɪ'tætʃ] *vt (remove)* separar
detachable [dɪ'tætʃəbəl] *adj* separable (**from** de)
detached [dɪ'tætʃt] *adj* (**a**) *(separated)* separado(a); **d. house** casa *f* independiente (**b**) *(impartial)* objetivo(a)
detachment [dɪ'tætʃmənt] *n* (**a**) *(impartiality)* objetividad *f*; *(aloofness)* desapego *m* (**b**) *Mil* destacamento *m*
detail ['diːteɪl] **1** *n* (**a**) detalle *m*, pormenor *m*; **without going into detail(s)** sin entrar en detalles; **details** *(information)* información *f* (**b**) *Mil* destacamento *m*
2 *vt* (**a**) *(list)* detallar, enumerar (**b**) *Mil (appoint)* destacar
detailed ['diːteɪld] *adj* detallado(a), minucioso(a)
detain [dɪ'teɪn] *vt* (**a**) *Jur* detener (**b**) *(delay)* retener
detainee [diːteɪ'niː] *n Pol* preso(a) *m,f*
detect [dɪ'tekt] *vt* (**a**) *(error, movement)* advertir; *(difference)* notar; *(smell, sound)* percibir (**b**) *(discover)* descubrir; *(enemy ship)* detectar; *(position)* localizar
detection [dɪ'tekʃən] *n* (**a**) descubrimiento *m*; *(of smell, sound)* percepción *f* (**b**) *(discovery) (of enemy ship)* detección *f*
detective [dɪ'tektɪv] *n* detective *mf*; **d. story** novela policíaca
detector [dɪ'tektə(r)] *n* aparato *m* detector
detention [dɪ'tenʃən] *n (of suspect etc)* detención *f*, arresto *m*; *Educ* **to get d.** quedarse castigado(a)
deter [dɪ'tɜː(r)] *vt (dissuade)* disuadir (**from** de); *(stop)* impedir

detergent [dɪ'tɜːdʒənt] *n* detergente *m*
deteriorate [dɪ'tɪərɪəreɪt] *vi* deteriorarse
deterioration [dɪtɪərɪə'reɪʃən] *n* empeoramiento *m*; *(of substance, friendship)* deterioro *m*
determination [dɪtɜːmɪ'neɪʃən] *n (resolution)* resolución *f*
determine [dɪ'tɜːmɪn] *vt* determinar
determined [dɪ'tɜːmɪnd] *adj (person)* decidido(a); *(effort)* enérgico(a)
deterrent [dɪ'terənt] **1** *adj* disuasivo(a)
2 *n* fuerza disuasoria
detest [dɪ'test] *vt* detestar, odiar
detonate ['detəneɪt] *vt & vi* detonar
detonation [detə'neɪʃən] *n* detonación *f*
detour ['diːtʊə(r)] *n* desvío *m*
detract [dɪ'trækt] *vi* quitar mérito (**from** a)
detractor [dɪ'træktə(r)] *n* detractor(a) *m,f*
detriment ['detrɪmənt] *n* perjuicio *m* (**to** de)
detrimental [detrɪ'mentəl] *adj* perjudicial (**to** para)
deuce [djuːs] *n (in tennis)* cuarenta iguales *mpl*
devaluation [diːvæljuː'eɪʃən] *n* devaluación *f*
devastate ['devəsteɪt] *vt (city, area)* asolar; *Fig (person)* desolar
devastating ['devəsteɪtɪŋ] *adj (fire)* devastador(a); *(wind, flood)* arrollador(a)
devastation [devə'steɪʃən] *n* asolación *f*
develop [dɪ'veləp] **1** *vt* (**a**) desarrollar; *(trade)* fomentar; *(skill)* perfeccionar; *(plan)* elaborar; *(habit)* contraer; *(interest)* mostrar (**b**) *(natural resources)* aprovechar; *Constr (site)* urbanizar (**c**) *Phot* revelar
2 *vi* (**a**) *(body, industry)* desarrollarse; *(system)* perfeccionarse; *(interest)* crecer (**b**) *(appear)* crearse; *(evolve)* evolucionar
developer [dɪ'veləpə(r)] *n* (**property**) **d.** inmobiliaria *f*
development [dɪ'veləpmənt] *n* (**a**) desarrollo *m*; *(of trade)* fomento *m*; *(of skill)* perfección *f*; *(of character)* formación *f*; **d. aid** ayuda *f* al desarrollo (**b**) *(advance)* avance *m* (**c**) **there are no new developments** no hay ninguna novedad (**d**) *(exploitation)* explotación *f* (**e**) *Constr* urbanización *f*
deviate ['diːvɪeɪt] *vi* desviarse (**from** de)
deviation [diːvɪ'eɪʃən] *n (from norm, route)* desviación *f* (**from** de); *(from truth)* alejamiento *m*

device [dɪˈvaɪs] n (**a**) aparato m; *(mechanism)* mecanismo m (**b**) *(trick, scheme)* ardid m

devil [ˈdevəl] n diablo m, demonio m; **d.'s advocate** abogado(a) m,f del diablo; *Fam* **where the d. did you put it?** ¿dónde demonios lo pusiste?; **you lucky d.!** ¡vaya suerte que tienes!

devious [ˈdiːvɪəs] adj (**a**) *(winding)* tortuoso(a) (**b**) *esp Pej (person)* taimado(a)

devise [dɪˈvaɪz] vt idear, concebir

devoid [dɪˈvɔɪd] adj desprovisto(a) (**of** de)

devolution [diːvəˈluːʃən] n Pol = transmisión de poderes a las regiones

devote [dɪˈvəʊt] vt dedicar; **she devoted her life to helping the poor** consagró su vida a la ayuda de los pobres

devoted [dɪˈvəʊtɪd] adj fiel, leal (**to** a)

devotee [devəˈtiː] n *(of religion)* devoto(a) m,f; *(of theatre, sport)* aficionado(a) m,f; Pol partidario(a) m,f

devotion [dɪˈvəʊʃən] n devoción f; *(to cause)* dedicación f

devour [dɪˈvaʊə(r)] vt devorar

devout [dɪˈvaʊt] adj devoto(a)

dew [djuː] n rocío m

dexterity [dekˈsterɪtɪ] n destreza f

dext(e)rous [ˈdekstrəs] adj diestro(a)

diabetes [daɪəˈbiːtiːz, daɪəˈbiːtɪs] n diabetes f

diabetic [daɪəˈbetɪk] adj & n diabético(a) (m,f)

diabolical [daɪəˈbɒlɪkəl] adj (**a**) *(evil)* diabólico(a) (**b**) *Fam (unbearable)* espantoso(a)

diagnose [ˈdaɪəgnəʊz] vt diagnosticar

diagnosis [daɪəgˈnəʊsɪs] n *(pl* **diagnoses** [daɪəgˈnəʊsiːz]) diagnóstico m

diagonal [daɪˈægənəl] adj & n diagonal (f)

diagonally [daɪˈægənəlɪ] adv en diagonal, diagonalmente

diagram [ˈdaɪəgræm] n diagrama m; *(of process, system)* esquema m; *(of workings)* gráfico m

dial [ˈdaɪəl, daɪl] **1** n *(of clock)* esfera f; *(of radio)* cuadrante m; *(of telephone)* disco m; *(of machine)* botón m selector

2 vt & vi Tel marcar; Br **dialling** or US **d. code** prefijo m; Br **dialling** or US **d. tone** señal f de marcar

dialect [ˈdaɪəlekt] n dialecto m

dialogue, US **dialog** [ˈdaɪəlɒg] n diálogo m

diameter [daɪˈæmɪtə(r)] n diámetro m

diametrically [daɪəˈmetrɪkəlɪ] adv diametralmente

diamond [ˈdaɪəmənd] n (**a**) diamante m (**b**) *(shape)* rombo m

diaper [ˈdaɪəpə(r)] n US pañal m

diaphragm [ˈdaɪəfræm] n diafragma m

diarrhoea, US **diarrhea** [daɪəˈrɪə] n diarrea f

diary [ˈdaɪərɪ] n (**a**) diario m; **to keep a d.** llevar un diario (**b**) Br *(for appointments)* agenda f

dice [daɪs] **1** n *(pl* **dice**) dado m

2 vt Culin cortar en cuadritos

dichotomy [daɪˈkɒtəmɪ] n dicotomía f

dictate 1 vt [dɪkˈteɪt] *(letter, order)* dictar

2 vi **to d. to sb** dar órdenes a algn

3 n [ˈdɪkteɪt] Fig **the dictates of conscience** los dictados de la conciencia

dictation [dɪkˈteɪʃən] n dictado m

dictator [dɪkˈteɪtə(r)] n dictador(a) m,f

dictatorship [dɪkˈteɪtəʃɪp] n dictadura f

diction [ˈdɪkʃən] n dicción f

dictionary [ˈdɪkʃənərɪ] n diccionario m

did [dɪd] pt of **do**

die [daɪ] vi (**a**) morir, morirse; *Fam Fig* **to be dying for sth/to do sth** morirse por algo/de ganas de hacer algo (**b**) *Fig (flame)* extinguirse; *Fig* **to d. hard** *(habit)* tardar en desaparecer (**c**) *(engine)* calarse; *(battery)* agotarse

▸ **die away** vi desvanecerse

▸ **die down** vi *(fire)* extinguirse; *(wind)* amainar; *(noise, excitement)* disminuir

▸ **die off** vi morir uno por uno

▸ **die out** vi extinguirse

die-hard [ˈdaɪhɑːd] n reaccionario(a) m,f

diesel [ˈdiːzəl] n (**a**) *(oil)* gasoil m; **d. engine** motor m diesel (**b**) *Fam (vehicle)* vehículo m diesel

diet [ˈdaɪət] **1** n *(normal food)* dieta f; *(selected food)* régimen m; **to be on a d.** estar a régimen

2 vi estar a régimen

dietician [daɪəˈtɪʃən] n especialista mf en dietética

differ [ˈdɪfə(r)] vi *(be unlike)* ser distinto(a); *(disagree)* discrepar

difference [ˈdɪfərəns] n (**a**) *(dissimilarity)* diferencia f; **it makes no d. (to me)** (me) da igual; **what d. does it make?** ¿qué más da? (**b**) *(disagreement)* desacuerdo m

different [ˈdɪfərənt] adj diferente, distinto(a); **you look d.** pareces otro(a)

differentiate [dɪfəˈrenʃɪeɪt] **1** vt distinguir, diferenciar (**from** de)

2 vi distinguir (**between** entre)

differently [ˈdɪfərəntlɪ] adv de otra manera

difficult [ˈdɪfɪkəlt] adj difícil

difficulty ['dɪfɪkəltɪ] *n* dificultad *f*; *(problem)* problema *m*; **to be in difficulties** estar en un apuro

diffident ['dɪfɪdənt] *adj* tímido(a)

diffuse 1 *adj* [dɪ'fjuːs] *(light)* difuso(a); *Fig* vago(a)
  2 *vt* [dɪ'fjuːz] difundir; *(heat)* desprender

dig [dɪg] **1** *n* (**a**) *(poke)* codazo *m* (**b**) *Fam (gibe)* pulla *f* (**c**) *(archaeological)* excavación *f* (**d**) *Br* **digs** *(lodgings)* alojamiento *m*; *(room)* habitación *f* alquilada
  2 *vt* *(pt & pp* **dug**) (**a**) *(earth)* cavar; *(tunnel)* excavar (**b**) *Fam Fig* **to d. one's heels in** mantenerse en sus trece
  3 *vi (person)* cavar; *(animal)* escarbar; *(excavate)* excavar
  ▸ **dig in** *vi Mil* atrincherarse
  ▸ **dig out** *vt sep Fig (old suit)* sacar; *(information)* descubrir
  ▸ **dig up** *vt sep (weeds)* arrancar; *(buried object)* desenterrar; *(road)* levantar; *Fig* sacar a relucir

digest 1 *n* ['daɪdʒest] *(summary)* resumen *m*
  2 *vt* [dɪ'dʒest] *(food)* digerir; *Fig (facts)* asimilar

digestion [dɪ'dʒestʃən] *n* digestión *f*

digestive [dɪ'dʒestɪv] *adj* digestivo(a); *Br* **d. biscuit** galleta *f* integral

digger ['dɪgə(r)] *n* excavadora *f*

digit ['dɪdʒɪt] *n* (**a**) *Math* dígito *m* (**b**) *Fml Anat* dedo *m*

digital ['dɪdʒɪtəl] *adj* digital; **d. television** televisión *f* digital

dignified ['dɪgnɪfaɪd] *adj (manner)* solemne, serio(a); *(appearance)* majestuoso(a)

dignitary ['dɪgnɪtərɪ] *n* dignatario *m*

dignity ['dɪgnɪtɪ] *n* dignidad *f*

digress [daɪ'gres] *vi* apartarse del tema

dike [daɪk] *n US* = **dyke**

dilapidated [dɪ'læpɪdeɪtɪd] *adj* en mal estado

dilemma [dɪ'lemə, daɪ'lemə] *n* dilema *m*

diligent ['dɪlɪdʒənt] *adj (worker)* diligente; *(inquiries, search)* esmerado(a)

dilute [daɪ'luːt] **1** *vt* diluir; *(wine, milk)* aguar; *Fig (effect, influence)* atenuar
  2 *vi* diluirse

dim [dɪm] **1** *adj* (**dimmer, dimmest**) (**a**) *(light)* débil, tenue; *(room)* oscuro(a); *(outline)* borroso(a); *(eyesight)* defectuoso(a); *Fig (memory)* vago(a); *Fig (future)* sombrío(a) (**b**) *Fam (stupid)* torpe
  2 *vt (light)* bajar
  3 *vi (light)* bajarse; *(sight)* nublarse; *Fig (joy)* extinguirse

dime [daɪm] *n US* moneda *f* de 10 centavos

dimension [daɪ'menʃən] *n* dimensión *f*

diminish [dɪ'mɪnɪʃ] *vt & vi* disminuir

diminutive [dɪ'mɪnjʊtɪv] **1** *adj* diminuto(a)
  2 *n Ling* diminutivo *m*

dimly ['dɪmlɪ] *adv* vagamente

dimmer ['dɪmə(r)] *n* **d. (switch)** regulador *m* de voltaje

dimple ['dɪmpəl] *n* hoyuelo *m*

din [dɪn] *n (of crowd)* alboroto *m*; *(of machinery)* estruendo *m*

dine [daɪn] *vi Fml* cenar; **to d. out** cenar fuera

diner ['daɪnə(r)] *n* (**a**) *(person)* comensal *mf* (**b**) *US (restaurant)* restaurante barato

dinghy ['dɪŋɪ] *n* bote *m*; **(rubber) d.** bote neumático

dingy ['dɪndʒɪ] *adj* (**dingier, dingiest**) (**a**) *(dark)* oscuro(a) (**b**) *(dirty)* sucio(a) (**c**) *(colour)* desteñido(a)

dining car ['daɪnɪŋkɑː(r)] *n* vagón *m* restaurante

dining room ['daɪnɪŋruːm] *n* comedor *m*

dinner ['dɪnə(r)] *n (at midday)* comida *f*; *(in evening)* cena *f*; **d. jacket** smoking *m*; **d. service** vajilla *f*; **d. table** mesa *f* de comedor

dinosaur ['daɪnəsɔː(r)] *n* dinosaurio *m*

dint [dɪnt] *n* **by d. of** a fuerza de

diocese ['daɪəsɪs] *n* diócesis *f inv*

dioxide [daɪ'ɒksaɪd] *n* bióxido *m*

dip [dɪp] **1** *n* (**a**) *Fam (bathe)* chapuzón *m* (**b**) *(of road)* pendiente *f*; *(in ground)* depresión *f* (**c**) *Culin* salsa *f*
  2 *vt* (**a**) bañar; *(spoon, hand)* meter (**b**) *Br Aut* **to d. one's lights** poner luces de cruce
  3 *vi (road)* bajar
  ▸ **dip into** *vt insep* (**a**) *(savings)* echar mano de (**b**) *(book)* hojear

diphthong ['dɪfθɒŋ] *n* diptongo *m*

diploma [dɪ'pləʊmə] *n* diploma *m*

diplomacy [dɪ'pləʊməsɪ] *n* diplomacia *f*

diplomat ['dɪpləmæt] *n* diplomático(a) *m,f*

diplomatic [dɪplə'mætɪk] *adj* diplomático(a)

dipstick ['dɪpstɪk] *n* indicador *m* de nivel del aceite

dire ['daɪə(r)] *adj (urgent)* extremo(a); *(serious)* grave

direct [dɪ'rekt, 'daɪrekt] **1** *adj* (**a**) directo(a); **d. current** corriente continua (**b**) **the d. opposite** todo lo contrario
  2 *adv* directamente
  3 *vt* (**a**) dirigir; **can you d. me to a bank?**

¿me puede indicar dónde hay un banco? (**b**) *Fml (order)* mandar

direction [dɪˈrekʃən, daɪˈrekʃən] *n* (**a**) dirección *f*; **sense of d.** sentido *m* de la orientación (**b**) **directions** *(to place)* señas *fpl*; **directions for use** modo *m* de empleo (**c**)*Th* puesta *f* en escena

directive [dɪˈrektɪv, daɪˈrektɪv] *n* directiva *f*

directly [dɪˈrektlɪ, daɪˈrektlɪ] **1** *adv* (**a**) *(above etc)* exactamente, justo (**b**) *(speak)* francamente (**c**) *(descend)* directamente (**d**) *(come)* en seguida
2 *conj Fam* en cuanto

director [dɪˈrektə(r), daɪˈrektə(r)] *n* director(a) *m,f*

directory [dɪˈrektərɪ, daɪˈrektərɪ] *n Tel* guía telefónica; **d. enquiries** (servicio *m* de) información *f*

dirt [dɜːt] *n* suciedad *f*

dirt-cheap [dɜːtˈtʃiːp] *adv & adj Fam* tirado(a)

dirty [ˈdɜːtɪ] **1** *adj* (**dirtier, dirtiest**) (**a**) sucio(a) (**b**) **to give sb a d. look** fulminar a algn con la mirada (**c**) *(joke)* verde; *(mind)* pervertido(a); **d. word** palabrota *f*; **d. old man** viejo *m* verde
2 *vt* ensuciar

disability [dɪsəˈbɪlɪtɪ] *n* incapacidad *f*, discapacidad *f*; **d. pension** pensión *f* por invalidez

disabled [dɪˈseɪbəld] **1** *adj* minusválido(a)
2 *npl* **the d.** los minusválidos

disadvantage [dɪsədˈvɑːntɪdʒ] *n* desventaja *f*; *(obstacle)* inconveniente *m*

disaffection [dɪsəˈfekʃən] *n* descontento *m*

disagree [dɪsəˈɡriː] *vi* (**a**) *(differ)* no estar de acuerdo (**with** con); **to d. on** *or* **over sth** reñir por algo (**b**) *(not match)* discrepar (**with** de *or* con) (**c**) **garlic disagrees with me** el ajo no me sienta bien

disagreeable [dɪsəˈɡriːəbəl] *adj* desagradable

disagreement [dɪsəˈɡriːmənt] *n* (**a**) desacuerdo *m*; *(argument)* riña *f* (**b**) *(non-correspondence)* discrepancia *f*

disallow [dɪsəˈlaʊ] *vt (goal)* anular; *(objection)* rechazar

disappear [dɪsəˈpɪə(r)] *vi* desaparecer

disappearance [dɪsəˈpɪərəns] *n* desaparición *f*

disappoint [dɪsəˈpɔɪnt] *vt (person)* decepcionar, defraudar; *(hope, ambition)* frustrar

disappointed [dɪsəˈpɔɪntɪd] *adj* decepcionado(a)

disappointing [dɪsəˈpɔɪntɪŋ] *adj* decepcionante

disappointment [dɪsəˈpɔɪntmənt] *n* decepción *f*

disapproval [dɪsəˈpruːvəl] *n* desaprobación *f*

disapprove [dɪsəˈpruːv] *vi* **to d. of** desaprobar

disarm [dɪsˈɑːm] **1** *vt* desarmar
2 *vi* desarmarse

disarmament [dɪsˈɑːməmənt] *n* desarme *m*

disarray [dɪsəˈreɪ] *n Fml* **in d.** *(room, papers)* en desorden; *(hair)* desarreglado(a); *(thoughts)* confuso(a)

disaster [dɪˈzɑːstə(r)] *n* desastre *m*

disastrous [dɪˈzɑːstrəs] *adj* desastroso(a)

disband [dɪsˈbænd] **1** *vt* disolver
2 *vi* disolverse

disbelief [dɪsbɪˈliːf] *n* incredulidad *f*

disc [dɪsk] *n* disco *m*; *Comput* disquete *m*; **d. jockey** disc-jockey *mf*, pinchadiscos *mf inv*

discard [dɪsˈkɑːd] *vt (old things)* deshacerse de; *(plan)* descartar

discern [dɪˈsɜːn] *vt (shape, difference)* percibir; *(truth)* darse cuenta de

discerning [dɪˈsɜːnɪŋ] *adj (person)* perspicaz; *(taste)* refinado(a)

discharge *Fml* **1** *vt* [dɪsˈtʃɑːdʒ] (**a**) *(smoke)* emitir; *(liquid)* echar; *(cargo)* descargar (**b**) *(prisoner)* soltar; *(patient)* dar de alta a; *(soldier)* licenciar; *(employee)* despedir (**c**) *(debt)* saldar (**d**) *(fulfil)* cumplir
2 *n* [ˈdɪstʃɑːdʒ] (**a**) *(of current, load)* descarga *f*; *(of gases)* escape *m* (**b**) *(of prisoner)* liberación *f*; *(of patient)* alta *f*; *(of soldier)* licencia *f* (**c**) *(of debt)* descargo *m* (**d**) *(of duty)* cumplimiento *m*

disciple [dɪˈsaɪpəl] *n* discípulo(a) *m,f*

discipline [ˈdɪsɪplɪn] **1** *n* disciplina *f*
2 *vt (child)* castigar; *(worker)* sancionar; *(official)* expedientar

disclaim [dɪsˈkleɪm] *vt Fml* negar tener

disclose [dɪsˈkləʊz] *vt* revelar

disclosure [dɪsˈkləʊʒə(r)] *n* revelación *f*

disco [ˈdɪskəʊ] *n Fam (abbr* **discotheque**) disco *f*

discolour, *US* **discolor** [dɪsˈkʌlə(r)] *vt* descolorir

discomfort [dɪsˈkʌmfət] *n* (**a**) *(lack of comfort)* incomodidad *f* (**b**) *(pain)* malestar *m* (**c**) *(unease)* inquietud *f*

disconcert [dɪskənˈsɜːt] *vt* desconcertar

disconcerting [dɪskənˈsɜːtɪŋ] *adj* desconcertante

disconnect [dɪskə'nekt] *vt* desconectar (**from** de); *(gas, electricity)* cortar

disconnected [dɪskə'nektɪd] *adj* inconexo(a)

disconsolate [dɪs'kɒnsəlɪt] *adj* desconsolado(a)

discontent [dɪskən'tent] *n* descontento *m*

discontented [dɪskən'tentɪd] *adj* descontento(a)

discontinue [dɪskən'tɪnjuː] *vt Fml* abandonar; *(work)* interrumpir

discord ['dɪskɔːd] *n* (**a**) *Fml* discordia *f* (**b**) *Mus* disonancia *f*

discordant [dɪs'kɔːdənt] *adj* discordante

discotheque ['dɪskətek] *n* discoteca *f*

discount 1 *n* ['dɪskaʊnt] descuento *m*
2 *vt* [dɪs'kaʊnt] (**a**) *(price)* rebajar (**b**) *(view, suggestion)* descartar

discourage [dɪs'kʌrɪdʒ] *vt (dishearten)* desanimar; *(advances)* rechazar

discouraging [dɪs'kʌrɪdʒɪŋ] *adj* desalentador(a)

discover [dɪ'skʌvə(r)] *vt* descubrir; *(missing person, object)* encontrar

discovery [dɪ'skʌvərɪ] *n* descubrimiento *m*

discredit [dɪs'kredɪt] 1 *n* descrédito *m*
2 *vt (person, régime)* desacreditar; *(theory)* poner en duda

discreet [dɪ'skriːt] *adj* discreto(a); *(distance, silence)* prudente; *(hat, house)* modesto(a)

discrepancy [dɪ'skrepənsɪ] *n* diferencia *f*

discretion [dɪ'skreʃən] *n* discreción *f*; *(prudence)* prudencia *f*; **at the d. of ...** a juicio de ...

discriminate [dɪ'skrɪmɪneɪt] *vi* discriminar (**between** entre); **to d. against sth/sb** discriminar algo/a algn

discriminating [dɪ'skrɪmɪneɪtɪŋ] *adj (person)* entendido(a); *(taste)* refinado(a)

discrimination [dɪskrɪmɪ'neɪʃən] *n* (**a**) *(bias)* discriminación *f* (**b**) *(distinction)* diferenciación *f*

discuss [dɪ'skʌs] *vt* discutir; *(in writing)* tratar de

discussion [dɪ'skʌʃən] *n* discusión *f*

disdain [dɪs'deɪn] *Fml* 1 *n* desdén *m*
2 *vt* desdeñar

disdainful [dɪs'deɪnfʊl] *adj Fml* desdeñoso(a)

disease [dɪ'ziːz] *n* enfermedad *f*; *Fig* mal *m*

disembark [dɪsɪm'bɑːk] *vt & vi* desembarcar

disenchanted [dɪsɪn'tʃɑːntɪd] *adj* desencantado(a), desilusionado(a)

disengage [dɪsɪn'geɪdʒ] *vt* soltar; *Aut* **to d. the clutch** soltar el embrague, desembragar

disentangle [dɪsɪn'tæŋgəl] *vt* desenredar

disfigure [dɪs'fɪgə(r)] *vt* desfigurar

disgrace [dɪs'greɪs] 1 *n* (**a**) *(disfavour)* desgracia *f*; **to be in d.** estar desacreditado(a); **to fall into d.** caer en desgracia (**b**) *(shame)* vergüenza *f*, escándalo *m*
2 *vt* deshonrar, desacreditar

disgraceful [dɪs'greɪsfʊl] *adj* vergonzoso(a)

disgruntled [dɪs'grʌntəld] *adj* contrariado(a), disgustado(a)

disguise [dɪs'gaɪz] 1 *n* disfraz *m*; **in d.** disfrazado(a)
2 *vt* (**a**) *(person)* disfrazar (**as** de) (**b**) *(feelings)* disimular

disgust [dɪs'gʌst] 1 *n* (**a**) *(loathing)* repugnancia *f*, asco *m* (**b**) *(strong disapproval)* indignación *f*
2 *vt* (**a**) *(revolt)* repugnar, dar asco a (**b**) *(offend)* indignar

---

*Note that the Spanish words **disgusto** and **disgustar** are false friends and are never a translation for the English word **disgust**. In Spanish, **disgusto** means "annoyance, trouble", and **disgustar** means "to upset".*

---

disgusting [dɪs'gʌstɪŋ] *adj* asqueroso(a), repugnante; *(behaviour, state of affairs)* intolerable

dish [dɪʃ] *n (for serving)* fuente *f*; *(course)* plato *m*; **to wash** *or* **do the dishes** fregar los platos
► **dish out** *vt sep Fam (food)* servir; *(books, advice)* repartir; **to d. it out (to sb)** *(criticize)* criticar (a algn)
► **dish up** *vt sep (meal)* servir

dishcloth ['dɪʃklɒθ] *n* trapo *m* de fregar

dishearten [dɪs'hɑːtən] *vt* desanimar

dishevelled, *US* **disheveled** [dɪ'ʃevəld] *adj (hair)* despeinado(a); *(appearance)* desaliñado(a)

dishonest [dɪs'ɒnɪst] *adj (person)* poco honrado(a); *(means)* fraudulento(a)

dishonesty [dɪs'ɒnɪstɪ] *n (of person)* falta *f* de honradez

dishonour, *US* **dishonor** [dɪs'ɒnə(r)] 1 *n Fml* deshonra *f*
2 *vt (name)* deshonrar

dishonourable, *US* **dishonorable** [dɪs'ɒnərəbəl] *adj* deshonroso(a)

dishtowel ['dɪʃtaʊəl] *n US* trapo *m* de cocina

dishwasher ['dɪʃwɒʃə(r)] *n* lavaplatos *m*

inv; *(person)* lavaplatos *mf inv*
disillusion [dɪsɪ'luːʒən] *vt* desilusionar
disincentive [dɪsɪn'sentɪv] *n* freno *m*
disinfect [dɪsɪn'fekt] *vt* desinfectar
disinfectant [dɪsɪn'fektənt] *n* desinfectante *m*
disinherit [dɪsɪn'herɪt] *vt* desheredar
disintegrate [dɪs'ɪntɪgreɪt] *vi* desintegrarse
disintegration [dɪsɪntɪ'greɪʃən] *n* desintegración *f*
disinterested [dɪs'ɪntrɪstɪd] *adj* desinteresado(a)
disjointed [dɪs'dʒɔɪntɪd] *adj* inconexo(a)
disk [dɪsk] *n US* disco *m*; *Comput* disquete *m*; **on d.** en disco; **d. drive** disquetera *f*, disketera *f*
diskette [dɪs'ket] *n Comput* disquete *m*
dislike [dɪs'laɪk] **1** *n* antipatía *f*, aversión *f* (**of** a *or* hacia)
 2 *vt* tener antipatía *or* aversión a *or* hacia
dislocate ['dɪsləkeɪt] *vt (joint)* dislocar
dislodge [dɪs'lɒdʒ] *vt* sacar
disloyal [dɪs'lɔɪəl] *adj* desleal
dismal ['dɪzməl] *adj* (**a**) *(prospect)* sombrío(a); *(place, weather)* deprimente; *(person)* triste (**b**) *(failure)* lamentable
dismantle [dɪs'mæntəl] *vt* desmontar
dismay [dɪs'meɪ] **1** *n* consternación *f*
 2 *vt* consternar
dismiss [dɪs'mɪs] *vt* (**a**) *(idea)* descartar (**b**) *(employee)* despedir; *(official)* destituir (**c**) **to d. sb** *(from room, presence)* dar permiso a algn para retirarse (**d**) *(reject)* rechazar; *Jur* desestimar; *(case)* sobreseer
dismissal [dɪs'mɪsəl] *n* (**a**) *(of employee)* despido *m*; *(of official)* destitución *f* (**b**) *(of claim)* rechazo *m*; *Jur* desestimación *f*
dismount [dɪs'maʊnt] *vi Fml* apearse (**from** de)
disobedience [dɪsə'biːdɪəns] *n* desobediencia *f*
disobedient [dɪsə'biːdɪənt] *adj* desobediente
disobey [dɪsə'beɪ] *vt & vi* desobedecer; *(law)* violar
disorder [dɪs'ɔːdə(r)] *n* (**a**) *(untidiness)* desorden *m* (**b**) *(riot)* disturbio *m* (**c**) *(of organ, mind)* trastorno *m*; *(of speech)* defecto *m*
disorderly [dɪs'ɔːdəlɪ] *adj* (**a**) *(untidy)* desordenado(a) (**b**) *(meeting)* alborotado(a); *(conduct)* escandaloso(a)
disorganized [dɪs'ɔːgənaɪzd] *adj* desorganizado(a)

disorient [dɪs'ɔːrɪənt], **disorientate** [dɪs'ɔːrɪenteɪt] *vt* desorientar
disown [dɪs'əʊn] *vt* desconocer
disparaging [dɪ'spærɪdʒɪŋ] *adj* despectivo(a)
disparity [dɪ'spærɪtɪ] *n Fml* disparidad *f*
dispassionate [dɪs'pæʃənɪt] *adj* desapasionado(a)
dispatch [dɪ'spætʃ] **1** *n* (**a**) *(official message)* despacho *m*; *(journalist's report)* reportaje *m*; *(military message)* parte *m* (**b**) *(of mail)* envío *m*; *(of goods)* consignación *f*
 2 *vt* (**a**) *(mail)* enviar; *(goods)* expedir (**b**) *Fam (food)* zamparse; *(job)* despachar
dispel [dɪ'spel] *vt* disipar
dispensary [dɪ'spensərɪ] *n* dispensario *m*
dispense [dɪ'spens] *vt (supplies)* repartir; *(justice)* administrar
 ▸ **dispense with** *vt insep (do without)* prescindir de
dispenser [dɪ'spensə(r)] *n* máquina expendedora; **cash d.** cajero automático; **soap d.** dosificador *m* de jabón
dispensing chemist [dɪspensɪŋ'kemɪst] *n Br* farmacéutico(a) *m,f*
dispersal [dɪ'spɜːsəl] *n* dispersión *f*
disperse [dɪ'spɜːs] **1** *vt* dispersar
 2 *vi* dispersarse; *(fog)* disiparse
dispirited [dɪ'spɪrɪtɪd] *adj* abatido(a)
displace [dɪs'pleɪs] *vt* (**a**) desplazar; **displaced person** desterrado(a) *m,f* (**b**) *(supplant)* sustituir
display [dɪ'spleɪ] **1** *n* *(exhibition)* exposición *f*; *Comput* visualización *f*; *(of feelings, skills)* demostración *f*; *(of force)* despliegue *m*; **d. window** escaparate *m*; **military d.** desfile *m* militar
 2 *vt* (**a**) mostrar; *(goods)* exponer; *Comput* visualizar (**b**) *(feelings)* manifestar
displease [dɪs'pliːz] *vt* disgustar; *(offend)* ofender
displeasure [dɪs'pleʒə(r)] *n* disgusto *m*
disposable [dɪ'spəʊzəbəl] *adj* (**a**) *(throwaway)* desechable (**b**) *(available)* disponible
disposal [dɪ'spəʊzəl] *n* (**a**) *(removal)* eliminación *f* (**b**) *(availability)* disponibilidad *f*; **at my d.** a mi disposición (**c**) *Fml (arrangement)* disposición *f* (**d**) *(sale)* venta *f*; *(of property)* traspaso *m*
dispose [dɪ'spəʊz] **1** *vi* **to d. of** *(remove)* eliminar; *(rubbish)* tirar; *(unwanted object)* deshacerse de; *(matter)* resolver; *(sell)* vender; *(property)* traspasar
 2 *vt Fml (arrange)* disponer

disposed [dɪˈspəʊzd] *adj (inclined)* dispuesto(a)

disposition [dɪspəˈzɪʃən] *n* (**a**) *(temperament)* genio *m* (**b**) *Fml (arrangement)* disposición *f*

disproportionate [dɪsprəˈpɔːʃənɪt] *adj* desproporcionado(a) (**to** a)

disprove [dɪsˈpruːv] *vt* refutar

dispute 1 *n* [ˈdɪspjuːt] *(disagreement)* discusión *f*; *(quarrel)* disputa *f*; **industrial d.** conflicto *m* laboral
2 *vt* [dɪˈspjuːt] *(claim)* refutar; *(territory)* disputar; *(matter)* discutir
3 *vi* discutir (**about** *or* **over** de *or* sobre)

disqualify [dɪsˈkwɒlɪfaɪ] *vt* (**a**) *Sport* descalificar (**b**) *(make ineligible)* incapacitar

disquiet [dɪsˈkwaɪət] *n* preocupación *f*, inquietud *f*

disregard [dɪsrɪˈgɑːd] **1** *n* indiferencia *f*; *(for safety)* despreocupación *f*
2 *vt* descuidar; *(ignore)* ignorar

disrepair [dɪsrɪˈpeə(r)] *n* mal estado *m*; **in (a state of) d.** en mal estado; **to fall into d.** deteriorarse

disreputable [dɪsˈrepjʊtəbəl] *adj (person, area)* de mala fama; *(behaviour)* vergonzoso(a)

disrepute [dɪsrɪˈpjuːt] *n* mala fama, oprobio *m*

disrespectful [dɪsrɪˈspektfʊl] *adj* irrespetuoso(a)

disrupt [dɪsˈrʌpt] *vt (meeting, traffic)* interrumpir; *(schedule etc)* desbaratar

disruption [dɪsˈrʌpʃən] *n (of meeting, traffic)* interrupción *f*; *(of schedule etc)* desbaratamiento *m*

dissatisfaction [dɪssætɪsˈfækʃən] *n* descontento *m*, insatisfacción *f*

dissatisfied [dɪsˈsætɪsfaɪd] *adj* descontento(a)

dissect [dɪˈsekt, daɪˈsekt] *vt* disecar

disseminate [dɪˈsemɪneɪt] *vt Fml* diseminar, difundir

dissent [dɪˈsent] **1** *n* disentimiento *m*
2 *vi* disentir

dissertation [dɪsəˈteɪʃən] *n* disertación *f*; *Univ* tesina *f* (**on** sobre)

disservice [dɪsˈsɜːvɪs] *n* perjuicio *m*; **to do sth/sb a d.** perjudicar algo/a algn

dissident [ˈdɪsɪdənt] *adj & n* disidente *(mf)*

dissimilar [dɪˈsɪmɪlə(r)] *adj* distinto(a)

dissipate [ˈdɪsɪpeɪt] **1** *vt* (**a**) disipar (**b**) *(waste)* derrochar
2 *vi* disiparse

dissociate [dɪˈsəʊʃɪeɪt] *vt* **to d. oneself** distanciarse

dissolute [ˈdɪsəluːt] *adj* disoluto(a)

dissolution [dɪsəˈluːʃən] *n* disolución *f*; *(of agreement)* rescisión *f*

dissolve [dɪˈzɒlv] **1** *vt* disolver
2 *vi* disolverse

dissuade [dɪˈsweɪd] *vt* disuadir (**from** de)

distance [ˈdɪstəns] **1** *n* distancia *f*; **in the d.** a lo lejos; *Fam* **to stay the d.** completar la prueba
2 *vt* **to d. oneself (from)** distanciarse (de)

distant [ˈdɪstənt] *adj* (**a**) *(place, time)* lejano(a); *(look)* distraído(a) (**b**) *(aloof)* distante, frío(a)

distaste [dɪsˈteɪst] *n* aversión *f*

distasteful [dɪsˈteɪstfʊl] *adj* desagradable

distend [dɪˈstend] *Fml* **1** *vt* dilatar
2 *vi* dilatarse

distil, *US* **distill** [dɪˈstɪl] *vt* destilar

distillery [dɪˈstɪlərɪ] *n* destilería *f*

distinct [dɪˈstɪŋkt] *adj* (**a**) *(different)* diferente; **as d. from** a diferencia de (**b**) *(smell, change)* marcado(a); *(idea, intention)* claro(a)

distinction [dɪˈstɪŋkʃən] *n* (**a**) *(difference)* diferencia *f* (**b**) *(excellence)* distinción *f* (**c**) *Educ* sobresaliente *m*

distinctive [dɪˈstɪŋktɪv] *adj* distintivo(a)

distinguish [dɪˈstɪŋgwɪʃ] *vt* distinguir

distinguished [dɪˈstɪŋgwɪʃt] *adj* distinguido(a)

distinguishing [dɪˈstɪŋgwɪʃɪŋ] *adj* distintivo(a), característico(a)

distort [dɪˈstɔːt] *vt (misrepresent)* deformar; *(words)* tergiversar

distortion [dɪˈstɔːʃən] *n* deformación *f*; *(of sound, image)* distorsión *f*

distract [dɪˈstrækt] *vt* distraer

distracted [dɪˈstræktɪd] *adj* distraído(a)

distraction [dɪˈstrækʃən] *n (interruption)* distracción *f*; *(confusion)* confusión *f*; **to drive sb to d.** sacar a algn de quicio

distraught [dɪˈstrɔːt] *adj (anguished)* afligido(a)

distress [dɪˈstres] **1** *n (mental)* angustia *f*; *(physical)* dolor *m*; **d. signal** señal *f* de socorro
2 *vt (upset)* apenar

distressing [dɪˈstresɪŋ] *adj* penoso(a)

distribute [dɪˈstrɪbjuːt] *vt* distribuir, repartir

distribution [dɪstrɪˈbjuːʃən] *n* distribución *f*

distributor [dɪˈstrɪbjʊtə(r)] *n* (**a**) *Com* distribuidor(a) *m,f* (**b**) *Aut* delco *m*

district [ˈdɪstrɪkt] *n (of country)* región *f*;

(of town) barrio *m; US* **d. attorney** fiscal *m;* **d. council** corporación *f* local; **d. nurse** practicante *mf*

distrust [dɪsˈtrʌst] **1** *n* recelo *m*
2 *vt* desconfiar de

disturb [dɪˈstɜːb] *vt* (**a**) *(inconvenience)* molestar (**b**) *(silence)* romper; *(sleep)* interrumpir (**c**) *(worry)* perturbar (**d**) *(papers)* desordenar

disturbance [dɪˈstɜːbəns] *n* (**a**) *(of routine)* alteración *f* (**b**) *(commotion)* disturbio *m*, alboroto *m*

disturbed [dɪˈstɜːbd] *adj (mentally)* inestable

disturbing [dɪˈstɜːbɪŋ] *adj* inquietante
disuse [dɪsˈjuːs] *n* desuso *m*
disused [dɪsˈjuːzd] *adj* abandonado(a)
ditch [dɪtʃ] **1** *n* zanja *f; (at roadside)* cuneta *f; (for irrigation)* acequia *f*
2 *vt Fam (plan, friend)* abandonar
dither [ˈdɪðə(r)] *vi Br Fam* vacilar, titubear
ditto [ˈdɪtəʊ] *adv* ídem, lo mismo
dive [daɪv] **1** *n* (**a**) *(into water)* salto *m* de cabeza; *(of submarine)* inmersión *f; (of plane)* picado *m; Sport* salto (**b**) *Fam (bar)* antro *m*
2 *vi* (**a**) *(from poolside, diving board)* tirarse de cabeza; *(submarine)* sumergirse; *(plane)* bajar en picado; *Sport* saltar (**b**) *(move quickly)* **he dived for the phone** se precipitó hacia el teléfono
diver [ˈdaɪvə(r)] *n (person)* buceador(a) *m,f; (professional)* buzo *m; Sport* saltador(a) *m,f*
diverge [daɪˈvɜːdʒ] *vi* divergir
diverse [daɪˈvɜːs] *adj (varied)* diverso(a), variado(a); *(different)* distinto(a), diferente
diversion [daɪˈvɜːʃən] *n* (**a**) *(distraction)* distracción *f* (**b**) *Br (detour)* desvío *m*
divert [daɪˈvɜːt] *vt* desviar
divide [dɪˈvaɪd] **1** *vt* dividir
2 *vi (road, stream)* bifurcarse
3 *n* división *f*, diferencia *f*
dividend [ˈdɪvɪdend] *n Com* dividendo *m; Fig* beneficio *m*
divine [dɪˈvaɪn] *adj* divino(a)
diving board [ˈdaɪvɪŋbɔːd] *n* trampolín *m*
divinity [dɪˈvɪnɪtɪ] *n* (**a**) divinidad *f* (**b**) *(subject)* teología *f*
division [dɪˈvɪʒən] *n* (**a**) división *f* (**b**) *(sharing)* reparto *m* (**c**) *(of organization)* sección *f*
divorce [dɪˈvɔːs] **1** *n* divorcio *m*
2 *vt* **she divorced him** se divorció de él
3 *vi* divorciarse

divorcé [dɪˈvɔːseɪ], **divorcée** [dɪvɔːˈsiː] *n* divorciado(a) *m,f*
divulge [daɪˈvʌldʒ] *vt Fml* divulgar, revelar
DIY [diːaɪˈwaɪ] *n Br (abbr* **do-it-yourself***)* bricolaje *m*
dizziness [ˈdɪzɪnɪs] *n* vértigo *m*
dizzy [ˈdɪzɪ] *adj* (**dizzier, dizziest**) (**a**) *(person) (unwell)* mareado(a) (**b**) *(height, pace)* vertiginoso(a)
DJ [ˈdiːdʒeɪ] *n Fam (abbr* **disc jockey***)* pinchadiscos *mf inv*, disc-jockey *mf*
DNA [diːenˈeɪ] *n (abbr* **deoxyribonucleic acid***)* ADN *m*
do [duː, *unstressed* dʊ, də] **1** *v aux*

> En el inglés hablado, y en el escrito en estilo coloquial, las formas negativas **do not**, **does not** y **did not** se transforman en **don't**, **doesn't** y **didn't**.

(3rd person sing pres **does***; pt* **did***; pp* **done***)* (**a**) *(in negatives and questions) (not translated in Spanish)* **do you want some coffee?** ¿quieres café?; **do you drive?** ¿tienes carnet de conducir?; **don't you want to come?** ¿no quieres venir?; **he doesn't smoke** no fuma
(**b**) *(emphatic) (not translated in Spanish)* **do come with us!** ¡ánimo, vente con nosotros!; **I do like your bag** me encanta tu bolso
(**c**) *(substituting main verb in sentence) (not translated in Spanish)* **I don't believe him – neither do I** no le creo – yo tampoco; **I'll go if you do** si vas tú, voy yo; **I think it's dear, but he doesn't** a mí me parece caro pero a él no; **who went? – I did** ¿quién asistió? – yo
(**d**) *(in question tags)* **he refused, didn't he?** dijo que no, ¿verdad?; **I don't like it, do you?** a mí no me gusta, ¿y a ti?
2 *vt* (**a**) hacer; *(task)* realizar; *(duty)* cumplir con; **to do one's best** hacer todo lo posible; **to do sth again** volver a hacer algo; **to do sth for sb** hacer algo por algn; **to do the cooking/cleaning** cocinar/limpiar; **to do the dishes** lavar los platos; **what can I do for you?** ¿en qué puedo servirle?; **what do you do (for a living)?** ¿a qué te dedicas?; **what's to be done?** ¿qué se puede hacer?; *Fam* **he's done it!** ¡lo ha conseguido!
(**b**) **do you do sportswear?** *(make, offer)* ¿(aquí) tienen ropa de deporte?
(**c**) *(distance)* recorrer; *(speed)* **we were doing 80** íbamos a 80; **this car can do 120** este coche puede alcanzar los 120

Do, unido a muchos nombres, expresa actividades, como **to do the gardening**, **to do the ironing**, etc. En este diccionario, estas estructuras se encuentran bajo los nombres respectivos.

3 *vi* (**a**) *(act)* hacer; **do as I tell you** haz lo que te digo; **you did right** hiciste bien

(**b**) **he did badly in the exams** los exámenes le salieron mal; **how are you doing?** ¿qué tal?; **how do you do?** *(greeting)* ¿cómo está usted?; *(answer)* mucho gusto; **to do well** *(person)* tener éxito; *(business)* ir bien

(**c**) **£5 will do** *(suffice)* con 5 libras será suficiente; *Fam* **that will do!** ¡basta ya!

(**d**) **this cushion will do as a pillow** *(be suitable)* este cojín servirá de almohada; **this won't do** esto no puede ser

4 *n Fam* (**a**) *Br (party)* fiesta *f*; *(event)* ceremonia *f*

(**b**) **do's and don'ts** reglas *fpl* de conducta

► **do away with** *vt insep* (**a**) *(abolish)* abolir; *(discard)* deshacerse de (**b**) *(kill)* asesinar

► **do down** *vt sep Fam (humiliate)* hacer quedar mal

► **do for** *vt insep Fam (destroy, ruin)* arruinar; *Fig* **I'm done for if I don't finish this** estoy perdido(a) si no acabo esto

► **do in** *vt sep Fam* (**a**) *(kill)* cargarse (**b**) **I'm done in** *(exhausted)* estoy hecho(a) polvo

► **do over** *vt sep Fam* (**a**) *US (repeat)* repetir (**b**) *Br (thrash)* dar una paliza a

► **do up** *vt sep* (**a**) *(wrap)* envolver (**b**) *(belt etc)* abrochar; *(laces)* atar (**c**) *(dress up)* arreglar (**d**) *Fam (redecorate)* renovar

► **do with** *vt insep* (**a**) **I could do with a rest** *(need)* un descanso no me vendría nada mal (**b**) **to have** *or* **be to do with** *(concern)* tener que ver con

► **do without** *vt insep* pasar sin, prescindir de

docile ['dəʊsaɪl] *adj* dócil; *(animal)* manso(a)

dock¹ [dɒk] **1** *n Naut* **the docks** el muelle

2 *vi* (**a**) *(ship)* atracar (**b**) *(spacecraft)* acoplarse

dock² [dɒk] *vt (reduce)* descontar

dock³ [dɒk] *n Jur* banquillo *m* (de los acusados)

docker ['dɒkə(r)] *n* estibador *m*

dockland ['dɒklænd] *n* zona *f* del puerto

dockyard ['dɒkjɑːd] *n* astillero *m*

doctor ['dɒktə(r)] **1** *n* (**a**) *Med* médico(a) *m,f* (**b**) *Univ* doctor(a) *m,f*; **D. of Law** doctor en derecho

2 *vt Pej (figures)* falsificar; *(text)* arreglar; *(drink etc)* adulterar

doctorate ['dɒktərɪt] *n* doctorado *m*

doctrine ['dɒktrɪn] *n* doctrina *f*

document ['dɒkjʊmənt] **1** *n* documento *m*; **documents** documentación *f*

2 *vt* documentar

documentary [dɒkjʊ'mentərɪ] *adj & n* documental *(m)*

dodge [dɒdʒ] **1** *vt* (**a**) *(blow)* esquivar; *(pursuer)* despistar; *Fig* eludir (**b**) *Fam* **to d. one's taxes** engañar a Hacienda

2 *vi (move aside)* echarse a un lado

3 *n* (**a**) *(movement)* regate *m* (**b**) *Fam (trick)* truco *m*

Dodgem® ['dɒdʒəm] *n Br* **D. (car)** coche *m* de choque

dodgy ['dɒdʒɪ] *adj* (**dodgier, dodgiest**) *Br Fam (risky)* arriesgado(a); *(tricky)* difícil; *(dishonest, not working properly)* chungo(a)

doe [dəʊ] *n (of deer)* gama *f*; *(of rabbit)* coneja *f*

does [dʌz] *3rd person sing pres of* **do**

doesn't ['dʌzənt] = **does not**

dog [dɒg] **1** *n* (**a**) *(animal)* perro(a) *m,f*; *Fam Fig* **a d.'s life** una vida de perros; **d. collar** *(of dog)* collar *m* de perro; *Fam Rel* alzacuello *m* (**b**) *(male canine)* macho *m*; *(fox)* zorro *m*; *(wolf)* lobo *m* (**c**) *Fam* **dirty d.** canalla *m* (**d**) *US Fam (disappointment)* desastre *m*

2 *vt* acosar; **to d. sb's footsteps** seguir los pasos de algn; *Fig* **dogged by bad luck** perseguido(a) por la mala suerte

dog-eared ['dɒgɪəd] *adj (book)* con los bordes de las páginas doblados; *(shabby)* sobado(a)

dogged ['dɒgɪd] *adj* obstinado(a), tenaz

doghouse ['dɒghaʊs] *n US Fam* perrera *f*; *Fig* **to be in the d.** estar castigado(a)

dogma ['dɒgmə] *n* dogma *m*

dogmatic [dɒg'mætɪk] *adj* dogmático(a)

dogsbody ['dɒgzbɒdɪ] *n Br Fam (drudge)* burro *m* de carga

doh [dəʊ] *n Mus* do *m*

doing ['duːɪŋ] *n* (**a**) *(action)* obra *f*; **it was none of my d.** yo no tuve nada que ver; *Fig* **it took some d.** costó trabajo hacerlo (**b**) **doings** *(activities)* actividades *fpl*

do-it-yourself [duːɪtjə'self] *n* bricolaje *m*

doldrums ['dɒldrəmz] *npl Fam Fig* **to be in the d.** *(person)* estar abatido(a); *(trade)* estar estancado(a)

dole [dəʊl] *Fam* **1** *n Br* **the d.** el paro; **to be on the d.** cobrar el paro; **to go on the d.**

apuntarse al paro; *Fig* **d. queue** los parados

  2 *vt* **to d. (out)** repartir

doleful ['dəʊlfʊl] *adj* triste, afligido(a)

doll [dɒl] **1** *n* (**a**) *(toy)* muñeca *f* (**b**) *US Fam (girl)* muñeca *f*

  2 *vt Fam* **to d. oneself up** ponerse guapa

dollar ['dɒlə(r)] *n* dólar *m*

dolphin ['dɒlfɪn] *n* delfín *m*

domain [də'meɪn] *n* (**a**) *(sphere)* campo *m*, esfera *f*; **that's not my d.** no es de mi competencia (**b**) *(territory)* dominio *m* (**c**) *Comput* dominio *m*; **d. name** nombre *m* de dominio

dome [dəʊm] *n (roof)* cúpula *f*; *(ceiling)* bóveda *f*

domestic [də'mestɪk] *adj* (**a**) *(appliance, pet)* doméstico(a); **d. science** economía doméstica (**b**) *(home-loving)* casero(a) (**c**) *(flight, news)* nacional; *(trade, policy)* interior

domesticate [də'mestɪkeɪt] *vt (make home-loving)* volver hogareño(a) *or* casero(a)

domicile ['dɒmɪsaɪl] *n* domicilio *m*

dominant ['dɒmɪnənt] *adj* dominante

dominate ['dɒmɪneɪt] *vt & vi* dominar

domineering [dɒmɪ'nɪərɪŋ] *adj* dominante

Dominican [də'mɪnɪkən] *adj & n (of Dominica)* dominicano(a) *(m,f)*; **D. Republic** República Dominicana

dominion [də'mɪnjən] *n* dominio *m*

domino ['dɒmɪnəʊ] *n (pl dominoes) (piece)* ficha *f* de dominó; **dominoes** *(game)* dominó *m*

don [dɒn] *n Br Univ* catedrático(a) *m,f*

donate [dəʊ'neɪt] *vt* donar

donation [dəʊ'neɪʃən] *n* donativo *m*

done [dʌn] **1** *adj* (**a**) *(finished)* terminado(a); **it's over and d. with** se acabó (**b**) *Fam (tired)* rendido(a) (**c**) *(meat)* hecho(a); *(vegetables)* cocido(a)

  2 *pp of* **do**

donkey ['dɒŋkɪ] *n* burro(a) *m,f*

donor ['dəʊnə(r)] *n* donante *m*

don't [dəʊnt] = **do not**

donut ['dəʊnʌt] *n US* dónut® *m*

doodle ['duːdəl] *vi Fam (write)* garabatear; *(draw)* hacer dibujos

doom [duːm] **1** *n (fate)* destino *m* (funesto); *(ruin)* perdición *f*; *(death)* muerte *f*

  2 *vt usu pass (destine)* destinar; **doomed to failure** condenado(a) al fracaso

doomsday ['duːmzdeɪ] *n* día *m* del juicio final

door [dɔː(r)] *n* puerta *f*; **front/back d.** puerta principal/trasera; *Fig* **behind**

closed doors a puerta cerrada; **d. handle** manilla *f* (de la puerta); **d. knocker** picaporte *m*; **next d. (to)** (en) la casa de al lado (de)

doorbell ['dɔːbel] *n* timbre *m* (de la puerta)

doorknob ['dɔːnɒb] *n* pomo *m*

doorman ['dɔːmən] *n* portero *m*

doormat ['dɔːmæt] *n* felpudo *m*, esterilla *f*; *Fam Fig (person)* trapo *m*

doorstep ['dɔːstep] *n* peldaño *m*; *Fig* **on one's d.** a la vuelta de la esquina

door-to-door ['dɔːtə'dɔː(r)] *adj* a domicilio

doorway ['dɔːweɪ] *n* portal *m*, entrada *f*

dope [dəʊp] **1** *n* (**a**) *Fam (drug)* chocolate *m* (**b**) *Fam (person)* imbécil *mf*

  2 *vt (food, drink)* adulterar con drogas; *Sport* dopar

dop(e)y ['dəʊpɪ] *adj* (**dopier, dopiest**) *Fam* (**a**) *(sleepy)* medio dormido(a); *(fuddled)* atontado(a) (**b**) *Fam (silly)* torpe

dork [dɔːk] *n US Fam* petardo(a) *m,f*

dormant ['dɔːmənt] *adj* inactivo(a); *Fig (rivalry)* latente

dormitory ['dɔːmɪtərɪ] *n* (**a**) *(in school)* dormitorio *m* (**b**) *US (in university)* colegio *m* mayor

dosage ['dəʊsɪdʒ] *n Fml (amount)* dosis *f inv*

dose [dəʊs] **1** *n* dosis *f inv*

  2 *vt (patient)* medicar

doss [dɒs] *vi Br Fam* sobar

dosshouse ['dɒshaʊs] *n Br Fam* pensión *f* de mala muerte

dossier ['dɒsɪeɪ] *n* expediente *m*

dot [dɒt] **1** *n* punto *m*; **on the d.** en punto; *Comput* **d. matrix printer** impresora *f* matricial *or* de agujas

  2 *vt* (**a**) *Fam* **to d. one's i's and cross one's t's** poner los puntos sobre las íes (**b**) *(scatter)* esparcir, salpicar

dote [dəʊt] *vi* **to d. on sb** chochear con algn

double ['dʌbəl] **1** *adj* doble; **it's d. the price** cuesta dos veces más; **d. bass** contrabajo *m*; **d. bed** cama *f* de matrimonio; **d. bill** programa *m* doble; *Br* **d. cream** nata *f* para montar; **d. glazing** ventana *f* doble

  2 *adv* doble; **folded d.** doblado(a) por la mitad

  3 *n* (**a**) vivo retrato *m*; *Cin & Th* doble *m* (**b**) **to earn d.** ganar el doble; *Fam* **at** *or* **on the d.** corriendo (**c**) **doubles** *(in chess)* *(partido m de)* dobles *mpl*

  4 *vt* doblar; *Fig (efforts)* redoblar

5 *vi* (**a**) *(increase)* doblarse (**b**) **to d. as** *(serve)* hacer las veces de

▸ **double back** *vi* **to d. back on one's tracks** volver sobre sus pasos

▸ **double up 1** *vt sep (bend)* doblar

2 *vi* (**a**) *(bend)* doblarse (**b**) *(share room)* compartir la habitación (**with** con)

double-barrelled ['dʌbəlbærəld] *adj* (**a**) *(gun)* de dos cañones (**b**) *Br (surname)* compuesto(a)

double-breasted ['dʌbəlbrestɪd] *adj* cruzado(a)

double-check [dʌbəl'tʃek] *vt & vi* repasar dos veces

double-cross [dʌbəl'krɒs] *Fam* **1** *vt* engañar, traicionar

2 *n* engaño *m*, traición *f*

double-decker [dʌbəl'dekə(r)] *n Br* **d. (bus)** autobús *m* de dos pisos

double-edged ['dʌbəledʒd] *adj* de doble filo

doubt [daʊt] **1** *n* duda *f*; **beyond (all) d.** sin duda alguna; **no d.** sin duda; **there's no d. about it** no cabe la menor duda; **to be in d. about sth** dudar algo; **to be open to d.** *(fact)* ser dudoso(a); *(outcome)* ser incierto(a)

2 *vt* (**a**) *(distrust)* desconfiar de (**b**) *(not be sure of)* dudar; **I d. if** *or* **whether he'll come** dudo que venga

doubtful ['daʊtfʊl] *adj* (**a**) *(future)* dudoso(a), *(look)* dubitativo(a); **I'm a bit d. about it** no me convence del todo; **it's d. whether ...** no se sabe seguro si ... (**b**) *(questionable)* sospechoso(a)

doubtless ['daʊtlɪs] *adv* sin duda, seguramente

dough [dəʊ] *n* (**a**) *(for bread)* masa *f*; *(for pastries)* pasta *f* (**b**) *Fam (money)* pasta *f*

doughnut ['dəʊnʌt] *n* rosquilla *f*, dónut® *m*

douse [daʊs] *vt* (**a**) *(soak)* mojar (**b**) *(extinguish)* apagar

dove [dʌv] *n* paloma *f*

dovetail ['dʌvteɪl] *vt Fig (plans)* sincronizar

dowdy ['daʊdɪ] *adj* (**dowdier, dowdiest**) poco elegante

down¹ [daʊn] **1** *prep* (**a**) *(to or at a lower level)* **d. the river** río abajo; **to go d. the road** bajar la calle

(**b**) *(along)* por

2 *adv* (**a**) *(to lower level)* (hacia) abajo; *(to floor)* al suelo; *(to ground)* a tierra; **to fall d.** caerse; **to go d.** *(price, person)* bajar; *(sun)* ponerse

(**b**) *(at lower level)* abajo; **d. there** allí abajo; **face d.** boca abajo; *Fig* **to be d.**

with a cold estar resfriado(a); *Fam Fig* **to feel d.** estar deprimido(a); *Fam Fig* **d. under** en/a Australia y Nueva Zelanda

(**c**) **I'm d. to my last stamp** no me queda más que un solo sello; **sales are d. by 5 percent** las ventas han bajado un 5 por ciento

(**d**) **to take sth d.** *(in writing)* apuntar algo

(**e**) **d. through the ages** a través de los siglos

3 *adj (payment)* al contado; *(on property)* de entrada

4 *vt Fam (drink)* tomarse de un trago; *(food)* zamparse

5 *n* **ups and downs** altibajos *mpl*

6 *interj* **d. with taxes!** ¡abajo los impuestos!

down² [daʊn] *n* (**a**) *(on bird)* plumón *m* (**b**) *(on cheek, peach)* pelusa *f*; *(on body)* vello *m*

down-and-out ['daʊnən'aʊt] **1** *adj* en las últimas

2 *n* vagabundo(a) *m,f*

downbeat ['daʊnbiːt] *adj Fam (gloomy)* deprimido(a)

downcast ['daʊnkɑːst] *adj* abatido(a)

downfall ['daʊnfɔːl] *n (of regime)* caída *f*; *(of person)* perdición *f*

downgrade ['daʊngreɪd] *vt* degradar

downhearted [daʊn'hɑːtɪd] *adj* desalentado(a)

downhill [daʊn'hɪl] **1** *adj (skiing)* de descenso; *Fam* **after his first exam, the rest were all d.** después del primer examen, los demás le fueron sobre ruedas

2 *adv* **to go d.** ir cuesta abajo; *Fig (standards)* deteriorarse

download ['daʊn'ləʊd] *vt Comput* bajar, descargar

down-market [daʊn'mɑːkɪt] **1** *adj* barato(a)

2 *adv* **to move d.** *(of company)* producir artículos más asequibles

downpour ['daʊnpɔː(r)] *n* chaparrón *m*

downright ['daʊnraɪt] *Fam* **1** *adj (blunt)* tajante; *(categorical)* categórico(a); **it's a d. lie** es una mentira y gorda

2 *adv (totally)* completamente

downsizing ['daʊnsaɪzɪŋ] *n Com* reajuste *m* de plantillas

downstairs 1 *adv* [daʊn'steəz] abajo; *(to ground floor)* a la planta baja; **to go d.** bajar la escalera

2 *adj* ['daʊnsteəz] *(on ground floor)* de la planta baja

downstream [daʊn'striːm] *adv* río abajo

down-to-earth [daʊntʊ'ɜːθ] *adj* realista
downtown [daʊn'taʊn] *adv US* en el centro (de la ciudad)
downturn ['daʊntɜːn] *n* baja *f*
downward ['daʊnwəd] **1** *adj (slope)* descendente; *(look)* hacia abajo; *Fin (tendency)* a la baja
   2 *adv* = **downwards**
downwards ['daʊnwədz] *adv* hacia abajo
dowry ['daʊrɪ] *n* dote *f*
doz (*abbr* **dozen**) docena *f*
doze [dəʊz] **1** *vi* dormitar
   2 *n* cabezada *f*; **to have a d.** echar una cabezada
   ▸ **doze off** *vi* quedarse dormido(a)
dozen ['dʌzən] *n* docena *f*; **half a d./a d. eggs** media docena/una docena de huevos; *Fam* **dozens of** un montón de
Dr (*abbr* **Doctor**) Dr., Dra.
drab [dræb] *adj* (**drabber, drabbest**) (**a**) *(ugly)* feo(a); *(dreary)* monótono(a), gris (**b**) *(colour)* pardo(a)
draft [drɑːft] **1** *n* (**a**) borrador *m* (**b**) *(bill of exchange)* giro *m* (**c**) *US* servicio militar obligatorio (**d**) *US* = **draught**
   2 *vt* (**a**) hacer un borrador de (**b**) *US Mil* reclutar
draftsman ['drɑːftsmən] *n US* = **draughtsman**
drag [dræg] **1** *vt* (**a**) *(pull)* arrastrar; *Fig* **to d. one's heels (over sth)** dar largas (a algo) (**b**) *(lake)* rastrear
   2 *vi* (**a**) *(trail)* arrastrarse (**b**) *(person)* rezagarse
   3 *n* (**a**) *Tech* resistencia *f* (aerodinámica) (**b**) *Fam (nuisance)* lata *f* (**c**) *Fam (on cigarette)* calada *f* (**d**) *Fam* **to be in d.** ir vestido de mujer (**e**) *US Fam* **the main d.** la calle mayor *or* principal
   ▸ **drag off** *vt sep* llevarse arrastrando
   ▸ **drag on** *vi (war, strike)* hacerse interminable
   ▸ **drag out** *vt sep (speech etc)* alargar
dragon ['drægən] *n* dragón *m*
dragonfly ['drægənflaɪ] *n* libélula *f*
drain [dreɪn] **1** *n* (**a**) *(for water)* desagüe *m*; *(for sewage)* alcantarilla *f* (**b**) *(grating)* sumidero *m* (**c**) *Fig* **the boys are a d. on her strength** los niños la dejan agotada
   2 *vt* (**a**) *(marsh etc)* avenar; *(reservoir)* desecar (**b**) *(crockery)* escurrir (**c**) *(empty) (glass)* apurar; *Fig (capital etc)* agotar
   3 *vi* (**a**) *(crockery)* escurrirse (**b**) **to d. (away)** *(liquid)* irse
drainage ['dreɪnɪdʒ] *n (of marsh)* drenaje *m*; *(of reservoir, building)* desagüe *m*; *(of town)* alcantarillado *m*

drainpipe ['dreɪnpaɪp] *n* tubo *m* de desagüe
dram [dræm] *n Fam* trago *m (de whisky)*
drama ['drɑːmə] *n* (**a**) *(play)* obra *f* de teatro; *Fig* drama *m* (**b**) *(subject)* teatro *m*
dramatic [drə'mætɪk] *adj* (**a**) *(change)* impresionante; *(moment)* emocionante (**b**) *Th* dramático(a), teatral
dramatist ['dræmətɪst] *n* dramaturgo(a) *m,f*
dramatization [dræmətaɪ'zeɪʃən] *n* adaptación *f* teatral
dramatize ['dræmətaɪz] *vt* (**a**) *(adapt)* hacer una adaptación teatral de (**b**) *(exaggerate)* dramatizar
drank [dræŋk] *pt of* **drink**
drape [dreɪp] **1** *vt* **to d. sth over sth** colgar algo sobre algo; **draped with** cubierto(a) de
   2 *n* (**a**) *(of fabric)* caída *f* (**b**) *US* cortina *f*
draper ['dreɪpə(r)] *n Br* pañero(a) *m,f*
drastic ['dræstɪk] *adj* (**a**) *(measures)* drástico(a), severo(a) (**b**) *(change)* radical
draught [drɑːft] **1** *n* (**a**) *(of cold air)* corriente *f* (de aire) (**b**) *(of liquid)* trago *m* (**c**) **d. (beer)** cerveza *f* de barril (**d**) *Br* **draughts** *(game)* damas *fpl* (**e**) *Naut* calado *m*
   2 *adj (animal)* de tiro
draughtboard ['drɑːftbɔːd] *n Br* tablero *m* de damas
draughtsman ['drɑːftsmən] *n* delineante *mf*
draw [drɔː] **1** *vt* (*pt* **drew**; *pp* **drawn**) (**a**) *(picture)* dibujar; *(line)* trazar
   (**b**) *(pull)* tirar de; *(train, carriage)* arrastrar; *(curtains) (open)* descorrer; *(close)* correr; *(blinds)* bajar
   (**c**) *(remove)* sacar; *(salary)* cobrar; *(cheque)* librar
   (**d**) *(attract)* atraer; *(attention)* llamar
   (**e**) *Fig (strength)* sacar
   (**f**) **to d. breath** respirar
   (**g**) **to d. lots** echar a suertes
   (**h**) *(comparison)* hacer; *(conclusion)* sacar
   2 *vi* (**a**) *(sketch)* dibujar
   (**b**) *(move)* **the train drew into/out of the station** el tren entró en/salió de la estación; **to d. apart (from)** separarse (de); **to d. to an end** acabarse
   (**c**) *Sport* **they drew two all** empataron a dos
   3 *n* (**a**) *(raffle)* sorteo *m*
   (**b**) *Sport* empate *m*
   (**c**) *Fig (attraction)* atracción *f*
   ▸ **draw in** *vi (days)* acortarse

▸**draw on** *vt insep (savings)* recurrir a; *(experience)* aprovecharse de

▸**draw out** *vt sep* (**a**) *(make long)* alargar (**b**) *(encourage to speak)* desatar la lengua a (**c**) *(from pocket, drawer etc)* sacar

▸**draw up** *vt sep (contract)* preparar; *(plan)* esbozar

drawback ['drɔːbæk] *n* desventaja *f*, inconveniente *m*

drawbridge ['drɔːbrɪdʒ] *n* puente levadizo

drawer ['drɔːə(r)] *n* cajón *m*

drawing ['drɔːɪŋ] *n* dibujo *m*; *Fam Fig* **to go back to the d. board** volver a empezar; *Br* **d. pin** chincheta *f*; *Fml* **d. room** sala *f* de estar

drawl [drɔːl] **1** *vi* hablar arrastrando las palabras

2 *n* voz cansina; *US* **a Southern d.** un acento sureño

drawn [drɔːn] **1** *adj (tired)* ojeroso(a)

2 *pp of* **draw**

dread [dred] **1** *vt* temer a, tener pavor a

2 *n* temor *m*

dreadful ['dredfʊl] *adj* (**a**) *(shocking)* espantoso(a) (**b**) *Fam (awful)* fatal; **how d.!** ¡qué horror!

dreadfully ['dredfʊlɪ] *adv Fam (horribly)* terriblemente; *(very)* muy, sumamente

dream [driːm] **1** *n* (**a**) sueño *m* (**b**) *(daydream)* ensueño *m* (**c**) *Fam (marvel)* maravilla *f*

2 *vt* (*pt & pp* **dreamed** *or* **dreamt**) soñar

3 *vi* soñar (**of** *or* **about** con)

dreamer ['driːmə(r)] *n* soñador(a) *m,f*

dreamt [dremt] *pt & pp of* **dream**

dreamy [driːmɪ] *adj* (**dreamier, dreamiest**) *(absent-minded)* distraído(a); *(wonderful)* de ensueño

dreary ['drɪərɪ] *adj* (**drearier, dreariest**) (**a**) *(gloomy)* triste (**b**) *Fam (boring)* aburrido(a), pesado(a)

dredge [dredʒ] *vt & vi* dragar, rastrear

▸**dredge up** *vt sep* (**a**) *(body)* sacar del agua (**b**) *Fam Fig* sacar a relucir

dregs [dregz] *npl* poso *m*

drench [drentʃ] *vt* empapar

dress [dres] **1** *n* (**a**) *(frock)* vestido *m* (**b**) *(clothing)* ropa *f*; **d. rehearsal** ensayo *m* general; **d. shirt** camisa *f* de etiqueta

2 *vt* (**a**) *(person)* vestir; **he was dressed in a grey suit** llevaba (puesto) un traje gris (**b**) *(salad)* aliñar (**c**) *(wound)* vendar

3 *vi* vestirse

▸**dress up 1** *vi* (**a**) *(in disguise)* disfrazarse (**as** de) (**b**) *(in best clothes)* vestirse elegante

2 *vt sep Fig* disfrazar

dresser ['dresə(r)] *n* (**a**) *Br (in kitchen)* aparador *m* (**b**) *US (in bedroom)* tocador *m* (**c**) *Th* ayudante *mf* de camerino

dressing ['dresɪŋ] *n* (**a**) *(bandage)* vendaje *m* (**b**) *(salad)* **d.** aliño *m* (**c**) **d. gown** bata *f*; **d. room** *Th* camerino *m*; *Sport* vestuario *m*; **d. table** tocador *m*

dressmaker ['dresmeɪkə(r)] *n* modista *mf*

dressy ['dresɪ] *adj* (**dressier, dressiest**) vistoso(a)

drew [druː] *pt of* **draw**

dribble ['drɪbəl] **1** *vi* (**a**) *(baby)* babear (**b**) *(liquid)* gotear

2 *vt Sport (ball)* driblar

3 *n (saliva)* saliva *f*; *(of water, blood)* gotas *fpl*

dried [draɪd] *adj (fruit)* seco(a); *(milk)* en polvo

drier ['draɪə(r)] *n* = **dryer**

drift [drɪft] **1** *vi* (**a**) *(boat)* ir a la deriva; *Fig (person)* ir sin rumbo, vagar; **they drifted away** se marcharon poco a poco (**b**) *(snow)* amontonarse

2 *n* (**a**) *(flow)* flujo *m* (**b**) *(of snow)* ventisquero *m*; *(of sand)* montón *m* (**c**) *Fig (meaning)* idea *f*

driftwood ['drɪftwʊd] *n* madera *f* flotante

drill [drɪl] **1** *n* (**a**) *(hand tool)* taladro *m*; *Min* barrena *f*; **dentist's d.** fresa *f*; **pneumatic d.** martillo neumático (**b**) *esp Mil* instrucción *f*

2 *vt* (**a**) *(wood etc)* taladrar (**b**) *(soldiers, children)* instruir

3 *vi (by hand)* taladrar; *(for oil, coal)* perforar, sondar

drink [drɪŋk] **1** *vt* (*pt* **drank**; *pp* **drunk**) beber

2 *vi* beber; **to have sth to d.** tomarse algo; **to d. to sth/sb** brindar por algo/algn

3 *n* bebida *f*; *(alcoholic)* copa *f*

drinker [drɪŋkə(r)] *n* bebedor(a) *m,f*

drinking ['drɪŋkɪŋ] *n* **d. water** agua *f* potable

drip [drɪp] **1** *n* (**a**) *(drop)* goteo *m* (**b**) *Med* gota a gota *m inv* (**c**) *Fam (person)* necio(a) *m,f*

2 *vi* gotear; **he was dripping with sweat** el sudor le caía a gotas

drip-dry ['drɪp'draɪ] *adj* que no necesita planchado

dripping ['drɪpɪŋ] *n Culin* pringue *f*

drive [draɪv] **1** *vt* (*pt* **drove**; *pp* **driven**) (**a**) *(vehicle)* conducir, *Am* manejar; *(person)* llevar

(**b**) *(power)* impulsar

(**c**) *(enemy)* acosar; *(ball)* mandar
(**d**) *(stake)* hincar; *(nail)* clavar
(**e**) *(compel)* forzar, obligar; **to d. sb mad**
volver loco(a) a algn
(**f**) **to d. (off)** rechazar
2 *vi Aut* conducir, *Am* manejar
3 *n* (**a**) *(trip)* paseo *m* en coche; **to go for
a d.** dar una vuelta en coche
(**b**) *(to house)* camino *m* de entrada
(**c**) *(transmission)* transmisión *f*; *Aut*
tracción *f*; *Aut* **left-hand d.** conducción *f*
por la izquierda
(**d**) *(in golf)* golpe *m* inicial
(**e**) *(campaign)* campaña *f*
(**f**) *(need)* necesidad *f*; *(energy)* energía
f, vigor *m*; **sex d.** instinto *m* sexual
(**g**) *Comput* unidad *f* de disco
drive-in ['draɪvɪn] *n US (cinema)* auto-
cine *m*
driven ['drɪvən] *pp of* **drive**
driver ['draɪvə(r)] *n (of car, bus)* conduc-
tor(a) *m,f*; *(of train)* maquinista *mf*; *(of
lorry)* camionero(a) *m,f*; *(of racing car)*
piloto *mf*; *US* **d.'s license** carnet *m* de
conducir
driveway ['draɪvweɪ] *n (to house)* camino *m* de entrada
driving ['draɪvɪŋ] **1** *n Br* **d. licence** carnet
m de conducir; **d. school** autoescuela *f*; **d.
test** examen *m* de conducir
2 *adj* (**a**) *(rain)* intenso(a) (**b**) **d. force**
fuerza *f* motriz
drizzle ['drɪzəl] **1** *n* llovizna *f*
2 *vi* lloviznar
droll [drəʊl] *adj* gracioso(a)
dromedary ['drɒmədərɪ] *n* dromedario
m
drone [drəʊn] *vi (bee etc)* zumbar
droop [druːp] *vi (flower)* marchitarse;
(eyelids) caerse
drop [drɒp] **1** *n* (**a**) *(of liquid)* gota *f*; **eye
drops** colirio *m*
(**b**) *(sweet)* pastilla *f*
(**c**) *(descent)* desnivel *m*
(**d**) *(in price)* bajada *f*; *(in temperature)*
descenso *m*
2 *vt* (**a**) *(let fall)* dejar caer; *(lower)*
bajar; *(reduce)* disminuir; **to d. a hint**
soltar una indirecta
(**b**) *(abandon) (subject, charge etc)* abandonar, dejar; *Sport* **he was dropped from
the team** le echaron del equipo
(**c**) *(omit) (spoken syllable)* comerse
3 *vi (object)* caerse; *(person)* tirarse;
(voice, price, temperature) bajar; *(wind)*
amainar; *(speed)* disminuir
▸ **drop by, drop in** *vi Fam (visit)* pasarse
(**at** por)

▸ **drop off 1** *vi Fam (fall asleep)* quedarse
dormido(a)
2 *vt sep (deliver)* dejar
▸ **drop out** *vi (from college)* dejar los
estudios; *(from society)* marginarse;
(from competition) retirarse
▸ **drop round** *vi Fam* = **drop by**
dropout ['drɒpaʊt] *n Fam Pej* automargi-
nado(a) *m,f*
dropper ['drɒpə(r)] *n* cuentagotas *m inv*
droppings ['drɒpɪŋz] *npl* excrementos
mpl
drought [draʊt] *n* sequía *f*
drove [drəʊv] **1** *n (of cattle)* manada *f*
2 *pt of* **drive**
drown [draʊn] **1** *vt* (**a**) ahogar (**b**) *(place)*
inundar
2 *vi* ahogarse; **he (was) drowned** murió
ahogado
drowsy ['draʊzɪ] *adj* (**drowsier, drow-
siest**) soñoliento(a); **to feel d.** tener sueño
drudgery ['drʌdʒərɪ] *n* trabajo duro y
pesado
drug [drʌg] **1** *n* (**a**) *(medicine)* medicamento *m* (**b**) *(narcotic)* droga *f*, estupefaciente *m*; **to be on drugs** drogarse; **d.
addict** drogadicto(a) *m,f*; **d. addiction**
drogadicción *f*; **d. squad** brigada *f* antidroga
2 *vt (person)* drogar; *(food, drink)* adulterar con drogas
druggist ['drʌgɪst] *n US* farmacéutico(a)
m,f
drugstore ['drʌgstɔːr] *n US* = establecimiento donde se compran medicamen-
tos, periódicos, etc.
drum [drʌm] **1** *n* (**a**) *(tambor m*; **to play
the drums** tocar la batería (**b**) *(container)*
bidón *m*
2 *vi Fig (with fingers)* tabalear
3 *vt Fig* **to d. sth into sb** enseñar algo a
algn a machamartillo
▸ **drum up** *vt sep Fam* solicitar
drummer ['drʌmə(r)] *n (in band)* tambor
mf; *(in pop group)* batería *mf*
drumstick ['drʌmstɪk] *n* (**a**) *Mus* baque-
ta *f* (**b**) *(chicken leg)* muslo *m*
drunk [drʌŋk] **1** *adj* borracho(a); **to get d.**
emborracharse
2 *n* borracho(a) *m,f*
3 *pp of* **drink**
drunkard ['drʌŋkəd] *n* borracho(a) *m,f*
dry [draɪ] **1** *adj* (**drier, driest** *or* **dryer,
dryest**) (**a**) seco(a); *US* **d. goods store**
mercería *f*, tienda *f* de confección (**b**)
(wry) socarrón(ona)
2 *vt (pt & pp* **dried** *)* secar

3 *vi* **to d. (off)** secarse

dry-clean [draɪˈkliːn] *vt* limpiar *or* lavar en seco

dryer [ˈdraɪə(r)] *n* secadora *f*

dub¹ [dʌb] *vt (subtitle)* doblar (**into** a)

dub² [dʌb] *vt* (**a**) *(give nickname to)* apodar (**b**) *(knight)* armar

dubious [ˈdjuːbɪəs] *adj* (**a**) *(morals etc)* dudoso(a); *(compliment)* equívoco(a) (**b**) *(doubting)* indeciso(a)

Dublin [ˈdʌblɪn] *n* Dublín

duchess [ˈdʌtʃɪs] *n* duquesa *f*

duck¹ [dʌk] *n* pato(a) *m,f*; *Culin* pato *m*

duck² [dʌk] **1** *vt* (**a**) *(submerge)* dar una ahogadilla a (**b**) *(evade)* esquivar

2 *vi* (**a**) *(evade blow)* esquivar (**b**) *Fam* **to d. (out)** rajarse

duckling [ˈdʌklɪŋ] *n* patito *m*

duct [dʌkt] *n (for fuel etc)* conducto *m*; *Anat* canal *m*

dud [dʌd] *Fam* **1** *adj* (**a**) *(useless)* inútil; *(defective)* estropeado(a) (**b**) *(banknote)* falso(a); *(cheque)* sin fondos

2 *n (useless thing)* engañifa *f*; *(person)* desastre *m*

dude [duːd] *n US Fam (man)* tipo *m*, tío *m*

due [djuː] **1** *adj* (**a**) *(expected)* esperado(a); **the train is d. (to arrive) at ten** el tren debe llegar a las diez (**b**) *Fml (proper)* debido(a); **in d. course** a su debido tiempo (**c**) *(owing)* pagadero(a); **how much are you d.?** *(owed)* ¿cuánto te deben? (**d**) **to be d. to** *(caused by)* deberse a; **d. to** *(because of)* debido de

2 *adv (north etc)* derecho hacia

3 *n* (**a**) **to give sb their d.** dar a algn su merecido (**b**) **dues** *(fee)* cuota *f*

duel [ˈdjuːəl] *n* duelo *m*

duet [djuːˈet] *n* dúo *m*

duffel [ˈdʌfəl] *n* **d. bag** petate *m*; **d. coat** trenca *f*

dug [dʌg] *pt & pp of* **dig**

duke [djuːk] *n* duque *m*

dull [dʌl] **1** *adj* (**a**) *(boring)* pesado(a); *(place)* sin interés (**b**) *(light)* apagado(a); *(weather)* gris (**c**) *(sound, ache)* sordo(a) (**d**) *Fig (slow-witted)* torpe

2 *vt* (**a**) *(pain)* aliviar (**b**) *Fig (faculty)* embotar

duly [ˈdjuːlɪ] *adv Fml (properly)* debidamente; *(as expected)* como era de esperar; *(in due course)* a su debido tiempo

dumb [dʌm] **1** *adj* (**a**) *Med* mudo(a) (**b**) *Fam (stupid)* tonto(a)

2 *npl* **the d.** los mudos

dumbbell [ˈdʌmbel] *n Sport* pesa *f*

dumbfounded [dʌmˈfaʊndɪd], **dumbstruck** [ˈdʌmstrʌk] *adj* pasmado(a)

dummy [ˈdʌmɪ] *n* (**a**) *(sham)* imitación *f* (**b**) *(in shop window)* maniquí *m*; *(of ventriloquist)* muñeco *m* (**c**) *Br (for baby)* chupete *m*

dump [dʌmp] **1** *n* (**a**) *(tip)* vertedero *m*; *(for old cars)* cementerio *m* (de coches) (**b**) *Fam Pej (place)* estercolero *m*; *(town)* poblacho *m*; *(dwelling)* tugurio *m* (**c**) *Mil* depósito *m*

2 *vt* (**a**) *(rubbish)* verter; *(truck contents)* descargar (**b**) *(person)* dejar; *Com* inundar el mercado con (**c**) *Comput (transfer)* copiar de memoria interna

dumping [ˈdʌmpɪŋ] *n* vertido *m*

dumpling [ˈdʌmplɪŋ] *n Culin* = bola de masa hervida

dumpy [ˈdʌmpɪ] *adj* (**dumpier, dumpiest**) *Fam* rechoncho(a)

dunce [dʌns] *n Fam* tonto(a) *m,f*

dune [djuːn] *n* **(sand) d.** duna *f*

dung [dʌŋ] *n* estiércol *m*

dungarees [dʌŋgəˈriːz] *npl* mono *m*

dungeon [ˈdʌndʒən] *n* calabozo *m*, mazmorra *f*

duo [ˈdjuːəʊ] *n Mus* dúo *m*; *Fam* pareja *f*

dupe [djuːp] **1** *vt* engañar

2 *n* ingenuo(a) *m,f*

duplex [ˈdjuːpleks] *n US (house)* casa adosada; **d. apartment** dúplex *m inv*

duplicate 1 *vt* [ˈdjuːplɪkeɪt] (**a**) *(copy)* duplicar; *(film, tape)* reproducir (**b**) *(repeat)* repetir

2 *n* [ˈdjuːplɪkɪt] duplicado *m*; **in d.** por duplicado

durable [ˈdjʊərəbəl] *adj* duradero(a)

duration [djʊˈreɪʃən] *n Fml* duración *f*

duress [djʊˈres] *n Fml* coacción *f*

> ✏ Note that the Spanish word **dureza** is a false friend and is never a translation for the English word **duress**. In Spanish, **dureza** means "hardness, harshness".

during [ˈdjʊərɪŋ] *prep* durante

dusk [dʌsk] *n Fml* crepúsculo *m*; **at d.** al anochecer

dust [dʌst] **1** *n* polvo *m*; **d. cloud** polvareda *f*; **d. jacket** sobrecubierta *f*

2 *vt* (**a**) *(furniture)* quitar el polvo a (**b**) *(cake)* espolvorear

dustbin [ˈdʌstbɪn] *n Br* cubo *m* de la basura

dustcart [ˈdʌstkɑːt] *n Br* camión *m* de la basura

duster [ˈdʌstə(r)] *n (for housework)* trapo *m or* paño *m* (del polvo); **feather d.** plumero *m*

dustman [ˈdʌstmən] *n Br* basurero *m*

dustpan [ˈdʌstpæn] *n* recogedor *m*

dusty [ˈdʌstɪ] *adj* (**dustier, dustiest**) polvoriento(a)

Dutch [dʌtʃ] **1** *adj* holandés(esa); *Fig* **D. cap** diafragma *m*

    2 *n* (**a**) *pl* **the D.** los holandeses (**b**) *(language)* holandés *m*; **it's double D. to me** me suena a chino

    3 *adv Fig* **to go D.** pagar cada uno lo suyo

Dutchman [ˈdʌtʃmən] *n* holandés *m*

Dutchwoman [ˈdʌtʃwʊmən] *n* holandesa *f*

duty [ˈdjuːtɪ] *n* (**a**) deber *m*; **to do one's d.** cumplir con su deber (**b**) *(task)* función *f* (**c**) **to be on d.** estar de servicio; *Med & Mil* estar de guardia; **d. chemist** farmacia *f* de guardia (**d**) *(tax)* impuesto *m*; **customs d.** derechos *mpl* de aduana

duty-free [djuːtɪˈfriː] **1** *adj* libre de impuestos

    2 *adv* sin pagar impuestos

    3 *n* duty-free *m*

duvet [ˈduːveɪ] *n* edredón *m*

DVD [diːviːˈdiː] *n Comput* (*abbr* **Digital Versatile Disk, Digital Video Disk**) DVD *m*

dwarf [dwɔːf] **1** *n* (*pl* **dwarves** [dwɔːvz]) *(person)* enano(a) *m,f*

    2 *vt* hacer parecer pequeño(a) a

dwell [dwel] *vi* (*pt & pp* **dwelt**) *Fml* morar
▶ **dwell on** *vt insep* hablar extensamente de; **let's not d. on it** olvidémoslo

dwelling [ˈdwelɪŋ] *n Fml & Hum* morada *f*, vivienda *f*

dwelt [dwelt] *pt & pp of* **dwell**

dwindle [ˈdwɪndəl] *vi* menguar, disminuir

dye [daɪ] **1** *n* tinte *m*

    2 *vt* (*pres p* **dyeing**; *pt & pp* **dyed**) teñir; **to d. one's hair black** teñirse el pelo de negro

dying [ˈdaɪɪŋ] *adj* (*person*) moribundo(a), agonizante; *Fig* (*custom*) en vías de desaparición

dyke [daɪk] *n* (**a**) *(bank)* dique *m*; *(causeway)* terraplén *m* (**b**) *very Fam Pej* tortillera *f*

dynamic [daɪˈnæmɪk] *adj* dinámico(a)

dynamics [daɪˈnæmɪks] *n sing* dinámica *f*

dynamism [ˈdaɪnəmɪzəm] *n* dinamismo *m*

dynamite [ˈdaɪnəmaɪt] *n* dinamita *f*

dynamo [ˈdaɪnəməʊ] *n* dínamo *f*

dynasty [ˈdɪnəstɪ] *n* dinastía *f*

dysentery [ˈdɪsəntrɪ] *n* disentería *f*

dyslexia [dɪsˈleksɪə] *n* dislexia *f*

E, e [i:] *n* (**a**) *(the letter)* E, e *f* (**b**) *Mus* E mi *m*
E [i:] *n* (**a**) *(abbr* **East**) E (**b**) *Fam (abbr*
ecstasy) *(drug)* éxtasis *m inv*
each [i:tʃ] **1** *adj* cada; **e. day/month** todos
los días/meses; **e. person** cada cual; **e.
time I see him** cada vez que lo veo
  2 *pron* (**a**) cada uno(a); **£2 e.** 2 libras
cada uno; **we bought one e.** nos compra-
mos uno cada uno (**b**) **e. other** el uno al
otro; **they hate e. other** se odian
eager ['i:gə(r)] *adj (anxious)* impaciente;
(desirous) deseoso(a); **e. to begin** impaciente por empezar; **to be e. for success**
codiciar el éxito
eagerly ['i:gəlɪ] *adv (anxiously)* con impaciencia; *(keenly)* con ilusión
eagle ['i:gəl] *n* águila *f*
ear [ɪə(r)] *n* (**a**) oreja *f*; *(sense of hearing)*
oído *m* (**b**) *(of corn etc)* espiga *f*
earache ['ɪəreɪk] *n* dolor *m* de oídos
eardrum ['ɪədrʌm] *n* tímpano *m*
earl [ɜ:l] *n* conde *m*
earlobe ['ɪələʊb] *n* lóbulo *m*
early ['ɜ:lɪ] (**earlier, earliest**) **1** *adj* (**a**)
(before the usual time) temprano(a); **to
have an e. night** acostarse pronto; **you're
e.!** ¡qué pronto has venido!
  (**b**) *(at first stage, period)* **at an e. age**
siendo joven; **in e. July** a principios de
julio; **e. work** obra de juventud; **in her e.
forties** a los cuarenta y pocos; **it's still e.
days** aún es pronto
  (**c**) *(in the near future)* **an e. reply** una
respuesta pronta; **at the earliest** cuanto
antes
  2 *adv* (**a**) *(before the expected time)*
temprano, pronto; **earlier on** antes; **five
minutes e.** con cinco minutos de adelanto; **to leave e.** irse pronto
  (**b**) *(near the beginning)* **as e. as 1914** ya
en 1914; **as e. as possible** tan pronto como
sea posible; **to book e.** reservar con
tiempo; **e. on** temprano
earmark ['ɪəmɑːk] *vt* destinar (**for** para
or a)
earn [ɜːn] *vt* (**a**) *(money)* ganar; **to e. one's
living** ganarse la vida (**b**) *(reputation)*
ganarse (**c**) **to e. interest** cobrar interés
or intereses

earnest ['ɜːnɪst] **1** *adj* serio(a), formal
  2 *n* **in e.** de veras, en serio
earnings ['ɜːnɪŋz] *npl* ingresos *mpl*
earring ['ɪərɪŋ] *n* pendiente *m*
earshot ['ɪəʃɒt] *n* **out of e.** fuera del
alcance del oído; **within e.** al alcance
del oído
earth [ɜːθ] **1** *n* (**a**) tierra *f*; *Fig* **to be down
to e.** ser práctico; *Fam* **where/why on e.
...?** ¿pero dónde/por qué demonios ...?
(**b**) *Br Elec* toma *f* de tierra
  2 *vt Br Elec* conectar a tierra
earthenware ['ɜːðənweə(r)] **1** *n* loza *f*
  2 *adj* de barro
earthquake ['ɜːθkweɪk] *n* terremoto *m*
earthshattering ['ɜːθʃætərɪŋ] *adj* trascendental; **e. news** noticia bomba
earthworm ['ɜːθwɜːm] *n* lombriz *f* de
tierra
earthy ['ɜːθɪ] *adj* (**earthier, earthiest**)
(**a**) *(taste)* terroso(a) (**b**) *(bawdy)* tos-
co(a)
earwig ['ɪəwɪg] *n* tijereta *f*
ease [iːz] **1** *n* (**a**) *(freedom from discomfort)* tranquilidad *f*; *Mil* posición *f* de
descanso; **at e.** relajado(a) (**b**) *(lack of
difficulty)* facilidad *f* (**c**) *(affluence)*
comodidad *f* (**d**) **e. of manner** naturalidad *f*
  2 *vt* (**a**) *(pain)* aliviar (**b**) *(move gently)*
deslizar con cuidado
  ▸ **ease off, ease up** *vi* (**a**) *(decrease)* disminuir (**b**) *(slow down)* ir más despacio
easel ['iːzəl] *n* caballete *m*
easily ['iːzɪlɪ] *adv* fácilmente; **e. the best**
con mucho el mejor
east [iːst] **1** *n* este *m*; **the Middle E.** el
Oriente Medio
  2 *adj* del este, oriental; **E. Germany**
Alemania Oriental
  3 *adv* al *or* hacia el este
Easter ['iːstə(r)] *n* Semana Santa, Pascua
f; **E. egg** huevo *m* de Pascua; **E. Sunday**
Domingo *m* de Resurrección
easterly ['iːstəlɪ] *adj (from the east)* del
este; *(to the east)* hacia al este
eastern ['iːstən] *adj* oriental, del este
eastward(s) ['iːstwəd(z)] *adv* hacia el
este

easy ['iːzɪ] (**easier, easiest**) **1** *adj* (**a**) *(simple)* fácil, sencillo(a) (**b**) *(unworried, comfortable)* cómodo(a), tranquilo(a); *Fam* **I'm e.!** ¡me da lo mismo!; **e. chair** butacón *m*
  2 *adv* **go e. on the wine** no te pases con el vino; *Fam* **to take things e.** tomarse las cosas con calma; *Fam* **take it e.!** ¡tranquilo!

easy-going [iːzɪ'gəʊɪŋ] *adj (calm)* tranquilo(a); *(lax)* despreocupado(a); *(undemanding)* poco exigente

eat [iːt] *vt* (*pt* **ate** [et, eɪt]; *pp* **eaten**) comer
  ▸ **eat away** *vt sep* desgastar; *(metal)* corroer
  ▸ **eat into** *vt insep* (**a**) *(wood)* roer (**b**) *Fig (savings)* consumir
  ▸ **eat out** *vi* comer fuera
  ▸ **eat up** *vt sep* (**a**) *(meal)* terminar (**b**) *Fig (petrol)* consumir; *(miles)* recorrer rápidamente

eatable ['iːtəbəl] *adj* comestible

eaten ['iːtən] *pp of* **eat**

eau de Cologne [əʊdəkə'ləʊn] *n* colonia *f*

eaves [iːvz] *npl* alero *m*

eavesdrop ['iːvzdrɒp] *vi* escuchar disimuladamente

ebb [eb] **1** *n* reflujo *m*; **e. and flow** flujo y reflujo; *Fig* **to be at a low e.** estar decaído
  2 *vi* (**a**) *(tide)* bajar; **to e. and flow** subir y bajar (**b**) *Fig* **to e. away** decaer

ebony ['ebənɪ] **1** *n* ébano *m*
  2 *adj* de ébano

eccentric [ɪk'sentrɪk] *adj & n* excéntrico(a) *(m,f)*

ecclesiastic [ɪkliːzɪ'æstɪk] *adj & n* eclesiástico(a) *(m,f)*

echelon ['eʃəlɒn] *n* escalafón *m*

echo ['ekəʊ] **1** *n* (*pl* **echoes**) eco *m*
  2 *vt (repeat)* repetir
  3 *vi* resonar, hacer eco

eclectic [ɪ'klektɪk] *adj* ecléctico(a)

eclipse [ɪ'klɪps] **1** *n* eclipse *m*
  2 *vt* eclipsar

ecological [iːkə'lɒdʒɪkəl] *adj* ecológico(a)

ecology [ɪ'kɒlədʒɪ] *n* ecología *f*

e-commerce [iː'kɒmɜːs] *n* comercio electrónico

economic [iːkə'nɒmɪk] *adj* económico(a); *(profitable)* rentable

economical [iːkə'nɒmɪkəl] *adj* económico(a)

economics [iːkə'nɒmɪks] *n sing (science)* economía *f*; *Educ* (ciencias *fpl*) económicas *fpl*

economist [ɪ'kɒnəmɪst] *n* economista *mf*

economize [ɪ'kɒnəmaɪz] *vi* economizar

economy [ɪ'kɒnəmɪ] *n* (**a**) *Pol* **the e.** la economía (**b**) *(saving)* ahorro *m*; **e. class** clase *f* turista

ecosystem ['iːkəʊsɪstəm] *n* ecosistema *m*

ecotax ['iːkəʊtæks] *n* ecotasa *f*

ecotourism ['iːkəʊtɔːrɪzəm] *n* ecoturismo *m*

ecstasy ['ekstəsɪ] *n* éxtasis *m*

ecstatic [ek'stætɪk] *adj* extático(a)

Ecuador ['ekwədɔː(r)] *n* Ecuador

eczema ['eksɪmə] *n* eczema *m*

eddy ['edɪ] **1** *n* remolino *m*
  2 *vi* arremolinarse

edge [edʒ] **1** *n* borde *m*; *(of knife)* filo *m*; *(of coin)* canto *m*; *(of water)* orilla *f*; **on the e. of town** en las afueras de la ciudad; **to have the e. on sb** llevar ventaja a algn; *Fig* **to be on e.** tener los nervios de punta
  2 *vt Sewing* ribetear
  3 *vi* **to e. closer** acercarse lentamente; **to e. forward** avanzar poco a poco

edgeways ['edʒweɪz], **edgewise** ['edʒwaɪz] *adv* de lado; *Fig* **I couldn't get a word in e.** no pude decir ni pío

edging ['edʒɪŋ] *n* borde *m*; *Sewing* ribete *m*

edgy ['edʒɪ] *adj* (**edgier, edgiest**) nervioso(a)

edible ['edɪbəl] *adj* comestible

edict ['iːdɪkt] *n Hist* edicto *m*; *Jur* decreto *m*

Edinburgh ['edɪnbrə] *n* Edimburgo

edit ['edɪt] *vt* (**a**) *(prepare for printing)* preparar para la imprenta (**b**) *(rewrite)* corregir; **to e. sth out** suprimir algo (**c**) *Press* ser redactor(a) de (**d**) *Cin, Rad & TV* montar; *(cut)* cortar

edition [ɪ'dɪʃən] *n* edición *f*

editor ['edɪtə(r)] *n (of book)* editor(a) *m,f*; *Press* redactor(a) *m,f*; *Cin & TV* montador(a) *m,f*

editorial [edɪ'tɔːrɪəl] **1** *adj* editorial; **e. staff** redacción *f*
  2 *n* editorial *m*

educate ['edjʊkeɪt] *vt* educar

educated ['edjʊkeɪtɪd] *adj* culto(a)

education [edjʊ'keɪʃən] *n* (**a**) *(schooling)* enseñanza *f*; **adult e.** educación *f* de adultos; **Ministry of E.** Ministerio *m* de Educación (**b**) *(training)* formación *f* (**c**) *(studies)* estudios *mpl* (**d**) *(culture)* cultura *f*

educational [edjʊ'keɪʃənəl] *adj* educativo(a), educacional

eel [iːl] *n* anguila *f*

eerie ['ɪərɪ] *adj* (**eerier, eeriest**) siniestro(a)

efface [ɪ'feɪs] *vt* borrar

effect [ɪ'fekt] **1** *n* (**a**) efecto *m*; **in e.** efectivamente; **to come into e.** entrar en vigor; **to have an e. on** afectar a; **to no e.** sin resultado alguno; **to take e.** *(drug)* surtir efecto; *(law)* entrar en vigor (**b**) *(impression)* impresión *f* (**c**) **effects** *(possessions)* efectos *mpl*
2 *vt Fml* provocar

effective [ɪ'fektɪv] *adj* (**a**) *(successful)* eficaz (**b**) *(real)* efectivo(a) (**c**) *(impressive)* impresionante

effectively [ɪ'fektɪvlɪ] *adv* (**a**) *(successfully)* eficazmente (**b**) *(in fact)* en efecto

effeminate [ɪ'femɪnɪt] *adj* afeminado(a)

effervescent [efə'vesənt] *adj* efervescente

efficiency [ɪ'fɪʃənsɪ] *n (of person)* eficacia *f*; *(of machine)* rendimiento *m*

efficient [ɪ'fɪʃənt] *adj* eficaz, eficiente; *(machine)* de buen rendimiento

effigy ['efɪdʒɪ] *n* efigie *f*

effluent ['efluənt] *n* vertidos *mpl*

effort ['efət] *n* (**a**) esfuerzo *m*; **to make an e.** hacer un esfuerzo, esforzarse (**b**) *(attempt)* intento *m*

effortless ['efətlɪs] *adj* sin esfuerzo

effrontery [ɪ'frʌntərɪ] *n* desfachatez *f*

effusive [ɪ'fjuːsɪv] *adj* efusivo(a)

eg [iː'dʒiː] *(abbr* **exempli gratia)** p. ej.

egalitarian [ɪgælɪ'teərɪən] *adj* igualitario(a)

egg [eg] **1** *n* huevo *m*; *Fam Fig* **to put all one's eggs in one basket** jugárselo todo a una carta; **e. cup** huevera *f*; **e. timer** reloj *m* de arena; **e. white** clara *f* de huevo
2 *vt* **to e. sb on (to do sth)** empujar a algn (a hacer algo)

eggplant ['egplɑːnt] *n US* berenjena *f*

eggshell ['egʃel] *n* cáscara *f* de huevo

ego ['iːgəʊ,'egəʊ] *n* (**a**) ego *m*; *Fam* **e. trip** autobombo *m* (**b**) *Fam* amor propio

egocentric(al) [iːgəʊ'sentrɪk(əl)] *adj* egocéntrico(a)

egoism ['iːgəʊɪzəm] *n* egoísmo *m*

egoist ['iːgəʊɪst] *n* egoísta *mf*

egotistic(al) [iːgəʊ'tɪstɪk(əl)] *adj* egotista

Egypt ['iːdʒɪpt] *n* Egipto *m*

Egyptian [ɪ'dʒɪpʃən] *adj & n* egipcio(a) *(m,f)*

eiderdown ['aɪdədaʊn] *n* edredón *m*

eight [eɪt] *adj & n* ocho *(m inv)*

eighteen [eɪ'tiːn] *adj & n* dieciocho *(m inv)*

eighteenth [eɪ'tiːnθ] **1** *adj & n* decimoctavo *(m,f)*
2 *n (fraction)* decimoctavo *m*

eighth [eɪtθ] **1** *adj & n* octavo(a) *(m,f)*
2 *n (fraction)* octavo *m*

eighty ['eɪtɪ] *adj & n* ochenta *(m inv)*

Eire ['eərə] *n* Eire

either ['aɪðə(r), 'iːðə(r)] **1** *pron* (**a**) *(affirmative)* cualquiera; **e. of them** cualquiera de los dos; **e. of us** cualquiera de nosotros dos (**b**) *(negative)* ninguno/ninguna, ni el uno ni el otro/ni la una ni la otra; **I don't want e. of them** no quiero ninguno de los dos
2 *adj (both)* cada, los dos/las dos; **on e. side** en ambos lados; **in e. case** en cualquier de los dos casos
3 *conj* o; **e. ... or ... or ...** o ... o ...; **e. Friday or Saturday** o (bien) el viernes o el sábado
4 *adv (after negative)* tampoco; **I don't want to do it e.** yo tampoco quiero hacerlo

ejaculate [ɪ'dʒækjʊleɪt] *vi (man)* eyacular

eject [ɪ'dʒekt] **1** *vt* expulsar
2 *vi Av* eyectarse

eke [iːk] *vt* **to e. out a living** ganarse la vida a duras penas

elaborate 1 *vt* [ɪ'læbəreɪt] (**a**) *(devise)* elaborar (**b**) *(explain)* explicar detalladamente
2 *vi* explicarse; **to e. on sth** explicar algo con más detalles
3 *adj* [ɪ'læbərɪt] (**a**) *(complicated)* complicado(a) (**b**) *(detailed)* detallado(a); *(style)* esmerado(a)

elapse [ɪ'læps] *vi* transcurrir, pasar

elastic [ɪ'læstɪk] **1** *adj* elástico(a); *Fig* flexible; **e. band** goma elástica
2 *n* elástico *m*

Elastoplast® [ɪ'lɑːstəplɑːst] *n* tirita *f*, *Am* curita *f*

elated [ɪ'leɪtɪd] *adj* eufórico(a)

elation [ɪ'leɪʃən] *n* regocijo *m*

elbow ['elbəʊ] **1** *n* (**a**) codo *m*; *Fig* **e. room** espacio *m* (**b**) *(bend)* recodo *m*
2 *vt* **to e. sb** dar un codazo a algn

elder¹ ['eldə(r)] **1** *adj* mayor
2 *n* **the elders** los ancianos

elder² ['eldə(r)] *n Bot* saúco *m*

elderly ['eldəlɪ] **1** *adj* anciano(a)
2 *npl* **the e.** los ancianos

eldest ['eldɪst] **1** *adj* mayor
2 *n* **the e.** el/la mayor

elect [ɪ'lekt] **1** *vt* (**a**) *Pol* elegir (**b**) **to e. to do sth** *(choose)* decidir hacer algo
2 *adj* **the president e.** el presidente electo

election [ɪ'lekʃən] **1** n elección f; **general e.** elecciones fpl generales
2 adj electoral
electioneering [ɪlekʃə'nɪərɪŋ] n electoralismo m
elector [ɪ'lektə(r)] n elector(a) m,f
electoral [ɪ'lektərəl] adj electoral
electorate [ɪ'lektərɪt] n electorado m
electric [ɪ'lektrɪk] adj (**a**) eléctrico(a); **e. blanket** manta eléctrica, Am frazada eléctrica; **e. chair** silla eléctrica; **e. shock** electrochoque m (**b**) Fig electrizante
electrical [ɪ'lektrɪkəl] adj eléctrico(a)
electrician [ɪlek'trɪʃən] n electricista mf
electricity [ɪlek'trɪsɪtɪ] n electricidad f; **e. bill** recibo m de la luz
electrify [ɪ'lektrɪfaɪ] vt (**a**) (railway line) electrificar (**b**) Fig (excite) electrizar
electrocute [ɪ'lektrəkjuːt] vt electrocutar
electron [ɪ'lektrɒn] n electrón m
electronic [ɪlek'trɒnɪk] adj electrónico(a); **e. banking** banca electrónica, telebanca f
electronics [ɪlek'trɒnɪks] **1** n sing (science) electrónica f
2 npl (of machine) componentes mpl electrónicos
elegant ['elɪgənt] adj elegante
element ['elɪmənt] n (**a**) elemento m (**b**) (part) parte f (**c**) (electrical) resistencia f (**d**) Fam Fig **to be in one's e.** estar en su salsa
elementary [elɪ'mentərɪ] adj (basic) elemental; (not developed) rudimentario(a); (easy) fácil; US **e. school** escuela primaria
elephant ['elɪfənt] n elefante m
elevate ['elɪveɪt] vt elevar; (in rank) ascender
elevation [elɪ'veɪʃən] n (**a**) elevación f (**b**) Archit alzado m (**c**) (above sea level) altitud f
elevator ['elɪveɪtər] n US ascensor m
eleven [ɪ'levən] adj & n once (m inv)
elevenses [ɪ'levənzɪz] npl Fam bocadillo m de las once
eleventh [ɪ'levənθ] **1** adj & n undécimo(a) (m,f)
2 n (fraction) undécimo m
elicit [ɪ'lɪsɪt] vt obtener
eligible ['elɪdʒəbəl] adj apto(a); **he isn't e. to vote** no tiene derecho al voto
eliminate [ɪ'lɪmɪneɪt] vt eliminar
elite [ɪ'liːt] n elite f
elitist [ɪ'liːtɪst] adj elitista
elm [elm] n olmo m
elocution [elə'kjuːʃən] n elocución f
elongate ['iːlɒŋgeɪt] vt alargar
elope [ɪ'ləʊp] vi fugarse para casarse

eloquent ['eləkwənt] adj elocuente
else [els] adv (**a**) **anyone e.** alguien más; **anything e.?** ¿algo más?; **everything e.** todo lo demás; **no one e.** nadie más; **someone e.** otro(a); **something e.** otra cosa, algo más; **somewhere e.** en otra parte; **what e.?** ¿qué más?; **where e.?** ¿en qué otro sitio? (**b**) **or e.** (otherwise) si no
elsewhere [els'weə(r)] adv en otra parte
elucidate [ɪ'luːsɪdeɪt] vt aclarar
elude [ɪ'luːd] vt (**a**) (escape) eludir; **his name eludes me** no consigo acordarme de su nombre (**b**) (avoid) esquivar
elusive [ɪ'luːsɪv] adj esquivo(a); (evasive) evasivo(a)
emaciated [ɪ'meɪsɪeɪtɪd] adj demacrado(a)
e-mail ['iːmeɪl] Comput **1** n (system) correo m electrónico; (message) (mensaje m por) correo electrónico; **e. address** dirección f de correo electrónico
2 vt (person) enviar un correo electrónico a; (file) enviar por correo electrónico
emanate ['eməneɪt] vi provenir (**from** de)
emancipate [ɪ'mænsɪpeɪt] vt emancipar
emancipation [ɪmænsɪ'peɪʃən] n emancipación f
embankment [ɪm'bæŋkmənt] n (**a**) (made of earth) terraplén m (**b**) (of river) dique m
embargo [em'bɑːgəʊ] n (pl embargoes) embargo m
embark [em'bɑːk] **1** vt (merchandise) embarcar
2 vi embarcar, embarcarse; Fig **to e. upon** emprender; (sth difficult) embarcarse en
embarkation [embɑː'keɪʃən] n embarque m
embarrass [ɪm'bærəs] vt avergonzar, Andes, CAm, Carib, Méx apenar
embarrassed [ɪm'bærəst] adj avergonzado(a), Andes, CAm, Carib, Méx apenado(a)

> 📝 Note that the Spanish word **embarazado** is a false friend and is never a translation for the English word **embarrassed**. In Spanish, **embarazado** means "pregnant".

embarrassing [ɪm'bærəsɪŋ] adj embarazoso(a), Andes, CAm, Carib, Méx penoso(a)
embarrassment [ɪm'bærəsmənt] n vergüenza f, Andes, CAm, Carib, Méx pena f
embassy ['embəsɪ] n embajada f

embed [ɪm'bed] *vt (jewels)* incrustar; *Fig* grabar

embellish [ɪm'belɪʃ] *vt* embellecer; *(story)* exagerar

ember ['embə(r)] *n* ascua *f*, rescoldo *m*

embezzle [ɪm'bezəl] *vt* desfalcar, malversar

embezzlement [ɪm'bezəlmənt] *n* malversación *f*

embitter [ɪm'bɪtə(r)] *vt* amargar

embittered [ɪm'bɪtəd] *adj* amargado(a), resentido(a)

emblem ['embləm] *n* emblema *m*

embody [ɪm'bɒdɪ] *vt* (**a**) *(include)* abarcar (**b**) *(personify)* encarnar

embossed [ɪm'bɒst] *adj* en relieve

embrace [ɪm'breɪs] **1** *vt* (**a**) abrazar (**b**) *(accept)* adoptar (**c**) *(include)* abarcar
2 *vi* abrazarse
3 *n* abrazo *m*

embroider [ɪm'brɔɪdə(r)] *vt* (**a**) *Sewing* bordar (**b**) *Fig (story, truth)* adornar, embellecer

embroidery [ɪm'brɔɪdərɪ] *n* bordado *m*

embryo ['embrɪəʊ] *n* embrión *m*

emerald ['emərəld] *n* esmeralda *f*

emerge [ɪ'mɜːdʒ] *vi* salir; *(problem)* surgir; **it emerged that ...** resultó que ...

emergence [ɪ'mɜːdʒəns] *n* aparición *f*

emergency [ɪ'mɜːdʒənsɪ] *n* emergencia *f*; *Med* urgencia *f*; **in an e.** en caso de emergencia; **e. exit** salida *f* de emergencia; **e. landing** aterrizaje forzoso; **e. measures** medidas *fpl* de urgencia; *US* **e. room** sala *f* de urgencias; *Aut* **e. stop** frenazo *m* en seco; *Pol* **state of e.** estado *m* de excepción

emery ['emərɪ] *n* **e. board** lima *f* de uñas

emigrant ['emɪgrənt] *n* emigrante *mf*

emigrate ['emɪgreɪt] *vi* emigrar

emigration [emɪ'greɪʃən] *n* emigración *f*

eminent ['emɪnənt] *adj* eminente

emission [ɪ'mɪʃən] *n* emisión *f*

emit [ɪ'mɪt] *vt (signals)* emitir; *(smells)* despedir; *(sound)* producir

emotion [ɪ'məʊʃən] *n* emoción *f*

emotional [ɪ'məʊʃənəl] *adj* (**a**) emocional (**b**) *(moving)* conmovedor(a)

emotive [ɪ'məʊtɪv] *adj* emotivo(a)

emperor ['empərə(r)] *n* emperador *m*

emphasis ['emfəsɪs] *n* (*pl* **emphases** ['emfəsiːz]) énfasis *m*; **to place e. on sth** hacer hincapié en algo

emphasize ['emfəsaɪz] *vt* subrayar, hacer hincapié en; *(insist)* insistir; *(highlight)* hacer resaltar

emphatic [em'fætɪk] *adj (forceful)* enfático(a); *(convinced)* categórico(a)

emphatically [em'fætɪklɪ] *adv* categóricamente

empire ['empaɪə(r)] *n* imperio *m*

employ [ɪm'plɔɪ] *vt* emplear; *(time)* ocupar

employee [em'plɔiː, emplɔɪ'iː] *n* empleado(a) *m,f*

employer [ɪm'plɔɪə(r)] *n* patrón(ona) *m,f*

employment [ɪm'plɔɪmənt] *n* empleo *m*; **e. agency** agencia *f* de colocaciones; **full e.** pleno empleo

empower [ɪm'paʊə(r)] *vt* autorizar

empress ['emprɪs] *n* emperatriz *f*

emptiness ['emptɪnɪs] *n* vacío *m*

empty ['emptɪ] **1** *adj* (**emptier, emptiest**) vacío(a); **an e. house** una casa deshabitada; **e. promises** promesas *fpl* vanas
2 *vt* vaciar
3 *vi* (**a**) vaciarse (**b**) *(river)* desembocar (**into** en)
4 *npl* **empties** envases vacíos

empty-handed [emptɪ'hændɪd] *adj* con las manos vacías

EMU [iːem'juː] *n Fin (abbr* **Economic and Monetary Union)** UEM *f*

emulate ['emjʊleɪt] *vt* emular

emulsion [ɪ'mʌlʃən] *n* emulsión *f*; **e. paint** pintura *f* mate

enable [ɪn'eɪbəl] *vt* permitir

enact [ɪ'nækt] *vt (play)* representar; *(law)* promulgar

enamel [ɪ'næməl] *n* esmalte *m*

enamoured, *US* **enamored** [ɪ'næməd] *adj* **to be e. of** estar enamorado(a) de; **I'm not greatly e. of the idea** no me entusiasma la idea

encase [ɪn'keɪs] *vt* **encased in** revestido de

enchant [ɪn'tʃɑːnt] *vt* encantar

enchanting [ɪn'tʃɑːntɪŋ] *adj* encantador(a)

encircle [ɪn'sɜːkəl] *vt* rodear

enclave ['enkleɪv] *n* enclave *m*

enclose [ɪn'kləʊz] *vt* (**a**) *(surround)* rodear (**b**) *(fence in)* cercar (**c**) *(in envelope)* adjuntar; **please find enclosed** le enviamos adjunto

enclosure [ɪn'kləʊʒə(r)] *n* (**a**) *(fenced area)* cercado *m* (**b**) *(in envelope)* documento adjunto (**c**) *(of racecourse)* recinto *m*

encompass [ɪn'kʌmpəs] *vt* abarcar

encore ['ɒŋkɔː(r)] **1** *interj* ¡otra!, ¡bis!
2 *n* repetición *f*, bis *m*

encounter [ɪn'kaʊntə(r)] **1** *n (meeting)* encuentro *m*
2 *vt* encontrar, encontrarse con; *(problems)* tropezar con

encourage [ɪnˈkʌrɪdʒ] *vt* (**a**) *(person)* animar (**b**) *(tourism, trade)* fomentar

encouragement [ɪnˈkʌrɪdʒmənt] *n* estímulo *m*

encroach [ɪnˈkrəʊtʃ] *vi* **to e. on** *(territory)* invadir; *(rights)* usurpar; *(time, freedom)* quitar

encrusted [ɪnˈkrʌstɪd] *adj* incrustado(a) (**with** de)

encumber [ɪnˈkʌmbə(r)] *vt* estorbar; *(with debts)* gravar

encyclop(a)edia [ensaɪkləʊˈpiːdɪə] *n* enciclopedia *f*

end [end] **1** *n* (**a**) *(of stick)* punta *f*; *(of street)* final *m*; *(of table)* extremo *m*; *Fig* **to make ends meet** llegar a final de mes; *Fig* **it makes my hair stand on e.** me pone el pelo de punta (**b**) *(conclusion)* fin *m*, final *m*; **in the e.** al final; **for hours on e.** hora tras hora; **no e. of** un sinfín de; **to bring an e. to sth** poner fin a algo; **to put an e. to** acabar con (**c**) *(aim)* objetivo *m*, fin *m*; **to no e.** en vano

   2 *vt* acabar, terminar

   3 *vi* acabarse, terminarse

  ▸ **end up** *vi* terminar; **it ended up in the dustbin** fue a parar al cubo de la basura; **to e. up doing sth** terminar por hacer algo

endanger [ɪnˈdeɪndʒə(r)] *vt* poner en peligro

endangered [ɪnˈdeɪndʒəd] *adj* en peligro

endearing [ɪnˈdɪərɪŋ] *adj* simpático(a)

endeavour, *US* **endeavor** [ɪnˈdevə(r)] **1** *n* esfuerzo *m*

   2 *vt* intentar, procurar

ending [ˈendɪŋ] *n* final *m*

endive [ˈendaɪv] *n Bot* (**a**) *(curly)* escarola *f* (**b**) *esp US (chicory)* endibia *f*

endless [ˈendlɪs] *adj* interminable

endorse [ɪnˈdɔːs] *vt* (**a**) *Fin* endosar (**b**) *(approve)* aprobar; *(support)* apoyar

endorsement [ɪnˈdɔːsmənt] *n* (**a**) *Fin* endoso *m* (**b**) *Aut* nota *f* de sanción (**c**) *(approval)* aprobación *f*

endow [ɪnˈdaʊ] *vt* dotar; **to be endowed with** estar dotado(a) de

endurance [ɪnˈdjʊərəns] *n* resistencia *f*

endure [ɪnˈdjʊə(r)] **1** *vt (bear)* aguantar, soportar

   2 *vi* perdurar

enemy [ˈenəmɪ] *adj & n* enemigo(a) *(m,f)*

energetic [enəˈdʒetɪk] *adj* enérgico(a)

energy [ˈenədʒɪ] *n* energía *f*

enforce [ɪnˈfɔːs] *vt (law)* hacer cumplir

enforcement [ɪnˈfɔːsmənt] *n* aplicación *f*

engage [ɪnˈɡeɪdʒ] *vt* (**a**) *(hire)* contratar (**b**) *(attention)* llamar (**c**) *(in conversation)* entablar (**d**) *Tech* engranar; *Aut* **to e. the clutch** pisar el embrague

engaged [ɪnˈɡeɪdʒd] *adj* (**a**) *(betrothed)* prometido(a); **to get e.** prometerse (**b**) *(busy)* ocupado(a); *Br Tel* **it's e.** está comunicando

engagement [ɪnˈɡeɪdʒmənt] *n* (**a**) *(betrothal)* petición *f* de mano; *(period)* noviazgo *m*; **e. ring** anillo *m* de compromiso (**b**) *(appointment)* cita *f* (**c**) *Mil* combate *m*

engaging [ɪnˈɡeɪdʒɪŋ] *adj* simpático(a), agradable

engender [ɪnˈdʒendə(r)] *vt* engendrar

engine [ˈendʒɪn] *n* motor *m*; *Rail* locomotora *f*; **e. room** sala *f* de máquinas; **e. driver** maquinista *mf*

engineer [endʒɪˈnɪə(r)] **1** *n* (**a**) ingeniero(a) *m,f*; **civil e.** ingeniero de caminos (**b**) *US Rail* maquinista *mf*

   2 *vt Fig (contrive)* maquinar

engineering [endʒɪˈnɪərɪŋ] *n* ingeniería *f*; **electrical e.** electrotecnia *f*; **civil e.** ingeniería civil

England [ˈɪŋɡlənd] *n* Inglaterra

English [ˈɪŋɡlɪʃ] **1** *adj* inglés(esa)

   2 *n* (**a**) *(language)* inglés *m* (**b**) *pl* **the E.** los ingleses

Englishman [ˈɪŋɡlɪʃmən] *n* inglés *m*

English-speaking [ˈɪŋɡlɪʃspiːkɪŋ] *adj* de habla inglesa

Englishwoman [ˈɪŋɡlɪʃwʊmən] *n* inglesa *f*

engraving [ɪnˈɡreɪvɪŋ] *n* grabado *m*

engrossed [ɪnˈɡrəʊst] *adj* absorto(a) (**in** en)

engulf [ɪnˈɡʌlf] *vt* tragarse

enhance [ɪnˈhɑːns] *vt (beauty)* realzar; *(power, chances)* aumentar

enigma [ɪˈnɪɡmə] *n* enigma *m*

enjoy [ɪnˈdʒɔɪ] *vt* (**a**) disfrutar de; **to e. oneself** pasarlo bien (**b**) *(benefit from)* gozar de

enjoyable [ɪnˈdʒɔɪəbəl] *adj* agradable; *(amusing)* divertido(a)

enjoyment [ɪnˈdʒɔɪmənt] *n* placer *m*, gusto *m*

enlarge [ɪnˈlɑːdʒ] **1** *vt* extender, ampliar; *Phot* ampliar

   2 *vi* **to e. upon a subject** extenderse sobre un tema

enlargement [ɪnˈlɑːdʒmənt] *n Phot* ampliación *f*

enlighten [ɪnˈlaɪtən] *vt* iluminar

enlightened [ɪnˈlaɪtənd] *adj* (**a**) *(learned)* culto(a); *(informed)* bien informado(a) (**b**) *Hist* ilustrado(a)

enlightenment [ɪn'laɪtənmənt] *n* **the Age of E.** el Siglo de las Luces
enlist [ɪn'lɪst] **1** *vt Mil* reclutar; **to e. sb's help** conseguir ayuda de algn
2 *vi Mil* alistarse
enmity ['enmɪtɪ] *n* enemistad *f*, hostilidad *f*
enormous [ɪ'nɔːməs] *adj* enorme
enormously [ɪ'nɔːməslɪ] *adv* enormemente; **I enjoyed myself e.** lo pasé genial
enough [ɪ'nʌf] **1** *adj* bastante, suficiente; **e. books** bastantes libros; **e. money** bastante dinero; **have we got e. petrol?** ¿tenemos suficiente gasolina?
2 *adv* bastante; **oddly e. ...** lo curioso es que ...; **sure e.** en efecto
3 *pron* lo bastante, lo suficiente; **e. to live on** lo suficiente para vivir; **it isn't e.** no basta; **more than e.** más que suficiente; *Fam* **e. is e.!** ¡ya está!; *Fam* **I've had e.!** ¡estoy harto!
enquire [ɪn'kwaɪə(r)] *vi* preguntar
enquiry [ɪn'kwaɪərɪ] *n* (**a**) *(question)* pregunta *f*; **to make an e.** preguntar; **enquiries** información *f* (**b**) *(investigation)* investigación *f*
enrage [ɪn'reɪdʒ] *vt* enfurecer
enrich [ɪn'rɪtʃ] *vt* enriquecer
enrol, *US* **enroll** [ɪn'rəʊl] **1** *vt* matricular, inscribir
2 *vi* matricularse, inscribirse

> ⚠ Note that the Spanish verb **enrollar** is a false friend and is never a translation for the English verb **to enrol**. In Spanish, **enrollar** means "to roll up".

enrolment [ɪn'rəʊlmənt] *n* matrícula *f*
en route [ɒn'ruːt] *adv* en *or* por el camino
ensign ['ensaɪn] *n* (**a**) *(flag)* bandera *f*; *Naut* pabellón *m* (**b**) *US (naval officer)* alférez *m* de fragata
enslave [ɪn'sleɪv] *vt* esclavizar
ensue [ɪn'sjuː] *vi* (**a**) *(follow)* seguir (**b**) *(result)* resultar (**from** de)
ensure [ɪn'ʃʊə(r)] *vt* asegurar
entail [ɪn'teɪl] *vt (involve)* suponer
entangle [ɪn'tæŋgəl] *vt* enredar
enter ['entə(r)] **1** *vt* (**a**) *(go into)* entrar en; *Fig (join)* ingresar en (**b**) *(write down)* apuntar, anotar (**c**) **to e. one's name for a course** *(register)* matricularse en un curso (**d**) *Comput* dar entrada a
2 *vi* entrar
▸**enter into** *vt insep* (**a**) *(agreement)* firmar; *(negotiations)* iniciar; *(bargain)* cerrar (**b**) *(relations)* establecer; *(conversation)* entablar

enterprise ['entəpraɪz] *n* empresa *f*; **free e.** libre empresa; **private e.** iniciativa privada; *(as a whole)* el sector privado; **public e.** el sector público
enterprising ['entəpraɪzɪŋ] *adj* emprendedor(a)
entertain [entə'teɪn] **1** *vt* (**a**) *(amuse)* divertir (**b**) *(consider)* considerar; **to e. an idea** abrigar una idea
2 *vi* tener invitados
entertainer [entə'teɪnə(r)] *n* artista *mf*
entertaining [entə'teɪnɪŋ] *adj* divertido(a)
entertainment [entə'teɪnmənt] *n* (**a**) diversión *f* (**b**) *Th* espectáculo *m*
enthralling [ɪn'θrɔːlɪŋ] *adj* fascinante
enthuse [ɪn'θjuːz] *vi* entusiasmarse (**over** por)
enthusiasm [ɪn'θjuːzɪæzəm] *n* entusiasmo *m*
enthusiast [ɪn'θjuːzɪæst] *n* entusiasta *mf*
enthusiastic [ɪnθjuːzɪ'æstɪk] *adj* entusiasta; *(praise)* caluroso(a); **to be e. about sth** entusiasmarse por algo
entice [ɪn'taɪs] *vt* seducir, atraer
enticing [ɪn'taɪsɪŋ] *adj* atractivo(a), tentador(a)
entire [ɪn'taɪə(r)] *adj* entero(a), todo(a)
entirely [ɪn'taɪəlɪ] *adv* (**a**) *(completely)* totalmente (**b**) *(solely)* exclusivamente
entirety [ɪn'taɪərɪtɪ] *n* **in its e.** en su totalidad
entitle [ɪn'taɪtəl] *vt* (**a**) dar derecho a; **to be entitled to** tener derecho a (**b**) *(book etc)* titular
entity ['entɪtɪ] *n* entidad *f*
entourage [ɒntʊ'rɑːʒ] *n* séquito *m*
entrails ['entreɪlz] *npl* tripas *fpl*; *Fig* entrañas *fpl*
entrance¹ ['entrəns] *n* (**a**) entrada *f*; **e. fee** *(to museum etc)* entrada; *(to organization)* cuota *f* (**b**) *(admission)* ingreso *m*; **e. examination** examen *m* de ingreso
entrance² [ɪn'trɑːns] *vt* encantar
entrant ['entrənt] *n* *(in competition)* participante *mf*; *(applicant)* aspirante *mf*
entreat [ɪn'triːt] *vt Fml* suplicar, rogar
entrée ['ɒntreɪ] *n Br (first course)* entrada *f*, primer plato *m*; *US (main course)* plato principal
entrenched [ɪn'trentʃt] *adj* firmemente enraizado(a)
entrepreneur [ɒntrəprə'nɜː(r)] *n* empresario(a) *m,f*
entrust [ɪn'trʌst] *vt* encargar (**with** de); **to e. sth to sb** dejar algo al cuidado de algn
entry ['entrɪ] *n* (**a**) *(entrance)* entrada *f*;

no e. *(sign)* dirección prohibida (**b**) *(in competition)* participante *mf*
enumerate [ɪ'njuːməreɪt] *vt* enumerar
enunciate [ɪ'nʌnsɪeɪt] *vt (words)* articular; *(ideas)* formular
envelop [ɪn'veləp] *vt* envolver
envelope ['envələʊp] *n* sobre *m*
envious ['envɪəs] *adj* envidioso(a); **to feel e.** tener envidia
environment [ɪn'vaɪərənmənt] *n* medio *m* ambiente
environmental [ɪnvaɪərən'mentəl] *adj* medioambiental
environmentally [ɪnvaɪərən'mentəlɪ] *adv* ecológicamente; **e. friendly** ecológico(a), que no daña el medio ambiente
envisage [ɪn'vɪzɪdʒ] *vt (imagine)* imaginarse; *(foresee)* prever
envoy ['envɔɪ] *n* enviado(a) *m,f*
envy ['envɪ] **1** *n* envidia *f*
 2 *vt* envidiar, tener envidia de
enzyme ['enzaɪm] *n* enzima *m*
ephemeral [ɪ'femərəl] *adj* efímero(a)
epic ['epɪk] **1** *n* epopeya *f*
 2 *adj* épico(a)
epidemic [epɪ'demɪk] *n* epidemia *f*; *Fig (of crime etc)* ola *f*
epilepsy ['epɪlepsɪ] *n* epilepsia *f*
epilogue, *US* **epilog** ['epɪlɒg] *n* epílogo *m*
episode ['epɪsəʊd] *n* episodio *m*
epistle [ɪ'pɪsəl] *n* epístola *f*
epitaph ['epɪtɑːf] *n* epitafio *m*
epitome [ɪ'pɪtəmɪ] *n Fml* personificación *f*
epitomize [ɪ'pɪtəmaɪz] *vt Fml* personificar
epoch ['iːpɒk] *n* época *f*
equable ['ekwəbəl] *adj* (**a**) *(person)* ecuánime (**b**) *(climate)* uniforme
equal ['iːkwəl] **1** *adj* igual; **to be e. to the occasion** estar a la altura de las circunstancias; **e. pay** igualdad *f* de salarios
 2 *n* igual *mf*; **to treat sb as an e.** tratar a algn de igual a igual
 3 *vt* (**a**) *Math* equivaler (**b**) *(match)* igualar
equality [iː'kwɒlɪtɪ] *n* igualdad *f*
equalize ['iːkwəlaɪz] **1** *vi Ftb* empatar
 2 *vt* igualar
equalizer ['iːkwəlaɪzə(r)] *n Ftb* gol *m* del empate; *(of sound)* ecualizador *m*
equally ['iːkwəlɪ] *adv* igualmente; **e. pretty** igual de bonito; **to share sth e.** dividir algo en partes iguales
equanimity [ekwə'nɪmɪtɪ] *n* ecuanimidad *f*
equate [ɪ'kweɪt] *vt* equiparar, comparar (**to** con)

equation [ɪ'kweɪʒən, ɪ'kweɪʃən] *n Math* ecuación *f*
equator [ɪ'kweɪtə(r)] *n* ecuador *m*
equatorial [ekwə'tɔːrɪəl] *adj* ecuatorial
equestrian [ɪ'kwestrɪən] *adj* ecuestre
equilibrium [iːkwɪ'lɪbrɪəm] *n* equilibrio *m*
equinox ['iːkwɪnɒks] *n* equinoccio *m*
equip [ɪ'kwɪp] *vt (with tools, machines)* equipar; *(with food)* proveer
equipment [ɪ'kwɪpmənt] *n (materials)* equipo *m*; **office e.** material *m* de oficina
equipped [ɪ'kwɪpt] *adj (with tools, machines)* equipado(a); *(with skills)* dotado(a)
equitable ['ekwɪtəbəl] *adj* equitativo(a)
equities ['ekwɪtɪz] *npl* acciones ordinarias
equivalent [ɪ'kwɪvələnt] *adj & n* equivalente *(m)*; **to be e. to** equivaler a, ser equivalente a
equivocal [ɪ'kwɪvəkəl] *adj* equívoco(a)
era ['ɪərə] *n* era *f*
eradicate [ɪ'rædɪkeɪt] *vt* erradicar
erase [ɪ'reɪz] *vt* borrar
eraser [*Br* ɪ'reɪzə(r), *US* ɪ'reɪsər] *n* goma *f* de borrar
erect [ɪ'rekt] **1** *adj* (**a**) *(upright)* erguido(a) (**b**) *(penis)* erecto(a)
 2 *vt (monument)* levantar, erigir
erection [ɪ'rekʃən] *n* (**a**) *(of building)* construcción *f* (**b**) *(penis)* erección *f*
ermine ['ɜːmɪn] *n* armiño *m*
erode [ɪ'rəʊd] *vt* (**a**) *(rock, soil)* erosionar (**b**) *(metal)* corroer, desgastar; *Fig (power, confidence)* hacer perder
erosion [ɪ'rəʊʒən] *n Geol* erosión *f*
erotic [ɪ'rɒtɪk] *adj* erótico(a)
err [ɜː(r)] *vi* errar; **to e. on the side of caution** pecar de prudente
errand ['erənd] *n* recado *m*; **e. boy** recadero *m*
erratic [ɪ'rætɪk] *adj (performance, behaviour)* irregular; *(weather)* muy variable; *(person)* caprichoso(a)
erroneous [ɪ'rəʊnɪəs] *adj* erróneo(a)
error ['erə(r)] *n* error *m*, equivocación *f*
erupt [ɪ'rʌpt] *vi* (**a**) *(volcano)* entrar en erupción; *(violence)* estallar (**b**) **his skin erupted in a rash** le salió una erupción
eruption [ɪ'rʌpʃən] *n* erupción *f*
escalate ['eskəleɪt] *vi (war)* intensificarse; *(prices)* aumentar; *(change)* convertirse (**into** en)
escalation [eskə'leɪʃən] *n (of war)* intensificación *f*, escalada *f*; *(of prices)* subida *f*
escalator ['eskəleɪtə(r)] *n* escalera mecánica

🖉 Note that the Spanish word **escalador** is a false friend and is never a translation for the English word **escalator**. In Spanish, **escalador** means "climber, mountaineer".

escalope ['eskəlɒp] *n* escalope *m*
escapade ['eskəpeɪd] *n* aventura *f*

🖉 Note that the Spanish word **escapada** is a false friend and is never a translation for the English word **escapade**. In Spanish, **escapada** means both "escape" and "quick trip".

escape [ɪ'skeɪp] **1** *n* huída *f*, fuga *f*; *(of gas)* escape *m*; **e. route** vía *f* de escape
2 *vi* escaparse
3 *vt* (**a**) *(avoid)* evitar, huir de; **to e. punishment** librarse del castigo (**b**) *Fig* **his name escapes me** no recuerdo su nombre
escapism [ɪ'skeɪpɪzəm] *n* evasión *f*
escort 1 *n* ['eskɔːt] (**a**) *(companion)* acompañante *mf* (**b**) *Mil* escolta *f*
2 *vt* [ɪ'skɔːt] (**a**) *(accompany)* acompañar (**b**) *(protect)* escoltar
Eskimo ['eskɪməʊ] *adj & n* esquimal *(mf)*
esoteric [esəʊ'terɪk] *adj* esotérico(a)
especial [ɪ'speʃəl] *adj* especial
especially [ɪ'speʃəlɪ] *adv* especialmente, sobre todo
espionage ['espɪənɑːʒ] *n* espionaje *m*
esplanade [esplə'neɪd] *n* paseo marítimo
espouse [ɪ'spaʊz] *vt Fml (cause)* abrazar, adoptar
espresso [e'spresəʊ] *n* **e. (coffee)** café *m* exprés
esquire [ɪ'skwaɪə(r)] *n Br* señor *m*; **Timothy Whiteman E.** Sr. Don Timothy Whiteman
essay ['eseɪ] *n Educ* redacción *f*
essence ['esəns] *n* esencia *f*; **in e.** esencialmente
essential [ɪ'senʃəl] **1** *adj* esencial, imprescindible
2 *n* necesidad básica; **the essentials** lo fundamental
essentially [ɪ'senʃəlɪ] *adv* esencialmente
establish [ɪ'stæblɪʃ] *vt* (**a**) *(found)* establecer; *(business)* montar (**b**) *Jur* **to e. a fact** probar un hecho; **to e. the truth** demostrar la verdad
established [ɪ'stæblɪʃt] *adj (person)* establecido(a); *(fact)* conocido(a)
establishment [ɪ'stæblɪʃmənt] *n* establecimiento *m*; **the E.** el sistema
estate [ɪ'steɪt] *n* (**a**) *(land)* finca *f*; *Br* **e.**

agent agente *mf* inmobiliario(a); *Br* **e. car** coche *m* modelo familiar (**b**) *(housing)* **e. zona** urbanizada (**c**) *(property)* bienes *mpl* (**d**) *(inheritance)* herencia *f*
esteem [ɪ'stiːm] **1** *n* **to hold sb in great e.** apreciar mucho a algn
2 *vt* estimar
esthetic [es'θetɪk] *adj US* estético(a)
estimate 1 *n* ['estɪmɪt] *(calculation)* cálculo *m*; *(likely cost of work)* presupuesto *m*; **rough e.** cálculo aproximado
2 *vt* ['estɪmeɪt] calcular; *Fig* pensar, creer
estimation [estɪ'meɪʃən] *n* (**a**) *(opinion)* juicio *m*, opinión *f* (**b**) *(esteem)* estima *f*
Estonia [e'stəʊnɪə] *n* Estonia
Estonian [e'stəʊnɪən] **1** *adj* estonio(a)
2 *n* (**a**) *(person)* estonio(a) *m,f* (**b**) *(language)* estonio *m*
estrange [ɪ'streɪndʒ] *vt* **to become estranged (from)** alejarse (de)
Estremadura [estreɪmə'dʊrə] *n* Extremadura
estuary ['estjʊərɪ] *n* estuario *m*
etching ['etʃɪŋ] *n* aguafuerte *m*
eternal [ɪ'tɜːnəl] *adj* eterno(a), incesante; **e. triangle** triángulo amoroso
eternity [ɪ'tɜːnɪtɪ] *n* eternidad *f*
ether ['iːθə(r)] *n* éter *m*
ethereal [ɪ'θɪərɪəl] *adj* etéreo(a)
ethical ['eθɪkəl] *adj* ético(a)
ethics ['eθɪks] *n* ética *f*
Ethiopia [iːθɪ'əʊpɪə] *n* Etiopía
ethnic ['eθnɪk] *adj* étnico(a)
ethos ['iːθɒs] *n* carácter distintivo
etiquette ['etɪket] *n* protocolo *m*, etiqueta *f*
etymology [etɪ'mɒlədʒɪ] *n* etimología *f*
EU [iː'juː] *n* (*abbr* **European Union**) UE *f*
eucalyptus [juːkə'lɪptəs] *n* eucalipto *m*
euphemism ['juːfɪmɪzəm] *n* eufemismo *m*
euphoria [juː'fɔːrɪə] *n* euforia *f*
euro ['jʊərəʊ] *n* (*pl* **euros**) *(European currency)* euro *m*
Eurocheque ['jʊərəʊtʃek] *n* eurocheque *m*
Eurocrat ['jʊərəʊkræt] *n* eurócrata *mf*
Euro-MP ['jʊərəʊempiː] *n* eurodiputado(a) *m,f*
Europe ['jʊərəp] *n* Europa
European [jʊərə'piːən] *adj & n* europeo(a) *(m,f)*; **E. Economic Community** Comunidad Económica Europea
Eurosceptic ['jʊərəʊskeptɪk] *n Br* euroescéptico(a) *m,f*
euthanasia [juːθə'neɪzɪə] *n* eutanasia *f*
evacuate [ɪ'vækjʊeɪt] *vt* evacuar

evacuation [ɪvækjʊ'eɪʃən] *n* evacuación *f*

evade [ɪ'veɪd] *vt* evadir

evaluate [ɪ'væljʊeɪt] *vt* evaluar

evaluation [ɪvæljʊ'eɪʃən] *n* evaluación *f*

evangelical [i:væn'dʒelɪkəl] *adj* evangélico(a)

evangelist [ɪ'vændʒɪlɪst] *n* evangelista *mf*

evaporate [ɪ'væpəreɪt] **1** *vt* evaporar; **evaporated milk** leche condensada sin endulzar
2 *vi* evaporarse; *Fig* desvanecerse

evasion [ɪ'veɪʒən] *n* (**a**) evasión *f* (**b**) *(evasive answer)* evasiva *f*

evasive [ɪ'veɪsɪv] *adj* evasivo(a)

eve [i:v] *n* víspera *f*; **on the e. of** en vísperas de

even ['i:vən] **1** *adj* (**a**) *(smooth)* liso(a); *(level)* llano(a)
(**b**) *(regular)* uniforme
(**c**) *(equally balanced)* igual; *Sport* **to be e.** ir empatados(as); **to get e. with sb** desquitarse con algn
(**d**) *(number)* par
(**e**) *(at the same level)* a nivel
(**f**) *(quantity)* exacto(a)
2 *adv* (**a**) incluso, hasta, aun; **e. now** incluso ahora; **e. so** aun así; **e. the children knew** hasta los niños lo sabían
(**b**) *(negative)* ni siquiera; **she can't e. write her name** ni siquiera sabe escribir su nombre; **without e. speaking** sin hablar siquiera
(**c**) *(before comparative)* aun, todavía; **e. worse** aun peor
(**d**) **e. as** mientras; **e. if** incluso si; **e. though** aunque
3 *vt* igualar

evening ['i:vnɪŋ] *n* (**a**) *(early)* tarde *f*; *(late)* noche *f*; **in the e.** por la tarde; **tomorrow e.** mañana por la tarde; **e. class** clase nocturna; **e. dress** *(for man)* traje *m* de etiqueta; *(for woman)* traje de noche; **e. paper** periódico vespertino (**b**) *(greeting)* **good e.!** *(early)* ¡buenas tardes!; *(late)* ¡buenas noches!

event [ɪ'vent] *n* (**a**) *(happening)* suceso *m*, acontecimiento *m* (**b**) *(case)* caso *m*; **at all events** en todo caso; **in the e. of fire** en caso de incendio (**c**) *Sport* prueba *f*

eventful [ɪ'ventfʊl] *adj* **an e. day** *(busy)* un día agitado; *(memorable)* un día memorable

eventual [ɪ'ventʃʊəl] *adj (ultimate)* final; *(resulting)* consiguiente

> ℓ Note that the Spanish word **eventual** is a false friend and is never a translation for the English word **eventual**. In Spanish, **eventual** means both "possible" and "temporary".

eventuality [ɪventʃʊ'ælɪtɪ] *n* eventualidad *f*

eventually [ɪ'ventʃʊəlɪ] *adv* finalmente

> ℓ Note that the Spanish word **eventualmente** is a false friend and is never a translation for the English word **eventually**. In Spanish, **eventualmente** means both "by chance" and "possibly".

ever ['evə(r)] *adv* (**a**) nunca, jamás; **stronger than e.** más fuerte que nunca (**b**) *(interrogative)* alguna vez; **have you e. been there?** ¿has estado allí alguna vez? (**c**) *(always)* siempre; **for e.** para siempre; **for e. and e.** para siempre jamás (**d**) *(emphasis)* **how e. did you manage it?** ¿cómo diablos lo conseguiste?; **why e. not?** ¿por qué no?; *Fam* **e. so expensive** tan carísimo; **e. such a lot of money** tantísimo dinero; **thank you e. so much** muchísimas gracias

evergreen ['evəgri:n] **1** *adj* de hoja perenne
2 *n* árbol *m*/planta *f* de hoja perenne

everlasting [evə'lɑ:stɪŋ] *adj* eterno(a)

evermore [evə'mɔ:(r)] *adv* **for e.** para siempre jamás

every ['evrɪ] *adj* (**a**) *(each)* cada; **e. now and then** de vez en cuando; **e. day** todos los días; **e. other day** cada dos días; **e. one of you** todos(as) vosotros(as); **e. citizen** todo ciudadano (**b**) **you had e. right to be angry** tenías toda la razón para estar enfadado

everybody ['evrɪbɒdɪ] *pron* todo el mundo, todos(as)

everyday ['evrɪdeɪ] *adj* diario(a), de todos los días; **an e. occurrence** un suceso cotidiano

everyone ['evrɪwʌn] *pron* todo el mundo, todos(as)

everyplace ['evrɪpleɪs] *adv US* = **everywhere**

everything ['evrɪθɪŋ] *pron* todo; **he eats e.** come de todo; **she means e. to me** ella lo es todo para mí

everywhere ['evrɪweə(r)] *adv* en todas partes, por todas partes

evict [ɪ'vɪkt] *vt* desahuciar

evidence ['evɪdəns] *n* (**a**) *(proof)* evidencia *f* (**b**) *Jur* testimonio *m*; **to give e.** prestar declaración (**c**) *(sign)* indicio *m*, señal *f*; **to be in e.** dejarse notar

evident ['evɪdənt] *adj* evidente, manifiesto(a)

evidently ['evɪdəntlɪ] *adv* evidentemente, al parecer

evil ['iːvəl] **1** *adj (wicked)* malo(a), malvado(a); *(harmful)* nocivo(a); *(unfortunate)* aciago(a)

2 *n* mal *m*

evocative [ɪ'vɒkətɪv] *adj* evocador(a)

evoke [ɪ'vəʊk] *vt* evocar

evolution [iːvə'luːʃən] *n* evolución *f*; *Biol* desarrollo *m*

evolve [ɪ'vɒlv] **1** *vi (species)* evolucionar; *(ideas)* desarrollarse

2 *vt* desarrollar

ewe [juː] *n* oveja *f*

ex [eks] *n* her ex su ex marido; his ex su ex mujer

ex- [eks] *pref* ex, antiguo(a); **ex-minister** ex ministro *m*

exacerbate [ɪg'zæsəbeɪt] *vt* exacerbar

exact [ɪg'zækt] **1** *adj (accurate)* exacto(a); *(definition)* preciso(a); **this e. spot** ese mismo lugar

2 *vt* exigir

exacting [ɪg'zæktɪŋ] *adj* exigente

exactly [ɪg'zæktlɪ] *adv* exactamente; precisamente; **e.!** ¡exacto!

exaggerate [ɪg'zædʒəreɪt] *vi & vt* exagerar

exaggeration [ɪgzædʒə'reɪʃən] *n* exageración *f*

exalt [ɪg'zɔːlt] *vt Fml* exaltar

exam [ɪg'zæm] *n Fam* examen *m*

examination [ɪgzæmɪ'neɪʃən] *n* (a) *Educ* examen *m*; **to sit an e.** hacer un examen (b) *Med* reconocimiento *m* (c) *Jur* interrogatorio *m*

examine [ɪg'zæmɪn] *vt Educ* examinar; *(customs)* registrar; *Med* hacer un reconocimiento médico a; *Jur* interrogar

examiner [ɪg'zæmɪnə(r)] *n* examinador(a) *m,f*

example [ɪg'zɑːmpəl] *n* ejemplo *m*; *(specimen)* ejemplar *m*; **for e.** por ejemplo

exasperate [ɪg'zɑːspəreɪt] *vt* exasperar

exasperation [ɪgzɑːspə'reɪʃən] *n* exasperación *f*

excavate ['ekskəveɪt] *vt* excavar

excavation [ekskə'veɪʃən] *n* excavación *f*

exceed [ek'siːd] *vt* exceder, sobrepasar

exceedingly [ek'siːdɪŋlɪ] *adv* extremadamente, sumamente

excel [ɪk'sel] **1** *vi* sobresalir

2 *vt* superar

excellency ['eksələnsɪ] *n* His E. Su Excelencia

excellent ['eksələnt] *adj* excelente

except [ɪk'sept] **1** *prep* excepto, salvo; **e. for the little ones** excepto los pequeños; **e. that ...** salvo que ...

2 *vt* exceptuar

exception [ɪk'sepʃən] *n* (a) excepción *f*; **with the e. of** a excepción de; **without e.** sin excepción (b) *(objection)* objeción *f*; **to take e. to sth** ofenderse por algo

exceptional [ɪk'sepʃənəl] *adj* excepcional

excerpt ['eksɜːpt] *n* extracto *m*

excess 1 *n* [ɪk'ses] exceso *m*

2 *adj* ['ekses] excedente; **e. baggage** exceso *m* de equipaje; **e. fare** suplemento *m*

excessive [ɪk'sesɪv] *adj* excesivo(a)

excessively [ɪk'sesɪvlɪ] *adv* excesivamente, en exceso

exchange [ɪks'tʃeɪndʒ] **1** *n* (a) cambio *m*; **e. of ideas** intercambio *m* de ideas; **in e. for** a cambio de (b) *Fin* **e. rate** tipo *m* de cambio (c) *(telephone)* **e.** central telefónica

2 *vt* (a) intercambiar; **to e. blows** golpearse (b) *(prisoners)* canjear

exchequer [ɪks'tʃekə(r)] *n Br* **the E.** Hacienda *f*; **Chancellor of the E.** Ministro *m* de Hacienda

excise ['eksaɪz] *n* impuesto *m* sobre el consumo; **e. duty** derechos *mpl* de aduana

excitable [ɪk'saɪtəbəl] *adj* excitable

excite [ɪk'saɪt] *vt (stimulate)* excitar; *(move)* emocionar; *(enthuse)* entusiasmar; *(arouse)* provocar

excitement [ɪk'saɪtmənt] *n (stimulation)* excitación *f*; *(emotion)* emoción *f*; *(commotion)* agitación *f*

exciting [ɪk'saɪtɪŋ] *adj* apasionante, emocionante

exclaim [ɪk'skleɪm] **1** *vi* exclamar

2 *vt* gritar

exclamation [eksklə'meɪʃən] *n* exclamación *f*; **e.** *Br* **mark** *or US* **point** signo *m* de admiración

exclude [ɪk'skluːd] *vt* excluir; *(from club)* no admitir

excluding [ɪk'skluːdɪŋ] *prep* excepto

exclusion [ɪk'skluːʒən] *n* exclusión *f*

exclusive [ɪk'skluːsɪv] **1** *adj* exclusivo(a); *(neighbourhood)* selecto(a); *(club)* cerrado(a)

2 *n Press* exclusiva *f*

exclusively [ɪk'skluːsɪvlɪ] *adv* exclusivamente

excommunicate [ekskə'mjuːnɪkeɪt] *vt* excomulgar

excrement ['ekskrɪmənt] *n* excremento *m*

excruciating [ɪk'skruːʃɪeɪtɪŋ] *adj* insoportable

excruciatingly [ɪk'skruːʃɪeɪtɪŋlɪ] *adv* horriblemente

excursion [ɪk'skɜːʃən] *n* excursión *f*

excusable [ɪk'skjuːzəbəl] *adj* perdonable

excuse 1 *vt* [ɪk'skjuːz] (**a**) perdonar, disculpar; **e. me!** *(to attract attention)* ¡perdón!, ¡oiga (por favor)!; *(when trying to get past)* con permiso; **may I be excused for a moment?** ¿puedo salir un momento? (**b**) *(exempt)* dispensar (**c**) *(justify)* justificar

　2 *n* [ɪk'skjuːs] excusa *f*; **to make an e.** dar excusas

ex-directory [eksdɪ'rektərɪ] *adj Br Tel* = que no se encuentra en la guía telefónica

execute ['eksɪkjuːt] *vt* (**a**) *(order)* cumplir; *(task)* realizar (**b**) *Jur* cumplir (**c**) *(person)* ejecutar

execution [eksɪ'kjuːʃən] *n* (**a**) *(of order)* cumplimiento *m*; *(of task)* realización *f* (**b**) *Jur* cumplimiento *m* (**c**) *(of person)* ejecución *f*

executioner [eksɪ'kjuːʃənə(r)] *n* verdugo *m*

executive [ɪg'zekjʊtɪv] **1** *adj* ejecutivo(a)
　2 *n* ejecutivo(a) *m,f*

executor [ɪg'zekjʊtə(r)] *n* albacea *m*

exemplary [ɪg'zemplərɪ] *adj* ejemplar

exemplify [ɪg'zemplɪfaɪ] *vt* ejemplificar

exempt [ɪg'zempt] **1** *vt* eximir (**from** de)
　2 *adj* exento(a); **e. from tax** libre de impuesto

exemption [ɪg'zempʃən] *n* exención *f*

exercise ['eksəsaɪz] **1** *n* ejercicio *m*; **e. book** cuaderno *m*
　2 *vt* (**a**) *(rights, duties)* ejercer (**b**) *(dog)* sacar de paseo
　3 *vi* hacer ejercicio

exert [ɪg'zɜːt] *vt (influence)* ejercer; **to e. oneself** esforzarse

exertion [ɪg'zɜːʃən] *n* esfuerzo *m*

exhale [eks'heɪl] **1** *vt (breathe)* exhalar
　2 *vi* espirar

exhaust [ɪg'zɔːst] **1** *vt* agotar
　2 *n (gas)* gases *mpl* de combustión; **e. pipe** tubo *m* de escape

exhausted [ɪg'zɔːstɪd] *adj* agotado(a)

exhaustion [ɪg'zɔːstʃən] *n* agotamiento *m*

exhaustive [ɪg'zɔːstɪv] *adj* exhaustivo(a)

exhibit [ɪg'zɪbɪt] **1** *n Art* objeto expuesto; *Jur* prueba *f* instrumental
　2 *vt Art* exponer; *(surprise etc)* mostrar

exhibition [eksɪ'bɪʃən] *n* exposición *f*

exhibitionist [eksɪ'bɪʃənɪst] *adj & n* exhibicionista *(mf)*

exhilarating [ɪg'zɪləreɪtɪŋ] *adj* estimulante

exhilaration [ɪgzɪlə'reɪʃən] *n* regocijo *m*

exhume [eks'hjuːm] *vt* exhumar

exile ['eksaɪl] **1** *n* (**a**) *(banishment)* exilio *m* (**b**) *(person)* exiliado(a) *m,f*
　2 *vt* exiliar

exist [ɪg'zɪst] *vi* existir; *(have little money)* malvivir

existence [ɪg'zɪstəns] *n* existencia *f*

existing [ɪg'zɪstɪŋ] *adj* existente, actual

exit ['eksɪt] **1** *n* (**a**) salida *f* (**b**) *Th* mutis *m*
　2 *vi Th* hacer mutis

> 🛈 Note that the Spanish word **éxito** is a false friend and is never a translation for the English word **exit**. In Spanish, **éxito** means "success".

exodus ['eksədəs] *n* éxodo *m*

exonerate [ɪg'zɒnəreɪt] *vt Fml* exonerar (**from** de)

exorbitant [ɪg'zɔːbɪtənt] *adj* exorbitante, desorbitado(a)

exotic [ɪg'zɒtɪk] *adj* exótico(a)

expand [ɪk'spænd] **1** *vt (enlarge)* ampliar; *(gas, metal)* dilatar
　2 *vi (grow)* ampliarse; *(metal)* dilatarse; *(become more friendly)* abrirse
　▸ **expand on** *vt insep* ampliar

expanse [ɪk'spæns] *n* extensión *f*

expansion [ɪk'spænʃən] *n (in size)* expansión *f*; *(of gas, metal)* dilatación *f*

expatriate 1 *adj & n* [eks'pætrɪt] expatriado(a) *(m,f)*
　2 *vt* [eks'pætrɪeɪt] expatriar

expect [ɪk'spekt] **1** *vt* (**a**) *(anticipate)* esperar; **I half-expected that to happen** suponía que iba a ocurrir (**b**) *(demand)* contar con (**c**) *(suppose)* suponer
　2 *vi Fam* **to be expecting** estar embarazada

expectancy [ɪk'spektənsɪ] *n* expectación *f*

expectant [ɪk'spektənt] *adj* ilusionado(a); **e. mother** mujer embarazada

expectation [ekspek'teɪʃən] *n* esperanza *f*; **contrary to e.** contrariamente a lo que se esperaba

expedient [ɪk'spiːdɪənt] **1** *adj* conveniente, oportuno(a)
　2 *n* expediente *m*, recurso *m*

expedition [ekspɪ'dɪʃən] *n* expedición *f*

expel [ɪk'spel] *vt* expulsar

expend [ɪk'spend] *vt* gastar

expendable [ɪk'spendəbəl] *adj* prescindible

expenditure [ɪk'spendɪtʃə(r)] *n* desembolso *m*

expense [ɪk'spens] *n* gasto *m*; **all expenses paid** con todos los gastos pagados; **to spare no e.** no escatimar gastos; *Fig* **at the e. of** a costa de; **e. account** cuenta *f* de gastos de representación

expensive [ɪk'spensɪv] *adj* caro(a), costoso(a)

experience [ɪk'spɪərɪəns] **1** *n* experiencia *f*
  2 *vt* (*sensation*) experimentar; (*difficulty, loss*) sufrir

experienced [ɪk'spɪərɪənst] *adj* experimentado(a)

experiment [ɪk'sperɪmənt] **1** *n* experimento *m*
  2 *vi* experimentar, hacer experimentos (**on** *or* **with** con)

experimental [ɪksperɪ'mentəl] *adj* experimental

expert ['ekspɜːt] **1** *adj* experto(a)
  2 *n* experto(a) *m,f*, especialista *mf*

expertise [ekspɜː'tiːz] *n* pericia *f*

expire [ɪk'spaɪə(r)] *vi* (**a**) (*die*) expirar; (*mandate*) terminar (**b**) *Com & Ins* vencer; (*ticket*) caducar

expiry [ɪk'spaɪərɪ] *n* vencimiento *m*; **e. date** fecha *f* de caducidad

explain [ɪk'spleɪn] **1** *vt* explicar; (*clarify*) aclarar; **to e. oneself** justificarse
  2 *vi* explicarse

explanation [eksplə'neɪʃən] *n* explicación *f*; (*clarification*) aclaración *f*

explanatory [ɪk'splænətərɪ] *adj* explicativo(a), aclaratorio(a)

explicit [ɪk'splɪsɪt] *adj* explícito(a)

explode [ɪk'spləʊd] **1** *vt* (**a**) (*bomb*) hacer explotar (**b**) *Fig* (*theory*) echar por tierra
  2 *vi* (*bomb*) estallar, explotar; *Fig* **to e. with** *or* **in anger** montar en cólera

exploit 1 *n* ['eksplɔɪt] proeza *f*, hazaña *f*
  2 *vt* [ek'splɔɪt] explotar

exploitation [eksplɔɪ'teɪʃən] *n* explotación *f*

exploratory [ek'splɒrətərɪ] *adj* exploratorio(a)

explore [ɪk'splɔː(r)] *vt* explorar

explorer [ɪk'splɔːrə(r)] *n* explorador(a) *m,f*

explosion [ɪk'spləʊʒən] *n* explosión *f*

explosive [ɪk'spləʊsɪv] **1** *adj* explosivo(a); **e. issue** asunto delicado
  2 *n* explosivo *m*

exponent [ɪk'spəʊnənt] *n* exponente *m*; (*supporter*) defensor(a) *m,f*

export 1 *vt* [ɪk'spɔːt] exportar
  2 *n* ['ekspɔːt] (**a**) (*trade*) exportación *f*

(**b**) (*commodity*) artículo *m* de exportación

exporter [ek'spɔːtə(r)] *n* exportador(a) *m,f*

expose [ɪk'spəʊz] *vt* (*uncover*) exponer; (*secret*) revelar; (*plot*) descubrir; **to e. oneself** exhibirse desnudo

exposed [ɪk'spəʊzd] *adj* expuesto(a)

exposure [ɪk'spəʊʒə(r)] *n* (**a**) (*to light, cold, heat*) exposición *f*; **to die of e.** morir de frío (**b**) *Phot* fotografía *f*; **e. meter** fotómetro *m* (**c**) (*of criminal*) descubrimiento *m*

expound [ɪk'spaʊnd] *vt* exponer

express [ɪk'spres] **1** *adj* (**a**) (*explicit*) expreso(a) (**b**) *Br* (*letter*) urgente; **e. train** expreso *m*
  2 *n Rail* expreso *m*
  3 *vt* expresar
  4 *adv* **send it e.** mándalo urgente

expression [ɪk'spreʃən] *n* expresión *f*

expressly [ɪk'spreslɪ] *adv Fml* expresamente

expressway [ɪk'spresweɪ] *n US* autopista *f*

expulsion [ɪk'spʌlʃən] *n* expulsión *f*

exquisite [ɪk'skwɪzɪt] *adj* exquisito(a)

extend [ɪk'stend] **1** *vt* (**a**) (*enlarge*) ampliar; (*lengthen*) alargar; (*increase*) aumentar; *Fig* **the prohibition was extended to cover cigarettes** extendieron la prohibición a los cigarrillos (**b**) (*give*) rendir, dar; **to e. a welcome to sb** recibir a algn (**c**) (*prolong*) prolongar
  2 *vi* (**a**) (*stretch*) extenderse (**b**) (*last*) prolongarse

extension [ɪk'stenʃən] *n* (**a**) extensión *f*; (*of time*) prórroga *f* (**b**) *Constr* anexo *m*

extensive [ɪk'stensɪv] *adj* extenso(a)

extent [ɪk'stent] *n* (**a**) (*area*) extensión *f* (**b**) **to some e.** hasta cierto punto; **to a large e.** en gran parte; **to a lesser e.** en menor grado; **to such an e.** hasta tal punto

extenuating [ɪk'stenjʊeɪtɪŋ] *adj* atenuante

exterior [ɪk'stɪərɪə(r)] **1** *adj* exterior, externo(a)
  2 *n* exterior *m*

exterminate [ɪk'stɜːmɪneɪt] *vt* exterminar

extermination [ɪkstɜːmɪ'neɪʃən] *n* exterminación *f*, exterminio *m*

external [ɪk'stɜːnəl] *adj* externo(a), exterior

extinct [ɪk'stɪŋkt] *adj* extinguido(a)

extinction [ɪk'stɪŋkʃən] *n* extinción *f*

extinguish [ɪk'stɪŋgwɪʃ] *vt* extinguir, apagar

extinguisher [ɪk'stɪŋgwɪʃə(r)] *n* extintor *m*

extol, *US* **extoll** [ɪk'stəʊl] *vt* ensalzar, alabar

extort [ɪk'stɔːt] *vt* arrancar; *(money)* sacar

extortion [ɪk'stɔːʃən] *n* extorsión *f*

extortionate [ɪk'stɔːʃənɪt] *adj* desorbitado(a)

extra ['ekstrə] **1** *adj* extra; *(spare)* de sobra; **e. time** *(in soccer match)* prórroga *f* **2** *adv* extra; **e. fine** extra fino **3** *n* *(additional charge)* suplemento *m*; *Cin* extra *mf*; *(newspaper)* edición *f* especial

extract 1 *n* ['ekstrækt] extracto *m* **2** *vt* [ɪk'strækt] *(tooth, information)* extraer; *(confession)* arrancar

extraction [ɪk'strækʃən] *n* extracción *f*

extracurricular [ekstrəkə'rɪkjʊlə(r)] *adj* extracurricular

extradite ['ekstrədaɪt] *vt* extraditar

extramarital [ekstrə'mærɪtəl] *adj* extramatrimonial

extramural [ekstrə'mjʊərəl] *adj* **e. course** = curso para estudiantes libres

extraordinary [ɪk'strɔːdənərɪ] *adj (meeting)* extraordinario(a); *(behaviour etc)* extraño(a)

extravagance [ɪk'strævəgəns] *n (with money)* derroche *m*; *(of behaviour)* extravagancia *f*

extravagant [ɪk'strævəgənt] *adj (wasteful)* derrochador(a); *(excessive)* exagerado(a); *(luxurious)* lujoso(a)

extreme [ɪk'striːm] **1** *adj* extremo(a); **an e. case** un caso excepcional; **to hold e. views** tener opiniones radicales **2** *n* extremo *m*; **in the e.** en sumo grado

extremely [ɪk'striːmlɪ] *adv* extremadamente; **I'm e. sorry** lo siento de veras

extremist [ɪk'striːmɪst] *n* extremista *mf*

extremity [ɪk'stremɪtɪ] *n* extremidad *f*

extricate ['ekstrɪkeɪt] *vt* sacar; **to e. oneself (from)** lograr salir (de)

extrovert ['ekstrəvɜːt] *adj & n* extrovertido(a) *(m,f)*

exuberant [ɪg'zjuːbərənt] *adj* exuberante

exude [ɪg'zjuːd] *vt & vi (moisture, sap)* exudar; *Fig* rebosar

exultant [ɪg'zʌltənt] *adj* jubiloso(a)

eye [aɪ] **1** *n* ojo *m*; *Fig* **I couldn't believe my eyes** no podía creerlo; *Fig* **in the eyes of** según; *Fig* **not to take one's eyes off sb/ sth** no quitar la vista de encima a algn/ algo; *Fig* **to catch sb's e.** llamar la atención a algn; *Fig* **to have an e. for** tener buen ojo para; *Fig* **to make eyes at sb** echar miraditas a algn; *Fig* **to see e. to e. with sb** estar de acuerdo con algn; *Fig* **to turn a blind e. (to)** hacer la vista gorda (a); *Fig* **with an e. to** con miras a; **to keep an e. on sb/sth** vigilar a algn/algo; **to keep an e. out for** estar pendiente de; **black e.** ojo morado; *US* **e. doctor** óptico(a) *m,f* **2** *vt* observar

eyeball ['aɪbɔːl] *n* globo *m* ocular

eyebrow ['aɪbraʊ] *n* ceja *f*

eyecatching ['aɪkætʃɪŋ] *adj* llamativo(a)

eye-drops ['aɪdrɒps] *npl (medicine)* colirio *m*

eyeglasses ['aɪglɑːsɪz] *npl US (spectacles)* gafas *fpl*, *Am* lentes *mpl*, anteojos *mpl*

eyelash ['aɪlæʃ] *n* pestaña *f*

eyelid ['aɪlɪd] *n* párpado *m*

eyeliner ['aɪlaɪnə(r)] *n* lápiz *m* de ojos

eye-opener ['aɪəʊpənə(r)] *n* revelación *f*, gran sorpresa *f*

eyeshadow ['aɪʃædəʊ] *n* sombra *f* de ojos

eyesight ['aɪsaɪt] *n* vista *f*

eyesore ['aɪsɔː(r)] *n* monstruosidad *f*

eyestrain ['aɪstreɪn] *n* vista cansada

eyewash ['aɪwɒʃ] *n* colirio *m*; *Fig* **it's all e.** eso son disparates

eyewitness ['aɪwɪtnɪs] *n* testigo *mf* ocular

F, f [ef] *n* (**a**) *(the letter)* F, f f (**b**) *Mus* F fa *m*
F [ef] *(abbr* **Fahrenheit**) F
fable ['feɪbəl] *n* fábula *f*
fabric ['fæbrɪk] *n* (**a**) *Tex* tejido *m* (**b**) *Constr* estructura *f*

> 🖉 Note that the Spanish word **fábrica** is a false friend and is never a translation for the English word **fabric**. In Spanish, **fábrica** means "factory".

fabricate ['fæbrɪkeɪt] *vt* fabricar
fabrication [fæbrɪ'keɪʃən] *n Fig* fabricación *f*
fabulous ['fæbjʊləs] *adj* fabuloso(a)
façade [fə'sɑːd, fæ'sɑːd] *n* fachada *f*
face [feɪs] **1** *n* (**a**) cara *f*, rostro *m*; **f. to f.** cara a cara; **I told him to his f.** se lo dije en la cara; **she slammed the door in my f.** me dió con la puerta en las narices; **to look sb in the f.** mirarle a algn a la cara; **f. cloth** paño *m*; **f. cream** crema *f* facial; **f. pack** mascarilla *f* facial
  (**b**) *(expression)* cara *f*, expresión *f*; **to pull a long f.** poner cara larga; **to pull faces** hacer muecas
  (**c**) *(surface)* superficie *f*; *(of card, coin)* cara *f*; *(of watch)* esfera *f*; **f. down/up** boca abajo/arriba; *Fig* **in the f. of danger** ante el peligro; **f. value** valor *m* nominal; **to take sth at f. value** entender algo sólo en su sentido literal
  (**d**) *(appearance)* aspecto *m*; **on the f. of it** a primera vista; **to lose f.** desprestigiarse; **to save f.** salvar las apariencias
  2 *vt* (**a**) *(look on to)* dar a; *(be opposite)* estar enfrente de
  (**b**) **to f. the wall/window** *(of person)* estar de cara a la pared/ventana
  (**c**) *(problem)* hacer frente a; **let's f. it** hay que reconocerlo; **to f. up to** hacer cara a
  (**d**) *(tolerate)* soportar, aguantar
  3 *vi* (**a**) *(show, film)* dar a; **to f. towards** mirar hacia; **f. this way** vuélvase de este lado
facelift ['feɪslɪft] *n Med* lifting *m*; *Fig* renovación *f*
facet ['fæsɪt] *n* faceta *f*
facetious [fə'siːʃəs] *adj* bromista

facial ['feɪʃəl] *adj* facial
facile ['fæsaɪl] *adj* superficial
facilitate [fə'sɪlɪteɪt] *vt* facilitar
facility [fə'sɪlɪtɪ] *n* (**a**) *(ease)* facilidad *f* (**b**) **facilities** *(means)* facilidades *fpl*; **credit facilities** facilidades de crédito (**c**) **facilities** *(rooms, equipment)* instalaciones *fpl*; **cooking facilities** derecho *m* a cocina
facing ['feɪsɪŋ] *adj* de enfrente
facsimile [fæk'sɪmɪlɪ] *n* (**a**) *(copy)* facsímil *m* (**b**) *(message)* telefax *m* (**c**) *(machine)* facsímil *m*
fact [fækt] *n* hecho *m*; **as a matter of f.** de hecho; **the f. that he confessed** el hecho de que confesara; **in f.** en realidad
fact-finding ['fæktfaɪndɪŋ] *adj* investigador(a)
faction ['fækʃən] *n (group)* facción *f*
factor ['fæktə(r)] *n* factor *m*
factory ['fæktərɪ] *n* fábrica *f*
factual ['fæktʃʊəl] *adj* **a f. error** un error de hecho
faculty ['fækəltɪ] *n* (**a**) facultad *f* (**b**) *US Univ* profesorado *m*, cuerpo *m* docente
fad [fæd] *n Fam (craze)* moda pasajera; *(whim)* capricho *m*
fade [feɪd] *vi (colour)* desteñirse; *(flower)* marchitarse; *(light)* apagarse
  ▸ **fade away** *vi* desvanecerse
  ▸ **fade in, fade out** *vt sep Cin & TV* fundir
faded ['feɪdɪd] *adj (colour)* desteñido(a); *(flower)* marchito(a)
fag [fæg] *n* (**a**) *Br Fam (cigarette)* pitillo *m* (**b**) *US very Fam (homosexual)* marica *m*
faggot ['fægət] *n* (**a**) *Br (meatball)* albóndiga *f* (**b**) *US very Fam (homosexual)* maricón *m*
fail [feɪl] **1** *n* (**a**) *Educ* suspenso *m* (**b**) **without f.** sin falta
  2 *vt* (**a**) **don't f. me** no me falles; **words f. me** no encuentro palabras (**b**) *(exam)* suspender (**c**) *(to be unable)* no lograr; **he failed to score** no logró marcar (**d**) *(neglect)* dejar de; **don't f. to come** no deje de venir
  3 *vi* (**a**) *(show, film)* fracasar; *(brakes)* fallar (**b**) *(business)* quebrar; *Educ* suspender (**c**) *(of health)* deteriorarse

failing ['feɪlɪŋ] **1** *n* (**a**) *(shortcoming)* defecto *m* (**b**) *(weakness)* punto *m* débil
2 *prep* a falta de
failure ['feɪljə(r)] *n* (**a**) fracaso *m* (**b**) *Com* quiebra *f* (**c**) *Educ* suspenso *m* (**d**) *(person)* fracasado(a) *m,f* (**e**) *(breakdown)* avería *f*; **brake f.** fallo *m* de los frenos; **power f.** apagón *m*; *Med* **heart f.** paro cardíaco (**f**) **her f. to answer** *(neglect)* el hecho de que no contestara
faint [feɪnt] **1** *adj* (**a**) *(sound)* débil; *(colour)* pálido(a); *(outline)* borroso(a); *(recollection)* vago(a); **I haven't the faintest idea** no tengo la más mínima idea (**b**) *(giddy)* mareado(a)
2 *n* desmayo *m*
3 *vi* desmayarse
faint-hearted [feɪnt'hɑːtɪd] *adj* temeroso(a)
fair¹ [feə(r)] **1** *adj* (**a**) *(impartial)* imparcial; *(just)* justo(a); **it's not f.** no hay derecho; *Fam* **f. enough!** ¡vale!; **f. trade** comercio justo (**b**) *(hair)* rubio(a) (**c**) *(weather)* bueno(a) (**d**) *(beautiful)* bello(a) (**e**) **a f. number** un buen número; **he has a f. chance** tiene bastantes probabilidades
2 *adv* **to play f.** jugar limpio
fair² [feə(r)] *n* feria *f*; **trade f.** feria de muestras
fairground ['feəɡraʊnd] *n* real *m* de la feria
fairly ['feəlɪ] *adv* (**a**) *(justly)* justamente (**b**) *(moderately)* bastante
fairness ['feənɪs] *n* justicia *f*, equidad *f*; **in all f.** para ser justo(a)
fairy ['feərɪ] *n* (**a**) hada *f*; **f. godmother** hada madrina; **f. tale** cuento *m* de hadas (**b**) *Fam Pej* marica *m*
fait accompli [feɪtə'kɒmpliː] *n Fml* hecho consumado
faith [feɪθ] *n* (**a**) *Rel* fe *f* (**b**) *(trust)* confianza *f*; **in good f.** de buena fe
faithful ['feɪθfʊl] **1** *adj* fiel
2 *npl* **the f.** los fieles
faithfully ['feɪθfʊlɪ] *adv* fielmente; **yours f.** *(in letter)* le saluda atentamente
fake [feɪk] **1** *adj* falso(a)
2 *n* (**a**) *(object)* falsificación *f* (**b**) *(person)* impostor(a) *m,f*
3 *vt* (**a**) *(forge)* falsificar (**b**) *(feign)* fingir
4 *vi* *(pretend)* fingir
falcon ['fɔːlkən] *n* halcón *m*
Falklands ['fɔːlkləndz] *npl* **the F.** las (Islas) Malvinas
fall [fɔːl] **1** *n* (**a**) caída *f* (**b**) *(of rock)* desprendimiento *m*; **f. of snow** nevada *f* (**c**) *(decrease)* baja *f* (**d**) *US* otoño *m* (**e**)

(usu pl) cascada *f*; **Niagara Falls** las cataratas del Niágara
2 *vi* *(pt* **fell**; *pp* **fallen**) (**a**) caer, caerse; **they f. into two categories** se dividen en dos categorías; *Fig* **night was falling** anochecía; *Fig* **to f. into line** aceptar las reglas; *Fig* **to f. short (of)** no alcanzar (**b**) *(in battle)* caer (**c**) *(temperature, prices)* bajar (**d**) **to f. asleep** dormirse; **to f. ill** caer enfermo(a); **to f. in love** enamorarse
▶**fall back** *vi* replegarse
▶**fall back on** *vt insep* echar mano a, recurrir a
▶**fall behind** *vi* *(in race)* quedarse atrás; **to f. behind with one's work** retrasarse en el trabajo
▶**fall down** *vi* (**a**) *(picture etc)* caerse (**b**) *(building)* derrumbarse (**c**) *(argument)* fallar
▶**fall for** *vt insep* (**a**) *(person)* enamorarse de (**b**) *(trick)* dejarse engañar por
▶**fall in** *vi* (**a**) *(roof)* desplomarse (**b**) *Mil* formar filas
▶**fall off** **1** *vi* (**a**) *(drop off)* caerse (**b**) *(part)* desprenderse (**c**) *(diminish)* disminuir
2 *vt insep* **to f. off sth** caerse de algo
▶**fall out** *vi* (**a**) *(hair)* caerse (**b**) *Mil* romper filas (**c**) *(quarrel)* pelearse
▶**fall over** *vi* caerse
▶**fall through** *vi* *(plan)* fracasar
fallacy ['fæləsɪ] *n* falacia *f*
fallen ['fɔːlən] *pp of* **fall**
fallible ['fælɪbəl] *adj* falible
fall-out ['fɔːlaʊt] *n* **(radioactive) f.** lluvia radioactiva; **f. shelter** refugio antiatómico
fallow ['fæləʊ] *adj Agr* en barbecho
false [fɔːls] *adj* falso(a); **f. step** paso *m* en falso; **f. start** salida nula; **f. teeth** dentadura postiza; **f. alarm** falsa alarma
falsehood ['fɔːlshʊd] *n* falsedad *f*
falsify ['fɔːlsɪfaɪ] *vt* *(records, accounts)* falsificar; *(story)* falsear
falter ['fɔːltə(r)] *vi* vacilar; *(voice)* fallar
faltering ['fɔːltərɪŋ] *adj* vacilante
fame [feɪm] *n* fama *f*
familiar [fə'mɪlɪə(r)] *adj* (**a**) *(common)* familiar, conocido(a); **his face is f.** su cara me suena (**b**) *(aware, knowledgeable)* enterado(a), al corriente (**with** de) (**c**) **to be on f. terms with sb** *(know well)* tener confianza con algn
familiarity [fəmɪlɪ'ærɪtɪ] *n* (**a**) *(awareness, knowledge)* familiaridad *f* (**with** con) (**b**) *(intimacy)* confianza *f*
familiarize [fə'mɪljəraɪz] *vt* (**a**) *(become acquainted)* familiarizar (**with** con); **to f.**

oneself with sth familiarizarse con algo (**b**) *(make widely known)* popularizar

family ['fæmɪlɪ] *n* familia *f*; **f. allowance** subsidio *m* familiar; **f. doctor** médico *m* de cabecera; **f. man** hombre hogareño; **f. planning** planificación *f* familiar; **f. tree** árbol genealógico

famine ['fæmɪn] *n* hambre *f*, escasez *f* de alimentos

famished ['fæmɪʃt] *adj Fam* muerto(a) de hambre

famous ['feɪməs] *adj* célebre, famoso(a) (**for** por)

famously ['feɪməslɪ] *adv Fam* estupendamente

fan [fæn] **1** *n* (**a**) abanico *m*; *Elec* ventilador *m* (**b**) *(person)* aficionado(a) *m,f*; *(of pop star etc)* fan *mf*; **f. club** club *m* de fans; **football f.** hincha *mf*
2 *vt* (**a**) abanicar (**b**) *(fire, passions)* avivar
▸ **fan out** *vi (troops)* desplegarse en abanico

fanatic [fə'nætɪk] *adj & n* fanático(a) *(m,f)*

fanatical [fə'nætɪkəl] *adj* fanático(a)

fanciful ['fænsɪfʊl] *adj* (**a**) *(person)* caprichoso(a) (**b**) *(idea)* fantástico(a)

fancy ['fænsɪ] **1** *adj* (**fancier, fanciest**) de fantasía; **f. dress** disfraz *m*; **f. dress ball** baile *m* de disfraces; **f. prices** precios *mpl* exorbitantes
2 *n* (**a**) *(imagination)* fantasía *f* (**b**) *(whim)* capricho *m*, antojo *m*; **to take a f. to sb** cogerle cariño a algn; **to take a f. to sth** encapricharse con algo; **what takes your f.?** ¿qué se le antoja?
3 *vt* (**a**) *(imagine)* imaginarse; *Fam* **f. that!** ¡fíjate!; *Fam* **f. seeing you here!** ¡qué casualidad verte por aquí! (**b**) *(like, want)* apetecer; **do you f. a drink?** ¿te apetece una copa?; *Fam* **I f. her** ella me gusta; *Fam* **to f. oneself** ser creído(a) *or* presumido(a)

fanfare ['fænfeə(r)] *n* fanfarria *f*

fang [fæŋ] *n* colmillo *m*

fanny ['fænɪ] *n* (**a**) *US Fam (buttocks)* culo *m*, *Am* cola *f* (**b**) *Br Vulg (vagina)* coño *m*, *Andes, RP* concha *f*

fantasize ['fæntəsaɪz] *vi* fantasear

fantastic [fæn'tæstɪk] *adj* fantástico(a)

fantasy ['fæntəsɪ] *n* fantasía *f*

far [fɑː(r)] (**farther** *or* **further, farthest** *or* **furthest**) **1** *adj* (**a**) *(distant)* lejano(a); **the F. East** el Lejano Oriente
(**b**) **at the f. end** en el otro extremo
(**c**) **the f. left** la extrema izquierda
2 *adv* (**a**) *(distant)* lejos; **f. and wide** por

todas partes; **f. off** a lo lejos; **farther back** más atrás; **farther north** más al norte; **how f. is it to Cardiff?** ¿cuánto hay de aquí a Cardiff?; *Fig* **as f. as I can** en lo que puedo; **as f. as I know** que yo sepa; **as f. as possible** en lo posible; *Fig* **f. from complaining, he seemed pleased** lejos de quejarse, parecía contento; *Fig* **he went so f. as to swear** llegó a jurar; *Fig* **I'm f. from satisfied** no estoy satisfecho(a) ni mucho menos; *Fig* **in so f. as ...** en la medida en que ...; *Fam* **to go too f.** pasarse de la raya
(**b**) *(in time)* **as f. back as the fifties** ya en los años cincuenta; **f. into the night** hasta muy entrada la noche; **so f.** hasta ahora
(**c**) *(much)* mucho; **by f.** con mucho; **f. cleverer** mucho más listo(a); **f. too much** demasiado; **you're not f. wrong** casi aciertas

faraway ['fɑːrəweɪ] *adj* lejano(a), remoto(a)

farce [fɑːs] *n* farsa *f*

farcical ['fɑːsɪkəl] *adj* absurdo(a)

fare [feə(r)] **1** *n* (**a**) *(ticket price)* tarifa *f*, precio *m* del billete; *(for boat)* pasaje *m*; **half f.** media tarifa (**b**) *(passenger)* pasajero(a) *m,f* (**c**) *(food)* comida *f*
2 *vi* **how did you f.?** ¿qué tal te fue?

farewell [feə'wel] **1** *interj Literary* ¡adiós!
2 *n* despedida *f*

far-fetched [fɑː'fetʃt] *adj* rebuscado(a)

farm [fɑːm] **1** *n* granja *f*, *Am* hacienda *f*
2 *vt* cultivar, labrar
▸ **farm out** *vt sep* encargar fuera

farmer ['fɑːmə(r)] *n* granjero(a) *m,f*, *Am* hacendado(a) *m,f*

farmhand ['fɑːmhænd] *n* peón *m*, labriego(a) *m,f*

farmhouse ['fɑːmhaʊs] *n* granja *f*, *Am* hacienda *f*

farming ['fɑːmɪŋ] **1** *n* (**a**) *(agriculture)* agricultura *f* (**b**) *(of land)* cultivo *m*, labranza *f*
2 *adj* agrícola

farmyard ['fɑːmjɑːd] *n* corral *m*

far-reaching [fɑː'riːtʃɪŋ] *adj* de gran alcance

far-sighted [fɑː'saɪtɪd] *adj* (**a**) *(person)* con visión de futuro (**b**) *(plan)* con miras al futuro

fart [fɑːt] *Fam* **1** *n* pedo *m*
2 *vi* echarse un pedo

farther ['fɑːðə(r)] *adj & adv comp of* **far**

farthest ['fɑːðɪst] *adj & adv superl of* **far**

fascinate ['fæsɪneɪt] *vt* fascinar

fascinating ['fæsɪneɪtɪŋ] *adj* fascinante

fascination [fæsɪ'neɪʃən] *n* fascinación *f*
fascism ['fæʃɪzəm] *n* fascismo *m*
fascist ['fæʃɪst] *adj & n* fascista *(mf)*
fashion ['fæʃən] **1** *n* (**a**) *(manner)* manera
f, modo *m*; **after a f.** más o menos (**b**)
(latest style) moda *f*; **to go/be out of f.**
pasar/no estar de moda; **f. designer** di-
señador(a) *m,f* de modas; **f. parade** desfile *m* de modelos
   2 *vt (metal)* labrar; *(clay)* formar
fashionable ['fæʃənəbəl] *adj* (**a**) de moda (**b**) *(area, hotel)* elegante
fast¹ [fɑːst] **1** *adj* (**a**) *(quick)* rápido(a) (**b**)
hard and f. rules reglas estrictas (**c**)
(clock) adelantado(a)
   2 *adv* (**a**) rápidamente, deprisa; **how f.?**
¿a qué velocidad? (**b**) *(securely)* firmemente; **f. asleep** profundamente dormi-
do(a)
fast² [fɑːst] **1** *n* ayuno *m*
   2 *vi* ayunar
fasten ['fɑːsən] **1** *vt* (**a**) *(attach)* sujetar;
(fix) fijar (**b**) *(belt)* abrochar; *(bag)* asegurar; *(shoelaces)* atar
   2 *vi (dress)* abrocharse
fastener ['fɑːsənə(r)] *n* cierre *m*
fastidious [fæ'stɪdɪəs] *adj* quisquillo-
so(a)
fat [fæt] **1** *adj* (**fatter, fattest**) (**a**) gor-
do(a) (**b**) *(book, file)* grueso(a) (**c**) *(meat)*
que tiene mucha grasa
   2 *n* grasa *f*; **cooking f.** manteca *f* de
cerdo
fatal ['feɪtəl] *adj* (**a**) *(accident, illness)*
mortal (**b**) *(ill-fated)* fatal, funesto(a) (**c**)
(fateful) fatídico(a)
fatalistic [feɪtə'lɪstɪk] *adj* fatalista
fatality [fə'tælɪtɪ] *n* víctima *f* mortal

> *Note that the Spanish word **fatalidad** is
> a false friend and is never a translation for
> the English word **fatality**. In Spanish, **fata-
> lidad** means both "fate" and "misfortune".*

fatally ['feɪtəlɪ] *adv* **f. wounded** mortalmente herido(a)
fate [feɪt] *n* destino *m*, suerte *f*
fateful ['feɪtfʊl] *adj* fatídico(a), acia-
go(a)
father ['fɑːðə(r)] *n* (**a**) padre *m*; **my f. and
mother** mis padres; **F. Christmas** Papá *m*
Noel (**b**) *Rel* padre *m*
father-in-law ['fɑːðərɪnlɔː] *n* suegro *m*
fatherland ['fɑːðəlænd] *n* patria *f*
fatherly ['fɑːðəlɪ] *adj* paternal
fathom ['fæðəm] **1** *n Naut* braza *f*
   2 *vt* comprender
▸ **fathom out** *vt sep* comprobar; **I can't f.
it out** no me lo explico

fatigue [fə'tiːg] *n* (**a**) *(tiredness)* fatiga *f*
(**b**) *Mil* faena *f*; **f. dress** traje *m* de faena
fatten ['fætən] *vt* engordar
fattening ['fætənɪŋ] *adj* que engorda
fatty ['fætɪ] **1** *adj (food)* graso(a); *Anat
(tissue)* adiposo(a)
   2 *n Fam (person)* gordinflón(ona) *m,f*
fatuous ['fætjʊəs] *adj* necio(a)
faucet ['fɔːsɪt] *n US* grifo *m*, *Chile, Méx*
llave *f*, *RP* canilla *f*
fault [fɔːlt] **1** *n* (**a**) *(defect)* defecto *m* (**b**)
(in merchandise) desperfecto *m*; **to find f.
with** poner reparos a (**c**) *(blame)* culpa *f*;
to be at f. tener la culpa (**d**) *(mistake)*
error *m* (**e**) *Geol* falla *f* (**f**) *(in tennis)* falta *f*
   2 *vt* criticar
faultless ['fɔːltlɪs] *adj* intachable
faulty ['fɔːltɪ] *adj* defectuoso(a)
fauna ['fɔːnə] *n* fauna *f*
faux pas [fəʊ'pɑː] *n (pl* **faux pas**) *Fml
(mistake)* paso *m* en falso; *(blunder)* metedura *f* de pata
favour, *US* **favor** ['feɪvə(r)] **1** *n* (**a**) favor
m; **in f. of** a favor de; **to be in f. with sb**
gozar del favor de algn; **to ask sb a f.**
pedirle un favor a algn (**b**) **1–0 in our f.**
(advantage) 1-0 a favor nuestro
   2 *vt* (**a**) *(person)* favorecer a (**b**) *(approve)* estar a favor de
favourable ['feɪvərəbəl] *adj* favorable
favourite ['feɪvərɪt] *adj & n* favorito(a)
(m,f)
favouritism ['feɪvərɪtɪzəm] *n* favoritismo
m
fawn¹ [fɔːn] **1** *adj* (de) color café claro
   2 *n* (**a**) *Zool* cervato *m* (**b**) color *m* café
claro
fawn² [fɔːn] *vi* adular (**on** a)
fax [fæks] **1** *n (machine, message)* fax *m*; **f.
modem** modem *m* fax
   2 *vt* mandar por fax
fear [fɪə(r)] **1** *n* miedo *m*, temor *m*; **for f. of**
por temor a; *Fam* **no f.!** ¡ni pensarlo!
   2 *vt* temer; **I f. it's too late** me temo que
ya es tarde
   3 *vi* temer (**for** por)
fearful ['fɪəfʊl] *adj* (**a**) *(person)* temero-
so(a) (**b**) *(frightening)* espantoso(a)
fearless ['fɪəlɪs] *adj* intrépido(a)
feasibility [fiːzə'bɪlɪtɪ] *n* viabilidad *f*
feasible ['fiːzəbəl] *adj (practicable)* factible; *(possible)* viable
feast [fiːst] *n* (**a**) banquete *m*; *Fam* comilona *f* (**b**) *Rel* **f. day** fiesta *f* de guardar
feat [fiːt] *n* hazaña *f*
feather ['feðə(r)] **1** *n* pluma *f*; **f. duster**
plumero *m*
   2 *vt Fam* **to f. one's nest** hacer su agosto

feature [ˈfiːtʃə(r)] **1** n (**a**) (of face) rasgo m, facción f (**b**) (characteristic) característica f (**c**) **f. film** largometraje m (**d**) Press crónica f especial

2 vt (**a**) poner de relieve (**b**) Cin tener como protagonista a

3 vi figurar

February [ˈfebrʊərɪ] n febrero m

fed [fed] **1** adj Fam **f. up (with)** harto(a) (de)

2 pt & pp of **feed**

federal [ˈfedərəl] adj federal

federation [fedəˈreɪʃən] n federación f

fee [fiː] n (of lawyer, doctor) honorarios mpl; Ftb **transfer f.** prima f de traslado; Univ **tuition fees** derechos mpl de matrícula

feeble [ˈfiːbəl] adj débil

feed [fiːd] **1** vt (pt & pp **fed**) (**a**) (give food to) dar de comer a; Fig (fire) alimentar; **to f. a baby** (breast-feed) amamantar a un bebé; (with bottle) dar el biberón a un bebé (**b**) Elec alimentar (**c**) (insert) introducir

2 vi (cows, sheep) pacer; **to f. on sth** (person) comer algo

3 n (**a**) (food) comida f; **cattle f.** pienso m (**b**) Tech alimentación f

▸ **feed up** vt sep cebar

feedback [ˈfiːdbæk] n (**a**) Tech feedback m (**b**) Fig reacción f

feeder [ˈfiːdə(r)] n Tech alimentador m

feeding [ˈfiːdɪŋ] n **f. bottle** biberón m

feel [fiːl] **1** vi (pt & pp **felt**) (**a**) (emotion, sensation) sentir; **how do you f.?** ¿qué tal te encuentras?; **I f. bad about it** me da pena; **I f. (sorry) for him** le compadezco; **to f. happy/uncomfortable** sentirse feliz/incómodo; **to f. cold/sleepy** tener frío/sueño; Fam **to f. up to (doing) sth** sentirse con ánimos para hacer algo

(**b**) (seem) **your hand feels cold** tienes la mano fría; **it feels like summer** parece verano

(**c**) (opinion) opinar; **I f. sure that ...** estoy seguro(a) de que ...

(**d**) **I f. like an ice cream** me apetece un helado; **to f. like doing sth** tener ganas de hacer algo

2 vt (**a**) (touch) tocar

(**b**) **she feels a failure** se siente inútil

(**c**) (notice, be aware of) notar

3 n (**a**) (touch, sensation) tacto m; Fig **to get the f. for sth** cogerle el truco a algo

(**b**) (atmosphere) ambiente m

▸ **feel for** vt insep (**a**) (search for) buscar (**b**) (have sympathy for) compadecer

feeler [ˈfiːlə(r)] n (of insect) antena f; Fig **to put one's feelers out** tantear el terreno

feeling [ˈfiːlɪŋ] **1** n (**a**) (emotion) sentimiento m; **ill f.** rencor m (**b**) (compassion) compasión f (**c**) **I had the f. that ...** (impression) tuve la impresión de que ... (**d**) (sensitivity) sensibilidad f (**e**) (opinion) opinión f; **to express one's feelings** expresar sus opiniones

2 adj sensible, compasivo(a)

feet [fiːt] pl of **foot**

feign [feɪn] vt fingir

feint [feɪnt] Sport **1** n finta f

2 vi fintar

fell¹ [fel] pt of **fall**

fell² [fel] vt (trees) talar; Fig (enemy) derribar

fellow [ˈfeləʊ] n (**a**) (companion) compañero(a) m,f; **f. citizen** conciudadano(a) m,f; **f. countryman/countrywoman** compatriota mf; **f. men** prójimos mpl; **f. passenger/student** compañero(a) m,f de viaje/estudios (**b**) Fam (chap) tipo m, tío m (**c**) (of society) socio(a) m,f

fellowship [ˈfeləʊʃɪp] n (**a**) (comradeship) camaradería f (**b**) Univ beca f de investigación

felony [ˈfelənɪ] n crimen m, delito m mayor

felt¹ [felt] pt & pp of **feel**

felt² [felt] n Tex fieltro m

felt-tip(ped) [ˈfelttɪp(t)] adj **f. pen** rotulador m

female [ˈfiːmeɪl] **1** adj (**a**) Zool hembra (**b**) femenino(a)

2 n (**a**) Zool hembra f (**b**) (woman) mujer f; (girl) chica f

feminine [ˈfemɪnɪn] adj femenino(a)

feminism [ˈfemɪnɪzəm] n feminismo m

feminist [ˈfemɪnɪst] adj & n feminista (mf)

fence [fens] **1** n cerca f, valla f; Fig **to sit on the f.** ver los toros desde la barrera

2 vi Sport practicar la esgrima

▸ **fence in** vt sep meter en un cercado

fencing [ˈfensɪŋ] n Sport esgrima f

fend [fend] vi **to f. for oneself** valerse por sí mismo

▸ **fend off** vt sep (blow) parar; (question) rehuir; (attack) rechazar

fender [ˈfendə(r)] n (**a**) (fireplace) pantalla f (**b**) US Aut guardabarros mpl (**c**) Naut defensa f

ferment 1 n [ˈfɜːment] Fig **in a state of f.** agitado(a)

2 vt & vi [fəˈment] fermentar

fern [fɜːn] n helecho m

ferocious [fəˈrəʊʃəs] adj feroz

ferocity [fəˈrɒsɪtɪ] n ferocidad f

ferret ['ferɪt] **1** n hurón m
  2 vi huronear, husmear
  ▸ **ferret out** vt sep descubrir
ferry ['ferɪ] **1** n (**a**) (small) barca f de
  pasaje (**b**) (large, for cars) transbordador
  m, ferry m
  2 vt transportar
fertile ['fɜːtaɪl] adj fértil
fertility [fə'tɪlɪtɪ] n (of soil) fertilidad f
fertilize ['fɜːtɪlaɪz] vt (**a**) (soil) abonar
  (**b**) (egg) fecundar
fertilizer ['fɜːtɪlaɪzə(r)] n abono m
fervent ['fɜːvənt] adj ferviente
fervour, US **fervor** ['fɜːvə(r)] n fervor m
fester ['festə(r)] vi supurar
festival ['festɪvəl] n (event) festival m;
  (celebration) fiesta f
festive ['festɪv] adj festivo(a); **the f. season** las fiestas de Navidad
festivity [fe'stɪvɪtɪ] n **the festivities** las
  fiestas
festoon [fe'stuːn] vt adornar
fetch [fetʃ] vt (**a**) (go for) ir a buscar (**b**)
  (bring) traer (**c**) **how much did it f.?** (sell
  for) ¿por cuánto se vendió?
fetching ['fetʃɪŋ] adj atractivo(a)
fete [feɪt] **1** n fiesta f
  2 vt festejar
fetish ['fetɪʃ, 'fiːtɪʃ] n fetiche m
fetus ['fiːtəs] n US = **foetus**
feud [fjuːd] **1** n enemistad duradera
  2 vi pelear
feudal ['fjuːdəl] adj feudal
fever ['fiːvə(r)] n fiebre f
feverish ['fiːvərɪʃ] adj febril
few [fjuː] **1** adj (**a**) (not many) pocos(as);
  as f. as solamente (**b**) (some) algu-
  nos(as), unos(as) cuantos(as); **a f. books**
  unos or algunos libros; **she has fewer
  books than I thought** tiene menos libros
  de lo que pensaba; **for the past f. years**
  durante estos últimos años; **in the next f.
  days** dentro de unos días; **quite a f.**
  bastantes
  2 pron (**a**) (not many) pocos(as); **there
  are too f.** no hay suficientes; **the fewer
  the better** cuantos menos mejor (**b**) **a
  f.** (some) algunos(as), unos(as) cuan-
  tos(as); **the chosen f.** los elegidos; **who
  has the fewest?** ¿quién tiene menos?
fiancé [fɪ'ɒnseɪ] n prometido m
fiancée [fɪ'ɒnseɪ] n prometida f
fiasco [fɪ'æskəʊ] n fiasco m
fib [fɪb] Fam **1** n trola f
  2 vi contar trolas
fibre, US **fiber** ['faɪbə(r)] n fibra f
fibreglass, US **fiberglass** ['faɪbəglɑːs] n
  fibra f de vidrio

fickle ['fɪkəl] adj inconstante, voluble
fiction ['fɪkʃən] n ficción f
fictional ['fɪkʃənəl] adj (**a**) Lit noveles-
  co(a) (**b**) (imaginative) ficticio(a)
fictitious [fɪk'tɪʃəs] adj ficticio(a)
fiddle ['fɪdəl] Fam **1** n (**a**) Mus violín m
  (**b**) (shady deal) trampa f
  2 vt estafar; (accounts) falsificar
  3 vi juguetear (**with** con)
  ▸ **fiddle about** vi perder tiempo
fiddly ['fɪdlɪ] adj Fam laborioso(a)
fidelity [fɪ'delətɪ] n fidelidad f
fidget ['fɪdʒɪt] vi (**a**) moverse; **stop fidgeting!** ¡estáte quieto! (**b**) jugar (**with**
  con)
field [fiːld] **1** n (**a**) campo m; **f. glasses**
  gemelos mpl; **f. marshal** mariscal m de
  campo (**b**) Geol & Min yacimiento m (**c**) **f.
  trip** viaje m de estudios; **f. work** trabajo m
  de campo
  2 vt Sport (**a**) (ball) parar y devolver (**b**)
  (team) presentar
fiend [fiːnd] n demonio m; Fam (fanatic)
  fanático(a) m,f
fiendish ['fiːndɪʃ] adj Fam diabólico(a)
fierce [fɪəs] adj (animal) feroz; (argument) acalorado(a); (heat, competition)
  intenso(a); (wind) violento(a)
fiery ['faɪərɪ] adj (temper) fogoso(a);
  (speech) acalorado(a); (colour) encendi-
  do(a)
fifteen [fɪf'tiːn] adj & n quince (m inv)
fifteenth [fɪf'tiːnθ] **1** adj & n decimo-
  quinto(a) (m,f)
  2 n (fraction) quinzavo m
fifth [fɪfθ] **1** adj & n quinto(a) (m,f)
  2 n (fraction) quinto m
fifty ['fɪftɪ] adj & n cincuenta (m inv)
fifty-fifty ['fɪftɪ'fɪftɪ] Fam **1** adj **a f.
chance** una probabilidad del cincuenta
  por ciento
  2 adv **to go f.** ir a medias
fig¹ [fɪg] n (fruit) higo m
fig² [fɪg] (abbr **figure**) fig
fight [faɪt] **1** vt (pt & pp **fought**) (**a**)
  pelear(se) con, luchar con; (of boxer)
  enfrentarse a, luchar con; (of bullfighter)
  lidiar; Fig (corruption) combatir (**b**)
  (battle) librar; (war) hacer (**c**) (decision)
  recurrir contra
  2 vi (**a**) pelear(se), luchar (**b**) (quarrel)
  reñir; **to f. over sth** disputarse la posesión de algo (**c**) Fig (struggle) luchar (**for/
  against** por/contra)
  3 n (**a**) pelea f, lucha f; (in boxing)
  combate m (**b**) (quarrel) riña f (**c**) Fig
  (struggle) lucha f (**d**) (spirit) combativi-
  dad f

▸ **fight back 1** *vt sep (tears)* contener
2 *vi* contraatacar
▸ **fight off** *vt sep* (**a**) *(attack)* rechazar (**b**) *(illness)* cortar
▸ **fight out** *vt sep* discutir
fighter ['faɪtə(r)] *n* (**a**) *(person)* combatiente *mf*; *(in boxing)* púgil *m* (**b**) *Fig* luchador(a) *m,f*; **f. (plane)** (avión *m* de) caza *m*; **f. bomber** cazabombardero *m*
fighting ['faɪtɪŋ] **1** *adj* **he's got a f. chance** tiene verdaderas posibilidades
2 *n* lucha *f*
figment ['fɪgmənt] *n* **it's a f. of your imagination** es un producto de tu imaginación
figurative ['fɪgərətɪv] *adj* figurado(a)
figure ['fɪgə(r), *US* 'fɪgjər] **1** *n* (**a**) *(form, outline)* forma *f*, silueta *f* (**b**) *(shape, statue, character)* figura *f*; **she has a good f.** tiene buen tipo; *Br* **f. of eight**, *US* **f. eight** ocho *m* (**c**) *(in book)* dibujo *m* (**d**) **f. of speech** figura retórica (**e**) *Math* cifra *f*
2 *vt US Fam* imaginarse
3 *vi* (**a**) *(appear)* figurar (**b**) *US Fam* **that figures** eso tiene sentido
▸ **figure out** *vt sep Fam* comprender; **I can't f. it out** no me lo explico
figurehead ['fɪgəhed] *n Fig* figura decorativa
filament ['fɪləmənt] *n* filamento *m*
filch [fɪltʃ] *vt Fam* mangar, birlar
file [faɪl] **1** *n* (**a**) *(tool)* lima *f* (**b**) *(folder)* carpeta *f* (**c**) *(archive, of computer)* archivo *m*; **on f.** archivado(a) (**d**) *(line)* fila *f*; **in single f.** en fila india
2 *vt* (**a**) *(smooth)* limar (**b**) *(put away)* archivar
3 *vi* **to f. past** desfilar
filing ['faɪlɪŋ] *n* clasificación *f*; **f. cabinet** archivador *m*; *(for cards)* fichero *m*
Filipino [fɪlɪ'piːnəʊ] *n* filipino(a) *m,f*
fill [fɪl] **1** *vt* (**a**) *(space, time)* llenar (**with** de) (**b**) *(post, requirements)* cubrir (**c**) *Culin* rellenar
2 *vi* llenarse (**with** de)
3 *n* **to eat one's f.** comer hasta hartarse
▸ **fill in 1** *vt sep* (**a**) *(space, form)* rellenar (**b**) *Fam (inform)* poner al corriente (**on** de) (**c**) *(time)* pasar
2 *vi* **to f. in for sb** sustituir a algn
▸ **fill out 1** *vt sep US (form)* llenar
2 *vi Fam* engordar
▸ **fill up 1** *vt sep* llenar hasta arriba; *Fam Aut* **f. her up!** ¡llénelo!
2 *vi* llenarse
fillet ['fɪlɪt] *n* filete *m*; **f. steak** filete *m*
filling ['fɪlɪŋ] **1** *adj* que llena mucho
2 *n* (**a**) *(stuffing)* relleno *m* (**b**) *(in tooth)*

empaste *m* (**c**) *Br* **f. station** gasolinera *f*, estación *f* de servicio, *Andes, Ven* bomba *f*, *Méx* gasolinería *f*, *Perú* grifo *m*
fillip ['fɪlɪp] *n Fam* estímulo *m*
film [fɪlm] **1** *n* (**a**) *Cin & Phot* película *f*; **f. star** estrella *f* de cine (**b**) *(layer)* capa *f*
2 *vt Cin* filmar
3 *vi Cin* rodar
film-strip ['fɪlmstrɪp] *n* cortometraje *m*
filter ['fɪltə(r)] **1** *n* filtro *m*; *Aut* **f. lane** carril *m* de acceso
2 *vt* filtrar
3 *vi Aut* **to f. to the right** girar a la derecha
▸ **filter through** *vi Fig* filtrarse (**to** a)
filter-tip ['fɪltətɪp] *n (cigarette)* cigarrillo *m* con filtro
filth [fɪlθ] *n (dirt)* porquería *f*; *Fig* porquerías *fpl*
filthy ['fɪlθɪ] *adj* (**filthier, filthiest**) (**a**) *(dirty)* asqueroso(a) (**b**) *(obscene)* obsceno(a)
fin [fɪn] *n Zool & Av* aleta *f*
final ['faɪnəl] **1** *adj* (**a**) *(last)* último(a), final (**b**) *(definitive)* definitivo(a)
2 *n* (**a**) *Sport* final *f* (**b**) *Univ* **finals** exámenes *mpl* de fin de carrera
finale [fɪ'nɑːlɪ] *n* final *m*
finalist ['faɪnəlɪst] *n* finalista *mf*
finalize ['faɪnəlaɪz] *vt* ultimar; *(date)* fijar
finally ['faɪnəlɪ] *adv (lastly)* por último; *(at last)* por fin
finance ['faɪnæns, fɪ'næns] **1** *n* (**a**) finanzas *fpl* (**b**) **finances** fondos *mpl*
2 *vt* financiar
financial [faɪ'nænʃəl, fɪ'nænʃəl] *adj* financiero(a); **f. crisis** crisis económica; **f. year** año económico
financier [faɪ'nænsɪə(r), fɪ'nænsɪə(r)] *n* financiero(a) *m,f*
finch [fɪntʃ] *n* pinzón *m*
find [faɪnd] **1** *vt* (*pt & pp* **found**) (**a**) *(locate)* encontrar (**b**) *(think)* encontrar (**c**) **this found its way into my bag** esto vino a parar a mi bolso (**d**) *(discover)* descubrir; **it has been found that ...** se ha comprobado que ... (**e**) *Jur* **to f. sb guilty/not guilty** declarar culpable/inocente a algn (**f**) **I can't f. the courage to tell him** no tengo valor para decírselo; **I found it impossible to get away** me resultó imposible irme
2 *n* hallazgo *m*
▸ **find out 1** *vt sep* (**a**) *(inquire)* averiguar (**b**) *(discover)* descubrir
2 *vi* (**a**) **to f. out about sth** informarse sobre algo (**b**) *(discover)* enterarse
findings ['faɪndɪŋz] *npl* conclusiones *fpl*

fine¹ [faɪn] **1** *n* multa *f*
2 *vt* multar

fine² [faɪn] **1** *adj* (**a**) *(delicate etc)* fino(a)
(**b**) *(subtle)* sutil (**c**) *(excellent)* excelente
(**d**) *(weather)* bueno(a); **it was f.** hacía
buen tiempo (**e**) **the f. arts** las bellas
artes (**f**) *(all right)* bien
2 *adv Fam* muy bien
3 *interj* ¡vale!

finely ['faɪnlɪ] *adv* (**a**) finamente; **f.
chopped** picado fino (**b**) **f. tuned** a
punto

finery ['faɪnərɪ] *n* galas *fpl*

finesse [fɪ'nes] *n* *(delicacy)* finura *f*;
(cunning) astucia *f*; *(tact)* sutileza *f*

finger ['fɪŋgə(r)] **1** *n* dedo *m* (de la mano);
Fam **to keep one's fingers crossed** esperar que todo salga bien; *Fam* **you've put
your f. on it** has dado en el clavo; **middle
f.** dedo corazón
2 *vt* tocar; *Pej* manosear

fingernail ['fɪŋgəneɪl] *n* uña *f*

fingerprint ['fɪŋgəprɪnt] *n* huella *f* dactilar

fingertip ['fɪŋgətɪp] *n* punta *f* or yema *f*
del dedo

finicky ['fɪnɪkɪ] *adj* *(person)* quisquillo-
so(a)

finish ['fɪnɪʃ] **1** *n* (**a**) fin *m*; *(of race)*
llegada *f* (**b**) *(surface)* acabado *m*
2 *vt* (**a**) *(complete)* acabar, terminar; **to f.
doing sth** terminar de hacer algo (**b**) *(use
up)* agotar
3 *vi* acabar, terminar; **to f. second** quedar el segundo
► **finish off** *vt sep* (**a**) *(complete)* terminar
completamente (**b**) *Fam (kill)* rematar
► **finish up 1** *vt sep* acabar, agotar
2 *vi* **to f. up in jail** ir a parar a la cárcel

finished ['fɪnɪʃt] *adj* (**a**) *(product)* aca-
bado(a) (**b**) *Fam (exhausted)* rendido(a)

finishing ['fɪnɪʃɪŋ] *adj* **to put the f.
touch(es) to sth** darle los últimos toques
a algo; **f. line** (línea *f* de) meta *f*; **f. school**
= escuela privada de modales para se-
ñoritas

finite ['faɪnaɪt] *adj* finito(a); *(verb)* conju-
gable

Finland ['fɪnlənd] *n* Finlandia

Finn [fɪn] *n* finlandés(esa) *m,f*

Finnish ['fɪnɪʃ] **1** *adj* finlandés(esa)
2 *n (language)* finlandés *m*

fir [fɜː(r)] *n* abeto *m*

fire ['faɪə(r)] **1** *n* (**a**) fuego *m* (**b**) *(accident
etc)* incendio *m*; **to be on f.** estar en
llamas; **to catch f.** incendiarse; **f. alarm**
alarma *f* de incendios; *Br* **f. brigade,** *US* **f.
department** (cuerpo *m* de) bomberos

mpl; **f. engine** coche *m* de bomberos; **f.
escape** escalera *f* de incendios; **f. exit**
salida *f* de emergencia; **f. extinguisher**
extintor *m*; **f. fighting** extinción *f* de
incendios; **f. station** parque *m* de bomberos (**c**) *(heater)* estufa *f* (**d**) *Mil* fuego *m*;
to open f. abrir fuego; *Fig* **to come under
f.** ser el blanco de las críticas
2 *vt* (**a**) *(gun)* disparar (**at** a); *(rocket)*
lanzar; *Fig* **to f. questions at sb** bombardear a algn a preguntas (**b**) *Fam (dismiss)*
despedir
3 *vi (shoot)* disparar (**at** sobre)

firearm ['faɪərɑːm] *n* arma *f* de fuego

fire-fighter ['faɪəfaɪtə(r)] *n US* bombero
m

fireman ['faɪəmən] *n* bombero *m*

fireplace ['faɪəpleɪs] *n* chimenea *f*;
(hearth) hogar *m*

fireside ['faɪəsaɪd] *n* hogar *m*; **by the f.** al
calor de la lumbre

firewood ['faɪəwʊd] *n* leña *f*

fireworks ['faɪəwɜːks] *npl* fuegos *mpl*
artificiales

firing ['faɪərɪŋ] *n Mil* tiroteo *m*; **f. line**
línea *f* de fuego; **f. squad** pelotón *m* de
fusilamiento

firm [fɜːm] **1** *adj* firme; **to be f. with sb**
(strict) tratar a algn con firmeza
2 *n Com* empresa *f*, firma *f*

firmly ['fɜːmlɪ] *adv* firmemente

firmness ['fɜːmnɪs] *n* firmeza *f*

first [fɜːst] **1** *adj* primero(a); *(before masculine singular noun)* primer; **Charles the
F.** Carlos Primero; **for the f. time** por
primera vez; **in the f. place** en primer
lugar; **f. aid** primeros auxilios; **f. aid box**
botiquín *m*; **f. floor** primer piso, *US* planta baja; **f. name** nombre *m* de pila
2 *adv (before anything else)* primero; **f.
and foremost** ante todo; **f. of all** en
primer lugar
3 *n* (**a**) **the f.** el primero/la primera; **the
f. of April** el uno or el primero de abril (**b**)
at f. al principio; **from the (very) f.** desde
el principio (**c**) *Aut* primera *f* (**d**) *Univ* **to
get a f.** sacar un sobresaliente

first-class ['fɜːst'klɑːs] **1** *adj* de primera
clase
2 *adv* **to travel f.** viajar en primera

first-hand ['fɜːst'hænd] *adv & adj* de
primera mano

firstly ['fɜːstlɪ] *adv* en primer lugar

first-rate ['fɜːstreɪt] *adj* de primera

fiscal ['fɪskəl] *adj* fiscal

fish [fɪʃ] **1** *n (pl* fish) (**a**) pez *m*; **f. shop**
pescadería *f* (**b**) *Culin* pescado *m*; **f. and
chips** = pescado frito con patatas or *Am*

papas fritas; **f.** *Br* **finger** *or US* **stick** palito *m* de pescado

   2 *vi* pescar; *Fig* **to f. in one's pocket for sth** buscar algo en el bolsillo

fishbone [ˈfɪʃbəʊn] *n* espina *f*, raspa *f*

fisherman [ˈfɪʃəmən] *n* pescador *m*

fishfinger [fɪʃˈfɪŋgə(r)] *n* palito *m* de pescado

fishing [ˈfɪʃɪŋ] *n* pesca *f*; **to go f.** ir de pesca; **f. net** red *f* de pesca; **f. rod** caña *f* de pescar; **f. tackle** aparejo *m* de pescar

fishmonger [ˈfɪʃmʌŋgə(r)] *n Br* pescadero(a) *m,f*; **fishmonger's (shop)** pescadería *f*

fishy [ˈfɪʃɪ] *adj* (**fishier, fishiest**) de pescado; *Fam Fig* **there's something f. going on** aquí hay gato encerrado

fist [fɪst] *n* puño *m*

fit¹ [fɪt] **1** *vt* (**a**) ir bien a; **that suit doesn't f. you** ese traje no te entalla
   (**b**) *Sewing* probar
   (**c**) **the key doesn't f. the lock** la llave no es de esta cerradura
   (**d**) *(install)* colocar; **a car fitted with a radio** un coche provisto de radio
   (**e**) *Fig* **she doesn't f. the description** no responde a la descripción

   2 *vi* (**a**) *(be of right size)* caber
   (**b**) *(facts etc)* cuadrar

   3 *adj* (**a**) *(suitable)* apto(a), adecuado(a) (**for** para); **are you f. to drive?** ¿estás en condiciones de conducir?
   (**b**) *(healthy)* en (plena) forma; **to keep f.** mantenerse en forma

   4 *n* ajuste *m*; *Sewing* corte *m*; **to be a good f.** encajar bien

   ▸ **fit in 1** *vi* (**a**) **he didn't f. in with his colleagues** no encajó con sus compañeros de trabajo (**b**) *(tally)* cuadrar (**with** con)

   2 *vt sep (find time for)* encontrar un hueco para

   ▸ **fit out** *vt sep* equipar

fit² [fɪt] *n* (**a**) *Med* ataque *m* (**b**) *Fig* arrebato *m*; **f. of anger** arranque *m* de cólera; *Fig* **by fits and starts** a trompicones

fitful [ˈfɪtfʊl] *adj* discontinuo(a)

fitness [ˈfɪtnɪs] *n* (**a**) *(aptitude)* aptitud *f*, capacidad *f* (**b**) *(health)* (buen) estado físico

fitted [ˈfɪtɪd] *adj* empotrado(a); **f. carpet** moqueta *f*; **f. cupboard** armario empotrado

fitter [ˈfɪtə(r)] *n* ajustador(a) *m,f*

fitting [ˈfɪtɪŋ] **1** *adj* apropiado(a)

   2 *n* (**a**) *(of dress)* prueba *f*; **f. room** probador *m* (**b**) *(usu pl)* accesorio *m*;

light fittings apliques eléctricos

five [faɪv] *adj & n* cinco *(m inv)*

fiver [ˈfaɪvə(r)] *n Fam* billete *m* de 5 libras/dólares

fix [fɪks] **1** *n* (**a**) *Fam* **to be in a f.** estar en un apuro (**b**) *Fam (drugs)* chute *m*

   2 *vt* (**a**) *(fasten)* fijar, asegurar (**b**) *(date, price)* fijar; *(limit)* señalar (**c**) **he'll f. it with the boss** *(arrange)* se las arreglará con el jefe (**d**) *(repair)* arreglar (**e**) *US (food, drink)* preparar

   ▸ **fix up** *vt sep (arrange)* arreglar; **to f. sb up with sth** proveer a algn de algo

fixation [fɪkˈseɪʃən] *n* idea fija

fixed [fɪkst] *adj* (**a**) fijo(a) (**b**) *Fam (match etc)* amañado(a)

fixture [ˈfɪkstʃə(r)] *n* (**a**) *Sport* encuentro *m* (**b**) **fixtures** *(in building)* accesorios *mpl*

fizz [fɪz] **1** *n* burbujeo *m*

   2 *vi* burbujear

   ▸ **fizzle out** [ˈfɪzəl] *vi* quedar en nada

fizzy [ˈfɪzɪ] *adj* (**fizzier, fizziest**) *(water)* con gas

flabbergasted [ˈflæbəgɑːstɪd] *adj* pasmado(a)

flabby [ˈflæbɪ] *adj* (**flabbier, flabbiest**) fofo(a)

flag [flæg] **1** *n* bandera *f*; *Naut* pabellón *m*

   2 *vt Fig* **to f. down a car** hacer señales a un coche para que pare

   3 *vi (interest)* decaer; *(conversation)* languidecer

flagpole [ˈflægpəʊl] *n* asta *f* de bandera

flagrant [ˈfleɪgrənt] *adj* flagrante

flagship [ˈflægʃɪp] *n* buque *m* insignia

flagstone [ˈflægstəʊn] *n* losa *f*

flair [fleə(r)] *n* facilidad *f*

flak [flæk] *n* (**a**) *Mil* fuego antiaéreo (**b**) *Fam* críticas *fpl*

flake [fleɪk] **1** *n* *(of snow)* copo *m*; *(of skin, soap)* escama *f*; *(of paint)* desconchón *m*

   2 *vi (skin)* descamarse; *(paint)* desconcharse

flamboyant [flæmˈbɔɪənt] *adj* extravagante

flame [fleɪm] *n* (**a**) *(of fire)* llama *f*; **to go up in flames** incendiarse (**b**) *Comput* llamarada *f*, = mensaje ofensivo

flameproof [ˈfleɪmpruːf] *adj* ininflamable

flamingo [fləˈmɪŋgəʊ] *n* flamenco *m*

flammable [ˈflæməbəl] *adj* inflamable

flan [flæn] *n* tarta *f*; **fruit f.** tarta de fruta

> ℓ Note that the Spanish word **flan** is a false friend and is never a translation for the English word **flan**. In Spanish, **flan** means "crème caramel".

flank [flæŋk] **1** n (**a**) (of animal) ijada f (**b**) Mil flanco m
  2 vt flanquear
flannel ['flænəl] n (**a**) Tex franela f (**b**) Br (face cloth) toallita f
flap [flæp] **1** vt (wings, arms) batir
  2 vi (wings) aletear; (flag) ondear
  3 n (**a**) (of envelope, pocket) solapa f; (of tent) faldón m (**b**) (of wing) aletazo m (**c**) Fam **to get into a f.** ponerse nervioso(a)
flare [fleə(r)] **1** n (**a**) (flame) llamarada f (**b**) Mil & Naut bengala f
  2 vi **to f. (up)** (fire) llamear; Fig (person) encolerizarse; (trouble) estallar
flared [fleəd] adj (trousers etc) acampanado(a)
flash [flæʃ] **1** n (**a**) (of light) destello m; (of lightning) relámpago m; Fig **in a f.** en un santiamén; Fig **a f. in the pan** un éxito fugaz (**b**) **news f.** noticia f de última hora (**c**) Phot flash m
  2 adj Fam chulo(a)
  3 vt (**a**) (torch) dirigir (**b**) Rad & TV transmitir (**c**) **he flashed his card** enseñó rápidamente su carnet
  4 vi (**a**) (light) destellar (**b**) **a car flashed past** un coche pasó como un rayo
flashback ['flæʃbæk] n flashback m
flashcube ['flæʃkjuːb] n cubo m flash
flashlight ['flæʃlaɪt] n US linterna f
flashy ['flæʃɪ] adj (flashier, flashiest) Fam chillón(ona)
flask [flɑːsk, flæsk] n frasco m; (Thermos®) **f.** termo m
flat [flæt] **1** adj (flatter, flattest) (**a**) (surface) llano(a) (**b**) (beer) sin gas (**c**) (battery) descargado(a); (tyre) desinflado(a) (**d**) (rate) fijo(a) (**e**) (categorical) rotundo(a) (**f**) (dull) soso(a) (**g**) Mus **B f.** si m bemol
  2 adv (**a**) **to fall f. on one's face** caerse de bruces (**b**) **in ten seconds f.** en diez segundos justos (**c**) Fam **to go f. out** ir a todo gas
  3 n (**a**) (apartment) piso m (**b**) US Aut pinchazo m (**c**) **mud flats** marismas fpl
flatly ['flætlɪ] adv rotundamente
flatmate ['flætmeɪt] n Br compañero(a) m,f de piso
flatten ['flætən] vt (**a**) (make level) allanar (**b**) (crush) aplastar
flatter ['flætə(r)] vt (**a**) adular, halagar (**b**) (clothes, portrait) favorecer (**c**) **to f. oneself** hacerse ilusiones
flattering ['flætərɪŋ] adj (**a**) (words) halagador(a) (**b**) (dress, portrait) favorecedor(a)
flattery ['flætərɪ] n adulación f, halago m

flaunt [flɔːnt] vt hacer alarde de
flavour, US **flavor** ['fleɪvə(r)] **1** n sabor m
  2 vt Culin sazonar (with con)
flavoured, US **flavored** ['fleɪvəd] adj **strawberry f.** con sabor a fresa, Bol, CSur, Ecuad frutilla
flavouring, US **flavoring** ['fleɪvərɪŋ] n condimento m; **artificial f.** aroma m artificial
flaw [flɔː] n (failing) defecto m; (fault) desperfecto m
flawless ['flɔːlɪs] adj perfecto(a)
flax [flæks] n lino m
flaxen ['flæksən] adj (hair) rubio pajizo
flea [fliː] n pulga f; **f. market** rastro m
fleck [flek] n (speck) mota f, punto m
fled [fled] pt & pp of **flee**
fledg(e)ling ['fledʒlɪŋ] adj Fig novato(a)
flee [fliː] **1** vt (pt & pp **fled**) huir de
  2 vi huir (from de)
fleece [fliːs] **1** n (**a**) (sheep's coat) lana f (**b**) (sheared) vellón m
  2 vt Fam (cheat) sangrar
fleet [fliːt] n flota f
fleeting ['fliːtɪŋ] adj fugaz
Flemish ['flemɪʃ] **1** adj flamenco(a)
  2 n (language) flamenco m
flesh [fleʃ] n (**a**) carne f; Fig **in the f.** en persona; Fig **to be of f. and blood** ser de carne y hueso; **f. wound** herida f superficial (**b**) (of fruit) pulpa f
flew [fluː] pt of **fly**
flex [fleks] **1** n Br Elec cable m
  2 vt (muscles) flexionar
flexibility [fleksɪ'bɪlɪtɪ] n flexibilidad f
flexible ['fleksɪbəl] adj flexible
flick [flɪk] **1** n movimiento rápido; (of finger) capirotazo m
  2 vt (with finger) dar un capirotazo a
  ▸ flick through vt insep (book) hojear
flicker ['flɪkə(r)] **1** n (**a**) parpadeo m; (of light) titileo m (**b**) Fig **a f. of hope** un destello de esperanza
  2 vi (eyes) parpadear; (flame) vacilar
flier ['flaɪə(r)] n aviador(a) m,f
flight [flaɪt] n (**a**) vuelo m; **f. path** trayectoria f de vuelo; **f. recorder** registrador m de vuelo (**b**) (of ball) trayectoria f (**c**) (escape) huida f, fuga f; **to take f.** darse a la fuga (**d**) (of stairs) tramo m
flight-deck ['flaɪtdek] n (cockpit) cabina f del piloto
flimsy ['flɪmzɪ] adj (flimsier, flimsiest) (cloth) ligero(a); (paper) fino(a); (structure) poco sólido(a); (excuse) poco convincente
flinch [flɪntʃ] vi (wince) estremecerse
fling [flɪŋ] **1** vt (pt & pp **flung**) arrojar

2 *n Fam* **to have a f.** echar una cana al aire

flint [flɪnt] *n* (**a**) *(stone)* pedernal *m* (**b**) *(in lighter)* piedra *f* de mechero

flip [flɪp] **1** *n (flick)* capirotazo *m*; **f. chart** flip chart *m*, pizarra *f* de conferencia *(con bloc)*

2 *vt (toss)* tirar (al aire); **to f. a coin** echar a cara o cruz

flip-flop ['flɪpflɒp] *n* (**a**) *Comput* báscula *f* biestable (**b**) *Br (footwear)* chancla *f*

flippant ['flɪpənt] *adj* frívolo(a)

flipper ['flɪpə(r)] *n* aleta *f*

flirt [flɜːt] **1** *n* coqueto(a) *m,f*

2 *vi* flirtear, coquetear; **to f. with death** jugar con la muerte

flirtation [flɜː'teɪʃən] *n* flirteo *m*, coqueteo *m*

flit [flɪt] *vi* revolotear

float [fləʊt] **1** *n* (**a**) flotador *m* (**b**) *(money)* cambio *m* (**c**) *(in procession)* carroza *f*

2 *vt* (**a**) poner a flote (**b**) *(shares)* emitir; *(currency, business)* hacer flotar

3 *vi* flotar

floating ['fləʊtɪŋ] *adj* flotante; *(voter)* indeciso(a)

flock [flɒk] **1** *n Zool* rebaño *m*; *Orn* bandada *f*; *Rel* grey *f*; *(crowd)* multitud *f*

2 *vi* acudir en masa

flog [flɒg] *vt* (**a**) azotar; *Fam Fig* **flogged to death** *(idea)* trillado(a) (**b**) *Fam (sell)* vender

flood [flʌd] **1** *n* inundación *f*; *(of river)* riada *f*; *Fig* torrente *m*

2 *vt* inundar

3 *vi (river)* desbordarse; *Fig* **to f. in** entrar a raudales

flooding ['flʌdɪŋ] *n* inundaciones *fpl*

floodlight ['flʌdlaɪt] *n* foco *m*

floor [flɔː(r)] **1** *n* (**a**) *(of room)* suelo *m*; **dance f.** pista *f* de baile (**b**) *(of ocean, forest)* fondo *m* (**c**) *(storey)* piso *m*; **first f.** *Br* primer piso, *US* planta baja; *Br* **ground f.** planta baja

2 *vt Fig* dejar perplejo(a)

floorboard ['flɔːbɔːd] *n* tabla *f* (del suelo)

flop [flɒp] **1** *n Fam* fracaso *m*

2 *vi* (**a**) **to f. down on the bed** tumbarse en la cama (**b**) *Fam* fracasar

floppy ['flɒpɪ] *adj* (**floppier, floppiest**) flojo(a); *Comput* **f. disk** disco *m* flexible

flora ['flɔːrə] *n* flora *f*

florid ['flɒrɪd] *adj (style)* florido(a)

florist ['flɒrɪst] *n* florista *mf*; **f.'s shop** floristería *f*

flounce¹ [flaʊns] *vi* **to f. in/out** entrar/ salir airadamente

flounce² [flaʊns] *n Sewing* volante *m*

flounder¹ ['flaʊndə(r)] *n (fish)* platija *f*

flounder² ['flaʊndə(r)] *vi* (**a**) *(struggle)* forcejear; *Fig* enredarse (**b**) *(be at a loss)* no saber que decir *or* hacer

flour ['flaʊə(r)] *n* harina *f*

flourish ['flʌrɪʃ] **1** *n* (**a**) *(gesture)* ademán *m* (teatral) (**b**) *(under signature)* rúbrica *f*

2 *vt (brandish)* agitar

3 *vi (thrive)* florecer; *(plant)* crecer

flourishing ['flʌrɪʃɪŋ] *adj* floreciente

flout [flaʊt] *vt Jur* desacatar

flow [fləʊ] **1** *n* flujo *m*; *(of river)* corriente *f*; *(of traffic)* circulación *f*; *(of capital)* movimiento *m*; *(of people, goods)* afluencia *f*; **f. chart** diagrama *m* de flujo; *Comput* organigrama *m*

2 *vi (blood, river)* fluir; *(sea)* subir; *(traffic)* circular

flower ['flaʊə(r)] **1** *n* flor *f*; **f. bed** arriate *m*

2 *vi* florecer

flowerpot ['flaʊəpɒt] *n* maceta *f*

flowery ['flaʊərɪ] *adj Fig* florido(a)

flowing ['fləʊɪŋ] *adj (hair)* suelto(a); *(dress)* de mucho vuelo; *(style)* fluido(a); *(shape, movement)* natural

flown [fləʊn] *pp of* **fly**

flu [fluː] *n (abbr* **influenza***)* gripe *f*

fluctuate ['flʌktjʊeɪt] *vi* fluctuar

fluctuation [flʌktjʊ'eɪʃən] *n* fluctuación *f*

flue [fluː] *n* conducto *m* de humos; *(chimney)* cañón *m*

fluent ['fluːənt] *adj* (**a**) **he speaks f. German** habla el alemán con soltura (**b**) *(eloquent)* fluido(a)

fluff [flʌf] **1** *n (down)* pelusa *f*

2 *vt Fam* **to f. sth** hacer algo mal

fluffy ['flʌfɪ] *adj* (**fluffier, fluffiest**) *(pillow)* mullido(a); *(toy)* de peluche; *(cake)* esponjoso(a)

fluid ['fluːɪd] **1** *adj (movement)* natural; *(style, prose)* fluido(a); *(situation)* incierto(a)

2 *n* fluido *m*, líquido *m*

fluke [fluːk] *n Fam* chiripa *f*; **by a f.** por chiripa

flummox ['flʌməks] *vt Fam* desconcertar

flung [flʌŋ] *pt & pp of* **fling**

flunk [flʌŋk] *vt & vi US Fam* catear

fluorescent [flʊə'resənt] *adj* fluorescente

fluoride ['flʊəraɪd] *n* fluoruro *m*

flurry ['flʌrɪ] *n* (**a**) *(of wind)* ráfaga *f*; *(of snow)* nevasca *f* (**b**) *Fig (bustle)* agitación *f*

flush [flʌʃ] **1** *adj* **f. with** *(level)* a ras de

2 *n (blush)* rubor *m*

. **3** *vt* **to f. the lavatory** tirar de la cadena
4 *vi* (**a**) **the loo won't f.** la cisterna del wáter no funciona (**b**) *(blush)* ruborizarse
flushed [flʌʃt] *adj (cheeks)* rojo(a), encendido(a); *Fig* **f. with success** emocionado(a) ante el éxito
fluster ['flʌstə(r)] *vt* **to get flustered** ponerse nervioso(a)
flute [fluːt] *n* flauta *f*
flutist ['fluːtɪst] *n US Mus* flautista *mf*
flutter ['flʌtə(r)] **1** *vi (leaves, birds)* revolotear; *(flag)* ondear
2 *n Fam (bet, gambling)* apuesta pequeña
flux [flʌks] *n (flow)* flujo *m*; *(instability)* inestabilidad *f*; *Fig* **to be in a state of f.** estar cambiando constantemente
fly¹ [flaɪ] **1** *vt (pt* **flew**; *pp* **flown**) (**a**) *Av* pilotar (**b**) *(merchandise, troops)* transportar (**c**) *(distance)* recorrer (**d**) *(kite)* hacer volar
2 *vi* (**a**) *(bird, plane)* volar (**b**) *(go by plane)* ir en avión (**c**) *(flag)* ondear (**d**) **to f. into a rage** montar en cólera (**e**) **the train flew past** el tren pasó volando (**f**) *Fam* **to go flying** *(fall)* caerse
3 *npl* **flies** bragueta *f*
fly² [flaɪ] *n (insect)* mosca *f*; **f. spray** spray *m* matamoscas
flying ['flaɪɪŋ] **1** *adj* volador(a); *(rapid)* rápido(a); **a f. visit** una visita relámpago; *Fig* **to come out of an affair with f. colours** salir airoso(a) de un asunto; *Fig* **to get off to a f. start** empezar con buen pie; **f. picket** piquete *m* (informativo); **f. saucer** platillo *m* volante
2 *n* (**a**) *(action)* vuelo *m* (**b**) *(aviation)* aviación *f*
flyleaf ['flaɪliːf] *n (of book)* guarda *f*
flyover ['flaɪəʊvə(r)] *n Br* paso elevado
flypast ['flaɪpɑːst] *n BrAv* desfile aéreo
flyweight ['flaɪweɪt] *n (in boxing)* peso *m* mosca
foal [fəʊl] *n* potro(a) *m,f*
foam [fəʊm] **1** *n* espuma *f*; **f. bath** espuma de baño; **f. rubber** goma espuma
2 *vi* hacer espuma
fob [fɒb] *n (chain)* cadena *f* (de reloj)
▸ **fob off** *vt sep Fam* **he fobbed off his old radio on a stranger** le colocó su radio vieja a un desconocido; **to f. sb off with excuses** darle largas a algn
focus ['fəʊkəs] **1** *vt* centrarse (**on** en)
2 *vi* enfocar; **to f. on sth** *Phot* enfocar algo; *Fig* centrarse en algo
3 *n (pl* **focuses**) foco *m*; **to be in f./out of f.** estar enfocado(a)/desenfocado(a);

Com & Pol **f. group** grupo *m* muestra
fodder ['fɒdə(r)] *n* pienso *m*
foe [fəʊ] *n Fml* enemigo(a) *m,f*
foetus ['fiːtəs] *n* feto *m*
fog [fɒg] *n* niebla *f*; *(at sea)* bruma *f*
fogey ['fəʊgɪ] *n Fam* **old f.** cascarrabias *mf inv*
foggy ['fɒgɪ] *adj* (**foggier, foggiest**) **it is f.** hay niebla; *Fam* **I haven't the foggiest (idea)** no tengo la más mínima idea
foghorn ['fɒghɔːn] *n* sirena *f* (de niebla)
foglamp ['fɒglæmp], *US* **foglight** ['fɒglaɪt] *n* faro *m* antiniebla
foil [fɔɪl] **1** *n* (**a**) **aluminium f.** papel *m* de aluminio (**b**) *(in fencing)* florete *m*
2 *vt (plot)* desbaratar
fold [fəʊld] **1** *n (crease)* pliegue *m*
2 *vt* plegar, doblar; **to f. one's arms** cruzar los brazos
3 *vi* **to f. (up)** *(chair etc)* plegarse; *Com* quebrar
folder ['fəʊldə(r)] *n* carpeta *f*
folding ['fəʊldɪŋ] *adj (chair etc)* plegable
foliage ['fəʊlɪdʒ] *n* follaje *m*
folk [fəʊk] **1** *npl* (**a**) *(people)* gente *f* (**b**) *Fam* **folks** *(family)* padres *mpl*; **one's folks** la familia
2 *adj* popular; **f. music** música *f* folk; **f. song** canción *f* popular
folklore ['fəʊklɔː(r)] *n* folklore *m*
follow ['fɒləʊ] **1** *vt* seguir; *(pursue)* perseguir; *(understand)* comprender; *(way of life)* llevar
2 *vi* (**a**) *(come after)* seguir; **as follows** como sigue (**b**) *(result)* resultar; **that doesn't f.** eso no es lógico (**c**) *(understand)* entender
▸ **follow through, follow up** *vt sep (idea)* llevar a cabo; *(clue)* investigar
follower ['fɒləʊə(r)] *n* seguidor(a) *m,f*
following ['fɒləʊɪŋ] **1** *adj* siguiente
2 *n* seguidores *mpl*
folly ['fɒlɪ] *n* locura *f*, desatino *m*
fond [fɒnd] *adj (loving)* cariñoso(a); **to be f. of sb** tenerle mucho cariño a algn; **to be f. of doing sth** ser aficionado(a) a hacer algo
fondle ['fɒndəl] *vt* acariciar
fondness ['fɒndnɪs] *n (love)* cariño *m* (**for** a); *(liking)* afición *f* (**for** a)
font [fɒnt] *n Rel* pila *f*
food [fuːd] *n* comida *f*; **f. chain** cadena trófica; **f. poisoning** intoxicación alimenticia
foodstuffs ['fuːdstʌfs] *npl* productos alimenticios
fool [fuːl] **1** *n* (**a**) tonto(a) *m,f*, imbécil *mf*; **to make a f. of sb** poner a algn en

ridículo; **to play the f.** hacer el tonto (**b**) *Culin* ≃ mousse *f* de fruta

2 *vt (deceive)* engañar

3 *vi (joke)* bromear; **to f. about** *or* **around** hacer el tonto

foolhardy ['fuːlhɑːdɪ] *adj* (**foolhardier, foolhardiest**) temerario(a); *(person)* intrépido(a)

foolish ['fuːlɪʃ] *adj* estúpido(a)

foolproof ['fuːlpruːf] *adj* infalible

foot [fʊt] **1** *n (pl* **feet**) pie *m*; *Zool* pata *f*; **on f.** a pie, andando; *Fig* **to find one's feet** acostumbrarse; *Fam Fig* **to put one's f. down** *(control)* imponerse; *(in car)* pisar a fondo; *Fam Fig* **to put one's f. in it** meter la pata; *Fam Fig* **to put one's feet up** descansar

2 *vt* **to f. the bill** *(pay)* pagar la cuenta

footage ['fʊtɪdʒ] *n Cin* metraje *m*

football ['fʊtbɔːl] *n* (**a**) *(soccer)* fútbol *m*; **bar f.** futbolín *m*; **f. ground** campo *m* de fútbol; **f. match** partido *m* de fútbol; **f. pools** quinielas *fpl* (**b**) *(ball)* balón *m*

footballer ['fʊtbɔːlə(r)] *n* futbolista *mf*

footbridge ['fʊtbrɪdʒ] *n* puente *m* para peatones

foothills ['fʊthɪlz] *npl* estribaciones *fpl*

foothold ['fʊthəʊld] *n Fig* **to gain a f.** afianzarse en una posición

footing ['fʊtɪŋ] *n* **to lose one's f.** perder el equilibrio; **on a friendly f.** en plan amistoso; **on an equal f.** en pie de igualdad

footlights ['fʊtlaɪts] *npl* candilejas *fpl*

footman ['fʊtmən] *n* lacayo *m*

footnote ['fʊtnəʊt] *n* nota *f* a pie de página

footpath ['fʊtpɑːθ] *n (track)* sendero *m*

footprint ['fʊtprɪnt] *n* pisada *f*

footsore ['fʊtsɔː(r)] *adj* con los pies doloridos

footstep ['fʊtstep] *n* paso *m*

footwear ['fʊtweə(r)] *n* calzado *m*

for [fɔː(r), *unstressed* fə(r)] **1** *prep* (**a**) *(intended)* para; **curtains f. the bedroom** cortinas para el dormitorio; **f. sale** en venta; **it's time f. bed** es hora de acostarse

(**b**) *(representing)* por; **a cheque f. £10** un cheque de 10 libras; **J f. John** J de Juan; **what's the Spanish f. "rivet"?** ¿cómo se dice "rivet" en español?

(**c**) *(purpose)* para; **it's good f. the digestion** es bueno para la digestión; **what's this f.?** ¿para qué sirve esto?

(**d**) *(because of)* por; **famous f. its cuisine** famoso(a) por su cocina; **to jump f. joy** saltar de alegría

(**e**) *(on behalf of)* por; **the campaign f.**

peace la campaña por la paz; **will you do it f. me?** ¿lo harás por mí?

(**f**) *(during)* por, durante; **I lent it to her f. a year** se lo presté por un año; **I shall stay f. two weeks** me quedaré dos semanas; **I was ill f. a month** estuve enfermo(a) durante un mes; **I've been here f. three months** hace tres meses que estoy aquí

(**g**) *(distance)* **I walked f. 10 km** caminé 10 km

(**h**) *(at a point in time)* para; **I can do it f. next Monday** puedo hacerlo para el lunes que viene; **f. the last time** por última vez

(**i**) *(destination)* para

(**j**) *(amount of money)* por; **I got the car f. £500** conseguí el coche por 500 libras

(**k**) *(in favour of)* a favor de; **are you f. or against?** ¿estás a favor o en contra?; **to vote f. sb** votar a algn

(**l**) *(to obtain)* para; **to run f. the bus** correr para coger al autobús; **to send sb f. water** mandar a algn a por agua

(**m**) *(with respect to)* en cuanto a; **as f. him** en cuanto a él; **f. all I care** por mí; **f. all I know** que yo sepa; **f. one thing** para empezar

(**n**) *(despite)* a pesar de; **f. all that** aún así; **he's tall f. his age** está muy alto para su edad

(**o**) *(instead of)* por; **can you go f. me?** ¿puede ir por mí?

(**p**) *(towards)* hacia, por; **affection f. sb** cariño hacia algn; **his love f. you** su amor por ti

(**q**) *(as)* por; **to leave sb f. dead** dar a algn por muerto(a); **what do you use f. fuel?** ¿qué utilizan como combustible?

(**r**) *(in exchange)* por; **to exchange one thing f. another** cambiar una cosa por otra; **how much did you sell it f.?** ¿por cuánto lo vendiste?

(**s**) *(+ object + infin)* **there's no reason f. us to quarrel** no hay motivo para que riñamos; **it's time f. you to go** es hora de que os marchéis; **it's easy f. him to say that** le es fácil decir eso

2 *conj (since, as)* ya que, puesto que

forage ['fɒrɪdʒ] **1** *n* forraje *m*

2 *vi* hurgar

foray ['fɒreɪ] *n* incursión *f*

forbade [fə'beɪd] *pt of* **forbid**

forbearance [fɔː'beərəns] *n* paciencia *f*

forbid [fə'bɪd] *vt (pt* **forbade**; *pp* **forbidden** [fə'bɪdən]) prohibir; **to f. sb to do sth** prohibirle a algn hacer algo

forbidding [fə'bɪdɪŋ] *adj (stern)* severo(a); *(bleak)* inhóspito(a)

force [fɔːs] **1** n (**a**) fuerza f; **by f.** por la fuerza; **to come into f.** entrar en vigor (**b**) Mil cuerpo m; **the (armed) forces** las fuerzas armadas; **the police f.** la policía **2** vt forzar; **to f. sb to do sth** forzar a algn a hacer algo

forced [fɔːst] adj forzado(a); **f. landing** aterrizaje forzoso

force-feed ['fɔːsfiːd] vt alimentar a la fuerza

forceful ['fɔːsfʊl] adj (**a**) (person) enérgico(a) (**b**) (argument) convincente

forceps ['fɔːseps] npl fórceps m

forcible ['fɔːsəbəl] adj **f. entry** allanamiento m de morada

forcibly ['fɔːsəblɪ] adv a or por la fuerza

ford [fɔːd] **1** n vado m **2** vt vadear

fore [fɔː(r)] n Fig **to come to the f.** empezar a destacar

forearm ['fɔːrɑːm] n antebrazo m

foreboding [fɔː'bəʊdɪŋ] n presentimiento m

forecast ['fɔːkɑːst] **1** n pronóstico m **2** vt (pt & pp **forecast** or **forecasted**) pronosticar

forecourt ['fɔːkɔːt] n (of garage) área f de servicio

forefathers ['fɔːfɑːðəz] npl antepasados mpl

forefront ['fɔːfrʌnt] n **in the f.** a la vanguardia

forego [fɔː'gəʊ] vt (pt **forewent**; pp **foregone** [fɔː'gɒn]) Fml sacrificar

foregone ['fɔːgɒn] adj **a f. conclusion** un resultado inevitable

foreground ['fɔːgraʊnd] n primer plano m

forehead ['fɒrɪd, 'fɔːhed] n frente f

foreign ['fɒrɪn] adj extranjero(a); (trade, policy) exterior; **f. exchange** divisas fpl; **the F. Office** el Ministerio de Asuntos Exteriores; **f. body** cuerpo extraño

foreigner ['fɒrɪnə(r)] n extranjero(a) m,f

foreman ['fɔːmən] n (**a**) Ind capataz m (**b**) Jur presidente m del jurado

foremost ['fɔːməʊst] adj principal; **first and f.** ante todo

forename ['fɔːneɪm] n nombre m de pila

forensic [fə'rensɪk] adj forense

forerunner ['fɔːrʌnə(r)] n precursor(a) m,f

foresee [fɔː'siː] vt (pt **foresaw** [fɔː'sɔː]; pp **foreseen**) prever

foreseeable [fɔː'siːəbəl] adj previsible; **in the f. future** en un futuro próximo

foreseen [fɔː'siːn] pp of **foresee**

foreshadow [fɔː'ʃædəʊ] vt presagiar

foresight ['fɔːsaɪt] n previsión f

forest ['fɒrɪst] n bosque m

forestall [fɔː'stɔːl] vt (plan) anticiparse a; (danger) prevenir

forestry ['fɒrɪstrɪ] n silvicultura f

foretaste ['fɔːteɪst] n anticipo m (**of** de)

foretell [fɔː'tel] vt (pt & pp **foretold** [fɔː'təʊld]) presagiar

forever [fə'revə(r)] adv (**a**) (eternally) siempre (**b**) (for good) para siempre (**c**) Fam (ages) siglos mpl

forewent [fɔː'went] pt of **forego**

foreword ['fɔːwɜːd] n prefacio m

forfeit ['fɔːfɪt] **1** n (penalty) pena f; (in games) prenda f **2** vt perder

forgave [fə'geɪv] pt of **forgive**

forge [fɔːdʒ] **1** n (**a**) (furnace) fragua f (**b**) (blacksmith's) herrería f **2** vt (**a**) (counterfeit) falsificar (**b**) (metal) forjar **3** vi **to f. ahead** hacer grandes progresos

forger ['fɔːdʒə(r)] n falsificador(a) m,f

forgery ['fɔːdʒərɪ] n falsificación f

forget [fə'get] **1** vt (pt **forgot**; pp **forgotten**) olvidar, olvidarse de; **I forgot to close the window** se me olvidó cerrar or me olvidé de cerrar la ventana; **I've forgotten my key** he olvidado la llave **2** vi olvidarse

forgetful [fə'getfʊl] adj olvidadizo(a)

forget-me-not [fə'getmɪnɒt] n nomeolvides f inv

forgive [fə'gɪv] vt (pt **forgave**; pp **forgiven** [fə'gɪvən]) perdonar; **to f. sb for sth** perdonarle algo a algn

forgiveness [fə'gɪvnɪs] n perdón m

forgo [fɔː'gəʊ] vt Fml = **forego**

forgot [fə'gɒt] pt of **forget**

forgotten [fə'gɒtən] pp of **forget**

fork [fɔːk] **1** n (**a**) Agr horca f (**b**) (cutlery) tenedor m (**c**) (in road) bifurcación f **2** vi (roads) bifurcarse ▸ **fork out** vt sep Fam (money) soltar

fork-lift truck [fɔːklɪft'trʌk] n carretilla f elevadora de horquilla

forlorn [fə'lɔːn] adj (forsaken) abandonado(a); (desolate) triste; (without hope) desesperado(a)

form [fɔːm] **1** n (**a**) (shape) forma f (**b**) (type) clase f (**c**) **for f.'s sake** para guardar las formas (**d**) (document) formulario m (**e**) **on/on top/off f.** en/en plena/en baja forma (**f**) Br Educ clase f; **the first f.** el primer curso **2** vt formar; **to f. an impression** formarse una impresión **3** vi formarse

formal ['fɔːməl] adj (**a**) (official) oficial;

a f. application una solicitud en forma (**b**) *(party, dress)* de etiqueta (**c**) *(ordered)* formal (**d**) *(person)* formalista

formality [fɔːˈmælɪtɪ] *n* formalidad *f*

formally [ˈfɔːməlɪ] *adv* oficialmente

format [ˈfɔːmæt] **1** *n* formato *m*
  2 *vt Comput* formatear

formation [fɔːˈmeɪʃən] *n* formación *f*

formative [ˈfɔːmətɪv] *adj* formativo(a)

former [ˈfɔːmə(r)] *adj* (**a**) *(time)* anterior (**b**) *(one-time)* antiguo(a); *(person)* ex; **the f. champion** el excampeón (**c**) *(first)* aquél/aquélla; **Peter and Lisa came, the f. wearing a hat** vinieron Peter y Lisa, aquél llevaba sombrero

formerly [ˈfɔːməlɪ] *adv* antiguamente

formidable [ˈfɔːmɪdəbəl] *adj (prodigious)* formidable; *(daunting)* terrible

formula [ˈfɔːmjʊlə] *n* fórmula *f*

forsake [fəˈseɪk] *vt* (*pt* **forsook** [fəˈsʊk]; *pp* **forsaken** [fəˈseɪkən]) *Literary* (**a**) *(abandon, desert)* abandonar (**b**) *(give up)* renunciar a

fort [fɔːt] *n* fortaleza *f*

forte [ˈfɔːteɪ] *n* fuerte *m*

forth [fɔːθ] *adv Fml* **and so f.** y así sucesivamente; **to go back and f.** ir de acá para allá

forthcoming [fɔːθˈkʌmɪŋ] *adj* (**a**) *(event)* próximo(a) (**b**) **no money was f.** no hubo oferta de dinero (**c**) *(communicative)* comunicativo(a)

forthright [ˈfɔːθraɪt] *adj* franco(a)

fortify [ˈfɔːtɪfaɪ] *vt* fortificar

fortitude [ˈfɔːtɪtjuːd] *n* fortaleza *f*, fuerza *f*

fortnight [ˈfɔːtnaɪt] *n Br* quincena *f*

fortnightly [ˈfɔːtnaɪtlɪ] *Br* **1** *adj* quincenal
  2 *adv* cada quince días

fortress [ˈfɔːtrɪs] *n* fortaleza *f*

fortunate [ˈfɔːtʃənɪt] *adj* afortunado(a); **it was f. that he came** fue una suerte que viniera

fortunately [ˈfɔːtʃənɪtlɪ] *adv* afortunadamente

fortune [ˈfɔːtʃən] *n* (**a**) *(luck, fate)* suerte *f*; **to tell sb's f.** echar la buenaventura a algn (**b**) *(money)* fortuna *f*

fortune-teller [ˈfɔːtʃəntelə(r)] *n* adivino(a) *m,f*

forty [ˈfɔːtɪ] *adj & n* cuarenta (*m inv*)

forum [ˈfɔːrəm] *n* foro *m*

forward [ˈfɔːwəd] **1** *adv* (**a**) *(also forwards)* *(direction and movement)* hacia adelante (**b**) *Fig* **to come f.** ofrecerse (**c**) **from this day f.** de ahora en adelante
  2 *adj* (**a**) *(movement)* hacia adelante; *(position)* delantero(a) (**b**) *(person)* fresco(a)
  3 *n Sport* delantero(a) *m,f*
  4 *vt* (**a**) *(send on)* remitir (**b**) *Fml (send goods)* expedir (**c**) *Fml (further)* fomentar

fossil [ˈfɒsəl] *n* fósil *m*; **f. fuel** combustible *m* fósil

foster [ˈfɒstə(r)] **1** *vt* (**a**) *(child)* criar (**b**) *Fml (hopes)* abrigar; *(relations)* fomentar
  2 *adj* **f. child** hijo(a) adoptivo(a); **f. father** padre adoptivo; **f. mother** madre adoptiva; **f. parents** padres adoptivos

fought [fɔːt] *pt & pp of* **fight**

foul [faʊl] **1** *adj* (**a**) *(smell)* fétido(a); *(taste)* asqueroso(a) (**b**) *(deed)* atroz; *(weather)* de perros (**c**) *(language)* grosero(a) (**d**) **to fall f. of** tener problemas con; *Sport* **f. play** juego sucio; *Jur* **f. play is suspected** se sospecha que se haya cometido un acto criminal
  2 *n Sport* falta *f*
  3 *vt* (**a**) *(dirty)* ensuciar; *(air)* contaminar (**b**) *Sport* cometer una falta contra

found¹ [faʊnd] *pt & pp of* **find**

found² [faʊnd] *vt (establish)* fundar

foundation [faʊnˈdeɪʃən] *n* (**a**) *(establishment)* fundación *f* (**b**) *(basis)* fundamento *m* (**c**) **f. (cream)** maquillaje *m* de fondo (**d**) *Constr* **foundations** cimientos *mpl*

founder¹ [ˈfaʊndə(r)] *n* fundador(a) *m,f*

founder² [ˈfaʊndə(r)] *vi* (**a**) *Fml (sink)* hundirse (**b**) *Fig (plan, hopes)* fracasar

foundry [ˈfaʊndrɪ] *n* fundición *f*

fountain [ˈfaʊntɪn] *n (structure)* fuente *f*; *(jet)* surtidor *m*; **f. pen** pluma estilográfica, *CSur* lapicera *f* fuente, *Perú* lapicero *m*

four [fɔː(r)] *adj & n* cuatro (*m inv*); **on all fours** a gatas

four-door [ˈfɔːdɔː(r)] *adj Aut* de cuatro puertas

four-poster [fɔːˈpəʊstə(r)] *adj & n* **f. (bed)** cama *f* con dosel

foursome [ˈfɔːsəm] *n* grupo *m* de cuatro personas

fourteen [fɔːˈtiːn] *adj & n* catorce (*m inv*)

fourteenth [fɔːˈtiːnθ] **1** *adj & n* decimocuarto(a) (*m,f*)
  2 *n (fraction)* catorceavo *m*

fourth [fɔːθ] **1** *adj & n* cuarto(a) (*m,f*)
  2 *n* (**a**) *(fraction)* cuarto *m* (**b**) *Aut* cuarta *f* (velocidad)

fowl [faʊl] *n* (*pl* **fowl**) ave *f* de corral

fox [fɒks] **1** *n* zorro(a) *m,f*
  2 *vt* (**a**) *(perplex)* dejar perplejo(a) (**b**) *(deceive)* engañar

foyer [ˈfɔɪeɪ, ˈfɔɪə(r)] *n* vestíbulo *m*

fracas ['frækɑ:] *n* gresca *f*, refriega *f*

> ⟨*ℓ*⟩ Note that the Spanish word **fracaso** is a false friend and is never a translation for the English word **fracas**. In Spanish, **fracaso** means "failure".

fraction ['frækʃən] *n* fracción *f*
fracture ['fræktʃə(r)] **1** *n* fractura *f*
   2 *vt* fracturar
fragile ['frædʒaɪl] *adj* frágil
fragment ['frægmənt] *n* fragmento *m*
fragrance ['freɪgrəns] *n* fragancia *f*, perfume *m*
fragrant ['freɪgrənt] *adj* fragante, aromático(a)
frail [freɪl] *adj* frágil, delicado(a)
frame [freɪm] **1** *n* (**a**) *(of window, door, picture)* marco *m*; *(of machine)* armazón *m*; *(of bicycle)* cuadro *m*; *(of spectacles)* montura *f*; *Fig* **f. of mind** estado *m* de ánimo (**b**) *Cin & TV* fotograma *m*
   2 *vt* (**a**) *(picture)* enmarcar (**b**) *(question)* formular (**c**) *Fam (innocent person)* incriminar
framework ['freɪmwɜ:k] *n Fig* **within the f. of ...** dentro del marco de ...
franc [fræŋk] *n* franco *m*
France [frɑ:ns] *n* Francia
franchise ['fræntʃaɪz] *n* (**a**) *Pol* derecho *m* al voto (**b**) *Com* concesión *f*, licencia *f*
frank [fræŋk] **1** *adj* franco(a)
   2 *vt (mail)* franquear
frankly ['fræŋklɪ] *adv* francamente
frankness ['fræŋknɪs] *n* franqueza *f*
frantic ['fræntɪk] *adj (anxious)* desesperado(a); *(hectic)* frenético(a)
fraternal [frə'tɜ:nəl] *adj* fraterno(a)
fraternity [frə'tɜ:nɪtɪ] *n (society)* asociación *f*; *Rel* cofradía *f*; *US Univ* club *m* de estudiantes
fraud [frɔ:d] *n* (**a**) fraude *m* (**b**) *(person)* impostor(a) *m,f*
fraught [frɔ:t] *adj* (**a**) *(full)* cargado(a) (**with** de) (**b**) *(tense)* nervioso(a)
fray¹ [freɪ] *vi* (**a**) *(cloth)* deshilacharse (**b**) *(nerves)* crisparse; **his temper frequently frayed** se irritaba a menudo
fray² [freɪ] *n* combate *m*
freak [fri:k] **1** *n* (**a**) *(monster)* monstruo *m* (**b**) *Fam (eccentric)* estrafalario(a) *m,f* (**c**) *Fam (fan)* fanático(a) *m,f*
   2 *adj* (**a**) *(unexpected)* inesperado(a) (**b**) *(unusual)* insólito(a)
freckle ['frekəl] *n* peca *f*
free [fri:] **1** *adj* (**a**) libre; **to set sb f.** poner en libertad a algn; **f. kick** tiro *m* libre; **f. speech** libertad *f* de expresión; **f. will** libre albedrío *m*; **f. trade** libre cambio *m*;

f. time tiempo *m* libre (**b**) **f. (of charge)** *(gratis)* gratuito(a); **f. gift** obsequio *m* (**c**) *(generous)* generoso(a)
   2 *adv* (**a**) **(for) f.** gratis (**b**) *(loose)* suelto(a)
   3 *vt* (**a**) *(liberate)* poner en libertad (**b**) *(let loose, work loose)* soltar (**c**) *(untie)* desatar (**d**) *(exempt)* eximir (**from** de)
freedom ['fri:dəm] *n* (**a**) *(liberty)* libertad *f*; **f. of the press** libertad de prensa (**b**) *(exemption)* exención *f*
free-for-all ['fri:fərɔ:l] *n* pelea *f*
freehold ['fri:həʊld] *adj* en propiedad absoluta
freelance ['fri:lɑ:ns] *adj* independiente
freely ['fri:lɪ] *adv* (**a**) libremente (**b**) *(openly)* abiertamente
freemason ['fri:meɪsən] *n* francmasón *m*
free-range ['fri:reɪndʒ] *adj Br* de granja
free-style ['fri:staɪl] *n* estilo *m* libre
freeway ['fri:weɪ] *n US* autopista *f*
freewheel [fri:'wi:l] *vi* ir en punto muerto
freeze [fri:z] **1** *vt* (*pt* **froze**; *pp* **frozen**) congelar
   2 *n Met* helada *f*; **price f.** congelación *f* de precios; *TV & Cin* **f. frame** imagen congelada
   3 *vi (liquid)* helarse; *(food)* congelarse
freeze-dried ['fri:zdraɪd] *adj* liofilizado(a)
freezer ['fri:zə(r)] *n* congelador *m*
freezing ['fri:zɪŋ] *adj* (**a**) glacial (**b**) **f. point** punto *m* de congelación; **above/below f. point** sobre/bajo cero
freight [freɪt] *n* (**a**) *(transport)* transporte *m* (**b**) *(goods, price)* flete *m*; *US* **f. car** vagón *m*; *US* **f. elevator** montacargas *m inv*; **f. train** tren *m* de mercancías
French [frentʃ] **1** *adj* francés(esa); **F. bean** judía *f* verde, *Bol, RP* chaucha *f*, *CAm* ejote *m*, *Col, Cuba* habichuela *f*, *Chile* poroto *m* verde, *Ven* vainita *f*; **F. dressing** vinagreta *f*; *US* **F. fries** patatas *fpl* or *Am* papas *fpl* fritas; **F. window** puerta *f* vidriera
   2 *n* (**a**) *(language)* francés *m* (**b**) *pl* **the F.** los franceses
Frenchman ['frentʃmən] *n* francés *m*
Frenchwoman ['frentʃwʊmən] *n* francesa *f*
frenetic [frɪ'netɪk] *adj* frenético(a)
frenzy ['frenzɪ] *n* frenesí *m*
frequency ['fri:kwənsɪ] *n* frecuencia *f*
frequent 1 *adj* ['fri:kwənt] frecuente
   2 *vt* [frɪ'kwent] frecuentar
frequently ['fri:kwəntlɪ] *adv* frecuentemente, a menudo

fresh [freʃ] *adj* (**a**) fresco(a); **f. water** agua *f* dulce; **f. bread** pan del día (**b**) *(new)* nuevo(a); **open a f. packet** abre otro paquete (**c**) *(air)* puro(a); **in the f. air** al aire libre (**d**) *US Fam (cheeky)* fresco(a)

freshen ['freʃən] *vi (wind)* refrescar
▸ **freshen up** *vi* asearse

fresher ['freʃə(r)] *n Univ* estudiante *mf* de primer año, novato(a) *m,f*

freshly ['freʃlɪ] *adv* recién, recientemente

freshman ['freʃmən] *n US* = fresher

freshness ['freʃnɪs] *n* frescura *f*

freshwater ['freʃwɔːtə(r)] *adj* de agua dulce

fret [fret] *vi* preocuparse (**about** por)

FRG [efɑːˈdʒiː] *n Hist (abbr Federal Republic of Germany)* RFA *f*

friar ['fraɪə(r)] *n* fraile *m*

friction ['frɪkʃən] *n* fricción *f*

Friday ['fraɪdɪ] *n* viernes *m*

fridge [frɪdʒ] *n* nevera *f*, frigorífico *m*, *Andes* frigider *m*, *RP* heladera *f*

friend [frend] *n* amigo(a) *m,f*; **a f. of mine** un(a) amigo(a) mío(a); **to make friends with sb** hacerse amigo(a) de algn; **to make friends again** hacer las paces

friendliness ['frendlɪnɪs] *n* amabilidad *f*, simpatía *f*

friendly ['frendlɪ] *adj* (**friendlier, friendliest**) *(person)* simpático(a); *(atmosphere)* acogedor(a); **f. advice** consejo *m* de amigo; **f. nation** nación amiga

friendship ['frendʃɪp] *n* amistad *f*

frieze [friːz] *n* friso *m*

frigate ['frɪgɪt] *n* fragata *f*

fright [fraɪt] *n* (**a**) *(fear)* miedo *m*; **to take f.** asustarse (**b**) *(shock)* susto *m*; **to get a f.** pegarse un susto

frighten ['fraɪtən] *vt* asustar
▸ **frighten away, frighten off** *vt sep* ahuyentar

frightened ['fraɪtənd] *adj* asustado(a); **to be f. of sb** tenerle miedo a algn

frightening ['fraɪtənɪŋ] *adj* espantoso(a)

frightful ['fraɪtfʊl] *adj* espantoso(a), horroroso(a)

frightfully ['fraɪtfʊlɪ] *adv* tremendamente, terriblemente

frigid ['frɪdʒɪd] *adj* frígido(a)

frill [frɪl] *n (on dress)* volante *m*; *Fig* **frills** *(decorations)* adornos *mpl*

fringe [frɪndʒ] *n* (**a**) *Br (of hair)* flequillo *m*, *Am* cerquillo *m* (**b**) *(edge)* borde *m*; *Fig* **on the f. of society** al margen de la sociedad; **f. theatre** teatro *m* experimental; **f. benefits** extras *mpl*

Frisbee® ['frɪzbɪ] *n* platillo *m*

frisk [frɪsk] *vt Fam (search)* registrar

frisky ['frɪskɪ] *adj* (**friskier, friskiest**) (**a**) *(children, animals)* juguetón(ona) (**b**) *(adult)* vivo(a)

fritter ['frɪtə(r)] *n* buñuelo *m*
▸ **fritter away** *vt sep* malgastar

frivolous ['frɪvələs] *adj* frívolo(a)

frizzy ['frɪzɪ] *adj* (**frizzier, frizziest**) crespo(a)

frock [frɒk] *n* vestido *m*; **f. coat** levita *f*

frog [frɒg] *n* rana *f*; **frogs' legs** ancas *fpl* de rana; *Fig* **to have a f. in one's throat** tener carraspera

frogman ['frɒgmən] *n* hombre *m* rana

frolic ['frɒlɪk] *vi* retozar, juguetear

from [frɒm, *unstressed* frəm] *prep* (**a**) *(time)* desde, a partir de; **f. now on** a partir de ahora; **f. Monday to Friday** de lunes a viernes; **f. the 8th to the 17th** desde el 8 hasta el 17; **f. time to time** de vez en cuando

(**b**) *(price, number)* desde, de; **dresses f. £5** vestidos desde 5 libras; **a number f. one to ten** un número del uno a diez

(**c**) *(origin)* de; **a letter f. her father** una carta de su padre; **f. English into Spanish** del inglés al español; **he's f. Malaga** es de Málaga; **the train f. Bilbao** el tren procedente de Bilbao; **to go f. door to door** ir de puerta en puerta; **her eyes were red f. crying** tenía los ojos rojos de llorar

(**d**) *(distance)* de; **the town is 4 miles f. the coast** el pueblo está a 4 millas de la costa

(**e**) *(out of)* de; **bread is made f. flour** el pan se hace con harina

(**f**) *(remove, subtract)* a; **he took the book f. the child** le quitó el libro al niño; **take three f. five** restar tres a cinco

(**g**) *(according to)* según, por; **f. what the author said** según lo que dijo el autor; **speaking f. my own experience** hablando por experiencia propia

(**h**) *(position)* desde, de; **f. here** desde aquí

(**i**) **can you tell margarine f. butter?** ¿puedes distinguir entre la margarina y la mantequilla?

front [frʌnt] **1** *n* (**a**) parte delantera; **in f. (of)** delante (de) (**b**) *(of building)* fachada *f* (**c**) *Mil, Pol & Met* frente *m* (**d**) *(seaside)* paseo marítimo (**e**) *Fig* **she put on a brave f.** hizo de tripas corazón

2 *adj* delantero(a), de delante; *Pol* **f. bench** = primera fila de escaños donde se sientan los ministros del Gobierno o de la Oposición; **f. door** puerta *f* principal; **f. room** salón *m*; **f. seat** asiento *m* de delante

frontier ['frʌntɪə(r)] *n* frontera *f*

front-page ['frʌntpeɪdʒ] *adj* de primera página

frost [frɒst] **1** *n* (**a**) *(covering)* escarcha *f* (**b**) *(freezing)* helada *f*
 2 *vt US Culin* recubrir con azúcar glas
 ▸ **frost over** *vi* escarchar

frostbite ['frɒstbaɪt] *n* congelación *f*

frosted ['frɒstɪd] *adj* (**a**) *(glass)* esmerilado(a) (**b**) *US Culin* recubierto(a) de azúcar glas

frosty ['frɒstɪ] *adj* (**frostier, frostiest**) (**a**) **it will be a f. night tonight** esta noche habrá helada (**b**) *Fig* glacial

froth [frɒθ] **1** *n* espuma *f*; *(from mouth)* espumarajos *mpl*
 2 *vi* espumar

frothy ['frɒθɪ] *adj* (**frothier, frothiest**) espumoso(a)

frown [fraʊn] *vi* fruncir el ceño
 ▸ **frown upon** *vt insep* desaprobar

froze [frəʊz] *pt of* **freeze**

frozen ['frəʊzən] **1** *adj (liquid, feet etc)* helado(a); *(food)* congelado(a)
 2 *pp of* **freeze**

frugal ['fruːgəl] *adj* frugal

fruit [fruːt] *n* (**a**) *Bot* fruto *m* (**b**) *(apple, orange etc)* fruta *f*; **f. cake** pastel *m* con fruto seco; **f. machine** máquina *f* tragaperras; **f. salad** macedonia *f* de frutas (**c**) **fruits** *(rewards)* frutos *mpl*

fruitful ['fruːtfʊl] *adj Fig* provechoso(a)

fruition [fruː'ɪʃən] *n Fml* **to come to f.** realizarse

frustrate [frʌ'streɪt] *vt* frustrar

frustrated [frʌ'streɪtɪd] *adj* frustrado(a)

frustration [frʌ'streɪʃən] *n* frustración *f*

fry¹ [fraɪ] **1** *vt (pt & pp* **fried***)* freír
 2 *vi Fig* asarse

fry² [fraɪ] *npl* **small f.** gente *f* de poca monta

frying pan ['fraɪŋpæn], *US* **fry-pan** ['fraɪpæn] *n* sartén *f*

ft *(abbr* **foot***)* pie *m*; *(abbr* **feet***)* pies *mpl*

fuck [fʌk] *vt & vi Vulg* joder; **f. (it)!** ¡joder!
 ▸ **fuck off** *vi Vulg* **f. off!** ¡vete a la mierda!
 ▸ **fuck up** *vt sep Vulg* joder

fucking ['fʌkɪŋ] *Vulg* **1** *adj* **f. idiot!** ¡gilipollas!; **where are my f. keys?** ¿dónde coño están las llaves?
 2 *adv* **a f. good film** una película de puta madre

fuddy-duddy ['fʌdɪdʌdɪ] *n Fam* **an old f.** un carcamal *or Am* carcamán

fudge [fʌdʒ] **1** *n Culin* = dulce hecho con azúcar, leche y mantequilla
 2 *vt (figures)* amañar

fuel ['fjʊəl] **1** *n* combustible *m*; *(for engines)* carburante *m*; **f. tank** depósito *m* de combustible
 2 *vt Fig (ambition)* estimular; *(difficult situation)* empeorar

fugitive ['fjuːdʒɪtɪv] *n Fml* fugitivo(a) *m,f*

fulfil, *US* **fulfill** [fʊl'fɪl] *vt* (**a**) *(task, ambition)* realizar; *(promise)* cumplir; *(role)* desempeñar (**b**) *(wishes)* satisfacer

fulfilment, *US* **fulfillment** [fʊl'fɪlmənt] *n* (**a**) *(of ambition)* realización *f* (**b**) *(of duty, promise)* cumplimiento *m*

full [fʊl] **1** *adj* (**a**) lleno(a); **f. of** lleno(a) de; **I'm f. (up)** no puedo más (**b**) *(complete)* completo(a); **at f. speed** a toda velocidad; **f. text** texto íntegro; *Fam* **in f. swing** en plena marcha; **f. board** pensión completa; **f. employment** pleno empleo; **f. house** lleno total; **f. moon** luna llena; **f. stop** punto *m*
 2 *n* **in f.** en su totalidad; **name in f.** nombre y apellidos completos
 3 *adv* **f. well** perfectamente

full-blown ['fʊlbləʊn] *adj* auténtico(a)

full-fledged ['fʊlfledʒd] *adj US* = **fully-fledged**

fullness ['fʊlnɪs] *n* **in the f. of time** con el tiempo

full-scale ['fʊlskeɪl] *adj* (**a**) *(model)* de tamaño natural (**b**) **f. search** registro *m* a fondo; **f. war** guerra generalizada *or* total

full-time ['fʊl'taɪm] **1** *adj* de jornada completa
 2 *adv* **to work f.** trabajar a tiempo completo

fully ['fʊlɪ] *adv* completamente

fully-fledged ['fʊlɪfledʒd] *adj* hecho(a) y derecho(a)

fulsome ['fʊlsəm] *adj* excesivo(a), exagerado(a)

fumble ['fʌmbəl] *vi* hurgar; **to f. for sth** buscar algo a tientas; **to f. with sth** manejar algo con torpeza

fume [fjuːm] **1** *n (usu pl)* humo *m*
 2 *vi* despedir humo

> ♬ Note that the Spanish verb **fumar** is a false friend and is never a translation for the English verb **to fume**. In Spanish, **fumar** means "to smoke".

fun [fʌn] **1** *n (amusement)* diversión *f*; **in** *or* **for f.** en broma; **to have f.** divertirse, pasarlo bien; **to make f. of sb** reírse de algn
 2 *adj* divertido(a)

function ['fʌŋkʃən] **1** *n* (**a**) función *f* (**b**) *(ceremony)* acto *m*; *(party)* recepción *f*
  2 *vi* funcionar
functional ['fʌŋkʃənəl] *adj* funcional
fund [fʌnd] **1** *n* (**a**) *Com* fondo *m* (**b**) **funds** fondos *mpl*
  2 *vt (finance)* financiar

> *Note that the Spanish verb* **fundar** *is a false friend and is never a translation for the English verb* **to fund**. *In Spanish,* **fundar** *means "to found".*

fundamental [fʌndə'mentəl] **1** *adj* fundamental
  2 *npl* **fundamentals** los fundamentos
funeral ['fjuːnərəl] *n* funeral *m*; *US* **f. home** funeraria *f*; **f. march** marcha *f* fúnebre; *Br* **f. parlour** funeraria; **f. service** misa *f* de cuerpo presente
funfair ['fʌnfeə(r)] *n Br* parque *m* de atracciones
fungus ['fʌŋgəs] *n (pl* **fungi** ['fʌŋgaɪ]) (**a**) *Bot* hongo *m* (**b**) *Med* fungo *m*
funnel ['fʌnəl] **1** *n* (**a**) *(for liquids)* embudo *m* (**b**) *Naut* chimenea *f*
  2 *vt Fig (funds, energy)* encauzar
funnily ['fʌnɪlɪ] *adv Fam* **f. enough** aunque parezca extraño
funny ['fʌnɪ] *adj* (**funnier, funniest**) (**a**) *(peculiar)* raro(a), extraño(a); **that's f.!** ¡qué raro! (**b**) *(amusing)* divertido(a), gracioso(a); **I found it very f.** me hizo mucha gracia (**c**) *Fam (ill)* mal (**d**) *Fam (dishonest)* dudoso(a)
fur [fɜː(r)] **1** *n* (**a**) *(of living animal)* pelo *m* (**b**) *(of dead animal)* piel *f* (**c**) *(in kettle, on tongue)* sarro *m*
  2 *adj* de piel; **f. coat** abrigo *m* de pieles
furious ['fjʊərɪəs] *adj* (**a**) *(angry)* furioso(a) (**b**) *(vigorous)* violento(a)
furlong ['fɜːlɒŋ] *n (measurement)* = aprox 201 m
furnace ['fɜːnɪs] *n* horno *m*
furnish ['fɜːnɪʃ] *vt* (**a**) *(house)* amueblar (**b**) *Fml (food)* suministrar; *(details)* facilitar
furnishings ['fɜːnɪʃɪŋz] *npl* (**a**) muebles *mpl* (**b**) *(fittings)* accesorios *mpl*
furniture ['fɜːnɪtʃə(r)] *n* muebles *mpl*; **a piece of f.** un mueble

furrow ['fʌrəʊ] *n Agr* surco *m*; *(on forehead)* arruga *f*
furry ['fɜːrɪ] *adj* (**furrier, furriest**) (**a**) *(hairy)* peludo(a) (**b**) *(tongue, kettle)* sarroso(a)
further ['fɜːðə(r)] **1** *adj* *(comp of* **far**) (**a**) *(new)* nuevo(a); **until f. notice** hasta nuevo aviso (**b**) *(additional)* otro(a), adicional (**c**) *(later)* posterior; **f. education** estudios *mpl* superiores
  2 *adv* (**a**) *(more)* más; **f. back** más atrás; **f. along** más adelante; **she heard nothing f.** no volvió a saber nada más (**b**) *Fml* **f. to your letter of the 9th** con referencia a su carta del 9 del corriente (**c**) *Fml (besides)* además
  3 *vt* fomentar
furthermore [fɜːðə'mɔː(r)] *adv Fml* además
furthest ['fɜːðɪst] *adj (superl of* **far**) más lejano(a)
furtive ['fɜːtɪv] *adj* furtivo(a)
fury ['fjʊərɪ] *n* furia *f*, furor *m*
fuse [fjuːz] **1** *n* (**a**) *Elec* fusible *m*; **f. box** caja *f* de fusibles (**b**) *(of bomb)* mecha *f*
  2 *vi* (**a**) *Elec* **the lights fused** se fundieron los plomos (**b**) *Fig (merge)* fusionarse (**c**) *(melt)* fundirse
  3 *vt* (**a**) *Elec* fundir los plomos de (**b**) *Fig (merge)* fusionar (**c**) *(melt)* fundir
fuselage ['fjuːzɪlaːʒ] *n* fuselaje *m*
fuss [fʌs] **1** *n (commotion)* jaleo *m*; **to kick up a f.** armar un escándalo; **stop making a f.** *(complaining)* deja ya de quejarte; **to make a f. of** *(pay attention to)* mimar a
  2 *vi* preocuparse (**about** por)
fussy ['fʌsɪ] *adj* (**fussier, fussiest**) exigente; *(nitpicking)* quisquilloso(a)
futile ['fjuːtaɪl] *adj* inútil, vano(a)
futility [fjuː'tɪlɪtɪ] *n* inutilidad *f*
future ['fjuːtʃə(r)] **1** *n* futuro *m*, porvenir *m*; **in the near f.** en un futuro próximo; **in f.** de aquí en adelante
  2 *adj* futuro(a)
futuristic [fjuːtʃə'rɪstɪk] *adj* futurista
fuze [fjuːz] *n, vi & vt US* = **fuse**
fuzzy ['fʌzɪ] *adj* (**fuzzier, fuzziest**) (**a**) *(hair)* muy rizado(a) (**b**) *(blurred)* borroso(a)

G, g [dʒiː] *n* (**a**) *(the letter)* G, g *f* (**b**) *Mus* **G** sol *m*

G [dʒiː] *adj US Cin* ≃ (apta) para todos los públicos

g *(abbr* **gramme**) g

gabble ['gæbəl] **1** *n* chapurreo *m*
 2 *vi* hablar atropelladamente

gable ['geɪbəl] *n* aguilón *m*

gadget ['gædʒɪt] *n* artilugio *m*, aparato *m*

Gaelic ['geɪlɪk] **1** *adj* gaélico(a)
 2 *n (language)* gaélico *m*

gaffe [gæf] *n* metedura *f* de pata, desliz *m*; **to make a g.** meter la pata, patinar

> ⚠ Note that the Spanish word **gafe** is a false friend and is never a translation for the English word **gaffe**. In Spanish, **gafe** means "jinxed person".

gag [gæg] **1** *n* (**a**) mordaza *f* (**b**) *Fam (joke)* chiste *m*
 2 *vt* amordazar

gage [geɪdʒ] *n & vt US =* **gauge**

gaiety ['geɪətɪ] *n* regocijo *m*

gaily ['geɪlɪ] *adv* alegremente

gain [geɪn] **1** *n* ganancia *f*, beneficio *m*; *(increase)* aumento *m*
 2 *vt* ganar; *Fig* **to g. ground** ganar terreno; **to g. speed** ganar velocidad, acelerar; **to g. weight** aumentar de peso

gait [geɪt] *n* (manera *f* de) andar *m*

gal (*pl* **gal** *or* **gals**) *(abbr* **gallon**) galón *m*

gala ['gɑːlə, 'geɪlə] *n* gala *f*, fiesta *f*

galaxy ['gæləksɪ] *n* galaxia *f*

gale [geɪl] *n* vendaval *m*

Galicia [gə'lɪʃə] *n* Galicia

Galician [gə'lɪʃɪən, gə'lɪʃən] **1** *adj* gallego(a)
 2 *n* (**a**) *(person)* gallego(a) *m,f* (**b**) *(language)* gallego *m*

gall [gɔːl] **1** *n Fam* descaro *m*
 2 *vt* molestar, irritar

gallant ['gælənt] *adj (brave)* valiente; *(also* [gə'lænt]) *(chivalrous)* galante

gallantry ['gæləntrɪ] *n (bravery)* gallardía *f*; *(politeness)* galantería *f*

galleon ['gælɪən] *n* galeón *m*

gallery ['gælərɪ] *n* (**a**) galería *f* (**b**) *Th*

gallinero *m* (**c**) *(court)* tribuna *f*

galley ['gælɪ] *n* (**a**) *(ship)* galera *f*; **g. slave** galeote *m* (**b**) *(kitchen)* cocina *f*

Gallicism ['gælɪsɪzəm] *n* galicismo *m*

gallivant ['gælɪvænt] *vi Fam* callejear

gallon ['gælən] *n* galón *m* (*Br* = 4,55 l; *US* = 3,79 l)

gallop ['gæləp] **1** *n* galope *m*
 2 *vi* galopar

gallows ['gæləʊz] *n sing* horca *f*, patíbulo *m*

gallstone ['gɔːlstəʊn] *n* cálculo *m* biliar

galore [gə'lɔː(r)] *adv Fam* en cantidad, en abundancia

galvanize ['gælvənaɪz] *vt (metal)* galvanizar; *Fig* **to g. sb into action** galvanizar a algn

galvanized ['gælvənaɪzd] *adj* galvanizado(a)

gambit ['gæmbɪt] *n (in chess)* gambito *m*; *Fig* táctica *f*

gamble ['gæmbəl] **1** *n (risk)* riesgo *m*; *(risky undertaking)* empresa arriesgada; *(bet)* apuesta *f*
 2 *vi (bet)* jugar; *(take a risk)* arriesgarse

gambler ['gæmblə(r)] *n* jugador(a) *m,f*

gambling ['gæmblɪŋ] *n* juego *m*

gambol ['gæmbəl] *vi* brincar

game [geɪm] **1** *n* (**a**) juego *m*; **g. of chance** juego de azar (**b**) *(match)* partido *m*; *(of bridge)* partida *f* (**c**) **games** *Sport* juegos *mpl*; *Br Educ* educación física (**d**) *(hunting)* caza *f*; *Fig* presa *f*; **g. reserve** coto *m* de caza
 2 *adj* **g. for anything** dispuesto(a) a todo

gamekeeper ['geɪmkiːpə(r)] *n* guardabosque *mf*

gamely ['geɪmlɪ] *adv* resueltamente

gammon ['gæmən] *n Br* jamón ahumado *or* curado

gamut ['gæmət] *n* gama *f*; **to run the g. of ...** experimentar todas las posibilidades de ...

gang [gæŋ] *n (of criminals)* banda *f*; *(of youths)* pandilla *f*; *(of workers)* cuadrilla *f*
 ▸**gang up** *vi Fam* confabularse (**on** contra)

gangplank ['gæŋplæŋk] *n* plancha *f*

gangrene ['gæŋgriːn] *n* gangrena *f*

gangster ['gæŋstə(r)] *n* gángster *m*
gangway ['gæŋweɪ] *n Naut* pasarela *f*; *Th* pasillo *m*
gantry ['gæntrɪ] *n* puente *m* transversal
gaol [dʒeɪl] *n & vt Br* = **jail**
gap [gæp] *n* (**a**) abertura *f*, hueco *m*; *(blank space)* blanco *m*; *(in traffic)* claro *m*; **to bridge a g.** rellenar un hueco (**b**) *(in time)* intervalo *m*; *(emptiness)* vacío *m* (**c**) *(gulf)* diferencia *f* (**d**) *(deficiency)* laguna *f*
gape [geɪp] *vi (person)* quedarse boquiabierto(a), mirar boquiabierto(a); *(thing)* estar abierto(a)
gaping ['geɪpɪŋ] *adj Fig* profundo(a)
garage ['gæraːʒ, 'gærɪdʒ] *n* garaje *m*; *(for repairs)* taller mecánico; *(filling station)* gasolinera *f*, estación *f* de servicio, *Andes, Ven* bomba *f*, *Méx* gasolinería *f*, *Perú* grifo *m*
garbage ['gaːbɪdʒ] *n US* basura *f*; *Fig* tonterías *fpl*; **g. can** cubo *m* de la basura; **g. dump** vertedero *m*; **g. man** basurero *m*; **g. truck** camión *m* de la basura
garbled ['gaːbəld] *adj* embrollado(a); **g. account** relato confuso
garden ['gaːdən] *n* jardín *m*; **g. centre** centro *m* de jardinería; **g. party** recepción *f* al aire libre
gardener ['gaːdənə(r)] *n* jardinero(a) *m,f*
gardenia [gaː'diːnɪə] *n* gardenia *f*
gardening ['gaːdənɪŋ] *n* jardinería *f*; **his mother does the g.** su madre es la que cuida el jardín
gargle ['gaːgəl] *vi* hacer gárgaras
gargoyle ['gaːgɔɪl] *n* gárgola *f*
garish ['geərɪʃ] *adj* chillón(ona)
garland ['gaːlənd] *n* guirnalda *f*
garlic ['gaːlɪk] *n* ajo *m*
garment ['gaːmənt] *n* prenda *f*
garnish ['gaːnɪʃ] *vt* guarnecer
garrison ['gærɪsən] *n* guarnición *f*
garrulous ['gærʊləs] *adj* locuaz
garter ['gaːtə(r)] *n* liga *f*
gas [gæs] **1** *n* (**a**) gas *m*; **g. chamber** cámara *f* de gas; **g. cooker** cocina *f* de gas; **g. fire** estufa *f* de gas; **g. mask** careta *f* antigás; **g. ring** hornillo *m* de gas (**b**) *US* gasolina *f*, *RP* nafta *f*; **g. pump** surtidor *m* de gasolina; **g. station** gasolinera *f*, estación *f* de servicio, *Andes, Ven* bomba *f*, *Méx* gasolinería *f*, *Perú* grifo *m*; **g. tank** depósito *m* de la gasolina
2 *vt (asphyxiate)* asfixiar con gas
3 *vi Fam (talk)* charlotear
gash [gæʃ] **1** *n* herida profunda
2 *vt* hacer un corte en; **he gashed his forehead** se hizo una herida en la frente
gasket ['gæskɪt] *n* junta *f*

gasoline ['gæsəliːn] *n US* gasolina *f*
gasp [gaːsp] **1** *n (cry)* grito sordo; *(breath)* bocanada *f*; *Fig* **to be at one's last g.** estar en las últimas
2 *vi (in surprise)* quedar boquiabierto(a); *(breathe)* jadear
gassy ['gæsɪ] *adj* (**gassier, gassiest**) gaseoso(a)
gastric ['gæstrɪk] *adj* gástrico(a)
gastronomic [gæstrə'nɒmɪk] *adj* gastronómico(a)
gate [geɪt] *n* (**a**) puerta *f* (**b**) *(at football ground)* entrada *f*; **g. (money)** taquilla *f* (**c**) *(attendance)* entrada *f*
gateau ['gætəʊ] *n (pl* **gateaux** ['gætəʊz]*)* pastel *m* con nata
gatecrash ['geɪtkræʃ] **1** *vt* colarse en
2 *vi* colarse
gateway ['geɪtweɪ] *n* puerta *f*; *Fig* pasaporte *m*
gather ['gæðə(r)] **1** *vt* (**a**) *(collect)* juntar; *(pick)* coger; *(pick up)* recoger (**b**) *(bring together)* reunir (**c**) *(harvest)* cosechar (**d**) **to g. speed** ir ganando velocidad; **to g. strength** cobrar fuerzas (**e**) *(understand)* suponer; **I g. that ...** tengo entendido que ... (**f**) *Sewing* fruncir
2 *vi* (**a**) *(come together)* reunirse (**b**) *(form)* formarse
► gather round *vi* agruparse
gathering ['gæðərɪŋ] **1** *adj* creciente
2 *n* reunión *f*
gauche [gəʊʃ] *adj (clumsy)* torpe; *(tactless)* sin tacto
gaudy ['gɔːdɪ] *adj* (**gaudier, gaudiest**) chillón(ona)
gauge [geɪdʒ] **1** *n* (**a**) medida *f* estándar; *(of gun, wire)* calibre *m* (**b**) *Rail* ancho *m* de vía (**c**) *(calibrator)* indicador *m* (**d**) *Fig (indication)* indicación *f*
2 *vt* (**a**) *(measure)* medir, calibrar (**b**) *Fig (judge)* juzgar
gaunt [gɔːnt] *adj (lean)* demacrado(a); *(desolate)* lúgubre
gauntlet ['gɔːntlɪt] *n* guantelete *m*; *Fig* **to run the g. of ...** estar sometido(a) a ...; *Fig* **to throw down the g.** arrojar el guante
gauze [gɔːz] *n* gasa *f*
gave [geɪv] *pt of* **give**
gawky ['gɔːkɪ] *adj* (**gawkier, gawkiest**) desgarbado(a)
gay [geɪ] *adj* (**a**) *(homosexual)* gay (**b**) *(happy)* alegre
gaze [geɪz] **1** *n* mirada fija
2 *vi* mirar fijamente
gazelle [gə'zel] *n* gacela *f*
gazette [gə'zet] *n* gaceta *f*; *US* periódico *m*
gazump [gə'zʌmp] *vi Br Fam* = romper

un compromiso de venta para vender a un precio más alto

GB [dʒiː'biː] (*abbr* **Great Britain**) GB

GCE [dʒiːsiː'iː] *n Br Formerly* (*abbr* **General Certificate of Education (A-Level)**) = certificado de enseñanza secundaria

GCSE [dʒiːsiːes'iː] *n Br* (*abbr* **General Certificate of Secondary Education**) = certificado de enseñanza secundaria

GDP [dʒiːdiː'piː] *n* (*abbr* **gross domestic product**) PIB *m*

GDR [dʒiːdiː'ɑː(r)] *n Hist* (*abbr* **German Democratic Republic**) RDA *f*

gear [gɪə(r)] *n* 1 (**a**) (*equipment*) equipo *m* (**b**) *Fam (belongings)* bártulos *mpl* (**c**) *Fam (clothing)* ropa *f* (**d**) *Tech* engranaje *m* (**e**) *Aut* velocidad *f*, marcha *f*; **first g.** primera *f* (velocidad *f*); **g. lever** *or US* **shift** palanca *f* de cambio

2 *vt* ajustar, adaptar

gearbox ['gɪəbɒks] *n* caja *f* de cambios

gearstick ['gɪəstɪk], *US* **gearshift** ['gɪəʃɪft] *n* palanca *f* de cambio

gee [dʒiː] *interj US* ¡caramba!

geese [giːs] *pl of* **goose**

gel [dʒel] 1 *n* gel *m*; (*for hair*) gomina *f* 2 *vi Fig (ideas etc)* cuajar 3 *vt (hair)* engominar

gelatin ['dʒelətɪn] *n* gelatina *f*

gelignite ['dʒelɪgnaɪt] *n* gelignita *f*

gem [dʒem] *n* piedra preciosa; *Fig (person)* joya *f*

Gemini ['dʒemɪnaɪ] *n* Géminis *m*

gen [dʒen] *n Fam* **to get the g. on sth** informarse sobre algo

gender ['dʒendə(r)] *n* género *m*

gene [dʒiːn] *n* gene *m*, gen *m*

general ['dʒenərəl] 1 *adj* general; **g. knowledge** conocimientos *mpl* generales; **in g.** en general; **the g. public** el público; **g. practitioner** médico *m* de cabecera

2 *n Mil* general *m*; *US* **g. of the army** mariscal *m* de campo

generalization [dʒenərəlaɪ'zeɪʃən] *n* generalización *f*

generalize ['dʒenərəlaɪz] *vt & vi* generalizar

generally ['dʒenərəlɪ] *adv* generalmente, en general

generate ['dʒenəreɪt] *vt* generar

generation [dʒenə'reɪʃən] *n* generación *f*; **g. gap** abismo *m or* conflicto *m* generacional

generator ['dʒenəreɪtə(r)] *n* generador *m*

generosity [dʒenə'rɒsɪtɪ] *n* generosidad *f*

generous ['dʒenərəs] *adj* generoso(a); *(plentiful)* copioso(a)

genetic [dʒɪ'netɪk] *adj* genético(a); **g. engineering** ingeniería genética

genetically [dʒɪ'netɪklɪ] *adv* **g. modified** *(plant, food)* modificado(a) genéticamente

genetics [dʒɪ'netɪks] *n sing* genética *f*

Geneva [dʒɪ'niːvə] *n* Ginebra

genial ['dʒiːnɪəl, 'dʒiːnjəl] *adj* cordial, amable

> Note that the Spanish word **genial** is a false friend and is never a translation for the English word **genial**. In Spanish, **genial** means both "brilliant" and "terrific".

genie ['dʒiːnɪ] *n* duende *m*, genio *m*

genitals ['dʒenɪtəlz] *npl* órganos *mpl* genitales

genius ['dʒiːnjəs, 'dʒiːnɪəs] *n* (**a**) *(person)* genio *m* (**b**) *(gift)* don *m*

genre ['ʒɑːnrə] *n* género *m*

gent [dʒent] *n Fam* (*abbr* **gentleman**) señor *m*, caballero *m*; **the gents** los servicios (de caballeros)

genteel [dʒen'tiːl] *adj* fino(a), distinguido(a)

> Note that the Spanish word **gentil** is a false friend and is never a translation for the English word **genteel**. In Spanish, **gentil** means "kind" and "pagan".

gentle ['dʒentəl] *adj* dulce, tierno(a); *(breeze)* suave

gentleman ['dʒentəlmən] *n* caballero ;b*m*; **g.'s agreement** pacto *m* de caballeros

gently ['dʒentlɪ] *adv* con cuidado

gentry ['dʒentrɪ] *n* pequeña nobleza, alta burguesía

genuine ['dʒenjʊɪn] *adj* auténtico(a), genuino(a); *(sincere)* sincero(a)

genuinely ['dʒenjʊɪnlɪ] *adv* auténticamente

geographic(al) [dʒɪə'græfɪk(əl)] *adj* geográfico(a)

geography [dʒɪ'ɒgrəfɪ, 'dʒɒgrəfɪ] *n* geografía *f*

geologic(al) [dʒɪə'lɒdʒɪk(əl)] *adj* geológico(a)

geology [dʒɪ'ɒlədʒɪ] *n* geología *f*

geometric(al) [dʒɪə'metrɪk(əl)] *adj* geométrico(a)

geometry [dʒɪ'ɒmɪtrɪ] *n* geometría *f*

geopolitical [dʒɪːəʊpə'lɪtɪkəl] *adj* geopolítico(a)

geranium [dʒɪ'reɪnɪəm] *n* geranio *m*

geriatric [dʒerɪ'ætrɪk] *adj* geriátrico(a)

germ [dʒɜːm] n (**a**) *Biol & Fig* germen m (**b**) *Med* microbio m

German ['dʒɜːmən] **1** adj alemán(ana); **G. measles** rubeola f
2 n (**a**) alemán(ana) m,f (**b**) *(language)* alemán m

Germany ['dʒɜːmənɪ] n Alemania

germinate ['dʒɜːmɪneɪt] vi germinar

gestation [dʒe'steɪʃən] n gestación f

gesticulate [dʒe'stɪkjʊleɪt] vi gesticular

gesture ['dʒestʃə(r)] **1** n gesto m, ademán m; **it's an empty g.** es pura formalidad
2 vi gesticular, hacer gestos

get [get] **1** vt (*pt & pp* **got**; *pp US also* **gotten**) (**a**) *(obtain)* obtener, conseguir; **to g. one's own way** salirse con la suya
(**b**) *(earn)* ganar
(**c**) *(fetch) (something)* traer; *(somebody)* ir a por; **g. the police!** ¡llama a la policía!; *Tel* **g. me Mr Brown** póngame con el Sr. Brown
(**d**) *(receive)* recibir; *Fam* **he got the sack** le despidieron
(**e**) *(bus, train, thief etc)* coger; *Am* agarrar
(**f**) *(prepare)* preparar; **can I g. you something to eat?** ¿quieres comer algo?
(**g**) *(ask)* pedir; **g. him to call me** dile que me llame
(**h**) **to g. sb to agree to sth** conseguir que algn acepte algo
(**i**) **when did you g. the house painted?** ¿cuándo os pintaron la casa?; **to g. one's hair cut** cortarse el pelo
(**j**) **they got him in the chest** le dieron en el pecho
(**k**) **have got, have got to** *see* **have**
(**l**) *Fam (understand)* entender
(**m**) *(record) (in writing)* apuntar; *(on tape)* grabar
2 vi (**a**) *(become)* ponerse; **to g. dark** anochecer; **to g. dressed** vestirse; **to g. drunk** emborracharse; **to g. late** hacerse tarde; **to g. married** casarse; **to g. used to doing sth** acostumbrarse a hacer algo; **to g. paid** cobrar
(**b**) *Fig* **we are not getting anywhere** así no vamos a ninguna parte
(**c**) *(arrive)* llegar
(**d**) **to g. to** *(come to)* llegar a; **to g. to know sb** llegar a conocer a algn
▸ **get about** vi *(person)* salir; *(news)* difundirse
▸ **get across** vt sep *(idea etc)* hacer comprender
▸ **get ahead** vi progresar
▸ **get along** vi (**a**) *(leave)* marcharse (**b**) *(manage)* arreglárselas (**c**) *(two people)* llevarse bien
▸ **get around** vi *(person)* salir; *(travel)* viajar; *(news)* difundirse
▸ **get at** vt insep (**a**) *(reach)* alcanzar (**b**) *(ascertain)* descubrir (**c**) *(insinuate)* insinuar; **what are you getting at?** ¿a dónde quieres llegar? (**d**) *(criticize)* criticar
▸ **get away** vi escaparse
▸ **get away with** vt insep salir impune de
▸ **get back 1** vi (**a**) *(return)* regresar, volver (**b**) **g. back!** *(move backwards)* ¡atrás!
2 vt sep *(recover)* recuperar; *Fam* **to g. one's own back on sb** vengarse de algn
▸ **get by** vi (**a**) *(manage)* arreglárselas; **she can g. by in French** sabe defenderse en francés (**b**) *(pass)* pasar
▸ **get down 1** vt sep *(depress)* deprimir
2 vi *(descend)* bajar
▸ **get down to** vt insep ponerse a; **to g. down to the facts** ir al grano
▸ **get in 1** vi (**a**) *(arrive)* llegar (**b**) *Pol* ser elegido(a)
2 vt sep (**a**) *(buy)* comprar (**b**) *(collect)* recoger; *Fam* **he couldn't g. a word in edgeways** no pudo decir ni pío
▸ **get into** vt insep *Fig* **to g. into bad habits** adquirir malas costumbres; **to g. into trouble** meterse en un lío
▸ **get off 1** vt insep *(bus etc)* bajarse de
2 vt sep *(remove)* quitarse
3 vi (**a**) bajarse; *Fam* **g. off!** ¡fuera! (**b**) **to g. off to a good start** *(begin)* empezar bien (**c**) *(escape)* escaparse; **to g. off lightly** salir bien librado(a)
▸ **get off with** vt insep *Fam* ligar
▸ **get on 1** vt insep *(board)* subir a
2 vi (**a**) *(board)* subirse (**b**) *(make progress)* hacer progresos; **how are you getting on?** ¿cómo te van las cosas? (**c**) **to g. on (well) (with sb)** llevarse bien (con algn) (**d**) *(continue)* seguir; **to g. on with one's work** seguir trabajando (**e**) **it's getting on for eleven** son casi las once; **time's getting on** se está haciendo tarde
▸ **get on to** vt insep (**a**) *(find a person)* localizar; *(find out)* descubrir (**b**) *(continue)* pasar a
▸ **get out 1** vt sep *(object)* sacar
2 vi (**a**) *(room etc)* salir (**of** de); *(train)* bajar (**of** de) (**b**) *(escape)* escaparse (**of** de); **to g. out of an obligation** librarse de un compromiso (**c**) *(news)* difundirse; *(secret)* hacerse público
▸ **get over 1** vt insep (**a**) *(illness)* recuperarse de; **I can't g. over him** no le puedo olvidar (**b**) *(difficulty)* vencer

2 *vt sep (convey)* hacer comprender
▸**get round** *vt insep* (**a**) *(problem)* salvar; *(difficulty)* vencer (**b**) *(rule)* soslayar (**c**) *(win over)* persuadir
▸**get round to** *vt insep* **if I g. round to it si tengo tiempo**
▸**get through 1** *vi* (**a**) *(message)* llegar (**b**) *Educ* aprobar (**c**) *Tel* **to g. through to sb** conseguir comunicar con algn
2 *vt insep* (**a**) **to g. through a lot of work** trabajar mucho (**b**) *(consume)* consumir (**c**) *Educ* aprobar
▸**get together 1** *vi (people)* juntarse, reunirse
2 *vt sep (people)* juntar, reunir
▸**get up 1** *vi (rise)* levantarse
2 *vt sep* (**a**) *(wake)* despertar (**b**) *(disguise)* **to g. oneself up as ...** disfrazarse de ...
▸**get up to** *vt insep* hacer; **to g. up to mischief** hacer de las suyas
getaway ['getəweɪ] *n* fuga *f*; **to make one's g.** fugarse
get-together ['gettəgeðə(r)] *n* reunión *f*
geyser ['giːzə(r), *US* 'gaɪzər] *n* (**a**) *Geog* géiser *m* (**b**) *(water heater)* calentador *m* de agua
ghastly ['gɑːstlɪ] *adj* (**ghastlier, ghastliest**) horrible, espantoso(a)
gherkin ['gɜːkɪn] *n* pepinillo *m*
ghetto ['getəʊ] *n* gueto *m*
ghost [gəʊst] *n* fantasma *m*; **g. story** cuento *m* de fantasmas; **g. town** pueblo *m* fantasma
ghost-writer ['gəʊstraɪtə(r)] *n* negro(a) *m,f*
ghoulish ['guːlɪʃ] *adj* macabro(a)
giant ['dʒaɪənt] *adj & n* gigante *(m)*
gibberish ['dʒɪbərɪʃ] *n* galimatías *m inv*
gibe [dʒaɪb] **1** *n* mofa *f*
2 *vi* mofarse (**at** de)
giblets ['dʒɪblɪts] *npl* menudillos *mpl*
Gibraltar [dʒɪ'brɔːltə(r)] *n* Gibraltar
Gibraltarian [dʒɪbrɔːl'teərɪən] *adj & n* gibraltareño(a) *(m,f)*
giddiness ['gɪdɪnɪs] *n* mareo *m*; *(vertigo)* vértigo *m*
giddy ['gɪdɪ] *adj* (**giddier, giddiest**) mareado(a); **it makes me g.** me da vértigo; **to feel g.** sentirse mareado(a)
gift [gɪft] *n* (**a**) regalo *m*; *Com* obsequio *m*; **g. token** vale *m* (**b**) *(talent)* don *m*; **to have a g. for music** estar muy dotado(a) para la música
gifted ['gɪftɪd] *adj* dotado(a)
gig [gɪg] *n Fam Mus* actuación *f*
gigantic [dʒaɪ'gæntɪk] *adj* gigantesco(a)

giggle ['gɪgəl] **1** *n* (**a**) risita *f* (**b**) *(lark)* broma *f*, diversión *f*
2 *vi* reírse tontamente
gild [gɪld] *vt* dorar
gill¹ [dʒɪl] *n (liquid measure)* = 0,142 l
gill² [gɪl] *n (of fish)* branquia *f*, agalla *f*
gilt [gɪlt] **1** *adj* dorado(a)
2 *n (colour)* dorado *m*
gilt-edged ['gɪltedʒd] *adj* **g. securities** valores *mpl* de máxima garantía
gimmick ['gɪmɪk] *n* truco *m*; *(in advertising)* reclamo *m*
gin [dʒɪn] *n* ginebra *f*; **g. and tonic** gin tonic *m*
ginger ['dʒɪndʒə(r)] **1** *n* jengibre *m*; **g. ale** ginger ale *m*
2 *adj* (**a**) de jengibre (**b**) *(hair)* pelirrojo(a)
gingerbread ['dʒɪndʒəbred] *n* pan *m* de jengibre
gingerly ['dʒɪndʒəlɪ] *adv* cautelosamente
gipsy ['dʒɪpsɪ] *adj & n* gitano(a) *(m,f)*
giraffe [dʒɪ'rɑːf] *n* jirafa *f*
girder ['gɜːdə(r)] *n* viga *f*
girdle ['gɜːdəl] *n* faja *f*
girl [gɜːl] *n* (**a**) chica *f*, joven *f*; *(child)* niña *f*; **g. guide**, *US* **g. scout** exploradora *f* (**b**) *(daughter)* hija *f* (**c**) *(sweetheart)* novia *f*
girlfriend ['gɜːlfrend] *n* (**a**) *(lover)* novia *f* (**b**) *(female friend)* amiga *f*
girlhood ['gɜːlhʊd] *n* niñez *f*
girlish ['gɜːlɪʃ] *adj* (**a**) de niña (**b**) *(effeminate)* afeminado(a)
giro ['dʒaɪrəʊ] *n Br* giro *m* (postal); **g. (cheque)** cheque *m* de giros postales
gist [dʒɪst] *n* esencia *f*; **did you get the g. of what he was saying?** ¿cogiste la idea de lo que decía?
give [gɪv] **1** *n (elasticity)* elasticidad *f*
2 *vt (pt* **gave**; *pp* **given**) (**a**) dar; **to g. sth to sb** dar algo a algn; **to g. a start** pegar un salto; **to g. sb a present** regalar algo a algn
(**b**) *(provide)* suministrar; **to g. sb sth to eat** dar de comer a algn
(**c**) *(pay)* pagar
(**d**) *(concert)* dar; *(speech)* pronunciar
(**e**) *(dedicate)* dedicar
(**f**) *(grant)* otorgar; **to g. sb one's attention** prestar atención a algn
(**g**) **to g. sb to understand that ...** dar a entender a algn que ...
(**h**) *(yield)* ceder; **to g. way** *Aut* ceder el paso; *Fig* ceder; *(of legs)* flaquear
3 *vi* (**a**) **to g. as good as one gets** devolver golpe por golpe
(**b**) *(yield)* ceder; *(fabric)* dar de sí

▸**give away** *vt sep* (**a**) repartir; *(present)* regalar (**b**) *(disclose)* revelar; **to g. the game away** descubrir el pastel (**c**) *(betray)* traicionar

▸**give back** *vt sep* devolver

▸**give in 1** *vi* (**a**) *(admit defeat)* darse por vencido(a); *(surrender)* rendirse (**b**) **to g. in to** ceder ante

2 *vt sep (hand in)* entregar

▸**give off** *vt sep (smell etc)* despedir

▸**give out** *vt sep* distribuir, repartir

▸**give over 1** *vt sep (hand over)* entregar; *(devote)* dedicar

2 *vi Fam* **g. over!** ¡basta ya!

▸**give up 1** *vt sep* (**a**) *(idea)* abandonar; **to g. up smoking** dejar de fumar (**b**) *(betray)* traicionar (**c**) *(hand over)* entregar; **to g. oneself up** entregarse

2 *vi (admit defeat)* darse por vencido(a), rendirse

▸**give up on** *vt insep* darse por vencido con

given ['gɪvən] **1** *adj* (**a**) *(particular)* dado(a); **at a g. time** en un momento dado (**b**) **g. to** dado(a) a

2 *conj* (**a**) *(considering)* dado(a) (**b**) *(if)* si

3 *pp of* **give**

glacial ['gleɪsɪəl] *adj* (**a**) *Geol* glaciar (**b**) *(icy)* glacial; *Fig* **g. look** mirada *f* glacial

glacier ['glæsɪə(r)] *n* glaciar *m*

glad [glæd] *adj* (**gladder, gladdest**) contento(a); *(happy)* alegre; **he'll be only too g. to help you** tendrá mucho gusto en ayudarle; **to be g.** alegrarse

gladiator ['glædɪeɪtə(r)] *n Hist* gladiador *m*

gladly ['glædlɪ] *adv* con mucho gusto

glamor ['glæmər] *n US* = **glamour**

glamorous ['glæmərəs] *adj* atractivo(a), encantador(a)

glamour ['glæmə(r)] *n* atractivo *m*; *(charm)* encanto *m*; **a g. girl** una belleza

glance [glɑːns] **1** *n* mirada *f*, vistazo *m*; **at a g.** de un vistazo; **at first g.** a primera vista

2 *vi* echar un vistazo (**at** a)

▸**glance off** *vt insep (of ball etc)* rebotar de

glancing ['glɑːnsɪŋ] *adj (blow)* oblicuo(a)

gland [glænd] *n* glándula *f*

glandular ['glændjʊlə(r)] *adj* glandular; **g. fever** mononucleosis infecciosa

glare [gleə(r)] **1** *n (light)* luz *f* deslumbrante; *(dazzle)* deslumbramiento *m*; *(look)* mirada *f* feroz

2 *vi (dazzle)* deslumbrar; *(look)* lanzar una mirada furiosa (**at** a)

glaring ['gleərɪŋ] *adj (light)* deslumbrante; *(colour)* chillón(ona); *(obvious)* evidente

glass [glɑːs] *n* (**a**) *(material)* vidrio *m*; **pane of g.** cristal *m* (**b**) *(drinking vessel)* vaso *m*; **wine g.** copa *f* (para vino) (**c**) **glasses** gafas *fpl*, *Am* lentes *mpl*, anteojos *mpl*; **to wear glasses** llevar gafas *or Am* lentes *or* anteojos

glasshouse ['glɑːshaʊs] *n* invernadero *m*

glassware ['glɑːsweə(r)] *n* cristalería *f*

glassy ['glɑːsɪ] *adj* (**glassier, glassiest**) *(water)* cristalino(a); *(eyes)* vidrioso(a)

glaze [gleɪz] **1** *n (varnish)* barniz *m*; *(for pottery)* vidriado *m*

2 *vt* (**a**) *(windows)* acristalar; (**b**) *(varnish)* barnizar; *(ceramics)* vidriar (**c**) *Culin* glasear

glazed [gleɪzd] *adj (eyes)* de mirada ausente

glazier ['gleɪzɪə(r)] *n* vidriero(a) *m,f*

gleam [gliːm] **1** *n* (**a**) destello *m* (**b**) *Fig (glimmer)* rayo *m*

2 *vi* brillar, relucir

gleaming ['gliːmɪŋ] *adj* brillante, reluciente

glean [gliːn] *vt Fig* recoger, cosechar

glee [gliː] *n* gozo *m*

gleeful ['gliːfʊl] *adj* gozoso(a)

glen [glen] *n* cañada *f*

glib [glɪb] *adj* (**glibber, glibbest**) *Pej* de mucha labia

glide [glaɪd] *vi* (**a**) *(slip, slide)* deslizarse (**b**) *Av* planear

glider ['glaɪdə(r)] *n* planeador *m*

gliding ['glaɪdɪŋ] *n* vuelo *m* sin motor

glimmer ['glɪmə(r)] *n* (**a**) *(light)* luz *f* tenue (**b**) *Fig (trace)* destello *m*

glimpse [glɪmps] **1** *n* atisbo *m*

2 *vt* atisbar

glint [glɪnt] **1** *n* destello *m*, centelleo *m*; **he had a g. in his eye** le brillaban los ojos

2 *vi* destellar, centellear

glisten ['glɪsən] *vi* relucir, brillar

glitter ['glɪtə(r)] **1** *n* brillo *m*

2 *vi* relucir

gloat [gləʊt] *vi* jactarse; **to g. over another's misfortune** recrearse con la desgracia de otro

global ['gləʊbəl] *adj* (**a**) *(of the world)* mundial (**b**) *(overall)* global

globe [gləʊb] *n* globo *m*, esfera *f*

gloom [gluːm] *n (obscurity)* penumbra *f*; *(melancholy)* melancolía *f*; *(despair)* desolación *f*

gloomy ['gluːmɪ] *adj* (**gloomier, gloomiest**) *(dark)* oscuro(a); *(weather)* gris;

(dismal) deprimente; *(despairing)* pesimista; *(sad)* triste

glorify [ˈglɔːrɪfaɪ] *vt* glorificar

glorious [ˈglɔːrɪəs] *adj (momentous)* glorioso(a); *(splendid)* magnífico(a), espléndido(a)

glory [ˈglɔːrɪ] *n* gloria *f*; *Fig (splendour)* esplendor *m*; *Fig (triumph)* triunfo *m*

gloss [glɒs] **1** *n* (a) *(explanation)* glosa *f* (b) *(sheen)* brillo *m*; **g. (paint)** pintura *f* brillante
  2 *vi* glosar
▸ **gloss over** *vt insep Fig* encubrir

glossary [ˈglɒsərɪ] *n* glosario *m*

glossy [ˈglɒsɪ] *adj* (**glossier, glossiest**) lustroso(a); **g. magazine** revista *f* de lujo

glove [glʌv] *n* guante *m*; *Aut* **g. compartment** guantera *f*

glow [gləʊ] **1** *n* brillo *m*; *(of fire)* incandescencia *f*; *(of sun)* arrebol *m*; *(heat)* calor *m*; *(light)* luz *f*; *(in cheeks)* rubor *m*
  2 *vi* brillar; *(fire)* arder; *Fig* rebosar de

glower [ˈglaʊə(r)] *vi* poner cara de enfadado(a)

glowing [ˈgləʊɪŋ] *adj* (a) *(fire)* incandescente; *(colour)* vivo(a); *(light)* brillante (b) *(cheeks)* encendido(a) (c) *Fig (report)* entusiasta

glucose [ˈgluːkəʊz] *n* glucosa *f*

glue [gluː] **1** *n* pegamento *m*, cola *f*
  2 *vt* pegar (**to** a)

glum [glʌm] *adj* (**glummer, glummest**) alicaído(a)

glut [glʌt] *n* superabundancia *f*, exceso *m*

glutton [ˈglʌtən] *n* glotón(ona) *m,f*; *Fam Fig* **you're a g. for punishment** eres masoquista

GM [dʒiːˈem] *adj (abbr* **genetically modified**) transgénico(a), modificado(a) genéticamente; **GM food** (alimentos) transgénicos

GMO [dʒiːemˈəʊ] *n (abbr* **genetically modified organism**) OMG *m*

GMT [dʒiːemˈtiː] *n (abbr* **Greenwich Mean Time**) hora *f* del meridiano de Greenwich

gnarled [nɑːld] *adj* nudoso(a)

gnash [næʃ] *vt* rechinar

gnat [næt] *n* mosquito *m*

gnaw [nɔː] *vt & vi (chew)* roer

gnome [nəʊm] *n* gnomo *m*

GNP [dʒiːenˈpiː] *n (abbr* **gross national product**) PNB *m*

go [gəʊ] **1** *vi (3rd person sing pres* **goes**; *pt* **went**; *pp* **gone**) (a) ir; **to go by car/on foot** ir en coche/a pie; **to go for a walk** (ir a) dar un paseo; **to g. on a journey** ir de viaje; **to go shopping** ir de compras; *Fig* **to go too far** pasarse (de la raya)

(b) *(depart)* irse, marcharse; *(bus)* salir

(c) *(disappear)* desaparecer

(d) *(function)* funcionar; *Fig* **to get things going** poner las cosas en marcha

(e) *(sell)* venderse; **shoes going cheap** zapatos a precios de rebaja

(f) *(become)* quedarse, volverse; **to go blind** quedarse ciego(a); **to go mad** volverse loco(a)

(g) *(progress)* ir, marchar; **everything went well** todo salió bien; **how's it going?** ¿qué tal (te van las cosas)?

(h) **to be going to** *(in the future)* ir a; *(on the point of)* estar a punto de

(i) *(fit)* caber

(j) *(be kept)* guardarse

(k) *(be available)* quedar; **I'll take whatever's going** me conformo con lo que hay

(l) *(be acceptable)* valer; **anything goes** todo vale

(m) *(break)* romperse; *(yield)* ceder

(n) **how does that song go?** ¿cómo es aquella canción?

(o) *(time)* pasar; **there are only two weeks to go** sólo quedan dos semanas

(p) *(be inherited)* pasar (**to** a)

(q) *(say)* decir; **as the saying goes** según el dicho

(r) **to let sth go** soltar algo

2 *vt* (a) *(travel)* hacer, recorrer

(b) **to go it alone** apañárselas solo

3 *n* (a) *(energy)* energía *f*, dinamismo *m*

(b) *(try)* intento *m*; **to have a go at sth** probar suerte con algo

(c) *(turn)* turno *m*; **it's your go** te toca a ti

(d) **to make a go of sth** tener éxito en algo

(e) **I knew from the word go** lo sabía desde el principio

(f) **to have a go at sb** criticar a algn

▸ **go about 1** *vt insep* (a) *(task)* emprender; **how do you go about it?** ¿cómo hay que hacerlo? (b) **to go about one's business** ocuparse de sus asuntos
  2 *vi (rumour)* correr

▸ **go after** *vt insep (pursue)* andar tras

▸ **go against** *vt insep (oppose)* ir en contra de; *(verdict)* ser desfavorable a

▸ **go ahead** *vi* (a) *(proceed)* proceder (b) **we'll go on ahead** iremos delante

▸ **go along 1** *vt insep (street)* pasar por
  2 *vi (progress)* progresar

▸ **go along with** *vt insep* (a) *(agree with)* estar de acuerdo con (b) *(accompany)* acompañar

▸ **go around** *vi* (a) *(rumour)* correr (b) **there's enough to go around** hay para todos

▶ **go away** *vi* marcharse

▶ **go back** *vi* (**a**) *(return)* volver, regresar (**b**) *Fig* **to go back to** *(date from)* datar de

▶ **go back on** *vt insep* **to go back on one's word** faltar a su palabra

▶ **go back to** *vt insep* volver a

▶ **go by** *vi* pasar; **as time goes by** con el tiempo

▶ **go down** *vi* (**a**) *(descend)* bajar; *(sun)* ponerse; *(ship)* hundirse (**b**) *(diminish)* disminuir; *(temperature)* bajar (**c**) *(be received)* ser acogido(a)

▶ **go down with** *vt insep (contract)* coger

▶ **go for** *vt insep* (**a**) *(attack)* lanzarse sobre; *Fam Fig* **go for it!** ¡a por ello! (**b**) *(fetch)* ir por (**c**) *Fam (like)* gustar

▶ **go in** *vi* entrar

▶ **go in for** *vt insep (exam)* presentarse a; *(hobby)* dedicarse a

▶ **go into** *vt insep* (**a**) *(enter)* entrar en; **to go into journalism** dedicarse al periodismo (**b**) *(study)* examinar; *(matter)* investigar (**c**) *(energy, money)* invertir en

▶ **go off 1** *vi* (**a**) *(leave)* irse, marcharse (**b**) *(bomb)* explotar; *(gun)* dispararse; *(alarm)* sonar (**c**) *(food)* pasarse (**d**) *(event)* resultar

2 *vt insep Fam* **to go off sth** perder el gusto *or* el interés por algo

▶ **go on** *vi* (**a**) *(continue)* seguir, continuar; **to go on talking** seguir hablando; *Fam* **to go on and on about sth** no parar de hablar sobre algo; *(complain)* quejarse constantemente de algo (**b**) *(happen)* pasar, ocurrir (**c**) *(time)* transcurrir, pasar (**d**) *(light)* encenderse

▶ **go out** *vi* (**a**) *(leave)* salir; **to go out for a meal** comer *or* cenar fuera (**b**) *(boy and girl)* salir juntos (**c**) *(fire, light)* apagarse (**d**) *(tide)* bajar (**e**) *TV & Rad* transmitirse (**f**) **to go (all) out** ir a por todas (**g**) *(in competition)* perder la eliminatoria

▶ **go over** *vt insep (revise)* repasar

▶ **go over to** *vt insep* (**a**) acercarse a; **to go over to the enemy** pasarse al enemigo (**b**) *(switch to)* pasar a

▶ **go round** *vi* (**a**) *(revolve)* dar vueltas (**b**) **to go round to sb's house** pasar por casa de algn

▶ **go through 1** *vi (bill)* ser aprobado(a)

2 *vt insep* (**a**) *(examine)* examinar; *(search)* registrar (**b**) *(rehearse)* ensayar (**c**) *(spend)* gastar (**d**) *(list etc)* explicar (**e**) *(endure)* sufrir

▶ **go through with** *vt insep* llevar a cabo

▶ **go under** *vi* (**a**) *(ship)* hundirse (**b**) *(business)* fracasar

▶ **go up** *vi* (**a**) *(price etc)* subir (**b**) **to go up**

to sb acercarse a algn (**c**) *(in a lift)* subir (**d**) **to go up in flames** quemarse (**e**) *Sport (be promoted)* subir

▶ **go with** *vt insep* (**a**) *(accompany)* ir con (**b**) *(colours)* hacer juego con

▶ **go without 1** *vt insep* (**a**) pasarse sin, prescindir de (**b**) *Fam* **that goes without saying** eso es evidente

2 *vi (not have)* aguantarse sin nada

goad [gəʊd] *vt* aguijonear

go-ahead ['gəʊəhed] *n Fam* **to give sb the g.** dar luz verde a algn

goal [gəʊl] *n* (**a**) *Sport* gol *m*; **g. kick** saque *m* de puerta; **g. post** poste *m*; **g. scorer** goleador(a) *m,f* (**b**) *(aim, objective)* meta *f*, objetivo *m*

goalkeeper ['gəʊlkiːpə(r)] *n* portero(a) *m,f*

goat [gəʊt] *n (female)* cabra *f*; *(male)* macho cabrío

gob [gɒb] *n Br Fam* boca *f*

gobble ['gɒbəl] *vt* engullir

go-between ['gəʊbɪtwiːn] *n* intermediario(a) *m,f*

goblet ['gɒblɪt] *n* copa *f*

god [gɒd] *n* dios *m*; **for G.'s sake!** ¡por Dios!; **G.** Dios; **(my) G.!** ¡Dios mío!; **G. forbid!** ¡Dios no lo quiera!; **G. only knows** sabe Dios

godchild ['gɒdtʃaɪld] *n* ahijado(a) *m,f*

goddam(n) ['gɒdæm] *US Fam* **1** *adj* maldito(a), dichoso(a), *Méx* pinche

2 *adv* **that was g. stupid!** ¡eso fue una auténtica estupidez!

goddaughter ['gɒddɔːtə(r)] *n* ahijada *f*

goddess ['gɒdɪs] *n* diosa *f*

godfather ['gɒdfɑːðə(r)] *n* padrino *m*

godforsaken ['gɒdfəseɪkən] *adj (place)* remoto(a)

godmother ['gɒdmʌðə(r)] *n* madrina *f*

godparents ['gɒdpeərənts] *npl* padrinos *mpl*

godsend ['gɒdsend] *n* regalo inesperado

godson ['gɒdsʌn] *n* ahijado *m*

goggles ['gɒgəlz] *npl* gafas *fpl* protectoras, *CSur* antiparras *fpl*

going ['gəʊɪŋ] **1** *adj* (**a**) *(price)* corriente; **the g. rate** el precio medio (**b**) **a g. concern** un negocio que marcha bien (**c**) **to get** *or* **be g.** marcharse (**d**) **to keep g.** resistir

2 *n* (**a**) **that was good g.!** ¡qué rápido! (**b**) *Fig* **to get out while the g. is good** retirarse antes que sea demasiado tarde

goings-on [gəʊɪŋz'ɒn] *npl Fam* tejemanejes *mpl*

go-kart ['gəʊkɑːt] *n Sport* kart *m*

gold [gəʊld] **1** *n* oro *m*; **g. leaf** pan *m* de

oro; **g. medal** medalla *f* de oro; **g. mine** mina *f* de oro

2 *adj* de oro; *(colour)* oro, dorado(a)

golden ['gəʊldən] *adj* de oro; *(colour)* dorado(a); *Fig* **a g. opportunity** una excelente oportunidad; *Orn* **g. eagle** águila *f* real; *Fig* **g. handshake** indemnización *f* por despido; **g. wedding** bodas *fpl* de oro

goldfish ['gəʊldfɪʃ] *n* pez *m* de colores

gold-plated [gəʊld'pleɪtɪd] *adj* chapado(a) en oro

goldsmith ['gəʊldsmɪθ] *n* orfebre *m*

golf [gɒlf] *n* golf *m*; **g. ball** pelota *f* de golf; **g. club** *(stick)* palo *m* de golf; *(place)* club *m* de golf; **g. course** campo *m* de golf

golfer ['gɒlfə(r)] *n* golfista *mf*

golly ['gɒlɪ] *interj* ¡vaya!

gone [gɒn] **1** *adj* desaparecido(a)

2 *pp of* **go**

gong [gɒŋ] *n* gong *m*

good [gʊd] **1** *adj* (**better, best**) (**a**) *(before noun)* buen(a); *(after noun)* bueno(a); **a g. book** un buen libro; **g. afternoon/evening** buenas tardes; **g. morning** buenos días; **g. night** buenas noches; **it looks g.** tiene buena pinta; **to be as g. as new** estar como nuevo(a); **to feel g.** sentirse bien; **to have a g. time** pasarlo bien; **to smell g.** oler bien; **G. Friday** Viernes *m* Santo

(**b**) *(kind)* amable; *(generous)* generoso(a)

(**c**) *(healthy)* sano(a)

(**d**) *(morally correct)* correcto(a); **be g.!** ¡pórtate bien!

(**e**) **he's g. at languages** tiene facilidad para los idiomas

(**f**) *(attractive)* bonito(a); **red looks g. on you** el rojo te favorece mucho; **g. looks** atractivo *m*, belleza *f*

(**g**) **it's as g. as an offer** equivale a una oferta; **it's as g. a way as any** es una manera como otra cualquiera

(**h**) *(at least)* como mínimo

(**i**) *(sufficient)* bastante

(**j**) **to make g.** *(injustice)* reparar; *(loss)* compensar; *(succeed in life)* triunfar

(**k**) *(reliable)* de confianza

(**l**) *(propitious)* propicio(a)

(**m**) **she comes from a g. family** es de buena familia

(**n**) *(character)* agradable; **he's in a g. mood** está de buen humor

2 *n* (**a**) bien *m*; **g. and evil** el bien y el mal; **to do g.** hacer el bien

(**b**) *(advantage)* bien *m*, provecho *m*; **for your own g.** para tu propio bien; **it's no g. waiting** no sirve de nada esperar; **it**

will do you g. te hará bien

(**c**) **goods** *(possessions)* bienes *mpl*

(**d**) *Com* **goods** artículos *mpl*, géneros *mpl*; **goods train** tren *m* de mercancías

3 *adv* **she's gone for g.** se ha ido para siempre

4 *interj* ¡muy bien!

goodbye [gʊd'baɪ] **1** *interj* ¡adiós!

2 *n* adiós *m*, despedida *f*; **to say g. to sb** despedirse de algn

good-for-nothing ['gʊdfənʌθɪŋ] *adj & n* inútil *(mf)*

good-hearted [gʊd'hɑːtɪd] *adj* de buen corazón

good-looking [gʊd'lʊkɪŋ] *adj* guapo(a)

good-natured [gʊd'neɪtʃəd] *adj* amable, bondadoso(a)

goodness ['gʊdnɪs] *n* bondad *f*; **my g.!** ¡Dios mío!; **thank g.!** ¡gracias a Dios!; **for g. sake!** ¡por Dios!

good-tempered [gʊd'tempəd] *adj* apacible

goodwill [gʊd'wɪl] *n* (**a**) buena voluntad *f* (**b**) *Com (reputation)* buen nombre *m*

goof [guːf] *US Fam* **1** *n* metedura *f* or *Am* metida *f* de pata

2 *vi* meter la pata

goose [guːs] *n* (*pl* **geese**) ganso *m*, oca *f*

gooseberry ['gʊzbərɪ, 'guːsbərɪ] *n* uva espina, grosella espinosa; *Fam* **to play g.** hacer de carabina

gooseflesh ['guːsfleʃ] *n*, **goosepimples** ['guːspɪmpəlz] *npl* carne *f* de gallina

goose-step ['guːsstep] *vi* ir a paso de la oca

gore¹ [gɔː(r)] *n* sangre derramada

gore² [gɔː(r)] *vt (of bull)* cornear, dar cornadas a

gorge [gɔːdʒ] **1** *n* desfiladero *m*

2 *vt & vi* **to g. (oneself) (on)** atiborrarse (de)

gorgeous ['gɔːdʒəs] *adj* magnífico(a), estupendo(a); *(person)* atractivo(a), guapo(a)

gorilla [gə'rɪlə] *n* gorila *m*

gorse [gɔːs] *n* aulaga *f*

gory ['gɔːrɪ] *adj* (**gorier, goriest**) sangriento(a)

gosh [gɒʃ] *interj Fam* ¡cielos!, ¡caray!

go-slow [gəʊ'sləʊ] *n* huelga *f* de celo

gospel ['gɒspəl] *n* **the G.** el Evangelio; *Fam* **it's the g. truth** es la pura verdad

gossip ['gɒsɪp] **1** *n* (**a**) *(rumour)* cotilleo *m*; **g. column** ecos *mpl* de sociedad (**b**) *(person)* chismoso(a) *m,f*, cotilla *mf*

2 *vi (natter)* cotillear, chismorrear

got [gɒt] *pt & pp of* **get**

Gothic ['gɒθɪk] *adj* gótico(a)

gotten ['gɒtən] *US pp of* **get**

gourmet ['gʊəmeɪ] *n* gourmet *mf*

gout [gaʊt] *n* gota *f*

govern ['gʌvən] *vt* (**a**) gobernar (**b**) *(determine)* determinar

governess ['gʌvənɪs] *n* institutriz *f*

governing ['gʌvənɪŋ] *adj* gobernante; **g. body** consejo *m* de administración

government ['gʌvənmənt] *n* gobierno *m*

governmental [gʌvən'mentəl] *adj* gubernamental

governor ['gʌvənə(r)] *n (ruler)* gobernador(a) *m,f; (of prison)* director(a) *m,f; (of school)* administrador(a) *m,f*

gown [gaʊn] *n (dress)* vestido largo; *Jur & Univ* toga *f*

GP [dʒiː'piː] *n (abbr* **general practitioner**) médico(a) *m,f* de familia *or* de cabecera

GPO [dʒiːpiː'əʊ] *n Br Formerly (abbr* **General Post Office**) ≃ (Administración *f* Central de) Correos *mpl*

grab [græb] **1** *n* agarrón *m; Fam* **to be up for grabs** estar disponible

2 *vt* (**a**) agarrar; **to g. hold of sb** agarrarse a algn (**b**) *Fig* **g. a bottle of wine** píllate una botella de vino (**c**) *Fig* **how does that g. you?** ¿qué te parece?

grace [greɪs] **1** *n* (**a**) gracia *f; Fig* **to fall from g.** caer en desgracia (**b**) **to say g.** bendecir la mesa (**c**) **to do sth with good g.** hacer algo de buena gana (**d**) **five days' g.** *(reprieve)* un plazo de cinco días (**e**) *(elegance)* elegancia *f* (**f**) **Your G.** (Su) Excelencia

2 *vt* (**a**) *(adorn)* adornar (**b**) *(honour)* honrar

graceful ['greɪsfʊl] *adj* elegante; *(movement)* garboso(a)

gracefully ['greɪsfʊlɪ] *adv* (**a**) *(beautifully)* con gracia, con elegancia (**b**) *(accept)* con cortesía

gracious ['greɪʃəs] **1** *adj* (**a**) *(elegant)* elegante (**b**) *(courteous)* cortés (**c**) *(kind)* amable

2 *interj* **good g. (me)!**, **goodness g.!** ¡santo cielo!

grade [greɪd] **1** *n* (**a**) *(quality)* grado *m; (rank)* categoría *f; Mil* rango *m* (**b**) *US Educ (mark)* nota *f* (**c**) *US Educ (class)* clase *f;* **g. school** escuela primaria (**d**) *(level)* nivel *m;* **to make the g.** llegar al nivel deseado (**e**) *US (slope)* pendiente *f* (**f**) *US* **g. crossing** paso *m* a nivel

2 *vt* clasificar

gradient ['greɪdɪənt] *n (graph)* declive *m; (hill)* cuesta *f*, pendiente *f*

gradual ['grædjʊəl] *adj* gradual, progresivo(a)

gradually ['grædjʊəlɪ] *adv* poco a poco

graduate 1 *n* ['grædjʊɪt] *Educ* titulado(a) *m,f; Univ* licenciado(a) *m,f; US* **g. school** escuela *f* para graduados

2 *vi* ['grædjʊeɪt] (**a**) *Educ* sacarse el título; *Univ* licenciarse (**in** en) (**b**) **to g. to** pasar a (**c**) *US (from high school)* ≃ sacar el bachillerato

graduation [grædjʊ'eɪʃən] *n* graduación *f; Univ* **g. ceremony** ceremonia *f* de entrega de los títulos

graffiti [grə'fiːtiː] *npl* grafiti *mpl*

graft [grɑːft] **1** *n* (**a**) *Med* injerto *m* (**b**) *Fam (work)* trabajo *m* (**c**) *US (bribery)* soborno *m*

2 *vt Med* injertar (**on to** en)

3 *vi Fam* trabajar duro

grain [greɪn] *n* (**a**) *(cereals)* cereales *mpl* (**b**) *(particle)* grano *m; Fig* **there's not a g. of truth in it** no tiene ni pizca de verdad (**c**) *(in wood)* fibra *f, (in stone)* veta *f, (in leather)* flor *f; Fig* **to go against the g.** ir a contrapelo

gram [græm] *n* gramo *m*

grammar ['græmə(r)] *n* gramática *f;* **g. (book)** libro *m* de gramática; *Br* **g. school** = instituto estatal de segunda enseñanza al que se ingresa por examen selectivo

grammatical [grə'mætɪkəl] *adj* gramatical

gramme [græm] *n* gramo *m*

gramophone ['græməfəʊn] *n* gramófono *m*

granary ['grænərɪ] *n* granero *m*

grand [grænd] **1** *adj* (**a**) grande; *(before singular noun)* gran; **g. piano** piano *m* de cola; **G. Prix** Gran Premio *m* (**b**) *(splendid)* grandioso(a), magnífico(a); *(impressive)* impresionante (**c**) **g. total** total *m* (**d**) *Fam (wonderful)* estupendo(a)

2 *n Fam* mil libras *fpl; US* mil dólares *mpl*

grandchild ['græntʃaɪld] *n* nieto(a) *m,f*

granddad ['grændæd] *n Fam* abuelo *m*

granddaughter ['grændɔːtə(r)] *n* nieta *f*

grandeur ['grændʒə(r)] *n* grandeza *f,* grandiosidad *f*

grandfather ['grænfɑːðə(r)] *n* abuelo *m;* **g. clock** reloj *m* de caja

grandiose ['grændɪəʊs] *adj* grandioso(a)

grandma ['grænmɑː] *n Fam* abuelita *f*

grandmother ['grænmʌðə(r)] *n* abuela *f*

grandpa ['grænpɑː] *n Fam* abuelito *m*

grandparents ['grænpeərənts] *npl* abuelos *mpl*

grandson ['grænsʌn] *n* nieto *m*

grandstand ['grænstænd] *n* tribuna *f*

granite ['grænɪt] *n* granito *m*

granny ['grænɪ] *n Fam* abuelita *f*
grant [grɑːnt] **1** *vt* (**a**) *(allow)* conceder, otorgar (**b**) *(admit)* admitir; **to take sb for granted** no apreciar a algn en lo que vale; **to take sth for granted** dar algo por sentado
2 *n Educ* beca *f*; *(subsidy)* subvención *f*
granulated ['grænjʊleɪtɪd] *adj* granulado(a)
granule ['grænjuːl] *n* gránulo *m*
grape [greɪp] *n* uva *f*; **g. juice** mosto *m*
grapefruit ['greɪpfruːt] *n* pomelo *m*
grapevine ['greɪpvaɪn] *n Bot* vid *f*; *(against wall)* parra *f*; *Fam* **I heard it on** *or* **through the g.** me enteré por ahí
graph [grɑːf, græf] *n* gráfica *f*
graphic ['græfɪk] *adj* gráfico(a); **g. arts** artes gráficas; **g. designer** grafista *mf*
graphics ['græfɪks] *n* (**a**) *(study)* grafismo *m* (**b**) *pl Comput* gráficas *fpl*
grapple ['græpəl] **1** *vi (struggle)* luchar cuerpo a cuerpo (**with** con); *Fig* **to g. with a problem** intentar resolver un problema
2 *n (hook)* garfio *m*
grasp [grɑːsp] **1** *vt* (**a**) agarrar (**b**) *(understand)* comprender
2 *n* (**a**) *(grip)* agarrón *m* (**b**) *(understanding)* comprensión *f*; **within sb's g.** al alcance de algn
grasping ['grɑːspɪŋ] *adj* avaro(a)
grass [grɑːs] **1** *n* (**a**) hierba *f*; *(lawn)* césped *m*; *(pasture)* pasto *m*; **keep off the g.** *(sign)* prohibido pisar el césped; **g. court** pista *f* de hierba; **g. roots** base *f*; **g. snake** culebra *f* (**b**) *Fam (drug)* hierba *f* (**c**) *Br Fam (informer)* soplón(ona) *m,f*, chivato(a) *m,f*
2 *vi Br Fam* chivarse (**on** a)
▸ **grass over** *vi* cubrirse de hierba
grasshopper ['grɑːshɒpə(r)] *n* saltamontes *m inv*
grassland ['grɑːslænd] *n* pradera *f*
grass-roots ['grɑːsruːts] *adj* de base; **at g. level** a nivel popular
grassy ['grɑːsɪ] *adj* (**grassier, grassiest**) cubierto(a) de hierba
grate¹ [greɪt] **1** *vt Culin* rallar
2 *vi* chirriar
grate² [greɪt] *n* (**a**) *(in fireplace)* rejilla *f* (**b**) *(fireplace)* chimenea *f* (**c**) *Constr* rejilla *f*, reja *f*
grateful ['greɪtfʊl] *adj* agradecido(a); **to be g. for** agradecer
grater ['greɪtə(r)] *n Culin* rallador *m*
gratification [grætɪfɪ'keɪʃən] *n (pleasure)* placer *m*, satisfacción *f*

gratify ['grætɪfaɪ] *vt* (**a**) *(please)* complacer (**b**) *(yield to)* sucumbir a
gratifying ['grætɪfaɪɪŋ] *adj* grato(a)
grating¹ ['greɪtɪŋ] *n* rejilla *f*, reja *f*
grating² ['greɪtɪŋ] *adj* chirriante; *(tone)* áspero(a)
gratis ['greɪtɪs, 'grætɪs] *adv* gratis
gratitude ['grætɪtjuːd] *n* agradecimiento *m*
gratuitous [grə'tjuːɪtəs] *adj* gratuito(a)
gratuity [grə'tjuːɪtɪ] *n* gratificación *f*
grave¹ [greɪv] *n* sepultura *f*, tumba *f*
grave² [greɪv] *adj (look etc)* serio(a); *(situation)* grave
gravel ['grævəl] *n* grava *f*, gravilla *f*
gravestone ['greɪvstəʊn] *n* lápida *f* sepulcral
graveyard ['greɪvjɑːd] *n* cementerio *m*
gravity ['grævɪtɪ] *n* gravedad *f*
gravy ['greɪvɪ] *n* salsa *f*, jugo *m* (de la carne)
gray [greɪ] *adj & n US* = **grey**
graze¹ [greɪz] *vi* pacer, pastar
graze² [greɪz] **1** *vt (scratch)* rasguñar; *(brush against)* rozar
2 *n* rasguño *m*
grease [griːs, griːz] **1** *n* grasa *f*
2 *vt* engrasar
greaseproof ['griːspruːf] *adj* **g. paper** papel graso
greasy ['griːsɪ, 'griːzɪ] *adj* (**greasier, greasiest**) (**a**) *(oily)* grasiento(a); *(hair, food)* graso(a) (**b**) *(slippery)* resbaladizo(a) (**c**) *Fam (ingratiating)* pelotillero(a)
great [greɪt] **1** *adj* (**a**) grande; *(before singular noun)* gran; *(pain, heat)* fuerte; **a g. many** muchos(as); **G. Britain** Gran Bretaña; *Br* **G. Bear** Osa *f* Mayor (**b**) *Fam (excellent)* estupendo(a), magnífico(a); **to have a g. time** pasarlo en grande
2 *adv Fam* muy bien, estupendamente
great-aunt [greɪt'ɑːnt] *n* tía abuela
great-grandchild [greɪt'græntʃaɪld] *n* bisnieto(a) *m,f*
great-grandfather [greɪt'grænfɑːðə(r)] *n* bisabuelo *m*
great-grandmother [greɪt'grænmʌðə(r)] *n* bisabuela *f*
greatly ['greɪtlɪ] *adv* muy, mucho
greatness ['greɪtnɪs] *n* grandeza *f*
great-uncle [greɪt'ʌŋkəl] *n* tío abuelo
Greece [griːs] *n* Grecia
greed [griːd], **greediness** ['griːdɪnɪs] *n (for food)* gula *f*; *(for money)* codicia *f*, avaricia *f*
greedy ['griːdɪ] *adj* (**greedier, greediest**) *(for food)* glotón(ona); *(for money)* codicioso(a) (**for** de)

Greek [griːk] **1** *adj* griego(a)
  2 *n* (**a**) *(person)* griego(a) *m,f* (**b**) *(language)* griego *m*
green [griːn] **1** *n* (**a**) *(colour)* verde *m* (**b**) *(in golf)* campo *m*; **village g.** plaza *f* (del pueblo) (**c**) **greens** verdura *f*, verduras *fpl*
  2 *adj* (**a**) verde; **g. bean** judía *f* verde, *Bol, RP* chaucha *f*, *CAm* ejote *m*, *Col, Cuba* habichuela *f*, *Chile* poroto *m* verde, *Ven* vainita *f*; **g. belt** zona *f* verde; *US* **g. card** *(work permit)* permiso *m* de trabajo; **g. pepper** pimiento *m* verde; **she was g. with envy** se la comía la envidia (**b**) *(inexperienced)* verde, novato(a); *(gullible)* crédulo(a) (**c**) *Pol* **G. Party** Partido *m* Verde
greenery ['griːnərɪ] *n* follaje *m*
greenfly ['griːnflaɪ] *n* pulgón *m*
greengage ['griːngeɪdʒ] *n* ciruela claudia
greengrocer ['griːngrəʊsə(r)] *n Br* verdulero(a) *m,f*
greenhouse ['griːnhaʊs] *n* invernadero *m*; **g. effect** efecto invernadero
greenish ['griːnɪʃ] *adj* verdoso(a)
Greenland ['griːnlənd] *n* Groenlandia
greet [griːt] *vt (wave at)* saludar; *(receive)* recibir; *(welcome)* dar la bienvenida a
greeting ['griːtɪŋ] *n* (**a**) saludo *m*; **greetings card** tarjeta *f* de felicitación (**b**) *(reception)* recibimiento *m*; *(welcome)* bienvenida *f*
gregarious [grɪ'geərɪəs] *adj* gregario(a), sociable
Grenada [gre'neɪdə] *n* Granada
grenade [grɪ'neɪd] *n* granada *f*
grew [gruː] *pt of* **grow**
grey [greɪ] **1** *adj (colour)* gris; *(hair)* cano(a); *(sky)* nublado(a); **g. matter** materia *f* gris
  2 *n* (**a**) *(colour)* gris *m* (**b**) *(horse)* caballo *m* tordo
grey-haired ['greɪheəd] *adj* canoso(a)
greyhound ['greɪhaʊnd] *n* galgo *m*
greyish ['greɪɪʃ] *adj* grisáceo(a)
grid [grɪd] *n* (**a**) *(on map)* cuadrícula *f* (**b**) *(of electricity etc)* red *f* nacional (**c**) = **gridiron**
gridiron ['grɪdaɪən] *n Culin* parrilla *f*
grief [griːf] *n* dolor *m*, pena *f*; *Fam* **to come to g.** *(car, driver)* sufrir un accidente; *(plans)* irse al traste
grievance ['griːvəns] *n (wrong)* agravio *m*; *(resentment)* queja *f*
grieve [griːv] **1** *vt* apenar, dar pena a
  2 *vi* apenarse, afligirse; **to g. for sb** llorar la muerte de algn
grievous ['griːvəs] *adj (offence)* grave; **g.**

bodily harm lesiones *fpl* corporales graves
grill [grɪl] **1** *vt* (**a**) *Culin* asar a la parrilla (**b**) *Fam (interrogate)* interrogar duramente
  2 *n* parrilla *f*; *(dish)* parrillada *f*
grill(e) [grɪl] *n (grating)* reja *f*
grim [grɪm] *adj* (**grimmer, grimmest**) (**a**) *(sinister)* macabro(a); *(landscape)* lúgubre; *(smile)* sardónico(a) (**b**) *(manner)* severo(a); *(person)* ceñudo(a) (**c**) *(resolute)* inexorable (**d**) *Fam (unpleasant)* desagradable; **g. reality** la dura realidad
grimace [grɪ'meɪs] **1** *n* mueca *f*
  2 *vi* hacer una mueca
grimy ['graɪmɪ] *adj* (**grimier, grimiest**) mugriento(a)
grin [grɪn] **1** *vi* sonreír abiertamente
  2 *n* sonrisa abierta
grind [graɪnd] **1** *vt* (*pt & pp* **ground**) *(mill)* moler; *(crush)* triturar; *(sharpen)* afilar; *US (meat)* picar; **to g. one's teeth** hacer rechinar los dientes
  2 *vi* (**a**) rechinar; *Fig* **to g. to a halt** *(vehicle)* pararse lentamente; *(production etc)* pararse poco a poco (**b**) *US Fam* empollar
  3 *n* (**a**) *Fam* **the daily g.** la rutina cotidiana; **what a g.!** ¡qué rollo! (**b**) *US Fam (studious pupil)* empollón(ona) *m,f*
  ▸ **grind down** *vt sep Fig* **to g. down the opposition** acabar con la oposición
grip [grɪp] **1** *n* (**a**) *(hold)* agarrón *m*; *(handshake)* apretón *m*; *(of tyre)* adherencia *f*; **get a g. on yourself!** ¡tranquilízate!; **to get to grips with a problem** superar un problema (**b**) *(handle)* asidero *m* (**c**) *(travel bag)* maletín *m* (**d**) *(hairgrip)* pasador *m*
  2 *vt* (**a**) agarrar, asir; *(hand)* apretar (**b**) *Fig (of film, story)* captar la atención de; **to be gripped by fear** ser presa del miedo
gripe [graɪp] **1** *vi Fam (complain)* quejarse
  2 *n* (**a**) *Med (pain)* retortijón *m* (**b**) *Fam (complaint)* queja *f*
gripping ['grɪpɪŋ] *adj (film, story)* apasionante
grisly ['grɪzlɪ] *adj* (**grislier, grisliest**) espeluznante
gristle ['grɪsəl] *n* cartílago *m*, ternilla *f*
grit [grɪt] **1** *n* (**a**) *(gravel)* grava *f* (**b**) *Fam (courage)* valor *m*
  2 *vt Fig* **to g. one's teeth** apretar los dientes
gritty ['grɪtɪ] *adj* (**grittier, grittiest**) valiente
grizzly ['grɪzlɪ] *adj* **g. bear** oso pardo

groan [grəʊn] **1** *n* (**a**) *(of pain)* gemido *m* (**b**) *Fam (of disapproval)* gruñido *m*
2 *vi* (**a**) *(in pain)* gemir (**b**) *Fam (complain)* quejarse (**about** de)

grocer ['grəʊsə(r)] *n* tendero(a) *m,f*; **g.'s (shop)** tienda *f* de comestibles, *CSur* almacén *m*, *Andes, CAm, Méx* tienda *f* de abarrotes

groceries ['grəʊsərɪz] *npl* comestibles *mpl*

grocery ['grəʊsərɪ] *n (shop)* tienda *f* de ultramarinos; *US* **g. store** supermercado *m*

groggy ['grɒgɪ] *adj* (**groggier, groggiest**) *Fam (boxer)* grogui; *Fig (unsteady)* atontado(a); *(weak)* débil

groin [grɔɪn] *n* ingle *f*

groom [gruːm] **1** *n* (**a**) mozo *m* de cuadra (**b**) *(bridegroom)* novio *m*
2 *vt (horse)* almohazar; *(clothes, appearance)* cuidar

groove [gruːv] *n (furrow etc)* ranura *f*; *(of record)* surco *m*

grope [grəʊp] *vi* (**a**) *(search about)* andar a tientas; **to g. for sth** buscar algo a tientas (**b**) *Fam (fondle)* meter mano

gross [grəʊs] **1** *adj* (**a**) grosero(a); *(joke)* verde (**b**) *(fat)* obeso(a) (**c**) *(flagrant)* flagrante; *(ignorance)* craso(a) (**d**) *Com & Econ* bruto(a); **g. national product** producto nacional bruto
2 *vt Com* recaudar (en bruto)

grossly ['grəʊslɪ] *adv* enormemente

grotesque [grəʊ'tesk] *adj* grotesco(a)

grotto ['grɒtəʊ] *n* gruta *f*

ground¹ [graʊnd] **1** *n* (**a**) suelo *m*, tierra *f*; **at g. level** al nivel del suelo; *Av* **to get off the g.** despegar; *Av* **g. control** control *m* de tierra; **g. floor** planta baja; *Av* **g. staff** personal *m* de tierra; *Fig* **g. swell** marejada *f* (**b**) *(terrain)* terreno *m*; **to gain/lose g.** ganar/perder terreno; *Fig* **to stand one's g.** mantenerse firme; **football g.** campo *m* de fútbol (**c**) *US Elec* toma *f* de tierra (**d**) **grounds** *(gardens)* jardines *mpl* (**e**) **grounds** *(reason)* motivo *m* (**f**) **grounds** *(sediment)* poso *m*
2 *vt* (**a**) *Av* obligar a quedarse en tierra; *Naut* varar (**b**) *US Elec* conectar con tierra

ground² [graʊnd] **1** *adj (coffee)* molido(a); *US (meat)* picado(a)
2 *pt & pp of* **grind**

grounding ['graʊndɪŋ] *n* base *f*; **to have a good g. in** tener buenos conocimientos de

groundless ['graʊndlɪs] *adj* infundado(a)

groundsheet ['graʊndʃiːt] *n* tela *f* impermeable

groundsman ['graʊndzmən] *n* encargado *m* de campo

groundwork ['graʊndwɜːk] *n* trabajo preparatorio

group [gruːp] **1** *n* grupo *m*, conjunto *m*
2 *vt* agrupar, juntar (**into** en)
3 *vi* **to g. (together)** agruparse, juntarse

grouse¹ [graʊs] *n Orn* urogallo *m*

grouse² [graʊs] *Fam* **1** *vi* quejarse (**about** de)
2 *n* queja *f*

grove [grəʊv] *n* arboleda *f*

grovel ['grɒvəl] *vi* humillarse (**to** ante); *(crawl)* arrastrarse (**to** ante)

grow [grəʊ] **1** *vt* (*pt* **grew**; *pp* **grown**) *(cultivate)* cultivar; **to g. a beard** dejarse (crecer) la barba
2 *vi* (**a**) crecer; *(increase)* aumentar (**b**) *(become)* hacerse, volverse; **to g. accustomed to** acostumbrarse a; **to g. dark** oscurecer; **to g. old** envejecer
▸ **grow out of** *vt insep* (**a**) **he's grown out of his shirt** se le ha quedado pequeña la camisa (**b**) *Fig (phase etc)* superar
▸ **grow up** *vi* crecer, hacerse mayor

grower ['grəʊə(r)] *n* cultivador(a) *m,f*

growing ['grəʊɪŋ] *adj (child)* que crece; *(problem etc)* creciente; **he's a g. boy** está dando el estirón

growl [graʊl] **1** *vi* gruñir
2 *n* gruñido *m*

grown [grəʊn] **1** *adj* crecido(a), adulto(a)
2 *pp of* **grow**

grown-up ['grəʊnʌp] *adj & n* adulto(a) *(m,f)*; **the grown-ups** los mayores

growth [grəʊθ] *n* (**a**) crecimiento *m*; *(increase)* aumento *m*; *(development)* desarrollo *m* (**b**) *Med* bulto *m*

grub [grʌb] *n* (**a**) *(larva)* gusano *m* (**b**) *Fam (food)* papeo *m*

grubby ['grʌbɪ] *adj* (**grubbier, grubbiest**) sucio(a)

grudge [grʌdʒ] **1** *n* rencor *m*; **to bear sb a g.** guardar rencor a algn
2 *vt (give unwillingly)* dar a regañadientes; **he grudges me my success** me envidia el éxito

grudgingly ['grʌdʒɪŋlɪ] *adv* a regañadientes

gruelling, *US* **grueling** ['gruːəlɪŋ] *adj* penoso(a)

gruesome ['gruːsəm] *adj* espantoso(a), horrible

gruff [grʌf] *adj (manner)* brusco(a); *(voice)* áspero(a)

grumble ['grʌmbəl] **1** *vi* refunfuñar
2 *n* queja *f*

grumpy ['grʌmpɪ] *adj* (**grumpier, grumpiest**) gruñón(ona)
grunt [grʌnt] **1** *vi* gruñir
  2 *n* gruñido *m*
guarantee [gærən'tiː] **1** *n* garantía *f; (certificate)* certificado *m* de garantía
  2 *vt* garantizar; *(assure)* asegurar
guard [gɑːd] **1** *vt* (**a**) *(protect)* defender, proteger; *(keep watch over)* vigilar (**b**) *(control)* guardar
  2 *vi* protegerse (**against** de *or* contra)
  3 *n* (**a**) **to be on one's g.** estar en guardia; **to catch sb off his g.** coger desprevenido a algn (**b**) *(sentry)* guardia *mf;* **g. of honour** guardia de honor; **to stand g.** montar la guardia; **g. dog** perro *m* guardián (**c**) *Br Rail* jefe *m* de tren; **g.'s van** furgón *m* de cola (**d**) *(on machine)* dispositivo *m* de seguridad; **fire g.** pantalla *f*
guarded ['gɑːdɪd] *adj* cauteloso(a), precavido(a)
guardhouse ['gɑːdhaʊs] *n Mil* (**a**) *(headquarters)* cuerpo *m* de guardia (**b**) *(prison)* prisión *f* militar
guardian ['gɑːdɪən] *n* (**a**) guardián(ana) *m,f;* **g. angel** ángel *m* de la guarda (**b**) *Jur (of minor)* tutor(a) *m,f*
Guatemala [gwɑːtə'mɑːlə] *n* Guatemala
Guatemalan [gwɑːtə'mɑːlən] *adj & n* guatemalteco(a) *(m,f)*
guava ['gwɑːvə] *n Bot* guayaba *f;* **g. tree** guayabo *m*
guer(r)illa [gə'rɪlə] *n* guerrillero(a) *m,f;* **g. warfare** guerra *f* de guerrillas
guess [ges] **1** *vt & vi* (**a**) adivinar; **I guessed as much** me lo imaginaba; **to g. right/wrong** acertar/no acertar (**b**) *US Fam* pensar, suponer; **I g. so** supongo que sí
  2 *n* conjetura *f; (estimate)* cálculo *m;* **at a rough g.** a ojo de buen cubero; **to have** *or* **make a g.** intentar adivinar
guesswork ['geswɜːk] *n* conjetura *f*
guest [gest] *n (at home)* invitado(a) *m,f; (in hotel)* cliente(a) *m,f,* huésped(a) *m,f;* **g. artist** artista *mf* invitado(a); **g. room** cuarto *m* de los invitados
guesthouse ['gesthaʊs] *n* casa *f* de huéspedes
guffaw [gʌ'fɔː] *vi* reírse a carcajadas
guidance ['gaɪdəns] *n* orientación *f,* consejos *mpl;* **for your g.** a título de información
guide [gaɪd] **1** *vt* guiar, dirigir
  2 *n* (**a**) *(person)* guía *mf; Br* **girl g.** exploradora *f;* **g. dog** perro lazarillo (**b**) *(guidebook)* guía *f*
guidebook ['gaɪdbʊk] *n* guía *f*

guided ['gaɪdɪd] *adj* dirigido(a); **g. tour** visita con guía; **g. missile** misil teledirigido
guideline ['gaɪdlaɪn] *n* pauta *f*
guild [gɪld] *n* gremio *m*
guile [gaɪl] *n* astucia *f*
guillotine ['gɪlətiːn] *n* guillotina *f*
guilt [gɪlt] *n* (**a**) culpa *f* (**b**) *Jur* culpabilidad *f*
guilty ['gɪltɪ] *adj* (**guiltier, guiltiest**) culpable (**of** de); **to have a g. conscience** remorderle a uno la conciencia
guinea¹ ['gɪnɪ] *n* **g. pig** conejillo *m* de Indias, cobayo *m; Fig* **to act as a g. pig** servir de conejillo de Indias
guinea² ['gɪnɪ] *n (coin)* guinea *f (= 21 chelines)*
guise [gaɪz] *n* **under the g. of** so pretexto de
guitar [gɪ'tɑː(r)] *n* guitarra *f*
guitarist [gɪ'tɑːrɪst] *n* guitarrista *mf*
gulf [gʌlf] *n* (**a**) golfo *m;* **G. of Mexico** Golfo de Méjico; **G. Stream** corriente *f* del Golfo de Méjico; **the G. War** la guerra del Golfo (**b**) *Fig* abismo *m*
gull [gʌl] *n* gaviota *f*
gulley ['gʌlɪ] *n* = **gully**
gullible ['gʌləbəl] *adj* crédulo(a)
gully ['gʌlɪ] *n* barranco *m,* hondonada *f*
gulp [gʌlp] **1** *n* trago *m*
  2 *vt* tragar; **to g. sth down** *(drink)* tomarse algo de un trago; *(food)* engullir algo
  3 *vi* (**a**) *(swallow air)* tragar aire (**b**) *Fig (with fear)* tragar saliva
gum¹ [gʌm] **1** *n* goma *f*
  2 *vt* pegar con goma
gum² [gʌm] *n Anat* encía *f*
gumboots ['gʌmbuːts] *npl* botas *fpl* de agua
gun [gʌn] *n* arma *f* de fuego; *(handgun)* pistola *f,* revólver *m; (rifle)* fusil *m,* escopeta *f; (cannon)* cañón *m; Fam* **the big guns** los peces gordos
  ► **gun down** *vt sep* matar a tiros
gunboat ['gʌnbəʊt] *n* cañonero *m*
gunfire ['gʌnfaɪə(r)] *n* tiros *mpl*
gunman ['gʌnmən] *n* pistolero *m,* gángster *m*
gunpoint ['gʌnpɔɪnt] *n* **at g.** a punta de pistola
gunpowder ['gʌnpaʊdə(r)] *n* pólvora *f*
gunrunner ['gʌnrʌnə(r)] *n* traficante *mf* de armas
gunshot ['gʌnʃɒt] *n* disparo *m,* tiro *m*
gunsmith ['gʌnsmɪθ] *n* armero *m*
gurgle ['gɜːgəl] *vi (baby)* gorjear; *(liquid)* gorgotear; *(stream)* murmurar

guru [ˈgʊruː, ˈguːruː] *n* gurú *m*

gush [gʌʃ] **1** *vi* (**a**) brotar (**b**) *Fig* **to g. over sb** enjabonar a algn
  2 *n (of water)* chorro *m*; *(of words)* torrente *m*

gushing [ˈgʌʃɪŋ] *adj Fig (person)* efusivo(a)

gusset [ˈgʌsɪt] *n* escudete *m*

gust [gʌst] *n (of wind)* ráfaga *f*, racha *f*

gusto [ˈgʌstəʊ] *n* entusiasmo *m*

gut [gʌt] **1** *n* (**a**) *Anat* intestino *m* (**b**) *(catgut)* cuerda *f* de tripa (**c**) **guts** *(entrails)* tripas *fpl*; *Fam* **to have guts** tener agallas
  2 *vt* (**a**) *(fish)* destripar (**b**) *(destroy)* destruir por dentro
  3 *adj Fam* **g. reaction** reacción *f* visceral

gutter [ˈgʌtə(r)] *n (in street)* arroyo *m*; *(on roof)* canalón *m*; *Fig* **g. press** prensa amarilla

guttural [ˈgʌtərəl] *adj* gutural

guy¹ [gaɪ] *n Fam* tipo *m*, tío *m*

guy² [gaɪ] *n (rope)* viento *m*, cuerda *f*

guzzle [ˈgʌzəl] *vt & vi Fam (food etc)* zamparse; *(car)* tragar mucho

gym [dʒɪm] *Fam* (**a**) *(gymnasium)* gimnasio *m* (**b**) *(gymnastics)* gimnasia *f*; **g. shoes** zapatillas *fpl* de deporte

gymnasium [dʒɪmˈneɪzɪəm] *n* gimnasio *m*

gymnast [ˈdʒɪmnæst] *n* gimnasta *mf*

gymnastics [dʒɪmˈnæstɪks] *n sing* gimnasia *f*

gynaecologist, *US* **gynecologist** [gaɪnɪˈkɒlədʒɪst] *n* ginecólogo(a) *m,f*

gypsy [ˈdʒɪpsɪ] *adj & n* gitano(a) *(m,f)*

gyrate [dʒaɪˈreɪt] *vi* girar

H, h [eɪtʃ] *n (the letter)* H, h *f*
haberdashery [hæbə'dæʃərɪ] *n* (**a**) *Br* artículos *mpl* de mercería (**b**) *US* ropa masculina
habit ['hæbɪt] *n* (**a**) costumbre *f* (**b**) *(garment)* hábito *m*
habitable ['hæbɪtəbəl] *adj* habitable
habitat ['hæbɪtæt] *n* hábitat *m*
habitual [hə'bɪtjʊəl] *adj* habitual; *(drinker, liar)* empedernido(a)
habitually [hə'bɪtjʊəlɪ] *adv* por costumbre
hack¹ [hæk] **1** *n (cut)* corte *m; (with an axe)* hachazo *m*
   2 *vt (with knife, axe)* cortar; *(kick)* dar un puntapié a
hack² [hæk] *n Fam (writer)* escritorzuelo(a) *m,f; (journalist)* gacetillero(a) *m,f*
hackneyed ['hæknɪd] *adj* trillado(a)
hacksaw ['hæksɔː] *n* sierra *f* para metales
had [hæd] *pt & pp of* **have**
haddock ['hædək] *n* abadejo *m*
haemophilia [hiːməʊ'fɪlɪə] *n* hemofilia *f*
haemophiliac [hiːməʊ'fɪlɪæk] *adj & n* hemofílico(a) *(m,f)*
haemorrhage ['hemərɪdʒ] *n* hemorragia *f*
haemorrhoids ['hemərɔɪdz] *npl* hemorroides *fpl*
hag [hæg] *n Pej* bruja *f*, arpía *f*
haggard ['hægəd] *adj* ojeroso(a)
haggle ['hægəl] *vi* regatear
Hague [heɪg] *n* **The H.** La Haya
hail¹ [heɪl] **1** *n* granizo *m; Fig* **a h. of bullets/insults** una lluvia de balas/insultos
   2 *vi* granizar
hail² [heɪl] **1** *vt* (**a**) *(taxi etc)* parar (**b**) *(acclaim)* aclamar
   2 *vi* **to h. from** *(originate)* ser nativo(a) de
hailstone ['heɪlstəʊn] *n* granizo *m*
hailstorm ['heɪlstɔːm] *n* granizada *f*
hair [heə(r)] *n (strand)* pelo *m*, cabello *m; (mass)* pelo, cabellos *mpl; (on arm, leg)* vello *m*; **to have long h.** tener el pelo largo
hairbrush ['heəbrʌʃ] *n* cepillo *m* (para el pelo)

haircut ['heəkʌt] *n* corte *m* de pelo; **to have a h.** cortarse el pelo
hairdo ['heəduː] *n Fam* peinado *m*
hairdresser ['heədresə(r)] *n* peluquero(a) *m,f*; **h.'s (shop)** peluquería *f*
hairdryer, hairdrier ['heədraɪə(r)] *n* secador *m* (de pelo)
hairgrip ['heəgrɪp] *n Br* horquilla *f*
hairline ['heəlaɪn] **1** *adj* muy fino(a)
   2 *n* nacimiento *m* del pelo; **receding h.** entradas *fpl*
hairnet ['heənet] *n* redecilla *f*
hairpiece ['heəpiːs] *n* postizo *m*
hairpin ['heəpɪn] *n* horquilla *f*; **h. bend** curva muy cerrada
hair-raising ['heəreɪzɪŋ] *adj* espeluznante
hair-remover ['heərɪmuːvə(r)] *n* depilatorio *m*
hairspray ['heəspreɪ] *n* laca *f* (para el pelo)
hairstyle ['heəstaɪl] *n* peinado *m*, corte *m* de pelo
hairy ['heərɪ] *adj* (**hairier, hairiest**) (**a**) *(with hair)* peludo(a) (**b**) *Fig (frightening)* enervante, espantoso(a)
hake [heɪk] *n* merluza *f; (young)* pescadilla *f*
half [hɑːf] **1** *n (pl* **halves)** mitad *f; Sport (period)* tiempo *m*; **he's four and a h.** tiene cuatro años y medio; **to cut in h.** cortar por la mitad
   2 *adj* medio(a); **h. a dozen/an hour** media docena/hora; **h. board** media pensión; **h. fare** media tarifa; **h. term** medio trimestre; **h. year** semestre *m*
   3 *adv* medio, a medias; **h. asleep** medio dormido(a)
half-caste ['hɑːfkɑːst] *adj & n* mestizo(a) *(m,f)*
half-day [hɑːf 'deɪ] *n* media jornada
half-hearted [hɑːf 'hɑːtɪd] *adj* poco entusiasta
half-hour [hɑːf 'aʊə(r)] *n* media hora
half-life ['hɑːflaɪf] *n* media vida
half-mast [hɑːf 'mɑːst] *n* **at h.** a media asta
half-price [hɑːf 'praɪs] *adv* a mitad de precio

half-time [hɑːf 'taɪm] *n* descanso *m*
half-way ['hɑːfweɪ] **1** *adj* intermedio(a)
 2 halfway [hɑːf 'weɪ] *adv* a medio camino, a mitad de camino
half-yearly ['hɑːfjɪəlɪ] *adj* semestral
halibut ['hælɪbət] *n* mero *m*
hall [hɔːl] *n* (**a**) *(lobby)* vestíbulo *m* (**b**) *(building)* sala *f*; *Univ* **h. of residence** colegio *m* mayor
hallmark ['hɔːlmɑːk] *n* (**a**) *(on gold, silver)* contraste *m* (**b**) *Fig* sello *m*
hallo [hə'ləʊ] *interj* ¡hola!
hallowed ['hæləʊd] *adj* santificado(a)
Hallowe(')en [hæləʊ'iːn] *n* víspera *f* de Todos los Santos
hallucinate [hə'luːsɪneɪt] *vi* alucinar
hallucination [həluːsɪ'neɪʃən] *n* alucinación *f*
hallucinogenic [həluːsɪnəʊ'dʒenɪk] *adj* alucinógeno(a)
hallway ['hɔːlweɪ] *n* vestíbulo *m*
halo ['heɪləʊ] *n* (**a**) *Rel* aureola *f* (**b**) *Astron* halo *m*
halt [hɔːlt] **1** *n* *(stop)* alto *m*, parada *f*; **to call a h. to sth** poner fin a algo
 2 *vt* parar
 3 *vi* pararse
halting ['hɔːltɪŋ] *adj* vacilante
halve [hɑːv] *vt* (**a**) partir por la mitad; *(reduce by half)* reducir a la mitad (**b**) *(share)* compartir
halves [hɑːvz] *pl of* **half**
ham [hæm] *n* jamón *m*; **boiled h.** jamón de York; **Parma** *or* **cured h.** jamón serrano
hamburger ['hæmbɜːgə(r)] *n* hamburguesa *f*
hamlet ['hæmlɪt] *n* aldea *f*
hammer ['hæmə(r)] **1** *n* (**a**) martillo *m*; **the h. and sickle** la hoz y el martillo (**b**) *(of gun)* percursor *m* (**c**) *Sport* lanzamiento *m* de martillo
 2 *vt* (**a**) martillar; *(nail)* clavar; *Fig* **to h. home** insistir sobre (**b**) *Fam (defeat)* dar una paliza a
 3 *vi* martillar, dar golpes
hammering ['hæmərɪŋ] *n Fam* paliza *f*
hammock ['hæmək] *n* hamaca *f*; *Naut* coy *m*
hamper¹ ['hæmpə(r)] *n* cesta *f*
hamper² ['hæmpə(r)] *vt* estorbar, dificultar
hamster ['hæmstə(r)] *n* hámster *m*
hamstring ['hæmstrɪŋ] *n* tendón *m* de la corva
hand [hænd] **1** *n* (**a**) mano *f*; **by h.** a mano; **(close) at h.** a mano; **hands up!** ¡manos arriba!; **on the one/other h.** por una/otra parte; *Fig* **to get out of h.** descontrolarse;

Fig **to be on h.** estar a mano; *Fig* **to have a h. in** intervenir en; *Fig* **to have time in h.** sobrarle a uno tiempo; *Fig* **to wash one's hands of sth** lavarse las manos de algo; *Fig* **to give sb a h.** echarle una mano a algn; **h. grenade** granada *f* de mano
 (**b**) *(worker)* trabajador(a) *m,f*; *Naut* tripulante *m*
 (**c**) *(of clock)* aguja *f*
 (**d**) **to give sb a big h.** *(applause)* dedicar a algn una gran ovación
 (**e**) *(handwriting)* letra *f*
 2 *vt* *(give)* dar, entregar; *Fam Fig* **I have to h. it to you** tengo que reconocerlo
▸ **hand back** *vt sep* devolver
▸ **hand down** *vt sep* dejar en herencia
▸ **hand in** *vt sep* *(homework)* entregar; *(resignation)* presentar
▸ **hand out** *vt sep* repartir
▸ **hand over** *vt sep* entregar
▸ **hand round** *vt sep* repartir
handbag ['hændbæg] *n Br* bolso *m*, cartera *f*, *Méx* bolsa *f*
handball ['hændbɔːl] *n Sport* balonmano *m*
handbook ['hændbʊk] *n* manual *m*
handbrake ['hændbreɪk] *n* freno *m* de mano
handcuff ['hændkʌf] **1** *vt* esposar
 2 *npl* **handcuffs** esposas *fpl*
handful ['hændfʊl] *n* puñado *m*
handicap ['hændɪkæp] **1** *n* (**a**) *Med* minusvalía *f* (**b**) *Sport* hándicap *m*, desventaja *f*
 2 *vt* impedir
handicapped ['hændɪkæpt] *adj* (**a**) *(physically)* minusválido(a); *(mentally)* retrasado(a) (**b**) *Sport* en desventaja (**c**) *Fig* desfavorecido(a)
handicraft ['hændɪkrɑːft] *n* artesanía *f*
handiwork ['hændɪwɜːk] *n (work)* obra *f*; *(craft)* artesanía *f*
handkerchief ['hæŋkətʃiːf] *n* pañuelo *m*
handle ['hændəl] **1** *n (of knife)* mango *m*; *(of cup)* asa *f*; *(of door)* pomo *m*; *(of lever)* palanca *f*; *(of drawer)* tirador *m*
 2 *vt* (**a**) manejar; **h. with care** *(sign)* frágil (**b**) *(problem)* encargarse de; *(people)* tratar; *Fam (put up with)* soportar
 3 *vi (car)* comportarse
handlebar ['hændəlbɑː(r)] *n* manillar *m*
handmade [hænd'meɪd] *adj* hecho(a) a mano
hand-out ['hændaʊt] *n* (**a**) *(leaflet)* folleto *m*; *Press* nota *f* de prensa (**b**) *(charity)* limosna *f*
hand-picked [hænd'pɪkt] *adj* selecto(a)
handrail ['hændreɪl] *n* pasamanos *m inv*

handshake ['hændʃeɪk] *n* apretón *m* de manos

handsome ['hænsəm] *adj* (**a**) *(person)* guapo(a) (**b**) *(substantial)* considerable

handwriting ['hændraɪtɪŋ] *n* letra *f*

handy ['hændɪ] *adj* (**handier, handiest**) (**a**) *(useful)* útil, práctico(a); *(nearby)* a mano (**b**) *(dextrous)* diestro(a)

hang [hæŋ] **1** *vt (pt & pp* **hung**) (**a**) colgar (**b**) *(head)* bajar (**c**) *(pt* **hanged**) ahorcar
2 *vi* (**a**) colgar (**from** de); *(in air)* flotar (**b**) *(criminal)* ser ahorcado(a); **to h. one-self** ahorcarse
► **hang about** *vi Fam* (**a**) perder el tiempo (**b**) *(wait)* esperar
► **hang around** *vi Fam* (**a**) esperar (**b**) frecuentar; **where does he h. around?** ¿a qué lugares suele ir?
► **hang on** *vi* (**a**) agarrarse (**b**) *(wait)* esperar
► **hang out 1** *vt sep (washing)* tender
2 *vi Fam (frequent)* frecuentar
► **hang round** *vi Fam* = **hang about**
► **hang together** *vi (ideas)* ser coherente
► **hang up** *vt sep (picture, telephone)* colgar

hangar ['hæŋə(r)] *n* hangar *m*

hanger ['hæŋə(r)] *n* percha *f*

hang-glider ['hæŋglaɪdə(r)] *n* ala delta

hang-gliding ['hæŋglaɪdɪŋ] *n* vuelo *m* libre

hangman ['hæŋmən] *n* verdugo *m*

hangover ['hæŋəʊvə(r)] *n* resaca *f*

hang-up ['hæŋʌp] *n Fam (complex)* complejo *m*

hanker ['hæŋkə(r)] *vi* **to h. after sth** anhelar algo

hankie, hanky ['hæŋkɪ] *n Fam* pañuelo *m*

haphazard [hæp'hæzəd] *adj* caótico(a), desordenado(a)

happen ['hæpən] *vi* suceder, ocurrir; **it so happens that** lo que pasa es que; **if you h. to see my friend** si por casualidad ves a mi amigo

happening ['hæpənɪŋ] *n* acontecimiento *m*

happily ['hæpɪlɪ] *adv (with pleasure)* felizmente; *(fortunately)* afortunadamente

happiness ['hæpɪnɪs] *n* felicidad *f*

happy ['hæpɪ] *adj* (**happier, happiest**) *(cheerful)* feliz, contento(a); *(fortunate)* afortunado(a); **h. birthday!** ¡feliz cumpleaños!

happy-go-lucky [hæpɪgəʊ'lʌkɪ] *adj* despreocupado(a); **a h. fellow** un viva la virgen

harangue [hə'ræŋ] **1** *vt* arengar
2 *n* arenga *f*

harass ['hærəs] *vt* acosar

harassment ['hærəsmənt, hə'ræsmənt] *n* hostigamiento *m*, acoso *m*

harbour, *US* **harbor** ['hɑːbə(r)] **1** *n* puerto *m*
2 *vt* (**a**) *(criminal)* encubrir (**b**) *(doubts)* abrigar

hard [hɑːd] **1** *adj* (**a**) duro(a); *(solid)* sólido(a); **h. court** pista (de tenis) rápida; *Comput* **h. disk** disco duro; *Br Aut* **h. shoulder** arcén *m*, *Andes* berma *f*, *Méx* acotamiento *m*, *RP* banquina *f*, *Ven* hombrillo *m*
(**b**) *(difficult)* difícil; **h. of hearing** duro(a) de oído; *Fam Fig* **to be h. up** estar sin blanca
(**c**) *(harsh)* severo(a); *(strict)* estricto(a); **to take a h. line** tomar medidas severas; **h. drugs** droga dura; *Pol* **h. left** extrema izquierda; **h. porn** pornografía dura; **h. sell** promoción *f* de venta agresiva
(**d**) **a h. drinker** un bebedor inveterado; **a h. worker** un trabajador concienzudo
(**e**) **h. luck!** ¡mala suerte!
(**f**) **h. evidence** pruebas definitivas; *Com* **h. cash** dinero *m* en metálico; **h. currency** divisa *f* fuerte
2 *adv* (**a**) *(hit)* fuerte
(**b**) *(work)* mucho, concienzudamente; *Fig* **to be h. on sb's heels** pisar los talones a algn
(**c**) **to be h. done by** ser tratado(a) injustamente

hardback ['hɑːdbæk] *n* edición *f* de tapas duras

hard-boiled ['hɑːdbɔɪld] *adj* duro(a)

hard-core ['hɑːdkɔː(r)] *adj* irreductible

harden ['hɑːdən] **1** *vt* endurecer
2 *vi* endurecerse

hardened ['hɑːdənd] *adj Fig* habitual

hard-headed [hɑːd'hedɪd] *adj* realista

hard-hearted [hɑːd'hɑːtɪd] *adj* insensible

hardliner [hɑːd'laɪnə(r)] *n* duro(a) *m,f*

hardly ['hɑːdlɪ] *adv* apenas; **h. anyone/ever** casi nadie/nunca; **he had h. begun when …** apenas había comenzado cuando …; **I can h. believe it** apenas lo puedo creer

hardship ['hɑːdʃɪp] *n* privación *f*, apuro *m*

hardware ['hɑːdweə(r)] *n* (**a**) *(goods)* ferretería *f*; **h. shop** ferretería (**b**) *Comput* hardware *m*

hardwearing [hɑːd'weərɪŋ] *adj* duradero(a)

hardworking ['hɑːdwɜːkɪŋ] *adj* muy trabajador(a)

hardy ['hɑːdɪ] *adj* (**hardier, hardiest**) *(person)* robusto(a), fuerte; *(plant)* resistente

hare [heə(r)] **1** *n* liebre *f*
  2 *vi* correr muy de prisa

haricot ['hærɪkəʊ] *n* **h. (bean)** alubia *f*

harm [hɑːm] **1** *n* daño *m*, perjuicio *m*; **to be out of h.'s way** estar a salvo
  2 *vt* hacer daño a, perjudicar

harmful ['hɑːmfʊl] *adj* perjudicial (**to** para)

harmless ['hɑːmlɪs] *adj* inofensivo(a)

harmonica [hɑːˈmɒnɪkə] *n* armónica *f*

harmonize ['hɑːmənaɪz] *vt & vi* armonizar

harmony ['hɑːmənɪ] *n* armonía *f*

harness ['hɑːnɪs] **1** *n* *(for horse)* arreos *mpl*
  2 *vt* (**a**) *(horse)* enjaezar (**b**) *Fig (resources etc)* aprovechar

harp [hɑːp] *n* arpa *f*
  ▸ **harp on** *vi Fam* hablar sin parar

harpoon [hɑːˈpuːn] **1** *n* arpón *m*
  2 *vt* arponear

harrowing ['hærəʊɪŋ] *adj* angustioso(a)

harsh [hɑːʃ] *adj* severo(a); *(voice)* áspero(a); *(sound)* discordante

harvest ['hɑːvɪst] **1** *n* cosecha *f*; *(of grapes)* vendimia *f*
  2 *vt* cosechar, recoger

harvester ['hɑːvɪstə(r)] *n* (**a**) *(person)* segador(a) *m,f* (**b**) *(machine)* cosechadora *f*

has [hæz] *3rd person sing pres of* **have**

hash¹ [hæʃ] *n Culin* sofrito *m* de carne; *Fam Fig* **to make a h. of sth** estropear algo

hash² [hæʃ] *n Fam* hachís *m*

hashish ['hæʃiːʃ] *n* hachís *m*

hassle ['hæsəl] *Fam* **1** *n* (**a**) *(nuisance)* rollo *m* (**b**) *(problem)* lío *m* (**c**) *(wrangle)* bronca *f*
  2 *vt* fastidiar

haste [heɪst] *n Fml* prisa *f*; **to make h.** darse prisa

hasten ['heɪsən] *vi* apresurarse

hastily ['heɪstɪlɪ] *adv (quickly)* de prisa

hasty ['heɪstɪ] *adj* (**hastier, hastiest**) apresurado(a); *(rash)* precipitado(a)

hat [hæt] *n* sombrero *m*

hatch¹ [hætʃ] *n* escotilla *f*; **serving h.** ventanilla *f*

hatch² [hætʃ] *vt* (**a**) *(eggs)* empollar (**b**) *Fig (plan)* tramar
  ▸ **hatch out** *vi* salirse del huevo

hatchback ['hætʃbæk] *n* coche *m* de 3/5 puertas

hatchet ['hætʃɪt] *n* hacha *f*; *Fam* **h. man** matón *m*

hate [heɪt] **1** *n* odio *m*
  2 *vt* odiar

hateful ['heɪtfʊl] *adj* odioso(a)

hatred ['heɪtrɪd] *n* odio *m*

haughty ['hɔːtɪ] *adj* (**haughtier, haughtiest**) altanero(a), arrogante

haul [hɔːl] **1** *n* (**a**) *(journey)* trayecto *m* (**b**) *(of fish)* redada *f* (**c**) *(loot)* botín *m*
  2 *vt* (**a**) tirar; *(drag)* arrastrar (**b**) *(transport)* acarrear
  ▸ **haul up** *vt sep Fam (to court)* llevar

haulage ['hɔːlɪdʒ] *n* transporte *m*

haulier ['hɔːljə(r)] *n* transportista *mf*

haunch [hɔːntʃ] *n* cadera *f*; *Culin* pernil *m*

haunt [hɔːnt] **1** *n* guarida *f*
  2 *vt* (**a**) *(of ghost)* aparecerse en (**b**) *Fig* atormentar (**c**) *(frequent)* frecuentar

haunted ['hɔːntɪd] *adj* encantado(a), embrujado(a)

Havana [həˈvænə] *n* La Habana; **H. cigar** habano *m*

have [hæv]

En el inglés hablado, y en el escrito en estilo coloquial, el verbo auxiliar **have** se contrae de forma que **I have** se transforma en **I've**, **he/she/it has** se transforman en **he's/she's/it's** y **you/we/they have** se transforman en **you've/we've/they've**. Las formas de pasado **I/you/he** *etc* **had** se transforman en **I'd, you'd, he'd** *etc*. Las formas negativas **has not, have not** y **had not** se transforman en **hasn't, haven't** y **hadn't**.

1 *vt* (*3rd person sing pres* **has**; *pt & pp* **had**) (**a**) *(possess)* tener; **h. you got a car?** ¿tienes coche?
  (**b**) *(get, experience, suffer)* tener; **to h. a holiday** tomarse unas vacaciones
  (**c**) *(partake of)* tomar; **to h. a cigarette** fumarse un cigarrillo; **to h. breakfast/lunch/tea/dinner** desayunar/comer/merendar/cenar
  (**d**) **to h. a bath/shave** bañarse/afeitarse; **to h. a nap** echar la siesta
  (**e**) **to h. to** *(obligation)* tener que, deber
  (**f**) *(make happen)* hacer que; **I'll h. someone come round** haré que venga alguien
  (**g**) *(receive)* recibir; **to h. people round** invitar a gente
  (**h**) **can I h. your pen a moment?** *(borrow)* ¿me dejas tu bolígrafo un momento?
  (**i**) *(party, meeting)* hacer, celebrar
  (**j**) **to h. a baby** tener un niño

(**k**) **we won't h. it** *(allow)* no lo consentiremos

(**l**) *(hold)* tener; *Fig* **to h. sth against sb** tener algo en contra de algn

(**m**) **legend has it that ...** según la leyenda ...

(**n**) *Fam (deceive)* engañar

(**o**) **you'd better stay** más vale que te quedes

2 *v aux* (**a**) *(compound)* haber; **I had been waiting for half an hour** hacía media hora que esperaba; **he hasn't eaten yet** no ha comido aún; **she had broken the window** había roto el cristal; **we h. lived here for ten years** hace diez años que vivimos aquí; **so I h.!** *(emphatic)* ¡ay, sí!, es verdad; **yes I h.!** ¡que sí!

(**b**) *(tag questions)* **you haven't seen my book, h. you?** no has visto mi libro, ¿verdad?; **he's been to France, hasn't he?** ha estado en Francia, ¿verdad? *or* ¿no?

(**c**) *(have + just)* acabar de

▶ **have on** *vt sep* (**a**) *(wear)* vestir (**b**) *Fam* **to h. sb on** tomarle el pelo a algn

▶ **have out** *vt sep Fam* **to h. it out with sb** ajustar cuentas con algn

▶ **have over** *vt sep (invite)* recibir

haven ['heɪvən] *n* puerto *m*; *Fig* refugio *m*
haversack ['hævəsæk] *n* mochila *f*
havoc ['hævək] *n* **to play h. with** hacer estragos en
hawk [hɔːk] *n Orn & Pol* halcón *m*
hawker ['hɔːkə(r)] *n* vendedor(a) *m,f* ambulante
hawthorn ['hɔːθɔːn] *n* espino *m* albar
hay [heɪ] *n* heno *m*; **h. fever** fiebre *f* del heno
haystack ['heɪstæk] *n* almiar *m*
haywire ['heɪwaɪə(r)] *adj Fam* en desorden; **to go h.** *(machine etc)* estropearse; *(person)* volverse loco(a)
hazard ['hæzəd] **1** *n* peligro *m*, riesgo *m*; *(in golf)* obstáculo *m*
2 *vt Fml* arriesgar; **to h. a guess** intentar adivinar
hazardous ['hæzədəs] *adj* arriesgado(a), peligroso(a)
haze [heɪz] *n (mist)* neblina *f*; *Fig (blur)* confusión *f*
hazel ['heɪzəl] *adj* (de color) avellana
hazelnut ['heɪzəlnʌt] *n* avellana *f*
hazy ['heɪzɪ] *adj* (hazier, haziest) nebuloso(a)
he [hiː] *pers pron* él *(usually omitted in Spanish, except for contrast)*; **he did it** ha sido él; **he who** el que
head [hed] **1** *n* (**a**) cabeza *f*; *(mind)* mente *f*; *Fig* **£3 a h.** 3 libras por cabeza; *Fig* **to be**

h. over heels in love estar locamente enamorado(a); *Fig* **to keep one's h.** mantener la calma; *Fig* **to lose one's h.** perder la cabeza; **success went to his h.** se le subió el éxito a cabeza; **h. start** ventaja *f*

(**b**) *(of nail)* cabeza *f*; *(of beer)* espuma *f*; *(of tape recorder)* cabezal *m*; *(of steam)* presión *f*; *Fig* **to come to a h.** llegar a un momento decisivo

(**c**) *(boss)* cabeza *m*; *(of company)* director(a) *m,f*; **h. teacher** director(a) *m,f*

(**d**) *(of coin)* cara *f*; **heads or tails** cara o cruz

2 *adj* principal; **h. office** oficina *f* central
3 *vt* (**a**) *(list etc)* encabezar
(**b**) *Ftb* cabecear
▶ **head for** *vt insep* dirigirse hacia
▶ **head off 1** *vi* irse
2 *vt sep (avert)* evitar
headache ['hedeɪk] *n* dolor *m* de cabeza; *Fig* quebradero *m* de cabeza
headcheese ['hedtʃiːz] *n US* queso *m* de cerdo
header ['hedə(r)] *n Ftb* cabezazo *m*
head-first [hed'fɜːst] *adv* de cabeza
head-hunter ['hedhʌntə(r)] *n Fig* cazatalentos *mf inv*
heading ['hedɪŋ] *n* título *m*; *(of letter)* membrete *m*
headlamp ['hedlæmp] *n* faro *m*
headland ['hedlənd] *n* punta *f*, cabo *m*
headlight ['hedlaɪt] *n* faro *m*
headline ['hedlaɪn] *n* titular *m*; **the headlines** *(on radio, TV)* los titulares
headlong ['hedlɒŋ] *adj & adv* de cabeza; **to rush h. into sth** lanzarse a hacer algo sin pensar
headmaster [hed'mɑːstə(r)] *n* director *m*
headmistress [hed'mɪstrɪs] *n* directora *f*
head-on ['hedɒn] *adj* **a h. collision** un choque frontal
headphones ['hedfəʊnz] *npl* auriculares *mpl*
headquarters ['hedkwɔːtəz] *npl* (**a**) oficina *f* central, sede *f* (**b**) *Mil* cuartel *m* general
headrest ['hedrest] *n Aut* apoyacabezas *m*
headroom ['hedruːm] *n* altura *f* libre
headscarf ['hedskɑːf] *n* pañuelo *m*
headstrong ['hedstrɒŋ] *adj* testarudo(a)
headway ['hedweɪ] *n* **to make h.** avanzar, progresar
headwind ['hedwɪnd] *n* viento *m* de proa
heady ['hedɪ] *adj* (headier, headiest) embriagador(a)
heal [hiːl] **1** *vi* cicatrizar
2 *vt (wound)* curar

health [helθ] *n* salud *f*; *Fig* prosperidad *f*; **to be in good/bad h.** estar bien/mal de salud; **your good h.!** ¡salud!; **h. foods** alimentos *mpl* naturales; **h. food shop** tienda *f* de alimentos naturales; *Br* **H. Service** ≃ Insalud *m*

healthy ['helθɪ] *adj* (**healthier, healthiest**) sano(a); *(good for health)* saludable; *(thriving)* próspero(a)

heap [hi:p] **1** *n* montón *m*

2 *vt* amontonar; *Fig* **to h. praise on sb** colmar a algn de alabanzas; **a heaped spoonful** una cucharada colmada

hear [hɪə(r)] **1** *vt* (*pt & pp* **heard** [hɜ:d]) (**a**) oír (**b**) *(listen to)* escuchar (**c**) **I won**'t h. of it! ¡ni hablar! (**d**) *(find out)* enterarse (**e**)*Jur* ver; *(evidence)* oír

2 *vi* **to h. from sb** tener noticias de algn

hearing ['hɪərɪŋ] *n* (**a**) oído *m*; **h. aid** audífono *m* (**b**) *Jur* audiencia *f*; *Fig* **to give sb a fair h.** escuchar a algn

hearsay ['hɪəseɪ] *n* rumores *mpl*

hearse [hɜ:s] *n* coche *m* fúnebre

heart [hɑ:t] *n* (**a**) corazón *m*; **h. attack** infarto *m* de miocardio; **h. transplant** trasplante *m* de corazón; **a broken h.** un corazón roto; **at h.** en el fondo; **to take sth to h.** tomarse algo a pecho; **to have a good h.** *(be kind)* tener buen corazón (**b**) *(courage)* valor *m*; **his h. wasn't in it** no ponía interés en ello; **to lose h.** desanimarse (**c**) *(core)* meollo *m*; *(of lettuce)* cogollo *m*

heartbeat ['hɑ:tbi:t] *n* latido *m* del corazón

heart-breaking ['hɑ:tbreɪkɪŋ] *adj* desgarrador(a)

heart-broken ['hɑ:tbrəʊkən] *adj* hundido(a); **he's h.** tiene el corazón destrozado

heartburn ['hɑ:tbɜ:n] *n* acedía *f*

heartening ['hɑ:tənɪŋ] *adj* alentador(a)

heartfelt ['hɑ:tfelt] *adj* sincero(a)

hearth [hɑ:θ] *n* (**a**) *(fireplace)* chimenea *f* (**b**) *Fml (home)* hogar *m*

heartless ['hɑ:tlɪs] *adj* cruel, insensible

heart-throb ['hɑ:tθrɒb] *n* ídolo *m*

hearty ['hɑ:tɪ] *adj* (**heartier, heartiest**) *(person)* francote; *(meal)* abundante; *(welcome)* cordial; **to have a h. appetite** ser de buen comer

heat [hi:t] **1** *n* (**a**) calor *m* (**b**) *Sport* eliminatoria *f* (**c**)*Zool* **on h.** en celo

2 *vt* calentar

▸ **heat up** *vi* (**a**) *(warm up)* calentarse (**b**) *(increase excitement)* acalorarse

heated ['hi:tɪd] *adj Fig (argument)* acalorado(a)

heater ['hi:tə(r)] *n* calentador *m*

heath [hi:θ] *n (land)* brezal *m*

heathen ['hi:ðən] *adj & n* pagano(a) *(m,f)*

heather ['heðə(r)] *n* brezo *m*

heating ['hi:tɪŋ] *n* calefacción *f*

heatwave ['hi:tweɪv] *n* ola *f* de calor

heave [hi:v] **1** *n (pull)* tirón *m*; *(push)* empujón *m*

2 *vt* (**a**) *(lift)* levantar; *(haul)* tirar; *(push)* empujar (**b**) *(throw)* arrojar

3 *vi* subir y bajar

heaven ['hevən] **1** *n* (**a**) cielo *m*; **for h.'s sake!** ¡por Dios!; **h. on earth** un paraíso en la tierra (**b**) **heavens** cielo *m*

2 *interj* **good heavens!** ¡por Dios!

heavenly ['hevənlɪ] *adj* celestial

heavily ['hevɪlɪ] *adv* **it rained h.** llovió mucho; **to sleep h.** dormir profundamente

heavy ['hevɪ] **1** *adj* (**heavier, heaviest**) pesado(a); *(rain, meal)* fuerte; *(traffic)* denso(a); *(loss)* grande; **h. going** duro(a); **is it h.?** ¿pesa mucho?; **a h. drinker/smoker** un(a) bebedor(a)/fumador(a) empedernido(a); *Mus* **h. metal** heavy metal *m*

2 *n Fam* gorila *m*

heavyweight ['hevɪweɪt] *n* peso pesado

Hebrew ['hi:bru:] **1** *adj* hebreo(a)

2 *n (language)* hebreo *m*

Hebrides ['hebrɪdi:z] *npl* **the H.** las (Islas) Hébridas

heckle ['hekəl] *vt* interrumpir

heckler ['heklə(r)] *n* altercador(a) *m,f*

hectare ['hektɑ:(r)] *n* hectárea *f*

hectic ['hektɪk] *adj* agitado(a)

hedge [hedʒ] **1** *n* seto *m*

2 *vt* cercar con un seto; *Fig* **to h. one's bets** cubrirse

hedgehog ['hedʒhɒg] *n* erizo *m*

hedgerow ['hedʒrəʊ] *n* seto vivo

heed [hi:d] *n* **to take h. of** hacer caso de

heedless ['hi:dlɪs] *adj* desatento(a)

heel [hi:l] *n (of foot)* talón *m*; *(of shoe)* tacón *m*; *(of palm)* pulpejo *m*; *Fig* **to be on sb's heels** pisarle los talones a algn; **high heels** zapatos *mpl* de tacón alto

heeled [hi:ld] *adj Fam Fig* **well-h.** adinerado(a)

hefty ['heftɪ] *adj* (**heftier, heftiest**) (**a**) *(person)* fornido(a); *(package)* pesado(a) (**b**) *(large)* grande

height [haɪt] *n* (**a**) altura *f*; *(of person)* estatura *f*; *Av* **to gain/lose h.** subir/bajar; **what h. are you?** ¿cuánto mides?; *Fig* **the h. of ignorance** el colmo de la ignorancia (**b**) *Geog* cumbre *f*

heighten ['haɪtən] *vt (intensify)* realzar; *(increase)* aumentar

heir [eə(r)] *n* heredero *m*
heiress ['eərɪs] *n* heredera *f*
heirloom ['eəluːm] *n* reliquia *f*/joya *f* de familia
held [held] *pt & pp of* **hold**
helicopter ['helɪkɒptə(r)] *n* helicóptero *m*
helium ['hiːlɪəm] *n* helio *m*
hell [hel] *n* infierno *m*; *Fam* **what the h. are you doing?** ¿qué diablos estás haciendo?; *Fam Pej* **go to h.!** ¡vete a hacer puñetas!; *Fam* **a h. of a party** una fiesta estupenda; *Fam* **she's had a h. of a day** ha tenido un día fatal
hellish ['helɪʃ] *adj Fam* infernal
hello [hə'ləʊ, he'ləʊ] *interj* ¡hola!; *Tel* ¡diga!; *(showing surprise)* ¡hala!
helm [helm] *n* timón *m*; **to be at the h.** llevar el timón
helmet ['helmɪt] *n* casco *m*
help [help] **1** *n* (**a**) ayuda *f*; **h.!** ¡socorro! (**b**) **(daily) h.** asistenta *f*
2 *vt* (**a**) ayudar; **can I h. you?** *(in shop)* ¿qué desea? (**b**) *(alleviate)* aliviar (**c**) **h. yourself!** *(to food etc)* ¡sírvete! (**d**) *(avoid)* evitar; **I can't h. it** no lo puedo remediar
► **help out** *vt sep* **to h. sb out** echarle una mano a algn
helper ['helpə(r)] *n* ayudante(a) *m,f*
helpful ['helpfʊl] *adj (person)* amable; *(thing)* útil
helping ['helpɪŋ] *n* ración *f*; **who wants a second h.?** ¿quién quiere repetir?
helpless ['helplɪs] *adj (defenceless)* desamparado(a); *(powerless)* incapaz
helplessly ['helplɪslɪ] *adv* inútilmente, en vano
helter-skelter [heltə'skeltə(r)] **1** *n* tobogán *m*
2 *adj* atropellado(a)
3 *adv* atropelladamente
hem [hem] **1** *n Sewing* dobladillo *m*
2 *vt Sewing* hacer un dobladillo a
► **hem in** *vt sep* cercar, rodear
hemisphere ['hemɪsfɪə(r)] *n* hemisferio *m*
hemophilia [hiːməʊ'fɪlɪə] *n US* = **haemophilia**
hemophiliac [hiːməʊ'fɪlɪæk] *adj & n* = **haemophiliac**
hemorrhage ['hemərɪdʒ] *n US* = **haemorrhage**
hen [hen] *n* gallina *f*; *Fam* **h. party** reunión *f* de mujeres
hence [hens] *adv Fml* (**a**) **six months h.** *(from now)* de aquí a seis meses (**b**) *(consequently)* por lo tanto

henceforth [hens'fɔːθ] *adv Fml* de ahora en adelante
henchman ['hentʃmən] *n Pej* secuaz *m*
henna ['henə] *n Bot* alheña *f*; *(dye)* henna *f*
henpecked ['henpekt] *adj Fam* **a h. husband** un calzonazos
hepatitis [hepə'taɪtɪs] *n* hepatitis *f*
her [hɜː(r), *unstressed* hə(r)] **1** *poss adj* *(one thing)* su; *(more than one)* sus; *(to distinguish)* de ella; **are they h. books or his?** ¿los libros son de ella o de él?; **she has cut h. finger** se ha cortado el dedo
2 *pron* (**a**) *(direct object)* la; **I saw h. recently** la vi hace poco (**b**) *(indirect object)* le; *(with other third person pronouns)* se; **he gave h. money** le dio dinero; **they handed it to h.** se lo entregaron (**c**) *(after prep)* ella; **for h.** para ella (**d**) *(as subject) Fam* ella; **look, it's h.!** ¡mira, es ella!
herald ['herəld] **1** *n* heraldo *m*
2 *vt* anunciar
heraldry ['herəldrɪ] *n* heráldica *f*
herb [hɜːb, *US* ɜːrb] *n* hierba *f*; **h. tea** infusión *f*
herbal ['hɜːbəl] *adj* herbario(a); **h. remedies** curas *fpl* de hierbas
herd [hɜːd] *n (of cattle)* manada *f*; *(of goats)* rebaño *m*; *Fig (large group)* multitud *f*
here [hɪə(r)] **1** *adv* aquí; **come h.** ven aquí; **h.!** ¡presente!; **h. goes!** ¡vamos a ver!; **here's to success!** ¡brindemos por el éxito!; **h. you are!** ¡toma!
2 *interj* **look h., you can't do that!** ¡oiga, que no se permite hacer eso!
hereafter [hɪər'ɑːftə(r)] *Fml* **1** *adv* de ahora en adelante
2 *n* **the h.** la otra vida, el más allá
hereby [hɪə'baɪ] *adv Fml* por la presente
hereditary [hɪ'redɪtərɪ] *adj* hereditario(a)
heresy ['herəsɪ] *n* herejía *f*
heretic ['herətɪk] *n* hereje *mf*
heritage ['herɪtɪdʒ] *n* patrimonio *m*; *Jur* herencia *f*
hermetically [hɜː'metɪklɪ] *adv* **h. sealed** herméticamente cerrado(a)
hermit ['hɜːmɪt] *n* ermitaño(a) *m,f*

📖 Note that the Spanish word **ermita** is a false friend and is never a translation for the English word **hermit**. In Spanish, **ermita** means "hermitage".

hermitage ['hɜːmɪtɪdʒ] *n* ermita *f*
hernia ['hɜːnɪə] *n* hernia *f*
hero ['hɪərəʊ] *n (pl* **heroes**) héroe *m*; *(in*

novel) protagonista *m;* **h. worship** idolatría *f*

heroic [hɪˈrəʊɪk] *adj* heroico(a)

heroin [ˈherəʊɪn] *n* heroína *f*

heroine [ˈherəʊɪn] *n* heroína *f; (in novel)* protagonista *f*

heron [ˈherən] *n* garza *f*

herring [ˈherɪŋ] *n* arenque *m*

hers [hɜːz] *poss pron* (**a**) *(attribute) (one thing)* suyo(a); *(more than one)* suyos(as); *(to distinguish)* de ella; **they are h.**, **not his** son de ella, no de él (**b**) *(noun reference) (one thing)* el suyo/la suya; *(more than one)* los suyos/las suyas; **my car is blue and h. is red** mi coche es azul y el suyo es rojo

herself [hɜːˈself] *pers pron* (**a**) *(reflexive)* se; **she dressed h.** se vistió (**b**) *(alone)* ella misma; **she was by h.** estaba sola (**c**) *(emphatic)* **she told me so h.** eso dijo ella

hesitant [ˈhezɪtənt] *adj* vacilante

hesitate [ˈhezɪteɪt] *vi* vacilar

hesitation [hezɪˈteɪʃən] *n* indecisión *f*

heterogeneous [hetərəʊˈdʒiːnɪəs] *adj* heterogéneo(a)

heterosexual [hetərəʊˈseksjʊəl] *adj & n* heterosexual *(mf)*

hey [heɪ] *interj* ¡oye!, ¡oiga!

heyday [ˈheɪdeɪ] *n* auge *m*, apogeo *m*

HGV [eɪtʃdʒiːˈviː] *n Br (abbr* **heavy goods vehicle***)* vehículo *m* de carga pesada

hi [haɪ] *interj Fam* ¡hola!

hiatus [haɪˈeɪtəs] *n Fml* laguna *f*

hibernate [ˈhaɪbəneɪt] *vi* hibernar

hibernation [haɪbəˈneɪʃən] *n* hibernación *f*

hibiscus [haɪˈbɪskəs] *n* hibisco *m*

hiccup, hiccough [ˈhɪkʌp] *n* hipo *m; Fam (minor problem)* problemilla *m;* **to have hiccups** tener hipo

hide¹ [haɪd] **1** *vt (pt* **hid** [hɪd]; *pp* **hidden** [ˈhɪdən]) *(conceal)* esconder; *(obscure)* ocultar

2 *vi* esconderse, ocultarse

3 *n* puesto *m*

hide² [haɪd] *n (of animal)* piel *f*

hide-and-seek [haɪdənˈsiːk] *n* escondite *m*

hideous [ˈhɪdɪəs] *adj (horrific)* horroroso(a); *(extremely ugly)* espantoso(a)

hide-out [ˈhaɪdaʊt] *n* escondrijo *m*, guarida *f*

hiding¹ [ˈhaɪdɪŋ] *n* **to go into h.** esconderse

hiding² [ˈhaɪdɪŋ] *n Fam* paliza *f*

hierarchy [ˈhaɪərɑːkɪ] *n* jerarquía *f*

hi-fi [ˈhaɪfaɪ] *n* hifi *m;* **h. equipment** equipo *m* de alta fidelidad

high [haɪ] **1** *adj* (**a**) alto(a); **how h. is that wall?** ¿qué altura tiene esa pared?; **it's 3 feet h.** tiene 3 pies de alto; **h. chair** silla alta para niños; **h. jump** salto *m* de altura (**b**) *(elevated)* elevado(a); **h. blood pressure** tensión alta; **h. prices** precios elevados; **to be in h. spirits** estar de buen humor (**c**) *(important)* importante; **h. wind** viento *m* fuerte; **to have a h. opinion of sb** tener muy buena opinión de algn; **H. Court** Tribunal Supremo; **h. fidelity** alta fidelidad; **h. road** carretera *f* principal; **h. school** instituto *m* de enseñanza media; **the H. Street** la Calle Mayor

(**d**) *Fam (drugged)* colocado(a)

2 *adv* alto; **to fly h.** volar a gran altura

3 *n (high point)* punto máximo

highbrow [ˈhaɪbraʊ] *adj & n* intelectual *(mf)*

high-class [ˈhaɪklɑːs] *adj* de alta categoría

higher [ˈhaɪə(r)] **1** *adj* superior; **h. education** enseñanza *f* superior

2 *n Scot Educ* **H.** = examen final de los estudios preuniversitarios

high-five [ˈhaɪfaɪv] *n US Fam* palmada *f* en el aire *(saludo entre dos)*

high-flier, high-flyer [haɪˈflaɪə(r)] *n Fig* = persona dotada y ambiciosa

high-handed [haɪˈhændɪd] *adj* déspotico(a)

high-heeled [ˈhaɪhiːld] *adj* de tacón alto

highlands [ˈhaɪləndz] *npl* tierras altas

highlight [ˈhaɪlaɪt] **1** *n* (**a**) *(in hair)* reflejo *m* (**b**) *(of event)* atracción *f* principal

2 *vt* (**a**) hacer resaltar (**b**) *(text)* marcar con un rotulador fosforescente

highly [ˈhaɪlɪ] *adv (very)* sumamente; **to speak h. of sb** hablar muy bien de algn

highly-strung [haɪlɪˈstrʌŋ] *adj* muy nervioso(a)

Highness [ˈhaɪnɪs] *n* alteza *mf;* **Your H.** Su Alteza

high-pitched [ˈhaɪpɪtʃt] *adj* estridente

high-powered [ˈhaɪpaʊəd] *adj (person)* dinámico(a)

high-ranking [ˈhaɪræŋkɪŋ] *adj* **h. official** alto funcionario

high-rise [ˈhaɪraɪz] *adj* **h. building** rascacielos *m inv*

high-speed [ˈhaɪspiːd] *adj* **h. lens** objetivo ultrarrápido; **h. train** tren *m* de alta velocidad

highway [ˈhaɪweɪ] *n US* carretera *f,* autopista *f; Br* **H. Code** código *m* de la circulación

highwayman [ˈhaɪweɪmən] *n* salteador *m* de caminos

hijack [ˈhaɪdʒæk] **1** *vt* secuestrar
2 *n* secuestro *m*
hijacker [ˈhaɪdʒækə(r)] *n* secuestrador(a) *m,f; (of planes)* pirata *mf* del aire
hike [haɪk] **1** *n* (**a**) *(walk)* excursión *f* (**b**)
price h. aumento *m* de precio
2 *vi* ir de excursión
hiker [ˈhaɪkə(r)] *n* excursionista *mf*
hilarious [hɪˈleərɪəs] *adj* graciosísimo(a)
hill [hɪl] *n* colina *f; (slope)* cuesta *f*
hillside [ˈhɪlsaɪd] *n* ladera *f*
hilltop [ˈhɪltɒp] *n* cima *f* de una colina
hilly [ˈhɪlɪ] *adj* (**hillier, hilliest**) accidentado(a)
hilt [hɪlt] *n* puño *m*, empuñadura *f;* **I'll support you up to the h.** te daré mi apoyo total
him [hɪm] *pron* (**a**) *(direct object)* lo, le; **hit h.!** ¡pégale!; **she loves h.** lo quiere (**b**) *(indirect object)* le; *(with other third person pronouns)* se; **give h. the money** dale el dinero; **give it to h.** dáselo (**c**) *(after prep)* él; **it's not like h. to say that** no es propio de él decir eso (**d**) *Fam (as subject)* él; **it's h.** es él
himself [hɪmˈself] *pers pron* (**a**) *(reflexive)* se; **he hurt h.** se hizo daño (**b**) *(alone)* solo, por sí mismo; **by h.** solo (**c**) *(emphatic)* él mismo
hind[1] [haɪnd] *adj* trasero(a); **h. legs** patas traseras
hind[2] [haɪnd] *n Zool* cierva *f*
hinder [ˈhɪndə(r)] *vt* dificultar, estorbar; **to h. sb from doing sth** impedir a algn hacer algo
hindrance [ˈhɪndrəns] *n* estorbo *m*
hindsight [ˈhaɪndsaɪt] *n* retrospectiva *f*
Hindu [hɪnˈduː, ˈhɪnduː] *adj & n* hindú *(mf)*
Hinduism [ˈhɪnduɪzəm] *n* hinduismo *m*
hinge [hɪndʒ] **1** *n* bisagra *f; Fig* eje *m*
2 *vt* engoznar
► **hinge on** *vt insep* depender de
hint [hɪnt] **1** *n* (**a**) indirecta *f;* **to take the h.** coger la indirecta (**b**) *(clue)* pista *f* (**c**) *(trace)* pizca *f* (**d**) *(advice)* consejo *m*
2 *vi* (**a**) lanzar indirectas (**b**) *(imply)* insinuar algo
hip[1] [hɪp] *n* cadera *f;* **h. flask** petaca *f*
hip[2] [hɪp] *adj Fam* en la onda
hippie [ˈhɪpɪ] *adj & n Fam* hippy *(mf)*
hippopotamus [hɪpəˈpɒtəməs] *n* hipopótamo *m*
hire [ˈhaɪə(r)] **1** *n* alquiler *m;* **bicycles for h.** se alquilan bicicletas; **taxi for h.** taxi *m* libre; **h. purchase** compra *f* a plazos
2 *vt* (**a**) *(rent)* alquilar, *Méx* rentar (**b**) *(employ)* contratar

► **hire out** *vt sep (car)* alquilar, *Méx* rentar; *(people)* contratar
his [hɪz] **1** *poss adj (one thing)* su; *(more than one)* sus; *(to distinguish)* de él; **he washed h. face** se lavó la cara; **is it h. dog or hers?** ¿el perro es de él o de ella?
2 *poss pron* (**a**) *(attribute) (one thing)* suyo(a); *(more than one)* suyos(as); *(to distinguish)* de él (**b**) *(noun reference) (one thing)* el suyo/la suya; *(more than one)* los suyos/las suyas; **my car is blue and h. is red** mi coche es azul y el suyo es rojo
Hispanic [hɪˈspænɪk] **1** *adj* hispánico(a)
2 *n US* hispano(a) *m,f,* latino(a) *m,f*
hiss [hɪs] **1** *n* siseo *m; Th* silbido *m*
2 *vt & vi* silbar
historian [hɪˈstɔːrɪən] *n* historiador(a) *m,f*
historic [hɪˈstɒrɪk] *adj* histórico(a)
historical [hɪˈstɒrɪkəl] *adj* histórico(a); **h. novel** novela histórica
history [ˈhɪstərɪ] *n* historia *f*
hit [hɪt] **1** *n* (**a**) *(blow)* golpe *m;* **direct h.** impacto directo; *Fam* **h. list** lista negra; *Fam* **h. man** asesino *m* a sueldo (**b**) *(success)* éxito *m;* **h. parade** lista *f* de éxitos (**c**) *Comput (visit to web site)* acceso *m*, visita *f*
2 *vt* (*pt & pp* **hit**) (**a**) *(strike)* golpear, pegar; **he was h. in the leg** le dieron en la pierna; **the car h. the kerb** el coche chocó contra el bordillo; *Fam Fig* **to h. the roof** poner el grito en el cielo (**b**) *(affect)* afectar (**c**) **to h. the headlines** ser noticia
► **hit back** *vi (reply to criticism)* replicar
► **hit on** *vt insep* dar con; **we h. on the idea of ...** se nos ocurrió la idea de ...
► **hit out** *vi* **to h. out at sb** atacar a algn
► **hit upon** *vt insep* = **hit on**
hit-and-run [hɪtənˈrʌn] *adj* **h. driver** = conductor que atropella a algn y no para
hitch [hɪtʃ] **1** *n* dificultad *f*
2 *vt (fasten)* atar
3 *vi Fam (hitch-hike)* hacer autostop
► **hitch up** *vt sep* remangarse
hitch-hike [ˈhɪtʃhaɪk] *vi* hacer autostop *or* dedo
hitch-hiker [ˈhɪtʃhaɪkə(r)] *n* autostopista *mf*
hitherto [hɪðəˈtuː] *adv Fml* hasta la fecha
HIV [eɪtʃaɪˈviː] *n (abbr* **human immunodeficiency virus**) VIH *m;* **to be diagnosed HIV positive/negative** dar seropositivo(a)/seronegativo(a) en la prueba del SIDA
hive [haɪv] *n* colmena *f; Fig* lugar muy activo

HM (*abbr* **His/Her Majesty**) SM
hoard [hɔːd] **1** *n* (*provisions*) reservas *fpl*; (*money etc*) tesoro *m*
  2 *vt* (*objects*) acumular; (*money*) atesorar
hoarding ['hɔːdɪŋ] *n* (*temporary fence*) valla *f*; *Br* (*billboard*) valla publicitaria
hoarfrost ['hɔːfrɒst] *n* escarcha *f*
hoarse [hɔːs] *adj* ronco(a); **to be h.** tener la voz ronca
hoax [həʊks] *n* (*joke*) broma pesada; (*trick*) engaño *m*
hob [hɒb] *n* (*of cooker*) encimera *f*
hobble ['hɒbəl] *vi* cojear
hobby ['hɒbɪ] *n* pasatiempo *m*, afición *f*
hobbyhorse ['hɒbɪhɔːs] *n* (*toy*) caballito *m* de juguete; *Fig* (*fixed idea*) idea fija, manía *f*
hobo ['həʊbəʊ] *n US* vagabundo(a) *m,f*
hockey ['hɒkɪ] *n* hockey *m*
hog [hɒg] **1** *n* cerdo *m*, puerco *m*; *Fam* **to go the whole h.** liarse la manta a la cabeza
  2 *vt Fam* acaparar
hoist [hɔɪst] **1** *n* (*crane*) grúa *f*; (*lift*) montacargas *m inv*
  2 *vt* levantar, subir; **to h. the flag** izar la bandera
hold [həʊld] **1** *vt* (*pt & pp* **held**) (**a**) (*keep in hand*) aguantar, tener (en la mano); (*grip*) agarrar; (*support*) (*weight*) soportar; (*opinion*) sostener; **to h. sb** abrazar a algn; **to h. sb's hand** cogerle la mano a algn; *Fig* **she can h. her own in French** se defiende en francés
  (**b**) (*contain*) dar cabida a; **the jug holds a litre** en la jarra cabe un litro
  (**c**) (*meeting*) celebrar; (*conversation*) mantener
  (**d**) (*reserve*) guardar
  (**e**) **to h. office** ocupar un puesto
  (**f**) (*consider*) considerar
  (**g**) **he was held for two hours at the police station** estuvo detenido durante dos horas en la comisaría; **to h. one's breath** contener la respiración; **to h. sb hostage** retener a algn como rehén
  (**h**) *Tel* **to h. the line** no colgar
  2 *vi* (**a**) (*rope*) aguantar
  (**b**) *Fig* (*offer*) ser válido(a)
  3 *n* (**a**) **to get h. of** (*grip*) coger, agarrar; *Fig* localizar; **can you get h. of a newspaper?** ¿puedes conseguir un periódico?
  (**b**) (*control*) control *m*
  (**c**) *Naut* bodega *f*
  (**d**) (*in wrestling*) llave *f*
▶ **hold back 1** *vt sep* (*crowd*) contener; (*feelings*) reprimir; (*truth*) ocultar; **I don't**

want to h. you back (*delay*) no quiero entretenerte
  2 *vi* (*hesitate*) vacilar
▶ **hold down** *vt sep* (**a**) (*control*) dominar (**b**) *Fam* (*job*) desempeñar
▶ **hold off** *vt sep* mantener a distancia
▶ **hold on** *vi* (**a**) (*keep a firm grasp*) agarrarse bien (**b**) (*wait*) esperar; *Tel* **h. on!** ¡no cuelgue!
▶ **hold out 1** *vt sep* (*hand*) tender
  2 *vi* (**a**) (*last*) (*things*) durar; (*person*) resistir (**b**) **to h. out for** insistir en
▶ **hold up** *vt sep* (**a**) (*rob*) (*train*) asaltar; (*bank*) atracar (**b**) (*delay*) retrasar; **we were held up for half an hour** sufrimos media hora de retraso (**c**) (*raise*) levantar (**d**) (*support*) apuntalar
holdall ['həʊldɔːl] *n Br* bolsa *f* de viaje
holder ['həʊldə(r)] *n* (**a**) (*receptacle*) recipiente *m* (**b**) (*owner*) poseedor(a) *m,f*; (*bearer*) portador(a) *m,f*; (*of passport*) titular *mf*; **record h.** plusmarquista *mf*
holding ['həʊldɪŋ] *n* (**a**) (*property*) propiedad *f* (**b**) *Fin* valor *m* en cartera; **h. company** holding *m*
hold-up ['həʊldʌp] *n* (**a**) (*robbery*) atraco *m* (**b**) (*delay*) retraso *m*; (*in traffic*) atasco *m*
hole [həʊl] *n* (**a**) agujero *m*; (*large*) hoyo *m*; (*in the road*) bache *m* (**b**) (*in golf*) hoyo *m* (**c**) *Fam* (*of place*) antro *m*
holiday ['hɒlɪdeɪ] **1** *n* (*one day*) día *m* de fiesta; *Br* (*several days*) vacaciones *fpl*; **to be/go on h.** estar/ir de vacaciones; **h. resort** lugar turístico
  2 *vi Br* pasar las vacaciones; (*in summer*) veranear
holiday-maker ['hɒlɪdeɪmeɪkə(r)] *n Br* turista *mf*; (*in summer*) veraneante *mf*
holiness ['həʊlɪnɪs] *n* santidad *f*
Holland ['hɒlənd] *n* Holanda
hollow ['hɒləʊ] **1** *adj* (**a**) hueco(a) (**b**) (*cheeks, eyes*) hundido(a) (**c**) *Fig* (*insincere*) falso(a); (*empty*) vacío(a)
  2 *n* hueco *m*; *Geog* hondonada *f*
  3 *vt* **to h. (out)** hacer un hueco en
holly ['hɒlɪ] *n* acebo *m*
holocaust ['hɒləkɔːst] *n* holocausto *m*
holster ['həʊlstə(r)] *n* pistolera *f*
holy ['həʊlɪ] *adj* sagrado(a), santo(a); (*blessed*) bendito(a); **H. Ghost** Espíritu Santo; **H. Land** Tierra Santa; **H. See** Santa Sede
homage ['hɒmɪdʒ] *n* homenaje *m*; **to pay h. to sb** rendir homenaje a algn
home [həʊm] **1** *n* (**a**) casa *f*, hogar *m*; **at h.** en casa; *Fig* **make yourself at h.!** ¡estás en tu casa!; *Fig* **to feel at h.** estar a gusto;

h. banking telebanco *m*; *Comput* **h. page** *(initial page)* portada *f*, página *f* inicial *or* de inicio; *(personal page)* página personal; **h. shopping** telecompra *f*; **h. shopping channel** teletienda *f*
 (**b**) *(institution)* asilo *m*; **old people's h.** asilo de ancianos
 (**c**) *(country)* patria *f*
 (**d**) *Sport* **to play at h.** jugar en casa; *US* **h. base** *(in baseball)* base *f* del bateador; **h. run** carrera completa
 2 *adj* (**a**) *(domestic)* del hogar; *Br* **h. help** asistenta *f*
 (**b**) *Pol* interior; **h. affairs** asuntos *mpl* interiores; *Br* **H. Office** Ministerio *m* del Interior; *Br* **H. Secretary** Ministro(a) *m,f* del Interior
 (**c**) *(native)* natal
 3 *adv* en casa; **to go h.** irse a casa; **to leave h.** irse de casa
homeland ['həʊmlænd] *n* patria *f*; *(birthplace)* tierra *f* natal
homeless ['həʊmlɪs] **1** *adj* sin techo
 2 *npl* **the h.** los sin techo
homely ['həʊmlɪ] *adj* (**homelier, homeliest**) (**a**) *Br (person)* casero(a); *(atmosphere)* familiar (**b**) *US (unattractive)* sin atractivo
home-made ['həʊmmeɪd] *adj* casero(a)
homeopathy [həʊmɪ'ɒpəθɪ] *n US* = **homoeopathy**
homesick ['həʊmsɪk] *adj* **to be h.** tener morriña
homeward(s) ['həʊmwəd(z)] *adv* hacia casa
homework ['həʊmwɜːk] *n* deberes *mpl*
homey ['həʊmɪ] *adj US Fam* hogareño(a)
homicide ['hɒmɪsaɪd] *n* homicidio *m*
homing ['həʊmɪŋ] *adj* (**a**) **h. device** cabeza buscadora (**b**) **h. pigeon** paloma mensajera
homoeopathy [həʊmɪ'ɒpəθɪ] *n* homeopatía *f*
homogeneous [hɒmə'dʒiːnɪəs] *adj* homogéneo(a)
homosexual [həʊməʊ'seksjʊəl] *adj & n* homosexual *(mf)*
Honduran [hɒn'djʊərən] *adj & n* hondureño(a) *(m,f)*
Honduras [hɒn'djʊərəs] *n* Honduras
honest ['ɒnɪst] *adj* honrado(a); *(sincere)* sincero(a), franco(a); *(fair)* justo(a); **the h. truth** la pura verdad
honestly ['ɒnɪstlɪ] *adv* honradamente; *(question)* ¿de verdad?; *(exclamation)* ¡hay que ver!; **h., it doesn't matter** de verdad, no tiene importancia
honesty ['ɒnɪstɪ] *n* honradez *f*

honey ['hʌnɪ] *n* miel *f*; *US Fam (endearment)* cariño *m*
honeycomb ['hʌnɪkəʊm] *n* panal *m*
honeymoon ['hʌnɪmuːn] *n* luna *f* de miel
honeysuckle ['hʌnɪsʌkəl] *n* madreselva *f*
honk [hɒŋk] *vi Aut* tocar la bocina
honor ['ɒnər] *n & vt US* = **honour**
honorary ['ɒnərərɪ] *adj (member)* honorario(a); *(duties)* honorífico(a)
honour ['ɒnə(r)] **1** *n* (**a**) honor *m* (**b**) *US Jur* **Her H./His H./Your H.** Su Señoría *f* (**c**) *Mil* **honours** honores *mpl* (**d**) **Honours degree** licenciatura *f* superior
 2 *vt* (**a**) *(respect)* honrar (**b**) *(obligation)* cumplir con
honourable ['ɒnərəbəl] *adj (person)* honrado(a); *(action)* honroso(a)
hood [hʊd] *n* (**a**) *(of garment)* capucha *f* (**b**) *(of car)* capota *f*; *US (bonnet)* capó *m* (**c**) *US Fam (gangster)* matón(ona) *m,f*
hoodlum ['huːdləm] *n* matón *m*
hoodwink ['hʊdwɪŋk] *vt* engañar
hoof [huːf] *n (pl* **hoofs** *or* **hooves**) *(of horse)* casco *m*; *(of cow, sheep)* pezuña *f*
hook [hʊk] **1** *n* (**a**) gancho *m*; *(in fishing)* anzuelo *m*; *Sewing* **hooks and eyes** corchetes *mpl*; **to take the phone off the h.** descolgar el teléfono (**b**) *(in boxing)* gancho *m*
 2 *vt* enganchar
 ▸ **hook up** *vt sep & vi Rad, TV & Comput* conectar (**with** con)
hooked [hʊkt] *adj* (**a**) *(nose)* aguileño(a) (**b**) *Fam (addicted)* enganchado(a) (**on** a); **to get h.** engancharse
hooker ['hʊkə(r)] *n US Fam (prostitute)* fulana *f*, puta *f*
hookey ['hʊkɪ] *n US Fam* **to play h.** hacer novillos
hook-up ['hʊkʌp] *n* (**a**) *Comput* conexión *f* (**b**) *Rad & TV* emisión *f* múltiple
hooky ['hʊkɪ] *n US Fam* = **hookey**
hooligan ['huːlɪgən] *n Fam* gamberro(a) *m,f*
hoop [huːp] *n* aro *m*; *(of barrel)* fleje *m*
hooray [huː'reɪ] *interj* ¡hurra!
hoot [huːt] **1** *n* (**a**) ululato *m*; *Fam* **hoots of laughter** carcajadas *fpl*; *Fam* **I don't care a h.** me importa un pepino (**b**) *(of car horn)* bocinazo *m*
 2 *vi* (**a**) *(owl)* ulular (**b**) *(car)* dar un bocinazo; *(train)* silbar; *(siren)* pitar
hooter ['huːtə(r)] *n esp Br (of car)* bocina *f*; *(siren)* sirena *f*
Hoover® ['huːvə(r)] *Br* **1** *n* aspiradora *f*
 2 *vt* **to h.** pasar la aspiradora por

hooves [huːvz] *pl of* **hoof**
hop¹ [hɒp] **1** *vi* saltar; **to h. on one leg** andar a la pata coja
2 *n (small jump)* brinco *m*
hop² [hɒp] *n Bot* lúpulo *m*
hope [həʊp] **1** *n* esperanza *f; (false)* ilusión *f;* **to have little h. of doing sth** tener pocas posibilidades de hacer algo
2 *vt & vi* esperar; **I h. so/not** espero que sí/no; **we h. you're well** esperamos que estés bien
hopeful [ˈhəʊpfʊl] *adj (confident)* optimista; *(promising)* prometedor(a)
hopefully [ˈhəʊpfʊlɪ] *adv* (**a**) *(confidently)* con optimismo (**b**) **h. the weather will be fine** *(it is hoped)* esperemos que haga buen tiempo
hopeless [ˈhəʊplɪs] *adj* desesperado(a); *Fam* **to be h. at sports** ser negado(a) para los deportes
hopelessly [ˈhəʊplɪslɪ] *adv* desesperadamente; **h. lost** completamente perdido(a)
horde [hɔːd] *n* multitud *f*
horizon [həˈraɪzən] *n* horizonte *m*
horizontal [hɒrɪˈzɒntəl] *adj* horizontal
hormone [ˈhɔːməʊn] *n* hormona *f*
horn [hɔːn] *n* (**a**) cuerno *m* (**b**) *Fam Mus* trompeta *f*; **French h.** trompa *f*; **hunting h.** cuerno *m* de caza (**c**) *Aut* bocina *f*
hornet [ˈhɔːnɪt] *n* avispón *m*
horny [ˈhɔːnɪ] *adj* (**hornier, horniest**) (**a**) *(hands)* calloso(a) (**b**) *very Fam (sexually aroused)* caliente, cachondo(a)
horoscope [ˈhɒrəskəʊp] *n* horóscopo *m*
horrendous [hɒˈrendəs] *adj* horrendo(a)
horrible [ˈhɒrəbəl] *adj* horrible
horrid [ˈhɒrɪd] *adj* horrible
horrific [həˈrɪfɪk] *adj* horrendo(a)
horrify [ˈhɒrɪfaɪ] *vt* horrorizar
horror [ˈhɒrə(r)] *n* horror *m; Fam* **a little h.** un diablillo; **h. film** película *f* de miedo *or* de terror
hors d'oeuvre [ɔːˈdɜːvr] *n* (*pl* **hors d'oeuvres**) entremés *m*
horse [hɔːs] *n* (**a**) caballo *m*; **h. race** carrera *f* de caballos (**b**) *(in gymnastics)* potro *m* (**c**) *Tech* caballete *m* (**d**) **h. chestnut** *(tree)* castaño *m* de Indias
horseback [ˈhɔːsbæk] *n* **on h.** a caballo; *US* **h. riding** equitación *f*
horseman [ˈhɔːsmən] *n* jinete *m*
horseplay [ˈhɔːspleɪ] *n* payasadas *fpl*
horsepower [ˈhɔːspaʊə(r)] *n* caballo *m* (de vapor)
horseradish [ˈhɔːsrædɪʃ] *n* rábano rusticano
horseshoe [ˈhɔːsʃuː] *n* herradura *f*

horsewoman [ˈhɔːswʊmən] *n* amazona *f*
horticulture [ˈhɔːtɪkʌltʃə(r)] *n* horticultura *f*
hose [həʊz] *n (pipe)* manguera *f*
hosiery [ˈhəʊzɪərɪ] *n* medias *fpl* y calcetines *mpl*
hospice [ˈhɒspɪs] *n* residencia *f* para enfermos terminales
hospitable [ˈhɒspɪtəbəl, hɒˈspɪtəbəl] *adj* hospitalario(a); **h. atmosphere** ambiente acogedor
hospital [ˈhɒspɪtəl] *n* hospital *m*
hospitality [hɒspɪˈtælɪtɪ] *n* hospitalidad *f*
Host [həʊst] *n Rel* hostia *f*
host¹ [həʊst] **1** *n* (**a**) *(at home)* anfitrión *m* (**b**) *Th & TV* presentador *m* (**c**) *Biol* huésped *m*
2 *vt Th & TV* presentar
host² [həʊst] *n (large number)* montón *m*
hostage [ˈhɒstɪdʒ] *n* rehén *m*
hostel [ˈhɒstəl] *n* hostal *m*
hostess [ˈhəʊstɪs] *n* (**a**) *(at home etc)* anfitriona *f* (**b**) *Th & TV* presentadora *f* (**c**) **(air) h.** azafata *f*
hostile [ˈhɒstaɪl] *adj* hostil
hostility [hɒˈstɪlɪtɪ] *n* hostilidad *f*
hot [hɒt] *adj* (**hotter, hottest**) (**a**) caliente; *Fig* **h. line** teléfono rojo; **h. spot** *(nightclub)* club nocturno (**b**) *(weather)* caluroso(a); **it's very h.** hace mucho calor; **to feel h.** tener calor (**c**) *(spicy)* picante; **h. dog** perrito *m* caliente (**d**) *(temper)* fuerte (**e**) *Fam (fresh)* de última hora (**f**) *Fam (good)* bueno(a); **it's not so h.** no es nada del otro mundo (**g**) *(popular)* popular (**h**) *(dangerous)* peligroso(a); *Fig* **to get oneself into h. water** meterse en un lío; *Fam* **h. seat** primera fila
► hot up *vi Fam* **things are hotting up** la cosa se está poniendo al rojo vivo
hotbed [ˈhɒtbed] *n Fig* hervidero *m*
hotel [həʊˈtel] *n* hotel *m*
hotelier [həʊˈteljeɪ] *n* hotelero(a) *m,f*
hot-headed [hɒtˈhedɪd] *adj* impetuoso(a)
hothouse [ˈhɒthaʊs] *n* invernadero *m*
hotplate [ˈhɒtpleɪt] *n (cooker)* placa *f* de cocina; *(to keep food warm)* calientaplatos *m inv*
hotshot [ˈhɒtʃɒt] *n Fam* as *m*
hot-water [hɒtˈwɔːtə(r)] *adj* **h. bottle** bolsa *f* de agua caliente
hound [haʊnd] **1** *n* perro *m* de caza
2 *vt* acosar
hour [ˈaʊə(r)] *n* hora *f*; **60 miles an h.** 60 millas por hora; **by the h.** por horas; **h. hand** manecilla *f*

hourly [ˈaʊəlɪ] **1** *adj* cada hora
2 *adv* por horas

house 1 *n* [haʊs] (**a**) casa *f*; **at my h.** en mi casa; *Fig* **on the h.** cortesía de la casa; **h. arrest** arresto domiciliario; **h. plant** planta *f* de interior (**b**) *Pol* **H. of Commons** Cámara *f* de los Comunes; **H. of Lords** Cámara de los Lores; *US* **H. of Representatives** Cámara de Representantes; **Houses of Parliament** Parlamento *m* (**c**) *(company)* empresa *f*; **publishing h.** editorial *f* (**d**) *Th* sala *f*
2 *vt* [haʊz] alojar; *(store)* guardar

houseboat [ˈhaʊsbəʊt] *n* casa *f* flotante

housebreaking [ˈhaʊsbreɪkɪŋ] *n* allanamiento *m* de morada

housebroken [ˈhaʊsbrəʊkən] *adj US (pet)* = que ya ha aprendido a no hacer sus necesidades en casa

housecoat [ˈhaʊskəʊt] *n* bata *f*

household [ˈhaʊshəʊld] *n* hogar *m*; **h. products** productos domésticos

housekeeper [ˈhaʊskiːpə(r)] *n* ama *f* de llaves

housekeeping [ˈhaʊskiːpɪŋ] *n* administración doméstica; **h. money** dinero *m* para los gastos domésticos

house-train [ˈhaʊstreɪn] *vt (pet)* educar

house-warming [ˈhaʊswɔːmɪŋ] *n* **h. (party)** = fiesta que se da al estrenar casa

housewife [ˈhaʊswaɪf] *n* ama *f* de casa

housework [ˈhaʊswɜːk] *n* trabajo doméstico

housing [ˈhaʊzɪŋ] *n* vivienda *f*; **h. estate** urbanización *f*

hovel [ˈhʌvəl, ˈhɒvəl] *n* casucha *f*

hover [ˈhɒvə(r)] *vi (bird)* cernerse; *(aircraft)* permanecer inmóvil (en el aire)

hovercraft [ˈhɒvəkrɑːft] *n* aerodeslizador *m*

how [haʊ] *adv* (**a**) *(direct question)* ¿cómo?; **h. are you?** ¿cómo estás?; *Fam* **h. come?** ¿por qué? (**b**) *(indirect question)* cómo; **I don't know h. to tell you** no sé cómo decírtelo (**c**) *(very)* qué; **h. funny!** ¡qué divertido! (**d**) *(suggestion)* **h. about going to the cinema?** ¿te apetece ir al cine?; **h. about a stroll?** ¿qué te parece un paseo? (**e**) *(quantity)* cuánto; **h. old is she?** ¿cuántos años tiene?; **h. tall are you?** ¿cuánto mides? (**f**) **h. many?** ¿cuántos(as)?; **h. much?** ¿cuánto(a)?; **I don't know h. many people there were** no sé cuánta gente había

however [haʊˈevə(r)] *adv* (**a**) *(nevertheless)* no obstante, sin embargo (**b**) *(with adjective)* **h. difficult it may be** por difícil que sea; **h. much** por mucho que *(+ subj)*

howl [haʊl] **1** *n* aullido *m*
2 *vi* aullar

howler [ˈhaʊlə(r)] *n Fam* despiste *m*

HP, hp [eɪtʃˈpiː] *n* (**a**) *Br (abbr* **hire purchase**) compra *f* a plazos (**b**) *(abbr* **horsepower**) cv *mpl*

HQ [eɪtʃˈkjuː] *n (abbr* **headquarters**) sede *f*, central *f*

hub [hʌb] *n Aut* cubo *m*; *Fig* eje *m*

hubbub [ˈhʌbʌb] *n* alboroto *m*

hubcap [ˈhʌbkæp] *n Aut* tapacubos *m inv*

huddle [ˈhʌdəl] **1** *n* grupo *m*
2 *vi* **to h. (up** *or* **together)** acurrucarse

hue¹ [hjuː] *n (colour)* tinte *m*; *(shade)* matiz *m*

hue² [hjuː] *n* **h. and cry** fuerte protesta *f*

huff [hʌf] *n* **to be in a h.** estar de mala uva

hug [hʌg] **1** *vt* abrazar
2 *n* abrazo *m*

huge [hjuːdʒ] *adj* enorme

hugely [ˈhjuːdʒlɪ] *adv* enormemente

hulk [hʌlk] *n* (**a**) *Naut* casco *m* (**b**) *(thing, person)* armatoste *m*

hull [hʌl] *n Naut* casco *m*

hullabal(l)oo [hʌləbəˈluː] *n Fam* follón *m*

hullo [hʌˈləʊ] *interj Br* ¡hola!

hum [hʌm] **1** *vt (tune)* tararear
2 *vi (bees, engine)* zumbar; *(sing)* tararear
3 *n (of bees)* zumbido *m*

human [ˈhjuːmən] **1** *adj* humano(a); **h. race** raza humana; **h. being** ser humano
2 *n* ser humano

humane [hjuːˈmeɪn] *adj* humano(a)

humanitarian [hjuːmænɪˈteərɪən] *adj* humanitario(a)

humanity [hjuːˈmænɪtɪ] *n* (**a**) humanidad *f* (**b**) *Univ* **the humanities** las humanidades

humble [ˈhʌmbəl] **1** *adj* humilde
2 *vt* humillar

humbug [ˈhʌmbʌg] *n* (**a**) *Fam* tonterías *fpl* (**b**) *Br (mint)* **h.** caramelo *m* de menta

humdrum [ˈhʌmdrʌm] *adj* monótono(a), aburrido(a)

humid [ˈhjuːmɪd] *adj* húmedo(a)

humidity [hjuːˈmɪdɪtɪ] *n* humedad *f*

humiliate [hjuːˈmɪlɪeɪt] *vt* humillar

humiliation [hjuːmɪlɪˈeɪʃən] *n* humillación *f*

humility [hjuːˈmɪlɪtɪ] *n* humildad *f*

humor [ˈhjuːmə(r)] *n US* = **humour**

humorous [ˈhjuːmərəs] *adj (writer)* humorístico(a); *(person, story)* gracioso(a), divertido(a)

humour [ˈhjuːmə(r)] **1** *n* humor *m*
2 *vt* seguir la corriente a

hump [hʌmp] **1** *n* (**a**) *(on back)* joroba *f*

(**b**) *(small hill)* montículo *m*
 2 *vt Br Fam (carry)* cargar (a la espalda)
humus ['hjuːməs] *n* mantillo *m*, humus *m*
hunch [hʌntʃ] *n Fam* corazonada *f*
hunchback ['hʌntʃbæk] *n* jorobado(a) *m,f*
hundred ['hʌndrəd] **1** *n* cien *m*, ciento *m*; *(rough number)* centenar *m*; **a h. and twenty-five** ciento veinticinco; **five h.** quinientos
 2 *adj* cien; **a h. people** cien personas; **a h. percent** cien por cien; **two h. chairs** doscientas sillas
hundredth ['hʌndrədθ] *adj & n* centésimo(a) *(m,f)*
hundredweight ['hʌndrədweɪt] *n Br* = 50,8 kg; *US* = 45,36 kg
hung [hʌŋ] **1** *adj Fam* (**a**) **h. over** con resaca (**b**) **h. up** acomplejado(a)
 2 *pt & pp of* **hang**
Hungarian [hʌŋ'geərɪən] *adj & n* húngaro(a) *(m,f)*
Hungary ['hʌŋgərɪ] *n* Hungría
hunger ['hʌŋgə(r)] **1** *n* hambre *f*; **h. strike** huelga *f* de hambre
 2 *vi Fig* tener hambre (**for** de)
hungry ['hʌŋgrɪ] *adj* (**hungrier, hungriest**) hambriento(a); **to be h.** tener hambre; **to go h.** pasar hambre
hunk [hʌŋk] *n* (**a**) *(piece)* buen pedazo *m* (**b**) *Fam (man)* machote *m*
hunt [hʌnt] **1** *vt* cazar
 2 *vi (for game)* cazar; *(search)* buscar
 3 *n* caza *f*; *(search)* búsqueda *f*
 ► **hunt down** *vt sep* perseguir
hunter ['hʌntə(r)] *n* cazador(a) *m,f*
hunting ['hʌntɪŋ] *n* caza *f*; *(expedition)* cacería *f*
hurdle ['hɜːdəl] *n Sport* valla *f*; *Fig* obstáculo *m*
hurl [hɜːl] *vt* arrojar, lanzar
hurrah [hʊ'rɑː], **hurray** [hʊ'reɪ] *interj* ¡hurra!; **h. for John!** ¡viva John!
hurricane ['hʌrɪkən, 'hʌrɪkeɪn] *n* huracán *m*
hurried ['hʌrɪd] *adj* apresurado(a); *(action etc)* hecho(a) de prisa
hurriedly ['hʌrɪdlɪ] *adv* deprisa, apresuradamente
hurry ['hʌrɪ] **1** *vi* darse prisa
 2 *vt* meter prisa a
 3 *n* **to be in a h.** tener prisa
hurt [hɜːt] **1** *vt (pt & pp* **hurt**) hacer daño a; *(wound)* herir; *(feelings)* ofender
 2 *vi* doler; **my arm hurts** me duele el brazo; *Fam* **it doesn't h. to go out once in a while** no viene mal salir de vez en cuando

3 *adj (physically)* herido(a); *(mentally)* dolido(a)
hurtful ['hɜːtfʊl] *adj* hiriente
hurtle ['hɜːtəl] *vi* lanzarse; **to h. down** desplomarse
husband ['hʌzbənd] *n* marido *m*, esposo *m*
hush [hʌʃ] **1** *vt* callar; **to h. sth up** echar tierra a un asunto
 2 *n* silencio *m*
 3 *interj* ¡silencio!
hush-hush [hʌʃ'hʌʃ] *adj Fam* confidencial
husky¹ ['hʌskɪ] *adj* (**huskier, huskiest**) ronco(a)
husky² ['hʌskɪ] *n (dog)* perro *m* esquimal
hustings ['hʌstɪŋz] *npl Pol* (**a**) *(platform)* tribuna *f* electoral (**b**) *(election)* elecciones *fpl*
hustle ['hʌsəl] **1** *vt* (**a**) *(jostle)* empujar (**b**) *Fam* meter prisa a
 2 *n* bullicio *m*; **h. and bustle** ajetreo *m*
hut [hʌt] *n* cabaña *f*; *(shed)* cobertizo *m*; *Mil* barraca *f*
hutch [hʌtʃ] *n* jaula *f*; **rabbit h.** conejera *f*
hyacinth ['haɪəsɪnθ] *n* jacinto *m*
hybrid ['haɪbrɪd] *adj & n* híbrido(a) *(m,f)*
hydrant ['haɪdrənt] *n* **fire h.** boca *f* de incendio
hydraulic [haɪ'drɒlɪk] *adj* hidráulico(a)
hydrocarbon [haɪdrəʊ'kɑːbən] *n* hidrocarburo *m*
hydrochloric [haɪdrəʊ'klɒrɪk] *adj* **h. acid** ácido clorhídrico
hydroelectric [haɪdrəʊɪ'lektrɪk] *adj* hidroeléctrico(a)
hydrofoil ['haɪdrəfɔɪl] *n* hidroala *f*
hydrogen ['haɪdrədʒən] *n* hidrógeno *m*
hydroplane ['haɪdrəpleɪn] *n US (seaplane)* hidroavión *m*
hyena [haɪ'iːnə] *n* hiena *f*
hygiene ['haɪdʒiːn] *n* higiene *f*
hygienic [haɪ'dʒiːnɪk] *adj* higiénico(a)
hymn [hɪm] *n* himno *m*; **h. book** cantoral *m*
hype [haɪp] *n Fam* campaña publicitaria, movida *f*
hyper- ['haɪpə(r)] *pref* hiper-; **hyperactive** hiperactivo(a)
hypermarket ['haɪpəmɑːkɪt] *n Br* hipermercado *m*
hypersensitive [haɪpə'sensɪtɪv] *adj* hipersensible
hyphen ['haɪfən] *n* guión *m*
hypnosis [hɪp'nəʊsɪs] *n* hipnosis *f*
hypnotist ['hɪpnətɪst] *n* hipnotizador(a) *m,f*

hypnotize ['hɪpnətaɪz] *vt* hipnotizar

hypochondriac [haɪpə'kɒndrɪæk] *adj &*
n hipocondríaco(a) *(m,f)*

hypocrisy [hɪ'pɒkrəsɪ] *n* hipocresía *f*

hypocrite ['hɪpəkrɪt] *n* hipócrita *mf*

hypocritical [hɪpə'krɪtɪkəl] *adj* hipócrita

hypodermic [haɪpə'dɜːmɪk] *adj Med* hi-
podérmico(a); **h. needle** aguja hipodér-
mica

hypothesis [haɪ'pɒθɪsɪs] *n* (*pl* **hypo-
theses** [haɪ'pɒθɪsiːz]) hipótesis *f*

hypothetic(al) [haɪpə'θetɪk(əl)] *adj* hi-
potético(a)

hysteria [hɪ'stɪərɪə] *n* histeria *f*

hysterical [hɪ'sterɪkəl] *adj* histérico(a)

hysterics [hɪ'sterɪks] *npl* (**a**) ataque *m* de
histeria (**b**) *Fam (of laughter)* ataque *m* de
risa

I, i [aɪ] *n (the letter)* I, i *f*
I [aɪ] *pers pron* yo *(usually omitted in Spanish, except for contrast)*; **I know her** (yo) la conozco
ICBM [aɪsiːbiːˈem] *n (abbr* **intercontinental ballistic missile**) misil *m* balístico intercontinental
ice [aɪs] **1** *n* hielo *m*; **i. axe** pico *m* (de alpinista); **i. cream** helado *m*; **i. cube** cubito *m* de hielo; **i. hockey** hockey *m* sobre hielo; *Br* **i. lolly** polo *m*; **i. rink** pista *f* de patinaje; **i. skate** patín *m* de cuchilla
  2 *vt (cake)* alcorzar
▸ **ice over, ice up** *vi (pond etc)* helarse; *(windscreen, plane wings)* cubrirse de hielo
iceberg [ˈaɪsbɜːɡ] *n* iceberg *m*
icebox [ˈaɪsbɒks] *n* (**a**) *(compartment of fridge)* congelador *m* (**b**) *US (fridge)* nevera *f*, frigorífico *m*, *Andes* frigider *m*, *RP* heladera *f*
icecap [ˈaɪskæp] *n* casquete *m* glaciar
Iceland [ˈaɪslənd] *n* Islandia
ice-skating [ˈaɪsskeɪtɪŋ] *n* patinaje *m* sobre hielo
icicle [ˈaɪsɪkəl] *n* carámbano *m*
icing [ˈaɪsɪŋ] *n* alcorza *f*; **i. sugar** azúcar *m* glas
icon [ˈaɪkɒn] *n* icono *m*
icy [ˈaɪsɪ] *adj* (**icier, iciest**) *(road etc)* helado(a); *Fig (smile)* glacial
ID [aɪˈdiː] *n US* documentación *f*; **ID card** DNI *m*
I'd [aɪd] = **I would**; **I had**
idea [aɪˈdɪə] *n* (**a**) idea *f* (**b**) *(aim)* intención *f* (**c**) *(impression)* impresión *f*
ideal [aɪˈdɪəl] *adj & n* ideal *(m)*
idealist [aɪˈdɪəlɪst] *n* idealista *mf*
idealistic [aɪdɪəˈlɪstɪk] *adj* idealista
idealize [aɪˈdɪəlaɪz] *vt* idealizar
ideally [aɪˈdɪəlɪ] *adv* (**a**) *(perfectly)* perfectamente (**b**) *(in the best conditions)* de ser posible
identical [aɪˈdentɪkəl] *adj* idéntico(a)
identification [aɪdentɪfɪˈkeɪʃən] *n* (**a**) identificación *f* (**b**) *(papers)* documentación *f*
identify [aɪˈdentɪfaɪ] **1** *vt (body)* identificar; *(cause)* descubrir
  2 *vi* identificarse (**with** con)

Identikit® [aɪˈdentɪkɪt] *n* **I. picture** retrato *m* robot
identity [aɪˈdentɪtɪ] *n* identidad *f*; **i. card** carné *m* de identidad; **proof of i.** prueba *f* de identidad
ideological [aɪdɪəˈlɒdʒɪkəl] *adj* ideológico(a)
ideology [aɪdɪˈɒlədʒɪ] *n* ideología *f*
idiom [ˈɪdɪəm] *n* modismo *m*; *Fig (style)* lenguaje *m*
idiomatic [ɪdɪəˈmætɪk] *adj* idiomático(a)
idiosyncrasy [ɪdɪəʊˈsɪŋkrəsɪ] *n* idiosincrasia *f*
idiot [ˈɪdɪət] *n* idiota *mf*, tonto(a) *m,f*
idiotic [ɪdɪˈɒtɪk] *adj (behaviour)* idiota, tonto(a); *(joke, plan)* estúpido(a)
idle [ˈaɪdəl] **1** *adj* holgazán(ana); *(not working) (person)* desempleado(a); *(machinery)* parado(a); *(gossip)* frívolo(a); *(threat)* vano(a)
  2 *vi (engine)* funcionar en vacío
▸ **idle away** *vt sep (time)* desperdiciar
idleness [ˈaɪdəlnɪs] *n (laziness)* holgazanería *f*; *(unemployment)* desempleo *m*; *(stoppage)* paro *m*
idol [ˈaɪdəl] *n* ídolo *m*
idolize [ˈaɪdəlaɪz] *vt* idolatrar
idyllic [ɪˈdɪlɪk] *adj* idílico(a)
i.e. *(abbr* **id est**) i.e.
if [ɪf] **1** *conj* (**a**) si; **if at all** si acaso; **rarely, if ever** raras veces; **if I were rich** si fuera rico(a); **if necessary** (en) caso de que sea necesario; **if not** si no; **if so** de ser así; **if I were you** yo en tu lugar (**b**) *(whenever)* si; **if you need help, ask** siempre que necesites ayuda, pídela (**c**) *(although)* aunque, si bien (**d**) *(exclamations)* **if only I'd known!** ¡de haberlo sabido!; **if only she were here!** ¡ojalá estuviera aquí!
  2 *n* **ifs and buts** pegas *fpl*
igloo [ˈɪgluː] *n* iglú *m*
ignite [ɪgˈnaɪt] **1** *vt* encender
  2 *vi* encenderse
ignition [ɪgˈnɪʃən] *n* ignición *f*; *Aut* encendido *m*; **i. key** llave *f* de contacto
ignorance [ˈɪgnərəns] *n* ignorancia *f*
ignorant [ˈɪgnərənt] *adj* ignorante (**of** de); **to be i. of the facts** ignorar *or* desconocer los hechos

ignore [ɪg'nɔː(r)] *vt (warning, remark)* no hacer caso de; *(behaviour, fact)* pasar por alto

ill [ɪl] **1** *adj* (**a**) enfermo(a); **to be taken i.** caer enfermo(a); **to feel i.** encontrarse mal (**b**) *(bad)* malo(a); **i. feeling** resentimiento *m*; **i. will** mala voluntad
 2 *n* mal *m*
 3 *adv* difícilmente

I'll [aɪl] = **I shall**; **I will**

ill-advised [ɪləd'vaɪzd] *adj (person)* imprudente; *(act)* desatinado(a); **you'd be i. to go** harías mal en ir

ill-disposed [ɪldɪ'spəʊzd] *adj* poco dispuesto(a)

illegal [ɪ'liːgəl] *adj* ilegal

illegible [ɪ'ledʒɪbəl] *adj* ilegible

illegitimate [ɪlɪ'dʒɪtɪmɪt] *adj* ilegítimo(a)

ill-fated [ɪl'feɪtɪd] *adj* abocado(a) al fracaso

ill-founded [ɪl'faʊndɪd] *adj* infundado(a)

illicit [ɪ'lɪsɪt] *adj* ilícito(a)

illiteracy [ɪ'lɪtərəsɪ] *n* analfabetismo *m*

illiterate [ɪ'lɪtərɪt] *adj (person)* analfabeto(a); *Fam (uneducated)* inculto(a)

illness ['ɪlnɪs] *n* enfermedad *f*

illogical [ɪ'lɒdʒɪkəl] *adj* ilógico(a)

ill-treat [ɪl'triːt] *vt* maltratar

illuminate [ɪ'luːmɪneɪt] *vt* (**a**) *(light up)* iluminar, alumbrar; *Fig (clarify)* aclarar (**b**) *(manuscript)* iluminar

illuminating [ɪ'luːmɪneɪtɪŋ] *adj (experience, book)* instructivo(a); *(remark)* revelador(a)

illumination [ɪluːmɪ'neɪʃən] *n* (**a**) iluminación *f*; *Fig (clarification)* aclaración *f* (**b**) *Br* **illuminations** iluminación *f*

illusion [ɪ'luːʒən] *n* ilusión *f*; **to be under the i. that ...** engañarse pensando que ...

illusory [ɪ'luːsərɪ] *adj* ilusorio(a)

illustrate ['ɪləstreɪt] *vt* ilustrar

illustration [ɪlə'streɪʃən] *n* ilustración *f*; *(example)* ejemplo *m*

illustrious [ɪ'lʌstrɪəs] *adj* ilustre

I'm [aɪm] = **I am**

image ['ɪmɪdʒ] *n* imagen *f*

imagery ['ɪmɪdʒərɪ] *n Lit* imágenes *fpl*

imaginary [ɪ'mædʒɪnərɪ] *adj* imaginario(a)

imagination [ɪmædʒɪ'neɪʃən] *n* imaginación *f*; *(inventiveness)* inventiva *f*

imaginative [ɪ'mædʒɪnətɪv] *adj* imaginativo(a)

imagine [ɪ'mædʒɪn] *vt (visualize)* imaginar; *(think)* suponer, imaginarse; **just i.!** ¡imagínate!

imbalance [ɪm'bæləns] *n* desequilibrio *m*

imbecile ['ɪmbɪsiːl] *n* imbécil *mf*

imitate ['ɪmɪteɪt] *vt* imitar

imitation [ɪmɪ'teɪʃən] **1** *n* imitación *f*, copia *f*; *Pej* remedo *m*
 2 *adj* de imitación

immaculate [ɪ'mækjʊlɪt] *adj (clean)* inmaculado(a); *(tidy)* perfectamente ordenado(a); *(clothes)* impecable; *(work)* perfecto(a); **the I. Conception** la Inmaculada Concepción

immaterial [ɪmə'tɪərɪəl] *adj* irrelevante; **it's i. to me whether ...** me trae sin cuidado si ...

immature [ɪmə'tjʊə(r)] *adj* inmaduro(a)

immediate [ɪ'miːdɪət] *adj* (**a**) inmediato(a); *(urgent)* urgente (**b**) *(close)* cercano(a); *(danger)* inminente (**c**) *(cause)* primero(a)

immediately [ɪ'miːdɪətlɪ] **1** *adv* (**a**) inmediatamente (**b**) *(directly)* directamente
 2 *conj* en cuanto

immense [ɪ'mens] *adj* inmenso(a), enorme

immensely [ɪ'menslɪ] *adv (rich)* enormemente; *(interesting, difficult)* sumamente

immerse [ɪ'mɜːs] *vt* sumergir (**in** en); *Fig* **to be immersed in sth** estar absorto(a) en algo

immersion [ɪ'mɜːʃən] *n* inmersión *f*; *Br* **i. heater** calentador *m* de inmersión; **i. course** cursillo intensivo

immigrant ['ɪmɪgrənt] *adj & n* inmigrante *(mf)*

immigration [ɪmɪ'greɪʃən] *n* inmigración *f*

imminent ['ɪmɪnənt] *adj* inminente

immobile [ɪ'məʊbaɪl] *adj* inmóvil

immobilize [ɪ'məʊbɪlaɪz] *vt* inmovilizar

immodest [ɪ'mɒdɪst] *adj* indecente

immoral [ɪ'mɒrəl] *adj* inmoral

immortal [ɪ'mɔːtəl] *adj* inmortal

immortality [ɪmɔː'tælɪtɪ] *n* inmortalidad *f*

immortalize [ɪ'mɔːtəlaɪz] *vt* inmortalizar

immune [ɪ'mjuːn] *adj* inmune; *(exempt)* exento(a)

immunity [ɪ'mjuːnɪtɪ] *n* inmunidad *f*

immunize ['ɪmjʊnaɪz] *vt* inmunizar (**against** contra)

impact ['ɪmpækt] *n* impacto *m*; *(crash)* choque *m*

impair [ɪm'peə(r)] *vt* perjudicar; *(sight etc)* dañar

impart [ɪm'pɑːt] *vt Fml (news)* comunicar; *(knowledge)* transmitir

impartial [ɪm'pɑːʃəl] *adj* imparcial

impassable [ɪm'pɑːsəbəl] *adj (road, ground)* intransitable; *(barrier)* infranqueable

impasse [æm'pɑːs] *n* punto muerto

impassive [ɪm'pæsɪv] *adj* impasible

impatience [ɪm'peɪʃəns] *n* impaciencia *f*

impatient [ɪm'peɪʃənt] *adj* impaciente; *(fretful)* irritable; **to get i.** perder la paciencia

impeccable [ɪm'pekəbəl] *adj* impecable

impede [ɪm'piːd] *vt (prevent)* impedir; *(hinder)* estorbar; *(obstruct)* poner trabas a

impediment [ɪm'pedɪmənt] *n* impedimento *m*; *(obstacle)* estorbo *m*; **speech i.** defecto *m* del habla

impending [ɪm'pendɪŋ] *adj Fml* inminente

impenetrable [ɪm'penɪtrəbəl] *adj* impenetrable; *Fig (mystery, thoughts)* insondable

imperative [ɪm'perətɪv] **1** *adj Fml* imperativo(a); *(tone)* imperioso(a); *(urgent)* urgente

2 *n Ling* imperativo *m*

imperceptible [ɪmpə'septəbəl] *adj* imperceptible

imperfect [ɪm'pɜːfɪkt] **1** *adj* imperfecto(a); *(goods)* defectuoso(a)

2 *n Ling* imperfecto *m*

imperfection [ɪmpə'fekʃən] *n* defecto *m*

imperial [ɪm'pɪərɪəl] *adj* (**a**) imperial (**b**) *(measure)* **i. gallon** galón británico *(aprox 4,546 l)*

imperialism [ɪm'pɪərɪəlɪzəm] *n* imperialismo *m*

imperialist [ɪm'pɪərɪəlɪst] *adj & n* imperialista *(mf)*

imperious [ɪm'pɪərɪəs] *adj* imperioso(a)

impersonal [ɪm'pɜːsənəl] *adj* impersonal

impersonate [ɪm'pɜːsəneɪt] *vt* hacerse pasar por; *(famous people)* imitar

impersonation [ɪmpɜːsə'neɪʃən] *n* imitación *f*

impertinent [ɪm'pɜːtɪnənt] *adj* impertinente

impervious [ɪm'pɜːvɪəs] *adj (rock)* impermeable; *Fig* **to be i. to reason** no atender a razones

impetuous [ɪm'petjʊəs] *adj* impetuoso(a)

impetus ['ɪmpɪtəs] *n* ímpetu *m*; *Fig* impulso *m*

impinge [ɪm'pɪndʒ] *vi Fml* afectar (**on** a)

implant *Med* **1** *vt* [ɪm'plɑːnt] implantar

2 *n* ['ɪmplɑːnt] implantación *f*

implement 1 *n* ['ɪmplɪmənt] *(tool)* herramienta *f*; *(instrument)* instrumento *m*; **farm implements** aperos *mpl* de labranza

2 *vt* ['ɪmplɪment] *(decision, plan)* llevar a cabo; *(law, policy)* aplicar

implicate ['ɪmplɪkeɪt] *vt* implicar (**in** en)

implication [ɪmplɪ'keɪʃən] *n* implicación *f*; *(consequence)* consecuencia *f*

implicit [ɪm'plɪsɪt] *adj (implied)* implícito(a); *(trust)* absoluto(a); *(faith)* incondicional

implore [ɪm'plɔː(r)] *vt* implorar, suplicar

imply [ɪm'plaɪ] *vt* (**a**) *(involve)* implicar (**b**) *(hint)* dar a entender; *(mean)* significar

impolite [ɪmpə'laɪt] *adj* maleducado(a)

import 1 *n* ['ɪmpɔːt] (**a**) *Com (usu pl)* importación *f*; **i. duty** derechos *mpl* de importación (**b**) *Fml (meaning)* sentido *m*

2 *vt* [ɪm'pɔːt] *Com* importar

importance [ɪm'pɔːtəns] *n* importancia *f*; *(standing)* envergadura *f*; **of little i.** de poca monta

important [ɪm'pɔːtənt] *adj* importante; **it's not i.** no importa

importer [ɪm'pɔːtə(r)] *n Com* importador(a) *m,f*

impose [ɪm'pəʊz] **1** *vt* imponer (**on** *or* **upon** a)

2 *vi* **to i. on** *or* **upon** *(take advantage of)* abusar de

imposing [ɪm'pəʊzɪŋ] *adj* imponente, impresionante

imposition [ɪmpə'zɪʃən] *n (of tax etc)* imposición *f*; *(unfair demand)* abuso *m*; **would it be an i. if ...?** ¿le molestaría si ...?

impossibility [ɪmpɒsə'bɪlɪtɪ] *n* imposibilidad *f*

impossible [ɪm'pɒsəbəl] **1** *adj* imposible; *(person)* insoportable

2 *n* **to do the i.** hacer lo imposible

impossibly [ɪm'pɒsəblɪ] *adv* de manera insoportable; **i. difficult** de una dificultad insuperable

impostor [ɪm'pɒstə(r)] *n* impostor(a) *m,f*

impotent ['ɪmpətənt] *adj* impotente

impound [ɪm'paʊnd] *vt* incautarse de

impoverished [ɪm'pɒvərɪʃt] *adj (person, country)* empobrecido(a); *(soil)* agotado(a)

impracticable [ɪm'præktɪkəbəl] *adj* impracticable, irrealizable

impractical [ɪm'præktɪkəl] *adj (person)* poco práctico(a); *(project, solution etc)* poco viable

imprecise [ɪmprɪ'saɪs] *adj* impreciso(a)

impregnable [ɪmˈpregnəbəl] *adj* inexpugnable

impregnate [ˈɪmpregneɪt] *vt* (**a**) *(soak)* impregnar (**with** de) (**b**) *Fml (fertilize)* fecundar

impress [ɪmˈpres] *vt* (**a**) impresionar; **to i. sb favourably/unfavourably** dar a algn buena/mala impresión (**b**) *(mark)* imprimir (**on** en); *(pattern)* estampar (**on** en); *Fig* **to i. sth on sb** convencer a algn de la importancia de algo

impression [ɪmˈpreʃən] *n* (**a**) impresión *f*; **to be under the i. that ...** tener la impresión de que ...; **to give the i. of ...** dar la impresión de ... (**b**) *(imprint)* marca *f*; *(in snow)* huella *f* (**c**) *(imitation)* imitación *f*

impressionist [ɪmˈpreʃənɪst] *adj & n* impresionista *(mf)*

impressive [ɪmˈpresɪv] *adj* impresionante

imprint 1 *vt* [ɪmˈprɪnt] *(mark)* dejar huella (**on** en)
2 *n* [ˈɪmprɪnt] (**a**) *(mark)* marca *f*; *(left by foot etc)* huella *f* (**b**) *(publisher's name)* pie *m* de imprenta

imprison [ɪmˈprɪzən] *vt* encarcelar

imprisonment [ɪmˈprɪzənmənt] *n* encarcelamiento *m*

improbable [ɪmˈprɒbəbəl] *adj (event)* improbable; *(story)* inverosímil

impromptu [ɪmˈprɒmptjuː] **1** *adj (speech)* improvisado(a); *(visit)* imprevisto(a)
2 *adv* de improviso

improper [ɪmˈprɒpə(r)] *adj* (**a**) impropio(a); *(method)* inadecuado(a) (**b**) *(indecent)*; *(behaviour)* deshonesto(a) (**c**) *(wrong)* incorrecto(a)

improve [ɪmˈpruːv] **1** *vt* mejorar; *(knowledge)* perfeccionar; *(mind)* cultivar; *(increase)* aumentar
2 *vi* mejorarse; *(increase)* aumentar
▸ **improve on** *vt insep* superar; *(offer, bid)* sobrepujar

improvement [ɪmˈpruːvmənt] *n* mejora *f*; *(in skill)* perfeccionamiento *m*; *(increase)* aumento *m*

improvise [ˈɪmprəvaɪz] *vt & vi* improvisar

imprudent [ɪmˈpruːdənt] *adj* imprudente

impudence [ˈɪmpjʊdəns] *n* insolencia *f*

impudent [ˈɪmpjʊdənt] *adj* insolente

impulse [ˈɪmpʌls] *n* impulso *m*; **to act on (an) i.** dejarse llevar por un impulso

impulsive [ɪmˈpʌlsɪv] *adj* irreflexivo(a)

impunity [ɪmˈpjuːnɪtɪ] *n* impunidad *f*

impure [ɪmˈpjʊə(r)] *adj* (**a**) *(act)* impuro(a); *(thought)* impúdico(a) (**b**) *(air)* contaminado(a)

impurity [ɪmˈpjʊərɪtɪ] *n* (**a**) *(of act)* deshonestidad *f* (**b**) *(usu pl) (in air, substance)* impureza *f*

in [ɪn] **1** *prep* (**a**) *(place)* en; *(within)* dentro de; **in bed** en la cama; **in England/Brazil/China** en Inglaterra/Brasil/China; **in prison** en la cárcel; **in the distance** a lo lejos
(**b**) *(motion)* en; **I threw it in the fire** lo eché al fuego; **she arrived in Paris** llegó a París
(**c**) *(time) (during)* en, durante; **I haven't seen her in years** hace años que no la veo; **in May/1945** en mayo/1945; **in spring** en primavera; **in the daytime** durante el día; **in the morning** por la mañana; **at ten in the morning** a las diez de la mañana
(**d**) *(time) (within)* dentro de; **I arrived in time** llegué a tiempo
(**e**) *(time) (after)* al cabo de
(**f**) *(manner)* en; **in alphabetical order** en orden alfabético; **in a loud/quiet voice** en voz alta/baja; **in fashion** de moda; **in French** en francés; **in an odd way** de una manera rara; **in writing** por escrito; **write in pencil** escribe con lápiz
(**g**) *(wearing)* en; **dressed in blue** vestido(a) de azul; **in uniform** de uniforme
(**h**) *(weather etc)* a, en; **in the rain** bajo la lluvia; **in the sun** al sol; **in darkness** en la oscuridad; **in daylight** a la luz del día; **in the shade** a la sombra
(**i**) *(state, emotion)* en; **carved in wood** tallado(a) en madera; **in bloom/danger/public/silence** en flor/peligro/público/silencio; **in love** enamorado(a); **in tears** llorando
(**j**) *(ratio, numbers)* de; **cut in half** cortado(a) por la mitad; **in threes** de tres en tres; **one in six** uno de cada seis; **2 m in length** 2 m de largo
(**k**) *(profession)* en; **to be in insurance** trabajar en seguros
(**l**) *(person)* en; **he has it in him to win** es capaz de ganar
(**m**) *(after superlative)* de; **the smallest car in the world** el coche más pequeño del mundo
(**n**) *(before present participle)* **in behaving this way** con su comportamiento; **in so doing** con ello
(**o**) *(phrases)* **in all** en total; **in itself/himself/herself** en sí; **in that ...** dado que ...

2 *adv* **in here/there** aquí/allí dentro; **let's go in** vamos adentro; **to be in** *(at home)* estar (en casa); *(at work)* estar; *(tide)* estar alta; *Fam (in fashion)* estar de moda; **the bus is in** el autobús ha llegado; **to invite sb in** invitar a algn a entrar; *Fam* **to be in on sth** estar enterado(a) de algo; *Fam* **we're in for a storm** vamos a tener tormenta
3 *adj Fam* (**a**) *(fashionable) (place)* de moda; *(clothes)* del último grito (**b**) **an in joke** una broma privada
4 *n Fam* **ins and outs** detalles *mpl*
inability [ɪnəˈbɪlɪtɪ] *n* incapacidad *f*
inaccessible [ɪnækˈsesəbəl] *adj* inaccesible
inaccurate [ɪnˈækjʊrɪt] *adj* inexacto(a); *(statement)* erróneo(a); *(figures, total)* incorrecto(a)
inactivity [ɪnækˈtɪvɪtɪ] *n* inactividad *f*
inadequate [ɪnˈædɪkwɪt] *adj* (**a**) *(lacking)* insuficiente (**b**) *(not capable)* incapaz; *(unsuitable)* inadecuado(a) (**c**) *(defective)* defectuoso(a)
inadvertent [ɪnədˈvɜːtənt] *adj* involuntario(a)
inadvertently [ɪnədˈvɜːtəntlɪ] *adv* involuntariamente
inadvisable [ɪnədˈvaɪzəbəl] *adj* imprudente
inane [ɪˈneɪn] *adj* necio(a), fatuo(a)
inanimate [ɪnˈænɪmɪt] *adj* inanimado(a)
inappropriate [ɪnəˈprəʊprɪɪt] *adj* inoportuno(a); *(behaviour)* poco apropiado(a)
inarticulate [ɪnɑːˈtɪkjʊlɪt] *adj (cry, sound)* inarticulado(a); *(words)* mal pronunciado(a)
inasmuch as [ɪnəzˈmʌtʃəz] *conj Fml* (**a**) *(since)* puesto que, ya que (**b**) *(in so far as)* en la medida en que
inattentive [ɪnəˈtentɪv] *adj* desatento(a)
inaudible [ɪnˈɔːdəbəl] *adj* inaudible
inaugural [ɪnˈɔːgjʊrəl] *adj* inaugural
inaugurate [ɪnˈɔːgjʊreɪt] *vt (building)* inaugurar; *(president)* investir
inauguration [ɪnɔːgjʊˈreɪʃən] *n (of building)* inauguración *f*; *(of president)* investidura *f*
inauspicious [ɪnɔːˈspɪʃəs] *adj (start)* poco prometedor(a); *(circumstances)* desfavorable
inborn [ˈɪnbɔːn] *adj* innato(a)
inbred [ˈɪnbred] *adj* (**a**) *(quality)* innato(a) (**b**) *(family)* endogámico(a)
Inc, inc *US Com* (*abbr* **Incorporated**) ≃ S.A.
incalculable [ɪnˈkælkjʊləbəl] *adj* incalculable

incapable [ɪnˈkeɪpəbəl] *adj* incapaz
incapacitate [ɪnkəˈpæsɪteɪt] *vt Fml* incapacitar
incapacity [ɪnkəˈpæsɪtɪ] *n* incapacidad *f*
incarcerate [ɪnˈkɑːsəreɪt] *vt Fml* encarcelar
incarnation [ɪnkɑːˈneɪʃən] *n* encarnación *f*
incendiary [ɪnˈsendɪərɪ] **1** *adj* incendiario(a)
2 *n* bomba incendiaria
incense¹ [ˈɪnsens] *n* incienso *m*
incense² [ɪnˈsens] *vt* enfurecer, sacar de quicio
incentive [ɪnˈsentɪv] *n* incentivo *m*
incessant [ɪnˈsesənt] *adj* incesante; *(demands)* constante
incessantly [ɪnˈsesəntlɪ] *adv* sin cesar
incest [ˈɪnsest] *n* incesto *m*
inch [ɪntʃ] *n* pulgada *f (aprox 2,54 cm)*; *Fig* **i. by i.** poco a poco; *Fig* **she wouldn't give an i.** no quería ceder ni un ápice
▸ **inch forward** *vt sep & vi* avanzar poco a poco
incidence [ˈɪnsɪdəns] *n* frecuencia *f*
incident [ˈɪnsɪdənt] *n* incidente *m*
incidental [ɪnsɪˈdentəl] *adj (accessory)* incidental, accesorio(a); *(risk)* inherente (**to** a); **i. music** música *f* de fondo
incidentally [ɪnsɪˈdentəlɪ] *adv* a propósito
incinerator [ɪnˈsɪnəreɪtə(r)] *n* incinerador *m*
incipient [ɪnˈsɪpɪənt] *adj Fml* incipiente
incision [ɪnˈsɪʒən] *n* incisión *f*
incisive [ɪnˈsaɪsɪv] *adj (comment)* incisivo(a); *(reply)* tajante; *(mind)* penetrante
incite [ɪnˈsaɪt] *vt* incitar; **to i. sb to do sth** incitar a algn a hacer algo
inclination [ɪnklɪˈneɪʃən] *n* inclinación *f*; **my i. is to stay** yo prefiero quedarme
incline [ɪnˈklaɪn] **1** *vt* (**a**) **I'm inclined to believe him** me inclino a creerlo; **if you feel so inclined** si quieres; **she's inclined to be aggressive** tiende a ser agresiva (**b**) *(head etc)* inclinar
2 *vi (slope)* inclinarse
3 *n* [ˈɪnklaɪn] *(slope)* pendiente *f*; **steep i.** cuesta empinada
include [ɪnˈkluːd] *vt* incluir (**in** en); *(in price)* comprender (**in** en); *(in list)* figurar (**in** en)
including [ɪnˈkluːdɪŋ] *prep* incluso, inclusive
inclusion [ɪnˈkluːʒən] *n* inclusión *f*
inclusive [ɪnˈkluːsɪv] *adj* inclusivo(a); **pages 6 to 10 i.** de la página 6 a la 10, ambas inclusive; **the rent is i. of bills** el

alquiler incluye las facturas
incognito [ɪnkɒgˈniːtəʊ] *adv* de incógnito
incoherent [ɪnkəʊˈhɪərənt] *adj* incoherente
income [ˈɪnkʌm] *n* ingresos *mpl*; *(from investment)* réditos *mpl*; **i. tax** impuesto *m* sobre la renta; **i. tax return** declaración *f* de la renta
incoming [ˈɪnkʌmɪŋ] *adj (flight, train)* de llegada; *(tide)* ascendente; *(mail, message, call)* recibido(a)
incomparable [ɪnˈkɒmpərəbəl] *adj* incomparable, sin par
incompatible [ɪnkəmˈpætəbəl] *adj* incompatible (**with** con)
incompetence [ɪnˈkɒmpɪtəns] *n* incompetencia *f*
incompetent [ɪnˈkɒmpɪtənt] *adj* incompetente
incomplete [ɪnkəmˈpliːt] *adj* incompleto(a)
incomprehensible [ɪnkɒmprɪˈhensəbəl] *adj* incomprensible
inconceivable [ɪnkənˈsiːvəbəl] *adj* inconcebible
inconclusive [ɪnkənˈkluːsɪv] *adj (vote)* no decisivo(a); *(proof)* no concluyente
incongruous [ɪnˈkɒŋgrʊəs] *adj* incongruente
inconsiderate [ɪnkənˈsɪdərɪt] *adj* desconsiderado(a); **how i. of you!** ¡qué falta de consideración por tu parte!
inconsistency [ɪnkənˈsɪstənsɪ] *n* inconsecuencia *f*; *(contradiction)* contradicción *f*
inconsistent [ɪnkənˈsɪstənt] *adj* inconsecuente; *(contradictory)* contradictorio(a); **your evidence is i. with the facts** su testimonio no concuerda con los hechos
inconspicuous [ɪnkənˈspɪkjʊəs] *adj* que pasa desapercibido(a); *(discreet)* discreto(a)
incontrovertible [ɪnkɒntrəˈvɜːtəbəl] *adj Fml* incontrovertible
inconvenience [ɪnkənˈviːnɪəns] **1** *n* inconveniente *f*; *(annoyance)* molestia *f*
2 *vt (annoy)* molestar; *(cause difficulty to)* incomodar
inconvenient [ɪnkənˈviːnɪənt] *adj* molesto(a); *(time)* inoportuno(a); *(design)* poco práctico(a)
incorporate [ɪnˈkɔːpəreɪt] *vt* incorporar (**in** *or* **into** a); *(include)* incluir; *(contain)* contener
incorporated [ɪnˈkɔːpəreɪtɪd] *adj US Com* **i. company** sociedad anónima

incorrect [ɪnkəˈrekt] *adj* incorrecto(a)
incorrigible [ɪnˈkɒrɪdʒəbəl] *adj* incorregible
increase 1 *n* [ˈɪnkriːs] aumento *m*; *(in number)* incremento *m*; *(in price etc)* subida *f*
2 *vt* [ɪnˈkriːs] aumentar; *(price etc)* subir
3 *vi* aumentar
increasing [ɪnˈkriːsɪŋ] *adj* creciente
increasingly [ɪnˈkriːsɪŋlɪ] *adv* cada vez más
incredible [ɪnˈkredəbəl] *adj* increíble
incredulous [ɪnˈkredjʊləs] *adj* incrédulo(a)
increment [ˈɪnkrɪmənt] *n* incremento *m*
incriminate [ɪnˈkrɪmɪneɪt] *vt* incriminar
incriminating [ɪnˈkrɪmɪneɪtɪŋ] *adj* incriminatorio(a)
incubation [ɪnkjʊˈbeɪʃən] *n* incubación *f*
incubator [ˈɪnkjʊbeɪtə(r)] *n* incubadora *f*
incumbent [ɪnˈkʌmbənt] **1** *n* titular *mf*
2 *adj Fml* **to be i. on sb to do sth** ser la obligación de algn hacer algo
incur [ɪnˈkɜː(r)] *vt (blame)* incurrir en; *(risk)* correr; *(debt)* contraer; *(loss)* sufrir
incurable [ɪnˈkjʊərəbəl] *adj* incurable
indebted [ɪnˈdetɪd] *adj* endeudado(a); *Fig (grateful)* agradecido(a); *Fig* **to be i. to sb** estar en deuda con algn
indecent [ɪnˈdiːsənt] *adj* indecente; **i. assault** atentado *m* contra el pudor; **i. exposure** exhibicionismo *m*
indecision [ɪndɪˈsɪʒən] *n* indecisión *f*
indecisive [ɪndɪˈsaɪsɪv] *adj (person)* indeciso(a); *(evidence)* poco concluyente; *(victory)* no decisivo(a)
indeed [ɪnˈdiːd] *adv* (**a**) *Fml (in fact)* efectivamente, en realidad (**b**) **I'm very sorry i.** lo siento de veras; **it's very hard i.** es verdaderamente difícil; **thank you very much i.** muchísimas gracias
indefinite [ɪnˈdefɪnɪt] *adj* indefinido(a)
indelible [ɪnˈdeləbəl] *adj* indeleble
indemnify [ɪnˈdemnɪfaɪ] *vt* indemnizar (**for** por)
indemnity [ɪnˈdemnɪtɪ] *n* (**a**) *(insurance)* indemnidad *f* (**b**) *(compensation)* indemnización *f*
indentation [ɪndenˈteɪʃən] *n* (**a**)*Typ* sangría *f* (**b**) *(of edge)* muesca *f*; *(of surface)* depresión *f*
independence [ɪndɪˈpendəns] *n* independencia *f*; *US* **I. Day** día *m* de la Independencia *(4 julio)*
independent [ɪndɪˈpendənt] *adj* independiente; *Br* **i. school** = colegio no subvencionado por el estado; **to become i.** independizarse

in-depth ['ɪndepθ] *adj* minucioso(a), exhaustivo(a)

indestructible [ɪndɪ'strʌktəbəl] *adj* indestructible

indeterminate [ɪndɪ'tɜːmɪnɪt] *adj* indeterminado(a)

index ['ɪndeks] **1** *n* (*pl* **indexes** *or* **indices**) (**a**) *(in book)* índice *m*; *(in library)* catálogo *m*; **i. card** ficha *f* (**b**) *Math* exponente *m*; *Econ* índice *m* (**c**) **i. finger** dedo *m* índice
2 *vt* catalogar

index-linked ['ɪndekslɪŋkt] *adj* sujeto(a) al aumento de la inflación

India ['ɪndɪə] *n* (la) India

Indian ['ɪndɪən] *adj & n* *(of America)* indio(a) *(m,f)*; *(of India)* hindú *(mf)*; **I. Ocean** Océano ndico; **I. Summer** veranillo *m* de San Martín

indicate ['ɪndɪkeɪt] **1** *vt* indicar
2 *vi Aut* poner el intermitente

indication [ɪndɪ'keɪʃən] *n* indicio *m*

indicative [ɪn'dɪkətɪv] **1** *adj* indicativo(a)
2 *n Ling* indicativo *m*

indicator ['ɪndɪkeɪtə(r)] *n* indicador *m*; *Br Aut* intermitente *m*

indices ['ɪndɪsiːz] *pl of* **index**

indict [ɪn'daɪt] *vt* acusar (**for** de)

indictment [ɪn'daɪtmənt] *n Jur* acusación *f*; *Fig* **a damning i. of his books** una crítica feroz de sus libros

indifference [ɪn'dɪfərəns] *n* indiferencia *f*

indifferent [ɪn'dɪfərənt] *adj* (**a**) *(uninterested)* indiferente (**b**) *(mediocre)* regular

indigenous [ɪn'dɪdʒɪnəs] *adj* indígena

indigestion [ɪndɪ'dʒestʃən] *n* indigestión *f*; **to suffer from i.** tener un empacho

indignant [ɪn'dɪgnənt] *adj* indignado(a); *(look)* de indignación; **to get i. about sth** indignarse por algo

indignity [ɪn'dɪgnɪtɪ] *n* indignidad *f*

indigo ['ɪndɪgəʊ] **1** *n* añil *m*
2 *adj* (de color) añil

indirect [ɪndɪ'rekt, ɪndaɪ'rekt] *adj* indirecto(a)

indiscreet [ɪndɪ'skriːt] *adj* indiscreto(a)

indiscretion [ɪndɪ'skreʃən] *n* indiscreción *f*

indiscriminate [ɪndɪ'skrɪmɪnɪt] *adj* *(punishment, shooting)* indiscriminado(a); *(praise, reading)* sin criterio

indispensable [ɪndɪ'spensəbəl] *adj* indispensable, imprescindible

indisposed [ɪndɪ'spəʊzd] *adj Fml* indispuesto(a)

indisputable [ɪndɪ'spjuːtəbəl] *adj* indiscutible, incontestable

indistinct [ɪndɪ'stɪŋkt] *adj* indistinto(a); *(memory)* confuso(a), vago(a); *(shape etc)* borroso(a)

indistinguishable [ɪndɪ'stɪŋgwɪʃəbəl] *adj* indistinguible

individual [ɪndɪ'vɪdjʊəl] **1** *adj* (**a**) *(separate)* individual; *(for one)* particular; *(personal)* personal (**b**) *(characteristic)* particular; *(original)* original
2 *n (person)* individuo *m*; **private i.** particular *m*

individualist [ɪndɪ'vɪdjʊəlɪst] *n* individualista *mf*

indoctrinate [ɪn'dɒktrɪneɪt] *vt* adoctrinar

indoctrination [ɪndɒktrɪ'neɪʃən] *n* adoctrinamiento *m*

indolent ['ɪndələnt] *adj Fml* indolente

Indonesia [ɪndəʊ'niːzɪə] *n* Indonesia

Indonesian [ɪndəʊ'niːzɪən] **1** *adj* indonesio(a)
2 *n* (**a**) *(person)* indonesio(a) *m,f* (**b**) *(language)* indonesio *m*

indoor ['ɪndɔː(r)] *adj (plant)* de interior; **i. football** fútbol *m* sala; **i. pool** piscina cubierta

indoors [ɪn'dɔːz] *adv (inside)* dentro (de casa); *(at home)* en casa; **let's go i.** vamos adentro

induce [ɪn'djuːs] *vt* (**a**) *(persuade)* inducir, persuadir (**b**) *(cause)* producir; *Med (labour)* provocar

inducement [ɪn'djuːsmənt] *n* incentivo *m*, aliciente *m*

induction [ɪn'dʌkʃən] *n* (**a**) *Med (of labour)* provocación *f* (**b**) *Elec* inducción *f* (**c**) *Educ* introducción *f*

indulge [ɪn'dʌldʒ] **1** *vt* (**a**) *(child)* consentir; *(person)* complacer; **to i. oneself** darse gusto (**b**) *(whim)* ceder a, satisfacer
2 *vi* darse el gusto (**in** de)

indulgence [ɪn'dʌldʒəns] *n* (**a**) *(of child)* mimo *m*; *(of attitude)* indulgencia *f* (**b**) *(of whim)* satisfacción *f*

indulgent [ɪn'dʌldʒənt] *adj* indulgente

industrial [ɪn'dʌstrɪəl] *adj* industrial; *(accident)* laboral; *(disease)* profesional; *Br* **to take i. action** declararse en huelga; *Br* **i. dispute** conflicto *m* laboral; **i.** *Br* **estate** *or US* **park** polígono *m* industrial; **i. relations** relaciones *fpl* laborales

industrialist [ɪn'dʌstrɪəlɪst] *n* industrial *mf*

industrialize [ɪn'dʌstrɪəlaɪz] *vt* industrializar; **to become industrialized** industrializarse

industrious [ɪn'dʌstrɪəs] *adj* trabajador(a)

industry ['ɪndəstrɪ] *n* (**a**) industria *f* (**b**) *(diligence)* aplicación *f*

inebriated [ɪn'iːbrɪeɪtɪd] *adj* embriagado(a)

inedible [ɪn'edəbəl] *adj* incomible

ineffective [ɪnɪ'fektɪv] *adj* ineficaz

ineffectual [ɪnɪ'fektʃʊəl] *adj (aim, protest)* ineficaz; *(person)* incompetente

inefficiency [ɪnɪ'fɪʃənsɪ] *n* ineficacia *f*; *(of person)* incompetencia *f*

inefficient [ɪnɪ'fɪʃənt] *adj* ineficaz; *(person)* inepto(a)

ineligible [ɪn'elɪdʒəbəl] *adj* no apto(a) (**for** para)

inept [ɪn'ept] *adj (person)* inepto(a); *(remark)* estúpido(a)

inequality [ɪnɪ'kwɒlɪtɪ] *n* desigualdad *f*

inert [ɪn'ɜːt] *adj* inerte

inertia [ɪn'ɜːʃə] *n* inercia *f*

inescapable [ɪnɪ'skeɪpəbəl] *adj* ineludible

inevitability [ɪnevɪtə'bɪlɪtɪ] *n* inevitabilidad *f*

inevitable [ɪn'evɪtəbəl] *adj* inevitable

inexcusable [ɪnɪk'skjuːzəbəl] *adj* inexcusable, imperdonable

inexhaustible [ɪnɪg'zɔːstəbəl] *adj* inagotable

inexorable [ɪn'eksərəbəl] *adj Fml* inexorable

inexpensive [ɪnɪk'spensɪv] *adj* económico(a)

inexperience [ɪnɪk'spɪərɪəns] *n* inexperiencia *f*

inexperienced [ɪnɪk'spɪərɪənst] *adj* inexperto(a)

inexplicable [ɪnɪk'splɪkəbəl] *adj* inexplicable

infallible [ɪn'fæləbəl] *adj* infalible

infamous ['ɪnfəməs] *adj* infame

infancy ['ɪnfənsɪ] *n* infancia *f*

infant ['ɪnfənt] *n* niño(a) *m,f*; *Br* **i. school** parvulario *m*

infantile ['ɪnfəntaɪl] *adj* infantil

infantry ['ɪnfəntrɪ] *n* infantería *f*

infatuated [ɪn'fætjʊeɪtɪd] *adj* encaprichado(a)

infatuation [ɪnfætjʊ'eɪʃən] *n* encaprichamiento *m*

infect [ɪn'fekt] *vt (cut)* infectar; *(water)* contaminar; *(person)* contagiar

infection [ɪn'fekʃən] *n (of cut)* infección *f*; *(of water)* contaminación *f*; *(with illness)* contagio *m*

infectious [ɪn'fekʃəs] *adj (disease)* infeccioso(a); *Fig* contagioso(a)

infer [ɪn'fɜː(r)] *vt* inferir (**from** de)

inference ['ɪnfərəns] *n* inferencia *f*

inferior [ɪn'fɪərɪə(r)] **1** *adj* inferior (**to** a) **2** *n Pej* inferior *mf*

inferiority [ɪnfɪərɪ'ɒrɪtɪ] *n* inferioridad *f*

inferno [ɪn'fɜːnəʊ] *n Literary* infierno *m*; *Fig* **the house was a raging i.** la casa ardía en llamas

infertile [ɪn'fɜːtaɪl] *adj* estéril

infertility [ɪnfə'tɪlɪtɪ] *n* esterilidad *f*

infest [ɪn'fest] *vt* infestar, plagar (**with** de)

infighting ['ɪnfaɪtɪŋ] *n Fig* luchas *fpl* internas

infiltrate ['ɪnfɪltreɪt] *vt* infiltrarse (**into** en)

infinite ['ɪnfɪnɪt] *adj* infinito(a)

infinitive [ɪn'fɪnɪtɪv] *n* infinitivo *m*

infinity [ɪn'fɪnɪtɪ] *n* infinidad *f*; *Math* infinito *m*

infirm [ɪn'fɜːm] **1** *adj (ailing)* enfermizo(a); *(weak)* débil **2** *npl* **the i.** los inválidos

infirmary [ɪn'fɜːmərɪ] *n* hospital *m*

infirmity [ɪn'fɜːmɪtɪ] *n Fml (ailment)* enfermedad *f*; *(weakness)* debilidad *f*

inflame [ɪn'fleɪm] *vt (passion)* encender; *(curiosity)* avivar; *(crowd)* excitar; **to be inflamed with rage** rabiar

inflamed [ɪn'fleɪmd] *adj* inflamado(a); **to become i.** inflamarse

inflammable [ɪn'flæməbəl] *adj (material)* inflamable; *Fig (situation)* explosivo(a)

inflammation [ɪnflə'meɪʃən] *n* inflamación *f*

inflatable [ɪn'fleɪtəbəl] *adj* inflable

inflate [ɪn'fleɪt] **1** *vt* inflar **2** *vi* inflarse

inflated [ɪn'fleɪtɪd] *adj* (**a**) *Fig (prices)* inflacionista (**b**) *Pej (view, idea)* exagerado(a)

inflation [ɪn'fleɪʃən] *n* inflación *f*

inflexible [ɪn'fleksəbəl] *adj* inflexible

inflict [ɪn'flɪkt] *vt (blow)* asestar (**on** a); *(damage)* causar (**on** a); *(defeat)* infligir (**on** a)

in-flight ['ɪnflaɪt] *adj* durante el vuelo

influence ['ɪnflʊəns] **1** *n* influencia *f*; *Fam* **to be under the i.** llevar una copa de más **2** *vt* influir en

influential [ɪnflʊ'enʃəl] *adj* influyente

influenza [ɪnflʊ'enzə] *n* gripe *f*

influx ['ɪnflʌks] *n* afluencia *f*

inform [ɪn'fɔːm] **1** *vt* informar (**of** *or* **about** de *or* sobre); *(police)* avisar (**of** *or* **about** de) **2** *vi* **to i. against** *or* **on** denunciar

informal [ɪn'fɔːməl] *adj* (**a**) *(occasion, behaviour)* informal; *(language, treatment)* familiar (**b**) *(unofficial)* no oficial

informality [ɪnfɔː'mælɪtɪ] *n (of occasion, behaviour)* sencillez *f; (of treatment)* familiaridad *f*

informant [ɪn'fɔːmənt] *n* informante *mf*

information [ɪnfə'meɪʃən] *n* información *f; (details)* detalles *mpl; (facts)* datos *mpl; (knowledge)* conocimientos *mpl; (news)* noticias *fpl*; **a piece of i.** un dato; **i. bureau** centro *m* de información; **i. (super)highway** autopista *f* de la información; **i. technology** informática *f*

informative [ɪn'fɔːmətɪv] *adj* informativo(a)

informed [ɪn'fɔːmd] *adj* enterado(a); **keep me i.** téngame al corriente

informer [ɪn'fɔːmə(r)] *n* delator(a) *m,f; (to the police)* soplón(ona) *m,f*

infrared [ɪnfrə'red] *adj* infrarrojo(a)

infrastructure ['ɪnfrəstrʌktʃə(r)] *n* infraestructura *f*

infringe [ɪn'frɪndʒ] **1** *vt (law, rule)* infringir; *(copyright)* no respetar

    2 *vi* **to i. on** *or* **upon** *(rights)* violar; *(privacy)* invadir

infringement [ɪn'frɪndʒmənt] *n (of law, rule)* infracción *f; (of rights)* violación *f*

infuriate [ɪn'fjʊərɪeɪt] *vt* poner furioso(a)

infuriating [ɪn'fjʊərɪeɪtɪŋ] *adj* exasperante

infusion [ɪn'fjuːʒən] *n* infusión *f*

ingenious [ɪn'dʒiːnɪəs] *adj* ingenioso(a)

ingenuity [ɪndʒɪ'njuːɪtɪ] *n* ingenio *m*

ingenuous [ɪn'dʒenjʊəs] *adj* ingenuo(a)

ingot ['ɪŋgət] *n* lingote *m*

ingrained [ɪn'greɪnd] *adj Fig* arraigado(a)

ingratiate [ɪn'greɪʃɪeɪt] *vt Pej* **to i. oneself with sb** congraciarse con algn

ingratiating [ɪn'greɪʃɪeɪtɪŋ] *adj* zalamero(a)

ingratitude [ɪn'grætɪtjuːd] *n* ingratitud *f*

ingredient [ɪn'griːdɪənt] *n* ingrediente *m*

inhabit [ɪn'hæbɪt] *vt* vivir en, ocupar

inhabitable [ɪn'hæbɪtəbəl] *adj* habitable

> *⃗* Note that the Spanish word **inhabitable** is a false friend and is never a translation for the English word **inhabitable**. In Spanish, **inhabitable** means "uninhabitable".

inhabitant [ɪn'hæbɪtənt] *n* habitante *mf*

inhale [ɪn'heɪl] **1** *vt (gas)* inhalar; *(air)* aspirar

    2 *vi* aspirar; *(smoker)* tragar el humo

inherent [ɪn'hɪərənt] *adj* inherente

inherit [ɪn'herɪt] *vt* heredar (**from** de)

inheritance [ɪn'herɪtəns] *n* herencia *f*

inhibit [ɪn'hɪbɪt] *vt (freedom)* limitar; *(person)* cohibir; **to i. sb from doing sth** impedir a algn hacer algo

inhibited [ɪn'hɪbɪtɪd] *adj* cohibido(a)

inhibition [ɪnhɪ'bɪʃən] *n* cohibición *f*

inhospitable [ɪnhɒ'spɪtəbəl] *adj* inhospitalario(a); *(climate, place)* inhóspito(a)

inhuman [ɪn'hjuːmən] *adj* inhumano(a)

iniquity [ɪ'nɪkwɪtɪ] *n Fml* iniquidad *f*

initial [ɪ'nɪʃəl] **1** *adj* inicial, primero(a)

    2 *n* (**a**) inicial *f* (**b**) **initials** *(of name)* iniciales *fpl; (of abbreviation)* siglas *fpl*

    3 *vt* firmar con las iniciales

initially [ɪ'nɪʃəlɪ] *adv* al principio

initiate [ɪ'nɪʃɪeɪt] *vt* (**a**) iniciar; *(reform)* promover; *(lawsuit)* entablar (**b**) *(into society)* admitir (**into** en); *(into knowledge)* iniciar (**into** en)

initiation [ɪnɪʃɪ'eɪʃən] *n* (**a**) *(start)* principio *m* (**b**) *(admission)* iniciación *f*

initiative [ɪ'nɪʃətɪv] *n* iniciativa *f*

inject [ɪn'dʒekt] *vt* (**a**) *(drug etc)* inyectar (**b**) *Fig (capital)* invertir; *(life, hope)* infundir

injection [ɪn'dʒekʃən] *n* (**a**) inyección *f* (**b**) *Fig (of capital)* inversión *f*

injunction [ɪn'dʒʌŋkʃən] *n* interdicto *m*

injure ['ɪndʒə(r)] *vt* herir; **to i. oneself** hacerse daño; *Fig (health, reputation)* perjudicar

injured ['ɪndʒəd] **1** *adj* herido(a); *Fig (look, tone)* ofendido(a)

    2 *npl* **the i.** los heridos

injury ['ɪndʒərɪ] *n (hurt)* herida *f; Fig (harm)* daño *m; Sport* **i. time** (tiempo *m* de) descuento *m*

injustice [ɪn'dʒʌstɪs] *n* injusticia *f*

ink [ɪŋk] *n* tinta *f*; **invisible i.** tinta simpática

inkjet printer ['ɪŋkdʒet'prɪntə(r)] *n Comput* impresora *f* de chorro de tinta

inkling ['ɪŋklɪŋ] *n (idea)* idea *f; (suspicion)* sospecha *f; (sign)* señal *f*

inkwell ['ɪŋkwel] *n* tintero *m*

inlaid [ɪn'leɪd] *adj (wood)* taraceado(a); *(ivory, gems)* incrustado(a)

inland 1 *adj* ['ɪnlənd] (del) interior; *Br* **I. Revenue** Hacienda *f*

    2 *adv* [ɪn'lænd] *(travel)* tierra adentro

in-laws ['ɪnlɔːz] *npl Fam* familia *f* política

inlet ['ɪnlet] *n* (**a**) *(in coastline)* ensenada *f*, cala *f* (**b**) *(in pipe, machine)* entrada *f*, admisión *f*

inline ['ɪnlaɪn] *adj* **i. skates** patines *mpl* en línea

inmate ['ɪnmeɪt] *n (of prison)* preso(a) *m,f; (of hospital)* enfermo(a) *m,f; (of asylum, camp)* internado(a) *m,f*

inn [ɪn] *n (with lodging)* posada *f*, mesón *m*
innate [ɪ'neɪt] *adj* innato(a)
inner ['ɪnə(r)] *adj* (**a**) *(region)* interior; *(structure)* interno(a); **i. city** zona urbana desfavorecida; **i. tube** cámara *f* de aire (**b**) *Fig (thoughts)* íntimo(a); *(peace etc)* interior
innermost ['ɪnəməʊst] *adj (room)* más interior; *Fig (thoughts)* más íntimo(a)
innings ['ɪnɪŋz] *npl (in cricket)* entrada *f*, turno *m*
innocence ['ɪnəsəns] *n* inocencia *f*
innocent ['ɪnəsənt] *adj & n* inocente *(mf)*
innocuous [ɪ'nɒkjʊəs] *adj* inocuo(a)
innovation [ɪnə'veɪʃən] *n* novedad *f*
innuendo [ɪnjʊ'endəʊ] *n* indirecta *f*
inoculate [ɪ'nɒkjʊleɪt] *vt* inocular
inoculation [ɪnɒkjʊ'leɪʃən] *n* inoculación *f*
inoffensive [ɪnə'fensɪv] *adj* inofensivo(a)
inopportune [ɪn'ɒpətjuːn, ɪnɒpə'tjuːn] *adj* inoportuno(a)
inordinate [ɪ'nɔːdɪnɪt] *adj* desmesurado(a)
inpatient ['ɪnpeɪʃənt] *n* interno(a) *m,f*
input ['ɪnpʊt] *n (of resources)* inversión *f*; *(of power)* entrada *f*; *Comput (of data)* input *m*, entrada
inquest ['ɪnkwest] *n* investigación *f* judicial
inquire [ɪn'kwaɪə(r)] **1** *vt* preguntar; *(find out)* averiguar
  2 *vi* preguntar (**about** por); *(find out)* informarse (**about** de)
  ▸ **inquire after** *vt insep* preguntar por
  ▸ **inquire into** *vt insep* investigar, indagar
inquiry [ɪn'kwaɪərɪ] *n* (**a**) pregunta *f*; **inquiries** *(sign)* información (**b**) *(investigation)* investigación *f*
inquisitive [ɪn'kwɪzɪtɪv] *adj (curious)* curioso(a); *(questioning)* preguntón(ona)
inroads ['ɪnrəʊdz] *npl* **the firm is making i. into the market** la empresa está ganando terreno en el mercado; **to make i. into one's capital** reducir su capital
insane [ɪn'seɪn] *adj* loco(a); *(act)* insensato(a); *Fig* **to drive sb i.** volver loco(a) a algn
insanity [ɪn'sænɪtɪ] *n* demencia *f*, locura *f*
insatiable [ɪn'seɪʃəbəl] *adj* insaciable
inscribe [ɪn'skraɪb] *vt Fml* inscribir; *(book)* dedicar
inscription [ɪn'skrɪpʃən] *n (on stone, coin)* inscripción *f*, *(in book, on photo)* dedicatoria *f*
inscrutable [ɪn'skruːtəbəl] *adj* inescrutable, insondable

insect ['ɪnsekt] *n* insecto *m*; **i. bite** picadura *f*
insecticide [ɪn'sektɪsaɪd] *n* insecticida *m*
insecure [ɪnsɪ'kjʊə(r)] *adj* inseguro(a)
insecurity [ɪnsɪ'kjʊərɪtɪ] *n* inseguridad *f*
insemination [ɪnsemɪ'neɪʃən] *n* inseminación *f*
insensible [ɪn'sensəbəl] *adj Fml* inconsciente
insensitive [ɪn'sensɪtɪv] *adj* insensible
inseparable [ɪn'sepərəbəl] *adj* inseparable
insert 1 *n* ['ɪnsɜːt] encarte *m*
  2 *vt* [ɪn'sɜːt] introducir
insertion [ɪn'sɜːʃən] *n* introducción *f*; *(of clause, text)* inserción *f*
inshore 1 *adj* ['ɪnʃɔː(r)] *(fishing)* de bajura
  2 *adv* [ɪn'ʃɔː(r)] cerca de la costa
inside [ɪn'saɪd] **1** *n* (**a**) interior *m*; **on the i.** por dentro; **to turn sth i. out** volver algo al revés (**b**) *Fam* **insides** tripas *fpl*
  2 ['ɪnsaɪd] *adj* interior; *Sport* **i. forward** interior *mf*; *Aut* **i. lane** carril *m* interior
  3 *adv (be)* dentro, adentro; *(run etc)* (hacia) adentro; **to come i.** entrar; *Br Fam* **he spent a year i.** pasó un año en chirona
  4 *prep* (**a**) *(place)* dentro de (**b**) *Fam* **i. (of)** *(time)* en menos de
insider [ɪn'saɪdə(r)] *n* **i. dealing** = uso indebido de información privilegiada y confidencial para operaciones comerciales
insidious [ɪn'sɪdɪəs] *adj* insidioso(a)
insight ['ɪnsaɪt] *n* perspicacia *f*
insignia [ɪn'sɪgnɪə] *n inv* insignia *f*
insignificant [ɪnsɪg'nɪfɪkənt] *adj* insignificante
insincere [ɪnsɪn'sɪə(r)] *adj* poco sincero(a)
insinuate [ɪn'sɪnjʊeɪt] *vt* insinuar
insipid [ɪn'sɪpɪd] *adj* soso(a), insulso(a)
insist [ɪn'sɪst] **1** *vi* insistir (**on** en); *(argue)* obstinarse (**on** en)
  2 *vt* **to i. that ...** insistir en que ...
insistence [ɪn'sɪstəns] *n* insistencia *f*
insistent [ɪn'sɪstənt] *adj* insistente
in so far as [ɪnsəʊ'fɑːrəz] *adv* en tanto que
insole ['ɪnsəʊl] *n (of shoe)* plantilla *f*
insolent ['ɪnsələnt] *adj* insolente
insoluble [ɪn'sɒljʊbəl] *adj* insoluble
insomnia [ɪn'sɒmnɪə] *n* insomnio *m*
insomniac [ɪn'sɒmnɪæk] *n* insomne *mf*
inspect [ɪn'spekt] *vt* inspeccionar, examinar; *(troops)* pasar revista a

inspection [ɪnˈspekʃən] *n* inspección *f*; *(of troops)* revista *f*

inspector [ɪnˈspektə(r)] *n* inspector(a) *m,f*; *(on bus, train)* revisor(a) *m,f*

inspiration [ɪnspɪˈreɪʃən] *n* inspiración *f*; **to get i. from sb/sth** inspirarse en algn/algo

inspire [ɪnˈspaɪə(r)] *vt* (**a**) inspirar; **to i. respect in sb** infundir respeto a algn (**b**) **to i. sb to do sth** animar a algn a hacer algo

inspired [ɪnˈspaɪəd] *adj* inspirado(a)

instability [ɪnstəˈbɪlɪtɪ] *n* inestabilidad *f*

install, *US* **instal** [ɪnˈstɔːl] *vt* instalar

installation [ɪnstəˈleɪʃən] *n* instalación *f*

instalment, *US* **installment** [ɪnˈstɔːlmənt] *n* (**a**) *(of payment)* plazo *m*; **to pay by instalments** pagar a plazos; *US* **i. plan** venta *f*/compra *f* a plazos (**b**) *(of novel, programme)* entrega *f*; *(of journal)* fascículo *m*

instance [ˈɪnstəns] *n* caso *m*, ejemplo *m*; **for i.** por ejemplo; **in the first i.** en primer lugar

> 🖉 Note that the Spanish word **instancia** is a false friend and is never a translation for the English word **instance**. In Spanish, **instancia** means "request".

instant [ˈɪnstənt] **1** *n (moment)* instante *m*, momento *m*; **in an i.** en un instante
    2 *adj* inmediato(a); *(coffee, meal)* instantáneo(a)

instantly [ˈɪnstəntlɪ] *adv* inmediatamente

instead [ɪnˈsted] **1** *adv* en cambio
    2 *prep* **i. of** en vez de, en lugar de

instep [ˈɪnstep] *n* empeine *m*

instigation [ɪnstɪˈgeɪʃən] *n* instigación *f*

instil, *US* **instill** [ɪnˈstɪl] *vt (idea, habit)* inculcar (**in** a *or* en); *(courage, respect)* infundir (**in** a)

instinct [ˈɪnstɪŋkt] *n* instinto *m*

instinctive [ɪnˈstɪŋktɪv] *adj* instintivo(a)

institute [ˈɪnstɪtjuːt] **1** *n* instituto *m*; *(centre)* centro *m*; *(professional body)* colegio *m*
    2 *vt Fml* (**a**) *(system)* establecer (**b**) *(start)* iniciar; *(proceedings)* entablar

institution [ɪnstɪˈtjuːʃən] *n* (**a**) institución *f* (**b**) *(home)* asilo *m*; *(asylum)* manicomio *m*

instruct [ɪnˈstrʌkt] *vt* instruir; *(order)* mandar; **I am instructed to say that ...** me han encargado decir que ...

instruction [ɪnˈstrʌkʃən] *n* (**a**) instrucción *f* (**b**) **instructions** instrucciones *fpl*; **instructions for use** modo de empleo

instructive [ɪnˈstrʌktɪv] *adj* instructivo(a)

instructor [ɪnˈstrʌktə(r)] *n* instructor(a) *m,f*; *(of driving)* profesor(a) *m,f*

instrument [ˈɪnstrəmənt] *n* instrumento *m*; **i. panel** tablero *m* de mandos

instrumental [ɪnstrəˈmentəl] *adj* (**a**) *Mus* instrumental (**b**) **to be i. in sth** contribuir decisivamente a algo

insubordinate [ɪnsəˈbɔːdɪnɪt] *adj* insubordinado(a)

insubstantial [ɪnsəbˈstænʃəl] *adj* insubstancial; *(structure)* poco sólido(a)

insufferable [ɪnˈsʌfərəbəl] *adj* insoportable

insufficient [ɪnsəˈfɪʃənt] *adj* insuficiente

insular [ˈɪnsjʊlə(r)] *adj* (**a**) *Geog* insular (**b**) *Fig Pej* estrecho(a) de miras

insulate [ˈɪnsjʊleɪt] *vt* aislar (**against** *or* **from** de)

insulating tape [ˈɪnsjʊleɪtɪŋteɪp] *n* cinta *f* aislante

insulation [ɪnsjʊˈleɪʃən] *n* aislamiento *m*

insulin [ˈɪnsjʊlɪn] *n* insulina *f*

insult 1 *n* [ˈɪnsʌlt] *(words)* insulto *m*; *(action)* afrenta *f*, ofensa *f*
    2 *vt* [ɪnˈsʌlt] insultar, ofender

insulting [ɪnˈsʌltɪŋ] *adj* insultante, ofensivo(a)

insuperable [ɪnˈsuːpərəbəl] *adj* insuperable

insurance [ɪnˈʃʊərəns] *n* seguro *m*; **fire i.** seguro contra incendios; **i. broker** agente *mf* de seguros; **i. company** compañía *f* de seguros; **i. policy** póliza *f* (de seguros); **private health i.** seguro médico privado

insure [ɪnˈʃʊə(r)] *vt* asegurar (**against** contra)

insurgent [ɪnˈsɜːdʒənt] *adj & n* insurrecto(a) *(m,f)*

insurmountable [ɪnsəˈmaʊntəbəl] *adj (problem etc)* insuperable; *(barrier)* infranqueable

intact [ɪnˈtækt] *adj* intacto(a)

intake [ˈɪnteɪk] *n* (**a**) *(of air, water)* entrada *f*; *(of electricity etc)* toma *f* (**b**) *(of food, calories)* consumo *m* (**c**) *(of students, recruits)* número *m* de admitidos

integral [ˈɪntɪgrəl] **1** *adj* (**a**) *(intrinsic)* integrante (**b**) *(whole)* íntegro(a) (**c**) *Math* integral
    2 *n Math* integral *f*

integrate [ˈɪntɪgreɪt] **1** *vt* integrar
    2 *vi* integrarse

integration [ɪntɪˈgreɪʃən] *n* integración *f*

integrity [ɪnˈtegrɪtɪ] *n* integridad *f*, honradez *f*

intellect [ˈɪntɪlekt] *n* intelecto *m*

intellectual [ɪntɪˈlektʃʊəl] *adj & n* intelectual *(mf)*
intelligence [ɪnˈtelɪdʒəns] *n* (**a**) inteligencia *f* (**b**) *(information)* información *f*
intelligent [ɪnˈtelɪdʒənt] *adj* inteligente
intelligentsia [ɪntelɪˈdʒentsɪə] *n* intelectualidad *f*
intelligible [ɪnˈtelɪdʒəbəl] *adj* inteligible
intend [ɪnˈtend] *vt* (**a**) *(mean)* tener la intención de (**b**) **to i. sth for sb** destinar algo a algn
intended [ɪnˈtendɪd] *adj (planned)* previsto(a)
intense [ɪnˈtens] *adj* intenso(a); *(person)* muy serio(a)
intensely [ɪnˈtenslɪ] *adv (extremely)* enormemente, sumamente
intensify [ɪnˈtensɪfaɪ] *vt (search)* intensificar; *(effort)* redoblar; *(production, pollution)* aumentar
intensity [ɪnˈtensɪtɪ] *n* intensidad *f*
intensive [ɪnˈtensɪv] *adj* intensivo(a); *Med* **i. care unit** unidad *f* de vigilancia intensiva
intent [ɪnˈtent] **1** *adj (absorbed)* absorto(a); *(gaze etc)* atento(a); **to be i. on doing sth** estar resuelto(a) a hacer algo
  2 *n Fml* intención *f*, propósito *m*; **to all intents and purposes** a todos los efectos
intention [ɪnˈtenʃən] *n* intención *f*
intentional [ɪnˈtenʃənəl] *adj* deliberado(a)
intentionally [ɪnˈtenʃənəlɪ] *adv* a propósito
interact [ɪntərˈækt] *vi (people)* interrelacionarse
interaction [ɪntərˈækʃən] *n* interacción *f*
interactive [ɪntərˈæktɪv] *adj* interactivo(a)
intercede [ɪntəˈsiːd] *vi* interceder (**with** ante)
intercept [ɪntəˈsept] *vt* interceptar
interchange **1** *n* [ˈɪntətʃeɪndʒ] (**a**) *(exchange)* intercambio *m* (**b**) *(on motorway)* cruce *m*
  2 *vt* [ɪntəˈtʃeɪndʒ] intercambiar (**with** con)
interchangeable [ɪntəˈtʃeɪndʒəbəl] *adj* intercambiable
intercity [ɪntəˈsɪtɪ] *adj Rail* de largo recorrido
intercom [ˈɪntəkɒm] *n* portero automático
intercontinental [ɪntəkɒntɪˈnentəl] *adj* **i. ballistic missile** misil balístico intercontinental
intercourse [ˈɪntəkɔːs] *n* (**a**) *(dealings)* trato *m* (**b**) *(sexual)* relaciones *fpl* sexuales

interest [ˈɪntrɪst] **1** *n* (**a**) interés *m* (**b**) *(advantage)* provecho *m*; **in the i. of** en pro de (**c**) *Com (share)* participación *f* (**d**) *Fin* interés *m*; **i. rate** tipo *m* de interés
  2 *vt* interesar; **he's interested in politics** le interesa la política
interesting [ˈɪntrɪstɪŋ] *adj* interesante
interface [ˈɪntəfeɪs] *n* interface *f*
interfere [ɪntəˈfɪə(r)] *vi* (**a**) *(meddle)* entrometerse (**in** en); **to i. with** *(hinder)* dificultar; *(spoil)* estropear; *(prevent)* impedir (**b**) *Rad & TV* interferir (**with** con)
interference [ɪntəˈfɪərəns] *n (meddling)* intromisión *f*; *(hindrance)* estorbo *m*; *Rad & TV* interferencia *f*
interim [ˈɪntərɪm] **1** *n Fml* **in the i.** en el ínterin
  2 *adj* interino(a), provisional
interior [ɪnˈtɪərɪə(r)] **1** *adj* interior
  2 *n* interior *m*; **i. design** diseño *m* de interiores
interlock [ɪntəˈlɒk] *vi* encajarse; *(fingers)* entrelazarse; *(cogs)* engranarse
interloper [ˈɪntələʊpə(r)] *n* intruso(a) *m,f*
interlude [ˈɪntəluːd] *n (break)* intervalo *m*; *Cin & Th* intermedio *m*; *Mus* interludio *m*
intermediary [ɪntəˈmiːdɪərɪ] *n* intermediario(a) *m,f*
intermediate [ɪntəˈmiːdɪət] *adj* intermedio(a)
interminable [ɪnˈtɜːmɪnəbəl] *adj* interminable
intermission [ɪntəˈmɪʃən] *n Cin & Th* intermedio *m*
intermittent [ɪntəˈmɪtənt] *adj* intermitente
intern **1** *vt* [ɪnˈtɜːn] internar
  2 *n* [ˈɪntɜːn] *US Med* interno(a) *m,f*
internal [ɪnˈtɜːnəl] *adj* interior; *(dispute, injury)* interno(a); *US* **I. Revenue Service** ≃ Hacienda *f*
internally [ɪnˈtɜːnəlɪ] *adv* interiormente; **not to be taken i.** *(on medicine)* uso externo
international [ɪntəˈnæʃənəl] **1** *adj* internacional
  2 *n Sport (player)* internacional *mf*; *(match)* partido *m* internacional
Internet [ˈɪntənet] *n Comput* **the I.** Internet; **it's on the I.** está en Internet; **I. access provider** proveedor *m* de acceso a Internet; **I. service provider** proveedor *m* de (acceso a) Internet
interplay [ˈɪntəpleɪ] *n* interacción *f*
interpret [ɪnˈtɜːprɪt] **1** *vt* interpretar
  2 *vi* actuar de intérprete

interpretation [ɪntɜːprɪˈteɪʃən] *n* interpretación *f*

interpreter [ɪnˈtɜːprɪtə(r)] *n* intérprete *mf*

interrelated [ɪntərɪˈleɪtɪd] *adj* estrechamente relacionado(a)

interrogate [ɪnˈterəgeɪt] *vt* interrogar

interrogation [ɪntɜrəˈgeɪʃən] *n* interrogatorio *m*

interrogative [ɪntəˈrɒgətɪv] *Ling* **1** *adj* interrogativo(a)
   2 *n (word)* palabra interrogativa

interrupt [ɪntəˈrʌpt] *vt & vi* interrumpir

interruption [ɪntəˈrʌpʃən] *n* interrupción *f*

intersect [ɪntəˈsekt] **1** *vt* cruzar
   2 *vi* cruzarse

intersection [ɪntəˈsekʃən] *n* (**a**) *(crossroads)* cruce *m* (**b**) *(of two lines)* intersección *f*

intersperse [ɪntəˈspɜːs] *vt* esparcir

intertwine [ɪntəˈtwaɪn] **1** *vt* entrelazar (**with** con)
   2 *vi* entrelazarse (**with** con)

interval [ˈɪntəvəl] *n* (**a**) *(of time, space)* intervalo *m*; **at intervals** *(time, space)* a intervalos; *(time)* de vez en cuando (**b**) *Br Cin & Th* intermedio *m*

intervene [ɪntəˈviːn] *vi* (**a**) *(person)* intervenir (**in** en) (**b**) *(event)* sobrevenir (**c**) *(time)* transcurrir

intervention [ɪntəˈvenʃən] *n* intervención *f*

interview [ˈɪntəvjuː] **1** *n* entrevista *f*; **to give an i.** conceder una entrevista
   2 *vt* entrevistar

interviewer [ˈɪntəvjuːə(r)] *n* entrevistador(a) *m,f*

intestine [ɪnˈtestɪn] *n (usu pl)* intestino *m*; **large/small i.** intestino grueso/delgado

intimacy [ˈɪntɪməsɪ] *n (closeness)* intimidad *f*; *Euph (sex)* relación íntima; **intimacies** intimidades *fpl*

intimate¹ [ˈɪntɪmɪt] *adj* íntimo(a); *(knowledge)* profundo(a)

intimate² [ˈɪntɪmeɪt] *vt Fml* dar a entender

intimidate [ɪnˈtɪmɪdeɪt] *vt* intimidar

intimidating [ɪnˈtɪmɪdeɪtɪŋ] *adj* atemorizante

into [ˈɪntuː, *unstressed* ˈɪntə] *prep* (**a**) *(motion)* en, a, con; **he fell i. the water** se cayó al agua; **I bumped i. a friend** me topé con un amigo; **to get i. a car** subir a un coche; **to go i. a house** entrar en una casa (**b**) *(state)* en, a; **he grew i. a man** se hizo un hombre; **to burst i. tears** echarse a llorar; **to change pounds i. pesetas** cambiar libras en *or* por pesetas; **to translate sth i. French** traducir algo al francés (**c**) **to work i. the night** trabajar hasta muy avanzada la noche (**d**) **to divide sth i. three** dividir algo en tres (**e**) *Fam* **to be i. sth** ser aficionado(a) a algo

intolerable [ɪnˈtɒlərəbəl] *adj* intolerable

intolerant [ɪnˈtɒlərənt] *adj* intolerante

intonation [ɪntəˈneɪʃən] *n* entonación *f*

intoxicated [ɪnˈtɒksɪkeɪtɪd] *adj* borracho(a)

> ℓ Note that the Spanish word **intoxicado** is a false friend and is never a translation for the English word **intoxicated**. In Spanish, **intoxicado** means "poisoned".

intoxicating [ɪnˈtɒksɪkeɪtɪŋ] *adj* embriagador(a); **i. liquor** bebida alcohólica

intoxication [ɪntɒksɪˈkeɪʃən] *n* embriaguez *f*

> ℓ Note that the Spanish word **intoxicación** is a false friend and is never a translation for the English word **intoxication**. In Spanish, **intoxicación** means "poisoning".

intractable [ɪnˈtræktəbəl] *adj Fml (person)* intratable; *(problem)* insoluble

intranet [ˈɪntrənet] *n Comput* intranet *f*

intransigent [ɪnˈtrænsɪdʒənt] *adj Fml* intransigente, intolerante

intransitive [ɪnˈtrænsɪtɪv] *adj* intransitivo(a)

intravenous [ɪntrəˈviːnəs] *adj* intravenoso(a)

in-tray [ˈɪntreɪ] *n* bandeja *f* de asuntos pendientes

intrepid [ɪnˈtrepɪd] *adj* intrépido(a), audaz

intricate [ˈɪntrɪkɪt] *adj* intrincado(a)

intrigue 1 *n* [ɪnˈtriːg, ˈɪntriːg] intriga *f*
   2 *vt* [ɪnˈtriːg] intrigar
   3 *vi* intrigar, conspirar

intriguing [ɪnˈtriːgɪŋ] *adj* intrigante

intrinsic [ɪnˈtrɪnsɪk] *adj Fml* intrínseco(a)

introduce [ɪntrəˈdjuːs] *vt* (**a**) *(person, programme)* presentar (**to** a) (**b**) *(bring in)* introducir (**into** *or* **to** en); *Com* lanzar (**into** *or* **to** a); *(topic)* proponer

introduction [ɪntrəˈdʌkʃən] *n* (**a**) *(of person, programme)* presentación *f*; *(in book)* introducción *f* (**b**) *(bringing in)* introducción *f*; *Com (of product)* lanzamiento *m*

introductory [ɪntrəˈdʌktərɪ] *adj* introductorio(a); *(remarks)* preliminar; *Com* de lanzamiento

introspective [ˌɪntrəˈspektɪv] *adj* introspectivo(a)

introvert [ˈɪntrəvɜːt] *n* introvertido(a) *m,f*

intrude [ɪnˈtruːd] *vi* entrometerse (**into** *or* **on** en); *(disturb)* molestar

intruder [ɪnˈtruːdə(r)] *n* intruso(a) *m,f*

intrusion [ɪnˈtruːʒən] *n* incursión *f*

intuition [ˌɪntjʊˈɪʃən] *n* intuición *f*

inundate [ˈɪnʌndeɪt] *vt* inundar (**with** de)

invade [ɪnˈveɪd] *vt* invadir

invader [ɪnˈveɪdə(r)] *n* invasor(a) *m,f*

invalid¹ [ˈɪnvəlɪd] *n (disabled person)* minusválido(a) *m,f*; *(sick person)* enfermo(a) *m,f*

invalid² [ɪnˈvælɪd] *adj* inválido(a), nulo(a)

invalidate [ɪnˈvælɪdeɪt] *vt* invalidar

invaluable [ɪnˈvæljʊəbəl] *adj* inestimable

invariable [ɪnˈveərɪəbəl] *adj* invariable

invasion [ɪnˈveɪʒən] *n* invasión *f*

invent [ɪnˈvent] *vt* inventar

invention [ɪnˈvenʃən] *n* invento *m*; *(creativity)* inventiva *f*; *(lie)* mentira *f*

inventive [ɪnˈventɪv] *adj* inventivo(a)

inventor [ɪnˈventə(r)] *n* inventor(a) *m,f*

inventory [ˈɪnvəntərɪ] *n* inventario *m*

invert [ɪnˈvɜːt] *vt* invertir

invertebrate [ɪnˈvɜːtɪbrɪt] **1** *adj* invertebrado(a)
2 *n* invertebrado *m*

inverted [ɪnˈvɜːtɪd] *adj* **(in) i. commas** (entre) comillas *fpl*

invest [ɪnˈvest] **1** *vt* invertir (**in** en); **to i. sb with sth** conferir algo a algn
2 *vi* invertir (**in** en)

investigate [ɪnˈvestɪgeɪt] *vt (crime, subject)* investigar; *(cause, possibility)* estudiar

investigation [ɪnˌvestɪˈgeɪʃən] *n (of crime)* investigación *f*; *(of cause)* examen *m*

investigator [ɪnˈvestɪgeɪtə(r)] *n* investigador(a) *m,f*; **private i.** detective privado

investment [ɪnˈvestmənt] *n* inversión *f*

investor [ɪnˈvestə(r)] *n* inversor(a) *m,f*

inveterate [ɪnˈvetərɪt] *adj* empedernido(a)

invidious [ɪnˈvɪdɪəs] *adj (task)* ingrato(a); *(comparison)* injusto(a)

> *♪* Note that the Spanish word **envidioso** is a false friend and is never a translation for the English word **invidious**. In Spanish, **envidioso** means "envious".

invigilator [ɪnˈvɪdʒɪleɪtə(r)] *n Br* vigilante *mf*

invigorating [ɪnˈvɪgəreɪtɪŋ] *adj* vigorizante

invincible [ɪnˈvɪnsəbəl] *adj* invencible

invisible [ɪnˈvɪzəbəl] *adj* invisible

invitation [ˌɪnvɪˈteɪʃən] *n* invitación *f*

invite [ɪnˈvaɪt] *vt* (**a**) invitar (**to** a) (**b**) *(comments etc)* solicitar; *(criticism)* provocar; **to i. trouble** buscarse problemas

inviting [ɪnˈvaɪtɪŋ] *adj (attractive)* atractivo(a); *(food)* apetitoso(a)

invoice [ˈɪnvɔɪs] **1** *n* factura *f*
2 *vt* facturar

invoke [ɪnˈvəʊk] *vt Fml* invocar

involuntary [ɪnˈvɒləntərɪ] *adj* involuntario(a)

involve [ɪnˈvɒlv] *vt* (**a**) *(concern)* implicar (**in** en); **the issues involved** las cuestiones en juego; **to be involved in an accident** sufrir un accidente (**b**) *(entail)* suponer, implicar; *(trouble, risk)* acarrear

involved [ɪnˈvɒlvd] *adj (complicated)* complicado(a); *Fam (romantically attached)* enredado(a), liado(a)

involvement [ɪnˈvɒlvmənt] *n (participation)* participación *f*; *(in crime)* implicación *f*

inward [ˈɪnwəd] **1** *adj* interior
2 *adv* = **inwards**

inwardly [ˈɪnwədlɪ] *adv* interiormente, por dentro

inwards [ˈɪnwədz] *adv* hacia dentro

in-your-face [ˈɪnjəˈfeɪs] *adj Fam (style)* descarado(a); *(movie, advert)* impactante, fuerte

iodine [ˈaɪədiːn] *n* yodo *m*

iota [aɪˈəʊtə] *n* pizca *f*, ápice *m*

IOU [aɪəʊˈjuː] *n (abbr* **I owe you**) pagaré *m*

IQ [aɪˈkjuː] *n (abbr* **intelligence quotient**) CI *m*

IRA [aɪɑːˈreɪ] *n (abbr* **Irish Republican Army**) IRA *m*

Iran [ɪˈrɑːn] *n* Irán

Iranian [ɪˈreɪnɪən] *adj & n* iraní *(mf)*

Iraq [ɪˈrɑːk] *n* Irak

Iraqi [ɪˈrɑːkɪ] *adj & n* iraquí *(mf)*

irascible [ɪˈræsɪbəl] *adj Fml* irascible

irate [aɪˈreɪt] *adj* airado(a), furioso(a)

Ireland [ˈaɪələnd] *n* Irlanda; **Republic of I.** República de Irlanda

iris [ˈaɪərɪs] *n* (**a**) *Anat* iris *m inv* (**b**) *Bot* lirio *m*

Irish [ˈaɪrɪʃ] **1** *adj* irlandés(esa); **I. coffee** café *m* irlandés; **I. Sea** Mar *m* de Irlanda
2 *n* (**a**) *(language)* irlandés *m* (**b**) *pl* **the I.** los irlandeses

Irishman [ˈaɪrɪʃmən] *n* irlandés *m*

Irishwoman [ˈaɪrɪʃwʊmən] *n* irlandesa *f*

irksome [ˈɜːksəm] *adj* fastidioso(a)

iron ['aɪən] **1** *n* (**a**) hierro *m*; **the i. and steel industry** la industria siderúrgica; **I. Curtain** Telón *m* de Acero; **i. ore** mineral *m* de hierro (**b**) *(for clothes)* plancha *f* (**c**) *(for golf)* hierro *m* (**d**) **irons** *(chains)* grillos *mpl*

2 *vt (clothes)* planchar

▸ **iron out** *vt sep* (**a**) *(crease)* planchar (**b**) *Fam Fig (problem)* resolver

ironic(al) [aɪ'rɒnɪk(əl)] *adj* irónico(a)

ironing ['aɪənɪŋ] *n* (**a**) **to do the i.** planchar; **i. board** mesa *f* de la plancha (**b**) *(clothes to be ironed)* ropa *f* para planchar; *(clothes ironed)* ropa planchada

ironmonger ['aɪənmʌŋgə(r)] *n Br* ferretero(a) *m,f*; **i.'s (shop)** ferretería *f*

irony ['aɪrənɪ] *n* ironía *f*

irrational [ɪ'ræʃənəl] *adj* irracional

irreconcilable [ɪrekən'saɪləbəl] *adj* irreconciliable

irrefutable [ɪrɪ'fjuːtəbəl] *adj Fml* irrefutable

irregular [ɪ'regjʊlə(r)] *adj* (**a**) irregular; *(abnormal)* anormal (**b**) *(uneven)* desigual

irrelevant [ɪ'reləvənt] *adj* no pertinente

irreparable [ɪ'repərəbəl] *adj* irreparable

irreplaceable [ɪrɪ'pleɪsəbəl] *adj* irremplazable

irrepressible [ɪrɪ'presəbəl] *adj* incontenible

irresistible [ɪrɪ'zɪstəbəl] *adj* irresistible

irresolute [ɪ'rezəluːt] *adj Fml* indeciso(a)

irrespective [ɪrɪ'spektɪv] *adj* **i. of** sin tener en cuenta

irresponsible [ɪrɪ'spɒnsəbəl] *adj* irresponsable

irreverent [ɪ'revərənt] *adj* irreverente

irrevocable [ɪ'revəkəbəl] *adj* irrevocable

irrigate ['ɪrɪgeɪt] *vt* regar

irrigation [ɪrɪ'geɪʃən] *n* riego *m*; **i. channel** acequia *f*; **i. system** sistema *m* de regadío

irritable ['ɪrɪtəbəl] *adj* irritable

irritate ['ɪrɪteɪt] *vt (annoy)* fastidiar; *Med* irritar

irritating ['ɪrɪteɪtɪŋ] *adj* irritante

irritation [ɪrɪ'teɪʃən] *n* (**a**) *(annoyance)* fastidio *m*; *(ill humour)* mal humor *m* (**b**) *Med* irritación *f*

is [ɪz] *3rd person sing pres of* **be**

Islam ['ɪzlɑːm] *n* Islam *m*

Islamic [ɪz'læmɪk] *adj* islámico(a)

island ['aɪlənd] *n* isla *f*; **(traffic) i.** isleta *f*

islander ['aɪləndə(r)] *n* isleño(a) *m,f*

isle [aɪl] *n* isla *f*

isn't ['ɪzənt] = **is not**

isolate ['aɪsəleɪt] *vt* aislar (**from** de)

isolated ['aɪsəleɪtɪd] *adj* aislado(a)

isolation [aɪsə'leɪʃən] *n* aislamiento *m*

ISP [aɪes'piː] *n Comput (abbr Internet Service Provider)* PSI *m*

Israel ['ɪzreɪəl] *n* Israel

Israeli [ɪz'reɪlɪ] *adj & n* israelí *(mf)*

issue ['ɪʃuː] **1** *n* (**a**) *(matter)* cuestión *f*; **to take i. with sb (over sth)** manifestar su desacuerdo con algn (en algo) (**b**) *(of banknotes etc)* emisión *f*; *(of passport)* expedición *f* (**c**) *(of journal etc)* ejemplar *m* (**d**) *(of supplies)* reparto *m* (**e**) *Fml (outcome)* resultado *m* (**f**) *Jur (offspring)* descendencia *f*

2 *vt* (**a**) *(book)* publicar; *(banknotes etc)* emitir; *(passport)* expedir (**b**) *(supplies)* repartir (**c**) *(order, instructions)* dar; *(warrant)* dictar

3 *vi Fml (blood)* brotar (**from** de); *(smoke)* salir (**from** de)

isthmus ['ɪsməs] *n* istmo *m*

it [ɪt] *pers pron* (**a**) *(subject)* él/ella/ello *(usually omitted in Spanish, except for contrast)*; **it's here** está aquí

(**b**) *(direct object)* lo/la; **I don't believe it** no me lo creo; **I liked the house and bought it** me gustó la casa y la compré

(**c**) *(indirect object)* le; **give it a kick** dale una patada

(**d**) *(after prep)* él/ella/ello; **I saw the beach and ran towards it** vi la playa y fui corriendo hacia ella; **we'll talk about it later** ya hablaremos de ello

(**e**) *(abstract)* ello; **let's get down to it!** ¡vamos a ello!

(**f**) *(impersonal)* **it's late** es tarde; **it's me** soy yo; **it's raining** está lloviendo; **it's said that ...** se dice que ...; **it's 2 miles to town** hay 2 millas de aquí al pueblo; **that's it!** *(agreeing)* ¡precisamente!; *(finishing)* ¡se acabó!; **this is it!** ¡ha llegado la hora!; **who is it?** ¿quién es?

Italian [ɪ'tæljən] **1** *adj* italiano(a)

2 *n* (**a**) *(person)* italiano(a) *m,f* (**b**) *(language)* italiano *m*

italic [ɪ'tælɪk] *n* cursiva *f*

Italy ['ɪtəlɪ] *n* Italia

itch [ɪtʃ] **1** *n* picor *m*; *Fig* **an i. to travel** unas ganas locas de viajar

2 *vi* (**a**) *(skin)* picar (**b**) *Fig* anhelar; *Fam* **to be itching to do sth** tener muchas ganas de hacer algo

itchy ['ɪtʃɪ] *adj* (**itchier, itchiest**) que pica

item ['aɪtəm] *n* (**a**) *(in list)* artículo *m*; *(in collection)* pieza *f*; **i. of clothing** prenda *f* de vestir (**b**) *(on agenda)* asunto *m*; *(in show)* número *m*; **news i.** noticia *f*

itemize ['aɪtəmaɪz] *vt* detallar

itinerant [ɪˈtɪnərənt] *adj Fml* itinerante

itinerary [aɪˈtɪnərərɪ] *n* itinerario *m*

it'll [ˈɪtəl] = **it will**

its [ɪts] *poss adj (one thing)* su; *(more than one)* sus

itself [ɪtˈself] *pers pron* (**a**) *(reflexive)* se; **the cat scratched i.** el gato se arañó (**b**) *(emphatic)* él mismo/ella misma/ello mismo; *(after prep)* sí (mismo(a)); **in i.** en sí

ITV [aɪtiːˈviː] *n Br* (*abbr* **Independent Television**) = canal privado de televisión británico

IUD [aɪjuːˈdiː] *n* (*abbr* **intrauterine (contraceptive) device**) DIU *m*

IVF [aɪviːˈef] *n Med* (*abbr* **in vitro fertilization**) fertilización *f* in vitro

ivory [ˈaɪvərɪ] *n* marfil *m*

ivy [ˈaɪvɪ] *n* hiedra *f*

J, j [dʒeɪ] *n (the letter)* J, j *f*
jab [dʒæb] **1** *n* pinchazo *m; (poke)* golpe seco
   2 *vt* pinchar; *(with fist)* dar un puñetazo a
jabber ['dʒæbə(r)] *vi Fam (chatter)* charlotear; *(speak quickly)* hablar atropelladamente
jack [dʒæk] *n* (**a**) *Aut* gato *m* (**b**) *Cards* sota *f* (**c**) *(bowls)* boliche *m*
   ▸**jack in** *vt sep Br Fam* dejar
   ▸**jack up** *vt sep Aut* levantar (con el gato); *Fig (prices)* aumentar
jackal ['dʒækɔːl] *n* chacal *m*
jackdaw ['dʒækdɔː] *n Orn* grajilla *f*
jacket ['dʒækɪt] *n* (**a**) chaqueta *f; (of suit)* americana *f; (bomber jacket)* cazadora *f* (**b**) *(of book)* sobrecubierta *f; US (of record)* funda *f* (**c**) **j. potatoes** patatas *fpl or Am* papas *fpl* al horno
jack-knife ['dʒæknaɪf] **1** *n* navaja *f*
   2 *vi* colear
jack-of-all-trades [dʒækəv'ɔːltreɪdz] *n* persona *f* mañosa *or* de muchos oficios
jackpot ['dʒækpɒt] *n* (premio *m*) gordo *m*
Jacuzzi® [dʒə'kuːzɪ] *n* jacuzzi® *m*
jade [dʒeɪd] *n* jade *m*
jaded ['dʒeɪdɪd] *adj (tired)* agotado(a); *(palate)* hastiado(a)
jagged ['dʒægɪd] *adj* dentado(a)
jaguar ['dʒægjʊə(r)] *n* jaguar *m*
jail [dʒeɪl] **1** *n* cárcel *f*, prisión *f*
   2 *vt* encarcelar
jailbreak ['dʒeɪlbreɪk] *n* fuga *f*, evasión *f*
jailer ['dʒeɪlə(r)] *n* carcelero(a) *m,f*
jam¹ [dʒæm] *n Culin* mermelada *f*
jam² [dʒæm] **1** *n* (**a**) *(blockage)* atasco *m; Fam (fix)* apuro *m* (**b**) *Mus* improvisación *f*
   2 *vt* (**a**) *(cram)* meter a la fuerza (**b**) *(block)* atascar; *Rad* interferir
   3 *vi (door)* atrancarse; *(brakes)* agarrotarse
Jamaica [dʒə'meɪkə] *n* Jamaica
jam-packed [dʒæm'pækt] *adj Fam (with people)* atestado(a); *(with things)* atiborrado(a)
jangle ['dʒæŋgəl] *vi* tintinear
janitor ['dʒænɪtə(r)] *n* portero *m*, conserje *m*

January ['dʒænjʊərɪ] *n* enero *m*
Japan [dʒə'pæn] *n* (el) Japón
Japanese [dʒæpə'niːz] **1** *adj* japonés(esa)
   2 *n (person)* japonés(esa) *m,f; (language)* japonés *m*
jar¹ [dʒɑː(r)] *n (glass)* tarro *m; (earthenware)* tinaja *f; (jug)* jarra *f; Br Fam* **to have a j.** tomar una copa
jar² [dʒɑː(r)] *vi (sounds)* chirriar; *(appearance)* chocar; *(colours)* desentonar; *Fig* **to j. on one's nerves** ponerle a uno los nervios de punta
jargon ['dʒɑːgən] *n* jerga *f*, argot *m*
jasmin(e) ['dʒæzmɪn] *n* jazmín *m*
jaundice ['dʒɔːndɪs] *n* ictericia *f*
jaundiced ['dʒɔːndɪst] *adj Med* ictérico(a); *Fig (bitter)* amargado(a)
jaunt [dʒɔːnt] *n (walk)* paseo *m; (trip)* excursión *f*
jaunty ['dʒɔːntɪ] *adj* (**jauntier, jauntiest**) *(sprightly)* garboso(a); *(lively)* vivaz
javelin ['dʒævəlɪn] *n* jabalina *f*
jaw [dʒɔː] **1** *n* mandíbula *f*
   2 *vi Fam* estar de palique
jay [dʒeɪ] *n Orn* arrendajo *m* (común)
jaywalker ['dʒeɪwɔːkə(r)] *n* peatón *m* imprudente
jazz [dʒæz] *n* jazz *m*
   ▸**jazz up** *vt sep* alegrar; *(premises)* arreglar
jazzy ['dʒæzɪ] *adj* (**jazzier, jazziest**) *Fam (showy)* llamativo(a); *(brightly coloured)* de colores chillones
jealous ['dʒeləs] *adj* celoso(a); *(envious)* envidioso(a); **to be j. of ...** tener celos de
jealousy ['dʒeləsɪ] *n* celos *mpl; (envy)* envidia *f*
jeans [dʒiːnz] *npl* vaqueros *mpl*, tejanos *mpl*
Jeep® [dʒiːp] *n* jeep *m*, todo terreno *m inv*
jeer [dʒɪə(r)] **1** *n (boo)* abucheo *m; (mocking)* mofa *f*
   2 *vi (boo)* abuchear; *(mock)* burlarse
jeering ['dʒɪərɪŋ] *adj* burlón(ona)
Jehovah [dʒɪ'həʊvə] *n* **J.'s Witness** testigo *mf* de Jehová
Jell-O®, **jello** ['dʒeləʊ] *n US* gelatina *f*

jelly ['dʒelɪ] *n* gelatina *f*

jellyfish ['dʒelɪfɪʃ] *n* medusa *f*

jeopardize ['dʒepədaɪz] *vt* poner en peligro; *(agreement etc)* comprometer

jeopardy ['dʒepədɪ] *n* riesgo *m*, peligro *m*

jerk [dʒɜːk] **1** *n* (**a**) *(jolt)* sacudida *f*; *(pull)* tirón *m* (**b**) *Pej (idiot)* imbécil *mf*
2 *vt (shake)* sacudir; *(pull)* dar un tirón a
3 *vi (move suddenly)* dar una sacudida; **the car jerked forward** el coche avanzaba a tirones

jerkin ['dʒɜːkɪn] *n* chaleco *m*

jersey ['dʒɜːzɪ] *n* jersey *m*, suéter *m*, pulóver *m*, *Andes* chompa *f*, *Urug* buzo *m*

jest [dʒest] **1** *n* broma *f*
2 *vi* bromear

Jesuit ['dʒezjʊɪt] *adj & n* jesuita *(m)*

Jesus ['dʒiːzəs] *n* Jesús *m*; **J. Christ** Jesucristo *m*

jet¹ [dʒet] **1** *n* (**a**) *(stream of water)* chorro *m* (**b**) *(spout)* surtidor *m* (**c**) *Av* reactor *m*; **j. engine** reactor *m*; **j. lag** = cansancio debido al desfase horario; **j. ski** moto náutica *or* acuática
2 *vi Fam* volar

jet² [dʒet] *n* **j. black** negro(a) como el azabache

jet-set ['dʒetset] *n* **the j.** la alta sociedad, la jet

jettison ['dʒetɪsən] *vt* echar al mar; *Fig* deshacerse de; *(project etc)* abandonar

jetty ['dʒetɪ] *n* muelle *m*, malecón *m*

Jew [dʒuː] *n* judío(a) *m,f*

jewel ['dʒuːəl] *n* joya *f*; *(stone)* piedra preciosa; *(in watch)* rubí *m*; *Fig (person)* joya

jeweller, jeweler ['dʒuːələ(r)] *n* joyero(a) *m,f*; **j.'s (shop)** joyería *f*

jewellery, jewelry ['dʒuːəlrɪ] *n* joyas *fpl*, alhajas *fpl*

Jewess ['dʒuːɪs] *n* judía *f*

Jewish ['dʒuːɪʃ] *adj* judío(a)

jibe [dʒaɪb] *n & vi* = **gibe**

jiffy ['dʒɪfɪ] *n Fam* momento *m*; **in a j.** en un santiamén; **just a j.!** ¡un momento!

jig [dʒɪg] *n Mus* giga *f*

jigsaw ['dʒɪgsɔː] *n (puzzle)* rompecabezas *m inv*

jilt [dʒɪlt] *vt Fam* dejar plantado(a)

jingle ['dʒɪŋgəl] **1** *n Rad & TV* = canción que acompaña un anuncio
2 *vi* tintinear

jingoistic [dʒɪŋgəʊ'ɪstɪk] *adj* patriotero(a)

jinx [dʒɪŋks] **1** *n (person)* gafe *mf*
2 *vt* gafar

jitters ['dʒɪtəz] *npl Fam* **to get the j.** tener canguelo

jive [dʒaɪv] **1** *n* swing *m*
2 *vi* bailar el swing

job [dʒɒb] *n* (**a**) trabajo *m*; *(task)* tarea *f*; **to give sth up as a bad j.** darse por vencido(a), *Fam* **just the j.!** ¡me viene de perlas! (**b**) *(occupation)* (puesto *m* de) trabajo *m*, empleo *m*; *(trade)* oficio *m*; *Br Fam* **jobs for the boys** enchufismo *m*; *US* **j. office** oficina *f* de empleo; **j. hunting** búsqueda *f* de empleo; **j. sharing** trabajo compartido a tiempo parcial (**c**) *Fam* **we had a j. to ...** nos costó (trabajo) ... (**d**) *(duty)* deber *m* (**e**) *Fam* **it's a good j. that ...** menos mal que ...

Jobcentre ['dʒɒbsentə(r)] *n Br* oficina *f* de empleo

jobless ['dʒɒblɪs] *adj* parado(a)

jockey ['dʒɒkɪ] **1** *n* jinete *m*, jockey *m*
2 *vi* **to j. for position** luchar para conseguir una posición aventajada

jocular ['dʒɒkjʊlə(r)] *adj* jocoso(a)

jog [dʒɒg] **1** *n* trote *m*
2 *vt* empujar; *Fig (memory)* refrescar
3 *vi Sport* hacer footing; *Fig* **to j. along** *(progress slowly)* avanzar poco a poco; *(manage)* ir tirando

jogging ['dʒɒgɪŋ] *n* footing *m*

john [dʒɒn] *n US Fam* **the j.** *(lavatory)* el váter

join [dʒɔɪn] **1** *vt* (**a**) juntar; **to j. forces with sb** unir fuerzas con algn (**b**) *(road)* empalmar con; *(river)* desembocar en (**c**) *(meet)* reunirse con (**d**) *(group)* unirse a; *(institution)* entrar; *(army)* alistarse a (**e**) *(party)* afiliarse a; *(club)* hacerse socio(a) de
2 *vi* (**a**) unirse (**b**) *(roads)* empalmar; *(rivers)* confluir (**c**) *(become member of political party)* afiliarse; *(become member of club)* hacerse socio(a)
3 *n* juntura *f*
▸ **join in 1** *vi* participar, tomar parte; *(debate)* intervenir
2 *vt insep* participar en, tomar parte en
▸ **join up 1** *vt sep* juntar
2 *vi (of roads)* unirse; *Mil* alistarse

joiner ['dʒɔɪnə(r)] *n Br* carpintero(a) *m,f*

joinery ['dʒɔɪnərɪ] *n* carpintería *f*

joint [dʒɔɪnt] **1** *n* (**a**) juntura *f*, unión *f*; *Tech & Anat* articulación *f*; **out of j.** dislocado(a) (**b**) *Culin* = corte de carne para asar; *(once roasted)* asado *m* (**c**) *Fam (nightclub etc)* garito *m* (**d**) *Fam (drug)* porro *m*
2 *adj* colectivo(a); **j. (bank) account** cuenta conjunta; **j. venture** empresa conjunta

jointly ['dʒɔɪntlɪ] *adv* conjuntamente, en común

joist [dʒɔɪst] *n* vigueta *f*

joke [dʒəʊk] **1** *n* (**a**) chiste *m*; *(prank)* broma *f*; **to play a j. on sb** gastarle una broma a algn; **to tell a j.** contar un chiste (**b**) *Fam (person)* hazmerreír *m*, payaso(a) *m,f*; **to be a j.** *(of thing)* ser de chiste
2 *vi* estar de broma; **you must be joking!** ¡no hablarás en serio!

joker ['dʒəʊkə(r)] *n* (**a**) bromista *mf* (**b**) *Cards* comodín *m*

jolly ['dʒɒlɪ] **1** *adj* (**jollier, jolliest**) alegre
2 *adv Fam (very)* muy; **she played j. well** jugó muy bien

jolt [dʒəʊlt] **1** *n* (**a**) sacudida *f*; *(pull)* tirón *m* (**b**) *Fig (fright)* susto *m*
2 *vi* moverse a sacudidas
3 *vt* sacudir

Jordan ['dʒɔːdən] *n* (**a**) *(river)* Jordán *m* (**b**) *(country)* Jordania

joss-stick ['dʒɒsstɪk] *n* varita *f* de incienso

jostle ['dʒɒsəl] **1** *vi* dar empujones
2 *vt* dar empujones a

jot [dʒɒt] *n* jota *f*, pizca *f*; **not a j.** ni jota
▸ **jot down** *vt sep* apuntar

jotter ['dʒɒtə(r)] *n Br* bloc *m*

journal ['dʒɜːnəl] *n* (**a**) revista *f* (**b**) *(diary)* diario *m* (**c**) *(newspaper)* periódico *m*

> 🖉 Note that the Spanish word **jornal** is a false friend and is never a translation for the English word **journal**. In Spanish, **jornal** means "day's wage".

journalism ['dʒɜːnəlɪzəm] *n* periodismo *m*

journalist ['dʒɜːnəlɪst] *n* periodista *mf*

journey ['dʒɜːnɪ] **1** *n* viaje *m*; *(distance)* trayecto *m*
2 *vi Fml* viajar

jovial ['dʒəʊvɪəl] *adj* jovial

jowl [dʒaʊl] *n* quijada *f*

joy [dʒɔɪ] *n* alegría *f*; *(pleasure)* placer *m*

joyful ['dʒɔɪfʊl] *adj* alegre, contento(a)

joyous ['dʒɔɪəs] *adj Literary* alegre

joyride ['dʒɔɪraɪd] *n Fam* = paseo en un coche robado

joystick ['dʒɔɪstɪk] *n Av* palanca *f* de mando; *(of video game)* joystick *m*

JP [dʒeɪ'piː] *n Br Law (abbr* **Justice of the Peace**) juez *mf* de paz

Jr *(abbr* **Junior**) Neil Smith, Jr Neil Smith, hijo

jubilant ['dʒuːbɪlənt] *adj* jubiloso(a)

jubilation [dʒuːbɪ'leɪʃən] *n* júbilo *m*

jubilee ['dʒuːbɪliː] *n* festejos *mpl*; **golden j.** quincuagésimo aniversario

judge [dʒʌdʒ] **1** *n* juez *mf*, jueza *f*; *(in competition)* jurado *m*
2 *vt* (**a**) *Jur* juzgar (**b**) *(estimate)* considerar (**c**) *(competition)* actuar de juez de (**d**) *(assess)* juzgar
3 *vi* juzgar; **judging from what you say** a juzgar por lo que dices

judg(e)ment ['dʒʌdʒmənt] *n* (**a**) *Jur* sentencia *f*, fallo *m*; **to pass j.** dictar sentencia (**b**) *(opinion)* juicio *m*; **to pass j. (on)** opinar (sobre); **to reserve j. (on)** no opinar (sobre) (**c**) *(ability)* buen juicio *m* (**d**) *(trial)* juicio *m*

judicial [dʒuː'dɪʃəl] *adj* judicial

judiciary [dʒuː'dɪʃərɪ] *n* magistratura *f*

judicious [dʒuː'dɪʃəs] *adj Fml* juicioso(a)

judo ['dʒuːdəʊ] *n* judo *m*

jug [dʒʌg] *n Br* jarra *f*; **milk j.** jarra de leche

juggernaut ['dʒʌgənɔːt] *n Br* camión pesado

juggle ['dʒʌgəl] *vi (perform)* hacer juegos malabares (**with** con); *Fig (responsibilities)* ajustar

juggler ['dʒʌglə(r)] *n* malabarista *mf*

juice [dʒuːs] *n* jugo *m*; *(of citrus fruits)* zumo *m*

juicy ['dʒuːsɪ] *adj* (**juicier, juiciest**) (**a**) jugoso(a) (**b**) *Fam Fig* picante

jukebox ['dʒuːkbɒks] *n* rocola *f*

July [dʒuː'laɪ, dʒə'laɪ] *n* julio *m*

jumble ['dʒʌmbəl] **1** *n* revoltijo *m*; **j. sale** mercadillo *m* de caridad
2 *vt* revolver

jumbo ['dʒʌmbəʊ] *n* **j. (jet)** jumbo *m*

jump [dʒʌmp] **1** *n* salto *m*; *(sudden increase)* subida repentina; **j. leads** cables *mpl* de emergencia; **j. suit** mono *m*
2 *vi* (**a**) saltar, dar un salto; *Fig* **to j. to conclusions** sacar conclusiones precipitadas (**b**) *Fig (start)* sobresaltarse (**c**) *(increase)* aumentar de golpe
3 *vt* saltar; *Fam Fig* **to j. the gun** precipitarse; **to j. the lights** saltarse el semáforo; *Br* **to j. the queue** colarse; *US* **to j. rope** saltar a la comba
▸ **jump at** *vt insep* aceptar sin pensarlo

jumper ['dʒʌmpə(r)] *n* (**a**) *Br (sweater)* jersey *m*, suéter *m*, pulóver *m*, *Andes* chompa *f*, *Urug* buzo *m* (**b**) *US (dress)* pichi *m*, falda *f* con peto (**c**) *US Aut* **j. cables** cables *mpl* de emergencia

jumpy ['dʒʌmpɪ] *adj* (**jumpier, jumpiest**) *Fam* nervioso(a)

junction ['dʒʌŋkʃən] *n (of roads)* cruce *m*; *Rail & Elec* empalme *m*

juncture ['dʒʌŋktʃə(r)] *n Fml* **at this j.** en esta coyuntura

June [dʒuːn] *n* junio *m*

jungle ['dʒʌŋgəl] *n* jungla *f*, selva *f*; *Fig* laberinto *m*; **the concrete j.** la jungla de asfalto

junior ['dʒuːnjə(r)] **1** *adj* (**a**) *(son of)* hijo; **David Hughes J.** David Hughes hijo (**b**) *US* **j. high (school)** *(between 11 and 15)* escuela secundaria; *Br* **j. school** *(between 7 and 11)* escuela primaria; **j. team** equipo *m* juvenil (**c**) *(lower in rank)* subalterno(a)

2 *n* (**a**) *(person of lower rank)* subalterno(a) *m,f* (**b**) *(younger person)* menor *mf*

junk [dʒʌŋk] *n* (**a**) *Fam* trastos *mpl*; **j. food** comida basura; **j. mail** propaganda *f* (por correo); **j. shop** tienda *f* de segunda mano (**b**) *(boat)* junco *m*

junkie ['dʒʌŋkɪ] *n Fam* yonqui *mf*

junkman ['dʒʌŋkmæn] *n US* trapero(a) *m,f*

junta ['dʒʌntə, *US* 'hʊntə] *n* junta *f* militar

jurisdiction [dʒʊərɪs'dɪkʃən] *n Fml* jurisdicción *f*

juror ['dʒʊərə(r)] *n* jurado(a) *m,f*

jury ['dʒʊərɪ] *n* jurado *m*

just [dʒʌst] **1** *adj (fair)* justo(a); *Fml (well-founded)* justificado(a)

2 *adv* (**a**) **he had j. arrived** acababa de llegar

(**b**) *(at this very moment)* ahora mismo, en este momento; **he was j. leaving when Rosa arrived** estaba a punto de salir cuando llegó Rosa; **I'm j. coming!** ¡ya voy!; **j. as ... cuando ...**, justo al ...; **j. as I**

thought me lo figuraba

(**c**) *(only)* solamente; **j. in case** por si acaso; **j. a minute!** ¡un momento!

(**d**) *(barely)* por poco; **I only j. caught the bus** cogí el autobús por los pelos; **j. about** casi; **j. enough** justo lo suficiente

(**e**) *(emphatic)* **it's j. fantastic!** ¡es sencillamente fantástico!; **you'll j. have to wait** tendrás que esperar

(**f**) *(exactly)* exactamente, justo; **that's j. it!** ¡precisamente!

(**g**) *(equally)* **j. as fast as** tan rápido como

justice ['dʒʌstɪs] *n* (**a**) justicia *f*; **he was brought to j.** lo llevaron ante los tribunales; **you didn't do yourself j.** no diste lo mejor de ti (**b**) *US (judge)* juez *mf*; *Br* **J. of the Peace** juez de paz

justifiable ['dʒʌstɪfaɪəbəl] *adj* justificable

justification [dʒʌstɪfɪ'keɪʃən] *n* justificación *f*

justified ['dʒʌstɪfaɪd] *adj* **to be j. in doing sth** tener razón en hacer algo

justify ['dʒʌstɪfaɪ] *vt* justificar

jut [dʒʌt] *vi* sobresalir; **to j. out over** proyectarse sobre

juvenile ['dʒuːvənaɪl] **1** *adj* (**a**) juvenil; **j. court** tribunal *m* de menores; **j. delinquent** delincuente *mf* juvenil (**b**) *(immature)* infantil

2 *n* menor *mf*, joven *mf*

juxtapose [dʒʌkstə'pəʊz] *vt* yuxtaponer

K, k [keɪ] *n (the letter)* K, k *f*
kaleidoscope [kəˈlaɪdəskəʊp] *n* caleidoscopio *m*
Kampuchea [kæmpʊˈtʃɪə] *n* Kampuchea
kangaroo [kæŋɡəˈruː] *n* canguro *m*
karat [ˈkærət] *n US* quilate *m*
karate [kəˈrɑːtɪ] *n* kárate *m*
kebab [kəˈbæb] *n Culin* pincho moruno, brocheta *f*
keel [kiːl] *n* quilla *f*; *Fig* **to be on an even k.** estar en calma
▸ **keel over** *vi Fam* desmayarse
keen [kiːn] *adj* (**a**) *(eager)* entusiasta (**b**) *(intense)* profundo(a) (**c**) *(mind, senses)* agudo(a); *(look)* penetrante; *(blade)* afilado(a); *(competition)* fuerte
keep [kiːp] **1** *n* (**a**) **to earn one's k.** ganarse el pan
(**b**) *(tower)* torreón *m*
(**c**) *Fam* **for keeps** para siempre
2 *vt* (*pt & pp* **kept**) (**a**) guardar; **to k. one's room tidy** mantener su cuarto limpio; **to k. sb informed** tener a algn al corriente; **to k. sth in mind** tener algo en cuenta
(**b**) *(not give back)* quedarse con
(**c**) *(detain)* detener; **to k. sb waiting** hacer esperar a algn
(**d**) *(maintain)* mantener; *(animals)* criar
(**e**) *(the law)* observar; *(a promise)* cumplir
(**f**) *(a secret)* guardar
(**g**) *(diary, accounts)* llevar
(**h**) *(prevent)* **to k. sb from doing sth** impedir a algn hacer algo
(**i**) *(own, manage)* tener; *(shop, hotel)* llevar
(**j**) *(stock)* tener
3 *vi* (**a**) *(remain)* seguir; **k. still!** ¡estáte quieto(a)!; **to k. fit** mantenerse en forma; **to k. going** seguir adelante; **to k. in touch** no perder el contacto
(**b**) *(do frequently)* no dejar de; **she keeps forgetting her keys** siempre se olvida las llaves
(**c**) *(food)* conservarse
▸ **keep at** *vt insep* perseverar en
▸ **keep away 1** *vt sep* mantener a distancia

2 *vi* mantenerse a distancia
▸ **keep back** *vt sep (information)* ocultar, callar; *(money etc)* retener
▸ **keep down** *vt sep* **to k. prices down** mantener los precios bajos
▸ **keep off** *vt insep* **k. off the grass** *(sign)* prohibido pisar la hierba
▸ **keep on 1** *vt sep* (**a**) *(clothes etc)* no quitarse; **to k. an eye on sth/sb** vigilar algo/a algn (**b**) *(continue to employ)* no despedir a
2 *vi (continue to do)* seguir
▸ **keep out 1** *vt sep* no dejar pasar
2 *vi* no entrar; **k. out!** *(sign)* ¡prohibida la entrada!
▸ **keep to** *vt insep (subject)* limitarse a; **to k. to one's room** quedarse en el cuatro; **k. to the point!** ¡cíñete a la cuestión!; **to k. to the left** circular por la izquierda
▸ **keep up** *vt sep* (**a**) mantener; **to k. up appearances** guardar las apariencias (**b**) **k. it up!** ¡sigue así! (**c**) *(prevent from sleeping)* mantener despierto(a)
▸ **keep up with** *vt insep* **to k. up with the times** estar al día
keeper [ˈkiːpə(r)] *n (in zoo)* guarda *mf*; *(in record office)* archivero(a) *m,f*; *(in museum)* conservador(a) *m,f*
keeping [ˈkiːpɪŋ] *n* (**a**) *(care)* cuidado *m* (**b**) **in k. with** en armonía con; **out of k. with** en desacuerdo con
keepsake [ˈkiːpseɪk] *n* recuerdo *m*
keg [keɡ] *n* barril *m*
kennel [ˈkenəl] *n* caseta *f* para perros; **kennels** hotel *m* de perros
Kenya [ˈkenjə, ˈkiːnjə] *n* Kenia
Kenyan [ˈkenjən, ˈkiːnjən] *adj & n* keniano(a) *(m,f)*
kept [kept] *pt & pp of* **keep**
kerb [kɜːb] *n Br* bordillo *m*
kernel [ˈkɜːnəl] *n (of fruit, nut)* pepita *f*; *(of wheat)* grano *m*; *Fig* meollo *m*
kerosene, kerosine [ˈkerəsiːn] *n US* queroseno *m*
ketchup [ˈketʃəp] *n* ketchup *m*, salsa *f* de tomate
kettle [ˈketəl] *n* hervidor *m*; **that's a different k. of fish** eso es harina de otro costal

key [kiː] **1** *n* (**a**) *(for lock)* llave *f*; **k. ring** llavero *m* (**b**) *(to code)* clave *f* (**c**) *(of piano, typewriter)* tecla *f* (**d**) *Mus* tono *m*
2 *adj* clave; *Br Educ* **k. stage** etapa educativa
3 *vt Comput* teclear
▸ **key in** *vt sep Comput* introducir
keyboard ['kiːbɔːd] *n* teclado *m*
keyed up [kiːd'ʌp] *adj* nervioso(a)
keyhole ['kiːhəʊl] *n* ojo *m* de la cerradura
keynote ['kiːnəʊt] *n Mus* tónica *f*; *Fig* nota *f* dominante
kg *(abbr* **kilogram(s))** kg
khaki ['kɑːkɪ] *adj & n* caqui *(m)*
kick [kɪk] **1** *n* (**a**) *(from person)* patada *f*, puntapié *m*; *(from horse etc)* coz *f*; *(from gun)* culatazo *m* (**b**) *Fam* **I get a k. out of it** eso me encanta; **to do sth for kicks** hacer algo por gusto
2 *vi (animal)* cocear; *(person)* dar patadas; *(gun)* dar un culatazo
3 *vt* dar un puntapié a
▸ **kick off** *vi Fam* empezar; *Ftb* sacar
▸ **kick out** *vt sep* echar a patadas
▸ **kick up** *vt insep Fam (fuss)* armar
kick-off ['kɪkɒf] *n Ftb* saque *m* inicial
kid¹ [kɪd] *n* (**a**) *Zool* cabrito *m*; *Fig* **to handle sb with k. gloves** tratar a algn con guante blanco (**b**) *Fam* niño(a) *m,f*, chiquillo(a) *m,f*; **the kids** los críos
kid² [kɪd] **1** *vi Fam* tomar el pelo; **no kidding!** ¡va en serio!
2 *vt* tomar el pelo a; **to k. oneself** *(fool)* hacerse ilusiones
kidnap ['kɪdnæp] *vt* secuestrar
kidnapper ['kɪdnæpə(r)] *n* secuestrador(a) *m,f*
kidnapping ['kɪdnæpɪŋ] *n* secuestro *m*
kidney ['kɪdnɪ] *n* riñón *m*
kill [kɪl] *vt* matar; *Fig* **to k. time** pasar el rato; *Fam* **my feet are killing me!** ¡cómo me duelen los pies!
▸ **kill off** *vt sep* exterminar
killer ['kɪlə(r)] *n* asesino(a) *m,f*; **k. whale** orca *f*
killing ['kɪlɪŋ] *n* asesinato *m*; *Fig* **to make a k.** forrarse de dinero
killjoy ['kɪldʒɔɪ] *n* aguafiestas *mf inv*
kiln [kɪln] *n* horno *m*
kilo ['kiːləʊ] *n* kilo *m*
kilogram(me) ['kɪləʊgræm] *n* kilogramo *m*
kilometre, *US* **kilometer** [kɪ'lɒmɪtə(r)] *n* kilómetro *m*
kilowatt ['kɪləʊwɒt] *n* kilovatio *m*
kilt [kɪlt] *n* falda escocesa, kilt *m*
kin [kɪn] *n* familiares *mpl*, parientes *mpl*

kind¹ [kaɪnd] **1** *n* tipo *m*, clase *f*; **they are two of a k.** son tal para cual; **in k.** *(payment)* en especie; *(treatment)* con la misma moneda
2 *adv Fam* **k. of** en cierta manera
kind² ['kaɪnd] *adj* amable, simpático(a); *Fml* **would you be so k. as to ...?** ¿me haría usted el favor de ...?
kindergarten ['kɪndəgɑːtən] *n* jardín *m* de infancia
kind-hearted [kaɪnd'hɑːtɪd] *adj* bondadoso(a)
kindle ['kɪndəl] *vt* encender
kindly ['kaɪndlɪ] **1** *adj* (**kindlier, kindliest**) amable, bondadoso(a)
2 *adv Fml (please)* por favor; **k. remit a cheque** sírvase enviar cheque; **to look k. on** aprobar
kindness ['kaɪndnɪs] *n* bondad *f*, amabilidad *f*
kindred ['kɪndrɪd] *adj* **k. spirits** almas gemelas
kinetic [kɪ'netɪk] *adj* cinético(a)
king [kɪŋ] *n* rey *m*; *(draughts)* dama *f*
kingdom ['kɪŋdəm] *n* reino *m*
kingfisher ['kɪŋfɪʃə(r)] *n Orn* martín *m* pescador
king-size ['kɪŋsaɪz] *adj* extralargo(a)
kink [kɪŋk] *n (in rope)* coca *f*; *(in hair)* rizo *m*
kinky ['kɪŋkɪ] *adj* (**kinkier, kinkiest**) *Fam* raro(a); *(sexually)* pervertido(a)
kiosk ['kiːɒsk] *n* quiosco *m*
kiss [kɪs] **1** *n* beso *m*
2 *vt* besar
3 *vi* besarse
kit [kɪt] *n* (**a**) *(gear)* equipo *m*; *Mil* avíos *mpl* (**b**) *(clothing)* ropa *f* (**c**) *(toy model)* maqueta *f*
▸ **kit out** *vt sep* equipar
kitchen ['kɪtʃɪn] *n* cocina *f*; **k. sink** fregadero *m*
kite [kaɪt] *n* (**a**) *(toy)* cometa *f* (**b**) *Orn* milano *m*
kitten ['kɪtən] *n* gatito(a) *m,f*
kitty ['kɪtɪ] *n (money)* fondo *m* común; *Cards* bote *m*
kiwi ['kiːwiː] *n Bot & Orn* kiwi *m*
km *(pl* **km** *or* **kms)** *(abbr* **kilometre(s))** km
knack [næk] *n* **to get the k. of doing sth** cogerle el truquillo a algo
knapsack ['næpsæk] *n* mochila *f*
knead [niːd] *vt* dar masaje a; *(bread etc)* amasar
knee [niː] **1** *n* rodilla *f*
2 *vt* dar un rodillazo a
kneecap ['niːkæp] **1** *n* rótula *f*
2 *vt* romper la rótula a

kneel [niːl] *vi* (*pt & pp* **knelt**) **to k. (down)** arrodillarse

knell [nel] *n Literary* toque *m* de difuntos

knelt [nelt] *pt & pp of* **kneel**

knew [njuː] *pt of* **know**

knickers ['nɪkəz] *npl Br* bragas *fpl*

knife [naɪf] **1** *n* (*pl* **knives**) cuchillo *m*
  2 *vt* apuñalar, dar una puñalada a

knight [naɪt] **1** *n Hist* caballero *m*; (*in chess*) caballo *m*
  2 *vt* armar caballero

knighthood ['naɪthʊd] *n* (*rank*) título *m* de caballero

knit [nɪt] **1** *vt* (*pt & pp* **knitted** *or* **knit**) (**a**) tejer (**b**) **to k. (together)** (*join*) juntar; *Fig* **to k. one's brow** fruncir el ceño
  2 *vi* (**a**) tejer, hacer punto (**b**) (*bone*) soldarse

knitting ['nɪtɪŋ] *n* punto *m*; **k. machine** máquina *f* de tejer; **k. needle** aguja *f* de tejer

knitwear ['nɪtweə(r)] *n* géneros *mpl* de punto

knives [naɪvz] *pl of* **knife**

knob [nɒb] *n* (**a**) (*of stick*) puño *m*; (*of drawer*) tirador *m*; (*button*) botón *m* (**b**) (*small portion*) trozo *m*

knock [nɒk] **1** *n* golpe *m*; *Fig* revés *m*
  2 *vt* (**a**) golpear (**b**) *Fam* (*criticize*) criticar
  3 *vi* chocar (**against** *or* **into** contra); (*at door*) llamar (**at** a)
  ▸**knock down** *vt sep* (**a**) (*demolish*) derribar (**b**) *Aut* atropellar (**c**) (*price*) rebajar
  ▸**knock off** *vt sep* (**a**) tirar (**b**) *Fam* (*steal*) birlar (**c**) *Fam* (*kill*) liquidar
  2 *vi Fam* **they k. off at five** se piran a las cinco
  ▸**knock out** *vt sep* (**a**) (*make unconscious*) dejar sin conocimiento; (*in boxing*) poner fuera de combate, derrotar por K.O. (**b**) (*surprise*) dejar pasmado(a)
  ▸**knock over** *vt sep* (*cup*) volcar; (*with car*) atropellar

knocker ['nɒkə(r)] *n* (*on door*) aldaba *f*

knock-kneed [nɒk'niːd] *adj* patizambo(a)

knockout ['nɒkaʊt] *n* (**a**) (*in boxing*) K.O. *m*, knock-out *m* (**b**) *Fam* maravilla *f*

knot [nɒt] **1** *n* nudo *m*; (*group*) grupo *m*
  2 *vt* anudar

knotty ['nɒtɪ] *adj* (**knottier**, **knottiest**) nudoso(a); *Fig* **a k. problem** un problema espinoso

know [nəʊ] *vt & vi* (*pt* **knew**; *pp* **known**) (**a**) saber; **as far as I k.** que yo sepa; **she knows how to ski** sabe esquiar; **to get to k. sth** enterarse de algo; **to let sb k.** avisar al algn (**b**) (*be acquainted with*) conocer; **we got to k. each other at the party** nos conocimos en la fiesta

know-all ['nəʊɔːl] *n Fam* sabelotodo *mf*

know-how ['nəʊhaʊ] *n Fam* conocimiento práctico

knowing ['nəʊɪŋ] *adj* (*deliberate*) deliberado(a); **a k. smile** una sonrisa de complicidad

knowingly ['nəʊɪŋlɪ] *adv* (*shrewdly*) a sabiendas; (*deliberately*) deliberadamente

knowledge ['nɒlɪdʒ] *n* (**a**) conocimiento *m*; **without my k.** sin saberlo yo (**b**) (*learning*) conocimientos *mpl*

knowledgeable ['nɒlɪdʒəbəl] *adj* erudito(a); **k. about** muy entendido(a) en

known [nəʊn] **1** *adj* conocido(a)
  2 *pp of* **know**

knuckle ['nʌkəl] *n Anat* nudillo *m*; *Culin* hueso *m*
  ▸**knuckle down** *vi Fam* ponerse a trabajar en serio

KO [keɪ'əʊ] *n Fam* (*abbr* **knockout**) K.O. *m*

Koran [kɔː'rɑːn] *n* Corán *m*

Korea [kə'riːə] *n* Corea

Korean [kə'riːən] *adj & n* coreano(a) (*m,f*)

Kurd [kɜːd] *n* curdo(a) *m,f*

Kuwait [kʊ'weɪt] *n* Kuwait

L

L, l [el] *n (the letter)* L, l *f*
lab [læb] *n Fam (abbr laboratory)* laboratorio *m*
label ['leɪbəl] **1** *n* etiqueta *f*; **record l.** ≃ casa discográfica
  2 *vt* poner etiqueta a
labor ['leɪbər] *n, adj, vt & vi US* = **labour**
laboratory [lə'bɒrətərɪ, *US* 'læbrətɔːrɪ] *n* laboratorio *m*
laborious [lə'bɔːrɪəs] *adj* penoso(a)
labour ['leɪbə(r)] **1** *n* (**a**) *(work)* trabajo *m*; *(task)* tarea *f* (**b**) *(workforce)* mano *f* de obra (**c**) **labours** esfuerzos *mpl* (**d**) **the L. Party** el Partido Laborista (**e**) *(childbirth)* parto *m*; **to be in l.** estar de parto
  2 *adj* laboral
  3 *vt (stress, linger on)* machacar; *(a point)* insistir en
  4 *vi* (**a**) *(work)* trabajar (duro) (**b**) *(move with difficulty)* avanzar penosamente
laboured ['leɪbəd] *adj (breathing)* fatigoso(a); *(style)* forzado(a)
labourer ['leɪbərə(r)] *n* peón *m*; **farm l.** peón *m* agrícola
labour-saving ['leɪbəseɪvɪŋ] *adj* **l. devices** electrodomésticos *mpl*
labyrinth ['læbərɪnθ] *n* laberinto *m*
lace [leɪs] **1** *n* (**a**) *(fabric)* encaje *m* (**b**) **laces** cordones *mpl*
  2 *vt* (**a**) *(shoes)* atar (los cordones de) (**b**) *(add spirits to)* echar licor a
  ▸ **lace up** *vt sep* atar con cordones
lacerate ['læsəreɪt] *vt* lacerar
lack [læk] **1** *n* falta *f*, escasez *f*; **for l. of** por falta de
  2 *vt* carecer de
  3 *vi* carecer (**in** de)
lackadaisical [lækə'deɪzɪkəl] *adj (lazy)* perezoso(a); *(indifferent)* indiferente
lacklustre, *US* **lackluster** ['læklʌstə(r)] *adj (eyes)* apagado(a); *(performance)* anodino(a)
laconic [lə'kɒnɪk] *adj* lacónico(a)
lacquer ['lækə(r)] **1** *n* laca *f*
  2 *vt (hair)* poner laca en
lad [læd] *n Fam* chaval *m*, muchacho *m*; *Fam* **the lads** los amigotes; **(stable) l.** mozo *m* de cuadra
ladder ['lædə(r)] **1** *n* (**a**) escalera *f* (de

mano); *Fig* escala *f* (**b**) *(in stocking)* carrera *f*
  2 *vt* **I've laddered my stocking** me he hecho una carrera en las medias
laden ['leɪdən] *adj* cargado(a) (**with** de)
ladle ['leɪdəl] *n* cucharón *m*
lady ['leɪdɪ] *n* señora *f*; *Pol* **First L.** primera dama; **Ladies** *(sign on WC)* Señoras; **ladies and gentlemen!** ¡señoras y señores!; **L. Brown** Lady Brown
ladybird ['leɪdɪbɜːd], *US* **ladybug** ['leɪdɪbʌg] *n* mariquita *f*
lady-in-waiting [leɪdɪn'weɪtɪŋ] *n* dama *f* de honor
ladylike ['leɪdɪlaɪk] *adj* elegante
ladyship ['leɪdɪʃɪp] *n* **her l./your l.** su señoría
lag [læg] **1** *n* **time l.** demora *f*
  2 *vi* **to l. (behind)** quedarse atrás, retrasarse
  3 *vt Tech* revestir
lager ['lɑːgə(r)] *n* cerveza rubia
lagoon [lə'guːn] *n* laguna *f*
laid [leɪd] *pt & pp of* **lay**
laid-back [leɪd'bæk] *adj Fam* tranquilo(a)
lain [leɪn] *pp of* **lie**²
lair [leə(r)] *n* guarida *f*
lake [leɪk] *n* lago *m*
lamb [læm] *n* cordero *m*; *(meat)* carne *f* de cordero; **l. chop** chuleta *f* de cordero; **l.'s wool** lana *f* de cordero
lame [leɪm] *adj* (**a**) cojo(a) (**b**) *Fig (excuse)* poco convincente; *(argument)* flojo(a)
lament [lə'ment] **1** *n Mus* elegia *f*
  2 *vt (death)* llorar, lamentar
  3 *vi* llorar (**for** a), lamentarse (**over** de)
lamentable ['læməntəbəl] *adj* lamentable
laminated ['læmɪneɪtɪd] *adj (metal)* laminado(a); *(glass)* inastillable; *(paper)* plastificado(a)
lamp [læmp] *n* lámpara *f*; *Aut* faro *m*
lampoon [læm'puːn] **1** *n* sátira *f*
  2 *vt* satirizar
lamp-post ['læmppəʊst] *n* farola *f*
lampshade ['læmpʃeɪd] *n* pantalla *f*
lance [lɑːns] **1** *n* lanza *f*; *Br Mil* **l. corporal**

cabo interino; *Med* lanceta *f*
2 *vt Med* abrir con lanceta

> *⌀* Note that the Spanish word **lance** is a false friend and is never a translation for the English word **lance**. In Spanish, **lance** means "event, incident".

land [lænd] **1** *n* (**a**) tierra *f*; *(soil)* suelo *m*; **by l.** por tierra; **farm l.** tierras *fpl* de cultivo (**b**) *(country)* país *m* (**c**) *(property)* tierras *fpl*; *(estate)* finca *f*; **piece of l.** terreno *m*
2 *vt* (**a**) *(plane)* hacer aterrizar (**b**) *(disembark)* desembarcar (**c**) *(fish)* pescar (**d**) *Fam (obtain)* conseguir; *(contract)* ganar (**e**) *Fam* **she got landed with the responsibility** tuvo que cargar con la responsabilidad (**f**) *Fam (blow)* asestar
3 *vi* (**a**) *(plane)* aterrizar (**b**) *(disembark)* desembarcar (**c**) *(after falling)* caer (**in** sobre)
▶ **land up** *vi Fam* ir a parar
landing ['lændɪŋ] *n* (**a**) *(of staircase)* rellano *m* (**b**) *(of plane)* aterrizaje *m*; **l. strip** pista *f* de aterrizaje (**c**) *(of passengers)* desembarco *m*; **l. stage** desembarcadero *m*
landlady ['lændleɪdɪ] *n (of flat)* dueña *f*, propietaria *f*; *(of boarding house)* patrona *f*; *(of pub)* dueña
landlord ['lændlɔːd] *n (of flat)* dueño *m*, propietario *m*; *(of pub)* patrón *m*, dueño
landmark ['lændmɑːk] *n* (**a**) señal *f*, marca *f*; *(well-known place)* lugar muy conocido (**b**) *Fig* hito *m*
landowner ['lændəʊnə(r)] *n* terrateniente *mf*
landscape ['lændskeɪp] **1** *n* paisaje *m*
2 *vt* ajardinar
landslide ['lændslaɪd] *n* desprendimiento *m* de tierras; **l. victory** victoria arrolladora
lane [leɪn] *n (in country)* camino *m*; *(in town)* callejón *m*; *(of motorway)* carril *m*; *Sport* calle *f*; *Naut* ruta *f*
language ['læŋgwɪdʒ] *n* (**a**) lenguaje *m*; **bad l.** palabrotas *fpl* (**b**) *(of a country)* idioma *m*, lengua *f*; **l. laboratory** laboratorio *m* de idiomas; **l. school** academia *f* de idiomas
languid ['læŋgwɪd] *adj* lánguido(a)
languish ['læŋgwɪʃ] *vi* languidecer; *(project, plan etc)* quedar abandonado(a); *(in prison)* pudrirse
lank [læŋk] *adj (hair)* lacio(a)
lanky ['læŋkɪ] *adj* (**lankier, lankiest**) larguirucho(a)
lantern ['læntən] *n* farol *m*

lap¹ [læp] *n Anat* regazo *m*
lap² [læp] **1** *n (circuit)* vuelta *f*; *Fig* etapa *f*
2 *vt (overtake)* doblar
lap³ [læp] **1** *vt* (*pt & pp* **lapped**) *(of cat)* beber a lengüetadas
2 *vi (waves)* lamer, besar
▶ **lap up** *vt sep* (**a**) *(of cat)* beber a lengüetadas (**b**) *Fig (wallow in)* disfrutar con; *(flattery)* recibir con estusiasmo (**c**) *Fig (believe)* tragar
lapel [lə'pel] *n* solapa *f*
Lapland ['læplænd] *n* Laponia
lapse [læps] **1** *n* (**a**) *(of time)* lapso *m* (**b**) *(error)* error *m*, desliz *m*; *(of memory)* fallo *m*
2 *vi* (**a**) *(time)* pasar, transcurrir (**b**) *(expire)* caducar (**c**) *(err)* cometer un error; *(fall back)* caer (**into** en) (**d**) *Rel* perder la fe
larceny ['lɑːsənɪ] *n Br* latrocinio *m*; *US* hurto *m*
larch [lɑːtʃ] *n* alerce *m*
lard [lɑːd] *n* manteca *f* de cerdo
larder ['lɑːdə(r)] *n* despensa *f*
large [lɑːdʒ] **1** *adj* grande; *(amount)* importante; *(extensive)* amplio(a); **by and l.** por lo general
2 *n* **to be at l.** andar suelto(a); **the public at l.** el público en general

> *⌀* Note that the Spanish word **largo** is a false friend and is never a translation for the English word **large**. In Spanish, **largo** means "long".

largely ['lɑːdʒlɪ] *adv (mainly)* en gran parte; *(chiefly)* principalmente
large-scale ['lɑːdʒskeɪl] *adj (project, problem etc)* de gran envergadura; *(map)* a gran escala
lark¹ [lɑːk] *n Orn* alondra *f*
lark² [lɑːk] *n Fam (joke)* broma *f*; **what a l.!** ¡qué risa!
▶ **lark about, lark around** *vi Fam* hacer el tonto
larva ['lɑːvə] *n* larva *f*
laryngitis [lærɪn'dʒaɪtɪs] *n* laringitis *f*
larynx ['lærɪŋks] *n Anat* laringe *f*
laser ['leɪzə(r)] *n* láser *m*; **l. printer** impresora *f* láser
lash [læʃ] **1** *n* (**a**) *(eyelash)* pestaña *f* (**b**) *(blow with whip)* latigazo *m*
2 *vt* (**a**) *(beat)* azotar (**b**) *(rain)* azotar (**c**) *(tie)* atar
▶ **lash out** *vi* (**a**) *(with fists)* repartir golpes a diestro y siniestro; *(verbally)* criticar (**at** a) (**b**) *Fam (spend money)* tirar la casa por la ventana
lass [læs] *n Fam* chavala *f*, muchacha *f*

lasso [læˈsuː] **1** *n* lazo *m*
2 *vt* coger con el lazo

last [lɑːst] **1** *adj* (**a**) *(final)* último(a), final;
Fam **the l. straw** el colmo (**b**) *(most recent)* último(a) (**c**) *(past)* pasado(a); *(previous)* anterior; **l. but one** penúltimo(a); **l. month** el mes pasado; **l. night** anoche;
the night before l. anteanoche
2 *adv* (**a**) **when l l. saw her** la última vez que la vi (**b**) *(at the end)* en último lugar;
(in race etc) último; **at (long) l.** por fin; **l. but not least** el último en orden pero no en importancia
3 *n* **the l.** el último/la última
4 *vi* (**a**) *(time)* durar; *(hold out)* aguantar (**b**) *(be enough for)* llegar, alcanzar

last-ditch [ˈlɑːstdɪtʃ] *adj (effort, attempt)* último(a) y desesperado(a)

lasting [ˈlɑːstɪŋ] *adj* duradero(a)

lastly [ˈlɑːstlɪ] *adv* por último, finalmente

last-minute [ˈlɑːstmɪnɪt] *adj* de última hora

latch [lætʃ] *n* picaporte *m*, pestillo *m*

late [leɪt] **1** *adj* (**a**) *(not on time)* tardío(a);
(hour) avanzado(a); **to be five minutes l.** llegar con cinco minutos de retraso (**b**) *(far on in time)* tarde; **in l. autumn** a finales del otoño; **in the l. afternoon** a última hora de la tarde; **she's in her l. twenties** ronda los treinta (**c**) *(dead)* difunto(a)
2 *adv* (**a**) *(not on time)* tarde; **to arrive l.** llegar tarde (**b**) *(far on in time)* tarde; **l. at night** a altas horas de la noche; **l. in life** a una edad avanzada (**c**) **as l. as 1950** todavía en 1950; **of l.** últimamente

latecomer [ˈleɪtkʌmə(r)] *n* tardón(ona) *m,f*

lately [ˈleɪtlɪ] *adv* últimamente, recientemente

latent [ˈleɪtənt] *adj* (**a**) latente (**b**) *(desire)* oculto(a)

later [ˈleɪtə(r)] **1** *adj* (**a**) *(subsequent)* más tarde; **in her l. novels** en sus novelas posteriores (**b**) *(more recent)* más reciente
2 *adv* más tarde, después; **l. on** más adelante, más tarde

lateral [ˈlætərəl] *adj* lateral

latest [ˈleɪtɪst] **1** *adj (superl of* **late)** *(most recent)* último(a), más reciente
2 *n* **the l.** lo último; **have you heard the l.?** ¿te enteraste de lo último?; **Friday at the l.** el viernes a más tardar

lathe [leɪð] *n Tech* torno *m*

lather [ˈlɑːðə(r)] **1** *n (of soap)* espuma *f*;
(horse's sweat) sudor *m*
2 *vt (with soap)* enjabonar

Latin [ˈlætɪn] **1** *adj & n* latino(a) *(m,f)*; **L. America** América Latina, Latinoamérica;
L. American latinoamericano(a) *(m,f)*
2 *n (language)* latín *m*

latitude [ˈlætɪtjuːd] *n* latitud *f*

latrine [ləˈtriːn] *n* letrina *f*

latter [ˈlætə(r)] **1** *adj* (**a**) *(last)* último(a) (**b**) *(second of two)* segundo(a)
2 *pron* éste(a); **the former ... the l.** aquél ... éste/aquélla ... ésta

lattice [ˈlætɪs] *n* enrejado *m*, rejilla *f*

laudable [ˈlɔːdəbəl] *adj* loable

laugh [lɑːf] **1** *n* risa *f*; *(guffaw)* carcajada *f*;
for a l. para divertirse
2 *vi* reír, reírse
► **laugh at** *vt insep* **to l. at sb/sth** reírse de algn/algo
► **laugh about** *vt insep* **to l. about sb/sth** reírse de algn/algo
► **laugh off** *vt sep* tomar a risa

laughable [ˈlɑːfəbəl] *adj (situation, suggestion)* ridículo(a); *(amount, offer)* irrisorio(a)

laughing-stock [ˈlɑːfɪŋstɒk] *n* hazmerreír *m inv*

laughter [ˈlɑːftə(r)] *n* risa *f*

launch [lɔːntʃ] **1** *n* (**a**) *(vessel)* lancha *f* (**b**) = **launching**
2 *vt* (**a**) *(attack, rocket, new product)* lanzar (**b**) *(ship)* botar (**c**) *(film, play)* estrenar (**d**) *(company)* fundar (**e**) *Fig (scheme)* iniciar

launching [ˈlɔːntʃɪŋ] *n* (**a**) *(of rocket, new product)* lanzamiento *m* (**b**) *(of ship)* botadura *f* (**c**) *(of film, play)* estreno *m* (**d**) *(of new company)* fundación *f*

launchpad [ˈlɔːntʃpæd] *n* plataforma *f* de lanzamiento

launder [ˈlɔːndə(r)] *vt* lavar y planchar;
Fig (money) blanquear

launderette [lɔːndəˈret], *US* **Laundromat**® [ˈlɔːndrəmæt] *n* lavandería automática

laundry [ˈlɔːndrɪ] *n* (**a**) *(place)* lavandería *f* (**b**) *(dirty clothes)* ropa sucia; **to do the l.** lavar la ropa

laurel [ˈlɒrəl] *n* laurel *m*; *Fam Fig* **to rest on one's laurels** dormirse en los laureles

lava [ˈlɑːvə] *n* lava *f*

lavatory [ˈlævətərɪ] *n* (**a**) excusado *m*, retrete *m* (**b**) *(room)* baño *m*; **public l.** servicios *mpl*, aseos *mpl*

lavender [ˈlævəndə(r)] *n* lavanda *f*

lavish [ˈlævɪʃ] **1** *adj* (**a**) *(generous)* pródigo(a) (**b**) *(abundant)* abundante (**c**) *(luxurious)* lujoso(a)
2 *vt* **to l. praise on sb** colmar de alabanzas a alguien; **to l. attention on sb**

prodigarse en atenciones con alguien

law [lɔː] *n* (**a**) ley *f*; **by l.** según la ley; **l. and order** el orden público; **to lay down the l.** dictar la ley (**b**) *(as subject)* derecho *m*; **l. court** tribunal *m* de justicia (**c**) *Fam* **the l.** los maderos

law-abiding [ˈlɔːəbaɪdɪŋ] *adj* respetuoso(a) de la ley

lawful [ˈlɔːfʊl] *adj* legal; *(permitted by law)* lícito(a); *(legitimate)* legítimo(a)

lawn [lɔːn] *n* césped *m*; **l. tennis** tenis *m* sobre hierba

lawnmower [ˈlɔːnməʊə(r)] *n* cortacésped *m*

lawsuit [ˈlɔːsjuːt] *n* pleito *m*

lawyer [ˈlɔːjə(r)] *n* abogado(a) *m,f*; **l.'s office** bufete *m* de abogados

lax [læks] *adj (not strict)* relajado(a); *(not demanding)* poco exigente; *(careless)* descuidado(a)

laxative [ˈlæksətɪv] *adj & n* laxante *(m)*

laxity [ˈlæksɪtɪ] *n* relajamiento *m*; *(carelessness)* descuido *m*; *(negligence)* negligencia *f*

lay¹ [leɪ] *adj* (**a**) *Rel* laico(a) (**b**) *(nonspecialist)* lego(a)

lay² [leɪ] *vt* (*pt & pp* **laid**) (**a**) *(place)* poner, colocar; *(cable, trap)* tender; *(foundations)* echar (**b**) *(fire)* preparar; *(table)* poner (**c**) *(leave)* dejar (**d**) *(eggs)* poner (**e**) *very Fam (have sex with)* follar (**f**) *(set down)* asentar; *(blame)* echar
▸ **lay aside** *vt sep* dejar a un lado
▸ **lay by** *vt sep (save)* guardar; *(money)* ahorrar
▸ **lay down** *vt sep* (**a**) *(put down)* poner; *(let go)* dejar; **to l. down one's arms** rendir las armas (**b**) *(plan)* formular (**c**) *(establish)* fijar, imponer; *(principles)* sentar
▸ **lay into** *vt insep Fam (physically)* dar una paliza a; *(verbally)* arremeter contra
▸ **lay off 1** *vt sep (dismiss)* despedir
  2 *vt insep Fam* dejar en paz
  3 *vi* **l. off!** ¡para ya!
▸ **lay on** *vt sep* (**a**) *(provide)* proveer de; *(food)* preparar (**b**) *(spread)* aplicar; *Fam* **to l. it on (thick)** cargar las tintas
▸ **lay out** *vt sep* (**a**) *(open out)* extender (**b**) *(arrange)* disponer (**c**) *(ideas)* exponer (**d**) *(plan)* trazar (**e**) *Fam (spend)* gastar (**f**) *Fam (knock out)* derribar
▸ **lay up** *vt sep* (**a**) *(store)* guardar (**b**) *(accumulate)* almacenar (**c**) *Fam* **to be laid up** tener que guardar cama

lay³ [leɪ] *pt of* **lie²**

layabout [ˈleɪəbaʊt] *n Fam* vago(a) *m,f*

lay-by [ˈleɪbaɪ] *n* área *f* de descanso

layer [ˈleɪə(r)] *n* capa *f*

layman [ˈleɪmən] *n* lego(a) *m,f*

layout [ˈleɪaʊt] *n (arrangement)* disposición *f*; *(presentation)* presentación *f*; *Typ* composición *f*; *(plan)* diseño *m*, trazado *m*

laze [leɪz] *vi* holgazanear, gandulear

laziness [ˈleɪzɪnɪs] *n* pereza *f*, holgazanería *f*

lazy [ˈleɪzɪ] *adj* (**lazier, laziest**) perezoso(a), holgazán(ana); **at a l. pace** a paso lento

lb *(abbr* **pound***)* libra *f*

lead¹ [led] *n* (**a**) *(metal)* plomo *m* (**b**) *(in pencil)* mina *f*

lead² [liːd] **1** *n* (**a**) *(front position)* delantera *f*; *(advantage)* ventaja *f*; **to take the l.** *(in race)* tomar la delantera; *(score)* adelantarse
  (**b**) *(clue)* pista *f*
  (**c**)*Th* primer papel *m*; **l. singer** cantante *mf* principal
  (**d**) *(leash)* correa *f*
  (**e**) *Elec* cable *m*
  2 *vt* (*pt & pp* **led**) (**a**) *(conduct)* llevar, conducir
  (**b**) *(be the leader of)* dirigir, encabezar
  (**c**) *(influence)* llevar a; **this leads me to believe that** esto me lleva a creer que; **she's easily led** se deja llevar fácilmente
  (**d**) *(life)* llevar
  3 *vi* (**a**) *(road)* llevar, conducir (**to** a)
  (**b**) *(go first)* ir delante; *(in race)* llevar la delantera
  (**c**) **to l. to** llevar a
▸ **lead away** *vt sep* llevar
▸ **lead on 1** *vi (go ahead)* ir adelante
  2 *vt sep (deceive)* engañar, timar
▸ **lead up to** *vt insep* llevar a

leaden [ˈledən] *adj (sky)* plomizo(a); *(food)* pesado(a)

leader [ˈliːdə(r)] *n* (**a**) jefe(a) *m,f*, líder *mf*; *(in race)* líder (**b**) *Press* editorial *m*, artículo *m* de fondo

leadership [ˈliːdəʃɪp] *n* (**a**) *(command)* dirección *f*, mando *m*; *Pol* liderazgo *m* (**b**) *(leaders)* dirigentes *mpl*, cúpula *f*

lead-free [ˈledfriː] *adj* sin plomo

leading [ˈliːdɪŋ] *adj* (**a**) *(main)* principal (**b**) *(outstanding)* destacado(a)

leaf [liːf] *n (pl* **leaves**) hoja *f*; **to turn over a new l.** hacer borrón y cuenta nueva
▸ **leaf through** *vt insep* hojear

leaflet [ˈliːflɪt] *n* folleto *m*

league [liːg] *n* (**a**) *(alliance)* alianza *f*; *(association)* sociedad *f*; *Fam* **to be in l. with sb** estar conchabado(a) con algn (**b**) *Sport* liga *f*

leak [liːk] **1** *n* (**a**) *(hole)* agujero *m*; *(in*

roof) gotera *f* (**b**) *(of gas, liquid)* fuga *f*, escape *m*; *(of information)* filtración *f*
2 *vi* (**a**) *(container)* tener un agujero; *(pipe)* tener un escape; *(roof)* gotear; *(boat)* hacer agua (**b**) *(gas, liquid)* escaparse; *(information)* filtrarse; *(news)* trascender
3 *vt (information)* filtrar (**to** a)
leaky ['liːkɪ] *adj* (**leakier, leakiest**) *(container)* agujereado(a); *(roof)* que tiene goteras; *(ship)* que hace agua
lean¹ [liːn] *adj (meat)* magro(a); *(person)* flaco(a); *(harvest)* escaso(a)
lean² [liːn] **1** *vi (pt & pp* **leaned** *or* **leant**) (**a**) inclinarse (**b**) **to l. on/against** apoyarse en/contra; *Fig* **to l. on sb** *(pressurize)* presionar a algn; *(depend)* depender de algn
2 *vt* apoyar (**on** en)
▸ **lean back** *vi* reclinarse
▸ **lean forward** *vi* inclinarse hacia delante
▸ **lean out** *vi* asomarse
▸ **lean over** *vi* inclinarse
leaning ['liːnɪŋ] **1** *adj* inclinado(a)
2 *n Fig (tendency)* inclinación *f*, tendencia *f*
leant [lent] *pt & pp of* **lean**
lean-to ['liːntuː] *n (hut)* cobertizo *m*
leap [liːp] **1** *n (jump)* salto *m*; *Fig* paso *m*; **l. year** año bisiesto
2 *vi (pt & pp* **leaped** *or* **leapt**) saltar; *Fig* **her heart leapt** su corazón dio un vuelco
▸ **leap at** *vt insep Fig (chance)* no dejar escapar
leapfrog ['liːpfrɒg] *n* pídola *f*
leapt [lept] *pt & pp of* **leap**
learn [lɜːn] **1** *vt (pt & pp* **learned** *or* **learnt**) (**a**) aprender; **to l. (how) to ski** aprender a esquiar (**b**) **to l. that** enterarse de que
2 *vi* (**a**) aprender (**b**) **to l. about** *or* **of** *(find out)* enterarse de
learned ['lɜːnɪd] *adj* erudito(a)
learner ['lɜːnə(r)] *n (beginner)* principiante *mf*; **l. driver** aprendiz(a) *m,f* de conductor
learning ['lɜːnɪŋ] *n (knowledge)* conocimientos *mpl*; *(erudition)* saber *m*
learnt [lɜːnt] *pt & pp of* **learn**
lease [liːs] **1** *n* contrato *m* de arrendamiento; *Fig* **to give sb a new l.** *Br* **of** *or US* **on life** dar nueva vida a algn
2 *vt* arrendar
leasehold ['liːshəʊld] **1** *n* derechos *mpl* de arrendamiento
2 *adj (property)* arrendado(a)
leash [liːʃ] *n* correa *f*
least [liːst] *(superl of* **little**) **1** *adj* menor,

mínimo(a); **he has the l. time** él es quien menos tiempo tiene
2 *adv* menos; **l. of all him** él menos que nadie
3 *n* **the l.** lo menos; **at l.** por lo menos, al menos; **not in the l.!** ¡en absoluto!; **to say the l.** por no decir más
leather ['leðə(r)] **1** *n* piel *f*, cuero *m*
2 *adj* de piel
leave¹ [liːv] **1** *vt (pt & pp* **left**) (**a**) dejar; *(go away from)* abandonar; *(go out of)* salir de (**b**) **l. him alone!** ¡déjale en paz!; *Fam* **l. it to me** yo me encargo (**c**) *(bequeath)* legar (**d**) *(forget)* dejarse, olvidarse (**e**) **I have two biscuits left** me quedan dos galletas (**f**) **to be left over** sobrar
2 *vi (go away)* irse, marcharse; *(go out)* salir; **the train leaves in five minutes** el tren sale dentro de cinco minutos
▸ **leave behind** *vt sep* (**a**) dejar atrás (**b**) *(forget)* olvidarse
▸ **leave on** *vt sep* (**a**) *(clothes)* dejar puesto(a) (**b**) *(lights, radio)* dejar encendido(a)
▸ **leave out** *vt sep (omit)* omitir; *Fig* **to feel left out** sentirse excluido(a)
leave² [liːv] *n* (**a**) *(permission)* permiso *m* (**b**) *(time off)* vacaciones *fpl*; *Mil* **on l.** de permiso; **l. of absence** excedencia *f* (**c**) **to take one's l. of sb** despedirse de algn
leaves [liːvz] *pl of* **leaf**
Lebanon ['lebənən] *n* (**the**) **L.** (el) Líbano
lecherous ['letʃərəs] *adj* lascivo(a)
lecture ['lektʃə(r)] **1** *n* (**a**) conferencia *f*; *Univ* clase *f*; **to give a l. (on)** dar una conferencia (sobre); **l. hall, l. room, l. theatre** sala *f* de conferencias; *Univ* aula *f* (**b**) *(rebuke)* sermón *m*
2 *vi* dar una conferencia; *Univ* dar clases
3 *vt (reproach)* sermonear
lecturer ['lektʃərə(r)] *n* conferenciante *mf*; *Univ* profesor(a) *m,f*
led [led] *pt & pp of* **lead**
ledge [ledʒ] *n* (**a**) *(shelf)* repisa *f*; *(of window)* alféizar *m* (**b**) *(on mountain)* saliente *m*
ledger ['ledʒə(r)] *n* libro *m* mayor
lee [liː] *n* (**a**) *Naut* sotavento *m* (**b**) *Fig* abrigo *m*
leech [liːtʃ] *n* sanguijuela *f*
leek [liːk] *n* puerro *m*
leer [lɪə(r)] *vi* mirar con lascivia
leeway ['liːweɪ] *n* libertad *f*; **this gives me a certain amount of l.** esto me da cierto margen de libertad
left¹ [left] **1** *adj* izquierdo(a); *Pol* **l. wing** izquierda *f*
2 *adv* a la izquierda

3 *n* (**a**) izquierda *f*; **on the l.** a mano izquierda (**b**) *Pol* **to be on the l.** ser de izquierdas
left² [left] *pt & pp of* **leave**
left-hand ['lefthænd] *adj* **l. drive** con el volante a la izquierda; **on the l. side** a mano izquierda
left-handed [left'hændɪd] *adj* zurdo(a)
left-luggage [left'lʌgɪdʒ] *n Br* **l. office** consigna *f*
leftovers ['leftəʊvəz] *npl* sobras *fpl*
left-wing ['leftwɪŋ] *adj* de izquierdas, izquierdista
leg [leg] *n* (**a**) *(of person)* pierna *f*; *(of animal, table)* pata *f*; *Culin (of lamb)* pierna; *(of trousers)* pernera *f* (**b**) *(stage)* etapa *f*
legacy ['legəsɪ] *n* herencia *f*, legado *m*
legal ['li:gəl] *adj* (**a**) legal; *(permitted by law)* lícito(a); **l. tender** moneda *f* de curso legal (**b**) *(relating to the law)* jurídico(a); **l. aid** asesoramiento jurídico gratuito; **l. dispute** contencioso *m*; *US* **l. holiday** fiesta *f* nacional
legalize ['li:gəlaɪz] *vt* legalizar
legally ['li:gəlɪ] *adv* legalmente
legend ['ledʒənd] *n* leyenda *f*
legendary ['ledʒəndərɪ] *adj* legendario(a)
leggings ['legɪŋz] *npl* polainas *fpl*
legible ['ledʒəbəl] *adj* legible
legion ['li:dʒən] *n* legión *f*
legislation [ledʒɪs'leɪʃən] *n* legislación *f*
legislative ['ledʒɪslətɪv] *adj* legislativo(a)
legislator ['ledʒɪsleɪtə(r)] *n* legislador(a) *m,f*
legislature ['ledʒɪsleɪtʃə(r)] *n* asamblea legislativa
legitimate [lɪ'dʒɪtɪmɪt] *adj* legítimo(a)
legroom ['legru:m] *n* espacio *m* para las piernas
leisure ['leʒə(r), *US* 'li:ʒər] *n* ocio *m*, tiempo *m* libre; **at l.** con calma; **do it at your l.** hazlo cuando tengas tiempo; **l. activities** pasatiempos *mpl*; **l. centre** centro recreativo
leisurely ['leʒəlɪ, *US* 'li:ʒərlɪ] *adj (unhurried)* tranquilo(a); *(slow)* lento(a)
lemon ['lemən] *n* limón *m*; **l. curd** crema *f* de limón; **l. juice** zumo *m* de limón; **l. tea** té *m* con limón
lemonade [lemə'neɪd] *n* limonada *f*
lend [lend] *vt (pt & pp* lent) prestar; **to l. oneself/itself to sth** prestarse a or para algo
lending ['lendɪŋ] *n* **l. library** biblioteca pública

length [leŋkθ, leŋθ] *n* (**a**) longitud *f*, largo *m*; **it is 5 m in l.** tiene 5 m de largo (**b**) *(duration)* duración *f* (**c**) *(of string)* trozo *m*; *(of cloth)* retal *m* (**d**) *(of swimming pool)* largo *m*; *Fig* **to go to any lengths to achieve sth** hacer lo que sea para conseguir algo (**e**) **at l.** *(finally)* finalmente; *(in depth)* a fondo
lengthen ['leŋkθən, 'leŋθən] **1** *vt* alargar; *(lifetime)* prolongar
   2 *vi* alargarse; *(lifetime)* prolongarse
lengthways ['leŋθweɪz] *adv* a lo largo
lengthy ['leŋkθɪ, 'leŋθɪ] *adj* (**lengthier**, **lengthiest**) largo(a); *(film, illness)* de larga duración; *(meeting, discussion)* prolongado(a)
lenient ['li:nɪənt] *adj* indulgente
lens [lenz] *n (of eye)* cristalino *m*; *(of spectacles)* lente *f*; *Phot* objetivo *m*
Lent [lent] *n* Cuaresma *f*
lent [lent] *pt & pp of* **lend**
lentil ['lentɪl] *n* lenteja *f*
Leo ['li:əʊ] *n* Leo *m*
leopard ['lepəd] *n* leopardo *m*
leotard ['li:ətɑ:d] *n* leotardo *m*
leper ['lepə(r)] *n* leproso(a) *m,f*
leprosy ['leprəsɪ] *n* lepra *f*
lesbian ['lezbɪən] *adj & n* lesbiana (*f*)
less [les] **1** *adj (comp of* **little**) menos
   2 *pron* menos; **the l. said about it, the better** cuanto menos se hable de eso mejor
   3 *adv* menos; **l. and l.** cada vez menos; **still l.** menos aún
   4 *prep* menos; **a year l. two days** un año menos dos días
lessen ['lesən] *vt & vi* disminuir
lesser ['lesə(r)] *adj* menor; **to a l. extent** en menor grado
lesson ['lesən] *n* (**a**) clase *f*; *(in book)* lección *f*; **Spanish lessons** clases de español (**b**) *Rel* lectura *f*
lest [lest] *conj Fml* (**a**) para (que) no; **l. we forget** para que no lo olvidemos (**b**) *(for fear that)* por miedo a que
let [let] **1** *vt (pt & pp* let) (**a**) dejar, permitir; **to l. go of sth** soltar algo; **to l. sb know** avisar a algn; *Fig* **to l. oneself go** dejarse ir (**b**) *(rent out)* alquilar, *Méx* rentar; **to l. (sign)** se alquila (**c**) **l. alone** ni mucho menos
   2 *v aux* **l. him wait** que espere; **l. me go!** ¡suéltame!; **l.'s go!** ¡vamos!, ¡vámonos!; **l.'s see** a ver
   ▸ **let down** *vt sep* (**a**) *(lower)* bajar; *(lengthen)* alargar; *Fam Fig* **to l. one's hair down** desmelenarse (**b**) *(deflate)* desinflar (**c**) *(fail)* fallar, defraudar

▸ **let in** *vt sep* (**a**) *(admit)* dejar entrar (**b**) **to l. oneself in for** meterse en

▸ **let off** *vt sep* (**a**) *(bomb)* hacer explotar; *(fireworks)* hacer estallar (**b**) *(liquid, air)* soltar (**c**) *Fam* **to l. sb off** *(pardon)* perdonar

▸ **let on** *vi Fam* **don't l. on** *(reveal information)* no se lo digas

▸ **let out** *vt sep* (**a**) *(release)* soltar; *(news)* divulgar; *(secret)* revelar (**b**) *(air, water)* dejar salir (**c**) *(cry)* soltar (**d**) *Sewing* ensanchar

▸ **let up** *vi* cesar, parar

letdown ['letdaʊn] *n* decepción *f*

lethal ['liːθəl] *adj* letal

lethargic [lɪ'θɑːdʒɪk] *adj* aletargado(a)

letter ['letə(r)] *n* (**a**) *(of alphabet)* letra *f*; *Fig* **to the l.** al pie de la letra (**b**) *(written message)* carta *f*; *Br* **l. box** buzón *m*; *Com* **l. of credit** carta de crédito

letterhead ['letəhed] *n* membrete *m*

lettering ['letərɪŋ] *n* rótulo *m*

lettuce ['letɪs] *n* lechuga *f*

let-up ['letʌp] *n Fam* descanso *m*, respiro *m*

leukaemia, *US* **leukemia** [luː'kiːmɪə] *n* leucemia *f*

level ['levəl] **1** *adj* (**a**) *(flat)* llano(a); *(even)* nivelado(a); *(equal)* igual, parejo(a); **a l. spoonful of** una cucharada rasa de; **to be l. with** estar a nivel de; *Br* **l. crossing** paso *m* a nivel (**b**) *(steady)* estable; *(tone)* uniforme

2 *vt* (**a**) nivelar, allanar (**b**) *(building)* arrasar (**c**) *(stare, criticism)* dirigir

3 *n* nivel *m*; **to be on a l. with** estar al mismo nivel que; *Fam* **to be on the l.** *(be honest)* ser de fiar; *(be truthful)* decir la verdad

▸ **level off, level out** *vi* estabilizarse

▸ **level with** *vt insep Fam* ser franco(a) con

level-headed [levəl'hedɪd] *adj* sensato(a)

lever ['liːvə(r)] **1** *n* palanca *f*

2 *vt* apalancar; **to l. sth out** sacar algo con palanca

leverage ['liːvərɪdʒ] *n Fig* influencia *f*

levy ['levɪ] **1** *vt* *(tax)* recaudar; *(fine)* imponer

2 *n* *(of tax)* recaudación *f*; *(of fine)* imposición *f*

lewd [luːd] *adj* *(person)* lascivo(a); *(story)* obsceno(a)

liability [laɪə'bɪlɪtɪ] *n* (**a**) *Jur* responsabilidad *f* (**b**) *(handicap)* estorbo *m* (**c**) *Fin* **liabilities** pasivo *m*

liable ['laɪəbəl] *adj* (**a**) *Jur* responsable; *(susceptible)* sujeto(a); **to be l. for** ser responsable de (**b**) **to be l. to do sth** ser propenso(a) a hacer algo; **it's l. to happen** es muy probable que (así) suceda

liaise [liː'eɪz] *vi* comunicarse (**with** con)

liaison [liː'eɪzɒn] *n* (**a**) enlace *m*; **l. officer** oficial *mf* de enlace (**b**) *(love affair)* amorío *m*

liar ['laɪə(r)] *n* mentiroso(a) *m,f*, embustero(a) *m,f*

libel ['laɪbəl] **1** *n* libelo *m*

2 *vt* difamar, calumniar

liberal ['lɪbərəl] **1** *adj* (**a**) liberal; **L. Party** Partido *m* Liberal (**b**) *(abundant)* abundante

2 *n Pol* **L.** liberal *mf*

liberate ['lɪbəreɪt] *vt* liberar; *(prisoner etc)* poner en libertad; **liberated woman** mujer liberada

liberation [lɪbə'reɪʃən] *n* liberación *f*

liberty ['lɪbətɪ] *n* libertad *f*; **to be at l. to say sth** ser libre de decir algo; **to take liberties** tomarse libertades

Libra ['liːbrə] *n* Libra *f*

librarian [laɪ'breərɪən] *n* bibliotecario(a) *m,f*

> *Note that the Spanish word **librero** is a false friend and is never a translation for the English word **librarian**. In Spanish, **librero** means "bookseller".*

library ['laɪbrərɪ] *n* biblioteca *f*

> *Note that the Spanish word **librería** is a false friend and is never a translation for the English word **library**. In Spanish, **librería** means "bookshop".*

Libya ['lɪbɪə] *n* Libia

Libyan ['lɪbɪən] *adj & n* libio(a) *(m,f)*

lice [laɪs] *pl of* **louse**

licence ['laɪsəns] *n* (**a**) *(permit)* licencia *f*, permiso *m*; *Aut* **l. number** matrícula *f*; *US* **l. plate** (placa *f* de la) matrícula (**b**) *(freedom)* libertad *f*; *(excessive freedom)* libertinaje *m*

license ['laɪsəns] **1** *vt* dar licencia a, autorizar

2 *n US* = **licence**

licensed ['laɪsənst] *adj* autorizado(a); **l. premises** = local autorizado para la venta de bebidas alcohólicas

licentious [laɪ'senʃəs] *adj* licencioso(a)

lichen ['laɪkən, 'lɪtʃən] *n* liquen *m*

lick [lɪk] **1** *vt* lamer; **to l. one's lips** relamerse

2 *n* lamedura *f*; *Fam* **a l. of paint** una mano de pintura

licorice ['lɪkərɪs, 'lɪkərɪʃ] *n US* = **liquorice**

lid [lɪd] *n* (**a**) *(cover)* tapa *f* (**b**) *(of eye)* párpado *m*

lie¹ [laɪ] **1** *vi* mentir
 2 *n* mentira *f*

lie² [laɪ] **1** *vi* (*pt* lay; *pp* lain) (**a**) *(act)* echarse, acostarse; *(state)* estar echado(a), estar acostado(a); *(be buried)* yacer (**b**) *(be situated)* encontrarse, hallarse; **the valley lay before us** el valle se extendía ante nosotros (**c**) *(remain)* quedarse
 2 *n* *(position)* situación *f*; *(direction)* orientación *f*
 ▸ **lie about, lie around** *vi* *(person)* estar tumbado(a); *(things)* estar tirado(a)
 ▸ **lie down** *vi* acostarse, echarse

lie-in ['laɪɪn] *n Fam* **to have a l.** levantarse tarde

lieu [ljuː, luː] *n* **in l. of** en lugar de

lieutenant [lefˈtenənt, *US* luːˈtenənt] *n* (**a**) *Mil* teniente *m* (**b**) *(non-military)* lugarteniente *m*

life [laɪf] *n* (*pl* lives) (**a**) vida *f*; **to come to l.** cobrar vida; **to take one's own l.** suicidarse; *Fam* **how's l.?** ¿qué tal?; **l. belt** cinturón *m* salvavidas; **l. imprisonment** cadena perpetua; **l. insurance** seguro *m* de vida; **l. jacket** chaleco *m* salvavidas; **l. style** estilo *m* de vida; **l. story** biografía *f* (**b**) *(liveliness)* vitalidad *f*; *Fam Fig* **to be the l. and soul of the party** ser el alma de la fiesta

lifeboat ['laɪfbəʊt] *n* *(on ship)* bote *m* salvavidas; *(on shore)* lancha *f* de socorro

lifeguard ['laɪfgɑːd] *n* socorrista *mf*

lifeless ['laɪflɪs] *adj* sin vida

lifelike ['laɪflaɪk] *adj* natural; *(portrait)* fiel

lifeline ['laɪflaɪn] *n Fig* cordón *m* umbilical

lifelong ['laɪflɒŋ] *adj* de toda la vida

life-size(d) ['laɪfsaɪz(d)] *adj* (de) tamaño natural

lifetime ['laɪftaɪm] *n* vida *f*; **in his l.** durante su vida; **it's the chance of a l.** es una ocasión única

lift [lɪft] **1** *vt* (**a**) levantar; *(head etc)* alzar; *(pick up)* coger (**b**) *(troops)* transportar (**c**) *Fam (steal)* birlar; *(plagiarize)* plagiar
 2 *vi* *(clouds, mist)* disiparse
 3 *n* (**a**) *Br (elevator)* ascensor *m* (**b**) **to give sb a l.** llevar a algn en coche (**c**) *Fig (boost)* estímulo *m*
 ▸ **lift up** *vt sep* levantar, alzar

lift-off ['lɪftɒf] *n* despegue *m*

light¹ [laɪt] **1** *n* (**a**) luz *f*; *Fig* **in the l. of** en vista de; *Fig* **to bring sth to l.** sacar algo a la luz; *Fig* **to come to l.** salir a la luz; **l.** **bulb** bombilla *f*; **l. meter** fotómetro *m*; **l. pen** lápiz óptico; **l. switch** interruptor *m* de la luz; **l. year** año *m* luz (**b**) *(lamp)* luz *f*, lámpara *f*; *(traffic light)* semáforo *m*; *(headlight)* faro *m* (**c**) *(flame)* lumbre *f*; **to set l. to sth** prender fuego a algo; *Fam* **have you got a l.?** ¿tiene fuego?
 2 *vt* (*pt & pp* lighted *or* lit) (**a**) *(illuminate)* iluminar, alumbrar (**b**) *(ignite)* encender
 3 *adj* claro(a); *(hair)* rubio(a)
 ▸ **light up 1** *vt sep* iluminar, alumbrar
 2 *vi* (**a**) iluminarse (**b**) *Fam* encender un cigarrillo

light² [laɪt] **1** *adj* ligero(a); *(rain)* fino(a); *(breeze)* suave; *Fig (sentence etc)* leve; *Fig* **to make l. of sth** dar poca importancia a algo
 2 *adv* **to travel l.** ir ligero(a) de equipaje

lighten¹ ['laɪtən] **1** *vt* (**a**) *(colour)* aclarar (**b**) *(illuminate)* iluminar
 2 *vi* aclararse

lighten² ['laɪtən] *vt* (**a**) *(weight)* aligerar (**b**) *Fig (mitigate)* aliviar; *(heart)* alegrar

lighter¹ ['laɪtə(r)] *n* (**cigarette**) **l.** encendedor *m*, mechero *m*

light-headed [laɪtˈhedɪd] *adj* (**a**) *(dizzy)* mareado(a) (**b**) *(frivolous)* frívolo(a)

light-hearted ['laɪthɑːtɪd] *adj* alegre

lighthouse ['laɪthaʊs] *n* faro *m*

lighting ['laɪtɪŋ] *n* (**a**) *(act)* iluminación *f* (**b**) *(system)* alumbrado *m*

lightly ['laɪtlɪ] *adv* (**a**) ligeramente (**b**) **to get off l.** salir casi indemne

lightness¹ ['laɪtnɪs] *n* luminosidad *f*, claridad *f*

lightness² ['laɪtnɪs] *n (of weight)* ligereza *f*

lightning ['laɪtnɪŋ] *n (flash)* relámpago *m*; *(stroke)* rayo *m*; **l. conductor** *or* **rod** pararrayos *m inv*; **l. strike** huelga *f* relámpago

lightweight ['laɪtweɪt] *adj (suit etc)* ligero(a); *(boxer)* de peso ligero; *Fig (person)* light

like¹ [laɪk] **1** *adj* (**a**) parecido(a), semejante (**b**) *(equal)* igual
 2 *adv* (**as**) **l. as not** a lo mejor
 3 *prep* (**a**) *(similar to)* como, parecido(a) a; *(the same as)* igual que; **it's not l. her to do that** no es propio de ella hacer eso; **I've never seen anything l. it** nunca he visto cosa igual; **l. that** así; **people l. that** ese tipo de gente; **what's he l.?** ¿cómo es?; *Fam* **that's more l. it!** ¡así se hace! (**b**) **to feel l.** *(want)* tener ganas de; **I feel l. a change** me apetece un cambio
 4 *n* **brushes, combs and the l.** cepillos,

peines y cosas por el estilo
like² [laɪk] **1** *vt* (**a**) **do you l. chocolate?** ¿te
gusta el chocolate?; **he likes dancing** le
gusta bailar; **she likes children** le gustan
los niños (**b**) *(want)* querer; **whether
you l. it or not** quieras o no (quieras);
would you l. a drink? ¿te apetece tomar
algo?
  2 *vi* querer, gustar; **as you l.** como quieras; **whenever you l.** cuando quieras
  3 *n* gusto *m*
likeable ['laɪkəbəl] *adj* simpático(a)
likelihood ['laɪklɪhʊd] *n* probabilidad *f*
likely ['laɪklɪ] **1** *adj* (**likelier, likeliest**)
probable; **he's l. to cause trouble** es probable que cause problemas; **where are
you l. to be this afternoon?** ¿dónde piensas estar esta tarde?
  2 *adv* probablemente; **not l.!** ¡ni hablar!
likeness ['laɪknɪs] *n* (**a**) semejanza *f*,
parecido *m* (**b**) *(portrait)* retrato *m*
likewise ['laɪkwaɪz] *adv* (**a**) *(also)* también, asimismo (**b**) *(the same)* lo mismo,
igual
liking ['laɪkɪŋ] *n (for thing)* afición *f*; *(for
person)* simpatía *f*; *(for friend)* cariño *m*;
to take a l. to sth cogerle el gusto a algo;
to take a l. to sb coger cariño a algn
lilac ['laɪlək] **1** *n* (**a**) *Bot* lila *f* (**b**) *(colour)*
lila *m*
  2 *adj* lila, de color lila
lilt [lɪlt] *n* melodía *f*
lily ['lɪlɪ] *n* lirio *m*, azucena *f*; **l. of the
valley** lirio de los valles
limb [lɪm] *n* miembro *m*; *Fig* **to be out on
a l.** *(in danger)* estar en peligro; *Br (isolated)* estar aislado(a)
  ▶ **limber up** ['lɪmbə(r)] *vi Sport* entrar en
calor; *Fig* prepararse (**for** para)
limbo ['lɪmbəʊ] *n* limbo *m*; *Fig* olvido *m*;
to be in l. caer en el olvido
lime¹ [laɪm] *n Chem* cal *f*
lime² [laɪm] *n (fruit)* lima *f*; *(tree)* limero *m*
limelight ['laɪmlaɪt] *n Fig* **to be in the l.**
estar en el candelero
limerick ['lɪmərɪk] *n* quintilla humorísti-
ca
limestone ['laɪmstəʊn] *n* piedra caliza
limit ['lɪmɪt] **1** *n* límite *m*; *(maximum)*
máximo *m*; *(minimum)* mínimo *m*
  2 *vt (restrict)* limitar
limitation [lɪmɪ'teɪʃən] *n* limitación *f*
limited ['lɪmɪtɪd] *adj* limitado(a); **l. edition** edición limitada; *Br* **l. (liability)
company** sociedad anónima
limitless ['lɪmɪtlɪs] *adj* ilimitado(a)
limousine ['lɪməziːn, lɪmə'ziːn] *n* limusi-
na *f*

limp¹ [lɪmp] **1** *vi* cojear
  2 *n* cojera *f*
limp² [lɪmp] *adj* (**a**) *(floppy)* flojo(a) (**b**)
(weak) débil
limpet ['lɪmpɪt] *n* lapa *f*
linchpin ['lɪntʃpɪn] *n Tech* pezonera *f*; *Fig*
eje *m*
line¹ [laɪn] *n* (**a**) línea *f*; *(straight)* raya *f*;
to be on the right lines ir por buen
camino; *US* **State l.** límite *m* de un Estado
  (**b**) *(of writing)* renglón *m*; *(of poetry)*
verso *m*; *Th* **to learn one's lines** apren-
derse el papel
  (**c**) *(row)* fila *f*; *(of trees)* hilera *f*; *US
(queue)* cola *f*; *Mil* **l. of fire** línea *f* de
fuego; *Mil* **to be in the front l.** estar en
primera línea; *Fig* **to be in l. (with)** coincidir (con); *Fam* **to bring sb into l.** pararle
los pies a algn; *US* **to stand in l.** *(queue)*
hacer cola; *Fam* **to step out of l.** salirse de
las reglas; *Fig* **sth along these lines** algo
por el estilo; **l. dancing** = baile al ritmo de
música country en el que los participan-
tes se colocan en hileras y se mueven
todos al mismo tiempo dando los mismos pasos
  (**d**) *(rope)* cuerda *f*; *(wire)* cable *m*; **fishing l.** sedal *m*
  (**e**) *Tel* línea *f*; **hold the l.!** ¡no cuelgue!
  (**f**) *Br Rail* vía *f*
  (**g**) *(range of goods)* surtido *m*; **a new l.**
una nueva línea
  (**h**) *(of descent)* linaje *m*
line² [laɪn] *vt (pipe etc)* revestir; *Sewing*
forrar; *Fam* **to l. one's pockets** forrarse
  ▶ **line up 1** *vt sep* (**a**) *(arrange in rows)*
poner en fila (**b**) **he has something lined
up for this evening** tiene algo organizado para esta noche
  2 *vi (people)* ponerse en fila; *(troops)*
formar; *(in queue)* hacer cola
linear ['lɪnɪə(r)] *adj* lineal
lined [laɪnd] *adj* (**a**) *(paper)* rayado(a);
(face) arrugado(a) (**b**) *(garment)* forra-
do(a)
linen ['lɪnɪn] *n* (**a**) *(cloth)* lino *m* (**b**)
(clothes) ropa *f*; *(sheets etc)* ropa blanca
liner ['laɪnə(r)] *n* transatlántico *m*
linesman ['laɪnzmən] *n Sport* juez *m* de
línea
line-up ['laɪnʌp] *n Sport* alineación *f*
linger ['lɪŋgə(r)] *vi* tardar; *(dawdle)* rezagarse; *(smell, doubt)* persistir; *Fig (memory)* perdurar
lingerie ['lænʒəriː] *n Fml* ropa *f* interior
(de mujer)
lingering ['lɪŋgərɪŋ] *adj (doubt)* persistente; *(look)* fijo(a)

lingo ['lɪŋgəʊ] *n* (*pl* **lingoes**) *Fam* (**a**) *(language)* lengua *f*, idioma *m* (**b**) *(jargon)* jerga *f*

linguist ['lɪŋgwɪst] *n* lingüista *mf*; **he's a good l.** se le dan bien los idiomas

linguistic [lɪŋ'gwɪstɪk] *adj* lingüístico(a)

linguistics [lɪŋ'gwɪstɪks] *n sing* lingüística *f*

lining ['laɪnɪŋ] *n* forro *m*

link [lɪŋk] **1** *n* (**a**) *(of chain)* eslabón *m* (**b**) *(connection)* conexión *f*; *Fig* vínculo *m*; **rail l.** enlace ferroviario (**c**) **links** campo *m* de golf
   2 *vt* unir
   ► **link up** *vi* unirse; *(meet)* encontrarse; *(spaceships)* acoplarse

link-up ['lɪŋkʌp] *n Tel & TV* conexión *f*; *(meeting)* encuentro *m*; *(of spaceships)* acoplamiento *m*

lino ['laɪnəʊ] *n Fam* linóleo *m*

linoleum [lɪ'nəʊlɪəm] *n* linóleo *m*, linóleum *m*

lion ['laɪən] *n* león *m*

lioness ['laɪənɪs] *n* leona *f*

lip [lɪp] *n* (**a**) labio *m* (**b**) *(of jug)* pico *m*

lip-read ['lɪpriːd] *vt & vi* leer en los labios

lip-service ['lɪpsɜːvɪs] *n* palabrería *f*

lipstick ['lɪpstɪk] *n* lápiz *m* de labios

liqueur [lɪ'kjʊə(r)] *n* licor *m*

liquid ['lɪkwɪd] *adj & n* líquido(a) *(m)*

liquidate ['lɪkwɪdeɪt] *vt* liquidar

liquidation [lɪkwɪ'deɪʃən] *n* liquidación *f*; **to go into l.** entrar en liquidación

liquidize ['lɪkwɪdaɪz] *vt* licuar

liquidizer ['lɪkwɪdaɪzə(r)] *n* licuadora *f*

liquor ['lɪkər] *n US* alcohol *m*, bebidas alcohólicas; **l. store** tienda *f* de bebidas alcohólicas

liquorice ['lɪkərɪs, 'lɪkərɪʃ] *n* regaliz *m*

Lisbon ['lɪzbən] *n* Lisboa *f*

lisp [lɪsp] **1** *n* ceceo *m*
   2 *vi* cecear

list¹ [lɪst] **1** *n* lista *f*; *(catalogue)* catálogo *m*
   2 *vt* *(make a list of)* hacer una lista de; *(put on a list)* poner en una lista; **it is not listed** no figura en la lista

list² [lɪst] *Naut* **1** *n* escora *f*
   2 *vi* escorar

listen ['lɪsən] *vi* escuchar; *(pay attention)* prestar atención
   ► **listen out for** *vt insep* estar atento(a) a

listener ['lɪsənə(r)] *n* oyente *mf*

listless ['lɪstlɪs] *adj* apático(a)

lit [lɪt] *pt & pp of* **light**

liter ['liːtər] *n US* = **litre**

literacy ['lɪtərəsɪ] *n* alfabetización *f*

literal ['lɪtərəl] *adj* literal

literally ['lɪtərəlɪ] *adv* literalmente

literary ['lɪtərərɪ] *adj* literario(a)

literate ['lɪtərɪt] *adj* alfabetizado(a)

> *Note that the Spanish word **literato** is a false friend and is never a translation for the English word **literate**. In Spanish, **literato** means "writer, author".*

literature ['lɪtərətʃə(r)] *n* (**a**) literatura *f* (**b**) *Fam (documentation)* folleto informativo

lithe [laɪð] *adj Fml* ágil

Lithuania [lɪθjʊ'eɪnɪə] *n* Lituania

Lithuanian [lɪθjʊ'eɪnɪən] **1** *adj* lituano(a)
   2 *n (person)* lituano(a) *m,f*; *(language)* lituano *m*

litigation [lɪtɪ'geɪʃən] *n* litigio *m*

litmus ['lɪtməs] *n Fig* **l. test** prueba *f* contundente

litre ['liːtə(r)] *n* litro *m*

litter ['lɪtə(r)] **1** *n* (**a**) *(rubbish)* basura *f*; *(papers)* papeles *mpl*; **l. bin** papelera *f* (**b**) *(offspring)* camada *f*
   2 *vt* ensuciar

littered ['lɪtəd] *adj* cubierto(a) (**with** de)

little ['lɪtəl] **1** *adj* (**a**) pequeño(a); **a l. dog** un perrito; **a l. house** una casita; **l. finger** dedo *m* meñique; **L.** *Br* **Bear** *or US* **Dipper** Osa *f* Menor (**b**) *(not much)* poco(a); **a l. cheese** un poco de queso
   2 *pron* poco *m*; **save me a l.** guárdame un poco
   3 *adv* poco; **l. by l.** poco a poco; **as l. as possible** lo menos posible; **they were a l. surprised** se quedaron algo sorprendidos

live¹ [lɪv] **1** *vi* vivir; **long l. the King!** ¡viva el Rey!
   2 *vt* vivir; **to l. an interesting life** vivir una vida interesante
   ► **live down** *vt sep* conseguir que se olvide
   ► **live for** *vt insep* vivir para
   ► **live off** *vt insep* vivir de
   ► **live on 1** *vt insep (food, money)* vivir de
   2 *vi (memory)* persistir
   ► **live through** *vt insep* vivir durante
   ► **live together** *vi* vivir juntos
   ► **live up** *vt sep Fam* **to l. it up** pegarse la gran vida
   ► **live up to** *vt insep (promises)* cumplir con; **it didn't l. up to expectations** no fue lo que se esperaba
   ► **live with** *vt insep* (**a**) vivir con (**b**) *Fig (accept)* aceptar

live² [laɪv] *adj* (**a**) *(living)* vivo(a) (**b**) *TV & Rad* en directo, en vivo (**c**) *(ammunition)* real; *(bomb)* sin explotar; *Elec* con corriente; *Fam* **he's a real l. wire!** ¡éste no para nunca!

livelihood [ˈlaɪvlɪhʊd] *n* sustento *m*
lively [ˈlaɪvlɪ] *adj* (**livelier, liveliest**) *(person)* vivo(a); *(place)* animado(a); *Fig (interest)* entusiástico(a)
liven [ˈlaɪvən] *vt* **to l. (up)** animar
liver [ˈlɪvə(r)] *n* hígado *m*
livery [ˈlɪvərɪ] *n* librea *f*
lives [laɪvz] *pl of* life
livestock [ˈlaɪvstɒk] *n* ganado *m*
livid [ˈlɪvɪd] *adj* lívido(a); *Fam (angry)* furioso(a)
living [ˈlɪvɪŋ] **1** *adj* vivo(a)
   2 *n* vida *f*; **l. conditions** condiciones *fpl* de vida; **l. expenses** dietas *fpl*; **to earn** *or* **make one's l.** ganarse la vida; **l. room** sala *f* de estar; **l. standards** nivel *m* de vida; **l. wage** sueldo mínimo
lizard [ˈlɪzəd] *n (large)* lagarto *m*; *(small)* lagartija *f*
llama [ˈlɑːmə] *n* llama *f*
load [ləʊd] **1** *n (cargo)* carga *f*; *(weight)* peso *m*; *Elec & Tech* carga; *Fam* **loads (of)** montones de; *Fam* **that's a l. of rubbish!** ¡no son más que tonterías!
   2 *vt* cargar
   ► load up *vi & vt sep* cargar
loaded [ˈləʊdɪd] *adj* (**a**) cargado(a) (**with** de); *Fig* **a l. question** una pregunta intencionada (**b**) *Fam* **to be l.** *(rich)* estar forrado(a) (**c**) *(dice)* trucado(a)
loading [ˈləʊdɪŋ] *n* carga *f*; **l. bay** cargadero *m*
loaf¹ [ləʊf] *n (pl* **loaves**) pan *m*; *(French stick)* barra *f* de pan; *(sliced)* pan de molde
loaf² [ləʊf] *vi* **to l. (about** *or* **around)** holgazanear
loan [ləʊn] **1** *n* préstamo *m*; *Fin* empréstito *m*; **on l.** prestado(a); *(footballer)* cedido(a)
   2 *vt* prestar
loath [ləʊθ] *adj* **to be l. to do sth** ser reacio(a) a hacer algo
loathe [ləʊð] *vt* aborrecer, odiar
loathing [ˈləʊðɪŋ] *n* aborrecimiento *m*, odio *m*
loathsome [ˈləʊðsəm] *adj* odioso(a), repugnante
loaves [ləʊvz] *pl of* loaf
lobby [ˈlɒbɪ] **1** *n* (**a**) *(hall)* vestíbulo *m* (**b**) *(pressure group)* grupo *m* de presión, lobby *m*
   2 *vt* presionar
   3 *vi* ejercer presiones
lobe [ləʊb] *n* lóbulo *m*
lobster [ˈlɒbstə(r)] *n* langosta *f*
local [ˈləʊkəl] **1** *adj* local; *(person)* del pueblo; *Med* **l. anaesthetic** anestesia *f*

local; *Tel* **l. call** llamada urbana; **l. government** gobierno *m* municipal
   2 *n Fam* (**a**) **the locals** los vecinos (**b**) *Br (pub)* bar *m* del barrio
locality [ləʊˈkælɪtɪ] *n* localidad *f*
locally [ˈləʊkəlɪ] *adv* en *or* de la localidad
locate [ləʊˈkeɪt] *vt (situate)* situar, ubicar; *(find)* localizar
location [ləʊˈkeɪʃən] *n* (**a**) lugar *m*, situación *f* (**b**) *Cin* **l. shots** exteriores *mpl*; **they're on l. in Australia** están rodando en Australia
loch [lɒx, lɒk] *n Scot* lago *m*
lock¹ [lɒk] **1** *n* (**a**) *(on door etc)* cerradura *f*; *(bolt)* cerrojo *m*; *(padlock)* candado *m* (**b**) *(on canal)* esclusa *f*
   2 *vt* cerrar con llave/cerrojo/candado
   3 *vi (door etc)* cerrarse; *(wheels)* trabarse
   ► lock up *vt sep (house)* cerrar; *(jail)* meter en la cárcel
lock² [lɒk] *n Literary (of hair)* mechón *m*
locker [ˈlɒkə(r)] *n (cupboard)* armario ropero; *US* **l. room** vestuario *m* con armarios roperos
locket [ˈlɒkɪt] *n* medallón *m*
lockout [ˈlɒkaʊt] *n* cierre *m* patronal
locksmith [ˈlɒksmɪθ] *n* cerrajero *m*
lockup [ˈlɒkʌp] *n (garage)* garaje alejado de la casa; *US (prison)* cárcel *f*
loco [ˈləʊkəʊ] *adj US Fam* pirado(a)
locomotive [ləʊkəˈməʊtɪv] *n* locomotora *f*
locust [ˈləʊkəst] *n* langosta *f*
lodge [lɒdʒ] **1** *n* (**a**) *(gamekeeper's)* casa *f* del guarda; *(porter's)* portería *f*; *(hunter's)* refugio *m* (**b**) *(masonic)* logia *f* (**c**) *(beaver's den)* madriguera *f*
   2 *vt* (**a**) *(accommodate)* alojar (**b**) *(complaint)* presentar
   3 *vi* (**a**) *(live)* alojarse (**b**) *(get stuck)* meterse (**in** en)
lodger [ˈlɒdʒə(r)] *n* huésped(a) *m,f*
lodging [ˈlɒdʒɪŋ] *n* alojamiento *m*; **l. house** casa *f* de huéspedes
loft [lɒft] *n* desván *m*
lofty [ˈlɒftɪ] *adj* (**loftier, loftiest**) *Literary (high)* alto(a); *Pej (haughty)* altivo(a)
log [lɒg] **1** *n* (**a**) tronco *m*; *(for fuel)* leño *m*; **l. cabin** cabaña *f* de troncos (**b**) *Naut* diario *m* a bordo
   2 *vt (record)* registrar
   ► log in, log on *vi Comput* entrar (en sistema)
   ► log out, log off *vi Comput* salir (del sistema)
logarithm [ˈlɒgərɪðəm] *n* logaritmo *m*
log-book [ˈlɒgbʊk] *n Naut* diario *m* de a

bordo; *Av* diario de vuelo; *Aut* documentación *f* (del coche)

loggerheads ['lɒgəhedz] *npl* **to be at l. with sb** estar a mal con algn

logic ['lɒdʒɪk] *n* lógica *f*

logical ['lɒdʒɪkəl] *adj* lógico(a)

logistics [lə'dʒɪstɪks] *npl* logística *f*

logo ['ləʊgəʊ] *n* logotipo *m*

loin [lɔɪn] *n (of animal)* ijada *f; Culin (of pork)* lomo *m; (of beef)* solomillo *m*

loiter ['lɔɪtə(r)] *vi (hang about)* holgazanear; *(lag behind)* rezagarse; *(prowl)* merodear

loll [lɒl] *vi (tongue, head)* colgar
▸ **loll about, loll around** *vi* repantigarse

lollipop ['lɒlɪpɒp] *n* pirulí *m*, chupachup® *m;* **ice(d) l.** polo *m; Br Fam* **l. lady/man** = guardia que para el tráfico para que crucen los colegiales

lolly ['lɒlɪ] *n Fam* (a) *(sweet)* pirulí *m,* chupachup® *m;* **ice(d) l.** polo *m* (b) *Fam (money)* pasta *f*

London ['lʌndən] *n* Londres

Londoner ['lʌndənə(r)] *n* londinense *mf*

lone [ləʊn] *adj (solitary)* solitario(a); *(single)* solo(a)

loneliness ['ləʊnlɪnɪs] *n* soledad *f*

lonely ['ləʊnlɪ] *adj* (**lonelier, loneliest**) solo(a), solitario(a)

long¹ [lɒŋ] **1** *adj* (a) *(size)* largo(a); **how l. is the table?** ¿cuánto tiene de largo la mesa?; **it's 3 m l.** tiene 3 m de largo; **l. jump** salto *m* de longitud (b) *(time)* mucho(a); **at l. last** por fin; **how l. is the film?** ¿cuánto tiempo dura la película?
    2 *adv* mucho, mucho tiempo; **all day l.** todo el día; **as l. as the exhibition lasts** mientras dure la exposición; **as l. as** *or* **so l. as you don't mind** con tal de que no te importe; **before l.** dentro de poco; **how l. have you been here?** ¿cuánto tiempo llevas aquí?

long² [lɒŋ] *vi* añorar; **to l. for** anhelar

long-distance ['lɒŋdɪstəns] *adj* de larga distancia; **l. call** conferencia interurbana; **l. runner** corredor(a) *m,f* de fondo

longhand ['lɒŋhænd] *n* escritura *f* a mano

longing ['lɒŋɪŋ] *n (desire)* anhelo *m; (nostalgia)* nostalgia *f*

longitude ['lɒndʒɪtjuːd] *n* longitud *f*

long-playing ['lɒŋpleɪɪŋ] *adj* de larga duración; **l. record** elepé *m*

long-range ['lɒŋreɪndʒ] *adj (missile etc)* de largo alcance; *(weather forecast)* de largo plazo

long-sighted [lɒŋ'saɪtɪd] *adj* (a) *Med* présbita (b) *Fig* previsor(a)

long-standing ['lɒŋstændɪŋ] *adj* antiguo(a), de mucho tiempo

long-suffering ['lɒŋsʌfərɪŋ] *adj* sufrido(a)

long-term ['lɒŋtɜːm] *adj* a largo plazo

long-winded [lɒŋ'wɪndɪd] *adj* prolijo(a)

loo [luː] *n Br Fam* wáter *m*

look [lʊk] **1** *n* (a) *(glance)* mirada *f;* **to take a l.** at *(peep)* echar un vistazo a; *(examine)* examinar (b) *(appearance)* aspecto *m,* apariencia *f;* **I don't like the l. of it** me da mala espina (c) *(fashion)* moda *f* (d) **(good) looks** belleza *f*
    2 *vi* (a) mirar (b) *(seem)* parecer; **he looks well** tiene buena cara; **it looks delicious** tiene un aspecto buenísimo; **she looks like her father** *(resembles)* se parece a su padre
    3 *vt* mirar
▸ **look after** *vt insep* cuidar a, ocuparse de
▸ **look at** *vt insep* mirar; *Fig* **whichever way you l. at it** desde cualquier punto de vista
▸ **look away** *vi* apartar la mirada
▸ **look back** *vi* (a) mirar hacia atrás; *Fig* **since then he has never looked back** desde entonces ha ido prosperando (b) *(remember)* recordar
▸ **look down** *vi Fig* **to l. down on sth/sb** despreciar algo/a algn
▸ **look for** *vt insep* buscar
▸ **look forward to** *vt insep* esperar con ansia; **I l. forward to hearing from you** *(in letter)* espero noticias suyas
▸ **look into** *vt insep* examinar, investigar
▸ **look on 1** *vt insep (consider)* considerar
    2 *vi* quedarse mirando
▸ **look onto** *vt insep* dar a
▸ **look out** *vi* (a) **the bedroom looks out onto the garden** el dormitorio da al jardín (b) **l. out!** *(take care)* ¡cuidado!, ¡ojo!
▸ **look over** *vt sep (examine)* revisar; *(place)* inspeccionar
▸ **look round 1** *vi* mirar alrededor; *(turn head)* volver la cabeza
    2 *vt insep (house, shop)* ver
▸ **look through** *vt insep* (a) *(window)* mirar por (b) *(leaf through)* hojear; *(examine)* revisar; *(check)* registrar
▸ **look to** *vt insep* (a) *(take care of)* velar por (b) *(turn to)* recurrir a
▸ **look up 1** *vi* (a) *(glance upwards)* alzar la vista (b) *Fam (improve)* mejorar
    2 *vt sep* (a) *(look for)* buscar (b) *(visit)* ir a visitar
▸ **look upon** *vt insep* considerar
▸ **look up to** *vt insep (person)* respetar

lookout ['lʊkaʊt] n (person) centinela mf; (place) mirador m; **to be on the l. for** estar al acecho de; Fam **that's his l.!** ¡eso es asunto suyo!

loom¹ [luːm] n telar m

loom² [luːm] vi alzarse; Fig (threaten) amenazar

loony ['luːnɪ] adj (**loonier, looniest**) Fam loco(a)

loop [luːp] **1** n (**a**) lazo m (**b**) Comput bucle m

2 vt (**a**) encordar (**b**) Av **to l. the loop** rizar el rizo

loophole ['luːphəʊl] n Fig escapatoria f

loose [luːs] adj (**a**) (not secure) flojo(a); (papers, hair, clothes) suelto(a); (tongue) desatado(a); (baggy) holgado(a); **to set sb l.** soltar a algn; Fam **to be at a l. end** no saber qué hacer (**b**) (not packaged) a granel; **l. tobacco** tabaco m en hebras; **l. change** suelto m (**c**) (not exact) vago(a); (translation) libre (**d**) (lax) relajado(a); **a l. woman** una mujer fácil

loosely ['luːslɪ] adv (**a**) (approximately) aproximadamente (**b**) (vaguely) vagamente

loosen ['luːsən] **1** vt aflojar; (belt) desabrochar; Fig (restrictions) flexibilizar

2 vi (slacken) aflojarse

loot [luːt] **1** n botín m

2 vt saquear

lop [lɒp] vt podar

▸ **lop off** vt sep cortar

lope [ləʊp] vi andar a zancadas

lopsided [lɒp'saɪdɪd] adj ladeado(a)

lord [lɔːd] n (**a**) señor m; (British peer) lord m; **the House of Lords** la Cámara de los Lores; **the L. Mayor** el señor alcalde (**b**) Rel **the L.** El Señor; **good L.!** ¡Dios mío!; **the L.'s Prayer** el Padrenuestro (**c**) (judge) señoría mf

lordship ['lɔːdʃɪp] n Br **his l./your l.** su señoría

lorry ['lɒrɪ] n Br camión m; **l. driver** camionero(a) m,f; **l. load** carga f

lose [luːz] **1** vt (pt & pp **lost**) perder; **to l. time** (of clock) atrasarse

2 vi perder; **to l. to sb** perder contra algn; **to l. out** salir perdiendo

loser ['luːzə(r)] n perdedor(a) m,f

loss [lɒs] n pérdida f; **to make a l.** perder; Fig **to be at a l. for words** quedarse de una pieza; **to be at a l. what to do** no saber qué hacer

lost [lɒst] **1** adj (**a**) perdido(a); **to get l.** perderse; Fam **get l.!** ¡vete a la porra!; **l. property office,** US **l. and found department** oficina f de objetos perdidos (**b**)

(disoriented) desorientado(a); (distracted) distraído(a); **l. in thought** ensimismado(a)

2 pt & pp of **lose**

lot [lɒt] n (**a**) (fate) suerte f (**b**) **to cast lots for sth** echar algo a suertes (**c**) US (plot of land) parcela f (**d**) (in an auction) lote m (**e**) (everything) todo m; **he ate the l.** se lo comió todo (**f**) **a l. of** (much) mucho(a); (many) muchos(as); **he feels a l. better** se encuentra mucho mejor; **she reads a l.** lee mucho; Fam **lots of** montones de, cantidad de

lotion ['ləʊʃən] n loción f

lottery ['lɒtərɪ] n lotería f; **l. ticket** ≃ décimo m de lotería

loud [laʊd] **1** adj (**a**) (voice) alto(a); (noise) fuerte; (laugh) estrepitoso(a); (applause) clamoroso(a); (protests, party) ruidoso(a) (**b**) (flashy) chillón(ona) (**c**) (vulgar) hortera

2 adv **to read/think out l.** leer/pensar en voz alta

loud-hailer [laʊd'heɪlə(r)] n megáfono m

loudspeaker [laʊd'spiːkə(r)] n altavoz m

lounge [laʊndʒ] **1** n Br salón m, sala f de estar

2 vi hacer el vago

louse [laʊs] n (pl **lice**) piojo m

lousy ['laʊzɪ] adj (**lousier, lousiest**) Fam fatal; **a l. trick** una cochinada

lout [laʊt] n gamberro m

lovable ['lʌvəbəl] adj adorable

love [lʌv] **1** n (**a**) amor m (**for** por); (passion) pasión f (**for** por); **to be in l. with sb** estar enamorado(a) de algn; **to fall in l.** enamorarse; **to make l.** hacer el amor; **(with) l. (from) Mary** (in letter) un abrazo, Mary; **l. affair** amorío m; **l. letter/story** carta f/historia f de amor; **l. life** vida f sentimental (**b**) (person) amor m, cariño m; Fam chato(a) m,f; **my l.** mi amor (**c**) (in tennis) **forty l.** cuarenta a cero

2 vt (person) querer a, amar a; **he loves cooking/football** le encanta cocinar/el fútbol

lovely ['lʌvlɪ] adj (**lovelier, loveliest**) (charming) encantador(a); (beautiful) hermoso(a), precioso(a); (delicious) riquísimo(a)

lover ['lʌvə(r)] n (**a**) (sexual partner) amante mf (**b**) (enthusiast) aficionado(a) m,f, amigo(a) m,f

loving ['lʌvɪŋ] adj cariñoso(a)

low¹ [ləʊ] **1** adj (**a**) bajo(a); (neckline) escotado(a); **the L. Countries** los Países Bajos (**b**) (in quantity) bajo(a) (**c**) (poor) pobre (**d**) *(battery)* gastado(a); **l. frequency** baja frecuencia (**e**) **to feel l.** sentirse deprimido(a) (**f**) *(reprehensible)* malo(a)

2 *adv* bajo

3 *n* (**a**) *Met* área *f* de baja presión (**b**) *(low point)* punto más bajo; **to reach an all-time l.** tocar fondo

low² [ləʊ] *vi (cow)* mugir

lowdown ['ləʊdaʊn] *n Fam* pormenores *mpl*

lower ['ləʊə(r)] **1** *adj (comp of* **low**) inferior; *Typ* **l. case** minúscula *f*; **l. class** clase baja

2 *adv comp of* **low**

3 *vt* bajar; *(flag)* arriar; *(reduce)* reducir; *(price)* rebajar

lower-class ['ləʊəklɑːs] *adj* de clase baja

lowest ['ləʊɪst] **1** *adj (superl of* **low**) más bajo(a); *(price, speed)* mínimo(a)

2 *n* **at the l.** como mínimo

low-key [ləʊ'kiː] *adj* sin ceremonia

lowlands ['ləʊləndz] *npl* tierras bajas

lowly ['ləʊlɪ] *adj* (**lowlier, lowliest**) humilde

low-necked ['ləʊnekt] *adj* escotado(a)

loyal ['lɔɪəl] *adj* leal, fiel

loyalty ['lɔɪəltɪ] *n* lealtad *f*, fidelidad *f*

lozenge ['lɒzɪndʒ] *n* pastilla *f*

LP [el'piː] *n (abbr* **long-playing record**) LP *m*

L-plate ['elpleɪt] *n Br* placa *f* de la "L"

LSD [eles'diː] *n (abbr* **lysergic acid diethylamide**) LSD *m*

Ltd *Br Com (abbr* **Limited (Liability)**) ≃ S.A.

lubricant ['luːbrɪkənt] *n* lubricante *m*

lubricate ['luːbrɪkeɪt] *vt* lubricar; *(engine)* engrasar

lubrication [luːbrɪ'keɪʃən] *n* engrase *m*

lucid ['luːsɪd] *adj* lúcido(a)

luck [lʌk] *n* suerte *f*; **bad l.!** ¡mala suerte!; **good l.!** ¡(buena) suerte!; **to be in l.** estar de suerte; **to be out of l.** no tener suerte; *Fig* **to push one's l.** tentar la suerte; *Fig* **to try one's l.** probar fortuna

luckily ['lʌkɪlɪ] *adv* por suerte, afortunadamente

lucky ['lʌkɪ] *adj* (**luckier, luckiest**) *(person)* afortunado(a); *(day)* de suerte; *(move)* oportuno(a); *(charm)* de la suerte; **a l. break** una oportunidad

lucrative ['luːkrətɪv] *adj* lucrativo(a)

ludicrous ['luːdɪkrəs] *adj* absurdo(a), ridículo(a)

lug [lʌg] *vt Fam* arrastrar

luggage ['lʌgɪdʒ] *n* equipaje *m*; **l. rack**

Aut baca *f*; *Rail* portaequipajes *m inv*

lukewarm ['luːkwɔːm] *adj (water etc)* tibio(a); *Fig (reception etc)* poco entusiasta

lull [lʌl] **1** *n (in storm)* calma chicha; *(in fighting)* tregua *f*

2 *vt (cause to sleep)* adormecer; **to l. sb into a false sense of security** infundir una falsa seguridad a algn

lullaby ['lʌləbaɪ] *n* canción *f* de cuna, nana *f*

lumbago [lʌm'beɪgəʊ] *n* lumbago *m*

lumber ['lʌmbə(r)] **1** *n* (**a**) *Br (junk)* trastos viejos (**b**) *US (timber)* maderos *mpl*

2 *vt Fam* cargar (**with** de)

lumberjack ['lʌmbədʒæk] *n* leñador *m*

luminous ['luːmɪnəs] *adj* luminoso(a)

lump [lʌmp] **1** *n (of coal etc)* trozo *m*; *(of sugar, earth)* terrón *m*; *(in sauce)* grumo *m*; *(swelling)* bulto *m*; *Fam Fig (in throat)* nudo *m*; **l. sum** cantidad *f* global

2 *vt Fam (endure)* aguantar

▸ **lump together** *vt sep* apelotonar

lumpy ['lʌmpɪ] *adj* (**lumpier, lumpiest**) *(bed)* lleno(a) de bultos; *(sauce)* grumoso(a)

lunacy ['luːnəsɪ] *n* locura *f*

lunar ['luːnə(r)] *adj* lunar

lunatic ['luːnətɪk] *adj & n* loco(a) *(m,f)*; **l. asylum** manicomio *m*

lunch [lʌntʃ] **1** *n* comida *f*, almuerzo *m*; **l. hour** hora *f* de comer

2 *vi* comer, almorzar

luncheon ['lʌntʃən] *n Old-fashioned Fml* almuerzo *m*; **l. voucher** vale *m* de comida; **(pork) l. meat** carne *f* de cerdo troceada, chopped *m*

lunchtime ['lʌntʃtaɪm] *n* hora *f* de comer

lung [lʌŋ] *n* pulmón *m*

lunge [lʌndʒ] **1** *n* arremetida *f*

2 *vi* **to l. (forward)** arremeter; **to l. (out) at sb** arremeter contra algn

lurch [lɜːtʃ] **1** *n* (**a**) *(of vehicle)* sacudida *f*; *(of person)* tambaleo *m* (**b**) *Fam* **to leave sb in the l.** dejar a algn en la cuneta

2 *vi (vehicle)* dar sacudidas; *(person)* tambalearse

lure [lʊə(r)] **1** *n (decoy)* señuelo *m*; *(bait)* cebo *m*; *Fig (charm)* aliciente *m*

2 *vt* atraer con engaños

lurid ['lʊərɪd] *adj* (**a**) *(gruesome)* espeluznante; *(sensational)* sensacionalista (**b**) *(gaudy)* chillón(ona)

lurk [lɜːk] *vi (lie in wait)* estar al acecho; *(hide)* esconderse

luscious ['lʌʃəs] *adj (food)* delicioso(a)

lush [lʌʃ] *adj (vegetation)* exuberante

lust [lʌst] **1** *n (sexual desire)* lujuria *f*; *(craving)* ansia *f*; *(greed)* codicia *f*
 2 *vi* **to l. after sth/sb** codiciar algo/ desear a algn
lustre, *US* **luster** [ˈlʌstə(r)] *n* lustre *m*
lusty [ˈlʌstɪ] *adj* (**lustier, lustiest**) robusto(a)
lute [luːt] *n* laúd *m*
Luxembourg [ˈlʌksəmbɜːg] *n* Luxemburgo
luxuriant [lʌgˈzjʊərɪənt] *adj (plants)* exuberante; *(hair etc)* abundante
luxurious [lʌgˈzjʊərɪəs] *adj* lujoso(a)
luxury [ˈlʌkʃərɪ] *n* lujo *m*; **l. flat** piso *m* de lujo

📝 Note that the Spanish word **lujuria** is a false friend and is never a translation for the English word **luxury**. In Spanish, **lujuria** means "lust".

lychee [ˈlaɪtʃiː] *n* lichi *m*
lying [ˈlaɪɪŋ] **1** *adj* mentiroso(a)
 2 *n* mentiras *fpl*
lynch [lɪntʃ] *vt* linchar
lyre [laɪə(r)] *n Mus* lira *f*
lyric [ˈlɪrɪk] **1** *adj* lírico(a)
 2 *n* (**a**) *(poem)* poema lírico (**b**) **lyrics** *(words of song)* letra *f*
lyrical [ˈlɪrɪkəl] *adj* lírico(a)

M, m [em] *n (the letter)* M, m *f*
m (**a**) (*abbr* **metre(s)**) m (**b**) (*abbr* **million(s)**) m
mac [mæk] *n Br Fam (raincoat)* impermeable *m*, gabardina *f*
macabre [mə'kɑːbrə] *adj* macabro(a)
mac(c)aroni [mækə'rəʊnɪ] *n* macarrones *mpl*
mace¹ [meɪs] *n (club, ceremonial staff)* maza *f*
mace² [meɪs] *n (spice)* macis *f inv*
machine [mə'ʃiːn] **1** *n* máquina *f*; **m. gun** ametralladora *f*; **m. language** lenguaje *m* máquina
    2 *vt* trabajar a máquina
machine-gun [mə'ʃiːngʌn] *vt* ametrallar
machine-readable [mə'ʃiːn'riːdəbəl] *adj Comput* para ser leído(a) por ordenador *or Am* computadora
machinery [mə'ʃiːnərɪ] *n (machines)* maquinaria *f*; *(workings of machine)* mecanismo *m*; *Fig* **the bureaucratic m.** la maquinaria burocrática
macintosh 'mækɪntɒʃ] *n* = **mackintosh**
mackerel ['mækrəl] *n (pl* **mackerel***)* caballa *f*
mackintosh ['mækɪntɒʃ] *n* impermeable *m*
macroeconomics [mækrəʊiːkə'nɒmɪks] *n sing* macroeconomía *f*
mad [mæd] *adj* (**madder, maddest**) (**a**) loco(a); *(animal)* furioso(a); *(dog)* rabioso(a); **to be m.** estar loco(a); **to drive sb m.** volver loco(a) a algn; **to go m.** volverse loco(a); **you must be m.!** ¿estás loco?; *Fam* **m. cow disease** el mal de las vacas locas (**b**) *(idea, plan)* disparatado(a) (**c**) *Fam* **to be m. about sth/sb** estar loco(a) por algo/algn (**d**) *esp US Fam* **to be m. at sb** estar enfadado(a) con algn (**e**) *(gallop, race etc)* desenfrenado(a)
madam ['mædəm] *n* (**a**) señora *f*; **Dear M.** *(in letter)* Muy señora mía, Estimada señora (**b**) *(of brothel)* madam *f*
madden ['mædən] *vt* volver loco(a)
maddening ['mædənɪŋ] *adj* exasperante
made [meɪd] *pt & pp of* **make**

Madeira [mə'dɪərə] *n* (**a**) *(island)* Madeira (**b**) *(wine)* madeira *m*; **M. cake** bizcocho *m*
made-to-measure ['meɪdtə'meʒə(r)] *adj* hecho(a) a (la) medida
made-up ['meɪdʌp] *adj* (**a**) *(face, person)* maquillado(a); *(eyes, lips)* pintado(a) (**b**) *(story, excuse)* inventado(a)
madly ['mædlɪ] *adv Fam (extremely)* terriblemente; **to be m. in love with sb** estar locamente enamorado(a) de algn
madman ['mædmən] *n* loco *m*
madness ['mædnɪs] *n* locura *f*
Madrid [mə'drɪd] *n* Madrid
Mafia ['mæfɪə] *n* mafia *f*
magazine [mægə'ziːn] *n* (**a**) *(periodical)* revista *f* (**b**) *(in rifle)* recámara *f* (**c**) *Mil (storehouse)* almacén *m*; *(for explosives)* polvorín *m*
maggot ['mægət] *n* larva *f*, gusano *m*
magic ['mædʒɪk] **1** *n* magia *f*
    2 *adj* (**a**) mágico(a); **m. wand** varita mágica (**b**) *Fam (wonderful)* estupendo(a)
magical ['mædʒɪkəl] *adj* mágico(a)
magician [mə'dʒɪʃən] *n* (**a**) *(wizard)* mago(a) *m,f* (**b**) *(conjurer)* prestidigitador(a) *m,f*
magistrate ['mædʒɪstreɪt] *n* juez *mf* de primera instancia; **magistrates' court** juzgado *m* de primera instancia
magnanimous [mæg'nænɪməs] *adj* magnánimo(a)
magnet ['mægnɪt] *n* imán *m*
magnetic [mæg'netɪk] *adj* magnético(a); *Fig (personality)* carismático(a); **m. tape** cinta magnetofónica
magnetism ['mægnɪtɪzəm] *n* magnetismo *m*
magnificence [mæg'nɪfɪsəns] *n* magnificencia *f*
magnificent [mæg'nɪfɪsənt] *adj* magnífico(a)
magnify ['mægnɪfaɪ] *vt* (**a**) *(enlarge)* aumentar (**b**) *Fig (exaggerate)* exagerar
magnifying glass ['mægnɪfaɪŋglɑːs] *n* lupa *f*
magnitude ['mægnɪtjuːd] *n* magnitud *f*
magpie ['mægpaɪ] *n* urraca *f*

mahogany [mə'hɒgənɪ] **1** *n* caoba *f*
2 *adj* de caoba

maid [meɪd] *n* (**a**) criada *f*, *Andes, RP*
mucama *f* (**b**) *Pej* old m. solterona *f*

maiden ['meɪdən] **1** *n Literary* doncella *f*
2 *adj* (**a**) *(unmarried)* soltera; **m. aunt** tía
soltera; **m. name** apellido *m* de soltera
(**b**) *(voyage, flight)* inaugural

mail [meɪl] **1** *n* correo *m*; **by m.** por correo;
m. order venta *f* por correo; **m. train** tren
m correo
2 *vt (post)* echar al buzón; *(send)* enviar
por correo

mailbox ['meɪlbɒks] *n US* buzón *m*

mailing list ['meɪlɪŋlɪst] *n* lista *f* de direcciones

mailman ['meɪlmæn] *n US* cartero *m*

maim [meɪm] *vt* lisiar

main [meɪn] **1** *adj (problem, door etc)*
principal; *(square, mast, sail)* mayor; *(office)* central; **the m. thing is to keep calm**
lo esencial es mantener la calma; *Culin*
m. course plato *m* principal; **m. road**
carretera *f* principal; *US* **M. Street** la
Calle Mayor
2 *n* (**a**) *(pipe, wire)* conducto *m* principal; **the mains** *(water or gas system)* la
cañería maestra; *Elec* la red eléctrica; **a
radio that works on battery or mains** una
radio que funciona con pilas o con corriente (**b**) **in the m.** por regla general

mainframe ['meɪnfreɪm] *n* **m. computer**
computer *or Am* ordenadora *f* central

mainland ['meɪnlənd] *n* continente *m*

mainly ['meɪnlɪ] *adv* principalmente, sobre todo; *(for the most part)* en su mayoría

mainstay ['meɪnsteɪ] *n Fig* sustento *m*,
sostén *m*

mainstream ['meɪnstriːm] *n* corriente *f*
principal

maintain [meɪn'teɪn] *vt* mantener;
(conversation) sostener; *(silence, appearances)* guardar; *(road, machine)* conservar en buen estado

maintenance ['meɪntənəns] *n* (**a**) mantenimiento *m* (**b**) *(divorce allowance)*
pensión *f*

maisonette [meɪzə'net] *n Br* dúplex *m*

maître d' ['meɪtrə'diː] *n US* maître *mf*

maize [meɪz] *n* maíz *m*

majestic [mə'dʒestɪk] *adj* majestuoso(a)

majesty ['mædʒɪstɪ] *n* majestad *f*

major ['meɪdʒə(r)] **1** *adj* (**a**) principal,
mayor; *(contribution, operation)* importante (**b**) *Mus* mayor
2 *n* (**a**) *Mil* comandante *m* (**b**) *US Univ*
especialidad *f*

3 *vi US Univ* **to m. in** especializarse en

Majorca [mə'jɔːkə] *n* Mallorca

Majorcan [mə'jɔːkən] *adj & n* mallor-
quín(ina) *(m,f)*

majority [mə'dʒɒrɪtɪ] *n* mayoría *f*; **to be
in the m.** ser (la) mayoría

make [meɪk] (*pt & pp* **made**) **1** *vt* (**a**)
hacer; *(manufacture)* fabricar; *(create)*
crear; *(clothes, curtains)* confeccionar;
(meal) preparar; *(payment)* efectuar;
(speech) pronunciar; *(decision)* tomar;
(mistake) cometer; **to be made of** ser de;
to m. a noise hacer ruido
(**b**) *(render)* poner, volver; *(convert)*
convertir (**into** en); *(appoint)* nombrar;
he made it clear that ... dejó claro que ...
(**c**) *(force, compel)* obligar; *(cause)* causar; **to m. do with sth** arreglárselas con
algo
(**d**) *(earn)* ganar; **to m. a living** ganarse
la vida; **to m. a name for oneself** hacerse
famoso(a); *Fig* **to m. the best of sth** sacar
partido de algo
(**e**) **7 and 5 m. 12** 7 y 5 son 12
(**f**) *(calculate, reckon)* calcular; **what
time do you m. it?** ¿qué hora tienes?
(**g**) *(think)* opinar; **I don't know what to
m. of it** no sé qué pensar de eso; **it
doesn't m. sense** no tiene sentido
(**h**) *(achieve)* alcanzar, conseguir
(**i**) **it will m. or break her** será su consagración o su ruina
(**j**) **to m. a fresh start** volver a empezar
2 *vi* (**a**) hacer; **to m. sure of sth** asegurarse de algo
(**b**) **she made as if to leave** hizo como si
quisiera marcharse
3 *n* (**a**) *(brand)* marca *f*
(**b**) *Fam* **to be on the m.** andar tras el
dinero

▸ **make for** *vt insep* (**a**) *(move towards)*
dirigirse hacia; *(attack)* atacar a (**b**) **this
makes for less work** esto ahorra trabajo

▸ **make out 1** *vt sep* (**a**) *(list, receipt)*
hacer; *(cheque)* extender (**b**) *(perceive)*
distinguir; *(writing)* descifrar (**c**) *(understand)* entender (**d**) *(claim)* pretender (**e**)
to m. out a case for doing sth exponer los
argumentos para hacer algo
2 *vi* **how did you m. out?** ¿qué tal te
fue?

▸ **make up 1** *vt sep* (**a**) *(parcel, list)* hacer;
(prescription) preparar; *(assemble)* montar (**b**) *(story)* inventar (**c**) *(apply
cosmetics to)* maquillar; *(one's face)* maquillarse (**d**) *(loss)* compensar; *(lost
time)* recuperar (**e**) *(constitute)* componer (**f**) **to m. it up (with sb)** hacer las

paces (con algn) (**g**) **to m. up one's mind** decidirse

2 *vi* maquillarse

▸ **make up to 1** *vt insep Br Fam* **to m. up to sb** congraciarse con algn

2 *vt sep* **to m. it up to sb for sth** compensar a algn por algo

make-believe ['meɪkbɪliːv] *n (fantasy)* fantasía *f; (pretence)* fingimiento *m;* **to live in a world of m.** vivir en un mundo de ensueño

maker ['meɪkə(r)] *n* fabricante *mf*

makeshift ['meɪkʃɪft] *adj (improvised)* improvisado(a); *(temporary)* provisional

make-up ['meɪkʌp] *n* (**a**) *(cosmetics)* maquillaje *m;* **m. remover** desmaquillador *m* (**b**) *(composition)* composición *f; (character)* carácter *m*

making ['meɪkɪŋ] *n* (**a**) *(manufacture)* fabricación *f; (preparation)* preparación *f* (**b**) **he has the makings of a politician** tiene madera de político

malaise [mæ'leɪz] *n* malestar *m*

malaria [mə'leərɪə] *n* malaria *f*

Malay [mə'leɪ] **1** *adj* malayo(a)

2 *n* (**a**) *(person)* malayo(a) *m,f* (**b**) *(language)* malayo *m*

Malaysia [mə'leɪzɪə] *n* Malasia

male [meɪl] **1** *adj (animal, plant)* macho; *(person)* varón; *(sex)* masculino; *Pej* **m. chauvinism** machismo *m*

2 *n (person)* varón *m; (animal, plant)* macho *m*

malevolent [mə'levələnt] *adj* malévolo(a)

malfunction [mæl'fʌŋkʃən] **1** *n* mal funcionamiento *m*

2 *vi* funcionar mal

malice ['mælɪs] *n* malicia *f; Jur* **with m. aforethought** con premeditación

malicious [mə'lɪʃəs] *adj* malévolo(a)

malign [mə'laɪn] **1** *adj* maligno(a); *(influence)* perjudicial

2 *vt* calumniar, difamar

malignant [mə'lɪgnənt] *adj* (**a**) *(person)* malvado(a) (**b**) *Med* maligno(a)

mall [mɔːl] *n US* centro *m* comercial

malleable ['mælɪəbəl] *adj* maleable

mallet ['mælɪt] *n* mazo *m*

malnutrition [mælnjuː'trɪʃən] *n* desnutrición *f*

malpractice [mæl'præktɪs] *n* procedimiento *m* ilegal; *Med* negligencia *f*

malt [mɔːlt] *n* malta *f*

Malta ['mɔːltə] *n* Malta

mammal ['mæməl] *n* mamífero *m*

mammary ['mæmərɪ] *adj* **m. gland** mama *f*

mammoth ['mæməθ] **1** *n Zool* mamut *m*

2 *adj* gigantesco(a)

man [mæn] **1** *n (pl* **men**) (**a**) *(adult male)* hombre *m;* **old m.** viejo *m;* **young m.** joven *m; Fig* **he's a m. of his word** es hombre de palabra; *Fig* **the m. in the street** el hombre de la calle; **m. Friday** factótum *m; Fam* **dirty old m.** viejo verde (**b**) *(humanity)* el hombre (**c**) *(husband)* marido *m; (partner)* pareja *f* (**d**) **our m. in Madrid** nuestro representante en Madrid (**e**) *(in chess)* pieza *f*

2 *vt (boat, plane)* tripular; *(post)* servir; **manned flight** vuelo tripulado

manage ['mænɪdʒ] **1** *vt* (**a**) *(company, household)* llevar; *(money, affairs, person)* manejar (**b**) *(succeed)* conseguir; **to m. to do sth** lograr hacer algo

2 *vi (cope physically)* poder; *(esp financially)* arreglárselas; **we're managing** vamos tirando

manageable ['mænɪdʒəbəl] *adj* manejable

management ['mænɪdʒmənt] *n* dirección *f*

manager ['mænɪdʒə(r)] *n* (**a**) *(of company, bank)* director(a) *m,f; (head of department)* jefe(a) *m,f* (**b**) *(of pop group etc)* mánager *m* (**c**) *Sport* entrenador *m*

manageress [mænɪdʒə'res] *n (of shop, restaurant)* encargada *f; (of company)* directora *f*

managerial [mænɪ'dʒɪərɪəl] *adj* directivo(a)

managing ['mænɪdʒɪŋ] *adj* directivo(a); **m. director** director(a) *m,f* gerente

mandarin ['mændərɪn] *n* **m. (orange)** mandarina *f*

mandate ['mændeɪt] *n* mandato *m*

mandatory ['mændətərɪ] *adj Fml* obligatorio(a)

mane [meɪn] *n (of horse)* crin *f; (of lion)* melena *f*

maneuver [mə'nuːvər] *n, vt & vi US =* manoeuvre

manfully ['mænfʊlɪ] *adv* valientemente

manger ['meɪndʒə(r)] *n* pesebre *m*

mangle¹ ['mæŋgəl] *n (for wringing)* rodillo *m*

mangle² ['mæŋgəl] *vt (crush)* aplastar; *(destroy by cutting)* despedazar

mango ['mæŋgəʊ] *n (pl* **mangoes**) mango *m*

mangy ['meɪndʒɪ] *adj* (**mangier, mangiest**) *(animal)* sarnoso(a); *Fam (carpet)* raído(a)

manhandle ['mænhændəl] *vt* maltratar

manhole ['mænhəʊl] *n* boca *f* de acceso

manhood ['mænhʊd] *n* (**a**) *(age)* mayoría

f de edad; **to reach m.** llegar a la edad viril
(**b**) *(manly qualities)* virilidad *f*
mania ['meɪnɪə] *n* manía *f*
maniac ['meɪnɪæk] *n* maníaco(a) *m,f*;
Fam loco(a) *m,f*
manic ['mænɪk] *adj* maníaco(a)
manic-depressive ['mænɪkdɪ'presɪv]
adj & n maníaco(a) *(m,f)* depresivo(a)
manicure ['mænɪkjʊə(r)] **1** *n* manicura *f*
2 *vt* **to m.** one's nails hacerse la manicura
manifest ['mænɪfest] *Fml* **1** *adj* manifies-
to(a)
2 *vt* manifestar
manifesto [mænɪ'festəʊ] *n* programa *m*
electoral
manifold ['mænɪfəʊld] *adj Fml (many)*
múltiples; *(varied)* diversos(as)
manipulate [mə'nɪpjʊleɪt] *vt* (**a**) manipular (**b**) *Fig (accounts etc)* falsificar
mankind [mæn'kaɪnd] *n* la humanidad,
el género humano
manly ['mænlɪ] *adj* (**manlier, manliest**)
varonil, viril
man-made ['mænmeɪd] *adj (lake)* artificial; *(fibres, fabric)* sintético(a)
manner ['mænə(r)] *n* (**a**) *(way, method)*
manera *f*, modo *m*; **in this m.** de esta
manera (**b**) *(way of behaving)* forma *f* de
ser (**c**) *Fml (type, class)* clase *f* (**d**) *(etiquette)* **(good) manners** buenos modales;
bad manners falta *f* de educación
mannerism ['mænərɪzəm] *n (gesture)*
gesto *m*; *(affectation)* amaneramiento *m*
manoeuvre [mə'nu:və(r)] **1** *n* maniobra *f*
2 *vt* maniobrar; *(person)* manejar
3 *vi* maniobrar
manor ['mænə(r)] *n* **m. house** casa solariega
manpower ['mænpaʊə(r)] *n* mano *f* de
obra
mansion ['mænʃən] *n* casa *f* grande; *(in
country)* casa solariega
manslaughter ['mænslɔːtə(r)] *n* homicidio involuntario
mantelpiece ['mæntəlpiːs] *n (shelf)* repisa *f* de chimenea; *(fireplace)* chimenea *f*
mantle ['mæntəl] *n Fig (of snow)* manto
m, capa *f*

> *𝒩* Note that the Spanish word **mantel** is a
> false friend and is never a translation for the
> English word **mantle**. In Spanish, **mantel**
> means "tablecloth".

manual ['mænjʊəl] *adj & n* manual *(m)*
manufacture [mænjʊ'fæktʃə(r)] **1** *vt* fabricar
2 *n* fabricación *f*

manufacturer [mænjʊ'fæktʃərə(r)] *n* fabricante *mf*
manure [mə'njʊə(r)] *n* abono *m*, estiércol *m*
manuscript ['mænjʊskrɪpt] *n* manuscrito *m*
many ['menɪ] **1** *adj* (**more, most**) mu-
cho(a)/muchos(as); **a great m.** muchísi-
mos(as); **as m. ... as ...** tantos(as) ... como
...; **how m. days?** ¿cuántos días?; **m. a
time** muchas veces; **so m. flowers!**
¡cuántas flores!; **too m.** demasiados(as)
2 *pron* muchos(as)
map [mæp] **1** *n (of country)* mapa *m*; *(of
town, bus route)* plano *m*
2 *vt* trazar un mapa de
▶ **map out** *vt sep (route)* trazar en un
mapa; *Fig (future etc)* planear
maple ['meɪpəl] *n* arce *m*
mar [mɑ:(r)] *vt* estropear; **to m. sb's enjoyment** aguarle la fiesta a algn
marathon ['mærəθən] *n* maratón *m*
marble ['mɑːbəl] **1** *n* (**a**) *(stone)* mármol
m (**b**) *(glass ball)* canica *f*
2 *adj* de mármol
March [mɑːtʃ] *n* marzo *m*
march [mɑːtʃ] **1** *n* (**a**) *Mil* marcha *f*; *Fig* **to
steal a m. on sb** tomar la delantera a algn;
m. past desfile *m* (**b**) *(demonstration)*
manifestación *f*
2 *vi* (**a**) marchar (**b**) *(demonstrate)* manifestarse
3 *vt Mil* hacer marchar
mare [meə(r)] *n* yegua *f*
margarine [mɑːdʒə'riːn] *n* margarina *f*
margin ['mɑːdʒɪn] *n* margen *m*; *Fig* **to
win by a narrow m.** ganar por escaso
margen; **m. of error** *(in statistics)* margen
de error
marginal ['mɑːdʒɪnəl] *adj* marginal; *Pol*
m. seat escaño *m* pendiente
marginally ['mɑːdʒɪnəlɪ] *adv* ligeramente
marigold ['mærɪɡəʊld] *n* caléndula *f*
marijuana, marihuana [mærɪ'hwɑːnə]
n marihuana *f*, marijuana *f*
marinate ['mærɪneɪt] *vt* adobar
marine [mə'riːn] **1** *adj* marino(a)
2 *n* soldado *m* de infantería de marina;
Br **the Marines,** *US* **the M. Corps** la infantería de marina
marital ['mærɪtəl] *adj* matrimonial; **m.
status** estado *m* civil
maritime ['mærɪtaɪm] *adj* marítimo(a)
marjoram ['mɑːdʒərəm] *n* mejorana *f*
mark¹ [mɑːk] **1** *n* (**a**) *(left by blow etc)*
señal *f*; *(stain)* mancha *f*; *Fig* **to make
one's m.** distinguirse (**b**) *(sign, token)*

señal *f*; *(indication)* indicio *m* (**c**) *Br (in exam etc)* nota *f*; **to get high marks** sacar buenas notas (**d**) *Fig* **to hit the m.** dar en el clavo; *Fig* **to be wide of the m.** estar lejos de la verdad
   2 *vt* (**a**) *(stain)* manchar (**b**) *(with tick, cross)* señalar (**c**) *(exam)* corregir; *(student)* dar notas a (**d**) **10 percent off marked price** *(sign)* descuento del 10 por ciento sobre el precio indicado (**e**) **m. my words** fíjate en lo que te digo (**f**) *Sport* marcar (**g**) **to m. time** *Mil* marcar el paso; *Fig* hacer tiempo
   ▸ **mark out** *vt sep* (**a**) *(area)* delimitar (**b**) **to m. sb out for** destinar a algn a
mark² [mɑːk] *n (unit of currency)* marco *m*
marked [mɑːkt] *adj (noticeable)* marcado(a), acusado(a)
marker ['mɑːkə(r)] *n* (**a**) *(bookmark)* registro *m* (**b**) *Sport* marcador(a) *m,f* (**c**) *(pen)* rotulador *m* fluorescente
market ['mɑːkɪt] **1** *n* mercado *m*; **on the m.** en venta; **m. forces** tendencias *fpl* del mercado; *Br* **m. garden** *(small)* huerto *m*; *(large)* huerta *f*; *Br* **m. gardener** hortelano(a) *m,f*; **m. price** precio *m* de mercado; **m. research** estudio *m* de mercado
   2 *vt (sell)* poner en venta; *(promote)* promocionar
marketable ['mɑːkɪtəbəl] *adj* comerciable
marketing ['mɑːkɪtɪŋ] *n* marketing *m*, mercadotecnia *f*
marketplace ['mɑːkɪtpleɪs] *n* mercado *m*
marksman ['mɑːksmən] *n* tirador *m*
marmalade ['mɑːməleɪd] *n* mermelada *f (de cítricos)*
maroon [mə'ruːn] *adj* (de color) granate
marooned [mə'ruːnd] *adj* bloqueado(a)
marquee [mɑː'kiː] *n* (**a**) *Br (tent)* carpa *f* (**b**) *US (of building)* marquesina *f*
marquess, marquis ['mɑːkwɪs] *n* marqués *m*
marriage ['mærɪdʒ] *n (state)* matrimonio *m*; *(wedding)* boda *f*; **m. bureau** agencia *f* matrimonial; **m. certificate** certificado *m* de matrimonio
married ['mærɪd] *adj* casado(a); **m. life** vida *f* conyugal
marrow ['mærəʊ] *n* (**a**) **(bone) m.** médula *f* (**b**) **(vegetable) m.** calabacín *m*
marry ['mærɪ] *vt (take in marriage)* casarse con; *(give in marriage)* casar (**to** con); *(unite in marriage)* casar; **to get married** casarse
Mars [mɑːz] *n* Marte *m*
marsh [mɑːʃ] *n* pantano *m*; **salt m.** marisma *f*

marshal ['mɑːʃəl] **1** *n* (**a**) *Mil* mariscal *m* (**b**) *Br (at sports event etc)* oficial *mf* (**c**) *US (sheriff)* alguacil *m* (**d**) *US (of police or fire department)* jefe *m*
   2 *vt* (**a**) *Mil* formar (**b**) *(facts etc)* ordenar
marshy ['mɑːʃɪ] *adj* (**marshier, marshiest**) pantanoso(a)
martial ['mɑːʃəl] *adj* marcial; **m. arts** artes *fpl* marciales; **m. law** ley *f* marcial
Martian ['mɑːʃən] *adj & n* marciano(a) *(m,f)*
martyr ['mɑːtə(r)] **1** *n* mártir *mf*
   2 *vt* martirizar
martyrdom ['mɑːtədəm] *n* martirio *m*
marvel ['mɑːvəl] **1** *n* maravilla *f*
   2 *vi* **to m. at** maravillarse de
marvellous, *US* **marvelous** ['mɑːvələs] *adj* maravilloso(a)
Marxism ['mɑːksɪzəm] *n* marxismo *m*
Marxist ['mɑːksɪst] *adj & n* marxista *(mf)*
marzipan ['mɑːzɪpæn] *n* mazapán *m*
mascara [mæ'skɑːrə] *n* rímel *m*

> Note that the Spanish word **máscara** is a false friend and is never a translation for the English word **mascara**. In Spanish, **máscara** means "mask".

mascot ['mæskət] *n* mascota *f*
masculine ['mæskjʊlɪn] *adj* masculino(a); *(woman)* hombruna
mash [mæʃ] **1** *n (for animals)* afrecho *m*
   2 *vt* **to m. (up)** machacar; **mashed potatoes** puré *m* de patatas *or Am* papas
mask [mɑːsk] **1** *n* máscara *f*; *(of doctor, dentist etc)* mascarilla *f*
   2 *vt* enmascarar; *Fig (conceal)* ocultar (**from** de)
masochist ['mæsəkɪst] *adj & n* masoquista *(mf)*
mason ['meɪsən] *n* (**a**) *(builder)* albañil *m* (**b**) *(freemason)* masón *m*, francmasón *m*
masonic [mə'sɒnɪk] *adj* masónico(a)
masonry ['meɪsənrɪ] *n (stonework)* albañilería *f*
masquerade [mæskə'reɪd] **1** *n (pretence)* farsa *f*
   2 *vi* **to m. as** hacerse pasar por
mass¹ [mæs] *n Rel* misa *f*; **to say m.** decir misa
mass² [mæs] **1** *n* (**a**) masa *f* (**b**) *(large quantity)* montón *m*; *(of people)* multitud *f* (**c**) **the masses** las masas
   2 *adj* masivo(a); **m. media** medios *mpl* de comunicación (de masas); **m. production** fabricación *f* en serie
   3 *vi (people)* congregarse; *Mil* concentrarse

massacre ['mæsəkə(r)] **1** *n* masacre *f*
2 *vt* masacrar
massage ['mæsɑːʒ, mə'sɑːdʒ] **1** *n* masaje *m*
2 *vt* (**a**) dar masajes a (**b**) *Fig (figures)* amañar
masseur [mæ'sɜː(r)] *n* masajista *m*
masseuse [mæ'sɜːz] *n* masajista *f*
massive ['mæsɪv] *adj* enorme; *(heart attack)* grave
mast [mɑːst] *n* (**a**) *Naut* mástil *m* (**b**) *Rad & TV* torre *f*
master ['mɑːstə(r)] **1** *n* (**a**) *(of dog, servant)* amo *m*; *(of household)* señor *m* (**b**) *Br (teacher)* profesor *m* (**c**) *Univ* **m.'s degree** ≃ máster *m* (**d**) *(expert)* maestro *m* (**e**) *(boy)* **M. James Brown** el señor James Brown
2 *adj* (**a**) **m. copy** original *m*; **m. key** llave *f* maestra (**b**) *(expert)* maestro(a)
3 *vt* (**a**) *(person, situation)* dominar (**b**) *(subject, skill)* llegar a dominar
masterful ['mɑːstəfʊl] *adj* autoritario(a); *(imperious)* imperioso(a); *(personality)* dominante
masterly ['mɑːstəlɪ] *adj* magistral
mastermind ['mɑːstəmaɪnd] **1** *n (person)* cerebro *m*
2 *vt* ser el cerebro de
masterpiece ['mɑːstəpiːs] *n* obra *f* maestra
mastery ['mɑːstərɪ] *n* (**a**) *(control)* dominio *m* (**of** de) (**b**) *(skill, expertise)* maestría *f*
masturbate ['mæstəbeɪt] *vi* masturbarse
mat¹ [mæt] *n (rug)* alfombrilla *f*; *(doormat)* felpudo *m*; *(rush mat)* estera *f*; *Sport* colchoneta *f*
mat² [mæt] *adj* mate
match¹ [mætʃ] *n* cerilla *f*, fósforo *m*
match² [mætʃ] **1** *n* (**a**) *Sport* partido *m*; *(in boxing)* combate *m* (**b**) *Fig* **to meet one's m.** *(equal)* encontrar uno la horma de su zapato
2 *vt* (**a**) *(equal, be the equal of)* igualar (**b**) *(be in harmony with)* armonizar; **they are well matched** *(teams)* van iguales; *(couple)* hacen buena pareja (**c**) *(colours, clothes)* hacer juego con; *(pair of socks, gloves)* ser el compañero de
3 *vi (harmonize)* hacer juego
matchbox ['mætʃbɒks] *n* caja *f* de cerillas
matching ['mætʃɪŋ] *adj* que hace juego
mate [meɪt] **1** *n* (**a**) *(at school, work)* compañero(a) *m,f*, colega *mf*; *Br Fam (friend)* amigo(a) *m,f* (**b**) *Zool (male)* macho *m*; *(female)* hembra *f* (**c**) *(assistant)*

ayudante *mf* (**d**) *Naut* **first/second m.** primer/segundo oficial
2 *vt Zool* aparear
3 *vi Zool* aparearse
material [mə'tɪərɪəl] **1** *n* (**a**) *(substance)* materia *f* (**b**) *(cloth)* tejido *m*, tela *f* (**c**) *(information)* material *m* (**d**) **materials** *(ingredients, equipment)* materiales *mpl*
2 *adj* (**a**) substancial (**b**) *(not spiritual)* material
materialistic [mətɪərɪə'lɪstɪk] *adj* materialista
materialize [mə'tɪərɪəlaɪz] *vi* (**a**) *(hopes)* realizarse; *(plan, idea)* concretarse (**b**) *(show up)* presentarse
maternal [mə'tɜːnəl] *adj* maternal; *(uncle etc)* materno(a)
maternity [mə'tɜːnɪtɪ] *n* maternidad *f*; **m. dress** vestido *m* premamá; **m. hospital** maternidad
math [mæθ] *n US* = **maths**
mathematical [mæθə'mætɪkəl] *adj* matemático(a)
mathematician [mæθəmə'tɪʃən] *n* matemático(a) *m,f*
mathematics [mæθə'mætɪks] *n sing* matemáticas *fpl*
maths [mæθs] *n sing Fam* matemáticas *fpl*
matinée ['mætɪneɪ] *n Cin* sesión *f* de tarde; *Th* función *f* de tarde
mating ['meɪtɪŋ] *n* apareamiento *m*; **m. call** reclamo *m*; **m. season** época *f* de celo
matrices ['meɪtrɪsiːz] *pl of* **matrix**
matriculation [mətrɪkjʊ'leɪʃən] *n Univ* matriculación *f*
matrimonial [mætrɪ'məʊnɪəl] *adj* matrimonial
matrimony ['mætrɪmənɪ] *n* matrimonio *m*; *(married life)* vida *f* conyugal
matrix ['meɪtrɪks] *n (pl* **matrices**) matriz *f*
matron ['meɪtrən] *n (in hospital)* enfermera *f* jefe
matronly ['meɪtrənlɪ] *adj* madura y recia
matt [mæt] *adj* mate
matted ['mætɪd] *adj* enmarañado(a)
matter ['mætə(r)] **1** *n* (**a**) *(affair, question)* asunto *m*; **as a m. of course** por rutina; **as a m. of fact** en realidad; **that's another m.** eso es otra cosa (**b**) *(problem)* **what's the m.?** ¿qué pasa? (**c**) **no m. what he does** haga lo que haga; **no m. when** no importa cuando; **no m. where you go** dondequiera que vayas; **no m. how clever he is** por muy inteligente que sea; **no m. how** como sea (**d**) *(substance)* materia *f*, sustancia *f* (**e**) *(content)* contenido *m*;

(subject) tema *m* (**f**) *Med (pus)* pus *m*

  2 *vi* importar; **it doesn't m.** no importa, da igual

matter-of-fact [ˈmætərəvˈfækt] *adj* *(person)* práctico(a); *(account)* realista; *(style)* prosaico(a)

mattress [ˈmætrɪs] *n* colchón *f*

mature [məˈtʃʊə(r)] **1** *adj* maduro(a); *Fin* vencido(a)

  2 *vi* madurar; *Fin* vencer

  3 *vt* madurar

maturity [məˈtʃʊərɪtɪ] *n* madurez *f*

maul [mɔːl] *vt* (**a**) *(wound)* agredir (**b**) *(handle roughly)* maltratar (**c**) *(touch in unpleasant way)* sobar

mauve [məʊv] *adj & n* malva *(m)*

max [mæks] *n* (*abbr* **maximum**) máx

maxim [ˈmæksɪm] *n* máxima *f*

maxima [ˈmæksɪmə] *pl of* **maximum**

maximize [ˈmæksɪmaɪz] *vt* maximizar

maximum [ˈmæksɪməm] **1** *n* (*pl* **maxima**) máximo *m*

  2 *adj* máximo(a)

May [meɪ] *n* mayo *m*; **M. Day** el Primero *or* el Uno de Mayo

may [meɪ] *v aux* (*pt* **might**)

> En el inglés hablado, y en el escrito en estilo coloquial, la forma negativa **might not** se transforma en **mightn't**. La forma **might have** se transforma en **might've**.

(**a**) *(expressing possibility)* poder, ser posible; **be that as it m.** sea como sea; **come what m.** pase lo que pase; **he m.** *or* **might come** puede que venga; **you m.** *or* **might as well stay** más vale que te quedes (**b**) *(permission)* poder; **m. I?** ¿me permite?; **you m. smoke** pueden fumar (**c**) *(wish)* ojalá (+ *subj*); **m. you always be happy!** ¡ojalá seas siempre feliz!

maybe [ˈmeɪbiː] *adv* quizá(s), tal vez

mayhem [ˈmeɪhem] *n* *(disturbance)* alboroto *m*; *(havoc)* estragos *mpl*

mayonnaise [meɪəˈneɪz] *n* mayonesa *f*, mahonesa *f*

mayor [meə(r)] *n* *(man)* alcalde *m*; *(woman)* alcaldesa *f*

mayoress [ˈmeərs] *n* alcaldesa *f*

maze [meɪz] *n* laberinto *m*

MD [emˈdiː] *n* (**a**) (*abbr* **Doctor of Medicine**) Dr. en Medicina (**b**) *Fam* (*abbr* **Managing Director**) director(a) *m,f* gerente

me [miː, *unstressed* mɪ] *pron* (**a**) *(as object)* me; **he gave it to me** me lo dio; **listen to me** escúchame; **she knows me** me conoce (**b**) *(after prep)* mí; **it's for me** es para mí; **with me** conmigo (**c**) *(emphatic)* yo; **it's me** soy yo; **what about me?** ¿y yo, qué?

meadow [ˈmedəʊ] *n* prado *m*, pradera *f*

meagre, *US* **meager** [ˈmiːgə(r)] *adj* exiguo(a)

meal¹ [miːl] *n* *(flour)* harina *f*

meal² [miːl] *n* *(food)* comida *f*

mealtime [ˈmiːltaɪm] *n* hora *f* de comer

mean¹ [miːn] *vt* (*pt & pp* **meant**) (**a**) *(signify)* significar, querer decir; **what do you m. by that?** ¿qué quieres decir con eso? (**b**) *(intend)* pensar, tener la intención de; **I m. it** (te) lo digo en serio; **she was meant to arrive on the 7th** tenía que *or* debía llegar el día 7; **they m. well** tienen buenas intenciones; **she didn't m. to do it** lo hizo sin querer (**c**) *(entail)* suponer (**d**) *(refer to)* referirse a (**e**) *(destine)* destinar (**for** a *or* para)

mean² [miːn] *adj* (**meaner, meanest**) (**a**) *(miserly)* tacaño(a) (**b**) *(unkind)* malo(a); *(petty)* mezquino(a); *US (bad-tempered)* malhumorado(a); **to be m. to sb** tratar mal a algn (**c**) *(inferior)* mediocre; *(origins)* humilde (**d**) **it was no m. feat** fue toda una hazaña

mean³ [miːn] **1** *adj* *(average)* medio(a)

  2 *n* *(average)* promedio *m*; *Math* media *f*

meander [mɪˈændə(r)] *vi* *(river)* serpentear; *(person)* vagar; *Fig (digress)* divagar

meaning [ˈmiːnɪŋ] *n* sentido *m*, significado *m*

meaningful [ˈmiːnɪŋfʊl] *adj* significativo(a)

meaningless [ˈmiːnɪŋlɪs] *adj* sin sentido

meanness [ˈmiːnnɪs] *n* (**a**) *(miserliness)* tacañería *f* (**b**) *(nastiness)* maldad *f*

means [miːnz] *n* (**a**) *sing or pl (method)* medio *m*, manera *f*; **by m. of** por medio de, mediante (**b**) *pl (resources, wealth)* medios *mpl* (de vida), recursos *mpl* (económicos); **to live beyond one's m.** vivir por encima de sus posibilidades (**c**) **by all m.!** ¡por supuesto!; **by no m.** de ninguna manera

meant [ment] *pt & pp of* **mean**

meantime [ˈmiːntaɪm] **1** *adv* mientras tanto

  2 *n* **in the m.** mientras tanto

meanwhile [ˈmiːnwaɪl] *adv* mientras tanto

measles [ˈmiːzəlz] *n sing* sarampión *m*

measure [ˈmeʒə(r)] **1** *n* (**a**) *(action, step)* medida *f* (**b**) *(ruler)* regla *f* (**c**) **in some m.** hasta cierto punto (**d**) *Mus* compás *m*

  2 *vt (object, area)* medir; *(person)* tomar las medidas de

---

📖 Note that the Spanish word **mesura** is a false friend and is never a translation for the English word **measure**. In Spanish, **mesura** means "moderation, restraint".

▸ **measure up** *vi* **to m. up (to sth)** estar a la altura (de algo)
measurement ['meʒəmənt] *n* medida *f*
meat [miːt] *n* carne *f*; *Culin* **m. pie** empanada *f* de carne
meatball ['miːtbɔːl] *n* albóndiga *f*
meaty ['miːtɪ] *adj* (**meatier, meatiest**) (**a**) carnoso(a) (**b**) *Fig (story)* jugoso(a)
Mecca ['mekə] *n* la Meca
mechanic [mɪ'kænɪk] *n (person)* mecánico(a) *m,f*
mechanical [mɪ'kænɪkəl] *adj* mecánico(a)
mechanics [mɪ'kænɪks] **1** *n sing (science)* mecánica *f*
 2 *npl (technical aspects)* mecanismo *m*
mechanism ['mekənɪzəm] *n* mecanismo *m*
medal ['medəl] *n* medalla *f*
medallion [mɪ'dæljən] *n* medallón *m*
medallist, US medalist ['medəlɪst] *n* medalla *f*
meddle ['medəl] *vi* entrometerse (**in** en); **to m. with sth** manosear algo
media ['miːdɪə] *npl* medios *mpl* de comunicación; **m. coverage** cobertura periodística

---

📖 Note that the Spanish word **media** is a false friend and is never a translation for the English word **media**. In Spanish, **media** means both "stocking, sock" and "average".

---

median ['miːdɪən] **1** *adj* mediano(a); *US Aut* **m. (strip)** mediana *f*, *Col, Méx* camellón *m*
 2 *n Geom* mediana *f*; *Math* valor mediano
mediate ['miːdɪeɪt] *vi* mediar
mediator ['miːdɪeɪtə(r)] *n* mediador(a) *m,f*
Medicaid ['medɪkeɪd] *n (in US)* = seguro médico estatal para personas con renta baja
medical ['medɪkəl] **1** *adj (treatment)* médico(a); *(book)* de medicina
 2 *n Fam* reconocimiento médico
Medicare ['medɪkeɪə(r)] *n (in US)* = seguro médico para ancianos y algunos discapacitados
medicated ['medɪkeɪtɪd] *adj* medicinal
medicine ['medsɪn] *n (science)* medicina *f*; *(drugs etc)* medicamento *m*
medieval [medɪ'iːvəl] *adj* medieval

mediocre [miːdɪ'əʊkə(r)] *adj* mediocre
meditate ['medɪteɪt] *vi* meditar (**on** sobre)
meditation [medɪ'teɪʃən] *n* meditación *f*
Mediterranean [medɪtə'reɪnɪən] **1** *adj* mediterráneo(a)
 2 *n* **the M.** el Mediterráneo
medium ['miːdɪəm] **1** *adj (average)* mediano(a); *Rad* **m. wave** onda media
 2 *n* (**a**) *(pl media) (means)* medio *m* (**b**) *(pl mediums) (spiritualist)* médium *mf*
medley ['medlɪ] *n (mixture)* mezcla *f*; *Mus* popurrí *m*
meek [miːk] *adj* manso(a), sumiso(a); *(humble)* humilde
meet [miːt] **1** *vt (pt & pp met)* (**a**) *(by chance)* encontrar, encontrarse con; *(by arrangement)* reunirse con; *(in formal meeting)* entrevistarse con
 (**b**) *(get to know)* conocer; **I'd like you to m. my mother** quiero presentarte a mi madre; **the first time I met him** cuando lo conocí; **pleased to m. you!** ¡mucho gusto!
 (**c**) *(await arrival of)* esperar; *(collect)* ir a buscar
 (**d**) *(danger)* encontrar; *(opponent)* enfrentarse con
 (**e**) *(satisfy)* satisfacer; *(obligations)* cumplir con; *(expenses)* hacer frente a
 2 *vi (by chance)* encontrarse; *(by arrangement)* reunirse; *(formal meeting)* entrevistarse; *(get to know each other)* conocerse; *Sport* enfrentarse; *(join)* unirse; *(rivers)* confluir; **their eyes met** cruzaron las miradas
 3 *n (sports event)* encuentro *m*; *(in athletics)* reunión *f* atlética
▸ **meet with** *vt insep (difficulty)* tropezar con; *(loss)* sufrir; *(success)* tener; *esp US (person)* reunirse con
meeting ['miːtɪŋ] *n (chance encounter)* encuentro *m*; *(prearranged)* cita *f*; *(formal)* entrevista *f*; *(of committee etc)* reunión *f*; *(of assembly)* sesión *f*; *(of shareholders)* junta *f*; *(rally)* mitin *m*; *Sport* encuentro *m*; *(of rivers)* confluencia *f*
mega ['megə] *adj Fam (excellent)* genial, guay, *Andes, CAm, Carib, Méx* chévere, *RP* bárbaro
megabyte ['megəbaɪt] *n Comput* megabyte *m*
megaphone ['megəfəʊn] *n* megáfono *m*
melancholy ['melənkəlɪ] **1** *n* melancolía *f*
 2 *adj* melancólico(a)
Melilla [me'liːjə] *n* Melilla
mellow ['meləʊ] **1** *adj* maduro(a); *(wine)*

añejo(a); *(colour, voice)* suave; *(person)* apacible

2 *vi (fruit)* madurar; *(colour, voice)* suavizarse

melodramatic [meladrə'mætɪk] *adj* melodramático(a)

melody ['melədɪ] *n* melodía *f*

melon ['melən] *n* melón *m*

melt [melt] **1** *vt (metal)* fundir; *Fig (sb's heart)* ablandar

2 *vi (snow)* derretirse; *(metal)* fundirse; *Fig* ablandarse

▸**melt away** *vi (snow)* derretirse; *Fig (money)* desaparecer; *Fig (confidence)* desvanecerse

▸**melt down** *vt sep (metal)* fundir

melting ['meltɪŋ] *n* fundición *f*; **m. point** punto *m* de fusión; **m. pot** crisol *m*

member ['membə(r)] *n* miembro *mf*; *(of a society)* socio(a) *m,f*; *(of party, union)* afiliado(a) *m,f*; *US* **M. of Congress** congresista *mf*; *Br* **M. of Parliament** diputado(a) *m,f*

membership ['membəʃɪp] *n (state)* calidad *f* de socio; *(entry)* ingreso *m*; *Pol* afiliación *f*; *(number of members)* número *m* de socios; **m. card** carnet *m* de socio

memento [mə'mentəʊ] *n* recuerdo *m*

memo ['meməʊ] *n (official note)* memorándum *m*; *(personal note)* nota *f*, apunte *m*

memoirs ['memwɑːz] *npl* memorias *fpl*

memorable ['memərəbəl] *adj* memorable

memorandum [memə'rændəm] *n (pl* **memoranda**) *(official note)* memorándum *m*; *(personal note)* nota *f*, apunte *m*

memorial [mɪ'mɔːrɪəl] **1** *adj (plaque etc)* conmemorativo(a)

2 *n* monumento conmemorativo

memorize ['meməraɪz] *vt* memorizar, aprender de memoria

memory ['memərɪ] *n* memoria *f*; *(recollection)* recuerdo *m*

men [men] *pl of* **man**

menace ['menɪs] **1** *n (threat)* amenaza *f*; *(danger)* peligro *m*; *Fam (person)* pesado(a) *m,f*

2 *vt* amenazar

menacing ['menɪsɪŋ] *adj* amenazador(a)

menagerie [mɪ'nædʒərɪ] *n* casa *f* de fieras

mend [mend] **1** *vt* reparar, arreglar; *(clothes)* remendar; *(socks etc)* zurcir

2 *vi (ill person)* reponerse

3 *n (patch)* remiendo *m*; *(darn)* zurcido *m*; *Fig* **to be on the m.** ir mejorando

mending ['mendɪŋ] *n (repair)* reparación

f; *(darning)* zurcido *m*; *(clothes for mending)* ropa *f* para remendar

menial ['miːnɪəl] *adj (task)* servil, bajo(a)

menopause ['menəpɔːz] *n* menopausia *f*

menstrual ['menstrʊəl] *adj* menstrual

menstruation [menstrʊ'eɪʃən] *n* menstruación *f*

mental ['mentəl] *adj* (**a**) mental; **m. home, m. hospital** hospital psiquiátrico; **m. illness** enfermedad *f* mental (**b**) *Fam (crazy)* chalado(a)

mentality [men'tælɪtɪ] *n* mentalidad *f*

mentally ['mentəlɪ] *adv* **m. ill** enfermo(a) mental; **to be m. handicapped** ser un(a) disminuido(a) psíquico(a)

mention ['menʃən] **1** *n* mención *f*

2 *vt* mencionar; **don't m. it!** ¡de nada!

mentor ['mentɔː(r)] *n* mentor *m*

menu ['menjuː] *n* (**a**) *(card)* carta *f*; *(fixed meal)* menú *m*; **today's m.** menú del día (**b**) *Comput* menú *m*

MEP [emiː'piː] *n* (*abbr* **Member of the European Parliament**) eurodiputado(a) *m,f*

mercenary ['mɜːsɪnərɪ] *adj & n* mercenario(a) *(m,f)*

merchandise ['mɜːtʃəndaɪz] *n* mercancías *fpl*, géneros *mpl*

merchant ['mɜːtʃənt] *n Com & Fin* comerciante *mf*; *(retailer)* detallista *mf*; **m. bank** banco *m* comercial; **m. navy** marina *f* mercante

merciful ['mɜːsɪfʊl] *adj* clemente, compasivo(a) (**towards** con)

merciless ['mɜːsɪlɪs] *adj* despiadado(a)

Mercury ['mɜːkjʊrɪ] *n* Mercurio *m*

mercury ['mɜːkjʊrɪ] *n* mercurio *m*

mercy ['mɜːsɪ] *n* misericordia *f*, compasión *f*; **at the m. of** a la merced de; **to have m. on** tener compasión de

mere [mɪə(r)] *adj* mero(a), simple

merely ['mɪəlɪ] *adv* simplemente

merge [mɜːdʒ] **1** *vt (blend)* unir (**with** con); *Com* fusionar

2 *vi* unirse; *(roads)* empalmar; *Com* fusionarse

merger ['mɜːdʒə(r)] *n Com* fusión *f*

meringue [mə'ræŋ] *n* merengue *m*

merit ['merɪt] **1** *n (of person)* mérito *m*; *(of plan etc)* ventaja *f*

2 *vt* merecer

mermaid ['mɜːmeɪd] *n* sirena *f*

merry ['merɪ] *adj* (**merrier, merriest**) alegre; *Fam (tipsy)* achispado(a); **m. Christmas!** ¡felices Navidades!

merry-go-round ['merɪɡəʊraʊnd] *n* tiovivo *m*

mesh [meʃ] **1** *n Tex* malla *f*; *Tech* engranaje *m*; *Fig* red *f*
  2 *vt Tech* engranar
mesmerize ['mezməraɪz] *vt* hipnotizar
mess [mes] **1** *n* (**a**) *(confusion)* confusión *f*; *(disorder)* desorden *m*; **to be in a m.** *(of room etc)* estar desordenado(a) (**b**) *(in life, affairs)* lío *m*; **to get into a m.** meterse en un lío (**c**) *(dirt)* suciedad *f* (**d**) *Mil (food)* rancho *m* (**e**) *Mil (room)* comedor *m*
  ▸ **mess about, mess around** *Fam* **1** *vt sep* fastidiar
    2 *vi (act the fool)* hacer el primo; *(idle)* gandulear; *(kill time)* pasar el rato
  ▸ **mess about with** *vt insep Fam (fiddle with)* manosear; **to m. about with sb** tener un lío con algn
  ▸ **mess up** *vt sep Fam (make untidy)* desordenar; *(dirty)* ensuciar; *(spoil)* estropear
message ['mesɪdʒ] *n (communication)* recado *m*; *(of story etc)* mensaje *m*; *Fam* **to get the m.** comprender
messenger ['mesɪndʒə(r)] *n* mensajero(a) *m,f*
Messrs ['mesəz] *npl (abbr* **Messieurs**) Sres.
messy ['mesɪ] *adj* (**messier, messiest**) *(untidy)* desordenado(a); *(confused)* enredado(a); *(dirty)* sucio(a)
met [met] *pt & pp of* **meet**
metabolism [me'tæbəlɪzəm] *n* metabolismo *m*
metal ['metəl] **1** *n* metal *m*
  2 *adj* metálico(a)
metallic [mɪ'tælɪk] *adj* metálico(a); **m. blue** azul metalizado
metallurgy [me'tælədʒɪ] *n* metalurgia *f*
metalwork ['metəlwɜːk] *n (craft)* metalistería *f*; *(objects)* objetos *mpl* de metal
metaphor ['metəfə(r)] *n* metáfora *f*
mete [miːt] *vt* **to m. out** imponer
meteor ['miːtɪə(r)] *n* bólido *m*
meteoric [miːtɪ'ɒrɪk] *adj* meteórico(a)
meteorite ['miːtɪəraɪt] *n* meteorito *m*
meteorology [miːtɪə'rɒlədʒɪ] *n* meteorología *f*
meter¹ ['miːtə(r)] *n* contador *m*
meter² ['miːtər] *n US* = **metre**
method ['meθəd] *n* método *m*
methodical [mɪ'θɒdɪkəl] *adj* metódico(a)
Methodist ['meθədɪst] *adj & n* metodista *(mf)*
meths [meθs] *n sing Br Fam* alcohol *m* de quemar
methylated spirits ['meθɪleɪtɪd'spɪrɪts] *n* alcohol metilado *or* desnaturalizado
meticulous [mə'tɪkjʊləs] *adj* meticuloso(a)
metre ['miːtə(r)] *n* metro *m*
metric ['metrɪk] *adj* métrico(a)
metropolis [mɪ'trɒpəlɪs] *n* metrópoli *f*
metropolitan [metrə'pɒlɪtən] *adj* metropolitano(a)
mettle ['metəl] *n* valor *m*
mew [mjuː] *vi (cat)* maullar
mews [mjuːz] *n sing (street)* callejuela *f*; **m. flat** = apartamento de lujo en unas caballerizas reconvertidas
Mexican ['meksɪkən] *adj & n* mejicano(a) *(m,f)*, mexicano(a) *(m,f)*
Mexico ['meksɪkəʊ] *n* Méjico, México
miaow [miː'aʊ] **1** *vi* maullar
  2 *n* maullido *m*
mice [maɪs] *pl of* **mouse**
mickey ['mɪkɪ] *n Fam* **to take the m. (out of sb)** tomar el pelo (a algn)
microbe ['maɪkrəʊb] *n* microbio *m*
microchip ['maɪkrəʊtʃɪp] *n* microplaqueta *f*, microchip *m*
microcomputer ['maɪkrəʊkəm'pjuːtə(r)] *n* microordenador *m*
microcosm ['maɪkrəʊkɒzəm] *n* microcosmo *m*
microfilm ['maɪkrəʊfɪlm] *n* microfilm *m*
microphone ['maɪkrəfəʊn] *n* micrófono *m*
microprocessor [maɪkrəʊ'prəʊsesə(r)] *n* microprocesador *m*
microscope ['maɪkrəskəʊp] *n* microscopio *m*
microwave ['maɪkrəʊweɪv] *n* microonda *f*; **m. (oven)** (horno *m*) microondas *m inv*
mid [mɪd] *adj* **(in) m. afternoon** a media tarde; **(in) m. April** a mediados de abril; **to be in one's m. thirties** tener unos treinta y cinco años
midair 1 *adj* ['mɪdeə(r)] *(collision, explosion)* en el aire
  2 *n* [mɪd'eə(r)] *Fig* **to leave sth in m.** dejar algo en el aire
midday 1 *n* [mɪd'deɪ] mediodía *m*
  2 *adj* ['mɪddeɪ] de mediodía
middle ['mɪdəl] **1** *adj* de en medio; **m. age** mediana edad; **the M. Ages** la Edad Media; **the m. class** la clase media
  2 *n* (**a**) *centro m*, medio *m*; **in the m. of** en medio de; **in the m. of winter** en pleno invierno; *Fam* **in the m. of nowhere** en el quinto pino (**b**) *Fam (waist)* cintura *f*
middle-aged [mɪdəl'eɪdʒd] *adj* de mediana edad
middle-class [mɪdəl'klɑːs] *adj* de clase media

middleman ['mɪdəlmæn] *n* intermediario *m*

middleweight ['mɪdəlweɪt] *n* peso medio

middling ['mɪdlɪŋ] *adj* mediano(a)

midfielder [mɪd'fiːldə(r)] *n Sport* centrocampista *mf*

midge [mɪdʒ] *n* mosca enana

midget ['mɪdʒɪt] *n* enano(a) *m,f*

Midlands ['mɪdləndz] *npl* **the M.** = la región central de Inglaterra

midnight ['mɪdnaɪt] *n* medianoche *f*

midst [mɪdst] *n* **in the m. of** en medio de

midsummer [mɪd'sʌmə(r)] *n* pleno verano; **M.'s Day** Día *m* de San Juan *(24 de junio)*

midway ['mɪdweɪ] *adv* a medio camino

midweek 1 *adv* [mɪd'wiːk] entre semana
2 *adj* ['mɪdwiːk] de entre semana

midwife ['mɪdwaɪf] *n* comadrona *f*, partera *f*

midwifery ['mɪdwɪfərɪ] *n* obstetricia *f*

midwinter [mɪd'wɪntə(r)] *n* pleno invierno *m*

might¹ [maɪt] *v aux see* **may**

might² [maɪt] *n Fml* fuerza *f*, poder *m*

mighty ['maɪtɪ] **1** *adj* (**mightier, mightiest**) *(strong)* fuerte; *(powerful)* poderoso(a); *(great)* enorme
2 *adv US Fam* cantidad de, muy

migraine ['miːgreɪn, 'maɪgreɪn] *n* jaqueca *f*

migrant ['maɪgrənt] **1** *adj* migratorio(a)
2 *n (person)* emigrante *mf*; *(bird)* ave migratoria

migrate [maɪ'greɪt] *vi* emigrar

migration [maɪ'greɪʃən] *n* migración *f*

mike [maɪk] *n Fam* micro *m*

mild [maɪld] *adj (person, character)* apacible; *(climate)* templado(a); *(punishment)* leve; *(tobacco, taste)* suave

mildew ['mɪldjuː] *n* moho *m*; *(on plants)* añublo *m*

mildly ['maɪldlɪ] *adv (softly, gently)* suavemente; *(slightly)* ligeramente; **and that's putting it m.** y esto es decir poco

mildness ['maɪldnɪs] *n (of character)* apacibilidad *f*; *(of climate, taste)* suavidad *f*; *(of punishment)* levedad *f*

mile [maɪl] *n* milla *f*; *Fam* **miles better** muchísimo mejor

mileage ['maɪlɪdʒ] *n* kilometraje *m*

milestone ['maɪlstəʊn] *n* hito *m*

milieu ['miːljɜː] *n* medio *m* ambiente

militant ['mɪlɪtənt] *adj & n* militante *(mf)*

military ['mɪlɪtərɪ] *adj* militar; **to do one's m. service** hacer el servicio militar

militia [mɪ'lɪʃə] *n* milicia *f*

milk [mɪlk] **1** *n* leche *f*; **m. chocolate** chocolate *m* con leche; **m. shake** batido *m*
2 *vt* (**a**) *(cow, goat)* ordeñar (**b**) *Fam* **they milked him of all his money** le sangraron hasta la última peseta

milkman ['mɪlkmən] *n* lechero *m*

milky ['mɪlkɪ] *adj* (**milkier, milkiest**) lechoso(a); *(colour)* pálido(a); **M. Way** Vía Láctea

mill [mɪl] **1** *n (grinder)* molino *m*; *(for coffee)* molinillo *m*; *(factory)* fábrica *f*; **cotton m.** hilandería *f*
2 *vt* moler
▸**mill about, mill around** *vi* arremolinarse

millennium [mɪ'lenɪəm] *n* (*pl* **millenniums** *or* **millennia** [mɪ'lenɪə]) milenio *m*

miller ['mɪlə(r)] *n* molinero(a) *m,f*

millet ['mɪlɪt] *n* mijo *m*

milligram(me) ['mɪlɪgræm] *n* miligramo *m*

millilitre, *US* **milliliter** ['mɪlɪliːtə(r)] *n* mililitro *m*

millimetre, *US* **millimeter** ['mɪlɪmiːtə(r)] *n* milímetro *m*

milliner ['mɪlɪnə(r)] *n* sombrerero(a) *m,f*

millinery ['mɪlɪnərɪ] *n* sombreros *mpl* de señora

million ['mɪljən] *n* millón *m*

millionaire [mɪljə'neə(r)] *n* millonario(a) *m,f*

millstone ['mɪlstəʊn] *n* muela *f*; *Fig* carga *f*

mime [maɪm] **1** *n (art)* mímica *f*; *(play)* pantomima *f*
2 *vt* representar con gestos

> ♪ Note that the Spanish verb **mimar** is a false friend and is never a translation for the English verb **to mime**. In Spanish, **mimar** means "to spoil, to pamper".

mimic ['mɪmɪk] **1** *adj & n* mímico(a) *(m,f)*
2 *vt* imitar

mimicry ['mɪmɪkrɪ] *n* imitación *f*

minaret ['mɪnərɛt] *n* alminar *m*, minarete *m*

mince [mɪns] **1** *n Br (meat)* carne picada; **m. pie** *(containing meat)* = especie de empanada de carne picada; *(containing fruit)* pastel *m* de picadillo de fruta
2 *vt* picar; *Fig* **he doesn't m. his words** no tiene pelos en la lengua
3 *vi (walk)* **to m. (along)** andar con pasos menuditos

mincemeat ['mɪnsmiːt] *n (dried fruit)* conserva *f* de picadillo de fruta; *(meat)* carne picada

mincer ['mɪnsə(r)] *n* picadora *f* de carne

mind [maɪnd] **1** *n* (**a**) *(intellect)* mente *f*; *(brain)* cabeza *f*; **what kind of car do you have in m.?** ¿en qué clase de coche estás pensando?; **to lose one's m.** perder el juicio; **it slipped my m.** lo olvidé por completo; **to call sth to m.** recordar algo (**b**) *(opinion)* **to be in two minds (about sth)** estar indeciso(a) (acerca de algo); **to my m.** a mi parecer
2 *vt* (**a**) *(child)* cuidar; *(house)* vigilar; *(be careful of)* tener cuidado con; **m. the step!** ¡ojo con el escalón!; **m. your own business!** ¡no te metas donde no te llaman!
(**b**) *(object to)* tener inconveniente en; **I wouldn't m. a cup of coffee** me vendría bien un café; **never m.** no importa
3 *vi* (**a**) **m. you, he is fifty** ten en cuenta que tiene cincuenta años
(**b**) *(object)* importar; **do you m. if I open the window?** ¿le importa que abra la ventana?
minder ['maɪndə(r)] *n Fam (bodyguard)* guardaespaldas *m inv*; *(for child)* niñera *f*, *(babysitter)* canguro *mf*
mindful ['maɪndfʊl] *adj* consciente
mindless ['maɪndlɪs] *adj (task)* de autómata; *(violence)* injustificable
mine¹ [maɪn] *poss pron* (el) mío/(la) mía/(los) míos, (las) mías, lo mío; **a friend of m.** un amigo mío; **these gloves are m.** estos guantes son míos; **which is m.?** ¿cuál es el mío?
mine² [maɪn] **1** *n* mina *f*; *Fig* **a m. of information** un pozo de información
2 *vt (coal etc)* extraer; *Mil* minar
minefield ['maɪnfiːld] *n* campo *m* de minas
miner ['maɪnə(r)] *n* minero(a) *m,f*
mineral ['mɪnərəl] **1** *adj* mineral; **m. water** agua *f* mineral
2 *n* mineral *m*
minesweeper ['maɪnswiːpə(r)] *n* dragaminas *m inv*
mingle ['mɪŋgəl] *vi* mezclarse
miniature ['mɪnɪtʃə(r)] **1** *n* miniatura *f*
2 *adj (railway)* en miniatura; *(camera, garden)* diminuto(a)
minibus ['mɪnɪbʌs] *n* microbús *m*
minim ['mɪnɪm] *n Mus* blanca *f*
minimal ['mɪnɪməl] *adj* mínimo(a)
minimum ['mɪnɪməm] **1** *adj* mínimo(a); **m. wage** salario mínimo
2 *n* mínimo *m*
mining ['maɪnɪŋ] **1** *n* minería *f*, explotación *f* de minas; *Mil & Naut* minado *m*
2 *adj* minero(a)
miniskirt ['mɪnɪskɜːt] *n* minifalda *f*

minister ['mɪnɪstə(r)] **1** *n* ministro(a) *m,f*; *Rel* pastor(a) *m,f*
2 *vi* **to m. to sb** atender a algn
ministerial [mɪnɪ'stɪərɪəl] *adj Pol* ministerial
ministry ['mɪnɪstrɪ] *n Pol* ministerio *m*; *Rel* sacerdocio *m*
mink [mɪŋk] *n* visón *m*; **m. coat** abrigo *m* de visón
minnow ['mɪnəʊ] *n* piscardo *m*
minor ['maɪnə(r)] **1** *adj (lesser)* menor; *(unimportant)* sin importancia; *(role)* secundario(a); *Mus* menor
2 *n Jur* menor *mf* de edad
Minorca [mɪ'nɔːkə] *n* Menorca
minority [maɪ'nɒrɪtɪ] *n* minoría *f*; **to be in the m.** ser (la) minoría; *Pol* **m. party** partido minoritario
mint¹ [mɪnt] **1** *n Fin* **the M.** la Casa de la Moneda; **in m. condition** en perfecto estado
2 *vt (coin, words)* acuñar
mint² [mɪnt] *n Bot* menta *f*; *(sweet)* pastilla *f* de menta
minus ['maɪnəs] **1** *prep* **5 m. 3** 5 menos 3; **m. 10 degrees** 10 grados bajo cero
2 *adj* negativo(a)
3 *n* **m. (sign)** signo *m* (de) menos
minute¹ ['mɪnɪt] *n* (**a**) *(time)* minuto *m*; **at the last m.** a última hora; **just a m.** (espera) un momento; **this very m.** ahora mismo
(**b**) **minutes** *(notes)* el acta
minute² [maɪ'njuːt] *adj (tiny)* diminuto(a); *(examination)* minucioso(a)
miracle ['mɪrəkəl] *n* milagro *m*
miraculous [mɪ'rækjʊləs] *adj* milagroso(a)
mirage [mɪ'rɑːʒ] *n* espejismo *m*
mire [maɪə(r)] *n* fango *m*, lodo *m*; *(muddy place)* lodazal *m*
mirror ['mɪrə(r)] **1** *n* espejo *m*; *Fig* reflejo *m*; **rear-view m.** retrovisor *m*; **m. image** réplica *f*
2 *vt* reflejar
mirth [mɜːθ] *n* alegría *f*; *(laughter)* risas *fpl*
misadventure [mɪsəd'ventʃə(r)] *n* desgracia *f*; **death by m.** muerte *f* accidental
misanthropist [mɪ'zænθrəpɪst] *n* misántropo(a) *m,f*
misapprehension [mɪsæprɪ'henʃən] *n* malentendido *m*
misbehave [mɪsbɪ'heɪv] *vi* portarse mal
miscalculate [mɪs'kælkjʊleɪt] *vt & vi* calcular mal
miscarriage ['mɪskærɪdʒ] *n Med* aborto *m* (espontáneo); **m. of justice** error *m* judicial

miscellaneous [mɪsɪ'leɪnɪəs] adj variado(a); **m. expenses** gastos diversos

mischief ['mɪstʃɪf] n (naughtiness) travesura f; Fml (evil) malicia f; Fam (harm) daño m; **to get up to m.** hacer travesuras

mischievous ['mɪstʃɪvəs] adj (naughty) travieso(a); (playful) juguetón(ona); Fml (wicked) malicioso(a)

misconception [mɪskən'sepʃən] n concepto erróneo

misconduct [mɪs'kɒndʌkt] n mala conducta; **professional m.** error m profesional

misconstrue [mɪskən'struː] vt interpretar mal

miscount [mɪs'kaʊnt] vt (votes etc) contar mal

misdeed [mɪs'diːd] n fechoría f

misdemeanour, US **misdemeanor** [mɪsdɪ'miːnə(r)] n (misdeed) fechoría f; Jur delito m menor

miser ['maɪzə(r)] n avaro(a) m,f

miserable ['mɪzərəbəl] adj (sad) triste; (unfortunate) desgraciado(a); (wretched) miserable

miserly ['maɪzəlɪ] adj avaro(a), tacaño(a)

misery ['mɪzərɪ] n (sadness) tristeza f; (wretchedness) desgracia f; (suffering) sufrimiento m; (poverty) miseria f; Fam (person) aguafiestas mf

misfire [mɪs'faɪə(r)] vi (engine, plan etc) fallar

misfit ['mɪsfɪt] n (person) inadaptado(a) m,f

misfortune [mɪs'fɔːtʃən] n desgracia f

misgiving [mɪs'gɪvɪŋ] n (doubt) recelo m; (fear) temor m

misguided [mɪs'gaɪdɪd] adj equivocado(a)

mishandle [mɪs'hændəl] vt llevar or manejar mal

mishap ['mɪshæp] n contratiempo m

misinform [mɪsɪn'fɔːm] vt informar mal

misinterpret [mɪsɪn'tɜːprɪt] vt interpretar mal

misjudge [mɪs'dʒʌdʒ] vt juzgar mal

mislay [mɪs'leɪ] vt extraviar

mislead [mɪs'liːd] vt despistar; (deliberately) engañar

misleading [mɪs'liːdɪŋ] adj (erroneous) erróneo(a); (deliberately) engañoso(a)

mismanagement [mɪs'mænɪdʒmənt] n mala administración f

misnomer [mɪs'nəʊmə(r)] n nombre equivocado

misogynist [mɪ'sɒdʒɪnɪst] n misógino(a) m,f

misplace [mɪs'pleɪs] vt (trust) encauzar mal; (book, spectacles etc) extraviar

misprint ['mɪsprɪnt] n errata f, error m de imprenta

misrepresent [mɪsreprɪ'zent] vt (facts) desvirtuar; (words) tergiversar

miss¹ [mɪs] n señorita f

miss² [mɪs] **1** n (throw etc) fallo m; Fam **to give sth a m.** pasar de algo

   2 vt (**a**) (when throwing) fallar; (when shooting) errar (**b**) (train etc) perder; (opportunity) dejar pasar; **you have missed the point** no has captado la idea; Fig **to m. the boat** perder el tren (**c**) (omit) saltarse (**d**) **I m. you** te echo de menos

   3 vi (when throwing) fallar; (when shooting) errar; **is anything missing?** ¿falta algo?

  ▸ **miss out 1** vt sep (omit) saltarse; (on purpose) pasar por alto

   2 vt insep **to m. out on** perderse

misshapen [mɪs'ʃeɪpən] adj deforme

missile ['mɪsaɪl, US 'mɪsəl] n Mil misil m; (object thrown) proyectil m

missing ['mɪsɪŋ] adj (object) perdido(a); (person) desaparecido(a); (from meeting etc) ausente; **m. person** desaparecido(a) m,f; **three cups are m.** faltan tres tazas

mission ['mɪʃən] n misión f

missionary ['mɪʃənərɪ] n misionero(a) m,f

misspent ['mɪsspent] adj (youth) malgastado(a)

mist [mɪst] **1** n neblina f; (thick) niebla f; (at sea) bruma f

   2 vi **to m. over** or **up** (countryside) cubrirse de neblina; (window etc) empañarse

mistake [mɪ'steɪk] **1** n error m; **by m.** por equivocación; **I hurt him by m.** le golpeé sin querer; **to make a m.** equivocarse, cometer un error

   2 vt (pt **mistook**; pp **mistaken**) (meaning) malentender; **to m. Jack for Bill** confundir a Jack con Bill

mistaken [mɪ'steɪkən] adj equivocado(a), erróneo(a); **you are m.** estás equivocado(a)

mister ['mɪstə(r)] n señor m

mistletoe ['mɪsəltəʊ] n muérdago m

mistook [mɪ'stʊk] pt of **mistake**

mistreat [mɪs'triːt] vt tratar mal

mistress ['mɪstrɪs] n (of house) señora f, ama f; (lover) amante f; Educ (primary school) maestra f; (secondary school) profesora f

mistrust [mɪs'trʌst] **1** n recelo m

   2 vt desconfiar de

misty ['mɪstɪ] *adj* (**mistier, mistiest**) *(day)* de niebla; *(window etc)* empañado(a)

misunderstand [mɪsʌndə'stænd] *vt & vi* malentender

misunderstanding [mɪsʌndə'stændɪŋ] *n* malentendido *m*; *(disagreement)* desavenencia *f*

misuse 1 *n* [mɪs'juːs] mal uso *m*; *(of funds)* malversación *f*; *(of power)* abuso *m*
 2 *vt* [mɪs'juːz] emplear mal; *(funds)* malversar; *(power)* abusar de

miter ['maɪtər] *n US* = **mitre**

mitigate ['mɪtɪgeɪt] *vt* atenuar

mitigating ['mɪtɪgeɪtɪŋ] *adj* **m. circumstances** circunstancias *fpl* atenuantes

mitre ['maɪtə(r)] *n* mitra *f*

mitten ['mɪtən] *n* manopla *f*; *(fingerless)* mitón *m*

mix [mɪks] **1** *n* mezcla *f*
 2 *vt* mezclar
 3 *vi* (*blend*) mezclarse (**with** con); *(go well together)* ir bien juntos
 ▸ **mix up** *vt sep (confuse)* confundir (**with** con); *(papers)* revolver; **to be mixed up in sth** estar involucrado(a) en algo

mixed [mɪkst] *adj (assorted)* surtido(a); *(varied)* variado(a); *(school)* mixto(a); *(feelings)* contradictorio(a)

mixed-up [mɪkst'ʌp] *adj (objects, papers etc)* revuelto(a); *(person)* confuso(a)

mixer ['mɪksə(r)] *n* (**a**) *Culin* batidora *f* (**b**) **to be a good m.** *(person)* tener don de gentes

mixture ['mɪkstʃə(r)] *n* mezcla *f*

mix-up ['mɪksʌp] *n Fam* confusión *f*, lío *m*

mm *(abbr* **millimetre(s)**) mm

moan [məʊn] **1** *n (groan)* gemido *m*, quejido *m*
 2 *vi (groan)* gemir; *(complain)* quejarse (**about** de)

moat [məʊt] *n* foso *m*

mob [mɒb] **1** *n* multitud *f*; *(riff-raff)* gentuza *f*; **the m.** el populacho
 2 *vt* acosar

mobile ['məʊbaɪl, *US* 'məʊbəl] **1** *adj* móvil; **m. home** caravana *f*; **m. phone** teléfono *m* móvil, *Am* teléfono *m* celular
 2 *n* (**a**) *(hanging ornament)* móvil *m* (**b**) *Fam (mobile phone)* móvil *m*, *Am* celular *m*

mobility [məʊ'bɪlɪtɪ] *n* movilidad *f*

mobilize ['məʊbɪlaɪz] *vt* movilizar

mock [mɒk] **1** *adj (sympathy etc)* fingido(a); *(objects)* de imitación
 2 *vt (make fun of)* burlarse de
 3 *vi* burlarse (**at** de)

mockery ['mɒkərɪ] *n* burla *f*

mode [məʊd] *n (manner)* modo *m*, estilo *m*; *(fashion)* moda *f*

model ['mɒdəl] **1** *n* modelo *m*; *(fashion model)* modelo *mf*, **(scale) m.** maqueta *f*
 2 *adj (railway)* en miniatura; *(pupil)* ejemplar; *(school)* modelo
 3 *vt (clay etc)* modelar; *(clothes)* presentar
 4 *vi (make models)* modelar; *(work as model)* trabajar de modelo

modem ['məʊdem] *n Comput* modem *m*

moderate¹ ['mɒdərɪt] **1** *adj* moderado(a); *(reasonable)* razonable; *(average)* regular; *(ability)* mediocre
 2 *n Pol* moderado(a) *m,f*

moderate² ['mɒdəreɪt] **1** *vt* moderar
 2 *vi* moderarse; *(wind)* calmarse; *(in debate)* arbitrar

moderately ['mɒdərɪtlɪ] *adv* medianamente

moderation [mɒdə'reɪʃən] *n* moderación *f*; **in m.** con moderación

modern ['mɒdən] *adj* moderno(a); *(history)* contemporáneo(a); **m. languages** lenguas modernas

modernize ['mɒdənaɪz] *vt* modernizar

modest ['mɒdɪst] *adj* modesto(a); *(chaste)* púdico(a); *(price)* módico(a); *(success)* discreto(a)

modesty ['mɒdɪstɪ] *n (humility)* modestia *f*; *(chastity)* pudor *m*

modification [mɒdɪfɪ'keɪʃən] *n* modificación *f*

modify ['mɒdɪfaɪ] *vt* modificar

module ['mɒdjuːl] *n* módulo *m*

mogul ['məʊgʌl] *n* magnate *m*

mohair ['məʊheə(r)] **1** *n* mohair *m*
 2 *adj* de mohair

moist [mɔɪst] *adj* húmedo(a)

moisten ['mɔɪsən] *vt* humedecer

moisture ['mɔɪstʃə(r)] *n* humedad *f*

moisturizer ['mɔɪstʃəraɪzə(r)] *n* crema *f or* leche *f* hidratante

molar ['məʊlə(r)] *n* muela *f*

molasses [mə'læsɪz] *n sing* melaza *f*

mold¹ [məʊld] *n US* = **mould¹**

mold² [məʊld] *n & vt US* = **mould²**

molder ['məʊldər] *vi US* = **moulder**

molding ['məʊldɪŋ] *n US* = **moulding**

moldy ['məʊldɪ] *adj US* = **mouldy**

mole¹ [məʊl] *n (beauty spot)* lunar *m*

mole² [məʊl] *n (animal)* topo *m*

molecule ['mɒlɪkjuːl] *n* molécula *f*

molest [mə'lest] *vt* importunar; *(sexually assault)* acosar (sexualmente)

mollycoddle ['mɒlɪkɒdəl] *vt Fam* mimar, consentir

molt [məʊlt] *vi US* = **moult**

molten ['məʊltən] *adj* fundido(a); *(lava)* líquido(a)

mom [mɒm] *n US Fam* mamá *f*

moment ['məʊmənt] *n* momento *m*; **at the m.** en este momento; **for the m.** de momento; **in a m.** dentro de un momento; **at any m.** de un momento a otro

momentarily ['məʊməntərɪlɪ] *adv* momentáneamente; *US (soon)* dentro de poco

momentary ['məʊməntərɪ] *adj* momentáneo(a)

momentous [məʊ'mentəs] *adj* trascendental

momentum [məʊ'mentəm] *n Phys* momento *m*; *(speed)* velocidad *f*; *Fig* **to gather m.** cobrar velocidad

mommy ['mɒmɪ] *n US Fam* mamá *f*

Monaco ['mɒnəkəʊ] *n* Mónaco

monarch ['mɒnək] *n* monarca *m*

monarchy ['mɒnəkɪ] *n* monarquía *f*

monastery ['mɒnəstərɪ] *n* monasterio *m*

Monday ['mʌndɪ] *n* lunes *m*

monetarism ['mʌnɪtərɪzəm] *n* monetarismo *m*

monetary ['mʌnɪtərɪ] *adj* monetario(a)

money ['mʌnɪ] *n* dinero *m*; *(currency)* moneda *f*; **to make m.** ganar dinero; **to put m. on** apostar por

moneylender ['mʌnɪlendə(r)] *n* prestamista *mf*

money-spinner ['mʌnɪspɪnə(r)] *n Fam* negocio *m* rentable

Mongolia [mɒŋ'gəʊlɪə] *n* Mongolia

mongolism ['mɒŋgəlɪzəm] *n* mongolismo *m*

mongrel ['mʌŋgrəl] *n* perro mestizo

monitor ['mɒnɪtə(r)] **1** *n (screen)* monitor *m*; *Educ* delegado(a) *m,f*
   2 *vt (check)* controlar; *(progress, events)* seguir de cerca

monk [mʌŋk] *n* monje *m*

monkey ['mʌŋkɪ] *n* mono *m*; **m. nut** cacahuete *m*, maní *m*, *Méx* cacahuate *m*; **m. wrench** llave inglesa

monochrome ['mɒnəkrəʊm] *adj* monocromo(a); *(television, photo)* en blanco y negro

monocle ['mɒnəkəl] *n* monóculo *m*

monologue, *US* **monolog** ['mɒnəlɒg] *n* monólogo *m*

monopolize [mə'nɒpəlaɪz] *vt Fin* monopolizar; *(attention etc)* acaparar

monopoly [mə'nɒpəlɪ] *n* monopolio *m*

monotone ['mɒnətəʊn] *n* **in a m.** con una voz monótona

monotonous [mə'nɒtənəs] *adj* monótono(a)

monotony [mə'nɒtənɪ] *n* monotonía *f*

monsoon [mɒn'suːn] *n* monzón *m*

monster ['mɒnstə(r)] *n* monstruo *m*

monstrosity [mɒn'strɒsɪtɪ] *n* monstruosidad *f*

monstrous ['mɒnstrəs] *adj (huge)* enorme; *(hideous)* monstruoso(a); *(outrageous)* escandaloso(a)

montage ['mɒntɑːʒ] *n* montaje *m*

month [mʌnθ] *n* mes *m*

monthly ['mʌnθlɪ] **1** *adj* mensual; **m. instalment** mensualidad *f*
   2 *n (periodical)* revista *f* mensual
   3 *adv* mensualmente, cada mes

monument ['mɒnjʊmənt] *n* monumento *m*

monumental [mɒnjʊ'mentəl] *adj* monumental; *Fam (huge)* enorme

moo [muː] **1** *n* mugido *m*
   2 *vi* mugir

mooch [muːtʃ] *Fam* **1** *vi* **to m. around** vagar, dar vueltas
   2 *vt* **to m. sth off sb** *(cadge)* gorronearle algo a algn

mood [muːd] *n* humor *m*; **to be in a good/bad m.** estar de buen/mal humor; **to be in the m. for (doing) sth** estar de humor para (hacer) algo

moody ['muːdɪ] *adj* (**moodier, moodiest**) *(changeable)* de humor variable; *(badtempered)* malhumorado(a)

moon [muːn] *n* luna *f*; *Fam* **over the m.** en el séptimo cielo

moonlight ['muːnlaɪt] *n* luz *f* de la luna

moonlighting ['muːnlaɪtɪŋ] *n Fam* pluriempleo *m*

moonlit ['muːnlɪt] *adj (night)* de luna

Moor [mʊə(r)] *n* moro(a) *m,f*

moor[1] [mʊə(r)] *n (heath)* páramo *m*

moor[2] [mʊə(r)] *vt Naut* amarrar

Moorish ['mʊərɪʃ] *adj* moro(a)

moorland ['mʊələnd] *n* páramo *m*

moose ['muːs] *n (pl* **moose**) alce *m*

moot [muːt] *adj* **it's a m. point** es discutible

mop [mɒp] **1** *n (for floor)* fregona *f*; *Fam* **m. of hair** melena *f*
   2 *vt* fregar
   ▸ **mop up** *vt sep (liquids)* enjugar; *(enemy forces)* acabar con

mope [məʊp] *vi* estar alicaído(a)
   ▸ **mope about, mope around** *vi* andar abatido(a)

moped ['məʊped] *n* ciclomotor *m*, vespa *f*

moral ['mɒrəl] **1** *adj* moral
   2 *n* moraleja *f*; **morals** moral *f*, moralidad *f*

morale [mə'rɑːl] *n* moral *f*, estado *m* de ánimo

morality [mə'rælɪtɪ] *n* moralidad *f*

morass [mə'ræs] *n* pantano *m*; *Fig* lío *m*

moratorium [mɒrə'tɔːrɪəm] *n* moratoria *f* (**on** en)

morbid ['mɔːbɪd] *adj Med* mórbido(a); *(mind)* morboso(a)

more [mɔː(r)] **1** *adj* más; **is there any m. tea?** ¿queda más té?; **I've no m. money** no me queda más dinero; **m. tourists** más turistas

2 *pron* más; **how many m.?** ¿cuántos más?; **I need some m.** necesito más; **it's m. than enough** es más que suficiente; **many/much m.** muchos(as)/mucho más; **m. than a hundred** más de cien; **the m. he has, the m. he wants** cuanto más tiene más quiere; **and what is m.** y lo que es más

3 *adv* más; **I won't do it any m.** no lo volveré a hacer; **she doesn't live here any m.** ya no vive aquí; **m. and m. difficult** cada vez más difícil; **m. or less** más o menos; **once m.** una vez más

moreover [mɔː'rəʊvə(r)] *adv* además

morgue [mɔːg] *n* depósito *m* de cadáveres

morning ['mɔːnɪŋ] **1** *n* mañana *f*; *(before dawn)* madrugada *f*; **in the m.** por la mañana; **on Monday mornings** los lunes por la mañana; **tomorrow m.** mañana por la mañana

2 *adj* matutino(a)

Moroccan [mə'rɒkən] *adj & n* marroquí *(mf)*

Morocco [mə'rɒkəʊ] *n* Marruecos

moron ['mɔːrɒn] *n Fam* imbécil *mf*

morose [mə'rəʊs] *adj* hosco(a), huraño(a)

> *Note that the Spanish word* **moroso** *is a false friend and is never a translation for the English word* **morose**. *In Spanish,* **moroso** *means "bad debtor".*

morphine ['mɔːfiːn] *n* morfina *f*

Morse [mɔːs] *n* **M. (code)** (alfabeto *m*) Morse *m*

morsel ['mɔːsəl] *n* *(of food)* bocado *m*; *Fig* trozo *m*

mortal ['mɔːtəl] **1** *adj* mortal

2 *n* mortal *mf*

mortality [mɔː'tælɪtɪ] *n* mortalidad *f*

mortally ['mɔːtəlɪ] *adv* mortalmente; **m. wounded** herido(a) de muerte

mortar ['mɔːtə(r)] *n* mortero *m*

mortgage ['mɔːgɪdʒ] **1** *n* hipoteca *f*

2 *vt* hipotecar

mortician [mɔː'tɪʃən] *n US (undertaker)* encargado(a) *m,f* de funeraria

mortify ['mɔːtɪfaɪ] *vt* mortificar; *Fam* **I was mortified** me sentí avergonzado(a)

mortuary ['mɔːtʃʊərɪ] *n* depósito *m* de cadáveres

mosaic [mə'zeɪk] *n* mosaico *m*

Moscow ['mɒskəʊ, US 'mɒskaʊ] *n* Moscú

Moslem ['mɒzləm] *adj & n* musulmán(a-na) *(m,f)*

mosque [mɒsk] *n* mezquita *f*

mosquito [mɒs'kiːtəʊ] *n (pl* **mosquitoes**) mosquito *m*; **m. net** mosquitero *m*

moss [mɒs] *n* musgo *m*

most [məʊst] **1** *adj* *(superl of* **much, many**) **(a)** *(greatest in quantity etc)* más; **this house suffered (the) m. damage** esta casa fue la más afectada; **who made (the) m. mistakes?** ¿quién cometió más errores?

(b) *(the majority of)* la mayoría de, la mayor parte de; **for the m. part** por lo general; **m. of the time** la mayor parte del tiempo; **m. people** la mayoría de la gente

2 *pron (greatest part)* la mayor parte; *(greatest number)* lo máximo, lo más; *(the majority of people)* la mayoría; **at the (very) m.** como máximo; **to make the m. of sth** aprovechar algo al máximo

3 *adv (superl of* **much**) **(a)** más; **the m. intelligent student** el estudiante más inteligente; **what I like m.** lo que más me gusta

(b) *(very)* muy; **m. likely** muy probablemente; **m. of all** sobre todo

mostly ['məʊstlɪ] *adv (chiefly)* en su mayor parte; *(generally)* generalmente; *(usually)* normalmente

MOT [eməʊ'tiː] *n Br (abbr* **Ministry of Transport**) **M. test** inspección técnica de vehículos, ≃ ITV

motel [məʊ'tel] *n* motel *m*

moth [mɒθ] *n* mariposa nocturna; **clothes m.** polilla *f*

mother ['mʌðə(r)] **1** *n* madre *f*; **unmarried m.** madre soltera; **M.'s Day** Día *m* de la Madre; **m. tongue** lengua materna

2 *vt* cuidar maternalmente

motherhood ['mʌðəhʊd] *n* maternidad *f*

mother-in-law ['mʌðərɪnlɔː] *n* suegra *f*

motherly ['mʌðəlɪ] *adj* maternal

mother-of-pearl [mʌðərəv'pɜːl] *n* madreperla *f*, nácar *m*

mother-to-be [mʌðətə'biː] *n* futura madre

motif [məʊ'tiːf] *n Art & Mus* motivo *m*; *(embroidered etc)* adorno *m*; *Fig (main subject)* tema *m*

motion ['məʊʃən] **1** *n (movement)* movimiento *m*; *(gesture)* ademán *m*; *(proposal)* moción *f*

  2 *vt & vi* hacer señas; **to m. (to) sb to do sth** hacer señas a algn para que haga algo

motionless ['məʊʃənlɪs] *adj* inmóvil

motivate ['məʊtɪveɪt] *vt* motivar

motivation [məʊtɪ'veɪʃən] *n* motivación *f*

motive ['məʊtɪv] **1** *adj (force)* motriz

  2 *n (reason)* motivo *m*; *Jur* móvil *m*; **with the best of motives** con la mejor intención

motley ['mɒtlɪ] *adj* (**motlier, motliest**) *(multicoloured)* abigarrado(a); *(varied)* variado(a)

motor ['məʊtə(r)] *n (engine)* motor *m*; *Fam (car)* máquina *f*; **m. racing** carreras *fpl* de coches

motorbike ['məʊtəbaɪk] *n Fam* motocicleta *f*, moto *f*

motorboat ['məʊtəbəʊt] *n* (lancha) motora *f*

motorcar ['məʊtəkɑː(r)] *n* coche *m*, automóvil *m*

motorcycle ['məʊtəsaɪkəl] *n* motocicleta *f*

motorcyclist ['məʊtəsaɪklɪst] *n* motociclista *mf*

motoring ['məʊtərɪŋ] *n* automovilismo *m*

motorist ['məʊtərɪst] *n* automovilista *mf*

motorway ['məʊtəweɪ] *n Br* autopista *f*

mottled ['mɒtəld] *adj (skin, animal)* con manchas; *(surface)* moteado(a)

motto ['mɒtəʊ] *n* lema *m*

mould¹ [məʊld] *n (fungus)* moho *m*

mould² [məʊld] **1** *n* molde *m*

  2 *vt* moldear; *(clay)* modelar

moulder ['məʊldə(r)] *vi* **to m. (away)** desmoronarse

moulding ['məʊldɪŋ] *n* moldura *f*

mouldy ['məʊldɪ] *adj* (**mouldier, mouldiest**) mohoso(a); **to go m.** enmohecerse

moult [məʊlt] *vi* mudar

mound [maʊnd] *n* montón *m*; *(small hill)* montículo *m*

mount¹ [maʊnt] *n* monte *m*; **M. Everest** (Monte) Everest *m*

mount² [maʊnt] **1** *n (horse)* montura *f*; *(support)* soporte *m*, base *f*; *(for photograph)* marco *m*; *(for jewel)* engaste *m*

  2 *vt (horse)* subirse *or* montar a; *(campaign)* organizar; *(photograph)* enmarcar; *(jewel)* engastar

  3 *vi (go up)* subir; *(get on horse, bike)* montar; *(increase)* subir

  ▸ **mount up** *vi (accumulate)* acumularse

mountain ['maʊntɪn] **1** *n* montaña *f*; *Fig (pile)* montón *m*

  2 *adj* de montaña, montañés(esa); **m. bike** bicicleta *f* de montaña; **m. range** sierra *f*, cordillera *f*

mountaineer [maʊntɪ'nɪə(r)] *n* alpinista *mf*, *Am* andinista *mf*

mountaineering [maʊntɪ'nɪərɪŋ] *n* alpinismo *m*, *Am* andinismo *m*

mountainous ['maʊntɪnəs] *adj* montañoso(a)

mourn [mɔːn] *vt & vi* **to m. (for) sb** llorar la muerte de algn

mourner ['mɔːnə(r)] *n* doliente *mf*

mournful ['mɔːnfʊl] *adj* triste; *(voice)* lúgubre

mourning ['mɔːnɪŋ] *n* luto *m*; **in m.** de luto

mouse [maʊs] *n (pl* **mice** *) also Comput* ratón *m*

mousetrap ['maʊstræp] *n* ratonera *f*

mousse [muːs] *n Culin* mousse *f*; *(for hair)* (**styling**) **m.** espuma *f* (moldeadora)

moustache [mə'stɑːʃ] *n* bigote *m*

mousy ['maʊsɪ] *adj* (**mousier, mousiest**) *(colour)* pardusco(a); *(hair)* castaño claro; *(shy)* tímido(a)

mouth [maʊθ] **1** *n (pl* **mouths** [maʊðz]) (**a**) boca *f*; *Fam* **down in the m.** deprimido(a) (**b**) *(of cave etc)* entrada *f*; *(of river)* desembocadura *f*

  2 *vt* [maʊð] pronunciar; *(insults)* proferir

mouthful ['maʊθfʊl] *n (of food)* bocado *m*; *(of drink)* sorbo *m*; **to be a bit of a m.** ser difícil de pronunciar

mouth organ ['maʊθɔːgən] *n* armónica *f*

mouthpiece ['maʊθpiːs] *n Mus* boquilla *f*; *(of telephone)* micrófono *m*; *Fig (spokesman)* portavoz *m*

mouthwash ['maʊθwɒʃ] *n* elixir *m*, enjuague *m* bucal

mouthwatering ['maʊθwɔːtərɪŋ] *adj* muy apetitoso(a), que le hace a uno la boca agua

movable ['muːvəbəl] *adj* movible, móvil

move [muːv] **1** *n* (**a**) *(movement)* movimiento *m*; **to be on the m.** estar en marcha; **we must make a m.** debemos irnos ya; *Fam* **get a m. on!** ¡date prisa!

  (**b**) *(in game)* jugada *f*; *(turn)* turno *m*

  (**c**) *(course of action)* medida *f*; **to make the first m.** dar el primer paso

  (**d**) *(to new home)* mudanza *f*; *(to new job)* traslado *m*

  2 *vt* (**a**) mover; *(furniture etc)* cambiar de

sitio; *(transfer)* trasladar; **to m. house** mudarse (de casa)

  (**b**) *(in game)* mover

  (**c**) *(motivate)* inducir; *(persuade)* persuadir; **I won't be moved** no me harán cambiar de parecer

  (**d**) *(affect emotionally)* conmover

  (**e**) *(resolution etc)* proponer

  3 *vi* (**a**) *(change position)* moverse, desplazarse; *(change house)* mudarse (de casa); *(change post)* trasladarse; **m. out of the way!** ¡quítate de en medio!

  (**b**) *(train etc)* estar en marcha; **to start moving** ponerse en marcha

  (**c**) *(travel)* ir

  (**d**) *(leave)* irse, marcharse

  (**e**) *(in game)* hacer una jugada

  (**f**) *(take action)* tomar medidas

▸ **move about 1** *vt sep* cambiar de sitio

  2 *vi (be restless)* ir y venir; *(travel)* viajar de un lugar a otro

▸ **move along 1** *vt sep (move forward)* hacer avanzar; *(keep moving)* hacer circular

  2 *vi (move forward)* avanzar; *(keep moving)* circular; **m. along!** *(to person on bench)* ¡haz sitio!

▸ **move around** *vt sep & vi* = move about

▸ **move away 1** *vt sep* alejar, apartar (**from** de)

  2 *vi (move aside)* alejarse, apartarse; *(leave)* irse; *(change house)* mudarse (de casa)

▸ **move back 1** *vt sep (to original place)* volver

  2 *vi (withdraw)* retirarse; *(to original place)* volver

▸ **move forward 1** *vt sep* avanzar; *(clock)* adelantar

  2 *vi* avanzar, adelantarse

▸ **move in** *vi (into new home)* instalarse

▸ **move off** *vi (go away)* irse, marcharse; *(train)* salir

▸ **move on** *vi (keep moving)* circular; *(go forward)* avanzar; *(time)* transcurrir

▸ **move out** *vi (leave)* irse, marcharse; *(leave house)* mudarse

▸ **move over** *vi* correrse

▸ **move up** *vi (go up)* subir; *Fig (be promoted)* ser ascendido(a), ascender; *(move along)* correrse, hacer sitio

movement ['muːvmənt] *n* (**a**) movimiento *m*; *(gesture)* gesto *m*, ademán *m* (**b**) *(of goods)* transporte *m*; *(of employees)* traslado *m* (**c**) *(trend)* corriente *f* (**d**) *(of machine)* mecanismo *m* (**e**) *(of goods, capital)* circulación *f*

movie ['muːvɪ] *n* película *f*; **to go to the** **movies** ir al cine; **m. star** estrella *f* de cine; *US* **m. theater** cine *m*

moving ['muːvɪŋ] *adj (that moves)* móvil; *(car etc)* en marcha; *Fig (touching)* conmovedor(a)

mow [məʊ] *vt (pt* **mowed***; pp* **mown** *or* **mowed***) (lawn)* cortar; *(corn, wheat)* segar; *Fig* **to m. down** segar

mower ['məʊə(r)] *n* cortacésped *m*

mown [məʊn] *pp of* mow

MP [em'piː] *n Br Pol (abbr* **Member of Parliament***)* diputado(a) *m,f*

mph [empiː'eɪtʃ] *(abbr* **miles per hour***)* millas *fpl* por hora

MPhil [em'fɪl] *n (abbr* **Master of Philosophy***)* = curso de posgrado de dos años de duración, superior a un máster e inferior a un doctorado

Mr ['mɪstə(r)] *(abbr* **Mister***)* Sr

Mrs ['mɪsɪz] *(abbr* **Missus***)* Sra

Ms [məz] *n* Sra/Srta

Ms es el equivalente femenino de **Mr**, y se utiliza para dirigirse a una mujer sin precisar su estado civil.

MSc [emes'siː] *n (abbr* **Master of Science***)* máster *m* en Ciencias

much [mʌtʃ] **1** *adj* mucho(a); **as m. ... as** tanto(a) ... como; **how m. chocolate?** ¿cuánto chocolate?; **m. admiration** mucha admiración; **so m.** tanto(a)

  2 *adv* mucho; **as m. as** tanto como; **as m. as possible** todo lo posible; **how m.?** ¿cuánto?; **how m. is it?** ¿cuánto es?, ¿cuánto vale?; **m. better** mucho mejor; **m. more** mucho más; **so m. the better!** ¡tanto mejor!; **thank you very m.** muchísimas gracias; **they are m. the same** son más o menos iguales; **too m.** demasiado; **without so m. as** ni siquiera

  3 *pron* mucho; **I thought as m.** lo suponía; **m. of the town was destroyed** gran parte de la ciudad quedó destruida; **m. remains to be done** queda mucho por hacer

muck [mʌk] *n (dirt)* suciedad *f*; *(mud)* lodo *m*; *Fig* porquería *f*

▸ **muck about, muck around** *Fam* **1** *vi (idle)* perder el tiempo; *(play the fool)* hacer el tonto

  2 *vt sep* **to m. sb about** fastidiar a algn

▸ **muck up** *vt sep (dirty)* ensuciar; *Fig (spoil)* echar a perder

mucky ['mʌkɪ] *adj (* **muckier, muckiest** *)* sucio(a)

mucus ['mjuːkəs] *n* moco *m*, mucosidad *f*

mud [mʌd] *n* lodo *m*, barro *m*; *(thick)* fango *m*; *Fig* **to sling m. at sb** poner a

algn por los suelos; **m. flat** marisma *f*
muddle ['mʌdəl] **1** *n* desorden *m*; *Fig*
(mix-up) embrollo *m*, lío *m*; **to get into a**
m. hacerse un lío
  2 *vt* confundir
▶ **muddle through** *vi* arreglárselas, ingeniárselas
▶ **muddle up** *vt sep* confundir
muddy ['mʌdɪ] *adj* (**muddier, muddiest**)
(lane) fangoso(a); *(hands)* cubierto(a) de
lodo; *(liquid)* turbio(a)
mudguard ['mʌdgɑːd] *n Br* guardabarros *m inv*
muff¹ [mʌf] *n* manguito *m*; **ear muffs**
orejeras *fpl*
muff² [mʌf] *vt Fam* pifiar; **to m. it (up)**
estropearlo
muffin ['mʌfɪn] *n* panecillo *m*
muffle ['mʌfəl] *vt (sound)* amortiguar; **to**
m. (up) *(person)* abrigar
muffler ['mʌflə(r)] *n US Aut* silenciador
m
mug¹ [mʌg] *n (large cup)* tazón *m*; *(beer*
tankard) jarra *f*
mug² [mʌg] **1** *n Fam (fool)* tonto(a) *m,f*;
(face) jeta *f*
  2 *vt* atracar, asaltar
mugging ['mʌgɪŋ] *n* asalto *m*
muggy ['mʌgɪ] *adj* (**muggier, muggiest**)
bochornoso(a)
mule [mjuːl] *n* mulo(a) *m,f*
mull [mʌl] *vt* **mulled wine** = vino caliente
con especias
▶ **mull over** *vt sep* **to m. over sth** reflexionar sobre algo
multicoloured, *US* **multicolored**
['mʌltɪkʌləd] *adj* multicolor
multinational [mʌltɪ'næʃənəl] *adj & n*
multinacional *(f)*
multiple ['mʌltɪpəl] **1** *adj* múltiple; **m.**
sclerosis esclerosis *f* múltiple
  2 *n* múltiplo *m*
multiplication [mʌltɪplɪ'keɪʃən] *n* multiplicación *f*; **m. sign** signo *m* de multiplicar
multiply ['mʌltɪplaɪ] **1** *vt* multiplicar (**by**
por)
  2 *vi* multiplicarse
multipurpose [mʌltɪ'pɜːpəs] *adj* multi-
uso *inv*
multistorey [mʌltɪ'stɔːrɪ] *adj (building)*
de varios pisos; **m. car park** parking *m* de
varias plantas
multitude ['mʌltɪtjuːd] *n* multitud *f*, muchedumbre *f*
mum¹ [mʌm] *n Fam* mamá *f*
mum² [mʌm] *adj* **to keep m.** no decir ni
pío

mumble ['mʌmbəl] **1** *vi* hablar entre
dientes
  2 *vt* decir entre dientes
mumbo-jumbo ['mʌmbəʊ'dʒʌmbəʊ] *n*
(nonsense) palabrería *f*, monsergas *fpl*
mummy¹ ['mʌmɪ] *n Fam (mother)* mamá
f, mami *f*
mummy² ['mʌmɪ] *n (body)* momia *f*
mumps [mʌmps] *n sing* paperas *fpl*
munch [mʌntʃ] *vt & vi* mascar
mundane [mʌn'deɪn] *adj Pej (ordinary)*
prosaico(a); *(job, life)* rutinario(a)

> *Note that the Spanish word* **mundano** *is
> a false friend and is never a translation for
> the English word* **mundane**. *In Spanish,*
> **mundano** *means "worldly".*

municipal [mjuː'nɪsɪpəl] *adj* municipal
municipality [mjuːnɪsɪ'pælɪtɪ] *n* municipio *m*
mural ['mjʊərəl] *adj & n* mural *(m)*
Murcia [muːˈsiːə] *n* Murcia
murder ['mɜːdə(r)] **1** *n* asesinato *m*, homicidio *m*
  2 *vt* asesinar
murderer ['mɜːdərə(r)] *n* asesino(a) *m,f*
murderess ['mɜːdərɪs] *n* asesina *f*
murderous ['mɜːdərəs] *adj* homicida
murky ['mɜːkɪ] *adj* (**murkier, murkiest**)
oscuro(a); *(water)* turbio(a)
murmur ['mɜːmə(r)] **1** *n* murmullo *m*; *(of*
traffic) ruido *m*; *(complaint)* queja *f*
  2 *vt & vi* murmurar
muscle ['mʌsəl] **1** *n* músculo *m*
  2 *vi Fam* **to m. in on sth** entrometerse en
asuntos ajenos
muscular ['mʌskjʊlə(r)] *adj (pain, tissue)*
muscular; *(person)* musculoso(a)
Muse [mjuːz] *n (in mythology)* musa *f*
muse [mjuːz] *vi* **to m. on** *or* **about sth**
meditar algo
museum [mjuːˈzɪəm] *n* museo *m*
mushroom ['mʌʃruːm] **1** *n* seta *f*, hongo
m; *Culin* champiñón *m*
  2 *vi Fig* crecer de la noche a la mañana
music ['mjuːzɪk] *n* música *f*; **m. hall** teatro
m de variedades; **m. library** fonoteca *f*;
Psy **m. therapy** musicoterapia *f*
musical ['mjuːzɪkəl] **1** *adj* musical; **to be**
m. estar dotado(a) para la música
  2 *n* musical *m*
musician [mjuːˈzɪʃən] *n* músico(a) *m,f*
Muslim ['mʊzlɪm] *adj & n* musulmán(a-
na) *(m,f)*
muslin ['mʌzlɪn] *n* muselina *f*
mussel ['mʌsəl] *n* mejillón *m*
must [mʌst] **1** *v aux* (**a**) *(obligation)* deber, tener que; **you m. arrive on time**

tienes que or debes llegar a la hora (**b**) *(probability)* deber de; **he m. be ill** debe de estar enfermo

2 *n Fam* **to be a m.** ser imprescindible

mustache ['mʌstæʃ] *n US* bigote *m*

mustard ['mʌstəd] *n* mostaza *f*

muster ['mʌstə(r)] **1** *vt Fig* **to m. (up) courage** cobrar fuerzas

2 *vi* reunirse, juntarse

mustn't ['mʌsənt] = **must not**

musty ['mʌstɪ] *adj* (**mustier, mustiest**) que huele a cerrado or a humedad

mute ['mjuːt] **1** *adj* mudo(a)

2 *n (person)* mudo(a) *m,f; Mus* sordina *f*

muted ['mjuːtɪd] *adj (sound)* sordo(a); *(colour)* suave

mutilate ['mjuːtɪleɪt] *vt* mutilar

mutiny ['mjuːtɪnɪ] **1** *n* motín *m*

2 *vi* amotinarse

mutter ['mʌtə(r)] **1** *n (mumble)* murmullo *m*

2 *vt* murmurar, decir entre dientes

3 *vi (angrily)* refunfuñar

mutton ['mʌtən] *n* (carne *f* de) cordero *m*

mutual ['mjuːtʃʊəl] *adj* mutuo(a); *(shared)* común

Muzak® ['mjuːzæk] *n* música *f* de supermercado

muzzle ['mʌzəl] **1** *n (snout)* hocico *m; (for dog)* bozal *m; (of gun)* boca *f*

2 *vt (dog)* abozalar; *Fig* amordazar

my [maɪ] *poss adj* mi; **my cousins** mis primos; **my father** mi padre; **one of my friends** un amigo mío; **I washed my hair** me lavé el pelo; **I twisted my ankle** me torcí el tobillo

myriad ['mɪrɪəd] *n Literary* miríada *f*

myself [maɪ'self] *pers pron* (**a**) *(emphatic)* yo mismo(a); **my husband and m.** mi marido y yo (**b**) *(reflexive)* me; **I hurt m.** me hice daño (**c**) *(after prep)* mí (mismo(a))

mysterious [mɪ'stɪərɪəs] *adj* misterioso(a)

mystery ['mɪstərɪ] *n* misterio *m*

mystical ['mɪstɪkəl] *adj* místico(a)

mystify ['mɪstɪfaɪ] *vt* dejar perplejo(a)

mystique [mɪ'stiːk] *n* mística *f*

myth [mɪθ] *n* mito *m*; **it's a complete m.** es pura fantasía

mythology [mɪ'θɒlədʒɪ] *n* mitología *f*

N

N, n [en] *n (the letter)* N, n *f*
N (*abbr* **North**) N
nab [næb] *vt Fam* pillar
naff [næf] *adj Br Fam* (**a**) *(tasteless)* hortera, cutre (**b**) *(for emphasis)* **n. all** nada de nada
NAFTA ['næftə] *n* (*abbr* **North American Free Trade Agreement**) NAFTA *f*, TLC *m*
nag [næg] **1** *vt* dar la tabarra a; **to n. sb to do sth** dar la tabarra a algn para que haga algo
2 *vi* quejarse
nagging ['nægɪŋ] *adj (persistent)* continuo(a)
nail [neɪl] **1** *n* (**a**) *(of finger, toe)* uña *f*; **n. clippers** cortaúñas *m inv*; **n. polish** *or* **varnish** esmalte *m or* laca *f* de uñas (**b**) *(metal)* clavo *m*; *Fig* **to hit the n. on the head** dar en el clavo
2 *vt* (**a**) clavar (**b**) *Fam (catch, trap)* pillar, coger
nailbrush ['neɪlbrʌʃ] *n* cepillo *m* de uñas
nailfile ['neɪlfaɪl] *n* lima *f* de uñas
nail-scissors ['neɪlsɪzəz] *npl* tijeras *fpl* de uñas
naïve [naɪ'iːv] *adj* ingenuo(a)
naked ['neɪkɪd] *adj* desnudo(a); *(flame)* sin protección; **the n. truth** la pura verdad
name [neɪm] **1** *n* (**a**) nombre *m*; *(surname)* apellido *m*; **what's your n.?** ¿cómo te llamas?; **to call sb names** poner verde a algn (**b**) *(reputation)* reputación *f*; **to have a bad/good n.** tener mala/buena reputación; **to make a n. for oneself** hacerse famoso(a)
2 *vt* (**a**) llamar; **to n. sb after** *or US* **for sb** poner a algn el nombre de algn (**b**) *(appoint)* nombrar (**c**) *(refer to)* mencionar
nameless ['neɪmlɪs] *adj* anónimo(a); **to remain n.** permanecer en el anonimato
namely ['neɪmlɪ] *adv* a saber
namesake ['neɪmseɪk] *n* tocayo(a) *m,f*
nanny ['nænɪ] *n* niñera *f*
nap [næp] **1** *n (sleep)* siesta *f*; **to have a n.** echar la *or* una siesta
2 *vi Fig* **to catch sb napping** coger a algn desprevenido(a)

napalm ['neɪpɑːm] *n* napalm *m*
nape [neɪp] *n* nuca *f*, cogote *m*
napkin ['næpkɪn] *n* (**table**) **n.** servilleta *f*
Naples ['neɪpəlz] *n* Nápoles
nappy ['næpɪ] *n Br* pañal *m*
narcissus [nɑː'sɪsəs] *n Bot* narciso *m*
narcotic [nɑː'kɒtɪk] **1** *adj* narcótico(a)
2 *n (usu pl)* narcótico *m*, estupefaciente *m*
narrate [nə'reɪt] *vt* narrar, relatar
narration [nə'reɪʃən] *n* narración *f*, relato *m*
narrative ['nærətɪv] **1** *n Lit* narrativa *f*; *(story)* narración *f*
2 *adj* narrativo(a)
narrator [nə'reɪtə(r)] *n* narrador(a) *m,f*
narrow ['nærəʊ] **1** *adj* (**a**) *(passage, road etc)* estrecho(a), angosto(a) (**b**) *(restricted)* reducido(a); *(sense)* estricto(a); **to have a n. escape** librarse por los pelos
2 *vi* estrecharse
narrowly ['nærəʊlɪ] *adv* (**a**) *(closely)* de cerca (**b**) *(by a small margin)* por poco
▸ **narrow down 1** *vt sep* reducir, limitar
2 *vi* **to n. down to** reducirse a
narrow-minded ['nærəʊ'maɪndɪd] *adj* de miras estrechas
nasal ['neɪzəl] *adj* nasal; *(voice)* gangoso(a)
nastiness ['nɑːstɪnɪs] *n* (**a**) *(unpleasantness)* carácter *m* desagradable (**b**) *(maliciousness)* mala intención
nasty ['nɑːstɪ] *adj* (**nastier, nastiest**) (**a**) *(person)* desagradable; **a n. business** un asunto feo; **a n. trick** una mala jugada *or* pasada; **cheap and n.** hortera; **to turn n.** *(of weather, situation)* ponerse feo(a) (**b**) *(unfriendly)* antipático(a); *(malicious)* mal intencionado(a); *Fam* **he's a n. piece of work** es un asco de tío (**c**) *(dirty)* sucio(a), asqueroso(a) (**d**) *(illness, accident)* grave
nation ['neɪʃən] *n* nación *f*
national ['næʃnəl] **1** *adj* nacional; **n. anthem** himno *m* nacional; **n. insurance** seguridad *f* social; *Br Mil* **n. service** servicio *m* militar
2 *n* súbdito(a) *m,f*
nationalism ['næʃnəlɪzəm] *n* nacionalismo *m*

nationalist ['næʃnəlɪst] *adj & n* nacionalista *(mf)*
nationality [næʃə'nælɪtɪ] *n* nacionalidad *f*
nationalization [næʃnəlaɪ'zeɪʃən] *n* na-
cionalización *f*
nationalize ['næʃnəlaɪz] *vt* nacionalizar
nationwide ['neɪʃənwaɪd] *adj* de ámbito
nacional
native ['neɪtɪv] **1** *adj* (**a**) *(place)* natal; **n.
land** patria *f*; **n. language** lengua materna
(**b**) *(innate)* innato(a) (**c**) *(plant, animal)*
originario(a) (**to** de)
 2 *n* nativo(a) *m,f*, natural *mf*; *(original
inhabitant)* indígena *mf*
NATO, Nato ['neɪtəʊ] *n* (*abbr* **North
Atlantic Treaty Organization**) OTAN *f*
natter ['nætə(r)] *Fam* **1** *vi* charlar
 2 *n* charla *f*
natural ['nætʃərəl] **1** *adj* (**a**) natural (**b**)
(normal) normal; **it's only n. that ...** es
lógico que ... (**c**) *(born)* nato(a)
 2 *n* (**a**) **she's a n. for the job** es la
persona ideal para el trabajo (**b**) *Mus*
becuadro *m*
naturalize ['nætʃərəlaɪz] *vt* **to become
naturalized** naturalizarse
naturally ['nætʃərəlɪ] *adv* (**a**) *(of course)*
naturalmente (**b**) *(by nature)* por naturaleza (**c**) *(in a relaxed manner)* con naturalidad
nature ['neɪtʃə(r)] *n* (**a**) naturaleza *f* (**b**)
(character) naturaleza *f*, carácter *m*; **by n.**
por naturaleza; **human n.** la naturaleza
humana (**c**) *(sort, kind)* índole *f*, clase *f*
naught [nɔːt] *n Literary* nada *f*; **to come
to n.** fracasar
naughtily ['nɔːtɪlɪ] *adv* **to behave n.** portarse mal
naughty ['nɔːtɪ] *adj* (**naughtier, naugh-
tiest**) (**a**) *(child)* travieso(a) (**b**) *(joke,
story)* atrevido(a), picante
nausea ['nɔːzɪə] *n Med (sickness)* náusea
f
nauseate ['nɔːzɪeɪt] *vt (disgust)* dar asco
a
nauseating ['nɔːzɪeɪtɪŋ] *adj* nauseabun-
do(a)
nautical ['nɔːtɪkəl] *adj* náutico(a); **n. mile**
milla marítima
naval ['neɪvəl] *adj* naval; **n. officer** oficial
mf de marina; **n. power** potencia marítima *or* naval
Navarre [nə'vɑː(r)] *n* Navarra
nave [neɪv] *n Archit* nave *f*
navel ['neɪvəl] *n Anat* ombligo *m*
navigate ['nævɪgeɪt] **1** *vt (river)* navegar
por; *Naut (ship)* gobernar

 2 *vi* navegar; *(in driving)* indicar la dirección
navigation [nævɪ'geɪʃən] *n Naut* navegación *f*
navigator ['nævɪgeɪtə(r)] *n* (**a**) *Naut* na-
vegante *mf*, oficial *mf* de derrota (**b**) *Aut
& Av* copiloto *mf*
navvy ['nævɪ] *n Br Fam* peón *m*
navy ['neɪvɪ] *n* marina *f*; **n. blue** azul
marino
Nazi ['nɑːtsɪ] *adj & n* nazi *(mf)*
Nazism ['nɑːtsɪzəm] *n* nazismo *m*
NB, nb [en'biː] (*abbr* **nota bene**) N.B.
neap [niːp] *n* **n. (tide)** marea muerta
near [nɪə(r)] **1** *adj (in space)* cercano(a);
(in time) próximo(a); **in the n. future** en
un futuro próximo; **it was a n. thing** poco
faltó
 2 *adv (in space)* cerca; **n. and far** por
todas partes; **that's n. enough** (ya) vale,
está bien
 3 *prep* cerca de; **n. the end of the film**
hacia el final de la película
 4 *vt* acercarse a
nearby [nɪə'baɪ] **1** *adj* cercano(a)
 2 *adv* cerca
nearly ['nɪəlɪ] *adv* casi; **very n.** casi, casi;
we haven't n. enough no alcanza ni con
mucho
nearside ['nɪəsaɪd] *n Aut (with left-hand
drive)* lado izquierdo; *(with right-hand
drive)* lado derecho
near-sighted [nɪə'saɪtɪd] *adj* miope
neat [niːt] *adj* (**a**) *(room, habits etc)* orde-
nado(a); *(handwriting)* claro(a); *(appearance)* pulcro(a) (**b**) *(idea)* ingenioso(a)
(**c**) *(whisky etc)* solo(a) (**d**) *US Fam (fine)*
chulísimo(a)
neatly ['niːtlɪ] *adv* (**a**) *(carefully)* cuidadosamente (**b**) *(cleverly)* hábilmente
necessarily [nesɪ'serəlɪ] *adv* necesaria-
mente, por fuerza
necessary ['nesɪsərɪ] **1** *adj* (**a**) *(essential)*
necesario(a); **to do what is n.** hacer lo
que haga falta; **if n.** si es preciso (**b**)
(unavoidable) inevitable
 2 *n* **the n.** lo necesario
necessitate [nɪ'sesɪteɪt] *vt* necesitar, exigir
necessity [nɪ'sesɪtɪ] *n* (**a**) necesidad *f*;
out of n. por necesidad (**b**) *(article)* requisito *m* indispensable; **necessities** artículos *mpl* de primera necesidad
neck [nek] **1** *n* cuello *m*; *(of animal)*
pescuezo *m*; **to be n. and n.** ir parejos;
to be up to one's n. in debt estar hasta el
cuello de deudas; **to risk one's n.** jugarse
el tipo; **to stick one's n. out** arriesgarse; **to**

win/lose by a n. *(in horse racing)* ganar/perder por una cabeza; **low n.** escote bajo
2 *vi Fam* magrearse
necklace ['neklɪs] *n* collar *m*
neckline ['neklaɪn] *n (of dress)* escote *m*
necktie ['nektaɪ] *n US* corbata *f*
nectar ['nektə(r)] *n* néctar *m*
nectarine ['nektəriːn] *n* nectarina *f*
née [neɪ] *adj* **n. Brown** de soltera Brown
need [niːd] **1** *n* (**a**) necesidad *f*; **if n. be** si fuera necesario; **there's no n. for you to do that** no hace falta que hagas eso (**b**) *(poverty)* indigencia *f*; **to be in n.** estar necesitado; **to help a friend in n.** sacar a un amigo de un apuro
2 *vt* (**a**) necesitar; **I n. to see him** tengo que verle; *Ironic* **that's all I n.** sólo me faltaba eso (**b**) *(action, solution etc)* requerir, exigir
3 *v aux* tener que, deber; **n. he go?** ¿tiene que ir?; **you needn't wait** no hace falta que esperes

Cuando se emplea como verbo modal sólo existe una forma, y los auxiliares **do/does** no se usan: **he need only worry about himself; need she go?; it needn't matter.**

needle ['niːdəl] **1** *n* (**a**) *(for sewing, knitting)* aguja *f* (**b**) *Bot* hoja *f* (**c**) *Br Fam* **to get the n.** picarse
2 *vt Fam* pinchar
needless ['niːdlɪs] *adj* innecesario(a); **n. to say** huelga decir
needlessly ['niːdlɪslɪ] *adv* innecesariamente
needlework ['niːdəlwɜːk] *n (sewing)* costura *f; (embroidery)* bordado *m*
needy ['niːdɪ] *adj* (**needier, neediest**) necesitado(a)
negate [nɪ'geɪt] *vt* (**a**) *(deny)* negar (**b**) *(nullify)* anular
negative ['negətɪv] **1** *adj* negativo(a)
2 *n* (**a**) *Ling* negación *f* (**b**) *Phot* negativo *m*
neglect [nɪ'glekt] **1** *vt* (**a**) *(child, duty etc)* descuidar, desatender (**b**) **to n. to do sth** *(omit to do)* no hacer algo
2 *n* dejadez *f*; **n. of duty** incumplimiento *m* del deber
neglectful [nɪ'glektfʊl] *adj* descuidado(a), negligente
negligée ['neglɪʒeɪ] *n* salto *m* de cama
negligence ['neglɪdʒəns] *n* negligencia *f*, descuido *m*
negligent ['neglɪdʒənt] *adj* negligente, descuidado(a)

negligible ['neglɪdʒɪbəl] *adj* insignificante
negotiate [nɪ'gəʊʃɪeɪt] **1** *vt* (**a**) *(contract)* negociar (**b**) *Fig (obstacle)* salvar, franquear
2 *vi* negociar
negotiation [nɪgəʊʃɪ'eɪʃən] *n* negociación *f*
negro ['niːgrəʊ] *n (pl* **negroes**) negro(a) *m,f*
neigh [neɪ] **1** *n* relincho *m*
2 *vi* relinchar
neighbour, *US* **neighbor** ['neɪbə(r)] *n* vecino(a) *m,f; Rel* prójimo *m*
neighbourhood, *US* **neighborhood** ['neɪbəhʊd] *n (district)* vecindad *f*, barrio *m; (people)* vecindario *m*
neighbouring, *US* **neighboring** ['neɪbərɪŋ] *adj* vecino(a)
neither ['naɪðə(r), 'niːðə(r)] **1** *adj & pron* ninguno de los dos/ninguna de las dos
2 *adv & conj* (**a**) ni; **n. ... nor** ni ... ni; *Fig* **it's n. here nor there** no viene al caso (**b**) tampoco; **she was not there and n. was her sister** ella no estaba, ni su hermana tampoco
neon ['niːɒn] *n* neón *m*; **n. light** luz *f* de neón
nephew ['nefjuː] *n* sobrino *m*
nerd [nɜːd] *n Fam* (**a**) *(boring person)* petardo(a) *m,f*, plasta *mf*, *Méx* sangrón(ona) *m,f*, *RP* nerd *mf* (**b**) *(as insult)* bobo(a) *m,f*, memo(a) *m,f*
nerve [nɜːv] *n* (**a**) *Anat* nervio *m*; **to get on sb's nerves** poner los nervios de punta a algn; **n. gas** gas nervioso (**b**) *(courage)* valor *m* (**c**) *Fam (cheek)* cara *f*, descaro *m*; **what a n.!** ¡qué cara!
nerve-racking ['nɜːvrækɪŋ] *adj* crispante, exasperante
nervous ['nɜːvəs] *adj* (**a**) nervioso(a); **n. breakdown** depresión nerviosa (**b**) *(afraid)* miedoso(a) (**c**) *(timid)* tímido(a)
nest [nest] **1** *n Orn* nido *m; (hen's)* nidal *m; (animal's)* madriguera *f; Fig* **n. egg** ahorros *mpl*
2 *vi (birds)* anidar
nestle ['nesəl] **1** *vt* recostar
2 *vi (settle comfortably)* acomodarse
Net [net] *n Fam Comput* **the N.** *(Internet)* la Red; **N. user** internauta *mf*
net¹ [net] *n* red *f; Br* **n. curtains** visillos *mpl*
net² [net] **1** *adj* neto(a); **n. weight** peso neto
2 *vt (earn)* ganar neto
netball ['netbɔːl] *n Sport* baloncesto femenino

Netherlands ['neðələndz] *npl* **the N.** los Países Bajos

netting ['netɪŋ] *n* redes *fpl*, malla *f*

nettle ['netəl] **1** *n Bot* ortiga *f*
2 *vt Fam* irritar

network ['netwɜːk] **1** *n* red *f*
2 *vi (establish contacts)* establecer contactos

neurosis [njʊ'rəʊsɪs] *n* neurosis *f*

neurotic [njʊ'rɒtɪk] *adj & n* neurótico(a) *(m,f)*

neuter ['njuːtə(r)] **1** *adj* neutro(a)
2 *n Ling* neutro *m*
3 *vt (geld)* castrar

neutral ['njuːtrəl] **1** *adj* neutro(a); *Pol* **to remain n.** permanecer neutral
2 *n Aut* punto muerto

neutrality [njuː'trælɪtɪ] *n* neutralidad *f*

neutralize ['njuːtrəlaɪz] *vt* neutralizar

neutron ['njuːtrɒn] *n Phys* neutrón *m*; **n. bomb** bomba *f* de neutrones

never ['nevə(r)] *adv* nunca, jamás; **he n. complains** nunca se queja, no se queja nunca; **n. again** nunca (ja)más; **n. in all my life** jamás en la vida; *Fam* **n. mind** da igual, no importa; *Fam* **well, I n. (did)!** ¡no me digas!

never-ending ['nevər'endɪŋ] *adj* sin fin, interminable

nevertheless [nevəðə'les] *adv* sin embargo, no obstante

new [njuː] *adj* nuevo(a); **as good as n.** como nuevo; **n. baby** recién nacido *m*; **n. moon** luna nueva; **N. Year** Año nuevo; **N. Year's Eve** Nochevieja *f*; **N. York** Nueva York; **N. Zealand** Nueva Zelanda

newborn ['njuːbɔːn] *adj* recién nacido(a)

newcomer ['njuːkʌmə(r)] *n* recién llegado(a) *m,f*; *(to job etc)* nuevo(a) *m,f*

newfangled ['njuːfæŋgəld] *adj* novedoso(a)

newly ['njuːlɪ] *adv* recién, recientemente

newlywed ['njuːlɪwed] *n* recién casado(a) *m,f*

news [njuːz] *n sing* noticias *fpl*; **a piece of n.** una noticia; *Fam* **it's n. to me** ahora me entero; **n. agency** agencia *f* de información; *US* **n. in brief** avance informativo; **n. bulletin** boletín informativo; **n. clipping** recorte *m* de periódico; **n. summary** avance informativo;

newsagent ['njuːzeɪdʒənt] *n* vendedor(a) *m,f* de periódicos

newsflash ['njuːzflæʃ] *n* noticia *f* de última hora

newsgroup ['njuːzgruːp] *n Comput* grupo *m* de noticias

newsletter ['njuːzletə(r)] *n* hoja informativa

newspaper ['njuːzpeɪpə(r)] *n* periódico *m*, diario *m*

newsprint ['njuːzprɪnt] *n* papel *m* de periódico

newsreader ['njuːzriːdə(r)] *n TV & Rad* presentador(a) *m,f* de los informativos

newsreel ['njuːzriːl] *n* noticiario *m*

news-stand ['njuːzstænd] *n* quiosco *m* de periódicos

newt [njuːt] *n Zool* tritón *m*

next [nekst] **1** *adj* (**a**) *(in place)* de al lado (**b**) *(in time)* próximo(a); **the n. day** el día siguiente; **n. Friday** el viernes que viene; **n. time** la próxima vez; **the week after n.** dentro de dos semanas (**c**) *(in order)* siguiente, próximo(a); **n. of kin** pariente *m* más cercano
2 *adv* después, luego; **what shall we do n.?** ¿qué hacemos ahora?
3 *prep* **n. to** al lado de, junto a; **n. to nothing** casi nada

next-door 1 *adj* ['neksdɔː(r)] de al lado; **our n. neighbour** el vecino/la vecina de al lado
2 *adv* [neks'dɔː(r)] al lado

NHS [eneɪtʃ'es] *n Br (abbr* **National Health Service)** Seguridad *f* Social

nib [nɪb] *n* plumilla *f*

nibble ['nɪbəl] *vt & vi* mordisquear

nice [naɪs] *adj* (**a**) *(person)* simpático(a); *(thing)* agradable; **n. and cool** fresquito(a); **to smell/taste n.** oler/saber bien (**b**) *(nice-looking)* bonito(a), *Am* lindo(a) (**c**) *Ironic* menudo(a); **a n. mess you've made!** ¡menudo lío has hecho! (**d**) *Fml (subtle)* sutil

nicely ['naɪslɪ] *adv* muy bien

niche [niːʃ] *n* (**a**) hornacina *f*, nicho *m* (**b**) *Fig* hueco *m*

nick [nɪk] **1** *n* (**a**) *(notch)* muesca *f*; *(cut)* herida pequeña; *Fam* **in the n. of time** en el momento preciso (**b**) *Br Fam* **the n.** *(prison)* chirona *f*
2 *vt Br Fam* (**a**) *(steal)* birlar (**b**) *(arrest)* pillar

nickel ['nɪkəl] *n* (**a**) níquel *m*; **n. silver** alpaca *f* (**b**) *US* moneda *f* de 5 centavos

nickname ['nɪkneɪm] **1** *n* apodo *m*
2 *vt* apodar

nicotine ['nɪkətiːn] *n* nicotina *f*

niece [niːs] *n* sobrina *f*

nifty ['nɪftɪ] *adj* (**niftier, niftiest**) (**a**) *(quick)* rápido(a); *(agile)* ágil (**b**) *(ingenious)* ingenioso(a)

Nigeria [naɪ'dʒɪərɪə] *n* Nigeria

nigger ['nɪgə(r)] *n Fam Pej* negro(a) *m,f*

niggling [ˈnɪgəlɪŋ] *adj (trifling)* insignificante; *(irritating)* molesto(a)

night [naɪt] *n* noche *f*; **at n.** de noche; **at twelve o'clock at n.** a las doce de la noche; **last n.** anoche; **to have a n. out** salir por la noche; **n. life** vida nocturna; *Fam* **n. owl** trasnochador(a) *m,f*; **n. school** escuela nocturna; **n. shift** turno *m* de noche

nightclub [ˈnaɪtklʌb] *n* sala *f* de fiestas; *(disco)* discoteca *f*

nightdress [ˈnaɪtdres] *n* camisón *m*

nightfall [ˈnaɪtfɔːl] *n* anochecer *m*

nightgown [ˈnaɪtgaʊn] *n* camisón *m*

nightingale [ˈnaɪtɪŋgeɪl] *n* ruiseñor *m*

nightly [ˈnaɪtlɪ] **1** *adj* de cada noche
2 *adv* todas las noches

nightmare [ˈnaɪtmeə(r)] *n* pesadilla *f*

nightshade [ˈnaɪtʃeɪd] *n Bot* **deadly n.** belladona *f*

night-time [ˈnaɪttaɪm] *n* noche *f*; **at n.** por la noche

nil [nɪl] *n* nada *f*; *Sport* cero *m*; **two n.** dos a cero

Nile [naɪl] *n* **the N.** el Nilo

nimble [ˈnɪmbəl] *adj* ágil, rápido(a)

nine [naɪn] *adj & n* nueve *(m inv)*; *Fam* **dressed up to the nines** de punta en blanco

nineteen [naɪnˈtiːn] *adj & n* diecinueve *(m inv)*

nineteenth [naɪnˈtiːnθ] *adj* decimonoveno(a)

ninety [ˈnaɪntɪ] *adj & n* noventa *(m inv)*

ninth [naɪnθ] **1** *adj & n* noveno(a) *(m,f)*
2 *n (fraction)* noveno *m*

nip [nɪp] **1** *vt* (**a**) *(pinch)* pellizcar (**b**) *(bite)* morder; **to n. sth in the bud** cortar algo de raíz
2 *n* (**a**) *(pinch)* pellizco *m* (**b**) *(bite)* mordisco *m*

nipple [ˈnɪpəl] *n* (**a**) *Anat (female)* pezón *m*; *(male)* tetilla *f* (**b**) *US (on baby's bottle)* tetilla *f*, tetina *f*

nippy [ˈnɪpɪ] *adj* (**nippier, nippiest**) *Fam* (**a**) *Br (quick)* rápido(a) (**b**) *(cold)* fresquito(a)

nit [nɪt] *n* liendre *f*

nitrogen [ˈnaɪtrədʒən] *n Chem* nitrógeno *m*

nitroglycerin(e) [naɪtrəʊˈglɪsəriːn] *n Chem* nitroglicerina *f*

nitty-gritty [ˈnɪtɪˈgrɪtɪ] *n Fam* **to get down to the n.** ir al grano

nitwit [ˈnɪtwɪt] *n Fam* imbécil *mf*

no [nəʊ] **1** *adv* no; **come here! – no!** ¡ven aquí! – ¡no!; **no longer** ya no; **no less than** no menos de

2 *adj* ninguno(a); **she has no children** no tiene hijos; **I have no idea** no tengo (ni) idea; **it's no good** *or* **use** no vale la pena; *Aut* **no parking** *(sign)* prohibido aparcar; **no sensible person** ninguna persona razonable; *Fam* **no way!** ¡ni hablar!

3 *n* no *m*; **she won't take no for an answer** no para hasta salirse con la suya; **to say no** decir que no

no. *(pl* **nos.**) *(abbr* **number**) n, núm.

nobility [nəʊˈbɪlɪtɪ] *n* nobleza *f*

noble [ˈnəʊbəl] *adj* noble

nobleman [ˈnəʊbəlmən] *n* noble *m*

noblewoman [ˈnəʊbəlwʊmən] *n* noble *f*

nobody [ˈnəʊbədɪ] **1** *pron* nadie; **there was n. there** no había nadie; **n. else** nadie más
2 *n* nadie *m*; **he's a n.** es un don nadie

nocturnal [nɒkˈtɜːnəl] *adj* nocturno(a)

nod [nɒd] **1** *n (of greeting)* saludo *m (con la cabeza)*; *(of agreement)* señal *f* de asentimiento
2 *vi (greet)* saludar con la cabeza; *(agree)* asentir con la cabeza
3 *vt* **to n. one's head** inclinar la cabeza
► **nod off** *vi* dormirse

no-go [ˈnəʊˈgəʊ] *adj* **n. area** zona prohibida

noise [nɔɪz] *n* ruido *m*; **to make a n.** hacer ruido

noiseless [ˈnɔɪzlɪs] *adj* silencioso(a), sin ruido

noisy [ˈnɔɪzɪ] *adj* (**noisier, noisiest**) ruidoso(a)

nomad [ˈnəʊmæd] *n* nómada *mf*

no-man's-land [ˈnəʊmænzlænd] *n* tierra *f* de nadie

nominal [ˈnɒmɪnəl] *adj* nominal; *(payment, rent)* simbólico(a)

nominate [ˈnɒmɪneɪt] *vt* (**a**) *(propose)* designar, proponer (**b**) *(appoint)* nombrar

nomination [nɒmɪˈneɪʃən] *n* (**a**) *(proposal)* propuesta *f* (**b**) *(appointment)* nombramiento *m*

nominative [ˈnɒmɪnətɪv] *n* nominativo *m*

nominee [nɒmɪˈniː] *n* persona propuesta

non- [nɒn] *pref* no

non-aggression [nɒnəˈgreʃən] *n Pol* no agresión *f*; **n. pact** pacto *m* de no agresión

non-alcoholic [nɒnælkəˈhɒlɪk] *adj* sin alcohol

non-aligned [nɒnəˈlaɪnd] *adj Pol* no alineado(a)

nonchalant [ˈnɒnʃələnt] *adj (indifferent)*

indiferente; *(calm)* imperturbable, impasible

noncommittal [ˈnɒnkəmɪtəl] *adj (person)* evasivo(a); *(answer)* que no compromete (a nada)

nonconformist [nɒnkənˈfɔːmɪst] *n* inconformista *mf*

nondescript [ˈnɒndɪskrɪpt] *adj* indescriptible; *(uninteresting)* soso(a)

none [nʌn] **1** *pron* ninguno(a); **I know n. of them** no conozco a ninguno de ellos; **n. at all** nada en absoluto; **n. other than ...** nada menos que ...

2 *adv* de ningún modo; **she's n. the worse for it** no se ha visto afectada *or* perjudicada por ello; **n. too soon** a buena hora

nonentity [nɒˈnentɪtɪ] *n (person)* cero *m* a la izquierda

nonetheless [nʌnðəˈles] *adv* no obstante, sin embargo

nonevent [nɒnɪˈvent] *n* fracaso *m*

nonexistent [nɒnɪgˈzɪstənt] *adj* inexistente

nonfiction [nɒnˈfɪkʃən] *n* no ficción *f*

no-nonsense [nəʊˈnɒnsəns] *adj (person)* recto(a), serio(a)

nonplussed [nɒnˈplʌst] *adj* perplejo(a)

non-profit(-making) [nɒnˈprɒfɪt(meɪkɪŋ)] *adj* sin fin lucrativo

nonreturnable [nɒnrɪˈtɜːnəbəl] *adj* no retornable

nonsense [ˈnɒnsəns] *n* tonterías *fpl*, disparates *mpl*; **that's n.** eso es absurdo

nonsmoker [nɒnˈsməʊkə(r)] *n* no fumador(a) *m,f*, persona *f* que no fuma

nonstarter [nɒnˈstɑːtə(r)] *n Fig* **to be a n.** *(person)* estar destinado a fracasar; *(plan)* ser irrealizable

nonstick [nɒnˈstɪk] *adj* antiadherente

nonstop [nɒnˈstɒp] **1** *adj* sin parar; *(train)* directo(a)

2 *adv* sin parar

noodles [ˈnuːdəlz] *npl Culin* fideos *mpl*

nook [nʊk] *n* recoveco *m*, rincón *m*

noon [nuːn] *n* mediodía *m*; **at n.** a mediodía

no one [ˈnəʊwʌn] *pron* nadie; **n. came** no vino nadie

noose [nuːs] *n* lazo *m*; *(hangman's)* soga *f*

nor [nɔː(r)] *conj* ni, ni tampoco; **neither ... n. ni ... ni; neither you n. I** ni tú ni yo; **n. do I** (ni) yo tampoco

norm [nɔːm] *n* norma *f*

normal [ˈnɔːməl] *adj* normal

normality [nɔːˈmælɪtɪ] *n* normalidad *f*

normally [ˈnɔːməlɪ] *adv* normalmente

Normandy [ˈnɔːməndɪ] *n* Normandía

north [nɔːθ] **1** *n* norte *m*; **the N.** el norte; **N. America** América del Norte, Norteamérica; **N. Korea** Corea del Norte; **N. Pole** Polo *m* Norte; **N. Sea** Mar *m* del Norte

2 *adv* hacia el norte, al norte

3 *adj* del norte; **n. wind** viento *m* del norte

northeast [nɔːθˈiːst] *n* nor(d)este *m*

northerly [ˈnɔːðəlɪ] *adj* norte, del norte

northern [ˈnɔːðən] *adj* del norte, septentrional; **n. hemisphere** hemisferio *m* norte; **N. Ireland** Irlanda del Norte

northerner [ˈnɔːðənə(r)] *n* norteño(a) *m,f*

northward [ˈnɔːθwəd] *adj & adv* hacia el norte

northwest [nɔːθˈwest] *n* noroeste *m*

Norway [ˈnɔːweɪ] *n* Noruega

Norwegian [nɔːˈwiːdʒən] **1** *adj* noruego(a)

2 *n* (**a**) *(person)* noruego(a) *m,f* (**b**) *(language)* noruego *m*

nose [nəʊz] *n* (**a**) nariz *f*; *Fig* **(right) under sb's n.** delante de las propias narices de algn; *Br Fam* **to get up sb's n.** hincharle a algn las narices (**b**) *(sense of smell)* olfato *m* (**c**) *(of car, plane)* morro *m*

▸ **nose about, nose around** *vi* curiosear

nosebleed [ˈnəʊzbliːd] *n* hemorragia *f* nasal

nosedive [ˈnəʊzdaɪv] *Av* **1** *n* picado *m*

2 *vi* descender en picado

nostalgia [nɒˈstældʒɪə] *n* nostalgia *f*

nostalgic [nɒˈstældʒɪk] *adj* nostálgico(a)

nostril [ˈnɒstrɪl] *n Anat* orificio *m* nasal

nosy [ˈnəʊzɪ] *adj* (**nosier, nosiest**) *Fam* entrometido(a)

not [nɒt] *adv* no; **he's n. in today** hoy no está; **I'm n. sorry to leave** no siento nada irme; **n. at all** en absoluto; **thank you – n. at all** gracias – no hay de qué; **n. one (of them) thanked me** nadie me dio las gracias; **n. that I don't want to come** no es que no quiera ir; **n. too well** bastante mal; **n. without reason** no sin razón; *Fam* **n. likely!** ¡ni hablar!

En el inglés hablado, y en el escrito en estilo coloquial, **not** se contrae después de verbos modales y auxiliares.

notable [ˈnəʊtəbəl] *adj* notable

notably [ˈnəʊtəblɪ] *adv* notablemente

notary [ˈnəʊtərɪ] *n* notario *m*

notch [nɒtʃ] *n* muesca *f*; *(cut)* corte *m*

▸ **notch up** *vt sep Fig* **to n. up a victory** apuntarse una victoria

note [nəʊt] **1** *n* (**a**) *Mus* nota *f*; *Fig* **to strike**

the right n. acertar (**b**) *(on paper)* nota *f*
(**c**) **to take n. of** *(notice)* prestar atención
a (**d**) *(banknote)* billete *m* (de banco) (**e**)
notes apuntes *mpl*; **to take n.** tomar
apuntes
  2 *vt* (**a**) *(write down)* apuntar, anotar (**b**)
(notice) notar, fijarse en
notebook ['nəʊtbʊk] *n* cuaderno *m*, libreta *f*
noted ['nəʊtɪd] *adj* notable, célebre
notepad ['nəʊtpæd] *n* bloc *m* de notas
notepaper ['nəʊtpeɪpə(r)] *n* papel *m* de
carta
noteworthy ['nəʊtwɜːðɪ] *adj* digno(a) de
mención
nothing ['nʌθɪŋ] **1** *n* nada; **I saw n.** no vi
nada; **for n.** *(free of charge)* gratis; **it's n.**
no es nada; **it's n. to do with you** no tiene
nada que ver contigo; **n. else** nada más;
there's n. in it no es cierto; *Fam* **n. much**
poca cosa; *Fam* **there's n. to it** es facilísimo
  2 *adv* **she looks n. like her sister** no se
parece en nada a su hermana
notice ['nəʊtɪs] **1** *n* (**a**) *(warning)* aviso *m*;
he gave a month's n. presentó la dimi-
sión con un mes de antelación; **at short
n.** con poca antelación; **until further n.**
hasta nuevo aviso (**b**) *(attention)* atención *f*; **to take
no n. of sth** no hacer caso de algo; **to take
n. of sth** prestar atención a algo; **it es-
caped my n.** se me escapó; **to come to
one's n.** llegar al conocimiento de uno (**c**)
(in newspaper etc) anuncio *m* (**d**) *(sign)*
letrero *m*, aviso *m*
  2 *vt* darse cuenta de, notar

  ⚬ Note that the Spanish word **noticia** is a
false friend and is never a translation for the
English word **notice**. In Spanish, **noticia**
means "(piece of) news".

noticeable ['nəʊtɪsəbəl] *adj* que se nota,
evidente
noticeboard ['nəʊtɪsbɔːd] *n Br* tablón *m*
de anuncios
notification [nəʊtɪfɪ'keɪʃən] *n* aviso *m*
notify ['nəʊtɪfaɪ] *vt* avisar
notion ['nəʊʃən] *n* (**a**) idea *f*, concepto *m*
(**b**) *(whim)* capricho *m* (**c**) *US Sewing*
notions artículos *mpl* de mercería
notorious [nəʊ'tɔːrɪəs] *adj Pej* triste-
mente célebre

  ⚬ Note that the Spanish word **notorio** is a
false friend and is never a translation for the
English word **notorious**. In Spanish, **notorio** means both "obvious" and "famous,
well-known".

notwithstanding [nɒtwɪθ'stændɪŋ] **1**
prep a pesar de
  2 *adv* sin embargo, no obstante
nougat ['nuːɡɑː] *n* turrón blando
nought [nɔːt] *n* cero *m*; *Br* **noughts and
crosses** *(game)* tres en raya *m*
noun [naʊn] *n* nombre *m*, sustantivo *m*
nourish ['nʌrɪʃ] *vt* nutrir; *Fig (hopes)*
abrigar
nourishing ['nʌrɪʃɪŋ] *adj* nutritivo(a)
nourishment ['nʌrɪʃmənt] *n* alimentación *f*, nutrición *f*
novel¹ ['nɒvəl] *n* novela *f*
novel² ['nɒvəl] *adj* original, novedoso(a)
novelist ['nɒvəlɪst] *n* novelista *mf*
novelty ['nɒvəltɪ] *n* novedad *f*
November [nəʊ'vembə(r)] *n* noviembre
m
novice ['nɒvɪs] *n* (**a**) *(beginner)* nova-
to(a) *m,f*, principiante *mf* (**b**) *Rel* novi-
cio(a) *m,f*
now [naʊ] **1** *adv* (**a**) *(at this moment)*
ahora; **just n., right n.** ahora mismo; **from
n. on** de ahora en adelante; **n. and then,
n. and again** de vez en cuando (**b**) *(for
events in past)* entonces (**c**) *(at present,
these days)* actualmente, hoy (en) día (**d**)
(not related to time) ahora bien; **n. (then)** ahora bien;
n., n.! ¡vamos!, ¡ya está bien!
  2 *conj* **n. (that)** ahora que, ya que
  3 *n* **until n.** hasta ahora; **he'll be home by
n.** ya habrá llegado a casa
nowadays ['naʊədeɪz] *adv* hoy (en) día,
actualmente
nowhere ['nəʊweə(r)] *adv* en ninguna
parte; **that will get you n.** eso no te
servirá de nada; **it's n. near ready** no está
preparado, ni mucho menos
noxious ['nɒkʃəs] *adj* nocivo(a)
nozzle ['nɒzəl] *n* boca *f*, boquilla *f*
nuance ['njuːɑːns] *n* matiz *m*
nub [nʌb] *n* **the n. of the matter** el quid
de la cuestión
nuclear ['njuːklɪə(r)] *adj* nuclear; **n. arms**
armas *fpl* nucleares; **n. disarmament** desarme *m* nuclear; **n. power** energía *f* nuclear; **n. power station** central *f* nuclear
nucleus ['njuːklɪəs] *n* núcleo *m*
nude [njuːd] **1** *adj* desnudo(a)
  2 *n Art & Phot* desnudo *m*; **in the n.** al
desnudo
nudge [nʌdʒ] **1** *vt* dar un codazo a
  2 *n* codazo *m*
nudist ['njuːdɪst] *adj & n* nudista *(mf)*
nudity ['njuːdɪtɪ] *n* desnudez *f*
nugget ['nʌɡɪt] *n Min* pepita *f*; **gold n.**
pepita de oro
nuisance ['njuːsəns] *n* (**a**) molestia *f*,

pesadez *f*; **what a n.!** ¡qué lata! (**b**) *(person)* pesado(a) *m,f*

nuke [njuːk] *Fam* **1** *n (bomb)* bomba *f* nuclear *or* atómica

2 *vt* atacar con armas nucleares

null [nʌl] *adj* nulo(a); **n. and void** nulo y sin valor

nullify [ˈnʌlɪfaɪ] *vt* anular

numb [nʌm] **1** *adj (without feeling)* entumecido(a); *Fig* paralizado(a); **n. with fear** paralizado de miedo

2 *vt (with cold)* entumecer (de frío); *(with anaesthetic)* adormecer

number [ˈnʌmbə(r)] **1** *n* (**a**) número *m*; *Tel* **have you got my n.?** ¿tienes mi (número de) teléfono?; *Fam* **to look after n. one** barrer para adentro (**b**) *(quantity)* **a n. of people** varias personas (**c**) *Br (of car)* matrícula *f*; **n. plate** (placa *f* de la) matrícula *f*

2 *vt* (**a**) *(put a number on)* numerar (**b**) *(count)* contar; **his days are numbered** tiene los días contados

numeral [ˈnjuːmərəl] *n* número *m*, cifra *f*

numerate [ˈnjuːmərət] *adj* **to be n.** tener un conocimiento básico de matemáticas

numerical [njuːˈmerɪkəl] *adj* numérico(a)

numerically [njuːˈmerɪkəlɪ] *adv* numéricamente

numerous [ˈnjuːmərəs] *adj* numeroso(a)

numismatics [njuːmɪzˈmætɪks] *n sing* numismática *f*

nun [nʌn] *n* monja *f*

nuptial [ˈnʌpʃəl] *adj* nupcial

nurse [nɜːs] **1** *n* enfermera *f*; *(male)* enfermero *m*; **children's n.** niñera *f*

2 *vt* (**a**) *(look after)* cuidar, atender (**b**) *(baby)* acunar (**c**) *(suckle)* amamantar (**d**) *Fig (grudge etc)* guardar

nursery [ˈnɜːsərɪ] *n* (**a**) *(institution)* guardería *f*; **n. school** jardín *m* de infancia (**b**) *(in house)* cuarto *m* de los niños; **n. rhyme** poema *m* infantil (**c**) *(garden centre)* vivero *m*

nursing [ˈnɜːsɪŋ] *n* **n. home** clínica *f*

nurture [ˈnɜːtʃə(r)] *vt (animal)* alimentar; *(feelings)* abrigar

nut [nʌt] *n* (**a**) *(fruit)* fruto seco; *Fig* **a tough n. to crack** un hueso duro de roer (**b**) *Fam (head)* coco *m* (**c**) *Fam (mad person)* loco(a) *m,f* (**d**) *Tech* tuerca *f*

nutcracker [ˈnʌtkrækə(r)] *n* cascanueces *m inv*

nutmeg [ˈnʌtmeg] *n* nuez moscada

nutrition [njuːˈtrɪʃən] *n* nutrición *f*

nutritious [njuːˈtrɪʃəs] *adj* nutritivo(a), alimenticio(a)

nuts [nʌts] *adj Fam* chalado(a); **to go n.** volverse loco; **he's n. about motorbikes** las motos le chiflan

nutshell [ˈnʌtʃel] *n* cáscara *f*; *Fig* **in a n.** en pocas palabras

nylon [ˈnaɪlɒn] **1** *n* (**a**) nilón *m*, nailon *m* (**b**) **nylons** medias *fpl* de nilón

2 *adj* de nilón

nymph [nɪmf] *n* ninfa *f*

nymphomaniac [nɪmfəˈmeɪnɪæk] *n* ninfómana *f*

O, o [əʊ] *n* (**a**) *(the letter)* O, o *f* (**b**) *Math & Tel* cero *m*

oak [əʊk] *n* roble *m*

OAP [əʊeɪ'piː] *n Br* (*abbr* **old-age pensioner**) pensionista *mf*, jubilado(a) *m,f*

oar [ɔː(r)] *n* remo *m*

oarsman ['ɔːzmən] *n* remero *m*

oasis [əʊ'eɪsɪs] *n* (*pl* **oases** [əʊ'eɪsiːz]) oasis *m inv*

oat [əʊt] *n* avena *f*; **rolled oats** copos *mpl* de avena

oath [əʊθ] *n* (*pl* **oaths** [əʊðz]) (**a**) *Jur* juramento *m*; **to take an o.** prestar juramento; *Fam* **on my o.** palabra de honor (**b**) *(swearword)* palabrota *f*

oatmeal ['əʊtmiːl] *n* harina *f* de avena

obedience [ə'biːdɪəns] *n* obediencia *f*

obedient [ə'biːdɪənt] *adj* obediente

obese [əʊ'biːs] *adj* obeso(a)

obey [ə'beɪ] *vt* obedecer; *(law)* cumplir con

obituary [ə'bɪtjʊərɪ] *n* necrología *f*

object¹ ['ɒbdʒɪkt] *n* (**a**) *(thing)* objeto *m* (**b**) *(aim, purpose)* fin *m*, objetivo *m* (**c**) **the o. of criticism** el blanco de las críticas (**d**) *(obstacle)* inconveniente *m* (**e**) *Ling* complemento *m*

object² [əb'dʒekt] *vi* oponerse (**to** a); **do you o. to my smoking?** ¿le molesta que fume?

objection [əb'dʒekʃən] *n* (**a**) objeción *f* (**b**) *(drawback)* inconveniente *m*; **provided there's no o.** si no hay inconveniente

objectionable [əb'dʒekʃənəbəl] *adj (unacceptable)* inaceptable; *(unpleasant)* ofensivo(a)

objective [əb'dʒektɪv] **1** *adj* objetivo(a) **2** *n* objetivo *m*

objector [əb'dʒektə(r)] *n* objetor(a) *m,f*

obligation [ɒblɪ'geɪʃən] *n* obligación *f*; **to be under an o. to sb** estarle muy agradecido(a) a algn

obligatory [ɒ'blɪgətərɪ] *adj* obligatorio(a)

oblige [ə'blaɪdʒ] *vt* (**a**) *(compel)* obligar; **I'm obliged to do it** me veo obligado(a) a hacerlo (**b**) *(do a favour for)* hacer un favor a (**c**) **to be obliged** *(grateful)* estar agradecido(a)

obliging [ə'blaɪdʒɪŋ] *adj* solícito(a)

oblique [ə'bliːk] *adj* oblicuo(a), inclinado(a); *Fig* **an o. reference** una alusión indirecta

obliterate [ə'blɪtəreɪt] *vt* (**a**) *(memory)* borrar (**b**) *(species, race)* eliminar; *(village)* arrasar

oblivion [ə'blɪvɪən] *n* olvido *m*; **to sink into o.** caer en el olvido

oblivious [ə'blɪvɪəs] *adj* inconsciente

oblong ['ɒblɒŋ] **1** *adj* oblongo(a) **2** *n* rectángulo *m*

obnoxious [əb'nɒkʃəs] *adj* repugnante

oboe ['əʊbəʊ] *n* oboe *m*

obscene [əb'siːn] *adj* obsceno(a)

obscure [əb'skjʊə(r)] **1** *adj* (**a**) oscuro(a); *(vague)* vago(a) (**b**) *(author, poet etc)* desconocido(a) **2** *vt (truth)* ocultar

obsequious [əb'siːkwɪəs] *adj* servil

observance [əb'zɜːvəns] *n* (**a**) observancia *f* (**b**) *Rel* **observances** prácticas religiosas

observant [əb'zɜːvənt] *adj* observador(a)

observation [ɒbzə'veɪʃən] *n* observación *f*; *(surveillance)* vigilancia *f*

observatory [əb'zɜːvətərɪ] *n* observatorio *m*

observe [əb'zɜːv] *vt* (**a**) observar; *(in surveillance)* vigilar (**b**) *(remark)* advertir (**c**) *(obey)* respetar

observer [əb'zɜːvə(r)] *n* observador(a) *m,f*

obsess [əb'ses] *vt* obsesionar; **to be obsessed (with** *or* **by)** estar obsesionado(a) (con)

obsession [əb'seʃən] *n* obsesión *f*

obsessive [əb'sesɪv] *adj* obsesivo(a)

obsolete ['ɒbsəliːt, ɒbsə'liːt] *adj* obsoleto(a)

obstacle ['ɒbstəkəl] *n* obstáculo *m*; *Fig* impedimento *m*; **o. race** carrera *f* de obstáculos

obstinate ['ɒbstɪnɪt] *adj* (**a**) *(person)* obstinado(a), terco(a) (**b**) *(pain)* persistente

obstruct [əb'strʌkt] *vt* (**a**) obstruir; *(pipe etc)* atascar; *(view)* tapar (**b**) *(hinder)* estorbar; *(progress)* dificultar

obstruction [əbˈstrʌkʃən] *n* (**a**) obstrucción *f* (**b**) *(hindrance)* obstáculo *m*

obtain [əbˈteɪn] *vt* obtener, conseguir

obtainable [əbˈteɪnəbəl] *adj* obtenible

obtrusive [əbˈtruːsɪv] *adj* (**a**) *(interfering)* entrometido(a) (**b**) *(noticeable)* llamativo(a)

obtuse [əbˈtjuːs] *adj* obtuso(a)

obviate [ˈɒbvɪeɪt] *vt Fml* obviar

obvious [ˈɒbvɪəs] *adj* obvio(a), evidente

obviously [ˈɒbvɪəslɪ] *adv* evidentemente; **o.!** ¡claro!, ¡por supuesto!

occasion [əˈkeɪʒən] **1** *n* (**a**) ocasión *f*; **on o.** de vez en cuando; **on the o. of** con motivo de (**b**) *(event)* acontecimiento *m* (**c**) *(cause)* motivo *m*
2 *vt Fml* ocasionar

occasional [əˈkeɪʒənəl] *adj* esporádico(a), eventual

occasionally [əˈkeɪʒənəlɪ] *adv* de vez en cuando

occupant [ˈɒkjʊpənt] *n* ocupante *mf*; *(tenant)* inquilino(a) *m,f*

occupation [ɒkjʊˈpeɪʃən] *n* (**a**) *(job, profession)* profesión *f*, ocupación *f* (**b**) *(pastime)* pasatiempo *m* (**c**) *(of building, house, country)* ocupación *f*

occupational [ɒkjʊˈpeɪʃənəl] *adj* profesional, laboral; **o. hazards** gajes *mpl* del oficio

occupied [ˈɒkjʊpaɪd] *adj* ocupado(a)

occupier [ˈɒkjʊpaɪə(r)] *n Br* ocupante *mf*; *(tenant)* inquilino(a) *m,f*

occupy [ˈɒkjʊpaɪ] *vt* (**a**) *(live in)* ocupar, habitar (**b**) *(time)* pasar; **to o. one's time in doing sth** dedicar su tiempo a hacer algo (**c**) *(building, factory etc in protest)* tomar posesión de

occur [əˈkɜː(r)] *vi* (**a**) *(event)* suceder, acaecer; *(change)* producirse (**b**) *(be found)* encontrarse (**c**) **it occurred to me that ...** se me ocurrió que ...

occurrence [əˈkʌrəns] *n* suceso *m*, incidencia *f*

> ℓ Note that the Spanish word **ocurrencia** is a false friend and is never a translation for the English word **occurrence**. In Spanish, **ocurrencia** means "witty remark" and "bright idea".

ocean [ˈəʊʃən] *n* océano *m*

ocean-going [ˈəʊʃəngəʊɪŋ] *adj* de alta mar

ochre, *US* **ocher** [ˈəʊkə(r)] **1** *n* ocre *m*; **red o.** almagre *m*; **yellow o.** ocre amarillo
2 *adj* (de color) ocre

o'clock [əˈklɒk] *adv* (**it's**) **one o.** (es) la una; (**it's**) **two o.** (son) las dos

octave [ˈɒktɪv] *n* octava *f*

October [ɒkˈtəʊbə(r)] *n* octubre *m*

octogenarian [ɒktəʊdʒɪˈneərɪən] *adj & n* octogenario(a) *(m,f)*

octopus [ˈɒktəpəs] *n* pulpo *m*

OD [əʊˈdiː] *(pt & pp* **OD'd** *or* **OD'ed)** *vi Fam* meterse una sobredosis

odd [ɒd] **1** *adj* (**a**) *(strange)* raro(a), extraño(a) (**b**) *(occasional)* esporádico(a); **at o. times** de vez en cuando; **the o. customer** algún que otro cliente; **o. job** trabajillo *m* (**c**) **an o. number** *(not even)* un impar (**d**) *(unpaired)* desparejado(a); **an o. sock** un calcetín suelto; *Fig* **to be the o. man out** estar de más
2 *adv* y pico; **twenty o. people** veinte y pico *or* y tantas personas

oddity [ˈɒdɪtɪ] *n* (**a**) *(thing)* curiosidad *f*; *(person)* estrafalario(a) *m,f* (**b**) *(quality)* rareza *f*

oddly [ˈɒdlɪ] *adv* extrañamente; **o. enough** por extraño que parezca

odds [ɒdz] *npl* (**a**) *(chances)* probabilidades *fpl*; **he's fighting against the o.** lleva las de perder; **the o. are that ...** lo más probable es que ... *(+ subj)* (**b**) *(in betting)* puntos *mpl* de ventaja; **the o. are five to one** las apuestas están cinco a uno (**c**) *Br* **it makes no o.** da lo mismo; *Fig* **at o. with sb** reñido(a) con algn (**d**) **o. and ends** *(small things)* cositas *fpl*; *(trinkets)* chucherías *fpl*

odds-on [ˈɒdzɒn] *adj* seguro(a); **o. favourite** *(horse)* caballo favorito

ode [əʊd] *n* oda *f*

odious [ˈəʊdɪəs] *adj* repugnante

odour, *US* **odor** [ˈəʊdə(r)] *n* olor *m*; *(fragrance)* perfume *m*

OECD [əʊiːsiːˈdiː] *n (abbr* **Organization for Economic Co-operation and Development)** OCDE *f*

of [ɒv, *unstressed* əv] *prep* (**a**) *(belonging to, part of)* de; **a friend of mine** un amigo mío; **the end of the novel** el final de la novela
(**b**) *(containing)* de; **a bottle of wine** una botella de vino
(**c**) *(origin)* de; **of good family** de buena familia
(**d**) *(by)* de, por; **beloved of all** amado(a) por todos
(**e**) *(quantity)* de; **there are four of us** somos cuatro; **two of them** dos de ellos
(**f**) *(from)* de; **free of** libre de; **south of** al sur de
(**g**) *(material)* de; **a dress (made) of silk** un vestido de seda

(**h**) *(apposition)* de; **the city of Lisbon** la ciudad de Lisboa

(**i**) *(characteristic)* de; **that's typical of her** es muy propio de ella; **that's very kind of you** es usted muy amable

(**j**) *(with adj)* de; **hard of hearing** duro(a) de oído

(**k**) *(after superlative)* de; **the thing she wanted most of all** lo que más quería

(**l**) *(cause)* por, de; **because of** a causa de; **of necessity** por necesidad

(**m**) *(concerning, about)* de, sobre; **to dream of sth/sb** soñar con algo/algn; **to think of sb** pensar en algn

(**n**) *(with dates)* de; **the 7th of November** el 7 de noviembre

off [ɒf] **1** *prep* (**a**) *(movement)* de; **she fell o. her horse** se cayó del caballo

(**b**) *(removal)* de; **I'll take sth o. the price for you** se lo rebajaré un poco

(**c**) *(distance, situation)* de; **a few kilometres o. the coast** a unos kilómetros de la costa; **a house o. the road** una casa apartada de la carretera

(**d**) **the ship went o. course** el barco se desvió; **to be o. form** no estar en forma

(**e**) **I'm o. wine** he perdido el gusto al vino

2 *adv* (**a**) **he turned o. the radio** apagó la radio

(**b**) *(absent)* fuera; **I have a day o.** tengo un día libre; **to be o. sick** estar de baja por enfermedad

(**c**) *(completely)* **this will kill o. any germs** esto rematará cualquier germen

(**d**) **his arrival is three days o.** faltan tres días para su llegada; **6 miles o.** a 6 millas

(**e**) **I'm o. to London** me voy a Londres; **she ran o.** se fue corriendo

(**f**) **10 percent o.** un descuento del 10 por ciento; **to take one's shoes o.** quitarse los zapatos

(**g**) **o. and on** de vez en cuando

3 *adj* (**a**) *(gas etc)* apagado(a); *(water)* cortado(a)

(**b**) *(cancelled)* cancelado(a)

(**c**) *(low)* bajo(a); *(unsatisfactory)* malo(a); **on the o. chance** por si acaso; **the o. season** la temporada baja

(**d**) **you're better o. like that** así estás mejor

(**e**) *(gone bad) (meat, fish)* malo(a), pasado(a); *(milk)* agrio(a)

offal ['ɒfəl] *n (of chicken etc)* menudillos *mpl*; *(of cattle, pigs)* asaduras *fpl*

off-colour, *US* **off-color** ['ɒf'kʌlə(r)] *adj* (**a**) *Br (ill)* indispuesto(a) (**b**) *(joke, story)* indecente

offence [ə'fens] *n* (**a**) *Jur* delito *m* (**b**) *(insult)* ofensa *f*; **to give o.** ofender; **to take o. at sth** ofenderse por algo (**c**) *Mil (attack)* ofensiva *f*

offend [ə'fend] *vt* ofender

offender [ə'fendə(r)] *n (criminal)* delincuente *mf*

offense [ə'fens] *n US* = **offence**

offensive [ə'fensɪv] **1** *adj* (**a**) *(insulting)* ofensivo(a) (**b**) *(repulsive)* repugnante

2 *n Mil* ofensiva *f*; **to be on the o.** estar a la ofensiva

offer ['ɒfə(r)] **1** *vt* (**a**) ofrecer; **to o. to do a job** ofrecerse para hacer un trabajo (**b**) *(propose)* proponer

2 *n* (**a**) oferta *f*; *(proposal)* propuesta *f*; **o. of marriage** proposición *f* de matrimonio (**b**) *Com* **on o.** de oferta

offering ['ɒfərɪŋ] *n* (**a**) ofrecimiento *m* (**b**) *Rel* ofrenda *f*

offhand 1 *adj* ['ɒfhænd] *(abrupt)* brusco(a); *(inconsiderate)* descortés

2 *adv* [ɒf'hænd] **I don't know o.** así sin pensarlo, no lo sé

office ['ɒfɪs] *n* (**a**) *(room)* despacho *m*; *(building)* oficina *f*; *(of lawyer)* despacho, bufete *m*; *US (of doctor, dentist)* consulta *f*; **o. hours** horas *fpl* de oficina (**b**) *Br Pol* ministerio *m* (**c**) *US (federal agency)* agencia *f* gubernamental (**d**) *(position)* cargo *m*; **to hold o.** ocupar un cargo (**e**) *Pol* **to be in o.** estar en el poder

officer ['ɒfɪsə(r)] *n* (**a**) *Mil* oficial *mf* (**b**) **(police) o.** agente *mf* de policía (**c**) *(government official)* funcionario(a) *m,f* (**d**) *(of company, society)* director(a) *m,f*

official [ə'fɪʃəl] **1** *adj* oficial

2 *n* funcionario(a) *m,f*

officiate [ə'fɪʃɪeɪt] *vi* (**a**) ejercer; **to o. as** ejercer de (**b**) *Rel* oficiar

officious [ə'fɪʃəs] *adj Pej* excesivamente celoso(a) *or* diligente

> ✐ Note that the Spanish word **oficioso** is a false friend and is never a translation for the English word **officious**. In Spanish, **oficioso** means "unofficial".

off-licence ['ɒflaɪsəns] *n Br* tienda *f* de bebidas alcohólicas

off-line ['ɒflaɪn] *adj Comput* desconectado(a)

off-peak [ɒf'piːk] *adj (flight)* de temporada baja; *(rate)* de fuera de las horas punta

off-putting ['ɒfpʊtɪŋ] *adj Br Fam* desconcertante

offset [ɒf'set] *vt (pt & pp offset) (balance out)* compensar

offshoot [ˈɒfʃuːt] n (**a**) Bot renuevo m (**b**) Fig (of organization) ramificación f

offshore [ˈɒfˈʃɔː(r)] adj (**a**) (breeze etc) terral (**b**) (oil rig) costa afuera (**c**) (overseas) en el extranjero; **o. investment** inversión f en el extranjero

offside 1 adv [ɒfˈsaɪd] Ftb fuera de juego **2** n [ˈɒfsaɪd] Aut (with left-hand drive) lado derecho; (with right-hand drive) lado izquierdo

offspring [ˈɒfsprɪŋ] n (pl **offspring**) (child) vástago m; (children) progenitura f

offstage [ɒfˈsteɪdʒ] adj & adv entre bastidores

often [ˈɒfən, ˈɒftən] adv a menudo, con frecuencia; **every so o.** de vez en cuando

ogle [ˈəʊɡəl] vt & vi **to o. (at) sb** comerse a algn con los ojos

oh [əʊ] interj ¡oh!, ¡ay!; **oh, my God!** ¡Dios mío!

oil [ɔɪl] **1** n (**a**) aceite m; **o. lamp** lámpara f de aceite, quinqué m; **o. slick** mancha f de aceite; **olive o.** aceite de oliva (**b**) (petroleum) petróleo m; **o. rig** plataforma petrolera; **o. tanker** petrolero m (**c**) (painting) pintura f al óleo; **o. paint** óleo m
2 vt engrasar

oilcan [ˈɔɪlkæn] n aceitera f

oilfield [ˈɔɪlfiːld] n yacimiento petrolífero

oilskin [ˈɔɪlskɪn] n (**a**) hule m (**b**) oilskins chubasquero m, impermeable m de hule

oily [ˈɔɪlɪ] adj (**oilier, oiliest**) aceitoso(a), grasiento(a); (hair, skin) graso(a)

ointment [ˈɔɪntmənt] n ungüento m, pomada f

O.K., okay [əʊˈkeɪ] Fam **1** interj ¡vale!, ¡de acuerdo!
2 adj bien; **is it O.K. if ...?** ¿está bien si ...?
3 vt dar el visto bueno a

old [əʊld] **1** adj (**a**) viejo(a); **an o. man** un anciano; **o. age** vejez f; **o.-age pensioner** pensionista mf; Br **o. boy** antiguo alumno; **o. hand** veterano(a) m,f; **good o. John!** ¡el bueno de John! (**b**) **how o. are you?** ¿cuántos años tienes?; **she's five years o.** tiene cinco años (**c**) (previous) antiguo(a)
2 n **of o.** de antaño

old-fashioned [əʊldˈfæʃənd] adj (outdated) a la antigua; (unfashionable) anticuado(a), pasado(a) de moda

olive [ˈɒlɪv] n (**a**) (tree) olivo m; **o. grove** olivar m (**b**) (fruit) aceituna f, oliva f (**c**) (wood) olivo m (**d**) **o. (green)** (colour) verde m oliva

Olympic [əˈlɪmpɪk] **1** adj olímpico(a); **O.**

Games Juegos Olímpicos
2 npl **the Olympics** las Olimpiadas

omelette, US **omelet** [ˈɒmlɪt] n tortilla f; **Spanish o.** tortilla española or de patatas or Am papas

omen [ˈəʊmen] n presagio m

ominous [ˈɒmɪnəs] adj de mal agüero

omission [əʊˈmɪʃən] n omisión f; Fig olvido m

omit [əʊˈmɪt] vt omitir; (accidentally) pasar por alto; (forget) olvidarse (**to** de)

omnipotent [ɒmˈnɪpətənt] **1** adj omnipotente
2 n **the O.** el Todopoderoso

on [ɒn] **1** prep (**a**) (location) sobre, encima de, en; **I hit him on the head** le di un golpe en la cabeza; **it's on the desk** está encima de or sobre el escritorio; **hanging on the wall** colgado de la pared; **on page 4** en la página 4; **have you got any money on you?** ¿llevas dinero?; **the drinks are on me/the house** invito yo/invita la casa
(**b**) (alongside) en; **a town on the coast** un pueblo en la costa
(**c**) (direction) en, a; **on the right** a la derecha; **on the way** en el camino
(**d**) (time) **on 3 April** el 3 de abril; **on a sunny day** un día de sol; **on Monday** el lunes; **on Mondays** los lunes; **on that occasion** en aquella ocasión; **on the following day** al día siguiente; **on time** a tiempo
(**e**) en; **on TV/the radio** en la tele/radio; **to play sth on the piano** tocar algo al piano; **on the phone** al teléfono
(**f**) (at the time of) a; **on his arrival** a su llegada; **on second thoughts** pensándolo bien; **on learning of this** al conocer esto
(**g**) **she lives on bread** vive de pan; **to depend on** depender de
(**h**) (transport) en/a; **on foot** a pie; **on the train/plane/bus** en el tren/avión/autobús; (travel by) en tren/avión/autobús
(**i**) (state, process) en/de; **on holiday** de vacaciones; **she is here on business** está aquí de negocios
(**j**) (regarding) sobre; **a lecture on numismatics** una conferencia sobre numismática; **they congratulated him on his success** le felicitaron por su éxito
(**k**) **on condition that** (subject to) bajo la condición de que
(**l**) (against) contra; **an attack on** un ataque contra
(**m**) **he's on the Times** (working for) trabaja para el Times
2 adv (**a**) (covering) encima, puesto; **she had a coat on** llevaba puesto un abrigo

(**b**) *Fam* **have you anything on tonight?** ¿tienes algún plan para esta noche?

(**c**) **and so on** y así sucesivamente; **go on!** ¡sigue!; **he talks on and on** habla sin parar; **to work on** seguir trabajando

(**d**) **from that day on** a partir de aquel día; **later on** más tarde

3 *adj Fam* (**a**) **to be on** *(TV, radio, light)* estar encendido(a); *(engine)* estar en marcha; *(film, play)* estar en cartelera; **that film was on last week** pusieron esa película la semana pasada

(**b**)*Th & TV* **you're on!** ¡a escena!

(**c**) *(definitely planned)* previsto(a); **you're on!** ¡trato hecho!

(**d**) **that isn't on** eso no vale

once [wʌns] **1** *adv* (**a**) *(one time)* una vez; **o. a week** una vez por semana; **o. in a while** de vez en cuando; **o. more** una vez más; **o. or twice** un par de veces; *Fig* **o. and for all** de una vez por todas (**b**) *(formerly)* en otro tiempo; **o. (upon a time) there was ...** érase una vez ... (**c**) **at o.** en seguida, inmediatamente; **don't all speak at o.** no habléis todos a la vez

2 *conj* una vez que *(+ subj)*, en cuanto *(+ subj)*

oncoming [ˈɒnkʌmɪŋ] *adj (car, traffic)* que viene en dirección contraria

one [wʌn] **1** *adj* (**a**) un/una; **for o. thing** primero; **you're the o. person who knows** tú eres el único que lo sabe; **the o. and only** el único/la única; **o. and the same** el mismo/la misma (**b**) *(indefinite)* un/una; **he'll come back o. day** un día volverá

2 *dem pron* **any o.** cualquiera; **that o.** ése/ésa; **this o.** éste/ésta; *(distant)* aquél/aquélla; **the blue ones** los azules/ las azules; **the o. on the table** la que está encima de la mesa; **the ones that, the ones who** los/las que

3 *indef pron* (**a**) uno(a) *m,f*; **I, for o., am against it** yo, por lo menos, estoy en contra; **I'm not o. to complain** no soy de los que se quejan; **o. at a time** de uno en uno; **o. by o.** uno tras otro; *Fig* **o. and all** todo el mundo

(**b**) *(indefinite person)* uno(a) *m,f*; **o. has to fight** hay que luchar; **o. hopes that will never happen** esperemos que no ocurra; **to break o.'s leg/arm** romperse la pierna/ el brazo

(**c**) **o. another** el uno al otro; **they love o. another** se aman

4 *n (digit)* uno *m*; **o. hundred/thousand** cien/mil

one-armed [ˈwʌnɑːmd] *adj Fig* **o.**

bandit máquina *f* tragaperras

one-man [ˈwʌnmæn] *adj* **a o. show** un espectáculo con un solo artista

one-man band [wʌnmænˈbænd] *n* hombre *m* orquesta

one-off [ˈwʌnɒf] *adj Br Fam* único(a), fuera de serie

oneself [wʌnˈself] *pron* (**a**) *(reflexive)* uno(a) mismo(a) *m,f*, sí mismo(a) *m,f*; **to talk to o.** hablar para sí (**b**) *(alone)* uno(a) mismo(a) *m,f*; **by o.** solo(a) (**c**) *(one's usual self)* el/la de siempre

one-sided [wʌnˈsaɪdɪd] *adj (bargain)* desigual; *(judgement)* parcial; *(decision)* unilateral

one-to-one [ˈwʌntəˈwʌn] *adj* **o. tuition** clase *f* individual

one-way [ˈwʌnweɪ] *adj* (**a**) *US (ticket)* de ida (**b**) *(street)* de dirección única

ongoing [ˈɒngəʊɪŋ] *adj* (**a**) *(in progress)* en curso, actual (**b**) *(developing)* en desarrollo

onion [ˈʌnjən] *n* cebolla *f*

on-line [ˈɒnlaɪn] *adj Comput* conectado(a)

onlooker [ˈɒnlʊkə(r)] *n* espectador(a) *m,f*

only [ˈəʊnlɪ] **1** *adj* único(a); **o. son** hijo único

2 *adv* (**a**) solamente, sólo; **staff o.** *(sign)* reservado al personal (**b**) *(not earlier than)* apenas; **he has o. just left** acaba de marcharse hace un momento; **o. yesterday** ayer mismo (**c**) **o. too glad!** ¡con mucho gusto!

3 *conj* pero

onset [ˈɒnset] *n (start)* comienzo *m*

onslaught [ˈɒnslɔːt] *n* embestida *f*

onto [ˈɒntʊ, *unstressed* ˈɒntə] *prep* = **on to**

onus [ˈəʊnəs] *n* responsabilidad *f*

onward [ˈɒnwəd] *adj* hacia adelante

onward(s) [ˈɒnwəd(z)] *adv* a partir de, en adelante; **from this time o.** de ahora en adelante

ooze [uːz] **1** *vi* rezumar

2 *vt* rebosar

opaque [əʊˈpeɪk] *adj* opaco(a)

OPEC [ˈəʊpek] *n* (*abbr* **Organization of Petroleum-Exporting Countries**) OPEP *f*

open [ˈəʊpən] **1** *adj* (**a**) abierto(a); **half o.** entreabierto; **wide o.** abierto de par en par; **in the o. air** al aire libre; **to be o. with sb** ser sincero(a) con algn; *Fig* **with o. arms** con los brazos abiertos; **to keep an o. mind** no tener prejuicios; **I am o. to suggestions** acepto cualquier sugerencia; **o. to criticism** susceptible a la crítica;

o. admiration franca admiración; *US* **o. house** fiesta *f* de inauguración de residencia; **an o. question** una cuestión sin resolver; **o. season** *(in hunting)* temporada *f* de caza; *Av & Rail* **o. ticket** billete abierto; *Br* **O. University** Universidad *f* a Distancia; **o. verdict** veredicto inconcluso
(**b**) *(car etc)* descubierto(a)
(**c**) *(opposition)* manifiesto(a)
2 *vt* (**a**) abrir; **to o. fire** abrir fuego; *Fig* **to o. one's heart to sb** sincerarse con algn
(**b**) *(exhibition etc)* inaugurar; *(negotiations, conversation)* entablar
3 *vi* (**a**) abrir, abrirse; **to o. onto** *(of door, window)* dar a
(**b**) *(start)* empezar; *Th & Cin* estrenarse
4 *n* (**a**) **in the o.** al aire libre; *Fig* **to bring into the o.** hacer público
(**b**) *Sport* open *m*
▸ **open out 1** *vt sep* abrir, desplegar
2 *vi (flowers)* abrirse; *(view)* extenderse
▸ **open up 1** *vt sep (market etc)* abrir; *(possibilities)* crear
2 *vi* (**a**) abrirse; *Fam* **o. up!** ¡abre la puerta! (**b**) *(start)* empezar
opener ['əʊpənə(r)] *n* **tin** *or US* **can o.** abrelatas *m inv*
opening ['əʊpənɪŋ] *n* (**a**) *(act)* apertura *f*; **o. night** noche *f* de estreno; *Br* **o. time** hora *f* de apertura de los bares (**b**) *(beginning)* comienzo *m* (**c**) *(aperture)* abertura *f*; *(gap)* brecha *f* (**d**) *Com* oportunidad *f* (**e**) *(vacancy)* vacante *f*
openly ['əʊpənlɪ] *adv* abiertamente
open-minded [əʊpən'maɪndɪd] *adj* sin prejuicios
openness ['əʊpənnɪs] *n* franqueza *f*
open-plan ['əʊpənplæn] *adj (office)* abierto(a)
opera ['ɒpərə] *n* ópera *f*; **o. house** ópera, teatro *m* de la ópera
operate ['ɒpəreɪt] **1** *vi* (**a**) *(function)* funcionar (**b**) *Med* operar; **to o. on sb for appendicitis** operar a algn de apendicitis
2 *vt* (**a**) *(control)* manejar (**b**) *(business)* dirigir
operatic [ɒpə'rætɪk] *adj* de ópera
operating ['ɒpəreɪtɪŋ] *n* (**a**) **o. costs** gastos *mpl* de funcionamiento (**b**) *Med* **o. table** mesa *f* de operaciones; **o. theatre** *or US* **room** quirófano *m*
operation [ɒpə'reɪʃən] *n* (**a**) *(of machine)* funcionamiento *m*; *(by person)* manejo *m* (**b**) *Mil* maniobra *f* (**c**) *Med* operación *f*, intervención quirúrgica; **to undergo an o. for** ser operado(a) de
operational [ɒpə'reɪʃənəl] *adj* (**a**) *(ready*

for use) operativo(a) (**b**) *Mil* operacional
operative ['ɒpərətɪv] *adj* (**a**) *Jur (in force)* vigente; **to become o.** entrar en vigor (**b**) *(significant)* clave, significativo(a); **the o. word** la palabra clave
operator ['ɒpəreɪtə(r)] *n* (**a**) *Ind* operario(a) *m,f* (**b**) *Tel* operador(a) *m,f* (**c**) *(dealer)* negociante *mf*, agente *mf*; **tour o.** agente de viajes
opinion [ə'pɪnjən] *n* opinión *f*; **in my o.** en mi opinión, a mi juicio; **it's a matter of o.** es cuestión de opiniones; **to have a high o. of sb** tener buen concepto de algn; **o. poll** encuesta *f*, sondeo *m*
opinionated [ə'pɪnjəneɪtɪd] *adj* dogmático(a)
opium ['əʊpɪəm] *n* opio *m*
opponent [ə'pəʊnənt] *n* adversario(a) *m,f*
opportune ['ɒpətjuːn] *adj* oportuno(a)
opportunist [ɒpə'tjuːnɪst] *adj & n* oportunista *(mf)*
opportunity [ɒpə'tjuːnɪtɪ] *n* (**a**) oportunidad *f*, ocasión *f* (**b**) *(prospect)* perspectiva *f*
oppose [ə'pəʊz] *vt* oponerse a
opposed [ə'pəʊzd] *adj* opuesto(a); **to be o. to sth** estar en contra de algo; **as o. to** comparado(a) con
opposing [ə'pəʊzɪŋ] *adj* adversario(a)
opposite ['ɒpəzɪt] **1** *adj* (**a**) *(facing)* de enfrente; *(page)* contiguo(a) (**b**) *(contrary)* opuesto(a), contrario(a); **in the o. direction** en dirección contraria
2 *n* **the o.** lo contrario; **quite the o.!** ¡al contrario!
3 *prep* enfrente de, frente a
4 *adv* enfrente
opposition [ɒpə'zɪʃən] *n* (**a**) oposición *f*; **in o. to** en contra de (**b**) *Pol* **the o.** la oposición
oppress [ə'pres] *vt* oprimir
oppression [ə'preʃən] *n* opresión *f*
oppressive [ə'presɪv] *adj* opresivo(a); *(atmosphere)* agobiante; *(heat)* sofocante
opt [ɒpt] *vi* optar; **to o. for** optar por; **to o. to do sth** optar por hacer algo
▸ **opt out** *vi* retirarse; **to o. out of doing sth** decidir no hacer algo
optical ['ɒptɪkəl] *adj* óptico(a)
optician [ɒp'tɪʃən] *n* óptico(a) *m,f*
optics ['ɒptɪks] *n sing* óptica *f*
optimist ['ɒptɪmɪst] *n* optimista *mf*
optimistic [ɒptɪ'mɪstɪk] *adj* optimista
optimistically [ɒptɪ'mɪstɪkəlɪ] *adv* con optimismo
optimum ['ɒptɪməm] **1** *n* grado óptimo
2 *adj* óptimo(a)

option [ˈɒpʃən] *n* opción *f*; **I have no o.** no tengo más remedio; **to keep one's options open** no comprometerse; **with the o. of** con opción a

optional [ˈɒpʃənəl] *adj* optativo(a), facultativo(a); *Educ* **o. subject** (asignatura *f*) optativa *f*

opulence [ˈɒpjʊləns] *n* opulencia *f*

or [ɔː(r), *unstressed* ə(r)] *conj* (**a**) o; *(before a word beginning with* **o** *or* **ho)** u; *(or else* si no, o bien; *whether you like it or not* tanto si te gusta como si no; **either a bun or a piece of cake** (o) una magdalena o un trozo de pastel (**b**) *(with negative)* ni; **he can't read or write** no sabe leer ni escribir; *see* **nor**

oral [ˈɔːrəl, ˈɒrəl] **1** *adj* oral
2 *n* examen *m* oral

orally [ˈɔːrəlɪ, ˈɒrəlɪ] *adv* **to be taken o.** *(on medicine)* por vía oral

orange [ˈɒrɪndʒ] **1** *n* naranja *f*; **o. juice** zumo *m* *or Am* jugo *m* de naranja
2 *adj* de color naranja

orator [ˈɒrətə(r)] *n* orador(a) *m,f*

oratory [ˈɒrətərɪ] *n* oratoria *f*

orbit [ˈɔːbɪt] **1** *n* *Astron* órbita *f*
2 *vt* girar alrededor de
3 *vi* girar

orchard [ˈɔːtʃəd] *n* huerto *m*

orchestra [ˈɔːkɪstrə] *n* orquesta *f*; *US (in theatre)* platea *f*

orchestral [ɔːˈkestrəl] *adj* orquestal

orchid [ˈɔːkɪd] *n* orquídea *f*

ordain [ɔːˈdeɪn] *vt* (**a**) *Rel* ordenar; **to be ordained** ordenarse (**b**) *(decree)* decretar

ordeal [ɔːˈdiːl] *n* mala experiencia

order [ˈɔːdə(r)] **1** *n* (**a**) *(sequence)* orden *m*; **in alphabetical o.** por orden alfabético; **to put in o.** ordenar
(**b**) *(condition)* estado *m*; **is your passport in o.?** ¿tienes el pasaporte en regla?; **out of o.** *(sign)* averiado(a)
(**c**) *(peace)* orden *m*; **to restore o.** restablecer el orden publico
(**d**) *(command)* orden *f*
(**e**) *Com* pedido *m*, encargo *m*; **to be on o.** estar pedido; **to o.** a la medida; **o. form** hoja *f* de pedido
(**f**) *Rel* orden *f*
(**g**) **of the highest o.** *(quality)* de primera calidad
(**h**) *(kind)* índole *f*, tipo *m*; *Biol* orden *m*
(**i**) **in the o. of** del orden de
(**j**) **in o. that** para que (+ *subj*), a fin de que (+ *subj*); **in o. to** (+ *infin*) para (+ *infin*), a fin de (+ *infin*)
2 *vt* (**a**) *(command)* ordenar, mandar; **to o. sb to do sth** mandar a algn hacer algo

(**b**) *Com* pedir, encargar; **to o. a dish** pedir un plato

orderly [ˈɔːdəlɪ] **1** *adj (tidy etc)* ordenado(a)
2 *n* (**a**) *Med* enfermero *m* (**b**) *Mil* ordenanza *m*

ordinary [ˈɔːdənrɪ] **1** *adj* usual, normal; *(average)* corriente, común; **the o. citizen** el ciudadano de a pie
2 **in the o.** lo corriente, lo normal; **out of the o.** fuera de lo común

ordnance [ˈɔːdnəns] *n Br* **O. Survey** = instituto británico de cartografía

ore [ɔː(r)] *n* mineral *m*

organ [ˈɔːgən] *n Mus & Anat etc* órgano *m*

organic [ɔːˈgænɪk] *adj* orgánico(a); *(farming, food)* biológico(a), ecológico(a)

organism [ˈɔːgənɪʒəm] *n* organismo *m*

organization [ɔːgənaɪˈzeɪʃən] *n* organización *f*

organize [ˈɔːgənaɪz] *vt* organizar

organizer [ˈɔːgənaɪzə(r)] *n* organizador(a) *m,f*

orgasm [ˈɔːgæzəm] *n* orgasmo *m*

orgy [ˈɔːdʒɪ] *n* orgía *f*

Orient [ˈɔːrɪənt] *n* **the O.** el Oriente

Oriental [ɔːrɪˈentəl] *adj & n* oriental *(mf)*

origin [ˈɒrɪdʒɪn] *n* origen *m*; **country of o.** país *m* natal *or* de origen

original [əˈrɪdʒɪnəl] **1** *adj* (**a**) original; *(first)* primero(a) (**b**) *(imaginative)* original
2 *n* original *m*

originality [ərɪdʒɪˈnælɪtɪ] *n* originalidad *f*

originally [əˈrɪdʒɪnəlɪ] *adv* (**a**) *(at first)* en un principio (**b**) *(with imagination)* con originalidad

originate [əˈrɪdʒɪneɪt] **1** *vt* originar
2 *vi* **to o. from** *or* **in** tener su origen en

Orkneys [ˈɔːknɪz] *npl* **the O.** las (Islas) Orcadas

ornament [ˈɔːnəmənt] *n* ornamento *m*, adorno *m*

ornamental [ɔːnəˈmentəl] *adj* decorativo(a)

ornate [ɔːˈneɪt] *adj* vistoso(a)

ornithology [ɔːnɪˈθɒlədʒɪ] *n* ornitología *f*

orphan [ˈɔːfən] **1** *n* huérfano(a) *m,f*
2 *vt* **she was orphaned** quedó huérfana

orphanage [ˈɔːfənɪdʒ] *n* orfanato *m*

orthodox [ˈɔːθədɒks] *adj* ortodoxo(a)

orthodoxy [ˈɔːθədɒksɪ] *n* ortodoxia *f*

orthopaedic, *US* **orthopedic** [ɔːθəʊˈpiːdɪk] *adj* ortopédico(a)

Oscar [ˈɒskə(r)] *n* Óscar *m*

oscillate [ˈɒsɪleɪt] *vi* oscilar
ostensible [ɒˈstensɪbəl] *adj* (**a**) *(apparent)* ostensible (**b**) *(pretended)* aparente
ostentatious [ɒstenˈteɪʃəs] *adj* ostentoso(a)
osteopath [ˈɒstɪəpæθ] *n* osteópata *mf*
ostracize [ˈɒstrəsaɪz] *vt (from society)* condenar al ostracismo; *(from group)* aislar, excluir
ostrich [ˈɒstrɪtʃ] *n* avestruz *f*
other [ˈʌðə(r)] **1** *adj* (**a**) otro(a); **every o. day** cada dos días; **on the o. hand** por otra parte; **o. people have seen it** otros lo han visto; **the o. four** los otros cuatro; **the o. one** el otro/la otra; **the o. thing** lo otro (**b**) **he must be somewhere or o.** debe estar en alguna parte
2 *pron* otro(a) *m,f*; **many others** otros muchos; **the others** los otros, los demás; **we see each o. quite often** nos vemos con bastante frecuencia
otherwise [ˈʌðəwaɪz] **1** *adv* (**a**) *(if not)* si no (**b**) *(differently)* de otra manera (**c**) *(in other respects)* por lo demás
2 *adj* distinto(a)
OTT [əʊtiːˈtiː] *adj Br Fam (abbr* **over the top***)* exagerado(a)
otter [ˈɒtə(r)] *n* nutria *f*
ought [ɔːt] *v aux*

En el inglés hablado, y en el escrito en estilo coloquial, la forma negativa **ought not** se transforma en **oughtn't**.

(**a**) *(obligation)* deber; **I thought I o. to tell you** creí que debía decírtelo; **she o. to do it** debería hacerlo (**b**) *(vague desirability)* tener que, deber; **you o. to see the exhibition** deberías ver la exposición (**c**) *(expectation)* **he o. to pass the exam** seguramente aprobará el examen; **that o. to do** con eso bastará
ounce [aʊns] *n* onza *f*
our [aʊə(r)] *poss adj* nuestro(a)
ours [aʊəz] *poss pron* (**a**) (el) nuestro/ (la) nuestra, (los) nuestros (**b**) **of o.** nuestro(a); **a friend of o.** un amigo nuestro
ourselves [aʊəˈselvz] *pers pron pl* (**a**) *(reflexive)* nos (**b**) *(emphatic)* nosotros mismos/nosotras mismas (**c**) **by o.** a solas
oust [aʊst] *vt* (**a**) *(from a post)* desbancar (**b**) *(from property etc)* desalojar
out [aʊt] **1** *adv* (**a**) *(outside, away)* fuera; **o. there** ahí fuera; **to go o.** salir (**b**) **I told him straight o.** se lo dije muy claramente; **o. loud** en voz alta (**c**) **hear me o.** escúchame hasta el final (**d**) **o. of** *(place)* fuera de; **move o. of the**

way! ¡quítate de en medio!; **o. of danger** fuera de peligro; **to go o. of the room** salir de la habitación; **o. of control** fuera de control; **o. of date** *(expired)* caducado(a); *(old-fashioned)* pasado(a) de moda
(**e**) **o. of** *(cause, motive)* por
(**f**) **o. of** *(made from)* de
(**g**) **o. of** *(short of, without)* sin; **I'm o. of money** se me ha acabado el dinero; **o. of breath** sin aliento
(**h**) **o. of** *(among)* entre; **forty o. of fifty** cuarenta de cada cincuenta; *(in exam etc)* cuarenta sobre cincuenta
2 *adj* (**a**) **the sun is o.** ha salido el sol
(**b**) *(unfashionable)* pasado(a) de moda
(**c**) *(fire)* apagado(a)
(**d**) *(not working)* estropeado(a)
(**e**) **she's o.** *(not in)* ha salido, no está
(**f**) **to be o. for sth** buscar algo; **to be o. to do sth** pretender hacer algo
(**g**) **the book is just o.** el libro acaba de salir
(**h**) *(inaccurate)* equivocado(a); **to be o. in one's calculations** equivocarse en los cálculos
(**i**) **before the week is o.** antes de que acabe la semana
3 *prep (out of)* por; **he jumped o. of the window** saltó por la ventana
out-and-out [ˈaʊtənaʊt] *adj* redomado(a)
outboard [ˈaʊtbɔːd] *adj* **o. motor** fueraborda *m*
outbreak [ˈaʊtbreɪk] *n (of war)* comienzo *m*; *(of spots)* erupción *f*; *(of disease)* brote *m*; *(of violence)* ola *f*; *(of anger)* arrebato *m*; **at the o. of war** cuando estalló la guerra
outbuilding [ˈaʊtbɪldɪŋ] *n* dependencia *f*
outburst [ˈaʊtbɜːst] *n (of anger)* arrebato *m*; *(of generosity)* arranque *m*
outcast [ˈaʊtkɑːst] *n* marginado(a) *m,f*
outcome [ˈaʊtkʌm] *n* resultado *m*
outcrop [ˈaʊtkrɒp] *n Geol* afloramiento *m*
outcry [ˈaʊtkraɪ] *n* **there was an o.** hubo fuertes protestas
outdated [aʊtˈdeɪtɪd] *adj* anticuado(a), obsoleto(a)
outdo [aʊtˈduː] *vt (pt* **outdid** [aʊtˈdɪd]*; pp* **outdone** [aʊtˈdʌn]*)* **to o. sb** superar a algn
outdoor [ˈaʊtdɔː(r)] *adj* (**a**) al aire libre (**b**) *(clothes)* de calle
outdoors [aʊtˈdɔːz] *adv* fuera, al aire libre

outer ['aʊtə(r)] *adj* exterior, externo(a)

outfit ['aʊtfɪt] *n* (**a**) *(kit, equipment)* equipo *m* (**b**) *(set of clothes)* conjunto *m* (**c**) *Fam (group)* grupo *m*

outgoing ['aʊtgəʊɪŋ] **1** *adj* (**a**) *(departing)* saliente (**b**) *(sociable)* extrovertido(a) **2** *npl* **outgoings** gastos *mpl*

outgrow [aʊt'grəʊ] *vt* (*pt* **outgrew** [aʊt'gruː]; *pp* **outgrown** [aʊt'grən]) **he's outgrowing all his clothes** toda la ropa se le está quedando pequeña; **she'll o. it** se le pasará con la edad

outhouse ['aʊthaʊs] *n* = outbuilding

outing ['aʊtɪŋ] *n* excursión *f*

outlandish [aʊt'lændɪʃ] *adj* estrafalario(a)

outlast [aʊt'lɑːst] *vt* durar más que

outlaw ['aʊtlɔː] **1** *n* proscrito(a) *m,f* **2** *vt* prohibir

outlet ['aʊtlet] *n* (**a**) *(opening)* salida *f* (**b**) *(for emotions)* válvula *f* de escape (**c**) *Com* mercado *m* (**d**) *(for water)* desagüe *m*

outline ['aʊtlaɪn] **1** *n* (**a**) *(draft)* bosquejo *m* (**b**) *(outer line)* contorno *m*; *(silhouette)* perfil *m*
2 *vt* (**a**) *(draw lines of)* perfilar (**b**) *(summarize)* resumir (**c**) *(describe roughly)* trazar las líneas generales de

outlive [aʊt'lɪv] *vt* sobrevivir a

outlook ['aʊtlʊk] *n* (**a**) *(point of view)* punto *m* de vista (**b**) *(prospect)* perspectiva *f*; *Met* previsión *f*

outlying ['aʊtlaɪɪŋ] *adj (remote)* aislado(a)

outmoded [aʊt'məʊdɪd] *adj* anticuado(a)

outnumber [aʊt'nʌmbə(r)] *vt* exceder en número

out-of-the-way ['aʊtəvðə'weɪ] *adj* (**a**) *(distant)* apartado(a), aislado(a) (**b**) *(uncommon)* poco corriente

outpatient ['aʊtpeɪʃənt] *n* paciente externo(a); **outpatients' department** clínica ambulatoria

outpost ['aʊtpəʊst] *n* avanzada *f*

output ['aʊtpʊt] *n* (**a**) producción *f*; *(of machine)* rendimiento *m* (**b**) *Elec* potencia *f* (**c**) *Comput* salida *f*

outrage ['aʊtreɪdʒ] **1** *n* ultraje *m*; **it's an o.!** ¡es un escándalo!
2 *vt* **to be outraged by sth** indignarse por algo

outrageous [aʊt'reɪdʒəs] *adj (behaviour)* escandaloso(a); *(clothes)* extravagante; *(price)* exorbitante

outright 1 *adj* ['aʊtraɪt] *(absolute)* absoluto(a)

2 *adv* [aʊt'raɪt] (**a**) *(completely)* por completo (**b**) *(directly)* directamente, sin reserva (**c**) *(immediately)* en el acto

outset ['aʊtset] *n* comienzo *m*, principio *m*

outside 1 *prep* [aʊt'saɪd, 'aʊtsaɪd] (**a**) fuera de (**b**) *(beyond)* más allá de (**c**) *(other than)* aparte de
2 *adj* ['aʊtsaɪd] (**a**) *(exterior)* exterior, externo(a) (**b**) *(remote)* remoto(a)
3 *adv* [aʊt'saɪd] fuera, afuera
4 *n* [aʊt'saɪd, 'aʊtsaɪd] exterior *m*; **on the o.** por fuera; *Fam* **at the o.** como mucho

outsider [aʊt'saɪdə(r)] *n* (**a**) *(stranger)* extraño(a) *m,f*, forastero(a) *m,f* (**b**) *Pol* = candidato(a) con pocas posibilidades de ganar

outsize(d) ['aʊtsaɪz(d)] *adj (clothes)* de talla muy grande

outskirts ['aʊtskɜːts] *npl* afueras *fpl*

outsourcing ['aʊtsɔːsɪŋ] *n Com* externalización *f*, subcontratación *f*, *Am* tercerización *f*

outspoken [aʊt'spəʊkən] *adj* directo(a), abierto(a)

outstanding [aʊt'stændɪŋ] *adj* (**a**) *(exceptional)* destacado(a) (**b**) *(unpaid, unresolved)* pendiente

outstretched [aʊt'stretʃt] *adj* extendido(a)

outward ['aʊtwəd] **1** *adj* (**a**) *(external)* exterior, externo(a) (**b**) **the o. journey** el viaje de ida
2 *adv* = outwards

outwardly ['aʊtwədlɪ] *adv* aparentemente

outwards ['aʊtwədz] *adv* hacia (a)fuera

outweigh [aʊt'weɪ] *vt* (**a**) *(prevail over)* prevalecer sobre (**b**) *(weigh more than)* pesar más que

oval ['əʊvəl] **1** *adj* oval, ovalado(a)
2 *n* óvalo *m*

ovary ['əʊvərɪ] *n* ovario *m*

ovation [əʊ'veɪʃən] *n* ovación *f*

oven ['ʌvən] *n* horno *m*

ovenproof ['ʌvənpruːf] *adj* refractario(a)

over ['əʊvə(r)] **1** *prep* (**a**) *(above)* encima de
(**b**) *(on top of)* sobre, encima de
(**c**) *(across)* al otro lado de; **the bridge o. the river** el puente que cruza el río
(**d**) *(during)* durante
(**e**) *(throughout)* por
(**f**) **all o.** por todo(a); **famous all o. the world** famoso en el mundo entero
(**g**) *(by the agency of)* por; **o. the phone** por teléfono

(**h**) *(more than)* más de; **men o. twenty-five** hombres mayores de veinticinco años; **o. and above** además de

(**i**) *(recovered from)* recuperado(a) de

2 *adv* (**a**) **o. there** allá; **why don't you come o. tomorrow?** ¿por qué no vienes a casa mañana?

(**b**) *(throughout)* por; **all o.** por todas partes

(**c**) *(more)* más

(**d**) *(again)* otra vez; **o. and o. (again)** una y otra vez; **twice o.** dos veces seguidas

(**e**) *(in excess)* de más

3 *adj (finished)* acabado(a); **it's (all) o.** se acabó; **the danger is o.** ha pasado el peligro

overall ['əʊvərɔːl] **1** *adj* total, global

2 *n* (**a**) *Br* guardapolvo *m* (**b**) **overalls** mono *m*

3 *adv* [əʊvər'ɔːl] *(on the whole)* por lo general, en conjunto

overawe [əʊvər'ɔː] *vt* **to be overawed** sobrecogerse

overbearing [əʊvə'beərɪŋ] *adj (domineering)* dominante; *(important)* significativo(a)

overboard ['əʊvəbɔːd] *adv* por la borda; **man o.!** ¡hombre al agua!; *Fam* **to go o.** pasarse

overcast ['əʊvəkɑːst] *adj* nublado(a)

overcharge [əʊvə'tʃɑːdʒ] *vt* (**a**) *(charge too much)* cobrar demasiado (**b**) *(overload)* sobrecargar

overcoat ['əʊvəkəʊt] *n* abrigo *m*

overcome [əʊvə'kʌm] *vt* (**a**) *(conquer)* vencer; **o. by grief** deshecho por el dolor (**b**) *(obstacle)* superar

overconfident [əʊvə'kɒnfɪdənt] *adj* presumido(a), creído(a)

overcrowded [əʊvə'kraʊdɪd] *adj (room)* atestado(a) (de gente); *(country)* superpoblado(a)

overcrowding [əʊvə'kraʊdɪŋ] *n (of prisons etc)* hacinamiento *m*; *(of country)* superpoblación *f*

overdo [əʊvə'duː] *vt* (*pt* **overdid** [əʊvə'dɪd]; *pp* **overdone** [əʊvə'dʌn]) (**a**) *(carry too far)* exagerar; **don't o. it** no te pases (**b**) *Culin* cocer *or* asar demasiado

overdose ['əʊvədəʊs] *n* sobredosis *f*

overdraft ['əʊvədrɑːft] *n* giro *m* en descubierto; *(amount)* saldo *m* deudor

overdraw [əʊvə'drɔː] *vt* **to be overdrawn** tener la cuenta en descubierto

overdue [əʊvə'djuː] *adj (rent, train etc)* atrasado(a); *(reform)* largamente esperado(a)

overestimate [əʊvər'estɪmeɪt] *vt* sobreestimar

overflow **1** *vi* [əʊvə'fləʊ] *(river)* desbordarse; *(cup etc)* derramarse

2 *n* ['əʊvəfləʊ] *(of river etc)* desbordamiento *m*; **o. pipe** cañería *f* de desagüe

overgrown [əʊvə'grəʊn] *adj* (**a**) *(with grass)* cubierto(a) (de hierba) (**b**) *(in size)* demasiado grande

overhaul **1** *vt* [əʊvə'hɔːl] revisar

2 *n* ['əʊvəhɔːl] revisión *f* y reparación *f*

overhead **1** *adj* ['əʊvəhed] *(por)* encima de la cabeza; **o. cable** cable aéreo

2 *adv* [əʊvə'hed] arriba, por encima de la cabeza

3 *n* ['əʊvərhed] *US* = **overheads**

overheads ['əʊvəhedz] *npl Br* gastos *mpl* generales

overhear [əʊvə'hɪə(r)] *vt* (*pt* & *pp* **overheard** [əʊvə'hɜːd]) oír por casualidad

overheat [əʊvə'hiːt] *vi* recalentarse

overjoyed [əʊvə'dʒɔɪd] *adj* rebosante de alegría

overlap [əʊvə'læp] *vi* superponerse; *Fig* **our plans o.** nuestros planes coinciden parcialmente

overleaf [əʊvə'liːf] *adv* al dorso

overload **1** *vt* [əʊvə'ləʊd] sobrecargar

2 *n* ['əʊvələʊd] sobrecarga *f*

overlook [əʊvə'lʊk] *vt* (**a**) *(fail to notice)* saltarse (**b**) *(ignore)* no hacer caso de; **we'll o. it this time** esta vez haremos la vista gorda (**c**) *(have a view of)* dar a, tener vista a

overmanning [əʊvə'mænɪŋ] *n Ind* exceso *m* de empleados

overnight **1** *adv* [əʊvə'naɪt] (**a**) *(during the night)* por la noche; **we stayed there o.** pasamos la noche allí (**b**) *(suddenly)* de la noche a la mañana

2 *adj* ['əʊvənaɪt] *(sudden)* repentino(a)

overpass ['əʊvəpɑːs] *n Br* paso *m* elevado

overpay [əʊvə'peɪ] *vt* (*pt* & *pp* **overpaid** [əʊvə'peɪd]) pagar demasiado

overpower [əʊvə'paʊə(r)] *vt* (**a**) *(subdue)* dominar (**b**) *(affect strongly)* abrumar

overrate [əʊvə'reɪt] *vt* sobreestimar, supervalorar

override [əʊvə'raɪd] *vt* (*pt* **overrode**; *pp* **overridden** [əʊvə'rɪdən]) (**a**) *(disregard)* hacer caso omiso de (**b**) *(annul, cancel out)* anular (**c**) *(be more important than)* contar más que

overriding [əʊvə'raɪdɪŋ] *adj* principal; *(importance)* primordial; *(need)* imperioso(a)

overrode [əʊvəˈrəʊd] *pt of* **override**

overrule [əʊvəˈruːl] *vt* invalidar; *Jur* denegar

overrun [əʊvəˈrʌn] *vt* (**a**) *(country)* invadir (**b**) *(allotted time)* excederse de

oversaw [əʊvəˈsɔː] *pt of* **oversee**

overseas 1 *adv* [əʊvəˈsiːz] en ultramar; **to live o.** vivir en el extranjero

 2 *adj* [ˈəʊvəsiːz] de ultramar; *(person)* extranjero(a); *(trade)* exterior

oversee [əʊvəˈsiː] *vt* (*pt* **oversaw**; *pp* **overseen** [əʊvəˈsiːn]) supervisar

overseer [ˈəʊvəsiːə(r)] *n* supervisor(a) *m,f; (foreman)* capataz *m*

overshadow [əʊvəˈʃædəʊ] *vt Fig* eclipsar

overshoot [əʊvəˈʃuːt] *vt* (*pt & pp* **overshot** [əʊvəˈʃɒt]) **to o. a turning** pasarse un cruce; *Fig* **to o. the mark** pasarse de la raya

oversight [ˈəʊvəsaɪt] *n* descuido *m*

oversleep [əʊvəˈsliːp] *vi* (*pt & pp* **overslept** [əʊvəˈslept]) quedarse dormido(a)

overspill [ˈəʊvəspɪl] *n* exceso *m* de población

overstate [əʊvəˈsteɪt] *vt* exagerar

overstep [əʊvəˈstep] *vt Fig* **to o. the mark** pasarse de la raya

overt [əʊˈvɜːt] *adj* patente

overtake [əʊvəˈteɪk] *vt* (*pt* **overtook**; *pp* **overtaken** [əʊvəˈteɪkən]) (**a**) *Br Aut* adelantar (**b**) *(surpass)* superar a (**c**) *(of night)* sorprender

overthrow [əʊvəˈθrəʊ] *vt* (*pt* **overthrew** [əʊvəˈθruː]; *pp* **overthrown** [əʊvəˈθrəʊn]) *(government)* derribar

overtime [ˈəʊvətaɪm] *n* (**a**) *(work)* horas *fpl* extra (**b**) *US* prórroga *f*

overtone [ˈəʊvətəʊn] *n* matiz *m*

overtook [əʊvəˈtʊk] *pt of* **overtake**

overture [ˈəʊvətjʊə(r)] *n* (**a**) *Mus* obertura *f; Fig (introduction)* introducción *f* (**b**) *(proposal)* propuesta *f*

overturn [əʊvəˈtɜːn] *vt & vi* volcar

overweight [əʊvəˈweɪt] *adj* demasiado pesado(a)

overwhelm [əʊvəˈwelm] *vt* (**a**) *(defeat)* aplastar; *(overpower)* abrumar; **I'm overwhelmed** estoy abrumado (**b**) *(with letters, work etc)* inundar

overwhelming [əʊvəˈwelmɪŋ] *adj (defeat)* aplastante; *(desire etc)* irresistible

overwork [əʊvəˈwɜːk] **1** *vi* trabajar demasiado

 2 *vt (person)* forzar; *(excuse etc)* abusar de

overwrought [əʊvəˈrɔːt] *adj* (**a**) *(tense)* muy nervioso(a) (**b**) *Literary (too elaborate)* forzado(a)

owe [əʊ] *vt* deber

owing [ˈəʊɪŋ] *adj* **o. to** debido a, a causa de

owl [aʊl] *n* lechuza *f*, búho *m*

own [əʊn] **1** *adj* propio(a); **it's his o. fault** es culpa suya

 2 *pron* (**a**) **my o./your o./his o.**/*etc* lo mío/lo tuyo/lo suyo/*etc; Fig* **to come into one's o.** realizarse; *Fam* **to get one's o. back** tomarse la revancha (**b**) **on one's o.** *(without help)* uno(a) mismo(a); *(alone)* solo(a)

 3 *vt* poseer, ser dueño(a) de

▸ **own up** *vi* **to o. up (to sth)** confesar (algo)

owner [ˈəʊnə(r)] *n* propietario(a) *m,f*, dueño(a) *m,f*

ownership [ˈəʊnəʃɪp] *n* propiedad *f*, posesión *f*

ox [ɒks] *n* (*pl* **oxen** [ˈɒksən]) buey *m*

oxide [ˈɒksaɪd] *n Chem* óxido *m*

oxtail [ˈɒksteɪl] *n* rabo *m* de buey

oxygen [ˈɒksɪdʒən] *n* oxígeno *m*; **o. mask** máscara *f* de oxígeno

oyster [ˈɔɪstə(r)] *n* ostra *f*

ozone [ˈəʊzəʊn] *n* ozono *m*; **o. layer** capa *f* de ozono

P, p [piː] *n (the letter)* P, p *f*

p (**a**) (*pl* **pp**) (*abbr* **page**) pág., p (**b**) [piː] *Br Fam* (*abbr* **penny, pence**) penique(s) *m(pl)*

PA [piːˈeɪ] *n Fam* (**a**) (*abbr* **personal assistant**) ayudante *mf* personal (**b**) (*abbr* **public-address (system)**) megafonía *f*

p.a. (*abbr* **per annum**) al año

pace [peɪs] **1** *n (step)* paso *m*; (*speed*) ritmo *m*; **to keep p. with** seguir a; *Fig* avanzar al mismo ritmo que; **to set the p.** marcar el paso; *Fig* marcar la pauta

2 *vi* **to p. up and down** ir de un lado a otro

pacemaker [ˈpeɪsmeɪkə(r)] *n Sport* liebre *f*; *Med* marcapasos *m inv*

Pacific [pəˈsɪfɪk] *adj* **the P. (Ocean)** el (océano) Pacífico

pacifier [ˈpæsɪfaɪə(r)] *n US (for baby)* chupete *m*

pacifist [ˈpæsɪfɪst] *adj & n* pacifista *(mf)*

pacify [ˈpæsɪfaɪ] *vt (person)* calmar; (*country*) pacificar

pack¹ [pæk] **1** *n (parcel)* paquete *m*; (*bundle*) bulto *m*; *US (of cigarettes)* paquete; *Br (of cards)* baraja *f*; (*of hounds*) jauría *f*

2 *vt* (**a**) (*goods*) embalar, envasar; (*in suitcase*) poner; **to p. one's bags** hacer las maletas; *Fig* marcharse (**b**) (*fill*) atestar (**c**) (*press down*) (*snow*) apretar

3 *vi* (**a**) hacer las maletas; *Fam* **to send sb packing** mandar a paseo a algn (**b**) (*of people*) apiñarse (**into** en)

▸ **pack in** *vt sep Br Fam (give up)* dejar

▸ **pack off** *vt sep Fam* mandar

▸ **pack up** *Fam* **1** *vt sep (give up)* dejar

2 *vi (stop working)* terminar; (*machine etc*) estropearse

pack² [pæk] *vt (meeting)* llenar de partidarios

package [ˈpækɪdʒ] **1** *n* (**a**) (*parcel*) paquete *m*; (*bundle*) bulto *m* (**b**) (*of proposals etc*) paquete *m*; (*agreement*) acuerdo *m*; **p. deal** convenio *m* general; **p. tour** viaje *m* todo incluido

2 *vt (goods)* envasar, embalar

packet [ˈpækɪt] *n* paquete *m*; *Fam (fortune)* dineral *m*

packing [ˈpækɪŋ] *n* embalaje *m*; **p. case** caja *f* de embalar; **to do one's p.** hacer las maletas

pact [pækt] *n* pacto *m*

pad¹ [pæd] **1** *n* (**a**) almohadilla *f*; (*of paper*) bloc *m*, taco *m* (**b**) **launch p.** plataforma *f* de lanzamiento (**c**) *Fam (flat)* piso *m*

2 *vt (chair)* acolchar

▸ **pad out** *vt sep Fig* meter paja en

pad² [pæd] *vi* **to p. about** *or* **around** andar silenciosamente

padding [ˈpædɪŋ] *n (material)* relleno *m*; *Fig (in speech etc)* paja *f*

paddle¹ [ˈpædəl] **1** *n* (**a**) *(oar)* pala *f*; **p. boat** *or* **steamer** vapor *m* de ruedas (**b**) *US (for table tennis)* pala *f*

2 *vt (boat)* remar con pala en

3 *vi (in boat)* remar con pala

paddle² [ˈpædəl] *vi* chapotear

paddling pool [ˈpædlɪŋpuːl] *n Br* piscina *f* para niños

paddock [ˈpædək] *n* potrero *m*; (*in race course*) paddock *m*

paddy [ˈpædɪ] *n* arrozal *m*

padlock [ˈpædlɒk] **1** *n* candado *m*

2 *vt* cerrar con candado

paediatrician [piːdɪəˈtrɪʃən] *n* pediatra *mf*

pagan [ˈpeɪgən] *adj & n* pagano(a) *(m,f)*

page¹ [peɪdʒ] *n* página *f*

page² [peɪdʒ] **1** *n (servant)* paje *m*; (*of knight*) escudero *m*; (*at club*) botones *m inv*

2 *vt (call)* llamar por altavoz

pageant [ˈpædʒənt] *n (show)* espectáculo *m*; (*procession*) desfile *m*; (*on horses*) cabalgata *f*

pageantry [ˈpædʒəntrɪ] *n* pompa *f*, boato *m*

paid [peɪd] **1** *adj* pagado(a); *Fig* **to put p. to sth** acabar con algo

2 *pt & pp of* **pay**

pail [peɪl] *n* cubo *m*; (*child's*) cubito *m*

pain [peɪn] **1** *n* (**a**) dolor *m*; (*grief*) sufrimiento *m*; *Fam* **he's a p. (in the neck)** es un pelmazo; **on p. of death** so pena de muerte (**b**) **to take pains over sth** esmerarse en algo

2 *vt (grieve)* dar pena a

pained [peɪnd] *adj* de reproche

painful ['peɪnfʊl] *adj* doloroso(a); *Fam (very bad)* malísimo(a)

painfully ['peɪnfʊlɪ] *adv* (**a**) **p. shy** lastimosamente tímido(a) (**b**) *Fam* terriblemente

painkiller ['peɪnkɪlə(r)] *n* analgésico *m*

painless ['peɪnlɪs] *adj* sin dolor; *Fig* sin dificultades

painstaking ['peɪnzteɪkɪŋ] *adj (person)* concienzudo(a); *(care, research)* esmerado(a)

paint [peɪnt] **1** *n* pintura *f*
   2 *vt* pintar; **to p. sth white** pintar algo de blanco
   3 *vi* pintar

paintbrush ['peɪntbrʌʃ] *n Art* pincel *m*; *(for walls)* brocha *f*

painter ['peɪntə(r)] *n* pintor(a) *m,f*

painting ['peɪntɪŋ] *n* cuadro *m*; *(activity)* pintura *f*

paintwork ['peɪntwɜːk] *n* pintura *f*

pair [peə(r)] *n (of gloves, shoes)* par *m*; *(of people, cards)* pareja *f*; **a p. of scissors** unas tijeras; **a p. of trousers** un pantalón, unos pantalones

pajamas [pə'dʒæməz] *npl US* = **pyjamas**

Pakistan [pɑːkɪ'stɑːn] *n* Paquistán

Pakistani [pɑːkɪ'stɑːnɪ] *adj & n* paquistaní *(mf)*

pal [pæl] *n Fam* amigo(a) *m,f*, colega *mf*

palace ['pælɪs] *n* palacio *m*

palatable ['pælətəbəl] *adj (tasty)* sabroso(a); *Fig* aceptable

palate ['pælɪt] *n* paladar *m*

palatial [pə'leɪʃəl] *adj* suntuoso(a), señorial

palaver [pə'lɑːvə(r)] *n Fam* lío *m*, follón *m*

pale¹ [peɪl] **1** *adj (skin)* pálido(a); *(colour)* claro(a); *(light)* tenue; **to turn p.** palidecer
   2 *vi* palidecer

pale² [peɪl] *n Fig* **to be beyond the p.** ser inaceptable

Palestine ['pælɪstaɪn] *n* Palestina

Palestinian [pælɪ'stɪnɪən] *adj & n* palestino(a) *(m,f)*

palette ['pælɪt] *n* paleta *f*; **p. knife** espátula *f*

paling ['peɪlɪŋ] *n* valla *f*

palisade [pælɪ'seɪd] *n* palizada *f*, estacada *f*

pall¹ [pɔːl] *n Fig* manto *m*; *(of smoke)* cortina *f*

pall² [pɔːl] *vi* aburrir; **it never palls** nunca cansa

pallet ['pælɪt] *n* plataforma *f* de carga

pallid ['pælɪd] *adj* pálido(a)

pallor ['pælə(r)] *n* palidez *f*

palm¹ [pɑːm] *n (tree)* palmera *f*; *(leaf)* palma *f*; **date p.** palma datilera; **P. Sunday** domingo *m* de Ramos

palm² [pɑːm] *n Anat* palma *f*
   ▸ **palm off** *vt sep* **to p. sth off on sb** colocar *or* endosar algo a algn

palmistry ['pɑːmɪstrɪ] *n* quiromancia *f*

palpable ['pælpəbəl] *adj* palpable

palpitate ['pælpɪteɪt] *vi* palpitar

palpitation [pælpɪ'teɪʃən] *n* palpitación *f*

paltry ['pɔːltrɪ] *adj* (**paltrier, paltriest**) insignificante

pamper ['pæmpə(r)] *vt* mimar, consentir

pamphlet ['pæmflɪt] *n* folleto *m*

pan¹ [pæn] **1** *n* (**a**) *(saucepan)* cazuela *f*, cacerola *f* (**b**) *(of scales)* platillo *m* (**c**) *(of lavatory)* taza *f*
   2 *vt Fam (criticize)* dejar por los suelos

pan² [pæn] *vi Cin* tomar vistas panorámicas

panacea [pænə'sɪə] *n* panacea *f*

panache [pə'næʃ] *n* garbo *m*, salero *m*

Panama ['pænəmɑː] *n* Panamá; **P. Canal** Canal *m* de Panamá

pancake ['pænkeɪk] *n* crepe *f*

panda ['pændə] *n* panda *m*; *Br* **p. car** coche *m* patrulla

pandemonium [pændɪ'məʊnɪəm] *n* alboroto *m*

pander ['pændə(r)] *vi* **to p. to** *(person)* complacer a; *(wishes)* acceder a

pane [peɪn] *n* cristal *m*, vidrio *m*

panel ['pænəl] *n* (**a**) *(of wall)* panel *m*; *(flat surface)* tabla *f*; *(of instruments)* tablero *m*; *(of ceiling)* artesón *m* (**b**) *(jury)* jurado *m*; *Rad & TV* concursantes *mpl*

panelling, *US* **paneling** ['pænəlɪŋ] *n* paneles *mpl*

pang [pæŋ] *n (of pain, hunger)* punzada *f*; *(of childbirth)* dolores *mpl*; *Fig (of conscience)* remordimiento *m*

panic ['pænɪk] **1** *n* pánico *m*; **to get into a p.** ponerse histérico(a)
   2 *vi* aterrarse

panicky ['pænɪkɪ] *adj* asustadizo(a)

panic-stricken ['pænɪkstrɪkən] *adj* aterrado(a)

panorama [pænə'rɑːmə] *n* panorama *m*

pansy ['pænzɪ] *n Bot* pensamiento *m*; *Fam Pej* mariquita *m*

pant [pænt] **1** *n* jadeo *m*
   2 *vi* jadear

panther ['pænθə(r)] *n* pantera *f*

panties ['pæntɪz] *npl* bragas *fpl*

*Note that the Spanish word **panty** is a false friend and is never a translation for the English word **panties**. In Spanish, **panty** means "(pair of) tights".*

pantomime ['pæntəmaɪm] *n Th (play)* función *f* musical navideña; *(mime)* pantomima *f*

pantry ['pæntrɪ] *n* despensa *f*

pants [pænts] *npl Br (underpants) (ladies')* bragas *fpl; (men's)* calzoncillos *mpl; US (trousers)* pantalones *mpl,* pantalón *m*

pantyhose ['pæntɪhəʊz] *n US* medias *fpl,* pantis *mpl*

papal ['peɪpəl] *adj* papal

paper ['peɪpə(r)] **1** *n* (**a**) papel *m; Fig* **on p.** en teoría; **p. money** papel moneda; **writing p.** papel de escribir (**b**) *(exam)* examen *m; (essay)* trabajo *m* (escrito) (**c**) *Pol* libro *m* (**d**) *(newspaper)* periódico *m;* **the papers** la prensa (**e**) **papers** *(documents)* documentos *mpl*
  2 *vt* empapelar

paperback ['peɪpəbæk] *n* libro *m* en rústica

paperclip ['peɪpəklɪp] *n* clip *m,* sujetapapeles *m inv*

paperweight ['peɪpəweɪt] *n* pisapapeles *m inv*

paperwork ['peɪpəwɜːk] *n* papeleo *m*

papier-mâché [pæpjeɪ'mæʃeɪ] *n* cartón *m* piedra

paprika ['pæprɪkə] *n* pimentón molido

par [pɑː(r)] *n (parity)* igualdad *f; (in golf)* par *m; Fig* **it's p. for the course** es lo normal en estos casos; *Fig* **to feel below p.** estar en baja forma

parable ['pærəbəl] *n* parábola *f*

paracetamol [pærə'siːtəmɒl] *n* paracetamol *m*

parachute ['pærəʃuːt] **1** *n* paracaídas *m inv*
  2 *vi* **to p. (down)** saltar *or* lanzarse en paracaídas

parade [pə'reɪd] **1** *n* desfile *m; Mil* **to be on p.** pasar revista
  2 *vt Mil* hacer desfilar; *Fig (flaunt)* hacer alarde de
  3 *vi (troops)* pasar revista; *(procession)* desfilar

paradise ['pærədaɪs] *n* paraíso *m*

paradox ['pærədɒks] *n* paradoja *f*

paradoxical [pærə'dɒksɪkəl] *adj* paradójico(a)

paraffin ['pærəfɪn] *n* parafina *f;* **liquid p.** aceite *m* de parafina; **p. lamp** lámpara *f* de petróleo

paragliding ['pærəglaɪdɪŋ] *n* parapente *m*

paragon ['pærəgən] *n* modelo *m*

paragraph ['pærəgrɑːf] *n* párrafo *m*

Paraguay ['pærəgwaɪ] *n* Paraguay

Paraguayan [pærə'gwaɪən] *adj & n* paraguayo(a) *(m,f)*

parallel ['pærəlel] **1** *adj* paralelo(a) (**to** *or* **with** a); *Fig* comparable (**to** *or* **with** a)
  2 *n Geog* paralelo *m; Geom* paralela *f; Fig* paralelo
  3 *vt Fig* ser paralelo(a) a

paralyse ['pærəlaɪz] *vt* paralizar

paralysis [pə'rælɪsɪs] *n* parálisis *f*

paralyze ['pærəlaɪz] *vt US* = **paralyse**

paramedic [pærə'medɪk] *n* auxiliar *mf* sanitario(a)

parameter [pə'ræmɪtə(r)] *n* parámetro *m*

paramilitary [pærə'mɪlɪtərɪ] *adj* paramilitar

paramount ['pærəmaʊnt] *adj* **of p. importance** de suma importancia

paranoid ['pærənɔɪd] *adj & n* paranoico(a) *(m,f)*

paraphernalia [pærəfə'neɪlɪə] *n* parafernalia *f*

paraphrase ['pærəfreɪz] *vt* parafrasear

parasite ['pærəsaɪt] *n* parásito *m*

parasol ['pærəsɒl] *n* sombrilla *f*

paratrooper ['pærətruːpə(r)] *n* paracaidista *mf*

parcel ['pɑːsəl] **1** *n* paquete *m;* **p. bomb** paquete bomba
  2 *vt* **to p. up** envolver, empaquetar

parched [pɑːtʃt] *adj (land)* reseco(a); *(lips, mouth)* seco(a); *Fig* **to be p.** estar muerto(a) de sed

parchment ['pɑːtʃmənt] *n* pergamino *m*

pardon ['pɑːdən] **1** *n* perdón *m; Jur* indulto *m;* **I beg your p.** (Usted) perdone; **(I beg your) p.?** ¿cómo (dice)?
  2 *vt* perdonar; *Jur* indultar; **p. me!** ¡Usted perdone!

parent ['peərənt] *n* **parents** padres *mpl*

*Note that the Spanish word **pariente** is a false friend and is never a translation for the English word **parent**. In Spanish, **pariente** means "relative, relation".*

parental [pə'rentəl] *adj* paternal; **p. guidance** consejos *mpl* paternales

parenthesis [pə'renθɪsɪs] *n* (*pl* **parentheses** [pə'renθɪsiːz]) paréntesis *m inv;* **in p.** entre paréntesis

pariah [pə'raɪə] *n* paria *mf*

Paris ['pærɪs] *n* París

parish ['pærɪʃ] *n* parroquia *f*

Parisian [pə'rɪzɪən] *adj & n* parisino(a) *(m,f)*

parity ['pærɪtɪ] *n* igualdad *f*; *(of shares)* paridad *f*

park [pɑːk] **1** *n* parque *m*
   2 *vt (car)* aparcar, *Carib, Col, Pan* parquear

parking ['pɑːkɪŋ] *n* aparcamiento *m*, estacionamiento *m*; **no p.** *(sign)* prohibido aparcar; *US* **p. lot** parking *m*, aparcamiento *m*; **p. meter** parquímetro *m*; **p. space** aparcamiento

parliament ['pɑːləmənt] *n* parlamento *m*

parliamentary [pɑːlə'mentərɪ] *adj* parlamentario(a)

parlour, *US* **parlor** ['pɑːlə(r)] *n* salón *m*

parochial [pə'rəʊkɪəl] *adj* parroquial; *Pej (narrow-minded)* de miras estrechas

parody ['pærədɪ] *n* parodia *f*

parole [pə'rəʊl] *n Jur* libertad *f* condicional; **on p.** en libertad bajo palabra

parquet ['pɑːkeɪ] *n* **p. floor** suelo *m* de parqué

parrot ['pærət] *n* loro *m*, papagayo *m*

parry ['pærɪ] *vt* parar

parsimonious [pɑːsɪ'məʊnɪəs] *adj* tacaño(a)

parsley ['pɑːslɪ] *n* perejil *m*

parsnip ['pɑːsnɪp] *n* chirivía *f*

parson ['pɑːsən] *n* cura *m*

part [pɑːt] **1** *n* (**a**) parte *f*, *(piece)* trozo *m*; *(episode)* capítulo *m*; *Tech* pieza *f*; **for the most p.** en la mayor parte (**b**) *Cin & Th* papel *m*; **to play a p. in sth** desempeñar un papel en algo; **to take p. in sth** participar en algo (**c**) *(place)* lugar *m*; **in these parts** por estos lugares (**d**) **for my p.** por mi parte; **to take sb's p.** tomar partido por algn; **to take sth in good p.** tomarse bien algo (**e**) *US (in hair)* raya *f*
   2 *adj (partial)* parcial; **in p. exchange** como parte del pago
   3 *adv (partly)* en parte
   4 *vt (separate)* separar; **to p. company with sb** separarse de algn; **to p. one's hair** hacerse la raya (en el pelo)
   5 *vi* separarse; *(say goodbye)* despedirse
   ▶ **part with** *vt insep* separarse de

partial ['pɑːʃəl] *adj* parcial; **to be p. to sth** ser aficionado(a) a algo

participant [pɑː'tɪsɪpənt] *n* participante *mf*; *(in competition)* concursante *mf*

participate [pɑː'tɪsɪpeɪt] *vi* participar (**in** en)

participation [pɑːtɪsɪ'peɪʃən] *n* participación *f*

participle ['pɑːtɪsɪpəl] *n* participio *m*

particle ['pɑːtɪkəl] *n* partícula *f*

particular [pə'tɪkjʊlə(r)] **1** *adj* (**a**) *(special)* particular, especial; **in this p. case** en este caso concreto; **that p. person** esa persona en particular (**b**) *(fussy)* exigente
   2 *npl* **particulars** pormenores *mpl*; **to take down sb's particulars** anotar los datos personales de algn

particularly [pə'tɪkjʊləlɪ] *adv* particularmente, especialmente

parting ['pɑːtɪŋ] **1** *n (separation)* separación *f*; *(farewell)* despedida *f*; *Br (in hair)* raya *f*
   2 *adj* de despedida

partisan [pɑːtɪ'zæn, 'pɑːtɪzæn] **1** *n Mil* guerrillero(a) *m,f*; *(supporter)* partidario(a) *m,f*
   2 *adj (supporter)* a ultranza; *(of party)* partidista

partition [pɑː'tɪʃən] **1** *n (wall)* tabique *m*; *(of country)* partición *f*
   2 *vt* dividir

partly ['pɑːtlɪ] *adv* en parte

partner ['pɑːtnə(r)] **1** *n* compañero(a) *m,f*; *(in dancing, tennis)* pareja *f*; *(husband)* marido *m*; *(wife)* mujer *f*; *Com* socio(a) *m,f*
   2 *vt* acompañar

partnership ['pɑːtnəʃɪp] *n (relationship)* vida *f* en común; *Com* sociedad *f*

partridge ['pɑːtrɪdʒ] *n* perdiz pardilla

part-time ['pɑːt'taɪm] **1** *adj (work etc)* de tiempo parcial
   2 *adv* a tiempo parcial

party ['pɑːtɪ] **1** *n* (**a**) *(celebration)* fiesta *f* (**b**) *(group)* grupo *m* (**c**) *Pol* partido *m*; **p. political broadcast** espacio *m* electoral (**d**) *Jur* parte *f*
   2 *adj* de fiesta; *Tel* **p. line** línea compartida

pass [pɑːs] **1** *n* (**a**) *(of mountain)* desfiladero *m*
   (**b**) *(permit)* permiso *m*; **bus p.** abono *m* de autobús
   (**c**) *Sport* pase *m*
   (**d**) *Fam* **to make a p. at sb** intentar ligar con algn
   2 *vt* (**a**) pasar; *(overtake)* adelantar
   (**b**) *(exam, law)* aprobar; *Jur* **to p. sentence** dictar sentencia
   3 *vi* (**a**) pasar; *(procession)* desfilar; *(car)* adelantar; *(people)* cruzarse; *Sport* hacer un pase; **we passed on the stairs** nos cruzamos en la escalera
   (**b**) *(pain)* remitir; *(opportunity)* perderse; *(time)* pasar
   (**c**) *(happen)* ocurrir, pasar

(**d**) *(in exam)* aprobar
▶**pass away** *vi Euph* pasar a mejor vida
▶**pass by 1** *vt sep* pasar de largo
   2 *vi* pasar
▶**pass for** *vt insep* pasar por
▶**pass off 1** *vt sep* hacer pasar; **to p.
oneself off as sth** hacerse pasar por algo
   2 *vi (happen)* transcurrir
▶**pass on 1** *vt sep (hand on)* transmitir
   2 *vi Euph* pasar a mejor vida
▶**pass out** *vi (faint)* desmayarse; *Mil* graduarse
▶**pass over** *vt insep* (**a**) *(aircraft)* volar por
(**b**) *(disregard)* pasar por alto
▶**pass up** *vt sep Fam (opportunity)* renunciar; *(offer)* rechazar

passable ['pɑːsəbəl] *adj (road)* transitable; *(acceptable)* pasable

passage ['pæsɪdʒ] *n* (**a**) *(alleyway)* callejón *m*; *(hallway)* pasillo *m* (**b**) *(movement)* tránsito *m*; *Naut* travesía *f* (**c**) *Mus & Lit* pasaje *m*

passageway ['pæsɪdʒweɪ] *n (interior)* pasillo *m*; *(exterior)* pasaje *m*

passbook ['pɑːsbʊk] *n* libreta *f* de banco

passenger ['pæsɪndʒə(r)] *n* pasajero(a) *m,f*

passer-by [pɑːsə'baɪ] *n* transeúnte *mf*

passing ['pɑːsɪŋ] **1** *n* (**a**) *(of time)* transcurso *m*; **in p.** de pasada (**b**) *(of law)* aprobación *f*
   2 *adj* que pasa; *(glance)* rápido(a); *(thought)* pasajero(a)

passion ['pæʃən] *n* pasión *f*; **p. fruit** granadilla *f*

passionate ['pæʃənɪt] *adj* apasionado(a)

passive ['pæsɪv] *adj* pasivo(a)

Passover ['pɑːsəʊvə(r)] *n* Pascua *f* de los judíos

passport ['pɑːspɔːt] *n* pasaporte *m*

password ['pɑːswɜːd] *n* contraseña *f*

past [pɑːst] **1** *n* pasado *m*; **in the p.** en el pasado; **to have a p.** tener antecedentes
   2 *adj* pasado(a); *(former)* anterior; **in the p. weeks** en las últimas semanas
   3 *adv* por delante; **to run p.** pasar corriendo
   4 *prep (beyond)* más allá de; *(more than)* más de; **he's p. forty** pasa de los cuarenta (años); **it's five p. ten** son las diez y cinco; *Fam* **to be p. it** estar muy carroza

pasta ['pæstə] *n* pasta *f*, pastas *fpl*

paste [peɪst] **1** *n* pasta *f*; *(glue)* engrudo *m*
   2 *vt (stick)* pegar; *(put paste on)* engomar

pastel ['pæstəl] *adj & n* pastel (*m*)

pasteurized ['pæstjəraɪzd] *adj* pasteurizado(a)

pastille ['pæstɪl] *n* pastilla *f*

pastime ['pɑːstaɪm] *n* pasatiempo *m*

pastor ['pɑːstə(r)] *n* pastor *m*

pastoral ['pɑːstərəl] *adj* pastoral

pastry ['peɪstrɪ] *n (dough)* pasta *f*; *(cake)* pastel *m*

pasture ['pɑːstʃə(r)] *n* pasto *m*

pasty[1] ['pæstɪ] *n Culin* empanada *f*, pastel *m* de carne

pasty[2] ['peɪstɪ] *adj* (**pastier, pastiest**) *(complexion)* pálido(a)

pat [pæt] **1** *n (caress)* caricia *f*; *(tap)* palmadita *f*; *Fig* **to give sb a p. on the back** felicitar a algn
   2 *vt* acariciar; **to p. sb on the back** dar a algn una palmadita en la espalda

patch [pætʃ] *n (of material)* parche *m*; *(of land)* terreno *m*; *(of colour)* mancha *f*; *Fig* **to go through a bad p.** pasar por una mala racha
▶**patch up** *vt sep (garment)* poner un parche en; **to p. things up** *(after argument)* limar asperezas

patchwork ['pætʃwɜːk] **1** *n* labor *f* de retales
   2 *adj (quilt etc)* hecho(a) con retales distintos

patchy ['pætʃɪ] *adj* (**patchier, patchiest**) *(colour, performance)* desigual; *(knowledge)* incompleto(a)

pâté ['pæteɪ] *n* paté *m*

patent[1] ['peɪtənt] **1** *n Com* patente *f*
   2 *adj (obvious)* patente, evidente; **p. medicine** específico *m*
   3 *vt Com* patentar

patent[2] ['peɪtənt] *n* **p. (leather)** charol *m*

patently ['peɪtəntlɪ] *adv* **it is p. obvious** está clarísimo

paternal [pə'tɜːnəl] *adj* paternal; *(grandmother etc)* paterno(a)

paternity [pə'tɜːnɪtɪ] *n* paternidad *f*

path [pɑːθ] *n* camino *m*, sendero *m*; *(route)* ruta *f*; *(of missile)* trayectoria *f*

pathetic [pə'θetɪk] *adj (pitiful)* patético(a); *Fam (hopeless)* malísimo(a); **she was a p. sight** daba lástima verla

pathological [pæθə'lɒdʒɪkəl] *adj* patológico(a)

pathologist [pə'θɒlədʒɪst] *n* patólogo(a) *m,f*

pathology [pə'θɒlədʒɪ] *n* patología *f*

pathos ['peɪθɒs] *n* patetismo *m*

pathway ['pɑːθweɪ] *n* camino *m*, sendero *m*

patience ['peɪʃəns] *n* (**a**) paciencia *f*; **to lose one's p. with sb** perder la paciencia con algn (**b**) *Br Cards* solitario *m*

patient ['peɪʃənt] **1** *adj* paciente; **to be p.**

with sb tener paciencia con algn
  2 *n Med* paciente *mf*
patio ['pætɪəʊ] *n* patio *m*
patriotic [pætrɪ'ɒtɪk] *adj (person)* patriota; *(speech, act)* patriótico(a)
patrol [pə'trəʊl] **1** *n* patrulla *f*; **p. car** coche *m* patrulla
  2 *vt* patrullar por
patrolman [pə'trəʊlmən] *n US* policía *m*
patron ['peɪtrən] *n* (**a**) *(of charity)* patrocinador(a) *m,f*; *(of arts)* mecenas *m inv*; **p. saint** (santo(a) *m,f*) patrón(ona) *m,f* (**b**) *(customer)* cliente(a) *m,f* habitual
patronize ['pætrənaɪz] *vt* (**a**) *(arts)* fomentar; *(shop)* ser cliente(a) *m,f* habitual de; *(club etc)* frecuentar (**b**) *Pej (person)* tratar con condescendencia
patronizing ['pætrənaɪzɪŋ] *adj Pej* condescendiente
patter¹ ['pætə(r)] **1** *n (of rain)* repiqueteo *m*; *(of feet)* pasito *m*
  2 *vi (rain)* repiquetear; *(feet)* hacer ruido sordo
patter² ['pætə(r)] *n Fam* labia *f*; *(of salesman)* discursillo preparado
pattern ['pætən] *n Sewing* patrón *m*; *(design)* dibujo *m*; *(on material)* estampado *m*; *Fig (of behaviour)* modelo *m*
paunch [pɔːntʃ] *n* panza *f*
pauper ['pɔːpə(r)] *n* pobre *mf*
pause [pɔːz] **1** *n* pausa *f*; *(silence)* silencio *m*
  2 *vi* hacer una pausa; *(be silent)* callarse
pave [peɪv] *vt* pavimentar; *(with stones)* empedrar; *Fig* **to p. the way for sb/sth** preparar el terreno para algn/algo
pavement ['peɪvmənt] *n* (**a**) *Br (beside road)* acera *f*, *CSur, Perú* vereda *f*, *CAm, Méx* banqueta *f* (**b**) *US (roadway)* calzada *f*, pavimento *m*
pavilion [pə'vɪljən] *n* pabellón *m*; *Br Sport (changing rooms)* vestuarios *mpl*
paving ['peɪvɪŋ] *n (on road)* pavimento *m*; *(on floor)* enlosado *m*; *(with stones)* empedrado *m*; **p. stone** losa *f*
paw [pɔː] **1** *n (foot)* pata *f*; *(of cat)* garra *f*; *(of lion)* zarpa *f*
  2 *vt (of lion)* dar zarpazos a; *Pej (of person)* manosear, sobar
pawn¹ [pɔːn] *n (in chess)* peón *m*; *Fig* **to be sb's p.** ser el juguete de algn
pawn² [pɔːn] *vt* empeñar
pawnbroker ['pɔːnbrəʊkə(r)] *n* prestamista *mf*
pawnshop ['pɔːnʃɒp] *n* casa *f* de empeños
pay [peɪ] **1** *n (wages)* paga *f*, sueldo *m*; **p.**

Br **packet** *or US* **envelope** sobre *m* de la paga; **p. rise** aumento *m* del sueldo; **p. slip** nómina *f*
  2 *vt (pt & pp* **paid**) (**a**) pagar; **to be** *or* **get paid** cobrar (**b**) *(attention)* prestar; *(homage)* rendir; *(visit)* hacer; **to p. sb a compliment** halagar a algn (**c**) *(be profitable for)* compensar
  3 *vi* (**a**) pagar; **to p. for sth** pagar (por) algo (**b**) *(be profitable)* ser rentable
  ▸ **pay back** *vt sep* reembolsar; *Fig* **to p. sb back** vengarse de algn
  ▸ **pay in** *vt sep (money)* ingresar
  ▸ **pay off 1** *vt sep (debt)* liquidar; *(mortgage)* cancelar
  2 *vi (be successful)* dar resultado
  ▸ **pay out** *vt sep (spend)* gastar (**on** en)
  ▸ **pay up** *vi* pagar
payable ['peɪəbəl] *adj* pagadero(a)
payday ['peɪdeɪ] *n* día *m* de pago
payee [peɪ'iː] *n* portador(a) *m,f*
payment ['peɪmənt] *n* pago *m*; *(of cheque)* cobro *m*; **advance p.** anticipo *m*; **down p.** entrada *f*; **monthly p.** mensualidad *f*
payoff ['peɪɒf] *n (reward)* recompensa *f*; *Fam (bribe)* soborno *m*
pay-per-view ['peɪpə'vjuː] *n* pago *m* por visión
payroll ['peɪrəʊl] *n* nómina *f*
PC ['piː'siː] **1** *n* (**a**) *Br (abbr* **Police Constable**) agente *mf* de policía (**b**) *(abbr* **personal computer**) PC *m*
  2 *adj (abbr* **politically correct**) políticamente correcto(a)
pc *(abbr* **per cent**) p.c.
PE ['piː'iː] *n Sch (abbr* **physical education**) educación *f* física
pea [piː] *n* guisante *m*, *Andes, Carib, RP* arveja *f*, *CAm, Méx* chícharo *m*
peace [piːs] *n* paz *f*; *(calm)* tranquilidad *f*; **at** *or* **in p.** en paz; **p. and quiet** tranquilidad; **to make p.** hacer las paces; *(of countries)* firmar la paz
peaceable ['piːsəbəl] *adj* pacífico(a)
peaceful ['piːsfʊl] *adj (demonstration)* pacífico(a); *(place)* tranquilo(a)
peace-keeping ['piːskiːpɪŋ] *adj* pacificador(a); **p. forces** fuerzas *fpl* de pacificación
peach [piːtʃ] *n* melocotón *m*, *Am* durazno *m*
peacock ['piːkɒk] *n* pavo *m* real
peak [piːk] *n (of cap)* visera *f*; *(of mountain)* pico *m*; *(summit)* cima *f*; *Fig* cumbre *f*; **p. hours** horas *fpl* punta; **p. period** horas de mayor consumo; **p. season** temporada alta

peal [pi:l] *n (of bells)* repique *m*; **p. of thunder** trueno *m*; **peals of laughter** carcajadas *fpl*

peanut ['pi:nʌt] *n* cacahuete *m*, maní *m*, *Méx* cacahuate *m*; **p. butter** mantequilla *f or* manteca *f* de cacahuete, maní, *Méx* cacahuate

pear [peə(r)] *n* pera *f*

pearl [pɜ:l] *n* perla *f*

peasant ['pezənt] *adj & n* campesino(a) *(m,f)*

peat [pi:t] *n* turba *f*; **p. bog** turbera *f*

pebble ['pebəl] *n* guijarro *m*; *(small)* china *f*

pecan [pɪ'kæn] *n (nut)* pacana *f*

peck [pek] **1** *n (of bird)* picotazo *m*; *Fam (kiss)* besito *m*
  2 *vt (bird)* picotear; *Fam (kiss)* dar un besito a
  3 *vi* **to p. at one's food** picar la comida

pecking order ['pekɪŋɔ:də(r)] *n Fig* jerarquía *f*

peckish ['pekɪʃ] *adj Fam* **to feel p.** empezar a tener hambre

peculiar [pɪ'kju:lɪə(r)] *adj (odd)* extraño(a); *(particular)* característico(a)

peculiarity [pɪkju:lɪ'ærɪtɪ] *n (oddity)* rareza *f*; *(characteristic)* característica *f*, peculiaridad *f*

pedal ['pedəl] **1** *n* pedal *m*
  2 *vi* pedalear

pedantic [pɪ'dæntɪk] *adj* pedante

peddle ['pedəl] *vt & vi Com* vender de puerta en puerta; **to p. drugs** traficar con drogas

peddler ['pedlə(r)] *n (of drugs)* traficante *mf*

pedestal ['pedɪstəl] *n* pedestal *m*; *Fig* **to put sb on a p.** poner a algn sobre un pedestal

pedestrian [pɪ'destrɪən] **1** *n* peatón(ona) *m,f*; **p. crossing** paso *m* de peatones
  2 *adj Pej* prosaico(a)

pediatrician [pi:dɪə'trɪʃən] *n US* = **paediatrician**

pedigree ['pedɪgri:] **1** *n* linaje *m*; *(family tree)* árbol genealógico; *(of animal)* pedigrí *m*
  2 *adj (animal)* de raza

pee [pi:] *Fam* **1** *n* pis *m*
  2 *vi* hacer pis

peek [pi:k] **1** *n* ojeada *f*
  2 *vi* **to p. at sth** mirar algo a hurtadillas

peel [pi:l] **1** *n* piel *f*; *(of orange, lemon)* cáscara *f*
  2 *vt (fruit)* pelar
  3 *vi (paint)* desconcharse; *(wallpaper)* despegarse; *(skin)* pelarse

peeler ['pi:lə(r)] *n* **potato p.** pelapatatas *m inv*

peelings ['pi:lɪŋz] *npl* peladuras *fpl*, mondaduras *fpl*

peep¹ [pi:p] *n (sound)* pío *m*

peep² [pi:p] **1** *n (glance)* ojeada *f*; *(furtive look)* mirada furtiva
  2 *vi* **to p. at sth** echar una ojeada a algo; **to p. out from behind sth** dejarse ver detrás de algo

peephole ['pi:phəʊl] *n* mirilla *f*

peer¹ [pɪə(r)] *n (noble)* par *m*; *(equal)* igual *mf*; **p. group** grupo parejo

peer² [pɪə(r)] *vi* mirar detenidamente; *(shortsightedly)* mirar con ojos de miope

peerage ['pɪərɪdʒ] *n* título *m* de nobleza

peeved [pi:vd] *adj Fam* fastidiado(a), de mal humor

peevish ['pi:vɪʃ] *adj* malhumorado(a)

peg [peg] **1** *n* clavija *f*; *(for coat, hat)* percha *f*
  2 *vt (clothes)* tender; *(prices)* fijar

pejorative [pɪ'dʒɒrətɪv] *adj* peyorativo(a)

Pekinese [pi:kə'ni:z] *adj & n* pequinés(esa) *(m,f)*

Peking [pi:'kɪŋ] *n* Pekín

pelican ['pelɪkən] *n* pelícano *m*; *Br* **p. crossing** paso *m* de peatones

pellet ['pelɪt] *n* bolita *f*; *(for gun)* perdigón *m*

pelt¹ [pelt] *n (skin)* pellejo *m*

pelt² [pelt] **1** *vt* **to p. sb with sth** tirar algo a algn
  2 *vi Fam* **(a) it's pelting (down)** *(raining)* llueve a cántaros **(b) to p. along** *(rush)* correr a toda prisa

pelvis ['pelvɪs] *n* pelvis *f*

pen¹ [pen] **1** *n* pluma *f*, *RP* birome *f*
  2 *vt* escribir

pen² [pen] **1** *n (enclosure)* corral *m*; *(for sheep)* redil *m*; *(for children)* corralito *m*
  2 *vt* **to p. in** acorralar

penal ['pi:nəl] *adj* penal

penalize ['pi:nəlaɪz] *vt* castigar; *Sport* penalizar

penalty ['penəltɪ] *n (punishment)* pena *f*; *Sport* castigo *m*; *Ftb* penalti *m*; **to pay the p. for sth** cargar con las consecuencias de algo; **p. area** área *f* de castigo

penance ['penəns] *n* penitencia *f*

pence [pens] *pl of* **penny**

pencil ['pensəl] *n* lápiz *m*; **p. case** estuche *m* de lápices; **p. sharpener** sacapuntas *m inv*

pendant ['pendənt] *n* colgante *m*

pending ['pendɪŋ] **1** *adj* pendiente
  2 *prep* a la espera de; **p. a decision** *(until)*

hasta que se tome una decisión
pendulum ['pendjʊləm] *n* péndulo *m*
penetrate ['penɪtreɪt] **1** *vt* penetrar; *Fig* adentrarse en
  2 *vi* atravesar; *(get inside)* penetrar
penetrating ['penɪtreɪtɪŋ] *adj (look)* penetrante; *(mind)* perspicaz; *(sound)* agudo(a)
penfriend ['penfrend] *n* amigo(a) *m,f* por carta
penguin ['peŋgwɪn] *n* pingüino *m*
penicillin [penɪ'sɪlɪn] *n* penicilina *f*
peninsula [pɪ'nɪnsjʊlə] *n* península *f*
penis ['piːnɪs] *n* pene *m*
penitent ['penɪtənt] *adj Rel* penitente; *(repentant)* arrepentido(a)
penitentiary [penɪ'tenʃərɪ] *n US* cárcel *f*, penal *m*
penknife ['pennaɪf] *n* navaja *f*, cortaplumas *m inv*
penniless ['penɪlɪs] *adj* sin dinero
penny ['penɪ] *n (pl* **pennies, pence***) Br* penique *m*; *US* centavo *m*
penpal ['penpæl] *n US* = **penfriend**
pension ['penʃən] *n* pensión *f*; **retirement p.** jubilación *f*
pensioner ['penʃənə(r)] *n* jubilado(a) *m,f*
pensive ['pensɪv] *adj* pensativo(a)
pentagon ['pentəgɒn] *n US Pol* **the P.** el Pentágono
Pentecost ['pentɪkɒst] *n* Pentecostés *m*
penthouse ['penthaʊs] *n* ático *m*
pent-up ['pentʌp] *adj* reprimido(a)
penultimate [pɪ'nʌltɪmɪt] *adj* penúltimo(a)
people ['piːpəl] *npl* **(a)** gente *f*; *(individuals)* personas *fpl*; **many p.** mucha gente; **old p.'s home** asilo *m* de ancianos; **p. say that ...** se dice que ...; **some p.** algunas personas **(b)** *(citizens)* ciudadanos *mpl*; *(inhabitants)* habitantes *mpl*; **the p.** el pueblo **(c)** *(nation)* pueblo *m*, nación *f*
pep [pep] *n Fam* ánimo *m*, energía *f*; **p. talk** discurso *m* enardecedor
  ► **pep up** *vt sep Fam* animar
pepper ['pepə(r)] **1** *n (spice)* pimienta *f*; *(fruit)* pimiento *m*; **black p.** pimienta negra; **p. pot** pimentero *m*; **red/green p.** pimiento rojo/verde; **p. mill** molinillo *m* de pimienta
  2 *vt Fig* **peppered with** salpicado(a) de
peppermint ['pepəmɪnt] *n* menta *f*; *(sweet)* pastilla *f* de menta
per [pɜː(r)] *prep* por; **five times p. week** cinco veces a la semana; **p. cent** por

ciento; **p. day/annum** al *or* por día/año; **p. capita** per cápita
perceive [pə'siːv] *vt (see)* percibir
percentage [pə'sentɪdʒ] *n* porcentaje *m*
perceptible [pə'septəbəl] *adj (visible)* perceptible; *(sound)* audible; *(improvement)* sensible
perception [pə'sepʃən] *n* percepción *f*
perceptive [pə'septɪv] *adj* perspicaz
perch¹ [pɜːtʃ] *n (fish)* perca *f*
perch² [pɜːtʃ] **1** *n (for bird)* percha *f*
  2 *vi (bird)* posarse (**on** en)
percolate ['pɜːkəleɪt] **1** *vt* filtrar; **percolated coffee** café *m* de cafetera
  2 *vi* filtrarse
percolator ['pɜːkəleɪtə(r)] *n* cafetera *f*
percussion [pə'kʌʃən] *n* percusión *f*
perennial [pə'renɪəl] *adj Bot* perenne
perfect 1 *adj* ['pɜːfɪkt] perfecto(a); **he's a p. stranger to us** nos es totalmente desconocido; **p. tense** tiempo perfecto
  2 *vt* [pə'fekt] perfeccionar
perfection [pə'fekʃən] *n* perfección *f*
perfectly ['pɜːfɪktlɪ] *adv* perfectamente; *(absolutely)* completamente
perforate ['pɜːfəreɪt] *vt* perforar
perforation [pɜːfə'reɪʃən] *n* perforación *f*; *(on stamps etc)* perforado *m*
perform [pə'fɔːm] **1** *vt (task)* ejecutar, realizar; *(piece of music)* interpretar; *Th* representar
  2 *vi (machine)* funcionar; *Mus* interpretar; *Th* actuar
performance [pə'fɔːməns] *n (of task)* ejecución *f*, realización *f*; *Mus* interpretación *f*; *Th* representación *f*; *Sport* actuación *f*; *(of machine etc)* rendimiento *m*
performer [pə'fɔːmə(r)] *n Mus* intérprete *mf*; *Th* actor *m*, actriz *f*
perfume ['pɜːfjuːm] *n* perfume *m*
perfunctory [pə'fʌŋktərɪ] *adj* superficial
perhaps [pə'hæps, præps] *adv* tal vez, quizá(s)
peril ['perɪl] *n (risk)* riesgo *m*; *(danger)* peligro *m*
perilous ['perɪləs] *adj (risky)* arriesgado(a); *(dangerous)* peligroso(a)
perilously ['perɪləslɪ] *adv* peligrosamente
perimeter [pə'rɪmɪtə(r)] *n* perímetro *m*
period ['pɪərɪəd] **1** *n* **(a)** período *m*; *(stage)* etapa *f* **(b)** *Educ* clase *f* **(c)** *US (full stop)* punto *m* **(d)** *(menstruation)* regla *f*
  2 *adj (dress, furniture)* de época
periodic [pɪərɪ'ɒdɪk] *adj* periódico(a)
periodical [pɪərɪ'ɒdɪkəl] **1** *adj* periódico(a)
  2 *n* revista *f*

periodically [pɪərɪ'ɒdɪklɪ] *adv* de vez en cuando

peripheral [pə'rɪfərəl] **1** *adj* periférico(a) **2** *n Comput* unidad periférica

perish ['perɪʃ] *vi* perecer; *(material)* echarse a perder

perishable ['perɪʃəbəl] *adj* perecedero(a)

perjury ['pɜːdʒərɪ] *n* perjurio *m*

perk [pɜːk] *n Fam* extra *m*
▸ **perk up** *vi (person)* animarse; *(after illness)* reponerse

perky ['pɜːkɪ] *adj* (**perkier, perkiest**) animado(a), alegre

perm [pɜːm] **1** *n* permanente *f* **2** *vt* **to have one's hair permed** hacerse la permanente

permanent ['pɜːmənənt] *adj* permanente; *(address, job)* fijo(a)

permeate ['pɜːmɪeɪt] *vt & vi* penetrar; *Fig* extenderse por

permissible [pə'mɪsəbəl] *adj* admisible

permission [pə'mɪʃən] *n* permiso *m*

permissive [pə'mɪsɪv] *adj* permisivo(a)

permit 1 *n* ['pɜːmɪt] permiso *m*; *Com* licencia *f*
2 *vt* [pə'mɪt] **to p. sb to do sth** permitir a algn hacer algo

pernicious [pə'nɪʃəs] *adj* pernicioso(a)

perpendicular [pɜːpən'dɪkjʊlə(r)] **1** *adj* perpendicular; *(cliff)* vertical **2** *n* perpendicular *f*

perpetrate ['pɜːpɪtreɪt] *vt* cometer

perpetual [pə'petʃʊəl] *adj (noise)* continuo(a); *(arguing)* interminable; *(snow)* perpetuo(a)

perplex [pə'pleks] *vt* dejar perplejo(a)

perplexing [pə'pleksɪŋ] *adj* desconcertante

persecute ['pɜːsɪkjuːt] *vt* perseguir; *(harass)* acosar

persecution [pɜːsɪ'kjuːʃən] *n* persecución *f*; *(harassment)* acoso *m*

perseverance [pɜːsɪ'vɪərəns] *n* perseverancia *f*

persevere [pɜːsɪ'vɪə(r)] *vi* perseverar

Persian ['pɜːʒən] *adj* persa; **P. Gulf** golfo Pérsico

persist [pə'sɪst] *vi* empeñarse (**in** en)

persistence [pə'sɪstəns] *n* empeño *m*

persistent [pə'sɪstənt] *adj (person)* perseverante; *(smell etc)* persistente; *(continual)* constante

person ['pɜːsən] *n* (*pl* **people**) persona *f*; *(individual)* individuo *m*; **in p.** en persona

personable ['pɜːsənəbəl] *adj (handsome)* bien parecido(a); *(pleasant)* amable

personal ['pɜːsənəl] (**a**) *adj (private)* personal; *(friend)* íntimo(a); **p. computer** ordenador *m* personal, *Am* computadora *f* personal; **p. column** anuncios *mpl* personales; **p. pronoun** pronombre *m* personal (**b**) *(in person)* en persona; **he will make a p. appearance** estará aquí en persona (**c**) *Pej (comment etc)* indiscreto(a)

personality [pɜːsə'nælɪtɪ] *n* personalidad *f*

personally ['pɜːsənəlɪ] *adv (for my part)* personalmente; *(in person)* en persona

personify [pɜː'sɒnɪfaɪ] *vt* personificar, encarnar

personnel [pɜːsə'nel] *n* personal *m*

perspective [pə'spektɪv] *n* perspectiva *f*

Perspex® ['pɜːspeks] *n* plexiglás® *m*

perspiration [pɜːspə'reɪʃən] *n* transpiración *f*

perspire [pə'spaɪə(r)] *vi* transpirar

persuade [pə'sweɪd] *vt* persuadir; **to p. sb to do sth** persuadir a algn para que haga algo

persuasion [pə'sweɪʒən] *n* persuasión *f*; *(opinion, belief)* credo *m*

persuasive [pə'sweɪsɪv] *adj* persuasivo(a)

pert [pɜːt] *adj* pizpireta, coqueto(a)

pertain [pə'teɪn] *vi* estar relacionado(a) (**to** con)

pertinent ['pɜːtɪnənt] *adj (relevant)* pertinente; **p. to** relacionado(a) con, a propósito de

perturbing [pə'tɜːbɪŋ] *adj* inquietante

Peru [pə'ruː] *n* Perú

peruse [pə'ruːz] *vt Fml* leer

Peruvian [pə'ruːvɪən] *adj & n* peruano(a) *(m,f)*

pervade [pɜː'veɪd] *vt (of smell)* penetrar; *(of light)* difundirse por; *Fig (of influence)* extenderse por

pervasive [pɜː'veɪsɪv] *adj (smell)* penetrante; *(influence)* extendido(a)

perverse [pə'vɜːs] *adj (wicked)* perverso(a); *(contrary)* contrario(a) a todo

perversion [pə'vɜːʃən] *n Med & Psy* perversión *f*; *(of justice, truth)* desvirtuación *f*

pervert 1 *n* ['pɜːvɜːt] *Med* pervertido(a) *m,f* (sexual)
2 *vt* [pə'vɜːt] pervertir; *(justice, truth)* desvirtuar

pessimist ['pesɪmɪst] *n* pesimista *mf*

pessimistic [pesɪ'mɪstɪk] *adj* pesimista

pest [pest] *n* (**a**) *Zool* animal nocivo; *Bot* planta nociva (**b**) *Fam (person)* pelma *mf*; *(thing)* lata *f*

pester ['pestə(r)] *vt* molestar, fastidiar

pet [pet] **1** *n* (**a**) animal doméstico (**b**) *(favourite)* preferido(a) *m,f*; *Fam* cariño *m*
  2 *adj (favourite)* preferido(a)
  3 *vt* acariciar
  4 *vi (sexually)* besuquearse
petal ['petəl] *n* pétalo *m*
peter ['piːtə(r)] *vi* **to p. out** agotarse
petite [pə'tiːt] *adj* menuda, chiquita
petition [pɪ'tɪʃən] *n* petición *f*
petrify ['petrɪfaɪ] *vt Literary* petrificar; *Fig* **they were petrified** se quedaron de piedra
petrol ['petrəl] *n Br* gasolina *f*, *RP* nafta *f*; **p. can** bidón *m* de gasolina; **p. pump** surtidor *m* de gasolina; **p. station** gasolinera *f*, estación *f* de servicio, *Andes, Ven* bomba *f*, *Méx* gasolinería *f*, *Perú* grifo *m*; **p. tank** depósito *m* de gasolina

> ✍ Note that the Spanish word **petróleo** is a false friend and is never a translation for the English word **petrol**. In Spanish, **petróleo** means "oil, petroleum".

petroleum [pə'trəʊlɪəm] *n* petróleo *m*
petticoat ['petɪkəʊt] *n* enaguas *fpl*
petty ['petɪ] *adj* (**pettier, pettiest**) *(trivial)* insignificante; *(small-minded)* mezquino(a); **p. cash** dinero *m* para gastos pequeños; *Naut* **p. officer** sargento *m* de marina
petulant ['petjʊlənt] *adj* malhumorado(a)

> ✍ Note that the Spanish word **petulante** is a false friend and is never a translation for the English word **petulant**. In Spanish, **petulante** means "opinionated, arrogant".

pew [pjuː] *n* banco *m* de iglesia; *Fam* **take a p.!** ¡siéntate!
pewter ['pjuːtə(r)] *n* peltre *m*
phantom ['fæntəm] *adj & n* fantasma *(m)*
pharmaceutical [faːmə'sjuːtɪkəl] *adj* farmacéutico(a)
pharmacist ['faːməsɪst] *n* farmacéutico(a) *m,f*
pharmacy ['faːməsɪ] *n* farmacia *f*
phase [feɪz] **1** *n* fase *f*
  2 *vt* **to p. sth in/out** introducir/retirar algo progresivamente
PhD [piːeɪtʃ'diː] *n* (*abbr* **Doctor of Philosophy**) *(person)* Doctor(a) *m,f* en Filosofía
pheasant ['fezənt] *n* faisán *m* (vulgar)
phenomena [fɪ'nɒmɪnə] *pl of* **phenomenon**
phenomenal [fɪ'nɒmɪnəl] *adj* fenomenal

phenomenon [fɪ'nɒmɪnən] *n* (*pl* **phenomena**) fenómeno *m*
phial [faɪəl] *n* frasco *m*
philanthropist [fɪ'lænθrəpɪst] *n* filántropo(a) *m,f*
philately [fɪ'lætəlɪ] *n* filatelia *f*
Philippines ['fɪlɪpiːnz] *npl* **the P.** las (Islas) Filipinas
philosopher [fɪ'lɒsəfə(r)] *n* filósofo(a) *m,f*
philosophical [fɪlə'sɒfɪkəl] *adj* filosófico(a)
philosophy [fɪ'lɒsəfɪ] *n* filosofía *f*
phlegm [flem] *n* flema *f*
phlegmatic [fleg'mætɪk] *adj* flemático(a)
phobia ['fəʊbɪə] *n* fobia *f*
phone [fəʊn] *n* = **telephone**
phone-in ['fəʊnɪn] *n Fam* = programa de radio o televisión con línea telefónica abierta
phonetic [fə'netɪk] **1** *adj* fonético(a)
  2 *n* **phonetics** fonética *f*
phoney ['fəʊnɪ] **1** *adj* (**phonier, phoniest**) *(thing)* falso(a); *(person)* farsante
  2 *n (person)* farsante *mf*
phonograph ['fəʊnəgraːf] *n US* tocadiscos *m inv*
phosphate ['fɒsfeɪt] *n* fosfato *m*
photo ['fəʊtəʊ] *n* foto *f*
photocopier ['fəʊtəʊkɒpɪə(r)] *n* fotocopiadora *f*
photocopy ['fəʊtəʊkɒpɪ] **1** *n* fotocopia *f*
  2 *vt* fotocopiar
photogenic [fəʊtəʊ'dʒenɪk] *adj* fotogénico(a)
photograph ['fəʊtəgræf, 'fəʊtəgraːf] **1** *n* fotografía *f*; **black and white/colour p.** fotografía en blanco y negro/en color
  2 *vt* fotografiar
photographer [fə'tɒgrəfə(r)] *n* fotógrafo(a) *m,f*
photography [fə'tɒgrəfɪ] *n* fotografía *f*
phrase [freɪz] **1** *n* frase *f*; **p. book** libro *m* de frases
  2 *vt* expresar
physical ['fɪzɪkəl] *adj* físico(a); **p. education** educación física
physically ['fɪzɪkəlɪ] *adv* físicamente; **p. handicapped** minusválido(a); **to be p. fit** estar en forma
physician [fɪ'zɪʃən] *n* médico(a) *m,f*
physicist ['fɪzɪsɪst] *n* físico(a) *m,f*
physics ['fɪzɪks] *n sing* física *f*
physiological [fɪzɪə'lɒdʒɪkəl] *adj* fisiológico(a)
physiotherapist [fɪzɪəʊ'θerəpɪst] *n* fisioterapeuta *mf*

physique [fɪ'ziːk] n físico m
pianist ['pɪənɪst] n pianista mf
piano [pɪ'ænəʊ] n piano m
piccolo ['pɪkələʊ] n flautín m
pick [pɪk] **1** n (a) (tool) pico m, piqueta f (b) **take your p.** (choice) elige el que quieras
 2 vt (a) (choose) escoger; (team) seleccionar (b) (flowers, fruit) coger, recoger (c) (scratch) hurgar; **to p. one's nose** hurgarse la nariz; **to p. one's teeth** mondarse los dientes (d) **to p. sb's pocket** robar algo del bolsillo de algn (e) (lock) forzar
 3 vi **to p. at one's food** comer sin ganas
 ▸**pick off** vt sep (a) (remove) quitar (b) (shoot) matar uno a uno
 ▸**pick on** vt insep (persecute) meterse con
 ▸**pick out** vt sep (choose) elegir; (distinguish) distinguir; (identify) identificar
 ▸**pick up 1** vt sep (a) (object on floor) recoger; (telephone) descolgar; **to p. oneself up** levantarse; Fig reponerse (b) (collect) recoger; (shopping, person) buscar; **to p. up speed** ganar velocidad (c) (acquire) conseguir; (learn) aprender
 2 vi (improve) mejorarse, ir mejorando; (prices) subir
pickaxe, US **pickax** ['pɪkæks] n piqueta f
picket ['pɪkɪt] **1** n piquete m; **p. line** piquete
 2 vt piquetear
 3 vi hacer piquete
pickle ['pɪkəl] **1** n (a) Br Culin salsa f picante (b) Fam (mess) lío m, apuro m
 2 vt Culin conservar en adobo or escabeche; **pickled onions** cebollas fpl en vinagre
pick-me-up ['pɪkmɪʌp] n Fam reconstituyente m, tónico m
pickpocket ['pɪkpɒkɪt] n carterista mf
pick-up ['pɪkʌp] n **p. (arm)** (on record player) brazo m; **p. (truck)** furgoneta f
picnic ['pɪknɪk] **1** n comida f de campo, picnic m
 2 vi hacer una comida de campo
pictorial [pɪk'tɔːrɪəl] adj ilustrado(a)
picture ['pɪktʃə(r)] **1** n (a) (painting) cuadro m; (drawing) dibujo m; (portrait) retrato m; (photo) foto f; (illustration) ilustración f; **p. book** libro ilustrado; **p. postcard** tarjeta f postal (b) TV imagen f; Cin película f; **to go to the pictures** ir al cine
 2 vt (imagine) imaginarse
picturesque [pɪktʃə'resk] adj pintoresco(a)
pie [paɪ] n (of fruit) tarta f, pastel m; (of meat etc) pastel, empanada f; (pasty) empanadilla f
piece [piːs] n (a) (of food) pedazo m, trozo m; (of paper) trozo; (part) pieza f; **a p. of advice** un consejo; **a p. of furniture** un mueble; **a p. of land** una parcela; **a p. of news** una noticia; **to break sth into pieces** hacer algo pedazos; Fig **to go to pieces** perder el control (de sí mismo) (b) Lit & Mus obra f, pieza f (c) (coin) moneda f (d) (in chess) pieza f; (in draughts) ficha f
 ▸**piece together** vt sep (facts) reconstruir; (jigsaw) hacer
piecemeal ['piːsmiːl] adv (by degrees) poco a poco, a etapas; (unsystematically) desordenadamente
piecework ['piːswɜːk] n trabajo m a destajo; **to be on p.** trabajar a destajo
pier [pɪə(r)] n embarcadero m, muelle m; (promenade) = paseo de madera que entra en el mar
pierce [pɪəs] vt perforar; (penetrate) penetrar en
piercing ['pɪəsɪŋ] adj (sound etc) penetrante
piety ['paɪtɪ] n piedad f
pig [pɪg] n (a) cerdo m (b) Fam (person) cochino m; (glutton) tragón(ona) m,f (c) Fam Pej (policeman) madero m
pigeon ['pɪdʒɪn] n paloma f; Culin & Sport pichón m
pigeonhole ['pɪdʒɪnhəʊl] n casilla f
piggy ['pɪgɪ] n **p. bank** = hucha en forma de cerdito
pigheaded [pɪg'hedɪd] adj terco(a), cabezota m
piglet ['pɪglɪt] n cerdito m, lechón m
pigment ['pɪgmənt] n pigmento m
pigskin ['pɪgskɪn] n piel f de cerdo
pigsty ['pɪgstaɪ] n pocilga f
pigtail ['pɪgteɪl] n trenza f; (bullfighter's) coleta f
pike [paɪk] n (fish) lucio m
pilchard ['pɪltʃəd] n sardina f
pile¹ [paɪl] **1** n montón m
 2 vt amontonar
 3 vi **to p. into** apiñarse en; **to p. on/off a bus** subir a/bajar de un autobús en tropel
 ▸**pile up 1** vt sep (things) amontonar; (riches, debts) acumular
 2 vi amontonarse
pile² [paɪl] n (on carpet) pelo m; **thick p.** pelo largo
piles [paɪlz] npl Med almorranas fpl, hemorroides fpl
pile-up ['paɪlʌp] n Aut choque m en cadena
pilfer ['pɪlfə(r)] vt & vi hurtar

pilgrim ['pɪlgrɪm] *n* peregrino(a) *m,f*
pilgrimage ['pɪlgrɪmɪdʒ] *n* peregrinación *f*
pill [pɪl] *n* píldora *f*, pastilla *f*; **to be on the p.** estar tomando la píldora (anticonceptiva)
pillage ['pɪlɪdʒ] *vt & vi* pillar, saquear
pillar ['pɪlə(r)] *n* pilar *m*, columna *f*; *Br* **p. box** buzón *m*
pillion ['pɪljən] *n* asiento trasero *(de una moto)*
pillow ['pɪləʊ] *n* almohada *f*
pillowcase ['pɪləʊkeɪs] *n* funda *f* de almohada
pilot ['paɪlət] **1** *n* piloto *m*
  2 *adj (trial)* piloto *inv*; **p. light** piloto *m*; **p. scheme** proyecto piloto
  3 *vt* pilotar
pimp [pɪmp] *n* chulo *m*
pimple ['pɪmpəl] *n* grano *m*, espinilla *f*
PIN [pɪn] *n* (*abbr* **personal identification number**) **P. (number)** PIN *m*
pin [pɪn] **1** *n* alfiler *m*; *Tech* clavija *f*; *(wooden)* espiga *f*; *(in plug)* polo *m*; *(in bowling)* bolo *m*; *US (brooch)* broche *m*; **pins and needles** hormigueo *m*
  2 *vt (on board)* clavar con chinchetas; *(garment etc)* sujetar con alfileres; **to p. sb against a wall** tener a algn contra una pared; *Fig* **to p. one's hopes on sth** poner sus esperanzas en algo; *Fam* **to p. a crime on sb** endosar un delito a algn
  ▸ **pin down** *vt sep Fig* **to p. sb down** hacer que algn se comprometa
pinafore ['pɪnəfɔː(r)] *n (apron)* delantal *m*; **p. dress** pichi *m*
pinball ['pɪnbɔːl] *n* flipper *m*, máquina *f* de petacos
pincers ['pɪnsəz] *npl (on crab)* pinzas *fpl*; *(tool)* tenazas *fpl*
pinch [pɪntʃ] **1** *n (nip)* pellizco *m*; *Fig Br* **at** or *US* **in a p.** en caso de apuro; **a p. of salt** una pizca de sal
  2 *vt* pellizcar; *Fam (steal)* birlar
  3 *vi (shoes)* apretar

> 🖉 Note that the Spanish verb **pinchar** is a false friend and is never a translation for the English verb **to pinch**. In Spanish, **pinchar** means "to prick, to puncture".

pincushion ['pɪnkʊʃən] *n* acerico *m*
pine¹ [paɪn] *n (tree)* pino *m*; **p. cone** piña *f*
pine² [paɪn] *vi* **to p. (away)** consumirse, morirse de pena; **to p. for sth/sb** añorar algo/a algn
pineapple ['paɪnæpəl] *n* piña *f*
ping [pɪŋ] *n* sonido metálico; *(of bullet)* silbido *m*

Ping-Pong® ['pɪŋpɒŋ] *n* ping-pong® *m*
pink [pɪŋk] **1** *n (colour)* rosa *m*; *Bot* clavel *m*
  2 *adj (colour)* rosa *inv*; *Pol Fam* rojillo(a)
pinnacle ['pɪnəkəl] *n (of building)* pináculo *m*; *(of mountain)* cima *f*, pico *m*; *Fig (of success)* cumbre *f*
pinpoint ['pɪnpɔɪnt] *vt* señalar
pinstripe ['pɪnstraɪp] *adj* a rayas
pint [paɪnt] *n* pinta *f*; *Br Fam* **a p. (of beer)** una pinta (de cerveza)
pioneer [paɪə'nɪə(r)] **1** *n (settler)* pionero(a) *m,f*; *(forerunner)* precursor(a) *m,f*
  2 *vt* ser pionero(a) en
pious ['paɪəs] *adj* piadoso(a), devoto(a); *Pej* beato(a)
pip¹ [pɪp] *n (seed)* pepita *f*
pip² [pɪp] *n (sound)* señal *f* (corta); *(on dice)* punto *m*
pipe [paɪp] **1** *n* (**a**) conducto *m*, tubería *f*; *(of organ)* caramillo *m*; *Fam* **the pipes** *(bagpipes)* la gaita (**b**) *(for smoking)* pipa *f*; **p. cleaner** limpiapipas *m inv*; *Fig* **p. dream** sueño *m* imposible
  2 *vt (water)* llevar por tubería; *(oil)* transportar por oleoducto; **piped music** hilo *m* musical
  ▸ **pipe down** *vi Fam* callarse
  ▸ **pipe up** *vi Fam* hacerse oír
pipeline ['paɪplaɪn] *n* tubería *f*, cañería *f*; *(for gas)* gasoducto *m*; *(for oil)* oleoducto *m*
piper ['paɪpə(r)] *n* gaitero(a) *m,f*
piping ['paɪpɪŋ] **1** *n (for water, gas etc)* tubería *f*, cañería *f*
  2 *adj* **p. hot** bien caliente
piquant ['piːkənt] *adj* picante; *(fig)* intrigante
pique [piːk] **1** *n* enojo *m*
  2 *vt* herir
pirate ['paɪrɪt] *n* pirata *m*; **p. edition** edición *f* pirata; **p. radio** emisora *f* pirata; **p. ship** barco *m* pirata
pirouette [pɪrʊ'et] **1** *n* pirueta *f*
  2 *vi* hacer piruetas
Pisces ['paɪsiːz] *n* Piscis *m*
piss [pɪs] *very Fam* **1** *vi* mear
  2 *n* meada *f*
pissed [pɪst] *adj very Fam* (**a**) *Br (drunk)* borracho(a) (**b**) *US (angry)* cabreado(a)
pistachio [pɪs'tɑːʃɪəʊ] *n (nut)* pistacho *m*
pistol ['pɪstəl] *n* pistola *f*
piston ['pɪstən] *n* pistón *m*
pit¹ [pɪt] **1** *n* hoyo *m*; *(large)* hoya *f*; *(coal mine)* mina *f* de carbón; *Th* platea *f*; *(in motor racing)* foso *m*, box *m*
  2 *vt* **to p. one's wits against sb** medirse con algn

pit² [pɪt] *n (of cherry)* hueso *m*, pipo *m*; *US (of peach, plum)* hueso

pitch¹ [pɪtʃ] **1** *vt* (**a**) *Mus (sound)* entonar (**b**) *(throw)* lanzar, arrojar (**c**) *(tent)* armar
   2 *vi (ship)* cabecear; **to p. forward** caerse hacia adelante
   3 *n* (**a**) *Mus (of sound)* tono *m* (**b**) *Sport* campo *m*, cancha *f* (**c**) *(in market etc)* puesto *m* (**d**) *(throw)* lanzamiento *m*

pitch² [pɪtʃ] *n (tar)* brea *f*, pez *f*

pitch-black [pɪtʃˈblæk], **pitch-dark** [pɪtʃˈdɑːk] *adj* negro(a) como la boca del lobo

pitched [pɪtʃt] *adj* **p. battle** batalla *f* campal

pitcher [ˈpɪtʃə(r)] *n (container)* cántaro *m*, jarro *m*

pitchfork [ˈpɪtʃfɔːk] *n* horca *f*

piteous [ˈpɪtɪəs] *adj* lastimoso(a)

pitfall [ˈpɪtfɔːl] *n* dificultad *f*, obstáculo *m*

pith [pɪθ] *n (of orange)* piel blanca; *Fig* meollo *m*

pithy [ˈpɪθɪ] *adj* (**pithier, pithiest**) *Fig* contundente

pitiful [ˈpɪtɪfʊl] *adj (producing pity)* lastimoso(a), *(terrible)* lamentable

pitiless [ˈpɪtɪlɪs] *adj* despiadado(a), implacable

pittance [ˈpɪtəns] *n* miseria *f*

pity [ˈpɪtɪ] **1** *n* (**a**) *(compassion)* compasión *f*, piedad *f*; **to take p. on sb** compadecerse de algn (**b**) *(shame)* lástima *f*, pena *f*; **what a p.!** ¡qué pena!, ¡qué lástima!
   2 *vt* compadecerse de; **I p. them** me dan pena

pivot [ˈpɪvət] **1** *n* pivote *m*
   2 *vi* girar sobre su eje

pizza [ˈpiːtsə] *n* pizza *f*; **p. parlour** pizzería *f*

placard [ˈplækɑːd] *n* pancarta *f*

placate [pləˈkeɪt] *vt* aplacar, apaciguar

place [pleɪs] **1** *n* (**a**) sitio *m*, lugar *m*; **to be in/out of p.** estar en/fuera de su sitio; **to take p.** tener lugar
   (**b**) *(seat)* sitio *m*; *(on bus)* asiento *m*; *(at university)* plaza *m*; **to change places with sb** intercambiar el sitio con algn; **to feel out of p.** encontrarse fuera de lugar; **to take sb's p.** sustituir a algn
   (**c**) *(position on scale)* posición *f*; *(social position)* rango *m*; **in the first p.** en primer lugar; **to take first p.** ganar el primer lugar
   (**d**) *(house)* casa *f*; *(building)* lugar *m*; **we're going to his p.** vamos a su casa
   2 *vt* (**a**) poner, colocar; **to p. a bet** hacer una apuesta; **to p. an order with sb** hacer un pedido a algn
   (**b**) *(face, person)* recordar; *(in job)* colocar en un empleo

placid [ˈplæsɪd] *adj* apacible

plagiarize [ˈpleɪdʒəraɪz] *vt* plagiar

plague [pleɪg] **1** *n (of insects)* plaga *f*; *Med* peste *f*
   2 *vt* **to p. sb with requests** acosar a algn a peticiones

plaice [pleɪs] *n (pl* **plaice**) *(fish)* platija *f*

plaid [plæd, pleɪd] *n (cloth)* tejido *m* escocés

plain [pleɪn] **1** *adj* (**a**) *(clear)* claro(a), evidente; *Fig* **he likes p. speaking** le gusta hablar con franqueza (**b**) *(simple)* sencillo(a); *(chocolate)* amargo(a); *(flour)* sin levadura; **in p. clothes** vestido(a) de paisano; **the p. truth** la verdad lisa y llana (**c**) *(unattractive)* poco atractivo(a)
   2 *n Geog* llanura *f*, llano *m*

plainly [ˈpleɪnlɪ] *adv* claramente; *(simply)* sencillamente; **to speak p.** hablar con franqueza

plaintiff [ˈpleɪntɪf] *n* demandante *mf*

plaintive [ˈpleɪntɪv] *adj* lastimero(a)

plait [plæt] **1** *n* trenza *f*
   2 *vt* trenzar

plan [plæn] **1** *n (scheme)* plan *m*, proyecto *m*; *(drawing)* plano *m*
   2 *vt* (**a**) *(for future)* planear, proyectar; *(economy)* planificar (**b**) *(intend)* pensar, tener la intención de; **it wasn't planned** no estaba previsto
   3 *vi* hacer planes; **to p. on doing sth** tener la intención de hacer algo

plane¹ [pleɪn] **1** *n* (**a**) *Math* plano *m*; *Fig* nivel *m* (**b**) *Fam Av* avión *m*
   2 *adj Geom* plano(a)
   3 *vi (glide)* planear

plane² [pleɪn] **1** *n (tool)* cepillo *m*
   2 *vt* cepillar

plane³ [pleɪn] *n Bot* **p. (tree)** plátano *m*

planet [ˈplænɪt] *n* planeta *m*

plank [plæŋk] *n* tabla *f*, tablón *m*

planner [ˈplænə(r)] *n* planificador(a) *m,f*

planning [ˈplænɪŋ] *n* planificación *f*; **family p.** planificación familiar; **p. permission** permiso *m* de obras

plant¹ [plɑːnt] **1** *n* planta *f*
   2 *vt (flowers)* plantar; *(seeds)* sembrar; *(bomb)* colocar

plant² [plɑːnt] *n (factory)* planta *f*, fábrica *f*; *(machinery)* maquinaria *f*

plantation [plænˈteɪʃən] *n* plantación *f*

plaque [plæk] *n* placa *f*; *(on teeth)* sarro *m*

plaster [ˈplɑːstə(r)] **1** *n Constr* yeso *m*;

Med escayola *f; Br* **sticking p.** esparadrapo *m,* tirita® *f, Am* curita *f;* **p. of Paris** yeso mate
2 *vt Constr* enyesar; *Fig (cover)* cubrir (**with** de)
plastered ['plɑːstəd] *adj Fam* borracho(a), trompa
plasterer ['plɑːstərə(r)] *n* yesero(a) *m,f*
plastic ['plæstɪk] **1** *n* plástico *m*
2 *adj (cup, bag)* de plástico; **p. surgery** cirugía plástica
Plasticine® ['plæstɪsiːn] *n* plastilina® *f*
plate [pleɪt] **1** *n* (**a**) plato *m* (**b**) *(sheet)* placa *f;* **gold p.** chapa *f* de oro; **p. glass** vidrio cilindrado (**c**) *(in book)* grabado *m,* lámina *f*
2 *vt* chapar
plateau ['plætəʊ] *n* meseta *f*
platform ['plætfɔːm] *n* (**a**) plataforma *f;* *(stage)* estrado *m; (at meeting)* tribuna *f* (**b**) *Rail* andén *m;* **p. ticket** billete *m* de andén (**c**) *Pol (programme)* programa *m*
platinum ['plætɪnəm] *n* platino *m*
platitude ['plætɪtjuːd] *n* lugar *m* común, tópico *m*
platoon [plə'tuːn] *n Mil* pelotón *m*
platter ['plætə(r)] *n* fuente *f*
plausible ['plɔːzəbəl] *adj* plausible
play [pleɪ] **1** *vt* (**a**) *(game)* jugar a
(**b**) *Sport (position)* jugar de; *(team)* jugar contra; **to p. a shot** *(in golf, tennis)* golpear
(**c**) *(instrument, tune)* tocar; **to p. a record** poner un disco
(**d**) *Th (part)* hacer (el papel) de; *(play)* representar; *Fig* **to p. a part in sth** participar en algo; *Fig* **to p. the fool** hacer el tonto
2 *vi* (**a**) *(children)* jugar (**with** con); *(animals)* juguetear
(**b**) *Sport* jugar; **to p. fair** jugar limpio; *Fig* **to p. for time** tratar de ganar tiempo
(**c**) *(joke)* bromear
(**d**) *Mus* tocar; *(instrument)* sonar
3 *n* (**a**)*Th* obra *f* de teatro
(**b**) *Sport* juego *m;* **fair/foul p.** juego limpio/sucio
(**c**) *Tech & Fig (movement)* juego *m; Fig* **to bring sth into p.** poner algo en juego; **a p. on words** un juego de palabras
▸ **play around** *vi (waste time)* gandulear; *(be unfaithful)* tener líos
▸ **play down** *vt sep* minimizar, quitar importancia a
▸ **play on** *vt insep (take advantage of)* aprovecharse de; *(nerves etc)* exacerbar
▸ **play up 1** *vt sep (annoy)* dar la lata a, fastidiar

2 *vi (child etc)* dar guerra
playboy ['pleɪbɔɪ] *n* playboy *m*
player ['pleɪə(r)] *n Sport* jugador(a) *m,f; Mus* músico(a) *m,f; Th (man)* actor *m; (woman)* actriz *f*
playful ['pleɪfʊl] *adj* juguetón(ona)
playground ['pleɪgraʊnd] *n* patio *m* de recreo
playgroup ['pleɪgruːp] *n* jardín *m* de infancia
playing ['pleɪɪŋ] *n* juego *m;* **p. card** carta *f,* naipe *m;* **p. field** campo *m* de deportes
playmate ['pleɪmeɪt] *n* compañero(a) *m,f* de juego
play-off ['pleɪɒf] *n Sport* partido *m* de desempate
playpen ['pleɪpen] *n* corralito *m* or parque *m* (de niños)
playschool ['pleɪskuːl] *n* jardín *m* de infancia
plaything ['pleɪθɪŋ] *n* juguete *m*
playwright ['pleɪraɪt] *n* dramaturgo(a) *m,f*
PLC, plc [piːel'siː] *n Br (abbr* **public limited company**) ≃ S.A.
plea [pliː] *n* (**a**) *(request)* petición *f,* súplica *f; (excuse)* pretexto *m,* disculpa *f* (**b**) *Jur* alegato *m*
plead [pliːd] **1** *vt* (**a**) *Jur & Fig* **to p. sb's cause** defender la causa de algn (**b**) **to p. ignorance** *(give as excuse)* alegar ignorancia
2 *vi* (**a**) *(beg)* rogar, suplicar; **to p. with sb to do sth** suplicar a algn que haga algo (**b**) *Jur* **to p. guilty/not guilty** declararse culpable/inocente
pleasant ['plezənt] *adj* agradable
pleasantry ['plezəntrɪ] *n* cumplido *m*
please [pliːz] **1** *vt (give pleasure to)* agradar, complacer; *(satisfy)* satisfacer; *Fam* **p. yourself** como quieras
2 *vi* complacer; *(give satisfaction)* satisfacer; **easy/hard to p.** poco/muy exigente
3 *adv* por favor; **may I? – p. do** ¿me permite? – desde luego; **p. do not smoke** *(sign)* se ruega no fumar; **yes, p.** sí, por favor
pleased [pliːzd] *adj (happy)* contento(a); *(satisfied)* satisfecho(a); **p. to meet you!** ¡encantado(a)!, ¡mucho gusto!; **to be p. about sth** alegrarse de algo
pleasing ['pliːzɪŋ] *adj (pleasant)* agradable, grato(a); *(satisfactory)* satisfactorio(a)
pleasure ['pleʒə(r)] *n* placer *m;* **it's a p. to talk to him** da gusto hablar con él; **to take great p. in doing sth** disfrutar mucho

haciendo algo; **with p.** con mucho gusto
pleat [pliːt] **1** *n* pliegue *m*
2 *vt* hacer pliegues en
pledge [pledʒ] **1** *n* promesa *f*; *(token of love etc)* señal *f*; *(guarantee)* prenda *f*
2 *vt (promise)* prometer; *(pawn)* empeñar
plentiful ['plentɪfʊl] *adj* abundante
plenty ['plentɪ] *n* abundancia *f*; **p. of books** muchos libros; **p. of time** tiempo de sobra; **we've got p.** tenemos de sobra
Plexiglas® ['pleksɪglɑːs] *n US* plexiglás® *m*
pliable ['plaɪəbəl] *adj* flexible
pliers ['plaɪəz] *npl* alicates *mpl*, tenazas *fpl*
plight [plaɪt] *n* situación *f* grave
plimsolls ['plɪmsəlz] *npl Br* zapatos *mpl* de tenis
plinth [plɪnθ] *n* plinto *m*
plod [plɒd] *vi* andar con paso pesado; *Fig* **to p. on** perseverar; *Fig* **to p. through a report** estudiar laboriosamente un informe
plodder ['plɒdə(r)] *n* trabajador(a) *m,f*/ estudiante *mf* tenaz
plonk¹ [plɒŋk] *vt Fam* dejar caer
plonk² [plɒŋk] *n Br Fam (wine)* vinazo *m*
plot¹ [plɒt] **1** *n* (**a**) *(conspiracy)* complot *m* (**b**) *Th & Lit (story)* argumento *m*, trama *f*
2 *vt* (**a**) *(course, route)* trazar (**b**) *(scheme)* fraguar
3 *vi* conspirar, tramar
plot² [plɒt] *n Agr* terreno *m*; *(for building)* solar *m*; **vegetable p.** campo *m* de hortalizas
plough [plaʊ] **1** *n* arado *m*
2 *vt* arar
3 *vi Fig* **the car ploughed through the fencing** el coche atravesó la valla; **to p. into sth** chocar contra algo; *Fig* **to p. through a book** leer un libro con dificultad
▸ **plough back** *vt sep (profits)* reinvertir
plow [plaʊ] *n, vt & vi US* = **plough**
ploy [plɔɪ] *n* estratagema *f*
pluck [plʌk] **1** *vt* (**a**) arrancar (**out of** de) (**b**) *(flowers)* coger (**c**) *(chicken)* desplumar (**d**) *(guitar)* puntear
2 *n (courage)* valor *m*, ánimo *m*
▸ **pluck up** *vt sep* **to p. up courage** armarse de valor
plucky ['plʌkɪ] *adj* (**pluckier, pluckiest**) valiente
plug [plʌg] **1** *n* (**a**) *(in bath etc)* tapón *m* (**b**) *Elec* enchufe *m*, clavija *f*; **two-/three-pin p.** clavija bipolar/tripolar

2 *vt* (**a**) *(hole)* tapar (**b**) *Fam (publicize)* dar publicidad a; *(idea etc)* hacer hincapié en
▸ **plug in** *vt sep & vi* enchufar
plum [plʌm] *n (fruit)* ciruela *f*; *Fig* **a p. job** un chollo
plumage ['pluːmɪdʒ] *n* plumaje *m*
plumb [plʌm] **1** *n* plomo *m*; **p. line** plomada *f*
2 *adj* vertical
3 *adv Fam* **p. in the middle** justo en medio; *US* **he's p. crazy** está completamente loco
4 *vt Fig* **to p. the depths** tocar fondo
plumber ['plʌmə(r)] *n* fontanero(a) *m,f*
plumbing ['plʌmɪŋ] *n (occupation)* fontanería *f*; *(system)* tuberías *fpl*, cañerías *fpl*
plume [pluːm] *n* penacho *m*
plummet ['plʌmɪt] *vi (bird, plane)* caer en picado; *Fig (prices)* bajar vertiginosamente; *(morale)* caer a plomo
plump¹ [plʌmp] *adj (person)* relleno(a); *(baby)* rechoncho(a)
plump² [plʌmp] *vi* **to p. for sth** optar por algo
▸ **plump down** *vt sep* dejar caer
▸ **plump up** *vt sep (cushions)* ahuecar
plunder ['plʌndə(r)] **1** *vt* saquear
2 *n (action)* saqueo *m*, pillaje *m*; *(loot)* botín *m*
plunge [plʌndʒ] **1** *vt (immerse)* sumergir; *(thrust)* arrojar
2 *vi (dive)* lanzarse, zambullirse; *Fig (fall)* caer, hundirse; *(prices)* desplomarse
3 *n (dive)* zambullida *f*, *Fig (fall)* desplome *m*; **to take the p.** dar el paso decisivo
plunger ['plʌndʒə(r)] *n Tech* émbolo *m*; *(for pipes)* desatascador *m*
pluperfect [pluː'pɜːfɪkt] *n* pluscuamperfecto *m*
plural ['plʊərəl] *adj & n* plural (*m*)
plus [plʌs] **1** *prep* más; **three p. four makes seven** tres más cuatro hacen siete
2 *n Math* signo *m* más; *Fig (advantage)* ventaja *f*
plush [plʌʃ] **1** *n* felpa *f*
2 *adj Fam* lujoso(a)
plutonium [pluː'təʊnɪəm] *n* plutonio *m*
ply [plaɪ] **1** *vt* **to p. one's trade** ejercer su oficio; **to p. sb with drinks** no parar de ofrecer copas a algn
2 *vi (ship)* ir y venir; **to p. for hire** ir en busca de clientes
plywood ['plaɪwʊd] *n* madera contrachapada

PM [piː'em] *n Br* (*abbr* **Prime Minister**) primer(a) ministro(a) *m,f*

p.m. [piː'em] (*abbr* **post meridiem**) después del mediodía; **at 2 p.m.** a las dos de la tarde

PMT [piːem'tiː] *n* (*abbr* **premenstrual tension**) tensión *f* premenstrual

pneumatic [njʊ'mætɪk] *adj* neumático(a)

pneumonia [njuː'məʊnɪə] *n* pulmonía *f*

PO [piː'əʊ] *n* (*abbr* **Post Office**) oficina *f* de correos; **PO Box** apartado *m* de correos, *CAm, Carib, Méx* casilla *f* postal, *Andes, RP* casilla de correos

poach¹ [pəʊtʃ] *vt* (**a**) **to p. fish/game** pescar/cazar furtivamente (**b**) *Fam Fig* (*steal*) birlar

poach² [pəʊtʃ] *vt Culin* (*egg*) escalfar; (*fish*) hervir

poacher ['pəʊtʃə(r)] *n* pescador/cazador furtivo

pocket ['pɒkɪt] **1** *n* (**a**) bolsillo *m*; *Fig* **to be £10 in/out of p.** salir ganando/perdiendo 10 libras; **p. money** dinero *m* de bolsillo (**b**) (*of air*) bolsa *f* (**c**) (*of resistance*) foco *m*
2 *vt* (*money*) embolsar

pocketbook ['pɒkɪtbʊk] *n US* bolso *m*

pocketknife ['pɒkɪtnaɪf] *n* navaja *f*

pod [pɒd] *n* vaina *f*

podgy ['pɒdʒɪ] *adj* (**podgier, podgiest**) gordinflón(ona), regordete

podiatrist [pə'daɪətrɪst] *n US* pedicuro(a) *m,f*

podium ['pəʊdɪəm] *n* podio *m*

poem ['pəʊɪm] *n* poema *m*

poet ['pəʊɪt] *n* poeta *mf*

poetic [pəʊ'etɪk] *adj* poético(a)

poetry ['pəʊɪtrɪ] *n* poesía *f*

poignant ['pɔɪnjənt] *adj* conmovedor(a)

point [pɔɪnt] **1** *n* (**a**) (*sharp end*) punta *f* (**b**) (*place*) punto *m*; *Fig* **p. of no return** punto sin retorno (**c**) (*quality*) **good/bad p.** cualidad buena/mala; **weak/strong p.** punto débil/fuerte (**d**) (*moment*) **at that p.** en aquel momento; **from that p. onwards** desde entonces; **to be on the p. of doing sth** estar a punto de hacer algo (**e**) (*score*) punto *m*, tanto *m*; **to win on points** ganar por puntos; **match p.** (*in tennis*) pelota *f* de match (**f**) (*in argument*) punto *m*; **to make one's p.** insistir en el argumento; **I take your p.** entiendo lo que quieres decir (**g**) (*purpose*) propósito *m*; **I don't see the p.** no veo el sentido; **that isn't the p.**, **it's beside the p.** eso no viene al caso; **there's no p. in going** no merece la pena ir; **to come to the p.** llegar al meollo de la cuestión (**h**) (*on scale*) punto *m*; (*in share index*) entero *m*; **six p. three** seis coma tres; *Fig* **up to a p.** hasta cierto punto (**i**) *Geog* punta *f* (**j**) **power p.** toma *f* de corriente (**k**) **points** *Aut* platinos *mpl*; *Rail* agujas *fpl*
2 *vt* (*way etc*) señalar, indicar; **to p. a gun at sb** apuntar a algn con una pistola
3 *vi* señalar, indicar; **to p. at sth/sb** señalar algo/a algn con el dedo
▶ **point out** *vt sep* indicar, señalar; (*mention*) hacer resaltar

point-blank ['pɔɪnt'blæŋk] **1** *adj* a quemarropa; (*refusal*) rotundo(a)
2 *adv* (*shoot*) a quemarropa; (*refuse*) rotundamente

pointed ['pɔɪntɪd] *adj* (*sharp*) puntiagudo(a); *Fig* (*comment*) intencionado(a); (*cutting*) mordaz

pointedly ['pɔɪntɪdlɪ] *adv Fig* (*significantly*) con intención; (*cuttingly*) con mordacidad

pointer ['pɔɪntə(r)] *n* (**a**) (*indicator*) indicador *m*, aguja *f*; (*for map*) puntero *m* (**b**) (*dog*) perro *m* de muestra

pointless ['pɔɪntlɪs] *adj* sin sentido

poise [pɔɪz] **1** *n* (*bearing*) porte *m*; (*self-assurance*) aplomo *m*
2 *vt Fig* **to be poised to do sth** estar listo(a) para hacer algo

poison ['pɔɪzən] **1** *n* veneno *m*
2 *vt* envenenar

poisoning ['pɔɪzənɪŋ] *n* envenenamiento *m*; (*by food etc*) intoxicación *f*

poisonous ['pɔɪzənəs] *adj* (*plant, snake*) venenoso(a); (*gas*) tóxico(a); *Fig* (*rumour*) pernicioso(a)

poke [pəʊk] *vt* (*with finger or stick*) dar con la punta del dedo/del bastón a; **to p. one's head out** asomar la cabeza; **to p. the fire** atizar el fuego
▶ **poke about, poke around** *vi* fisgonear, hurgar
▶ **poke out** *vt sep* (*eye*) sacar

poker¹ ['pəʊkə(r)] *n* (*for fire*) atizador *m*

poker² ['pəʊkə(r)] *n Cards* póquer *m*

poker-faced ['pəʊkəfeɪst] *adj Fam* de cara impasible

poky ['pəʊkɪ] *adj* (**pokier, pokiest**) *Fam Pej* minúsculo(a); **a p. little room** un cuartucho

Poland ['pəʊlənd] *n* Polonia

polar [ˈpəʊlə(r)] *adj* polar; **p. bear** oso *m* polar

Pole [pəʊl] *n* polaco(a) *m,f*

pole¹ [pəʊl] *n* palo *m*; **p. vault** salto *m* con pértiga

pole² [pəʊl] *n Geog* polo *m*; *Fig* **to be poles apart** ser polos opuestos

police [pəˈliːs] **1** *npl* policía *f*; **p. car** coche *m* patrulla; **p. constable** policía *m*; **p. force** cuerpo *m* de policía; **p. record** antecedentes *mpl* penales; **p. state** estado *m* policial; **p. station** comisaría *f*
2 *vt* vigilar

policeman [pəˈliːsmən] *n* policía *m*

policewoman [pəˈliːswʊmən] *n* (mujer *f*) policía *f*

policy [ˈpɒlɪsɪ] *n Pol* política *f*; *(of company)* norma *f*, principio *m*; *Ins* póliza *f* (de seguros)

polio [ˈpəʊlɪəʊ] *n* poliomielitis *f*

Polish [ˈpəʊlɪʃ] **1** *adj* polaco(a)
2 *n* (**a**) **the P.** los polacos (**b**) *(language)* polaco *m*

polish [ˈpɒlɪʃ] **1** *vt* pulir; *(furniture)* encerar; *(shoes)* limpiar; *(silver)* sacar brillo a
2 *n* (**a**) *(for furniture)* cera *f*; *(for shoes)* betún *m*; *(for nails)* esmalte *m* (**b**) *(shine)* brillo *m*; *Fig (refinement)* refinamiento *m*
▸ **polish off** *vt sep Fam (work)* despachar; *(food)* zamparse
▸ **polish up** *vt sep Fig* perfeccionar

polished [ˈpɒlɪʃt] *adj Fig (manners)* refinado(a); *(style)* pulido(a); *(performance)* impecable

polite [pəˈlaɪt] *adj* educado(a)

politeness [pəˈlaɪtnɪs] *n* educación *f*

politic [ˈpɒlɪtɪk] *adj* prudente

political [pəˈlɪtɪkəl] *adj* político(a)

politically [pəˈlɪtɪklɪ] *adv* políticamente; **p. correct** políticamente correcto(a)

politician [pɒlɪˈtɪʃən] *n* político(a) *m,f*

politics [ˈpɒlɪtɪks] *n sing* política *f*

polka [ˈpɒlkə] *n (dance)* polca *f*; **p. dot** lunar *m*

poll [pəʊl] **1** *n* (**a**) votación *f*; **the polls** las elecciones; **to go to the polls** acudir a las urnas (**b**) *(survey)* encuesta *f*
2 *vt (votes)* obtener

pollen [ˈpɒlən] *n* polen *m*

polling [ˈpəʊlɪŋ] *n* votación *f*; **p. booth** cabina *f* electoral; **p. station** colegio *m* electoral

pollute [pəˈluːt] *vt* contaminar

pollution [pəˈluːʃən] *n* contaminación *f*, polución *f*; **environmental p.** contaminación ambiental

polo [ˈpəʊləʊ] *n Sport* polo *m*; **p. neck** *(sweater)* jersey *m* de cuello vuelto

polyester [pɒlɪˈestə(r)] *n* poliéster *m*

polyethylene [pɒlɪˈeθəliːn] *n US* polietileno *m*

polymer [ˈpɒlɪmə(r)] *n Chem* polímero *m*

Polynesia [pɒlɪˈniːʒɪə] *n* Polinesia

polystyrene [pɒlɪˈstaɪriːn] *n* poliestireno *m*

polytechnic [pɒlɪˈteknɪk] *n* escuela politécnica, politécnico *m*

polythene [ˈpɒlɪθiːn] *n Br* polietileno *m*

pomegranate [ˈpɒmɪgrænɪt] *n* granada *f*

pomp [pɒmp] *n* pompa *f*

pompom [ˈpɒmpɒm], **pompon** [ˈpɒmpɒn] *n* borla *f*, pompón *m*

pompous [ˈpɒmpəs] *adj (person)* presumido(a); *(speech)* rimbombante

pond [pɒnd] *n* estanque *m*

ponder [ˈpɒndə(r)] **1** *vt* considerar
2 *vi* **to p. over sth** meditar sobre algo

ponderous [ˈpɒndərəs] *adj* pesado(a)

pong [pɒŋ] *n Br Fam* hedor *m*

pontoon¹ [pɒnˈtuːn] *n Constr* pontón *m*

pontoon² [pɒnˈtuːn] *n Cards* veintiuna *f*

pony [ˈpəʊnɪ] *n* poney *m*

ponytail [ˈpəʊnɪteɪl] *n* cola *f* de caballo

poodle [ˈpuːdəl] *n* caniche *m*

poof [pʊf] *n Br Fam Pej* marica *m*

pool¹ [puːl] *n (of water, oil etc)* charco *m*; *(pond)* estanque *m*; *(in river)* pozo *m*; **swimming p.** piscina *f*

pool² [puːl] **1** *n* (**a**) *(common fund)* fondo *m* común (**b**) **typing p.** servicio *m* de mecanografía (**c**) *US (snooker)* billar americano (**d**) *Br* **football pools** quinielas *fpl*
2 *vt (funds)* reunir; *(ideas, resources)* juntar

poor [pʊə(r)] **1** *adj* pobre; *(quality)* malo(a); *Fam* **you p. thing!** ¡pobrecito!
2 *npl* **the p.** los pobres

poorly [ˈpʊəlɪ] **1** *adv (badly)* mal
2 *adj* (**poorlier, poorliest**) *(ill)* mal, malo(a)

pop [pɒp] **1** *vt (burst)* hacer reventar; *(cork)* hacer saltar
2 *vi (burst)* reventar; *(cork)* saltar; *Fam* **I'm just popping over to Ian's** voy un momento a casa de Ian
3 *n* (**a**) *(noise)* pequeña explosión (**b**) *Fam (drink)* gaseosa *f* (**c**) *US Fam (father)* papá *m* (**d**) *Fam Mus* música *f* pop; **p. singer** cantante *mf* pop
▸ **pop in** *vi Fam* entrar un momento, pasar

popcorn [ˈpɒpkɔːn] *n* palomitas *fpl*

Pope [pəʊp] *n* **the P.** el Papa

poplar [ˈpɒplə(r)] *n* álamo *m*

poppy [ˈpɒpɪ] *n* amapola *f*

Popsicle® ['pɒpsɪkəl] *n US* polo *m*
populace ['pɒpjʊləs] *n (people)* pueblo *m*
popular ['pɒpjʊlə(r)] *adj* popular; *(fashionable)* de moda; *(common)* corriente
popularity [pɒpjʊ'lærɪtɪ] *n* popularidad *f*
popularize ['pɒpjʊləraɪz] *vt* popularizar
populate ['pɒpjʊleɪt] *vt* poblar
population [pɒpjʊ'leɪʃən] *n* población *f*; **the p. explosion** la explosión demográfica
porcelain ['pɔːsəlɪn] *n* porcelana *f*
porch [pɔːtʃ] *n (of church)* pórtico *m*; *(of house)* porche *m*, entrada *f*; *US (veranda)* terraza *f*
porcupine ['pɔːkjʊpaɪn] *n* puerco *m* espín
pore¹ [pɔː(r)] *vi* **to p. over sth** leer *or* estudiar algo detenidamente
pore² [pɔː(r)] *n Anat* poro *m*
pork [pɔːk] *n* carne *f* de cerdo
pornography [pɔː'nɒgrəfɪ] *n* pornografía *f*
porous ['pɔːrəs] *adj* poroso(a)
porpoise ['pɔːpəs] *n* marsopa *f*
porridge ['pɒrɪdʒ] *n* gachas *fpl* de avena
port¹ [pɔːt] *n (harbour)* puerto *m*; **p. of call** puerto de escala
port² [pɔːt] *n Naut & Av* babor *m*
port³ [pɔːt] *n (wine)* vino *m* de Oporto, oporto *m*
portable ['pɔːtəbəl] *adj* portátil
portal ['pɔːtəl] *n Comput (web page)* portal *m*
portent ['pɔːtent] *n Fml* augurio *m*
porter ['pɔːtə(r)] *n (in hotel etc)* portero(a) *m,f*; *Rail* mozo *m* de estación; *US* mozo de los coches-cama
portfolio [pɔːt'fəʊlɪəʊ] *n (file)* carpeta *f*; *(of artist, politician)* cartera *f*
porthole ['pɔːthəʊl] *n* portilla *f*
portion ['pɔːʃən] *n (part, piece)* parte *f*, porción *f*; *(of food)* ración *f*
▸ **portion out** *vt sep* repartir
portly ['pɔːtlɪ] *adj* (**portlier, portliest**) corpulento(a)
portrait ['pɔːtreɪt] *n* retrato *m*
portray [pɔː'treɪ] *vt (paint portrait of)* retratar; *(describe)* describir; *Th* representar
Portugal ['pɔːtjʊgəl] *n* Portugal
Portuguese [pɔːtjʊ'giːz] **1** *adj* portugués(esa)
2 *n (person)* portugués(esa) *m,f*; *(language)* portugués *m*
pose [pəʊz] **1** *vt (problem)* plantear; *(threat)* representar
2 *vi (for painting)* posar; *Pej (behave*

affectedly) hacer pose; **to p. as** hacerse pasar por
3 *n (stance)* postura *f*; *Pej (affectation)* pose *f*
posh [pɒʃ] *adj Br Fam* elegante, de lujo; *(person)* presumido(a); *(accent)* de clase alta
position [pə'zɪʃən] **1** *n* (**a**) posición *f*; *(location)* situación *f*; *(rank)* rango *m*; **to be in a p. to do sth** estar en condiciones de hacer algo (**b**) *(opinion)* postura *f* (**c**) *(job)* puesto *m*
2 *vt* colocar
positive ['pɒzɪtɪv] *adj* positivo(a); *(sign)* favorable; *(proof)* incontrovertible; *(sure)* seguro(a); *Fam (absolute)* auténtico(a)
possess [pə'zes] *vt* poseer; *(of fear)* apoderarse de
possessed [pə'zest] *adj* poseído(a)
possession [pə'zeʃən] *n* posesión *f*; **possessions** bienes *mpl*
possessive [pə'zesɪv] *adj* posesivo(a)
possibility [pɒsɪ'bɪlɪtɪ] *n* posibilidad *f*; **possibilities** *(potential)* potencial *m*
possible ['pɒsɪbəl] *adj* posible; **as much as p.** todo lo posible; **as often as p.** cuanto más mejor; **as soon as p.** cuanto antes
possibly ['pɒsɪblɪ] *adv* posiblemente; *(perhaps)* tal vez, quizás; **I can't p. come** no puedo venir de ninguna manera
post¹ [pəʊst] **1** *n (of wood)* poste *m*
2 *vt (fix)* fijar
post² [pəʊst] **1** *n (job)* puesto *m*; *US* **trading p.** factoría *f*
2 *vt* enviar
post³ [pəʊst] *Br* **1** *n (mail)* correo *m*; **by p.** por correo; **p. office** oficina *f* de correos; **P. Office Box** apartado *m* de correos
2 *vt (letter)* echar al correo; **to p. sth to sb** mandar algo por correo a algn
postage ['pəʊstɪdʒ] *n* franqueo *m*
postal ['pəʊstəl] *adj* postal, de correos; *Br* **p. code** código *m* postal **p. order** giro *m* postal; **p. vote** voto *m* por correo
postbox ['pəʊstbɒks] *n Br* buzón *m*
postcard ['pəʊstkɑːd] *n* (tarjeta *f*) postal *f*
postcode ['pəʊstkəʊd] *n Br* código *m* postal
postdate [pəʊst'deɪt] *vt (cheque)* extender con fecha posterior
poster ['pəʊstə(r)] *n* póster *m*; *(advertising)* cartel *m*
posterior [pɒ'stɪərɪə(r)] **1** *n Hum* trasero *m*, pompis *m*
2 *adj* posterior
posterity [pɒ'sterɪtɪ] *n* posteridad *f*

postgraduate [pəʊst'grædjʊɪt] **1** *n* posgraduado(a) *m,f*
2 *adj* de posgraduado
posthumous ['pɒstjʊməs] *adj* póstumo(a)
postman ['pəʊstmən] *n Br* cartero *m*
postmark ['pəʊstmɑːk] *n* matasellos *m inv*
postmaster ['pəʊstmɑːstə(r)] *n* administrador *m* de correos; **p. general** director *m* general de correos
postmortem [pəʊst'mɔːtəm] *n* autopsia *f*
postpone [pəs'pəʊn] *vt* aplazar
postscript ['pəʊsskrɪpt] *n* posdata *f*
posture ['pɒstʃə(r)] **1** *n* postura *f*; *(affected)* pose *f*
2 *vi* adoptar una pose
postwar ['pəʊstwɔː(r)] *adj* de la posguerra
posy ['pəʊzɪ] *n* ramillete *m*
pot [pɒt] **1** *n (container)* tarro *m*, pote *m*; *(for cooking)* olla *f*; *(for flowers)* maceta *f*; *Fam* **to go to p.** irse al traste; **p. shot** tiro *m* al azar
2 *vt (plant)* poner en una maceta
potassium [pə'tæsɪəm] *n* potasio *m*
potato [pə'teɪtəʊ] *n (pl* **potatoes***)* patata *f, Am* papa *f*
potent ['pəʊtənt] *adj* potente
potential [pə'tenʃəl] **1** *adj* potencial, posible
2 *n* potencial *m*
potentially [pə'tenʃəlɪ] *adv* en potencia
pothole ['pɒthəʊl] *n Geol* cueva *f*; *(in road)* bache *m*
potholing ['pɒthəʊlɪŋ] *n Br* espeleología *f*
potion ['pəʊʃən] *n* poción *f*, pócima *f*
potluck [pɒt'lʌk] *n Fam* **to take p.** conformarse con lo que haya
potted ['pɒtɪd] *adj (food)* en conserva; *(plant)* en maceta *or* tiesto
potter ¹ ['pɒtə(r)] *n* alfarero(a) *m,f*
potter ² ['pɒtə(r)] *vi Br* **to p. about** *or* **around** entretenerse
pottery ['pɒtərɪ] *n (craft, place)* alfarería *f*, *(objects)* cerámica *f*
potty ¹ ['pɒtɪ] *adj (***pottier, pottiest***) Br Fam* chiflado(a)
potty ² ['pɒtɪ] *n Fam* orinal *m*
pouch [paʊtʃ] *n (***a***)* bolsa pequeña; *(for ammunition)* morral *m*; *(for tobacco)* petaca *f (***b***) Zool* bolsa *f* abdominal
poultry ['pəʊltrɪ] *n (live)* aves *fpl* de corral; *(food)* pollos *mpl*
pounce [paʊns] *vi* **to p. on** abalanzarse encima de

pound ¹ [paʊnd] **1** *vt (strike)* aporrear
2 *vi (heart)* palpitar; *(walk heavily)* andar con paso pesado
pound ² [paʊnd] *n (money, weight)* libra *f*
pound ³ [paʊnd] *n (for dogs)* perrera *f*; *(for cars)* depósito *m* de coches
pour [pɔː(r)] **1** *vt* echar, verter; **to p. sb a drink** servirle una copa a algn
2 *vi* correr, fluir; **it's pouring with rain** está lloviendo a cántaros
▸ **pour out** *vt sep* echar, verter; *Fig* **to p. one's heart out to sb** desahogarse con algn
pouring ['pɔːrɪŋ] *adj (rain)* torrencial
pout [paʊt] **1** *vi* hacer pucheros
2 *n* puchero *m*
poverty ['pɒvətɪ] *n* pobreza *f*
poverty-stricken ['pɒvətɪstrɪkən] *adj* necesitado(a); **to be p.** vivir en la miseria
powder ['paʊdə(r)] **1** *n* polvo *m*; **p. compact** polvera *f*; **p. keg** polvorín *m*; **p. puff** borla *f*; **p. room** servicios *mpl* de señoras
2 *vt* **to p. one's nose** ponerse polvos en la cara; *Euph* ir a los servicios *or* al tocador
powdered ['paʊdəd] *adj (milk)* en polvo
power ['paʊə(r)] **1** *n (***a***)* fuerza *f*; *(energy)* energía *f*; *Elec* **to cut off the p.** cortar la corriente; **p. point** enchufe *m*; **p. station** central eléctrica (**b**) *(ability)* poder *m* (**c**) *(authority)* poder *m*; *(nation)* potencia *f*; *(influence)* influencia *f*; **to be in p.** estar en el poder; *Pol* **to come into p.** subir al poder; **the p. of veto** el derecho de veto (**d**) *Tech* potencia *f*; *(output)* rendimiento *m*
2 *vt* propulsar, impulsar
powerboat ['paʊəbəʊt] *n* lancha *f* (motora)
powerful ['paʊəfʊl] *adj (strong)* fuerte; *(influential)* poderoso(a); *(remedy)* eficaz; *(engine, machine)* potente; *(emotion)* fuerte; *(speech)* conmovedor(a)
powerless ['paʊəlɪs] *adj* impotente, ineficaz
pp *(abbr* **pages***)* págs., pp
PR [piː'ɑː(r)] *(abbr* **public relations***)* relaciones *fpl* públicas
practicable ['præktɪkəbəl] *adj* factible
practical ['præktɪkəl] *adj* práctico(a); *(useful)* útil; *(sensible)* adecuado(a)
practicality [præktɪ'kælɪtɪ] *n (of suggestion, plan)* factibilidad *f*; **practicalities** detalles prácticos
practically ['præktɪkəlɪ] *adv (almost)* casi
practice ['præktɪs] **1** *n (***a***) (habit)* costumbre *f (***b***) (exercise)* práctica *f*; *Sport*

entrenamiento *m*; *Mus* ensayo *m*; **to be out of p.** no estar en forma (**c**) *(way of doing sth)* práctica *f*; **in p.** en la práctica; **to put sth into p.** poner algo en práctica (**d**) *(of profession)* ejercicio *m* (**e**) *(place) (of doctors)* consultorio *m*; *(of lawyers)* bufete *m* (**f**) *(clients) (of doctors)* pacientes *mpl*; *(of lawyers)* clientela *f*

2 *vt & vi US* = **practise**

practicing ['præktɪsɪŋ] *adj US* = **practising**

practise ['præktɪs] **1** *vt* practicar; *(method)* seguir; *(principle)* poner en práctica; *Mus* ensayar; *(profession)* ejercer

2 *vi* practicar; *Sport* entrenar; *Mus* ensayar; *(doctor)* practicar; *(lawyer)* ejercer

practising ['præktɪsɪŋ] *adj (doctor etc)* en ejercicio; *(Christian etc)* practicante

practitioner [præk'tɪʃənə(r)] *n Br Med* **general p.** médico(a) *m,f* de cabecera; **medical p.** médico(a) *m,f*

pragmatic [præg'mætɪk] *adj* pragmático(a)

prairie ['preərɪ] *n* pradera *f*; *US* llanura *f*

praise [preɪz] **1** *n* alabanza *f*

2 *vt* alabar, elogiar

praiseworthy ['preɪzwɜ:ðɪ] *adj* loable

pram [præm] *n Br* cochecito *m* de niño

prance [prɑːns] *vi (horse)* encabritarse; **to p. about** *(person)* pegar brincos

prank [præŋk] *n* broma *f*; *(of child)* travesura *f*

prat [præt] *n Br Fam* soplagaitas *mf inv*, *Am* pendejo(a) *m,f*

prawn [prɔːn] *n* gamba *f*

pray [preɪ] *vi* rezar, orar

prayer [preə(r)] *n* rezo *m*, oración *f*; *(entreaty)* súplica *f*; **p. book** misal *m*

preach [priːtʃ] *vi* predicar

preacher ['priːtʃə(r)] *n* predicador(a) *m,f*

precarious [prɪ'keərɪəs] *adj* precario(a)

precaution [prɪ'kɔːʃən] *n* precaución *f*

precede [prɪ'siːd] *vt* preceder

precedence ['presɪdəns] *n* preferencia *f*, prioridad *f*; **to take p. over sth/sb** tener prioridad sobre algo/algn

precedent ['presɪdənt] *n* precedente *m*

preceding [prɪ'siːdɪŋ] *adj* precedente

precinct ['priːsɪŋkt] *n* (**a**) *(area)* recinto *m*; **pedestrian/shopping p.** zona *f* peatonal/comercial (**b**) *US (administrative, police division)* distrito *m*; *(police station)* comisaría *f* (de policía)

---

*Note that the Spanish word **precinto** is a false friend and is never a translation for the English word **precinct**. In Spanish, **precinto** means "seal".*

---

precious ['preʃəs] **1** *adj* precioso(a); **p. stones** piedras preciosas

2 *adv Fam* **p. little/few** muy poco/pocos

precipice ['presɪpɪs] *n* precipicio *m*

precipitate 1 *vt* [prɪ'sɪpɪteɪt] precipitar; *Fig* arrojar

2 *adj* [prɪ'sɪpɪtət] precipitado(a)

precise [prɪ'saɪs] *adj* preciso(a), exacto(a); *(meticulous)* meticuloso(a)

precisely [prɪ'saɪslɪ] *adv (exactly)* precisamente, exactamente; **p.!** ¡eso es!, ¡exacto!

precision [prɪ'sɪʒən] *n* precisión *f*

preclude [prɪ'kluːd] *vt* excluir; *(misunderstanding)* evitar

precocious [prɪ'kəʊʃəs] *adj* precoz

preconceived [priːkən'siːvd] *adj* preconcebido(a)

precondition [priːkən'dɪʃən] *n* condición previa

precursor [priː'kɜːsə(r)] *n* precursor(a) *m,f*

predator ['predətə(r)] *n* depredador *m*

predecessor ['priːdɪsesə(r)] *n* antecesor(a) *m,f*

predetermine [priːdɪ'tɜːmɪn] *vt* predeterminar

predicament [prɪ'dɪkəmənt] *n* apuro *m*, aprieto *m*

predict [prɪ'dɪkt] *vt* predecir, pronosticar

predictable [prɪ'dɪktəbəl] *adj* previsible

prediction [prɪ'dɪkʃən] *n* pronóstico *m*

predispose [priːdɪ'spəʊz] *vt* **to be predisposed to doing sth** estar predispuesto(a) a hacer algo

predominant [prɪ'dɒmɪnənt] *adj* predominante

predominantly [prɪ'dɒmɪnəntlɪ] *adv* en su mayoría

predominate [prɪ'dɒmɪneɪt] *vi* predominar

pre-empt [prɪ'empt] *vt* adelantarse a

preen [priːn] *vt* **to p. oneself** *(of bird)* arreglarse las plumas; *Fig (of person)* pavonearse

prefab ['priːfæb] *n Br Fam (house)* casa prefabricada

prefabricated [priː'fæbrɪkeɪtɪd] *adj* prefabricado(a)

preface ['prefɪs] **1** *n* prefacio *m*

2 *vt* prologar

prefect ['priːfekt] *n Br Educ* monitor(a) *m,f*

prefer [prɪ'fɜː(r)] *vt* preferir; **I p. coffee to tea** prefiero el café al té

preferable ['prefərəbəl] *adj* preferible (**to** a)

preferably ['prefərəblı] *adv* preferente-
mente

preference ['prefərəns] *n* preferencia *f*;
(priority) prioridad *f*; **to give p. to sth** dar
prioridad a algo

preferential [prefə'renʃəl] *adj* preferente

prefix ['pri:fıks] *n* prefijo *m*

pregnancy ['pregnənsı] *n* embarazo *m*

pregnant ['pregnənt] *adj (woman)* embarazada; *(animal)* preñada; *Fig* **a p.
pause** una pausa cargada de significado

prehistoric(al) [pri:hı'stɒrık(əl)] *adj*
prehistórico(a)

prejudice ['predʒʊdıs] **1** *n (bias)* prejuicio *m*; *(harm)* perjuicio *m*
   2 *vt (bias)* predisponer; *(harm)* perjudicar

prejudiced ['predʒʊdıst] *adj* parcial; **to
be p. against/in favour of** estar predis-
puesto(a) en contra/a favor de

preliminary [prı'lımınərı] **1** *adj* preliminar; *Sport (round)* eliminatorio(a)
   2 *n* **preliminaries** preliminares *mpl*

prelude ['prelju:d] *n* preludio *m*

premarital [pri:'mærıtəl] *adj* prematrimonial

premature [premə'tjʊə(r), 'premətjʊə(r)]
adj prematuro(a)

prematurely [premə'tjʊəlı, 'premətjʊəlı]
adv antes de tiempo

premeditate [prı'medıteıt] *vt (crime)*
premeditar

premenstrual [pri:'menstrʊəl] *adj* **p.
tension** tensión *f* premenstrual

premier ['premjə(r)] **1** *n Pol* primer(a)
ministro(a) *m,f*
   2 *adj* primer, primero(a)

premiere ['premıeə(r)] *n Cin* estreno *m*

premise ['premıs] *n* premisa *f*

premises ['premısız] *npl* local *m*; **on the
p.** en el local

premium ['pri:mıəm] *n Com, Fin & Ind*
prima *f*; **to be at a p.** tener sobreprecio;
Fig estar muy solicitado(a); *Br* **p. bonds** =
bonos numerados emitidos por el Gobierno británico, cuyo comprador entra
en un sorteo mensual de premios en
metálico

premonition [premə'nıʃən] *n* presentimiento *m*

preoccupied [pri:'ɒkjʊpaıd] *adj* preocu-
pado(a); **to be p. with sth** preocuparse
por algo

prep [prep] *n Br Fam* deberes *mpl*; **p.
school** = colegio privado para alumnos
de entre 7 y 13 años

prepacked [pri:'pækt] *adj* empaqueta-
do(a)

prepaid [pri:'peıd] *adj* con el porte pagado

preparation [prepə'reıʃən] *n* preparación *f*; *(plan)* preparativo *m*

preparatory [prı'pærətərı] *adj* prepara-
torio(a), preliminar; **p. school** *Br* = colegio privado para alumnos de entre 7 y
13 años; *US* = escuela secundaria privada

prepare [prı'peə(r)] **1** *vt* preparar; **to p. to
do sth** prepararse para hacer algo
   2 *vi* prepararse (**for** para)

prepared [prı'peəd] *adj (ready)* prepara-
do(a); **to be p. to do sth** *(willing)* estar
dispuesto(a) a hacer algo

preponderance [prı'pɒndərəns] *n* pre-
ponderancia *f*

preposition [prepə'zıʃən] *n* preposición
f

preposterous [prı'pɒstərəs] *adj* absur-
do(a), ridículo(a)

prerequisite [pri:'rekwızıt] *n* condición *f*
previa

prerogative [prı'rɒgətıv] *n* prerrogativa
f

preschool [pri:'sku:l] *adj* preescolar

prescribe [prı'skraıb] *vt (set down)* prescribir; *Med* recetar; *Fig (recommend)* recomendar

prescription [prı'skrıpʃən] *n Med* receta
f

presence ['prezəns] *n* presencia *f*; *(attendance)* asistencia *f*; *Fig* **p. of mind**
presencia de ánimo

present¹ ['prezənt] **1** *adj* (**a**) *(in attendance)* presente; *Ling* **p. tense** (tiempo *m*)
presente *m*; **to be p. at** estar presente en
(**b**) *(current)* actual
   2 *n (time)* presente *m*, actualidad *f*; **at p.**
actualmente; **for the p.** de momento; **up
to the p.** hasta ahora

present² **1** *vt* [prı'zent] (**a**) *(give as gift)*
regalar; *(medals, prizes etc)* entregar; **to
p. sb with sth** obsequiar a algn con algo
(**b**) *(report etc)* presentar; *(opportunity)*
ofrecer; *(problems)* plantear (**c**) *(introduce) (person, programme)* presentar
   2 *n* ['prezənt] *(gift)* regalo *m*; *(formal)*
obsequio *m*

presentable [prı'zentəbəl] *adj* presentable; **to make oneself p.** arreglarse

presentation [prezən'teıʃən] *n* (**a**) presentación *f*; **p. ceremony** ceremonia *f* de
entrega (**b**) *Rad & TV* representación *f*

present-day ['prezəntdeı] *adj* actual, de
hoy en día

presenter [prı'zentə(r)] *n Rad* locutor(a)
m,f; *TV* presentador(a) *m,f*

presently ['prezəntlɪ] *adv (soon)* dentro de poco; *US (now)* ahora

preservation [prezə'veɪʃən] *n* conservación *f*

preservative [prɪ'zɜːvətɪv] *n* conservante *m*

preserve [prɪ'zɜːv] **1** *vt* (**a**) *(keep)* mantener (**b**) *Culin* conservar
2 *n* (**a**) *(hunting)* coto *m* (**b**) *Culin* conserva *f*

preside [prɪ'zaɪd] *vi* presidir

president ['prezɪdənt] *n Pol* presidente(a) *m,f*; *US Com* director(a) *m,f*, gerente *mf*

presidential [prezɪ'denʃəl] *adj* presidencial

press [pres] **1** *vt* (**a**) apretar; *(button)* pulsar; *(grapes)* pisar; *(trousers etc)* planchar
(**b**) *(urge)* presionar; **to p. sb to do sth** acosar a algn para que haga algo
2 *vi* (**a**) *(push)* apretar; **to p. against sb/ sth** apretarse contra algn/algo; **to p. (down) on sth** hacer presión sobre algo
(**b**) *(urge)* apremiar; **time presses** el tiempo apremia
3 *n* (**a**) **p. stud** botón *m* de presión
(**b**) *(machine)* prensa *f*; **to go to p.** *(of newspaper)* entrar en prensa
(**c**) *Press* prensa *f*; **the p.** la prensa; **to get a good/bad p.** tener buena/mala prensa; **p. agency** agencia *f* de prensa; **p. conference** rueda *f* de prensa; **p. cutting** recorte *m* de prensa
▸ **press on** *vi* seguir adelante

pressed [prest] *adj* **to be (hard) p. for** andar escaso(a) de; **I'd be hard p. to do it** me costaría mucho hacerlo

pressing ['presɪŋ] *adj* apremiante, urgente

press-up ['presʌp] *n Br* flexión *f* (de brazos)

pressure ['preʃə(r)] *n* presión *f*; *Med & Met* **high/low p.** altas/bajas presiones; **p. cooker** olla *f* a presión; **p. gauge** manómetro *m*; *Fig* **to bring p. (to bear) on sb** ejercer presión sobre algn

pressurize ['preʃəraɪz] *vt Fig* presionar; **pressurized cabin** cabina presurizada

prestige [pre'stiːʒ] *n* prestigio *m*

presumably [prɪ'zjuːməblɪ] *adv* es de suponer que

presume [prɪ'zjuːm] **1** *vt* suponer, presumir
2 *vi (suppose)* suponer; **we p. so/not** suponemos que sí/no

presumption [prɪ'zʌmpʃən] *n* (**a**) *(supposition)* suposición *f* (**b**) *(boldness)* osadía *f*; *(conceit)* presunción *f*

presumptuous [prɪ'zʌmptjʊəs] *adj* impertinente

> *Note that the Spanish word **presuntuoso** is a false friend and is never a translation for the English word **presumptuous**. In Spanish, **presuntuoso** means "vain" and "pretentious".*

presuppose [priːsə'pəʊz] *vt* presuponer

pretence [prɪ'tens] *n* (**a**) *(deception)* fingimiento *m*; **false pretences** estafa *f*; **under the p. of** so pretexto de (**b**) *(claim)* pretensión *f*

pretend [prɪ'tend] **1** *vt (feign)* fingir, aparentar; *(claim)* pretender
2 *vi (feign)* fingir

pretense [prɪ'tens] *n US* = **pretence**

pretention [prɪ'tenʃən] *n* pretensión *f*

pretentious [prɪ'tenʃəs] *adj* presuntuoso(a), pretencioso(a)

pretext ['priːtekst] *n* pretexto *m*; **on the p. of** so pretexto de

pretty ['prɪtɪ] **1** *adj* (**prettier, prettiest**) bonito(a), guapo(a)
2 *adv Fam* bastante; **p. much the same** más o menos lo mismo

prevail [prɪ'veɪl] *vi* (**a**) predominar (**b**) *(win through)* prevalecer (**c**) **to p. upon** *or* **on sb to do sth** *(persuade)* persuadir *or* convencer a algn para que haga algo

prevailing [prɪ'veɪlɪŋ] *adj (wind)* predominante; *(opinion)* general; *(condition, fashion)* actual

prevalent ['prevələnt] *adj* predominante; *(illness)* extendido(a)

prevaricate [prɪ'værɪkeɪt] *vi* andar con ambages

prevent [prɪ'vent] *vt* impedir; *(accident)* evitar; *(illness)* prevenir; **to p. sb from doing sth** impedir a algn hacer algo; **to p. sth from happening** evitar que pase algo

prevention [prɪ'venʃən] *n* prevención *f*

preventive [prɪ'ventɪv] *adj* preventivo(a)

preview ['priːvjuː] *n (of film etc)* preestreno *m*

previous ['priːvɪəs] **1** *adj* anterior, previo(a); **p. conviction** antecedente *m* penal
2 *adv* **p. to going** antes de ir

previously ['priːvɪəslɪ] *adv* anteriormente, previamente

prewar ['priːwɔː(r)] *adj* de antes de la guerra

prey [preɪ] **1** *n* presa *f*; *Fig* víctima *f*
2 *vi* **to p. on** alimentarse de

price [praɪs] **1** *n* precio *m*; **what p. is that**

coat? ¿cuánto cuesta el abrigo?; **p. list** lista *f* de precios; **p. tag** etiqueta *f*
   2 *vt (put price on)* poner un precio a; *(value)* valorar
priceless ['praɪslɪs] *adj* que no tiene precio
prick [prɪk] **1** *vt* picar; **to p. one's finger** pincharse el dedo; *Fig* **to p. up one's ears** aguzar el oído
   2 *n* (**a**) *(with pin)* pinchazo *m* (**b**) *very Fam (penis)* polla *f* (**c**) *very Fam Pej (person)* gilipollas *mf inv*
prickle ['prɪkəl] **1** *n* espina *f*; *(spike)* pincho *m*; *(sensation)* picor *m*
   2 *vt & vi* pinchar, picar
prickly ['prɪklɪ] *adj* (**pricklier, prickliest**) espinoso(a); *Fig (touchy)* enojadizo(a); **p. heat** = sarpullido por causa del calor; **p. pear** higo chumbo
pride [praɪd] **1** *n* orgullo *m*; *(arrogance)* soberbia *f*; **to take p. in sth** enorgullecerse de algo
   2 *vt* **to p. oneself on** enorgullecerse de
priest [priːst] *n* sacerdote *m*, cura *m*
priestess ['priːstɪs] *n* sacerdotisa *f*
priesthood ['priːsthʊd] *n (clergy)* clero *m*; *(office)* sacerdocio *m*
prig [prɪg] *n* gazmoño(a) *m,f*, mojigato(a) *m,f*
prim [prɪm] *adj* (**primmer, primmest**) **p. (and proper)** remilgado(a)
primaeval [praɪˈmiːvəl] *adj* primitivo(a)
primarily ['praɪmərɪlɪ] *adv* ante todo
primary ['praɪmərɪ] **1** *adj* fundamental, principal; **of p. importance** primordial; **p. colour** color primario; **p. education/school** enseñanza/escuela primaria
   2 *n US Pol* (elección *f*) primaria *f*
primate¹ ['praɪmeɪt] *n Rel* primado *m*
primate² ['praɪmeɪt] *n Zool* primate *m*
prime [praɪm] **1** *adj* (**a**) principal; *(major)* primordial; **P. Minister** primer(a) ministro(a) *m,f* (**b**) *(first-rate)* de primera; **p. number** número primo
   2 *n* **in the p. of life** en la flor de la vida
   3 *vt (pump, engine)* cebar; *(surface)* imprimar; *Fig (prepare)* preparar
primer¹ ['praɪmə(r)] *n (textbook)* cartilla *f*
primer² ['praɪmə(r)] *n (paint)* imprimación *f*
primeval [praɪˈmiːvəl] *adj* = **primaeval**
primitive ['prɪmɪtɪv] *adj* primitivo(a); *(method, tool)* rudimentario(a)
primrose ['prɪmrəʊz] *n* primavera *f*
Primus® ['praɪməs] *n* hornillo *m* de camping
prince [prɪns] *n* príncipe *m*; **P. Charming** Príncipe Azul

princess [prɪnˈses] *n* princesa *f*
principal ['prɪnsɪpəl] **1** *adj* principal
   2 *n Educ* director(a) *m,f*; *Th (in play)* protagonista *mf* principal
principle ['prɪnsɪpəl] *n* principio *m*; **in p.** en principio; **on p.** por principio
print [prɪnt] **1** *vt* (**a**) imprimir; *(publish)* publicar; *Fig* grabar; **printed matter** impresos *mpl* (**b**) *(write)* escribir con letra de imprenta
   2 *n* (**a**) *(of hand, foot)* huella *f* (**b**) *(written text)* letra *f*; **out of p.** agotado(a) (**c**) *Tex* estampado *m*; **p. skirt** falda estampada (**d**) *Art* grabado *m*; *Phot* copia *f*
   ▸ **print out** *vt sep Comput* imprimir
printer ['prɪntə(r)] *n (person)* impresor(a) *m,f*; *(machine)* impresora *f*
printing ['prɪntɪŋ] *n (industry)* imprenta *f*; *(process)* impresión *f*; *(print run)* tirada *f*; **p. press** prensa *f*
print-out ['prɪntaʊt] *n Comput* impresión *f*; *(copy)* copia impresa
prior ['praɪə(r)] *adj* previo(a), anterior; **p. to leaving** antes de salir
priority [praɪˈɒrɪtɪ] *n* prioridad *f*
prise [praɪz] *vt* **to p. sth open** abrir algo con palanca; **to p. sth off** arrancar algo
prism ['prɪzəm] *n* prisma *f*
prison ['prɪzən] *n* cárcel *f*, prisión *f*
prisoner ['prɪzənə(r)] *n* preso(a) *m,f*; **to hold sb p.** detener a algn; **p. of war** prisionero(a) *m,f* de guerra
privacy ['praɪvəsɪ, 'prɪvəsɪ] *n* intimidad *f*
private ['praɪvɪt] **1** *adj* privado(a); *(secretary)* particular; *(matter)* personal; *(letter)* confidencial; **one's p. life** la vida privada de uno; **p.** *(notice) (on road)* carretera privada; *(on gate)* propiedad privada; *(on envelope)* confidencial; **p. detective, Fam p. eye** detective *mf* privado(a); **p. school** escuela privada
   2 *n Mil* soldado raso
privately ['praɪvɪtlɪ] *adv* en privado; *(personally)* personalmente
privet ['prɪvɪt] *n* alheña *f*
privilege ['prɪvɪlɪdʒ] *n* privilegio *m*
privileged ['prɪvɪlɪdʒd] *adj* privilegiado(a)
privy ['prɪvɪ] **1** *adj Br* **P. Council** Consejo Privado; **to be p. to sth** estar enterado(a) de algo
   2 *n (lavatory)* retrete *m*
prize [praɪz] **1** *n* premio *m*
   2 *adj (first-class)* de primera (categoría *or* clase)
   3 *vt (value)* apreciar, valorar
prize-giving ['praɪzgɪvɪŋ] *n* distribución *f* de premios

prizewinner [ˈpraɪzwɪnə(r)] *n* premiado(a) *m,f*

pro¹ [prəʊ] *n* pro *m*; **the pros and cons of an issue** los pros y los contras de una cuestión

pro² [prəʊ] *n Fam* profesional *mf*

pro- [prəʊ] *pref (in favour of)* pro-

probability [prɒbəˈbɪlɪtɪ] *n* probabilidad *f*

probable [ˈprɒbəbəl] *adj* probable

probably [ˈprɒbəblɪ] *adv* probablemente

probation [prəˈbeɪʃən] *n Jur* **to be on p.** estar en libertad condicional; **to be on two months' p.** *(at work)* trabajar dos meses de prueba

probe [prəʊb] **1** *n Med & (in outer space)* sonda *f*; *(investigation)* sondeo *m*
2 *vt Med* sondar; *(investigate)* investigar
▸ **probe into** *vt insep* investigar

problem [ˈprɒbləm] *n* problema *m*

problematic(al) [prɒbləˈmætɪk(əl)] *adj* problemático(a); **it's p.** tiene sus problemas

procedure [prəˈsiːdʒə(r)] *n* procedimiento *m*; *(legal, business)* gestión *f*, trámite *m*

proceed [prəˈsiːd] *vi* seguir, proceder; **to p. to do sth** ponerse a hacer algo; **to p. to the next matter** pasar a la siguiente cuestión

proceedings [prəˈsiːdɪŋz] *npl (of meeting)* actas *fpl*; *(measures)* medidas *fpl*; *Jur* proceso *m*

proceeds [ˈprəʊsiːdz] *npl* ganancias *fpl*

process [ˈprəʊses] **1** *n* proceso *m*; *(method)* método *m*, sistema *m*; **in the p. of** en vías de
2 *vt (information)* tramitar; *(food)* tratar; *Comput* procesar

processing [ˈprəʊsesɪŋ] *n (of information)* evaluación *f*; *Comput* tratamiento *m*

procession [prəˈseʃən] *n* desfile *m*; *Rel* procesión *f*

proclaim [prəˈkleɪm] *vt* proclamar, declarar

proclamation [prɒkləˈmeɪʃən] *n* proclamación *f*

procrastinate [prəʊˈkræstɪneɪt] *vi* dejar las cosas para después

procure [prəˈkjʊə(r)] *vt* conseguir, procurarse

prod [prɒd] *vt (with stick etc)* golpear; *(push)* empujar

prodigal [ˈprɒdɪgəl] *adj* pródigo(a)

prodigious [prəˈdɪdʒəs] *adj* prodigioso(a)

prodigy [ˈprɒdɪdʒɪ] *n* prodigio *m*

produce 1 *vt* [prəˈdjuːs] **(a)** producir; *Ind* fabricar **(b)** *Th* dirigir; *Rad & TV* realizar; *Cin* producir **(c)** *(give birth to)* dar a luz a **(d)** *(document)* enseñar; *(bring out)* sacar
2 *n* [ˈprɒdjuːs] productos *mpl*; **p. of Spain** producto *m* de España

producer [prəˈdjuːsə(r)] *n* **(a)** productor(a) *m,f*; *Ind* fabricante *mf* **(b)** *Th* director(a) *m,f* de escena; *Rad & TV* realizador(a) *m,f*; *Cin* productor(a) *m,f*

product [ˈprɒdʌkt] *n* producto *m*

production [prəˈdʌkʃən] *n* **(a)** producción *f*; *Ind* fabricación *f* **(b)** *Th* representación *f*; *Rad & TV* realización *f*; *Cin* producción *f*; **p. line** cadena *f* de montaje

productive [prəˈdʌktɪv] *adj* productivo(a)

productivity [prɒdʌkˈtɪvɪtɪ] *n* productividad *f*

profane [prəˈfeɪn] *adj (secular)* profano(a); *(language)* blasfemo(a)

profess [prəˈfes] *vt (faith)* profesar; *(opinion)* expresar; *(claim)* pretender

profession [prəˈfeʃən] *n* profesión *f*

professional [prəˈfeʃənəl] **1** *adj* profesional; *(soldier)* de profesión; *(polished)* de gran calidad
2 *n* profesional *mf*

professor [prəˈfesə(r)] *n Univ Br* catedrático(a) *m,f*; *US* profesor(a) *m,f*

proficiency [prəˈfɪʃənsɪ] *n (in language)* capacidad *f*; *(in skill)* pericia *f*

proficient [prəˈfɪʃənt] *adj (in language)* experto(a); *(in skill)* hábil

profile [ˈprəʊfaɪl] *n* perfil *m*; **in p.** de perfil

profit [ˈprɒfɪt] **1** *n* **(a)** beneficio *m*, ganancia *f*; **to make a p. on** sacar beneficios de **(b)** *Fml (benefit)* provecho *m*
2 *vi Fig* sacar provecho; **to p. from** aprovecharse de

profitability [prɒfɪtəˈbɪlɪtɪ] *n* rentabilidad *f*

profitable [ˈprɒfɪtəbəl] *adj Com* rentable; *Fig (worthwhile)* provechoso(a)

profiteer [prɒfɪˈtɪə(r)] **1** *n* especulador(a) *m,f*
2 *vi* obtener beneficios excesivos

profound [prəˈfaʊnd] *adj* profundo(a)

profuse [prəˈfjuːs] *adj* profuso(a), abundante

profusely [prəˈfjuːslɪ] *adv* con profusión; **to sweat p.** sudar mucho

profusion [prəˈfjuːʒən] *n* profusión *f*, abundancia *f*

prognosis [prɒgˈnəʊsɪs] *n Med* pronóstico *m*; *Fig (prediction)* augurio *m*

program ['prəʊgræm] *Comput* **1** *n* programa *m*
    2 *vi & vt* programar
    3 *US* = **programme**
programer ['prəʊgræmər] *n US* = **programmer**
programme ['prəʊgræm] **1** *n* programa *m; (plan)* plan *m*
    2 *vt* (**a**) *(plan)* planear, planificar (**b**) *(computer)* programar
programmer ['prəʊgræmə(r)] *n* programador(a) *m,f*
progress 1 *n* ['prəʊgres] progreso *m; (development)* desarrollo *m; Med* mejora *f;* **to make p.** hacer progresos; **in p.** en curso
    2 *vi* [prəʊ'gres] avanzar; *(develop)* desarrollar; *(improve)* hacer progresos; *Med* mejorar
progressive [prə'gresɪv] *adj (increasing)* progresivo(a); *Pol* progresista
progressively [prə'gresɪvlɪ] *adv* progresivamente
prohibit [prə'hɪbɪt] *vt* prohibir; **to p. sb from doing sth** prohibir a algn hacer algo
prohibitive [prə'hɪbɪtɪv] *adj* prohibitivo(a)
project 1 *n* ['prɒdʒekt] proyecto *m; (plan)* plan *m; Educ* trabajo *m; US* **(housing) p.** = urbanización con viviendas de protección oficial
    2 *vt* [prə'dʒekt] proyectar, planear
    3 *vi (stick out)* sobresalir
projectile [prə'dʒektaɪl] *n Fml* proyectil *m*
projection [prə'dʒekʃən] *n* (**a**) *(overhang)* saliente *m* (**b**) *Cin* proyección *f* (**c**) *(forecast)* proyección *f*
projector [prə'dʒektə(r)] *n Cin* proyector *m*
proletariat [prəʊlɪ'eərɪət] *n* proletariado *m*
prolific [prə'lɪfɪk] *adj* prolífico(a)
prologue ['prəʊlɒg] *n* prólogo *m*
prolong [prə'lɒŋ] *vt* prolongar
prom [prɒm] *n Br Fam (seafront)* paseo marítimo; *Br (concert)* = concierto sinfónico en que parte del público está de pie; *US (school dance)* = baile de fin de curso
promenade [prɒmə'nɑːd] **1** *n (at seaside)* paseo marítimo
    2 *vi* pasearse
prominence ['prɒmɪnəns] *n* prominencia *f; Fig (importance)* importancia *f*
prominent ['prɒmɪnənt] *adj (standing out)* saliente; *Fig (important)* importante; *(famous)* eminente

promiscuous [prə'mɪskjʊəs] *adj* promiscuo(a)
promise ['prɒmɪs] **1** *n* promesa *f;* **to show p.** ser prometedor(a)
    2 *vt & vi* prometer
promising ['prɒmɪsɪŋ] *adj* prometedor(a)
promontory ['prɒməntərɪ] *n* promontorio *m*
promote [prə'məʊt] *vt* ascender; *(product)* promocionar; *(ideas)* fomentar; *Ftb* **they've been promoted** han subido
promoter [prə'məʊtə(r)] *n* promotor(a) *m,f*
promotion [prə'məʊʃən] *n (in rank)* promoción *f*, ascenso *m; (of product)* promoción; *(of arts etc)* fomento *m*
prompt ['prɒmpt] **1** *adj (quick)* rápido(a); *(punctual)* puntual
    2 *adv* **at two o'clock p.** a las dos en punto
    3 *vt* (**a**) *(motivate)* incitar; **to p. sb to do sth** instar a algn a hacer algo (**b**) *(actor)* apuntar
promptly ['prɒmptlɪ] *adv (quickly)* rápidamente; *(punctually)* puntualmente
prone [prəʊn] *adj* (**a**) **to be p. to do sth** ser propenso(a) a hacer algo (**b**) *Fml (face down)* boca abajo
prong [prɒŋ] *n* punta *f*, diente *m*
pronoun ['prəʊnaʊn] *n* pronombre *m*
pronounce [prə'naʊns] **1** *vt* pronunciar; *Fml (declare)* declarar
    2 *vi Fml* **to p. on sth** opinar sobre algo
pronounced [prə'naʊnst] *adj* pronunciado(a)
pronouncement [prə'naʊnsmənt] *n Fml* declaración *f*
pronunciation [prənʌnsɪ'eɪʃən] *n* pronunciación *f*
proof [pruːf] **1** *n* prueba *f*
    2 *adj* (**a**) *(secure)* a prueba de (**b**) **this rum is 70 percent p.** este ron tiene 70 grados
    3 *vt* impermeabilizar
prop¹ [prɒp] **1** *n (support)* puntal *m; Fig* sostén *m*
    2 *vt (support)* apoyar; *Fig* sostener
    ▸ **prop up** *vt sep* apoyar
prop² [prɒp] *n Fam Th* accesorio *m*
propaganda [prɒpə'gændə] *n* propaganda *f*
propel [prə'pel] *vt* propulsar
propeller [prə'pelə(r)] *n* hélice *f*
propelling pencil [prə'pelɪŋ'pensəl] *n* portaminas *m inv*
propensity [prə'pensɪtɪ] *n Fml* propensión *f*
proper ['prɒpə(r)] *adj* (**a**) adecuado(a),

correcto(a); **the p. time** el momento oportuno (**b**) *(real)* real, auténtico(a); *(actual, exact)* propiamente dicho(a) (**c**) *(characteristic)* propio(a); *Ling* **p. noun** nombre propio

properly ['prɒpəlɪ] *adv (suitably, correctly, decently)* correctamente; **it wasn't p. closed** no estaba bien cerrado(a); **she refused, quite p.** se negó, y con razón

property ['prɒpətɪ] *n* (**a**) *(quality)* propiedad *f* (**b**) *(possession)* propiedad *f*, posesión *f*; **personal p.** bienes *mpl*; **public p.** dominio público (**c**) *(estate)* finca *f*

prophecy ['prɒfɪsɪ] *n* profecía *f*

prophesy ['prɒfɪsaɪ] *vt (predict)* predecir; *Rel* profetizar

prophet ['prɒfɪt] *n* profeta *mf*

proportion [prə'pɔːʃən] *n* proporción *f*; *(part, quantity)* parte *f*; **in p. to** *or* **with** en proporción a

proportional [prə'pɔːʃənəl] *adj* proporcional (**to** a); *Pol* **p. representation** representación *f* proporcional

proportionate [prə'pɔːʃənɪt] *adj* proporcional

proposal [prə'pəʊzəl] *n* propuesta *f*; *(suggestion)* sugerencia *f*; **p. of marriage** propuesta de matrimonio

propose [prə'pəʊz] **1** *vt* proponer; *(suggest)* sugerir; *Fml (intend)* tener la intención de
   2 *vi* declararse

proposition [prɒpə'zɪʃən] *n* propuesta *f*; *Math* proposición *f*

proprietor [prə'praɪətə(r)] *n* propietario(a) *m,f*

propriety [prə'praɪətɪ] *n (decency)* decoro *m*

propulsion [prə'pʌlʃən] *n* propulsión *f*

prosaic [prəʊ'zeɪɪk] *adj* prosaico(a)

prose [prəʊz] *n Lit* prosa *f*; *Educ* texto *m* para traducir

prosecute ['prɒsɪkjuːt] *vt* procesar

prosecution [prɒsɪ'kjuːʃən] *n (action)* proceso *m*, juicio *m*; **the p.** la acusación

prosecutor ['prɒsɪkjuːtə(r)] *n* acusador(a) *m,f*

prospect 1 *n* ['prɒspekt] *(outlook)* perspectiva *f*; *(hope)* esperanza *f*; **the job has prospects** es un trabajo con porvenir
   2 *vt* [prə'spekt] explorar
   3 *vi* **to p. for gold/oil** buscar oro/petróleo

prospective [prə'spektɪv] *adj (future)* futuro(a); *(possible)* eventual, probable

prospector [prə'spektə(r)] *n* **gold p.** buscador(a) *m,f* del oro

prospectus [prə'spektəs] *n* prospecto *m*

prosper ['prɒspə(r)] *vi* prosperar

prosperity [prɒ'sperɪtɪ] *n* prosperidad *f*

prosperous ['prɒspərəs] *adj* próspero(a)

prostitute ['prɒstɪtjuːt] *n* prostituta *f*

prostitution [prɒstɪ'tjuːʃən] *n* prostitución *f*

prostrate ['prɒstreɪt] *adj (face down)* boca abajo; **p. with grief** deshecho(a) de dolor

protagonist [prəʊ'tægənɪst] *n* protagonista *mf*

protect [prə'tekt] *vt* proteger; *(interests etc)* salvaguardar; **to p. sb from sth** proteger a algn de algo

protection [prə'tekʃən] *n* protección *f*

protective [prə'tektɪv] *adj* protector(a)

protégé ['prɒtəʒeɪ] *n* protegido *m*

protégée ['prɒtəʒeɪ] *n* protegida *f*

protein ['prəʊtiːn] *n* proteína *f*

protest 1 *n* ['prəʊtest] protesta *f*; *(complaint)* queja *f*
   2 *vt* [prə'test] *US* protestar en contra de
   3 *vi Br* protestar

Protestant ['prɒtɪstənt] *adj & n* protestante *(mf)*

protester [prə'testə(r)] *n* manifestante *mf*

protocol ['prəʊtəkɒl] *n* protocolo *m*

prototype ['prəʊtətaɪp] *n* prototipo *m*

protracted [prə'træktɪd] *adj* prolongado(a)

protrude [prə'truːd] *vi Fml* sobresalir

protuberance [prə'tjuːbərəns] *n Fml* protuberancia *f*

proud [praʊd] *adj* orgulloso(a); *(arrogant)* soberbio(a)

prove [pruːv] *vt* (**a**) probar, demostrar; *Math* comprobar; **to p. oneself** dar pruebas de valor (**b**) **it proved to be disastrous** *(turned out)* resultó ser desastroso(a)

proverb ['prɒvɜːb] *n* refrán *m*, proverbio *m*

provide [prə'vaɪd] **1** *vt* proporcionar; *(supplies)* suministrar, proveer
   2 *vi* proveer; **to p. for sb** mantener a algn

provided [prə'vaɪdɪd] *conj* **p. (that)** con tal de que

providing [prə'vaɪdɪŋ] *conj* = **provided**

province ['prɒvɪns] *n* provincia *f*; *Fig (field of knowledge)* campo *m*

provincial [prə'vɪnʃəl] **1** *adj* provincial; *Pej* provinciano(a)
   2 *n Pej (person)* provinciano(a) *m,f*

provision [prə'vɪʒən] *n* provisión *f*; *(supply)* suministro *m*; **provisions** *(food)* provisiones *fpl*, víveres *mpl*

provisional [prə'vɪʒənəl] *adj* provisional
proviso [prə'vaɪzəʊ] *n* with the p. that a condición de que
provocation [prɒvə'keɪʃən] *n* provocación *f*
provocative [prə'vɒkətɪv] *adj* provocador(a); *(flirtatious)* provocativo(a)
provoke [prə'vəʊk] *vt* provocar
prow [praʊ] *n* proa *f*
prowess ['praʊɪs] *n* destreza *f*
prowl [praʊl] **1** *n* merodeo *m*; **to be on the p.** merodear, rondar
  2 *vi* merodear; *Fam* **to p. about** *or* **around** rondar
prowler ['praʊlə(r)] *n Fam* merodeador *m*
proximity [prɒk'sɪmɪtɪ] *n* proximidad *f*; **in p. to, in the p. of** cerca de
proxy ['prɒksɪ] *n Jur (power)* poderes *mpl*; *(person)* apoderado(a) *m,f*; **by p.** por poderes
prudence ['pruːdəns] *n* prudencia *f*
prudent ['pruːdənt] *adj* prudente
prudish ['pruːdɪʃ] *adj* remilgado(a)
prune¹ [pruːn] *n* ciruela pasa
prune² [pruːn] *vt (roses etc)* podar; *Fig* acortar
pry [praɪ] *vi* curiosear, husmear; **to p. into sb's affairs** meterse en asuntos ajenos
PS, ps [piː'es] *(abbr* **postscript)** P.S., P.D.
psalm [sɑːm] *n* salmo *m*
pseudo- ['sjuːdəʊ] *pref* pseudo-, seudo-
pseudonym ['sjuːdənɪm] *n* (p)seudónimo *m*
psyche ['saɪkɪ] *n* psique *f*
psychiatric [saɪkɪ'ætrɪk] *adj* psiquiátrico(a)
psychiatrist [saɪ'kaɪətrɪst] *n* psiquiatra *mf*
psychiatry [saɪ'kaɪətrɪ] *n* psiquiatría *f*
psychic ['saɪkɪk] **1** *adj* psíquico(a)
  2 *n* médium *mf*
psychoanalysis [saɪkəʊə'nælɪsɪs] *n* psicoanálisis *f*
psychoanalyst [saɪkəʊ'ænəlɪst] *n* psicoanalista *mf*
psychological [saɪkə'lɒdʒɪkəl] *adj* psicológico(a)
psychologist [saɪ'kɒlədʒɪst] *n* psicólogo(a) *m,f*
psychology [saɪ'kɒlədʒɪ] *n* psicología *f*
psychopath ['saɪkəʊpæθ] *n* psicópata *mf*
psychotherapist ['saɪkəʊ'θerəpɪst] *n* psicoterapeuta *mf*
psychotherapy ['saɪkəʊ'θerəpɪ] *n* psicoterapia *f*

psychotic [saɪ'kɒtɪk] *adj & n* psicótico(a) *(m,f)*
PT [piː'tiː] *n (abbr* **physical training)** educación *f* física
PTA [piːtiː'eɪ] *n (abbr* **Parent-Teacher Association)** = asociación de padres de alumnos y profesores, ≃ APA *f*
PTO, pto [piːtiː'əʊ] *(abbr* **please turn over)** sigue
pub [pʌb] *n Br Fam* bar *m*, pub *m*
puberty ['pjuːbətɪ] *n* pubertad *f*
pubic ['pjuːbɪk] *adj* púbico(a)
public ['pʌblɪk] **1** *adj* público(a); **to make sth p.** hacer público algo; *Com* **to go p.** *(of company)* pasar a cotizar en Bolsa; **p. company** empresa pública; **p. convenience** servicios *mpl*, aseos *mpl*; **p. holiday** fiesta *f* nacional; *Br* **p. house** pub *m*, taberna *f*; *Br* **p. limited company** sociedad anónima; **p. opinion** opinión pública; *Br* **p. prosecutor** fiscal *m*; **p. relations** relaciones públicas; **p. school** *Br* colegio privado; *US* colegio público; **p. transport** transporte público
  2 *n* **the p.** el público; **in p.** en público
public-address system ['pʌblɪkə'dresɪstəm] *n* megafonía *f*
publican ['pʌblɪkən] *n* tabernero(a) *m,f*
publication [pʌblɪ'keɪʃən] *n* publicación *f*
publicity [pʌ'blɪsɪtɪ] *n* publicidad *f*
publicize ['pʌblɪsaɪz] *vt (make public)* hacer público(a); *(advertise)* hacer publicidad a
public-spirited [pʌblɪk'spɪrɪtɪd] *adj* de espíritu cívico
publish ['pʌblɪʃ] *vt* publicar, editar
publisher ['pʌblɪʃə(r)] *n (person)* editor(a) *m,f*; *(firm)* (casa *f*) editorial *f*
publishing ['pʌblɪʃɪŋ] *n (business)* industria *f* editorial; **p. company** *or* **house** casa *f* editorial
pucker ['pʌkə(r)] *vt (lips, brow)* fruncir, arrugar
pudding ['pʊdɪŋ] *n Culin* pudín *m*; *(dessert)* postre *m*; **Christmas p.** = pudín a base de frutos secos típico de Navidad; **p. basin** cuenco *m*; **steamed p.** budín *m*
puddle ['pʌdəl] *n* charco *m*
Puerto Rican ['pweətəʊ'riːkən] *adj & n* portorriqueño(a) *(m,f)*, puertorriqueño(a) *(m,f)*
Puerto Rico ['pweətəʊ'riːkəʊ] *n* Puerto Rico
puff [pʌf] **1** *n (of wind)* racha *f*; *(of smoke)* bocanada *f*; **p. pastry** pasta *f* de hojaldre
  2 *vi (person)* jadear, resoplar; *(train)* echar humo; **to p. on one's pipe** chupar la pipa

3 *vt (cigarette)* dar una calada a
▸ **puff up** *vi* hincharse
puffy ['pʌfɪ] *adj* (**puffier, puffiest**) hinchado(a)
pugnacious [pʌg'neɪʃəs] *adj* belicoso(a)
pull [pʊl] **1** *n* (**a**) **to give sth a p.** *(tug)* dar un tirón a algo (**b**) *(of engine)* tracción *f*; *Fig (attraction)* atracción *f*; *(influence)* enchufe *m*
2 *vt* (**a**) *(tug)* dar un tirón a; **to p. a muscle** sufrir un tirón en un músculo; **to p. the trigger** apretar el gatillo; **to p. to pieces** hacer pedazos; *Fig* poner algo por los suelos; *Fig* **to p. sb's leg** tomar el pelo a algn (**b**) *(draw)* tirar, arrastrar; *Fig* **to p. one's weight** hacer su parte del trabajo (**c**) *(draw out)* sacar (**d**) *Fam (people)* atraer
3 *vi (drag)* tirar; **to p. alongside sb** acercarse a algn
▸ **pull apart** *vt sep* desmontar; *Fig (criticize)* poner por los suelos
▸ **pull down** *vt sep (building)* derribar
▸ **pull in 1** *vt sep (crowds)* atraer
2 *vi (train)* entrar en la estación; *(stop)* parar
▸ **pull off 1** *vt sep Fam (carry out)* llevar a cabo
2 *vi (vehicle)* arrancar
▸ **pull out 1** *vt sep (withdraw)* retirar
2 *vi Aut* **to p. out to overtake** salir para adelantar
▸ **pull over** *vi* hacerse a un lado
▸ **pull through** *vi* reponerse, restablecerse
▸ **pull together** *vt sep* **to p. oneself together** calmarse
▸ **pull up 1** *vt sep* (**a**) *(uproot)* desarraigar; **to p. up one's socks** subirse los calcetines; *Fig* espabilarse (**b**) *(chair)* acercar
2 *vi (stop)* pararse
pulley ['pʊlɪ] *n* polea *f*
pullover ['pʊləʊvə(r)] *n* jersey *m*, suéter *m*, pulóver *m*, *Andes* chompa *f*, *Urug* buzo *m*
pulp [pʌlp] **1** *n (of paper, wood)* pasta *f*; *(of fruit)* pulpa *f*; *Fam Fig (book etc)* basura *f*
2 *vt* reducir a pulpa
pulpit ['pʊlpɪt] *n* púlpito *m*
pulsate [pʌl'seɪt] *vi* vibrar, palpitar
pulse¹ [pʌls] *n Anat* pulso *m*
pulse² [pʌls] *n Bot & Culin* legumbre *f*
pumice ['pʌmɪs] *n* **p. (stone)** piedra *f* pómez
pummel ['pʌməl] *vt* aporrear
pump¹ [pʌmp] **1** *n* bomba *f*
2 *vt* bombear; **to p. sth in/out** meter/

sacar algo con una bomba; *Fam Fig* **to p. sb for information** sonsacar información a algn
▸ **pump out** *vt sep (empty)* vaciar
▸ **pump up** *vt sep (tyre)* inflar
pump² [pʌmp] *n (shoe)* zapatilla *f*
pumpkin ['pʌmpkɪn] *n* calabaza *f*
pun [pʌn] *n* juego *m* de palabras
punch¹ [pʌntʃ] **1** *n (for making holes)* perforadora *f*; *(for tickets)* taladradora *f*; *(for leather etc)* punzón *m*
2 *vt (make hole in)* perforar; *(ticket)* picar; *(leather)* punzar
punch² [pʌntʃ] **1** *n (blow)* puñetazo *m*; *(in boxing)* pegada *f*; *Fig* **it lacks p.** le falta fuerza; **p. line** remate *m (de un chiste)*
2 *vt (with fist)* dar un puñetazo a
punch³ [pʌntʃ] *n (drink)* ponche *m*
punch-up ['pʌntʃʌp] *n Fam* pelea *f*
punctual ['pʌŋktjʊəl] *adj* puntual
punctuate ['pʌŋktjʊeɪt] *vt* puntuar; *Fig* salpicar
punctuation [pʌŋktjʊ'eɪʃən] *n* puntuación *f*
puncture ['pʌŋktʃə(r)] **1** *n* pinchazo *m*
2 *vt (tyre)* pinchar
pundit ['pʌndɪt] *n Fam* experto(a) *m,f*
pungent ['pʌndʒənt] *adj (smell)* acre; *(taste)* fuerte
punish ['pʌnɪʃ] *vt* castigar
punishable ['pʌnɪʃəbəl] *adj* castigable, punible
punishment ['pʌnɪʃmənt] *n* castigo *m*
punk [pʌŋk] *n Fam* (**a**) punk *mf*; **p. music** música *f* punk (**b**) *US* mamón *m*
punt [pʌnt] **1** *n (boat)* batea *f*
2 *vi* ir en batea
punter ['pʌntə(r)] *n Br (gambler)* jugador(a) *m,f*, *(customer)* cliente(a) *m,f*
puny ['pjuːnɪ] *adj* (**punier, puniest**) enclenque, endeble
pup [pʌp] *n* cachorro(a) *m,f*
pupil¹ ['pjuːpəl] *n Educ* alumno(a) *m,f*
pupil² ['pjuːpəl] *n Anat* pupila *f*
puppet ['pʌpɪt] *n* títere *m*
puppy ['pʌpɪ] *n* cachorro(a) *m,f*, perrito *m*
purchase ['pɜːtʃɪs] **1** *n* compra *f*
2 *vt* comprar; **purchasing power** poder adquisitivo
purchaser ['pɜːtʃɪsə(r)] *n* comprador(a) *m,f*
pure [pjʊə(r)] *adj* puro(a)
purée ['pjʊəreɪ] *n* puré *m*
purely [pjʊəlɪ] *adv* simplemente
purge [pɜːdʒ] **1** *n* purga *f*
2 *vt* purgar
purify ['pjʊərɪfaɪ] *vt* purificar

purl [pɜːl] *vt (in knitting)* hacer punto del revés

purple ['pɜːpəl] *adj* morado(a), purpúreo(a); **to go p. (in the face)** ponerse morado(a)

purport [pɜːˈpɔːt] *vi Fml* pretender; **to p. to be sth** pretender ser algo

purpose ['pɜːpəs] *n* (**a**) propósito *m*, intención *f*; **on p.** a propósito (**b**) *(use)* utilidad *f*

purposeful ['pɜːpəsfʊl] *adj (resolute)* decidido(a), resoluto(a)

purr [pɜː(r)] *vi (cat)* ronronear; *(engine)* zumbar

purse [pɜːs] **1** *n Br* monedero *m*; *US (bag)* bolso *m*, cartera *f*, *Méx* bolsa *f*; *(prize money)* premio *m* en metálico

2 *vt* **to p. one's lips** apretarse los labios

purser ['pɜːsə(r)] *n* contador(a) *m,f*

pursue [pəˈsjuː] *vt (criminal)* perseguir; *(person)* seguir; *(pleasure)* buscar; *(career)* ejercer

pursuer [pəˈsjuːə(r)] *n Fml* perseguidor(a) *m,f*

pursuit [pəˈsjuːt] *n (of criminal)* persecución *f*; *(of animal)* caza *f*; *(of pleasure)* búsqueda *f*; *(pastime)* pasatiempo *m*

purveyor [pəˈveɪə(r)] *n Fml* proveedor(a) *m,f*

pus [pʌs] *n* pus *m*

push [pʊʃ] **1** *n* empujón *m*; *Fig (drive)* brío *m*, dinamismo *m*

2 *vt* (**a**) empujar; *(button)* pulsar, apretar; **to p. one's finger into a hole** meter el dedo en un agujero (**b**) *Fig (pressurize)* instar; *(harass)* acosar; *Fam* **to be (hard) pushed for time** andar justo(a) de tiempo (**c**) *Fam (product)* promover; **to p. drugs** pasar droga

3 *vi* empujar

▸ **push aside** *vt sep (object)* apartar

▸ **push in** *vi* colarse

▸ **push off** *vi (in boat)* desatracar; *Fam* **p. off!** ¡lárgate!

▸ **push on** *vi (continue)* seguir adelante

▸ **push through** *vt sep* abrirse paso entre

pushchair ['pʊʃtʃeə(r)] *n Br* sillita *f* (de ruedas)

pusher ['pʊʃə(r)] *n Fam (of drugs)* camello *m*

pushover ['pʊʃəʊvə(r)] *n Fam* **it's a p.** está chupado; **she's a p.** es un ligue fácil

push-up ['pʊʃʌp] *n* flexión *f* (de brazos)

pushy ['pʊʃɪ] *adj* (**pushier, pushiest**) *Fam* agresivo(a)

puss [pʊs], **pussy** ['pʊsɪ] *n Fam* minino *m*

put [pʊt] **1** *vt* (*pt & pp* **put**) (**a**) poner; *(place)* colocar; *(insert)* meter; **to p. to bed** acostar a; **to p. a picture up on the wall** colgar un cuadro en la pared; **to p. a stop to sth** poner término a algo; *Fig* **to p. one's foot in it** meter la pata

(**b**) *(present)* presentar, exponer; **to p. a question to sb** hacer una pregunta a algn

(**c**) *(express)* expresar, decir; **to p. it mildly** y me quedo corto; **to p. sth simply** explicar algo de manera sencilla

(**d**) *(estimate)* calcular

(**e**) *(money)* ingresar; *(invest)* invertir

2 *vi Naut* **to p. to sea** zarpar

3 *adv* **to stay p.** quedarse quieto(a)

▸ **put about** *vt sep (rumour)* hacer correr

▸ **put across** *vt sep (idea etc)* comunicar

▸ **put aside** *vt sep (money)* ahorrar; *(time)* reservar

▸ **put away** *vt sep (tidy away)* recoger; *Fam (eat)* zamparse; *(save money)* ahorrar

▸ **put back** *vt sep (postpone)* aplazar; **to p. the clock back** retrasar la hora

▸ **put by** *vt sep (money)* ahorrar

▸ **put down** *vt sep (set down)* dejar; *(suppress)* sofocar; *(humiliate)* humillar; *(criticize)* criticar; *(animal)* provocar la muerte de; *(write down)* apuntar

▸ **put down to** *vt sep* achacar a

▸ **put forward** *vt sep (theory)* exponer; *(proposal)* hacer; **to p. one's name forward for sth** presentarse como candidato(a) para algo

▸ **put in 1** *vt sep (install)* instalar; *(complaint, request)* presentar; *(time)* pasar

2 *vi Naut* hacer escala (**at** en)

▸ **put off** *vt sep (postpone)* aplazar; **to p. sb off (doing) sth** *(dissuade)* disuadir a algn de (hacer) algo

▸ **put on** *vt sep (clothes)* poner, ponerse; *(show)* montar; *(concert)* dar; *(switch on) (radio)* poner; *(light)* encender; *(water, gas)* abrir; **to p. on weight** aumentar de peso; **to p. on the brakes** frenar; *Fig* **to p. on a straight face** poner cara de serio(a)

▸ **put out** *vt sep (light, fire)* apagar; *(place outside)* sacar; *(extend) (arm)* extender; *(tongue)* sacar; *(hand)* tender; *(spread) (rumour)* hacer correr; *(annoy)* molestar; *(inconvenience)* incordiar; *(anger)* **to be p. out by sth** enojarse por algo

▸ **put through** *vt sep Tel* **p. me through to Pat, please** póngame con Pat, por favor

▸ **put together** *vt sep (join)* unir, reunir; *(assemble)* armar, montar

▸ **put up** *vt sep (raise)* levantar, subir; *(picture)* colocar; *(curtains)* colgar; *(building)* construir; *(tent)* armar; *(prices)*

subir, aumentar; *(accommodate)* alojar, hospedar; **to p. up a fight** ofrecer resistencia

▸ **put up to** *vt sep* **to p. sb up to sth** incitar a algn a hacer algo

▸ **put up with** *vt insep* aguantar, soportar

putrid ['pjuːtrɪd] *adj Fml* putrefacto(a)

putt [pʌt] **1** *n* tiro *m* al hoyo

　2 *vt & vi* tirar al hoyo

putting ['pʌtɪŋ] *n* **p. green** minigolf *m*

putty ['pʌtɪ] *n* masilla *f*

puzzle ['pʌzəl] **1** *n* rompecabezas *m inv*; *(crossword)* crucigrama *m*; *Fig (mystery)* misterio *m*

　2 *vt* dejar perplejo(a); **to be puzzled about sth** no entender algo

▸ **puzzle over** *vt insep* **to p. over sth** dar vueltas a algo (en la cabeza)

puzzling ['pʌzlɪŋ] *adj* extraño(a), curioso(a)

PVC [piːviːˈsiː] *n* (*abbr* **polyvinyl chloride**) PVC *m*

pygmy ['pɪgmɪ] *n* pigmeo(a) *m,f*; *Fig* enano(a) *m,f*

pyjamas [pəˈdʒɑːməz] *npl* pijama *m*

pylon ['paɪlən] *n* torre *f* (de conducción eléctrica)

pyramid ['pɪrəmɪd] *n* pirámide *f*

Pyrenees [pɪrəˈniːz] *npl* **the P.** los Pirineos

Pyrex® ['paɪreks] *n* pírex® *m*

python ['paɪθən] *n* pitón *m*

Q, q [kjuː] *n (the letter)* Q, q *f*
quack [kwæk] **1** *n* (**a**) *(of duck)* graznido *m* (**b**) *Fam (doctor)* curandero(a) *m,f*
  2 *vi* graznar
quad [kwɒd] *n Fam* (**a**) *Br (of school, university)* patio *m* interior (**b**) *(quadruplet)* cuatrillizo(a) *m,f*
quadrangle [ˈkwɒdræŋgəl] *n* (**a**) *Geom* cuadrángulo *m* (**b**) *(courtyard)* patio *m* interior
quadruple [ˈkwɒdrʊpəl, kwɒˈdruːpəl] **1** *n* cuádruplo *m*
  2 *adj* cuádruple
  3 *vt* cuadruplicar
  4 *vi* cuadruplicarse
quadruplet [ˈkwɒdrʊplɪt, kwɒˈdruːplɪt] *n* cuatrillizo(a) *m,f*
quagmire [ˈkwægmaɪə(r), ˈkwɒgmaɪə(r)] *n (land)* cenagal *m*
quail¹ [kweɪl] *n Orn* codorniz *f*
quail² [kweɪl] *vi Fig* encogerse
quaint [kweɪnt] *adj (picturesque)* pintoresco(a); *(original)* singular
quake [kweɪk] **1** *vi* temblar
  2 *n Fam* temblor *m* de tierra
Quaker [ˈkweɪkə(r)] *n* cuáquero(a) *m,f*
qualification [kwɒlɪfɪˈkeɪʃən] *n* (**a**) *(ability)* aptitud *f* (**b**) *(requirement)* requisito *m* (**c**) *(diploma etc)* título *m* (**d**) *(reservation)* reserva *f*
qualified [ˈkwɒlɪfaɪd] *adj* (**a**) capacitado(a); **q. teacher** profesor titulado (**b**) **q. approval** *(modified)* aprobación *f* condicional
qualify [ˈkwɒlɪfaɪ] **1** *vt* (**a**) *(entitle)* capacitar (**b**) *(modify)* modificar; *(statement)* matizar; *Ling* calificar
  2 *vi* (**a**) **to q. as** *(doctor etc)* sacar el título de; **when did you q.?** ¿cuándo terminaste la carrera? (**b**) *(in competition)* quedar clasificado(a)
qualifying [ˈkwɒlɪfaɪŋ] *adj (round, exam)* eliminatorio(a)
quality [ˈkwɒlɪtɪ] *n* (**a**) *(excellence)* calidad *f*, **q. control** control *m* de calidad; *Br* **q. newspapers** prensa *f* no sensacionalista (**b**) *(attribute)* cualidad *f*
qualm [kwɑːm] *n* (**a**) *(scruple)* escrúpulo *m* (**b**) *(doubt)* duda *f*

quandary [ˈkwɒndərɪ, ˈkwɒndrɪ] *n* **to be in a q.** estar en un dilema
quango [ˈkwæŋgəʊ] *n* = organización semi-autónoma paralela
quantity [ˈkwɒntɪtɪ] *n* cantidad *f*
quarantine [ˈkwɒrəntiːn] *n* cuarentena *f*
quarrel [ˈkwɒrəl] **1** *n (argument)* riña *f*, pelea *f*; *(disagreement)* desacuerdo *m*
  2 *vi (argue)* pelearse, reñir; **to q. with sth** discrepar de algo
quarrelsome [ˈkwɒrəlsəm] *adj* camorrista
quarry¹ [ˈkwɒrɪ] *Min* **1** *n* cantera *f*
  2 *vt* extraer
quarry² [ˈkwɒrɪ] *n* presa *f*
quart [kwɔːt] *n (measurement)* = cuarto de galón *(Br = 1,13 l; US = 0,94 l)*
quarter [ˈkwɔːtə(r)] **1** *n* (**a**) cuarto *m*, cuarta parte; **a q. of an hour** un cuarto de hora; **a q. of a cake** la cuarta parte de un pastel
  (**b**) **it's a q.** *Br* **to** *or US* **of three** son las tres menos cuarto; **it's a q.** *Br* **past** *or US* **after six** son las seis y cuarto
  (**c**) *(three months)* trimestre *m*
  (**d**) *Br (weight)* cuarto *m* de libra
  (**e**) *US (coin)* cuarto *m* (de dólar)
  (**f**) *(district)* barrio *m*
  (**g**) **there was criticism from all quarters** *(areas, people)* todos lo criticaron
  (**h**) *(of moon)* cuarto *m*
  (**i**) **quarters** *(lodgings)* alojamiento *m*; *Mil* **officers' quarters** residencia *f* de oficiales; **at close quarters** muy cerca
  (**j**) *US Mus* **q. note** negra *f*
  2 *vt* (**a**) *(cut into quarters)* dividir en cuartos
  (**b**) *(accommodate)* alojar
quarterfinal [ˈkwɔːtəfaɪnəl] *n Sport* cuarto *m* de final
quarterly [ˈkwɔːtəlɪ] **1** *adj* trimestral
  2 *n* publicación *f* trimestral
  3 *adv* trimestralmente
quartermaster [ˈkwɔːtəmɑːstə(r)] *n* (**a**) *Mil* oficial *m* de intendencia (**b**) *Naut* cabo *m* de la Marina
quartet(te) [kwɔːˈtet] *n* cuarteto *m*
quartz [kwɔːts] *n* cuarzo *m*; **q. watch** reloj *m* de cuarzo

quash [kwɒʃ] *vt Jur* anular; *(uprising)* aplastar

quasi ['kwɑːzɪ, 'kweɪzaɪ, 'kweɪsaɪ] *pref* cuasi

quaver ['kweɪvə(r)] **1** *n* (**a**) *Mus* corchea *f* (**b**) *(in voice)* temblor *m*
2 *vi (voice)* temblar

quay(side) ['kiː(saɪd)] *n* muelle *m*

queasy ['kwiːzɪ] *adj* (**queasier, queasiest**) **to feel q.** *(ill)* tener náuseas

queen [kwiːn] *n* (**a**) reina *f* (**b**) *Fam Pej* loca *f*, marica *m*

queer [kwɪə(r)] **1** *adj* (**a**) *(strange)* extraño(a), raro(a) (**b**) *Fam (mad)* loco(a) (**c**) *Fam (unwell)* mareado(a) (**d**) *Fam Pej* maricón
2 *n Fam Pej* marica *m*, maricón *m*

quell [kwel] *vt* reprimir

quench [kwentʃ] *vt* apagar

querulous ['kweruːləs, 'kwerjuːləs] *adj Fml* quejumbroso(a)

query ['kwɪərɪ] **1** *n (question)* pregunta *f*
2 *vt (ask questions about)* preguntar acerca de; *(have doubts about)* poner en duda

quest [kwest] *n Literary* búsqueda *f*, busca *f*

question ['kwestʃən] **1** *n* (**a**) *(interrogative)* pregunta *f*; **to ask sb a q.** hacer una pregunta a algn; **he did it without q.** lo hizo sin rechistar; **q. mark** signo *m* de interrogación; *Fig* interrogante *m*
(**b**) *(problem, issue)* asunto *m*, cuestión *f*; **it's a q. of two hours** es cuestión de dos horas
(**c**) *(doubt)* duda *f*; **beyond q.** fuera de duda; **in q.** en duda; **to call sth into q.** poner algo en duda
(**d**) **out of the q.** imposible; **that's out of the q.!** ¡ni hablar!
(**e**) *Educ* problema *m*
2 *vt (ask questions of)* hacer preguntas a; *(interrogate)* interrogar; *(query)* poner en duda

questionable ['kwestʃənəbəl] *adj (doubtful)* dudoso(a); *(debatable)* discutible

questionnaire [kwestʃə'neə(r)] *n* cuestionario *m*

queue [kjuː] *Br* **1** *n* cola *f*
2 *vi* **to q. (up)** hacer cola

quibble ['kwɪbəl] **1** *n* pega *f*
2 *vi* poner pegas (**with** a); *Fam* buscarle tres pies al gato

quiche [kiːʃ] *n* quiche *m or f*

quick [kwɪk] *adj* (**a**) *(fast)* rápido(a); **a q. look** un vistazo; **a q. snack** un bocado; **be q.!** ¡date prisa! (**b**) *(clever)* espabilado(a);

(wit) agudo(a) (**c**) **she has a q. temper** se enfada con nada

quicken ['kwɪkən] **1** *vt* acelerar; **to q. one's pace** acelerar el paso
2 *vi (speed up)* acelerarse

quickly ['kwɪklɪ] *adv* rápidamente, de prisa

quickness ['kwɪknɪs] *n* (**a**) *(speed)* rapidez *f* (**b**) *(of wit)* agudeza *f*, viveza *f*

quicksand ['kwɪksænd] *n* arenas movedizas

quicksilver ['kwɪksɪlvə(r)] *n* mercurio *m*

quick-witted [kwɪk'wɪtɪd] *adj* agudo(a)

quid [kwɪd] *n* (*pl* **quid**) *Br Fam* libra *f* (esterlina)

quiet ['kwaɪət] **1** *n* (**a**) *(silence)* silencio *m* (**b**) *(calm)* tranquilidad *f*
2 *adj* (**a**) *(silent)* silencioso(a); *(street)* tranquilo(a); **a q. voice** una voz suave; **keep q.!** ¡silencio! (**b**) *(calm)* tranquilo(a) (**c**) *Com & Fin* **business is q. today** hoy hay poco negocio (**d**) *(person)* reservado(a) (**e**) *(secret)* confidencial (**f**) *(not showy) (clothes)* sobrio(a); *(colours)* apagado(a) (**g**) *(ceremony, dinner)* intimo(a)
2 *vt US* calmar
3 *vi US* calmarse

quieten ['kwaɪətən] **1** *vt (silence)* callar; *(calm)* calmar
2 *vi (silence)* callarse; *(calm)* calmarse
▸ **quieten down** *Br* **1** *vt sep* calmar
2 *vi* calmarse

quietly ['kwaɪətlɪ] *adv* (**a**) *(silently)* silenciosamente; **he spoke q.** habló en voz baja (**b**) *(calmly)* tranquilamente (**c**) *(discreetly)* discretamente

quietness ['kwaɪətnɪs] *n* (**a**) *(silence)* silencio *m* (**b**) *(calm)* tranquilidad *f*

quill [kwɪl] *n (feather, pen)* pluma *f*; *(of porcupine)* púa *f*

quilt [kwɪlt] **1** *n* edredón *m*
2 *vt* acolchar

quin [kwɪn] *n Fam* quintillizo(a) *m,f*

quinine ['kwɪniːn, *US* 'kwamaɪn] *n* quinina *f*

quint [kwɪnt] *n Fam US* = **quin**

quintessential [kwɪntɪ'senʃəl] *adj* fundamental

quintet(te) [kwɪn'tet] *n* quinteto *m*

quintuple ['kwɪntjʊpəl, kwɪn'tjuːpəl] **1** *adj* quíntuplo(a)
2 *n* quíntuplo *m*
3 *vt* quintuplicar

quintuplet ['kwɪntjʊplɪt, kwɪn'tjuːplɪt] *n* quintillizo(a) *m,f*

quip [kwɪp] **1** *n* salida *f*; *(joke)* chiste *m*
2 *vi* bromear

quirk [kwɜːk] *n* (**a**) *(peculiarity)* manía *f*

(**b**) *(of fate)* arbitrariedad *f*

quit [kwɪt] **1** *vt* (*pt & pp* **quitted** *or* **quit**) (**a**) *(leave)* dejar, abandonar (**b**) **q. making that noise!** ¡deja de hacer ese ruido!

2 *vi* (**a**) *(go)* irse; *(give up)* dimitir (**b**) *(cease)* dejar de hacer algo

3 *adj* **let's call it quits** dejémoslo estar

> Note that the Spanish verb **quitar** is a false friend and is never a translation for the English verb **to quit**. In Spanish, **quitar** means both "to remove" and "to take away".

quite [kwaɪt] *adv* (**a**) *(entirely)* totalmente; **she's q. right** tiene toda la razón (**b**) *(rather)* bastante; **q. a few** bastantes; **q. a while** un buen rato; **q. often** con bastante frecuencia; **that's q. enough!** ¡ya está bien! (**c**) **he's q. a character** es un tipo original; **it's q. something** es increíble (**d**) *(exactly)* exactamente; **q.**

(**so**)! ¡en efecto!, ¡exacto!

quiver¹ ['kwɪvə(r)] *vi* temblar

quiver² ['kwɪvə(r)] *n (for arrows)* aljaba *f*, carcaj *m*

quiz [kwɪz] **1** *n Rad & TV* **q. show** concurso *m*

2 *vt* hacer preguntas a

quizzical ['kwɪzɪkəl] *adj* (**a**) *(bemused)* burlón(ona) (**b**) *(enquiring)* curioso(a)

quota ['kwəʊtə] *n* (**a**) *(proportional share)* cuota *f*, parte *f* (**b**) *(prescribed amount, number)* cupo *m*

quotation [kwəʊ'teɪʃən] *n* (**a**) *Lit* cita *f*; **q. marks** comillas *fpl* (**b**) *Fin* cotización *f*

quote [kwəʊt] **1** *vt* (**a**) *(cite)* citar (**b**) *Com* **to q. a price** dar un presupuesto (**c**) *Fin* cotizar

2 *n* (**a**) *Lit* cita *f* (**b**) *Com* presupuesto *m*

quotient ['kwəʊʃənt] *n* cociente *m*

R, r [ɑ:(r)] *n (the letter)* R, r *f*
rabbi ['ræbaɪ] *n* rabí *m*, rabino *m*
rabbit ['ræbɪt] **1** *n* conejo(a) *m,f*; **r. hutch**
conejera *f*
   2 *vi Fam* **to r. (on)** enrollarse
rabble ['ræbəl] *n Pej* **the r.** el populacho
rabies ['reɪbi:z] *n* rabia *f*
RAC [ɑ:reɪ'si:] *n Br (abbr* **Royal Automobile Club**) = organización británica de
ayuda al automovilista, ≃ RACE *m*
race¹ [reɪs] **1** *n* (**a**) *Sport* carrera *f* (**b**) *Br*
the races las carreras (de caballos)
   2 *vt* (**a**) **I'll r. you!** ¡te echo una carrera!
(**b**) *(car, horse)* hacer correr (**c**) *(engine)*
acelerar
   3 *vi (go quickly)* correr; *(pulse)* acelerarse
race² [reɪs] *n (people)* raza *f*
racecourse ['reɪskɔ:s] *n Br* hipódromo
m
racehorse ['reɪshɔ:s] *n* caballo *m* de carreras
racer ['reɪsə(r)] *n Sport* (**a**) *(person)* co-
rredor(a) *m,f* (**b**) *(bicycle)* bicicleta *f* de
carreras; *(car)* coche *m* de carreras
racetrack ['reɪstræk] *n (for cars, people,
bikes)* pista *f*; *US (for horses)* hipódromo
m
racial ['reɪʃəl] *adj* racial
racing ['reɪsɪŋ] **1** *n* carreras *fpl*
   2 *adj* de carreras; **r. car/bike** coche *m*/
moto *f* de carreras
racism ['reɪsɪzəm] *n* racismo *m*
racist ['reɪsɪst] *adj & n* racista *(mf)*
rack [ræk] **1** *n* (**a**) *(shelf)* estante *m*; *(for
clothes)* percha *f*; **luggage r.** portaequipajes *m inv*; **roof r.** baca *f* (**b**) *(for torture)*
potro *m*
   2 *vt Literary (torment)* atormentar; *Fam
Fig* **to r. one's brains** devanarse los sesos
racket¹ ['rækɪt] *n* (**a**) *(din)* ruido *m*, jaleo
m (**b**) *(swindle)* timo *m*; *(shady business)*
chanchullo *m*
racket² ['rækɪt] *n Sport* raqueta *f*
racquet ['rækɪt] *n* = **racket²**
racy ['reɪsɪ] *adj* (**racier, raciest**) *(lively)*
vivo(a); *(risqué)* atrevido(a)
radar ['reɪdɑ:(r)] *n* radar *m*
radiance ['reɪdɪəns] *n* resplandor *m*

radiant ['reɪdɪənt] *adj* radiante, resplandeciente
radiate ['reɪdɪeɪt] *vt* irradiar; *Fig* **she ra-
diated happiness** rebosaba de alegría
radiation [reɪdɪ'eɪʃən] *n* radiación *f*
radiator ['reɪdɪeɪtə(r)] *n* radiador *m*
radical ['rædɪkəl] *adj* radical
radio ['reɪdɪəʊ] *n* radio *f*; **on the r.** en *or*
por la radio; **r. station** emisora *f* (de radio)
radioactive [reɪdɪəʊ'æktɪv] *adj* radiacti-
vo(a)
radio-controlled [reɪdɪəʊkən'trəʊld]
adj teledirigido(a)
radiography [reɪdɪ'ɒgrəfɪ] *n* radiografía
f
radiology [reɪdɪ'ɒlədʒɪ] *n* radiología *f*
radiotherapy [reɪdɪəʊ'θerəpɪ] *n* radiote-
rapia *f*
radish ['rædɪʃ] *n* rábano *m*
radius ['reɪdɪəs] *n* radio *m*; **within a r. of**
en un radio de
RAF [ɑ:reɪ'ef] *n Br (abbr* **Royal Air Force**)
= fuerzas aéreas británicas
raffle ['ræfəl] **1** *n* rifa *f*
   2 *vt* rifar
raft [rɑ:ft] *n* balsa *f*
rafter ['rɑ:ftə(r)] *n* viga *f* de madera
rag¹ [ræg] *n* (**a**) *(torn piece)* harapo *m*; **r.
doll** muñeca *f* de trapo (**b**) *(for cleaning)*
trapo *m* (**c**) *Fam* **rags** *(clothes)* trapos *mpl*
(**d**) *Pej Press* periodicucho *m*
rag² [ræg] **1** *n Br Univ* función benéfica
   2 *vt* gastar bromas a
rag-and-bone ['rægən'bəʊn] *adj Br* **r.
man** trapero *m*
rage [reɪdʒ] **1** *n* (**a**) *(fury)* cólera *f* (**b**) *Fam*
it's all the r. hace furor
   2 *vi* (**a**) *(person)* rabiar, estar furioso(a)
(**b**) *Fig (storm, sea)* rugir; *(wind)* bramar
ragged ['rægɪd] *adj* (**a**) *(clothes)* he-
cho(a) jirones (**b**) *(person)* harapiento(a)
(**c**) *(edge)* mellado(a) (**d**) *Fig (uneven)*
desigual
raging ['reɪdʒɪŋ] *adj* (**a**) *(angry)* furio-
so(a) (**b**) *Fig (sea)* embravecido(a) (**c**)
(intense) feroz; *(storm)* violento(a)
raid [reɪd] **1** *n Mil* incursión *f*; *(by police)*
redada *f*; *(robbery etc)* atraco *m*
   2 *vt Mil* hacer una incursión en; *(police)*

hacer una redada en; *(rob)* asaltar; *Fam*
to r. the larder vaciar la despensa
raider ['reɪdə(r)] *n (invader)* invasor(a)
m,f
rail [reɪl] *n* (**a**) barra *f* (**b**) *(railing)* barandilla *f* (**c**) *Rail* carril *f*; **by r.** *(send sth)* por
ferrocarril; *(travel)* en tren
railcard ['reɪlkɑːd] *n Br* abono *m*
railing ['reɪlɪŋ] *n (usu pl)* verja *f*
railroad ['reɪlrəʊd] *n US* ferrocarril *m*
railway ['reɪlweɪ] *n Br* ferrocarril *m*; **r.
line, r. track** vía férrea; **r. station** estación
f de ferrocarril
railwayman ['reɪlweɪmən] *n Br* ferroviario *m*
rain [reɪn] **1** *n* lluvia *f*; **in the r.** bajo la
lluvia
   2 *vi* llover; **it's raining** llueve
rainbow ['reɪnbəʊ] *n* arco *m* iris
raincoat ['reɪnkəʊt] *n* impermeable *m*
raindrop ['reɪndrɒp] *n* gota *f* de lluvia
rainfall ['reɪnfɔːl] *n (falling of rain)* precipitación *f*; *(amount)* pluviosidad *f*
rainforest ['reɪnfɒrɪst] *n* selva *f* tropical
rainy ['reɪnɪ] *adj* (**rainier, rainiest**) lluvio-
so(a)
raise [reɪz] **1** *n US* aumento *m* (de sueldo)
   2 *vt* (**a**) levantar; *(glass)* brindar; *(voice)*
subir; *(building)* erigir (**b**) *(prices)* aumentar (**c**) *(money, help)* reunir (**d**) *(issue)* plantear (**e**) *(crops, children)* criar
(**f**) *Rad* comunicar con (**g**) *(standards)*
mejorar (**h**) *(laugh)* provocar
raisin ['reɪzən] *n* pasa *f*
rake¹ [reɪk] **1** *n (garden tool)* rastrillo *m*;
(for fire) hurgón *m*
   2 *vt (leaves)* rastrillar; *(fire)* hurgar; *(with
machine gun)* barrer
rake² [reɪk] *n (dissolute man)* calavera *m*,
libertino *m*
rally ['rælɪ] **1** *n* (**a**) *(gathering)* reunión *f*;
Pol mitin *m* (**b**) *Aut* rallye *m* (**c**) *(in tennis)*
jugada *f*
   2 *vt (support)* reunir
   3 *vi* recuperarse
   ► **rally round** *vi* formar una piña
RAM [ræm] *n Comput (abbr* **random access memory**) RAM *f*
ram [ræm] **1** *n* (**a**) *Zool* carnero *m* (**b**) *Tech*
maza *f*
   2 *vt* (**a**) *(drive into place)* hincar; *(cram)*
embutir; *Fam* **to r. sth home** hacer algo
patente (**b**) *(crash into)* chocar con
ramble ['ræmbəl] **1** *n (walk)* caminata *f*
   2 *vi* (**a**) *(walk)* hacer una excursión a pie
(**b**) *Fig (digress)* divagar
rambler ['ræmblə(r)] *n* (**a**) *(person)* excursionista *mf* (**b**) *Bot* rosal *m* trepador

rambling ['ræmblɪŋ] *adj* (**a**) *(incoherent)*
incoherente (**b**) *(house)* laberíntico(a)
(**c**) *Bot* trepador(a)
ramp [ræmp] *n* (**a**) rampa *f* (**b**) *Av (movable stairway)* escalerilla *f*
rampage **1** *n* ['ræmpeɪdʒ] **to be on the r.**
desmandarse
   2 *vi* [ræm'peɪdʒ] **to r. about** comportarse como un loco
rampant ['ræmpənt] *adj* incontrola-
do(a); **corruption is r.** la corrupción está
muy extendida
rampart ['ræmpɑːt] *n* muralla *f*
ramshackle ['ræmʃækəl] *adj* destartala-
do(a)
ran [ræn] *pt of* **run**
ranch [rɑːntʃ] *n US* rancho *m*, hacienda *f*
rancher ['rɑːntʃə(r)] *n US* ranchero(a)
m,f
rancid ['rænsɪd] *adj* rancio(a)
rancour, *US* **rancor** ['ræŋkə(r)] *n Fml*
rencor *m*
R & D [ɑːrən'diː] *n (abbr* **Research and
Development**) I+D
random ['rændəm] **1** *n* **at r.** al azar
   2 *adj* fortuito(a); **r. selection** selección
hecha al azar
randy ['rændɪ] *adj* (**randier, randiest**) *Br
Fam* cachondo(a), caliente
rang [ræŋ] *pt of* **ring**
range [reɪndʒ] **1** *n* (**a**) *(of mountains)*
cordillera *f*, sierra *f* (**b**) *US (open land)*
pradera *f* (**c**) *(choice)* surtido *m*; *(of products)* gama *f* (**d**) *Mus* registro *m* (**e**)
firing r. campo *m* de tiro (**f**) *(of missile)*
alcance *m*; **at close r.** de cerca; **long-/
short-r. missiles** mísiles *mpl* de largo/
corto alcance (**g**) *Culin* cocina *f* de carbón
   2 *vi (extend)* extenderse (**to** hasta);
prices r. from £5 to £20 pounds los precios oscilan entre 5 y 20 libras
   3 *vt Literary (wander)* vagar por
ranger ['reɪndʒə(r)] *n* (**a**) **(forest) r.** guar-
dabosques *mf inv* (**b**) *US (mounted policeman)* policía montado
rank¹ [ræŋk] **1** *n* (**a**) *Mil (row)* fila *f*; **the
ranks** los soldados rasos; **the r. and file** la
base (**b**) *(position in army)* graduación *f*;
(in society) rango *m* (**c**) **(taxi) r.** parada *f*
de taxis
   2 *vt (classify)* clasificar
   3 *vi (figure)* figurar; **to r. above/below
sb** figurar por encima/debajo de algn; **to
r. with** estar al mismo nivel que
rank² [ræŋk] *adj Fml* (**a**) *(vegetation)*
exuberante (**b**) *(foul-smelling)* fétido(a)
(**c**) *(thorough)* total, absoluto(a)

ransack ['rænsæk] *vt (plunder)* saquear; *(rummage in)* registrar

ransom ['rænsəm] *n* rescate *m*; **to hold sb to r.** pedir rescate por algn; *Fig* poner a algn entre la espada y la pared

rant [rænt] *vi* vociferar; *Fam* **to r. and rave** pegar gritos

rap [ræp] **1** *n* (**a**) *(blow)* golpe *m* seco; *(on door)* golpecito *m* (**b**) *Mus* rap *m*
2 *vt & vi (knock)* golpear

rape¹ [reɪp] *Jur* **1** *n* violación *f*
2 *vt* violar

rape² [reɪp] *n Bot* colza *f*

rapeseed ['reɪpsiːd] *n* **r. oil** aceite *m* de colza

rapid ['ræpɪd] **1** *adj* rápido(a)
2 *n* **rapids** *(in river)* rápidos *mpl*

rapidity [rə'pɪdɪtɪ] *n* rapidez *f*

rapist ['reɪpɪst] *n* violador(a) *m,f*

rapport [ræ'pɔː(r)] *n* compenetración *f*

rapture ['ræptʃə(r)] *n* éxtasis *m*

rapturous ['ræptʃərəs] *adj* muy entusiasta

rare¹ [reə(r)] *adj* raro(a), poco común

rare² [reə(r)] *adj (steak)* poco hecho(a)

rarefied ['reərɪfaɪd] *adj* enrarecido(a)

rarely ['reəlɪ] *adv* raras veces

raring ['reərɪŋ] *adj Fam* **to be r. to do sth** morirse de ganas de hacer algo

rarity ['reərɪtɪ] *n* rareza *f*

rascal ['rɑːskəl] *n* granuja *mf*

rash¹ [ræʃ] *n* (**a**) *Med* erupción *f*, sarpullido *m* (**b**) *Fig (of robberies etc)* racha *f*

rash² [ræʃ] *adj (reckless)* impetuoso(a); *(words, actions)* precipitado(a), imprudente

rasher ['ræʃə(r)] *n* loncha *f*

raspberry ['rɑːzbərɪ] *n* frambuesa *f*

rasping ['rɑːspɪŋ] *adj* áspero(a)

rat [ræt] *n* (**a**) *(animal)* rata *f*; **r. poison** raticida *m* (**b**) *US Fam (informer)* soplón(ona) *m,f*, chivato(a) *m,f*

rate [reɪt] **1** *n* (**a**) *(ratio)* índice *m*, tasa *f*; **at any r.** *(at least)* al menos; *(anyway)* en cualquier caso (**b**) *(cost)* precio *m*; *Fin (of interest, exchange)* tipo *m* (**c**) **at the r. of** *(speed)* a la velocidad de; *(quantity)* a razón de (**d**) **first r.** de primera categoría (**e**) *Br* **rates** impuestos *mpl* municipales
2 *vt* (**a**) *(estimate)* estimar (**b**) *(evaluate)* tasar (**c**) *(consider)* considerar

rateable ['reɪtəbəl] *adj Br* **r. value** valor *m* catastral

ratepayer ['reɪtpeɪə(r)] *n Br* contribuyente *mf*

rather ['rɑːðə(r)] *adv* (**a**) *(quite)* más bien, bastante; *(very much so)* muy (**b**) *(more accurately)* mejor dicho; **r. than**

(instead of) en vez de; *(more than)* más que (**c**) **she would r. stay here** *(prefer to)* prefiere quedarse aquí

ratify ['rætɪfaɪ] *vt* ratificar

rating ['reɪtɪŋ] *n* (**a**) *(valuation)* tasación *f*; *(score)* valoración *f* (**b**) *TV* **(programme) ratings** índice *m* de audiencia (**c**) *Naut* marinero *m* sin graduación

ratio ['reɪʃɪəʊ] *n* razón *f*; **in the r. of** a razón de

ration ['ræʃən] **1** *n* (**a**) *(allowance)* ración *f* (**b**) **rations** víveres *mpl*
2 *vt* racionar

rational ['ræʃənəl] *adj* racional

rationale [ræʃə'nɑːl] *n* base *f*

rationalize ['ræʃənəlaɪz] *vt* racionalizar

rattle ['rætəl] **1** *n* (**a**) *(of train, cart)* traqueteo *m*; *(of metal)* repiqueteo *m*; *(of glass)* tintineo *m* (**b**) *(toy)* sonajero *m*; *(instrument)* carraca *f*
2 *vt* (**a**) *(keys etc)* hacer sonar (**b**) *Fam (unsettle)* poner nervioso(a)
3 *vi* sonar; *(metal)* repiquetear; *(glass)* tintinear

rattlesnake ['rætəlsneɪk] *n* serpiente *f* de cascabel

raucous ['rɔːkəs] *adj* estridente

ravage ['rævɪdʒ] *Fml* **1** *n (usu pl)* estragos *mpl*
2 *vt* asolar, devastar

rave [reɪv] **1** *vi* (**a**) *(be delirious)* delirar (**b**) *(be angry)* enfurecerse (**at** con) (**c**) *Fam (show enthusiasm)* entusiasmarse (**about** por)
2 *n Fam* **r. review** crítica *f* muy favorable

raven ['reɪvən] *n* cuervo *m*

ravenous ['rævənəs] *adj* **I'm r.** tengo un hambre que no veo

ravine [rə'viːn] *n* barranco *m*

raving ['reɪvɪŋ] *n Fam* **r. mad** loco(a) de atar

ravishing ['rævɪʃɪŋ] *adj (person)* encantador(a)

raw [rɔː] *adj* (**a**) *(uncooked)* crudo(a) (**b**) *(not processed)* bruto(a); *(alcohol)* puro(a); **r. material** materia prima (**c**) *(emotion)* instintivo(a) (**d**) *(weather)* crudo(a) (**e**) **r. deal** trato injusto (**f**) *(wound)* abierto(a); **r. flesh** carne viva (**g**) *US (inexperienced)* novato(a) (**h**) *(frank)* franco(a)

ray¹ [reɪ] *n* rayo *m*; *Fig* **r. of hope** rayo de esperanza

ray² [reɪ] *n (fish)* raya *f*

rayon ['reɪɒn] *n* rayón *m*

raze [reɪz] *vt* arrasar

razor ['reɪzə(r)] *n (for shaving)* maquinilla *f* de afeitar; **r. blade** hoja *f* de afeitar

Rd *(abbr* **Road)** calle *f*, c/

re [riː] *prep* respecto a, con referencia a

reach [riːtʃ] **1** *vt* (**a**) *(arrive at)* llegar a (**b**) *(contact)* localizar

2 *vi* alcanzar; **to r. for sth** intentar coger algo; **to r. out** extender la mano

3 *n* (**a**) *(range)* alcance *m*; **out of r.** fuera del alcance; **within r.** al alcance (**b**) *(in boxing)* extensión *f* del brazo (**c**) **reaches** *(on a river)* recta *f*

react [rɪˈækt] *vi* reaccionar

reaction [rɪˈækʃən] *n* reacción *f*

reactor [rɪˈæktə(r)] *n* reactor *m*

read [riːd] **1** *vt* (*pt & pp* **read** [red]) (**a**) leer (**b**) *(decipher)* descifrar (**c**) *(understand)* entender; *(interpret)* interpretar (**d**) *Univ* estudiar (**e**) *(of dial)* marcar (**f**) *(of signpost, text)* decir

2 *vi* leer

▸ **read out** *vt sep* leer en voz alta

readable [ˈriːdəbəl] *adj* (**a**) *(interesting)* interesante (**b**) *(legible)* legible

reader [ˈriːdə(r)] *n* (**a**) lector(a) *m,f* (**b**) *(book)* libro *m* de lectura (**c**) *Br Univ* profesor(a) *m,f* adjunto(a)

readership [ˈriːdəʃɪp] *n Press* lectores *mpl*

readily [ˈredɪlɪ] *adv* (**a**) *(easily)* fácilmente; **r. available** disponible en el acto (**b**) *(willingly)* de buena gana

readiness [ˈredɪnɪs] *n* (**a**) *(preparedness)* preparación *f* (**b**) *(willingness)* buena disposición

reading [ˈriːdɪŋ] *n* (**a**) lectura *f* (**b**) *Fig* interpretación *f* (**c**) *(of laws, bill)* presentación *f*

readjust [riːəˈdʒʌst] **1** *vt* reajustar

2 *vi* *(adapt oneself)* adaptarse

ready [ˈredɪ] *adj* (**a**) *(prepared)* listo(a), preparado(a); **r., steady, go!** ¡preparados, listos, ya! (**b**) **r. to** *(about to)* a punto de (**c**) *(to hand)* a mano; **r. cash** dinero *m* en efectivo (**d**) *(willing)* dispuesto(a)

ready-cooked [ˈredɪˈkʊkt] *adj* precocinado(a)

ready-made [ˈredɪˈmeɪd] *adj* confeccionado(a); *(food)* preparado(a)

real [rɪəl] *adj* (**a**) real, verdadero(a); *Fam* **for r.** de veras (**b**) *(genuine)* auténtico(a); **r. leather** piel legítima (**c**) *US Com* **r. estate** bienes *mpl* inmuebles; **r. estate agent** agente inmobiliario

realism [ˈrɪəlɪzəm] *n* realismo *m*

realistic [ˈrɪəlɪstɪk] *adj* realista

reality [rɪˈælɪtɪ] *n* realidad *f*; **in r.** en realidad

realization [rɪəlaɪˈzeɪʃən] *n* (**a**) *(understanding)* comprensión *f* (**b**) *(of plan, assets)* realización *f*

realize [ˈrɪəlaɪz] *vt* (**a**) *(become aware of)* darse cuenta de (**b**) *(assets, plan)* realizar

really [ˈrɪəlɪ] *adv* verdaderamente, realmente; **I r. don't know** no lo sé de verdad; **r.?** ¿de veras?

realm [relm] *n* *(kingdom)* reino *m*; *Fig (field)* terreno *m*

realtor [ˈrɪəltə(r)] *n US* agente *mf* inmobiliario(a)

ream [riːm] *n* *(of paper)* resma *f*

reap [riːp] *vt Agr* cosechar; *Fig* **to r. the benefits** llevarse los beneficios

reappear [riːəˈpɪə(r)] *vi* reaparecer

reappraisal [riːəˈpreɪzəl] *n* revaluación *f*

rear¹ [rɪə(r)] **1** *n* (**a**) *(back part)* parte *f* de atrás (**b**) *Fam (buttocks)* trasero *m*

2 *adj* trasero(a); **r. entrance** puerta *f* de atrás

rear² [rɪə(r)] **1** *vt* (**a**) *(breed, raise)* criar (**b**) *(lift up)* levantar

2 *vi* **to r. up** *(horse)* encabritarse

rearguard [ˈrɪəɡɑːd] *n* retaguardia *f*

rearmament [riːˈɑːməmənt] *n* rearme *m*

rearrange [riːəˈreɪndʒ] *vt* (**a**) *(furniture)* colocar de otra manera (**b**) *(appointment)* fijar otra fecha para

rear-view [ˈrɪəvjuː] *adj* **r. mirror** (espejo *m*) retrovisor *m*

reason [ˈriːzən] **1** *n* (**a**) motivo *m*, razón *f*; **for no r.** sin razón; **for some r.** por algún motivo (**b**) *(good sense)* razón *f*; **it stands to r.** es lógico; **to listen to r.** atender a razones

2 *vi* (**a**) **to r. with sb** convencer a algn (**b**) *(argue, work out)* razonar

reasonable [ˈriːzənəbəl] *adj* (**a**) *(fair)* razonable (**b**) *(sensible)* sensato(a) (**c**) *(average)* regular

reasonably [ˈriːzənəblɪ] *adv (fairly)* bastante

reasoning [ˈriːzənɪŋ] *n* razonamiento *m*

reassurance [riːəˈʃʊərəns] *n* consuelo *m*

reassure [riːəˈʃʊə(r)] *vt* (**a**) *(comfort)* tranquilizar (**b**) *(restore confidence)* dar confianza a

reassuring [riːəˈʃʊərɪŋ] *adj* consolador(a)

rebate [ˈriːbeɪt] *n* devolución *f*; **tax r.** devolución fiscal

> *📝* Note that the Spanish verb **rebatir** is a false friend and is never a translation for the English verb **to rebate**. In Spanish, **rebatir** means "to refute".

rebel 1 *adj & n* [ˈrebəl] rebelde *(mf)*

2 *vi* [rɪˈbel] rebelarse, sublevarse (**against** contra)

rebellion [rɪˈbeljən] *n* rebelión *f*

rebellious [rɪ'beljəs] *adj* rebelde
rebound 1 *n* ['riːbaʊnd] *(of ball)* rebote *m*;
Fig **on the r.** de rebote
  2 *vi* [rɪ'baʊnd] *(ball)* rebotar
rebuff [rɪ'bʌf] **1** *n* desaire *m*
  2 *vt* desairar
rebuild [riː'bɪld] *vt* reconstruir
rebuke [rɪ'bjuːk] **1** *n* reproche *m*
  2 *vt* reprochar
rebut [rɪ'bʌt] *vt* refutar
recalcitrant [rɪ'kælsɪtrənt] *adj Fml* recalcitrante
recall [rɪ'kɔːl] *vt* (**a**) *(soldiers, products)* hacer volver; *(ambassador)* retirar (**b**) *(remember)* recordar
recant [rɪ'kænt] *vi Fml* retractarse
recap 1 *vt & vi* [riː'kæp] resumir; **to r.** en resumen
  2 *n* ['riːkæp] recapitulación *f*
recapitulate [riːkə'pɪtjʊleɪt] *vt & vi Fml* recapitular
recapture [riː'kæptʃə(r)] *vt Fig* recuperar
recd *Com (abbr* **received***)* recibido(a)
recede [rɪ'siːd] *vi* retroceder; *(fade)* desvanecerse
receipt [rɪ'siːt] *n* (**a**) *(act)* recepción *f*; **to acknowledge r. of sth** acusar recibo de algo (**b**) *Com (paper)* recibo *m* (**c**) **receipts** *(takings)* recaudación *f*
receive [rɪ'siːv] *vt* (**a**) recibir (**b**) *Jur (stolen goods)* ocultar (**c**) *(welcome)* acoger (**d**) *TV & Rad* captar
receiver [rɪ'siːvə(r)] *n* (**a**) *(person)* receptor(a) *m,f* (**b**) *Jur (of stolen goods)* perista *mf* (**c**) *Br Jur* **official r.** síndico *m* (**d**) *Tel* auricular *m* (**e**) *Rad* receptor *m*
recent ['riːsənt] *adj* reciente; **in r. years** en los últimos años
recently ['riːsəntlɪ] *adv* hace poco, recientemente
receptacle [rɪ'septəkəl] *n* receptáculo *m*
reception [rɪ'sepʃən] *n* (**a**) *(welcome)* acogida *f* (**b**) *(party)* recepción *f*; **wedding r.** banquete *m* de bodas (**c**) **r. (desk)** recepción *f* (**d**) *Rad & TV* recepción *f*
receptionist [rɪ'sepʃənɪst] *n* recepcionista *mf*
recess ['riːses, rɪ'ses] *n* (**a**) *(in a wall)* hueco *m* (**b**) *(secret place)* escondrijo *m* (**c**) *US Educ* recreo *m*; *Pol* período *m* de vacaciones
recession [rɪ'seʃən] *n* recesión *f*
recharge [riː'tʃɑːdʒ] *vt (battery)* recargar
rechargeable [riː'tʃɑːdʒəbəl] *adj* recargable
recipe ['resɪpɪ] *n Culin* receta *f*; *Fig* fórmula *f*

recipient [rɪ'sɪpɪənt] *n* receptor(a) *m,f*; *(of letter)* destinatario(a) *m,f*

> *♪* Note that the Spanish word **recipiente** is a false friend and is never a translation for the English word **recipient**. In Spanish, **recipiente** means "receptacle, container".

reciprocate [rɪ'sɪprəkeɪt] **1** *vt (favour etc)* devolver
  2 *vi* hacer lo mismo
recital [rɪ'saɪtəl] *n* recital *m*
recite [rɪ'saɪt] *vt & vi* recitar
reckless ['reklɪs] *adj (unwise)* imprudente; *(fearless)* temerario(a)
reckon ['rekən] *vt & vi* (**a**) *(calculate)* calcular; *(count)* contar (**b**) *Fam (think)* creer; *(consider)* considerar
  ▶ **reckon on** *vt insep* contar con
reckoner ['rekənə(r)] *n* **ready r.** tabla *f* de cálculo
reckoning ['rekənɪŋ] *n* cálculo *m*; **by my r. ...** según mis cálculos ...; *Fig* **day of r.** día *m* del juicio final
reclaim [rɪ'kleɪm] *vt* (**a**) *(recover)* recuperar; *(demand back)* reclamar (**b**) *(marshland etc)* convertir
recline [rɪ'klaɪn] *vi* recostarse, reclinarse
reclining [rɪ'klaɪnɪŋ] *adj* recostado(a); **r. seat** asiento *m* abatible
recluse [rɪ'kluːs] *n* solitario(a) *m,f*

> *♪* Note that the Spanish word **recluso** is a false friend and is never a translation for the English word **recluse**. In Spanish, **recluso** means "prisoner".

recognition [rekəg'nɪʃən] *n* reconocimiento *m*; *(appreciation)* apreciación *f*; **changed beyond all r.** irreconocible
recognizable [rekəg'naɪzəbəl] *adj* reconocible
recognize ['rekəgnaɪz] *vt* reconocer
recoil 1 *n* ['riːkɔɪl] *(of gun)* culatazo *m*; *(of spring)* aflojamiento *m*
  2 *vi* [rɪ'kɔɪl] (**a**) *(gun)* dar un culatazo; *(spring)* aflojarse (**b**) *(in fear)* espantarse
recollect [rekə'lekt] *vt* recordar
recollection [rekə'lekʃən] *n* recuerdo *m*

> *♪* Note that the Spanish word **recolección** is a false friend and is never a translation for the English word **recollection**. In Spanish, **recolección** means "harvest, collection".

recommend [rekə'mend] *vt* recomendar
recommendation [rekəmen'deɪʃən] *n* recomendación *f*
recompense ['rekəmpens] **1** *n* recompensa *f*; *Jur* indemnización *f*
  2 *vt* recompensar; *Jur* indemnizar

reconcile ['rekənsaıl] *vt (two people)* reconciliar; *(two ideas)* conciliar; **to r. oneself to** resignarse a

recondition [riːkən'dıʃən] *vt (engine)* revisar

reconnaissance [rı'kɒnısəns] *n Mil* reconocimiento *m*

reconnoitre, *US* **reconnoiter** [rekə'nɔıtə(r)] *vt Mil* reconocer

reconsider [riːkən'sıdə(r)] *vt* reconsiderar

reconstruct [riːkən'strʌkt] *vt* reconstruir

reconstruction [riːkən'strʌkʃən] *n* reconstrucción *f*

record 1 *n* ['rekɔːd] (**a**) *(account)* relación *f*; *(of meeting)* actas *fpl*; **off the r.** confidencialmente (**b**) *(document)* documento *m*; **r. of attendance** registro *m* de asistencia; **public records** archivos *mpl* (**c**) *Med* historial médico (**d**) *Mus* disco *m*; **r. player** tocadiscos *m inv* (**e**) *Sport* récord *m*

2 *vt* [rı'kɔːd] (**a**) *(relate)* hacer constar; *(note down)* apuntar (**b**) *(record, voice)* grabar (**c**) *(of thermometer etc)* marcar

recorded [rı'kɔːdıd] *adj* **r. delivery** correo certificado; **r. message** mensaje grabado

recorder [rı'kɔːdə(r)] *n* (**a**) *(person)* registrador(a) *m,f*; *Jur* magistrado(a) *m,f* (**b**) *Mus* flauta *f*

recording [rı'kɔːdıŋ] *n (registering)* registro *m*; *(recorded music, message etc)* grabación *f*

recount [rı'kaʊnt] *vt (tell)* contar

re-count 1 *vi* [riː'kaʊnt] *Pol* hacer un recuento

2 *n* ['riːkaʊnt] *Pol* recuento *m*

recoup [rı'kuːp] *vt (losses etc)* recuperar

recourse [rı'kɔːs] *n* **to have r. to** recurrir a

recover [rı'kʌvə(r)] **1** *vt (items, lost time)* recuperar; *(consciousness)* recobrar

2 *vi (from illness etc)* reponerse

recovery [rı'kʌvərı] *n* (**a**) *(retrieval)* recuperación *f* (**b**) *(from illness)* restablecimiento *m*

recreation [rekrı'eıʃən] *n* (**a**) diversión *f* (**b**) *Educ (playtime)* recreo *m*; **r. ground** terreno *m* de juegos

recreational [rekrı'eıʃənəl] *adj* recreativo(a)

recrimination [rıkrımı'neıʃən] *n* reproche *m*

recruit [rı'kruːt] **1** *n* recluta *m*

2 *vt (soldiers)* reclutar; *(workers)* contratar

recruitment [rı'kruːtmənt] *n (of soldiers)* reclutamiento *m*; *(of employees)* contratación *f*

rectangle ['rektæŋgəl] *n* rectángulo *m*

rectangular [rek'tæŋgjʊlə(r)] *adj* rectangular

rectify ['rektıfaı] *vt* rectificar

rector ['rektə(r)] *n* (**a**) *Rel* párroco *m* (**b**) *Scot Educ* director(a) *m,f*

recuperate [rı'kuːpəreıt] *vi* reponerse

recur [rı'kɜː(r)] *vi* repetirse

Note that the Spanish verb **recurrir** *is a false friend and is never a translation for the English verb* **to recur***. In Spanish,* **recurrir** *means "to appeal, to resort".*

recurrence [rı'kʌrəns] *n* repetición *f*, reaparición *f*

recurrent [rı'kʌrənt] *adj* constante; *Med* recurrente

recycle [riː'saıkəl] *vt* reciclar

recycling [riː'saıklıŋ] *n* reciclaje *m*

red [red] **1** *adj (redder, reddest)* rojo(a); **r. light** semáforo *m* en rojo; **r. wine** vino tinto; **to go r.** ponerse colorado(a); **to have r. hair** ser pelirrojo(a); *Fig* **r. herring** truco *m* para despistar; *Fam* **to roll out the r. carpet for sb** recibir a algn con todos los honores; **R. Cross** Cruz Roja; **R. Indian** piel roja *mf*; **R. Riding Hood** Caperucita Roja; **R. Sea** Mar Rojo; **r. tape** papeleo *m*

2 *n* (**a**) *(colour)* rojo *m* (**b**) *Fin* **to be in the r.** estar en números rojos

redcurrant ['redkʌrənt] *n* grosella roja

redden ['redən] **1** *vi (blush)* enrojecerse, ponerse colorado(a)

2 *vt (make red)* teñir de rojo

reddish ['redıʃ] *adj* rojizo(a)

redeem [rı'diːm] *vt* (**a**) *(regain)* recobrar; *(from pawn)* desempeñar; *(voucher)* canjear (**b**) *(debt)* amortizar (**c**) *(film, novel etc)* salvar (**d**) *Rel* redimir; *Fig* **to r. oneself** redimirse

redeeming [rı'diːmıŋ] *adj* compensatorio(a); **his only r. feature** lo único que le salva

redemption [rı'dempʃən] *n Fml* (**a**) *(of debt)* amortización *f* (**b**) *Rel* redención *f*; **beyond r.** sin remedio

redeploy [riːdı'plɔı] *vt* redistribuir

red-handed [red'hændıd] *adj* **to catch sb r.** coger a algn con las manos en la masa

redhead ['redhed] *n* pelirrojo(a) *m,f*

red-hot [red'hɒt] *adj* (**a**) candente; **r. news** noticia(s) *f(pl)* de última hora (**b**) *Fam (passionate)* ardiente

redial [riː'daıəl] *n Tel (facility)* rellamada *f*

redirect [riːdı'rekt] *vt* (**a**) *(funds)* redistribuir (**b**) *(letter)* remitir a la nueva dirección

red-light [red'laɪt] *adj Fam* **r. district** barrio chino

redouble [riː'dʌbəl] *vt* redoblar

redress [rɪ'dres] *Fml* **1** *n* reparación *f*
2 *vt* reparar

redskin ['redskɪn] *n* piel roja *mf*

reduce [rɪ'djuːs] *vt* (**a**) reducir (**b**) *(in rank)* degradar (**c**) *Culin (sauce)* espesar (**d**) *Med* recomponer

reduction [rɪ'dʌkʃən] *n* reducción *f*; *Com (in purchase price)* descuento *m*, rebaja *f*

redundancy [rɪ'dʌndənsɪ] *n* despido *m*

redundant [rɪ'dʌndənt] *adj* (**a**) *(superfluous)* redundante (**b**) *Ind* **to be made r.** perder el empleo; **to make sb r.** despedir a algn

reed [riːd] *n* (**a**) *Bot* caña *f* (**b**) *Mus* caramillo *m*

reef [riːf] *n* arrecife *m*

reek [riːk] **1** *n* tufo *m*
2 *vi* apestar

reel [riːl] **1** *n* (**a**) *(spool)* bobina *f*, carrete *m* (**b**) *Scot Mus* danza *f* tradicional
2 *vi (stagger)* tambalearse

re-elect [riːɪ'lekt] *vt* reelegir

ref [ref] *n* (**a**) *Fam Sport* árbitro *m* (**b**) *Com (abbr* **reference)** ref

refectory [rɪ'fektərɪ] *n* refectorio *m*

refer [rɪ'fɜː(r)] **1** *vt* mandar, enviar; **to r. a matter to a tribunal** remitir un asunto a un tribunal
2 *vi* (**a**) *(allude)* referirse, aludir (**to** a) (**b**) **to r. to** *(consult)* consultar

referee [refə'riː] **1** *n* (**a**) *Sport* árbitro(a) *m,f* (**b**) *(for job application)* garante *mf*
2 *vt Sport* arbitrar

reference ['refərəns] *n* (**a**) referencia *f*; **with r. to** referente a, con referencia a; **r. book** libro *m* de consulta; **r. library** biblioteca *f* de consulta (**b**) *(character report)* informe *m*, referencia *f*

referendum [refə'rendəm] *n* referéndum *m*

refill 1 *n* ['riːfɪl] (**a**) *(replacement)* recambio *m*, carga *f* (**b**) *Fam (drink)* otra copa
2 *vt* [riː'fɪl] rellenar

refine [rɪ'faɪn] *vt* refinar

refined [rɪ'faɪnd] *adj* refinado(a)

refinement [rɪ'faɪnmənt] *n* refinamiento *m*

refinery [rɪ'faɪnərɪ] *n* refinería *f*

reflect [rɪ'flekt] **1** *vt (light, attitude)* reflejar
2 *vi (think)* reflexionar; **to r. on sth** meditar sobre algo

reflection [rɪ'flekʃən] *n* (**a**) *(indication, mirror image)* reflejo *m* (**b**) *(thought)* reflexión *f*; **on r.** pensándolo bien (**c**) *(criticism)* crítica *f*

reflector [rɪ'flektə(r)] *n (of vehicle)* catafaro *m*

reflex ['riːfleks] *n* reflejo *m*

reflexive [rɪ'fleksɪv] *adj* reflexivo(a)

reform [rɪ'fɔːm] **1** *n* reforma *f*; **r. school** reformatorio *m*
2 *vt* reformar

reformation [refə'meɪʃən] *n* reforma *f*

reformatory [rɪ'fɔːmətərɪ] *n* reformatorio *m*

reformer [rɪ'fɔːmə(r)] *n* reformador(a) *m,f*

refrain [rɪ'freɪn] **1** *n Mus* estribillo *m*; *Fig* lema *m*
2 *vi* abstenerse (**from** de)

refresh [rɪ'freʃ] *vt* refrescar

refresher [rɪ'freʃə(r)] *n* **r. course** cursillo *m* de reciclaje

refreshing [rɪ'freʃɪŋ] *adj* refrescante; **a r. change** un cambio muy agradable

refreshment [rɪ'freʃmənt] *n* refresco *m*

refrigerator [rɪ'frɪdʒəreɪtə(r)] *n* nevera *f*, frigorífico *m*, *Andes* frigider *m*, *RP* heladera *f*

refuel [riː'fjuːəl] *vi* repostar combustible

refuge ['refjuːdʒ] *n* refugio *m*, cobijo *m*; **to take r.** refugiarse

refugee [refjʊ'dʒiː] *n* refugiado(a) *m,f*

refund 1 *n* ['riːfʌnd] reembolso *m*
2 *vt* [rɪ'fʌnd] reembolsar, devolver

refurbish [riː'fɜːbɪʃ] *vt* redecorar

refusal [rɪ'fjuːzəl] *n* negativa *f*; **to have first r. on sth** tener la primera opción en algo

refuse¹ [rɪ'fjuːz] **1** *vt* rechazar; **to r. sb sth** negar algo a algn
2 *vi* negarse

refuse² ['refjuːs] *n* basura *f*; **r. collector** basurero *m*

refute [rɪ'fjuːt] *vt* refutar, rebatir

regain [rɪ'geɪn] *vt* recuperar; *(consciousness)* recobrar

regal ['riːgəl] *adj* regio(a)

regard [rɪ'gɑːd] **1** *n* (**a**) *(concern)* consideración *f*, respeto *m*; **with r. to** respecto a (**b**) *(esteem)* estima *f* (**c**) **regards** *(good wishes)* recuerdos *mpl*; **give him my regards** dale recuerdos de mi parte
2 *vt* (**a**) *(consider)* considerar (**b**) **as regards** *(regarding)* respecto a

regarding [rɪ'gɑːdɪŋ] *prep* respecto a

regardless [rɪ'gɑːdlɪs] **1** *prep* **r. of** sin tener en cuenta; **r. of the outcome** pase lo que pase
2 *adv* a toda costa

regime [reɪ'ʒiːm] *n* régimen *m*

regiment [ˈredʒɪmənt] **1** n regimiento m **2** vt regimentar

regimental [redʒɪˈmentəl] adj del regimiento

region [ˈriːdʒən] n (**a**) región f (**b**) **in the r. of** aproximadamente

regional [ˈriːdʒənəl] adj regional

regionalism [ˈriːdʒənəlɪzəm] n regionalismo m

register [ˈredʒɪstə(r)] **1** n registro m **2** vt (**a**) (record) registrar (**b**) (letter) certificar (**c**) (show) mostrar; **his face registered fear** en su rostro se reflejaba el miedo
3 vi (for course) inscribirse; Univ matricularse

registered [ˈredʒɪstəd] adj certificado(a); **r. letter** carta certificada; **r. trademark** marca registrada

registrar [redʒɪˈstrɑː(r), ˈredʒɪstrɑː(r)] n (**a**) (record keeper) registrador(a) m,f (**b**) Br Med interno(a) m,f (**c**) Univ secretario(a) m,f general

registration [redʒɪˈstreɪʃən] n inscripción f; Univ matrícula f; Br Aut **r. number** matrícula f

registry [ˈredʒɪstrɪ] n registro m; **to get married in a r. office** casarse por lo civil; **r. office** registro civil

regret [rɪˈgret] **1** n (remorse) remordimiento m; (sadness) pesar m; **regrets** (excuses) excusas fpl; **to have no regrets** no arrepentirse de nada
2 vt arrepentirse de, lamentar

regretful [rɪˈgretfʊl] adj arrepentido(a)

regrettable [rɪˈgretəbəl] adj lamentable

regroup [riːˈgruːp] **1** vt reagrupar
2 vi reagruparse

regular [ˈregjʊlə(r)] **1** adj (**a**) regular (**b**) (usual) normal (**c**) (staff) permanente (**d**) (frequent) frecuente (**e**) **r. army** tropas fpl regulares (**f**) US Fam **a r. guy** un tío legal, Am un tipo derecho
2 n (**a**) (customer) cliente mf habitual (**b**) Mil militar m de carrera

regularity [regjʊˈlærɪtɪ] n regularidad f

regularly [ˈregjʊləlɪ] adv con regularidad

regulate [ˈregjʊleɪt] vt regular

regulation [regjʊˈleɪʃən] **1** n (**a**) (control) regulación f (**b**) (rule) regla f
2 adj reglamentario(a)

rehabilitation [riːəbɪlɪˈteɪʃən] n rehabilitación f; **r. centre** centro m de reinserción

rehearsal [rɪˈhɜːsəl] n ensayo m

rehearse [rɪˈhɜːs] vt & vi ensayar

reign [reɪn] **1** n reinado m
2 vi reinar

reigning [ˈreɪnɪŋ] adj **r. champion** campeón m actual

reimburse [riːɪmˈbɜːs] vt reembolsar

rein [reɪn] n (for horse) rienda f; Fig **he gave free r. to his emotions** dio rienda suelta a sus emociones

reindeer [ˈreɪndɪə(r)] n reno m

reinforce [riːɪnˈfɔːs] vt (strengthen) reforzar; (support) apoyar; **reinforced concrete** hormigón armado

reinforcement [riːɪnˈfɔːsmənt] n (**a**) refuerzo m; Constr armazón m (**b**) Mil **reinforcements** refuerzos mpl

reinstate [riːɪnˈsteɪt] vt (to job) reincorporar

reiterate [riːˈɪtəreɪt] vt & vi reiterar

reject 1 n [ˈriːdʒekt] (**a**) desecho m (**b**) Com **rejects** artículos defectuosos
2 vt [rɪˈdʒekt] rechazar

rejection [rɪˈdʒekʃən] n rechazo m

rejoice [rɪˈdʒɔɪs] vi regocijarse (**at** or **over** de)

rejuvenate [rɪˈdʒuːvɪneɪt] vt rejuvenecer; Fig revitalizar

relapse [rɪˈlæps] **1** n (**a**) Med recaída f; **to have a r.** sufrir una recaída (**b**) (into crime, alcoholism) reincidencia f
2 vi recaer

relate [rɪˈleɪt] **1** vt (**a**) (connect) relacionar (**b**) (tell) relatar
2 vi relacionarse

related [rɪˈleɪtɪd] adj (**a**) (linked) relacionado(a) (**to** con) (**b**) **to be r. to sb** ser pariente de algn

relation [rɪˈleɪʃən] n (**a**) (link) relación f; **in** or **with r. to** respecto a; **it bears no r. to what we said** no tiene nada que ver con lo que dijimos (**b**) (member of family) pariente(a) m,f

relationship [rɪˈleɪʃənʃɪp] n (**a**) (link) relación f (**b**) (between people) relaciones fpl; **to have a good/bad r. with sb** llevarse bien/mal con algn

relative [ˈrelətɪv] **1** n pariente mf
2 adj relativo(a)

relatively [ˈrelətɪvlɪ] adv relativamente

relax [rɪˈlæks] **1** vt (muscles, rules) relajar
2 vi relajarse

relaxation [riːlækˈseɪʃən] n (**a**) (rest) descanso m, relajación f (**b**) (of rules) relajación f (**c**) (pastime) distracción f

relaxed [rɪˈlækst] adj relajado(a); (peaceful) tranquilo(a)

relaxing [rɪˈlæksɪŋ] adj relajante

relay 1 n [ˈriːleɪ] (**a**) relevo m; **r. (race)** carrera f de relevos (**b**) Rad & TV retransmisión f

2 vt [rɪ'leɪ] (**a**) (pass on) difundir (**b**) Rad & TV retransmitir

release [rɪ'liːs] **1** n (**a**) (of prisoner) liberación f, puesta f en libertad; (of gas) escape m (**b**) Com puesta f en venta (**c**) Cin estreno m (**d**) (record) disco m (**e**) Press comunicado m
2 vt (**a**) (let go) soltar; (prisoner) poner en libertad; (gas) despedir (**b**) Com poner en venta (**c**) Cin estrenar (**d**) (record) editar (**e**) (publish) publicar

relegate ['relɪgeɪt] vt (**a**) relegar (**b**) Ftb **to be relegated** bajar a una división inferior

relent [rɪ'lent] vi ceder; (storm) aplacarse

relentless [rɪ'lentlɪs] adj implacable

relevant ['reləvənt] adj pertinente (**to** a); **it is not r.** no viene al caso

> ⟋ Note that the Spanish word **relevante** is a false friend and is never a translation for the English word **relevant**. In Spanish, **relevante** means "outstanding, important".

reliability [rɪlaɪə'bɪlɪtɪ] n (**a**) (of person) formalidad f (**b**) (of car, machine) fiabilidad f

reliable [rɪ'laɪəbəl] adj (person) de fiar; **a r. car** un coche seguro; **a r. source** una fuente fidedigna

reliably [rɪ'laɪəblɪ] adv **to be r. informed that** saber de buena tinta que

reliant [rɪ'laɪənt] adj **to be r. on** depender de

relic ['relɪk] n (**a**) Rel reliquia f (**b**) (reminder of past) vestigio m

relief [rɪ'liːf] n (**a**) alivio m (**b**) (help) auxilio m, ayuda f; US **to be on r.** cobrar un subsidio (**c**) Art & Geog relieve m

relieve [rɪ'liːv] vt (**a**) aliviar; (monotony) romper (**b**) (take over from) relevar (**c**) Euph **to r. oneself** hacer sus necesidades (**d**) **to r. sb of sth** coger algo a algn

relieved [rɪ'liːvd] adj aliviado(a), tranquilizado(a)

religion [rɪ'lɪdʒən] n religión f

religious [rɪ'lɪdʒəs] adj religioso(a)

relinquish [rɪ'lɪŋkwɪʃ] vt renunciar a; **to r. one's hold on sth** soltar algo

relish ['relɪʃ] **1** n (**a**) (enjoyment) deleite m (**b**) Culin condimento m
2 vt agradar

relocate [riːləʊ'keɪt] vt trasladar

reluctance [rɪ'lʌktəns] n desgana f

reluctant [rɪ'lʌktənt] adj reacio(a); **to be r. to do sth** estar poco dispuesto(a) a hacer algo

reluctantly [rɪ'lʌktəntlɪ] adv de mala gana, a regañadientes

rely [rɪ'laɪ] vi contar (**on** con), confiar (**on** en)

remain [rɪ'meɪn] **1** vi (**a**) (stay) permanecer, quedarse (**b**) (be left) quedar; **it remains to be seen** está por ver
2 npl **remains** restos mpl

remainder [rɪ'meɪndə(r)] n resto m

remaining [rɪ'meɪnɪŋ] adj restante

remand [rɪ'mɑːnd] Jur **1** vt remitir; **remanded in custody** en prevención
2 n detención f; **on r.** detenido(a)

remark [rɪ'mɑːk] **1** n comentario m
2 vt comentar, observar

> ⟋ Note that the Spanish verb **remarcar** is a false friend and is never a translation for the English verb **to remark**. In Spanish, **remarcar** means "to stress, to underline".

remarkable [rɪ'mɑːkəbəl] adj extraordinario(a); (strange) curioso(a)

remedial [rɪ'miːdɪəl] adj reparador(a); **r. classes** clases fpl para niños atrasados en los estudios

remedy ['remɪdɪ] **1** n remedio m
2 vt remediar

remember [rɪ'membə(r)] **1** vt (**a**) acordarse de, recordar (**b**) **r. me to your mother** dale recuerdos a tu madre
2 vi acordarse, recordar; **I don't r.** no me acuerdo

remembrance [rɪ'membrəns] n **in r. of** en recuerdo de; Br **R. Day** or **Sunday** = día en que se conmemora el armisticio de 1918

remind [rɪ'maɪnd] vt recordar; **r. me to do it** recuérdame que lo haga; **she reminds me of your sister** me recuerda a tu hermana; **that reminds me** ahora que me acuerdo

reminder [rɪ'maɪndə(r)] n recordatorio m, aviso m

reminisce [remɪ'nɪs] vi rememorar

reminiscent [remɪ'nɪsənt] adj Fml nostálgico(a); **to be r. of** recordar

remiss [rɪ'mɪs] adj (negligent) descuidado(a)

remission [rɪ'mɪʃən] n (**a**) Med remisión f (**b**) Jur perdón m

remit [rɪ'mɪt] vt (**a**) (send) remitir (**b**) Jur referir a otro tribunal

remittance [rɪ'mɪtəns] n (**a**) (sending) envío m (**b**) (payment) giro m, pago m

remnant ['remnənt] n resto m; **remnants** (of cloth) retales mpl

remold ['riːməʊld] n US = remould

remorse [rɪ'mɔːs] n remordimiento m

remorseful [rɪ'mɔːsfʌl] adj lleno(a) de remordimiento

remorseless [rɪ'mɔːslɪs] *adj* despiadado(a)

remote [rɪ'məʊt] *adj* (**a**) *(far away)* remoto(a); **r. control** mando *m* a distancia (**b**) *(isolated)* aislado(a) (**c**) *(possibility)* remoto(a); **I haven't the remotest idea** no tengo la más mínima idea

remote-controlled [rɪ'məʊtkən'trəʊld] *adj* teledirigido(a)

remotely [rɪ'məʊtlɪ] *adv* (**a**) *(vaguely)* vagamente (**b**) *(distantly)* en lugar aislado

remould ['riːməʊld] *n Aut* neumático recauchutado

removable [rɪ'muːvəbəl] *adj (detachable)* que se puede quitar

removal [rɪ'muːvəl] *n* (**a**) *(moving house)* mudanza *f*; **r. van** camión *m* de mudanzas (**b**) *(of stain etc)* eliminación *f*

remove [rɪ'muːv] *vt* (**a**) *(move)* quitar; **to r. one's make-up** desmaquillarse; **to r. one's name from a list** tachar su nombre de una lista (**b**) *(from office)* despedir

> 🖉 Note that the Spanish verb **remover** is a false friend and is never a translation for the English verb **to remove**. In Spanish, **remover** means "to move over, to turn over, to stir".

removed [rɪ'muːvd] *adj* **far r. from** muy diferente de

remover [rɪ'muːvə(r)] *n* **make-up r.** desmaquillador *m*; **nail varnish r.** quitaesmalte *m*; **stain r.** quitamanchas *m inv*

remuneration [rɪmjuːnə'reɪʃən] *n Fml* remuneración *f*

renaissance [rə'neɪsəns] **1** *n* renacimiento *m*; **the R.** el Renacimiento
  2 *adj* renacentista

rend [rend] *vt (pt & pp rent) Fml* rasgar

render ['rendə(r)] *vt Fml* (**a**) *(give)* dar (**b**) *(make)* hacer (**c**) *Com* presentar (**d**) *(translate)* traducir

rendering ['rendərɪŋ] *n* (**a**) *(of song, piece of music)* interpretación *f* (**b**) *(translation)* traducción *f*

rendezvous ['rɒndɪvuː] **1** *n* (**a**) *(meeting)* cita *f* (**b**) *(place)* lugar *m* de reunión
  2 *vi* reunirse

renegade ['renɪgeɪd] *n* renegado(a) *m,f*

renew [rɪ'njuː] *vt (contract etc)* renovar; *(talks etc)* reanudar; **with renewed vigour** con renovadas fuerzas

renewal [rɪ'njuːəl] *n (of contract etc)* renovación *f*; *(of talks etc)* reanudación *f*

renounce [rɪ'naʊns] *vt Fml* renunciar

renovate ['renəveɪt] *vt* renovar, hacer reformas en

renown [rɪ'naʊn] *n* renombre *m*

renowned [rɪ'naʊnd] *adj* renombrado(a)

rent [rent] **1** *n* (**a**) *(for building, car, TV)* alquiler *m* (**b**) *(for land)* arriendo *m*
  2 *vt* (**a**) *(building, car, TV)* alquilar, *Méx* rentar (**b**) *(land)* arrendar
  3 *pt & pp of* **rend**

rental ['rentəl] *n (of house etc)* alquiler *m*

renunciation [rɪnʌnsɪ'eɪʃən] *n Fml* renuncia *f*

reorganize [riː'ɔːgənaɪz] *vt* reorganizar

rep [rep] *n Fam* (**a**) *Com* representante *mf* (**b**) *Th* teatro *m* de repertorio

repaid [riː'peɪd] *pt & pp of* **repay**

repair [rɪ'peə(r)] **1** *n* reparación *f*, arreglo *m*; **in good/bad r.** en buen/mal estado
  2 *vt* (**a**) arreglar; *(car)* reparar; *(clothes)* remendar (**b**) *(make amends for)* reparar

repartee [repɑː'tiː] *n* réplica aguda

repatriate [riː'pætrɪeɪt] *vt* repatriar

repay [riː'peɪ] *vt (pt & pp repaid)* devolver; **to r. a debt** liquidar una deuda; **to r. a kindness** devolver un favor

repayment [riː'peɪmənt] *n* pago *m*

repeal [rɪ'piːl] *Jur* **1** *n* revocación *f*
  2 *vt* revocar

repeat [rɪ'piːt] **1** *vt* repetir; **to r. oneself** repetirse
  2 *n (repetition)* repetición *f*; *TV* reposición *f*

repeated [rɪ'piːtɪd] *adj* repetido(a)

repeatedly [rɪ'piːtɪdlɪ] *adv* repetidas veces

repel [rɪ'pel] *vt* (**a**) *(fight off)* repeler (**b**) *(disgust)* repugnar

repellent [rɪ'pelənt] **1** *adj* repelente; **water-r.** impermeable
  2 *n* **(insect) r.** loción *f or* spray *m* antiinsectos

repent [rɪ'pent] *vt & vi* arrepentirse (de)

repentance [rɪ'pentəns] *n* arrepentimiento *m*

repercussion [riːpə'kʌʃən] *n (usu pl)* repercusión *f*

repertoire ['repətwɑː(r)] *n* repertorio *m*

repertory ['repətrɪ] *n Th* teatro *m* de repertorio

repetition [repɪ'tɪʃən] *n* repetición *f*

repetitive [rɪ'petɪtɪv] *adj* repetitivo(a)

replace [rɪ'pleɪs] *vt* (**a**) *(put back)* volver a poner en su sitio (**b**) *(substitute for)* sustituir, reemplazar

replacement [rɪ'pleɪsmənt] *n* (**a**) *(returning)* reemplazo *m* (**b**) *(person)* sustituto(a) *m,f* (**c**) *(part)* pieza *f* de recambio

replay ['riːpleɪ] *n* repetición *f*

replenish [rɪ'plenɪʃ] *vt* (**a**) *(fill up)* rellenar (**b**) **to r. stocks** reponer las existencias

replete [rɪ'pliːt] *adj Fml* repleto(a)
replica ['replɪkə] *n* réplica *f*
reply [rɪ'plaɪ] **1** *n* respuesta *f*, contestación *f*
   2 *vi* responder, contestar
report [rɪ'pɔːt] **1** *n* (**a**) informe *m*; **medical r.** parte médico; *Br* **school r.** informe escolar (**b**) *(piece of news)* noticia *f* (**c**) *Press, Rad & TV* reportaje *m* (**d**) *(rumour)* rumor *m* (**e**) *Fml (of gun)* estampido *m*
   2 *vt* (**a**) **it is reported that ...** se dice que ... (**b**) *(tell authorities about)* denunciar (**c**) *Press* hacer un reportaje sobre
   3 *vi* (**a**) *(of committee member etc)* hacer un informe (**b**) *Press* hacer un reportaje (**c**) *(for duty etc)* presentarse; *Mil* **to r. sick** coger la baja por enfermedad
reported [rɪ'pɔːtɪd] *adj* **r. speech** estilo indirecto
reportedly [rɪ'pɔːtɪdlɪ] *adv Fml* según se dice
reporter [rɪ'pɔːtə(r)] *n* periodista *mf*
repose [rɪ'pəʊz] *Fml* **1** *n* reposo *m*
   2 *vt & vi* reposar
repossess [riːpə'zes] *vt* **our house has been repossessed** el banco ha ejecutado la hipoteca de nuestra casa
reprehensible [reprɪ'hensəbəl] *adj* reprensible, censurable
represent [reprɪ'zent] *vt* representar
representation [reprɪzen'teɪʃən] *n* (**a**) representación *f* (**b**) *Fml* **representations** queja *f*
representative [reprɪ'zentətɪv] **1** *adj* representativo(a)
   2 *n* (**a**) representante *mf* (**b**) *US Pol* diputado(a) *m,f*
repress [rɪ'pres] *vt* reprimir, contener
repressed [rɪ'prest] *adj* **to be r.** estar reprimido(a)
repression [rɪ'preʃən] *n* represión *f*
repressive [rɪ'presɪv] *adj* represivo(a)
reprieve [rɪ'priːv] **1** *n* (**a**) *Jur* indulto *m* (**b**) *Fig* alivio *m*
   2 *vt Jur* indultar
reprimand ['reprɪmɑːnd] **1** *n* reprimenda *f*
   2 *vt* reprender
reprisal [rɪ'praɪzəl] *n* represalia *f*
reproach [rɪ'prəʊtʃ] **1** *n* reproche *m*; **beyond r.** intachable
   2 *vt* reprochar
reproachful [rɪ'prəʊtʃfʊl] *adj* reprobador(a)
reproduce [riːprə'djuːs] **1** *vt* reproducir
   2 *vi* reproducirse
reproduction [riːprə'dʌkʃən] *n* reproducción *f*

reproof [rɪ'pruːf] *n Fml* reprobación *f*, censura *f*
reprove [rɪ'pruːv] *vt Fml* reprobar, censurar
reptile ['reptaɪl] *n* reptil *m*
republic [rɪ'pʌblɪk] *n* república *f*
republican [rɪ'pʌblɪkən] *adj & n* republicano(a) *(m,f)*; *US Pol* **R. Party** Partido Republicano
repudiate [rɪ'pjuːdɪeɪt] *vt Fml* (**a**) *(reject)* rechazar (**b**) *(not acknowledge)* negarse a reconocer
repugnant [rɪ'pʌgnənt] *adj* repugnante
repulse [rɪ'pʌls] *vt* rechazar
repulsive [rɪ'pʌlsɪv] *adj* repulsivo(a)
reputable ['repjʊtəbəl] *adj (company etc)* acreditado(a); *(person, products)* de toda confianza
reputation [repjʊ'teɪʃən] *n* reputación *f*
repute [rɪ'pjuːt] *n Fml* reputación *f*
reputed [rɪ'pjuːtɪd] *adj* supuesto(a); **to be r. to be** ser considerado(a) como
reputedly [rɪ'pjuːtɪdlɪ] *adv* según se dice
request [rɪ'kwest] **1** *n* petición *f*, solicitud *f*; **available on r.** disponible a petición de los interesados; *Br* **r. stop** *(for bus)* parada *f* discrecional
   2 *vt* pedir, solicitar
require [rɪ'kwaɪə(r)] *vt* (**a**) *(need)* necesitar, requerir (**b**) *(demand)* exigir
requirement [rɪ'kwaɪəmənt] *n* (**a**) *(need)* necesidad *f* (**b**) *(demand)* requisito *m*

> ℓ Note that the Spanish word **requerimiento** is a false friend and is never a translation for the English word **requirement**. In Spanish, **requerimiento** means both "entreaty" and "writ, injunction".

requisite ['rekwɪzɪt] *Fml* **1** *adj* requerido(a)
   2 *n* requisito *m*
requisition [rekwɪ'zɪʃən] **1** *n* requisición *f*
   2 *vt* requisar
rescind [rɪ'sɪnd] *vt Fml (contract)* rescindir; *(law)* abrogar
rescue ['reskjuː] **1** *n* rescate *m*; **r. team** equipo *m* de rescate
   2 *vt* rescatar
rescuer ['reskjʊə(r)] *n* rescatador(a) *m,f*
research [rɪ'sɜːtʃ] **1** *n* investigación *f*; **R. and Development** Investigación más Desarrollo
   2 *vt & vi* investigar
researcher [rɪ'sɜːtʃə(r)] *n* investigador(a) *m,f*
resemblance [rɪ'zembləns] *n* semejanza *f*

resemble [rɪ'zembəl] *vt* parecerse a
resent [rɪ'zent] *vt* ofenderse por
resentful [rɪ'zentfʊl] *adj* ofendido(a)
resentment [rɪ'zentmənt] *n* resentimiento *m*
reservation [rezə'veɪʃən] *n* reserva *f*
reserve [rɪ'zɜːv] **1** *n* (**a**) reserva *f*; **to keep sth in r.** guardar algo de reserva (**b**) *Sport* suplente *mf* (**c**) *Mil* **reserves** reservas *fpl*
2 *vt* reservar
reserved [rɪ'zɜːvd] *adj* reservado(a)
reservoir ['rezəvwɑː(r)] *n* embalse *m*, pantano *m*; *Fig* reserva *f*
reshape [riː'ʃeɪp] *vt* rehacer; *Fig* reorganizar
reshuffle [riː'ʃʌfəl] *n* *Pol* remodelación *f*
reside [rɪ'zaɪd] *vi* *Fml* residir
residence ['rezɪdəns] *n* *Fml* (*home*) residencia *f*; (*address*) domicilio *m*; (*period of time*) permanencia *f*
resident ['rezɪdənt] *adj & n* residente (*mf*); *US Med* = médico que ha cumplido la residencia y prosigue con su especialización; **to be r. in** estar domiciliado(a) en
residential [rezɪ'denʃəl] *adj* residencial
residual [rɪ'zɪdjʊəl] *adj* residual
residue ['rezɪdjuː] *n* residuo *m*
resign [rɪ'zaɪn] **1** *vt* (**a**) (*give up*) dimitir (**b**) **to r. oneself to sth** resignarse a algo
2 *vi* (*from job*) dimitir
resignation [rezɪg'neɪʃən] *n* (**a**) (*from a job*) dimisión *f* (**b**) (*acceptance*) resignación *f*
resigned [rɪ'zaɪnd] *adj* resignado(a)
resilience [rɪ'zɪlɪəns] *n* resistencia *f*
resilient [rɪ'zɪlɪənt] *adj* (*strong*) resistente
resin ['rezɪn] *n* resina *f*
resist [rɪ'zɪst] **1** *vt* (**a**) (*not yield to*) resistir (**b**) (*oppose*) oponerse a
2 *vi* resistir
resistance [rɪ'zɪstəns] *n* resistencia *f*
resit [riː'sɪt] *vt* (*exam*) volver a presentarse a
resolute ['rezəluːt] *adj* resuelto(a), decidido(a)
resolution [rezə'luːʃən] *n* resolución *f*
resolve [rɪ'zɒlv] **1** *n* resolución *f*
2 *vt* resolver; **to r. to do** resolverse a hacer
3 *vi* resolverse
resonant ['rezənənt] *adj* resonante
resort [rɪ'zɔːt] **1** *n* (**a**) (*place*) lugar *m* de vacaciones; **tourist r.** centro turístico (**b**) (*recourse*) recurso *m*; **as a last r.** como último recurso
2 *vi* recurrir (**to** a)

📝 Note that the Spanish word **resorte** is a false friend and is never a translation for the English word **resort**. In Spanish, **resorte** means both "spring" and "means".

resound [rɪ'zaʊnd] *vi* resonar; *Fig* tener resonancia
resounding [rɪ'zaʊndɪŋ] *adj* **a r. failure** un fracaso total; **a r. success** un éxito rotundo
resource [rɪ'sɔːs] *n* recurso *m*
resourceful [rɪ'sɔːsfʊl] *adj* ingenioso(a)
respect [rɪ'spekt] **1** *n* (**a**) (*deference*) respeto *m*; **to pay one's respects to sb** presentar sus respetos a algn (**b**) (*relation, reference*) respecto *m*; **in that r.** a ese respecto; **with r. to** con referencia a
2 *vt* respetar
respectable [rɪ'spektəbəl] *adj* respetable; (*clothes*) decente
respectful [rɪ'spektfʊl] *adj* respetuoso(a)
respective [rɪ'spektɪv] *adj* respectivo(a)
respectively [rɪ'spektɪvlɪ] *adv* respectivamente
respite ['respaɪt] *n* *Fml* respiro *m*
resplendent [rɪ'splendənt] *adj* resplandeciente
respond [rɪ'spɒnd] *vi* responder
response [rɪ'spɒns] *n* (**a**) (*reply*) respuesta *f* (**b**) (*reaction*) reacción *f*
responsibility [rɪspɒnsə'bɪlɪtɪ] *n* responsabilidad *f*
responsible [rɪ'spɒnsəbəl] *adj* responsable (**for** de); **to be r. to sb** tener que dar cuentas a algn
responsive [rɪ'spɒnsɪv] *adj* sensible
rest¹ [rest] **1** *n* (**a**) (*break*) descanso *m*; **r. cure** cura *f* de reposo; *US* **r. room** aseos *mpl* (**b**) (*peace*) tranquilidad *f*; **at r.** (*object*) inmóbil (**c**) (*support*) apoyo *m* (**d**) *Mus* pausa *f*
2 *vt* (**a**) descansar (**b**) (*lean*) apoyar; **to r. a ladder against a wall** apoyar una escalera contra una pared
3 *vi* (**a**) descansar (**b**) (*be calm*) quedarse tranquilo(a) (**c**) **it doesn't r. with me** no depende de mí; **we'll let the matter r.** dejémoslo estar
rest² [rest] *n* **the r.** (*remainder*) el resto, lo demás; **the r. of the day** el resto del día; **the r. of the girls** las demás chicas; **the r. of us** los demás
restaurant ['restərɒnt] *n* restaurante *m*; *Rail* **r. car** coche *m* restaurante
restful ['restfʊl] *adj* relajante
restitution [restɪ'tjuːʃən] *n* *Fml* restitución *f*; **to make r.** restituir

restive [ˈrestɪv] *adj* inquieto(a), nervioso(a)

restless [ˈrestlɪs] *adj* agitado(a), inquieto(a)

restoration [restəˈreɪʃən] *n* (**a**) *(giving back)* devolución *f* (**b**) *Br Hist* **the R.** la Restauración (**c**) *(of building, piece of furniture)* restauración *f*

restore [rɪˈstɔː(r)] *vt* (**a**) *(give back)* devolver (**b**) *(re-establish)* restablecer (**c**) *(building etc)* restaurar

restrain [rɪˈstreɪn] *vt* contener; **to r. one's anger** reprimir la cólera; **to r. oneself** contenerse

restrained [rɪˈstreɪnd] *adj* *(person)* moderado(a); *(emotion)* contenido(a)

restraint [rɪˈstreɪnt] *n* (**a**) *(restriction)* restricción *f*; *(hindrance)* traba *f* (**b**) *(moderation)* moderación *f*

restrict [rɪˈstrɪkt] *vt* restringir, limitar

restriction [rɪˈstrɪkʃən] *n* restricción *f*, limitación *f*

restrictive [rɪˈstrɪktɪv] *adj* restrictivo(a)

result [rɪˈzʌlt] **1** *n* (**a**) resultado *m* (**b**) *(consequence)* consecuencia *f*; **as a r. of** como consecuencia de
2 *vi* (**a**) resultar; **to r. from** resultar de (**b**) **to r. in** causar

resume [rɪˈzjuːm] **1** *vt* *(journey, work, conversation)* reanudar; *(control)* reasumir
2 *vi* recomenzar

> ⟋ Note that the Spanish verb **resumir** is a false friend and is never a translation for the English verb **to resume**. In Spanish, **resumir** means "to sum up, to summarize".

résumé [ˈrezjʊmeɪ] *n* (**a**) *(summary)* resumen *m* (**b**) *US (curriculum vitae)* currículum (vitae) *m*

resumption [rɪˈzʌmpʃən] *n* *(of journey, work, conversation)* reanudación *f*

resurface [riːˈsɜːfɪs] **1** *vt* *(road)* rehacer el firme de
2 *vi Fig* resurgir

resurgence [rɪˈsɜːdʒəns] *n* resurgimiento *m*

resurrection [rezəˈrekʃən] *n* resurrección *f*

resuscitate [rɪˈsʌsɪteɪt] *vt Med* reanimar

retail [ˈriːteɪl] **1** *n* venta *f* al por menor; **r. outlet** punto *m* de venta; **r. price** precio *m* de venta al público; **R. Price Index** Indice *m* de Precios al Consumo
2 *vt* vender al por menor
3 *vi* venderse al por menor
4 *adv* al por menor

retailer [ˈriːteɪlə(r)] *n* detallista *mf*

retain [rɪˈteɪn] *vt* (**a**) *(heat)* conservar; *(personal effects)* guardar (**b**) *(water)* retener (**c**) *(facts, information)* recordar (**d**) **to r. the services of a lawyer** contratar a un abogado

retainer [rɪˈteɪnə(r)] *n* (**a**) *(payment)* anticipo *m* sobre los honorarios (**b**) *(servant)* criado(a) *m,f*

retaliate [rɪˈtælieɪt] *vi* tomar represalias (**against** contra)

retaliation [rɪtælɪˈeɪʃən] *n* represalias *fpl*; **in r.** en represalia

retarded [rɪˈtɑːdɪd] *adj* retrasado(a)

retch [retʃ] *vi* tener náuseas

retentive [rɪˈtentɪv] *adj* retentivo(a)

rethink [ˈriːθɪŋk] *n Fam* **to have a r. about sth** volver a reflexionar sobre algo

reticent [ˈretɪsənt] *adj* reticente

retina [ˈretɪnə] *n* retina *f*

retinue [ˈretɪnjuː] *n* séquito *m*

retire [rɪˈtaɪə(r)] **1** *vt* jubilar
2 *vi* (**a**) *(stop working)* jubilarse (**b**) *(from race)* retirarse; **to r. for the night** irse a la cama, acostarse

retired [rɪˈtaɪəd] *adj* jubilado(a)

retiree [rɪtaɪəˈriː] *n US* retirado(a) *m,f*

retirement [rɪˈtaɪəmənt] *n* jubilación *f*

retiring [rɪˈtaɪərɪŋ] *adj* (**a**) *(reserved)* reservado(a) (**b**) *(official)* saliente

retort [rɪˈtɔːt] **1** *n* réplica *f*
2 *vi* replicar

retrace [riːˈtreɪs] *vt* *(recall)* reconstruir; **to r. one's steps** volver sobre sus pasos

retract [rɪˈtrækt] **1** *vt* (**a**) *(claws)* retraer; *(landing gear)* replegar (**b**) *(statement)* retirar
2 *vi* (**a**) *(claws)* retraerse; *(landing gear)* replegarse (**b**) *Fml* retractarse

retread [ˈriːtred] *n Aut* neumático recauchutado

retreat [rɪˈtriːt] **1** *n* (**a**) *Mil* retirada *f* (**b**) *(shelter)* refugio *m* (**c**) *Rel* retiro *m*
2 *vi* retirarse (**from** de)

retrial [ˈriːtraɪəl] *n Jur* nuevo juicio

retribution [retrɪˈbjuːʃən] *n* represalias *fpl*

> ⟋ Note that the Spanish word **retribución** is a false friend and is never a translation for the English word **retribution**. In Spanish, **retribución** means "payment, reward".

retrieval [rɪˈtriːvəl] *n* recuperación *f*; *Comput* **information r. system** sistema *m* de recuperación de datos

retrieve [rɪˈtriːv] *vt* (**a**) *(recover)* recuperar; *(of dog)* cobrar; *Comput* recoger (**b**) *(rescue)* salvar

retriever [rɪˈtriːvə(r)] *n* perro *m* cazador

retrograde ['retrəʊgreɪd] *adj* retrógrado(a)

retrospect ['retrəʊspekt] *n* **in r.** retrospectivamente

retrospective [retrəʊ'spektɪv] **1** *adj* retrospectivo(a)

2 *n Art* (exposición *f*) retrospectiva *f*

return [rɪ'tɜːn] **1** *n* (**a**) *(of person)* regreso *m*, vuelta *f*; **by r. of post** a vuelta de correo; **in r. for** a cambio de; **many happy returns!** ¡felicidades!; **r. match** partido *m* de vuelta; *Br* **r. (ticket)** billete *m* de ida y vuelta (**b**) *(of sth borrowed, stolen)* devolución *f* (**c**) *(profit)* beneficio *m*, ganancia *f* (**d**) *(interest)* interés *m*

2 *vt* (**a**) *(give back)* devolver; **r. to sender** *(on envelope)* devuélvase al remitente; **to r. a favour/sb's love** corresponder a un favor/al amor de algn (**b**) *Br Pol* elegir (**c**) *Jur (verdict)* pronunciar

3 *vi* (**a**) *(come or go back)* volver, regresar (**b**) *(reappear)* reaparecer

returnable [rɪ'tɜːnəbəl] *adj (bottle)* retornable

reunion [riː'juːnjən] *n* reunión *f*

reunite [riːjuː'naɪt] *vt* **to be reunited with** *(after separation)* reunirse con

rev [rev] *Fam Aut* **1** *n* revolución *f*

2 *vi* **to r. (up)** acelerar el motor

revamp [riː'væmp] *vt Fam* modernizar, renovar

reveal [rɪ'viːl] *vt (make known)* revelar; *(show)* dejar ver

revealing [rɪ'viːlɪŋ] *adj* revelador(a)

reveille [rɪ'vælɪ] *n* diana *f*

revel ['revəl] *vi* disfrutar (**in** con); **to r. in doing sth** gozar muchísimo haciendo algo

revelation [revə'leɪʃən] *n* revelación *f*

revelry ['revəlrɪ] *n* jarana *f*, juerga *f*

revenge [rɪ'vendʒ] *n* venganza *f*; **to take r. on sb for sth** vengarse de algo en algn

revenue ['revɪnjuː] *n* renta *f*

reverberate [rɪ'vɜːbəreɪt] *vi* (**a**) *(sound)* reverberar (**b**) *(ideas, news)* resonar

reverberation [rɪvɜːbə'reɪʃən] *n* resonancia *f*

revere [rɪ'vɪə(r)] *vt* reverenciar

reverence ['revərəns] *n* reverencia *f*

reverend ['revərənd] *Rel* **1** *adj* reverendo(a); **R. Mother** reverenda madre

2 *n* (Protestant) pastor *m*; (Catholic) padre *m*

reverie ['revərɪ] *n* ensueño *m*

reversal [rɪ'vɜːsəl] *n* (**a**) *(of order)* inversión *f* (**b**) *(of attitude, policy)* cambio *m* total (**c**) *Jur* revocación *f*

reverse [rɪ'vɜːs] **1** *adj* inverso(a); *Br*

r.-charge call llamada *f or Am* llamado *m* a cobro revertido

2 *n* (**a**) **quite the r.** todo lo contrario (**b**) *(other side) (of cloth)* revés *m*; *(of coin)* cruz *f*; *(of page)* dorso *m* (**c**) *Aut* **r. gear** marcha *f* atrás

3 *vt* (**a**) *(order)* invertir (**b**) *(turn round)* volver del revés (**c**) *(change)* cambiar totalmente (**d**) *Jur* revocar (**e**) *Br Tel* **to r. the charges** poner una conferencia a cobro revertido

4 *vi Aut* dar marcha atrás

revert [rɪ'vɜːt] *vi* volver (**to** a)

review [rɪ'vjuː] **1** *n* (**a**) *(examination)* examen *m* (**b**) *Mil* revista *f* (**c**) *Press* crítica *f*, reseña *f* (**d**) *(magazine)* revista *f*

2 *vt* (**a**) *(examine)* examinar (**b**) *Mil* **to r. the troops** pasar revista a las tropas (**c**) *(book etc)* hacer una crítica de

reviewer [rɪ'vjuːə(r)] *n* crítico(a) *m,f*

revile [rɪ'vaɪl] *vt Fml* injuriar

revise [rɪ'vaɪz] *vt* (**a**) *(look over)* revisar; *(at school)* repasar (**b**) *(change)* modificar (**c**) *(proofs)* corregir

revision [rɪ'vɪʒən] *n* (**a**) revisión *f*; *(at school)* repaso *m* (**b**) *(change)* modificación *f* (**c**) *(of proofs)* corrección *f*

revitalize [riː'vaɪtəlaɪz] *vt* revivificar

revival [rɪ'vaɪvəl] *n* (**a**) *(of interest)* renacimiento *m*; *(of economy, industry)* reactivación *f*; *(of a country)* resurgimiento *m* (**b**) *Th* reestreno *m* (**c**) *Med* reanimación *f*

revive [rɪ'vaɪv] *vt* (**a**) *(interest)* renovar; *(a law)* restablecer; *(economy, industry)* reactivar; *(hopes)* despertar (**b**) *Th* reestrenar (**c**) *Med* reanimar

2 *vi* (**a**) *(interest, hopes)* renacer (**b**) *Med* volver en sí

revoke [rɪ'vəʊk] *vt* revocar; *(permission)* suspender

revolt [rɪ'vəʊlt] **1** *n* rebelión *f*, sublevación *f*

2 *vi* rebelarse, sublevarse

3 *vt* repugnar, dar asco a

revolting [rɪ'vəʊltɪŋ] *adj* repugnante

revolution [revə'luːʃən] *n* revolución *f*

revolutionary [revə'luːʃənərɪ] *adj & n* revolucionario(a) *(m,f)*

revolve [rɪ'vɒlv] **1** *vi* girar; *Fig* **to r. around** girar en torno a

2 *vt* hacer girar

Note that the Spanish verb **revolver** *is a false friend and is never a translation for the English verb* **to revolve**. *In Spanish,* **revolver** *means* "to stir, to mix" *and* "to mess up".

---

revolver [rɪ'vɒlvə(r)] *n* revólver *m*

revolving [rɪ'vɒlvɪŋ] *adj* giratorio(a)

revue [rɪ'vjuː] *n* revista *f*
revulsion [rɪ'vʌlʃən] *n* repulsión *f*
reward [rɪ'wɔːd] **1** *n* recompensa *f*
  2 *vt* recompensar
rewarding [rɪ'wɔːdɪŋ] *adj* provechoso(a)
rewire [riː'waɪə(r)] *vt Elec* **to r. a house**
  poner nueva instalación eléctrica a una
  casa
reword [riː'wɜːd] *vt* expresar con otras
  palabras
rewrite [riː'raɪt] *vt* (*pt* **rewrote** [riː'rəʊt];
  pp **rewritten** [riː'rɪtən]) escribir de nuevo
rhapsody ['ræpsədɪ] *n Mus* rapsodia *f*
rhetoric ['retərɪk] *n* retórica *f*
rhetorical [rɪ'tɒrɪkəl] *adj* retórico(a)
rheumatism ['ruːmətɪzəm] *n* reuma *m*
rheumatoid ['ruːmətɔɪd] *adj* **r. arthritis**
  reuma *m* articular
Rhine [raɪn] *n* **the R.** el Rin
rhinoceros [raɪ'nɒsərəs] *n* rinoceronte *m*
rhododendron [rəʊdə'dendrən] *n* rododendro *m*
Rhone [rəʊn] *n* **the R.** el Ródano
rhubarb ['ruːbɑːb] *n* ruibarbo *m*
rhyme [raɪm] **1** *n* rima *f*; (*poem*) poema *m*
  2 *vi* rimar
rhythm ['rɪðəm] *n* ritmo *m*
rib¹ [rɪb] *n* (**a**) *Anat* costilla *f*; **r. cage** caja
  torácica (**b**) (*in knitting*) canalé *m* (**c**) (*of
  umbrella*) varilla *f* (**d**) *Bot* (*of leaf*) nervio
  m
rib² [rɪb] *vt Fam* burlarse de
ribald ['rɪbəld] *adj* (*humour*) verde
ribbon ['rɪbən] *n* cinta *f*; (*in hair etc*) lazo
  m; **torn to ribbons** hecho(a) jirones
rice [raɪs] *n* arroz *m*; **brown r.** arroz integral; **r. paper** papel de arroz; **r. pudding**
  arroz con leche
rich [rɪtʃ] **1** *adj* (*person, food*) rico(a);
  (*soil*) fértil; (*voice*) sonoro(a); (*colour*)
  vivo(a)
  2 *npl* **the r.** los ricos
riches ['rɪtʃɪz] *npl* riquezas *fpl*
richly ['rɪtʃlɪ] *adv* ricamente; **r. deserved**
  bien merecido(a)
richness ['rɪtʃnɪs] *n* riqueza *f*; (*of soil*)
  fertilidad *f*; (*of voice*) sonoridad *f*; (*of
  colour*) viveza *f*
rickets ['rɪkɪts] *n sing Med* raquitismo *m*
rickety ['rɪkətɪ] *adj* (*chair etc*) cojo(a);
  (*car*) desvencijado(a)
ricochet ['rɪkəʃeɪ, 'rɪkəʃet] **1** *n* rebote *m*
  2 *vi* rebotar
rid [rɪd] *vt* (*pt & pp* **rid**) librar; **to get r. of
  sth** deshacerse de algo; **to r. oneself of**
  librarse de
riddance ['rɪdəns] *n Fam* **good r.!** ¡ya era
  hora!

ridden ['rɪdən] *pp of* **ride**
riddle¹ ['rɪdəl] *n* (**a**) (*puzzle*) acertijo *m*,
  adivinanza *f* (**b**) (*mystery*) enigma *m*
riddle² ['rɪdəl] *vt* (*with bullets*) acribillar
ride [raɪd] **1** *n* paseo *m*, vuelta *f*; **a short
  bus r.** un corto trayecto en autobús; *Fam*
  to take sb for a r. tomar el pelo a algn;
  horse r. paseo a caballo
  2 *vt* (*pt* **rode**; *pp* **ridden**) (*bicycle, horse*)
  montar en; **can you r. a bike?** ¿sabes
  montar en bici?
  3 *vi* (**a**) (*on horse*) montar a caballo (**b**)
  (*travel*) (*in bus, train etc*) viajar (**c**) *Naut* **to
  r. at anchor** estar anclado(a)
  ▸ **ride out** *vt sep* sobrevivir; **to r. out the
  storm** capear el temporal
rider ['raɪdə(r)] *n* (*of horse*) (*man*) jinete
  m; (*woman*) amazona *f*; (*of bicycle*) ciclista *mf*; (*of motorbike*) motociclista *mf*
ridge [rɪdʒ] *n* (*crest of a hill*) cresta *f*;
  (*hillock*) loma *f*; (*of roof*) caballete *m*;
  Met área *m*
ridicule ['rɪdɪkjuːl] **1** *n* burla *f*
  2 *vt* burlarse de
ridiculous [rɪ'dɪkjʊləs] *adj* ridículo(a)
riding ['raɪdɪŋ] *n* equitación *f*; **r. breeches**
  pantalones *mpl* de montar; **r. school** escuela hípica
rife [raɪf] *adj* abundante; **rumour is r. that
  ...** corre la voz de que ...; **to be r. with**
  abundar en
riffraff ['rɪfræf] *n Fam* chusma *f*, gentuza
  f
rifle¹ ['raɪfəl] *n* fusil *m*, rifle *m*; **r. range**
  campo *m* de tiro
rifle² ['raɪfəl] *vt* desvalijar
rift [rɪft] *n* (**a**) *Geol* falla *f* (**b**) *Fig* (*in
  friendship*) ruptura *f*; *Pol* (*in party*) escisión *f*; (*quarrel*) desavenencia *f*
rig [rɪg] **1** *n* (**a**) *Naut* aparejo *m* (**b**) (**oil**) **r.**
  (*onshore*) torre *f* de perforación; (*off-
  shore*) plataforma petrolífera
  2 *vt Pej* amañar
  ▸ **rig out** *vt sep Fam* ataviar
  ▸ **rig up** *vt sep* improvisar
rigging ['rɪgɪŋ] *n* aparejo *m*, jarcia *f*
right [raɪt] **1** *adj* (**a**) (*not left*) derecho(a);
  the r. hand la mano derecha
   (**b**) (*correct*) correcto(a); (*time*) exac-
  to(a); **to be r.** tener razón; **all r.** de acuerdo; **r.?** ¿vale?; **that's r.** eso es; **the r. word**
  la palabra justa
   (**c**) (*true*) cierto(a)
   (**d**) (*suitable*) adecuado(a); **the r. time** el
  momento oportuno
   (**e**) (*proper*) apropiado(a)
   (**f**) *Fam* (*healthy*) bien
   (**g**) *Fam* (*complete*) auténtico(a)

(**h**) *(in order)* en orden
(**i**) **r. angle** ángulo recto
2 *n* (**a**) *(right side)* derecha *f*
(**b**) *(right hand)* mano derecha
(**c**) *Pol* **the R.** la derecha
(**d**) *(lawful claim)* derecho *m*; **in one's own r.** por derecho propio; **r. of way** *(across land)* derecho de paso; *(on roads)* prioridad *f*; **civil rights** derechos civiles
(**e**) **r. and wrong** el bien y el mal
3 *adv* (**a**) *(correctly)* bien; **it's just r.** es justo lo que hace falta
(**b**) **r. away** *(immediately)* en seguida
(**c**) *(to the right)* a la derecha; **r. and left** a diestro y siniestro; **to turn r.** girar a la derecha
(**d**) *(directly)* directamente; **go r. on** sigue recto; **r. at the top** en todo lo alto; **r. in the middle** justo en medio; **r. to the end** hasta el final
4 *vt* (**a**) *(correct)* corregir
(**b**) *(put straight)* enderezar
righteous ['raɪtʃəs] *adj (upright)* recto(a)
rightful ['raɪtfʊl] *adj* legítimo(a)
right-hand ['raɪthænd] *adj* derecho(a); **r. drive** conducción *f* por la derecha; **r. side** lado derecho; *Fam* **r. man** brazo derecho
right-handed [raɪt'hændɪd] *adj (person)* que usa la mano derecha; *(tool)* para la mano derecha
rightly ['raɪtlɪ] *adv* debidamente; **and r. so** y con razón
right-wing ['raɪtwɪŋ] *adj* de derechas, derechista
right-winger [raɪt'wɪŋə(r)] *n* derechista *mf*
rigid ['rɪdʒɪd] *adj* rígido(a), inflexible
rigidity [rɪ'dʒɪdɪtɪ] *n* rigidez *f*, inflexibilidad *f*
rigmarole ['rɪgmərəʊl] *n Fam* galimatías *m inv*
rigor ['rɪgər] *n US =* **rigour**
rigorous ['rɪgərəs] *adj* riguroso(a)
rigour ['rɪgə(r)] *n* rigor *m*, severidad *f*
rile [raɪl] *vt Fam* irritar, sacar de quicio
rim [rɪm] *n (edge)* borde *m*; *(of wheel)* llanta *f*; *(of spectacles)* montura *f*
rind [raɪnd] *n (of fruit, cheese)* corteza *f*
ring¹ [rɪŋ] **1** *n* (**a**) *(sound of bell)* toque *m*; *(of doorbell, alarm clock)* timbre *m* (**b**) *Tel* llamada *f*
2 *vt* (*pt* **rang**; *pp* **rung**) (**a**) *(bell)* tocar; *Fig* **it rings a bell** me suena (**b**) *Br Tel* llamar por teléfono
3 *vi* (**a**) *(bell, phone etc)* sonar (**b**) **my ears are ringing** tengo un pitido en los oídos (**c**) *Tel* llamar

▸ **ring back** *vt sep Br Tel* volver a llamar
▸ **ring off** *vi Br Tel* colgar
▸ **ring out** *vi* resonar
▸ **ring up** *vt sep Br Tel* llamar por teléfono a
ring² [rɪŋ] **1** *n* (**a**) *(metal hoop)* aro *m*; **curtain r.** anilla *f*; **r. binder** carpeta *f* de anillas (**b**) *(for finger)* anillo *m*, sortija *f*; **r. finger** dedo *m* anular (**c**) *(circle)* círculo *m*; *Br* **r. road** carretera *f* de circunvalación (**d**) **rings** *(in gymnastics)* anillas *fpl* (**e**) *(group of people)* corro *m*; *(of spies)* red *f*; *(of thieves)* banda *f* (**f**) *(arena)* pista *f*; *(for boxing)* cuadrilátero *m*; *(for bullfights)* ruedo *m*; **circus r.** pista de circo
2 *vt* (**a**) *(bird, animal)* anillar (**b**) *(surround)* rodear
ringing ['rɪŋɪŋ] *n (of bell)* toque *m*, repique *m*; *(in ears)* pitido *m*
ringleader ['rɪŋliːdə(r)] *n* cabecilla *mf*
ringlet ['rɪŋlɪt] *n* tirabuzón *m*
rink [rɪŋk] *n* pista *f*; **ice r.** pista de hielo
rinse [rɪns] **1** *n* (**a**) *(of clothes, hair)* aclarado *m*, enjuague *m*; *(of dishes)* enjuagado *m* (**b**) *(tint for hair)* reflejo *m*
2 *vt* (**a**) aclarar; *(the dishes)* enjuagar (**b**) **to r. one's hair** *(tint)* darse reflejos en el pelo
riot ['raɪət] **1** *n* (**a**) disturbio *m*, motín *m*; **to run r.** desmandarse; **r. police** policía *f* antidisturbios (**b**) *Fig (of colour)* profusión *f*
2 *vi* amotinarse
rioter ['raɪətə(r)] *n* amotinado(a) *m,f*
riotous ['raɪətəs] *adj* (**a**) amotinado(a) (**b**) *(noisy)* bullicioso(a) (**c**) *(unrestrained)* desenfrenado(a)
rip [rɪp] **1** *n (tear)* rasgón *m*
2 *vt* rasgar, rajar; **to r. one's trousers** rajarse los pantalones
3 *vi* rasgarse, rajarse
▸ **rip off** *vt sep Fam* **to r. sb off** timar a algn
▸ **rip up** *vt sep* hacer pedacitos
ripcord ['rɪpkɔːd] *n* cuerda *f* de apertura
ripe [raɪp] *adj* (**a**) maduro(a) (**b**) *(ready)* listo(a); **the time is r.** es el momento oportuno
ripen ['raɪpən] *vt & vi* madurar
rip-off ['rɪpɒf] *n Fam* timo *m*
ripple ['rɪpəl] **1** *n* (**a**) *(on water, fabric)* onda *f* (**b**) *(sound)* murmullo *m*
2 *vt (water)* ondular
3 *vi* (**a**) *(water)* ondularse (**b**) *(applause)* extenderse
rise [raɪz] **1** *n* (**a**) *(of slope, hill)* cuesta *f*
(**b**) *(of waters)* crecida *f*
(**c**) *(in status)* ascenso *m*

(**d**) *(in prices, temperature)* subida *f; (in wages)* aumento *m*
(**e**) *(in sound)* aumento *m*
(**f**) **to give r. to** ocasionar
 2 *vi (pt* **rose**; *pp* **risen** ['rɪzən]) (**a**) *(land etc)* elevarse
(**b**) *(waters)* crecer; *(river)* nacer; *(tide)* subir; *(wind)* levantarse
(**c**) *(sun, moon)* salir
(**d**) *(voice)* alzarse
(**e**) *(in rank)* ascender
(**f**) *(prices, temperature)* subir; *(wages)* aumentar
(**g**) *(curtain)* subir
(**h**) *(from bed)* levantarse
(**i**) *(stand up)* levantarse; *Fig (city, building)* erguirse
(**j**) **to r. to a challenge** aceptar un reto; **to r. to the occasion** ponerse a la altura de las circunstancias
▸ **rise above** *vt insep* estar por encima de
▸ **rise up** *vi (rebel)* sublevarse
rising ['raɪzɪŋ] **1** *adj (sun)* naciente; *(tide)* creciente; *(prices)* en aumento; **r. damp** humedad *f*
 2 *n* (**a**) *(of sun)* salida *f* (**b**) *(rebellion)* levantamiento *m*
risk [rɪsk] **1** *n* riesgo *m*; **at r.** en peligro; **at your own r.** por su cuenta y riesgo; **to take risks** arriesgarse
 2 *vt* arriesgar; **I'll r. it** correré el riesgo
risky ['rɪskɪ] *adj* (**riskier, riskiest**) arriesgado(a)
risqué ['rɪskeɪ] *adj* atrevido(a); *(joke)* picante
rite [raɪt] *n* rito *m*; **the last rites** la extremaunción
ritual ['rɪtjʊəl] *adj & n* ritual *(m)*
rival ['raɪvəl] **1** *adj & n* rival *(mf)*
 2 *vt* rivalizar con
rivalry ['raɪvəlrɪ] *n* rivalidad *f*
river ['rɪvə(r)] *n* río *m*; **down/up r.** río abajo/arriba
river-bank ['rɪvəbæŋk] *n* orilla *f*, ribera *f*
river-bed ['rɪvəbed] *n* lecho *m*
rivet ['rɪvɪt] **1** *n Tech* remache *m*, roblón *m*
 2 *vt Tech* remachar; *Fig* cautivar
riveting ['rɪvɪtɪŋ] *adj Fig* fascinante
roach [rəʊtʃ] *n US Fam (cockroach)* cucaracha *f*
road [rəʊd] *n* (**a**) carretera *f*; *Br* **A/B r.** carretera nacional/secundaria; **main r.** carretera principal; **r. accident** accidente *m* de tráfico; **r. safety** seguridad *f* vial; **r. sign** señal *f* de tráfico; **r.** *Br* **works** *or US* **work** obras *fpl* (**b**) *(street)* calle *f* (**c**) *(way)* camino *m*

roadblock ['rəʊdblɒk] *n* control *m* policial
roadhog ['rəʊdhɒg] *n Fam* loco(a) *m,f* del volante, dominguero(a) *m,f*
roadside ['rəʊdsaɪd] *n* borde *m* de la carretera; **r. restaurant/café** restaurante *m*/cafetería *f* de carretera
roadway ['rəʊdweɪ] *n* calzada *f*
roadworthy ['rəʊdwɜːðɪ] *adj (vehicle)* en buen estado
roam [rəʊm] **1** *vt* vagar por, rondar
 2 *vi* vagar
roar [rɔː(r)] **1** *n (of lion)* rugido *m*; *(of bull, sea, wind)* bramido *m*; *(of crowd)* clamor *m*
 2 *vi (lion, crowd)* rugir; *(bull, sea, wind)* bramar; *(crowd)* clamar; *Fig* **to r. with laughter** reírse a carcajadas
roaring ['rɔːrɪŋ] *adj Fam Fig* **a r. success** un éxito clamoroso; **to do a r. trade** hacer un negocio redondo
roast [rəʊst] **1** *adj (meat)* asado(a); **r. beef** rosbif *m*
 2 *n Culin* asado *m*
 3 *vt (meat)* asar; *(coffee, nuts)* tostar
 4 *vi* asarse; *Fam Fig* **I'm roasting** me aso de calor
rob [rɒb] *vt* robar; *(bank)* atracar
robber ['rɒbə(r)] *n* ladrón(ona) *m,f*; **bank r.** atracador(a) *m,f*
robbery ['rɒbərɪ] *n* robo *m*
robe [rəʊb] *n (ceremonial)* toga *f*; *(dressing gown)* bata *f*
robin ['rɒbɪn] *n* petirrojo *m*
robot ['rəʊbɒt] *n* robot *m*
robust [rəʊ'bʌst] *adj (sturdy)* robusto(a)
rock [rɒk] **1** *n* (**a**) roca *f; Fig* **to be on the rocks** *(of marriage)* estar a punto de fracasar; *Fig* **whisky on the rocks** whisky *m* con hielo (**b**) *US (stone)* piedra *f* (**c**) *Br (sweet)* **stick of r.** barra *f* de caramelo (**d**) *Mus* música *f* rock; **r. and roll** rock and roll *m*
 2 *vt* (**a**) *(chair)* mecer; *(baby)* acunar (**b**) *(shake)* hacer temblar; *Fig (shock)* conmover
 3 *vi* (**a**) *(move to and fro)* mecerse (**b**) *(shake)* vibrar
rock-bottom ['rɒk'bɒtəm] *adj* bajísimo(a); **r. prices** precios regalados
rockery ['rɒkərɪ] *n* jardín *m* de rocas
rocket ['rɒkɪt] **1** *n* cohete *m*; **r. launcher** lanzacohetes *m inv*
 2 *vi Fam (prices)* dispararse
rocking-chair ['rɒkɪŋtʃeə(r)] *n* mecedora *f*
rocking-horse ['rɒkɪŋhɔːs] *n* caballito *m* de balancín

rocky ['rɒkɪ] *adj* (**rockier, rockiest**) roco-so(a); *Fam Fig (unsteady)* inseguro(a); **the R. Mountains** las Montañas Rocosas

rod [rɒd] *n (of metal)* barra *f*; *(stick)* vara *f*; **fishing r.** caña *f* de pescar

rode [rəʊd] *pt of* **ride**

rodent ['rəʊdənt] *n* roedor *m*

roe¹ [rəʊ] *n Zool* **r. (deer)** corzo(a) *m,f*

roe² [rəʊ] *n (fish eggs)* hueva *f*

rogue [rəʊg] *n* granuja *m*

role, rôle [rəʊl] *n* papel *m*; **to play a r.** desempeñar un papel

roll [rəʊl] **1** *n* (**a**) rollo *m*; **r. of banknotes** fajo *m* de billetes; *Fam Fig* **rolls of fat** michelines *mpl* (**b**) **(bread) r.** bollo *m* (**c**) *(list of names)* lista *f*, nómina *f*; **to call the r.** pasar lista (**d**) *(movement of ship)* balanceo *m* (**e**) *(of drum)* redoble *m*; *(of thunder)* fragor *m*
2 *vt* (**a**) *(ball)* hacer rodar (**b**) *(cigarette)* liar (**c**) *(move)* mover (**d**) *(push)* empujar (**e**) *(lawn, road)* allanar
3 *vi* (**a**) *(ball)* rodar; *Fam* **to be rolling in money** estar forrado(a) (**b**) *(animal)* revolcarse (**c**) *(ship)* balancearse (**d**) *(drum)* redoblar; *(thunder)* retumbar
▸ **roll about, roll around** *vi* rodar (de acá para allá)
▸ **roll by** *vi (years)* pasar
▸ **roll in** *vi Fam* (**a**) *(arrive)* llegar (**b**) *(money)* llegar a raudales
▸ **roll over** *vi* dar una vuelta
▸ **roll up 1** *vt sep* enrollar; *(blinds)* subir; **to r. up one's sleeves** (ar)remangarse
2 *vi Fam (arrive)* llegar

roll-call ['rəʊlkɔːl] *n* **to have a r.** pasar lista

roller ['rəʊlə(r)] *n* (**a**) *Tech* rodillo *m*; **r. blades** patines *mpl* en línea; **r. coaster** montaña rusa; **r. skates** patines *mpl* (de ruedas) (**b**) *(large wave)* ola *f* grande (**c**) *(for hair)* rulo *m*

rolling ['rəʊlɪŋ] **1** *adj* (**a**) *Rail* **r. stock** material *m* rodante (**b**) *(countryside)* ondulado(a)
2 *n* rodamiento *m*; *(of ground)* apisonamiento *m*; **r. pin** rodillo *m* (de cocina)

ROM [rɒm] *n Comput (abbr* **read-only memory**) ROM *f*

Roman ['rəʊmən] *adj & n* romano(a) *(m,f)*; **R. Catholic** católico(a) *m,f* (romano(a)); **R. law** derecho romano; **R. numerals** números romanos

Romance [rəʊ'mæns] *adj Ling* románico(a), romance; **R. languages** lenguas románicas

romance [rəʊ'mæns] **1** *n* (**a**) *(tale)* novela romántica (**b**) *(love affair)* aventura amorosa (**c**) *(romantic quality)* lo romántico
2 *vi* fantasear

Romania [rə'meɪnɪə] *n* Rumanía

Romanian [rə'meɪnɪən] **1** *adj* rumano(a)
2 *n (person)* rumano(a) *m,f*; *(language)* rumano *m*

romantic [rəʊ'mæntɪk] *adj & n* romántico(a) *(m,f)*

Rome [rəʊm] *n* Roma

romp [rɒmp] **1** *n* jugueteo *m*
2 *vi* juguetear

rompers ['rɒmpəz] *npl* pelele *m*

roof [ruːf] **1** *n (pl* **roofs** [ruːfs, ruːvz]) (**a**) tejado *m*; *Fam Fig* **to go through the r.** *(of prices)* estar por las nubes; *(with anger)* subirse por las paredes (**b**) *Aut* techo *m*; **r. rack** baca *f* (**c**) *(of mouth)* cielo *m*
2 *vt* techar

roofing ['ruːfɪŋ] *n* materiales *mpl* usados para techar

rook [rʊk] *n* (**a**) *Orn* grajo *m* (**b**) *(in chess)* torre *f*

rookie ['rʊkɪ] *n US Fam (novice)* novato(a) *m,f*

room [ruːm] *n* (**a**) habitación *f*, cuarto *m*; **single r.** habitación individual; **r. service** servicio *m* de habitación (**b**) *(space)* sitio *m*, espacio *m*; **make r. for me** hazme sitio

rooming-house ['ruːmɪŋhaʊs] *n US* pensión *f*

roommate ['ruːmmeɪt] *n* compañero(a) *m,f* de habitación

roomy ['ruːmɪ] *adj* (**roomier, roomiest**) amplio(a)

roost [ruːst] **1** *n* palo *m*, percha *f*; *(hen)* **r.** gallinero *m*; *Fig* **to rule the r.** llevar la batuta
2 *vi* posarse

rooster ['ruːstə(r)] *n esp US* gallo *m*

root¹ [ruːt] **1** *n* raíz *f*; **to take r.** echar raíces
2 *vt* arraigar
3 *vi* arraigar
▸ **root out, root up** *vt sep* arrancar de raíz

root² [ruːt] *vi (search)* buscar; **to r. about** *or* **around for sth** hurgar en busca de algo

root³ [ruːt] *vi Fam* **to r. for a team** animar a un equipo

rope [rəʊp] **1** *n* (**a**) *(thin)* cuerda *f*; *(thick)* soga *f*; *Naut* cabo *m* (**b**) *Fig* **to have sb on the ropes** tener a algn contra las cuerdas; *Fam Fig* **to know the ropes** estar al tanto
2 *vt (package)* atar; *(climbers)* encordar

> ℓ Note that the Spanish word **ropa** is a false friend and is never a translation for the English word **rope**. In Spanish, **ropa** means "clothes".

▸**rope in** *vt sep Fam* enganchar
▸**rope off** *vt sep* acordonar
rop(e)y ['rəʊpɪ] *adj* (**ropier, ropiest**) *Br Fam* chungo(a)
rosary ['rəʊzərɪ] *n* rosario *m*
rose¹ [rəʊz] *pt of* **rise**
rose² [rəʊz] *n* (**a**) *Bot* rosa *f*; **r. bed** rosaleda *f*; **r. bush** rosal *m* (**b**) (*colour*) rosa *m* (**c**) (*of watering can*) alcachofa *f*
rosé ['rəʊzeɪ] *n* (vino *m*) rosado *m*
rosebud ['rəʊzbʌd] *n* capullo *m* de rosa
rosemary ['rəʊzmərɪ] *n* romero *m*
rosette [rəʊ'zet] *n* (*of ribbons*) escarapela *f*
roster ['rɒstə(r)] *n* lista *f*
rostrum ['rɒstrəm] *n* estrado *m*

🖉 Note that the Spanish word **rostro** is a false friend and is never a translation for the English word **rostrum**. In Spanish, **rostro** means "face".

rosy ['rəʊzɪ] *adj* (**rosier, rosiest**) (**a**) (*complexion*) sonrosado(a) (**b**) *Fig* (*future*) prometedor(a)
rot [rɒt] **1** *n* (**a**) (*decay*) putrefacción *f*; **dry r.** putrefacción de la madera (**b**) *Fam* (*nonsense*) tonterías *fpl*
 2 *vt* pudrir
 ▸**rot away** *vi* pudrirse
rota ['rəʊtə] *n esp Br* lista *f*
rotary ['rəʊtərɪ] **1** *n US* (*for traffic*) rotonda *f*
 2 *adj* rotatorio(a), giratorio(a)
rotate [rəʊ'teɪt] **1** *vt* (**a**) (*revolve*) hacer girar (**b**) (*jobs, crops*) alternar
 2 *vi* (*revolve*) girar
rotating [rəʊ'teɪtɪŋ] *adj* rotativo(a)
rotation [rəʊ'teɪʃən] *n* rotación *f*
rote [rəʊt] *n* **by r.** de memoria
rotten ['rɒtən] *adj* (**a**) (*decayed*) podrido(a); (*tooth*) picado(a) (**b**) *Fam* (*very bad*) malísimo(a); *Fam* **I feel r.** me encuentro fatal
rouble ['ruːbəl] *n* rublo *m*
rouge [ruːʒ] **1** *n* colorete *m*
 2 *vt* poner colorete a
rough [rʌf] **1** *adj* (**a**) (*surface, skin*) áspero(a); (*terrain*) accidentado(a); (*road*) desigual; (*sea*) agitado(a); (*weather*) tempestuoso(a)
 (**b**) (*rude*) grosero(a); (*violent*) violento(a)
 (**c**) (*voice*) bronco(a)
 (**d**) (*wine*) áspero(a)
 (**e**) (*bad*) malo(a); *Fam* **to feel r.** encontrarse fatal
 (**f**) (*approximate*) aproximado(a)
 (**g**) (*plan etc*) preliminar; **r. draft**

borrador *m*; **r. sketch** esbozo *m*
 (**h**) (*harsh*) severo(a)
 2 *adv* duramente; *Fam Fig* **to sleep r.** dormir a la intemperie
 3 *n* (**a**) *Fam* (*person*) matón *m*
 (**b**) **the r.** (*in golf*) la hierba alta
 4 *vt Fam* **to r. it** vivir sin comodidades
roughage ['rʌfɪdʒ] *n* (*substance*) fibra *f*
rough-and-ready ['rʌfən'redɪ] *adj* improvisado(a)
roughen ['rʌfən] *vt* poner áspero(a)
roughly ['rʌflɪ] *adv* (**a**) (*crudely*) toscamente (**b**) (*clumsily*) torpemente (**c**) (*not gently*) bruscamente (**d**) (*approximately*) aproximadamente
roulette [ruː'let] *n* ruleta *f*
Roumania [ruː'meɪnɪə] *n* = **Romania**
round [raʊnd] **1** *adj* redondo(a); **in r. figures** en números redondos; **r. table** mesa redonda; **r. trip** viaje *m* de ida y vuelta
 2 *n* (**a**) (*circle*) círculo *m*
 (**b**) (*series*) serie *f*; **r. of talks** ronda *f* de negociaciones
 (**c**) (*of ammunition*) cartucho *m*; (*salvo*) salva *f*
 (**d**) **a r. of toast** una tostada
 (**e**) (*of drinks*) ronda *f*
 (**f**) **the daily r.** (*routine*) la rutina diaria
 (**g**) (*in golf*) partido *m*; *Cards* partida *f*
 (**h**) (*in boxing*) round *m*
 (**i**) (*in a competition*) eliminatoria *f*
 (**j**) **rounds** (*doctor's*) visita *f*; (*of salesman*) recorrido *m*
 3 *adv* **all year r.** durante todo el año; **to invite sb r.** invitar a algn a casa
 4 *prep* alrededor de; **r. here** por aquí; **r. the clock** día y noche; **r. the corner** a la vuelta de la esquina
 5 *vt* (*turn*) dar la vuelta a
 ▸**round off** *vt sep* acabar, concluir
 ▸**round on** *vt insep* (*attack*) atacar
 ▸**round up** *vt sep* (*cattle*) acorralar, rodear; (*people*) reunir
roundabout ['raʊndəbaʊt] **1** *n* (**a**) (*merry-go-round*) tiovivo *m* (**b**) *Br Aut* rotonda *f*
 2 *adj* indirecto(a)
rounders ['raʊndəz] *n Br* = juego parecido al béisbol
roundly ['raʊndlɪ] *adv* completamente, totalmente
round-shouldered ['raʊnd'ʃəʊldəd] *adj* cargado(a) de espaldas
round-trip ['raʊnd'trɪp] *US* **1** *n* billete *m* de ida y vuelta
 2 *adj* (*ticket*) de ida y vuelta
round-up ['raʊndʌp] *n* (**a**) (*of cattle*)

rodeo *m*; *(of suspects)* redada *f* (**b**) *(summary)* resumen *m*

rouse [raʊz] *vt* despertar; *(stir up)* suscitar

rousing ['raʊzɪŋ] *adj (cheer)* entusiasta; *(applause)* caluroso(a); *(speech, song)* conmovedor(a)

rout [raʊt] **1** *n* aniquilación *f*
2 *vt* aniquilar

route [ruːt] **1** *n* (**a**) ruta *f*; *(of bus)* línea *f*; *Naut* derrota *f*; *Fig* camino *m*; **r. map** mapa *m* de carreteras (**b**) *US* **R.** ≃ carretera *f* nacional
2 *vt* encaminar

routine [ruːˈtiːn] **1** *n* (**a**) rutina *f* (**b**) *Th* número *m*
2 *adj* rutinario(a)

roving ['rəʊvɪŋ] *adj* errante; **r. reporter** enviado(a) *m,f* especial

row¹ [rəʊ] *n* fila *f*, hilera *f*; *Fig* **three times in a r.** tres veces seguidas

row² [rəʊ] *vt & vi (in a boat)* remar

row³ [raʊ] **1** *n* (**a**) *(quarrel)* pelea *f*, bronca *f* (**b**) *(noise)* jaleo *m*; *(protest)* escándalo *m*
2 *vi* pelearse

rowboat ['rəʊbəʊt] *n US* bote *m* de remos

rowdy ['raʊdɪ] **1** *adj* (**rowdier, rowdiest**) (**a**) *(noisy)* ruidoso(a); *(disorderly)* alborotador(a) (**b**) *(quarrelsome)* camorrista
2 *n* camorrista *mf*

rowing ['rəʊɪŋ] *n* remo *m*; **r. boat** bote *m* de remos

royal ['rɔɪəl] **1** *adj* real; **r. blue** azul marino; **the R. Family** la Familia Real
2 *npl* **the Royals** los miembros de la Familia Real

royally ['rɔɪəlɪ] *adv Fig* magníficamente

royalty ['rɔɪəltɪ] *n* (**a**) *(royal persons)* miembro(s) *m(pl)* de la Familia Real (**b**) **royalties** derechos *mpl* de autor

RPI [ɑːpiːˈaɪ] *n* *(abbr* **Retail Price Index**) IPC *m*

rpm [ɑːpiːˈem] *n* *(abbr* **revolutions per minute**) r.p.m.

RSPCA [ɑːrespiːsiːˈeɪ] *n Br (abbr* **Royal Society for the Prevention of Cruelty to Animals**) ≃ Sociedad *f* Protectora de Animales

RSVP [ɑːresviːˈpiː] *(abbr* **répondez s'il vous plaît**) se ruega contestación, S.R.C.

Rt Hon *Br Pol (abbr* **(the) Right Honourable**) su Señoría

rub [rʌb] **1** *n* **to give sth a r.** frotar algo
2 *vt* frotar; *(hard)* restregar; *(massage)* friccionar
3 *vi* rozar (**against** contra)
▸ **rub down** *vt sep* rotar; *(horse)* almohazar; *(surface)* raspar

▸ **rub in** *vt sep* (**a**) *(cream etc)* frotar con (**b**) *Fam* **don't r. it in** no me lo refriegues

▸ **rub off 1** *vt sep (erase)* borrar
2 *vi Fig* **to r. off on sb** influir en algn

▸ **rub out** *vt sep* borrar

▸ **rub up** *vt sep Fam Fig* **to r. up the wrong way** fastidiar a algn

rubber¹ ['rʌbə(r)] *n* (**a**) *(substance)* caucho *m*, goma *f*; **r. band** goma; **r. plant** gomero *m*; **r. stamp** tampón *m* (**b**) *Br (eraser)* goma *f* (de borrar) (**c**) *Fam (condom)* goma *f*

rubber² ['rʌbə(r)] *n (in bridge)* rubber *m*

rubbery ['rʌbərɪ] *adj (elastic)* elástico(a)

rubbish ['rʌbɪʃ] *n* (**a**) *Br (refuse)* basura *f*; **r. bin** cubo *m* de la basura; **r. dump** *or* **tip** vertedero *m* (**b**) *Fam (worthless thing)* birria *f* (**c**) *Fam (nonsense)* tonterías *fpl*

rubble ['rʌbəl] *n* escombros *mpl*

rubric ['ruːbrɪk] *n* rúbrica *f*

ruby ['ruːbɪ] *n* rubí *m*

rucksack ['rʌksæk] *n* mochila *f*

ructions ['rʌkʃənz] *npl Fam* jaleo *m*

rudder ['rʌdə(r)] *n* timón *m*

ruddy ['rʌdɪ] *adj* (**ruddier, ruddiest**) (**a**) *(complexion)* rojizo(a), colorado(a) (**b**) *Br Fam (damned)* maldito(a)

rude [ruːd] *adj* (**a**) *(impolite)* maleducado(a); *(foul-mouthed)* grosero(a); **don't be r. to your mother** no le faltes al respeto a tu madre (**b**) *(abrupt)* **a r. awakening** un despertar repentino

rudimentary [ruːdɪˈmentərɪ] *adj* rudimentario(a)

rudiments ['ruːdɪmənts] *npl* rudimentos *mpl*

rue [ruː] *vt* arrepentirse de

rueful ['ruːfʊl] *adj (regretful)* arrepentido(a); *(sad)* triste

ruff [rʌf] *n (collar)* gorguera *f*

ruffian ['rʌfɪən] *n* canalla *m*

ruffle ['rʌfəl] *vt* (**a**) *(water)* agitar (**b**) *(feathers)* encrespar; *(hair)* despeinar (**c**) *Fig (annoy)* hacer perder la calma a

ruffled ['rʌfəld] *adj* (**a**) *(hair)* alborotado(a); *(clothes)* en desorden (**b**) *(perturbed)* perturbado(a)

rug [rʌg] *n* alfombra *f*, alfombrilla *f*

rugby ['rʌgbɪ] *n* rugby *m*; **r. league** rugby a trece; **r. union** rugby a quince

rugged ['rʌgɪd] *adj* (**a**) *(terrain)* accidentado(a) (**b**) *(features)* marcado(a) (**c**) *(character)* vigoroso(a)

rugger ['rʌgə(r)] *n Fam* rugby *m*

ruin ['ruːɪn] **1** *n* (**a**) ruina *f* (**b**) **ruins** ruinas *fpl*, restos *mpl*; **in ruins** en ruinas
2 *vt* arruinar; *(spoil)* estropear

rule [ruːl] **1** *n* (**a**) regla *f*, norma *f*; **to work**

to r. hacer una huelga de celo; **as a r.** por regla general (**b**) *(government)* dominio *m*; *(of monarch)* reinado *m*; **r. of law** imperio *m* de la ley

2 *vt & vi* (**a**) *(govern)* gobernar; *(of monarch)* reinar (**b**) *(decide)* decidir; *(decree)* decretar (**c**) *(draw)* tirar

▸ **rule out** *vt sep* descartar

ruled [ruːld] *adj* rayado(a)

ruler ['ruːlə(r)] *n* (**a**) dirigente *mf*; *(monarch)* soberano(a) *m,f* (**b**) *(for measuring)* regla *f*

ruling ['ruːlɪŋ] **1** *adj (in charge)* dirigente; *Fig (predominant)* predominante; **the r. party** el partido en el poder

2 *n Jur* fallo *m*

rum [rʌm] *n* ron *m*

Rumania [ruːˈmeɪnɪə] *n* = **Romania**

Rumanian [ruːˈmeɪnɪən] *adj & n* = **Romanian**

rumble ['rʌmbəl] **1** *n* (**a**) ruido sordo; *(of thunder)* estruendo *m* (**b**) *(of stomach)* ruido *m*

2 *vi* (**a**) hacer un ruido sordo; *(thunder)* retumbar (**b**) *(stomach etc)* hacer ruidos

ruminate ['ruːmɪneɪt] *vi (chew, ponder)* rumiar

rummage ['rʌmɪdʒ] *vi* revolver (**through** en); *US* **r. sale** *(in store)* = venta de productos discontinuados o sin salida en un almacén; *(for charity)* rastrillo benéfico

rumour, *US* **rumor** ['ruːmə(r)] **1** *n* rumor *m*; **r. has it that ...** se dice que ...

2 *vt* **it is rumoured that** se rumorea que

rump [rʌmp] *n (of animal)* ancas *fpl*; *Fam Hum (of person)* trasero *m*; **r. steak** filete *m* de lomo

rumpus ['rʌmpəs] *n Fam* jaleo *m*

run [rʌn] **1** *n* (**a**) carrera *f*; **on the r.** fugado(a); **to go for a r.** hacer footing; *Fig* **in the long r.** a largo plazo

(**b**) *(trip)* paseo *m*, vuelta *f*

(**c**) *(sequence)* serie *f*

(**d**) **ski r.** pista *f* de esquí

(**e**) *(demand)* gran demanda *f*; **a r. on** una gran demanda de

(**f**) **to give sb the r. of a house** poner una casa a disposición de algn

(**g**) *(print run)* tirada *f*

(**h**) *(in stocking)* carrera *f*

2 *vt (pt* **ran**; *pp* **run**) (**a**) correr; **to r. a race** correr en una carrera; **to r. errands** hacer recados

(**b**) *(drive)* llevar

(**c**) *(house, business)* llevar; *(company)* dirigir; *(organize)* organizar

(**d**) *(fingers)* pasar

(**e**) **it's a cheap car to r.** *(operate)* es un coche económico; *Comput* **to r. a program** pasar un programa

(**f**) *Press* publicar

3 *vi* (**a**) correr

(**b**) *(colour)* desteñirse

(**c**) *(water, river)* correr; **to leave the tap running** dejar el grifo abierto; *Fam* **your nose is running** se te caen los mocos

(**d**) *(operate) (machine)* funcionar (**on** con); **trains r. every two hours** hay trenes cada dos horas

(**e**) *Naut* **to r. aground** encallar

(**f**) *Pol* **to r. for president** presentarse como candidato a la presidencia

(**g**) **so the story runs** según lo que se dice

(**h**) *(range)* oscilar (**between** entre)

(**i**) **we're running low on milk** nos queda poca leche

(**j**) **shyness runs in the family** la timidez le viene de familia

(**k**) *Cin & Th* estar en cartel

(**l**) *(last)* durar

(**m**) *(stocking)* tener una carrera

▸ **run about** *vi* corretear

▸ **run across** *vt insep (meet)* tropezar con

▸ **run away** *vi* fugarse; *(horse)* desbocarse

▸ **run down 1** *vt insep (stairs)* bajar corriendo

2 *vt sep* (**a**) *(in car)* atropellar (**b**) *(criticize)* criticar

3 *vi (battery)* agotarse; *(clock)* pararse

▸ **run in** *vt sep Aut* rodar

▸ **run into** *vt insep* (**a**) *(room)* entrar corriendo en (**b**) *(people, problems)* tropezar con (**c**) *(crash into)* chocar contra

▸ **run off 1** *vt sep (print)* tirar

2 *vi* escaparse

▸ **run on 1** *vt sep Typ* enlazar

2 *vi (meeting)* continuar

▸ **run out** *vi* (**a**) *(exit)* salir corriendo (**b**) *(come to an end)* agotarse; *(of contract)* vencer; **to r. out of** quedarse sin

▸ **run over 1** *vt sep (in car)* atropellar

2 *vt insep (rehearse)* ensayar

3 *vi (overflow)* rebosar

▸ **run through** *vt insep* (**a**) *(of river)* pasar por (**b**) *(read quickly)* echar un vistazo a (**c**) *(rehearse)* ensayar

▸ **run up** *vt sep* (**a**) *(flag)* izar (**b**) *(debts)* acumular

▸ **run up against** *vt insep* tropezar con

runaway ['rʌnəweɪ] **1** *n* fugitivo(a) *m,f*

2 *adj (person)* huido(a); *(horse)* desbocado(a); *(vehicle)* incontrolado(a); *(inflation)* galopante; *(success)* clamoroso(a)

rundown ['rʌndaʊn] *n Fam* **to give sb a r.** poner a algn al corriente

run-down [rʌn'daʊn] *adj* (**a**) *(exhausted)* agotado(a) (**b**) *(dilapidated)* ruinoso(a)

rung¹ [rʌŋ] *pp of* **ring**

rung² [rʌŋ] *n (of ladder)* escalón *m*, peldaño *m*

runner ['rʌnə(r)] *n* (**a**) *(person)* corredor(a) *m,f* (**b**) *(horse)* caballo *m* de carreras (**c**) *(of skate)* cuchilla *f* (**d**) *(on table)* tapete *m* (**e**) **r. bean** judía escarlata

runner-up [rʌnər'ʌp] *n* subcampeón(ona) *m,f*

running ['rʌnɪŋ] **1** *n* (**a**) **he likes r.** le gusta correr; *Fig* **to be in the r. for sth** tener posibilidades de conseguir algo (**b**) *(of company)* dirección *f* (**c**) *(of machine)* funcionamiento *m*
2 *adj* (**a**) **r. commentary** comentario *m* en directo; **r. costs** gastos *mpl* de mantenimiento; *Pol* **r. mate** candidato *m* a la vicepresidencia; **r. water** agua *f* corriente (**b**) **three weeks r.** tres semanas seguidas

runny ['rʌnɪ] *adj* (**runnier, runniest**) blando(a); *(egg)* crudo(a); *(butter)* derretido(a); *(nose)* que moquea

run-of-the-mill ['rʌnəvðə'mɪl] *adj* corriente y moliente

runt [rʌnt] *n Fam* enano(a) *m,f*

run-up ['rʌnʌp] *n (to elections)* preliminares *mpl*

runway ['rʌnweɪ] *n Av* pista *f* (de aterrizaje y despegue)

rupee [ruː'piː] *n* rupia *f*

rupture ['rʌptʃə(r)] **1** *n* (**a**) *Med* hernia *f* (**b**) *Fig* ruptura *f*
2 *vt* (**a**) **to r. oneself** herniarse (**b**) *(break)* romper

rural ['rʊərəl] *adj* rural

ruse [ruːz] *n* ardid *m*, astucia *f*

rush¹ [rʌʃ] *n Bot* junco *m*

rush² [rʌʃ] **1** *n* (**a**) *(hurry)* prisa *f*; *(hustle and bustle)* ajetreo *m*; **there's no r.** no corre prisa; **r. hour** hora punta (**b**) *(demand)* demanda *f* (**c**) *(of wind)* ráfaga *f* (**d**) *(of water)* torrente *m* (**e**) *Mil* ataque *m*
2 *vt* (**a**) *(task)* hacer de prisa; *(person)* meter prisa a; **to r. sb to hospital** llevar a algn urgentemente al hospital (**b**) *(attack)* abalanzarse sobre; *Mil* tomar por asalto
3 *vi (go quickly)* precipitarse
► **rush about** *vi* correr de un lado a otro
► **rush into** *vt insep Fig* **to r. into sth** hacer algo sin pensarlo bien
► **rush off** *vi* irse corriendo

rusk [rʌsk] *n* = galleta dura para niños

Russia ['rʌʃə] *n* Rusia

Russian ['rʌʃən] **1** *adj* ruso(a)
2 *n* (**a**) *(person)* ruso(a) *m,f* (**b**) *(language)* ruso *m*

rust [rʌst] **1** *n* (**a**) *(substance)* herrumbre *f* (**b**) *(colour)* pardo rojizo
2 *vt* oxidar
3 *vi* oxidarse

rustic ['rʌstɪk] *adj* rústico(a)

rustle ['rʌsəl] **1** *n* crujido *m*
2 *vt (papers etc)* hacer crujir
3 *vi (steal cattle)* robar ganado

rustproof ['rʌstpruːf] *adj* inoxidable

rusty ['rʌstɪ] *adj* (**rustier, rustiest**) oxidado(a); *Fam Fig* **my French is a bit r.** tengo el francés un poco oxidado

rut [rʌt] *n* (**a**) *(furrow)* surco *m*; *(groove)* ranura *f* (**b**) *Fig* **to be in a r.** ser esclavo de la rutina (**c**) *Zool* celo *m*

ruthless ['ruːθlɪs] *adj* despiadado(a)

rye [raɪ] *n* centeno *m*; **r. bread** pan *m* de centeno; **r. grass** ballica *f*; *US* **r. (whiskey)** whisky *m* de centeno

S, s [es] *n (the letter)* S, s *f*
Sabbath ['sæbəθ] *n (Jewish)* sábado *m*; *(Christian)* domingo *m*
sabbatical [sə'bætɪkəl] *adj* sabático(a)
sabotage ['sæbətɑːʒ] **1** *n* sabotaje *m*
   2 *vt* sabotear
saccharin ['sækərɪn] *n* sacarina *f*
sachet ['sæʃeɪ] *n* bolsita *f*, sobrecito *m*
sack [sæk] **1** *n* (**a**) *(bag)* saco *m* (**b**) *Br Fam* **to get the s.** ser despedido(a); *Fam* **to give sb the s.** despedir a algn
   2 *vt* (**a**) *Br Fam* despedir (**b**) *Mil* saquear
sacking ['sækɪŋ] *n Tex* arpillera *f*
sacrament ['sækrəmənt] *n* sacramento *m*
sacred ['seɪkrɪd] *adj* sagrado(a)
sacrifice ['sækrɪfaɪs] **1** *n* sacrificio *m*
   2 *vt* sacrificar
sacrificial [sækrɪ'fɪʃəl] *adj* **s. lamb** chivo expiatorio
sacrilege ['sækrɪlɪdʒ] *n* sacrilegio *m*
sacrosanct ['sækrəʊsæŋkt] *adj* sacrosanto(a)
sad [sæd] *adj* (**sadder, saddest**) triste; **how s.!** ¡qué pena!
sadden ['sædən] *vt* entristecer
saddle ['sædəl] **1** *n (for horse)* silla *f* (de montar); *(of bicycle etc)* sillín *m*
   2 *vt (horse)* ensillar; *Fam* **to s. sb with sth** cargarle a algn con algo
saddlebag ['sædəlbæg] *n* alforja *f*
sadist ['seɪdɪst] *n* sádico(a) *m,f*
sadistic [sə'dɪstɪk] *adj* sádico(a)
sadness ['sædnɪs] *n* tristeza *f*
sadomasochism [seɪdəʊ'mæsəkɪzəm] *n* sadomasoquismo *m*
sae [eseɪ'iː] *n Br (abbr* **stamped addressed envelope**) = sobre franqueado con la dirección del remitente
safari [sə'fɑːrɪ] *n* safari *m*; **s. park** reserva *f*
safe [seɪf] **1** *adj* (**a**) *(unharmed)* ileso(a); *(out of danger)* a salvo; **s. and sound** sano(a) y salvo(a) (**b**) *(not dangerous)* inocuo(a) (**c**) *(secure, sure)* seguro(a); **to be on the s. side** para mayor seguridad; **s. house** *(for spies etc)* piso franco (**d**) *(driver)* prudente
   2 *n (for money etc)* caja *f* fuerte

safe-conduct [seɪf'kɒndʌkt] *n* salvoconducto *m*
safe-deposit [seɪfdɪ'pɒzɪt] *n* **s. (box)** cámara blindada
safeguard ['seɪfgɑːd] **1** *n (protection)* salvaguarda *f*; *(guarantee)* garantía *f*
   2 *vt* proteger, salvaguardar
safekeeping [seɪf'kiːpɪŋ] *n* custodia *f*
safely ['seɪflɪ] *adv* (**a**) con toda seguridad (**b**) **to arrive s.** llegar sin incidentes
safety ['seɪftɪ] *n* seguridad *f*; **s. first!** ¡la seguridad ante todo!; **s. belt** cinturón *m* de seguridad; **s. net** red *f* de protección; **s. pin** imperdible *m*
saffron ['sæfrən] *n* azafrán *m*
sag [sæg] *vi* (**a**) *(roof)* hundirse; *(wall)* pandear; *(wood, iron)* combarse; *(flesh)* colgar (**b**) *Fig (spirits)* flaquear
sage¹ [seɪdʒ] **1** *adj (wise)* sabio(a)
   2 *n (person)* sabio(a) *m,f*
sage² [seɪdʒ] *n* salvia *f*
Sagittarius [sædʒɪ'teərɪəs] *n* Sagitario *m*
Sahara [sə'hɑːrə] *n* **the S.** el Sahara
Saharan [sə'hɑːrən] *adj* saharaui, sahariano(a)
said [sed] **1** *adj* dicho(a)
   2 *pt & pp of* **say**
sail [seɪl] **1** *n* (**a**) *(canvas)* vela *f*; **to set s.** zarpar (**b**) *(trip)* paseo *m* en barco
   2 *vt (ship)* gobernar; *Literary* navegar
   3 *vi* (**a**) ir en barco (**b**) *(set sail)* zarpar
   ▸ **sail through** *vt insep Fam* **he sailed through university** en la universidad todo le fue sobre ruedas
sailboat ['seɪlbəʊt] *n US* velero *m*
sailing ['seɪlɪŋ] *n* navegación *f*; *(yachting)* vela *f*; *Fam* **it's all plain s.** es todo coser y cantar; *Br* **s. boat** *or* **ship** velero *m*, barco *m* de vela
sailor ['seɪlə(r)] *n* marinero *m*
saint [seɪnt] *n* santo(a) *m,f*; *(before all masculine names except those beginning* **Do** *or* **To**) San; *(before feminine names)* Santa; **S. Dominic** Santo Domingo; **S. Helen** Santa Elena; **S. John** San Juan; **All Saints' Day** Día *m* de Todos los Santos
saintly ['seɪntlɪ] *adj* (**saintlier, saintliest**) santo(a)
sake [seɪk] *n* **for the s. of** por (el bien de);

for your own s. por tu propio bien

salad ['sæləd] *n* ensalada *f*; **potato s.** ensalada de patatas *or Am* papas; **s. bowl** ensaladera *f*; **s. cream** salsa *f* tipo mahonesa; **s. dressing** vinagreta *f*, aliño *m*

salami [sə'lɑːmɪ] *n* salchichón *m*, salami *m*

salary ['sælərɪ] *n* salario *m*, sueldo *m*

sale [seɪl] *n* (**a**) venta *f*; **for** *or* **on s.** en venta; **sales department** departamento *m* comercial; **sales manager** jefe(a) *m,f* de ventas (**b**) *(at low prices)* rebajas *fpl*

salesclerk ['seɪlzklɑːk] *n US* dependiente(a) *m,f*

salesman ['seɪlzmən] *n* (**a**) vendedor *m*; *(in shop)* dependiente *m* (**b**) *(commercial traveller)* representante *m*

salesroom ['seɪlzruːm] *n* sala *f* de subastas

saleswoman ['seɪlzwʊmən] *n* (**a**) vendedora *f*; *(in shop)* dependienta *f* (**b**) *(commercial traveller)* representante *f*

salient ['seɪlɪənt] *adj Fig* sobresaliente

saliva [sə'laɪvə] *n* saliva *f*

sallow ['sæləʊ] *adj* cetrino(a)

salmon ['sæmən] **1** *n* salmón *m*
 2 *adj* (de color) salmón

salmonella [sælmə'nelə] *n Biol & Med (bacteria)* salmonela *f*; *(food poisoning)* salmonelosis *f*

salon ['sælɒn] *n* salón *m*

saloon [sə'luːn] *n* (**a**) *(on ship)* cámara *f* (**b**) *US (bar)* taberna *f*, bar *m*; *Br* **s. (bar)** bar de lujo (**c**) *(car)* turismo *m*

salt [sɔːlt] **1** *n* sal *f*; *Fig* **to take sth with a pinch of s.** creer algo con reservas; **bath salts** sales de baño; **smelling salts** sales aromáticas
 2 *adj* salado(a)
 3 *vt* (**a**) *(cure)* salar (**b**) *(add salt to)* echar sal a

saltcellar ['sɔːltselə(r)] *n* salero *m*

saltwater ['sɔːltwɔːtə(r)] *adj* de agua salada

salty ['sɔːltɪ] *adj* (**saltier, saltiest**) salado(a)

salubrious [sə'luːbrɪəs] *adj* salubre, sano(a)

salutary ['sæljʊtərɪ] *adj (experience)* beneficioso(a); *(warning)* útil

salute [sə'luːt] **1** *n (greeting)* saludo *m*
 2 *vt* (**a**) *Mil* saludar (**b**) *Fig (achievement etc)* aplaudir
 3 *vi Mil* saludar

salvage ['sælvɪdʒ] **1** *n* (**a**) *(of ship etc)* salvamento *m*, rescate *m* (**b**) *(objects recovered)* objetos recuperados (**c**) *Jur* derecho *m* de salvamento
 2 *vt (from ship etc)* rescatar

salvation [sæl'veɪʃən] *n* salvación *f*; **S. Army** Ejército *m* de Salvación

Samaritan [sə'mærɪtən] *n* samaritano(a) *m,f*; **the Samaritans** ≃ el teléfono de la Esperanza

same [seɪm] **1** *adj* mismo(a); **at that very s. moment** en ese mismísimo momento; **at the s. time** *(simultaneously)* al mismo tiempo; *(however)* sin embargo; **in the s. way** del mismo modo; **the two cars are the s.** los dos coches son iguales
 2 *pron* **the s.** el mismo/la misma/lo mismo; *Fam* **the s. here** lo mismo digo yo; *Fam* **the s. to you!** ¡igualmente!
 3 *adv* del mismo modo, igual; **all the s., just the s.** sin embargo, aun así; **it's all the s. to me** (a mí) me da igual *or* lo mismo

sample ['sɑːmpəl] **1** *n* muestra *f*
 2 *vt (wines)* catar; *(dish)* probar

sanatorium [sænə'tɔːrɪəm] *n* sanatorio *m*

sanctimonious [sæŋktɪ'məʊnɪəs] *adj* beato(a)

sanction ['sæŋkʃən] **1** *n* (**a**) *(authorization)* permiso *m* (**b**) *(penalty)* sanción *f* (**c**) *Pol* **sanctions** sanciones *fpl*
 2 *vt* sancionar

sanctity ['sæŋktɪtɪ] *n (sacredness)* santidad *f*; *(of marriage)* indisolubilidad *f*

sanctuary ['sæŋktjʊərɪ] *n* (**a**) *Rel* santuario *m* (**b**) *Pol* asilo *m* (**c**) *(for birds, animals)* reserva *f*

sand [sænd] **1** *n* arena *f*; **s. castle** castillo *m* de arena; **s. dune** duna *f*
 2 *vt* **to s. (down)** lijar

sandal ['sændəl] *n* sandalia *f*

sandalwood ['sændəlwʊd] *n* sándalo *m*

sandbag ['sændbæg] *n* saco terrero

sandbox ['sændbɒks] *n US* arenal *m*

sandpaper ['sændpeɪpə(r)] *n* papel *m* de lija

sandpit ['sændpɪt] *n Br (in playground etc)* arenal *m*

sandshoe ['sændʃuː] *n Br* playera *f*

sandstone ['sændstəʊn] *n* arenisca *f*

sandwich ['sænwɪdʒ, 'sænwɪtʃ] **1** *n (bread roll)* bocadillo *m*; *(sliced bread)* sándwich *m*; *Educ* **s. course** curso teórico-práctico
 2 *vt* intercalar; **it was sandwiched between two lorries** quedó encajonado entre dos camiones

sandy ['sændɪ] *adj* (**sandier, sandiest**) (**a**) *(earth, beach)* arenoso(a) (**b**) *(hair)* rubio rojizo

307

sane [seɪn] *adj (not mad)* cuerdo(a); *(sensible)* sensato(a)

> 🖉 Note that the Spanish word **sano** is a false friend and is never a translation for the English word **sane**. In Spanish, **sano** means "healthy".

sang [sæŋ] *pt of* sing
sanitarium [sænɪ'teərɪəm] *n US* sanatorio *m*
sanitary ['sænɪtərɪ] *adj* sanitario(a); *(hygienic)* higiénico(a); **s. Br towel** *or US* **napkin** compresa *f*
sanitation [sænɪ'teɪʃən] *n* sanidad *f* (pública); *(plumbing)* sistema *m* de saneamiento
sanity ['sænɪtɪ] *n* cordura *f*, juicio *m*; *(good sense)* sensatez *f*

> 🖉 Note that the Spanish word **sanidad** is a false friend and is never a translation for the English word **sanity**. In Spanish, **sanidad** means "health".

sank [sæŋk] *pt of* sink
Santa Claus ['sæntə'klɔːz] *n* Papá Noel *m*, San Nicolás *m*
sap¹ [sæp] *n Bot* savia *f*
sap² [sæp] *vt (undermine)* minar; *Fig* agotar
sapling ['sæplɪŋ] *n Bot* árbol *m* joven
sapphire ['sæfaɪə(r)] *n* zafiro *m*
sarcasm ['sɑːkæzəm] *n* sarcasmo *m*
sarcastic [sɑː'kæstɪk] *adj* sarcástico(a)
sardine [sɑː'diːn] *n* sardina *f*
Sardinia [sɑː'dɪnɪə] *n* Cerdeña
sardonic [sɑː'dɒnɪk] *adj* sardónico(a)
SASE [eseɪes'iː] *n US* (*abbr* **self-addressed stamped envelope**) = sobre franqueado con la dirección del remitente
sash¹ [sæʃ] *n* faja *f*
sash² [sæʃ] *n* **s. window** ventana *f* de guillotina
sat [sæt] *pt & pp of* sit
Satan ['seɪtən] *n* Satán *m*, Satanás *m*
satanic [sə'tænɪk] *adj* satánico(a)
satchel ['sætʃəl] *n* cartera *f* de colegial
satellite ['sætəlaɪt] *n* satélite *m*; **s. dish (aerial)** antena parabólica
satin ['sætɪn] *n* satén *m*; **s. finish** (acabado *m*) satinado *m*
satire ['sætaɪə(r)] *n* sátira *f*
satirical [sə'tɪrɪkəl] *adj* satírico(a)
satisfaction [sætɪs'fækʃən] *n* satisfacción *f*
satisfactory [sætɪs'fæktərɪ] *adj* satisfactorio(a)
satisfied ['sætɪsfaɪd] *adj* satisfecho(a)
satisfy ['sætɪsfaɪ] *vt* (**a**) satisfacer (**b**)

(fulfil) cumplir con (**c**) *(convince)* convencer
satisfying ['sætɪsfaɪɪŋ] *adj* satisfactorio(a); *(pleasing)* agradable; *(meal)* que llena
saturate ['sætʃəreɪt] *vt* saturar (**with** de)
Saturday ['sætədɪ] *n* sábado *m*
sauce [sɔːs] *n* (**a**) salsa *f* (**b**) *Fam (impudence)* descaro *m*
saucepan ['sɔːspən] *n* cacerola *f*; *(large)* olla *f*
saucer ['sɔːsə(r)] *n* platillo *m*
saucy ['sɔːsɪ] *adj* (**saucier, sauciest**) *Fam* fresco(a)
Saudi Arabia ['saʊdɪə'reɪbɪə] *n* Arabia *f* Saudita *or* Saudí
Saudi Arabian ['saʊdɪə'reɪbɪən] *adj & n* saudita *(mf)*, saudí *(mf)*
sauna ['sɔːnə] *n* sauna *f*
saunter ['sɔːntə(r)] **1** *n* paseo *m*
  2 *vi* pasearse
sausage ['sɒsɪdʒ] *n (raw)* salchicha *f*; *(cured)* salchichón *m*; *(spicy)* chorizo *m*; *Fam* **s. dog** perro *m* salchicha; *Br* **s. roll** empanada *f* de carne
sauté ['sɔʊteɪ] **1** *adj* salteado(a)
  2 *vt* saltear
savage ['sævɪdʒ] **1** *adj* (**a**) *(ferocious)* feroz; *(cruel)* cruel; *(violent)* salvaje (**b**) *(primitive)* salvaje
  2 *n* salvaje *mf*
  3 *vt (attack)* embestir; *Fig (criticize)* criticar despiadadamente
save [seɪv] **1** *vt* (**a**) *(rescue)* salvar, rescatar; *Fig* **to s. face** salvar las apariencias (**b**) *(put by)* guardar; *(money, energy, time)* ahorrar; *(food)* almacenar; **it saved him a lot of trouble** le evitó muchos problemas
  2 *vi* (**a**) **to s. (up)** ahorrar (**b**) **to s. on paper** *(economize)* ahorrar papel
  3 *n Ftb* parada *f*
  4 *prep Literary* salvo, excepto
saving ['seɪvɪŋ] **1** *n* (**a**) *(of time, money)* ahorro *m* (**b**) **savings** ahorros *mpl*; **savings account** cuenta *f* de ahorros; **savings bank** caja *f* de ahorros
  2 *adj* **it's his only s. grace** es el único mérito que tiene
saviour, *US* **savior** ['seɪvjə(r)] *n* salvador(a) *m,f*
savour, *US* **savor** ['seɪvə(r)] **1** *n* sabor *m*, gusto *m*
  2 *vi* saborear
savoury, *US* **savory** ['seɪvərɪ] *adj (tasty)* sabroso(a); *(salted)* salado(a); *(spicy)* picante
saw¹ [sɔː] **1** *n (tool)* sierra *f*

2 vt & vi (pt **sawed**; pp **sawed** or **sawn**) serrar

▶ **saw up** vt sep serrar (**into** en)

saw² [sɔː] pt of **see**

sawdust ['sɔːdʌst] n (a)serrín m

sawmill ['sɔːmɪl] n aserradero m, serrería f

sawn [sɔːn] pp of **saw**

sawn-off ['sɔːnɒf], US **sawed-off** ['sɔːdɒf] adj recortado(a); **s. shotgun** escopeta f de cañones recortados

saxophone ['sæksəfəʊn] n saxofón m

say [seɪ] **1** vt (pt & pp **said**) (**a**) decir; **it goes without saying that ...** huelga decir que ...; **it is said that ...** se dice que ...; **not to s. ...** por no decir ...; **that is to s.** es decir; **to s. yes/no** decir que sí/no; Fam **I s.!** ¡oiga!; **what does the sign s.?** ¿qué pone en el letrero? (**b**) (think) pensar (**c**) **shall we s. Friday then?** ¿quedamos el viernes, pues?

2 n **I have no s. in the matter** no tengo ni voz ni voto en el asunto; **to have one's s.** dar su opinión

saying ['seɪɪŋ] n refrán m, dicho m

scab [skæb] n (**a**)Med costra f (**b**) Fam Pej esquirol mf

scaffold ['skæfəld] n (for execution) patíbulo m

scaffolding ['skæfəldɪŋ] n Constr andamio n

scald [skɔːld] **1** n escaldadura f

2 vt escaldar

scale¹ [skeɪl] n (of fish, on skin) escama f; (in boiler) incrustaciones fpl

scale² [skeɪl] **1** n (**a**) escala f; **on a large s.** a gran escala; **to s.** a escala; **s. model** maqueta f (**b**) (extent) alcance m (**c**) Mus escala f

2 vt (climb) escalar

▶ **scale down** vt sep (drawing) reducir a escala; (production) reducir

scales [skeɪlz] npl (**pair of**) **s.** (shop, kitchen) balanza f; (bathroom) báscula f

scallop ['skɒləp] n (**a**) (mollusc) vieira f (**b**) (shell) venera f

scalp [skælp] **1** n cuero cabelludo

2 vt arrancar el cuero cabelludo a

scalpel ['skælpəl] n bisturí m

scamper ['skæmpə(r)] vi corretear

scampi ['skæmpɪ] n gambas empanadas

scan [skæn] **1** vt (**a**) (scrutinize) escrutar; (horizon) otear (**b**) (glance at) ojear (**c**) (of radar) explorar

2 n Med exploración ultrasónica; (in gynaecology etc) ecografía f

scandal ['skændəl] n (**a**) escándalo m;

what a s.! ¡qué vergüenza! (**b**) (gossip) chismes mpl

Scandinavia [skændɪ'neɪvɪə] n Escandinavia

Scandinavian [skændɪ'neɪvɪən] adj & n escandinavo(a) (m,f)

scanner ['skænə(r)] n Med & Comput escáner m

scant [skænt] adj escaso(a)

scanty ['skæntɪ] adj (**scantier, scantiest**) escaso(a); (meal) insuficiente; (clothes) ligero(a)

scapegoat ['skeɪpgəʊt] n chivo expiatorio

scar [skɑː(r)] n cicatriz f

scarce [skeəs] adj escaso(a); Fig **to make oneself s.** largarse

scarcely ['skeəslɪ] adv apenas

scarcity ['skeəsɪtɪ] n escasez f; (rarity) rareza f

scare [skeə(r)] **1** n (fright) susto m; (widespread alarm) pánico m; **bomb s.** amenaza f de bomba

2 vt asustar, espantar; Fam **to be scared stiff** estar muerto(a) de miedo

▶ **scare away, scare off** vt sep ahuyentar

scarecrow ['skeəkrəʊ] n espantapájaros m inv

scarf [skɑːf] n (pl **scarfs** or **scarves**) (long, woollen) bufanda f; (square) pañuelo m; (silk) fular m

scarlet ['skɑːlɪt] **1** adj escarlata

2 n escarlata f; **s. fever** escarlatina f

scarves [skɑːvz] pl of **scarf**

scathing ['skeɪðɪŋ] adj mordaz, cáustico(a)

scatter ['skætə(r)] **1** vt (**a**) (papers etc) esparcir, desparramar (**b**) (crowd) dispersar

2 vi dispersarse

scatterbrained ['skætəbreɪnd] adj Fam ligero(a) de cascos; (forgetful) despistado(a)

scattered ['skætəd] adj **s. showers** chubascos aislados

scavenger ['skævɪndʒə(r)] n (**a**) (person) rebuscador(a) m,f, trapero m (**b**) (animal) (animal m) carroñero(a) mf

scenario [sɪ'nɑːrɪəʊ] n (**a**) Cin guión m (**b**) (situation) situación f hipotética

scene [siːn] n (**a**) Th, Cin & TV escena f; **behind the scenes** entre bastidores (**b**) (place) lugar m, escenario m; **a change of s.** un cambio de aires (**c**) (view) panorama m (**d**) **to make a s.** (fuss) montar un espectáculo

scenery ['siːnərɪ] n (**a**) (landscape) paisaje m (**b**) Th decorado m

scenic ['si:nɪk] *adj (picturesque)* pintoresco(a)

scent [sent] **1** *n* (**a**) *(smell)* olor *m*; *(of food)* aroma *m* (**b**) *(perfume)* perfume *m* (**c**) *(in hunting)* pista *f*
  2 *vt (add perfume to)* perfumar; *(smell)* olfatear; *Fig* presentir

sceptic ['skeptɪk] *n* escéptico(a) *m,f*

sceptical ['skeptɪkəl] *adj* escéptico(a)

scepticism ['skeptɪsɪzəm] *n* escepticismo *m*

sceptre ['septə(r)] *n* cetro *m*

schedule ['ʃedju:l, *US* 'skedʒʊəl] **1** *n* (**a**) *(plan, agenda)* programa *m*; *(timetable)* horario *m*; **on s.** a la hora (prevista); **to be behind s.** llevar retraso (**b**) *(list)* lista *f*; *(inventory)* inventario *m*
  2 *vt (plan)* programar, fijar

scheduled ['ʃedju:ld, *US* 'skedʒʊəld] *adj* previsto(a), fijo(a); **s. flight** vuelo regular

scheme [ski:m] **1** *n* (**a**) *(plan)* plan *m*; *(project)* proyecto *m*; *(idea)* idea *f*; **colour s.** combinación *f* de colores (**b**) *(plot)* intriga *f*; *(trick)* ardid *m*
  2 *vi (plot)* tramar, intrigar

scheming ['ski:mɪŋ] *adj* intrigante, maquinador(a)

schism ['sɪzəm] *n* cisma *m*

schizophrenic [skɪtsəʊ'frenɪk] *adj & n* esquizofrénico(a) *(m,f)*

scholar ['skɒlə(r)] *n (learned person)* erudito(a) *m,f*; *(pupil)* alumno(a) *m,f*

scholarship ['skɒləʃɪp] *n* (**a**) *(learning)* erudición *f* (**b**) *(grant)* beca *f*; **s. holder** becario(a) *m,f*

school [sku:l] **1** *n* (**a**) escuela *f*, colegio *m*; **drama s.** academia *f* de arte dramático; **of s. age** en edad escolar; **s. year** año *m* escolar (**b**) *US (university)* universidad *f* (**c**) *(university department)* facultad *f* (**d**) *(group of artists)* escuela *f*; **s. of thought** corriente *f* de opinión
  2 *vt (teach)* enseñar; *(train)* formar

schoolbook ['sku:lbʊk] *n* libro *m* de texto

schoolboy ['sku:lbɔɪ] *n* alumno *m*

schoolchild ['sku:ltʃaɪld] *n* alumno(a) *m,f*

schooldays ['sku:ldeɪz] *npl* años *mpl* de colegio

schoolgirl ['sku:lgɜ:l] *n* alumna *f*

schooling ['sku:lɪŋ] *n* educación *f*, estudios *mpl*

schoolmaster ['sku:lmɑ:stə(r)] *n* profesor *m*; *(primary school)* maestro *m*

schoolmistress ['sku:lmɪstrɪs] *n* profesora *f*; *(primary school)* maestra *f*

schoolteacher ['sku:lti:tʃə(r)] *n* profesor(a) *m,f*; *(primary school)* maestro(a) *m,f*

schooner ['sku:nə(r)] *n Naut* goleta *f*

sciatica [saɪ'ætɪkə] *n* ciática *f*

science ['saɪəns] *n* ciencia *f*; *(school subject)* ciencias; **s. fiction** ciencia-ficción *f*

scientific [saɪən'tɪfɪk] *adj* científico(a)

scientist ['saɪəntɪst] *n* científico(a) *m,f*

scintillating ['sɪntɪleɪtɪŋ] *adj* brillante

scissors ['sɪzəz] *npl* tijeras *fpl*; **a pair of s.** unas tijeras

scoff[1] [skɒf] *vi (mock)* mofarse (**at** de)

scoff[2] [skɒf] *vt Fam (eat)* zamparse

scold [skəʊld] *vt* regañar, reñir

scone [skəʊn, skɒn] *n* bollo *m*, pastelito *m*

scoop [sku:p] *n* (**a**) *(for flour)* pala *f*; *(for ice cream)* cucharón *m*; *(amount)* palada *f*, cucharada *f* (**b**) *Press* exclusiva *f*
  ▶ **scoop out** *vt sep (flour etc)* sacar con pala; *(water) (from boat)* achicar
  ▶ **scoop up** *vt sep* recoger

scooter ['sku:tə(r)] *n (child's)* patinete *m*; *(adult's)* Vespa® *f*

scope [skəʊp] *n* (**a**) *(range)* alcance *m*; *(of undertaking)* ámbito *m* (**b**) *(freedom)* libertad *f*

scorch [skɔ:tʃ] *vt (singe)* chamuscar

scorching ['skɔ:tʃɪŋ] *adj Fam* abrasador(a)

score [skɔ:(r)] **1** *n* (**a**) *Sport* tanteo *m*; *Cards & (in golf)* puntuación *f*; *(result)* resultado *m*
  (**b**) *(notch)* muesca *f*
  (**c**) **I have a s. to settle with you** tengo que ajustar las cuentas contigo
  (**d**) **on that s.** a ese respecto
  (**e**) *(twenty)* veintena *f*
  (**f**) *Mus (of opera)* partitura *f*; *(of film)* música *f*
  2 *vt* (**a**) *(goal)* marcar; *(points)* conseguir
  (**b**) *(wood)* hacer una muesca en; *(paper)* rayar
  3 *vi* (**a**) *Sport* marcar un tanto; *Ftb* marcar un gol; *(keep the score)* llevar el marcador
  (**b**) *(have success)* tener éxito (**with** con); *Fam* ligar (**with** con)
  ▶ **score out** *vt sep (word etc)* tachar

scoreboard ['skɔ:bɔ:d] *n* marcador *m*

scorer ['skɔ:rə(r)] *n* (**a**) *(goal striker)* goleador *m* (**b**) *(scorekeeper)* encargado(a) *m,f* del marcador

scorn [skɔ:n] **1** *n* desprecio *m*
  2 *vt* despreciar

scornful ['skɔ:nfʊl] *adj* desdeñoso(a)

Scorpio ['skɔːpɪəʊ] *n* Escorpión *m*

scorpion ['skɔːpɪən] *n* alacrán *m*, escorpión *m*

Scot [skɒt] *n* escocés(esa) *m,f*

Scotch [skɒtʃ] **1** *adj* escocés(esa); *US* **S. tape**® cinta adhesiva, celo® *m*

  2 *n (whisky)* whisky *m* escocés

scotch [skɒtʃ] *vt (plot)* frustrar; *(rumour)* negar, desmentir

scot-free ['skɒt'friː] *adj* impune

Scotland ['skɒtlənd] *n* Escocia

Scots [skɒts] **1** *adj* escocés(esa)

  2 *n* (dialecto *m*) escocés *m*

Scotsman ['skɒtsmən] *n* escocés *m*

Scotswoman ['skɒtswʊmən] *n* escocesa *f*

Scottish ['skɒtɪʃ] *adj* escocés(esa)

scoundrel ['skaʊndrəl] *n* sinvergüenza *mf*, canalla *m*

scour¹ [skaʊə(r)] *vt (clean)* fregar, restregar

scour² [skaʊə(r)] *vt (search) (countryside)* rastrear; *(building)* registrar

scourge [skɜːdʒ] *n Fig* azote *m*

scout [skaʊt] **1** *n Mil* explorador(a) *m,f*; *Sport & Cin* cazatalentos *m inv*; **boy s.** boy *m* scout

  2 *vi Mil* reconocer el terreno; **to s. around for sth** andar en busca de algo

scowl [skaʊl] **1** *vi* fruncir el ceño; **to s. at sb** mirar a algn con ceño

  2 *n* ceño *m*

scrabble ['skræbəl] *vi* escarbar; *Fig* **to s. around for sth** revolver todo para encontrar algo

scraggy ['skrægɪ] *adj* (**scraggier, scraggiest**) delgado(a), flacucho(a)

scramble ['skræmbəl] **1** *vi* trepar; **to s. for** pelearse por; **to s. up a tree** trepar a un árbol

  2 *vt* (**a**) *Culin* **scrambled eggs** huevos revueltos (**b**) *Rad & Tel (message)* codificar; *(broadcast)* interferir

  3 *n (climb)* subida *f*; *Fig* **it's going to be a s.** *(rush)* va a ser muy apresurado

scrap¹ [skræp] **1** *n* (**a**) *(small piece)* pedazo *m*; **there isn't a s. of truth in it** no tiene ni un ápice de verdad; **s. (metal)** chatarra *f*; **s. dealer** *or* **merchant** chatarrero(a) *m,f*; **s. paper** papel *m* de borrador; **s. yard** *(for cars)* cementerio *m* de coches (**b**) **scraps** restos *mpl*; *(of food)* sobras *fpl*

  2 *vt (discard)* desechar; *Fig (idea)* descartar

scrap² [skræp] *Fam* **1** *n (fight)* pelea *f*

  2 *vi* pelearse (**with** con)

scrapbook ['skræpbʊk] *n* álbum *m* de recortes

scrape [skreɪp] **1** *vt (paint, wood)* raspar; *(knee)* arañarse, hacerse un rasguño en

  2 *vi (make noise)* chirriar; *(rub)* rozar

  3 *n Fam (trouble)* lío *m*

  ▸ **scrape through** *vi Fam (exam)* aprobar por los pelos

  ▸ **scrape together** *vt sep* reunir a duras penas

scraper ['skreɪpə(r)] *n* rasqueta *f*

scrapheap ['skræphiːp] *n (dump)* vertedero *m*

scratch [skrætʃ] **1** *n* (**a**) *(on skin, paintwork)* arañazo *m*; *(on record)* raya *f* (**b**) *(noise)* chirrido *m* (**c**) *Fig* **to be up to s.** dar la talla; *Fig* **to start from s.** partir de cero

  2 *adj* **s. team** equipo improvisado

  3 *vt* (**a**) *(with nail, claw)* arañar, rasguñar; *(paintwork)* rayar (**b**) *(to relieve itching)* rascarse

scrawl [skrɔːl] **1** *n* garabatos *mpl*

  2 *vt (message etc)* garabatear

  3 *vi* hacer garabatos

scrawny ['skrɔːnɪ] *adj* (**scrawnier, scrawniest**) flaco(a)

scream [skriːm] **1** *n* chillido *m*; **screams of laughter** carcajadas *fpl*

  2 *vt (insults etc)* gritar

  3 *vi* chillar; **to s. at sb** chillar a algn

scree [skriː] *n* pedregal *m*

screech [skriːtʃ] **1** *n (of person)* chillido *m*; *(of tyres, brakes)* chirrido *m*

  2 *vi (person)* chillar; *(tyres)* chirriar

screen [skriːn] **1** *n* (**a**) *(movable partition)* biombo *m* (**b**) *Fig* cortina *f* (**c**) *Cin, TV & Comput* pantalla *f*; **s. test** casting *m*

  2 *vt* (**a**) *(protect)* proteger; *(conceal)* tapar (**b**) *(sieve) (coal etc)* tamizar; *Fig (candidates)* seleccionar (**c**) *(show) (film)* proyectar; *(for first time)* estrenar (**d**) *Med* examinar

screening ['skriːnɪŋ] *n* (**a**) *(of film)* proyección *f*; *(for first time)* estreno *m* (**b**) *Med* exploración *f*

screenplay ['skriːnpleɪ] *n* guión *m*

screw [skruː] **1** *n* (**a**) *(writing)* tornillo *m* (**b**) *(propeller)* hélice *f*

  2 *vt* (**a**) atornillar; **to s. sth down** *or* **in** *or* **on** fijar algo con tornillos (**b**) *Vulg* joder

  ▸ **screw up** *vt sep* (**a**) *(piece of paper)* arrugar; *(one's face)* torcer (**b**) *very Fam (ruin)* joder

screwdriver ['skruːdraɪvə(r)] *n* destornillador *m*

scribble ['skrɪbəl] **1** *n* garabatos *mpl*

  2 *vt (message etc)* garabatear

  3 *vi* hacer garabatos

script [skrɪpt] *n* (**a**) *(writing)* escritura *f*; *(handwriting)* letra *f*; *Typ* letra cursiva (**b**) *(in exam)* escrito *m* (**c**) *Cin* guión *m*

Scripture ['skrɪptʃə(r)] *n* Holy S. Sagrada Escritura

scroll [skrəʊl] *n* rollo *m* de pergamino

scrounge [skraʊndʒ] *Fam* **1** *vi* gorronear; **to s. (around) for** buscar; **to s. off sb** vivir a costa de algn
  2 *vt* gorronear

scrounger ['skraʊndʒə(r)] *n Fam* gorrón(ona) *m,f*

scrub¹ [skrʌb] *n (undergrowth)* maleza *f*

scrub² [skrʌb] **1** *vt* (**a**) frotar (**b**) *Fam (cancel)* borrar
  2 *n (cleaning)* fregado *m*

scruff [skrʌf] *n* pescuezo *m*, cogote *m*

scruffy ['skrʌfɪ] *adj* (**scruffier, scruffiest**) *Fam* desaliñado(a)

scrum [skrʌm] *n* melée *f*; **s. half** medio *m* melée

scruple ['skruːpəl] *n* escrúpulo *m*

scrupulous ['skruːpjʊləs] *adj* escrupuloso(a)

scrupulously ['skruːpjʊləslɪ] *adv* **s. honest** sumamente honrado(a)

scrutinize ['skruːtɪnaɪz] *vt* escudriñar

scrutiny ['skruːtɪnɪ] *n* escrutinio *m*

scuff [skʌf] *vt (the floor)* rayar; *(one's feet)* arrastrar

scuffle ['skʌfəl] **1** *n* pelea *f*
  2 *vi* pelearse (**with** con)

scullery ['skʌlərɪ] *n* cuarto *m* de pila

sculptor ['skʌlptə(r)] *n* escultor(a) *m,f*

sculpture ['skʌlptʃə(r)] *n* escultura *f*

scum [skʌm] *n* (**a**) *(on liquid)* espuma *f* (**b**) *Fig* escoria *f*

scupper ['skʌpə(r)] *vt Br Fam (plan etc)* desbaratar

scurrilous ['skʌrɪləs] *adj (abusive)* difamatorio(a)

scurry ['skʌrɪ] *vi (run)* corretear; *(hurry)* apresurarse; **to s. away** *or* **off** escabullirse

scuttle¹ ['skʌtəl] *n* cubo *m*; **coal s.** cubo del carbón

scuttle² ['skʌtəl] *vt (ship)* barrenar

scuttle³ ['skʌtəl] *vi* **to s. away** *or* **off** escabullirse

scythe [saɪð] **1** *n* guadaña *f*
  2 *vt* guadañar

SDI [esdiː'aɪ] *n (abbr Strategic Defence Initiative)* Iniciativa *f* para la Defensa Estratégica

sea [siː] *n* mar *m or f*; **by the s.** a orillas del mar; **out at s.** en alta mar; **to go by s.** ir en barco; **to put to s.** zarpar; *Fig* **to be all at s.** estar desorientado(a); **s. breeze** brisa marina; *Fig* **s. change** metamorfosis *f*; **s. level** nivel *m* del mar; **s. lion** león marino; **s. water** agua *f* de mar

seabed ['siːbed] *n* fondo *m* del mar

seaboard ['siːbɔːd] *n US* costa *f*, litoral *m*

seafood ['siːfuːd] *n* mariscos *mpl*

seafront ['siːfrʌnt] *n* paseo marítimo

seagull ['siːgʌl] *n* gaviota *f*

seal¹ [siːl] *n Zool* foca *f*

seal² [siːl] **1** *n* (**a**) *(official stamp)* sello *m* (**b**) *(airtight closure)* cierre hermético; *(on bottle)* precinto *m*
  2 *vt* (**a**) *(with official stamp)* sellar; *(with wax)* lacrar (**b**) *(close)* cerrar; *(make airtight)* cerrar herméticamente (**c**) *(determine)* **this sealed his fate** esto decidío su destino
  ▸ **seal off** *vt sep (pipe etc)* cerrar; *(area)* acordonar

seam [siːm] *n* (**a**) *Sewing* costura *f*; *Tech* juntura *f*; *Fam* **to be bursting at the seams** *(room)* rebosar de gente (**b**) *Geol & Min* veta *f*, filón *m*

seaman ['siːmən] *n* marinero *m*

seamy ['siːmɪ] *adj* (**seamier, seamiest**) *Fig* sórdido(a)

séance ['seɪɑːns] *n* sesión *f* de espiritismo

seaplane ['siːpleɪn] *n* hidroavión *m*

seaport ['siːpɔːt] *n* puerto marítimo

search [sɜːtʃ] **1** *vt (files etc)* buscar en; *(building, suitcase)* registrar; *(person)* cachear; *(one's conscience)* examinar
  2 *vi* buscar; **to s. through** registrar
  3 *n* búsqueda *f*; *(of building etc)* registro *m*; *(of person)* cacheo *m*; **in s. of** en busca de; *Comput* **s. engine** motor *m* de búsqueda; **s. party** equipo *m* de salvamento; **s. warrant** orden *f* de registro

searching ['sɜːtʃɪŋ] *adj (look)* penetrante; *(question)* indagatorio(a)

searchlight ['sɜːtʃlaɪt] *n* reflector *m*

seashell ['siːʃel] *n* concha marina

seashore ['siːʃɔː(r)] *n (beach)* playa *f*

seasick ['siːsɪk] *adj* mareado(a); **to get s.** marearse

seaside ['siːsaɪd] *n* playa *f*, costa *f*; **s. resort** lugar turístico de veraneo; **s. town** pueblo costero

season¹ ['siːzən] *n* época *f*; *(of year)* estación *f*; *(for sport etc)* temporada *f*; **the busy s.** la temporada alta; **the rainy s.** la estación de lluvias; **in s.** *(fruit)* en sazón; *(animal)* en celo; *Br* **s. ticket** abono *m*

season² ['siːzən] *vt Culin* sazonar

seasonal ['siːzənəl] *adj* estacional

seasoned ['siːzənd] *adj* (**a**) *Culin* sazonado(a) (**b**) *Fig (campaigner)* curtido(a), avezado(a)

seasoning ['siːzənɪŋ] *n* condimento *m*, aderezo *m*

seat [siːt] **1** n (**a**) asiento m; (place) plaza f; Cin & Th localidad f; **to take a s.** sentarse; Aut **s. belt** cinturón m de seguridad (**b**) (of cycle) sillín m; Fam (buttocks) trasero m (**c**) (of power, learning) centro m, sede f (**d**) Parl escaño m
 2 vt (**a**) (guests etc) sentar (**b**) (accommodate) tener cabida para
seating [ˈsiːtɪŋ] n asientos mpl; **s. capacity** cabida f, aforo m
seaweed [ˈsiːwiːd] n alga f (marina)
seaworthy [ˈsiːwɜːðɪ] adj en condiciones de navegar
sec [sek] n Fam (abbr **second**) segundo m
secede [sɪˈsiːd] vi separarse (**from** de)
secluded [sɪˈkluːdɪd] adj retirado(a), apartado(a)
second¹ [ˈsekənd] **1** adj segundo(a); **every s. day** cada dos días; **it's the s. highest mountain** es la segunda montaña más alta; **on s. thought(s)** ... pensándolo bien ...; **to have s. thoughts about sth** dudar de algo; **to settle for s. best** conformarse con lo que hay
 2 n (**a**) (in series) segundo(a) m,f; **Charles the S.** Carlos Segundo; **the s. of October** el dos de octubre (**b**) Aut (gear) segunda f (**c**) Com **seconds** artículos defectuosos
 3 vt (motion) apoyar
 4 adv **to come s.** terminar en segundo lugar
second² [ˈsekənd] n (time) segundo m; Fam **in a s.** enseguida; Fam **just a s.!** ¡un momentito!; **s. hand** (of watch, clock) segundero m
secondary [ˈsekəndərɪ] adj secundario(a); Br **s. school** escuela secundaria
second-class [ˈsekəndˈklɑːs] **1** adj de segunda clase
 2 adv **to travel s.** viajar en segunda
second-hand [ˈsekəndˈhænd] adj & adv de segunda mano
secondly [ˈsekəndlɪ] adv en segundo lugar
secondment [sɪˈkɒndmənt] n Br traslado m temporal
second-rate [ˈsekəndˈreɪt] adj de segunda categoría
secrecy [ˈsiːkrəsɪ] n secreto m; **in s.** en secreto
secret [ˈsiːkrɪt] **1** adj secreto(a); **to keep sth s.** mantener algo en secreto; **s. ballot** votación secreta
 2 n secreto m; Fig clave f; **in s.** en secreto; **to keep a s.** guardar un secreto
secretarial [sekrɪˈteərɪəl] adj de secretaria(a)

secretary [ˈsekrətrɪ] n secretario(a) m,f; **S. of State** Br ministro(a) m,f con cartera; US ministro(a) m,f de Asuntos Exteriores
secretion [sɪˈkriːʃən] n secreción f
secretive [ˈsiːkrɪtɪv] adj reservado(a)
secretly [ˈsiːkrɪtlɪ] adv en secreto
sect [sekt] n secta f
sectarian [sekˈteərɪən] adj & n sectario(a) (m,f)
section [ˈsekʃən] n (**a**) (part) sección f, parte f; (of law) artículo m; (of community) sector m; (of orchestra, department) sección (**b**) (cut) corte m
sector [ˈsektə(r)] n sector m
secular [ˈsekjʊlə(r)] adj (school, teaching) laico(a); (music, art) profano(a); (priest) seglar, secular
secure [sɪˈkjʊə(r)] **1** adj seguro(a); (window, door) bien cerrado(a); (ladder etc) firme
 2 vt (**a**) (make safe) asegurar (**b**) (fix) (rope, knot) sujetar, fijar; (object to floor) afianzar; (window, door) cerrar bien (**c**) (obtain) conseguir, obtener (**d**) Fin (guarantee) avalar
security [sɪˈkjʊərɪtɪ] n (**a**) seguridad f; **national s.** seguridad nacional; **S. Council** (of United Nations) Consejo m de Seguridad (**b**) Fin (guarantee) fianza f; (guarantor) fiador(a) m,f (**c**) Fin **securities** valores mpl
sedan [sɪˈdæn] n (**a**) Hist **s. chair** silla f de manos (**b**) US Aut turismo m
sedate [sɪˈdeɪt] **1** adj sosegado(a)
 2 vt sedar
sedation [sɪˈdeɪʃən] n sedación f
sedative [ˈsedətɪv] adj & n sedante (m)
sediment [ˈsedɪmənt] n sedimento m; (of wine) poso m
seduce [sɪˈdjuːs] vt seducir
seduction [sɪˈdʌkʃən] n seducción f
seductive [sɪˈdʌktɪv] adj seductor(a)
see¹ [siː] vt & vi (pt **saw**; pp **seen**) (**a**) ver; **I'll s. what can be done** veré lo que se puede hacer; **let's s.** a ver; **that remains to be seen** eso queda por ver; **s. page 10** véase la página 10; **s. you (later)/soon!** ¡hasta luego/pronto!
 (**b**) (meet with) ver, tener cita con; **they are seeing each other** (of couple) salen juntos
 (**c**) (visit) ver; **to s. the world** recorrer el mundo
 (**d**) (understand) entender; **as far as I can s.** por lo visto; **I s.** ya veo; **you s., he hasn't got a car** es que no tiene coche, ¿sabes?

(**e**) **he sees himself as a second Caruso** se cree otro Caruso

(**f**) *(ensure)* asegurarse de (**g**) **to s. sb home** acompañar a algn a casa

▶ **see about** *vt insep (deal with)* ocuparse de

▶ **see off** *vt sep (say goodbye to)* despedirse de

▶ **see out** *vt sep* (**a**) *(show out)* acompañar hasta la puerta (**b**) *(survive)* sobrevivir

▶ **see through 1** *vt insep Fam* **to s. through sb** verle el plumero a algn

2 *vt sep* (**a**) **I'll s. you through** puedes contar con mi ayuda; **£20 should s. me through** con 20 libras me las apaño (**b**) **to s. sth through** *(carry out)* llevar algo a cabo

▶ **see to** *vt insep (deal with)* ocuparse de

see² [siː] *n Rel* sede *f;* **the Holy S.** la Santa Sede

seed [siːd] **1** *n* (**a**) *Bot* semilla *f; (of fruit)* pepita *f;* **to go to s.** *(of plant)* granar; *Fig (of person)* descuidarse (**b**) *(in tennis) (player)* cabeza *mf* de serie

2 *vt* (**a**) *(sow with seed)* sembrar (**b**) *(grapes)* despepitar (**c**) *(in tennis)* preseleccionar

seedling ['siːdlɪŋ] *n* plantón *m*

seedy ['siːdɪ] *adj* (**seedier, seediest**) *Fam (bar etc)* sórdido(a); *(clothes)* raído(a); *(appearance)* desaseado(a)

seeing ['siːɪŋ] *conj* **s. that** visto que, dado que

seeing-eye dog ['siːɪŋaɪˈdɒg] *n US* perro *m* lazarillo

seek [siːk] **1** *vt (pt & pp sought)* (**a**) *(look for)* buscar (**b**) *(advice, help)* solicitar

2 *vt* buscar; **to s. to do sth** procurar hacer algo

▶ **seek after** *vt insep* buscar; **much sought after** *(person)* muy solicitado(a); *(thing)* muy cotizado(a)

seem [siːm] *vi* parecer; **I s. to remember his name was Colin** creo recordar que su nombre era Colin; **it seems to me that** me parece que; **so it seems** eso parece

seeming ['siːmɪŋ] *adj* aparente

seemingly ['siːmɪŋlɪ] *adv* aparentemente, según parece

seen [siːn] *pp of* **see**

seep [siːp] *vi* **to s. through/into/out** filtrarse por/en/de

seesaw ['siːsɔː] **1** *n* balancín *m*, subibaja *m*

2 *vi* (**a**) columpiarse, balancearse (**b**) *Fig* vacilar, oscilar

seethe [siːð] *vi* bullir, hervir; *Fig* **to s.**

with anger rabiar; **to s. with people** rebosar de gente

see-through ['siːθruː] *adj* transparente

segment ['segmənt] *n* segmento *m; (of orange)* gajo *m*

segregate ['segrɪgeɪt] *vt* segregar (**from** de)

segregation [segrɪ'geɪʃən] *n* segregación *f*

seize [siːz] *vt (grab)* agarrar, asir; *Jur (property, drugs)* incautar; *(assets)* secuestrar; *(territory)* tomar; *(arrest)* detener; **to s. an opportunity** aprovechar una ocasión; **to s. power** hacerse con el poder

▶ **seize on** *vt insep (chance)* agarrar; *(idea)* aferrarse a

▶ **seize up** *vi* agarrotarse

seizure ['siːʒə(r)] *n* (**a**) *Jur (of property, drugs)* incautación *f; (of newspaper)* secuestro *m; (arrest)* detención *f* (**b**) *Med* ataque *m* (de apoplejía)

seldom ['seldəm] *adv* rara vez, raramente

select [sɪ'lekt] **1** *vt (thing)* escoger, elegir; *(team)* seleccionar

2 *adj* selecto(a)

selected [sɪ'lektɪd] *adj* selecto(a), escogido(a); *(team, player)* seleccionado(a); *Lit* **s. works** obras escogidas

selection [sɪ'lekʃən] *n (choosing)* elección *f; (people or things chosen)* selección *f; (range)* surtido *m*

selective [sɪ'lektɪv] *adj* selectivo(a)

self [self] *n (pl selves)* uno(a) mismo(a), sí mismo(a); *Psy* **the s.** el yo

self- [self] *pref* auto-

self-adhesive [selfəd'hiːsɪv] *adj* autoadhesivo(a)

self-assured [selfə'ʃʊəd] *adj* seguro(a) de sí mismo(a)

self-catering [self'keɪtərɪŋ] *adj* sin servicio de comida

self-centred, *US* **self-centered** [self-'sentəd] *adj* egocéntrico(a)

self-confessed [selfkən'fest] *adj* confeso(a)

self-confidence [self'kɒnfɪdəns] *n* confianza *f* en sí mismo(a)

self-confident [self'kɒnfɪdənt] *adj* seguro(a) de sí mismo(a)

self-conscious [self'kɒnʃəs] *adj* cohibido(a)

self-contained [selfkən'teɪnd] *adj (flat)* con entrada propia; *(person)* independiente

self-control [selfkən'trəʊl] *n* autocontrol *m*

self-defence, US **self-defense** [self-dɪ'fens] n autodefensa f
self-discipline [self'dɪsɪplɪn] n autodisciplina f
self-employed [selfɪm'plɔɪd] adj (worker) autónomo(a)
self-esteem [selfɪ'stiːm] n amor propio, autoestima f
self-evident [self'evɪdənt] adj evidente, patente
self-governing [self'gʌvənɪŋ] adj autónomo(a)
self-important [selfɪm'pɔːtənt] adj engreído(a), presumido(a)
self-indulgent [selfɪn'dʌldʒənt] adj inmoderado(a)
self-interest [self'ɪntrɪst] n egoísmo m
selfish ['selfɪʃ] adj egoísta
selfishness ['selfɪʃnɪs] n egoísmo m
selfless ['selflɪs] adj desinteresado(a)
self-made ['selfmeɪd] adj **s. man** hombre m que se ha hecho a sí mismo
self-pity [self'pɪtɪ] n autocompasión f
self-portrait [self'pɔːtreɪt] n autorretrato m
self-possessed [selfpə'zest] adj sereno(a), dueño(a) de sí mismo(a)
self-preservation [selfprezə'veɪʃən] n (instinct of) s. instinto m de conservación
self-raising ['selfreɪzɪŋ] adj **s. flour** harina f con levadura
self-reliant [selfrɪ'laɪənt] adj autosuficiente
self-respect [selfrɪ'spekt] n amor propio, dignidad f
self-righteous [self'raɪtʃəs] adj santurrón(ona)
self-rising ['selfraɪzɪŋ] adj US = **self-raising**
self-satisfied [self'sætɪsfaɪd] adj satisfecho(a) de sí mismo(a)
self-service [self'sɜːvɪs] **1** n (in shop etc) autoservicio m
  2 adj de autoservicio
self-sufficient [selfsə'fɪʃənt] adj autosuficiente
self-taught [self'tɔːt] adj autodidacta
sell [sel] **1** vt (pt & pp sold) vender
  2 vi venderse; **this record is selling well** este disco se vende bien
  3 n hard/soft s. (in advertising) publicidad agresiva/discreta
  ► **sell off** vt sep vender; (goods) liquidar
  ► **sell out 1** vi to s. out to the enemy claudicar ante el enemigo
  2 vt sep Com **we're sold out of sugar** se nos ha agotado el azúcar; Th **sold out**

(sign) agotadas las localidades
seller ['selə(r)] n vendedor(a) m,f
selling ['selɪŋ] n venta f; **s. point** atractivo m comercial; **s. price** precio m de venta
Sellotape® ['seləteɪp] **1** n celo® m, cinta adhesiva
  2 vt pegar or fijar con celo®
sell-out ['selaʊt] n (**a**) Th éxito m de taquilla (**b**) (act of disloyalty) claudicación f
selves [selvz] pl of **self**
semaphore ['seməfɔː(r)] n semáforo m
semblance ['sembləns] n apariencia f; **there was some s. of truth in it** había algo de verdad en ello
semen ['siːmen] n semen m
semester [sɪ'mestə(r)] n semestre m
semi- ['semɪ] pref semi-
semicircle ['semɪsɜːkəl] n semicírculo m
semicolon [semɪ'kəʊlən] n punto y coma m
semiconductor ['semɪkən'dʌktə(r)] n semiconductor m
semidetached [semɪdɪ'tætʃt] Br **1** adj adosado(a)
  2 n chalé adosado, casa adosada
semifinal [semɪ'faɪnəl] n semifinal f
seminar ['semɪnɑː(r)] n seminario m
seminary ['semɪnərɪ] n seminario m
semitrailer ['semɪtreɪlə(r)] n US camión articulado
semolina [semə'liːnə] n sémola f
senate ['senɪt] n (**a**) Pol senado m (**b**) Univ claustro m
senator ['senətə(r)] n senador(a) m,f
send [send] **1** vt (pt & pp sent) (**a**) (letter) enviar, mandar; (radio signal) transmitir; (rocket, ball) lanzar; **he was sent to prison** lo mandaron a la cárcel; **to s. sth flying** tirar algo (**b**) **to s. sb mad** (cause to become) volver loco(a) a algn
  2 vi to s. for sb mandar llamar a algn; to s. for sth encargar algo
  ► **send away 1** vt sep (dismiss) despedir
  2 vi to s. away for sth escribir pidiendo algo
  ► **send back** vt sep (goods etc) devolver; (person) hacer volver
  ► **send in** vt sep (application etc) mandar; (troops) enviar
  ► **send off** vt sep (**a**) (letter etc) enviar; (goods) despachar (**b**) Ftb (player) expulsar
  ► **send on** vt sep (luggage) (ahead) facturar; (later) mandar (más tarde)
  ► **send out** vt sep (**a**) (person) echar (**b**) (invitations) enviar (**c**) (emit) emitir
  ► **send up** vt sep (**a**) hacer subir; (rocket)

lanzar; *(smoke)* echar (**b**) *Br Fam (make fun of) (person)* burlarse de; *(book etc)* satirizar
sender ['sendə(r)] *n* remitente *mf*
sendoff ['sendɒf] *n Fam* despedida *f*
senile ['siːnaɪl] *adj* senil
senior ['siːnjə(r)] **1** *adj* (**a**) *(in age)* mayor; **William Armstrong S.** William Armstrong padre; **s. citizen** jubilado(a) *m,f* (**b**) *(in rank)* superior; *(with longer service)* más antiguo(a); *Mil* **s. officer** oficial *mf* de alta graduación
2 *n* (**a**) **she's three years my s.** *(in age)* me lleva tres años (**b**) *US Educ* estudiante *mf* del último curso
seniority [siːnɪ'ɒrɪtɪ] *n* antigüedad *f*
sensation [sen'seɪʃən] *n* sensación *f*; **to be a s.** ser un éxito; **to cause a s.** causar sensación
sensational [sen'seɪʃənəl] *adj (marvellous)* sensacional; *(exaggerated)* sensacionalista
sense [sens] **1** *n* (**a**) *(faculty)* sentido *m*; *(feeling)* sensación *f*; **s. of direction/humour** sentido *m* de la orientación/del humor (**b**) *(wisdom)* sentido *m* común, juicio *m*; **common s.** sentido común (**c**) *(meaning)* sentido *m*; *(of word)* significado *m*; **in a s.** en cierto sentido; **it doesn't make s.** no tiene sentido (**d**) **to come to one's senses** recobrar el juicio
2 *vt* sentir, percatarse de
senseless ['senslɪs] *adj* (**a**) *(absurd)* insensato(a), absurdo(a) (**b**) *(unconscious)* sin conocimiento
sensibility [sensɪ'bɪlɪtɪ] *n* (**a**) *(sensitivity)* sensibilidad *f* (**b**) **sensibilities** susceptibilidad *f*
sensible ['sensɪbəl] *adj* (**a**) *(wise)* sensato(a) (**b**) *(choice)* acertado(a) (**c**) *(clothes, shoes)* práctico(a), cómodo(a)

> 🖉 Note that the Spanish word **sensible** is a false friend and is never a translation for the English word **sensible**. In Spanish, **sensible** means both "sensitive" and "perceptible".

sensitive ['sensɪtɪv] *adj* (**a**) *(person)* sensible; *(touchy)* susceptible (**b**) *(skin)* delicado(a); *(document)* confidencial
sensor ['sensə(r)] *n* sensor *m*
sensual ['sensjʊəl] *adj* sensual
sensuous ['sensjʊəs] *adj* sensual
sent [sent] *pt & pp of* **send**
sentence ['sentəns] **1** *n* (**a**) frase *f*; *Ling* oración *f* (**b**) *Jur* sentencia *f*; **to pass s. on sb** imponer una pena a algn; **life s.** cadena perpetua
2 *vt Jur* condenar

sentiment ['sentɪmənt] *n* (**a**) *(sentimentality)* sensiblería *f* (**b**) *(feeling)* sentimiento *m* (**c**) *(opinion)* opinión *f*
sentimental [sentɪ'mentəl] *adj* sentimental
sentry ['sentrɪ] *n* centinela *m*
separate 1 *vt* ['sepəreɪt] separar (**from** de); *(divide)* dividir (**into** en); *(distinguish)* distinguir
2 *vi* separarse
3 *adj* ['sepərɪt] separado(a); *(different)* distinto(a); *(entrance)* particular
4 *npl* **separates** ['sepərɪts] *(clothes)* piezas *fpl*
separately ['sepərətlɪ] *adv* por separado
separation [sepə'reɪʃən] *n* separación *f*
separatist ['sepərətɪst] *n* separatista *mf*
September [sep'tembə(r)] *n* se(p)tiembre *m*
septic ['septɪk] *adj* séptico(a); **to become s.** *(of wound)* infectarse; **s. tank** fosa séptica
sequel ['siːkwəl] *n* secuela *f*; *(of film etc)* continuación *f*
sequence ['siːkwəns] *n* (**a**) *(order)* secuencia *f*, orden *m* (**b**) *(series)* serie *f*, sucesión *f*; *Cin* **film s.** secuencia *f*
serenade [serɪ'neɪd] *n* serenata *f*
serene [sɪ'riːn] *adj* sereno(a), tranquilo(a)
sergeant ['saːdʒənt] *n Mil* sargento *mf*; *(of police)* ≃ oficial *mf* de policía; **s. major** sargento *mf* mayor
serial ['sɪərɪəl] *n* (**a**) *Rad & TV* serial *m*; *(soap opera)* radionovela *f*, telenovela *f* (**b**) **s. number** número *m* de serie
series ['sɪəriːz] *n* (*pl* **series**) serie *f*; *(of books)* colección *f*; *(of concerts, lectures)* ciclo *m*
serious ['sɪərɪəs] *adj* (**a**) *(solemn, earnest)* serio(a); **I am s.** hablo en serio (**b**) *(causing concern)* grave
seriously ['sɪərɪəslɪ] *adv* (**a**) *(in earnest)* en serio (**b**) *(dangerously, severely)* gravemente
seriousness ['sɪərɪəsnɪs] *n* gravedad *f*, seriedad *f*; **in all s.** hablando en serio
sermon ['saːmən] *n* sermón *m*
serpent ['saːpənt] *n* serpiente *f*
serrated [sɪ'reɪtɪd] *adj* dentado(a)
serum ['sɪərəm] *n* suero *m*
servant ['saːvənt] *n (domestic)* criado(a) *m,f*; *Fig* servidor(a) *m,f*
serve [saːv] **1** *vt* (**a**) servir (**b**) *(customer)* atender a (**c**) *(in tennis)* servir (**d**) **if my memory serves me right** si mal no recuerdo; **it serves him right** bien merecido lo tiene (**e**) *Fam* **to s. time** cumplir una

condena; **to s. one's apprenticeship** hacer el aprendizaje
2 *vi* (**a**) *(serve)*; **to s. on a committee** ser miembro de una comisión (**b**) *(in tennis)* servir (**c**) *(be useful)* servir (**as** de)
3 *n (in tennis)* servicio *m*
▸ **serve out, serve up** *vt sep* servir
service ['sɜːvɪs] **1** *n* (**a**) servicio *m*; **at your s.!** ¡a sus órdenes!; **how can I be of s. to you?** ¿en qué puedo servirle?; **s. (charge) included** servicio incluido; **s. area** área *m* de servicio; **s. industry** sector *m* de servicios; *Br* **s. lift** montacargas *m inv*; **s. station** estación *f* de servicio (**b**) **medical s.** servicios médicos; *Mil* **the Services** las Fuerzas Armadas; **the train s. to Bristol** la línea de trenes a Bristol (**c**) *(maintenance)* revisión *f* (**d**) *Rel* oficio *m*; *(mass)* misa *f* (**e**) *(in tennis)* servicio *m*; **s. line** línea *f* de saque (**f**) *(set of dishes)* juego *m*
2 *vt (car, machine)* revisar
serviceable ['sɜːvɪsəbəl] *adj* (**a**) *(fit for use)* útil, servible (**b**) *(practical)* práctico(a)
serviceman ['sɜːvɪsmən] *n* militar *m*
serviette [sɜːvɪ'et] *n Br* servilleta *f*
sesame ['sesəmɪ] *n* sésamo *m*
session ['seʃən] *n* (**a**) sesión *f*; **to be in s.** estar reunido(a); *(of Parliament, court)* celebrar una sesión (**b**) *Educ (academic year)* año académico
set¹ [set] **1** *vt (pt & pp set)* (**a**) *(put, place)* poner, colocar; *(trap)* poner (**for** para); **the novel is s. in Moscow** la novela se desarrolla en Moscú; **to s. fire to sth** prender fuego a algo
(**b**) *(time, price)* fijar; *(record)* establecer; *(trend)* imponer
(**c**) *(mechanism etc)* ajustar; *(bone)* encajar; **to s. one's watch** poner el reloj en hora
(**d**) *(arrange)* arreglar; **he s. the words to music** puso música a la letra; **to s. the table** poner la mesa
(**e**) *(exam, homework)* poner; *(example)* dar; *(precedent)* sentar
(**f**) **to s. sail** zarpar; **to s. sb free** poner en libertad a algn; **to s. sth going** poner algo en marcha
(**g**) *(pearl, diamond etc)* engastar
(**h**) *Typ* componer
2 *vi* (**a**) *(sun, moon)* ponerse
(**b**) *(jelly, jam)* cuajar; *(cement)* fraguar; *(bone)* encajarse
(**c**) **to s. to** *(begin)* ponerse a
3 *n* (**a**) **shampoo and s.** lavar y marcar
(**b**) *(stage) Cin* plató *m*; *Th* escenario

m; *(scenery)* decorado *m*
4 *adj* (**a**) *(task, idea)* fijo(a); *(date, time)* señalado(a); *(opinion)* inflexible; *(smile)* rígido(a); *(gaze)* fijo(a); **s. phrase** frase hecha; **to be s. on doing sth** estar empeñado(a) en hacer algo; **s. square** cartabón *m*
(**b**) *(ready)* listo(a)
▸ **set about** *vt insep* (**a**) *(begin)* empezar (**b**) *(attack)* agredir
▸ **set aside** *vt sep (time, money)* reservar; *(differences)* dejar de lado
▸ **set back** *vt sep* (**a**) *(delay)* retrasar; *(hinder)* entorpecer (**b**) *Fam (cost)* costar
▸ **set down** *vt sep (luggage etc)* dejar (en el suelo); *Br (passengers)* dejar
▸ **set in** *vi (winter, rain)* comenzar; **panic s. in** cundió el pánico
▸ **set off 1** *vi (depart)* salir
2 *vt sep* (**a**) *(bomb)* hacer estallar; *(burglar alarm)* hacer sonar; *(reaction)* desencadenar (**b**) *(enhance)* hacer resaltar
▸ **set out 1** *vi* (**a**) *(depart)* salir; **to s. out for ...** partir hacia ... (**b**) **to s. out to do sth** proponerse hacer algo
2 *vt sep (arrange)* disponer; *(present)* presentar
▸ **set up 1** *vt sep* (**a**) *(position)* colocar; *(statue, camp)* levantar; *(tent, stall)* montar (**b**) *(business etc)* establecer; *Fam* montar; *(committee)* constituir; *Fam* **you've been s. up!** ¡te han timado!
2 *vi* establecerse
set² [set] *n* (**a**) *(series)* serie *f*; *(of golf clubs etc)* juego *m*; *(of tools)* estuche *m*; *(of turbines etc)* equipo *m*; *(of books, poems)* colección *f*; *(of teeth)* dentadura *f*; **chess s.** juego de ajedrez; **s. of cutlery** cubertería *f*; **s. of kitchen utensils** batería *f* de cocina (**b**) *(of people)* grupo *m*; *Pej (clique)* camarilla *f* (**c**) *Math* conjunto *m* (**d**) *(in tennis)* set *m* (**e**) *TV* **s.** televisor *m*
setback ['setbæk] *n* revés *m*, contratiempo *m*
settee [se'tiː] *n* sofá *m*
setting ['setɪŋ] *n* (**a**) *(background)* marco *m*; *(of novel, film)* escenario *m* (**b**) *(of jewel)* engaste *m*
settle ['setəl] **1** *vt* (**a**) *(put in position)* colocar
(**b**) *(decide on)* acordar; *(date, price)* fijar; *(problem)* resolver; *(differences)* arreglar
(**c**) *(debt)* pagar; *(account)* saldar
(**d**) *(nerves)* calmar; *(stomach)* asentar
(**e**) *Fam (put an end to)* acabar con
(**f**) *(establish) (person)* instalar
(**g**) *(colonize)* asentarse en

2 *vi* (**a**) *(bird, insect)* posarse; *(dust)* depositarse; *(snow)* cuajar; *(sediment)* precipitarse; *(liquid)* asentarse; **to s. into an armchair** acomodarse en un sillón (**b**) *(put down roots)* afincarse; *(in a colony)* asentarse

(**c**) *(weather)* serenarse

(**d**) *(child, nerves)* calmarse

(**e**) *(pay)* pagar; **to s. out of court** llegar a un acuerdo amistoso

▸ **settle down** *vi* (**a**) *(put down roots)* instalarse; *(marry)* casarse (**b**) **to s. down to work** ponerse a trabajar (**c**) *(child)* calmarse; *(situation)* normalizarse

▸ **settle for** *vt insep* conformarse con

▸ **settle in** *vi (move in)* instalarse; *(become adapted)* adaptarse

▸ **settle with** *vt sep (pay debt to)* ajustar cuentas con

settlement ['setəlmənt] *n* (**a**) *(agreement)* acuerdo *m* (**b**) *(of debt)* pago *m*; *(of account)* liquidación *f* (**c**) *(dowry)* dote *m* (**d**) *(colonization)* colonización *f* (**e**) *(colony)* asentamiento *m*; *(village)* poblado *m*

settler ['setlə(r)] *n* colono *m*

setup ['setʌp] *n (system)* sistema *m*; *(situation)* situación *f*; *Fam* montaje *m*

seven ['sevən] *adj & n* siete *(m inv)*

seventeen [sevən'tiːn] *adj & n* diecisiete *(m inv)*, diez y siete *(m inv)*

seventeenth [sevən'tiːnθ] **1** *adj & n* decimoséptimo(a) *(m,f)*

2 *n (fraction)* decimoséptima parte

seventh ['sevənθ] **1** *adj & n* séptimo(a) *(m,f)*

2 *n* séptimo *m*

seventy ['sevəntɪ] *adj & n* setenta *(m inv)*

sever ['sevə(r)] *vt (cut)* cortar; *Fig (relations)* romper

several ['sevərəl] **1** *adj* (**a**) *(more than a few)* varios(as) (**b**) *(different)* distintos(as)

2 *pron* algunos(as)

severance ['sevərəns] *n (of relations etc)* ruptura *f*; **s. pay** indemnización *f* por despido

severe [sɪ'vɪə(r)] *adj* severo(a); *(climate, blow)* duro(a); *(illness, loss)* grave; *(pain)* intenso(a)

severity [sɪ'verɪtɪ] *n (of person, criticism, punishment)* severidad *f*; *(of climate)* rigor *m*; *(of illness)* gravedad *f*; *(of pain)* intensidad *f*; *(of style)* austeridad *f*

Seville [sə'vɪl] *n* Sevilla

sew [səʊ] *vt & vi (pt* **sewed**; *pp* **sewed** *or* **sewn**) coser

▸ **sew up** *vt sep (stitch together)* coser; *(mend)* remendar

sewage ['suːɪdʒ] *n* aguas *fpl* residuales

sewer ['suːə(r)] *n* alcantarilla *f*, cloaca *f*

sewerage ['suːərɪdʒ] *n* alcantarillado *m*

sewing ['səʊɪŋ] *n* costura *f*; **s. machine** máquina *f* de coser

sewn [səʊn] *pp of* **sew**

sex [seks] *n* sexo *m*; **s. education** educación *f* sexual; **to have s. with sb** tener relaciones sexuales con algn; **s. appeal** sex-appeal *m*

sexist ['seksɪst] *adj & n* sexista *(mf)*

sexual ['seksjʊəl] *adj* sexual

sexuality [seksjʊ'ælɪtɪ] *n* sexualidad *f*

sexy ['seksɪ] *adj* (**sexier, sexiest**) *Fam* sexi, erótico(a)

shabby ['ʃæbɪ] *adj* (**shabbier, shabbiest**) (**a**) *(garment)* raído(a); *(house)* desvencijado(a); *(person)* *(in rags)* harapiento(a); *(unkempt)* desaseado(a) (**b**) *(treatment)* mezquino(a)

shack [ʃæk] *n* choza *f*

shackles ['ʃækəlz] *npl* grilletes *mpl*, grillos *mpl*; *Fig* trabas *fpl*

shade [ʃeɪd] **1** *n* (**a**) *(shadow)* sombra *f*; **in the s.** a la sombra (**b**) *(eyeshade)* visera *f*; *(lampshade)* pantalla *f*; *US (blind)* persiana *f* (**c**) *(of colour)* tono *m*, matiz *m*; *Fig (of meaning)* matiz (**d**) *(small amount)* poquito *m* (**e**) *Fam* **shades** gafas *fpl or Am* anteojos *mpl* de sol

2 *vt (from sun)* proteger contra el sol

shadow ['ʃædəʊ] **1** *n* (**a**) *(shade)* sombra *f*; *(darkness)* oscuridad *f*; *Fig* **without a s. of a doubt** sin lugar a dudas (**b**) *Br* **the S. Cabinet** el gabinete de la oposición

2 *vt Fig* seguir la pista a

shadowy ['ʃædəʊɪ] *adj (dark)* oscuro(a); *(hazy)* vago(a)

shady ['ʃeɪdɪ] *adj* (**shadier, shadiest**) *(place)* a la sombra; *(suspicious)* *(person)* sospechoso(a); *(deal)* turbio(a)

shaft [ʃɑːft] *n* (**a**) *(of tool, golf club)* mango *m*; *(of lance)* asta *f*; *(of arrow)* astil *m* (**b**) *Tech* eje *m* (**c**) *(of mine)* pozo *m*; *(of lift, elevator)* hueco *m* (**d**) *(beam of light)* rayo *m*

shaggy ['ʃægɪ] *adj* (**shaggier, shaggiest**) *(hairy)* peludo(a); *(long-haired)* melenudo(a); *(beard)* desgreñado(a)

shake [ʃeɪk] **1** *n* sacudida *f*

2 *vt (pt* **shook**; *pp* **shaken** ['ʃeɪkən]) *(carpet etc)* sacudir; *(bottle)* agitar; *(dice)* mover; *(building)* hacer temblar; **the news shook him** la noticia le conmocionó; **to s. hands with sb** estrechar la mano a algn; **to s. one's head** negar con la cabeza

3 *vi (person, building)* temblar; **to s. with cold** tiritar de frío
▸ **shake off** *vt sep* (**a**) *(dust etc)* sacudirse (**b**) *Fig (bad habit)* librarse de; *(cough, cold)* quitarse de encima; *(pursuer)* dar esquinazo a
▸ **shake up** *vt sep Fig (shock)* trastornar; *(reorganize)* reorganizar

shake-up [ˈʃeɪkʌp] *n Fig* reorganización *f*

shaky [ˈʃeɪkɪ] *adj* (**shakier, shakiest**) *(hand, voice)* tembloroso(a); *(step)* inseguro(a); *(handwriting)* temblón(ona)

shall [ʃæl, *unstressed* ʃəl] *v aux*

> En el inglés hablado, y en el escrito en estilo coloquial, el verbo **shall** se contrae de manera que **I/you/he** *etc* **shall** se transforman en **I'll/you'll/he'll** *etc*. La forma negativa **shall not** se transforma en **shan't**.

(**a**) *(used to form future tense) (first person only)* **I s.** *or* **I'll buy it** lo compraré; **I s. not** *or* **I shan't say anything** no diré nada (**b**) *(used to form questions) (usu first person)* **s. I close the door?** ¿cierro la puerta?; **s. I mend it for you?** ¿quieres que te lo repare?; **s. we go?** ¿nos vamos? (**c**) *(emphatic, command, threat) (all persons)* **we s. overcome** venceremos; **you s. leave immediately** te irás enseguida

shallow [ˈʃæləʊ] *adj* poco profundo(a); *Fig* superficial

sham [ʃæm] **1** *adj* falso(a); *(illness etc)* fingido(a)
2 *n* (**a**) *(pretence)* engaño *m*, farsa *f* (**b**) *(person)* fantoche *m*
3 *vt* fingir, simular
4 *vi* fingir

shambles [ˈʃæmbəlz] *n sing* confusión *f*; **the performance was a s.** la función fue un desastre

shame [ʃeɪm] **1** *n* (**a**) *(person)* vergüenza *f*; *Andes, CAm, Carib, Méx* pena *f*; **to put to s.** *(far outdo)* eclipsar, sobrepasar (**b**) *(pity)* pena *f*, lástima *f*; **what a s.!** ¡qué pena!, ¡qué lástima!
2 *vt* avergonzar, *Andes, CAm, Carib, Méx* apenar; *(disgrace)* deshonrar

shamefaced [ˈʃeɪmfeɪst] *adj* avergonzado(a), *Andes, CAm, Carib, Méx* apenado(a)

shameful [ˈʃeɪmfʊl] *adj* vergonzoso(a)

shameless [ˈʃeɪmlɪs] *adj* descarado(a)

shampoo [ʃæmˈpuː] **1** *n* champú *m*
2 *vt* lavar con champú; **to s. one's hair** lavarse el pelo

shamrock [ˈʃæmrɒk] *n* trébol *m*

shandy [ˈʃændɪ] *n Br* clara *f*, cerveza *f* con gaseosa

shantytown [ˈʃæntɪtaʊn] *n* barrio *m* de chabolas, *Arg* villa *f* miseria, *Chile* población *f* callampa, *Méx* ciudad *f* perdida, *Urug* cantegril *m*, *Ven* rancho *m*

shape [ʃeɪp] **1** *n* (**a**) forma *f*; *(shadow)* silueta *m*; **to take s.** tomar forma (**b**) **in good/bad s.** *(condition)* en buen/mal estado; **to be in good s.** *(health)* estar en forma
2 *vt* dar forma a; *(clay)* modelar; *(stone)* tallar; *(character)* formar; *(destiny)* determinar; **star-shaped** con forma de estrella
3 *vi* (*also* **s. up**) tomar forma; **to s. up well** *(events)* tomar buen cariz; *(person)* hacer progresos

shapeless [ˈʃeɪplɪs] *adj* amorfo(a), informe

shapely [ˈʃeɪplɪ] *adj* (**shapelier, shapeliest**) escultural

share [ˈʃeə(r)] **1** *n* (**a**) *(portion)* parte *f* (**b**) *Fin* acción *f*; **s. index** índice *m* de la Bolsa; **s. prices** cotizaciones *fpl*
2 *vt* (**a**) *(divide)* dividir (**b**) *(have in common)* compartir
3 *vi* compartir
▸ **share out** *vt sep* repartir

shareholder [ˈʃeəhəʊldə(r)] *n* accionista *mf*

shark [ʃɑːk] *n* (**a**) *(fish)* tiburón *m* (**b**) *Fam (swindler)* estafador(a) *m,f*; **loan s.** usurero(a) *m,f*

sharp [ʃɑːp] **1** *adj* (**a**) *(razor, knife)* afilado(a); *(needle, pencil)* puntiagudo(a)
(**b**) *(angle)* agudo(a); *(features)* anguloso(a); *(bend)* cerrado(a)
(**c**) *(outline)* definido(a); *(contrast)* marcado(a)
(**d**) *(observant)* perspicaz; *(clever)* listo(a); *(quick-witted)* avispado(a); *(cunning)* astuto(a)
(**e**) *(sudden)* brusco(a)
(**f**) *(pain, cry)* agudo(a); *(wind)* penetrante
(**g**) *(sour)* acre
(**h**) *(criticism)* mordaz; *(temper)* arisco(a); *(tone)* seco(a)
(**i**) *Mus* sostenido(a); *(out of tune)* desafinado(a)
2 *adv* **at two o'clock s.** *(exactly)* a las dos en punto
3 *n Mus* sostenido *m*

sharpen [ˈʃɑːpən] *vt* (**a**) *(knife)* afilar; *(pencil)* sacar punta a (**b**) *Fig (desire, intelligence)* agudizar

sharpener [ˈʃɑːpənə(r)] *n (for knife)* afilador *m*; *(for pencil)* sacapuntas *m inv*

sharp-eyed ['ʃɑːpaɪd] *adj* con ojos de lince

sharply ['ʃɑːplɪ] *adv* (**a**) *(abruptly)* bruscamente (**b**) *(clearly)* marcadamente

shatter ['ʃætə(r)] **1** *vt* hacer añicos; *(nerves)* destrozar; *(hopes)* frustrar
  2 *vi* hacerse añicos

shave [ʃeɪv] **1** *n* afeitado *m*; **to have a s.** afeitarse; *Fig* **to have a close s.** escaparse por los pelos
  2 *vt* (*pt* **shaved**; *pp* **shaved** *or* **shaven** ['ʃeɪvən]) *(person)* afeitar; *(wood)* cepillar
  3 *vi* afeitarse

shaver ['ʃeɪvə(r)] *n* (**electric**) **s.** máquina *f* de afeitar

shaving ['ʃeɪvɪŋ] *n* (**a**) *(of wood)* viruta *f* (**b**) **s. brush** brocha *f* de afeitar; **s. cream** crema *f* de afeitar; **s. foam** espuma *f* de afeitar

shawl [ʃɔːl] *n* chal *m*

she [ʃiː] *pers pron* ella *(usually omitted in Spanish, except for contrast)*

she- [ʃiː] *pref (of animal)* hembra; **s.-cat** gata *f*

sheaf [ʃiːf] *n* (*pl* **sheaves**) *Agr* gavilla *f*; *(of arrows)* haz *m*; *(of papers, banknotes)* fajo *m*

shear [ʃɪə(r)] **1** *vt* (*pt* **sheared**; *pp* **shorn** *or* **sheared**) *(sheep)* esquilar; **to s. off** cortar
  2 *vi* esquilar ovejas

shears [ʃɪəz] *npl* tijeras *fpl* (grandes)

sheath [ʃiːθ] *n* (**a**) *(for sword)* vaina *f*; *(for knife, scissors)* funda *f* (**b**) *(contraceptive)* preservativo *m*

sheaves [ʃiːvz] *pl of* **sheaf**

shed¹ [ʃed] *n (in garden)* cobertizo *m*; *(workmen's hut)* barraca *f*; *(for cattle)* establo *m*; *(in factory)* nave *f*

shed² [ʃed] *vt* (*pt & pp* **shed**) (**a**) *(clothes)* despojarse de; *(unwanted thing)* deshacerse de; **the snake s. its skin** la serpiente mudó de piel (**b**) *(blood, tears)* derramar

sheen [ʃiːn] *n* brillo *m*

sheep [ʃiːp] *n* (*pl* **sheep**) oveja *f*

sheepdog ['ʃiːpdɒg] *n* perro *m* pastor

sheepish ['ʃiːpɪʃ] *adj* avergonzado(a)

sheepskin ['ʃiːpskɪn] *n* piel *f* de carnero

sheer [ʃɪə(r)] *adj* (**a**) *(utter)* total, puro(a) (**b**) *(cliff)* escarpado(a); *(drop)* vertical (**c**) *(stockings, cloth)* fino(a)

sheet [ʃiːt] *n* (**a**) *(on bed)* sábana *f* (**b**) *(of paper)* hoja *f*; *(of tin, glass, plastic)* lámina *f*; *(of ice)* capa *f*

sheik(h) [ʃeɪk] *n* jeque *m*

shelf [ʃelf] *n* (*pl* **shelves**) *(on bookcase)* estante *m*; *(in cupboard)* tabla *f*; **shelves** estantería *f*

shell [ʃel] **1** *n* (**a**) *(of egg, nut)* cáscara *f*; *(of pea)* vaina *f*; *(of tortoise etc)* caparazón *m*; *(of snail etc)* concha *f* (**b**) *(of building)* armazón *m* (**c**) *(mortar etc)* obús *m*, proyectil *m*; *(cartridge)* cartucho *m*; **s. shock** neurosis *f* de guerra
  2 *vt* (**a**) *(peas)* desvainar; *(nuts)* pelar (**b**) *Mil* bombardear

shellfish ['ʃelfɪʃ] *n* (*pl* **shellfish**) marisco *m*, mariscos *mpl*

shelter ['ʃeltə(r)] **1** *n* (**a**) *(protection)* abrigo *m*, amparo *m*; **to take s. (from)** refugiarse (de) (**b**) *(place)* refugio *m*; *(for homeless)* asilo *m*; **bus s.** marquesina *f*
  2 *vt* (**a**) *(protect)* abrigar, proteger (**b**) *(take into one's home)* ocultar
  3 *vi* refugiarse

sheltered ['ʃeltəd] *adj (place)* abrigado(a); **to lead a s. life** vivir apartado(a) del mundo

shelve [ʃelv] *vt Fig (postpone)* dar carpetazo a

shelves [ʃelvz] *pl of* **shelf**

shepherd ['ʃepəd] **1** *n* pastor *m*; **s.'s pie** = pastel de carne picada con puré de patatas *or Am* papas
  2 *vt Fig* **to s. sb in** hacer entrar a algn

sheriff ['ʃerɪf] *n Br* gobernador *m* civil; *Scot* juez *m* presidente; *US* sheriff *m*

sherry ['ʃerɪ] *n* jerez *m*

Shetland ['ʃetlənd] *n* **the S. Isles, S.** las Islas Shetland; **S. wool** lana *f* Shetland

shield [ʃiːld] **1** *n* (**a**) *(of policeman)* escudo *m*; *(of policeman)* placa *f* (**b**) *(on machinery)* blindaje *m*
  2 *vt* proteger (**from** de)

shift [ʃɪft] **1** *n* (**a**) *(change)* cambio *m*; *US Aut* (**gear**) **s.** cambio de velocidades (**b**) *(period of work, group of workers)* turno *m*; **to be on the day s.** hacer el turno de día
  2 *vt (change)* cambiar; *(move)* cambiar de sitio, trasladar
  3 *vi (move)* moverse; *(change place)* cambiar de sitio; *(opinion)* cambiar; *(wind)* cambiar de dirección

shiftless ['ʃɪftlɪs] *n* perezoso(a), vago(a)

shiftwork ['ʃɪftwɜːk] *n* trabajo *m* por turnos

shifty ['ʃɪftɪ] *adj* (**shiftier**, **shiftiest**) *(look)* furtivo(a); *(person)* sospechoso(a)

shilling ['ʃɪlɪŋ] *n* chelín *m*

shimmer ['ʃɪmə(r)] **1** *vi* relucir; *(shine)* brillar
  2 *n* luz trémula, reflejo trémulo; *(shining)* brillo *m*

shin [ʃɪn] *n* espinilla *f*; **s. pad** espinillera *f*

shine [ʃaɪn] **1** *vi* (*pt & pp* **shone**) (**a**) *(light)* brillar; *(metal)* relucir (**b**) *Fig (excel)* sobresalir (**at** en)

   2 *vt* (**a**) *(lamp)* dirigir (**b**) *(pt & pp* **shined**) *(polish)* sacar brillo a; *(shoes)* limpiar

   3 *n* brillo *m*, lustre *m*

shingle ['ʃɪŋgəl] *n* (**a**) *(pebbles)* guijarros *mpl* (**b**) *(roof tile)* tablilla *f*

shingles ['ʃɪŋgəlz] *n sing Med* herpes *m*

shining ['ʃaɪnɪŋ] *adj Fig (outstanding)* ilustre

shiny ['ʃaɪnɪ] *adj* (**shinier, shiniest**) brillante

ship [ʃɪp] **1** *n* barco *m*, buque *m*

   2 *vt* (**a**) *(take on board)* embarcar (**b**) *(transport)* transportar (en barco); *(send)* enviar, mandar

shipbuilding ['ʃɪpbɪldɪŋ] *n* construcción *f* naval

shipment ['ʃɪpmənt] *n* (**a**) *(act)* transporte *m* (**b**) *(load)* consignación *f*, envío *m*

shipper ['ʃɪpə(r)] *n (person)* cargador(a) *m,f*

shipping ['ʃɪpɪŋ] *n* (**a**) *(ships)* barcos *mpl*; **s. lane** vía *f* de navegación (**b**) *(loading)* embarque *m*; *(transporting)* transporte *m* (en barco); **s. company** compañía naviera

shipshape ['ʃɪpʃeɪp] *adj & adv* en perfecto orden

shipwreck ['ʃɪprek] **1** *n* naufragio *m*

   2 *vt* **to be shipwrecked** naufragar

shipyard ['ʃɪpjɑːd] *n* astillero *m*

shire [ʃaɪə(r)] *n Br* condado *m*

shirk [ʃɜːk] **1** *vt (duty)* faltar a; *(problem)* eludir

   2 *vi* gandulear

shirt [ʃɜːt] *n* camisa *f*; **in s. sleeves** en mangas de camisa; *Fam* **keep your s. on!** ¡no te sulfures!

shit [ʃɪt] *Vulg* **1** *n* mierda *f*; **in the s.** jodido(a)

   2 *interj* ¡mierda!

   3 *vi* cagar

shiver ['ʃɪvə(r)] **1** *vi (with cold)* tiritar; *(with fear)* temblar, estremecerse

   2 *n (with cold, fear)* escalofrío *m*

shoal [ʃəʊl] *n (of fish)* banco *m*

shock [ʃɒk] **1** *n* (**a**) *(jolt)* choque *m*; **s. absorber** amortiguador *m*; **s. wave** onda expansiva (**b**) *(upset)* conmoción *f*; *(scare)* susto *m* (**c**) *Med* shock *m*

   2 *vt (upset)* conmover; *(startle)* sobresaltar; *(scandalize)* escandalizar

shocking ['ʃɒkɪŋ] *adj* (**a**) *(causing horror)* espantoso(a); *Fam (very bad)* horroroso(a) (**b**) *(disgraceful)* escandaloso(a) (**c**) **s. pink** rosa chillón

shod [ʃɒd] *pt & pp of* **shoe**

shoddy ['ʃɒdɪ] *adj* (**shoddier, shoddiest**) *(goods)* de mala calidad; *(work)* chapucero(a)

shoe [ʃuː] **1** *n* (**a**) zapato *m*; *(for horse)* herradura *f*; **brake s.** zapata *f*; **s. polish** betún *m*; **s. repair (shop)** remiendo *m* de zapatos; **s. shop**, *US* **s. store** zapatería *f* (**b**) **shoes** calzado *m*

   2 *vt (pt & pp* **shod**) *(horse)* herrar

shoebrush ['ʃuːbrʌʃ] *n* cepillo *m* para los zapatos

shoehorn ['ʃuːhɔːn] *n* calzador *m*

shoelace ['ʃuːleɪs] *n* cordón *m* (de zapatos)

shoestring ['ʃuːstrɪŋ] *n Fig* **to do sth on a s.** hacer algo con poquísimo dinero

shone [ʃɒn, *US* ʃəʊn] *pt & pp of* **shine**

shoo [ʃuː] **1** *interj* ¡fuera!

   2 *vt* **to s. (away)** espantar

shook [ʃʊk] *pt of* **shake**

shoot [ʃuːt] **1** *n Bot* retoño *m*; *(of vine)* sarmiento *m*

   2 *vt (pt & pp* **shot**) (**a**) pegar un tiro a; *(kill)* matar; *(execute)* fusilar; *(hunt)* cazar; **to s. dead** matar a tiros (**b**) *(missile, glance)* lanzar; *(bullet, ball)* disparar (**c**) *(film)* rodar, filmar; *Phot* fotografiar

   3 *vi* (**a**) *(with gun)* disparar (**at sb** a algn); **to s. at a target** tirar al blanco; *Ftb* **to s. at the goal** chutar a puerta (**b**) **to s. past** *or* **by** pasar flechado(a)

  ▸ **shoot down** *vt sep (aircraft)* derribar

  ▸ **shoot out** *vi (person)* salir disparado(a); *(water)* brotar; *(flames)* salir

  ▸ **shoot up** *vi* (**a**) *(flames)* salir; *(water)* brotar; *(prices)* dispararse (**b**) *Fam (inject drugs)* chutarse

shooting ['ʃuːtɪŋ] **1** *n* (**a**) *(shots)* tiros *mpl*; *(murder)* asesinato *m*; *(hunting)* caza *f*; **s. star** estrella *f* fugaz (**b**) *(of film)* rodaje *m*

   2 *adj (pain)* punzante

shoot-out ['ʃuːtaʊt] *n* tiroteo *m*

shop [ʃɒp] **1** *n* (**a**) tienda *f*; *(large store)* almacén *m*; **s. assistant** dependiente(a) *m,f*; **s. window** escaparate *m* (**b**) *(workshop)* taller *m*; **s. floor** *(place)* planta *f*; *(workers)* obreros *mpl*; **s. steward** enlace *mf* sindical

   2 *vi* hacer compras; **to go shopping** ir de compras

shopkeeper ['ʃɒpkiːpə(r)] *n* tendero(a) *m,f*

shoplifter ['ʃɒplɪftə(r)] *n* ladrón(ona) *m,f* (de tiendas)

shopper ['ʃɒpə(r)] *n* comprador(a) *m,f*

shopping ['ʃɒpɪŋ] *n (purchases)* compras *fpl*; **s. bag/basket** bolsa *f*/cesta *f* de la compra; **s. centre** or **precinct** centro *m* comercial

shopsoiled ['ʃɒpsɔɪld], *US* **shopworn** ['ʃɒpwɔːn] *adj* deteriorado(a)

shore [ʃɔː(r)] *n (of sea, lake)* orilla *f*; *US (beach)* playa *f*; *(coast)* costa *f*; **to go on s.** desembarcar
▶ **shore up** *vt sep* apuntalar

shorn [ʃɔːn] *pp of* **shear**

short [ʃɔːt] **1** *adj* (**a**) corto(a); *(not tall)* bajo(a); **in a s. while** dentro de un rato; **in the s. term** a corto plazo; **s. circuit** corto-circuito *m*; **s. cut** atajo *m*; *Br* **s. list** lista *f* de seleccionados; **s. story** relato corto, cuento *m*; **s. wave** onda corta
(**b**) *(brief)* corto(a), breve; **"Bob" is s. for "Robert"** "Bob" es el diminutivo de "Robert"; **for s.** para abreviar; **in s.** en pocas palabras
(**c**) **to be s. of breath** faltarle a uno la respiración; **to be s. of food** andar esca-so(a) de comida
(**d**) *(curt)* brusco(a), seco(a)
2 *adv* (**a**) **to pull up s.** pararse en seco
(**b**) **to cut s.** *(holiday)* interrumpir; *(meeting)* suspender; **we're running s. of coffee** se nos está acabando el café
(**c**) **s. of** *(except)* excepto, menos
3 *n* (**a**) *Cin* cortometraje *m*
(**b**) *Fam (drink)* copa *f*
4 *vi* **to s. (out)** tener un cortocircuito

shortage ['ʃɔːtɪdʒ] *n* escasez *f*

shortbread ['ʃɔːtbred] *n* mantecado *m*

short-change [ʃɔːt'tʃeɪndʒ] *vt* **to s. sb** no devolver el cambio completo a algn; *Fig* timar a algn

short-circuit [ʃɔːt'sɜːkɪt] **1** *vt* provocar un cortocircuito en
2 *vi* tener un cortocircuito

shortcomings ['ʃɔːtkʌmɪŋz] *npl* defec-tos *mpl*

shortcrust ['ʃɔːtkrʌst] *n* **s. pastry** pasta brisa

shorten ['ʃɔːtən] *vt (skirt, visit)* acortar; *(word)* abreviar; *(text)* resumir

shortfall ['ʃɔːtfɔːl] *n* déficit *m*

shorthand ['ʃɔːthænd] *n* taquigrafía *f*; *Br* **s. typist** taquimecanógrafo(a) *m,f*

short-list ['ʃɔːtlɪst] *vt* poner en la lista de seleccionados

short-lived [ʃɔːt'lɪvd] *adj* efímero(a)

shortly ['ʃɔːtlɪ] *adv (soon)* dentro de poco; **s. after** poco después

short-range ['ʃɔːtreɪndʒ] *adj* de corto alcance

shorts [ʃɔːts] *npl* (**a**) pantalones *mpl* cortos; **a pair of s.** un pantalón corto (**b**) *US (underpants)* calzoncillos *mpl*

short-sighted [ʃɔːt'saɪtɪd] *adj (person)* miope; *Fig (plan etc)* sin visión de futuro

short-staffed [ʃɔːt'stɑːft] *adj* escaso(a) de personal

short-tempered [ʃɔːt'tempəd] *adj* de mal genio

short-term ['ʃɔːttɜːm] *adj* a corto plazo

shot¹ [ʃɒt] *n* (**a**) *(act, sound)* tiro *m*, dis-paro *m* (**b**) *(projectile)* bala *f*; *(pellets)* perdigones *mpl*; *Fig* **he was off like a s.** salió disparado; *Sport* **s. put** lanzamiento *m* de peso (**c**) *(person)* tirador(a) *m,f* (**d**) *Ftb (kick)* tiro *m* (a puerta); *(in billiards, cricket, golf)* golpe *m* (**e**) *(attempt)* tenta-tiva *f*; **to have a s. at sth** intentar hacer algo (**f**) *(injection)* inyección *f*; *Fam* pin-chazo *m* (**g**) *(drink)* trago *m* (**h**) *Phot* foto *f*; *Cin* toma *f*

shot² [ʃɒt] *pt & pp of* **shoot**

shotgun ['ʃɒtgʌn] *n* escopeta *f*

should [ʃʊd, *unstressed* ʃəd] *v aux* (**a**) *(duty)* deber; **all employees s. wear hel-mets** todos los empleados deben llevar casco; **he s. have been an architect** de-bería haber sido arquitecto (**b**) *(probab-ility)* deber de; **he s. have finished by now** ya debe de haber acabado; **this s. be interesting** esto promete ser interesante (**c**) *(conditional use)* **if anything strange s. happen** si pasara algo raro (**d**) **I s. like to ask a question** quisiera hacer una pregunta

La forma negativa **should not** se transfor-ma en **shouldn't**.

shoulder ['ʃəʊldə(r)] **1** *n* (**a**) hombro *m*; **s. blade** omóplato *m*; **s. strap** *(of garment)* tirante *m*; *(of bag)* correa *f*; *Br Aut* **hard s.** arcén *m*, *Andes* berma *f*, *Méx* acotamien-to *m*, *RP* banquina *f*, *Ven* hombrillo *m* (**b**) *Culin* paletilla *f* (**c**) *US Aut* arcén *m*, *Andes* berma *f*, *Méx* acotamiento *m*, *RP* banqui-na *f*, *Ven* hombrillo *m*
2 *vt Fig (responsibilities)* cargar con

shout [ʃaʊt] **1** *n* grito *m*
2 *vt* gritar
3 *vi* gritar; **to s. at sb** gritar a algn
▶ **shout down** *vt sep* abuchear

shouting ['ʃaʊtɪŋ] *n* gritos *mpl*, vocerío *m*

shove [ʃʌv] **1** *n Fam* empujón *m*
2 *vt* empujar; **to s. sth into one's pocket** meterse algo en el bolsillo a empellones
3 *vi* empujar; *(jostle)* dar empellones
▶ **shove off** *vi Fam* largarse
▶ **shove up** *vi Fam (move along)* correrse

shovel ['ʃʌvəl] **1** *n* pala *f*; **mechanical s.** excavadora *f*

2 *vt* mover con pala *or* a paladas

show [ʃəʊ] **1** *vt* (*pt* **showed**; *pp* **shown** *or* **showed**) (**a**) (*ticket etc*) mostrar; (*painting etc*) exponer; (*film*) poner; (*latest plans etc*) presentar

(**b**) (*display*) demostrar; **to s. oneself to be** comportarse como

(**c**) (*teach*) enseñar; (*explain*) explicar

(**d**) (*temperature, way etc*) indicar; (*profit etc*) registrar

(**e**) (*prove*) demostrar

(**f**) (*conduct*) llevar; **to s. sb in** hacer pasar a algn; **to s. sb to the door** acompañar a algn hasta la puerta

2 *vi* (**a**) (*be visible*) notarse

(**b**) *Fam* (*turn up*) aparecer

(**c**) *Cin* **what's showing?** ¿qué ponen?

3 *n* (**a**) (*display*) demostración *f*

(**b**) (*outward appearance*) apariencia *f*

(**c**) (*exhibition*) exposición *f*; **on s.** expuesto(a); **boat s.** salón náutico; **motor s.** salón del automóvil

(**d**) *Th* (*entertainment*) espectáculo *m*; (*performance*) función *f*; *Rad & TV* programa *m*; **s. business** *or Fam* **biz** el mundo del espectáculo

▸ **show off 1** *vt sep* (**a**) (*highlight*) hacer resaltar (**b**) *Fam* (*flaunt*) hacer alarde de

2 *vi Fam* farolear

▸ **show up 1** *vt sep* (**a**) (*reveal*) sacar a luz; (*highlight*) hacer resaltar (**b**) *Fam* (*embarrass*) dejar en evidencia

2 *vi* (**a**) (*stand out*) destacarse (**b**) *Fam* (*arrive*) aparecer

showdown [ˈʃəʊdaʊn] *n* enfrentamiento *m*

shower [ˈʃaʊə(r)] **1** *n* (**a**) (*rain*) chubasco *m*, chaparrón *m* (**b**) *Fig* (*of stones, blows etc*) lluvia *f* (**c**) (*bath*) ducha *f*, *Col, Méx, Ven* regadera *f*; **to have a s.** ducharse

2 *vt* (**a**) (*spray*) rociar (**b**) *Fig* **to s. gifts/praise on sb** colmar a algn de regalos/elogios

3 *vi* ducharse

showerproof [ˈʃaʊəpruːf] *adj* impermeable

showing [ˈʃəʊɪŋ] *n* (*of film*) proyección *f*

showjumping [ˈʃəʊdʒʌmpɪŋ] *n* hípica *f*

shown [ʃəʊn] *pp of* **show**

show-off [ˈʃəʊɒf] *n Fam* farolero(a) *m,f*

showpiece [ˈʃəʊpiːs] *n* (*in exhibition etc*) obra maestra; *Fig* (*at school etc*) modelo *m*

showroom [ˈʃəʊruːm] *n Com* exposición *f*; *Art* galería *f*

shrank [ʃræŋk] *pt of* **shrink**

shrapnel [ˈʃræpnəl] *n* metralla *f*

shred [ʃred] **1** *n* triza *f*; (*of cloth*) jirón *m*; (*of paper*) tira *f*

2 *vt* (*paper*) hacer trizas; (*vegetables*) rallar

shredder [ˈʃredə(r)] *n* (*for waste paper*) trituradora *f*; (*for vegetables*) rallador *m*

shrew [ʃruː] *n* (**a**) *Zool* musaraña *f* (**b**) *Fig* (*woman*) arpía *f*

shrewd [ʃruːd] *adj* astuto(a); (*clear-sighted*) perspicaz; (*wise*) sabio(a); (*decision*) acertado(a)

shriek [ʃriːk] **1** *n* chillido *m*; **shrieks of laughter** carcajadas *fpl*

2 *vi* chillar

shrill [ʃrɪl] *adj* agudo(a), estridente

shrimp [ʃrɪmp] **1** *n* camarón *m*

2 *vi* pescar camarones

shrine [ʃraɪn] *n* (*tomb*) sepulcro *m*; (*chapel*) capilla *f*; (*holy place*) lugar sagrado

shrink [ʃrɪŋk] **1** *vt* (*pt* **shrank**; *pp* **shrunk**) encoger

2 *vi* (**a**) (*clothes*) encoger(se) (**b**) (*savings*) disminuir (**c**) **to s. (back)** echarse atrás; **to s. from doing sth** no tener valor para hacer algo

2 *n Fam* (*psychiatrist*) psiquiatra *mf*

shrinkage [ˈʃrɪŋkɪdʒ] *n* (**a**) (*of cloth*) encogimiento *m*; (*of metal*) contracción *f* (**b**) (*of savings etc*) disminución *f*

shrink-wrapped [ˈʃrɪŋkræpt] *adj* envuelto(a) en plástico

shrivel [ˈʃrɪvəl] **1** *vt* **to s. (up)** encoger; (*plant*) secar; (*skin*) arrugar

2 *vi* encogerse; (*plant*) secarse; (*skin*) arrugarse

shroud [ʃraʊd] **1** *n Rel* sudario *m*

2 *vt Fig* envolver

Shrove Tuesday [ˈʃrəʊvˈtjuːzdɪ] *n* martes *m* de carnaval

shrub [ʃrʌb] *n* arbusto *m*

shrubbery [ˈʃrʌbərɪ] *n* arbustos *mpl*

shrug [ʃrʌg] **1** *vt* **to s. one's shoulders** encogerse de hombros

2 *vi* encogerse de hombros

3 *n* encogimiento *m* de hombros

▸ **shrug off** *vt sep* no dejarse desanimar por

shrunk [ʃrʌŋk] *pp of* **shrink**

shudder [ˈʃʌdə(r)] **1** *n* (**a**) escalofrío *m*, estremecimiento *m* (**b**) (*of machinery*) sacudida *f*

2 *vi* (**a**) (*person*) estremecerse (**b**) (*machinery*) dar sacudidas

shuffle [ˈʃʌfəl] **1** *vt* (**a**) (*feet*) arrastrar (**b**) (*papers etc*) revolver; (*cards*) barajar

2 *vi* (**a**) (*walk*) andar arrastrando los pies (**b**) *Cards* barajar

shun [ʃʌn] *vt* (*person*) esquivar; (*responsibility*) rehuir

shunt [ʃʌnt] *vt Rail* cambiar de vía; *Elec* derivar

shut [ʃʌt] **1** *vt (pt & pp* **shut**) cerrar
2 *vi* cerrarse
3 *adj* cerrado(a)
▸ **shut down 1** *vt sep (factory)* cerrar
2 *vi (factory)* cerrar
▸ **shut off** *vt sep (gas, water etc)* cortar
▸ **shut out** *vt sep* (**a**) *(lock out)* dejar fuera a (**b**) *(exclude)* excluir
▸ **shut up 1** *vt sep* (**a**) *(close)* cerrar (**b**) *(imprison)* encerrar (**c**) *Fam (silence)* callar
2 *vi Fam (keep quiet)* callarse

shutdown [ˈʃʌtdaʊn] *n* cierre *m*

shutter [ˈʃʌtə(r)] *n* (**a**) *(on window)* contraventana *f*, postigo *m* (**b**) *Phot* obturador *m*

shuttle [ˈʃʌtəl] **1** *n* (**a**) *(in weaving)* lanzadera *f* (**b**) *Av* puente aéreo; **(space) s.** transbordador *m* espacial
2 *vi* ir y venir

shuttlecock [ˈʃʌtəlkɒk] *n* volante *m*

shy [ʃaɪ] **1** *adj* (**shyer, shyest** *or* **shier, shiest**) *(timid)* tímido(a), *Andes, CAm, Carib, Méx* penoso(a); *(reserved)* reservado(a)
2 *vi (horse)* espantarse (**at** de); *Fig* **to s. away from doing sth** negarse a hacer algo

shyness [ˈʃaɪnɪs] *n* timidez *f*

Siberia [saɪˈbɪərɪə] *n* Siberia

sibling [ˈsɪblɪŋ] *n Fml (brother)* hermano *m*; *(sister)* hermana *f*; **siblings** hermanos

Sicily [ˈsɪsɪlɪ] *n* Sicilia

sick [sɪk] *adj* (**a**) *(ill)* enfermo(a); **s. leave** baja *f* por enfermedad; **s. pay** subsidio *m* de enfermedad (**b**) **to feel s.** *(about to vomit)* tener ganas de devolver; **to be s.** devolver (**c**) *Fam (fed up)* harto(a) (**d**) *Fam (mind, joke)* morboso(a); **s. humour** humor negro

sickbay [ˈsɪkbeɪ] *n* enfermería *f*

sicken [ˈsɪkən] **1** *vt (make ill)* poner enfermo; *(revolt)* dar asco a
2 *vi (fall ill)* enfermar

sickening [ˈsɪkənɪŋ] *adj* nauseabundo(a); *(revolting)* repugnante; *(horrifying)* escalofriante

sickle [ˈsɪkəl] *n* hoz *f*

sickly [ˈsɪklɪ] *adj* (**sicklier, sickliest**) (**a**) *(person)* enfermizo(a) (**b**) *(taste)* empalagoso(a) (**c**) *(smile)* forzado(a)

sickness [ˈsɪknɪs] *n* (**a**) *(illness)* enfermedad *f* (**b**) *(nausea)* náuseas *fpl*

side [saɪd] **1** *n* (**a**) lado *m*; *(of coin etc)* cara *f*; *(of hill)* ladera *f*; **by the s. of** junto a (**b**) *(of body)* costado *m*; *(of animal)* ijar *m*; **a s. of bacon** una pieza de tocino; **by my s.** a mi lado; **s. by s.** juntos (**c**) *(edge)* borde *m*; *(of lake, river)* orilla *f* (**d**) *Fig (aspect)* aspecto *m* (**e**) *(team)* equipo *m*; *Pol* partido *m*; **she's on our s.** está de nuestro lado; **to take sides with sb** ponerse de parte de algn; **s. dish** plato *m* de guarnición; **s. effect** efecto secundario; **s. entrance** entrada *f* lateral; **s. street** calle *f* lateral
2 *vi* **to s. with sb** ponerse de parte de algn

sideboard [ˈsaɪdbɔːd] *n* aparador *m*

sideboards [ˈsaɪdbɔːdz], **sideburns** [ˈsaɪdbɜːnz] *npl* patillas *fpl*

sidelight [ˈsaɪdlaɪt] *n Aut* luz *f* lateral, piloto *m*

sideline [ˈsaɪdlaɪn] *n* (**a**) *Sport* línea *f* de banda (**b**) *Com (product)* línea suplementaria; *(job)* empleo suplementario

sidelong [ˈsaɪdlɒŋ] *adj* de reojo

side-saddle [ˈsaɪdsædəl] **1** *n* silla *f* de amazona
2 *adv* **to ride s.** montar a la inglesa

sideshow [ˈsaɪdʃəʊ] *n* atracción secundaria

sidestep [ˈsaɪdstep] *vt (issue)* esquivar

sidetrack [ˈsaɪdtræk] *vt Fig (person)* despistar

sidewalk [ˈsaɪdwɔːk] *n US* acera *f*, *CSur, Perú* vereda *f*, *CAm, Méx* banqueta *f*

sideways [ˈsaɪdweɪz] **1** *adj (movement)* lateral; *(look)* de reojo
2 *adv* de lado

siding [ˈsaɪdɪŋ] *n Rail* apartadero *m*, vía muerta

sidle [ˈsaɪdəl] *vi* **to s. up to sb** acercarse furtivamente a algn

siege [siːdʒ] *n* sitio *m*, cerco *m*; **to lay s. to** sitiar

sieve [sɪv] **1** *n (fine)* tamiz *m*; *(coarse)* criba *f*
2 *vt (fine)* tamizar; *(coarse)* cribar

sift [sɪft] *vt (sieve)* tamizar; *Fig* **to s. through** examinar cuidadosamente

sigh [saɪ] **1** *vi* suspirar
2 *n* suspiro *m*

sight [saɪt] **1** *n* (**a**) *(faculty)* vista *f*; **at first s.** a primera vista; **to catch s. of** divisar; **to know by s.** conocer de vista; **to lose s. of sth/sb** perder algo/a algn de vista (**b**) *(range of vision)* vista *f*; **within s.** a la vista; **to come into s.** aparecer (**c**) *(spectacle)* espectáculo *m* (**d**) *(on gun)* mira *f*; *Fig* **to set one's sights on** tener la mira puesta en (**e**) **sights** monumentos *mpl*
2 *vt* ver; *(land)* divisar

sightseeing [ˈsaɪtsiːɪŋ] *n* turismo *m*; **to go s.** hacer turismo

sign [saɪn] **1** *n* (**a**) *(symbol)* signo *m* (**b**) *(gesture)* gesto *m*, seña *f*; *(signal)* señal *f* (**c**) *(indication)* señal *f*; *(trace)* rastro *m*, huella *f*; **as a s. of** como muestra de (**d**) *(notice)* anuncio *m*; *(board)* letrero *m*
   2 *vt* (**a**) *(letter etc)* firmar (**b**) *Ftb* fichar
   3 *vi* firmar
► **sign on 1** *vt sep (worker)* contratar
   2 *vi (worker)* firmar un contrato; *Br Fam* apuntarse al paro; *(regularly)* firmar el paro
► **sign up 1** *vt sep (soldier)* reclutar; *(worker)* contratar
   2 *vi (soldier)* alistarse; *(worker)* firmar un contrato
signal [ˈsɪgnəl] **1** *n* señal *f*; *Rad & TV* sintonía *f*; *Rail* **s. box** garita *f* de señales
   2 *vt* (**a**) *(message)* transmitir por señales (**b**) *(direction etc)* indicar
   3 *vi (with hands)* hacer señales; *(in car)* señalar
signalman [ˈsɪgnəlmən] *n* guardavía *m*
signature [ˈsɪgnɪtʃə(r)] *n (name)* firma *f*; *Rad & TV* **s. tune** sintonía *f*
signet [ˈsɪgnɪt] *n* **s. ring** (anillo *m* de) sello *m*
significance [sɪgˈnɪfɪkəns] *n (meaning)* significado *m*; *(importance)* importancia *f*
significant [sɪgˈnɪfɪkənt] *adj (meaningful)* significativo(a); *(important)* importante
significantly [sɪgˈnɪfɪkəntlɪ] *adv (markedly)* sensiblemente
signify [ˈsɪgnɪfaɪ] *vt* (**a**) *(mean)* significar (**b**) *(show, make known)* indicar
signpost [ˈsaɪnpəʊst] *n* poste *m* indicador
silence [ˈsaɪləns] **1** *n* silencio *m*
   2 *vt* acallar; *(engine)* silenciar
silencer [ˈsaɪlənsə(r)] *n* (**a**) *(on gun)* silenciador *m* (**b**) *Br (on car)* silenciador *m*
silent [ˈsaɪlənt] *adj* silencioso(a); *(not talkative)* callado(a); *(film)* mudo(a); **be s.!** ¡cállate!; **to remain s.** guardar silencio
silently [ˈsaɪləntlɪ] *adv* silenciosamente
silhouette [sɪluːˈet] *n* silueta *f*
silicon [ˈsɪlɪkən] *n* silicio *m*; **s. chip** chip *m* (de silicio)
silk [sɪlk] **1** *n* seda *f*
   2 *adj* de seda
silky [ˈsɪlkɪ] *adj* (**silkier, silkiest**) *(cloth)* sedoso(a); *(voice etc)* aterciopelado(a)
sill [sɪl] *n (of window)* alféizar *m*
silly [ˈsɪlɪ] *adj* (**sillier, silliest**) tonto(a)
silo [ˈsaɪləʊ] *n* silo *m*
silt [sɪlt] *n* cieno *m*
► **silt up** *vi* obstruirse con cieno

silver [ˈsɪlvə(r)] **1** *n* (**a**) *(metal)* plata *f* (**b**) *(coins)* monedas *fpl* (de plata) (**c**) *(tableware)* vajilla *f* de plata
   2 *adj* de plata; **s. foil** *(tinfoil)* papel *m* de aluminio; **s. paper** papel de plata; **s. wedding** bodas *fpl* de plata
silver-plated [sɪlvəˈpleɪtɪd] *adj* plateado(a)
silversmith [ˈsɪlvəsmɪθ] *n* platero(a) *m,f*
silverware [ˈsɪlvəweə(r)] *n* vajilla *f* de plata
silvery [ˈsɪlvərɪ] *adj* plateado(a)
similar [ˈsɪmɪlə(r)] *adj* parecido(a), semejante (**to** a); **to be s.** parecerse
similarity [sɪmɪˈlærɪtɪ] *n* semejanza *f*
similarly [ˈsɪmɪləlɪ] *adv* (**a**) *(as well)* igualmente (**b**) *(likewise)* del mismo modo, asimismo
simile [ˈsɪmɪlɪ] *n* símil *m*
simmer [ˈsɪmə(r)] **1** *vt* cocer a fuego lento
   2 *vi* cocerse a fuego lento
► **simmer down** *vi Fam* calmarse
simpering [ˈsɪmpərɪŋ] *adj* melindroso(a)
simple [ˈsɪmpəl] *adj* (**a**) sencillo(a); **s. interest** interés *m* simple (**b**) *(natural)* natural (**c**) *(foolish)* simple; *(naïve)* ingenuo(a); *(dim)* de pocas luces
simplicity [sɪmˈplɪsɪtɪ] *n* (**a**) sencillez *f* (**b**) *(naïveté)* ingenuidad *f*
simplify [ˈsɪmplɪfaɪ] *vt* simplificar
simply [ˈsɪmplɪ] *adv* (**a**) *(plainly)* sencillamente (**b**) *(only)* simplemente, sólo
simulate [ˈsɪmjʊleɪt] *vt* simular
simulator [ˈsɪmjʊleɪtə(r)] *n* **flight s.** simulador de vuelo
simultaneous [sɪməlˈteɪnɪəs] *adj* simultáneo(a)
simultaneously [sɪməlˈteɪnɪəslɪ] *adv* simultáneamente
sin [sɪn] **1** *n* pecado *m*
   2 *vi* pecar
since [sɪns] **1** *adv* (**ever**) **s.** desde entonces; **long s.** hace mucho tiempo; **it has s. come out that ...** desde entonces se ha sabido que ...
   2 *prep* desde; **she has been living here s. 1975** vive aquí desde 1975
   3 *conj* (**a**) *(time)* desde que; **how long is it s. you last saw him?** ¿cuánto tiempo hace que lo viste por última vez? (**b**) *(because, as)* ya que, puesto que
sincere [sɪnˈsɪə(r)] *adj* sincero(a)
sincerely [sɪnˈsɪəlɪ] *adv* sinceramente; **Yours s.** *(in letter)* (le saluda) atentamente
sincerity [sɪnˈserɪtɪ] *n* sinceridad *f*
sinew [ˈsɪnjuː] *n (tendon)* tendón *m*; *(in meat)* nervio *m*

sinful [ˈsɪnfʊl] *adj (person)* pecador(a); *(act, thought)* pecaminoso(a); *Fig (waste etc)* escandaloso(a)

sing [sɪŋ] **1** *vt (pt* sang; *pp* sung) cantar **2** *vi (person, bird)* cantar; *(kettle, bullets)* silbar

singe [sɪndʒ] *vt* chamuscar

singer [ˈsɪŋə(r)] *n* cantante *mf*

singing [ˈsɪŋɪŋ] *n (art)* canto *m*; *(songs)* canciones *fpl*; *(of kettle)* silbido *m*

single [ˈsɪŋɡəl] **1** *adj* (**a**) *(solitary)* solo(a) (**b**) *(only one)* único(a) (**c**) *(not double)* sencillo(a); **s. bed/room** cama *f*/habitación *f* individual (**d**) *(unmarried)* soltero(a) **2** *n* (**a**) *Br Rail* billete *m or Am* boleto *m or Am* pasaje *m* sencillo *or* de ida (**b**) *(record)* single *m* (**c**) *Sport* **singles** individuales *mpl*
▸ **single out** *vt sep (choose)* escoger; *(distinguish)* distinguir

single-breasted [ˈsɪŋɡəlˈbrestɪd] *adj (suit, jacket)* recto(a)

single-handed [ˈsɪŋɡəlˈhændɪd] *adj & adv* sin ayuda

single-minded [ˈsɪŋɡəlˈmaɪndɪd] *adj* resuelto(a)

singlet [ˈsɪŋɡlɪt] *n Br* camiseta *f*

singly [ˈsɪŋɡlɪ] *adv (individually)* por separado; *(one by one)* uno por uno

singular [ˈsɪŋɡjʊlə(r)] **1** *adj* (**a**) *Ling* singular (**b**) *Fml (outstanding)* excepcional (**c**) *Fml (unique)* único(a) **2** *n Ling* singular *m*

singularly [ˈsɪŋɡjʊləlɪ] *adv* excepcionalmente

sinister [ˈsɪnɪstə(r)] *adj* siniestro(a)

sink¹ [sɪŋk] *n (in kitchen)* fregadero *m*

sink² [sɪŋk] **1** *vt (pt* sank; *pp* sunk) (**a**) *(ship)* hundir, echar a pique; *Fig (hopes)* acabar con (**b**) *(hole, well)* cavar; *(post, knife, teeth)* hincar **2** *vi* (**a**) *(ship)* hundirse (**b**) *Fig* **my heart sank** se me cayó el alma a los pies (**c**) *(sun)* ponerse (**d**) **to s. to one's knees** hincarse de rodillas
▸ **sink in** *vi (penetrate)* penetrar; *Fig* **it hasn't sunk in yet** todavía no me he/se ha/*etc* hecho a la idea

sinner [ˈsɪnə(r)] *n* pecador(a) *m,f*

sinus [ˈsaɪnəs] *n* seno *m* (nasal)

sip [sɪp] **1** *n* sorbo *m* **2** *vt* sorber, beber a sorbos

siphon [ˈsaɪfən] *n* sifón *m*
▸ **siphon off** *vt sep (liquid)* sacar con sifón; *Fig (funds, traffic)* desviar

sir [sɜː(r)] *n Fml* (**a**) señor *m*; **yes, s.** sí, señor (**b**) *(title)* sir; **S. Walter Raleigh** Sir Walter Raleigh

siren [ˈsaɪrən] *n* sirena *f*

sirloin [ˈsɜːlɔɪn] *n* solomillo *m*

sissy [ˈsɪsɪ] *n Fam (coward)* miedica *mf*

sister [ˈsɪstə(r)] *n* (**a**) *(relation)* hermana *f* (**b**) *Br Med* enfermera *f* jefe (**c**) *Rel* hermana *f*; *(before name)* sor

sister-in-law [ˈsɪstərɪnlɔː] *n* cuñada *f*

sit [sɪt] **1** *vt (pt & pp* sat) (**a**) *(child etc)* sentar (**in/on** en) (**b**) *Br (exam)* presentarse a **2** *vi* (**a**) *(action)* sentarse (**b**) *(be seated)* estar sentado(a) (**c**) *(object)* estar; *(be situated)* hallarse; *(person)* quedarse (**d**) *(assembly)* reunirse
▸ **sit back** *vi* recostarse
▸ **sit down** *vi* sentarse
▸ **sit in on** *vt insep* asistir sin participar a
▸ **sit out** *vt sep* aguantar hasta el final
▸ **sit through** *vt insep* aguantar
▸ **sit up** *vi* (**a**) incorporarse (**b**) *(stay up late)* quedarse levantado(a)

site [saɪt] **1** *n* (**a**) *(area)* lugar *m*; **building s.** solar *m*; *(under construction)* obra *f* (**b**) *(location)* situación *f*; **nuclear testing s.** zona *f* de pruebas nucleares **2** *vt* situar

sit-in [ˈsɪtɪn] *n Fam (demonstration)* sentada *f*; *(strike)* huelga *f* de brazos caídos

sitting [ˈsɪtɪŋ] **1** *n (of committee)* sesión *f*; *(in canteen)* turno *m* **2** *adj* **s. room** sala *f* de estar

situated [ˈsɪtjʊeɪtɪd] *adj* situado(a), ubicado(a)

situation [sɪtjʊˈeɪʃən] *n* (**a**) situación *f* (**b**) *(job)* puesto *m*; *Br* **situations vacant** *(in newspaper)* ofertas de trabajo

six [sɪks] *adj & n* seis *(m inv)*

sixteen [sɪksˈtiːn] *adj & n* dieciséis *(m inv)*, diez y seis *(m inv)*

sixteenth [sɪksˈtiːnθ] **1** *adj & n* decimosexto(a) *(m,f)* **2** *n (fraction)* dieciseisavo *m*

sixth [sɪksθ] **1** *adj* sexto(a); *Br Educ* **s. form** ≃ COU; **s. former** ≃ estudiante de COU **2** *n* (**a**) *(in series)* sexto(a) *m,f* (**b**) *(fraction)* sexto *m*, sexta parte

sixty [ˈsɪkstɪ] *adj & n* sesenta *(m inv)*

sizable [ˈsaɪzəbəl] *adj* = sizeable

size [saɪz] *n* tamaño *m*; *(of garment)* talla *f*; *(of shoes)* número *m*; *(of person)* estatura *f*; *(scope)* alcance *m*; **what s. do you take?** *(garment)* ¿qué talla tienes?; *(shoes)* ¿qué número calzas?
▸ **size up** *vt sep (person)* juzgar; *(situation, problem)* evaluar

sizeable [ˈsaɪzəbəl] *adj (building etc)*

(bastante) grande; *(sum)* considerable; *(problem)* importante

sizzle ['sɪzəl] *vi* chisporrotear

skate¹ [skeɪt] **1** *n* patín *m*
  2 *vi* patinar

skate² [skeɪt] *n (fish)* raya *f*

skateboard ['skeɪtbɔːd] *n* monopatín *m*

skater ['skeɪtə(r)] *n* patinador(a) *m,f*

skating ['skeɪtɪŋ] *n* patinaje *m*; **s. rink** pista *f* de patinaje

skeleton ['skelɪtən] **1** *n* (**a**) esqueleto *m* (**b**) *(of building)* armazón *m* (**c**) *(outline)* esquema *m*
  2 *adj (staff, service)* reducido(a); **s. key** llave maestra

skeptic ['skeptɪk] *n US* = sceptic

sketch [sketʃ] **1** *n* (**a**) *(preliminary drawing)* bosquejo *m*, esbozo *m*; *(drawing)* dibujo *m*; *(outline)* esquema *m*; *(rough draft)* boceto *m* (**b**) *Th & TV* sketch *m*
  2 *vt (draw)* dibujar; *(preliminary drawing)* bosquejar, esbozar

sketch-book ['sketʃbʊk], **sketch-pad** ['sketʃpæd] *n* bloc *m* de dibujo

sketchy ['sketʃɪ] *adj* (**sketchier, sketchiest**) *(incomplete)* incompleto(a); *(not detailed)* vago(a)

skewer ['skjʊə(r)] *n* pincho *m*, broqueta *f*

ski [skiː] **1** *n* esquí *m*
  2 *adj* de esquí; **s. boots** botas *fpl* de esquiar; **s. jump** *(action)* salto *m* con esquís; **s. lift** telesquí *m*; *(with seats)* telesilla *f*; **s. pants** pantalón *m* de esquiar; **s. resort** estación *f* de esquí; **s. stick** *or* **pole** bastón *m* de esquiar
  3 *vi* esquiar; **to go skiing** ir a esquiar

skid [skɪd] **1** *n* patinazo *m*
  2 *vi* patinar

skier ['skiːə(r)] *n* esquiador(a) *m,f*

skiing ['skiːɪŋ] *n* esquí *m*

skilful ['skɪlfʊl] *adj* hábil, diestro(a)

skill [skɪl] *n* (**a**) *(ability)* habilidad *f*, destreza *f*; *(talent)* don *m* (**b**) *(technique)* técnica *f*

skilled [skɪld] *adj* (**a**) *(dextrous)* hábil, diestro(a); *(expert)* experto(a) (**b**) *(worker)* cualificado(a)

skillet ['skɪlɪt] *n US* sartén *f*

skillful ['skɪlfʊl] *adj US* = skilful

skim [skɪm] **1** *vt* (**a**) *(milk)* desnatar; **skimmed milk** leche desnatada (**b**) *(brush against)* rozar; **to s. the ground** *(bird, plane)* volar a ras de suelo
  2 *vi Fig* **to s. through a book** hojear un libro

skimp [skɪmp] *vt & vi (food, material)* escatimar; *(work)* chapucear

skimpy ['skɪmpɪ] *adj* (**skimpier,**

skimpiest) *(shorts)* muy corto(a); *(meal)* escaso(a)

skin [skɪn] **1** *n* (**a**) piel *f*; *(of face)* cutis *m*; *(complexion)* tez *f*; **s. cream** crema *f* de belleza (**b**) *(of fruit)* piel *f*; *(of lemon)* cáscara *f*; *(peeling)* mondadura *f* (**c**) *(of sausage)* pellejo *m* (**d**) *(on milk etc)* nata *f*
  2 *vt* (**a**) *(animal)* despellejar (**b**) *(graze)* arañar

skin-deep ['skɪn'diːp] *adj* superficial

skin-diving ['skɪndaɪvɪŋ] *n* buceo *m*, submarinismo *m*

skinhead ['skɪnhed] *n Fam* cabeza *mf* rapada

skinny ['skɪnɪ] *adj* (**skinnier, skinniest**) *Fam* flaco(a)

skin-tight ['skɪntaɪt] *adj (clothing)* muy ajustado(a)

skip¹ [skɪp] **1** *n (jump)* salto *m*, brinco *m*
  2 *vi (jump)* saltar, brincar; *(with rope)* saltar a la comba; *Fig* **to s. over sth** saltarse algo
  3 *vt Fig* saltarse

skip² [skɪp] *n Br (for rubbish)* contenedor *m*

skipper ['skɪpə(r)] *n Naut & Sport Fam* capitán(ana) *m,f*

skipping ['skɪpɪŋ] *n* comba *f*; **s. rope** comba

skirmish ['skɜːmɪʃ] *n* escaramuza *f*

skirt [skɜːt] **1** *n* falda *f*
  2 *vt (town etc)* rodear; *(coast)* bordear; *Fig (problem)* esquivar

skirting ['skɜːtɪŋ] *n Br* **s. (board)** zócalo *m*

skit [skɪt] *n* sátira *f*, parodia *f*

skittle ['skɪtəl] *n* (**a**) *(pin)* bolo *m* (**b**) **skittles** *(game)* (juego *m* de los) bolos *mpl*, boliche *m*

skive [skaɪv] *vi Br Fam* escaquearse

skulk [skʌlk] *vi (hide)* esconderse; *(prowl)* merodear; *(lie in wait)* estar al acecho

skull [skʌl] *n Anat* cráneo *m*; *Fam* calavera *f*

skunk [skʌŋk] *n* mofeta *f*

sky [skaɪ] *n* cielo *m*; **s. blue** azul *m* celeste

skylight ['skaɪlaɪt] *n* tragaluz *m*, claraboya *f*

skyline ['skaɪlaɪn] *n (of city)* perfil *m*

skyscraper ['skaɪskreɪpə(r)] *n* rascacielos *m inv*

slab [slæb] *n (of stone)* losa *f*; *(of chocolate)* tableta *f*; *(of cake)* trozo *m*

slack [slæk] **1** *adj* (**a**) *(not taut)* flojo(a) (**b**) *(lax)* descuidado(a); *(lazy)* vago(a) (**c**) *(market)* flojo(a); **business is s.** hay poco negocio
  2 *n (in rope)* parte floja

slacken ['slækən] **1** *vt* (**a**) *(rope)* aflojar (**b**) *(speed)* reducir
2 *vi* (**a**) *(rope)* aflojarse; *(wind)* amainar (**b**) *(trade)* aflojar
▸ **slacken off** *vi* disminuirse
slacks [slæks] *npl* pantalones *mpl* ajustados
slag [slæg] *n* (**a**) *Min* escoria *f*; **s. heap** escorial *m* (**b**) *Br very Fam (woman)* puta *f*
▸ **slag off** *vt sep Br* poner verde a
slain [sleɪn] **1** *npl* **the s.** los caídos
2 *pp of* **slay**
slam [slæm] **1** *n (of door)* portazo *m*
2 *vt (bang)* cerrar de golpe; **to s. sth down on the table** soltar algo sobre la mesa de un palmetazo; **to s. the door** dar un portazo; **to s. on the brakes** dar un frenazo
3 *vi (door)* cerrarse de golpe
slander ['slɑːndə(r)] **1** *n* difamación *f*, calumnia *f*
2 *vt* difamar, calumniar
slang [slæŋ] *n* argot *m*, jerga *f*
slant [slɑːnt] **1** *n* (**a**) inclinación *f*; *(slope)* pendiente *f* (**b**) *Fig (point of view)* punto *m* de vista
2 *vt Fig (problem etc)* enfocar subjetivamente
3 *vi* inclinarse
slanting ['slɑːntɪŋ] *adj* inclinado(a)
slap [slæp] **1** *n* palmada *f*; *(in face)* bofetada *f*
2 *adv Fam* **he ran s. into the fence** se dio de lleno contra la valla; **s. in the middle of ...** justo en medio de ...
3 *vt* pegar con la mano; *(hit in face)* dar una bofetada a; **to s. sb on the back** dar a algn una palmada en la espalda
slapdash [slæp'dæʃ] *adj Fam* descuidado(a); *(work)* chapucero(a)
slapstick ['slæpstɪk] *n* bufonadas *fpl*, payasadas *fpl*
slap-up ['slæpʌp] *adj Fam* **s. meal** comilona *f*
slash [slæʃ] **1** *n Fam Typ* barra oblicua
2 *vt* (**a**) *(with knife)* acuchillar; *(with sword)* dar un tajo a (**b**) *Fig (prices)* rebajar
slat [slæt] *n* tablilla *f*, listón *m*
slate [sleɪt] **1** *n* pizarra *f*; *Fig* **to wipe the s. clean** hacer borrón y cuenta nueva
2 *vt Br Fam* criticar duramente
slaughter ['slɔːtə(r)] **1** *n (of animals)* matanza *f*; *(of people)* carnicería *f*
2 *vt (animals)* matar; *(people)* matar brutalmente; *(in large numbers)* masacrar

slaughterhouse ['slɔːtəhaʊs] *n* matadero *m*
Slav [slɑːv] *adj & n* eslavo(a) *(m,f)*
slave [sleɪv] **1** *n* esclavo(a) *m,f*; **s. trade** trata *f* de esclavos
2 *vi* **to s. (away)** dar el callo
slavery ['sleɪvərɪ] *n* esclavitud *f*
Slavonic [slə'vɒnɪk] *adj* eslavo(a)
slay [sleɪ] *vt (pt* **slew**; *pp* **slain)** matar
sleazy ['sliːzɪ] *adj* (**sleazier, sleaziest**) sórdido(a)
sled [sled] **1** *n US* trineo *m*
2 *vi* ir en trineo
sledge [sledʒ] *n Br* trineo *m*
sledgehammer ['sledʒhæmə(r)] *n* almádena *f*
sleek [sliːk] *adj (hair)* lustroso(a); *(appearance)* impecable
sleep [sliːp] **1** *n* sueño *m*
2 *vi (pt & pp* **slept)** (**a**) dormir; **to go to s.** dormirse; *Fig* **to send to s.** (hacer) dormir; *Fam* **to s. like a log** dormir como un lirón (**b**) **my foot has gone to s.** se me ha dormido el pie
▸ **sleep in** *vi Br (oversleep)* quedarse dormido(a); *(have a lie-in)* quedarse en la cama
▸ **sleep with** *vt insep Fam* **to s. with sb** acostarse con algn
sleeper ['sliːpə(r)] *n* (**a**) *(person)* durmiente *mf*; **to be a heavy s.** tener el sueño pesado (**b**) *Br Rail (on track)* traviesa *f* (**c**) *Rail (coach)* coche-cama *m*; *(berth)* litera *f*
sleeping ['sliːpɪŋ] *adj* **s. bag** saco *m* de dormir; **S. Beauty** la Bella durmiente; **s. car** coche-cama *m*; *Br Com* **s. partner** socio(a) *m,f* comanditario(a); **s. pill** somnífero *m*
sleepless ['sliːplɪs] *adj* **to have a s. night** pasar la noche en blanco
sleepwalker ['sliːpwɔːkə(r)] *n* sonámbulo(a) *m,f*
sleepy ['sliːpɪ] *adj* (**sleepier, sleepiest**) soñoliento(a); **to be** *or* **feel s.** tener sueño
sleet [sliːt] **1** *n* aguanieve *f*
2 *vi* **it's sleeting** cae aguanieve
sleeve [sliːv] *n (of garment)* manga *f*; *(of record)* funda *f*
sleigh [sleɪ] *n* trineo *m*; **s. bell** cascabel *m*
sleight [slaɪt] *n* **s. of hand** juego *m* de manos
slender ['slendə(r)] *adj* (**a**) *(thin)* delgado(a) (**b**) *Fig (hope, chance)* remoto(a)
slept [slept] *pt & pp of* **sleep**
slew [sluː] *pt of* **slay**
slice [slaɪs] **1** *n* (**a**) *(of bread)* rebanada *f*; *(of ham)* loncha *f*; *(of beef etc)* tajada *f*; *(of*

lemon etc) rodaja *f; (of cake)* trozo *m* (**b**) *(utensil)* pala *f*

2 *vt (food)* cortar a rebanadas/tajos/ rodajas; *(divide)* partir

slick [slɪk] **1** *adj* (**a**) *(programme, show)* logrado(a) (**b**) *(skilful)* hábil, mañoso(a) **2** *n* (**oil**) **s.** marea negra

slide [slaɪd] **1** *n* (**a**) *(act)* resbalón *m* (**b**) *(in prices etc)* baja *f* (**c**) *(in playground)* tobogán *m* (**d**) *Phot* diapositiva *f*; **s. projector** proyector *m* de diapositivas (**e**) **s. rule** regla *f* de cálculo (**f**) *Br (for hair)* pasador *m*

2 *vt (pt & pp* **slid** [slɪd]) deslizar; *(furniture)* correr

3 *vi (on purpose)* deslizarse; *(slip)* resbalar

sliding ['slaɪdɪŋ] *adj (door, window)* corredizo(a); *Fin* **s. scale** escala *f* móvil

slight [slaɪt] **1** *adj* (**a**) *(small)* pequeño(a); **not in the slightest** en absoluto (**b**) *(build)* menudo(a); *(slim)* delgado(a); *(frail)* delicado(a) (**c**) *(trivial)* leve

2 *n (affront)* desaire *m*

3 *vt* (**a**) *(scorn)* despreciar (**b**) *(snub)* desairar

slightly ['slaɪtlɪ] *adv (a little)* ligeramente, algo

slim [slɪm] **1** *adj* (**slimmer, slimmest**) (**a**) *(person)* delgado(a) (**b**) *Fig (resources)* escaso(a); *(hope, chance)* remoto(a)

2 *vi* adelgazar

slime [slaɪm] *n (mud)* lodo *m*, cieno *m; (of snail)* baba *f*

slimming ['slɪmɪŋ] **1** *adj (diet, pills)* para adelgazar; *(food)* que no engorda

2 *n (process)* adelgazamiento *m*

slimy ['slaɪmɪ] *adj* (**slimier, slimiest**) (**a**) *(muddy)* lodoso(a); *(snail)* baboso(a) (**b**) *Fig (person)* zalamero(a)

sling [slɪŋ] **1** *n* (**a**) *(catapult)* honda *f; (child's)* tirador *m* (**b**) *Med* cabestrillo *m*

2 *vt (pt & pp* **slung**) *(throw)* tirar

slingshot ['slɪŋʃɒt] *n US* tirachinas *m inv*

slink [slɪŋk] *vi (pt & pp* **slunk**) **to s. off** escabullirse

slip [slɪp] **1** *n* (**a**) *(slide)* resbalón *m; Fam Fig* **to give sb the s.** dar esquinazo a algn (**b**) *(mistake)* error *m; (moral)* desliz *m;* **a s. of the tongue** un lapsus linguae (**c**) *(underskirt)* combinación *f* (**d**) *(of paper)* trocito *m*

2 *vi* (**a**) *(slide)* resbalar (**b**) *Med* dislocarse; **slipped disc** vértebra dislocada (**c**) *(move quickly)* ir de prisa (**d**) *(standards etc)* deteriorarse

3 *vt* (**a**) *(slide)* dar a escondidas (**b**) **it slipped my memory** se me fue de la cabeza

▸ **slip away** *vi (person)* escabullirse

▸ **slip off** *vt sep (clothes)* quitarse rápidamente

▸ **slip on** *vt sep (clothes)* ponerse rápidamente

▸ **slip out** *vi* (**a**) *(leave)* salir (**b**) *Fig* **the secret slipped out** se le escapó el secreto

▸ **slip up** *vi Fam (blunder)* cometer un desliz

slipper ['slɪpə(r)] *n* zapatilla *f*

slippery ['slɪpərɪ] *adj* resbaladizo(a)

slip-road ['slɪprəʊd] *n Br* vía *f* de acceso

slipshod ['slɪpʃɒd] *adj* descuidado(a); *(work)* chapucero(a)

slip-up ['slɪpʌp] *n Fam (blunder)* desliz *m*

slipway ['slɪpweɪ] *n* grada *f*

slit [slɪt] **1** *n (opening)* hendidura *f; (cut)* corte *m*, raja *f*

2 *vt (pt & pp* **slit**) cortar, rajar

slither ['slɪðə(r)] *vi* deslizarse

sliver ['slɪvə(r)] *n (of wood, glass)* astilla *f; (of ham)* loncha *f*

slob [slɒb] *n Fam* dejado(a) *m,f*

slog [slɒg] **1** *n Fam* **it was a hard s.** costó un montón

2 *vi* (**a**) *Fam* **to s. away** sudar tinta (**b**) *(walk)* caminar trabajosamente

3 *vt (hit)* golpear fuerte

slogan ['sləʊgən] *n* (e)slogan *m*, lema *m*

slop [slɒp] **1** *vi* **to s. (over)** derramarse; **to s. about** chapotear

2 *vt* derramar

slope [sləʊp] **1** *n (incline)* cuesta *f*, pendiente *f; (up)* subida *f; (down)* bajada *f; (of mountain)* ladera *f; (of roof)* vertiente *f*

2 *vi* inclinarse; **to s. up/down** subir/ bajar en pendiente

▸ **slope off** *vi Fam* largarse

sloping ['sləʊpɪŋ] *adj* inclinado(a)

sloppy ['slɒpɪ] *adj* (**sloppier, sloppiest**) *Fam* descuidado(a); *(work)* chapucero(a); *(appearance)* desaliñado(a)

slot [slɒt] **1** *n* (**a**) *(for coin)* ranura *f; (opening)* rendija *f;* **s. machine** *(for gambling)* (máquina *f*) tragaperras *f inv; (vending machine)* distribuidor automático (**b**) *Rad & TV* espacio *m*

2 *vt (place)* meter; *(put in)* introducir

3 *vi* **to s. in** *or* **together** encajar

sloth [sləʊθ] *n Fml (laziness)* pereza *f*

slouch [slaʊtʃ] *vi* andar *or* sentarse con los hombros caídos

Slovakia [sləʊˈvækɪə] *n* Eslovaquia

Slovakian [sləʊˈvækɪən] *adj & n* eslovaco(a) *(m,f)*

Slovene ['sləʊviːn] **1** *n* (**a**) *(person)* esloveno(a) *m,f* (**b**) *(language)* esloveno *m*

2 *adj* esloveno(a)

Slovenia [sləʊˈviːnɪə] *n* Eslovenia
slovenly [ˈslʌvənlɪ] *adj* descuidado(a); *(appearance)* desaliñado(a); *(work)* chapucero(a)
slow [sləʊ] **1** *adj* (**a**) lento(a); **in s. motion** a cámara lenta; **to be s. to do sth** tardar en hacer algo (**b**) *(clock)* atrasado(a) (**c**) *(stupid)* lento(a), torpe
    2 *adv* despacio, lentamente
    3 *vt (car)* reducir la marcha de; *(progress)* retrasar
    4 *vi* **to s. down** *or* **up** ir más despacio; *(in car)* reducir la velocidad
slowly [ˈsləʊlɪ] *adv* despacio, lentamente
sludge [slʌdʒ] *n (mud)* fango *m*, lodo *m*
slug [slʌg] **1** *n* (**a**) *Zool* babosa *f* (**b**) *US Fam (bullet)* posta *f* (**c**) *Fam (blow)* porrazo *m*
    2 *vt Fam (hit)* aporrear
sluggish [ˈslʌgɪʃ] *adj* (**a**) *(river, engine)* lento(a); *Com* flojo(a) (**b**) *(lazy)* perezoso(a)
sluice [sluːs] *n (waterway)* canal *m*
sluicegate [ˈsluːsgeɪt] *n* esclusa *f*
slumber [ˈslʌmbə(r)] *Fml* **1** *n (sleep)* sueño *m*
    2 *vi* dormir
slump [slʌmp] **1** *n* (**a**) *(drop in sales etc)* bajón *m* (**b**) *(economic depression)* crisis económica
    2 *vi* (**a**) *(sales etc)* caer de repente; *(prices)* desplomarse; *(the economy)* hundirse; *Fig (morale)* hundirse (**b**) *(fall)* caer
slums [slʌmz] *npl* barrios bajos
slung [slʌŋ] *pt & pp of* **sling**
slunk [slʌŋk] *pt & pp of* **slink**
slur [slɜː(r)] **1** *n (stigma)* mancha *f*; *(slanderous remark)* calumnia *f*
    2 *vt (word)* tragarse
slush [slʌʃ] *n* (**a**) *(melting snow)* nieve medio fundida (**b**) *Fam* sentimentalismo *m* (**c**) *US Fam* **s. fund** fondos *mpl* para sobornos
slut [slʌt] *n very Fam Pej* (**a**) *(untidy woman)* marrana *f* (**b**) *(whore)* fulana *f*
sly [slaɪ] *adj* (**slyer, slyest** *or* **slier, sliest**) (**a**) *(cunning)* astuto(a) (**b**) *(secretive)* furtivo(a) (**c**) *(mischievous)* travieso(a) (**d**) *(underhand)* malicioso(a)
smack¹ [smæk] **1** *n* (**a**) *(slap)* bofetada *f* (**b**) *(sharp sound)* ruido sonoro
    2 *vt* (**a**) *(slap)* dar una bofetada a (**b**) *(hit)* golpear; *Fig* **to s. one's lips** relamerse
smack² [smæk] *vi Fig* **to s. of** oler a
small [smɔːl] **1** *adj* (**a**) pequeño(a); **a s.**

table una mesita; **in s. letters** en minúsculas; **in the s. hours** a altas horas de la noche; **s. ads** anuncios *mpl* por palabras; *Fig* **s. print** letra pequeña (**b**) *(in height)* bajo(a) (**c**) *(scant)* escaso(a); **s. change** cambio *m*, suelto *m* (**d**) *(minor)* insignificante; **s. businessmen** pequeños comerciantes; **s. talk** charloteo *m* (**e**) *(increase)* ligero(a)
    2 *n* (**a**) **s. of the back** región *f* lumbar (**b**) *Br Fam* **smalls** *(underwear)* paños *mpl* menores
smallholder [ˈsmɔːlhəʊldə(r)] *n* minifundista *mf*
smallpox [ˈsmɔːlpɒks] *n* viruela *f*
smarmy [ˈsmɑːmɪ] *adj* (**smarmier, smarmiest**) *Fam* cobista, zalamero(a)
smart [smɑːt] **1** *adj* (**a**) *(elegant)* elegante (**b**) *(clever)* listo(a), inteligente; *Fam* **s. alec(k)** listillo (**c**) *(quick)* rápido(a); *(pace)* ligero(a)
    2 *vi* (**a**) *(sting)* picar, escocer (**b**) *Fig* sufrir
smarten [ˈsmɑːtən] **1** *vt* **to s. (up)** arreglar
    2 *vi* **to s. (oneself) up** arreglarse
smash [smæʃ] **1** *n* (**a**) *(loud noise)* estrépito *m*; *(collision)* choque violento (**b**) *(in tennis)* smash *m*
    2 *vt* (**a**) *(break)* romper; *(shatter)* hacer pedazos; *(crush)* aplastar (**b**) *(destroy)* destrozar; *(defeat)* aplastar (**c**) *(record)* fulminar
    3 *vi (break)* romperse; *(shatter)* hacerse pedazos; *(crash)* estrellarse; *(in tennis)* hacer un mate
    ▸ **smash up** *vt sep Fam (car)* hacer pedazos; *(place)* destrozar
smashing [ˈsmæʃɪŋ] *adj Br Fam* estupendo(a)
smattering [ˈsmætərɪŋ] *n* **he had a s. of French** hablaba un poquito de francés
smear [smɪə(r)] **1** *n* (**a**) *(smudge)* mancha *f*; **s. (test)** citología *f* (**b**) *Fig (defamation)* calumnia *f*
    2 *vt* (**a**) *(butter etc)* untar; *(grease)* embadurnar (**b**) *(make dirty)* manchar (**c**) *Fig (defame)* calumniar, difamar
smell [smel] **1** *n* (**a**) *(sense)* olfato *m* (**b**) *(odour)* olor *m*
    2 *vt* (*pt & pp* **smelled** *or* **smelt**) oler; *Fig* olfatear
    3 *vi* oler (**of** a); **it smells good/like lavender** huele bien/a lavanda; **he smelt of whisky** olía a whisky
smelly [ˈsmelɪ] *adj* (**smellier, smelliest**) *Fam* maloliente, apestoso(a)
smelt¹ [smelt] *vt (ore)* fundir
smelt² [smelt] *pt & pp of* **smell**

smidgen ['smɪdʒən] *n Fam* pizca *f*

smile [smaɪl] **1** *n* sonrisa *f*

  2 *vi* sonreír; **to s. at sb** sonreír a algn; **to s. at sth** reírse de algo

smiling ['smaɪlɪŋ] *adj* sonriente, risueño(a)

smirk [smɜːk] **1** *n (conceited)* sonrisa satisfecha; *(foolish)* sonrisa boba

  2 *vi (conceitedly)* sonreír con satisfacción; *(foolishly)* sonreír bobamente

smith [smɪθ] *n* herrero *m*

smithereens [smɪðəˈriːnz] *npl* **to smash/ blow sth to s.** hacer algo añicos

smithy ['smɪðɪ] *n* herrería *f*

smitten ['smɪtən] *adj Fam* **to be s. with sb** estar enamorado(a) de algn

smock [smɒk] *n (blouse)* blusón *m*; *(worn in pregnancy)* blusón de premamá; *(overall)* bata *f*

smog [smɒg] *n* niebla tóxica, smog *m*

smoke [sməʊk] **1** *n* humo *m*; **s. bomb** bomba *f* de humo; **s. screen** cortina *f* de humo

  2 *vi* fumar; *(chimney etc)* echar humo

  3 *vt* **(a)** *(tobacco)* fumar; **to s. a pipe** fumar en pipa **(b)** *(fish, meat)* ahumar

smoked [sməʊkt] *adj* ahumado(a)

smokeless ['sməʊklɪs] *adj* **s. fuel** combustible sin humo; **s. zone** zona libre de humos

smoker ['sməʊkə(r)] *n* **(a)** *(person)* fumador(a) *m,f* **(b)** *Rail* vagón *m* de fumadores

smoking ['sməʊkɪŋ] *n* **no s.** *(sign)* prohibido fumar

smoky ['sməʊkɪ] *adj* (**smokier, smokiest**) **(a)** *(chimney)* humeante; *(room)* lleno(a) de humo; *(atmosphere)* cargado(a) (de humo); *(taste)* ahumado(a) **(b)** *(colour)* ahumado(a)

smolder ['sməʊldə(r)] *vi US* = **smoulder**

smooth [smuːð] **1** *adj* **(a)** *(surface)* liso(a); *(skin)* suave; *(road)* llano(a); *(sea)* tranquilo(a) **(b)** *(beer, wine)* suave **(c)** *(flowing)* fluido(a) **(d)** *(flight)* tranquilo(a); *(transition)* sin problemas **(e)** *Pej (slick)* zalamero(a)

  2 *vt* **(a)** *(hair etc)* alisar **(b)** *(plane down)* limar

  ▸ **smooth out** *vt sep (creases)* alisar; *Fig (difficulties)* allanar; *(problems)* resolver

  ▸ **smooth over** *vt sep Fig* **to s. things over** limar asperezas

smoothly ['smuːðlɪ] *adv* sobre ruedas

smother ['smʌðə(r)] *vt* **(a)** *(asphyxiate)* asfixiar; *(suffocate)* sofocar **(b)** *Fig (cover)* cubrir (**with** de)

smoulder ['sməʊldə(r)] *vi (fire)* arder sin llama; *Fig (passions)* arder; **smouldering hatred** odio latente

smudge [smʌdʒ] **1** *n (stain)* mancha *f*; *(of ink)* borrón *m*

  2 *vt* manchar; *(piece of writing)* emborronar

smug [smʌg] *adj* (**smugger, smuggest**) engreído(a)

smuggle ['smʌgəl] *vt* pasar de contrabando

smuggler ['smʌglə(r)] *n* contrabandista *mf*

smuggling ['smʌgəlɪŋ] *n* contrabando *m*

smutty ['smʌtɪ] *adj* (**smuttier, smuttiest**) *Fam* obsceno(a); *(joke)* verde; *(book, film etc)* pornográfico(a)

snack [snæk] *n* bocado *m*; **s. bar** cafetería *f*

snag [snæg] **1** *n (difficulty)* pega *f*, problemilla *m*

  2 *vt (clothing)* enganchar

snail [sneɪl] *n* caracol *m*

snake [sneɪk] *n (big)* serpiente *f*; *(small)* culebra *f*

snap [snæp] **1** *n* **(a)** *(noise)* ruido seco; *(of branch, fingers)* chasquido *m* **(b)** *(bite)* mordisco *m* **(c)** *Phot* (foto *f*) instantánea *f*

  2 *adj (sudden)* repentino(a)

  3 *vt* **(a)** *(branch etc)* partir (en dos) **(b)** *(make noise)* **to s. one's fingers** chasquear los dedos; **to s. sth shut** cerrar algo de golpe **(c)** *Phot* sacar una foto de

  4 *vi* **(a)** *(break)* romperse **(b)** *(make noise)* hacer un ruido seco **(c)** *(whip)* chasquear; **to s. shut** cerrarse de golpe **(d)** **to s. at sb** *(dog)* intentar morder a algn; *Fam (person)* regañar a algn

  ▸ **snap off 1** *vt sep (branch etc)* arrancar

  2 *vi (branch etc)* separarse

  ▸ **snap up** *vt sep Fam* **to s. up a bargain** llevarse una ganga

snappy ['snæpɪ] *adj* (**snappier, snappiest**) *Fam* **(a)** *(quick)* rápido(a); **look s.!, make it s.!** ¡date prisa! **(b)** *(stylish)* elegante **(c)** *(short-tempered)* irritable

snapshot ['snæpʃɒt] *n* (foto *f*) instantánea *f*

snare [sneə(r)] **1** *n* trampa *f*

  2 *vt (animal)* cazar con trampa; *Fig (person)* hacer caer en la trampa

snarl¹ [snɑːl] **1** *n* gruñido *m*

  2 *vi* gruñir

snarl² [snɑːl] **1** *n (in wool)* maraña *f*

  2 *vt* **to s. (up)** *(wool)* enmarañar; *(traffic)* atascar; *(plans)* enredar

snatch [snætʃ] **1** *n* **(a)** *Fam (theft)* robo *m*; **bag s.** tirón *m* **(b)** *(fragment)* fragmentos *mpl*

2 *vt* (**a**) *(grab)* arrebatar (**b**) *Fam (steal)* robar; *(kidnap)* secuestrar

3 *vi* **to s. at sth** intentar agarrar algo

sneak [sniːk] **1** *n Fam* chivato(a) *m,f*

2 *(pt & pp* **sneaked** *or US* **snuck)** *vt* **to s. sth out of a place** sacar algo de un lugar a escondidas

3 *vi* (**a**) **to s. off** escabullirse; **to s. in/out** entrar/salir a hurtadillas (**b**) *Fam* **to s. on sb** *(tell tales)* chivarse de algn

sneaker ['sniːkə(r)] *n US* playera *f*

sneaky ['sniːkɪ] *adj* (**sneakier, sneakiest**) solapado(a)

sneer [snɪə(r)] *vi* **to s. at** hacer un gesto de desprecio a

sneeze [sniːz] **1** *n* estornudo *m*
2 *vi* estornudar

sniff [snɪf] **1** *n* *(by person)* aspiración *f*; *(by dog)* husmeo *m*
2 *vt (flower etc)* oler; *(suspiciously)* husmear; *(snuff etc)* aspirar; *(glue)* esnifar
3 *vi* aspirar por la nariz

snigger ['snɪgə(r)] **1** *n* risa disimulada
2 *vi* reír disimuladamente; **to s. at sth** burlarse de algo

snip [snɪp] **1** *n* (**a**) *(cut)* tijeretada *f*; *(small piece)* recorte *m* (**b**) *Br Fam (bargain)* ganga *f*
2 *vt* cortar a tijeretazos

sniper ['snaɪpə(r)] *n* francotirador(a) *m,f*

snippet ['snɪpɪt] *n (of cloth, paper)* recorte *m*; *(of conversation)* fragmento *m*

snivel ['snɪvəl] *vi* lloriquear

snivelling ['snɪvəlɪŋ] *adj* llorón(ona)

snob [snɒb] *n* (e)snob *mf*

snobbery ['snɒbərɪ] *n* (e)snobismo *m*

snobbish ['snɒbɪʃ] *adj* (e)snob

snooker ['snuːkə(r)] *n* snooker *m*, billar ruso

snoop [snuːp] *vi* fisgar, fisgonear

snooty ['snuːtɪ] *adj* (**snootier, snootiest**) *Fam* (e)snob

snooze [snuːz] *Fam* **1** *n* cabezada *f*
2 *vi* echar una cabezada

snore [snɔː(r)] **1** *n* ronquido *m*
2 *vi* roncar

snoring ['snɔːrɪŋ] *n* ronquidos *mpl*

snorkel ['snɔːkəl] *n (of swimmer)* tubo *m* de respiración; *(of submarine)* esnórquel *m*

snort [snɔːt] **1** *n* resoplido *m*
2 *vi* resoplar

snout [snaʊt] *n (of animal, gun etc)* morro *m*

snow [snəʊ] **1** *n* nieve *f*; **s. shower** nevada *f*
2 *vi* nevar; **it's snowing** está nevando
3 *vt Fig* **to be snowed under with work** estar agobiado(a) de trabajo

snowball ['snəʊbɔːl] **1** *n* bola *f* de nieve
2 *vi Fig* aumentar rápidamente

snowbound ['snəʊbaʊnd] *adj* aislado(a) por la nieve

snowdrift ['snəʊdrɪft] *n* ventisquero *m*

snowdrop ['snəʊdrɒp] *n* campanilla *f* de invierno

snowfall ['snəʊfɔːl] *n* nevada *f*

snowflake ['snəʊfleɪk] *n* copo *m* de nieve

snowman ['snəʊmæn] *n* hombre *m* de nieve

snowplough, *US* **snowplow** ['snəʊplaʊ] *n* quitanieves *m inv*

snowshoe ['snəʊʃuː] *n* raqueta *f* (de nieve)

snowstorm ['snəʊstɔːm] *n* nevasca *f*

snowy ['snəʊɪ] *adj* (**snowier, snowiest**) *(mountain)* nevado(a); *(climate)* nevoso(a); *(day)* de nieve

Snr *(abbr* **Senior**) **Neil Smith S.** Neil Smith padre

snub [snʌb] **1** *n (of person)* desaire *m*; *(of offer)* rechazo *m*
2 *vt (person)* desairar; *(offer)* rechazar

snub-nosed ['snʌbnəʊzd] *adj* de nariz respingona

snuck [snʌk] *US pt & pp of* **sneak**

snuff [snʌf] *n* rapé *m*

snug [snʌg] *adj* (**snugger, snuggest**) (**a**) *(cosy)* cómodo(a) (**b**) *(tightfitting)* ajustado(a)

snuggle ['snʌgəl] *vi* **to s. down in bed** acurrucarse en la cama; **to s. up to sb** arrimarse a algn

snugly ['snʌglɪ] *adv* **to fit s.** *(clothes)* quedar ajustado(a); *(object in box etc)* encajar

so [səʊ] **1** *adv* (**a**) *(to such an extent)* tanto; **he was so tired that ...** estaba tan cansado que ...; **it's so long since ...** hace tanto tiempo que ...; **he isn't so nice as his sister** no es tan agradable como su hermana; *Fam* **so long!** ¡hasta luego!

(**b**) *(degree)* tanto; **a week or so** una semana más o menos; **twenty or so** una veintena; **we loved her so (much)** la queríamos tanto; **so many books** tantos libros; *Fam* **he's ever so handsome!** ¡es tan guapo!; *Ironic* **so much for that** ¿qué le vamos a hacer?

(**c**) *(thus, in this way)* así, de esta manera; **and so on, and so forth** y así sucesivamente; **if so** en este caso; **I think/hope so** creo/espero que sí; **I told you so** ya te lo dije; **it so happens that ...** da la casualidad de que ...; **so be it!** ¡así sea!; **so far** hasta ahora *or* allí; **so it seems** eso parece; **so they say** eso dicen; **you're late!** – **so I am!** ¡llegas tarde! – ¡tienes razón!

(**d**) *(also)* I'm going to Spain – **so am I** voy a España – yo también

2 *conj* (**a**) *(expresses result)* así que; **so you like England, do you?** ¿así que te gusta Inglaterra, pues?; *Fam* **so what?** ¿y qué?

(**b**) *(expresses purpose)* para que; **I'll put the key here so (that) everyone can see it** pongo la llave aquí para que todos la vean

soak [səʊk] **1** *vt (washing, food)* remojar; *(cotton, wool)* empapar (**in** en)

2 *vi (washing, food)* estar en remojo

▸ **soak in** *vi* penetrar

▸ **soak up** *vt sep* absorber

soaking [ˈsəʊkɪŋ] *adj (object)* empapado(a); *(person)* calado(a) hasta los huesos

so-and-so [ˈsəʊənsəʊ] *n Fam* **Mr So-and-so** Don Fulano (de tal); *Pej* **an old so-and-so** un viejo imbécil

soap [səʊp] **1** *n* (**a**) jabón *m*; **s. flakes** jabón en escamas; **s. powder** jabón en polvo (**b**) *TV* **s. opera** culebrón *m*

2 *vt* enjabonar

soapy [ˈsəʊpɪ] *adj* (**soapier, soapiest**) jabonoso(a); *(hands)* cubierto(a) de jabón

soar [sɔː(r)] *vi (bird, plane)* remontar el vuelo; *Fig (skyscraper)* elevarse; *(hopes, prices)* aumentar

sob [sɒb] **1** *n* sollozo *m*

2 *vi* sollozar

sober [ˈsəʊbə(r)] *adj (not drunk, moderate)* sobrio(a); *(sensible)* sensato(a); *(serious)* serio(a); *(colour)* discreto(a)

▸ **sober up** *vi* **he sobered up** se le pasó la borrachera

so-called [ˈsəʊkɔːld] *adj* supuesto(a), llamado(a)

soccer [ˈsɒkə(r)] *n* fútbol *m*

sociable [ˈsəʊʃəbəl] *adj (gregarious)* sociable; *(friendly)* amistoso(a)

social [ˈsəʊʃəl] *adj* social; **s. class** clase *f* social; **s. climber** arribista *mf*; **S. Democratic** socialdemócrata; *US* **s. insurance** seguro *m* social; **s. security** seguridad *f* social; **the s. services** los servicios sociales; **s. work** asistencia *f* social; **s. worker** asistente(a) *m,f* social

socialist [ˈsəʊʃəlɪst] *adj & n* socialista *(mf)*

socialite [ˈsəʊʃəlaɪt] *n* vividor(a) *m,f*

socialize [ˈsəʊʃəlaɪz] **1** *vi* alternar, mezclarse con la gente

2 *vt* socializar

socially [ˈsəʊʃəlɪ] *adv* socialmente

society [səˈsaɪətɪ] **1** *n* (**a**) sociedad *f*; **the consumer s.** la sociedad de consumo; **(high) s.** la alta sociedad (**b**) *(club)* asociación *f* (**c**) *(companionship)* compañía *f*

2 *adj* de sociedad; **s. column** ecos *mpl* de sociedad

sociologist [səʊsɪˈɒlədʒɪst] *n* sociólogo(a) *m,f*

sociology [səʊsɪˈɒlədʒɪ] *n* sociología *f*

sock [sɒk] *n* calcetín *m*, *CSur* zoquete *m*

socket [ˈsɒkɪt] *n* (**a**) *(of eye)* cuenca *f* (**b**) *Elec* enchufe *m*

sod¹ [sɒd] *n Fml (piece of turf)* terrón *m*

sod² [sɒd] *very Fam* **1** *n* (**a**) *Pej (bastard)* cabrón(ona) *m,f*; **the lazy s.!** ¡qué tío más vago! (**b**) *(wretch)* desgraciado(a) *m,f*; **the poor s.** el pobrecito (**c**) **I've done s. all today** hoy no he pegado ni golpe

2 *vt* **s. it!** ¡maldita sea!

soda [ˈsəʊdə] *n* (**a**) *Chem* sosa *f*; **baking s.** bicarbonato sódico (**b**) **s. water** soda *f* (**c**) *US (fizzy drink)* gaseosa *f*

sodden [ˈsɒdən] *adj* empapado(a)

sodium [ˈsəʊdɪəm] *n* sodio *m*

sofa [ˈsəʊfə] *n* sofá *m*; **s. bed** sofá cama

soft [sɒft] *adj* (**a**) *(not hard)* blando(a); **s. toy** muñeco *m* de peluche (**b**) *(skin, colour, hair, light, music)* suave; *(breeze, steps)* ligero(a) (**c**) *(lenient)* permisivo(a) (**d**) *(voice)* bajo(a) (**e**) *(foolish)* lelo(a); **to be a s. touch** ser fácil de engañar (**f**) **to have a s. spot for sb** tener debilidad por algn (**g**) *(easy)* fácil; **s. job** chollo *m* (**h**) *(drink)* no alcohólico(a); **s. drinks** refrescos *mpl* (**i**) **s. drugs** drogas blandas; **s. porn** pornografía blanda

soften [ˈsɒfən] **1** *vt (leather, heart)* ablandar; *(skin)* suavizar; *Fig (blow)* amortiguar

2 *vi (leather, heart)* ablandarse; *(skin)* suavizarse

softly [ˈsɒftlɪ] *adv (gently)* suavemente; *(quietly)* silenciosamente

softness [ˈsɒftnɪs] *n* (**a**) blandura *f* (**b**) *(of hair, skin)* suavidad *f* (**c**) *(foolishness)* estupidez *f*

software [ˈsɒftweə(r)] *n Comput* software *m*; **s. package** paquete *m*

soggy [ˈsɒgɪ] *adj* (**soggier, soggiest**) empapado(a); *(bread)* pastoso(a)

soil [sɔɪl] **1** *n (earth)* tierra *f*

2 *vt (dirty)* ensuciar; *Fig (reputation)* manchar

soiled [sɔɪld] *adj* sucio(a)

solace [ˈsɒlɪs] *n Fml* consuelo *m*

solar [ˈsəʊlə(r)] *adj* solar

sold [səʊld] *pt & pp of* **sell**

solder [ˈsɒldə(r)] **1** n soldadura f
2 vt soldar
soldier [ˈsəʊldʒə(r)] n soldado m; (officer) militar m; **toy s.** soldadito m de plomo
▸ **soldier on** vi Fig continuar contra viento y marea
sole¹ [səʊl] n (of foot) planta f; (of shoe, sock) suela f
sole² [səʊl] n (fish) lenguado m
sole³ [səʊl] adj (only) único(a)
solemn [ˈsɒləm] adj solemne
solicit [səˈlɪsɪt] **1** vt (request) solicitar
2 vi (prostitute) abordar a los clientes
solicitor [səˈlɪsɪtə(r)] n abogado(a) m,f; (for wills) notario(a) m,f
solid [ˈsɒlɪd] **1** adj (**a**) (not liquid) sólido(a); (firm) firme (**b**) (not hollow, pure) (metal) macizo(a) (**c**) (fog etc) espeso(a); (of strong material) resistente; **a man of s. build** un hombre fornido (**d**) (reliable) formal (**e**) (unanimous) unánime
2 n sólido m
solidarity [sɒlɪˈdærɪtɪ] n solidaridad f
solidify [səˈlɪdɪfaɪ] vi solidificarse
solidly [ˈsɒlɪdlɪ] adv sólidamente; **s. built** (house etc) de construcción sólida; **to work s.** trabajar sin descanso
soliloquy [səˈlɪləkwɪ] n soliloquio m
solitaire [ˈsɒlɪteə(r)] n solitario m
solitary [ˈsɒlɪtərɪ] adj (**a**) (alone) solitario(a); (secluded) apartado(a) (**b**) (only) solo(a)
solitude [ˈsɒlɪtjuːd] n soledad f
solo [ˈsəʊləʊ] n solo m
soloist [ˈsəʊləʊɪst] n solista mf
solstice [ˈsɒlstɪs] n solsticio m
solution [səˈluːʃən] n solución f
solve [sɒlv] vt resolver, solucionar
solvent [ˈsɒlvənt] adj & n solvente (m)
sombre, US **somber** [ˈsɒmbə(r)] adj (dark) sombrío(a); (gloomy) lúgubre; (pessimistic) pesimista
some [sʌm] **1** adj (**a**) (with plural nouns) unos(as), algunos(as); (several) varios(as); (a few) unos(as) cuantos(as); **did she bring s. flowers?** ¿trajo flores?; **there were s. roses** había unas rosas; **s. more peas** más guisantes
(**b**) (with singular nouns) algún/alguna; (a little) un poco de; **if you need s. help** si necesitas ayuda; **there's s. wine left** queda un poco de vino; **would you like s. coffee?** ¿quiere café?
(**c**) (certain) cierto(a), alguno(a); **in s. ways** en cierto modo; **to s. extent** hasta cierto punto; **s. people say that ...** algunas personas dicen que ...
(**d**) (unspecified) algún/alguna; **for s.**

reason or other por una razón o por otra; **in s. book or other** en algún libro que otro; **s. day** algún día; **s. other time** otro día
(**e**) (quite a lot of) bastante; **it's s. distance away** queda bastante lejos; **s. years ago** hace algunos años
2 pron (**a**) (people) algunos(as), unos(as); **s. go by bus and s. by train** unos van en autobús y otros en tren
(**b**) (objects) algunos(as); (a few) unos(as) cuantos(as); (a little) algo, un poco; (certain ones) algunos(as)
3 adv **s. thirty cars** unos treinta coches
somebody [ˈsʌmbədɪ] pron alguien; **s. else** otro(a)
somehow [ˈsʌmhaʊ] adv (**a**) (in some way) de alguna forma (**b**) (for some reason) por alguna razón
someone [ˈsʌmwʌn] pron = **somebody**
someplace [ˈsʌmpleɪs] adv US = **somewhere**
somersault [ˈsʌməsɔːlt] **1** n voltereta f; (by acrobat etc) salto m mortal; (by car) vuelta f de campana
2 vi dar volteretas; (acrobat etc) dar un salto mortal; (car) dar una vuelta de campana
something [ˈsʌmθɪŋ] pron & n algo; **s. to eat/drink** algo de comer/beber; **are you drunk or s.?** ¿estás borracho o qué?; **s. must be done** hay que hacer algo; **she has a certain s.** tiene un no sé qué; **is s. the matter?** ¿le pasa algo?; **s. else** otra cosa; **s. of the kind** algo por el estilo
sometime [ˈsʌmtaɪm] adv algún día; **s. last week** un día de la semana pasada; **s. next year** durante el año que viene
sometimes [ˈsʌmtaɪmz] adv a veces, de vez en cuando
somewhat [ˈsʌmwɒt] adv Fml algo, un tanto
somewhere [ˈsʌmweə(r)] adv (**a**) (in some place) en alguna parte; (to some place) a alguna parte; **s. else** (in some other place) en otra parte; (to some other place) a otra parte; **s. or other** no sé dónde (**b**) **s. in the region of** (approximately) más o menos
son [sʌn] n hijo m; **eldest/youngest s.** hijo mayor/menor
song [sɒŋ] n canción f; (of bird) canto m
songwriter [ˈsɒŋraɪtə(r)] n compositor(a) m,f (de canciones)
sonic [ˈsɒnɪk] adj sónico(a)
son-in-law [ˈsʌnɪnlɔː] n yerno m
sonnet [ˈsɒnɪt] n soneto m
sonny [ˈsʌnɪ] n Fam hijo m, hijito m

soon [suːn] *adv* (**a**) *(within a short time)* pronto, dentro de poco; *(quickly)* rápidamente; **see you s.!** ¡hasta pronto!; **s. after midnight** poco después de medianoche; **s. afterwards** poco después (**b**) **as s. as I arrived** en cuanto llegué; **as s. as possible** cuanto antes (**c**) *(early)* pronto; *Fig* **don't speak too s.** no cantes victoria (**d**) *(preference)* **I would just as s. stay at home** prefiero quedarme en casa (**e**) *(indifference)* **I would (just) as s. read as watch TV** tanto me da leer como ver la tele

sooner [ˈsuːnə(r)] *adv* (**a**) *(earlier)* más temprano; **s. or later** tarde o temprano; **the s. the better** cuanto antes mejor (**b**) **no s. had he finished than he fainted** *(immediately after)* nada más acabar se desmayó (**c**) **I would s. do it alone** *(rather)* prefiero hacerlo yo solo

soot [sʊt] *n* hollín *m*

soothe [suːð] *vt (calm)* tranquilizar; *(pain)* aliviar

sop [sɒp] *n (concession)* favor *m*; *(bribe)* soborno *m*
▸ **sop up** *vt sep* empapar

sophisticated [səˈfɪstɪkeɪtɪd] *adj* sofisticado(a)

sophomore [ˈsɒfəmɔː(r)] *n US Univ* = estudiante de segundo curso

soporific [sɒpəˈrɪfɪk] *adj* soporífero(a)

sopping [ˈsɒpɪŋ] *adj Fam* **s. (wet)** como una sopa

soppy [ˈsɒpɪ] *adj* (**soppier, soppiest**) *Fam* sentimentaloide

soprano [səˈprɑːnəʊ] *n* soprano *mf*

sorcerer [ˈsɔːsərə(r)] *n* brujo *m*

sorceress [ˈsɔːsərɪs] *n* bruja *f*

sordid [ˈsɔːdɪd] *adj* sórdido(a)

sore [sɔː(r)] **1** *adj* (**a**) dolorido(a); **to have a s. throat** tener dolor de garganta (**b**) *Fam (angry)* enfadado(a); **to feel s. about sth** estar resentido(a) por algo **2** *n* llaga *f*

sorely [ˈsɔːlɪ] *adv (very)* muy; *(a lot)* mucho; *(deeply)* profundamente

sorrow [ˈsɒrəʊ] *n* pena *f*, dolor *m*

sorrowful [ˈsɒrəʊfʊl] *adj* afligido(a)

sorry [ˈsɒrɪ] **1** *adj* (**sorrier, sorriest**) (**a**) **I feel very s. for her** me da mucha pena (**b**) *(pitiful)* triste (**c**) **to be s. (about sth)** sentir (algo); **I'm s. I'm late** siento llegar tarde **2** *interj* (**a**) *(apology)* ¡perdón! (**b**) *Br (for repetition)* ¿cómo?

sort [sɔːt] **1** *n* (**a**) *(kind)* clase *f*, tipo *m*; *(brand)* marca *f*; **it's a s. of teapot** es una especie de tetera (**b**) **he is a musician of sorts** tiene algo de músico; **there's an office of sorts** hay una especie de despacho (**c**) **s. of** en cierto modo **2** *vt (classify)* clasificar
▸ **sort out** *vt sep* (**a**) *(classify)* clasificar; *(put in order)* ordenar (**b**) *(problem)* arreglar, solucionar

sorting [ˈsɔːtɪŋ] *n* **s. office** sala *f* de batalla

SOS [esəʊˈes] *n (abbr* **save our souls**) S.O.S. *m*

so-so [ˈsəʊsəʊ] *adv Fam* así así, regular

soufflé [ˈsuːfleɪ] *n* soufflé *m*, suflé *m*

sought [sɔːt] *pt & pp of* **seek**

soul [səʊl] *n* (**a**) alma *f* (**b**) **he's a good s.** *(person)* es muy buena persona (**c**) *Mus (música f)* soul *m*

soul-destroying [ˈsəʊldɪstrɔɪɪŋ] *adj (boring)* monótono(a); *(demoralizing)* desmoralizador(a)

soulful [ˈsəʊlfʊl] *adj* conmovedor(a)

sound¹ [saʊnd] **1** *n* sonido *m*; *(noise)* ruido *m*; *Fig* **I don't like the s. of it** no me gusta nada la idea; **s. barrier** barrera *f* del sonido; **s. effects** efectos sonoros **2** *vt (bell, trumpet)* tocar; **to s. the alarm** dar la señal de alarma **3** *vi* (**a**) *(trumpet, bell, alarm)* sonar (**b**) *(give an impression)* parecer; **how does it s. to you?** ¿qué te parece?; **it sounds interesting** parece interesante

sound² [saʊnd] **1** *adj* (**a**) *(healthy)* sano(a); *(in good condition)* en buen estado (**b**) *(safe, dependable)* seguro(a); *(correct)* acertado(a); *(logical)* lógico(a) (**c**) *(basis etc)* sólido(a) (**d**) *(defeat etc)* rotundo(a) (**e**) *(sleep)* profundo(a) **2** *adv* **to be s. asleep** estar profundamente dormido(a)

sound³ [saʊnd] *vt Naut & Med* sondar
▸ **sound out** *vt sep* sondear

sound⁴ [saʊnd] *n Geog* estrecho *m*

sounding [ˈsaʊndɪŋ] *n Naut* sondeo *m*

soundproof [ˈsaʊndpruːf] *adj* insonorizado(a)

soundtrack [ˈsaʊndtræk] *n* banda sonora

soup [suːp] *n* sopa *f*; *(thin, clear)* caldo *m*; *Fam* **in the s.** en un apuro; **s. dish** plato hondo; **s. spoon** cuchara *f* sopera

sour [saʊə(r)] *adj* (**a**) *(fruit, wine)* agrio(a); *(milk)* cortado(a); **to go s.** *(milk)* cortarse; *(wine)* agriarse; *Fig (situation)* empeorar (**b**) *Fig (person)* amargado(a)

source [sɔːs] *n* fuente *f*; *(of infection)* foco *m*

south [saʊθ] **1** *n* sur *m*; **in the s. of England** en el sur de Inglaterra; **to the s. of York** al sur de York

2 *adj* del sur; **S. Africa** Sudáfrica; **S. African** sudafricano(a) *(m,f)*; **S. Korea** Corea del Sur; **S. Pole** Polo *m* Sur

3 *adv (location)* al sur; *(direction)* hacia el sur

southeast [saʊθ'iːst] **1** *n* sudeste *m*

2 *adv (location)* al sudeste; *(direction)* hacia el sudeste

southeasterly [saʊθ'iːstəlɪ] *adj* del sudeste

southerly ['sʌðəlɪ] *adj (direction)* hacia el sur; *(point)* al sur; *(wind)* del sur

southern ['sʌðən] *adj* del sur, meridional; **S. Europe** Europa del Sur; **the s. hemisphere** el hemisferio sur

southerner ['sʌðənə(r)] *n* sureño(a) *m,f*

southward ['saʊθwəd] *adj & adv* hacia el sur

southwest [saʊθ'west] **1** *n* suroeste *m*

2 *adj* suroeste

3 *adv (location)* al suroeste; *(direction)* hacia el suroeste

souvenir [suːvə'nɪə(r)] *n* recuerdo *m*, souvenir *m*

sovereign ['sɒvrɪn] **1** *n* (a) *(monarch)* soberano(a) *m,f* (b) *Hist (coin)* soberano *m*

2 *adj* soberano(a)

soviet ['səʊvɪət] **1** *n* (a) *(council)* soviet *m* (b) **the Soviets** los soviéticos

2 *adj* soviético(a); *Hist* **S. Union** Unión Soviética

sow¹ [səʊ] *vt (pt* **sowed***; pp* **sowed** *or* **sown**) sembrar

sow² [saʊ] *n Zool* cerda *f*

sown [səʊn] *pp of* **sow**

soy [sɔɪ] *n* soja *f*; **s. sauce** salsa *f* de soja

soya ['sɔɪə] *n* soja *f*; **s. bean** semilla *f* de soja

spa [spɑː] *n* balneario *m*

space [speɪs] **1** *n* (a) espacio *m*; **s. age** era *f* espacial; **s. shuttle** transbordador *m* espacial; **s. station** estación *f* espacial (b) *(room)* sitio *m*; **in a confined s.** en un espacio reducido

2 *vt (also* **s. out***)* espaciar, separar

spacecraft ['speɪskrɑːft] *n (pl* **spacecraft***)* nave *f* espacial

spaceman ['speɪsmən] *n* astronauta *m*, cosmonauta *m*

spacing ['speɪsɪŋ] *n* **double s.** doble espacio

spacious ['speɪʃəs] *adj* espacioso(a), amplio(a)

spade¹ [speɪd] *n (for digging)* pala *f*

> ✍ Note that the Spanish word **espada** is a false friend and is never a translation for the English word **spade**. In Spanish, **espada** means "sword".

spade² [speɪd] *n Cards* pica *f*

spaghetti [spə'getɪ] *n* espaguetis *mpl*

Spain [speɪn] *n* España

span [spæn] **1** *n (of wing)* envergadura *f*; *(of hand)* palmo *m*; *(of arch)* luz *f*; *(of road)* tramo *m*; *(of time)* lapso *m*; **life s.** vida *f*

2 *vt (river etc)* extenderse sobre, atravesar; *(period of time etc)* abarcar

3 *pt of* **spin**

Spaniard ['spænjəd] *n* español(a) *m,f*

spaniel ['spænjəl] *n* perro *m* de aguas

Spanish ['spænɪʃ] **1** *adj* español(a)

2 *n* (a) **the S.** los españoles (b) *(language)* español *m*, castellano *m*

Spanish-speaking ['spænɪʃspiːkɪŋ] *adj* de habla española, hispanohablante

spank [spæŋk] *vt* zurrar

spanner ['spænə(r)] *n* llave *f* (para tuercas); *Br Fam* **to throw a s. in the works** estropear los planes

spar¹ [spɑː(r)] *n Naut* palo *m*, verga *f*

spar² [spɑː(r)] *vi* (a) *(boxers)* entrenarse (b) *(argue)* discutir

spare [speə(r)] **1** *vt* (a) *(do without)* prescindir de; **can you s. me ten?** ¿me puedes dejar diez?; **I can't s. the time** no tengo tiempo; **there's none to s.** no sobra nada (b) *(begrudge)* escatimar (c) *(show mercy to)* perdonar (d) **s. me the details** ahórrate los detalles

2 *adj* (a) *(left over)* sobrante; *(surplus)* de sobra, de más; **a s. moment** un momento libre; **s. part** (pieza *f* de) recambio *m*; **s. room** cuarto *m* de los invitados; **s. tyre** *Aut* neumático *m* de recambio; *Br Fam (on body)* michelines *mpl*; **s. wheel** rueda *f* de recambio (b) *(thin)* enjuto(a)

3 *n Aut (pieza f de)* recambio *m*

sparing ['speərɪŋ] *adj* **to be s. with praise** escatimar elogios; **to be s. with words** ser parco(a) en palabras

sparingly ['speərɪŋlɪ] *adv* en poca cantidad

spark [spɑːk] **1** *n* chispa *f*; *Aut* **s. plug** bujía *f*

2 *vi* echar chispas

▸ **spark off** *vt sep* desatar

sparking ['spɑːkɪŋ] *adj* **s. plug** bujía *f*

sparkle ['spɑːkəl] **1** *vi (diamond, glass)* centellear, destellar; *(eyes)* brillar

2 *n (of diamond, glass)* centelleo *m*,

destello *m*; *(of eyes)* brillo *m*
sparkling ['spɑːklɪŋ] *adj* (**a**) *(diamond, glass)* centelleante; *(eyes)* brillante; **s. wine** vino espumoso (**b**) *Fig (person, conversation)* vivaz
sparrow ['spærəʊ] *n* gorrión *m*
sparse [spɑːs] *adj (thin)* escaso(a); *(scattered)* esparcido(a); *(hair)* ralo(a)
Spartan ['spɑːtən] *adj & n* espartano(a) *(m,f)*
spasm ['spæzəm] *n* (**a**) *Med* espasmo *m*; *(of coughing)* acceso *m* (**b**) *(of anger, activity)* arrebato *m*
spasmodic [spæz'mɒdɪk] *adj* (**a**) *Med* espasmódico(a) (**b**) *(irregular)* irregular
spastic ['spæstɪk] *adj & n Med* espástico(a) *(m,f)*
spat [spæt] *pt & pp of* **spit**
spate [speɪt] *n* (**a**) *(of letters)* avalancha *f*; *(of words)* torrente *m*; *(of accidents)* racha *f* (**b**) *Br (river)* desbordamiento *m*; **to be in full s.** estar crecido(a)
spatter ['spætə(r)] *vt* salpicar (**with** de)
spatula ['spætjʊlə] *n* espátula *f*
spawn [spɔːn] **1** *n (of fish, frogs)* huevas *fpl*
2 *vi (fish, frogs)* frezar
3 *vt Fig Pej* generar
speak [spiːk] **1** *vt (pt* spoke; *pp* spoken) (**a**) *(utter)* decir; **to s. the truth** decir la verdad
(**b**) *(language)* hablar
2 *vi* (**a**) *(gen)* hablar; **roughly speaking** a grandes rasgos; **so to s.** por así decirlo; **speaking of ...** a propósito de ...; **to s. to sb** hablar con algn
(**b**) *(make a speech)* pronunciar un discurso; *(take the floor)* tomar la palabra
(**c**)*Tel* hablar; **speaking!** ¡al habla!; **who's speaking, please?** ¿de parte de quién?
▸ **speak for** *vt insep (person, group)* hablar en nombre de; **it speaks for itself** es evidente
▸ **speak out** *vi* **to s. out against sth** denunciar algo
▸ **speak up** *vi* hablar más fuerte; *Fig* **to s. up for sb** intervenir a favor de algn
speaker ['spiːkə(r)] *n* (**a**) *(in dialogue)* interlocutor(a) *m,f*; *(lecturer)* conferenciante *mf*; (**public**) **s.** orador(a) *m,f* (**b**) *(of language)* hablante *mf* (**c**) *Br Pol* **the S.** el Presidente de la Cámara de los Comunes; *US* **the S. of the House** el Presidente de la Cámara de los Representantes (**d**) *(loudspeaker)* altavoz *m*
spear [spɪə(r)] *n* lanza *f*; *(javelin)* jabalina *f*; *(harpoon)* arpón *m*
spearhead ['spɪəhed] *vt* encabezar

spec [spek] *n Fam* **on s.** sin garantías
special ['speʃəl] **1** *adj* especial; *(specific)* específico(a); *(exceptional)* extraordinario(a); **s. delivery** *(letter)* exprés; *(parcel)* de entrega inmediata; **s. edition** número *m* especial; **s. effects** efectos *mpl* especiales
2 *n Rad & TV* programa *m* especial
specialist ['speʃəlɪst] *n* especialista *mf*
speciality [speʃɪ'ælɪtɪ] *n esp Br* especialidad *f*
specialize ['speʃəlaɪz] *vi* especializarse (**in** en)
specially ['speʃəlɪ] *adv (specifically)* especialmente; *(on purpose)* a propósito
specialty ['speʃəltɪ] *n US =* **speciality**
species ['spiːʃiːz] *n (pl* **species**) especie *f*
specific [spɪ'sɪfɪk] *adj* específico(a); *(definite)* concreto(a); *(precise)* preciso(a); **to be s.** concretar
specifically [spɪ'sɪfɪklɪ] *adv (exactly)* específicamente; *(expressly)* expresamente; *(namely)* en concreto
specifications [spesɪfɪ'keɪʃənz] *npl* datos específicos
specify ['spesɪfaɪ] *vt* especificar, precisar
specimen ['spesɪmɪn] *n (sample)* muestra *f*; *(example)* ejemplar *m*; **urine/tissue s.** espécimen de orina/tejido
speck [spek] *n (of dust)* mota *f*; *(stain)* manchita *f*; *(small trace)* pizca *f*
speckled ['spekəld] *adj* moteado(a)
specs [speks] *npl Fam (spectacles)* gafas *fpl*
spectacle ['spektəkəl] *n* (**a**) *(display)* espectáculo *m* (**b**) **spectacles** *(glasses)* gafas *fpl*, *Am* lentes *mpl*, anteojos *mpl*
spectacular [spek'tækjʊlə(r)] **1** *adj* espectacular, impresionante
2 *n Cin & TV* (gran) espectáculo *m*
spectator [spek'teɪtə(r)] *n* espectador(a) *m,f*
spectre, *US* **specter** ['spektə(r)] *n* espectro *m*, fantasma *m*
spectrum ['spektrəm] *n* espectro *m*
speculate ['spekjʊleɪt] *vi* especular
speculation [spekjʊ'leɪʃən] *n* especulación *f*
sped [sped] *pt & pp of* **speed**
speech [spiːtʃ] *n* (**a**) *(faculty)* habla *f*; *(pronunciation)* pronunciación *f*; **freedom of s.** libertad *f* de expresión (**b**) *(address)* discurso *m*; **to give a s.** pronunciar un discurso (**c**) *Ling* **part of s.** parte *f* de la oración
speechless ['spiːtʃlɪs] *adj* mudo(a), boquiabierto(a)
speed [spiːd] **1** *n* velocidad *f*; *(rapidity)*

rapidez *f*; **at top s.** a toda velocidad; **s. limit** límite *m* de velocidad

2 *vi* (**a**) (*pt & pp* **sped**) (*go fast*) ir corriendo; (*hurry*) apresurarse; **to s. along** (*car etc*) ir a toda velocidad; **to s. past** pasar volando (**b**) (*pt & pp* **speeded**) (*exceed speed limit*) conducir con exceso de velocidad

▸ **speed up 1** *vt sep* acelerar; (*person*) meter prisa a

2 *vi* (*person*) darse prisa

speedboat ['spi:dbəʊt] *n* lancha rápida

speeding ['spi:dɪŋ] *n* exceso *m* de velocidad

speedometer [spɪ'dɒmɪtə(r)] *n* velocímetro *m*

speedway ['spi:dweɪ] *n* (**a**) (*racing*) carreras *fpl* de motos (**b**) (*track*) pista *f* de carreras

speedy ['spi:dɪ] *adj* (**speedier, speediest**) veloz, rápido(a)

spell¹ [spel] **1** *vt* (*pt & pp* **spelt** *or* **spelled**) (*letter by letter*) deletrear; *Fig* (*denote*) significar; **how do you s. your name?** ¿cómo se escribe su nombre?

2 *vi* **she can't s.** comete faltas de ortografía

▸ **spell out** *vt sep Fig* explicar con detalle

spell² [spel] *n* (*magical*) hechizo *m*, encanto *m*

spell³ [spel] *n* (**a**) (*period*) período *m*; (*short period*) rato *m*; *Met* **cold s.** ola *f* de frío (**b**) (*shift*) turno *m*

spellbound ['spelbaʊnd] *adj* hechizado(a), embelesado(a)

spelling ['spelɪŋ] *n* ortografía *f*

spelt [spelt] *pt & pp of* **spell**

spend [spend] *vt* (*pt & pp* **spent**) (**a**) (*money*) gastar (**on** en) (**b**) (*time*) pasar; **to s. time on sth** dedicar tiempo a algo

spending ['spendɪŋ] *n* gastos *mpl*; **s. money** dinero *m* de bolsillo; **s. power** poder adquisitivo

spendthrift ['spendθrɪft] *adj & n* derrochador(a) (*m,f*)

spent [spent] **1** *adj* gastado(a)

2 *pt & pp of* **spend**

sperm [spɜ:m] *n* esperma *m*; **s. bank** banco *m* de esperma; **s. whale** cachalote *m*

spew [spju:] *vt* **to s. (up)** vomitar

sphere [sfɪə(r)] *n* esfera *f*

spice [spaɪs] **1** *n* (**a**) especia *f* (**b**) *Fig* sal *f*

2 *vt* (**a**) *Culin* sazonar (**b**) **to s. (up)** (*story etc*) salpimentar

spick-and-span [spɪkən'spæn] *adj* (*very clean*) limpísimo(a); (*well-groomed*) acicalado(a)

spicy ['spaɪsɪ] *adj* (**spicier, spiciest**) (**a**) *Culin* sazonado(a); (*hot*) picante (**b**) *Fig* (*story etc*) picante

spider ['spaɪdə(r)] *n* araña *f*; **s.'s web** telaraña *f*

spike¹ [spaɪk] *n* (*sharp point*) punta *f*; (*metal rod*) pincho *m*; (*on railing*) barrote *m*; *Sport* (*on shoes*) clavo *m*

spike² [spaɪk] *n Bot* espiga *f*

spiky ['spaɪkɪ] *adj* (**spikier, spikiest**) puntiagudo(a); (*hairstyle*) de punta

spill [spɪl] **1** *vt* (*pt & pp* **spilled** *or* **spilt** [spɪlt]) derramar

2 *vi* (*liquid*) derramarse

▸ **spill over** *vi* desbordarse

spin [spɪn] **1** *vt* (*pt* **span** *or* **spun**; *pp* **spun**) (**a**) (*wheel etc*) hacer girar; (*washing*) centrifugar (**b**) (*cotton, wool*) hilar; (*spider's web*) tejer

2 *vi* (*wheel etc*) girar; *Av* caer en barrena; *Aut* patinar

3 *n* (**a**) (*turn*) vuelta *f*, giro *m* (**b**) *Sport* efecto *m* (**c**) *Av* barrena *f*; *Aut* patinazo *m* (**d**) *Br* **to go for a s.** (*ride*) dar una vuelta (**e**) *Pol* (*on news story*) sesgo *m*; **s. doctor** asesor(a) *m,f* político(a) (*para dar buena prensa a un partido o político*)

spinach ['spɪnɪtʃ] *n* espinacas *fpl*

spinal ['spaɪnəl] *adj* espinal, vertebral; **s. column** columna *f* vertebral; **s. cord** médula *f* espinal

spindly ['spɪndlɪ] *adj* (**spindlier, spindliest**) *Fam* (*long-bodied*) larguirucho(a); (*long-legged*) zanquilargo(a)

spin-dryer [spɪn'draɪə(r)] *n* secador centrífugo

spine [spaɪn] *n* (**a**) *Anat* columna *f* vertebral, espinazo *m*; (*of book*) lomo *m* (**b**) *Zool* púa *f*; *Bot* espina *f*

spineless ['spaɪnlɪs] *adj Fig* (*weak*) sin carácter

spinning ['spɪnɪŋ] *n* (**a**) (*of cotton etc*) (*act*) hilado *m*; (*art*) hilandería *f*; **s. wheel** rueca *f* (**b**) **s. top** peonza *f*

spin-off ['spɪnɒf] *n* (*by-product*) derivado *m*; *Fig* efecto secundario

spinster ['spɪnstə(r)] *n* soltera *f*

spiral ['spaɪərəl] **1** *n* espiral *f*

2 *adj* en espiral; **s. staircase** escalera *f* de caracol

spirit¹ ['spɪrɪt] *n* (**a**) (*soul*) espíritu *m*, alma *f*; (*ghost*) fantasma *m* (**b**) (*attitude*) espíritu *m*; (*mood*) humor *m*; **to take sth in the right s.** tomar algo a bien; **community s.** civismo *m* (**c**) (*courage*) valor *m*; (*liveliness*) ánimo *m*; (*vitality*) vigor *m*; **to break sb's s.** quebrar la voluntad de algn (**d**) **spirits** (*mood*) humor *m*; **to be in**

good spirits estar de buen humor; **to be in high/low spirits** estar muy animado/desanimado

spirit² ['spɪrɪt] *n* (**a**) *Chem* alcohol *m*; **s. level** nivel *m* de aire (**b**) **spirits** *(alcoholic drinks)* licores *mpl*

spirited ['spɪrɪtɪd] *adj (person, attempt)* valiente; *(horse)* fogoso(a); *(attack)* enérgico(a)

spiritual ['spɪrɪtjʊəl] *adj* espiritual

spit¹ [spɪt] **1** *vt (pt & pp* **spat)** escupir

2 *vi* escupir; *Fam* **he's the spitting image of his father** es el vivo retrato de su padre

3 *n (saliva)* saliva *f*

spit² [spɪt] *n Culin* asador *m*

spite [spaɪt] **1** *n* (**a**) *(ill will)* rencor *m*, ojeriza *f* (**b**) **in s. of** a pesar de, pese a; **in s. of the fact that** a pesar de que, pese a que

2 *vt (annoy)* fastidiar

spiteful ['spaɪtfʊl] *adj (person)* rencoroso(a); *(remark)* malévolo(a); *(tongue)* viperino(a)

spittle ['spɪtəl] *n* saliva *f*

spittoon [spɪ'tuːn] *n* escupidera *f*

splash [splæʃ] **1** *vt* salpicar

2 *vi* (**a**) **(about)** *(in water)* chapotear (**b**) *(water etc)* salpicar

3 *n* (**a**) *(noise)* chapoteo *m* (**b**) *(spray)* salpicadura *f*; *Fig (of colour)* mancha *f*

▸ **splash out** *vi Fam* tirar la casa por la ventana

spleen [spliːn] *n Anat* bazo *m*

splendid ['splendɪd] *adj* espléndido(a)

splendour, *US* **splendor** ['splendə(r)] *n* esplendor *m*

splint [splɪnt] *n* tablilla *f*

splinter ['splɪntə(r)] **1** *n (wood)* astilla *f*; *(bone, stone)* esquirla *f*; *(glass)* fragmento *m*; **s. group** grupo *m* disidente

2 *vi* (**a**) *(wood etc)* astillarse (**b**) *Pol* escindirse

split [splɪt] **1** *n* (**a**) *(crack)* grieta *f*, hendidura *f*; *(tear)* desgarrón *m*; *Fig (division)* cisma *m*; *Pol* escisión *f* (**b**) **to do the splits** abrir las piernas en cruz

2 *adj* partido(a); **in a s. second** en una fracción de segundo; **s. personality** desdoblamiento *m* de personalidad

3 *vt (pt & pp* **split)** (**a**) *(crack)* agrietar; *(cut)* partir; *(tear)* rajar; *(atom)* desintegrar; *Fig* **to s. hairs** buscarle tres pies al gato (**b**) *(divide)* dividir (**c**) *(share out)* repartir (**d**) *Pol* escindir

4 *vi* (**a**) *(crack)* agrietarse; *(into two parts)* partirse; *(garment)* rajarse (**b**) *(divide)* dividirse (**c**) *Pol* escindirse

▸ **split up** **1** *vt sep (break up)* partir; *(divide up)* dividir; *(share out)* repartir

2 *vi (couple)* separarse

splutter ['splʌtə(r)] *vi (person)* balbucear; *(candle, fat)* chisporrotear; *(engine)* petardear

spoil [spɔɪl] **1** *vt (pt & pp* **spoiled** *or* **spoilt)** (**a**) *(ruin)* estropear, echar a perder (**b**) *(child)* mimar a; **to be spoilt for choice** tener demasiadas cosas para elegir

2 *vi (food)* estropearse

spoilsport ['spɔɪlspɔːt] *n Fam* aguafiestas *mf inv*

spoilt [spɔɪlt] **1** *adj* (**a**) *(food, merchandise)* estropeado(a) (**b**) *(child)* mimado(a)

2 *pt & pp of* **spoil**

spoke¹ [spəʊk] *pt of* **speak**

spoke² [spəʊk] *n (of wheel)* radio *m*, rayo *m*

spoken ['spəʊkən] *pp of* **speak**

spokesman ['spəʊksmən] *n* portavoz *m*

spokeswoman ['spəʊkswʊmən] *n* portavoz *f*

sponge [spʌndʒ] **1** *n* esponja *f*; *Fig* **to throw in the s.** arrojar la toalla; *Br* **s. cake** bizcocho *m*

2 *vt (wash)* lavar con esponja

3 *vi Fam* vivir de gorra

▸ **sponge off, sponge on** *vt insep* vivir a costa de

spongy ['spʌndʒɪ] *adj* (**spongier, spongiest**) esponjoso(a)

sponsor ['spɒnsə(r)] **1** *vt* patrocinar; *Fin* avalar; *(support)* respaldar

2 *n* patrocinador(a) *m,f*; *Fin* avalador(a) *m,f*

sponsorship ['spɒnsəʃɪp] *n* patrocinio *m*; *Fin* aval *m*; *(support)* respaldo *m*

spontaneous [spɒn'teɪnɪəs] *adj* espontáneo(a)

spoof [spuːf] *n Fam* (**a**) *(parody)* burla *f* (**b**) *(hoax)* engaño *m*

spooky ['spuːkɪ] *adj* (**spookier, spookiest**) *Fam* espeluznante

spool [spuːl] *n* bobina *f*, carrete *m*

spoon [spuːn] **1** *n* cuchara *f*; *(small)* cucharita *f*

2 *vt* sacar con cuchara; *(serve)* servir con cuchara

spoon-feed ['spuːnfiːd] *vt (baby)* dar de comer con cuchara a; *Fig (spoil)* mimar

spoonful ['spuːnfʊl] *n* cucharada *f*

sporadic [spə'rædɪk] *adj* esporádico(a)

sport [spɔːt] **1** *n* (**a**) deporte *m* (**b**) *Fam* **he's a good s.** es buena persona; **be a s.!** ¡sé amable!

2 *vt (display)* lucir

sporting ['spɔːtɪŋ] *adj* deportivo(a)

sports [spɔːts] **1** *npl* deportes *mpl*, deporte *m*
2 *adj* **s. car** coche deportivo; **s. jacket** chaqueta *f* (de) sport
sportsman ['spɔːtsmən] *n* deportista *m*
sportsmanlike ['spɔːtsmənlaɪk] *adj* deportivo(a)
sportsmanship ['spɔːtsmənʃɪp] *n* deportividad *f*
sportswear ['spɔːtsweə(r)] *n* (for sport) ropa *f* de deporte; *(casual clothes)* ropa (de) sport
sportswoman ['spɔːtswʊmən] *n* deportista *f*
sporty ['spɔːtɪ] *adj* (**sportier, sportiest**) *Fam* deportivo(a)
spot [spɒt] **1** *n* (**a**) *(dot)* punto *m*; *(on fabric)* lunar *m*
 (**b**) *(stain)* mancha *f*
 (**c**) *(pimple)* grano *m*
 (**d**) *(place)* sitio *m*, lugar *m*; **on the s.** *(person)* allí, presente; **to decide sth on the s.** decidir algo en el acto; **s. check** chequeo rápido; *Fig* **weak s.** punto débil; **to be in a tight s.** estar en un apuro; **to put sb on the s.** poner a algn en un aprieto
 (**e**) *Fam (small amount)* poquito *m*; **a s. of bother** unos problemillas
 (**f**) *Rad, TV & Th (in show)* espacio *m*; *(advertisement)* spot *m*, anuncio *m*
 2 *vt (notice)* darse cuenta de, notar; *(see)* ver
spotless ['spɒtlɪs] *adj (very clean)* impecable; *Fig (reputation etc)* intachable
spotlight ['spɒtlaɪt] *n* foco *m*; *Aut* faro *m* auxiliar; *Fig* **to be in the s.** ser objeto de la atención pública
spot-on [spɒt'ɒn] *adj Fam* exacto(a)
spotted ['spɒtɪd] *adj (with dots)* con puntos, *(fabric)* con lunares; *(speckled)* moteado(a)
spotty ['spɒtɪ] *adj* (**spottier, spottiest**) *Pej* con granos
spouse [spaʊs] *n* cónyuge *mf*
spout [spaʊt] **1** *n* (of jug) pico *m*; *(of teapot)* pitorro *m*
 2 *vt Fam (nonsense)* soltar
 3 *vi* **to s. out/up** *(liquid)* brotar
sprain [spreɪn] **1** *n* esguince *m*
 2 *vt* torcer; **to s. one's ankle** torcerse el tobillo
sprang [spræŋ] *pt of* **spring**
sprawl [sprɔːl] **1** *vi* (**a**) *(sit, lie)* tumbarse
 (**b**) *(city, plant)* extenderse
 2 *n (of city)* extensión *f*
spray¹ [spreɪ] **1** *n* (**a**) *(of water)* rociada *f*; *(from sea)* espuma *f*; *(from aerosol)* pulverización *f* (**b**) *(aerosol)* spray *m*; *(for plants)* pulverizador *m*; **s. can** aerosol *m*
 2 *vt (water)* rociar; *(insecticide, perfume)* pulverizar
spray² [spreɪ] *n (of flowers)* ramita *f*
spread [spred] **1** *n* (**a**) extensión *f*; *(of ideas)* difusión *f*; *(of disease, fire)* propagación *f*; *(of terrorism)* generalización *f*
 (**b**) *(range)* gama *f*
 (**c**) *(of wings)* envergadura *f*
 (**d**) *(for bread)* pasta *f*; **cheese s.** queso *m* para untar
 (**e**) *Fam (large meal)* banquetazo *m*
 (**f**) *Press* **full-page s.** plana entera; **two-page s.** doble página *f*
 2 *vt (pt & pp* **spread**) (**a**) *(unfold)* desplegar; *(lay out)* extender; *Fig* **to s. one's wings** desplegar las alas
 (**b**) *(butter etc)* untar
 (**c**) *(news)* difundir; *(rumour)* hacer correr; *(disease, fire)* propagar; *(panic)* sembrar
 3 *vi* (**a**) *(stretch out)* extenderse; *(unfold)* desplegarse
 (**b**) *(news)* difundirse; *(rumour)* correr; *(disease)* propagarse
spread-eagled [spred'iːgəld] *adj* despatarrado(a)
spreadsheet ['spredʃiːt] *n Comput* hoja *f* de cálculo
spree [spriː] *n* juerga *f*; **to go on a s.** ir de juerga
sprig [sprɪg] *n* ramita *f*
sprightly ['spraɪtlɪ] *adj* (**sprightlier, sprightliest**) *(nimble)* ágil; *(energetic)* enérgico(a); *(lively)* animado(a)
spring¹ [sprɪŋ] **1** *n (season)* primavera *f*
 2 *adj* primaveral; **s. onion** cebolleta *f*; **s. roll** rollo *m* de primavera
spring² [sprɪŋ] **1** *n* (**a**) *(of water)* manantial *m*, fuente *f* (**b**) *(of watch etc)* resorte *m*; *(of mattress)* muelle *m*; *Aut* ballesta *f*
 2 *vi* (*pt* **sprang**; *pp* **sprung**) (**a**) *(jump)* saltar; **the lid sprang open** la tapa se abrió de golpe (**b**) *(appear)* aparecer (de repente)
 3 *vt* (**a**) **to s. a leak** hacer agua (**b**) *Fig (news, surprise)* dar de golpe
 ▸ **spring up** *vi* aparecer; *(plants)* brotar; *(buildings)* elevarse; *(problems)* surgir
springboard ['sprɪŋbɔːd] *n* trampolín *m*
spring-clean [sprɪŋ'kliːn] *vt* limpiar a fondo
springtime ['sprɪŋtaɪm] *n* primavera *f*
springy ['sprɪŋɪ] *adj* (**springier, springiest**) *(bouncy)* elástico(a); *Fig (step)* saltarín
sprinkle ['sprɪŋkəl] *vt (with water)* rociar

(**with** de); *(with sugar)* espolvorear (**with** de)

sprint [sprɪnt] **1** *n* esprint *m*
    2 *vi* esprintar

sprinter [ˈsprɪntə(r)] *n* esprínter *mf*, velocista *mf*

sprout [spraʊt] **1** *vi (bud)* brotar; *Fig* crecer rápidamente
    2 *n* (**Brussels**) **sprouts** coles *fpl* de Bruselas

spruce¹ [spruːs] *n Bot* picea *f*

spruce² [spruːs] *adj (neat)* pulcro(a); *(smart)* apuesto(a)
    ▸ **spruce up** *vt sep* acicalar

sprung [sprʌŋ] *pp of* **spring**

spry [spraɪ] *adj* (**sprier, spriest**) *(nimble)* ágil; *(active)* activo(a); *(lively)* vivaz

spun [spʌn] *pt & pp of* **spin**

spur [spɜː(r)] **1** *n* (**a**) *(a)* espuela *f* (**b**) *Fig (stimulus)* acicate *m*; **on the s. of the moment** sin pensarlo
    2 *vt* (**a**) *(horse)* espolear (**b**) *Fig* incitar

spurious [ˈspjʊərɪəs] *adj* falso(a), espurio(a)

spurn [spɜːn] *vt Fml* desdeñar, rechazar

spurt [spɜːt] **1** *n* (**a**) *(of liquid)* chorro *m* (**b**) *Fig (of activity etc)* racha *f*; *(effort)* esfuerzo *m*
    2 *vi* (**a**) *(liquid)* chorrear (**b**) *(make an effort)* hacer un último esfuerzo; *(accelerate)* acelerar

spy [spaɪ] **1** *n* espía *mf*
    2 *vt Fml (see)* divisar
    3 *vi* espiar (**on** a)

spyhole [ˈspaɪhəʊl] *n* mirilla *f*

spying [ˈspaɪɪŋ] *n* espionaje *m*

squabble [ˈskwɒbəl] **1** *n* riña *f*, pelea *f*
    2 *vi* reñir, pelearse (**over** *or* **about** por)

squad [skwɒd] *n Mil* pelotón *m*; *(of police)* brigada *f*; *Sport* equipo *m*; **drugs s.** brigada antidroga

squadron [ˈskwɒdrən] *n Mil* escuadrón *m*; *Av* escuadrilla *f*; *Naut* escuadra *f*

squalid [ˈskwɒlɪd] *adj (very dirty)* asqueroso(a); *(poor)* miserable; *(motive)* vil

squall¹ [skwɔːl] *n (wind)* ráfaga *f*

squall² [skwɔːl] *vi* chillar, berrear

squalor [ˈskwɒlə(r)] *n (dirtiness)* mugre *f*; *(poverty)* miseria *f*

squander [ˈskwɒndə(r)] *vt (money)* derrochar, despilfarrar; *(time)* desperdiciar

square [skweə(r)] **1** *n* (**a**) *(a)* cuadro *m*; *(on chessboard, crossword)* casilla *f*; *Fig* **we're back to s. one!** ¡volvemos a partir desde cero!
    (**b**) *(in town)* plaza *f*
    (**c**) *Math* cuadrado *m*
    2 *adj* (**a**) *(in shape)* cuadrado(a)

(**b**) *Math* cuadrado(a); **s. metre** metro cuadrado; **s. root** raíz cuadrada
    (**c**) *Fam (fair)* justo(a); **to be s. with sb** *(honest)* ser franco(a) con algn
    (**d**) **a s. meal** una buena comida
    (**e**) *(old-fashioned)* carroza; *(conservative)* carca
    3 *vt* (**a**) *(make square)* cuadrar; **to s. one's shoulders** sacar el pecho
    (**b**) *Math* elevar al cuadrado
    (**c**) *(settle)* arreglar
    4 *vi (agree)* cuadrar (**with** con)

squarely [ˈskweəlɪ] *adv (directly)* directamente, de lleno

squash¹ [skwɒʃ] **1** *n Br (drink)* concentrado *m*
    2 *vt* (**a**) *(crush)* aplastar (**b**) *Fig (objection)* echar por tierra
    3 *vi (crush)* aplastarse

squash² [skwɒʃ] *n Sport* squash *m*

squash³ [skwɒʃ] *n US (vegetable)* calabacín *m*

squat [skwɒt] **1** *adj (person)* rechoncho(a)
    2 *vi* (**a**) *(crouch)* agacharse, sentarse en cuclillas (**b**) *(in building)* ocupar ilegalmente
    3 *n (building)* edificio *m* ocupado ilegalmente

squatter [ˈskwɒtə(r)] *n* ocupante *mf* ilegal, okupa *mf*

squawk [skwɔːk] **1** *n* graznido *m*
    2 *vi* graznar

squeak [skwiːk] **1** *n (of mouse)* chillido *m*; *(of hinge, wheel)* chirrido *m*; *(of shoes)* crujido *m*
    2 *vi (mouse)* chillar; *(hinge, wheel)* chirriar, rechinar; *(shoes)* crujir

squeaky [ˈskwiːkɪ] *adj* (**squeakier, squeakiest**) chirriante; *(voice)* chillón(ona); *(shoes)* que crujen

squeal [skwiːl] **1** *n (of animal, person)* chilli-do *m*
    2 *vi* (**a**) *(animal, person)* chillar (**b**) *Fam (inform)* chivarse

squeamish [ˈskwiːmɪʃ] *adj* muy sensible

squeeze [skwiːz] **1** *vt* apretar; *(lemon etc)* exprimir; *(sponge)* estrujar; **to s. paste out of a tube** sacar pasta de un tubo apretando
    2 *vi* **to s. in** apretujarse
    3 *n* (**a**) *(pressure)* estrujón *m*; **a s. of lemon** unas gotas de limón (**b**) *(of hand)* apretón *m*; *(hug)* abrazo *m*; *(crush)* apiñamiento *m*; **credit s.** reducción *f* de créditos

squelch [skweltʃ] *vi* chapotear

squid [skwɪd] *n* calamar *m*; *(small)* chipirón *m*

squiggle ['skwɪgəl] *n* garabato *m*

squint [skwɪnt] **1** *n* (**a**) bizquera *f*; **to have a s.** ser bizco(a) (**b**) *Fig (quick look)* vistazo *m*

  2 *vi* (**a**) ser bizco(a) (**b**) **to s. at sth** *(glance)* echar un vistazo a algo; *(with eyes half-closed)* mirar algo con los ojos entrecerrados

squirm [skwɜːm] *vi* retorcerse; *Fig (feel embarrassed)* sentirse incómodo(a)

squirrel ['skwɪrəl] *n* ardilla *f*

squirt [skwɜːt] **1** *n (of liquid)* chorro *m*

  2 *vt* lanzar a chorro

  3 *vi* **to s. out** salir a chorros

Sr (*abbr* **Senior**)Thomas Smith, Sr Thomas Smith, padre

Sri Lanka [sriːˈlæŋkə] *n* Sri Lanka

St (**a**) (*abbr* **Saint**) S./Sto./Sta. (**b**) (*abbr* **Street**) c/

st *Br* (*abbr* **stone**) = peso que equivale a 6,348 kg

stab [stæb] **1** *n (with knife)* puñalada *f*; *(of pain)* punzada *f*; *Fam Fig* **to have a s. at doing sth** intentar hacer algo

  2 *vt* apuñalar

stabbing ['stæbɪŋ] *adj (pain)* punzante

stability [stəˈbɪlɪtɪ] *n* estabilidad *f*

stable¹ ['steɪbəl] *adj* estable

stable² ['steɪbəl] *n* cuadra *f*, caballeriza *f*

stack [stæk] **1** *n (pile)* montón *m*; *Fam* **he's got stacks of money** está forrado

  2 *vt (pile up)* amontonar, apilar; *Fig* **the odds are stacked against us** todo está en contra nuestra

stadium ['steɪdɪəm] *n* estadio *m*

staff [stɑːf] **1** *n* (**a**) *(personnel)* personal *m*; *Mil* estado *m* mayor; **s. meeting** claustro *m*; *Br* **s. nurse** enfermera cualificada (**b**) *(stick)* bastón *m*; *(of shepherd)* cayado *m*

  2 *vt* proveer de personal

staffroom ['stɑːfruːm] *n* sala *f* de profesores

stag [stæg] *n* ciervo *m*, venado *m*; *Fam* **s. party** despedida *f* de soltero

stage [steɪdʒ] **1** *n* (**a**) *(platform)* plataforma *f* (**b**) *(in theatre)* escenario *m*; **s. door** entrada *f* de artistas; **s. fright** miedo escénico; **s. manager** director(a) *m,f* de escena (**c**) *(phase) (of development, journey, rocket)* etapa *f*; *(of road, pipeline)* tramo *m*; **at this s. of the negotiations** a estas alturas de las negociaciones; **in stages** por etapas

  2 *vt* (**a**) *(play)* poner en escena, montar (**b**) *(arrange)* organizar; *(carry out)* llevar a cabo

stagecoach ['steɪdʒkəʊtʃ] *n* diligencia *f*

stagger ['stægə(r)] **1** *vi* tambalearse

  2 *vt* (**a**) *(amaze)* asombrar (**b**) *(hours, work)* escalonar

staggering ['stægərɪŋ] *adj* asombroso(a)

stagnant ['stægnənt] *adj* estancado(a)

stagnate [stægˈneɪt] *vi* estancarse

staid [steɪd] *adj (person)* conservador(a); *(manner, clothes)* serio(a), formal

stain [steɪn] **1** *n* (**a**) mancha *f*; **s. remover** quitamanchas *m inv* (**b**) *(dye)* tinte *m*

  2 *vt* (**a**) manchar (**b**) *(dye)* teñir

  3 *vi* mancharse

stained [steɪnd] *adj* **s. glass window** vidriera *f* de colores

stainless ['steɪnlɪs] *adj (steel)* inoxidable

stair [steə(r)] *n* escalón *m*, peldaño *m*; **stairs** escalera *f*

staircase ['steəkeɪs] *n* escalera *f*

stake¹ [steɪk] **1** *n (stick)* estaca *f*; *(for plant)* rodrigón *m*; *(post)* poste *m*

  2 *vt* **to s. (out)** cercar con estacas

stake² [steɪk] **1** *n* (**a**) *(bet)* apuesta *f*; **the issue at s.** el tema en cuestión; **to be at s.** *(at risk)* estar en juego (**b**) *(investment)* interés *m*

  2 *vt (bet)* apostar; *(invest)* invertir; **to s. a claim to sth** reivindicar algo

stale [steɪl] *adj (food)* pasado(a); *(bread)* duro(a)

stalemate ['steɪlmeɪt] *n (in chess)* tablas *fpl*; *Fig* **to reach s.** llegar a un punto muerto

stalk¹ [stɔːk] *n (of plant)* tallo *m*; *(of fruit)* rabo *m*

stalk² [stɔːk] **1** *vt (of hunter)* cazar al acecho; *(of animal)* acechar

  2 *vi* **he stalked out** salió airado

stall¹ [stɔːl] **1** *n* (**a**) *(in market)* puesto *m*; *(at fair)* caseta *f* (**b**) *(stable)* establo *m*; *(stable compartment)* casilla *f* de establo (**c**) *BrTh* **stalls** platea *f*

  2 *vt Aut* calar

  3 *vi Aut* calarse; *Av* perder velocidad

stall² [stɔːl] *vi* **to s. (for time)** intentar ganar tiempo

stallion ['stæljən] *n* semental *m*

stalwart ['stɔːlwət] *n* incondicional *mf*

stamina ['stæmɪnə] *n* resistencia *f*

stammer ['stæmə(r)] **1** *n* tartamudeo *m*

  2 *vi* tartamudear

stamp [stæmp] **1** *n* (**a**) *(postage stamp)* sello *m*; **s. album** álbum *m* de sellos; **s. collector** filatelista *mf*; *Br* **s. duty** póliza *f* (**b**) *(rubber stamp)* tampón *m*; *(for metals)* cuño *m* (**c**) *(with foot)* patada *f*

  2 *vt* (**a**) *(with postage stamp)* poner el sello a; *Br* **stamped addressed envelope,**

US **self-addressed stamped envelope** sobre franqueado con la dirección del remitente (**b**) *(with rubber stamp)* sellar (**c**) **to s. one's feet** patear; *(in dancing)* zapatear

3 *vi* patear

🖉 Note that the Spanish word **estampa** is a false friend and is never a translation for the English word **stamp**. In Spanish, **estampa** means "print, image".

▸ **stamp out** *vt sep Fig (racism etc)* acabar con; *(rebellion)* sofocar

stampede [stæm'piːd] **1** *n* estampida *f*; *Fig (rush)* desbandada *f*

2 *vi* desbandarse; *Fig (rush)* precipitarse

stance [stæns] *n* postura *f*

stand [stænd] **1** *n* (**a**) *(position)* posición *f*, postura *f*; **to make a s.** resistir

(**b**) *(of lamp, sculpture)* pie *m*

(**c**) *(market stall)* puesto *m*; *(at fair)* caseta *f*; *(at exhibition)* stand *m*; **newspaper s.** quiosco *m*

(**d**) *(platform)* plataforma *f*, *(in stadium)* tribuna *f*, *US (witness box)* estrado *m*

2 *vt (pt & pp* **stood**) (**a**) *(place)* poner, colocar

(**b**) *(tolerate)* aguantar, soportar

(**c**) **to s. one's ground** mantenerse firme

3 *vi* (**a**) *(be upright)* estar de pie; *(get up)* levantarse; *(remain upright)* quedarse de pie; **s. still!** ¡estáte quieto(a)!

(**b**) *(measure)* medir

(**c**) *(be situated)* estar, encontrarse

(**d**) *(remain unchanged)* permanecer

(**e**) *(remain valid)* seguir vigente

(**f**) **as things s.** tal como están las cosas

(**g**) *Pol* presentarse

▸ **stand back** *vi (allow sb to pass)* abrir paso

▸ **stand by 1** *vi* (**a**) *(do nothing)* quedarse sin hacer nada (**b**) *(be ready)* estar listo(a)

2 *vt insep (person)* apoyar a; *(promise)* cumplir con; *(decision)* atenerse a

▸ **stand down** *vi Fig* retirarse

▸ **stand for** *vt insep* (**a**) *(mean)* significar (**b**) *(represent)* representar (**c**) *(tolerate)* aguantar

▸ **stand in** *vi* sustituir

▸ **stand in for** *vt insep* sustituir

▸ **stand out** *vi (mountain etc)* destacarse (**against** contra); *Fig (person)* destacar

▸ **stand up** *vi (get up)* ponerse de pie; *(be standing)* estar de pie; *Fig* **it will s. up to wear and tear** es muy resistente; *Fig* **to s. up for sb** defender a algn; *Fig* **to s. up to sb** hacer frente a algn

standard ['stændəd] **1** *n* (**a**) *(level)* nivel *m*; **s. of living** nivel de vida (**b**) *(criterion)* criterio *m* (**c**) *(norm)* norma *f*, estándar *m* (**d**) *(flag)* estandarte *m*

2 *adj* normal, estándar; **s. lamp** lámpara *f* de pie

standardize ['stændədaɪz] *vt* normalizar

standby ['stændbaɪ] *n* (**a**) *(thing)* recurso *m* (**b**) *(person)* suplente *mf*; **to be on s.** *Mil* estar de retén; *Av* estar en la lista de espera; **s. ticket** billete *m* sin reserva

stand-in ['stændɪn] *n* suplente *mf*; *Cin* doble *mf*

standing ['stændɪŋ] **1** *adj* (**a**) *(not sitting)* de pie; *(upright)* recto(a); **to give sb a s. ovation** ovacionar a algn de pie; **there was s. room only** no quedaban asientos (**b**) *(committee)* permanente; *(invitation)* permanente; *Br* **s. order** pago fijo

2 *n* (**a**) *(social position)* rango *m* (**b**) *(duration)* duración *f*; *(in job)* antigüedad *f*

stand-offish [stænd'ɒfɪʃ] *adj Fam* distante

standpoint ['stændpɔɪnt] *n* punto *m* de vista

standstill ['stændstɪl] *n* **at a s.** *(car, traffic)* parado(a); *(industry)* paralizado(a); **to come to a s.** *(car, traffic)* pararse; *(industry)* paralizarse

stand-up ['stændʌp] *adj* **s. comic** *or* **comedian** = humorista que basa su actuación en contar chistes al público solo desde el escenario

stank [stæŋk] *pt of* **stink**

staple¹ ['steɪpəl] **1** *n (fastener)* grapa *f*

2 *vt* grapar

staple² ['steɪpəl] **1** *adj (food)* básico(a); *(product)* de primera necesidad

2 *n (food)* alimento básico

stapler ['steɪpələ(r)] *n* grapadora *f*

star [stɑː(r)] **1** *n* estrella *f*

2 *adj* estelar

3 *vt Cin* tener como protagonista a

4 *vi Cin* **to s. in a film** protagonizar una película

starboard ['stɑːbəd] *n* estribor *m*

starch [stɑːtʃ] **1** *n* almidón *m*

2 *vt* almidonar

stardom ['stɑːdəm] *n* estrellato *m*

stare [steə(r)] **1** *n* mirada fija

2 *vi* mirar fijamente

starfish ['stɑːfɪʃ] *n* estrella *f* de mar

stark [stɑːk] *adj (landscape)* desolado(a); *(décor)* austero(a); **the s. truth** la dura realidad; **s. poverty** la miseria

stark-naked ['stɑːkneɪkɪd] *adj Fam* en cueros

starling ['stɑːlɪŋ] *n* estornino *m*

starry ['stɑːrɪ] *adj* (**starrier, starriest**) estrellado(a)

starry-eyed [stɑːrɪ'aɪd] *adj (idealistic)* idealista; *(in love)* enamorado(a)

start [stɑːt] **1** *n* (**a**) *(beginning)* principio *m*, comienzo *m*; *(of race)* salida *f*; **at the s.** al principio; **for a s.** para empezar; **from the s.** desde el principio; **to make a fresh s.** volver a empezar

(**b**) *(advantage)* ventaja *f*

(**c**) *(jump)* sobresalto *m*

2 *vt* (**a**) *(begin)* empezar, comenzar; **to s. doing sth** empezar a hacer algo

(**b**) *(cause)* causar, provocar

(**c**) *(found)* fundar; **to s. a business** montar un negocio

(**d**) *(set in motion)* arrancar

3 *vi* (**a**) *(begin)* empezar, comenzar; *(engine)* arrancar; **starting from Monday** a partir del lunes

(**b**) *(take fright)* asustarse, sobresaltarse

▶ **start off** *vi* (**a**) *(begin)* empezar, comenzar; **to s. off by/with** empezar por/con

(**b**) *(leave)* salir, ponerse en camino

▶ **start up 1** *vt sep (engine)* arrancar

2 *vi* empezar; *(car)* arrancar

starter ['stɑːtə(r)] *n* (**a**) *Sport (official)* juez *mf* de salida; *(competitor)* competidor(a) *m,f* (**b**) *Aut* motor *m* de arranque (**c**) *Culin* entrada *f*

starting ['stɑːtɪŋ] *n* **s. block** taco *m* de salida; **s. point** punto *m* de partida; **s. post** línea *f* de salida

startle ['stɑːtəl] *vt* asustar

startling ['stɑːtlɪŋ] *adj* (**a**) *(frightening)* alarmante (**b**) *(news etc)* asombroso(a); *(coincidence)* extraordinario(a)

starvation [stɑː'veɪʃən] *n* hambre *f*

starve [stɑːv] **1** *vt* privar de comida; *Fig* **he was starved of affection** fue privado de cariño

2 *vi* pasar hambre; **to s. to death** morirse de hambre

starving ['stɑːvɪŋ] *adj* hambriento(a); *Fam* **I'm s.!** ¡estoy muerto(a) de hambre!

state [steɪt] **1** *n* (**a**) estado *m*; **s. of emergency** estado de emergencia; **s. of mind** estado de ánimo; **to be in no fit s. to do sth** no estar en condiciones de hacer algo (**b**) **the States** los Estados Unidos; *US* **s. highway** ≃ carretera *f* nacional; *US* **the S. Department** el Ministerio de Asuntos Exteriores

2 *adj* (**a**) *Pol* estatal; **s. education** enseñanza pública; **s. ownership** propiedad *f* del Estado (**b**) *(ceremonial)* de gala; **s. visit** visita *f* oficial

3 *vt* declarar, afirmar; *(case)* exponer; *(problem)* plantear

stated ['steɪtɪd] *adj* indicado(a)

stately ['steɪtlɪ] *adj* (**statelier, stateliest**) majestuoso(a); **s. home** casa solariega

statement ['steɪtmənt] *n* (**a**) declaración *f*; **official s.** comunicado *m* oficial; *Jur* **to make a s.** prestar declaración (**b**) *Fin* **estado** *m* de cuenta; **monthly s.** balance *m* mensual

statesman ['steɪtsmən] *n* estadista *m*

static ['stætɪk] **1** *adj* estático(a)

2 *n Rad* ruido *m*

station ['steɪʃən] **1** *n* (**a**) estación *f*; *US* **s. wagon** camioneta *f* (**b**) *(position)* puesto *m* (**c**) *(social standing)* rango *m*

2 *vt (place)* colocar; *Mil* apostar

stationary ['steɪʃənərɪ] *adj (not moving)* inmóvil; *(unchanging)* estacionario(a)

stationer ['steɪʃənə(r)] *n* papelero(a) *m,f*; **s.'s (shop)** papelería *f*

stationery ['steɪʃənərɪ] *n (paper)* papel *m* de escribir; *(pens, ink etc)* artículos *mpl* de escritorio

stationmaster ['steɪʃənmɑːstə(r)] *n* jefe *m* de estación

statistic [stə'tɪstɪk] *n* estadística *f*

statistical [stə'tɪstɪkəl] *adj* estadístico(a)

statistics [stə'tɪstɪks] **1** *n sing (science)* estadística *f*

2 *npl (data)* estadísticas *fpl*

statue ['stætjuː] *n* estatua *f*

status ['steɪtəs] *n* estado *m*; **social s.** estatus *m*; **s. symbol** signo *m* de prestigio; **s. quo** status quo *m*

statute ['stætjuːt] *n* estatuto *m*

statutory ['stætjʊtərɪ] *adj* reglamentario(a); *(offence)* contemplado(a) por la ley; *(right)* legal; *(holiday)* oficial

staunch [stɔːntʃ] *adj* incondicional, acérrimo

stave [steɪv] *n Mus* pentagrama *m*

▶ **stave off** *vt sep (repel)* rechazar; *(avoid)* evitar; *(delay)* aplazar

stay¹ [steɪ] **1** *n* estancia *f*

2 *vi* (**a**) *(remain)* quedarse, permanecer (**b**) *(reside temporarily)* alojarse; **she's staying with us for a few days** ha venido a pasar unos días con nosotros

3 *vt Fig* **to s. the course** aguantar hasta el final; **staying power** resistencia *f*

▶ **stay in** *vi* quedarse en casa

▶ **stay on** *vi* quedarse

▶ **stay out** *vi* **to s. out all night** no volver a casa en toda la noche

▶ **stay up** *vi* no acostarse

stay² [steɪ] *n (rope)* estay *m*, viento *m*

stead [sted] *n* **in sb's s.** en lugar de algn; **to**

stand sb in good s. resultar muy útil a algn

steadfast ['stedfəst, 'stedfɑːst] *adj* firme

steadily ['stedɪlɪ] *adv (improve)* constantemente; *(walk)* con paso seguro; *(gaze)* fijamente; *(rain, work)* sin parar

steady ['stedɪ] **1** *adj* (**steadier, steadiest**) firme, seguro(a); *(gaze)* fijo(a); *(prices)* estable; *(demand, speed)* constante; *(pace)* regular; *(worker)* aplicado(a); **s. job** empleo fijo

2 *vt (table etc)* estabilizar; *(nerves)* calmar

3 *vi (market)* estabilizarse

steak [steɪk] *n* bistec *m*

steal [stiːl] *(pt* stole; *pp* stolen) **1** *vt* robar; **to s. a glance at sth** echar una mirada furtiva a algo; **to s. the show** llevarse todos los aplausos

2 *vi* (**a**) *(rob)* robar (**b**) *(move quietly)* moverse con sigilo; **to s. away** escabullirse

stealth [stelθ] *n* sigilo *m*

stealthily ['stelθɪlɪ] *adv* a hurtadillas

stealthy ['stelθɪ] *adj* (**stealthier, stealthiest**) sigiloso(a), furtivo(a)

steam [stiːm] **1** *n* vapor *m*; *Fam* **to let off s.** desahogarse; **s. engine** máquina *f* de vapor

2 *vt Culin* cocer al vapor

3 *vi (give off steam)* echar vapor; *(bowl of soup etc)* humear

▸ **steam up** *vi (window etc)* empañarse

steamer ['stiːmə(r)] *n Naut* vapor *m*

steamroller ['stiːmrəʊlə(r)] *n* apisonadora *f*

steamship ['stiːmʃɪp] *n* vapor *m*

steamy ['stiːmɪ] *adj* (**steamier, steamiest**) lleno(a) de vapor

steel [stiːl] **1** *n* acero *m*; **s. industry** industria siderúrgica

2 *vt Fig* **to s. oneself to do sth** armarse de valor para hacer algo

steelworks ['stiːlwɜːks] *npl* acería *f*

steep¹ [stiːp] *adj (hill etc)* empinado(a); *Fig (price, increase)* excesivo(a)

steep² [stiːp] *vt (washing)* remojar; *(food)* poner en remojo

steeple ['stiːpəl] *n* aguja *f*

steeplechase ['stiːpəltʃeɪs] *n* carrera *f* de obstáculos

steer [stɪə(r)] **1** *vt* dirigir; *(car)* conducir; *(ship)* gobernar

2 *vi (car)* conducirse; *Fig* **to s. clear of sth** evitar algo

steering ['stɪərɪŋ] *n* dirección *f*; **assisted s.** dirección asistida; **s. wheel** volante *m*

stem [stem] **1** *n* (**a**) *(of plant)* tallo *m*; *(of glass)* pie *m*; *(of pipe)* tubo *m* (**b**) *(of word)* raíz *f*

2 *vi* **to s. from** derivarse de

3 *vt (blood)* restañar; *(flood, attack)* contener

stench [stentʃ] *n* hedor *m*

stencil ['stensəl] *n* (**a**) *(for artwork etc)* plantilla *f* (**b**) *(for typing)* cliché *m*

step [step] **1** *n* (**a**) paso *m*; *(sound)* paso, pisada *f*; **s. by s.** poco a poco (**b**) *(measure)* medida *f*; **a s. in the right direction** un paso acertado (**c**) *(stair)* peldaño *m*, escalón *m* (**d**) **steps** escalera *f*

2 *vi* dar un paso; **s. this way, please** haga el favor de pasar por aquí; **to s. aside** apartarse

▸ **step down** *vi* dimitir

▸ **step forward** *vi (volunteer)* ofrecerse

▸ **step in** *vi* intervenir

▸ **step up** *vt sep* aumentar

stepbrother ['stepbrʌðə(r)] *n* hermanastro *m*

stepchild ['steptʃaɪld] *n* hijastro(a) *m,f*

stepdaughter ['stepdɔːtə(r)] *n* hijastra *f*

stepfather ['stepfɑːðə(r)] *n* padrastro *m*

stepladder ['steplædə(r)] *n* escalera *f* de tijera

stepmother ['stepmʌðə(r)] *n* madrastra *f*

stepping-stone ['stepɪŋstəʊn] *n* pasadera *f*; *Fig* trampolín *m*

stepsister ['stepsɪstə(r)] *n* hermanastra *f*

stepson ['stepsʌn] *n* hijastro *m*

stereo ['sterɪəʊ] **1** *n* estéreo *m*

2 *adj* estereo(fónico(a))

stereotype ['sterɪətaɪp] *n* estereotipo *m*

sterile ['steraɪl] *adj (barren)* estéril

sterilize ['sterɪlaɪz] *vt* esterilizar

sterling ['stɜːlɪŋ] **1** *n* libras *fpl* esterlinas; **s. silver** plata *f* de ley; **the pound s.** la libra esterlina

2 *adj (person, quality)* excelente

stern¹ [stɜːn] *adj (severe)* severo(a)

stern² [stɜːn] *n Naut* popa *f*

steroid ['sterɔɪd] *n* esteroide *m*

stethoscope ['steθəskəʊp] *n* estetoscopio *m*

stew [stjuː] **1** *n* estofado *m*, cocido *m*

2 *vt (meat)* guisar, estofar; *(fruit)* cocer

steward ['stjʊəd] *n (on estate)* administrador *m*; *(on ship)* camarero *m*; *(on plane)* auxiliar *m* de vuelo

stewardess ['stjʊədɪs] *n (on ship)* camarera *f*; *(on plane)* azafata *f*

stick¹ [stɪk] *n* (**a**) palo *m*; *(walking stick)* bastón *m*; *(of dynamite)* cartucho *m*; *Fam* **to give sb s.** dar caña a algn (**b**) *Fam* **to live in the sticks** vivir en el quinto pino

stick² [stɪk] **1** vt (pt & pp **stuck**) (**a**) (push) meter; (knife) clavar; **he stuck his head out of the window** asomó la cabeza por la ventana (**b**) Fam (put) meter (**c**) (with glue etc) pegar (**d**) Fam (tolerate) soportar, aguantar

2 vi (**a**) (become attached) pegarse (**b**) (window, drawer) atrancarse; (machine part) encasquillarse

► **stick at** vt insep perseverar en

► **stick by** vt insep (friend) ser fiel a; (promise) cumplir con

► **stick out 1** vi (project) sobresalir; (be noticeable) resaltar

2 vt sep (tongue) sacar; Fig **to s. one's neck out** jugarse el tipo

► **stick to** vt insep (principles) atenerse a

► **stick up 1** vi (project) sobresalir; (hair) ponerse de punta

2 vt sep (**a**) (poster) fijar (**b**) (hand etc) levantar

► **stick up for** vt insep defender

sticker ['stɪkə(r)] n (label) etiqueta adhesiva; (with slogan) pegatina f

sticking-plaster ['stɪkɪŋ'plɑːstə(r)] n Br tirita® f, Am curita f

stickler ['stɪklə(r)] n meticuloso(a) m,f; **to be a s. for detail** ser muy detallista

stick-up ['stɪkʌp] n US Fam atraco m, asalto m

sticky ['stɪkɪ] adj (**stickier, stickiest**) pegajoso(a); (label) engomado(a); (weather) bochornoso(a); Fam (situation) difícil

stiff [stɪf] **1** adj (**a**) rígido(a), tieso(a); (collar, lock) duro(a); (joint) entumecido(a); (machine part) atascado(a); **to have a s. neck** tener tortícolis (**b**) Fig (test) difícil; (punishment) severo(a); (price) excesivo(a); (drink) fuerte; (person) (unnatural) estirado(a)

2 n Fam (corpse) fiambre m

stiffen ['stɪfən] **1** vt (fabric) reforzar; (collar) almidonar; Fig (resistance) fortalecer

2 vi (person) ponerse tieso(a); (joints) entumecerse; Fig (resistance) fortalecerse

stiffness ['stɪfnɪs] n rigidez f

stifle ['staɪfəl] **1** vt sofocar; (yawn) reprimir

2 vi ahogarse, sofocarse

stifling ['staɪflɪŋ] adj sofocante, agobiante

stigma ['stɪgmə] n estigma m

stile [staɪl] n = escalones para pasar por encima de una valla

stiletto [stɪ'letəʊ] n zapato m con tacón de aguja

still¹ [stɪl] **1** adv (**a**) (up to this time) todavía, aún

(**b**) (with comp adj & adv) (even) aún; **s. colder** aún más frío

(**c**) (nonetheless) no obstante, con todo

(**d**) (however) sin embargo

(**e**) (motionless) quieto; **to stand s.** no moverse

2 adj (calm) tranquilo(a); (peaceful) sosegado(a); (silent) silencioso(a); (motionless) inmóvil

3 n Cin fotograma m; Art **s. life** naturaleza muerta

4 vt Fml (fears etc) calmar

still² [stɪl] n (apparatus) alambique m

stillborn ['stɪlbɔːn] adj nacido(a) muerto(a)

stillness ['stɪlnɪs] n calma f; (silence) silencio m

stilt [stɪlt] n zanco m

stilted ['stɪltɪd] adj afectado(a)

stimulant ['stɪmjʊlənt] n estimulante m

stimulate ['stɪmjʊleɪt] vt estimular

stimulating ['stɪmjʊleɪtɪŋ] adj estimulante

stimulus ['stɪmjʊləs] n (pl **stimuli** ['stɪmjʊlaɪ]) estímulo m; Fig incentivo m

sting [stɪŋ] **1** n (part of bee, wasp) aguijón m; (wound) picadura f; (burning) escozor m; Fig (of remorse) punzada f; Fig (of remark) sarcasmo m

2 vt (pt & pp **stung**) picar; Fig (conscience) remorder; Fig (remark) herir en lo vivo

3 vi picar

stingy ['stɪndʒɪ] adj (**stingier, stingiest**) Fam (person) tacaño(a); (amount) escaso(a); **to be s. with** escatimar

stink [stɪŋk] **1** n peste m, hedor m

2 vi (pt **stank** or **stunk**; pp **stunk**) apestar, heder (**of** a)

stinking ['stɪŋkɪŋ] **1** adj (smelly) apestoso(a); Fam **to have a s. cold** tener un catarro bestial

2 adv Fam **he's s. rich** está podrido de dinero

stint [stɪnt] **1** n (period) período m, temporada f; (shift) turno m; **he did a two-year s. in the navy** sirvió durante dos años en la Marina

2 vt escatimar

stipulate ['stɪpjʊleɪt] vt estipular

stipulation [stɪpjʊ'leɪʃən] n estipulación f

stir [stɜː(r)] **1** n Fig revuelo m

2 vt (**a**) (liquid) remover (**b**) (move) agitar (**c**) Fig (curiosity, interest) despertar; (anger) provocar

3 vi (move) rebullirse

▸ **stir up** *vt sep Fig (memories, curiosity)* despertar; *(passions)* excitar; *(anger)* provocar; *(revolt)* fomentar

stirring ['stɜːrɪŋ] *adj* conmovedor(a)

stirrup ['stɪrəp] *n* estribo *m*

stitch [stɪtʃ] **1** *n* (**a**) *Sewing* puntada *f*; *(in knitting)* punto *m*; *Med* punto (de sutura); *Fam* **we were in stitches** nos tronchábamos de risa (**b**) *(pain)* punzada *f*
2 *vt Sewing* coser; *Med* suturar, dar puntos a

stoat [stəʊt] *n* armiño *m*

stock [stɒk] **1** *n* (**a**) *(supply)* reserva *f*; *Com (goods)* existencias *fpl*, stock *m*; *(selection)* surtido *m*; **out of s.** agotado(a); **to have sth in s.** tener existencias de algo; *Fig* **to take s. of** evaluar (**b**) *Fin* capital *m* social; **stocks and shares** acciones *fpl*, valores *mpl*; **S. Exchange** Bolsa *f* (de valores); **s. market** bolsa (**c**) *Agr* ganado *m*; **s. farming** ganadería *f* (**d**) *Culin* caldo *m*; **s. cube** cubito *m* de caldo (**e**) *(descent)* estirpe *f*
2 *adj* (**a**) *(goods)* corriente (**b**) *(excuse, response)* de siempre; *(phrase)* gastado(a)
3 *vt* (**a**) *(have in stock)* tener existencias de (**b**) *(provide)* abastecer, surtir (**with** de); *(cupboard)* llenar (**with** de)

▸ **stock up** *vi* abastecerse (**on** *or* **with** de)

stockbroker ['stɒkbrəʊkə(r)] *n* corredor(a) *m,f* de Bolsa

stockholder ['stɒkhəʊldə(r)] *n US* accionista *mf*

stocking ['stɒkɪŋ] *n* media *f*; **a pair of stockings** unas medias

stockist ['stɒkɪst] *n* distribuidor(a) *m,f*

stockpile ['stɒkpaɪl] **1** *n* reservas *fpl*
2 *vt* almacenar; *(accumulate)* acumular

stocks [stɒks] *npl Hist* cepo *m*

stocktaking ['stɒkteɪkɪŋ] *n Com* inventario *m*

stocky ['stɒkɪ] *adj* (**stockier, stockiest**) *(squat)* rechoncho(a); *(heavily built)* fornido(a)

stodgy ['stɒdʒɪ] *adj* (**stodgier, stodgiest**) *(food)* indigesto(a); *Fig (book, person)* pesado(a)

stoical ['stəʊɪkəl] *adj* estoico(a)

stoke [stəʊk] *vt (poke)* atizar; **to s. (up)** *(feed)* alimentar

stole¹ [stəʊl] *pt of* **steal**

stole² [stəʊl] *n* estola *f*

stolen ['stəʊlən] *pp of* **steal**

stolid ['stɒlɪd] *adj* impasible

stomach ['stʌmək] **1** *n* estómago *m*; **s. ache** dolor *m* de estómago; **s. upset** trastorno gástrico
2 *vt Fig* aguantar

stone [stəʊn] **1** *n* (**a**) piedra *f*; *(on grave)* lápida *f*; *Fig* **at a s.'s throw** a tiro de piedra (**b**) *Med* cálculo *m* (**c**) *(of fruit)* hueso *m* (**d**) *(weight)* = 6,348 kg
2 *adj* de piedra; **the S. Age** la Edad de Piedra
3 *vt (kill)* lapidar

stone-cold [stəʊn'kəʊld] *adj* helado(a)

stoned [stəʊnd] *adj Fam (drugged)* colocado(a); *(drunk)* como una cuba

stone-deaf [stəʊn'def] *adj* sordo(a) como una tapia

stonework ['stəʊnwɜːk] *n* mampostería *f*

stony ['stəʊnɪ] *adj* (**stonier, stoniest**) *(ground)* pedregoso(a); *Fig (look, silence)* glacial

stood [stʊd] *pt & pp of* **stand**

stool [stuːl] *n* (**a**) *(seat)* taburete *m* (**b**) *Med* heces *fpl*

stoop [stuːp] *vi* (**a**) *(have a stoop)* andar encorvado(a) (**b**) *(bend)* **to s. down** inclinarse, agacharse (**c**) *Fig* **to s. to** rebajarse a; **he wouldn't s. so low** no se rebajaría tanto

stop [stɒp] **1** *n* (**a**) *(halt)* parada *f*, alto *m*; **to come to a s.** pararse; **to put a s. to sth** poner fin a algo (**b**) *(break)* pausa *f*; *(for refuelling etc)* escala *f* (**c**) *(for bus, tram)* parada *f* (**d**) *(punctuation mark)* punto *m*
2 *vt* (**a**) parar; *(conversation)* interrumpir; *(pain, abuse etc)* poner fin a (**b**) *(payments)* suspender; *(cheque)* anular (**c**) **to s. doing sth** dejar de hacer algo; **s. singing** deja de cantar; **s. it!** ¡basta ya! (**d**) *(prevent)* evitar; **to s. sb from doing sth** impedir a algn hacer algo (**e**) *(hole)* tapar; *(gap)* rellenar
3 *vi* (**a**) *(person, moving vehicle)* pararse, detenerse; **my watch has stopped** se me ha parado el reloj; **to s. dead** pararse en seco (**b**) *(cease)* acabarse, terminar (**c**) *Fam (stay)* pararse

▸ **stop by** *vi Fam* visitar

▸ **stop off** *vi* pararse un rato

▸ **stop over** *vi (spend the night)* pasar la noche; *(for refuelling etc)* hacer escala

▸ **stop up** *vt sep (hole)* tapar

stopgap ['stɒpgæp] *n (thing)* medida *f* provisional; *(person)* sustituto(a) *m,f*

stopover ['stɒpəʊvə(r)] *n* parada *f*; *Av* escala *f*

stoppage ['stɒpɪdʒ] *n* (**a**) *(of game, payments)* suspensión *f*; *(of work)* paro *m*; *(strike)* huelga *f*; *(deduction)* deducción *f* (**b**) *(blockage)* obstrucción *f*

stopper ['stɒpə(r)] *n* tapón *m*

stop-press [stɒp'pres] *n* noticias *fpl* de última hora

stopwatch ['stɒpwɒtʃ] *n* cronómetro *m*

storage ['stɔːrɪdʒ] *n* almacenaje *m*, almacenamiento *m*; **s. battery** acumulador *m*; **s. heater** placa acumuladora

store [stɔː(r)] **1** *n* (**a**) *(stock)* provisión *f*; *Fig (of wisdom)* reserva *f* (**b**) **stores** víveres *mpl* (**c**) *(warehouse)* almacén *m* (**d**) *esp US (shop)* tienda *f*; **department s.** gran almacén *m*
2 *vt* (**a**) *(furniture, computer data)* almacenar; *(keep)* guardar (**b**) **to s. (up)** acumular

storekeeper ['stɔːkiːpə(r)] *n US* tendero(a) *m,f*

storeroom ['stɔːruːm] *n* despensa *f*

storey ['stɔːrɪ] *n* piso *m*

stork [stɔːk] *n* cigüeña *f*

storm [stɔːm] **1** *n* tormenta *f*; *(with wind)* vendaval *m*; *Fig (uproar)* revuelo *m*; *Fig* **she has taken New York by s.** ha cautivado a todo Nueva York
2 *vt* tomar por asalto
3 *vi (with rage)* echar pestes

stormy ['stɔːmɪ] *adj* (**stormier, stormiest**) *(weather)* tormentoso(a); *Fig (discussion)* acalorado(a); *(relationship)* tempestuoso(a)

story¹ ['stɔːrɪ] *n* historia *f*; *(tale, account)* relato *m*; *(article)* artículo *m*; *(plot)* trama *f*; *(joke)* chiste *m*; *(rumour)* rumor *m*; **it's a long s.** sería largo de contar; **tall s.** cuento chino

story² ['stɔːrɪ] *n US* = **storey**

storybook ['stɔːrɪbʊk] *n* libro *m* de cuentos

storyteller ['stɔːrɪtelə(r)] *n* cuentista *mf*

stout [staʊt] **1** *adj* (**a**) *(fat)* gordo(a), corpulento(a) (**b**) *(strong)* fuerte (**c**) *(brave)* valiente; *(determined)* firme
2 *n (beer)* cerveza negra

stoutly ['staʊtlɪ] *adv* resueltamente

stove [stəʊv] *n* (**a**) *(for heating)* estufa *f* (**b**) *(cooker)* cocina *f*

stow [stəʊ] *vt* (**a**) *(cargo)* estibar (**b**) *(put away)* guardar
▶ **stow away** *vi (on ship, plane)* viajar de polizón

stowaway ['stəʊəweɪ] *n* polizón *mf*

straddle ['strædəl] *vt* (**a**) *(horse etc)* sentarse a horcajadas sobre (**b**) *Fig (embrace)* abarcar

straggle ['strægəl] *vi* (**a**) *(lag behind)* rezagarse (**b**) *(spread untidily)* desparramarse

straggler ['stræglə(r)] *n* rezagado(a) *m,f*

straight [streɪt] **1** *adj* (**a**) *(not bent)* recto(a), derecho(a); *(hair)* liso(a); **to keep a s. face** contener la risa
(**b**) **I work eight hours s.** trabajo ocho horas seguidas
(**c**) *(honest)* honrado(a); *(answer)* sincero(a); *(refusal)* rotundo(a); **let's get things s.** pongamos las cosas claras
(**d**) *(drink)* solo(a), sin mezcla
2 *adv* (**a**) *(in a straight line)* en línea recta
(**b**) *(directly)* directamente, derecho; **keep s. ahead** sigue todo recto; **she walked s. in** entró sin llamar
(**c**) **s. away** en seguida; **s. off** en el acto
(**d**) *(frankly)* francamente
3 *n Br Sport* **the home s.** la recta final

straighten ['streɪtən] *vt (sth bent)* enderezar, poner derecho(a); *(tie, picture)* poner bien; *(hair)* alisar
▶ **straighten out** *vt sep (problem)* resolver

straight-faced ['streɪt'feɪst] *adj* con la cara seria

straightforward [streɪt'fɔːwəd] *adj* (**a**) *(honest)* honrado(a); *(sincere)* franco(a) (**b**) *Br (simple)* sencillo(a)

strain¹ [streɪn] **1** *vt* (**a**) *(rope etc)* estirar; *Fig* crear tensiones en (**b**) *Med* torcer(se); *(eyes, voice)* forzar; *(heart)* cansar (**c**) *(liquid)* filtrar; *(vegetables, tea)* colar
2 *vi (pull)* tirar (**at** de); *Fig* **to s. to do sth** esforzarse por hacer algo
3 *n* (**a**) tensión *f*; *(effort)* esfuerzo *m* (**b**) *(exhaustion)* agotamiento *m* (**c**) *Med* torcedura *f* (**d**) *Mus* **strains** son *m*

strain² [streɪn] *n* (**a**) *(breed)* raza *f* (**b**) *(streak)* vena *f*

strained ['streɪnd] *adj* (**a**) *(muscle)* torcido(a); *(eyes)* cansado(a); *(voice)* forzado(a) (**b**) *(atmosphere)* tenso(a)

strainer ['streɪnə(r)] *n* colador *m*

strait [streɪt] *n* (**a**) *Geog* estrecho *m* (**b**) *(usu pl) (difficulty)* aprieto *m*; **in dire straits** en un gran aprieto

straitjacket ['streɪtdʒækɪt] *n* camisa *f* de fuerza

strait-laced [streɪt'leɪst] *adj* remilgado(a)

strand¹ [strænd] *vt Fig (person)* abandonar; **to leave stranded** dejar plantado(a)

strand² [strænd] *n (of thread)* hebra *f*; *(of hair)* pelo *m*

strange [streɪndʒ] *adj* (**a**) *(unknown)* desconocido(a); *(unfamiliar)* nuevo(a) (**b**) *(odd)* raro(a), extraño(a)

stranger ['streɪndʒə(r)] *n (unknown person)* desconocido(a) *m,f*; *(outsider)* forastero(a) *m,f*

strangle ['stræŋgəl] *vt* estrangular

stranglehold ['stræŋgəlhəʊld] *n* **to have a s. on sb** tener a algn agarrado(a) por el cuello

strangulation [stræŋgjʊ'leɪʃən] *n* estrangulación *f*

strap [stræp] **1** *n (of leather)* correa *f*; *(on bag)* bandolera *f*; *(on dress)* tirante *m*
2 *vt* atar con correa

strapping ['stræpɪŋ] *adj Fam* fornido(a), robusto(a)

strata ['strɒːtə] *pl of* **stratum**

strategic [strə'tiːdʒɪk] *adj* estratégico(a)

strategy ['strætɪdʒɪ] *n* estrategia *f*

stratosphere ['strætəsfɪə(r)] *n* estratosfera *f*

stratum ['strɒːtəm] *n (pl* **strata**) estrato *m*

straw [strɔː] *n* (**a**) paja *f*; *Fig* **to clutch at straws** agarrarse a un clavo ardiente; *Fam* **that's the last s.!** ¡eso ya es el colmo! (**b**) *(for drinking)* pajita *f*

strawberry ['strɔːbərɪ] *n* fresa *f*, *Bol, CSur, Ecuad* frutilla *f*; *(large)* fresón *m*

stray [streɪ] **1** *vi (from path)* desviarse; *(get lost)* extraviarse
2 *n* animal extraviado
3 *adj (bullet)* perdido(a); *(animal)* callejero(a)

streak [striːk] **1** *n* (**a**) *(line)* raya *f*; **s. of lightning** rayo *m* (**b**) *(in hair)* reflejo *m* (**c**) *Fig (of genius etc)* vena *f*; *Fig (of luck)* racha *f*
2 *vt* rayar (**with** de)
3 *vi* **to s. past** pasar como un rayo

stream [striːm] **1** *n* (**a**) *(brook)* arroyo *m*, riachuelo *m* (**b**) *(current)* corriente *f* (**c**) *(of water, air)* flujo *m*; *(of tears)* torrente *m*; *(of blood)* chorro *m*; *(of light)* raudal *m* (**d**) *Fig (of abuse)* sarta *f*; *(of people)* oleada *f* (**e**) *Br Educ* clase *f*
2 *vt Br Educ* poner en grupos
3 *vi* (**a**) *(liquid)* correr (**b**) *Fig* **to s. in/out/past** *(people etc)* entrar/salir/pasar en tropel (**c**) *(hair, banner)* ondear

streamer ['striːmə(r)] *n (paper ribbon)* serpentina *f*

streamlined ['striːmlaɪnd] *adj* (**a**) *(car)* aerodinámico(a) (**b**) *(system, method)* racionalizado(a)

street [striːt] *n* calle *f*; **the man in the s.** el hombre de la calle; **s. map, s. plan** (plano *m*) callejero *m*

streetcar ['striːtkɑː(r)] *n US* tranvía *m*

streetlamp ['striːtlæmp] *n* farol *m*

streetwise ['striːtwaɪz] *adj* espabilado(a)

strength [streŋθ] *n* (**a**) fuerza *f*; *(of rope etc)* resistencia *f*; *(of emotion, colour)* intensidad *f*; *(of alcohol)* graduación *f* (**b**) *(power)* poder *m*; **on the s. of** a base de (**c**) *(ability)* punto *m* fuerte (**d**) **to be at full s./below s.** tener/no tener completo el cupo

strengthen ['streŋθən] **1** *vt* (**a**) reforzar; *(character)* fortalecer (**b**) *(intensify)* intensificar
2 *vi* (**a**) *(gen)* reforzarse (**b**) *(intensify)* intensificarse

strenuous ['strenjʊəs] *adj* (**a**) *(denial)* enérgico(a); *(effort, life)* intenso(a) (**b**) *(exhausting)* fatigoso(a), cansado(a)

stress [stres] **1** *n* (**a**) *Tech* tensión *f* (**b**) *Med* estrés *m* (**c**) *(emphasis)* hincapié *m*; *(on word)* acento *m*
2 *vt (emphasize)* subrayar; *(word)* acentuar

stretch [stretʃ] **1** *vt (elastic)* estirar; *(wings)* desplegar
2 *vi (elastic)* estirarse; *Fig* **my money won't s. to it** mi dinero no me llegará para eso
3 *n* (**a**) *(length)* trecho *m*, tramo *m* (**b**) *(of land)* extensión *f*; *(of time)* intervalo *m*

> 🖉 Note that the Spanish verb **estrechar** is a false friend and is never a translation for the English verb **to stretch**. In Spanish, **estrechar** means "to make narrow, to tighten".

▸ **stretch out 1** *vt sep (arm, hand)* alargar; *(legs)* estirar
2 *vi* (**a**) *(person)* estirarse (**b**) *(countryside, years etc)* extenderse

stretcher ['stretʃə(r)] *n* camilla *f*

strew [struː] *vt (pt* **strewed**; *pp* **strewed** *or* **strewn** [struːn]) esparcir

stricken ['strɪkən] *adj (with grief)* afligido(a); *(with illness)* aquejado(a); *(by disaster etc)* afectado(a); *(damaged)* dañado(a)

strict [strɪkt] *adj* (**a**) estricto(a) (**b**) *(absolute)* absoluto(a)

strictly ['strɪktlɪ] *adv* (**a**) *(categorically)* terminantemente (**b**) *(precisely)* estrictamente; **s. speaking** en sentido estricto

stride [straɪd] **1** *n* zancada *f*, tranco *m*; *Fig (progress)* progresos *mpl*
2 *vi (pt* **strode**; *pp* **stridden** ['strɪdən]) **to s. (along)** andar a zancadas

strident ['straɪdənt] *adj (voice, sound)*

estridente; *(protest etc)* enérgico(a)

strife [straɪf] *n* conflictos *mpl*

strike [straɪk] **1** *vt* (*pt & pp* **struck**) (**a**) *(hit)* pegar, golpear

(**b**) *(collide with)* chocar contra; *(of bullet, lightning)* alcanzar

(**c**) *(match)* encender

(**d**) *(pose)* adoptar

(**e**) *(bargain)* cerrar; *(balance)* encontrar

(**f**) **the clock struck three** el reloj dio las tres

(**g**) *(oil, gold)* descubrir; *Fam* **to s. it lucky/rich** tener suerte/hacerse rico(a)

(**h**) *(impress)* impresionar; **it strikes me ...** me parece ...

2 *vi* (**a**) *(attack)* atacar; *(disaster)* sobrevenir

(**b**) *(clock)* dar la hora

(**c**) *(workers)* declararse en huelga

3 *n* (**a**) *(by workers)* huelga *f*; **on s.** en huelga; **to call a s.** convocar una huelga

(**b**) *(of oil, gold)* descubrimiento *m*

(**c**) *(blow)* golpe *m*

(**d**) *Mil* ataque *m*

▸ **strike back** *vi* devolver el golpe

▸ **strike down** *vt sep* fulminar, abatir

▸ **strike out 1** *vt sep (cross out)* tachar

2 *vi* **to s. out at sb** arremeter contra algn

▸ **strike up** *vt insep* (**a**) *(friendship)* trabar; *(conversation)* entablar (**b**) *(tune)* empezar a tocar

striker ['straɪkə(r)] *n* (**a**) *(worker)* huelguista *mf* (**b**) *Fam Ftb* marcador(a) *m,f*

striking ['straɪkɪŋ] *adj (eye-catching)* llamativo(a); *(noticeable)* notable; *(impressive)* impresionante

string [strɪŋ] **1** *n* (**a**) *(cord)* cuerda *f*; *Fig* **to pull strings for sb** enchufar a algn; **s. bean** judía *f* verde, *Bol, RP* chaucha *f*, *CAm* ejote *m*, *Col, Cuba* habichuela *f*, *Chile* poroto *m* verde, *Ven* vainita *f* (**b**) *(of events)* cadena *f*; *(of lies)* sarta *f* (**c**) *(of racket, guitar)* cuerda *f*; *Mus* **the strings** los instrumentos de cuerda

2 *vt* (*pt & pp* **strung**) (**a**) *(beads)* ensartar (**b**) *(racket etc)* encordar (**c**) *(beans)* quitar la hebra a

stringent ['strɪndʒənt] *adj* severo(a), estricto(a)

strip¹ [strɪp] **1** *vt* (**a**) *(person)* desnudar; *(bed)* quitar la ropa de; *(paint)* quitar (**b**) *Tech* **to s. (down)** desmontar

2 *vi* *(undress)* desnudarse; *(perform striptease)* hacer un striptease

▸ **strip off 1** *vt sep* quitar

2 *vi* *(undress)* desnudarse

strip² [strɪp] *n* tira *f*; *(of land)* franja *f*; *(of*

metal) fleje *m*; **s. cartoon** historieta *f*; **s. lighting** alumbrado *m* fluorescente; **to tear sb off a s.** echar una bronca a algn

stripe [straɪp] *n* raya *f*; *Mil* galón *m*

striped [straɪpt] *adj* rayado(a), a rayas

stripper ['strɪpə(r)] *n* artista *mf* de striptease

strive [straɪv] *vi* (*pt* **strove**; *pp* **striven** ['strɪvən]) **to s. to do sth** esforzarse por hacer algo

strobe [strəʊb] *n* **s. lighting** luces estroboscópicas

strode [strəʊd] *pt of* **stride**

stroke [strəʊk] **1** *n* (**a**) **a s. of luck** un golpe de suerte (**b**) *(in golf, cricket)* golpe *m*; *(in rowing)* remada *f*; *(in swimming)* brazada *f* (**c**) *(of pen)* trazo *m*; *(of brush)* pincelada *f* (**d**) *(caress)* caricia *f* (**e**) *Med* apoplejía *f*

2 *vt* acariciar

stroll [strəʊl] **1** *vi* dar un paseo

2 *n* paseo *m*

stroller ['strəʊlə(r)] *n* *US (for baby)* cochecito *m*

strong [strɒŋ] **1** *adj* (**a**) fuerte (**b**) *(durable)* sólido(a) (**c**) *(firm, resolute)* firme (**d**) *(colour)* intenso(a); *(light)* brillante (**e**) *(incontestable)* convincente (**f**) **to be twenty s.** contar con veinte miembros

2 *adv* fuerte; **to be going s.** *(business)* ir fuerte; *(elderly person)* conservarse bien

strongbox ['strɒŋbɒks] *n* caja *f* fuerte

stronghold ['strɒŋhəʊld] *n* *Mil* fortaleza *f*; *Fig* baluarte *m*

strongly ['strɒŋlɪ] *adv* fuertemente

strongroom ['strɒŋruːm] *n* cámara acorazada

stroppy ['strɒpɪ] *adj* (**stroppier, stroppiest**) *Br Fam* de mala uva

strove [strəʊv] *pt of* **strive**

struck [strʌk] *pt & pp of* **strike**

structural ['strʌktʃərəl] *adj* estructural

structure ['strʌktʃə(r)] *n* estructura *f*; *(constructed thing)* construcción *f*; *(building)* edificio *m*

struggle ['strʌɡəl] **1** *vi* luchar

2 *n* lucha *f*; *(physical fight)* pelea *f*

strum [strʌm] *vt (guitar)* rasguear

strung [strʌŋ] *pt & pp of* **string**

strut [strʌt] *vi* pavonearse

stub [stʌb] **1** *n* *(of cigarette)* colilla *f*; *(of pencil)* cabo *m*; *(of cheque)* matriz *f*

2 *vt* (**a**) *(strike)* golpear (**b**) **to s. (out)** apagar

stubble ['stʌbəl] *n* *(in field)* rastrojo *m*; *(on chin)* barba *f* de tres días

stubborn ['stʌbən] *adj* (**a**) terco(a),

testarudo(a) (**b**) *(stain)* difícil (**c**) *(refusal)* rotundo(a)

stucco ['stʌkəʊ] *n* estuco *m*

stuck [stʌk] *pt & pp of* **stick**

stuck-up [stʌk'ʌp] *adj Fam* creído(a)

stud¹ [stʌd] **1** *n (on clothing)* tachón *m*; *(on football boots)* taco *m*; *(on shirt)* botonadura *f*

  2 *vt (decorate)* tachonar (**with** de); *Fig (dot, cover)* salpicar (**with** de)

stud² [stʌd] *n (horse)* semental *m*

student ['stju:dənt] *n* estudiante *mf*; **s. teacher** profesor(a) *m,f* en prácticas

studio ['stju:dɪəʊ] *n TV & Cin* estudio *m*; *(artist's)* taller *m*; **s. (apartment** *or Br* **flat)** estudio

studious ['stju:dɪəs] *adj* estudioso(a)

studiously ['stju:dɪəslɪ] *adv* cuidadosamente

study ['stʌdɪ] **1** *vt* estudiar; *(facts etc)* examinar, investigar; *(behaviour)* observar

  2 *vi* estudiar; **to s. to be a doctor** estudiar para médico

  3 *n* (**a**) estudio *m*; **s. group** grupo *m* de trabajo (**b**) *(room)* despacho *m*, estudio *m*

stuff [stʌf] **1** *vt* (**a**) *(container)* llenar (**with** de); *Culin* rellenar (**with** con *or* de); *(animal)* disecar (**b**) *(cram)* atiborrar (**with** de)

  2 *n Fam* (**a**) *(substance)* cosa *f* (**b**) *(things)* cosas *fpl*

stuffing ['stʌfɪŋ] *n Culin* relleno *m*

stuffy ['stʌfɪ] *adj* (**stuffier, stuffiest**) (**a**) *(room)* mal ventilado(a); *(atmosphere)* cargado(a) (**b**) *(pompous)* estirado(a); *(narrow-minded)* de miras estrechas

stumble ['stʌmbəl] *vi* tropezar, dar un traspié; *Fig* **to s. across** *or* **on** *or* **upon** tropezar *or* dar con

stumbling ['stʌmblɪŋ] *n* **s. block** escollo *m*

stump [stʌmp] **1** *n* (**a**) *(of pencil)* cabo *m*; *(of tree)* tocón *m*; *(of arm, leg)* muñón *m* (**b**) *(in cricket)* estaca *f*

  2 *vt (puzzle)* confundir; **to be stumped** estar perplejo(a)

stun [stʌn] *vt (of blow)* aturdir; *Fig (of news etc)* sorprender

stung [stʌŋ] *pt & pp of* **sting**

stunk [stʌŋk] *pt & pp of* **stink**

stunning ['stʌnɪŋ] *adj (blow)* duro(a); *(news)* sorprendente; *Fam (woman, outfit)* fenomenal

stunt¹ [stʌnt] *vt (growth)* atrofiar

stunt² [stʌnt] *n* (**a**) *Av* acrobacia *f* (**b**) **publicity s.** truco publicitario (**c**) *Cin*

escena peligrosa; **s. man** doble *m*

stunted ['stʌntɪd] *adj* enano(a), mal desarrollado(a)

stupefy ['stju:pɪfaɪ] *vt (alcohol, drugs)* aturdir; *Fig (news etc)* dejar pasmado(a)

stupendous [stju:'pendəs] *adj (wonderful)* estupendo(a)

stupid ['stju:pɪd] *adj* estúpido(a), imbécil

stupidity [stju:'pɪdɪtɪ] *n* estupidez *f*

stupor ['stju:pə(r)] *n* estupor *m*

sturdy ['stɜ:dɪ] *adj* (**sturdier, sturdiest**) robusto(a), fuerte; *(resistance)* enérgico(a)

stutter ['stʌtə(r)] **1** *vi* tartamudear

  2 *n* tartamudeo *m*

sty [staɪ] *n (pen)* pocilga *f*

sty(e) [staɪ] *n Med* orzuelo *m*

style [staɪl] **1** *n* (**a**) estilo *m*; *(of dress)* modelo *m* (**b**) *(fashion)* moda *f* (**c**) **to live in s.** *(elegance)* vivir a lo grande

  2 *vt (hair)* marcar

stylish ['staɪlɪʃ] *adj* con estilo

stylist ['staɪlɪst] *n (hairdresser)* peluquero(a) *mf*

stylus ['staɪləs] *n (of record player)* aguja *f*

suave [swɑ:v] *adj* amable, afable; *Pej* zalamero(a)

> ℐ Note that the Spanish word **suave** is a false friend and is never a translation for the English word **suave**. In Spanish, **suave** means both "smooth" and "soft".

sub [sʌb] *n Fam* (**a**) *(to magazine)* suscripción *f*; *(to club)* cuota *f* (**b**) *(substitute)* suplente *mf*

sub- [sʌb] *pref* sub-

subconscious [sʌb'kɒnʃəs] **1** *adj* subconsciente

  2 *n* **the s.** el subconsciente

subcontract [sʌbkən'trækt] *vt* subcontratar

subcontractor [sʌbkən'træktə(r)] *n* subcontratista *mf*

subdivide [sʌbdɪ'vaɪd] *vt* subdividir (**into** en)

subdue [səb'dju:] *vt* (**a**) *(nation, people)* sojuzgar (**b**) *(feelings)* dominar (**c**) *(colour, light)* atenuar

subdued [səb'dju:d] *adj* (**a**) *(person, emotion)* callado(a) (**b**) *(voice, tone)* bajo(a) (**c**) *(light)* tenue; *(colour)* apagado(a)

subject ['sʌbdʒɪkt] **1** *n* (**a**) *(citizen)* súbdito *m* (**b**) *(topic)* tema *m*; **s. matter** materia *f*; *(contents)* contenido *m* (**c**) *Educ* asignatura *f* (**d**) *Ling* sujeto *m*

  2 *adj* **s. to** *(law, tax)* sujeto(a) a; *(charge)*

expuesto(a) a; *(changes, delays)* susceptible de; *(illness)* propenso(a) a; *(conditional upon)* previo(a)
3 *vt* [səb'dʒekt] someter
subjective [səb'dʒektɪv] *adj* subjetivo(a)
subjunctive [səb'dʒʌŋktɪv] **1** *adj* subjun-
tivo(a)
2 *n* subjuntivo *m*
sublet [sʌb'let] *vt & vi* subarrendar
sublime [sə'blaɪm] *adj* sublime
submachine-gun [sʌbmə'ʃiːngʌn] *n*
metralleta *f*
submarine ['sʌbməriːn] *n* submarino *m*
submerge [səb'mɜːdʒ] *vt* sumergir;
(flood) inundar; *Fig* **submerged in ...**
sumido(a) en ...
submission [səb'mɪʃən] *n* (**a**) *(yielding)*
sumisión *f* (**b**) *(of documents)* presentación *f* (**c**) *(report)* informe *m*
submissive [səb'mɪsɪv] *adj* sumiso(a)
submit [səb'mɪt] **1** *vt* (**a**) *(present)* presentar (**b**) *(subject)* someter (**to** a)
2 *vi (surrender)* rendirse
subnormal [sʌb'nɔːməl] *adj* subnormal
subordinate [sə'bɔːdɪnɪt] *adj & n* subor-
dinado(a) *(m,f)*
subpoena [səb'piːnə] *Jur* **1** *n* citación *f*
2 *vt* citar
subscribe [səb'skraɪb] *vi (magazine)*
suscribirse (**to** a); *(opinion, theory)* adherirse (**to** a)
subscriber [səb'skraɪbə(r)] *n* abona-
do(a) *m,f*
subscription [səb'skrɪpʃən] *n (to magazine)* suscripción *f*; *(to club)* cuota *f*
subsequent ['sʌbsɪkwənt] *adj* subsi-
guiente
subsequently ['sʌbsɪkwəntlɪ] *adv* posteriormente
subside [səb'saɪd] *vi (land)* hundirse;
(floodwater) bajar; *(wind, anger)* amainar
subsidence [səb'saɪdəns] *n (of land)*
hundimiento *m*; *(of floodwater)* bajada *f*;
(of wind) amaine *m*
subsidiary [sʌb'sɪdɪərɪ] **1** *adj (role)* se-
cundario(a)
2 *n Com* sucursal *f*, filial *f*
subsidize ['sʌbsɪdaɪz] *vt* subvencionar
subsidy ['sʌbsɪdɪ] *n* subvención *f*
subsistence [səb'sɪstəns] *n* subsistencia
f
substance ['sʌbstəns] *n* (**a**) sustancia *f*
(**b**) *(essence)* esencia *f* (**c**) **a woman of s.**
(wealth) una mujer acaudalada
substantial [səb'stænʃəl] *adj* (**a**) *(solid)*
sólido(a) (**b**) *(sum, loss)* importante; *(difference, improvement)* notable; *(meal)*
abundante

substantiate [səb'stænʃɪeɪt] *vt* respaldar
substitute ['sʌbstɪtjuːt] **1** *vt* sustituir; **to
s. X for Y** sustituir X por Y
2 *n (person)* suplente *mf*; *(thing)* sucedáneo *m*
subtitle ['sʌbtaɪtəl] *n* subtítulo *m*
subtle ['sʌtəl] *adj* sutil; *(taste)* delica-
do(a); *(remark)* ingenioso(a); *(irony)* fi-
no(a)
subtlety ['sʌtəltɪ] *n* sutileza *f*; *(of remark)*
ingeniosidad *f*; *(of irony, joke)* finura *f*
subtract [səb'trækt] *vt* restar
subtraction [səb'trækʃən] *n* resta *f*
suburb ['sʌbɜːb] *n* barrio periférico; **the
suburbs** las afueras
suburban [sə'bɜːbən] *adj* suburbano(a)
suburbia [sə'bɜːbɪə] *n* barrios residen-
ciales periféricos
subversive [səb'vɜːsɪv] *adj & n* subversi-
vo(a) *(m,f)*
subway ['sʌbweɪ] *n* (**a**) *Br (underpass)*
paso subterráneo (**b**) *US (underground
railway)* metro *m*
succeed [sək'siːd] **1** *vi* (**a**) *(person)* tener
éxito; *(plan)* salir bien; **to s. in doing sth**
conseguir hacer algo (**b**) *(follow after)*
suceder; **to s. to** *(throne)* suceder a
2 *vt (monarch)* suceder a
succeeding [sək'siːdɪŋ] *adj* sucesivo(a)
success [sək'ses] *n* éxito *m*

> Note that the Spanish word **suceso** is a
> false friend and is never a translation for the
> English word **success**. In Spanish, **suceso**
> means both "event" and "incident".

successful [sək'sesfʊl] *adj* de éxito, exi-
toso(a); *(business)* próspero(a); *(marriage)* feliz; **to be s. in doing sth** lograr
hacer algo
successfully [sək'sesfʊlɪ] *adv* con éxito
succession [sək'seʃən] *n* sucesión *f*, serie *f*; **in s.** sucesivamente
successive [sək'sesɪv] *adj* sucesivo(a),
consecutivo(a)
successor [sək'sesə(r)] *n* sucesor(a) *m,f*
succinct [sək'sɪŋkt] *adj* sucinto(a)
succumb [sə'kʌm] *vi* sucumbir (**to** a)
such [sʌtʃ] **1** *adj* (**a**) *(of that sort)* tal,
semejante; **artists s. as Monet** artistas
como Monet; **at s. and s. a time** a tal hora;
in s. a way that de tal manera que (**b**) *(so
much, so great)* tanto(a); **he's always in s.
a hurry** siempre anda con tanta prisa;
she was in s. pain sufría tanto
2 *adv (so very)* tan; **it's s. a long time ago**
hace tanto tiempo; **she's s. a clever woman** es una mujer tan inteligente; **s. a lot
of books** tantos libros; **we had s. good**

weather hizo un tiempo tan bueno
suchlike ['sʌtʃlaɪk] **1** *adj* tal

2 *pron (things)* cosas *fpl* por el estilo; *(people)* gente *f* por el estilo

suck [sʌk] **1** *vt (by pump)* aspirar; *(liquid)* sorber; *(lollipop, blood)* chupar

2 *vi (person)* chupar; *(baby)* mamar
▸ **suck in** *vt sep (of whirlpool)* tragar

sucker ['sʌkə(r)] *n* (**a**) *Fam* primo(a) *m,f*, bobo(a) *m,f* (**b**) *Zool* ventosa *f*; *Bot* chupón *m*

suckle ['sʌkəl] *vt (mother)* amamantar

suction ['sʌkʃən] *n* succión *f*

sudden ['sʌdən] *adj* (**a**) *(hurried)* súbito(a), repentino(a) (**b**) *(unexpected)* imprevisto(a) (**c**) *(abrupt)* brusco(a); **all of a s.** de repente

suddenly ['sʌdənlɪ] *adv* de repente

suds [sʌdz] *npl* espuma *f* de jabón, jabonaduras *fpl*

sue [suː, sjuː] *Jur* **1** *vt* demandar

2 *vi* presentar una demanda; **to s. for divorce** solicitar el divorcio

suede [sweɪd] *n* ante *m*, gamuza *f*; *(for gloves)* cabritilla *f*

suet ['suːɪt] *n* sebo *m*

suffer ['sʌfə(r)] **1** *vt* (**a**) sufrir (**b**) *(tolerate)* aguantar, soportar

2 *vi* sufrir; **to s. from** sufrir de

sufferer ['sʌfərə(r)] *n Med* enfermo(a) *m,f*

suffering ['sʌfərɪŋ] *n (affliction)* sufrimiento *m*; *(pain, torment)* dolor *m*

suffice [sə'faɪs] *vi Fml* bastar, ser suficiente

sufficient [sə'fɪʃənt] *adj* suficiente, bastante

sufficiently [sə'fɪʃəntlɪ] *adv* suficientemente, bastante

suffocate ['sʌfəkeɪt] **1** *vt* asfixiar

2 *vi* asfixiarse

suffocating ['sʌfəkeɪtɪŋ] *adj (heat)* agobiante, sofocante

suffrage ['sʌfrɪdʒ] *n* sufragio *m*

suffuse [sə'fjuːz] *vt Literary* bañar, cubrir (**with** de)

sugar ['ʃʊɡə(r)] **1** *n* azúcar *m* or *f*; **s. beet** remolacha *f* (azucarera); **s. bowl** azucarero *m*; **s. cane** caña *f* de azúcar

2 *vt* azucarar, echar azúcar a

sugary ['ʃʊɡərɪ] *adj* (**a**) *(like sugar)* azucarado(a) (**b**) *Fig (insincere)* zalamero(a); *(over-sentimental)* sentimentaloide

suggest [sə'dʒest] *vt* (**a**) *(propose)* sugerir (**b**) *(advise)* aconsejar (**c**) *(indicate, imply)* indicar

suggestion [sə'dʒestʃən] *n* (**a**) *(proposal)* sugerencia *f* (**b**) *(trace)* sombra *f*;

(small amount) toque *m*

suggestive [sə'dʒestɪv] *adj* (**a**) *(reminiscent, thought-provoking)* sugerente (**b**) *(remark)* insinuante

suicidal [sjuːɪ'saɪdəl] *adj* suicida

suicide ['sjuːɪsaɪd] *n* suicidio *m*

suit [suːt, sjuːt] **1** *n* (**a**) *(clothes)* traje *m* de chaqueta (**b**) *Jur* pleito *m* (**c**) *Cards* palo *m*; *Fig* **to follow s.** seguir el ejemplo

2 *vt* (**a**) *(be convenient to)* convenir a, venir bien a (**b**) *(be right, appropriate for)* ir bien a; **red really suits you** el rojo te favorece mucho; **they are well suited** están hechos el uno para el otro (**c**) *(adapt)* adaptar a (**d**) *(please)* **s. yourself!** ¡como quieras!

suitable ['sjuːtəbəl] *adj (convenient)* conveniente; *(appropriate)* adecuado(a); **the most s. woman for the job** la mujer más indicada para el puesto

suitably ['sjuːtəblɪ] *adv (correctly)* correctamente; *(properly)* adecuadamente

suitcase ['suːtkeɪs] *n* maleta *f*, *Méx* petaca *f*, *RP* valija *f*

suite [swiːt] *n* (**a**) *(of furniture)* juego *m* (**b**) *(of hotel rooms, music)* suite *f*

suitor ['sjuːtə(r)] *n Literary (wooer)* pretendiente *m*

sulfur ['sʌlfə(r)] *n US* = **sulphur**

sulk [sʌlk] *vi* enfurruñarse

sulky ['sʌlkɪ] *adj* (**sulkier, sulkiest**) malhumorado(a), enfurruñado(a)

sullen ['sʌlən] *adj* hosco(a); *(sky)* plomizo(a)

sulphur ['sʌlfər] *n* azufre *m*

sulphuric [sʌl'fjʊərɪk] *adj* sulfúrico(a)

sultan ['sʌltən] *n* sultán *m*

sultana [sʌl'tɑːnə] *n (raisin)* pasa *f* de Esmirna

sultry ['sʌltrɪ] *adj* (**sultrier, sultriest**) (**a**) *(muggy)* bochornoso(a) (**b**) *(seductive)* sensual

sum [sʌm] *n* (**a**) *(arithmetic problem, amount)* suma *f* (**b**) *(total amount)* total *m*; *(of money)* importe *m*
▸ **sum up 1** *vt sep* resumir

2 *vi* resumir; **to s. up ...** en resumidas cuentas ...

summarize ['sʌməraɪz] *vt & vi* resumir

summary ['sʌmərɪ] **1** *n* resumen *m*

2 *adj* sumario(a)

summer ['sʌmə(r)] **1** *n* verano *m*

2 *adj (holiday etc)* de verano; *(weather)* veraniego(a); *(resort)* de veraneo

summerhouse ['sʌməhaʊs] *n* cenador *m*, glorieta *f*

summertime ['sʌmətaɪm] *n* verano *m*

summit ['sʌmɪt] *n* (**a**) *(of mountain)* cima

f, cumbre *f* (**b**) *Pol* **s. (meeting)** cumbre *f*
summon ['sʌmən] *vt* (**a**) *(meeting, person)* convocar (**b**) *(aid)* pedir (**c**) *Jur* citar
▶ **summon up** *vt sep (resources)* reunir; **to s. up one's courage** armarse de valor
summons ['sʌmənz] **1** *n sing* (**a**) *(call)* llamada *f*, llamamiento *m* (**b**)*Jur* citación *f* judicial
  2 *vt Jur* citar
sumptuous ['sʌmptjʊəs] *adj* suntuoso(a)
sun [sʌn] **1** *n* sol *m*
  2 *vt* **to s. oneself** tomar el sol
sunbathe ['sʌnbeɪð] *vi* tomar el sol
sunbed ['sʌnbed] *n (in garden)* tumbona *f*; *(with sunlamp)* solario *m*
sunburn ['sʌnbɜːn] *n (burn)* quemadura *f* de sol
sunburnt ['sʌnbɜːnt] *adj (burnt)* quemado(a) por el sol; *(tanned)* bronceado(a)
Sunday ['sʌndɪ] *n* domingo *m inv*; **S. newspaper** periódico *m* del domingo; **S. school** catequesis *f*
sundial ['sʌndaɪəl] *n* reloj *m* de sol
sundown ['sʌndaʊn] *n US* anochecer *m*
sundry ['sʌndrɪ] **1** *adj* diversos(as), varios(as); *Fam* **all and s.** todos sin excepción
  2 *npl Com* **sundries** artículos *mpl* diversos; *(expenses)* gastos diversos
sunflower ['sʌnflaʊə(r)] *n* girasol *m*
sung [sʌŋ] *pp of* **sing**
sunglasses ['sʌnɡlɑːsɪz] *npl* gafas *fpl* de sol, *Am* lentes *mpl* de sol, anteojos *mpl* de sol
sunk [sʌŋk] *pp of* **sink**
sunlamp ['sʌnlæmp] *n* lámpara *f* solar
sunlight ['sʌnlaɪt] *n* sol *m*, luz *f* del sol
sunlit ['sʌnlɪt] *adj* iluminado(a) por el sol
sunny ['sʌnɪ] *adj* (**sunnier, sunniest**) (**a**) *(day)* de sol; *(place)* soleado(a); **it is s.** hace sol (**b**) *Fig (smile, disposition)* alegre; *(future)* prometedor(a)
sunrise ['sʌnraɪz] *n* salida *f* del sol
sunroof ['sʌnruːf] *n Aut* techo corredizo
sunset ['sʌnset] *n* puesta *f* del sol
sunshade ['sʌnʃeɪd] *n* sombrilla *f*
sunshine ['sʌnʃaɪn] *n* sol *m*, luz *f* del sol
sunstroke ['sʌnstrəʊk] *n* insolación *f*
suntan ['sʌntæn] *n* bronceado *m*; **s. oil** crema protectora; **s. lotion** (aceite *m*) bronceador *m*
super ['suːpə(r)] *adj Fam* fenomenal
super- ['suːpə(r)] *pref* super-, sobre-
superannuation [suːpərænjʊ'eɪʃən] *n Br* jubilación *f*, pensión *f*
superb [sʊ'pɜːb] *adj* espléndido(a)

supercilious [suːpə'sɪlɪəs] *adj (condescending)* altanero(a); *(disdainful)* desdeñoso(a)
superficial [suːpə'fɪʃəl] *adj* superficial
superfluous [suː'pɜːflʊəs] *adj* sobrante, superfluo(a); **to be s.** sobrar
superglue ['suːpəɡluː] *n* pegamento rápido
superhuman [suːpə'hjuːmən] *adj* sobrehumano(a)
superimpose [suːpərɪm'pəʊz] *vt* sobreponer
superintendent [suːpərɪn'tendənt] *n* director(a) *m,f*; **police s.** subjefe(a) *m,f* de policía
superior [suː'pɪərɪə(r)] **1** *adj* (**a**) superior (**b**) *(haughty)* altivo(a)
  2 *n* superior(a) *m,f*
superiority [suːpɪərɪ'ɒrɪtɪ] *n* superioridad *f*
superlative [suː'pɜːlətɪv] **1** *adj* superlativo(a)
  2 *n Ling* superlativo *m*
superman ['suːpəmæn] *n* superhombre *m*, supermán *m*
supermarket ['suːpəmɑːkɪt] *n* supermercado *m*
supernatural [suːpə'nætʃərəl] **1** *adj* sobrenatural
  2 *n* **the s.** lo sobrenatural
superpower ['suːpəpaʊə(r)] *n Pol* superpotencia *f*
supersede [suːpə'siːd] *vt Fml* suplantar
supersonic [suːpə'sɒnɪk] *adj* supersónico(a)
superstitious [suːpə'stɪʃəs] *adj* supersticioso(a)
supertanker ['suːpətæŋkə(r)] *n* superpetrolero *m*
supervise ['suːpəvaɪz] *vt* supervisar; *(watch over)* vigilar
supervision [suːpə'vɪʒən] *n* supervisión *f*
supervisor ['suːpəvaɪzə(r)] *n* supervisor(a) *m,f*
supper ['sʌpə(r)] *n* cena *f*; **to have s.** cenar
supplant [sə'plɑːnt] *vt* suplantar
supple ['sʌpəl] *adj* flexible
supplement 1 *n* ['sʌplɪmənt] suplemento *m*
  2 *vt* ['sʌplɪment] complementar
supplementary [sʌplɪ'mentərɪ] *adj* adicional
supplier [sə'plaɪə(r)] *n* suministrador(a) *m,f*; *Com* proveedor(a) *m,f*
supply [sə'plaɪ] **1** *n* (**a**) suministro *m*; *Com* provisión *f*; *(stock)* surtido *m*; **s. and**

demand oferta *f* y demanda (**b**) **supplies** *(food)* víveres *mpl; Mil* pertrechos *mpl;* **office supplies** material *m* para oficina

　2 *vt* (**a**) *(provide)* suministrar (**b**) *(with provisions)* aprovisionar (**c**) *(information)* facilitar (**d**) *Com* surtir

support [sə'pɔːt] **1** *n* (**a**) *(moral)* apoyo *m* (**b**) *(funding)* ayuda económica

　2 *vt* (**a**) *(weight etc)* sostener (**b**) *Fig (back)* apoyar; *(substantiate)* respaldar (**c**) *Sport* ser (hincha) de (**d**) *(sustain)* mantener; *(feed)* alimentar

supporter [sə'pɔːtə(r)] *n Pol* partidario(a) *m,f; Sport* hincha *mf*

suppose [sə'pəʊz] *vt* suponer; *(presume)* creer; **I** s. **not/so** supongo que no/sí; **you're not supposed to smoke in here** no está permitido fumar aquí dentro; **you're supposed to be in bed** deberías estar acostado(a) ya

supposed [sə'pəʊzd] *adj* supuesto(a)

supposedly [sə'pəʊzdlɪ] *adv* teóricamente

suppress [sə'pres] *vt* suprimir; *(feelings, laugh etc)* contener; *(news, truth)* callar; *(revolt)* sofocar

supremacy [sʊ'preməsɪ] *n* supremacía *f*

supreme [sʊ'priːm] *adj* supremo(a); **with** s. **indifference** con total indiferencia; *US Law* **S. Court** Tribunal *m* Supremo, *Am* Corte *f* Suprema

supremely [sʊ'priːmlɪ] *adv* sumamente

surcharge ['sɜːtʃɑːdʒ] *n* recargo *m*

sure [ʃʊə(r)] **1** *adj* (**a**) seguro(a); **I'm** s. **(that)** ... estoy seguro(a) de que ...; **make** s. **that it's ready** asegúrate de que esté listo; **s. of oneself** seguro(a) de sí mismo(a) (**b**) *Fam* s. **thing!** ¡claro!; *US* **it** s. **is cold** qué frío que hace

　2 *adv* (**a**) *(of course)* claro (**b**) *(certainly)* seguro (**c**) s. **enough** efectivamente

surely ['ʃʊəlɪ] *adv (without a doubt)* sin duda; s. **not!** ¡no puede ser!

surety ['ʃʊərɪtɪ] *n* (**a**) *(sum)* fianza *f* (**b**) *(person)* fiador(a) *m,f;* **to stand** s. **for sb** ser fiador de algn

surf [sɜːf] **1** *n (waves)* oleaje *m; (foam)* espuma *f*

　2 *vt Comput* **to** s. **the Net** navegar por Internet

　3 *vi Sport* hacer surf

surface ['sɜːfɪs] **1** *n* superficie *f; (of road)* firme *m*

　2 *adj* superficial; s. **area** área *f* de la superficie; **by** s. **mail** por vía terrestre *or* marítima

　3 *vt (road)* revestir

　4 *vi (submarine etc)* salir a la superficie;

Fam (wake up) levantarse

surface-to-air ['sɜːfɪstʊ'eə(r)] *adj* s. **missile** misil *m* tierra-aire

surfboard ['sɜːfbɔːd] *n* tabla *f* de surf

surfeit ['sɜːfɪt] *n Fml* exceso *m*

surfer ['sɜːfə(r)] *n* surfista *mf*

surfing ['sɜːfɪŋ] *n* surf *m*, surfing *m*

surge [sɜːdʒ] **1** *n* (**a**) *(growth)* alza *f* (**b**) *(of sea, sympathy)* oleada *f; Fig (of anger, energy)* arranque *m*

　2 *vi* **to** s. **forward** *(people)* avanzar en tropel

surgeon ['sɜːdʒən] *n* cirujano(a) *m,f*

surgery ['sɜːdʒərɪ] *n* (**a**) *(operation)* cirugía *f* (**b**) *Br (consulting room)* consultorio *m;* s. **hours** horas *fpl* de consulta

surgical ['sɜːdʒɪkəl] *adj* quirúrgico(a); s. **spirit** alcohol *m* de 90°

surly ['sɜːlɪ] *adj* (**surlier, surliest**) *(bad-tempered)* hosco(a), malhumorado(a); *(rude)* maleducado(a)

surmount [sɜː'maʊnt] *vt* superar, vencer

surname ['sɜːneɪm] *n* apellido *m*

surpass [sɜː'pɑːs] *vt* superar

surplus ['sɜːpləs] **1** *n (of goods)* excedente *m; (of budget)* superávit *m*

　2 *adj* excedente

surprise [sə'praɪz] **1** *n* sorpresa *f;* **to take sb by** s. coger desprevenido(a) a algn

　2 *adj (visit)* inesperado(a); s. **attack** ataque *m* sorpresa

　3 *vt* sorprender

surprising [sə'praɪzɪŋ] *adj* sorprendente

surprisingly [sə'praɪzɪŋlɪ] *adv* sorprendentemente, de modo sorprendente

surrealist [sə'rɪəlɪst] *adj & n* surrealista *(mf)*

surrender [sə'rendə(r)] **1** *n Mil* rendición *f; (of weapons)* entrega *f; Ins* rescate *m*

　2 *vt Mil* rendir; *(right)* renunciar a

　3 *vi (give in)* rendirse

surreptitious [sʌrəp'tɪʃəs] *adj* subrepticio(a)

surrogate ['sʌrəgɪt] *n Fml* sustituto(a) *m,f;* s. **mother** madre *f* de alquiler

surround [sə'raʊnd] **1** *n* marco *m*, borde *m*

　2 *vt* rodear

surrounding [sə'raʊndɪŋ] **1** *adj* circundante

　2 *npl* **surroundings** *(of place)* alrededores *mpl*, cercanías *fpl*

surveillance [sɜː'veɪləns] *n* vigilancia *f*

survey 1 *n* ['sɜːveɪ] (**a**) *(of building)* inspección *f; (of land)* reconocimiento *m* (**b**) *(of trends etc)* encuesta *f* (**c**) *(overall view)* panorama *m*

　2 *vt* [sə'veɪ] (**a**) *(building)* inspeccionar;

(land) medir (**b**) *(trends etc)* hacer una encuesta sobre (**c**) *(look at)* contemplar

surveyor [sə'veɪə(r)] *n* agrimensor(a) *m,f*; **quantity s.** aparejador(a) *m,f*

survival [sə'vaɪvəl] *n* supervivencia *f*

survive [sə'vaɪv] **1** *vi* sobrevivir; *(remain)* perdurar

2 *vt* sobrevivir a

survivor [sə'vaɪvə(r)] *n* superviviente *mf*

susceptible [sə'septəbəl] *adj (to attack)* susceptible (**to** a); *(to illness)* propenso(a) (**to** a)

suspect ['sʌspekt] **1** *adj (dubious)* sospechoso(a)

2 *n* sospechoso(a) *m,f*

3 *vt* [sə'spekt] (**a**) *(person)* sospechar (**of** de); *(plot, motives)* recelar de (**b**) *(think likely)* imaginar, creer

suspend [sə'spend] *vt* suspender; *(pupil)* expulsar por un tiempo

suspended [sə'spendɪd] *adj* (**a**) suspendido(a); *Jur* **s. sentence** condena *f* condicional (**b**) *Sport* sancionado(a)

suspender [sə'spendə(r)] *n* (**a**) *Br (for stocking)* liga *f*; **s. belt** liguero *m* (**b**) *US* **suspenders** tirantes *mpl*

suspense [sə'spens] *n* incertidumbre *f*; *Cin & Th* suspense *m*; **to keep sb in s.** mantener a algn en la incertidumbre

suspension [sə'spenʃən] *n* (**a**) suspensión *f* (**b**) *Sport* sanción *f* (**c**) *(of pupil, employee)* expulsión *f* temporal (**d**) **s. bridge** puente *m* colgante

suspicion [sə'spɪʃən] *n* (**a**) sospecha *f*; *(mistrust)* recelo *m*; *(doubt)* duda *f* (**b**) *(trace)* pizca *f*

suspicious [sə'spɪʃəs] *adj* (**a**) *(arousing suspicion)* sospechoso(a) (**b**) *(distrustful)* receloso(a); **to be s. of sb** desconfiar de algn

▸ **suss out** [sʌs] *vt sep Br Fam (person)* calar; *(system)* coger *or Am* agarrar el truco a; **I haven't sussed out how it works yet** todavía no me he enterado de cómo funciona

sustain [sə'steɪn] *vt* (**a**) sostener (**b**) *(nourish)* sustentar (**c**) *Jur (objection)* admitir (**d**) *(injury etc)* sufrir

sustained [sə'steɪnd] *adj* sostenido(a)

sustenance ['sʌstənəns] *n* sustento *m*

swab [swɒb] **1** *n (cotton wool)* algodón *m*; *(for specimen)* frotis *m*

2 *vt (wound)* limpiar

swagger ['swægə(r)] **1** *n* pavoneo *m*

2 *vi* pavonearse

swallow¹ ['swɒləʊ] **1** *n (of drink, food)* trago *m*

2 *vt* (**a**) *(drink, food)* tragar (**b**) *Fig (believe)* tragarse

3 *vi* tragar

▸ **swallow up** *vt sep Fig* (**a**) *(engulf)* tragar (**b**) *(eat up)* consumir

swallow² ['swɒləʊ] *n Orn* golondrina *f*

swam [swæm] *pt of* **swim**

swamp [swɒmp] **1** *n* ciénaga *f*

2 *vt* (**a**) *(boat)* hundir (**b**) *Fig* inundar (**with** *or* **by** de)

swan [swɒn] **1** *n* cisne *m*

2 *vi Fam* **to s. around** pavonearse; **to s. around doing nothing** hacer el vago

swap [swɒp] **1** *n Fam* intercambio *m*

2 *vt* cambiar

▸ **swap round, swap over** *vt sep (switch)* cambiar

swarm [swɔːm] **1** *n* enjambre *m*

2 *vi (bees)* enjambrar; *Fig* **Neath was swarming with tourists** Neath estaba lleno de turistas

swarthy ['swɔːðɪ] *adj* (**swarthier, swarthiest**) moreno(a)

swastika ['swɒstɪkə] *n* esvástica *f*, cruz gamada

swat [swɒt] *vt* aplastar

swathe [sweɪð] *vt (bind up)* envolver

sway [sweɪ] **1** *n* (**a**) *(movement)* balanceo *m* (**b**) **to hold s. over sb** dominar a algn

2 *vi* (**a**) *(swing)* balancearse, mecerse (**b**) *(totter)* tambalearse

3 *vt Fig (persuade)* convencer

swear [sweə(r)] **1** *vt (pt* **swore**; *pp* **sworn**) *(vow)* jurar; **to s. an oath** prestar juramento

2 *vi* (**a**) *(formally)* jurar, prestar juramento (**b**) *(curse)* soltar tacos, decir palabrotas; *(blaspheme)* jurar; **to s. at sb** echar pestes contra algn

swear-word ['sweəwɜːd] *n* palabrota *f*

sweat [swet] **1** *n (perspiration)* sudor *m*; *Fam (hard work)* trabajo duro

2 *vi (perspire)* sudar; *Fig (work hard)* sudar la gota gorda

3 *vt Fam* **to s. it out** aguantar

sweater ['swetə(r)] *n* suéter *m*

sweatshirt ['swetʃɜːt] *n* sudadera *f*

sweaty ['swetɪ] *adj* (**sweatier, sweatiest**) sudoroso(a)

Swede [swiːd] *n (person)* sueco(a) *m,f*

swede [swiːd] *n Bot* nabo sueco

Sweden ['swiːdən] *n* Suecia

Swedish ['swiːdɪʃ] **1** *adj* sueco(a)

2 *n* (**a**) *(language)* sueco *m* (**b**) **the S.** los suecos

sweep [swiːp] **1** *n* (**a**) *(with broom)* barrido *m*; *Fig* **to make a clean s. of things** hacer tabla rasa (**b**) *(of arm)* gesto amplio (**c**) *(of river, road)* curva *f* (**d**) **(chimney) s.** deshollinador(a) *m,f*

2 *vt* (*pt & pp* **swept**) (**a**) *(floor etc)* barrer (**b**) *(of searchlight)* recorrer; *(minefield)* rastrear (**c**) *(spread throughout)* extenderse por

3 *vi* (**a**) *(with broom)* barrer (**b**) **to s. in/out/past** entrar/salir/pasar rápidamente

▸ **sweep aside** *vt sep* apartar bruscamente; *Fig (objections)* rechazar
▸ **sweep away** *vt sep* (**a**) *(dust)* barrer (**b**) *(of storm)* arrastrar
▸ **sweep up** *vi* barrer

sweeper ['swiːpə(r)] *n* (**a**) *(machine)* barredora *f* (**b**) *Ftb* líbero *m*

sweeping ['swiːpɪŋ] *adj* (**a**) *(broad)* amplio(a); **a s. statement** una declaración demasiado general (**b**) *(victory)* aplastante (**c**) *(reforms, changes etc)* radical

sweet [swiːt] **1** *adj* (**a**) dulce; *(sugary)* azucarado(a); **to have a s. tooth** ser goloso(a); **s. pea** guisante *m* de olor; **s. shop** confitería *f* (**b**) *(pleasant)* agradable; *(smell)* fragante; *(sound)* melodioso(a) (**c**) *(person, animal)* encantador(a)
2 *n* (**a**) *Br (chocolate)* bombón *m*; **(boiled) s.** caramelo *m* (**b**) *(dessert)* postre *m*

sweet-and-sour ['swiːtən'saʊə(r)] *adj* agridulce

sweetcorn ['swiːtkɔːn] *n* maíz tierno

sweeten ['swiːtən] *vt* (**a**) *(tea etc)* azucarar (**b**) *Fig (temper)* aplacar; **to s. the pill** suavizar el golpe

sweetener ['swiːtənə(r)] *n (for tea, coffee)* edulcorante *m*

sweetheart ['swiːthɑːt] *n* (**a**) *(boyfriend)* novio *m*; *(girlfriend)* novia *f* (**b**) *(dear, love)* cariño *m*, amor *m*

sweetness ['swiːtnɪs] *n* dulzura *f*; *(of smell)* fragancia *f*; *(of sound)* suavidad *f*

swell [swel] **1** *n (of sea)* marejada *f*, oleaje *m*
2 *adj US Fam* fenomenal
3 *vi* (*pt* **swelled**; *pp* **swollen**) *(part of body)* hincharse; *(river)* subir
▸ **swell up** *vi* hincharse

swelling ['swelɪŋ] *n* hinchazón *f*, *Med* tumefacción *f*

sweltering ['sweltərɪŋ] *adj* agobiante

swept [swept] *pt & pp of* **sweep**

swerve [swɜːv] **1** *n* (**a**) *(by car)* viraje *m* (**b**) *Sport (by player)* regate *m*
2 *vi* (**a**) *(car)* dar un viraje brusco (**b**) *Sport (player)* dar un regate

swift [swɪft] **1** *adj* rápido(a), veloz
2 *n Orn* vencejo *m* (común)

swiftly ['swɪftlɪ] *adv* rápidamente

swig [swɪg] *Fam* **1** *n* trago *m*
2 *vt* beber a tragos

swill [swɪl] **1** *n* (**a**) bazofia *f* (**b**) *(rinse)* enjuague *m*
2 *vt* (**a**) *(rinse)* enjuagar (**b**) *Fam (drink)* beber a grandes tragos
▸ **swill out** *vt sep* enjuagar

swim [swɪm] **1** *vi* (*pt* **swam**; *pp* **swum**) nadar; **to go swimming** ir a nadar; *Fam* **my head is swimming** la cabeza me da vueltas
2 *vt (the Channel)* pasar a nado
3 *n* baño *m*; **to go for a s.** ir a nadar *or* bañarse

swimmer ['swɪmə(r)] *n* nadador(a) *m,f*

swimming ['swɪmɪŋ] *n* natación *f*; **s. cap** gorro *m* de baño; **s. costume** traje *m* de baño, bañador *m*; **s. pool** piscina *f*; **s. trunks** bañador

swimsuit ['swɪmsuːt] *n* traje *m* de baño, bañador *m*

swindle ['swɪndəl] **1** *n* estafa *f*
2 *vt* estafar

swindler ['swɪndlə(r)] *n* estafador(a) *m,f*

swine [swaɪn] *n* (**a**) *(pl* **swine**) *(pig)* cerdo *m*, puerco *m* (**b**) *(pl* **swines**) *Fam (person)* canalla *mf*, cochino(a) *m,f*

swing [swɪŋ] **1** *n* (**a**) balanceo *m*, vaivén *m*; *Fig (in votes etc)* viraje *m*; **s. bridge** puente giratorio; **s. door** puerta giratoria (**b**) *(in golf)* swing *m* (**c**) *(plaything)* columpio *m* (**d**) *(rhythm)* ritmo *m*; *(jazz style)* swing *m*; **in full s.** en plena marcha
2 *vi* (*pt & pp* **swung**) (**a**) *(move to and fro)* balancearse; *(arms, legs)* menearse; *(on swing)* columpiarse; **to s. open/shut** abrirse/cerrarse de golpe (**b**) *(turn)* girar; **he swung round** dio media vuelta
3 *vt* (**a**) *(cause to move to and fro)* balancear; *(arms, legs)* menear; *(on swing)* columpiar (**b**) *(turn)* hacer girar; **she swung the sack onto her back** se echó el saco a los hombros

swingeing ['swɪndʒɪŋ] *adj* drástico(a)

swipe [swaɪp] **1** *n* golpe *m*
2 *vt* (**a**) *(hit)* dar un tortazo a (**b**) *Fam (steal)* birlar

swirl [swɜːl] **1** *n* remolino *m*; *(of cream, smoke)* voluta *f*
2 *vi* arremolinarse

swish [swɪʃ] **1** *adj Fam (smart)* elegante
2 *vt (tail)* menear
3 *vi (whip)* dar un chasquido; *(skirt)* crujir

Swiss [swɪs] **1** *adj* suizo(a)
  2 *n* (*pl* **Swiss**) *(person)* suizo(a) *m,f*; **the S.** los suizos
switch [swɪtʃ] **1** *n* (**a**) *Elec* interruptor *m* (**b**) *(changeover)* cambio repentino; *(exchange)* intercambio *m* (**c**) *(stick)* vara *f*; *(riding whip)* fusta *f* (**d**) *US Rail* agujas *fpl*
  2 *vt* (**a**) *(jobs, direction)* cambiar de (**b**) *(allegiance)* cambiar (**to** por); *(attention)* desviar (**to** hacia)
  ▸ **switch off** *vt sep* apagar
  ▸ **switch on** *vt sep* encender
  ▸ **switch over** *vi* cambiar (**to** a)
switchboard ['swɪtʃbɔːd] *n* centralita *f*
Switzerland ['swɪtsələnd] *n* Suiza
swivel ['swɪvəl] **1** *n* **s. chair** silla giratoria
  2 *vt & vi* girar
swollen ['swəʊlən] **1** *adj (ankle, face)* hinchado(a); *(river, lake)* crecido(a)
  2 *pp of* **swell**
swoon [swuːn] **1** *n* desmayo *m*
  2 *vi* desmayarse
swoop [swuːp] **1** *n* (**a**) *(of bird)* calada *f*; *(of plane)* descenso *m* en picado (**b**) *(by police)* redada *f*
  2 *vi* (**a**) **to s. down** *(bird)* abalanzarse (**on** sobre); *(plane)* bajar en picado (**b**) *(police)* hacer una redada
swop [swɒp] *n & vt* = **swap**
sword [sɔːd] *n* espada *f*
swordfish ['sɔːdfɪʃ] *n* pez *m* espada
swore [swɔː(r)] *pt of* **swear**
sworn [swɔːn] **1** *adj* jurado(a)
  2 *pp of* **swear**
swot [swɒt] *vi Br Fam* empollar
swum [swʌm] *pp of* **swim**
swung [swʌŋ] *pt & pp of* **swing**
sycamore ['sɪkəmɔː(r)] *n* (**a**) *Br* sicomoro *m* (**b**) *US (plane tree)* plátano *m*
syllable ['sɪləbəl] *n* sílaba *f*
syllabus ['sɪləbəs] *n* programa *m* de estudios
symbol ['sɪmbəl] *n* símbolo *m*
symbolic [sɪm'bɒlɪk] *adj* simbólico(a)
symbolize ['sɪmbəlaɪz] *vt* simbolizar
symmetry ['sɪmɪtrɪ] *n* simetría *f*
sympathetic [sɪmpə'θetɪk] *adj* (**a**) *(showing pity)* compasivo(a) (**b**) *(understanding)* comprensivo(a); *(kind)* amable

  🖉 Note that the Spanish word **simpático** is a false friend and is never a translation for the English word **sympathetic**. In Spanish, **simpático** means "nice, likeable".

sympathize ['sɪmpəθaɪz] *vi* (**a**) *(show pity)* compadecerse (**with** de) (**b**) *(understand)* comprender
sympathizer ['sɪmpəθaɪzə(r)] *n* simpatizante *mf*
sympathy ['sɪmpəθɪ] *n* (**a**) *(pity)* compasión *f* (**b**) *(condolences)* pésame *m*; **letter of s.** pésame; **to express one's s.** dar el pésame (**c**) *(understanding)* comprensión *f*

  🖉 Note that the Spanish word **simpatía** is a false friend and is never a translation for the English word **sympathy**. In Spanish, **simpatía** means "liking, affection".

symphony ['sɪmfənɪ] *n* sinfonía *f*
symposium [sɪm'pəʊzɪəm] *n* simposio *m*
symptom ['sɪmptəm] *n* síntoma *m*
symptomatic [sɪmptə'mætɪk] *adj* sintomático(a)
synagogue ['sɪnəgɒg] *n* sinagoga *f*
synchronize ['sɪŋkrənaɪz] *vt* sincronizar
syndicate ['sɪndɪkɪt] *n* corporación *f*; **newspaper s.** sindicato periodístico
syndrome ['sɪndrəʊm] *n* síndrome *m*
synonym ['sɪnənɪm] *n* sinónimo *m*
synopsis [sɪ'nɒpsɪs] *n* sinopsis *f inv*
syntax ['sɪntæks] *n* sintaxis *f inv*
synthesis ['sɪnθɪsɪs] *n* (*pl* **syntheses** ['sɪnθɪsiːz]) síntesis *f inv*
synthesizer ['sɪnθɪsaɪzə(r)] *n* sintetizador *m*
synthetic [sɪn'θetɪk] *adj* sintético(a)
syphilis ['sɪfɪlɪs] *n* sífilis *f*
syphon ['saɪfən] *n* = **siphon**
Syria ['sɪrɪə] *n* Siria
Syrian ['sɪrɪən] *adj & n* sirio(a) *(m,f)*
syringe [sɪ'rɪndʒ] *n* jeringa *f*, jeringuilla *f*
syrup ['sɪrəp] *n* jarabe *m*, almíbar *m*
system ['sɪstəm] *n* sistema *m*; *Fam* **the s.** el orden establecido; *Comput* **systems analyst** analista *mf* de sistemas
systematic [sɪstɪ'mætɪk] *adj* sistemático(a)

T, t [tiː] *n (the letter)* T, t *f*

t (*abbr* **ton(s)**) tonelada(s) *f(pl)*

ta [tɑː] *interj Br Fam* gracias

tab [tæb] *n* (**a**) *(flap)* lengüeta *f*; *(label)* etiqueta *f*; *Fam* **to keep tabs on sb** vigilar a algn (**b**) *US Fam (bill)* cuenta *f*

tabby ['tæbɪ] *n* **t.** (**cat**) gato(a) *m,f* romano(a)

table ['teɪbəl] **1** *n* (**a**) mesa *f*; **to lay** *or* **set the t.** poner la mesa; **t. lamp** lámpara *f* de mesa; **t. mat** salvamanteles *m inv*; **t. tennis** ping-pong® *m*, tenis *m* de mesa; **t. wine** vino *m* de mesa (**b**) *(of figures)* tabla *f*, cuadro *m*; **t. of contents** índice *m* de materias

2 *vt (motion, proposal) Br* presentar; *US* posponer

tablecloth ['teɪbəlklɒθ] *n* mantel *m*

tablespoon ['teɪbəlspuːn] *n* cucharón *m*

tablespoonful ['teɪbəlspuːnfʊl] *n* cucharada *f* grande

tablet ['tæblɪt] *n* (**a**) *Med* pastilla *f* (**b**) *(of stone)* lápida *f* (**c**) *(of soap)* pastilla *f*; *(of chocolate)* tableta *f* (**d**) *US (of writing paper)* bloc *m*

tableware ['teɪbəlweə(r)] *n* vajilla *f*

tabloid ['tæblɔɪd] *n* periódico *m* de pequeño formato; **t. press** prensa sensacionalista

taboo [tə'buː] *adj & n* tabú *(m)*

tabulate ['tæbjʊleɪt] *vt* disponer en listas

tacit ['tæsɪt] *adj* tácito(a)

taciturn ['tæsɪtɜːn] *adj* taciturno(a)

tack [tæk] **1** *n* (**a**) *(small nail)* tachuela *f* (**b**) *Sewing* hilván *m* (**c**) *Naut* amura *f*; *(distance)* bordada *f*; *Fig* **to change t.** cambiar de rumbo

2 *vt* (**a**) **to t. sth down** clavar algo con tachuelas (**b**) *Sewing* hilvanar

3 *vi Naut* virar de bordo

▸ **tack on** *vt sep (add)* añadir

tackle ['tækəl] **1** *n* (**a**) *(equipment)* aparejos *mpl*; **fishing t.** aparejos de pescar (**b**) *Sport* placaje *m*; *Ftb* entrada *f*

2 *vt* agarrar; *(task)* emprender; *(problem)* abordar; *Sport* placar; *Ftb* entrar a

tacky¹ ['tækɪ] *adj* (**tackier, tackiest**) pegajoso(a)

tacky² ['tækɪ] *adj Fam (shoddy)* cutre

tact [tækt] *n* tacto *m*, diplomacia *f*

tactful ['tæktfʊl] *adj* diplomático(a)

tactic ['tæktɪk] *n* táctica *f*; **tactics** táctica *f*

tactical ['tæktɪkəl] *adj* táctico(a)

tactless ['tæktlɪs] *adj (person)* poco diplomático(a); *(question)* indiscreto(a)

tadpole ['tædpəʊl] *n* renacuajo *m*

taffy ['tæfɪ] *n US* caramelo *m* de melaza

tag [tæg] *n* (**a**) *(label)* etiqueta *f* (**b**) *(saying)* coletilla *f*

▸ **tag along** *vi Fam* pegarse

▸ **tag on** *vt sep (add to end)* añadir

tail [teɪl] **1** *n* (**a**) cola *f*; **t. end** cola (**b**) *(of shirt)* faldón *m*; **to wear tails** ir de frac; **t. coat** frac *m* (**c**) **tails** *(of coin)* cruz *f*

2 *vt Fam (follow)* seguir de cerca

▸ **tail away, tail off** *vi* desvanecerse

tailback ['teɪlbæk] *n Br* caravana *f*

tail-gate ['teɪlgeɪt] **1** *n Aut* puerta trasera

2 *vt US* conducir *or Am* manejar pegado a, pisar los talones a

tailor ['teɪlə(r)] **1** *n* sastre *m*; **t.'s (shop)** sastrería *f*

2 *vt (suit)* confeccionar; *Fig* adaptar

tailor-made [teɪlə'meɪd] *adj* hecho(a) a la medida

tailwind ['teɪlwɪnd] *n* viento *m* de cola

taint [teɪnt] *vt* contaminar; *Fig* corromper

tainted ['teɪntɪd] *adj* contaminado(a); *(reputation)* manchado(a)

take [teɪk] **1** *vt (pt* **took**; *pp* **taken**) (**a**) tomar, coger; **to t. an opportunity** aprovechar una oportunidad; **to t. hold of sth** agarrar algo; **to t. sth from one's pocket** sacarse algo del bolsillo; **t. your time!** ¡tómate el tiempo que quieras!; **to t. a bath** bañarse; **to t. care (of oneself)** cuidarse; **his car takes six people** caben seis personas en su coche; **is this seat taken?** ¿está ocupado este asiento?; **to t. a decision** tomar una decisión; **to t. a liking/dislike to sb** tomar cariño/antipatía a algn; **to t. a photograph** sacar una fotografía; **t. the first road on the left** coja la primera a la izquierda; **to t. the train** coger el tren

(**b**) *(accept)* aceptar; *(earn)* **to t. so much per week** recaudar tanto por semana

(**c**) *(win)* ganar; *(prize)* llevarse
(**d**) *(eat, drink)* tomar; **to t. drugs** drogarse
(**e**) **she's taking (a degree in) law** estudia derecho; **to t. an exam (in ...)** examinarse (de ...)
(**f**) *(person to a place)* llevar
(**g**) *(endure)* aguantar
(**h**) *(consider)* considerar
(**i**) **I t. it that ...** supongo que ...; **what do you t. me for?** ¿por quién me tomas?
(**j**) *(require)* requerir; **it takes an hour to get there** se tarda una hora en llegar hasta allí
(**k**) **to be taken ill** enfermar
2 *n Cin* toma *f*
▸ **take after** *vt insep* parecerse a
▸ **take apart** *vt sep (machine)* desmontar
▸ **take away** *vt sep* (**a**) *(carry off)* llevarse (**b**) **to t. sth away from sb** quitarle algo a algn (**c**) *Math* restar
▸ **take back** *vt sep* (**a**) *(give back)* devolver; *(receive back)* recuperar (**b**) *(withdraw)* retractarse
▸ **take down** *vt sep* (**a**) *(lower)* bajar (**b**) *(demolish)* derribar (**c**) *(write)* apuntar
▸ **take in** *vt sep* (**a**) *(shelter, lodge)* alojar, acoger (**b**) *Sewing* meter (**c**) *(include)* abarcar (**d**) *(understand)* entender (**e**) *(deceive)* engañar
▸ **take off 1** *vt sep* (**a**) *(quitar)* quitar; **he took off his jacket** se quitó la chaqueta (**b**) *(lead or carry away)* llevarse (**c**) *(deduct)* descontar (**d**) *(imitate)* imitar burlonamente
2 *vi Av* despegar
▸ **take on** *vt sep* (**a**) *(undertake)* encargarse de (**b**) *(acquire)* tomar (**c**) *(employ)* contratar (**d**) *(compete with)* competir con
▸ **take out** *vt sep* sacar, quitar; **he's taking me out to dinner** me ha invitado a cenar fuera
▸ **take over 1** *vt sep Com & Pol* tomar posesión de; **the rebels took over the country** los rebeldes se apoderaron del país
2 *vi* **to t. over from sb** relevar a algn
▸ **take to** *vt insep (become fond of)* coger cariño a; **to t. to drink** darse a la bebida
▸ **take up** *vt sep* (**a**) *Sewing* acortar (**b**) *(accept)* aceptar; *(adopt)* adoptar (**c**) **I've taken up the piano/French** he empezado a tocar el piano/a aprender francés (**d**) *(occupy)* ocupar

takeaway ['teɪkəweɪ] *Br* **1** *n (food)* comida *f* para llevar; *(restaurant)* restaurante *m* que vende comida para llevar
2 *adj (food)* para llevar

take-home pay ['teɪkhəʊm'peɪ] *n* sueldo neto
taken ['teɪkən] *pp of* **take**
takeoff ['teɪkɒf] *n* (**a**) *Av* despegue *m* (**b**) *(imitation)* imitación burlona
takeout ['teɪkaʊt] *US* **1** *n (food)* comida *f* para llevar
2 *adj (food)* para llevar
takeover ['teɪkəʊvə(r)] *n Com* absorción *f*; *military* **t.** golpe *m* de estado; **t. bid** oferta pública de adquisición, OPA *f*
takings ['teɪkɪŋz] *npl Com* recaudación *f*
talc [tælk] *n* talco *m*
talcum powder ['tælkəmpaʊdə(r)] *n* (polvos *mpl* de) talco *m*
tale [teɪl] *n* cuento *m*; **to tell tales** contar chismes
talent ['tælənt] *n* talento *m*
talented ['tæləntɪd] *adj* dotado(a)
talk [tɔːk] **1** *vi* hablar; *(chat)* charlar; *(gossip)* chismorrear; *Fam* **now you're talking!** ¡eso sí que me interesa!
2 *vt* **to t. nonsense** decir tonterías; **to t. sense** hablar con sentido común; **to t. shop** hablar del trabajo
3 *n* (**a**) *(conversation)* conversación *f* (**b**) *(words)* palabras *fpl*; **all t.** no hace más que hablar (**c**) *(rumour)* rumor *m*; *(gossip)* chismes *mpl* (**d**) *(lecture)* charla *f*
▸ **talk into** *vt sep* **to t. sb into sth** convencer a algn para que haga algo
▸ **talk out of** *vt sep* **to t. sb out of sth** disuadir a algn de que haga algo
▸ **talk over** *vt sep* discutir
talkative ['tɔːkətɪv] *adj* hablador(a)
talking ['tɔːkɪŋ] *n* **no t. please!** ¡silencio, por favor!; **t. point** tema *m* de conversación
talking-to ['tɔːkɪŋtuː] *n Fam* bronca *f*
tall [tɔːl] *adj* alto(a); **a tree 10 m t.** un árbol de 10 m (de alto); **how t. are you?** ¿cuánto mides?; *Fig* **that's a t. order** eso es mucho pedir
tally ['tælɪ] **1** *vi* **to t. with sth** corresponderse con algo
2 *n Com* apunte *m*; **to keep a t. of** llevar la cuenta de
talon ['tælən] *n* garra *f*

> *Note that the Spanish word* **talón** *is a false friend and is never a translation for the English word* **talon**. *In Spanish,* **talón** *means both "heel" and "cheque".*

tambourine [tæmbə'riːn] *n* pandereta *f*
tame [teɪm] **1** *adj* (**a**) *(animal)* domado(a); *(by nature)* manso(a); *(person)* dócil (**b**) *(style)* soso(a)
2 *vt* domar

tamper [ˈtæmpə(r)] *vi* **to t. with** *(text)* adulterar; *(records, an entry)* falsificar; *(lock)* intentar forzar

tampon [ˈtæmpɒn] *n* tampón *m*

tan [tæn] **1** *n* (**a**) *(colour)* marrón rojizo (**b**) *(of skin)* bronceado *m*
  2 *adj (colour)* marrón rojizo
  3 *vt* (**a**) *(leather)* curtir (**b**) *(skin)* broncear
  4 *vi* ponerse moreno(a)

tang [tæŋ] *n* sabor *m* fuerte

tangent [ˈtændʒənt] *n* tangente *f*; *Fig* **to go off at a t.** salirse por la tangente

tangerine [tændʒəˈriːn] *n* clementina *f*

tangible [ˈtændʒəbəl] *adj* tangible

tangle [ˈtæŋɡəl] *n (of thread)* maraña *f*; *Fig* lío *m*; *Fig* **to get into a t.** hacerse un lío

tank [tæŋk] *n* (**a**) *(container)* depósito *m* (**b**) *Mil* tanque *m*

tanker [ˈtæŋkə(r)] *n Naut* tanque *m*; *(for oil)* petrolero *m*; *Aut* camión *m* cisterna

Tannoy® [ˈtænɔɪ] *n* sistema *m* de megafonía

tantalize [ˈtæntəlaɪz] *vt* atormentar

tantalizing [ˈtæntəlaɪzɪŋ] *adj* atormentador(a)

tantamount [ˈtæntəmaʊnt] *adj* **t. to** equivalente a

tantrum [ˈtæntrəm] *n* rabieta *f*

tap¹ [tæp] **1** *vt* golpear suavemente; *(with hand)* dar una palmadita a
  2 *vi* **to t. at the door** llamar suavemente a la puerta
  3 *n* golpecito *m*; **t. dancing** claqué *m*

tap² [tæp] **1** *n Br (for water)* grifo *m*, *Chile, Méx* llave *f*, *RP* canilla *f*; *Fig* **funds on t.** fondos *mpl* disponibles
  2 *vt* (**a**) *(tree)* sangrar; *Fig* **to t. new markets** explotar nuevos mercados (**b**) *(phone)* pinchar

tape [teɪp] **1** *n* (**a**) *(tree)* cinta *f*; **sticky t.** cinta adhesiva; **t. measure** cinta métrica (**b**) *(for recording)* cinta *f* (magnetofónica); **t. recorder** magnetófono *m*, cassette *m*; **t. recording** grabación *f*
  2 *vt* (**a**) pegar (con cinta adhesiva) (**b**) *(record)* grabar (en cinta)

taper [ˈteɪpə(r)] **1** *vi* estrecharse; *(to a point)* afilarse
  2 *n (candle)* vela *f*
  ▸ **taper off** *vi* ir disminuyendo

tapestry [ˈtæpɪstrɪ] *n* tapiz *m*

tapping [ˈtæpɪŋ] *n* (**a**) *(of tree)* sangría *f*; *(of resources)* explotación *f* (**b**) *Tel* intervención *f* ilegal de un teléfono

tar [tɑː(r)] *n* alquitrán *m*

target [ˈtɑːɡɪt] *n* (**a**) *(object aimed at)* blanco *m*; **t. practice** tiro *m* al blanco (**b**) *(purpose)* meta *f*

tariff [ˈtærɪf] *n* tarifa *f*, arancel *m*

tarmac® [ˈtɑːmæk] **1** *n* (**a**) *(substance)* alquitrán *m* (**b**) *Av* pista *f* de aterrizaje
  2 *vt* alquitranar

tarnish [ˈtɑːnɪʃ] *vt* deslustrar

tarpaulin [tɑːˈpɔːlɪn] *n* lona *f*

tart¹ [tɑːt] *n Br Culin* tarta *f*

tart² [tɑːt] *adj (taste)* ácido(a), agrio(a)

tart³ [tɑːt] *Fam* **1** *n* puta *f*
  2 *vt Br* **to t. oneself up** emperifollarse

tartan [ˈtɑːtən] *n* tartán *m*

tartar [ˈtɑːtə(r)] *n* (**a**) *Chem* tártaro *m* (**b**) *Culin* **t. sauce** salsa tártara

task [tɑːsk] *n* tarea *f*; **to take sb to t.** reprender a algn; *Mil* **t. force** destacamento *m* (de fuerzas)

tassel [ˈtæsəl] *n* borla *f*

taste [teɪst] **1** *n* (**a**) *(sense)* gusto *m*; *(flavour)* sabor *m*; **it has a burnt t.** sabe a quemado (**b**) *(sample) (of food)* bocado *m*; *(of drink)* trago *m*; **to give sb a t. of his own medicine** pagar a algn con la misma moneda (**c**) *(liking)* afición *f*; **to have a t. for sth** gustarle a uno algo (**d**) **in bad t.** de mal gusto; **to have (good) t.** tener (buen) gusto
  2 *vt (sample)* probar
  3 *vi* **to t. of sth** saber a algo

tasteful [ˈteɪstfʊl] *adj* de buen gusto

tasteless [ˈteɪstlɪs] *adj* (**a**) *(food)* soso(a) (**b**) *(in bad taste)* de mal gusto

tasty [ˈteɪstɪ] *adj* (**tastier, tastiest**) sabroso(a)

tattered [ˈtætəd] *adj* hecho(a) jirones

tatters [ˈtætəz] *npl* **in t.** hecho(a) jirones

tattoo¹ [tæˈtuː] *n Mil* retreta *f*

tattoo² [tæˈtuː] **1** *n (mark)* tatuaje *m*
  2 *vt* tatuar

tatty [ˈtætɪ] *adj* (**tattier, tattiest**) *Br* en mal estado; *(material, clothing)* raído(a); *(décor)* deslustrado(a)

taught [tɔːt] *pt & pp of* teach

taunt [tɔːnt] **1** *vt* **to t. sb with sth** echar algo en cara a algn
  2 *n* pulla *f*

Taurus [ˈtɔːrəs] *n* Tauro *m*

taut [tɔːt] *adj* tenso(a), tirante

tavern [ˈtævən] *n* taberna *f*

tawdry [ˈtɔːdrɪ] *adj* (**tawdrier, tawdriest**) hortera

tawn(e)y [ˈtɔːnɪ] *adj* leonado(a), rojizo(a)

tax [tæks] **1** *n* impuesto *m*; **t. free** exento(a) de impuestos; **t. collector** recaudador(a) *m,f* (de impuestos); **t. evasion** evasión *f* fiscal; **t. return** declaración *f* de renta

2 *vt* (**a**) gravar (**b**) *(patience etc)* poner a prueba

taxable ['tæksəbəl] *adj* imponible

taxation [tæk'seɪʃən] *n* impuestos *mpl*

taxi ['tæksɪ] **1** *n* taxi *m*; **t. driver** taxista *mf*; **t.** *Br* **rank** *or US* **stand** parada *f* de taxis
2 *vi (aircraft)* rodar por la pista

taxidermy ['tæksɪdɜːmɪ] *n* taxidermia *f*

taxing ['tæksɪŋ] *adj* exigente

taxpayer ['tækspeɪə(r)] *n* contribuyente *mf*

TB [tiː'biː] *n (tuberculosis)* tuberculosis *f inv*

tea [tiː] *n* (**a**) té *m*; **t. bag** bolsita *f* de té; **t. break** descanso *m*; **t. cosy** cubretetera *f*; **t. leaf** hoja *f* de té; **t. service** *or* **set** juego *m* de té; **t. towel** paño *m* (de cocina) (**b**) *(snack)* merienda *f*; **(high) t.** merienda-cena *f*

teach [tiːtʃ] **1** *vt (pt & pp* **taught**) enseñar; *(subject)* dar clases de; **to t. sb (how) to do sth** enseñar a algn a hacer algo; *US* **to t. school** ser profesor(a)
2 *vi* dar clases, ser profesor(a)

teacher ['tiːtʃə(r)] *n* profesor(a) *m,f*; *(in primary school)* maestro(a) *m,f*

teaching ['tiːtʃɪŋ] *n* enseñanza *f*

teacup ['tiːkʌp] *n* taza *f* de té

teak [tiːk] *n* teca *f*

team [tiːm] *n* equipo *m*; *(of oxen)* yunta *f*

team-mate ['tiːmmeɪt] *n* compañero(a) *m,f* de equipo

teamwork ['tiːmwɜːk] *n* trabajo *m* en equipo

teapot ['tiːpɒt] *n* tetera *f*

tear¹ [tɪə(r)] *n* lágrima *f*; **to be in tears** estar llorando; **t. gas** gas lacrimógeno

tear² [teə(r)] **1** *vt (pt* **tore**; *pp* **torn**) (**a**) rajar, desgarrar (**b**) **to t. sth out of sb's hands** arrancarle algo de las manos a algn
2 *vi* (**a**) *(cloth)* rajarse (**b**) **to t. along** ir a toda velocidad
3 *n* desgarrón *m*; *(in clothes)* rasgón *m*
▶ **tear down** *vt sep* derribar
▶ **tear off** *vt sep* arrancar
▶ **tear out** *vt sep* arrancar
▶ **tear up** *vt sep* (**a**) romper, hacer pedazos (**b**) *(uproot)* arrancar de raiz

tearful ['tɪəfʊl] *adj* lloroso(a)

tearoom ['tiːruːm] *n Br* = **teashop**

tease [tiːz] **1** *vt* tomar el pelo a
2 *n* bromista *mf*

teashop ['tiːʃɒp] *n Br* salón *m* de té

teaspoon ['tiːspuːn] *n* cucharilla *f*

teaspoonful ['tiːspuːnfʊl] *n* cucharadita *f*

teat [tiːt] *n (of animal)* teta *f*; *(of bottle)* tetina *f*

teatime ['tiːtaɪm] *n* hora *f* del té

technical ['teknɪkəl] *adj* técnico(a); **t. college** instituto *m* de formación profesional

technicality [teknɪ'kælɪtɪ] *n* detalle técnico

technically ['teknɪkəlɪ] *adv (theoretically)* en teoría

technician [tek'nɪʃən] *n* técnico(a) *m,f*

technique [tek'niːk] *n* técnica *f*

technological [teknə'lɒdʒɪkəl] *adj* tecnológico(a)

technology [tek'nɒlədʒɪ] *n* tecnología *f*

teddy bear ['tedɪbeə(r)] *n* oso *m* de felpa

tedious ['tiːdɪəs] *adj* tedioso(a), aburrido(a)

tee [tiː] *n (in golf)* tee *m*

teem [tiːm] *vi* **to t. with** rebosar de; *Fam* **it was teeming down** llovía a cántaros

teenage ['tiːneɪdʒ] *adj* adolescente

teenager ['tiːneɪdʒə(r)] *n* adolescente *mf*

teens [tiːnz] *npl* adolescencia *f*

tee-shirt ['tiːʃɜːt] *n* camiseta *f*

teeter ['tiːtə(r)] *vi* balancearse

teeth [tiːθ] *pl of* **tooth**

teethe [tiːð] *vi* echar los dientes

teething ['tiːðɪŋ] *n* **t. ring** chupador *m*; *Fig* **t. troubles** dificultades *fpl* iniciales

teetotaller [tiː'təʊtələ(r)] *n* abstemio(a) *m,f*

telecommunications ['telɪkəmjuːnɪ'keɪʃənz] *n sing* telecomunicaciones *fpl*

telegram ['telɪgræm] *n* telegrama *m*

telegraph ['telɪgrɑːf] **1** *n* telégrafo *m*; **t. pole** poste telegráfico
2 *vt & vi* telegrafiar

telepathy [tɪ'lepəθɪ] *n* telepatía *f*

telephone ['telɪfəʊn] **1** *n* teléfono *m*; **t. banking** telebanca *f*; *Br* **t. booth** *or* **box** cabina *f* (telefónica); **t. call** llamada telefónica; **t. directory** guía telefónica; **t. number** número *m* de teléfono
2 *vt* telefonear, llamar por teléfono

telephonist [tɪ'lefənɪst] *n Br* telefonista *mf*

telephoto ['telɪfəʊtəʊ] *adj* **t. lens** teleobjetivo *m*

teleprinter ['telɪprɪntə(r)] *n* teletipo *m*

telescope ['telɪskəʊp] **1** *n* telescopio *m*
2 *vi* plegarse (como un catalejo)
3 *vt* plegar

telescopic [telɪ'skɒpɪk] *adj (umbrella)* plegable

televise ['telɪvaɪz] *vt* televisar

television ['telɪvɪʒən] *n* televisión *f*; **t. programme** programa *m* de televisión; **t. (set)** televisor *m*

teleworker [ˈtelɪwɜːkə(r)] *n* teletrabajador(a) *m,f*

teleworking [ˈtelɪwɜːkɪŋ] *n* teletrabajo *m*

telex [ˈteleks] **1** *n* télex *m*
2 *vt* enviar por télex

tell [tel] **1** *vt* (*pt & pp* **told**) (**a**) (*say*) decir; (*relate*) contar; (*inform*) comunicar; **to t. lies** mentir; **to t. sb about sth** contarle algo a algn; **you're telling me!** ¡a mí me lo vas a contar! (**b**) (*order*) mandar; **to t. sb to do sth** decir a algn que haga algo (**c**) (*distinguish*) distinguir; **to know how to t. the time** saber decir la hora (**d**) **all told** en total
2 *vi* (**a**) (*reveal*) reflejar (**b**) **who can t.?** (*know*) ¿quién sabe? (**c**) (*have effect*) notarse; **the pressure is telling on her** está acusando la presión
▶ **tell off** *vt sep Fam* regañar, reñir

teller [ˈtelə(r)] *n* (*in bank etc*) cajero(a) *m,f*

telling [ˈtelɪŋ] *adj* (*action*) eficaz; (*blow, argument*) contundente

telltale [ˈtelteɪl] *n* chivato(a) *m,f*; **t. signs** señales reveladoras

telly [ˈtelɪ] *n Br Fam* **the t.** la tele

temp [temp] *n Fam* trabajador(a) *m,f* temporal

temper [ˈtempə(r)] **1** *n* (**a**) (*mood*) humor *m*; **to keep one's t.** no perder la calma; **to lose one's t.** perder los estribos (**b**) (*temperament*) **to have a bad t.** tener (mal) genio
2 *vt* (*in metallurgy*) templar; *Fig* suavizar

temperament [ˈtempərəmənt] *n* temperamento *m*

temperamental [tempərəmentəl] *adj* temperamental

temperate [ˈtempərɪt] *adj* (**a**) mesurado(a) (**b**) (*climate*) templado(a)

temperature [ˈtemprɪtʃə(r)] *n* temperatura *f*; **to have a t.** tener fiebre

tempest [ˈtempɪst] *n* tempestad *f*

temple¹ [ˈtempəl] *n Archit* templo *m*

temple² [ˈtempəl] *n Anat* sien *f*

tempo [ˈtempəʊ] *n* tempo *m*

temporary [ˈtempərərɪ] *adj* provisional; (*setback, improvement*) momentáneo(a); (*staff*) temporal

tempt [tempt] *vt* tentar; **to t. providence** tentar la suerte; **to t. sb to do sth** incitar a algn a hacer algo

temptation [tempˈteɪʃən] *n* tentación *f*

tempting [ˈtemptɪŋ] *adj* tentador(a)

ten [ten] *adj & n* diez (*m inv*)

tenable [ˈtenəbəl] *adj* (*opinion*) sostenible

tenacious [tɪˈneɪʃəs] *adj* tenaz

tenancy [ˈtenənsɪ] *n* (*of house*) alquiler *m*; (*of land*) arrendamiento *m*

tenant [ˈtenənt] *n* (*of house*) inquilino(a) *m,f*; (*of farm*) arrendatario(a) *m,f*

tend¹ [tend] *vi* (*be inclined*) tender, tener tendencia (**to** a)

tend² [tend] *vt* (*care for*) cuidar

tendency [ˈtendənsɪ] *n* tendencia *f*

tender¹ [ˈtendə(r)] *adj* (*affectionate*) cariñoso(a); (*compassionate*) compasivo(a); (*meat*) tierno(a)

tender² [ˈtendə(r)] **1** *vt* ofrecer; **to t. one's resignation** presentar la dimisión
2 *vi Com* **to t. for** sacar a concurso
3 *n* (**a**) *Com* oferta *f* (**b**) **legal t.** moneda *f* de curso legal

tenderness [ˈtendənɪs] *n* ternura *f*

tendon [ˈtendən] *n* tendón *m*

tenement [ˈtenɪmənt] *n* casa *f* de vecindad

tenet [ˈtenɪt] *n* principio *m*

tennis [ˈtenɪs] *n* tenis *m*; **t. ball** pelota *f* de tenis; **t. court** pista *f* de tenis; **t. player** tenista *mf*; **t. racket** raqueta *f* de tenis; **t. shoe** zapatilla *f* de tenis

tenor [ˈtenə(r)] *n Mus* tenor *m*

tense¹ [tens] *adj* tenso(a)

tense² [tens] *n Gram* tiempo *m*

tension [ˈtenʃən] *n* tensión *f*

tent [tent] *n* tienda *f* de campaña; **t. peg** estaca *f*

tentacle [ˈtentəkəl] *n* tentáculo *m*

tentative [ˈtentətɪv] *adj* (**a**) (*not definite*) de prueba (**b**) (*hesitant*) indeciso(a)

tenterhooks [ˈtentəhʊks] *npl Fig* **on t.** sobre ascuas

tenth [tenθ] **1** *adj & n* décimo(a) (*m,f*)
2 *n* (*fraction*) décimo *m*

tenuous [ˈtenjʊəs] *adj* (**a**) tenue (**b**) (*argument*) flojo(a)

tenure [ˈtenjʊə(r)] *n* (**a**) (*of office*) ocupación *f* (**b**) (*of property*) arrendamiento *m*

tepid [ˈtepɪd] *adj* tibio(a)

term [tɜːm] **1** *n* (**a**) (*period*) período *m*; *Educ* trimestre *m*; **t. of office** mandato *m*, legislatura *f*; **in the long/short t.** a largo/corto plazo (**b**) (*word*) término *m*; *Fig* **in terms of money** en cuanto al dinero (**c**) **terms** (*conditions*) condiciones *fpl*; **to come to terms with** hacerse a la idea de (**d**) **to be on good/bad terms with sb** tener buenas/malas relaciones con algn
2 *vt* calificar de

terminal [ˈtɜːmɪnəl] **1** *adj* terminal; **t. cancer** cáncer incurable
2 *n* terminal *f*

terminate ['tɜːmɪneɪt] **1** vt terminar; **to t. a pregnancy** abortar
2 vi terminarse
termini ['tɜːmɪnaɪ] pl of **terminus**
terminology [tɜːmɪ'nɒlədʒɪ] n terminología f
terminus ['tɜːmɪnəs] n (pl **termini**) terminal m
terrace ['terəs] n (**a**) Agr bancal m (**b**) Br (of houses) hilera f de casas (**c**) (patio) terraza f (**d**) Ftb **the terraces** las gradas
terraced ['terəst] adj Br **t. houses** casas fpl (de estilo uniforme) en hilera
terrain [tə'reɪn] n terreno m
terrible ['terəbəl] adj terrible; Fig **I feel t.** (ill) me encuentro fatal
terribly ['terəblɪ] adv terriblemente
terrier ['terɪə(r)] n terrier m
terrific [tə'rɪfɪk] adj (**a**) Fam (excellent) fenomenal (**b**) (extreme) tremendo(a)
terrify ['terɪfaɪ] vt aterrorizar
terrifying ['terɪfaɪɪŋ] adj aterrador(a)
territory ['terɪtərɪ] n territorio m
terror ['terə(r)] n terror m
terrorism ['terərɪzəm] n terrorismo m
terrorist ['terərɪst] adj & n terrorista (mf)
terrorize ['terəraɪz] vt aterrorizar
terry ['terɪ] n **t. towel** toalla f de rizo
terse [tɜːs] adj (curt) lacónico(a)
test [test] **1** vt probar, someter a una prueba; (analyse) analizar; Med hacer un análisis de
2 n prueba f, examen m; **to put to the t.** poner a prueba; **to stand the t.** pasar la prueba; **t. match** partido m internacional; **t. pilot** piloto m de pruebas; **t. tube** probeta f; **t.-tube baby** niño m probeta
testament ['testəmənt] n testamento m; **Old/New T.** Antiguo/Nuevo Testamento
testicle ['testɪkəl] n testículo m
testify ['testɪfaɪ] **1** vt declarar
2 vi Fig **to t. to sth** atestiguar algo
testimonial [testɪ'məʊnɪəl] n recomendación f
testimony ['testɪmənɪ] n testimonio m, declaración f
tetanus ['tetənəs] n tétano(s) m inv
tether ['teðə(r)] **1** n ronzal m; Fig **to be at the end of one's t.** estar hasta la coronilla
2 vt (animal) atar
Texas ['teksəs] n Tejas
text [tekst] n texto m
textbook ['tekstbʊk] n libro m de texto
textile ['tekstaɪl] **1** n tejido m
2 adj textil
texture ['tekstʃə(r)] n textura f
Thai [taɪ] adj & n tailandés(esa) (m,f)
Thailand ['taɪlænd] n Tailandia

Thames [temz] n **the T.** el Támesis
than [ðæn, unstressed ðən] conj que; (with numbers) de; **he's older t. me** es mayor que yo; **I have more/less t. you** tengo más/menos que tú; **more interesting t. we thought** más interesante de lo que creíamos; **more t. once** más de una vez; **more t. ten people** más de diez personas
thank [θæŋk] vt agradecer a; **t. you** gracias
thankful ['θæŋkfʊl] adj agradecido(a)
thankless ['θæŋklɪs] adj (task) ingrato(a)
thanks [θæŋks] npl gracias fpl; **no t.** no gracias; **many t.** muchas gracias; **t. for phoning** gracias por llamar; **t. to** gracias a
thanksgiving [θæŋks'gɪvɪŋ] n US **T. Day** Día m de Acción de Gracias
that [ðæt, unstressed ðət] **1** dem pron (pl **those**) (**a**) ése m, ésa f; (further away) aquél m, aquélla f; **this one is new but t. is old** éste es nuevo pero ése es viejo
(**b**) (indefinite) eso; (remote) aquello; **after t.** después de eso; **like t.** así; **t.'s right** eso es; **t.'s where I live** allí vivo yo; **what's t.?** ¿qué es eso?; **who's t.?** ¿quién es?
(**c**) (with relative) el/la; **all those I saw** todos los que vi
2 dem adj (pl **those**) (masculine) ese; (feminine) esa; (further away) (masculine) aquel; (feminine) aquella; **at t. time** en aquella época; **t. book** ese/aquel libro; **t. one** ése/aquél
3 rel pron (**a**) (subject, direct object) que; **all (t.) you said** todo lo que dijiste; **the letter (t.) I sent you** la carta que te envié
(**b**) (governed by preposition) que, el/la que, los/las que, el/la cual, los/las cuales; **the car (t.) they came in** el coche en el que vinieron
(**c**) (when) que, en que; **the moment (t.) you arrived** el momento en que llegaste

---
El pronombre relativo **that** puede omitirse salvo cuando es sujeto de la oración subordinada.
---

4 conj que; **come here so (t.) I can see you** ven aquí (para) que te vea; **he said (t.) he would come** dijo que vendría

---
La conjunción **that** se puede omitir cuando introduce una oración subordinada.
---

5 adv así de, tanto, tan; **cut off t. much** córteme un trozo así de grande; **I don't think it can be t. old** no creo que sea tan viejo; **we haven't got t. much money**

no tenemos tanto dinero

thatched [θætʃt] *adj* cubierto(a) con paja; **t. cottage** casita *f* con techo de paja; **t. roof** techo *m* de paja

thaw [θɔː] **1** *vt* (*snow*) derretir; (*food, freezer*) descongelar

2 *vi* descongelarse; (*snow*) derretirse

3 *n* deshielo *m*

the [ðə, *before vowel sound* ðɪ, *emphatic* ðiː] **1** *def art* (**a**) el/la; *pl* los/las; **at/to t.** al/a la; *pl* a los/a las; **of** *or* **from t.** del/de la; *pl* de los/de las; **t. Alps** los Alpes; **t. right time** la hora exacta; **t. voice of t. people** la voz del pueblo

(**b**) (*omitted*) **George t. Sixth** Jorge Sexto

(**c**) **by t. day** al día; **by t. dozen** a docenas

(**d**) (*with adjectives used as nouns*) **t. elderly** los ancianos

(**e**) (*indicating kind*) **he's not t. person to do that** no es de los que hacen tales cosas

(**f**) (*enough*) **he hasn't t. patience to wait** no tiene suficiente paciencia para esperar

2 *adv* **t. more t. merrier** cuantos más mejor; **t. sooner t. better** cuanto antes mejor

theatre, *US* **theater** [ˈθɪətə(r)] *n* teatro *m*

theatre-goer, *US* **theater-goer** [ˈθɪətə-gəʊə(r)] *n* aficionado(a) *m,f* al teatro

theatrical [θɪˈætrɪkəl] *adj* teatral

theft [θeft] *n* robo *m*; **petty t.** hurto *m*

their [ðeə(r)] *poss adj* (*one thing*) su; (*various things*) sus

theirs [ðeəz] *poss pron* (el) suyo/(la) suya; *pl* (los) suyos/(las) suyas

them [ðem, *unstressed* ðəm] *pers pron pl* (**a**) (*direct object*) los/las; (*indirect object*) les; **I know t.** los/las conozco; **I shall tell t. so** se lo diré (a ellos/ellas); **it's t.!** ¡son ellos!; **speak to t.** hábleles (**b**) (*with preposition*) ellos/ellas; **walk in front of t.** camine delante de ellos; **they took the keys away with t.** se llevaron las llaves; **both of t., the two of t.** los dos; **neither of t.** ninguno de los dos; **none of t.** ninguno de ellos

theme [θiːm] *n* tema *m*; **t. tune** sintonía *f*

themselves [ðəmˈselvz] *pers pron pl* (*as subject*) ellos mismos/ellas mismas; (*as direct or indirect object*) se; (*after a preposition*) sí mismos/sí mismas; **they did it by t.** lo hicieron ellos solos

then [ðen] **1** *adv* (**a**) (*at that time*) entonces; **since t.** desde entonces; **there and t.** en el acto; **till t.** hasta entonces (**b**) (*next, afterwards*) luego (**c**) (*anyway*) de todas

formas (**d**) (*in that case*) entonces; **go t.** pues vete

2 *conj* entonces

3 *adj* **the t. president** el entonces presidente

theology [θɪˈɒlədʒɪ] *n* teología *f*

theoretic(al) [θɪəˈretɪk(əl)] *adj* teórico(a)

theoretically [θɪəˈretɪklɪ)] *adv* teóricamente

theory [ˈθɪərɪ] *n* teoría *f*

therapist [ˈθerəpɪst] *n* terapeuta *mf*

therapy [ˈθerəpɪ] *n* terapia *f*

there [ðeə(r), *unstressed* ðə(r)] **1** *adv* (**a**) (*indicating place*) allí, allá; (*nearer speaker*) ahí; **here and t.** acá y allá; **in t.** ahí dentro; **is Peter t.?** ¿está Peter? (**b**) (*emphatic*) **that man t.** aquel hombre (**c**) (*unstressed*) **t. is .../t. are ...** hay...; **t. were many cars** había muchos coches; **t. were six of us** éramos seis (**d**) (*in respect*) **t.'s the difficulty** ahí está la dificultad

2 *interj* **so t.!** ¡ea!; **t., t.** bien, bien

thereabouts [ˈðeərəbaʊts], *US* **thereabout** [ˈðeərəbaʊt] *adv* **in Cambridge or t.** en Cambridge o por allí cerca; **at four o'clock or t.** a las cuatro o así

thereafter [ðeərˈɑːftə(r)] *adv* a partir de entonces

thereby [ˈðeəbaɪ] *adv* por eso *or* ello

therefore [ˈðeəfɔː(r)] *adv* por lo tanto, por eso

thermal [ˈθɜːməl] **1** *adj* (*spring*) termal; *Phys* térmico(a)

2 *n Met* corriente térmica

thermometer [θəˈmɒmɪtə(r)] *n* termómetro *m*

Thermos® [ˈθɜːməs] *n* **T. (flask)** termo *m*

thermostat [ˈθɜːməstæt] *n* termostato *m*

thesaurus [θɪˈsɔːrəs] *n* diccionario *m* de sinónimos

these [ðiːz] **1** *dem adj pl* estos(as)

2 *dem pron pl* éstos(as); *see* **this**

thesis [ˈθiːsɪs] *n* (*pl* **theses** [ˈθiːsiːz]) tesis *f inv*

they [ðeɪ] *pron pl* (**a**) ellos/ellas (*usually omitted in Spanish, except for contrast*); **t. are dancing** están bailando; **t. are rich** son ricos (**b**) (*stressed*) **t. alone** ellos solos; **t. themselves told me** me lo dijeron ellos mismos (**c**) (*with relative*) los/las (**d**) (*indefinite*) **that's what t. say** eso es lo que se dice; **t. say that ...** se dice que ...

thick [θɪk] **1** *adj* (**a**) (*book etc*) grueso(a); **a wall 2 m t.** un muro de 2 m de espesor (**b**) (*dense*) espeso(a) (**c**) *Fam* (*stupid*) tonto(a)

2 *adv* densamente

3 *n* **to be in the t. of it** estar metido(a) de lleno

thicken ['θɪkən] **1** *vt* espesar

2 *vi* espesarse; *Fig (plot)* complicarse

thickness ['θɪknɪs] *n (of wall etc)* espesor *m*; *(of wire, lips)* grueso *m*; *(of liquid, woodland)* espesura *f*

thickset [θɪk'set] *adj (person)* rechoncho(a)

thick-skinned [θɪk'skɪnd] *adj Fig* poco sensible

thief [θiːf] *n* (*pl* **thieves** [θiːvz]) ladrón(ona) *m,f*

thigh [θaɪ] *n* muslo *m*

thimble ['θɪmbəl] *n* dedal *m*

thin [θɪn] **1** *adj* (**thinner, thinnest**) (**a**) delgado(a); **a t. slice** una loncha fina (**b**) *(hair, vegetation)* ralo(a); *(liquid)* claro(a); *(population)* escaso(a) (**c**) *Fig (voice)* débil; **a t. excuse** un pobre pretexto

2 *vt* **to t. (down)** *(paint)* diluir

thing [θɪŋ] *n* (**a**) cosa *f*; **my things** *(clothing)* mi ropa *f*; *(possessions)* mis cosas *fpl*; **for one t.** en primer lugar; **the t. is ...** resulta que ...; **what with one t. and another** entre unas cosas y otras; **as things are** tal como están las cosas (**b**) **poor little t.!** ¡pobrecito(a)!

think [θɪŋk] **1** *vt* (*pt & pp* **thought**) (**a**) *(believe)* pensar, creer; **I t. so/not** creo que sí/no (**b**) **I thought as much** yo me lo imaginaba

2 *vi* (**a**) pensar (**of** *or* **about** en); **give me time to t.** dame tiempo para reflexionar; **to t. ahead** prevenir (**b**) *(have as opinion)* opinar, pensar; **to t. highly of sb** apreciar a algn; **what do you t.?** ¿a ti qué te parece? (**c**) **just t.!** ¡imagínate!

▸ **think out** *vt sep* meditar; **a carefully thought-out answer** una respuesta razonada

▸ **think over** *vt sep* reflexionar; **we'll have to t. it over** lo tendremos que pensar

▸ **think up** *vt sep* imaginar, idear

thinking ['θɪŋkɪŋ] *adj* racional

think-tank ['θɪŋktæŋk] *n Fam* grupo *m* de expertos

thinly ['θɪnlɪ] *adv* poco, ligeramente

third [θɜːd] **1** *adj* tercero(a); *(before masculine singular noun)* tercer; **(on) the t. of March** el tres de marzo; **the T. World** el Tercer Mundo; **t. party insurance** seguro *m* a terceros

2 *n* (**a**) *(in series)* tercero(a) *m,f* (**b**) *(fraction)* tercio *m*, tercera parte

thirdly ['θɜːdlɪ] *adv* en tercer lugar

third-rate ['θɜːdreɪt] *adj* de calidad inferior

thirst [θɜːst] *n* sed *f*

thirsty ['θɜːstɪ] *adj* (**thirstier, thirstiest**) sediento(a); **to be t.** tener sed

thirteen [θɜː'tiːn] *adj & n* trece *(m inv)*

thirteenth [θɜː'tiːnθ] **1** *adj & n* decimotercero(a) *(m,f)*

2 *n (fraction)* decimotercera parte

thirtieth ['θɜːtɪɪθ] **1** *adj & n* trigésimo(a) *(m,f)*

2 *n (fraction)* trigésima parte

thirty ['θɜːtɪ] *adj & n* treinta *(m inv)*

this [ðɪs] **1** *dem adj* (*pl* **these**) *(masculine)* este; *(feminine)* esta; **t. book/these books** este libro/estos libros; **t. one** éste/ésta

2 *dem pron* (*pl* **these**) (**a**) *(indefinite)* esto; **it was like t.** fue así (**b**) *(place)* **t. is where we met** fue aquí donde nos conocimos (**c**) *(time)* **it should have come before t.** debería haber llegado ya (**d**) *(specific person or thing)* éste *m*, ésta *f*; **I prefer these to those** me gustan más éstos que aquéllos; *(introduction)* **t. is Mr Álvarez** le presento al Sr. Álvarez; *Tel* **t. is Julia (speaking)** soy Julia

3 *adv* **he got it. far** llegó hasta aquí; **t. small/big** así de pequeño/grande

thistle ['θɪsəl] *n* cardo *m*

thong [θɒŋ] *n* (**a**) *(for fastening)* correa *f* (**b**) *US & Austral (sandal)* chancla *f*

thorax ['θɔːræks] *n* tórax *m*

thorn [θɔːn] *n* espina *f*

thorough ['θʌrə] *adj (careful)* minucioso(a); *(work)* concienzudo(a); *(knowledge)* profundo(a); **to carry out a t. enquiry into a matter** investigar a fondo un asunto

thoroughbred ['θʌrəbred] **1** *adj (horse)* de pura sangre

2 *n (horse)* pura sangre *mf*

thoroughfare ['θʌrəfeə(r)] *n (road)* carretera *f*; *(street)* calle *f*

thoroughly ['θʌrəlɪ] *adv (carefully)* a fondo; *(wholly)* completamente

those [ðəʊz] **1** *dem pron pl* ésos(as); *(remote)* aquéllos(as); **t. who** los que/las que

2 *dem adj pl* esos(as); *(remote)* aquellos(as); *see* **that**

though [ðəʊ] **1** *conj* (**a**) aunque; **strange t. it may seem** por (muy) extraño que parezca (**b**) **as t.** como si; **it looks as t. he's gone** parece que se ha ido

2 *adv* sin embargo

thought [θɔːt] **1** *n* (**a**) *(act of thinking)* pensamiento *m*; **what a tempting t.!** ¡qué idea más tentadora! (**b**) *(reflection)* reflexión *f* (**c**) **it's the t. that counts** *(intention)* lo que cuenta es la intención

2 *pt & pp of* **think**

thoughtful ['θɔːtfʊl] *adj (pensive)* pensativo(a); *(considerate)* atento(a)

thoughtless ['θɔːtlɪs] *adj (person)* desconsiderado(a); *(action)* irreflexivo(a)

thousand ['θaʊzənd] *adj & n* mil *(m inv)*; **thousands of people** miles de personas

thousandth ['θaʊzənθ] **1** *adj* milésimo(a)

2 *n* (**a**) *(in series)* milésimo(a) *m,f* (**b**) *(fraction)* milésima parte

thrash [θræʃ] **1** *vt* dar una paliza a

2 *vi* **to t. about** *or* **around** agitarse

▸ **thrash out** *vt sep* discutir a fondo

thread [θred] **1** *n* (**a**) hilo *m*; **length of t.** hebra *f* (**b**) *(of screw)* rosca *f*

2 *vt* (**a**) *(needle)* enhebrar (**b**) **to t. one's way (through)** colarse (por)

threadbare ['θredbeə(r)] *adj* raído(a)

threat [θret] *n* amenaza *f*

threaten ['θretən] *vt* amenazar; **to t. to do sth** amenazar con hacer algo

threatening ['θretənɪŋ] *adj* amenazador(a)

threateningly ['θretənɪŋlɪ] *adv* de modo amenazador

three [θriː] *adj & n* tres *(m inv)*

three-dimensional [ˌθriːdɪˈmenʃənəl] *adj* tridimensional

threefold ['θriːfəʊld] **1** *adj* triple

2 *adv* tres veces; **to increase t.** triplicarse

three-piece ['θriːpiːs] *adj* **t. suit** traje *m* de tres piezas; **t. suite** tresillo *m*

three-ply ['θriːplaɪ] *adj* de tres hebras

three-wheeler [θriːˈwiːlə(r)] *n Aut* coche *m* de tres ruedas; *(tricycle)* triciclo *m*

thresh [θreʃ] *vt* trillar

threshold ['θreʃəʊld] *n* umbral *m*; *Fig* **to be on the t. of** estar a las puertas *or* en los umbrales de

threw [θruː] *pt of* **throw**

thrifty ['θrɪftɪ] *adj* (**thriftier, thriftiest**) económico(a), ahorrador(a)

thrill [θrɪl] **1** *n* (**a**) *(excitement)* emoción *f* (**b**) *(quiver)* estremecimiento *m*

2 *vt (excite)* emocionar; *(audience)* entusiasmar

thriller ['θrɪlə(r)] *n* novela *f*/película *f* de suspense

thrilling ['θrɪlɪŋ] *adj* emocionante

thrive [θraɪv] *vi (pt* **thrived** *or* **throve**; *pp* **thrived** *or* **thriven** ['θrɪvən]) (**a**) *(person)* rebosar de salud (**b**) *Fig (business)* prosperar; **he thrives on it** le viene de maravilla

thriving ['θraɪvɪŋ] *adj Fig* próspero(a)

throat [θrəʊt] *n* garganta *f*

throb [θrɒb] **1** *n (of heart)* latido *m*; *(of machine)* zumbido *m*

2 *vi (heart)* latir; *(machine)* zumbar; **my head is throbbing** me va a estallar la cabeza

throes [θrəʊz] *npl* **to be in one's death t.** estar agonizando; *Fig* **in the t. of ...** en pleno(a) ...

thrombosis [θrɒmˈbəʊsɪs] *n Med* trombosis *f inv*

throne [θrəʊn] *n* trono *m*

throng [θrɒŋ] **1** *n* multitud *f*, gentío *m*

2 *vi* apiñarse

3 *vt* atestar

throttle ['θrɒtəl] **1** *n* **t. (valve)** *(of engine)* válvula reguladora

2 *vt (person)* estrangular

▸ **throttle back** *vt sep (engine)* desacelerar

through [θruː] **1** *prep* (**a**) *(place)* a través de, por; **to look t. the window** mirar por la ventana

(**b**) *(time)* a lo largo de; **all t. his life** durante toda su vida; *US* **Tuesday t. Thursday** desde el martes hasta el jueves inclusive

(**c**) *(by means of)* por, mediante; **I learnt of it t. Jack** me enteré por Jack

(**d**) *(because of)* a *or* por causa de; **t. ignorance** por ignorancia

2 *adj* **a t. train** un tren directo; **t. traffic** tránsito *m*

3 *adv* (**a**) *(from one side to the other)* de un lado a otro; **to let sb t.** dejar pasar a algn; *Fig* **socialist/French t. and t.** socialista/francés por los cuatro costados

(**b**) **I'm t. with him** he terminado con él

(**c**) *Tel* **to get t. to sb** comunicar con algn; **you're t.** ¡hablen!

throughout [θruːˈaʊt] **1** *prep* por todo(a); **t. the year** durante todo el año

2 *adv (place)* en todas partes; *(time)* todo el tiempo

throve [θrəʊv] *pt of* **thrive**

throw [θrəʊ] **1** *vt (pt* **threw**; *pp* **thrown**) (**a**) tirar, arrojar; *(to the ground)* derribar; *(rider)* desmontar; *Fig* **he threw a fit** le dio un ataque; *Fig* **to t. a party** dar una fiesta (**b**) *(disconcert)* desconcertar

2 *n* tiro *m*, lanzamiento *m*; *(in wrestling)* derribo *m*

▸ **throw away** *vt sep (rubbish)* tirar; *(money)* malgastar; *(opportunity)* perder

▸ **throw in** *vt sep* (**a**) tirar; *Sport* sacar de banda; *Fig* **to t. in the towel** arrojar la toalla (**b**) *(include)* añadir; *(in deal)* incluir (gratis)

▶**throw off** *vt sep (person, thing)* deshacerse de; *(clothes)* quitarse

▶**throw out** *vt sep (rubbish)* tirar; *(person)* echar

▶**throw up 1** *vt sep* (**a**) lanzar al aire (**b**) *Constr* construir rápidamente
2 *vi Fam* vomitar, devolver

throwaway ['θrəʊəweɪ] *adj* desechable

throw-in ['θrəʊɪn] *n Sport* saque *m* de banda

thrown [θrəʊn] *pp of* **throw**

thru [θruː] *prep, adj & adv US Fam* = **through**

thrush [θrʌʃ] *n Orn* tordo *m*, zorzal *m*

thrust [θrʌst] **1** *vt (pt & pp* **thrust**) empujar con fuerza; **he t. a letter into my hand** me puso una carta violentamente en la mano
2 *n (push)* empujón *m*; *Av & Phys* empuje *m*

thud [θʌd] *n* ruido sordo

thug [θʌg] *n (lout)* gamberro *m*; *(criminal)* criminal *m*

thumb [θʌm] **1** *n* pulgar *m*
2 *vt* (**a**) manosear (**b**) **to t. a lift** hacer autostop

▶**thumb through** *vt insep (book)* hojear

thumbtack ['θʌmtæk] *n US* chincheta *f*

thump [θʌmp] **1** *n* (**a**) *(sound)* ruido sordo (**b**) *(blow)* golpazo *m*; *Fam* torta *f*
2 *vt* golpear
3 *vi* (**a**) **to t. on the table** golpear la mesa (**b**) *(heart)* latir ruidosamente

thunder ['θʌndə(r)] **1** *n* trueno *m*; **t. of applause** estruendo *m* de aplausos
2 *vi* tronar

thunderbolt ['θʌndəbəʊlt] *n (lighting)* rayo *m*; *Fig (news)* bomba *f*

thunderclap ['θʌndəklæp] *n* trueno *m*

thunderous ['θʌndərəs] *adj Fig* ensordecedor(a)

thunderstorm ['θʌndəstɔːm] *n* tormenta *f*

thundery ['θʌndərɪ] *adj (weather)* tormentoso(a)

Thursday ['θɜːzdɪ] *n* jueves *m*

thus [ðʌs] *adv* así, de esta manera; **and t. ...** así que ...

thwart [θwɔːt] *vt* frustrar, desbaratar

thyme [taɪm] *n* tomillo *m*

thyroid ['θaɪrɔɪd] *n* tiroides *f inv*

tiara [tɪ'ɑːrə] *n* diadema *f*; *Rel* tiara *f*

tic [tɪk] *n* tic *m*

tick[1] [tɪk] **1** *n* (**a**) *(sound)* tic-tac *m* (**b**) *Br Fam* **I'll do it in a t.** ahora mismo lo hago (**c**) *(mark)* marca *f* de visto bueno
2 *vi* hacer tic-tac
3 *vt* marcar

▶**tick off** *vt sep* (**a**) *(mark)* marcar (**b**) *Br Fam (reprimand)* regañar

▶**tick over** *vi Aut* funcionar al ralentí

tick[2] [tɪk] *n (insect)* garrapata *f*

ticket ['tɪkɪt] *n* (**a**) *(for bus etc)* billete *m*, *Am* boleto *m*; *(for theatre, cinema)* entrada *f*, *Méx* boleto; *(for lottery)* décimo *m*, *Am* boleto; **t. collector** revisor(a) *m,f*; **t. office** taquilla *f*; **t.** *Br* **tout** *or US* **scalper** revendedor *m* de entradas (**b**) *(receipt)* recibo *m* (**c**) *(label)* etiqueta *f* (**d**) *Aut* multa *f*

tickle ['tɪkəl] **1** *vt* hacer cosquillas a
2 *vi* hacer cosquillas
3 *n* cosquillas *fpl*

ticklish ['tɪklɪʃ] *adj* **to be t.** tener cosquillas

tick-tack-toe ['tɪktæk'təʊ] *n US* tres en raya *m*

tidal ['taɪdəl] *adj* de la marea; **t. wave** ola *f* gigante

tidbit ['tɪdbɪt] *n US* = **titbit**

tiddlywinks ['tɪdlɪwɪŋks] *n sing (game)* pulga *f*

tide [taɪd] *n* (**a**) marea *f*; **high/low t.** marea alta/baja (**b**) *Fig (of events)* curso *m*; **the t. has turned** han cambiado las cosas; **to go against the t.** ir contra corriente

tidings ['taɪdɪŋz] *npl Fml* noticias *fpl*

tidy ['taɪdɪ] **1** *adj* (**tidier, tidiest**) (**a**) *(room, habits)* ordenado(a) (**b**) *(appearance)* arreglado(a)
2 *vt* arreglar; **to t. away** poner en su sitio
3 *vi* **to t. (up)** ordenar las cosas

tie [taɪ] **1** *vt (shoelaces etc)* atar; **to t. a knot** hacer un nudo
2 *vi Sport* empatar (**with** con)
3 *n* (**a**) *(bond)* lazo *m*, vínculo *m* (**b**) *Fig (hindrance)* atadura *f* (**c**) *(clothing)* corbata *f* (**d**) *Sport (match)* partido *m*; *(draw)* empate *m*

▶**tie down** *vt sep* sujetar; *Fig* **to be tied down** estar atado(a); *Fig* **to t. sb down to a promise** obligar a algn a cumplir una promesa

▶**tie up** *vt sep* (**a**) *(parcel, dog)* atar (**b**) *(deal)* concluir (**c**) *(capital)* inmovilizar; *Fig* **I'm tied up just now** de momento estoy muy ocupado(a)

tiebreaker ['taɪbreɪkə(r)] *n* tie-break *m*

tiepin ['taɪpɪn] *n* alfiler *m* de corbata

tier [tɪə(r)] *n (of seats)* fila *f*; *(in stadium)* grada *f*; **four-t. cake** pastel *m* de cuatro pisos

tiger ['taɪgə(r)] *n* tigre *m*

tight [taɪt] **1** *adj* (**a**) apretado(a); *(clothing)* ajustado(a); *(seal)* hermético(a);

my shoes are too t. me aprietan los zapatos; *Fig* **to be in a t. corner** estar en un apuro (**b**) *(scarce)* escaso(a); **money's a bit t.** estamos escasos de dinero (**c**) *(mean)* agarrado(a) (**d**) *Fam (drunk)* borracho(a)

  2 *adv* estrechamente; *(seal)* herméticamente; **hold t.** agárrate fuerte; **shut t.** bien cerrado(a); **to sit t.** no moverse de su sitio

tighten ['taɪtən] **1** *vt (screw)* apretar, *(rope)* tensar; *Fig* **to t. (up) restrictions** intensificar las restricciones

  2 *vi* apretarse; *(cable)* tensarse

tightfisted [taɪt'fɪstɪd] *adj* tacaño(a)

tightrope ['taɪtrəʊp] *n* cuerda floja; **t. walker** funámbulo(a) *m,f*

tights [taɪts] *npl (thick)* leotardos *mpl*; *(of dancer)* mallas *fpl*; *Br (thin)* medias *fpl*, pantis *mpl*

tile [taɪl] **1** *n (of roof)* teja *f*; *(glazed)* azulejo *m*; *(for floor)* baldosa *f*

  2 *vt (roof)* tejar; *(wall)* azulejar; *(floor)* embaldosar

tiled [taɪld] *adj (roof)* de *or* con tejas; *(wall)* revestido(a) de azulejos; *(floor)* embaldosado(a)

till¹ [tɪl] *n (for cash)* caja *f*

till² [tɪl] *vt (field)* labrar, cultivar

till³ [tɪl] **1** *prep* hasta; **from morning t. night** de la mañana a la noche; **t. then** hasta entonces

  2 *conj* hasta que

tiller ['tɪlə(r)] *n Naut* caña *f* del timón

tilt [tɪlt] **1** *n* (**a**) *(angle)* inclinación *f* (**b**) **(at) full t.** *(speed)* a toda velocidad

  2 *vi* **to t. over** volcarse; **to t. (up)** inclinarse

  3 *vt* inclinar

timber ['tɪmbə(r)] *n (wood)* madera *f* (de construcción); *(trees)* árboles *mpl*; **(piece of) t.** viga *f*

time [taɪm] **1** *n* (**a**) tiempo *m*; **all the t.** todo el tiempo; **for some t. (past)** desde hace algún tiempo; **I haven't seen him for a long t.** hace mucho (tiempo) que no lo veo; **in a short t.** en poco tiempo; **in no t.** en un abrir y cerrar de ojos; **in t.** a tiempo; **in three weeks' t.** dentro de tres semanas; **to take one's t. over sth** hacer algo con calma; *Fam* **to do t.** cumplir una condena; **t. bomb** bomba *f* de relojería; **t. limit** límite *m* de tiempo; *(for payment etc)* plazo *m*; **t. switch** interruptor *m* electrónico automático; **t. zone** huso horario

  (**b**) *(era)* época *f*, tiempos *mpl*; **a sign of the times** un signo de los tiempos; **to be**

behind the times tener ideas anticuadas (**c**) *(point in time)* momento *m*; **(at) any t. (you like)** cuando quiera; **at no t.** en ningún momento; **at that t.** (en aquel) entonces; **at the same t.** al mismo tiempo; **at times** a veces; **from t. to t.** de vez en cuando; **he may turn up at any t.** puede llegar en cualquier momento

  (**d**) *(time of day)* hora *f*; **and about t. too!** ¡ya era hora!; **in good t.** con anticipación; **on t.** puntualmente; **what's the t.?** ¿qué hora es?

  (**e**) **t. of year** época *f* del año

  (**f**) **to have a good/bad t.** pasarlo bien/mal

  (**g**) *(occasion)* vez *f*; **four at a t.** cuatro a la vez; **next t.** la próxima vez; **several times over** varias veces; **three times running** tres veces seguidas; **t. after t.** una y otra vez

  (**h**) *(in multiplication)* **three times four** tres (multiplicado) por cuatro; **four times as big** cuatro veces más grande

  (**i**) *Mus* compás *m*; **in t.** al compás

  2 *vt* (**a**) *(speech)* calcular la duración de; *Sport (race)* cronometrar

  (**b**) *(choose the time of)* escoger el momento oportuno para

time-consuming ['taɪmkənsjuːmɪŋ] *adj* que ocupa mucho tiempo

time-lag ['taɪmlæg] *n* intervalo *m*

timeless ['taɪmlɪs] *adj* eterno(a)

timely ['taɪmlɪ] *adj* (**timelier, timeliest**) oportuno(a)

timer ['taɪmə(r)] *n (device)* temporizador *m*

timetable ['taɪmteɪbəl] *n* horario *m*

timid ['tɪmɪd] *adj* tímido(a)

timing ['taɪmɪŋ] *n* (**a**) *(timeliness)* oportunidad *f*; *(coordination)* coordinación *f*; **your t. was wrong** no calculaste bien (**b**) *Sport* cronometraje *m*

tin [tɪn] **1** *n* (**a**) *(metal)* estaño *m*; **t. plate** hojalata *f* (**b**) *(container)* lata *f*

  2 *vt (tins)* enlatar; **tinned food** conservas *fpl*

tinfoil ['tɪnfɔɪl] *n* papel *m* de estaño

tinge [tɪndʒ] **1** *n* tinte *m*, matiz *m*

  2 *vt* teñir

tingle ['tɪŋgəl] *vi* **my feet are tingling** siento un hormigueo en los pies

tinker ['tɪŋkə(r)] **1** *n Pej* calderero(a) *mf*

  2 *vi* **stop tinkering with the radio** deja de toquetear la radio

tinkle ['tɪŋkəl] *vi* tintinear

tin-opener ['tɪnəʊpənə(r)] *n* abrelatas *m inv*

tinsel ['tɪnsəl] *n* oropel *m*

tint [tɪnt] **1** *n* tinte *m*, matiz *m*
 2 *vt* teñir; **to t. one's hair** teñirse el pelo
tiny ['taɪnɪ] *adj* (**tinier, tiniest**) pequeñito(a); **a t. bit** un poquitín
tip¹ [tɪp] **1** *n* (*end*) punta *f*; (*of cigarette*) colilla *f*; **it's on the t. of my tongue** lo tengo en la punta de la lengua
 2 *vt* poner cantera a; **tipped with steel** con punta de acero
tip² [tɪp] **1** *n* (**a**) (*gratuity*) propina *f* (**b**) (*advice*) consejo *m* (**c**) *Sport* (*racing*) pronóstico *m*
 2 *vt* (**a**) dar una propina a (**b**) *Sport* pronosticar
 ► **tip off** *vt sep* (*police*) dar el chivatazo a
tip³ [tɪp] **1** *n Br* **rubbish t.** vertedero *m*
 2 *vt* inclinar; *Br* (*rubbish*) verter
 3 *vi* **to t. (up)** ladearse; (*cart*) bascular
 ► **tip over 1** *vt sep* volcar
 2 *vi* volcarse
tipple ['tɪpəl] *Fam* **1** *vi* empinar el codo
 2 *n* bebida alcohólica; **what's your t.?** ¿qué te gusta beber?
tipsy ['tɪpsɪ] *adj* (**tipsier, tipsiest**) contentillo(a)
tiptoe ['tɪptəʊ] **1** *vi* andar de puntillas; **to t. in/out** entrar/salir de puntillas
 2 *n* **on t.** de puntillas
tiptop ['tɪptɒp] *adj Fam* de primera
tire¹ [taɪə(r)] *n US* = **tyre**
tire² [taɪə(r)] **1** *vt* cansar; **to t. sb out** agotar a algn
 2 *vi* cansarse; **to t. of doing sth** cansarse de hacer algo
tired ['taɪəd] *adj* cansado(a); **t. out** rendido(a); **to be t.** estar cansado(a); **to be t. of sth** estar harto(a) de algo
tireless ['taɪəlɪs] *adj* incansable
tiresome ['taɪəsəm] *adj* pesado(a)
tiring ['taɪərɪŋ] *adj* agotador(a)
tissue ['tɪʃuː, 'tɪsjuː] *n* (**a**) *Biol* tejido *m* (**b**) *Tex* tisú *m*; **t. paper** papel *m* de seda (**c**) (*handkerchief*) pañuelo *m* de papel, kleenex® *m*
tit¹ [tɪt] *n* **to give t. for tat** devolver la pelota
tit² [tɪt] *n very Fam* (*breast*) teta *f*
titbit ['tɪtbɪt] *n* golosina *f*
titillate ['tɪtɪleɪt] *vt* excitar
title ['taɪtəl] *n* (**a**) título *m*; *Cin* **credit titles** ficha técnica; **t. page** portada *f*; **t. role** papel *m* principal (**b**) *Jur* título *m*
titter ['tɪtə(r)] **1** *vi* reírse nerviosamente; (*foolishly*) reírse tontamente
 2 *n* risa ahogada; (*foolish*) risilla tonta
titular ['tɪtjʊlə(r)] *adj* titular
TM *n* (*abbr* **trademark**) marca registrada
to [tuː, *unstressed before vowels* tʊ, *before*

consonants tə] **1** *prep* (**a**) (*with place*) a; (*expressing direction*) hacia; **from town to town** de ciudad en ciudad; **he went to France/Japan** fue a Francia/Japón; **I'm going to Mary's** voy a casa de Mary; **it is 30 miles to London** Londres está a 30 millas; **the train to Madrid** el tren de Madrid; **to the east** hacia el este; **to the right** a la derecha; **what school do you go to?** ¿a qué escuela vas?
 (**b**) (*time*) a; **from day to day** de día en día; **from two to four** de dos a cuatro; **ten (minutes) to six** las seis menos diez
 (**c**) (*as far as*) hasta; **accurate to a millimetre** exacto(a) hasta el milímetro
 (**d**) (*with indirect object*) **he gave it to his cousin** se lo dio a su primo; **what's that to you?** ¿qué te importa a ti?
 (**e**) (*towards a person*) **he was very kind to me** se portó muy bien conmigo
 (**f**) (*of*) **de; heir to an estate** heredero *m* de una propiedad; **adviser to the president** consejero *m* del presidente
 (**g**) **to come to sb's assistance** acudir en ayuda de algn; **to everyone's surprise** para sorpresa de todos; **to this end** con este fin
 (**h**) **to the best of my knowledge** que yo sepa
 (**i**) (*compared to*) **that's nothing to what I've seen** eso no es nada en comparación con lo que he visto yo
 (**j**) (*in proportion*) **one house to the square kilometre** una casa por kilómetro cuadrado; **six votes to four** seis votos contra cuatro
 (**k**) (*about*) **what did he say to my suggestion?** ¿qué contestó a mi sugerencia?
 2 *with infin* (**a**) *with simple infinitives* **to** *is not translated but is shown by the verb endings;* **to buy** comprar; **to come** venir
 (**b**) (*in order to*) para; (*with verbs of motion or purpose*) a, por; **he did it to help me** lo hizo para ayudarme; **he stopped to talk** se detuvo a hablar; **he fought to convince them** luchó por convencerlos
 (**c**) *various verbs followed by dependent infinitives take particular prepositions* (a, de, en, por, con, para *etc*) *and others take no preposition; see the entry of the verb in question*
 (**d**) (*with adj and infin*) a, de; **difficult to do** difícil de hacer; **ready to listen** dispuesto(a) a escuchar; **too hot to drink** demasiado caliente para bebérselo
 (**e**) (*with noun and infin*) **the first to complain** el primero en quejarse; **this is**

the time to do it éste es el momento de hacerlo; **to have a great deal to do** tener mucho que hacer

(**f**) *(expressing following action)* **he awoke to find the light still on** al despertarse encontró la lámpara todavía encendida

(**g**) *(with verbs of ordering, wishing etc)* **he asked me to do it** me pidió que lo hiciera

(**h**) *(expressing obligation)* **fifty employees are to go** cincuenta empleados deben ser despedidos; **to have to do sth** tener que hacer algo

(**i**) *(replacing infin)* **go if you want to** váyase si quiere

3 *adv* **to go to and fro** ir y venir; **to push the door to** encajar la puerta

toad [təʊd] *n* sapo *m*

toadstool [ˈtəʊdstuːl] *n* hongo *m* (venenoso)

toast¹ [təʊst] *Culin* **1** *n* pan tostado; **a slice of t.** una tostada

2 *vt* tostar

toast² [təʊst] **1** *n (drink)* brindis *m inv*; **to drink a t. to** brindar por

2 *vt* brindar por

toaster [ˈtəʊstə(r)] *n* tostador *m* (de pan)

tobacco [təˈbækəʊ] *n* tabaco *m*

tobacconist [təˈbækənɪst] *n Br* estanquero(a) *m,f*; *Br* **t.'s (shop)** estanco *m*

toboggan [təˈbɒgən] *n* tobogán *m*

today [təˈdeɪ] **1** *n* hoy *m*

2 *adv* hoy; *(nowadays)* hoy en día; **a week t.** justo dentro de una semana

toddler [ˈtɒdlə(r)] *n* niño(a) *m,f* que empieza a andar; **the toddlers** los pequeñitos

toddy [ˈtɒdɪ] *n (drink)* ponche *m*

to-do [təˈduː] *n* lío *m*, jaleo *m*

toe [təʊ] **1** *n* dedo *m* del pie; **big t.** dedo gordo

2 *vt* **to t. the line** conformarse

toenail [ˈtəʊneɪl] *n* uña *f* del dedo del pie

toffee [ˈtɒfɪ] *n* caramelo *m*

together [təˈgeðə(r)] *adv* junto, juntos(as); **all t.** todos juntos; **t. with** junto con; **to bring t.** reunir

toil [tɔɪl] **1** *n* trabajo duro

2 *vi* afanarse, trabajar (duro); **to t. up a hill** subir penosamente una cuesta

toilet [ˈtɔɪlɪt] *n* (**a**) wáter *m*, retrete *m*; *(for public)* servicios *mpl*; **t. paper** *or* **tissue** papel higiénico; **t. roll** rollo *m* de papel higiénico (**b**) *(washing etc)* aseo *m* (personal); **t. bag** neceser *m*; **t. soap** jabón *m* de tocador

toiletries [ˈtɔɪlɪtrɪz] *npl* artículos *mpl* de aseo

token [ˈtəʊkən] **1** *n* (**a**) *(sign)* señal *f*; **as a t. of respect** en señal de respeto (**b**) *Com* vale *m*; **book t.** vale para comprar libros

2 *adj* simbólico(a)

told [təʊld] *pt & pp of* **tell**

tolerable [ˈtɒlərəbəl] *adj* tolerable

tolerance [ˈtɒlərəns] *n* tolerancia *f*

tolerant [ˈtɒlərənt] *adj* tolerante

tolerate [ˈtɒləreɪt] *vt* tolerar

toll¹ [təʊl] **1** *vt* tocar

2 *vi* doblar

toll² [təʊl] *n* (**a**) *Aut* peaje *m* (**b**) *(loss)* pérdidas *fpl*; **the death t.** el número de víctimas mortales

toll-free [təʊlˈfriː] *US* **1** *adj* **t. number** (número *m* de) teléfono *m* gratuito

2 *adv (call)* gratuitamente

tomato [təˈmɑːtəʊ, *US* təˈmeɪtəʊ] *n (pl* **tomatoes)** tomate *m*; **t. sauce** salsa *f* de tomate

tomb [tuːm] *n* tumba *f*, sepulcro *m*

tomboy [ˈtɒmbɔɪ] *n* marimacho *f*

tombstone [ˈtuːmstəʊn] *n* lápida *f* sepulcral

tomcat [ˈtɒmkæt] *n* gato *m* (macho)

tomorrow [təˈmɒrəʊ] **1** *n* mañana *m*; **the day after t.** pasado mañana; **t. night** mañana por la noche

2 *adv* mañana; **see you t.!** ¡hasta mañana!; **t. week** dentro de ocho días a partir de mañana

ton [tʌn] *n* tonelada *f*; *Fam* **tons of** montones de

tone [təʊn] **1** *n* tono *m*

2 *vi* **to t. (in) with sth** armonizar con algo

▸ **tone down** *vt sep* atenuar

tone-deaf [ˈtəʊnˈdef] *adj* **to be t.** no tener oído

tongs [tɒŋz] *npl (for sugar, hair)* tenacillas *fpl*; **(fire) t.** tenazas *fpl*

tongue [tʌŋ] *n* (**a**) lengua *f*; *Fig* **to say sth t. in cheek** decir algo con la boca pequeña; *Fig* **t. twister** trabalenguas *m inv* (**b**) *(of shoe)* lengüeta *f*; *(of bell)* badajo *m*

tongue-tied [ˈtʌŋtaɪd] *adj* mudo(a) *(por la timidez)*

tonic [ˈtɒnɪk] **1** *n* (**a**) *Med* tónico *m* (**b**) *(drink)* tónica *f*

2 *adj* tónico(a)

tonight [təˈnaɪt] *adv & n* esta noche

tonnage [ˈtʌnɪdʒ] *n (of ship)* tonelaje *m*

tonne [tʌn] *n* = **ton**

tonsil [ˈtɒnsəl] *n* amígdala *f*; **to have one's tonsils out** ser operado(a) de las amígdalas

tonsillitis [tɒnsɪˈlaɪtɪs] *n* amigdalitis *f*

too [tuː] *adv* (**a**) *(besides)* además (**b**)

(also) también (**c**) *(excessively)* demasiado; **t. much money** demasiado dinero; **£10 t. much** 10 libras de más; **t. frequently** con demasiada frecuencia; **t. old** demasiado viejo

took [tʊk] *pt of* **take**

tool [tuːl] *n (utensil)* herramienta *f*

toolbox ['tuːlbɒks] *n* caja *f* de herramientas

toot [tuːt] *Aut* **1** *vt* tocar
2 *vi* tocar la bocina

tooth [tuːθ] *n (pl* **teeth**) (**a**) diente *m*; *(molar)* muela *f*; *Fig* **to fight t. and nail** luchar a brazo partido (**b**) *(of saw)* diente *m*; *(of comb)* púa *f*

toothache ['tuːθeɪk] *n* dolor *m* de muelas

toothbrush ['tuːθbrʌʃ] *n* cepillo *m* de dientes

toothpaste ['tuːθpeɪst] *n* pasta dentífrica

toothpick ['tuːθpɪk] *n* mondadientes *m inv*

top¹ [tɒp] **1** *n* (**a**) *(upper part)* parte *f* de arriba; *(of hill)* cumbre *f*, cima *f*; *(of tree)* copa *f*; **from t. to bottom** de arriba a abajo; **on t. of** encima de; *Fig* **on t. of it all ...** para colmo ...; **t. hat** sombrero *m* de copa
(**b**) *(surface)* superficie *f*
(**c**) *(of list etc)* cabeza *f*
(**d**) *(of bottle etc)* tapa *f*, tapón *m*
(**e**) *(garment)* camiseta *f*
(**f**) *(best)* lo mejor
(**g**) *Fig* **at the t. of one's voice** a voz en grito
2 *adj* (**a**) *(part)* superior, de arriba; **the t. floor** el último piso; **t. coat** *(of paint)* última mano
(**b**) *(highest)* más alto(a); *Aut* **t. gear** directa *f*
(**c**) *(best)* mejor
3 *vt* (**a**) *(place on top of)* coronar
(**b**) *Th* **to t. the bill** encabezar el reparto
▸ **top up** *vt sep* llenar hasta el tope; **to t. up the petrol tank** llenar el depósito; *Fig* **and to t. it all** y para colmo

top² [tɒp] *n (toy)* peonza *f*

topic ['tɒpɪk] *n* tema *m*

> 🖉 Note that the Spanish word **tópico** is a false friend and is never a translation for the English word **topic**. In Spanish, **tópico** means "cliché".

topical ['tɒpɪkəl] *adj* de actualidad

top-level ['tɒplevəl] *adj* de alto nivel

topmost ['tɒpməʊst] *adj* (el) más alto/(la) más alta

topple ['tɒpəl] **1** *vi (building)* venirse abajo; **to t. (over)** volcarse
2 *vt* volcar; *Fig (government)* derrocar

top-secret ['tɒp'siːkrɪt] *adj* de alto secreto

topsy-turvy ['tɒpsɪ'tɜːvɪ] *adj & adv* al revés; *(in confusion)* en desorden, patas arriba

torch [tɔːtʃ] *n (electric)* linterna *f*

tore [tɔː(r)] *pt of* **tear**

torment 1 *vt* [tɔː'ment] atormentar
2 *n* ['tɔːment] tormento *m*, suplicio *m*

torn [tɔːn] *pp of* **tear**

tornado [tɔː'neɪdəʊ] *n* tornado *m*

torpedo [tɔː'piːdəʊ] *n* torpedo *m*

torrent ['tɒrənt] *n* torrente *m*

torrential [tɒ'renʃəl] *adj* torrencial

torrid ['tɒrɪd] *adj* tórrido(a)

torso ['tɔːsəʊ] *n* torso *m*

tortoise ['tɔːtəs] *n* tortuga *f* (de tierra)

tortoiseshell ['tɔːtəsʃel] *adj* de carey

torture ['tɔːtʃə(r)] **1** *vt* torturar; *Fig* atormentar
2 *n* tortura *f*; *Fig* tormento *m*

Tory ['tɔːrɪ] *adj & n Br Pol* conservador(a) *(m,f)*

toss [tɒs] **1** *vt* (**a**) *(ball)* tirar; **to t. a coin** echar a cara o cruz (**b**) *(throw about)* sacudir
2 *vi* (**a**) **to t. about** agitarse; **to t. and turn** dar vueltas en la cama (**b**) *Sport* **to t. (up)** sortear
3 *n* (**a**) *(of ball)* lanzamiento *m*; *(of coin)* sorteo *m* (a cara o cruz) (**b**) *(of head)* sacudida *f*

tot¹ [tɒt] *n* (**a**) **(tiny) t.** *(child)* nene(a) *m,f* (**b**) *(of whisky etc)* trago *m*

tot² [tɒt] *vt Br* **to t. up** sumar

total ['təʊtəl] **1** *n* total *m*; *(in bill)* importe *m*; **grand t.** suma *f* total
2 *adj* total
3 *vt* sumar
4 *vi* **to t. up to** ascender a

totalitarian [təʊtælɪ'teərɪən] *adj* totalitario(a)

totally ['təʊtəlɪ] *adv* totalmente

tote [təʊt] *n Fam Sport* totalizador *m*

tote bag ['təʊtbæg] *n US* petate *m*

totem ['təʊtəm] *n* tótem *m*

totter ['tɒtə(r)] *vi* tambalearse

touch [tʌtʃ] **1** *vt* (**a**) tocar; *Fig* **to t. on a subject** tocar un tema
(**b**) *(equal)* igualar
(**c**) *(move)* conmover
2 *vi* tocarse; *Fig* **it was t. and go whether we caught the train** estuvimos a punto de perder el tren
3 *n* (**a**) toque *m*
(**b**) *(sense of touch)* tacto *m*

(**c**) **it was a nice t. of his** fue un detalle de su parte; **to put the finishing touches to sth** dar los últimos toques a algo (**d**) *(ability)* habilidad *f* (**e**) *(contact)* contacto *m*; **to be/get/ keep in t. with sb** estar/ponerse/mantenerse en contacto con algn; **to be out of t. with sth** no estar al tanto de algo (**f**) *(small amount)* pizca *f* (**g**)*Sport* **in t.** fuera de banda
▶ **touch down** *vi (plane)* aterrizar
▶ **touch off** *vt sep* desencadenar
▶ **touch up** *vt sep (picture)* retocar

touchdown ['tʌtʃdaʊn] *n* (**a**) *(of plane)* aterrizaje *m*; *(of space capsule)* amerizaje *m* (**b**) *(in American football)* ensayo *m*

touched [tʌtʃt] *adj* (**a**) *(moved)* emocionado(a) (**b**) *Fam (crazy)* tocado(a)

touching ['tʌtʃɪŋ] *adj* conmovedor(a)

touchline ['tʌtʃlaɪn] *n* línea *f* de banda

touchy ['tʌtʃɪ] *adj* (**touchier, touchiest**) *Fam (person)* susceptible; *(subject)* delicado(a)

tough [tʌf] **1** *adj (material, competitor etc)* fuerte, resistente; *(test, criminal, meat)* duro(a); *(punishment)* severo(a); *(problem)* difícil
2 *n (person)* matón *m*

toughen ['tʌfən] *vt* endurecer

toupee ['tuːpeɪ] *n* tupé *m*

tour [tʊə(r)] **1** *n* (**a**) *(journey)* viaje *m*; **package t.** viaje organizado (**b**) *(of monument etc)* visita *f*; *(of city)* recorrido turístico (**c**) *Sport & Th* gira *f*; **on t.** de gira
2 *vt* (**a**) *(country)* viajar por (**b**) *(building)* visitar (**c**)*Th* estar de gira en
3 *vi* estar de viaje

tourism ['tʊərɪzəm] *n* turismo *m*

tourist ['tʊərɪst] *n* turista *mf*; **t. centre** centro *m* de información turística; *Av* **t. class** clase *f* turista

tournament ['tʊənəmənt] *n* torneo *m*

tousled ['taʊzəld] *adj (hair)* despeinado(a)

tout [taʊt] **1** *vt Com* tratar de vender; *(tickets)* revender
2 *vi* = salir a la caza y captura de compradores
3 *n Com* gancho *m*

tow [təʊ] **1** *n* **to take a car in t.** remolcar un coche; *US* **t. truck** grúa *f*
2 *vt* remolcar

towards [tə'wɔːdz, tɔːdz] *prep* (**a**) *(direction, time)* hacia (**b**) *(with regard to)* hacia, (para) con; **our duty t. others** nuestro deber para con los demás; **what is your attitude t. religion?** ¿cuál es su actitud respecto a la religión?

towel ['taʊəl] **1** *n* toalla *f*; **hand t.** toallita *f*; **t.** *Br* **rail** *or US* **bar** toallero *m*
2 *vt* **to t. dry** secar con una toalla

towelling ['taʊəlɪŋ] *n* felpa *f*

tower ['taʊə(r)] **1** *n* torre *f*
2 *vi* **to t. over** *or* **above sth** dominar algo

towering ['taʊərɪŋ] *adj* impresionante, enorme

town [taʊn] *n* ciudad *f*; *(small)* pueblo *m*; **to go into t.** ir al centro; *Fam* **to go to t.** tirar la casa por la ventana; **t. council** ayuntamiento *m*; **t. councillor** concejal(a) *m,f*; **t. hall** ayuntamiento *m*; **t. planning** urbanismo *m*

townspeople ['taʊnzpiːpəl] *npl* ciudadanos *mpl*

towpath ['təʊpɑːθ] *n* sendero *m* a lo largo de un canal

towrope ['təʊrəʊp] *n* cable *m* de remolque

toxic ['tɒksɪk] *adj* tóxico(a)

toy [tɔɪ] **1** *n* juguete *m*
2 *vi* **to t. with an idea** acariciar una idea; **to t. with one's food** comer sin gana

toyshop ['tɔɪʃɒp] *n* juguetería *f*

trace [treɪs] **1** *n* (**a**) *(sign)* indicio *m*, vestigio *m* (**b**) *(tracks)* huella(s) *f(pl)*
2 *vt* (**a**) *(drawing)* calcar (**b**) *(plan)* bosquejar (**c**) *(locate)* seguir la pista de

tracing ['treɪsɪŋ] *n* **t. paper** papel *m* de calco

track [træk] **1** *n* (**a**) *(trail)* huellas *fpl*, pista *f*; **to keep/lose t. of sb** no perder/perder de vista a algn
(**b**) *(pathway)* camino *m*; **to be on the right/wrong t.** ir por el buen/mal camino
(**c**) *Sport* pista *f*; *(for motor racing)* circuito *m*; *Fig* **t. record** historial *m*
(**d**) *Rail* vía *f*; *Fig* **he has a one-t. mind** tiene una única obsesión
(**e**) *(on record, CD)* canción *f*
(**f**) *US Educ* = cada una de las divisiones del alumnado en grupos por niveles de aptitud
2 *vt* seguir la pista de; *(with radar)* seguir la trayectoria de
▶ **track down** *vt sep (locate)* localizar

tracksuit ['træksuːt] *n* chándal *m*, *Arg* buzo *m*, *Méx* pants *m*, *Urug* jogging *m*, *Ven* mono *m*

tract¹ [trækt] *n (expanse)* extensión *f*

tract² [trækt] *n (treatise)* tratado *m*; *(pamphlet)* folleto *m*

traction ['trækʃən] *n* tracción *f*

tractor ['træktə(r)] *n* tractor *m*

trade [treɪd] **1** *n* (**a**) *(profession)* oficio *m*; **by t.** de oficio (**b**) *Com* comercio *m*; **it's good for t.** es bueno para los negocios;

the building t. (la industria de) la construcción; **t. name** nombre *m* comercial; **t. union** sindicato *m*; **t. unionist** sindicalista *mf*
2 *vi* comerciar (**in** en)
3 *vt* **to t. sth for sth** trocar algo por algo
▸ **trade in** *vt sep* dar como entrada
trademark ['treɪdmɑːk] *n* marca *f* (de fábrica); **registered t.** marca registrada
trader ['treɪdə(r)] *n* comerciante *mf*
tradesman ['treɪdzmən] *n (shopkeeper)* tendero *m*
trading ['treɪdɪŋ] *n* comercio *m*; *Br* **t. estate** polígono *m* industrial
tradition [trə'dɪʃən] *n* tradición *f*
traditional [trə'dɪʃənəl] *adj* tradicional
traffic ['træfɪk] **1** *n* (**a**) tráfico *m*, circulación *f*; *US* **t. circle** rotonda *f*; **t. island** isleta *f*; **t. jam** atasco *m*; **t. lights** semáforo *m*; *Br* **t. warden** ≃ guardia *mf* urbano(a) (**b**) *(trade)* tráfico *m*
2 *vi* (*pt & pp* **trafficked**) **to t. in drugs** traficar con droga
trafficker ['træfɪkə(r)] *n* traficante *mf*
tragedy ['trædʒɪdɪ] *n* tragedia *f*
tragic ['trædʒɪk] *adj* trágico(a)
trail [treɪl] **1** *vt* (**a**) *(drag)* arrastrar (**b**) *(follow)* rastrear
2 *vi* (**a**) *(drag)* arrastrarse (**b**) **to t. behind** rezagarse
3 *n* (**a**) *(track)* pista *f*, rastro *m* (**b**) *(path)* senda *f*, camino *m* (**c**) *(of smoke)* estela *f*
trailer ['treɪlə(r)] *n* (**a**) *Aut* remolque *m* (**b**) *US Aut (caravan)* caravana *f* (**c**) *Cin* trailer *m*, avance *m*
train [treɪn] **1** *n* (**a**) *Rail* tren *m* (**b**) *(of vehicles)* convoy *m*; *(of followers)* séquito *m*; *(of events)* serie *f* (**c**) *(of dress)* cola *f*
2 *vt* (**a**) *(teach)* formar; *Sport* entrenar; *(animal)* amaestrar; *(voice etc)* educar (**b**) *(gun)* apuntar (**on** a); *(camera)* enfocar (**on** a)
3 *vi* prepararse; *Sport* entrenarse
trainee [treɪ'niː] *n* aprendiz(a) *m,f*
trainer ['treɪnə(r)] *n* (**a**) *Sport* entrenador(a) *m,f*; *(of dogs)* amaestrador(a) *m,f*; *(of lions)* domador(a) *m,f* (**b**) **trainers** *(shoes)* zapatillas *fpl* de deporte
training ['treɪnɪŋ] *n (instruction)* formación *f*; *Sport* entrenamiento *m*; *(of animals)* amaestramiento *m*; *(of lions)* doma *f*; **to go into t.** empezar el entrenamiento; **vocational t.** formación profesional
traipse [treɪps] *vi Fam* vagar
trait [treɪt] *n* rasgo *m*
traitor ['treɪtə(r)] *n* traidor(a) *m,f*
trajectory [trə'dʒektərɪ] *n* trayectoria *f*

tram [træm], **tramcar** ['træmkɑː(r)] *n Br* tranvía *m*
tramp [træmp] **1** *vi* (**a**) *(travel on foot)* caminar (**b**) *(walk heavily)* andar con pasos pesados
2 *n (person)* vagabundo(a) *m,f*; *Pej* **she's a t.** es una fulana

> ⚬ Note that the Spanish word **trampa** is a false friend and is never a translation for the English word **tramp**. In Spanish, **trampa** means both "trap" and "trick".

trample ['træmpəl] *vt* **to t. down the grass** pisotear la hierba; **to t. sth underfoot** pisotear algo
trampoline ['træmpəliːn] *n* cama elástica

> ⚬ Note that the Spanish word **trampolín** is a false friend and is never a translation for the English word **trampoline**. In Spanish, **trampolín** means both "diving board" and "ski jump".

trance [trɑːns] *n* trance *m*
tranquil ['træŋkwɪl] *adj* tranquilo(a)
tranquillity [træŋ'kwɪlɪtɪ] *n* tranquilidad *f*
tranquillizer ['træŋkwɪlaɪzə(r)] *n* tranquilizante *m*
transact [træn'zækt] *vt* negociar
transaction [træn'zækʃən] *n (procedure)* tramitación *f*; *(deal)* transacción *f*
transatlantic [trænzət'læntɪk] *adj* transatlántico(a)
transcend [træn'send] *vt* trascender
transcribe [træn'skraɪb] *vt* transcribir
transcript ['trænskrɪpt] *n* transcripción *f*
transcription [træn'skrɪpʃən] *n* transcripción *f*
transfer 1 *vt* [træns'fɜː(r)] trasladar; *(funds)* trasferir; *Jur* ceder; *Ftb* traspasar; *US Rail* hacer transbordo
2 *n* ['trænsfɜː(r)] (**a**) traslado *m*; *(of funds)* transferencia *f*; *Jur* cesión *f*; *Ftb* traspaso *m* (**b**) *(picture, design)* calcomanía *f* (**c**) *US Rail* transbordo *m*
transform [træns'fɔːm] *vt* trasformar
transformation [trænsfə'meɪʃən] *n* trasformación *f*
transfusion [træns'fjuːʒən] *n Med* transfusión *f* (de sangre)
transgenic [trænz'dʒiːnɪk] *adj* transgénico(a)
transgress [trænz'gres] *vi Fml* transgredir
transient ['trænzɪənt] *adj* transitorio(a)
transistor [træn'zɪstə(r)] *n* transistor *m*
transit ['trænzɪt] *n* tránsito *m*; **in t.** de tránsito

transition [træn'zɪʃən] n transición f
transitive ['trænzɪtɪv] adj transitivo(a)
transitory ['trænzɪtərɪ] adj transitorio(a)
translate [træns'leɪt] vt traducir
translation [træns'leɪʃən] n traducción f
translator [træns'leɪtə(r)] n traductor(a) m,f
translucent [trænz'luːsənt] adj translúcido(a)
transmission [trænz'mɪʃən] n transmisión f
transmit [trænz'mɪt] vt transmitir
transmitter [trænz'mɪtə(r)] n Rad (set) transmisor m; Rad & TV (station) emisora f
transparency [træns'pærənsɪ] n Phot diapositiva f
transparent [træns'pærənt] adj transparente
transpire [træn'spaɪə(r)] vi (happen) ocurrir; **it transpired that ...** ocurrió que ...
transplant 1 vt [træns'plɑːnt] trasplantar
2 n ['trænsplɑːnt] trasplante m
transport 1 vt [træns'pɔːt] transportar
2 n ['trænspɔːt] transporte m; **t. aircraft/ship** avión m/buque m de transporte; Br **t. café** bar m de carretera
transportation [trænspɔː'teɪʃən] n transporte m
transvestite [trænz'vestaɪt] n Fam travestí mf
trap [træp] **1** n trampa f; **t. door** trampilla f; Th escotillón m
2 vt atrapar
trapeze [trə'piːz] n trapecio m
trappings ['træpɪŋz] npl parafernalia f
trash [træʃ] n (inferior goods) bazofia f; US (rubbish) basura f; Fig **to talk a lot of t.** decir tonterías; US **t. can** cubo m de la basura
trashy ['træʃɪ] adj (trashier, trashiest) de ínfima calidad
trauma ['trɔːmə] n trauma m
traumatic [trɔː'mætɪk] adj traumático(a)
travel ['trævəl] **1** vi (a) viajar; **to t. through** recorrer (b) (vehicle, electric current) ir; Fig (news) propagarse
2 vt recorrer
3 n viajar m; **t. agency** agencia f de viajes
traveller, US **traveler** ['trævələ(r)] n viajero(a) m,f; **t.'s** Br **cheque** or US **check** cheque m de viaje
travelling, US **traveling** ['trævəlɪŋ] **1** adj (salesman) ambulante
2 n viajes mpl, (el) viajar m; **I'm fond of t.** me gusta viajar; **t. expenses** gastos mpl de viaje

travel-sick ['trævəlsɪk] adj **to be t.** estar mareado(a)
travesty ['trævɪstɪ] n parodia f burda

🖉 Note that the Spanish word **travesti** is a false friend and is never a translation for the English word **travesty**. In Spanish, **travesti** means "transvestite".

trawler [trɔːlə(r)] n barco m de arrastre
tray [treɪ] n (for food) bandeja f; (for letters) cesta f (para la correspondencia)
treacherous ['tretʃərəs] adj (a) (person) traidor(a); (action) traicionero(a) (b) (dangerous) peligroso(a)
treachery ['tretʃərɪ] n traición f
treacle ['triːkəl] n Br melaza f
tread [tred] **1** vi (pt **trod**; pp **trod** or **trodden**) pisar; **to t. on** pisar
2 vt (a) (step on) pisar (b) **to t. water** mantenerse a flote verticalmente
3 n (a) (step) paso m; (sound) ruido m de pasos (b) (of tyre) banda f de rodadura
treadmill ['tredmɪl] n Fig rutina f
treason ['triːzən] n traición f
treasure ['treʒə(r)] **1** n tesoro m
2 vt (keep) guardar como oro en paño; (value) apreciar muchísimo
treasurer ['treʒərə(r)] n tesorero(a) m,f
treasury ['treʒərɪ] n Pol Br **the T.**, US **the Department of the T.** ≃ el Ministerio de Hacienda; **T. bill** bono m del Tesoro
treat [triːt] **1** n (a) (present) regalo m (b) (pleasure) placer m
2 vt (a) tratar; **to t. badly** maltratar (b) (regard) considerar (c) **he treated them to dinner** les invitó a cenar
treatise ['triːtɪz] n tratado m
treatment ['triːtmənt] n (a) (of person) trato m (b) (of subject, of patient) tratamiento m
treaty ['triːtɪ] n tratado m
treble ['trebəl] **1** adj (a) (triple) triple (b) Mus **t. clef** clave f de sol; **t. voice** voz f tiple
2 vt triplicar
3 vi triplicarse
tree [triː] n árbol m; **apple/cherry t.** manzano m/cerezo m
treetop ['triːtɒp] n copa f
trek [trek] **1** n (journey) viaje m (largo y difícil); Fam (walk) caminata f
2 vi (pt & pp **trekked**) hacer un viaje largo y difícil; Fam (walk) ir caminando
trellis ['trelɪs] n enrejado m
tremble ['trembəl] vi temblar, estremecerse
trembling ['tremblɪŋ] adj tembloroso(a)
tremendous [trɪ'mendəs] adj (huge) enorme; (success) arrollador(a); (shock

etc) tremendo(a); *Fam (marvellous)* estupendo(a)

tremor ['tremə(r)] *n* temblor *m*

trench [trentʃ] *n* (**a**) *(ditch)* zanja *f*; *Mil* trinchera *f* (**b**) **t. coat** trinchera *f*

trend [trend] **1** *n (tendency)* tendencia *f*; *(fashion)* moda *f*
　2 *vi* tender (**to** *or* **towards** hacia)

trendy ['trendɪ] *adj* (**trendier, trendiest**) *Fam (person)* moderno(a); *(clothes)* a la última

trepidation [trepɪ'deɪʃən] *n* turbación *f*

trespass ['trespəs] *vi* entrar sin autorización

> 🖉 Note that the Spanish verb **traspasar** is a false friend and is never a translation for the English verb **to trespass**. In Spanish, **traspasar** means "to go through, to cross, to transfer" and "to exceed".

trespasser ['trespəsə(r)] *n* intruso(a) *m,f*

trestle ['tresəl] *n* caballete *m*

trial ['traɪəl] *n* (**a**) *Jur* proceso *m*, juicio *m* (**b**) *(test)* prueba *f*; **on t.** a prueba; **by t. and error** a fuerza de equivocarse (**c**) **trials** *(competition)* concurso *m* (**d**) **trials** *(suffering)* sufrimiento *m*; **trials and tribulations** tribulaciones *fpl*

triangle ['traɪæŋgəl] *n* triángulo *m*

tribe [traɪb] *n* tribu *f*

tribunal [traɪ'bjuːnəl] *n* tribunal *m*

tributary ['trɪbjʊtərɪ] *n (river)* afluente *m*

tribute ['trɪbjuːt] *n* (**a**) *(payment)* tributo *m* (**b**) *(mark of respect)* homenaje *m*; **to pay t. to** rendir homenaje a

trice [traɪs] *n Fam* **in a t.** en un abrir y cerrar de ojos

trick [trɪk] **1** *n* (**a**) *(ruse)* ardid *m*; *(dishonest)* engaño *m*; *(in question)* trampa *f* (**b**) *(practical joke)* broma *f*; **to play a t. on sb** gastarle una broma a algn; *(malicious)* jugar una mala pasada a algn (**c**) *(of magic, knack)* truco *m*; **that'll do the t.!** ¡eso es exactamente lo que hace falta! (**d**) *Cards* baza *f*
　2 *vt* engañar; **to t. sb out of sth** estafar algo a algn

trickery ['trɪkərɪ] *n* engaños *mpl*, trampas *fpl*

trickle ['trɪkəl] **1** *vi* discurrir; *(water)* gotear
　2 *n* hilo *m*

tricky ['trɪkɪ] *adj* (**trickier, trickiest**) *(person)* astuto(a); *(situation, mechanism)* delicado(a)

tricycle ['traɪsɪkəl] *n* triciclo *m*

tried [traɪd] *pt & pp of* **try**

trifle ['traɪfəl] **1** *n* (**a**) *(insignificant thing)*

bagatela *f*; **he's a t. optimistic** es ligeramente optimista (**b**) *Br Culin* = postre de bizcocho, gelatina, frutas y nata
　2 *vi* **to t. with** tomar a la ligera

trifling ['traɪflɪŋ] *adj* insignificante, trivial

trigger ['trɪgə(r)] **1** *n (of gun)* gatillo *m*; *(of mechanism)* disparador *m*
　2 *vt* **to t. (off)** desencadenar

trill [trɪl] *n (of music, bird)* trino *m*; *Ling* vibración *f*

trilogy ['trɪlədʒɪ] *n* trilogía *f*

trim [trɪm] **1** *adj* (**trimmer, trimmest**) *(neat)* aseado(a); **to have a t. figure** tener buen tipo
　2 *vt* (**a**) *(cut)* recortar; *Fig (expenses)* disminuir (**b**) *(decorate)* adornar
　3 *n* (**a**) *(condition)* estado *m*; *Naut* asiento *m* (**b**) *(cut)* recorte *m*

trimming ['trɪmɪŋ] *n* (**a**) *(cut)* recorte *m* (**b**) *(on clothes)* adorno *m* (**c**) *Culin* **trimmings** guarnición *f*

trinket ['trɪŋkɪt] *n* baratija *f*

trio ['triːəʊ] *n* trío *m*

trip [trɪp] **1** *n* (**a**) *(journey)* viaje *m*; *(excursion)* excursión *f*; **to go on a t.** ir de excursión (**b**) *Fam* **to be on a t.** *(on drugs)* estar colocado(a)
　2 *vi* (**a**) **to t. (up)** *(stumble)* tropezar (**over** con); *Fig (err)* equivocarse (**b**) **to t. along** ir con paso ligero
　3 *vt* **to t. sb (up)** poner la zancadilla a algn; *Fig* coger *or* pillar a algn

tripe [traɪp] *n* (**a**) *Culin* callos *mpl* (**b**) *Fam* bobadas *fpl*

triple ['trɪpəl] **1** *adj* triple
　2 *vt* triplicar
　3 *vi* triplicarse

triplet ['trɪplɪt] *n* trillizo(a) *m,f*

triplicate ['trɪplɪkɪt] *adj* **in t.** por triplicado

tripod ['traɪpɒd] *n* trípode *m*

trite [traɪt] *adj (sentiment)* banal; *(subject)* trillado(a)

triumph ['traɪəmf] **1** *n* triunfo *m*
　2 *vi* triunfar

triumphant [traɪ'ʌmfənt] *adj* triunfante

trivia ['trɪvɪə] *npl* trivialidades *fpl*

trivial ['trɪvɪəl] *adj* trivial, banal

trod [trɒd] *pt & pp of* **tread**

trodden ['trɒdən] *pp of* **tread**

trolley ['trɒlɪ] *n Br* carro *m*

trombone [trɒm'bəʊn] *n* trombón *m*

troop [truːp] **1** *n* (**a**) *(of people)* grupo *m* (**b**) *Mil* **troops** tropas *fpl*
　2 *vi* **to t. in/out/off** entrar/salir/marcharse en tropel

trooper ['truːpə(r)] *n* (**a**) *(soldier)* soldado

m de caballería (**b**) *US (policeman)* policía *mf*

trooping ['tru:pɪŋ] *n Br* **t. the colour** = ceremonia de homenaje a la bandera de un regimiento

trophy ['trəʊfɪ] *n* trofeo *m*

tropic ['trɒpɪk] *n* trópico *m*

tropical ['trɒpɪkəl] *adj* tropical

trot [trɒt] **1** *vi* trotar

2 *n* trote *m*; **to go at a t.** ir al trote; *Fam* **on the t.** *(in succession)* seguidos(as)

trouble ['trʌbəl] **1** *n* (**a**) *(misfortune)* desgracia *f*

(**b**) *(problems)* problemas *mpl*; **to be in t.** estar en un lío; **to cause sb t.** ocasionar problemas a algn; **to get sb out of t.** sacar a algn de un apuro; **the t. is that ...** lo que pasa es que ...

(**c**) *(effort)* esfuerzo *m*; **it's no t.** no es ninguna molestia; **it's not worth the t.** no merece la pena; **to take the t. to do sth** molestarse en hacer algo

(**d**) *(conflict)* conflicto *m*

(**e**) *Med* enfermedad *f*; **to have liver t.** tener problemas de hígado

2 *vt* (**a**) *(affect)* afligir; *(worry)* preocupar; **that doesn't t. him at all** eso le tiene sin cuidado

(**b**) *(bother)* molestar

3 *vi* molestarse

troubled ['trʌbəld] *adj* agitado(a)

troublemaker ['trʌbəlmeɪkə(r)] *n* alborotador(a) *m,f*

troubleshooter ['trʌbəlʃuːtə(r)] *n Ind* = persona encargada de solucionar problemas

troublesome ['trʌbəlsəm] *adj* molesto(a)

trough [trɒf] *n* (**a**) **(drinking) t.** abrevadero *m*; **(feeding) t.** pesebre *m* (**b**) *(of wave)* seno *m* (**c**) *Geog & Met* depresión *f*

trounce [traʊns] *vt* dar una paliza a

troupe [truːp] *n Th* compañía *f*

trousers ['traʊzəz] *npl* pantalón *m*, pantalones *mpl*

trousseau ['truːsəʊ] *n* ajuar *m*

trout [traʊt] *n* trucha *f*

trowel ['traʊəl] *n* (**a**) *(builder's)* palustre *m* (**b**) *(for gardening)* desplantador *m*

truant ['truːənt] *n Br* **to play t.** hacer novillos

truce [truːs] *n* tregua *f*

truck¹ [trʌk] *n* (**a**) *Br Rail* vagón *m* (**b**) *Aut* camión *m*; **t. driver** camionero(a) *m,f*, *US* **t. farm** huerta *f*; *US* **t. farmer** hortelano(a) *m,f*

truck² [trʌk] *n* (**a**) **to have no t. with** no

estar dispuesto a tolerar (**b**) *US* verduras *fpl*; **t. farm** huerta *f*; **t. farming** cultivo *m* de hortalizas

truculent ['trʌkjʊlənt] *adj* agresivo(a), airado(a)

> 🖉 Note that the Spanish word **truculento** is a false friend and is never a translation for the English word **truculent**. In Spanish, **truculento** means "horrifying, terrifying".

trudge [trʌdʒ] *vi* caminar con dificultad

true [truː] *adj* (**truer, truest**) (**a**) verdadero(a); **it's t. that ...** es verdad que ...; **to come t.** cumplirse, hacerse realidad (**b**) *(faithful)* fiel (**c**) *(aim)* acertado(a)

truffle ['trʌfəl] *n* trufa *f*

truly ['truːlɪ] *adv* (**a**) de verdad; **really and t.?** ¿de veras? (**b**) *(faithfully)* fielmente; **yours t.** atentamente

trump [trʌmp] *Cards* **1** *n* triunfo *m*

2 *vt* fallar

trumped-up ['trʌmptʌp] *adj* inventado(a)

trumpet ['trʌmpɪt] *n* trompeta *f*

trumpeting ['trʌmpɪtɪŋ] *n (of elephant)* berrido *m*

truncheon ['trʌntʃən] *n Br* porra *f (de policía)*

trundle ['trʌndəl] *vi* rodar

trunk [trʌŋk] *n* (**a**) *(of tree, body)* tronco *m* (**b**) *(of elephant)* trompa *f* (**c**) *(luggage)* baúl *m* (**d**) *Br Tel* **t. call** conferencia interurbana; *Br* **t. road** carretera *f* principal (**e**) *US (of car)* maletero *m*, *CAm, Méx* cajuela *f*, *RP* baúl *m*

trunks [trʌŋks] *npl* **(bathing) t.** bañador *m*

truss [trʌs] **1** *vt (tie)* atar

2 *n* (**a**) *Constr* cuchillo *m* de armadura (**b**) *Med* braguero *m*

trust [trʌst] **1** *n* (**a**) confianza *f*; **breach of t.** abuso *m* de confianza (**b**) *Jur* fideicomiso *m* (**c**) *Fin* trust *m*

2 *vt* (**a**) *(hope)* esperar (**b**) *(rely upon)* fiarse de; **to t. sb with sth** confiar algo a algn

3 *vi* confiar (**in** en)

trusted ['trʌstɪd] *adj* de fiar

trustee [trʌsˈtiː] *n Jur* fideicomisario(a) *m,f*; *(in bankruptcy)* síndico *m*

trustful ['trʌstfʊl], **trusting** ['trʌstɪŋ] *adj* confiado(a)

trustworthy ['trʌstwɜːðɪ] *adj (person)* de confianza; *(information)* fidedigno(a)

trusty ['trʌstɪ] *adj* (**trustier, trustiest**) fiel, leal

truth [truːθ] *n* verdad *f*; **to tell the t.** decir la verdad

truthful ['trʊːθfʊl] *adj (person)* veraz, sincero(a); *(testimony)* verídico(a)

truthfully ['trʊːθfʊlɪ] *adv* sinceramente

try [traɪ] **1** *vt (pt & pp tried)* (**a**) *(attempt)* intentar; **to t. to do sth** tratar de *or* intentar hacer algo (**b**) *(test)* probar, ensayar; **to t. sb's patience** poner a prueba la paciencia de algn (**c**)*Jur* juzgar

2 *vi* intentar

3 *n* (**a**) *(attempt)* tentativa *f*, intento *m* (**b**)*Sport* ensayo *m*

▶ **try on** *vt sep (dress)* probarse

▶ **try out** *vt sep* probar

trying ['traɪɪŋ] *adj (person)* molesto(a), pesado(a); **to have a t. time** pasar un mal rato

tsar [zɑː(r)] *n* zar *m*

T-shirt ['tiːʃɜːt] *n* camiseta *f*

tub [tʌb] *n* (**a**) *(container)* tina *f*, cuba *f* (**b**) *(bath)* bañera *f*

tuba ['tjuːbə] *n* tuba *f*

tubby ['tʌbɪ] *adj* (**tubbier, tubbiest**) rechoncho(a)

tube [tjuːb] *n* (**a**) tubo *m*; *Anat* conducto *m*; *(of bicycle)* cámara *f* (de aire) (**b**) *Br Fam* **the t.** *(underground)* el metro

tuberculosis [tjʊbɜːkjʊ'ləʊsɪs] *n* tuberculosis *f*

tubing ['tjuːbɪŋ] *n* tubería *f*; **(piece of) t.** (trozo *m* de) tubo *m*

tubular ['tjuːbjʊlə(r)] *adj* tubular

tuck [tʌk] **1** *vt* **to t. in the bedclothes** remeter la ropa de la cama; **to t. sb in** arropar a algn; **to t. one's shirt into one's trousers** meterse la camisa por dentro (de los pantalones)

2 *n Sewing* pliegue *m*

▶ **tuck in** *vi Fam* devorar

Tuesday ['tjuːzdɪ] *n* martes *m*

tuft [tʌft] *n (of hair)* mechón *m*

tug [tʌg] **1** *vt (pull at)* tirar de; *(haul along)* arrastrar; *Naut* remolcar

2 *n* (**a**) *(pull)* tirón *m*; **t. of war** *(game)* lucha *f* de la cuerda; *Fig* lucha encarnizada (**b**) *Naut* remolcador *m*

tugboat ['tʌgbəʊt] *n* remolcador *m*

tuition [tjuː'ɪʃən] *n* instrucción *f*; **private t.** clases *fpl* particulares; **t. fees** honorarios *mpl*

tulip ['tjuːlɪp] *n* tulipán *m*

tumble ['tʌmbəl] **1** *vi (person)* caerse; *(acrobat)* dar volteretas; *(building)* venirse abajo

2 *vt* volcar

3 *n* (**a**) caída *f* (**b**) **t. dryer** secadora *f*

tumbledown ['tʌmbəldaʊn] *adj* en ruinas

tumbler ['tʌmblə(r)] *n* vaso *m*

tummy ['tʌmɪ] *n Fam* estómago *m*, barriga *f*

tumour, *US* **tumor** ['tjuːmə(r)] *n* tumor *m*

tumult ['tjuːmʌlt] *n* tumulto *m*

tuna ['tjuːnə] *n* atún *m*, bonito *m*

> 🖉 Note that the Spanish word **tuna** is a false friend and is never a translation for the English word **tuna**. In Spanish, **tuna** means "group of student minstrels".

tune [tjuːn] **1** *n* (**a**) *(melody)* melodía *f*; *Fig* **to change one's t.** cambiar de tono (**b**) *Mus* tono *m*; **in/out of t.** afinado/desafinado; **to sing out of t.** desafinar

2 *vt Mus* afinar

3 *vi Rad & TV* **to t. in to a station** sintonizar una emisora

▶ **tune up** *vi* afinar los instrumentos

tuneful ['tjuːnfʊl] *adj* melodioso(a)

tuner ['tjuːnə(r)] (**a**) *(of pianos)* afinador(a) *m,f* (**b**) *Rad & TV (knob)* sintonizador *m*

tunic ['tjuːnɪk] *n* túnica *f*

tuning ['tjuːnɪŋ] *n* (**a**) *Mus* afinación *f*; **t. fork** diapasón *m* (**b**) *Rad & TV* **t. in** sintonización *f*

Tunisia [tjuː'nɪzɪə] *n* Túnez

Tunisian [tjuː'nɪzɪən] *adj & n* tunecino(a) *(m,f)*

tunnel ['tʌnəl] **1** *n* túnel *m*; *Min* galería *f*

2 *vt* **to t. through** abrir un túnel a través de

turban ['tɜːbən] *n* turbante *m*

turbine ['tɜːbaɪn] *n* turbina *f*

turbulent ['tɜːbjʊlənt] *adj* turbulento(a)

tureen [tə'riːn] *n* sopera *f*

turf [tɜːf] *n* (**a**) *(grass)* césped *m*; *(peat)* turba *f* (**b**) *Br* **t. accountant** *(in horse racing)* corredor(a) *m,f* de apuestas

▶ **turf out** *vt sep Br Fam* **to t. sb out** poner a algn de patitas en la calle

Turk [tɜːk] *n* turco(a) *m,f*

Turkey ['tɜːkɪ] *n* Turquía

turkey ['tɜːkɪ] *n* pavo *m*

Turkish ['tɜːkɪʃ] **1** *adj* turco(a)

2 *n (language)* turco *m*

turmoil ['tɜːmɔɪl] *n* confusión *f*

turn [tɜːn] **1** *vt* (**a**) volver; *(rotate)* girar, hacer girar; **to t. sth inside out** volver algo del revés; **to t. a page** volver una hoja; **to t. one's head/gaze** volver la cabeza/mirada (**towards** hacia); **to t. the corner** doblar la esquina; *Fig* **he's turned forty** ha cumplido los cuarenta (**b**) *(change)* transformar (**into** en) (**c**) *(on lathe)* tornear

2 *vi* (**a**) *(rotate)* girar

(**b**) *(turn round)* volverse, dar la vuelta; **to t. to sb** volverse hacia algn; *Fig (for help)* acudir a algn; **to t. upside down** volcarse; *Fig* **to t. on sb** volverse contra algn

(**c**) *(become)* volverse; **the milk has turned sour** la leche se ha cortado

3 *n* (**a**) *(of wheel)* vuelta *f*; **done to a t.** *(meat)* en su punto

(**b**) *(change of direction)* cambio *m* de dirección; *(in road)* curva *f*; **to take a t. for the better** empezar a mejorar; **left/ right t.** giro *m* al izquierdo/a la derecha; *US Aut* **t. signal** intermitente *m*

(**c**) **to do sb a good t.** hacer un favor a algn

(**d**) *Med* ataque *m*

(**e**) *(in game, queue)* turno *m*, vez *f*; **it's your t.** te toca a ti; **to take it in turns to do sth** turnarse para hacer algo

(**f**) *Th* número *m*

(**g**) **t. of phrase** giro *m*

▸ **turn aside 1** *vt sep* desviar

2 *vi* desviarse

▸ **turn away 1** *vt sep (person)* rechazar

2 *vi* volver la cabeza

▸ **turn back 1** *vt sep (person)* hacer retroceder; *(clock)* retrasar

2 *vi* volverse

▸ **turn down** *vt sep* (**a**) *(gas, radio etc)* bajar (**b**) *(reject)* rechazar (**c**) *(fold)* doblar

▸ **turn in** *Fam* **1** *vt sep (person)* entregar a la policía

2 *vi* acostarse

▸ **turn off 1** *vt sep (electricity)* desconectar; *(gas, light)* apagar; *(water)* cerrar

2 *vi* desviarse

▸ **turn on** *vt sep (electricity)* encender; *(tap, gas)* abrir; *(machine)* poner en marcha; *Fam* **it turns me on** me encanta

▸ **turn out 1** *vt sep* (**a**) *(extinguish)* apagar (**b**) *(eject)* echar; *(empty)* vaciar (**c**) *(produce)* producir

2 *vi* (**a**) *(attend)* asistir (**b**) **it turns out that ...** resulta que ...; **things have turned out well** las cosas han salido bien

▸ **turn over 1** *vt sep (turn upside down)* poner al revés; *(page)* dar la vuelta a

2 *vi* volverse

▸ **turn round 1** *vt sep* volver

2 *vi (rotate)* girar, dar vueltas

▸ **turn up 1** *vt sep* (**a**) *(collar)* levantar; **to t. up one's shirt sleeves** arremangarse; **turned-up nose** nariz respingona (**b**) *Rad & TV* subir

2 *vi* (**a**) *Fig* **something is sure to t. up** algo saldrá (**b**) *(arrive)* llegar, presentarse;

nobody turned up nadie se presentó (**c**) *(attend)* asistir

turning ['tɜːnɪŋ] *n* (**a**) *Fig* **t. point** punto decisivo (**b**) *(in road)* salida *f*

turnip ['tɜːnɪp] *n* nabo *m*

turnout ['tɜːnaʊt] *n* asistencia *f*

turnover ['tɜːnəʊvə(r)] *n Com (sales)* facturación *f*; *(of goods)* movimiento *m*

turnpike ['tɜːnpaɪk] *n US* autopista *f* de peaje

turnstile ['tɜːnstaɪl] *n* torniquete *m*

turntable ['tɜːnteɪbəl] *n (for record)* plato *m* (giratorio)

turn-up ['tɜːnʌp] *n Br* (**a**) *(of trousers)* vuelta *f* (**b**) *Fam Fig* **what a t. for the books!** ¡vaya sorpresa!

turpentine ['tɜːpəntaɪn] *n* (esencia *f* de) trementina *f*

turquoise ['tɜːkwɔɪz] **1** *n (colour, stone)* turquesa *f*

2 *adj* **t. (blue)** azul turquesa

turret ['tʌrɪt] *n* torrecilla *f*

turtle ['tɜːtəl] *n* tortuga *f*; *US (tortoise)* tortuga *f*

turtledove ['tɜːtəldʌv] *n* tórtola *f*

turtleneck ['tɜːtəlnek] *n* **a t. (sweater)** un jersey de cuello alto

tusk [tʌsk] *n* colmillo *m*

tussle ['tʌsəl] *n* pelea *f*, lucha *f*

tutor ['tjuːtə(r)] *n Univ* tutor(a) *m,f*; **private t.** profesor(a) *m,f* particular

tutorial [tjuːˈtɔːrɪəl] *n Univ* tutoría *f*, seminario *m*

tuxedo [tʌkˈsiːdəʊ] *n US* smoking *m*

TV [tiːˈviː] *n (abbr* **television***)* televisión *f*

twang [twæŋ] **1** *n* (**a**) *(of instrument)* sonido *m* vibrante (**b**) **nasal t.** gangueo *m*

2 *vt* puntear

3 *vi (string)* vibrar

tweak [twiːk] *vt* pellizcar

tweed [twiːd] *n* cheviot *m*

tweezers ['twiːzəz] *npl* pinzas *fpl*

twelfth [twelfθ] **1** *adj & n* duodécimo(a) *(m,f)*

2 *n (fraction)* duodécimo *m*

twelve [twelv] *adj & n* doce *(m inv)*

twentieth ['twentɪθ] **1** *adj & n* vigésimo(a) *(m,f)*

2 *n (fraction)* vigésimo *m*

twenty ['twentɪ] *adj & n* veinte *(m inv)*

twice [twaɪs] *adv* dos veces; **he's t. as old as I am** tiene el doble de años que yo

twiddle ['twɪdəl] **1** *vt* dar vueltas a; **to t. one's moustache** mesarse el bigote; **to t. one's thumbs** estar mano sobre mano

2 *vi* **to t. with sth** juguetear con algo

twig[1] [twɪg] *n* ramilla *f*

twig[2] [twɪg] *vi Br Fam* caer en la cuenta

twilight ['twaɪlaɪt] *n* crepúsculo *m*
twin [twɪn] **1** *n* mellizo(a) *m,f*; **identical twins** gemelos (idénticos); **t. brother/ sister** hermano gemelo/hermana gemela; **t. beds** camas *fpl* gemelas
  2 *vt* hermanar
twine [twaɪn] **1** *n* bramante *m*
  2 *vt* entretejer
  3 *vi* **to t. round sth** enroscarse alrededor de algo
twinge [twɪndʒ] *n (of pain)* punzada *f*; *Fig* **t. of conscience** remordimiento *m*
twinkle ['twɪŋkəl] *vi (stars)* centellear; *(eyes)* brillar
twinkling ['twɪŋklɪŋ] *n (of stars)* centelleo *m*; *Fig* **in the t. of an eye** en un abrir y cerrar de ojos
twirl [twɜːl] **1** *vt* girar rápidamente
  2 *vi (spin)* girar rápidamente; *(dancer)* piruetear
  3 *n (movement)* giro rápido; *(of dancer)* pirueta *f*
twist [twɪst] **1** *vt* torcer; *(sense)* tergiversar; **to t. one's ankle** torcerse el tobillo
  2 *vi (smoke)* formar volutas; *(path)* serpentear
  3 *n* (**a**) *(of yarn)* torzal *m* (**b**) *(movement)* torsión *f*; *Med* torcedura *f*; *Fig* **to give a new t. to sth** dar un nuevo enfoque a algo (**c**) *(in road)* vuelta *f* (**d**) *(dance)* twist *m*
twit [twɪt] *n Br Fam* memo(a) *m,f*
twitch [twɪtʃ] **1** *vt* dar un tirón a
  2 *vi* crisparse; **his face twitches** tiene un tic en la cara
twitter ['twɪtə(r)] **1** *vi* gorjear
  2 *n* gorjeo *m*
two [tuː] **1** *adj* dos *inv*; *Fig* **to be in** *or* **of t. minds about sth** estar indeciso(a) respecto a algo
  2 *n* dos *m inv*; *Fig* **to put t. and t. together** atar cabos
two-faced ['tuːˈfeɪst] *adj* hipócrita

two-party ['tuːˈpɑːtɪ] *adj* **t. system** bipartidismo *m*
twopence ['tʌpəns] *n Br* dos peniques
two-piece ['tuːˈpiːs] **1** *adj* de dos piezas
  2 *n (suit)* traje *m* de dos piezas
two-seater ['tuːˈsiːtə(r)] *adj & n* biplaza *(f)*
twosome ['tuːsəm] *n* pareja *f*
two-time ['tuːtaɪm] *vt Fam* poner los cuernos a
two-way ['tuːweɪ] *adj* (**a**) *(street)* de dos direcciones (**b**) **t. radio** aparato *m* emisor y receptor
tycoon [taɪˈkuːn] *n* magnate *m*
type [taɪp] **1** *n* (**a**) *(kind)* tipo *m*, clase *f*; *(brand)* marca *f*; *(of car)* modelo *m* (**b**) *Typ* carácter *m*; *(print)* caracteres *mpl*
  2 *vt & vi* escribir a máquina
typecast ['taɪpkɑːst] *vt* encasillar
typescript ['taɪpskrɪpt] *n* texto *m* escrito a máquina
typeset ['taɪpset] *vt* componer
typesetter ['taɪpsetə(r)] *n* (**a**) *(person)* cajista *mf* (**b**) *(machine)* máquina *f* para componer tipos
typewriter ['taɪpraɪtə(r)] *n* máquina *f* de escribir
typewritten ['taɪprɪtən] *adj* escrito(a) a máquina
typhoid ['taɪfɔɪd] *n* **t. (fever)** fiebre tifoidea
typhoon [taɪˈfuːn] *n* tifón *m*
typical ['tɪpɪkəl] *adj* típico(a)
typify ['tɪpɪfaɪ] *vt* tipificar
typing ['taɪpɪŋ] *n* mecanografía *f*
typist ['taɪpɪst] *n* mecanógrafo(a) *m,f*
tyrannical [tɪˈrænɪkəl] *adj* tiránico(a)
tyrannize ['tɪrənaɪz] *vt* tiranizar
tyranny ['tɪrənɪ] *n* tiranía *f*
tyrant ['taɪrənt] *n* tirano(a) *m,f*
tyre [taɪə(r)] *n* neumático *m*; **t. pressure** presión *f* de los neumáticos

U, u [ju:] *n (the letter)* U, u *f*
U [ju:] *adj (film)* ≃ (apta) para todos los públicos
ubiquity [ju:'bɪkwɪtɪ] *n* ubicuidad *f*
udder ['ʌdə(r)] *n* ubre *f*
UFO, ufo ['ju:ef'əʊ, 'ju:fəʊ] *n (abbr unidentified flying object)* OVNI *m*
ugh [ʌx] *interj* ¡uf!, ¡puf!
ugly ['ʌglɪ] *adj* (**uglier, ugliest**) feo(a); *(situation)* desagradable; *Fig* **u. duckling** patito feo
UK [ju:'keɪ] *n (abbr* **United Kingdom**) R.U. *m*
Ukraine [ju:'kreɪn] *n* **the U.** Ucrania
ulcer ['ʌlsə(r)] *n (sore)* llaga *f; (internal)* úlcera *f*
ulterior [ʌl'tɪərɪə(r)] *adj (motive)* oculto(a)
ultimate ['ʌltɪmɪt] *adj* (**a**) *(final)* último(a); *(aim)* final (**b**) *(basic)* esencial
ultimately ['ʌltɪmɪtlɪ] *adv* (**a**) *(finally)* finalmente (**b**) *(basically)* en el fondo
ultimatum [ʌltɪ'meɪtəm] *n* ultimátum *m*
ultrasound ['ʌltrəsaʊnd] *n* ultrasonido *m*
ultraviolet [ʌltrə'vaɪəlɪt] *adj* ultravioleta
umbilical [ʌm'bɪlɪkəl] *adj* **u. cord** cordón *m* umbilical
umbrella [ʌm'brelə] *n* paraguas *m inv*
umpire ['ʌmpaɪə(r)] **1** *n* árbitro *m*
2 *vt* arbitrar
umpteen [ʌmp'ti:n] *adj Fam* muchísimos(as), la tira de
umpteenth [ʌmp'ti:nθ] *adj* enésimo(a)
UN [ju:'en] *n (abbr* **United Nations (Organization)**) ONU *f*
unabashed [ʌnə'bæʃt] *adj* (**a**) *(unperturbed)* inmutable, imperturbable (**b**) *(shameless)* desvergonzado(a), descarado(a)
unable [ʌn'eɪbəl] *adj* incapaz; **to be u. to do sth/anything** no poder hacer algo/nada
unacceptable [ʌnək'septəbəl] *adj* inaceptable
unaccompanied [ʌnə'kʌmpənɪd] *adj* solo(a)
unaccountable [ʌnə'kaʊntəbəl] *adj* inexplicable

unaccounted-for [ʌnə'kaʊntɪdfɔ:(r)] *adj* **to be u.** faltar
unaccustomed [ʌnə'kʌstəmd] *adj* **he's u. to this climate** no está muy acostumbrado a este clima
unaffected [ʌnə'fektɪd] *adj* (**a**) no afectado(a) (**by** por) (**b**) *(indifferent)* indiferente (**by** a) (**c**) *(natural) (person)* natural; *(style)* llano(a)
unaided [ʌn'eɪdɪd] *adj* sin ayuda, solo(a)
unanimous [ju:'nænɪməs] *adj* unánime
unannounced [ʌnə'naʊnst] *adj* sin avisar
unanswered [ʌn'ɑ:nsəd] *adj* sin contestar
unapproachable [ʌnə'prəʊtʃəbəl] *adj* inabordable, inaccesible
unarmed [ʌn'ɑ:md] *adj* desarmado(a)
unashamed [ʌnə'ʃeɪmd] *adj* desvergonzado(a)
unasked [ʌn'ɑ:skt] *adv* **u. (for)** *(unrequested)* no solicitado(a); *(spontaneous)* espontáneo(a)
unassuming [ʌnə'sju:mɪŋ] *adj* sin pretensiones
unattached [ʌnə'tætʃt] *adj* (**a**) *(independent)* libre; *(loose)* suelto(a) (**b**) *(person)* soltero(a) y sin compromiso
unattended [ʌnə'tendɪd] *adj (counter etc)* desatendido(a); **to leave a child u.** dejar a un niño solo
unauthorized [ʌn'ɔ:θəraɪzd] *adj* (**a**) *(person)* no autorizado(a) (**b**) *(trade etc)* ilícito(a), ilegal
unavoidable [ʌnə'vɔɪdəbəl] *adj* inevitable; *(accident)* imprevisible
unaware [ʌnə'weə(r)] *adj* **to be u. of sth** ignorar algo
unawares [ʌnə'weəz] *adv* (**a**) *(unexpectedly)* desprevenido(a) (**b**) *(without knowing)* inconscientemente
unbalanced [ʌn'bælənst] *adj* desequilibrado(a)
unbearable [ʌn'beərəbəl] *adj* insoportable
unbeatable [ʌn'bi:təbəl] *adj (team)* invencible; *(price, quality)* inmejorable
unbelievable [ʌnbɪ'li:vəbəl] *adj* increíble

unbend [ʌnˈbend] *vi Fam Fig* relajarse
unbia(s)sed [ʌnˈbaɪəst] *adj* imparcial
unborn [ʌnˈbɔːn] *adj* sin nacer, nonato(a)
unbreakable [ʌnˈbreɪkəbəl] *adj* irrompible; *Fig* inquebrantable
unbroken [ʌnˈbrəʊkən] *adj* (a) *(whole)* intacto(a) (b) *(uninterrupted)* continuo(a) (c) *(record)* imbatido(a)
unbutton [ʌnˈbʌtən] *vt* desabrochar
uncalled-for [ʌnˈkɔːldfɔː(r)] *adj (inappropriate)* insensato(a); *(unjustified)* inmerecido(a)
uncanny [ʌnˈkænɪ] *adj* misterioso(a), extraño(a)
unceasing [ʌnˈsiːsɪŋ] *adj* incesante
uncertain [ʌnˈsɜːtən] *adj* (a) *(not certain)* incierto(a); *(doubtful)* dudoso(a); **in no u. terms** claramente (b) *(hesitant)* indeciso(a)
uncertainty [ʌnˈsɜːtəntɪ] *n* incertidumbre *f*
unchanged [ʌnˈtʃeɪndʒd] *adj* igual
unchecked [ʌnˈtʃekt] *adj* (a) *(unrestrained)* desenfrenado(a) (b) *(not examined)* no comprobado(a)
uncivilized [ʌnˈsɪvɪlaɪzd] *adj (tribe)* incivilizado(a), salvaje; *(not cultured)* inculto(a)
uncle [ˈʌŋkəl] *n* tío *m*
uncomfortable [ʌnˈkʌmftəbəl] *adj* incómodo(a); **to make things u. for** complicarle la vida a
uncommon [ʌnˈkɒmən] *adj* (a) *(rare)* poco común; *(unusual)* extraordinario(a) (b) *(excessive)* excesivo(a)
uncommonly [ʌnˈkɒmənlɪ] *adv* **not u.** con cierta frecuencia
uncompromising [ʌnˈkɒmprəmaɪzɪŋ] *adj* intransigente; **u. honesty** sinceridad absoluta
unconcerned [ʌnkənˈsɜːnd] *adj* indiferente (**about** a)
unconditional [ʌnkənˈdɪʃənəl] *adj* incondicional; **u. refusal** negativa rotunda
unconnected [ʌnkəˈnektɪd] *adj* no relacionado(a)
unconscious [ʌnˈkɒnʃəs] **1** *adj* (a) inconsciente (**of** de) (b) *(unintentional)* involuntario(a)
2 *n* **the u.** el inconsciente
unconsciousness [ʌnˈkɒnʃəsnɪs] *n Med* pérdida *f* del conocimiento
uncontested [ʌnkənˈtestɪd] *adj Pol* **u. seat** escaño *m* ganado sin oposición
uncontrollable [ʌnkənˈtrəʊləbəl] *adj* incontrolable; *(desire)* irresistible
unconventional [ʌnkənˈvenʃənəl] *adj* poco convencional, original
uncooperative [ʌnkəʊˈɒpərətɪv] *adj* poco cooperativo(a)
uncouth [ʌnˈkuːθ] *adj (rude)* grosero(a)
uncover [ʌnˈkʌvə(r)] *vt* destapar; *Fig* descubrir
undamaged [ʌnˈdæmɪdʒd] *adj (article etc)* sin desperfectos; *(person)* indemne; *(reputation)* intacto(a)
undaunted [ʌnˈdɔːntɪd] *adj* firme, impávido(a)
undecided [ʌndɪˈsaɪdɪd] *adj* (a) *(person)* indeciso(a) (b) *(issue)* pendiente; **it's still u.** está aún por decidir
undefeated [ʌndɪˈfiːtɪd] *adj* invicto(a)
undefined [ʌndɪˈfaɪnd] *adj* indeterminado(a)
undeniable [ʌndɪˈnaɪəbəl] *adj* innegable
under [ˈʌndə(r)] **1** *prep* (a) debajo de; **u. the sun** bajo el sol (b) *(less than)* menos de; **incomes u. £1,000** ingresos inferiores a 1.000 libras; **u. age** menor de edad (c) *(of rank)* de rango inferior a (d) **u. Caesar** bajo César (e) *(subject to)* bajo; **u. arrest** detenido(a); **u. cover** a cubierto; **u. obligation to** en la obligación de; **u. the circumstances** dadas las circunstancias; *Fig* **I was u. the impression that ...** tenía la impresión de que ... (f) *(according to)* según, conforme a
2 *adv* abajo, debajo
under- [ˈʌndə(r)] *pref (below)* sub-, infra-; *(insufficiently)* insuficientemente
underarm [ˈʌndərɑːm] **1** *adj* **u. deodorant** desodorante *m* para las axilas
2 *adv Sport* por debajo del hombro
undercarriage [ˈʌndəkærɪdʒ] *n* tren *m* de aterrizaje
undercharge [ʌndəˈtʃɑːdʒ] *vt* cobrar menos de lo debido
underclothes [ˈʌndəkləʊðz] *npl* ropa *f* interior
undercoat [ˈʌndəkəʊt] *n (of paint)* primera mano
undercover [ʌndəˈkʌvə(r)] *adj* secreto(a)
undercurrent [ˈʌndəkʌrənt] *n* (a) *(in sea)* corriente submarina (b) *Fig* sentimiento *m* latente
undercut [ʌndəˈkʌt] *vt (pt & pp* **undercut**) *Com* vender más barato que
underdeveloped [ʌndədɪˈveləpt] *adj* subdesarrollado(a)
underdog [ˈʌndədɒg] *n* desvalido(a) *m,f*
underestimate [ʌndərˈestɪmeɪt] *vt* infravalorar
underexposure [ʌndərɪkˈspəʊʒə(r)] *n Phot* subexposición *f*

underfed [ʌndə'fed] *adj* subalimentado(a)

underfoot [ʌndə'fʊt] *adv* en el suelo

undergo [ʌndə'gəʊ] *vt* (*pt* **underwent**; *pp* **undergone** [ʌndə'gɒn]) experimentar; *(change)* sufrir; *(test etc)* pasar por

undergraduate [ʌndə'grædjɔɪt] *n* estudiante *mf* universitario(a)

underground [ʌndə'graʊnd] **1** *adj* subterráneo(a); *Fig* clandestino(a)
  2 *n* (**a**) *Pol* movimiento clandestino (**b**) *Br* **the u.** *(train)* el metro
  3 *adv* [ʌndə'graʊnd] *Fig* **to go u.** pasar a la clandestinidad

undergrowth ['ʌndəgrəʊθ] *n* maleza *f*

underhand **1** *adj* ['ʌndəhænd] *(method)* ilícito(a); *(person)* solapado(a)
  2 *adv* [ʌndə'hænd] bajo cuerda

underline [ʌndə'laɪn] *vt* subrayar

underling ['ʌndəlɪŋ] *n Pej* mandado(a) *m,f*

underlying [ʌndə'laɪɪŋ] *adj (basic)* fundamental

undermine [ʌndə'maɪn] *vt* socavar, minar

underneath [ʌndə'niːθ] **1** *prep* debajo de, bajo
  2 *adv* abajo, debajo
  3 *adj* de abajo
  4 *n* parte *f* inferior

undernourished [ʌndə'nʌrɪʃt] *adj* desnutrido(a)

underpaid [ʌndə'peɪd] *adj* mal pagado(a)

underpass ['ʌndəpɑːs] *n* paso subterráneo

underprivileged [ʌndə'prɪvɪlɪdʒd] **1** *adj* desfavorecido(a)
  2 *npl* **the u.** los menos favorecidos

under-secretary [ʌndə'sekrətərɪ] *n* subsecretario(a) *m,f*

undershirt ['ʌndəʃɜːt] *n US* camiseta *f*

underskirt ['ʌndəskɜːt] *n* combinación *f*

understand [ʌndə'stænd] *vt & vi* (*pt & pp* **understood**) (**a**) *(comprehend)* entender, comprender; **do I make myself understood?** ¿me explico? (**b**) *(assume, believe)* entender; **she gave me to u. that ...** me dio a entender que ... (**c**) *(hear)* tener entendido (**d**) **to u. one another** entenderse

understandable [ʌndə'stændəbəl] *adj* comprensible

understanding [ʌndə'stændɪŋ] **1** *n* (**a**) *(intellectual grasp)* entendimiento *m*, comprensión *f* (**b**) *(interpretation)* interpretación *f* (**c**) *(agreement)* acuerdo *m*

(**d**) **on the u. that ...** a condición de que ...
  2 *adj* comprensivo(a)

understatement [ʌndə'steɪtmənt] *n* **to make an u.** minimizar, subestimar; **to say that the boy is rather clever is an u.** decir que el chico es bastante listo es quedarse corto

understood [ʌndə'stʊd] **1** *adj* (**a**) **I wish it to be u. that ...** que conste que ... (**b**) *(agreed on)* convenido(a) (**c**) *(implied)* sobreentendido(a)
  2 *pt & pp of* **understand**

understudy ['ʌndəstʌdɪ] *n* suplente *mf*

undertake [ʌndə'teɪk] *vt* (*pt* **undertook**; *pp* **undertaken** [ʌndə'teɪkən]) (**a**) *(responsibility)* asumir; *(task, job)* encargarse de (**b**) *(promise)* comprometerse a

undertaker ['ʌndəteɪkə(r)] *n* empresario(a) *m,f* de pompas fúnebres; **u.'s** funeraria *f*

undertaking [ʌndə'teɪkɪŋ] *n* (**a**) *(task)* empresa *f* (**b**) *(promise)* compromiso *m*

undertone ['ʌndətəʊn] *n* **in an u.** en voz baja

undertook [ʌndə'tʊk] *pt of* **undertake**

underwater [ʌndə'wɔːtə(r)] **1** *adj* submarino(a)
  2 *adv* bajo el agua

underwear ['ʌndəweə(r)] *n* ropa *f* interior

underwent [ʌndə'went] *pt of* **undergo**

underworld ['ʌndəwɜːld] *n (criminals)* hampa *f*, bajos fondos

underwrite [ʌndə'raɪt] *vt* (*pt* **underwrote**; *pp* **underwritten**) (**a**) *(guarantee)* garantizar, avalar (**b**) *(insure)* asegurar

underwriter ['ʌndəraɪtə(r)] *n* (**a**) *Fin* suscriptor(a) *m,f* (**b**) *(insurer)* asegurador(a) *m,f*

underwritten [ʌndə'rɪtən] *pp of* **underwrite**

underwrote [ʌndə'rəʊt] *pt of* **underwrite**

undesirable [ʌndɪ'zaɪrəbəl] *adj & n* indeseable *(mf)*

undeterred [ʌndɪ'tɜːd] *adj* sin inmutarse; **u. by** sin arredrarse ante

undid [ʌn'dɪd] *pt of* **undo**

undies ['ʌndɪz] *npl Fam* bragas *fpl*

undignified [ʌn'dɪgnɪfaɪd] *adj (attitude etc)* indecoroso(a)

undisciplined [ʌn'dɪsɪplɪnd] *adj* indisciplinado(a)

undisclosed [ʌndɪs'kləʊzd] *adj* sin revelar

undiscovered [ʌndɪ'skʌvəd] *adj* sin descubrir

undisguised [ʌndɪs'gaɪzd] *adj Fig* no disimulado(a)

undisputed [ʌndɪ'spjuːtɪd] *adj (unchallenged)* incontestable; *(unquestionable)* indiscutible

undivided [ʌndɪ'vaɪdɪd] *adj* **to give one's u. attention** prestar toda la atención

undo [ʌn'duː] *vt (pt undid; pp undone)* **(a)** deshacer; *(button)* desabrochar **(b)** *(put right)* enmendar

undone¹ [ʌn'dʌn] *adj (unfinished)* inacabado(a)

undone² [ʌn'dʌn] **1** *adj (knot etc)* deshecho(a); **to come u.** *(shoelace)* desatarse; *(button, blouse)* desabrocharse; *(necklace etc)* soltarse
2 *pp of* **undo**

undoubted [ʌn'daʊtɪd] *adj* indudable

undress [ʌn'dres] **1** *vt* desnudar
2 *vi* desnudarse

undressed [ʌn'drest] *adj (naked)* desnudo(a)

undue [ʌn'djuː] **(a)** *adj (excessive)* excesivo(a) **(b)** *(improper)* indebido(a)

undulate ['ʌndjʊleɪt] *vi* ondular, ondear

unearth [ʌn'ɜːθ] *vt* desenterrar

unearthly [ʌn'ɜːθlɪ] *adj* **(a)** *(being)* sobrenatural **(b)** *Fam (din)* espantoso(a); **at an u. hour** a una hora intempestiva

uneasy [ʌn'iːzɪ] *adj* **(a)** *(worried)* preocupado(a); *(disturbing)* inquietante **(b)** *(uncomfortable)* incómodo(a)

uneconomic(al) [ʌniːkə'nɒmɪk(əl)] *adj* poco económico(a)

uneducated [ʌn'edjʊkeɪtɪd] *adj* inculto(a)

unemployed [ʌnɪm'plɔɪd] **1** *adj* en paro, parado(a); **to be u.** estar en paro
2 *npl* **the u.** los parados

unemployment [ʌnɪm'plɔɪmənt] *n* paro *m*, desempleo *m*; **u. benefit**, *US* **u. compensation** subsidio *m* de desempleo

unending [ʌn'endɪŋ] *adj* interminable

unenviable [ʌn'envɪəbəl] *adj* poco envidiable

unequal [ʌn'iːkwəl] *adj* desigual

unequivocal [ʌnɪ'kwɪvəkəl] *adj* inequívoco(a)

uneven [ʌn'iːvən] *adj* **(a)** *(not level)* desigual; *(bumpy)* accidentado(a) **(b)** *(variable)* irregular

uneventful [ʌnɪ'ventfʊl] *adj* sin acontecimientos

unexceptional [ʌnɪk'sepʃənəl] *adj* ordinario(a)

unexpected [ʌnɪk'spektɪd] *adj (unhoped for)* inesperado(a); *(event)* imprevisto(a)

unfailing [ʌn'feɪlɪŋ] *adj* indefectible; *(incessant)* constante; *(patience)* inagotable

unfair [ʌn'feə(r)] *adj* injusto(a); *Sport* sucio(a)

unfaithful [ʌn'feɪθfʊl] *adj (friend)* desleal; *(husband, wife)* infiel

unfamiliar [ʌnfə'mɪljə(r)] *adj (unknown)* desconocido(a); *(not conversant)* no familiarizado(a) (**with** con)

unfashionable [ʌn'fæʃənəbəl] *adj* pasado(a) de moda; *(ideas etc)* poco popular

unfasten [ʌn'fɑːsən] *vt (knot)* desatar; *(clothing, belt)* desabrochar

unfavourable, *US* **unfavorable** [ʌn'feɪvərəbəl] *adj* desfavorable; *(criticism)* adverso(a); *(winds)* contrario(a)

unfeeling [ʌn'fiːlɪŋ] *adj* insensible

unfinished [ʌn'fɪnɪʃt] *adj* inacabado(a); **u. business** un asunto pendiente

unfit [ʌn'fɪt] *adj* **(a)** *(thing)* inadecuado(a); *(person)* no apto(a) (**for** para) **(b)** *(incompetent)* incompetente **(c)** *(physically)* incapacitado(a); **to be u.** no estar en forma

unflinching [ʌn'flɪntʃɪŋ] *adj* **(a)** *(determined)* resuelto(a) **(b)** *(fearless)* impávido(a)

unfold [ʌn'fəʊld] **1** *vt* **(a)** *(sheet)* desdoblar; *(newspaper)* abrir **(b)** *(plan, secret)* revelar
2 *vi* **(a)** *(open up)* abrirse; *(landscape)* extenderse **(b)** *(plot)* desarrollarse **(c)** *(secret)* descubrirse

unforeseen [ʌnfɔː'siːn] *adj* imprevisto(a)

unforgettable [ʌnfə'getəbəl] *adj* inolvidable

unforgivable [ʌnfə'gɪvəbəl] *adj* imperdonable

unfortunate [ʌn'fɔːtʃənɪt] *adj (person, event)* desgraciado(a); *(remark)* desafortunado(a); **how u.!** ¡qué mala suerte!

unfortunately [ʌn'fɔːtʃənɪtlɪ] *adv* desgraciadamente, por desgracia

unfounded [ʌn'faʊndɪd] *adj* infundado(a)

unfriendly [ʌn'frendlɪ] *adj* (**unfriendlier, unfriendliest**) antipático(a), poco amistoso(a)

unfurl [ʌn'fɜːl] *vi* desplegarse

unfurnished [ʌn'fɜːnɪʃt] *adj* sin amueblar

ungainly [ʌn'geɪnlɪ] *adj (gait)* desgarbado(a)

ungodly [ʌn'gɒdlɪ] *adj* (**ungodlier, ungodliest**) *(behaviour)* impío(a); *Fam Fig* **at an u. hour** a una hora intempestiva

ungrateful [ʌn'greɪtfʊl] *adj (person)* desagradecido(a); *(task)* ingrato(a)

unguarded [ʌnˈgɑːdɪd] *adj* (**a**) *(unprotected)* desatendido(a); *(imprudent)* desprevenido(a) (**b**) *(frank)* franco(a)

unhappiness [ʌnˈhæpɪnɪs] *n* (**a**) *(sadness)* tristeza *f* (**b**) *(wretchedness)* desdicha *f*

unhappy [ʌnˈhæpɪ] *adj* (**unhappier, unhappiest**) (**a**) *(sad)* triste (**b**) *(wretched)* desgraciado(a), infeliz; *(unfortunate)* desafortunado(a)

unharmed [ʌnˈhɑːmd] *adj* ileso(a), indemne

unhealthy [ʌnˈhelθɪ] *adj* (**unhealthier, unhealthiest**) (**a**) *(ill)* enfermizo(a) (**b**) *(unwholesome)* malsano(a)

unheard [ʌnˈhɜːd] *adj* (**a**) **her request went u.** su petición no fue atendida (**b**) **u. of** *(outrageous)* inaudito(a); *(without precedent)* sin precedente

unhesitating [ʌnˈhezɪteɪtɪŋ] *adj* resuelto(a)

unhook [ʌnˈhʊk] *vt (from hook)* descolgar; *(clothing)* desabrochar

unhurt [ʌnˈhɜːt] *adj* ileso(a), indemne

unhygienic [ʌnhaɪˈdʒiːnɪk] *adj* antihigiénico(a)

unidentified [ʌnaɪˈdentɪfaɪd] *adj* **u. flying object** objeto volador no identificado, ovni *m*

unification [juːnɪfɪˈkeɪʃən] *n* unificación *f*

uniform [ˈjuːnɪfɔːm] *adj & n* uniforme (*m*)

uniformity [juːnɪˈfɔːmɪtɪ] *n* uniformidad *f*

unify [ˈjuːnɪfaɪ] *vt* unificar

unilateral [juːnɪˈlætərəl] *adj* unilateral

unimportant [ʌnɪmˈpɔːtənt] *adj* poco importante

uninformed [ʌnɪnˈfɔːmd] *adj (opinion)* sin fundamento

uninhabited [ʌnɪnˈhæbɪtɪd] *adj* despoblado(a)

uninhibited [ʌnɪnˈhɪbɪtɪd] *adj* sin inhibición

uninspired [ʌnɪnˈspaɪəd] *adj (person)* falto(a) de inspiración; *(performance)* insulso(a)

uninspiring [ʌnɪnˈspaɪərɪŋ] *adj* que no inspira

unintelligible [ʌnɪnˈtelɪdʒəbəl] *adj* ininteligible, incomprensible

unintentional [ʌnɪnˈtenʃənəl] *adj* involuntario(a)

unintentionally [ʌnɪnˈtenʃənəlɪ] *adv* sin querer

uninteresting [ʌnˈɪntrɪstɪŋ] *adj* poco interesante

uninterrupted [ʌnɪntəˈrʌptɪd] *adj* ininterrumpido(a)

union [ˈjuːnjən] **1** *n* (**a**) unión *f* (**b**) *(organization)* sindicato *m* (**c**) *US* **the U.** los Estados Unidos; *Br* **U. Jack** bandera *f* del Reino Unido
2 *adj* sindical

unique [juːˈniːk] *adj* único(a)

unison [ˈjuːnɪsən] *n Mus* unisonancia *f*; *Fig (harmony)* armonía *f*; **in u.** al unísono

unit [ˈjuːnɪt] *n* (**a**) unidad *f*; **monetary u.** unidad monetaria; *Br Fin* **u. trust** sociedad *f* de inversiones (**b**) *(piece of furniture)* módulo *m*; **kitchen u.** mueble *m* de cocina (**c**) *Tech* grupo *m*; *Comput* **central processing u.** procesador *m* central; **visual display u.** monitor *m* (**d**) *(department)* servicio *m* (**e**) *(team)* equipo *m*

unite [juːˈnaɪt] **1** *vt* unir
2 *vi* unirse

united [juːˈnaɪtɪd] *adj* unido(a); **U. Kingdom** Reino Unido; **U. States (of America)** Estados Unidos (de América); **U. Nations** Naciones Unidas

unity [ˈjuːnɪtɪ] *n* unidad *f*; *(harmony)* armonía *f*

universal [juːnɪˈvɜːsəl] *adj* universal

universe [ˈjuːnɪvɜːs] *n* universo *m*

university [juːnɪˈvɜːsɪtɪ] **1** *n* universidad *f*
2 *adj* universitario(a)

unjust [ʌnˈdʒʌst] *adj* injusto(a)

unkempt [ʌnˈkempt] *adj* descuidado(a); *(hair)* despeinado(a); *(appearance)* desaliñado(a)

unkind [ʌnˈkaɪnd] *adj (not nice)* poco amable; *(cruel)* despiadado(a)

unknown [ʌnˈnəʊn] **1** *adj* desconocido(a); **u. quantity** incógnita *f*
2 *n* **the u.** lo desconocido

unlawful [ʌnˈlɔːfʊl] *adj (not legal)* ilegal

unleash [ʌnˈliːʃ] *vt* (**a**) *(dog)* soltar (**b**) *Fig (release)* liberar; *(provoke)* desencadenar

unless [ʌnˈles] *conj* a menos que, a no ser que

unlike [ʌnˈlaɪk] **1** *adj* diferente, distinto(a)
2 *prep* a diferencia de

unlikely [ʌnˈlaɪklɪ] *adj* (**a**) *(improbable)* poco probable (**b**) *(unusual)* raro(a)

unlimited [ʌnˈlɪmɪtɪd] *adj* ilimitado(a)

unlisted [ʌnˈlɪstɪd] *adj US Tel* que no se encuentra en la guía telefónica

unload [ʌnˈləʊd] *vt & vi* descargar

unlock [ʌnˈlɒk] *vt* abrir (con llave)

unluckily [ʌnˈlʌkɪlɪ] *adv* desafortunadamente, por desgracia

unlucky [ʌnˈlʌkɪ] *adj* (**unluckier, unluckiest**) *(unfortunate)* desgraciado(a); **to be**

u. *(person)* tener mala suerte; *(thing)* traer mala suerte

unmanageable [ʌnˈmænɪdʒəbəl] *adj (people)* ingobernable; *(child, hair)* incontrolable

unmanned [ʌnˈmænd] *adj (spacecraft etc)* no tripulado(a)

unmarried [ʌnˈmærɪd] *adj* soltero(a)

unmask [ʌnˈmɑːsk] *vt Fig (plot)* descubrir

unmistak(e)able [ʌnmɪsˈteɪkəbəl] *adj* inconfundible

unmistak(e)ably [ʌnmɪsˈteɪkəblɪ] *adv* sin lugar a dudas

unmitigated [ʌnˈmɪtɪɡeɪtɪd] *adj* (**a**) *(absolute)* absoluto(a); *(liar)* rematado(a) (**b**) *(grief)* profundo(a)

unnamed [ʌnˈneɪmd] *adj (anonymous)* anónimo(a)

unnatural [ʌnˈnætʃərəl] *adj* (**a**) *(against nature)* antinatural; *(abnormal)* anormal (**b**) *(affected)* afectado(a)

unnecessary [ʌnˈnesɪsərɪ] *adj* innecesario(a), inútil; **it's u. to add that ...** sobra añadir que ...

unnoticed [ʌnˈnəʊtɪst] *adj* desapercibido(a); **to let sth pass u.** pasar algo por alto

unobserved [ʌnɒbˈzɜːvd] *adj* inadvertido(a)

unobtainable [ʌnəbˈteɪnəbəl] *adj* inasequible, inalcanzable

unobtrusive [ʌnəbˈtruːsɪv] *adj* discreto(a)

unoccupied [ʌnˈɒkjʊpaɪd] *adj (house)* desocupado(a); *(seat)* libre

unofficial [ʌnəˈfɪʃəl] *adj* no oficial; *Ind* **u. strike** huelga *f* no apoyada por los sindicatos

unorthodox [ʌnˈɔːθədɒks] *adj* (**a**) *(behaviour etc)* poco ortodoxo(a) (**b**) *Rel* heterodoxo(a)

unpack [ʌnˈpæk] **1** *vt (boxes)* desembalar; *(suitcase)* deshacer
  2 *vi* deshacer la(s) maleta(s)

unpalatable [ʌnˈpælətəbəl] *adj* desagradable

unparalleled [ʌnˈpærəleld] *adj* (**a**) *(in quality)* incomparable (**b**) *(without precedent)* sin precedente

unpardonable [ʌnˈpɑːdənəbəl] *adj* imperdonable

unperturbed [ʌnpəˈtɜːbd] *adj* impasible

unpleasant [ʌnˈplezənt] *adj* desagradable (**to** con)

unpleasantness [ʌnˈplezəntnɪs] *n* disgusto *m*

unplug [ʌnˈplʌɡ] *vt* desenchufar

unpopular [ʌnˈpɒpjʊlə(r)] *adj* impopular; **to make oneself u.** ganarse la antipatía de todos

unprecedented [ʌnˈpresɪdentɪd] *adj* sin precedente

unpredictable [ʌnprɪˈdɪktəbəl] *adj* imprevisible

unprepared [ʌnprɪˈpeəd] *adj (speech etc)* improvisado(a); *(person)* desprevenido(a)

unprincipled [ʌnˈprɪnsɪpəld] *adj* sin escrúpulos

unprintable [ʌnˈprɪntəbəl] *adj (word, comment)* malsonante

unproductive [ʌnprəˈdʌktɪv] *adj (inefficient)* improductivo(a); *(fruitless)* infructuoso(a)

unprofessional [ʌnprəˈfeʃənəl] *adj (unethical)* poco profesional; *(substandard)* de aficionado(a)

unprotected [ʌnprəˈtektɪd] *adj* indefenso(a)

unprovoked [ʌnprəˈvəʊkt] *adj* gratuito(a)

unpunished [ʌnˈpʌnɪʃt] *adj* impune

unqualified [ʌnˈkwɒlɪfaɪd] *adj* (**a**) *(without qualification)* sin título; *(incompetent)* incompetente (**b**) *(unconditional)* incondicional; *(denial)* rotundo(a); *(endorsement)* sin reserva; *(success)* total

unquestionable [ʌnˈkwestʃənəbəl] *adj* indiscutible

unquestioning [ʌnˈkwestʃənɪŋ] *adj* incondicional; *(obedience)* ciego(a)

unravel [ʌnˈrævəl] **1** *vt* desenmarañar
  2 *vi* desenmarañarse

unreadable [ʌnˈriːdəbəl] *adj* (**a**) *(handwriting)* ilegible (**b**) *(book)* imposible de leer

unreal [ʌnˈrɪəl] *adj* irreal

unrealistic [ʌnrɪəˈlɪstɪk] *adj* poco realista

unreasonable [ʌnˈriːzənəbəl] *adj* poco razonable; *(demands)* desmedido(a); *(prices)* exorbitante; *(hour)* inoportuno(a)

unrefined [ʌnrɪˈfaɪnd] *adj* (**a**) *(sugar, oil etc)* sin refinar (**b**) *(person)* tosco(a), basto(a)

unrelated [ʌnrɪˈleɪtɪd] *adj (not connected)* no relacionado(a)

unrelenting [ʌnrɪˈlentɪŋ] *adj (behaviour)* implacable; *(struggle)* encarnizado(a)

unreliable [ʌnrɪˈlaɪəbəl] *adj* (**a**) *(person)* de poca confianza (**b**) *(information)* que no es de fiar; *(machine)* poco fiable

unrelieved [ʌnrɪˈliːvd] *adj (boredom)* total

unremitting [ʌnrɪ'mɪtɪŋ] *adj* (**a**) *(efforts etc)* incesante (**b**) *(person)* incansable

unrepentant [ʌnrɪ'pentənt] *adj* impenitente

unreserved [ʌnrɪ'zɜːvd] *adj (praise, support)* sin reserva

unreservedly [ʌnrɪ'zɜːvɪdlɪ] *adv* sin reserva

unrest [ʌn'rest] *n (social etc)* malestar *m*; **political u.** agitación política

unrivalled, *US* **unrivaled** [ʌn'raɪvəld] *adj* sin par, sin rival

unroll [ʌn'rəʊl] *vt* desenrollar

unruffled [ʌn'rʌfəld] *adj Fig* tranquilo(a)

unruly [ʌn'ruːlɪ] *adj* (**unrulier, unruliest**) (**a**) *(child)* revoltoso(a) (**b**) *(hair)* rebelde

unsafe [ʌn'seɪf] *adj (dangerous)* peligroso(a); *(risky)* inseguro(a); **to feel u.** sentirse expuesto(a)

unsaid [ʌn'sed] *adj* **it's better left u.** más vale no decir nada; **much was left u.** quedó mucho por decir

unsatisfactory [ʌnsætɪs'fæktərɪ] *adj* insatisfactorio(a); **it's most u.** deja mucho que desear

unsavoury, *US* **unsavory** [ʌn'seɪvərɪ] *adj* desagradable

unscathed [ʌn'skeɪðd] *adj* ileso(a), indemne

unscrew [ʌn'skruː] *vt* destornillar

unscrupulous [ʌn'skruːpjʊləs] *adj* sin escrúpulos

unseemly [ʌn'siːmlɪ] *adj* impropio(a)

unseen [ʌn'siːn] **1** *adj* invisible; *(unnoticed)* inadvertido(a)
2 *n Br Educ* = texto no trabajado en clase

unselfish [ʌn'selfɪʃ] *adj* desinteresado(a)

unsettle [ʌn'setəl] *vt* perturbar

unsettled [ʌn'setəld] *adj* (**a**) *(person)* nervioso(a); *(situation)* inestable (**b**) *(weather)* inestable (**c**) *(matter, debt)* pendiente (**d**) *(land)* sin colonizar

unshaven [ʌn'ʃeɪvən] *adj* sin afeitar

unsightly [ʌn'saɪtlɪ] *adj* feo(a), desagradable

unskilled [ʌn'skɪld] *adj (worker)* no cualificado(a); *(work)* no especializado(a)

unsociable [ʌn'səʊʃəbəl] *adj* insociable, huraño(a)

unsophisticated [ʌnsə'fɪstɪkeɪtɪd] *adj* (**a**) *(naïve)* ingenuo(a) (**b**) *(simple)* poco sofisticado(a)

unsound [ʌn'saʊnd] *adj* (**a**) *(unstable)* inestable; **of u. mind** demente (**b**) *(fallacious)* falso(a)

unspeakable [ʌn'spiːkəbəl] *adj* (**a**) indecible (**b**) *Fig (evil)* atroz

unspoken [ʌn'spəʊkən] *adj* (**a**) *(tacit)* tácito(a) (**b**) *(feeling)* interior, secreto(a)

unstable [ʌn'steɪbəl] *adj* inestable

unsteady [ʌn'stedɪ] *adj (not firm)* inestable; *(table, chair)* cojo(a); *(hand, voice)* tembloroso(a)

unstinting [ʌn'stɪntɪŋ] *adj* pródigo(a) (**in** en)

unstuck [ʌn'stʌk] *adj* **to come u.** despegarse; *Fig* venirse abajo

unsuccessful [ʌnsək'sesfʊl] *adj* (**a**) *(fruitless)* fracasado(a); *(useless)* vano(a) (**b**) *(businessman etc)* fracasado(a); *(candidate)* derrotado(a); **to be u. at sth** no tener éxito con algo

unsuccessfully [ʌnsək'sesfʊlɪ] *adv* sin éxito, en vano

unsuitable [ʌn'suːtəbəl] *adj* (**a**) *(person)* no apto(a) (**b**) *(thing)* inadecuado(a); *(remark)* inoportuno(a); *(time)* inconveniente

unsuited [ʌn'suːtɪd] *adj* (**a**) *(person)* no apto(a); *(thing)* impropio(a) (**to** para) (**b**) *(incompatible)* incompatible

unsure [ʌn'ʃʊə(r)] *adj* poco seguro(a)

unsuspecting [ʌnsə'spektɪŋ] *adj* confiado(a); **he went in u.** entró sin sospechar nada

unswerving [ʌn'swɜːvɪŋ] *adj* firme

unsympathetic [ʌnsɪmpə'θetɪk] *adj (unfeeling)* impasible; *(not understanding)* poco comprensivo(a)

untapped [ʌn'tæpt] *adj (resource)* sin explotar

untarnished [ʌn'tɑːnɪʃt] *adj Fig* sin mancha

untenable [ʌn'tenəbəl] *adj* insostenible

unthinkable [ʌn'θɪŋkəbəl] *adj* impensable, inconcebible

untidy [ʌn'taɪdɪ] *adj* (**untidier, untidiest**) *(room, person)* desordenado(a); *(hair)* despeinado(a); *(appearance)* desaseado(a)

untie [ʌn'taɪ] *vt* desatar; *(free)* soltar

until [ʌn'tɪl] **1** *conj* hasta que; **she worked u. she collapsed** trabajó hasta desfallecer; **u. she gets back** hasta que vuelva
2 *prep* hasta; **u. now** hasta ahora; **u. ten o'clock** hasta las diez; **not u. Monday** hasta el lunes no

untimely [ʌn'taɪmlɪ] *adj* (**a**) *(premature)* prematuro(a) (**b**) *(inopportune)* inoportuno(a); *(hour)* intempestivo(a)

untold [ʌn'təʊld] *adj* (**a**) *(indescribable)* indecible (**b**) *Fig (loss, wealth)* incalculable (**c**) *(not told)* sin contar

untouchable [ʌnˈtʌtʃəbəl] *adj & n* intocable *(mf)*

untoward [ʌntəˈwɔːd] *adj* (**a**) *(unfortunate)* desafortunado(a) (**b**) *(adverse)* adverso(a)

untrained [ʌnˈtreɪnd] *adj* (**a**) *(unskilled)* sin preparación profesional (**b**) *(inexpert)* inexperto(a)

untrue [ʌnˈtruː] *adj* (**a**) *(false)* falso(a) (**b**) *(unfaithful)* infiel (**c**) *(inexact)* inexacto(a)

untrustworthy [ʌnˈtrʌstwɜːðɪ] *adj* (**a**) *(person)* de poca confianza (**b**) *(source)* no fidedigno(a)

unused [ʌnˈjuːzd] *adj* (**a**) *(car)* sin usar; *(flat etc)* sin estrenar; *(stamp)* sin matar (**b**) *(not in use)* que ya no se utiliza (**c**) [ʌnˈjuːst] *(unaccustomed)* desacostumbrado(a) (**to** a)

unusual [ʌnˈjuːʒʊəl] *adj (rare)* insólito(a), poco común; *(original)* original; *(exceptional)* excepcional

unusually [ʌnˈjuːʒʊəlɪ] *adv* excepcionalmente

unveil [ʌnˈveɪl] *vt* descubrir

unwarranted [ʌnˈwɒrəntɪd] *adj* injustificado(a); *(remark)* gratuito(a)

unwavering [ʌnˈweɪvərɪŋ] *adj (loyalty)* constante, firme; *(courage)* inquebrantable

unwelcome [ʌnˈwelkəm] *adj (visitor)* molesto(a); *(visit)* inoportuno(a); *Fig (news etc)* desagradable

unwell [ʌnˈwel] *adj* malo(a), indispuesto(a)

unwieldy [ʌnˈwiːldɪ] *adj (difficult to handle)* poco manejable; *(clumsy)* torpe

unwilling [ʌnˈwɪlɪŋ] *adj* **to be u. to do sth** no estar dispuesto a hacer algo

unwillingly [ʌnˈwɪlɪŋlɪ] *adv* de mala gana

unwind [ʌnˈwaɪnd] **1** *vt (pt & pp* **unwound)** desenrollar
2 *vi* (**a**) desenrollarse (**b**) *(relax)* relajarse

unwise [ʌnˈwaɪz] *adj* imprudente, desaconsejable

unwitting [ʌnˈwɪtɪŋ] *adj* involuntario(a)

unworkable [ʌnˈwɜːkəbəl] *adj (not feasible)* impracticable; *(suggestion)* irrealizable

unworthy [ʌnˈwɜːðɪ] *adj* indigno(a)

unwound [ʌnˈwaʊnd] *pt & pp of* **unwind**

unwrap [ʌnˈræp] *vt (gift)* desenvolver; *(package)* deshacer

unwritten [ʌnˈrɪtən] *adj* no escrito(a); *(agreement)* verbal

unyielding [ʌnˈjiːldɪŋ] *adj* inflexible

up [ʌp] **1** *prep* (**a**) *(movement)* **to climb up the mountain** escalar la montaña; **to walk up the street** ir calle arriba
(**b**) *(position)* en lo alto de; **further up the street** más adelante (en la misma calle); **halfway up the ladder** a mitad de la escalera
2 *adv* (**a**) *(upwards)* arriba, hacia arriba; *(position)* arriba; **from £10 up** de 10 libras para arriba; **halfway up** a medio camino; **right up (to the top)** hasta arriba (del todo); **to go/come up** subir; **this side up** *(sign)* este lado hacia arriba
(**b**) **the moon is up** ha salido la luna
(**c**) *(towards)* hacia; **to come** *or* **go up to sb** acercarse a algn; **to walk up and down** ir de un lado a otro
(**d**) *(in, to)* **he's up in Yorkshire** está en Yorkshire
(**e**) *(increased)* **bread is up** el pan ha subido
(**f**) **it's up for discussion** se está discutiendo; **up for sale** en venta
(**g**) *Fam* **something's up** pasa algo; **what's up (with you)?** ¿qué pasa (contigo)?
(**h**) **to be up against sth** enfrentarse con algo
(**i**) **up to** *(as far as, until)* hasta; **I can spend up to £5** puedo gastar un máximo de 5 libras; **up to here** hasta aquí; **up to now** hasta ahora
(**j**) **to be up to** *(depend on)* depender de; *(be capable of)* estar a la altura de; **I don't feel up to doing it today** hoy no me encuentro con fuerzas para hacerlo; **it's not up to much** no vale gran cosa
(**k**) **he's up to sth** está tramando algo
3 *adj* (**a**) *(out of bed)* levantado(a)
(**b**) *(finished)* terminado(a); **time's up** (ya) es la hora
4 *vt Fam* aumentar
5 *n Fig* **ups and downs** altibajos *mpl*

up-and-coming [ˈʌpənˈkʌmɪŋ] *adj* prometedor(a)

upbringing [ˈʌpbrɪŋɪŋ] *n* educación *f*

update [ʌpˈdeɪt] *vt* actualizar, poner al día

upgrade 1 *vt* [ʌpˈgreɪd] (**a**) *(promote)* ascender (**b**) *(improve)* mejorar la calidad de (**c**) *Comput (software, hardware)* actualizar
2 *n* [ˈʌpgreɪd] *Comput* actualización *f*

upheaval [ʌpˈhiːvəl] *n* trastorno *m*

upheld [ʌpˈheld] *pt & pp of* **uphold**

uphill 1 *adj* [ˈʌphɪl] ascendente; *Fig* arduo(a)
2 *adv* [ʌpˈhɪl] cuesta arriba

uphold [ʌp'həʊld] *vt* (*pt & pp* **upheld**) sostener

upholstery [ʌp'həʊlstərɪ] *n* tapizado *m*, tapicería *f*

upkeep ['ʌpkiːp] *n* mantenimiento *m*

up-market ['ʌpmɑːkɪt] *adj* de categoría

upon [ə'pɒn] *prep Fml* en, sobre; **once u. a time ...** érase una vez ...; **u. my word** (mi) palabra de honor

upper ['ʌpə(r)] **1** *adj* (**a**) (*position*) superior; **u. storey** piso de arriba; *Fig* **to have the u. hand** llevar la delantera (**b**) (*in rank*) alto(a); **the u. class** la clase alta; **the U. House** la Cámara Alta
2 *n* (*of shoe*) pala *f*

upper-class ['ʌpə'klæs] *adj* de la clase alta

uppermost ['ʌpəməʊst] *adj* más alto(a); *Fig* **it was u. in my mind** era lo que me preocupaba más

upright ['ʌpraɪt] **1** *adj* (**a**) (*vertical*) vertical (**b**) (*honest*) honrado(a)
2 *adv* derecho
3 *n Ftb* (*post*) poste *m*

uprising ['ʌpraɪzɪŋ] *n* sublevación *f*

uproar ['ʌprɔː(r)] *n* tumulto *m*, alboroto *m*

uproot [ʌp'ruːt] *vt* (*plant*) arrancar de raíz

upset [ʌp'set] **1** *vt* (*pt & pp* **upset**) (**a**) (*overturn*) volcar; (*spill*) derramar (**b**) (*shock*) trastornar; (*worry*) preocupar; (*displease*) disgustar (**c**) (*spoil*) desbaratar (**d**) (*make ill*) sentar mal a
2 *adj* (*shocked*) alterado(a); (*displeased*) disgustado(a); **to have an u. stomach** sentirse mal del estómago
3 *n* ['ʌpset] (**a**) (*reversal*) revés *m* (**b**) *Sport* resultado inesperado

upshot ['ʌpʃɒt] *n* resultado *m*

upside ['ʌpsaɪd] *n* **u. down** al revés

upstage [ʌp'steɪdʒ] *vt Fam* eclipsar

upstairs [ʌp'steəz] **1** *adv* al piso de arriba; **she lives u.** vive en el piso de arriba
2 *n* piso *m* de arriba

upstart ['ʌpstɑːt] *n* advenedizo(a) *m,f*

upstream [ʌp'striːm] *adv* río arriba

uptake ['ʌpteɪk] *n Fam* **to be quick on the u.** cogerlas al vuelo

uptight [ʌp'taɪt] *adj Fam* nervioso(a)

up-to-date [ʌptə'deɪt] *adj* (**a**) (*current*) al día (**b**) (*modern*) moderno(a)

upturn ['ʌptɜːn] *n* mejora *f*

upward ['ʌpwəd] *adj* ascendente

upward(s) ['ʌpwəd(z)] *adv* hacia arriba; **from ten (years) up.** a partir de los diez años; *Fam* **u. of** algo más de

uranium [jʊ'reɪnɪəm] *n* uranio *m*

urban ['ɜːbən] *adj* urbano(a)

urbane [ɜː'beɪn] *adj* urbano(a), cortés

urchin ['ɜːtʃɪn] *n* (**a**) (*child*) pilluelo(a) *m,f* (**b**) **sea u.** erizo *m* de mar

urge [ɜːdʒ] **1** *vt* (**a**) instar; (*plead*) exhortar (**b**) (*advocate*) preconizar; **to u. that sth should be done** insistir en que se haga algo
2 *n* impulso *m*
► **urge on** *vt sep* animar a

urgency ['ɜːdʒənsɪ] *n* urgencia *f*

urgent ['ɜːdʒənt] *adj* urgente; (*need, tone*) apremiante

urinal [jʊ'raɪnəl] *n* (*toilet*) urinario *m*; (*bowl*) orinal *m*

urinate ['jʊərɪneɪt] *vi* orinar

urine ['jʊərɪn] *n* orina *f*

URL [juːɑː'rel] *n Comput* (*abbr* **uniform resource locator**) URL *m*

urn [ɜːn] *n* (**a**) urna *f* (**b**) **tea u.** tetera *f* grande

Uruguay ['jʊərəgwaɪ] *n* Uruguay

Uruguayan [jʊərə'gwaɪən] *adj & n* uruguayo(a) (*m,f*)

US [juː'es] *n* (*abbr* **United States**) EE.UU. *mpl*

us [ʌs, *unstressed* əs] *pers pron* (**a**) (*as object*) nos; **let's forget it** olvidémoslo (**b**) (*after prep*) nosotros(as); **both of us** nosotros dos; **he's one of us** es de los nuestros (**c**) (*after v* **to be**) nosotros(as); **she wouldn't believe it was us** no creía que fueramos nosotros (**d**) *Fam* me; **give us a kiss!** ¡dame un beso!

USA [juːes'eɪ] *n* (*abbr* **United States of America**) EE.UU. *mpl*

usage ['juːsɪdʒ] *n* (**a**) (*habit, custom*) costumbre *f* (**b**) *Ling* uso *m*

use [juːz] **1** *vt* (**a**) emplear, utilizar; **what is it used for?** ¿para qué sirve?; **to u. force** hacer uso de la fuerza
(**b**) (*consume*) consumir, gastar
(**c**) (*take unfair advantage of*) aprovecharse de
(**d**) *Fam* **I could u. a drink** no me vendría mal un trago
2 *v aux* **used to** ['juːstə] soler, acostumbrar; **where did you u. to live?** ¿dónde vivías (antes)?

> Como verbo auxiliar, aparece siempre en la forma **used to**. Se traduce al español por el verbo principal en pretérito imperfecto, o por el pretérito imperfecto de **soler** más infinitivo.

3 *n* [juːs] (**a**) uso *m*, empleo *m*; (*handling*) manejo *m*; **directions for u.** modo de empleo; **in u.** en uso; **not in u.** (*on* *lift)* no funciona; **ready for u.** listo para usar; **to make (good) u. of sth** aprovechar algo; **to put to good u.** sacar partido de

(**b**) *(application)* aplicación *f*
(**c**) *(usefulness)* utilidad *f*; **it's no u.** es inútil; **what's the u.?** ¿para qué?; *Fam* **it's no u. crying** no sirve de nada llorar; **of u.** útil; **to be of u.** servir
▸ **use up** *vt sep* acabar

used *adj* (**a**) [juːzd] *(second-hand)* usado(a) (**b**) [juːst] **to be u. to** estar acostumbrado(a) a

useful [ˈjuːsfʊl] *adj* útil; *(practical)* práctico(a); **to come in u.** venir bien

usefulness [ˈjuːsfʊlnɪs] *n* utilidad *f*

useless [ˈjuːslɪs] *adj* inútil

user [ˈjuːzə(r)] *n* (**a**) usuario(a) *m,f* (**b**) *Fam (of drugs)* drogadicto(a) *m,f*

usher [ˈʌʃə(r)] **1** *n* (**a**) *Cin & Th* acomodador(a) *m,f* (**b**) *(in court etc)* ujier *m*
2 *vt* **to u. in** *Cin & Th* acomodar; *(at home)* hacer pasar; **to u. out** acompañar hasta la puerta

USSR [juːeseⁱˈɑː(r)] *n Hist (abbr* **Union of Soviet Socialist Republics**) URSS *f*

usual [ˈjuːʒʊəl] **1** *adj* corriente, normal; **as u.** como siempre; **at the u. hour** a la hora habitual; **earlier than u.** más pronto que de costumbre; **the u. problems** los problemas de siempre
2 *n* lo habitual; **out of the u.** fuera de lo común

usually [ˈjuːʒʊəlɪ] *adv* normalmente

usurp [juːˈzɜːp] *vt* usurpar

utensil [juːˈtensəl] *n* utensilio *m*; **kitchen utensils** batería *f* de cocina

uterus [ˈjuːtərəs] *n* útero *m*

utilitarian [juːtɪlɪˈteərɪən] *adj* (**a**) *(in philosophy)* utilitarista (**b**) *(useful)* utilitario(a)

utility [juːˈtɪlɪtɪ] *n* (**a**) utilidad *f*; **u. room** cuarto *m* de planchar; *(for storage)* trascocina *f* (**b**) **(public) u.** empresa *f* de servicio público

utilize [ˈjuːtɪlaɪz] *vt* utilizar

utmost [ˈʌtməʊst] **1** *adj* sumo(a); **of the u. importance** de suma importancia
2 *n* máximo *m*; **to do** *or* **try one's u.** hacer todo lo posible; **to the u.** al máximo, a más no poder

utopian [juːˈtəʊpɪən] *adj* utópico(a)

utter ¹ [ˈʌtə(r)] *vt (words)* pronunciar; *(sigh)* dar; *(cry, threat)* lanzar

utter ² [ˈʌtə(r)] *adj* total, completo(a)

utterance [ˈʌtərəns] *n* declaración *f*

U-turn [ˈjuːtɜːn] *n* cambio *m* de sentido; *Pol* giro *m* de 180 grados

V, v [viː] *n (the letter)* V, v *f*
V *(abbr* **volt(s))** V
v (**a**) *(abbr* **verse)** v (**b**) *(also* **vs)** *(abbr* **versus)** contra
vacancy ['veɪkənsɪ] *n* (**a**) *(job)* vacante *f* (**b**) *(room)* habitación *f* libre; **no vacancies** *(sign)* completo
vacant ['veɪkənt] *adj* (**a**) *(empty)* vacío(a) (**b**) *(job)* vacante; *Br* **situations v.** *(in newspaper)* ofertas de trabajo (**c**) *(free, not in use)* libre
vacate [vəˈkeɪt] *vt (flat)* desalojar
vacation [vəˈkeɪʃən] *US* **1** *n* vacaciones *fpl*; **on v.** de vacaciones
  2 *vi* pasar las vacaciones (**in/at** en)
vacationer [vəˈkeɪʃənə(r)], **vacationist** [vəˈkeɪʃənɪst] *n US* **summer v.** veraneante *mf*
vaccinate ['væksɪneɪt] *vt* vacunar
vaccine ['væksiːn] *n* vacuna *f*
vacuum ['vækjʊəm] **1** *n* vacío *m*; **v. cleaner** aspiradora *f*; **v. flask** termo *m*
  2 *vt (carpet, room)* pasar la aspiradora por
vacuum-packed ['vækjʊəm'pækt] *adj* envasado(a) al vacío
vagina [vəˈdʒaɪnə] *n* vagina *f*
vagrant ['veɪgrənt] *adj & n* vagabundo(a) *(m,f)*
vague [veɪg] *adj (imprecise)* vago(a), impreciso(a); *(indistinct)* borroso(a)
vain [veɪn] *adj* (**a**) *(proud)* vanidoso(a), presumido(a) (**b**) *(hopeless)* vano(a); **in v.** en vano
valentine ['væləntaɪn] *n* (**a**) *(card)* = tarjeta que se manda el Día de los Enamorados (**b**) *(sweetheart)* novio(a) *m,f*
valet ['vælɪt, 'væleɪ] *n* ayuda *m* de cámara
valiant ['væljənt] *adj* valiente
valid ['vælɪd] *adj* válido(a); **no longer v.** caducado(a)
valley ['vælɪ] *n* valle *m*
valour, *US* **valor** ['vælə(r)] *n* valor *m*, valentía *f*
valuable ['væljʊəbəl] **1** *adj* valioso(a), de valor
  2 *npl* **valuables** objetos *mpl* de valor

valuation [væljʊ'eɪʃən] *n* (**a**) *(act)* valoración *f* (**b**) *(price)* valor *m*
value ['væljuː] **1** *n* valor *m*; **50 pence is good v.** 50 peniques es un buen precio; **to get good v. for money** sacarle jugo al dinero; **v.-added tax** impuesto *m* sobre el valor añadido
  2 *vt* valorar
valve [vælv] *n* (**a**) *Anat & Tech* válvula *f* (**b**) *Rad* lámpara *f*
vampire ['væmpaɪə(r)] *n* vampiro *m*
van [væn] *n Br* (**a**) *Aut* furgoneta *f* (**b**) *Rail* furgón *m*
vandal ['vændəl] *n* vándalo(a) *m,f*
vandalism ['vændəlɪzəm] *n* vandalismo *m*
vandalize ['vændəlaɪz] *vt* destruir, destrozar
vanguard ['vængɑːd] *n* vanguardia *f*
vanilla [vəˈnɪlə] *n* vainilla *f*
vanish ['vænɪʃ] *vi* desaparecer
vanity ['vænɪtɪ] *n* vanidad *f*; **v. bag** *or* **case** neceser *m*
vantage ['vɑːntɪdʒ] *n* ventaja *f*; **v. point** posición estratégica
vapor ['veɪpər] *n US* = **vapour**
vaporizer ['veɪpəraɪzə(r)] *n (device)* vaporizador *m*; *(spray)* pulverizador *m*
vapour ['veɪpə(r)] *n* vapor *m*; *(on windowpane)* vaho *m*; **v. trail** estela *f* de humo
variable ['veərɪəbəl] *adj & n* variable *(f)*
variance ['veərɪəns] *n Fml* **to be at v.** no concordar; **to be at v. with sb** estar en desacuerdo con algn
variation [veərɪ'eɪʃən] *n* variación *f*
varicose ['værɪkəʊs] *adj* **v. veins** varices *fpl*
varied ['veərɪd] *adj* variado(a), diverso(a)
variety [vəˈraɪtɪ] *n* (**a**) *(diversity)* variedad *f*; *(assortment)* surtido *m*; **for a v. of reasons** por razones diversas (**b**) **v. show** espectáculo *m* de variedades
various ['veərɪəs] *adj* diversos(as), varios(as)
varnish ['vɑːnɪʃ] **1** *n* barniz *m*; *Br* **nail v.** esmalte *m* de uñas
  2 *vt* barnizar; *(nails)* esmaltar
vary ['veərɪ] *vi* variar; **prices v. from £2 to**

£4 los precios oscilan entre 2 y 4 libras; **to v. in size** variar de tamaño

varying ['veərɪɪŋ] *adj* **with v. degrees of success** con más o menos éxito

vase [*Br* vɑːz, *US* veɪs] *n* jarrón *m*

🖉 Note that the Spanish word **vaso** is a false friend and is never a translation for the English word **vase**. In Spanish, **vaso** means both "glass" and "vessel".

---

vasectomy [və'sektəmɪ] *n Med* vasectomía *f*

Vaseline® ['væsɪliːn] *n* vaselina *f*

vast [vɑːst] *adj* vasto(a); *(majority)* inmenso(a)

VAT [viːeɪ'tiː, væt] *n* (*abbr* **value-added tax**) IVA *m*

vat [væt] *n* cuba *f*, tina *f*

Vatican ['vætɪkən] *n* **the V.** el Vaticano

vault¹ [vɔːlt] *n* bóveda *f; (for wine)* bodega *f; (tomb)* cripta *f; (of bank)* cámara acorazada

vault² [vɔːlt] **1** *vt & vi* saltar
   2 *n* salto *m*

vaunt [vɔːnt] *vt Fml* jactarse de, hacer alarde de

VCR [viːsiː'ɑː(r)] *n* (*abbr* **video cassette recorder**) (aparato *m* de) vídeo *m*

VD [viː'diː] *n* (*abbr* **venereal disease**) enfermedad venérea

VDU [viːdiː'juː] *n* (*abbr* **visual display unit**) monitor *m*

veal [viːl] *n* ternera *f*

veer [vɪə(r)] *vi (ship)* virar; *(car)* girar

vegan ['viːgən] *n* vegetaliano(a) *m,f,* = vegetariano estricto que no come ningún producto de origen animal

vegeburger ['vedʒɪbɜːgə(r)] *n* hamburguesa vegetariana

vegetable ['vedʒtəbəl] *n (food)* verdura *f*, hortaliza *f;* **v. garden** huerta *f,* huerto *m*

vegetarian [vedʒɪ'teərɪən] *adj & n* vegetariano(a) *(m,f)*

vegetation [vedʒɪ'teɪʃən] *n* vegetación *f*

vehement ['viːɪmənt] *adj* vehemente

vehicle ['viːɪkəl] *n* vehículo *m*

veil [veɪl] **1** *n* velo *m*
   2 *vt* velar

vein [veɪn] *n* vena *f*

velocity [vɪ'lɒsɪtɪ] *n* velocidad *f*

velvet ['velvɪt] *n* terciopelo *m*

velvety ['velvɪtɪ] *adj* aterciopelado(a)

vendetta [ven'detə] *n* vendetta *f*

vending ['vendɪŋ] *n* **v. machine** máquina expendedora

vendor ['vendɔː(r)] *n* vendedor(a) *m,f*

veneer [vɪ'nɪə(r)] *n* (**a**) *(covering)* chapa *f*
   (**b**) *Fig* apariencia *f*

venerable ['venərəbəl] *adj* venerable

venereal [vɪ'nɪərɪəl] *adj* venéreo(a)

Venetian [vɪ'niːʃən] *adj & n* veneciano(a) *(m,f);* **v. blind** persiana *f* graduable

Venezuela [venɪ'zweɪlə] *n* Venezuela

Venezuelan [venɪ'zweɪlən] *adj & n* venezolano(a) *(m,f)*

vengeance ['vendʒəns] *n* venganza *f; Fam* **it was raining with a v.** llovía con ganas

Venice ['venɪs] *n* Venecia

venison ['venɪsən] *n* carne *f* de venado

venom ['venəm] *n* veneno *m*

venomous ['venəməs] *adj* venenoso(a); *Fig* **v. tongue** lengua viperina

vent [vent] **1** *n* (**a**) *(opening)* abertura *f,* orificio *m; (grille)* rejilla *f* de ventilación; **air v.** respiradero *m* (**b**) *(of volcano)* chimenea *f*
   2 *vt Fig (feelings)* descargar

ventilate ['ventɪleɪt] *vt* ventilar

ventilation [ventɪ'leɪʃən] *n* ventilación *f*

ventilator ['ventɪleɪtə(r)] *n* ventilador *m*

ventriloquist [ven'trɪləkwɪst] *n* ventrílocuo(a) *m,f*

venture ['ventʃə(r)] **1** *vt* arriesgar, aventurar; **he didn't v. to ask** no se atrevió a preguntarlo
   2 *vi* arriesgarse; **to v. out of doors** atreverse a salir
   3 *n* empresa arriesgada, aventura *f; Com* **business/joint v.** empresa comercial/colectiva

venue ['venjuː] *n* (**a**) *(meeting place)* lugar *m* de reunión (**b**) *(for concert etc)* local *m*

Venus ['viːnəs] *n (goddess)* Venus *f; (planet)* Venus *m*

veranda(h) [və'rændə] *n* porche *m,* terraza *f*

verb [vɜːb] *n* verbo *m*

verbal ['vɜːbəl] *adj* verbal

verbatim [vɜː'beɪtɪm] **1** *adj* textual
   2 *adv* textualmente

verbose [vɜː'bəʊs] *adj* prodigo(a) en palabras

verdict ['vɜːdɪkt] *n* (**a**) *Jur* veredicto *m,* fallo *m* (**b**) *(opinion)* opinión *f,* juicio *m*

verge [vɜːdʒ] **1** *n* (**a**) *(margin)* borde *m; Fig* **on the v. of** al borde de; *Fig* **to be on the v. of doing sth** estar a punto de hacer algo (**b**) *Br (of road)* arcén *m, Andes* berma *f, Méx* acotamiento *m, RP* banquina *f, Ven* hombrillo *m*
   2 *vi* rayar (**on** en)

verification [verɪfɪ'keɪʃən] *n* verificación *f,* comprobación *f*

verify ['verɪfaɪ] *vt* verificar, comprobar

veritable ['verɪtəbəl] *adj* auténtico(a)
vermicelli [vɜːmɪ'tʃelɪ] *n* fideos *mpl*
vermin ['vɜːmɪn] *npl* (**a**) *(animals)* bichos *mpl*, sabandijas *fpl* (**b**) *Fig* gentuza *f*
vermouth ['vɜːməθ] *n* vermú *m*, vermut *m*
verruca [və'ruːkə] *n* verruga *f*
versatile ['vɜːsətaɪl] *adj (person)* polifacético(a); *(object)* versátil
verse [vɜːs] *n* (**a**) *(stanza)* estrofa *f* (**b**) *(poetry)* versos *mpl*, poesía *f* (**c**) *(of song)* copla *f* (**d**) *(of Bible)* versículo *m*
versed [vɜːst] *adj* **to be (well) v. in** ser (muy) versado en
version ['vɜːʃən, 'vɜːʒən] *n* (**a**) versión *f*; **stage v.** adaptación *f* teatral (**b**) *Aut* modelo *m*
versus ['vɜːsəs] *prep* contra
vertebra ['vɜːtɪbrə] *n* (*pl* **vertebras** *or* **vertebrae** ['vɜːtɪbriː]) vértebra *f*
vertical ['vɜːtɪkəl] *adj & n* vertical *(f)*
vertigo ['vɜːtɪɡəʊ] *n* vértigo *m*
verve [vɜːv] *n* vigor *m*, brío *m*
very ['verɪ] **1** *adv* (**a**) *(extremely)* muy; **to be v. hungry** tener mucha hambre; **v. much** muchísimo; **v. well** muy bien (**b**) *(emphatic)* **at the v. latest** como máximo; **at the v. least** como mínimo; **the v. best** el mejor de todos; **the v. first/last** el primero/último de todos; **the v. same day** el mismo día
  2 *adj* (**a**) **at the v. end/beginning** al final/principio de todo (**b**) *(precise)* **at this v. moment** en este mismo momento; **her v. words** sus palabras exactas; **in the v. middle** justo en medio (**c**) *(mere)* **the v. thought of it!** ¡sólo con pensarlo!
vespers ['vespəz] *npl* vísperas *fpl*
vessel ['vesəl] *n* (**a**) *(container)* vasija *f* (**b**) *Naut* buque *m*, nave *f* (**c**) *Anat & Bot* vaso *m*
vest [vest] **1** *n* (**a**) *Br (undershirt)* camiseta *f* de tirantes (**b**) *US* chaleco *m*
  2 *vt Jur* **by the power vested in me ...** por los poderes que se me han conferido ...
vested ['vestɪd] *adj Jur & Fin* **v. interests** derechos adquiridos; *Fig* intereses *mpl* personales
vestibule ['vestɪbjuːl] *n* vestíbulo *m*
vestige ['vestɪdʒ] *n* vestigio *m*
vestry ['vestrɪ] *n* sacristía *f*
vet [vet] **1** *n* veterinario(a) *m,f*
  2 *vt Br* someter a investigación, examinar
veteran ['vetərən] *n* (**a**) veterano(a) *m,f* (**b**) *US* **(war) v.** ex combatiente *mf*
veterinarian [vetərɪ'neərɪən] *n US* veterinario(a) *m,f*

veterinary ['vetərɪnərɪ] *adj* veterinario(a); **v. medicine** veterinaria *f*; *Br* **v. surgeon** veterinario(a) *m,f*
veto ['viːtəʊ] **1** *n* (*pl* **vetoes**) veto *m*
  2 *vt Pol* vetar; *(suggestion etc)* descartar
vexed [vekst] *adj* (**a**) *(annoyed)* disgustado(a) (**b**) *(debated)* controvertido(a)
VHF [viːeɪtʃ'ef] *(abbr* **very high frequency**) VHF
via ['vaɪə] *prep* por, vía
viable ['vaɪəbəl] *adj* viable, factible
viaduct ['vaɪədʌkt] *n* viaducto *m*
vibrant ['vaɪbrənt] *adj* (**a**) *(sound)* vibrante (**b**) *Fig (personality)* vital; *(city)* animado(a)
vibrate [vaɪ'breɪt] *vi* vibrar (**with** de)
vibration [vaɪ'breɪʃən] *n* vibración *f*
vicar ['vɪkə(r)] *n* párroco *m*
vicarage ['vɪkərɪdʒ] *n* casa *f* del párroco
vicarious [vɪ'keərɪəs] *adj* experimentado(a) por otro; *(punishment)* sufrido(a) por otro
vice¹ [vaɪs] *n* vicio *m*
vice² [vaɪs] *n Br (tool)* torno *m* de banco
vice- [vaɪs] *pref* vice-; **v.-chancellor** rector(a) *m,f*; **v.-president** vicepresidente(a) *m,f*
vice-chairman [vaɪs'tʃeəmən] *n* vicepresidente *m*
vice versa [vaɪsɪ'vɜːsə] *adv* viceversa
vicinity [vɪ'sɪnɪtɪ] *n (area)* vecindad *f*; **in the v. of** *(geographic location)* cerca de, en las inmediaciones de; *(amount)* alrededor de
vicious ['vɪʃəs] *adj (violent)* violento(a); *(malicious)* malintencionado(a); *(cruel)* cruel; **v. circle** círculo vicioso
victim ['vɪktɪm] *n* víctima *f*
victimize ['vɪktɪmaɪz] *vt* perseguir, tratar injustamente
victor ['vɪktə(r)] *n* vencedor(a) *m,f*
victorious [vɪk'tɔːrɪəs] *adj* victorioso(a)
victory ['vɪktərɪ] *n* victoria *f*
video ['vɪdɪəʊ] *n* vídeo *m*; **v. camera** videocámara *f*; **v. cassette** videocasete *m*; **v. club** videoclub *m*; **v. game** videojuego *m*; **v. (cassette) recorder** vídeo *m*; **v. tape** cinta *f* de vídeo
video-tape ['vɪdɪəʊteɪp] *vt* grabar (en vídeo)
vie [vaɪ] *vi* competir (**against** *or* **with** con)
Vienna [vɪ'enə] *n* Viena
Viennese [vɪə'niːz] *adj & n* vienés(esa) *(m,f)*
Vietnam [vjet'næm] *n* Vietnam
view [vjuː] **1** *n* (**a**) *(sight)* vista *f*, panorama *m*; **in full v.** completamente visible; **on v.** a la vista; **to come into v.** aparecer;

Fig **in v. of the fact that ...** dado que ... (**b**) *(opinion)* opinión *f*; **point of v.** punto *m* de vista; **to take a dim v. of** ver con malos ojos (**c**) *(aim)* fin *m*; **with a v. to** con la intención de
　2 *vt* (**a**) *(look at)* mirar; *(house etc)* visitar (**b**) *(consider)* contemplar; *(topic, problem)* enfocar

viewer ['vju:ə(r)] *n* (**a**) *TV* televidente *mf* (**b**) *Phot* visionador *m*

viewfinder ['vju:faɪndə(r)] *n* visor *m*

viewpoint ['vju:pɔɪnt] *n* punto *m* de vista

vigil ['vɪdʒɪl] *n* vigilia *f*

vigilante [vɪdʒɪ'læntɪ] *n* **v. group** patrulla ciudadana

vigorous ['vɪgərəs] *adj* vigoroso(a), enérgico(a)

vigour, *US* **vigor** ['vɪgə(r)] *n* vigor *m*

vile [vaɪl] *adj* (**a**) *(evil)* vil, infame (**b**) *(disgusting)* repugnante (**c**) *Fam (awful)* horrible

vilify ['vɪlɪfaɪ] *vt* denigrar

villa ['vɪlə] *n* (**a**) *(in country)* casa *f* de campo (**b**) *Br* chalet *m*

village ['vɪlɪdʒ] *n* *(small)* aldea *f*; *(larger)* pueblo *m*

villager ['vɪlɪdʒə(r)] *n* aldeano(a) *m,f*

villain ['vɪlən] *n* villano(a) *m,f*; *Cin & Th* malo(a) *m,f*

vinaigrette [vɪneɪ'gret] *n* vinagreta *f*

vindicate ['vɪndɪkeɪt] *vt* justificar, vindicar

vindictive [vɪn'dɪktɪv] *adj* vengativo(a)

vine [vaɪn] *n* vid *f*; *(climbing)* parra *f*

vinegar ['vɪnɪgə(r)] *n* vinagre *m*

vineyard ['vɪnjəd] *n* viña *f*, viñedo *m*

vintage ['vɪntɪdʒ] **1** *n* (**a**) *(crop, year)* cosecha *f* (**b**) *(season)* vendimia *f* (**c**) *(era)* era *f*
　2 *adj* (**a**) *(wine)* añejo(a) (**b**) *(classic)* clásico(a); **v. car** coche *m* de época

vinyl ['vaɪnɪl] *n* vinilo *m*

viola [vɪ'əʊlə] *n* viola *f*

violate ['vaɪəleɪt] *vt* violar

violence ['vaɪələns] *n* violencia *f*

violent ['vaɪələnt] *adj* (**a**) violento(a) (**b**) *(intense)* intenso(a)

violet ['vaɪələt] **1** *n* (**a**) *Bot* violeta *f* (**b**) *(colour)* violeta *m*
　2 *adj* violeta

violin [vaɪə'lɪn] *n* violín *m*

violinist [vaɪə'lɪnɪst] *n* violinista *mf*

VIP [vi:aɪ'pi:] *n* *Fam* (*abbr* **very important person**) personaje *m* muy importante

viper ['vaɪpə(r)] *n* víbora *f*

virgin ['vɜːdʒɪn] **1** *n* virgen *f*; **the V. Mary** la Virgen María; **to be a v.** ser virgen
　2 *adj* virgen

virginity [və'dʒɪnɪtɪ] *n* virginidad *f*

Virgo ['vɜːgəʊ] *n* Virgo *m*

virile ['vɪraɪl] *adj* viril

virtual ['vɜːtjʊəl] *adj* virtual; *Comput* **v. reality** realidad *f* virtual

virtually ['vɜːtjʊəlɪ] *adv* *(almost)* prácticamente

virtue ['vɜːtjuː] *n* virtud *f*; **by v. of** en virtud de

virtuous ['vɜːtjʊəs] *adj* virtuoso(a)

virulent ['vɪrʊlənt] *adj* virulento(a)

virus ['vaɪrəs] *n* virus *m inv*; *Comput* **v. check** detección *m* de virus

visa ['viːzə] *n* visado *m*, *Am* visa *f*

vis-à-vis [viːzɑː'viː] *prep* (**a**) *(regarding)* respecto a (**b**) *(opposite)* frente a

viscose ['vɪskəʊs] *n* viscosa *f*

viscount ['vaɪkaʊnt] *n* vizconde *m*

vise [vaɪs] *n* *US (tool)* torno *m* de banco

visibility [vɪzɪ'bɪlɪtɪ] *n* visibilidad *f*

visible ['vɪzɪbəl] *adj* visible

vision ['vɪʒən] *n* (**a**) visión *f* (**b**) *(eyesight)* vista *f*

visit ['vɪzɪt] **1** *vt* (**a**) *(person)* visitar, hacer una visita a (**b**) *(place)* visitar, ir a
　2 *n* visita *f*; **to pay sb a v.** hacerle una visita a algn

visiting ['vɪzɪtɪŋ] *adj* **v. card** tarjeta *f* de visita; *Med* **v. hours** horas *fpl* de visita; *Sport* **v. team** equipo *m* visitante

visitor ['vɪzɪtə(r)] *n* (**a**) *(guest)* invitado(a) *m,f*; **we've got visitors** tenemos visita (**b**) *(in hotel)* cliente(a) *m,f* (**c**) *(tourist)* turista *mf*

visor ['vaɪzə(r)] *n* visera *f*

> ℓ Note that the Spanish word **visor** is a false friend and is never a translation for the English word **visor**. In Spanish, **visor** means ;viewfinder".

vista ['vɪstə] *n* vista *f*, panorama *m*

visual ['vɪʒʊəl] *adj* visual; **v. aids** medios *mpl* visuales

visualize ['vɪʒʊəlaɪz] *vt* (**a**) *(imagine)* imaginar(se) (**b**) *(foresee)* prever

vital ['vaɪtəl] *adj* (**a**) *(lively)* enérgico(a) (**b**) *(essential)* fundamental (**c**) *(decisive)* decisivo(a); *Fam* **v. statistics** medidas *fpl* del cuerpo de la mujer (**d**) *Med (function, sign)* vital

vitality [vaɪ'tælɪtɪ] *n* vitalidad *f*

vitally ['vaɪtəlɪ] *adv* **it's v. important** es de vital importancia

vitamin ['vɪtəmɪn, *US* 'vaɪtəmɪn] *n* vitamina *f*

viva ['vaɪvə] *n* *Br* examen *m* oral

vivacious [vɪ'veɪʃəs] *adj* vivaz

vivacity [vɪ'væsɪtɪ] *n* viveza *f*, vivacidad *f*

vivid ['vɪvɪd] *adj* (**a**) *(bright, lively)* vivo(a), intenso(a) (**b**) *(graphic)* gráfico(a)
vixen ['vɪksən] *n* zorra *f*
V-neck(ed) ['viːnek(t)] *adj* con el cuello en pico
vocabulary [və'kæbjʊlərɪ] *n* vocabulario *m*
vocal ['vəʊkəl] *adj* vocal; **v. cords** cuerdas *fpl* vocales
vocalist ['vəʊkəlɪst] *n* cantante *mf*
vocation [vəʊ'keɪʃən] *n* vocación *f*
vocational [vəʊ'keɪʃənəl] *adj* profesional; **v. training** formación *f* profesional
vociferous [vəʊ'sɪfərəs] *adj* (**a**) *(protest)* enérgico(a) (**b**) *(noisy)* clamoroso(a)
vodka ['vɒdkə] *n* vodka *m*
vogue [vəʊg] *n* boga *f*, moda *f*; **in v.** de moda
voice [vɔɪs] **1** *n* voz *f*; **to lose one's v.** quedarse afónico; *Fig* **at the top of one's v.** a voz en grito; *Comput* **v. mail** buzon *m* de voz
  2 *vt* (**a**) *(express)* manifestar (**b**) *Ling* sonorizar
void [vɔɪd] **1** *adj* (**a**) **v. of** sin (**b**) *Jur* nulo(a), inválido(a)
  2 *n* vacío *m*
volatile ['vɒlətaɪl] *adj* volátil
volcanic [vɒl'kænɪk] *adj* volcánico(a)
volcano [vɒl'keɪnəʊ] *n* (*pl* **volcanoes**) volcán *m*
volition [və'lɪʃən] *n* *Fml* **of one's own v.** por voluntad propia
volley ['vɒlɪ] **1** *n* (**a**) *(of shots)* descarga *f* (**b**) *Fig (of stones, insults)* lluvia *f* (**c**) *(in tennis, football)* volea *f*
  2 *vt (in tennis, football)* volear
volleyball ['vɒlɪbɔːl] *n* voleibol *m*
volt [vəʊlt] *n* voltio *m*
voltage ['vəʊltɪdʒ] *n* voltaje *m*
voluble ['vɒljʊbəl] *adj* locuaz

> 📙 Note that the Spanish word **voluble** is a false friend and is never a translation for the English word **voluble**. In Spanish, **voluble** means "fickle, changeable".

volume ['vɒljuːm] *n* (**a**) volumen *m* (**b**) *(book)* volumen *m*, tomo *m*; *Fig* **to speak volumes** decirlo todo
voluntary ['vɒləntərɪ] *adj* voluntario(a); **v. organization** organización benéfica
volunteer [vɒlən'tɪə(r)] **1** *n* voluntario(a) *m,f*
  2 *vt (help etc)* ofrecer
  3 *vi* (**a**) ofrecerse (**for** para) (**b**) *Mil* alistarse como voluntario
voluptuous [və'lʌptjʊəs] *adj* voluptuoso(a)
vomit ['vɒmɪt] **1** *vt & vi* vomitar
  2 *n* vómito *m*
voracious [vɒ'reɪʃəs] *adj* voraz
vortex ['vɔːteks] *n* (*pl* **vortices** ['vɔːtɪsiːz]) vórtice *m*; *Fig* vorágine *f*
vote [vəʊt] **1** *n* voto *m*; *(voting)* votación *f*; **v. of confidence** voto de confianza; **to take a v. on sth** someter algo a votacíon; **to have the v.** tener derecho al voto
  2 *vt* (**a**) votar (**b**) *(elect)* elegir (**c**) *Fam* proponer
  3 *vi* votar; **to v. for sb** votar a algn
voter ['vəʊtə(r)] *n* votante *mf*
voting ['vəʊtɪŋ] *n* votación *f*
vouch [vaʊtʃ] *vi* **to v. for sth/sb** responder de algo/por algn
voucher ['vaʊtʃə(r)] *n* *Br* vale *m*
vow [vaʊ] **1** *n* voto *m*
  2 *vt* jurar
vowel ['vaʊəl] *n* vocal *f*
voyage ['vɔɪɪdʒ] *n* viaje *m*; *(crossing)* travesía *f*; **to go on a v.** hacer un viaje (en barco)
vulgar ['vʌlgə(r)] *adj* *(coarse)* vulgar, ordinario(a); *(in poor taste)* de mal gusto
vulgarity [vʌl'gærɪtɪ] *n* *(coarseness)* vulgaridad *f*, ordinariez *f*; *(poor taste)* mal gusto *m*
vulnerable ['vʌlnərəbəl] *adj* vulnerable
vulture ['vʌltʃə(r)] *n* buitre *m*
vulva ['vʌlvə] *n* vulva *f*

W, w ['dʌbəljuː] *n (the letter)* W, w *f*
W (**a**) (*abbr* **West**) O (**b**) (*abbr* **Watt(s)**) W
wad [wɒd] *n (of paper)* taco *m*; *(of cotton wool)* bolita *f*; *(of banknotes)* fajo *m*
waddle ['wɒdəl] *vi* andar como los patos
wade [weɪd] *vi* caminar por el agua; **to w. across a river** vadear un río
▸ **wade through** *vt insep* hacer con dificultad; **I'm wading through the book** me cuesta mucho terminar el libro
wading pool ['weɪdɪŋpuːl] *n US* piscina *f* para niños
wafer ['weɪfə(r)] *n* barquillo *m*; *Rel* hostia *f*
waffle¹ ['wɒfəl] *n Culin* = tipo de barquillo
waffle² ['wɒfəl] *Br Fam* **1** *vi* meter mucha paja; **to w. on** parlotear
2 *n* paja *f*
waft [wɑːft, wɒft] **1** *vt* llevar por el aire
2 *vi* flotar (por *or* en el aire)
wag [wæg] **1** *vt* menear
2 *vi (tail)* menearse
wage [weɪdʒ] **1** *n* (*also* **wages**) salario *m*, sueldo *m*; **w. earner** asalariado(a) *m,f*; **w. freeze** congelación *f* salarial
2 *vt (campaign)* realizar (**against** contra); **to w. war (on)** hacer la guerra (a)
wage-packet ['weɪdʒpækɪt] *n* sueldo *m*
wager ['weɪdʒə(r)] **1** *n* apuesta *f*
2 *vt* apostar
waggle ['wægəl] **1** *vt* menear
2 *vi* menearse
wa(g)gon ['wægən] *n (horse-drawn)* carro *m*; *Br Rail* vagón *m*
wail [weɪl] **1** *n* lamento *m*, gemido *m*
2 *vi (person)* lamentar, gemir
waist [weɪst] *n Anat* cintura *f*; *Sewing* talle *m*
waistcoat ['weɪstkəʊt] *n Br* chaleco *m*
waistline ['weɪstlaɪn] *n Anat* cintura; *Sewing* talle *m*
wait [weɪt] **1** *n* espera *f*; *(delay)* demora *f*; **to lie in w.** estar al acecho
2 *vi* (**a**) esperar, aguardar; **I can't w. to see her** me muero de ganas de verla; **while you w.** en el acto; **to keep sb waiting** hacer esperar a algn (**b**) **to w. at table** servir la mesa

▸ **wait about, wait around** *vi* esperar
▸ **wait on** *vt insep* servir
waiter ['weɪtə(r)] *n* camarero *m*, *CAm, Col, Méx* mesero *m*, *Chile, Ven* mesonero *m*, *Perú, RP* mozo *m*
waiting ['weɪtɪŋ] *n* **no w.** *(sign)* prohibido aparcar; **w. list** lista *f* de espera; **w. room** sala *f* de espera
waitress ['weɪtrɪs] *n* camarera *f*, *CAm, Col, Méx* mesera *f*, *Chile, Ven* mesonera *f*, *Perú, RP* moza *f*
waive [weɪv] *vt Fml (rule)* no aplicar
wake¹ [weɪk] **1** *vt (pt* woke; *pp* woken) **to w. sb (up)** despertar a algn
2 *vi* **to w. (up)** despertar(se)
3 *n (for dead)* velatorio *m*
wake² [weɪk] *n (in water)* estela *f*; *Fig* **in the w. of** tras
waken ['weɪkən] *vt Literary* despertar
Wales [weɪlz] *n* (el país de) Gales
walk [wɔːk] **1** *n* (**a**) *(long)* caminata *m*; *(short)* paseo *m*; **it's an hour's w.** está a una hora de camino; **to go for a w.** dar un paseo; **to take the dog for a w.** sacar a pasear al perro (**b**) *(gait)* modo *m* de andar (**c**) **people from all walks of life** gente *f* de toda condición
2 *vt* (**a**) **we walked her home** la acompañamos a casa (**b**) *(dog)* pasear
3 *vi* (**a**) andar (**b**) *(go on foot)* ir andando
▸ **walk away** *vi* alejarse; *Fig* **to w. away with a prize** llevarse un premio
▸ **walk into** *vt insep* (**a**) *(place)* entrar en; *Fig (trap)* caer en (**b**) *(bump into)* chocarse contra
▸ **walk out** *vi* salir; *Ind* declararse en huelga; **to w. out on sb** abandonar a algn
▸ **walk up** *vi* **to w. up to sb** abordar a algn
walkabout ['wɔːkəbaʊt] *n (by Queen etc)* = paseo informal entre la gente
walker ['wɔːkə(r)] *n* paseante *mf*; *Sport* marchador(a) *m,f*
walkie-talkie [wɔːkɪ'tɔːkɪ] *n* walkie-talkie *m*
walking ['wɔːkɪŋ] **1** *n* andar *m*; *(hiking)* excursionismo *m*
2 *adj* **at w. pace** a paso de marcha; **w. shoes** zapatos *mpl* de andar; **w. stick** bastón *m*

Walkman® ['wɔːkmən] *n* (*pl* **Walkmans**) walkman® *m*

walkout ['wɔːkaʊt] *n Ind* huelga *f*

walkover ['wɔːkəʊvə(r)] *n* it was a w. fue pan comido

walkway ['wɔːkweɪ] *n* paso *m* de peatones

wall [wɔːl] *n* (**a**) *(freestanding, exterior)* muro *m*; *Fig* **to have one's back to the w.** estar entre la espada y la pared; **city w.** muralla *f*; **garden w.** tapia *f* (**b**) *(interior)* pared *f*; **w. map** mapa *m* mural (**c**) *Ftb* barrera *f*

► **wall up** *vt sep (door, fireplace)* tabicar

walled [wɔːld] *adj (city)* amurallado(a); *(garden)* cercado(a) con tapia

wallet ['wɒlɪt] *n* cartera *f*

wallflower ['wɔːlflaʊə(r)] *n* (**a**) *Bot* alhelí *m* (**b**) *Fam* **to be a w.** ser un convidado de piedra

wallop ['wɒləp] *Fam* **1** *n* golpazo *m*
2 *vt* (**a**) *(hit)* pegar fuerte (**b**) *(defeat)* dar una paliza a

wallow ['wɒləʊ] *vi* revolcarse (**en** in); *Fig* **to w. in self-pity** sumirse en la autocompasión

wallpaper ['wɔːlpeɪpə(r)] **1** *n* papel pintado
2 *vt* empapelar

wally ['wɒlɪ] *n Fam* idiota *mf*

walnut ['wɔːlnʌt] *n* nuez *f*; *(tree, wood)* nogal *m*

walrus ['wɔːlrəs] *n* morsa *f*

waltz [wɔːls] **1** *n* vals *m*
2 *vi* bailar un vals

wan [wɒn] *adj* (**wanner, wannest**) pálido(a); *(look, smile)* apagado(a)

wand [wɒnd] *n* (**magic**) **w.** varita *f* (mágica)

wander ['wɒndə(r)] **1** *vt* **to w. the streets** vagar por las calles
2 *vi* (**a**) *(aimlessly)* vagar, errar; **to w. about** deambular; **to w. in/out** entrar/salir sin prisas (**b**) *(stray)* desviarse; *(mind)* divagar; **his glance wandered round the room** recorrió el cuarto con la mirada

wandering ['wɒndərɪŋ] *adj* errante; *(tribe)* nómada; *(speech)* divagador(a)

wane [weɪn] *vi* menguar; *(interest)* decaer

wangle ['wæŋgəl] *vt Fam* agenciarse

wank [wæŋk] *Br Vulg* **1** *n* paja *f*
2 *vi* hacerse una paja

wanker ['wæŋkə(r)] *n Br Vulg* mamón(ona) *m,f*

want [wɒnt] **1** *n* (**a**) *(lack)* falta *f*; **for w. of** por falta de (**b**) *(poverty)* miseria *f*

2 *vt* (**a**) *(desire)* querer, desear; **to w. to do sth** querer hacer algo (**b**) *Fam (need)* necesitar; **the grass wants cutting** hace falta cortar el césped (**c**) *(seek)* buscar; **you're wanted on the phone** te llaman al teléfono

► **want for** *vt insep* carecer de; **to w. for nothing** tenerlo todo

wanting ['wɒntɪŋ] *adj* (**a**) **she is w. in tact** le falta tacto (**b**) **he was found w.** no daba la talla

wanton ['wɒntən] *adj* (**a**) *(motiveless)* sin motivo; **w. cruelty** crueldad gratuita (**b**) *(unrestrained)* desenfrenado(a); *(licentious)* lascivo(a)

war [wɔː(r)] *n* guerra *f*; **to be at w. (with)** estar en guerra (con); *Fig* **to declare/wage w. on** declarar/hacer la guerra a; **w. crime** crimen *m* de guerra

warble ['wɔːbəl] *vi* gorjear

ward [wɔːd] *n* (**a**) *(of hospital)* sala *f* (**b**) *Jur* pupilo(a) *m,f*; **w. of court** pupilo(a) bajo tutela judicial (**c**) *Br Pol* distrito *m* electoral

► **ward off** *vt sep (blow)* parar, desviar; *(attack)* rechazar; *(danger)* evitar; *(illness)* prevenir

warden ['wɔːdən] *n (of residence)* guardián(ana) *m,f*; **game w.** guardia *m* de coto

warder ['wɔːdə(r)] *n Br* carcelero(a) *m,f*

wardrobe ['wɔːdrəʊb] *n* (**a**) armario *m*, ropero *m* (**b**) *(clothes)* guardarropa *m* (**c**) *Th* vestuario *m*

warehouse ['weəhaʊs] *n* almacén *m*

wares [weəz] *npl* mercancías *fpl*

warfare ['wɔːfeə(r)] *n* guerra *f*

warhead ['wɔːhed] *n* (**nuclear**) **w.** ojiva *f* nuclear

warm [wɔːm] **1** *adj* (**a**) *(water)* tibio(a); *(hands)* caliente; *(climate)* cálido(a); **a w. day** un día de calor; **I am w.** tengo calor; **it is (very) w. today** hoy hace (mucho) calor; **w. clothing** ropa *f* de abrigo (**b**) *(welcome, applause)* cálido(a)
2 *vt* calentar; *Fig* alegrar
3 *vi* calentarse; **to w. to sb** cogerle simpatía a algn

► **warm up 1** *vt sep* (**a**) calentar; *(soup)* (re)calentar (**b**) *(audience)* animar
2 *vi* (**a**) calentarse; *(food)* (re)calentarse; *(person)* entrar en calor (**b**) *(athlete)* hacer ejercicios de calentamiento (**c**) *Fig (audience, party)* animarse

warm-blooded [wɔːm'blʌdɪd] *adj* de sangre caliente

warm-hearted [wɔːm'hɑːtɪd] *adj* afectuoso(a)

warmly [ˈwɔːmlɪ] *adv Fig* calurosamente; *(thank)* con efusión

warmth [wɔːmθ] *n (heat)* calor *m*; *Fig* cordialidad *f*

warn [wɔːn] *vt* avisar (**of** de), advertir (**about/against** sobre/contra); **he warned me not to go** me advirtió que no fuera; **to w. sb that** advertir a algn que

warning [ˈwɔːnɪŋ] **1** *adj* **w. light** piloto *m*; **w. sign** señal *f* de aviso
2 *n* (**a**) *(of danger)* advertencia *f*, aviso *m* (**b**) *(replacing punishment)* amonestación *f* (**c**) *(notice)* aviso *m*; **without w.** sin previo aviso

warp [wɔːp] **1** *vt* (**a**) *(wood)* alabear, combar (**b**) *Fig (mind)* pervertir
2 *vi* alabearse, combarse

warrant [ˈwɒrənt] **1** *n* (**a**) *Jur* orden *f* judicial; **death w.** sentencia *f* de muerte (**b**) *(authorization note)* cédula *f*; *Com* bono *m*
2 *vt* (**a**) *(justify)* justificar (**b**) *(guarantee)* garantizar

warranty [ˈwɒrəntɪ] *n Com* garantía *f*

warren [ˈwɒrən] *n* conejera *f*; *Fig* laberinto *m*

warrior [ˈwɒrɪə(r)] *n* guerrero(a) *m,f*

Warsaw [ˈwɔːsɔː] *n* Varsovia

warship [ˈwɔːʃɪp] *n* buque *m or* barco *m* de guerra

wart [wɔːt] *n* verruga *f*

wartime [ˈwɔːtaɪm] *n* tiempos *mpl* de guerra

wary [ˈweərɪ] *adj* (**warier, wariest**) cauteloso(a); **to be w. of doing sth** dudar en hacer algo; **to be w. of sb/sth** recelar de algn/algo

was [wɒz] *pt of* be

wash [wɒʃ] **1** *n* (**a**) lavado *m*; **to have a w.** lavarse (**b**) *(of ship)* estela *f*; *(sound)* chapoteo *m*
2 *vt* (**a**) lavar; *(dishes)* fregar; **to w. one's hair** lavarse el pelo (**b**) *(of sea, river)* arrastrar
3 *vi* (**a**) *(person)* lavarse; *(do the laundry)* hacer la colada (**b**) *(lap)* batir
▸ **wash away** *vt sep (of sea)* llevarse; *(traces)* borrar
▸ **wash off** *vi* quitarse lavando
▸ **wash out 1** *vt sep* (**a**) *(stain)* quitar lavando (**b**) *(bottle)* enjuagar
2 *vi* quitarse lavando
▸ **wash up 1** *vt sep Br (dishes)* fregar
2 *vi* (**a**) *Br* fregar los platos (**b**) *US* lavarse rápidamente

washable [ˈwɒʃəbəl] *adj* lavable

washbasin [ˈwɒʃbeɪsən], *US* **washbowl** [ˈwɒʃbəʊl] *n* palangana *f*

washcloth [ˈwɒʃklɒθ] *n US* manopla *f*

washer [ˈwɒʃə(r)] *n (on tap)* junta *f*

washing [ˈwɒʃɪŋ] *n (action)* lavado *m*; *(of clothes)* colada *f*; **(dirty) w.** ropa sucia; **to do the w.** hacer la colada; **w. line** tendedero *m*; **w. machine** lavadora *f*; **w. powder** detergente *m*

washing-up [wɒʃɪŋˈʌp] *n Br* (**a**) *(action)* fregado *m*; **w. bowl** barreño *m*; **w. liquid** (detergente *m*) lavavajillas (**b**) *(dishes)* platos *mpl* (para fregar)

washout [ˈwɒʃaʊt] *n Fam* fracaso *m*

washroom [ˈwɒʃruːm] *n US* servicios *mpl*

wasp [wɒsp] *n* avispa *f*

wastage [ˈweɪstɪdʒ] *n* pérdidas *fpl*

waste [weɪst] **1** *adj* (**a**) *(unwanted)* desechado(a); **w. food** restos *mpl* de comida; **w. products** productos *mpl* de desecho (**b**) *(ground)* baldío(a)
2 *n* (**a**) *(unnecessary use)* desperdicio *m*; *(of resources, effort, money)* derroche *m*; *(of time)* pérdida *f*; **to go to w.** echarse a perder (**b**) *(leftovers)* desperdicios *mpl*; *(rubbish)* basura *f*; **radioactive w.** desechos radioactivos; **w. disposal unit** trituradora *f* (de desperdicios); **w. pipe** tubo *m* de desagüe
3 *vt (squander)* desperdiciar, malgastar; *(resources)* derrochar; *(money)* despilfarrar; *(time)* perder
▸ **waste away** *vi* consumirse

wasteful [ˈweɪstfʊl] *adj* derrochador(a)

wasteland [ˈweɪstlænd] *n* baldío *m*

wastepaper [weɪstˈpeɪpə(r)] *n* papeles usados; **w. basket** papelera *f*

watch [wɒtʃ] **1** *n* (**a**) *(look-out)* vigilancia *f*; **to keep a close w. on sth/sb** vigilar algo/a algn muy atentamente (**b**) *Mil (body)* guardia *f*; *(individual)* centinela *m*; **to be on w.** estar de guardia (**c**) *(timepiece)* reloj *m*
2 *vt* (**a**) *(observe)* mirar, observar (**b**) *(keep an eye on)* vigilar; *(with suspicion)* acechar (**c**) *(be careful of)* tener cuidado con; *Fig* **to w. one's step** ir con pies de plomo
3 *vi (look)* mirar, observar; **w. out!** ¡cuidado!
▸ **watch out for** *vt insep (be careful of)* tener cuidado con

watchband [ˈwɒtʃbænd] *n US* = **watchstrap**

watchdog [ˈwɒtʃdɒg] *n* perro *m* guardián; *Fig* guardián(ana) *m,f*

watchful [ˈwɒtʃfʊl] *adj* vigilante

watchmaker [ˈwɒtʃmeɪkə(r)] *n* relojero(a) *m,f*

watchman ['wɒtʃmən] *n* vigilante *m*; **night w.** *(of site)* vigilante nocturno

watchstrap ['wɒtʃstræp] *n* correa *f* (de reloj)

watchtower ['wɒtʃtaʊə(r)] *n* atalaya *f*

water ['wɔːtə(r)] **1** *n* (**a**) agua *f*; **w. bottle** cantimplora *f*; **w. lily** nenúfar *m*; **w. main** conducción *f* de aguas; **w. polo** water polo *m*; **w. sports** deportes acuáticos; **w. tank** depósito *m* de agua; **territorial waters** aguas jurisdiccionales; *Fig* **it's all w. under the bridge** ha llovido mucho desde entonces (**b**) **to pass w.** orinar

2 *vt (plants)* regar

3 *vi* **my eyes are watering** me lloran los ojos; **my mouth watered** se me hizo la boca agua

► **water down** *vt sep (drink)* aguar

watercolour, *US* **watercolor** ['wɔːtəkʌlə(r)] *n* acuarela *f*

watercress ['wɔːtəkres] *n* berro *m*

waterfall ['wɔːtəfɔːl] *n* cascada *f*; *(very big)* catarata *f*

waterfront ['wɔːtəfrʌnt] *n (shore)* orilla *f* del agua; *(harbour)* puerto *m*

watering ['wɔːtərɪŋ] *n (of plants)* riego *m*; **w. can** regadera *f*; **w. place** abrevadero *m*

waterline ['wɔːtəlaɪn] *n* línea *f* de flotación

waterlogged ['wɔːtəlɒgd] *adj* anegado(a)

watermark ['wɔːtəmɑːk] *n* filigrana *f*

watermelon ['wɔːtəmelən] *n* sandía *f*

waterproof ['wɔːtəpruːf] **1** *adj (material)* impermeable; *(watch)* sumergible

2 *n (coat)* impermeable *m*

watershed ['wɔːtəʃed] *n Geog* línea divisoria de aguas; *Fig* punto decisivo

water-skiing ['wɔːtəskiːɪŋ] *n* esquí acuático

watertight ['wɔːtətaɪt] *adj* hermético(a)

waterway ['wɔːtəweɪ] *n* vía *f* fluvial

waterworks ['wɔːtəwɜːks] *npl* central *f* de abastecimiento de agua; *Fig* **to turn on the w.** empezar a llorar

watery ['wɔːtərɪ] *adj* (**a**) *(soup)* aguado(a); *(coffee)* flojo(a) (**b**) *(eyes)* lacrimoso(a) (**c**) *(pale)* pálido(a)

watt [wɒt] *n* vatio *m*

wave [weɪv] **1** *n* (**a**) *(at sea)* ola *f* (**b**) *(in hair)* & *Rad* onda *f* (**c**) *Fig (of anger, strikes etc)* oleada *f* (**d**) *(gesture)* saludo *m* con la mano)

2 *vt* (**a**) agitar; *(brandish)* blandir (**b**) *(hair)* ondular

3 *vi* (**a**) agitar el brazo; **she waved (to me)** *(greeting)* me saludó con la mano; *(goodbye)* se despidió (de mí) con la

mano; *(signal)* me hizo señas con la mano (**b**) *(flag)* ondear; *(corn)* ondular

wavelength ['weɪvleŋθ] *n* longitud *f* de onda

waver ['weɪvə(r)] *vi (hesitate)* vacilar (**between** entre); *(voice)* temblar; *(courage)* flaquear

wavy ['weɪvɪ] *adj* (**wavier, waviest**) ondulado(a)

wax¹ [wæks] **1** *n* cera *f*

2 *vt* encerar

wax² [wæks] *vi* (**a**) *(moon)* crecer (**b**) **to w. lyrical** exaltarse

waxworks ['wækswɜːks] *n sing* museo *m* de cera

way [weɪ] **1** *n* (**a**) *(route)* camino *m*; *(road)* vía *f*, camino; **a letter is on the w.** una carta está en camino; **on the w.** en el camino; **on the w. here** de camino para aquí; **out of the w.** apartado(a); **to ask the w.** preguntar el camino; **to go the wrong w.** ir por el camino equivocado; **to lose one's w.** perderse; **to make one's w. through the crowd** abrirse camino entre la multitud; **which is the w. to the station?** ¿por dónde se va a la estación?; *Fig* **she went out of her w. to help** se desvivió por ayudar; **w. in** entrada *f*; **w. out** salida *f*; *Fig* **the easy w. out** la solución fácil; **I can't find my w. out** no encuentro la salida; **on the w. back** en el viaje de regreso; **on the w. up/down** en la subida/bajada; **there's no w. through** el paso está cerrado; **you're in the w.** estás estorbando; **(get) out of the w.!** ¡quítate de en medio!; *Fig* **to get sb/sth out of the w.** desembarazarse de algn/algo; **I kept out of the w.** me mantuve a distancia; *Aut* **right of w.** prioridad *f*; **there's a wall in the w.** hay un muro en medio; **to give w.** ceder; *Aut* ceder el paso

(**b**) *(direction)* dirección *f*; **come this w.** venga por aquí; **which w. did he go?** ¿por dónde se fue?; **that w.** por allá; **the other w. round** al revés

(**c**) *(distance)* distancia *f*; **a long w. off** lejos; *Fig* **he'll go a long w.** llegará lejos; *Fig* **we've come a long w.** hemos hecho grandes progresos

(**d**) **to get under w.** *(travellers, work)* ponerse en marcha; *(meeting, match)* empezar

(**e**) *(means, method)* método *m*, manera *f*; **do it any w. you like** hazlo como quieras; **I'll do it my w.** lo haré a mi manera

(**f**) *(manner)* modo *m*, manera *f*; **in a friendly w.** de modo amistoso; **one w. or**

another de un modo o de otro; **the French w. of life** el estilo de vida francés; **the w. things are going** tal como van las cosas; **to my w. of thinking** a mi modo de ver; *Fam* **no w.!** ¡ni hablar!; **she has a w. with children** tiene un don para los niños; **by w. of** a modo de; **either w.** en cualquier caso; **in a w.** en cierto sentido; **in many ways** desde muchos puntos de vista; **in some ways** en algunos aspectos; **in no w.** de ninguna manera

(**g**) *(custom)* hábito *m*, costumbre *f*; **to be set in one's ways** tener costumbres arraigadas

(**h**) *(state)* estado *m*; **leave it the w.** **it is** déjalo tal como está; **he is in a bad w.** está bastante mal

(**i**) **by the w.** a propósito; **in the w. of business** en el curso de los negocios

2 *adv Fam* mucho, muy; **it was w. off target** cayó muy desviado del blanco; **w. back in 1940** allá en 1940

waylay ['weɪ'leɪ] *vt* (*pt & pp* **waylaid** [weɪ'leɪd]) (**a**) *(attack)* atacar por sorpresa (**b**) *Fig (intercept)* abordar, detener

wayside ['weɪsaɪd] *n Fig* **to fall by the w.** quedarse en el camino

wayward ['weɪwəd] *adj* rebelde; *(capricious)* caprichoso(a)

WC [dʌblju:'si:] *n* (*abbr* **water closet**) wáter *m*, WC *m*

we [wi:] *pers pron* nosotros(as) *(usually omitted in Spanish, except for contrast)*

weak [wi:k] *adj* débil; *(argument, excuse)* pobre; *(team, piece of work, tea)* flojo(a)

weaken ['wi:kən] **1** *vt* debilitar; *(argument)* quitar fuerza a

2 *vi* (**a**) debilitarse (**b**) *(concede ground)* ceder

weakling ['wi:klɪŋ] *n* enclenque *mf*

weakness ['wi:knɪs] *n* debilidad *f*, *(character flaw)* punto flaco

wealth [welθ] *n* riqueza *f*; *Fig* abundancia *f*

wealthy ['welθɪ] *adj* (**wealthier, wealthiest**) rico(a)

wean [wi:n] *vt (child)* destetar; *Fig* **to w. sb from a habit** desacostumbrar (gradualmente) a algn de un hábito

weapon ['wepən] *n* arma *f*

wear [weə(r)] **1** *vt* (*pt* **wore**; *pp* **worn**) (**a**) *(clothes)* llevar puesto, vestir; *(shoes)* llevar puestos, calzar; **he wears glasses** lleva gafas; **to w. black** vestirse de negro (**b**) *(erode)* desgastar

2 *vi* **to w. (thin/smooth)** desgastarse (con el roce); *Fig* **my patience is wearing thin** se me está acabando la paciencia

3 *n* (**a**) ropa *f*; **leisure w.** ropa de sport (**b**) *(use) (clothes)* uso *m* (**c**) *(deterioration)* desgaste *m*; **normal w. and tear** desgaste natural

▸ **wear away 1** *vt sep* erosionar

2 *vi (stone etc)* erosionarse; *(inscription)* borrarse

▸ **wear down 1** *vt sep (heels)* desgastar; *Fig* **to w. sb down** vencer la resistencia de algn

2 *vi* desgastarse

▸ **wear off** *vi (effect, pain)* pasar, desaparecer

▸ **wear out 1** *vt sep* gastar; *Fig* agotar

2 *vi* gastarse

wearily ['wɪərɪlɪ] *adv* con cansancio

wearisome ['wɪərɪsəm] *adj* fatigoso(a)

weary ['wɪərɪ] **1** *adj* (**wearier, weariest**) (**a**) *(tired)* cansado(a) (**b**) *(fed up)* harto(a)

2 *vt* cansar

3 *vi* cansarse (**of** de)

weasel ['wi:zəl] *n* comadreja *f*

weather ['weðə(r)] **1** *n* tiempo *m*; **the w. is fine** hace buen tiempo; *Fig* **to feel under the w.** no encontrarse bien; **w. chart** mapa meteorológico; **w. forecast** parte meteorológico; **w. vane** veleta *f*

2 *vt Fig (crisis)* aguantar; *Fig* **to w. the storm** capear el temporal

weather-beaten ['weðəbi:tən] *adj* curtido(a)

weathercock ['weðəkɒk] *n* veleta *f*

weatherman ['weðəmæn] *n* hombre *m* del tiempo

weave [wi:v] **1** *n* tejido *m*

2 *vt* (*pt* **wove**; *pp* **woven**) (**a**) *Tex* tejer (**b**) *(intertwine)* entretejer (**c**) *(intrigues)* tramar

3 *vi (person, road)* zigzaguear

weaver ['wi:və(r)] *n* tejedor(a) *m,f*

web [web] *n* (**a**) *(of spider)* telaraña *f* (**b**) *(of lies)* sarta *f* (**c**) *Comput* **the W.** la Web; **w. page** página *f* web; **w. site** sitio *m* web

webbed [webd] *adj Orn* palmeado(a)

wed [wed] *vt Literary* (*pt & pp* **wed** *or* **wedded**) casarse con

wedding ['wedɪŋ] *n* boda *f*, casamiento *m*; **w. cake** tarta *f* nupcial; **w. day** día *m* de la boda; **w. dress** traje *m* de novia; **w. present** regalo *m* de boda; **w. ring** alianza *f*

wedge [wedʒ] **1** *n* (**a**) cuña *f*; *(for table leg)* calce *m* (**b**) *(of cake, cheese)* trozo *m* grande

2 *vt* calzar; **to be wedged tight** *(object)* estar completamente atrancado(a)

Wednesday ['wenzdɪ] *n* miércoles *m*

wee¹ [wiː] *adj esp Scot* pequeñito(a)

wee² [wiː] *Fam* **1** *n* pipí *m*

2 *vi* hacer pipí

weed [wiːd] **1** *n Bot* mala hierba

2 *vt* (**a**) *(garden)* escardar (**b**) *Fig* **to w. out** eliminar

3 *vi* escardar

weedkiller ['wiːdkɪlə(r)] *n* herbicida *m*

weedy ['wiːdɪ] *adj* (**weedier, weediest**) *Pej* debilucho(a)

week [wiːk] *n* semana *f*; **a w. (ago) to-day/yesterday** hoy hace/ayer hizo una semana; **a w. today** justo dentro de una semana; **last/next w.** la semana pasada/que viene; **once a w.** una vez por semana; **w. in, w. out** semana tras semana

weekday ['wiːkdeɪ] *n* día *m* laborable

weekend [wiːk'end] *n* fin *m* de semana

weekly ['wiːklɪ] **1** *adj* semanal

2 *adv* semanalmente; **twice w.** dos veces por semana

3 *n Press* semanario *m*

weep [wiːp] **1** *vi* (*pt & pp* **wept**) llorar; **to w. for sb** llorar la muerte de algn

2 *vt (tears)* derramar

weeping ['wiːpɪŋ] *adj* **w. willow** sauce *m* llorón

weigh [weɪ] **1** *vt* (**a**) pesar (**b**) *Fig (consider)* ponderar (**c**) **to w. anchor** levar anclas

2 *vi* (**a**) pesar (**b**) *Fig (influence)* influir

▸ **weigh down** *vt sep* sobrecargar

▸ **weigh in** *vi* (**a**) *Sport* pesarse (**b**) *Fam (join in)* intervenir

▸ **weigh up** *vt sep (matter)* evaluar; *(person)* formar una opinión sobre; **to w. up the pros and cons** sopesar los pros y los contras

weight [weɪt] *n* (**a**) peso *m*; **to lose w.** adelgazar; **to put on w.** subir de peso; *Fam Fig* **to pull one's w.** poner de su parte (**b**) *(of clock, scales)* pesa *f* (**c**) *Fig* **that's a w. off my mind** eso me quita un peso de encima

weighting ['weɪtɪŋ] *n Br (on salary)* suplemento *m* de salario

weightlifter ['weɪtlɪftə(r)] *n* halterófilo(a) *m,f*

weighty ['weɪtɪ] *adj* (**weightier, weightiest**) pesado(a); *Fig (problem, matter)* importante, grave; *(argument)* de peso

weir [wɪə(r)] *n* presa *f*

weird [wɪəd] *adj* raro(a), extraño(a)

welcome ['welkəm] **1** *adj (person)* bienvenido(a); *(news)* grato(a); *(change)* oportuno(a); **to make sb w.** acoger a algn calurosamente; **you're w.!** ¡no hay de qué!

2 *n (greeting)* bienvenida *f*

3 *vt* acoger; *(more formally)* darle la bienvenida a; *(news)* acoger con agrado; *(decision)* aplaudir

welcoming ['welkəmɪŋ] *adj (person)* acogedor(a); *(smile)* de bienvenida

weld [weld] *vt* soldar

welfare ['welfeə(r)] *n* (**a**) *(well-being)* bienestar *m*; **animal/child w.** protección *f* de animales/de menores; **w. work** asistencia *f* social; **w. worker** asistente *mf* social (**b**) *US (social security)* seguridad *f* social

well¹ [wel] *n* (**a**) pozo *m* (**b**) *(of staircase, lift)* hueco *m* (**c**) *(of court, hall)* hemiciclo *m*

▸ **well up** *vi* brotar

well² [wel] **1** *adj* (**a**) *(healthy)* bien; **are you keeping w.?** ¿estás bien de salud?; **to get w.** reponerse (**b**) *(satisfactory)* bien; **all is w.** todo va bien; **it's just as w.** menos mal (**c**) **it is as w. to remember that** conviene recordar que

2 *adv* (**better, best**) (**a**) *(properly)* bien; **he has done w. (for himself)** ha prosperado; **the business is doing w.** el negocio marcha bien; **she did w. in the exam** el examen le fue bien; **w. done!** ¡muy bien!; **he took it w.** lo tomó a bien (**b**) *(thoroughly)* bien; **I know it only too w.** lo sé de sobra; *Culin* **w. done** muy hecho(a) (**c**) **he's w. over thirty** tiene treinta años bien cumplidos; **w. after six o'clock** mucho después de las seis (**d**) *(easily, with good reason)* **he couldn't very w. say no** difícilmente podía decir que no; **I may w. do that** puede que haga eso (**e**) **as w.** también; **as w. as** así como; **children as w. as adults** tanto niños como adultos

3 *interj* (**a**) *(surprise)* ¡bueno!, ¡vaya!; **w. I never!** ¡no me digas! (**b**) *(agreement, interrogation, resignation)* bueno; **very w.** bueno; **w.?** ¿y bien? (**c**) *(doubt)* pues; **w., I don't know** pues no sé (**d**) *(resumption)* **w., as I was saying** pues (bien), como iba diciendo

well-behaved ['welbɪheɪvd] *adj (child)* formal, educado(a)

well-being ['welbiːŋ] *n* bienestar *m*

well-built ['welbɪlt] *adj (building etc)* de construcción sólida; *(person)* fornido(a)

well-earned ['welɜːnd] *adj* merecido(a)

well-educated [wel'edʊkeɪtɪd] *adj* culto(a)

well-heeled ['welhiːld] *adj Fam* adinerado(a)

well-informed ['welɪnfɔːmd] *adj* bien informado(a)

wellingtons [ˈwelɪŋtənz] *npl* botas *fpl* de goma

well-known [ˈwelnəʊn] *adj* (bien) conocido(a)

well-mannered [ˈwelmænəd] *adj* educado(a)

well-meaning [welˈmiːnɪŋ] *adj* bien intencionado(a)

well-off [welˈɒf] *adj (rich)* acomodado(a)

well-read [welˈred] *adj* culto(a)

well-spoken [welˈspəʊkən] *adj* con acento culto

well-to-do [weltəˈduː] *adj* acomodado(a)

well-wisher [ˈwelwɪʃə(r)] *n* admirador(a) *m,f*

Welsh [welʃ] **1** *adj* galés(esa); **W. rarebit** = tostada con queso fundido
2 *n* (**a**) *(language)* galés *m* (**b**) **the W.** los galeses

Welshman [ˈwelʃmən] *n* galés *m*

Welshwoman [ˈwelʃwʊmən] *n* galesa *f*

welterweight [ˈwelterweɪt] *n* (peso *m*) wélter *m*

wench [wentʃ] *n Old-fashioned* moza *f*

went [went] *pt of* **go**

wept [wept] *pt & pp of* **weep**

were [wɜː(r), *unstressed* wə(r)] *pt of* **be**

west [west] **1** *n* oeste *m*, occidente *m*; **in/to the w.** al oeste; *Pol* **the W.** los países occidentales
2 *adj* del oeste, occidental; **the W. Indies** las Antillas; **W. Indian** antillano(a)
3 *adv* al oeste, hacia el oeste

westerly [ˈwestəlɪ] *adj (wind)* del oeste

western [ˈwestən] **1** *adj* del oeste, occidental; **W. Europe** Europa Occidental
2 *n Cin* western *m*, película *f* del oeste

westward [ˈwestwəd] *adj* **in a w. direction** hacia el oeste

westwards [ˈwestwəds] *adv* hacia el oeste

wet [wet] **1** *adj* (**wetter, wettest**) (**a**) mojado(a); *(slightly)* húmedo(a); **w. paint** *(sign)* recién pintado; **w. through** *(person)* calado(a) hasta los huesos; *(thing)* empapado(a); **w. suit** traje isotérmico (**b**) *(rainy)* lluvioso(a) (**c**) *Fam (person)* soso(a); **w. blanket** aguafiestas *mf inv*
2 *n Fam* apocado(a) *m,f*
3 *vt (pt & pp* **wet**) mojar; **to w. oneself** orinarse

whack [wæk] **1** *vt (hit hard)* golpear fuertemente
2 *n* (**a**) *(blow)* porrazo *m* (**b**) *Fam (share)* parte *f*, porción *f*

whale [weɪl] *n* ballena *f*

wharf [wɔːf] *n* (*pl* **wharves** [wɔːvz]) muelle *m*

what [wɒt, *unstressed* wət] **1** *adj* (**a**) *(direct question)* qué; **w. (sort of) bird is that?** ¿qué tipo de ave es ésa?; **w. good is that?** ¿para qué sirve eso?
(**b**) *(indirect question)* qué; **ask her w. colour she likes** pregúntale qué color le gusta
2 *pron* (**a**) *(direct question)* qué; **w. are you talking about?** ¿de qué estás hablando?; **w. about your father?** ¿y tu padre (qué)?; **w. about going tomorrow?** ¿qué te parece si vamos mañana?; **w. can I do for you?** ¿en qué puedo servirle?; **w. did it cost?** ¿cuánto costó?; **w. did you do that for?** ¿por qué hiciste eso?; **w. (did you say)?** ¿cómo?; **w. does it sound like?** ¿cómo suena?; **w. is happening?** ¿qué pasa?; **w. is it?** *(definition)* ¿qué es?; *(what's the matter)* ¿qué pasa?; **w.'s it called?** ¿cómo se llama?; **w.'s this for?** ¿para qué sirve esto?
(**b**) *(indirect question)* qué, lo que; **he asked me w. I thought** me preguntó lo que pensaba; **I didn't know w. to say** no sabía qué decir
(**c**) **(and) w.'s more** y además; **come w. may** pase lo que pase; **guess w.!** ¿sabes qué?; **it's just w. I need** es exactamente lo que necesito
(**d**) *(in exclamations)* **w. a goal!** ¡qué *or* vaya golazo!; **w. a lovely picture!** ¡qué cuadro más bonito!
3 *interj (surprise, indignation)* ¡cómo!; **w., no dessert?** ¿cómo, no hay postre?

whatever [wɒtˈevə(r), *unstressed* wətˈevə(r)] **1** *adj* (**a**) *(any)* cualquiera que; **at w. time you like** a la hora que quieras; **of w. colour** no importa de qué color (**b**) *(with negative)* **nothing w.** nada en absoluto; **with no interest w.** sin interés alguno
2 *pron* (**a**) *(what)* **w. happened?** ¿qué pasó? (**b**) *(anything, all that)* (todo) lo que; **do w. you like** haz lo que quieras (**c**) *(no matter what)* **don't tell him, w. you do** no se te ocurra decírselo; **w. (else) you find** cualquier (otra) cosa que encuentres; **he goes out w. the weather** sale haga el tiempo que haga

whatsoever [wɒtsəʊˈevə(r)] *adj* **anything w.** cualquier cosa; **nothing w.** nada en absoluto

wheat [wiːt] *n* trigo *m*; **w. germ** germen *m* de trigo

wheedle [ˈwiːdəl] *vt* **to w. sb into doing sth** engatusar a algn para que haga algo;

to **w. sth out of sb** sonsacar algo a algn halagándole

wheel [wiːl] **1** n rueda f

2 vt (bicycle) empujar

3 vi (**a**) (bird) revolotear (**b**) **to w. round** girar sobre los talones

wheelbarrow ['wiːlbærəʊ] n carretilla f

wheelchair ['wiːltʃeə(r)] n silla f de ruedas

wheeze [wiːz] vi respirar con dificultad, resollar

when [wen] **1** adv (**a**) (direct question) cuándo; **since w.?** ¿desde cuándo?; **w. did he arrive?** ¿cuándo llegó? (**b**) (indirect question) cuándo; **tell me w. to go** dime cuándo debo irme (**c**) (on which) cuando, en que; **the days w. I work** los días en que trabajo

2 conj (**a**) cuando; **I'll tell you w. she comes** se lo diré cuando llegue; **w. he was a boy...** de niño... (**b**) (whenever) cuando (**c**) (given that, if) si (**d**) (although) aunque

whence [wens] adv Fml Literary (from where) de dónde

whenever [wen'evə(r)] **1** conj (when) cuando; (every time) siempre que

2 adv **w. that might be** sea cuando sea

where [weə(r)] adv (**a**) (direct question) dónde; (direction) adónde; **w. are you going?** ¿adónde vas?; **w. did we go wrong?** ¿en qué nos equivocamos?; **w. do you come from?** ¿de dónde es usted? (**b**) (indirect question) dónde; (direction) adónde; **tell me w. you went** dime adónde fuiste (**c**) (at, in which) donde; (direction) adonde, a donde (**d**) (when) cuando

whereabouts 1 adv [weərə'baʊts] **w. do you live?** ¿por dónde vives?

2 n ['weərəbaʊts] paradero m

whereas [weər'æz] conj (**a**) (but, while) mientras que (**b**) Jur considerando que

whereby [weə'baɪ] adv por el/la/lo cual

whereupon [weərə'pɒn] conj Fml después de lo cual

wherever [weər'evə(r)] **1** conj dondequiera que; **I'll find him w. he is** le encontraré dondequiera que esté; **sit w. you like** siéntate donde quieras

2 adv (direct question) adónde

wherewithal ['weəwɪðɔːl] n Fam pelas fpl

whet [wet] vt **to w. sb's appetite** abrir el apetito a algn

whether ['weðə(r)] conj (**a**) (if) si; **I don't know w. it is true** no sé si es verdad; **I doubt w. he'll win** dudo que gane (**b**) **w.**

he comes or not venga o no

which [wɪtʃ] **1** adj (**a**) (direct question) qué; **w. colour do you prefer?** ¿qué color prefieres?; **w. one?** ¿cuál?; **w. way?** ¿por dónde?

(**b**) (indirect question) qué; **tell me w. dress you like** dime qué vestido te gusta

(**c**) **by w. time** y para entonces; **in w. case** en cuyo caso

2 pron (**a**) (direct question) cuál/cuáles; **w. of you did it?** ¿quién de vosotros lo hizo?

(**b**) (indirect question) cuál/cuáles; **I don't know w.** I'd rather have no sé cuál prefiero

(**c**) (defining relative) que; (after preposition) que, el/la cual, los/las cuales, el/la que, los/las que; **here are the books (w.) I have read** aquí están los libros que he leído; **the accident (w.) I told you about** el accidente del que te hablé; **the car in w. he was travelling** el coche en (el) que viajaba; **this is the one (w.) I like** éste es el que me gusta

(**d**) (non-defining relative) el/la cual, los/las cuales; **I played three sets, all of w. I lost** jugué tres sets, todos los cuales perdí

(**e**) (referring to a clause) lo cual, lo que; **he won, w. made me very happy** ganó, lo cual or lo que me alegró mucho

whichever [wɪtʃ'evə(r)] **1** adj el/la que, cualquiera que; **I'll take w. books you don't want** tomaré los libros que no quieras; **w. system you choose** cualquiera que sea el sistema que elijas

2 pron el/la que

whiff [wɪf] n (**a**) (quick smell) ráfaga f; (of air, smoke) bocanada f (**b**) Fam (bad smell) tufo m

while [waɪl] **1** n (**a**) (length of time) rato m, tiempo m; **in a little w.** dentro de poco; **once in a w.** de vez en cuando (**b**) **it's not worth your w. staying** no merece la pena que te quedes

2 conj (**a**) (time) mientras; **he fell asleep w. driving** se durmió mientras conducía (**b**) (although) aunque (**c**) (whereas) mientras que

▸ **while away** vt sep **to w. away the time** pasar el rato

whilst [waɪlst] conj = **while**

whim [wɪm] n capricho m, antojo m

whimper ['wɪmpə(r)] **1** n quejido m

2 vi lloriquear

whine [waɪn] vi (**a**) (child) lloriquear; (with pain) dar quejidos (**b**) (complain) quejarse (**c**) (engine) chirriar

whip [wɪp] **1** *n* (**a**) *(for punishment)* látigo *m*; *(for riding)* fusta *f* (**b**) *Br Pol* = oficial encargado(a) de la disciplina de un partido
2 *vt* (**a**) *(as punishment)* azotar; *(horse)* fustigar (**b**) *Culin* batir; **whipped cream** nata montada (**c**) *Fam (steal)* mangar
▸ **whip away** *vt sep* arrebatar
▸ **whip up** *vt sep (passions, enthusiasm)* avivar; *(support)* incrementar
whipping ['wɪpɪŋ] *n Fig* **w. boy** cabeza *f* de turco
whip-round ['wɪpraʊnd] *n Fam* colecta *f*
whir [wɜː(r)] *vi* = **whirr**
whirl [wɜːl] **1** *n* giro *m*; *Fig* torbellino *m*
2 *vt* **to w. sth round** dar vueltas a *or* hacer girar algo
3 *vi* **to w. round** girar con rapidez; *(leaves etc)* arremolinarse; **my head's whirling** me está dando vueltas la cabeza
whirlpool ['wɜːlpuːl] *n* remolino *m*
whirlwind ['wɜːlwɪnd] *n* torbellino *m*
whirr [wɜː(r)] *vi* zumbar, runrunear
whisk [wɪsk] **1** *n Culin* batidor *m*; *(electric)* batidora *f*
2 *vt Culin* batir
▸ **whisk away, whisk off** *vt sep* quitar bruscamente, llevarse de repente
whisker ['wɪskə(r)] *n* **whiskers** *(of person)* patillas *fpl*; *(of cat)* bigotes *mpl*
whisky, *US* **whiskey** ['wɪskɪ] *n* whisky *m*
whisper ['wɪspə(r)] **1** *n* (**a**) *(sound)* susurro *m* (**b**) *(rumour)* rumor *m*
2 *vt* decir en voz baja
3 *vi* susurrar
whistle ['wɪsəl] **1** *n* (**a**) *(instrument)* pito *m* (**b**) *(sound)* silbido *m*, pitido *m*
2 *vt (tune)* silbar
3 *vi (person, kettle, wind)* silbar; *(train)* pitar
white [waɪt] **1** *adj* blanco(a); **to go w.** *(face)* palidecer; *(hair)* encanecer; **w. coffee** café *m* con leche; **w. hair** pelo cano; **a w. Christmas** una Navidad con nieve; *Fig* **a w. lie** una mentira piadosa; *US* **the W. House** la Casa Blanca; *Pol* **w. paper** libro blanco; **w. sauce** bechamel *f*
2 *n* (**a**) *(colour, person, of eye)* blanco *m* (**b**) *(of egg)* clara *f* (**c**) **whites** ropa *f* blanca
white-collar ['waɪtkɒlə(r)] *adj* **w. worker** empleado *m* de oficina
whiteness ['waɪtnɪs] *n* blancura *f*
whitewash ['waɪtwɒʃ] **1** *n* (**a**) cal *f* (**b**) *Fig (cover-up)* encubrimiento *m* (**c**) *Fig (defeat)* paliza *f*
2 *vt* (**a**) *(wall)* enjalbegar, blanquear (**b**) *Fig* encubrir

whiting ['waɪtɪŋ] *n* (*pl* **whiting**) *(fish)* pescadilla *f*
Whitsun(tide) ['wɪtsən(taɪd)] *n* pentecostés *m*
whittle ['wɪtəl] *vt* cortar en pedazos; **to w. away at** roer; *Fig* **to w. down** reducir poco a poco
whiz(z) [wɪz] *vi* (**a**) *(sound)* silbar (**b**) **to w. past** pasar volando; *Fam* **w. kid** joven *mf* dinámico(a) y emprendedor(a)
who [huː] *pron* (**a**) *(direct question)* quién/quiénes; **w. are they?** ¿quiénes son?; **w. is it?** ¿quién es? (**b**) *(indirect question)* quién; **I don't know w. did it** no sé quién lo hizo (**c**) *rel (defining)* que; **those w. don't know** los que no saben (**d**) *rel (nondefining)* quien/quienes, el/la cual, los/las cuales; **Elena's mother, w. is very rich …** la madre de Elena, la cual es muy rica …
whodun(n)it [huː'dʌnɪt] *n Fam* novela *f/* obra *f* de teatro/película *f* de suspense
whoever [huː'evə(r)] *pron* (**a**) quienquiera que; **give it to w. you like** dáselo a quien quieras; **w. said that is a fool** el que dijo eso es un tonto; **w. you are** quienquiera que seas (**b**) *(direct question)* **w. told you that?** ¿quién te dijo eso?
whole [həʊl] **1** *adj* (**a**) *(entire)* entero(a), íntegro(a); **a w. week** una semana entera; **he took the w. lot** se los llevó todos (**b**) *(in one piece)* intacto(a)
2 *n* (**a**) *(single unit)* todo *m*, conjunto *m*; **as a w.** en su totalidad (**b**) *(all)* totalidad *f*; **the w. of London** todo Londres (**c**) **on the w.** en general
wholefood ['həʊlfuːd] *n* alimentos *mpl* integrales
wholehearted [həʊl'hɑːtɪd] *adj (enthusiastic)* entusiasta; *(sincere)* sincero(a); *(unreserved)* incondicional
wholemeal ['həʊlmiːl] *adj Br* integral
wholesale ['həʊlseɪl] *Com* **1** *n* venta *f* al por mayor
2 *adj* al por mayor; *Fig* total
3 *adv* al por mayor; *Fig* en su totalidad
wholesaler ['həʊlseɪlə(r)] *n* mayorista *mf*
wholesome ['həʊlsəm] *adj* sano(a)
wholly ['həʊllɪ] *adv* enteramente, completamente
whom [huːm] *pron Fml* (**a**) *(direct question) (accusative)* a quién; **w. did you talk to?** ¿con quién hablaste?; *(after preposition)* **of/from w.?** ¿de quién?; **to w. are you referring?** ¿a quién te refieres? (**b**) *rel (accusative)* que, a quien/a quienes; **those w. I have seen** aquéllos a quien he

visto (**c**) *rel (after preposition)* quien/
quienes, el/la cual, los/las cuales; **my
brothers, both of w. are miners** mis hermanos, que son mineros los dos

En la actualidad, sólo aparece en contextos
formales. **Whom** se puede sustituir por
who en todos los casos salvo cuando va
después de preposición.

whooping cough ['huːpɪŋkɒf] *n* tos ferina
whopping ['wɒpɪŋ] *adj Fam* enorme
whore [hɔː(r)] *n very Fam Pej* puta *f*
whose [huːz] **1** *pron* (**a**) *(direct question)*
de quién/de quiénes; **w. are these gloves?; w. is this?**
¿de quién son estos guantes?; **w. is this?**
¿de quién es esto? (**b**) *(indirect question)*
de quién/de quiénes; **I don't know w.
these coats are** no sé de quién son estos
abrigos (**c**) *rel* cuyo(s)/cuya(s); **the man
w. children we saw** el hombre a cuyos
hijos vimos
2 *adj* **w. car/house is this?** ¿de quién es
este coche/esta casa?
why [waɪ] **1** *adv* por qué; *(for what purpose)* para qué; **w. did you do that?** ¿por
qué hiciste eso?; **w. not go to bed?** ¿por
qué no te acuestas?; **I don't know w. he
did it** no sé por qué lo hizo; **that is w. I
didn't come** por eso no vine; **there's no
reason w. you shouldn't go** no hay motivo para que no vayas
2 *interj* (**a**) *(fancy that!)* ¡toma!, ¡vaya!;
w., it's David! ¡sí es David! (**b**) *(protest,
assertion)* sí, vamos
wick [wɪk] *n* mecha *f*
wicked ['wɪkɪd] *adj* (**a**) malvado(a) (**b**)
Fam malísimo(a); *(temper)* de perros
wicker ['wɪkə(r)] **1** *n* mimbre *m*
2 *adj* de mimbre
wickerwork ['wɪkəwɜːk] *n (material)*
mimbre *m*; *(articles)* artículos *mpl* de
mimbre
wicket ['wɪkɪt] *n (in cricket) (stumps)*
palos *mpl*
wide [waɪd] **1** *adj* (**a**) *(road, trousers)*
ancho(a); *(gap, interval)* grande; **it is 10
m w.** tiene 10 m de ancho (**b**) *(area,
knowledge, support, range)* amplio(a); **w.
interests** intereses muy diversos (**c**) *(off
target)* desviado(a)
2 *adv* **from far and w.** de todas partes; **to
open one's eyes w.** abrir los ojos de par en
par; **w. apart** muy separados(as); **w.
awake** completamente despierto(a); **w.
open** abierto(a) de par en par; **with
mouth w. open** boquiabierto(a)
wide-angle ['waɪdæŋgəl] *adj Phot* **w.**

lens objetivo *m* gran angular
widely ['waɪdlɪ] *adv (travel etc)* extensamente; *(believed)* generalmente; **he is w.
known** es muy conocido
widen ['waɪdən] **1** *vt* ensanchar; *(interests)* ampliar
2 *vi* ensancharse
wide-ranging ['waɪd'reɪndʒɪŋ] *adj (interests)* muy diversos(as); *(discussion)*
amplio(a); *(study)* de gran alcance
widespread ['waɪdspred] *adj (unrest, belief)* general; *(damage)* extenso(a); **to
become w.** generalizarse
widow ['wɪdəʊ] *n* viuda *f*
widowed ['wɪdəʊd] *adj* enviudado(a)
widower ['wɪdəʊə(r)] *n* viudo *m*
width [wɪdθ] *n* (**a**) anchura *f* (**b**) *(of
material, swimming pool)* ancho *m*
wield [wiːld] *vt (weapon)* blandir; *Fig
(power)* ejercer
wife [waɪf] *n (pl* **wives**) mujer *f*, esposa *f*
wig [wɪg] *n* peluca *f*
wiggle ['wɪgəl] **1** *vt (finger etc)* menear;
to w. one's hips contonearse
2 *vi* menearse
Wight [waɪt] *n* Isle of W. Isla *f* de Wight
wild [waɪld] **1** *adj* (**a**) *(animal, tribe)* salvaje; **w. beast** fiera *f*; *Fig* **w. goose chase**
búsqueda *f* inútil
(**b**) *(plant)* silvestre
(**c**) *(landscape)* agreste; **the W. West** el
Salvaje Oeste
(**d**) *(temperament, behaviour)* aloca-
do(a); *(appearance)* desordenado(a);
(passions etc) desenfrenado(a); *(laughter, thoughts)* loco(a); *(applause)* fervoro-
so(a); **to make a w. guess** adivinar al
azar; *Fam Fig* **she is w. about him/about
tennis** está loca por él/por el tenis
(**e**) *Br Fam Fig (angry)* furioso(a)
2 *adv Fig* **to run w.** *(children)* desmandarse
3 *n* **in the w.** en el estado salvaje; *Fig* **to
live out in the wilds** vivir en el quinto pino
wildcat ['waɪldkæt] *n* **w. strike** huelga *f*
salvaje
wilderness ['wɪldənɪs] *n* desierto *m*
wildfire ['waɪldfaɪə(r)] *n* **to spread like
w.** correr como la pólvora
wildlife ['waɪldlaɪf] *n* fauna *f*; **w. park**
parque *m* natural
wildly ['waɪldlɪ] *adv* (**a**) *(rush round etc)*
como un(a) loco(a); *(shoot)* sin apuntar;
(hit out) a tontas y a locas (**b**) **w. enthusiastic** loco(a) de entusiasmo; **w. inaccurate** totalmente erróneo(a)
wilful, *US* **wilfull** ['wɪlfʊl] *adj* (**a**) *(stubborn)* terco(a) (**b**) *Jur* premeditado(a)

will¹ [wɪl] **1** *n* (**a**) voluntad *f*; **good/ill w.**
buena/mala voluntad; **of my own free w.**
por mi propia voluntad (**b**) *Jur (testament)* testamento *m*; **to make one's w.**
hacer testamento
　　2 *vt* **fate willed that ...** el destino quiso
que ...

will² [wɪl] *v aux* (*pt* **would**)

> En el inglés hablado, y en el escrito en estilo
> coloquial, el verbo **will** se contrae de manera que **I/you/he** *etc* **will** se transforman
> en **I'll, you'll, he'll** *etc* y el verbo **would** se
> contrae de manera que **I/you/he** *etc*
> **would** se transforman en **I'd, you'd, he'd**
> *etc*. Las formas negativas **will not** y **would**
> **not** se transforman en **won't** y **wouldn't**.

　　(**a**) *(future) (esp 2nd & 3rd person)*
they'll come vendrán; **w. he be there? –**
yes, he w. ¿estará allí? – sí(, estará);
you'll tell him, won't you? se lo dirás,
¿verdad?; **don't forget, w. you!** ¡que no
se te olvide, vale!; **she won't do it** no lo
hará
　　(**b**) *(command)* **you w. be here at**
eleven! ¡debes estar aquí a las once!
　　(**c**) *(future perfect)* **they'll have finished**
by tomorrow habrán terminado para
mañana
　　(**d**) *(willingness)* **be quiet, w. you! – no, I**
won't! ¿quiere callarse? – no quiero; **I**
won't have it! ¡no lo permito!; **w. you**
have a drink? – yes, I w. ¿quiere tomar
algo? – sí, por favor; **won't you sit down?**
¿quiere sentarse?
　　(**e**) *(custom)* **accidents w. happen**
siempre habrá accidentes
　　(**f**) *(persistence)* **if you w. go out without a coat ...** si te empeñas en salir sin
abrigo ...
　　(**g**) *(probability)* **he'll be on holiday now**
ahora estará de vacaciones
　　(**h**) *(ability)* **the lift w. hold ten people**
en el ascensor caben diez personas

willing ['wɪlɪŋ] *adj (obliging)* complaciente; **I'm quite w. to do it** lo haré con
mucho gusto; **to be w. to do sth** estar
dispuesto(a) a hacer algo

willingly ['wɪlɪŋlɪ] *adv* de buena gana

willingness ['wɪlɪŋnɪs] *n* buena voluntad

willow ['wɪləʊ] *n* **w. (tree)** sauce *m*

willpower ['wɪlpaʊə(r)] *n* (fuerza *f* de)
voluntad *f*

willy-nilly ['wɪlɪ'nɪlɪ] *adv* por gusto o por
fuerza

wilt [wɪlt] *vi* marchitarse

wily ['waɪlɪ] *adj* (**wilier, wiliest**) astuto(a)

wimp [wɪmp] *n Fam (physically)* debilucho(a) *m,f*; *(lacking character)* blandengue *mf*

win [wɪn] **1** *n* victoria *f*
　　2 *vt* (*pt & pp* **won**) (**a**) ganar; *(prize)*
llevarse; *(victory)* conseguir (**b**) *Fig (sympathy, friendship)* ganarse; *(praise)* cosechar; **to w. sb's love** conquistar a algn
　　3 *vi* ganar
　　▸ **win back** *vt sep* recuperar
　　▸ **win over** *vt sep (to cause, idea)* atraer
(**to** a); *(voters, support)* ganarse
　　▸ **win through** *vi* conseguir triunfar

wince [wɪns] *vi* tener un rictus de dolor

winch [wɪntʃ] *n* cigüeña *f*, torno *m*

wind¹ [wɪnd] **1** *n* (**a**) viento *m*; *Fig* **to get**
w. of sth olerse algo; **w. farm** parque
eólico; **w. tunnel** túnel aerodinámico (**b**)
(breath) aliento *m*; **to get one's second w.**
recobrar el aliento (**c**) *Med* flato *m*, gases
mpl (**d**) **w. instrument** instrumento *m* de
viento
　　2 *vt* **to be winded** quedarse sin aliento

wind² [waɪnd] **1** *vt* (*pt & pp* **wound**) (**a**)
(on to a reel) enrollar; **to w. a bandage**
round one's finger vendarse el dedo (**b**)
to w. on/back *(film, tape)* avanzar/rebobinar (**c**) *(clock)* dar cuerda a
　　2 *vi (road, river)* serpentear
　　▸ **wind down 1** *vt sep (window)* bajar
　　2 *vi Fam (person)* relajarse
　　▸ **wind up 1** *vt sep (a) (roll up)* enrollar (**b**)
(business etc) cerrar; *(debate)* clausurar
(**c**) *(clock)* dar cuerda a
　　2 *vi (meeting)* terminar

windfall ['wɪndfɔːl] *n Fig* ganancia inesperada

winding ['waɪndɪŋ] *adj (road, river)* sinuoso(a); *(staircase)* de caracol

windmill ['wɪndmɪl] *n* molino *m* (de
viento)

window ['wɪndəʊ] *n* ventana *f*; *(of vehicle, ticket office etc)* ventanilla *f*; **(shop) w.**
escaparate *m*; **to clean the windows** limpiar los cristales; **w. box** jardinera *f*; **w.**
cleaner limpiacristales *mf inv*

windowpane ['wɪndəʊpeɪn] *n* cristal *m*

window-shopping ['wɪndəʊʃɒpɪŋ] *n* **to**
go w. ir a mirar escaparates

windowsill ['wɪndəʊsɪl] *n* alféizar *m*

windpipe ['wɪndpaɪp] *n* tráquea *f*

windscreen ['wɪndskriːn], *US* **windshield** ['wɪndʃiːld] *n* parabrisas *m inv*;
w. washer lavaparabrisas *m inv*; **w. wiper**
limpiaparabrisas *m inv*

windswept ['wɪndswept] *adj (landscape)* expuesto(a) a los vientos; *(person, hair)* despeinado(a) (por el viento)

windy ['wɪndɪ] *adj* (**windier, windiest**) *(weather)* ventoso(a); *(place)* desprotegido(a) del viento; **it is very w. today** hoy hace mucho viento

wine [waɪn] *n* vino *m*; **w. cellar** bodega *f*; **w. list** lista *f* de vinos; **w. merchant** vinatero(a) *m,f*; **w. tasting** cata *f* de vinos; **w. vinegar** vinagre *m* de vino

wineglass ['waɪnglɑːs] *n* copa *f* (para vino)

wing [wɪŋ] *n* (**a**) *Orn & Av* ala *f* (**b**) *(of building)* ala *f* (**c**) *Aut* aleta *f*; **w. mirror** retrovisor *m* externo (**d**) *Th* (**in the**) **wings** (entre) bastidores *mpl* (**e**) *Ftb* banda *f* (**f**) *Pol* ala *f*; **the left w.** la izquierda

winger ['wɪŋə(r)] *n Ftb* extremo *m*

wink [wɪŋk] **1** *n* guiño *m*; *Fam Fig* **I didn't get a w.** (**of sleep**) no pegué ojo

2 *vi* (**a**) *(person)* guiñar (el ojo) (**b**) *(light)* parpadear

winner ['wɪnə(r)] *n* ganador(a) *m,f*

winning ['wɪnɪŋ] *adj (person, team)* ganador(a); *(number)* premiado(a); *(goal)* decisivo(a); **w. post** meta *f*

winnings ['wɪnɪŋz] *npl* ganancias *fpl*

winter ['wɪntə(r)] **1** *n* invierno *m*

2 *adj* de invierno; **w. sports** deportes *mpl* de invierno

3 *vi* invernar

wintry ['wɪntrɪ] *adj* (**wintrier, wintriest**) invernal

wipe [waɪp] *vt* limpiar; **to w. one's brow** enjugarse la frente; **to w. one's feet/nose** limpiarse los pies/las narices

▸ **wipe away** *vt sep (tear)* enjugar

▸ **wipe off** *vt sep* quitar frotando; **to w. sth off the blackboard/the tape** borrar algo de la pizarra/de la cinta

▸ **wipe out** *vt sep* (**a**) *(erase)* borrar (**b**) *(army)* aniquilar; *(species etc)* exterminar

▸ **wipe up** *vt sep* limpiar

wire [waɪə(r)] **1** *n* (**a**) alambre *m*; *Elec* cable *m*; *Tel* hilo; **w. cutters** cizalla *f* (**b**) *(telegram)* telegrama *m*

2 *vt* (**a**) **to w. (up) a house** poner la instalación eléctrica de una casa; **to w. (up) an appliance to the mains** conectar un aparato a la toma eléctrica (**b**) *(information)* enviar por telegrama

wireless ['waɪəlɪs] *n* radio *f*

wiring ['waɪərɪŋ] *n (network)* cableado *m*; *(action)* instalación *f* del cableado

wiry ['waɪərɪ] *adj* (**wirier, wiriest**) *(hair)* estropajoso(a); *(person)* nervudo(a)

wisdom ['wɪzdəm] *n* (**a**) *(learning)* sabiduría *f*, saber *m* (**b**) *(good sense) (of person)* cordura *f*; *(of action)* sensatez *f* (**c**) **w. tooth** muela *f* del juicio

wise [waɪz] *adj* (**a**) sabio(a); **a w. man** un sabio; **the Three W. Men** los Reyes Magos (**b**) *(remark)* juicioso(a); *(decision)* acertado(a); **it would be w. to keep quiet** sería prudente callarse

wisecrack ['waɪzkræk] *n Fam* salida *f*, ocurrencia *f*

wisely ['waɪzlɪ] *adv (with prudence)* prudentemente

wish [wɪʃ] **1** *n* (**a**) *(desire)* deseo *m* (**for** de); **to make a w.** pedir un deseo

(**b**) **best wishes** felicitaciones *fpl*; **give your mother my best wishes** salude a su madre de mi parte; **with best wishes, Peter** *(at end of letter)* saludos cordiales, Peter

2 *vt* (**a**) *(want)* querer, desear; **I w. I could stay longer** me gustaría poder quedarme más tiempo; **I w. you had told me!** ¡ojalá me lo hubieras dicho!; **to w. to do sth** querer hacer algo

(**b**) **to w. sb goodnight** darle las buenas noches a algn; **to w. sb well** desearle a algn mucha suerte

3 *vi (want)* desear; **as you w.** como quieras; **do as you w.** haga lo que quiera; **to w. for sth** desear algo

wishful ['wɪʃfʊl] *adj* **it's w. thinking** es hacerse ilusiones

wishy-washy ['wɪʃɪwɒʃɪ] *adj Fam (person)* soso(a); *(ideas)* poco definido(a)

wisp [wɪsp] *n (of wool, hair)* mechón *m*; *(of smoke)* voluta *f*

wistful ['wɪstfʊl] *adj* melancólico(a)

wit [wɪt] *n* (**a**) *(intelligence) (often pl)* inteligencia *f*; *Fig* **to be at one's wits' end** estar para volverse loco(a); *Fam Fig* **to have one's wits about one** ser despabilado(a) (**b**) *(humour)* ingenio *m* (**c**) *(person)* ingenioso(a) *m,f*

witch [wɪtʃ] *n* bruja *f*; *Fig* **w. hunt** caza *f* de brujas

witchcraft ['wɪtʃkrɑːft] *n* brujería *f*

with [wɪð, wɪθ] *prep* con; **a room w. a bath** un cuarto con baño; **do you have any money w. you?** ¿traes dinero?; **the man w. the glasses** el hombre de las gafas; **he went w. me/you** fue conmigo/contigo; *Fam* **w. (sugar) or without (sugar)?** ¿con o sin azúcar?; **I have six w. this one** con éste tengo seis; **w. all his faults, I admire him** le admiro con todos sus defectos; **w. your permission** con su permiso; **we're all w. you** *(support)* todos estamos contigo; **you're not w. me, are you?** *(understand)* no me entiendes, ¿verdad?; **he's w. Lloyds** trabaja para Lloyds; **she is popular w. her colleagues**

todos sus colegas la estiman mucho; **to fill a vase w. water** llenar un jarrón de agua; **it is made w. butter** está hecho con mantequilla; **she put on weight w. so much eating** engordó de tanto comer; **to be paralysed w. fear** estar paralizado(a) de miedo; **w. experience** con la experiencia

withdraw [wɪð'drɔː] 1 vt (pt **withdrew**; pp **withdrawn**) (**a**) retirar, sacar; **to w. money from the bank** sacar dinero del banco (**b**) (go back on) retirar; (statement) retractarse de; (plan, claim) renunciar a

2 vi (**a**) retirarse (**b**) (drop out) renunciar

withdrawal [wɪð'drɔːəl] n retirada f; (of statement) retractación f; (of complaint, plan) renuncia f; **w. symptoms** síndrome m de abstinencia

withdrawn [wɪð'drɔːn] 1 adj (person) introvertido(a)

2 pp of **withdraw**

withdrew [wɪð'druː] pt of **withdraw**

wither ['wɪðə(r)] vi marchitarse

withering ['wɪðərɪŋ] adj (look) fulminante; (criticism) mordaz

withhold [wɪð'həʊld] vt (pt & pp **withheld** [wɪð'held]) (money) retener; (decision) aplazar; (consent) negar; (information) ocultar

within [wɪ'ðɪn] 1 prep (**a**) (inside) dentro de (**b**) (range) **the house is w. walking distance** se puede ir andando a la casa; **situated w. 5 km of the town** situado(a) a menos de 5 km de la ciudad; **w. sight of the sea** con vistas al mar; Fig **w. an inch of death** a dos dedos de la muerte (**c**) (time) **they arrived w. a few days of each other** llegaron con pocos días de diferencia; **w. the hour** dentro de una hora; **w. the next five years** durante los cinco próximos años

2 adv dentro; **from w.** desde dentro

with-it ['wɪðɪt] adj Fam **she is very w.** tiene ideas muy modernas; **to get w.** ponerse de moda

without [wɪ'ðaʊt] prep sin; **he did it w. my knowing** lo hizo sin que lo supiera yo; Fig **to do** or **go w. sth** (voluntarily) prescindir de algo; (forcibly) pasar(se) sin algo

withstand [wɪð'stænd] vt (pt & pp **withstood** [wɪð'stʊd]) resistir a; (pain) aguantar

witness ['wɪtnɪs] 1 n (**a**) (person) testigo mf; **w. box**, US **w. stand** barra f de los testigos (**b**) (evidence) **to bear w. to sth** dar fe de algo

2 vt (**a**) (see) presenciar, ser testigo de (**b**) Fig (notice) notar (**c**) Jur **to w. a document** firmar un documento como testigo

witticism ['wɪtɪsɪzəm] n ocurrencia f, salida f

witty ['wɪtɪ] adj (**wittier, wittiest**) ingenioso(a), agudo(a)

wives [waɪvz] pl of **wife**

wizard ['wɪzəd] n hechicero m, mago m

wizened ['wɪzənd] adj (face) arrugado(a)

wobble ['wɒbəl] vi (table, ladder etc) tambalearse; (jelly) temblar

woe [wəʊ] n Literary infortunio m; **w. betide you if I catch you!** ¡ay de ti si te cojo!

woeful ['wəʊfʊl] adj (**a**) (person) afligido(a) (**b**) (sight) penoso(a); **w. ignorance** una ignorancia lamentable

woke [wəʊk] pt of **wake**

woken ['wəʊkən] pp of **wake**

wolf [wʊlf] n (pl **wolves** [wʊlvz]) lobo m; Fig **a w. in sheep**'s clothing un lobo con piel de cordero

woman ['wʊmən] n (pl **women**) mujer f; **old w.** vieja f; Fam **women's libber** feminista mf; Fam **women's lib** movimiento m feminista; **women's rights** derechos mpl de la mujer

womanhood ['wʊmənhʊd] n (adult) edad adulta de la mujer

womanizer ['wʊmənaɪzə(r)] n mujeriego m

womanly ['wʊmənlɪ] adj femenino(a)

womb [wuːm] n matriz f, útero m

women ['wɪmɪn] pl of **woman**

won [wʌn] pt & pp of **win**

wonder ['wʌndə(r)] 1 n (**a**) (miracle) milagro m; **no w. he hasn't come** no es de extrañar que no haya venido (**b**) (amazement) admiración f, asombro m

2 vt (**a**) (be surprised) sorprenderse (**b**) (ask oneself) preguntarse; **I w. why** ¿por qué será?

3 vi (**a**) (marvel) maravillarse; **to w. at sth** admirarse de algo (**b**) **it makes you w.** (reflect) te da qué pensar

wonderful ['wʌndəfʊl] adj maravilloso(a)

wonderfully ['wʌndəfʊlɪ] adv maravillosamente

wont [wəʊnt] Fml 1 adj **to be w. to** soler

2 n costumbre f; **it is his w. to ...** tiene la costumbre de ...

woo [wuː] vt Literary (court) cortejar; Fig intentar congraciarse con

wood [wʊd] n (**a**) (forest) bosque m (**b**)

woodcarving ▸ working

(material) madera *f*; *(for fire)* leña *f*; *Fam Fig* **touch w.!** ¡toca madera! (**c**) *(in golf)* palo *m* de madera (**d**) *(bowling)* bola *f*

woodcarving ['wʊdkɑːvɪŋ] *n* (**a**) *(craft)* tallado *m* en madera (**b**) *(object)* talla *f* en madera

woodcutter ['wʊdkʌtə(r)] *n* leñador(a) *m,f*

wooded ['wʊdɪd] *adj* arbolado(a)

wooden ['wʊdən] *adj* (**a**) de madera; **w. spoon/leg** cuchara *f*/pata *f* de palo (**b**) *Fig* rígido(a); *(acting)* sin expresión

woodlouse ['wʊdlaʊs] *n* cochinilla *f*

woodpecker ['wʊdpekə(r)] *n* pájaro carpintero

woodwind ['wʊdwɪnd] *n* **w. (instruments)** instrumentos *mpl* de viento de madera

woodwork ['wʊdwɜːk] *n* (**a**) *(craft)* carpintería *f* (**b**) *(of building)* maderaje *m*

woodworm ['wʊdwɜːm] *n* carcoma *f*

wool [wʊl] **1** *n* lana *f*; *Fig* **to pull the w. over sb's eyes** dar gato por liebre a algn
2 *adj* de lana

woollen, *US* **woolen** ['wʊlən] **1** *adj* (**a**) de lana (**b**) *(industry)* lanero(a)
2 *npl* **woollens** géneros *mpl* de lana or de punto

woolly, *US* **wooly** ['wʊlɪ] *adj* (**woollier, woolliest,** *US* **woolier, wooliest**) (**a**) *(made of wool)* de lana (**b**) *Fig (unclear)* confuso(a)

word [wɜːd] **1** *n* (**a**) *(spoken, written)* palabra *f*; **in other words ...** es decir ..., o sea ...; **words failed me** me quedé sin habla; *Fig* **a w. of advice** un consejo; *Fig* **I'd like a w. with you** quiero hablar contigo un momento; *Fig* **she didn't say it in so many words** no lo dijo de modo tan explícito; **in the words of the poet ...** como dice el poeta ...; *Fig* **w. for w.** palabra por palabra; **w. processing** tratamiento *m* de textos; **w. processor** procesador *m* de textos
(**b**) *Fig (message)* mensaje *m*; **by w. of mouth** de palabra; **is there any w. from him?** ¿hay noticias de él?; **to send w.** mandar recado
(**c**) *Fig (rumour)* voz *f*, rumor *m*
(**d**) *Fig (promise)* palabra *f*; **he's a man of his w.** es hombre de palabra
2 *vt (express)* formular; **a badly worded letter** una carta mal redactada

wording ['wɜːdɪŋ] *n* expresión *f*; **I changed the w. slightly** cambié algunas palabras

word-perfect [wɜːd'pɜːfekt] *adj* **to be w.** saberse el papel perfectamente

wore [wɔː(r)] *pt of* **wear**

work [wɜːk] **1** *n* (**a**) trabajo *m*; **his w. in the field of physics** su labor en el campo de la física; **it's hard w.** cuesta trabajo
(**b**) *(employment)* trabajo *m*, empleo *m*; **out of w.** parado(a)
(**c**) *(action)* obra *f*, acción *f*; **keep up the good w.!** ¡que siga así!
(**d**) **a piece of w.** un trabajo; **a w. of art** una obra de arte
(**e**) **works** obras *fpl*; **public works** obras (públicas)
(**f**) **works** *(machinery)* mecanismo *m*
(**g**) *Br* **works** *(factory)* fábrica *f*
2 *vt* (**a**) *(drive)* hacer trabajar; **to w. one's way up/down** subir/bajar a duras penas; *Fig* **to w. one's way up in a firm** trabajarse el ascenso en una empresa
(**b**) *(machine)* manejar; *(mechanism)* accionar
(**c**) *(miracles, changes)* operar, hacer
(**d**) *(land)* cultivar; *(mine)* explotar
(**e**) *(wood, metal etc)* trabajar
3 *vi* (**a**) trabajar (**on** *or* **at** en); **to w. as a gardener** trabajar de jardinero
(**b**) *(machine)* funcionar; **it works on gas** funciona con gas
(**c**) *(drug)* surtir efecto; *(system)* funcionar bien; *(plan, trick)* salir bien
(**d**) *(operate)* obrar; **to w. loose** soltarse; **we have no data to w. on** no tenemos datos en que basarnos
▸ **work off** *vt sep (fat)* eliminar trabajando; *(anger)* desahogar
▸ **work out 1** *vt sep* (**a**) *(plan)* idear; *(itinerary)* planear; *(details)* desarrollar (**b**) *(problem)* solucionar; *(solution)* encontrar; *(amount)* calcular; **I can't w. out how he did it** no me explico cómo lo hizo
2 *vi* (**a**) **things didn't w. out for her** las cosas no le salieron bien (**b**) **it works out at five each** sale a cinco cada uno (**c**) *Sport* hacer ejercicio
▸ **work through** *vi* penetrar (**to** hasta)
▸ **work up** *vt sep (excite)* acalorar; **to get worked up** excitarse; **to w. up enthusiasm (for)** entusiasmarse (con)

workable ['wɜːkəbəl] *adj* factible

workaholic [wɜːkə'hɒlɪk] *n Fam* trabajoadicto(a) *m,f*

workbench ['wɜːkbentʃ] *n* obrador *m*

worker ['wɜːkə(r)] *n* trabajador(a) *m,f*; *(manual)* obrero(a) *m,f*

workforce ['wɜːkfɔːs] *n* mano *f* de obra

working ['wɜːkɪŋ] **1** *adj* (**a**) *(population, capital)* activo(a); **w. class** clase obrera; **w. man** obrero *m* (**b**) *(clothes, conditions, hours)* de trabajo; **w. day** día *m* laborable;

(number of hours) jornada *f* laboral (**c**) **it is in w. order** funciona (**d**) *(majority)* suficiente; **w. knowledge** conocimientos básicos
  2 *n* **workings** *(mechanics)* funcionamiento *m*; *Min* explotación *f*

workman ['wɜːkmən] *n (manual)* obrero *m*

workmanship ['wɜːkmənʃɪp] *n (appearance)* acabado *m*; *(skill)* habilidad *f*, arte *m*; **a fine piece of w.** un trabajo excelente

workmate ['wɜːkmeɪt] *n* compañero(a) *m,f* de trabajo

work-out ['wɜːkaʊt] *n* entrenamiento *m*

worksheet ['wɜːkʃiːt] *n* plan *m* de trabajo

workshop ['wɜːkʃɒp] *n* taller *m*

worktop ['wɜːktɒp] *n* encimera *f*

work-to-rule ['wɜːktə'ruːl] *n* huelga *f* de celo

world [wɜːld] *n* mundo *m*; **all over the w.** en todo el mundo; **the best in the w.** el mejor del mundo; *Fig* **there is a w. of difference between A and B** hay un mundo de diferencia entre A y B; *Fig* **to feel on top of the w.** sentirse fenomenal; *Fig* **to think the w. of sb** adorar a algn; *Fam Fig* **it is out of this w.** es una maravilla; **the W. Bank** el Banco Mundial; *Ftb* **the W. Cup** los Mundiales; **w. record** récord *m* mundial; **w. war** guerra *f* mundial

world-class ['wɜːld'klɑːs] *adj* de categoría mundial

world-famous ['wɜːld'feɪməs] *adj* de fama mundial

worldly ['wɜːldlɪ] *adj* mundano(a)

worldwide ['wɜːldwaɪd] *adj* mundial

worm [wɜːm] **1** *n* (**a**) gusano *m*; **(earth) w.** lombriz *f* (**b**) *Med* **worms** lombrices *fpl*
  2 *vt* **to w. a secret out of sb** sonsacarle un secreto a algn

worn [wɔːn] **1** *adj* gastado(a), usado(a)
  2 *pp of* **wear**

worn-out ['wɔːnaʊt] *adj (thing)* gastado(a); *(person)* rendido(a), agotado(a)

worried ['wʌrɪd] *adj* inquieto(a), preocupado(a)

worry ['wʌrɪ] **1** *vt* (**a**) preocupar, inquietar; **it doesn't w. me** me trae sin cuidado (**b**) *(pester)* molestar
  2 *vi* preocuparse (**about** por); **don't w.** no te preocupes
  3 *n (state)* inquietud *f*; *(cause)* preocupación *f*

worrying ['wʌrɪɪŋ] *adj* inquietante, preocupante

worse [wɜːs] **1** *adj (comp of* **bad**) peor; **he gets w. and w.** va de mal en peor; **to get w.** empeorar; *Fam* **w. luck!** ¡mala suerte!
  2 *n* **a change for the w.** un empeoramiento; *Fig* **to take a turn for the w.** empeorar
  3 *adv (comp of* **badly**) peor; **w. than ever** peor que nunca

worship ['wɜːʃɪp] **1** *vt* adorar
  2 *n* (**a**) adoración *f* (**b**) *(ceremony)* culto *m* (**c**) *Br* **his W. the Mayor** el señor alcalde; *Jur* **your W.** señoría

worshipper ['wɜːʃɪpə(r)] *n* devoto(a) *m,f*

worst [wɜːst] **1** *adj (superl of* **bad**) peor; **the w. part about it is that …** lo peor es que …
  2 *n* (**a**) *(person)* el/la peor, los/las peores (**b**) **the w. of the storm is over** ya ha pasado lo peor de la tormenta
  3 *adv (superl of* **badly**) peor; *Fig* **to come off w.** salir perdiendo

worth [wɜːθ] **1** *adj* (**a**) **to be w. £3** valer 3 libras; **a house w. £50,000** una casa que vale 50.000 libras (**b**) *(deserving of)* merecedor(a) de; **a book w. reading** un libro que merece la pena leer; **for what it's w.** por si sirve de algo; **it's w. your while, it's w. it** vale *or* merece la pena; **it's w. mentioning** es digno de mención
  2 *n* (**a**) *(in money)* valor *m*; **£5 w. of petrol** gasolina por valor de 5 libras (**b**) *(of person)* valía *f*

worthless ['wɜːθlɪs] *adj* sin valor; *(person)* despreciable

worthwhile [wɜːθ'waɪl] *adj* valioso(a), que vale la pena

worthy ['wɜːðɪ] *adj* (**worthier, worthiest**) (**a**) *(deserving)* digno(a) (**of** de); *(winner, cause)* justo(a) (**b**) *(citizen)* respetable; *(effort, motives, action)* loable

would [wʊd, *unstressed* wəd] *v aux* (**a**) *(conditional)* **I w. go if I had time** iría si tuviera tiempo; **he w. have won but for that** habría ganado su no hubiera sido por eso; **we w. if we could** lo haríamos si pudieramos; **you w. have to choose me!** ¡tenías que elegirme precisamente a mí!
  (**b**) *(reported speech)* **he said that he w. come** dijo que vendría
  (**c**) *(willingness)* **the car wouldn't start** el coche no arrancaba; **they asked him to come but he wouldn't** le invitaron a venir pero no quiso; **w. you do me a favour?** ¿quiere hacerme un favor?
  (**d**) *(wishing)* **he w. like to know why** quisiera saber por qué; **I'd rather go home** preferiría ir a casa; **w. you like a cigarette?** ¿quiere un cigarrillo?

(**e**) *(custom)* **we w. go for walks** solíamos dar un paseo

(**f**) **try as I w.** por mucho que lo intentara

(**g**) *(conjecture)* **it w. have been about three weeks ago** debe haber sido hace unas tres semanas; **w. this be your cousin?** ¿será éste tu primo?

(**h**) *(expectation)* **so it w. appear** según parece

would-be ['wʊdbiː] *adj* en potencia; **a w. politician** un aspirante a político; *Pej* **a w. poet** un supuesto poeta

wound¹ [waʊnd] *pt & pp of* **wind²**

wound² [wuːnd] **1** *n* herida *f*

2 *vt* herir

wove [wəʊv] *pt of* **weave**

woven ['wəʊvən] *pp of* **weave**

wow [waʊ] *Fam* **1** *vt* encandilar

2 *interj* ¡caramba!

WP *n* (**a**) *(abbr* **word processor**) procesador *m* de textos (**b**) *(abbr* **word processing**) tratamiento *m* de textos

wrangle ['ræŋgəl] **1** *n* disputa *f*

2 *vi* disputar (**over** por)

wrap [ræp] **1** *vt* **to w. (up)** envolver; **he wrapped his arms around her** la estrechó entre sus brazos; *Fam* **we wrapped up the deal** concluimos el negocio

2 *vi Fam* **w. up well** abrígate

3 *n (shawl)* chal *m*; *(cape)* capa *f*

wrapper ['ræpə(r)] *n (of sweet)* envoltorio *m*; *(of book)* sobrecubierta *f*

wrapping ['ræpɪŋ] *n* **w. paper** papel *m* de envolver

wreath [riːθ] *n (pl* **wreaths** [riːðz, riːθs]) *(of flowers)* corona *f*; **laurel w.** corona de laurel

wreck [rek] **1** *n* (**a**) *Naut* naufragio *m*; *(ship)* barco naufragado (**b**) *(of car, plane)* restos *mpl*; *(of building)* ruinas *fpl* (**c**) *Fig (person)* ruina *f*

2 *vt* (**a**) *(ship)* hacer naufragar (**b**) *(car, machine)* destrozar (**c**) *Fig (health, life)* arruinar; *(plans, hopes)* desbaratar; *(chances)* echar a perder

wreckage ['rekɪdʒ] *n (of ship, car, plane)* restos *mpl*; *(of building)* ruinas *fpl*

wren [ren] *n* chochín *m*

wrench [rentʃ] **1** *n* (**a**) *(pull)* tirón *m* (**b**) *Med* torcedura *f* (**c**) *(tool) Br* llave inglesa; *US* llave

2 *vt* **to w. oneself free** soltarse de un tirón; **to w. sth off sb** arrebatarle algo a algn; **to w. sth off/open** quitar/abrir algo de un tirón

wrestle ['resəl] *vi* luchar

wrestler ['reslə(r)] *n* luchador(a) *m,f*

wrestling ['reslɪŋ] *n* lucha *f*

wretch [retʃ] *n* (**poor**) **w.** desgraciado(a) *m,f*

wretched ['retʃɪd] *adj* (**a**) desdichado(a); *(conditions)* deplorable; *Fam (bad, poor)* horrible (**b**) **I feel w.** *(ill)* me siento fatal (**c**) *(contemptible)* despreciable (**d**) *Fam (damned)* maldito(a), condenado(a)

wriggle ['rɪgəl] **1** *vt* menear

2 *vi* **to w. (about)** *(worm)* serpentear; *(restless child)* moverse nerviosamente; **to w. free** escapar deslizándose

wring [rɪŋ] *vt (pt & pp* **wrung**) (**a**) *(clothes)* escurrir; *(hands)* retorcer (**b**) *Fig (extract)* arrancar, sacar

wringing ['rɪŋɪŋ] *adj* **to be w. wet** estar empapado(a)

wrinkle ['rɪŋkəl] **1** *n* arruga *f*

2 *vt* arrugar

3 *vi* arrugarse

wrist [rɪst] *n* muñeca *f*

wristwatch ['rɪstwɒtʃ] *n* reloj *m* de pulsera

writ [rɪt] *n* orden *f* judicial

write [raɪt] **1** *vt (pt* **wrote**; *pp* **written**) escribir; *(article)* redactar; *(cheque)* extender

2 *vi* escribir (**about** sobre); **to w. for a paper** colaborar en un periódico

▸ **write back** *vi* contestar

▸ **write down** *vt sep* poner por escrito; *(note)* apuntar

▸ **write in** *vi* escribir

▸ **write off 1** *vt sep (debt)* condonar; *(car)* destrozar

2 *vi* **to w. off for sth** pedir algo por escrito

▸ **write out** *vt sep (cheque, recipe)* extender

▸ **write up** *vt sep (notes)* redactar; *(diary, journal)* poner al día

write-off ['raɪtɒf] *n* **the car's a w.** el coche está hecho una ruina

writer ['raɪtə(r)] *n (by profession)* escritor(a) *m,f*; *(of book, letter)* autor(a) *m,f*

writhe [raɪð] *vi* retorcerse

writing ['raɪtɪŋ] *n* (**a**) *(script)* escritura *f*; *(handwriting)* letra *f*; **in w.** por escrito (**b**) **writings** escritos *mpl* (**c**) *(action)* escritura *f*; **w. desk** escritorio *m*

written ['rɪtən] *pp of* **write**

wrong [rɒŋ] **1** *adj* (**a**) *(person)* equivocado(a); **I was w. about that boy** me equivoqué con ese chico; **to be w.** no tener razón; **you're w. in thinking that ...** te equivocas si piensas que ...

(**b**) *(answer, way)* incorrecto(a), equivocado(a); **my watch is w.** mi reloj anda mal; **to drive on the w. side of the road** conducir por el lado contrario de la carretera; **to go the w. way** equivocarse de camino; *Tel* **I've got the w. number** me he confundido de número

(**c**) *(unsuitable)* impropio(a), inadecuado(a); *(time)* inoportuno(a); **to say the w. thing** decir algo inoportuno

(**d**) *(immoral etc)* malo(a); **there's nothing w. in that** no hay nada malo en ello; **what's w. with smoking?** ¿qué tiene de malo fumar?

(**e**) **is anything w.?** ¿pasa algo?; **something's w.** hay algo que no está bien; **what's w.?** ¿qué pasa?; **what's w. with you?** ¿qué te pasa?

2 *adv* mal, incorrectamente; **to get it w.** equivocarse; *Fam* **to go w.** *(plan)* fallar, salir mal

3 *n* (**a**) *(evil, bad action)* mal *m*; **you did w. to hit him** hiciste mal en pegarle

(**b**) *(injustice)* injusticia *f*; *(offence)* agravio *m*; **the rights and wrongs of a matter** lo justo y lo injusto de un asunto

(**c**) **to be in the w.** *(be to blame)* tener la culpa

4 *vt* *(treat unfairly)* ser injusto(a) con; *(offend)* agraviar

wrongdoing ['rɒŋduːɪŋ] *n* maldad *f*

wrongful ['rɒŋfʊl] *adj* injusto(a)

wrongly ['rɒŋlɪ] *adv* (**a**) *(incorrectly)* incorrectamente (**b**) *(mistakenly)* equivocadamente (**c**) *(unjustly)* injustamente

wrote [rəʊt] *pt of* **write**

wrung [rʌŋ] *pt & pp of* **wring**

wry [raɪ] *adj* (**wrier, wriest** *or* **wryer, wryest**) sardónico(a)

xenophobia [zenə'fəʊbɪə] *n* xenofobia *f*
Xerox® ['zɪərɒks] **1** *n* fotocopia *f*, xeroco-
pia *f*
  2 *vt* fotocopiar
Xmas ['krɪsməs, 'eksməs] *n* (*abbr* **Christmas**) Navidad *f*
X-ray ['eksreɪ] **1** *n* (*radiation*) rayo *m* X;
(*picture*) radiografía *f*; **to have an X.** hacerse una radiografía
  2 *vt* radiografiar

Y, y [waɪ] *n* (*the letter*) Y, y *f*
yacht [jɒt] *n* yate *m*; **y. club** club náutico
yachting ['jɒtɪŋ] *n Sport* navegación *f* a
vela; (*competition*) regatas *fpl*
yachtsman ['jɒtsmən] *n* balandrista *m*
yachtswoman ['jɒtswʊmən] *n* balandrista *f*
yam [jæm] *n* (**a**) ñame *m* (**b**) *US* (*sweet
potato*) boniato *m*, batata *f*, *Andes, CAm,
Carib, Méx* camote *m*
Yank [jæŋk] *n Br Pej* yanqui *mf*
yank [jæŋk] *vt Fam* tirar; (*tooth*) arrancar
Yankee ['jæŋkɪ] *adj & n Pej* yanqui (*mf*)
yap [jæp] *vi* (*dog*) aullar; *Fam* (*person*)
darle al pico
yard¹ [jɑːd] *n* (*measure*) yarda *f* (*aprox
0,914 m*)
yard² [jɑːd] *n* patio *m*; *US* jardín *m*
yardstick ['jɑːdstɪk] *n Fig* criterio *m*, norma *f*
yarn [jɑːn] *n* (**a**) *Sewing* hilo *m* (**b**) (*story*)
historia *f*, cuento *m*; **to spin a y.** (*lie*)
inventarse una historia
yawn [jɔːn] **1** *vi* bostezar
  2 *n* bostezo *m*
yawning ['jɔːnɪŋ] *adj* (*gap*) profundo(a)
yd (*pl* **yds**) (*abbr* **yard**) yarda *f*
yeah [jeə] *adv Fam* sí
year [jɪə(r)] *n* (**a**) año *m*; **all y. round**
durante todo el año; **last y.** el año pasado; **next y.** el año que viene; **y. in, y. out**
año tras año; **I'm ten years old** tengo diez
años (**b**) *Educ* curso *m*; **first-y. student**
estudiante *mf* de primero
yearly ['jɪəlɪ] **1** *adj* anual
  2 *adv* anualmente, cada año
yearn [jɜːn] *vi* **to y. for sth** anhelar algo
yearning ['jɜːnɪŋ] *n* anhelo *m* (**for** de)

yeast [jiːst] *n* levadura *f*
yell [jel] **1** *vi* gritar
  2 *n* grito *m*, alarido *m*
yellow ['jeləʊ] **1** *adj* amarillo(a); *Fam Fig*
(*cowardly*) cobarde; *Tel* **Y. Pages**® páginas
amarillas
  2 *n* amarillo *m*
yelp [jelp] **1** *vi* aullar
  2 *n* aullido *m*
yen [jen] *n* (**a**) (*currency*) yen *m* (**b**) **to
have a y. for sth** tener ganas de algo
yeoman ['jəʊmən] *n Br* **Y. of the Guard** =
alabardero de la Casa Real británica
yes [jes] **1** *adv* sí; **you said y.** dijiste que sí
  2 *n* sí *m*
yesterday ['jestədeɪ] *adv & n* ayer *m*; **the
day before y.** anteayer; **y. morning** ayer
por la mañana
yet [jet] **1** *adv* (**a**) **not y.** aún no, todavía
no; **as y.** hasta ahora; **I haven't eaten y.** no
he comido todavía (**b**) (*in questions*) ya;
has he arrived y.? ¿ha venido ya? (**c**)
(*even*) más; **y. again** otra vez; **y. more**
todavía más (**d**) (*eventually*) todavía,
aún; **he'll win y.** todavía puede ganar
  2 *conj* sin embargo
yew [juː] *n* tejo *m*
yield [jiːld] **1** *n* (**a**) rendimiento *m* (**b**) *Agr*
cosecha *f* (**c**) *Fin* beneficio *m*
  2 *vt* producir; *Agr* dar; (*money*) producir
  3 *vi* (**a**) (*surrender, break*) ceder (**b**) *US
Aut* ceder el paso
YMCA [waɪemsiː'eɪ] *n* (*abbr* **Young Men's
Christian Association**) ACJ *f*, Asociación *f*
Cristiana de Jóvenes (*que regenta hostales económicos*)
yob(bo) ['jɒb(əʊ)] *n Fam* gamberro(a) *m,f*
yoga ['jəʊgə] *n* yoga *m*
yog(h)urt ['jɒgət] *n* yogur *m*
yoke [jəʊk] **1** *n* yugo *m*
  2 *vt* (*oxen*) uncir; *Fig* unir
yokel ['jəʊkəl] *n Pej* paleto(a) *m,f*
yolk [jəʊk] *n* yema *f*
yonder ['jɒndə(r)] *adv* más allá
you [juː, *unstressed* jʊ] *pers pron* (**a**)
(*subject*) (*usually omitted in Spanish, except for contrast*) (*familiar use*) (*singular*)
tú; (*pl*) vosotros(as); **how are y.?** ¿cómo
estás?, ¿cómo estáis?

(**b**) *(subject) (polite use) (singular)* usted; *(pl)* ustedes; **how are y.?** ¿cómo está?, ¿cómo están?

(**c**) *(subject) (impers use)* **y. never know** nunca se sabe

(**d**) *(object) (familiar use) (singular) (before verb)* te; *(after preposition)* ti; *(pl) (before verb)* os; *(after preposition)* vosotros(as); **I saw y.** te vi/os vi; **it's for y.** es para ti/es para vosotros(as); **with y.** contigo/con vosotros(as)

(**e**) *(object) (polite use) (singular) (before verb)* le; *(after preposition)* usted; *(pl) (before verb)* les; *(after preposition)* ustedes; **I saw y.** le vi/les vi; **it's for y.** es para usted/es para ustedes; **with y.** con usted/con ustedes

(**f**) *(object) (impers use)* **alcohol makes y. drunk** el alcohol emborracha

> In Spanish, the formal form **usted** takes a third person singular verb, and **ustedes** takes a third person plural verb. In many Latin American countries, **ustedes** is the standard form of the second person plural (**vosotros**) and is not considered formal. Note also that in some of those countries **usted** is used in the second person singular (**tú**), and is likewise not considered formal.

young [jʌŋ] **1** *adj (age)* joven; *(brother etc)* pequeño(a); **y. lady** señorita *f*; **y. man** joven *m*

2 *npl* (**a**) *(people)* **the y.** los jóvenes, la juventud (**b**) *(animals)* crías *fpl*

youngster ['jʌŋstə(r)] *n* muchacho(a) *m,f*

your [jɔː(r), *unstressed* jə(r)] *poss adj* (**a**) *(familiar use) (singular)* tu/tus; *(pl)* vuestro(a)/vuestros(as) (**b**) *(polite use)* su/sus (**c**) *(impers use)* **the house is on y. right** la casa queda a la derecha; **they clean y. shoes for you** te limpian los zapatos (**d**) *(formal address)* Su; **Y. Majesty** Su Majestad

yours [jɔːz] *poss pron* (**a**) *(familiar use) (singular)* el tuyo/la tuya/los tuyos/las tuyas; *(pl)* el vuestro/la vuestra/los vuestros/las vuestras; **the house is y.** la casa es tuya (**b**) *(polite use) (singular)* el suyo/la suya; *(pl)* los suyos/las suyas; **the house is y.** la casa es suya (**c**) *(in letters)* **y. faithfully** le(s) saluda atentamente; **y. sincerely** reciba un cordial saludo de

> In Spanish, the forms **tuyo(a)**, **suyo(a)** and **vuestro(a)** require a definite article in the singular and in the plural when they are the subject of the phrase.

yourself [jɔː'self, *unstressed* jə'self] (*pl* **yourselves** [jɔː'selvz]) **1** *pers pron* (**a**) *(familiar use) (singular)* tú mismo(a); *(pl)* vosotros(as) mismos(as); **by y.** (tú) solo; **by yourselves** vosotros(as) solos(as) (**b**) *(polite use) (singular)* usted mismo(a); *(pl)* ustedes mismos(as); **by y.** (usted) solo(a); **by yourselves** (ustedes) solos(as)

2 *reflexive pron* (**a**) *(familiar use) (singular)* te; *(pl)* (familiar use) os; **enjoy y.!** ¡diviértete!; **enjoy yourselves!** ¡divertíos! (**b**) *(polite use)* se; **enjoy y.!** ¡diviértase!; **enjoy yourselves!** ¡diviértanse!

> In many Latin American countries, **se/ustedes** is the standard form of the second person plural and is not considered formal.

youth [juːθ] *n* (**a**) juventud *f* (**b**) *(young man)* joven *m*; **y. club** club *m* juvenil; **y. hostel** albergue *m* juvenil

youthful ['juːθfʊl] *adj* juvenil, joven

Yugoslav ['juːɡəʊslɑːv] *adj & n* yugoslavo(a) *(m,f)*

Yugoslavia [juːɡəʊ'slɑːvɪə] *n* Yugoslavia

Yugoslavian [juːɡəʊ'slɑːvɪən] *adj & n* yugoslavo(a) *(m,f)*

YWCA ['waɪdʌbəljuːsiː'eɪ] *n* (*abbr* **Young Women's Christian Association**) ACJ *f*, Asociación *f* Cristiana de Jóvenes *(que regenta hostales económicos)*

Z, z [zed, *US* ziː] *n (the letter)* Z, z *f*

zany ['zeɪnɪ] *adj* (**zanier, zaniest**) *Fam* (**a**) *(mad)* chiflado(a) (**b**) *(eccentric)* estrafalario(a)

zap [zæp] **1** *interj* ¡zas!

2 *vt Fam* (**a**) *(hit)* pegar (**b**) *(kill)* cargarse a

3 *vi TV* hacer zapping

zeal [ziːl] *n (enthusiasm)* entusiasmo *m*

zealous ['zeləs] *adj (enthusiastic)* entusiasta

zebra ['ziːbrə, 'zebrə] *n* cebra *f*; *Br* **z. crossing** paso *m* de cebra

zenith ['zenɪθ] *n Astron* cenit *m*; *Fig* apogeo *m*

zero ['zɪərəʊ] *n* cero *m*; **z. hour** hora *f* cero

zest [zest] *n (eagerness)* entusiasmo *m*

zigzag ['zɪɡzæg] **1** *n* zigzag *m*

2 *vi* zigzaguear

Zimbabwe [zɪm'bɑːbweɪ] *n* Zimbabue

zinc [zɪŋk] *n* cinc *m*, zinc *m*

zip [zɪp] **1** *n* (**a**) *Br* **z. (fastener)** cremallera *f* (**b**) *Fam* brío *m*; *US* **z. code** código *m* postal

2 *vi* cerrarse con cremallera

▸ **zip by** *vi* pasar como un rayo

▸ **zip up** *vt sep* cerrar con cremallera; **to z. sb up** cerrar la cremallera a algn

zipper ['zɪpə(r)] *n US* cremallera *f*

zodiac ['zəʊdɪæk] *n* zodiaco *m*, zodíaco *m*

zombie ['zɒmbɪ] *n* zombie *mf*

zone [zəʊn] **1** *n* zona *f*
   2 *vt* dividir en zonas

zoo [zuː] *n* zoo *m*

zoological [zuːə'lɒdʒɪkəl] *adj* zoológico(a)

zoologist [zuː'ɒlədʒɪst] *n* zoólogo(a) *m,f*

zoology [zuː'ɒlədʒɪ] *n* zoología *f*

zoom [zuːm] **1** *n* (a) *(buzz)* zumbido *m* (b) **z. lens** zoom *m*, teleobjetivo *m*
   2 *vi* (a) *(buzz)* zumbar (b) **to z. past** pasar volando
▸ **zoom in** *vi (camera)* acercarse rápidamente

zucchini [zuː'kiːnɪ] *n US* calabacín *m*, *CSur* zapallito *m*

Zulu ['zuːluː] *adj & n* zulú *(mf)*